The
BIBLE
in
ONE YEAR

The
BIBLE

in

ONE YEAR

NEW INTERNATIONAL VERSION

HODDER & STOUGHTON

LONDON   SYDNEY   AUCKLAND   TORONTO

The Holy Bible, New International Version
Copyright © 1973, 1978, 1984 by International Bible Society
First published in Great Britain 1979
This edition 1989
This impression 1992

British Library Cataloguing in Publication Data

The Bible in one year: New International Version.
  1. Bible—Daily readings
  242′.2

FOREWORD

THE BIBLE IN ONE YEAR is a new arrangement of the Bible designed to let the reader get the most out of reading the complete Bible methodically in the space of one year. For every day in the year, readings are given from the Old Testament, the New Testament, and from Psalms or Proverbs. Reading may begin at any time during the year; but the Old Testament books are placed in broadly chronological order, starting on January 1st. However, in the interests of smooth reading, and to keep the individual character of different books, the books themselves are not broken up but are generally read in sequence. For the same reason, the New Testament is presented in traditional Bible order. A time chart is included in the notes and maps at the end of the book, and reference to this will help the reader to see the flow of biblical history.

Psalms and Proverbs have been divided evenly over the whole year. Because of the poetic nature of the Psalms, and the pithy wisdom of Proverbs, they are presented in regular, short sections to encourage reflection at the end of the day's reading.

This Bible may also be used for reference, and the contents pages show where each book begins.

The notes and maps at the end of the book will be especially useful to those who are less familiar with the Bible. The section called *What is the Bible* is a helpful introduction to Bible reading, and other sections give background information, a summary of the individual books, an index to well known passages, and five useful Bible maps.

FOREWORD

PREFACE

TO THE NEW INTERNATIONAL VERSION

THE NEW INTERNATIONAL VERSION is a completely new translation of the Holy Bible made by over a hundred scholars working directly from the best available Hebrew, Aramaic and Greek texts. It had its beginning in 1965 when, after several years of exploratory study by committees from the Christian Reformed Church and the National Association of Evangelicals, a group of scholars met at Palos Heights, Illinois, and concurred in the need for a new translation of the Bible in contemporary English. This group, though not made up of official church representatives, was transdenominational. Its conclusion was endorsed by a large number of leaders from many denominations who met in Chicago in 1966.

Responsibility for the new version was delegated by the Palos Heights group to a self-governing body of fifteen, the Committee on Bible Translation, composed for the most part of biblical scholars from colleges, universities and seminaries. In 1967 the New York Bible Society (now the International Bible Society) generously undertook the financial sponsorship of the project—a sponsorship that made it possible to enlist the help of many distinguished scholars. The fact that participants from the United States, Great Britain, Canada, Australia and New Zealand worked together gave the project its international scope. That they were from many denominations—including Anglican, Assemblies of God, Baptist, Brethren, Christian Reformed, Church of Christ, Evangelical Free, Lutheran, Mennonite, Methodist, Nazarene, Presbyterian, Wesleyan and other churches—helped to safeguard the translation from sectarian bias.

How it was made helps to give the New International Version its distinctiveness. The translation of each book was assigned to a team of scholars. Next, one of the Intermediate Editorial Committees revised the initial translation, with constant reference to the Hebrew, Aramaic or Greek. Their work then went to one of the General Editorial Committees, which checked it in detail and made another thorough revision. This revision in turn was carefully reviewed by the Committee on Bible Translation, which made further changes and then released the final version for publication. In this way the entire Bible underwent three revisions, during each of which the translation was examined for its faithfulness to the original languages and for its English style.

All this involved many thousands of hours of research and discussion regarding the meaning of the texts and the precise way of putting them into English. It may well be that no other translation has been made by a more thorough process of review and revision from committee to committee than this one.

From the beginning of the project, the Committee on Bible Translation held to certain goals for the New International Version: that it would be an accurate translation and one that would have clarity and literary quality and so prove suitable for public and private reading, teaching, preaching, memorising and liturgical use. The Committee also sought to preserve some measure of continuity with the long tradition of translating the Scriptures into English.

In working towards these goals, the translators were united in their commitment to the authority and infallibility of the Bible as God's Word in written form. They believe that it contains the divine answer to the deepest needs of humanity, that it sheds unique light on our path in a dark world, and that it sets forth the way to our eternal well-being.

The first concern of the translators has been the accuracy of the translation and its fidelity to the thought of the biblical writers. They have weighed the significance of the lexical and grammatical details of the Hebrew, Aramaic and Greek texts. At the same time, they have striven for more than a word-for-word translation. Because thought patterns and syntax differ from language to language, faithful communication of the meaning of the writers of the Bible demands frequent modifications in sentence structure and constant regard for the contextual meanings of words.

A sensitive feeling for style does not always accompany scholarship. Accordingly the Committee on Bible Translation submitted the developing version to a number of stylistic consultants. Two of them read every book of both Old and New Testaments twice—once before and once after the last major revision—and made invaluable suggestions. Samples of the translation were tested for clarity and ease of reading by various kinds of people—young and old, highly educated and less well educated, ministers and laymen.

Concern for clear and natural English—that the New International Version should be idiomatic but not idiosyncratic, contemporary but not dated—motivated the translators and consultants. At the same time, they tried to reflect the differing styles of the biblical writers. In view of the international use of English, the translators sought to avoid obvious Americanisms on the one hand and obvious Anglicisms on the other. A British edition reflects the comparatively few differences of significant idiom and of spelling.

As for the traditional pronouns "thou", "thee" and "thine" in reference to the Deity, the translators judged that to use these archaisms (along with old verb forms such as "doest", "wouldest" and "hadst") would violate accuracy in translation. Neither Hebrew, Aramaic nor Greek uses special pronouns for the persons of the Godhead. A present-day translation is not enhanced by forms that in the time of the King James Version were used in everyday speech, whether referring to God or man.

For the Old Testament the standard Hebrew text, the Masoretic Text as published in the latest editions of *Biblia Hebraica*, was used throughout. The Dead Sea Scrolls contain material bearing on an earlier stage of the Hebrew text. They were consulted, as were the Samaritan Pentateuch and the ancient scribal traditions relating to textual changes. Sometimes a variant Hebrew reading in the margin of the Masoretic Text was followed instead of the text itself. Such instances, being variants within the Masoretic tradition, are not specified by footnotes. In rare cases, words in the consonantal text were divided differently from the way they appear in the Masoretic Text. Footnotes indicate this. The translators also consulted the more important early versions—the Septuagint; Aquila, Symmachus and Theodotion; the Vulgate; the Syriac Peshitta; the Targums; and for the Psalms the *Juxta Hebraica* of Jerome. Readings from these versions were occasionally followed where the Masoretic Text seemed doubtful and where accepted principles of textual criticism showed that one or more of these textual witnesses appeared to provide the correct reading. Such instances are footnoted. Sometimes vowel letters and vowel signs did not, in the judgment of the translators, represent the correct vowels for the original consonantal text. Accordingly some words were read with a different set of vowels. These instances are usually not indicated by footnotes.

The Greek text used in translating the New Testament was an eclectic one. No other piece of ancient literature has such an abundance of manuscript witnesses as does the New Testament. Where existing manuscripts differ, the translators made their choice of readings according to accepted principles of New Testament textual criticism. Footnotes call attention to places where there was uncertainty about what the original text was. The best current printed texts of the Greek New Testament were used.

There is a sense in which the work of translation is never wholly finished. This applies to all great literature and uniquely so to the Bible. In 1973 the New Testament in the New International Version was published. Since then, suggestions for corrections and revisions have been received from various sources. The Committee on Bible Translation carefully considered the suggestions and adopted a number of them. These were incorporated in the first printing of the entire Bible in 1978. Additional revisions were made by the Committee on Bible Translation in 1983 and appear in printings after that date.

As in other ancient documents, the precise meaning of the biblical texts is sometimes uncertain. This is more often the case with the Hebrew and Aramaic texts than with the Greek text. Although archaeological and linguistic discoveries in this century aid in understanding difficult passages, some uncertainties remain. The more significant of these have been called to the reader's attention in the footnotes.

In regard to the divine name *YHWH*, commonly referred to as the *Tetragrammaton*, the translators adopted the device used in most English versions of rendering that name as "Lord" in capital letters to distinguish it from *Adonai*, another Hebrew word rendered "Lord", for which small letters are used. Wherever the two names stand together in the Old Testament as a compound name of God, they are rendered "Sovereign Lord".

Because for most readers today the phrases "the Lord of hosts" and "God of hosts" have little meaning, this version renders them "the Lord Almighty" and "God Almighty". These renderings convey the sense of the Hebrew, namely, "he who is sovereign over all the 'hosts' (powers) in heaven and on earth, especially over the 'hosts' (armies) of Israel." For readers unacquainted with Hebrew this does not make clear the distinction between *Sabaoth* ("hosts" or "Almighty") and *Shaddai* (which can also be translated "Almighty"), but the latter occurs infrequently and is always footnoted. When *Adonai* and *YHWH Sabaoth* occur together, they are rendered "the Lord, the Lord Almighty".

As for other proper nouns, the familiar spellings of the Authorised Version are generally retained. Names traditionally spelled with "ch", except where it is final, are usually spelled in this translation with "k" or "c", since the biblical languages do not have the sound that "ch" frequently indicates in English—for example, in *chant*. For well-known names such as Zechariah, however, the traditional spelling has been retained. Variation in the spelling of names in the original languages has usually not been indicated. Where a person or place has two or more different names in the Hebrew, Aramaic or Greek texts, the more familiar one has generally been used, with footnotes where needed.

To achieve clarity the translators sometimes supplied words not in the original texts but required by the context. If there was uncertainty about such material, it is enclosed in brackets. Also for the sake of clarity or style, nouns, including some proper nouns, are sometimes substituted for pronouns, and vice versa. And though the Hebrew writers often shifted back and forth between first, second and third personal pronouns without change of antecedent, this translation often makes them uniform, in accordance with English style and without the use of footnotes.

Poetical passages are printed as poetry, that is, with indentation of lines and with separate stanzas. These are generally designed to reflect the structure of Hebrew poetry. This poetry is normally characterised by parallelism in balanced lines. Most of the poetry in the Bible is in the Old Testament, and scholars differ regarding the scansion of Hebrew lines. The translators determined the stanza divisions for the most part by analysis of the subject matter. The stanzas therefore serve as poetic paragraphs.

As an aid to the reader, italicised sectional headings are inserted in most of the books. They are not to be regarded as part of the NIV text, are not for oral reading, and are not intended to dictate the interpretation of the sections they head.

The footnotes in this version are of several kinds, most of which need no explanation. Those giving alternative translations begin with "Or" and generally introduce the alternative with the last word preceding it in the text, except when it is a single-word alternative; in poetry quoted in a footnote a slant mark indicates a line division. Footnotes introduced by "Or" do not have uniform significance. In some cases two possible translations were considered to have about equal validity. In other cases, though the translators were convinced that the translation in the text was correct, they judged that another interpretation was possible and of sufficient importance to be represented in a footnote.

In the New Testament, footnotes that refer to uncertainty regarding the original text are introduced by "Some manuscripts" or similar expressions. In the Old Testament, evidence for the reading chosen is given first and evidence for the alternative is added after a semicolon (for example: Septuagint; Hebrew *father*). In such notes the term "Hebrew" refers to the Masoretic Text.

It should be noted that minerals, flora and fauna, architectural details, articles of clothing and jewellery, musical instruments and other articles cannot always be identified with precision. Also measures of capacity in the biblical period are particularly uncertain (see the table of weights and measures following the text).

Like all translations of the Bible, made as they are by imperfect man, this one undoubtedly falls short of its goals. Yet we are grateful to God for the extent to which he has enabled us to realise these goals and for the strength he has given us and our colleagues to complete our task. We offer this version of the Bible to him in whose name and for whose glory it has been made. We pray that it will lead many into a better understanding of the Holy Scriptures and a fuller knowledge of Jesus Christ the incarnate Word, of whom the Scriptures so faithfully testify.

The Committee on Bible Translation

June 1978
(Revised August 1983)

Names of the translators and editors may be secured
from the International Bible Society
PO Box 62970, Colorado Springs CO80962-2970, U.S.A.

Note   The footnotes to the New International Version are not included in this edition, which is intended for general Bible reading. They are to be found in other editions of this Bible, also available from Hodder and Stoughton.

CONTENTS

The page numbers given indicate where the first reading from a particular book begins. Psalms and Proverbs are spread throughout the year – see separate index overleaf.

INDEX TO PSALMS AND PROVERBS

OLD TESTAMENT READING
Genesis 1:1–2:17

The Beginning

1 In the beginning God created the heavens and the earth. ²Now the earth was formless and empty, darkness was over the surface of the deep, and the Spirit of God was hovering over the waters.

³And God said, "Let there be light," and there was light. ⁴God saw that the light was good, and he separated the light from the darkness. ⁵God called the light "day", and the darkness he called "night". And there was evening, and there was morning—the first day.

⁶And God said, "Let there be an expanse between the waters to separate water from water." ⁷So God made the expanse and separated the water under the expanse from the water above it. And it was so. ⁸God called the expanse "sky". And there was evening, and there was morning—the second day.

⁹And God said, "Let the water under the sky be gathered to one place, and let dry ground appear." And it was so. ¹⁰God called the dry ground "land", and the gathered waters he called "seas". And God saw that it was good.

¹¹Then God said, "Let the land produce vegetation: seed-bearing plants and trees on the land that bear fruit with seed in it, according to their various kinds." And it was so. ¹²The land produced vegetation: plants bearing seed according to their kinds and trees bearing fruit with seed in it according to their kinds. And God saw that it was good. ¹³And there

was evening, and there was morning—the third day.

¹⁴And God said, "Let there be lights in the expanse of the sky to separate the day from the night, and let them serve as signs to mark seasons and days and years, ¹⁵and let them be lights in the expanse of the sky to give light on the earth." And it was so. ¹⁶God made two great lights—the greater light to govern the day and the lesser light to govern the night. He also made the stars. ¹⁷God set them in the expanse of the sky to give light on the earth, ¹⁸to govern the day and the night, and to separate light from darkness. And God saw that it was good. ¹⁹And there was evening, and there was morning—the fourth day.

²⁰And God said, "Let the water teem with living creatures, and let birds fly above the earth across the expanse of the sky." ²¹So God created the great creatures of the sea and every living and moving thing with which the water teems, according to their kinds, and every winged bird according to its kind. And God saw that it was good. ²²God blessed them and said, "Be fruitful and increase in number and fill the water in the seas, and let the birds increase on the earth." ²³And there was evening, and there was morning—the fifth day.

²⁴And God said, "Let the land produce living creatures according to their kinds: livestock, creatures that move along the ground, and wild animals, each according to its kind." And it was so. ²⁵God made the wild animals according to their kinds, the livestock according to their kinds, and all the creatures that move along the ground

according to their kinds. And God saw that it was good.

26Then God said, "Let us make man in our image, in our likeness, and let them rule over the fish of the sea and the birds of the air, over the livestock, over all the earth, and over all the creatures that move along the ground."

27So God created man
　in his own image,
　in the image of God
　　he created him;
　male and female
　　he created them.

28God blessed them and said to them, "Be fruitful and increase in number; fill the earth and subdue it. Rule over the fish of the sea and the birds of the air and over every living creature that moves on the ground."

29Then God said, "I give you every seed-bearing plant on the face of the whole earth and every tree that has fruit with seed in it. They will be yours for food. 30And to all the beasts of the earth and all the birds of the air and all the creatures that move on the ground—everything that has the breath of life in it—I give every green plant for food." And it was so.

31God saw all that he had made, and it was very good. And there was evening, and there was morning—the sixth day.

2 　Thus the heavens and the earth were completed in all their vast array.

2By the seventh day God had finished the work he had been doing; so on the seventh day he rested from all his work. 3And God blessed the seventh day and made it holy, because on it he rested from all the work of creating that he had done.

Adam and Eve

4This is the account of the heavens and the earth when they were created.

When the LORD God made the earth and the heavens—5and no shrub of the field had yet appeared on the earth and no plant of the field had yet sprung up, for the LORD God had not sent rain on the earth and there was no man to work the ground, 6but streams came up from the earth and watered the whole surface of the ground—7the LORD God formed the man from the dust of the ground and breathed into his nostrils the breath of life, and the man became a living being.

8Now the LORD God had planted a garden in the east, in Eden; and there he put the man he had formed. 9And the LORD God made all kinds of trees grow out of the ground—trees that were pleasing to the eye and good for food. In the middle of the garden were the tree of life and the tree of the knowledge of good and evil.

10A river watering the garden flowed from Eden; from there it was separated into four headwaters. 11The name of the first is the Pishon; it winds through the entire land of Havilah, where there is gold. 12(The gold of that land is good; aromatic resin and onyx are also there.) 13The name of the second river is the Gihon; it winds through the entire land of Cush. 14The name of the third river is the Tigris; it runs along the east side of Asshur. And the fourth river is the Euphrates.

15The LORD God took the man and put him in the Garden of Eden to work it and take care of it. 16And the LORD God commanded the man, "You are free to eat from any tree in the garden; 17but you must not eat from the tree of the knowledge of good and evil, for when you eat of it you will surely die."

NEW TESTAMENT READING
Matthew 1:1–25

The Genealogy of Jesus

1 A record of the genealogy of Jesus Christ the son of David, the son of Abraham:

²Abraham was the father of Isaac,
  Isaac the father of Jacob,
  Jacob the father of Judah and his brothers,
³Judah the father of Perez and Zerah, whose mother was Tamar,
  Perez the father of Hezron,
  Hezron the father of Ram,
⁴Ram the father of Amminadab,
  Amminadab the father of Nahshon,
  Nahshon the father of Salmon,
⁵Salmon the father of Boaz, whose mother was Rahab,
  Boaz the father of Obed, whose mother was Ruth,
  Obed the father of Jesse,
⁶and Jesse the father of King David.

David was the father of Solomon, whose mother had been Uriah's wife,
⁷Solomon the father of Rehoboam,
  Rehoboam the father of Abijah,
  Abijah the father of Asa,
⁸Asa the father of Jehoshaphat,
  Jehoshaphat the father of Jehoram,
  Jehoram the father of Uzziah,
⁹Uzziah the father of Jotham,
  Jotham the father of Ahaz,
  Ahaz the father of Hezekiah,
¹⁰Hezekiah the father of Manasseh,
  Manasseh the father of Amon,
  Amon the father of Josiah,
¹¹and Josiah the father of Jeconiah and his brothers at the time of the exile to Babylon.

¹²After the exile to Babylon:
  Jeconiah was the father of Shealtiel,
  Shealtiel the father of Zerubbabel,
¹³Zerubbabel the father of Abiud,
  Abiud the father of Eliakim,
  Eliakim the father of Azor,
¹⁴Azor the father of Zadok,
  Zadok the father of Akim,
  Akim the father of Eliud,
¹⁵Eliud the father of Eleazar,
  Eleazar the father of Matthan,
  Matthan the father of Jacob,
¹⁶and Jacob the father of Joseph, the husband of Mary, of whom was born Jesus, who is called Christ.

¹⁷Thus there were fourteen generations in all from Abraham to David, fourteen from David to the exile to Babylon, and fourteen from the exile to the Christ.

The Birth of Jesus Christ

¹⁸This is how the birth of Jesus Christ came about: His mother Mary was pledged to be married to Joseph, but before they came together, she was found to be with child through the Holy Spirit. ¹⁹Because Joseph her husband was a righteous man and did not want to expose her to public disgrace, he had in mind to divorce her quietly. ²⁰But after he had considered this, an angel of the Lord appeared to him in a dream and said, "Joseph son of David, do not be afraid to take Mary home as your wife, because what is conceived in her is from the Holy Spirit. ²¹She will give birth to a son, and you are to give him the name Jesus, because he will save his people from their sins."

²²All this took place to fulfil what the Lord had said through the prophet: ²³"The virgin will be with child and will give birth to a son, and they will call him Immanuel"—which means, "God with us."

²⁴When Joseph woke up, he did what

the angel of the Lord had commanded him and took Mary home as his wife. 25But he had no union with her until she gave birth to a son. And he gave him the name Jesus.

READING FROM PSALMS
Psalm 1:1–6

1Blessed is the man
  who does not walk in the counsel
    of the wicked
or stand in the way of sinners
  or sit in the seat of mockers.
2But his delight is in the law of the
    LORD,
  and on his law he meditates day
    and night.

3He is like a tree planted by streams of
    water,
  which yields its fruit in season
and whose leaf does not wither.
  Whatever he does prospers.

4Not so the wicked!
  They are like chaff
    that the wind blows away.
5Therefore the wicked will not stand
    in the judgment,
  nor sinners in the assembly of the
    righteous.

6For the LORD watches over the way
    of the righteous,
  but the way of the wicked will
    perish.

DAY 2

JANUARY 2

OLD TESTAMENT READING
Genesis 2:18–4:16

18The LORD God said, "It is not good for the man to be alone. I will make a helper suitable for him."

19Now the LORD God had formed out of the ground all the beasts of the field and all the birds of the air. He brought them to the man to see what he would name them; and whatever the man called each living creature, that was its name. 20So the man gave names to all the livestock, the birds of the air and all the beasts of the field.

But for Adam no suitable helper was found. 21So the LORD God caused the man to fall into a deep sleep; and while he was sleeping, he took one of the man's ribs and closed up the place with flesh. 22Then the LORD God made a woman from the rib he had taken out of the man, and he brought her to the man.

23The man said,

"This is now bone of my bones
  and flesh of my flesh;

she shall be called 'woman',
  for she was taken out of man."

24For this reason a man will leave his father and mother and be united to his wife, and they will become one flesh. 25The man and his wife were both naked, and they felt no shame.

The Fall of Man

3 Now the serpent was more crafty than any of the wild animals the LORD God had made. He said to the woman, "Did God really say, 'You must not eat from any tree in the garden'?"

2The woman said to the serpent, "We may eat fruit from the trees in the garden, 3but God did say, 'You must not eat fruit from the tree that is in the middle of the garden, and you must not touch it, or you will die.'"

4"You will not surely die," the serpent said to the woman. 5"For God knows that when you eat of it your eyes will be opened, and you will be like God, knowing good and evil."

⁶When the woman saw that the fruit of the tree was good for food and pleasing to the eye, and also desirable for gaining wisdom, she took some and ate it. She also gave some to her husband, who was with her, and he ate it. ⁷Then the eyes of both of them were opened, and they realised that they were naked; so they sewed fig leaves together and made coverings for themselves.

⁸Then the man and his wife heard the sound of the LORD God as he was walking in the garden in the cool of the day, and they hid from the LORD God among the trees of the garden. ⁹But the LORD God called to the man, "Where are you?"

¹⁰He answered, "I heard you in the garden, and I was afraid because I was naked; so I hid."

¹¹And he said, "Who told you that you were naked? Have you eaten from the tree from which I commanded you not to eat?"

¹²The man said, "The woman you put here with me—she gave me some fruit from the tree, and I ate it."

¹³Then the LORD God said to the woman, "What is this you have done?"

The woman said, "The serpent deceived me, and I ate."

¹⁴So the LORD God said to the serpent, "Because you have done this,

"Cursed are you above all the
    livestock
    and all the wild animals!
You will crawl on your belly
    and you will eat dust
    all the days of your life.
¹⁵And I will put enmity
    between you and the woman,
    and between your offspring and
        hers;
he will crush your head,
    and you will strike his heel."

¹⁶To the woman he said,

"I will greatly increase your pains in
    childbearing;

with pain you will give birth to
    children.
Your desire will be for your husband,
    and he will rule over you."

¹⁷To Adam he said, "Because you listened to your wife and ate from the tree about which I commanded you, 'You must not eat of it,'

"Cursed is the ground because of
    you;
    through painful toil you will eat of
        it
    all the days of your life.
¹⁸It will produce thorns and thistles for
    you,
    and you will eat the plants of the
        field.
¹⁹By the sweat of your brow
    you will eat your food
until you return to the ground,
    since from it you were taken;
for dust you are
    and to dust you will return."

²⁰Adam named his wife Eve, because she would become the mother of all the living.

²¹The LORD God made garments of skin for Adam and his wife and clothed them. ²²And the LORD God said, "The man has now become like one of us, knowing good and evil. He must not be allowed to reach out his hand and take also from the tree of life and eat, and live for ever." ²³So the LORD God banished him from the Garden of Eden to work the ground from which he had been taken. ²⁴After he drove the man out, he placed on the east side of the Garden of Eden cherubim and a flaming sword flashing back and forth to guard the way to the tree of life.

Cain and Abel

4 Adam lay with his wife Eve, and she became pregnant and gave birth to Cain. She said, "With the help of the LORD I have brought forth a

man." 2Later she gave birth to his brother Abel.

Now Abel kept flocks, and Cain worked the soil. 3In the course of time Cain brought some of the fruits of the soil as an offering to the LORD. 4But Abel brought fat portions from some of the firstborn of his flock. The LORD looked with favour on Abel and his offering, 5but on Cain and his offering he did not look with favour. So Cain was very angry, and his face was downcast.

6Then the LORD said to Cain, "Why are you angry? Why is your face downcast? 7If you do what is right, will you not be accepted? But if you do not do what is right, sin is crouching at your door; it desires to have you, but you must master it."

8Now Cain said to his brother Abel, "Let's go out to the field." And while they were in the field, Cain attacked his brother Abel and killed him.

9Then the LORD said to Cain, "Where is your brother Abel?"

"I don't know," he replied. "Am I my brother's keeper?"

10The LORD said, "What have you done? Listen! Your brother's blood cries out to me from the ground. 11Now you are under a curse and driven from the ground, which opened its mouth to receive your brother's blood from your hand. 12When you work the ground, it will no longer yield its crops for you. You will be a restless wanderer on the earth."

13Cain said to the LORD, "My punishment is more than I can bear. 14Today you are driving me from the land, and I will be hidden from your presence; I will be a restless wanderer on the earth, and whoever finds me will kill me."

15But the LORD said to him, "Not so; if anyone kills Cain, he will suffer vengeance seven times over." Then the LORD put a mark on Cain so that no-one who found him would kill him. 16So Cain went out from the LORD's presence and lived in the land of Nod, east of Eden.

NEW TESTAMENT READING
Matthew 2:1–18

The Visit of the Magi

2 After Jesus was born in Bethlehem in Judea, during the time of King Herod, Magi from the east came to Jerusalem 2and asked, "Where is the one who has been born king of the Jews? We saw his star in the east and have come to worship him."

3When King Herod heard this he was disturbed, and all Jerusalem with him. 4When he had called together all the people's chief priests and teachers of the law, he asked them where the Christ was to be born. 5"In Bethlehem in Judea," they replied, "for this is what the prophet has written:

6"'But you, Bethlehem, in the land of Judah,
    are by no means least among the rulers of Judah;
for out of you will come a ruler
    who will be the shepherd of my people Israel.'"

7Then Herod called the Magi secretly and found out from them the exact time the star had appeared. 8He sent them to Bethlehem and said, "Go and make a careful search for the child. As soon as you find him, report to me, so that I too may go and worship him."

9After they had heard the king, they went on their way, and the star they had seen in the east went ahead of them until it stopped over the place where the child was. 10When they saw the star, they were overjoyed. 11On coming to the house, they saw the child with his mother Mary, and they bowed down and worshipped him. Then they opened their treasures and presented him with gifts of gold and of incense and of myrrh. 12And having been warned in a dream not to go back to Herod, they returned to their country by another route.

The Escape to Egypt

¹³When they had gone, an angel of the Lord appeared to Joseph in a dream. "Get up," he said, "take the child and his mother and escape to Egypt. Stay there until I tell you, for Herod is going to search for the child to kill him."

¹⁴So he got up, took the child and his mother during the night and left for Egypt, ¹⁵where he stayed until the death of Herod. And so was fulfilled what the Lord had said through the prophet: "Out of Egypt I called my son."

¹⁶When Herod realised that he had been outwitted by the Magi, he was furious, and he gave orders to kill all the boys in Bethlehem and its vicinity who were two years old and under, in accordance with the time he had learned from the Magi. ¹⁷Then what was said through the prophet Jeremiah was fulfilled:

¹⁸"A voice is heard in Ramah,
    weeping and great mourning,
Rachel weeping for her children
    and refusing to be comforted,
because they are no more."

READING FROM PSALMS
Psalm 2:1–12

¹Why do the nations conspire
    and the peoples plot in vain?
²The kings of the earth take their
        stand
and the rulers gather together
        against the LORD
    and against his Anointed One.
³"Let us break their chains," they say,
    "and throw off their fetters."

⁴The One enthroned in heaven
        laughs;
    the Lord scoffs at them.
⁵Then he rebukes them in his anger
    and terrifies them in his wrath,
        saying,
⁶"I have installed my King
    on Zion, my holy hill."

⁷I will proclaim the decree of the LORD:

He said to me, "You are my Son;
    today I have become your Father.
⁸Ask of me,
    and I will make the nations your
        inheritance,
    the ends of the earth your
        possession.
⁹You will rule them with an iron
        sceptre;
    you will dash them to pieces like
        pottery."

¹⁰Therefore, you kings, be wise;
    be warned, you rulers of the earth.
¹¹Serve the LORD with fear
    and rejoice with trembling.
¹²Kiss the Son, lest he be angry
    and you be destroyed in your way,
for his wrath can flare up in a
        moment.
    Blessed are all who take refuge in
        him.

JANUARY 3

OLD TESTAMENT READING
Genesis 4:17–6:22

17Cain lay with his wife, and she became pregnant and gave birth to Enoch. Cain was then building a city, and he named it after his son Enoch. 18To Enoch was born Irad, and Irad was the father of Mehujael, and Mehujael was the father of Methushael, and Methushael was the father of Lamech.

19Lamech married two women, one named Adah and the other Zillah. 20Adah gave birth to Jabal; he was the father of those who live in tents and raise livestock. 21His brother's name was Jubal; he was the father of all who play the harp and flute. 22Zillah also had a son, Tubal-Cain, who forged all kinds of tools out of bronze and iron. Tubal-Cain's sister was Naamah.

23Lamech said to his wives,

"Adah and Zillah, listen to me;
    wives of Lamech, hear my words.
I have killed a man for wounding me,
    a young man for injuring me.
24If Cain is avenged seven times,
    then Lamech seventy-seven
        times."

25Adam lay with his wife again, and she gave birth to a son and named him Seth, saying, "God has granted me another child in place of Abel, since Cain killed him." 26Seth also had a son, and he named him Enosh.

At that time men began to call on the name of the LORD.

From Adam to Noah

5 This is the written account of Adam's line.

When God created man, he made him in the likeness of God. 2He created them male and female and blessed them. And when they were created, he called them "man".

3When Adam had lived 130 years, he had a son in his own likeness, in his own image; and he named him Seth. 4After Seth was born, Adam lived 800 years and had other sons and daughters. 5Altogether, Adam lived 930 years, and then he died.

6When Seth had lived 105 years, he became the father of Enosh. 7And after he became the father of Enosh, Seth lived 807 years and had other sons and daughters. 8Altogether, Seth lived 912 years, and then he died.

9When Enosh had lived 90 years, he became the father of Kenan. 10And after he became the father of Kenan, Enosh lived 815 years and had other sons and daughters. 11Altogether, Enosh lived 905 years, and then he died.

12When Kenan had lived 70 years, he became the father of Mahalalel. 13And after he became the father of Mahalalel, Kenan lived 840 years and had other sons and daughters. 14Altogether, Kenan lived 910 years, and then he died.

15When Mahalalel had lived 65 years, he became the father of Jared. 16And after he became the father of Jared, Mahalalel lived 830 years and had other sons and daughters. 17Altogether, Mahalalel lived 895 years, and then he died.

18When Jared had lived 162 years, he became the father of Enoch. 19And after he became the father of Enoch, Jared lived 800 years and had other sons and daughters. 20Altogether, Jared lived 962 years, and then he died.

21When Enoch had lived 65 years, he became the father of Methuselah. 22And after he became the father of Methuselah, Enoch walked with God 300 years and had other sons and daughters. 23Altogether, Enoch lived 365 years. 24Enoch walked with God; then he was no more, because God took him away.

25When Methuselah had lived 187 years, he became the father of Lamech. 26And after he became the father of Lamech, Methuselah lived 782 years and had other sons and daughters. 27Altogether, Methuselah lived 969 years, and then he died.

28When Lamech had lived 182 years, he had a son. 29He named him Noah and said, "He will comfort us in the labour and painful toil of our hands caused by the ground the LORD has cursed." 30After Noah was born, Lamech lived 595 years and had other sons and daughters. 31Altogether, Lamech lived 777 years, and then he died.

32After Noah was 500 years old, he became the father of Shem, Ham and Japheth.

The Flood

6 When men began to increase in number on the earth and daughters were born to them, 2the sons of God saw that the daughters of men were beautiful, and they married any of them they chose. 3Then the LORD said, "My Spirit will not contend with man for ever, for he is mortal; his days will be a hundred and twenty years."

4The Nephilim were on the earth in those days—and also afterwards—when the sons of God went to the daughters of men and had children by them. They were the heroes of old, men of renown.

5The LORD saw how great man's wickedness on the earth had become, and that every inclination of the thoughts of his heart was only evil all the time. 6The LORD was grieved that he had made man on the earth, and his heart was filled with pain. 7So the LORD said, "I will wipe mankind, whom I have created, from the face of the earth—men and animals, and creatures that move along the ground, and birds of the air—for I am grieved that I have made them." 8But Noah found favour in the eyes of the LORD.

9This is the account of Noah.

Noah was a righteous man, blameless among the people of his time, and he walked with God. 10Noah had three sons: Shem, Ham and Japheth.

11Now the earth was corrupt in God's sight and was full of violence. 12God saw how corrupt the earth had become, for all the people on earth had corrupted their ways. 13So God said to Noah, "I am going to put an end to all people, for the earth is filled with violence because of them. I am surely going to destroy both them and the earth. 14So make yourself an ark of cypress wood; make rooms in it and coat it with pitch inside and out. 15This is how you are to build it: The ark is to be 450 feet long, 75 feet wide and 45 feet high. 16Make a roof for it and finish the ark to within 18 inches of the top. Put a door in the side of the ark and make lower, middle and upper decks. 17I am going to bring floodwaters on the earth to destroy all life under the heavens, every creature that has the breath of life in it. Everything on earth will perish. 18But I will establish my covenant with you, and you will enter the ark—you and your sons and your wife and your sons' wives with you. 19You are to bring into the ark two of all living creatures, male and female, to keep them alive with you. 20Two of every kind of bird, of every kind of animal and of every kind of creature that moves along the ground will come to you to be kept alive. 21You are to take every kind of food that is to be eaten and store it away as food for you and for them."

22Noah did everything just as God commanded him.

NEW TESTAMENT READING
Matthew 2:19–3:17

The Return to Nazareth

19After Herod died, an angel of the Lord appeared in a dream to Joseph in Egypt 20and said, "Get up, take the child and his mother and go to the land of Israel, for those who were trying to take the child's life are dead."

²¹So he got up, took the child and his mother and went to the land of Israel. ²²But when he heard that Archelaus was reigning in Judea in place of his father Herod, he was afraid to go there. Having been warned in a dream, he withdrew to the district of Galilee, ²³and he went and lived in a town called Nazareth. So was fulfilled what was said through the prophets: "He will be called a Nazarene."

John the Baptist Prepares the Way

3 In those days John the Baptist came, preaching in the Desert of Judea ²and saying, "Repent, for the kingdom of heaven is near." ³This is he who was spoken of through the prophet Isaiah:

"A voice of one calling in the desert,
   'Prepare the way for the Lord,
      make straight paths for him.'"

⁴John's clothes were made of camel's hair, and he had a leather belt round his waist. His food was locusts and wild honey. ⁵People went out to him from Jerusalem and all Judea and the whole region of the Jordan. ⁶Confessing their sins, they were baptised by him in the Jordan River.

⁷But when he saw many of the Pharisees and Sadducees coming to where he was baptising, he said to them: "You brood of vipers! Who warned you to flee from the coming wrath? ⁸Produce fruit in keeping with repentance. ⁹And do not think you can say to yourselves, 'We have Abraham as our father.' I tell you that out of these stones God can raise up children for Abraham. ¹⁰The axe is already at the root of the trees, and every tree that does not produce good fruit will be cut down and thrown into the fire.

¹¹"I baptise you with water for repentance. But after me will come one who is more powerful than I, whose sandals I am not fit to carry. He will baptise you with the Holy Spirit and with fire. ¹²His winnowing fork is in his hand, and he will clear his threshing-floor, gathering his wheat into the barn and burning up the chaff with unquenchable fire."

The Baptism of Jesus

¹³Then Jesus came from Galilee to the Jordan to be baptised by John. ¹⁴But John tried to deter him, saying, "I need to be baptised by you, and do you come to me?"

¹⁵Jesus replied, "Let it be so now; it is proper for us to do this to fulfil all righteousness." Then John consented.

¹⁶As soon as Jesus was baptised, he went up out of the water. At that moment heaven was opened, and he saw the Spirit of God descending like a dove and lighting on him. ¹⁷And a voice from heaven said, "This is my Son, whom I love; with him I am well pleased."

READING FROM PSALMS
Psalm 3:1–8

A psalm of David. When he fled from his son Absalom.

¹O Lord, how many are my foes!
   How many rise up against me!
²Many are saying of me,
   "God will not deliver him."
                  Selah

³But you are a shield around me, O
      Lord;
   you bestow glory on me and lift up
      my head.
⁴To the Lord I cry aloud,
   and he answers me from his holy
      hill.   *Selah*

⁵I lie down and sleep;
   I wake again, because the Lord
      sustains me.

6I will not fear the tens of thousands
  drawn up against me on every
      side.

7Arise, O LORD!
  Deliver me, O my God!

Strike all my enemies on the jaw;
  break the teeth of the wicked.

8From the LORD comes deliverance.
  May your blessing be on your
      people.   *Selah*

JANUARY 4   DAY 4

OLD TESTAMENT READING
Genesis 7:1–9:17

7 The LORD then said to Noah, "Go into the ark, you and your whole family, because I have found you righteous in this generation. 2Take with you seven of every kind of clean animal, a male and its mate, and two of every kind of unclean animal, a male and its mate, 3and also seven of every kind of bird, male and female, to keep their various kinds alive throughout the earth. 4Seven days from now I will send rain on the earth for forty days and forty nights, and I will wipe from the face of the earth every living creature I have made."

5And Noah did all that the LORD commanded him.

6Noah was six hundred years old when the floodwaters came on the earth. 7And Noah and his sons and his wife and his sons' wives entered the ark to escape the waters of the flood. 8Pairs of clean and unclean animals, of birds and of all creatures that move along the ground, 9male and female, came to Noah and entered the ark, as God had commanded Noah. 10And after the seven days the floodwaters came on the earth.

11In the six hundredth year of Noah's life, on the seventeenth day of the second month—on that day all the springs of the great deep burst forth, and the floodgates of the heavens were opened. 12And rain fell on the earth for forty days and forty nights.

13On that very day Noah and his sons, Shem, Ham and Japheth, together with his wife and the wives of his three sons, entered the ark. 14They had with them every wild animal according to its kind, all livestock according to their kinds, every creature that moves along the ground according to its kind and every bird according to its kind, everything with wings. 15Pairs of all creatures that have the breath of life in them came to Noah and entered the ark. 16The animals going in were male and female of every living thing, as God had commanded Noah. Then the LORD shut him in.

17For forty days the flood kept coming on the earth, and as the waters increased they lifted the ark high above the earth. 18The waters rose and increased greatly on the earth, and the ark floated on the surface of the water. 19They rose greatly on the earth, and all the high mountains under the entire heavens were covered. 20The waters rose and covered the mountains to a depth of more than twenty feet. 21Every living thing that moved on the earth perished—birds, livestock, wild animals, all the creatures that swarm over the earth, and all mankind. 22Everything on dry land that had the breath of life in its nostrils died. 23Every living thing on the face of the earth was wiped out; men and animals and the creatures that move along the ground and the birds of the air were wiped from the earth. Only Noah was left, and those with him in the ark.

24The waters flooded the earth for a hundred and fifty days.

8 But God remembered Noah and all the wild animals and the livestock that were with him in the ark, and he sent a wind over the earth, and the waters receded. 2Now the springs of the deep and the floodgates of the heavens had been closed, and the rain had stopped falling from the sky. 3The water receded steadily from the earth. At the end of the hundred and fifty days the water had gone down, 4and on the seventeenth day of the seventh month the ark came to rest on the mountains of Ararat. 5The waters continued to recede until the tenth month, and on the first day of the tenth month the tops of the mountains became visible.

6After forty days Noah opened the window he had made in the ark 7and sent out a raven, and it kept flying back and forth until the water had dried up from the earth. 8Then he sent out a dove to see if the water had receded from the surface of the ground. 9But the dove could find no place to set its feet because there was water over all the surface of the earth; so it returned to Noah in the ark. He reached out his hand and took the dove and brought it back to himself in the ark. 10He waited seven more days and again sent out the dove from the ark. 11When the dove returned to him in the evening, there in its beak was a freshly plucked olive leaf! Then Noah knew that the water had receded from the earth. 12He waited seven more days and sent the dove out again, but this time it did not return to him.

13By the first day of the first month of Noah's six hundred and first year, the water had dried up from the earth. Noah then removed the covering from the ark and saw that the surface of the ground was dry. 14By the twenty-seventh day of the second month the earth was completely dry.

15Then God said to Noah, 16"Come out of the ark, you and your wife and your sons and their wives. 17Bring out every kind of living creature that is with you—the birds, the animals, and all the creatures that move along the ground —so they can multiply on the earth and be fruitful and increase in number upon it."

18So Noah came out, together with his sons and his wife and his sons' wives. 19All the animals and all the creatures that move along the ground and all the birds—everything that moves on the earth—came out of the ark, one kind after another.

20Then Noah built an altar to the LORD and, taking some of all the clean animals and clean birds, he sacrificed burnt offerings on it. 21The LORD smelled the pleasing aroma and said in his heart: "Never again will I curse the ground because of man, even though every inclination of his heart is evil from childhood. And never again will I destroy all living creatures, as I have done.

22"As long as the earth endures,
  seedtime and harvest,
  cold and heat,
  summer and winter,
  day and night
  will never cease."

God's Covenant With Noah

9 Then God blessed Noah and his sons, saying to them, "Be fruitful and increase in number and fill the earth. 2The fear and dread of you will fall upon all the beasts of the earth and all the birds of the air, upon every creature that moves along the ground, and upon all the fish of the sea; they are given into your hands. 3Everything that lives and moves will be food for you. Just as I gave you the green plants, I now give you everything.

4"But you must not eat meat that has its lifeblood still in it. 5And for your lifeblood I will surely demand an accounting. I will demand an accounting from every animal. And from each man, too, I will demand an accounting for the life of his fellow man.

6"Whoever sheds the blood of man,
by man shall his blood be shed;
for in the image of God
has God made man.

7As for you, be fruitful and increase in number; multiply on the earth and increase upon it."

8Then God said to Noah and to his sons with him: 9"I now establish my covenant with you and with your descendants after you 10and with every living creature that was with you—the birds, the livestock and all the wild animals, all those that came out of the ark with you—every living creature on earth. 11I establish my covenant with you: Never again will all life be cut off by the waters of a flood; never again will there be a flood to destroy the earth."

12And God said, "This is the sign of the covenant I am making between me and you and every living creature with you, a covenant for all generations to come: 13I have set my rainbow in the clouds, and it will be the sign of the covenant between me and the earth. 14Whenever I bring clouds over the earth and the rainbow appears in the clouds, 15I will remember my covenant between me and you and all living creatures of every kind. Never again will the waters become a flood to destroy all life. 16Whenever the rainbow appears in the clouds, I will see it and remember the everlasting covenant between God and all living creatures of every kind on the earth."

17So God said to Noah, "This is the sign of the covenant I have established between me and all life on the earth."

NEW TESTAMENT READING
Matthew 4:1–22

The Temptation of Jesus

4 Then Jesus was led by the Spirit into the desert to be tempted by the devil. 2After fasting for forty days and forty nights, he was hungry. 3The tempter came to him and said, "If you are the Son of God, tell these stones to become bread."

4Jesus answered, "It is written: 'Man does not live on bread alone, but on every word that comes from the mouth of God.'"

5Then the devil took him to the holy city and had him stand on the highest point of the temple. 6"If you are the Son of God," he said, "throw yourself down. For it is written:

" 'He will command his angels
concerning you,
and they will lift you up in their
hands,
so that you will not strike your foot
against a stone.'"

7Jesus answered him, "It is also written: 'Do not put the Lord your God to the test.'"

8Again, the devil took him to a very high mountain and showed him all the kingdoms of the world and their splendour. 9"All this I will give you," he said, "if you will bow down and worship me."

10Jesus said to him, "Away from me, Satan! For it is written: 'Worship the Lord your God, and serve him only.'"

11Then the devil left him, and angels came and attended him.

Jesus Begins to Preach

12When Jesus heard that John had been put in prison, he returned to Galilee. 13Leaving Nazareth, he went and lived in Capernaum, which was by the lake in the area of Zebulun and Naphtali—14to fulfil what was said through the prophet Isaiah:

15"Land of Zebulun and land of
Naphtali,
the way to the sea, along the
Jordan,
Galilee of the Gentiles—

[16]the people living in darkness
    have seen a great light;
on those living in the land of the
        shadow of death
    a light has dawned."

[17]From that time on Jesus began to
preach, "Repent, for the kingdom of
heaven is near."

The Calling of the First Disciples

[18]As Jesus was walking beside the Sea
of Galilee, he saw two brothers, Simon
called Peter and his brother Andrew.
They were casting a net into the lake,
for they were fishermen. [19]"Come, follow me," Jesus said, "and I will make
you fishers of men." [20]At once they left
their nets and followed him.

[21]Going on from there, he saw two
other brothers, James son of Zebedee
and his brother John. They were in a
boat with their father Zebedee, preparing their nets. Jesus called them,
[22]and immediately they left the boat and
their father and followed him.

READING FROM PROVERBS
Proverbs 1:1–7

Prologue: Purpose and Theme

1 The proverbs of Solomon son of
  David, king of Israel:

[2]for attaining wisdom and discipline;
    for understanding words of insight;
[3]for acquiring a disciplined and
        prudent life,
    doing what is right and just and
        fair;
[4]for giving prudence to the simple,
    knowledge and discretion to the
        young—
[5]let the wise listen and add to their
        learning,
    and let the discerning get
        guidance—
[6]for understanding proverbs and
        parables,
    the sayings and riddles of the wise.

[7]The fear of the LORD is the beginning
        of knowledge,
    but fools despise wisdom and
        discipline.

DAY 5

JANUARY 5

OLD TESTAMENT READING
Genesis 9:18—11:9

The Sons of Noah

[18]The sons of Noah who came out of
the ark were Shem, Ham and Japheth.
(Ham was the father of Canaan.)
[19]These were the three sons of Noah,
and from them came the people who
were scattered over the earth.

[20]Noah, a man of the soil, proceeded
to plant a vineyard. [21]When he drank
some of its wine, he became drunk and
lay uncovered inside his tent. [22]Ham,
the father of Canaan, saw his father's

nakedness and told his two brothers
outside. [23]But Shem and Japheth took a
garment and laid it across their shoulders; then they walked in backwards
and covered their father's nakedness.
Their faces were turned the other way
so that they would not see their father's
nakedness.

[24]When Noah awoke from his wine
and found out what his youngest son
had done to him, [25]he said,

"Cursed be Canaan!
    The lowest of slaves
        will he be to his brothers."

26He also said,

"Blessed be the LORD, the God of
    Shem!
  May Canaan be the slave of Shem.
27May God extend the territory of
    Japheth;
  may Japheth live in the tents of
    Shem,
  and may Canaan be his slave."

28After the flood Noah lived 350
years. 29Altogether, Noah lived 950
years, and then he died.

The Table of Nations

10 This is the account of Shem,
Ham and Japheth, Noah's sons,
who themselves had sons after the
flood.

The Japhethites

2The sons of Japheth:
  Gomer, Magog, Madai, Javan,
  Tubal, Meshech and Tiras.
3The sons of Gomer:
  Ashkenaz, Riphath and Togarmah.
4The sons of Javan:
  Elishah, Tarshish, the Kittim
  and the Rodanim. 5(From these
  the maritime peoples spread out
  into their territories by their
  clans within their nations, each
  with its own language.)

The Hamites

6The sons of Ham:
  Cush, Mizraim, Put and Canaan.
7The sons of Cush:
  Seba, Havilah, Sabtah, Raamah
  and Sabteca.
The sons of Raamah:
  Sheba and Dedan.

8Cush was the father of Nimrod, who
grew to be a mighty warrior on the
earth. 9He was a mighty hunter before
the LORD; that is why it is said, "Like
Nimrod, a mighty hunter before the
LORD." 10The first centres of his kingdom were Babylon, Erech, Akkad and
Calneh, in Shinar. 11From that land he
went to Assyria, where he built
Nineveh, Rehoboth Ir, Calah 12and Re-
sen, which is between Nineveh and
Calah; that is the great city.

13Mizraim was the father of
  the Ludites, Anamites, Lehabites, Naphtuhites, 14Pathrusites,
  Casluhites (from whom the Philistines came) and Caphtorites.
15Canaan was the father of
  Sidon his firstborn, and of the
  Hittites, 16Jebusites, Amorites,
  Girgashites, 17Hivites, Arkites,
  Sinites, 18Arvadites, Zemarites
  and Hamathites.

Later the Canaanite clans scattered
19and the borders of Canaan reached
from Sidon towards Gerar as far as
Gaza, and then towards Sodom,
Gomorrah, Admah and Zeboiim, as far
as Lasha.

20These are the sons of Ham by their
clans and languages, in their territories
and nations.

The Semites

21Sons were also born to Shem,
whose older brother was Japheth; Shem
was the ancestor of all the sons of Eber.

22The sons of Shem:
  Elam, Asshur, Arphaxad, Lud
  and Aram.
23The sons of Aram:
  Uz, Hul, Gether and Meshech.
24Arphaxad was the father of Shelah,
  and Shelah the father of Eber.
25Two sons were born to Eber:
  One was named Peleg, because
  in his time the earth was divided;
  his brother was named Joktan.
26Joktan was the father of
  Almodad, Sheleph, Hazarmaveth, Jerah, 27Hadoram,

Uzal, Diklah, 28Obal, Abimael, Sheba, 29Ophir, Havilah and Jobab. All these were sons of Joktan.

30The region where they lived stretched from Mesha towards Sephar, in the eastern hill country.

31These are the sons of Shem by their clans and languages, in their territories and nations.

32These are the clans of Noah's sons, according to their lines of descent, within their nations. From these the nations spread out over the earth after the flood.

The Tower of Babel

11 Now the whole world had one language and a common speech. 2As men moved eastward, they found a plain in Shinar and settled there.

3They said to each other, "Come, let's make bricks and bake them thoroughly." They used brick instead of stone, and bitumen for mortar. 4Then they said, "Come, let us build ourselves a city, with a tower that reaches to the heavens, so that we may make a name for ourselves and not be scattered over the face of the whole earth."

5But the LORD came down to see the city and the tower that the men were building. 6The LORD said, "If as one people speaking the same language they have begun to do this, then nothing they plan to do will be impossible for them. 7Come, let us go down and confuse their language so they will not understand each other."

8So the LORD scattered them from there over all the earth, and they stopped building the city. 9That is why it was called Babel—because there the LORD confused the language of the whole world. From there the LORD scattered them over the face of the whole earth.

NEW TESTAMENT READING
Matthew 4:23–5:20

Jesus Heals the Sick

23Jesus went throughout Galilee, teaching in their synagogues, preaching the good news of the kingdom, and healing every disease and sickness among the people. 24News about him spread all over Syria, and people brought to him all who were ill with various diseases, those suffering severe pain, the demon-possessed, those having seizures, and the paralysed, and he healed them. 25Large crowds from Galilee, the Decapolis, Jerusalem, Judea and the region across the Jordan followed him.

The Beatitudes

5 Now when he saw the crowds, he went up on a mountainside and sat down. His disciples came to him, 2and he began to teach them, saying:

3"Blessed are the poor in spirit,
   for theirs is the kingdom of
     heaven.
4Blessed are those who mourn,
   for they will be comforted.
5Blessed are the meek,
   for they will inherit the earth.
6Blessed are those who hunger and
    thirst for righteousness,
   for they will be filled.
7Blessed are the merciful,
   for they will be shown mercy.
8Blessed are the pure in heart,
   for they will see God.
9Blessed are the peacemakers,
   for they will be called sons of God.
10Blessed are those who are persecuted
    because of righteousness,
   for theirs is the kingdom of heaven.

11"Blessed are you when people insult you, persecute you and falsely say all kinds of evil against you because of me. 12Rejoice and be glad, because great is your reward in heaven, for in the same way they persecuted the prophets who were before you.

Salt and Light

13"You are the salt of the earth. But if the salt loses its saltiness, how can it be made salty again? It is no longer good for anything, except to be thrown out and trampled by men. 14"You are the light of the world. A city on a hill cannot be hidden. 15Neither do people light a lamp and put it under a bowl. Instead they put it on its stand, and it gives light to everyone in the house. 16In the same way, let your light shine before men, that they may see your good deeds and praise your Father in heaven.

The Fulfilment of the Law

17"Do not think that I have come to abolish the Law or the Prophets; I have not come to abolish them but to fulfil them. 18I tell you the truth, until heaven and earth disappear, not the smallest letter, not the least stroke of a pen, will by any means disappear from the Law until everything is accomplished. 19Anyone who breaks one of the least of these commandments and teaches others to do the same will be called least in the kingdom of heaven, but whoever practises and teaches these commands will be called great in the kingdom of heaven. 20For I tell you that unless your righteousness surpasses that of the Pharisees and the teachers of the law, you will certainly not enter the kingdom of heaven.

READING FROM PSALMS
Psalm 4:1–8

For the director of music. With stringed instruments. A psalm of David.

1Answer me when I call to you,
    O my righteous God.
Give me relief from my distress;
    be merciful to me and hear my prayer.

2How long, O men, will you turn my glory into shame?
    How long will you love delusions and seek false gods?   *Selah*
3Know that the LORD has set apart the godly for himself;
    the LORD will hear when I call to him.

4In your anger do not sin;
    when you are on your beds,
    search your hearts and be silent.
                                            Selah
5Offer right sacrifices
    and trust in the LORD.

6Many are asking, "Who can show us any good?"
    Let the light of your face shine upon us, O LORD.
7You have filled my heart with greater joy
    than when their grain and new wine abound.
8I will lie down and sleep in peace,
    for you alone, O LORD,
    make me dwell in safety.

JANUARY 6

OLD TESTAMENT READING
Genesis 11:10–13:18

From Shem to Abram

10This is the account of Shem.

Two years after the flood, when Shem was 100 years old, he became the father of Arphaxad. 11And after he became the father of Arphaxad, Shem lived 500 years and had other sons and daughters.

12When Arphaxad had lived 35 years, he became the father of Shelah. 13And after he became the father of Shelah, Arphaxad lived 403 years and had other sons and daughters.

14When Shelah had lived 30 years, he became the father of Eber. 15And after he became the father of Eber, Shelah lived 403 years and had other sons and daughters.

16When Eber had lived 34 years, he became the father of Peleg. 17And after he became the father of Peleg, Eber lived 430 years and had other sons and daughters.

18When Peleg had lived 30 years, he became the father of Reu. 19And after he became the father of Reu, Peleg lived 209 years and had other sons and daughters.

20When Reu had lived 32 years, he became the father of Serug. 21And after he became the father of Serug, Reu lived 207 years and had other sons and daughters.

22When Serug had lived 30 years, he became the father of Nahor. 23And after he became the father of Nahor, Serug lived 200 years and had other sons and daughters.

24When Nahor had lived 29 years, he became the father of Terah. 25And after he became the father of Terah, Nahor lived 119 years and had other sons and daughters.

26After Terah had lived 70 years, he became the father of Abram, Nahor and Haran.

27This is the account of Terah.

Terah became the father of Abram, Nahor and Haran. And Haran became the father of Lot. 28While his father Terah was still alive, Haran died in Ur of the Chaldeans, in the land of his birth. 29Abram and Nahor both married. The name of Abram's wife was Sarai, and the name of Nahor's wife was Milcah; she was the daughter of Haran, the father of both Milcah and Iscah. 30Now Sarai was barren; she had no children.

31Terah took his son Abram, his grandson Lot son of Haran, and his daughter-in-law Sarai, the wife of his son Abram, and together they set out from Ur of the Chaldeans to go to Canaan. But when they came to Haran, they settled there.

32Terah lived 205 years, and he died in Haran.

The Call of Abram

12 The LORD had said to Abram, "Leave your country, your people and your father's household and go to the land I will show you.

2"I will make you into a great nation
    and I will bless you;
I will make your name great,
    and you will be a blessing.
3I will bless those who bless you,
    and whoever curses you I will
        curse;
and all peoples on earth
    will be blessed through you."

4So Abram left, as the LORD had told him; and Lot went with him. Abram was seventy-five years old when he set out from Haran. 5He took his wife

Sarai, his nephew Lot, all the possessions they had accumulated and the people they had acquired in Haran, and they set out for the land of Canaan, and they arrived there.

6Abram travelled through the land as far as the site of the great tree of Moreh at Shechem. At that time the Canaanites were in the land. 7The LORD appeared to Abram and said, "To your offspring I will give this land." So he built an altar there to the LORD, who had appeared to him.

8From there he went on towards the hills east of Bethel and pitched his tent, with Bethel on the west and Ai on the east. There he built an altar to the LORD and called on the name of the LORD. 9Then Abram set out and continued towards the Negev.

Abram in Egypt

10Now there was a famine in the land, and Abram went down to Egypt to live there for a while because the famine was severe. 11As he was about to enter Egypt, he said to his wife Sarai, "I know what a beautiful woman you are. 12When the Egyptians see you, they will say, 'This is his wife.' Then they will kill me but will let you live. 13Say you are my sister, so that I will be treated well for your sake and my life will be spared because of you."

14When Abram came to Egypt, the Egyptians saw that she was a very beautiful woman. 15And when Pharaoh's officials saw her, they praised her to Pharaoh, and she was taken into his palace. 16He treated Abram well for her sake, and Abram acquired sheep and cattle, male and female donkeys, menservants and maidservants, and camels.

17But the LORD inflicted serious diseases on Pharaoh and his household because of Abram's wife Sarai. 18So Pharaoh summoned Abram. "What have you done to me?" he said. "Why didn't you tell me she was your wife? 19Why did you say, 'She is my sister,' so that I took her to be my wife? Now then,

here is your wife. Take her and go!" 20Then Pharaoh gave orders about Abram to his men, and they sent him on his way, with his wife and everything he had.

Abram and Lot Separate

13 So Abram went up from Egypt to the Negev, with his wife and everything he had, and Lot went with him. 2Abram had become very wealthy in livestock and in silver and gold.

3From the Negev he went from place to place until he came to Bethel, to the place between Bethel and Ai where his tent had been earlier 4and where he had first built an altar. There Abram called on the name of the LORD.

5Now Lot, who was moving about with Abram, also had flocks and herds and tents. 6But the land could not support them while they stayed together, for their possessions were so great that they were not able to stay together. 7And quarrelling arose between Abram's herdsmen and the herdsmen of Lot. The Canaanites and Perizzites were also living in the land at that time.

8So Abram said to Lot, "Let's not have any quarrelling between you and me, or between your herdsmen and mine, for we are brothers. 9Is not the whole land before you? Let's part company. If you go to the left, I'll go to the right; if you go to the right, I'll go to the left."

10Lot looked up and saw that the whole plain of the Jordan was well watered, like the garden of the LORD, like the land of Egypt, towards Zoar. (This was before the LORD destroyed Sodom and Gomorrah.) 11So Lot chose for himself the whole plain of the Jordan and set out towards the east. The two men parted company: 12Abram lived in the land of Canaan, while Lot lived among the cities of the plain and pitched his tents near Sodom. 13Now the men of Sodom were wicked and were sinning greatly against the LORD.

14The LORD said to Abram after Lot

had parted from him, "Lift up your eyes from where you are and look north and south, east and west. 15All the land that you see I will give to you and your offspring for ever. 16I will make your offspring like the dust of the earth, so that if anyone could count the dust, then your offspring could be counted. 17Go, walk through the length and breadth of the land, for I am giving it to you."

18So Abram moved his tents and went to live near the great trees of Mamre at Hebron, where he built an altar to the LORD.

NEW TESTAMENT READING
Matthew 5:21–42

Murder

21"You have heard that it was said to the people long ago, 'Do not murder, and anyone who murders will be subject to judgment.' 22But I tell you that anyone who is angry with his brother will be subject to judgment. Again, anyone who says to his brother, 'Raca,' is answerable to the Sanhedrin. But anyone who says, 'You fool!' will be in danger of the fire of hell.

23"Therefore, if you are offering your gift at the altar and there remember that your brother has something against you, 24leave your gift there in front of the altar. First go and be reconciled to your brother; then come and offer your gift.

25"Settle matters quickly with your adversary who is taking you to court. Do it while you are still with him on the way, or he may hand you over to the judge, and the judge may hand you over to the officer, and you may be thrown into prison. 26I tell you the truth, you will not get out until you have paid the last penny.

Adultery

27"You have heard that it was said, 'Do not commit adultery.' 28But I tell you that anyone who looks at a woman lustfully has already committed adultery with her in his heart. 29If your right eye causes you to sin, gouge it out and throw it away. It is better for you to lose one part of your body than for your whole body to be thrown into hell. 30And if your right hand causes you to sin, cut it off and throw it away. It is better for you to lose one part of your body than for your whole body to go into hell.

Divorce

31"It has been said, 'Anyone who divorces his wife must give her a certificate of divorce.' 32But I tell you that anyone who divorces his wife, except for marital unfaithfulness, causes her to become an adulteress, and anyone who marries the divorced woman commits adultery.

Oaths

33"Again, you have heard that it was said to the people long ago, 'Do not break your oath, but keep the oaths you have made to the Lord.' 34But I tell you, Do not swear at all: either by heaven, for it is God's throne; 35or by the earth, for it is his footstool; or by Jerusalem, for it is the city of the Great King. 36And do not swear by your head, for you cannot make even one hair white or black. 37Simply let your 'Yes' be 'Yes', and your 'No', 'No'; anything beyond this comes from the evil one.

An Eye for an Eye

38"You have heard that it was said, 'Eye for eye, and tooth for tooth.' 39But I tell you, Do not resist an evil person. If someone strikes you on the right cheek, turn to him the other also. 40And if someone wants to sue you and take your tunic, let him have your cloak as well. 41If someone forces you to go one mile, go with him two miles. 42Give to the one who asks you, and do not turn away from the one who wants to borrow from you.

READING FROM PSALMS
Psalm 5:1–12

For the director of music. For flutes.
A psalm of David.

¹Give ear to my words, O LORD,
    consider my sighing.
²Listen to my cry for help,
    my King and my God,
    for to you I pray.
³In the morning, O LORD, you hear
    my voice;
    in the morning I lay my requests
      before you
    and wait in expectation.

⁴You are not a God who takes
    pleasure in evil;
    with you the wicked cannot dwell.
⁵The arrogant cannot stand in your
    presence;
    you hate all who do wrong.
⁶You destroy those who tell lies;
    bloodthirsty and deceitful men
    the LORD abhors.

⁷But I, by your great mercy,
    will come into your house;
in reverence will I bow down
    towards your holy temple.
⁸Lead me, O LORD, in your
    righteousness
    because of my enemies—
    make straight your way before me.

⁹Not a word from their mouth can be
    trusted;
    their heart is filled with
      destruction.
Their throat is an open grave;
    with their tongue they speak
      deceit.
¹⁰Declare them guilty, O God!
    Let their intrigues be their
      downfall.
Banish them for their many sins,
    for they have rebelled against you.

¹¹But let all who take refuge in you be
    glad;
    let them ever sing for joy.
Spread your protection over them,
    that those who love your name may
      rejoice in you.
¹²For surely, O LORD, you bless the
    righteous;
    you surround them with your
    favour as with a shield.

JANUARY 7   DAY 7

OLD TESTAMENT READING
Genesis 14:1–16:16

Abram Rescues Lot

14 At this time Amraphel king of
Shinar, Arioch king of Ellasar,
Kedorlaomer king of Elam and Tidal
king of Goiim ²went to war against Bera
king of Sodom, Birsha king of Gomorrah, Shinab king of Admah, Shemeber
king of Zeboiim, and the king of Bela
(that is, Zoar). ³All these latter kings
joined forces in the Valley of Siddim
(the Salt Sea). ⁴For twelve years they
had been subject to Kedorlaomer, but
in the thirteenth year they rebelled.

⁵In the fourteenth year, Kedorlaomer and the kings allied with him
went out and defeated the Rephaites in
Ashteroth Karnaim, the Zuzites in
Ham, the Emites in Shaveh Kiriathaim
⁶and the Horites in the hill country of
Seir, as far as El Paran near the desert.
⁷Then they turned back and went to En
Mishpat (that is, Kadesh), and they
conquered the whole territory of the
Amalekites, as well as the Amorites
who were living in Hazezon Tamar.
⁸Then the king of Sodom, the king of

Gomorrah, the king of Admah, the king of Zeboiim and the king of Bela (that is, Zoar) marched out and drew up their battle lines in the Valley of Siddim ⁹against Kedorlaomer king of Elam, Tidal king of Goiim, Amraphel king of Shinar and Arioch king of Ellasar—four kings against five. ¹⁰Now the Valley of Siddim was full of tar pits, and when the kings of Sodom and Gomorrah fled, some of the men fell into them and the rest fled to the hills. ¹¹The four kings seized all the goods of Sodom and Gomorrah and all their food; then they went away. ¹²They also carried off Abram's nephew Lot and his possessions, since he was living in Sodom.

¹³One who had escaped came and reported this to Abram the Hebrew. Now Abram was living near the great trees of Mamre the Amorite, a brother of Eshcol and Aner, all of whom were allied with Abram. ¹⁴When Abram heard that his relative had been taken captive, he called out the 318 trained men born in his household and went in pursuit as far as Dan. ¹⁵During the night Abram divided his men to attack them and he routed them, pursuing them as far as Hobah, north of Damascus. ¹⁶He recovered all the goods and brought back his relative Lot and his possessions, together with the women and the other people.

¹⁷After Abram returned from defeating Kedorlaomer and the kings allied with him, the king of Sodom came out to meet him in the Valley of Shaveh (that is, the King's Valley).

¹⁸Then Melchizedek king of Salem brought out bread and wine. He was priest of God Most High, ¹⁹and he blessed Abram, saying,

> "Blessed be Abram by God Most
>   High,
>   Creator of heaven and earth.
> ²⁰And blessed be God Most High,
>   who delivered your enemies into
>   your hand."

Then Abram gave him a tenth of everything.

²¹The king of Sodom said to Abram, "Give me the people and keep the goods for yourself."

²²But Abram said to the king of Sodom, "I have raised my hand to the LORD, God Most High, Creator of heaven and earth, and have taken an oath ²³that I will accept nothing belonging to you, not even a thread or the thong of a sandal, so that you will never be able to say, 'I made Abram rich.' ²⁴I will accept nothing but what my men have eaten and the share that belongs to the men who went with me—to Aner, Eshcol and Mamre. Let them have their share."

God's Covenant With Abram

15 After this, the word of the LORD came to Abram in a vision:

> "Do not be afraid, Abram.
>   I am your shield,
>   your very great reward."

²But Abram said, "O Sovereign LORD, what can you give me since I remain childless and the one who will inherit my estate is Eliezer of Damascus?" ³And Abram said, "You have given me no children; so a servant in my household will be my heir." ⁴Then the word of the LORD came to him: "This man will not be your heir, but a son coming from your own body will be your heir." ⁵He took him outside and said, "Look up at the heavens and count the stars—if indeed you can count them." Then he said to him, "So shall your offspring be."

⁶Abram believed the LORD, and he credited it to him as righteousness.

⁷He also said to him, "I am the LORD, who brought you out of Ur of the Chaldeans to give you this land to take possession of it."

⁸But Abram said, "O Sovereign LORD, how can I know that I shall gain possession of it?"

⁹So the LORD said to him, "Bring me a heifer, a goat and a ram, each three

years old, along with a dove and a young pigeon."

¹⁰Abram brought all these to him, cut them in two and arranged the halves opposite each other; the birds, however, he did not cut in half. ¹¹Then birds of prey came down on the carcasses, but Abram drove them away.

¹²As the sun was setting, Abram fell into a deep sleep, and a thick and dreadful darkness came over him. ¹³Then the LORD said to him, "Know for certain that your descendants will be strangers in a country not their own, and they will be enslaved and ill-treated four hundred years. ¹⁴But I will punish the nation they serve as slaves, and afterwards they will come out with great possessions. ¹⁵You, however, will go to your fathers in peace and be buried at a good old age. ¹⁶In the fourth generation your descendants will come back here, for the sin of the Amorites has not yet reached its full measure."

¹⁷When the sun had set and darkness had fallen, a smoking brazier with a blazing torch appeared and passed between the pieces. ¹⁸On that day the LORD made a covenant with Abram and said, "To your descendants I give this land, from the river of Egypt to the great river, the Euphrates—¹⁹the land of the Kenites, Kenizzites, Kadmonites, ²⁰Hittites, Perizzites, Rephaites, ²¹Amorites, Canaanites, Girgashites and Jebusites."

Hagar and Ishmael

16 Now Sarai, Abram's wife, had borne him no children. But she had an Egyptian maidservant named Hagar; ²so she said to Abram, "The LORD has kept me from having children. Go, sleep with my maidservant; perhaps I can build a family through her."

Abram agreed to what Sarai said. ³So after Abram had been living in Canaan ten years, Sarai his wife took her Egyptian maidservant Hagar and gave her to her husband to be his wife. ⁴He slept with Hagar, and she conceived.

When she knew she was pregnant, she began to despise her mistress. ⁵Then Sarai said to Abram, "You are responsible for the wrong I am suffering. I put my servant in your arms, and now that she knows she is pregnant, she despises me. May the LORD judge between you and me."

⁶"Your servant is in your hands," Abram said. "Do with her whatever you think best." Then Sarai ill-treated Hagar; so she fled from her.

⁷The angel of the LORD found Hagar near a spring in the desert; it was the spring that is beside the road to Shur. ⁸And he said, "Hagar, servant of Sarai, where have you come from, and where are you going?"

"I'm running away from my mistress Sarai," she answered.

⁹Then the angel of the LORD told her, "Go back to your mistress and submit to her." ¹⁰The angel added, "I will so increase your descendants that they will be too numerous to count."

¹¹The angel of the LORD also said to her:

"You are now with child
    and you will have a son.
You shall name him Ishmael,
    for the LORD has heard of your
        misery.
¹²He will be a wild donkey of a man;
    his hand will be against everyone
    and everyone's hand against him,
and he will live in hostility
    towards all his brothers."

¹³She gave this name to the LORD who spoke to her: "You are the God who sees me," for she said, "I have now seen the One who sees me." ¹⁴That is why the well was called Beer Lahai Roi; it is still there, between Kadesh and Bered.

¹⁵So Hagar bore Abram a son, and Abram gave the name Ishmael to the son she had borne. ¹⁶Abram was eighty-six years old when Hagar bore him Ishmael.

NEW TESTAMENT READING
Matthew 5:43–6:24

Love for Enemies

43"You have heard that it was said, 'Love your neighbour and hate your enemy.' 44But I tell you: Love your enemies and pray for those who persecute you, 45that you may be sons of your Father in heaven. He causes his sun to rise on the evil and the good, and sends rain on the righteous and the unrighteous. 46If you love those who love you, what reward will you get? Are not even the tax collectors doing that? 47And if you greet only your brothers, what are you doing more than others? Do not even pagans do that? 48Be perfect, therefore, as your heavenly Father is perfect.

Giving to the Needy

6 "Be careful not to do your 'acts of righteousness' before men, to be seen by them. If you do, you will have no reward from your Father in heaven.

2"So when you give to the needy, do not announce it with trumpets, as the hypocrites do in the synagogues and on the streets, to be honoured by men. I tell you the truth, they have received their reward in full. 3But when you give to the needy, do not let your left hand know what your right hand is doing, 4so that your giving may be in secret. Then your Father, who sees what is done in secret, will reward you.

Prayer

5"And when you pray, do not be like the hypocrites, for they love to pray standing in the synagogues and on the street corners to be seen by men. I tell you the truth, they have received their reward in full. 6But when you pray, go into your room, close the door and pray to your Father, who is unseen. Then your Father, who sees what is done in secret, will reward you. 7And when you pray, do not keep on babbling like pagans, for they think they will be heard because of their many words. 8Do not be like them, for your Father knows what you need before you ask him.

9"This, then, is how you should pray:

"'Our Father in heaven,
  hallowed be your name,
10your kingdom come,
  your will be done
    on earth as it is in heaven.
11Give us today our daily bread.
12Forgive us our debts,
    as we also have forgiven our
      debtors.
13And lead us not into temptation,
  but deliver us from the evil one.'

14For if you forgive men when they sin against you, your heavenly Father will also forgive you. 15But if you do not forgive men their sins, your Father will not forgive your sins.

Fasting

16"When you fast, do not look sombre as the hypocrites, for they disfigure their faces to show men they are fasting. I tell you the truth, they have received their reward in full. 17But when you fast, put oil on your head and wash your face, 18so that it will not be obvious to men that you are fasting, but only to your Father, who is unseen; and your Father, who sees what is done in secret, will reward you.

Treasures in Heaven

19"Do not store up for yourselves treasures on earth, where moth and rust destroy, and where thieves break in and steal. 20But store up for yourselves treasures in heaven, where moth and rust do not destroy, and where thieves do not break in and steal. 21For where your treasure is, there your heart will be also. 22"The eye is the lamp of the body. If your eyes are good, your whole body will be full of light. 23But if your eyes are bad, your whole body will be full of darkness. If then the light within you is darkness, how great is that darkness!

²⁴"No-one can serve two masters. Either he will hate the one and love the other, or he will be devoted to the one and despise the other. You cannot serve both God and Money.

READING FROM PSALMS
Psalm 6:1–10

For the director of music. With stringed instruments. According to sheminith. *A psalm of David.*

¹O LORD, do not rebuke me in your anger
  or discipline me in your wrath.
²Be merciful to me, LORD, for I am faint;
  O LORD, heal me, for my bones are in agony.
³My soul is in anguish.
  How long, O LORD, how long?

⁴Turn, O LORD, and deliver me;
  save me because of your unfailing love.
⁵No-one remembers you when he is dead.
  Who praises you from his grave?

⁶I am worn out from groaning;
  all night long I flood my bed with weeping
  and drench my couch with tears.
⁷My eyes grow weak with sorrow;
  they fail because of all my foes.

⁸Away from me, all you who do evil,
  for the LORD has heard my weeping.
⁹The LORD has heard my cry for mercy;
  the LORD accepts my prayer.
¹⁰All my enemies will be ashamed and dismayed;
  they will turn back in sudden disgrace.

JANUARY 8   DAY 8

OLD TESTAMENT READING
Genesis 17:1–18:33

The Covenant of Circumcision

17 When Abram was ninety-nine years old, the LORD appeared to him and said, "I am God Almighty; walk before me and be blameless. ²I will confirm my covenant between me and you and will greatly increase your numbers."

³Abram fell face down, and God said to him, ⁴"As for me, this is my covenant with you: You will be the father of many nations. ⁵No longer will you be called Abram; your name will be Abraham, for I have made you a father of many nations. ⁶I will make you very fruitful; I will make nations of you, and kings will come from you. ⁷I will establish my covenant as an everlasting covenant between me and you and your descendants after you for the generations to come, to be your God and the God of your descendants after you. ⁸The whole land of Canaan, where you are now an alien, I will give as an everlasting possession to you and your descendants after you; and I will be their God."

⁹Then God said to Abraham, "As for you, you must keep my covenant, you and your descendants after you for the generations to come. ¹⁰This is my covenant with you and your descendants after you, the covenant you are to keep: Every male among you shall be circumcised. ¹¹You are to undergo circumcision, and it will be the sign of the covenant between me and you. ¹²For

the generations to come every male among you who is eight days old must be circumcised, including those born in your household or bought with money from a foreigner—those who are not your offspring. 13Whether born in your household or bought with your money, they must be circumcised. My covenant in your flesh is to be an everlasting covenant. 14Any uncircumcised male, who has not been circumcised in the flesh, will be cut off from his people; he has broken my covenant."

15God also said to Abraham, "As for Sarai your wife, you are no longer to call her Sarai; her name will be Sarah. 16I will bless her and will surely give you a son by her. I will bless her so that she will be the mother of nations; kings of peoples will come from her."

17Abraham fell face down; he laughed and said to himself, "Will a son be born to a man a hundred years old? Will Sarah bear a child at the age of ninety?" 18And Abraham said to God, "If only Ishmael might live under your blessing!"

19Then God said, "Yes, but your wife Sarah will bear you a son, and you will call him Isaac. I will establish my covenant with him as an everlasting covenant for his descendants after him. 20And as for Ishmael, I have heard you: I will surely bless him; I will make him fruitful and will greatly increase his numbers. He will be the father of twelve rulers, and I will make him into a great nation. 21But my covenant I will establish with Isaac, whom Sarah will bear to you by this time next year." 22When he had finished speaking with Abraham, God went up from him.

23On that very day Abraham took his son Ishmael and all those born in his household or bought with his money, every male in his household, and circumcised them, as God told him. 24Abraham was ninety-nine years old when he was circumcised, 25and his son Ishmael was thirteen; 26Abraham and his son Ishmael were both circumcised on that same day. 27And every male in

Abraham's household, including those born in his household or bought from a foreigner, was circumcised with him.

The Three Visitors

18 The LORD appeared to Abraham near the great trees of Mamre while he was sitting at the entrance to his tent in the heat of the day. 2Abraham looked up and saw three men standing nearby. When he saw them, he hurried from the entrance of his tent to meet them and bowed low to the ground.

3He said, "If I have found favour in your eyes, my lord, do not pass your servant by. 4Let a little water be brought, and then you may all wash your feet and rest under this tree. 5Let me get you something to eat, so you can be refreshed and then go on your way—now that you have come to your servant."

"Very well," they answered, "do as you say."

6So Abraham hurried into the tent to Sarah. "Quick," he said, "get three seahs of fine flour and knead it and bake some bread."

7Then he ran to the herd and selected a choice, tender calf and gave it to a servant, who hurried to prepare it. 8He then brought some curds and milk and the calf that had been prepared, and set these before them. While they ate, he stood near them under a tree.

9"Where is your wife Sarah?" they asked him.

"There, in the tent," he said.

10Then the LORD said, "I will surely return to you about this time next year, and Sarah your wife will have a son."

Now Sarah was listening at the entrance to the tent, which was behind him. 11Abraham and Sarah were already old and well advanced in years, and Sarah was past the age of childbearing. 12So Sarah laughed to herself as she thought, "After I am worn out and my master is old, will I now have this pleasure?"

¹³Then the LORD said to Abraham, "Why did Sarah laugh and say, 'Will I really have a child, now that I am old?' ¹⁴Is anything too hard for the LORD? I will return to you at the appointed time next year and Sarah will have a son."

¹⁵Sarah was afraid, so she lied and said, "I did not laugh."

But he said, "Yes, you did laugh."

Abraham Pleads for Sodom

¹⁶When the men got up to leave, they looked down towards Sodom, and Abraham walked along with them to see them on their way. ¹⁷Then the LORD said, "Shall I hide from Abraham what I am about to do? ¹⁸Abraham will surely become a great and powerful nation, and all nations on earth will be blessed through him. ¹⁹For I have chosen him, so that he will direct his children and his household after him to keep the way of the LORD by doing what is right and just, so that the LORD will bring about for Abraham what he has promised him."

²⁰Then the LORD said, "The outcry against Sodom and Gomorrah is so great and their sin so grievous ²¹that I will go down and see if what they have done is as bad as the outcry that has reached me. If not, I will know."

²²The men turned away and went towards Sodom, but Abraham remained standing before the LORD. ²³Then Abraham approached him and said: "Will you sweep away the righteous with the wicked? ²⁴What if there are fifty righteous people in the city? Will you really sweep it away and not spare the place for the sake of the fifty righteous people in it? ²⁵Far be it from you to do such a thing—to kill the righteous with the wicked, treating the righteous and the wicked alike. Far be it from you! Will not the Judge of all the earth do right?"

²⁶The LORD said, "If I find fifty righteous people in the city of Sodom, I will spare the whole place for their sake."

²⁷Then Abraham spoke up again: "Now that I have been so bold as to speak to the Lord, though I am nothing but dust and ashes, ²⁸what if the number of the righteous is five less than fifty? Will you destroy the whole city because of five people?"

"If I find forty-five there," he said, "I will not destroy it."

²⁹Once again he spoke to him, "What if only forty are found there?"

He said, "For the sake of forty, I will not do it."

³⁰Then he said, "May the Lord not be angry, but let me speak. What if only thirty can be found there?"

He answered, "I will not do it if I find thirty there."

³¹Abraham said, "Now that I have been so bold as to speak to the Lord, what if only twenty can be found there?"

He said, "For the sake of twenty, I will not destroy it."

³²Then he said, "May the Lord not be angry, but let me speak just once more. What if only ten can be found there?"

He answered, "For the sake of ten, I will not destroy it."

³³When the LORD had finished speaking with Abraham, he left, and Abraham returned home.

NEW TESTAMENT READING
Matthew 6:25–7:23

Do Not Worry

²⁵"Therefore I tell you, do not worry about your life, what you will eat or drink; or about your body, what you will wear. Is not life more important than food, and the body more important than clothes? ²⁶Look at the birds of the air; they do not sow or reap or store away in barns, and yet your heavenly Father feeds them. Are you not much more valuable than they? ²⁷Who of you by worrying can add a single hour to his life?

²⁸"And why do you worry about clothes? See how the lilies of the field grow. They do not labour or spin. ²⁹Yet

I tell you that not even Solomon in all his splendour was dressed like one of these. ³⁰If that is how God clothes the grass of the field, which is here today and tomorrow is thrown into the fire, will he not much more clothe you, O you of little faith? ³¹So do not worry, saying, 'What shall we eat?' or 'What shall we drink?' or 'What shall we wear?' ³²For the pagans run after all these things, and your heavenly Father knows that you need them. ³³But seek first his kingdom and his righteousness, and all these things will be given to you as well. ³⁴Therefore do not worry about tomorrow, for tomorrow will worry about itself. Each day has enough trouble of its own.

Judging Others

7 "Do not judge, or you too will be judged. ²For in the same way as you judge others, you will be judged, and with the measure you use, it will be measured to you.

³"Why do you look at the speck of sawdust in your brother's eye and pay no attention to the plank in your own eye? ⁴How can you say to your brother, 'Let me take the speck out of your eye,' when all the time there is a plank in your own eye? ⁵You hypocrite, first take the plank out of your own eye, and then you will see clearly to remove the speck from your brother's eye.

⁶"Do not give dogs what is sacred; do not throw your pearls to pigs. If you do, they may trample them under their feet, and then turn and tear you to pieces.

Ask, Seek, Knock

⁷"Ask and it will be given to you; seek and you will find; knock and the door will be opened to you. ⁸For everyone who asks receives; he who seeks finds; and to him who knocks, the door will be opened.

⁹"Which of you, if his son asks for bread, will give him a stone? ¹⁰Or if he asks for a fish, will give him a snake? ¹¹If you, then, though you are evil, know how to give good gifts to your children, how much more will your Father in heaven give good gifts to those who ask him! ¹²So in everything, do to others what you would have them do to you, for this sums up the Law and the Prophets.

The Narrow and Wide Gates

¹³"Enter through the narrow gate. For wide is the gate and broad is the road that leads to destruction, and many enter through it. ¹⁴But small is the gate and narrow the road that leads to life, and only a few find it.

A Tree and Its Fruit

¹⁵"Watch out for false prophets. They come to you in sheep's clothing, but inwardly they are ferocious wolves. ¹⁶By their fruit you will recognise them. Do people pick grapes from thorn-bushes, or figs from thistles? ¹⁷Likewise every good tree bears good fruit, but a bad tree bears bad fruit. ¹⁸A good tree cannot bear bad fruit, and a bad tree cannot bear good fruit. ¹⁹Every tree that does not bear good fruit is cut down and thrown into the fire. ²⁰Thus, by their fruit you will recognise them.

²¹"Not everyone who says to me, 'Lord, Lord,' will enter the kingdom of heaven, but only he who does the will of my Father who is in heaven. ²²Many will say to me on that day, 'Lord, Lord, did we not prophesy in your name, and in your name drive out demons and perform many miracles?' ²³Then I will tell them plainly, 'I never knew you. Away from me, you evildoers!'

READING FROM PROVERBS
Proverbs 1:8–19

Exhortations to Embrace Wisdom
Warning Against Enticement

⁸Listen, my son, to your father's
    instruction

and do not forsake your mother's
teaching.
⁹They will be a garland to grace your
head
and a chain to adorn your neck.

¹⁰My son, if sinners entice you,
do not give in to them.
¹¹If they say, "Come along with us;
let's lie in wait for someone's
blood,
let's waylay some harmless soul;
¹²let's swallow them alive, like the
grave,
and whole, like those who go down
to the pit;
¹³we will get all sorts of valuable things

and fill our houses with plunder;
¹⁴throw in your lot with us,
and we will share a common
purse"—
¹⁵my son, do not go along with them,
do not set foot on their paths;
¹⁶for their feet rush into sin,
they are swift to shed blood.
¹⁷How useless to spread a net
in full view of all the birds!
¹⁸These men lie in wait for their own
blood;
they waylay only themselves!
¹⁹Such is the end of all who go after
ill-gotten gain;
it takes away the lives of those who
get it.

JANUARY 9 DAY 9

OLD TESTAMENT READING
Genesis 19:1–20:18

Sodom and Gomorrah Destroyed

19 The two angels arrived at
Sodom in the evening, and Lot
was sitting in the gateway of the city.
When he saw them, he got up to meet
them and bowed down with his face to
the ground. ²"My lords," he said,
"please turn aside to your servant's
house. You can wash your feet and
spend the night and then go on your way
early in the morning."

"No," they answered, "we will spend
the night in the square."

³But he insisted so strongly that they
did go with him and entered his house.
He prepared a meal for them, baking
bread without yeast, and they ate.
⁴Before they had gone to bed, all the
men from every part of the city of
Sodom—both young and old—
surrounded the house. ⁵They called to
Lot, "Where are the men who came

to you tonight? Bring them out to us so
that we can have sex with them."

⁶Lot went outside to meet them and
shut the door behind him ⁷and said,
"No, my friends. Don't do this wicked
thing. ⁸Look, I have two daughters who
have never slept with a man. Let me
bring them out to you, and you can do
what you like with them. But don't do
anything to these men, for they have
come under the protection of my roof."

⁹"Get out of our way," they replied.
And they said, "This fellow came here
as an alien, and now he wants to play the
judge! We'll treat you worse than
them." They kept bringing pressure on
Lot and moved forward to break down
the door.

¹⁰But the men inside reached out and
pulled Lot back into the house and shut
the door. ¹¹Then they struck the men
who were at the door of the house,
young and old, with blindness so that
they could not find the door.

¹²The two men said to Lot, "Do you
have anyone else here—sons-in-law,
sons or daughters, or anyone else in the

city who belongs to you? Get them out of here, 13because we are going to destroy this place. The outcry to the LORD against its people is so great that he has sent us to destroy it."

14So Lot went out and spoke to his sons-in-law, who were pledged to marry his daughters. He said, "Hurry and get out of this place, because the LORD is about to destroy the city!" But his sons-in-law thought he was joking.

15With the coming of dawn, the angels urged Lot, saying, "Hurry! Take your wife and your two daughters who are here, or you will be swept away when the city is punished."

16When he hesitated, the men grasped his hand and the hands of his wife and of his two daughters and led them safely out of the city, for the LORD was merciful to them. 17As soon as they had brought them out, one of them said, "Flee for your lives! Don't look back, and don't stop anywhere in the plain! Flee to the mountains or you will be swept away!"

18But Lot said to them, "No, my lords, please! 19Your servant has found favour in your eyes, and you have shown great kindness to me in sparing my life. But I can't flee to the mountains; this disaster will overtake me, and I'll die. 20Look, here is a town near enough to run to, and it is small. Let me flee to it—it is very small, isn't it? Then my life will be spared."

21He said to him, "Very well, I will grant this request too; I will not overthrow the town you speak of. 22But flee there quickly, because I cannot do anything until you reach it." (That is why the town was called Zoar.)

23By the time Lot reached Zoar, the sun had risen over the land. 24Then the LORD rained down burning sulphur on Sodom and Gomorrah—from the LORD out of the heavens. 25Thus he overthrew those cities and the entire plain, including all those living in the cities—and also the vegetation in the land. 26But Lot's wife looked back, and she became a pillar of salt.

27Early the next morning Abraham got up and returned to the place where he had stood before the LORD. 28He looked down towards Sodom and Gomorrah, towards all the land of the plain, and he saw dense smoke rising from the land, like smoke from a furnace.

29So when God destroyed the cities of the plain, he remembered Abraham, and he brought Lot out of the catastrophe that overthrew the cities where Lot had lived.

Lot and His Daughters

30Lot and his two daughters left Zoar and settled in the mountains, for he was afraid to stay in Zoar. He and his two daughters lived in a cave. 31One day the older daughter said to the younger, "Our father is old, and there is no man around here to lie with us, as is the custom all over the earth. 32Let's get our father to drink wine and then lie with him and preserve our family line through our father."

33That night they got their father to drink wine, and the older daughter went in and lay with him. He was not aware of it when she lay down or when she got up.

34The next day the older daughter said to the younger, "Last night I lay with my father. Let's get him to drink wine again tonight, and you go in and lie with him so we can preserve our family line through our father." 35So they got their father to drink wine that night also, and the younger daughter went and lay with him. Again he was not aware of it when she lay down or when she got up.

36So both of Lot's daughters became pregnant by their father. 37The older daughter had a son, and she named him Moab; he is the father of the Moabites of today. 38The younger daughter also had a son, and she named him Ben-Ammi; he is the father of the Ammonites of today.

Abraham and Abimelech

20 Now Abraham moved on from there into the region of the Negev and lived between Kadesh and Shur. For a while he stayed in Gerar, 2and there Abraham said of his wife Sarah, "She is my sister." Then Abimelech king of Gerar sent for Sarah and took her.

3But God came to Abimelech in a dream one night and said to him, "You are as good as dead because of the woman you have taken; she is a married woman."

4Now Abimelech had not gone near her, so he said, "Lord, will you destroy an innocent nation? 5Did he not say to me, 'She is my sister,' and didn't she also say, 'He is my brother'? I have done this with a clear conscience and clean hands."

6Then God said to him in the dream, "Yes, I know you did this with a clear conscience, and so I have kept you from sinning against me. That is why I did not let you touch her. 7Now return the man's wife, for he is a prophet, and he will pray for you and you will live. But if you do not return her, you may be sure that you and all yours will die."

8Early the next morning Abimelech summoned all his officials, and when he told them all that had happened, they were very much afraid. 9Then Abimelech called Abraham in and said, "What have you done to us? How have I wronged you that you have brought such great guilt upon me and my kingdom? You have done things to me that should not be done." 10And Abimelech asked Abraham, "What was your reason for doing this?"

11Abraham replied, "I said to myself, 'There is surely no fear of God in this place, and they will kill me because of my wife.' 12Besides, she really is my sister, the daughter of my father though not of my mother; and she became my wife. 13And when God caused me to wander from my father's household, I said to her, 'This is how you can show

your love to me: Everywhere we go, say of me, "He is my brother." '"

14Then Abimelech brought sheep and cattle and male and female slaves and gave them to Abraham, and he returned Sarah his wife to him. 15And Abimelech said, "My land is before you; live wherever you like."

16To Sarah he said, "I am giving your brother a thousand shekels of silver. This is to cover the offence against you before all who are with you; you are completely vindicated."

17Then Abraham prayed to God, and God healed Abimelech, his wife and his slave girls so they could have children again, 18for the LORD had closed up every womb in Abimelech's household because of Abraham's wife Sarah.

NEW TESTAMENT READING
Matthew 7:24–8:22

The Wise and Foolish Builders

24"Therefore everyone who hears these words of mine and puts them into practice is like a wise man who built his house on the rock. 25The rain came down, the streams rose, and the winds blew and beat against that house; yet it did not fall, because it had its foundation on the rock. 26But everyone who hears these words of mine and does not put them into practice is like a foolish man who built his house on sand. 27The rain came down, the streams rose, and the winds blew and beat against that house, and it fell with a great crash."

28When Jesus had finished saying these things, the crowds were amazed at his teaching, 29because he taught as one who had authority, and not as their teachers of the law.

The Man With Leprosy

8 When he came down from the mountainside, large crowds followed him. 2A man with leprosy came and knelt before him and said, "Lord, if you are willing, you can make me clean."

³Jesus reached out his hand and touched the man. "I am willing," he said. "Be clean!" Immediately he was cured of his leprosy. ⁴Then Jesus said to him, "See that you don't tell anyone. But go, show yourself to the priest and offer the gift Moses commanded, as a testimony to them."

The Faith of the Centurion

⁵When Jesus had entered Capernaum, a centurion came to him, asking for help. ⁶"Lord," he said, "my servant lies at home paralysed and in terrible suffering."

⁷Jesus said to him, "I will go and heal him."

⁸The centurion replied, "Lord, I do not deserve to have you come under my roof. But just say the word, and my servant will be healed. ⁹For I myself am a man under authority, with soldiers under me. I tell this one, 'Go,' and he goes; and that one, 'Come,' and he comes. I say to my servant, 'Do this,' and he does it."

¹⁰When Jesus heard this, he was astonished and said to those following him, "I tell you the truth, I have not found anyone in Israel with such great faith. ¹¹I say to you that many will come from the east and the west, and will take their places at the feast with Abraham, Isaac and Jacob in the kingdom of heaven. ¹²But the subjects of the kingdom will be thrown outside, into the darkness, where there will be weeping and gnashing of teeth."

¹³Then Jesus said to the centurion, "Go! It will be done just as you believed it would." And his servant was healed at that very hour.

Jesus Heals Many

¹⁴When Jesus came into Peter's house, he saw Peter's mother-in-law lying in bed with a fever. ¹⁵He touched her hand and the fever left her, and she got up and began to wait on him.

¹⁶When evening came, many who were demon-possessed were brought to him, and he drove out the spirits with a word and healed all the sick. ¹⁷This was to fulfil what was spoken through the prophet Isaiah:

"He took up our infirmities
　　and carried our diseases."

The Cost of Following Jesus

¹⁸When Jesus saw the crowd around him, he gave orders to cross to the other side of the lake. ¹⁹Then a teacher of the law came to him and said, "Teacher, I will follow you wherever you go."

²⁰Jesus replied, "Foxes have holes and birds of the air have nests, but the Son of Man has nowhere to lay his head."

²¹Another disciple said to him, "Lord, first let me go and bury my father."

²²But Jesus told him, "Follow me, and let the dead bury their own dead."

READING FROM PSALMS
Psalm 7:1–9

A *shiggaion* of David, which he sang to the LORD concerning Cush, a Benjamite.

¹O LORD my God, I take refuge in
　　you;
　　save and deliver me from all who
　　　　pursue me,
²or they will tear me like a lion
　　and rip me to pieces with no-one to
　　　　rescue me.

³O LORD my God, if I have done this
　　and there is guilt on my hands—
⁴if I have done evil to him who is at
　　peace with me
　　or without cause have robbed my
　　　　foe—
⁵then let my enemy pursue and
　　overtake me;

let him trample my life to the
   ground
and make me sleep in the dust.
                              Selah

6Arise, O Lord, in your anger;
   rise up against the rage of my
      enemies.
   Awake, my God; decree justice.
7Let the assembled peoples gather
   round you.

Rule over them from on high;
8   let the Lord judge the peoples.
Judge me, O Lord, according to my
      righteousness,
   according to my integrity, O Most
      High.
9O righteous God,
   who searches minds and hearts,
bring to an end the violence of the
      wicked
   and make the righteous secure.

JANUARY 10   DAY 10

OLD TESTAMENT READING
Genesis 21:1–23:20

The Birth of Isaac

21 Now the Lord was gracious to
Sarah as he had said, and the
Lord did for Sarah what he had promised. 2Sarah became pregnant and bore
a son to Abraham in his old age, at the
very time God had promised him.
3Abraham gave the name Isaac to the
son Sarah bore him. 4When his son
Isaac was eight days old, Abraham circumcised him, as God commanded him.
5Abraham was a hundred years old
when his son Isaac was born to him.

6Sarah said, "God has brought me
laughter, and everyone who hears
about this will laugh with me." 7And
she added, "Who would have said to
Abraham that Sarah would nurse children? Yet I have borne him a son in his
old age."

Hagar and Ishmael Sent Away

8The child grew and was weaned, and
on the day Isaac was weaned Abraham
held a great feast. 9But Sarah saw that
the son whom Hagar the Egyptian had
borne to Abraham was mocking, 10and
she said to Abraham, "Get rid of that
slave woman and her son, for that slave

woman's son will never share in the
inheritance with my son Isaac."

11The matter distressed Abraham
greatly because it concerned his son.
12But God said to him, "Do not be so
distressed about the boy and your maidservant. Listen to whatever Sarah tells
you, because it is through Isaac that
your offspring will be reckoned. 13I will
make the son of the maidservant into a
nation also, because he is your
offspring."

14Early the next morning Abraham
took some food and a skin of water and
gave them to Hagar. He set them on her
shoulders and then sent her off with the
boy. She went on her way and wandered
in the desert of Beersheba.

15When the water in the skin was
gone, she put the boy under one of the
bushes. 16Then she went off and sat
down nearby, about a bow-shot away,
for she thought, "I cannot watch the
boy die." And as she sat there nearby,
she began to sob.

17God heard the boy crying, and the
angel of God called to Hagar from
heaven and said to her, "What is the
matter, Hagar? Do not be afraid; God
has heard the boy crying as he lies there.
18Lift the boy up and take him by the
hand, for I will make him into a great
nation."

¹⁹Then God opened her eyes and she saw a well of water. So she went and filled the skin with water and gave the boy a drink.

²⁰God was with the boy as he grew up. He lived in the desert and became an archer. ²¹While he was living in the Desert of Paran, his mother got a wife for him from Egypt.

The Treaty at Beersheba

²²At that time Abimelech and Phicol the commander of his forces said to Abraham, "God is with you in everything you do. ²³Now swear to me here before God that you will not deal falsely with me or my children or my descendants. Show to me and the country where you are living as an alien the same kindness that I have shown to you."

²⁴Abraham said, "I swear it."

²⁵Then Abraham complained to Abimelech about a well of water that Abimelech's servants had seized. ²⁶But Abimelech said, "I don't know who has done this. You did not tell me, and I heard about it only today."

²⁷So Abraham brought sheep and cattle and gave them to Abimelech, and the two men made a treaty. ²⁸Abraham set apart seven ewe lambs from the flock, ²⁹and Abimelech asked Abraham, "What is the meaning of these seven ewe lambs you have set apart by themselves?"

³⁰He replied, "Accept these seven lambs from my hand as a witness that I dug this well."

³¹So that place was called Beersheba, because the two men swore an oath there.

³²After the treaty had been made at Beersheba, Abimelech and Phicol the commander of his forces returned to the land of the Philistines. ³³Abraham planted a tamarisk tree in Beersheba, and there he called upon the name of the LORD, the Eternal God. ³⁴And Abraham stayed in the land of the Philistines for a long time.

Abraham Tested

22 Some time later God tested Abraham. He said to him, "Abraham!"

"Here I am," he replied.

²Then God said, "Take your son, your only son, Isaac, whom you love, and go to the region of Moriah. Sacrifice him there as a burnt offering on one of the mountains I will tell you about."

³Early the next morning Abraham got up and saddled his donkey. He took with him two of his servants and his son Isaac. When he had cut enough wood for the burnt offering, he set out for the place God had told him about. ⁴On the third day Abraham looked up and saw the place in the distance. ⁵He said to his servants, "Stay here with the donkey while I and the boy go over there. We will worship and then we will come back to you."

⁶Abraham took the wood for the burnt offering and placed it on his son Isaac, and he himself carried the fire and the knife. As the two of them went on together, ⁷Isaac spoke up and said to his father Abraham, "Father?"

"Yes, my son?" Abraham replied.

"The fire and wood are here," Isaac said, "but where is the lamb for the burnt offering?"

⁸Abraham answered, "God himself will provide the lamb for the burnt offering, my son." And the two of them went on together.

⁹When they reached the place God had told him about, Abraham built an altar there and arranged the wood on it. He bound his son Isaac and laid him on the altar, on top of the wood. ¹⁰Then he reached out his hand and took the knife to slay his son. ¹¹But the angel of the LORD called out to him from heaven, "Abraham! Abraham!"

"Here I am," he replied.

¹²"Do not lay a hand on the boy," he said. "Do not do anything to him. Now I know that you fear God, because you have not withheld from me your son, your only son."

13Abraham looked up and there in a thicket he saw a ram caught by its horns. He went over and took the ram and sacrificed it as a burnt offering instead of his son. 14So Abraham called that place The LORD Will Provide. And to this day it is said, "On the mountain of the LORD it will be provided."

15The angel of the LORD called to Abraham from heaven a second time 16and said, "I swear by myself, declares the LORD, that because you have done this and have not withheld your son, your only son, 17I will surely bless you and make your descendants as numerous as the stars in the sky and as the sand on the seashore. Your descendants will take possession of the cities of their enemies, 18and through your offspring all nations on earth will be blessed, because you have obeyed me."

19Then Abraham returned to his servants, and they set off together for Beersheba. And Abraham stayed in Beersheba.

Nahor's Sons

20Some time later Abraham was told, "Milcah is also a mother; she has borne sons to your brother Nahor: 21Uz the firstborn, Buz his brother, Kemuel (the father of Aram), 22Kesed, Hazo, Pildash, Jidlaph and Bethuel." 23Bethuel became the father of Rebekah. Milcah bore these eight sons to Abraham's brother Nahor. 24His concubine, whose name was Reumah, also had sons: Tebah, Gaham, Tahash and Maacah.

The Death of Sarah

23 Sarah lived to be a hundred and twenty-seven years old. 2She died at Kiriath Arba (that is, Hebron) in the land of Canaan, and Abraham went to mourn for Sarah and to weep over her.

3Then Abraham rose from beside his dead wife and spoke to the Hittites. He said, 4"I am an alien and a stranger among you. Sell me some property for a burial site here so that I can bury my dead."

5The Hittites replied to Abraham, 6"Sir, listen to us. You are a mighty prince among us. Bury your dead in the choicest of our tombs. None of us will refuse you his tomb for burying your dead."

7Then Abraham rose and bowed down before the people of the land, the Hittites. 8He said to them, "If you are willing to let me bury my dead, then listen to me and intercede with Ephron son of Zohar on my behalf 9so that he will sell me the cave of Machpelah, which belongs to him and is at the end of his field. Ask him to sell it to me for the full price as a burial site among you."

10Ephron the Hittite was sitting among his people and he replied to Abraham in the hearing of all the Hittites who had come to the gate of his city. 11"No, my lord," he said. "Listen to me; I give you the field, and I give you the cave that is in it. I give it to you in the presence of my people. Bury your dead."

12Again Abraham bowed down before the people of the land 13and he said to Ephron in their hearing, "Listen to me, if you will. I will pay the price of the field. Accept it from me so that I can bury my dead there."

14Ephron answered Abraham, 15"Listen to me, my lord; the land is worth four hundred shekels of silver, but what is that between me and you? Bury your dead."

16Abraham agreed to Ephron's terms and weighed out for him the price he had named in the hearing of the Hittites: four hundred shekels of silver, according to the weight current among the merchants.

17So Ephron's field in Machpelah near Mamre—both the field and the cave in it, and all the trees within the borders of the field—was legally made over 18to Abraham as his property in the presence of all the Hittites who had come to the gate of the city. [19]Afterwards Abraham buried his wife Sarah in the cave in the field of Machpelah near Mamre (which is at Hebron) in the land of Canaan. [20]So the field and the cave in it were legally made over to Abraham by the Hittites as a burial site.

NEW TESTAMENT READING
Matthew 8:23—9:13

Jesus Calms the Storm

[23]Then he got into the boat and his disciples followed him. [24]Without warning, a furious storm came up on the lake, so that the waves swept over the boat. But Jesus was sleeping. [25]The disciples went and woke him, saying, "Lord, save us! We're going to drown!"

[26]He replied, "You of little faith, why are you so afraid?" Then he got up and rebuked the winds and the waves, and it was completely calm.

[27]The men were amazed and asked, "What kind of man is this? Even the winds and the waves obey him!"

The Healing of Two Demon-possessed Men

[28]When he arrived at the other side in the region of the Gadarenes, two demon-possessed men coming from the tombs met him. They were so violent that no-one could pass that way. [29]"What do you want with us, Son of God?" they shouted. "Have you come here to torture us before the appointed time?"

[30]Some distance from them a large herd of pigs was feeding. [31]The demons begged Jesus, "If you drive us out, send us into the herd of pigs."

[32]He said to them, "Go!" So they came out and went into the pigs, and the whole herd rushed down the steep bank into the lake and died in the water. [33]Those tending the pigs ran off, went into the town and reported all this, including what had happened to the demon-possessed men. [34]Then the whole town went out to meet Jesus. And when they saw him, they pleaded with him to leave their region.

Jesus Heals a Paralytic

9 Jesus stepped into a boat, crossed over and came to his own town. [2]Some men brought to him a paralytic, lying on a mat. When Jesus saw their faith, he said to the paralytic, "Take heart, son; your sins are forgiven."

[3]At this, some of the teachers of the law said to themselves, "This fellow is blaspheming!"

[4]Knowing their thoughts, Jesus said, "Why do you entertain evil thoughts in your hearts? [5]Which is easier: to say, 'Your sins are forgiven,' or to say, 'Get up and walk'? [6]But so that you may know that the Son of Man has authority on earth to forgive sins. . . ." Then he said to the paralytic, "Get up, take your mat and go home." [7]And the man got up and went home. [8]When the crowd saw this, they were filled with awe; and they praised God, who had given such authority to men.

The Calling of Matthew

[9]As Jesus went on from there, he saw a man named Matthew sitting at the tax collector's booth. "Follow me," he told him, and Matthew got up and followed him.

[10]While Jesus was having dinner at Matthew's house, many tax collectors and "sinners" came and ate with him and his disciples. [11]When the Pharisees saw this, they asked his disciples, "Why does your teacher eat with tax collectors and 'sinners'?"

[12]On hearing this, Jesus said, "It is not the healthy who need a doctor, but the sick. [13]But go and learn what this means: 'I desire mercy, not sacrifice.' For I have not come to call the righteous, but sinners."

READING FROM PSALMS
Psalm 7:10–17

10My shield is God Most High,
    who saves the upright in heart.
11God is a righteous judge,
    a God who expresses his wrath
        every day.
12If he does not relent,
    he will sharpen his sword;
    he will bend and string his bow.
13He has prepared his deadly
        weapons;
    he makes ready his flaming arrows.

14He who is pregnant with evil
    and conceives trouble gives birth to
        disillusionment.
15He who digs a hole and scoops it out
    falls into the pit he has made.
16The trouble he causes recoils on
        himself;
    his violence comes down on his
        own head.

17I will give thanks to the LORD
    because of his righteousness
    and will sing praise to the name of
        the LORD Most High.

JANUARY 11   DAY 11

OLD TESTAMENT READING
Genesis 24:1–67

Isaac and Rebekah

24 Abraham was now old and well
advanced in years, and the LORD
had blessed him in every way. 2He said
to the chief servant in his household, the
one in charge of all that he had, "Put
your hand under my thigh. 3I want you
to swear by the LORD, the God of
heaven and the God of earth, that you
will not get a wife for my son from the
daughters of the Canaanites, among
whom I am living, 4but will go to my
country and my own relatives and get a
wife for my son Isaac."

5The servant asked him, "What if the
woman is unwilling to come back with
me to this land? Shall I then take your
son back to the country you came
from?"

6"Make sure that you do not take my
son back there," Abraham said. 7"The
LORD, the God of heaven, who brought
me out of my father's household and my
native land and who spoke to me and
promised me on oath, saying, 'To your
offspring I will give this land'—he will
send his angel before you so that you

can get a wife for my son from there. 8If
the woman is unwilling to come back
with you, then you will be released from
this oath of mine. Only do not take my
son back there." 9So the servant put his
hand under the thigh of his master
Abraham and swore an oath to him
concerning this matter.

10Then the servant took ten of his
master's camels and left, taking with
him all kinds of good things from his
master. He set out for Aram Naharaim
and made his way to the town of Nahor.
11He made the camels kneel down near
the well outside the town; it was towards evening, the time the women go
out to draw water.

12Then he prayed, "O LORD, God of
my master Abraham, give me success
today, and show kindness to my master
Abraham. 13See, I am standing beside
this spring, and the daughters of the
townspeople are coming out to draw
water. 14May it be that when I say to a
girl, 'Please let down your jar that I may
have a drink,' and she says, 'Drink, and
I'll water your camels too'—let her be
the one you have chosen for your servant Isaac. By this I will know that you
have shown kindness to my master."

¹⁵Before he had finished praying, Rebekah came out with her jar on her shoulder. She was the daughter of Bethuel son of Milcah, who was the wife of Abraham's brother Nahor. ¹⁶The girl was very beautiful, a virgin; no man had ever lain with her. She went down to the spring, filled her jar and came up again.

¹⁷The servant hurried to meet her and said, "Please give me a little water from your jar."

¹⁸"Drink, my lord," she said, and quickly lowered the jar to her hands and gave him a drink.

¹⁹After she had given him a drink, she said, "I'll draw water for your camels too, until they have finished drinking."

²⁰So she quickly emptied her jar into the trough, ran back to the well to draw more water, and drew enough for all his camels. ²¹Without saying a word, the man watched her closely to learn whether or not the LORD had made his journey successful.

²²When the camels had finished drinking, the man took out a gold nose ring weighing a beka and two gold bracelets weighing ten shekels. ²³Then he asked, "Whose daughter are you? Please tell me, is there room in your father's house for us to spend the night?"

²⁴She answered him, "I am the daughter of Bethuel, the son that Milcah bore to Nahor." ²⁵And she added, "We have plenty of straw and fodder, as well as room for you to spend the night."

²⁶Then the man bowed down and worshipped the LORD, ²⁷saying, "Praise be to the LORD, the God of my master Abraham, who has not abandoned his kindness and faithfulness to my master. As for me, the LORD has led me on the journey to the house of my master's relatives."

²⁸The girl ran and told her mother's household about these things. ²⁹Now Rebekah had a brother named Laban, and he hurried out to the man at the spring. ³⁰As soon as he had seen the nose ring, and the bracelets on his sister's arms, and had heard Rebekah tell what the man said to her, he went out to the man and found him standing by the camels near the spring. ³¹"Come, you who are blessed by the LORD," he said. "Why are you standing out here? I have prepared the house and a place for the camels."

³²So the man went to the house, and the camels were unloaded. Straw and fodder were brought for the camels, and water for him and his men to wash their feet. ³³Then food was set before him, but he said, "I will not eat until I have told you what I have to say."

"Then tell us," Laban said.

³⁴So he said, "I am Abraham's servant. ³⁵The LORD has blessed my master abundantly, and he has become wealthy. He has given him sheep and cattle, silver and gold, menservants and maidservants, and camels and donkeys. ³⁶My master's wife Sarah has borne him a son in her old age, and he has given him everything he owns. ³⁷And my master made me swear an oath, and said, 'You must not get a wife for my son from the daughters of the Canaanites, in whose land I live, ³⁸but go to my father's family and to my own clan, and get a wife for my son.'

³⁹"Then I asked my master, 'What if the woman will not come back with me?'

⁴⁰"He replied, 'The LORD, before whom I have walked, will send his angel with you and make your journey a success, so that you can get a wife for my son from my own clan and from my father's family. ⁴¹Then, when you go to my clan, you will be released from my oath even if they refuse to give her to you—you will be released from my oath.'

⁴²"When I came to the spring today, I said, 'O LORD, God of my master Abraham, if you will, please grant success to the journey on which I have come. ⁴³See, I am standing beside this spring; if a maiden comes out to draw water and I say to her, "Please let me drink a little water from your jar," ⁴⁴and if she says

to me, "Drink, and I'll draw water for your camels too," let her be the one the LORD has chosen for my master's son.'

45"Before I finished praying in my heart, Rebekah came out, with her jar on her shoulder. She went down to the spring and drew water, and I said to her, 'Please give me a drink.'

46"She quickly lowered her jar from her shoulder and said, 'Drink, and I'll water your camels too.' So I drank, and she watered the camels also.

47"I asked her, 'Whose daughter are you?'

"She said, 'The daughter of Bethuel son of Nahor, whom Milcah bore to him.'

"Then I put the ring in her nose and the bracelets on her arms, 48and I bowed down and worshipped the LORD. I praised the LORD, the God of my master Abraham, who had led me on the right road to get the granddaughter of my master's brother for his son. 49Now if you will show kindness and faithfulness to my master, tell me; and if not, tell me, so I may know which way to turn."

50Laban and Bethuel answered, "This is from the LORD; we can say nothing to you one way or the other. 51Here is Rebekah; take her and go, and let her become the wife of your master's son, as the LORD has directed."

52When Abraham's servant heard what they said, he bowed down to the ground before the LORD. 53Then the servant brought out gold and silver jewellery and articles of clothing and gave them to Rebekah; he also gave costly gifts to her brother and to her mother. 54Then he and the men who were with him ate and drank and spent the night there.

When they got up the next morning, he said, "Send me on my way to my master."

55But her brother and her mother replied, "Let the girl remain with us ten days or so; then you may go."

56But he said to them, "Do not detain me, now that the LORD has granted success to my journey. Send me on my way so I may go to my master."

57Then they said, "Let's call the girl and ask her about it." 58So they called Rebekah and asked her, "Will you go with this man?"

"I will go," she said.

59So they sent their sister Rebekah on her way, along with her nurse and Abraham's servant and his men. 60And they blessed Rebekah and said to her,

"Our sister, may you increase
    to thousands upon thousands;
may your offspring possess
    the gates of their enemies."

61Then Rebekah and her maids got ready and mounted their camels and went back with the man. So the servant took Rebekah and left.

62Now Isaac had come from Beer Lahai Roi, for he was living in the Negev. 63He went out to the field one evening to meditate, and as he looked up, he saw camels approaching. 64Rebekah also looked up and saw Isaac. She got down from her camel 65and asked the servant, "Who is that man in the field coming to meet us?"

"He is my master," the servant answered. So she took her veil and covered herself.

66Then the servant told Isaac all he had done. 67Isaac brought her into the tent of his mother Sarah, and he married Rebekah. So she became his wife, and he loved her; and Isaac was comforted after his mother's death.

NEW TESTAMENT READING
Matthew 9:14–38

Jesus Questioned About Fasting

14Then John's disciples came and asked him, "How is it that we and the Pharisees fast, but your disciples do not fast?"

15Jesus answered, "How can the guests of the bridegroom mourn while he is with them? The time will come when the bridegroom will be taken from them; then they will fast.

16"No-one sews a patch of unshrunk cloth on an old garment, for the patch will pull away from the garment, making the tear worse. 17Neither do men pour new wine into old wineskins. If they do, the skins will burst, the wine will run out and the wineskins will be ruined. No, they pour new wine into new wineskins, and both are preserved."

A Dead Girl and a Sick Woman

18While he was saying this, a ruler came and knelt before him and said, "My daughter has just died. But come and put your hand on her, and she will live." 19Jesus got up and went with him, and so did his disciples.

20Just then a woman who had been subject to bleeding for twelve years came up behind him and touched the edge of his cloak. 21She said to herself, "If I only touch his cloak, I will be healed."

22Jesus turned and saw her. "Take heart, daughter," he said, "your faith has healed you." And the woman was healed from that moment.

23When Jesus entered the ruler's house and saw the flute players and the noisy crowd, 24he said, "Go away. The girl is not dead but asleep." But they laughed at him. 25After the crowd had been put outside, he went in and took the girl by the hand, and she got up. 26News of this spread through all that region.

Jesus Heals the Blind and Mute

27As Jesus went on from there, two blind men followed him, calling out, "Have mercy on us, Son of David!"

28When he had gone indoors, the blind men came to him, and he asked them, "Do you believe that I am able to do this?"

"Yes, Lord," they replied.

29Then he touched their eyes and said, "According to your faith will it be done to you"; 30and their sight was restored. Jesus warned them sternly, "See that no-one knows about this." 31But they went out and spread the news about him all over that region.

32While they were going out, a man who was demon-possessed and could not talk was brought to Jesus. 33And when the demon was driven out, the man who had been mute spoke. The crowd was amazed and said, "Nothing like this has ever been seen in Israel."

34But the Pharisees said, "It is by the prince of demons that he drives out demons."

The Workers Are Few

35Jesus went through all the towns and villages, teaching in their synagogues, preaching the good news of the kingdom and healing every disease and sickness. 36When he saw the crowds, he had compassion on them, because they were harassed and helpless, like sheep without a shepherd. 37Then he said to his disciples, "The harvest is plentiful but the workers are few. 38Ask the Lord of the harvest, therefore, to send out workers into his harvest field."

READING FROM PSALMS
Psalm 8:1–9

For the director of music. According to *gittith*. A psalm of David.

1O LORD, our Lord,
   how majestic is your name in all
     the earth!

You have set your glory
   above the heavens.
2From the lips of children and infants
   you have ordained praise
because of your enemies,
   to silence the foe and the avenger.

³When I consider your heavens,
   the work of your fingers,
the moon and the stars,
   which you have set in place,
⁴what is man that you are mindful of
   him,
   the son of man that you care for
   him?
⁵You made him a little lower than the
   heavenly beings
   and crowned him with glory and
   honour.

⁶You made him ruler over the works
   of your hands;
   you put everything under his feet:
⁷all flocks and herds,
   and the beasts of the field,
⁸the birds of the air,
   and the fish of the sea,
   all that swim the paths of the seas.

⁹O LORD, our Lord,
   how majestic is your name in all
   the earth!

JANUARY 12   DAY 12

OLD TESTAMENT READING
Genesis 25:1–26:35

The Death of Abraham

25 Abraham took another wife, whose name was Keturah. ²She bore him Zimran, Jokshan, Medan, Midian, Ishbak and Shuah. ³Jokshan was the father of Sheba and Dedan; the descendants of Dedan were the Asshurites, the Letushites and the Leummites. ⁴The sons of Midian were Ephah, Epher, Hanoch, Abida and Eldaah. All these were descendants of Keturah.

⁵Abraham left everything he owned to Isaac. ⁶But while he was still living, he gave gifts to the sons of his concubines and sent them away from his son Isaac to the land of the east.

⁷Altogether, Abraham lived a hundred and seventy-five years. ⁸Then Abraham breathed his last and died at a good old age, an old man and full of years; and he was gathered to his people. ⁹His sons Isaac and Ishmael buried him in the cave of Machpelah near Mamre, in the field of Ephron son of Zohar the Hittite, ¹⁰the field Abraham had bought from the Hittites. There Abraham was buried with his wife

Sarah. ¹¹After Abraham's death, God blessed his son Isaac, who then lived near Beer Lahai Roi.

Ishmael's Sons

¹²This is the account of Abraham's son Ishmael, whom Sarah's maidservant, Hagar the Egyptian, bore to Abraham.

¹³These are the names of the sons of Ishmael, listed in the order of their birth: Nebaioth the firstborn of Ishmael, Kedar, Adbeel, Mibsam, ¹⁴Mishma, Dumah, Massa, ¹⁵Hadad, Tema, Jetur, Naphish and Kedemah. ¹⁶These were the sons of Ishmael, and these are the names of the twelve tribal rulers according to their settlements and camps. ¹⁷Altogether, Ishmael lived a hundred and thirty-seven years. He breathed his last and died, and he was gathered to his people. ¹⁸His descendants settled in the area from Havilah to Shur, near the border of Egypt, as you go towards Asshur. And they lived in hostility towards all their brothers.

Jacob and Esau

¹⁹This is the account of Abraham's son Isaac.

Abraham became the father of Isaac, [20]and Isaac was forty years old when he married Rebekah daughter of Bethuel the Aramean from Paddan Aram and sister of Laban the Aramean.

[21]Isaac prayed to the LORD on behalf of his wife, because she was barren. The LORD answered his prayer, and his wife Rebekah became pregnant. [22]The babies jostled each other within her, and she said, "Why is this happening to me?" So she went to enquire of the LORD.

[23]The LORD said to her,

"Two nations are in your womb,
     and two peoples from within you
         will be separated;
one people will be stronger than the
         other,
     and the older will serve the
         younger."

[24]When the time came for her to give birth, there were twin boys in her womb. [25]The first to come out was red, and his whole body was like a hairy garment; so they named him Esau. [26]After this, his brother came out, with his hand grasping Esau's heel; so he was named Jacob. Isaac was sixty years old when Rebekah gave birth to them.

[27]The boys grew up, and Esau became a skilful hunter, a man of the open country, while Jacob was a quiet man, staying among the tents. [28]Isaac, who had a taste for wild game, loved Esau, but Rebekah loved Jacob.

[29]Once when Jacob was cooking some stew, Esau came in from the open country, famished. [30]He said to Jacob, "Quick, let me have some of that red stew! I'm famished!" (That is why he was also called Edom.)

[31]Jacob replied, "First sell me your birthright."

[32]"Look, I am about to die," Esau said. "What good is the birthright to me?"

[33]But Jacob said, "Swear to me first." So he swore an oath to him, selling his birthright to Jacob.

[34]Then Jacob gave Esau some bread and some lentil stew. He ate and drank, and then got up and left.

So Esau despised his birthright.

Isaac and Abimelech

26 Now there was a famine in the land—besides the earlier famine of Abraham's time—and Isaac went to Abimelech king of the Philistines in Gerar. [2]The LORD appeared to Isaac and said, "Do not go down to Egypt; live in the land where I tell you to live. [3]Stay in this land for a while, and I will be with you and will bless you. For to you and your descendants I will give all these lands and will confirm the oath I swore to your father Abraham. [4]I will make your descendants as numerous as the stars in the sky and will give them all these lands, and through your offspring all nations on earth will be blessed, [5]because Abraham obeyed me and kept my requirements, my commands, my decrees and my laws." [6]So Isaac stayed in Gerar.

[7]When the men of that place asked him about his wife, he said, "She is my sister," because he was afraid to say, "She is my wife." He thought, "The men of this place might kill me on account of Rebekah, because she is beautiful."

[8]When Isaac had been there a long time, Abimelech king of the Philistines looked down from a window and saw Isaac caressing his wife Rebekah. [9]So Abimelech summoned Isaac and said, "She is really your wife! Why did you say, 'She is my sister'?"

Isaac answered him, "Because I thought I might lose my life on account of her."

[10]Then Abimelech said, "What is this you have done to us? One of the men might well have slept with your wife, and you would have brought guilt upon us."

[11]So Abimelech gave orders to all the people: "Anyone who molests this man or his wife shall surely be put to death."

¹²Isaac planted crops in that land and the same year reaped a hundredfold, because the LORD blessed him. ¹³The man became rich, and his wealth continued to grow until he became very wealthy. ¹⁴He had so many flocks and herds and servants that the Philistines envied him. ¹⁵So all the wells that his father's servants had dug in the time of his father Abraham, the Philistines stopped up, filling them with earth.

¹⁶Then Abimelech said to Isaac, "Move away from us; you have become too powerful for us."

¹⁷So Isaac moved away from there and encamped in the Valley of Gerar and settled there. ¹⁸Isaac reopened the wells that had been dug in the time of his father Abraham, which the Philistines had stopped up after Abraham died, and he gave them the same names his father had given them.

¹⁹Isaac's servants dug in the valley and discovered a well of fresh water there. ²⁰But the herdsmen of Gerar quarrelled with Isaac's herdsmen and said, "The water is ours!" So he named the well Esek, because they disputed with him. ²¹Then they dug another well, but they quarrelled over that one also; so he named it Sitnah. ²²He moved on from there and dug another well, and no-one quarrelled over it. He named it Rehoboth, saying, "Now the LORD has given us room and we will flourish in the land."

²³From there he went up to Beersheba. ²⁴That night the LORD appeared to him and said, "I am the God of your father Abraham. Do not be afraid, for I am with you; I will bless you and will increase the number of your descendants for the sake of my servant Abraham."

²⁵Isaac built an altar there and called on the name of the LORD. There he pitched his tent, and there his servants dug a well.

²⁶Meanwhile, Abimelech had come to him from Gerar, with Ahuzzath his personal adviser and Phicol the commander of his forces. ²⁷Isaac asked them, "Why have you come to me, since you were hostile to me and sent me away?"

²⁸They answered, "We saw clearly that the LORD was with you; so we said, 'There ought to be a sworn agreement between us'—between us and you. Let us make a treaty with you ²⁹that you will do us no harm, just as we did not molest you but always treated you well and sent you away in peace. And now you are blessed by the LORD."

³⁰Isaac then made a feast for them, and they ate and drank. ³¹Early the next morning the men swore an oath to each other. Then Isaac sent them on their way, and they left him in peace.

³²That day Isaac's servants came and told him about the well they had dug. They said, "We've found water!" ³³He called it Shibah, and to this day the name of the town has been Beersheba.

³⁴When Esau was forty years old, he married Judith daughter of Beeri the Hittite, and also Basemath daughter of Elon the Hittite. ³⁵They were a source of grief to Isaac and Rebekah.

NEW TESTAMENT READING
Matthew 10:1–31

Jesus Sends Out the Twelve

10 He called his twelve disciples to him and gave them authority to drive out evil spirits and to heal every disease and sickness.

²These are the names of the twelve apostles: first, Simon (who is called Peter) and his brother Andrew; James son of Zebedee, and his brother John; ³Philip and Bartholomew; Thomas and Matthew the tax collector; James son of Alphaeus, and Thaddaeus; ⁴Simon the Zealot and Judas Iscariot, who betrayed him.

⁵These twelve Jesus sent out with the following instructions: "Do not go among the Gentiles or enter any town of the Samaritans. ⁶Go rather to the lost sheep of Israel. ⁷As you go, preach this

message: 'The kingdom of heaven is near.' 8Heal the sick, raise the dead, cleanse those who have leprosy, drive out demons. Freely you have received, freely give. 9Do not take along any gold or silver or copper in your belts; 10take no bag for the journey, or extra tunic, or sandals or a staff; for the worker is worth his keep.

11"Whatever town or village you enter, search for some worthy person there and stay at his house until you leave. 12As you enter the home, give it your greeting. 13If the home is deserving, let your peace rest on it; if it is not, let your peace return to you. 14If anyone will not welcome you or listen to your words, shake the dust off your feet when you leave that home or town. 15I tell you the truth, it will be more bearable for Sodom and Gomorrah on the day of judgment than for that town. 16I am sending you out like sheep among wolves. Therefore be as shrewd as snakes and as innocent as doves.

17"Be on your guard against men; they will hand you over to the local councils and flog you in their synagogues. 18On my account you will be brought before governors and kings as witnesses to them and to the Gentiles. 19But when they arrest you, do not worry about what to say or how to say it. At that time you will be given what to say, 20for it will not be you speaking, but the Spirit of your Father speaking through you.

21"Brother will betray brother to death, and a father his child; children will rebel against their parents and have them put to death. 22All men will hate you because of me, but he who stands firm to the end will be saved. 23When you are persecuted in one place, flee to another. I tell you the truth, you will not finish going through the cities of Israel before the Son of Man comes.

24"A student is not above his teacher, nor a servant above his master. 25It is enough for the student to be like his teacher, and the servant like his master. If the head of the house has been called Beelzebub, how much more the members of his household!

26"So do not be afraid of them. There is nothing concealed that will not be disclosed, or hidden that will not be made known. 27What I tell you in the dark, speak in the daylight; what is whispered in your ear, proclaim from the roofs. 28Do not be afraid of those who kill the body but cannot kill the soul. Rather, be afraid of the One who can destroy both soul and body in hell. 29Are not two sparrows sold for a penny? Yet not one of them will fall to the ground apart from the will of your Father. 30And even the very hairs of your head are all numbered. 31So don't be afraid; you are worth more than many sparrows.

READING FROM PROVERBS
Proverbs 1:20–33

Warning Against Rejecting Wisdom

20Wisdom calls aloud in the street,
　　she raises her voice in the public
　　　　squares;
21at the head of the noisy streets she
　　　　cries out,
　　in the gateways of the city she
　　　　makes her speech:

22"How long will you simple ones love
　　your simple ways?
　　How long will mockers delight in
　　　　mockery
　　and fools hate knowledge?
23If you had responded to my rebuke,
　　I would have poured out my heart
　　　　to you
　　and made my thoughts known to
　　　　you.
24But since you rejected me when I
　　called
　　and no-one gave heed when I
　　　　stretched out my hand,
25since you ignored all my advice
　　and would not accept my rebuke,
26I in turn will laugh at your disaster;
　　I will mock when calamity
　　　　overtakes you—

27when calamity overtakes you like a
    storm,
  when disaster sweeps over you like
    a whirlwind,
  when distress and trouble
    overwhelm you.

28"Then they will call to me but I will
    not answer;
  they will look for me but will not
    find me.
29Since they hated knowledge
  and did not choose to fear the
    LORD,

30since they would not accept my
    advice
  and spurned my rebuke,
31they will eat the fruit of their ways
  and be filled with the fruit of their
    schemes.
32For the waywardness of the simple
    will kill them,
  and the complacency of fools will
    destroy them;
33but whoever listens to me will live in
    safety
  and be at ease, without fear of
    harm."

JANUARY 13   DAY 13

OLD TESTAMENT READING
Genesis 27:1–28:22

Jacob Gets Isaac's Blessing

27 When Isaac was old and his eyes
were so weak that he could no
longer see, he called for Esau his older
son and said to him, "My son."

"Here I am," he answered.

2Isaac said, "I am now an old man
and don't know the day of my death.
3Now then, get your weapons—your
quiver and bow—and go out to the
open country to hunt some wild game
for me. 4Prepare me the kind of tasty
food I like and bring it to me to eat, so
that I may give you my blessing before I
die."

5Now Rebekah was listening as Isaac
spoke to his son Esau. When Esau left
for the open country to hunt game and
bring it back, 6Rebekah said to her son
Jacob, "Look, I overheard your father
say to your brother Esau, 7'Bring me
some game and prepare me some tasty
food to eat, so that I may give you my
blessing in the presence of the LORD
before I die.' 8Now, my son, listen carefully and do what I tell you: 9Go out to
the flock and bring me two choice young

goats, so that I can prepare some tasty
food for your father, just the way he
likes it. 10Then take it to your father to
eat, so that he may give you his blessing
before he dies."

11Jacob said to Rebekah his mother,
"But my brother Esau is a hairy man,
and I'm a man with smooth skin. 12What
if my father touches me? I would appear
to be tricking him and would bring
down a curse on myself rather than a
blessing."

13His mother said to him, "My son,
let the curse fall on me. Just do what I
say; go and get them for me."

14So he went and got them and
brought them to his mother, and she
prepared some tasty food, just the way
his father liked it. 15Then Rebekah took
the best clothes of Esau her older son,
which she had in the house, and put
them on her younger son Jacob. 16She
also covered his hands and the smooth
part of his neck with the goatskins.
17Then she handed to her son Jacob the
tasty food and the bread she had made.

18He went to his father and said, "My
father."

"Yes, my son," he answered. "Who
is it?"

¹⁹Jacob said to his father, "I am Esau your firstborn. I have done as you told me. Please sit up and eat some of my game so that you may give me your blessing."

²⁰Isaac asked his son, "How did you find it so quickly, my son?"

"The LORD your God gave me success," he replied.

²¹Then Isaac said to Jacob, "Come near so I can touch you, my son, to know whether you really are my son Esau or not."

²²Jacob went close to his father Isaac, who touched him and said, "The voice is the voice of Jacob, but the hands are the hands of Esau." ²³He did not recognise him, for his hands were hairy like those of his brother Esau; so he blessed him. ²⁴"Are you really my son Esau?" he asked.

"I am," he replied.

²⁵Then he said, "My son, bring me some of your game to eat, so that I may give you my blessing."

Jacob brought it to him and he ate; and he brought some wine and he drank. ²⁶Then his father Isaac said to him, "Come here, my son, and kiss me."

²⁷So he went to him and kissed him. When Isaac caught the smell of his clothes, he blessed him and said,

"Ah, the smell of my son
    is like the smell of a field
    that the LORD has blessed.
²⁸May God give you of heaven's dew
    and of earth's richness—
      an abundance of grain and new
      wine.
²⁹May nations serve you
    and peoples bow down to you.
Be lord over your brothers,
    and may the sons of your mother
      bow down to you.
May those who curse you be cursed
    and those who bless you be
      blessed."

³⁰After Isaac finished blessing him and Jacob had scarcely left his father's presence, his brother Esau came in from hunting. ³¹He too prepared some tasty food and brought it to his father. Then he said to him, "My father, sit up and eat some of my game, so that you may give me your blessing."

³²His father Isaac asked him, "Who are you?"

"I am your son," he answered, "your firstborn, Esau."

³³Isaac trembled violently and said, "Who was it, then, that hunted game and brought it to me? I ate it just before you came and I blessed him—and indeed he will be blessed!"

³⁴When Esau heard his father's words, he burst out with a loud and bitter cry and said to his father, "Bless me—me too, my father!"

³⁵But he said, "Your brother came deceitfully and took your blessing."

³⁶Esau said, "Isn't he rightly named Jacob? He has deceived me these two times: He took my birthright, and now he's taken my blessing!" Then he asked, "Haven't you reserved any blessing for me?"

³⁷Isaac answered Esau, "I have made him lord over you and have made all his relatives his servants, and I have sustained him with grain and new wine. So what can I possibly do for you, my son?"

³⁸Esau said to his father, "Do you have only one blessing, my father? Bless me too, my father!" Then Esau wept aloud.

³⁹His father Isaac answered him,

"Your dwelling will be
    away from the earth's richness,
    away from the dew of heaven
      above.
⁴⁰You will live by the sword
    and you will serve your brother.
But when you grow restless,
    you will throw his yoke
    from off your neck."

Jacob Flees to Laban

⁴¹Esau held a grudge against Jacob because of the blessing his father had

given him. He said to himself, "The days of mourning for my father are near; then I will kill my brother Jacob."

⁴²When Rebekah was told what her older son Esau had said, she sent for her younger son Jacob and said to him, "Your brother Esau is consoling himself with the thought of killing you. ⁴³Now then, my son, do what I say: Flee at once to my brother Laban in Haran. ⁴⁴Stay with him for a while until your brother's fury subsides. ⁴⁵When your brother is no longer angry with you and forgets what you did to him, I'll send word for you to come back from there. Why should I lose both of you in one day?"

⁴⁶Then Rebekah said to Isaac, "I'm disgusted with living because of these Hittite women. If Jacob takes a wife from among the women of this land, from Hittite women like these, my life will not be worth living."

28 So Isaac called for Jacob and blessed him and commanded him: "Do not marry a Canaanite woman. ²Go at once to Paddan Aram, to the house of your mother's father Bethuel. Take a wife for yourself there, from among the daughters of Laban, your mother's brother. ³May God Almighty bless you and make you fruitful and increase your numbers until you become a community of peoples. ⁴May he give you and your descendants the blessing given to Abraham, so that you may take possession of the land where you now live as an alien, the land God gave to Abraham." ⁵Then Isaac sent Jacob on his way, and he went to Paddan Aram, to Laban son of Bethuel the Aramean, the brother of Rebekah, who was the mother of Jacob and Esau.

⁶Now Esau learned that Isaac had blessed Jacob and had sent him to Paddan Aram to take a wife from there, and that when he blessed him he commanded him, "Do not marry a Canaanite woman," ⁷and that Jacob had obeyed his father and mother and had gone to Paddan Aram. ⁸Esau then realised how displeasing the Canaanite women were

to his father Isaac; ⁹so he went to Ishmael and married Mahalath, the sister of Nebaioth and daughter of Ishmael son of Abraham, in addition to the wives he already had.

Jacob's Dream at Bethel

¹⁰Jacob left Beersheba and set out for Haran. ¹¹When he reached a certain place, he stopped for the night because the sun had set. Taking one of the stones there, he put it under his head and lay down to sleep. ¹²He had a dream in which he saw a stairway resting on the earth, with its top reaching to heaven, and the angels of God were ascending and descending on it. ¹³There above it stood the LORD, and he said: "I am the LORD, the God of your father Abraham and the God of Isaac. I will give you and your descendants the land on which you are lying. ¹⁴Your descendants will be like the dust of the earth, and you will spread out to the west and to the east, to the north and to the south. All peoples on earth will be blessed through you and your offspring. ¹⁵I am with you and will watch over you wherever you go, and I will bring you back to this land. I will not leave you until I have done what I have promised you."

¹⁶When Jacob awoke from his sleep, he thought, "Surely the LORD is in this place, and I was not aware of it." ¹⁷He was afraid and said, "How awesome is this place! This is none other than the house of God; this is the gate of heaven."

¹⁸Early the next morning Jacob took the stone he had placed under his head and set it up as a pillar and poured oil on top of it. ¹⁹He called that place Bethel, though the city used to be called Luz.

²⁰Then Jacob made a vow, saying, "If God will be with me and will watch over me on this journey I am taking and will give me food to eat and clothes to wear ²¹so that I return safely to my father's house, then the LORD will be my God ²²and this stone that I have set up as a pillar will be God's house, and of all that you give me I will give you a tenth."

NEW TESTAMENT READING
Matthew 10:32–11:15

32"Whoever acknowledges me before men, I will also acknowledge him before my Father in heaven. 33But whoever disowns me before men, I will disown him before my Father in heaven.

34"Do not suppose that I have come to bring peace to the earth. I did not come to bring peace, but a sword. 35For I have come to turn

" 'a man against his father,
a daughter against her mother,
a daughter-in-law against her
mother-in-law—
36 a man's enemies will be the
members of his own
household.'

37"Anyone who loves his father or mother more than me is not worthy of me; anyone who loves his son or daughter more than me is not worthy of me; 38and anyone who does not take his cross and follow me is not worthy of me. 39Whoever finds his life will lose it, and whoever loses his life for my sake will find it.

40"He who receives me receives me, and he who receives me receives the one who sent me. 41Anyone who receives a prophet because he is a prophet will receive a prophet's reward, and anyone who receives a righteous man because he is a righteous man will receive a righteous man's reward. 42And if anyone gives even a cup of cold water to one of these little ones because he is my disciple, I tell you the truth, he will certainly not lose his reward."

Jesus and John the Baptist

11 After Jesus had finished instructing his twelve disciples, he went on from there to teach and preach in the towns of Galilee.

2When John heard in prison what Christ was doing, he sent his disciples 3to ask him, "Are you the one who was to come, or should we expect someone else?"

4Jesus replied, "Go back and report to John what you hear and see: 5The blind receive sight, the lame walk, those who have leprosy are cured, the deaf hear, the dead are raised, and the good news is preached to the poor. 6Blessed is the man who does not fall away on account of me."

7As John's disciples were leaving, Jesus began to speak to the crowd about John: "What did you go out into the desert to see? A reed swayed by the wind? 8If not, what did you go out to see? A man dressed in fine clothes? No, those who wear fine clothes are in kings' palaces. 9Then what did you go out to see? A prophet? Yes, I tell you, and more than a prophet. 10This is the one about whom it is written:

" 'I will send my messenger ahead of
you,
who will prepare your way before
you.'

11I tell you the truth: Among those born of women there has not risen anyone greater than John the Baptist; yet he who is least in the kingdom of heaven is greater than he. 12From the days of John the Baptist until now, the kingdom of heaven has been forcefully advancing, and forceful men lay hold of it. 13For all the Prophets and the Law prophesied until John. 14And if you are willing to accept it, he is the Elijah who was to come. 15He who has ears, let him hear.

READING FROM PSALMS
Psalm 9:1–6

For the director of music. To ⌐the tune of⌐ "The Death of the Son". A psalm of David.

1I will praise you, O LORD, with all my
heart;
I will tell of all your wonders.
2I will be glad and rejoice in you;

I will sing praise to your name, O
　　Most High.

³My enemies turn back;
　　they stumble and perish before
　　　　you.
⁴For you have upheld my right and my
　　cause;
　　you have sat on your throne,
　　　　judging righteously.

⁵You have rebuked the nations and
　　destroyed the wicked;
　　you have blotted out their name
　　　　for ever and ever.
⁶Endless ruin has overtaken the
　　enemy,
　　you have uprooted their
　　　　cities;
　　even the memory of them has
　　　　perished.

JANUARY 14　　　　DAY 14

OLD TESTAMENT READING
Genesis 29:1–30:43

Jacob Arrives in Paddan Aram

29 Then Jacob continued on his
journey and came to the land of
the eastern peoples. ²There he saw a
well in the field, with three flocks of
sheep lying near it because the flocks
were watered from that well. The stone
over the mouth of the well was large.
³When all the flocks were gathered
there, the shepherds would roll the
stone away from the well's mouth and
water the sheep. Then they would return the stone to its place over the
mouth of the well.

⁴Jacob asked the shepherds, "My
brothers, where are you from?"

"We're from Haran," they replied.

⁵He said to them, "Do you know
Laban, Nahor's grandson?"

"Yes, we know him," they answered.

⁶Then Jacob asked them, "Is he
well?"

"Yes, he is," they said, "and here
comes his daughter Rachel with the
sheep."

⁷"Look," he said, "the sun is still
high; it is not time for the flocks to be
gathered. Water the sheep and take
them back to pasture."

⁸"We can't," they replied, "until all
the flocks are gathered and the stone

has been rolled away from the mouth of
the well. Then we will water the sheep."

⁹While he was still talking with them,
Rachel came with her father's sheep,
for she was a shepherdess. ¹⁰When
Jacob saw Rachel daughter of Laban,
his mother's brother, and Laban's
sheep, he went over and rolled the
stone away from the mouth of the well
and watered his uncle's sheep. ¹¹Then
Jacob kissed Rachel and began to weep
aloud. ¹²He had told Rachel that he
was a relative of her father and a son
of Rebekah. So she ran and told her
father.

¹³As soon as Laban heard the news
about Jacob, his sister's son, he hurried
to meet him. He embraced him and
kissed him and brought him to his
home, and there Jacob told him all
these things. ¹⁴Then Laban said to him,
"You are my own flesh and blood."

Jacob Marries Leah and Rachel

After Jacob had stayed with him for
a whole month, ¹⁵Laban said to him,
"Just because you are a relative of
mine, should you work for me for
nothing? Tell me what your wages
should be."

¹⁶Now Laban had two daughters; the
name of the older was Leah, and the
name of the younger was Rachel.
¹⁷Leah had weak eyes, but Rachel was

lovely in form, and beautiful. ¹⁸Jacob was in love with Rachel and said, "I'll work for you seven years in return for your younger daughter Rachel."

¹⁹Laban said, "It's better that I give her to you than to some other man. Stay here with me." ²⁰So Jacob served seven years to get Rachel, but they seemed like only a few days to him because of his love for her.

²¹Then Jacob said to Laban, "Give me my wife. My time is completed, and I want to lie with her."

²²So Laban brought together all the people of the place and gave a feast. ²³But when evening came, he took his daughter Leah and gave her to Jacob, and Jacob lay with her. ²⁴And Laban gave his servant girl Zilpah to his daughter as her maidservant.

²⁵When morning came, there was Leah! So Jacob said to Laban, "What is this you have done to me? I served you for Rachel, didn't I? Why have you deceived me?"

²⁶Laban replied, "It is not our custom here to give the younger daughter in marriage before the older one. ²⁷Finish this daughter's bridal week; then we will give you the younger one also, in return for another seven years of work."

²⁸And Jacob did so. He finished the week with Leah, and then Laban gave him his daughter Rachel to be his wife. ²⁹Laban gave his servant girl Bilhah to his daughter Rachel as her maidservant. ³⁰Jacob lay with Rachel also, and he loved Rachel more than Leah. And he worked for Laban another seven years.

Jacob's Children

³¹When the LORD saw that Leah was not loved, he opened her womb, but Rachel was barren. ³²Leah became pregnant and gave birth to a son. She named him Reuben, for she said, "It is because the LORD has seen my misery. Surely my husband will love me now."

³³She conceived again, and when she gave birth to a son she said, "Because the LORD heard that I am not loved, he gave me this one too." So she named him Simeon.

³⁴Again she conceived, and when she gave birth to a son she said, "Now at last my husband will become attached to me, because I have borne him three sons." So he was named Levi.

³⁵She conceived again, and when she gave birth to a son she said, "This time I will praise the LORD." So she named him Judah. Then she stopped having children.

30 When Rachel saw that she was not bearing Jacob any children, she became jealous of her sister. So she said to Jacob, "Give me children, or I'll die!"

²Jacob became angry with her and said, "Am I in the place of God, who has kept you from having children?"

³Then she said, "Here is Bilhah, my maidservant. Sleep with her so that she can bear children for me and that through her I too can build a family."

⁴So she gave him her servant Bilhah as a wife. Jacob slept with her, ⁵and she became pregnant and bore him a son. ⁶Then Rachel said, "God has vindicated me; he has listened to my plea and given me a son." Because of this she named him Dan.

⁷Rachel's servant Bilhah conceived again and bore Jacob a second son. ⁸Then Rachel said, "I have had a great struggle with my sister, and I have won." So she named him Naphtali.

⁹When Leah saw that she had stopped having children, she took her maidservant Zilpah and gave her to Jacob as a wife. ¹⁰Leah's servant Zilpah bore Jacob a son. ¹¹Then Leah said, "What good fortune!" So she named him Gad.

¹²Leah's servant Zilpah bore Jacob a second son. ¹³Then Leah said, "How happy I am! The women will call me happy." So she named him Asher.

¹⁴During wheat harvest, Reuben went out into the fields and found some mandrake plants, which he brought to his mother Leah. Rachel said to Leah, "Please give me some of your son's mandrakes."

¹⁵But she said to her, "Wasn't it enough that you took away my husband? Will you take my son's mandrakes too?"

"Very well," Rachel said, "he can sleep with you tonight in return for your son's mandrakes."

¹⁶So when Jacob came in from the fields that evening, Leah went out to meet him. "You must sleep with me," she said. "I have hired you with my son's mandrakes." So he slept with her that night.

¹⁷God listened to Leah, and she became pregnant and bore Jacob a fifth son. ¹⁸Then Leah said, "God has rewarded me for giving my maidservant to my husband." So she named him Issachar.

¹⁹Leah conceived again and bore Jacob a sixth son. ²⁰Then Leah said, "God has presented me with a precious gift. This time my husband will treat me with honour, because I have borne him six sons." So she named him Zebulun.

²¹Some time later she gave birth to a daughter and named her Dinah.

²²Then God remembered Rachel; he listened to her and opened her womb. ²³She became pregnant and gave birth to a son and said, "God has taken away my disgrace." ²⁴She named him Joseph, and said, "May the LORD add to me another son."

Jacob's Flocks Increase

²⁵After Rachel gave birth to Joseph, Jacob said to Laban, "Send me on my way so that I can go back to my own homeland. ²⁶Give me my wives and children, for whom I have served you, and I will be on my way. You know how much work I've done for you."

²⁷But Laban said to him, "If I have found favour in your eyes, please stay. I have learned by divination that the LORD has blessed me because of you." ²⁸He added, "Name your wages, and I will pay them."

²⁹Jacob said to him, "You know how I have worked for you and how your livestock has fared under my care. ³⁰The little you had before I came has increased greatly, and the LORD has blessed you wherever I have been. But now, when may I do something for my own household?"

³¹"What shall I give you?" he asked.

"Don't give me anything," Jacob replied. "But if you will do this one thing for me, I will go on tending your flocks and watching over them: ³²Let me go through all your flocks today and remove from them every speckled or spotted sheep, every dark-coloured lamb and every spotted or speckled goat. They will be my wages. ³³And my honesty will testify for me in the future, whenever you check on the wages you have paid me. Any goat in my possession that is not speckled or spotted, or any lamb that is not dark-coloured, will be considered stolen."

³⁴"Agreed," said Laban. "Let it be as you have said." ³⁵That same day he removed all the male goats that were streaked or spotted, and all the speckled or spotted female goats (all that had white on them) and all the dark-coloured lambs, and he placed them in the care of his sons. ³⁶Then he put a three-day journey between himself and Jacob, while Jacob continued to tend the rest of Laban's flocks.

³⁷Jacob, however, took fresh-cut branches from poplar, almond and plane trees and made white stripes on them by peeling the bark and exposing the white inner wood of the branches. ³⁸Then he placed the peeled branches in all the watering troughs, so that they would be directly in front of the flocks when they came to drink. When the flocks were in heat and came to drink, ³⁹they mated in front of the branches. And they bore young that were streaked or speckled or spotted. ⁴⁰Jacob set apart the young of the flock by themselves, but made the rest face the streaked and dark-coloured animals that belonged to Laban. Thus he made separate flocks for himself and did not put them with Laban's animals.

41Whenever the stronger females were in heat, Jacob would place the branches in the troughs in front of the animals so that they would mate near the branches, 42but if the animals were weak, he would not place them there. So the weak animals went to Laban and the strong ones to Jacob. 43In this way the man grew exceedingly prosperous and came to own large flocks, and maidservants and menservants, and camels and donkeys.

NEW TESTAMENT READING
Matthew 11:16–30

16"To what can I compare this generation? They are like children sitting in the market-places and calling out to others:

17"'We played the flute for you,
    and you did not dance;
we sang a dirge,
    and you did not mourn.'

18For John came neither eating nor drinking, and they say, 'He has a demon.' 19The Son of Man came eating and drinking, and they say, 'Here is a glutton and a drunkard, a friend of tax collectors and "sinners".' But wisdom is proved right by her actions."

Woe on Unrepentant Cities

20Then Jesus began to denounce the cities in which most of his miracles had been performed, because they did not repent. 21"Woe to you, Korazin! Woe to you, Bethsaida! If the miracles that were performed in you had been performed in Tyre and Sidon, they would have repented long ago in sackcloth and ashes. 22But I tell you, it will be more bearable for Tyre and Sidon on the day of judgment than for you. 23And you, Capernaum, will you be lifted up to the skies? No, you will go down to the depths. If the miracles that were performed in you had been performed in Sodom, it would have remained to this day. 24But I tell you that it will be more bearable for Sodom on the day of judgment than for you."

Rest for the Weary

25At that time Jesus said, "I praise you, Father, Lord of heaven and earth, because you have hidden these things from the wise and learned, and revealed them to little children. 26Yes, Father, for this was your good pleasure.

27"All things have been committed to me by my Father. No-one knows the Son except the Father, and no-one knows the Father except the Son and those to whom the Son chooses to reveal him.

28"Come to me, all you who are weary and burdened, and I will give you rest. 29Take my yoke upon you and learn from me, for I am gentle and humble in heart, and you will find rest for your souls. 30For my yoke is easy and my burden is light."

READING FROM PSALMS
Psalm 9:7–12

7The LORD reigns for ever;
    he has established his throne for
        judgment.
8He will judge the world in
        righteousness;
    he will govern the peoples with
        justice.
9The LORD is a refuge for the
        oppressed,
    a stronghold in times of trouble.
10Those who know your name will trust
        in you,
    for you, LORD, have never
        forsaken those who seek you.

11Sing praises to the LORD, enthroned
        in Zion;
    proclaim among the nations what
        he has done.
12For he who avenges blood
        remembers;
    he does not ignore the cry of the
        afflicted.

OLD TESTAMENT READING
Genesis 31:1–55

Jacob Flees From Laban

31 Jacob heard that Laban's sons were saying, "Jacob has taken everything our father owned and has gained all this wealth from what belonged to our father." ²And Jacob noticed that Laban's attitude towards him was not what it had been.

³Then the LORD said to Jacob, "Go back to the land of your fathers and to your relatives, and I will be with you."

⁴So Jacob sent word to Rachel and Leah to come out to the fields where his flocks were. ⁵He said to them, "I see that your father's attitude towards me is not what it was before, but the God of my father has been with me. ⁶You know that I've worked for your father with all my strength, ⁷yet your father has cheated me by changing my wages ten times. However, God has not allowed him to harm me. ⁸If he said, 'The speckled ones will be your wages,' then all the flocks gave birth to speckled young; and if he said, 'The streaked ones will be your wages,' then all the flocks bore streaked young. ⁹So God has taken away your father's livestock and has given them to me.

¹⁰"In the breeding season I once had a dream in which I looked up and saw that the male goats mating with the flock were streaked, speckled or spotted. ¹¹The angel of God said to me in the dream, 'Jacob.' I answered, 'Here I am.' ¹²And he said, 'Look up and see that all the male goats mating with the flock are streaked, speckled or spotted, for I have seen all that Laban has been doing to you. ¹³I am the God of Bethel, where you anointed a pillar and where you made a vow to me. Now leave this land at once and go back to your native land.'"

¹⁴Then Rachel and Leah replied, "Do we still have any share in the inheritance of our father's estate? ¹⁵Does he not regard us as foreigners? Not only has he sold us, but he has used up what was paid for us. ¹⁶Surely all the wealth that God took away from our father belongs to us and our children. So do whatever God has told you."

¹⁷Then Jacob put his children and his wives on camels, ¹⁸and he drove all his livestock ahead of him, along with all the goods he had accumulated in Paddan Aram, to go to his father Isaac in the land of Canaan.

¹⁹When Laban had gone to shear his sheep, Rachel stole her father's household gods. ²⁰Moreover, Jacob deceived Laban the Aramean by not telling him he was running away. ²¹So he fled with all he had, and crossing the River, he headed for the hill country of Gilead.

Laban Pursues Jacob

²²On the third day Laban was told that Jacob had fled. ²³Taking his relatives with him, he pursued Jacob for seven days and caught up with him in the hill country of Gilead. ²⁴Then God came to Laban the Aramean in a dream at night and said to him, "Be careful not to say anything to Jacob, either good or bad."

²⁵Jacob had pitched his tent in the hill country of Gilead when Laban overtook him, and Laban and his relatives camped there too. ²⁶Then Laban said to Jacob, "What have you done? You've deceived me, and you've carried off my daughters like captives in war. ²⁷Why did you run off secretly and deceive me? Why didn't you tell me, so that I could send you away with joy and singing to the music of tambourines and harps? ²⁸You didn't even let me kiss my grandchildren and my daughters good-bye. You have done a foolish thing. ²⁹I have

the power to harm you; but last night the God of your father said to me, 'Be careful not to say anything to Jacob, either good or bad.' ³⁰Now you have gone off because you longed to return to your father's house. But why did you steal my gods?"

³¹Jacob answered Laban, "I was afraid, because I thought you would take your daughters away from me by force. ³²But if you find anyone who has your gods, he shall not live. In the presence of our relatives, see for yourself whether there is anything of yours here with me; and if so, take it." Now Jacob did not know that Rachel had stolen the gods.

³³So Laban went into Jacob's tent and into Leah's tent and into the tent of the two maidservants, but he found nothing. After he came out of Leah's tent, he entered Rachel's tent. ³⁴Now Rachel had taken the household gods and put them inside her camel's saddle and was sitting on them. Laban searched through everything in the tent but found nothing.

³⁵Rachel said to her father, "Don't be angry, my lord, that I cannot stand up in your presence; I'm having my period." So he searched but could not find the household gods.

³⁶Jacob was angry and took Laban to task. "What is my crime?" he asked Laban. "What sin have I committed that you hunt me down? ³⁷Now that you have searched through all my goods, what have you found that belongs to your household? Put it here in front of your relatives and mine, and let them judge between the two of us.

³⁸"I have been with you for twenty years now. Your sheep and goats have not miscarried, nor have I eaten rams from your flocks. ³⁹I did not bring you animals torn by wild beasts; I bore the loss myself. And you demanded payment from me for whatever was stolen by day or night. ⁴⁰This was my situation: The heat consumed me in the daytime and the cold at night, and sleep fled from my eyes. ⁴¹It was like this for the

twenty years I was in your household. I worked for you fourteen years for your two daughters and six years for your flocks, and you changed my wages ten times. ⁴²If the God of my father, the God of Abraham and the Fear of Isaac, had not been with me, you would surely have sent me away empty-handed. But God has seen my hardship and the toil of my hands, and last night he rebuked you."

⁴³Laban answered Jacob, "The women are my daughters, the children are my children, and the flocks are my flocks. All you see is mine. Yet what can I do today about these daughters of mine, or about the children they have borne? ⁴⁴Come now, let's make a covenant, you and I, and let it serve as a witness between us."

⁴⁵So Jacob took a stone and set it up as a pillar. ⁴⁶He said to his relatives, "Gather some stones." So they took stones and piled them in a heap, and they ate there by the heap. ⁴⁷Laban called it Jegar Sahadutha, and Jacob called it Galeed.

⁴⁸Laban said, "This heap is a witness between you and me today." That is why it was called Galeed. ⁴⁹It was also called Mizpah, because he said, "May the LORD keep watch between you and me when we are away from each other. ⁵⁰If you ill-treat my daughters or if you take any wives besides my daughters, even though no-one is with us, remember that God is a witness between you and me."

⁵¹Laban also said to Jacob, "Here is this heap, and here is this pillar I have set up between you and me. ⁵²This heap is a witness, and this pillar is a witness, that I will not go past this heap to your side to harm you and that you will not go past this heap and pillar to my side to harm me. ⁵³May the God of Abraham and the God of Nahor, the God of their father, judge between us."

So Jacob took an oath in the name of the Fear of his father Isaac. ⁵⁴He offered a sacrifice there in the hill country and invited his relatives to a meal.

After they had eaten, they spent the night there.

⁵⁵Early the next morning Laban kissed his grandchildren and his daughters and blessed them. Then he left and returned home.

NEW TESTAMENT READING
Matthew 12:1–21

Lord of the Sabbath

12 At that time Jesus went through the cornfields on the Sabbath. His disciples were hungry and began to pick some ears of corn and eat them. ²When the Pharisees saw this, they said to him, "Look! Your disciples are doing what is unlawful on the Sabbath."

³He answered, "Haven't you read what David did when he and his companions were hungry? ⁴He entered the house of God, and he and his companions ate the consecrated bread—which was not lawful for them to do, but only for the priests. ⁵Or haven't you read in the Law that on the Sabbath the priests in the temple desecrate the day and yet are innocent? ⁶I tell you that one greater than the temple is here. ⁷If you had known what these words mean, 'I desire mercy, not sacrifice,' you would not have condemned the innocent. ⁸For the Son of Man is Lord of the Sabbath."

⁹Going on from that place, he went into their synagogue, and ¹⁰a man with a shrivelled hand was there. Looking for a reason to accuse Jesus, they asked him, "Is it lawful to heal on the Sabbath?"

¹¹He said to them, "If any of you has a sheep and it falls into a pit on the Sabbath, will you not take hold of it and lift it out? ¹²How much more valuable is a man than a sheep! Therefore it is lawful to do good on the Sabbath."

¹³Then he said to the man, "Stretch out your hand." So he stretched it out and it was completely restored, just as sound as the other. ¹⁴But the Pharisees went out and plotted how they might kill Jesus.

God's Chosen Servant

¹⁵Aware of this, Jesus withdrew from that place. Many followed him, and he healed all their sick, ¹⁶warning them not to tell who he was. ¹⁷This was to fulfil what was spoken through the prophet Isaiah:

¹⁸"Here is my servant whom I have
    chosen,
  the one I love, in whom I delight;
I will put my Spirit on him,
    and he will proclaim justice to the
    nations.
¹⁹He will not quarrel or cry out;
  no-one will hear his voice in the
    streets.
²⁰A bruised reed he will not break,
    and a smouldering wick he will not
    snuff out,
till he leads justice to victory.
²¹ In his name the nations will put
    their hope."

READING FROM PSALMS
Psalm 9:13–20

¹³O LORD, see how my enemies
    persecute me!
  Have mercy and lift me up from
    the gates of death,
¹⁴that I may declare your praises
  in the gates of the Daughter of
    Zion
  and there rejoice in your salvation.
¹⁵The nations have fallen into the pit
    they have dug;
  their feet are caught in the net they
    have hidden.
¹⁶The LORD is known by his justice;
  the wicked are ensnared by the
    work of their hands.
            Higgaion. Selah

¹⁷The wicked return to the grave,
  all the nations that forget God.
¹⁸But the needy will not always be
    forgotten,
  nor the hope of the afflicted ever
    perish.

¹⁹Arise, O LORD, let not man triumph;
   let the nations be judged in your
     presence.

²⁰Strike them with terror, O LORD;
   let the nations know they are but
     men.   *Selah*

DAY 16

JANUARY 16

OLD TESTAMENT READING
Genesis 32:1–33:20

Jacob Prepares to Meet Esau

32 Jacob also went on his way, and the angels of God met him. ²When Jacob saw them, he said, "This is the camp of God!" So he named that place Mahanaim.

³Jacob sent messengers ahead of him to his brother Esau in the land of Seir, the country of Edom. ⁴He instructed them: "This is what you are to say to my master Esau: 'Your servant Jacob says, I have been staying with Laban and have remained there till now. ⁵I have cattle and donkeys, sheep and goats, menservants and maidservants. Now I am sending this message to my lord, that I may find favour in your eyes.'"

⁶When the messengers returned to Jacob, they said, "We went to your brother Esau, and now he is coming to meet you, and four hundred men are with him."

⁷In great fear and distress Jacob divided the people who were with him into two groups, and the flocks and herds and camels as well. ⁸He thought, "If Esau comes and attacks one group, the group that is left may escape."

⁹Then Jacob prayed, "O God of my father Abraham, God of my father Isaac, O LORD, who said to me, 'Go back to your country and your relatives, and I will make you prosper,' ¹⁰I am unworthy of all the kindness and faithfulness you have shown your servant. I had only my staff when I crossed this Jordan, but now I have become two groups. ¹¹Save me, I pray, from the hand of my brother Esau, for I am afraid he will come and attack me, and also the mothers with their children. ¹²But you have said, 'I will surely make you prosper and will make your descendants like the sand of the sea, which cannot be counted.'"

¹³He spent the night there, and from what he had with him he selected a gift for his brother Esau: ¹⁴two hundred female goats and twenty male goats, two hundred ewes and twenty rams, ¹⁵thirty female camels with their young, forty cows and ten bulls, and twenty female donkeys and ten male donkeys. ¹⁶He put them in the care of his servants, each herd by itself, and said to his servants, "Go ahead of me, and keep some space between the herds."

¹⁷He instructed the one in the lead: "When my brother Esau meets you and asks, 'To whom do you belong, and where are you going, and who owns all these animals in front of you?' ¹⁸then you are to say, 'They belong to your servant Jacob. They are a gift sent to my lord Esau, and he is coming behind us.'"

¹⁹He also instructed the second, the third and all the others who followed the herds: "You are to say the same thing to Esau when you meet him. ²⁰And be sure to say, 'Your servant Jacob is coming behind us.'" For he thought, "I will pacify him with these gifts I am sending on ahead; later, when I see him, perhaps he will receive me." ²¹So Jacob's gifts went on ahead of him, but he himself spent the night in the camp.

Jacob Wrestles with God

22That night Jacob got up and took his two wives, his two maidservants and his eleven sons and crossed the ford of the Jabbok. 23After he had sent them across the stream, he sent over all his possessions. 24So Jacob was left alone, and a man wrestled with him till daybreak. 25When the man saw that he could not overpower him, he touched the socket of Jacob's hip so that his hip was wrenched as he wrestled with the man. 26Then the man said, "Let me go, for it is daybreak."

But Jacob replied, "I will not let you go unless you bless me."

27The man asked him, "What is your name?"

"Jacob," he answered.

28Then the man said, "Your name will no longer be Jacob, but Israel, because you have struggled with God and with men and have overcome."

29Jacob said, "Please tell me your name."

But he replied, "Why do you ask my name?" Then he blessed him there.

30So Jacob called the place Peniel, saying, "It is because I saw God face to face, and yet my life was spared."

31The sun rose above him as he passed Peniel, and he was limping because of his hip. 32Therefore to this day the Israelites do not eat the tendon attached to the socket of the hip, because the socket of Jacob's hip was touched near the tendon.

Jacob Meets Esau

33 Jacob looked up and there was Esau, coming with his four hundred men; so he divided the children among Leah, Rachel and the two maidservants. 2He put the maidservants and their children in front, Leah and her children next, and Rachel and Joseph in the rear. 3He himself went on ahead and bowed down to the ground seven times as he approached his brother.

4But Esau ran to meet Jacob and embraced him; he threw his arms around his neck and kissed him. And they wept. 5Then Esau looked up and saw the women and children. "Who are these with you?" he asked.

Jacob answered, "They are the children God has graciously given your servant."

6Then the maidservants and their children approached and bowed down. 7Next, Leah and her children came and bowed down. Last of all came Joseph and Rachel, and they too bowed down.

8Esau asked, "What do you mean by all these droves I met?"

"To find favour in your eyes, my lord," he said.

9But Esau said, "I already have plenty, my brother. Keep what you have for yourself."

10"No, please!" said Jacob. "If I have found favour in your eyes, accept this gift from me. For to see your face is like seeing the face of God, now that you have received me favourably. 11Please accept the present that was brought to you, for God has been gracious to me and I have all I need." And because Jacob insisted, Esau accepted it.

12Then Esau said, "Let us be on our way; I'll accompany you."

13But Jacob said to him, "My lord knows that the children are tender and that I must care for the ewes and cows that are nursing their young. If they are driven hard just one day, all the animals will die. 14So let my lord go on ahead of his servant, while I move along slowly at the pace of the droves before me and that of the children, until I come to my lord in Seir."

15Esau said, "Then let me leave some of my men with you."

"But why do that?" Jacob asked. "Just let me find favour in the eyes of my lord."

16So that day Esau started on his way back to Seir. 17Jacob, however, went to Succoth, where he built a place for himself and made shelters for his livestock. That is why the place is called Succoth.

18After Jacob came from Paddan

Aram, he arrived safely at the city of Shechem in Canaan and camped within sight of the city. 19For a hundred pieces of silver, he bought from the sons of Hamor, the father of Shechem, the plot of ground where he pitched his tent. 20There he set up an altar and called it El Elohe Israel.

NEW TESTAMENT READING
Matthew 12:22–45

Jesus and Beelzebub

22Then they brought him a demon-possessed man who was blind and mute, and Jesus healed him, so that he could both talk and see. 23All the people were astonished and said, "Could this be the Son of David?"

24But when the Pharisees heard this, they said, "It is only by Beelzebub, the prince of demons, that this fellow drives out demons."

25Jesus knew their thoughts and said to them, "Every kingdom divided against itself will be ruined, and every city or household divided against itself will not stand. 26If Satan drives out Satan, he is divided against himself. How then can his kingdom stand? 27And if I drive out demons by Beelzebub, by whom do your people drive them out? So then, they will be your judges. 28But if I drive out demons by the Spirit of God, then the kingdom of God has come upon you.

29"Or again, how can anyone enter a strong man's house and carry off his possessions unless he first ties up the strong man? Then he can rob his house.

30"He who is not with me is against me, and he who does not gather with me scatters. 31And so I tell you, every sin and blasphemy will be forgiven men, but the blasphemy against the Spirit will not be forgiven. 32Anyone who speaks a word against the Son of Man will be forgiven, but anyone who speaks against the Holy Spirit will not be forgiven, either in this age or in the age to come.

33"Make a tree good and its fruit will be good, or make a tree bad and its fruit will be bad, for a tree is recognised by its fruit. 34You brood of vipers, how can you who are evil say anything good? For out of the overflow of the heart the mouth speaks. 35The good man brings good things out of the good stored up in him, and the evil man brings evil things out of the evil stored up in him. 36But I tell you that men will have to give account on the day of judgment for every careless word they have spoken. 37For by your words you will be acquitted, and by your words you will be condemned."

The Sign of Jonah

38Then some of the Pharisees and teachers of the law said to him, "Teacher, we want to see a miraculous sign from you."

39He answered, "A wicked and adulterous generation asks for a miraculous sign! But none will be given it except the sign of the prophet Jonah. 40For as Jonah was three days and three nights in the belly of a huge fish, so the Son of Man will be three days and three nights in the heart of the earth. 41The men of Nineveh will stand up at the judgment with this generation and condemn it; for they repented at the preaching of Jonah, and now one greater than Jonah is here. 42The Queen of the South will rise at the judgment with this generation and condemn it; for she came from the ends of the earth to listen to Solomon's wisdom, and now one greater than Solomon is here.

43"When an evil spirit comes out of a man, it goes through arid places seeking rest and does not find it. 44Then it says, 'I will return to the house I left.' When it arrives, it finds the house unoccupied, swept clean and put in order. 45Then it goes and takes with it seven other spirits more wicked than itself, and they go in and live there. And the final condition of that man is worse than the first. That is how it will be with this wicked generation."

READING FROM PROVERBS
Proverbs 2:1–11

Moral Benefits of Wisdom

2 My son, if you accept my words
  and store up my commands within
    you,
²turning your ear to wisdom
  and applying your heart to
    understanding,
³and if you call out for insight
  and cry aloud for understanding,
⁴and if you look for it as for silver
  and search for it as for hidden
    treasure,
⁵then you will understand the fear of
    the LORD
  and find the knowledge of God.

⁶For the LORD gives wisdom,
  and from his mouth come
    knowledge and understanding.
⁷He holds victory in store for the
    upright,
  he is a shield to those whose walk is
    blameless,
⁸for he guards the course of the just
  and protects the way of his faithful
    ones.

⁹Then you will understand what is
    right and just
  and fair—every good path.
¹⁰For wisdom will enter your heart,
  and knowledge will be pleasant to
    your soul.
¹¹Discretion will protect you,
  and understanding will guard you.

JANUARY 17   DAY 17

OLD TESTAMENT READING
Genesis 34:1–35:29

Dinah and the Shechemites

34 Now Dinah, the daughter Leah
  had borne to Jacob, went out to
visit the women of the land. ²When
Shechem son of Hamor the Hivite, the
ruler of that area, saw her, he took her
and raped her. ³His heart was drawn to
Dinah daughter of Jacob, and he loved
the girl and spoke tenderly to her. ⁴And
Shechem said to his father Hamor,
"Get me this girl as my wife."

⁵When Jacob heard that his daughter
Dinah had been defiled, his sons were in
the fields with his livestock; so he kept
quiet about it until they came home.

⁶Then Shechem's father Hamor went
out to talk with Jacob. ⁷Now Jacob's
sons had come in from the fields as soon
as they heard what had happened. They
were filled with grief and fury, because
Shechem had done a disgraceful thing in

Israel by lying with Jacob's daughter
—a thing that should not be done.
⁸But Hamor said to them, "My son
Shechem has his heart set on your
daughter. Please give her to him as his
wife. ⁹Intermarry with us; give us your
daughters and take our daughters for
yourselves. ¹⁰You can settle among us;
the land is open to you. Live in it, trade
in it, and acquire property in it."

¹¹Then Shechem said to Dinah's
father and brothers, "Let me find
favour in your eyes, and I will give you
whatever you ask. ¹²Make the price for
the bride and the gift I am to bring as
great as you like, and I'll pay whatever
you ask me. Only give me the girl as my
wife."

¹³Because their sister Dinah had been
defiled, Jacob's sons replied deceitfully
as they spoke to Shechem and his father
Hamor. ¹⁴They said to them, "We can't
do such a thing; we can't give our sister
to a man who is not circumcised. That
would be a disgrace to us. ¹⁵We will give

our consent to you on one condition only: that you become like us by circumcising all your males. ¹⁶Then we will give you our daughters and take your daughters for ourselves. We'll settle among you and become one people with you. ¹⁷But if you will not agree to be circumcised, we'll take our sister and go."

¹⁸Their proposal seemed good to Hamor and his son Shechem. ¹⁹The young man, who was the most honoured of all his father's household, lost no time in doing what they said, because he was delighted with Jacob's daughter. ²⁰So Hamor and his son Shechem went to the gate of their city to speak to their fellow townsmen. ²¹"These men are friendly towards us," they said. "Let them live in our land and trade in it; the land has plenty of room for them. We can marry their daughters and they can marry ours. ²²But the men will consent to live with us as one people only on the condition that our males be circumcised, as they themselves are. ²³Won't their livestock, their property and all their other animals become ours? So let us give our consent to them, and they will settle among us."

²⁴All the men who went out of the city gate agreed with Hamor and his son Shechem, and every male in the city was circumcised.

²⁵Three days later, while all of them were still in pain, two of Jacob's sons, Simeon and Levi, Dinah's brothers, took their swords and attacked the unsuspecting city, killing every male. ²⁶They put Hamor and his son Shechem to the sword and took Dinah from Shechem's house and left. ²⁷The sons of Jacob came upon the dead bodies and looted the city where their sister had been defiled. ²⁸They seized their flocks and herds and donkeys and everything else of theirs in the city and out in the fields. ²⁹They carried off all their wealth and all their women and children, taking as plunder everything in the houses.

³⁰Then Jacob said to Simeon and Levi, "You have brought trouble on me by making me a stench to the Canaanites and Perizzites, the people living in this land. We are few in number, and if they join forces against me and attack me, I and my household will be destroyed."

³¹But they replied, "Should he have treated our sister like a prostitute?"

Jacob Returns to Bethel

35 Then God said to Jacob, "Go up to Bethel and settle there, and build an altar there to God, who appeared to you when you were fleeing from your brother Esau."

²So Jacob said to his household and to all who were with him, "Get rid of the foreign gods you have with you, and purify yourselves and change your clothes. ³Then come, let us go up to Bethel, where I will build an altar to God, who answered me in the day of my distress and who has been with me wherever I have gone." ⁴So they gave Jacob all the foreign gods they had and the rings in their ears, and Jacob buried them under the oak at Shechem. ⁵Then they set out, and the terror of God fell upon the towns all around them so that no-one pursued them.

⁶Jacob and all the people with him came to Luz (that is, Bethel) in the land of Canaan. ⁷There he built an altar, and he called the place El Bethel, because it was there that God revealed himself to him when he was fleeing from his brother.

⁸Now Deborah, Rebekah's nurse, died and was buried under the oak below Bethel. So it was named Allon Bacuth.

⁹After Jacob returned from Paddan Aram, God appeared to him again and blessed him. ¹⁰God said to him, "Your name is Jacob, but you will no longer be called Jacob; your name will be Israel." So he named him Israel.

¹¹And God said to him, "I am God Almighty; be fruitful and increase in number. A nation and a community of

nations will come from you, and kings will come from your body. ¹²The land I gave to Abraham and Isaac I also give to you, and I will give this land to your descendants after you." ¹³Then God went up from him at the place where he had talked with him.

¹⁴Jacob set up a stone pillar at the place where God had talked with him, and he poured out a drink offering on it; he also poured oil on it. ¹⁵Jacob called the place where God had talked with him Bethel.

The Deaths of Rachel and Isaac

¹⁶Then they moved on from Bethel. While they were still some distance from Ephrath, Rachel began to give birth and had great difficulty. ¹⁷And as she was having great difficulty in childbirth, the midwife said to her, "Don't be afraid, for you have another son." ¹⁸As she breathed her last—for she was dying—she named her son Ben-Oni. But his father named him Benjamin.

¹⁹So Rachel died and was buried on the way to Ephrath (that is, Bethlehem). ²⁰Over her tomb Jacob set up a pillar, and to this day that pillar marks Rachel's tomb.

²¹Israel moved on again and pitched his tent beyond Migdal Eder. ²²While Israel was living in that region, Reuben went in and slept with his father's concubine Bilhah, and Israel heard of it.

Jacob had twelve sons:

²³The sons of Leah:

Reuben the firstborn of Jacob, Simeon, Levi, Judah, Issachar and Zebulun.

²⁴The sons of Rachel:

Joseph and Benjamin.

²⁵The sons of Rachel's maidservant Bilhah:

Dan and Naphtali.

²⁶The sons of Leah's maidservant Zilpah:

Gad and Asher.

These were the sons of Jacob, who were born to him in Paddan Aram.

²⁷Jacob came home to his father Isaac in Mamre, near Kiriath Arba (that is, Hebron), where Abraham and Isaac had stayed. ²⁸Isaac lived a hundred and eighty years. ²⁹Then he breathed his last and died and was gathered to his people, old and full of years. And his sons Esau and Jacob buried him.

NEW TESTAMENT READING
Matthew 12:46–13:17

Jesus' Mother and Brothers

⁴⁶While Jesus was still talking to the crowd, his mother and brothers stood outside, wanting to speak to him. ⁴⁷Someone told him, "Your mother and brothers are standing outside, wanting to speak to you."

⁴⁸He replied to him, "Who is my mother, and who are my brothers?" ⁴⁹Pointing to his disciples, he said, "Here are my mother and my brothers. ⁵⁰For whoever does the will of my Father in heaven is my brother and sister and mother."

The Parable of the Sower

13 That same day Jesus went out of the house and sat by the lake. ²Such large crowds gathered round him that he got into a boat and sat in it, while all the people stood on the shore. ³Then he told them many things in parables, saying: "A farmer went out to sow his seed. ⁴As he was scattering the seed, some fell along the path, and the birds came and ate it up. ⁵Some fell on rocky places, where it did not have much soil. It sprang up quickly, because the soil was shallow. ⁶But when the sun came up, the plants were scorched, and they withered because they had no root. ⁷Other seed fell among thorns, which grew up and choked the plants. ⁸Still other seed fell on good soil, where it produced a crop—a hundred, sixty or thirty times what was sown. ⁹He who has ears, let him hear."

¹⁰The disciples came to him and asked, "Why do you speak to the people in parables?"

¹¹He replied, "The knowledge of the secrets of the kingdom of heaven has been given to you, but not to them. ¹²Whoever has will be given more, and he will have an abundance. Whoever does not have, even what he has will be taken from him. ¹³This is why I speak to them in parables:

"Though seeing, they do not see;
    though hearing, they do not hear
    or understand.'

¹⁴In them is fulfilled the prophecy of Isaiah:

"'You will be ever hearing but never
    understanding;
 you will be ever seeing but never
    perceiving.
¹⁵For this people's heart has become
    calloused;
 they hardly hear with their ears,
    and they have closed their eyes.
 Otherwise they might see with their
    eyes,
 hear with their ears,
 understand with their hearts
 and turn, and I would heal them.'

¹⁶"But blessed are your eyes because they see, and your ears because they hear. ¹⁷For I tell you the truth, many prophets and righteous men longed to see what you see but did not see it, and to hear what you hear but did not hear it.

READING FROM PSALMS
Psalm 10:1–11

¹Why, O LORD, do you stand far off?
    Why do you hide yourself in times
        of trouble?

²In his arrogance the wicked man
        hunts down the weak,
    who are caught in the schemes he
        devises.
³He boasts of the cravings of his heart;
    he blesses the greedy and reviles
        the LORD.
⁴In his pride the wicked does not seek
        him;
    in all his thoughts there is no room
        for God.
⁵His ways are always prosperous;
    he is haughty and your laws are far
        from him;
    he sneers at all his enemies.
⁶He says to himself, "Nothing will
        shake me;
    I'll always be happy and never
        have trouble."
⁷His mouth is full of curses and lies
        and threats;
    trouble and evil are under his
        tongue.
⁸He lies in wait near the villages;
    from ambush he murders the
        innocent,
    watching in secret for his victims.
⁹He lies in wait like a lion in cover;
    he lies in wait to catch the helpless;
    he catches the helpless and drags
        them off in his net.
¹⁰His victims are crushed, they
        collapse;
    they fall under his strength.
¹¹He says to himself, "God has
        forgotten;
    he covers his face and never sees."

OLD TESTAMENT READING
Genesis 36:1–37:36

Esau's Descendants

36 This is the account of Esau (that is, Edom).

²Esau took his wives from the women of Canaan: Adah daughter of Elon the Hittite, and Oholibamah daughter of Anah and granddaughter of Zibeon the Hivite— ³also Basemath daughter of Ishmael and sister of Nebaioth.

⁴Adah bore Eliphaz to Esau, Basemath bore Reuel, ⁵and Oholibamah bore Jeush, Jalam and Korah. These were the sons of Esau, who were born to him in Canaan.

⁶Esau took his wives and sons and daughters and all the members of his household, as well as his livestock and all his other animals and all the goods he had acquired in Canaan, and moved to a land some distance from his brother Jacob. ⁷Their possessions were too great for them to remain together; the land where they were staying could not support them both because of their livestock. ⁸So Esau (that is, Edom) settled in the hill country of Seir.

⁹This is the account of Esau the father of the Edomites in the hill country of Seir.

¹⁰These are the names of Esau's sons:
   Eliphaz, the son of Esau's wife Adah, and Reuel, the son of Esau's wife Basemath.
¹¹The sons of Eliphaz:
   Teman, Omar, Zepho, Gatam and Kenaz.

¹²Esau's son Eliphaz also had a concubine named Timna, who bore him Amalek. These were grandsons of Esau's wife Adah.
¹³The sons of Reuel:
   Nahath, Zerah, Shammah and Mizzah. These were grandsons of Esau's wife Basemath.
¹⁴The sons of Esau's wife Oholibamah daughter of Anah and granddaughter of Zibeon, whom she bore to Esau:
   Jeush, Jalam and Korah.

¹⁵These were the chiefs among Esau's descendants:
   The sons of Eliphaz the firstborn of Esau:
   Chiefs Teman, Omar, Zepho, Kenaz, ¹⁶Korah, Gatam and Amalek. These were the chiefs descended from Eliphaz in Edom; they were grandsons of Adah.
¹⁷The sons of Esau's son Reuel:
   Chiefs Nahath, Zerah, Shammah and Mizzah. These were the chiefs descended from Reuel in Edom; they were grandsons of Esau's wife Basemath.
¹⁸The sons of Esau's wife Oholibamah:
   Chiefs Jeush, Jalam and Korah. These were the chiefs descended from Esau's wife Oholibamah daughter of Anah.
¹⁹These were the sons of Esau (that is, Edom), and these were their chiefs.

²⁰These were the sons of Seir the Horite, who were living in the region:
   Lotan, Shobal, Zibeon, Anah, ²¹Dishon, Ezer and Dishan. These sons of Seir in Edom were Horite chiefs.
²²The sons of Lotan:
   Hori and Homam. Timna was Lotan's sister.

23The sons of Shobal:

Alvan, Manahath, Ebal, Shepho and Onam.

24The sons of Zibeon:

Aiah and Anah. This is the Anah who discovered the hot springs in the desert while he was grazing the donkeys of his father Zibeon.

25The children of Anah:

Dishon and Oholibamah daughter of Anah.

26The sons of Dishon:

Hemdan, Eshban, Ithran and Keran.

27The sons of Ezer:

Bilhan, Zaavan and Akan.

28The sons of Dishan:

Uz and Aran.

29These were the Horite chiefs:

Lotan, Shobal, Zibeon, Anah, 30Dishon, Ezer and Dishan. These were the Horite chiefs, according to their divisions, in the land of Seir.

The Rulers of Edom

31These were the kings who reigned in Edom before any Israelite king reigned:

32Bela son of Beor became king of Edom. His city was named Dinhabah.

33When Bela died, Jobab son of Zerah from Bozrah succeeded him as king.

34When Jobab died, Husham from the land of the Temanites succeeded him as king.

35When Husham died, Hadad son of Bedad, who defeated Midian in the country of Moab, succeeded him as king. His city was named Avith.

36When Hadad died, Samlah from Masrekah succeeded him as king.

37When Samlah died, Shaul from Rehoboth on the river succeeded him as king.

38When Shaul died, Baal-Hanan son of Acbor succeeded him as king.

39When Baal-Hanan son of Acbor died, Hadad succeeded him as king. His city was named Pau, and his wife's name was Mehetabel daughter of Matred, the daughter of Me-Zahab.

40These were the chiefs descended from Esau, by name, according to their clans and regions:

Timna, Alvah, Jetheth, 41Oholibamah, Elah, Pinon, 42Kenaz, Teman, Mibzar, 43Magdiel and Iram. These were the chiefs of Edom, according to their settlements in the land they occupied.

This was Esau the father of the Edomites.

Joseph's Dreams

37 Jacob lived in the land where his father had stayed, the land of Canaan.

2This is the account of Jacob.

Joseph, a young man of seventeen, was tending the flocks with his brothers, the sons of Bilhah and the sons of Zilpah, his father's wives, and he brought their father a bad report about them.

3Now Israel loved Joseph more than any of his other sons, because he had been born to him in his old age; and he made a richly ornamented robe for him. 4When his brothers saw that their father loved him more than any of them, they hated him and could not speak a kind word to him.

5Joseph had a dream, and when he told it to his brothers, they hated him all the more. 6He said to them, "Listen to this dream I had: 7We were binding sheaves of corn out in the field when suddenly my sheaf rose and stood upright, while your sheaves gathered round mine and bowed down to it."

8His brothers said to him, "Do you

intend to reign over us? Will you actually rule us?" And they hated him all the more because of his dream and what he had said.

9Then he had another dream, and he told it to his brothers. "Listen," he said, "I had another dream, and this time the sun and moon and eleven stars were bowing down to me."

10When he told his father as well as his brothers, his father rebuked him and said, "What is this dream you had? Will your mother and I and your brothers actually come and bow down to the ground before you?" 11His brothers were jealous of him, but his father kept the matter in mind.

Joseph Sold by His Brothers

12Now his brothers had gone to graze their father's flocks near Shechem, 13and Israel said to Joseph, "As you know, your brothers are grazing the flocks near Shechem. Come, I am going to send you to them."

"Very well," he replied.

14So he said to him, "Go and see if all is well with your brothers and with the flocks, and bring word back to me." Then he sent him off from the Valley of Hebron.

When Joseph arrived at Shechem, 15a man found him wandering around in the fields and asked him, "What are you looking for?"

16He replied, "I'm looking for my brothers. Can you tell me where they are grazing their flocks?"

17"They have moved on from here," the man answered. "I heard them say, 'Let's go to Dothan.'"

So Joseph went after his brothers and found them near Dothan. 18But they saw him in the distance, and before he reached them, they plotted to kill him.

19"Here comes that dreamer!" they said to each other. 20"Come now, let's kill him and throw him into one of these cisterns and say that a ferocious animal devoured him. Then we'll see what comes of his dreams."

21When Reuben heard this, he tried to rescue him from their hands. "Let's not take his life," he said. 22"Don't shed any blood. Throw him into this cistern here in the desert, but don't lay a hand on him." Reuben said this to rescue him from them and take him back to his father.

23So when Joseph came to his brothers, they stripped him of his robe —the richly ornamented robe he was wearing—24and they took him and threw him into the cistern. Now the cistern was empty; there was no water in it.

25As they sat down to eat their meal, they looked up and saw a caravan of Ishmaelites coming from Gilead. Their camels were loaded with spices, balm and myrrh, and they were on their way to take them down to Egypt.

26Judah said to his brothers, "What will we gain if we kill our brother and cover up his blood? 27Come, let's sell him to the Ishmaelites and not lay our hands on him; after all, he is our brother, our own flesh and blood." His brothers agreed.

28So when the Midianite merchants came by, his brothers pulled Joseph up out of the cistern and sold him for twenty shekels of silver to the Ishmaelites, who took him to Egypt.

29When Reuben returned to the cistern and saw that Joseph was not there, he tore his clothes. 30He went back to his brothers and said, "The boy isn't there! Where can I turn now?"

31Then they got Joseph's robe, slaughtered a goat and dipped the robe in the blood. 32They took the ornamented robe back to their father and said, "We found this. Examine it to see whether it is your son's robe."

33He recognised it and said, "It is my son's robe! Some ferocious animal has devoured him. Joseph has surely been torn to pieces."

34Then Jacob tore his clothes, put on sackcloth and mourned for his son many days. 35All his sons and daughters came to comfort him, but he refused to be comforted. "No," he said, "in mourning will I go down to the grave to my son." So his father wept for him. ³⁶Meanwhile, the Midianites sold Joseph in Egypt to Potiphar, one of Pharaoh's officials, the captain of the guard.

NEW TESTAMENT READING
Matthew 13:18–35

¹⁸"Listen then to what the parable of the sower means: ¹⁹When anyone hears the message about the kingdom and does not understand it, the evil one comes and snatches away what was sown in his heart. This is the seed sown along the path. ²⁰The one who received the seed that fell on rocky places is the man who hears the word and at once receives it with joy. ²¹But since he has no root, he lasts only a short time. When trouble or persecution comes because of the word, he quickly falls away. ²²The one who received the seed that fell among the thorns is the man who hears the word, but the worries of this life and the deceitfulness of wealth choke it, making it unfruitful. ²³But the one who received the seed that fell on good soil is the man who hears the word and understands it. He produces a crop, yielding a hundred, sixty or thirty times what was sown."

The Parable of the Weeds

²⁴Jesus told them another parable: "The kingdom of heaven is like a man who sowed good seed in his field. ²⁵But while everyone was sleeping, his enemy came and sowed weeds among the wheat, and went away. ²⁶When the wheat sprouted and formed ears, then the weeds also appeared.

²⁷"The owner's servants came to him and said, 'Sir, didn't you sow good seed in your field? Where then did the weeds come from?'

²⁸"'An enemy did this,' he replied.

"The servants asked him, 'Do you want us to go and pull them up?'

²⁹"'No,' he answered, 'because while you are pulling the weeds, you may root up the wheat with them. ³⁰Let both grow together until the harvest. At that time I will tell the harvesters: First collect the weeds and tie them in bundles to be burned; then gather the wheat and bring it into my barn.'"

The Parables of the Mustard Seed and the Yeast

³¹He told them another parable: "The kingdom of heaven is like a mustard seed, which a man took and planted in his field. ³²Though it is the smallest of all your seeds, yet when it grows, it is the largest of garden plants and becomes a tree, so that the birds of the air come and perch in its branches."

³³He told them still another parable: "The kingdom of heaven is like yeast that a woman took and mixed into a large amount of flour until it worked all through the dough."

³⁴Jesus spoke all these things to the crowd in parables; he did not say anything to them without using a parable. ³⁵So was fulfilled what was spoken through the prophet:

"I will open my mouth in parables,
    I will utter things hidden since the
        creation of the world."

READING FROM PSALMS
Psalm 10:12–18

¹²Arise, LORD! Lift up your hand, O
        God.
    Do not forget the helpless.
¹³Why does the wicked man revile
        God?
    Why does he say to himself,
        "He won't call me to account"?
¹⁴But you, O God, do see trouble and
        grief;

you consider it to take it in hand.
The victim commits himself to you;
you are the helper of the fatherless.
15Break the arm of the wicked and evil
man;
call him to account for his
wickedness
that would not be found out.

16The LORD is King for ever and ever;

the nations will perish from his
land.
17You hear, O LORD, the desire of the
afflicted;
you encourage them, and you
listen to their cry,
18defending the fatherless and the
oppressed,
in order that man, who is of the
earth, may terrify no more.

JANUARY 19 DAY 19

OLD TESTAMENT READING
Genesis 38:1–39:23

Judah and Tamar

38 At that time, Judah left his
brothers and went down to stay
with a man of Adullam named Hirah.
2There Judah met the daughter of a
Canaanite man named Shua. He married
her and lay with her; 3she became
pregnant and gave birth to a son, who
was named Er. 4She conceived again
and gave birth to a son and named him
Onan. 5She gave birth to still another
son and named him Shelah. It was at
Kezib that she gave birth to him.

6Judah got a wife for Er, his firstborn,
and her name was Tamar. 7But Er,
Judah's firstborn, was wicked in the
LORD's sight; so the LORD put him to
death.

8Then Judah said to Onan, "Lie with
your brother's wife and fulfil your duty
to her as a brother-in-law to produce
offspring for your brother." 9But Onan
knew that the offspring would not be
his; so whenever he lay with his
brother's wife, he spilled his semen on
the ground to keep from producing
offspring for his brother. 10What he did
was wicked in the LORD's sight; so he
put him to death also.

11Judah then said to his daughter-in-
law Tamar, "Live as a widow in your

father's house until my son Shelah
grows up." For he thought, "He may
die too, just like his brothers." So
Tamar went to live in her father's
house.

12After a long time Judah's wife, the
daughter of Shua, died. When Judah
had recovered from his grief, he went
up to Timnah, to the men who were
shearing his sheep, and his friend Hirah
the Adullamite went with him.

13When Tamar was told, "Your
father-in-law is on his way to Timnah to
shear his sheep," 14she took off her
widow's clothes, covered herself with a
veil to disguise herself, and then sat
down at the entrance to Enaim, which is
on the road to Timnah. For she saw
that, though Shelah had now grown up,
she had not been given to him as his
wife.

15When Judah saw her, he thought
she was a prostitute, for she had
covered her face. 16Not realising that
she was his daughter-in-law, he went
over to her by the roadside and said,
"Come now, let me sleep with you."

"And what will you give me to sleep
with you?" she asked.

17"I'll send you a young goat from my
flock," he said.

"Will you give me something as a
pledge until you send it?" she asked.

18He said, "What pledge should I give
you?"

"Your seal and its cord, and the staff in your hand," she answered. So he gave them to her and slept with her, and she became pregnant by him. ¹⁹After she left, she took off her veil and put on her widow's clothes again.

²⁰Meanwhile Judah sent the young goat by his friend the Adullamite in order to get his pledge back from the woman, but he did not find her. ²¹He asked the men who lived there, "Where is the shrine-prostitute who was beside the road at Enaim?"

"There hasn't been any shrine-prostitute here," they said.

²²So he went back to Judah and said, "I didn't find her. Besides, the men who lived there said, 'There hasn't been any shrine-prostitute here.'"

²³Then Judah said, "Let her keep what she has, or we will become a laughing-stock. After all, I did send her this young goat, but you didn't find her."

²⁴About three months later Judah was told, "Your daughter-in-law Tamar is guilty of prostitution, and as a result she is now pregnant."

Judah said, "Bring her out and have her burned to death!"

²⁵As she was being brought out, she sent a message to her father-in-law. "I am pregnant by the man who owns these," she said. And she added, "See if you recognise whose seal and cord and staff these are."

²⁶Judah recognised them and said, "She is more righteous than I, since I wouldn't give her to my son Shelah." And he did not sleep with her again.

²⁷When the time came for her to give birth, there were twin boys in her womb. ²⁸As she was giving birth, one of them put out his hand; so the midwife took a scarlet thread and tied it on his wrist and said, "This one came out first." ²⁹But when he drew back his hand, his brother came out, and she said, "So this is how you have broken out!" And he was named Perez. ³⁰Then his brother, who had the scarlet thread

on his wrist, came out and he was given the name Zerah.

Joseph and Potiphar's Wife

39 Now Joseph had been taken down to Egypt. Potiphar, an Egyptian who was one of Pharaoh's officials, the captain of the guard, bought him from the Ishmaelites who had taken him there.

²The LORD was with Joseph and he prospered, and he lived in the house of his Egyptian master. ³When his master saw that the LORD was with him and that the LORD gave him success in everything he did, ⁴Joseph found favour in his eyes and became his attendant. Potiphar put him in charge of his household, and he entrusted to his care everything he owned. ⁵From the time he put him in charge of his household and of all that he owned, the LORD blessed the household of the Egyptian because of Joseph. The blessing of the LORD was on everything Potiphar had, both in the house and in the field. ⁶So he left in Joseph's care everything he had; with Joseph in charge, he did not concern himself with anything except the food he ate.

Now Joseph was well-built and handsome, ⁷and after a while his master's wife took notice of Joseph and said, "Come to bed with me!"

⁸But he refused. "With me in charge," he told her, "my master does not concern himself with anything in the house; everything he owns he has entrusted to my care. ⁹No-one is greater in this house than I am. My master has withheld nothing from me except you, because you are his wife. How then could I do such a wicked thing and sin against God?" ¹⁰And though she spoke to Joseph day after day, he refused to go to bed with her or even to be with her.

¹¹One day he went into the house to attend to his duties, and none of the household servants was inside. ¹²She caught him by his cloak and said, "Come to bed with me!" But he left his

cloak in her hand and ran out of the house. 13When she saw that he had left his cloak in her hand and had run out of the house, 14she called her household servants. "Look," she said to them, "this Hebrew has been brought to us to make sport of us! He came in here to sleep with me, but I screamed. 15When he heard me scream for help, he left his cloak beside me and ran out of the house."

16She kept his cloak beside her until his master came home. 17Then she told him this story: "That Hebrew slave you brought us came to me to make sport of me. 18But as soon as I screamed for help, he left his cloak beside me and ran out of the house."

19When his master heard the story his wife told him, saying, "This is how your slave treated me," he burned with anger. 20Joseph's master took him and put him in prison, the place where the king's prisoners were confined.

But while Joseph was there in the prison, 21the LORD was with him; he showed him kindness and granted him favour in the eyes of the prison warder. 22So the warder put Joseph in charge of all those held in the prison, and he was made responsible for all that was done there. 23The warder paid no attention to anything under Joseph's care, because the LORD was with Joseph and gave him success in whatever he did.

NEW TESTAMENT READING
Matthew 13:36–58

The Parable of the Weeds Explained

36Then he left the crowd and went into the house. His disciples came to him and said, "Explain to us the parable of the weeds in the field." 37He answered, "The one who sowed the good seed is the Son of Man. 38The field is the world, and the good seed stands for the sons of the kingdom. The weeds are the sons of the evil one, 39and

the enemy who sows them is the devil. The harvest is the end of the age, and the harvesters are angels.

40"As the weeds are pulled up and burned in the fire, so it will be at the end of the age. 41The Son of Man will send out his angels, and they will weed out of his kingdom everything that causes sin and all who do evil. 42They will throw them into the fiery furnace, where there will be weeping and gnashing of teeth. 43Then the righteous will shine like the sun in the kingdom of their Father. He who has ears, let him hear.

The Parables of the Hidden Treasure and the Pearl

44"The kingdom of heaven is like treasure hidden in a field. When a man found it, he hid it again, and then in his joy went and sold all he had and bought that field.

45"Again, the kingdom of heaven is like a merchant looking for fine pearls. 46When he found one of great value, he went away and sold everything he had and bought it.

The Parable of the Net

47"Once again, the kingdom of heaven is like a net that was let down into the lake and caught all kinds of fish. 48When it was full, the fishermen pulled it up on the shore. Then they sat down and collected the good fish in baskets, but threw the bad away. 49This is how it will be at the end of the age. The angels will come and separate the wicked from the righteous 50and throw them into the fiery furnace, where there will be weeping and gnashing of teeth.

51"Have you understood all these things?" Jesus asked.

"Yes," they replied.

52He said to them, "Therefore every teacher of the law who has been instructed about the kingdom of heaven is like the owner of a house who brings out of his storeroom new treasures as well as old."

A Prophet Without Honour

53When Jesus had finished these parables, he moved on from there.
54Coming to his home town, he began
teaching the people in their synagogue,
and they were amazed. "Where did this
man get this wisdom and these miraculous powers?" they asked. 55"Isn't this
the carpenter's son? Isn't his mother's
name Mary, and aren't his brothers
James, Joseph, Simon and Judas?
56Aren't all his sisters with us? Where
then did this man get all these things?"
57And they took offence at him.

But Jesus said to them, "Only in his
home town and in his own house is a
prophet without honour."

58And he did not do many miracles
there because of their lack of faith.

READING FROM PSALMS
Psalm 11:1–7

For the director of music. Of David.

1In the LORD I take refuge.
   How then can you say to me:
   "Flee like a bird to your mountain.

2For look, the wicked bend their
      bows;
   they set their arrows against the
      strings
 to shoot from the shadows
   at the upright in heart.
3When the foundations are being
      destroyed,
   what can the righteous do?"

4The LORD is in his holy temple;
   the LORD is on his heavenly
      throne.
 He observes the sons of men;
   his eyes examine them.
5The LORD examines the righteous,
   but the wicked and those who love
      violence
   his soul hates.
6On the wicked he will rain
   fiery coals and burning sulphur;
   a scorching wind will be their
      lot.

7For the LORD is righteous,
   he loves justice;
   upright men will see his face.

JANUARY 20

OLD TESTAMENT READING
Genesis 40:1–41:40

The Cupbearer and the Baker

40 Some time later, the cupbearer
   and the baker of the king of
Egypt offended their master, the king of
Egypt. 2Pharaoh was angry with his two
officials, the chief cupbearer and the
chief baker, 3and put them in custody in
the house of the captain of the guard, in
the same prison where Joseph was confined. 4The captain of the guard

assigned them to Joseph, and he
attended them.

After they had been in custody for
some time, 5each of the two men—the
cupbearer and the baker of the king of
Egypt, who were being held in prison
—had a dream the same night, and each
dream had a meaning of its own.

6When Joseph came to them the next
morning, he saw that they were dejected. 7So he asked Pharaoh's officials
who were in custody with him in his
master's house, "Why are your faces so
sad today?"

8"We both had dreams," they

answered, "but there is no-one to interpret them."

Then Joseph said to them, "Do not interpretations belong to God? Tell me your dreams."

⁹So the chief cupbearer told Joseph his dream. He said to him, "In my dream I saw a vine in front of me, ¹⁰and on the vine were three branches. As soon as it budded, it blossomed, and its clusters ripened into grapes. ¹¹Pharaoh's cup was in my hand, and I took the grapes, squeezed them into Pharaoh's cup and put the cup in his hand."

¹²"This is what it means," Joseph said to him. "The three branches are three days. ¹³Within three days Pharaoh will lift up your head and restore you to your position, and you will put Pharaoh's cup in his hand, just as you used to do when you were his cupbearer. ¹⁴But when all goes well with you, remember me and show me kindness; mention me to Pharaoh and get me out of this prison. ¹⁵For I was forcibly carried off from the land of the Hebrews, and even here I have done nothing to deserve being put in a dungeon."

¹⁶When the chief baker saw that Joseph had given a favourable interpretation, he said to Joseph, "I too had a dream: On my head were three baskets of bread. ¹⁷In the top basket were all kinds of baked goods for Pharaoh, but the birds were eating them out of the basket on my head."

¹⁸"This is what it means," Joseph said. "The three baskets are three days. ¹⁹Within three days Pharaoh will lift off your head and hang you on a tree. And the birds will eat away your flesh."

²⁰Now the third day was Pharaoh's birthday, and he gave a feast for all his officials. He lifted up the heads of the chief cupbearer and the chief baker in the presence of his officials: ²¹He restored the chief cupbearer to his position, so that he once again put the cup into Pharaoh's hand, ²²but he hanged the chief baker, just as Joseph had said to them in his interpretation.

²³The chief cupbearer, however, did not remember Joseph; he forgot him.

Pharaoh's Dreams

41 When two full years had passed, Pharaoh had a dream: He was standing by the Nile, ²when out of the river there came up seven cows, sleek and fat, and they grazed among the reeds. ³After them, seven other cows, ugly and gaunt, came up out of the Nile and stood beside those on the riverbank. ⁴And the cows that were ugly and gaunt ate up the seven sleek, fat cows. Then Pharaoh woke up.

⁵He fell asleep again and had a second dream: Seven ears of corn, healthy and good, were growing on a single stalk. ⁶After them, seven other ears of corn sprouted—thin and scorched by the east wind. ⁷The thin ears of corn swallowed up the seven healthy, full ears. Then Pharaoh woke up; it had been a dream.

⁸In the morning his mind was troubled, so he sent for all the magicians and wise men of Egypt. Pharaoh told them his dreams, but no-one could interpret them for him.

⁹Then the chief cupbearer said to Pharaoh, "Today I am reminded of my shortcomings. ¹⁰Pharaoh was once angry with his servants, and he imprisoned me and the chief baker in the house ‧ of the captain of the guard. ¹¹Each of us had a dream the same night, and each dream had a meaning of its own. ¹²Now a young Hebrew was there with us, a servant of the captain of the guard. We told him our dreams, and he interpreted them for us, giving each man the interpretation of his dream. ¹³And things turned out exactly as he interpreted them to us: I was restored to my position, and the other man was hanged."

¹⁴So Pharaoh sent for Joseph, and he was quickly brought from the dungeon. When he had shaved and changed his clothes, he came before Pharaoh. ¹⁵Pharaoh said to Joseph, "I had a

dream, and no-one can interpret it. But I have heard it said of you that when you hear a dream you can interpret it."

16"I cannot do it," Joseph replied to Pharaoh, "but God will give Pharaoh the answer he desires."

17Then Pharaoh said to Joseph, "In my dream I was standing on the bank of the Nile, 18when out of the river there came up seven cows, fat and sleek, and they grazed among the reeds. 19After them, seven other cows came up—scrawny and very ugly and lean. I had never seen such ugly cows in all the land of Egypt. 20The lean, ugly cows ate up the seven fat cows that came up first. 21But even after they ate them, no-one could tell that they had done so; they looked just as ugly as before. Then I woke up.

22"In my dreams I also saw seven ears of corn, full and good, growing on a single stalk. 23After them, seven other ears sprouted—withered and thin and scorched by the east wind. 24The thin ears of corn swallowed up the seven good ears. I told this to the magicians, but none could explain it to me."

25Then Joseph said to Pharaoh, "The dreams of Pharaoh are one and the same. God has revealed to Pharaoh what he is about to do. 26The seven good cows are seven years, and the seven good ears of corn are seven years; it is one and the same dream. 27The seven lean, ugly cows that came up afterwards are seven years, and so are the seven worthless ears of corn scorched by the east wind: They are seven years of famine.

28"It is just as I said to Pharaoh: God has shown Pharaoh what he is about to do. 29Seven years of great abundance are coming throughout the land of Egypt, 30but seven years of famine will follow them. Then all the abundance in Egypt will be forgotten, and the famine will ravage the land. 31The abundance in the land will not be remembered, because the famine that follows it will be so severe. 32The reason the dream was given to Pharaoh in two forms is

that the matter has been firmly decided by God, and God will do it soon.

33"And now let Pharaoh look for a discerning and wise man and put him in charge of the land of Egypt. 34Let Pharaoh appoint commissioners over the land to take a fifth of the harvest of Egypt during the seven years of abundance. 35They should collect all the food of these good years that are coming and store up the grain under the authority of Pharaoh, to be kept in the cities for food. 36This food should be held in reserve for the country, to be used during the seven years of famine that will come upon Egypt, so that the country may not be ruined by the famine."

37The plan seemed good to Pharaoh and to all his officials. 38So Pharaoh asked them, "Can we find anyone like this man, one in whom is the spirit of God?"

39Then Pharaoh said to Joseph, "Since God has made all this known to you, there is no-one so discerning and wise as you. 40You shall be in charge of my palace, and all my people are to submit to your orders. Only with respect to the throne will I be greater than you."

NEW TESTAMENT READING
Matthew 14:1–21

John the Baptist Beheaded

14 At that time Herod the tetrarch heard the reports about Jesus, 2and he said to his attendants, "This is John the Baptist; he has risen from the dead! That is why miraculous powers are at work in him."

3Now Herod had arrested John and bound him and put him in prison because of Herodias, his brother Philip's wife, 4for John had been saying to him: "It is not lawful for you to have her." 5Herod wanted to kill John, but he was afraid of the people, because they considered him a prophet.

6On Herod's birthday the daughter of

Herodias danced for them and pleased Herod so much 7that he promised with an oath to give her whatever she asked. 8Prompted by her mother, she said, "Give me here on a platter the head of John the Baptist." 9The king was distressed, but because of his oaths and his dinner guests, he ordered that her request be granted 10and had John beheaded in the prison. 11His head was brought in on a platter and given to the girl, who carried it to her mother. 12John's disciples came and took his body and buried it. Then they went and told Jesus.

Jesus Feeds the Five Thousand

13When Jesus heard what had happened, he withdrew by boat privately to a solitary place. Hearing of this, the crowds followed him on foot from the towns. 14When Jesus landed and saw a large crowd, he had compassion on them and healed their sick.

15As evening approached, the disciples came to him and said, "This is a remote place, and it's already getting late. Send the crowds away, so that they can go to the villages and buy themselves some food."

16Jesus replied, "They do not need to go away. You give them something to eat."

17"We have here only five loaves of bread and two fish," they answered.

18"Bring them here to me," he said. 19And he directed the people to sit down on the grass. Taking the five loaves and the two fish and looking up to heaven, he gave thanks and broke the loaves. Then he gave them to the disciples, and the disciples gave them to the people. 20They all ate and were satisfied, and the disciples picked up twelve basketfuls of broken pieces that were left over. 21The number of those who ate was about five thousand men, besides women and children.

READING FROM PROVERBS
Proverbs 2:12–22

12Wisdom will save you from the ways
 of wicked men,
 from men whose words are
  perverse,
13who leave the straight paths
 to walk in dark ways,
14who delight in doing wrong
 and rejoice in the perverseness of
  evil,
15whose paths are crooked
 and who are devious in their ways.

16It will save you also from the
 adulteress,
 from the wayward wife with her
  seductive words,
17who has left the partner of her youth
 and ignored the covenant she made
  before God.
18For her house leads down to death
 and her paths to the spirits of the
  dead.
19None who go to her return
 or attain the paths of life.

20Thus you will walk in the ways of
 good men
 and keep to the paths of the
  righteous.
21For the upright will live in the land,
 and the blameless will remain in it;
22but the wicked will be cut off from
 the land,
 and the unfaithful will be torn from
  it.

JANUARY 21

OLD TESTAMENT READING
Genesis 41:41–42:38

Joseph in Charge of Egypt

41So Pharaoh said to Joseph, "I hereby put you in charge of the whole land of Egypt." 42Then Pharaoh took his signet ring from his finger and put it on Joseph's finger. He dressed him in robes of fine linen and put a gold chain around his neck. 43He had him ride in a chariot as his second-in-command, and men shouted before him, "Make way!" Thus he put him in charge of the whole land of Egypt.

44Then Pharaoh said to Joseph, "I am Pharaoh, but without your word no-one will lift hand or foot in all Egypt." 45Pharaoh gave Joseph the name Zaphenath-Paneah and gave him Asenath daughter of Potiphera, priest of On, to be his wife. And Joseph went throughout the land of Egypt.

46Joseph was thirty years old when he entered the service of Pharaoh king of Egypt. And Joseph went out from Pharaoh's presence and travelled throughout Egypt. 47During the seven years of abundance the land produced plentifully. 48Joseph collected all the food produced in those seven years of abundance in Egypt and stored it in the cities. In each city he put the food grown in the fields surrounding it. 49Joseph stored up huge quantities of grain, like the sand of the sea; it was so much that he stopped keeping records because it was beyond measure.

50Before the years of famine came, two sons were born to Joseph by Asenath daughter of Potiphera, priest of On. 51Joseph named his firstborn Manasseh and said, "It is because God has made me forget all my trouble and all my father's household." 52The second son he named Ephraim and said, "It is

because God has made me fruitful in the land of my suffering."

53The seven years of abundance in Egypt came to an end, 54and the seven years of famine began, just as Joseph had said. There was famine in all the other lands, but in the whole land of Egypt there was food. 55When all Egypt began to feel the famine, the people cried to Pharaoh for food. Then Pharaoh told all the Egyptians, "Go to Joseph and do what he tells you."

56When the famine had spread over the whole country, Joseph opened the storehouses and sold grain to the Egyptians, for the famine was severe throughout Egypt. 57And all the countries came to Egypt to buy grain from Joseph, because the famine was severe in all the world.

Joseph's Brothers Go to Egypt

42 When Jacob learned that there was grain in Egypt, he said to his sons, "Why do you just keep looking at each other?" 2He continued, "I have heard that there is grain in Egypt. Go down there and buy some for us, so that we may live and not die."

3Then ten of Joseph's brothers went down to buy grain from Egypt. 4But Jacob did not send Benjamin, Joseph's brother, with the others, because he was afraid that harm might come to him. 5So Israel's sons were among those who went to buy grain, for the famine was in the land of Canaan also.

6Now Joseph was the governor of the land, the one who sold grain to all its people. So when Joseph's brothers arrived, they bowed down to him with their faces to the ground. 7As soon as Joseph saw his brothers, he recognised them, but he pretended to be a stranger and spoke harshly to them. "Where do you come from?" he asked.

"From the land of Canaan," they replied, "to buy food."

⁸Although Joseph recognised his brothers, they did not recognise him. ⁹Then he remembered his dreams about them and said to them, "You are spies! You have come to see where our land is unprotected."

¹⁰"No, my lord," they answered. "Your servants have come to buy food. ¹¹We are all the sons of one man. Your servants are honest men, not spies."

¹²"No!" he said to them. "You have come to see where our land is unprotected."

¹³But they replied, "Your servants were twelve brothers, the sons of one man, who lives in the land of Canaan. The youngest is now with our father, and one is no more."

¹⁴Joseph said to them, "It is just as I told you: You are spies! ¹⁵And this is how you will be tested: As surely as Pharaoh lives, you will not leave this place unless your youngest brother comes here. ¹⁶Send one of your number to get your brother; the rest of you will be kept in prison, so that your words may be tested to see if you are telling the truth. If you are not, then as surely as Pharaoh lives, you are spies!" ¹⁷And he put them all in custody for three days.

¹⁸On the third day, Joseph said to them, "Do this and you will live, for I fear God: ¹⁹If you are honest men, let one of your brothers stay here in prison, while the rest of you go and take grain back for your starving households. ²⁰But you must bring your youngest brother to me, so that your words may be verified and that you may not die." This they proceeded to do.

²¹They said to one another, "Surely we are being punished because of our brother. We saw how distressed he was when he pleaded with us for his life, but we would not listen; that's why this distress has come upon us."

²²Reuben replied, "Didn't I tell you not to sin against the boy? But you wouldn't listen! Now we must give an accounting for his blood." ²³They did not realise that Joseph could understand them, since he was using an interpreter.

²⁴He turned away from them and began to weep, but then turned back and spoke to them again. He had Simeon taken from them and bound before their eyes.

²⁵Joseph gave orders to fill their bags with grain, to put each man's silver back in his sack, and to give them provisions for their journey. After this was done for them, ²⁶they loaded their grain on their donkeys and left.

²⁷At the place where they stopped for the night one of them opened his sack to get feed for his donkey, and he saw his silver in the mouth of his sack. ²⁸"My silver has been returned," he said to his brothers. "Here it is in my sack."

Their hearts sank and they turned to each other trembling and said, "What is this that God has done to us?"

²⁹When they came to their father Jacob in the land of Canaan, they told him all that had happened to them. They said, ³⁰"The man who is lord over the land spoke harshly to us and treated us as though we were spying on the land. ³¹But we said to him, 'We are honest men; we are not spies. ³²We were twelve brothers, sons of one father. One is no more, and the youngest is now with our father in Canaan.'

³³"Then the man who is lord over the land said to us, 'This is how I will know whether you are honest men: Leave one of your brothers here with me, and take food for your starving households and go. ³⁴But bring your youngest brother to me so I will know that you are not spies but honest men. Then I will give your brother back to you, and you can trade in the land.'"

³⁵As they were emptying their sacks, there in each man's sack was his pouch of silver! When they and their father saw the money pouches, they were frightened. ³⁶Their father Jacob said to them, "You have deprived me of my children. Joseph is no more and Simeon

is no more, and now you want to take Benjamin. Everything is against me!"

[37] Then Reuben said to his father, "You may put both of my sons to death if I do not bring him back to you. Entrust him to my care, and I will bring him back."

[38] But Jacob said, "My son will not go down there with you; his brother is dead and he is the only one left. If harm comes to him on the journey you are taking, you will bring my grey head down to the grave in sorrow."

NEW TESTAMENT READING
Matthew 14:22–15:9

Jesus Walks on the Water

[22] Immediately Jesus made the disciples get into the boat and go on ahead of him to the other side, while he dismissed the crowd. [23] After he had dismissed them, he went up on a mountainside by himself to pray. When evening came, he was there alone, [24] but the boat was already a considerable distance from land, buffeted by the waves because the wind was against it.

[25] During the fourth watch of the night Jesus went out to them, walking on the lake. [26] When the disciples saw him walking on the lake, they were terrified. "It's a ghost," they said, and cried out in fear.

[27] But Jesus immediately said to them: "Take courage! It is I. Don't be afraid."

[28] "Lord, if it's you," Peter replied, "tell me to come to you on the water."

[29] "Come," he said.

Then Peter got down out of the boat, walked on the water and came towards Jesus. [30] But when he saw the wind, he was afraid and, beginning to sink, cried out, "Lord, save me!"

[31] Immediately Jesus reached out his hand and caught him. "You of little faith," he said, "why did you doubt?"

[32] And when they climbed into the boat, the wind died down. [33] Then those who were in the boat worshipped him, saying, "Truly you are the Son of God."

[34] When they had crossed over, they landed at Gennesaret. [35] And when the men of that place recognised Jesus, they sent word to all the surrounding country. People brought all their sick to him [36] and begged him to let the sick just touch the edge of his cloak, and all who touched him were healed.

Clean and Unclean

15 Then some Pharisees and teachers of the law came to Jesus from Jerusalem and asked, [2] "Why do your disciples break the tradition of the elders? They don't wash their hands before they eat!"

[3] Jesus replied, "And why do you break the command of God for the sake of your tradition? [4] For God said, 'Honour your father and mother' and 'Anyone who curses his father or mother must be put to death.' [5] But you say that if a man says to his father or mother, 'Whatever help you might otherwise have received from me is a gift devoted to God,' [6] he is not to 'honour his father' with it. Thus you nullify the word of God for the sake of your tradition. [7] You hypocrites! Isaiah was right when he prophesied about you:

[8] "'These people honour me with their lips,
    but their hearts are far from me.
[9] They worship me in vain;
    their teachings are but rules taught
      by men.'"

READING FROM PSALMS
Psalm 12:1–8

For the director of music. According to *sheminith*. A psalm of David.

[1] Help, LORD, for the godly are no more;
    the faithful have vanished from
      among men.

²Everyone lies to his neighbour;
    their flattering lips speak with
        deception.

³May the LORD cut off all flattering
        lips
    and every boastful tongue
⁴that says, "We will triumph with our
        tongues;
    we own our lips—who is our
        master?"

⁵"Because of the oppression of the
        weak
    and the groaning of the needy,

I will now arise," says the LORD.
    "I will protect them from those
        who malign them."
⁶And the words of the LORD are
        flawless,
    like silver refined in a furnace of
        clay,
    purified seven times.

⁷O LORD, you will keep us safe
    and protect us from such people
        for ever.
⁸The wicked freely strut about
    when what is vile is honoured
        among men.

JANUARY 22   DAY 22

OLD TESTAMENT READING
Genesis 43:1–44:34

The Second Journey to Egypt

43 Now the famine was still severe
in the land. ²So when they had
eaten all the grain they had brought
from Egypt, their father said to them,
"Go back and buy us a little more
food."

³But Judah said to him, "The man
warned us solemnly, 'You will not see
my face again unless your brother is
with you.' ⁴If you will send our brother
along with us, we will go down and buy
food for you. ⁵But if you will not send
him, we will not go down, because the
man said to us, 'You will not see my face
again unless your brother is with you.'"

⁶Israel asked, "Why did you bring
this trouble on me by telling the man
you had another brother?"

⁷They replied, "The man questioned
us closely about ourselves and our family. 'Is your father still living?' he asked
us. 'Do you have another brother?' We
simply answered his questions. How
were we to know he would say, 'Bring
your brother down here'?"

⁸Then Judah said to Israel his father,
"Send the boy along with me and we
will go at once, so that we and you and
our children may live and not die. ⁹I
myself will guarantee his safety; you can
hold me personally responsible for him.
If I do not bring him back to you and set
him here before you, I will bear the
blame before you all my life. ¹⁰As it is, if
we had not delayed, we could have gone
and returned twice."

¹¹Then their father Israel said to
them, "If it must be, then do this: Put
some of the best products of the land in
your bags and take them down to the
man as a gift—a little balm and a little
honey, some spices and myrrh, some
pistachio nuts and almonds. ¹²Take
double the amount of silver with you,
for you must return the silver that was
put back into the mouths of your sacks.
Perhaps it was a mistake. ¹³Take your
brother also and go back to the man at
once. ¹⁴And may God Almighty grant
you mercy before the man so that he will
let your other brother and Benjamin
come back with you. As for me, if I am
bereaved, I am bereaved."

¹⁵So the men took the gifts and
double the amount of silver, and

Benjamin also. They hurried down to Egypt and presented themselves to Joseph. [16]When Joseph saw Benjamin with them, he said to the steward of his house, "Take these men to my house, slaughter an animal and prepare dinner; they are to eat with me at noon."

[17]The man did as Joseph told him and took the men to Joseph's house. [18]Now the men were frightened when they were taken to his house. They thought, "We were brought here because of the silver that was put back into our sacks the first time. He wants to attack us and overpower us and seize us as slaves and take our donkeys."

[19]So they went up to Joseph's steward and spoke to him at the entrance to the house. [20]"Please, sir," they said, "we came down here the first time to buy food. [21]But at the place where we stopped for the night we opened our sacks and each of us found his silver—the exact weight—in the mouth of his sack. So we have brought it back with us. [22]We have also brought additional silver with us to buy food. We don't know who put our silver in our sacks."

[23]"It's all right," he said. "Don't be afraid. Your God, the God of your father, has given you treasure in your sacks; I received your silver." Then he brought Simeon out to them.

[24]The steward took the men into Joseph's house, gave them water to wash their feet and provided fodder for their donkeys. [25]They prepared their gifts for Joseph's arrival at noon, because they had heard that they were to eat there.

[26]When Joseph came home, they presented to him the gifts they had brought into the house, and they bowed down before him to the ground. [27]He asked them how they were, and then he said, "How is your aged father you told me about? Is he still living?"

[28]They replied, "Your servant our father is still alive and well." And they bowed low to pay him honour.

[29]As he looked about and saw his brother Benjamin, his own mother's son, he asked, "Is this your youngest brother, the one you told me about?" And he said, "God be gracious to you, my son." [30]Deeply moved at the sight of his brother, Joseph hurried out and looked for a place to weep. He went into his private room and wept there.

[31]After he had washed his face, he came out and, controlling himself, said, "Serve the food."

[32]They served him by himself, the brothers by themselves, and the Egyptians who ate with him by themselves, because Egyptians could not eat with Hebrews, for that is detestable to Egyptians. [33]The men had been seated before him in the order of their ages, from the firstborn to the youngest; and they looked at each other in astonishment. [34]When portions were served to them from Joseph's table, Benjamin's portion was five times as much as anyone else's. So they feasted and drank freely with him.

A Silver Cup in a Sack

44 Now Joseph gave these instructions to the steward of his house: "Fill the men's sacks with as much food as they can carry, and put each man's silver in the mouth of his sack. [2]Then put my cup, the silver one, in the mouth of the youngest one's sack, along with the silver for his grain." And he did as Joseph said.

[3]As morning dawned, the men were sent on their way with their donkeys. [4]They had not gone far from the city when Joseph said to his steward, "Go after those men at once, and when you catch up with them, say to them, 'Why have you repaid good with evil? [5]Isn't this the cup my master drinks from and also uses for divination? This is a wicked thing you have done.'"

[6]When he caught up with them, he repeated these words to them. [7]But they said to him, "Why does my lord say such things? Far be it from your servants to do anything like that! [8]We even brought back to you from the land of

Canaan the silver we found inside the mouths of our sacks. So why would we steal silver or gold from your master's house? ⁹If any of your servants is found to have it, he will die; and the rest of us will become my lord's slaves."

¹⁰"Very well, then," he said, "let it be as you say. Whoever is found to have it will become my slave; the rest of you will be free from blame."

¹¹Each of them quickly lowered his sack to the ground and opened it. ¹²Then the steward proceeded to search, beginning with the oldest and ending with the youngest. And the cup was found in Benjamin's sack. ¹³At this, they tore their clothes. Then they all loaded their donkeys and returned to the city.

¹⁴Joseph was still in the house when Judah and his brothers came in, and they threw themselves to the ground before him. ¹⁵Joseph said to them, "What is this you have done? Don't you know that a man like me can find things out by divination?"

¹⁶"What can we say to my lord?" Judah replied. "What can we say? How can we prove our innocence? God has uncovered your servants' guilt. We are now my lord's slaves—we ourselves and the one who was found to have the cup."

¹⁷But Joseph said, "Far be it from me to do such a thing! Only the man who was found to have the cup will become my slave. The rest of you, go back to your father in peace."

¹⁸Then Judah went up to him and said: "Please, my lord, let your servant speak a word to my lord. Do not be angry with your servant, though you are equal to Pharaoh himself. ¹⁹My lord asked his servants, 'Do you have a father or a brother?' ²⁰And we answered, 'We have an aged father, and there is a young son born to him in his old age. His brother is dead, and he is the only one of his mother's sons left, and his father loves him.'

²¹"Then you said to your servants, 'Bring him down to me so I can see him

for myself.' ²²And we said to my lord, 'The boy cannot leave his father; if he leaves him, his father will die.' ²³But you told your servants, 'Unless your youngest brother comes down with you, you will not see my face again.' ²⁴When we went back to your servant my father, we told him what my lord had said.

²⁵"Then our father said, 'Go back and buy a little more food.' ²⁶But we said, 'We cannot go down. Only if our youngest brother is with us will we go. We cannot see the man's face unless our youngest brother is with us.'

²⁷"Your servant my father said to us, 'You know that my wife bore me two sons. ²⁸One of them went away from me, and I said, "He has surely been torn to pieces." And I have not seen him since. ²⁹If you take this one from me too and harm comes to him, you will bring my grey head down to the grave in misery.'

³⁰"So now, if the boy is not with us when I go back to your servant my father and if my father, whose life is closely bound up with the boy's life, ³¹sees that the boy isn't there, he will die. Your servants will bring the grey head of our father down to the grave in sorrow. ³²Your servant guaranteed the boy's safety to my father. I said, 'If I do not bring him back to you, I will bear the blame before you, my father, all my life!'

³³"Now then, please let your servant remain here as my lord's slave in place of the boy, and let the boy return with his brothers. ³⁴How can I go back to my father if the boy is not with me? No! Do not let me see the misery that would come upon my father."

NEW TESTAMENT READING
Matthew 15:10–39

¹⁰Jesus called the crowd to him and said, "Listen and understand. ¹¹What goes into a man's mouth does not make him 'unclean', but what comes out of

his mouth, that is what makes him 'unclean'."

12Then the disciples came to him and asked, "Do you know that the Pharisees were offended when they heard this?"

13He replied, "Every plant that my heavenly Father has not planted will be pulled up by the roots. 14Leave them; they are blind guides. If a blind man leads a blind man, both will fall into a pit."

15Peter said, "Explain the parable to us."

16"Are you still so dull?" Jesus asked them. 17"Don't you see that whatever enters the mouth goes into the stomach and then out of the body? 18But the things that come out of the mouth come from the heart, and these make a man 'unclean'. 19For out of the heart come evil thoughts, murder, adultery, sexual immorality, theft, false testimony, slander. 20These are what make a man 'unclean'; but eating with unwashed hands does not make him 'unclean'."

The Faith of the Canaanite Woman

21Leaving that place, Jesus withdrew to the region of Tyre and Sidon. 22A Canaanite woman from that vicinity came to him, crying out, "Lord, Son of David, have mercy on me! My daughter is suffering terribly from demon-possession."

23Jesus did not answer a word. So his disciples came to him and urged him, "Send her away, for she keeps crying out after us."

24He answered, "I was sent only to the lost sheep of Israel."

25The woman came and knelt before him. "Lord, help me!" she said.

26He replied, "It is not right to take the children's bread and toss it to their dogs."

27"Yes, Lord," she said, "but even the dogs eat the crumbs that fall from their masters' table."

28Then Jesus answered, "Woman, you have great faith! Your request is granted." And her daughter was healed from that very hour.

Jesus Feeds the Four Thousand

29Jesus left there and went along the Sea of Galilee. Then he went up on a mountainside and sat down. 30Great crowds came to him, bringing the lame, the blind, the crippled, the mute and many others, and laid them at his feet; and he healed them. 31The people were amazed when they saw the mute speaking, the crippled made well, the lame walking and the blind seeing. And they praised the God of Israel.

32Jesus called his disciples to him and said, "I have compassion for these people; they have already been with me three days and have nothing to eat. I do not want to send them away hungry, or they may collapse on the way."

33His disciples answered, "Where could we get enough bread in this remote place to feed such a crowd?"

34"How many loaves do you have?" Jesus asked.

"Seven," they replied, "and a few small fish."

35He told the crowd to sit down on the ground. 36Then he took the seven loaves and the fish, and when he had given thanks, he broke them and gave them to the disciples, and they in turn to the people. 37They all ate and were satisfied. Afterwards the disciples picked up seven basketfuls of broken pieces that were left over. 38The number of those who ate was four thousand, besides women and children. 39After Jesus had sent the crowd away, he got into the boat and went to the vicinity of Magadan.

READING FROM PSALMS
Psalm 13:1–6

For the director of music. A psalm of David.

1How long, O LORD? Will you forget me for ever?
How long will you hide your face from me?

²How long must I wrestle with my
   thoughts
   and every day have sorrow in my
   heart?
   How long will my enemy triumph
   over me?

³Look on me and answer, O LORD my
   God.
   Give light to my eyes, or I will
   sleep in death;

⁴my enemy will say, "I have overcome
   him,"
   and my foes will rejoice when I
   fall.

⁵But I trust in your unfailing love;
   my heart rejoices in your
   salvation.
⁶I will sing to the LORD,
   for he has been good to me.

JANUARY 23   DAY 23

OLD TESTAMENT READING
Genesis 45:1–47:12

Joseph Makes Himself Known

45 Then Joseph could no longer
control himself before all his
attendants, and he cried out, "Make
everyone leave my presence!" So there
was no-one with Joseph when he made
himself known to his brothers. ²And he
wept so loudly that the Egyptians heard
him, and Pharaoh's household heard
about it.

³Joseph said to his brothers, "I am
Joseph! Is my father still living?" But
his brothers were not able to answer
him, because they were terrified at his
presence.

⁴Then Joseph said to his brothers,
"Come close to me." When they had
done so, he said, "I am your brother
Joseph, the one you sold into Egypt!
⁵And now, do not be distressed and do
not be angry with yourselves for selling
me here, because it was to save lives
that God sent me ahead of you. ⁶For
two years now there has been famine in
the land, and for the next five years
there will not be ploughing and reaping.
⁷But God sent me ahead of you to preserve for you a remnant on earth and to
save your lives by a great deliverance.

⁸"So then, it was not you who sent me
here, but God. He made me father to
Pharaoh, lord of his entire household
and ruler of all Egypt. ⁹Now hurry back
to my father and say to him, 'This is
what your son Joseph says: God has
made me lord of all Egypt. Come down
to me; don't delay. ¹⁰You shall live in
the region of Goshen and be near me
—you, your children and grandchildren, your flocks and herds, and all you
have. ¹¹I will provide for you there,
because five years of famine are still to
come. Otherwise you and your household and all who belong to you will
become destitute.'

¹²"You can see for yourselves, and so
can my brother Benjamin, that it is
really I who am speaking to you. ¹³Tell
my father about all the honour accorded
me in Egypt and about everything you
have seen. And bring my father down
here quickly."

¹⁴Then he threw his arms around his
brother Benjamin and wept, and Benjamin embraced him, weeping. ¹⁵And
he kissed all his brothers and wept over
them. Afterwards his brothers talked
with him.

¹⁶When the news reached Pharaoh's
palace that Joseph's brothers had come,
Pharaoh and all his officials were
pleased. ¹⁷Pharaoh said to Joseph,

"Tell your brothers, 'Do this: Load your animals and return to the land of Canaan, [18]and bring your father and your families back to me. I will give you the best of the land of Egypt and you can enjoy the fat of the land.'

[19]"You are also directed to tell them, 'Do this: Take some carts from Egypt for your children and your wives, and get your father and come. [20]Never mind about your belongings, because the best of all Egypt will be yours.'"

[21]So the sons of Israel did this. Joseph gave them carts, as Pharaoh had commanded, and he also gave them provisions for their journey. [22]To each of them he gave new clothing, but to Benjamin he gave three hundred shekels of silver and five sets of clothes. [23]And this is what he sent to his father: ten donkeys loaded with the best things of Egypt, and ten female donkeys loaded with grain and bread and other provisions for his journey. [24]Then he sent his brothers away, and as they were leaving he said to them, "Don't quarrel on the way!"

[25]So they went up out of Egypt and came to their father Jacob in the land of Canaan. [26]They told him, "Joseph is still alive! In fact, he is ruler of all Egypt." Jacob was stunned; he did not believe them. [27]But when they told him everything Joseph had said to them, and when he saw the carts Joseph had sent to carry him back, the spirit of their father Jacob revived. [28]And Israel said, "I'm convinced! My son Joseph is still alive. I will go and see him before I die."

Jacob Goes to Egypt

46 So Israel set out with all that was his, and when he reached Beersheba, he offered sacrifices to the God of his father Isaac.

[2]And God spoke to Israel in a vision at night and said, "Jacob! Jacob!"

"Here I am," he replied.

[3]"I am God, the God of your father," he said. "Do not be afraid to go down to Egypt, for I will make you into a great nation there. [4]I will go down to Egypt

with you, and I will surely bring you back again. And Joseph's own hand will close your eyes."

[5]Then Jacob left Beersheba, and Israel's sons took their father Jacob and their children and their wives in the carts that Pharaoh had sent to transport him. [6]They also took with them their livestock and the possessions they had acquired in Canaan, and Jacob and all his offspring went to Egypt. [7]He took with him to Egypt his sons and grandsons and his daughters and granddaughters—all his offspring.

[8]These are the names of the sons of Israel (Jacob and his descendants) who went to Egypt:

Reuben the firstborn of Jacob.
[9]The sons of Reuben:
Hanoch, Pallu, Hezron and Carmi.
[10]The sons of Simeon:
Jemuel, Jamin, Ohad, Jakin, Zohar and Shaul the son of a Canaanite woman.
[11]The sons of Levi:
Gershon, Kohath and Merari.
[12]The sons of Judah:
Er, Onan, Shelah, Perez and Zerah (but Er and Onan had died in the land of Canaan). The sons of Perez:
Hezron and Hamul.
[13]The sons of Issachar:
Tola, Puah, Jashub and Shimron.
[14]The sons of Zebulun:
Sered, Elon and Jahleel.
[15]These were the sons Leah bore to Jacob in Paddan Aram, besides his daughter Dinah. These sons and daughters of his were thirty-three in all.

[16]The sons of Gad:
Zephon, Haggi, Shuni, Ezbon, Eri, Arodi and Areli.
[17]The sons of Asher:
Imnah, Ishvah, Ishvi and Beriah.
Their sister was Serah.

The sons of Beriah:
>Heber and Malkiel.

¹⁸These were the children born to Jacob by Zilpah, whom Laban had given to his daughter Leah—sixteen in all.

¹⁹The sons of Jacob's wife Rachel:
>Joseph and Benjamin. ²⁰In Egypt, Manasseh and Ephraim were born to Joseph by Asenath daughter of Potiphera, priest of On.

²¹The sons of Benjamin:
>Bela, Beker, Ashbel, Gera, Naaman, Ehi, Rosh, Muppim, Huppim and Ard.

²²These were the sons of Rachel who were born to Jacob—fourteen in all.

²³The son of Dan:
>Hushim.

²⁴The sons of Naphtali:
>Jahziel, Guni, Jezer and Shillem.

²⁵These were the sons born to Jacob by Bilhah, whom Laban had given to his daughter Rachel—seven in all.

²⁶All those who went to Egypt with Jacob—those who were his direct descendants, not counting his sons' wives—numbered sixty-six persons. ²⁷With the two sons who had been born to Joseph in Egypt, the members of Jacob's family, which went to Egypt, were seventy in all.

²⁸Now Jacob sent Judah ahead of him to Joseph to get directions to Goshen. When they arrived in the region of Goshen, ²⁹Joseph had his chariot made ready and went to Goshen to meet his father Israel. As soon as Joseph appeared before him, he threw his arms around his father and wept for a long time.

³⁰Israel said to Joseph, "Now I am ready to die, since I have seen for myself that you are still alive."

³¹Then Joseph said to his brothers and to his father's household, "I will go up and speak to Pharaoh and will say to him, 'My brothers and my father's household, who were living in the land of Canaan, have come to me. ³²The men are shepherds; they tend livestock, and they have brought along their flocks and herds and everything they own.' ³³When Pharaoh calls you in and asks, 'What is your occupation?' ³⁴you should answer, 'Your servants have tended livestock from our boyhood on, just as our fathers did.' Then you will be allowed to settle in the region of Goshen, for all shepherds are detestable to the Egyptians."

47 Joseph went and told Pharaoh, "My father and brothers, with their flocks and herds and everything they own, have come from the land of Canaan and are now in Goshen." ²He chose five of his brothers and presented them before Pharaoh.

³Pharaoh asked the brothers, "What is your occupation?"

"Your servants are shepherds," they replied to Pharaoh, "just as our fathers were." ⁴They also said to him, "We have come to live here awhile, because the famine is severe in Canaan and your servants' flocks have no pasture. So now, please let your servants settle in Goshen."

⁵Pharaoh said to Joseph, "Your father and your brothers have come to you, ⁶and the land of Egypt is before you; settle your father and your brothers in the best part of the land. Let them live in Goshen. And if you know of any among them with special ability, put them in charge of my own livestock."

⁷Then Joseph brought his father Jacob in and presented him before Pharaoh. After Jacob blessed Pharaoh, ⁸Pharaoh asked him, "How old are you?"

⁹And Jacob said to Pharaoh, "The years of my pilgrimage are a hundred and thirty. My years have been few and difficult, and they do not equal the years of the pilgrimage of my fathers." ¹⁰Then Jacob blessed Pharaoh and went out from his presence.

11So Joseph settled his father and his brothers in Egypt and gave them property in the best part of the land, the district of Rameses, as Pharaoh directed. 12Joseph also provided his father and his brothers and all his father's household with food, according to the number of their children.

NEW TESTAMENT READING
Matthew 16:1–20

The Demand for a Sign

16 The Pharisees and Sadducees came to Jesus and tested him by asking him to show them a sign from heaven.

2He replied, "When evening comes, you say, 'It will be fair weather, for the sky is red,' 3and in the morning, 'Today it will be stormy, for the sky is red and overcast.' You know how to interpret the appearance of the sky, but you cannot interpret the signs of the times. 4A wicked and adulterous generation looks for a miraculous sign, but none will be given it except the sign of Jonah." Jesus then left them and went away.

The Yeast of the Pharisees and Sadducees

5When they went across the lake, the disciples forgot to take bread. 6"Be careful," Jesus said to them. "Be on your guard against the yeast of the Pharisees and Sadducees."

7They discussed this among themselves and said, "It is because we didn't bring any bread."

8Aware of their discussion, Jesus asked, "You of little faith, why are you talking among yourselves about having no bread? 9Do you still not understand? Don't you remember the five loaves for the five thousand, and how many basketfuls you gathered? 10Or the seven loaves for the four thousand, and how many basketfuls you gathered? 11How is it you don't understand that I was not talking to you about bread? But be on your guard against the yeast of the Pharisees and Sadducees." 12Then they understood that he was not telling them to guard against the yeast used in bread, but against the teaching of the Pharisees and Sadducees.

Peter's Confession of Christ

13When Jesus came to the region of Caesarea Philippi, he asked his disciples, "Who do people say the Son of Man is?"

14They replied, "Some say John the Baptist; others say Elijah; and still others, Jeremiah or one of the prophets."

15"But what about you?" he asked. "Who do you say I am?"

16Simon Peter answered, "You are the Christ, the Son of the living God."

17Jesus replied, "Blessed are you, Simon son of Jonah, for this was not revealed to you by man, but by my Father in heaven. 18And I tell you that you are Peter, and on this rock I will build my church, and the gates of Hades will not overcome it. 19I will give you the keys of the kingdom of heaven; whatever you bind on earth will be bound in heaven, and whatever you loose on earth will be loosed in heaven." 20Then he warned his disciples not to tell anyone that he was the Christ.

READING FROM PSALMS
Psalm 14:1–7

For the director of music. Of David.

1The fool says in his heart,
  "There is no God."
They are corrupt, their deeds are vile;
  there is no-one who does good.

2The LORD looks down from heaven
  on the sons of men
to see if there are any who understand,
  any who seek God.

³All have turned aside,
  they have together become
    corrupt;
there is no-one who does good,
  not even one.

⁴Will evildoers never learn—
  those who devour my people as
    men eat bread
  and who do not call on the LORD?
⁵There they are, overwhelmed with
    dread,

for God is present in the company
  of the righteous.
⁶You evildoers frustrate the plans of
    the poor,
  but the LORD is their refuge.

⁷Oh, that salvation for Israel would
    come out of Zion!
  When the LORD restores the
    fortunes of his people,
  let Jacob rejoice and Israel be
    glad!

JANUARY 24   DAY 24

OLD TESTAMENT READING
Genesis 47:13–48:22

Joseph and the Famine

¹³There was no food, however, in the
whole region because the famine was
severe; both Egypt and Canaan wasted
away because of the famine. ¹⁴Joseph
collected all the money that was to be
found in Egypt and Canaan in payment
for the grain they were buying, and he
brought it to Pharaoh's palace. ¹⁵When
the money of the people of Egypt and
Canaan was gone, all Egypt came to
Joseph and said, "Give us food. Why
should we die before your eyes? Our
money is used up."

¹⁶"Then bring your livestock," said
Joseph. "I will sell you food in exchange
for your livestock, since your money is
gone." ¹⁷So they brought their livestock
to Joseph, and he gave them food in
exchange for their horses, their sheep
and goats, their cattle and donkeys.
And he brought them through that
year with food in exchange for all their
livestock.

¹⁸When that year was over, they
came to him the following year and
said, "We cannot hide from our lord the
fact that since our money is gone and

our livestock belongs to you, there is
nothing left for our lord except our
bodies and our land. ¹⁹Why should we
perish before your eyes—we and our
land as well? Buy us and our land in
exchange for food, and we with our
land will be in bondage to Pharaoh.
Give us seed so that we may live and
not die, and that the land may not
become desolate."

²⁰So Joseph bought all the land in
Egypt for Pharaoh. The Egyptians, one
and all, sold their fields, because the
famine was too severe for them. The
land became Pharaoh's, ²¹and Joseph
reduced the people to servitude, from
one end of Egypt to the other. ²²However, he did not buy the land of
the priests, because they received a regular allotment from Pharaoh and had
food enough from the allotment Pharaoh gave them. That is why they did not
sell their land.

²³Joseph said to the people, "Now
that I have bought you and your land
today for Pharaoh, here is seed for you
so you can plant the ground. ²⁴But when
the crop comes in, give a fifth of it to
Pharaoh. The other four-fifths you may
keep as seed for the fields and as food
for yourselves and your households and
your children."

25"You have saved our lives," they said. "May we find favour in the eyes of our lord; we will be in bondage to Pharaoh."

26So Joseph established it as a law concerning land in Egypt—still in force today—that a fifth of the produce belongs to Pharaoh. It was only the land of the priests that did not become Pharaoh's.

27Now the Israelites settled in Egypt in the region of Goshen. They acquired property there and were fruitful and increased greatly in number.

28Jacob lived in Egypt seventeen years, and the years of his life were a hundred and forty-seven. 29When the time drew near for Israel to die, he called for his son Joseph and said to him, "If I have found favour in your eyes, put your hand under my thigh and promise that you will show me kindness and faithfulness. Do not bury me in Egypt, 30but when I rest with my fathers, carry me out of Egypt and bury me where they are buried."

"I will do as you say," he said.

31"Swear to me," he said. Then Joseph swore to him, and Israel worshipped as he leaned on the top of his staff.

Manasseh and Ephraim

48 Some time later Joseph was told, "Your father is ill." So he took his two sons Manasseh and Ephraim along with him. 2When Jacob was told, "Your son Joseph has come to you," Israel rallied his strength and sat up on the bed.

3Jacob said to Joseph, "God Almighty appeared to me at Luz in the land of Canaan, and there he blessed me 4and said to me, 'I am going to make you fruitful and will increase your numbers. I will make you a community of peoples, and I will give this land as an everlasting possession to your descendants after you.'

5"Now then, your two sons born to you in Egypt before I came to you here will be reckoned as mine; Ephraim and Manasseh will be mine, just as Reuben and Simeon are mine. 6Any children born to you after them will be yours; in the territory they inherit they will be reckoned under the names of their brothers. 7As I was returning from Paddan, to my sorrow Rachel died in the land of Canaan while we were still on the way, a little distance from Ephrath. So I buried her there beside the road to Ephrath" (that is, Bethlehem).

8When Israel saw the sons of Joseph, he asked, "Who are these?"

9"They are the sons God has given me here," Joseph said to his father.

Then Israel said, "Bring them to me so that I may bless them."

10Now Israel's eyes were failing because of old age, and he could hardly see. So Joseph brought his sons close to him, and his father kissed them and embraced them.

11Israel said to Joseph, "I never expected to see your face again, and now God has allowed me to see your children too."

12Then Joseph removed them from Israel's knees and bowed down with his face to the ground. 13And Joseph took both of them, Ephraim on his right towards Israel's left hand and Manasseh on his left towards Israel's right hand, and brought them close to him. 14But Israel reached out his right hand and put it on Ephraim's head, though he was the younger, and crossing his arms, he put his left hand on Manasseh's head, even though Manasseh was the firstborn.

15Then he blessed Joseph and said,

"May the God before whom my
     fathers
   Abraham and Isaac walked,
the God who has been my
     shepherd
   all my life to this day,
16the Angel who has delivered me
     from all harm
   —may he bless these boys.

May they be called by my name
and the names of my fathers
Abraham and Isaac,
and may they increase greatly
upon the earth."

17When Joseph saw his father placing his right hand on Ephraim's head he was displeased; so he took hold of his father's hand to move it from Ephraim's head to Manasseh's head. 18Joseph said to him, "No, my father, this one is the firstborn; put your right hand on his head."

19But his father refused and said, "I know, my son, I know. He too will become a people, and he too will become great. Nevertheless, his younger brother will be greater than he, and his descendants will become a group of nations." 20He blessed them that day and said,

"In your name will Israel pronounce this blessing:
'May God make you like Ephraim and Manasseh.'"

So he put Ephraim ahead of Manasseh.

21Then Israel said to Joseph, "I am about to die, but God will be with you and take you back to the land of your fathers. 22And to you, as one who is over your brothers, I give the ridge of land I took from the Amorites with my sword and my bow."

NEW TESTAMENT READING
Matthew 16:21–17:13

Jesus Predicts His Death

21From that time on Jesus began to explain to his disciples that he must go to Jerusalem and suffer many things at the hands of the elders, chief priests and teachers of the law, and that he must be killed and on the third day be raised to life.

22Peter took him aside and began to rebuke him. "Never, Lord!" he said. "This shall never happen to you!"

23Jesus turned and said to Peter, "Get behind me, Satan! You are a stumbling-block to me; you do not have in mind the things of God, but the things of men."

24Then Jesus said to his disciples, "If anyone would come after me, he must deny himself and take up his cross and follow me. 25For whoever wants to save his life will lose it, but whoever loses his life for me will find it. 26What good will it be for a man if he gains the whole world, yet forfeits his soul? Or what can a man give in exchange for his soul? 27For the Son of Man is going to come in his Father's glory with his angels, and then he will reward each person according to what he has done. 28I tell you the truth, some who are standing here will not taste death before they see the Son of Man coming in his kingdom."

The Transfiguration

17 After six days Jesus took with him Peter, James and John the brother of James, and led them up a high mountain by themselves. 2There he was transfigured before them. His face shone like the sun, and his clothes became as white as the light. 3Just then there appeared before them Moses and Elijah, talking with Jesus.

4Peter said to Jesus, "Lord, it is good for us to be here. If you wish, I will put up three shelters—one for you, one for Moses and one for Elijah."

5While he was still speaking, a bright cloud enveloped them, and a voice from the cloud said, "This is my Son, whom I love; with him I am well pleased. Listen to him!"

6When the disciples heard this, they fell face down to the ground, terrified. 7But Jesus came and touched them. "Get up," he said. "Don't be afraid." 8When they looked up, they saw no-one except Jesus.

9As they were coming down the mountain, Jesus instructed them,

"Don't tell anyone what you have seen, until the Son of Man has been raised from the dead."

¹⁰The disciples asked him, "Why then do the teachers of the law say that Elijah must come first?"

¹¹Jesus replied, "To be sure, Elijah comes and will restore all things. ¹²But I tell you, Elijah has already come, and they did not recognise him, but have done to him everything they wished. In the same way the Son of Man is going to suffer at their hands." ¹³Then the disciples understood that he was talking to them about John the Baptist.

READING FROM PROVERBS
Proverbs 3:1–10

Further Benefits of Wisdom

3 My son, do not forget my teaching,
  but keep my commands in your heart,
²for they will prolong your life many years
  and bring you prosperity.

³Let love and faithfulness never leave you;
  bind them around your neck,
  write them on the tablet of your heart.
⁴Then you will win favour and a good name
  in the sight of God and man.

⁵Trust in the LORD with all your heart
  and lean not on your own understanding;
⁶in all your ways acknowledge him,
  and he will make your paths straight.

⁷Do not be wise in your own eyes;
  fear the LORD and shun evil.
⁸This will bring health to your body
  and nourishment to your bones.

⁹Honour the LORD with your wealth,
  with the firstfruits of all your crops;
¹⁰then your barns will be filled to overflowing,
  and your vats will brim over with new wine.

DAY 25

JANUARY 25

OLD TESTAMENT READING
Genesis 49:1–50:26

Jacob Blesses His Sons

49 Then Jacob called for his sons and said: "Gather round so that I can tell you what will happen to you in days to come.

²"Assemble and listen, sons of Jacob;
  listen to your father Israel.

³"Reuben, you are my firstborn,
  my might, the first sign of my strength,

excelling in honour, excelling in power.
⁴Turbulent as the waters, you will no longer excel,
  for you went up onto your father's bed,
  onto my couch and defiled it.

⁵"Simeon and Levi are brothers—
  their swords are weapons of violence.
⁶Let me not enter their council,
  let me not join their assembly,
  for they have killed men in their anger
  and hamstrung oxen as they pleased.

⁷Cursed be their anger, so fierce,
    and their fury, so cruel!
I will scatter them in Jacob
    and disperse them in Israel.

⁸"Judah, your brothers will praise
    you;
    your hand will be on the neck of
      your enemies;
    your father's sons will bow down to
      you.
⁹You are a lion's cub, O Judah;
    you return from the prey, my son.
Like a lion he crouches and lies
    down,
    like a lioness—who dares to rouse
      him?
¹⁰The sceptre will not depart from
    Judah,
    nor the ruler's staff from between
      his feet,
until he comes to whom it belongs
    and the obedience of the nations is
      his.
¹¹He will tether his donkey to a vine,
    his colt to the choicest branch;
he will wash his garments in wine,
    his robes in the blood of grapes.
¹²His eyes will be darker than wine,
    his teeth whiter than milk.

¹³"Zebulun will live by the seashore
    and become a haven for ships;
    his border will extend towards
      Sidon.

¹⁴"Issachar is a scrawny donkey
    lying down between two
      saddlebags.
¹⁵When he sees how good is his resting
      place
    and how pleasant is his land,
he will bend his shoulder to the
      burden
    and submit to forced labour.

¹⁶"Dan will provide justice for his
      people
    as one of the tribes of Israel.
¹⁷Dan will be a serpent by the roadside,
    a viper along the path,

that bites the horse's heels
    so that its rider tumbles backwards.

¹⁸"I look for your deliverance, O
    Lord.

¹⁹"Gad will be attacked by a band of
      raiders,
    but he will attack them at their
      heels.

²⁰"Asher's food will be rich;
    he will provide delicacies fit for a
      king.

²¹"Naphtali is a doe set free
    that bears beautiful fawns.

²²"Joseph is a fruitful vine,
    a fruitful vine near a spring,
    whose branches climb over a wall.
²³With bitterness archers attacked him;
    they shot at him with hostility.
²⁴But his bow remained steady,
    his strong arms stayed supple,
because of the hand of the Mighty
      One of Jacob,
    because of the Shepherd, the Rock
      of Israel,
²⁵because of your father's God, who
      helps you,
    because of the Almighty, who
      blesses you
with blessings of the heavens above,
    blessings of the deep that lies
      below,
    blessings of the breast and womb.
²⁶Your father's blessings are greater
    than the blessings of the ancient
      mountains,
    than the bounty of the age-old
      hills.
Let all these rest on the head of
      Joseph,
    on the brow of the prince among
      his brothers.

²⁷"Benjamin is a ravenous wolf;
    in the morning he devours the
      prey,
    in the evening he divides the
      plunder."

28All these are the twelve tribes of Israel, and this is what their father said to them when he blessed them, giving each the blessing appropriate to him.

The Death of Jacob

29Then he gave them these instructions: "I am about to be gathered to my people. Bury me with my fathers in the cave in the field of Ephron the Hittite, 30the cave in the field of Machpelah, near Mamre in Canaan, which Abraham bought as a burial place from Ephron the Hittite, along with the field. 31There Abraham and his wife Sarah were buried, there Isaac and his wife Rebekah were buried, and there I buried Leah. 32The field and the cave in it were bought from the Hittites."

33When Jacob had finished giving instructions to his sons, he drew his feet up into the bed, breathed his last and was gathered to his people.

50 Joseph threw himself upon his father and wept over him and kissed him. 2Then Joseph directed the physicians in his service to embalm his father Israel. So the physicians embalmed him, 3taking a full forty days, for that was the time required for embalming. And the Egyptians mourned for him seventy days.

4When the days of mourning had passed, Joseph said to Pharaoh's court, "If I have found favour in your eyes, speak to Pharaoh for me. Tell him, 5'My father made me swear an oath and said, "I am about to die; bury me in the tomb I dug for myself in the land of Canaan." Now let me go up and bury my father; then I will return.'"

6Pharaoh said, "Go up and bury your father, as he made you swear to do."

7So Joseph went up to bury his father. All Pharaoh's officials accompanied him—the dignitaries of his court and all the dignitaries of Egypt—8besides all the members of Joseph's household and his brothers and those belonging to his father's household. Only their children and their flocks and herds were left in Goshen. 9Chariots and horsemen also went up with him. It was a very large company.

10When they reached the threshing-floor of Atad, near the Jordan, they lamented loudly and bitterly; and there Joseph observed a seven-day period of mourning for his father. 11When the Canaanites who lived there saw the mourning at the threshing-floor of Atad, they said, "The Egyptians are holding a solemn ceremony of mourning." That is why that place near the Jordan is called Abel Mizraim.

12So Jacob's sons did as he had commanded them: 13They carried him to the land of Canaan and buried him in the cave in the field of Machpelah, near Mamre, which Abraham had bought as a burial place from Ephron the Hittite, along with the field. 14After burying his father, Joseph returned to Egypt, together with his brothers and all the others who had gone with him to bury his father.

Joseph Reassures His Brothers

15When Joseph's brothers saw that their father was dead, they said, "What if Joseph holds a grudge against us and pays us back for all the wrongs we did to him?" 16So they sent word to Joseph, saying, "Your father left these instructions before he died: 17'This is what you are to say to Joseph: I ask you to forgive your brothers the sins and the wrongs they committed in treating you so badly.' Now please forgive the sins of the servants of the God of your father." When their message came to him, Joseph wept.

18His brothers then came and threw themselves down before him. "We are your slaves," they said.

19But Joseph said to them, "Don't be afraid. Am I in the place of God? 20You intended to harm me, but God intended it for good to accomplish what is now being done, the saving of many lives. 21So then, don't be afraid. I will provide for you and your children." And he reassured them and spoke kindly to them.

The Death of Joseph

22Joseph stayed in Egypt, along with all his father's family. He lived a hundred and ten years 23and saw the third generation of Ephraim's children. Also the children of Makir son of Manasseh were placed at birth on Joseph's knees.

24Then Joseph said to his brothers, "I am about to die. But God will surely come to your aid and take you up out of this land to the land he promised on oath to Abraham, Isaac and Jacob." 25And Joseph made the sons of Israel swear an oath and said, "God will surely come to your aid, and then you must carry my bones up from this place."

26So Joseph died at the age of a hundred and ten. And after they embalmed him, he was placed in a coffin in Egypt.

NEW TESTAMENT READING
Matthew 17:14–18:9

The Healing of a Boy With a Demon

14When they came to the crowd, a man approached Jesus and knelt before him. 15"Lord, have mercy on my son," he said. "He has seizures and is suffering greatly. He often falls into the fire or into the water. 16I brought him to your disciples, but they could not heal him."

17"O unbelieving and perverse generation," Jesus replied, "how long shall I stay with you? How long shall I put up with you? Bring the boy here to me." 18Jesus rebuked the demon, and it came out of the boy, and he was healed from that moment.

19Then the disciples came to Jesus in private and asked, "Why couldn't we drive it out?"

20He replied, "Because you have so little faith. I tell you the truth, if you have faith as small as a mustard seed, you can say to this mountain, 'Move from here to there' and it will move. Nothing will be impossible for you."

22When they came together in Galilee, he said to them, "The Son of Man is going to be betrayed into the hands of men. 23They will kill him, and on the third day he will be raised to life." And the disciples were filled with grief.

The Temple Tax

24After Jesus and his disciples arrived in Capernaum, the collectors of the two-drachma tax came to Peter and asked, "Doesn't your teacher pay the temple tax?"

25"Yes, he does," he replied.

When Peter came into the house, Jesus was the first to speak. "What do you think, Simon?" he asked. "From whom do the kings of the earth collect duty and taxes—from their own sons or from others?"

26"From others," Peter answered.

"Then the sons are exempt," Jesus said to him. 27"But so that we may not offend them, go to the lake and throw out your line. Take the first fish you catch; open its mouth and you will find a four-drachma coin. Take it and give it to them for my tax and yours."

The Greatest in the Kingdom of Heaven

18 At that time the disciples came to Jesus and asked, "Who is the greatest in the kingdom of heaven?"

2He called a little child and had him stand among them. 3And he said: "I tell you the truth, unless you change and become like little children, you will never enter the kingdom of heaven. 4Therefore, whoever humbles himself like this child is the greatest in the kingdom of heaven.

5"And whoever welcomes a little child like this in my name welcomes me. 6But if anyone causes one of these little ones who believe in me to sin, it would be better for him to have a large millstone hung around his neck and to be drowned in the depths of the sea.

7"Woe to the world because of the things that cause people to sin! Such things must come, but woe to the man through whom they come! ⁸If your hand or your foot causes you to sin, cut it off and throw it away. It is better for you to enter life maimed or crippled than to have two hands or two feet and be thrown into eternal fire. ⁹And if your eye causes you to sin, gouge it out and throw it away. It is better for you to enter life with one eye than to have two eyes and be thrown into the fire of hell.

READING FROM PSALMS
Psalm 15:1–5

A psalm of David.

¹LORD, who may dwell in your
　　sanctuary?
　Who may live on your holy hill?

²He whose walk is blameless
　　and who does what is righteous,
　who speaks the truth from his
　　　heart
³　and has no slander on his
　　　tongue,
　who does his neighbour no wrong
　　and casts no slur on his
　　　fellow-man,
⁴who despises a vile man
　　but honours those who fear the
　　　LORD,
　who keeps his oath
　　even when it hurts,
⁵who lends his money without usury
　　and does not accept a bribe against
　　　the innocent.

He who does these things
　will never be shaken.

JANUARY 26

OLD TESTAMENT READING
Job 1:1–3:26

Prologue

1 In the land of Uz there lived a man whose name was Job. This man was blameless and upright; he feared God and shunned evil. ²He had seven sons and three daughters, ³and he owned seven thousand sheep, three thousand camels, five hundred yoke of oxen and five hundred donkeys, and had a large number of servants. He was the greatest man among all the people of the East.

⁴His sons used to take turns holding feasts in their homes, and they would invite their three sisters to eat and drink with them. ⁵When a period of feasting had run its course, Job would send and have them purified. Early in the morning he would sacrifice a burnt offering for each of them, thinking, "Perhaps my children have sinned and cursed

God in their hearts." This was Job's regular custom.

Job's First Test

⁶One day the angels came to present themselves before the LORD, and Satan also came with them. ⁷The LORD said to Satan, "Where have you come from?"

Satan answered the LORD, "From roaming through the earth and going to and fro in it."

⁸Then the LORD said to Satan, "Have you considered my servant Job? There is no-one on earth like him; he is blameless and upright, a man who fears God and shuns evil."

⁹"Does Job fear God for nothing?" Satan replied. ¹⁰"Have you not put a hedge around him and his household and everything he has? You have blessed the work of his hands, so that his flocks and herds are spread throughout the land. ¹¹But stretch out your hand

and strike everything he has, and he will surely curse you to your face."

¹²The LORD said to Satan, "Very well, then, everything he has is in your hands, but on the man himself do not lay a finger."

Then Satan went out from the presence of the LORD.

¹³One day when Job's sons and daughters were feasting and drinking wine at the oldest brother's house, ¹⁴a messenger came to Job and said, "The oxen were ploughing and the donkeys were grazing nearby, ¹⁵and the Sabeans attacked and carried them off. They put the servants to the sword, and I am the only one who has escaped to tell you!"

¹⁶While he was still speaking, another messenger came and said, "The fire of God fell from the sky and burned up the sheep and the servants, and I am the only one who has escaped to tell you!"

¹⁷While he was still speaking, another messenger came and said, "The Chaldeans formed three raiding parties and swept down on your camels and carried them off. They put the servants to the sword, and I am the only one who has escaped to tell you!"

¹⁸While he was still speaking, yet another messenger came and said, "Your sons and daughters were feasting and drinking wine at the oldest brother's house, ¹⁹when suddenly a mighty wind swept in from the desert and struck the four corners of the house. It collapsed on them and they are dead, and I am the only one who has escaped to tell you!"

²⁰At this, Job got up and tore his robe and shaved his head. Then he fell to the ground in worship ²¹and said:

"Naked I came from my mother's womb,
    and naked I shall depart.
The LORD gave and the LORD has taken away;
    may the name of the LORD be praised."

²²In all this, Job did not sin by charging God with wrongdoing.

Job's Second Test

2 On another day the angels came to present themselves before the LORD, and Satan also came with them to present himself before him. ²And the LORD said to Satan, "Where have you come from?"

Satan answered the LORD, "From roaming through the earth and going to and fro in it."

³Then the LORD said to Satan, "Have you considered my servant Job? There is no-one on earth like him; he is blameless and upright, a man who fears God and shuns evil. And he still maintains his integrity, though you incited me against him to ruin him without any reason."

⁴"Skin for skin!" Satan replied. "A man will give all he has for his own life. ⁵But stretch out your hand and strike his flesh and bones, and he will surely curse you to your face."

⁶The LORD said to Satan, "Very well, then, he is in your hands; but you must spare his life."

⁷So Satan went out from the presence of the LORD and afflicted Job with painful sores from the soles of his feet to the top of his head. ⁸Then Job took a piece of broken pottery and scraped himself with it as he sat among the ashes.

⁹His wife said to him, "Are you still holding on to your integrity? Curse God and die!"

¹⁰He replied, "You are talking like a foolish woman. Shall we accept good from God, and not trouble?"

In all this, Job did not sin in what he said.

Job's Three Friends

¹¹When Job's three friends, Eliphaz the Temanite, Bildad the Shuhite and Zophar the Naamathite, heard about all the troubles that had come upon him, they set out from their homes and met together by agreement to go and sympathise with him and comfort him. ¹²When they saw him from a distance,

they could hardly recognise him; they began to weep aloud, and they tore their robes and sprinkled dust on their heads. ¹³Then they sat on the ground with him for seven days and seven nights. No-one said a word to him, because they saw how great his suffering was.

Job Speaks

3 After this, Job opened his mouth and cursed the day of his birth. ²He said:

³"May the day of my birth perish,
    and the night it was said, 'A boy is
        born!'
⁴That day—may it turn to darkness;
    may God above not care about it;
    may no light shine upon it.
⁵May darkness and deep shadow claim
        it once more;
    may a cloud settle over it;
    may blackness overwhelm its light.
⁶That night—may thick darkness seize
        it;
    may it not be included among the
        days of the year
    nor be entered in any of the
        months.
⁷May that night be barren;
    may no shout of joy be heard in it.
⁸May those who curse days curse that
        day,
    those who are ready to rouse
        Leviathan.
⁹May its morning stars become dark;
    may it wait for daylight in vain
    and not see the first rays of dawn,
¹⁰for it did not shut the doors of the
        womb on me
    to hide trouble from my eyes.

¹¹"Why did I not perish at birth,
    and die as I came from the womb?
¹²Why were there knees to receive me
    and breasts that I might be nursed?
¹³For now I would be lying down in
        peace;
    I would be asleep and at rest

¹⁴with kings and counsellors of the
        earth,
    who built for themselves places
        now lying in ruins,
¹⁵with rulers who had gold,
    who filled their houses with silver.
¹⁶Or why was I not hidden in the
        ground like a stillborn child,
    like an infant who never saw the
        light of day?
¹⁷There the wicked cease from turmoil,
    and there the weary are at rest.
¹⁸Captives also enjoy their ease;
    they no longer hear the slave
        driver's shout.
¹⁹The small and the great are there,
    and the slave is freed from his
        master.

²⁰"Why is light given to those in
        misery,
    and life to the bitter of soul,
²¹to those who long for death that does
        not come,
    who search for it more than for
        hidden treasure,
²²who are filled with gladness
    and rejoice when they reach the
        grave?
²³Why is life given to a man
    whose way is hidden,
    whom God has hedged in?
²⁴For sighing comes to me instead of
        food;
    my groans pour out like water.
²⁵What I feared has come upon me;
    what I dreaded has happened to
        me.
²⁶I have no peace, no quietness;
    I have no rest, but only turmoil."

NEW TESTAMENT READING
Matthew 18:10–35

The Parable of the Lost Sheep

¹⁰"See that you do not look down on one of these little ones. For I tell you that their angels in heaven always see the face of my Father in heaven.
¹²"What do you think? If a man owns

a hundred sheep, and one of them wanders away, will he not leave the ninety-nine on the hills and go to look for the one that wandered off? 13And if he finds it, I tell you the truth, he is happier about that one sheep than about the ninety-nine that did not wander off. 14In the same way your Father in heaven is not willing that any of these little ones should be lost.

A Brother Who Sins Against You

15"If your brother sins against you, go and show him his fault, just between the two of you. If he listens to you, you have won your brother over. 16But if he will not listen, take one or two others along, so that 'every matter may be established by the testimony of two or three witnesses.' 17If he refuses to listen to them, tell it to the church; and if he refuses to listen even to the church, treat him as you would a pagan or a tax collector.

18"I tell you the truth, whatever you bind on earth will be bound in heaven, and whatever you loose on earth will be loosed in heaven.

19"Again, I tell you that if two of you on earth agree about anything you ask for, it will be done for you by my Father in heaven. 20For where two or three come together in my name, there am I with them."

The Parable of the Unmerciful Servant

21Then Peter came to Jesus and asked, "Lord, how many times shall I forgive my brother when he sins against me? Up to seven times?"

22Jesus answered, "I tell you, not seven times, but seventy-seven times.

23"Therefore, the kingdom of heaven is like a king who wanted to settle accounts with his servants. 24As he began the settlement, a man who owed him ten thousand talents was brought to him. 25Since he was not able to pay, the master ordered that he and his wife and his children and all that he had be sold to repay the debt.

26"The servant fell on his knees before him. 'Be patient with me,' he begged, 'and I will pay back everything.' 27The servant's master took pity on him, cancelled the debt and let him go.

28"But when that servant went out, he found one of his fellow-servants who owed him a hundred denarii. He grabbed him and began to choke him. 'Pay back what you owe me!' he demanded.

29"His fellow-servant fell to his knees and begged him, 'Be patient with me, and I will pay you back.'

30"But he refused. Instead, he went off and had the man thrown into prison until he could pay the debt. 31When the other servants saw what had happened, they were greatly distressed and went and told their master everything that had happened.

32"Then the master called the servant in. 'You wicked servant,' he said, 'I cancelled all that debt of yours because you begged me to. 33Shouldn't you have had mercy on your fellow-servant just as I had on you?' 34In anger his master turned him over to the jailers to be tortured, until he should pay back all he owed.

35"This is how my heavenly Father will treat each of you unless you forgive your brother from your heart."

READING FROM PSALMS
Psalm 16:1–11

A *miktam* of David.

1Keep me safe, O God,
    for in you I take refuge.

2I said to the LORD, "You are my
    Lord;
    apart from you I have no good
      thing."
3As for the saints who are in the land,
    they are the glorious ones in whom
      is all my delight.

[4]The sorrows of those will increase
    who run after other gods.
I will not pour out their libations of
    blood
    or take up their names on my lips.

[5]LORD, you have assigned me my
    portion and my cup;
    you have made my lot secure.
[6]The boundary lines have fallen for
    me in pleasant places;
    surely I have a delightful
        inheritance.

[7]I will praise the LORD, who counsels
    me;
    even at night my heart instructs
        me.

[8]I have set the LORD always before
    me.
    Because he is at my right hand,
    I shall not be shaken.

[9]Therefore my heart is glad and my
    tongue rejoices;
    my body also will rest secure,
[10]because you will not abandon me to
    the grave,
    nor will you let your Holy One see
        decay.
[11]You have made known to me the
    path of life;
    you will fill me with joy in your
        presence,
    with eternal pleasures at your right
        hand.

DAY 27

JANUARY 27

OLD TESTAMENT READING
Job 4:1–7:21

Eliphaz

4 Then Eliphaz the Temanite replied:

[2]"If someone ventures a word with
    you, will you be impatient?
    But who can keep from speaking?
[3]Think how you have instructed
    many,
    how you have strengthened feeble
        hands.
[4]Your words have supported those
    who stumbled;
    you have strengthened faltering
        knees.
[5]But now trouble comes to you, and
    you are discouraged;
    it strikes you, and you are
        dismayed.
[6]Should not your piety be your
    confidence

and your blameless ways your
    hope?

[7]"Consider now: Who, being
    innocent, has ever perished?
    Where were the upright ever
        destroyed?
[8]As I have observed, those who
    plough evil
    and those who sow trouble reap it.
[9]At the breath of God they are
    destroyed;
    at the blast of his anger they
        perish.
[10]The lions may roar and growl,
    yet the teeth of the great lions are
        broken.
[11]The lion perishes for lack of prey,
    and the cubs of the lioness are
        scattered.

[12]"A word was secretly brought to me,
    my ears caught a whisper of it.
[13]Amid disquieting dreams in the
    night,
    when deep sleep falls on men,

¹⁴fear and trembling seized me
and made all my bones shake.
¹⁵A spirit glided past my face,
and the hair on my body stood on
end.
¹⁶It stopped,
but I could not tell what it was.
A form stood before my eyes,
and I heard a hushed voice:
¹⁷'Can a mortal be more righteous than
God?
Can a man be more pure than his
Maker?
¹⁸If God places no trust in his servants,
if he charges his angels with error,
¹⁹how much more those who live in
houses of clay,
whose foundations are in the dust,
who are crushed more readily than
a moth!
²⁰Between dawn and dusk they are
broken to pieces;
unnoticed, they perish for ever.
²¹Are not the cords of their tent pulled
up,
so that they die without wisdom?'

5 "Call if you will, but who will
answer you?
To which of the holy ones will you
turn?
²Resentment kills a fool,
and envy slays the simple.
³I myself have seen a fool taking root,
but suddenly his house was cursed.
⁴His children are far from safety,
crushed in court without a
defender.
⁵The hungry consume his harvest,
taking it even from among thorns,
and the thirsty pant after his
wealth.
⁶For hardship does not spring from
the soil,
nor does trouble sprout from the
ground.
⁷Yet man is born to trouble
as surely as sparks fly upward.

⁸"But if it were I, I would appeal to
God;
I would lay my cause before him.

⁹He performs wonders that cannot be
fathomed,
miracles that cannot be counted.
¹⁰He bestows rain on the earth;
he sends water upon the
countryside.
¹¹The lowly he sets on high,
and those who mourn are lifted to
safety.
¹²He thwarts the plans of the crafty,
so that their hands achieve no
success.
¹³He catches the wise in their
craftiness,
and the schemes of the wily are
swept away.
¹⁴Darkness comes upon them in the
daytime;
at noon they grope as in the night.
¹⁵He saves the needy from the sword in
their mouth;
he saves them from the clutches of
the powerful.
¹⁶So the poor have hope,
and injustice shuts its mouth.

¹⁷"Blessed is the man whom God
corrects;
so do not despise the discipline of
the Almighty.
¹⁸For he wounds, but he also binds up;
he injures, but his hands also
heal.
¹⁹From six calamities he will rescue
you;
in seven no harm will befall you.
²⁰In famine he will ransom you from
death,
and in battle from the stroke of the
sword.
²¹You will be protected from the lash
of the tongue,
and need not fear when destruction
comes.
²²You will laugh at destruction and
famine,
and need not fear the beasts of the
earth.
²³For you will have a covenant with the
stones of the field,
and the wild animals will be at
peace with you.

24You will know that your tent is
secure;
you will take stock of your
property and find nothing
missing.
25You will know that your children will
be many,
and your descendants like the grass
of the earth.
26You will come to the grave in full
vigour,
like sheaves gathered in season.

27"We have examined this, and it is
true.
So hear it and apply it to yourself."

Job

6 Then Job replied:

2"If only my anguish could be weighed
and all my misery be placed on the
scales!
3It would surely outweigh the sand of
the seas—
no wonder my words have been
impetuous.
4The arrows of the Almighty are in
me,
my spirit drinks in their poison;
God's terrors are marshalled
against me.
5Does a wild donkey bray when it has
grass,
or an ox bellow when it has
fodder?
6Is tasteless food eaten without salt,
or is there flavour in the white of
an egg?
7I refuse to touch it;
such food makes me ill.

8"Oh, that I might have my request,
that God would grant what I hope
for,
9that God would be willing to crush
me,
to let loose his hand and cut me
off!
10Then I would still have this
consolation—

my joy in unrelenting pain—
that I had not denied the words of
the Holy One.

11"What strength do I have, that I
should still hope?
What prospects, that I should be
patient?
12Do I have the strength of stone?
Is my flesh bronze?
13Do I have any power to help myself,
now that success has been driven
from me?

14"A despairing man should have the
devotion of his friends,
even though he forsakes the fear of
the Almighty.
15But my brothers are as undependable
as intermittent streams,
as the streams that overflow
16when darkened by thawing ice
and swollen with melting snow,
17but that cease to flow in the dry
season,
and in the heat vanish from their
channels.
18Caravans turn aside from their
routes;
they go up into the wasteland and
perish.
19The caravans of Tema look for water,
the travelling merchants of Sheba
look in hope.
20They are distressed, because they had
been confident;
they arrive there, only to be
disappointed.
21Now you too have proved to be of no
help;
you see something dreadful and are
afraid.
22Have I ever said, 'Give something on
my behalf,
pay a ransom for me from your
wealth,
23deliver me from the hand of the
enemy,
ransom me from the clutches of the
ruthless'?

24"Teach me, and I will be quiet;
show me where I have been wrong.

25How painful are honest words!
    But what do your arguments
        prove?
26Do you mean to correct what I say,
    and treat the words of a despairing
        man as wind?
27You would even cast lots for the
        fatherless
    and barter away your friend.

28"But now be so kind as to look at me.
    Would I lie to your face?
29Relent, do not be unjust;
    reconsider, for my integrity is at
        stake.
30Is there any wickedness on my lips?
    Can my mouth not discern malice?

7   "Does not man have hard service
        on earth?
    Are not his days like those of a
        hired man?
2Like a slave longing for the evening
        shadows,
    or a hired man waiting eagerly for
        his wages,
3so I have been allotted months of
        futility,
    and nights of misery have been
        assigned to me.
4When I lie down I think, 'How long
        before I get up?'
    The night drags on, and I toss till
        dawn.
5My body is clothed with worms and
        scabs,
    my skin is broken and festering.

6"My days are swifter than a weaver's
        shuttle,
    and they come to an end without
        hope.
7Remember, O God, that my life is
        but a breath;
    my eyes will never see happiness
        again.
8The eye that now sees me will see me
        no longer;
    you will look for me, but I will be
        no more.
9As a cloud vanishes and is gone,
    so he who goes down to the grave
        does not return.

10He will never come to his house
        again;
    his place will know him no more.

11"Therefore I will not keep silent;
    I will speak out in the anguish of
        my spirit,
    I will complain in the bitterness of
        my soul.
12Am I the sea, or the monster of the
        deep,
    that you put me under guard?
13When I think my bed will comfort me
    and my couch will ease my
        complaint,
14even then you frighten me with
        dreams
    and terrify me with visions,
15so that I prefer strangling and death,
    rather than this body of mine.
16I despise my life; I would not live for
        ever.
    Let me alone; my days have no
        meaning.

17"What is man that you make so much
        of him,
    that you give him so much
        attention,
18that you examine him every morning
    and test him every moment?
19Will you never look away from me,
    or let me alone even for an instant?
20If I have sinned, what have I done to
        you,
    O watcher of men?
    Why have you made me your target?
    Have I become a burden to you?
21Why do you not pardon my offences
    and forgive my sins?
    For I shall soon lie down in the dust;
    you will search for me, but I shall
        be no more."

NEW TESTAMENT READING
Matthew 19:1–15

Divorce

19 When Jesus had finished saying
    these things, he left Galilee and
went into the region of Judea to the

other side of the Jordan. [2]Large crowds followed him, and he healed them there.

[3]Some Pharisees came to him to test him. They asked, "Is it lawful for a man to divorce his wife for any and every reason?"

[4]"Haven't you read," he replied, "that at the beginning the Creator 'made them male and female', [5]and said, 'For this reason a man will leave his father and mother and be united to his wife, and the two will become one flesh'? [6]So they are no longer two, but one. Therefore what God has joined together, let man not separate."

[7]"Why then," they asked, "did Moses command that a man give his wife a certificate of divorce and send her away?"

[8]Jesus replied, "Moses permitted you to divorce your wives because your hearts were hard. But it was not this way from the beginning. [9]I tell you that anyone who divorces his wife, except for marital unfaithfulness, and marries another woman commits adultery."

[10]The disciples said to him, "If this is the situation between a husband and wife, it is better not to marry."

[11]Jesus replied, "Not everyone can accept this word, but only those to whom it has been given. [12]For some are eunuchs because they were born that way; others were made that way by men; and others have renounced marriage because of the kingdom of heaven. The one who can accept this should accept it."

The Little Children and Jesus

[13]Then little children were brought to Jesus for him to place his hands on them and pray for them. But the disciples rebuked those who brought them.

[14]Jesus said, "Let the little children come to me, and do not hinder them, for the kingdom of heaven belongs to such as these." [15]When he had placed his hands on them, he went on from there.

READING FROM PSALMS
Psalm 17:1–5

A prayer of David.

[1]Hear, O LORD, my righteous plea;
  listen to my cry.
Give ear to my prayer—
  it does not rise from deceitful lips.
[2]May my vindication come from you;
  may your eyes see what is right.

[3]Though you probe my heart and
    examine me at night,
  though you test me, you will find
    nothing;
  I have resolved that my mouth will
    not sin.
[4]As for the deeds of men—
    by the word of your lips
  I have kept myself
  from the ways of the violent.
[5]My steps have held to your paths;
  my feet have not slipped.

OLD TESTAMENT READING
Job 8:1–10:22

Bildad

8 Then Bildad the Shuhite replied:

2"How long will you say such things?
    Your words are a blustering wind.
3Does God pervert justice?
    Does the Almighty pervert what is
      right?
4When your children sinned against
      him,
    he gave them over to the penalty of
      their sin.
5But if you will look to God
    and plead with the Almighty,
6if you are pure and upright,
    even now he will rouse himself on
      your behalf
    and restore you to your rightful
      place.
7Your beginnings will seem humble,
    so prosperous will your future be.

8"Ask the former generations
    and find out what their fathers
      learned,
9for we were born only yesterday and
      know nothing,
    and our days on earth are but a
      shadow.
10Will they not instruct you and tell
      you?
    Will they not bring forth words
      from their understanding?
11Can papyrus grow tall where there is
      no marsh?
    Can reeds thrive without water?
12While still growing and uncut,
    they wither more quickly than
      grass.
13Such is the destiny of all who forget
      God;
    so perishes the hope of the godless.
14What he trusts in is fragile;
    what he relies on is a spider's web.

15He leans on his web, but it gives way;
    he clings to it, but it does not hold.
16He is like a well-watered plant in the
      sunshine,
    spreading its shoots over the
      garden;
17it entwines its roots around a pile of
      rocks
    and looks for a place among the
      stones.
18But when it is torn from its spot,
    that place disowns it and says, 'I
      never saw you.'
19Surely its life withers away,
    and from the soil other plants grow.

20"Surely God does not reject a
      blameless man
    or strengthen the hands of
      evildoers.
21He will yet fill your mouth with
      laughter
    and your lips with shouts of joy.
22Your enemies will be clothed in
      shame,
    and the tents of the wicked will be
      no more."

Job

9 Then Job replied:

2"Indeed, I know that this is true.
    But how can a mortal be righteous
      before God?
3Though one wished to dispute with
      him,
    he could not answer him one time
      out of a thousand.
4His wisdom is profound, his power is
      vast.
    Who has resisted him and come
      out unscathed?
5He moves mountains without their
      knowing it
    and overturns them in his anger.
6He shakes the earth from its place
    and makes its pillars tremble.

7He speaks to the sun and it does not
    shine;
  he seals off the light of the stars.
8He alone stretches out the heavens
    and treads on the waves of the sea.
9He is the Maker of the Bear and
    Orion,
  the Pleiades and the constellations
    of the south.
10He performs wonders that cannot be
    fathomed,
  miracles that cannot be counted.
11When he passes me, I cannot see him;
  when he goes by, I cannot perceive
    him.
12If he snatches away, who can stop
    him?
  Who can say to him, 'What are you
    doing?'
13God does not restrain his anger;
  even the cohorts of Rahab cowered
    at his feet.

14"How then can I dispute with him?
  How can I find words to argue with
    him?
15Though I were innocent, I could not
    answer him;
  I could only plead with my Judge
    for mercy.
16Even if I summoned him and he
    responded,
  I do not believe he would give me a
    hearing.
17He would crush me with a storm
  and multiply my wounds for no
    reason.
18He would not let me regain my breath
  but would overwhelm me with
    misery.
19If it is a matter of strength, he is
    mighty!
  And if it is a matter of justice, who
    will summon him?
20Even if I were innocent, my mouth
    would condemn me;
  if I were blameless, it would
    pronounce me guilty.

21"Although I am blameless,
  I have no concern for myself;
  I despise my own life.

22It is all the same; that is why I say,
  'He destroys both the blameless
    and the wicked.'
23When a scourge brings sudden death,
  he mocks the despair of the
    innocent.
24When a land falls into the hands of
    the wicked,
  he blindfolds its judges.
  If it is not he, then who is it?

25"My days are swifter than a runner;
  they fly away without a glimpse of
    joy.
26They skim past like boats of papyrus,
  like eagles swooping down on their
    prey.
27If I say, 'I will forget my complaint,
  I will change my expression, and
    smile,'
28I still dread all my sufferings,
  for I know you will not hold me
    innocent.
29Since I am already found guilty,
  why should I struggle in vain?
30Even if I washed myself with soap
  and my hands with washing soda,
31you would plunge me into a slime pit
  so that even my clothes would
    detest me.

32"He is not a man like me that I might
    answer him,
  that we might confront each other
    in court.
33If only there were someone to
    arbitrate between us,
  to lay his hand upon us both,
34someone to remove God's rod from
    me,
  so that his terror would frighten me
    no more.
35Then I would speak up without fear
    of him,
  but as it now stands with me, I
    cannot.

10 "I loathe my very life;
    therefore I will give free rein to
    my complaint
  and speak out in the bitterness of
    my soul.

²I will say to God: Do not condemn
me,
but tell me what charges you have
against me.
³Does it please you to oppress me,
to spurn the work of your hands,
while you smile on the schemes of
the wicked?
⁴Do you have eyes of flesh?
Do you see as a mortal sees?
⁵Are your days like those of a mortal
or your years like those of a man,
⁶that you must search out my faults
and probe after my sin—
⁷though you know that I am not guilty
and that no-one can rescue me
from your hand?

⁸"Your hands shaped me and made
me.
Will you now turn and destroy me?
⁹Remember that you moulded me like
clay.
Will you now turn me to dust
again?
¹⁰Did you not pour me out like milk
and curdle me like cheese,
¹¹clothe me with skin and flesh
and knit me together with bones
and sinews?
¹²You gave me life and showed me
kindness,
and in your providence watched
over my spirit.

¹³"But this is what you concealed in
your heart,
and I know that this was in your
mind:
¹⁴If I sinned, you would be watching
me
and would not let my offence go
unpunished.
¹⁵If I am guilty—woe to me!
Even if I am innocent, I cannot lift
my head,
for I am full of shame
and drowned in my affliction.
¹⁶If I hold my head high, you stalk me
like a lion

and again display your awesome
power against me.
¹⁷You bring new witnesses against me
and increase your anger towards
me;
your forces come against me wave
upon wave.

¹⁸"Why then did you bring me out of
the womb?
I wish I had died before any eye
saw me.
¹⁹If only I had never come into being,
or had been carried straight from
the womb to the grave!
²⁰Are not my few days almost over?
Turn away from me so that I can
have a moment's joy
²¹before I go to the place of no return,
to the land of gloom and deep
shadow,
²²to the land of deepest night,
of deep shadow and disorder,
where even the light is like
darkness."

NEW TESTAMENT READING
Matthew 19:16–30

The Rich Young Man

¹⁶Now a man came up to Jesus and
asked, "Teacher, what good thing must
I do to get eternal life?"
¹⁷"Why do you ask me about what is
good?" Jesus replied. "There is only
One who is good. If you want to enter
life, obey the commandments."
¹⁸"Which ones?" the man enquired.
Jesus replied, "'Do not murder, do
not commit adultery, do not steal, do
not give false testimony, ¹⁹honour your
father and mother,' and 'love your
neighbour as yourself.'"
²⁰"All these I have kept," the young
man said. "What do I still lack?"
²¹Jesus answered, "If you want to be
perfect, go, sell your possessions and
give to the poor, and you will have

treasure in heaven. Then come, follow me."

²²When the young man heard this, he went away sad, because he had great wealth.

²³Then Jesus said to his disciples, "I tell you the truth, it is hard for a rich man to enter the kingdom of heaven. ²⁴Again I tell you, it is easier for a camel to go through the eye of a needle than for a rich man to enter the kingdom of God."

²⁵When the disciples heard this, they were greatly astonished and asked, "Who then can be saved?"

²⁶Jesus looked at them and said, "With man this is impossible, but with God all things are possible."

²⁷Peter answered him, "We have left everything to follow you! What then will there be for us?"

²⁸Jesus said to them, "I tell you the truth, at the renewal of all things, when the Son of Man sits on his glorious throne, you who have followed me will also sit on twelve thrones, judging the twelve tribes of Israel. ²⁹And everyone who has left houses or brothers or sisters or father or mother or children or fields for my sake will receive a hundred times as much and will inherit eternal life. ³⁰But many who are first will be last, and many who are last will be first.

READING FROM PROVERBS
Proverbs 3:11–20

¹¹My son, do not despise the LORD's discipline
    and do not resent his rebuke,
¹²because the LORD disciplines those he loves,
    as a father the son he delights in.

¹³Blessed is the man who finds wisdom,
    the man who gains understanding,
¹⁴for she is more profitable than silver
    and yields better returns than gold.
¹⁵She is more precious than rubies;
    nothing you desire can compare with her.
¹⁶Long life is in her right hand;
    in her left hand are riches and honour.
¹⁷Her ways are pleasant ways,
    and all her paths are peace.
¹⁸She is a tree of life to those who embrace her;
    those who lay hold of her will be blessed.

¹⁹By wisdom the LORD laid the earth's foundations,
    by understanding he set the heavens in place;
²⁰by his knowledge the deeps were divided,
    and the clouds let drop the dew.

DAY 29

JANUARY 29

OLD TESTAMENT READING
Job 11:1–14:22

Zophar

11 Then Zophar the Naamathite replied:

²"Are all these words to go unanswered?
    Is this talker to be vindicated?

³Will your idle talk reduce men to silence?
    Will no-one rebuke you when you mock?
⁴You say to God, 'My beliefs are flawless
    and I am pure in your sight.'
⁵Oh, how I wish that God would speak,
    that he would open his lips against you

6and disclose to you the secrets of
wisdom,
  for true wisdom has two sides.
  Know this: God has even forgotten
  some of your sin.

7"Can you fathom the mysteries of
God?
  Can you probe the limits of the
  Almighty?
8They are higher than the
heavens—what can you do?
  They are deeper than the depths of
  the grave—what can you
  know?
9Their measure is longer than the
earth
  and wider than the sea.

10"If he comes along and confines you
in prison
  and convenes a court, who can
  oppose him?
11Surely he recognises deceitful men;
  and when he sees evil, does he not
  take note?
12But a witless man can no more
become wise
  than a wild donkey's colt can be
  born a man.

13"Yet if you devote your heart to him
and stretch out your hands to him,
14if you put away the sin that is in your
hand
  and allow no evil to dwell in your
  tent,
15then you will lift up your face without
shame;
  you will stand firm and without
  fear.
16You will surely forget your trouble,
  recalling it only as waters gone by.
17Life will be brighter than noonday,
  and darkness will become like
  morning.
18You will be secure, because there is
hope;
  you will look about you and take
  your rest in safety.
19You will lie down, with no-one to
make you afraid,
  and many will court your favour.

20But the eyes of the wicked will fail,
  and escape will elude them;
  their hope will become a dying
  gasp."

Job

12 Then Job replied:

2"Doubtless you are the people,
  and wisdom will die with you!
3But I have a mind as well as you;
  I am not inferior to you.
  Who does not know all these
  things?

4"I have become a laughing-stock to
my friends,
  though I called upon God and he
  answered—
  a mere laughing-stock, though
  righteous and blameless!
5Men at ease have contempt for
misfortune
  as the fate of those whose feet are
  slipping.
6The tents of marauders are
undisturbed,
  and those who provoke God are
  secure—
  those who carry their god in their
  hands.

7"But ask the animals, and they will
teach you,
  or the birds of the air, and they will
  tell you;
8or speak to the earth, and it will teach
you,
  or let the fish of the sea inform
  you.
9Which of all these does not know
  that the hand of the LORD has done
  this?
10In his hand is the life of every
creature
  and the breath of all mankind.
11Does not the ear test words
  as the tongue tastes food?
12Is not wisdom found among the
aged?
  Does not long life bring
  understanding?

¹³"To God belong wisdom and power;
  counsel and understanding are his.
¹⁴What he tears down cannot be
    rebuilt;
  the man he imprisons cannot be
    released.
¹⁵If he holds back the waters, there is
    drought;
  if he lets them loose, they
    devastate the land.
¹⁶To him belong strength and victory;
  both deceived and deceiver are his.
¹⁷He leads counsellors away stripped
  and makes fools of judges.
¹⁸He takes off the shackles put on by
    kings
  and ties a loincloth round their
    waist.
¹⁹He leads priests away stripped
  and overthrows men long
    established.
²⁰He silences the lips of trusted advisers
  and takes away the discernment of
    elders.
²¹He pours contempt on nobles
  and disarms the mighty.
²²He reveals the deep things of
    darkness
  and brings deep shadows into the
    light.
²³He makes nations great, and destroys
    them;
  he enlarges nations, and disperses
    them.
²⁴He deprives the leaders of the earth
    of their reason;
  he sends them wandering through a
    trackless waste.
²⁵They grope in darkness with no light;
  he makes them stagger like
    drunkards.

13 "My eyes have seen all this,
      my ears have heard and
      understood it.
²What you know, I also know;
  I am not inferior to you.
³But I desire to speak to the Almighty
  and to argue my case with God.
⁴You, however, smear me with lies;
  you are worthless physicians, all of
    you!

⁵If only you would be altogether
    silent!
  For you, that would be wisdom.
⁶Hear now my argument;
  listen to the plea of my lips.
⁷Will you speak wickedly on God's
    behalf?
  Will you speak deceitfully for him?
⁸Will you show him partiality?
  Will you argue the case for God?
⁹Would it turn out well if he examined
    you?
  Could you deceive him as you
    might deceive men?
¹⁰He would surely rebuke you
  if you secretly showed partiality.
¹¹Would not his splendour terrify you?
  Would not the dread of him fall on
    you?
¹²Your maxims are proverbs of ashes;
  your defences are defences of clay.

¹³"Keep silent and let me speak;
  then let come to me what may.
¹⁴Why do I put myself in jeopardy
  and take my life in my hands?
¹⁵Though he slay me, yet will I hope in
    him;
  I will surely defend my ways to his
    face.
¹⁶Indeed, this will turn out for my
    deliverance,
  for no godless man would dare
    come before him!
¹⁷Listen carefully to my words;
  let your ears take in what I say.
¹⁸Now that I have prepared my case,
  I know I will be vindicated.
¹⁹Can anyone bring charges against me?
  If so, I will be silent and die.

²⁰"Only grant me these two things, O
    God,
  and then I will not hide from you:
²¹Withdraw your hand far from me,
  and stop frightening me with your
    terrors.
²²Then summon me and I will answer,
  or let me speak, and you reply.
²³How many wrongs and sins have I
    committed?
  Show me my offence and my sin.

²⁴Why do you hide your face
  and consider me your enemy?
²⁵Will you torment a wind-blown leaf?
  Will you chase after dry chaff?
²⁶For you write down bitter things
        against me
  and make me inherit the sins of my
        youth.
²⁷You fasten my feet in shackles;
  you keep close watch on all my
        paths
  by putting marks on the soles of my
        feet.

²⁸"So man wastes away like something
        rotten,
  like a garment eaten by moths.

14 "Man born of woman
      is of few days and full of
      trouble.
²He springs up like a flower and
      withers away;
  like a fleeting shadow, he does not
      endure.
³Do you fix your eye on such a one?
  Will you bring him before you for
      judgment?
⁴Who can bring what is pure from the
      impure?
  No-one!
⁵Man's days are determined;
  you have decreed the number of
      his months
  and have set limits he cannot
      exceed.
⁶So look away from him and let him
      alone,
  till he has put in his time like a
      hired man.

⁷"At least there is hope for a tree:
  If it is cut down, it will sprout
      again,
  and its new shoots will not fail.
⁸Its roots may grow old in the ground
  and its stump die in the soil,
⁹yet at the scent of water it will bud
  and put forth shoots like a plant.
¹⁰But man dies and is laid low;
  he breathes his last and is no more.
¹¹As water disappears from the sea

  or a river bed becomes parched
      and dry,
¹²so man lies down and does not rise;
  till the heavens are no more, men
      will not awake
  or be roused from their sleep.

¹³"If only you would hide me in the
      grave
  and conceal me till your anger has
      passed!
  If only you would set me a time
    and then remember me!
¹⁴If a man dies, will he live again?
  All the days of my hard service
  I will wait for my renewal to come.
¹⁵You will call and I will answer you;
  you will long for the creature your
      hands have made.
¹⁶Surely then you will count my steps
  but not keep track of my sin.
¹⁷My offences will be sealed up in a
      bag;
  you will cover over my sin.

¹⁸"But as a mountain erodes and
      crumbles
  and as a rock is moved from its
      place,
¹⁹as water wears away stones
  and torrents wash away the soil,
  so you destroy man's hope.
²⁰You overpower him once for all, and
      he is gone;
  you change his countenance and
      send him away.
²¹If his sons are honoured, he does not
      know it;
  if they are brought low, he does not
      see it.
²²He feels but the pain of his own body
  and mourns only for himself."

NEW TESTAMENT READING
Matthew 20:1–19

*The Parable of the Workers in the
Vineyard*

20 "For the kingdom of heaven is
      like a landowner who went out
early in the morning to hire men to work

in his vineyard. [2]He agreed to pay them a denarius for the day and sent them into his vineyard.

[3]"About the third hour he went out and saw others standing in the market-place doing nothing. [4]He told them, 'You also go and work in my vineyard, and I will pay you whatever is right.' [5]So they went.

"He went out again about the sixth hour and the ninth hour and did the same thing. [6]About the eleventh hour he went out and found still others standing around. He asked them, 'Why have you been standing here all day long doing nothing?'

[7]"'Because no-one has hired us,' they answered.

"He said to them, 'You also go and work in my vineyard.'

[8]"When evening came, the owner of the vineyard said to his foreman, 'Call the workers and pay them their wages, beginning with the last ones hired and going on to the first.'

[9]"The workers who were hired about the eleventh hour came and each received a denarius. [10]So when those came who were hired first, they expected to receive more. But each one of them also received a denarius. [11]When they received it, they began to grumble against the landowner. [12]"These men who were hired last worked only one hour,' they said, 'and you have made them equal to us who have borne the burden of the work and the heat of the day.'

[13]"But he answered one of them, 'Friend, I am not being unfair to you. Didn't you agree to work for a denarius? [14]Take your pay and go. I want to give the man who was hired last the same as I gave you. [15]Don't I have the right to do what I want with my own

money? Or are you envious because I am generous?'

[16]"So the last will be first, and the first will be last."

Jesus Again Predicts His Death

[17]Now as Jesus was going up to Jerusalem, he took the twelve disciples aside and said to them, [18]"We are going up to Jerusalem, and the Son of Man will be betrayed to the chief priests and the teachers of the law. They will condemn him to death [19]and will turn him over to the Gentiles to be mocked and flogged and crucified. On the third day he will be raised to life!"

READING FROM PSALMS
Psalm 17:6–12

[6]I call on you, O God, for you will answer me;
    give ear to me and hear my prayer.
[7]Show the wonder of your great love,
    you who save by your right hand
    those who take refuge in you from
        their foes.
[8]Keep me as the apple of your eye;
    hide me in the shadow of your
        wings
[9]from the wicked who assail me,
    from my mortal enemies who
        surround me.

[10]They close up their callous hearts,
    and their mouths speak with
        arrogance.
[11]They have tracked me down, they
        now surround me,
    with eyes alert, to throw me to the
        ground.
[12]They are like a lion hungry for prey,
    like a great lion crouching in cover.

OLD TESTAMENT READING
Job 15:1–18:21

Eliphaz

15 Then Eliphaz the Temanite replied:

2"Would a wise man answer with
empty notions
   or fill his belly with the hot east
   wind?
3Would he argue with useless words,
   with speeches that have no value?
4But you even undermine piety
   and hinder devotion to God.
5Your sin prompts your mouth;
   you adopt the tongue of the crafty.
6Your own mouth condemns you, not
   mine;
   your own lips testify against you.

7"Are you the first man ever born?
   Were you brought forth before the
   hills?
8Do you listen in on God's council?
   Do you limit wisdom to yourself?
9What do you know that we do not
   know?
   What insights do you have that we
   do not have?
10The grey-haired and the aged are on
   our side,
   men even older than your father.
11Are God's consolations not enough
   for you,
   words spoken gently to you?
12Why has your heart carried you
   away,
   and why do your eyes flash,
13so that you vent your rage against
   God
   and pour out such words from your
   mouth?

14"What is man, that he could be pure,
   or one born of woman, that he
   could be righteous?

15If God places no trust in his holy
   ones,
   if even the heavens are not pure in
   his eyes,
16how much less man, who is vile and
   corrupt,
   who drinks up evil like water!

17"Listen to me and I will explain to
   you;
   let me tell you what I have seen,
18what wise men have declared,
   hiding nothing received from their
   fathers
19(to whom alone the land was given
   when no alien passed among
   them):
20All his days the wicked man suffers
   torment,
   the ruthless through all the years
   stored up for him.
21Terrifying sounds fill his ears;
   when all seems well, marauders
   attack him.
22He despairs of escaping the darkness;
   he is marked for the sword.
23He wanders about—food for
   vultures;
   he knows the day of darkness is at
   hand.
24Distress and anguish fill him with
   terror;
   they overwhelm him, like a king
   poised to attack,
25because he shakes his fist at God
   and vaunts himself against the
   Almighty,
26defiantly charging against him
   with a thick, strong shield.

27"Though his face is covered with fat
   and his waist bulges with flesh,
28he will inhabit ruined towns
   and houses where no-one lives,
   houses crumbling to rubble.
29He will no longer be rich and his
   wealth will not endure,

nor will his possessions spread over
the land.
30He will not escape the darkness;
a flame will wither his shoots,
and the breath of God's mouth will
carry him away.
31Let him not deceive himself by
trusting what is worthless,
for he will get nothing in return.
32Before his time he will be paid in full,
and his branches will not flourish.
33He will be like a vine stripped of its
unripe grapes,
like an olive tree shedding its
blossoms.
34For the company of the godless will
be barren,
and fire will consume the tents of
those who love bribes.
35They conceive trouble and give birth
to evil;
their womb fashions deceit."

Job

16

Then Job replied:

2"I have heard many things like these;
miserable comforters are you all!
3Will your long-winded speeches
never end?
What ails you that you keep on
arguing?
4I also could speak like you,
if you were in my place;
I could make fine speeches against
you
and shake my head at you.
5But my mouth would encourage you;
comfort from my lips would bring
you relief.

6"Yet if I speak, my pain is not
relieved;
and if I refrain, it does not go
away.
7Surely, O God, you have worn me
out;
you have devastated my entire
household.
8You have bound me—and it has
become a witness;

my gauntness rises up and testifies
against me.
9God assails me and tears me in his
anger
and gnashes his teeth at me;
my opponent fastens on me his
piercing eyes.
10Men open their mouths to jeer at me;
they strike my cheek in scorn
and unite together against me.
11God has turned me over to evil men
and thrown me into the clutches of
the wicked.
12All was well with me, but he
shattered me;
he seized me by the neck and
crushed me.
He has made me his target;
13 his archers surround me.
Without pity, he pierces my kidneys
and spills my gall on the ground.
14Again and again he bursts upon me;
he rushes at me like a warrior.

15"I have sewed sackcloth over my skin
and buried my brow in the dust.
16My face is red with weeping,
deep shadows ring my eyes;
17yet my hands have been free of
violence
and my prayer is pure.

18"O earth, do not cover my blood;
may my cry never be laid to rest!
19Even now my witness is in heaven;
my advocate is on high.
20My intercessor is my friend
as my eyes pour out tears to God;
21on behalf of a man he pleads with
God
as a man pleads for his friend.

22"Only a few years will pass
before I go on the journey of no
return.

17

1My spirit is broken,
my days are cut short,
the grave awaits me.
2Surely mockers surround me;
my eyes must dwell on their
hostility.

³"Give me, O God, the pledge you
    demand.
  Who else will put up security for
    me?
⁴You have closed their minds to
    understanding;
  therefore you will not let them
    triumph.
⁵If a man denounces his friends for
    reward,
  the eyes of his children will fail.

⁶"God has made me a byword to
    everyone,
  a man in whose face people spit.
⁷My eyes have grown dim with grief;
  my whole frame is but a shadow.
⁸Upright men are appalled at this;
  the innocent are aroused against
    the ungodly.
⁹Nevertheless, the righteous will hold
    to their ways,
  and those with clean hands will
    grow stronger.

¹⁰"But come on, all of you, try again!
  I will not find a wise man among
    you.
¹¹My days have passed, my plans are
    shattered,
  and so are the desires of my heart.
¹²These men turn night into day;
  in the face of darkness they say,
    'Light is near.'
¹³If the only home I hope for is the
    grave,
  if I spread out my bed in darkness,
¹⁴if I say to corruption, 'You are my
    father,'
  and to the worm, 'My mother' or
    'My sister',
¹⁵where then is my hope?
  Who can see any hope for me?
¹⁶Will it go down to the gates of death?
  Will we descend together into the
    dust?"

Bildad

18 Then Bildad the Shuhite replied:

²"When will you end these speeches?
  Be sensible, and then we can talk.

³Why are we regarded as cattle
  and considered stupid in your
    sight?
⁴You who tear yourself to pieces in
    your anger,
  is the earth to be abandoned for
    your sake?
  Or must the rocks be moved from
    their place?

⁵"The lamp of the wicked is snuffed
    out;
  the flame of his fire stops burning.
⁶The light in his tent becomes dark;
  the lamp beside him goes out.
⁷The vigour of his step is weakened;
  his own schemes throw him down.
⁸His feet thrust him into a net
  and he wanders into its mesh.
⁹A trap seizes him by the heel;
  a snare holds him fast.
¹⁰A noose is hidden for him on the
    ground;
  a trap lies in his path.
¹¹Terrors startle him on every side
  and dog his every step.
¹²Calamity is hungry for him;
  disaster is ready for him when he
    falls.
¹³It eats away parts of his skin;
  death's firstborn devours his limbs.
¹⁴He is torn from the security of his
    tent
  and marched off to the king of
    terrors.
¹⁵Fire resides in his tent;
  burning sulphur is scattered over
    his dwelling.
¹⁶His roots dry up below
  and his branches wither above.
¹⁷The memory of him perishes from the
    earth;
  he has no name in the land.
¹⁸He is driven from light into darkness
  and is banished from the world.
¹⁹He has no offspring or descendants
    among his people,
  no survivor where once he lived.
²⁰Men of the west are appalled at his
    fate;
  men of the east are seized with
    horror.

21Surely such is the dwelling of an evil
　　man;
　　　such is the place of one who knows
　　　　not God."

NEW TESTAMENT READING
Matthew 20:20–34

A Mother's Request

20Then the mother of Zebedee's sons
came to Jesus with her sons and, kneeling down, asked a favour of him.
21"What is it you want?" he asked.

She said, "Grant that one of these
two sons of mine may sit at your right
and the other at your left in your
kingdom."

22"You don't know what you are
asking," Jesus said to them. "Can you
drink the cup I am going to drink?"

"We can," they answered.

23Jesus said to them, "You will indeed drink from my cup, but to sit at
my right or left is not for me to grant.
These places belong to those for
whom they have been prepared by my
Father."

24When the ten heard about this, they
were indignant with the two brothers.
25Jesus called them together and said,
"You know that the rulers of the
Gentiles lord it over them, and
their high officials exercise authority
over them. 26Not so with you. Instead, whoever wants to become great
among you must be your servant, 27and
whoever wants to be first must be your
slave—28just as the Son of Man did
not come to be served, but to serve,
and to give his life as a ransom for
many."

Two Blind Men Receive Sight

29As Jesus and his disciples were leaving Jericho, a large crowd followed him.
30Two blind men were sitting by the
roadside, and when they heard that
Jesus was going by, they shouted,
"Lord, Son of David, have mercy on
us!"

31The crowd rebuked them and told
them to be quiet, but they shouted all
the louder, "Lord, Son of David, have
mercy on us!"

32Jesus stopped and called them.
"What do you want me to do for you?"
he asked.

33"Lord," they answered, "we want
our sight."

34Jesus had compassion on them and
touched their eyes. Immediately they
received their sight and followed him.

READING FROM PSALMS
Psalm 17:13–15

13Rise up, O LORD, confront them,
　　bring them down;
　　　rescue me from the wicked by your
　　　　sword.
14O LORD, by your hand save me from
　　such men,
　　from men of this world whose
　　　reward is in this life.

You still the hunger of those you
　　cherish;
　　their sons have plenty,
　　and they store up wealth for their
　　　children.
15And I—in righteousness I shall see
　　your face;
　　when I awake, I shall be satisfied
　　　with seeing your likeness.

OLD TESTAMENT READING
Job 19:1–21:34

Job

19 Then Job replied:

2"How long will you torment me
   and crush me with words?
3Ten times now you have reproached
   me;
   shamelessly you attack me.
4If it is true that I have gone astray,
   my error remains my concern
   alone.
5If indeed you would exalt yourselves
   above me
   and use my humiliation against me,
6then know that God has wronged me
   and drawn his net around me.

7"Though I cry, 'I've been wronged!' I
   get no response;
   though I call for help, there is no
   justice.
8He has blocked my way so that I
   cannot pass;
   he has shrouded my paths in
   darkness.
9He has stripped me of my honour
   and removed the crown from my
   head.
10He tears me down on every side till I
   am gone;
   he uproots my hope like a tree.
11His anger burns against me;
   he counts me among his enemies.
12His troops advance in force;
   they build a siege ramp against me
   and encamp around my tent.

13"He has alienated my brothers from
   me;
   my acquaintances are completely
   estranged from me.
14My kinsmen have gone away;
   my friends have forgotten me.

15My guests and my maidservants
   count me a stranger;
   they look upon me as an alien.
16I summon my servant, but he does
   not answer,
   though I beg him with my own
   mouth.
17My breath is offensive to my wife;
   I am loathsome to my own
   brothers.
18Even the little boys scorn me;
   when I appear, they ridicule me.
19All my intimate friends detest me;
   those I love have turned against
   me.
20I am nothing but skin and bones;
   I have escaped by only the skin of
   my teeth.

21"Have pity on me, my friends, have
   pity,
   for the hand of God has struck me.
22Why do you pursue me as God does?
   Will you never get enough of my
   flesh?

23"Oh, that my words were recorded,
   that they were written on a scroll,
24that they were inscribed with an iron
   tool on lead,
   or engraved in rock for ever!
25I know that my Redeemer lives,
   and that in the end he will stand
   upon the earth.
26And after my skin has been
   destroyed,
   yet in my flesh I will see God;
27I myself will see him
   with my own eyes—I, and not
   another.
   How my heart yearns within me!

28"If you say, 'How we will hound him,
   since the root of the trouble lies in
   him,'
29you should fear the sword yourselves;
   for wrath will bring punishment by
   the sword,

and then you will know that there
is judgment.''

Zophar

20 Then Zophar the Naamathite
replied:

²"My troubled thoughts prompt me to
answer
because I am greatly disturbed.
³I hear a rebuke that dishonours me,
and my understanding inspires me
to reply.

⁴"Surely you know how it has been
from of old,
ever since man was placed on the
earth,
⁵that the mirth of the wicked is brief,
the joy of the godless lasts but a
moment.
⁶Though his pride reaches to the
heavens
and his head touches the clouds,
⁷he will perish for ever, like his own
dung;
those who have seen him will say,
'Where is he?'
⁸Like a dream he flies away, no more
to be found,
banished like a vision of the night.
⁹The eye that saw him will not see him
again;
his place will look on him no more.
¹⁰His children must make amends to
the poor;
his own hands must give back his
wealth.
¹¹The youthful vigour that fills his
bones
will lie with him in the dust.

¹²"Though evil is sweet in his mouth
and he hides it under his tongue,
¹³though he cannot bear to let it go
and keeps it in his mouth,
¹⁴yet his food will turn sour in his
stomach;
it will become the venom of
serpents within him.

¹⁵He will spit out the riches he
swallowed;
God will make his stomach vomit
them up.
¹⁶He will suck the poison of serpents;
the fangs of an adder will kill him.
¹⁷He will not enjoy the streams,
the rivers flowing with honey and
cream.
¹⁸What he toiled for he must give back
uneaten;
he will not enjoy the profit from his
trading.
¹⁹For he has oppressed the poor and
left them destitute;
he has seized houses he did not
build.

²⁰"Surely he will have no respite from
his craving;
he cannot save himself by his
treasure.
²¹Nothing is left for him to devour;
his prosperity will not endure.
²²In the midst of his plenty, distress will
overtake him;
the full force of misery will come
upon him.
²³When he has filled his belly,
God will vent his burning anger
against him
and rain down his blows upon him.
²⁴Though he flees from an iron
weapon,
a bronze-tipped arrow pierces
him.
²⁵He pulls it out of his back,
the gleaming point out of his liver.
Terrors will come over him;
²⁶   total darkness lies in wait for his
treasures.
A fire unfanned will consume him
and devour what is left in his tent.
²⁷The heavens will expose his guilt;
the earth will rise up against him.
²⁸A flood will carry off his house,
rushing waters on the day of God's
wrath.
²⁹Such is the fate God allots the
wicked,
the heritage appointed for them by
God.''

Job

21

Then Job replied:

2"Listen carefully to my words;
  let this be the consolation you give
    me.
3Bear with me while I speak,
  and after I have spoken, mock on.

4"Is my complaint directed to man?
  Why should I not be impatient?
5Look at me and be astonished;
  clap your hand over your mouth.
6When I think about this, I am
    terrified;
  trembling seizes my body.
7Why do the wicked live on,
  growing old and increasing in
    power?
8They see their children established
    around them,
  their offspring before their eyes.
9Their homes are safe and free from
    fear;
  the rod of God is not upon them.
10Their bulls never fail to breed;
  their cows calve and do not
    miscarry.
11They send forth their children as a
    flock;
  their little ones dance about.
12They sing to the music of tambourine
    and harp;
  they make merry to the sound of
    the flute.
13They spend their years in prosperity
  and go down to the grave in peace.
14Yet they say to God, 'Leave us alone!
  We have no desire to know your
    ways.
15Who is the Almighty, that we should
    serve him?
  What would we gain by praying to
    him?'
16But their prosperity is not in their
    own hands,
  so I stand aloof from the counsel of
    the wicked.

17"Yet how often is the lamp of the
    wicked snuffed out?

How often does calamity come
    upon them,
  the fate God allots in his anger?
18How often are they like straw before
    the wind,
  like chaff swept away by a gale?
19It is said, 'God stores up a man's
    punishment for his sons.'
  Let him repay the man himself, so
    that he will know it!
20Let his own eyes see his destruction;
  let him drink of the wrath of the
    Almighty.
21For what does he care about the
    family he leaves behind
  when his allotted months come to
    an end?

22"Can anyone teach knowledge to
    God,
  since he judges even the highest?
23One man dies in full vigour,
  completely secure and at ease,
24his body well nourished,
  his bones rich with marrow.
25Another man dies in bitterness of
    soul,
  never having enjoyed anything
    good.
26Side by side they lie in the dust,
  and worms cover them both.

27"I know full well what you are
    thinking,
  the schemes by which you would
    wrong me.
28You say, 'Where now is the great
    man's house,
  the tents where wicked men lived?'
29Have you never questioned those
    who travel?
  Have you paid no regard to their
    accounts—
30that the evil man is spared from the
    day of calamity,
  that he is delivered from the day of
    wrath?
31Who denounces his conduct to his
    face?
  Who repays him for what he has
    done?

³²He is carried to the grave,
and watch is kept over his tomb.
³³The soil in the valley is sweet to him;
all men follow after him,
and a countless throng goes before
him.

³⁴"So how can you console me with
your nonsense?
Nothing is left of your answers but
falsehood!"

NEW TESTAMENT READING
Matthew 21:1–17

The Triumphal Entry

21 As they approached Jerusalem
and came to Bethphage on the
Mount of Olives, Jesus sent two disci-
ples, ²saying to them, "Go to the village
ahead of you, and at once you will find a
donkey tied there, with her colt by her.
Untie them and bring them to me. ³If
anyone says anything to you, tell him
that the Lord needs them, and he will
send them right away."

⁴This took place to fulfil what was
spoken through the prophet:

⁵"Say to the Daughter of Zion,
'See, your king comes to you,
gentle and riding on a donkey,
on a colt, the foal of a donkey.'"

⁶The disciples went and did as Jesus
had instructed them. ⁷They brought the
donkey and the colt, placed their cloaks
on them, and Jesus sat on them. ⁸A very
large crowd spread their cloaks on the
road, while others cut branches from
the trees and spread them on the road.
⁹The crowds that went ahead of him and
those that followed shouted,

"Hosanna to the Son of David!"

"Blessed is he who comes in the
name of the Lord!"

"Hosanna in the highest!"

¹⁰When Jesus entered Jerusalem, the
whole city was stirred and asked, "Who
is this?"

¹¹The crowds answered, "This is
Jesus, the prophet from Nazareth in
Galilee."

Jesus at the Temple

¹²Jesus entered the temple area and
drove out all who were buying and selling there. He overturned the tables of
the money changers and the benches of
those selling doves. ¹³"It is written," he
said to them, "'My house will be called
a house of prayer,'but you are making it
a 'den of robbers'."

¹⁴The blind and the lame came to him
at the temple, and he healed them.
¹⁵But when the chief priests and the
teachers of the law saw the wonderful
things he did and the children shouting
in the temple area, "Hosanna to the Son
of David," they were indignant.

¹⁶"Do you hear what these children
are saying?" they asked him.

"Yes," replied Jesus, "have you
never read,

"'From the lips of children and
infants
you have ordained praise'?"

¹⁷And he left them and went out of
the city to Bethany, where he spent the
night.

READING FROM PSALMS
Psalm 18:1–6

For the director of music. Of David the
servant of the LORD. He sang to the LORD
the words of this song when the LORD
delivered him from the hand of all his
enemies and from the hand of Saul. He said:

¹I love you, O LORD, my strength.

²The LORD is my rock, my fortress and
my deliverer;

my God is my rock, in whom I take
refuge.
He is my shield and the horn of my
salvation, my stronghold.
³I call to the LORD, who is worthy of
praise,
and I am saved from my enemies.

⁴The cords of death entangled
me;

the torrents of destruction
overwhelmed me.
⁵The cords of the grave coiled around
me;
the snares of death confronted me.
⁶In my distress I called to the LORD;
I cried to my God for help.
From his temple he heard my voice;
my cry came before him, into his
ears.

FEBRUARY 1 DAY 32

OLD TESTAMENT READING
Job 22:1–24:25

Eliphaz

22 Then Eliphaz the Temanite replied:

²"Can a man be of benefit to God?
Can even a wise man benefit him?
³What pleasure would it give the
Almighty if you were
righteous?
What would he gain if your ways
were blameless?

⁴"Is it for your piety that he rebukes
you
and brings charges against you?
⁵Is not your wickedness great?
Are not your sins endless?
⁶You demanded security from your
brothers for no reason;
you stripped men of their clothing,
leaving them naked.
⁷You gave no water to the weary
and you withheld food from the
hungry,
⁸though you were a powerful man,
owning land—
an honoured man, living on it.
⁹And you sent widows away
empty-handed
and broke the strength of the
fatherless.

¹⁰That is why snares are all around you,
why sudden peril terrifies you,
¹¹why it is so dark that you cannot see,
and why a flood of water covers
you.

¹²"Is not God in the heights of heaven?
And see how lofty are the highest
stars!
¹³Yet you say, 'What does God know?
Does he judge through such
darkness?
¹⁴Thick clouds veil him, so he does not
see us
as he goes about in the vaulted
heavens.'
¹⁵Will you keep to the old path
that evil men have trod?
¹⁶They were carried off before their
time,
their foundations washed away by
a flood.
¹⁷They said to God, 'Leave us alone!
What can the Almighty do to us?'
¹⁸Yet it was he who filled their houses
with good things,
so I stand aloof from the counsel of
the wicked.

¹⁹"The righteous see their ruin and
rejoice;
the innocent mock them, saying,
²⁰'Surely our foes are destroyed,
and fire devours their wealth.'

²¹"Submit to God and be at peace with
    him;
  in this way prosperity will come to
    you.
²²Accept instruction from his mouth
  and lay up his words in your heart.
²³If you return to the Almighty, you
    will be restored:
  If you remove wickedness far from
    your tent
²⁴and assign your nuggets to the dust,
  your gold of Ophir to the rocks in
    the ravines,
²⁵then the Almighty will be your gold,
  the choicest silver for you.
²⁶Surely then you will find delight in
    the Almighty
  and will lift up your face to God.
²⁷You will pray to him, and he will hear
    you,
  and you will fulfil your vows.
²⁸What you decide on will be done,
  and light will shine on your ways.
²⁹When men are brought low and you
    say, 'Lift them up!'
  then he will save the downcast.
³⁰He will deliver even one who is not
    innocent,
  who will be delivered through the
    cleanness of your hands."

Job

23

Then Job replied:

²"Even today my complaint is bitter;
  his hand is heavy in spite of my
    groaning.
³If only I knew where to find him;
  if only I could go to his dwelling!
⁴I would state my case before him
  and fill my mouth with arguments.
⁵I would find out what he would
    answer me,
  and consider what he would say.
⁶Would he oppose me with great
    power?
  No, he would not press charges
    against me.
⁷There an upright man could present
    his case before him,
  and I would be delivered for ever
    from my judge.

⁸"But if I go to the east, he is not
    there;
  if I go to the west, I do not find him.
⁹When he is at work in the north, I do
    not see him;
  when he turns to the south, I catch
    no glimpse of him.
¹⁰But he knows the way that I take;
  when he has tested me, I shall
    come forth as gold.
¹¹My feet have closely followed his
    steps;
  I have kept to his way without
    turning aside.
¹²I have not departed from the
    commands of his lips;
  I have treasured the words of his
    mouth more than my daily
    bread.

¹³"But he stands alone, and who can
    oppose him?
  He does whatever he pleases.
¹⁴He carries out his decree against me,
  and many such plans he still has in
    store.
¹⁵That is why I am terrified before him;
  when I think of all this, I fear him.
¹⁶God has made my heart faint;
  the Almighty has terrified me.
¹⁷Yet I am not silenced by the
    darkness,
  by the thick darkness that covers
    my face.

24

"Why does the Almighty not
    set times for judgment?
  Why must those who know him
    look in vain for such days?
²Men move boundary stones;
  they pasture flocks they have
    stolen.
³They drive away the orphan's donkey
  and take the widow's ox in pledge.
⁴They thrust the needy from the path
  and force all the poor of the land
    into hiding.
⁵Like wild donkeys in the desert,
  the poor go about their labour of
    foraging food;
  the wasteland provides food for
    their children.

⁶They gather fodder in the fields
    and glean in the vineyards of the
        wicked.
⁷Lacking clothes, they spend the night
        naked;
    they have nothing to cover
        themselves in the cold.
⁸They are drenched by mountain rains
    and hug the rocks for lack of
        shelter.
⁹The fatherless child is snatched from
        the breast;
    the infant of the poor is seized for a
        debt.
¹⁰Lacking clothes, they go about naked;
    they carry the sheaves, but still go
        hungry.
¹¹They crush olives among the terraces;
    they tread the winepresses, yet
        suffer thirst.
¹²The groans of the dying rise from the
        city,
    and the souls of the wounded cry
        out for help.
    But God charges no-one with
        wrongdoing.

¹³"There are those who rebel against
        the light,
    who do not know its ways
    or stay in its paths.
¹⁴When daylight is gone, the murderer
        rises up
    and kills the poor and needy;
    in the night he steals forth like a
        thief.
¹⁵The eye of the adulterer watches for
        dusk;
    he thinks, 'No eye will see me,'
    and he keeps his face concealed.
¹⁶In the dark, men break into houses,
    but by day they shut themselves in;
    they want nothing to do with the
        light.
¹⁷For all of them, deep darkness is their
        morning;
    they make friends with the terrors
        of darkness.

¹⁸"Yet they are foam on the surface of
        the water;
    their portion of the land is cursed,
    so that no-one goes to the
        vineyards.
¹⁹As heat and drought snatch away the
        melted snow,
    so the grave snatches away those
        who have sinned.
²⁰The womb forgets them,
    the worm feasts on them;
    evil men are no longer remembered
    but are broken like a tree.
²¹They prey on the barren and childless
        woman,
    and to the widow show no
        kindness.
²²But God drags away the mighty by
        his power;
    though they become established,
        they have no assurance of life.
²³He may let them rest in a feeling of
        security,
    but his eyes are on their ways.
²⁴For a little while they are exalted,
        and then they are gone;
    they are brought low and gathered
        up like all others;
    they are cut off like ears of corn.

²⁵"If this is not so, who can prove me
        false
    and reduce my words to nothing?"

NEW TESTAMENT READING
Matthew 21:18–32

The Fig-Tree Withers

¹⁸Early in the morning, as he was on
his way back to the city, he was hungry.
¹⁹Seeing a fig-tree by the road, he went
up to it but found nothing on it except
leaves. Then he said to it, "May you
never bear fruit again!" Immediately
the tree withered.

²⁰When the disciples saw this, they
were amazed. "How did the fig-tree
wither so quickly?" they asked.

²¹Jesus replied, "I tell you the truth, if
you have faith and do not doubt, not
only can you do what was done to the
fig-tree, but also you can say to this
mountain, 'Go, throw yourself into the

sea,' and it will be done. ²²If you believe, you will receive whatever you ask for in prayer.''

The Authority of Jesus Questioned

²³Jesus entered the temple courts, and, while he was teaching, the chief priests and the elders of the people came to him. ''By what authority are you doing these things?'' they asked. ''And who gave you this authority?''

²⁴Jesus replied, ''I will also ask you one question. If you answer me, I will tell you by what authority I am doing these things. ²⁵John's baptism—where did it come from? Was it from heaven, or from men?''

They discussed it among themselves and said, ''If we say, 'From heaven', he will ask, 'Then why didn't you believe him?' ²⁶But if we say, 'From men'—we are afraid of the people, for they all hold that John was a prophet.''

²⁷So they answered Jesus, ''We don't know.''

Then he said, ''Neither will I tell you by what authority I am doing these things.

The Parable of the Two Sons

²⁸''What do you think? There was a man who had two sons. He went to the first and said, 'Son, go and work today in the vineyard.'

²⁹'''I will not,' he answered, but later he changed his mind and went.

³⁰''Then the father went to the other son and said the same thing. He answered, 'I will, sir,' but he did not go.

³¹''Which of the two did what his father wanted?''

''The first,'' they answered.

Jesus said to them, ''I tell you the truth, the tax collectors and the prostitutes are entering the kingdom of God ahead of you. ³²For John came to you to show you the way of righteousness, and you did not believe him, but the tax collectors and the prostitutes did. And even after you saw this, you did not repent and believe him.

READING FROM PROVERBS
Proverbs 3:21–35

²¹My son, preserve sound judgment
 and discernment,
  do not let them out of your sight;
²²they will be life for you,
  an ornament to grace your neck.
²³Then you will go on your way in
   safety,
  and your foot will not stumble;
²⁴when you lie down, you will not be
   afraid;
  when you lie down, your sleep will
   be sweet.
²⁵Have no fear of sudden disaster
  or of the ruin that overtakes the
   wicked,
²⁶for the LORD will be your confidence
  and will keep your foot from being
   snared.

²⁷Do not withhold good from those
   who deserve it,
  when it is in your power to act.
²⁸Do not say to your neighbour,
   ''Come back later; I'll give it
    tomorrow''—
  when you now have it with you.

²⁹Do not plot harm against your
   neighbour,
  who lives trustfully near you.
³⁰Do not accuse a man for no reason—
  when he has done you no harm.

³¹Do not envy a violent man
  or choose any of his ways,
³²for the LORD detests a perverse man
  but takes the upright into his
   confidence.

³³The LORD's curse is on the house of
   the wicked,
  but he blesses the home of the
   righteous.
³⁴He mocks proud mockers
  but gives grace to the humble.
³⁵The wise inherit honour,
  but fools he holds up to shame.

OLD TESTAMENT READING
Job 25:1–29:25

Bildad

25 Then Bildad the Shuhite replied:

²"Dominion and awe belong to God;
  he establishes order in the heights
    of heaven.
³Can his forces be numbered?
  Upon whom does his light not rise?
⁴How then can a man be righteous
    before God?
  How can one born of woman be
    pure?
⁵If even the moon is not bright
  and the stars are not pure in his
    eyes,
⁶how much less man, who is but a
    maggot—
  a son of man, who is only a worm!"

Job

26 Then Job replied:

²"How you have helped the
    powerless!
  How you have saved the arm that
    is feeble!
³What advice you have offered to one
    without wisdom!
  And what great insight you have
    displayed!
⁴Who has helped you utter these
    words?
  And whose spirit spoke from your
    mouth?

⁵"The dead are in deep anguish,
  those beneath the waters and all
    that live in them.
⁶Death is naked before God;
  Destruction lies uncovered.
⁷He spreads out the northern ˻skies˼
    over empty space;

he suspends the earth over
    nothing.
⁸He wraps up the waters in his clouds,
  yet the clouds do not burst under
    their weight.
⁹He covers the face of the full moon,
  spreading his clouds over it.
¹⁰He marks out the horizon on the face
    of the waters
  for a boundary between light and
    darkness.
¹¹The pillars of the heavens quake,
  aghast at his rebuke.
¹²By his power he churned up the sea;
  by his wisdom he cut Rahab to
    pieces.
¹³By his breath the skies became fair;
  his hand pierced the gliding
    serpent.
¹⁴And these are but the outer fringe of
    his works;
  how faint the whisper we hear of
    him!
  Who then can understand the
    thunder of his power?"

27 And Job continued his dis-
    course:

²"As surely as God lives, who has
    denied me justice,
  the Almighty, who has made me
    taste bitterness of soul,
³as long as I have life within me,
  the breath of God in my nostrils,
⁴my lips will not speak wickedness,
  and my tongue will utter no deceit.
⁵I will never admit you are in the
    right;
  till I die, I will not deny my
    integrity.
⁶I will maintain my righteousness and
    never let go of it;
  my conscience will not reproach
    me as long as I live.

⁷"May my enemies be like the wicked,
  my adversaries like the unjust!

⁸For what hope has the godless when
    he is cut off,
    when God takes away his life?
⁹Does God listen to his cry
    when distress comes upon him?
¹⁰Will he find delight in the Almighty?
    Will he call upon God at all times?

¹¹"I will teach you about the power of
    God;
    the ways of the Almighty I will not
    conceal.
¹²You have all seen this yourselves.
    Why then this meaningless talk?

¹³"Here is the fate God allots to the
    wicked,
    the heritage a ruthless man
    receives from the Almighty:
¹⁴However many his children, their
    fate is the sword;
    his offspring will never have
    enough to eat.
¹⁵The plague will bury those who
    survive him,
    and their widows will not weep for
    them.
¹⁶Though he heaps up silver like dust
    and clothes like piles of clay,
¹⁷what he lays up the righteous will
    wear,
    and the innocent will divide his
    silver.
¹⁸The house he builds is like a moth's
    cocoon,
    like a hut made by a watchman.
¹⁹He lies down wealthy, but will do so
    no more;
    when he opens his eyes, all is gone.
²⁰Terrors overtake him like a flood;
    a tempest snatches him away in the
    night.
²¹The east wind carries him off, and he
    is gone;
    it sweeps him out of his place.
²²It hurls itself against him without
    mercy
    as he flees headlong from its
    power.
²³It claps its hands in derision
    and hisses him out of his place.

28 "There is a mine for silver
    and a place where gold is
    refined.
²Iron is taken from the earth,
    and copper is smelted from ore.
³Man puts an end to the darkness;
    he searches the farthest recesses
    for ore in the blackest darkness.
⁴Far from where people dwell he cuts
    a shaft,
    in places forgotten by the foot of
    man;
    far from men he dangles and
    sways.
⁵The earth, from which food comes,
    is transformed below as by fire;
⁶sapphires come from its rocks,
    and its dust contains nuggets of
    gold.
⁷No bird of prey knows that hidden
    path,
    no falcon's eye has seen it.
⁸Proud beasts do not set foot on it,
    and no lion prowls there.
⁹Man's hand assaults the flinty rock
    and lays bare the roots of the
    mountains.
¹⁰He tunnels through the rock;
    his eyes see all its treasures.
¹¹He searches the sources of the rivers
    and brings hidden things to light.

¹²"But where can wisdom be found?
    Where does understanding dwell?
¹³Man does not comprehend its worth;
    it cannot be found in the land of
    the living.
¹⁴The deep says, 'It is not in me';
    the sea says, 'It is not with me.'
¹⁵It cannot be bought with the finest
    gold,
    nor can its price be weighed in
    silver.
¹⁶It cannot be bought with the gold of
    Ophir,
    with precious onyx or sapphires.
¹⁷Neither gold nor crystal can compare
    with it,
    nor can it be had for jewels of
    gold.
¹⁸Coral and jasper are not worthy of
    mention;

the price of wisdom is beyond
rubies.
19The topaz of Cush cannot compare
with it;
it cannot be bought with pure gold.

20"Where then does wisdom come
from?
Where does understanding dwell?
21It is hidden from the eyes of every
living thing,
concealed even from the birds of
the air.
22Destruction and Death say,
'Only a rumour of it has reached
our ears.'
23God understands the way to it
and he alone knows where it
dwells,
24for he views the ends of the earth
and sees everything under the
heavens.
25When he established the force of the
wind
and measured out the waters,
26when he made a decree for the rain
and a path for the thunderstorm,
27then he looked at wisdom and
appraised it;
he confirmed it and tested it.
28And he said to man,
'The fear of the Lord—that is
wisdom,
and to shun evil is
understanding.'"

29 Job continued his discourse:

2"How I long for the months gone by,
for the days when God watched
over me,
3when his lamp shone upon my head
and by his light I walked through
darkness!
4Oh, for the days when I was in my
prime,
when God's intimate friendship
blessed my house,
5when the Almighty was still with me
and my children were around me,
6when my path was drenched with
cream

and the rock poured out for me
streams of olive oil.

7"When I went to the gate of the city
and took my seat in the public
square,
8the young men saw me and stepped
aside
and the old men rose to their feet;
9the chief men refrained from
speaking
and covered their mouths with
their hands;
10the voices of the nobles were hushed,
and their tongues stuck to the roof
of their mouths.
11Whoever heard me spoke well of me,
and those who saw me commended
me,
12because I rescued the poor who cried
for help,
and the fatherless who had none to
assist him.
13The man who was dying blessed me;
I made the widow's heart sing.
14I put on righteousness as my clothing;
justice was my robe and my turban.
15I was eyes to the blind
and feet to the lame.
16I was a father to the needy;
I took up the case of the stranger.
17I broke the fangs of the wicked
and snatched the victims from
their teeth.

18"I thought, 'I shall die in my own
house,
my days as numerous as the grains
of sand.
19My roots will reach to the water,
and the dew will lie all night on my
branches.
20My glory will remain fresh in me,
the bow ever new in my hand.'

21"Men listened to me expectantly,
waiting in silence for my counsel.
22After I had spoken, they spoke no
more;
my words fell gently on their ears.
23They waited for me as for showers
and drank in my words as the
spring rain.

^{24}When I smiled at them, they scarcely
believed it;
the light of my face was precious to
them.
^{25}I chose the way for them and sat as
their chief;
I dwelt as a king among his troops;
I was like one who comforts
mourners.

NEW TESTAMENT READING
Matthew 21:33–22:14

The Parable of the Tenants

^{33}"Listen to another parable: There
was a landowner who planted a
vineyard. He put a wall around it, dug a
winepress in it and built a watchtower.
Then he rented the vineyard to some
farmers and went away on a journey.
^{34}When the harvest time approached,
he sent his servants to the tenants to
collect his fruit.

^{35}"The tenants seized his servants;
they beat one, killed another, and
stoned a third. ^{36}Then he sent other
servants to them, more than the first
time, and the tenants treated them in
the same way. ^{37}Last of all, he sent his
son to them. 'They will respect my son,'
he said.

^{38}"But when the tenants saw the son,
they said to each other, 'This is the heir.
Come, let's kill him and take his inheritance.' ^{39}So they took him and threw him
out of the vineyard and killed him.

^{40}"Therefore, when the owner of the
vineyard comes, what will he do to
those tenants?"

^{41}"He will bring those wretches to a
wretched end," they replied, "and he
will rent the vineyard to other tenants,
who will give him his share of the crop at
harvest time."

^{42}Jesus said to them, "Have you
never read in the Scriptures:

" 'The stone the builders rejected
has become the capstone;
the Lord has done this,
and it is marvellous in our eyes'?

^{43}"Therefore I tell you that the kingdom of God will be taken away from
you and given to a people who will
produce its fruit. ^{44}He who falls on this
stone will be broken to pieces, but he on
whom it falls will be crushed."

^{45}When the chief priests and the
Pharisees heard Jesus' parables, they
knew he was talking about them. ^{46}They
looked for a way to arrest him, but
they were afraid of the crowd because
the people held that he was a prophet.

The Parable of the Wedding Banquet

22 Jesus spoke to them again in
parables, saying: ^{2}"The kingdom of heaven is like a king who prepared a wedding banquet for his son.
^{3}He sent his servants to those who had
been invited to the banquet to tell them
to come, but they refused to come.

^{4}"Then he sent some more servants
and said, 'Tell those who have been
invited that I have prepared my dinner:
My oxen and fattened cattle have been
slaughtered, and everything is ready.
Come to the wedding banquet.'

^{5}"But they paid no attention and
went off—one to his field, another to
his business. ^{6}The rest seized his servants, ill-treated them and killed them.
^{7}The king was enraged. He sent his
army and destroyed those murderers
and burned their city.

^{8}"Then he said to his servants, 'The
wedding banquet is ready, but those I
invited did not deserve to come. ^{9}Go to
the street corners and invite to the banquet anyone you find.' ^{10}So the servants
went out into the streets and gathered
all the people they could find, both good
and bad, and the wedding hall was filled
with guests.

^{11}"But when the king came in to see
the guests, he noticed a man there who
was not wearing wedding clothes.
^{12}'Friend,' he asked, 'how did you get in
here without wedding clothes?' The
man was speechless.

^{13}"Then the king told the attendants,
'Tie him hand and foot, and throw him

outside, into the darkness, where there
will be weeping and gnashing of teeth.'
¹⁴"For many are invited, but few are
chosen."

READING FROM PSALMS
Psalm 18:7–15

⁷The earth trembled and quaked,
and the foundations of the
mountains shook;
they trembled because he was
angry.
⁸Smoke rose from his nostrils;
consuming fire came from his
mouth,
burning coals blazed out of it.
⁹He parted the heavens and came
down;
dark clouds were under his feet.

¹⁰He mounted the cherubim and flew;
he soared on the wings of the wind.
¹¹He made darkness his covering, his
canopy around him—
the dark rain clouds of the sky.
¹²Out of the brightness of his presence
clouds advanced,
with hailstones and bolts of
lightning.
¹³The LORD thundered from heaven;
the voice of the Most High
resounded.
¹⁴He shot his arrows and scattered ⌐the
enemies⌐,
great bolts of lightning and routed
them.
¹⁵The valleys of the sea were exposed
and the foundations of the earth
laid bare
at your rebuke, O LORD,
at the blast of breath from your
nostrils.

FEBRUARY 3   DAY 34

OLD TESTAMENT READING
Job 30:1–32:22

30 "But now they mock me,
men younger than I,
whose fathers I would have disdained
to put with my sheep dogs.
²Of what use was the strength of their
hands to me,
since their vigour had gone from
them?
³Haggard from want and hunger,
they roamed the parched land
in desolate wastelands at night.
⁴In the brush they gathered salt herbs,
and their food was the root of the
broom tree.
⁵They were banished from their
fellow-men,
shouted at as if they were thieves.
⁶They were forced to live in the dry
stream beds,

among the rocks and in holes in the
ground.
⁷They brayed among the bushes
and huddled in the undergrowth.
⁸A base and nameless brood,
they were driven out of the
land.

⁹"And now their sons mock me in
song;
I have become a byword among
them.
¹⁰They detest me and keep their
distance;
they do not hesitate to spit in my
face.
¹¹Now that God has unstrung my bow
and afflicted me,
they throw off restraint in my
presence.
¹²On my right the tribe attacks;
they lay snares for my feet,

they build their siege ramps against
me.
13They break up my road;
they succeed in destroying me—
without anyone's helping them.
14They advance as through a gaping
breach;
amid the ruins they come rolling in.
15Terrors overwhelm me;
my dignity is driven away as by the
wind,
my safety vanishes like a cloud.

16"And now my life ebbs away;
days of suffering grip me.
17Night pierces my bones;
my gnawing pains never rest.
18In his great power ⌊God⌋ becomes
like clothing to me;
he binds me like the neck of my
garment.
19He throws me into the mud,
and I am reduced to dust and
ashes.

20"I cry out to you, O God, but you do
not answer;
I stand up, but you merely look at
me.
21You turn on me ruthlessly;
with the might of your hand you
attack me.
22You snatch me up and drive me
before the wind;
you toss me about in the storm.
23I know you will bring me down to
death,
to the place appointed for all the
living.

24"Surely no-one lays a hand on a
broken man
when he cries for help in his
distress.
25Have I not wept for those in trouble?
Has not my soul grieved for the
poor?
26Yet when I hoped for good, evil
came;
when I looked for light, then came
darkness.
27The churning inside me never stops;
days of suffering confront me.

28I go about blackened, but not by the
sun;
I stand up in the assembly and cry
for help.
29I have become a brother of jackals,
a companion of owls.
30My skin grows black and peels;
my body burns with fever.
31My harp is tuned to mourning,
and my flute to the sound of
wailing.

31 "I made a covenant with my
eyes
not to look lustfully at a girl.
2For what is man's lot from God
above,
his heritage from the Almighty on
high?
3Is it not ruin for the wicked,
disaster for those who do wrong?
4Does he not see my ways
and count my every step?

5"If I have walked in falsehood
or my foot has hurried after
deceit—
6let God weigh me in honest scales
and he will know that I am
blameless—
7if my steps have turned from the
path,
if my heart has been led by my
eyes,
or if my hands have been defiled,
8then may others eat what I have
sown,
and may my crops be uprooted.

9"If my heart has been enticed by a
woman,
or if I have lurked at my
neighbour's door,
10then may my wife grind another
man's grain,
and may other men sleep with her.
11For that would have been shameful,
a sin to be judged.
12It is a fire that burns to Destruction;
it would have uprooted my harvest.

13"If I have denied justice to my
menservants and maidservants

when they had a grievance against
me,
¹⁴what will I do when God confronts
me?
What will I answer when called to
account?
¹⁵Did not he who made me in the
womb make them?
Did not the same one form us both
within our mothers?

¹⁶"If I have denied the desires of the
poor
or let the eyes of the widow grow
weary,
¹⁷if I have kept my bread to myself,
not sharing it with the fatherless—
¹⁸but from my youth I reared him as
would a father,
and from my birth I guided the
widow—
¹⁹if I have seen anyone perishing for
lack of clothing,
or a needy man without a garment,
²⁰and his heart did not bless me
for warming him with the fleece
from my sheep,
²¹if I have raised my hand against the
fatherless,
knowing that I had influence in
court,
²²then let my arm fall from the
shoulder,
let it be broken off at the joint.
²³For I dreaded destruction from God,
and for fear of his splendour I
could not do such things.

²⁴"If I have put my trust in gold
or said to pure gold, 'You are my
security,'
²⁵if I have rejoiced over my great
wealth,
the fortune my hands had gained,
²⁶if I have regarded the sun in its
radiance
or the moon moving in splendour,
²⁷so that my heart was secretly enticed
and my hand offered them a kiss of
homage,
²⁸then these also would be sins to be
judged,

for I would have been unfaithful to
God on high.

²⁹"If I have rejoiced at my enemy's
misfortune
or gloated over the trouble that
came to him—
³⁰I have not allowed my mouth to sin
by invoking a curse against his
life—
³¹if the men of my household have
never said,
'Who has not had his fill of Job's
meat?'—
³²but no stranger had to spend the
night in the street,
for my door was always open to the
traveller—
³³if I have concealed my sin as men do,
by hiding my guilt in my heart
³⁴because I so feared the crowd
and so dreaded the contempt of the
clans
that I kept silent and would not go
outside—

³⁵("Oh, that I had someone to hear
me!
I sign now my defence—let the
Almighty answer me;
let my accuser put his indictment in
writing.
³⁶Surely I would wear it on my
shoulder,
I would put it on like a crown.
³⁷I would give him an account of my
every step;
like a prince I would approach
him.)—

³⁸"if my land cries out against me
and all its furrows are wet with
tears,
³⁹if I have devoured its yield without
payment
or broken the spirit of its tenants,
⁴⁰then let briers come up instead of
wheat
and weeds instead of barley."

The words of Job are ended.

Elihu

32 So these three men stopped answering Job, because he was righteous in his own eyes. [2]But Elihu son of Barakel the Buzite, of the family of Ram, became very angry with Job for justifying himself rather than God. [3]He was also angry with the three friends, because they had found no way to refute Job, and yet had condemned him. [4]Now Elihu had waited before speaking to Job because they were older than he. [5]But when he saw that the three men had nothing more to say, his anger was aroused.

[6]So Elihu son of Barakel the Buzite said:

"I am young in years,
　and you are old;
that is why I was fearful,
　not daring to tell you what I know.
[7]I thought, 'Age should speak;
　advanced years should teach
　　wisdom.'
[8]But it is the spirit in a man,
　the breath of the Almighty, that
　　gives him understanding.
[9]It is not only the old who are wise,
　not only the aged who understand
　　what is right.

[10]"Therefore I say: Listen to me;
　I too will tell you what I know.
[11]I waited while you spoke,
　I listened to your reasoning,
while you were searching for words,
[12]　I gave you my full attention.
But not one of you has proved Job
　　wrong;
　none of you has answered his
　　arguments.
[13]Do not say, 'We have found wisdom;
　let God refute him, not man.'
[14]But Job has not marshalled his words
　　against me,
　and I will not answer him with your
　　arguments.

[15]"They are dismayed and have no
　　more to say;
　words have failed them.
[16]Must I wait, now that they are silent,

now that they stand there with no
　　reply?
[17]I too will have my say;
　I too will tell you what I know.
[18]For I am full of words,
　and the spirit within me compels
　　me;
[19]inside I am like bottled-up wine,
　like new wineskins ready to burst.
[20]I must speak and find relief;
　I must open my lips and reply.
[21]I will show partiality to no-one,
　nor will I flatter any man;
[22]for if I were skilled in flattery,
　my Maker would soon take me
　　away.

NEW TESTAMENT READING
Matthew 22:15-46

Paying Taxes to Caesar

[15]Then the Pharisees went out and laid plans to trap him in his words. [16]They sent their disciples to him along with the Herodians. "Teacher," they said, "we know you are a man of integrity and that you teach the way of God in accordance with the truth. You aren't swayed by men, because you pay no attention to who they are. [17]Tell us then, what is your opinion? Is it right to pay taxes to Caesar or not?"

[18]But Jesus, knowing their evil intent, said, "You hypocrites, why are you trying to trap me? [19]Show me the coin used for paying the tax." They brought him a denarius, [20]and he asked them, "Whose portrait is this? And whose inscription?"

[21]"Caesar's," they replied.

Then he said to them, "Give to Caesar what is Caesar's, and to God what is God's."

[22]When they heard this, they were amazed. So they left him and went away.

Marriage at the Resurrection

[23]That same day the Sadducees, who say there is no resurrection, came to

him with a question. 24"Teacher," they said, "Moses told us that if a man dies without having children, his brother must marry the widow and have children for him. 25Now there were seven brothers among us. The first one married and died, and since he had no children, he left his wife to his brother. 26The same thing happened to the second and third brother, right on down to the seventh. 27Finally, the woman died. 28Now then, at the resurrection, whose wife will she be of the seven, since all of them were married to her?"

29Jesus replied, "You are in error because you do not know the Scriptures or the power of God. 30At the resurrection people will neither marry nor be given in marriage; they will be like the angels in heaven. 31But about the resurrection of the dead—have you not read what God said to you, 32'I am the God of Abraham, the God of Isaac, and the God of Jacob'? He is not the God of the dead but of the living."

33When the crowds heard this, they were astonished at his teaching.

The Greatest Commandment

34Hearing that Jesus had silenced the Sadducees, the Pharisees got together. 35One of them, an expert in the law, tested him with this question: 36"Teacher, which is the greatest commandment in the Law?"

37Jesus replied: "'Love the Lord your God with all your heart and with all your soul and with all your mind.' 38This is the first and greatest commandment. 39And the second is like it: 'Love your neighbour as yourself.' 40All the Law and the Prophets hang on these two commandments."

Whose Son Is the Christ?

41While the Pharisees were gathered together, Jesus asked them, 42"What do you think about the Christ? Whose son is he?"

"The son of David," they replied.

43He said to them, "How is it then that David, speaking by the Spirit, calls him 'Lord'? For he says,

44"'The Lord said to my Lord:
    "Sit at my right hand
until I put your enemies
    under your feet."'

45If then David calls him 'Lord', how can he be his son?" 46No-one could say a word in reply, and from that day on no-one dared to ask him any more questions.

READING FROM PSALMS
Psalm 18:16–24

16He reached down from on high and
        took hold of me;
    he drew me out of deep waters.
17He rescued me from my powerful
        enemy,
    from my foes, who were too strong
        for me.
18They confronted me in the day of my
        disaster,
    but the LORD was my support.
19He brought me out into a spacious
        place;
    he rescued me because he
        delighted in me.

20The LORD has dealt with me
        according to my righteousness;
    according to the cleanness of my
        hands he has rewarded me.
21For I have kept the ways of the LORD;
    I have not done evil by turning
        from my God.
22All his laws are before me;
    I have not turned away from his
        decrees.
23I have been blameless before him
    and have kept myself from sin.
24The LORD has rewarded me
        according to my righteousness,
    according to the cleanness of my
        hands in his sight.

FEBRUARY 4

OLD TESTAMENT READING
Job 33:1–34:37

33 "But now, Job, listen to my words;
pay attention to everything I say.
²I am about to open my mouth;
my words are on the tip of my tongue.
³My words come from an upright heart;
my lips sincerely speak what I know.
⁴The Spirit of God has made me;
the breath of the Almighty gives me life.
⁵Answer me then, if you can;
prepare yourself and confront me.
⁶I am just like you before God;
I too have been taken from clay.
⁷No fear of me should alarm you,
nor should my hand be heavy upon you.

⁸"But you have said in my hearing—
I heard the very words—
⁹'I am pure and without sin;
I am clean and free from guilt.
¹⁰Yet God has found fault with me;
he considers me his enemy.
¹¹He fastens my feet in shackles;
he keeps close watch on all my paths.'

¹²"But I tell you, in this you are not right,
for God is greater than man.
¹³Why do you complain to him
that he answers none of man's words?
¹⁴For God does speak—now one way, now another—
though man may not perceive it.
¹⁵In a dream, in a vision of the night,
when deep sleep falls on men
as they slumber in their beds,
¹⁶he may speak in their ears
and terrify them with warnings,

¹⁷to turn man from wrongdoing
and keep him from pride,
¹⁸to preserve his soul from the pit,
his life from perishing by the sword.
¹⁹Or a man may be chastened on a bed of pain
with constant distress in his bones,
²⁰so that his very being finds food repulsive
and his soul loathes the choicest meal.
²¹His flesh wastes away to nothing,
and his bones, once hidden, now stick out.
²²His soul draws near to the pit,
and his life to the messengers of death.

²³"Yet if there is an angel on his side
as a mediator, one out of a thousand,
to tell a man what is right for him,
²⁴to be gracious to him and say,
'Spare him from going down to the pit;
I have found a ransom for him'—
²⁵then his flesh is renewed like a child's;
it is restored as in the days of his youth.
²⁶He prays to God and finds favour with him,
he sees God's face and shouts for joy;
he is restored by God to his righteous state.
²⁷Then he comes to men and says,
'I have sinned, and perverted what was right,
but I did not get what I deserved.
²⁸He redeemed my soul from going down to the pit,
and I shall live to enjoy the light.'

²⁹"God does all these things to a man—
twice, even three times—

30to turn back his soul from the pit,
    that the light of life may shine on
    him.

31"Pay attention, Job, and listen to me;
    be silent, and I will speak.
32If you have anything to say, answer
    me;
    speak up, for I want you to be
    cleared.
33But if not, then listen to me;
    be silent, and I will teach you
    wisdom."

34 Then Elihu said:

2"Hear my words, you wise men;
    listen to me, you men of learning.
3For the ear tests words
    as the tongue tastes food.
4Let us discern for ourselves what is
    right;
    let us learn together what is good.

5"Job says, 'I am innocent,
    but God denies me justice.
6Although I am right,
    I am considered a liar;
    although I am guiltless,
    his arrow inflicts an incurable
    wound.'
7What man is like Job,
    who drinks scorn like water?
8He keeps company with evildoers;
    he associates with wicked men.
9For he says, 'It profits a man nothing
    when he tries to please God.'

10"So listen to me, you men of
    understanding.
    Far be it from God to do evil,
    from the Almighty to do wrong.
11He repays a man for what he has
    done;
    he brings upon him what his
    conduct deserves.
12It is unthinkable that God would do
    wrong,
    that the Almighty would pervert
    justice.
13Who appointed him over the earth?

Who put him in charge of the
    whole world?
14If it were his intention
    and he withdrew his spirit and
    breath,
15all mankind would perish together
    and man would return to the dust.

16"If you have understanding, hear
    this;
    listen to what I say.
17Can he who hates justice govern?
    Will you condemn the just and
    mighty One?
18Is he not the One who says to kings,
    'You are worthless,'
    and to nobles, 'You are wicked,'
19who shows no partiality to princes
    and does not favour the rich over
    the poor,
    for they are all the work of his
    hands?
20They die in an instant, in the middle
    of the night;
    the people are shaken and they
    pass away;
    the mighty are removed without
    human hand.

21"His eyes are on the ways of men;
    he sees their every step.
22There is no dark place, no deep
    shadow,
    where evildoers can hide.
23God has no need to examine men
    further,
    that they should come before him
    for judgment.
24Without enquiry he shatters the
    mighty
    and sets up others in their place.
25Because he takes note of their deeds,
    he overthrows them in the night
    and they are crushed.
26He punishes them for their
    wickedness
    where everyone can see them,
27because they turned from following
    him
    and had no regard for any of his
    ways.

28They caused the cry of the poor to
 come before him,
 so that he heard the cry of the
 needy.
29But if he remains silent, who can
 condemn him?
 If he hides his face, who can see
 him?
 Yet he is over man and nation alike,
30 to keep a godless man from ruling,
 from laying snares for the people.

31"Suppose a man says to God,
 'I am guilty but will offend no
 more.
32Teach me what I cannot see;
 if I have done wrong, I will not do
 so again.'
33Should God then reward you on your
 terms,
 when you refuse to repent?
 You must decide, not I;
 so tell me what you know.

34"Men of understanding declare,
 wise men who hear me say to me,
35'Job speaks without knowledge;
 his words lack insight.'
36Oh, that Job might be tested to the
 utmost
 for answering like a wicked man!
37To his sin he adds rebellion;
 scornfully he claps his hands
 among us
 and multiplies his words against
 God.''

NEW TESTAMENT READING
Matthew 23:1–39

Seven Woes

23 Then Jesus said to the crowds
 and to his disciples: 2"The
teachers of the law and the Pharisees sit
in Moses' seat. 3So you must obey them
and do everything they tell you. But do
not do what they do, for they do not
practise what they preach. 4They tie up
heavy loads and put them on men's
shoulders, but they themselves are not
willing to lift a finger to move them.

5"Everything they do is done for men
to see: They make their phylacteries
wide and the tassels on their garments
long; 6they love the place of honour at
banquets and the most important seats
in the synagogues; 7they love to be
greeted in the market-places and to
have men call them 'Rabbi'.

8"But you are not to be called
'Rabbi', for you have only one Master
and you are all brothers. 9And do not
call anyone on earth 'father', for you
have one Father, and he is in heaven.
10Nor are you to be called 'teacher', for
you have one Teacher, the Christ. 11The
greatest among you will be your servant. 12For whoever exalts himself will
be humbled, and whoever humbles
himself will be exalted.

13"Woe to you, teachers of the law
and Pharisees, you hypocrites! You
shut the kingdom of heaven in men's
faces. You yourselves do not enter, nor
will you let those enter who are trying
to.

15"Woe to you, teachers of the law
and Pharisees, you hypocrites! You
travel over land and sea to win a single
convert, and when he becomes one, you
make him twice as much a son of hell as
you are.

16"Woe to you, blind guides! You
say, 'If anyone swears by the temple, it
means nothing; but if anyone swears by
the gold of the temple, he is bound by
his oath.' 17You blind fools! Which is
greater: the gold, or the temple that
makes the gold sacred? 18You also say,
'If anyone swears by the altar, it means
nothing; but if anyone swears by the gift
on it, he is bound by his oath.' 19You
blind men! Which is greater: the gift, or
the altar that makes the gift sacred?
20Therefore, he who swears by the altar
swears by it and by everything on it.
21And he who swears by the temple
swears by it and by the one who dwells
in it. 22And he who swears by heaven
swears by God's throne and by the one
who sits on it.

23"Woe to you, teachers of the law
and Pharisees, you hypocrites! You give

a tenth of your spices—mint, dill and cummin. But you have neglected the more important matters of the law—justice, mercy and faithfulness. You should have practised the latter, without neglecting the former. 24You blind guides! You strain out a gnat but swallow a camel.

25"Woe to you, teachers of the law and Pharisees, you hypocrites! You clean the outside of the cup and dish, but inside they are full of greed and self-indulgence. 26Blind Pharisee! First clean the inside of the cup and dish, and then the outside also will be clean.

27"Woe to you, teachers of the law and Pharisees, you hypocrites! You are like whitewashed tombs, which look beautiful on the outside but on the inside are full of dead men's bones and everything unclean. 28In the same way, on the outside you appear to people as righteous but on the inside you are full of hypocrisy and wickedness.

29"Woe to you, teachers of the law and Pharisees, you hypocrites! You build tombs for the prophets and decorate the graves of the righteous. 30And you say, 'If we had lived in the days of our forefathers, we would not have taken part with them in shedding the blood of the prophets.' 31So you testify against yourselves that you are the descendants of those who murdered the prophets. 32Fill up, then, the measure of the sin of your forefathers!

33"You snakes! You brood of vipers! How will you escape being condemned to hell? 34Therefore I am sending you prophets and wise men and teachers. Some of them you will kill and crucify; others you will flog in your synagogues and pursue from town to town. 35And so upon you will come all the righteous blood that has been shed on earth, from the blood of righteous Abel to the blood of Zechariah son of Berakiah, whom you murdered between the temple and the altar. 36I tell you the truth, all this will come upon this generation.

37"O Jerusalem, Jerusalem, you who kill the prophets and stone those sent to you, how often I have longed to gather your children together, as a hen gathers her chicks under her wings, but you were not willing. 38Look, your house is left to you desolate. 39For I tell you, you will not see me again until you say, 'Blessed is he who comes in the name of the Lord.'"

READING FROM PSALMS
Psalm 18:25–36

25To the faithful you show yourself faithful,
   to the blameless you show yourself blameless,
26to the pure you show yourself pure,
   but to the crooked you show yourself shrewd.
27You save the humble
   but bring low those whose eyes are haughty.
28You, O Lord, keep my lamp burning;
   my God turns my darkness into light.
29With your help I can advance against a troop;
   with my God I can scale a wall.

30As for God, his way is perfect;
   the word of the Lord is flawless.
He is a shield
   for all who take refuge in him.
31For who is God besides the Lord?
   And who is the Rock except our God?
32It is God who arms me with strength
   and makes my way perfect.
33He makes my feet like the feet of a deer;
   he enables me to stand on the heights.
34He trains my hands for battle;
   my arms can bend a bow of bronze.
35You give me your shield of victory,
   and your right hand sustains me;
   you stoop down to make me great.
36You broaden the path beneath me,
   so that my ankles do not turn over.

FEBRUARY 5

OLD TESTAMENT READING
Job 35:1–37:24

35 Then Elihu said:

2"Do you think this is just?
  You say, 'I shall be cleared by
    God.'
3Yet you ask him, 'What profit is it to
    me,
  and what do I gain by not sinning?'

4"I would like to reply to you
  and to your friends with you.
5Look up at the heavens and see;
  gaze at the clouds so high above
    you.
6If you sin, how does that affect him?
  If your sins are many, what does
    that do to him?
7If you are righteous, what do you
    give to him,
  or what does he receive from your
    hand?
8Your wickedness affects only a man
    like yourself,
  and your righteousness only the
    sons of men.

9"Men cry out under a load of
    oppression;
  they plead for relief from the arm
    of the powerful.
10But no-one says, 'Where is God my
    Maker,
  who gives songs in the night,
11who teaches more to us than to the
    beasts of the earth
  and makes us wiser than the birds
    of the air?'
12He does not answer when men cry
    out
  because of the arrogance of the
    wicked.
13Indeed, God does not listen to their
    empty plea;
  the Almighty pays no attention to
    it.

14How much less, then, will he listen
  when you say that you do not see
    him,
that your case is before him
  and you must wait for him,
15and further, that his anger never
    punishes
  and he does not take the least
    notice of wickedness.
16So Job opens his mouth with empty
    talk;
  without knowledge he multiplies
    words."

36 Elihu continued:

2"Bear with me a little longer and I
    will show you
  that there is more to be said on
    God's behalf.
3I get my knowledge from afar;
  I will ascribe justice to my Maker.
4Be assured that my words are not
    false;
  one perfect in knowledge is with
    you.

5"God is mighty, but does not despise
    men;
  he is mighty, and firm in his
    purpose.
6He does not keep the wicked alive
  but gives the afflicted their rights.
7He does not take his eyes off the
    righteous;
  he enthrones them with kings
  and exalts them for ever.
8But if men are bound in chains,
  held fast by cords of affliction,
9he tells them what they have done—
  that they have sinned arrogantly.
10He makes them listen to correction
  and commands them to repent of
    their evil.
11If they obey and serve him,
  they will spend the rest of their
    days in prosperity
  and their years in contentment.

12But if they do not listen,
 they will perish by the sword
 and die without knowledge.

13"The godless in heart harbour
   resentment;
 even when he fetters them, they do
   not cry for help.
14They die in their youth,
 among male prostitutes of the
   shrines.
15But those who suffer he delivers in
   their suffering;
 he speaks to them in their
   affliction.

16"He is wooing you from the jaws of
   distress
 to a spacious place free from
   restriction,
 to the comfort of your table laden
   with choice food.
17But now you are laden with the
   judgment due to the wicked;
 judgment and justice have taken
   hold of you.
18Be careful that no-one entices you by
   riches;
 do not let a large bribe turn you
 • aside.
19Would your wealth
 or even all your mighty efforts
 sustain you so you would not be in
   distress?
20Do not long for the night,
 to drag people away from their
   homes.
21Beware of turning to evil,
 which you seem to prefer to
   affliction.

22"God is exalted in his power.
 Who is a teacher like him?
23Who has prescribed his ways for him,
 or said to him, 'You have done
   wrong'?
24Remember to extol his work,
 which men have praised in song.
25All mankind has seen it;
 men gaze on it from afar.
26How great is God—beyond our
   understanding!

The number of his years is past
 finding out.

27"He draws up the drops of water,
 which distil as rain to the streams;
28the clouds pour down their moisture
 and abundant showers fall on
   mankind.
29Who can understand how he spreads
   out the clouds,
 how he thunders from his pavilion?
30See how he scatters his lightning
   about him,
 bathing the depths of the sea.
31This is the way he governs the nations
 and provides food in abundance.
32He fills his hands with lightning
 and commands it to strike its mark.
33His thunder announces the coming
   storm;
 even the cattle make known its
   approach.

37 "At this my heart pounds
   and leaps from its place.
2Listen! Listen to the roar of his voice,
 to the rumbling that comes from
   his mouth.
3He unleashes his lightning beneath
   the whole heaven
 and sends it to the ends of the
   earth.
4After that comes the sound of his
   roar;
 he thunders with his majestic
   voice.
 When his voice resounds,
 he holds nothing back.
5God's voice thunders in marvellous
   ways;
 he does great things beyond our
   understanding.
6He says to the snow, 'Fall on the
   earth,'
 and to the rain shower, 'Be a
   mighty downpour.'
7So that all men he has made may
   know his work,
 he stops every man from his
   labour.
8The animals take cover;
 they remain in their dens.

⁹The tempest comes out from its
　　chamber,
　the cold from the driving winds.
¹⁰The breath of God produces ice,
　　and the broad waters become
　　frozen.
¹¹He loads the clouds with moisture;
　he scatters his lightning through
　　them.
¹²At his direction they swirl around
　　over the face of the whole earth
　to do whatever he commands
　　them.
¹³He brings the clouds to punish men,
　or to water his earth and show his
　　love.

¹⁴"Listen to this, Job;
　stop and consider God's wonders.
¹⁵Do you know how God controls the
　　clouds
　and makes his lightning flash?
¹⁶Do you know how the clouds hang
　　poised,
　those wonders of him who is
　　perfect in knowledge?
¹⁷You who swelter in your clothes
　when the land lies hushed under
　　the south wind,
¹⁸can you join him in spreading out the
　　skies,
　hard as a mirror of cast bronze?

¹⁹"Tell us what we should say to him;
　we cannot draw up our case
　　because of our darkness.
²⁰Should he be told that I want to
　　speak?
　Would any man ask to be
　　swallowed up?
²¹Now no-one can look at the sun,
　bright as it is in the skies
　after the wind has swept them
　　clean.
²²Out of the north he comes in golden
　　splendour;
　God comes in awesome majesty.
²³The Almighty is beyond our reach
　　and exalted in power;
　in his justice and great
　　righteousness, he does not
　　oppress.

²⁴Therefore, men revere him,
　for does he not have regard for all
　　the wise in heart?"

NEW TESTAMENT READING
Matthew 24:1–31

Signs of the End of the Age

24 Jesus left the temple and was
walking away when his disciples
came up to him to call his attention to its
buildings. ²"Do you see all these
things?" he asked. "I tell you the truth,
not one stone here will be left on
another; every one will be thrown
down."

³As Jesus was sitting on the Mount of
Olives, the disciples came to him privately. "Tell us," they said, "when will
this happen, and what will be the sign of
your coming and of the end of the age?"

⁴Jesus answered: "Watch out that no-
one deceives you. ⁵For many will come
in my name, claiming, 'I am the Christ,'
and will deceive many. ⁶You will hear of
wars and rumours of wars, but see to it
that you are not alarmed. Such things
must happen, but the end is still to
come. ⁷Nation will rise against nation,
and kingdom against kingdom. There
will be famines and earthquakes in
various places. ⁸All these are the
beginning of birth-pains.

⁹"Then you will be handed over to be
persecuted and put to death, and you
will be hated by all nations because of
me. ¹⁰At that time many will turn away
from the faith and will betray and hate
each other, ¹¹and many false prophets
will appear and deceive many people.
¹²Because of the increase of wickedness, the love of most will grow cold,
¹³but he who stands firm to the end will
be saved. ¹⁴And this gospel of the kingdom will be preached in the whole
world as a testimony to all nations, and
then the end will come.

¹⁵"So when you see standing in the
holy place 'the abomination that causes
desolation', spoken of through the

prophet Daniel—let the reader understand—16then let those who are in Judea flee to the mountains. 17Let no-one on the roof of his house go down to take anything out of the house. 18Let no-one in the field go back to get his cloak. 19How dreadful it will be in those days for pregnant women and nursing mothers! 20Pray that your flight will not take place in winter or on the Sabbath. 21For then there will be great distress, unequalled from the beginning of the world until now—and never to be equalled again. 22If those days had not been cut short, no-one would survive, but for the sake of the elect those days will be shortened. 23At that time if anyone says to you, 'Look, here is the Christ!' or, 'There he is!' do not believe it. 24For false Christs and false prophets will appear and perform great signs and miracles to deceive even the elect—if that were possible. 25See, I have told you ahead of time.

26"So if anyone tells you, 'There he is, out in the desert,' do not go out; or, 'Here he is, in the inner rooms,' do not believe it. 27For as lightning that comes from the east is visible even in the west, so will be the coming of the Son of Man. 28Wherever there is a carcass, there the vultures will gather.

29"Immediately after the distress of those days

"'the sun will be darkened,
    and the moon will not give its light;
the stars will fall from the sky,
    and the heavenly bodies will be
        shaken.'

30"At that time the sign of the Son of Man will appear in the sky, and all the nations of the earth will mourn. They will see the Son of Man coming on the clouds of the sky, with power and great glory. 31And he will send his angels with a loud trumpet call, and they will gather his elect from the four winds, from one end of the heavens to the other.

READING FROM PROVERBS
Proverbs 4:1–9

Wisdom Is Supreme

4 Listen, my sons, to a father's instruction;
    pay attention and gain
        understanding.
2I give you sound learning,
    so do not forsake my teaching.
3When I was a boy in my father's
        house,
    still tender, and an only child of my
        mother,
4he taught me and said,
    "Lay hold of my words with all
        your heart;
    keep my commands and you will
        live.
5Get wisdom, get understanding;
    do not forget my words or swerve
        from them.
6Do not forsake wisdom, and she will
        protect you;
    love her, and she will watch over
        you.
7Wisdom is supreme; therefore get
        wisdom.
    Though it cost all you have, get
        understanding.
8Esteem her, and she will exalt you;
    embrace her, and she will honour
        you.
9She will set a garland of grace on
        your head
    and present you with a crown of
        splendour."

OLD TESTAMENT READING
Job 38:1–40:2

The LORD Speaks

38 Then the LORD answered Job out of the storm. He said:

2"Who is this that darkens my counsel
   with words without knowledge?
3Brace yourself like a man;
   I will question you,
   and you shall answer me.

4"Where were you when I laid the
      earth's foundation?
   Tell me, if you understand.
5Who marked off its dimensions?
      Surely you know!
   Who stretched a measuring line
      across it?
6On what were its footings set,
   or who laid its cornerstone—
7while the morning stars sang together
   and all the angels shouted for joy?

8"Who shut up the sea behind doors
      when it burst forth from the womb,
9when I made the clouds its garment
   and wrapped it in thick darkness,
10when I fixed limits for it
   and set its doors and bars in place,
11when I said, 'This far you may come
      and no farther;
   here is where your proud waves
      halt'?

12"Have you ever given orders to the
      morning,
   or shown the dawn its place,
13that it might take the earth by the
      edges
   and shake the wicked out of it?
14The earth takes shape like clay under
      a seal;
   its features stand out like those of a
      garment.
15The wicked are denied their light,
   and their upraised arm is broken.

16"Have you journeyed to the springs
      of the sea
   or walked in the recesses of the
      deep?
17Have the gates of death been shown
      to you?
   Have you seen the gates of the
      shadow of death?
18Have you comprehended the vast
      expanses of the earth?
   Tell me, if you know all this.

19"What is the way to the abode of
      light?
   And where does darkness reside?
20Can you take them to their places?
   Do you know the paths to their
      dwellings?
21Surely you know, for you were
      already born!
   You have lived so many years!

22"Have you entered the storehouses
      of the snow
   or seen the storehouses of the
      hail,
23which I reserve for times of trouble,
   for days of war and battle?
24What is the way to the place where
      the lightning is dispersed,
   or the place where the east winds
      are scattered over the earth?
25Who cuts a channel for the torrents of
      rain,
   and a path for the thunderstorm,
26to water a land where no man lives,
   a desert with no-one in it,
27to satisfy a desolate wasteland
   and make it sprout with grass?
28Does the rain have a father?
   Who fathers the drops of dew?
29From whose womb comes the ice?
   Who gives birth to the frost from
      the heavens
30when the waters become hard as
      stone,
   when the surface of the deep is
      frozen?

³¹"Can you bind the beautiful
       Pleiades?
   Can you loose the cords of Orion?
³²Can you bring forth the constellations
       in their seasons
   or lead out the Bear with its cubs?
³³Do you know the laws of the
       heavens?
   Can you set up ⌜God's⌝ dominion
       over the earth?

³⁴"Can you raise your voice to the
       clouds
   and cover yourself with a flood of
       water?
³⁵Do you send the lightning bolts on
       their way?
   Do they report to you, 'Here we
       are'?
³⁶Who endowed the heart with wisdom
   or gave understanding to the mind?
³⁷Who has the wisdom to count the
       clouds?
   Who can tip over the water jars of
       the heavens
³⁸when the dust becomes hard
   and the clods of earth stick
       together?

³⁹"Do you hunt the prey for the lioness
   and satisfy the hunger of the lions
⁴⁰when they crouch in their dens
   or lie in wait in a thicket?
⁴¹Who provides food for the raven
   when its young cry out to God
   and wander about for lack of food?

39 "Do you know when the
       mountain goats give birth?
   Do you watch when the doe bears
       her fawn?
²Do you count the months till they
       bear?
   Do you know the time they give
       birth?
³They crouch down and bring forth
       their young;
   their labour pains are ended.
⁴Their young thrive and grow strong
       in the wilds;
   they leave and do not return.

⁵"Who let the wild donkey go free?
   Who untied his ropes?
⁶I gave him the wasteland as his home,
   the salt flats as his habitat.
⁷He laughs at the commotion in the
       town;
   he does not hear a driver's shout.
⁸He ranges the hills for his pasture
   and searches for any green thing.

⁹"Will the wild ox consent to serve
       you?
   Will he stay by your manger at
       night?
¹⁰Can you hold him to the furrow with
       a harness?
   Will he till the valleys behind you?
¹¹Will you rely on him for his great
       strength?
   Will you leave your heavy work to
       him?
¹²Can you trust him to bring in your
       grain
   and gather it to your
       threshing-floor?

¹³"The wings of the ostrich flap
       joyfully,
   but they cannot compare with the
       pinions and feathers of the
       stork.
¹⁴She lays her eggs on the ground
   and lets them warm in the sand,
¹⁵unmindful that a foot may crush
       them,
   that some wild animal may trample
       them.
¹⁶She treats her young harshly, as if
       they were not hers;
   she cares not that her labour was in
       vain,
¹⁷for God did not endow her with
       wisdom
   or give her a share of good sense.
¹⁸Yet when she spreads her feathers to
       run,
   she laughs at horse and rider.

¹⁹"Do you give the horse his strength
   or clothe his neck with a flowing
       mane?
²⁰Do you make him leap like a locust,

striking terror with his proud
  snorting?
21He paws fiercely, rejoicing in his
  strength,
  and charges into the fray.
22He laughs at fear, afraid of nothing;
  he does not shy away from the
  sword.
23The quiver rattles against his side,
  along with the flashing spear and
  lance.
24In frenzied excitement he eats up the
  ground;
  he cannot stand still when the
  trumpet sounds.
25At the blast of the trumpet he snorts,
  'Aha!'
  He catches the scent of battle from
  afar,
  the shout of commanders and the
  battle cry.

26"Does the hawk take flight by your
  wisdom
  and spread his wings towards the
  south?
27Does the eagle soar at your command
  and build his nest on high?
28He dwells on a cliff and stays there at
  night;
  a rocky crag is his stronghold.
29From there he seeks out his food;
  his eyes detect it from afar.
30His young ones feast on blood,
  and where the slain are, there is
  he."

40 The LORD said to Job:

2"Will the one who contends with the
  Almighty correct him?
  Let him who accuses God answer
  him!"

NEW TESTAMENT READING
Matthew 24:32–25:13

32"Now learn this lesson from the
fig-tree: As soon as its twigs get tender
and its leaves come out, you know that
summer is near. 33Even so, when you
see all these things, you know that it is
near, right at the door. 34I tell you the
truth, this generation will certainly not
pass away until all these things have
happened. 35Heaven and earth will pass
away, but my words will never pass
away.

The Day and Hour Unknown

36"No-one knows about that day or
hour, not even the angels in heaven, nor
the Son, but only the Father. 37As it was
in the days of Noah, so it will be at the
coming of the Son of Man. 38For in the
days before the flood, people were eating and drinking, marrying and giving in
marriage, up to the day Noah entered
the ark; 39and they knew nothing about
what would happen until the flood came
and took them all away. That is how it
will be at the coming of the Son of Man.
40Two men will be in the field; one will
be taken and the other left. 41Two
women will be grinding with a hand
mill; one will be taken and the other
left.

42"Therefore keep watch, because
you do not know on what day your Lord
will come. 43But understand this: If the
owner of the house had known at what
time of night the thief was coming, he
would have kept watch and would not
have let his house be broken into. 44So
you also must be ready, because the Son
of Man will come at an hour when you
do not expect him.

45"Who then is the faithful and wise
servant, whom the master has put in
charge of the servants in his household
to give them their food at the proper
time? 46It will be good for that servant
whose master finds him doing so when
he returns. 47I tell you the truth, he will
put him in charge of all his possessions.
48But suppose that servant is wicked
and says to himself, 'My master is
staying away a long time,' 49and he then
begins to beat his fellow-servants and to
eat and drink with drunkards. 50The
master of that servant will come on a
day when he does not expect him and at

an hour he is not aware of. ⁵¹He will cut him to pieces and assign him a place with the hypocrites, where there will be weeping and gnashing of teeth.

The Parable of the Ten Virgins

25 "At that time the kingdom of heaven will be like ten virgins who took their lamps and went out to meet the bridegroom. ²Five of them were foolish and five were wise. ³The foolish ones took their lamps but did not take any oil with them. ⁴The wise, however, took oil in jars along with their lamps. ⁵The bridegroom was a long time in coming, and they all became drowsy and fell asleep.

⁶"At midnight the cry rang out: 'Here's the bridegroom! Come out to meet him!'

⁷"Then all the virgins woke up and trimmed their lamps. ⁸The foolish ones said to the wise, 'Give us some of your oil; our lamps are going out.'

⁹"'No,' they replied, 'there may not be enough for both us and you. Instead, go to those who sell oil and buy some for yourselves.'

¹⁰"But while they were on their way to buy the oil, the bridegroom arrived. The virgins who were ready went in with him to the wedding banquet. And the door was shut.

¹¹"Later the others also came. 'Sir! Sir!' they said. 'Open the door for us!'

¹²"But he replied, 'I tell you the truth, I don't know you.'

¹³"Therefore keep watch, because you do not know the day or the hour.

READING FROM PSALMS
Psalm 18:37–42

³⁷I pursued my enemies and overtook them;
    I did not turn back till they were destroyed.
³⁸I crushed them so that they could not rise;
    they fell beneath my feet.
³⁹You armed me with strength for battle;
    you made my adversaries bow at my feet.
⁴⁰You made my enemies turn their backs in flight,
    and I destroyed my foes.
⁴¹They cried for help, but there was no-one to save them—
    to the LORD, but he did not answer.
⁴²I beat them as fine as dust borne on the wind;
    I poured them out like mud in the streets.

FEBRUARY 7   DAY 38

OLD TESTAMENT READING
Job 40:3–42:17

³Then Job answered the LORD:

⁴"I am unworthy—how can I reply to you?
    I put my hand over my mouth.
⁵I spoke once, but I have no answer—
    twice, but I will say no more."

⁶Then the LORD spoke to Job out of the storm:

⁷"Brace yourself like a man;
    I will question you,
    and you shall answer me.

⁸"Would you discredit my justice?
    Would you condemn me to justify yourself?

9Do you have an arm like God's,
 and can your voice thunder like
  his?
10Then adorn yourself with glory and
  splendour,
 and clothe yourself in honour and
  majesty.
11Unleash the fury of your wrath,
 look at every proud man and bring
  him low,
12look at every proud man and humble
  him,
 crush the wicked where they
  stand.
13Bury them all in the dust together;
 shroud their faces in the grave.
14Then I myself will admit to you
 that your own right hand can save
  you.

15"Look at the behemoth,
 which I made along with you
 and which feeds on grass like an
  ox.
16What strength he has in his loins,
 what power in the muscles of his
  belly!
17His tail sways like a cedar;
 the sinews of his thighs are
  close-knit.
18His bones are tubes of bronze,
 his limbs like rods of iron.
19He ranks first among the works of
  God,
 yet his Maker can approach him
  with his sword.
20The hills bring him their produce,
 and all the wild animals play
  nearby.
21Under the lotus plant he lies,
 hidden among the reeds in the
  marsh.
22The lotuses conceal him in their
  shadow;
 the poplars by the stream surround
  him.
23When the river rages, he is not
  alarmed;
 he is secure, though the Jordan
  should surge against his mouth.
24Can anyone capture him by the eyes,
 or trap him and pierce his nose?

41 "Can you pull in the leviathan
  with a fishhook
 or tie down his tongue with a rope?
2Can you put a cord through his nose
 or pierce his jaw with a hook?
3Will he keep begging you for mercy?
 Will he speak to you with gentle
  words?
4Will he make an agreement with you
 for you to take him as your slave
  for life?
5Can you make a pet of him like a bird
 or put him on a leash for your
  girls?
6Will traders barter for him?
 Will they divide him up among the
  merchants?
7Can you fill his hide with harpoons
 or his head with fishing spears?
8If you lay a hand on him,
 you will remember the struggle and
  never do it again!
9Any hope of subduing him is false;
 the mere sight of him is
  overpowering.
10No-one is fierce enough to rouse him.
 Who then is able to stand against
  me?
11Who has a claim against me that I
  must pay?
 Everything under heaven belongs
  to me.

12"I will not fail to speak of his limbs,
 his strength and his graceful form.
13Who can strip off his outer coat?
 Who would approach him with a
  bridle?
14Who dares open the doors of his
  mouth,
 ringed about with his fearsome
  teeth?
15His back has rows of shields
 tightly sealed together;
16each is so close to the next
 that no air can pass between.
17They are joined fast to one another;
 they cling together and cannot be
  parted.
18His snorting throws out flashes of
  light;
 his eyes are like the rays of dawn.

19Firebrands stream from his mouth;
sparks of fire shoot out.
20Smoke pours from his nostrils
as from a boiling pot over a fire of
reeds.
21His breath sets coals ablaze,
and flames dart from his mouth.
22Strength resides in his neck;
dismay goes before him.
23The folds of his flesh are tightly
joined;
they are firm and immovable.
24His chest is hard as rock,
hard as a lower millstone.
25When he rises up, the mighty are
terrified;
they retreat before his thrashing.
26The sword that reaches him has no
effect,
nor does the spear or the dart or
the javelin.
27Iron he treats like straw
and bronze like rotten wood.
28Arrows do not make him flee;
slingstones are like chaff to him.
29A club seems to him but a piece of
straw;
he laughs at the rattling of the
lance.
30His undersides are jagged potsherds,
leaving a trail in the mud like a
threshing-sledge.
31He makes the depths churn like a
boiling cauldron
and stirs up the sea like a pot of
ointment.
32Behind him he leaves a glistening
wake;
one would think the deep had
white hair.
33Nothing on earth is his equal—
a creature without fear.
34He looks down on all that are
haughty;
he is king over all that are proud."

Job

42 Then Job replied to the LORD:
2"I know that you can do all things;
no plan of yours can be thwarted.

3⌐You asked,⌐ 'Who is this that
obscures my counsel without
knowledge?'
Surely I spoke of things I did not
understand,
things too wonderful for me to
know.

4⌐"You said,⌐ 'Listen now, and I will
speak;
I will question you,
and you shall answer me.'
5My ears had heard of you
but now my eyes have seen you.
6Therefore I despise myself
and repent in dust and ashes."

Epilogue

7After the LORD had said these things
to Job, he said to Eliphaz the Temanite,
"I am angry with you and your two
friends, because you have not spoken of
me what is right, as my servant Job has.
8So now take seven bulls and seven
rams and go to my servant Job and
sacrifice a burnt offering for yourselves.
My servant Job will pray for you, and I
will accept his prayer and not deal with
you according to your folly. You have
not spoken of me what is right, as my
servant Job has." 9So Eliphaz the
Temanite, Bildad the Shuhite and
Zophar the Naamathite did what the
LORD told them; and the LORD accepted
Job's prayer.

10After Job had prayed for his
friends, the LORD made him prosperous
again and gave him twice as much as he
had before. 11All his brothers and sisters and everyone who had known him
before came and ate with him in his
house. They comforted and consoled
him over all the trouble the LORD had
brought upon him, and each one gave
him a piece of silver and a gold ring.

12The LORD blessed the latter part of
Job's life more than the first. He had
fourteen thousand sheep, six thousand
camels, a thousand yoke of oxen and a
thousand donkeys. 13And he also had

seven sons and three daughters. 14The first daughter he named Jemimah, the second Keziah and the third Keren-Happuch. 15Nowhere in all the land were there found women as beautiful as Job's daughters, and their father granted them an inheritance along with their brothers.

16After this, Job lived a hundred and forty years; he saw his children and their children to the fourth generation. 17And so he died, old and full of years.

NEW TESTAMENT READING
Matthew 25:14–46

The Parable of the Talents

14"Again, it will be like a man going on a journey, who called his servants and entrusted his property to them. 15To one he gave five talents of money, to another two talents, and to another one talent, each according to his ability. Then he went on his journey. 16The man who had received the five talents went at once and put his money to work and gained five more. 17So also, the one with the two talents gained two more. 18But the man who had received the one talent went off, dug a hole in the ground and hid his master's money.

19"After a long time the master of those servants returned and settled accounts with them. 20The man who had received the five talents brought the other five. 'Master,' he said, 'you entrusted me with five talents. See, I have gained five more.'

21"His master replied, 'Well done, good and faithful servant! You have been faithful with a few things; I will put you in charge of many things. Come and share your master's happiness!'

22"The man with the two talents also came. 'Master,' he said, 'you entrusted me with two talents; see, I have gained two more.'

23"His master replied, 'Well done, good and faithful servant! You have been faithful with a few things; I will put

you in charge of many things. Come and share your master's happiness!'

24"Then the man who had received the one talent came. 'Master,' he said, 'I knew that you are a hard man, harvesting where you have not sown and gathering where you have not scattered seed. 25So I was afraid and went out and hid your talent in the ground. See, here is what belongs to you.'

26"His master replied, 'You wicked, lazy servant! So you knew that I harvest where I have not sown and gather where I have not scattered seed? 27Well then, you should have put my money on deposit with the bankers, so that when I returned I would have received it back with interest.

28"'Take the talent from him and give it to the one who has the ten talents. 29For everyone who has will be given more, and he will have an abundance. Whoever does not have, even what he has will be taken from him. 30And throw that worthless servant outside, into the darkness, where there will be weeping and gnashing of teeth.'

The Sheep and the Goats

31"When the Son of Man comes in his glory, and all the angels with him, he will sit on his throne in heavenly glory. 32All the nations will be gathered before him, and he will separate the people one from another as a shepherd separates the sheep from the goats. 33He will put the sheep on his right and the goats on his left.

34"Then the King will say to those on his right, 'Come, you who are blessed by my Father; take your inheritance, the kingdom prepared for you since the creation of the world. 35For I was hungry and you gave me something to eat, I was thirsty and you gave me something to drink, I was a stranger and you invited me in, 36I needed clothes and you clothed me, I was sick and you looked after me, I was in prison and you came to visit me.'

37"Then the righteous will answer him, 'Lord, when did we see you hungry and feed you, or thirsty and give you something to drink? 38When did we see you a stranger and invite you in, or needing clothes and clothe you? 39When did we see you sick or in prison and go to visit you?'

40"The King will reply, 'I tell you the truth, whatever you did for one of the least of these brothers of mine, you did for me.'

41"Then he will say to those on his left, 'Depart from me, you who are cursed, into the eternal fire prepared for the devil and his angels. 42For I was hungry and you gave me nothing to eat, I was thirsty and you gave me nothing to drink, 43I was a stranger and you did not invite me in, I needed clothes and you did not clothe me, I was sick and in prison and you did not look after me.'

44"They also will answer, 'Lord, when did we see you hungry or thirsty or a stranger or needing clothes or sick or in prison, and did not help you?'

45"He will reply, 'I tell you the truth, whatever you did not do for one of the least of these, you did not do for me.'

46"Then they will go away to eternal punishment, but the righteous to eternal life.'"

READING FROM PSALMS
Psalm 18:43–50

43You have delivered me from the
    attacks of the people;
  you have made me the head of
    nations;
  people I did not know are subject
    to me.
44As soon as they hear me, they obey
    me;
  foreigners cringe before me.
45They all lose heart;
  they come trembling from their
    strongholds.

46The LORD lives! Praise be to my
    Rock!
  Exalted be God my Saviour!
47He is the God who avenges me,
  who subdues nations under me,
48 who saves me from my enemies.
You exalted me above my foes;
  from violent men you rescued me.
49Therefore I will praise you among the
    nations, O LORD;
  I will sing praises to your name.
50He gives his king great victories;
  he shows unfailing kindness to his
    anointed,
  to David and his descendants for
    ever.

FEBRUARY 8   DAY 39

OLD TESTAMENT READING
Exodus 1:1–3:22

The Israelites Oppressed

1 These are the names of the sons of Israel who went to Egypt with Jacob, each with his family: 2Reuben, Simeon, Levi and Judah; 3Issachar, Zebulun and Benjamin; 4Dan and Naphtali; Gad and Asher. 5The descendants of Jacob numbered seventy in all; Joseph was already in Egypt.

6Now Joseph and all his brothers and all that generation died, 7but the Israelites were fruitful and multiplied greatly and became exceedingly numerous, so that the land was filled with them.

8Then a new king, who did not know about Joseph, came to power in Egypt. 9"Look," he said to his people, "the Israelites have become much too numerous for us. 10Come, we must deal shrewdly with them or they will become even more numerous and, if war breaks out, will join our enemies, fight against us and leave the country."

11So they put slave masters over them to oppress them with forced labour, and they built Pithom and Rameses as store cities for Pharaoh. 12But the more they were oppressed, the more they multiplied and spread; so the Egyptians came to dread the Israelites 13and worked them ruthlessly. 14They made their lives bitter with hard labour in brick and mortar and with all kinds of work in the fields; in all their hard labour the Egyptians used them ruthlessly.

15The king of Egypt said to the Hebrew midwives, whose names were Shiphrah and Puah, 16"When you help the Hebrew women in childbirth and observe them on the delivery stool, if it is a boy, kill him; but if it is a girl, let her live." 17The midwives, however, feared God and did not do what the king of Egypt had told them to do; they let the boys live. 18Then the king of Egypt summoned the midwives and asked them, "Why have you done this? Why have you let the boys live?"

19The midwives answered Pharaoh, "Hebrew women are not like Egyptian women; they are vigorous and give birth before the midwives arrive."

20So God was kind to the midwives and the people increased and became even more numerous. 21And because the midwives feared God, he gave them families of their own.

22Then Pharaoh gave this order to all his people: "Every boy that is born you must throw into the Nile, but let every girl live."

The Birth of Moses

2 Now a man of the house of Levi married a Levite woman, 2and she became pregnant and gave birth to a son. When she saw that he was a fine child, she hid him for three months. 3But when she could hide him no longer, she got a papyrus basket for him and coated it with tar and pitch. Then she placed the child in it and put it among the reeds along the bank of the Nile. 4His sister stood at a distance to see what would happen to him.

5Then Pharaoh's daughter went down to the Nile to bathe, and her attendants were walking along the river bank. She saw the basket among the reeds and sent her slave girl to get it. 6She opened it and saw the baby. He was crying, and she felt sorry for him. "This is one of the Hebrew babies," she said.

7Then his sister asked Pharaoh's daughter, "Shall I go and get one of the Hebrew women to nurse the baby for you?"

8"Yes, go," she answered. And the girl went and got the baby's mother. 9Pharaoh's daughter said to her, "Take this baby and nurse him for me, and I will pay you." So the woman took the baby and nursed him. 10When the child grew older, she took him to Pharaoh's daughter and he became her son. She named him Moses, saying, "I drew him out of the water."

Moses Flees to Midian

11One day, after Moses had grown up, he went out to where his own people were and watched them at their hard labour. He saw an Egyptian beating a Hebrew, one of his own people. 12Glancing this way and that and seeing no-one, he killed the Egyptian and hid him in the sand. 13The next day he went out and saw two Hebrews fighting. He asked the one in the wrong, "Why are you hitting your fellow Hebrew?"

14The man said, "Who made you ruler and judge over us? Are you thinking of killing me as you killed the Egyptian?" Then Moses was afraid and thought, "What I did must have become known."

15When Pharaoh heard of this, he tried to kill Moses, but Moses fled from Pharaoh and went to live in Midian, where he sat down by a well. 16Now a priest of Midian had seven daughters, and they came to draw water and fill the troughs to water their father's flock. [17]Some shepherds came along and drove them away, but Moses got up and came to their rescue and watered their flock.

[18]When the girls returned to Reuel their father, he asked then, "Why have you returned so early today?"

[19]They answered, "An Egyptian rescued us from the shepherds. He even drew water for us and watered the flock."

[20]"And where is he?" he asked his daughters. "Why did you leave him? Invite him to have something to eat."

[21]Moses agreed to stay with the man, who gave his daughter Zipporah to Moses in marriage. [22]Zipporah gave birth to a son, and Moses named him Gershom, saying, "I have become an alien in a foreign land."

[23]During that long period, the king of Egypt died. The Israelites groaned in their slavery and cried out, and their cry for help because of their slavery went up to God. [24]God heard their groaning and he remembered his covenant with Abraham, with Isaac and with Jacob. [25]So God looked on the Israelites and was concerned about them.

Moses and the Burning Bush

3 Now Moses was tending the flock of Jethro his father-in-law, the priest of Midian, and he led the flock to the far side of the desert and came to Horeb, the mountain of God. [2]There the angel of the LORD appeared to him in flames of fire from within a bush. Moses saw that though the bush was on fire it did not burn up. [3]So Moses thought, "I will go over and see this strange sight—why the bush does not burn up."

[4]When the LORD saw that he had gone over to look, God called to him from within the bush, "Moses! Moses!"

And Moses said, "Here I am."

[5]"Do not come any closer," God said. "Take off your sandals, for the place where you are standing is holy ground." [6]Then he said, "I am the God of your father, the God of Abraham, the God of Isaac and the God of Jacob." At this, Moses hid his face, because he was afraid to look at God.

[7]The LORD said, "I have indeed seen the misery of my people in Egypt. I have heard them crying out because of their slave drivers, and I am concerned about their suffering. [8]So I have come down to rescue them from the hand of the Egyptians and to bring them up out of that land into a good and spacious land, a land flowing with milk and honey—the home of the Canaanites, Hittites, Amonites, Perizzites, Hivites and Jebusites. [9]And now the cry of the Israelites has reached me, and I have seen the way the Egyptians are oppressing them. [10]So now, go. I am sending you to Pharaoh to bring my people the Israelites out of Egypt."

[11]But Moses said to God, "Who am I, that I should go to Pharaoh and bring the Israelites out of Egypt?"

[12]And God said, "I will be with you. And this will be the sign to you that it is I who have sent you: When you have brought the people out of Egypt, you will worship God on this mountain."

[13]Moses said to God, "Suppose I go to the Israelites and say to them, 'The God of your fathers has sent me to you,' and they ask me, 'What is his name?' Then what shall I tell them?"

[14]God said to Moses, "I AM WHO I AM. This is what you are to say to the Israelites: 'I AM has sent me to you.'"

[15]God also said to Moses, "Say to the Israelites, 'The LORD, the God of your fathers—the God of Abraham, the God of Isaac and the God of Jacob —has sent me to you.' This is my name for ever, the name by which I am to be remembered from generation to generation.

[16]"Go, assemble the elders of Israel and say to them, 'The LORD, the God of your fathers—the God of Abraham, Isaac and Jacob—appeared to me and said: I have watched over you and have seen what has been done to you in

Egypt. ¹⁷And I have promised to bring you up out of your misery in Egypt into the land of the Canaanites, Hittites, Amorites, Perizzites, Hivites and Jebusites—a land flowing with milk and honey.'

¹⁸"The elders of Israel will listen to you. Then you and the elders are to go to the king of Egypt and say to him, 'The LORD, the God of the Hebrews, has met with us. Let us take a three-day journey into the desert to offer sacrifices to the LORD our God.' ¹⁹But I know that the king of Egypt will not let you go unless a mighty hand compels him. ²⁰So I will stretch out my hand and strike the Egyptians with all the wonders that I will perform among them. After that, he will let you go.

²¹"And I will make the Egyptians favourably disposed towards this people, so that when you leave you will not go empty-handed. ²²Every woman is to ask her neighbour and any woman living in her house for articles of silver and gold and for clothing, which you will put on your sons and daughters. And so you will plunder the Egyptians."

NEW TESTAMENT READING
Matthew 26:1–30

The Plot Against Jesus

26 When Jesus had finished saying all these things, he said to his disciples, ²"As you know, the Passover is two days away—and the Son of Man will be handed over to be crucified."

³Then the chief priests and the elders of the people assembled in the palace of the high priest, whose name was Caiaphas, ⁴and they plotted to arrest Jesus in some sly way and kill him. ⁵"But not during the Feast," they said, "or there may be a riot among the people."

Jesus Anointed at Bethany

⁶While Jesus was in Bethany in the home of a man known as Simon the Leper, ⁷a woman came to him with an alabaster jar of very expensive perfume, which she poured on his head as he was reclining at the table.

⁸When the disciples saw this, they were indignant. "Why this waste?" they asked. ⁹"This perfume could have been sold at a high price and the money given to the poor."

¹⁰Aware of this, Jesus said to them, "Why are you bothering this woman? She has done a beautiful thing to me. ¹¹The poor you will always have with you, but you will not always have me. ¹²When she poured this perfume on my body, she did it to prepare me for burial. ¹³I tell you the truth, wherever this gospel is preached throughout the world, what she has done will also be told, in memory of her."

Judas Agrees to Betray Jesus

¹⁴Then one of the Twelve—the one called Judas Iscariot—went to the chief priests ¹⁵and asked, "What are you willing to give me if I hand him over to you?" So they counted out for him thirty silver coins. ¹⁶From then on Judas watched for an opportunity to hand him over.

The Lord's Supper

¹⁷On the first day of the Feast of Unleavened Bread, the disciples came to Jesus and asked, "Where do you want us to make preparations for you to eat the Passover?"

¹⁸He replied, "Go into the city to a certain man and tell him, 'The Teacher says: My appointed time is near. I am going to celebrate the Passover with my disciples at your house.'" ¹⁹So the disciples did as Jesus had directed them and prepared the Passover.

²⁰When evening came, Jesus was reclining at the table with the Twelve. ²¹And while they were eating, he said, "I tell you the truth, one of you will betray me."

²²They were very sad and began to say to him one after the other, "Surely not I, Lord?"

²³Jesus replied, "The one who has dipped his hand into the bowl with me will betray me. ²⁴The Son of Man will go just as it is written about him. But woe to that man who betrays the Son of Man! It would be better for him if he had not been born."

²⁵Then Judas, the one who would betray him, said, "Surely not I, Rabbi?"

Jesus answered, "Yes, it is you."

²⁶While they were eating, Jesus took bread, gave thanks and broke it, and gave it to his disciples, saying, "Take and eat; this is my body."

²⁷Then he took the cup, gave thanks and offered it to them, saying, "Drink from it, all of you. ²⁸This is my blood of the covenant, which is poured out for many for the forgiveness of sins. ²⁹I tell you, I will not drink of this fruit of the vine from now on until that day when I drink it anew with you in my Father's kingdom."

³⁰When they had sung a hymn, they went out to the Mount of Olives.

READING FROM PSALMS
Psalm 19:1–6

For the director of music. A psalm of David.

¹The heavens declare the glory of God;
the skies proclaim the work of his hands.
²Day after day they pour forth speech;
night after night they display knowledge.
³There is no speech or language where their voice is not heard.
⁴Their voice goes out into all the earth,
their words to the ends of the world.

In the heavens he has pitched a tent for the sun,
5 which is like a bridegroom coming forth from his pavilion,
like a champion rejoicing to run his course.
⁶It rises at one end of the heavens and makes its circuit to the other;
nothing is hidden from its heat.

FEBRUARY 9   DAY 40

OLD TESTAMENT READING
Exodus 4:1–6:12

Signs for Moses

4 Moses answered, "What if they do not believe me or listen to me and say, 'The LORD did not appear to you'?"

²Then the LORD said to him, "What is that in your hand?"

"A staff," he replied.

³The LORD said, "Throw it on the ground."

Moses threw it on the ground and it became a snake, and he ran from it. ⁴Then the LORD said to him, "Reach out your hand and take it by the tail." So Moses reached out and took hold of the snake and it turned back into a staff in his hand. ⁵"This," said the LORD, "is so that they may believe that the LORD, the God of their fathers—the God of Abraham, the God of Isaac and the God of Jacob—has appeared to you."

⁶Then the LORD said, "Put your hand inside your cloak." So Moses put his hand into his cloak, and when he took it out, it was leprous, like snow.

⁷"Now put it back into your cloak,"

he said. So Moses put his hand back into his cloak, and when he took it out, it was restored, like the rest of his flesh.

8Then the LORD said, "If they do not believe you or pay attention to the first miraculous sign, they may believe the second. 9But if they do not believe these two signs or listen to you, take some water from the Nile and pour it on the dry ground. The water you take from the river will become blood on the ground."

10Moses said to the LORD, "O Lord, I have never been eloquent, neither in the past nor since you have spoken to your servant. I am slow of speech and tongue."

11The LORD said to him, "Who gave man his mouth? Who makes him deaf or mute? Who gives him sight or makes him blind? Is it not I, the LORD? 12Now go; I will help you speak and will teach you what to say."

13But Moses said, "O Lord, please send someone else to do it."

14Then the LORD's anger burned against Moses and he said, "What about your brother, Aaron the Levite? I know he can speak well. He is already on his way to meet you, and his heart will be glad when he sees you. 15You shall speak to him and put words in his mouth; I will help both of you speak and will teach you what to do. 16He will speak to the people for you, and it will be as if he were your mouth and as if you were God to him. 17But take this staff in your hand so that you can perform miraculous signs with it."

Moses Returns to Egypt

18Then Moses went back to Jethro his father-in-law and said to him, "Let me go back to my own people in Egypt to see if any of them are still alive."

Jethro said, "Go, and I wish you well."

19Now the LORD had said to Moses in Midian, "Go back to Egypt, for all the men who wanted to kill you are dead."

20So Moses took his wife and sons, put them on a donkey and started back to Egypt. And he took the staff of God in his hand.

21The LORD said to Moses, "When you return to Egypt, see that you perform before Pharaoh all the wonders I have given you the power to do. But I will harden his heart so that he will not let the people go. 22Then say to Pharaoh, 'This is what the LORD says: Israel is my firstborn son, 23and I told you, "Let my son go, so that he may worship me." But you refused to let him go; so I will kill your firstborn son.'"

24At a lodging place on the way, the LORD met ⌊Moses⌋ and was about to kill him. 25But Zipporah took a flint knife, cut off her son's foreskin and touched ⌊Moses'⌋ feet with it. "Surely you are a bridegroom of blood to me," she said. 26So the LORD let him alone. (At that time she said "bridegroom of blood", referring to circumcision.)

27The LORD said to Aaron, "Go into the desert to meet Moses." So he met Moses at the mountain of God and kissed him. 28Then Moses told Aaron everything the LORD had sent him to say, and also about all the miraculous signs he had commanded him to perform.

29Moses and Aaron brought together all the elders of the Israelites, 30and Aaron told them everything the LORD had said to Moses. He also performed the signs before the people, 31and they believed. And when they heard that the LORD was concerned about them and had seen their misery, they bowed down and worshipped.

Bricks Without Straw

5 Afterwards Moses and Aaron went to Pharaoh and said, "This is what the LORD, the God of Israel, says: 'Let my people go, so that they may hold a festival to me in the desert.'"

2Pharaoh said, "Who is the LORD, that I should obey him and let Israel go?

I do not know the LORD and I will not let Israel go."

³Then they said, "The God of the Hebrews has met with us. Now let us take a three-day journey into the desert to offer sacrifices to the LORD our God, or he may strike us with plagues or with the sword."

⁴But the king of Egypt said, "Moses and Aaron, why are you taking the people away from their labour? Get back to your work!" ⁵Then Pharaoh said, "Look, the people of the land are now numerous, and you are stopping them from working."

⁶That same day Pharaoh gave this order to the slave drivers and foremen in charge of the people: ⁷"You are no longer to supply the people with straw for making bricks; let them go and gather their own straw. ⁸But require them to make the same number of bricks as before; don't reduce the quota. They are lazy; that is why they are crying out, 'Let us go and sacrifice to our God.' ⁹Make the work harder for the men so that they keep working and pay no attention to lies."

¹⁰Then the slave drivers and the foremen went out and said to the people, "This is what Pharaoh says: 'I will not give you any more straw. ¹¹Go and get your own straw wherever you can find it, but your work will not be reduced at all.'" ¹²So the people scattered all over Egypt to gather stubble to use for straw. ¹³The slave drivers kept pressing them, saying, "Complete the work required of you for each day, just as when you had straw." ¹⁴The Israelite foremen appointed by Pharaoh's slave drivers were beaten and were asked, "Why didn't you meet your quota of bricks yesterday or today, as before?"

¹⁵Then the Israelite foremen went and appealed to Pharaoh: "Why have you treated your servants this way? ¹⁶Your servants are given no straw, yet we are told, 'Make bricks!' Your servants are being beaten, but the fault is with your own people."

¹⁷Pharaoh said, "Lazy, that's what you are—lazy! That is why you keep saying, 'Let us go and sacrifice to the LORD.' ¹⁸Now get to work. You will not be given any straw, yet you must produce your full quota of bricks."

¹⁹The Israelite foremen realised they were in trouble when they were told, "You are not to reduce the number of bricks required of you for each day." ²⁰When they left Pharaoh, they found Moses and Aaron waiting to meet them, ²¹and they said, "May the LORD look upon you and judge you! You have made us a stench to Pharaoh and his officials and have put a sword in their hand to kill us."

God Promises Deliverance

²²Moses returned to the LORD and said, "O Lord, why have you brought trouble upon this people? Is this why you sent me? ²³Ever since I went to Pharaoh to speak in your name, he has brought trouble upon this people, and you have not rescued your people at all."

6 Then the LORD said to Moses, "Now you will see what I will do to Pharaoh: Because of my mighty hand he will let them go; because of my mighty hand he will drive them out of his country."

²God also said to Moses, "I am the LORD. ³I appeared to Abraham, to Isaac and to Jacob as God Almighty, but by my name the LORD I did not make myself known to them. ⁴I also established my covenant with them to give them the land of Canaan, where they lived as aliens. ⁵Moreover, I have heard the groaning of the Israelites, whom the Egyptians are enslaving, and I have remembered my covenant.

⁶"Therefore, say to the Israelites: 'I am the LORD, and I will bring you out from under the yoke of the Egyptians. I will free you from being slaves to them, and I will redeem you with an outstretched arm and with mighty acts of judgment. ⁷I will take you as my own people, and I will be your God. Then

you will know that I am the LORD your God, who brought you out from under the yoke of the Egyptians. 8And I will bring you to the land I swore with uplifted hand to give to Abraham, to Isaac and to Jacob. I will give it to you as a possession. I am the LORD.'"

9Moses reported this to the Israelites, but they did not listen to him because of their discouragement and cruel bondage.

10Then the LORD said to Moses, 11"Go, tell Pharaoh king of Egypt to let the Israelites go out of his country."

12But Moses said to the LORD, "If the Israelites will not listen to me, why would Pharaoh listen to me, since I speak with faltering lips?"

NEW TESTAMENT READING
Matthew 26:31–46

Jesus Predicts Peter's Denial

31Then Jesus told them, "This very night you will all fall away on account of me, for it is written:

"'I will strike the shepherd,
    and the sheep of the flock will be
      scattered.'

32But after I have risen, I will go ahead of you into Galilee."

33Peter replied, "Even if all fall away on account of you, I never will."

34"I tell you the truth," Jesus answered, "this very night, before the cock crows, you will disown me three times."

35But Peter declared, "Even if I have to die with you, I will never disown you." And all the other disciples said the same.

Gethsemane

36Then Jesus went with his disciples to a place called Gethsemane, and he said to them, "Sit here while I go over there and pray." 37He took Peter and the two sons of Zebedee along with him, and he began to be sorrowful and troubled. 38Then he said to them, "My soul is overwhelmed with sorrow to the point of death. Stay here and keep watch with me."

39Going a little farther, he fell with his face to the ground and prayed, "My Father, if it is possible, may this cup be taken from me. Yet not as I will, but as you will."

40Then he returned to his disciples and found them sleeping. "Could you men not keep watch with me for one hour?" he asked Peter. 41"Watch and pray so that you will not fall into temptation. The spirit is willing, but the body is weak."

42He went away a second time and prayed, "My Father, if it is not possible for this cup to be taken away unless I drink it, may your will be done."

43When he came back, he again found them sleeping, because their eyes were heavy. 44So he left them and went away once more and prayed the third time, saying the same thing.

45Then he returned to the disciples and said to them, "Are you still sleeping and resting? Look, the hour is near, and the Son of Man is betrayed into the hands of sinners. 46Rise, let us go! Here comes my betrayer!"

READING FROM PROVERBS
Proverbs 4:10–19

10Listen, my son, accept what I say,
    and the years of your life will be
      many.
11I guide you in the way of wisdom
    and lead you along straight paths.
12When you walk, your steps will not
      be hampered;
    when you run, you will not
      stumble.
13Hold on to instruction, do not let it
      go;
    guard it well, for it is your life.
14Do not set foot on the path of the
      wicked

or walk in the way of evil men.
¹⁵Avoid it, do not travel on it;
     turn from it and go on your way.
¹⁶For they cannot sleep till they do evil;
     they are robbed of slumber till they
          make someone fall.
¹⁷They eat the bread of wickedness
     and drink the wine of violence.

¹⁸The path of the righteous is like the
     first gleam of dawn,
     shining ever brighter till the full
          light of day.
¹⁹But the way of the wicked is like deep
     darkness;
     they do not know what makes them
          stumble.

FEBRUARY 10   DAY 41

OLD TESTAMENT READING
Exodus 6:13–8:32

Family Record of Moses and Aaron

¹³Now the LORD spoke to Moses and Aaron about the Israelites and Pharaoh king of Egypt, and he commanded them to bring the Israelites out of Egypt.

¹⁴These were the heads of their families:

The sons of Reuben the firstborn son of Israel were Hanoch and Pallu, Hezron and Carmi. These were the clans of Reuben.

¹⁵The sons of Simeon were Jemuel, Jamin, Ohad, Jakin, Zohar and Shaul the son of a Canaanite woman. These were the clans of Simeon.

¹⁶These were the names of the sons of Levi according to their records: Gershon, Kohath and Merari. Levi lived 137 years.

¹⁷The sons of Gershon, by clans, were Libni and Shimei.

¹⁸The sons of Kohath were Amram, Izhar, Hebron and Uzziel. Kohath lived 133 years.

¹⁹The sons of Merari were Mahli and Mushi.

These were the clans of Levi according to their records.

²⁰Amram married his father's sister Jochebed, who bore him Aaron and Moses. Amram lived 137 years.

²¹The sons of Izhar were Korah, Nepheg and Zicri.

²²The sons of Uzziel were Mishael, Elzaphan and Sithri.

²³Aaron married Elisheba, daughter of Amminadab and sister of Nahshon, and she bore him Nadab and Abihu, Eleazar and Ithamar.

²⁴The sons of Korah were Assir, Elkanah and Abiasaph. These were the Korahite clans.

²⁵Eleazar son of Aaron married one of the daughters of Putiel, and she bore him Phinehas.

These were the heads of the Levite families, clan by clan.

²⁶It was this same Aaron and Moses to whom the LORD said, "Bring the Israelites out of Egypt by their divisions." ²⁷They were the ones who spoke to Pharaoh king of Egypt about bringing the Israelites out of Egypt. It was the same Moses and Aaron.

Aaron to Speak for Moses

²⁸Now when the LORD spoke to Moses in Egypt, ²⁹he said to him, "I am the LORD. Tell Pharaoh king of Egypt everything I tell you."

³⁰But Moses said to the LORD, "Since

I speak with faltering lips, why would Pharaoh listen to me?''

7 Then the LORD said to Moses, "See, I have made you like God to Pharaoh, and your brother Aaron will be your prophet. ²You are to say everything I command you, and your brother Aaron is to tell Pharaoh to let the Israelites go out of his country. ³But I will harden Pharaoh's heart, and though I multiply my miraculous signs and wonders in Egypt, ⁴he will not listen to you. Then I will lay my hand on Egypt and with mighty acts of judgment I will bring out my divisions, my people the Israelites. ⁵And the Egyptians will know that I am the LORD when I stretch out my hand against Egypt and bring the Israelites out of it.''

⁶Moses and Aaron did just as the LORD commanded them. ⁷Moses was eighty years old and Aaron eighty-three when they spoke to Pharaoh.

Aaron's Staff Becomes a Snake

⁸The LORD said to Moses and Aaron, ⁹"When Pharaoh says to you, 'Perform a miracle,' then say to Aaron, 'Take your staff and throw it down before Pharaoh,' and it will become a snake.''

¹⁰So Moses and Aaron went to Pharaoh and did just as the LORD commanded. Aaron threw his staff down in front of Pharaoh and his officials, and it became a snake. ¹¹Pharaoh then summoned the wise men and sorcerers, and the Egyptian magicians also did the same things by their secret arts: ¹²Each one threw down his staff and it became a snake. But Aaron's staff swallowed up their staffs. ¹³Yet Pharaoh's heart became hard and he would not listen to them, just as the LORD had said.

The Plague of Blood

¹⁴Then the LORD said to Moses, "Pharaoh's heart is unyielding; he refuses to let the people go. ¹⁵Go to Pharaoh in the morning as he goes out to the water. Wait on the bank of the Nile to meet him, and take in your hand the staff that was changed into a snake. ¹⁶Then say to him, 'The LORD, the God of the Hebrews, has sent me to say to you: Let my people go, so that they may worship me in the desert. But until now you have not listened. ¹⁷This is what the LORD says: By this you will know that I am the LORD: With the staff that is in my hand I will strike the water of the Nile, and it will be changed into blood. ¹⁸The fish in the Nile will die, and the river will stink; the Egyptians will not be able to drink its water.' ''

¹⁹The LORD said to Moses, "Tell Aaron, 'Take your staff and stretch out your hand over the waters of Egypt —over the streams and canals, over the ponds and all the reservoirs'—and they will turn to blood. Blood will be everywhere in Egypt, even in the wooden buckets and stone jars.''

²⁰Moses and Aaron did just as the LORD had commanded. He raised his staff in the presence of Pharaoh and his officials and struck the water of the Nile, and all the water was changed into blood. ²¹The fish in the Nile died, and the river smelled so bad that the Egyptians could not drink its water. Blood was everywhere in Egypt.

²²But the Egyptian magicians did the same things by their secret arts, and Pharaoh's heart became hard; he would not listen to Moses and Aaron, just as the LORD had said. ²³Instead, he turned and went into his palace, and did not take even this to heart. ²⁴And all the Egyptians dug along the Nile to get drinking water, because they could not drink the water of the river.

The Plague of Frogs

²⁵Seven days passed after the LORD struck the Nile. ¹Then the LORD 8 said to Moses, "Go to Pharaoh and say to him, 'This is what the LORD says: Let my people go, so that they may worship me. ²If you refuse to let them go, I will plague your whole country with frogs. ³The Nile will teem with

frogs. They will come up into your palace and your bedroom and onto your bed, into the houses of your officials and on your people, and into your ovens and kneading troughs. 4The frogs will go up on you and your people and all your officials.'"

5Then the LORD said to Moses, "Tell Aaron, 'Stretch out your hand with your staff over the streams and canals and ponds, and make frogs come up on the land of Egypt.'"

6So Aaron stretched out his hand over the waters of Egypt, and the frogs came up and covered the land. 7But the magicians did the same things by their secret arts; they also made frogs come up on the land of Egypt.

8Pharaoh summoned Moses and Aaron and said, "Pray to the LORD to take the frogs away from me and my people, and I will let your people go to offer sacrifices to the LORD."

9Moses said to Pharaoh, "I leave to you the honour of setting the time for me to pray for you and your officials and your people that you and your houses may be rid of the frogs, except for those that remain in the Nile."

10"Tomorrow," Pharaoh said.

Moses replied, "It will be as you say, so that you may know there is no-one like the LORD our God. 11The frogs will leave you and your houses, your officials and your people; they will remain only in the Nile."

12After Moses and Aaron left Pharaoh, Moses cried out to the LORD about the frogs he had brought on Pharaoh. 13And the LORD did what Moses asked. The frogs died in the houses, in the courtyards and in the fields. 14They were piled into heaps, and the land reeked of them. 15But when Pharaoh saw that there was relief, he hardened his heart and would not listen to Moses and Aaron, just as the LORD had said.

The Plague of Gnats

16Then the LORD said to Moses, "Tell Aaron, 'Stretch out your staff and strike the dust of the ground,' and throughout the land of Egypt the dust will become gnats." 17They did this, and when Aaron stretched out his hand with the staff and struck the dust of the ground, gnats came upon men and animals. All the dust throughout the land of Egypt became gnats. 18But when the magicians tried to produce gnats by their secret arts, they could not. And the gnats were on men and animals.

19The magicians said to Pharaoh, "This is the finger of God." But Pharaoh's heart was hard and he would not listen, just as the LORD had said.

The Plague of Flies

20Then the LORD said to Moses, "Get up early in the morning and confront Pharaoh as he goes to the water and say to him, 'This is what the LORD says: Let my people go, so that they may worship me. 21If you do not let my people go, I will send swarms of flies on you and your officials, on your people and into your houses. The houses of the Egyptians will be full of flies, and even the ground where they are.

22" 'But on that day I will deal differently with the land of Goshen, where my people live; no swarms of flies will be there, so that you will know that I, the LORD, am in this land. 23I will make a distinction between my people and your people. This miraculous sign will occur tomorrow.'"

24And the LORD did this. Dense swarms of flies poured into Pharaoh's palace and into the houses of his officials, and throughout Egypt the land was ruined by the flies.

25Then Pharaoh summoned Moses and Aaron and said, "Go, sacrifice to your God here in the land."

26But Moses said, "That would not be right. The sacrifices we offer the LORD our God would be detestable to the Egyptians. And if we offer sacrifices that are detestable in their eyes, will they not stone us? 27We must take a three-day journey into the desert to offer sacrifices to the LORD our God, as he commands us."

²⁸Pharaoh said, "I will let you go to offer sacrifices to the LORD your God in the desert, but you must not go very far. Now pray for me."

²⁹Moses answered, "As soon as I leave you, I will pray to the LORD, and tomorrow the flies will leave Pharaoh and his officials and his people. Only be sure that Pharaoh does not act deceitfully again by not letting the people go to offer sacrifices to the LORD."

³⁰Then Moses left Pharaoh and prayed to the LORD, ³¹and the LORD did what Moses asked: The flies left Pharaoh and his officials and his people; not a fly remained. ³²But this time also Pharaoh hardened his heart and would not let the people go.

NEW TESTAMENT READING
Matthew 26:47–68

Jesus Arrested

⁴⁷While he was still speaking, Judas, one of the Twelve, arrived. With him was a large crowd armed with swords and clubs, sent from the chief priests and the elders of the people. ⁴⁸Now the betrayer had arranged a signal with them: "The one I kiss is the man; arrest him." ⁴⁹Going at once to Jesus, Judas said, "Greetings, Rabbi!" and kissed him.

⁵⁰Jesus replied, "Friend, do what you came for."

Then the men stepped forward, seized Jesus and arrested him. ⁵¹With that, one of Jesus' companions reached for his sword, drew it out and struck the servant of the high priest, cutting off his ear.

⁵²"Put your sword back in its place," Jesus said to him, "for all who draw the sword will die by the sword. ⁵³Do you think I cannot call on my Father, and he will at once put at my disposal more than twelve legions of angels? ⁵⁴But how then would the Scriptures be fulfilled that say it must happen in this way?"

⁵⁵At that time Jesus said to the crowd, "Am I leading a rebellion, that you have come out with swords and clubs to capture me? Every day I sat in the temple courts teaching, and you did not arrest me. ⁵⁶But this has all taken place that the writings of the prophets might be fulfilled." Then all the disciples deserted him and fled.

Before the Sanhedrin

⁵⁷Those who had arrested Jesus took him to Caiaphas, the high priest, where the teachers of the law and the elders had assembled. ⁵⁸But Peter followed him at a distance, right up to the courtyard of the high priest. He entered and sat down with the guards to see the outcome.

⁵⁹The chief priests and the whole Sanhedrin were looking for false evidence against Jesus so that they could put him to death. ⁶⁰But they did not find any, though many false witnesses came forward.

Finally two came forward ⁶¹and declared, "This fellow said, 'I am able to destroy the temple of God and rebuild it in three days.'"

⁶²Then the high priest stood up and said to Jesus, "Are you not going to answer? What is this testimony that these men are bringing against you?" ⁶³But Jesus remained silent.

The high priest said to him, "I charge you under oath by the living God: Tell us if you are the Christ, the Son of God."

⁶⁴"Yes, it is as you say," Jesus replied. "But I say to all of you: In the future you will see the Son of Man sitting at the right hand of the Mighty One and coming on the clouds of heaven."

⁶⁵Then the high priest tore his clothes and said, "He has spoken blasphemy! Why do we need any more witnesses? Look, now you have heard the blasphemy. ⁶⁶What do you think?"

"He is worthy of death," they answered.

⁶⁷Then they spat in his face and struck him with their fists. Others slapped him ⁶⁸and said, "Prophesy to us, Christ. Who hit you?"

READING FROM PSALMS
Psalm 19:7–14

⁷The law of the LORD is perfect,
    reviving the soul.
The statutes of the LORD are
        trustworthy,
    making wise the simple.
⁸The precepts of the LORD are right,
    giving joy to the heart.
The commands of the LORD are
        radiant,
    giving light to the eyes.
⁹The fear of the LORD is pure,
    enduring for ever.

The ordinances of the LORD are sure
    and altogether righteous.
¹⁰They are more precious than gold,
    than much pure gold;
they are sweeter than honey,
    than honey from the comb.
¹¹By them is your servant warned;
    in keeping them there is great
        reward.

¹²Who can discern his errors?
    Forgive my hidden faults.
¹³Keep your servant also from wilful
        sins;
    may they not rule over me.
Then will I be blameless,
    innocent of great transgression.

¹⁴May the words of my mouth and the
        meditation of my heart
    be pleasing in your sight,
    O LORD, my Rock and my
        Redeemer.

FEBRUARY 11

DAY 42

OLD TESTAMENT READING
Exodus 9:1–10:29

The Plague on Livestock

9 Then the LORD said to Moses, "Go to Pharaoh and say to him, 'This is what the LORD, the God of the Hebrews, says: "Let my people go, so that they may worship me." ²If you refuse to let them go and continue to hold them back, ³the hand of the LORD will bring a terrible plague on your livestock in the field—on your horses and donkeys and camels and on your cattle and sheep and goats. ⁴But the LORD will make a distinction between the livestock of Israel and that of Egypt, so that no animal belonging to the Israelites will die.'"

⁵The LORD set a time and said, "Tomorrow the LORD will do this in the land." ⁶And the next day the LORD did it: All the livestock of the Egyptians died, but not one animal belonging to the Israelites died. ⁷Pharaoh sent men to investigate and found that not even one of the animals of the Israelites had died. Yet his heart was unyielding and he would not let the people go.

The Plague of Boils

⁸Then the LORD said to Moses and Aaron, "Take handfuls of soot from a furnace and have Moses toss it into the air in the presence of Pharaoh. ⁹It will become fine dust over the whole land of Egypt, and festering boils will break out on men and animals throughout the land."

¹⁰So they took soot from a furnace and stood before Pharaoh. Moses

tossed it into the air, and festering boils broke out on men and animals. [11]The magicians could not stand before Moses because of the boils that were on them and on all the Egyptians. [12]But the LORD hardened Pharaoh's heart and he would not listen to Moses and Aaron, just as the LORD had said to Moses.

The Plague of Hail

[13]Then the LORD said to Moses, "Get up early in the morning, confront Pharaoh and say to him, 'This is what the LORD, the God of the Hebrews, says: Let my people go, so that they may worship me, [14]or this time I will send the full force of my plagues against you and against your officials and your people, so you may know that there is no-one like me in all the earth. [15]For by now I could have stretched out my hand and struck you and your people with a plague that would have wiped you off the earth. [16]But I have raised you up for this very purpose, that I might show you my power and that my name might be proclaimed in all the earth. [17]You still set yourself against my people and will not let them go. [18]Therefore, at this time tomorrow I will send the worst hailstorm that has ever fallen on Egypt, from the day it was founded till now. [19]Give an order now to bring your livestock and everything you have in the field to a place of shelter, because the hail will fall on every man and animal that has not been brought in and is still out in the field, and they will die.'"

[20]Those officials of Pharaoh who feared the word of the LORD hurried to bring their slaves and their livestock inside. [21]But those who ignored the word of the LORD left their slaves and livestock in the field.

[22]Then the LORD said to Moses, "Stretch out your hand towards the sky so that hail will fall all over Egypt—on men and animals and on everything growing in the fields of Egypt." [23]When Moses stretched out his staff towards the sky, the LORD sent thunder and hail, and lightning flashed down to the ground. So the LORD rained hail on the land of Egypt; [24]hail fell and lightning flashed back and forth. It was the worst storm in all the land of Egypt since it had become a nation. [25]Throughout Egypt hail struck everything in the fields—both men and animals; it beat down everything growing in the fields and stripped every tree. [26]The only place it did not hail was the land of Goshen, where the Israelites were.

[27]Then Pharaoh summoned Moses and Aaron. "This time I have sinned," he said to them. "The LORD is in the right, and I and my people are in the wrong. [28]Pray to the LORD, for we have had enough thunder and hail. I will let you go; you don't have to stay any longer."

[29]Moses replied, "When I have gone out of the city, I will spread out my hands in prayer to the LORD. The thunder will stop and there will be no more hail, so you may know that the earth is the LORD's. [30]But I know that you and your officials still do not fear the LORD God."

[31](The flax and barley were destroyed, since the barley was in the ear and the flax was in bloom. [32]The wheat and spelt, however, were not destroyed, because they ripen later.)

[33]Then Moses left Pharaoh and went out of the city. He spread out his hands towards the LORD; the thunder and hail stopped, and the rain no longer poured down on the land. [34]When Pharaoh saw that the rain and hail and thunder had stopped, he sinned again: He and his officials hardened their hearts. [35]So Pharaoh's heart was hard and he would not let the Israelites go, just as the LORD had said through Moses.

The Plague of Locusts

10 Then the LORD said to Moses, "Go to Pharaoh, for I have hardened his heart and the hearts of his officials so that I may perform these miraculous signs of mine among them [2]that you may tell your children and grandchildren how I dealt harshly with the Egyptians and how I performed my signs among them, and that you may know that I am the LORD."

[3]So Moses and Aaron went to Pharaoh and said to him, "This is what the LORD, the God of the Hebrews, says: 'How long will you refuse to humble yourself before me? Let my people go, so that they may worship me. [4]If you refuse to let them go, I will bring locusts into your country tomorrow. [5]They will cover the face of the ground so that it cannot be seen. They will devour what little you have left after the hail, including every tree that is growing in your fields. [6]They will fill your houses and those of all your officials and all the Egyptians—something neither your fathers nor your forefathers have ever seen from the day they settled in this land till now.'" Then Moses turned and left Pharaoh.

[7]Pharaoh's officials said to him, "How long will this man be a snare to us? Let the people go, so that they may worship the LORD their God. Do you not yet realise that Egypt is ruined?"

[8]Then Moses and Aaron were brought back to Pharaoh. "Go, worship the LORD your God," he said. "But just who will be going?"

[9]Moses answered, "We will go with our young and old, with our sons and daughters, and with our flocks and herds, because we are to celebrate a festival to the LORD."

[10]Pharaoh said, "The LORD be with you—if I let you go, along with your women and children! Clearly you are bent on evil. [11]No! Let only the men go; and worship the LORD, since that's what you have been asking for." Then Moses and Aaron were driven out of Pharaoh's presence.

[12]And the LORD said to Moses, "Stretch out your hand over Egypt so that locusts will swarm over the land and devour everything growing in the fields, everything left by the hail."

[13]So Moses stretched out his staff over Egypt, and the LORD made an east wind blow across the land all that day and all that night. By morning the wind had brought the locusts; [14]they invaded all Egypt and settled down in every area of the country in great numbers. Never before had there been such a plague of locusts, nor will there ever be again. [15]They covered all the ground until it was black. They devoured all that was left after the hail—everything growing in the fields and the fruit on the trees. Nothing green remained on tree or plant in all the land of Egypt.

[16]Pharaoh quickly summoned Moses and Aaron and said, "I have sinned against the LORD your God and against you. [17]Now forgive my sin once more and pray to the LORD your God to take this deadly plague away from me."

[18]Moses then left Pharaoh and prayed to the LORD. [19]And the LORD changed the wind to a very strong west wind, which caught up the locusts and carried them into the Red Sea. Not a locust was left anywhere in Egypt. [20]But the LORD hardened Pharaoh's heart, and he would not let the Israelites go.

The Plague of Darkness

[21]Then the LORD said to Moses, "Stretch out your hand towards the sky so that darkness will spread over Egypt —darkness that can be felt." [22]So Moses stretched out his hand towards the sky, and total darkness covered all Egypt for three days. [23]No-one could see anyone else or leave his place for three days. Yet all the Israelites had light in the places where they lived.

[24]Then Pharaoh summoned Moses and said, "Go, worship the LORD. Even your women and children may go with you; only leave your flocks and herds behind."

[25]But Moses said, "You must allow us to have sacrifices and burnt offerings to present to the LORD our God. [26]Our livestock too must go with us; not a hoof is to be left behind. We have to use

some of them in worshipping the LORD our God, and until we get there we will not know what we are to use to worship the LORD."

27But the LORD hardened Pharaoh's heart, and he was not willing to let them go. 28Pharaoh said to Moses, "Get out of my sight! Make sure you do not appear before me again! The day you see my face you will die."

29"Just as you say," Moses replied, "I will never appear before you again."

NEW TESTAMENT READING
Matthew 26:69–27:10

Peter Disowns Jesus

69Now Peter was sitting out in the courtyard, and a servant girl came to him. "You also were with Jesus of Galilee," she said.

70But he denied it before them all. "I don't know what you're talking about," he said.

71Then he went out to the gateway, where another girl saw him and said to the people there, "This fellow was with Jesus of Nazareth."

72He denied it again, with an oath: "I don't know the man!"

73After a little while, those standing there went up to Peter and said, "Surely you are one of them, for your accent gives you away."

74Then he began to call down curses on himself and he swore to them, "I don't know the man!"

Immediately a cock crowed. 75Then Peter remembered the word Jesus had spoken: "Before the cock crows, you will disown me three times." And he went outside and wept bitterly.

Judas Hangs Himself

27 Early in the morning, all the chief priests and the elders of the people came to the decision to put Jesus to death. 2They bound him, led him

away and handed him over to Pilate, the governor.

3When Judas, who had betrayed him, saw that Jesus was condemned, he was seized with remorse and returned the thirty silver coins to the chief priests and the elders. 4"I have sinned," he said, "for I have betrayed innocent blood."

"What is that to us?" they replied. "That's your responsibility."

5So Judas threw the money into the temple and left. Then he went away and hanged himself.

6The chief priests picked up the coins and said, "It is against the law to put this into the treasury, since it is blood money." 7So they decided to use the money to buy the potter's field as a burial place for foreigners. 8That is why it has been called the Field of Blood to this day. 9Then what was spoken by Jeremiah the prophet was fulfilled: "They took the thirty silver coins, the price set on him by the people of Israel, 10and they used them to buy the potter's field, as the Lord commanded me."

READING FROM PSALMS
Psalm 20:1–9

For the director of music. A psalm of David.

1May the LORD answer you when you
    are in distress;
    may the name of the God of Jacob
    protect you.
2May he send you help from the
    sanctuary
    and grant you support from Zion.
3May he remember all your sacrifices
    and accept your burnt offerings.
        Selah
4May he give you the desire of your
    heart
    and make all your plans succeed.
5We will shout for joy when you are
    victorious
    and will lift up our banners in the
    name of our God.
May the LORD grant all your
    requests.

⁶Now I know that the LORD saves his
    anointed;
  he answers him from his holy
    heaven
  with the saving power of his right
    hand.
⁷Some trust in chariots and some in
    horses,

but we trust in the name of the
    LORD our God.
⁸They are brought to their knees and
    fall,
  but we rise up and stand firm.

⁹O LORD, save the king!
  Answer us when we call!

FEBRUARY 12   DAY 43

OLD TESTAMENT READING
Exodus 11:1–12:51

The Plague on the Firstborn

11 Now the LORD said to Moses, "I
will bring one more plague on
Pharaoh and on Egypt. After that, he
will let you go from here, and when he
does, he will drive you out completely.
²Tell the people that men and women
alike are to ask their neighbours for
articles of silver and gold." ³(The LORD
made the Egyptians favourably disposed towards the people, and Moses
himself was highly regarded in Egypt by
Pharaoh's officials and by the people.)

⁴So Moses said, "This is what the
LORD says: 'About midnight I will go
throughout Egypt. ⁵Every firstborn son
in Egypt will die, from the firstborn son
of Pharaoh, who sits on the throne, to
the firstborn son of the slave girl, who is
at her hand mill, and all the firstborn of
the cattle as well. ⁶There will be loud
wailing throughout Egypt—worse than
there has ever been or ever will be
again. ⁷But among the Israelites not a
dog will bark at any man or animal.'
Then you will know that the LORD
makes a distinction between Egypt and
Israel. ⁸All these officials of yours will
come to me, bowing down before me
and saying, 'Go, you and all the people
who follow you!' After that I will
leave." Then Moses, hot with anger,
left Pharaoh.

⁹The LORD had said to Moses, "Pharaoh will refuse to listen to you—so that
my wonders may be multiplied in
Egypt." ¹⁰Moses and Aaron performed
all these wonders before Pharaoh, but
the LORD hardened Pharaoh's heart,
and he would not let the Israelites go
out of his country.

The Passover

12 The LORD said to Moses and
Aaron in Egypt, ²"This month is
to be for you the first month, the first
month of your year. ³Tell the whole
community of Israel that on the tenth
day of this month each man is to take a
lamb for his family, one for each household. ⁴If any household is too small for a
whole lamb, they must share one with
their nearest neighbour, having taken
into account the number of people there
are. You are to determine the amount
of lamb needed in accordance with what
each person will eat. ⁵The animals you
choose must be year-old males without
defect, and you may take them from the
sheep or the goats. ⁶Take care of them
until the fourteenth day of the month,
when all the people of the community of
Israel must slaughter them at twilight.
⁷Then they are to take some of the
blood and put it on the sides and tops of
the door-frames of the houses where
they eat the lambs. ⁸That same night
they are to eat the meat roasted over the

fire, along with bitter herbs, and bread made without yeast. ⁹Do not eat the meat raw or cooked in water, but roast it over the fire—head, legs and inner parts. ¹⁰Do not leave any of it till morning; if some is left till morning, you must burn it. ¹¹This is how you are to eat it: with your cloak tucked into your belt, your sandals on your feet and your staff in your hand. Eat it in haste; it is the LORD's Passover.

¹²"On that same night I will pass through Egypt and strike down every firstborn—both men and animals—and I will bring judgment on all the gods of Egypt. I am the LORD. ¹³The blood will be a sign for you on the houses where you are; and when I see the blood, I will pass over you. No destructive plague will touch you when I strike Egypt.

¹⁴"This is a day you are to commemorate; for the generations to come you shall celebrate it as a festival to the LORD—a lasting ordinance. ¹⁵For seven days you are to eat bread made without yeast. On the first day remove the yeast from your houses, for whoever eats anything with yeast in it from the first day until the seventh day must be cut off from Israel. ¹⁶On the first day hold a sacred assembly, and another one on the seventh day. Do no work at all on these days, except to prepare food for everyone to eat—that is all you may do.

¹⁷"Celebrate the Feast of Unleavened Bread, because it was on this very day that I brought your divisions out of Egypt. Celebrate this day as a lasting ordinance for the generations to come. ¹⁸In the first month you are to eat bread made without yeast, from the evening of the fourteenth day until the evening of the twenty-first day. ¹⁹For seven days no yeast is to be found in your houses. And whoever eats anything with yeast in it must be cut off from the community of Israel, whether he is an alien or native-born. ²⁰Eat nothing made with yeast. Wherever you live, you must eat unleavened bread."

²¹Then Moses summoned all the elders of Israel and said to them, "Go at once and select the animals for your families and slaughter the Passover lamb. ²²Take a bunch of hyssop, dip it into the blood in the basin and put some of the blood on the top and on both sides of the door-frame. Not one of you shall go out of the door of his house until morning. ²³When the LORD goes through the land to strike down the Egyptians, he will see the blood on the top and sides of the door-frame and will pass over that doorway, and he will not permit the destroyer to enter your houses and strike you down.

²⁴"Obey these instructions as a lasting ordinance for you and your descendants. ²⁵When you enter the land that the LORD will give you as he promised, observe this ceremony. ²⁶And when your children ask you, 'What does this ceremony mean to you?' ²⁷then tell them, 'It is the Passover sacrifice to the LORD, who passed over the houses of the Israelites in Egypt and spared our homes when he struck down the Egyptians.'" Then the people bowed down and worshipped. ²⁸The Israelites did just what the LORD commanded Moses and Aaron.

²⁹At midnight the LORD struck down all the firstborn in Egypt, from the firstborn of Pharaoh, who sat on the throne, to the firstborn of the prisoner, who was in the dungeon, and the firstborn of all the livestock as well. ³⁰Pharaoh and all his officials and all the Egyptians got up during the night, and there was loud wailing in Egypt, for there was not a house without someone dead.

The Exodus

³¹During the night Pharaoh summoned Moses and Aaron and said, "Up! Leave my people, you and the Israelites! Go, worship the LORD as you have requested. ³²Take your flocks and herds, as you have said, and go. And also bless me."

³³The Egyptians urged the people to hurry and leave the country. "For otherwise," they said, "we will all die!"

34So the people took their dough before the yeast was added, and carried it on their shoulders in kneading troughs wrapped in clothing. 35The Israelites did as Moses instructed and asked the Egyptians for articles of silver and gold and for clothing. 36The Lord had made the Egyptians favourably disposed towards the people, and they gave them what they asked for; so they plundered the Egyptians.

37The Israelites journeyed from Rameses to Succoth. There were about six hundred thousand men on foot, besides women and children. 38Many other people went up with them, as well as large droves of livestock, both flocks and herds. 39With the dough they had brought from Egypt, they baked cakes of unleavened bread. The dough was without yeast because they had been driven out of Egypt and did not have time to prepare food for themselves.

40Now the length of time the Israelite people lived in Egypt was 430 years. 41At the end of the 430 years, to the very day, all the Lord's divisions left Egypt. 42Because the Lord kept vigil that night to bring them out of Egypt, on this night all the Israelites are to keep vigil to honour the Lord for the generations to come.

Passover Restrictions

43The Lord said to Moses and Aaron, "These are the regulations for the Passover:

"No foreigner is to eat of it. 44Any slave you have bought may eat of it after you have circumcised him, 45but a temporary resident and a hired worker may not eat of it.

46"It must be eaten inside one house; take none of the meat outside the house. Do not break any of the bones. 47The whole community of Israel must celebrate it.

48"An alien living among you who wants to celebrate the Lord's Passover must have all the males in his household circumcised; then he may take part like one born in the land. No uncircumcised

male may eat of it. 49The same law applies to the native-born and to the alien living among you."

50All the Israelites did just what the Lord had commanded Moses and Aaron. 51And on that very day the Lord brought the Israelites out of Egypt by their divisions.

NEW TESTAMENT READING
Matthew 27:11–44

Jesus Before Pilate

11Meanwhile Jesus stood before the governor, and the governor asked him, "Are you the king of the Jews?"

"Yes, it is as you say," Jesus replied.

12When he was accused by the chief priests and the elders, he gave no answer. 13Then Pilate asked him, "Don't you hear the testimony they are bringing against you?" 14But Jesus made no reply, not even to a single charge—to the great amazement of the governor.

15Now it was the governor's custom at the Feast to release a prisoner chosen by the crowd. 16At that time they had a notorious prisoner, called Barabbas. 17So when the crowd had gathered, Pilate asked them, "Which one do you want me to release to you: Barabbas, or Jesus who is called Christ?" 18For he knew it was out of envy that they had handed Jesus over to him.

19While Pilate was sitting on the judge's seat, his wife sent him this message: "Don't have anything to do with that innocent man, for I have suffered a great deal today in a dream because of him."

20But the chief priests and the elders persuaded the crowd to ask for Barabbas and to have Jesus executed.

21"Which of the two do you want me to release to you?" asked the governor.

"Barabbas," they answered.

22"What shall I do, then, with Jesus who is called Christ?" Pilate asked.

They all answered, "Crucify him!"

23"Why? What crime has he committed?" asked Pilate.

But they shouted all the louder, "Crucify him!"

24When Pilate saw that he was getting nowhere, but that instead an uproar was starting, he took water and washed his hands in front of the crowd. "I am innocent of this man's blood," he said. "It is your responsibility!"

25All the people answered, "Let his blood be on us and on our children!"

26Then he released Barabbas to them. But he had Jesus flogged, and handed him over to be crucified.

The Soldiers Mock Jesus

27Then the governor's soldiers took Jesus into the Praetorium and gathered the whole company of soldiers round him. 28They stripped him and put a scarlet robe on him, 29and then twisted together a crown of thorns and set it on his head. They put a staff in his right hand and knelt in front of him and mocked him. "Hail, king of the Jews!" they said. 30They spat on him, and took the staff and struck him on the head again and again. 31After they had mocked him, they took off the robe and put his own clothes on him. Then they led him away to crucify him.

The Crucifixion

32As they were going out, they met a man from Cyrene, named Simon, and they forced him to carry the cross. 33They came to a place called Golgotha (which means The Place of the Skull). 34There they offered Jesus wine to drink, mixed with gall; but after tasting it, he refused to drink it. 35When they had crucified him, they divided up his clothes by casting lots. 36And sitting down, they kept watch over him there. 37Above his head they placed the written charge against him: THIS IS JESUS, THE KING OF THE JEWS. 38Two robbers were crucified with him, one on his right and one on his left. 39Those who passed

by hurled insults at him, shaking their heads 40and saying, "You who are going to destroy the temple and build it in three days, save yourself! Come down from the cross, if you are the Son of God!"

41In the same way the chief priests, the teachers of the law and the elders mocked him. 42"He saved others," they said, "but he can't save himself! He's the King of Israel! Let him come down now from the cross, and we will believe in him. 43He trusts in God. Let God rescue him now if he wants him, for he said, 'I am the Son of God.'" 44In the same way the robbers who were crucified with him also heaped insults on him.

READING FROM PSALMS
Psalm 21:1–7

For the director of music. A psalm of David.

1O LORD, the king rejoices in your
    strength.
  How great is his joy in the victories
      you give!
2You have granted him the desire of
    his heart
  and have not withheld the request
      of his lips.   *Selah*
3You welcomed him with rich
    blessings
  and placed a crown of pure gold on
      his head.
4He asked you for life, and you gave it
    to him—
  length of days, for ever and ever.
5Through the victories you gave, his
    glory is great;
  you have bestowed on him
      splendour and majesty.
6Surely you have granted him eternal
    blessings
  and made him glad with the joy of
      your presence.
7For the king trusts in the LORD;
  through the unfailing love of the
      Most High
  he will not be shaken.

OLD TESTAMENT READING
Exodus 13:1–14:31

Consecration of the Firstborn

13 The LORD said to Moses, 2"Consecrate to me every firstborn male. The first offspring of every womb among the Israelites belongs to me, whether man or animal."

3Then Moses said to the people, "Commemorate this day, the day you came out of Egypt, out of the land of slavery, because the LORD brought you out of it with a mighty hand. Eat nothing containing yeast. 4Today, in the month of Abib, you are leaving. 5When the LORD brings you into the land of the Canaanites, Hittites, Amorites, Hivites and Jebusites—the land he swore to your forefathers to give you, a land flowing with milk and honey—you are to observe this ceremony in this month: 6For seven days eat bread made without yeast and on the seventh day hold a festival to the LORD. 7Eat unleavened bread during those seven days; nothing with yeast in it is to be seen among you, nor shall any yeast be seen anywhere within your borders. 8On that day tell your son, 'I do this because of what the LORD did for me when I came out of Egypt.' 9This observance will be for you like a sign on your hand and a reminder on your forehead that the law of the LORD is to be on your lips. For the LORD brought you out of Egypt with his mighty hand. 10You must keep this ordinance at the appointed time year after year.

11"After the LORD brings you into the land of the Canaanites and gives it to you, as he promised on oath to you and your forefathers, 12you are to give over to the LORD the first offspring of every womb. All the firstborn males of your livestock belong to the LORD. 13Redeem with a lamb every firstborn donkey, but if you do not redeem it, break its neck. Redeem every firstborn among your sons.

14"In days to come when your son asks you, 'What does this mean?' say to him, 'With a mighty hand the LORD brought us out of Egypt, out of the land of slavery. 15When Pharaoh stubbornly refused to let us go, the LORD killed every firstborn in Egypt, both man and animal. This is why I sacrifice to the LORD the first male offspring of every womb and redeem each of my firstborn sons.' 16And it will be like a sign on your hand and a symbol on your forehead that the LORD brought us out of Egypt with his mighty hand."

Crossing the Sea

17When Pharaoh let the people go, God did not lead them on the road through the Philistine country, though that was shorter. For God said, "If they face war, they might change their minds and return to Egypt." 18So God led the people around by the desert road towards the Red Sea. The Israelites went up out of Egypt armed for battle.

19Moses took the bones of Joseph with him because Joseph had made the sons of Israel swear an oath. He had said, "God will surely come to your aid, and then you must carry my bones up with you from this place."

20After leaving Succoth they camped at Etham on the edge of the desert. 21By day the LORD went ahead of them in a pillar of cloud to guide them on their way and by night in a pillar of fire to give them light, so that they could travel by day or night. 22Neither the pillar of cloud by day nor the pillar of fire by night left its place in front of the people.

14 Then the LORD said to Moses, 2"Tell the Israelites to turn back and camp near Pi Hahiroth, between Migdol and the sea. They are to camp by the sea, directly opposite Baal

Zephon. ³Pharaoh will think, 'The Israelites are wandering around the land in confusion, hemmed in by the desert.' ⁴And I will harden Pharaoh's heart, and he will pursue them. But I will gain glory for myself through Pharaoh and all his army, and the Egyptians will know that I am the LORD." So the Israelites did this.

⁵When the king of Egypt was told that the people had fled, Pharaoh and his officials changed their minds about them and said, "What have we done? We have let the Israelites go and have lost their services!" ⁶So he had his chariot made ready and took his army with him. ⁷He took six hundred of the best chariots, along with all the other chariots of Egypt, with officers over all of them. ⁸The LORD hardened the heart of Pharaoh king of Egypt, so that he pursued the Israelites, who were marching out boldly. ⁹The Egyptians—all Pharaoh's horses and chariots, horsemen and troops—pursued the Israelites and overtook them as they camped by the sea near Pi Hahiroth, opposite Baal Zephon.

¹⁰As Pharaoh approached, the Israelites looked up, and there were the Egyptians, marching after them. They were terrified and cried out to the LORD. ¹¹They said to Moses, "Was it because there were no graves in Egypt that you brought us to the desert to die? What have you done to us by bringing us out of Egypt? ¹²Didn't we say to you in Egypt, 'Leave us alone; let us serve the Egyptians'? It would have been better for us to serve the Egyptians than to die in the desert!"

¹³Moses answered the people, "Do not be afraid. Stand firm and you will see the deliverance the LORD will bring you today. The Egyptians you see today you will never see again. ¹⁴The LORD will fight for you; you need only to be still."

¹⁵Then the LORD said to Moses, "Why are you crying out to me? Tell the Israelites to move on. ¹⁶Raise your staff and stretch out your hand over the sea to divide the water so that the Israelites can go through the sea on dry ground. ¹⁷I will harden the hearts of the Egyptians so that they will go in after them. And I will gain glory through Pharaoh and all his army, through his chariots and his horsemen. ¹⁸The Egyptians will know that I am the LORD when I gain glory through Pharaoh, his chariots and his horsemen."

¹⁹Then the angel of God, who had been travelling in front of Israel's army, withdrew and went behind them. The pillar of cloud also moved from in front and stood behind them, ²⁰coming between the armies of Egypt and Israel. Throughout the night the cloud brought darkness to the one side and light to the other; so neither went near the other all night long.

²¹Then Moses stretched out his hand over the sea, and all that night the LORD drove the sea back with a strong east wind and turned it into dry land. The waters were divided, ²²and the Israelites went through the sea on dry ground, with a wall of water on their right and on their left.

²³The Egyptians pursued them, and all Pharaoh's horses and chariots and horsemen followed them into the sea. ²⁴During the last watch of the night the LORD looked down from the pillar of fire and cloud at the Egyptian army and threw it into confusion. ²⁵He made the wheels of their chariots come off so that they had difficulty driving. And the Egyptians said, "Let's get away from the Israelites! The LORD is fighting for them against Egypt."

²⁶Then the LORD said to Moses, "Stretch out your hand over the sea so that the waters may flow back over the Egyptians and their chariots and horsemen." ²⁷Moses stretched out his hand over the sea, and at daybreak the sea went back to its place. The Egyptians were fleeing towards it, and the LORD swept them into the sea. ²⁸The water flowed back and covered the chariots and horsemen—the entire army of Pharaoh that had followed the Israelites

into the sea. Not one of them survived. ²⁹But the Israelites went through the sea on dry ground, with a wall of water on their right and on their left. ³⁰That day the LORD saved Israel from the hands of the Egyptians, and Israel saw the Egyptians lying dead on the shore. ³¹And when the Israelites saw the great power the LORD displayed against the Egyptians, the people feared the LORD and put their trust in him and in Moses his servant.

NEW TESTAMENT READING
Matthew 27:45–66

The Death of Jesus

⁴⁵From the sixth hour until the ninth hour darkness came over all the land. ⁴⁶About the ninth hour Jesus cried out in a loud voice, *"Eloi, Eloi, lama sabachthani?"*—which means, "My God, my God, why have you forsaken me?"

⁴⁷When some of those standing there heard this, they said, "He's calling Elijah."

⁴⁸Immediately one of them ran and got a sponge. He filled it with wine vinegar, put it on a stick, and offered it to Jesus to drink. ⁴⁹The rest said, "Now leave him alone. Let's see if Elijah comes to save him."

⁵⁰And when Jesus had cried out again in a loud voice, he gave up his spirit.

⁵¹At that moment the curtain of the temple was torn in two from top to bottom. The earth shook and the rocks split. ⁵²The tombs broke open and the bodies of many holy people who had died were raised to life. ⁵³They came out of the tombs, and after Jesus' resurrection they went into the holy city and appeared to many people.

⁵⁴When the centurion and those with him who were guarding Jesus saw the earthquake and all that had happened, they were terrified, and exclaimed, "Surely he was the Son of God!"

⁵⁵Many women were there, watching from a distance. They had followed Jesus from Galilee to care for his needs. ⁵⁶Among them were Mary Magdalene, Mary the mother of James and Joses, and the mother of Zebedee's sons.

The Burial of Jesus

⁵⁷As evening approached, there came a rich man from Arimathea, named Joseph, who had himself become a disciple of Jesus. ⁵⁸Going to Pilate, he asked for Jesus' body, and Pilate ordered that it be given to him. ⁵⁹Joseph took the body, wrapped it in a clean linen cloth, ⁶⁰and placed it in his own new tomb that he had cut out of the rock. He rolled a big stone in front of the entrance to the tomb and went away. ⁶¹Mary Magdalene and the other Mary were sitting there opposite the tomb.

The Guard at the Tomb

⁶²The next day, the one after Preparation Day, the chief priests and the Pharisees went to Pilate. ⁶³"Sir," they said, "we remember that while he was still alive that deceiver said, 'After three days I will rise again.' ⁶⁴So give the order for the tomb to be made secure until the third day. Otherwise, his disciples may come and steal the body and tell the people that he has been raised from the dead. This last deception will be worse than the first."

⁶⁵"Take a guard," Pilate answered. "Go, make the tomb as secure as you know how." ⁶⁶So they went and made the tomb secure by putting a seal on the stone and posting the guard.

READING FROM PROVERBS
Proverbs 4:20–27

²⁰My son, pay attention to what I say;
    listen closely to my words.
²¹Do not let them out of your sight,
    keep them within your heart;

²²for they are life to those who find
   them
   and health to a man's whole
   body.
²³Above all else, guard your heart,
   for it is the wellspring of life.
²⁴Put away perversity from your
   mouth;

   keep corrupt talk far from your
      lips.
²⁵Let your eyes look straight ahead,
   fix your gaze directly before you.
²⁶Make level paths for your feet
   and take only ways that are firm.
²⁷Do not swerve to the right or the left;
   keep your foot from evil.

FEBRUARY 14

OLD TESTAMENT READING
Exodus 15:1–16:36

The Song of Moses and Miriam

15 Then Moses and the Israelites
     sang this song to the LORD:

"I will sing to the LORD,
   for he is highly exalted.
The horse and its rider
   he has hurled into the sea.
²The LORD is my strength and my
      song;
   he has become my salvation.
He is my God, and I will praise him,
   my father's God, and I will exalt
      him.
³The LORD is a warrior;
   the LORD is his name.
⁴Pharaoh's chariots and his army
   he has hurled into the sea.
The best of Pharaoh's officers
   are drowned in the Red Sea.
⁵The deep waters have covered them;
   they sank to the depths like a
      stone.

⁶"Your right hand, O LORD,
   was majestic in power.
Your right hand, O LORD,
   shattered the enemy.
⁷In the greatness of your majesty
   you threw down those who
      opposed you.

You unleashed your burning anger;
   it consumed them like stubble.
⁸By the blast of your nostrils
   the waters piled up.
The surging waters stood firm like a
      wall;
   the deep waters congealed in the
      heart of the sea.

⁹"The enemy boasted,
   'I will pursue, I will overtake them.
I will divide the spoils;
   I will gorge myself on them.
I will draw my sword
   and my hand will destroy them.'
¹⁰But you blew with your breath,
   and the sea covered them.
They sank like lead
   in the mighty waters.

¹¹"Who among the gods is like you, O
      LORD?
   Who is like you—
   majestic in holiness,
   awesome in glory,
   working wonders?
¹²You stretched out your right hand
   and the earth swallowed them.

¹³"In your unfailing love you will lead
   the people you have redeemed.
In your strength you will guide them
   to your holy dwelling.
¹⁴The nations will hear and tremble;
   anguish will grip the people of
      Philistia.

15The chiefs of Edom will be terrified,
the leaders of Moab will be seized
with trembling,
the people of Canaan will melt away;
16 terror and dread will fall upon
them.
By the power of your arm
they will be as still as a stone—
until your people pass by, O LORD,
until the people you bought pass
by.
17You will bring them in and plant
them
on the mountain of your
inheritance—
the place, O LORD, you made for
your dwelling,
the sanctuary, O Lord, your hands
established.
18The LORD will reign
for ever and ever."

19When Pharaoh's horses, chariots
and horsemen went into the sea, the
LORD brought the waters of the sea back
over them, but the Israelites walked
through the sea on dry ground. 20Then
Miriam the prophetess, Aaron's sister,
took a tambourine in her hand, and all
the women followed her, with tambourines and dancing. 21Miriam sang to
them:

"Sing to the LORD,
for he is highly exalted.
The horse and its rider
he has hurled into the sea."

The Waters of Marah and Elim

22Then Moses led Israel from the Red
Sea and they went into the Desert of
Shur. For three days they travelled in
the desert without finding water.
23When they came to Marah, they could
not drink its water because it was bitter.
(That is why the place is called Marah.)
24So the people grumbled against
Moses, saying, "What are we to drink?"
25Then Moses cried out to the LORD,
and the LORD showed him a piece of

wood. He threw it into the water, and
the water became sweet.
There the LORD made a decree and a
law for them, and there he tested them.
26He said, "If you listen carefully to the
voice of the LORD your God and do
what is right in his eyes, if you pay
attention to his commands and keep all
his decrees, I will not bring on you any
of the diseases I brought on the Egyptians, for I am the LORD, who heals
you."
27Then they came to Elim, where
there were twelve springs and seventy
palm trees, and they camped there near
the water.

Manna and Quail

16 The whole Israelite community
set out from Elim and came to
the Desert of Sin, which is between
Elim and Sinai, on the fifteenth day of
the second month after they had come
out of Egypt. 2In the desert the whole
community grumbled against Moses
and Aaron. 3The Israelites said to them,
"If only we had died by the LORD's hand
in Egypt! There we sat round pots of
meat and ate all the food we wanted,
but you have brought us out into this
desert to starve this entire assembly to
death."
4Then the LORD said to Moses, "I will
rain down bread from heaven for you.
The people are to go out each day and
gather enough for that day. In this way I
will test them and see whether they will
follow my instructions. 5On the sixth
day they are to prepare what they bring
in, and that is to be twice as much as
they gather on the other days."
6So Moses and Aaron said to all the
Israelites, "In the evening you will
know that it was the LORD who brought
you out of Egypt, 7and in the morning
you will see the glory of the LORD,
because he has heard your grumbling
against him. Who are we, that you
should grumble against us?" 8Moses
also said, "You will know that it was the

LORD when he gives you meat to eat in the evening and all the bread you want in the morning, because he has heard your grumbling against him. Who are we? You are not grumbling against us, but against the LORD."

9Then Moses told Aaron, "Say to the entire Israelite community, 'Come before the LORD, for he has heard your grumbling.'"

10While Aaron was speaking to the whole Israelite community, they looked towards the desert, and there was the glory of the LORD appearing in the cloud.

11The LORD said to Moses, 12"I have heard the grumbling of the Israelites. Tell them, 'At twilight you will eat meat, and in the morning you will be filled with bread. Then you will know that I am the LORD your God.'"

13That evening quail came and covered the camp, and in the morning there was a layer of dew around the camp. 14When the dew was gone, thin flakes like frost on the ground appeared on the desert floor. 15When the Israelites saw it, they said to each other, "What is it?" For they did not know what it was.

Moses said to them, "It is the bread the LORD has given you to eat. 16This is what the LORD has commanded: 'Each one is to gather as much as he needs. Take an omer for each person you have in your tent.'"

17The Israelites did as they were told; some gathered much, some little. 18And when they measured it by the omer, he who gathered much did not have too much, and he who gathered little did not have too little. Each one gathered as much as he needed.

19Then Moses said to them, "No-one is to keep any of it until morning."

20However, some of them paid no attention to Moses; they kept part of it until morning, but it was full of maggots and began to smell. So Moses was angry with them.

21Each morning everyone gathered as much as he needed, and when the sun grew hot, it melted away. 22On the sixth day, they gathered twice as much—two omers for each person—and the leaders of the community came and reported this to Moses. 23He said to them, "This is what the LORD commanded: 'Tomorrow is to be a day of rest, a holy Sabbath to the LORD. So bake what you want to bake and boil what you want to boil. Save whatever is left and keep it until morning.'"

24So they saved it until morning, as Moses commanded, and it did not stink or get maggots in it. 25"Eat it today," Moses said, "because today is a Sabbath to the LORD. You will not find any of it on the ground today. 26Six days you are to gather it, but on the seventh day, the Sabbath, there will not be any."

27Nevertheless, some of the people went out on the seventh day to gather it, but they found none. 28Then the LORD said to Moses, "How long will you refuse to keep my commands and my instructions? 29Bear in mind that the LORD has given you the Sabbath; that is why on the sixth day he gives you bread for two days. Everyone is to stay where he is on the seventh day; no-one is to go out." 30So the people rested on the seventh day.

31The people of Israel called the bread manna. It was white like coriander seed and tasted like wafers made with honey. 32Moses said, "This is what the LORD has commanded: 'Take an omer of manna and keep it for the generations to come, so they can see the bread I gave you to eat in the desert when I brought you out of Egypt.'"

33So Moses said to Aaron, "Take a jar and put an omer of manna in it. Then place it before the LORD to be kept for the generations to come."

34As the LORD commanded Moses, Aaron put the manna in front of the Testimony, that it might be kept. 35The Israelites ate manna for forty years, until they came to a land that was settled; they ate manna until they reached the border of Canaan.

36(An omer is one tenth of an ephah.)

NEW TESTAMENT READING
Matthew 28:1–20

The Resurrection

28 After the Sabbath, at dawn on the first day of the week, Mary Magdalene and the other Mary went to look at the tomb.

²There was a violent earthquake, for an angel of the Lord came down from heaven and, going to the tomb, rolled back the stone and sat on it. ³His appearance was like lightning, and his clothes were white as snow. ⁴The guards were so afraid of him that they shook and became like dead men.

⁵The angel said to the women, "Do not be afraid, for I know that you are looking for Jesus, who was crucified. ⁶He is not here; he has risen, just as he said. Come and see the place where he lay. ⁷Then go quickly and tell his disciples: 'He has risen from the dead and is going ahead of you into Galilee. There you will see him.' Now I have told you."

⁸So the women hurried away from the tomb, afraid yet filled with joy, and ran to tell his disciples. ⁹Suddenly Jesus met them. "Greetings," he said. They came to him, clasped his feet and worshipped him. ¹⁰Then Jesus said to them, "Do not be afraid. Go and tell my brothers to go to Galilee; there they will see me."

The Guards' Report

¹¹While the women were on their way, some of the guards went into the city and reported to the chief priests everything that had happened. ¹²When the chief priests had met with the elders and devised a plan, they gave the soldiers a large sum of money, ¹³telling them, "You are to say, 'His disciples came during the night and stole him away while we were asleep.' ¹⁴If this report gets to the governor, we will satisfy him and keep you out of trouble." ¹⁵So the soldiers took the money and did as they were instructed. And this story has been widely circulated among the Jews to this very day.

The Great Commission

¹⁶Then the eleven disciples went to Galilee, to the mountain where Jesus had told them to go. ¹⁷When they saw him, they worshipped him; but some doubted. ¹⁸Then Jesus came to them and said, "All authority in heaven and on earth has been given to me. ¹⁹Therefore go and make disciples of all nations, baptising them in the name of the Father and of the Son and of the Holy Spirit, ²⁰and teaching them to obey everything I have commanded you. And surely I am with you always, to the very end of the age."

READING FROM PSALMS
Psalm 21:8–13

⁸Your hand will lay hold on all your
　　enemies;
　your right hand will seize your
　　foes.
⁹At the time of your appearing
　you will make them like a fiery
　　furnace.
In his wrath the LORD will swallow
　　them up,
　and his fire will consume them.
¹⁰You will destroy their descendants
　　from the earth,
　their posterity from mankind.
¹¹Though they plot evil against you
　and devise wicked schemes, they
　　cannot succeed;
¹²for you will make them turn their
　　backs
　when you aim at them with drawn
　　bow.

¹³Be exalted, O LORD, in your
　　strength;
　we will sing and praise your might.

OLD TESTAMENT READING
Exodus 17:1–18:27

Water From the Rock

17 The whole Israelite community set out from the Desert of Sin, travelling from place to place as the LORD commanded. They camped at Rephidim, but there was no water for the people to drink. ²So they quarrelled with Moses and said, "Give us water to drink."

Moses replied, "Why do you quarrel with me? Why do you put the LORD to the test?"

³But the people were thirsty for water there, and they grumbled against Moses. They said, "Why did you bring us up out of Egypt to make us and our children and livestock die of thirst?"

⁴Then Moses cried out to the LORD, "What am I to do with these people? They are almost ready to stone me."

⁵The LORD answered Moses, "Walk on ahead of the people. Take with you some of the elders of Israel and take in your hand the staff with which you struck the Nile, and go. ⁶I will stand there before you by the rock at Horeb. Strike the rock, and water will come out of it for the people to drink." So Moses did this in the sight of the elders of Israel. ⁷And he called the place Massah and Meribah because the Israelites quarrelled and because they tested the LORD saying, "Is the LORD among us or not?"

The Amalekites Defeated

⁸The Amalekites came and attacked the Israelites at Rephidim. ⁹Moses said to Joshua, "Choose some of our men and go out to fight the Amalekites. Tomorrow I will stand on top of the hill with the staff of God in my hands."

¹⁰So Joshua fought the Amalekites as Moses had ordered, and Moses, Aaron and Hur went to the top of the hill. ¹¹As long as Moses held up his hands, the Israelites were winning, but whenever he lowered his hands, the Amalekites were winning. ¹²When Moses' hands grew tired, they took a stone and put it under him and he sat on it. Aaron and Hur held his hands up—one on one side, one on the other—so that his hands remained steady till sunset. ¹³So Joshua overcame the Amalekite army with the sword.

¹⁴Then the LORD said to Moses, "Write this on a scroll as something to be remembered and make sure that Joshua hears it, because I will completely blot out the memory of Amalek from under heaven."

¹⁵Moses built an altar and called it The LORD is my Banner. ¹⁶He said, "For hands were lifted up to the throne of the LORD. The LORD will be at war against the Amalekites from generation to generation."

Jethro Visits Moses

18 Now Jethro, the priest of Midian and father-in-law of Moses, heard of everything God had done for Moses and for his people Israel, and how the LORD had brought Israel out of Egypt.

²After Moses had sent away his wife Zipporah, his father-in-law Jethro received her ³and her two sons. One son was named Gershom, for Moses said, "I have become an alien in a foreign land"; ⁴and the other was named Eliezer, for he said, "My father's God was my helper; he saved me from the sword of Pharaoh."

⁵Jethro, Moses' father-in-law, together with Moses' sons and wife, came to him in the desert, where he was camped near the mountain of God.

[6]Jethro had sent word to him, "I, your father-in-law Jethro, am coming to you with your wife and her two sons."

[7]So Moses went out to meet his father-in-law and bowed down and kissed him. They greeted each other and then went into the tent. [8]Moses told his father-in-law about everything the LORD had done to Pharaoh and the Egyptians for Israel's sake and about all the hardships they had met along the way and how the LORD had saved them.

[9]Jethro was delighted to hear about all the good things the LORD had done for Israel in rescuing them from the hand of the Egyptians. [10]He said, "Praise be to the LORD, who rescued you from the hand of the Egyptians and of Pharaoh, and who rescued the people from the hand of the Egyptians. [11]Now I know that the LORD is greater than all other gods, for he did this to those who had treated Israel arrogantly." [12]Then Jethro, Moses' father-in-law, brought a burnt offering and other sacrifices to God, and Aaron came with all the elders of Israel to eat bread with Moses' father-in-law in the presence of God.

[13]The next day Moses took his seat to serve as judge for the people, and they stood round him from morning till evening. [14]When his father-in-law saw all that Moses was doing for the people, he said, "What is this you are doing for the people? Why do you alone sit as judge, while all these people stand round you from morning till evening?"

[15]Moses answered him, "Because the people come to me to seek God's will. [16]Whenever they have a dispute, it is brought to me, and I decide between the parties and inform them of God's decrees and laws."

[17]Moses' father-in-law replied, "What you are doing is not good. [18]You and these people who come to you will only wear yourselves out. The work is too heavy for you; you cannot handle it alone. [19]Listen now to me and I will give you some advice, and may God be with you. You must be the people's representative before God and bring their disputes to him. [20]Teach them the decrees and laws, and show them the way to live and the duties they are to perform. [21]But select capable men from all the people—men who fear God, trustworthy men who hate dishonest gain—and appoint them as officials over thousands, hundreds, fifties and tens. [22]Have them serve as judges for the people at all times, but have them bring every difficult case to you; the simple cases they can decide themselves. That will make your load lighter, because they will share it with you. [23]If you do this and God so commands, you will be able to stand the strain, and all these people will go home satisfied."

[24]Moses listened to his father-in-law and did everything he said. [25]He chose capable men from all Israel and made them leaders of the people, officials over thousands, hundreds, fifties and tens. [26]They served as judges for the people at all times. The difficult cases they brought to Moses, but the simple ones they decided themselves.

[27]Then Moses sent his father-in-law on his way, and Jethro returned to his own country.

NEW TESTAMENT READING
Mark 1:1–28

John the Baptist Prepares the Way

1 The beginning of the gospel about Jesus Christ, the Son of God.

[2]It is written in Isaiah the prophet:

"I will send my messenger ahead of you,
    who will prepare your way"—
[3]"a voice of one calling in the desert,
'Prepare the way for the Lord,
    make straight paths for him.' "

[4]And so John came, baptising in the desert region and preaching a baptism of repentance for the forgiveness of sins. [5]The whole Judean countryside

and all the people of Jerusalem went out to him. Confessing their sins, they were baptised by him in the Jordan River. 6John wore clothing made of camel's hair, with a leather belt round his waist, and he ate locusts and wild honey. 7And this was his message: "After me will come one more powerful than I, the thongs of whose sandals I am not worthy to stoop down and untie. 8I baptise you with water, but he will baptise you with the Holy Spirit."

The Baptism and Temptation of Jesus

9At that time Jesus came from Nazareth in Galilee and was baptised by John in the Jordan. 10As Jesus was coming up out of the water, he saw heaven being torn open and the Spirit descending on him like a dove. 11And a voice came from heaven: "You are my Son, whom I love; with you I am well pleased."

12At once the Spirit sent him out into the desert, 13and he was in the desert for forty days, being tempted by Satan. He was with the wild animals, and angels attended him.

The Calling of the First Disciples

14After John was put in prison, Jesus went into Galilee, proclaiming the good news of God. 15"The time has come," he said. "The kingdom of God is near. Repent and believe the good news!"

16As Jesus walked beside the Sea of Galilee, he saw Simon and his brother Andrew casting a net into the lake, for they were fishermen. 17"Come, follow me," Jesus said, "and I will make you fishers of men." 18At once they left their nets and followed him.

19When he had gone a little farther, he saw James son of Zebedee and his brother John in a boat, preparing their nets. 20Without delay he called them, and they left their father Zebedee in the boat with the hired men and followed him.

Jesus Drives Out an Evil Spirit

21They went to Capernaum, and when the Sabbath came, Jesus went into the synagogue and began to teach. 22The people were amazed at his teaching, because he taught them as one who had authority, not as the teachers of the law. 23Just then a man in their synagogue who was possessed by an evil spirit cried out, 24"What do you want with us, Jesus of Nazareth? Have you come to destroy us? I know who you are—the Holy One of God!"

25"Be quiet!" said Jesus sternly. "Come out of him!" 26The evil spirit shook the man violently and came out of him with a shriek.

27The people were all so amazed that they asked each other, "What is this? A new teaching—and with authority! He even gives orders to evil spirits and they obey him." 28News about him spread quickly over the whole region of Galilee.

READING FROM PSALMS
Psalm 22:1–11

For the director of music. To ⌊the tune of⌋ "The Doe of the Morning". A psalm of David.

1My God, my God, why have you
     forsaken me?
   Why are you so far from saving
     me,
   so far from the words of my
     groaning?
2O my God, I cry out by day, but you
     do not answer,
   by night, and am not silent.

3Yet you are enthroned as the Holy
     One;
   you are the praise of Israel.
4In you our fathers put their trust;
   they trusted and you delivered
     them.
5They cried to you and were saved;
   in you they trusted and were not
     disappointed.

⁶But I am a worm and not a man,
 scorned by men and despised by
  the people.
⁷All who see me mock me;
 they hurl insults, shaking their
  heads:
⁸"He trusts in the LORD;
 let the LORD rescue him.
 Let him deliver him,
  since he delights in him."

⁹Yet you brought me out of the
 womb;
 you made me trust in you
 even at my mother's breast.
¹⁰From birth I was cast upon you;
 from my mother's womb you have
  been my God.
¹¹Do not be far from me,
 for trouble is near
 and there is no-one to help.

FEBRUARY 16

DAY 47

OLD TESTAMENT READING
Exodus 19:1–20:26

At Mount Sinai

19 In the third month after the Israelites left Egypt—on the very day—they came to the Desert of Sinai. ²After they set out from Rephidim, they entered the Desert of Sinai, and Israel camped there in the desert in front of the mountain.

³Then Moses went up to God, and the LORD called to him from the mountain and said, "This is what you are to say to the house of Jacob and what you are to tell the people of Israel: ⁴'You yourselves have seen what I did to Egypt, and how I carried you on eagles' wings and brought you to myself. ⁵Now if you obey me fully and keep my covenant, then out of all nations you will be my treasured possession. Although the whole earth is mine, ⁶you will be for me a kingdom of priests and a holy nation.' These are the words you are to speak to the Israelites."

⁷So Moses went back and summoned the elders of the people and set before them all the words the LORD had commanded him to speak. ⁸The people all responded together, "We will do everything the LORD has said." So Moses brought their answer back to the LORD.

⁹The LORD said to Moses, "I am going to come to you in a dense cloud, so that the people will hear me speaking with you and will always put their trust in you." Then Moses told the LORD what the people had said.

¹⁰And the LORD said to Moses, "Go to the people and consecrate them today and tomorrow. Make them wash their clothes ¹¹and be ready by the third day, because on that day the LORD will come down on Mount Sinai in the sight of all the people. ¹²Put limits for the people around the mountain and tell them, 'Be careful that you do not go up the mountain or touch the foot of it. Whoever touches the mountain shall surely be put to death. ¹³He shall surely be stoned or shot with arrows; not a hand is to be laid on him. Whether man or animal, he shall not be permitted to live.' Only when the ram's horn sounds a long blast may they go up to the mountain."

¹⁴After Moses had gone down the mountain to the people, he consecrated them, and they washed their clothes. ¹⁵Then he said to the people, "Prepare yourselves for the third day. Abstain from sexual relations."

¹⁶On the morning of the third day there was thunder and lightning, with a thick cloud over the mountain, and a very loud trumpet blast. Everyone in

the camp trembled. ¹⁷Then Moses led the people out of the camp to meet with God, and they stood at the foot of the mountain. ¹⁸Mount Sinai was covered with smoke, because the LORD descended on it in fire. The smoke billowed up from it like smoke from a furnace, the whole mountain trembled violently, ¹⁹and the sound of the trumpet grew louder and louder. Then Moses spoke and the voice of God answered him.

²⁰The LORD descended to the top of Mount Sinai and called Moses to the top of the mountain. So Moses went up ²¹and the LORD said to him, "Go down and warn the people so they do not force their way through to see the LORD and many of them perish. ²²Even the priests, who approach the LORD, must consecrate themselves, or the LORD will break out against them."

²³Moses said to the LORD, "The people cannot come up Mount Sinai, because you yourself warned us, 'Put limits around the mountain and set it apart as holy.'"

²⁴The LORD replied, "Go down and bring Aaron up with you. But the priests and the people must not force their way through to come up to the LORD, or he will break out against them."

²⁵So Moses went down to the people and told them.

The Ten Commandments

20 And God spoke all these words:

²"I am the LORD your God, who brought you out of Egypt, out of the land of slavery.

³"You shall have no other gods before me.

⁴"You shall not make for yourself an idol in the form of anything in heaven above or on the earth beneath or in the waters below. ⁵You shall not bow down to them or worship them; for I, the LORD your God, am a jealous God, punishing the children for the sin of the fathers to the third and fourth generation of those who hate me, ⁶but showing love to a thousand ⌊generations⌋ of those who love me and keep my commandments.

⁷"You shall not misuse the name of the LORD your God, for the LORD will not hold anyone guiltless who misuses his name.

⁸"Remember the Sabbath day by keeping it holy. ⁹Six days you shall labour and do all your work, ¹⁰but the seventh day is a Sabbath to the LORD your God. On it you shall not do any work, neither you, nor your son or daughter, nor your manservant or maidservant, nor your animals, nor the alien within your gates. ¹¹For in six days the LORD made the heavens and the earth, the sea, and all that is in them, but he rested on the seventh day. Therefore the LORD blessed the Sabbath day and made it holy.

¹²"Honour your father and your mother, so that you may live long in the land the LORD your God is giving you.

¹³"You shall not murder.

¹⁴"You shall not commit adultery.

¹⁵"You shall not steal.

¹⁶"You shall not give false testimony against your neighbour.

¹⁷"You shall not covet your neighbour's house. You shall not covet your neighbour's wife, or his manservant or maidservant, his ox or donkey, or anything that belongs to your neighbour."

¹⁸When the people saw the thunder and lightning and heard the trumpet

and saw the mountain in smoke, they trembled with fear. They stayed at a distance 19and said to Moses, "Speak to us yourself and we will listen. But do not have God speak to us or we will die."

20Moses said to the people, "Do not be afraid. God has come to test you, so that the fear of God will be with you to keep you from sinning."

21The people remained at a distance, while Moses approached the thick darkness where God was.

Idols and Altars

22Then the LORD said to Moses, "Tell the Israelites this: 'You have seen for yourselves that I have spoken to you from heaven: 23Do not make any gods to be alongside me; do not make for yourselves gods of silver or gods of gold. 24"'Make an altar of earth for me and sacrifice on it your burnt offerings and fellowship offerings, your sheep and goats and your cattle. Wherever I cause my name to be honoured, I will come to you and bless you. 25If you make an altar of stones for me, do not build it with dressed stones, for you will defile it if you use a tool on it. 26And do not go up to my altar on steps, lest your nakedness be exposed on it.'

NEW TESTAMENT READING
Mark 1:29–2:17

Jesus Heals Many

29As soon as they left the synagogue, they went with James and John to the home of Simon and Andrew. 30Simon's mother-in-law was in bed with a fever, and they told Jesus about her. 31So he went to her, took her hand and helped her up. The fever left her and she began to wait on them.

32That evening after sunset the people brought to Jesus all the sick and demon-possessed. 33The whole town gathered at the door, 34and Jesus healed

many who had various diseases. He also drove out many demons, but he would not let the demons speak because they knew who he was.

Jesus Prays in a Solitary Place

35Very early in the morning, while it was still dark, Jesus got up, left the house and went off to a solitary place, where he prayed. 36Simon and his companions went to look for him, 37and when they found him, they exclaimed: "Everyone is looking for you!"

38Jesus replied, "Let us go somewhere else—to the nearby villages—so that I can preach there also. That is why I have come." 39So he travelled throughout Galilee, preaching in their synagogues and driving out demons.

A Man With Leprosy

40A man with leprosy came to him and begged him on his knees, "If you are willing, you can make me clean."

41Filled with compassion, Jesus reached out his hand and touched the man. "I am willing," he said. "Be clean!" 42Immediately the leprosy left him and he was cured.

43Jesus sent him away at once with a strong warning: 44"See that you don't tell this to anyone. But go, show yourself to the priest and offer the sacrifices that Moses commanded for your cleansing, as a testimony to them." 45Instead he went out and began to talk freely, spreading the news. As a result, Jesus could no longer enter a town openly but stayed outside in lonely places. Yet the people still came to him from everywhere.

Jesus Heals a Paralytic

2 A few days later, when Jesus again entered Capernaum, the people heard that he had come home. 2So many gathered that there was no room left, not even outside the door, and he preached the word to them. 3Some men

came, bringing to him a paralytic, carried by four of them. [4]Since they could not get him to Jesus because of the crowd, they made an opening in the roof above Jesus and, after digging through it, lowered the mat the paralysed man was lying on. [5]When Jesus saw their faith, he said to the paralytic, "Son, your sins are forgiven."

[6]Now some teachers of the law were sitting there, thinking to themselves, [7]"Why does this fellow talk like that? He's blaspheming! Who can forgive sins but God alone?"

[8]Immediately Jesus knew in his spirit that this was what they were thinking in their hearts, and he said to them, "Why are you thinking these things? [9]Which is easier: to say to the paralytic, 'Your sins are forgiven,' or to say, 'Get up, take your mat and walk'? [10]But that you may know that the Son of Man has authority on earth to forgive sins. . . ." He said to the paralytic, [11]"I tell you, get up, take your mat and go home." [12]He got up, took his mat and walked out in full view of them all. This amazed everyone and they praised God, saying, "We have never seen anything like this!"

The Calling of Levi

[13]Once again Jesus went out beside the lake. A large crowd came to him, and he began to teach them. [14]As he walked along, he saw Levi son of Alphaeus sitting at the tax collector's booth. "Follow me," Jesus told him, and Levi got up and followed him.

[15]While Jesus was having dinner at Levi's house, many tax collectors and "sinners" were eating with him and his disciples, for there were many who followed him. [16]When the teachers of the law who were Pharisees saw him eating with the "sinners" and tax collectors, they asked his disciples: "Why does he eat with tax collectors and 'sinners'?"

[17]On hearing this, Jesus said to them, "It is not the healthy who need a doctor, but the sick. I have not come to call the righteous, but sinners."

READING FROM PSALMS
Psalm 22:12–21

[12]Many bulls surround me;
　　strong bulls of Bashan encircle me.
[13]Roaring lions tearing their prey
　　open their mouths wide against
　　　me.
[14]I am poured out like water,
　　and all my bones are out of joint.
My heart has turned to wax;
　　it has melted away within me.
[15]My strength is dried up like a
　　　potsherd,
　　and my tongue sticks to the roof of
　　　my mouth;
　　you lay me in the dust of death.
[16]Dogs have surrounded me;
　　a band of evil men has encircled
　　　me,
　　they have pierced my hands and my
　　　feet.
[17]I can count all my bones;
　　people stare and gloat over me.
[18]They divide my garments among
　　　them
　　and cast lots for my clothing.

[19]But you, O LORD, be not far off;
　　O my Strength, come quickly to
　　　help me.
[20]Deliver my life from the sword,
　　my precious life from the power of
　　　the dogs.
[21]Rescue me from the mouth of the
　　　lions;
　　save me from the horns of the wild
　　　oxen.

OLD TESTAMENT READING
Exodus 21:1–22:31

21 "These are the laws you are to set before them:

Hebrew Servants

2"If you buy a Hebrew servant, he is to serve you for six years. But in the seventh year, he shall go free, without paying anything. 3If he comes alone, he is to go free alone; but if he has a wife when he comes, she is to go with him. 4If his master gives him a wife and she bears him sons or daughters, the woman and her children shall belong to her master, and only the man shall go free.

5"But if the servant declares, 'I love my master and my wife and children and do not want to go free,' 6then his master must take him before the judges. He shall take him to the door or the doorpost and pierce his ear with an awl. Then he will be his servant for life.

7"If a man sells his daughter as a servant, she is not to go free as menservants do. 8If she does not please the master who has selected her for himself, he must let her be redeemed. He has no right to sell her to foreigners, because he has broken faith with her. 9If he selects her for his son, he must grant her the rights of a daughter. 10If he marries another woman, he must not deprive the first one of her food, clothing and marital rights. 11If he does not provide her with these three things, she is to go free, without any payment of money.

Personal Injuries

12"Anyone who strikes a man and kills him shall surely be put to death. 13However, if he does not do it intentionally, but God lets it happen, he is to flee to a place I will designate. 14But if a man schemes and kills another man deliberately, take him away from my altar and put him to death.

15"Anyone who attacks his father or his mother must be put to death.

16"Anyone who kidnaps another and either sells him or still has him when he is caught must be put to death.

17"Anyone who curses his father or mother must be put to death.

18"If men quarrel and one hits the other with a stone or with his fist and he does not die but is confined to bed, 19the one who struck the blow will not be held responsible if the other gets up and walks around outside with his staff; however, he must pay the injured man for the loss of his time and see that he is completely healed.

20"If a man beats his male or female slave with a rod and the slave dies as a direct result, he must be punished, 21but he is not to be punished if the slave gets up after a day or two, since the slave is his property.

22"If men who are fighting hit a pregnant woman and she gives birth prematurely but there is no serious injury, the offender must be fined whatever the woman's husband demands and the court allows. 23But if there is serious injury, you are to take life for life, 24eye for eye, tooth for tooth, hand for hand, foot for foot, 25burn for burn, wound for wound, bruise for bruise.

26"If a man hits a manservant or maidservant in the eye and destroys it, he must let the servant go free to compensate for the eye. 27And if he knocks out the tooth of a manservant or maidservant, he must let the servant go free to compensate for the tooth.

28"If a bull gores a man or a woman to death, the bull must be stoned to death, and its meat must not be eaten. But the owner of the bull will not be held responsible. 29If, however, the bull has had the habit of goring and the owner has been warned but has not kept it penned up and it kills a man or woman, the bull must be stoned and the owner also must be put to death. ³⁰However, if payment is demanded of him, he may redeem his life by paying whatever is demanded. ³¹This law also applies if the bull gores a son or a daughter. ³²If the bull gores a male or female slave, the owner must pay thirty shekels of silver to the master of the slave, and the bull must be stoned.

³³"If a man uncovers a pit or digs one and fails to cover it and an ox or a donkey falls into it, ³⁴the owner of the pit must pay for the loss; he must pay its owner, and the dead animal will be his.

³⁵"If a man's bull injures the bull of another and it dies, they are to sell the live one and divide both the money and the dead animal equally. ³⁶However, if it was known that the bull had the habit of goring, yet the owner did not keep it penned up, the owner must pay, animal for animal, and the dead animal will be his.

Protection of Property

22 "If a man steals an ox or a sheep and slaughters it or sells it, he must pay back five head of cattle for the ox and four sheep for the sheep.

²"If a thief is caught breaking in and is struck so that he dies, the defender is not guilty of bloodshed; ³but if it happens after sunrise, he is guilty of bloodshed.

"A thief must certainly make restitution, but if he has nothing, he must be sold to pay for his theft.

⁴"If the stolen animal is found alive in his possession—whether ox or donkey or sheep—he must pay back double.

⁵"If a man grazes his livestock in a field or vineyard and lets them stray and they graze in another man's field, he must make restitution from the best of his own field or vineyard.

⁶"If a fire breaks out and spreads into thornbushes so that it burns shocks of grain or standing corn or the whole field, the one who started the fire must make restitution.

⁷"If a man gives his neighbour silver or goods for safekeeping and they are stolen from the neighbour's house, the thief, if he is caught, must pay back double. ⁸But if the thief is not found, the owner of the house must appear before the judges to determine whether he has laid his hands on the other man's property. ⁹In all cases of illegal possession of an ox, a donkey, a sheep, a garment, or any other lost property about which somebody says, 'This is mine,' both parties are to bring their cases before the judges. The one whom the judges declare guilty must pay back double to his neighbour.

¹⁰"If a man gives a donkey, an ox, a sheep or any other animal to his neighbour for safekeeping and it dies or is injured or is taken away while no-one is looking, ¹¹the issue between them will be settled by the taking of an oath before the LORD that the neighbour did not lay hands on the other person's property. The owner is to accept this, and no restitution is required. ¹²But if the animal was stolen from the neighbour, he must make restitution to the owner. ¹³If it was torn to pieces by a wild animal, he shall bring in the remains as evidence and he will not be required to pay for the torn animal.

¹⁴"If a man borrows an animal from his neighbour and it is injured or dies while the owner is not present, he must make restitution. ¹⁵But if the owner is with the animal, the borrower will not have to pay. If the animal was hired, the money paid for the hire covers the loss.

Social Responsibility

¹⁶"If a man seduces a virgin who is not pledged to be married and sleeps with her, he must pay the bride-price, and she shall be his wife. ¹⁷If her father absolutely refuses to give her to him, he must still pay the bride-price for virgins.

¹⁸"Do not allow a sorceress to live.

¹⁹"Anyone who has sexual relations with an animal must be put to death.

²⁰"Whoever sacrifices to any god other than the LORD must be destroyed.

²¹"Do not ill-treat an alien or oppress him, for you were aliens in Egypt.

²²"Do not take advantage of a widow or an orphan. ²³If you do and they cry out to me, I will certainly hear their cry. ²⁴My anger will be aroused, and I will kill you with the sword; your wives will become widows and your children fatherless.

²⁵"If you lend money to one of my people among you who is needy, do not be like a money-lender; charge him no interest. ²⁶If you take your neighbour's cloak as a pledge, return it to him by sunset, ²⁷because his cloak is the only covering he has for his body. What else will he sleep in? When he cries out to me, I will hear, for I am compassionate.

²⁸"Do not blaspheme God or curse the ruler of your people.

²⁹"Do not hold back offerings from your granaries or your vats.

"You must give me the firstborn of your sons. ³⁰Do the same with your cattle and your sheep. Let them stay with their mothers for seven days, but give them to me on the eighth day.

³¹"You are to be my holy people. So do not eat the meat of an animal torn by wild beasts; throw it to the dogs.

NEW TESTAMENT READING
Mark 2:18–3:30

Jesus Questioned About Fasting

¹⁸Now John's disciples and the Pharisees were fasting. Some people came and asked Jesus, "How is it that John's disciples and the disciples of the Pharisees are fasting, but yours are not?"

¹⁹Jesus answered, "How can the guests of the bridegroom fast while he is with them? They cannot, so long as they have him with them. ²⁰But the time will come when the bridegroom will be taken from them, and on that day they will fast.

²¹"No-one sews a patch of unshrunk cloth on an old garment. If he does, the new piece will pull away from the old, making the tear worse. ²²And no-one pours new wine into old wineskins. If he does, the wine will burst the skins, and both the wine and the wineskins will be ruined. No, he pours new wine into new wineskins."

Lord of the Sabbath

²³One Sabbath Jesus was going through the cornfields, and as his disciples walked along, they began to pick some ears of corn. ²⁴The Pharisees said to him, "Look, why are they doing what is unlawful on the Sabbath?"

²⁵He answered, "Have you never read what David did when he and his companions were hungry and in need? ²⁶In the days of Abiathar the high priest, he entered the house of God and ate the consecrated bread, which is lawful only for priests to eat. And he also gave some to his companions."

²⁷Then he said to them, "The Sabbath was made for man, not man for the Sabbath. ²⁸So the Son of Man is Lord even of the Sabbath."

3 Another time he went into the synagogue, and a man with a shrivelled hand was there. ²Some of them were looking for a reason to accuse Jesus, so they watched him closely to see if he would heal him on the Sabbath. ³Jesus said to the man with the shrivelled hand, "Stand up in front of everyone."

⁴Then Jesus asked them, "Which is lawful on the Sabbath: to do good or to do evil, to save life or to kill?" But they remained silent.

⁵He looked round at them in anger and, deeply distressed at their stubborn hearts, said to the man, "Stretch out your hand." He stretched it out, and his hand was completely restored. ⁶Then the Pharisees went out and began to

plot with the Herodians how they might kill Jesus.

Crowds Follow Jesus

7Jesus withdrew with his disciples to the lake, and a large crowd from Galilee followed. 8When they heard all he was doing, many people came to him from Judea, Jerusalem, Idumea, and the regions across the Jordan and around Tyre and Sidon. 9Because of the crowd he told his disciples to have a small boat ready for him, to keep the people from crowding him. 10For he had healed many, so that those with diseases were pushing forward to touch him. 11Whenever the evil spirits saw him, they fell down before him and cried out, "You are the Son of God." 12But he gave them strict orders not to tell who he was.

The Appointing of the Twelve Apostles

13Jesus went up on a mountainside and called to him those he wanted, and they came to him. 14He appointed twelve—designating them apostles—that they might be with him and that he might send them out to preach 15and to have authority to drive out demons. 16These are the twelve he appointed: Simon (to whom he gave the name Peter); 17James son of Zebedee and his brother John (to them he gave the name Boanerges, which means Sons of Thunder); 18Andrew, Philip, Bartholomew, Matthew, Thomas, James son of Alphaeus, Thaddaeus, Simon the Zealot 19and Judas Iscariot, who betrayed him.

Jesus and Beelzebub

20Then Jesus entered a house, and again a crowd gathered, so that he and his disciples were not even able to eat. 21When his family heard about this, they went to take charge of him, for they said, "He is out of his mind."

22And the teachers of the law who came down from Jerusalem said, "He is possessed by Beelzebub! By the prince of demons he is driving out demons."

23So Jesus called them and spoke to them in parables: "How can Satan drive out Satan? 24If a kingdom is divided against itself, that kingdom cannot stand. 25If a house is divided against itself, that house cannot stand. 26And if Satan opposes himself and is divided, he cannot stand; his end has come. 27In fact, no-one can enter a strong man's house and carry off his possessions unless he first ties up the strong man. Then he can rob his house. 28I tell you the truth, all the sins and blasphemies of men will be forgiven them. 29But whoever blasphemes against the Holy Spirit will never be forgiven; he is guilty of an eternal sin."

30He said this because they were saying, "He has an evil spirit."

READING FROM PROVERBS
Proverbs 5:1–14

Warning Against Adultery

5 My son, pay attention to my wisdom,
  listen well to my words of insight,
2that you may maintain discretion
  and your lips may preserve knowledge.
3For the lips of an adulteress drip honey,
  and her speech is smoother than oil;
4but in the end she is bitter as gall,
  sharp as a double-edged sword.
5Her feet go down to death;
  her steps lead straight to the grave.
6She gives no thought to the way of life;
  her paths are crooked, but she knows it not.

7Now then, my sons, listen to me;
  do not turn aside from what I say.

8Keep to a path far from her,
　　do not go near the door of her
　　　house,
9lest you give your best strength to
　　others
　　and your years to one who is cruel,
10lest strangers feast on your wealth
　　and your toil enrich another man's
　　　house.
11At the end of your life you will groan,
　　when your flesh and body are
　　　spent.
12You will say, "How I hated
　　discipline!
　　How my heart spurned correction!
13I would not obey my teachers
　　or listen to my instructors.
14I have come to the brink of utter ruin
　　in the midst of the whole
　　　assembly."

FEBRUARY 18   DAY 49

OLD TESTAMENT READING
Exodus 23:1–24:18

Laws of Justice and Mercy

23 "Do not spread false reports.
Do not help a wicked man by
being a malicious witness.

2"Do not follow the crowd in doing
wrong. When you give testimony in a
lawsuit, do not pervert justice by siding
with the crowd, 3and do not show
favouritism to a poor man in his lawsuit.

4"If you come across your enemy's ox
or donkey wandering off, be sure to
take it back to him. 5If you see the
donkey of someone who hates you
fallen down under its load, do not leave
it there; be sure you help him with it.

6"Do not deny justice to your poor
people in their lawsuits. 7Have nothing
to do with a false charge and do not put
an innocent or honest person to death,
for I will not acquit the guilty.

8"Do not accept a bribe, for a bribe
blinds those who see and twists the
words of the righteous.

9"Do not oppress an alien; you
yourselves know how it feels to be
aliens, because you were aliens in
Egypt.

Sabbath Laws

10"For six years you are to sow your
fields and harvest the crops, 11but
during the seventh year let the land lie
unploughed and unused. Then the poor
among your people may get food from
it, and the wild animals may eat what
they leave. Do the same with your
vineyard and your olive grove.

12"Six days do your work, but on the
seventh day do not work, so that your
ox and your donkey may rest and the
slave born in your household, and the
alien as well, may be refreshed.

13"Be careful to do everything I have
said to you. Do not invoke the names of
other gods; do not let them be heard on
your lips.

The Three Annual Festivals

14"Three times a year you are to celebrate a festival to me.

15"Celebrate the Feast of Unleavened Bread; for seven days eat
bread made without yeast, as I commanded you. Do this at the appointed
time in the month of Abib, for in that
month you came out of Egypt.

"No-one is to appear before me
empty-handed.

16"Celebrate the Feast of Harvest
with the firstfruits of the crops you sow
in your field.

"Celebrate the Feast of Ingathering
at the end of the year, when you gather
in your crops from the field.

17"Three times a year all the men are to appear before the Sovereign LORD.

18"Do not offer the blood of a sacrifice to me along with anything containing yeast.

"The fat of my festival offerings must not be kept until morning.

19"Bring the best of the firstfruits of your soil to the house of the LORD your God.

"Do not cook a young goat in its mother's milk.

God's Angel to Prepare the Way

20"See, I am sending an angel ahead of you to guard you along the way and to bring you to the place I have prepared. 21Pay attention to him and listen to what he says. Do not rebel against him; he will not forgive your rebellion, since my Name is in him. 22If you listen carefully to what he says and do all that I say, I will be an enemy to your enemies and will oppose those who oppose you. 23My angel will go ahead of you and bring you into the land of the Amorites, Hittites, Perizzites, Canaanites, Hivites and Jebusites, and I will wipe them out. 24Do not bow down before their gods or worship them or follow their practices. You must demolish them and break their sacred stones to pieces. 25Worship the LORD your God, and his blessing will be on your food and water. I will take away sickness from among you, 26and none will miscarry or be barren in your land. I will give you a full life span.

27"I will send my terror ahead of you and throw into confusion every nation you encounter. I will make all your enemies turn their backs and run. 28I will send the hornet ahead of you to drive the Hivites, Canaanites and Hittites out of your way. 29But I will not drive them out in a single year, because the land would become desolate and the wild animals too numerous for you. 30Little by little I will drive them out before you, until you have increased enough to take possession of the land. 31"I will establish your borders from the Red Sea to the Sea of the Philistines, and from the desert to the River. I will hand over to you the people who live in the land and you will drive them out before you. 32Do not make a covenant with them or with their gods. 33Do not let them live in your land, or they will cause you to sin against me, because the worship of their gods will certainly be a snare to you."

The Covenant Confirmed

24 Then he said to Moses, "Come up to the LORD, you and Aaron, Nadab and Abihu, and seventy of the elders of Israel. You are to worship at a distance, 2but Moses alone is to approach the LORD; the others must not come near. And the people may not come up with him."

3When Moses went and told the people all the LORD's words and laws, they responded with one voice, "Everything the LORD has said we will do." 4Moses then wrote down everything the LORD had said.

He got up early the next morning and built an altar at the foot of the mountain and set up twelve stone pillars representing the twelve tribes of Israel. 5Then he sent young Israelite men, and they offered burnt offerings and sacrificed young bulls as fellowship offerings to the LORD. 6Moses took half of the blood and put it in bowls, and the other half he sprinkled on the altar. 7Then he took the Book of the Covenant and read it to the people. They responded, "We will do everything the LORD has said; we will obey."

8Moses then took the blood, sprinkled it on the people and said, "This is the blood of the covenant that the LORD has made with you in accordance with all these words."

9Moses and Aaron, Nadab and Abihu, and the seventy elders of Israel went up 10and saw the God of Israel. Under his feet was something like a pavement made of sapphire, clear as the sky itself. 11But God did not raise his hand against these leaders of the Israelites; they saw God, and they ate and drank.

12The LORD said to Moses, "Come up to me on the mountain and stay here, and I will give you the tablets of stone, with the law and commands I have written for their instruction."

13Then Moses set out with Joshua his assistant, and Moses went up on the mountain of God. 14He said to the elders, "Wait here for us until we come back to you. Aaron and Hur are with you, and anyone involved in a dispute can go to them."

15When Moses went up on the mountain, the cloud covered it, 16and the glory of the LORD settled on Mount Sinai. For six days the cloud covered the mountain, and on the seventh day the LORD called to Moses from within the cloud. 17To the Israelites the glory of the LORD looked like a consuming fire on top of the mountain. 18Then Moses entered the cloud as he went on up the mountain. And he stayed on the mountain forty days and forty nights.

NEW TESTAMENT READING
Mark 3:31–4:29

Jesus' Mother and Brothers

31Then Jesus' mother and brothers arrived. Standing outside, they sent someone in to call him. 32A crowd was sitting around him, and they told him, "Your mother and brothers are outside looking for you."

33"Who are my mother and my brothers?" he asked.

34Then he looked at those seated in a circle around him and said, "Here are my mother and my brothers! 35Whoever does God's will is my brother and sister and mother."

The Parable of the Sower

4 Again Jesus began to teach by the lake. The crowd that gathered round him was so large that he got into a

boat and sat in it out on the lake, while all the people were along the shore at the water's edge. 2He taught them many things by parables, and in his teaching said: 3"Listen! A farmer went out to sow his seed. 4As he was scattering the seed, some fell along the path, and the birds came and ate it up. 5Some fell on rocky places, where it did not have much soil. It sprang up quickly, because the soil was shallow. 6But when the sun came up, the plants were scorched, and they withered because they had no root. 7Other seed fell among thorns, which grew up and choked the plants, so that they did not bear grain. 8Still other seed fell on good soil. It came up, grew and produced a crop, multiplying thirty, sixty, or even a hundred times."

9Then Jesus said, "He who has ears to hear, let him hear."

10When he was alone, the Twelve and the others around him asked him about the parables. 11He told them, "The secret of the kingdom of God has been given to you. But to those on the outside everything is said in parables 12so that,

" 'they may be ever seeing but never
        perceiving,
    and ever hearing but never
        understanding;
otherwise they might turn and be
        forgiven!' "

13Then Jesus said to them, "Don't you understand this parable? How then will you understand any parable? 14The farmer sows the word. 15Some people are like seed along the path, where the word is sown. As soon as they hear it, Satan comes and takes away the word that was sown in them. 16Others, like seed sown on rocky places, hear the word and at once receive it with joy. 17But since they have no root, they last only a short time. When trouble or persecution comes because of the word, they quickly fall away. 18Still others, like seed sown among thorns, hear the word; [19]but the worries of this life, the deceitfulness of wealth and the desires for other things come in and choke the word, making it unfruitful. [20]Others, like seed sown on good soil, hear the word, accept it, and produce a crop —thirty, sixty or even a hundred times what was sown."

A Lamp on a Stand

[21]He said to them, "Do you bring in a lamp to put it under a bowl or a bed? Instead, don't you put it on its stand? [22]For whatever is hidden is meant to be disclosed, and whatever is concealed is meant to be brought out into the open. [23]If anyone has ears to hear, let him hear."

[24]"Consider carefully what you hear," he continued. "With the measure you use, it will be measured to you—and even more. [25]Whoever has will be given more; whoever does not have, even what he has will be taken from him."

The Parable of the Growing Seed

[26]He also said, "This is what the kingdom of God is like. A man scatters seed on the ground. [27]Night and day, whether he sleeps or gets up, the seed sprouts and grows, though he does not know how. [28]All by itself the soil produces corn—first the stalk, then the ear, then the full grain in the ear. [29]As soon as the grain is ripe, he puts the sickle to it, because the harvest has come."

READING FROM PSALMS
Psalm 22:22–31

[22]I will declare your name to my brothers;
    in the congregation I will praise you.
[23]You who fear the LORD, praise him!
    All you descendants of Jacob, honour him!
    Revere him, all you descendants of Israel!
[24]For he has not despised or disdained
    the suffering of the afflicted one;
he has not hidden his face from him
    but has listened to his cry for help.

[25]From you comes the theme of my
    praise in the great assembly;
    before those who fear you will I fulfil my vows.
[26]The poor will eat and be satisfied;
    they who seek the LORD will praise him—
    may your hearts live for ever!
[27]All the ends of the earth
    will remember and turn to the LORD,
and all the families of the nations
    will bow down before him,
[28]for dominion belongs to the LORD
    and he rules over the nations.

[29]All the rich of the earth will feast and
    worship;
all who go down to the dust will
    kneel before him—
    those who cannot keep themselves alive.
[30]Posterity will serve him;
    future generations will be told about the Lord.
[31]They will proclaim his righteousness
    to a people yet unborn—
    for he has done it.

OLD TESTAMENT READING
Exodus 25:1–26:37

Offerings for the Tabernacle

25 The LORD said to Moses, 2"Tell the Israelites to bring me an offering. You are to receive the offering for me from each man whose heart prompts him to give. 3These are the offerings you are to receive from them: gold, silver and bronze; 4blue, purple and scarlet yarn and fine linen; goat hair; 5ram skins dyed red and hides of sea cows; acacia wood; 6olive oil for the light; spices for the anointing oil and for the fragrant incense; 7and onyx stones and other gems to be mounted on the ephod and breastpiece.

8"Then have them make a sanctuary for me, and I will dwell among them. 9Make this tabernacle and all its furnishings exactly like the pattern I will show you.

The Ark

10"Have them make a chest of acacia wood—two and a half cubits long, a cubit and a half wide, and a cubit and a half high. 11Overlay it with pure gold, both inside and out, and make a gold moulding around it. 12Cast four gold rings for it and fasten them to its four feet, with two rings on one side and two rings on the other. 13Then make poles of acacia wood and overlay them with gold. 14Insert the poles into the rings on the sides of the chest to carry it. 15The poles are to remain in the rings of this ark; they are not to be removed. 16Then put in the ark the Testimony, which I will give you.

17"Make an atonement cover of pure gold—two and a half cubits long and a cubit and a half wide. 18And make two cherubim out of hammered gold at the ends of the cover. 19Make one cherub on one end and the second cherub on the other; make the cherubim of one piece with the cover, at the two ends. 20The cherubim are to have their wings spread upwards, overshadowing the cover with them. The cherubim are to face each other, looking towards the cover. 21Place the cover on top of the ark and put in the ark the Testimony, which I will give you. 22There, above the cover between the two cherubim that are over the ark of the Testimony, I will meet with you and give you all my commands for the Israelites.

The Table

23"Make a table of acacia wood—two cubits long, a cubit wide and a cubit and a half high. 24Overlay it with pure gold and make a gold moulding around it. 25Also make around it a rim a handbreadth wide and put a gold moulding on the rim. 26Make four gold rings for the table and fasten them to the four corners, where the four legs are. 27The rings are to be close to the rim to hold the poles used in carrying the table. 28Make the poles of acacia wood, overlay them with gold and carry the table with them. 29And make its plates and dishes of pure gold, as well as its pitchers and bowls for the pouring out of offerings. 30Put the bread of the Presence on this table to be before me at all times.

The Lampstand

31"Make a lampstand of pure gold and hammer it out, base and shaft; its flowerlike cups, buds and blossoms shall be of one piece with it. 32Six branches are to extend from the sides of the lampstand—three on one side and three on the other. 33Three cups shaped like almond flowers with buds and blossoms are to be on one branch, three on the next branch, and the same for all six branches extending from the lampstand. ³⁴And on the lampstand there are to be four cups shaped like almond flowers with buds and blossoms. ³⁵One bud shall be under the first pair of branches extending from the lampstand, a second bud under the second pair, and a third bud under the third pair—six branches in all. ³⁶The buds and branches shall all be of one piece with the lampstand, hammered out of pure gold.

³⁷"Then make its seven lamps and set them up on it so that they light the space in front of it. ³⁸Its wick trimmers and trays are to be of pure gold. ³⁹A talent of pure gold is to be used for the lampstand and all these accessories. ⁴⁰See that you make them according to the pattern shown you on the mountain.

The Tabernacle

26 "Make the tabernacle with ten curtains of finely twisted linen and blue, purple and scarlet yarn, with cherubim worked into them by a skilled craftsman. ²All the curtains are to be the same size—twenty-eight cubits long and four cubits wide. ³Join five of the curtains together, and do the same with the other five. ⁴Make loops of blue material along the edge of the end curtain in one set, and do the same with the end curtain in the other set. ⁵Make fifty loops on one curtain and fifty loops on the end curtain of the other set, with the loops opposite each other. ⁶Then make fifty gold clasps and use them to fasten the curtains together so that the tabernacle is a unit.

⁷"Make curtains of goat hair for the tent over the tabernacle—eleven altogether. ⁸All eleven curtains are to be the same size—thirty cubits long and four cubits wide. ⁹Join five of the curtains together into one set and the other six into another set. Fold the sixth curtain double at the front of the tent. ¹⁰Make fifty loops along the edge of the end curtain in one set and also along the

edge of the end curtain in the other set. ¹¹Then make fifty bronze clasps and put them in the loops to fasten the tent together as a unit. ¹²As for the additional length of the tent curtains, the half curtain that is left over is to hang down at the rear of the tabernacle. ¹³The tent curtains will be a cubit longer on both sides; what is left will hang over the sides of the tabernacle so as to cover it. ¹⁴Make for the tent a covering of ram skins dyed red, and over that a covering of hides of sea cows.

¹⁵"Make upright frames of acacia wood for the tabernacle. ¹⁶Each frame is to be ten cubits long and a cubit and a half wide, ¹⁷with two projections set parallel to each other. Make all the frames of the tabernacle in this way. ¹⁸Make twenty frames for the south side of the tabernacle ¹⁹and make forty silver bases to go under them—two bases for each frame, one under each projection. ²⁰For the other side, the north side of the tabernacle, make twenty frames ²¹and forty silver bases—two under each frame. ²²Make six frames for the far end, that is, the west end of the tabernacle, ²³and make two frames for the corners at the far end. ²⁴At these two corners they must be double from the bottom all the way to the top, and fitted into a single ring; both shall be like that. ²⁵So there will be eight frames and sixteen silver bases—two under each frame.

²⁶"Also make crossbars of acacia wood: five for the frames on one side of the tabernacle, ²⁷five for those on the other side, and five for the frames on the west, at the far end of the tabernacle. ²⁸The centre crossbar is to extend from end to end at the middle of the frames. ²⁹Overlay the frames with gold and make gold rings to hold the crossbars. Also overlay the crossbars with gold.

³⁰"Set up the tabernacle according to the plan shown you on the mountain.

³¹"Make a curtain of blue, purple and scarlet yarn and finely twisted linen, with cherubim worked into it by a skilled craftsman. ³²Hang it with gold

hooks on four posts of acacia wood overlaid with gold and standing on four silver bases. ³³Hang the curtain from the clasps and place the ark of the Testimony behind the curtain. The curtain will separate the Holy Place from the Most Holy Place. ³⁴Put the atonement cover on the ark of the Testimony in the Most Holy Place. ³⁵Place the table outside the curtain on the north side of the tabernacle and put the lampstand opposite it on the south side.

³⁶"For the entrance to the tent make a curtain of blue, purple and scarlet yarn and finely twisted linen—the work of an embroiderer. ³⁷Make gold hooks for this curtain and five posts of acacia wood overlaid with gold. And cast five bronze bases for them.

NEW TESTAMENT READING
Mark 4:30–5:20

The Parable of the Mustard Seed

³⁰Again he said, "What shall we say the kingdom of God is like, or what parable shall we use to describe it? ³¹It is like a mustard seed, which is the smallest seed you plant in the ground. ³²Yet when planted, it grows and becomes the largest of all garden plants, with such big branches that the birds of the air can perch in its shade."

³³With many similar parables Jesus spoke the word to them, as much as they could understand. ³⁴He did not say anything to them without using a parable. But when he was alone with his own disciples, he explained everything.

Jesus Calms the Storm

³⁵That day when evening came, he said to his disciples, "Let us go over to the other side." ³⁶Leaving the crowd behind, they took him along, just as he was, in the boat. There were also other boats with him. ³⁷A furious squall came up, and the waves broke over the boat, so that it was nearly swamped. ³⁸Jesus was in the stern, sleeping on a cushion. The disciples woke him and said to him, "Teacher, don't you care if we drown?"

³⁹He got up, rebuked the wind and said to the waves, "Quiet! Be still!" Then the wind died down and it was completely calm.

⁴⁰He said to his disciples, "Why are you so afraid? Do you still have no faith?"

⁴¹They were terrified and asked each other, "Who is this? Even the wind and the waves obey him!"

The Healing of a Demon-possessed Man

5 They went across the lake to the region of the Gerasenes. ²When Jesus got out of the boat, a man with an evil spirit came from the tombs to meet him. ³This man lived in the tombs, and no-one could bind him any more, not even with a chain. ⁴For he had often been chained hand and foot, but he tore the chains apart and broke the irons on his feet. No-one was strong enough to subdue him. ⁵Night and day among the tombs and in the hills he would cry out and cut himself with stones.

⁶When he saw Jesus from a distance, he ran and fell on his knees in front of him. ⁷He shouted at the top of his voice, "What do you want with me, Jesus, Son of the Most High God? Swear to God that you won't torture me!" ⁸For Jesus had said to him, "Come out of this man, you evil spirit!"

⁹Then Jesus asked him, "What is your name?"

"My name is Legion," he replied, "for we are many." ¹⁰And he begged Jesus again and again not to send them out of the area.

¹¹A large herd of pigs was feeding on the nearby hillside. ¹²The demons begged Jesus, "Send us among the pigs;

allow us to go into them." ¹³He gave them permission, and the evil spirits came out and went into the pigs. The herd, about two thousand in number, rushed down the steep bank into the lake and were drowned.

¹⁴Those tending the pigs ran off and reported this in the town and countryside, and the people went out to see what had happened. ¹⁵When they came to Jesus, they saw the man who had been possessed by the legion of demons, sitting there, dressed and in his right mind; and they were afraid. ¹⁶Those who had seen it told the people what had happened to the demon-possessed man—and told about the pigs as well. ¹⁷Then the people began to plead with Jesus to leave their region.

¹⁸As Jesus was getting into the boat, the man who had been demon-possessed begged to go with him. ¹⁹Jesus did not let him, but said, "Go home to your family and tell them how much the Lord has done for you, and how he has had mercy on you." ²⁰So the man went away and began to tell in the Decapolis how much Jesus had done for him. And all the people were amazed.

READING FROM PSALMS
Psalm 23:1–6

A psalm of David.

¹The LORD is my shepherd,
    I shall not be in want.
2   He makes me lie down in green
        pastures,
he leads me beside quiet waters,
3   he restores my soul.
He guides me in paths of
        righteousness
    for his name's sake.
⁴Even though I walk
    through the valley of the shadow of
        death,
I will fear no evil,
    for you are with me;
your rod and your staff,
    they comfort me.

⁵You prepare a table before me
    in the presence of my enemies.
You anoint my head with oil;
    my cup overflows.
⁶Surely goodness and love will follow
        me
    all the days of my life,
and I will dwell in the house of the
        LORD
    for ever.

DAY 51

FEBRUARY 20

OLD TESTAMENT READING
Exodus 27:1–28:43

The Altar of Burnt Offering

27 "Build an altar of acacia wood, three cubits high; it is to be square, five cubits long and five cubits wide. ²Make a horn at each of the four corners, so that the horns and the altar are of one piece, and overlay the altar with bronze. ³Make all its utensils of bronze—its pots to remove the ashes, and its shovels, sprinkling bowls, meat forks and firepans. ⁴Make a grating for it, a bronze network, and make a bronze ring at each of the four corners of the network. ⁵Put it under the ledge of the altar so that it is halfway up the altar. ⁶Make poles of acacia wood for the altar and overlay them with bronze. ⁷The poles are to be inserted into the rings so they will be on two sides of the altar when it is carried. ⁸Make the altar hollow, out of boards. It is to be made just as you were shown on the mountain.

The Courtyard

9"Make a courtyard for the tabernacle. The south side shall be a hundred cubits long and is to have curtains of finely twisted linen, 10with twenty posts and twenty bronze bases and with silver hooks and bands on the posts. 11The north side shall be a hundred cubits long and is to have curtains, with twenty posts and twenty bronze bases and with silver hooks and bands on the posts.

12"The west end of the courtyard shall be fifty cubits wide and have curtains, with ten posts and ten bases. 13On the east end, towards the sunrise, the courtyard shall also be fifty cubits wide. 14Curtains fifteen cubits long are to be on one side of the entrance, with three posts and three bases, 15and curtains fifteen cubits long are to be on the other side, with three posts and three bases.

16"For the entrance to the courtyard, provide a curtain twenty cubits long, of blue, purple and scarlet yarn and finely twisted linen—the work of an embroiderer—with four posts and four bases. 17All the posts around the courtyard are to have silver bands and hooks, and bronze bases. 18The courtyard shall be a hundred cubits long and fifty cubits wide, with curtains of finely twisted linen five cubits high, and with bronze bases. 19All the other articles used in the service of the tabernacle, whatever their function, including all the tent pegs for it and those for the courtyard, are to be of bronze.

Oil for the Lampstand

20"Command the Israelites to bring you clear oil of pressed olives for the light so that the lamps may be kept burning. 21In the Tent of Meeting, outside the curtain that is in front of the Testimony, Aaron and his sons are to keep the lamps burning before the LORD from evening till morning. This is to be a lasting ordinance among the Israelites for the generations to come.

The Priestly Garments

28 "Have Aaron your brother brought to you from among the Israelites, with his sons Nadab and Abihu, Eleazar and Ithamar, so that they may serve me as priests. 2Make sacred garments for your brother Aaron, to give him dignity and honour. 3Tell all the skilled men to whom I have given wisdom in such matters that they are to make garments for Aaron, for his consecration, so that he may serve me as priest. 4These are the garments they are to make: a breastpiece, an ephod, a robe, a woven tunic, a turban and a sash. They are to make these sacred garments for your brother Aaron and his sons, so that they may serve me as priests. 5Make them use gold, and blue, purple and scarlet yarn, and fine linen.

The Ephod

6"Make the ephod of gold, and of blue, purple and scarlet yarn, and of finely twisted linen—the work of a skilled craftsman. 7It is to have two shoulder pieces attached to two of its corners, so that it can be fastened. 8Its skilfully woven waistband is to be like it—of one piece with the ephod and made with gold, and with blue, purple and scarlet yarn, and with finely twisted linen.

9"Take two onyx stones and engrave on them the names of the sons of Israel 10in the order of their birth—six names on one stone and the remaining six on the other. 11Engrave the names of the sons of Israel on the two stones the way a gem cutter engraves a seal. Then mount the stones in gold filigree settings 12and fasten them on the shoulder pieces of the ephod as memorial stones for the sons of Israel. Aaron is to bear the names on his shoulders as a memorial before the LORD. ¹³Make gold filigree settings ¹⁴and two braided chains of pure gold, like a rope, and attach the chains to the settings.

The Breastpiece

¹⁵"Fashion a breastpiece for making decisions—the work of a skilled craftsman. Make it like the ephod: of gold, and of blue, purple and scarlet yarn, and of finely twisted linen. ¹⁶It is to be square—a span long and a span wide —and folded double. ¹⁷Then mount four rows of precious stones on it. In the first row there shall be a ruby, a topaz and a beryl; ¹⁸in the second row a turquoise, a sapphire and an emerald; ¹⁹in the third row a jacinth, an agate and an amethyst; ²⁰in the fourth row a chrysolite, an onyx and a jasper. Mount them in gold filigree settings. ²¹There are to be twelve stones, one for each of the names of the sons of Israel, each engraved like a seal with the name of one of the twelve tribes.

²²"For the breastpiece make braided chains of pure gold, like a rope. ²³Make two gold rings for it and fasten them to two corners of the breastpiece. ²⁴Fasten the two gold chains to the rings at the corners of the breastpiece, ²⁵and the other ends of the chains to the two settings, attaching them to the shoulder pieces of the ephod at the front. ²⁶Make two gold rings and attach them to the other two corners of the breastpiece on the inside edge next to the ephod. ²⁷Make two more gold rings and attach them to the bottom of the shoulder pieces on the front of the ephod, close to the seam just above the waistband of the ephod. ²⁸The rings of the breastpiece are to be tied to the rings of the ephod with blue cord, connecting it to the waistband, so that the breastpiece will not swing out from the ephod.

²⁹"Whenever Aaron enters the Holy Place, he will bear the names of the sons of Israel over his heart on the breastpiece of decision as a continuing memorial before the LORD. ³⁰Also put the Urim and the Thummim in the breastpiece, so they may be over Aaron's heart whenever he enters the presence of the LORD. Thus Aaron will always bear the means of making decisions for the Israelites over his heart before the LORD.

Other Priestly Garments

³¹"Make the robe of the ephod entirely of blue cloth, ³²with an opening for the head in its centre. There shall be a woven edge like a collar around this opening, so that it will not tear. ³³Make pomegranates of blue, purple and scarlet yarn around the hem of the robe, with gold bells between them. ³⁴The gold bells and the pomegranates are to alternate around the hem of the robe. ³⁵Aaron must wear it when he ministers. The sound of the bells will be heard when he enters the Holy Place before the LORD and when he comes out, so that he will not die.

³⁶"Make a plate of pure gold and engrave on it as on a seal: HOLY TO THE LORD. ³⁷Fasten a blue cord to it to attach it to the turban; it is to be on the front of the turban. ³⁸It will be on Aaron's forehead, and he will bear the guilt involved in the sacred gifts the Israelites consecrate, whatever their gifts may be. It will be on Aaron's forehead continually so that they will be acceptable to the LORD.

³⁹"Weave the tunic of fine linen and make the turban of fine linen. The sash is to be the work of an embroiderer. ⁴⁰Make tunics, sashes and headbands for Aaron's sons, to give them dignity and honour. ⁴¹After you put these clothes on your brother Aaron and his sons, anoint and ordain them. Consecrate them so they may serve me as priests.

⁴²"Make linen undergarments as a covering for the body, reaching from the waist to the thigh. ⁴³Aaron and his

sons must wear them whenever they enter the Tent of Meeting or approach the altar to minister in the Holy Place, so that they will not incur guilt and die.

"This is to be a lasting ordinance for Aaron and his descendants.

NEW TESTAMENT READING
Mark 5:21–6:6a

A Dead Girl and a Sick Woman

21When Jesus had again crossed over by boat to the other side of the lake, a large crowd gathered round him while he was by the lake. 22Then one of the synagogue rulers, named Jairus, came there. Seeing Jesus, he fell at his feet 23and pleaded earnestly with him, "My little daughter is dying. Please come and put your hands on her so that she will be healed and live." 24So Jesus went with him.

A large crowd followed and pressed around him. 25And a woman was there who had been subject to bleeding for twelve years. 26She had suffered a great deal under the care of many doctors and had spent all she had, yet instead of getting better she grew worse. 27When she heard about Jesus, she came up behind him in the crowd and touched his cloak, 28because she thought, "If I just touch his clothes, I will be healed." 29Immediately her bleeding stopped and she felt in her body that she was freed from her suffering.

30At once Jesus realised that power had gone out from him. He turned around in the crowd and asked, "Who touched my clothes?"

31"You see the people crowding against you," his disciples answered, "and yet you can ask, 'Who touched me?'"

32But Jesus kept looking around to see who had done it. 33Then the woman, knowing what had happened to her, came and fell at his feet and, trembling with fear, told him the whole truth. 34He said to her, "Daughter, your faith

has healed you. Go in peace and be freed from your suffering."

35While Jesus was still speaking, some men came from the house of Jairus, the synagogue ruler. "Your daughter is dead," they said. "Why bother the teacher any more?"

36Ignoring what they said, Jesus told the synagogue ruler, "Don't be afraid; just believe."

37He did not let anyone follow him except Peter, James and John the brother of James. 38When they came to the home of the synagogue ruler, Jesus saw a commotion, with people crying and wailing loudly. 39He went in and said to them, "Why all this commotion and wailing? The child is not dead but asleep." 40But they laughed at him.

After he put them all out, he took the child's father and mother and the disciples who were with him, and went in where the child was. 41He took her by the hand and said to her, *"Talitha koum!"* (which means, "Little girl, I say to you, get up!"). 42Immediately the girl stood up and walked around (she was twelve years old). At this they were completely astonished. 43He gave strict orders not to let anyone know about this, and told them to give her something to eat.

A Prophet Without Honour

6 Jesus left there and went to his home town, accompanied by his disciples. 2When the Sabbath came, he began to teach in the synagogue, and many who heard him were amazed.

"Where did this man get these things?" they asked. "What's this wisdom that has been given him, that he even does miracles! 3Isn't this the carpenter? Isn't this Mary's son and the brother of James, Joseph, Judas and Simon? Aren't his sisters here with us?" And they took offence at him.

4Jesus said to them, "Only in his home town, among his relatives and in his own house is a prophet without honour." 5He could not do any miracles there, except lay his hands on a few sick people and heal them. ⁶And he was amazed at their lack of faith.

READING FROM PSALMS
Psalm 24:1–10

Of David. A psalm.

¹The earth is the LORD's, and
  everything in it,
  the world, and all who live in it;
²for he founded it upon the seas
  and established it upon the waters.

³Who may ascend the hill of the
  LORD?
  Who may stand in his holy place?
⁴He who has clean hands and a pure
  heart,
  who does not lift up his soul to an
  idol

or swear by what is false.
⁵He will receive blessing from the
  LORD
  and vindication from God his
  Saviour.
⁶Such is the generation of those who
  seek him,
  who seek your face, O God of
  Jacob.   *Selah*

⁷Lift up your heads, O you gates;
  be lifted up, you ancient doors,
  that the King of glory may come in.
⁸Who is this King of glory?
  The LORD strong and mighty,
  the LORD mighty in battle.
⁹Lift up your heads, O you gates;
  lift them up, you ancient doors,
  that the King of glory may come in.
¹⁰Who is he, this King of glory?
  The LORD Almighty—
  he is the King of glory.   *Selah*

DAY 52 | **FEBRUARY 21**

OLD TESTAMENT READING
Exodus 29:1–30:38

Consecration of the Priests

29 "This is what you are to do to consecrate them, so that they may serve me as priests: Take a young bull and two rams without defect. ²And from fine wheat flour, without yeast, make bread, and cakes mixed with oil, and wafers spread with oil. ³Put them in a basket and present them in it—along with the bull and the two rams. ⁴Then bring Aaron and his sons to the entrance to the Tent of Meeting and wash them with water. ⁵Take the garments and dress Aaron with the tunic, the robe of the ephod, the ephod itself and the breastpiece. Fasten the ephod on him by its skilfully woven waistband. ⁶Put

the turban on his head and attach the sacred diadem to the turban. ⁷Take the anointing oil and anoint him by pouring it on his head. ⁸Bring his sons and dress them in tunics ⁹and put headbands on them. Then tie sashes on Aaron and his sons. The priesthood is theirs by a lasting ordinance. In this way you shall ordain Aaron and his sons.

¹⁰"Bring the bull to the front of the Tent of Meeting, and Aaron and his sons shall lay their hands on its head. ¹¹Slaughter it in the LORD's presence at the entrance to the Tent of Meeting. ¹²Take some of the bull's blood and put it on the horns of the altar with your finger, and pour out the rest of it at the base of the altar. ¹³Then take all the fat around the inner parts, the covering of the liver, and both kidneys with the fat on them, and burn them on the altar. ¹⁴But burn the bull's flesh and its hide

and its offal outside the camp. It is a sin offering.

15"Take one of the rams, and Aaron and his sons shall lay their hands on its head. 16Slaughter it and take the blood and sprinkle it against the altar on all sides. 17Cut the ram into pieces and wash the inner parts and the legs, putting them with the head and the other pieces. 18Then burn the entire ram on the altar. It is a burnt offering to the LORD, a pleasing aroma, an offering made to the LORD by fire.

19"Take the other ram, and Aaron and his sons shall lay their hands on its head. 20Slaughter it, take some of its blood and put it on the lobes of the right ears of Aaron and his sons, on the thumbs of their right hands, and on the big toes of their right feet. Then sprinkle blood against the altar on all sides. 21And take some of the blood on the altar and some of the anointing oil and sprinkle it on Aaron and his garments and on his sons and their garments. Then he and his sons and their garments will be consecrated.

22"Take from this ram the fat, the fat tail, the fat around the inner parts, the covering of the liver, both kidneys with the fat on them, and the right thigh. (This is the ram for the ordination.) 23From the basket of bread made without yeast, which is before the LORD, take a loaf, and a cake made with oil, and a wafer. 24Put all these in the hands of Aaron and his sons and wave them before the LORD as a wave offering. 25Then take them from their hands and burn them on the altar along with the burnt offering for a pleasing aroma to the LORD, an offering made to the LORD by fire. 26After you take the breast of the ram for Aaron's ordination, wave it before the LORD as a wave offering, and it will be your share.

27"Consecrate those parts of the ordination ram that belong to Aaron and his sons: the breast that was waved and the thigh that was presented. 28This is always to be the regular share from the Israelites for Aaron and his sons. It

is the contribution the Israelites are to make to the LORD from their fellowship offerings.

29"Aaron's sacred garments will belong to his descendants so that they can be anointed and ordained in them. 30The son who succeeds him as priest and comes to the Tent of Meeting to minister in the Holy Place is to wear them seven days.

31"Take the ram for the ordination and cook the meat in a sacred place. 32At the entrance to the Tent of Meeting, Aaron and his sons are to eat the meat of the ram and the bread that is in the basket. 33They are to eat these offerings by which atonement was made for their ordination and consecration. But no-one else may eat them, because they are sacred. 34And if any of the meat of the ordination ram or any bread is left over till morning, burn it up. It must not be eaten, because it is sacred.

35"Do for Aaron and his sons everything I have commanded you, taking seven days to ordain them. 36Sacrifice a bull each day as a sin offering to make atonement. Purify the altar by making atonement for it, and anoint it to consecrate it. 37For seven days make atonement for the altar and consecrate it. Then the altar will be most holy, and whatever touches it will be holy.

38"This is what you are to offer on the altar regularly each day: two lambs a year old. 39Offer one in the morning and the other at twilight. 40With the first lamb offer a tenth of an ephah of fine flour mixed with a quarter of a hin of oil from pressed olives, and a quarter of a hin of wine as a drink offering. 41Sacrifice the other lamb at twilight with the same grain offering and its drink offering as in the morning—a pleasing aroma, an offering made to the LORD by fire.

42"For the generations to come this burnt offering is to be made regularly at the entrance to the Tent of Meeting before the LORD. There I will meet you and speak to you; 43there also I will meet with the Israelites, and the place will be consecrated by my glory.

44"So I will consecrate the Tent of Meeting and the altar and will consecrate Aaron and his sons to serve me as priests. 45Then I will dwell among the Israelites and be their God. 46They will know that I am the LORD their God, who brought them out of Egypt so that I might dwell among them. I am the LORD their God.

The Altar of Incense

30 "Make an altar of acacia wood for burning incense. 2It is to be square, a cubit long and a cubit wide, and two cubits high—its horns of one piece with it. 3Overlay the top and all the sides and the horns with pure gold, and make a gold moulding around it. 4Make two gold rings for the altar below the moulding—two on opposite sides —to hold the poles used to carry it. 5Make the poles of acacia wood and overlay them with gold. 6Put the altar in front of the curtain that is before the ark of the Testimony—before the atonement cover that is over the Testimony —where I will meet with you.

7"Aaron must burn fragrant incense on the altar every morning when he tends the lamps. 8He must burn incense again when he lights the lamps at twilight so that incense will burn regularly before the LORD for the generations to come. 9Do not offer on this altar any other incense or any burnt offering or grain offering, and do not pour a drink offering on it. 10Once a year Aaron shall make atonement on its horns. This annual atonement must be made with the blood of the atoning sin offering for the generations to come. It is most holy to the LORD."

Atonement Money

11Then the LORD said to Moses, 12"When you take a census of the Israelites to count them, each one must pay the LORD a ransom for his life at the time he is counted. Then no plague will come on them when you number them. 13Each one who crosses over to those already counted is to give a half shekel, according to the sanctuary shekel, which weighs twenty gerahs. This half shekel is an offering to the LORD. 14All who cross over, those twenty years old or more, are to give an offering to the LORD. 15The rich are not to give more than a half shekel and the poor are not to give less when you make the offering to the LORD to atone for your lives. 16Receive the atonement money from the Israelites and use it for the service of the Tent of Meeting. It will be a memorial for the Israelites before the LORD, making atonement for your lives."

Basin for Washing

17Then the LORD said to Moses, 18"Make a bronze basin, with its bronze stand, for washing. Place it between the Tent of Meeting and the altar, and put water in it. 19Aaron and his sons are to wash their hands and feet with water from it. 20Whenever they enter the Tent of Meeting, they shall wash with water so that they will not die. Also, when they approach the altar to minister by presenting an offering made to the LORD by fire, 21they shall wash their hands and feet so that they will not die. This is to be a lasting ordinance for Aaron and his descendants for the generations to come."

Anointing Oil

22Then the LORD said to Moses, 23"Take the following fine spices: 500 shekels of liquid myrrh, half as much (that is, 250 shekels) of fragrant cinnamon, 250 shekels of fragrant cane, 24500 shekels of cassia—all according to the sanctuary shekel—and a hin of olive oil. 25Make these into a sacred anointing oil, a fragrant blend, the work of a perfumer. It will be the sacred anointing oil. 26Then use it to anoint the Tent of

Meeting, the ark of the Testimony, 27the table and all its articles, the lampstand and its accessories, the altar of incense, 28the altar of burnt offering and all its utensils, and the basin with its stand. 29You shall consecrate them so they will be most holy, and whatever touches them will be holy.

30"Anoint Aaron and his sons and consecrate them so they may serve me as priests. 31Say to the Israelites, 'This is to be my sacred anointing oil for the generations to come. 32Do not pour it on men's bodies and do not make any oil with the same formula. It is sacred, and you are to consider it sacred. 33Whoever makes perfume like it and whoever puts it on anyone other than a priest must be cut off from his people.'"

Incense

34Then the LORD said to Moses, "Take fragrant spices—gum resin, onycha and galbanum—and pure frankincense, all in equal amounts, 35and make a fragrant blend of incense, the work of a perfumer. It is to be salted and pure and sacred. 36Grind some of it to powder and place it in front of the Testimony in the Tent of Meeting, where I will meet with you. It shall be most holy to you. 37Do not make any incense with this formula for yourselves; consider it holy to the LORD. 38Whoever makes any like it to enjoy its fragrance must be cut off from his people."

NEW TESTAMENT READING
Mark 6:6b–29

Jesus Sends Out the Twelve

Then Jesus went round teaching from village to village. 7Calling the Twelve to him, he sent them out two by two and gave them authority over evil spirits.

8These were his instructions: "Take nothing for the journey except a staff —no bread, no bag, no money in your belts. 9Wear sandals but not an extra tunic. 10Whenever you enter a house, stay there until you leave that town. 11And if any place will not welcome you or listen to you, shake the dust off your feet when you leave, as a testimony against them."

12They went out and preached that people should repent. 13They drove out many demons and anointed many sick people with oil and healed them.

John the Baptist Beheaded

14King Herod heard about this, for Jesus' name had become well known. Some were saying, "John the Baptist has been raised from the dead, and that is why miraculous powers are at work in him."

15Others said, "He is Elijah."

And still others claimed, "He is a prophet, like one of the prophets of long ago."

16But when Herod heard this, he said, "John, the man I beheaded, has been raised from the dead!"

17For Herod himself had given orders to have John arrested, and he had him bound and put in prison. He did this because of Herodias, his brother Philip's wife, whom he had married. 18For John had been saying to Herod, "It is not lawful for you to have your brother's wife." 19So Herodias nursed a grudge against John and wanted to kill him. But she was not able to, 20because Herod feared John and protected him, knowing him to be a righteous and holy man. When Herod heard John, he was greatly puzzled; yet he liked to listen to him.

21Finally the opportune time came. On his birthday Herod gave a banquet for his high officials and military commanders and the leading men of Galilee. 22When the daughter of Herodias came in and danced, she pleased Herod and his dinner guests.

The king said to the girl, "Ask me for anything you want, and I'll give it to you." 23And he promised her with an oath, "Whatever you ask I will give you, up to half my kingdom."

24She went out and said to her mother, "What shall I ask for?"

"The head of John the Baptist," she answered.

25At once the girl hurried in to the king with the request: "I want you to give me right now the head of John the Baptist on a platter."

26The king was greatly distressed, but because of his oaths and his dinner guests, he did not want to refuse her. 27So he immediately sent an executioner with orders to bring John's head. The man went, beheaded John in the prison, 28and brought back his head on a platter. He presented it to the girl, and she gave it to her mother. 29On hearing of this, John's disciples came and took his body and laid it in a tomb.

READING FROM PROVERBS
Proverbs 5:15–23

15Drink water from your own cistern,
    running water from your own well.
16Should your springs overflow in the
        streets,
    your streams of water in the public
        squares?
17Let them be yours alone,
    never to be shared with strangers.
18May your fountain be blessed,
    and may you rejoice in the wife of
        your youth.
19A loving doe, a graceful deer—
    may her breasts satisfy you always,
    may you ever be captivated by her
        love.
20Why be captivated, my son, by an
        adulteress?
    Why embrace the bosom of
        another man's wife?

21For a man's ways are in full view of
        the LORD,
    and he examines all his paths.
22The evil deeds of a wicked man
        ensnare him;
    the cords of his sin hold him fast.
23He will die for lack of discipline,
    led astray by his own great folly.

DAY 53

FEBRUARY 22

OLD TESTAMENT READING
Exodus 31:1–33:6

Bezalel and Oholiab

31 Then the LORD said to Moses, 2"See I have chosen Bezalel son of Uri, the son of Hur, of the tribe of Judah, 3and I have filled him with the Spirit of God, with skill, ability and knowledge in all kinds of crafts—4to make artistic designs for work in gold, silver and bronze, 5to cut and set stones, to work in wood, and to engage in all kinds of craftsmanship. 6Moreover, I have appointed Oholiab son of Ahisamach, of the tribe of Dan, to help him.

Also I have given skill to all the craftsmen to make everything I have commanded you: 7the Tent of Meeting, the ark of the Testimony with the atonement cover on it, and all the other furnishings of the tent—8the table and its articles, the pure gold lampstand and all its accessories, the altar of incense, 9the altar of burnt offering and all its utensils, the basin with its stand—10and also the woven garments, both the sacred garments for Aaron the priest and the garments for his sons when they serve as priests, 11and the anointing oil and fragrant incense for the Holy Place. They are to make them just as I commanded you."

The Sabbath

¹²Then the LORD said to Moses, ¹³"Say to the Israelites, 'You must observe my Sabbaths. This will be a sign between me and you for the generations to come, so that you may know that I am the LORD, who makes you holy.

¹⁴"'Observe the Sabbath, because it is holy to you. Anyone who desecrates it must be put to death; whoever does any work on that day must be cut off from his people. ¹⁵For six days, work is to be done, but the seventh day is a Sabbath of rest, holy to the LORD. Whoever does any work on the Sabbath day must be put to death. ¹⁶The Israelites are to observe the Sabbath, celebrating it for the generations to come as a lasting covenant. ¹⁷It will be a sign between me and the Israelites for ever, for in six days the LORD made the heavens and the earth, and on the seventh day he abstained from work and rested.'"

¹⁸When the LORD finished speaking to Moses on Mount Sinai, he gave him the two tablets of the Testimony, the tablets of stone inscribed by the finger of God.

The Golden Calf

32 When the people saw that Moses was so long in coming down from the mountain, they gathered round Aaron and said, "Come, make us gods who will go before us. As for this fellow Moses who brought us up out of Egypt, we don't know what has happened to him."

²Aaron answered them, "Take off the gold ear-rings that your wives, your sons and your daughters are wearing, and bring them to me." ³So all the people took off their ear-rings and brought them to Aaron. ⁴He took what they handed him and made it into an idol cast in the shape of a calf, fashioning it with a tool. Then they said, "These are your gods, O Israel, who brought you up out of Egypt."

⁵When Aaron saw this, he built an altar in front of the calf and announced, "Tomorrow there will be a festival to the LORD." ⁶So the next day the people rose early and sacrificed burnt offerings and presented fellowship offerings. Afterwards they sat down to eat and drink and got up to indulge in revelry.

⁷Then the LORD said to Moses, "Go down, because your people, whom you brought up out of Egypt, have become corrupt. ⁸They have been quick to turn away from what I commanded them and have made themselves an idol cast in the shape of a calf. They have bowed down to it and sacrificed to it and have said, 'These are your gods, O Israel, who brought you up out of Egypt.'

⁹"I have seen these people," the LORD said to Moses, "and they are a stiff-necked people. ¹⁰Now leave me alone so that my anger may burn against them and that I may destroy them. Then I will make you into a great nation."

¹¹But Moses sought the favour of the LORD his God. "O LORD," he said, "why should your anger burn against your people, whom you brought out of Egypt with great power and a mighty hand? ¹²Why should the Egyptians say, 'It was with evil intent that he brought them out, to kill them in the mountains and to wipe them off the face of the earth'? Turn from your fierce anger; relent and do not bring disaster on your people. ¹³Remember your servants Abraham, Isaac and Israel, to whom you swore by your own self: 'I will make your descendants as numerous as the stars in the sky and I will give your descendants all this land I promised them, and it will be their inheritance for ever.'" ¹⁴Then the LORD relented and did not bring on his people the disaster he had threatened.

¹⁵Moses turned and went down the mountain with the two tablets of the Testimony in his hands. They were inscribed on both sides, front and back. ¹⁶The tablets were the work of God; the writing was the writing of God, engraved on the tablets.

17When Joshua heard the noise of the people shouting, he said to Moses, "There is the sound of war in the camp."

18Moses replied:

"It is not the sound of victory,
    it is not the sound of defeat;
    it is the sound of singing that I
        hear."

19When Moses approached the camp and saw the calf and the dancing, his anger burned and he threw the tablets out of his hands, breaking them to pieces at the foot of the mountain. 20And he took the calf they had made and burned it in the fire; then he ground it to powder, scattered it on the water and made the Israelites drink it.

21He said to Aaron, "What did these people do to you, that you led them into such great sin?"

22"Do not be angry, my lord," Aaron answered. "You know how prone these people are to evil. 23They said to me, 'Make us gods who will go before us. As for this fellow Moses who brought us up out of Egypt, we don't know what has happened to him.' 24So I told them, 'Whoever has any gold jewellery, take it off.' Then they gave me the gold, and I threw it into the fire, and out came this calf!"

25Moses saw that the people were running wild and that Aaron had let them get out of control and so become a laughing-stock to their enemies. 26So he stood at the entrance to the camp and said, "Whoever is for the LORD, come to me." And all the Levites rallied to him.

27Then he said to them, "This is what the LORD, the God of Israel, says: 'Each man strap a sword to his side. Go back and forth through the camp from one end to the other, each killing his brother and friend and neighbour.'" 28The Levites did as Moses commanded, and that day about three thousand of the people died. 29Then Moses said, "You have been set apart to the LORD today, for you were against your own sons and brothers, and he has blessed you this day."

30The next day Moses said to the people, "You have committed a great sin. But now I will go up to the LORD; perhaps I can make atonement for your sin."

31So Moses went back to the LORD and said, "Oh, what a great sin these people have committed! They have made themselves gods of gold. 32But now, please forgive their sin—but if not, then blot me out of the book you have written."

33The LORD replied to Moses, "Whoever has sinned against me I will blot out of my book. 34Now go, lead the people to the place I spoke of, and my angel will go before you. However, when the time comes for me to punish, I will punish them for their sin."

35And the LORD struck the people with a plague because of what they did with the calf Aaron had made.

33 Then the LORD said to Moses, "Leave this place, you and the people you brought up out of Egypt, and go up to the land I promised on oath to Abraham, Isaac and Jacob, saying, 'I will give it to your descendants.' 2I will send an angel before you and drive out the Canaanites, Amorites, Hittites, Perizzites, Hivites and Jebusites. 3Go up to the land flowing with milk and honey. But I will not go with you, because you are a stiff-necked people and I might destroy you on the way."

4When the people heard these distressing words, they began to mourn and no-one put on any ornaments. 5For the LORD had said to Moses, "Tell the Israelites, 'You are a stiff-necked people. If I were to go with you even for a moment, I might destroy you. Now take off your ornaments and I will decide what to do with you.'" 6So the Israelites stripped off their ornaments at Mount Horeb.

NEW TESTAMENT READING
Mark 6:30-56

Jesus Feeds the Five Thousand

³⁰The apostles gathered round Jesus and reported to him all they had done and taught. ³¹Then, because so many people were coming and going that they did not even have a chance to eat, he said to them, "Come with me by yourselves to a quiet place and get some rest."

³²So they went away by themselves in a boat to a solitary place. ³³But many who saw them leaving recognised them and ran on foot from all the towns and got there ahead of them. ³⁴When Jesus landed and saw a large crowd, he had compassion on them, because they were like sheep without a shepherd. So he began teaching them many things.

³⁵By this time it was late in the day, so his disciples came to him. "This is a remote place," they said, "and it's already very late. ³⁶Send the people away so that they can go to the surrounding countryside and villages and buy themselves something to eat."

³⁷But he answered, "You give them something to eat."

They said to him, "That would take eight months of a man's wages! Are we to go and spend that much on bread and give it to them to eat?"

³⁸"How many loaves do you have?" he asked. "Go and see."

When they found out, they said, "Five—and two fish."

³⁹Then Jesus directed them to have all the people sit down in groups on the green grass. ⁴⁰So they sat down in groups of hundreds and fifties. ⁴¹Taking the five loaves and the two fish and looking up to heaven, he gave thanks and broke the loaves. Then he gave them to his disciples to set before the people. He also divided the two fish among them all. ⁴²They all ate and were satisfied, ⁴³and the disciples picked up twelve basketfuls of broken pieces of bread and fish. ⁴⁴The number of the men who had eaten was five thousand.

Jesus Walks on the Water

⁴⁵Immediately Jesus made his disciples get into the boat and go on ahead of him to Bethsaida, while he dismissed the crowd. ⁴⁶After leaving them, he went up on a mountainside to pray.

⁴⁷When evening came, the boat was in the middle of the lake, and he was alone on land. ⁴⁸He saw the disciples straining at the oars, because the wind was against them. About the fourth watch of the night he went out to them, walking on the lake. He was about to pass by them, ⁴⁹but when they saw him walking on the lake, they thought he was a ghost. They cried out, ⁵⁰because they all saw him and were terrified.

Immediately he spoke to them and said, "Take courage! It is I. Don't be afraid." ⁵¹Then he climbed into the boat with them, and the wind died down. They were completely amazed, ⁵²for they had not understood about the loaves; their hearts were hardened.

⁵³When they had crossed over, they landed at Gennesaret and anchored there. ⁵⁴As soon as they got out of the boat, people recognised Jesus. ⁵⁵They ran throughout that whole region and carried the sick on mats to wherever they heard he was. ⁵⁶And wherever he went—into villages, towns or countryside—they placed the sick in the market-places. They begged him to let them touch even the edge of his cloak, and all who touched him were healed.

READING FROM PSALMS
Psalm 25:1-7

Of David.

¹To you, O LORD, I lift up my soul;
² in you I trust, O my God.
Do not let me be put to shame,
    nor let my enemies triumph over
    me.
³No-one whose hope is in you
    will ever be put to shame,

but they will be put to shame
who are treacherous without
excuse.

⁴Show me your ways, O LORD,
teach me your paths;
⁵guide me in your truth and teach me,
for you are God my Saviour,

and my hope is in you all day long.
⁶Remember, O LORD, your great
mercy and love,
for they are from of old.
⁷Remember not the sins of my youth
and my rebellious ways;
according to your love remember me,
for you are good, O LORD.

DAY 54

FEBRUARY 23

OLD TESTAMENT READING
Exodus 33:7–34:35

The Tent of Meeting

⁷Now Moses used to take a tent and
pitch it outside the camp some distance
away, calling it the "tent of meeting".
Anyone enquiring of the LORD would
go to the tent of meeting outside the
camp. ⁸And whenever Moses went out
to the tent, all the people rose and stood
at the entrances to their tents, watching
Moses until he entered the tent. ⁹As
Moses went into the tent, the pillar of
cloud would come down and stay at the
entrance, while the LORD spoke with
Moses. ¹⁰Whenever the people saw the
pillar of cloud standing at the entrance
to the tent, they all stood and worshipped, each at the entrance to his tent.
¹¹The LORD would speak to Moses face
to face, as a man speaks with his friend.
Then Moses would return to the camp,
but his young assistant Joshua son of
Nun did not leave the tent.

Moses and the Glory of the LORD

¹²Moses said to the LORD, "You have
been telling me, 'Lead these people,'
but you have not let me know whom you
will send with me. You have said, 'I
know you by name and you have found
favour with me.' ¹³If you are pleased
with me, teach me your ways so I may
know you and continue to find favour

with you. Remember that this nation is
your people."

¹⁴The LORD replied, "My Presence
will go with you, and I will give you
rest."

¹⁵Then Moses said to him, "If your
Presence does not go with us, do not
send us up from here. ¹⁶How will anyone know that you are pleased with me
and with your people unless you go with
us? What else will distinguish me and
your people from all the other people
on the face of the earth?"

¹⁷And the LORD said to Moses, "I will
do the very thing you have asked, because I am pleased with you and I know
you by name."

¹⁸Then Moses said, "Now show me
your glory."

¹⁹And the LORD said, "I will cause all
my goodness to pass in front of you, and
I will proclaim my name, the LORD, in
your presence. I will have mercy on
whom I will have mercy, and I will have
compassion on whom I will have compassion. ²⁰But," he said, "you cannot
see my face, for no-one may see me and
live."

²¹Then the LORD said, "There is a
place near me where you may stand on a
rock. ²²When my glory passes by, I will
put you in a cleft in the rock and cover
you with my hand until I have passed
by. ²³Then I will remove my hand and
you will see my back; but my face must
not be seen."

The New Stone Tablets

34 The LORD said to Moses, "Chisel out two stone tablets like the first ones, and I will write on them the words that were on the first tablets, which you broke. [2]Be ready in the morning, and then come up on Mount Sinai. Present yourself to me there on top of the mountain. [3]No-one is to come with you or be seen anywhere on the mountain; not even the flocks and herds may graze in front of the mountain."

[4]So Moses chiselled out two stone tablets like the first ones and went up Mount Sinai early in the morning, as the LORD had commanded him; and he carried the two stone tablets in his hands. [5]Then the LORD came down in the cloud and stood there with him and proclaimed his name, the LORD. [6]And he passed in front of Moses, proclaiming, "The LORD, the LORD, the compassionate and gracious God, slow to anger, abounding in love and faithfulness, [7]maintaining love to thousands, and forgiving wickedness, rebellion and sin. Yet he does not leave the guilty unpunished; he punishes the children and their children for the sin of the fathers to the third and fourth generation."

[8]Moses bowed to the ground at once and worshipped. [9]"O Lord, if I have found favour in your eyes," he said, "then let the Lord go with us. Although this is a stiff-necked people, forgive our wickedness and our sin, and take us as your inheritance."

[10]Then the LORD said: "I am making a covenant with you. Before all your people I will do wonders never before done in any nation in all the world. The people you live among will see how awesome is the work that I, the LORD, will do for you. [11]Obey what I command you today. I will drive out before you the Amorites, Canaanites, Hittites, Perizzites, Hivites and Jebusites. [12]Be careful not to make a treaty with those who live in the land where you are going, or they will be a snare among

you. [13]Break down their altars, smash their sacred stones and cut down their Asherah poles. [14]Do not worship any other god, for the LORD, whose name is Jealous, is a jealous God.

[15]"Be careful not to make a treaty with those who live in the land; for when they prostitute themselves to their gods and sacrifice to them, they will invite you and you will eat their sacrifices. [16]And when you choose some of their daughters as wives for your sons and those daughters prostitute themselves to their gods, they will lead your sons to do the same.

[17]"Do not make cast idols.

[18]"Celebrate the Feast of Unleavened Bread. For seven days eat bread made without yeast, as I commanded you. Do this at the appointed time in the month of Abib, for in that month you came out of Egypt.

[19]"The first offspring of every womb belongs to me, including all the firstborn males of your livestock, whether from herd or flock. [20]Redeem the firstborn donkey with a lamb, but if you do not redeem it, break its neck. Redeem all your firstborn sons.

"No-one is to appear before me empty-handed.

[21]"Six days you shall labour, but on the seventh day you shall rest; even during the ploughing season and harvest you must rest.

[22]"Celebrate the Feast of Weeks with the firstfruits of the wheat harvest, and the Feast of Ingathering at the turn of the year. [23]Three times a year all your men are to appear before the Sovereign LORD, the God of Israel. [24]I will drive out nations before you and enlarge your territory, and no-one will covet your land when you go up three times each year to appear before the LORD your God.

[25]"Do not offer the blood of a sacrifice to me along with anything containing yeast, and do not let any of the sacrifice from the Passover Feast remain until morning.

[26]"Bring the best of the firstfruits of

your soil to the house of the LORD your God.

"Do not cook a young goat in its mother's milk."

27Then the LORD said to Moses, "Write down these words, for in accordance with these words I have made a covenant with you and with Israel." 28Moses was there with the LORD forty days and forty nights without eating bread or drinking water. And he wrote on the tablets the words of the covenant —the Ten Commandments.

The Radiant Face of Moses

29When Moses came down from Mount Sinai with the two tablets of the Testimony in his hands, he was not aware that his face was radiant because he had spoken with the LORD. 30When Aaron and all the Israelites saw Moses, his face was radiant, and they were afraid to come near him. 31But Moses called to them; so Aaron and all the leaders of the community came back to him, and he spoke to them. 32Afterwards all the Israelites came near him, and he gave them all the commands the LORD had given him on Mount Sinai.

33When Moses finished speaking to them, he put a veil over his face. 34But whenever he entered the LORD's presence to speak with him, he removed the veil until he came out. And when he came out and told the Israelites what he had been commanded, 35they saw that his face was radiant. Then Moses would put the veil back over his face until he went in to speak with the LORD.

NEW TESTAMENT READING
Mark 7:1–30

Clean and Unclean

7 The Pharisees and some of the teachers of the law who had come from Jerusalem gathered round Jesus and 2saw some of his disciples eating food with hands that were "unclean",

that is, unwashed. 3(The Pharisees and all the Jews do not eat unless they give their hands a ceremonial washing, holding to the tradition of the elders. 4When they come from the market-place they do not eat unless they wash. And they observe many other traditions, such as the washing of cups, pitchers and kettles.)

5So the Pharisees and teachers of the law asked Jesus, "Why don't your disciples live according to the tradition of the elders instead of eating their food with 'unclean' hands?"

6He replied, "Isaiah was right when he prophesied about you hypocrites; as it is written:

" 'These people honour me with their lips,
   but their hearts are far from me.
7They worship me in vain;
   their teachings are but rules taught by men.'

8You have let go of the commands of God and are holding on to the traditions of men."

9And he said to them: "You have a fine way of setting aside the commands of God in order to observe your own traditions! 10For Moses said, 'Honour your father and your mother,' and, 'Anyone who curses his father or mother must be put to death.' 11But you say that if a man says to his father or mother: 'Whatever help you might otherwise have received from me is Corban' (that is, a gift devoted to God), 12then you no longer let him do anything for his father or mother. 13Thus you nullify the word of God by your tradition that you have handed down. And you do many things like that."

14Again Jesus called the crowd to him and said, "Listen to me, everyone, and understand this. 15Nothing outside a man can make him 'unclean' by going into him. Rather, it is what comes out of a man that makes him 'unclean'."

17After he had left the crowd and entered the house, his disciples asked him about this parable. 18"Are you so dull?" he asked. "Don't you see that nothing that enters a man from the outside can make him 'unclean'? 19For it doesn't go into his heart but into his stomach, and then out of his body." (In saying this, Jesus declared all foods "clean".)

20He went on: "What comes out of a man is what makes him 'unclean'. 21For from within, out of men's hearts, come evil thoughts, sexual immorality, theft, murder, adultery, 22greed, malice, deceit, lewdness, envy, slander, arrogance and folly. 23All these evils come from inside and make a man 'unclean'."

The Faith of a Syro-Phoenician Woman

24Jesus left that place and went to the vicinity of Tyre. He entered a house and did not want anyone to know it; yet he could not keep his presence secret. 25In fact, as soon as she heard about him, a woman whose little daughter was possessed by an evil spirit came and fell at his feet. 26The woman was a Greek, born in Syrian Phoenicia. She begged Jesus to drive the demon out of her daughter.

27"First let the children eat all they want," he told her, "for it is not right to take the children's bread and toss it to their dogs."

28"Yes, Lord," she replied, "but even the dogs under the table eat the children's crumbs."

29Then he told her, "For such a reply, you may go; the demon has left your daughter."

30She went home and found her child lying on the bed, and the demon gone.

READING FROM PSALMS
Psalm 25:8–15

8Good and upright is the LORD;
therefore he instructs sinners in his ways.
9He guides the humble in what is right and teaches them his way.
10All the ways of the LORD are loving and faithful
for those who keep the demands of his covenant.
11For the sake of your name, O LORD, forgive my iniquity, though it is great.
12Who, then, is the man that fears the LORD?
He will instruct him in the way chosen for him.
13He will spend his days in prosperity, and his descendants will inherit the land.
14The LORD confides in those who fear him;
he makes his covenant known to them.
15My eyes are ever on the LORD, for only he will release my feet from the snare.

OLD TESTAMENT READING
Exodus 35:1—36:38

Sabbath Regulations

35 Moses assembled the whole Israelite community and said to them, "These are the things the LORD has commanded you to do: ²For six days, work is to be done, but the seventh day shall be your holy day, a Sabbath of rest to the LORD. Whoever does any work on it must be put to death. ³Do not light a fire in any of your dwellings on the Sabbath day."

Materials for the Tabernacle

⁴Moses said to the whole Israelite community, "This is what the LORD has commanded: ⁵From what you have, take an offering for the LORD. Everyone who is willing is to bring to the LORD an offering of gold, silver and bronze; ⁶blue, purple and scarlet yarn and fine linen; goat hair; ⁷ram skins dyed red and hides of sea cows; acacia wood; ⁸olive oil for the light; spices for the anointing oil and for the fragrant incense; ⁹and onyx stones and other gems to be mounted on the ephod and breastpiece.

¹⁰"All who are skilled among you are to come and make everything the LORD has commanded: ¹¹the tabernacle with its tent and its covering, clasps, frames, crossbars, posts and bases; ¹²the ark with its poles and the atonement cover and the curtain that shields it; ¹³the table with its poles and all its articles and the bread of the Presence; ¹⁴the lampstand that is for light with its accessories, lamps and oil for the light; ¹⁵the altar of incense with its poles, the anointing oil and the fragrant incense; the curtain for the doorway at the entrance to the tabernacle; ¹⁶the altar of burnt offering with its bronze grating, its poles and all its utensils; the bronze basin with its stand; ¹⁷the curtains of the courtyard with its posts and bases, and the curtain for the entrance to the courtyard; ¹⁸the tent pegs for the tabernacle and for the courtyard, and their ropes; ¹⁹the woven garments worn for ministering in the sanctuary—both the sacred garments for Aaron the priest and the garments for his sons when they serve as priests."

²⁰Then the whole Israelite community withdrew from Moses' presence, ²¹and everyone who was willing and whose heart moved him came and brought an offering to the LORD for the work on the Tent of Meeting, for all its service, and for the sacred garments. ²²All who were willing, men and women alike, came and brought gold jewellery of all kinds: brooches, ear-rings, rings and ornaments. They all presented their gold as a wave offering to the LORD. ²³Everyone who had blue, purple or scarlet yarn or fine linen, or goat hair, ram skins dyed red or hides of sea cows brought them. ²⁴Those presenting an offering of silver or bronze brought it as an offering to the LORD, and everyone who had acacia wood for any part of the work brought it. ²⁵Every skilled woman spun with her hands and brought what she had spun—blue, purple or scarlet yarn or fine linen. ²⁶And all the women who were willing and had the skill spun the goat hair. ²⁷The leaders brought onyx stones and other gems to be mounted on the ephod and breastpiece. ²⁸They also brought spices and olive oil for the light and for the anointing oil and for the fragrant incense. ²⁹All the Israelite men and women who were willing brought to the LORD freewill offerings for all the work the LORD through Moses had commanded them to do.

Bezalel and Oholiab

30Then Moses said to the Israelites, "See, the LORD has chosen Bezalel son of Uri, the son of Hur, of the tribe of Judah, 31and he has filled him with the Spirit of God, with skill, ability and knowledge in all kinds of crafts—32to make artistic designs for work in gold, silver and bronze, 33to cut and set stones, to work in wood and to engage in all kinds of artistic craftsmanship. 34And he has given both him and Oholiab son of Ahisamach, of the tribe of Dan, the ability to teach others. 35He has filled them with skill to do all kinds of work as craftsmen, designers, embroiderers in blue, purple and scarlet yarn and fine linen, and weavers—all of them master craftsmen and designers.

36 1So Bezalel, Oholiab and every skilled person to whom the LORD has given skill and ability to know how to carry out all the work of constructing the sanctuary are to do the work just as the LORD has commanded."

2Then Moses summoned Bezalel and Oholiab and every skilled person to whom the LORD had given ability and who was willing to come and do the work. 3They received from Moses all the offerings the Israelites had brought to carry out the work of constructing the sanctuary. And the people continued to bring freewill offerings morning after morning. 4So all the skilled craftsmen who were doing all the work on the sanctuary left their work 5and said to Moses, "The people are bringing more than enough for doing the work the LORD commanded to be done."

6Then Moses gave an order and they sent this word throughout the camp: "No man or woman is to make anything else as an offering for the sanctuary." And so the people were restrained from bringing more, 7because what they already had was more than enough to do all the work.

The Tabernacle

8All the skilled men among the workmen made the tabernacle with ten curtains of finely twisted linen and blue, purple and scarlet yarn, with cherubim worked into them by a skilled craftsman. 9All the curtains were the same size—twenty-eight cubits long and four cubits wide. 10They joined five of the curtains together and did the same with the other five. 11Then they made loops of blue material along the edge of the end curtain in one set, and the same was done with the end curtain in the other set. 12They also made fifty loops on one curtain and fifty loops on the end curtain of the other set, with the loops opposite each other. 13Then they made fifty gold clasps and used them to fasten the two sets of curtains together so that the tabernacle was a unit.

14They made curtains of goat hair for the tent over the tabernacle—eleven altogether. 15All eleven curtains were the same size—thirty cubits long and four cubits wide. 16They joined five of the curtains into one set and the other six into another set. 17Then they made fifty loops along the edge of the end curtain in one set and also along the edge of the end curtain in the other set. 18They made fifty bronze clasps to fasten the tent together as a unit. 19Then they made for the tent a covering of ram skins dyed red, and over that a covering of hides of sea cows.

20They made upright frames of acacia wood for the tabernacle. 21Each frame was ten cubits long and a cubit and a half wide, 22with two projections set parallel to each other. They made all the frames of the tabernacle in this way. 23They made twenty frames for the south side of the tabernacle 24and made forty silver bases to go under them—two bases for each frame, one under each projection. 25For the other side, the north side of the tabernacle, they made twenty frames 26and forty silver bases—two under each frame. 27They made six frames for the far end, that is, the west end of the tabernacle, 28and two frames were made for the corners of the tabernacle at the far end. 29At these two corners the frames were double from the bottom all the way to the top and fitted into a single ring; both were made alike. 30So there were eight frames and sixteen silver bases—two under each frame.

31They also made crossbars of acacia wood: five for the frames on one side of the tabernacle, 32five for those on the other side, and five for the frames on the west, at the far end of the tabernacle. 33They made the centre crossbar so that it extended from end to end at the middle of the frames. 34They overlaid the frames with gold and made gold rings to hold the crossbars. They also overlaid the crossbars with gold.

35They made the curtain of blue, purple and scarlet yarn and finely twisted linen, with cherubim worked into it by a skilled craftsman. 36They made four posts of acacia wood for it and overlaid them with gold. They made gold hooks for them and cast their four silver bases. 37For the entrance to the tent they made a curtain of blue, purple and scarlet yarn and finely twisted linen—the work of an embroiderer; 38and they made five posts with hooks for them. They overlaid the tops of the posts and their bands with gold and made their five bases of bronze.

NEW TESTAMENT READING
Mark 7:31–8:13

The Healing of a Deaf and Mute Man

31Then Jesus left the vicinity of Tyre and went through Sidon, down to the Sea of Galilee and into the region of the Decapolis. 32There some people brought to him a man who was deaf and could hardly talk, and they begged him to place his hand on the man.

33After he took him aside, away from the crowd, Jesus put his fingers into the man's ears. Then he spat and touched the man's tongue. 34He looked up to heaven and with a deep sigh said to him, *"Ephphatha!"* (which means, "Be opened!"). 35At this, the man's ears were opened, his tongue was loosened and he began to speak plainly.

36Jesus commanded them not to tell anyone. But the more he did so, the more they kept talking about it. 37People were overwhelmed with amazement. "He has done everything well," they said. "He even makes the deaf hear and the mute speak."

Jesus Feeds the Four Thousand

8 During those days another large crowd gathered. Since they had nothing to eat, Jesus called his disciples to him and said, 2"I have compassion for these people; they have already been with me three days and have nothing to eat. 3If I send them home hungry, they will collapse on the way, because some of them have come a long distance."

4His disciples answered, "But where in this remote place can anyone get enough bread to feed them?"

5"How many loaves do you have?" Jesus asked.

"Seven," they replied.

6He told the crowd to sit down on the ground. When he had taken the seven loaves and given thanks, he broke them and gave them to his disciples to set before the people, and they did so. 7They had a few small fish as well; he gave thanks for them also and told the disciples to distribute them. 8The people ate and were satisfied. Afterwards the disciples picked up seven basketfuls of broken pieces that were left over. 9About four thousand men were present. And having sent them away, 10he got into the boat with his disciples and went to the region of Dalmanutha.

11The Pharisees came and began to question Jesus. To test him, they asked him for a sign from heaven. 12He sighed deeply and said, "Why does this generation ask for a miraculous sign? I tell you

the truth, no sign will be given to it."
13Then he left them, got back into the
boat and crossed to the other side.

READING FROM PSALMS
Psalm 25:16–22

16Turn to me and be gracious to me,
    for I am lonely and afflicted.
17The troubles of my heart have
        multiplied;
    free me from my anguish.

18Look upon my affliction and my
        distress
    and take away all my sins.
19See how my enemies have increased
    and how fiercely they hate me!
20Guard my life and rescue me;
    let me not be put to shame,
    for I take refuge in you.
21May integrity and uprightness protect
        me,
    because my hope is in you.

22Redeem Israel, O God,
    from all their troubles!

FEBRUARY 25   DAY 56

OLD TESTAMENT READING
Exodus 37:1–38:31

The Ark

37 Bezalel made the ark of acacia
wood—two and a half cubits
long, a cubit and a half wide, and a cubit
and a half high. 2He overlaid it with pure
gold, both inside and out, and made
a gold moulding around it. 3He cast
four gold rings for it and fastened them
to its four feet, with two rings on one
side and two rings on the other. 4Then
he made poles of acacia wood and overlaid them with gold. 5And he inserted
the poles into the rings on the sides of
the ark to carry it.
6He made the atonement cover of
pure gold—two and a half cubits long
and a cubit and a half wide. 7Then he
made two cherubim out of hammered
gold at the ends of the cover. 8He made
one cherub on one end and the second
cherub on the other; at the two ends he
made them of one piece with the cover.
9The cherubim had their wings spread
upwards, overshadowing the cover with
them. The cherubim faced each other,
looking towards the cover.

The Table

10They made the table of acacia wood
—two cubits long, a cubit wide, and a
cubit and a half high. 11Then they overlaid it with pure gold and made a gold
moulding around it. 12They also made
around it a rim a handbreadth wide and
put a gold moulding on the rim. 13They
cast four gold rings for the table and
fastened them to the four corners,
where the four legs were. 14The rings
were put close to the rim to hold the
poles used in carrying the table. 15The
poles for carrying the table were made
of acacia wood and were overlaid with
gold. 16And they made from pure gold
the articles for the table—its plates and
dishes and bowls and its pitchers for the
pouring out of drink offerings.

The Lampstand

17They made the lampstand of pure
gold and hammered it out, base and
shaft; its flowerlike cups, buds and blossoms were of one piece with it. 18Six
branches extended from the sides of the
lampstand—three on one side and
three on the other. 19Three cups shaped

like almond flowers with buds and blossoms were on one branch, three on the next branch and the same for all six branches extending from the lampstand. 20And on the lampstand were four cups shaped like almond flowers with buds and blossoms. 21One bud was under the first pair of branches extending from the lampstand, a second bud under the second pair, and a third bud under the third pair—six branches in all. 22The buds and the branches were all of one piece with the lampstand, hammered out of pure gold.

23They made its seven lamps, as well as its wick trimmers and trays, of pure gold. 24They made the lampstand and all its accessories from one talent of pure gold.

The Altar of Incense

25They made the altar of incense out of acacia wood. It was square, a cubit long and a cubit wide, and two cubits high—its horns of one piece with it. 26They overlaid the top and all the sides and the horns with pure gold, and made a gold moulding around it. 27They made two gold rings below the moulding—two on opposite sides—to hold the poles used to carry it. 28They made the poles of acacia wood and overlaid them with gold.

29They also made the sacred anointing oil and the pure, fragrant incense —the work of a perfumer.

The Altar of Burnt Offering

38 They built the altar of burnt offering of acacia wood, three cubits high; it was square, five cubits long and five cubits wide. 2They made a horn at each of the four corners, so that the horns and the altar were of one piece, and they overlaid the altar with bronze. 3They made all its utensils of bronze—its pots, shovels, sprinkling bowls, meat forks and firepans. 4They made a grating for the altar, a bronze

network, to be under its ledge, halfway up the altar. 5They cast bronze rings to hold the poles for the four corners of the bronze grating. 6They made the poles of acacia wood and overlaid them with bronze. 7They inserted the poles into the rings so they would be on the sides of the altar for carrying it. They made it hollow, out of boards.

Basin for Washing

8They made the bronze basin and its bronze stand from the mirrors of the women who served at the entrance to the Tent of Meeting.

The Courtyard

9Next they made the courtyard. The south side was a hundred cubits long and had curtains of finely twisted linen, 10with twenty posts and twenty bronze bases, and with silver hooks and bands on the posts. 11The north side was also a hundred cubits long and had twenty posts and twenty bronze bases, with silver hooks and bands on the posts.

12The west end was fifty cubits wide and had curtains, with ten posts and ten bases, with silver hooks and bands on the posts. 13The east end, towards the sunrise, was also fifty cubits wide. 14Curtains fifteen cubits long were on one side of the entrance, with three posts and three bases, 15and curtains fifteen cubits long were on the other side of the entrance to the courtyard, with three posts and three bases. 16All the curtains around the courtyard were of finely twisted linen. 17The bases for the posts were bronze. The hooks and bands on the posts were silver, and their tops were overlaid with silver; so all the posts of the courtyard had silver bands.

18The curtain for the entrance to the courtyard was of blue, purple and scarlet yarn and finely twisted linen—the work of an embroiderer. It was twenty cubits long and, like the curtains of the courtyard, five cubits high, 19with four posts and four bronze bases. Their hooks and bands were silver, and their tops were overlaid with silver. ²⁰All the tent pegs of the tabernacle and of the surrounding courtyard were bronze.

The Materials Used

²¹These are the amounts of the materials used for the tabernacle, the tabernacle of the Testimony, which were recorded at Moses' command by the Levites under the direction of Ithamar son of Aaron, the priest. ²²(Bezalel son of Uri, the son of Hur, of the tribe of Judah, made everything the LORD commanded Moses; ²³with him was Oholiab son of Ahisamach, of the tribe of Dan —a craftsman and designer, and an embroiderer in blue, purple and scarlet yarn and fine linen.) ²⁴The total amount of the gold from the wave offering used for all the work on the sanctuary was 29 talents and 730 shekels, according to the sanctuary shekel.

²⁵The silver obtained from those of the community who were counted in the census was 100 talents and 1,775 shekels, according to the sanctuary shekel—²⁶one beka per person, that is, half a shekel, according to the sanctuary shekel, from everyone who had crossed over to those counted, twenty years old or more, a total of 603,550 men. ²⁷The 100 talents of silver were used to cast the bases for the sanctuary and for the curtain—100 bases from the 100 talents, one talent for each base. ²⁸They used the 1,775 shekels to make the hooks for the posts, to overlay the tops of the posts, and to make their bands.

²⁹The bronze from the wave offering was 70 talents and 2,400 shekels. ³⁰They used it to make the bases for the entrance to the Tent of Meeting, the bronze altar with its bronze grating and all its utensils, ³¹the bases for the surrounding courtyard and those for its entrance and all the tent pegs for the tabernacle and those for the surrounding courtyard.

NEW TESTAMENT READING
Mark 8:14–9:1

The Yeast of the Pharisees and Herod

¹⁴The disciples had forgotten to bring bread, except for one loaf they had with them in the boat. ¹⁵"Be careful," Jesus warned them. "Watch out for the yeast of the Pharisees and that of Herod."

¹⁶They discussed this with one another and said, "It is because we have no bread."

¹⁷Aware of their discussion, Jesus asked them: "Why are you talking about having no bread? Do you still not see or understand? Are your hearts hardened? ¹⁸Do you have eyes but fail to see, and ears but fail to hear? And don't you remember? ¹⁹When I broke the five loaves for the five thousand, how many basketfuls of pieces did you pick up?"

"Twelve," they replied.

²⁰"And when I broke the seven loaves for the four thousand, how many basketfuls of pieces did you pick up?"

They answered, "Seven."

²¹He said to them, "Do you still not understand?"

The Healing of a Blind Man at Bethsaida

²²They came to Bethsaida, and some people brought a blind man and begged Jesus to touch him. ²³He took the blind man by the hand and led him outside the village. When he had spat on the man's eyes and put his hands on him, Jesus asked, "Do you see anything?"

²⁴He looked up and said, "I see people; they look like trees walking around."

²⁵Once more Jesus put his hands on the man's eyes. Then his eyes were opened, his sight was restored, and he saw everything clearly. ²⁶Jesus sent him home, saying, "Don't go into the village."

Peter's Confession of Christ

²⁷Jesus and his disciples went on to the villages around Caesarea Philippi.

On the way he asked them, "Who do people say I am?"

²⁸They replied, "Some say John the Baptist; others say Elijah; and still others, one of the prophets."

²⁹"But what about you?" he asked. "Who do you say I am?"

Peter answered, "You are the Christ."

³⁰Jesus warned them not to tell anyone about him.

Jesus Predicts His Death

³¹He then began to teach them that the Son of Man must suffer many things and be rejected by the elders, chief priests and teachers of the law, and that he must be killed and after three days rise again. ³²He spoke plainly about this, and Peter took him aside and began to rebuke him.

³³But when Jesus turned and looked at his disciples, he rebuked Peter. "Get behind me, Satan!" he said. "You do not have in mind the things of God, but the things of men."

³⁴Then he called the crowd to him along with his disciples and said: "If anyone would come after me, he must deny himself and take up his cross and follow me. ³⁵For whoever wants to save his life will lose it, but whoever loses his life for me and for the gospel will save it. ³⁶What good is it for a man to gain the whole world, yet forfeit his soul? ³⁷Or what can a man give in exchange for his soul? ³⁸If anyone is ashamed of me and my words in this adulterous and sinful generation, the Son of Man will be ashamed of him when he comes in his Father's glory with the holy angels."

9 And he said to them, "I tell you the truth, some who are standing here will not taste death before they see the kingdom of God come with power."

READING FROM PROVERBS
Proverbs 6:1–11

Warnings Against Folly

6 My son, if you have put up
  security for your neighbour,
   if you have struck hands in pledge
     for another,
²if you have been trapped by what you
     said,
   ensnared by the words of your
     mouth,
³then do this, my son, to free
     yourself,
   since you have fallen into your
     neighbour's hands:
 Go and humble yourself;
   press your plea with your
     neighbour!
⁴Allow no sleep to your eyes,
   no slumber to your eyelids.
⁵Free yourself, like a gazelle from the
     hand of the hunter,
   like a bird from the snare of the
     fowler.

⁶Go to the ant, you sluggard;
   consider its ways and be wise!
⁷It has no commander,
   no overseer or ruler,
⁸yet it stores its provisions in summer
   and gathers its food at harvest.

⁹How long will you lie there, you
     sluggard?
   When will you get up from your
     sleep?
¹⁰A little sleep, a little slumber,
   a little folding of the hands to
     rest—
¹¹and poverty will come on you like a
     bandit
   and scarcity like an armed man.

OLD TESTAMENT READING
Exodus 39:1–40:38

The Priestly Garments

39 From the blue, purple and scarlet yarn they made woven garments for ministering in the sanctuary. They also made sacred garments for Aaron, as the LORD commanded Moses.

The Ephod

²They made the ephod of gold, and of blue, purple and scarlet yarn, and of finely twisted linen. ³They hammered out thin sheets of gold and cut strands to be worked into the blue, purple and scarlet yarn and fine linen—the work of a skilled craftsman. ⁴They made shoulder pieces for the ephod, which were attached to two of its corners, so that it could be fastened. ⁵Its skilfully woven waistband was like it—of one piece with the ephod and made with gold, and with blue, purple and scarlet yarn, and with finely twisted linen, as the LORD commanded Moses.

⁶They mounted the onyx stones in gold filigree settings and engraved them like a seal with the names of the sons of Israel. ⁷Then they fastened them on the shoulder pieces of the ephod as memorial stones for the sons of Israel, as the LORD commanded Moses.

The Breastpiece

⁸They fashioned the breastpiece—the work of a skilled craftsman. They made it like the ephod: of gold, and of blue, purple and scarlet yarn, and of finely twisted linen. ⁹It was square—a span long and a span wide—and folded double. ¹⁰Then they mounted four rows of precious stones on it. In the first row there was a ruby, a topaz and a beryl; ¹¹in the second row a turquoise, a sapphire and an emerald; ¹²in the third row a jacinth, an agate and an amethyst; ¹³in the fourth row a chrysolite, an onyx and a jasper. They were mounted in gold filigree settings. ¹⁴There were twelve stones, one for each of the names of the sons of Israel, each engraved like a seal with the name of one of the twelve tribes.

¹⁵For the breastpiece they made braided chains of pure gold, like a rope. ¹⁶They made two gold filigree settings and two gold rings, and fastened the rings to two of the corners of the breastpiece. ¹⁷They fastened the two gold chains to the rings at the corners of the breastpiece, ¹⁸and the other ends of the chains to the two settings, attaching them to the shoulder pieces of the ephod at the front. ¹⁹They made two gold rings and attached them to the other two corners of the breastpiece on the inside edge next to the ephod. ²⁰Then they made two more gold rings and attached them to the bottom of the shoulder pieces on the front of the ephod, close to the seam just above the waistband of the ephod. ²¹They tied the rings of the breastpiece to the rings of the ephod with blue cord, connecting it to the waistband so that the breastpiece would not swing out from the ephod—as the LORD commanded Moses.

Other Priestly Garments

²²They made the robe of the ephod entirely of blue cloth—the work of a weaver—²³with an opening in the centre of the robe like the opening of a collar, and a band around this opening, so that it would not tear. ²⁴They made pomegranates of blue, purple and scarlet yarn and finely twisted linen around the hem of the robe. ²⁵And they made bells of pure gold and attached them

around the hem between the pomegranates. [26]The bells and pomegranates alternated around the hem of the robe to be worn for ministering, as the LORD commanded Moses.

[27]For Aaron and his sons, they made tunics of fine linen—the work of a weaver—[28]and the turban of fine linen, the linen headbands and the undergarments of finely twisted linen. [29]The sash was of finely twisted linen and blue, purple and scarlet yarn—the work of an embroiderer—as the LORD commanded Moses.

[30]They made the plate, the sacred diadem, out of pure gold and engraved on it, like an inscription on a seal: HOLY TO THE LORD. [31]Then they fastened a blue cord to it to attach it to the turban, as the LORD commanded Moses.

Moses Inspects the Tabernacle

[32]So all the work on the tabernacle, the Tent of Meeting, was completed. The Israelites did everything just as the LORD commanded Moses. [33]Then they brought the tabernacle to Moses: the tent and all its furnishings, its clasps, frames, crossbars, posts and bases; [34]the covering of ram skins dyed red, the covering of hides of sea cows and the shielding curtain; [35]the ark of the Testimony with its poles and the atonement cover; [36]the table with all its articles and the bread of the Presence; [37]the pure gold lampstand with its row of lamps and all its accessories, and the oil for the light; [38]the gold altar, the anointing oil, the fragrant incense, and the curtain for the entrance to the tent; [39]the bronze altar with its bronze grating, its poles and all its utensils; the basin with its stand; [40]the curtains of the courtyard with its posts and bases, and the curtain for the entrance to the courtyard; the ropes and tent pegs for the courtyard; all the furnishings for the tabernacle, the Tent of Meeting; [41]and the woven garments worn for ministering in the sanctuary, both the sacred garments for Aaron the priest and the garments for his sons when serving as priests.

[42]The Israelites had done all the work just as the LORD had commanded Moses. [43]Moses inspected the work and saw that they had done it just as the LORD had commanded. So Moses blessed them.

Setting Up the Tabernacle

40 Then the LORD said to Moses: [2]"Set up the tabernacle, the Tent of Meeting, on the first day of the first month. [3]Place the ark of the Testimony in it and shield the ark with the curtain. [4]Bring in the table and set out what belongs on it. Then bring in the lampstand and set up its lamps. [5]Place the gold altar of incense in front of the ark of the Testimony and put the curtain at the entrance to the tabernacle.

[6]"Place the altar of burnt offering in front of the entrance to the tabernacle, the Tent of Meeting; [7]place the basin between the Tent of Meeting and the altar and put water in it. [8]Set up the courtyard around it and put the curtain at the entrance to the courtyard.

[9]"Take the anointing oil and anoint the tabernacle and everything in it; consecrate it and all its furnishings, and it will be holy. [10]Then anoint the altar of burnt offering and all its utensils; consecrate the altar, and it will be most holy. [11]Anoint the basin and its stand and consecrate them.

[12]"Bring Aaron and his sons to the entrance to the Tent of Meeting and wash them with water. [13]Then dress Aaron in the sacred garments, anoint him and consecrate him so that he may serve me as priest. [14]Bring his sons and dress them in tunics. [15]Anoint them just as you anointed their father, so that they may serve me as priests. Their anointing will be to a priesthood that will continue for all generations to come." [16]Moses did everything just as the LORD commanded him.

[17]So the tabernacle was set up on the first day of the first month in the second year. [18]When Moses set up the tabernacle, he put the bases in place, erected

the frames, inserted the crossbars and set up the posts. 19Then he spread the tent over the tabernacle and put the covering over the tent, as the LORD commanded him.

20He took the Testimony and placed it in the ark, attached the poles to the ark and put the atonement cover over it. 21Then he brought the ark into the tabernacle and hung the shielding curtain and shielded the ark of the Testimony, as the LORD commanded him.

22Moses placed the table in the Tent of Meeting on the north side of the tabernacle outside the curtain 23and set out the bread on it before the LORD, as the LORD commanded him.

24He placed the lampstand in the Tent of Meeting opposite the table on the south side of the tabernacle 25and set up the lamps before the LORD, as the LORD commanded him.

26Moses placed the gold altar in the Tent of Meeting in front of the curtain 27and burned fragrant incense on it, as the LORD commanded him. 28Then he put up the curtain at the entrance to the tabernacle.

29He set the altar of burnt offering near the entrance to the tabernacle, the Tent of Meeting, and offered on it burnt offerings and grain offerings, as the LORD commanded him.

30He placed the basin between the Tent of Meeting and the altar and put water in it for washing, 31and Moses and Aaron and his sons used it to wash their hands and feet. 32They washed whenever they entered the Tent of Meeting or approached the altar, as the LORD commanded Moses.

33Then Moses set up the courtyard around the tabernacle and altar and put up the curtain at the entrance to the courtyard. And so Moses finished the work.

The Glory of the LORD

34Then the cloud covered the Tent of Meeting, and the glory of the LORD filled the tabernacle. 35Moses could not enter the Tent of Meeting because the cloud had settled upon it, and the glory of the LORD filled the tabernacle.

36In all the travels of the Israelites, whenever the cloud lifted from above the tabernacle, they would set out; 37but if the cloud did not lift, they did not set out—until the day it lifted. 38So the cloud of the LORD was over the tabernacle by day, and fire was in the cloud by night, in the sight of all the house of Israel during all their travels.

NEW TESTAMENT READING
Mark 9:2–32

The Transfiguration

2After six days Jesus took Peter, James and John with him and led them up a high mountain, where they were all alone. There he was transfigured before them. 3His clothes became dazzling white, whiter than anyone in the world could bleach them. 4And there appeared before them Elijah and Moses, who were talking with Jesus.

5Peter said to Jesus, "Rabbi, it is good for us to be here. Let us put up three shelters—one for you, one for Moses and one for Elijah." 6(He did not know what to say, they were so frightened.)

7Then a cloud appeared and enveloped them, and a voice came from the cloud: "This is my Son, whom I love. Listen to him!"

8Suddenly, when they looked round, they no longer saw anyone with them except Jesus.

9As they were coming down the mountain, Jesus gave them orders not to tell anyone what they had seen until the Son of Man had risen from the dead. 10They kept the matter to themselves, discussing what "rising from the dead" meant.

11And they asked him, "Why do the teachers of the law say that Elijah must come first?"

12Jesus replied, "To be sure, Elijah

does come first, and restores all things. Why then is it written that the Son of Man must suffer much and be rejected? 13But I tell you, Elijah has come, and they have done to him everything they wished, just as it is written about him."

The Healing of a Boy With an Evil Spirit

14When they came to the other disciples, they saw a large crowd around them and the teachers of the law arguing with them. 15As soon as all the people saw Jesus, they were overwhelmed with wonder and ran to greet him.

16"What are you arguing with them about?" he asked.

17A man in the crowd answered, "Teacher, I brought you my son, who is possessed by a spirit that has robbed him of speech. 18Whenever it seizes him, it throws him to the ground. He foams at the mouth, gnashes his teeth and becomes rigid. I asked your disciples to drive out the spirit, but they could not."

19"O unbelieving generation," Jesus replied, "how long shall I stay with you? How long shall I put up with you? Bring the boy to me."

20So they brought him. When the spirit saw Jesus, it immediately threw the boy into a convulsion. He fell to the ground and rolled around, foaming at the mouth.

21Jesus asked the boy's father, "How long has he been like this?"

"From childhood," he answered. 22"It has often thrown him into fire or water to kill him. But if you can do anything, take pity on us and help us."

23"'If you can'?" said Jesus. "Everything is possible for him who believes."

24Immediately the boy's father exclaimed, "I do believe; help me overcome my unbelief!"

25When Jesus saw that a crowd was running to the scene, he rebuked the evil spirit. "You deaf and mute spirit," he said, "I command you, come out of him and never enter him again."

26The spirit shrieked, convulsed him violently and came out. The boy looked so much like a corpse that many said, "He's dead." 27But Jesus took him by the hand and lifted him to his feet, and he stood up.

28After Jesus had gone indoors, his disciples asked him privately, "Why couldn't we drive it out?"

29He replied, "This kind can come out only by prayer."

30They left that place and passed through Galilee. Jesus did not want anyone to know where they were, 31because he was teaching his disciples. He said to them, "The Son of Man is going to be betrayed into the hands of men. They will kill him, and after three days he will rise." 32But they did not understand what he meant and were afraid to ask him about it.

READING FROM PSALMS
Psalm 26:1–12

Of David.

1Vindicate me, O LORD,
  for I have led a blameless life;
I have trusted in the LORD
  without wavering.

2Test me, O LORD, and try me,
  examine my heart and my mind;
3for your love is ever before me,
  and I walk continually in your
    truth.

4I do not sit with deceitful men,
  nor do I consort with hypocrites;
5I abhor the assembly of evildoers
  and refuse to sit with the wicked.
6I wash my hands in innocence,
  and go about your altar, O LORD,
7proclaiming aloud your praise
  and telling of all your wonderful
    deeds.

8I love the house where you live, O
    LORD,
  the place where your glory dwells.

⁹Do not take away my soul along with
  sinners,
  my life with bloodthirsty men,
¹⁰in whose hands are wicked schemes,
  whose right hands are full of
  bribes.

¹¹But I lead a blameless life;
  redeem me and be merciful to me.

¹²My feet stand on level ground;
  in the great assembly I will praise
  the LORD.

FEBRUARY 27 DAY 58

OLD TESTAMENT READING
Leviticus 1:1–3:17

The Burnt Offering

1 The LORD called to Moses and
spoke to him from the Tent of
Meeting. He said, ²"Speak to the
Israelites and say to them: 'When any of
you brings an offering to the LORD,
bring as your offering an animal from
either the herd or the flock.

³"'If the offering is a burnt offering
from the herd, he is to offer a male
without defect. He must present it at the
entrance to the Tent of Meeting so that
it will be acceptable to the LORD. ⁴He is
to lay his hand on the head of the burnt
offering, and it will be accepted on his
behalf to make atonement for him. ⁵He
is to slaughter the young bull before the
LORD, and then Aaron's sons the priests
shall bring the blood and sprinkle it
against the altar on all sides at the entrance to the Tent of Meeting. ⁶He is to
skin the burnt offering and cut it into
pieces. ⁷The sons of Aaron the priest
are to put fire on the altar and arrange
wood on the fire. ⁸Then Aaron's sons
the priests shall arrange the pieces, including the head and the fat, on the
burning wood that is on the altar. ⁹He is
to wash the inner parts and the legs with
water, and the priest is to burn all of it
on the altar. It is a burnt offering, an
offering made by fire, an aroma pleasing to the LORD.

¹⁰"'If the offering is a burnt offering
from the flock, from either the sheep or
the goats, he is to offer a male without
defect. ¹¹He is to slaughter it at the
north side of the altar before the LORD,
and Aaron's sons the priests shall
sprinkle its blood against the altar on all
sides. ¹²He is to cut it into pieces, and
the priest shall arrange them, including
the head and the fat, on the burning
wood that is on the altar. ¹³He is to wash
the inner parts and the legs with water,
and the priest is to bring all of it and
burn it on the altar. It is a burnt offering, an offering made by fire, an aroma
pleasing to the LORD.

¹⁴"'If the offering to the LORD is a
burnt offering of birds, he is to offer a
dove or a young pigeon. ¹⁵The priest
shall bring it to the altar, wring off the
head and burn it on the altar; its blood
shall be drained out on the side of the
altar. ¹⁶He is to remove the crop with its
contents and throw it to the east side of
the altar, where the ashes are. ¹⁷He
shall tear it open by the wings, not
severing it completely, and then the
priest shall burn it on the wood that is on
the fire on the altar. It is a burnt offering, an offering made by fire, an aroma
pleasing to the LORD.

The Grain Offering

2 "'When someone brings a grain
offering to the LORD, his offering is
to be of fine flour. He is to pour oil on it,

put incense on it ²and take it to Aaron's sons the priests. The priest shall take a handful of the fine flour and oil, together with all the incense, and burn this as a memorial portion on the altar, an offering made by fire, an aroma pleasing to the LORD. ³The rest of the grain offering belongs to Aaron and his sons; it is a most holy part of the offerings made to the LORD by fire.

⁴"'If you bring a grain offering baked in an oven, it is to consist of fine flour: cakes made without yeast and mixed with oil, or wafers made without yeast and spread with oil. ⁵If your grain offering is prepared on a griddle, it is to be made of fine flour mixed with oil, and without yeast. ⁶Crumble it and pour oil on it; it is a grain offering. ⁷If your grain offering is cooked in a pan, it is to be made of fine flour and oil. ⁸Bring the grain offering made of these things to the LORD; present it to the priest, who shall take it to the altar. ⁹He shall take out the memorial portion from the grain offering and burn it on the altar as an offering made by fire, an aroma pleasing to the LORD. ¹⁰The rest of the grain offering belongs to Aaron and his sons; it is a most holy part of the offerings made to the LORD by fire.

¹¹"'Every grain offering you bring to the LORD must be made without yeast, for you are not to burn any yeast or honey in an offering made to the LORD by fire. ¹²You may bring them to the LORD as an offering of the firstfruits, but they are not to be offered on the altar as a pleasing aroma. ¹³Season all your grain offerings with salt. Do not leave the salt of the covenant of your God out of your grain offerings; add salt to all your offerings.

¹⁴"'If you bring a grain offering of firstfruits to the LORD, offer crushed heads of new grain roasted in the fire. ¹⁵Put oil and incense on it; it is a grain offering. ¹⁶The priest shall burn the memorial portion of the crushed grain and the oil, together with all the incense, as an offering made to the LORD by fire.

The Fellowship Offering

3 "'If someone's offering is a fellowship offering, and he offers an animal from the herd, whether male or female, he is to present before the LORD an animal without defect. ²He is to lay his hand on the head of his offering and slaughter it at the entrance to the Tent of Meeting. Then Aaron's sons the priests shall sprinkle the blood against the altar on all sides. ³From the fellowship offering he is to bring a sacrifice made to the LORD by fire: all the fat that covers the inner parts or is connected to them, ⁴both kidneys with the fat on them near the loins, and the covering of the liver, which he will remove with the kidneys. ⁵Then Aaron's sons are to burn it on the altar on top of the burnt offering that is on the burning wood, as an offering made by fire, an aroma pleasing to the LORD.

⁶"'If he offers an animal from the flock as a fellowship offering to the LORD, he is to offer a male or female without defect. ⁷If he offers a lamb, he is to present it before the LORD. ⁸He is to lay his hand on the head of his offering and slaughter it in front of the Tent of Meeting. Then Aaron's sons shall sprinkle its blood against the altar on all sides. ⁹From the fellowship offering he is to bring a sacrifice made to the LORD by fire: its fat, the entire fat tail cut off close to the backbone, all the fat that covers the inner parts or is connected to them, ¹⁰both kidneys with the fat on them near the loins, and the covering of the liver, which he will remove with the kidneys. ¹¹The priest shall burn them on the altar as food, an offering made to the LORD by fire.

¹²"'If his offering is a goat, he is to present it before the LORD. ¹³He is to lay his hand on its head and slaughter it in front of the Tent of Meeting. Then Aaron's sons shall sprinkle its blood against the altar on all sides. ¹⁴From what he offers he is to make this offering to the LORD by fire: all the fat that covers the inner parts or is connected to

them, 15both kidneys with the fat on them near the loins, and the covering of the liver, which he will remove with the kidneys. 16The priest shall burn them on the altar as food, an offering made by fire, a pleasing aroma. All the fat is the LORD's.

17" 'This is a lasting ordinance for the generations to come, wherever you live: You must not eat any fat or any blood.' "

NEW TESTAMENT READING
Mark 9:33–10:12

Who Is the Greatest?

33They came to Capernaum. When he was in the house, he asked them, "What were you arguing about on the road?" 34But they kept quiet because on the way they had argued about who was the greatest. 35Sitting down, Jesus called the Twelve and said, "If anyone wants to be first, he must be the very last, and the servant of all."

36He took a little child and had him stand among them. Taking him in his arms, he said to them, 37"Whoever welcomes one of these little children in my name welcomes me; and whoever welcomes me does not welcome me but the one who sent me."

Whoever Is Not Against Us Is for Us

38"Teacher," said John, "we saw a man driving out demons in your name and we told him to stop, because he was not one of us."

39"Do not stop him," Jesus said. "No-one who does a miracle in my name can in the next moment say anything bad about me, 40for whoever is not against us is for us. 41I tell you the truth, anyone who gives you a cup of water in my name because you belong to Christ will certainly not lose his reward.

Causing to Sin

42"And if anyone causes one of these little ones who believe in me to sin, it would be better for him to be thrown into the sea with a large millstone tied around his neck. 43If your hand causes you to sin, cut it off. It is better for you to enter life maimed than with two hands to go into hell, where the fire never goes out. 45And if your foot causes you to sin, cut it off. It is better for you to enter life crippled than to have two feet and be thrown into hell. 47And if your eye causes you to sin, pluck it out. It is better for you to enter the kingdom of God with one eye than to have two eyes and be thrown into hell, 48where

" 'their worm does not die,
    and the fire is not quenched.'

49Everyone will be salted with fire.

50"Salt is good, but if it loses its saltiness, how can you make it salty again? Have salt in yourselves, and be at peace with each other."

Divorce

10 Jesus then left that place and went into the region of Judea and across the Jordan. Again crowds of people came to him, and as was his custom, he taught them.

2Some Pharisees came and tested him by asking, "Is it lawful for a man to divorce his wife?"

3"What did Moses command you?" he replied.

4They said, "Moses permitted a man to write a certificate of divorce and send her away."

5"It was because your hearts were hard that Moses wrote you this law," Jesus replied. 6"But at the beginning of creation God 'made them male and female'. 7'For this reason a man will leave his father and mother and be united to his wife, 8and the two will become one flesh.' So they are no longer two, but one. ⁹Therefore what God has joined together, let man not separate."

¹⁰When they were in the house again, the disciples asked Jesus about this. ¹¹He answered, "Anyone who divorces his wife and marries another woman commits adultery against her. ¹²And if she divorces her husband and marries another man, she commits adultery."

READING FROM PSALMS
Psalm 27:1–6

Of David.

¹The LORD is my light and my
    salvation—
    whom shall I fear?
The LORD is the stronghold of my
    life—
    of whom shall I be afraid?
²When evil men advance against me
    to devour my flesh,
when my enemies and my foes attack
    me,

they will stumble and fall.
³Though an army besiege me,
    my heart will not fear;
though war break out against me,
    even then will I be confident.

⁴One thing I ask of the LORD,
    this is what I seek:
that I may dwell in the house of the
    LORD
    all the days of my life,
to gaze upon the beauty of the LORD
    and to seek him in his temple.
⁵For in the day of trouble
    he will keep me safe in his
        dwelling;
he will hide me in the shelter of his
        tabernacle
    and set me high upon a rock.
⁶Then my head will be exalted
    above the enemies who surround
        me;
at his tabernacle will I sacrifice with
        shouts of joy;
    I will sing and make music to the
        LORD.

DAY 59   # FEBRUARY 28

OLD TESTAMENT READING
Leviticus 4:1–5:13

The Sin Offering

4 The LORD said to Moses, ²"Say to the Israelites: 'When anyone sins unintentionally and does what is forbidden in any of the LORD's commands—

³"'If the anointed priest sins, bringing guilt on the people, he must bring to the LORD a young bull without defect as a sin offering for the sin he has committed. ⁴He is to present the bull at the entrance to the Tent of Meeting before the LORD. He is to lay his hand on its head and slaughter it before the LORD.

⁵Then the anointed priest shall take some of the bull's blood and carry it into the Tent of Meeting. ⁶He is to dip his finger into the blood and sprinkle some of it seven times before the LORD, in front of the curtain of the sanctuary. ⁷The priest shall then put some of the blood on the horns of the altar of fragrant incense that is before the LORD in the Tent of Meeting. The rest of the bull's blood he shall pour out at the base of the altar of burnt offering at the entrance to the Tent of Meeting. ⁸He shall remove all the fat from the bull of the sin offering—the fat that covers the inner parts or is connected to them, ⁹both kidneys with the fat on them near the loins, and the covering of the liver,

which he will remove with the kidneys —10just as the fat is removed from the ox sacrificed as a fellowship offering. Then the priest shall burn them on the altar of burnt offering. 11But the hide of the bull and all its flesh, as well as the head and legs, the inner parts and offal —12that is, all the rest of the bull—he must take outside the camp to a place ceremonially clean, where the ashes are thrown, and burn it in a wood fire on the ash heap.

13"If the whole Israelite community sins unintentionally and does what is forbidden in any of the LORD's commands, even though the community is unaware of the matter, they are guilty. 14When they become aware of the sin they committed, the assembly must bring a young bull as a sin offering and present it before the Tent of Meeting. 15The elders of the community are to lay their hands on the bull's head before the LORD, and the bull shall be slaughtered before the LORD. 16Then the anointed priest is to take some of the bull's blood into the Tent of Meeting. 17He shall dip his finger into the blood and sprinkle it before the LORD seven times in front of the curtain. 18He is to put some of the blood on the horns of the altar that is before the LORD in the Tent of Meeting. The rest of the blood he shall pour out at the base of the altar of burnt offering at the entrance to the Tent of Meeting. 19He shall remove all the fat from it and burn it on the altar, 20and do with this bull just as he did with the bull for the sin offering. In this way the priest will make atonement for them, and they will be forgiven. 21Then he shall take the bull outside the camp and burn it as he burned the first bull. This is the sin offering for the community.

22"When a leader sins unintentionally and does what is forbidden in any of the commands of the LORD his God, he is guilty. 23When he is made aware of the sin he committed, he must bring as his offering a male goat

without defect. 24He is to lay his hand on the goat's head and slaughter it at the place where the burnt offering is slaughtered before the LORD. It is a sin offering. 25Then the priest shall take some of the blood of the sin offering with his finger and put it on the horns of the altar of burnt offering and pour out the rest of the blood at the base of the altar. 26He shall burn all the fat on the altar as he burned the fat of the fellowship offering. In this way the priest will make atonement for the man's sin, and he will be forgiven.

27"If a member of the community sins unintentionally and does what is forbidden in any of the LORD's commands, he is guilty. 28When he is made aware of the sin he committed, he must bring as his offering for the sin he committed a female goat without defect. 29He is to lay his hand on the head of the sin offering and slaughter it at the place of the burnt offering. 30Then the priest is to take some of the blood with his finger and put it on the horns of the altar of burnt offering and pour out the rest of the blood at the base of the altar. 31He shall remove all the fat, just as the fat is removed from the fellowship offering, and the priest shall burn it on the altar as an aroma pleasing to the LORD. In this way the priest will make atonement for him, and he will be forgiven.

32"If he brings a lamb as his sin offering, he is to bring a female without defect. 33He is to lay his hand on its head and slaughter it for a sin offering at the place where the burnt offering is slaughtered. 34Then the priest shall take some of the blood of the sin offering with his finger and put it on the horns of the altar of burnt offering and pour out the rest of the blood at the base of the altar. 35He shall remove all the fat, just as the fat is removed from the lamb of the fellowship offering, and the priest shall burn it on the altar on top of the offerings made to the LORD by fire. In this way the priest will make atonement for him for the sin he has committed, and he will be forgiven.

5 " 'If a person sins because he does not speak up when he hears a public charge to testify regarding something he has seen or learned about, he will be held responsible.

2" 'Or if a person touches anything ceremonially unclean—whether the carcasses of unclean wild animals or of unclean livestock or of unclean creatures that move along the ground—even though he is unaware of it, he has become unclean and is guilty.

3" 'Or if he touches human uncleanness—anything that would make him unclean—even though he is unaware of it, when he learns of it he will be guilty.

4" 'Or if a person thoughtlessly takes an oath to do anything, whether good or evil—in any matter one might carelessly swear about—even though he is unaware of it, in any case when he learns of it he will be guilty.

5" 'When anyone is guilty in any of these ways, he must confess in what way he has sinned 6and, as a penalty for the sin he has committed, he must bring to the LORD a female lamb or goat from the flock as a sin offering; and the priest shall make atonement for him for his sin.

7" 'If he cannot afford a lamb, he is to bring two doves or two young pigeons to the LORD as a penalty for his sin—one for a sin offering and the other for a burnt offering. 8He is to bring them to the priest, who shall first offer the one for the sin offering. He is to wring its head from its neck, not severing it completely, 9and is to sprinkle some of the blood of the sin offering against the side of the altar; the rest of the blood must be drained out at the base of the altar. It is a sin offering. 10The priest shall then offer the other as a burnt offering in the prescribed way and make atonement for him for the sin he has committed, and he will be forgiven.

11" 'If, however, he cannot afford two doves or two young pigeons, he is to bring as an offering for his sin a tenth of an ephah of fine flour for a sin offering. He must not put oil or incense on it, because it is a sin offering. 12He is to bring it to the priest, who shall take a handful of it as a memorial portion and burn it on the altar on top of the offerings made to the LORD by fire. It is a sin offering. 13In this way the priest will make atonement for him for any of these sins he has committed, and he will be forgiven. The rest of the offering will belong to the priest, as in the case of the grain offering.' "

NEW TESTAMENT READING
Mark 10:13–31

The Little Children and Jesus

13People were bringing little children to Jesus to have him touch them, but the disciples rebuked them. 14When Jesus saw this, he was indignant. He said to them, "Let the little children come to me, and do not hinder them, for the kingdom of God belongs to such as these. 15I tell you the truth, anyone who will not receive the kingdom of God like a little child will never enter it." 16And he took the children in his arms, put his hands on them and blessed them.

The Rich Young Man

17As Jesus started on his way, a man ran up to him and fell on his knees before him. "Good teacher," he asked, "what must I do to inherit eternal life?"

18"Why do you call me good?" Jesus answered. "No-one is good—except God alone. 19You know the commandments: 'Do not murder, do not commit adultery, do not steal, do not give false testimony, do not defraud, honour your father and mother.' "

20"Teacher," he declared, "all these I have kept since I was a boy."

21Jesus looked at him and loved him. "One thing you lack," he said. "Go, sell everything you have and give to the poor, and you will have treasure in heaven. Then come, follow me."

²²At this the man's face fell. He went away sad, because he had great wealth.

²³Jesus looked around and said to his disciples, "How hard it is for the rich to enter the kingdom of God!" ²⁴The disciples were amazed at his words. But Jesus said again, "Children, how hard it is to enter the kingdom of God! ²⁵It is easier for a camel to go through the eye of a needle than for a rich man to enter the kingdom of God."

²⁶The disciples were even more amazed, and said to each other, "Who then can be saved?"

²⁷Jesus looked at them and said, "With man this is impossible, but not with God; all things are possible with God."

²⁸Peter said to him, "We have left everything to follow you!"

²⁹"I tell you the truth," Jesus replied, "no-one who has left home or brothers or sisters or mother or father or children or fields for me and the gospel ³⁰will fail to receive a hundred times as much in this present age (homes, brothers, sisters, mothers, children and fields—and with them, persecutions) and in the age to come, eternal life. ³¹But many who are first will be last, and the last first."

READING FROM PSALMS
Psalm 27:7–14

⁷Hear my voice when I call, O LORD;
  be merciful to me and answer me.
⁸My heart says of you, "Seek his
    face!"
  Your face, LORD, I will seek.
⁹Do not hide your face from me,
  do not turn your servant away in
    anger;
  you have been my helper.
Do not reject me or forsake me,
  O God my Saviour.
¹⁰Though my father and mother
    forsake me,
  the LORD will receive me.
¹¹Teach me your way, O LORD;
  lead me in a straight path
  because of my oppressors.
¹²Do not hand me over to the desire of
    my foes,
  for false witnesses rise up against
    me,
  breathing out violence.

¹³I am still confident of this:
  I will see the goodness of the LORD
  in the land of the living.
¹⁴Wait for the LORD;
  be strong and take heart
  and wait for the LORD.

MARCH 1   DAY 60

OLD TESTAMENT READING
Leviticus 5:14–7:10

The Guilt Offering

¹⁴The LORD said to Moses: ¹⁵"When a person commits a violation and sins unintentionally in regard to any of the LORD's holy things, he is to bring to the LORD as a penalty a ram from the flock, one without defect and of the proper value in silver, according to the sanctuary shekel. It is a guilt offering. ¹⁶He

must make restitution for what he has failed to do in regard to the holy things, add a fifth of the value to that and give it all to the priest, who will make atonement for him with the ram as a guilt offering, and he will be forgiven.

¹⁷"If a person sins and does what is forbidden in any of the LORD's commands, even though he does not know it, he is guilty and will be held responsible. ¹⁸He is to bring to the priest as a guilt offering a ram from the flock, one without defect and of the proper value.

In this way the priest will make atonement for him for the wrong he has committed unintentionally, and he will be forgiven. [19]It is a guilt offering; he has been guilty of wrongdoing against the LORD."

6 The LORD said to Moses: [2]"If anyone sins and is unfaithful to the LORD by deceiving his neighbour about something entrusted to him or left in his care or stolen, or if he cheats him, [3]or if he finds lost property and lies about it, or if he swears falsely, or if he commits any such sin that people may do— [4]when he thus sins and becomes guilty, he must return what he has stolen or taken by extortion, or what was entrusted to him, or the lost property he found, [5]or whatever it was he swore falsely about. He must make restitution in full, add a fifth of the value to it and give it all to the owner on the day he presents his guilt offering. [6]And as a penalty he must bring to the priest, that is, to the LORD, his guilt offering, a ram from the flock, one without defect and of the proper value. [7]In this way the priest will make atonement for him before the LORD, and he will be forgiven for any of these things he did that made him guilty."

The Burnt Offering

[8]The LORD said to Moses: [9]"Give Aaron and his sons this command: 'These are the regulations for the burnt offering: The burnt offering is to remain on the altar hearth throughout the night, till morning, and the fire must be kept burning on the altar. [10]The priest shall then put on his linen clothes, with linen undergarments next to his body, and shall remove the ashes of the burnt offering that the fire has consumed on the altar and place them beside the altar. [11]Then he is to take off these clothes and put on others, and carry the ashes outside the camp to a place that is ceremonially clean. [12]The fire on the altar must be kept burning; it must not

go out. Every morning the priest is to add firewood and arrange the burnt offering on the fire and burn the fat of the fellowship offerings on it. [13]The fire must be kept burning on the altar continuously; it must not go out.

The Grain Offering

[14]"'These are the regulations for the grain offering: Aaron's sons are to bring it before the LORD, in front of the altar. [15]The priest is to take a handful of fine flour and oil, together with all the incense on the grain offering, and burn the memorial portion on the altar as an aroma pleasing to the LORD. [16]Aaron and his sons shall eat the rest of it, but it is to be eaten without yeast in a holy place; they are to eat it in the courtyard of the Tent of Meeting. [17]It must not be baked with yeast; I have given it as their share of the offerings made to me by fire. Like the sin offering and the guilt offering, it is most holy. [18]Any male descendant of Aaron may eat it. It is his regular share of the offerings made to the LORD by fire for the generations to come. Whatever touches it will become holy.'"

[19]The LORD also said to Moses, [20]"This is the offering Aaron and his sons are to bring to the LORD on the day he is anointed: a tenth of an ephah of fine flour as a regular grain offering, half of it in the morning and half in the evening. [21]Prepare it with oil on a griddle; bring it well-mixed and present the grain offering broken in pieces as an aroma pleasing to the LORD. [22]The son who is to succeed him as anointed priest shall prepare it. It is the LORD's regular share and is to be burned completely. [23]Every grain offering of a priest shall be burned completely; it must not be eaten."

The Sin Offering

[24]The LORD said to Moses, [25]"Say to Aaron and his sons: 'These are the

regulations for the sin offering: The sin offering is to be slaughtered before the LORD in the place where the burnt offering is slaughtered; it is most holy. 26The priest who offers it shall eat it; it is to be eaten in a holy place, in the courtyard of the Tent of Meeting. 27Whatever touches any of the flesh will become holy, and if any of the blood is spattered on a garment, you must wash it in a holy place. 28The clay pot that the meat is cooked in must be broken; but if it is cooked in a bronze pot, the pot is to be scoured and rinsed with water. 29Any male in a priest's family may eat it; it is most holy. 30But any sin offering whose blood is brought into the Tent of Meeting to make atonement in the Holy Place must not be eaten; it must be burned.

The Guilt Offering

7 "'These are the regulations for the guilt offering, which is most holy: 2The guilt offering is to be slaughtered in the place where the burnt offering is slaughtered, and its blood is to be sprinkled against the altar on all sides. 3All its fat shall be offered: the fat tail and the fat that covers the inner parts, 4both kidneys with the fat on them near the loins, and the covering of the liver, which is to be removed with the kidneys. 5The priest shall burn them on the altar as an offering made to the LORD by fire. It is a guilt offering. 6Any male in a priest's family may eat it, but it must be eaten in a holy place; it is most holy.

7"'The same law applies to both the sin offering and the guilt offering: They belong to the priest who makes atonement with them. 8The priest who offers a burnt offering for anyone may keep its hide for himself. 9Every grain offering baked in an oven or cooked in a pan or on a griddle belongs to the priest who offers it, 10and every grain offering, whether mixed with oil or dry, belongs equally to all the sons of Aaron.

NEW TESTAMENT READING
Mark 10:32–52

Jesus Again Predicts His Death

32They were on their way up to Jerusalem, with Jesus leading the way, and the disciples were astonished, while those who followed were afraid. Again he took the Twelve aside and told them what was going to happen to him. 33"We are going up to Jerusalem," he said, "and the Son of Man will be betrayed to the chief priests and teachers of the law. They will condemn him to death and will hand him over to the Gentiles, 34who will mock him and spit on him, flog him and kill him. Three days later he will rise."

The Request of James and John

35Then James and John, the sons of Zebedee, came to him. "Teacher," they said, "we want you to do for us whatever we ask."
36"What do you want me to do for you?" he asked.
37They replied, "Let one of us sit at your right and the other at your left in your glory."
38"You don't know what you are asking," Jesus said. "Can you drink the cup I drink or be baptised with the baptism I am baptised with?"
39"We can," they answered.
Jesus said to them, "You will drink the cup I drink and be baptised with the baptism I am baptised with, 40but to sit at my right or left is not for me to grant. These places belong to those for whom they have been prepared."
41When the ten heard about this, they became indignant with James and John. 42Jesus called them together and said, "You know that those who are regarded as rulers of the Gentiles lord it over them, and their high officials exercise authority over them. 43Not so with you. Instead, whoever wants to become great among you must be your servant, 44and whoever wants to be first must be

slave of all. 45For even the Son of Man did not come to be served, but to serve, and to give his life as a ransom for many."

Blind Bartimaeus Receives His Sight

46Then they came to Jericho. As Jesus and his disciples, together with a large crowd, were leaving the city, a blind man, Bartimaeus (that is, the Son of Timaeus), was sitting by the roadside begging. 47When he heard that it was Jesus of Nazareth, he began to shout, "Jesus, Son of David, have mercy on me!"

48Many rebuked him and told him to be quiet, but he shouted all the more, "Son of David, have mercy on me!"

49Jesus stopped and said, "Call him."

So they called to the blind man, "Cheer up! On your feet! He's calling you." 50Throwing his cloak aside, he jumped to his feet and came to Jesus.

51"What do you want me to do for you?" Jesus asked him.

The blind man said, "Rabbi, I want to see."

52"Go," said Jesus, "your faith has healed you." Immediately he received his sight and followed Jesus along the road.

READING FROM PROVERBS
Proverbs 6:12–19

12A scoundrel and villain,
     who goes about with a corrupt
          mouth,
13   who winks with his eye,
     signals with his feet
     and motions with his fingers,
14   who plots evil with deceit in his
          heart—
     he always stirs up dissension.
15Therefore disaster will overtake him
          in an instant;
     he will suddenly be destroyed—
          without remedy.

16There are six things the LORD
          hates,
     seven that are detestable to him:
17   haughty eyes,
     a lying tongue,
     hands that shed innocent
          blood,
18   a heart that devises wicked
          schemes,
     feet that are quick to rush into
          evil,
19   a false witness who pours out lies
     and a man who stirs up
          dissension among brothers.

DAY 61

MARCH 2

OLD TESTAMENT READING
Leviticus 7:11–8:36

The Fellowship Offering

11"'These are the regulations for the fellowship offering a person may present to the LORD:

12"'If he offers it as an expression of thankfulness, then along with this thank-offering he is to offer cakes of bread made without yeast and mixed with oil, wafers made without yeast and spread with oil, and cakes of fine flour well-kneaded and mixed with oil. 13Along with his fellowship offering of thanksgiving he is to present an offering with cakes of bread made with yeast. 14He is to bring one of each kind as an offering, a contribution to the LORD; it belongs to the priest who sprinkles the blood of the fellowship offerings. 15The meat of his fellowship offering of thanksgiving must be eaten on the day it is offered; he must leave none of it till morning.

16"'If, however, his offering is the result of a vow or is a freewill offering, the sacrifice shall be eaten on the day he offers it, but anything left over may be eaten on the next day. 17Any meat of the sacrifice left over till the third day must be burned up. 18If any meat of the fellowship offering is eaten on the third day, it will not be accepted. It will not be credited to the one who offered it, for it is impure; the person who eats any of it will be held responsible.

19"'Meat that touches anything ceremonially unclean must not be eaten; it must be burned up. As for other meat, anyone ceremonially clean may eat it. 20But if anyone who is unclean eats any meat of the fellowship offering belonging to the LORD, that person must be cut off from his people. 21If anyone touches something unclean—whether human uncleanness or an unclean animal or any unclean, detestable thing—and then eats any of the meat of the fellowship offering belonging to the LORD, that person must be cut off from his people.'"

Eating Fat and Blood Forbidden

22The LORD said to Moses, 23"Say to the Israelites: 'Do not eat any of the fat of cattle, sheep or goats. 24The fat of an animal found dead or torn by wild animals may be used for any other purpose, but you must not eat it. 25Anyone who eats the fat of an animal from which an offering by fire may be made to the LORD must be cut off from his people. 26And wherever you live, you must not eat the blood of any bird or animal. 27If anyone eats blood, that person must be cut off from his people.'"

The Priests' Share

28The LORD said to Moses, 29"Say to the Israelites: 'Anyone who brings a fellowship offering to the LORD is to bring part of it as his sacrifice to the LORD. 30With his own hands he is to bring the offering made to the LORD by fire; he is to bring the fat, together with the breast, and wave the breast before the LORD as a wave offering. 31The priest shall burn the fat on the altar, but the breast belongs to Aaron and his sons. 32You are to give the right thigh of your fellowship offerings to the priest as a contribution. 33The son of Aaron who offers the blood and the fat of the fellowship offering shall have the right thigh as his share. 34From the fellowship offerings of the Israelites, I have taken the breast that is waved and the thigh that is presented and have given them to Aaron the priest and his sons as their regular share from the Israelites.'"

35This is the portion of the offerings made to the LORD by fire that were allotted to Aaron and his sons on the day they were presented to serve the LORD as priests. 36On the day they were anointed, the LORD commanded that the Israelites give this to them as their regular share for the generations to come.

37These, then, are the regulations for the burnt offering, the grain offering, the sin offering, the guilt offering, the ordination offering and the fellowship offering, 38which the LORD gave Moses on Mount Sinai on the day he commanded the Israelites to bring their offerings to the LORD, in the Desert of Sinai.

The Ordination of Aaron and His Sons

8 The LORD said to Moses, 2"Bring Aaron and his sons, their garments, the anointing oil, the bull for the sin offering, the two rams and the basket containing bread made without yeast, 3and gather the entire assembly at the entrance to the Tent of Meeting." 4Moses did as the LORD commanded him, and the assembly gathered at the entrance to the Tent of Meeting.

5Moses said to the assembly, "This is what the LORD has commanded to be done." 6Then Moses brought Aaron and his sons forward and washed them with water. 7He put the tunic on Aaron, tied the sash around him, clothed him with the robe and put the ephod on him. He also tied the ephod to him by its skilfully woven waistband; so it was fastened on him. 8He placed the breastpiece on him and put the Urim and Thummim in the breastpiece. 9Then he placed the turban on Aaron's head and set the gold plate, the sacred diadem, on the front of it, as the LORD commanded Moses.

10Then Moses took the anointing oil and anointed the tabernacle and everything in it, and so consecrated them. 11He sprinkled some of the oil on the altar seven times, anointing the altar and all its utensils and the basin with its stand, to consecrate them. 12He poured some of the anointing oil on Aaron's head and anointed him to consecrate him. 13Then he brought Aaron's sons forward, put tunics on them, tied sashes around them and put headbands on them, as the LORD commanded Moses.

14He then presented the bull for the sin offering, and Aaron and his sons laid their hands on its head. 15Moses slaughtered the bull and took some of the blood, and with his finger he put it on all the horns of the altar to purify the altar. He poured out the rest of the blood at the base of the altar. So he consecrated it to make atonement for it. 16Moses also took all the fat around the inner parts, the covering of the liver, and both kidneys and their fat, and burned it on the altar. 17But the bull with its hide and its flesh and its offal he burned up outside the camp, as the LORD commanded Moses.

18He then presented the ram for the burnt offering, and Aaron and his sons laid their hands on its head. 19Then Moses slaughtered the ram and sprinkled the blood against the altar on all sides. 20He cut the ram into pieces and burned the head, the pieces and the fat. 21He washed the inner parts and the legs with water and burned the whole ram on the altar as a burnt offering, a pleasing aroma, an offering made to the

LORD by fire, as the LORD commanded Moses.

22He then presented the other ram, the ram for the ordination, and Aaron and his sons laid their hands on its head. 23Moses slaughtered the ram and took some of its blood and put it on the lobe of Aaron's right ear, on the thumb of his right hand and on the big toe of his right foot. 24Moses also brought Aaron's sons forward and put some of the blood on the lobes of their right ears, on the thumbs of their right hands and on the big toes of their right feet. Then he sprinkled blood against the altar on all sides. 25He took the fat, the fat tail, all the fat around the inner parts, the covering of the liver, both kidneys and their fat and the right thigh. 26Then from the basket of bread made without yeast, which was before the LORD, he took a cake of bread, and one made with oil, and a wafer; he put these on the fat portions and on the right thigh. 27He put all these in the hands of Aaron and his sons and waved them before the LORD as a wave offering. 28Then Moses took them from their hands and burned them on the altar on top of the burnt offering as an ordination offering, a pleasing aroma, an offering made to the LORD by fire. 29He also took the breast —Moses' share of the ordination ram —and waved it before the LORD as a wave offering, as the LORD commanded Moses.

30Then Moses took some of the anointing oil and some of the blood from the altar and sprinkled them on Aaron and his garments and on his sons and their garments. So he consecrated Aaron and his garments and his sons and their garments.

31Moses then said to Aaron and his sons, "Cook the meat at the entrance to the Tent of Meeting and eat it there with the bread from the basket of ordination offerings, as I commanded, saying, 'Aaron and his sons are to eat it.' 32Then burn up the rest of the meat and the bread. 33Do not leave the entrance to the Tent of Meeting for seven days, until the days of your ordination are completed, for your ordination will last seven days. 34What has been done today was commanded by the LORD to make atonement for you. 35You must stay at the entrance to the Tent of Meeting day and night for seven days and do what the LORD requires, so that you will not die; for that is what I have been commanded." 36So Aaron and his sons did everything the LORD commanded through Moses.

NEW TESTAMENT READING
Mark 11:1–25

The Triumphal Entry

11 As they approached Jerusalem and came to Bethphage and Bethany at the Mount of Olives, Jesus sent two of his disciples, 2saying to them, "Go to the village ahead of you, and just as you enter it, you will find a colt tied there, which no-one has ever ridden. Untie it and bring it here. 3If anyone asks you, 'Why are you doing this?' tell him, 'The Lord needs it and will send it back here shortly.'"

4They went and found a colt outside in the street, tied at a doorway. As they untied it, 5some people standing there asked, "What are you doing, untying that colt?" 6They answered as Jesus had told them to, and the people let them go. 7When they brought the colt to Jesus and threw their cloaks over it, he sat on it. 8Many people spread their cloaks on the road, while others spread branches they had cut in the fields. 9Those who went ahead and those who followed shouted,

"Hosanna!"

"Blessed is he who comes in the
    name of the Lord!"

10"Blessed is the coming kingdom of
    our father David!"

"Hosanna in the highest!"

11Jesus entered Jerusalem and went to the temple. He looked around at everything, but since it was already late, he went out to Bethany with the Twelve.

Jesus Clears the Temple

12The next day as they were leaving Bethany, Jesus was hungry. 13Seeing in the distance a fig-tree in leaf, he went to find out if it had any fruit. When he reached it, he found nothing but leaves, because it was not the season for figs. 14Then he said to the tree, "May no-one ever eat fruit from you again." And his disciples heard him say it.

15On reaching Jerusalem, Jesus entered the temple area and began driving out those who were buying and selling there. He overturned the tables of the money changers and the benches of those selling doves, 16and would not allow anyone to carry merchandise through the temple courts. 17And as he taught them, he said, "Is it not written:

"'My house will be called
    a house of prayer for all nations'?

But you have made it 'a den of robbers'."

18The chief priests and the teachers of the law heard this and began looking for a way to kill him, for they feared him, because the whole crowd was amazed at his teaching.

19When evening came, they went out of the city.

The Withered Fig-Tree

20In the morning, as they went along, they saw the fig-tree withered from the roots. 21Peter remembered and said to Jesus, "Rabbi, look! The fig-tree you cursed has withered!"

22"Have faith in God," Jesus answered. 23"I tell you the truth, if anyone says to this mountain, 'Go, throw yourself into the sea,' and does not doubt in his heart but believes that what he says will happen, it will be done for him. 24Therefore I tell you, whatever you ask for in prayer, believe that you have received it, and it will be yours. 25And when you stand praying, if you hold anything against anyone, forgive him, so that your Father in heaven may forgive you your sins."

READING FROM PSALMS
Psalm 28:1–9

Of David.

1To you I call, O LORD my Rock;
    do not turn a deaf ear to me.
For if you remain silent,
    I shall be like those who have gone
        down to the pit.
2Hear my cry for mercy
    as I call to you for help,
as I lift up my hands
    towards your Most Holy Place.

3Do not drag me away with the
        wicked,
    with those who do evil,
who speak cordially with their
        neighbours
    but harbour malice in their hearts.

4Repay them for their deeds
    and for their evil work;
repay them for what their hands have
        done
    and bring back upon them what
        they deserve.
5Since they show no regard for the
        works of the LORD
    and what his hands have done,
he will tear them down
    and never build them up again.

6Praise be to the LORD,
    for he has heard my cry for mercy.
7The LORD is my strength and my
        shield;
    my heart trusts in him, and I am
        helped.
My heart leaps for joy
    and I will give thanks to him in
        song.

8The LORD is the strength of his
        people,
    a fortress of salvation for his
        anointed one.
9Save your people and bless your
        inheritance;
    be their shepherd and carry them
        for ever.

DAY 62   # MARCH 3

OLD TESTAMENT READING
Leviticus 9:1–10:20

The Priests Begin Their Ministry

9 On the eighth day Moses summoned Aaron and his sons and the elders of Israel. 2He said to Aaron, "Take a bull calf for your sin offering and a ram for your burnt offering, both without defect, and present them before the LORD. 3Then say to the Israelites: 'Take a male goat for a sin offering, a calf and a lamb—both a year old and without defect—for a burnt offering, 4and an ox and a ram for a fellowship offering to sacrifice before the LORD, together with a grain offering mixed with oil. For today the LORD will appear to you.'"

5They took the things Moses commanded to the front of the Tent of Meeting, and the entire assembly came near and stood before the LORD. 6Then Moses said, "This is what the LORD has commanded you to do, so that the glory of the LORD may appear to you."

7Moses said to Aaron, "Come to the

altar and sacrifice your sin offering and your burnt offering and make atonement for yourself and the people; sacrifice the offering that is for the people and make atonement for them, as the LORD has commanded.''

⁸So Aaron came to the altar and slaughtered the calf as a sin offering for himself. ⁹His sons brought the blood to him, and he dipped his finger into the blood and put it on the horns of the altar; the rest of the blood he poured out at the base of the altar. ¹⁰On the altar he burned the fat, the kidneys and the covering of the liver from the sin offering, as the LORD commanded Moses; ¹¹the flesh and the hide he burned up outside the camp.

¹²Then he slaughtered the burnt offering. His sons handed him the blood, and he sprinkled it against the altar on all sides. ¹³They handed him the burnt offering piece by piece, including the head, and he burned them on the altar. ¹⁴He washed the inner parts and the legs and burned them on top of the burnt offering on the altar.

¹⁵Aaron then brought the offering that was for the people. He took the goat for the people's sin offering and slaughtered it and offered it for a sin offering as he did with the first one.

¹⁶He brought the burnt offering and offered it in the prescribed way. ¹⁷He also brought the grain offering, took a handful of it and burned it on the altar in addition to the morning's burnt offering.

¹⁸He slaughtered the ox and the ram as the fellowship offering for the people. His sons handed him the blood, and he sprinkled it against the altar on all sides. ¹⁹But the fat portions of the ox and the ram—the fat tail, the layer of fat, the kidneys and the covering of the liver—²⁰these they laid on the breasts, and then Aaron burned the fat on the altar. ²¹Aaron waved the breasts and the right thigh before the LORD as a wave offering, as Moses commanded.

²²Then Aaron lifted his hands towards the people and blessed them.

And having sacrificed the sin offering, the burnt offering and the fellowship offering, he stepped down.

²³Moses and Aaron went into the Tent of Meeting. When they came out, they blessed the people; and the glory of the LORD appeared to all the people. ²⁴Fire came out from the presence of the LORD and consumed the burnt offering and the fat portions on the altar. And when all the people saw it, they shouted for joy and fell face down.

The Death of Nadab and Abihu

10 Aaron's sons Nadab and Abihu took their censers, put fire in them and added incense; and they offered unauthorised fire before the LORD, contrary to his command. ²So fire came out from the presence of the LORD and consumed them, and they died before the LORD. ³Moses then said to Aaron, "This is what the LORD spoke of when he said:

"'Among those who approach me
    I will show myself holy;
in the sight of all the people
    I will be honoured.'"

Aaron remained silent.

⁴Moses summoned Mishael and Elzaphan, sons of Aaron's uncle Uzziel, and said to them, "Come here; carry your cousins outside the camp, away from the front of the sanctuary." ⁵So they came and carried them, still in their tunics, outside the camp, as Moses ordered.

⁶Then Moses said to Aaron and his sons Eleazar and Ithamar, "Do not let your hair become unkempt, and do not tear your clothes, or you will die and the LORD will be angry with the whole community. But your relatives, all the house of Israel, may mourn for those the LORD has destroyed by fire. ⁷Do not leave the entrance to the Tent of Meeting or you will die, because the LORD's anointing oil is on you." So they did as Moses said.

⁸Then the LORD said to Aaron, ⁹"You and your sons are not to drink wine or other fermented drink whenever you go into the Tent of Meeting, or you will die. This is a lasting ordinance for the generations to come. ¹⁰You must distinguish between the holy and the common, between the unclean and the clean, ¹¹and you must teach the Israelites all the decrees the LORD has given them through Moses."

¹²Moses said to Aaron and his remaining sons, Eleazar and Ithamar, "Take the grain offering left over from the offerings made to the LORD by fire and eat it prepared without yeast beside the altar, for it is most holy. ¹³Eat it in a holy place, because it is your share and your sons' share of the offerings made to the LORD by fire; for so I have been commanded. ¹⁴But you and your sons and your daughters may eat the breast that was waved and the thigh that was presented. Eat them in a ceremonially clean place; they have been given to you and your children as your share of the Israelites' fellowship offerings. ¹⁵The thigh that was presented and the breast that was waved must be brought with the fat portions of the offerings made by fire, to be waved before the LORD as a wave offering. This will be the regular share for you and your children, as the LORD has commanded."

¹⁶When Moses enquired about the goat of the sin offering and found that it had been burned up, he was angry with Eleazar and Ithamar, Aaron's remaining sons, and asked, ¹⁷"Why didn't you eat the sin offering in the sanctuary area? It is most holy; it was given to you to take away the guilt of the community by making atonement for them before the LORD. ¹⁸Since its blood was not taken into the Holy Place, you should have eaten the goat in the sanctuary area, as I commanded."

¹⁹Aaron replied to Moses, "Today they sacrificed their sin offering and their burnt offering before the LORD, but such things as this have happened to me. Would the LORD have been pleased

if I had eaten the sin offering today?" ²⁰When Moses heard this, he was satisfied.

NEW TESTAMENT READING
Mark 11:27–12:12

The Authority of Jesus Questioned

²⁷They arrived again in Jerusalem, and while Jesus was walking in the temple courts, the chief priests, the teachers of the law and the elders came to him. ²⁸"By what authority are you doing these things?" they asked. "And who gave you authority to do this?"

²⁹Jesus replied, "I will ask you one question. Answer me, and I will tell you by what authority I am doing these things. ³⁰John's baptism—was it from heaven, or from men? Tell me!"

³¹They discussed it among themselves and said, "If we say, 'From heaven', he will ask, 'Then why didn't you believe him?' ³²But if we say, 'From men'. . . .'" (They feared the people, for everyone held that John really was a prophet.)

³³So they answered Jesus, "We don't know."

Jesus said, "Neither will I tell you by what authority I am doing these things."

The Parable of the Tenants

12 He then began to speak to them in parables: "A man planted a vineyard. He put a wall around it, dug a pit for the winepress and built a watchtower. Then he rented the vineyard to some farmers and went away on a journey. ²At harvest time he sent a servant to the tenants to collect from them some of the fruit of the vineyard. ³But they seized him, beat him and sent him away empty-handed. ⁴Then he sent another servant to them; they struck this man on the head and treated him shamefully. ⁵He sent still another, and that one they

killed. He sent many others; some of them they beat, others they killed.

⁶"He had one left to send, a son, whom he loved. He sent him last of all, saying, 'They will respect my son.'

⁷"But the tenants said to one another, 'This is the heir. Come, let's kill him, and the inheritance will be ours.' ⁸So they took him and killed him, and threw him out of the vineyard.

⁹"What then will the owner of the vineyard do? He will come and kill those tenants and give the vineyard to others. ¹⁰Haven't you read this scripture:

" 'The stone the builders rejected
    has become the capstone;
¹¹the Lord has done this,
    and it is marvellous in our eyes'?"

¹²Then they looked for a way to arrest him because they knew he had spoken the parable against them. But they were afraid of the crowd; so they left him and went away.

READING FROM PSALMS
Psalm 29:1–11

A psalm of David.

¹Ascribe to the LORD, O mighty ones,
    ascribe to the LORD glory and
    strength.

²Ascribe to the LORD the glory due to
    his name;
    worship the LORD in the splendour
    of his holiness.

³The voice of the LORD is over the
    waters;
    the God of glory thunders,
    the LORD thunders over the mighty
    waters.

⁴The voice of the LORD is powerful;
    the voice of the LORD is majestic.

⁵The voice of the LORD breaks the
    cedars;
    the LORD breaks in pieces the
    cedars of Lebanon.

⁶He makes Lebanon skip like a calf,
    Sirion like a young wild ox.

⁷The voice of the LORD strikes
    with flashes of lightning.

⁸The voice of the LORD shakes the
    desert;
    the LORD shakes the Desert of
    Kadesh.

⁹The voice of the LORD twists the oaks
    and strips the forests bare.
    And in his temple all cry, "Glory!"

¹⁰The LORD sits enthroned over the
    flood;
    the LORD is enthroned as King for
    ever.

¹¹The LORD gives strength to his
    people;
    the LORD blesses his people with
    peace.

MARCH 4

OLD TESTAMENT READING
Leviticus 11:1–12:8

Clean and Unclean Food

11 The LORD said to Moses and Aaron, 2"Say to the Israelites: 'Of all the animals that live on land, these are the ones you may eat: 3You may eat any animal that has a split hoof completely divided and that chews the cud.

4" 'There are some that only chew the cud or only have a split hoof, but you must not eat them. The camel, though it chews the cud, does not have a split hoof; it is ceremonially unclean for you. 5The coney, though it chews the cud, does not have a split hoof; it is unclean for you. 6The rabbit, though it chews the cud, does not have a split hoof; it is unclean for you. 7And the pig, though it has a split hoof completely divided, does not chew the cud; it is unclean for you. 8You must not eat their meat or touch their carcasses; they are unclean for you.

9" 'Of all the creatures living in the water of the seas and the streams, you may eat any that have fins and scales. 10But all creatures in the seas or streams that do not have fins and scales— whether among all the swarming things or among all the other living creatures in the water—you are to detest them. 11And since you are to detest them, you must not eat their meat and you must detest their carcasses. 12Anything living in the water that does not have fins and scales is to be detestable to you.

13" 'These are the birds you are to detest and not eat because they are detestable: the eagle, the vulture, the black vulture, 14the red kite, any kind of black kite, 15any kind of raven, 16the horned owl, the screech owl, the gull, any kind of hawk, 17the little owl, the cormorant, the great owl, 18the white owl, the desert owl, the osprey, 19the stork, any kind of heron, the hoopoe and the bat.

20" 'All flying insects that walk on all fours are to be detestable to you. 21There are, however, some winged creatures that walk on all fours that you may eat: those that have jointed legs for hopping on the ground. 22Of these you may eat any kind of locust, katydid, cricket or grasshopper. 23But all other winged creatures that have four legs you are to detest.

24" 'You will make yourselves unclean by these; whoever touches their carcasses will be unclean till evening. 25Whoever picks up one of their carcasses must wash his clothes, and he will be unclean till evening.

26" 'Every animal that has a split hoof not completely divided or that does not chew the cud is unclean for you; whoever touches ⌊the carcass of⌋ any of them will be unclean. 27Of all the animals that walk on all fours, those that walk on their paws are unclean for you; whoever touches their carcasses will be unclean till evening. 28Anyone who picks up their carcasses must wash his clothes, and he will be unclean till evening. They are unclean for you.

29" 'Of the animals that move about on the ground, these are unclean for you: the weasel, the rat, any kind of great lizard, 30the gecko, the monitor lizard, the wall lizard, the skink and the chameleon. 31Of all those that move along the ground, these are unclean for you. Whoever touches them when they are dead will be unclean till evening. 32When one of them dies and falls on something, that article, whatever its use, will be unclean, whether it is made of wood, cloth, hide or sackcloth. Put it in water; it will be unclean till evening, and then it will be clean. 33If one of them falls into a clay pot, everything in it will be unclean, and you must break the pot. 34Any food that could be eaten but has water on it from such a pot is unclean, and any liquid that could be drunk from it is unclean. 35Anything that one of their carcasses falls on becomes unclean; an oven or cooking pot must be broken up. They are unclean, and you are to regard them as unclean. 36A spring, however, or a cistern for collecting water remains clean, but anyone who touches one of these carcasses is unclean. 37If a carcass falls on any seeds that are to be planted, they remain clean. 38But if water has been put on the seed and a carcass falls on it, it is unclean for you.

39"'If an animal that you are allowed to eat dies, anyone who touches the carcass will be unclean till evening. 40Anyone who eats some of the carcass must wash his clothes, and he will be unclean till evening. Anyone who picks up the carcass must wash his clothes, and he will be unclean till evening.

41"'Every creature that moves about on the ground is detestable; it is not to be eaten. 42You are not to eat any creature that moves about on the ground, whether it moves on its belly or walks on all fours or on many feet; it is detestable. 43Do not defile yourselves by any of these creatures. Do not make yourselves unclean by means of them or be made unclean by them. 44I am the LORD your God; consecrate yourselves and be holy, because I am holy. Do not make yourselves unclean by any creature that moves about on the ground. 45I am the LORD who brought you up out of Egypt to be your God; therefore be holy, because I am holy.

46"'These are the regulations concerning animals, birds, every living thing that moves in the water and every creature that moves about on the ground. 47You must distinguish between the unclean and the clean, between living creatures that may be eaten and those that may not be eaten.'"

Purification After Childbirth

12 The LORD said to Moses, 2"Say to the Israelites: 'A woman who becomes pregnant and gives birth to a son will be ceremonially unclean for seven days, just as she is unclean during her monthly period. 3On the eighth day the boy is to be circumcised. 4Then the woman must wait thirty-three days to be purified from her bleeding. She must not touch anything sacred or go to the sanctuary until the days of her purification are over. 5If she gives birth to a daughter, for two weeks the woman will be unclean, as during her period. Then she must wait sixty-six days to be purified from her bleeding.

6"'When the days of her purification for a son or daughter are over, she is to bring to the priest at the entrance to the Tent of Meeting a year-old lamb for a burnt offering and a young pigeon or a dove for a sin offering. 7He shall offer them before the LORD to make atonement for her, and then she will be ceremonially clean from her flow of blood.

"'These are the regulations for the woman who gives birth to a boy or a girl. 8If she cannot afford a lamb, she is to bring two doves or two young pigeons, one for a burnt offering and the other for a sin offering. In this way the priest will make atonement for her, and she will be clean.'"

NEW TESTAMENT READING
Mark 12:13–27

Paying Taxes to Caesar

13Later they sent some of the Pharisees and Herodians to Jesus to catch him in his words. 14They came to him and said, "Teacher, we know you are a man of integrity. You aren't swayed by men, because you pay no attention to who they are; but you teach the way of God in accordance with the truth. Is it right to pay taxes to Caesar or not? 15Should we pay or shouldn't we?"

But Jesus knew their hypocrisy. "Why are you trying to trap me?" he asked. "Bring me a denarius and let me look at it." 16They brought the coin, and he asked them, "Whose portrait is this? And whose inscription?"

"Caesar's," they replied.

17Then Jesus said to them, "Give to Caesar what is Caesar's and to God what is God's."

And they were amazed at him.

Marriage at the Resurrection

18Then the Sadducees, who say there is no resurrection, came to him with a question. 19"Teacher," they said, "Moses wrote for us that if a man's brother dies and leaves a wife but no children, the man must marry the widow and have children for his brother. 20Now there were seven brothers. The first one married and died without leaving any children. 21The second one married the widow, but he also died, leaving no child. It was the same with the third. 22In fact, none of the seven left any children. Last of all, the woman died too. 23At the resurrection whose wife will she be, since the seven were married to her?"

24Jesus replied, "Are you not in error because you do not know the Scriptures or the power of God? 25When the dead rise, they will neither marry nor be given in marriage; they will be like the angels in heaven. 26Now about the dead rising—have you not read in the book of Moses, in the account of the bush,

how God said to him, 'I am the God of Abraham, the God of Isaac, and the God of Jacob'? 27He is not the God of the dead, but of the living. You are badly mistaken!"

READING FROM PSALMS
Psalm 30:1–7

A psalm. A song. For the dedication of the temple. Of David.

1I will exalt you, O LORD,
 for you lifted me out of the depths
 and did not let my enemies gloat
  over me.
2O LORD my God, I called to you for
  help
 and you healed me.
3O LORD, you brought me up from the
  grave;
 you spared me from going down
  into the pit.

4Sing to the LORD, you saints of his;
 praise his holy name.
5For his anger lasts only a moment,
 but his favour lasts a lifetime;
weeping may remain for a night,
 but rejoicing comes in the
  morning.

6When I felt secure, I said,
 "I shall never be shaken."
7O LORD, when you favoured me,
 you made my mountain stand firm;
but when you hid your face,
 I was dismayed.

OLD TESTAMENT READING
Leviticus 13:1–59

Regulations About Infectious Skin Diseases

13 The LORD said to Moses and Aaron, [2]"When anyone has a swelling or a rash or a bright spot on his skin that may become an infectious skin disease, he must be brought to Aaron the priest or to one of his sons who is a priest. [3]The priest is to examine the sore on his skin, and if the hair in the sore has turned white and the sore appears to be more than skin deep, it is an infectious skin disease. When the priest examines him, he shall pronounce him ceremonially unclean. [4]If the spot on his skin is white but does not appear to be more than skin deep and the hair in it has not turned white, the priest is to put the infected person in isolation for seven days. [5]On the seventh day the priest is to examine him, and if he sees that the sore is unchanged and has not spread in the skin, he is to keep him in isolation another seven days. [6]On the seventh day the priest is to examine him again, and if the sore has faded and has not spread in the skin, the priest shall pronounce him clean; it is only a rash. The man must wash his clothes, and he will be clean. [7]But if the rash does spread in his skin after he has shown himself to the priest to be pronounced clean, he must appear before the priest again. [8]The priest is to examine him, and if the rash has spread in the skin, he shall pronounce him unclean; it is an infectious disease.

[9]"When anyone has an infectious skin disease, he must be brought to the priest. [10]The priest is to examine him, and if there is a white swelling in the skin that has turned the hair white and if there is raw flesh in the swelling, [11]it is a chronic skin disease and the priest shall pronounce him unclean. He is not to put him in isolation, because he is already unclean.

[12]"If the disease breaks out all over his skin and, so far as the priest can see, it covers all the skin of the infected person from head to foot, [13]the priest is to examine him, and if the disease has covered his whole body, he shall pronounce that person clean. Since it has all turned white, he is clean. [14]But whenever raw flesh appears on him, he will be unclean. [15]When the priest sees the raw flesh, he shall pronounce him unclean. The raw flesh is unclean; he has an infectious skin disease. [16]Should the raw flesh change and turn white, he must go to the priest. [17]The priest is to examine him, and if the sores have turned white, the priest shall pronounce the infected person clean; then he will be clean.

[18]"When someone has a boil on his skin and it heals, [19]and in the place where the boil was, a white swelling or reddish-white spot appears, he must present himself to the priest. [20]The priest is to examine it, and if it appears to be more than skin deep and the hair in it has turned white, the priest shall pronounce him unclean. It is an infectious skin disease that has broken out where the boil was. [21]But if, when the priest examines it, there is no white hair in it and it is not more than skin deep and has faded, then the priest is to put him in isolation for seven days. [22]If it is spreading in the skin, the priest shall pronounce him unclean; it is infectious. [23]But if the spot is unchanged and has not spread, it is only a scar from the boil, and the priest shall pronounce him clean.

[24]"When someone has a burn on his skin and a reddish-white or white spot appears in the raw flesh of the burn,

25the priest is to examine the spot, and if the hair in it has turned white, and it appears to be more than skin deep, it is an infectious disease that has broken out in the burn. The priest shall pronounce him unclean; it is an infectious skin disease. 26But if the priest examines it and there is no white hair in the spot and if it is not more than skin deep and has faded, then the priest is to put him in isolation for seven days. 27On the seventh day the priest is to examine him, and if it is spreading in the skin, the priest shall pronounce him unclean; it is an infectious skin disease. 28If, however, the spot is unchanged and has not spread in the skin but has faded, it is a swelling from the burn, and the priest shall pronounce him clean; it is only a scar from the burn.

29"If a man or woman has a sore on the head or on the chin, 30the priest is to examine the sore, and if it appears to be more than skin deep and the hair in it is yellow and thin, the priest shall pronounce that person unclean; it is an itch, an infectious disease of the head or chin. 31But if, when the priest examines this kind of sore, it does not seem to be more than skin deep and there is no black hair in it, then the priest is to put the infected person in isolation for seven days. 32On the seventh day the priest is to examine the sore, and if the itch has not spread and there is no yellow hair in it and it does not appear to be more than skin deep, 33he must be shaved except for the diseased area, and the priest is to keep him in isolation another seven days. 34On the seventh day the priest is to examine the itch, and if it has not spread in the skin and appears to be no more than skin deep, the priest shall pronounce him clean. He must wash his clothes, and he will be clean. 35But if the itch does spread in the skin after he is pronounced clean, 36the priest is to examine him, and if the itch has spread in the skin, the priest does not need to look for yellow hair; the person is unclean. 37If, however, in his judgment it is unchanged and black hair has grown in it, the itch is healed. He is clean, and the priest shall pronounce him clean.

38"When a man or woman has white spots on the skin, 39the priest is to examine them, and if the spots are dull white, it is a harmless rash that has broken out on the skin; that person is clean.

40"When a man has lost his hair and is bald, he is clean. 41If he has lost his hair from the front of his scalp and has a bald forehead, he is clean. 42But if he has a reddish-white sore on his bald head or forehead, it is an infectious disease breaking out on his head or forehead. 43The priest is to examine him, and if the swollen sore on his head or forehead is reddish-white like an infectious skin disease, 44the man is diseased and is unclean. The priest shall pronounce him unclean because of the sore on his head.

45"The person with such an infectious disease must wear torn clothes, let his hair be unkempt, cover the lower part of his face and cry out, 'Unclean! Unclean!' 46As long as he has the infection he remains unclean. He must live alone; he must live outside the camp.

Regulations About Mildew

47"If any clothing is contaminated with mildew—any woollen or linen clothing, 48any woven or knitted material of linen or wool, any leather or anything made of leather—49and if the contamination in the clothing, or leather, or woven or knitted material, or any leather article, is greenish or reddish, it is a spreading mildew and must be shown to the priest. 50The priest is to examine the mildew and isolate the affected article for seven days. 51On the seventh day he is to examine it, and if the mildew has spread in the clothing, or the woven or knitted material, or the leather, whatever its use, it is a destructive mildew; the article is unclean. 52He must burn up the clothing, or the woven or knitted material of wool or linen, or any leather article that has the contamination in it, because the mildew is destructive; the article must be burned up.

53"But if, when the priest examines it, the mildew has not spread in the clothing, or the woven or knitted material, or the leather article, 54he shall order that the contaminated article be washed. Then he is to isolate it for another seven days. 55After the affected article has been washed, the priest is to examine it, and if the mildew has not changed its appearance, even though it has not spread, it is unclean. Burn it with fire, whether the mildew has affected one side or the other. 56If, when the priest examines it, the mildew has faded after the article has been washed, he is to tear the contaminated part out of the clothing, or the leather, or the woven or knitted material. 57But if it reappears in the clothing, or in the woven or knitted material, or in the leather article, it is spreading, and whatever has the mildew must be burned with fire. 58The clothing, or the woven or knitted material, or any leather article that has been washed and is rid of the mildew, must be washed again, and it will be clean."

59These are the regulations concerning contamination by mildew in woollen or linen clothing, woven or knitted material, or any leather article, for pronouncing them clean or unclean.

NEW TESTAMENT READING
Mark 12:28–44

The Greatest Commandment

28One of the teachers of the law came and heard them debating. Noticing that Jesus had given them a good answer, he asked him, "Of all the commandments, which is the most important?"

29"The most important one," answered Jesus, "is this: 'Hear, O Israel, the Lord our God, the Lord is one. 30Love the Lord your God with all your heart and with all your soul and with all your mind and with all your strength.' 31The second is this: 'Love your neighbour as yourself.' There is no commandment greater than these."

32"Well said, teacher," the man replied. "You are right in saying that God is one and there is no other but him. 33To love him with all your heart, with all your understanding and with all your strength, and to love your neighbour as yourself is more important than all burnt offerings and sacrifices."

34When Jesus saw that he had answered wisely, he said to him, "You are not far from the kingdom of God." And from then on no-one dared ask him any more questions.

Whose Son Is the Christ?

35While Jesus was teaching in the temple courts, he asked, "How is it that the teachers of the law say that the Christ is the son of David? 36David himself, speaking by the Holy Spirit, declared:

"'The Lord said to my Lord:
    "Sit at my right hand
until I put your enemies
    under your feet."'

37David himself calls him 'Lord'. How then can he be his son?"

The large crowd listened to him with delight.

38As he taught, Jesus said, "Watch out for the teachers of the law. They like to walk around in flowing robes and be greeted in the market-places, 39and have the most important seats in the synagogues and the places of honour at banquets. 40They devour widows' houses and for a show make lengthy prayers. Such men will be punished most severely."

The Widow's Offering

41Jesus sat down opposite the place where the offerings were put and watched the crowd putting their money into the temple treasury. Many rich people threw in large amounts. ⁴²But a poor widow came and put in two very small copper coins, worth only a fraction of a penny.

⁴³Calling his disciples to him, Jesus said, "I tell you the truth, this poor widow has put more into the treasury than all the others. ⁴⁴They all gave out of their wealth; but she, out of her poverty, put in everything—all she had to live on."

READING FROM PROVERBS
Proverbs 6:20–29

Warning Against Adultery

²⁰My son, keep your father's
        commands
    and do not forsake your mother's
        teaching.
²¹Bind them upon your heart for ever;
    fasten them around your neck.
²²When you walk, they will guide you;
    when you sleep, they will watch
        over you;
    when you awake, they will speak to
        you.
²³For these commands are a lamp,
    this teaching is a light,
    and the corrections of discipline
        are the way to life,
²⁴keeping you from the immoral
        woman,
    from the smooth tongue of the
        wayward wife.
²⁵Do not lust in your heart after her
        beauty
    or let her captivate you with her
        eyes,
²⁶for the prostitute reduces you to a
        loaf of bread,
    and the adulteress preys upon your
        very life.
²⁷Can a man scoop fire into his lap
    without his clothes being burned?
²⁸Can a man walk on hot coals
    without his feet being scorched?
²⁹So is he who sleeps with another
        man's wife;
    no-one who touches her will go
        unpunished.

DAY 65

MARCH 6

OLD TESTAMENT READING
Leviticus 14:1–57

*Cleansing From Infectious Skin
Diseases*

14 The LORD said to Moses, ²"These are the regulations for the diseased person at the time of his ceremonial cleansing, when he is brought to the priest: ³The priest is to go outside the camp and examine him. If the person has been healed of his infectious skin disease, ⁴the priest shall order that two live clean birds and some cedar wood, scarlet yarn and hyssop be brought for the one to be cleansed.

⁵Then the priest shall order that one of the birds be killed over fresh water in a clay pot. ⁶He is then to take the live bird and dip it, together with the cedar wood, the scarlet yarn and the hyssop, into the blood of the bird that was killed over the fresh water. ⁷Seven times he shall sprinkle the one to be cleansed of the infectious disease and pronounce him clean. Then he is to release the live bird in the open fields.

⁸"The person to be cleansed must wash his clothes, shave off all his hair and bathe with water; then he will be ceremonially clean. After this he may come into the camp, but he must stay outside his tent for seven days. ⁹On the

seventh day he must shave off all his hair; he must shave his head, his beard, his eyebrows and the rest of his hair. He must wash his clothes and bathe himself with water, and he will be clean.

10"On the eighth day he must bring two male lambs and one ewe lamb a year old, each without defect, along with three-tenths of an ephah of fine flour mixed with oil for a grain offering, and one log of oil. 11The priest who pronounces him clean shall present both the one to be cleansed and his offerings before the Lord at the entrance to the Tent of Meeting.

12"Then the priest is to take one of the male lambs and offer it as a guilt offering, along with the log of oil; he shall wave them before the Lord as a wave offering. 13He is to slaughter the lamb in the holy place where the sin offering and the burnt offering are slaughtered. Like the sin offering, the guilt offering belongs to the priest; it is most holy. 14The priest is to take some of the blood of the guilt offering and put it on the lobe of the right ear of the one to be cleansed, on the thumb of his right hand and on the big toe of his right foot. 15The priest shall then take some of the log of oil, pour it in the palm of his own left hand, 16dip his right forefinger into the oil in his palm, and with his finger sprinkle some of it before the Lord seven times. 17The priest is to put some of the oil remaining in his palm on the lobe of the right ear of the one to be cleansed, on the thumb of his right hand and on the big toe of his right foot, on top of the blood of the guilt offering. 18The rest of the oil in his palm the priest shall put on the head of the one to be cleansed and make atonement for him before the Lord.

19"Then the priest is to sacrifice the sin offering and make atonement for the one to be cleansed from his uncleanness. After that, the priest shall slaughter the burnt offering 20and offer it on the altar, together with the grain offering, and make atonement for him, and he will be clean.

21"If, however, he is poor and cannot afford these, he must take one male lamb as a guilt offering to be waved to make atonement for him, together with a tenth of an ephah of fine flour mixed with oil for a grain offering, a log of oil, 22and two doves or two young pigeons, which he can afford, one for a sin offering and the other for a burnt offering.

23"On the eighth day he must bring them for his cleansing to the priest at the entrance to the Tent of Meeting, before the Lord. 24The priest is to take the lamb for the guilt offering, together with the log of oil, and wave them before the Lord as a wave offering. 25He shall slaughter the lamb for the guilt offering and take some of its blood and put it on the lobe of the right ear of the one to be cleansed, on the thumb of his right hand and on the big toe of his right foot. 26The priest is to pour some of the oil into the palm of his own left hand, 27and with his right forefinger sprinkle some of the oil from his palm seven times before the Lord. 28Some of the oil in his palm he is to put on the same places he put the blood of the guilt offering—on the lobe of the right ear of the one to be cleansed, on the thumb of his right hand and on the big toe of his right foot. 29The rest of the oil in his palm the priest shall put on the head of the one to be cleansed, to make atonement for him before the Lord. 30Then he shall sacrifice the doves or the young pigeons, which the person can afford, 31one as a sin offering and the other as a burnt offering, together with the grain offering. In this way the priest will make atonement before the Lord on behalf of the one to be cleansed."

32These are the regulations for anyone who has an infectious skin disease and who cannot afford the regular offerings for his cleansing.

Cleansing From Mildew

33The Lord said to Moses and Aaron, 34"When you enter the land of Canaan, which I am giving you as your possession, and I put a spreading mildew in a house in that land, 35the owner of the house must go and tell the priest, 'I have seen something that looks like mildew in my house.' 36The priest is to order the house to be emptied before he goes in to examine the mildew, so that nothing in the house will be pronounced unclean. After this the priest is to go in and inspect the house. 37He is to examine the mildew on the walls, and if it has greenish or reddish depressions that appear to be deeper than the surface of the wall, 38the priest shall go out of the doorway of the house and close it up for seven days. 39On the seventh day the priest shall return to inspect the house. If the mildew has spread on the walls, 40he is to order that the contaminated stones be torn out and thrown into an unclean place outside the town. 41He must have all the inside walls of the house scraped and the material that is scraped off dumped into an unclean place outside the town. 42Then they are to take other stones to replace these and take new clay and plaster the house.

43"If the mildew reappears in the house after the stones have been torn out and the house scraped and plastered, 44the priest is to go and examine it and, if the mildew has spread in the house, it is a destructive mildew; the house is unclean. 45It must be torn down —its stones, timbers and all the plaster —and taken out of the town to an unclean place.

46"Anyone who goes into the house while it is closed up will be unclean till evening. 47Anyone who sleeps or eats in the house must wash his clothes.

48"But if the priest comes to examine it and the mildew has not spread after the house has been plastered, he shall pronounce the house clean, because the mildew is gone. 49To purify the house he is to take two birds and some cedar wood, scarlet yarn and hyssop. 50He shall kill one of the birds over fresh water in a clay pot. 51Then he is to take the cedar wood, the hyssop, the scarlet yarn and the live bird, dip them into the blood of the dead bird and the fresh water, and sprinkle the house seven times. 52He shall purify the house with the bird's blood, the fresh water, the live bird, the cedar wood, the hyssop and the scarlet yarn. 53Then he is to release the live bird in the open fields outside the town. In this way he will make atonement for the house, and it will be clean."

54These are the regulations for any infectious skin disease, for an itch, 55for mildew in clothing or in a house, 56and for a swelling, a rash or a bright spot, 57to determine when something is clean or unclean.

These are the regulations for infectious skin diseases and mildew.

NEW TESTAMENT READING
Mark 13:1–31

Signs of the End of the Age

13 As he was leaving the temple, one of his disciples said to him, "Look, Teacher! What massive stones! What magnificent buildings!"

2"Do you see all these great buildings?" replied Jesus. "Not one stone here will be left on another; every one will be thrown down."

3As Jesus was sitting on the Mount of Olives opposite the temple, Peter, James, John and Andrew asked him privately, 4"Tell us, when will these things happen? And what will be the sign that they are all about to be fulfilled?"

5Jesus said to them: "Watch out that no-one deceives you. 6Many will come in my name, claiming, 'I am he,' and will deceive many. 7When you hear of wars and rumours of wars, do not be alarmed. Such things must happen, but the end is still to come. 8Nation will rise against nation, and kingdom against kingdom. There will be earthquakes in various places, and famines. These are the beginning of birth-pains.

9"You must be on your guard. You

will be handed over to the local councils and flogged in the synagogues. On account of me you will stand before governors and kings as witnesses to them. ¹⁰And the gospel must first be preached to all nations. ¹¹Whenever you are arrested and brought to trial, do not worry beforehand about what to say. Just say whatever is given you at the time, for it is not you speaking, but the Holy Spirit.

¹²"Brother will betray brother to death, and a father his child. Children will rebel against their parents and have them put to death. ¹³All men will hate you because of me, but he who stands firm to the end will be saved.

¹⁴"When you see 'the abomination that causes desolation' standing where it does not belong—let the reader understand—then let those who are in Judea flee to the mountains. ¹⁵Let no-one on the roof of his house go down or enter the house to take anything out. ¹⁶Let no-one in the field go back to get his cloak. ¹⁷How dreadful it will be in those days for pregnant women and nursing mothers! ¹⁸Pray that this will not take place in winter, ¹⁹because those will be days of distress unequalled from the beginning, when God created the world, until now—and never to be equalled again. ²⁰If the Lord had not cut short those days, no-one would survive. But for the sake of the elect, whom he has chosen, he has shortened them. ²¹At that time if anyone says to you, 'Look, here is the Christ!' or, 'Look, there he is!' do not believe it. ²²For false Christs and false prophets will appear and perform signs and miracles to deceive the elect—if that were possible. ²³So be on your guard; I have told you everything ahead of time.

²⁴"But in those days, following that distress,

" 'the sun will be darkened,
      and the moon will not give its light;
²⁵the stars will fall from the sky,
      and the heavenly bodies will be shaken.'

²⁶"At that time men will see the Son of Man coming in clouds with great power and glory. ²⁷And he will send his angels and gather his elect from the four winds, from the ends of the earth to the ends of the heavens.

²⁸"Now learn this lesson from the fig-tree: As soon as its twigs get tender and its leaves come out, you know that summer is near. ²⁹Even so, when you see these things happening, you know that it is near, right at the door. ³⁰I tell you the truth, this generation will certainly not pass away until all these things have happened. ³¹Heaven and earth will pass away, but my words will never pass away.

READING FROM PSALMS
Psalm 30:8–12

⁸To you, O LORD, I called;
      to the Lord I cried for mercy:
⁹"What gain is there in my
            destruction,
      in my going down into the pit?
      Will the dust praise you?
      Will it proclaim your faithfulness?
¹⁰Hear, O LORD, and be merciful to
            me;
      O LORD, be my help."

¹¹You turned my wailing into dancing;
      you removed my sackcloth and
            clothed me with joy,
¹²that my heart may sing to you and not
            be silent.
      O LORD my God, I will give you
            thanks for ever.

OLD TESTAMENT READING
Leviticus 15:1–16:34

Discharges Causing Uncleanness

15 The LORD said to Moses and Aaron, 2"Speak to the Israelites and say to them: 'When any man has a bodily discharge, the discharge is unclean. 3Whether it continues flowing from his body or is blocked, it will make him unclean. This is how his discharge will bring about uncleanness:

4"'Any bed the man with a discharge lies on will be unclean, and anything he sits on will be unclean. 5Anyone who touches his bed must wash his clothes and bathe with water, and he will be unclean till evening. 6Whoever sits on anything that the man with a discharge sat on must wash his clothes and bathe with water, and he will be unclean till evening.

7"'Whoever touches the man who has a discharge must wash his clothes and bathe with water, and he will be unclean till evening.

8"'If the man with the discharge spits on someone who is clean, that person must wash his clothes and bathe with water, and he will be unclean till evening.

9"'Everything the man sits on when riding will be unclean, 10and whoever touches any of the things that were under him will be unclean till evening; whoever picks up those things must wash his clothes and bathe with water, and he will be unclean till evening.

11"'Anyone the man with a discharge touches without rinsing his hands with water must wash his clothes and bathe with water, and he will be unclean till evening.

12"'A clay pot that the man touches must be broken, and any wooden article is to be rinsed with water.

13"'When a man is cleansed from his discharge, he is to count off seven days for his ceremonial cleansing; he must wash his clothes and bathe himself with fresh water, and he will be clean. 14On the eighth day he must take two doves or two young pigeons and come before the LORD to the entrance to the Tent of Meeting and give them to the priest. 15The priest is to sacrifice them, the one for a sin offering and the other for a burnt offering. In this way he will make atonement before the LORD for the man because of his discharge.

16"'When a man has an emission of semen, he must bathe his whole body with water, and he will be unclean till evening. 17Any clothing or leather that has semen on it must be washed with water, and it will be unclean till evening. 18When a man lies with a woman and there is an emission of semen, both must bathe with water, and they will be unclean till evening.

19"'When a woman has her regular flow of blood, the impurity of her monthly period will last seven days, and anyone who touches her will be unclean till evening.

20"'Anything she lies on during her period will be unclean, and anything she sits on will be unclean. 21Whoever touches her bed must wash his clothes and bathe with water, and he will be unclean till evening. 22Whoever touches anything she sits on must wash his clothes and bathe with water, and he will be unclean till evening. 23Whether it is the bed or anything she was sitting on, when anyone touches it, he will be unclean till evening.

24"'If a man lies with her and her monthly flow touches him, he will be unclean for seven days; any bed he lies on will be unclean.

25"'When a woman has a discharge of blood for many days at a time other than her monthly period or has a discharge that continues beyond her period, she will be unclean as long as she has the discharge, just as in the days of her period. 26Any bed she lies on while her discharge continues will be unclean, as is her bed during her monthly period, and anything she sits on will be unclean, as during her period. 27Whoever touches them will be unclean; he must wash his clothes and bathe with water, and he will be unclean till evening.

28"When she is cleansed from her discharge, she must count off seven days, and after that she will be ceremonially clean. 29On the eighth day she must take two doves or two young pigeons and bring them to the priest at the entrance to the Tent of Meeting. 30The priest is to sacrifice one for a sin offering and the other for a burnt offering. In this way he will make atonement for her before the LORD for the uncleanness of her discharge.

31"You must keep the Israelites separate from things that make them unclean, so they will not die in their uncleanness for defiling my dwelling-place, which is among them.'"

32These are the regulations for a man with a discharge, for anyone made unclean by an emission of semen, 33for a woman in her monthly period, for a man or a woman with a discharge, and for a man who lies with a woman who is ceremonially unclean.

The Day of Atonement

16 The LORD spoke to Moses after the death of the two sons of Aaron who died when they approached the LORD. 2The LORD said to Moses: "Tell your brother Aaron not to come whenever he chooses into the Most Holy Place behind the curtain in front of the atonement cover on the ark, or else he will die, because I appear in the cloud over the atonement cover.

3"This is how Aaron is to enter the sanctuary area: with a young bull for a sin offering and a ram for a burnt offering. 4He is to put on the sacred linen

tunic, with linen undergarments next to his body; he is to tie the linen sash around him and put on the linen turban. These are sacred garments; so he must bathe himself with water before he puts them on. 5From the Israelite community he is to take two male goats for a sin offering and a ram for a burnt offering.

6"Aaron is to offer the bull for his own sin offering to make atonement for himself and his household. 7Then he is to take the two goats and present them before the LORD at the entrance to the Tent of Meeting. 8He is to cast lots for the two goats—one lot for the LORD and the other for the scapegoat. 9Aaron shall bring the goat whose lot falls to the LORD and sacrifice it for a sin offering. 10But the goat chosen by lot as the scapegoat shall be presented alive before the LORD to be used for making atonement by sending it into the desert as a scapegoat.

11"Aaron shall bring the bull for his own sin offering to make atonement for himself and his household, and he is to slaughter the bull for his own sin offering. 12He is to take a censer full of burning coals from the altar before the LORD and two handfuls of finely ground fragrant incense and take them behind the curtain. 13He is to put the incense on the fire before the LORD, and the smoke of the incense will conceal the atonement cover above the Testimony, so that he will not die. 14He is to take some of the bull's blood and with his finger sprinkle it on the front of the atonement cover; then he shall sprinkle some of it with his finger seven times before the atonement cover.

15"He shall then slaughter the goat for the sin offering for the people and take its blood behind the curtain and do with it as he did with the bull's blood: He shall sprinkle it on the atonement cover and in front of it. 16In this way he will make atonement for the Most Holy Place because of the uncleanness and rebellion of the Israelites, whatever their sins have been. He is to do the same for the Tent of Meeting, which is among them in the midst of their uncleanness. ¹⁷No-one is to be in the Tent of Meeting from the time Aaron goes in to make atonement in the Most Holy Place until he comes out, having made atonement for himself, his household and the whole community of Israel.

¹⁸"Then he shall come out to the altar that is before the LORD and make atonement for it. He shall take some of the bull's blood and some of the goat's blood and put it on all the horns of the altar. ¹⁹He shall sprinkle some of the blood on it with his finger seven times to cleanse it and consecrate it from the uncleanness of the Israelites.

²⁰"When Aaron has finished making atonement for the Most Holy Place, the Tent of Meeting and the altar, he shall bring forward the live goat. ²¹He is to lay both hands on the head of the live goat and confess over it all the wickedness and rebellion of the Israelites—all their sins—and put them on the goat's head. He shall send the goat away into the desert in the care of a man appointed for the task. ²²The goat will carry on itself all their sins to a solitary place; and the man shall release it in the desert.

²³"Then Aaron is to go into the Tent of Meeting and take off the linen garments he put on before he entered the Most Holy Place, and he is to leave them there. ²⁴He shall bathe himself with water in a holy place and put on his regular garments. Then he shall come out and sacrifice the burnt offering for himself and the burnt offering for the people, to make atonement for himself and for the people. ²⁵He shall also burn the fat of the sin offering on the altar.

²⁶"The man who releases the goat as a scapegoat must wash his clothes and bathe himself with water; afterwards he may come into the camp. ²⁷The bull and the goat for the sin offerings, whose blood was brought into the Most Holy Place to make atonement, must be taken outside the camp; their hides, flesh and offal are to be burned up.

²⁸The man who burns them must wash his clothes and bathe himself with water; afterwards he may come into the camp.

²⁹"This is to be a lasting ordinance for you: On the tenth day of the seventh month you must deny yourselves and not do any work—whether native-born or an alien living among you—³⁰because on this day atonement will be made for you, to cleanse you. Then, before the LORD, you will be clean from all your sins. ³¹It is a sabbath of rest, and you must deny yourselves; it is a lasting ordinance. ³²The priest who is anointed and ordained to succeed his father as high priest is to make atonement. He is to put on the sacred linen garments ³³and make atonement for the Most Holy Place, for the Tent of Meeting and the altar, and for the priests and all the people of the community.

³⁴"This is to be a lasting ordinance for you: Atonement is to be made once a year for all the sins of the Israelites."

And it was done, as the LORD commanded Moses.

NEW TESTAMENT READING
Mark 13:32–14:16

The Day and Hour Unknown

³²"No-one knows about that day or hour, not even the angels in heaven, nor the Son, but only the Father. ³³Be on guard! Be alert! You do not know when that time will come. ³⁴It's like a man going away: He leaves his house and puts his servants in charge, each with his assigned task, and tells the one at the door to keep watch.

³⁵"Therefore keep watch because you do not know when the owner of the house will come back—whether in the evening, or at midnight, or when the cock crows, or at dawn. ³⁶If he comes suddenly, do not let him find you sleeping. ³⁷What I say to you, I say to everyone: 'Watch!'"

Jesus Anointed at Bethany

14 Now the Passover and the Feast of Unleavened Bread were only two days away, and the chief priests and the teachers of the law were looking for some sly way to arrest Jesus and kill him. 2"But not during the Feast," they said, "or the people may riot."

3While he was in Bethany, reclining at the table in the home of a man known as Simon the Leper, a woman came with an alabaster jar of very expensive perfume, made of pure nard. She broke the jar and poured the perfume on his head.

4Some of those present were saying indignantly to one another, "Why this waste of perfume? 5It could have been sold for more than a year's wages and the money given to the poor." And they rebuked her harshly.

6"Leave her alone," said Jesus. "Why are you bothering her? She has done a beautiful thing to me. 7The poor you will always have with you, and you can help them any time you want. But you will not always have me. 8She did what she could. She poured perfume on my body beforehand to prepare for my burial. 9I tell you the truth, wherever the gospel is preached throughout the world, what she has done will also be told, in memory of her."

10Then Judas Iscariot, one of the Twelve, went to the chief priests to betray Jesus to them. 11They were delighted to hear this and promised to give him money. So he watched for an opportunity to hand him over.

The Lord's Supper

12On the first day of the Feast of Unleavened Bread, when it was customary to sacrifice the Passover lamb, Jesus' disciples asked him, "Where do you want us to go and make preparations for you to eat the Passover?"

13So he sent two of his disciples, telling them, "Go into the city, and a man carrying a jar of water will meet you. Follow him. 14Say to the owner of the house he enters, 'The Teacher asks: Where is my guest room, where I may eat the Passover with my disciples?' 15He will show you a large upper room, furnished and ready. Make preparations for us there."

16The disciples left, went into the city and found things just as Jesus had told them. So they prepared the Passover.

READING FROM PSALMS
Psalm 31:1–8

For the director of music. A psalm of David.

1In you, O LORD, I have taken refuge;
    let me never be put to shame;
    deliver me in your righteousness.
2Turn your ear to me,
    come quickly to my rescue;
be my rock of refuge,
    a strong fortress to save me.
3Since you are my rock and my
        fortress,
    for the sake of your name lead and
        guide me.
4Free me from the trap that is set for
        me,
    for you are my refuge.
5Into your hands I commit my spirit;
    redeem me, O LORD, the God of
        truth.

6I hate those who cling to worthless
        idols;
    I trust in the LORD.
7I will be glad and rejoice in your love,
    for you saw my affliction
    and knew the anguish of my soul.
8You have not handed me over to the
        enemy
    but have set my feet in a spacious
        place.

OLD TESTAMENT READING
Leviticus 17:1–18:30

Eating Blood Forbidden

17 The LORD said to Moses, 2"Speak to Aaron and his sons and to all the Israelites and say to them: 'This is what the LORD has commanded: 3Any Israelite who sacrifices an ox, a lamb or a goat in the camp or outside of it 4instead of bringing it to the entrance to the Tent of Meeting to present it as an offering to the LORD in front of the tabernacle of the LORD—that man shall be considered guilty of bloodshed; he has shed blood and must be cut off from his people. 5This is so that the Israelites will bring to the LORD the sacrifices they are now making in the open fields. They must bring them to the priest, that is, to the LORD, at the entrance to the Tent of Meeting and sacrifice them as fellowship offerings. 6The priest is to sprinkle the blood against the altar of the LORD at the entrance to the Tent of Meeting and burn the fat as an aroma pleasing to the LORD. 7They must no longer offer any of their sacrifices to the goat idols to whom they prostitute themselves. This is to be a lasting ordinance for them and for the generations to come.'

8"Say to them: 'Any Israelite or any alien living among them who offers a burnt offering or sacrifice 9and does not bring it to the entrance to the Tent of Meeting to sacrifice it to the LORD—that man must be cut off from his people.

10"'Any Israelite or any alien living among them who eats any blood—I will set my face against that person who eats blood and will cut him off from his people. 11For the life of a creature is in the blood, and I have given it to you to make atonement for yourselves on the altar; it is the blood that makes atonement for one's life. 12Therefore I say to the Israelites, "None of you may eat blood, nor may an alien living among you eat blood."

13"'Any Israelite or any alien living among you who hunts any animal or bird that may be eaten must drain out the blood and cover it with earth, 14because the life of every creature is its blood. That is why I have said to the Israelites, "You must not eat the blood of any creature, because the life of every creature is its blood; anyone who eats it must be cut off."

15"'Anyone, whether native-born or alien, who eats anything found dead or torn by wild animals must wash his clothes and bathe with water, and he will be ceremonially unclean till evening; then he will be clean. 16But if he does not wash his clothes and bathe himself, he will be held responsible.'"

Unlawful Sexual Relations

18 The LORD said to Moses, 2"Speak to the Israelites and say to them: 'I am the LORD your God. 3You must not do as they do in Egypt, where you used to live, and you must not do as they do in the land of Canaan, where I am bringing you. Do not follow their practices. 4You must obey my laws and be careful to follow my decrees. I am the LORD your God. 5Keep my decrees and laws, for the man who obeys them will live by them. I am the LORD.

6"'No-one is to approach any close relative to have sexual relations. I am the LORD.

7"'Do not dishonour your father by having sexual relations with your mother. She is your mother; do not have relations with her.

8"'Do not have sexual relations with your father's wife; that would dishonour your father.

9"'Do not have sexual relations with your sister, either your father's daughter or your mother's daughter, whether she was born in the same home or elsewhere.

10"'Do not have sexual relations with your son's daughter or your daughter's daughter; that would dishonour you.

11"'Do not have sexual relations with the daughter of your father's wife, born to your father; she is your sister.

12"'Do not have sexual relations with your father's sister; she is your father's close relative.

13"'Do not have sexual relations with your mother's sister, because she is your mother's close relative.

14"'Do not dishonour your father's brother by approaching his wife to have sexual relations; she is your aunt.

15"'Do not have sexual relations with your daughter-in-law. She is your son's wife; do not have relations with her.

16"'Do not have sexual relations with your brother's wife; that would dishonour your brother.

17"'Do not have sexual relations with both a woman and her daughter. Do not have sexual relations with either her son's daughter or her daughter's daughter; they are her close relatives. That is wickedness.

18"'Do not take your wife's sister as a rival wife and have sexual relations with her while your wife is living.

19"'Do not approach a woman to have sexual relations during the uncleanness of her monthly period.

20"'Do not have sexual relations with your neighbour's wife and defile yourself with her.

21"'Do not give any of your children to be sacrificed to Molech, for you must not profane the name of your God. I am the LORD.

22"'Do not lie with a man as one lies with a woman; that is detestable.

23"'Do not have sexual relations with an animal and defile yourself with it. A woman must not present herself to an animal to have sexual relations with it; that is a perversion.

24"'Do not defile yourselves in any of these ways, because this is how the nations that I am going to drive out before you became defiled. 25Even the land was defiled; so I punished it for its sin, and the land vomited out its inhabitants. 26But you must keep my decrees and my laws. The native-born and the aliens living among you must not do any of these detestable things, 27for all these things were done by the people who lived in the land before you, and the land became defiled. 28And if you defile the land, it will vomit you out as it vomited out the nations that were before you.

29"'Everyone who does any of these detestable things—such persons must be cut off from their people. 30Keep my requirements and do not follow any of the detestable customs that were practised before you came and do not defile yourselves with them. I am the LORD your God.'"

NEW TESTAMENT READING
Mark 14:17–42

17When evening came, Jesus arrived with the Twelve. 18While they were reclining at the table eating, he said, "I tell you the truth, one of you will betray me—one who is eating with me."

19They were saddened, and one by one they said to him, "Surely not I?"

20"It is one of the Twelve," he replied, "one who dips bread into the bowl with me. 21The Son of Man will go just as it is written about him. But woe to that man who betrays the Son of Man! It would be better for him if he had not been born."

22While they were eating, Jesus took bread, gave thanks and broke it, and gave it to his disciples, saying, "Take it; this is my body."

23Then he took the cup, gave thanks and offered it to them, and they all drank from it.

24"This is my blood of the covenant, which is poured out for many," he said to them. 25"I tell you the truth, I will not drink again of the fruit of the vine until that day when I drink it anew in the kingdom of God."

26When they had sung a hymn, they went out to the Mount of Olives.

Jesus Predicts Peter's Denial

27"You will all fall away," Jesus told them, "for it is written:

"'I will strike the shepherd,
 and the sheep will be scattered.'

28But after I have risen, I will go ahead of you into Galilee."

29Peter declared, "Even if all fall away, I will not."

30"I tell you the truth," Jesus answered, "today—yes, tonight—before the cock crows twice you yourself will disown me three times."

31But Peter insisted emphatically, "Even if I have to die with you, I will never disown you." And all the others said the same.

Gethsemane

32They went to a place called Gethsemane, and Jesus said to his disciples, "Sit here while I pray." 33He took Peter, James and John along with him, and he began to be deeply distressed and troubled. 34"My soul is overwhelmed with sorrow to the point of death," he said to them. "Stay here and keep watch."

35Going a little farther, he fell to the ground and prayed that if possible the hour might pass from him. 36"Abba, Father," he said, "everything is possible for you. Take this cup from me. Yet not what I will, but what you will."

37Then he returned to his disciples and found them sleeping. "Simon," he said to Peter, "are you asleep? Could you not keep watch for one hour? 38Watch and pray so that you will not fall into temptation. The spirit is willing, but the body is weak."

39Once more he went away and prayed the same thing. 40When he came back, he again found them sleeping, because their eyes were heavy. They did not know what to say to him.

41Returning the third time, he said to them, "Are you still sleeping and resting? Enough! The hour has come. Look, the Son of Man is betrayed into the hands of sinners. 42Rise! Let us go! Here comes my betrayer!"

READING FROM PSALMS
Psalm 31:9–18

9Be merciful to me, O Lord, for I am
    in distress;
  my eyes grow weak with sorrow,
  my soul and my body with grief.
10My life is consumed by anguish
    and my years by groaning;
  my strength fails because of my
    affliction,
  and my bones grow weak.
11Because of all my enemies,
  I am the utter contempt of my
    neighbours;
  I am a dread to my friends—
  those who see me on the street flee
    from me.
12I am forgotten by them as though I
    were dead;
  I have become like broken pottery.
13For I hear the slander of many;
  there is terror on every side;
  they conspire against me
    and plot to take my life.

14But I trust in you, O Lord;
  I say, "You are my God."
15My times are in your hands;
  deliver me from my enemies
    and from those who pursue me.
16Let your face shine on your servant;
  save me in your unfailing love.
17Let me not be put to shame, O Lord,
  for I have cried out to you;
  but let the wicked be put to shame
    and lie silent in the grave.
18Let their lying lips be silenced,
  for with pride and contempt
    they speak arrogantly against the
    righteous.

OLD TESTAMENT READING
Leviticus 19:1–20:27

Various Laws

19 The LORD said to Moses, 2"Speak to the entire assembly of Israel and say to them: 'Be holy because I, the LORD your God, am holy.

3"'Each of you must respect his mother and father, and you must observe my Sabbaths. I am the LORD your God.

4"'Do not turn to idols or make gods of cast metal for yourselves. I am the LORD your God.

5"'When you sacrifice a fellowship offering to the LORD, sacrifice it in such a way that it will be accepted on your behalf. 6It shall be eaten on the day you sacrifice it or on the next day; anything left over until the third day must be burned up. 7If any of it is eaten on the third day, it is impure and will not be accepted. 8Whoever eats it will be held responsible because he has desecrated what is holy to the LORD; that person must be cut off from his people.

9"'When you reap the harvest of your land, do not reap to the very edges of your field or gather the gleanings of your harvest. 10Do not go over your vineyard a second time or pick up the grapes that have fallen. Leave them for the poor and the alien. I am the LORD your God.

11"'Do not steal.

"'Do not lie.

"'Do not deceive one another.

12"'Do not swear falsely by my name and so profane the name of your God. I am the LORD.

13"'Do not defraud your neighbour or rob him.

"'Do not hold back the wages of a hired man overnight.

14"'Do not curse the deaf or put a stumbling-block in front of the blind, but fear your God. I am the LORD.

15"'Do not pervert justice; do not show partiality to the poor or favouritism to the great, but judge your neighbour fairly.

16"'Do not go about spreading slander among your people.

"'Do not do anything that endangers your neighbour's life. I am the LORD.

17"'Do not hate your brother in your heart. Rebuke your neighbour frankly so that you will not share in his guilt.

18"'Do not seek revenge or bear a grudge against one of your people, but love your neighbour as yourself. I am the LORD.

19"'Keep my decrees.

"'Do not mate different kinds of animals.

"'Do not plant your field with two kinds of seed.

"'Do not wear clothing woven of two kinds of material.

20"'If a man sleeps with a woman who is a slave girl promised to another man but who has not been ransomed or given her freedom, there must be due punishment. Yet they are not to be put to death, because she had not been freed. 21The man, however, must bring a ram to the entrance to the Tent of Meeting for a guilt offering to the LORD. 22With the ram of the guilt offering the priest is to make atonement for him before the LORD for the sin he has committed, and his sin will be forgiven.

23"'When you enter the land and plant any kind of fruit tree, regard its fruit as forbidden. For three years you are to consider it forbidden; it must not be eaten. 24In the fourth year all its fruit will be holy, an offering of praise to the LORD. 25But in the fifth year you may eat its fruit. In this way your harvest will be increased. I am the LORD your God.

26"'Do not eat any meat with the blood still in it.

"'Do not practise divination or sorcery.

27" 'Do not cut the hair at the sides of your head or clip off the edges of your beard.

28" 'Do not cut your bodies for the dead or put tattoo marks on yourselves. I am the LORD.

29" 'Do not degrade your daughter by making her a prostitute, or the land will turn to prostitution and be filled with wickedness.

30" 'Observe my Sabbaths and have reverence for my sanctuary. I am the LORD.

31" 'Do not turn to mediums or seek out spiritists, for you will be defiled by them. I am the LORD your God.

32" 'Rise in the presence of the aged, show respect for the elderly and revere your God. I am the LORD.

33" 'When an alien lives with you in your land, do not ill-treat him. ³⁴The alien living with you must be treated as one of your native-born. Love him as yourself, for you were aliens in Egypt. I am the LORD your God.

35" 'Do not use dishonest standards when measuring length, weight or quantity. ³⁶Use honest scales and honest weights, an honest ephah and an honest hin. I am the LORD your God, who brought you out of Egypt.

37" 'Keep all my decrees and all my laws and follow them. I am the LORD.'"

Punishments for Sin

20 The LORD said to Moses, ²"Say to the Israelites: 'Any Israelite or any alien living in Israel who gives any of his children to Molech must be put to death. The people of the community are to stone him. ³I will set my face against that man and I will cut him off from his people; for by giving his children to Molech, he has defiled my sanctuary and profaned my holy name. ⁴If the people of the community close their eyes when that man gives one of his children to Molech and they fail to put him to death, ⁵I will set my face against that man and his family and will cut off from their people both him and

all who follow him in prostituting themselves to Molech.

6" 'I will set my face against the person who turns to mediums and spiritists to prostitute himself by following them, and I will cut him off from his people.

7" 'Consecrate yourselves and be holy, because I am the LORD your God. ⁸Keep my decrees and follow them. I am the LORD, who makes you holy.

9" 'If anyone curses his father or mother, he must be put to death. He has cursed his father or his mother, and his blood will be on his own head.

10" 'If a man commits adultery with another man's wife—with the wife of his neighbour—both the adulterer and the adulteress must be put to death.

11" 'If a man sleeps with his father's wife, he has dishonoured his father. Both the man and the woman must be put to death; their blood will be on their own heads.

12" 'If a man sleeps with his daughter-in-law, both of them must be put to death. What they have done is a perversion; their blood will be on their own heads.

13" 'If a man lies with a man as one lies with a woman, both of them have done what is detestable. They must be put to death; their blood will be on their own heads.

14" 'If a man marries both a woman and her mother, it is wicked. Both he and they must be burned in the fire, so that no wickedness will be among you.

15" 'If a man has sexual relations with an animal, he must be put to death, and you must kill the animal.

16" 'If a woman approaches an animal to have sexual relations with it, kill both the woman and the animal. They must be put to death; their blood will be on their own heads.

17" 'If a man marries his sister, the daughter of either his father or his mother, and they have sexual relations, it is a disgrace. They must be cut off before the eyes of their people. He has dishonoured his sister and will be held responsible.

18"'If a man lies with a woman during her monthly period and has sexual relations with her, he has exposed the source of her flow, and she has also uncovered it. Both of them must be cut off from their people.

19"'Do not have sexual relations with the sister of either your mother or your father, for that would dishonour a close relative; both of you would be held responsible.

20"'If a man sleeps with his aunt, he has dishonoured his uncle. They will be held responsible; they will die childless.

21"'If a man marries his brother's wife, it is an act of impurity; he has dishonoured his brother. They will be childless.

22"'Keep all my decrees and laws and follow them, so that the land where I am bringing you to live may not vomit you out. 23You must not live according to the customs of the nations I am going to drive out before you. Because they did all these things, I abhorred them. 24But I said to you, "You will possess their land; I will give it to you as an inheritance, a land flowing with milk and honey." I am the LORD your God, who has set you apart from the nations.

25"'You must therefore make a distinction between clean and unclean animals and between unclean and clean birds. Do not defile yourselves by any animal or bird or anything that moves along the ground—those which I have set apart as unclean for you. 26You are to be holy to me because I, the LORD, am holy, and I have set you apart from the nations to be my own.

27"'A man or woman who is a medium or spiritist among you must be put to death. You are to stone them; their blood will be on their own heads.'"

NEW TESTAMENT READING
Mark 14:43–72
Jesus Arrested

43Just as he was speaking, Judas, one of the Twelve, appeared. With him was a crowd armed with swords and clubs, sent from the chief priests, the teachers of the law, and the elders.

44Now the betrayer had arranged a signal with them: "The one I kiss is the man; arrest him and lead him away under guard." 45Going at once to Jesus, Judas said, "Rabbi!" and kissed him. 46The men seized Jesus and arrested him. 47Then one of those standing near drew his sword and struck the servant of the high priest, cutting off his ear.

48"Am I leading a rebellion," said Jesus, "that you have come out with swords and clubs to capture me? 49Every day I was with you, teaching in the temple courts, and you did not arrest me. But the Scriptures must be fulfilled." 50Then everyone deserted him and fled.

51A young man, wearing nothing but a linen garment, was following Jesus. When they seized him, 52he fled naked, leaving his garment behind.

Before the Sanhedrin

53They took Jesus to the high priest, and all the chief priests, elders and teachers of the law came together. 54Peter followed him at a distance, right into the courtyard of the high priest. There he sat with the guards and warmed himself at the fire.

55The chief priests and the whole Sanhedrin were looking for evidence against Jesus so that they could put him to death, but they did not find any. 56Many testified falsely against him, but their statements did not agree.

57Then some stood up and gave this false testimony against him: 58"We heard him say, 'I will destroy this man-made temple and in three days will build another, not made by man.'" 59Yet even then their testimony did not agree.

60Then the high priest stood up before them and asked Jesus, "Are you not going to answer? What is this testimony that these men are bringing against you?" 61But Jesus remained silent and gave no answer.

Again the high priest asked him, "Are you the Christ, the Son of the Blessed One?"

62"I am," said Jesus. "And you will see the Son of Man sitting at the right hand of the Mighty One and coming on the clouds of heaven."

63The high priest tore his clothes. "Why do we need any more witnesses?" he asked. 64"You have heard the blasphemy. What do you think?"

They all condemned him as worthy of death. 65Then some began to spit at him; they blindfolded him, struck him with their fists, and said, "Prophesy!" And the guards took him and beat him.

Peter Disowns Jesus

66While Peter was below in the courtyard, one of the servant girls of the high priest came by. 67When she saw Peter warming himself, she looked closely at him.

"You also were with that Nazarene, Jesus," she said.

68But he denied it. "I don't know or understand what you're talking about," he said, and went out into the entrance.

69When the servant girl saw him there, she said again to those standing around, "This fellow is one of them." 70Again he denied it.

After a little while, those standing near said to Peter, "Surely you are one of them, for you are a Galilean."

71He began to call down curses on himself, and he swore to them, "I don't know this man you're talking about."

72Immediately the cock crowed the second time. Then Peter remembered the word Jesus had spoken to him: "Before the cock crows twice you will disown me three times." And he broke down and wept.

READING FROM PROVERBS
Proverbs 6:30–35

30Men do not despise a thief if he steals
    to satisfy his hunger when he is
    starving.
31Yet if he is caught, he must pay
    sevenfold,
    though it costs him all the wealth of
    his house.
32But a man who commits adultery
    lacks judgment;
    whoever does so destroys himself.
33Blows and disgrace are his lot,
    and his shame will never be wiped
    away;
34for jealousy arouses a husband's fury,
    and he will show no mercy when he
    takes revenge.
35He will not accept any compensation;
    he will refuse the bribe, however
    great it is.

DAY 69   # MARCH 10

OLD TESTAMENT READING
Leviticus 21:1–22:33

Rules for Priests

21 The LORD said to Moses, "Speak to the priests, the sons of Aaron, and say to them: 'A priest must not make himself ceremonially unclean for any of his people who die, 2except

for a close relative, such as his mother or father, his son or daughter, his brother, 3or an unmarried sister who is dependent on him since she has no husband—for her he may make himself unclean. 4He must not make himself unclean for people related to him by marriage, and so defile himself.

5"'Priests must not shave their heads or shave off the edges of their beards or cut their bodies. ⁶They must be holy to their God and must not profane the name of their God. Because they present the offerings made to the LORD by fire, the food of their God, they are to be holy.

⁷"They must not marry women defiled by prostitution or divorced from their husbands, because priests are holy to their God. ⁸Regard them as holy, because they offer up the food of your God. Consider them holy, because I the LORD am holy—I who make you holy.

⁹"'If a priest's daughter defiles herself by becoming a prostitute, she disgraces her father; she must be burned in the fire.

¹⁰"'The high priest, the one among his brothers who has had the anointing oil poured on his head and who has been ordained to wear the priestly garments, must not let his hair become unkempt or tear his clothes. ¹¹He must not enter a place where there is a dead body. He must not make himself unclean, even for his father or mother, ¹²nor leave the sanctuary of his God or desecrate it, because he has been dedicated by the anointing oil of his God. I am the LORD.

¹³"'The woman he marries must be a virgin. ¹⁴He must not marry a widow, a divorced woman, or a woman defiled by prostitution, but only a virgin from his own people, ¹⁵so that he will not defile his offspring among his people. I am the LORD, who makes him holy.'"

¹⁶The LORD said to Moses, ¹⁷"Say to Aaron: 'For the generations to come none of your descendants who has a defect may come near to offer the food of his God. ¹⁸No man who has any defect may come near: no man who is blind or lame, disfigured or deformed; ¹⁹no man with a crippled foot or hand, ²⁰or who is hunchbacked or dwarfed, or who has any eye defect, or who has festering or running sores or damaged testicles. ²¹No descendant of Aaron the priest who has any defect is to come near to present the offerings made to the LORD by fire. He has a defect; he must not come near to offer the food of

his God. ²²He may eat the most holy food of his God, as well as the holy food; ²³yet because of his defect, he must not go near the curtain or approach the altar, and so desecrate my sanctuary. I am the LORD, who makes them holy.'"

²⁴So Moses told this to Aaron and his sons and to all the Israelites.

22 The LORD said to Moses, ²"Tell Aaron and his sons to treat with respect the sacred offerings the Israelites consecrate to me, so that they will not profane my holy name. I am the LORD.

³"Say to them: 'For the generations to come, if any of your descendants is ceremonially unclean and yet comes near the sacred offerings that the Israelites consecrate to the LORD, that person must be cut off from my presence. I am the LORD.

⁴"'If a descendant of Aaron has an infectious skin disease or a bodily discharge, he may not eat the sacred offerings until he is cleansed. He will also be unclean if he touches something defiled by a corpse or by anyone who has an emission of semen, ⁵or if he touches any crawling thing that makes him unclean, or any person who makes him unclean, whatever the uncleanness may be. ⁶The one who touches any such thing will be unclean till evening. He must not eat any of the sacred offerings unless he has bathed himself with water. ⁷When the sun goes down, he will be clean, and after that he may eat the sacred offerings, for they are his food. ⁸He must not eat anything found dead or torn by wild animals, and so become unclean through it. I am the LORD.

⁹"'The priests are to keep my requirements so that they do not become guilty and die for treating them with contempt. I am the LORD, who makes them holy.

¹⁰"'No-one outside a priest's family may eat the sacred offering, nor may the guest of a priest or his hired worker eat it. ¹¹But if a priest buys a slave with

money, or if a slave is born in his household, that slave may eat his food. ¹²If a priest's daughter marries anyone other than a priest, she may not eat any of the sacred contributions. ¹³But if a priest's daughter becomes a widow or is divorced, yet has no children, and she returns to live in her father's house as in her youth, she may eat of her father's food. No unauthorised person, however, may eat any of it.

¹⁴"'If anyone eats a sacred offering by mistake, he must make restitution to the priest for the offering and add a fifth of the value to it. ¹⁵The priests must not desecrate the sacred offerings the Israelites present to the LORD ¹⁶by allowing them to eat the sacred offerings and so bring upon them guilt requiring payment. I am the LORD, who makes them holy.'"

Unacceptable Sacrifices

¹⁷The LORD said to Moses, ¹⁸"Speak to Aaron and his sons and to all the Israelites and say to them: 'If any of you—either an Israelite or an alien living in Israel—presents a gift for a burnt offering to the LORD, either to fulfil a vow or as a freewill offering, ¹⁹you must present a male without defect from the cattle, sheep or goats in order that it may be accepted on your behalf. ²⁰Do not bring anything with a defect, because it will not be accepted on your behalf. ²¹When anyone brings from the herd or flock a fellowship offering to the LORD to fulfil a special vow or as a freewill offering, it must be without defect or blemish to be acceptable. ²²Do not offer to the LORD the blind, the injured or the maimed, or anything with warts or festering or running sores. Do not place any of these on the altar as an offering made to the LORD by fire. ²³You may, however, present as a freewill offering an ox or a sheep that is deformed or stunted, but it will not be accepted in fulfilment of a vow. ²⁴You must not offer to the LORD an animal whose testicles are bruised, crushed,

torn or cut. You must not do this in your own land, ²⁵and you must not accept such animals from the hand of a foreigner and offer them as the food of your God. They will not be accepted on your behalf, because they are deformed and have defects.'"

²⁶The LORD said to Moses, ²⁷"When a calf, a lamb or a goat is born, it is to remain with its mother for seven days. From the eighth day on, it will be acceptable as an offering made to the LORD by fire. ²⁸Do not slaughter a cow or a sheep and its young on the same day.

²⁹"When you sacrifice a thank-offering to the LORD, sacrifice it in such a way that it will be accepted on your behalf. ³⁰It must be eaten that same day; leave none of it till morning. I am the LORD.

³¹"Keep my commands and follow them. I am the LORD. ³²Do not profane my holy name. I must be acknowledged as holy by the Israelites. I am the LORD, who makes you holy ³³and who brought you out of Egypt to be your God. I am the LORD."

NEW TESTAMENT READING
Mark 15:1–32

Jesus Before Pilate

15 Very early in the morning, the chief priests, with the elders, the teachers of the law and the whole Sanhedrin, reached a decision. They bound Jesus, led him away and turned him over to Pilate.

²"Are you the king of the Jews?" asked Pilate.

"Yes, it is as you say," Jesus replied.

³The chief priests accused him of many things. ⁴So again Pilate asked him, "Aren't you going to answer? See how many things they are accusing you of."

⁵But Jesus still made no reply, and Pilate was amazed.

⁶Now it was the custom at the Feast to

release a prisoner whom the people requested. ⁷A man called Barabbas was in prison with the insurrectionists who had committed murder in the uprising. ⁸The crowd came up and asked Pilate to do for them what he usually did.

⁹"Do you want me to release to you the king of the Jews?" asked Pilate, ¹⁰knowing it was out of envy that the chief priests had handed Jesus over to him. ¹¹But the chief priests stirred up the crowd to have Pilate release Barabbas instead.

¹²"What shall I do, then, with the one you call the king of the Jews?" Pilate asked them.

¹³"Crucify him!" they shouted.

¹⁴"Why? What crime has he committed?" asked Pilate.

But they shouted all the louder, "Crucify him!"

¹⁵Wanting to satisfy the crowd, Pilate released Barabbas to them. He had Jesus flogged, and handed him over to be crucified.

The Soldiers Mock Jesus

¹⁶The soldiers led Jesus away into the palace (that is, the Praetorium) and called together the whole company of soldiers. ¹⁷They put a purple robe on him, then twisted together a crown of thorns and set it on him. ¹⁸And they began to call out to him, "Hail, king of the Jews!" ¹⁹Again and again they struck him on the head with a staff and spat on him. Falling on their knees, they paid homage to him. ²⁰And when they had mocked him, they took off the purple robe and put his own clothes on him. Then they led him out to crucify him.

The Crucifixion

²¹A certain man from Cyrene, Simon, the father of Alexander and Rufus, was passing by on his way in from the country, and they forced him to carry the cross. ²²They brought Jesus to the place called Golgotha (which means The Place of the Skull). ²³Then they offered him wine mixed with myrrh, but he did not take it. ²⁴And they crucified him. Dividing up his clothes, they cast lots to see what each would get.

²⁵It was the third hour when they crucified him. ²⁶The written notice of the charge against him read: THE KING OF THE JEWS. ²⁷They crucified two robbers with him, one on his right and one on his left. ²⁹Those who passed by hurled insults at him, shaking their heads and saying, "So! You who are going to destroy the temple and build it in three days, ³⁰come down from the cross and save yourself!"

³¹In the same way the chief priests and the teachers of the law mocked him among themselves. "He saved others," they said, "but he can't save himself! ³²Let this Christ, this King of Israel, come down now from the cross, that we may see and believe." Those crucified with him also heaped insults on him.

READING FROM PSALMS
Psalm 31:19–24

¹⁹How great is your goodness,
    which you have stored up for those
        who fear you,
    which you bestow in the sight of men
        on those who take refuge in you.
²⁰In the shelter of your presence you
        hide them
    from the intrigues of men;
in your dwelling you keep them safe
    from accusing tongues.

²¹Praise be to the LORD,
    for he showed his wonderful love
        to me
    when I was in a besieged city.
²²In my alarm I said,
    "I am cut off from your sight!"
Yet you heard my cry for mercy
    when I called to you for help.

²³Love the LORD, all his saints!
    The LORD preserves the faithful,
    but the proud he pays back in full.
²⁴Be strong and take heart,
    all you who hope in the LORD.

MARCH 11

OLD TESTAMENT READING
Leviticus 23:1–24:23

23 The LORD said to Moses, [2]"Speak to the Israelites and say to them: 'These are my appointed feasts, the appointed feasts of the LORD, which you are to proclaim as sacred assemblies.

The Sabbath

[3]"'There are six days when you may work, but the seventh day is a Sabbath of rest, a day of sacred assembly. You are not to do any work; wherever you live, it is a Sabbath to the LORD.

The Passover and Unleavened Bread

[4]"'These are the LORD's appointed feasts, the sacred assemblies you are to proclaim at their appointed times: [5]The LORD's Passover begins at twilight on the fourteenth day of the first month. [6]On the fifteenth day of that month the LORD's Feast of Unleavened Bread begins; for seven days you must eat bread made without yeast. [7]On the first day hold a sacred assembly and do no regular work. [8]For seven days present an offering made to the LORD by fire. And on the seventh day hold a sacred assembly and do no regular work.'"

Firstfruits

[9]The LORD said to Moses, [10]"Speak to the Israelites and say to them: 'When you enter the land I am going to give you and you reap its harvest, bring to the priest a sheaf of the first grain you harvest. [11]He is to wave the sheaf before the LORD so that it will be accepted on your behalf; the priest is to wave it on the day after the Sabbath. [12]On the day you wave the sheaf, you must sacrifice

as a burnt offering to the LORD a lamb a year old without defect, [13]together with its grain offering of two-tenths of an ephah of fine flour mixed with oil—an offering made to the LORD by fire, a pleasing aroma—and its drink offering of a quarter of a hin of wine. [14]You must not eat any bread, or roasted or new grain, until the very day you bring this offering to your God. This is to be a lasting ordinance for the generations to come, wherever you live.

Feast of Weeks

[15]"'From the day after the Sabbath, the day you brought the sheaf of the wave offering, count off seven full weeks. [16]Count off fifty days up to the day after the seventh Sabbath, and then present an offering of new grain to the LORD. [17]From wherever you live, bring two loaves made of two-tenths of an ephah of fine flour, baked with yeast, as a wave offering of firstfruits to the LORD. [18]Present with this bread seven male lambs, each a year old and without defect, one young bull and two rams. They will be a burnt offering to the LORD, together with their grain offerings and drink offerings—an offering made by fire, an aroma pleasing to the LORD. [19]Then sacrifice one male goat for a sin offering and two lambs, each a year old, for a fellowship offering. [20]The priest is to wave the two lambs before the LORD as a wave offering, together with the bread of the firstfruits. They are a sacred offering to the LORD for the priest. [21]On that same day you are to proclaim a sacred assembly and do no regular work. This is to be a lasting ordinance for the generations to come, wherever you live.

[22]"'When you reap the harvest of your land, do not reap to the very edges of your field or gather the gleanings of your harvest. Leave them for the poor

and the alien. I am the LORD your God.'"

Feast of Trumpets

23The LORD said to Moses, 24"Say to the Israelites: 'On the first day of the seventh month you are to have a day of rest, a sacred assembly commemorated with trumpet blasts. 25Do no regular work, but present an offering made to the LORD by fire.'"

Day of Atonement

26The LORD said to Moses, 27"The tenth day of this seventh month is the Day of Atonement. Hold a sacred assembly and deny yourselves, and present an offering made to the LORD by fire. 28Do no work on that day, because it is the Day of Atonement, when atonement is made for you before the LORD your God. 29Anyone who does not deny himself on that day must be cut off from his people. 30I will destroy from among his people anyone who does any work on that day. 31You shall do no work at all. This is to be a lasting ordinance for the generations to come, wherever you live. 32It is a sabbath of rest for you, and you must deny yourselves. From the evening of the ninth day of the month until the following evening you are to observe your sabbath."

Feast of Tabernacles

33The LORD said to Moses, 34"Say to the Israelites: 'On the fifteenth day of the seventh month the LORD's Feast of Tabernacles begins, and it lasts for seven days. 35The first day is a sacred assembly; do no regular work. 36For seven days present offerings made to the LORD by fire, and on the eighth day hold a sacred assembly and present an offering made to the LORD by fire. It is the closing assembly; do no regular work.

37("These are the LORD's appointed feasts, which you are to proclaim as sacred assemblies for bringing offerings made to the LORD by fire—the burnt offerings and grain offerings, sacrifices and drink offerings required for each day. 38These offerings are in addition to those for the LORD's Sabbaths and in addition to your gifts and whatever you have vowed and all the freewill offerings you give to the LORD.)

39"So beginning with the fifteenth day of the seventh month, after you have gathered the crops of the land, celebrate the festival to the LORD for seven days; the first day is a day of rest, and the eighth day also is a day of rest. 40On the first day you are to take choice fruit from the trees, and palm fronds, leafy branches and poplars, and rejoice before the LORD your God for seven days. 41Celebrate this as a festival to the LORD for seven days each year. This is to be a lasting ordinance for the generations to come; celebrate it in the seventh month. 42Live in booths for seven days: All native-born Israelites are to live in booths 43so that your descendants will know that I made the Israelites live in booths when I brought them out of Egypt. I am the LORD your God.'"

44So Moses announced to the Israelites the appointed feasts of the LORD.

Oil and Bread Set Before the LORD

24 The LORD said to Moses, 2"Command the Israelites to bring you clear oil of pressed olives for the light so that the lamps may be kept burning continually. 3Outside the curtain of the Testimony in the Tent of Meeting, Aaron is to tend the lamps before the LORD from evening till morning, continually. This is to be a lasting ordinance for the generations to come. 4The lamps on the pure gold lampstand before the LORD must be tended continually.

5"Take fine flour and bake twelve loaves of bread, using two-tenths of an ephah for each loaf. 6Set them in two rows, six in each row, on the table of pure gold before the LORD. 7Along each row put some pure incense as a memorial portion to represent the bread and to be an offering made to the LORD by fire. 8This bread is to be set out before the LORD regularly, Sabbath after Sabbath, on behalf of the Israelites, as a lasting covenant. 9It belongs to Aaron and his sons, who are to eat it in a holy place, because it is a most holy part of their regular share of the offerings made to the LORD by fire."

A Blasphemer Stoned

10Now the son of an Israelite mother and an Egyptian father went out among the Israelites, and a fight broke out in the camp between him and an Israelite. 11The son of the Israelite woman blasphemed the Name with a curse; so they brought him to Moses. (His mother's name was Shelomith, the daughter of Dibri the Danite.) 12They put him in custody until the will of the LORD should be made clear to them.

13Then the LORD said to Moses: 14"Take the blasphemer outside the camp. All those who heard him are to lay their hands on his head, and the entire assembly is to stone him. 15Say to the Israelites: 'If anyone curses his God, he will be held responsible; 16anyone who blasphemes the name of the LORD must be put to death. The entire assembly must stone him. Whether an alien or native-born, when he blasphemes the Name, he must be put to death.

17"'If anyone takes the life of a human being, he must be put to death. 18Anyone who takes the life of someone's animal must make restitution—life for life. 19If anyone injures his neighbour, whatever he has done must be done to him: 20fracture for fracture, eye for eye, tooth for tooth. As he has injured the other, so he is to be injured. 21Whoever kills an animal must make restitution, but whoever kills a man must be put to death. 22You are to have the same law for the alien and the native-born. I am the LORD your God.'"

23Then Moses spoke to the Israelites, and they took the blasphemer outside the camp and stoned him. The Israelites did as the LORD commanded Moses.

NEW TESTAMENT READING
Mark 15:33–47

The Death of Jesus

33At the sixth hour darkness came over the whole land until the ninth hour. 34And at the ninth hour Jesus cried out in a loud voice, "*Eloi, Eloi, lama sabachthani?*"—which means, "My God, my God, why have you forsaken me?"

35When some of those standing near heard this, they said, "Listen, he's calling Elijah."

36One man ran, filled a sponge with wine vinegar, put it on a stick, and offered it to Jesus to drink. "Now leave him alone. Let's see if Elijah comes to take him down," he said.

37With a loud cry, Jesus breathed his last.

38The curtain of the temple was torn in two from top to bottom. 39And when the centurion, who stood there in front of Jesus, heard his cry and saw how he died, he said, "Surely this man was the Son of God!"

40Some women were watching from a distance. Among them were Mary Magdalene, Mary the mother of James the younger and of Joses, and Salome. 41In Galilee these women had followed him and cared for his needs. Many other women who had come up with him to Jerusalem were also there.

The Burial of Jesus

42It was Preparation Day (that is, the day before the Sabbath). So as evening approached, 43Joseph of Arimathea, a prominent member of the Council, who was himself waiting for the kingdom of God, went boldly to Pilate and asked for Jesus' body. 44Pilate was surprised to hear that he was already dead. Summoning the centurion, he asked him if Jesus had already died. [45]When he learned from the centurion that it was so, he gave the body to Joseph. [46]So Joseph bought some linen cloth, took down the body, wrapped it in the linen, and placed it in a tomb cut out of rock. Then he rolled a stone against the entrance of the tomb. [47]Mary Magdalene and Mary the mother of Joses saw where he was laid.

READING FROM PSALMS
Psalm 32:1–11

Of David. A maskil.

[1]Blessed is he
    whose transgressions are forgiven,
    whose sins are covered.
[2]Blessed is the man
    whose sin the LORD does not count
        against him
    and in whose spirit is no deceit.

[3]When I kept silent,
    my bones wasted away
    through my groaning all day long.
[4]For day and night
    your hand was heavy upon me;
my strength was sapped
    as in the heat of summer.   *Selah*

[5]Then I acknowledged my sin to you
    and did not cover up my iniquity.
I said, "I will confess
    my transgressions to the LORD"—
and you forgave
    the guilt of my sin.   *Selah*

[6]Therefore let everyone who is godly
        pray to you
    while you may be found;
surely when the mighty waters rise,
    they will not reach him.
[7]You are my hiding-place;
    you will protect me from trouble
    and surround me with songs of
        deliverance.   *Selah*

[8]I will instruct you and teach you in
        the way you should go;
    I will counsel you and watch over
        you.
[9]Do not be like the horse or the mule,
    which have no understanding
but must be controlled by bit and
        bridle
    or they will not come to you.
[10]Many are the woes of the wicked,
    but the LORD's unfailing love
    surrounds the man who trusts in
        him.

[11]Rejoice in the LORD and be glad, you
        righteous;
    sing, all you who are upright in
        heart!

MARCH 12   DAY 71

OLD TESTAMENT READING
Leviticus 25:1–26:13

The Sabbath Year

25 The LORD said to Moses on Mount Sinai, [2]"Speak to the Israelites and say to them: 'When you enter the land I am going to give you, the land itself must observe a sabbath to the LORD. [3]For six years sow your fields, and for six years prune your vineyards and gather their crops. [4]But in the seventh year the land is to have a sabbath of rest, a sabbath to the LORD. Do not sow your fields or prune your vineyards. [5]Do not reap what grows of itself or harvest the grapes of your untended vines. The land is to have a year of rest. [6]Whatever the land yields during the sabbath year will be food for you—for yourself, your manservant and maidservant, and the hired worker and temporary resident who live among you, 7as well as for your livestock and the wild animals in your land. Whatever the land produces may be eaten.

The Year of Jubilee

8"'Count off seven sabbaths of years —seven times seven years—so that the seven sabbaths of years amount to a period of forty-nine years. 9Then have the trumpet sounded everywhere on the tenth day of the seventh month; on the Day of Atonement sound the trumpet throughout your land. 10Consecrate the fiftieth year and proclaim liberty throughout the land to all its inhabitants. It shall be a jubilee for you; each one of you is to return to his family property and each to his own clan. 11The fiftieth year shall be a jubilee for you; do not sow and do not reap what grows of itself or harvest the untended vines. 12For it is a jubilee and is to be holy for you; eat only what is taken directly from the fields.

13"'In this Year of Jubilee everyone is to return to his own property.

14"'If you sell land to one of your countrymen or buy any from him, do not take advantage of each other. 15You are to buy from your countryman on the basis of the number of years since the Jubilee. And he is to sell to you on the basis of the number of years left for harvesting crops. 16When the years are many, you are to increase the price, and when the years are few, you are to decrease the price, because what he is really selling you is the number of crops. 17Do not take advantage of each other, but fear your God. I am the LORD your God.

18"'Follow my decrees and be careful to obey my laws, and you will live safely in the land. 19Then the land will yield its fruit, and you will eat your fill and live there in safety. 20You may ask, "What will we eat in the seventh year if we do not plant or harvest our crops?" 21I will send you such a blessing in the sixth year that the land will yield enough for three years. 22While you plant during the eighth year, you will eat from the old crop and will continue to eat from it until the harvest of the ninth year comes in.

23"'The land must not be sold permanently, because the land is mine and you are but aliens and my tenants. 24Throughout the country that you hold as a possession, you must provide for the redemption of the land.

25"'If one of your countrymen becomes poor and sells some of his property, his nearest relative is to come and redeem what his countryman has sold. 26If, however, a man has no-one to redeem it for him but he himself prospers and acquires sufficient means to redeem it, 27he is to determine the value for the years since he sold it and refund the balance to the man to whom he sold it; he can then go back to his own property. 28But if he does not acquire the means to repay him, what he sold will remain in the possession of the buyer until the Year of Jubilee. It will be returned in the Jubilee, and he can then go back to his property.

29"'If a man sells a house in a walled city, he retains the right of redemption a full year after its sale. During that time he may redeem it. 30If it is not redeemed before a full year has passed, the house in the walled city shall belong permanently to the buyer and his descendants. It is not to be returned in the Jubilee. 31But houses in villages without walls round them are to be considered as open country. They can be redeemed, and they are to be returned in the Jubilee.

32"'The Levites always have the right to redeem their houses in the Levitical towns, which they possess. 33So the property of the Levites is redeemable —that is, a house sold in any town they hold—and is to be returned in the Jubilee, because the houses in the towns of the Levites are their property among the Israelites. ³⁴But the pasture-land belonging to their towns must not be sold; it is their permanent possession.

³⁵"If one of your countrymen becomes poor and is unable to support himself among you, help him as you would an alien or a temporary resident, so that he can continue to live among you. ³⁶Do not take interest of any kind from him, but fear your God, so that your countryman may continue to live among you. ³⁷You must not lend him money at interest or sell him food at a profit. ³⁸I am the LORD your God, who brought you out of Egypt to give you the land of Canaan and to be your God.

³⁹"If one of your countrymen becomes poor among you and sells himself to you, do not make him work as a slave. ⁴⁰He is to be treated as a hired worker or a temporary resident among you; he is to work for you until the Year of Jubilee. ⁴¹Then he and his children are to be released, and he will go back to his own clan and to the property of his forefathers. ⁴²Because the Israelites are my servants, whom I brought out of Egypt, they must not be sold as slaves. ⁴³Do not rule over them ruthlessly, but fear your God.

⁴⁴"Your male and female slaves are to come from the nations around you; from them you may buy slaves. ⁴⁵You may also buy some of the temporary residents living among you and members of their clans born in your country, and they will become your property. ⁴⁶You can will them to your children as inherited property and can make them slaves for life, but you must not rule over your fellow Israelites ruthlessly.

⁴⁷"If an alien or a temporary resident among you becomes rich and one of your countrymen becomes poor and sells himself to the alien living among you or to a member of the alien's clan, ⁴⁸he retains the right of redemption after he has sold himself. One of his relatives may redeem him: ⁴⁹An uncle or a cousin or any blood-relative in his clan may redeem him. Or if he prospers, he may redeem himself. ⁵⁰He and his

buyer are to count the time from the year he sold himself up to the Year of Jubilee. The price for his release is to be based on the rate paid to a hired man for that number of years. ⁵¹If many years remain, he must pay for his redemption a larger share of the price paid for him. ⁵²If only a few years remain until the Year of Jubilee, he is to compute that and pay for his redemption accordingly. ⁵³He is to be treated as a man hired from year to year; you must see to it that his owner does not rule over him ruthlessly.

⁵⁴"Even if he is not redeemed in any of these ways, he and his children are to be released in the Year of Jubilee, ⁵⁵for the Israelites belong to me as servants. They are my servants, whom I brought out of Egypt. I am the LORD your God.

Reward for Obedience

26 "'Do not make idols or set up an image or a sacred stone for yourselves, and do not place a carved stone in your land to bow down before it. I am the LORD your God.

²"Observe my Sabbaths and have reverence for my sanctuary. I am the LORD.

³"If you follow my decrees and are careful to obey my commands, ⁴I will send you rain in its season, and the ground will yield its crops and the trees of the field their fruit. ⁵Your threshing will continue until grape harvest and the grape harvest will continue until planting, and you will eat all the food you want and live in safety in your land.

⁶"I will grant peace in the land, and you will lie down and no-one will make you afraid. I will remove savage beasts from the land, and the sword will not pass through your country. ⁷You will pursue your enemies, and they will fall by the sword before you. ⁸Five of you will chase a hundred, and a hundred of you will chase ten thousand, and your enemies will fall by the sword before you.

⁹"I will look on you with favour and

make you fruitful and increase your numbers, and I will keep my covenant with you. [10]You will still be eating last year's harvest when you will have to move it out to make room for the new. [11]I will put my dwelling-place among you, and I will not abhor you. [12]I will walk among you and be your God, and you will be my people. [13]I am the LORD your God, who brought you out of Egypt so that you would no longer be slaves to the Egyptians; I broke the bars of your yoke and enabled you to walk with heads held high.

NEW TESTAMENT READING
Mark 16:1–20

The Resurrection

16 When the Sabbath was over, Mary Magdalene, Mary the mother of James, and Salome bought spices so that they might go to anoint Jesus' body. [2]Very early on the first day of the week, just after sunrise, they were on their way to the tomb [3]and they asked each other, "Who will roll the stone away from the entrance of the tomb?"

[4]But when they looked up, they saw that the stone, which was very large, had been rolled away. [5]As they entered the tomb, they saw a young man dressed in a white robe sitting on the right side, and they were alarmed.

[6]"Don't be alarmed," he said. "You are looking for Jesus the Nazarene, who was crucified. He has risen! He is not here. See the place where they laid him. [7]But go, tell his disciples and Peter, 'He is going ahead of you into Galilee. There you will see him, just as he told you.'"

[8]Trembling and bewildered, the women went out and fled from the tomb. They said nothing to anyone, because they were afraid.

[The most reliable early manuscripts and other ancient witnesses do not have Mark 16:9–20.]

[9]When Jesus rose early on the first day of the week, he appeared first to Mary Magdalene, out of whom he had driven seven demons. [10]She went and told those who had been with him and who were mourning and weeping. [11]When they heard that Jesus was alive and that she had seen him, they did not believe it.

[12]Afterwards Jesus appeared in a different form to two of them while they were walking in the country. [13]These returned and reported it to the rest; but they did not believe them either.

[14]Later Jesus appeared to the Eleven as they were eating; he rebuked them for their lack of faith and their stubborn refusal to believe those who had seen him after he had risen.

[15]He said to them, "Go into all the world and preach the good news to all creation. [16]Whoever believes and is baptised will be saved, but whoever does not believe will be condemned. [17]And these signs will accompany those who believe: In my name they will drive out demons; they will speak in new tongues; [18]they will pick up snakes with their hands; and when they drink deadly poison, it will not hurt them at all; they will place their hands on sick people, and they will get well."

[19]After the Lord Jesus had spoken to them, he was taken up into heaven and he sat at the right hand of God. [20]Then the disciples went out and preached everywhere, and the Lord worked with them and confirmed his word by the signs that accompanied it.

READING FROM PSALMS
Psalm 33:1–11

[1]Sing joyfully to the LORD, you righteous;
　　it is fitting for the upright to praise him.
[2]Praise the LORD with the harp;

make music to him on the
    ten-stringed lyre.
³Sing to him a new song;
    play skilfully, and shout for joy.

⁴For the word of the LORD is right and
        true;
    he is faithful in all he does.
⁵The LORD loves righteousness and
        justice;
    the earth is full of his unfailing
        love.

⁶By the word of the LORD were the
        heavens made,
    their starry host by the breath of
        his mouth.

⁷He gathers the waters of the sea into
        jars;
    he puts the deep into storehouses.
⁸Let all the earth fear the LORD;
    let all the people of the world
        revere him.
⁹For he spoke, and it came to be;
    he commanded, and it stood firm.
¹⁰The LORD foils the plans of the
        nations;
    he thwarts the purposes of the
        peoples.
¹¹But the plans of the LORD stand firm
        for ever,
    the purposes of his heart through
        all generations.

MARCH 13   DAY 72

OLD TESTAMENT READING
Leviticus 26:14–27:34

Punishment for Disobedience

¹⁴" 'But if you will not listen to me and
carry out all these commands, ¹⁵and if
you reject my decrees and abhor my
laws and fail to carry out all my commands and so violate my covenant,
¹⁶then I will do this to you: I will bring
upon you sudden terror, wasting diseases and fever that will destroy your
sight and drain away your life. You will
plant seed in vain, because your enemies will eat it. ¹⁷I will set my face
against you so that you will be defeated
by your enemies; those who hate you
will rule over you, and you will flee even
when no-one is pursuing you.

¹⁸" 'If after all this you will not listen
to me, I will punish you for your sins
seven times over. ¹⁹I will break down
your stubborn pride and make the sky
above you like iron and the ground
beneath you like bronze. ²⁰Your
strength will be spent in vain, because
your soil will not yield its crops, nor will
the trees of the land yield their fruit.

²¹" 'If you remain hostile towards me
and refuse to listen to me, I will multiply
your afflictions seven times over, as
your sins deserve. ²²I will send wild
animals against you, and they will rob
you of your children, destroy your cattle
and make you so few in number that
your roads will be deserted.

²³" 'If in spite of these things you do
not accept my correction but continue
to be hostile towards me, ²⁴I myself will
be hostile towards you and will afflict
you for your sins seven times over.
²⁵And I will bring the sword upon you to
avenge the breaking of the covenant.
When you withdraw into your cities, I
will send a plague among you, and you
will be given into enemy hands. ²⁶When
I cut off your supply of bread, ten
women will be able to bake your bread
in one oven, and they will dole out the
bread by weight. You will eat, but you
will not be satisfied.

²⁷" 'If in spite of this you still do not
listen to me but continue to be hostile
towards me, ²⁸then in my anger I will be
hostile towards you, and I myself will
punish you for your sins seven times

over. ²⁹You will eat the flesh of your sons and the flesh of your daughters. ³⁰I will destroy your high places, cut down your incense altars and pile your dead bodies on the lifeless forms of your idols, and I will abhor you. ³¹I will turn your cities into ruins and lay waste your sanctuaries, and I will take no delight in the pleasing aroma of your offerings. ³²I will lay waste the land, so that your enemies who live there will be appalled. ³³I will scatter you among the nations and will draw out my sword and pursue you. Your land will be laid waste, and your cities will lie in ruins. ³⁴Then the land will enjoy its sabbath years all the time that it lies desolate and you are in the country of your enemies; then the land will rest and enjoy its sabbaths. ³⁵All the time that it lies desolate, the land will have the rest it did not have during the sabbaths you lived in it.

³⁶"'As for those of you who are left, I will make their hearts so fearful in the lands of their enemies that the sound of a wind-blown leaf will put them to flight. They will run as though fleeing from the sword, and they will fall, even though no-one is pursuing them. ³⁷They will stumble over one another as though fleeing from the sword, even though no-one is pursuing them. So you will not be able to stand before your enemies. ³⁸You will perish among the nations; the land of your enemies will devour you. ³⁹Those of you who are left will waste away in the lands of their enemies because of their sins; also because of their fathers' sins they will waste away.

⁴⁰"'But if they will confess their sins and the sins of their fathers—their treachery against me and their hostility towards me, ⁴¹which made me hostile towards them so that I sent them into the land of their enemies—then when their uncircumcised hearts are humbled and they pay for their sin, ⁴²I will remember my covenant with Jacob and my covenant with Isaac and my covenant with Abraham, and I will remember the land. ⁴³For the land will be deserted by them and will enjoy its sabbaths while it lies desolate without them. They will pay for their sins because they rejected my laws and abhorred my decrees. ⁴⁴Yet in spite of this, when they are in the land of their enemies, I will not reject them or abhor them so as to destroy them completely, breaking my covenant with them. I am the LORD their God. ⁴⁵But for their sake I will remember the covenant with their ancestors whom I brought out of Egypt in the sight of the nations to be their God. I am the LORD.'"

⁴⁶These are the decrees, the laws and the regulations that the LORD established on Mount Sinai between himself and the Israelites through Moses.

Redeeming What Is the LORD's

27 The LORD said to Moses, ²"Speak to the Israelites and say to them: 'If anyone makes a special vow to dedicate persons to the LORD by giving equivalent values, ³set the value of a male between the ages of twenty and sixty at fifty shekels of silver, according to the sanctuary shekel; ⁴and if it is a female, set her value at thirty shekels. ⁵If it is a person between the ages of five and twenty, set the value of a male at twenty shekels and of a female at ten shekels. ⁶If it is a person between one month and five years, set the value of a male at five shekels of silver and that of a female at three shekels of silver. ⁷If it is a person sixty years old or more, set the value of a male at fifteen shekels and of a female at ten shekels. ⁸If anyone making the vow is too poor to pay the specified amount, he is to present the person to the priest, who will set the value for him according to what the man making the vow can afford.

⁹"'If what he vowed is an animal that is acceptable as an offering to the LORD, such an animal given to the LORD becomes holy. ¹⁰He must not exchange it or substitute a good one for a bad one, or a bad one for a good one; if he should substitute one animal for another, both it and the substitute become holy. ¹¹If

what he vowed is a ceremonially unclean animal—one that is not acceptable as an offering to the LORD—the animal must be presented to the priest, 12who will judge its quality as good or bad. Whatever value the priest then sets, that is what it will be. 13If the owner wishes to redeem the animal, he must add a fifth to its value.

14"If a man dedicates his house as something holy to the LORD, the priest will judge its quality as good or bad. Whatever value the priest then sets, so it will remain. 15If the man who dedicates his house redeems it, he must add a fifth to its value, and the house will again become his.

16"If a man dedicates to the LORD part of his family land, its value is to be set according to the amount of seed required for it—fifty shekels of silver to a homer of barley seed. 17If he dedicates his field during the Year of Jubilee, the value that has been set remains. 18But if he dedicates his field after the Jubilee, the priest will determine the value according to the number of years that remain until the next Year of Jubilee, and its set value will be reduced. 19If the man who dedicates the field wishes to redeem it, he must add a fifth to its value, and the field will again become his. 20If, however, he does not redeem the field, or if he has sold it to someone else, it can never be redeemed. 21When the field is released in the Jubilee, it will become holy, like a field devoted to the LORD; it will become the property of the priests.

22"If a man dedicates to the LORD a field he has bought, which is not part of his family land, 23the priest will determine its value up to the Year of Jubilee, and the man must pay its value on that day as something holy to the LORD. 24In the Year of Jubilee the field will revert to the person from whom he bought it, the one whose land it was. 25Every value is to be set according to the sanctuary shekel, twenty gerahs to the shekel.

26"No-one, however, may dedicate the firstborn of an animal, since the firstborn already belongs to the LORD; whether an ox or a sheep, it is the LORD's. 27If it is one of the unclean animals, he may buy it back at its set value, adding a fifth of the value to it. If he does not redeem it, it is to be sold at its set value.

28"But nothing that a man owns and devotes to the LORD—whether man or animal or family land—may be sold or redeemed; everything so devoted is most holy to the LORD.

29"No person devoted to destruction may be ransomed; he must be put to death.

30"A tithe of everything from the land, whether grain from the soil or fruit from the trees, belongs to the LORD; it is holy to the LORD. 31If a man redeems any of his tithe, he must add a fifth of the value to it. 32The entire tithe of the herd and flock—every tenth animal that passes under the shepherd's rod—will be holy to the LORD. 33He must not pick out the good from the bad or make any substitution. If he does make a substitution, both the animal and its substitute become holy and cannot be redeemed.'"

34These are the commands the LORD gave Moses on Mount Sinai for the Israelites.

NEW TESTAMENT READING
Luke 1:1–25

Introduction

1 Many have undertaken to draw up an account of the things that have been fulfilled among us, 2just as they were handed down to us by those who from the first were eye-witnesses and servants of the word. 3Therefore, since I myself have carefully investigated everything from the beginning, it seemed good also to me to write an orderly account for you, most excellent Theophilus, 4so that you may know the certainty of the things you have been taught.

The Birth of John the Baptist Foretold

5In the time of Herod king of Judea there was a priest named Zechariah, who belonged to the priestly division of Abijah; his wife Elizabeth was also a descendant of Aaron. 6Both of them were upright in the sight of God, observing all the Lord's commandments and regulations blamelessly. 7But they had no children, because Elizabeth was barren; and they were both well on in years.

8Once when Zechariah's division was on duty and he was serving as priest before God, 9he was chosen by lot, according to the custom of the priesthood, to go into the temple of the Lord and burn incense. 10And when the time for the burning of incense came, all the assembled worshippers were praying outside.

11Then an angel of the Lord appeared to him, standing at the right side of the altar of incense. 12When Zechariah saw him, he was startled and was gripped with fear. 13But the angel said to him: "Do not be afraid, Zechariah; your prayer has been heard. Your wife Elizabeth will bear you a son, and you are to give him the name John. 14He will be a joy and delight to you, and many will rejoice because of his birth, 15for he will be great in the sight of the Lord. He is never to take wine or other fermented drink, and he will be filled with the Holy Spirit even from birth. 16Many of the people of Israel will he bring back to the Lord their God. 17And he will go on before the Lord, in the spirit and power of Elijah, to turn the hearts of the fathers to their children and the disobedient to the wisdom of the righteous—to make ready a people prepared for the Lord."

18Zechariah asked the angel, "How can I be sure of this? I am an old man and my wife is well on in years."

19The angel answered, "I am Gabriel. I stand in the presence of God, and I have been sent to speak to you and to tell you this good news. 20And now you will be silent and not able to speak until the day this happens, because you did not believe my words, which will come true at their proper time."

21Meanwhile, the people were waiting for Zechariah and wondering why he stayed so long in the temple. 22When he came out, he could not speak to them. They realised he had seen a vision in the temple, for he kept making signs to them but remained unable to speak.

23When his time of service was completed, he returned home. 24After this his wife Elizabeth became pregnant and for five months remained in seclusion. 25"The Lord has done this for me," she said. "In these days he has shown his favour and taken away my disgrace among the people."

READING FROM PROVERBS
Proverbs 7:1–5

Warning Against the Adulteress

7 My son, keep my words
  and store up my commands
    within you.
2Keep my commands and you will
    live;
  guard my teachings as the apple of
    your eye.
3Bind them on your fingers;
  write them on the tablet of your
    heart.
4Say to wisdom, "You are my sister,"
  and call understanding your
    kinsman.
5they will keep you from the
    adulteress,
  from the wayward wife with her
    seductive words.

OLD TESTAMENT READING
Numbers 1:1–2:9

The Census

1 The LORD spoke to Moses in the Tent of Meeting in the Desert of Sinai on the first day of the second month of the second year after the Israelites came out of Egypt. He said: [2] "Take a census of the whole Israelite community by their clans and families, listing every man by name, one by one. [3] You and Aaron are to number by their divisions all the men in Israel twenty years old or more who are able to serve in the army. [4] One man from each tribe, each the head of his family, is to help you. [5] These are the names of the men who are to assist you:

from Reuben, Elizur son of Shedeur;
[6] from Simeon, Shelumiel son of Zurishaddai;
[7] from Judah, Nahshon son of Amminadab;
[8] from Issachar, Nethanel son of Zuar;
[9] from Zebulun, Eliab son of Helon;
[10] from the sons of Joseph:
from Ephraim, Elishama son of Ammihud;
from Manasseh, Gamaliel son of Pedahzur;
[11] from Benjamin, Abidan son of Gideoni;
[12] from Dan, Ahiezer son of Ammishaddai;
[13] from Asher, Pagiel son of Ocran;
[14] from Gad, Eliasaph son of Deuel;
[15] from Naphtali, Ahira son of Enan."

[16] These were the men appointed from the community, the leaders of their ancestral tribes. They were the heads of the clans of Israel.

[17] Moses and Aaron took these men whose names had been given, [18] and they called the whole community together on the first day of the second month. The people indicated their ancestry by their clans and families, and the men twenty years old or more were listed by name, one by one, [19] as the LORD commanded Moses. And so he counted them in the Desert of Sinai:

[20] From the descendants of Reuben the firstborn son of Israel:
All the men twenty years old or more who were able to serve in the army were listed by name, one by one, according to the records of their clans and families. [21] The number from the tribe of Reuben was 46,500.

[22] From the descendants of Simeon:
All the men twenty years old or more who were able to serve in the army were counted and listed by name, one by one, according to the records of their clans and families. [23] The number from the tribe of Simeon was 59,300.

[24] From the descendants of Gad:
All the men twenty years old or more who were able to serve in the army were listed by name, according to the records of their clans and families. [25] The number from the tribe of Gad was 45,650.

[26] From the descendants of Judah:
All the men twenty years old or more who were able to serve in the army were listed by name, according to the records of their clans and families. [27] The number from the tribe of Judah was 74,600.

28From the descendants of Issachar:
All the men twenty years old or more who were able to serve in the army were listed by name, according to the records of their clans and families. 29The number from the tribe of Issachar was 54,400.

30From the descendants of Zebulun:
All the men twenty years old or more who were able to serve in the army were listed by name, according to the records of their clans and families. 31The number from the tribe of Zebulun was 57,400.

32From the sons of Joseph:
From the descendants of Ephraim:
All the men twenty years old or more who were able to serve in the army were listed by name, according to the records of their clans and families. 33The number from the tribe of Ephraim was 40,500.

34From the descendants of Manasseh:
All the men twenty years old or more who were able to serve in the army were listed by name, according to the records of their clans and families. 35The number from the tribe of Manasseh was 32,200.

36From the descendants of Benjamin:
All the men twenty years old or more who were able to serve in the army were listed by name, according to the records of their clans and families. 37The number from the tribe of Benjamin was 35,400.

38From the descendants of Dan:
All the men twenty years old or more who were able to serve in the army were listed by name, according to the records of their clans and families. 39The number from the tribe of Dan was 62,700.

40From the descendants of Asher:
All the men twenty years old or more who were able to serve in the army were listed by name, according to the records of their clans and families. 41The number from the tribe of Asher was 41,500.

42From the descendants of Naphtali:
All the men twenty years old or more who were able to serve in the army were listed by name, according to the records of their clans and families. 43The number from the tribe of Naphtali was 53,400.

44These were the men counted by Moses and Aaron and the twelve leaders of Israel, each one representing his family. 45All the Israelites twenty years old or more who were able to serve in Israel's army were counted according to their families. 46The total number was 603,550.

47The families of the tribe of Levi, however, were not counted along with the others. 48The LORD had said to Moses: 49"You must not count the tribe of Levi or include them in the census of the other Israelites. 50Instead, appoint the Levites to be in charge of the tabernacle of the Testimony—over all its furnishings and everything belonging to it. They are to carry the tabernacle and all its furnishings; they are to take care of it and encamp round it. 51Whenever the tabernacle is to move, the Levites are to take it down, and whenever the tabernacle is to be set up, the Levites shall do it. Anyone else who goes near it shall be put to death. 52The Israelites are to set up their tents by divisions, each man in his own camp under his own standard. 53The Levites, however, are to set up their tents round the tabernacle of the Testimony so that wrath will not fall on the Israelite community. The Levites are to be responsible for the care of the tabernacle of the Testimony."

⁵⁴The Israelites did all this just as the LORD commanded Moses.

The Arrangement of the Tribal Camps

2 The LORD said to Moses and Aaron: ²"The Israelites are to camp round the Tent of Meeting some distance from it, each man under his standard with the banners of his family."

³On the east, towards the sunrise, the divisions of the camp of Judah are to encamp under their standard. The leader of the people of Judah is Nahshon son of Amminadab. ⁴His division numbers 74,600.

⁵The tribe of Issachar will camp next to them. The leader of the people of Issachar is Nethanel son of Zuar. ⁶His division numbers 54,400.

⁷The tribe of Zebulun will be next. The leader of the people of Zebulun is Eliab son of Helon. ⁸His division numbers 57,400.

⁹All the men assigned to the camp of Judah, according to their divisions, number 186,400. They will set out first.

NEW TESTAMENT READING
Luke 1:26–38

The Birth of Jesus Foretold

²⁶In the sixth month, God sent the angel Gabriel to Nazareth, a town in Galilee, ²⁷to a virgin pledged to be married to a man named Joseph, a descendant of David. The virgin's name was Mary. ²⁸The angel went to her and said, "Greetings, you who are highly favoured! The Lord is with you."

²⁹Mary was greatly troubled at his words and wondered what kind of greeting this might be. ³⁰But the angel said to her, "Do not be afraid, Mary, you have found favour with God. ³¹You will be with child and give birth to a son, and you are to give him the name Jesus. ³²He will be great and will be called the Son of the Most High. The Lord God will give him the throne of his father David, ³³and he will reign over the house of Jacob for ever; his kingdom will never end."

³⁴"How will this be," Mary asked the angel, "since I am a virgin?"

³⁵The angel answered, "The Holy Spirit will come upon you, and the power of the Most High will overshadow you. So the holy one to be born will be called the Son of God. ³⁶Even Elizabeth your relative is going to have a child in her old age, and she who was said to be barren is in her sixth month. ³⁷For nothing is impossible with God."

³⁸"I am the Lord's servant," Mary answered. "May it be to me as you have said." Then the angel left her.

READING FROM PSALMS
Psalm 33:12–22

¹²Blessed is the nation whose God is
　　the LORD,
　　the people he chose for his
　　　inheritance.
¹³From heaven the LORD looks down
　　and sees all mankind;
¹⁴from his dwelling-place he watches
　　all who live on earth—
¹⁵he who forms the hearts of all,
　　who considers everything they do.
¹⁶No king is saved by the size of his
　　army;
　　no warrior escapes by his great
　　　strength.
¹⁷A horse is a vain hope for
　　deliverance;
　　despite all its great strength it
　　　cannot save.
¹⁸But the eyes of the LORD are on those
　　who fear him,

on those whose hope is in his
unfailing love,
19to deliver them from death
and keep them alive in famine.

20We wait in hope for the LORD;

he is our help and our shield.
21In him our hearts rejoice,
for we trust in his holy name.
22May your unfailing love rest upon us,
O LORD,
even as we put our hope in you.

DAY 74

MARCH 15

OLD TESTAMENT READING
Numbers 2:10–3:51

10On the south will be the divisions of the camp of Reuben under their standard. The leader of the people of Reuben is Elizur son of Shedeur. 11His division numbers 46,500.
12The tribe of Simeon will camp next to them. The leader of the people of Simeon is Shelumiel son of Zurishaddai. 13His division numbers 59,300.
14The tribe of Gad will be next. The leader of the people of Gad is Eliasaph son of Deuel. 15His division numbers 45,650.
16All the men assigned to the camp of Reuben, according to their divisions, number 151,450. They will set out second.

17Then the Tent of Meeting and the camp of the Levites will set out in the middle of the camps. They will set out in the same order as they encamp, each in his own place under his standard.

18On the west will be the divisions of the camp of Ephraim under their standard. The leader of the people of Ephraim is Elishama son of Ammihud. 19His division numbers 40,500.
20The tribe of Manasseh will be

next to them. The leader of the people of Manasseh is Gamaliel son of Pedahzur. 21His division numbers 32,200.
22The tribe of Benjamin will be next. The leader of the people of Benjamin is Abidan son of Gideoni. 23His division numbers 35,400.
24All the men assigned to the camp of Ephraim, according to their divisions, number 108,100. They will set out third.

25On the north will be the divisions of the camp of Dan, under their standard. The leader of the people of Dan is Ahiezer son of Ammishaddai. 26His division numbers 62,700.
27The tribe of Asher will camp next to them. The leader of the people of Asher is Pagiel son of Ocran. 28His division numbers 41,500.
29The tribe of Naphtali will be next. The leader of the people of Naphtali is Ahira son of Enan. 30His division numbers 53,400.
31All the men assigned to the camp of Dan number 157,600. They will set out last, under their standards.

32These are the Israelites, counted according to their families. All those in the camps, by their divisions, number 603,550. [33]The Levites, however, were not counted along with the other Israelites, as the LORD commanded Moses.

[34]So the Israelites did everything the LORD commanded Moses; that is the way they encamped under their standards, and that is the way they set out, each with his clan and family.

The Levites

3 This is the account of the family of Aaron and Moses at the time the LORD talked with Moses on Mount Sinai.

[2]The names of the sons of Aaron were Nadab the firstborn and Abihu, Eleazar and Ithamar. [3]Those were the names of Aaron's sons, the anointed priests, who were ordained to serve as priests. [4]Nadab and Abihu, however, fell dead before the LORD when they made an offering with unauthorised fire before him in the Desert of Sinai. They had no sons; so only Eleazar and Ithamar served as priests during the lifetime of their father Aaron.

[5]The LORD said to Moses, [6]"Bring the tribe of Levi and present them to Aaron the priest to assist him. [7]They are to perform duties for him and for the whole community at the Tent of Meeting by doing the work of the tabernacle. [8]They are to take care of all the furnishings of the Tent of Meeting, fulfilling the obligations of the Israelites by doing the work of the tabernacle. [9]Give the Levites to Aaron and his sons; they are the Israelites who are to be given wholly to him. [10]Appoint Aaron and his sons to serve as priests; anyone else who approaches the sanctuary must be put to death."

[11]The LORD also said to Moses, [12]"I have taken the Levites from among the Israelites in place of the first male offspring of every Israelite woman. The Levites are mine, [13]for all the firstborn are mine. When I struck down all the firstborn in Egypt, I set apart for myself every firstborn in Israel, whether man or animal. They are to be mine. I am the LORD."

[14]The LORD said to Moses in the Desert of Sinai, [15]"Count the Levites by their families and clans. Count every male a month old or more." [16]So Moses counted them, as he was commanded by the word of the LORD.

[17]These were the names of the sons of Levi:
  Gershon, Kohath and Merari.
[18]These were the names of the Gershonite clans:
  Libni and Shimei.
[19]The Kohathite clans:
  Amram, Izhar, Hebron and Uzziel.
[20]The Merarite clans:
  Mahli and Mushi.
These were the Levite clans, according to their families.

[21]To Gershon belonged the clans of the Libnites and Shimeites; these were the Gershonite clans. [22]The number of all the males a month old or more who were counted was 7,500. [23]The Gershonite clans were to camp on the west, behind the tabernacle. [24]The leader of the families of the Gershonites was Eliasaph son of Lael. [25]At the Tent of Meeting the Gershonites were responsible for the care of the tabernacle and tent, its coverings, the curtain at the entrance to the Tent of Meeting, [26]the curtains of the courtyard, the curtain at the entrance to the courtyard surrounding the tabernacle and altar, and the ropes—and everything related to their use.

[27]To Kohath belonged the clans of the Amramites, Izharites, Hebronites and Uzzielites; these were the Kohathite clans. [28]The number of all the males a month old or more was 8,600. The Kohathites were responsible for the care of the sanctuary. [29]The

Kohathite clans were to camp on the south side of the tabernacle. [30]The leader of the families of the Kohathite clans was Elizaphan son of Uzziel. [31]They were responsible for the care of the ark, the table, the lampstand, the altars, the articles of the sanctuary used in ministering, the curtain, and everything related to their use. [32]The chief leader of the Levites was Eleazar son of Aaron, the priest. He was appointed over those who were responsible for the care of the sanctuary.

[33]To Merari belonged the clans of the Mahlites and the Mushites; these were the Merarite clans. [34]The number of all the males a month old or more who were counted was 6,200. [35]The leader of the families of the Merarite clans was Zuriel son of Abihail; they were to camp on the north side of the tabernacle. [36]The Merarites were appointed to take care of the frames of the tabernacle, its crossbars, posts, bases, all its equipment, and everything related to their use, [37]as well as the posts of the surrounding courtyard with their bases, tent pegs and ropes.

[38]Moses and Aaron and his sons were to camp to the east of the tabernacle, towards the sunrise, in front of the Tent of Meeting. They were responsible for the care of the sanctuary on behalf of the Israelites. Anyone else who approached the sanctuary was to be put to death.

[39]The total number of Levites counted at the LORD's command by Moses and Aaron according to their clans, including every male a month old or more, was 22,000.

[40]The LORD said to Moses, "Count all the firstborn Israelite males who are a month old or more and make a list of their names. [41]Take the Levites for me in place of all the firstborn of the Israelites, and the livestock of the Levites in place of all the firstborn of the livestock of the Israelites. I am the LORD."

[42]So Moses counted all the firstborn of the Israelites, as the LORD commanded him. [43]The total number of firstborn males a month old or more, listed by name, was 22,273.

[44]The LORD also said to Moses, [45]"Take the Levites in place of all the firstborn of Israel, and the livestock of the Levites in place of their livestock. The Levites are to be mine. I am the LORD. [46]To redeem the 273 firstborn Israelites who exceed the number of the Levites, [47]collect five shekels for each one, according to the sanctuary shekel, which weighs twenty gerahs. [48]Give the money for the redemption of the additional Israelites to Aaron and his sons."

[49]So Moses collected the redemption money from those who exceeded the number redeemed by the Levites. [50]From the firstborn of the Israelites he collected silver weighing 1,365 shekels, according to the sanctuary shekel. [51]Moses gave the redemption money to Aaron and his sons, as he was commanded by the word of the LORD.

NEW TESTAMENT READING
Luke 1:39–56

Mary Visits Elizabeth

[39]At that time Mary got ready and hurried to a town in the hill country of Judea, [40]where she entered Zechariah's home and greeted Elizabeth. [41]When Elizabeth heard Mary's greeting, the baby leaped in her womb, and Elizabeth was filled with the Holy Spirit. [42]In a loud voice she exclaimed: "Blessed are you among women, and blessed is the child you will bear! [43]But why am I so favoured, that the mother of my Lord should come to me? [44]As soon as the sound of your greeting reached my ears, the baby in my womb leaped for joy. [45]Blessed is she who has believed that what the Lord has said to her will be accomplished!"

Mary's Song

46And Mary said:

> "My soul glorifies the Lord
> 47   and my spirit rejoices in God my
>   Saviour,
> 48for he has been mindful
>   of the humble state of his servant.
>   From now on all generations will call
>   me blessed,
> 49   for the Mighty One has done great
>   things for me—
>   holy is his name.
> 50His mercy extends to those who fear
>   him,
>   from generation to generation.
> 51He has performed mighty deeds with
>   his arm;
>   he has scattered those who are
>   proud in their inmost thoughts.
> 52He has brought down rulers from
>   their thrones
>   but has lifted up the humble.
> 53He has filled the hungry with good
>   things
>   but has sent the rich away empty.
> 54He has helped his servant Israel,
>   remembering to be merciful
> 55to Abraham and his descendants for
>   ever,
>   even as he said to our fathers."

56Mary stayed with Elizabeth for about three months and then returned home.

READING FROM PSALMS
Psalm 34:1–10

Of David. When he pretended to be insane before Abimelech, who drove him away, and he left.

> 1I will extol the LORD at all times;
>   his praise will always be on my lips.
> 2My soul will boast in the LORD;
>   let the afflicted hear and rejoice.
> 3Glorify the LORD with me:
>   let us exalt his name together.
>
> 4I sought the LORD, and he answered
>   me;
>   he delivered me from all my fears.
> 5Those who look to him are radiant;
>   their faces are never covered with
>   shame.
> 6This poor man called, and the LORD
>   heard him;
>   he saved him out of all his troubles.
> 7The angel of the LORD encamps
>   around those who fear him,
>   and he delivers them.
>
> 8Taste and see that the LORD is good;
>   blessed is the man who takes
>   refuge in him.
> 9Fear the LORD, you his saints,
>   for those who fear him lack
>   nothing.
> 10The lions may grow weak and
>   hungry,
>   but those who seek the LORD lack
>   no good thing.

OLD TESTAMENT READING
Numbers 4:1–5:10

The Kohathites

4 The LORD said to Moses and Aaron: ²"Take a census of the Kohathite branch of the Levites by their clans and families. ³Count all the men from thirty to fifty years of age who come to serve in the work in the Tent of Meeting.

⁴"This is the work of the Kohathites in the Tent of Meeting: the care of the most holy things. ⁵When the camp is to move, Aaron and his sons are to go in and take down the shielding curtain and cover the ark of the Testimony with it. ⁶Then they are to cover this with hides of sea cows, spread a cloth of solid blue over that and put the poles in place.

⁷"Over the table of the Presence they are to spread a blue cloth and put on it the plates, dishes and bowls, and the jars for drink offerings; the bread that is continually there is to remain on it. ⁸Over these they are to spread a scarlet cloth, cover that with hides of sea cows and put its poles in place.

⁹"They are to take a blue cloth and cover the lampstand that is for light, together with its lamps, its wick trimmers and trays, and all its jars for the oil used to supply it. ¹⁰Then they are to wrap it and all its accessories in a covering of hides of sea cows and put it on a carrying frame.

¹¹"Over the gold altar they are to spread a blue cloth and cover that with hides of sea cows and put its poles in place.

¹²"They are to take all the articles used for ministering in the sanctuary, wrap them in a blue cloth, cover that with hides of sea cows and put them on a carrying frame.

¹³"They are to remove the ashes from the bronze altar and spread a purple cloth over it. ¹⁴Then they are to place on

it all the utensils used for ministering at the altar, including the firepans, meat forks, shovels and sprinkling bowls. Over it they are to spread a covering of hides of sea cows and put its poles in place.

¹⁵"After Aaron and his sons have finished covering the holy furnishings and all the holy articles, and when the camp is ready to move, the Kohathites are to come to do the carrying. But they must not touch the holy things or they will die. The Kohathites are to carry those things that are in the Tent of Meeting.

¹⁶"Eleazar son of Aaron, the priest, is to have charge of the oil for the light, the fragrant incense, the regular grain offering and the anointing oil. He is to be in charge of the entire tabernacle and everything in it, including its holy furnishings and articles."

¹⁷The LORD said to Moses and Aaron, ¹⁸"See that the Kohathite tribal clans are not cut off from the Levites. ¹⁹So that they may live and not die when they come near the most holy things, do this for them: Aaron and his sons are to go into the sanctuary and assign to each man his work and what he is to carry. ²⁰But the Kohathites must not go in to look at the holy things, even for a moment, or they will die."

The Gershonites

²¹The LORD said to Moses, ²²"Take a census also of the Gershonites by their families and clans. ²³Count all the men from thirty to fifty years of age who come to serve in the work at the Tent of Meeting.

²⁴"This is the service of the Gershonite clans as they work and carry burdens: ²⁵They are to carry the curtains of the tabernacle, the Tent of Meeting, its covering and the outer covering of hides of sea cows, the curtains for the entrance to the Tent of Meeting, ²⁶the

curtains of the courtyard surrounding the tabernacle and altar, the curtain for the entrance, the ropes and all the equipment used in its service. The Gershonites are to do all that needs to be done with these things. 27All their service, whether carrying or doing other work, is to be done under the direction of Aaron and his sons. You shall assign to them as their responsibility all they are to carry. 28This is the service of the Gershonite clans at the Tent of Meeting. Their duties are to be under the direction of Ithamar son of Aaron, the priest.

The Merarites

29"Count the Merarites by their clans and families. 30Count all the men from thirty to fifty years of age who come to serve in the work at the Tent of Meeting. 31This is their duty as they perform service at the Tent of Meeting: to carry the frames of the tabernacle, its crossbars, posts and bases, 32as well as the posts of the surrounding courtyard with their bases, tent pegs, ropes, all their equipment and everything related to their use. Assign to each man the specific things he is to carry. 33This is the service of the Merarite clans as they work at the Tent of Meeting under the direction of Ithamar son of Aaron, the priest."

The Numbering of the Levite Clans

34Moses, Aaron and the leaders of the community counted the Kohathites by their clans and families. 35All the men from thirty to fifty years of age who came to serve in the work in the Tent of Meeting, 36counted by clans, were 2,750. 37This was the total of all those in the Kohathite clans who served in the Tent of Meeting. Moses and Aaron counted them according to the LORD's command through Moses.

38The Gershonites were counted by their clans and families. 39All the men from thirty to fifty years of age who came to serve in the work at the Tent of Meeting, 40counted by their clans and families, were 2,630. 41This was the total of those in the Gershonite clans who served at the Tent of Meeting. Moses and Aaron counted them according to the LORD's command.

42The Merarites were counted by their clans and families. 43All the men from thirty to fifty years of age who came to serve in the work at the Tent of Meeting, 44counted by their clans, were 3,200. 45This was the total of those in the Merarite clans. Moses and Aaron counted them according to the LORD's command through Moses.

46So Moses, Aaron and the leaders of Israel counted all the Levites by their clans and families. 47All the men from thirty to fifty years of age who came to do the work of serving and carrying the Tent of Meeting 48numbered 8,580. 49At the LORD's command through Moses, each was assigned his work and told what to carry.

Thus they were counted, as the LORD commanded Moses.

The Purity of the Camp

5 The LORD said to Moses, 2"Command the Israelites to send away from the camp anyone who has an infectious skin disease or a discharge of any kind, or who is ceremonially unclean because of a dead body. 3Send away male and female alike; send them outside the camp so that they will not defile their camp, where I dwell among them." 4The Israelites did this; they sent them outside the camp. They did just as the LORD had instructed Moses.

Restitution for Wrongs

5The LORD said to Moses, 6"Say to the Israelites: 'When a man or woman wrongs another in any way and so is unfaithful to the LORD, that person is guilty 7and must confess the sin he has committed. He must make full restitution for his wrong, add one fifth to it and give it all to the person he has wronged. 8But if that person has no close relative to whom restitution can be made for the wrong, the restitution belongs to the LORD and must be given to the priest, along with the ram with which atonement is made for him. 9All the sacred contributions the Israelites bring to a priest will belong to him. 10Each man's sacred gifts are his own, but what he gives to the priest will belong to the priest.'"

NEW TESTAMENT READING
Luke 1:57–80

The Birth of John the Baptist

57When it was time for Elizabeth to have her baby, she gave birth to a son. 58Her neighbours and relatives heard that the Lord had shown her great mercy, and they shared her joy.

59On the eighth day they came to circumcise the child, and they were going to name him after his father Zechariah, 60but his mother spoke up and said, "No! He is to be called John." 61They said to her, "There is no-one among your relatives who has that name."

62Then they made signs to his father, to find out what he would like to name the child. 63He asked for a writing tablet, and to everyone's astonishment he wrote, "His name is John." 64Immediately his mouth was opened and his tongue was loosed, and he began to speak, praising God. 65The neighbours were all filled with awe, and throughout the hill country of Judea people were talking about all these things. 66Everyone who heard this wondered about it, asking, "What then is this child going to be?" For the Lord's hand was with him.

Zechariah's Song

67His father Zechariah was filled with the Holy Spirit and prophesied:

68"Praise be to the Lord, the God of Israel,

because he has come and has redeemed his people.
69He has raised up a horn of salvation for us
    in the house of his servant David
70(as he said through his holy prophets of long ago),
71salvation from our enemies
    and from the hand of all who hate us—
72to show mercy to our fathers
    and to remember his holy covenant,
73   the oath he swore to our father Abraham:
74to rescue us from the hand of our enemies,
    and to enable us to serve him without fear
75   in holiness and righteousness before him all our days.

76And you, my child, will be called a prophet of the Most High;
    for you will go on before the Lord to prepare the way for him,
77to give his people the knowledge of salvation
    through the forgiveness of their sins,
78because of the tender mercy of our God,
    by which the rising sun will come to us from heaven
79to shine on those living in darkness and in the shadow of death,
    to guide our feet into the path of peace."

80And the child grew and became strong in spirit; and he lived in the desert until he appeared publicly to Israel.

READING FROM PSALMS
Psalm 34:11–22

11Come, my children, listen to me;
    I will teach you the fear of the LORD.
12Whoever of you loves life
    and desires to see many good days,

¹³keep your tongue from evil
    and your lips from speaking lies.
¹⁴Turn from evil and do good;
    seek peace and pursue it.

¹⁵The eyes of the LORD are on the
    righteous
    and his ears are attentive to their
        cry;
¹⁶the face of the LORD is against those
    who do evil,
    to cut off the memory of them from
        the earth.

¹⁷The righteous cry out, and the LORD
    hears them;
    he delivers them from all their
        troubles.

¹⁸The LORD is close to the
    broken-hearted
    and saves those who are crushed in
        spirit.

¹⁹A righteous man may have many
    troubles,
    but the LORD delivers him from
        them all;
²⁰he protects all his bones,
    not one of them will be broken.

²¹Evil will slay the wicked;
    the foes of the righteous will be
        condemned.
²²The LORD redeems his servants;
    no-one will be condemned who
        takes refuge in him.

MARCH 17   DAY 76

OLD TESTAMENT READING
Numbers 5:11–6:27

The Test for an Unfaithful Wife

¹¹Then the LORD said to Moses,
¹²"Speak to the Israelites and say to
them: 'If a man's wife goes astray and is
unfaithful to him ¹³by sleeping with
another man, and this is hidden from
her husband and her impurity is un-
detected (since there is no witness
against her and she has not been caught
in the act), ¹⁴and if feelings of jealousy
come over her husband and he suspects
his wife and she is impure—or if he is
jealous and suspects her even though
she is not impure—¹⁵then he is to take
his wife to the priest. He must also take
an offering of a tenth of an ephah of
barley flour on her behalf. He must not
pour oil on it or put incense on it, because it is a grain offering for jealousy, a
reminder offering to draw attention to
guilt.

¹⁶"'The priest shall bring her and

make her stand before the LORD.
¹⁷Then he shall take some holy water in
a clay jar and put some dust from the
tabernacle floor into the water. ¹⁸After
the priest has made the woman stand
before the LORD, he shall loosen her
hair and place in her hands the reminder
offering, the grain offering for jealousy,
while he himself holds the bitter water
that brings a curse. ¹⁹Then the priest
shall put the woman under oath and say
to her, "If no other man has slept with
you and you have not gone astray and
become impure while married to your
husband, may this bitter water that
brings a curse not harm you. ²⁰But if you
have gone astray while married to your
husband and you have defiled yourself
by sleeping with a man other than your
husband"—²¹here the priest is to put
the woman under this curse of the oath
—"may the LORD cause your people to
curse and denounce you when he causes
your thigh to waste away and your
abdomen to swell. ²²May this water that
brings a curse enter your body so that

your abdomen swells and your thigh wastes away."

"'Then the woman is to say, "Amen. So be it."

23"'The priest is to write these curses on a scroll and then wash them off into the bitter water. 24He shall make the woman drink the bitter water that brings a curse, and this water will enter her and cause bitter suffering. 25The priest is to take from her hands the grain offering for jealousy, wave it before the LORD and bring it to the altar. 26The priest is then to take a handful of the grain offering as a memorial offering and burn it on the altar; after that, he is to make the woman drink the water. 27If she has defiled herself and been unfaithful to her husband, then when she is made to drink the water that brings a curse, it will go into her and cause bitter suffering; her abdomen will swell and her thigh waste away, and she will become accursed among her people. 28If, however, the woman has not defiled herself and is free from impurity, she will be cleared of guilt and will be able to have children.

29"'This, then, is the law of jealousy when a woman goes astray and defiles herself while married to her husband, 30or when feelings of jealousy come over a man because he suspects his wife. The priest is to make her stand before the LORD and is to apply this entire law to her. 31The husband will be innocent of any wrongdoing, but the woman will bear the consequences of her sin.'"

The Nazirite

6 The LORD said to Moses, 2"Speak to the Israelites and say to them: 'If a man or woman wants to make a special vow, a vow of separation to the LORD as a Nazirite, 3he must abstain from wine and other fermented drink and must not drink vinegar made from wine or from other fermented drink. He must not drink grape juice or eat grapes or raisins. 4As long as he is a Nazirite, he must not eat anything that comes

from the grapevine, not even the seeds or skins.

5"'During the entire period of his vow of separation no razor may be used on his head. He must be holy until the period of his separation to the LORD is over; he must let the hair of his head grow long. 6Throughout the period of his separation to the LORD he must not go near a dead body. 7Even if his own father or mother or brother or sister dies, he must not make himself ceremonially unclean on account of them, because the symbol of his separation to God is on his head. 8Throughout the period of his separation he is consecrated to the LORD.

9"'If someone dies suddenly in his presence, thus defiling the hair he has dedicated, he must shave his head on the day of his cleansing—the seventh day. 10Then on the eighth day he must bring two doves or two young pigeons to the priest at the entrance to the Tent of Meeting. 11The priest is to offer one as a sin offering and the other as a burnt offering to make atonement for him because he sinned by being in the presence of the dead body. That same day he is to consecrate his head. 12He must dedicate himself to the LORD for the period of his separation and must bring a year-old male lamb as a guilt offering. The previous days do not count, because he became defiled during his separation.

13"'Now this is the law for the Nazirite when the period of his separation is over. He is to be brought to the entrance to the Tent of Meeting. 14There he is to present his offerings to the LORD: a year-old male lamb without defect for a burnt offering, a year-old ewe lamb without defect for a sin offering, a ram without defect for a fellowship offering, 15together with their grain offerings and drink offerings, and a basket of bread made without yeast—cakes made of fine flour mixed with oil, and wafers spread with oil.

16"'The priest is to present them before the LORD and make the sin offering and the burnt offering. [17]He is to present the basket of unleavened bread and is to sacrifice the ram as a fellowship offering to the LORD, together with its grain offering and drink offering.

[18]"Then at the entrance to the Tent of Meeting, the Nazirite must shave off the hair that he dedicated. He is to take the hair and put it in the fire that is under the sacrifice of the fellowship offering.

[19]"After the Nazirite has shaved off the hair of his dedication, the priest is to place in his hands a boiled shoulder of the ram, and a cake and a wafer from the basket, both made without yeast. [20]The priest shall then wave them before the LORD as a wave offering; they are holy and belong to the priest, together with the breast that was waved and the thigh that was presented. After that, the Nazirite may drink wine.

[21]"This is the law of the Nazirite who vows his offering to the LORD in accordance with his separation, in addition to whatever else he can afford. He must fulfil the vow he has made, according to the law of the Nazirite.' "

The Priestly Blessing

[22]The LORD said to Moses, [23]"Tell Aaron and his sons, 'This is how you are to bless the Israelites. Say to them:

[24]" 'The LORD bless you
  and keep you;
[25]the LORD make his face shine upon
    you
  and be gracious to you;
[26]the LORD turn his face towards you
  and give you peace.' "

[27]"So they will put my name on the Israelites, and I will bless them."

NEW TESTAMENT READING
Luke 2:1–20

The Birth of Jesus

2 In those days Caesar Augustus issued a decree that a census should be taken of the entire Roman world.

([2]This was the first census that took place while Quirinius was governor of Syria.) [3]And everyone went to his own town to register.

[4]So Joseph also went up from the town of Nazareth in Galilee to Judea, to Bethlehem the town of David, because he belonged to the house and line of David. [5]He went there to register with Mary, who was pledged to be married to him and was expecting a child. [6]While they were there, the time came for the baby to be born, [7]and she gave birth to her firstborn, a son. She wrapped him in cloths and placed him in a manger, because there was no room for them in the inn.

The Shepherds and the Angels

[8]And there were shepherds living out in the fields near by, keeping watch over their flocks at night. [9]An angel of the Lord appeared to them, and the glory of the Lord shone around them, and they were terrified. [10]But the angel said to them, "Do not be afraid. I bring you good news of great joy that will be for all the people. [11]Today in the town of David a Saviour has been born to you; he is Christ the Lord. [12]This will be a sign to you: You will find a baby wrapped in cloths and lying in a manger."

[13]Suddenly a great company of the heavenly host appeared with the angel, praising God and saying,

[14]"Glory to God in the highest,
  and on earth peace to men on
    whom his favour rests."

[15]When the angels had left them and gone into heaven, the shepherds said to one another, "Let's go to Bethlehem and see this thing that has happened, which the Lord has told us about."

[16]So they hurried off and found Mary and Joseph, and the baby, who was lying in the manger. [17]When they had seen him, they spread the word concerning what had been told them about

this child, 18and all who heard it were amazed at what the shepherds said to them. 19But Mary treasured up all these things and pondered them in her heart. 20The shepherds returned, glorifying and praising God for all the things they had heard and seen, which were just as they had been told.

READING FROM PROVERBS
Proverbs 7:6–20

6At the window of my house
    I looked out through the lattice.
7I saw among the simple,
    I noticed among the young men,
    a youth who lacked judgment.
8He was going down the street near
        her corner,
    walking along in the direction of
        her house
9at twilight, as the day was fading,
    as the dark of night set in.

10Then out came a woman to meet him,
    dressed like a prostitute and with
        crafty intent.
11(She is loud and defiant,
    her feet never stay at home;
12now in the street, now in the squares,
    at every corner she lurks.)
13She took hold of him and kissed him
    and with a brazen face she said:

14"I have fellowship offerings at home;
    today I fulfilled my vows.
15So I came out to meet you;
    I looked for you and have found
        you!
16I have covered my bed
    with coloured linens from Egypt.
17I have perfumed my bed
    with myrrh, aloes and cinnamon.
18Come, let's drink deep of love till
        morning;
    let's enjoy ourselves with love!
19My husband is not at home;
    he has gone on a long journey.
20He took his purse filled with money
    and will not be home till full
        moon."

DAY 77

MARCH 18

OLD TESTAMENT READING
Numbers 7:1–65

Offerings at the Dedication of the Tabernacle

7 When Moses finished setting up the tabernacle, he anointed it and consecrated it and all its furnishings. He also anointed and consecrated the altar and all its utensils. 2Then the leaders of Israel, the heads of families who were the tribal leaders in charge of those who were counted, made offerings. 3They brought as their gifts before the LORD six covered carts and twelve oxen—an ox from each leader and a cart from every two. These they presented before the tabernacle.

4The LORD said to Moses, 5"Accept these from them, that they may be used in the work at the Tent of Meeting. Give them to the Levites as each man's work requires."

6So Moses took the carts and oxen and gave them to the Levites. 7He gave two carts and four oxen to the Gershonites, as their work required, 8and he gave four carts and eight oxen to the Merarites, as their work required. They were all under the direction of Ithamar son of Aaron, the priest. 9But Moses did not give any to the Kohathites, because they were to carry on their shoulders the holy things, for which they were responsible.

10When the altar was anointed, the

leaders brought their offerings for its dedication and presented them before the altar. [11]For the LORD had said to Moses, "Each day one leader is to bring his offering for the dedication of the altar."

[12]The one who brought his offering on the first day was Nahshon son of Amminadab of the tribe of Judah.

[13]His offering was one silver plate weighing a hundred and thirty shekels, and one silver sprinkling bowl weighing seventy shekels, both according to the sanctuary shekel, each filled with fine flour mixed with oil as a grain offering; [14]one gold dish weighing ten shekels, filled with incense; [15]one young bull, one ram and one male lamb a year old, for a burnt offering; [16]one male goat for a sin offering; [17]and two oxen, five rams, five male goats and five male lambs a year old, to be sacrificed as a fellowship offering. This was the offering of Nahshon son of Amminadab.

[18]On the second day Nethanel son of Zuar, the leader of Issachar, brought his offering.

[19]The offering he brought was one silver plate weighing a hundred and thirty shekels, and one silver sprinkling bowl weighing seventy shekels, both according to the sanctuary shekel, each filled with fine flour mixed with oil as a grain offering; [20]one gold dish weighing ten shekels, filled with incense; [21]one young bull, one ram and one male lamb a year old, for a burnt offering; [22]one male goat for a sin offering; [23]and two oxen, five rams, five male goats and five male lambs a year old, to be sacrificed as a fellowship offering. This was the offering of Nethanel son of Zuar.

[24]On the third day, Eliab son of Helon, the leader of the people of Zebulun, brought his offering.

[25]His offering was one silver plate weighing a hundred and thirty shekels, and one silver sprinkling bowl weighing seventy shekels, both according to the sanctuary shekel, each filled with fine flour mixed with oil as a grain offering; [26]one gold dish weighing ten shekels, filled with incense; [27]one young bull, one ram and one male lamb a year old, for a burnt offering; [28]one male goat for a sin offering; [29]and two oxen, five rams, five male goats and five male lambs a year old, to be sacrificed as a fellowship offering. This was the offering of Eliab son of Helon.

[30]On the fourth day Elizur son of Shedeur, the leader of the people of Reuben, brought his offering.

[31]His offering was one silver plate weighing a hundred and thirty shekels, and one silver sprinkling bowl weighing seventy shekels, both according to the sanctuary shekel, each filled with fine flour mixed with oil as a grain offering; [32]one gold dish weighing ten shekels, filled with incense; [33]one young bull, one ram and one male lamb a year old, for a burnt offering; [34]one male goat for a sin offering; [35]and two oxen, five rams, five male goats and five male lambs a year old, to be sacrificed as a fellowship offering. This was the offering of Elizur son of Shedeur.

[36]On the fifth day Shelumiel son of Zurishaddai, the leader of the people of Simeon, brought his offering.

[37]His offering was one silver plate weighing a hundred and thirty shekels, and one silver sprinkling bowl weighing seventy shekels, both according to the sanctuary shekel, each filled with fine flour mixed with oil as a grain offering; [38]one gold dish weighing ten shekels, filled with incense; [39]one young bull, one ram and one male

lamb a year old, for a burnt offering; ⁴⁰one male goat for a sin offering; ⁴¹and two oxen, five rams, five male goats and five male lambs a year old, to be sacrificed as a fellowship offering. This was the offering of Shelumiel son of Zurishaddai.

⁴²On the sixth day Eliasaph son of Deuel, the leader of the people of Gad, brought his offering.

⁴³His offering was one silver plate weighing a hundred and thirty shekels, and one silver sprinkling bowl weighing seventy shekels, both according to the sanctuary shekel, each filled with fine flour mixed with oil as a grain offering; ⁴⁴one gold dish weighing ten shekels, filled with incense; ⁴⁵one young bull, one ram and one male lamb a year old, for a burnt offering; ⁴⁶one male goat for a sin offering; ⁴⁷and two oxen, five rams, five male goats and five male lambs a year old, to be sacrificed as a fellowship offering. This was the offering of Eliasaph son of Deuel.

⁴⁸On the seventh day Elishama son of Ammihud, the leader of the people of Ephraim, brought his offering.

⁴⁹His offering was one silver plate weighing a hundred and thirty shekels, and one silver sprinkling bowl weighing seventy shekels, both according to the sanctuary shekel, each filled with fine flour mixed with oil as a grain offering; ⁵⁰one gold dish weighing ten shekels, filled with incense; ⁵¹one young bull, one ram and one male lamb a year old, for a burnt offering; ⁵²one male goat for a sin offering; ⁵³and two oxen, five rams, five male goats and five male lambs a year old, to be sacrificed as a fellowship offering. This was the offering of Elishama son of Ammihud.

⁵⁴On the eighth day Gamaliel son of Pedahzur, the leader of the people of Manasseh, brought his offering.

⁵⁵His offering was one silver plate weighing a hundred and thirty shekels, and one silver sprinkling bowl weighing seventy shekels, both according to the sanctuary shekel, each filled with fine flour mixed with oil as a grain offering; ⁵⁶one gold dish weighing ten shekels, filled with incense; ⁵⁷one young bull, one ram and one male lamb a year old, for a burnt offering; ⁵⁸one male goat for a sin offering; ⁵⁹and two oxen, five rams, five male goats and five male lambs a year old, to be sacrificed as a fellowship offering. This was the offering of Gamaliel son of Pedahzur.

⁶⁰On the ninth day Abidan son of Gideoni, the leader of the people of Benjamin, brought his offering.

⁶¹His offering was one silver plate weighing a hundred and thirty shekels, and one silver sprinkling bowl weighing seventy shekels, both according to the sanctuary shekel, each filled with fine flour mixed with oil as a grain offering; ⁶²one gold dish weighing ten shekels, filled with incense; ⁶³one young bull, one ram and one male lamb a year old, for a burnt offering; ⁶⁴one male goat for a sin offering; ⁶⁵and two oxen, five rams, five male goats and five male lambs a year old, to be sacrificed as a fellowship offering. This was the offering of Abidan son of Gideoni.

NEW TESTAMENT READING
Luke 2:21–40

Jesus Presented in the Temple

²¹On the eighth day, when it was time to circumcise him, he was named Jesus, the name the angel had given him before he had been conceived.

²²When the time of their purification according to the Law of Moses had been completed, Joseph and Mary took him to Jerusalem to present him to the Lord ²³(as it is written in the Law of the Lord, "Every firstborn male is to be consecrated to the Lord"), ²⁴and to offer a sacrifice in keeping with what is said in the Law of the Lord: "a pair of doves or two young pigeons".

²⁵Now there was a man in Jerusalem called Simeon, who was righteous and devout. He was waiting for the consolation of Israel, and the Holy Spirit was upon him. ²⁶It had been revealed to him by the Holy Spirit that he would not die before he had seen the Lord's Christ. ²⁷Moved by the Spirit, he went into the temple courts. When the parents brought in the child Jesus to do for him what the custom of the Law required, ²⁸Simeon took him in his arms and praised God, saying:

²⁹"Sovereign Lord, as you have
        promised,
    you now dismiss your servant in
        peace.
³⁰For my eyes have seen your
        salvation,
³¹   which you have prepared in the
        sight of all people,
³²a light for revelation to the Gentiles
    and for glory to your people
        Israel."

³³The child's father and mother marvelled at what was said about him. ³⁴Then Simeon blessed them and said to Mary, his mother: "This child is destined to cause the falling and rising of many in Israel, and to be a sign that will be spoken against, ³⁵so that the thoughts of many hearts will be revealed. And a sword will pierce your own soul too."

³⁶There was also a prophetess, Anna, the daughter of Phanuel, of the tribe of Asher. She was very old; she had lived with her husband seven years after her marriage, ³⁷and then was a widow until she was eighty-four. She never left the temple but worshipped night and day, fasting and praying. ³⁸Coming up to them at that very moment, she gave thanks to God and spoke about the child to all who were looking forward to the redemption of Jerusalem.

³⁹When Joseph and Mary had done everything required by the Law of the Lord, they returned to Galilee to their own town of Nazareth. ⁴⁰And the child grew and became strong; he was filled with wisdom, and the grace of God was upon him.

READING FROM PSALMS
Psalm 35:1–10

Of David.

¹Contend, O LORD, with those who
        contend with me;
    fight against those who fight
        against me.
²Take up shield and buckler;
    arise and come to my aid.
³Brandish spear and javelin
    against those who pursue me.
Say to my soul,
    "I am your salvation."

⁴May those who seek my life
    be disgraced and put to shame;
may those who plot my ruin
    be turned back in dismay.
⁵May they be like chaff before the
        wind,
    with the angel of the LORD driving
        them away;
⁶may their path be dark and slippery,
    with the angel of the LORD
        pursuing them.
⁷Since they hid their net for me
        without cause
    and without cause dug a pit for me,
⁸may ruin overtake them by
        surprise—
    may the net they hid entangle
        them,
    may they fall into the pit, to their
        ruin.

⁹Then my soul will rejoice in the LORD
   and delight in his salvation.
¹⁰My whole being will exclaim,
   "Who is like you, O LORD?

You rescue the poor from those too
   strong for them,
   the poor and needy from those who
   rob them."

MARCH 19

OLD TESTAMENT READING
Numbers 7:66–9:14

⁶⁶On the tenth day Ahiezer son of Ammishaddai, the leader of the people of Dan, brought his offering.

⁶⁷His offering was one silver plate weighing a hundred and thirty shekels, and one silver sprinkling bowl weighing seventy shekels, both according to the sanctuary shekel, each filled with fine flour mixed with oil as a grain offering; ⁶⁸one gold dish weighing ten shekels, filled with incense; ⁶⁹one young bull, one ram and one male lamb a year old, for a burnt offering; ⁷⁰one male goat for a sin offering; ⁷¹and two oxen, five rams, five male goats and five male lambs a year old, to be sacrificed as a fellowship offering. This was the offering of Ahiezer son of Ammishaddai.

⁷²On the eleventh day Pagiel son of Ocran, the leader of the people of Asher, brought his offering.

⁷³His offering was one silver plate weighing a hundred and thirty shekels, and one silver sprinkling bowl weighing seventy shekels, both according to the sanctuary shekel, each filled with fine flour mixed with oil as a grain offering; ⁷⁴one gold dish weighing ten shekels, filled with incense; ⁷⁵one young bull, one ram and one male lamb a year old, for a burnt offering; ⁷⁶one male goat for a sin offering; ⁷⁷and two oxen, five rams, five

male goats and five male lambs a year old, to be sacrificed as a fellowship offering. This was the offering of Pagiel son of Ocran.

⁷⁸On the twelfth day Ahira son of Enan, the leader of the people of Naphtali, brought his offering.

⁷⁹His offering was one silver plate weighing a hundred and thirty shekels, and one silver sprinkling bowl weighing seventy shekels, both according to the sanctuary shekel, each filled with fine flour mixed with oil as a grain offering; ⁸⁰one gold dish weighing ten shekels, filled with incense; ⁸¹one young bull, one ram and one male lamb a year old, for a burnt offering; ⁸²one male goat for a sin offering; ⁸³and two oxen, five rams, five male goats and five male lambs a year old, to be sacrificed as a fellowship offering. This was the offering of Ahira son of Enan.

⁸⁴These were the offerings of the Israelite leaders for the dedication of the altar when it was anointed: twelve silver plates, twelve silver sprinkling bowls and twelve gold dishes. ⁸⁵Each silver plate weighed a hundred and thirty shekels, and each sprinkling bowl seventy shekels. Altogether, the silver dishes weighed two thousand four hundred shekels, according to the sanctuary shekel. ⁸⁶The twelve gold dishes filled with incense weighed ten shekels each, according to the sanctuary shekel. Altogether, the gold dishes weighed a hundred and twenty shekels. ⁸⁷The total

number of animals for the burnt offering came to twelve young bulls, twelve rams and twelve male lambs a year old, together with their grain offering. Twelve male goats were used for the sin offering. [88]The total number of animals for the sacrifice of the fellowship offering came to twenty-four oxen, sixty rams, sixty male goats and sixty male lambs a year old. These were the offerings for the dedication of the altar after it was anointed.

[89]When Moses entered the Tent of Meeting to speak with the LORD, he heard the voice speaking to him from between the two cherubim above the atonement cover on the ark of the Testimony. And he spoke with him.

Setting Up the Lamps

8 The LORD said to Moses, [2]"Speak to Aaron and say to him, 'When you set up the seven lamps, they are to light the area in front of the lampstand.'"

[3]Aaron did so; he set up the lamps so that they faced forward on the lampstand, just as the LORD commanded Moses. [4]This is how the lampstand was made: It was made of hammered gold —from its base to its blossoms. The lampstand was made exactly like the pattern the LORD had shown Moses.

The Setting Apart of the Levites

[5]The LORD said to Moses: [6]"Take the Levites from among the other Israelites and make them ceremonially clean. [7]To purify them, do this: Sprinkle the water of cleansing on them; then make them shave their whole bodies and wash their clothes, and so purify themselves. [8]Make them take a young bull with its grain offering of fine flour mixed with oil; then you are to take a second young bull for a sin offering. [9]Bring the Levites to the front of the Tent of Meeting and assemble the whole Israelite community. [10]You are to bring the Levites before the LORD, and the Israelites are to

lay their hands on them. [11]Aaron is to present the Levites before the LORD as a wave offering from the Israelites, so that they may be ready to do the work of the LORD.

[12]"After the Levites lay their hands on the heads of the bulls, use the one for a sin offering to the LORD and the other for a burnt offering, to make atonement for the Levites. [13]Make the Levites stand in front of Aaron and his sons and then present them as a wave offering to the LORD. [14]In this way you are to set the Levites apart from the other Israelites, and the Levites will be mine.

[15]"After you have purified the Levites and presented them as a wave offering, they are to come to do their work at the Tent of Meeting. [16]They are the Israelites who are to be given wholly to me. I have taken them as my own in place of the firstborn, the first male offspring from every Israelite woman. [17]Every firstborn male in Israel, whether man or animal, is mine. When I struck down all the firstborn in Egypt, I set them apart for myself. [18]And I have taken the Levites in place of all the firstborn sons in Israel. [19]Of all the Israelites, I have given the Levites as gifts to Aaron and his sons to do the work at the Tent of Meeting on behalf of the Israelites and to make atonement for them so that no plague will strike the Israelites when they go near the sanctuary."

[20]Moses, Aaron and the whole Israelite community did with the Levites just as the LORD commanded Moses. [21]The Levites purified themselves and washed their clothes. Then Aaron presented them as a wave offering before the LORD and made atonement for them to purify them. [22]After that, the Levites came to do their work at the Tent of Meeting under the supervision of Aaron and his sons. They did with the Levites just as the LORD commanded Moses.

[23]The LORD said to Moses, [24]"This applies to the Levites: Men twenty-five years old or more shall come to take

part in the work at the Tent of Meeting, ²⁵but at the age of fifty, they must retire from their regular service and work no longer. ²⁶They may assist their brothers in performing their duties at the Tent of Meeting, but they themselves must not do the work. This, then, is how you are to assign the responsibilities of the Levites."

The Passover

9 The LORD spoke to Moses in the Desert of Sinai in the first month of the second year after they came out of Egypt. He said, ²"Make the Israelites celebrate the Passover at the appointed time. ³Celebrate it at the appointed time, at twilight on the fourteenth day of this month, in accordance with all its rules and regulations."

⁴So Moses told the Israelites to celebrate the Passover, ⁵and they did so in the Desert of Sinai at twilight on the fourteenth day of the first month. The Israelites did everything just as the LORD commanded Moses.

⁶But some of them could not celebrate the Passover on that day because they were ceremonially unclean on account of a dead body. So they came to Moses and Aaron that same day ⁷and said to Moses, "We have become unclean because of a dead body, but why should we be kept from presenting the LORD's offering with the other Israelites at the appointed time?"

⁸Moses answered them, "Wait until I find out what the LORD commands concerning you."

⁹Then the LORD said to Moses, ¹⁰"Tell the Israelites: 'When any of you or your descendants are unclean because of a dead body or are away on a journey, they may still celebrate the LORD's Passover. ¹¹They are to celebrate it on the fourteenth day of the second month at twilight. They are to eat the lamb, together with unleavened bread and bitter herbs. ¹²They must not leave any of it till morning or break any of its bones. When they celebrate the

Passover, they must follow all the regulations. ¹³But if a man who is ceremonially clean and not on a journey fails to celebrate the Passover, that person must be cut off from his people because he did not present the LORD's offering at the appointed time. That man will bear the consequences of his sin.

¹⁴"'An alien living among you who wants to celebrate the LORD's Passover must do so in accordance with its rules and regulations. You must have the same regulations for the alien and the native-born.'"

NEW TESTAMENT READING
Luke 2:41–52

The Boy Jesus at the Temple

⁴¹Every year his parents went to Jerusalem for the Feast of the Passover. ⁴²When he was twelve years old, they went up to the Feast, according to the custom. ⁴³After the Feast was over, while his parents were returning home, the boy Jesus stayed behind in Jerusalem, but they were unaware of it. ⁴⁴Thinking he was in their company, they travelled on for a day. Then they began looking for him among their relatives and friends. ⁴⁵When they did not find him, they went back to Jerusalem to look for him. ⁴⁶After three days they found him in the temple courts, sitting among the teachers, listening to them and asking them questions. ⁴⁷Everyone who heard him was amazed at his understanding and his answers. ⁴⁸When his parents saw him, they were astonished. His mother said to him, "Son, why have you treated us like this? Your father and I have been anxiously searching for you."

⁴⁹"Why were you searching for me?" he asked. "Didn't you know I had to be in my Father's house?" ⁵⁰But they did not understand what he was saying to them.

⁵¹Then he went down to Nazareth

with them and was obedient to them. But his mother treasured all these things in her heart. 52And Jesus grew in wisdom and stature, and in favour with God and men.

READING FROM PSALMS
Psalm 35:11–18

11Ruthless witnesses come forward;
    they question me on things I know
      nothing about.
12They repay me evil for good
    and leave my soul forlorn.
13Yet when they were ill, I put on
      sackcloth
    and humbled myself with fasting.
    When my prayers returned to me
      unanswered,

14 I went about mourning
    as though for my friend or brother.
  I bowed my head in grief
    as though weeping for my mother.
15But when I stumbled, they gathered
      in glee;
    attackers gathered against me
      when I was unaware.
    They slandered me without
      ceasing.
16Like the ungodly they maliciously
      mocked;
    they gnashed their teeth at me.
17O Lord, how long will you look on?
    Rescue my life from their ravages,
    my precious life from these lions.
18I will give you thanks in the great
      assembly;
    among throngs of people I will
      praise you.

MARCH 20   DAY 79

OLD TESTAMENT READING
Numbers 9:15–11:3

The Cloud Above the Tabernacle

15On the day the tabernacle, the Tent of the Testimony, was set up, the cloud covered it. From evening till morning the cloud above the tabernacle looked like fire. 16That is how it continued to be; the cloud covered it, and at night it looked like fire. 17Whenever the cloud lifted from above the Tent, the Israelites set out; wherever the cloud settled, the Israelites encamped. 18At the LORD's command the Israelites set out, and at his command they encamped. As long as the cloud stayed over the tabernacle, they remained in camp. 19When the cloud remained over the tabernacle a long time, the Israelites obeyed the LORD's order and did not set out. 20Sometimes the cloud was over the tabernacle only a few days; at the

LORD's command they would encamp, and then at his command they would set out. 21Sometimes the cloud stayed only from evening till morning, and when it lifted in the morning, they set out. Whether by day or by night, whenever the cloud lifted, they set out. 22Whether the cloud stayed over the tabernacle for two days or a month or a year, the Israelites would remain in camp and not set out; but when it lifted, they would set out. 23At the LORD's command they encamped, and at the LORD's command they set out. They obeyed the LORD's order, in accordance with his command through Moses.

The Silver Trumpets

10 The LORD said to Moses: 2"Make two trumpets of hammered silver, and use them for calling the community together and for having the camps set out. 3When both are

sounded, the whole community is to assemble before you at the entrance to the Tent of Meeting. 4If only one is sounded, the leaders—the heads of the clans of Israel—are to assemble before you. 5When a trumpet blast is sounded, the tribes camping on the east are to set out. 6At the sounding of a second blast, the camps on the south are to set out. The blast will be the signal for setting out. 7To gather the assembly, blow the trumpets, but not with the same signal.

8"The sons of Aaron, the priests, are to blow the trumpets. This is to be a lasting ordinance for you and the generations to come. 9When you go into battle in your own land against an enemy who is oppressing you, sound a blast on the trumpets. Then you will be remembered by the LORD your God and rescued from your enemies. 10Also at your times of rejoicing—your appointed feasts and New Moon festivals —you are to sound the trumpets over your burnt offerings and fellowship offerings, and they will be a memorial for you before your God. I am the LORD your God."

The Israelites Leave Sinai

11On the twentieth day of the second month of the second year, the cloud lifted from above the tabernacle of the Testimony. 12Then the Israelites set out from the Desert of Sinai and travelled from place to place until the cloud came to rest in the Desert of Paran. 13They set out, this first time, at the LORD's command through Moses.

14The divisions of the camp of Judah went first, under their standard. Nahshon son of Amminadab was in command. 15Nethanel son of Zuar was over the division of the tribe of Issachar, 16and Eliab son of Helon was over the division of the tribe of Zebulun. 17Then the tabernacle was taken down, and the Gershonites and Merarites, who carried it, set out.

18The divisions of the camp of Reuben went next, under their standard. Elizur son of Shedeur was in command. 19Shelumiel son of Zurishaddai was over the division of the tribe of Simeon, 20and Eliasaph son of Deuel was over the division of the tribe of Gad. 21Then the Kohathites set out, carrying the holy things. The tabernacle was to be set up before they arrived.

22The divisions of the camp of Ephraim went next, under their standard. Elishama son of Ammihud was in command. 23Gamaliel son of Pedahzur was over the division of the tribe of Manasseh, 24and Abidan son of Gideoni was over the division of the tribe of Benjamin.

25Finally, as the rear guard for all the units, the divisions of the camp of Dan set out, under their standard. Ahiezer son of Ammishaddai was in command. 26Pagiel son of Ocran was over the division of the tribe of Asher, 27and Ahira son of Enan was over the division of the tribe of Naphtali. 28This was the order of march for the Israelite divisions as they set out.

29Now Moses said to Hobab son of Reuel the Midianite, Moses' father-in-law, "We are setting out for the place about which the LORD said, 'I will give it to you.' Come with us and we will treat you well, for the LORD has promised good things to Israel."

30He answered, "No, I will not go; I am going back to my own land and my own people."

31But Moses said, "Please do not leave us. You know where we should camp in the desert, and you can be our eyes. 32If you come with us, we will share with you whatever good things the LORD gives us."

33So they set out from the mountain of the LORD and travelled for three days. The ark of the covenant of the LORD went before them during those three days to find them a place to rest. 34The cloud of the LORD was over them by day when they set out from the camp.

35Whenever the ark set out, Moses said,

"Rise up, O LORD!
    May your enemies be scattered;
    may your foes flee before you."

36Whenever it came to rest, he said,

"Return, O LORD,
    to the countless thousands of
        Israel."

Fire From the LORD

11 Now the people complained about their hardships in the hearing of the LORD, and when he heard them his anger was aroused. Then fire from the LORD burned among them and consumed some of the outskirts of the camp. 2When the people cried out to Moses, he prayed to the LORD and the fire died down. 3So that place was called Taberah, because fire from the LORD had burned among them.

NEW TESTAMENT READING
Luke 3:1–22

John the Baptist Prepares the Way

3 In the fifteenth year of the reign of Tiberius Caesar—when Pontius Pilate was governor of Judea, Herod tetrarch of Galilee, his brother Philip tetrarch of Iturea and Traconitis, and Lysanias tetrarch of Abilene—2during the high priesthood of Annas and Caiaphas, the word of God came to John son of Zechariah in the desert. 3He went into all the country around the Jordan, preaching a baptism of repentance for the forgiveness of sins. 4As is written in the book of the words of Isaiah the prophet:

"A voice of one calling in the desert,
'Prepare the way for the Lord,
    make straight paths for him.
5Every valley shall be filled in,
    every mountain and hill made low.
The crooked roads shall become
        straight,
    the rough ways smooth.

6And all mankind will see God's salvation.'"

7John said to the crowds coming out to be baptised by him, "You brood of vipers! Who warned you to flee from the coming wrath? 8Produce fruit in keeping with repentance. And do not begin to say to yourselves, 'We have Abraham as our father.' For I tell you that out of these stones God can raise up children for Abraham. 9The axe is already at the root of the trees, and every tree that does not produce good fruit will be cut down and thrown into the fire."

10"What should we do then?" the crowd asked.

11John answered, "The man with two tunics should share with him who has none, and the one who has food should do the same."

12Tax collectors also came to be baptised. "Teacher," they asked, "what should we do?"

13"Don't collect any more than you are required to," he told them.

14Then some soldiers asked him, "And what should we do?"

He replied, "Don't extort money and don't accuse people falsely—be content with your pay."

15The people were waiting expectantly and were all wondering in their hearts if John might possibly be the Christ. 16John answered them all, "I baptise you with water. But one more powerful than I will come, the thongs of whose sandals I am not worthy to untie. He will baptise you with the Holy Spirit and with fire. 17His winnowing fork is in his hand to clear his threshing-floor and to gather the wheat into his barn, but he will burn up the chaff with unquenchable fire." 18And with many other words John exhorted the people and preached the good news to them.

19But when John rebuked Herod the tetrarch because of Herodias, his brother's wife, and all the other evil things he had done, 20Herod added this to them all: He locked John up in prison.

The Baptism and Genealogy of Jesus

²¹When all the people were being baptised, Jesus was baptised too. And as he was praying, heaven was opened ²²and the Holy Spirit descended on him in bodily form like a dove. And a voice came from heaven: "You are my Son, whom I love; with you I am well pleased."

READING FROM PSALMS
Psalm 35:19–28

¹⁹Let not those gloat over me
    who are my enemies without cause;
let not those who hate me without
        reason
    maliciously wink the eye.
²⁰They do not speak peaceably,
    but devise false accusations
    against those who live quietly in
        the land.
²¹They gape at me and say, "Aha!
        Aha!

With our own eyes we have seen
    it."

²²O LORD, you have seen this; be not
    silent.
    Do not be far from me, O Lord.
²³Awake, and rise to my defence!
    Contend for me, my God and
        Lord.
²⁴Vindicate me in your righteousness,
        O LORD my God;
    do not let them gloat over me.
²⁵Do not let them think, "Aha, just
        what we wanted!"
    or say, "We have swallowed him
        up."

²⁶May all who gloat over my distress
    be put to shame and confusion;
may all who exalt themselves over me
    be clothed with shame and
        disgrace.
²⁷May those who delight in my
        vindication
    shout for joy and gladness;
may they always say, "The LORD be
        exalted,
    who delights in the well-being of
        his servant."
²⁸My tongue will speak of your
        righteousness
    and of your praises all day long.

DAY 80

MARCH 21

OLD TESTAMENT READING
Numbers 11:4–13:25

Quail From the LORD

⁴The rabble with them began to crave other food, and again the Israelites started wailing and said, "If only we had meat to eat! ⁵We remember the fish we ate in Egypt at no cost—also the cucumbers, melons, leeks, onions and garlic. ⁶But now we have lost our appetite; we never see anything but this manna!"

⁷The manna was like coriander seed and looked like resin. ⁸The people went around gathering it, and then ground it in a hand mill or crushed it in a mortar. They cooked it in a pot or made it into cakes. And it tasted like something made with olive oil. ⁹When the dew settled on the camp at night, the manna also came down.

¹⁰Moses heard the people of every family wailing, each at the entrance to

his tent. The LORD became exceedingly angry, and Moses was troubled. [11]He asked the LORD, "Why have you brought this trouble on your servant? What have I done to displease you that you put the burden of all these people on me? [12]Did I conceive all these people? Did I give them birth? Why do you tell me to carry them in my arms, as a nurse carries an infant, to the land you promised on oath to their forefathers? [13]Where can I get meat for all these people? They keep wailing to me, 'Give us meat to eat!' [14]I cannot carry all these people by myself; the burden is too heavy for me. [15]If this is how you are going to treat me, put me to death right now—if I have found favour in your eyes—and do not let me face my own ruin."

[16]The LORD said to Moses: "Bring me seventy of Israel's elders who are known to you as leaders and officials among the people. Make them come to the Tent of Meeting, that they may stand there with you. [17]I will come down and speak with you there, and I will take of the Spirit that is on you and put the Spirit on them. They will help you carry the burden of the people so that you will not have to carry it alone.

[18]"Tell the people: 'Consecrate yourselves in preparation for tomorrow, when you will eat meat. The LORD heard you when you wailed, "If only we had meat to eat! We were better off in Egypt!" Now the LORD will give you meat, and you will eat it. [19]You will not eat it for just one day, or two days, or five, ten or twenty days, [20]but for a whole month—until it comes out of your nostrils and you loathe it—because you have rejected the LORD, who is among you, and have wailed before him, saying, "Why did we ever leave Egypt?" '"

[21]But Moses said, "Here I am among six hundred thousand men on foot, and you say, 'I will give them meat to eat for a whole month!' [22]Would they have enough if flocks and herds were slaughtered for them? Would they have

enough if all the fish in the sea were caught for them?"

[23]The LORD answered Moses, "Is the LORD's arm too short? You will now see whether or not what I say will come true for you."

[24]So Moses went out and told the people what the LORD had said. He brought together seventy of their elders and made them stand round the Tent. [25]Then the LORD came down in the cloud and spoke with him, and he took of the Spirit that was on him and put the Spirit on the seventy elders. When the Spirit rested on them, they prophesied, but they did not do so again.

[26]However, two men, whose names were Eldad and Medad, had remained in the camp. They were listed among the elders, but did not go out to the Tent. Yet the Spirit also rested on them, and they prophesied in the camp. [27]A young man ran and told Moses, "Eldad and Medad are prophesying in the camp."

[28]Joshua son of Nun, who had been Moses' assistant since youth, spoke up and said, "Moses, my lord, stop them!"

[29]But Moses replied, "Are you jealous for my sake? I wish that all the LORD's people were prophets and that the LORD would put his Spirit on them!" [30]Then Moses and the elders of Israel returned to the camp.

[31]Now a wind went out from the LORD and drove quail in from the sea. It brought them down all around the camp to about three feet above the ground, as far as a day's walk in any direction. [32]All that day and night and all the next day the people went out and gathered quail. No-one gathered less than ten homers. Then they spread them out all around the camp. [33]But while the meat was still between their teeth and before it could be consumed, the anger of the LORD burned against the people, and he struck them with a severe plague. [34]Therefore the place was named Kibroth Hattaavah, because there they buried the people who had craved other food.

³⁵From Kibroth Hattaavah the people travelled to Hazeroth and stayed there.

Miriam and Aaron Oppose Moses

12 Miriam and Aaron began to talk against Moses because of his Cushite wife, for he had married a Cushite. ²"Has the LORD spoken only through Moses?" they asked. "Hasn't he also spoken through us?" And the LORD heard this.

³(Now Moses was a very humble man, more humble than anyone else on the face of the earth.)

⁴At once the LORD said to Moses, Aaron and Miriam, "Come out to the Tent of Meeting, all three of you." So the three of them came out. ⁵Then the LORD came down in a pillar of cloud; he stood at the entrance to the Tent and summoned Aaron and Miriam. When both of them stepped forward, ⁶he said,

"Listen to my words:

"When a prophet of the LORD is
among you,
I reveal myself to him in visions,
I speak to him in dreams.
⁷But this is not true of my servant
Moses;
he is faithful in all my house.
⁸With him I speak face to face,
clearly and not in riddles;
he sees the form of the LORD.
Why then were you not afraid
to speak against my servant
Moses?"

⁹The anger of the LORD burned against them, and he left them.

¹⁰When the cloud lifted from above the Tent, there stood Miriam—leprous, like snow. Aaron turned towards her and saw that she had leprosy; ¹¹and he said to Moses, "Please, my lord, do not hold against us the sin we have so foolishly committed. ¹²Do not let her be like a stillborn infant coming from its mother's womb with its flesh half eaten away."

¹³So Moses cried out to the LORD, "O God, please heal her!"

¹⁴The LORD replied to Moses, "If her father had spat in her face, would she not have been in disgrace for seven days? Confine her outside the camp for seven days; after that she can be brought back." ¹⁵So Miriam was confined outside the camp for seven days, and the people did not move on till she was brought back.

¹⁶After that, the people left Hazeroth and encamped in the Desert of Paran.

Exploring Canaan

13 The LORD said to Moses, ²"Send some men to explore the land of Canaan, which I am giving to the Israelites. From each ancestral tribe send one of its leaders."

³So at the LORD's command Moses sent them out from the Desert of Paran. All of them were leaders of the Israelites. ⁴These are their names:

from the tribe of Reuben, Shammua son of Zaccur;
⁵from the tribe of Simeon, Shaphat son of Hori;
⁶from the tribe of Judah, Caleb son of Jephunneh;
⁷from the tribe of Issachar, Igal son of Joseph;
⁸from the tribe of Ephraim, Hoshea son of Nun;
⁹from the tribe of Benjamin, Palti son of Raphu;
¹⁰from the tribe of Zebulun, Gaddiel son of Sodi;
¹¹from the tribe of Manasseh (a tribe of Joseph), Gaddi son of Susi;
¹²from the tribe of Dan, Ammiel son of Gemalli;
¹³from the tribe of Asher, Sethur son of Michael;
¹⁴from the tribe of Naphtali, Nahbi son of Vophsi;
¹⁵from the tribe of Gad, Geuel son of Maki.

¹⁶These are the names of the men Moses sent to explore the land. (Moses gave Hoshea son of Nun the name Joshua.)

17When Moses sent them to explore Canaan, he said, "Go up through the Negev and on into the hill country. 18See what the land is like and whether the people who live there are strong or weak, few or many. 19What kind of land do they live in? Is it good or bad? What kind of towns do they live in? Are they unwalled or fortified? 20How is the soil? Is it fertile or poor? Are there trees on it or not? Do your best to bring back some of the fruit of the land." (It was the season for the first ripe grapes.)

21So they went up and explored the land from the Desert of Zin as far as Rehob, towards Lebo Hamath. 22They went up through the Negev and came to Hebron, where Ahiman, Sheshai and Talmai, the descendants of Anak, lived. (Hebron had been built seven years before Zoan in Egypt.) 23When they reached the Valley of Eshcol, they cut off a branch bearing a single cluster of grapes. Two of them carried it on a pole between them, along with some pomegranates and figs. 24That place was called the Valley of Eshcol because of the cluster of grapes the Israelites cut off there. 25At the end of forty days they returned from exploring the land.

NEW TESTAMENT READING
Luke 3:23–4:13

23Now Jesus himself was about thirty years old when he began his ministry. He was the son, so it was thought, of Joseph,

the son of Heli, 24the son of Matthat,
the son of Levi, the son of Melki,
the son of Jannai, the son of Joseph,
25the son of Mattathias, the son of
    Amos,
the son of Nahum, the son of Esli,
the son of Naggai, 26the son of
    Maath,
the son of Mattathias, the son of
    Semein,
the son of Josech, the son of Joda,
27the son of Joanan, the son of Rhesa,

the son of Zerubbabel, the son of
    Shealtiel,
the son of Neri, 28the son of Melki,
the son of Addi, the son of Cosam,
the son of Elmadam, the son of Er,
29the son of Joshua, the son of Eliezer,
the son of Jorim, the son of Matthat,
the son of Levi, 30the son of Simeon,
the son of Judah, the son of Joseph,
the son of Jonam, the son of Eliakim,
31the son of Melea, the son of Menna,
the son of Mattatha, the son of
    Nathan,
the son of David, 32the son of Jesse,
the son of Obed, the son of Boaz,
the son of Salmon, the son of
    Nahshon,
33the son of Amminadab, the son of
    Ram,
the son of Hezron, the son of Perez,
the son of Judah, 34the son of Jacob,
the son of Isaac, the son of Abraham,
the son of Terah, the son of Nahor,
35the son of Serug, the son of Reu,
the son of Peleg, the son of Eber,
the son of Shelah, 36the son of
    Cainan,
the son of Arphaxad, the son of
    Shem,
the son of Noah, the son of Lamech,
37the son of Methuselah, the son of
    Enoch,
the son of Jared, the son of
    Mahalalel,
the son of Kenan, 38the son of Enosh,
the son of Seth, the son of Adam,
the son of God.

The Temptation of Jesus

4 Jesus, full of the Holy Spirit, returned from the Jordan and was led by the Spirit in the desert, 2where for forty days he was tempted by the devil. He ate nothing during those days, and at the end of them he was hungry.

3The devil said to him, "If you are the Son of God, tell this stone to become bread."

4Jesus answered, "It is written: 'Man does not live on bread alone.'"

5The devil led him up to a high place

and showed him in an instant all the kingdoms of the world. 6And he said to him, "I will give you all their authority and splendour, for it has been given to me, and I can give it to anyone I want to. 7So if you worship me, it will all be yours."

8Jesus answered, "It is written: 'Worship the Lord your God and serve him only.'"

9The devil led him to Jerusalem and had him stand on the highest point of the temple. "If you are the Son of God," he said, "throw yourself down from here. 10For it is written:

"'He will command his angels
        concerning you
    to guard you carefully;
11they will lift you up in their hands,
    so that you will not strike your foot
        against a stone.'"

12Jesus answered, "It says: 'Do not put the Lord your God to the test.'"

13When the devil had finished all this tempting, he left him until an opportune time.

READING FROM PROVERBS
Proverbs 7:21–27

21With persuasive words she led him
        astray;
    she seduced him with her smooth
        talk.
22All at once he followed her
    like an ox going to the slaughter,
    like a deer stepping into a noose
23   till an arrow pierces his liver,
    like a bird darting into a snare,
        little knowing it will cost him his
            life.

24Now then, my sons, listen to me;
    pay attention to what I say.
25Do not let your heart turn to her ways
    or stray into her paths.
26Many are the victims she has brought
        down;
    her slain are a mighty throng.
27Her house is a highway to the grave,
    leading down to the chambers of
        death.

DAY 81

MARCH 22

OLD TESTAMENT READING
Numbers 13:26–14:45

Report on the Exploration

26They came back to Moses and Aaron and the whole Israelite community at Kadesh in the Desert of Paran. There they reported to them and to the whole assembly and showed them the fruit of the land. 27They gave Moses this account: "We went into the land to which you sent us, and it does flow with milk and honey! Here is its fruit. 28But the people who live there are powerful, and the cities are fortified and very large. We even saw descendants of

Anak there. 29The Amalekites live in the Negev; the Hittites, Jebusites and Amorites live in the hill country; and the Canaanites live near the sea and along the Jordan."

30Then Caleb silenced the people before Moses and said, "We should go up and take possession of the land, for we can certainly do it."

31But the men who had gone up with him said, "We can't attack those people; they are stronger than we are." 32And they spread among the Israelites a bad report about the land they had explored. They said, "The land we explored devours those living in it. All the people we saw there are of great size.

³³We saw the Nephilim there (the descendants of Anak come from the Nephilim). We seemed like grasshoppers in our own eyes, and we looked the same to them."

The People Rebel

14 That night all the people of the community raised their voices and wept aloud. ²All the Israelites grumbled against Moses and Aaron, and the whole assembly said to them, "If only we had died in Egypt! Or in this desert! ³Why is the LORD bringing us to this land only to let us fall by the sword? Our wives and children will be taken as plunder. Wouldn't it be better for us to go back to Egypt?" ⁴And they said to each other, "We should choose a leader and go back to Egypt."

⁵Then Moses and Aaron fell face down in front of the whole Israelite assembly gathered there. ⁶Joshua son of Nun and Caleb son of Jephunneh, who were among those who had explored the land, tore their clothes ⁷and said to the entire Israelite assembly, "The land we passed through and explored is exceedingly good. ⁸If the LORD is pleased with us, he will lead us into that land, a land flowing with milk and honey, and will give it to us. ⁹Only do not rebel against the LORD. And do not be afraid of the people of the land, because we will swallow them up. Their protection is gone, but the LORD is with us. Do not be afraid of them."

¹⁰But the whole assembly talked about stoning them. Then the glory of the LORD appeared at the Tent of Meeting to all the Israelites. ¹¹The LORD said to Moses, "How long will these people treat me with contempt? How long will they refuse to believe in me, in spite of all the miraculous signs I have performed among them? ¹²I will strike them down with a plague and destroy them, but I will make you into a nation greater and stronger than they."

¹³Moses said to the LORD, "Then the Egyptians will hear about it! By your power you brought these people up from among them. ¹⁴And they will tell the inhabitants of this land about it. They have already heard that you, O LORD, are with these people and that you, O LORD, have been seen face to face, that your cloud stays over them, and that you go before them in a pillar of cloud by day and a pillar of fire by night. ¹⁵If you put these people to death all at one time, the nations who have heard this report about you will say, ¹⁶'The LORD was not able to bring these people into the land he promised them on oath; so he slaughtered them in the desert.'

¹⁷"Now may the Lord's strength be displayed, just as you have declared: ¹⁸'The LORD is slow to anger, abounding in love and forgiving sin and rebellion. Yet he does not leave the guilty unpunished; he punishes the children for the sin of the fathers to the third and fourth generation.' ¹⁹In accordance with your great love, forgive the sin of these people, just as you have pardoned them from the time they left Egypt until now."

²⁰The LORD replied, "I have forgiven them, as you asked. ²¹Nevertheless, as surely as I live and as surely as the glory of the LORD fills the whole earth, ²²not one of the men who saw my glory and the miraculous signs I performed in Egypt and in the desert but who disobeyed me and tested me ten times —²³not one of them will ever see the land I promised on oath to their forefathers. No-one who has treated me with contempt will ever see it. ²⁴But because my servant Caleb has a different spirit and follows me wholeheartedly, I will bring him into the land he went to, and his descendants will inherit it. ²⁵Since the Amalekites and Canaanites are living in the valleys, turn back tomorrow and set out towards the desert along the route to the Red Sea."

²⁶The LORD said to Moses and Aaron: ²⁷"How long will this wicked community grumble against me? I have

heard the complaints of these grumbling Israelites. 28So tell them, 'As surely as I live, declares the LORD, I will do to you the very things I heard you say: 29In this desert your bodies will fall—every one of you twenty years old or more who was counted in the census and who has grumbled against me. 30Not one of you will enter the land I swore with uplifted hand to make your home, except Caleb son of Jephunneh and Joshua son of Nun. 31As for your children that you said would be taken as plunder, I will bring them in to enjoy the land you have rejected. 32But you —your bodies will fall in this desert. 33Your children will be shepherds here for forty years, suffering for your unfaithfulness, until the last of your bodies lies in the desert. 34For forty years— one year for each of the forty days you explored the land—you will suffer for your sins and know what it is like to have me against you.' 35I, the LORD, have spoken, and I will surely do these things to this whole wicked community, which has banded together against me. They will meet their end in this desert; here they will die."

36So the men Moses had sent to explore the land, who returned and made the whole community grumble against him by spreading a bad report about it—37these men responsible for spreading the bad report about the land were struck down and died of a plague before the LORD. 38Of the men who went to explore the land, only Joshua son of Nun and Caleb son of Jephunneh survived.

39When Moses reported this to all the Israelites, they mourned bitterly. 40Early the next morning they went up towards the high hill country. "We have sinned," they said. "We will go up to the place the LORD promised."

41But Moses said, "Why are you disobeying the LORD's command? This will not succeed! 42Do not go up, because the LORD is not with you. You will be defeated by your enemies, 43for the Amalekites and Canaanites will face you there. Because you have turned away from the LORD, he will not be with you and you will fall by the sword."

44Nevertheless, in their presumption they went up towards the high hill country, though neither Moses nor the ark of the LORD's covenant moved from the camp. 45Then the Amalekites and Canaanites who lived in that hill country came down and attacked them and beat them down all the way to Hormah.

NEW TESTAMENT READING
Luke 4:14–37

Jesus Rejected at Nazareth

14Jesus returned to Galilee in the power of the Spirit, and news about him spread through the whole countryside. 15He taught in their synagogues, and everyone praised him.

16He went to Nazareth, where he had been brought up, and on the Sabbath day he went into the synagogue, as was his custom. And he stood up to read. 17The scroll of the prophet Isaiah was handed to him. Unrolling it, he found the place where it is written:

18"The Spirit of the Lord is on me,
　　because he has anointed me
　　to preach good news to the poor.
He has sent me to proclaim freedom
　　for the prisoners
　　and recovery of sight for the blind,
to release the oppressed,
19　to proclaim the year of the Lord's
　　　favour."

20Then he rolled up the scroll, gave it back to the attendant and sat down. The eyes of everyone in the synagogue were fastened on him, 21and he began by saying to them, "Today this scripture is fulfilled in your hearing."

22All spoke well of him and were amazed at the gracious words that came from his lips. "Isn't this Joseph's son?" they asked.

23Jesus said to them, "Surely you will quote this proverb to me: 'Physician, heal yourself! Do here in your home town what we have heard that you did in Capernaum.' "

24"I tell you the truth," he continued, "no prophet is accepted in his home town. 25I assure you that there were many widows in Israel in Elijah's time, when the sky was shut for three and a half years and there was a severe famine throughout the land. 26Yet Elijah was not sent to any of them, but to a widow in Zarephath in the region of Sidon. 27And there were many in Israel with leprosy in the time of Elisha the prophet, yet not one of them was cleansed—only Naaman the Syrian."

28All the people in the synagogue were furious when they heard this. 29They got up, drove him out of the town, and took him to the brow of the hill on which the town was built, in order to throw him down the cliff. 30But he walked right through the crowd and went on his way.

Jesus Drives Out an Evil Spirit

31Then he went down to Capernaum, a town in Galilee, and on the Sabbath began to teach the people. 32They were amazed at his teaching, because his message had authority.

33In the synagogue there was a man possessed by a demon, an evil spirit. He cried out at the top of his voice, 34"Ha! What do you want with us, Jesus of Nazareth? Have you come to destroy us? I know who you are—the Holy One of God!"

35"Be quiet!" Jesus said sternly. "Come out of him!" Then the demon threw the man down before them all and came out without injuring him.

36All the people were amazed and said to each other, "What is this teaching? With authority and power he gives orders to evil spirits and they come out!" 37And the news about him spread throughout the surrounding area.

READING FROM PSALMS
Psalm 36:1–12

For the director of music. Of David the servant of the LORD.

1An oracle is within my heart
  concerning the sinfulness of the wicked:
There is no fear of God
  before his eyes.

2For in his own eyes he flatters himself
  too much to detect or hate his sin.

3The words of his mouth are wicked and deceitful;
  he has ceased to be wise and to do good.

4Even on his bed he plots evil;
  he commits himself to a sinful course
  and does not reject what is wrong.

5Your love, O LORD, reaches to the heavens,
  your faithfulness to the skies.

6Your righteousness is like the mighty mountains,
  your justice like the great deep.
O LORD, you preserve both man and beast.

7 How priceless is your unfailing love!
Both high and low among men
  find refuge in the shadow of your wings.

8They feast in the abundance of your house;
  you give them drink from your river of delights.

9For with you is the fountain of life;
  in your light we see light.

10Continue your love to those who know you,
  your righteousness to the upright in heart.

11May the foot of the proud not come against me,
  nor the hand of the wicked drive me away.

12See how the evildoers lie fallen—
  thrown down, not able to rise!

OLD TESTAMENT READING
Numbers 15:1–16:35

Supplementary Offerings

15 The LORD said to Moses, 2"Speak to the Israelites and say to them: 'After you enter the land I am giving you as a home 3and you present to the LORD offerings made by fire, from the herd or the flock, as an aroma pleasing to the LORD—whether burnt offerings or sacrifices, for special vows or freewill offerings or festival offerings—4then the one who brings his offering shall present to the LORD a grain offering of a tenth of an ephah of fine flour mixed with a quarter of a hin of oil. 5With each lamb for the burnt offering or the sacrifice, prepare a quarter of a hin of wine as a drink offering.

6"'With a ram prepare a grain offering of two-tenths of an ephah of fine flour mixed with a third of a hin of oil, 7and a third of a hin of wine as a drink offering. Offer it as an aroma pleasing to the LORD.

8"'When you prepare a young bull as a burnt offering or sacrifice, for a special vow or a fellowship offering to the LORD, 9bring with the bull a grain offering of three-tenths of an ephah of fine flour mixed with half a hin of oil. 10Also bring half a hin of wine as a drink offering. It will be an offering made by fire, an aroma pleasing to the LORD. 11Each bull or ram, each lamb or young goat, is to be prepared in this manner. 12Do this for each one, for as many as you prepare.

13"'Everyone who is native-born must do these things in this way when he brings an offering made by fire as an aroma pleasing to the LORD. 14For the generations to come, whenever an alien or anyone else living among you presents an offering made by fire as an aroma pleasing to the LORD, he must do exactly as you do. 15The community is to have the same rules for you and for the alien living among you; this is a lasting ordinance for the generations to come. You and the alien shall be the same before the LORD: 16The same laws and regulations will apply both to you and to the alien living among you.'"

17The LORD said to Moses, 18"Speak to the Israelites and say to them: 'When you enter the land to which I am taking you 19and you eat the food of the land, present a portion as an offering to the LORD. 20Present a cake from the first of your ground meal and present it as an offering from the threshing-floor. 21Throughout the generations to come you are to give this offering to the LORD from the first of your ground meal.

Offerings for Unintentional Sins

22"'Now if you unintentionally fail to keep any of these commands the LORD gave Moses—23any of the LORD's commands to you through him, from the day the LORD gave them and continuing through the generations to come—24and if this is done unintentionally without the community being aware of it, then the whole community is to offer a young bull for a burnt offering as an aroma pleasing to the LORD, along with its prescribed grain offering and drink offering, and a male goat for a sin offering. 25The priest is to make atonement for the whole Israelite community, and they will be forgiven, for it was not intentional and they have brought to the LORD for their wrong an offering made by fire and a sin offering. 26The whole Israelite community and the aliens living among them will be forgiven, because all the people were involved in the unintentional wrong.

27"'But if just one person sins unintentionally, he must bring a year-old female goat for a sin offering. 28The priest is to make atonement before the LORD for the one who erred by sinning unintentionally, and when atonement has been made for him, he will be forgiven. 29One and the same law applies to everyone who sins unintentionally, whether he is a native-born Israelite or an alien.

30"'But anyone who sins defiantly, whether native-born or alien, blasphemes the LORD, and that person must be cut off from his people. 31Because he has despised the LORD's word and broken his commands, that person must surely be cut off; his guilt remains on him.'"

The Sabbath-Breaker Put to Death

32While the Israelites were in the desert, a man was found gathering wood on the Sabbath day. 33Those who found him gathering wood brought him to Moses and Aaron and the whole assembly, 34and they kept him in custody, because it was not clear what should be done to him. 35Then the LORD said to Moses, "The man must die. The whole assembly must stone him outside the camp." 36So the assembly took him outside the camp and stoned him to death, as the LORD commanded Moses.

Tassels on Garments

37The LORD said to Moses, 38"Speak to the Israelites and say to them: 'Throughout the generations to come you are to make tassels on the corners of your garments, with a blue cord on each tassel. 39You will have these tassels to look at and so you will remember all the commands of the LORD, that you may obey them and not prostitute yourselves by going after the lusts of your own hearts and eyes. 40Then you will remember to obey all my commands and will be consecrated to your God. 41I am the LORD your God, who brought you out of Egypt to be your God. I am the LORD your God.'"

Korah, Dathan and Abiram

16 Korah son of Izhar, the son of Kohath, the son of Levi, and certain Reubenites—Dathan and Abiram, sons of Eliab, and On son of Peleth—became insolent 2and rose up against Moses. With them were 250 Israelite men, well-known community leaders who had been appointed members of the council. 3They came as a group to oppose Moses and Aaron and said to them, "You have gone too far! The whole community is holy, every one of them, and the LORD is with them. Why then do you set yourselves above the LORD's assembly?"

4When Moses heard this, he fell face down. 5Then he said to Korah and all his followers: "In the morning the LORD will show who belongs to him and who is holy, and he will make that person come near him. The man he chooses he will cause to come near him. 6You, Korah, and all your followers are to do this: Take censers 7and tomorrow put fire and incense in them before the LORD. The man the LORD chooses will be the one who is holy. You Levites have gone too far!"

8Moses also said to Korah, "Now listen, you Levites! 9Isn't it enough for you that the God of Israel has separated you from the rest of the Israelite community and brought you near himself to do the work at the LORD's tabernacle and to stand before the community and minister to them? 10He has brought you and all your fellow Levites near himself, but now you are trying to get the priesthood too. 11It is against the LORD that you and all your followers have banded together. Who is Aaron that you should grumble against him?"

12Then Moses summoned Dathan and Abiram, the sons of Eliab. But they said, "We will not come! 13Isn't it enough that you have brought us up out of a land flowing with milk and honey to kill us in the desert? And now you also want to lord it over us? 14Moreover, you haven't brought us into a land flowing with milk and honey or given us an inheritance of fields and vineyards. Will you gouge out the eyes of these men? No, we will not come!"

15Then Moses became very angry and said to the LORD, "Do not accept their offering. I have not taken so much as a donkey from them, nor have I wronged any of them."

16Moses said to Korah, "You and all your followers are to appear before the LORD tomorrow—you and they and Aaron. 17Each man is to take his censer and put incense in it—250 censers in all—and present it before the LORD. You and Aaron are to present your censers also." 18So each man took his censer, put fire and incense in it, and stood with Moses and Aaron at the entrance to the Tent of Meeting. 19When Korah had gathered all his followers in opposition to them at the entrance to the Tent of Meeting, the glory of the LORD appeared to the entire assembly. 20The LORD said to Moses and Aaron, 21"Separate yourselves from this assembly so that I can put an end to them at once."

22But Moses and Aaron fell face down and cried out, "O God, God of the spirits of all mankind, will you be angry with the entire assembly when only one man sins?"

23Then the LORD said to Moses, 24"Say to the assembly, 'Move away from the tents of Korah, Dathan and Abiram.'"

25Moses got up and went to Dathan and Abiram, and the elders of Israel followed him. 26He warned the assembly, "Move back from the tents of these wicked men! Do not touch anything belonging to them, or you will be swept away because of all their sins." 27So they moved away from the tents of Korah, Dathan and Abiram. Dathan and Abiram had come out and were standing with their wives, children and little ones at the entrances to their tents.

28Then Moses said, "This is how you will know that the LORD has sent me to do all these things and that it was not my idea: 29If these men die a natural death and experience only what usually happens to men, then the LORD has not sent me. 30But if the LORD brings about something totally new, and the earth opens its mouth and swallows them, with everything that belongs to them, and they go down alive into the grave, then you will know that these men have treated the LORD with contempt."

31As soon as he finished saying all this, the ground under them split apart 32and the earth opened its mouth and swallowed them, with their households and all Korah's men and all their possessions. 33They went down alive into the grave, with everything they owned; the earth closed over them, and they perished and were gone from the community. 34At their cries, all the Israelites around them fled, shouting, "The earth is going to swallow us too!"

35And fire came out from the LORD and consumed the 250 men who were offering the incense.

NEW TESTAMENT READING
Luke 4:38—5:16

Jesus Heals Many

38Jesus left the synagogue and went to the home of Simon. Now Simon's mother-in-law was suffering from a high fever, and they asked Jesus to help her. 39So he bent over her and rebuked the fever, and it left her. She got up at once and began to wait on them.

40When the sun was setting, the people brought to Jesus all who had various kinds of sickness, and laying his hands on each one, he healed them. 41Moreover, demons came out of many people, shouting, "You are the Son of God!" But he rebuked them and would not allow them to speak, because they knew he was the Christ.

42At daybreak Jesus went out to a solitary place. The people were looking for him and when they came to where he was, they tried to keep him from leaving them. 43But he said, "I must preach the good news of the kingdom of God to the other towns also, because that is why I was sent." 44And he kept on preaching in the synagogues of Judea.

The Calling of the First Disciples

5 One day as Jesus was standing by the Lake of Gennesaret, with the people crowding round him and listening to the word of God, 2he saw at the water's edge two boats, left there by the fishermen, who were washing their nets. 3He got into one of the boats, the one belonging to Simon, and asked him to put out a little from shore. Then he sat down and taught the people from the boat.

4When he had finished speaking, he said to Simon, "Put out into deep water, and let down the nets for a catch."

5Simon answered, "Master, we've worked hard all night and haven't caught anything. But because you say so, I will let down the nets."

6When they had done so, they caught such a large number of fish that their nets began to break. 7So they signalled to their partners in the other boat to come and help them, and they came and filled both boats so full that they began to sink.

8When Simon Peter saw this, he fell at Jesus' knees and said, "Go away from me, Lord; I am a sinful man!" 9For he and all his companions were astonished at the catch of fish they had taken, 10and so were James and John, the sons of Zebedee, Simon's partners.

Then Jesus said to Simon, "Don't be afraid; from now on you will catch men." 11So they pulled their boats up on shore, left everything and followed him.

The Man With Leprosy

12While Jesus was in one of the towns, a man came along who was covered with leprosy. When he saw Jesus, he fell with his face to the ground and begged him, "Lord, if you are willing, you can make me clean."

13Jesus reached out his hand and touched the man. "I am willing," he said. "Be clean!" And immediately the leprosy left him.

14Then Jesus ordered him, "Don't tell anyone, but go, show yourself to the priest and offer the sacrifices that Moses commanded for your cleansing, as a testimony to them."

15Yet the news about him spread all the more, so that crowds of people came to hear him and to be healed of their sicknesses. 16But Jesus often withdrew to lonely places and prayed.

READING FROM PSALMS
Psalm 37:1–9

Of David.

1Do not fret because of evil men
  or be envious of those who do
    wrong;
2for like the grass they will soon
    wither,
  like green plants they will soon die
    away.

3Trust in the LORD and do good;
  dwell in the land and enjoy safe
    pasture.
4Delight yourself in the LORD
  and he will give you the desires of
    your heart.

5Commit your way to the LORD;
  trust in him and he will do this:
6He will make your righteousness
    shine like the dawn,
  the justice of your cause like the
    noonday sun.

7Be still before the LORD and wait
    patiently for him;
  do not fret when men succeed in
    their ways,
  when they carry out their wicked
    schemes.

8Refrain from anger and turn from
    wrath;
  do not fret—it leads only to evil.
9For evil men will be cut off,
  but those who hope in the LORD
    will inherit the land.

OLD TESTAMENT READING
Numbers 16:36–18:32

³⁶The LORD said to Moses, ³⁷"Tell Eleazar son of Aaron, the priest, to take the censers out of the smouldering remains and scatter the coals some distance away, for the censers are holy —³⁸the censers of the men who sinned at the cost of their lives. Hammer the censers into sheets to overlay the altar, for they were presented before the LORD and have become holy. Let them be a sign to the Israelites."

³⁹So Eleazar the priest collected the bronze censers brought by those who had been burned up, and he had them hammered out to overlay the altar, ⁴⁰as the LORD directed him through Moses. This was to remind the Israelites that no-one except a descendant of Aaron should come to burn incense before the LORD, or he would become like Korah and his followers.

⁴¹The next day the whole Israelite community grumbled against Moses and Aaron. "You have killed the LORD's people," they said.

⁴²But when the assembly gathered in opposition to Moses and Aaron and turned towards the Tent of Meeting, suddenly the cloud covered it and the glory of the LORD appeared. ⁴³Then Moses and Aaron went to the front of the Tent of Meeting, ⁴⁴and the LORD said to Moses, ⁴⁵"Get away from this assembly so that I can put an end to them at once." And they fell face down.

⁴⁶Then Moses said to Aaron, "Take your censer and put incense in it, along with fire from the altar, and hurry to the assembly to make atonement for them. Wrath has come out from the LORD; the plague has started." ⁴⁷So Aaron did as Moses said, and ran into the midst of the assembly. The plague had already started among the people, but Aaron offered the incense and made atonement for them. ⁴⁸He stood between the living and the dead, and the plague stopped. ⁴⁹But 14,700 people died from the plague, in addition to those who had died because of Korah. ⁵⁰Then Aaron returned to Moses at the entrance to the Tent of Meeting, for the plague had stopped.

The Budding of Aaron's Staff

17 The LORD said to Moses, ²"Speak to the Israelites and get twelve staffs from them, one from the leader of each of their ancestral tribes. Write the name of each man on his staff. ³On the staff of Levi write Aaron's name, for there must be one staff for the head of each ancestral tribe. ⁴Place them in the Tent of Meeting in front of the Testimony, where I meet with you. ⁵The staff belonging to the man I choose will sprout, and I will rid myself of this constant grumbling against you by the Israelites."

⁶So Moses spoke to the Israelites, and their leaders gave him twelve staffs, one for the leader of each of their ancestral tribes, and Aaron's staff was among them. ⁷Moses placed the staffs before the LORD in the Tent of the Testimony.

⁸The next day Moses entered the Tent of the Testimony and saw that Aaron's staff, which represented the house of Levi, had not only sprouted but had budded, blossomed and produced almonds. ⁹Then Moses brought out all the staffs from the LORD's presence to all the Israelites. They looked at them, and each man took his own staff.

¹⁰The LORD said to Moses, "Put back Aaron's staff in front of the Testimony, to be kept as a sign to the rebellious. This will put an end to their grumbling against me, so that they will not die." ¹¹Moses did just as the LORD commanded him.

¹²The Israelites said to Moses, "We shall die! We are lost, we are all lost! ¹³Anyone who even comes near the tabernacle of the LORD will die. Are we all going to die?"

Duties of Priests and Levites

18 The LORD said to Aaron, "You, your sons and your father's family are to bear the responsibility for offences against the sanctuary, and you and your sons are to bear the responsibility for offences against the priesthood. ²Bring your fellow Levites from your ancestral tribe to join you and assist you when you and your sons minister before the Tent of the Testimony. ³They are to be responsible to you and are to perform all the duties of the Tent, but they must not go near the furnishings of the sanctuary or the altar, or both they and you will die. ⁴They are to join you and be responsible for the care of the Tent of Meeting—all the work at the Tent—and no-one else may come near where you are.

⁵"You are to be responsible for the care of the sanctuary and the altar, so that wrath will not fall on the Israelites again. ⁶I myself have selected your fellow Levites from among the Israelites as a gift to you, dedicated to the LORD to do the work at the Tent of Meeting. ⁷But only you and your sons may serve as priests in connection with everything at the altar and inside the curtain. I am giving you the service of the priesthood as a gift. Anyone else who comes near the sanctuary must be put to death."

Offerings for Priests and Levites

⁸Then the LORD said to Aaron, "I myself have put you in charge of the offerings presented to me; all the holy offerings the Israelites give me I give to you and your sons as your portion and regular share. ⁹You are to have the part of the most holy offerings that is kept from the fire. From all the gifts they bring me as most holy offerings, whether grain or sin or guilt offerings, that part belongs to you and your sons. ¹⁰Eat it as something most holy; every male shall eat it. You must regard it as holy.

¹¹"This also is yours: whatever is set aside from the gifts of all the wave offerings of the Israelites. I give this to you and your sons and daughters as your regular share. Everyone in your household who is ceremonially clean may eat it.

¹²"I give you all the finest olive oil and all the finest new wine and grain they give to the LORD as the firstfruits of their harvest. ¹³All the land's firstfruits that they bring to the LORD will be yours. Everyone in your household who is ceremonially clean may eat it.

¹⁴"Everything in Israel that is devoted to the LORD is yours. ¹⁵The first offspring of every womb, both man and animal, that is offered to the LORD is yours. But you must redeem every firstborn son and every firstborn male of unclean animals. ¹⁶When they are a month old, you must redeem them at the redemption price set at five shekels of silver, according to the sanctuary shekel, which weighs twenty gerahs.

¹⁷"But you must not redeem the firstborn of an ox, a sheep or a goat; they are holy. Sprinkle their blood on the altar and burn their fat as an offering made by fire, an aroma pleasing to the LORD. ¹⁸Their meat is to be yours, just as the breast of the wave offering and the right thigh are yours. ¹⁹Whatever is set aside from the holy offerings the Israelites present to the LORD I give to you and your sons and daughters as your regular share. It is an everlasting covenant of salt before the LORD for both you and your offspring."

²⁰The LORD said to Aaron, "You will have no inheritance in their land, nor will you have any share among them; I am your share and your inheritance among the Israelites.

²¹"I give to the Levites all the tithes in Israel as their inheritance in return for the work they do while serving at the

Tent of Meeting. 22From now on the Israelites must not go near the Tent of Meeting, or they will bear the consequences of their sin and will die. 23It is the Levites who are to do the work at the Tent of Meeting and bear the responsibility for offences against it. This is a lasting ordinance for the generations to come. They will receive no inheritance among the Israelites. 24Instead, I give to the Levites as their inheritance the tithes that the Israelites present as an offering to the LORD. That is why I said concerning them: 'They will have no inheritance among the Israelites.'"

25The LORD said to Moses, 26"Speak to the Levites and say to them: 'When you receive from the Israelites the tithe I give you as your inheritance, you must present a tenth of that tithe as the LORD's offering. 27Your offering will be reckoned to you as grain from the threshing-floor or juice from the winepress. 28In this way you also will present an offering to the LORD from all the tithes you receive from the Israelites. From these tithes you must give the LORD's portion to Aaron the priest. 29You must present as the LORD's portion the best and holiest part of everything given to you.'

30"Say to the Levites: 'When you present the best part, it will be reckoned to you as the product of the threshing-floor or the winepress. 31You and your households may eat the rest of it anywhere, for it is your wages for your work at the Tent of Meeting. 32By presenting the best part of it you will not be guilty in this matter; then you will not defile the holy offerings of the Israelites, and you will not die.'"

NEW TESTAMENT READING
Luke 5:17–32

Jesus Heals a Paralytic

17One day as he was teaching, Pharisees and teachers of the law, who had come from every village of Galilee and from Judea and Jerusalem, were sitting there. And the power of the Lord was present for him to heal the sick. 18Some men came carrying a paralytic on a mat and tried to take him into the house to lay him before Jesus. 19When they could not find a way to do this because of the crowd, they went up on the roof and lowered him on his mat through the tiles into the middle of the crowd, right in front of Jesus.

20When Jesus saw their faith, he said, "Friend, your sins are forgiven."

21The Pharisees and the teachers of the law began thinking to themselves, "Who is this fellow who speaks blasphemy? Who can forgive sins but God alone?"

22Jesus knew what they were thinking and asked, "Why are you thinking these things in your hearts? 23Which is easier: to say, 'Your sins are forgiven,' or to say, 'Get up and walk'? 24But that you may know that the Son of Man has authority on earth to forgive sins. . . ." He said to the paralysed man, "I tell you, get up, take your mat and go home." 25Immediately he stood up in front of them, took what he had been lying on and went home praising God. 26Everyone was amazed and gave praise to God. They were filled with awe and said, "We have seen remarkable things today."

The Calling of Levi

27After this, Jesus went out and saw a tax collector by the name of Levi sitting at his tax booth. "Follow me," Jesus said to him, 28and Levi got up, left everything and followed him.

29Then Levi held a great banquet for Jesus at his house, and a large crowd of tax collectors and others were eating with them. 30But the Pharisees and the teachers of the law who belonged to their sect complained to his disciples, "Why do you eat and drink with tax collectors and 'sinners'?"

31Jesus answered them, "It is not the

healthy who need a doctor, but the sick. ³²I have not come to call the righteous, but sinners to repentance."

READING FROM PSALMS
Psalm 37:10–20

¹⁰A little while, and the wicked will be
no more;
though you look for them, they will
not be found.
¹¹But the meek will inherit the land
and enjoy great peace.

¹²The wicked plot against the righteous
and gnash their teeth at them;
¹³but the Lord laughs at the wicked,
for he knows their day is coming.

¹⁴The wicked draw the sword
and bend the bow
to bring down the poor and needy,
to slay those whose ways are
upright.

¹⁵But their swords will pierce their own
hearts,
and their bows will be broken.

¹⁶Better the little that the righteous
have
than the wealth of many wicked;
¹⁷for the power of the wicked will be
broken,
but the LORD upholds the
righteous.

¹⁸The days of the blameless are known
to the LORD,
and their inheritance will endure
for ever.
¹⁹In times of disaster they will not
wither;
in days of famine they will enjoy
plenty.

²⁰But the wicked will perish:
The LORD's enemies will be like
the beauty of the fields,
they will vanish—vanish like
smoke.

MARCH 25   DAY 84

OLD TESTAMENT READING
Numbers 19:1–21:3

The Water of Cleansing

19 The LORD said to Moses and Aaron: ²"This is a requirement of the law that the LORD has commanded: Tell the Israelites to bring you a red heifer without defect or blemish and that has never been under a yoke. ³Give it to Eleazar the priest; it is to be taken outside the camp and slaughtered in his presence. ⁴Then Eleazar the priest is to take some of its blood on his finger and sprinkle it seven times towards the front of the Tent of Meeting. ⁵While he watches, the heifer is to be burned—its hide, flesh, blood and offal. ⁶The priest

is to take some cedar wood, hyssop and scarlet wool and throw them onto the burning heifer. ⁷After that, the priest must wash his clothes and bathe himself with water. He may then come into the camp, but he will be ceremonially unclean till evening. ⁸The man who burns it must also wash his clothes and bathe with water, and he too will be unclean till evening.

⁹"A man who is clean shall gather up the ashes of the heifer and put them in a ceremonially clean place outside the camp. They shall be kept by the Israelite community for use in the water of cleansing; it is for purification from sin. ¹⁰The man who gathers up the ashes of the heifer must also wash his clothes, and he too will be unclean till evening.

This will be a lasting ordinance both for the Israelites and for the aliens living among them.

11"Whoever touches the dead body of anyone will be unclean for seven days. 12He must purify himself with the water on the third day and on the seventh day; then he will be clean. But if he does not purify himself on the third and seventh days, he will not be clean. 13Whoever touches the dead body of anyone and fails to purify himself defiles the LORD's tabernacle. That person must be cut off from Israel. Because the water of cleansing has not been sprinkled on him, he is unclean; his uncleanness remains on him.

14"This is the law that applies when a person dies in a tent: Anyone who enters the tent and anyone who is in it will be unclean for seven days, 15and every open container without a lid fastened on it will be unclean.

16"Anyone out in the open who touches someone who has been killed with a sword or someone who has died a natural death, or anyone who touches a human bone or a grave, will be unclean for seven days.

17"For the unclean person, put some ashes from the burned purification offering into a jar and pour fresh water over them. 18Then a man who is ceremonially clean is to take some hyssop, dip it in the water and sprinkle the tent and all the furnishings and the people who were there. He must also sprinkle anyone who has touched a human bone or a grave or someone who has been killed or someone who has died a natural death. 19The man who is clean is to sprinkle the unclean person on the third and seventh days, and on the seventh day he is to purify him. The person being cleansed must wash his clothes and bathe with water, and that evening he will be clean. 20But if a person who is unclean does not purify himself, he must be cut off from the community, because he has defiled the sanctuary of the LORD. The water of cleansing has not been sprinkled on him, and he is unclean. 21This is a lasting ordinance for them.

"The man who sprinkles the water of cleansing must also wash his clothes, and anyone who touches the water of cleansing will be unclean till evening. 22Anything that an unclean person touches becomes unclean, and anyone who touches it becomes unclean till evening."

Water From the Rock

20 In the first month the whole Israelite community arrived at the Desert of Zin, and they stayed at Kadesh. There Miriam died and was buried.

2Now there was no water for the community, and the people gathered in opposition to Moses and Aaron. 3They quarrelled with Moses and said, "If only we had died when our brothers fell dead before the LORD! 4Why did you bring the LORD's community into this desert, that we and our livestock should die here? 5Why did you bring us up out of Egypt to this terrible place? It has no grain or figs, grapevines or pomegranates. And there is no water to drink!"

6Moses and Aaron went from the assembly to the entrance to the Tent of Meeting and fell face down, and the glory of the LORD appeared to them. 7The LORD said to Moses, 8"Take the staff, and you and your brother Aaron gather the assembly together. Speak to that rock before their eyes and it will pour out its water. You will bring water out of the rock for the community so that they and their livestock can drink."

9So Moses took the staff from the LORD's presence, just as he commanded him. 10He and Aaron gathered the assembly together in front of the rock and Moses said to them, "Listen, you rebels, must we bring you water out of this rock?" 11Then Moses raised his arm and struck the rock twice with his staff. Water gushed out, and the community and their livestock drank.

¹²But the LORD said to Moses and Aaron, "Because you did not trust in me enough to honour me as holy in the sight of the Israelites, you will not bring this community into the land I give them."

¹³These were the waters of Meribah, where the Israelites quarrelled with the LORD and where he showed himself holy among them.

Edom Denies Israel Passage

¹⁴Moses sent messengers from Kadesh to the king of Edom, saying:

"This is what your brother Israel says: You know about all the hardships that have come upon us. ¹⁵Our forefathers went down into Egypt, and we lived there many years. The Egyptians ill-treated us and our fathers, ¹⁶but when we cried out to the LORD, he heard our cry and sent an angel and brought us out of Egypt.

"Now we are here at Kadesh, a town on the edge of your territory. ¹⁷Please let us pass through your country. We will not go through any field or vineyard, or drink water from any well. We will travel along the king's highway and not turn to the right or to the left until we have passed through your territory."

¹⁸But Edom answered:

"You may not pass through here; if you try, we will march out and attack you with the sword."

¹⁹The Israelites replied:

"We will go along the main road, and if we or our livestock drink any of your water, we will pay for it. We only want to pass through on foot—nothing else."

²⁰Again they answered:

"You may not pass through."

Then Edom came out against them with a large and powerful army. ²¹Since Edom refused to let them go through their territory, Israel turned away from them.

The Death of Aaron

²²The whole Israelite community set out from Kadesh and came to Mount Hor. ²³At Mount Hor, near the border of Edom, the LORD said to Moses and Aaron, ²⁴"Aaron will be gathered to his people. He will not enter the land I give the Israelites, because both of you rebelled against my command at the waters of Meribah. ²⁵Call Aaron and his son Eleazar and take them up Mount Hor. ²⁶Remove Aaron's garments and put them on his son Eleazar, for Aaron will be gathered to his people; he will die there."

²⁷Moses did as the LORD commanded: They went up Mount Hor in the sight of the whole community. ²⁸Moses removed Aaron's garments and put them on his son Eleazar. And Aaron died there on top of the mountain. Then Moses and Eleazar came down from the mountain, ²⁹and when the whole community learned that Aaron had died, the entire house of Israel mourned for him thirty days.

Arad Destroyed

21 When the Canaanite king of Arad, who lived in the Negev, heard that Israel was coming along the road to Atharim, he attacked the Israelites and captured some of them. ²Then Israel made this vow to the LORD: "If you will deliver these people into our hands, we will totally destroy their cities." ³The LORD listened to Israel's plea and gave the Canaanites over to them. They completely destroyed them and their towns; so the place was named Hormah.

NEW TESTAMENT READING
Luke 5:33–6:11

Jesus Questioned About Fasting

³³They said to him, "John's disciples often fast and pray, and so do the disciples of the Pharisees, but yours go on eating and drinking."

³⁴Jesus answered, "Can you make the guests of the bridegroom fast while he is with them? ³⁵But the time will come when the bridegroom will be taken from them; in those days they will fast."

³⁶He told them this parable: "No-one tears a patch from a new garment and sews it on an old one. If he does, he will have torn the new garment, and the patch from the new will not match the old. ³⁷And no-one pours new wine into old wineskins. If he does, the new wine will burst the skins, the wine will run out and the wineskins will be ruined. ³⁸No, new wine must be poured into new wineskins. ³⁹And no-one after drinking old wine wants the new, for he says, 'The old is better.'"

Lord of the Sabbath

6 One Sabbath Jesus was going through the cornfields, and his disciples began to pick some ears of corn, rub them in their hands and eat the grain. ²Some of the Pharisees asked, "Why are you doing what is unlawful on the Sabbath?"

³Jesus answered them, "Have you never read what David did when he and his companions were hungry? ⁴He entered the house of God, and taking the consecrated bread, he ate what is lawful only for priests to eat. And he also gave some to his companions." ⁵Then Jesus said to them, "The Son of Man is Lord of the Sabbath."

⁶On another Sabbath he went into the synagogue and was teaching, and a man was there whose right hand was shrivelled. ⁷The Pharisees and the teachers of the law were looking for a reason to accuse Jesus, so they watched him closely to see if he would heal on the Sabbath. ⁸But Jesus knew what they were thinking and said to the man with the shrivelled hand, "Get up and stand in front of everyone." So he got up and stood there.

⁹Then Jesus said to them, "I ask you, which is lawful on the Sabbath: to do good or to do evil, to save life or to destroy it?"

¹⁰He looked round at them all, and then said to the man, "Stretch out your hand." He did so, and his hand was completely restored. ¹¹But they were furious and began to discuss with one another what they might do to Jesus.

READING FROM PROVERBS
Proverbs 8:1–11

Wisdom's Call

8 Does not wisdom call out?
  Does not understanding raise her voice?
²On the heights along the way,
  where the paths meet, she takes her stand;
³beside the gates leading into the city,
  at the entrances, she cries aloud:
⁴"To you, O men, I call out;
  I raise my voice to all mankind.
⁵You who are simple, gain prudence;
  you who are foolish, gain understanding.
⁶Listen, for I have worthy things to say;
  I open my lips to speak what is right.
⁷My mouth speaks what is true,
  for my lips detest wickedness.
⁸All the words of my mouth are just;
  none of them is crooked or perverse.
⁹To the discerning all of them are right;
  they are faultless to those who have knowledge.
¹⁰Choose my instruction instead of silver,
  knowledge rather than choice gold,
¹¹for wisdom is more precious than rubies,
  and nothing you desire can compare with her.

OLD TESTAMENT READING
Numbers 21:4–22:20

The Bronze Snake

⁴They travelled from Mount Hor along the route to the Red Sea, to go round Edom. But the people grew impatient on the way; ⁵they spoke against God and against Moses, and said, "Why have you brought us up out of Egypt to die in the desert? There is no bread! There is no water! And we detest this miserable food!"

⁶Then the LORD sent venomous snakes among them; they bit the people and many Israelites died. ⁷The people came to Moses and said, "We sinned when we spoke against the LORD and against you. Pray that the LORD will take the snakes away from us." So Moses prayed for the people.

⁸The LORD said to Moses, "Make a snake and put it up on a pole; anyone who is bitten can look at it and live." ⁹So Moses made a bronze snake and put it up on a pole. Then when anyone was bitten by a snake and looked at the bronze snake, he lived.

The Journey to Moab

¹⁰The Israelites moved on and camped at Oboth. ¹¹Then they set out from Oboth and camped in Iye Abarim, in the desert that faces Moab towards the sunrise. ¹²From there they moved on and camped in the Zered Valley. ¹³They set out from there and camped alongside the Arnon, which is in the desert extending into Amorite territory. The Arnon is the border of Moab, between Moab and the Amorites. ¹⁴That is why the Book of the Wars of the LORD says:

". . . Waheb in Suphah and the ravines,

the Arnon ¹⁵and the slopes of the ravines
that lead to the site of Ar
and lie along the border of Moab."

¹⁶From there they continued on to Beer, the well where the LORD said to Moses, "Gather the people together and I will give them water." ¹⁷Then Israel sang this song:

"Spring up, O well!
    Sing about it,
¹⁸about the well that the princes dug,
    that the nobles of the people sank—
    the nobles with sceptres and staffs."

Then they went from the desert to Mattanah, ¹⁹from Mattanah to Nahaliel, from Nahaliel to Bamoth, ²⁰and from Bamoth to the valley in Moab where the top of Pisgah overlooks the wasteland.

Defeat of Sihon and Og

²¹Israel sent messengers to say to Sihon king of the Amorites:

²²"Let us pass through your country. We will not turn aside into any field or vineyard, or drink water from any well. We will travel along the king's highway until we have passed through your territory."

²³But Sihon would not let Israel pass through his territory. He mustered his entire army and marched out into the desert against Israel. When he reached Jahaz, he fought with Israel. ²⁴Israel, however, put him to the sword and took over his land from the Arnon to the Jabbok, but only as far as the Ammonites, because their border was fortified. ²⁵Israel captured all the cities of the Amorites and occupied them, including Heshbon and all its surrounding settlements. ²⁶Heshbon was the city of

Sihon king of the Amorites, who had fought against the former king of Moab and had taken from him all his land as far as the Arnon.

27That is why the poets say:

"Come to Heshbon and let it be rebuilt;
let Sihon's city be restored.

28"Fire went out from Heshbon,
a blaze from the city of Sihon.
It consumed Ar of Moab,
the citizens of Arnon's heights.

29Woe to you, O Moab!
You are destroyed, O people of Chemosh!
He has given up his sons as fugitives
and his daughters as captives
to Sihon king of the Amorites.

30"But we have overthrown them;
Heshbon is destroyed all the way to Dibon.
We have demolished them as far as Nophah,
which extends to Medeba."

31So Israel settled in the land of the Amorites.

32After Moses had sent spies to Jazer, the Israelites captured its surrounding settlements and drove out the Amorites who were there. 33Then they turned and went up along the road towards Bashan, and Og king of Bashan and his whole army marched out to meet them in battle at Edrei.

34The LORD said to Moses, "Do not be afraid of him, for I have handed him over to you, with his whole army and his land. Do to him what you did to Sihon king of the Amorites, who reigned in Heshbon."

35So they struck him down, together with his sons and his whole army, leaving them no survivors. And they took possession of his land.

Balak Summons Balaam

22 Then the Israelites travelled to the plains of Moab and camped along the Jordan across from Jericho.

2Now Balak son of Zippor saw all that Israel had done to the Amorites, 3and Moab was terrified because there were so many people. Indeed, Moab was filled with dread because of the Israelites.

4The Moabites said to the elders of Midian, "This horde is going to lick up everything around us, as an ox licks up the grass of the field."

So Balak son of Zippor, who was king of Moab at that time, 5sent messengers to summon Balaam son of Beor, who was at Pethor, near the River, in his native land. Balak said:

"A people has come out of Egypt; they cover the face of the land and have settled next to me. 6Now come and put a curse on these people, because they are too powerful for me. Perhaps then I will be able to defeat them and drive them out of the country. For I know that those you bless are blessed, and those you curse are cursed."

7The elders of Moab and Midian left, taking with them the fee for divination. When they came to Balaam, they told him what Balak had said.

8"Spend the night here," Balaam said to them, "and I will bring you back the answer the LORD gives me." So the Moabite princes stayed with him.

9God came to Balaam and asked, "Who are these men with you?"

10Balaam said to God, "Balak son of Zippor, king of Moab, sent me this message: 11'A people that has come out of Egypt covers the face of the land. Now come and put a curse on them for me. Perhaps then I will be able to fight them and drive them away.'"

12But God said to Balaam, "Do not go with them. You must not put a curse on those people, because they are blessed."

13The next morning Balaam got up and said to Balak's princes, "Go back to your own country, for the LORD has refused to let me go with you."

14So the Moabite princes returned to Balak and said, "Balaam refused to come with us."

15Then Balak sent other princes, more numerous and more distinguished than the first. 16They came to Balaam and said:

"This is what Balak son of Zippor says: Do not let anything keep you from coming to me, 17because I will reward you handsomely and do whatever you say. Come and put a curse on these people for me."

18But Balaam answered them, "Even if Balak gave me his palace filled with silver and gold, I could not do anything great or small to go beyond the command of the LORD my God. 19Now stay here tonight as the others did, and I will find out what else the LORD will tell me."

20That night God came to Balaam and said, "Since these men have come to summon you, go with them, but do only what I tell you."

NEW TESTAMENT READING
Luke 6:12–36

The Twelve Apostles

12One of those days Jesus went out to a mountainside to pray, and spent the night praying to God. 13When morning came, he called his disciples to him and chose twelve of them, whom he also designated apostles: 14Simon (whom he named Peter), his brother Andrew, James, John, Philip, Bartholomew, 15Matthew, Thomas, James son of Alphaeus, Simon who was called the Zealot, 16Judas son of James, and Judas Iscariot, who became a traitor.

Blessings and Woes

17He went down with them and stood on a level place. A large crowd of his disciples was there and a great number of people from all over Judea, from Jerusalem, and from the coast of Tyre and Sidon, 18who had come to hear him and to be healed of their diseases. Those troubled by evil spirits were cured, 19and the people all tried to touch him, because power was coming from him and healing them all.

20Looking at his disciples, he said:

"Blessed are you who are poor,
 for yours is the kingdom of God.
21Blessed are you who hunger now,
 for you will be satisfied.
Blessed are you who weep now,
 for you will laugh.
22Blessed are you when men hate you,
 when they exclude you and insult
  you
 and reject your name as evil,
 because of the Son of Man.

23"Rejoice in that day and leap for joy, because great is your reward in heaven. For that is how their fathers treated the prophets.

24"But woe to you who are rich,
 for you have already received your
  comfort.
25Woe to you who are well fed now,
 for you will go hungry.
Woe to you who laugh now,
 for you will mourn and weep.
26Woe to you when all men speak well
  of you,
 for that is how their fathers treated
  the false prophets.

Love for Enemies

27"But I tell you who hear me: Love your enemies, do good to those who hate you, 28bless those who curse you, pray for those who ill-treat you. 29If someone strikes you on one cheek, turn to him the other also. If someone takes your cloak, do not stop him from taking your tunic. 30Give to everyone who asks you, and if anyone takes what belongs to you, do not demand it back. 31Do to others as you would have them do to you.

³²"If you love those who love you, what credit is that to you? Even 'sinners' love those who love them. ³³And if you do good to those who are good to you, what credit is that to you? Even 'sinners' do that. ³⁴And if you lend to those from whom you expect repayment, what credit is that to you? Even 'sinners' lend to 'sinners', expecting to be repaid in full. ³⁵But love your enemies, do good to them, and lend to them without expecting to get anything back. Then your reward will be great, and you will be sons of the Most High, because he is kind to the ungrateful and wicked. ³⁶Be merciful, just as your Father is merciful.

READING FROM PSALMS
Psalm 37:21–31

²¹The wicked borrow and do not repay,
> but the righteous give generously;
²²those the LORD blesses will inherit
> the land,
> but those he curses will be cut off.

²³If the LORD delights in a man's way,
> he makes his steps firm;

²⁴though he stumble, he will not fall,
> for the LORD upholds him with his hand.

²⁵I was young and now I am old,
> yet I have never seen the righteous forsaken
> or their children begging bread.
²⁶They are always generous and lend freely;
> their children will be blessed.

²⁷Turn from evil and do good;
> then you will dwell in the land for ever.
²⁸For the LORD loves the just
> and will not forsake his faithful ones.

They will be protected for ever,
> but the offspring of the wicked will be cut off;
²⁹the righteous will inherit the land
> and dwell in it for ever.

³⁰The mouth of the righteous man utters wisdom,
> and his tongue speaks what is just.
³¹The law of his God is in his heart;
> his feet do not slip.

DAY 86

MARCH 27

OLD TESTAMENT READING
Numbers 22:21–23:26

Balaam's Donkey

²¹Balaam got up in the morning, saddled his donkey and went with the princes of Moab. ²²But God was very angry when he went, and the angel of the LORD stood in the road to oppose him. Balaam was riding on his donkey, and his two servants were with him. ²³When the donkey saw the angel of the LORD standing in the road with a drawn sword in his hand, she turned off the road into a field. Balaam beat her to get her back on the road.

²⁴Then the angel of the LORD stood in a narrow path between two vineyards, with walls on both sides. ²⁵When the donkey saw the angel of the LORD, she pressed close to the wall, crushing Balaam's foot against it. So he beat her again.

²⁶Then the angel of the LORD moved on ahead and stood in a narrow place where there was no room to turn, either to the right or to the left. ²⁷When the donkey saw the angel of the LORD, she lay down under Balaam, and he was

angry and beat her with his staff. ²⁸Then the LORD opened the donkey's mouth, and she said to Balaam, "What have I done to you to make you beat me these three times?"

²⁹Balaam answered the donkey, "You have made a fool of me! If I had a sword in my hand, I would kill you right now."

³⁰The donkey said to Balaam, "Am I not your own donkey, which you have always ridden, to this day? Have I been in the habit of doing this to you?"

"No," he said.

³¹Then the LORD opened Balaam's eyes, and he saw the angel of the LORD standing in the road with his sword drawn. So he bowed low and fell face down.

³²The angel of the LORD asked him, "Why have you beaten your donkey these three times? I have come here to oppose you because your path is a reckless one before me. ³³The donkey saw me and turned away from me these three times. If she had not turned away, I would certainly have killed you by now, but I would have spared her."

³⁴Balaam said to the angel of the LORD, "I have sinned. I did not realise you were standing in the road to oppose me. Now if you are displeased, I will go back."

³⁵The angel of the LORD said to Balaam, "Go with the men, but speak only what I tell you." So Balaam went with the princes of Balak.

³⁶When Balak heard that Balaam was coming, he went out to meet him at the Moabite town on the Arnon border, at the edge of his territory. ³⁷Balak said to Balaam, "Did I not send you an urgent summons? Why didn't you come to me? Am I really not able to reward you?"

³⁸"Well, I have come to you now," Balaam replied. "But can I say just anything? I must speak only what God puts in my mouth."

³⁹Then Balaam went with Balak to Kiriath Huzoth. ⁴⁰Balak sacrificed cattle and sheep, and gave some to Balaam and the princes who were with him.

⁴¹The next morning Balak took Balaam up to Bamoth Baal, and from there he saw part of the people.

Balaam's First Oracle

23 Balaam said, "Build me seven altars here, and prepare seven bulls and seven rams for me." ²Balak did as Balaam said, and the two of them offered a bull and a ram on each altar.

³Then Balaam said to Balak, "Stay here beside your offering while I go aside. Perhaps the LORD will come to meet with me. Whatever he reveals to me I will tell you." Then he went off to a barren height.

⁴God met with him, and Balaam said, "I have prepared seven altars, and on each altar I have offered a bull and a ram."

⁵The LORD put a message in Balaam's mouth and said, "Go back to Balak and give him this message."

⁶So he went back to him and found him standing beside his offering, with all the princes of Moab. ⁷Then Balaam uttered his oracle:

"Balak brought me from Aram,
    the king of Moab from the eastern
        mountains.
'Come,' he said, 'curse Jacob for me;
    come, denounce Israel.'
⁸How can I curse
    those whom God has not cursed?
How can I denounce
    those whom the LORD has not
        denounced?
⁹From the rocky peaks I see them,
    from the heights I view them.
I see people who live apart
    and do not consider themselves
        one of the nations.
¹⁰Who can count the dust of Jacob
    or number the fourth part of
        Israel?
Let me die the death of the righteous,
    and may my end be like theirs!"

¹¹Balak said to Balaam, "What have you done to me? I brought you to curse

my enemies, but you have done nothing but bless them!"

¹²He answered, "Must I not speak what the LORD puts in my mouth?"

Balaam's Second Oracle

¹³Then Balak said to him, "Come with me to another place where you can see them; you will see only a part but not all of them. And from there, curse them for me." ¹⁴So he took him to the field of Zophim on the top of Pisgah, and there he built seven altars and offered a bull and a ram on each altar.

¹⁵Balaam said to Balak, "Stay here beside your offering while I meet with him over there."

¹⁶The LORD met with Balaam and put a message in his mouth and said, "Go back to Balak and give him this message."

¹⁷So he went to him and found him standing beside his offering, with the princes of Moab. Balak asked him, "What did the LORD say?"

¹⁸Then he uttered his oracle:

"Arise, Balak, and listen;
    hear me, son of Zippor.
¹⁹God is not a man, that he should lie,
    nor a son of man, that he should
      change his mind.
Does he speak and then not act?
    Does he promise and not fulfil?
²⁰I have received a command to bless;
    he has blessed, and I cannot
      change it.

²¹"No misfortune is seen in Jacob,
    no misery observed in Israel.
The LORD their God is with them;
    the shout of the King is among
      them.
²²God brought them out of Egypt;
    they have the strength of a wild ox.
²³There is no sorcery against Jacob,
    no divination against Israel.
It will now be said of Jacob
    and of Israel, 'See what God has
      done!'
²⁴The people rise like a lioness;

they rouse themselves like a lion
that does not rest till he devours his
    prey
   and drinks the blood of his
    victims."

²⁵Then Balak said to Balaam, "Neither curse them at all nor bless them at all!"

²⁶Balaam answered, "Did I not tell you I must do whatever the LORD says?"

NEW TESTAMENT READING
Luke 6:37–7:10

Judging Others

³⁷"Do not judge, and you will not be judged. Do not condemn, and you will not be condemned. Forgive, and you will be forgiven. ³⁸Give, and it will be given to you. A good measure, pressed down, shaken together and running over, will be poured into your lap. For with the measure you use, it will be measured to you."

³⁹He also told them this parable: "Can a blind man lead a blind man? Will they not both fall into a pit? ⁴⁰A student is not above his teacher, but everyone who is fully trained will be like his teacher.

⁴¹"Why do you look at the speck of sawdust in your brother's eye and pay no attention to the plank in your own eye? ⁴²How can you say to your brother, 'Brother, let me take the speck out of your eye,' when you yourself fail to see the plank in your own eye? You hypocrite, first take the plank out of your eye, and then you will see clearly to remove the speck from your brother's eye.

A Tree and Its Fruit

⁴³"No good tree bears bad fruit, nor does a bad tree bear good fruit. ⁴⁴Each tree is recognised by its own fruit. People do not pick figs from thornbushes, or grapes from briers. ⁴⁵The good man

brings good things out of the good stored up in his heart, and the evil man brings evil things out of the evil stored up in his heart. For out of the overflow of his heart his mouth speaks.

The Wise and Foolish Builders

46"Why do you call me, 'Lord, Lord,' and do not do what I say? 47I will show you what he is like who comes to me and hears my words and puts them into practice. 48He is like a man building a house, who dug down deep and laid the foundation on rock. When the flood came, the torrent struck that house but could not shake it, because it was well built. 49But the one who hears my words and does not put them into practice is like a man who built a house on the ground without a foundation. The moment the torrent struck that house, it collapsed and its destruction was complete."

The Faith of the Centurion

7 When Jesus had finished saying all this in the hearing of the people, he entered Capernaum. 2There a centurion's servant, whom his master valued highly, was sick and about to die. 3The centurion heard of Jesus and sent some elders of the Jews to him, asking him to come and heal his servant. 4When they came to Jesus, they pleaded earnestly with him, "This man deserves to have you do this, 5because he loves our nation and has built our synagogue." 6So Jesus went with them.

He was not far from the house when the centurion sent friends to say to him: "Lord, don't trouble yourself, for I do not deserve to have you come under my roof. 7That is why I did not even consider myself worthy to come to you. But say the word, and my servant will be healed. 8For I myself am a man under authority, with soldiers under me. I tell this one, 'Go', and he goes; and that one, 'Come', and he comes. I say to my servant, 'Do this', and he does it."

9When Jesus heard this, he was amazed at him, and turning to the crowd following him, he said, "I tell you, I have not found such great faith even in Israel." 10Then the men who had been sent returned to the house and found the servant well.

READING FROM PSALMS
Psalm 37:32–40

32The wicked lie in wait for the
    righteous,
    seeking their very lives;
33but the LORD will not leave them in
    their power
    or let them be condemned when
    brought to trial.

34Wait for the LORD
    and keep his way.
He will exalt you to inherit the land;
    when the wicked are cut off, you
    will see it.

35I have seen a wicked and ruthless
    man
    flourishing like a green tree in its
    native soil,
36but he soon passed away and was no
    more;
    though I looked for him, he could
    not be found.

37Consider the blameless, observe the
    upright;
    there is a future for the man of
    peace.
38But all sinners will be destroyed;
    the future of the wicked will be cut
    off.

39The salvation of the righteous comes
    from the LORD;
    he is their stronghold in time of
    trouble.
40The LORD helps them and delivers
    them;
    he delivers them from the wicked
    and saves them,
    because they take refuge in him.

OLD TESTAMENT READING
Numbers 23:27–26:11

Balaam's Third Oracle

²⁷Then Balak said to Balaam, "Come, let me take you to another place. Perhaps it will please God to let you curse them for me from there." ²⁸And Balak took Balaam to the top of Peor, overlooking the wasteland. ²⁹Balaam said, "Build me seven altars here, and prepare seven bulls and seven rams for me." ³⁰Balak did as Balaam had said, and offered a bull and a ram on each altar.

24 Now when Balaam saw that it pleased the LORD to bless Israel, he did not resort to sorcery as at other times, but turned his face towards the desert. ²When Balaam looked out and saw Israel encamped tribe by tribe, the Spirit of God came upon him ³and he uttered his oracle:

"The oracle of Balaam son of Beor,
  the oracle of one whose eye sees
    clearly,
⁴the oracle of one who hears the
    words of God,
  who sees a vision from the
    Almighty,
  who falls prostrate, and whose eyes
    are opened:

⁵"How beautiful are your tents, O
    Jacob,
  your dwelling-places, O Israel!

⁶"Like valleys they spread out,
  like gardens beside a river,
  like aloes planted by the LORD,
  like cedars beside the waters.
⁷Water will flow from their buckets;
  their seed will have abundant
    water.

"Their king will be greater than
    Agag;
  their kingdom will be exalted.

⁸"God brought them out of Egypt;
  they have the strength of a wild ox.
They devour hostile nations
  and break their bones in pieces;
  with their arrows they pierce them.
⁹Like a lion they crouch and lie down,
  like a lioness—who dares to rouse
    them?

"May those who bless you be blessed
  and those who curse you be
    cursed!"

¹⁰Then Balak's anger burned against Balaam. He struck his hands together and said to him, "I summoned you to curse my enemies, but you have blessed them these three times. ¹¹Now leave at once and go home! I said I would reward you handsomely, but the LORD has kept you from being rewarded."

¹²Balaam answered Balak, "Did I not tell the messengers you sent me, ¹³'Even if Balak gave me his palace filled with silver and gold, I could not do anything of my own accord, good or bad, to go beyond the command of the LORD—and I must say only what the LORD says'? ¹⁴Now I am going back to my people, but come, let me warn you of what this people will do to your people in days to come."

Balaam's Fourth Oracle

¹⁵Then he uttered his oracle:

"The oracle of Balaam son of Beor,
  the oracle of one whose eye sees
    clearly,
¹⁶the oracle of one who hears the words
    of God,
  who has knowledge from the Most
    High,
  who sees a vision from the Almighty,
  who falls prostrate, and whose eyes
    are opened:

17"I see him, but not now;
  I behold him, but not near.
A star will come out of Jacob;
  a sceptre will rise out of Israel.
He will crush the foreheads of Moab,
  the skulls of all the sons of Sheth.
18Edom will be conquered;
  Seir, his enemy, will be conquered,
  but Israel will grow strong.
19A ruler will come out of Jacob
  and destroy the survivors of the
    city."

Balaam's Final Oracles

20Then Balaam saw Amalek and uttered his oracle:

"Amalek was first among the
    nations,
  but he will come to ruin at last."

21Then he saw the Kenites and uttered his oracle:

"Your dwelling-place is secure,
  your nest is set in a rock;
22yet you Kenites will be destroyed
  when Asshur takes you captive."

23Then he uttered his oracle:

"Ah, who can live when God does
    this?
24 Ships will come from the shores of
    Kittim;
they will subdue Asshur and Eber,
  but they too will come to ruin."

25Then Balaam got up and returned home and Balak went his own way.

Moab Seduces Israel

25 While Israel was staying in Shittim, the men began to indulge in sexual immorality with Moabite women, 2who invited them to the sacrifices to their gods. The people ate and bowed down before these gods. 3So Israel joined in worshipping the Baal of Peor. And the LORD's anger burned against them.

4The LORD said to Moses, "Take all the leaders of these people, kill them and expose them in broad daylight before the LORD, so that the LORD's fierce anger may turn away from Israel."

5So Moses said to Israel's judges, "Each of you must put to death those of your men who have joined in worshipping the Baal of Peor."

6Then an Israelite man brought to his family a Midianite woman right before the eyes of Moses and the whole assembly of Israel while they were weeping at the entrance to the Tent of Meeting. 7When Phinehas son of Eleazar, the son of Aaron, the priest, saw this, he left the assembly, took a spear in his hand 8and followed the Israelite into the tent. He drove the spear through both of them —through the Israelite and into the woman's body. Then the plague against the Israelites was stopped; 9but those who died in the plague numbered 24,000.

10The LORD said to Moses, 11"Phinehas son of Eleazar, the son of Aaron, the priest, has turned my anger away from the Israelites; for he was as zealous as I am for my honour among them, so that in my zeal I did not put an end to them. 12Therefore tell him I am making my covenant of peace with him. 13He and his descendants will have a covenant of a lasting priesthood, because he was zealous for the honour of his God and made atonement for the Israelites."

14The name of the Israelite who was killed with the Midianite woman was Zimri son of Salu, the leader of a Simeonite family. 15And the name of the Midianite woman who was put to death was Cozbi daughter of Zur, a tribal chief of a Midianite family.

16The LORD said to Moses, 17"Treat the Midianites as enemies and kill them, 18because they treated you as enemies when they deceived you in the affair of Peor and their sister Cozbi, the daughter of a Midianite leader, the woman who was killed when the plague came as a result of Peor."

The Second Census

26 After the plague the LORD said to Moses and Eleazar son of Aaron, the priest, [2]"Take a census of the whole Israelite community by families—all those twenty years old or more who are able to serve in the army of Israel." [3]So on the plains of Moab by the Jordan across from Jericho, Moses and Eleazar the priest spoke with them and said, [4]"Take a census of men twenty years or more, as the LORD commanded Moses."

These were the Israelites who came out of Egypt:

[5]The descendants of Reuben, the firstborn son of Israel, were:

through Hanoch, the Hanochite clan;
through Pallu, the Palluite clan;
[6]through Hezron, the Hezronite clan;
through Carmi, the Carmite clan.
[7]These were the clans of Reuben; those numbered were 43,730.

[8]The son of Pallu was Eliab, [9]and the sons of Eliab were Nemuel, Dathan and Abiram. The same Dathan and Abiram were the community officials who rebelled against Moses and Aaron and were among Korah's followers when they rebelled against the LORD. [10]The earth opened its mouth and swallowed them along with Korah, whose followers died when the fire devoured the 250 men. And they served as a warning sign. [11]The line of Korah, however, did not die out.

NEW TESTAMENT READING
Luke 7:11–35

Jesus Raises a Widow's Son

[11]Soon afterwards, Jesus went to a town called Nain, and his disciples and a large crowd went along with him. [12]As he approached the town gate, a dead person was being carried out—the only son of his mother, and she was a widow. And a large crowd from the town was with her. [13]When the Lord saw her, his heart went out to her and he said, "Don't cry."

[14]Then he went up and touched the coffin, and those carrying it stood still. He said, "Young man, I say to you, get up!" [15]The dead man sat up and began to talk, and Jesus gave him back to his mother.

[16]They were all filled with awe and praised God. "A great prophet has appeared among us," they said. "God has come to help his people." [17]This news about Jesus spread throughout Judea and the surrounding country.

Jesus and John the Baptist

[18]John's disciples told him about all these things. Calling two of them, [19]he sent them to the Lord to ask, "Are you the one who was to come, or should we expect someone else?"

[20]When the men came to Jesus, they said, "John the Baptist sent us to you to ask, 'Are you the one who was to come, or should we expect someone else?'"

[21]At that very time Jesus cured many who had diseases, sicknesses and evil spirits, and gave sight to many who were blind. [22]So he replied to the messengers, "Go back and report to John what you have seen and heard: The blind receive sight, the lame walk, those who have leprosy are cured, the deaf hear, the dead are raised, and the good news is preached to the poor. [23]Blessed is the man who does not fall away on account of me."

[24]After John's messengers left, Jesus began to speak to the crowd about John: "What did you go out into the desert to see? A reed swayed by the wind? [25]If not, what did you go out to see? A man dressed in fine clothes? No, those who wear expensive clothes and indulge in luxury are in palaces. [26]But

what did you go out to see? A prophet? Yes, I tell you, and more than a prophet. ²⁷This is the one about whom it is written:

> "'I will send my messenger ahead of you,
> who will prepare your way before you.'

²⁸I tell you, among those born of women there is no-one greater than John; yet the one who is least in the kingdom of God is greater than he."

(²⁹All the people, even the tax collectors, when they heard Jesus' words, acknowledged that God's way was right, because they had been baptised by John. ³⁰But the Pharisees and experts in the law rejected God's purpose for themselves, because they had not been baptised by John.)

³¹"To what, then, can I compare the people of this generation? What are they like? ³²They are like children sitting in the market-place and calling out to each other:

> "'We played the flute for you,
> and you did not dance;
> we sang a dirge,
> and you did not cry.'

³³For John the Baptist came neither eating bread nor drinking wine, and you say, 'He has a demon.' ³⁴The Son of Man came eating and drinking, and you say, 'Here is a glutton and a drunkard, a friend of tax collectors and "sinners".' ³⁵But wisdom is proved right by all her children."

READING FROM PSALMS
Psalm 38:1–12

A psalm of David. A petition.

¹O LORD, do not rebuke me in your anger
    or discipline me in your wrath.
²For your arrows have pierced me,
    and your hand has come down upon me.
³Because of your wrath there is no health in my body;
    my bones have no soundness because of my sin.
⁴My guilt has overwhelmed me
    like a burden too heavy to bear.

⁵My wounds fester and are loathsome
    because of my sinful folly.
⁶I am bowed down and brought very low;
    all day long I go about mourning.
⁷My back is filled with searing pain;
    there is no health in my body.
⁸I am feeble and utterly crushed;
    I groan in anguish of heart.

⁹All my longings lie open before you, O Lord;
    my sighing is not hidden from you.
¹⁰My heart pounds, my strength fails me;
    even the light has gone from my eyes.
¹¹My friends and companions avoid me because of my wounds;
    my neighbours stay far away.
¹²Those who seek my life set their traps,
    those who would harm me talk of my ruin;
    all day long they plot deception.

MARCH 29

OLD TESTAMENT READING
Numbers 26:12–27:11

12The descendants of Simeon by their clans were:
   through Nemuel, the Nemuelite clan;
   through Jamin, the Jaminite clan;
   through Jakin, the Jakinite clan;
13through Zerah, the Zerahite clan;
   through Shaul, the Shaulite clan.
14These were the clans of Simeon; there were 22,200 men.

15The descendants of Gad by their clans were:
   through Zephon, the Zephonite clan;
   through Haggi, the Haggite clan;
   through Shuni, the Shunite clan;
16through Ozni, the Oznite clan;
   through Eri, the Erite clan;
17through Arodi, the Arodite clan;
   through Areli, the Arelite clan.
18These were the clans of Gad; those numbered were 40,500.

19Er and Onan were sons of Judah, but they died in Canaan.
20The descendants of Judah by their clans were:
   through Shelah, the Shelanite clan;
   through Perez, the Perezite clan;
   through Zerah, the Zerahite clan.
21The descendants of Perez were:
   through Hezron, the Hezronite clan;
   through Hamul, the Hamulite clan.
22These were the clans of Judah; those numbered were 76,500.

23The descendants of Issachar by their clans were:
   through Tola, the Tolaite clan;
   through Puah, the Puite clan;
24through Jashub, the Jashubite clan;
   through Shimron, the Shimronite clan.

25These were the clans of Issachar; those numbered were 64,300.

26The descendants of Zebulun by their clans were:
   through Sered, the Seredite clan;
   through Elon, the Elonite clan;
   through Jahleel, the Jahleelite clan.
27These were the clans of Zebulun; those numbered were 60,500.

28The descendants of Joseph by their clans through Manasseh and Ephraim were:

29The descendants of Manasseh:
   through Makir, the Makirite clan
      (Makir was the father of Gilead);
   through Gilead, the Gileadite clan.
30These were the descendants of Gilead:
   through Iezer, the Iezerite clan;
   through Helek, the Helekite clan;
31through Asriel, the Asrielite clan;
   through Shechem, the Shechemite clan;
32through Shemida, the Shemidaite clan;
   through Hepher, the Hepherite clan.
33(Zelophehad son of Hepher had no sons; he had only daughters, whose names were Mahlah, Noah, Hoglah, Milcah and Tirzah.)
34These were the clans of Manasseh; those numbered were 52,700.

35These were the descendants of Ephraim by their clans:
   through Shuthelah, the Shuthelahite clan;
   through Beker, the Bekerite clan;
   through Tahan, the Tahanite clan.
36These were the descendants of Shuthelah:
   through Eran, the Eranite clan.

37These were the clans of Ephraim; those numbered were 32,500.

These were the descendants of Joseph by their clans.

38The descendants of Benjamin by their clans were:

through Bela, the Belaite clan;
through Ashbel, the Ashbelite clan;
through Ahiram, the Ahiramite clan;
39through Shupham, the Shuphamite clan;
through Hupham, the Huphamite clan.
40The descendants of Bela through Ard and Naaman were:
through Ard, the Ardite clan;
through Naaman, the Naamite clan.
41These were the clans of Benjamin; those numbered were 45,600.

42These were the descendants of Dan by their clans:

through Shuham, the Shuhamite clan.
These were the clans of Dan: 43All of them were Shuhamite clans; and those numbered were 64,400.

44The descendants of Asher by their clans were:

through Imnah, the Imnite clan;
through Ishvi, the Ishvite clan;
through Beriah, the Beriite clan;
45and through the descendants of Beriah:
through Heber, the Heberite clan;
through Malkiel, the Malkielite clan.
46(Asher had a daughter named Serah.)
47These were the clans of Asher; those numbered were 53,400.

48The descendants of Naphtali by their clans were:

through Jahzeel, the Jahzeelite clan;
through Guni, the Gunite clan;
49through Jezer, the Jezerite clan;
through Shillem, the Shillemite clan.

50These were the clans of Naphtali; those numbered were 45,400.

51The total number of the men of Israel was 601,730.

52The LORD said to Moses, 53"The land is to be allotted to them as an inheritance based on the number of names. 54To a larger group give a larger inheritance, and to a smaller group a smaller one; each is to receive its inheritance according to the number of those listed. 55Be sure that the land is distributed by lot. What each group inherits will be according to the names for its ancestral tribe. 56Each inheritance is to be distributed by lot among the larger and smaller groups."

57These were the Levites who were counted by their clans:

through Gershon, the Gershonite clan;
through Kohath, the Kohathite clan;
through Merari, the Merarite clan.
58These also were Levite clans:
the Libnite clan,
the Hebronite clan,
the Mahlite clan,
the Mushite clan,
the Korahite clan.
(Kohath was the forefather of Amram; 59the name of Amram's wife was Jochebed, a descendant of Levi, who was born to the Levites in Egypt. To Amram she bore Aaron, Moses and their sister Miriam. 60Aaron was the father of Nadab and Abihu, Eleazar and Ithamar. 61But Nadab and Abihu died when they made an offering before the LORD with unauthorised fire.)

62All the male Levites a month old or more numbered 23,000. They were not counted along with the other Israelites because they received no inheritance among them.

63These are the ones counted by Moses and Eleazar the priest when they counted the Israelites on the plains of Moab by the Jordan across from Jericho. 64Not one of them was among those counted by Moses and Aaron the priest when they counted the Israelites in the Desert of Sinai. 65For the LORD had told those Israelites they would surely die in the desert, and not one of them was left except Caleb son of Jephunneh and Joshua son of Nun.

Zelophehad's Daughters

27 The daughters of Zelophehad son of Hepher, the son of Gilead, the son of Makir, the son of Manasseh, belonged to the clans of Manasseh son of Joseph. The names of the daughters were Mahlah, Noah, Hoglah, Milcah and Tirzah. They approached 2the entrance to the Tent of Meeting and stood before Moses, Eleazar the priest, the leaders and the whole assembly, and said, 3"Our father died in the desert. He was not among Korah's followers, who banded together against the LORD, but he died for his own sin and left no sons. 4Why should our father's name disappear from his clan because he had no son? Give us property among our father's relatives."

5So Moses brought their case before the LORD 6and the LORD said to him, 7"What Zelophehad's daughters are saying is right. You must certainly give them property as an inheritance among their father's relatives and give their father's inheritance over to them.

8"Say to the Israelites, 'If a man dies and leaves no son, give his inheritance over to his daughter. 9If he has no daughter, give his inheritance to his brothers. 10If he has no brothers, give his inheritance to his father's brothers. 11If his father had no brothers, give his inheritance to the nearest relative in his clan, that he may possess it. This is to be a legal requirement for the Israelites, as the LORD commanded Moses.'"

NEW TESTAMENT READING
Luke 7:36–50

Jesus Anointed by a Sinful Woman

36Now one of the Pharisees invited Jesus to have dinner with him, so he went to the Pharisee's house and reclined at the table. 37When a woman who had lived a sinful life in that town learned that Jesus was eating at the Pharisee's house, she brought an alabaster jar of perfume, 38and as she stood behind him at his feet weeping, she began to wet his feet with her tears. Then she wiped them with her hair, kissed them and poured perfume on them.

39When the Pharisee who had invited him saw this, he said to himself, "If this man were a prophet, he would know who is touching him and what kind of woman she is—that she is a sinner."

40Jesus answered him, "Simon, I have something to tell you."

"Tell me, teacher," he said.

41"Two men owed money to a certain money-lender. One owed him five hundred denarii, and the other fifty. 42Neither of them had the money to pay him back, so he cancelled the debts of both. Now which of them will love him more?"

43Simon replied, "I suppose the one who had the bigger debt cancelled."

"You have judged correctly," Jesus said.

44Then he turned towards the woman and said to Simon, "Do you see this woman? I came into your house. You did not give me any water for my feet, but she wet my feet with her tears and wiped them with her hair. 45You did not give me a kiss, but this woman, from the time I entered has not stopped kissing my feet. 46You did not put oil on my head, but she has poured perfume on my feet. 47Therefore, I tell you, her many sins have been forgiven—for she loved much. But he who has been forgiven little loves little."

48Then Jesus said to her, "Your sins are forgiven."

⁴⁹The other guests began to say among themselves, "Who is this who even forgives sins?"

⁵⁰Jesus said to the woman, "Your faith has saved you; go in peace."

READING FROM PROVERBS
Proverbs 8:12–21

¹²"I, wisdom, dwell together with
        prudence;
    I possess knowledge and
        discretion.
¹³To fear the LORD is to hate evil;
    I hate pride and arrogance,
        evil behaviour and perverse
        speech.

¹⁴Counsel and sound judgment are
        mine;
    I have understanding and power.
¹⁵By me kings reign
    and rulers make laws that are just;
¹⁶by me princes govern,
    and all nobles who rule on earth.
¹⁷I love those who love me,
    and those who seek me find me.
¹⁸With me are riches and honour,
    enduring wealth and prosperity.
¹⁹My fruit is better than fine gold;
    what I yield surpasses choice silver.
²⁰I walk in the way of righteousness,
    along the paths of justice,
²¹bestowing wealth on those who love
        me
    and making their treasuries full.

MARCH 30   DAY 89

OLD TESTAMENT READING
Numbers 27:12–29:11

Joshua to Succeed Moses

¹²Then the LORD said to Moses, "Go up this mountain in the Abarim Range and see the land I have given the Israelites. ¹³After you have seen it, you too will be gathered to your people, as your brother Aaron was, ¹⁴for when the community rebelled at the waters in the Desert of Zin, both of you disobeyed my command to honour me as holy before their eyes." (These were the waters of Meribah Kadesh, in the Desert of Zin.)

¹⁵Moses said to the LORD, ¹⁶"May the LORD, the God of the spirits of all mankind, appoint a man over this community ¹⁷to go out and come in before them, one who will lead them out and bring them in, so that the LORD's people will not be like sheep without a shepherd."

¹⁸So the LORD said to Moses, "Take Joshua son of Nun, a man in whom is the spirit, and lay your hand on him.

¹⁹Make him stand before Eleazar the priest and the entire assembly and commission him in their presence. ²⁰Give him some of your authority so that the whole Israelite community will obey him. ²¹He is to stand before Eleazar the priest, who will obtain decisions for him by enquiring of the Urim before the LORD. At his command he and the entire community of the Israelites will go out, and at his command they will come in."

²²Moses did as the LORD commanded him. He took Joshua and made him stand before Eleazar the priest and the whole assembly. ²³Then he laid his hands on him and commissioned him, as the LORD instructed through Moses.

Daily Offerings

28 The LORD said to Moses, ²"Give this command to the Israelites and say to them: 'See that you present to me at the appointed time the food for my offerings made by fire, as an aroma pleasing to me.' ³Say to them: 'This is the offering made by fire that you are to present to the LORD: two lambs a year old without defect, as a regular burnt offering each day. ⁴Prepare one lamb in the morning and the other at twilight, ⁵together with a grain offering of a tenth of an ephah of fine flour mixed with a quarter of a hin of oil from pressed olives. ⁶This is the regular burnt offering instituted at Mount Sinai as a pleasing aroma, an offering made to the LORD by fire. ⁷The accompanying drink offering is to be a quarter of a hin of fermented drink with each lamb. Pour out the drink offering to the LORD at the sanctuary. ⁸Prepare the second lamb at twilight, along with the same kind of grain offering and drink offering that you prepare in the morning. This is an offering made by fire, an aroma pleasing to the LORD.

Sabbath Offerings

⁹"On the Sabbath day, make an offering of two lambs a year old without defect, together with its drink offering and a grain offering of two-tenths of an ephah of fine flour mixed with oil. ¹⁰This is the burnt offering for every Sabbath, in addition to the regular burnt offering and its drink offering.

Monthly Offerings

¹¹"On the first of every month, present to the LORD a burnt offering of two young bulls, one ram and seven male lambs a year old, all without defect. ¹²With each bull there is to be a grain offering of three-tenths of an ephah of fine flour mixed with oil; with the ram, a grain offering of two-tenths of an ephah of fine flour mixed with oil; ¹³and with each lamb, a grain offering of a tenth of an ephah of fine flour mixed with oil. This is for a burnt offering, a pleasing aroma, an offering made to the LORD by fire. ¹⁴With each bull there is to be a drink offering of half a hin of wine; with the ram, a third of a hin; and with each lamb, a quarter of a hin. This is the

monthly burnt offering to be made at each new moon during the year. ¹⁵Besides the regular burnt offering with its drink offering, one male goat is to be presented to the LORD as a sin offering.

The Passover

¹⁶"On the fourteenth day of the first month the LORD's Passover is to be held. ¹⁷On the fifteenth day of this month there is to be a festival; for seven days eat bread made without yeast. ¹⁸On the first day hold a sacred assembly and do no regular work. ¹⁹Present to the LORD an offering made by fire, a burnt offering of two young bulls, one ram and seven male lambs a year old, all without defect. ²⁰With each bull prepare a grain offering of three-tenths of an ephah of fine flour mixed with oil; with the ram, two-tenths; ²¹and with each of the seven lambs, one-tenth. ²²Include one male goat as a sin offering to make atonement for you. ²³Prepare these in addition to the regular morning burnt offering. ²⁴In this way prepare the food for the offering made by fire every day for seven days as an aroma pleasing to the LORD; it is to be prepared in addition to the regular burnt offering and its drink offering. ²⁵On the seventh day hold a sacred assembly and do no regular work.

Feast of Weeks

²⁶"On the day of firstfruits, when you present to the LORD an offering of new grain during the Feast of Weeks, hold a sacred assembly and do no regular work. ²⁷Present a burnt offering of two young bulls, one ram and seven male lambs a year old as an aroma pleasing to the LORD. ²⁸With each bull there is to be a grain offering of three-tenths of an ephah of fine flour mixed with oil; with the ram, two-tenths; ²⁹and with each of the seven lambs, one-tenth. ³⁰Include one male goat to make atonement for you. ³¹Prepare these together with their drink offerings, in

addition to the regular burnt offering and its grain offering. Be sure the animals are without defect.

Feast of Trumpets

29 "'On the first day of the seventh month hold a sacred assembly and do no regular work. It is a day for you to sound the trumpets. ²As an aroma pleasing to the LORD, prepare a burnt offering of one young bull, one ram and seven male lambs a year old, all without defect. ³With the bull prepare a grain offering of three-tenths of an ephah of fine flour mixed with oil; with the ram, two-tenths; ⁴and with each of the seven lambs, one-tenth. ⁵Include one male goat as a sin offering to make atonement for you. ⁶These are in addition to the monthly and daily burnt offerings with their grain offerings and drink offerings as specified. They are offerings made to the LORD by fire—a pleasing aroma.

Day of Atonement

7"'On the tenth day of this seventh month hold a sacred assembly. You must deny yourselves and do no work. ⁸Present as an aroma pleasing to the LORD a burnt offering of one young bull, one ram and seven male lambs a year old, all without defect. ⁹With the bull prepare a grain offering of three-tenths of an ephah of fine flour mixed with oil; with the ram, two-tenths; ¹⁰and with each of the seven lambs, one-tenth. ¹¹Include one male goat as a sin offering, in addition to the sin offering for atonement and the regular burnt offering with its grain offering, and their drink offerings.

NEW TESTAMENT READING
Luke 8:1–18

The Parable of the Sower

8 After this, Jesus travelled about from one town and village to another, proclaiming the good news of the kingdom of God. The Twelve were with him, ²and also some women who had been cured of evil spirits and diseases: Mary (called Magdalene) from whom seven demons had come out; ³Joanna the wife of Chuza, the manager of Herod's household; Susanna; and many others. These women were helping to support them out of their own means.

⁴While a large crowd was gathering and people were coming to Jesus from town after town, he told this parable: ⁵"A farmer went out to sow his seed. As he was scattering the seed, some fell along the path; it was trampled on, and the birds of the air ate it up. ⁶Some fell on rock, and when it came up, the plants withered because they had no moisture. ⁷Other seed fell among thorns, which grew up with it and choked the plants. ⁸Still other seed fell on good soil. It came up and yielded a crop, a hundred times more than was sown."

When he said this, he called out, "He who has ears to hear, let him hear."

⁹His disciples asked him what this parable meant. ¹⁰He said, "The knowledge of the secrets of the kingdom of God has been given to you, but to others I speak in parables, so that,

"'though seeing, they may not see;
though hearing, they may not
understand.'

¹¹"This is the meaning of the parable: The seed is the word of God. ¹²Those along the path are the ones who hear, and then the devil comes and takes away the word from their hearts, so that they may not believe and be saved. ¹³Those on the rock are the ones who receive the word with joy when they hear it, but they have no root. They believe for a while, but in the time of testing they fall away. ¹⁴The seed that fell among thorns stands for those who hear, but as they go on their way they are choked by life's worries, riches and pleasures, and they do not mature. ¹⁵But the seed on good soil stands for

those with a noble and good heart, who hear the word, retain it, and by persevering produce a crop.

A Lamp on a Stand

16"No-one lights a lamp and hides it in a jar or puts it under a bed. Instead, he puts it on a stand, so that those who come in can see the light. 17For there is nothing hidden that will not be disclosed, and nothing concealed that will not be known or brought out into the open. 18Therefore consider carefully how you listen. Whoever has will be given more; whoever does not have, even what he thinks he has will be taken from him."

READING FROM PSALMS
Psalm 38:13–22

13I am like a deaf man, who cannot hear,
　　like a mute, who cannot open his mouth;

14I have become like a man who does not hear,
　　whose mouth can offer no reply.
15I wait for you, O LORD;
　　you will answer, O Lord my God.
16For I said, "Do not let them gloat
　　or exalt themselves over me when my foot slips."

17For I am about to fall,
　　and my pain is ever with me.
18I confess my iniquity;
　　I am troubled by my sin.
19Many are those who are my vigorous enemies;
　　those who hate me without reason are numerous.
20Those who repay my good with evil slander me when I pursue what is good.

21O LORD, do not forsake me;
　　be not far from me, O my God.
22Come quickly to help me,
　　O Lord my Saviour.

DAY 90

MARCH 31

OLD TESTAMENT READING
Numbers 29:12–31:24

Feast of Tabernacles

12"'On the fifteenth day of the seventh month, hold a sacred assembly and do no regular work. Celebrate a festival to the LORD for seven days. 13Present an offering made by fire as an aroma pleasing to the LORD, a burnt offering of thirteen young bulls, two rams and fourteen male lambs a year old, all without defect. 14With each of the thirteen bulls prepare a grain offering of three-tenths of an ephah of fine flour mixed with oil; with each of the two rams, two-tenths; 15and with each of the fourteen lambs, one-tenth.

16Include one male goat as a sin offering, in addition to the regular burnt offering with its grain offering and drink offering.

17"'On the second day prepare twelve young bulls, two rams and fourteen male lambs a year old, all without defect. 18With the bulls, rams and lambs, prepare their grain offerings and drink offerings according to the number specified. 19Include one male goat as a sin offering, in addition to the regular burnt offering with its grain offering, and their drink offerings.

20"'On the third day prepare eleven bulls, two rams and fourteen male lambs a year old, all without defect. 21With the bulls, rams and lambs, prepare their grain offerings and drink offerings according to the number specified. ²²Include one male goat as a sin offering, in addition to the regular burnt offering with its grain offering and drink offering.

²³"On the fourth day prepare ten bulls, two rams and fourteen male lambs a year old, all without defect. ²⁴With the bulls, rams and lambs, prepare their grain offerings and drink offerings according to the number specified. ²⁵Include one male goat as a sin offering, in addition to the regular burnt offering with its grain offering and drink offering.

²⁶"On the fifth day prepare nine bulls, two rams and fourteen male lambs a year old, all without defect. ²⁷With the bulls, rams and lambs, prepare their grain offerings and drink offerings according to the number specified. ²⁸Include one male goat as a sin offering, in addition to the regular burnt offering with its grain offering and drink offering.

²⁹"On the sixth day prepare eight bulls, two rams and fourteen male lambs a year old, all without defect. ³⁰With the bulls, rams and lambs, prepare their grain offerings and drink offerings according to the number specified. ³¹Include one male goat as a sin offering, in addition to the regular burnt offering with its grain offering and drink offering.

³²"On the seventh day prepare seven bulls, two rams and fourteen male lambs a year old, all without defect. ³³With the bulls, rams and lambs, prepare their grain offerings and drink offerings according to the number specified. ³⁴Include one male goat as a sin offering, in addition to the regular burnt offering with its grain offering and drink offering.

³⁵"On the eighth day hold an assembly and do no regular work. ³⁶Present an offering made by fire as an aroma pleasing to the LORD, a burnt offering of one bull, one ram and seven male lambs a year old, all without defect. ³⁷With the bull, the ram and the lambs, prepare

their grain offerings and drink offerings according to the number specified. ³⁸Include one male goat as a sin offering, in addition to the regular burnt offering with its grain offering and drink offering.

³⁹"In addition to what you vow and your freewill offerings, prepare these for the LORD at your appointed feasts: your burnt offerings, grain offerings, drink offerings and fellowship offerings.'"

⁴⁰Moses told the Israelites all that the LORD commanded him.

Vows

30 Moses said to the heads of the tribes of Israel: "This is what the LORD commands: ²When a man makes a vow to the LORD or takes an oath to bind himself by a pledge, he must not break his word but must do everything he said.

³"When a young woman still living in her father's house makes a vow to the LORD or binds herself by a pledge ⁴and her father hears about her vow or pledge but says nothing to her, then all her vows and every pledge by which she bound herself will stand. ⁵But if her father forbids her when he hears about it, none of her vows or the pledges by which she bound herself will stand; the LORD will release her because her father has forbidden her.

⁶"If she marries after she makes a vow or after her lips utter a rash promise by which she binds herself ⁷and her husband hears about it but says nothing to her, then her vows or the pledges by which she bound herself will stand. ⁸But if her husband forbids her when he hears about it, he nullifies the vow that binds her or the rash promise by which she binds herself, and the LORD will release her.

⁹"Any vow or obligation taken by a widow or divorced woman will be binding on her.

¹⁰"If a woman living with her husband makes a vow or binds herself by a

pledge under oath 11and her husband hears about it but says nothing to her and does not forbid her, then all her vows or the pledges by which she bound herself will stand. 12But if her husband nullifies them when he hears about them, then none of the vows or pledges that came from her lips will stand. Her husband has nullified them, and the LORD will release her. 13Her husband may confirm or nullify any vow she makes or any sworn pledge to deny herself. 14But if her husband says nothing to her about it from day to day, then he confirms all her vows or the pledges binding on her. He confirms them by saying nothing to her when he hears about them. 15If, however, he nullifies them some time after he hears about them, then he is responsible for her guilt."

16These are the regulations the LORD gave Moses concerning relationships between a man and his wife, and between a father and his young daughter still living in his house.

Vengeance on the Midianites

31 The LORD said to Moses, 2"Take vengeance on the Midianites for the Israelites. After that, you will be gathered to your people."

3So Moses said to the people, "Arm some of your men to go to war against the Midianites and to carry out the LORD's vengeance on them. 4Send into battle a thousand men from each of the tribes of Israel." 5So twelve thousand men armed for battle, a thousand from each tribe, were supplied from the clans of Israel. 6Moses sent them into battle, a thousand from each tribe, along with Phinehas son of Eleazar, the priest, who took with him articles from the sanctuary and the trumpets for signalling.

7They fought against Midian, as the LORD commanded Moses, and killed every man. 8Among their victims were Evi, Rekem, Zur, Hur and Reba—the five kings of Midian. They also killed Balaam son of Beor with the sword. 9The Israelites captured the Midianite women and children and took all the Midianite herds, flocks and goods as plunder. 10They burned all the towns where the Midianites had settled, as well as all their camps. 11They took all the plunder and spoils, including the people and animals, 12and brought the captives, spoils and plunder to Moses and Eleazar the priest and the Israelite assembly at their camp on the plains of Moab, by the Jordan across from Jericho.

13Moses, Eleazar the priest and all the leaders of the community went to meet them outside the camp. 14Moses was angry with the officers of the army —the commanders of thousands and commanders of hundreds—who returned from the battle.

15"Have you allowed all the women to live?" he asked them. 16"They were the ones who followed Balaam's advice and were the means of turning the Israelites away from the LORD in what happened at Peor, so that a plague struck the LORD's people. 17Now kill all the boys. And kill every woman who has slept with a man, 18but save for yourselves every girl who has never slept with a man.

19"All of you who have killed anyone or touched anyone who was killed must stay outside the camp seven days. On the third and seventh days you must purify yourselves and your captives. 20Purify every garment as well as everything made of leather, goat hair or wood." 21Then Eleazar the priest said to the soldiers who had gone into battle, "This is the requirement of the law that the LORD gave Moses: 22Gold, silver, bronze, iron, tin, lead 23and anything else that can withstand fire must be put through the fire, and then it will be clean. But it must also be purified with the water of cleansing. And whatever cannot withstand fire must be put through that water. 24On the seventh day wash your clothes and you will be clean. Then you may come into the camp."

NEW TESTAMENT READING
Luke 8:19–39

Jesus' Mother and Brothers

19Now Jesus' mother and brothers came to see him, but they were not able to get near him because of the crowd. 20Someone told him, "Your mother and brothers are standing outside, wanting to see you."

21He replied, "My mother and brothers are those who hear God's word and put it into practice."

Jesus Calms the Storm

22One day Jesus said to his disciples, "Let's go over to the other side of the lake." So they got into a boat and set out. 23As they sailed, he fell asleep. A squall came down on the lake, so that the boat was being swamped, and they were in great danger.

24The disciples went and woke him, saying, "Master, Master, we're going to drown!"

He got up and rebuked the wind and the raging waters; the storm subsided, and all was calm. 25"Where is your faith?" he asked his disciples.

In fear and amazement they asked one another, "Who is this? He commands even the winds and the water, and they obey him."

The Healing of a Demon-possessed Man

26They sailed to the region of the Gerasenes, which is across the lake from Galilee. 27When Jesus stepped ashore, he was met by a demon-possessed man from the town. For a long time this man had not worn clothes or lived in a house, but had lived in the tombs. 28When he saw Jesus, he cried out and fell at his feet, shouting at the top of his voice, "What do you want with me, Jesus, Son of the Most High God? I beg you, don't torture me!" 29For Jesus had commanded the evil spirit to come out of the man. Many times it had seized him, and

though he was chained hand and foot and kept under guard, he had broken his chains and had been driven by the demon into solitary places.

30Jesus asked him, "What is your name?"

"Legion," he replied, because many demons had gone into him. 31And they begged him repeatedly not to order them to go into the Abyss.

32A large herd of pigs was feeding there on the hillside. The demons begged Jesus to let them go into them, and he gave them permission. 33When the demons came out of the man, they went into the pigs, and the herd rushed down the steep bank into the lake and was drowned.

34When those tending the pigs saw what had happened, they ran off and reported this in the town and countryside, 35and the people went out to see what had happened. When they came to Jesus, they found the man from whom the demons had gone out, sitting at Jesus' feet, dressed and in his right mind; and they were afraid. 36Those who had seen it told the people how the demon-possessed man had been cured. 37Then all the people of the region of the Gerasenes asked Jesus to leave them, because they were overcome with fear. So he got into the boat and left.

38The man from whom the demons had gone out begged to go with him, but Jesus sent him away, saying, 39"Return home and tell how much God has done for you." So the man went away and told all over the town how much Jesus had done for him.

READING FROM PSALMS
Psalm 39:1–13

For the director of music. For Jeduthun. A psalm of David.

1I said, "I will watch my ways
     and keep my tongue from sin;
I will put a muzzle on my mouth
     as long as the wicked are in my
          presence."

²But when I was silent and still,
    not even saying anything good,
    my anguish increased.
³My heart grew hot within me,
    and as I meditated, the fire burned;
    then I spoke with my tongue:

⁴"Show me, O LORD, my life's end
    and the number of my days;
    let me know how fleeting is my life.
⁵You have made my days a mere
    handbreadth;
    the span of my years is as nothing
    before you.
    Each man's life is but a breath.
                                    Selah
⁶Man is a mere phantom as he goes to
    and fro:
    He bustles about, but only in vain;
    he heaps up wealth, not knowing
    who will get it.

⁷"But now, Lord, what do I look for?
    My hope is in you.

⁸Save me from all my transgressions;
    do not make me the scorn of fools.
⁹I was silent; I would not open my
    mouth,
    for you are the one who has done
    this.
¹⁰Remove your scourge from me;
    I am overcome by the blow of your
    hand.
¹¹You rebuke and discipline men for
    their sin;
    you consume their wealth like a
    moth—
    each man is but a breath.   *Selah*

¹²"Hear my prayer, O LORD,
    listen to my cry for help;
    be not deaf to my weeping.
    For I dwell with you as an alien,
    a stranger, as all my fathers were.
¹³Look away from me, that I may
    rejoice again
    before I depart and am no more."

APRIL 1

OLD TESTAMENT READING
Numbers 31:25–32:42

Dividing the Spoils

²⁵The LORD said to Moses, ²⁶"You
and Eleazar the priest and the family
heads of the community are to count all
the people and animals that were captured. ²⁷Divide the spoils between the
soldiers who took part in the battle and
the rest of the community. ²⁸From the
soldiers who fought in the battle, set
apart as tribute for the LORD one out of
every five hundred, whether persons,
cattle, donkeys, sheep or goats. ²⁹Take
this tribute from their half share and
give it to Eleazar the priest as the
LORD's part. ³⁰From the Israelites' half,
select one out of every fifty, whether
persons, cattle, donkeys, sheep, goats

or other animals. Give them to the Levites, who are responsible for the care
of the LORD's tabernacle." ³¹So Moses
and Eleazar the priest did as the LORD
commanded Moses.

³²The plunder remaining from the
spoils that the soldiers took was 675,000
sheep, ³³72,000 cattle, ³⁴61,000 donkeys
³⁵and 32,000 women who had never
slept with a man.

³⁶The half share of those who fought
in the battle was:

    337,500 sheep, ³⁷of which the tribute
        for the LORD was 675;
³⁸36,000 cattle, of which the tribute for
        the LORD was 72;
³⁹30,500 donkeys, of which the tribute
        for the LORD was 61;
⁴⁰16,000 people, of which the tribute
        for the LORD was 32.

⁴¹Moses gave the tribute to Eleazar the priest as the LORD's part, as the LORD commanded Moses.

⁴²The half belonging to the Israelites, which Moses set apart from that of the fighting men— ⁴³the community's half —was 337,500 sheep, ⁴⁴36,000 cattle, ⁴⁵30,500 donkeys ⁴⁶and 16,000 people. ⁴⁷From the Israelites' half, Moses selected one out of every fifty persons and animals, as the LORD commanded him, and gave them to the Levites, who were responsible for the care of the LORD's tabernacle.

⁴⁸Then the officers who were over the units of the army—the commanders of thousands and commanders of hundreds—went to Moses ⁴⁹and said to him, "Your servants have counted the soldiers under our command, and not one is missing. ⁵⁰So we have brought as an offering to the LORD the gold articles each of us acquired—armlets, bracelets, signet rings, ear-rings and necklaces—to make atonement for ourselves before the LORD."

⁵¹Moses and Eleazar the priest accepted from them the gold—all the handcrafted articles. ⁵²All the gold from the commanders of thousands and commanders of hundreds that Moses and Eleazar presented as a gift to the LORD weighed 16,750 shekels. ⁵³Each soldier had taken plunder for himself. ⁵⁴Moses and Eleazar the priest accepted the gold from the commanders of thousands and commanders of hundreds and brought it into the Tent of Meeting as a memorial for the Israelites before the LORD.

The Transjordan Tribes

32 The Reubenites and Gadites, who had very large herds and flocks, saw that the lands of Jazer and Gilead were suitable for livestock. ²So they came to Moses and Eleazar the priest and to the leaders of the community, and said, ³"Ataroth, Dibon, Jazer, Nimrah, Heshbon, Elealeh, Sebam, Nebo and Beon—⁴the land the LORD subdued before the people of Israel—

are suitable for livestock, and your servants have livestock. ⁵If we have found favour in your eyes," they said, "let this land be given to your servants as our possession. Do not make us cross the Jordan."

⁶Moses said to the Gadites and Reubenites, "Shall your countrymen go to war while you sit here? ⁷Why do you discourage the Israelites from going over into the land the LORD has given them? ⁸This is what your fathers did when I sent them from Kadesh Barnea to look over the land. ⁹After they went up to the Valley of Eshcol and viewed the land, they discouraged the Israelites from entering the land the LORD had given them. ¹⁰The LORD's anger was aroused that day and he swore this oath: ¹¹'Because they have not followed me wholeheartedly, not one of the men twenty years old or more who came up out of Egypt will see the land I promised on oath to Abraham, Isaac and Jacob —¹²not one except Caleb son of Jephunneh the Kenizzite and Joshua son of Nun, for they followed the LORD wholeheartedly.' ¹³The LORD's anger burned against Israel and he made them wander in the desert for forty years, until the whole generation of those who had done evil in his sight was gone.

¹⁴"And here you are, a brood of sinners, standing in the place of your fathers and making the LORD even more angry with Israel. ¹⁵If you turn away from following him, he will again leave all this people in the desert, and you will be the cause of their destruction."

¹⁶Then they came up to him and said, "We would like to build pens here for our livestock and cities for our women and children. ¹⁷But we are ready to arm ourselves and go ahead of the Israelites until we have brought them to their place. Meanwhile our women and children will live in fortified cities, for protection from the inhabitants of the land. ¹⁸We will not return to our homes until every Israelite has received his inheritance. ¹⁹We will not receive any inheritance with them on the other side of

the Jordan, because our inheritance has come to us on the east side of the Jordan."

²⁰Then Moses said to them, "If you will do this—if you will arm yourselves before the LORD for battle, ²¹and if all of you will go armed over the Jordan before the LORD until he has driven his enemies out before him—²²then when the land is subdued before the LORD, you may return and be free from your obligation to the LORD and to Israel. And this land will be your possession before the LORD.

²³"But if you fail to do this, you will be sinning against the LORD; and you may be sure that your sin will find you out. ²⁴Build cities for your women and children, and pens for your flocks, but do what you have promised."

²⁵The Gadites and Reubenites said to Moses, "We your servants will do as our lord commands. ²⁶Our children and wives, our flocks and herds will remain here in the cities of Gilead. ²⁷But your servants, every man armed for battle, will cross over to fight before the LORD, just as our lord says."

²⁸Then Moses gave orders about them to Eleazar the priest and Joshua son of Nun and to the family heads of the Israelite tribes. ²⁹He said to them, "If the Gadites and Reubenites, every man armed for battle, cross over the Jordan with you before the LORD, then when the land is subdued before you, give them the land of Gilead as their possession. ³⁰But if they do not cross over with you armed, they must accept their possession with you in Canaan."

³¹The Gadites and Reubenites answered, "Your servants will do what the LORD has said. ³²We will cross over before the LORD into Canaan armed, but the property we inherit will be on this side of the Jordan."

³³Then Moses gave to the Gadites, the Reubenites and the half-tribe of Manasseh son of Joseph the kingdom of Sihon king of the Amorites and the kingdom of Og king of Bashan—the whole land with its cities and the territory around them.

³⁴The Gadites built up Dibon, Ataroth, Aroer, ³⁵Atroth Shophan, Jazer, Jogbehah, ³⁶Beth Nimrah and Beth Haran as fortified cities, and built pens for their flocks. ³⁷And the Reubenites rebuilt Heshbon, Elealeh and Kiriathaim, ³⁸as well as Nebo and Baal Meon (these names were changed) and Sibmah. They gave names to the cities they rebuilt.

³⁹The descendants of Makir son of Manasseh went to Gilead, captured it and drove out the Amorites who were there. ⁴⁰So Moses gave Gilead to the Makirites, the descendants of Manasseh, and they settled there. ⁴¹Jair, a descendant of Manasseh, captured their settlements and called them Havvoth Jair. ⁴²And Nobah captured Kenath and its surrounding settlements and called it Nobah after himself.

NEW TESTAMENT READING
Luke 8:40–9:9

A Dead Girl and a Sick Woman

⁴⁰Now when Jesus returned, a crowd welcomed him, for they were all expecting him. ⁴¹Then a man named Jairus, a ruler of the synagogue, came and fell at Jesus' feet, pleading with him to come to his house ⁴²because his only daughter, a girl of about twelve, was dying.

As Jesus was on his way, the crowds almost crushed him. ⁴³And a woman was there who had been subject to bleeding for twelve years, but no-one could heal her. ⁴⁴She came up behind him and touched the edge of his cloak, and immediately her bleeding stopped.

⁴⁵"Who touched me?" Jesus asked.

When they all denied it, Peter said, "Master, the people are crowding and pressing against you."

⁴⁶But Jesus said, "Someone touched me; I know that power has gone out from me."

⁴⁷Then the woman, seeing that she

could not go unnoticed, came trembling and fell at his feet. In the presence of all the people, she told why she had touched him and how she had been instantly healed. 48Then he said to her, "Daughter, your faith has healed you. Go in peace."

49While Jesus was still speaking, someone came from the house of Jairus, the synagogue ruler. "Your daughter is dead," he said. "Don't bother the teacher any more."

50Hearing this, Jesus said to Jairus, "Don't be afraid; just believe, and she will be healed."

51When he arrived at the house of Jairus, he did not let anyone go in with him except Peter, John and James, and the child's father and mother. 52Meanwhile, all the people were wailing and mourning for her. "Stop wailing," Jesus said. "She is not dead but asleep."

53They laughed at him, knowing that she was dead. 54But he took her by the hand and said, "My child, get up!" 55Her spirit returned, and at once she stood up. Then Jesus told them to give her something to eat. 56Her parents were astonished, but he ordered them not to tell anyone what had happened.

Jesus Sends Out the Twelve

9 When Jesus had called the Twelve together, he gave them power and authority to drive out all demons and to cure diseases, 2and he sent them out to preach the kingdom of God and to heal the sick. 3He told them: "Take nothing for the journey—no staff, no bag, no bread, no money, no extra tunic. 4Whatever house you enter, stay there until you leave that town. 5If people do not welcome you, shake the dust off your feet when you leave their town, as a testimony against them." 6So they set out and went from village to village, preaching the gospel and healing people everywhere.

7Now Herod the tetrarch heard about all that was going on. And he was perplexed, because some were saying that John had been raised from the dead, 8others that Elijah had appeared, and still others that one of the prophets of long ago had come back to life. 9But Herod said, "I beheaded John. Who, then, is this I hear such things about?" And he tried to see him.

READING FROM PSALMS
Psalm 40:1–8

*For the director of music. Of David.
A psalm.*

1I waited patiently for the LORD;
   he turned to me and heard my cry.
2He lifted me out of the slimy pit,
   out of the mud and mire;
he set my feet on a rock
   and gave me a firm place to stand.
3He put a new song in my mouth,
   a hymn of praise to our God.
Many will see and fear
   and put their trust in the LORD.

4Blessed is the man
   who makes the LORD his trust,
who does not look to the proud,
   to those who turn aside to false
      gods.
5Many, O LORD my God,
   are the wonders you have done.
The things you planned for us
   no-one can recount to you;
were I to speak and tell of them,
   they would be too many to declare.

6Sacrifice and offering you did not
      desire,
   but my ears you have pierced;
burnt offerings and sin offerings
   you did not require.
7Then I said, "Here I am, I have
      come—
   it is written about me in the scroll.
8I desire to do your will, O my God;
   your law is within my heart."

APRIL 2

OLD TESTAMENT READING
Numbers 33:1–34:29

Stages in Israel's Journey

33 Here are the stages in the journey of the Israelites when they came out of Egypt by divisions under the leadership of Moses and Aaron. ²At the LORD's command Moses recorded the stages in their journey. This is their journey by stages:

³The Israelites set out from Rameses on the fifteenth day of the first month, the day after the Passover. They marched out boldly in full view of all the Egyptians, ⁴who were burying all their firstborn, whom the LORD had struck down among them; for the LORD had brought judgment on their gods.

⁵The Israelites left Rameses and camped at Succoth.

⁶They left Succoth and camped at Etham, on the edge of the desert.

⁷They left Etham, turned back to Pi Hahiroth, to the east of Baal Zephon, and camped near Migdol.

⁸They left Pi Hahiroth and passed through the sea into the desert, and when they had travelled for three days in the Desert of Etham, they camped at Marah.

⁹They left Marah and went to Elim, where there were twelve springs and seventy palm trees, and they camped there.

¹⁰They left Elim and camped by the Red Sea.

¹¹They left the Red Sea and camped in the Desert of Sin.

¹²They left the Desert of Sin and camped at Dophkah.

¹³They left Dophkah and camped at Alush.

¹⁴They left Alush and camped at Rephidim, where there was no water for the people to drink.

¹⁵They left Rephidim and camped in the Desert of Sinai.

¹⁶They left the Desert of Sinai and camped at Kibroth Hattaavah.

¹⁷They left Kibroth Hattaavah and camped at Hazeroth.

¹⁸They left Hazeroth and camped at Rithmah.

¹⁹They left Rithmah and camped at Rimmon Perez.

²⁰They left Rimmon Perez and camped at Libnah.

²¹They left Libnah and camped at Rissah.

²²They left Rissah and camped at Kehelathah.

²³They left Kehelathah and camped at Mount Shepher.

²⁴They left Mount Shepher and camped at Haradah.

²⁵They left Haradah and camped at Makheloth.

²⁶They left Makheloth and camped at Tahath.

²⁷They left Tahath and camped at Terah.

²⁸They left Terah and camped at Mithcah.

²⁹They left Mithcah and camped at Hashmonah.

³⁰They left Hashmonah and camped at Moseroth.

³¹They left Moseroth and camped at Bene Jaakan.

³²They left Bene Jaakan and camped at Hor Haggidgad.

³³They left Hor Haggidgad and camped at Jotbathah.

³⁴They left Jotbathah and camped at Abronah.

³⁵They left Abronah and camped at Ezion Geber.

³⁶They left Ezion Geber and camped at Kadesh, in the Desert of Zin.

³⁷They left Kadesh and camped at Mount Hor, on the border of Edom. ³⁸At the LORD's command Aaron the priest went up Mount Hor, where he died on the first day of the fifth month of the fortieth year after the Israelites came out of Egypt. ³⁹Aaron was a hundred and twenty-three years old when he died on Mount Hor.

⁴⁰The Canaanite king of Arad, who lived in the Negev of Canaan, heard that the Israelites were coming.

⁴¹They left Mount Hor and camped at Zalmonah.

⁴²They left Zalmonah and camped at Punon.

⁴³They left Punon and camped at Oboth.

⁴⁴They left Oboth and camped at Iye Abarim, on the border of Moab.

⁴⁵They left Iyim and camped at Dibon Gad.

⁴⁶They left Dibon Gad and camped at Almon Diblathaim.

⁴⁷They left Almon Diblathaim and camped in the mountains of Abarim, near Nebo.

⁴⁸They left the mountains of Abarim and camped on the plains of Moab by the Jordan across from Jericho. ⁴⁹There on the plains of Moab they camped along the Jordan from Beth Jeshimoth to Abel Shittim.

⁵⁰On the plains of Moab by the Jordan across from Jericho the LORD said to Moses, ⁵¹"Speak to the Israelites and say to them: 'When you cross the Jordan into Canaan, ⁵²drive out all the inhabitants of the land before you. Destroy all their carved images and their cast idols, and demolish all their high places. ⁵³Take possession of the land and settle in it, for I have given you the land to possess. ⁵⁴Distribute the land by lot, according to your clans. To a larger group give a larger inheritance, and to a smaller group a smaller one. Whatever

falls to them by lot will be theirs. Distribute it according to your ancestral tribes.

⁵⁵"'But if you do not drive out the inhabitants of the land, those you allow to remain will become barbs in your eyes and thorns in your sides. They will give you trouble in the land where you will live. ⁵⁶And then I will do to you what I plan to do to them.'"

Boundaries of Canaan

34 The LORD said to Moses, ²"Command the Israelites and say to them: 'When you enter Canaan, the land that will be allotted to you as an inheritance will have these boundaries:

³"'Your southern side will include some of the Desert of Zin along the border of Edom. On the east, your southern boundary will start from the end of the Salt Sea, ⁴cross south of Scorpion Pass, continue on to Zin and go south of Kadesh Barnea. Then it will go to Hazar Addar and over to Azmon, ⁵where it will turn, join the Wadi of Egypt and end at the Sea.

⁶"'Your western boundary will be the coast of the Great Sea. This will be your boundary on the west.

⁷"'For your northern boundary, run a line from the Great Sea to Mount Hor ⁸and from Mount Hor to Lebo Hamath. Then the boundary will go to Zedad, ⁹continue to Ziphron and end at Hazar Enan. This will be your boundary on the north.

¹⁰"'For your eastern boundary, run a line from Hazar Enan to Shepham. ¹¹The boundary will go down from Shepham to Riblah on the east side of Ain and continue along the slopes east of the Sea of Kinnereth. ¹²Then the boundary will go down along the Jordan and end at the Salt Sea.

"'This will be your land, with its boundaries on every side.'"

¹³Moses commanded the Israelites: "Assign this land by lot as an inheritance. The LORD has ordered that it be given to the nine and a half tribes,

14because the families of the tribe of Reuben, the tribe of Gad and the half-tribe of Manasseh have received their inheritance. 15These two and a half tribes have received their inheritance on the east side of the Jordan of Jericho, towards the sunrise."

16The LORD said to Moses, 17"These are the names of the men who are to assign the land for you as an inheritance: Eleazar the priest and Joshua son of Nun. 18And appoint one leader from each tribe to help assign the land. 19These are their names:

Caleb son of Jephunneh,
    from the tribe of Judah;
20Shemuel son of Ammihud,
    from the tribe of Simeon;
21Elidad son of Kislon,
    from the tribe of Benjamin;
22Bukki son of Jogli,
    the leader from the tribe of Dan;
23Hanniel son of Ephod,
    the leader from the tribe of Manasseh son of Joseph;
24Kemuel son of Shiphtan,
    the leader from the tribe of Ephraim son of Joseph;
25Elizaphan son of Parnach,
    the leader from the tribe of Zebulun;
26Paltiel son of Azzan,
    the leader from the tribe of Issachar;
27Ahihud son of Shelomi,
    the leader from the tribe of Asher;
28Pedahel son of Ammihud,
    the leader from the tribe of Naphtali."

29These are the men the LORD commanded to assign the inheritance to the Israelites in the land of Canaan.

NEW TESTAMENT READING
Luke 9:10–27

Jesus Feeds the Five Thousand

10When the apostles returned, they reported to Jesus what they had done. Then he took them with him and they withdrew by themselves to a town called Bethsaida, 11but the crowds learned about it and followed him. He welcomed them and spoke to them about the kingdom of God, and healed those who needed healing.

12Late in the afternoon the Twelve came to him and said, "Send the crowd away so they can go to the surrounding villages and countryside and find food and lodging, because we are in a remote place here."

13He replied, "You give them something to eat."

They answered, "We have only five loaves of bread and two fish—unless we go and buy food for all this crowd." 14(About five thousand men were there.)

But he said to his disciples, "Make them sit down in groups of about fifty each." 15The disciples did so, and everybody sat down. 16Taking the five loaves and the two fish and looking up to heaven, he gave thanks and broke them. Then he gave them to the disciples to set before the people. 17They all ate and were satisfied, and the disciples picked up twelve basketfuls of broken pieces that were left over.

Peter's Confession of Christ

18Once when Jesus was praying in private and his disciples were with him, he asked them, "Who do the crowds say I am?"

19They replied, "Some say John the Baptist; others say Elijah; and still others, that one of the prophets of long ago has come back to life."

20"But what about you?" he asked. "Who do you say I am?"

Peter answered, "The Christ of God."

21Jesus strictly warned them not to tell this to anyone. 22And he said, "The Son of Man must suffer many things and be rejected by the elders, chief priests and teachers of the law, and he must be killed and on the third day be raised to life."

23Then he said to them all: "If anyone would come after me, he must deny himself and take up his cross daily and follow me. 24For whoever wants to save his life will lose it, but whoever loses his life will save it. 25What good is it for a man to gain the whole world, and yet lose or forfeit his very self? 26If anyone is ashamed of me and my words, the Son of Man will be ashamed of him when he comes in his glory and in the glory of the Father and of the holy angels. 27I tell you the truth, some who are standing here will not taste death before they see the kingdom of God."

READING FROM PROVERBS
Proverbs 8:22–31

22"The LORD brought me forth as the
    first of his works,
  before his deeds of old;
23I was appointed from eternity,
  from the beginning, before the
    world began.

24When there were no oceans, I was
    given birth,
  when there were no springs
    abounding with water;
25before the mountains were settled in
    place,
  before the hills, I was given birth,
26before he made the earth or its fields
  or any of the dust of the world.
27I was there when he set the heavens
    in place,
  when he marked out the horizon
    on the face of the deep,
28when he established the clouds above
  and fixed securely the fountains of
    the deep,
29when he gave the sea its boundary
    so that the waters would not
      overstep his command,
  and when he marked out the
    foundations of the earth.
30   Then I was the craftsman at his
      side.
  I was filled with delight day after day,
    rejoicing always in his presence,
31rejoicing in his whole world
  and delighting in mankind.

APRIL 3   DAY 93

OLD TESTAMENT READING
Numbers 35:1–36:13

Towns for the Levites

35 On the plains of Moab by the Jordan across from Jericho, the LORD said to Moses, 2"Command the Israelites to give the Levites towns to live in from the inheritance the Israelites will possess. And give them pasture-lands around the towns. 3Then they will have towns to live in and pasture-lands for their cattle, flocks and all their other livestock.

4"The pasture-lands around the towns that you give the Levites will extend out fifteen hundred feet from the town wall. 5Outside the town, measure three thousand feet on the east side, three thousand on the south side, three thousand on the west and three thousand on the north, with the town in the centre. They will have this area as pasture-land for the towns.

Cities of Refuge

6"Six of the towns you give the Levites will be cities of refuge, to which a person who has killed someone may flee. In addition, give them forty-two other towns. 7In all you must give the Levites forty-eight towns, together with their pasture-lands. ⁸The towns you give the Levites from the land the Israelites possess are to be given in proportion to the inheritance of each tribe: Take many towns from a tribe that has many, but few from one that has few."

⁹Then the LORD said to Moses: ¹⁰"Speak to the Israelites and say to them: 'When you cross the Jordan into Canaan, ¹¹select some towns to be your cities of refuge, to which a person who has killed someone accidentally may flee. ¹²They will be places of refuge from the avenger, so that a person accused of murder may not die before he stands trial before the assembly. ¹³These six towns you give will be your cities of refuge. ¹⁴Give three on this side of the Jordan and three in Canaan as cities of refuge. ¹⁵These six towns will be a place of refuge for Israelites, aliens and any other people living among them, so that anyone who has killed another accidentally can flee there.

¹⁶"If a man strikes someone with an iron object so that he dies, he is a murderer; the murderer shall be put to death. ¹⁷Or if anyone has a stone in his hand that could kill, and he strikes someone so that he dies, he is a murderer; the murderer shall be put to death. ¹⁸Or if anyone has a wooden object in his hand that could kill, and he hits someone so that he dies, he is a murderer; the murderer shall be put to death. ¹⁹The avenger of blood shall put the murderer to death; when he meets him, he shall put him to death. ²⁰If anyone with malice aforethought pushes another or throws something at him intentionally so that he dies ²¹or if in hostility he hits him with his fist so that he dies, that person shall be put to death; he is a murderer. The avenger of blood shall put the murderer to death when he meets him.

²²"But if without hostility someone suddenly pushes another or throws something at him unintentionally ²³or, without seeing him, drops a stone on him that could kill him, and he dies,

then since he was not his enemy and he did not intend to harm him, ²⁴the assembly must judge between him and the avenger of blood according to these regulations. ²⁵The assembly must protect the one accused of murder from the avenger of blood and send him back to the city of refuge to which he fled. He must stay there until the death of the high priest, who was anointed with holy oil.

²⁶"But if the accused ever goes outside the limits of the city of refuge to which he has fled ²⁷and the avenger of blood finds him outside the city, the avenger of blood may kill the accused without being guilty of murder. ²⁸The accused must stay in his city of refuge until the death of the high priest; only after the death of the high priest may he return to his own property.

²⁹"These are to be legal requirements for you throughout the generations to come, wherever you live.

³⁰"Anyone who kills a person is to be put to death as a murderer only on the testimony of witnesses. But no-one is to be put to death on the testimony of only one witness.

³¹"Do not accept a ransom for the life of a murderer, who deserves to die. He must surely be put to death.

³²"Do not accept a ransom for anyone who has fled to a city of refuge and so allow him to go back and live on his own land before the death of the high priest.

³³"Do not pollute the land where you are. Bloodshed pollutes the land, and atonement cannot be made for the land on which blood has been shed, except by the blood of the one who shed it. ³⁴Do not defile the land where you live and where I dwell, for I, the LORD, dwell among the Israelites.'"

Inheritance of Zelophehad's Daughters

36 The family heads of the clan of Gilead son of Makir, the son of Manasseh, who were from the clans of the descendants of Joseph, came and spoke before Moses and the leaders, the heads of the Israelite families. ²They said, "When the LORD commanded my lord to give the land as an inheritance to the Israelites by lot, he ordered you to give the inheritance of our brother Zelophehad to his daughters. ³Now suppose they marry men from other Israelite tribes; then their inheritance will be taken from our ancestral inheritance and added to that of the tribe they marry into. And so part of the inheritance allotted to us will be taken away. ⁴When the Year of Jubilee for the Israelites comes, their inheritance will be added to that of the tribe into which they marry, and their property will be taken from the tribal inheritance of our forefathers."

⁵Then at the LORD's command Moses gave this order to the Israelites: "What the tribe of the descendants of Joseph is saying is right. ⁶This is what the LORD commands for Zelophehad's daughters: They may marry anyone they please as long as they marry within the tribal clan of their father. ⁷No inheritance in Israel is to pass from tribe to tribe, for every Israelite shall keep the tribal land inherited from his forefathers. ⁸Every daughter who inherits land in any Israelite tribe must marry someone in her father's tribal clan, so that every Israelite will possess the inheritance of his fathers. ⁹No inheritance may pass from tribe to tribe, for each Israelite tribe is to keep the land it inherits."

¹⁰So Zelophehad's daughters did as the LORD commanded Moses. ¹¹Zelophehad's daughters—Mahlah, Tirzah, Hoglah, Milcah and Noah—married their cousins on their father's side. ¹²They married within the clans of the descendants of Manasseh son of Joseph, and their inheritance remained in their father's clan and tribe.

¹³These are the commands and regulations the LORD gave through Moses to the Israelites on the plains of Moab by the Jordan across from Jericho.

NEW TESTAMENT READING
Luke 9:28–56

The Transfiguration

²⁸About eight days after Jesus said this, he took Peter, John and James with him and went up onto a mountain to pray. ²⁹As he was praying, the appearance of his face changed, and his clothes became as bright as a flash of lightning. ³⁰Two men, Moses and Elijah, ³¹appeared in glorious splendour, talking with Jesus. They spoke about his departure, which he was about to bring to fulfilment at Jerusalem. ³²Peter and his companions were very sleepy, but when they became fully awake, they saw his glory and the two men standing with him. ³³As the men were leaving Jesus, Peter said to him, "Master, it is good for us to be here. Let us put up three shelters—one for you, one for Moses and one for Elijah." (He did not know what he was saying.)

³⁴While he was speaking, a cloud appeared and enveloped them, and they were afraid as they entered the cloud. ³⁵A voice came from the cloud, saying, "This is my Son, whom I have chosen; listen to him." ³⁶When the voice had spoken, they found that Jesus was alone. The disciples kept this to themselves, and told no-one at that time what they had seen.

The Healing of a Boy With an Evil Spirit

³⁷The next day, when they came down from the mountain, a large crowd met him. ³⁸A man in the crowd called out, "Teacher, I beg you to look at my son, for he is my only child. ³⁹A spirit seizes him and he suddenly screams; it throws him into convulsions so that he foams at the mouth. It scarcely ever leaves him and is destroying him. ⁴⁰I begged your disciples to drive it out, but they could not."

⁴¹"O unbelieving and perverse generation," Jesus replied, "how long shall

I stay with you and put up with you? Bring your son here."

42Even while the boy was coming, the demon threw him to the ground in a convulsion. But Jesus rebuked the evil spirit, healed the boy and gave him back to his father. 43And they were all amazed at the greatness of God.

While everyone was marvelling at all that Jesus did, he said to his disciples, 44"Listen carefully to what I am about to tell you: The Son of Man is going to be betrayed into the hands of men." 45But they did not understand what this meant. It was hidden from them, so that they did not grasp it, and they were afraid to ask him about it.

Who Will Be the Greatest?

46An argument started among the disciples as to which of them would be the greatest. 47Jesus, knowing their thoughts, took a little child and made him stand beside him. 48Then he said to them, "Whoever welcomes this little child in my name welcomes me; and whoever welcomes me welcomes the one who sent me. For he who is least among you all—he is the greatest."

49"Master," said John, "we saw a man driving out demons in your name and we tried to stop him, because he is not one of us."

50"Do not stop him," Jesus said, "for whoever is not against you is for you."

Samaritan Opposition

51As the time approached for him to be taken up to heaven, Jesus resolutely set out for Jerusalem. 52And he sent messengers on ahead, who went into a Samaritan village to get things ready for him; 53but the people there did not welcome him, because he was heading for Jerusalem. 54When the disciples James and John saw this, they asked, "Lord, do you want us to call fire down from

heaven to destroy them?" 55But Jesus turned and rebuked them, 56and they went to another village.

READING FROM PSALMS
Psalm 40:9–17

9I proclaim righteousness in the great assembly;
  I do not seal my lips,
    as you know, O LORD.
10I do not hide your righteousness in my heart;
  I speak of your faithfulness and salvation.
  I do not conceal your love and your truth
    from the great assembly.

11Do not withhold your mercy from me, O LORD;
  may your love and your truth always protect me.
12For troubles without number surround me;
  my sins have overtaken me, and I cannot see.
  They are more than the hairs of my head,
    and my heart fails within me.

13Be pleased, O LORD, to save me;
  O LORD, come quickly to help me.
14May all who seek to take my life be put to shame and confusion;
  may all who desire my ruin be turned back in disgrace.
15May those who say to me, "Aha! Aha!"
  be appalled at their own shame.
16But may all who seek you rejoice and be glad in you;
  may those who love your salvation always say,
    "The LORD be exalted!"

17Yet I am poor and needy;
  may the Lord think of me.
  You are my help and my deliverer;
  O my God, do not delay.

OLD TESTAMENT READING
Deuteronomy 1:1–2:23

The Command to Leave Horeb

1 These are the words Moses spoke to all Israel in the desert east of the Jordan—that is, in the Arabah—opposite Suph, between Paran and Tophel, Laban, Hazeroth and Dizahab. ²(It takes eleven days to go from Horeb to Kadesh Barnea by the Mount Seir road.)

³In the fortieth year, on the first day of the eleventh month, Moses proclaimed to the Israelites all that the LORD had commanded him concerning them. ⁴This was after he had defeated Sihon king of the Amorites, who reigned in Heshbon, and at Edrei had defeated Og king of Bashan, who reigned in Ashtaroth.

⁵East of the Jordan in the territory of Moab, Moses began to expound this law, saying:

⁶The LORD our God said to us at Horeb, "You have stayed long enough at this mountain. ⁷Break camp and advance into the hill country of the Amorites; go to all the neighbouring peoples in the Arabah, in the mountains, in the western foothills, in the Negev and along the coast, to the land of the Canaanites and to Lebanon, as far as the great river, the Euphrates. ⁸See, I have given you this land. Go in and take possession of the land that the LORD swore he would give to your fathers—to Abraham, Isaac and Jacob—and to their descendants after them."

The Appointment of Leaders

⁹At that time I said to you, "You are too heavy a burden for me to carry alone. ¹⁰The LORD your God has increased your numbers so that today you are as many as the stars in the sky.

¹¹May the LORD, the God of your fathers, increase you a thousand times and bless you as he has promised! ¹²But how can I bear your problems and your burdens and your disputes all by myself? ¹³Choose some wise, understanding and respected men from each of your tribes, and I will set them over you."

¹⁴You answered me, "What you propose to do is good."

¹⁵So I took the leading men of your tribes, wise and respected men, and appointed them to have authority over you—as commanders of thousands, of hundreds, of fifties and of tens and as tribal officials. ¹⁶And I charged your judges at that time: Hear the disputes between your brothers and judge fairly, whether the case is between brother Israelites or between one of them and an alien. ¹⁷Do not show partiality in judging; hear both small and great alike. Do not be afraid of any man, for judgment belongs to God. Bring me any case too hard for you, and I will hear it. ¹⁸And at that time I told you everything you were to do.

Spies Sent Out

¹⁹Then, as the LORD our God commanded us, we set out from Horeb and went towards the hill country of the Amorites through all that vast and dreadful desert that you have seen, and so we reached Kadesh Barnea. ²⁰Then I said to you, "You have reached the hill country of the Amorites, which the LORD our God is giving us. ²¹See, the LORD your God has given you the land. Go up and take possession of it as the LORD, the God of your fathers, told you. Do not be afraid; do not be discouraged."

²²Then all of you came to me and said, "Let us send men ahead to spy out the land for us and bring back a report

about the route we are to take and the towns we will come to."

23The idea seemed good to me; so I selected twelve of you, one man from each tribe. 24They left and went up into the hill country, and came to the Valley of Eshcol and explored it. 25Taking with them some of the fruit of the land, they brought it down to us and reported, "It is a good land that the LORD our God is giving us."

Rebellion Against the LORD

26But you were unwilling to go up; you rebelled against the command of the LORD your God. 27You grumbled in your tents and said, "The LORD hates us; so he brought us out of Egypt to deliver us into the hands of the Amorites to destroy us. 28Where can we go? Our brothers have made us lose heart. They say, 'The people are stronger and taller than we are; the cities are large, with walls up to the sky. We even saw the Anakites there.'"

29Then I said to you, "Do not be terrified; do not be afraid of them. 30The LORD your God, who is going before you, will fight for you, as he did for you in Egypt, before your very eyes, 31and in the desert. There you saw how the LORD your God carried you, as a father carries his son, all the way you went until you reached this place."

32In spite of this, you did not trust in the LORD your God, 33who went ahead of you on your journey, in fire by night and in a cloud by day, to search out places for you to camp and to show you the way you should go.

34When the LORD heard what you said, he was angry and solemnly swore: 35"Not a man of this evil generation shall see the good land I swore to give your forefathers, 36except Caleb son of Jephunneh. He will see it, and I will give him and his descendants the land he set his feet on, because he followed the LORD wholeheartedly."

37Because of you the LORD became angry with me also and said, "You shall not enter it, either. 38But your assistant,

Joshua son of Nun, will enter it. Encourage him, because he will lead Israel to inherit it. 39And the little ones that you said would be taken captive, your children who do not yet know good from bad—they will enter the land. I will give it to them and they will take possession of it. 40But as for you, turn round and set out towards the desert along the route to the Red Sea."

41Then you replied, "We have sinned against the LORD. We will go up and fight, as the LORD our God commanded us." So every one of you put on his weapons, thinking it easy to go up into the hill country.

42But the LORD said to me, "Tell them, 'Do not go up and fight, because I will not be with you. You will be defeated by your enemies.'"

43So I told you, but you would not listen. You rebelled against the LORD's command and in your arrogance you marched up into the hill country. 44The Amorites who lived in those hills came out against you; they chased you like a swarm of bees and beat you down from Seir all the way to Hormah. 45You came back and wept before the LORD, but he paid no attention to your weeping and turned a deaf ear to you. 46And so you stayed in Kadesh many days—all the time you spent there.

Wanderings in the Desert

2 Then we turned back and set out towards the desert along the route to the Red Sea, as the LORD had directed me. For a long time we made our way around the hill country of Seir.

2Then the LORD said to me, 3"You have made your way around this hill country long enough; now turn north. 4Give the people these orders: 'You are about to pass through the territory of your brothers the descendants of Esau, who live in Seir. They will be afraid of you, but be very careful. 5Do not provoke them to war, for I will not give you any of their land, not even enough to put your foot on. I have given Esau the hill country of Seir as his own. 6You are to pay them in silver for the food you eat and the water you drink.'"

7The LORD your God has blessed you in all the work of your hands. He has watched over your journey through this vast desert. These forty years the LORD your God has been with you, and you have not lacked anything.

8So we went on past our brothers the descendants of Esau, who live in Seir. We turned from the Arabah road, which comes up from Elath and Ezion Geber, and travelled along the desert road of Moab.

9Then the LORD said to me, "Do not harass the Moabites or provoke them to war, for I will not give you any part of their land. I have given Ar to the descendants of Lot as a possession."

10(The Emites used to live there—a people strong and numerous, and as tall as the Anakites. 11Like the Anakites, they too were considered Rephaites, but the Moabites called them Emites. 12Horites used to live in Seir, but the descendants of Esau drove them out. They destroyed the Horites from before them and settled in their place, just as Israel did in the land the LORD gave them as their possession.)

13And the LORD said, "Now get up and cross the Zered Valley." So we crossed the valley.

14Thirty-eight years passed from the time we left Kadesh Barnea until we crossed the Zered Valley. By then, that entire generation of fighting men had perished from the camp, as the LORD had sworn to them. 15The LORD's hand was against them until he had completely eliminated them from the camp.

16Now when the last of these fighting men among the people had died, 17the LORD said to me, 18"Today you are to pass by the region of Moab at Ar. 19When you come to the Ammonites, do not harass them or provoke them to war, for I will not give you possession of any land belonging to the Ammonites. I have given it as a possession to the descendants of Lot."

20(That too was considered a land of the Rephaites, who used to live there; but the Ammonites called them Zamzummites. 21They were a people strong and numerous, and as tall as the Anakites. The LORD destroyed them from before the Ammonites, who drove them out and settled in their place. 22The LORD had done the same for the descendants of Esau, who lived in Seir, when he destroyed the Horites from before them. They drove them out and have lived in their place to this day. 23And as for the Avvites who lived in villages as far as Gaza, the Caphtorites coming out from Caphtor destroyed them and settled in their place.)

NEW TESTAMENT READING
Luke 9:57–10:24

The Cost of Following Jesus

57As they were walking along the road, a man said to him, "I will follow you wherever you go."

58Jesus replied, "Foxes have holes and birds of the air have nests, but the Son of Man has nowhere to lay his head."

59He said to another man, "Follow me."

But the man replied, "Lord, first let me go and bury my father."

60Jesus said to him, "Let the dead bury their own dead, but you go and proclaim the kingdom of God."

61Still another said, "I will follow you, Lord; but first let me go back and say good-bye to my family."

62Jesus replied, "No-one who puts his hand to the plough and looks back is fit for service in the kingdom of God."

Jesus Sends Out the Seventy-two

10 After this the Lord appointed seventy-two others and sent them two by two ahead of him to every town and place where he was about to go. 2He told them, "The harvest is plentiful, but the workers are few. Ask the Lord of the harvest, therefore, to send out workers into his harvest field. ³Go! I am sending you out like lambs among wolves. ⁴Do not take a purse or bag or sandals; and do not greet anyone on the road.

⁵"When you enter a house, first say, 'Peace to this house.' ⁶If a man of peace is there, your peace will rest on him; if not, it will return to you. ⁷Stay in that house, eating and drinking whatever they give you, for the worker deserves his wages. Do not move around from house to house.

⁸"When you enter a town and are welcomed, eat what is set before you. ⁹Heal the sick who are there and tell them, 'The kingdom of God is near you.' ¹⁰But when you enter a town and are not welcomed, go into its streets and say, ¹¹'Even the dust of your town that sticks to our feet we wipe off against you. Yet be sure of this: The kingdom of God is near.' ¹²I tell you, it will be more bearable on that day for Sodom than for that town.

¹³"Woe to you, Korazin! Woe to you, Bethsaida! For if the miracles that were performed in you had been performed in Tyre and Sidon, they would have repented long ago, sitting in sackcloth and ashes. ¹⁴But it will be more bearable for Tyre and Sidon at the judgment than for you. ¹⁵And you, Capernaum, will you be lifted up to the skies? No, you will go down to the depths.

¹⁶"He who listens to you listens to me; he who rejects you rejects me; but he who rejects me rejects him who sent me."

¹⁷The seventy-two returned with joy and said, "Lord, even the demons submit to us in your name."

¹⁸He replied, "I saw Satan fall like lightning from heaven. ¹⁹I have given you authority to trample on snakes and scorpions and to overcome all the power of the enemy; nothing will harm you. ²⁰However, do not rejoice that the spirits submit to you, but rejoice that your names are written in heaven."

²¹At that time Jesus, full of joy through the Holy Spirit, said, "I praise you, Father, Lord of heaven and earth, because you have hidden these things from the wise and learned, and revealed them to little children. Yes, Father, for this was your good pleasure.

²²"All things have been committed to me by my Father. No-one knows who the Son is except the Father, and no-one knows who the Father is except the Son and those to whom the Son chooses to reveal him."

²³Then he turned to his disciples and said privately, "Blessed are the eyes that see what you see. ²⁴For I tell you that many prophets and kings wanted to see what you see but did not see it, and to hear what you hear but did not hear it."

READING FROM PSALMS
Psalm 41:1–6

For the director of music. A psalm of David.

¹Blessed is he who has regard for the weak;
the LORD delivers him in times of trouble.
²The LORD will protect him and preserve his life;
he will bless him in the land
and not surrender him to the desire of his foes.
³The LORD will sustain him on his sick-bed
and restore him from his bed of illness.

⁴I said, "O LORD, have mercy on me;
heal me, for I have sinned against you."
⁵My enemies say of me in malice,
"When will he die and his name perish?"
⁶Whenever one comes to see me,
he speaks falsely, while his heart gathers slander;
then he goes out and spreads it abroad.

OLD TESTAMENT READING
Deuteronomy 2:24—4:14

Defeat of Sihon King of Heshbon

24"Set out now and cross the Arnon Gorge. See, I have given into your hand Sihon the Amorite, king of Heshbon, and his country. Begin to take possession of it and engage him in battle. 25This very day I will begin to put the terror and fear of you on all the nations under heaven. They will hear reports of you and will tremble and be in anguish because of you."

26From the desert of Kedemoth I sent messengers to Sihon king of Heshbon offering peace and saying, 27"Let us pass through your country. We will stay on the main road; we will not turn aside to the right or to the left. 28Sell us food to eat and water to drink for their price in silver. Only let us pass through on foot—29as the descendants of Esau, who live in Seir, and the Moabites, who live in Ar, did for us—until we cross the Jordan into the land the LORD our God is giving us." 30But Sihon king of Heshbon refused to let us pass through. For the LORD your God had made his spirit stubborn and his heart obstinate in order to give him into your hands, as he has now done.

31The LORD said to me, "See, I have begun to deliver Sihon and his country over to you. Now begin to conquer and possess his land."

32When Sihon and all his army came out to meet us in battle at Jahaz, 33the LORD our God delivered him over to us and we struck him down, together with his sons and his whole army. 34At that time we took all his towns and completely destroyed them—men, women and children. We left no survivors. 35But the livestock and the plunder from the towns we had captured we carried off for ourselves. 36From Aroer

on the rim of the Arnon Gorge, and from the town in the gorge, even as far as Gilead, not one town was too strong for us. The LORD our God gave us all of them. 37But in accordance with the command of the LORD our God, you did not encroach on any of the land of the Ammonites, neither the land along the course of the Jabbok nor that around the towns in the hills.

Defeat of Og King of Bashan

3 Next we turned and went up along the road towards Bashan, and Og king of Bashan with his whole army marched out to meet us in battle at Edrei. 2The LORD said to me, "Do not be afraid of him, for I have handed him over to you with his whole army and his land. Do to him what you did to Sihon king of the Amorites, who reigned in Heshbon."

3So the LORD our God also gave into our hands Og king of Bashan and all his army. We struck them down, leaving no survivors. 4At that time we took all his cities. There was not one of the sixty cities that we did not take from them —the whole region of Argob, Og's kingdom in Bashan. 5All these cities were fortified with high walls and with gates and bars, and there were also a great many unwalled villages. 6We completely destroyed them, as we had done with Sihon king of Heshbon, destroying every city—men, women and children. 7But all the livestock and the plunder from their cities we carried off for ourselves.

8So at that time we took from these two kings of the Amorites the territory east of the Jordan, from the Arnon Gorge as far as Mount Hermon. 9(Hermon is called Sirion by the Sidonians; the Amorites call it Senir.) 10We took all the towns on the plateau, and all Gilead, and all Bashan as far as

Salecah and Edrei, towns of Og's kingdom in Bashan. [11](Only Og king of Bashan was left of the remnant of the Rephaites. His bed was made of iron and was more than thirteen feet long and six feet wide. It is still in Rabbah of the Ammonites.)

Division of the Land

[12]Of the land that we took over at that time, I gave the Reubenites and the Gadites the territory north of Aroer by the Arnon Gorge, including half the hill country of Gilead, together with its towns. [13]The rest of Gilead and also all of Bashan, the kingdom of Og, I gave to the half-tribe of Manasseh. (The whole region of Argob in Bashan used to be known as a land of the Rephaites. [14]Jair, a descendant of Manasseh, took the whole region of Argob as far as the border of the Geshurites and the Maacathites; it was named after him, so that to this day Bashan is called Havvoth Jair.) [15]And I gave Gilead to Makir. [16]But to the Reubenites and the Gadites I gave the territory extending from Gilead down to the Arnon Gorge (the middle of the gorge being the border) and out to the Jabbok River, which is the border of the Ammonites. [17]Its western border was the Jordan in the Arabah, from Kinnereth to the Sea of the Arabah (the Salt Sea), below the slopes of Pisgah.

[18]I commanded you at that time: "The LORD your God has given you this land to take possession of it. But all your able-bodied men, armed for battle, must cross over ahead of your brother Israelites. [19]However, your wives, your children and your livestock (I know you have much livestock) may stay in the towns I have given you, [20]until the LORD gives rest to your brothers as he has to you, and they too have taken over the land that the LORD your God is giving them, across the Jordan. After that, each of you may go back to the possession I have given you."

Moses Forbidden to Cross the Jordan

[21]At that time I commanded Joshua: "You have seen with your own eyes all that the LORD your God has done to these two kings. The LORD will do the same to all the kingdoms over there where you are going. [22]Do not be afraid of them; the LORD your God himself will fight for you."

[23]At that time I pleaded with the LORD: [24]"O Sovereign LORD, you have begun to show to your servant your greatness and your strong hand. For what god is there in heaven or on earth who can do the deeds and mighty works you do? [25]Let me go over and see the good land beyond the Jordan—that fine hill country and Lebanon."

[26]But because of you the LORD was angry with me and would not listen to me. "That is enough," the LORD said. "Do not speak to me any more about this matter. [27]Go up to the top of Pisgah and look west and north and south and east. Look at the land with your own eyes, since you are not going to cross this Jordan. [28]But commission Joshua, and encourage and strengthen him, for he will lead this people across and will cause them to inherit the land that you will see." [29]So we stayed in the valley near Beth Peor.

Obedience Commanded

4 Hear now, O Israel, the decrees and laws I am about to teach you. Follow them so that you may live and may go in and take possession of the land that the LORD, the God of your fathers, is giving you. [2]Do not add to what I command you and do not subtract from it, but keep the commands of the LORD your God that I give you.

[3]You saw with your own eyes what the LORD did at Baal Peor. The LORD your God destroyed from among you everyone who followed the Baal of Peor, [4]but all of you who held fast to the LORD your God are still alive today.

[5]See, I have taught you decrees and

laws as the LORD my God commanded me, so that you may follow them in the land you are entering to take possession of it. 6Observe them carefully, for this will show your wisdom and understanding to the nations, who will hear about all these decrees and say, "Surely this great nation is a wise and understanding people." 7What other nation is so great as to have their gods near them the way the LORD our God is near us whenever we pray to him? 8And what other nation is so great as to have such righteous decrees and laws as this body of laws I am setting before you today?

9Only be careful, and watch yourselves closely so that you do not forget the things your eyes have seen or let them slip from your heart as long as you live. Teach them to your children and to their children after them. 10Remember the day you stood before the LORD your God at Horeb, when he said to me, "Assemble the people before me to hear my words so that they may learn to revere me as long as they live in the land and may teach them to their children." 11You came near and stood at the foot of the mountain while it blazed with fire to the very heavens, with black clouds and deep darkness. 12Then the LORD spoke to you out of the fire. You heard the sound of words but saw no form; there was only a voice. 13He declared to you his covenant, the Ten Commandments, which he commanded you to follow and then wrote them on two stone tablets. 14And the LORD directed me at that time to teach you the decrees and laws you are to follow in the land that you are crossing the Jordan to possess.

NEW TESTAMENT READING
Luke 10:25–11:4

The Parable of the Good Samaritan

25On one occasion an expert in the law stood up to test Jesus. "Teacher," he asked, "what must I do to inherit eternal life?"

26"What is written in the Law?" he replied. "How do you read it?"

27He answered: "'Love the Lord your God with all your heart and with all your soul and with all your strength and with all your mind'; and, 'Love your neighbour as yourself.'"

28"You have answered correctly," Jesus replied. "Do this and you will live."

29But he wanted to justify himself, so he asked Jesus, "And who is my neighbour?"

30In reply Jesus said: "A man was going down from Jerusalem to Jericho, when he fell into the hands of robbers. They stripped him of his clothes, beat him and went away, leaving him half-dead. 31A priest happened to be going down the same road, and when he saw the man, he passed by on the other side. 32So too, a Levite, when he came to the place and saw him, passed by on the other side. 33But a Samaritan, as he travelled, came where the man was; and when he saw him, he took pity on him. 34He went to him and bandaged his wounds, pouring on oil and wine. Then he put the man on his own donkey, brought him to an inn and took care of him. 35The next day he took out two silver coins and gave them to the innkeeper. 'Look after him,' he said, 'and when I return, I will reimburse you for any extra expense you may have.'

36"Which of these three do you think was a neighbour to the man who fell into the hands of robbers?"

37The expert in the law replied, "The one who had mercy on him."

Jesus told him, "Go and do likewise."

At the Home of Martha and Mary

38As Jesus and his disciples were on their way, he came to a village where a woman named Martha opened her home to him. 39She had a sister called Mary, who sat at the Lord's feet listening to what he said. 40But Martha was distracted by all the preparations that had to be made. She came to him and asked, "Lord, don't you care that my sister has left me to do the work by myself? Tell her to help me!"

⁴¹"Martha, Martha," the Lord answered, "you are worried and upset about many things, ⁴²but only one thing is needed. Mary has chosen what is better, and it will not be taken away from her."

Jesus' Teaching on Prayer

11 One day Jesus was praying in a certain place. When he finished, one of his disciples said to him, "Lord, teach us to pray, just as John taught his disciples."

²He said to them, "When you pray, say:

" 'Father,
hallowed be your name,
   your kingdom come.
³Give us each day our daily bread.
⁴Forgive us our sins,
   for we also forgive everyone who
      sins against us.
And lead us not into temptation.' "

READING FROM PSALMS
Psalm 41:7–13

⁷All my enemies whisper together
      against me;
   they imagine the worst for me,
      saying,
⁸"A vile disease has beset him;
   he will never get up from the place
      where he lies."
⁹Even my close friend, whom I
      trusted,
   he who shared my bread,
   has lifted up his heel against me.

¹⁰But you, O LORD, have mercy on me;
   raise me up, that I may repay
      them.
¹¹I know that you are pleased with me,
   for my enemy does not triumph
      over me.
¹²In my integrity you uphold me
   and set me in your presence for
      ever.

¹³Praise be to the LORD, the God of
      Israel,
   from everlasting to everlasting.
            Amen and Amen.

DAY 96

APRIL 6

OLD TESTAMENT READING
Deuteronomy 4:15–5:33

Idolatry Forbidden

¹⁵You saw no form of any kind the day the LORD spoke to you at Horeb out of the fire. Therefore watch yourselves very carefully, ¹⁶so that you do not become corrupt and make for yourselves an idol, an image of any shape, whether formed like a man or a woman, ¹⁷or like any animal on earth or any bird that flies in the air, ¹⁸or like any creature that moves along the ground or any fish in

the waters below. ¹⁹And when you look up to the sky and see the sun, the moon and the stars—all the heavenly array —do not be enticed into bowing down to them and worshiping things the LORD your God has apportioned to all the nations under heaven. ²⁰But as for you, the LORD took you and brought you out of the iron-smelting furnace, out of Egypt, to be the people of his inheritance, as you now are.

²¹The LORD was angry with me because of you, and he solemnly swore that I would not cross the Jordan and enter the good land the LORD your God

is giving you as your inheritance. ²²I will die in this land; I will not cross the Jordan; but you are about to cross over and take possession of that good land. ²³Be careful not to forget the covenant of the LORD your God that he made with you; do not make for yourselves an idol in the form of anything the LORD your God has forbidden. ²⁴For the LORD your God is a consuming fire, a jealous God.

²⁵After you have had children and grandchildren and have lived in the land a long time—if you then become corrupt and make any kind of idol, doing evil in the eyes of the LORD your God and provoking him to anger, ²⁶I call heaven and earth as witnesses against you this day that you will quickly perish from the land that you are crossing the Jordan to possess. You will not live there long but will certainly be destroyed. ²⁷The LORD will scatter you among the peoples, and only a few of you will survive among the nations to which the LORD will drive you. ²⁸There you will worship man-made gods of wood and stone, which cannot see or hear or eat or smell. ²⁹But if from there you seek the LORD your God, you will find him if you look for him with all your heart and with all your soul. ³⁰When you are in distress and all these things have happened to you, then in later days you will return to the LORD your God and obey him. ³¹For the LORD your God is a merciful God; he will not abandon or destroy you or forget the covenant with your forefathers, which he confirmed to them by oath.

The LORD Is God

³²Ask now about the former days, long before your time, from the day God created man on the earth; ask from one end of the heavens to the other. Has anything so great as this ever happened, or has anything like it ever been heard of? ³³Has any other people heard the voice of God speaking out of fire, as you have, and lived? ³⁴Has any god ever

tried to take for himself one nation out of another nation, by testings, by miraculous signs and wonders, by war, by a mighty hand and an outstretched arm, or by great and awesome deeds, like all the things the LORD your God did for you in Egypt before your very eyes?

³⁵You were shown these things so that you might know that the LORD is God; besides him there is no other. ³⁶From heaven he made you hear his voice to discipline you. On earth he showed you his great fire, and you heard his words from out of the fire. ³⁷Because he loved your forefathers and chose their descendants after them, he brought you out of Egypt by his Presence and his great strength, ³⁸to drive out before you nations greater and stronger than you and to bring you into their land to give it to you for your inheritance, as it is today.

³⁹Acknowledge and take to heart this day that the LORD is God in heaven above and on the earth below. There is no other. ⁴⁰Keep his decrees and commands, which I am giving you today, so that it may go well with you and your children after you and that you may live long in the land the LORD your God gives you for all time.

Cities of Refuge

⁴¹Then Moses set aside three cities east of the Jordan, ⁴²to which anyone who had killed a person could flee if he had unintentionally killed his neighbour without malice aforethought. He could flee into one of these cities and save his life. ⁴³The cities were these: Bezer in the desert plateau, for the Reubenites; Ramoth in Gilead, for the Gadites; and Golan in Bashan, for the Manassites.

Introduction to the Law

⁴⁴This is the law Moses set before the Israelites. ⁴⁵These are the stipulations, decrees and laws Moses gave them when they came out of Egypt ⁴⁶and

were in the valley near Beth Peor east of the Jordan, in the land of Sihon king of the Amorites, who reigned in Heshbon and was defeated by Moses and the Israelites as they came out of Egypt. 47They took possession of his land and the land of Og king of Bashan, the two Amorite kings east of the Jordan. 48This land extended from Aroer on the rim of the Arnon Gorge to Mount Siyon (that is, Hermon), 49and included all the Arabah east of the Jordan, as far as the Sea of the Arabah, below the slopes of Pisgah.

The Ten Commandments

5 Moses summoned all Israel and said:
Hear, O Israel, the decrees and the laws I declare in your hearing today. Learn them and be sure to follow them. 2The LORD our God made a covenant with us at Horeb. 3It was not with our fathers that the LORD made this covenant, but with us, with all of us who are alive here today. 4The LORD spoke to you face to face out of the fire on the mountain. 5(At that time I stood between the LORD and you to declare to you the word of the LORD, because you were afraid of the fire and did not go up the mountain.) And he said:

6"I am the LORD your God, who brought you out of Egypt, out of the land of slavery.

7"You shall have no other gods before me.

8"You shall not make for yourself an idol in the form of anything in heaven above or on the earth beneath or in the waters below. 9You shall not bow down to them or worship them; for I, the LORD your God, am a jealous God, punishing the children for the sin of the fathers to the third and fourth generation of those who hate me, 10but

showing love to a thousand ⌊generations⌋ of those who love me and keep my commandments.

11"You shall not misuse the name of the LORD your God, for the LORD will not hold anyone guiltless who misuses his name.

12"Observe the Sabbath day by keeping it holy, as the LORD your God has commanded you. 13Six days you shall labour and do all your work, 14but the seventh day is a Sabbath to the LORD your God. On it you shall not do any work, neither you, nor your son or daughter, nor your manservant or maidservant, nor your ox, your donkey or any of your animals, nor the alien within your gates, so that your manservant and maidservant may rest, as you do. 15Remember that you were slaves in Egypt and that the LORD your God brought you out of there with a mighty hand and an outstretched arm. Therefore the LORD your God has commanded you to observe the Sabbath day.

16"Honour your father and your mother, as the LORD your God has commanded you, so that you may live long and that it may go well with you in the land the LORD your God is giving you.

17"You shall not murder.

18"You shall not commit adultery.

19"You shall not steal.

20"You shall not give false testimony against your neighbour.

21"You shall not covet your neighbour's wife. You shall not set your desire on your neighbour's house or land, his manservant or maidservant, his ox or donkey, or anything that belongs to your neighbour."

²²These are the commandments the LORD proclaimed in a loud voice to your whole assembly there on the mountain from out of the fire, the cloud and the deep darkness; and he added nothing more. Then he wrote them on two stone tablets and gave them to me.

²³When you heard the voice out of the darkness, while the mountain was ablaze with fire, all the leading men of your tribes and your elders came to me. ²⁴And you said, "The LORD our God has shown us his glory and his majesty, and we have heard his voice from the fire. Today we have seen that a man can live even if God speaks with him. ²⁵But now, why should we die? This great fire will consume us, and we will die if we hear the voice of the LORD our God any longer. ²⁶For what mortal man has ever heard the voice of the living God speaking out of fire, as we have, and survived? ²⁷Go near and listen to all that the LORD our God says. Then tell us whatever the LORD our God tells us. We will listen and obey."

²⁸The LORD heard you when you spoke to me and the LORD said to me, "I have heard what this people said to you. Everything they said was good. ²⁹Oh, that their hearts would be inclined to fear me and keep all my commands always, so that it might go well with them and their children for ever!

³⁰"Go, tell them to return to their tents. ³¹But you stay here with me so that I may give you all the commands, decrees and laws that you are to teach them to follow in the land I am giving them to possess."

³²So be careful to do what the LORD your God has commanded you; do not turn aside to the right or to the left. ³³Walk in all the way that the LORD your God has commanded you, so that you may live and prosper and prolong your days in the land that you will possess.

NEW TESTAMENT READING
Luke 11:5–32

⁵Then he said to them, "Suppose one of you has a friend, and he goes to him at midnight and says, 'Friend, lend me three loaves of bread, ⁶because a friend of mine on a journey has come to me, and I have nothing to set before him.'

⁷"Then the one inside answers, 'Don't bother me. The door is already locked, and my children are with me in bed. I can't get up and give you anything.' ⁸I tell you, though he will not get up and give him the bread because he is his friend, yet because of the man's boldness he will get up and give him as much as he needs.

⁹"So I say to you: Ask and it will be given to you; seek and you will find; knock and the door will be opened to you. ¹⁰For everyone who asks receives; he who seeks finds; and to him who knocks, the door will be opened.

¹¹"Which of you fathers, if your son asks for a fish, will give him a snake instead? ¹²Or if he asks for an egg, will give him a scorpion? ¹³If you then, though you are evil, know how to give good gifts to your children, how much more will your Father in heaven give the Holy Spirit to those who ask him!"

Jesus and Beelzebub

¹⁴Jesus was driving out a demon that was mute. When the demon left, the man who had been mute spoke, and the crowd was amazed. ¹⁵But some of them said, "By Beelzebub, the prince of demons, he is driving out demons." ¹⁶Others tested him by asking for a sign from heaven.

¹⁷Jesus knew their thoughts and said to them: "Any kingdom divided against itself will be ruined, and a house divided against itself will fall. ¹⁸If Satan is divided against himself, how can his kingdom stand? I say this because you claim that I drive out demons by Beelzebub. ¹⁹Now if I drive out demons by Beelzebub, by whom do your followers drive

them out? So then, they will be your judges. 20But if I drive out demons by the finger of God, then the kingdom of God has come to you.

21"When a strong man, fully armed, guards his own house, his possessions are safe. 22But when someone stronger attacks and overpowers him, he takes away the armour in which the man trusted and divides up the spoils.

23"He who is not with me is against me, and he who does not gather with me, scatters.

24"When an evil spirit comes out of a man, it goes through arid places seeking rest and does not find it. Then it says, 'I will return to the house I left.' 25When it arrives, it finds the house swept clean and put in order. 26Then it goes and takes seven other spirits more wicked than itself, and they go in and live there. And the final condition of that man is worse than the first."

27As Jesus was saying these things, a woman in the crowd called out, "Blessed is the mother who gave you birth and nursed you."

28He replied, "Blessed rather are those who hear the word of God and obey it."

The Sign of Jonah

29As the crowds increased, Jesus said, "This is a wicked generation. It asks for a miraculous sign, but none will be given it except the sign of Jonah. 30For as Jonah was a sign to the Ninevites, so also will the Son of Man be to this generation. 31The Queen of the South will rise at the judgment with the men of this generation and condemn them; for she came from the ends of the earth to listen to Solomon's wisdom, and now one greater than Solomon is here. 32The men of Nineveh will stand up at the judgment with this generation and condemn it; for they repented at the preaching of Jonah, and now one greater than Jonah is here.

READING FROM PROVERBS
Proverbs 8:32–36

32"Now then, my sons, listen to me;
    blessed are those who keep my
    ways.
33Listen to my instruction and be wise;
    do not ignore it.
34Blessed is the man who listens to me,
    watching daily at my doors,
    waiting at my doorway.
35For whoever finds me finds life
    and receives favour from the
    LORD.
36But whoever fails to find me harms
    himself;
    all who hate me love death."

DAY 97

APRIL 7

OLD TESTAMENT READING
Deuteronomy 6:1–8:20

Love the LORD Your God

6 These are the commands, decrees and laws the LORD your God directed me to teach you to observe in the land that you are crossing the Jordan to possess, 2so that you, your children and their children after them may fear the LORD your God as long as you live by keeping all his decrees and commands that I give you, and so that you may enjoy long life. 3Hear, O Israel, and be careful to obey so that it may go well with you and that you may increase greatly in a land flowing with

milk and honey, just as the LORD, the God of your fathers, promised you.

⁴Hear, O Israel: The LORD our God, the LORD is one. ⁵Love the LORD your God with all your heart and with all your soul and with all your strength. ⁶These commandments that I give you today are to be upon your hearts. ⁷Impress them on your children. Talk about them when you sit at home and when you walk along the road, when you lie down and when you get up. ⁸Tie them as symbols on your hands and bind them on your foreheads. ⁹Write them on the door-frames of your houses and on your gates.

¹⁰When the LORD your God brings you into the land he swore to your fathers, to Abraham, Isaac and Jacob, to give you—a land with large, flourishing cities you did not build, ¹¹houses filled with all kinds of good things you did not provide, wells you did not dig, and vineyards and olive groves you did not plant—then when you eat and are satisfied, ¹²be careful that you do not forget the LORD, who brought you out of Egypt, out of the land of slavery.

¹³Fear the LORD your God, serve him only and take your oaths in his name. ¹⁴Do not follow other gods, the gods of the peoples around you; ¹⁵for the LORD your God, who is among you, is a jealous God and his anger will burn against you, and he will destroy you from the face of the land. ¹⁶Do not test the LORD your God as you did at Massah. ¹⁷Be sure to keep the commands of the LORD your God and the stipulations and decrees he has given you. ¹⁸Do what is right and good in the LORD's sight, so that it may go well with you and you may go in and take over the good land that the LORD promised on oath to your forefathers, ¹⁹thrusting out all your enemies before you, as the LORD said.

²⁰In the future, when your son asks you, "What is the meaning of the stipulations, decrees and laws the LORD our God has commanded you?" ²¹tell him:

"We were slaves of Pharaoh in Egypt, but the LORD brought us out of Egypt with a mighty hand. ²²Before our eyes the LORD sent miraculous signs and wonders—great and terrible—upon Egypt and Pharaoh and his whole household. ²³But he brought us out from there to bring us in and give us the land that he promised on oath to our forefathers. ²⁴The LORD commanded us to obey all these decrees and to fear the LORD our God, so that we might always prosper and be kept alive, as is the case today. ²⁵And if we are careful to obey all this law before the LORD our God, as he has commanded us, that will be our righteousness."

Driving Out the Nations

7 When the LORD your God brings you into the land you are entering to possess and drives out before you many nations—the Hittites, Girgashites, Amorites, Canaanites, Perizzites, Hivites and Jebusites, seven nations larger and stronger than you —²and when the LORD your God has delivered them over to you and you have defeated them, then you must destroy them totally. Make no treaty with them, and show them no mercy. ³Do not intermarry with them. Do not give your daughters to their sons or take their daughters for your sons, ⁴for they will turn your sons away from following me to serve other gods, and the LORD's anger will burn against you and will quickly destroy you. ⁵This is what you are to do to them: Break down their altars, smash their sacred stones, cut down their Asherah poles and burn their idols in the fire. ⁶For you are a people holy to the LORD your God. The LORD your God has chosen you out of all the peoples on the face of the earth to be his people, his treasured possession.

⁷The LORD did not set his affection on you and choose you because you were more numerous than other peoples, for you were the fewest of all peoples. ⁸But it was because the LORD loved you and

kept the oath he swore to your fore-fathers that he brought you out with a mighty hand and redeemed you from the land of slavery, from the power of Pharaoh king of Egypt. 9Know there-fore that the LORD your God is God; he is the faithful God, keeping his cov-enant of love to a thousand generations of those who love him and keep his commands. 10But

those who hate him he will repay to
their face by destruction;
he will not be slow to repay to their
face those who hate him.

11Therefore, take care to follow the commands, decrees and laws I give you today.

12If you pay attention to these laws and are careful to follow them, then the LORD your God will keep his covenant of love with you, as he swore to your forefathers. 13He will love you and bless you and increase your numbers. He will bless the fruit of your womb, the crops of your land—your grain, new wine and oil—the calves of your herds and the lambs of your flocks in the land that he swore to your forefathers to give you. 14You will be blessed more than any other people; none of your men or women will be childless, nor any of your livestock without young. 15The LORD will keep you free from every disease. He will not inflict on you the horrible diseases you knew in Egypt, but he will inflict them on all who hate you. 16You must destroy all the peoples the LORD your God gives over to you. Do not look on them with pity and do not serve their gods, for that will be a snare to you.

17You may say to yourselves, "These nations are stronger than we are. How can we drive them out?" 18But do not be afraid of them; remember well what the LORD your God did to Pharaoh and to all Egypt. 19You saw with your own eyes the great trials, the miraculous signs and wonders, the mighty hand and out-stretched arm, with which the LORD your God brought you out. The LORD your God will do the same to all the peoples you now fear. 20Moreover, the LORD your God will send the hornet among them until even the survivors who hide from you have perished. 21Do not be terrified by them, for the LORD your God, who is among you, is a great and awesome God. 22The LORD your God will drive out those nations before you, little by little. You will not be allowed to eliminate them all at once, or the wild animals will multiply around you. 23But the LORD your God will de-liver them over to you, throwing them into great confusion until they are de-stroyed. 24He will give their kings into your hand, and you will wipe out their names from under heaven. No-one will be able to stand up against you; you will destroy them. 25The images of their gods you are to burn in the fire. Do not covet the silver and gold on them, and do not take it for yourselves, or you will be ensnared by it, for it is detestable to the LORD your God. 26Do not bring a detestable thing into your house or you, like it, will be set apart for destruction. Utterly abhor and detest it, for it is set apart for destruction.

Do Not Forget the Lord

8 Be careful to follow every com-mand I am giving you today, so that you may live and increase and may en-ter and possess the land that the LORD promised on oath to your forefathers. 2Remember how the LORD your God led you all the way in the desert these forty years, to humble you and to test you in order to know what was in your heart, whether or not you would keep his commands. 3He humbled you, caus-ing you to hunger and then feeding you with manna, which neither you nor your fathers had known, to teach you that man does not live on bread alone but on every word that comes from the mouth of the LORD. 4Your clothes did not wear out and your feet did not swell during these forty years. 5Know then in your heart that as a man disciplines his son, so the LORD your God disciplines you.

⁶Observe the commands of the LORD your God, walking in his ways and revering him. ⁷For the LORD your God is bringing you into a good land—a land with streams and pools of water, with springs flowing in the valleys and hills; ⁸a land with wheat and barley, vines and fig-trees, pomegranates, olive oil and honey; ⁹a land where bread will not be scarce and you will lack nothing; a land where the rocks are iron and you can dig copper out of the hills.

¹⁰When you have eaten and are satisfied, praise the LORD your God for the good land he has given you. ¹¹Be careful that you do not forget the LORD your God, failing to observe his commands, his laws and his decrees that I am giving you this day. ¹²Otherwise, when you eat and are satisfied, when you build fine houses and settle down, ¹³and when your herds and flocks grow large and your silver and gold increase and all you have is multiplied, ¹⁴then your heart will become proud and you will forget the LORD your God, who brought you out of Egypt, out of the land of slavery. ¹⁵He led you through the vast and dreadful desert, that thirsty and waterless land, with its venomous snakes and scorpions. He brought you water out of hard rock. ¹⁶He gave you manna to eat in the desert, something your fathers had never known, to humble and to test you so that in the end it might go well with you. ¹⁷You may say to yourself, "My power and the strength of my hands have produced this wealth for me." ¹⁸But remember the LORD your God, for it is he who gives you the ability to produce wealth, and so confirms his covenant, which he swore to your forefathers, as it is today.

¹⁹If you ever forget the LORD your God and follow other gods and worship and bow down to them, I testify against you today that you will surely be destroyed. ²⁰Like the nations the LORD destroyed before you, so you will be destroyed for not obeying the LORD your God.

NEW TESTAMENT READING
Luke 11:33–54

The Lamp of the Body

³³"No-one lights a lamp and puts it in a place where it will be hidden, or under a bowl. Instead he puts it on its stand, so that those who come in may see the light. ³⁴Your eye is the lamp of your body. When your eyes are good, your whole body also is full of light. But when they are bad, your body also is full of darkness. ³⁵See to it, then, that the light within you is not darkness. ³⁶Therefore, if your whole body is full of light, and no part of it is dark, it will be completely lighted, as when the light of a lamp shines on you."

Six Woes

³⁷When Jesus had finished speaking, a Pharisee invited him to eat with him; so he went in and reclined at the table. ³⁸But the Pharisee, noticing that Jesus did not first wash before the meal, was surprised.

³⁹Then the Lord said to him, "Now then, you Pharisees clean the outside of the cup and dish, but inside you are full of greed and wickedness. ⁴⁰You foolish people! Did not the one who made the outside make the inside also? ⁴¹But give what is inside₁the dish₁to the poor, and everything will be clean for you.

⁴²"Woe to you Pharisees, because you give God a tenth of your mint, rue and all other kinds of garden herbs, but you neglect justice and the love of God. You should have practised the latter without leaving the former undone.

⁴³"Woe to you Pharisees, because you love the most important seats in the synagogues and greetings in the market-places.

⁴⁴"Woe to you, because you are like unmarked graves, which men walk over without knowing it."

⁴⁵One of the experts in the law answered him, "Teacher, when you say these things, you insult us also."

⁴⁶Jesus replied, "And you experts in

the law, woe to you, because you load people down with burdens they can hardly carry, and you yourselves will not lift one finger to help them.

47"Woe to you, because you build tombs for the prophets, and it was your forefathers who killed them. 48So you testify that you approve of what your forefathers did; they killed the prophets, and you build their tombs. 49Because of this, God in his wisdom said, 'I will send them prophets and apostles, some of whom they will kill and others they will persecute.' 50Therefore this generation will be held responsible for the blood of all the prophets that has been shed since the beginning of the world, 51from the blood of Abel to the blood of Zechariah, who was killed between the altar and the sanctuary. Yes, I tell you, this generation will be held responsible for it all.

52"Woe to you experts in the law, because you have taken away the key to knowledge. You yourselves have not entered, and you have hindered those who were entering."

53When Jesus left there, the Pharisees and the teachers of the law began to oppose him fiercely and to besiege him with questions, 54waiting to catch him in something he might say.

READING FROM PSALMS
Psalm 42:1–6a

For the director of music. A *maskil* of the Sons of Korah.

1As the deer pants for streams of water,
   so my soul pants for you, O God.
2My soul thirsts for God, for the living God.
   When can I go and meet with God?
3My tears have been my food day and night,
while men say to me all day long,
   "Where is your God?"
4These things I remember as I pour out my soul:
how I used to go with the multitude,
   leading the procession to the house of God,
with shouts of joy and thanksgiving among the festive throng.

5Why are you downcast, O my soul?
   Why so disturbed within me?
Put your hope in God,
   for I will yet praise him,
   my Saviour and 6my God.

DAY 98

APRIL 8

OLD TESTAMENT READING
Deuteronomy 9:1–10:22

Not Because of Israel's Righteousness

9 Hear, O Israel. You are now about to cross the Jordan to go in and dispossess nations greater and stronger than you, with large cities that have walls up to the sky. 2The people are strong and tall—Anakites! You know about them and have heard it said: "Who can stand up against the Anakites?" 3But be assured today that the LORD your God is the one who goes across ahead of you like a devouring fire. He will destroy them; he will subdue them before you. And you will drive them out and annihilate them quickly, as the LORD has promised you.

4After the LORD your God has driven them out before you, do not say to yourself, "The LORD has brought me here to take possession of this land because of my righteousness." No, it is on account of the wickedness of these nations that the LORD is going to drive them out before you. 5It is not because of your righteousness or your integrity that you are going in to take possession of their land; but on account of the wickedness of these nations, the LORD your God will drive them out before you, to accomplish what he swore to your fathers, to Abraham, Isaac and Jacob. 6Understand, then, that it is not because of your righteousness that the LORD your God is giving you this good land to possess, for you are a stiff-necked people.

The Golden Calf

7Remember this and never forget how you provoked the LORD your God to anger in the desert. From the day you left Egypt until you arrived here, you have been rebellious against the LORD. 8At Horeb you aroused the LORD's wrath so that he was angry enough to destroy you. 9When I went up on the mountain to receive the tablets of stone, the tablets of the covenant that the LORD had made with you, I stayed on the mountain forty days and forty nights; I ate no bread and drank no water. 10The LORD gave me two stone tablets inscribed by the finger of God. On them were all the commandments the LORD proclaimed to you on the mountain out of the fire, on the day of the assembly.

11At the end of the forty days and forty nights, the LORD gave me the two stone tablets, the tablets of the covenant. 12Then the LORD told me, "Go down from here at once, because your people whom you brought out of Egypt have become corrupt. They have turned away quickly from what I commanded them and have made a cast idol for themselves."

13And the LORD said to me, "I have seen this people, and they are a stiff-necked people indeed! 14Let me alone, so that I may destroy them and blot out their name from under heaven. And I will make you into a nation stronger and more numerous than they."

15So I turned and went down from the mountain while it was ablaze with fire. And the two tablets of the covenant were in my hands. 16When I looked, I saw that you had sinned against the LORD your God; you had made for yourselves an idol cast in the shape of a calf. You had turned aside quickly from the way that the LORD had commanded you. 17So I took the two tablets and threw them out of my hands, breaking them to pieces before your eyes.

18Then once again I fell prostrate before the LORD for forty days and forty nights; I ate no bread and drank no water, because of all the sin you had committed, doing what was evil in the LORD's sight and so provoking him to anger. 19I feared the anger and wrath of the LORD, for he was angry enough with you to destroy you. But again the LORD listened to me. 20And the LORD was angry enough with Aaron to destroy him, but at that time I prayed for Aaron too. 21Also I took that sinful thing of yours, the calf you had made, and burned it in the fire. Then I crushed it and ground it to powder as fine as dust and threw the dust into a stream that flowed down the mountain.

22You also made the LORD angry at Taberah, at Massah and at Kibroth Hattaavah.

23And when the LORD sent you out from Kadesh Barnea, he said, "Go up and take possession of the land I have given you." But you rebelled against the command of the LORD your God. You did not trust him or obey him. 24You have been rebellious against the LORD ever since I have known you.

25I lay prostrate before the LORD those forty days and forty nights because the LORD had said he would destroy you. 26I prayed to the LORD and said, "O Sovereign LORD, do not destroy your people, your own inheritance that you redeemed by your great power and brought out of Egypt with a mighty hand. 27Remember your servants Abraham, Isaac and Jacob. Overlook the stubbornness of this people, their wickedness and their sin. 28Otherwise, the country from which you brought us will say, 'Because the LORD was not able to take them into the land he had promised them, and because he hated them, he brought them out to put them to death in the desert.' ²⁹But they are your people, your inheritance that you brought out by your great power and your outstretched arm."

Tablets Like the First Ones

10 At that time the LORD said to me, "Chisel out two stone tablets like the first ones and come up to me on the mountain. Also make a wooden chest. ²I will write on the tablets the words that were on the first tablets, which you broke. Then you are to put them in the chest."

³So I made the ark out of acacia wood and chiselled out two stone tablets like the first ones, and I went up on the mountain with the two tablets in my hands. ⁴The LORD wrote on these tablets what he had written before, the Ten Commandments he had proclaimed to you on the mountain, out of the fire, on the day of the assembly. And the LORD gave them to me. ⁵Then I came back down the mountain and put the tablets in the ark I had made, as the LORD commanded me, and they are there now.

⁶(The Israelites travelled from the wells of the Jaakanites to Moserah. There Aaron died and was buried, and Eleazar his son succeeded him as priest. ⁷From there they travelled to Gudgodah and on to Jotbathah, a land with streams of water. ⁸At that time the LORD set apart the tribe of Levi to carry the ark of the covenant of the LORD, to stand before the LORD to minister and to pronounce blessings in his name, as they still do today. ⁹That is why the Levites have no share or inheritance among their brothers; the LORD is their inheritance, as the LORD your God told them.)

¹⁰Now I had stayed on the mountain forty days and nights, as I did the first time, and the LORD listened to me at this time also. It was not his will to destroy you. ¹¹"Go," the LORD said to me, "and lead the people on their way, so that they may enter and possess the land that I swore to their fathers to give them."

Fear the LORD

¹²And now, O Israel, what does the LORD your God ask of you but to fear the LORD your God, to walk in all his ways, to love him, to serve the LORD your God with all your heart and with all your soul, ¹³and to observe the LORD's commands and decrees that I am giving you today for your own good?

¹⁴To the LORD your God belong the heavens, even the highest heavens, the earth and everything in it. ¹⁵Yet the LORD set his affection on your forefathers and loved them, and he chose you, their descendants, above all the nations, as it is today. ¹⁶Circumcise your hearts, therefore, and do not be stiff-necked any longer. ¹⁷For the LORD your God is God of gods and Lord of lords, the great God, mighty and awesome, who shows no partiality and accepts no bribes. ¹⁸He defends the cause of the fatherless and the widow, and loves the alien, giving him food and clothing. ¹⁹And you are to love those who are aliens, for you yourselves were aliens in Egypt. ²⁰Fear the LORD your God and serve him. Hold fast to him and take your oaths in his name. ²¹He is your praise; he is your God, who performed for you those great and awesome wonders you saw with your own eyes. ²²Your forefathers who went down into Egypt were seventy in all, and now the LORD your God has made you as numerous as the stars in the sky.

NEW TESTAMENT READING
Luke 12:1–34

Warnings and Encouragements

12 Meanwhile, when a crowd of many thousands had gathered, so that they were trampling on one another, Jesus began to speak first to his disciples, saying: "Be on your guard against the yeast of the Pharisees, which is hypocrisy. ²There is nothing concealed that will not be disclosed, or hidden that will not be made known. ³What you have said in the dark will be heard in the daylight, and what you have whispered in the ear in the inner rooms will be proclaimed from the roofs.

⁴"I tell you, my friends, do not be afraid of those who kill the body and after that can do no more. ⁵But I will show you whom you should fear: Fear him who, after the killing of the body, has power to throw you into hell. Yes, I tell you, fear him. ⁶Are not five sparrows sold for two pennies? Yet not one of them is forgotten by God. ⁷Indeed, the very hairs of your head are all numbered. Don't be afraid; you are worth more than many sparrows.

⁸"I tell you, whoever acknowledges me before men, the Son of Man will also acknowledge him before the angels of God. ⁹But he who disowns me before men will be disowned before the angels of God. ¹⁰And everyone who speaks a word against the Son of Man will be forgiven, but anyone who blasphemes against the Holy Spirit will not be forgiven.

¹¹"When you are brought before synagogues, rulers and authorities, do not worry about how you will defend yourselves or what you will say, ¹²for the Holy Spirit will teach you at that time what you should say."

The Parable of the Rich Fool

¹³Someone in the crowd said to him, "Teacher, tell my brother to divide the inheritance with me."

¹⁴Jesus replied, "Man, who appointed me a judge or an arbiter between you?" ¹⁵Then he said to them, "Watch out! Be on your guard against all kinds of greed; a man's life does not consist in the abundance of his possessions."

¹⁶And he told them this parable: "The ground of a certain rich man produced a good crop. ¹⁷He thought to himself, 'What shall I do? I have no place to store my crops.'

¹⁸"Then he said, 'This is what I'll do. I will tear down my barns and build bigger ones, and there I will store all my grain and my goods. ¹⁹And I'll say to myself, "You have plenty of good things laid up for many years. Take life easy; eat, drink and be merry."'

²⁰"But God said to him, 'You fool! This very night your life will be demanded from you. Then who will get what you have prepared for yourself?'

²¹"This is how it will be with anyone who stores up things for himself but is not rich towards God."

Do Not Worry

²²Then Jesus said to his disciples: "Therefore I tell you, do not worry about your life, what you will eat; or about your body, what you will wear. ²³Life is more than food, and the body more than clothes. ²⁴Consider the ravens: They do not sow or reap, they have no storeroom or barn; yet God feeds them. And how much more valuable you are than birds! ²⁵Who of you by worrying can add a single hour to his life? ²⁶Since you cannot do this very little thing, why do you worry about the rest?

²⁷"Consider how the lilies grow. They do not labour or spin. Yet I tell you, not even Solomon in all his splendour was dressed like one of these. ²⁸If that is how God clothes the grass of the field, which is here today, and tomorrow is thrown into the fire, how much more will he clothe you, O you of little faith! ²⁹And do not set your heart on what you will eat or drink; do not worry about it. ³⁰For the pagan world runs after all such things, and your Father knows that you need them. ³¹But seek his kingdom, and these things will be given to you as well.

³²"Do not be afraid, little flock, for your Father has been pleased to give

you the kingdom. ³³Sell your possessions and give to the poor. Provide purses for yourselves that will not wear out, a treasure in heaven that will not be exhausted, where no thief comes near and no moth destroys. ³⁴For where your treasure is, there your heart will be also.

READING FROM PSALMS
Psalm 42:6b–11

My soul is downcast within me;
  therefore I will remember you
from the land of the Jordan,
  the heights of Hermon—from
    Mount Mizar.
⁷Deep calls to deep
  in the roar of your waterfalls;

all your waves and breakers
  have swept over me.

⁸By day the LORD directs his love,
  at night his song is with me—
  a prayer to the God of my life.

⁹I say to God my Rock,
  "Why have you forgotten me?
Why must I go about mourning,
  oppressed by the enemy?"
¹⁰My bones suffer mortal agony
  as my foes taunt me,
saying to me all day long,
  "Where is your God?"

¹¹Why are you downcast, O my soul?
  Why so disturbed within me?
Put your hope in God,
  for I will yet praise him,
  my Saviour and my God.

DAY 99

APRIL 9

OLD TESTAMENT READING
Deuteronomy 11:1–12:32

Love and Obey the LORD

11 Love the LORD your God and keep his requirements, his decrees, his laws and his commands always. ²Remember today that your children were not the ones who saw and experienced the discipline of the LORD your God: his majesty, his mighty hand, his outstretched arm; ³the signs he performed and the things he did in the heart of Egypt, both to Pharaoh king of Egypt and to his whole country; ⁴what he did to the Egyptian army, to its horses and chariots, how he overwhelmed them with the waters of the Red Sea as they were pursuing you, and how the LORD brought lasting ruin on them. ⁵It was not your children who saw what he did for you in the desert until

you arrived at this place, ⁶and what he did to Dathan and Abiram, sons of Eliab the Reubenite, when the earth opened its mouth right in the middle of all Israel and swallowed them up with their households, their tents and every living thing that belonged to them. ⁷But it was your own eyes that saw all these great things the LORD has done.

⁸Observe therefore all the commands I am giving you today, so that you may have the strength to go in and take over the land that you are crossing the Jordan to possess, ⁹and so that you may live long in the land that the LORD swore to your forefathers to give to them and their descendants, a land flowing with milk and honey. ¹⁰The land you are entering to take over is not like the land of Egypt, from which you have come, where you planted your seed and irrigated it by foot as in a vegetable garden. ¹¹But the land you are crossing the Jordan to take possession of is a land of

mountains and valleys that drinks rain from heaven. [12]It is a land the LORD your God cares for; the eyes of the LORD your God are continually on it from the beginning of the year to its end.

[13]So if you faithfully obey the commands I am giving you today—to love the LORD your God and to serve him with all your heart and with all your soul—[14]then I will send rain on your land in its season, both autumn and spring rains, so that you may gather in your grain, new wine and oil. [15]I will provide grass in the fields for your cattle, and you will eat and be satisfied.

[16]Be careful, or you will be enticed to turn away and worship other gods and bow down to them. [17]Then the LORD's anger will burn against you, and he will shut the heavens so that it will not rain and the ground will yield no produce, and you will soon perish from the good land the LORD is giving you. [18]Fix these words of mine in your hearts and minds; tie them as symbols on your hands and bind them on your foreheads. [19]Teach them to your children, talking about them when you sit at home and when you walk along the road, when you lie down and when you get up. [20]Write them on the door-frames of your houses and on your gates, [21]so that your days and the days of your children may be many in the land that the LORD swore to give your forefathers, as many as the days that the heavens are above the earth.

[22]If you carefully observe all these commands I am giving you to follow —to love the LORD your God, to walk in all his ways and to hold fast to him —[23]then the LORD will drive out all these nations before you, and you will dispossess nations larger and stronger than you. [24]Every place where you set your foot will be yours: Your territory will extend from the desert to Lebanon, and from the Euphrates River to the western sea. [25]No man will be able to stand against you. The LORD your God, as he promised you, will put the terror

and fear of you on the whole land, wherever you go.

[26]See, I am setting before you today a blessing and a curse—[27]the blessing if you obey the commands of the LORD your God that I am giving you today; [28]the curse if you disobey the commands of the LORD your God and turn from the way that I command you today by following other gods, which you have not known. [29]When the LORD your God has brought you into the land you are entering to possess, you are to proclaim on Mount Gerizim the blessings, and on Mount Ebal the curses. [30]As you know, these mountains are across the Jordan, west of the road, towards the setting sun, near the great trees of Moreh, in the territory of those Canaanites living in the Arabah in the vicinity of Gilgal. [31]You are about to cross the Jordan to enter and take possession of the land the LORD your God is giving you. When you have taken it over and are living there, [32]be sure that you obey all the decrees and laws I am setting before you today.

The One Place of Worship

12 These are the decrees and laws you must be careful to follow in the land that the LORD, the God of your fathers, has given you to possess—as long as you live in the land. [2]Destroy completely all the places on the high mountains and on the hills and under every spreading tree where the nations you are dispossessing worship their gods. [3]Break down their altars, smash their sacred stones and burn their Asherah poles in the fire; cut down the idols of their gods and wipe out their names from these places.

[4]You must not worship the LORD your God in their way. [5]But you are to seek the place the LORD your God will choose from among all your tribes to put his Name there for his dwelling. To that place you must go; [6]there bring your burnt offerings and sacrifices, your tithes and special gifts, what you have

vowed to give and your freewill offerings, and the firstborn of your herds and flocks. 7There, in the presence of the LORD your God, you and your families shall eat and shall rejoice in everything you have put your hand to, because the LORD your God has blessed you.

8You are not to do as we do here today, everyone as he sees fit, 9since you have not yet reached the resting place and the inheritance the LORD your God is giving you. 10But you will cross the Jordan and settle in the land the LORD your God is giving you as an inheritance, and he will give you rest from all your enemies around you so that you will live in safety. 11Then to the place the LORD your God will choose as a dwelling for his Name—there you are to bring everything I command you: your burnt offerings and sacrifices, your tithes and special gifts, and all the choice possessions you have vowed to the LORD. 12And there rejoice before the LORD your God, you, your sons and daughters, your menservants and maidservants, and the Levites from your towns, who have no allotment or inheritance of their own. 13Be careful not to sacrifice your burnt offerings anywhere you please. 14Offer them only at the place the LORD will choose in one of your tribes, and there observe everything I command you.

15Nevertheless, you may slaughter your animals in any of your towns and eat as much of the meat as you want, as if it were gazelle or deer, according to the blessing the LORD your God gives you. Both the ceremonially unclean and the clean may eat it. 16But you must not eat the blood; pour it out on the ground like water. 17You must not eat in your own towns the tithe of your grain and new wine and oil, or the firstborn of your herds and flocks, or whatever you have vowed to give, or your freewill offerings or special gifts. 18Instead, you are to eat them in the presence of the LORD your God at the place the LORD your God will choose—you, your sons and daughters, your menservants and

maidservants, and the Levites from your towns—and you are to rejoice before the LORD your God in everything you put your hand to. 19Be careful not to neglect the Levites as long as you live in your land.

20When the LORD your God has enlarged your territory as he promised you, and you crave meat and say, "I would like some meat," then you may eat as much of it as you want. 21If the place where the LORD your God chooses to put his Name is too far away from you, you may slaughter animals from the herds and flocks the LORD has given you, as I have commanded you, and in your own towns you may eat as much of them as you want. 22Eat them as you would gazelle or deer. Both the ceremonially unclean and the clean may eat. 23But be sure you do not eat the blood, because the blood is the life, and you must not eat the life with the meat. 24You must not eat the blood; pour it out on the ground like water. 25Do not eat it, so that it may go well with you and your children after you, because you will be doing what is right in the eyes of the LORD.

26But take your consecrated things and whatever you have vowed to give, and go to the place the LORD will choose. 27Present your burnt offerings on the altar of the LORD your God, both the meat and the blood. The blood of your sacrifices must be poured beside the altar of the LORD your God, but you may eat the meat. 28Be careful to obey all these regulations I am giving you, so that it may always go well with you and your children after you, because you will be doing what is good and right in the eyes of the LORD your God.

29The LORD your God will cut off before you the nations you are about to invade and dispossess. But when you have driven them out and settled in their land, 30and after they have been destroyed before you, be careful not to be ensnared by enquiring about their gods, saying, "How do these nations serve their gods? We will do the same."

³¹You must not worship the LORD your God in their way, because in worshipping their gods, they do all kinds of detestable things the LORD hates. They even burn their sons and daughters in the fire as sacrifices to their gods.

³²See that you do all I command you; do not add to it or take away from it.

NEW TESTAMENT READING
Luke 12:35–59

Watchfulness

³⁵"Be dressed ready for service and keep your lamps burning, ³⁶like men waiting for their master to return from a wedding banquet, so that when he comes and knocks they can immediately open the door for him. ³⁷It will be good for those servants whose master finds them watching when he comes. I tell you the truth, he will dress himself to serve, will have them recline at the table and will come and wait on them. ³⁸It will be good for those servants whose master finds them ready, even if he comes in the second or third watch of the night. ³⁹But understand this: If the owner of the house had known at what hour the thief was coming, he would not have let his house be broken into. ⁴⁰You also must be ready, because the Son of Man will come at an hour when you do not expect him."

⁴¹Peter asked, "Lord, are you telling this parable to us, or to everyone?"

⁴²The Lord answered, "Who then is the faithful and wise manager, whom the master puts in charge of his servants to give them their food allowance at the proper time? ⁴³It will be good for that servant whom the master finds doing so when he returns. ⁴⁴I tell you the truth, he will put him in charge of all his possessions. ⁴⁵But suppose the servant says to himself, 'My master is taking a long time in coming,' and he then begins to beat the menservants and maidservants and to eat and drink and get drunk. ⁴⁶The master of that servant will come on a day when he does not expect him and at an hour he is not aware of. He will cut him to pieces and assign him a place with the unbelievers.

⁴⁷"That servant who knows his master's will and does not get ready or does not do what his master wants will be beaten with many blows. ⁴⁸But the one who does not know and does things deserving punishment will be beaten with few blows. From everyone who has been given much, much will be demanded; and from the one who has been entrusted with much, much more will be asked.

Not Peace but Division

⁴⁹"I have come to bring fire on the earth, and how I wish it were already kindled! ⁵⁰But I have a baptism to undergo, and how distressed I am until it is completed! ⁵¹Do you think I came to bring peace on earth? No, I tell you, but division. ⁵²From now on there will be five in one family divided against each other, three against two and two against three. ⁵³They will be divided, father against son and son against father, mother against daughter and daughter against mother, mother-in-law against daughter-in-law and daughter-in-law against mother-in-law."

Interpreting the Times

⁵⁴He said to the crowd: "When you see a cloud rising in the west, immediately you say, 'It's going to rain,' and it does. ⁵⁵And when the south wind blows, you say, 'It's going to be hot,' and it is. ⁵⁶Hypocrites! You know how to interpret the appearance of the earth and the sky. How is it that you don't know how to interpret this present time?

⁵⁷"Why don't you judge for yourselves what is right? ⁵⁸As you are going with your adversary to the magistrate, try hard to be reconciled to him on the way, or he may drag you off to

the judge, and the judge turn you over to the officer, and the officer throw you into prison. ⁵⁹I tell you, you will not get out until you have paid the last penny.''

READING FROM PSALMS
Psalm 43:1–5

¹Vindicate me, O God,
  and plead my cause against an
    ungodly nation;
  rescue me from deceitful and
    wicked men.
²You are God my stronghold.
  Why have you rejected me?

Why must I go about mourning,
  oppressed by the enemy?
³Send forth your light and your truth,
  let them guide me;
  let them bring me to your holy
    mountain,
  to the place where you dwell.
⁴Then will I go to the altar of God,
  to God, my joy and my delight.
  I will praise you with the harp,
    O God, my God.

⁵Why are you downcast, O my soul?
  Why so disturbed within me?
  Put your hope in God,
  for I will yet praise him,
    my Saviour and my God.

DAY 100

APRIL 10

OLD TESTAMENT READING
Deuteronomy 13:1–14:29

Worshipping Other Gods

13 If a prophet, or one who foretells by dreams, appears among you and announces to you a miraculous sign or wonder, ²and if the sign or wonder of which he has spoken takes place, and he says, ''Let us follow other gods'' (gods you have not known) ''and let us worship them,'' ³you must not listen to the words of that prophet or dreamer. The LORD your God is testing you to find out whether you love him with all your heart and with all your soul. ⁴It is the LORD your God you must follow, and him you must revere. Keep his commands and obey him; serve him and hold fast to him. ⁵That prophet or dreamer must be put to death, because he preached rebellion against the LORD your God, who brought you out of Egypt and redeemed you from the land of slavery; he has tried to turn you from the way the LORD your God commanded you to follow. You must purge the evil from among you.

⁶If your very own brother, or your son or daughter, or the wife you love, or your closest friend secretly entices you, saying, ''Let us go and worship other gods'' (gods that neither you nor your fathers have known, ⁷gods of the peoples around you, whether near or far, from one end of the land to the other), ⁸do not yield to him or listen to him. Show him no pity. Do not spare him or shield him. ⁹You must certainly put him to death. Your hand must be the first in putting him to death, and then the hands of all the people. ¹⁰Stone him to death, because he tried to turn you away from the LORD your God, who brought you out of Egypt, out of the land of slavery. ¹¹Then all Israel will hear and be afraid, and no-one among you will do such an evil thing again.

¹²If you hear it said about one of the towns the LORD your God is giving you to live in ¹³that wicked men have arisen among you and have led the people of their town astray, saying, ''Let us go and worship other gods'' (gods you have not known), ¹⁴then you must enquire, probe and investigate it thoroughly.

And if it is true and it has been proved that this detestable thing has been done among you, 15you must certainly put to the sword all who live in that town. Destroy it completely, both its people and its livestock. 16Gather all the plunder of the town into the middle of the public square and completely burn the town and all its plunder as a whole burnt offering to the LORD your God. It is to remain a ruin for ever, never to be rebuilt. 17None of those condemned things shall be found in your hands, so that the LORD will turn from his fierce anger; he will show you mercy, have compassion on you, and increase your numbers, as he promised on oath to your forefathers, 18because you obey the LORD your God, keeping all his commands that I am giving you today and doing what is right in his eyes.

Clean and Unclean Food

14 You are the children of the LORD your God. Do not cut yourselves or shave the front of your heads for the dead, 2for you are a people holy to the LORD your God. Out of all the peoples on the face of the earth, the LORD has chosen you to be his treasured possession.

3Do not eat any detestable thing. 4These are the animals you may eat: the ox, the sheep, the goat, 5the deer, the gazelle, the roe deer, the wild goat, the ibex, the antelope and the mountain sheep. 6You may eat any animal that has a split hoof divided in two and that chews the cud. 7However, of those that chew the cud or that have a split hoof completely divided you may not eat the camel, the rabbit or the coney. Although they chew the cud, they do not have a split hoof; they are ceremonially unclean for you. 8The pig is also unclean; although it has a split hoof, it does not chew the cud. You are not to eat their meat or touch their carcasses.

9Of all the creatures living in the water, you may eat any that has fins and scales. 10But anything that does not have fins and scales you may not eat; for you it is unclean.

11You may eat any clean bird. 12But these you may not eat: the eagle, the vulture, the black vulture, 13the red kite, the black kite, any kind of falcon, 14any kind of raven, 15the horned owl, the screech owl, the gull, any kind of hawk, 16the little owl, the great owl, the white owl, 17the desert owl, the osprey, the cormorant, 18the stork, any kind of heron, the hoopoe and the bat.

19All flying insects that swarm are unclean to you; do not eat them. 20But any winged creature that is clean you may eat.

21Do not eat anything you find already dead. You may give it to an alien living in any of your towns, and he may eat it, or you may sell it to a foreigner. But you are a people holy to the LORD your God.

Do not cook a young goat in its mother's milk.

Tithes

22Be sure to set aside a tenth of all that your fields produce each year. 23Eat the tithe of your grain, new wine and oil, and the firstborn of your herds and flocks in the presence of the LORD your God at the place he will choose as a dwelling for his Name, so that you may learn to revere the LORD your God always. 24But if that place is too distant and you have been blessed by the LORD your God and cannot carry your tithe (because the place where the LORD will choose to put his Name is so far away), 25then exchange your tithe for silver, and take the silver with you and go to the place the LORD your God will choose. 26Use the silver to buy whatever you like: cattle, sheep, wine or other fermented drink, or anything you wish. Then you and your household shall eat there in the presence of the LORD your God and rejoice. 27And do not neglect the Levites living in your towns, for they have no allotment or inheritance of their own.

28At the end of every three years, bring all the tithes of that year's produce and store it in your towns, 29so that the Levites (who have no allotment or inheritance of their own) and the aliens, the fatherless and the widows who live in your towns may come and eat and be satisfied, and so that the LORD your God may bless you in all the work of your hands.

NEW TESTAMENT READING
Luke 13:1–30

Repent or Perish

13 Now there were some present at that time who told Jesus about the Galileans whose blood Pilate had mixed with their sacrifices. 2Jesus answered, "Do you think that these Galileans were worse sinners than all the other Galileans because they suffered this way? 3I tell you, no! But unless you repent, you too will all perish. 4Or those eighteen who died when the tower in Siloam fell on them —do you think they were more guilty than all the others living in Jerusalem? 5I tell you, no! But unless you repent, you too will all perish."

6Then he told this parable: "A man had a fig-tree, planted in his vineyard, and he went to look for fruit on it, but did not find any. 7So he said to the man who took care of the vineyard, 'For three years now I've been coming to look for fruit on this fig-tree and haven't found any. Cut it down! Why should it use up the soil?'

8"'Sir,' the man replied, 'leave it alone for one more year, and I'll dig round it and fertilise it. 9If it bears fruit next year, fine! If not, then cut it down.'"

A Crippled Woman Healed on the Sabbath

10On a Sabbath Jesus was teaching in one of the synagogues, 11and a woman was there who had been crippled by a spirit for eighteen years. She was bent over and could not straighten up at all. 12When Jesus saw her, he called her forward and said to her, "Woman, you are set free from your infirmity." 13Then he put his hands on her, and immediately she straightened up and praised God.

14Indignant because Jesus had healed on the Sabbath, the synagogue ruler said to the people, "There are six days for work. So come and be healed on those days, not on the Sabbath."

15The Lord answered him, "You hypocrites! Doesn't each of you on the Sabbath untie his ox or donkey from the stall and lead it out to give it water? 16Then should not this woman, a daughter of Abraham, whom Satan has kept bound for eighteen long years, be set free on the Sabbath day from what bound her?"

17When he said this, all his opponents were humiliated, but the people were delighted with all the wonderful things he was doing.

The Parables of the Mustard Seed and the Yeast

18Then Jesus asked, "What is the kingdom of God like? What shall I compare it to? 19It is like a mustard seed, which a man took and planted in his garden. It grew and became a tree, and the birds of the air perched in its branches."

20Again he asked, "What shall I compare the kingdom of God to? 21It is like yeast that a woman took and mixed into a large amount of flour until it worked all through the dough."

The Narrow Door

22Then Jesus went through the towns and villages, teaching as he made his way to Jerusalem. 23Someone asked him, "Lord, are only a few people going to be saved?"

He said to them, 24"Make every

effort to enter through the narrow door, because many, I tell you, will try to enter and will not be able to. 25Once the owner of the house gets up and closes the door, you will stand outside knocking and pleading, 'Sir, open the door for us.'

"But he will answer, 'I don't know you or where you come from.'

26"Then you will say, 'We ate and drank with you, and you taught in our streets.'

27"But he will reply, 'I don't know you or where you come from. Away from me, all you evildoers!'

28"There will be weeping there, and gnashing of teeth, when you see Abraham, Isaac and Jacob and all the prophets in the kingdom of God, but you yourselves thrown out. 29People will come from east and west and north and south, and will take their places at the feast in the kingdom of God. 30Indeed there are those who are last who will be first, and first who will be last."

READING FROM PROVERBS
Proverbs 9:1–12

Invitations of Wisdom and of Folly

9 Wisdom has built her house; she has hewn out its seven pillars. 2She has prepared her meat and mixed her wine; she has also set her table.

3She has sent out her maids, and she calls from the highest point of the city.
4"Let all who are simple come in here!" she says to those who lack judgment.
5"Come, eat my food and drink the wine I have mixed.
6Leave your simple ways and you will live; walk in the way of understanding.

7"Whoever corrects a mocker invites insult; whoever rebukes a wicked man incurs abuse.
8Do not rebuke a mocker or he will hate you; rebuke a wise man and he will love you.
9Instruct a wise man and he will be wiser still; teach a righteous man and he will add to his learning.

10"The fear of the LORD is the beginning of wisdom, and knowledge of the Holy One is understanding.
11For through me your days will be many, and years will be added to your life.
12If you are wise, your wisdom will reward you; if you are a mocker, you alone will suffer."

APRIL 11

OLD TESTAMENT READING
Deuteronomy 15:1–16:20

The Year for Cancelling Debts

15 At the end of every seven years you must cancel debts. ²This is how it is to be done: Every creditor shall cancel the loan he has made to his fellow Israelite. He shall not require payment from his fellow Israelite or brother, because the LORD's time for cancelling debts has been proclaimed. ³You may require payment from a foreigner, but you must cancel any debt your brother owes you. ⁴However, there should be no poor among you, for in the land the LORD your God is giving you to possess as your inheritance, he will richly bless you, ⁵if only you fully obey the LORD your God and are careful to follow all these commands I am giving you today. ⁶For the LORD your God will bless you as he has promised, and you will lend to many nations but will borrow from none. You will rule over many nations but none will rule over you.

⁷If there is a poor man among your brothers in any of the towns of the land that the LORD your God is giving you, do not be hard-hearted or tight-fisted towards your poor brother. ⁸Rather be open-handed and freely lend him whatever he needs. ⁹Be careful not to harbour this wicked thought: "The seventh year, the year for cancelling debts, is near," so that you do not show ill will towards your needy brother and give him nothing. He may then appeal to the LORD against you, and you will be found guilty of sin. ¹⁰Give generously to him and do so without a grudging heart; then because of this the LORD your God will bless you in all your work and in everything you put your hand to. ¹¹There will always be poor people in the land. Therefore I command you to be open-handed towards your brothers and towards the poor and needy in your land.

Freeing Servants

¹²If a fellow Hebrew, a man or woman, sells himself to you and serves you six years, in the seventh year you must let him go free. ¹³And when you release him, do not send him away empty-handed. ¹⁴Supply him liberally from your flock, your threshing-floor and your winepress. Give to him as the LORD your God has blessed you. ¹⁵Remember that you were slaves in Egypt and the LORD your God redeemed you. That is why I give you this command today.

¹⁶But if your servant says to you, "I do not want to leave you," because he loves you and your family and is well off with you, ¹⁷then take an awl and push it through his ear lobe into the door, and he will become your servant for life. Do the same for your maidservant.

¹⁸Do not consider it a hardship to set your servant free, because his service to you these six years has been worth twice as much as that of a hired hand. And the LORD your God will bless you in everything you do.

The Firstborn Animals

¹⁹Set apart for the LORD your God every firstborn male of your herds and flocks. Do not put the firstborn of your oxen to work, and do not shear the firstborn of your sheep. ²⁰Each year you and your family are to eat them in the presence of the LORD your God at the place he will choose. ²¹If an animal has a defect, is lame or blind, or has any serious flaw, you must not sacrifice it to the LORD your God. ²²You are to eat it in your own towns. Both the ceremonially unclean and the clean may eat it, as if it were gazelle or deer. ²³But you

must not eat the blood; pour it out on the ground like water.

Passover

16 Observe the month of Abib and celebrate the Passover of the LORD your God, because in the month of Abib he brought you out of Egypt by night. ²Sacrifice as the Passover to the LORD your God an animal from your flock or herd at the place the LORD will choose as a dwelling for his Name. ³Do not eat it with bread made with yeast, but for seven days eat unleavened bread, the bread of affliction, because you left Egypt in haste—so that all the days of your life you may remember the time of your departure from Egypt. ⁴Let no yeast be found in your possession in all your land for seven days. Do not let any of the meat you sacrifice on the evening of the first day remain until morning.

⁵You must not sacrifice the Passover in any town the LORD your God gives you ⁶except in the place he will choose as a dwelling for his Name. There you must sacrifice the Passover in the evening, when the sun goes down, on the anniversary of your departure from Egypt. ⁷Roast it and eat it at the place the LORD your God will choose. Then in the morning return to your tents. ⁸For six days eat unleavened bread and on the seventh day hold an assembly to the LORD your God and do no work.

Feast of Weeks

⁹Count off seven weeks from the time you begin to put the sickle to the standing corn. ¹⁰Then celebrate the Feast of Weeks to the LORD your God by giving a freewill offering in proportion to the blessings the LORD your God has given you. ¹¹And rejoice before the LORD your God at the place he will choose as a dwelling for his Name—you, your sons and daughters, your menservants and maidservants, the Levites in your towns, and the aliens, the fatherless

and the widows living among you. ¹²Remember that you were slaves in Egypt, and follow carefully these decrees.

Feast of Tabernacles

¹³Celebrate the Feast of Tabernacles for seven days after you have gathered the produce of your threshing-floor and your winepress. ¹⁴Be joyful at your Feast—you, your sons and daughters, your menservants and maidservants, and the Levites, the aliens, the fatherless and the widows who live in your towns. ¹⁵For seven days celebrate the Feast to the LORD your God at the place the LORD will choose. For the LORD your God will bless you in all your harvest and in all the work of your hands, and your joy will be complete.

¹⁶Three times a year all your men must appear before the LORD your God at the place he will choose: at the Feast of Unleavened Bread, the Feast of Weeks and the Feast of Tabernacles. No man should appear before the LORD empty-handed: ¹⁷Each of you must bring a gift in proportion to the way the LORD your God has blessed you.

Judges

¹⁸Appoint judges and officials for each of your tribes in every town the LORD your God is giving you, and they shall judge the people fairly. ¹⁹Do not pervert justice or show partiality. Do not accept a bribe, for a bribe blinds the eyes of the wise and twists the words of the righteous. ²⁰Follow justice and justice alone, so that you may live and possess the land the LORD your God is giving you.

NEW TESTAMENT READING
Luke 13:31–14:14

Jesus' Sorrow for Jerusalem

³¹At that time some Pharisees came to Jesus and said to him, "Leave this

place and go somewhere else. Herod wants to kill you."

32He replied, "Go tell that fox, 'I will drive out demons and heal people today and tomorrow, and on the third day I will reach my goal.' 33In any case, I must keep going today and tomorrow and the next day—for surely no prophet can die outside Jerusalem!

34"O Jerusalem, Jerusalem, you who kill the prophets and stone those sent to you, how often I have longed to gather your children together, as a hen gathers her chicks under her wings, but you were not willing! 35Look, your house is left to you desolate. I tell you, you will not see me again until you say, 'Blessed is he who comes in the name of the Lord.'"

Jesus at a Pharisee's House

14 One Sabbath, when Jesus went to eat in the house of a prominent Pharisee, he was being carefully watched. 2There in front of him was a man suffering from dropsy. 3Jesus asked the Pharisees and experts in the law, "Is it lawful to heal on the Sabbath or not?" 4But they remained silent. So taking hold of the man, he healed him and sent him away.

5Then he asked them, "If one of you has a son or an ox that falls into a well on the Sabbath day, will you not immediately pull him out?" 6And they had nothing to say.

7When he noticed how the guests picked the places of honour at the table, he told them this parable: 8"When someone invites you to a wedding feast, do not take the place of honour, for a person more distinguished than you may have been invited. 9If so, the host who invited both of you will come and say to you, 'Give this man your seat.' Then, humiliated, you will have to take the least important place. 10But when you are invited, take the lowest place, so that when your host comes, he will say to you, 'Friend, move up to a better place.' Then you will be honoured in the presence of all your fellow guests. 11For everyone who exalts himself will be humbled, and he who humbles himself will be exalted."

12Then Jesus said to his host, "When you give a luncheon or dinner, do not invite your friends, your brothers or relatives, or your rich neighbours; if you do, they may invite you back and so you will be repaid. 13But when you give a banquet, invite the poor, the crippled, the lame, the blind, 14and you will be blessed. Although they cannot repay you, you will be repaid at the resurrection of the righteous."

READING FROM PSALMS
Psalm 44:1–12

For the director of music. Of the Sons of Korah. A *maskil*.

1We have heard with our ears, O God;
   our fathers have told us
what you did in their days,
   in days long ago.
2With your hand you drove out the nations
   and planted our fathers;
you crushed the peoples
   and made our fathers flourish.
3It was not by their sword that they won the land,
   nor did their arm bring them victory;
it was your right hand, your arm,
   and the light of your face, for you loved them.

4You are my King and my God,
   who decrees victories for Jacob.
5Through you we push back our enemies;
   through your name we trample our foes.
6I do not trust in my bow,
   my sword does not bring me victory;
7but you give us victory over our enemies,
   you put our adversaries to shame.

8In God we make our boast all day
   long,
   and we will praise your name for
      ever.   *Selah*

9But now you have rejected and
   humbled us;
   you no longer go out with our
      armies.

10You made us retreat before the
   enemy,
   and our adversaries have
      plundered us.
11You gave us up to be devoured like
   sheep
   and have scattered us among the
      nations.
12You sold your people for a pittance,
   gaining nothing from their sale.

APRIL 12   DAY 102

OLD TESTAMENT READING
Deuteronomy 16:21–18:22

Worshipping Other Gods

21Do not set up any wooden Asherah
pole beside the altar you build to the
LORD your God, 22and do not erect a
sacred stone, for these the LORD your
God hates.

17 Do not sacrifice to the LORD
your God an ox or a sheep that
has any defect or flaw in it, for that
would be detestable to him.

2If a man or woman living among you
in one of the towns the LORD gives you
is found doing evil in the eyes of the
LORD your God in violation of his covenant, 3and contrary to my command
has worshipped other gods, bowing
down to them or to the sun or the moon
or the stars of the sky, 4and this has been
brought to your attention, then you
must investigate it thoroughly. If it is
true and it has been proved that this
detestable thing has been done in Israel,
5take the man or woman who has done
this evil deed to your city gate and stone
that person to death. 6On the testimony
of two or three witnesses a man shall be
put to death, but no-one shall be put to
death on the testimony of only one witness. 7The hands of the witnesses must
be the first in putting him to death, and

then the hands of all the people. You
must purge the evil from among you.

Law Courts

8If cases come before your courts that
are too difficult for you to judge—
whether bloodshed, lawsuits or assaults
—take them to the place the LORD your
God will choose. 9Go to the priests,
who are Levites, and to the judge who is
in office at that time. Enquire of them
and they will give you the verdict. 10You
must act according to the decisions they
give you at the place the LORD will
choose. Be careful to do everything
they direct you to do. 11Act according to
the law they teach you and the decisions
they give you. Do not turn aside from
what they tell you, to the right or to the
left. 12The man who shows contempt for
the judge or for the priest who stands
ministering there to the LORD your God
must be put to death. You must purge
the evil from Israel. 13All the people will
hear and be afraid, and will not be
contemptuous again.

The King

14When you enter the land the LORD
your God is giving you and have taken
possession of it and settled in it, and you
say, "Let us set a king over us like all the

nations around us," [15]be sure to appoint over you the king the LORD your God chooses. He must be from among your own brothers. Do not place a foreigner over you, one who is not a brother Israelite. [16]The king, moreover, must not acquire great numbers of horses for himself or make the people return to Egypt to get more of them, for the LORD has told you, "You are not to go back that way again." [17]He must not take many wives, or his heart will be led astray. He must not accumulate large amounts of silver and gold.

[18]When he takes the throne of his kingdom, he is to write for himself on a scroll a copy of this law, taken from that of the priests, who are Levites. [19]It is to be with him, and he is to read it all the days of his life so that he may learn to revere the LORD his God and follow carefully all the words of this law and these decrees [20]and not consider himself better than his brothers and turn from the law to the right or to the left. Then he and his descendants will reign a long time over his kingdom in Israel.

Offerings for Priests and Levites

18 The priests, who are Levites— indeed the whole tribe of Levi —are to have no allotment or inheritance with Israel. They shall live on the offerings made to the LORD by fire, for that is their inheritance. [2]They shall have no inheritance among their brothers; the LORD is their inheritance, as he promised them.

[3]This is the share due to the priests from the people who sacrifice a bull or a sheep: the shoulder, the jowls and the inner parts. [4]You are to give them the firstfruits of your grain, new wine and oil, and the first wool from the shearing of your sheep, [5]for the LORD your God has chosen them and their descendants out of all your tribes to stand and minister in the LORD's name always.

[6]If a Levite moves from one of your towns anywhere in Israel where he is living, and comes in all earnestness to the place the LORD will choose, [7]he may minister in the name of the LORD his God like all his fellow Levites who serve there in the presence of the LORD. [8]He is to share equally in their benefits even though he has received money from the sale of family possessions.

Detestable Practices

[9]When you enter the land the LORD your God is giving you, do not learn to imitate the detestable ways of the nations there. [10]Let no-one be found among you who sacrifices his son or daughter in the fire, who practises divination or sorcery, interprets omens, engages in witchcraft, [11]or casts spells, or who is a medium or spiritist or who consults the dead. [12]Anyone who does these things is detestable to the LORD, and because of these detestable practices the LORD your God will drive out those nations before you. [13]You must be blameless before the LORD your God.

The Prophet

[14]The nations you will dispossess listen to those who practise sorcery or divination. But as for you, the LORD your God has not permitted you to do so. [15]The LORD your God will raise up for you a prophet like me from among your own brothers. You must listen to him. [16]For this is what you asked of the LORD your God at Horeb on the day of the assembly when you said, "Let us not hear the voice of the LORD our God nor see this great fire any more, or we will die."

[17]The LORD said to me: "What they say is good. [18]I will raise up for them a prophet like you from among their brothers; I will put my words in his mouth, and he will tell them everything I command him. [19]If anyone does not listen to my words that the prophet speaks in my name, I myself will call him to account. [20]But a prophet who presumes to speak in my name anything

I have not commanded him to say, or a prophet who speaks in the name of other gods, must be put to death."

21You may say to yourselves, "How can we know when a message has not been spoken by the LORD?" 22If what a prophet proclaims in the name of the LORD does not take place or come true, that is a message the LORD has not spoken. That prophet has spoken presumptuously. Do not be afraid of him.

NEW TESTAMENT READING
Luke 14:15–35

The Parable of the Great Banquet

15When one of those at the table with him heard this, he said to Jesus, "Blessed is the man who will eat at the feast in the kingdom of God."

16Jesus replied: "A certain man was preparing a great banquet and invited many guests. 17At the time of the banquet he sent his servant to tell those who had been invited, 'Come, for everything is now ready.'

18"But they all alike began to make excuses. The first said, 'I have just bought a field, and I must go and see it. Please excuse me.'

19"Another said, 'I have just bought five yoke of oxen, and I'm on my way to try them out. Please excuse me.'

20"Still another said, 'I have just got married, so I can't come.'

21"The servant came back and reported this to his master. Then the owner of the house became angry and ordered his servant, 'Go out quickly into the streets and alleys of the town and bring in the poor, the crippled, the blind and the lame.'

22"'Sir,' the servant said, 'what you ordered has been done, but there is still room.'

23"Then the master told his servant, 'Go out to the roads and country lanes and make them come in, so that my house will be full. 24I tell you, not one of those men who were invited will get a taste of my banquet.'"

The Cost of Being a Disciple

25Large crowds were travelling with Jesus, and turning to them he said: 26"If anyone comes to me and does not hate his father and mother, his wife and children, his brothers and sisters—yes, even his own life—he cannot be my disciple. 27And anyone who does not carry his cross and follow me cannot be my disciple.

28"Suppose one of you wants to build a tower. Will he not first sit down and estimate the cost to see if he has enough money to complete it? 29For if he lays the foundation and is not able to finish it, everyone who sees it will ridicule him, 30saying, 'This fellow began to build and was not able to finish.'

31"Or suppose a king is about to go to war against another king. Will he not first sit down and consider whether he is able with ten thousand men to oppose the one coming against him with twenty thousand? 32If he is not able, he will send a delegation while the other is still a long way off and will ask for terms of peace. 33In the same way, any of you who does not give up everything he has cannot be my disciple.

34"Salt is good, but if it loses its saltiness, how can it be made salty again? 35It is fit neither for the soil nor for the manure heap; it is thrown out.

"He who has ears to hear, let him hear."

READING FROM PSALMS
Psalm 44:13–26

13You have made us a reproach to our
  neighbours,
   the scorn and derision of those
     around us.
14You have made us a byword among
   the nations;
   the peoples shake their heads at us.
15My disgrace is before me all day long,
   and my face is covered with shame
16at the taunts of those who reproach
     and revile me,

because of the enemy, who is bent
on revenge.

17All this happened to us,
though we had not forgotten you
or been false to your covenant.
18Our hearts had not turned back;
our feet had not strayed from your
path.
19But you crushed us and made us a
haunt for jackals
and covered us over with deep
darkness.

20If we had forgotten the name of our
God
or spread out our hands to a
foreign god,
21would not God have discovered it,
since he knows the secrets of the
heart?
22Yet for your sake we face death all
day long;
we are considered as sheep to be
slaughtered.

23Awake, O Lord! Why do you sleep?
Rouse yourself! Do not reject us
for ever.
24Why do you hide your face
and forget our misery and
oppression?

25We are brought down to the dust;
our bodies cling to the ground.
26Rise up and help us;
redeem us because of your
unfailing love.

DAY 103

APRIL 13

OLD TESTAMENT READING
Deuteronomy 19:1–20:20

Cities of Refuge

19 When the LORD your God has
destroyed the nations whose
land he is giving you, and when you
have driven them out and settled in
their towns and houses, 2then set aside
for yourselves three cities centrally lo-
cated in the land the LORD your God is
giving you to possess. 3Build roads to
them and divide into three parts the
land the LORD your God is giving you as
an inheritance, so that anyone who kills
a man may flee there.

4This is the rule concerning the man
who kills another and flees there to save
his life—one who kills his neighbour
unintentionally, without malice aforethought. 5For instance, a man may go
into the forest with his neighbour to cut
wood, and as he swings his axe to fell a
tree, the head may fly off and hit his
neighbour and kill him. That man may
flee to one of these cities and save his
life. 6Otherwise, the avenger of blood
might pursue him in a rage, overtake
him if the distance is too great, and kill
him even though he is not deserving of
death, since he did it to his neighbour
without malice aforethought. 7This is
why I command you to set aside for
yourselves three cities.

8If the LORD your God enlarges your
territory, as he promised on oath to
your forefathers, and gives you the
whole land he promised them, 9because
you carefully follow all these laws I
command you today—to love the LORD
your God and to walk always in his
ways—then you are to set aside three
more cities. 10Do this so that innocent
blood will not be shed in your land,
which the LORD your God is giving you
as your inheritance, and so that you will
not be guilty of bloodshed.

11But if a man hates his neighbour
and lies in wait for him, assaults and
kills him, and then flees to one of these

cities, 12the elders of his town shall send for him, bring him back from the city, and hand him over to the avenger of blood to die. 13Show him no pity. You must purge from Israel the guilt of shedding innocent blood, so that it may go well with you.

14Do not move your neighbour's boundary stone set up by your predecessors in the inheritance you receive in the land the LORD your God is giving you to possess.

Witnesses

15One witness is not enough to convict a man accused of any crime or offence he may have committed. A matter must be established by the testimony of two or three witnesses.

16If a malicious witness takes the stand to accuse a man of a crime, 17the two men involved in the dispute must stand in the presence of the LORD before the priests and the judges who are in office at the time. 18The judges must make a thorough investigation, and if the witness proves to be a liar, giving false testimony against his brother, 19then do to him as he intended to do to his brother. You must purge the evil from among you. 20The rest of the people will hear of this and be afraid, and never again will such an evil thing be done among you. 21Show no pity: life for life, eye for eye, tooth for tooth, hand for hand, foot for foot.

Going to War

20 When you go to war against your enemies and see horses and chariots and an army greater than yours, do not be afraid of them, because the LORD your God, who brought you up out of Egypt, will be with you. 2When you are about to go into battle, the priest shall come forward and address the army. 3He shall say: "Hear, O Israel, today you are going into battle against your enemies. Do not be fainthearted or afraid; do not be terrified or give way to panic before them. 4For the LORD your God is the one who goes with you to fight for you against your enemies to give you victory."

5The officers shall say to the army: "Has anyone built a new house and not dedicated it? Let him go home, or he may die in battle and someone else may dedicate it. 6Has anyone planted a vineyard and not begun to enjoy it? Let him go home, or he may die in battle and someone else enjoy it. 7Has anyone become pledged to a woman and not married her? Let him go home, or he may die in battle and someone else marry her." 8Then the officers shall add, "Is any man afraid or fainthearted? Let him go home so that his brothers will not become disheartened too." 9When the officers have finished speaking to the army, they shall appoint commanders over it.

10When you march up to attack a city, make its people an offer of peace. 11If they accept and open its gates, all the people in it shall be subject to forced labour and shall work for you. 12If they refuse to make peace and they engage you in battle, lay siege to that city. 13When the LORD your God delivers it into your hand, put to the sword all the men in it. 14As for the women, the children, the livestock and everything else in the city, you may take these as plunder for yourselves. And you may use the plunder the LORD your God gives you from your enemies. 15This is how you are to treat all the cities that are at a distance from you and do not belong to the nations nearby.

16However, in the cities of the nations the LORD your God is giving you as an inheritance, do not leave alive anything that breathes. 17Completely destroy them—the Hittites, Amorites, Canaanites, Perizzites, Hivites and Jebusites—as the LORD your God has commanded you. 18Otherwise, they will teach you to follow all the detestable things they do in worshipping their gods, and you will sin against the LORD your God.

19When you lay siege to a city for a long time, fighting against it to capture it, do not destroy its trees by putting an axe to them, because you can eat their fruit. Do not cut them down. Are the trees of the field people, that you should besiege them? 20However, you may cut down trees that you know are not fruit trees and use them to build siege works until the city at war with you falls.

NEW TESTAMENT READING
Luke 15:1–32

The Parable of the Lost Sheep

15 Now the tax collectors and "sinners" were all gathering round to hear him. 2But the Pharisees and the teachers of the law muttered, "This man welcomes sinners, and eats with them."

3Then Jesus told them this parable: 4"Suppose one of you has a hundred sheep and loses one of them. Does he not leave the ninety-nine in the open country and go after the lost sheep until he finds it? 5And when he finds it, he joyfully puts it on his shoulders 6and goes home. Then he calls his friends and neighbours together and says, 'Rejoice with me; I have found my lost sheep.' 7I tell you that in the same way there will be more rejoicing in heaven over one sinner who repents than over ninety-nine righteous persons who do not need to repent.

The Parable of the Lost Coin

8"Or suppose a woman has ten silver coins and loses one. Does she not light a lamp, sweep the house and search carefully until she finds it? 9And when she finds it, she calls her friends and neighbours together and says, 'Rejoice with me; I have found my lost coin.' 10In the same way, I tell you, there is rejoicing in the presence of the angels of God over one sinner who repents."

The Parable of the Lost Son

11Jesus continued: "There was a man who had two sons. 12The younger one said to his father, 'Father, give me my share of the estate.' So he divided his property between them.

13"Not long after that, the younger son got together all he had, set off for a distant country and there squandered his wealth in wild living. 14After he had spent everything, there was a severe famine in that whole country, and he began to be in need. 15So he went and hired himself out to a citizen of that country, who sent him to his fields to feed pigs. 16He longed to fill his stomach with the pods that the pigs were eating, but no-one gave him anything.

17"When he came to his senses, he said, 'How many of my father's hired men have food to spare, and here I am starving to death! 18I will set out and go back to my father and say to him: Father, I have sinned against heaven and against you. 19I am no longer worthy to be called your son; make me like one of your hired men.' 20So he got up and went to his father.

"But while he was still a long way off, his father saw him and was filled with compassion for him; he ran to his son, threw his arms around him and kissed him.

21"The son said to him, 'Father, I have sinned against heaven and against you. I am no longer worthy to be called your son.'

22"But the father said to his servants, 'Quick! Bring the best robe and put it on him. Put a ring on his finger and sandals on his feet. 23Bring the fattened calf and kill it. Let's have a feast and celebrate. 24For this son of mine was dead and is alive again; he was lost and is found.' So they began to celebrate.

25"Meanwhile, the older son was in the field. When he came near the house, he heard music and dancing. 26So he called one of the servants and asked him what was going on. 27'Your brother has come,' he replied, 'and your father has killed the fattened calf because he has him back safe and sound.'

28"The older brother became angry and refused to go in. So his father went out and pleaded with him. 29But he answered his father, 'Look! All these years I've been slaving for you and never disobeyed your orders. Yet you never gave me even a young goat so I could celebrate with my friends. 30But when this son of yours who has squandered your property with prostitutes comes home, you kill the fattened calf for him!'

31"'My son,' the father said, 'you are always with me, and everything I have is yours. 32But we had to celebrate and be glad, because this brother of yours was dead and is alive again; he was lost and is found.'"

READING FROM PSALMS
Psalm 45:1–9

For the director of music. To ⌊the tune of⌋ "Lilies". Of the Sons of Korah. A *maskil*. A wedding song.

1My heart is stirred by a noble theme
    as I recite my verses for the king;
    my tongue is the pen of a skilful
      writer.

2You are the most excellent of men
    and your lips have been anointed
      with grace,

since God has blessed you for
      ever.
3Gird your sword upon your side, O
    mighty one;
    clothe yourself with splendour and
      majesty.
4In your majesty ride forth
    victoriously
    on behalf of truth, humility and
      righteousness;
    let your right hand display
      awesome deeds.
5Let your sharp arrows pierce the
    hearts of the king's enemies;
    let the nations fall beneath your
      feet.
6Your throne, O God, will last for
    ever and ever;
    a sceptre of justice will be the
      sceptre of your kingdom.
7You love righteousness and hate
    wickedness;
    therefore God, your God, has set
      you above your companions
    by anointing you with the oil of
      joy.
8All your robes are fragrant with
    myrrh and aloes and cassia;
    from palaces adorned with ivory
    the music of the strings makes you
      glad.
9Daughters of kings are among your
    honoured women;
    at your right hand is the royal bride
      in gold of Ophir.

APRIL 14   DAY 104

OLD TESTAMENT READING
Deuteronomy 21:1–22:30

Atonement for an Unsolved Murder

21 If a man is found slain, lying in a field in the land the LORD your God is giving you to possess, and it is not known who killed him, 2your elders and judges shall go out and measure the

distance from the body to the neighbouring towns. 3Then the elders of the town nearest the body shall take a heifer that has never been worked and has never worn a yoke 4and lead her down to a valley that has not been ploughed or planted and where there is a flowing stream. There in the valley they are to break the heifer's neck. 5The priests, the sons of Levi, shall step forward, for the LORD your God has chosen them to minister and to pronounce blessings in the name of the LORD and to decide all cases of dispute and assault. ⁶Then all the elders of the town nearest the body shall wash their hands over the heifer whose neck was broken in the valley, ⁷and they shall declare: "Our hands did not shed this blood, nor did our eyes see it done. ⁸Accept this atonement for your people Israel, whom you have redeemed, O LORD, and do not hold your people guilty of the blood of an innocent man." And the bloodshed will be atoned for. ⁹So you will purge from yourselves the guilt of shedding innocent blood, since you have done what is right in the eyes of the LORD.

Marrying a Captive Woman

¹⁰When you go to war against your enemies and the LORD your God delivers them into your hands and you take captives, ¹¹if you notice among the captives a beautiful woman and are attracted to her, you may take her as your wife. ¹²Bring her into your home and make her shave her head, trim her nails ¹³and put aside the clothes she was wearing when captured. After she has lived in your house and mourned her father and mother for a full month, then you may go to her and be her husband and she shall be your wife. ¹⁴If you are not pleased with her, let her go wherever she wishes. You must not sell her or treat her as a slave, since you have dishonoured her.

The Right of the Firstborn

¹⁵If a man has two wives, and he loves one but not the other, and both bear him sons but the firstborn is the son of the wife he does not love, ¹⁶when he wills his property to his sons, he must not give the rights of the firstborn to the son of the wife he loves in preference to his actual firstborn, the son of the wife he does not love. ¹⁷He must acknowledge the son of his unloved wife as the firstborn by giving him a double share of all he has. That son is the first sign of his father's strength. The right of the firstborn belongs to him.

A Rebellious Son

¹⁸If a man has a stubborn and rebellious son who does not obey his father and mother and will not listen to them when they discipline him, ¹⁹his father and mother shall take hold of him and bring him to the elders at the gate of his town. ²⁰They shall say to the elders, "This son of ours is stubborn and rebellious. He will not obey us. He is a profligate and a drunkard." ²¹Then all the men of his town shall stone him to death. You must purge the evil from among you. All Israel will hear of it and be afraid.

Various Laws

²²If a man guilty of a capital offence is put to death and his body is hung on a tree, ²³you must not leave his body on the tree overnight. Be sure to bury him that same day, because anyone who is hung on a tree is under God's curse. You must not desecrate the land the LORD your God is giving you as an inheritance.

22 If you see your brother's ox or sheep straying, do not ignore it but be sure to take it back to him. ²If the brother does not live near you or if you do not know who he is, take it home with you and keep it until he comes looking for it. Then give it back to him. ³Do the same if you find your brother's donkey or his cloak or anything he loses. Do not ignore it.

⁴If you see your brother's donkey or his ox fallen on the road, do not ignore it. Help him to get it to its feet.

⁵A woman must not wear men's clothing, nor a man wear women's clothing, for the LORD your God detests anyone who does this.

⁶If you come across a bird's nest beside the road, either in a tree or on the ground, and the mother is sitting on the young or on the eggs, do not take the mother with the young. ⁷You may take the young, but be sure to let the mother go, so that it may go well with you and you may have a long life.

⁸When you build a new house, make a parapet around your roof so that you may not bring the guilt of bloodshed on your house if someone falls from the roof.

⁹Do not plant two kinds of seed in your vineyard; if you do, not only the crops you plant but also the fruit of the vineyard will be defiled.

¹⁰Do not plough with an ox and a donkey yoked together.

¹¹Do not wear clothes of wool and linen woven together.

¹²Make tassels on the four corners of the cloak you wear.

Marriage Violations

¹³If a man takes a wife and, after lying with her, dislikes her ¹⁴and slanders her and gives her a bad name, saying, "I married this woman, but when I approached her, I did not find proof of her virginity," ¹⁵then the girl's father and mother shall bring proof that she was a virgin to the town elders at the gate. ¹⁶The girl's father will say to the elders, "I gave my daughter in marriage to this man, but he dislikes her. ¹⁷Now he has slandered her and said, 'I did not find your daughter to be a virgin.' But here is the proof of my daughter's virginity." Then her parents shall display the cloth before the elders of the town, ¹⁸and the elders shall take the man and punish him. ¹⁹They shall fine him a hundred shekels of silver and give them to the girl's father, because this man has given an Israelite virgin a bad name. She shall continue to be his wife; he must not divorce her as long as he lives.

²⁰If, however, the charge is true and no proof of the girl's virginity can be found, ²¹she shall be brought to the door of her father's house and there the men of her town shall stone her to death. She has done a disgraceful thing in Israel by being promiscuous while still in her father's house. You must purge the evil from among you.

²²If a man is found sleeping with another man's wife, both the man who slept with her and the woman must die. You must purge the evil from Israel.

²³If a man happens to meet in a town a virgin pledged to be married and he sleeps with her, ²⁴you shall take both of them to the gate of that town and stone them to death—the girl because she was in a town and did not scream for help, and the man because he violated another man's wife. You must purge the evil from among you.

²⁵But if out in the country a man happens to meet a girl pledged to be married and rapes her, only the man who has done this shall die. ²⁶Do nothing to the girl; she has committed no sin deserving death. This case is like that of someone who attacks and murders his neighbour, ²⁷for the man found the girl out in the country, and though the betrothed girl screamed, there was no-one to rescue her.

²⁸If a man happens to meet a virgin who is not pledged to be married and rapes her and they are discovered, ²⁹he shall pay the girl's father fifty shekels of silver. He must marry the girl, for he has violated her. He can never divorce her as long as he lives.

³⁰A man is not to marry his father's wife; he must not dishonour his father's bed.

NEW TESTAMENT READING
Luke 16:1–18

The Parable of the Shrewd Manager

16 Jesus told his disciples: "There was a rich man whose manager was accused of wasting his possessions. ²So he called him in and asked him, 'What is this I hear about you? Give an account of your management, because you cannot be manager any longer.'

3"The manager said to himself, 'What shall I do now? My master is taking away my job. I'm not strong enough to dig, and I'm ashamed to beg —4I know what I'll do so that, when I lose my job here, people will welcome me into their houses.'

5"So he called in each one of his master's debtors. He asked the first, 'How much do you owe my master?'

6"'Eight hundred gallons of olive oil,' he replied.

"The manager told him, 'Take your bill, sit down quickly, and make it four hundred.'

7"Then he asked the second, 'And how much do you owe?'

"'A thousand bushels of wheat,' he replied.

"He told him, 'Take your bill and make it eight hundred.'

8"The master commended the dishonest manager because he had acted shrewdly. For the people of this world are more shrewd in dealing with their own kind than are the people of the light. 9I tell you, use worldly wealth to gain friends for yourselves, so that when it is gone, you will be welcomed into eternal dwellings.

10"Whoever can be trusted with very little can also be trusted with much, and whoever is dishonest with very little will also be dishonest with much. 11So if you have not been trustworthy in handling worldly wealth, who will trust you with true riches? 12And if you have not been trustworthy with someone else's property, who will give you property of your own?

13"No servant can serve two masters. Either he will hate the one and love the other, or he will be devoted to the one and despise the other. You cannot serve both God and Money."

14The Pharisees, who loved money, heard all this and were sneering at Jesus. 15He said to them, "You are the ones who justify yourselves in the eyes of men, but God knows your hearts. What is highly valued among men is detestable in God's sight.

Additional Teachings

16"The Law and the Prophets were proclaimed until John. Since that time, the good news of the kingdom of God is being preached, and everyone is forcing his way into it. 17It is easier for heaven and earth to disappear than for the least stroke of a pen to drop out of the Law.

18"Anyone who divorces his wife and marries another woman commits adultery, and the man who marries a divorced woman commits adultery.

READING FROM PROVERBS
Proverbs 9:13–18

13The woman Folly is loud;
    she is undisciplined and without knowledge.
14She sits at the door of her house,
    on a seat at the highest point of the city,
15calling out to those who pass by,
    who go straight on their way.
16"Let all who are simple come in here!"
    she says to those who lack judgment.
17"Stolen water is sweet;
    food eaten in secret is delicious!"
18But little do they know that the dead are there,
    that her guests are in the depths of the grave.

OLD TESTAMENT READING
Deuteronomy 23:1–25:19

Exclusion From the Assembly

23 No-one who has been emasculated by crushing or cutting may enter the assembly of the LORD.

²No-one born of a forbidden marriage nor any of his descendants may enter the assembly of the LORD, even down to the tenth generation.

³No Ammonite or Moabite or any of his descendants may enter the assembly of the LORD, even down to the tenth generation. ⁴For they did not come to meet you with bread and water on your way when you came out of Egypt, and they hired Balaam son of Beor from Pethor in Aram Naharaim to pronounce a curse on you. ⁵However, the LORD your God would not listen to Balaam but turned the curse into a blessing for you, because the LORD your God loves you. ⁶Do not seek a treaty of friendship with them as long as you live.

⁷Do not abhor an Edomite, for he is your brother. Do not abhor an Egyptian, because you lived as an alien in his country. ⁸The third generation of children born to them may enter the assembly of the LORD.

Uncleanness in the Camp

⁹When you are encamped against your enemies, keep away from everything impure. ¹⁰If one of your men is unclean because of a nocturnal emission, he is to go outside the camp and stay there. ¹¹But as evening approaches he is to wash himself, and at sunset he may return to the camp.

¹²Designate a place outside the camp where you can go to relieve yourself. ¹³As part of your equipment have something to dig with, and when you relieve yourself, dig a hole and cover up your excrement. ¹⁴For the LORD your God moves about in your camp to protect you and to deliver your enemies to you. Your camp must be holy, so that he will not see among you anything indecent and turn away from you.

Miscellaneous Laws

¹⁵If a slave has taken refuge with you, do not hand him over to his master. ¹⁶Let him live among you wherever he likes and in whatever town he chooses. Do not oppress him.

¹⁷No Israelite man or woman is to become a shrine-prostitute. ¹⁸You must not bring the earnings of a female prostitute or of a male prostitute into the house of the LORD your God to pay any vow, because the LORD your God detests them both.

¹⁹Do not charge your brother interest, whether on money or food or anything else that may earn interest. ²⁰You may charge a foreigner interest, but not a brother Israelite, so that the LORD your God may bless you in everything you put your hand to in the land you are entering to possess.

²¹If you make a vow to the LORD your God, do not be slow to pay it, for the LORD your God will certainly demand it of you and you will be guilty of sin. ²²But if you refrain from making a vow, you will not be guilty. ²³Whatever your lips utter you must be sure to do, because you made your vow freely to the LORD your God with your own mouth.

²⁴If you enter your neighbour's vineyard, you may eat all the grapes you want, but do not put any in your basket. ²⁵If you enter your neighbour's cornfield, you may pick the ears with your hands, but you must not put a sickle to his standing corn.

24 If a man marries a woman who becomes displeasing to him because he finds something indecent about her, and he writes her a certificate of divorce, gives it to her and sends her from his house, 2and if after she leaves his house she becomes the wife of another man, 3and her second husband dislikes her and writes her a certificate of divorce, gives it to her and sends her from his house, or if he dies, 4then her first husband, who divorced her, is not allowed to marry her again after she has been defiled. That would be detestable in the eyes of the LORD. Do not bring sin upon the land the LORD your God is giving you as an inheritance.

5If a man has recently married, he must not be sent to war or have any other duty laid on him. For one year he is to be free to stay at home and bring happiness to the wife he has married.

6Do not take a pair of millstones—not even the upper one—as security for a debt, because that would be taking a man's livelihood as security.

7If a man is caught kidnapping one of his brother Israelites and treats him as a slave or sells him, the kidnapper must die. You must purge the evil from among you.

8In cases of leprous diseases be very careful to do exactly as the priests, who are Levites, instruct you. You must follow carefully what I have commanded them. 9Remember what the LORD your God did to Miriam along the way after you came out of Egypt.

10When you make a loan of any kind to your neighbour, do not go into his house to get what he is offering as a pledge. 11Stay outside and let the man to whom you are making the loan bring the pledge out to you. 12If the man is poor, do not go to sleep with his pledge in your possession. 13Return his cloak to him by sunset so that he may sleep in it. Then he will thank you, and it will be regarded as a righteous act in the sight of the LORD your God.

14Do not take advantage of a hired man who is poor and needy, whether he is a brother Israelite or an alien living in one of your towns. 15Pay him his wages each day before sunset, because he is poor and is counting on it. Otherwise he

may cry to the LORD against you, and you will be guilty of sin.

16Fathers shall not be put to death for their children, nor children put to death for their fathers; each is to die for his own sin.

17Do not deprive the alien or the fatherless of justice, or take the cloak of the widow as a pledge. 18Remember that you were slaves in Egypt and the LORD your God redeemed you from there. That is why I command you to do this.

19When you are harvesting in your field and you overlook a sheaf, do not go back to get it. Leave it for the alien, the fatherless and the widow, so that the LORD your God may bless you in all the work of your hands. 20When you beat the olives from your trees, do not go over the branches a second time. Leave what remains for the alien, the fatherless and the widow. 21When you harvest the grapes in your vineyard, do not go over the vines again. Leave what remains for the alien, the fatherless and the widow. 22Remember that you were slaves in Egypt. That is why I command you to do this.

25 When men have a dispute, they are to take it to court and the judges will decide the case, acquitting the innocent and condemning the guilty. 2If the guilty man deserves to be beaten, the judge shall make him lie down and have him flogged in his presence with the number of lashes his crime deserves, 3but he must not give him more than forty lashes. If he is flogged more than that, your brother will be degraded in your eyes.

4Do not muzzle an ox while it is treading out the grain.

5If brothers are living together and one of them dies without a son, his widow must not marry outside the family. Her husband's brother shall take her and marry her and fulfil the duty of a brother-in-law to her. 6The first son she bears shall carry on the name of the dead brother so that his name will not be blotted out from Israel.

7However, if a man does not want to marry his brother's wife, she shall go to the elders at the town gate and say, "My husband's brother refuses to carry on his brother's name in Israel. He will not fulfil the duty of a brother-in-law to me." 8Then the elders of his town shall summon him and talk to him. If he persists in saying, "I do not want to marry her," 9his brother's widow shall go up to him in the presence of the elders, take off one of his sandals, spit in his face and say, "This is what is done to the man who will not build up his brother's family line." 10That man's line shall be known in Israel as The Family of the Unsandalled.

11If two men are fighting and the wife of one of them comes to rescue her husband from his assailant, and she reaches out and seizes him by his private parts, 12you shall cut off her hand. Show her no pity.

13Do not have two differing weights in your bag—one heavy, one light. 14Do not have two differing measures in your house—one large, one small. 15You must have accurate and honest weights and measures, so that you may live long in the land the LORD your God is giving you. 16For the LORD your God detests anyone who does these things, anyone who deals dishonestly.

17Remember what the Amalekites did to you along the way when you came out of Egypt. 18When you were weary and worn out, they met you on your journey and cut off all who were lagging behind; they had no fear of God. 19When the LORD your God gives you rest from all the enemies around you in the land he is giving you to possess as an inheritance, you shall blot out the memory of Amalek from under heaven. Do not forget!

NEW TESTAMENT READING
Luke 16:19–17:10

The Rich Man and Lazarus

19"There was a rich man who was dressed in purple and fine linen and lived in luxury every day. 20At his gate was laid a beggar named Lazarus, covered with sores 21and longing to eat what fell from the rich man's table. Even the dogs came and licked his sores.

22"The time came when the beggar died and the angels carried him to Abraham's side. The rich man also died and was buried. 23In hell, where he was in torment, he looked up and saw Abraham far away, with Lazarus by his side. 24So he called to him, 'Father Abraham, have pity on me and send Lazarus to dip the tip of his finger in water and cool my tongue, because I am in agony in this fire.'

25"But Abraham replied, 'Son, remember that in your lifetime you received your good things, while Lazarus received bad things, but now he is comforted here and you are in agony. 26And besides all this, between us and you a great chasm has been fixed, so that those who want to go from here to you cannot, nor can anyone cross over from there to us.'

27"He answered, 'Then I beg you, father, send Lazarus to my father's house, 28for I have five brothers. Let him warn them, so that they will not also come to this place of torment.'

29"Abraham replied, 'They have Moses and the Prophets; let them listen to them.'

30" 'No, father Abraham,' he said, 'but if someone from the dead goes to them, they will repent.'

31"He said to him, 'If they do not listen to Moses and the Prophets, they will not be convinced even if someone rises from the dead.' "

Sin, Faith, Duty

17 Jesus said to his disciples: "Things that cause people to sin are bound to come, but woe to that person through whom they come. 2It would be better for him to be thrown into the sea with a millstone tied round his neck than for him to cause one of

these little ones to sin. ³So watch yourselves.

"If your brother sins, rebuke him, and if he repents, forgive him. ⁴If he sins against you seven times in a day, and seven times comes back to you and says, 'I repent,' forgive him."

⁵The apostles said to the Lord, "Increase our faith!"

⁶He replied, "If you have faith as small as a mustard seed, you can say to this mulberry tree, 'Be uprooted and planted in the sea,' and it will obey you.

⁷"Suppose one of you had a servant ploughing or looking after the sheep. Would he say to the servant when he comes in from the field, 'Come along now and sit down to eat'? ⁸Would he not rather say, 'Prepare my supper, get yourself ready and wait on me while I eat and drink; after that you may eat and drink'? ⁹Would he thank the servant because he did what he was told to do? ¹⁰So you also, when you have done everything you were told to do, should say, 'We are unworthy servants; we have only done our duty.'"

READING FROM PSALMS
Psalm 45:10–17

¹⁰Listen, O daughter, consider and give ear:

Forget your people and your
    father's house.
¹¹The king is enthralled by your
    beauty;
  honour him, for he is your lord.
¹²The Daughter of Tyre will come with
    a gift,
  men of wealth will seek your
    favour.

¹³All glorious is the princess within
    ⌐her chamber⌐;
  her gown is interwoven with gold.
¹⁴In embroidered garments she is led to
    the king;
  her virgin companions follow her
    and are brought to you.
¹⁵They are led in with joy and
    gladness;
  they enter the palace of the
    king.

¹⁶Your sons will take the place of your
    fathers;
  you will make them princes
    throughout the land.
¹⁷I will perpetuate your memory
    through all generations;
  therefore the nations will praise
    you for ever and ever.

DAY 106

APRIL 16

OLD TESTAMENT READING
Deuteronomy 26:1–28:14

Firstfruits and Tithes

26 When you have entered the land that the LORD your God is giving you as an inheritance and have taken possession of it and settled in it, ²take some of the firstfruits of all that you produce from the soil of the land that the LORD your God is giving you and put them in a basket. Then go to the place that the LORD your God will choose as a dwelling for his Name ³and say to the priest in office at the time, "I declare today to the LORD your God that I have come to the land that the LORD swore to our forefathers to give us." ⁴The priest shall take the basket from your hands and set it down in front of the altar of the LORD your God. ⁵Then you shall declare before the LORD your God: "My father was a wandering Aramean, and he went down into Egypt with a few people and lived there and became a great nation, powerful and numerous. 6But the Egyptians ill-treated us and made us suffer, putting us to hard labour. 7Then we cried out to the LORD, the God of our fathers, and the LORD heard our voice and saw our misery, toil and oppression. 8So the LORD brought us out of Egypt with a mighty hand and an outstretched arm, with great terror and with miraculous signs and wonders. 9He brought us to this place and gave us this land, a land flowing with milk and honey; 10and now I bring the firstfruits of the soil that you, O LORD, have given me." Place the basket before the LORD your God and bow down before him. 11And you and the Levites and the aliens among you shall rejoice in all the good things the LORD your God has given to you and your household.

12When you have finished setting aside a tenth of all your produce in the third year, the year of the tithe, you shall give it to the Levite, the alien, the fatherless and the widow, so that they may eat in your towns and be satisfied. 13Then say to the LORD your God: "I have removed from my house the sacred portion and have given it to the Levite, the alien, the fatherless and the widow, according to all you commanded. I have not turned aside from your commands nor have I forgotten any of them. 14I have not eaten any of the sacred portion while I was in mourning, nor have I removed any of it while I was unclean, nor have I offered any of it to the dead. I have obeyed the LORD my God; I have done everything you commanded me. 15Look down from heaven, your holy dwelling-place, and bless your people Israel and the land you have given us as you promised on oath to our forefathers, a land flowing with milk and honey."

Follow the LORD's Commands

16The LORD your God commands you this day to follow these decrees and laws; carefully observe them with all your heart and with all your soul. 17You have declared this day that the LORD is your God and that you will walk in his ways, that you will keep his decrees, commands and laws, and that you will obey him. 18And the LORD has declared this day that you are his people, his treasured possession as he promised, and that you are to keep all his commands. 19He has declared that he will set you in praise, fame and honour high above all the nations he has made and that you will be a people holy to the LORD your God, as he promised.

The Altar on Mount Ebal

27 Moses and the elders of Israel commanded the people: "Keep all these commands that I give you today. 2When you have crossed the Jordan into the land the LORD your God is giving you, set up some large stones and coat them with plaster. 3Write on them all the words of this law when you have crossed over to enter the land the LORD your God is giving you, a land flowing with milk and honey, just as the LORD, the God of your fathers, promised you. 4And when you have crossed the Jordan, set up these stones on Mount Ebal, as I command you today, and coat them with plaster. 5Build there an altar to the LORD your God, an altar of stones. Do not use any iron tool upon them. 6Build the altar of the LORD your God with stones from the field and offer burnt offerings on it to the LORD your God. 7Sacrifice fellowship offerings there, eating them and rejoicing in the presence of the LORD your God. 8And you shall write very clearly all the words of this law on these stones you have set up."

Curses From Mount Ebal

9Then Moses and the priests, who are Levites, said to all Israel, "Be silent, O Israel, and listen! You have now become the people of the LORD your God. 10Obey the LORD your God and follow his commands and decrees that I give you today."

¹¹On the same day Moses commanded the people:

¹²When you have crossed the Jordan, these tribes shall stand on Mount Gerizim to bless the people: Simeon, Levi, Judah, Issachar, Joseph and Benjamin. ¹³And these tribes shall stand on Mount Ebal to pronounce curses: Reuben, Gad, Asher, Zebulun, Dan and Naphtali.

¹⁴The Levites shall recite to all the people of Israel in a loud voice:

¹⁵"Cursed is the man who carves an image or casts an idol—a thing detestable to the LORD, the work of the craftsman's hands—and sets it up in secret."

Then all the people shall say,
"Amen!"

¹⁶"Cursed is the man who dishonours his father or his mother."

Then all the people shall say,
"Amen!"

¹⁷"Cursed is the man who moves his neighbour's boundary stone."

Then all the people shall say,
"Amen!"

¹⁸"Cursed is the man who leads the blind astray on the road."

Then all the people shall say,
"Amen!"

¹⁹"Cursed is the man who withholds justice from the alien, the fatherless or the widow."

Then all the people shall say,
"Amen!"

²⁰"Cursed is the man who sleeps with his father's wife, for he dishonours his father's bed."

Then all the people shall say,
"Amen!"

²¹"Cursed is the man who has sexual relations with any animal."

Then all the people shall say,
"Amen!"

²²"Cursed is the man who sleeps with his sister, the daughter of his father or the daughter of his mother."

Then all the people shall say,
"Amen!"

²³"Cursed is the man who sleeps with his mother-in-law."

Then all the people shall say,
"Amen!"

²⁴"Cursed is the man who kills his neighbour secretly."

Then all the people shall say,
"Amen!"

²⁵"Cursed is the man who accepts a bribe to kill an innocent person."

Then all the people shall say,
"Amen!"

²⁶"Cursed is the man who does not uphold the words of this law by carrying them out."

Then all the people shall say,
"Amen!"

Blessings for Obedience

28 If you fully obey the LORD your God and carefully follow all his commands that I give you today, the LORD your God will set you high above all the nations on earth. ²All these blessings will come upon you and accompany you if you obey the LORD your God:

³You will be blessed in the city and blessed in the country.

⁴The fruit of your womb will be blessed, and the crops of your land and the young of your livestock —the calves of your herds and the lambs of your flocks.

⁵Your basket and your kneading trough will be blessed.

⁶You will be blessed when you come in and blessed when you go out.

⁷The LORD will grant that the enemies who rise up against you will be defeated before you. They will come at you from one direction but flee from you in seven.

⁸The LORD will send a blessing on your barns and on everything you put your hand to. The LORD your God will bless you in the land he is giving you.

⁹The LORD will establish you as his holy people, as he promised you on oath, if you keep the commands of the LORD your God and walk in his ways. ¹⁰Then all the peoples on earth will see that you are called by the name of the LORD, and they will fear you. ¹¹The LORD will grant you abundant prosperity—in the fruit of your womb, the young of your livestock and the crops of your ground—in the land he swore to your forefathers to give you.

¹²The LORD will open the heavens, the storehouse of his bounty, to send rain on your land in season and to bless all the work of your hands. You will lend to many nations but will borrow from none. ¹³The LORD will make you the head, not the tail. If you pay attention to the commands of the LORD your God that I give you this day and carefully follow them, you will always be at the top, never at the bottom. ¹⁴Do not turn aside from any of the commands I give you today, to the right or to the left, following other gods and serving them.

NEW TESTAMENT READING
Luke 17:11–37

Ten Healed of Leprosy

¹¹Now on his way to Jerusalem, Jesus travelled along the border between Samaria and Galilee. ¹²As he was going into a village, ten men who had leprosy met him. They stood at a distance ¹³and called out in a loud voice, "Jesus, Master, have pity on us!"

¹⁴When he saw them, he said, "Go, show yourselves to the priests." And as they went, they were cleansed.

¹⁵One of them, when he saw he was healed, came back, praising God in a loud voice. ¹⁶He threw himself at Jesus' feet and thanked him—and he was a Samaritan.

¹⁷Jesus asked, "Were not all ten cleansed? Where are the other nine? ¹⁸Was no-one found to return and give praise to God except this foreigner?"

¹⁹Then he said to him, "Rise and go; your faith has made you well."

The Coming of the Kingdom of God

²⁰Once, having been asked by the Pharisees when the kingdom of God would come, Jesus replied, "The kingdom of God does not come with your careful observation, ²¹nor will people say, 'Here it is,' or 'There it is,' because the kingdom of God is within you."

²²Then he said to his disciples, "The time is coming when you will long to see one of the days of the Son of Man, but you will not see it. ²³Men will tell you, 'There he is!' or 'Here he is!' Do not go running off after them. ²⁴For the Son of Man in his day will be like the lightning, which flashes and lights up the sky from one end to the other. ²⁵But first he must suffer many things and be rejected by this generation.

²⁶"Just as it was in the days of Noah, so also will it be in the days of the Son of Man. ²⁷People were eating, drinking, marrying and being given in marriage up to the day Noah entered the ark. Then the flood came and destroyed them all.

²⁸"It was the same in the days of Lot. People were eating and drinking, buying and selling, planting and building. ²⁹But the day Lot left Sodom, fire and sulphur rained down from heaven and destroyed them all.

³⁰"It will be just like this on the day the Son of Man is revealed. ³¹On that day no-one who is on the roof of his house, with his goods inside, should go down to get them. Likewise, no-one in the field should go back for anything. ³²Remember Lot's wife! ³³Whoever tries to keep his life will lose it, and whoever loses his life will preserve it. ³⁴I tell you, on that night two people will be in one bed; one will be taken and the other left. ³⁵Two women will be grinding grain together; one will be taken and the other left."

³⁷"Where, Lord?" they asked.

He replied, "Where there is a dead body, there the vultures will gather."

READING FROM PSALMS
Psalm 46:1–11

For the director of music. Of the Sons of
Korah. According to *alamoth*. A song.

¹God is our refuge and strength,
   an ever-present help in trouble.
²Therefore we will not fear, though
      the earth give way
   and the mountains fall into the
      heart of the sea,
³though its waters roar and foam
   and the mountains quake with
      their surging.   *Selah*

⁴There is a river whose streams make
   glad the city of God,
   the holy place where the Most
      High dwells.
⁵God is within her, she will not fall;
   God will help her at break of day.

⁶Nations are in uproar, kingdoms fall;
   he lifts his voice, the earth melts.

⁷The LORD Almighty is with us;
   the God of Jacob is our fortress.
                           Selah

⁸Come and see the works of the LORD,
   the desolations he has brought on
      the earth.
⁹He makes wars cease to the ends of
      the earth;
   he breaks the bow and shatters the
      spear,
   he burns the shields with fire.
¹⁰"Be still, and know that I am God;
   I will be exalted among the
      nations,
   I will be exalted in the earth."

¹¹The LORD Almighty is with us;
   the God of Jacob is our fortress.
                           Selah

DAY 107

APRIL 17

OLD TESTAMENT READING
Deuteronomy 28:15–68

Curses for Disobedience

¹⁵However, if you do not obey the
LORD your God and do not carefully
follow all his commands and decrees I
am giving you today, all these curses
will come upon you and overtake you:

¹⁶You will be cursed in the city
and cursed in the country.

¹⁷Your basket and your kneading trough will be cursed.

¹⁸The fruit of your womb will be
cursed, and the crops of your land,
and the calves of your herds and
the lambs of your flocks.

¹⁹You will be cursed when you
come in and cursed when you go
out.

²⁰The LORD will send on you curses,
confusion and rebuke in everything you
put your hand to, until you are destroyed and come to sudden ruin because of the evil you have done in forsaking him. ²¹The LORD will plague you
with diseases until he has destroyed you
from the land you are entering to possess. ²²The LORD will strike you with
wasting disease, with fever and in-
flammation, with scorching heat and
drought, with blight and mildew, which
will plague you until you perish. ²³The
sky over your head will be bronze, the
ground beneath you iron. ²⁴The LORD
will turn the rain of your country into
dust and powder; it will come down
from the skies until you are destroyed.

²⁵The LORD will cause you to be defeated before your enemies. You will
come at them from one direction but
flee from them in seven, and you will

become a thing of horror to all the kingdoms on earth. ²⁶Your carcasses will be food for all the birds of the air and the beasts of the earth, and there will be no-one to frighten them away. ²⁷The LORD will afflict you with the boils of Egypt and with tumours, festering sores and the itch, from which you cannot be cured. ²⁸The LORD will afflict you with madness, blindness and confusion of mind. ²⁹At midday you will grope about like a blind man in the dark. You will be unsuccessful in everything you do; day after day you will be oppressed and robbed, with no-one to rescue you.

³⁰You will be pledged to be married to a woman, but another will take her and ravish her. You will build a house, but you will not live in it. You will plant a vineyard, but you will not even begin to enjoy its fruit. ³¹Your ox will be slaughtered before your eyes, but you will eat none of it. Your donkey will be forcibly taken from you and will not be returned. Your sheep will be given to your enemies, and no-one will rescue them. ³²Your sons and daughters will be given to another nation, and you will wear out your eyes watching for them day after day, powerless to lift a hand. ³³A people that you do not know will eat what your land and labour produce, and you will have nothing but cruel oppression all your days. ³⁴The sights you see will drive you mad. ³⁵The LORD will afflict your knees and legs with painful boils that cannot be cured, spreading from the soles of your feet to the top of your head.

³⁶The LORD will drive you and the king you set over you to a nation unknown to you or your fathers. There you will worship other gods, gods of wood and stone. ³⁷You will become a thing of horror and an object of scorn and ridicule to all the nations where the LORD will drive you.

³⁸You will sow much seed in the field but you will harvest little, because locusts will devour it. ³⁹You will plant vineyards and cultivate them but you will not drink the wine or gather the grapes, because worms will eat them. ⁴⁰You will have olive trees throughout your country but you will not use the oil, because the olives will drop off. ⁴¹You will have sons and daughters but you will not keep them, because they will go into captivity. ⁴²Swarms of locusts will take over all your trees and the crops of your land.

⁴³The alien who lives among you will rise above you higher and higher, but you will sink lower and lower. ⁴⁴He will lend to you, but you will not lend to him. He will be the head, but you will be the tail.

⁴⁵All these curses will come upon you. They will pursue you and overtake you until you are destroyed, because you did not obey the LORD your God and observe the commands and decrees he gave you. ⁴⁶They will be a sign and a wonder to you and your descendants for ever. ⁴⁷Because you did not serve the LORD your God joyfully and gladly in the time of prosperity, ⁴⁸therefore in hunger and thirst, in nakedness and dire poverty, you will serve the enemies the LORD sends against you. He will put an iron yoke on your neck until he has destroyed you.

⁴⁹The LORD will bring a nation against you from far away, from the ends of the earth, like an eagle swooping down, a nation whose language you will not understand, ⁵⁰a fierce-looking nation without respect for the old or pity for the young. ⁵¹They will devour the young of your livestock and the crops of your land until you are destroyed. They will leave you no grain, new wine or oil, nor any calves of your herds or lambs of your flocks until you are ruined. ⁵²They will lay siege to all the cities throughout your land until the high fortified walls in which you trust fall down. They will besiege all the cities throughout the land the LORD your God is giving you.

⁵³Because of the suffering that your enemy will inflict on you during the siege, you will eat the fruit of the womb, the flesh of the sons and daughters the

LORD your God has given you. ⁵⁴Even the most gentle and sensitive man among you will have no compassion on his own brother or the wife he loves or his surviving children, ⁵⁵and he will not give to one of them any of the flesh of his children that he is eating. It will be all he has left because of the suffering that your enemy will inflict on you during the siege of all your cities. ⁵⁶The most gentle and sensitive woman among you—so sensitive and gentle that she would not venture to touch the ground with the sole of her foot—will begrudge the husband she loves and her own son or daughter ⁵⁷the afterbirth from her womb and the children she bears. For she intends to eat them secretly during the siege and in the distress that your enemy will inflict on you in your cities.

⁵⁸If you do not carefully follow all the words of this law, which are written in this book, and do not revere this glorious and awesome name—the LORD your God—⁵⁹the LORD will send fearful plagues on you and your descendants, harsh and prolonged disasters, and severe and lingering illnesses. ⁶⁰He will bring upon you all the diseases of Egypt that you dreaded, and they will cling to you. ⁶¹The LORD will also bring on you every kind of sickness and disaster not recorded in this Book of the Law, until you are destroyed. ⁶²You who were as numerous as the stars in the sky will be left but few in number, because you did not obey the LORD your God. ⁶³Just as it pleased the LORD to make you prosper and increase in number, so it will please him to ruin and destroy you. You will be uprooted from the land you are entering to possess.

⁶⁴Then the LORD will scatter you among all nations, from one end of the earth to the other. There you will worship other gods—gods of wood and stone, which neither you nor your fathers have known. ⁶⁵Among those nations you will find no repose, no resting place for the sole of your foot. There the LORD will give you an anxious mind, eyes weary with longing, and a despairing heart. ⁶⁶You will live in constant suspense, filled with dread both night and day, never sure of your life. ⁶⁷In the morning you will say, "If only it were evening!" and in the evening, "If only it were morning!"—because of the terror that will fill your hearts and the sights that your eyes will see. ⁶⁸The LORD will send you back in ships to Egypt on a journey I said you should never make again. There you will offer yourselves for sale to your enemies as male and female slaves, but no-one will buy you.

NEW TESTAMENT READING
Luke 18:1–30

The Parable of the Persistent Widow

18 Then Jesus told his disciples a parable to show them that they should always pray and not give up. ²He said: "In a certain town there was a judge who neither feared God nor cared about men. ³And there was a widow in that town who kept coming to him with the plea, 'Grant me justice against my adversary.'

⁴"For some time he refused. But finally he said to himself, 'Even though I don't fear God or care about men, ⁵yet because this widow keeps bothering me, I will see that she gets justice, so that she won't eventually wear me out with her coming!'"

⁶And the Lord said, "Listen to what the unjust judge says. ⁷And will not God bring about justice for his chosen ones, who cry out to him day and night? Will he keep putting them off? ⁸I tell you, he will see that they get justice, and quickly. However, when the Son of Man comes, will he find faith on the earth?"

The Parable of the Pharisee and the Tax Collector

⁹To some who were confident of their own righteousness and looked down on

everybody else, Jesus told this parable: [10]"Two men went up to the temple to pray, one a Pharisee and the other a tax collector. [11]The Pharisee stood up and prayed about himself: 'God, I thank you that I am not like other men— robbers, evildoers, adulterers—or even like this tax collector. [12]I fast twice a week and give a tenth of all I get.'

[13]"But the tax collector stood at a distance. He would not even look up to heaven, but beat his breast and said, 'God, have mercy on me, a sinner.'

[14]"I tell you that this man, rather than the other, went home justified before God. For everyone who exalts himself will be humbled, and he who humbles himself will be exalted."

The Little Children and Jesus

[15]People were also bringing babies to Jesus to have him touch them. When the disciples saw this, they rebuked them. [16]But Jesus called the children to him and said, "Let the little children come to me, and do not hinder them, for the kingdom of God belongs to such as these. [17]I tell you the truth, anyone who will not receive the kingdom of God like a little child will never enter it."

The Rich Ruler

[18]A certain ruler asked him, "Good teacher, what must I do to inherit eternal life?"

[19]"Why do you call me good?" Jesus answered. "No-one is good—except God alone. [20]You know the commandments: 'Do not commit adultery, do not murder, do not steal, do not give false testimony, honour your father and mother.'"

[21]"All these I have kept since I was a boy," he said.

[22]When Jesus heard this, he said to him, "You still lack one thing. Sell everything you have and give to the poor, and you will have treasure in heaven. Then come, follow me."

[23]When he heard this, he became very sad, because he was a man of great wealth. [24]Jesus looked at him and said, "How hard it is for the rich to enter the kingdom of God! [25]Indeed, it is easier for a camel to go through the eye of a needle than for a rich man to enter the kingdom of God."

[26]Those who heard this asked, "Who then can be saved?"

[27]Jesus replied, "What is impossible with men is possible with God."

[28]Peter said to him, "We have left all we had to follow you!"

[29]"I tell you the truth," Jesus said to them, "no-one who has left home or wife or brothers or parents or children for the sake of the kingdom of God [30]will fail to receive many times as much in this age and, in the age to come, eternal life."

READING FROM PSALMS
Psalm 47:1–9

For the director of music. Of the Sons of Korah. A psalm.

[1]Clap your hands, all you nations;
    shout to God with cries of joy.
[2]How awesome is the LORD Most High,
    the great King over all the earth!
[3]He subdued nations under us,
    peoples under our feet.
[4]He chose our inheritance for us,
    the pride of Jacob, whom he loved.
                                    Selah

[5]God has ascended amid shouts of joy,
    the LORD amid the sounding of trumpets.
[6]Sing praises to God, sing praises;
    sing praises to our King, sing praises.

[7]For God is the King of all the earth;
    sing to him a psalm of praise.
[8]God reigns over the nations;
    God is seated on his holy throne.

⁹The nobles of the nations assemble
as the people of the God of
Abraham,

for the kings of the earth belong to
God;
he is greatly exalted.

DAY 108

APRIL 18

OLD TESTAMENT READING
Deuteronomy 29:1–30:10

Renewal of the Covenant

29 These are the terms of the covenant the LORD commanded Moses to make with the Israelites in Moab, in addition to the covenant he had made with them at Horeb.

²Moses summoned all the Israelites and said to them:

Your eyes have seen all that the LORD did in Egypt to Pharaoh, to all his officials and to all his land. ³With your own eyes you saw those great trials, those miraculous signs and great wonders. ⁴But to this day the LORD has not given you a mind that understands or eyes that see or ears that hear. ⁵During the forty years that I led you through the desert, your clothes did not wear out, nor did the sandals on your feet. ⁶You ate no bread and drank no wine or other fermented drink. I did this so that you might know that I am the LORD your God.

⁷When you reached this place, Sihon king of Heshbon and Og king of Bashan came out to fight against us, but we defeated them. ⁸We took their land and gave it as an inheritance to the Reubenites, the Gadites and the half-tribe of Manasseh.

⁹Carefully follow the terms of this covenant, so that you may prosper in everything you do. ¹⁰All of you are standing today in the presence of the LORD your God—your leaders and chief men, your elders and officials, and

all the other men of Israel, ¹¹together with your children and your wives, and the aliens living in your camps who chop your wood and carry your water. ¹²You are standing here in order to enter into a covenant with the LORD your God, a covenant the LORD is making with you this day and sealing with an oath, ¹³to confirm you this day as his people, that he may be your God as he promised you and as he swore to your fathers, Abraham, Isaac and Jacob. ¹⁴I am making this covenant, with its oath, not only with you ¹⁵who are standing here with us today in the presence of the LORD our God but also with those who are not here today.

¹⁶You yourselves know how we lived in Egypt and how we passed through the countries on the way here. ¹⁷You saw among them their detestable images and idols of wood and stone, of silver and gold. ¹⁸Make sure there is no man or woman, clan or tribe among you today whose heart turns away from the LORD our God to go and worship the gods of those nations; make sure there is no root among you that produces such bitter poison.

¹⁹When such a person hears the words of this oath, he invokes a blessing on himself and therefore thinks, "I will be safe, even though I persist in going my own way." This will bring disaster on the watered land as well as the dry. ²⁰The LORD will never be willing to forgive him; his wrath and zeal will burn against that man. All the curses written in this book will fall upon him, and the LORD will blot out his name from under heaven. ²¹The LORD will single him out

from all the tribes of Israel for disaster, according to all the curses of the covenant written in this Book of the Law.

²²Your children who follow you in later generations and foreigners who come from distant lands will see the calamities that have fallen on the land and the diseases with which the LORD has afflicted it. ²³The whole land will be a burning waste of salt and sulphur—nothing planted, nothing sprouting, no vegetation growing on it. It will be like the destruction of Sodom and Gomorrah, Admah and Zeboiim, which the LORD overthrew in fierce anger. ²⁴All the nations will ask: "Why has the LORD done this to this land? Why this fierce, burning anger?"

²⁵And the answer will be: "It is because this people abandoned the covenant of the LORD, the God of their fathers, the covenant he made with them when he brought them out of Egypt. ²⁶They went off and worshipped other gods and bowed down to them, gods they did not know, gods he had not given them. ²⁷Therefore the LORD's anger burned against this land, so that he brought on it all the curses written in this book. ²⁸In furious anger and in great wrath the LORD uprooted them from their land and thrust them into another land, as it is now."

²⁹The secret things belong to the LORD our God, but the things revealed belong to us and to our children for ever, that we may follow all the words of this law.

Prosperity After Turning to the LORD

30 When all these blessings and curses I have set before you come upon you and you take them to heart wherever the LORD your God disperses you among the nations, ²and when you and your children return to the LORD your God and obey him with all your heart and with all your soul according to everything I command you today, ³then the LORD your God will restore your fortunes and have compassion on you and gather you again from all the nations where he scattered you. ⁴Even if you have been banished to the most distant land under the heavens, from there the LORD your God will gather you and bring you back. ⁵He will bring you to the land that belonged to your fathers, and you will take possession of it. He will make you more prosperous and numerous than your fathers. ⁶The LORD your God will circumcise your hearts and the hearts of your descendants, so that you may love him with all your heart and with all your soul, and live. ⁷The LORD your God will put all these curses on your enemies who hate and persecute you. ⁸You will again obey the LORD and follow all his commands I am giving you today. ⁹Then the LORD your God will make you most prosperous in all the work of your hands and in the fruit of your womb, the young of your livestock and the crops of your land. The LORD will again delight in you and make you prosperous, just as he delighted in your fathers, ¹⁰if you obey the LORD your God and keep his commands and decrees that are written in this Book of the Law and turn to the LORD your God with all your heart and with all your soul.

NEW TESTAMENT READING
Luke 18:31–19:10

Jesus Again Predicts His Death

³¹Jesus took the Twelve aside and told them, "We are going up to Jerusalem, and everything that is written by the prophets about the Son of Man will be fulfilled. ³²He will be turned over to the Gentiles. They will mock him, insult him, spit on him, flog him and kill him. ³³On the third day he will rise again."

³⁴The disciples did not understand any of this. Its meaning was hidden from them, and they did not know what he was talking about.

A Blind Beggar Receives His Sight

35As Jesus approached Jericho, a blind man was sitting by the roadside begging. 36When he heard the crowd going by, he asked what was happening. 37They told him, "Jesus of Nazareth is passing by."

38He called out, "Jesus, Son of David, have mercy on me!"

39Those who led the way rebuked him and told him to be quiet, but he shouted all the more, "Son of David, have mercy on me!"

40Jesus stopped and ordered the man to be brought to him. When he came near, Jesus asked him, 41"What do you want me to do for you?"

"Lord, I want to see," he replied.

42Jesus said to him, "Receive your sight; your faith has healed you." 43Immediately he received his sight and followed Jesus, praising God. When all the people saw it, they also praised God.

Zacchaeus the Tax Collector

19 Jesus entered Jericho and was passing through. 2A man was there by the name of Zacchaeus; he was a chief tax collector and was wealthy. 3He wanted to see who Jesus was, but being a short man he could not, because of the crowd. 4So he ran ahead and climbed a sycamore-fig tree to see him, since Jesus was coming that way.

5When Jesus reached the spot, he looked up and said to him, "Zacchaeus, come down immediately. I must stay at your house today." 6So he came down at once and welcomed him gladly.

7All the people saw this and began to mutter, "He has gone to be the guest of a 'sinner'."

8But Zacchaeus stood up and said to the Lord, "Look, Lord! Here and now I give half of my possessions to the poor, and if I have cheated anybody out of anything, I will pay back four times the amount."

9Jesus said to him, "Today salvation has come to this house, because this man, too, is a son of Abraham. 10For the Son of Man came to seek and to save what was lost."

READING FROM PROVERBS
Proverbs 10:1–10

Proverbs of Solomon

10 The proverbs of Solomon:

A wise son brings joy to his father,
  but a foolish son grief to his
    mother.

2Ill-gotten treasures are of no value,
  but righteousness delivers from
    death.

3The LORD does not let the righteous
    go hungry
  but he thwarts the craving of the
    wicked.

4Lazy hands make a man poor,
  but diligent hands bring wealth.

5He who gathers crops in summer is a
    wise son,
  but he who sleeps during harvest is
    a disgraceful son.

6Blessings crown the head of the
    righteous,
  but violence overwhelms the
    mouth of the wicked.

7The memory of the righteous will be
    a blessing,
  but the name of the wicked will
    rot.

8The wise in heart accept commands,
  but a chattering fool comes to ruin.

9The man of integrity walks securely,
  but he who takes crooked paths
    will be found out.

10He who winks maliciously causes
    grief,
  and a chattering fool comes to ruin.

OLD TESTAMENT READING
Deuteronomy 30:11–31:29

The Offer of Life or Death

¹¹Now what I am commanding you today is not too difficult for you or beyond your reach. ¹²It is not up in heaven, so that you have to ask, "Who will ascend into heaven to get it and proclaim it to us so that we may obey it?" ¹³Nor is it beyond the sea, so that you have to ask, "Who will cross the sea to get it and proclaim it to us so that we may obey it?" ¹⁴No, the word is very near you; it is in your mouth and in your heart so that you may obey it.

¹⁵See, I set before you today life and prosperity, death and destruction. ¹⁶For I command you today to love the LORD your God, to walk in his ways, and to keep his commands, decrees and laws; then you will live and increase, and the LORD your God will bless you in the land you are entering to possess.

¹⁷But if your heart turns away and you are not obedient, and if you are drawn away to bow down to other gods and worship them, ¹⁸I declare to you this day that you will certainly be destroyed. You will not live long in the land you are crossing the Jordan to enter and possess.

¹⁹This day I call heaven and earth as witnesses against you that I have set before you life and death, blessings and curses. Now choose life, so that you and your children may live ²⁰and that you may love the LORD your God, listen to his voice, and hold fast to him. For the LORD is your life, and he will give you many years in the land he swore to give to your fathers, Abraham, Isaac and Jacob.

Joshua to Succeed Moses

31 Then Moses went out and spoke these words to all Israel: ²"I am now a hundred and twenty years old and I am no longer able to lead you. The LORD has said to me, 'You shall not cross the Jordan.' ³The LORD your God himself will cross over ahead of you. He will destroy these nations before you, and you will take possession of their land. Joshua also will cross over ahead of you, as the LORD said. ⁴And the LORD will do to them what he did to Sihon and Og, the kings of the Amorites, whom he destroyed along with their land. ⁵The LORD will deliver them to you, and you must do to them all that I have commanded you. ⁶Be strong and courageous. Do not be afraid or terrified because of them, for the LORD your God goes with you; he will never leave you nor forsake you."

⁷Then Moses summoned Joshua and said to him in the presence of all Israel, "Be strong and courageous, for you must go with this people into the land that the LORD swore to their forefathers to give them, and you must divide it among them as their inheritance. ⁸The LORD himself goes before you and will be with you; he will never leave you nor forsake you. Do not be afraid; do not be discouraged."

The Reading of the Law

⁹So Moses wrote down this law and gave it to the priests, the sons of Levi, who carried the ark of the covenant of the LORD, and to all the elders of Israel. ¹⁰Then Moses commanded them: "At the end of every seven years, in the year for cancelling debts, during the Feast of Tabernacles, ¹¹when all Israel comes to appear before the LORD your God at the place he will choose, you shall read this law before them in their hearing. ¹²Assemble the people—men, women and children, and the aliens living in your towns—so that they can listen and learn to fear the LORD your God and follow carefully all the words of this law. ¹³Their children, who do not know this

law, must hear it and learn to fear the LORD your God as long as you live in the land you are crossing the Jordan to possess."

Israel's Rebellion Predicted

14The LORD said to Moses, "Now the day of your death is near. Call Joshua and present yourselves at the Tent of Meeting, where I will commission him." So Moses and Joshua came and presented themselves at the Tent of Meeting.

15Then the LORD appeared at the Tent in a pillar of cloud, and the cloud stood over the entrance to the Tent. 16And the LORD said to Moses: "You are going to rest with your fathers, and these people will soon prostitute themselves to the foreign gods of the land they are entering. They will forsake me and break the covenant I made with them. 17On that day I will become angry with them and forsake them; I will hide my face from them, and they will be destroyed. Many disasters and difficulties will come upon them, and on that day they will ask, 'Have not these disasters come upon us because our God is not with us?' 18And I will certainly hide my face on that day because of all their wickedness in turning to other gods.

19"Now write down for yourselves this song and teach it to the Israelites and make them sing it, so that it may be a witness for me against them. 20When I have brought them into the land flowing with milk and honey, the land I promised on oath to their forefathers, and when they eat their fill and thrive, they will turn to other gods and worship them, rejecting me and breaking my covenant. 21And when many disasters and difficulties come upon them, this song will testify against them, because it will not be forgotten by their descendants. I know what they are disposed to do, even before I bring them into the land I promised them on oath." 22So Moses wrote down this song that day and taught it to the Israelites.

23The LORD gave this command to Joshua son of Nun: "Be strong and courageous, for you will bring the Israelites into the land I promised them on oath, and I myself will be with you."

24After Moses finished writing in a book the words of this law from beginning to end, 25he gave this command to the Levites who carried the ark of the covenant of the LORD: 26"Take this Book of the Law and place it beside the ark of the covenant of the LORD your God. There it will remain as a witness against you. 27For I know how rebellious and stiff-necked you are. If you have been rebellious against the LORD while I am still alive and with you, how much more will you rebel after I die! 28Assemble before me all the elders of your tribes and all your officials, so that I can speak these words in their hearing and call heaven and earth to testify against them. 29For I know that after my death you are sure to become utterly corrupt and to turn from the way I have commanded you. In days to come, disaster will fall upon you because you will do evil in the sight of the LORD and provoke him to anger by what your hands have made."

NEW TESTAMENT READING
Luke 19:11–44

The Parable of the Ten Minas

11While they were listening to this, he went on to tell them a parable, because he was near Jerusalem and the people thought that the kingdom of God was going to appear at once. 12He said: "A man of noble birth went to a distant country to have himself appointed king and then to return. 13So he called ten of his servants and gave them ten minas. 'Put this money to work,' he said, 'until I come back.'

14"But his subjects hated him and sent a delegation after him to say, 'We don't want this man to be our king.'

15"He was made king, however, and returned home. Then he sent for the servants to whom he had given the money, in order to find out what they had gained with it.

16"The first one came and said, 'Sir, your mina has earned ten more.'

17"'Well done, my good servant!' his master replied. 'Because you have been trustworthy in a very small matter, take charge of ten cities.'

18"The second one came and said, 'Sir, your mina has earned five more.'

19"His master answered, 'You take charge of five cities.'

20"Then another servant came and said, 'Sir, here is your mina; I have kept it laid away in a piece of cloth. 21I was afraid of you, because you are a hard man. You take out what you did not put in and reap what you did not sow.'

22"His master replied, 'I will judge you by your own words, you wicked servant! You knew, did you, that I am a hard man, taking out what I did not put in, and reaping what I did not sow? 23Why then didn't you put my money on deposit, so that when I came back, I could have collected it with interest?'

24"Then he said to those standing by, 'Take his mina away from him and give it to the one who has ten minas.'

25"'Sir,' they said, 'he already has ten!'

26"He replied, 'I tell you that to everyone who has, more will be given, but as for the one who has nothing, even what he has will be taken away. 27But those enemies of mine who did not want me to be a king over them—bring them here and kill them in front of me.'"

The Triumphal Entry

28After Jesus had said this, he went on ahead, going up to Jerusalem. 29As he approached Bethphage and Bethany at the hill called the Mount of Olives, he sent two of his disciples, saying to them, 30"Go to the village ahead of you, and as you enter it, you will find a colt tied there, which no-one has ever ridden. Untie it and bring it here. 31If anyone asks you, 'Why are you untying it?' tell him, 'The Lord needs it.'"

32Those who were sent ahead went and found it just as he had told them. 33As they were untying the colt, its owners asked them, "Why are you untying the colt?"

34They replied, "The Lord needs it."

35They brought it to Jesus, threw their cloaks on the colt and put Jesus on it. 36As he went along, people spread their cloaks on the road.

37When he came near the place where the road goes down the Mount of Olives, the whole crowd of disciples began joyfully to praise God in loud voices for all the miracles they had seen:

38"Blessed is the king who comes in the
    name of the Lord!"

"Peace in heaven and glory in the
    highest!"

39Some of the Pharisees in the crowd said to Jesus, "Teacher, rebuke your disciples!"

40"I tell you," he replied, "if they keep quiet, the stones will cry out."

41As he approached Jerusalem and saw the city, he wept over it 42and said, "If you, even you, had only known on this day what would bring you peace —but now it is hidden from your eyes. 43The days will come upon you when your enemies will build an embankment against you and encircle you and hem you in on every side. 44They will dash you to the ground, you and the children within your walls. They will not leave one stone on another, because you did not recognise the time of God's coming to you."

READING FROM PSALMS
Psalm 48:1–8

A song. A psalm of the Sons of Korah.

1Great is the LORD, and most worthy
    of praise,
  in the city of our God, his holy
    mountain.

²It is beautiful in its loftiness,
   the joy of the whole earth.
Like the utmost heights of Zaphon is
   Mount Zion,
   the city of the Great King.
³God is in her citadels;
   he has shown himself to be her
      fortress.

⁴When the kings joined forces,
   when they advanced together,
⁵they saw ⌐her⌐ and were astounded;
   they fled in terror.

⁶Trembling seized them there,
   pain like that of a woman in
      labour.
⁷You destroyed them like ships of
   Tarshish
   shattered by an east wind.

⁸As we have heard,
   so have we seen
in the city of the LORD Almighty,
   in the city of our God:
   God makes her secure for ever.
                                    Selah

DAY 110

APRIL 20

OLD TESTAMENT READING
Deuteronomy 31:30–32:52

The Song of Moses

   ³⁰And Moses recited the words of this
song from beginning to end in the hearing of the whole assembly of Israel:

32 Listen, O heavens, and I will
         speak;
      hear, O earth, the words of my
         mouth.
²Let my teaching fall like rain
   and my words descend like dew,
like showers on new grass,
   like abundant rain on tender
      plants.

³I will proclaim the name of the LORD.
   Oh, praise the greatness of our
      God!
⁴He is the Rock, his works are perfect,
   and all his ways are just.
A faithful God who does no wrong,
   upright and just is he.

⁵They have acted corruptly towards
      him;
   to their shame they are no longer
      his children,

but a warped and crooked
   generation.
⁶Is this the way you repay the LORD,
   O foolish and unwise people?
Is he not your Father, your Creator,
   who made you and formed you?

⁷Remember the days of old;
   consider the generations long past.
Ask your father and he will tell you,
   your elders, and they will explain
      to you.
⁸When the Most High gave the
      nations their inheritance,
   when he divided all mankind,
he set up boundaries for the peoples
   according to the number of the
      sons of Israel.
⁹For the LORD's portion is his people,
   Jacob his allotted inheritance.

¹⁰In a desert land he found him,
   in a barren and howling waste.
He shielded him and cared for him;
   he guarded him as the apple of his
      eye,
¹¹like an eagle that stirs up its nest
   and hovers over its young,
that spreads its wings to catch them
   and carries them on its pinions.
¹²The LORD alone led him;
   no foreign god was with him.

¹³He made him ride on the heights of
the land
and fed him with the fruit of the
fields.
He nourished him with honey from
the rock,
and with oil from the flinty crag,
¹⁴with curds and milk from herd and
flock
and with fattened lambs and goats,
with choice rams of Bashan
and the finest grains of wheat.
You drank the foaming blood of the
grape.

¹⁵Jeshurun grew fat and kicked;
filled with food, he became heavy
and sleek.
He abandoned the God who made
him
and rejected the Rock his Saviour.
¹⁶They made him jealous with their
foreign gods
and angered him with their
detestable idols.
¹⁷They sacrificed to demons, which are
not God—
gods they had not known,
gods that recently appeared,
gods your fathers did not fear.
¹⁸You deserted the Rock, who fathered
you;
you forgot the God who gave you
birth.

¹⁹The LORD saw this and rejected them
because he was angered by his sons
and daughters.
²⁰"I will hide my face from them," he
said,
"and see what their end will be;
for they are a perverse generation,
children who are unfaithful.
²¹They made me jealous by what is no
god
and angered me with their
worthless idols.
I will make them envious by those
who are not a people;
I will make them angry by a nation
that has no understanding.

²²For a fire has been kindled by my
wrath,
one that burns to the realm of
death below.
It will devour the earth and its
harvests
and set on fire the foundations of
the mountains.

²³"I will heap calamities upon them
and expend my arrows against
them.
²⁴I will send wasting famine against
them,
consuming pestilence and deadly
plague;
I will send against them the fangs of
wild beasts,
the venom of vipers that glide in
the dust.
²⁵In the street the sword will make
them childless;
in their homes terror will reign.
Young men and young women will
perish,
infants and grey-haired men.
²⁶I said I would scatter them
and blot out their memory from
mankind,
²⁷but I dreaded the taunt of the enemy,
lest the adversary misunderstand
and say, 'Our hand has triumphed;
the LORD has not done all this.' "

²⁸They are a nation without sense,
there is no discernment in them.
²⁹If only they were wise and would
understand this
and discern what their end will be!
³⁰How could one man chase a
thousand,
or two put ten thousand to flight,
unless their Rock had sold them,
unless the LORD had given them
up?
³¹For their rock is not like our Rock,
as even our enemies concede.
³²Their vine comes from the vine of
Sodom
and from the fields of Gomorrah.
Their grapes are filled with poison,
and their clusters with bitterness.

³³Their wine is the venom of serpents,
   the deadly poison of cobras.

³⁴"Have I not kept this in reserve
   and sealed it in my vaults?
³⁵It is mine to avenge; I will repay.
   In due time their foot will slip;
their day of disaster is near
   and their doom rushes upon
      them."

³⁶The LORD will judge his people
   and have compassion on his
      servants
when he sees their strength is gone
   and no-one is left, slave or free.
³⁷He will say: "Now where are their
      gods,
   the rock they took refuge in,
³⁸the gods who ate the fat of their
      sacrifices
   and drank the wine of their drink
      offerings?
Let them rise up to help you!
   Let them give you shelter!

³⁹"See now that I myself am He!
   There is no god besides me.
I put to death and I bring to life,
   I have wounded and I will heal,
   and no-one can deliver out of my
      hand.
⁴⁰I lift my hand to heaven and declare:
   As surely as I live for ever,
⁴¹when I sharpen my flashing sword
   and my hand grasps it in judgment,
I will take vengeance on my
      adversaries
   and repay those who hate me.
⁴²I will make my arrows drunk with
      blood,
   while my sword devours flesh:
the blood of the slain and the
      captives,
   the heads of the enemy leaders."

⁴³Rejoice, O nations, with his people,
   for he will avenge the blood of his
      servants;
he will take vengeance on his enemies
   and make atonement for his land
      and people.

⁴⁴Moses came with Joshua son of Nun and spoke all the words of this song in the hearing of the people. ⁴⁵When Moses finished reciting all these words to all Israel, ⁴⁶he said to them, "Take to heart all the words I have solemnly declared to you this day, so that you may command your children to obey carefully all the words of this law. ⁴⁷They are not just idle words for you—they are your life. By them you will live long in the land you are crossing the Jordan to possess."

Moses to Die on Mount Nebo

⁴⁸On that same day the LORD told Moses, ⁴⁹"Go up into the Abarim Range to Mount Nebo in Moab, across from Jericho, and view Canaan, the land I am giving the Israelites as their own possession. ⁵⁰There on the mountain that you have climbed you will die and be gathered to your people, just as your brother Aaron died on Mount Hor and was gathered to his people. ⁵¹This is because both of you broke faith with me in the presence of the Israelites at the waters of Meribah Kadesh in the Desert of Zin and because you did not uphold my holiness among the Israelites. ⁵²Therefore, you will see the land only from a distance; you will not enter the land I am giving to the people of Israel."

NEW TESTAMENT READING
Luke 19:45–20:26

Jesus at the Temple

⁴⁵Then he entered the temple area and began driving out those who were selling. ⁴⁶"It is written," he said to them, "'My house will be a house of prayer'; but you have made it 'a den of robbers'."

⁴⁷Every day he was teaching at the temple. But the chief priests, the teachers of the law and the leaders among the people were trying to kill

him. [48]Yet they could not find any way to do it, because all the people hung on his words.

The Authority of Jesus Questioned

20 One day as he was teaching the people in the temple courts and preaching the gospel, the chief priests and the teachers of the law, together with the elders, came up to him. [2]"Tell us by what authority you are doing these things," they said. "Who gave you this authority?"

[3]He replied, "I will also ask you a question. Tell me, [4]John's baptism—was it from heaven, or from men?"

[5]They discussed it among themselves and said, "If we say, 'From heaven', he will ask, 'Why didn't you believe him?' [6]But if we say, 'From men', all the people will stone us, because they are persuaded that John was a prophet."

[7]So they answered, "We don't know where it was from."

[8]Jesus said, "Neither will I tell you by what authority I am doing these things."

The Parable of the Tenants

[9]He went on to tell the people this parable: "A man planted a vineyard, rented it to some farmers and went away for a long time. [10]At harvest time he sent a servant to the tenants so they would give him some of the fruit of the vineyard. But the tenants beat him and sent him away empty-handed. [11]He sent another servant, but that one also they beat and treated shamefully and sent away empty-handed. [12]He sent still a third, and they wounded him and threw him out.

[13]"Then the owner of the vineyard said, 'What shall I do? I will send my son, whom I love; perhaps they will respect him.'

[14]"But when the tenants saw him, they talked the matter over. 'This is the heir,' they said. 'Let's kill him, and the inheritance will be ours.' [15]So they threw him out of the vineyard and killed him.

"What then will the owner of the vineyard do to them? [16]He will come and kill these tenants and give the vineyard to others."

When the people heard this, they said, "May this never be!"

[17]Jesus looked directly at them and asked, "Then what is the meaning of that which is written:

" 'The stone the builders rejected
has become the capstone' ?

[18]Everyone who falls on that stone will be broken to pieces, but he on whom it falls will be crushed."

[19]The teachers of the law and the chief priests looked for a way to arrest him immediately, because they knew he had spoken this parable against them. But they were afraid of the people.

Paying Taxes to Caesar

[20]Keeping a close watch on him, they sent spies, who pretended to be honest. They hoped to catch Jesus in something he said so that they might hand him over to the power and authority of the governor. [21]So the spies questioned him: "Teacher, we know that you speak and teach what is right, and that you do not show partiality but teach the way of God in accordance with the truth. [22]Is it right for us to pay taxes to Caesar or not?"

[23]He saw through their duplicity and said to them, [24]"Show me a denarius. Whose portrait and inscription are on it?"

[25]"Caesar's," they replied.

He said to them, "Then give to Caesar what is Caesar's, and to God what is God's."

[26]They were unable to trap him in what he had said there in public. And astonished by his answer, they became silent.

READING FROM PSALMS
Psalm 48:9–14

⁹Within your temple, O God,
  we meditate on your unfailing
    love.
¹⁰Like your name, O God,
  your praise reaches to the ends of
    the earth;
  your right hand is filled with
    righteousness.
¹¹Mount Zion rejoices,

the villages of Judah are glad
  because of your judgments.

¹²Walk about Zion, go round her,
  count her towers,
¹³consider well her ramparts,
  view her citadels,
  that you may tell of them to the
    next generation.
¹⁴For this God is our God for ever and
    ever;
  he will be our guide even to the
    end.

DAY 111

APRIL 21

OLD TESTAMENT READING
Deuteronomy 33:1–34:12

Moses Blesses the Tribes

33 This is the blessing that Moses
the man of God pronounced on
the Israelites before his death. ²He said:

"The LORD came from Sinai
  and dawned over them from Seir;
  he shone forth from Mount Paran.
He came with myriads of holy ones
  from the south, from his mountain
    slopes.
³Surely it is you who love the people;
  all the holy ones are in your hand.
At your feet they all bow down,
  and from you receive instruction,
⁴the law that Moses gave us,
  the possession of the assembly of
    Jacob.
⁵He was king over Jeshurun
  when the leaders of the people
    assembled,
  along with the tribes of Israel.

⁶"Let Reuben live and not die,
  nor his men be few."

⁷And this he said about Judah:

"Hear, O LORD, the cry of Judah;
  bring him to his people.
With his own hands he defends his
    cause.
  Oh, be his help against his foes!"

⁸About Levi he said:

"Your Thummim and Urim belong
  to the man you favoured.
You tested him at Massah;
  you contended with him at the
    waters of Meribah.
⁹He said of his father and mother,
  'I have no regard for them.'
He did not recognise his brothers
  or acknowledge his own children,
but he watched over your word
  and guarded your covenant.
¹⁰He teaches your precepts to Jacob
  and your law to Israel.
He offers incense before you
  and whole burnt offerings on your
    altar.
¹¹Bless all his skills, O LORD,
  and be pleased with the work of his
    hands.
Smite the loins of those who rise up
  against him;
  strike his foes till they rise no
    more."

12About Benjamin he said:

"Let the beloved of the LORD rest
secure in him,
for he shields him all day long,
and the one the LORD loves rests
between his shoulders."

13About Joseph he said:

"May the LORD bless his land
with the precious dew from heaven
above
and with the deep waters that lie
below;
14with the best the sun brings forth
and the finest the moon can yield;
15with the choicest gifts of the ancient
mountains
and the fruitfulness of the
everlasting hills;
16with the best gifts of the earth and its
fulness
and the favour of him who dwelt in
the burning bush.
Let all these rest on the head of
Joseph,
on the brow of the prince among
his brothers.
17In majesty he is like a firstborn bull;
his horns are the horns of a wild ox.
With them he will gore the nations,
even those at the ends of the earth.
Such are the ten thousands of
Ephraim;
such are the thousands of
Manasseh."

18About Zebulun he said:

"Rejoice, Zebulun, in your going
out,
and you, Issachar, in your tents.
19They will summon peoples to the
mountain
and there offer sacrifices of
righteousness;
they will feast on the abundance of
the seas,
on the treasures hidden in the
sand."

20About Gad he said:

"Blessed is he who enlarges Gad's
domain!
Gad lives there like a lion,
tearing at arm or head.
21He chose the best land for himself;
the leader's portion was kept for
him.
When the heads of the people
assembled,
he carried out the LORD's righteous
will,
and his judgments concerning
Israel."

22About Dan he said:

"Dan is a lion's cub,
springing out of Bashan."

23About Naphtali he said:

"Naphtali is abounding with the
favour of the LORD
and is full of his blessing;
he will inherit southward to the
lake."

24About Asher he said:

"Most blessed of sons is Asher;
let him be favoured by his
brothers,
and let him bathe his feet in oil.
25The bolts of your gates will be iron
and bronze,
and your strength will equal your
days.

26"There is no-one like the God of
Jeshurun,
who rides on the heavens to help
you
and on the clouds in his majesty.
27The eternal God is your refuge,
and underneath are the everlasting
arms.
He will drive out your enemy before
you,
saying, 'Destroy him!'

²⁸So Israel will live in safety alone;
Jacob's spring is secure
in a land of grain and new wine,
where the heavens drop dew.
²⁹Blessed are you, O Israel!
Who is like you,
a people saved by the LORD?
He is your shield and helper
and your glorious sword.
Your enemies will cower before you,
and you will trample down their
high places."

The Death of Moses

34 Then Moses climbed Mount Nebo from the plains of Moab to the top of Pisgah, across from Jericho. There the LORD showed him the whole land—from Gilead to Dan, ²all of Naphtali, the territory of Ephraim and Manasseh, all the land of Judah as far as the western sea, ³the Negev and the whole region from the Valley of Jericho, the City of Palms, as far as Zoar. ⁴Then the LORD said to him, "This is the land I promised on oath to Abraham, Isaac and Jacob when I said, 'I will give it to your descendants.' I have let you see it with your eyes, but you will not cross over into it."

⁵And Moses the servant of the LORD died there in Moab, as the LORD had said. ⁶He buried him in Moab, in the valley opposite Beth Peor, but to this day no-one knows where his grave is. ⁷Moses was a hundred and twenty years old when he died, yet his eyes were not weak nor his strength gone. ⁸The Israelites grieved for Moses in the plains of Moab thirty days, until the time of weeping and mourning was over.

⁹Now Joshua son of Nun was filled with the spirit of wisdom because Moses had laid his hands on him. So the Israelites listened to him and did what the LORD had commanded Moses.

¹⁰Since then, no prophet has risen in Israel like Moses, whom the LORD knew face to face, ¹¹who did all those miraculous signs and wonders the LORD sent him to do in Egypt—to Pharaoh and to all his officials and to his whole land. ¹²For no-one has ever shown the mighty power or performed the awesome deeds that Moses did in the sight of all Israel.

NEW TESTAMENT READING
Luke 20:27–21:4

The Resurrection and Marriage

²⁷Some of the Sadducees, who say there is no resurrection, came to Jesus with a question. ²⁸"Teacher," they said, "Moses wrote for us that if a man's brother dies and leaves a wife but no children, the man must marry the widow and have children for his brother. ²⁹Now there were seven brothers. The first one married a woman and died childless. ³⁰The second ³¹and then the third married her, and in the same way the seven died, leaving no children. ³²Finally, the woman died too. ³³Now then, at the resurrection whose wife will she be, since the seven were married to her?"

³⁴Jesus replied, "The people of this age marry and are given in marriage. ³⁵But those who are considered worthy of taking part in that age and in the resurrection from the dead will neither marry nor be given in marriage, ³⁶and they can no longer die; for they are like the angels. They are God's children, since they are children of the resurrection. ³⁷But in the account of the bush, even Moses showed that the dead rise, for he calls the Lord 'the God of Abraham, and the God of Isaac, and the God of Jacob'. ³⁸He is not the God of the dead, but of the living, for to him all are alive."

³⁹Some of the teachers of the law responded, "Well said, teacher!" ⁴⁰And no-one dared to ask him any more questions.

Whose Son Is the Christ?

⁴¹Then Jesus said to them, "How is it that they say the Christ is the Son of

David? ⁴²David himself declares in the Book of Psalms:

" 'The Lord said to my Lord:
  "Sit at my right hand
⁴³until I make your enemies
  a footstool for your feet." '

⁴⁴David calls him 'Lord'. How then can he be his son?"

⁴⁵While all the people were listening, Jesus said to his disciples, ⁴⁶"Beware of the teachers of the law. They like to walk around in flowing robes and love to be greeted in the market-places and have the most important seats in the synagogues and the places of honour at banquets. ⁴⁷They devour widows' houses and for a show make lengthy prayers. Such men will be punished most severely."

The Widow's Offering

21 As he looked up, Jesus saw the rich putting their gifts into the temple treasury. ²He also saw a poor widow put in two very small copper coins. ³"I tell you the truth," he said, "this poor widow has put in more than all the others. ⁴All these people gave their gifts out of their wealth; but she out of her poverty put in all she had to live on."

READING FROM PSALMS
Psalm 49:1–20

For the director of music. Of the Sons of
  Korah. A psalm.

¹Hear this, all you peoples;
  listen, all who live in this world,
²both low and high,
  rich and poor alike:
³My mouth will speak words of
    wisdom;
  the utterance from my heart will
    give understanding.

⁴I will turn my ear to a proverb;
  with the harp I will expound my
    riddle:

⁵Why should I fear when evil days
    come,
  when wicked deceivers surround
    me—
⁶those who trust in their wealth
  and boast of their great riches?
⁷No man can redeem the life of
    another
  or give to God a ransom for him—
⁸the ransom for a life is costly,
  no payment is ever enough—
⁹that he should live on for ever
  and not see decay.

¹⁰For all can see that wise men die;
  the foolish and the senseless alike
    perish
  and leave their wealth to others.
¹¹Their tombs will remain their houses
    for ever,
  their dwellings for endless
    generations,
  though they had named lands after
    themselves.

¹²But man, despite his riches, does not
    endure;
  he is like the beasts that perish.

¹³This is the fate of those who trust in
    themselves,
  and of their followers, who
    approve their sayings.   *Selah*
¹⁴Like sheep they are destined for the
    grave,
  and death will feed on them.
  The upright will rule over them in the
    morning;
  their forms will decay in the grave,
  far from their princely mansions.
¹⁵But God will redeem my life from the
    grave;
  he will surely take me to himself.
                            Selah

¹⁶Do not be overawed when a man
    grows rich,
  when the splendour of his house
    increases;

17for he will take nothing with him
    when he dies,
  his splendour will not descend with
    him.
18Though while he lived he counted
    himself blessed—
  and men praise you when you
    prosper—

19he will join the generation of his
    fathers,
  who will never see the light ⌊of
    life⌋.

20A man who has riches without
    understanding
  is like the beasts that perish.

DAY 112   # APRIL 22

OLD TESTAMENT READING
Joshua 1:1–2:24

The LORD Commands Joshua

1 After the death of Moses the servant of the LORD, the LORD said to
Joshua son of Nun, Moses' assistant:
2"Moses my servant is dead. Now then,
you and all these people, get ready to
cross the Jordan River into the land I
am about to give to them—to the
Israelites. 3I will give you every place
where you set your foot, as I promised
Moses. 4Your territory will extend from
the desert to Lebanon, and from the
great river, the Euphrates—all the Hittite country—to the Great Sea on the
west. 5No-one will be able to stand up
against you all the days of your life. As I
was with Moses, so I will be with you; I
will never leave you nor forsake you.

6"Be strong and courageous, because
you will lead these people to inherit the
land I swore to their forefathers to give
them. 7Be strong and very courageous.
Be careful to obey all the law my servant
Moses gave you; do not turn from it to
the right or to the left, that you may be
successful wherever you go. 8Do not let
this Book of the Law depart from your
mouth; meditate on it day and night, so
that you may be careful to do everything
written in it. Then you will be prosperous and successful. 9Have I not
commanded you? Be strong and
courageous. Do not be terrified; do not

be discouraged, for the LORD your God
will be with you wherever you go."

10So Joshua ordered the officers of
the people: 11"Go through the camp
and tell the people, 'Get your supplies
ready. Three days from now you will
cross the Jordan here to go in and take
possession of the land the LORD your
God is giving you for your own.'"

12But to the Reubenites, the Gadites
and the half-tribe of Manasseh, Joshua
said, 13"Remember the command that
Moses the servant of the LORD gave
you: 'The LORD your God is giving you
rest and has granted you this land.'
14Your wives, your children and your
livestock may stay in the land that
Moses gave you east of the Jordan, but
all your fighting men, fully armed, must
cross over ahead of your brothers. You
are to help your brothers 15until the
LORD gives them rest, as he has done for
you, and until they too have taken possession of the land that the LORD your
God is giving them. After that, you may
go back and occupy your own land,
which Moses the servant of the LORD
gave you east of the Jordan towards the
sunrise."

16Then they answered Joshua,
"Whatever you have commanded us we
will do, and wherever you send us we
will go. 17Just as we fully obeyed Moses,
so we will obey you. Only may the LORD
your God be with you as he was with
Moses. 18Whoever rebels against your

word and does not obey your words, whatever you may command them, will be put to death. Only be strong and courageous!"

Rahab and the Spies

2 Then Joshua son of Nun secretly sent two spies from Shittim. "Go, look over the land," he said, "especially Jericho." So they went and entered the house of a prostitute named Rahab and stayed there.

²The king of Jericho was told, "Look! Some of the Israelites have come here tonight to spy out the land." ³So the king of Jericho sent this message to Rahab: "Bring out the men who came to you and entered your house, because they have come to spy out the whole land."

⁴But the woman had taken the two men and hidden them. She said, "Yes, the men came to me, but I did not know where they had come from. ⁵At dusk, when it was time to close the city gate, the men left. I don't know which way they went. Go after them quickly. You may catch up with them." ⁶(But she had taken them up to the roof and hidden them under the stalks of flax she had laid out on the roof.) ⁷So the men set out in pursuit of the spies on the road that leads to the fords of the Jordan, and as soon as the pursuers had gone out, the gate was shut.

⁸Before the spies lay down for the night, she went up on the roof ⁹and said to them, "I know that the LORD has given this land to you and that a great fear of you has fallen on us, so that all who live in this country are melting in fear because of you. ¹⁰We have heard how the LORD dried up the water of the Red Sea for you when you came out of Egypt, and what you did to Sihon and Og, the two kings of the Amorites east of the Jordan, whom you completely destroyed. ¹¹When we heard of it, our hearts sank and everyone's courage failed because of you, for the LORD your God is God in heaven above and on the earth below. ¹²Now then, please swear to me by the LORD that you will show kindness to my family, because I have shown kindness to you. Give me a sure sign ¹³that you will spare the lives of my father and mother, my brothers and sisters, and all who belong to them, and that you will save us from death."

¹⁴"Our lives for your lives!" the men assured her. "If you don't tell what we are doing, we will treat you kindly and faithfully when the LORD gives us the land."

¹⁵So she let them down by a rope through the window, for the house she lived in was part of the city wall. ¹⁶Now she had said to them, "Go to the hills so that the pursuers will not find you. Hide yourselves there three days until they return, and then go on your way."

¹⁷The men said to her, "This oath you made us swear will not be binding on us ¹⁸unless, when we enter the land, you have tied this scarlet cord in the window through which you let us down, and unless you have brought your father and mother, your brothers and all your family into your house. ¹⁹If anyone goes outside your house into the street, his blood will be on his own head; we will not be responsible. As for anyone who is in the house with you, his blood will be on our head if a hand is laid on him. ²⁰But if you tell what we are doing, we will be released from the oath you made us swear."

²¹"Agreed," she replied. "Let it be as you say." So she sent them away and they departed. And she tied the scarlet cord in the window.

²²When they left, they went into the hills and stayed there three days, until the pursuers had searched all along the road and returned without finding them. ²³Then the two men started back. They went down out of the hills, forded the river and came to Joshua son of Nun and told him everything that had happened to them. ²⁴They said to Joshua, "The LORD has surely given the whole land into our hands; all the people are melting in fear because of us."

NEW TESTAMENT READING
Luke 21:5-38

Signs of the End of the Age

⁵Some of his disciples were remarking about how the temple was adorned with beautiful stones and with gifts dedicated to God. But Jesus said, ⁶"As for what you see here, the time will come when not one stone will be left on another; every one of them will be thrown down."

⁷"Teacher," they asked, "when will these things happen? And what will be the sign that they are about to take place?"

⁸He replied: "Watch out that you are not deceived. For many will come in my name, claiming, 'I am he,' and 'The time is near.' Do not follow them. ⁹When you hear of wars and revolutions, do not be frightened. These things must happen first, but the end will not come right away."

¹⁰Then he said to them: "Nation will rise against nation, and kingdom against kingdom. ¹¹There will be great earthquakes, famines and pestilences in various places, and fearful events and great signs from heaven.

¹²"But before all this, they will lay hands on you and persecute you. They will deliver you to synagogues and prisons, and you will be brought before kings and governors, and all on account of my name. ¹³This will result in your being witnesses to them. ¹⁴But make up your mind not to worry beforehand how you will defend yourselves. ¹⁵For I will give you words and wisdom that none of your adversaries will be able to resist or contradict. ¹⁶You will be betrayed even by parents, brothers, relatives and friends, and they will put some of you to death. ¹⁷All men will hate you because of me. ¹⁸But not a hair of your head will perish. ¹⁹By standing firm you will gain life.

²⁰"When you see Jerusalem being surrounded by armies, you will know that its desolation is near. ²¹Then let those who are in Judea flee to the mountains, let those in the city get out, and let those in the country not enter the city. ²²For this is the time of punishment in fulfilment of all that has been written. ²³How dreadful it will be in those days for pregnant women and nursing mothers! There will be great distress in the land and wrath against this people. ²⁴They will fall by the sword and will be taken as prisoners to all the nations. Jerusalem will be trampled on by the Gentiles until the times of the Gentiles are fulfilled.

²⁵"There will be signs in the sun, moon and stars. On the earth, nations will be in anguish and perplexity at the roaring and tossing of the sea. ²⁶Men will faint from terror, apprehensive of what is coming on the world, for the heavenly bodies will be shaken. ²⁷At that time they will see the Son of Man coming in a cloud with power and great glory. ²⁸When these things begin to take place, stand up and lift up your heads, because your redemption is drawing near."

²⁹He told them this parable: "Look at the fig-tree and all the trees. ³⁰When they sprout leaves, you can see for yourselves and know that summer is near. ³¹Even so, when you see these things happening, you know that the kingdom of God is near.

³²"I tell you the truth, this generation will certainly not pass away until all these things have happened. ³³Heaven and earth will pass away, but my words will never pass away.

³⁴"Be careful, or your hearts will be weighed down with dissipation, drunkenness and the anxieties of life, and that day will close on you unexpectedly like a trap. ³⁵For it will come upon all those who live on the face of the whole earth. ³⁶Be always on the watch, and pray that you may be able to escape all that is about to happen, and that you may be able to stand before the Son of Man."

³⁷Each day Jesus was teaching at the temple, and each evening he went out to spend the night on the hill called the

Mount of Olives, 38and all the people came early in the morning to hear him at the temple.

READING FROM PROVERBS
Proverbs 10:11–20

11The mouth of the righteous is a
    fountain of life,
  but violence overwhelms the
    mouth of the wicked.

12Hatred stirs up dissension,
  but love covers over all wrongs.

13Wisdom is found on the lips of the
    discerning,
  but a rod is for the back of him who
    lacks judgment.

14Wise men store up knowledge,
  but the mouth of a fool invites ruin.

15The wealth of the rich is their
    fortified city,

but poverty is the ruin of the
    poor.

16The wages of the righteous bring
    them life,
  but the income of the wicked
    brings them punishment.

17He who heeds discipline shows the
    way to life,
  but whoever ignores correction
    leads others astray.

18He who conceals his hatred has lying
    lips,
  and whoever spreads slander is a
    fool.

19When words are many, sin is not
    absent,
  but he who holds his tongue is
    wise.

20The tongue of the righteous is choice
    silver,
  but the heart of the wicked is of
    little value.

APRIL 23   DAY 113

OLD TESTAMENT READING
Joshua 3:1–5:12

Crossing the Jordan

3 Early in the morning Joshua and all the Israelites set out from Shittim and went to the Jordan, where they camped before crossing over. 2After three days the officers went throughout the camp, 3giving orders to the people: "When you see the ark of the covenant of the LORD your God, and the priests, who are Levites, carrying it, you are to move out from your positions and follow it. 4Then you will know which way to go, since you have never been this way before. But keep a distance of

about a thousand yards between you and the ark; do not go near it."

5Joshua told the people, "Consecrate yourselves, for tomorrow the LORD will do amazing things among you."

6Joshua said to the priests, "Take up the ark of the covenant and pass on ahead of the people." So they took it up and went ahead of them.

7And the LORD said to Joshua, "Today I will begin to exalt you in the eyes of all Israel, so that they may know that I am with you as I was with Moses. 8Tell the priests who carry the ark of the covenant: 'When you reach the edge of the Jordan's waters, go and stand in the river.'"

9Joshua said to the Israelites, "Come

here and listen to the words of the LORD your God. [10]This is how you will know that the living God is among you and that he will certainly drive out before you the Canaanites, Hittites, Hivites, Perizzites, Girgashites, Amorites and Jebusites. [11]See, the ark of the covenant of the Lord of all the earth will go into the Jordan ahead of you. [12]Now then, choose twelve men from the tribes of Israel, one from each tribe. [13]And as soon as the priests who carry the ark of the LORD—the Lord of all the earth —set foot in the Jordan, its waters flowing downstream will be cut off and stand up in a heap."

[14]So when the people broke camp to cross the Jordan, the priests carrying the ark of the covenant went ahead of them. [15]Now the Jordan is in flood all during harvest. Yet as soon as the priests who carried the ark reached the Jordan and their feet touched the water's edge, [16]the water from upstream stopped flowing. It piled up in a heap a great distance away, at a town called Adam in the vicinity of Zarethan, while the water flowing down to the Sea of the Arabah (the Salt Sea) was completely cut off. So the people crossed over opposite Jericho. [17]The priests who carried the ark of the covenant of the LORD stood firm on dry ground in the middle of the Jordan, while all Israel passed by until the whole nation had completed the crossing on dry ground.

4 When the whole nation had finished crossing the Jordan, the LORD said to Joshua, [2]"Choose twelve men from among the people, one from each tribe, [3]and tell them to take up twelve stones from the middle of the Jordan from right where the priests stood and to carry them over with you and put them down at the place where you stay tonight."

[4]So Joshua called together the twelve men he had appointed from the Israelites, one from each tribe, [5]and said to them, "Go over before the ark of the LORD your God into the middle of the Jordan. Each of you is to take up a stone on his shoulder, according to the number of the tribes of the Israelites, [6]to serve as a sign among you. In the future, when your children ask you, 'What do these stones mean?' [7]tell them that the flow of the Jordan was cut off before the ark of the covenant of the LORD. When it crossed the Jordan, the waters of the Jordan were cut off. These stones are to be a memorial to the people of Israel for ever."

[8]So the Israelites did as Joshua commanded them. They took twelve stones from the middle of the Jordan, according to the number of the tribes of the Israelites, as the LORD had told Joshua; and they carried them over with them to their camp, where they put them down. [9]Joshua set up the twelve stones that had been in the middle of the Jordan at the spot where the priests who carried the ark of the covenant had stood. And they are there to this day.

[10]Now the priests who carried the ark remained standing in the middle of the Jordan until everything the LORD had commanded Joshua was done by the people, just as Moses had directed Joshua. The people hurried over, [11]and as soon as all of them had crossed, the ark of the LORD and the priests came to the other side while the people watched. [12]The men of Reuben, Gad and the half-tribe of Manasseh crossed over, armed, in front of the Israelites, as Moses had directed them. [13]About forty thousand armed for battle crossed over before the LORD to the plains of Jericho for war.

[14]That day the LORD exalted Joshua in the sight of all Israel; and they revered him all the days of his life, just as they had revered Moses.

[15]Then the LORD said to Joshua, [16]"Command the priests carrying the ark of the Testimony to come up out of the Jordan."

[17]So Joshua commanded the priests, "Come up out of the Jordan."

[18]And the priests came up out of the river carrying the ark of the covenant of the LORD. No sooner had they set their

feet on the dry ground than the waters of the Jordan returned to their place and ran in flood as before.

[19]On the tenth day of the first month the people went up from the Jordan and camped at Gilgal on the eastern border of Jericho. [20]And Joshua set up at Gilgal the twelve stones they had taken out of the Jordan. [21]He said to the Israelites, "In the future when your descendants ask their fathers, 'What do these stones mean?' [22]tell them, 'Israel crossed the Jordan on dry ground.' [23]For the LORD your God dried up the Jordan before you until you had crossed over. The LORD your God did to the Jordan just what he had done to the Red Sea when he dried it up before us until we had crossed over. [24]He did this so that all the peoples of the earth might know that the hand of the LORD is powerful and so that you might always fear the LORD your God."

Circumcision at Gilgal

5 Now when all the Amorite kings west of the Jordan and all the Canaanite kings along the coast heard how the LORD had dried up the Jordan before the Israelites until we had crossed over, their hearts sank and they no longer had the courage to face the Israelites.

[2]At that time the LORD said to Joshua, "Make flint knives and circumcise the Israelites again." [3]So Joshua made flint knives and circumcised the Israelites at Gibeath Haaraloth. [4]Now this is why he did so: All those who came out of Egypt—all the men of military age—died in the desert on the way after leaving Egypt. [5]All the people that came out had been circumcised, but all the people born in the desert during the journey from Egypt had not. [6]The Israelites had moved about in the desert forty years until all the men who were of military age when they left Egypt had died, since they had not obeyed the LORD. For the LORD had sworn to them that they would not see

the land that he had solemnly promised their fathers to give us, a land flowing with milk and honey. [7]So he raised up their sons in their place, and these were the ones Joshua circumcised. They were still uncircumcised because they had not been circumcised on the way. [8]And after the whole nation had been circumcised, they remained where they were in camp until they were healed.

[9]Then the LORD said to Joshua, "Today I have rolled away the reproach of Egypt from you." So the place has been called Gilgal to this day.

[10]On the evening of the fourteenth day of the month, while camped at Gilgal on the plains of Jericho, the Israelites celebrated the Passover. [11]The day after the Passover, that very day, they ate some of the produce of the land: unleavened bread and roasted grain. [12]The manna stopped the day after they ate this food from the land; there was no longer any manna for the Israelites, but that year they ate of the produce of Canaan.

NEW TESTAMENT READING
Luke 22:1–38

Judas Agrees to Betray Jesus

22 Now the Feast of Unleavened Bread, called the Passover, was approaching, [2]and the chief priests and the teachers of the law were looking for some way to get rid of Jesus, for they were afraid of the people. [3]Then Satan entered Judas, called Iscariot, one of the Twelve. [4]And Judas went to the chief priests and the officers of the temple guard and discussed with them how he might betray Jesus. [5]They were delighted and agreed to give him money. [6]He consented, and watched for an opportunity to hand Jesus over to them when no crowd was present.

The Last Supper

[7]Then came the day of Unleavened Bread on which the Passover lamb had

to be sacrificed. [8]Jesus sent Peter and John, saying, "Go and make preparations for us to eat the Passover."

[9]"Where do you want us to prepare for it?" they asked.

[10]He replied, "As you enter the city, a man carrying a jar of water will meet you. Follow him to the house that he enters, [11]and say to the owner of the house, 'The Teacher asks: Where is the guest room, where I may eat the Passover with my disciples?' [12]He will show you a large upper room, all furnished. Make preparations there."

[13]They left and found things just as Jesus had told them. So they prepared the Passover.

[14]When the hour came, Jesus and his apostles reclined at the table. [15]And he said to them, "I have eagerly desired to eat this Passover with you before I suffer. [16]For I tell you, I will not eat it again until it finds fulfilment in the kingdom of God."

[17]After taking the cup, he gave thanks and said, "Take this and divide it among you. [18]For I tell you I will not drink again of the fruit of the vine until the kingdom of God comes."

[19]And he took bread, gave thanks and broke it, and gave it to them, saying, "This is my body given for you; do this in remembrance of me."

[20]In the same way, after the supper he took the cup, saying, "This cup is the new covenant in my blood, which is poured out for you. [21]But the hand of him who is going to betray me is with mine on the table. [22]The Son of Man will go as it has been decreed, but woe to that man who betrays him." [23]They began to question among themselves which of them it might be who would do this.

[24]Also a dispute arose among them as to which of them was considered to be greatest. [25]Jesus said to them, "The kings of the Gentiles lord it over them; and those who exercise authority over them call themselves Benefactors. [26]But you are not to be like that. Instead, the greatest among you should be like the youngest, and the one who rules like the one who serves. [27]For who is greater, the one who is at the table or the one who serves? Is it not the one who is at the table? But I am among you as one who serves. [28]You are those who have stood by me in my trials. [29]And I confer on you a kingdom, just as my Father conferred one on me, [30]so that you may eat and drink at my table in my kingdom and sit on thrones, judging the twelve tribes of Israel.

[31]"Simon, Simon, Satan has asked to sift you as wheat. [32]But I have prayed for you, Simon, that your faith may not fail. And when you have turned back, strengthen your brothers."

[33]But he replied, "Lord, I am ready to go with you to prison and to death."

[34]Jesus answered, "I tell you, Peter, before the cock crows today, you will deny three times that you know me."

[35]Then Jesus asked them, "When I sent you without purse, bag or sandals, did you lack anything?"

"Nothing," they answered.

[36]He said to them, "But now if you have a purse, take it, and also a bag; and if you don't have a sword, sell your cloak and buy one. [37]It is written: 'And he was numbered with the transgressors'; and I tell you that this must be fulfilled in me. Yes, what is written about me is reaching its fulfilment."

[38]The disciples said, "See, Lord, here are two swords."

"That is enough," he replied.

READING FROM PSALMS
Psalm 50:1–15

A psalm of Asaph.

[1]The Mighty One, God, the LORD, speaks and summons the earth from the rising of the sun to the place where it sets.
[2]From Zion, perfect in beauty, God shines forth.
[3]Our God comes and will not be silent;

a fire devours before him,
and around him a tempest rages.
⁴He summons the heavens above,
and the earth, that he may judge
his people:
⁵"Gather to me my consecrated
ones,
who made a covenant with me by
sacrifice."
⁶And the heavens proclaim his
righteousness,
for God himself is judge.   *Selah*

⁷"Hear, O my people, and I will
speak,
O Israel, and I will testify against
you:
I am God, your God.
⁸I do not rebuke you for your
sacrifices

or your burnt offerings, which are
ever before me.
⁹I have no need of a bull from your
stall
or of goats from your pens,
¹⁰for every animal of the forest is mine,
and the cattle on a thousand hills.
¹¹I know every bird in the mountains,
and the creatures of the field are
mine.
¹²If I were hungry I would not tell you,
for the world is mine, and all that is
in it.
¹³Do I eat the flesh of bulls
or drink the blood of goats?
¹⁴Sacrifice thank-offerings to God,
fulfil your vows to the Most High,
¹⁵and call upon me in the day of
trouble;
I will deliver you, and you will
honour me."

APRIL 24   DAY 114

OLD TESTAMENT READING
Joshua 5:13–7:26

The Fall of Jericho

¹³Now when Joshua was near Jericho,
he looked up and saw a man standing in
front of him with a drawn sword in his
hand. Joshua went up to him and asked,
"Are you for us or for our enemies?"

¹⁴"Neither," he replied, "but as commander of the army of the LORD I have
now come." Then Joshua fell face down
to the ground in reverence, and asked
him, "What message does my Lord
have for his servant?"

¹⁵The commander of the LORD's
army replied, "Take off your sandals,
for the place where you are standing is
holy." And Joshua did so.

6 Now Jericho was tightly shut up
because of the Israelites. No-one
went out and no-one came in.

²Then the LORD said to Joshua, "See,

I have delivered Jericho into your
hands, along with its king and its
fighting men. ³March around the city
once with all the armed men. Do this for
six days. ⁴Make seven priests carry
trumpets of rams' horns in front of the
ark. On the seventh day, march around
the city seven times, with the priests
blowing the trumpets. ⁵When you hear
them sound a long blast on the trumpets, make all the people give a loud
shout; then the wall of the city will
collapse and the people will go up,
every man straight in."

⁶So Joshua son of Nun called the
priests and said to them, "Take up the
ark of the covenant of the LORD and
make seven priests carry trumpets in
front of it." ⁷And he ordered the people, "Advance! March around the city,
with the armed guard going ahead of the
ark of the LORD."

⁸When Joshua had spoken to the people, the seven priests carrying the seven

trumpets before the LORD went forward, blowing their trumpets, and the ark of the LORD's covenant followed them. ⁹The armed guard marched ahead of the priests who blew the trumpets, and the rear guard followed the ark. All this time the trumpets were sounding. ¹⁰But Joshua had commanded the people, "Do not give a war cry, do not raise your voices, do not say a word until the day I tell you to shout. Then shout!" ¹¹So he had the ark of the LORD carried around the city, circling it once. Then the people returned to camp and spent the night there.

¹²Joshua got up early the next morning and the priests took up the ark of the LORD. ¹³The seven priests carrying the seven trumpets went forward, marching before the ark of the LORD and blowing the trumpets. The armed men went ahead of them and the rear guard followed the ark of the LORD, while the trumpets kept sounding. ¹⁴So on the second day they marched around the city once and returned to the camp. They did this for six days.

¹⁵On the seventh day, they got up at daybreak and marched around the city seven times in the same manner, except that on that day they circled the city seven times. ¹⁶The seventh time around, when the priests sounded the trumpet blast, Joshua commanded the people, "Shout! For the LORD has given you the city! ¹⁷The city and all that is in it are to be devoted to the LORD. Only Rahab the prostitute and all who are with her in her house shall be spared, because she hid the spies we sent. ¹⁸But keep away from the devoted things, so that you will not bring about your own destruction by taking any of them. Otherwise you will make the camp of Israel liable to destruction and bring trouble on it. ¹⁹All the silver and gold and the articles of bronze and iron are sacred to the LORD and must go into his treasury."

²⁰When the trumpets sounded, the people shouted, and at the sound of the trumpet, when the people gave a loud shout, the wall collapsed; so every man charged straight in, and they took the city. ²¹They devoted the city to the LORD and destroyed with the sword every living thing in it—men and women, young and old, cattle, sheep and donkeys.

²²Joshua said to the two men who had spied out the land, "Go into the prostitute's house and bring her out and all who belong to her, in accordance with your oath to her." ²³So the young men who had done the spying went in and brought out Rahab, her father and mother and brothers and all who belonged to her. They brought out her entire family and put them in a place outside the camp of Israel.

²⁴Then they burned the whole city and everything in it, but they put the silver and gold and the articles of bronze and iron into the treasury of the LORD's house. ²⁵But Joshua spared Rahab the prostitute, with her family and all who belonged to her, because she hid the men Joshua had sent as spies to Jericho —and she lives among the Israelites to this day.

²⁶At that time Joshua pronounced this solemn oath: "Cursed before the LORD is the man who undertakes to rebuild this city, Jericho:

"At the cost of his firstborn son
    will he lay its foundations;
at the cost of his youngest
    will he set up its gates."

²⁷So the LORD was with Joshua, and his fame spread throughout the land.

Achan's Sin

7 But the Israelites acted unfaithfully in regard to the devoted things; Achan son of Carmi, the son of Zimri, the son of Zerah, of the tribe of Judah, took some of them. So the LORD's anger burned against Israel.

²Now Joshua sent men from Jericho to Ai, which is near Beth Aven to the east of Bethel, and told them, "Go up

and spy out the region." So the men went up and spied out Ai.

³When they returned to Joshua, they said, "Not all the people will have to go up against Ai. Send two or three thousand men to take it and do not weary all the people, for only a few men are there." ⁴So about three thousand men went up; but they were routed by the men of Ai, ⁵who killed about thirty-six of them. They chased the Israelites from the city gate as far as the stone quarries and struck them down on the slopes. At this the hearts of the people melted and became like water.

⁶Then Joshua tore his clothes and fell face down to the ground before the ark of the LORD, remaining there till evening. The elders of Israel did the same, and sprinkled dust on their heads. ⁷And Joshua said, "Ah, Sovereign LORD, why did you ever bring this people across the Jordan to deliver us into the hands of the Amorites to destroy us? If only we had been content to stay on the other side of the Jordan! ⁸O Lord, what can I say, now that Israel has been routed by its enemies? ⁹The Canaanites and the other people of the country will hear about this and they will surround us and wipe out our name from the earth. What then will you do for your own great name?"

¹⁰The LORD said to Joshua, "Stand up! What are you doing down on your face? ¹¹Israel has sinned; they have violated my covenant, which I commanded them to keep. They have taken some of the devoted things; they have stolen, they have lied, they have put them with their own possessions. ¹²That is why the Israelites cannot stand against their enemies; they turn their backs and run because they have been made liable to destruction. I will not be with you any more unless you destroy whatever among you is devoted to destruction.

¹³"Go, consecrate the people. Tell them, 'Consecrate yourselves in preparation for tomorrow; for this is what the LORD, the God of Israel, says: That which is devoted is among you, O Israel. You cannot stand against your enemies until you remove it.

¹⁴"'In the morning, present yourselves tribe by tribe. The tribe that the LORD takes shall come forward clan by clan; the clan that the LORD takes shall come forward family by family; and the family that the LORD takes shall come forward man by man. ¹⁵He who is caught with the devoted things shall be destroyed by fire, along with all that belongs to him. He has violated the covenant of the LORD and has done a disgraceful thing in Israel!'"

¹⁶Early the next morning Joshua had Israel come forward by tribes, and Judah was taken. ¹⁷The clans of Judah came forward, and he took the Zera-hites. He had the clan of the Zerahites come forward by families, and Zimri was taken. ¹⁸Joshua had his family come forward man by man, and Achan son of Carmi, the son of Zimri, the son of Zerah, of the tribe of Judah, was taken.

¹⁹Then Joshua said to Achan, "My son, give glory to the LORD, the God of Israel, and give him the praise. Tell me what you have done; do not hide it from me."

²⁰Achan replied, "It is true! I have sinned against the LORD, the God of Israel. This is what I have done: ²¹When I saw in the plunder a beautiful robe from Babylonia, two hundred shekels of silver and a wedge of gold weighing fifty shekels, I coveted them and took them. They are hidden in the ground inside my tent, with the silver underneath."

²²So Joshua sent messengers, and they ran to the tent, and there it was, hidden in his tent, with the silver underneath. ²³They took the things from the tent, brought them to Joshua and all the Israelites and spread them out before the LORD.

²⁴Then Joshua, together with all Israel, took Achan son of Zerah, the silver, the robe, the gold wedge, his sons and daughters, his cattle, donkeys and sheep, his tent and all that he had, to the Valley of Achor. ²⁵Joshua said,

"Why have you brought this trouble on us? The LORD will bring trouble on you today."

Then all Israel stoned him, and after they had stoned the rest, they burned them. ²⁶Over Achan they heaped up a large pile of rocks, which remains to this day. Then the LORD turned from his fierce anger. Therefore that place has been called the Valley of Achor ever since.

NEW TESTAMENT READING
Luke 22:39–62

Jesus Prays on the Mount of Olives

³⁹Jesus went out as usual to the Mount of Olives, and his disciples followed him. ⁴⁰On reaching the place, he said to them, "Pray that you will not fall into temptation." ⁴¹He withdrew about a stone's throw beyond them, knelt down and prayed, ⁴²"Father, if you are willing, take this cup from me; yet not my will, but yours be done." ⁴³An angel from heaven appeared to him and strengthened him. ⁴⁴And being in anguish, he prayed more earnestly, and his sweat was like drops of blood falling to the ground.

⁴⁵When he rose from prayer and went back to the disciples, he found them asleep, exhausted from sorrow. ⁴⁶"Why are you sleeping?" he asked them. "Get up and pray so that you will not fall into temptation."

Jesus Arrested

⁴⁷While he was still speaking a crowd came up, and the man who was called Judas, one of the Twelve, was leading them. He approached Jesus to kiss him, ⁴⁸but Jesus asked him, "Judas, are you betraying the Son of Man with a kiss?"

⁴⁹When Jesus' followers saw what was going to happen, they said, "Lord, should we strike with our swords?" ⁵⁰And one of them struck the servant of the high priest, cutting off his right ear.

⁵¹But Jesus answered, "No more of this!" And he touched the man's ear and healed him.

⁵²Then Jesus said to the chief priests, the officers of the temple guard, and the elders, who had come for him, "Am I leading a rebellion, that you have come with swords and clubs? ⁵³Every day I was with you in the temple courts, and you did not lay a hand on me. But this is your hour—when darkness reigns."

Peter Disowns Jesus

⁵⁴Then seizing him, they led him away and took him into the house of the high priest. Peter followed at a distance. ⁵⁵But when they had kindled a fire in the middle of the courtyard and had sat down together, Peter sat down with them. ⁵⁶A servant girl saw him seated there in the firelight. She looked closely at him and said, "This man was with him."

⁵⁷But he denied it. "Woman, I don't know him," he said.

⁵⁸A little later someone else saw him and said, "You also are one of them."

"Man, I am not!" Peter replied.

⁵⁹About an hour later another asserted, "Certainly this fellow was with him, for he is a Galilean."

⁶⁰Peter replied, "Man, I don't know what you're talking about!" Just as he was speaking, the cock crowed. ⁶¹The Lord turned and looked straight at Peter. Then Peter remembered the word the Lord had spoken to him: "Before the cock crows today, you will disown me three times." ⁶²And he went outside and wept bitterly.

READING FROM PSALMS
Psalm 50:16–23

¹⁶But to the wicked, God says:

"What right have you to recite my
     laws
     or take my covenant on your lips?

17You hate my instruction
    and cast my words behind you.
18When you see a thief, you join with
    him;
    you throw in your lot with
    adulterers.
19You use your mouth for evil
    and harness your tongue to deceit.
20You speak continually against your
    brother
    and slander your own mother's
    son.
21These things you have done and I
    kept silent;

you thought I was altogether like
    you.
But I will rebuke you
    and accuse you to your face.

22"Consider this, you who forget God,
    or I will tear you to pieces, with
    none to rescue:
23He who sacrifices thank-offerings
    honours me,
    and he prepares the way
    so that I may show him the
    salvation of God."

APRIL 25   DAY 115

OLD TESTAMENT READING
Joshua 8:1–9:15

Ai Destroyed

8 Then the LORD said to Joshua, "Do not be afraid; do not be discouraged. Take the whole army with you, and go up and attack Ai. For I have delivered into your hands the king of Ai, his people, his city and his land. 2You shall do to Ai and its king as you did to Jericho and its king, except that you may carry off their plunder and livestock for yourselves. Set an ambush behind the city."

3So Joshua and the whole army moved out to attack Ai. He chose thirty thousand of his best fighting men and sent them out at night 4with these orders: "Listen carefully. You are to set an ambush behind the city. Don't go very far from it. All of you be on the alert. 5I and all those with me will advance on the city, and when the men come out against us, as they did before, we will flee from them. 6They will pursue us until we have lured them away from the city, for they will say, 'They are running away from us as they did before.' So when we flee from them,

7you are to rise up from ambush and take the city. The LORD your God will give it into your hand. 8When you have taken the city, set it on fire. Do what the LORD has commanded. See to it; you have my orders."

9Then Joshua sent them off, and they went to the place of ambush and lay in wait between Bethel and Ai, to the west of Ai—but Joshua spent that night with the people.

10Early the next morning Joshua mustered his men, and he and the leaders of Israel marched before them to Ai. 11The entire force that was with him marched up and approached the city and arrived in front of it. They set up camp north of Ai, with the valley between them and the city. 12Joshua had taken about five thousand men and set them in ambush between Bethel and Ai, to the west of the city. 13They had the soldiers take up their positions—all those in the camp to the north of the city and the ambush to the west of it. That night Joshua went into the valley.

14When the king of Ai saw this, he and all the men of the city hurried out early in the morning to meet Israel in battle at a certain place overlooking the

Arabah. But he did not know that an ambush had been set against him behind the city. 15Joshua and all Israel let themselves be driven back before them, and they fled towards the desert. 16All the men of Ai were called to pursue them, and they pursued Joshua and were lured away from the city. 17Not a man remained in Ai or Bethel who did not go after Israel. They left the city open and went in pursuit of Israel.

18Then the LORD said to Joshua, "Hold out towards Ai the javelin that is in your hand, for into your hand I will deliver the city." So Joshua held out his javelin towards Ai. 19As soon as he did this, the men in the ambush rose quickly from their position and rushed forward. They entered the city and captured it and quickly set it on fire.

20The men of Ai looked back and saw the smoke of the city rising against the sky, but they had no chance to escape in any direction, for the Israelites who had been fleeing towards the desert had turned back against their pursuers. 21For when Joshua and all Israel saw that the ambush had taken the city and that smoke was going up from the city, they turned round and attacked the men of Ai. 22The men of the ambush also came out of the city against them, so that they were caught in the middle, with Israelites on both sides. Israel cut them down, leaving them neither survivors nor fugitives. 23But they took the king of Ai alive and brought him to Joshua.

24When Israel had finished killing all the men of Ai in the fields and in the desert where they had chased them, and when every one of them had been put to the sword, all the Israelites returned to Ai and killed those who were in it. 25Twelve thousand men and women fell that day—all the people of Ai. 26For Joshua did not draw back the hand that held out his javelin until he had destroyed all who lived in Ai. 27But Israel did carry off for themselves the livestock and plunder of this city, as the LORD had instructed Joshua.

28So Joshua burned Ai and made it a permanent heap of ruins, a desolate place to this day. 29He hung the king of Ai on a tree and left him there until evening. At sunset, Joshua ordered them to take his body from the tree and throw it down at the entrance of the city gate. And they raised a large pile of rocks over it, which remains to this day.

The Covenant Renewed at Mount Ebal

30Then Joshua built on Mount Ebal an altar to the LORD, the God of Israel, 31as Moses the servant of the LORD had commanded the Israelites. He built it according to what is written in the Book of the Law of Moses—an altar of uncut stones, on which no iron tool had been used. On it they offered to the LORD burnt offerings and sacrificed fellowship offerings. 32There, in the presence of the Israelites, Joshua copied on stones the law of Moses, which he had written. 33All Israel, aliens and citizens alike, with their elders, officials and judges, were standing on both sides of the ark of the covenant of the LORD, facing those who carried it—the priests, who were Levites. Half of the people stood in front of Mount Gerizim and half of them in front of Mount Ebal, as Moses the servant of the LORD had formerly commanded when he gave instructions to bless the people of Israel.

34Afterwards, Joshua read all the words of the law—the blessings and the curses—just as it is written in the Book of the Law. 35There was not a word of all that Moses had commanded that Joshua did not read to the whole assembly of Israel, including the women and children, and the aliens who lived among them.

The Gibeonite Deception

9 Now when all the kings west of the Jordan heard about these things —those in the hill country, in the western foothills, and along the entire coast of the Great Sea as far as Lebanon

(the kings of the Hittites, Amorites, Canaanites, Perizzites, Hivites and Jebusites)—²they came together to make war against Joshua and Israel.

³However, when the people of Gibeon heard what Joshua had done to Jericho and Ai, ⁴they resorted to a ruse: They went as a delegation whose donkeys were loaded with worn-out sacks and old wineskins, cracked and mended. ⁵The men put worn and patched sandals on their feet and wore old clothes. All the bread of their food supply was dry and mouldy. ⁶Then they went to Joshua in the camp at Gilgal and said to him and the men of Israel, "We have come from a distant country; make a treaty with us."

⁷The men of Israel said to the Hivites, "But perhaps you live near us. How then can we make a treaty with you?"

⁸"We are your servants," they said to Joshua.

But Joshua asked, "Who are you and where do you come from?"

⁹They answered: "Your servants have come from a very distant country because of the fame of the LORD your God. For we have heard reports of him: all that he did in Egypt, ¹⁰and all that he did to the two kings of the Amorites east of the Jordan—Sihon king of Heshbon, and Og king of Bashan, who reigned in Ashtaroth. ¹¹And our elders and all those living in our country said to us, 'Take provisions for your journey; go and meet them and say to them, "We are your servants; make a treaty with us."' ¹²This bread of ours was warm when we packed it at home on the day we left to come to you. But now see how dry and mouldy it is. ¹³And these wineskins we filled were new, but see how cracked they are. And our clothes and sandals are worn out by the very long journey."

¹⁴The men of Israel sampled their provisions but did not enquire of the LORD. ¹⁵So Joshua made a treaty of peace with them to let them live, and the leaders of the assembly ratified it by oath.

NEW TESTAMENT READING
Luke 22:63–23:25

The Guards Mock Jesus

⁶³The men who were guarding Jesus began mocking and beating him. ⁶⁴They blindfolded him and demanded, "Prophesy! Who hit you?" ⁶⁵And they said many other insulting things to him.

Jesus Before Pilate and Herod

⁶⁶At daybreak the council of the elders of the people, both the chief priests and teachers of the law, met together, and Jesus was led before them. ⁶⁷"If you are the Christ," they said, "tell us."

Jesus answered, "If I tell you, you will not believe me, ⁶⁸and if I asked you, you would not answer. ⁶⁹But from now on, the Son of Man will be seated at the right hand of the mighty God."

⁷⁰They all asked, "Are you then the Son of God?"

He replied, "You are right in saying I am."

⁷¹Then they said, "Why do we need any more testimony? We have heard it from his own lips."

23 Then the whole assembly rose and led him off to Pilate. ²And they began to accuse him, saying, "We have found this man subverting our nation. He opposes payment of taxes to Caesar and claims to be Christ, a king."

³So Pilate asked Jesus, "Are you the king of the Jews?"

"Yes, it is as you say," Jesus replied.

⁴Then Pilate announced to the chief priests and the crowd, "I find no basis for a charge against this man."

⁵But they insisted, "He stirs up the people all over Judea by his teaching. He started in Galilee and has come all the way here."

⁶On hearing this, Pilate asked if the man was a Galilean. ⁷When he learned that Jesus was under Herod's jurisdiction, he sent him to Herod, who was also in Jerusalem at that time.

⁸When Herod saw Jesus, he was greatly pleased, because for a long time he had been wanting to see him. From what he had heard about him, he hoped to see him perform some miracle. ⁹He plied him with many questions, but Jesus gave him no answer. ¹⁰The chief priests and the teachers of the law were standing there, vehemently accusing him. ¹¹Then Herod and his soldiers ridiculed and mocked him. Dressing him in an elegant robe, they sent him back to Pilate. ¹²That day Herod and Pilate became friends—before this they had been enemies.

¹³Pilate called together the chief priests, the rulers and the people, ¹⁴and said to them, "You brought me this man as one who was inciting the people to rebellion. I have examined him in your presence and have found no basis for your charges against him. ¹⁵Neither has Herod, for he sent him back to us; as you can see, he has done nothing to deserve death. ¹⁶Therefore, I will punish him and then release him."

¹⁸With one voice they cried out, "Away with this man! Release Barabbas to us!" (¹⁹Barabbas had been thrown into prison for an insurrection in the city, and for murder.)

²⁰Wanting to release Jesus, Pilate appealed to them again. ²¹But they kept shouting, "Crucify him! Crucify him!"

²²For the third time he spoke to them: "Why? What crime has this man committed? I have found in him no grounds for the death penalty. Therefore I will have him punished and then release him."

²³But with loud shouts they insistently demanded that he be crucified, and their shouts prevailed. ²⁴So Pilate decided to grant their demand. ²⁵He released the man who had been thrown into prison for insurrection and murder, the one they asked for, and surrendered Jesus to their will.

READING FROM PSALMS
Psalm 51:1–9

For the director of music. A psalm of David. When the prophet Nathan came to him after David had committed adultery with Bathsheba.

¹Have mercy on me, O God,
  according to your unfailing love;
according to your great compassion
  blot out my transgressions.
²Wash away all my iniquity
  and cleanse me from my sin.

³For I know my transgressions,
  and my sin is always before me.
⁴Against you, you only, have I sinned
  and done what is evil in your sight,
so that you are proved right when
    you speak
  and justified when you judge.
⁵Surely I was sinful at birth,
  sinful from the time my mother
    conceived me.
⁶Surely you desire truth in the inner
    parts;
  you teach me wisdom in the inmost
    place.

⁷Cleanse me with hyssop, and I shall
    be clean;
  wash me, and I shall be whiter than
    snow.
⁸Let me hear joy and gladness;
  let the bones you have crushed
    rejoice.
⁹Hide your face from my sins
  and blot out all my iniquity.

OLD TESTAMENT READING
Joshua 9:16–10:43

16Three days after they made the treaty with the Gibeonites, the Israelites heard that they were neighbours, living near them. 17So the Israelites set out and on the third day came to their cities: Gibeon, Kephirah, Beeroth and Kiriath Jearim. 18But the Israelites did not attack them, because the leaders of the assembly had sworn an oath to them by the LORD, the God of Israel.

The whole assembly grumbled against the leaders, 19but all the leaders answered, "We have given them our oath by the LORD, the God of Israel, and we cannot touch them now. 20This is what we will do to them: We will let them live, so that wrath will not fall on us for breaking the oath we swore to them." 21They continued, "Let them live, but let them be woodcutters and water-carriers for the entire community." So the leaders' promise to them was kept.

22Then Joshua summoned the Gibeonites and said, "Why did you deceive us by saying, 'We live a long way from you,' while actually you live near us? 23You are now under a curse: You will never cease to serve as woodcutters and water-carriers for the house of my God."

24They answered Joshua, "Your servants were clearly told how the LORD your God had commanded his servant Moses to give you the whole land and to wipe out all its inhabitants from before you. So we feared for our lives because of you, and that is why we did this. 25We are now in your hands. Do to us whatever seems good and right to you."

26So Joshua saved them from the Israelites, and they did not kill them. 27That day he made the Gibeonites woodcutters and water-carriers for the community and for the altar of the LORD at the place the LORD would choose. And that is what they are to this day.

The Sun Stands Still

10 Now Adoni-Zedek king of Jerusalem heard that Joshua had taken Ai and totally destroyed it, doing to Ai and its king as he had done to Jericho and its king, and that the people of Gibeon had made a treaty of peace with Israel and were living near them. 2He and his people were very much alarmed at this, because Gibeon was an important city, like one of the royal cities; it was larger than Ai, and all its men were good fighters. 3So Adoni-Zedek king of Jerusalem appealed to Hoham king of Hebron, Piram king of Jarmuth, Japhia king of Lachish and Debir king of Eglon. 4"Come up and help me attack Gibeon," he said, "because it has made peace with Joshua and the Israelites."

5Then the five kings of the Amorites —the kings of Jerusalem, Hebron, Jarmuth, Lachish and Eglon—joined forces. They moved up with all their troops and took up positions against Gibeon and attacked it.

6The Gibeonites then sent word to Joshua in the camp at Gilgal: "Do not abandon your servants. Come up to us quickly and save us! Help us, because all the Amorite kings from the hill country have joined forces against us."

7So Joshua marched up from Gilgal with his entire army, including all the best fighting men. 8The LORD said to Joshua, "Do not be afraid of them; I have given them into your hand. Not one of them will be able to withstand you."

9After an all-night march from Gilgal, Joshua took them by surprise.

¹⁰The LORD threw them into confusion before Israel, who defeated them in a great victory at Gibeon. Israel pursued them along the road going up to Beth Horon and cut them down all the way to Azekah and Makkedah. ¹¹As they fled before Israel on the road down from Beth Horon to Azekah, the LORD hurled large hailstones down on them from the sky, and more of them died from the hailstones than were killed by the swords of the Israelites.

¹²On the day the LORD gave the Amorites over to Israel, Joshua said to the LORD in the presence of Israel:

"O sun, stand still over Gibeon,
    O moon, over the Valley of
        Aijalon."
¹³So the sun stood still,
    and the moon stopped,
    till the nation avenged itself on its
        enemies,

as it is written in the Book of Jashar.

The sun stopped in the middle of the sky and delayed going down about a full day. ¹⁴There has never been a day like it before or since, a day when the LORD listened to a man. Surely the LORD was fighting for Israel!

¹⁵Then Joshua returned with all Israel to the camp at Gilgal.

Five Amorite Kings Killed

¹⁶Now the five kings had fled and hidden in the cave at Makkedah. ¹⁷When Joshua was told that the five kings had been found hiding in the cave at Makkedah, ¹⁸he said, "Roll large rocks up to the mouth of the cave, and post some men there to guard it. ¹⁹But don't stop! Pursue your enemies, attack them from the rear and don't let them reach their cities, for the LORD your God has given them into your hand."

²⁰So Joshua and the Israelites destroyed them completely—almost to a man—but the few who were left reached their fortified cities. ²¹The whole army then returned safely to Joshua in the camp at Makkedah, and no-one uttered a word against the Israelites.

²²Joshua said, "Open the mouth of the cave and bring those five kings out to me." ²³So they brought the five kings out of the cave—the kings of Jerusalem, Hebron, Jarmuth, Lachish and Eglon. ²⁴When they had brought these kings to Joshua, he summoned all the men of Israel and said to the army commanders who had come with him, "Come here and put your feet on the necks of these kings." So they came forward and placed their feet on their necks.

²⁵Joshua said to them, "Do not be afraid; do not be discouraged. Be strong and courageous. This is what the LORD will do to all the enemies you are going to fight." ²⁶Then Joshua struck and killed the kings and hung them on five trees, and they were left hanging on the trees until evening.

²⁷At sunset Joshua gave the order and they took them down from the trees and threw them into the cave where they had been hiding. At the mouth of the cave they placed large rocks, which are there to this day.

²⁸That day Joshua took Makkedah. He put the city and its king to the sword and totally destroyed everyone in it. He left no survivors. And he did to the king of Makkedah as he had done to the king of Jericho.

Southern Cities Conquered

²⁹Then Joshua and all Israel with him moved on from Makkedah to Libnah and attacked it. ³⁰The LORD also gave that city and its king into Israel's hand. The city and everyone in it Joshua put to the sword. He left no survivors there. And he did to its king as he had done to the king of Jericho.

³¹Then Joshua and all Israel with him moved on from Libnah to Lachish; he took up positions against it and attacked it. ³²The LORD handed Lachish over to Israel, and Joshua took it on the second

day. The city and everyone in it he put to the sword, just as he had done to Libnah. 33Meanwhile, Horam king of Gezer had come up to help Lachish, but Joshua defeated him and his army—until no survivors were left.

34Then Joshua and all Israel with him moved on from Lachish to Eglon; they took up positions against it and attacked it. 35They captured it that same day and put it to the sword and totally destroyed everyone in it, just as they had done to Lachish.

36Then Joshua and all Israel with him went up from Eglon to Hebron and attacked it. 37They took the city and put it to the sword, together with its king, its villages and everyone in it. They left no survivors. Just as at Eglon, they totally destroyed it and everyone in it.

38Then Joshua and all Israel with him turned round and attacked Debir. 39They took the city, its king and its villages, and put them to the sword. Everyone in it they totally destroyed. They left no survivors. They did to Debir and its king as they had done to Libnah and its king and to Hebron.

40So Joshua subdued the whole region, including the hill country, the Negev, the western foothills and the mountain slopes, together with all their kings. He left no survivors. He totally destroyed all who breathed, just as the LORD, the God of Israel, had commanded. 41Joshua subdued them from Kadesh Barnea to Gaza and from the whole region of Goshen to Gibeon. 42All these kings and their lands Joshua conquered in one campaign, because the LORD, the God of Israel, fought for Israel.

43Then Joshua returned with all Israel to the camp at Gilgal.

NEW TESTAMENT READING
Luke 23:26–56

The Crucifixion

26As they led him away, they seized Simon from Cyrene, who was on his way in from the country, and put the cross on him and made him carry it behind Jesus. 27A large number of people followed him, including women who mourned and wailed for him. 28Jesus turned and said to them, "Daughters of Jerusalem, do not weep for me; weep for yourselves and for your children. 29For the time will come when you will say, 'Blessed are the barren women, the wombs that never bore and the breasts that never nursed!' 30Then

"'they will say to the mountains,
    "Fall on us!"
  and to the hills "Cover us!"'

31For if men do these things when the tree is green, what will happen when it is dry?"

32Two other men, both criminals, were also led out with him to be executed. 33When they came to the place called the Skull, there they crucified him, along with the criminals—one on his right, the other on his left. 34Jesus said, "Father, forgive them, for they do not know what they are doing." And they divided up his clothes by casting lots.

35The people stood watching, and the rulers even sneered at him. They said, "He saved others; let him save himself if he is the Christ of God, the Chosen One."

36The soldiers also came up and mocked him. They offered him wine vinegar 37and said, "If you are the king of the Jews, save yourself."

38There was a written notice above him, which read: THIS IS THE KING OF THE JEWS.

39One of the criminals who hung there hurled insults at him: "Aren't you the Christ? Save yourself and us!"

40But the other criminal rebuked him. "Don't you fear God," he said, "since you are under the same sentence? 41We are punished justly, for we are getting what our deeds deserve. But this man has done nothing wrong."

42Then he said, "Jesus, remember me when you come into your kingdom."

43Jesus answered him, "I tell you the truth, today you will be with me in paradise."

Jesus' Death

44It was now about the sixth hour, and darkness came over the whole land until the ninth hour, 45for the sun stopped shining. And the curtain of the temple was torn in two. 46Jesus called out with a loud voice, "Father, into your hands I commit my spirit." When he had said this, he breathed his last.

47The centurion, seeing what had happened, praised God and said, "Surely this was a righteous man." 48When all the people who had gathered to witness this sight saw what took place, they beat their breasts and went away. 49But all those who knew him, including the women who had followed him from Galilee, stood at a distance, watching these things.

Jesus' Burial

50Now there was a man named Joseph, a member of the Council, a good and upright man, 51who had not consented to their decision and action. He came from the Judean town of Arimathea and he was waiting for the kingdom of God. 52Going to Pilate, he asked for Jesus' body. 53Then he took it down, wrapped it in linen cloth and placed it in a tomb cut in the rock, one in which no-one had yet been laid. 54It was Preparation Day, and the Sabbath was about to begin.

55The women who had come with Jesus from Galilee followed Joseph and saw the tomb and how his body was laid in it. 56Then they went home and prepared spices and perfumes. But they rested on the Sabbath in obedience to the commandment.

READING FROM PROVERBS
Proverbs 10:21–30

21The lips of the righteous nourish many,
    but fools die for lack of judgment.

22The blessing of the LORD brings wealth,
    and he adds no trouble to it.

23A fool finds pleasure in evil conduct,
    but a man of understanding delights in wisdom.

24What the wicked dreads will overtake him;
    what the righteous desire will be granted.

25When the storm has swept by, the wicked are gone,
    but the righteous stand firm for ever.

26As vinegar to the teeth and smoke to the eyes,
    so is a sluggard to those who send him.

27The fear of the LORD adds length to life,
    but the years of the wicked are cut short.

28The prospect of the righteous is joy,
    but the hopes of the wicked come to nothing.

29The way of the LORD is a refuge for the righteous,
    but it is the ruin of those who do evil.

30The righteous will never be uprooted,
    but the wicked will not remain in the land.

OLD TESTAMENT READING
Joshua 11:1–12:24

Northern Kings Defeated

11 When Jabin king of Hazor heard of this, he sent word to Jobab king of Madon, to the kings of Shimron and Acshaph, ²and to the northern kings who were in the mountains, in the Arabah south of Kinnereth, in the western foothills and in Naphoth Dor on the west; ³to the Canaanites in the east and west; to the Amorites, Hittites, Perizzites and Jebusites in the hill country; and to the Hivites below Hermon in the region of Mizpah. ⁴They came out with all their troops and a large number of horses and chariots—a huge army, as numerous as the sand on the seashore. ⁵All these kings joined forces and made camp together at the Waters of Merom, to fight against Israel.

⁶The LORD said to Joshua, "Do not be afraid of them, because by this time tomorrow I will hand all of them over to Israel, slain. You are to hamstring their horses and burn their chariots."

⁷So Joshua and his whole army came against them suddenly at the Waters of Merom and attacked them, ⁸and the LORD gave them into the hand of Israel. They defeated them and pursued them all the way to Greater Sidon, to Misrephoth Maim, and to the Valley of Mizpah on the east, until no survivors were left. ⁹Joshua did to them as the LORD had directed: He hamstrung their horses and burned their chariots.

¹⁰At that time Joshua turned back and captured Hazor and put its king to the sword. (Hazor had been the head of all these kingdoms.) ¹¹Everyone in it they put to the sword. They totally destroyed them, not sparing anything that breathed, and he burned up Hazor itself.

¹²Joshua took all these royal cities and their kings and put them to the sword. He totally destroyed them, as Moses the servant of the LORD had commanded. ¹³Yet Israel did not burn any of the cities built on their mounds—except Hazor, which Joshua burned. ¹⁴The Israelites carried off for themselves all the plunder and livestock of these cities, but all the people they put to the sword until they completely destroyed them, not sparing anyone that breathed. ¹⁵As the LORD commanded his servant Moses, so Moses commanded Joshua, and Joshua did it; he left nothing undone of all that the LORD commanded Moses.

¹⁶So Joshua took this entire land: the hill country, all the Negev, the whole region of Goshen, the western foothills, the Arabah and the mountains of Israel with their foothills, ¹⁷from Mount Halak, which rises towards Seir, to Baal Gad in the Valley of Lebanon below Mount Hermon. He captured all their kings and struck them down, putting them to death. ¹⁸Joshua waged war against all these kings for a long time. ¹⁹Except for the Hivites living in Gibeon, not one city made a treaty of peace with the Israelites, who took them all in battle. ²⁰For it was the LORD himself who hardened their hearts to wage war against Israel, so that he might destroy them totally, exterminating them without mercy, as the LORD had commanded Moses.

²¹At that time Joshua went and destroyed the Anakites from the hill country: from Hebron, Debir and Anab, from all the hill country of Judah, and from all the hill country of Israel. Joshua totally destroyed them and their towns. ²²No Anakites were left in Israelite territory; only in Gaza, Gath and Ashdod did any survive. ²³So Joshua took the entire land, just as the LORD had directed Moses, and he gave

it as an inheritance to Israel according to their tribal divisions.

Then the land had rest from war.

List of Defeated Kings

12 These are the kings of the land whom the Israelites had defeated and whose territory they took over east of the Jordan, from the Arnon Gorge to Mount Hermon, including all the eastern side of the Arabah:

²Sihon king of the Amorites,
who reigned in Heshbon. He ruled from Aroer on the rim of the Arnon Gorge—from the middle of the gorge—to the Jabbok River, which is the border of the Ammonites. This included half of Gilead. ³He also ruled over the eastern Arabah from the Sea of Kinnereth to the Sea of the Arabah (the Salt Sea), to Beth Jeshimoth, and then southward below the slopes of Pisgah.

⁴And the territory of Og king of Bashan,
one of the last of the Rephaites, who reigned in Ashtaroth and Edrei. ⁵He ruled over Mount Hermon, Salecah, all of Bashan to the border of the people of Geshur and Maacah, and half of Gilead to the border of Sihon king of Heshbon.

⁶Moses, the servant of the LORD, and the Israelites conquered them. And Moses the servant of the LORD gave their land to the Reubenites, the Gadites and the half-tribe of Manasseh to be their possession.

⁷These are the kings of the land that Joshua and the Israelites conquered on the west side of the Jordan, from Baal Gad in the Valley of Lebanon to Mount Halak, which rises towards Seir (their lands Joshua gave as an inheritance to the tribes of Israel according to their tribal divisions—⁸the hill country, the western foothills, the Arabah, the mountain slopes, the desert and the Negev—the lands of the Hittites, Amorites, Canaanites, Perizzites, Hivites and Jebusites):

⁹the king of Jericho	one
the king of Ai (near Bethel)	one
¹⁰the king of Jerusalem	one
the king of Hebron	one
¹¹the king of Jarmuth	one
the king of Lachish	one
¹²the king of Eglon	one
the king of Gezer	one
¹³the king of Debir	one
the king of Geder	one
¹⁴the king of Hormah	one
the king of Arad	one
¹⁵the king of Libnah	one
the king of Adullam	one
¹⁶the king of Makkedah	one
the king of Bethel	one
¹⁷the king of Tappuah	one
the king of Hepher	one
¹⁸the king of Aphek	one
the king of Lasharon	one
¹⁹the king of Madon	one
the king of Hazor	one
²⁰the king of Shimron Meron	one
the king of Acshaph	one
²¹the king of Taanach	one
the king of Megiddo	one
²²the king of Kedesh	one
the king of Jokneam in Carmel	one
²³the king of Dor (in Naphoth Dor)	one
the king of Goyim in Gilgal	one
²⁴the king of Tirzah	one

thirty-one kings in all.

NEW TESTAMENT READING
Luke 24:1–35

The Resurrection

24 On the first day of the week, very early in the morning, the women took the spices they had prepared and went to the tomb. ²They found the stone rolled away from the tomb, 3but when they entered, they did not find the body of the Lord Jesus. 4While they were wondering about this, suddenly two men in clothes that gleamed like lightning stood beside them. 5In their fright the women bowed down with their faces to the ground, but the men said to them, "Why do you look for the living among the dead? 6He is not here; he has risen! Remember how he told you, while he was still with you in Galilee: 7'The Son of Man must be delivered into the hands of sinful men, be crucified and on the third day be raised again.'" 8Then they remembered his words.

9When they came back from the tomb, they told all these things to the Eleven and to all the others. 10It was Mary Magdalene, Joanna, Mary the mother of James, and the others with them who told this to the apostles. 11But they did not believe the women, because their words seemed to them like nonsense. 12Peter, however, got up and ran to the tomb. Bending over, he saw the strips of linen lying by themselves, and he went away, wondering to himself what had happened.

On the Road to Emmaus

13Now that same day two of them were going to a village called Emmaus, about seven miles from Jerusalem. 14They were talking with each other about everything that had happened. 15As they talked and discussed these things with each other, Jesus himself came up and walked along with them; 16but they were kept from recognising him.

17He asked them, "What are you discussing together as you walk along?"

They stood still, their faces downcast. 18One of them, named Cleopas, asked him, "Are you only a visitor to Jerusalem and do not know the things that have happened there in these days?"

19"What things?" he asked.

"About Jesus of Nazareth," they replied. "He was a prophet, powerful in word and deed before God and all the people. 20The chief priests and our rulers handed him over to be sentenced to death, and they crucified him; 21but we had hoped that he was the one who was going to redeem Israel. And what is more, it is the third day since all this took place. 22In addition, some of our women amazed us. They went to the tomb early this morning 23but didn't find his body. They came and told us that they had seen a vision of angels, who said he was alive. 24Then some of our companions went to the tomb and found it just as the women had said, but him they did not see."

25He said to them, "How foolish you are, and how slow of heart to believe all that the prophets have spoken! 26Did not the Christ have to suffer these things and then enter his glory?" 27And beginning with Moses and all the Prophets, he explained to them what was said in all the Scriptures concerning himself.

28As they approached the village to which they were going, Jesus acted as if he were going further. 29But they urged him strongly, "Stay with us, for it is nearly evening; the day is almost over." So he went in to stay with them.

30When he was at the table with them, he took bread, gave thanks, broke it and began to give it to them. 31Then their eyes were opened and they recognised him, and he disappeared from their sight. 32They asked each other, "Were not our hearts burning within us while he talked with us on the road and opened the Scriptures to us?"

33They got up and returned at once to Jerusalem. There they found the Eleven and those with them, assembled together 34and saying, "It is true! The Lord has risen and has appeared to Simon." 35Then the two told what had happened on the way, and how Jesus was recognised by them when he broke the bread.

READING FROM PSALMS
Psalm 51:10–19

¹⁰Create in me a pure heart, O God,
      and renew a steadfast spirit within
         me.
¹¹Do not cast me from your presence
      or take your Holy Spirit from me.
¹²Restore to me the joy of your
         salvation
      and grant me a willing spirit, to
         sustain me.

¹³Then I will teach transgressors your
         ways,
      and sinners will turn back to you.
¹⁴Save me from bloodguilt, O God,
      the God who saves me,
      and my tongue will sing of your
         righteousness.

¹⁵O Lord, open my lips,
      and my mouth will declare your
         praise.
¹⁶You do not delight in sacrifice, or I
         would bring it;
      you do not take pleasure in burnt
         offerings.
¹⁷The sacrifices of God are a broken
         spirit;
      a broken and contrite heart,
      O God, you will not despise.

¹⁸In your good pleasure make Zion
         prosper;
      build up the walls of Jerusalem.
¹⁹Then there will be righteous
         sacrifices,
      whole burnt offerings to delight
         you;
      then bulls will be offered on your
         altar.

DAY 118

APRIL 28

OLD TESTAMENT READING
Joshua 13:1–14:15

Land Still to Be Taken

13 When Joshua was old and well advanced in years, the LORD said to him, "You are very old, and there are still very large areas of land to be taken over.

²"This is the land that remains: all the regions of the Philistines and Geshurites: ³from the Shihor River on the east of Egypt to the territory of Ekron on the north, all of it counted as Canaanite (the territory of the five Philistine rulers in Gaza, Ashdod, Ashkelon, Gath and Ekron—that of the Avvites); ⁴from the south, all the land of the Canaanites, from Arah of the Sidonians as far as Aphek, the region of the Amorites, ⁵the area of the

Gebalites; and all Lebanon to the east, from Baal Gad below Mount Hermon to Lebo Hamath.

⁶"As for all the inhabitants of the mountain regions from Lebanon to Misrephoth Maim, that is, all the Sidonians, I myself will drive them out before the Israelites. Be sure to allocate this land to Israel for an inheritance, as I have instructed you, ⁷and divide it as an inheritance among the nine tribes and half of the tribe of Manasseh."

Division of the Land East of the Jordan

⁸The other half of Manasseh, the Reubenites and the Gadites had received the inheritance that Moses had given them east of the Jordan, as he, the servant of the LORD, had assigned it to them.

⁹It extended from Aroer on the rim of the Arnon Gorge, and from the

town in the middle of the gorge, and included the whole plateau of Medeba as far as Dibon, 10and all the towns of Sihon king of the Amorites, who ruled in Heshbon, out to the border of the Ammonites. 11It also included Gilead, the territory of the people of Geshur and Maacah, all of Mount Hermon and all Bashan as far as Salecah —12that is, the whole kingdom of Og in Bashan, who had reigned in Ashtaroth and Edrei and had survived as one of the last of the Rephaites. Moses had defeated them and taken over their land. 13But the Israelites did not drive out the people of Geshur and Maacah, so they continue to live among the Israelites to this day.

14But to the tribe of Levi he gave no inheritance, since the offerings made by fire to the LORD, the God of Israel, are their inheritance, as he promised them.

15This is what Moses had given to the tribe of Reuben, clan by clan:

16The territory from Aroer on the rim of the Arnon Gorge, and from the town in the middle of the gorge, and the whole plateau past Medeba 17to Heshbon and all its towns on the plateau, including Dibon, Bamoth Baal, Beth Baal Meon, 18Jahaz, Kedemoth, Mephaath, 19Kiriathaim, Sibmah, Zereth Shahar on the hill in the valley, 20Beth Peor, the slopes of Pisgah, and Beth Jeshimoth 21—all the towns on the plateau and the entire realm of Sihon king of the Amorites, who ruled at Heshbon. Moses had defeated him and the Midianite chiefs, Evi, Rekem, Zur, Hur and Reba—princes allied with Sihon —who lived in that country. 22In addition to those slain in battle, the Israelites had put to the sword Balaam son of Beor, who practised divination. 23The boundary of the Reubenites was the bank of the

Jordan. These towns and their villages were the inheritance of the Reubenites, clan by clan.

24This is what Moses had given to the tribe of Gad, clan by clan:

25The territory of Jazer, all the towns of Gilead and half the Ammonite country as far as Aroer, near Rabbah; 26and from Heshbon to Ramath Mizpah and Betonim, and from Mahanaim to the territory of Debir; 27and in the valley, Beth Haram, Beth Nimrah, Succoth and Zaphon with the rest of the realm of Sihon king of Heshbon (the east side of the Jordan, the territory up to the end of the Sea of Kinnereth). 28These towns and their villages were the inheritance of the Gadites, clan by clan.

29This is what Moses had given to the half-tribe of Manasseh, that is, to half the family of the descendants of Manasseh, clan by clan:

30The territory extending from Mahanaim and including all of Bashan, the entire realm of Og king of Bashan—all the settlements of Jair in Bashan, sixty towns, 31half of Gilead, and Ashtaroth and Edrei (the royal cities of Og in Bashan). This was for the descendants of Makir son of Manasseh—for half of the sons of Makir, clan by clan.

32This is the inheritance Moses had given when he was in the plains of Moab across the Jordan east of Jericho. 33But to the tribe of Levi, Moses had given no inheritance; the LORD, the God of Israel, is their inheritance, as he promised them.

Division of the Land West of the Jordan

14 Now these are the areas the Israelites received as an inheritance in the land of Canaan, which

Eleazar the priest, Joshua son of Nun and the heads of the tribal clans of Israel allotted to them. ²Their inheritances were assigned by lot to the nine-and-a-half tribes, as the LORD had commanded through Moses. ³Moses had granted the two-and-a-half tribes their inheritance east of the Jordan but had not granted the Levites an inheritance among the rest, ⁴for the sons of Joseph had become two tribes—Manasseh and Ephraim. The Levites received no share of the land but only towns to live in, with pasture-lands for their flocks and herds. ⁵So the Israelites divided the land, just as the LORD had commanded Moses.

Hebron Given to Caleb

⁶Now the men of Judah approached Joshua at Gilgal, and Caleb son of Jephunneh the Kenizzite said to him, "You know what the LORD said to Moses the man of God at Kadesh Barnea about you and me. ⁷I was forty years old when Moses the servant of the LORD sent me from Kadesh Barnea to explore the land. And I brought him back a report according to my convictions, ⁸but my brothers who went up with me made the hearts of the people sink. I, however, followed the LORD my God wholeheartedly. ⁹So on that day Moses swore to me, 'The land on which your feet have walked will be your inheritance and that of your children for ever, because you have followed the LORD my God wholeheartedly.'

¹⁰"Now then, just as the LORD promised, he has kept me alive for forty-five years since the time he said this to Moses, while Israel moved about in the desert. So here I am today, eighty-five years old! ¹¹I am still as strong today as the day Moses sent me out; I'm just as vigorous to go out to battle now as I was then. ¹²Now give me this hill country that the LORD promised me that day. You yourself heard then that the Anakites were there and their cities were

large and fortified, but, the LORD helping me, I will drive them out just as he said."

¹³Then Joshua blessed Caleb son of Jephunneh and gave him Hebron as his inheritance. ¹⁴So Hebron has belonged to Caleb son of Jephunneh the Kenizzite ever since, because he followed the LORD, the God of Israel, wholeheartedly. ¹⁵(Hebron used to be called Kiriath Arba after Arba, who was the greatest man among the Anakites.)

Then the land had rest from war.

NEW TESTAMENT READING
Luke 24:36–53

Jesus Appears to the Disciples

³⁶While they were still talking about this, Jesus himself stood among them and said to them, "Peace be with you."

³⁷They were startled and frightened, thinking they saw a ghost. ³⁸He said to them, "Why are you troubled, and why do doubts rise in your minds? ³⁹Look at my hands and my feet. It is I myself! Touch me and see; a ghost does not have flesh and bones, as you see I have."

⁴⁰When he had said this, he showed them his hands and feet. ⁴¹And while they still did not believe it because of joy and amazement, he asked them, "Do you have anything here to eat?" ⁴²They gave him a piece of broiled fish, ⁴³and he took it and ate it in their presence.

⁴⁴He said to them, "This is what I told you while I was still with you: Everything must be fulfilled that is written about me in the Law of Moses, the Prophets and the Psalms."

⁴⁵Then he opened their minds so they could understand the Scriptures. ⁴⁶He told them, "This is what is written: The Christ will suffer and rise from the dead on the third day, ⁴⁷and repentance and forgiveness of sins will be preached in his name to all nations, beginning at Jerusalem. ⁴⁸You are witnesses of these

things. ⁴⁹I am going to send you what my Father has promised; but stay in the city until you have been clothed with power from on high."

The Ascension

⁵⁰When he had led them out to the vicinity of Bethany, he lifted up his hands and blessed them. ⁵¹While he was blessing them, he left them and was taken up into heaven. ⁵²Then they worshipped him and returned to Jerusalem with great joy. ⁵³And they stayed continually at the temple, praising God.

READING FROM PSALMS
Psalm 52:1–9

For the director of music. A *maskil* of David. When Doeg the Edomite had gone to Saul and told him: "David has gone to the house of Ahimelech."

¹Why do you boast of evil, you mighty man?
    Why do you boast all day long,
    you who are a disgrace in the eyes of God?
²Your tongue plots destruction;
    it is like a sharpened razor,
    you who practise deceit.

³You love evil rather than good,
    falsehood rather than speaking the truth.   *Selah*
⁴You love every harmful word,
    O you deceitful tongue!

⁵Surely God will bring you down to everlasting ruin:
    He will snatch you up and tear you from your tent;
    he will uproot you from the land of the living.   *Selah*
⁶The righteous will see and fear;
    they will laugh at him, saying,
⁷"Here now is the man
    who did not make God his stronghold
but trusted in his great wealth
    and grew strong by destroying others!"

⁸But I am like an olive tree
    flourishing in the house of God;
I trust in God's unfailing love
    for ever and ever.
⁹I will praise you for ever for what you have done;
    in your name I will hope, for your name is good.
    I will praise you in the presence of your saints.

APRIL 29   DAY 119

OLD TESTAMENT READING
Joshua 15:1–16:10

Allotment for Judah

15 The allotment for the tribe of Judah, clan by clan, extended down to the territory of Edom, to the Desert of Zin in the extreme south.

²Their southern boundary started from the bay at the southern end of the Salt Sea, ³crossed south of Scorpion Pass, continued on to Zin and went over to the south of Kadesh Barnea. Then it ran past Hezron up to Addar and curved around to Karka. ⁴It then passed along to Azmon and joined the Wadi of Egypt, ending at the sea. This is their southern boundary.

⁵The eastern boundary is the Salt Sea as far as the mouth of the Jordan.

The northern boundary started from the bay of the sea at the mouth of the Jordan, [6]went up to Beth Hoglah and continued north of Beth Arabah to the Stone of Bohan son of Reuben. [7]The boundary then went up to Debir from the Valley of Achor and turned north to Gilgal, which faces the Pass of Adummim south of the gorge. It continued along to the waters of En Shemesh and came out at En Rogel. [8]Then it ran up the Valley of Ben Hinnom along the southern slope of the Jebusite city (that is, Jerusalem). From there it climbed to the top of the hill west of the Hinnom Valley at the northern end of the Valley of Rephaim. [9]From the hilltop the boundary headed towards the spring of the waters of Nephtoah, came out at the towns of Mount Ephron and went down towards Baalah (that is, Kiriath Jearim). [10]Then it curved westward from Baalah to Mount Seir, ran along the northern slope of Mount Jearim (that is, Kesalon), continued down to Beth Shemesh and crossed to Timnah. [11]It went to the northern slope of Ekron, turned towards Shikkeron, passed along to Mount Baalah and reached Jabneel. The boundary ended at the sea.

[12]The western boundary is the coastline of the Great Sea.

These are the boundaries around the people of Judah by their clans.

[13]In accordance with the LORD's command to him, Joshua gave to Caleb son of Jephunneh a portion in Judah—Kiriath Arba, that is, Hebron. (Arba was the forefather of Anak.) [14]From Hebron Caleb drove out the three Anakites—Sheshai, Ahiman and Talmai—descendants of Anak. [15]From there he marched against the people living in Debir (formerly called Kiriath Sepher). [16]And Caleb said, "I will give my daughter Acsah in marriage to the man who attacks and captures Kiriath Sepher." [17]Othniel son of Kenaz,

Caleb's brother, took it; so Caleb gave his daughter Acsah to him in marriage.

[18]One day when she came to Othniel, she urged him to ask her father for a field. When she got off her donkey, Caleb asked her, "What can I do for you?"

[19]She replied, "Do me a special favour. Since you have given me land in the Negev, give me also springs of water." So Caleb gave her the upper and lower springs.

[20]This is the inheritance of the tribe of Judah, clan by clan:

[21]The southernmost towns of the tribe of Judah in the Negev towards the boundary of Edom were:

Kabzeel, Eder, Jagur, [22]Kinah, Dimonah, Adadah, [23]Kedesh, Hazor, Ithnan, [24]Ziph, Telem, Bealoth, [25]Hazor Hadattah, Kerioth Hezron (that is, Hazor), [26]Amam, Shema, Moladah, [27]Hazar Gaddah, Heshmon, Beth Pelet, [28]Hazar Shual, Beersheba, Biziothiah, [29]Baalah, Iim, Ezem, [30]Eltolad, Kesil, Hormah, [31]Ziklag, Madmannah, Sansannah, [32]Lebaoth, Shilhim, Ain and Rimmon—a total of twenty-nine towns and their villages.

[33]In the western foothills:

Eshtaol, Zorah, Ashnah, [34]Zanoah, En Gannim, Tappuah, Enam, [35]Jarmuth, Adullam, Socoh, Azekah, [36]Shaaraim, Adithaim and Gederah (or Gederothaim)—fourteen towns and their villages.

[37]Zenan, Hadashah, Migdal Gad, [38]Dilean, Mizpah, Joktheel, [39]Lachish, Bozkath, Eglon, [40]Cabbon, Lahmas, Kitlish, [41]Gederoth, Beth Dagon, Naamah and Makkedah—sixteen towns and their villages.

[42]Libnah, Ether, Ashan, [43]Iphtah, Ashnah, Nezib, [44]Keilah, Aczib and Mareshah—nine towns and their villages.

45Ekron, with its surrounding settlements and villages; 46west of Ekron, all that were in the vicinity of Ashdod, together with their villages; 47Ashdod, its surrounding settlements and villages; and Gaza, its settlements and villages, as far as the Wadi of Egypt and the coastline of the Great Sea.

48In the hill country:

Shamir, Jattir, Socoh, 49Dannah, Kiriath Sannah (that is, Debir), 50Anab, Eshtemoh, Anim, 51Goshen, Holon and Giloh—eleven towns and their villages.

52Arab, Dumah, Eshan, 53Janim, Beth Tappuah, Aphekah, 54Humtah, Kiriath Arba (that is, Hebron) and Zior—nine towns and their villages.

55Maon, Carmel, Ziph, Juttah, 56Jezreel, Jokdeam, Zanoah, 57Kain, Gibeah and Timnah—ten towns and their villages.

58Halhul, Beth Zur, Gedor, 59Maarath, Beth Anoth and Eltekon—six towns and their villages.

60Kiriath Baal (that is, Kiriath Jearim) and Rabbah—two towns and their villages.

61In the desert:

Beth Arabah, Middin, Secacah, 62Nibshan, the City of Salt and En Gedi—six towns and their villages.

63Judah could not dislodge the Jebusites, who were living in Jerusalem; to this day the Jebusites live there with the people of Judah.

Allotment for Ephraim and Manasseh

16 The allotment for Joseph began at the Jordan of Jericho, east of the waters of Jericho, and went up from there through the desert into the hill country of Bethel. 2It went on from Bethel (that is, Luz), crossed over to the territory of the Arkites in Ataroth, 3descended westward to the territory of the Japhletites as far as the region of Lower Beth Horon and on to Gezer, ending at the sea.

4So Manasseh and Ephraim, the descendants of Joseph, received their inheritance.

5This was the territory of Ephraim, clan by clan:

The boundary of their inheritance went from Ataroth Addar in the east to Upper Beth Horon 6and continued to the sea. From Micmethath on the north it curved eastward to Taanath Shiloh, passing by it to Janoah on the east. 7Then it went down from Janoah to Ataroth and Naarah, touched Jericho and came out at the Jordan. 8From Tappuah the border went west to the Kanah Ravine and ended at the sea. This was the inheritance of the tribe of the Ephraimites, clan by clan. 9It also included all the towns and their villages that were set aside for the Ephraimites within the inheritance of the Manassites.

10They did not dislodge the Canaanites living in Gezer; to this day the Canaanites live among the people of Ephraim but are required to do forced labour.

NEW TESTAMENT READING
John 1:1–28

The Word Became Flesh

1 In the beginning was the Word, and the Word was with God, and the Word was God. 2He was with God in the beginning.

3Through him all things were made; without him nothing was made that has been made. 4In him was life, and that life was the light of men. 5The light shines in the darkness, but the darkness has not understood it.

6There came a man who was sent from God; his name was John. 7He came as a witness to testify concerning that light, so that through him all men might believe. [8]He himself was not the light; he came only as a witness to the light. [9]The true light that gives light to every man was coming into the world.

[10]He was in the world, and though the world was made through him, the world did not recognise him. [11]He came to that which was his own, but his own did not receive him. [12]Yet to all who received him, to those who believed in his name, he gave the right to become children of God—[13]children born not of natural descent, nor of human decision or a husband's will, but born of God.

[14]The Word became flesh and made his dwelling among us. We have seen his glory, the glory of the One and Only, who came from the Father, full of grace and truth.

[15]John testifies concerning him. He cries out, saying, "This was he of whom I said, 'He who comes after me has surpassed me because he was before me.'" [16]From the fulness of his grace we have all received one blessing after another. [17]For the law was given through Moses; grace and truth came through Jesus Christ. [18]No-one has ever seen God, but God the One and Only, who is at the Father's side, has made him known.

John the Baptist Denies Being the Christ

[19]Now this was John's testimony when the Jews of Jerusalem sent priests and Levites to ask him who he was. [20]He did not fail to confess, but confessed freely, "I am not the Christ."

[21]They asked him, "Then who are you? Are you Elijah?"

He said, "I am not."

"Are you the Prophet?"

He answered, "No."

[22]Finally they said, "Who are you? Give us an answer to take back to those who sent us. What do you say about yourself?"

[23]John replied in the words of Isaiah the prophet, "I am the voice of one calling in the desert, 'Make straight the way for the Lord.'"

[24]Now some Pharisees who had been sent [25]questioned him, "Why then do you baptise if you are not the Christ, nor Elijah, nor the Prophet?"

[26]"I baptise with water," John replied, "but among you stands one you do not know. [27]He is the one who comes after me, the thongs of whose sandals I am not worthy to untie."

[28]This all happened at Bethany on the other side of the Jordan, where John was baptising.

READING FROM PSALMS
Psalm 53:1–6

For the director of music. According to mahalath. A maskil of David.

[1]The fool says in his heart,
  "There is no God."
They are corrupt, and their ways are vile;
  there is no-one who does good.

[2]God looks down from heaven
  on the sons of men
to see if there are any who understand,
  any who seek God.
[3]Everyone has turned away,
  they have together become corrupt;
there is no-one who does good,
  not even one.

[4]Will the evildoers never learn—
  those who devour my people as men eat bread
and who do not call on God?
[5]There they were, overwhelmed with dread,
  where there was nothing to dread.
God scattered the bones of those who attacked you;
  you put them to shame, for God despised them.

[6]Oh, that salvation for Israel would come out of Zion!
  When God restores the fortunes of his people,
  let Jacob rejoice and Israel be glad!

OLD TESTAMENT READING
Joshua 17:1–18:28

17 This was the allotment for the tribe of Manasseh as Joseph's firstborn, that is, for Makir, Manasseh's firstborn. Makir was the ancestor of the Gileadites, who had received Gilead and Bashan because the Makirites were great soldiers. ²So this allotment was for the rest of the people of Manasseh—the clans of Abiezer, Helek, Asriel, Shechem, Hepher and Shemida. These are the other male descendants of Manasseh son of Joseph by their clans.

³Now Zelophehad son of Hepher, the son of Gilead, the son of Makir, the son of Manasseh, had no sons but only daughters, whose names were Mahlah, Noah, Hoglah, Milcah and Tirzah. ⁴They went to Eleazar the priest, Joshua son of Nun, and the leaders and said, "The LORD commanded Moses to give us an inheritance among our brothers." So Joshua gave them an inheritance along with the brothers of their father, according to the LORD's command. ⁵Manasseh's share consisted of ten tracts of land besides Gilead and Bashan east of the Jordan, ⁶because the daughters of the tribe of Manasseh received an inheritance among the sons. The land of Gilead belonged to the rest of the descendants of Manasseh.

⁷The territory of Manasseh extended from Asher to Micmethath east of Shechem. The boundary ran southward from there to include the people living at En Tappuah. ⁸(Manasseh had the land of Tappuah, but Tappuah itself, on the boundary of Manasseh, belonged to the Ephraimites.) ⁹Then the boundary continued south to the Kanah Ravine. There were towns belonging to Ephraim lying among the towns of Manasseh, but the boundary of Manasseh was the northern side of the ravine and ended at the sea. ¹⁰On the south the land belonged to Ephraim, on the north to Manasseh. The territory of Manasseh reached the sea and bordered Asher on the north and Issachar on the east.

¹¹Within Issachar and Asher, Manasseh also had Beth Shan, Ibleam and the people of Dor, Endor, Taanach and Megiddo, together with their surrounding settlements (the third in the list is Naphoth).

¹²Yet the Manassites were not able to occupy these towns, for the Canaanites were determined to live in that region. ¹³However, when the Israelites grew stronger, they subjected the Canaanites to forced labour but did not drive them out completely.

¹⁴The people of Joseph said to Joshua, "Why have you given us only one allotment and one portion for an inheritance? We are a numerous people and the LORD has blessed us abundantly."

¹⁵"If you are so numerous," Joshua answered, "and if the hill country of Ephraim is too small for you, go up into the forest and clear land for yourselves there in the land of the Perizzites and Rephaites."

¹⁶The people of Joseph replied, "The hill country is not enough for us, and all the Canaanites who live in the plain have iron chariots, both those in Beth Shan and its settlements and those in the Valley of Jezreel."

¹⁷But Joshua said to the house of Joseph—to Ephraim and Manasseh— "You are numerous and very powerful. You will have not only one allotment ¹⁸but the forested hill country as well. Clear it, and its farthest limits will be yours; though the Canaanites have iron

chariots and though they are strong, you can drive them out."

Division of the Rest of the Land

18 The whole assembly of the Israelites gathered at Shiloh and set up the Tent of Meeting there. The country was brought under their control, 2but there were still seven Israelite tribes who had not yet received their inheritance.

3So Joshua said to the Israelites: "How long will you wait before you begin to take possession of the land that the LORD, the God of your fathers, has given you? 4Appoint three men from each tribe. I will send them out to make a survey of the land and to write a description of it, according to the inheritance of each. Then they will return to me. 5You are to divide the land into seven parts. Judah is to remain in its territory on the south and the house of Joseph in its territory on the north. 6After you have written descriptions of the seven parts of the land, bring them here to me and I will cast lots for you in the presence of the LORD our God. 7The Levites, however, do not get a portion among you, because the priestly service of the LORD is their inheritance. And Gad, Reuben and the half-tribe of Manasseh have already received their inheritance on the east side of the Jordan. Moses the servant of the LORD gave it to them."

8As the men started on their way to map out the land, Joshua instructed them, "Go and make a survey of the land and write a description of it. Then return to me, and I will cast lots for you here at Shiloh in the presence of the LORD." 9So the men left and went through the land. They wrote its description on a scroll, town by town, in seven parts, and returned to Joshua in the camp at Shiloh. 10Joshua then cast lots for them in Shiloh in the presence of the LORD, and there he distributed the land to the Israelites according to their tribal divisions.

Allotment for Benjamin

11The lot came up for the tribe of Benjamin, clan by clan. Their allotted territory lay between the tribes of Judah and Joseph:

12On the north side their boundary began at the Jordan, passed the northern slope of Jericho and headed west into the hill country, coming out at the desert of Beth Aven. 13From there it crossed to the south slope of Luz (that is, Bethel) and went down to Ataroth Addar on the hill south of Lower Beth Horon.

14From the hill facing Beth Horon on the south the boundary turned south along the western side and came out at Kiriath Baal (that is, Kiriath Jearim), a town of the people of Judah. This was the western side.

15The southern side began at the outskirts of Kiriath Jearim on the west, and the boundary came out at the spring of the waters of Nephtoah. 16The boundary went down to the foot of the hill facing the Valley of Ben Hinnom, north of the Valley of Rephaim. It continued down the Hinnom Valley along the southern slope of the Jebusite city and so to En Rogel. 17It then curved north, went to En Shemesh, continued to Geliloth, which faces the Pass of Adummim, and ran down to the Stone of Bohan son of Reuben. 18It continued to the northern slope of Beth Arabah and on down into the Arabah. 19It then went to the northern slope of Beth Hoglah and came out at the northern bay of the Salt Sea, at the mouth of the Jordan in the south. This was the southern boundary.

20The Jordan formed the boundary on the eastern side.

These were the boundaries that marked out the inheritance of the clans of Benjamin on all sides.

²¹The tribe of Benjamin, clan by clan, had the following cities:

Jericho, Beth Hoglah, Emek Keziz, ²²Beth Arabah, Zemaraim, Bethel, ²³Avvim, Parah, Ophrah, ²⁴Kephar Ammoni, Ophni and Geba—twelve towns and their villages.

²⁵Gibeon, Ramah, Beeroth, ²⁶Mizpah, Kephirah, Mozah, ²⁷Rekem, Irpeel, Taralah, ²⁸Zelah, Haeleph, the Jebusite city (that is, Jerusalem), Gibeah and Kiriath—fourteen towns and their villages.

This was the inheritance of Benjamin for its clans.

NEW TESTAMENT READING
John 1:29–51

Jesus the Lamb of God

²⁹The next day John saw Jesus coming towards him and said, "Look, the Lamb of God, who takes away the sin of the world! ³⁰This is the one I meant when I said, 'A man who comes after me has surpassed me because he was before me.' ³¹I myself did not know him, but the reason I came baptising with water was that he might be revealed to Israel."

³²Then John gave this testimony: "I saw the Spirit come down from heaven as a dove and remain on him. ³³I would not have known him, except that the one who sent me to baptise with water told me, 'The man on whom you see the Spirit come down and remain is he who will baptise with the Holy Spirit.' ³⁴I have seen and I testify that this is the Son of God."

Jesus' First Disciples

³⁵The next day John was there again with two of his disciples. ³⁶When he saw Jesus passing by, he said, "Look, the Lamb of God!"

³⁷When the two disciples heard him say this, they followed Jesus. ³⁸Turning round, Jesus saw them following and asked, "What do you want?"

They said, "Rabbi" (which means Teacher), "where are you staying?"

³⁹"Come," he replied, "and you will see."

So they went and saw where he was staying, and spent that day with him. It was about the tenth hour.

⁴⁰Andrew, Simon Peter's brother, was one of the two who heard what John had said and who had followed Jesus. ⁴¹The first thing Andrew did was to find his brother Simon and tell him, "We have found the Messiah" (that is, the Christ). ⁴²And he brought him to Jesus.

Jesus looked at him and said, "You are Simon son of John. You will be called Cephas" (which, when translated, is Peter).

Jesus Calls Philip and Nathanael

⁴³The next day Jesus decided to leave for Galilee. Finding Philip, he said to him, "Follow me."

⁴⁴Philip, like Andrew and Peter, was from the town of Bethsaida. ⁴⁵Philip found Nathanael and told him, "We have found the one Moses wrote about in the Law, and about whom the prophets also wrote—Jesus of Nazareth, the son of Joseph."

⁴⁶"Nazareth! Can anything good come from there?" Nathanael asked.

"Come and see," said Philip.

⁴⁷When Jesus saw Nathanael approaching, he said of him, "Here is a true Israelite, in whom there is nothing false."

⁴⁸"How do you know me?" Nathanael asked.

Jesus answered, "I saw you while you were still under the fig-tree before Philip called you."

⁴⁹Then Nathanael declared, "Rabbi, you are the Son of God; you are the King of Israel."

⁵⁰Jesus said, "You believe because I told you I saw you under the fig-tree. You shall see greater things than that."

51He then added, "I tell you the truth, you shall see heaven open, and the angels of God ascending and descending on the Son of Man."

READING FROM PROVERBS
Proverbs 10:31–11:8

31The mouth of the righteous brings
forth wisdom,
but a perverse tongue will be cut
out.

32The lips of the righteous know what is
fitting,
but the mouth of the wicked only
what is perverse.

11 The LORD abhors dishonest
scales,
but accurate weights are his
delight.

2When pride comes, then comes
disgrace,
but with humility comes wisdom.

3The integrity of the upright guides
them,
but the unfaithful are destroyed by
their duplicity.

4Wealth is worthless in the day of
wrath,
but righteousness delivers from
death.

5The righteousness of the blameless
makes a straight way for them,
but the wicked are brought down
by their own wickedness.

6The righteousness of the upright
delivers them,
but the unfaithful are trapped by
evil desires.

7When a wicked man dies, his hope
perishes;
all he expected from his power
comes to nothing.

8The righteous man is rescued from
trouble,
and it comes on the wicked
instead.

DAY 121

MAY 1

OLD TESTAMENT READING
Joshua 19:1–21:19

Allotment for Simeon

19 The second lot came out for the
tribe of Simeon, clan by clan.
Their inheritance lay within the territory of Judah. 2It included:
Beersheba (or Sheba), Moladah,
3Hazar Shual, Balah, Ezem,
4Eltolad, Bethul, Hormah,
5Ziklag, Beth Marcaboth, Hazar
Susah, 6Beth Lebaoth and Shar-
uhen—thirteen towns and their
villages;
7Ain, Rimmon, Ether and
Ashan—four towns and their

villages—8and all the villages
around these towns as far as Baalath
Beer (Ramah in the Negev).
This was the inheritance of the tribe of
the Simeonites, clan by clan. 9The inheritance of the Simeonites was taken
from the share of Judah, because
Judah's portion was more than they
needed. So the Simeonites received
their inheritance within the territory of
Judah.

Allotment for Zebulun

10The third lot came up for Zebulun,
clan by clan:
The boundary of their inheritance went as far as Sarid. 11Going

west it ran to Maralah, touched Dabbesheth, and extended to the ravine near Jokneam. [12]It turned east from Sarid towards the sunrise to the territory of Kisloth Tabor and went on to Daberath and up to Japhia. [13]Then it continued eastward to Gath Hepher and Eth Kazin; it came out at Rimmon and turned towards Neah. [14]There the boundary went round on the north to Hannathon and ended at the Valley of Iphtah El. [15]Included were Kattath, Nahalal, Shimron, Idalah and Bethlehem. There were twelve towns and their villages.

[16]These towns and their villages were the inheritance of Zebulun, clan by clan.

Allotment for Issachar

[17]The fourth lot came out for Issachar, clan by clan. [18]Their territory included:

Jezreel, Kesulloth, Shunem, [19]Hapharaim, Shion, Anaharath, [20]Rabbith, Kishion, Ebez, [21]Remeth, En Gannim, En Haddah and Beth Pazzez. [22]The boundary touched Tabor, Shahazumah and Beth Shemesh, and ended at the Jordan. There were sixteen towns and their villages.

[23]These towns and their villages were the inheritance of the tribe of Issachar, clan by clan.

Allotment for Asher

[24]The fifth lot came out for the tribe of Asher, clan by clan. [25]Their territory included:

Helkath, Hali, Beten, Acshaph, [26]Allammelech, Amad and Mishal. On the west the boundary touched Carmel and Shihor Libnath. [27]It then turned east towards Beth Dagon, touched Zebulun and the Valley of Iphtah El, and went north to Beth Emek and Neiel, passing Cabul on the left. [28]It went to Abdon, Rehob, Hammon and Kanah, as far as Greater Sidon. [29]The boundary then turned back towards Ramah and went to the fortified city of Tyre, turned towards Hosah and came out at the sea in the region of Aczib, [30]Ummah, Aphek and Rehob. There were twenty-two towns and their villages.

[31]These towns and their villages were the inheritance of the tribe of Asher, clan by clan.

Allotment for Naphtali

[32]The sixth lot came out for Naphtali, clan by clan:

[33]Their boundary went from Heleph and the large tree in Zaanannim, passing Adami Nekeb and Jabneel to Lakkum and ending at the Jordan. [34]The boundary ran west through Aznoth Tabor and came out at Hukkok. It touched Zebulun on the south, Asher on the west and the Jordan on the east. [35]The fortified cities were Ziddim, Zer, Hammath, Rakkath, Kinnereth, [36]Adamah, Ramah, Hazor, [37]Kedesh, Edrei, En Hazor, [38]Iron, Migdal El, Horem, Beth Anath and Beth Shemesh. There were nineteen towns and their villages.

[39]These towns and their villages were the inheritance of the tribe of Naphtali, clan by clan.

Allotment for Dan

[40]The seventh lot came out for the tribe of Dan, clan by clan. [41]The territory of their inheritance included:

Zorah, Eshtaol, Ir Shemesh, [42]Shaalabbin, Aijalon, Ithlah, [43]Elon, Timnah, Ekron, [44]Eltekeh, Gibbethon, Baalath, [45]Jehud, Bene Berak, Gath Rimmon, [46]Me Jarkon and Rakkon, with the area facing Joppa.

[47](But the Danites had difficulty taking possession of their territory, so

they went up and attacked Leshem, took it, put it to the sword and occupied it. They settled in Leshem and named it Dan after their forefather.)

48These towns and their villages were the inheritance of the tribe of Dan, clan by clan.

Allotment for Joshua

49When they had finished dividing the land into its allotted portions, the Israelites gave Joshua son of Nun an inheritance among them, 50as the LORD had commanded. They gave him the town he asked for—Timnath Serah in the hill country of Ephraim. And he built up the town and settled there.

51These are the territories that Eleazar the priest, Joshua son of Nun and the heads of the tribal clans of Israel assigned by lot at Shiloh in the presence of the LORD at the entrance to the Tent of Meeting. And so they finished dividing the land.

Cities of Refuge

20 Then the LORD said to Joshua: 2"Tell the Israelites to designate the cities of refuge, as I instructed you through Moses, 3so that anyone who kills a person accidentally and unintentionally may flee there and find protection from the avenger of blood.

4"When he flees to one of these cities, he is to stand in the entrance of the city gate and state his case before the elders of that city. Then they are to admit him into their city and give him a place to live with them. 5If the avenger of blood pursues him, they must not surrender the one accused, because he killed his neighbour unintentionally and without malice aforethought. 6He is to stay in that city until he has stood trial before the assembly and until the death of the high priest who is serving at that time. Then he may go back to his own home in the town from which he fled."

7So they set apart Kedesh in Galilee in the hill country of Naphtali, Shechem in the hill country of Ephraim, and Kiriath Arba (that is, Hebron) in the hill country of Judah. 8On the east side of the Jordan of Jericho they designated Bezer in the desert on the plateau in the tribe of Reuben, Ramoth in Gilead in the tribe of Gad, and Golan in Bashan in the tribe of Manasseh. 9Any of the Israelites or any alien living among them who killed someone accidentally could flee to these designated cities and not be killed by the avenger of blood prior to standing trial before the assembly.

Towns for the Levites

21 Now the family heads of the Levites approached Eleazar the priest, Joshua son of Nun, and the heads of the other tribal families of Israel 2at Shiloh in Canaan and said to them, "The LORD commanded through Moses that you give us towns to live in, with pasture-lands for our livestock." 3So, as the LORD had commanded, the Israelites gave the Levites the following towns and pasture-lands out of their own inheritance:

4The first lot came out for the Kohathites, clan by clan. The Levites who were descendants of Aaron the priest were allotted thirteen towns from the tribes of Judah, Simeon and Benjamin. 5The rest of Kohath's descendants were allotted ten towns from the clans of the tribes of Ephraim, Dan and half of Manasseh.

6The descendants of Gershon were allotted thirteen towns from the clans of the tribes of Issachar, Asher, Naphtali and the half-tribe of Manasseh in Bashan.

7The descendants of Merari, clan by clan, received twelve towns from the tribes of Reuben, Gad and Zebulun.

8So the Israelites allotted to the Levites these towns and their pasture-lands, as the LORD had commanded through Moses.

9From the tribes of Judah and Simeon they allotted the following towns by name [10](these towns were assigned to the descendants of Aaron who were from the Kohathite clans of the Levites, because the first lot fell to them):

[11]They gave them Kiriath Arba (that is, Hebron), with its surrounding pasture-land, in the hill country of Judah. (Arba was the forefather of Anak.) [12]But the fields and villages around the city they had given to Caleb son of Jephunneh as his possession.

[13]So to the descendants of Aaron the priest they gave Hebron (a city of refuge for one accused of murder), Libnah, [14]Jattir, Eshtemoa, [15]Holon, Debir, [16]Ain, Juttah and Beth Shemesh, together with their pasture-lands—nine towns from these two tribes.

[17]And from the tribe of Benjamin they gave them Gibeon, Geba, [18]Anathoth and Almon, together with their pasture-lands —four towns.

[19]All the towns for the priests, the descendants of Aaron, were thirteen, together with their pasture-lands.

NEW TESTAMENT READING
John 2:1–25

Jesus Changes Water to Wine

2 On the third day a wedding took place at Cana in Galilee. Jesus' mother was there, [2]and Jesus and his disciples had also been invited to the wedding. [3]When the wine was gone, Jesus' mother said to him, "They have no more wine."

[4]"Dear woman, why do you involve me?" Jesus replied, "My time has not yet come."

[5]His mother said to the servants, "Do whatever he tells you."

[6]Nearby stood six stone water jars, the kind used by the Jews for ceremonial washing, each holding from twenty to thirty gallons.

[7]Jesus said to the servants, "Fill the jars with water"; so they filled them to the brim.

[8]Then he told them, "Now draw some out and take it to the master of the banquet."

They did so, [9]and the master of the banquet tasted the water that had been turned into wine. He did not realise where it had come from, though the servants who had drawn the water knew. Then he called the bridegroom aside [10]and said, "Everyone brings out the choice wine first and then the cheaper wine after the guests have had too much to drink; but you have saved the best till now."

[11]This, the first of his miraculous signs, Jesus performed at Cana in Galilee. He thus revealed his glory, and his disciples put their faith in him.

Jesus Clears the Temple

[12]After this he went down to Capernaum with his mother and brothers and his disciples. There they stayed for a few days.

[13]When it was almost time for the Jewish Passover, Jesus went up to Jerusalem. [14]In the temple courts he found men selling cattle, sheep and doves, and others sitting at tables exchanging money. [15]So he made a whip out of cords, and drove all from the temple area, both sheep and cattle; he scattered the coins of the money changers and overturned their tables. [16]To those who sold doves he said, "Get these out of here! How dare you turn my Father's house into a market!"

[17]His disciples remembered that it is written, "Zeal for your house will consume me."

[18]Then the Jews demanded of him, "What miraculous sign can you show us to prove your authority to do all this?"

[19]Jesus answered them, "Destroy this temple, and I will raise it again in three days."

[20]The Jews replied, "It has taken forty-six years to build this temple, and you are going to raise it in three days?"

21But the temple he had spoken of was his body. 22After he was raised from the dead, his disciples recalled what he had said. Then they believed the Scripture and the words that Jesus had spoken.

23Now while he was in Jerusalem at the Passover Feast, many people saw the miraculous signs he was doing and believed in his name. 24But Jesus would not entrust himself to them, for he knew all men. 25He did not need man's testimony about man, for he knew what was in a man.

READING FROM PSALMS
Psalm 54:1–7

For the director of music. With stringed instruments. A *maskil* of David. When the Ziphites had gone to Saul and said, "Is not David hiding among us?"

1Save me, O God, by your name;
   vindicate me by your might.

2Hear my prayer, O God;
   listen to the words of my mouth.

3Strangers are attacking me;
   ruthless men seek my life—
   men without regard for God. *Selah*

4Surely God is my help;
   the Lord is the one who sustains
   me.

5Let evil recoil on those who slander
   me;
   in your faithfulness destroy
   them.

6I will sacrifice a freewill offering to
   you;
   I will praise your name, O LORD,
   for it is good.
7For he has delivered me from all my
   troubles,
   and my eyes have looked in
   triumph on my foes.

DAY 122

MAY 2

OLD TESTAMENT READING
Joshua 21:20–22:34

20The rest of the Kohathite clans of the Levites were allotted towns from the tribe of Ephraim:

21In the hill country of Ephraim they were given Shechem (a city of refuge for one accused of murder) and Gezer, 22Kibzaim and Beth Horon, together with their pasture-lands—four towns.

23Also from the tribe of Dan they received Eltekeh, Gibbethon, 24Aijalon and Gath Rimmon, together with their pasture-lands —four towns.

25From half the tribe of Manasseh they received Taanach and Gath Rimmon, together with their pasture-lands—two towns.

26All these ten towns and their pasture-lands were given to the rest of the Kohathite clans.

27The Levite clans of the Gershonites were given:

from the half-tribe of Manasseh, Golan in Bashan (a city of refuge for one accused of murder) and Be Eshtarah, together with their pasture-lands—two towns;
28from the tribe of Issachar, Kishion, Daberath, 29Jarmuth and En Gannim, together with their pasture-lands—four towns;
30from the tribe of Asher, Mishal, Abdon, 31Helkath and Rehob, together with their pasture-lands—four towns;
32from the tribe of Naphtali, Kedesh in Galilee (a city of refuge

for one accused of murder), Hammoth Dor and Kartan, together with their pasture-lands—three towns.

³³All the towns of the Gershonite clans were thirteen, together with their pasture-lands.

³⁴The Merarite clans (the rest of the Levites) were given:

from the tribe of Zebulun,
Jokneam, Kartah, ³⁵Dimnah and Nahalal, together with their pasture-lands—four towns;

³⁶from the tribe of Reuben,
Bezer, Jahaz, ³⁷Kedemoth and Mephaath, together with their pasture-lands—four towns;

³⁸from the tribe of Gad,
Ramoth in Gilead (a city of refuge for one accused of murder), Mahanaim, ³⁹Heshbon and Jazer, together with their pasture-lands—four towns in all.

⁴⁰All the towns allotted to the Merarite clans, who were the rest of the Levites, were twelve.

⁴¹The towns of the Levites in the territory held by the Israelites were forty-eight in all, together with their pasture-lands. ⁴²Each of these towns had pasture-lands surrounding it; this was true for all these towns.

⁴³So the LORD gave Israel all the land he had sworn to give their forefathers, and they took possession of it and settled there. ⁴⁴The LORD gave them rest on every side, just as he had sworn to their forefathers. Not one of their enemies withstood them; the LORD handed all their enemies over to them. ⁴⁵Not one of all the LORD's good promises to the house of Israel failed; every one was fulfilled.

Eastern Tribes Return Home

22 Then Joshua summoned the Reubenites, the Gadites and the half-tribe of Manasseh ²and said to them, "You have done all that Moses the servant of the LORD commanded, and you have obeyed me in everything I commanded. ³For a long time now—to this very day—you have not deserted your brothers but have carried out the mission the LORD your God gave you. ⁴Now that the LORD your God has given your brothers rest as he promised, return to your homes in the land that Moses the servant of the LORD gave you on the other side of the Jordan. ⁵But be very careful to keep the commandment and the law that Moses the servant of the LORD gave you: to love the LORD your God, to walk in all his ways, to obey his commands, to hold fast to him and to serve him with all your heart and all your soul."

⁶Then Joshua blessed them and sent them away, and they went to their homes. ⁷(To the half-tribe of Manasseh Moses had given land in Bashan, and to the other half of the tribe Joshua gave land on the west side of the Jordan with their brothers.) When Joshua sent them home, he blessed them, ⁸saying, "Return to your homes with your great wealth—with large herds of livestock, with silver, gold, bronze and iron, and a great quantity of clothing—and divide with your brothers the plunder from your enemies."

⁹So the Reubenites, the Gadites and the half-tribe of Manasseh left the Israelites at Shiloh in Canaan to return to Gilead, their own land, which they had acquired in accordance with the command of the LORD through Moses.

¹⁰When they came to Geliloth near the Jordan in the land of Canaan, the Reubenites, the Gadites and the half-tribe of Manasseh built an imposing altar there by the Jordan. ¹¹And when the Israelites heard that they had built the altar on the border of Canaan at Geliloth near the Jordan on the Israelite side, ¹²the whole assembly of Israel gathered at Shiloh to go to war against them.

¹³So the Israelites sent Phinehas son of Eleazar, the priest, to the land of

Gilead—to Reuben, Gad and the half-tribe of Manasseh. ¹⁴With him they sent ten of the chief men, one for each of the tribes of Israel, each the head of a family division among the Israelite clans.

¹⁵When they went to Gilead—to Reuben, Gad and the half-tribe of Manasseh—they said to them: ¹⁶"The whole assembly of the LORD says: 'How could you break faith with the God of Israel like this? How could you turn away from the LORD and build yourselves an altar in rebellion against him now? ¹⁷Was not the sin of Peor enough for us? Up to this very day we have not cleansed ourselves from that sin, even though a plague fell on the community of the LORD! ¹⁸And are you now turning away from the LORD?

"'If you rebel against the LORD today, tomorrow he will be angry with the whole community of Israel. ¹⁹If the land you possess is defiled, come over to the LORD's land, where the LORD's tabernacle stands, and share the land with us. But do not rebel against the LORD or against us by building an altar for yourselves, other than the altar of the LORD our God. ²⁰When Achan son of Zerah acted unfaithfully regarding the devoted things, did not wrath come upon the whole community of Israel? He was not the only one who died for his sin.'"

²¹Then Reuben, Gad and the half-tribe of Manasseh replied to the heads of the clans of Israel: ²²"The Mighty One, God, the LORD! The Mighty One, God, the LORD! He knows! And let Israel know! If this has been in rebellion or disobedience to the LORD, do not spare us this day. ²³If we have built our own altar to turn away from the LORD and to offer burnt offerings and grain offerings, or to sacrifice fellowship offerings on it, may the LORD himself call us to account.

²⁴"No! We did it for fear that some day your descendants might say to ours, 'What do you have to do with the LORD, the God of Israel? ²⁵The LORD has made the Jordan a boundary between us and you—you Reubenites and Gadites! You have no share in the LORD.' So your descendants might cause ours to stop fearing the LORD.

²⁶"That is why we said, 'Let us get ready and build an altar—but not for burnt offerings or sacrifices.' ²⁷On the contrary, it is to be a witness between us and you and the generations that follow, that we will worship the LORD at his sanctuary with our burnt offerings, sacrifices and fellowship offerings. Then in the future your descendants will not be able to say to ours, 'You have no share in the LORD.'

²⁸"And we said, 'If they ever say this to us, or to our descendants, we will answer: Look at the replica of the LORD's altar, which our fathers built, not for burnt offerings or sacrifices, but as a witness between us and you.'

²⁹"Far be it from us to rebel against the LORD and turn away from him today by building an altar for burnt offerings, grain offerings and sacrifices, other than the altar of the LORD our God that stands before his tabernacle."

³⁰When Phinehas the priest and the leaders of the community—the heads of the clans of the Israelites—heard what Reuben, Gad and Manasseh had to say, they were pleased. ³¹And Phinehas son of Eleazar, the priest, said to Reuben, Gad and Manasseh, "Today we know that the LORD is with us, because you have not acted unfaithfully towards the LORD in this matter. Now you have rescued the Israelites from the LORD's hand."

³²Then Phinehas son of Eleazar, the priest, and the leaders returned to Canaan from their meeting with the Reubenites and Gadites in Gilead and reported to the Israelites. ³³They were glad to hear the report and praised God. And they talked no more about going to war against them to devastate the country where the Reubenites and the Gadites lived.

³⁴And the Reubenites and the Gadites gave the altar this name: A Witness Between Us that the LORD is God.

NEW TESTAMENT READING
John 3:1–21

Jesus Teaches Nicodemus

3 Now there was a man of the Pharisees named Nicodemus, a member of the Jewish ruling council. ²He came to Jesus at night and said, "Rabbi, we know you are a teacher who has come from God. For no-one could perform the miraculous signs you are doing if God were not with him."

³In reply Jesus declared, "I tell you the truth, no-one can see the kingdom of God unless he is born again."

⁴"How can a man be born when he is old?" Nicodemus asked. "Surely he cannot enter a second time into his mother's womb to be born!"

⁵Jesus answered, "I tell you the truth, no-one can enter the kingdom of God unless he is born of water and the Spirit. ⁶Flesh gives birth to flesh, but the Spirit gives birth to spirit. ⁷You should not be surprised at my saying, 'You must be born again.' ⁸The wind blows wherever it pleases. You hear its sound, but you cannot tell where it comes from or where it is going. So it is with everyone born of the Spirit."

⁹"How can this be?" Nicodemus asked.

¹⁰"You are Israel's teacher," said Jesus, "and do you not understand these things? ¹¹I tell you the truth, we speak of what we know, and we testify to what we have seen, but still you people do not accept our testimony. ¹²If I have spoken to you of earthly things and you do not believe; how then will you believe if I speak of heavenly things? ¹³No-one has ever gone into heaven except the one who came from heaven—the Son of Man. ¹⁴Just as Moses lifted up the snake in the desert, so the Son of Man must be lifted up, ¹⁵that everyone who believes in him may have eternal life.

¹⁶"For God so loved the world that he gave his one and only Son, that whoever believes in him shall not perish but have eternal life. ¹⁷For God did not send his Son into the world to condemn the world, but to save the world through him. ¹⁸Whoever believes in him is not condemned, but whoever does not believe stands condemned already because he has not believed in the name of God's one and only Son. ¹⁹This is the verdict: Light has come into the world, but men loved darkness instead of light because their deeds were evil. ²⁰Everyone who does evil hates the light, and will not come into the light for fear that his deeds will be exposed. ²¹But whoever lives by the truth comes into the light, so that it may be seen plainly that what he has done has been done through God."

READING FROM PSALMS
Psalm 55:1–11

For the director of music. With stringed instruments. A *maskil* of David.

¹Listen to my prayer, O God,
   do not ignore my plea;
² hear me and answer me.
   My thoughts trouble me and I am distraught
³ at the voice of the enemy,
   at the stares of the wicked;
for they bring down suffering upon me
   and revile me in their anger.

⁴My heart is in anguish within me;
   the terrors of death assail me.
⁵Fear and trembling have beset me;
   horror has overwhelmed me.
⁶I said, "Oh, that I had the wings of a dove!
   I would fly away and be at rest—
⁷I would flee far away
   and stay in the desert;   *Selah*
⁸I would hurry to my place of shelter,
   far from the tempest and storm."

⁹Confuse the wicked, O Lord,
   confound their speech,
for I see violence and strife in the city.

¹⁰Day and night they prowl about on its
walls;
malice and abuse are within
it.

¹¹Destructive forces are at work in the
city;
threats and lies never leave its
streets.

MAY 3

OLD TESTAMENT READING
Joshua 23:1–24:33

Joshua's Farewell to the Leaders

23 After a long time had passed and the LORD had given Israel rest from all their enemies around them, Joshua, by then old and well advanced in years, ²summoned all Israel—their elders, leaders, judges and officials—and said to them: "I am old and well advanced in years. ³You yourselves have seen everything the LORD your God has done to all these nations for your sake; it was the LORD your God who fought for you. ⁴Remember how I have allotted as an inheritance for your tribes all the land of the nations that remain—the nations I conquered—between the Jordan and the Great Sea in the west. ⁵The LORD your God himself will drive them out of your way. He will push them out before you, and you will take possession of their land, as the LORD your God promised you.

⁶"Be very strong; be careful to obey all that is written in the Book of the Law of Moses, without turning aside to the right or to the left. ⁷Do not associate with these nations that remain among you; do not invoke the names of their gods or swear by them. You must not serve them or bow down to them. ⁸But you are to hold fast to the LORD your God, as you have until now.

⁹"The LORD has driven out before you great and powerful nations; to this day no-one has been able to withstand you. ¹⁰One of you routs a thousand, because the LORD your God fights for

you, just as he promised. ¹¹So be very careful to love the LORD your God.

¹²"But if you turn away and ally yourselves with the survivors of these nations that remain among you and if you intermarry with them and associate with them, ¹³then you may be sure that the LORD your God will no longer drive out these nations before you. Instead, they will become snares and traps for you, whips on your backs and thorns in your eyes, until you perish from this good land, which the LORD your God has given you.

¹⁴"Now I am about to go the way of all the earth. You know with all your heart and soul that not one of all the good promises the LORD your God gave you has failed. Every promise has been fulfilled; not one has failed. ¹⁵But just as every good promise of the LORD your God has come true, so the LORD will bring on you all the evil he has threatened, until he has destroyed you from this good land he has given you. ¹⁶If you violate the covenant of the LORD your God, which he commanded you, and go and serve other gods and bow down to them, the LORD's anger will burn against you, and you will quickly perish from the good land he has given you."

The Covenant Renewed at Shechem

24 Then Joshua assembled all the tribes of Israel at Shechem. He summoned the elders, leaders, judges and officials of Israel, and they presented themselves before God.

2Joshua said to all the people, "This is what the LORD, the God of Israel, says: 'Long ago your forefathers, including Terah the father of Abraham and Nahor, lived beyond the River and worshipped other gods. 3But I took your father Abraham from the land beyond the River and led him throughout Canaan and gave him many descendants. I gave him Isaac, 4and to Isaac I gave Jacob and Esau. I assigned the hill country of Seir to Esau, but Jacob and his sons went down to Egypt.

5" 'Then I sent Moses and Aaron, and I afflicted the Egyptians by what I did there, and I brought you out. 6When I brought your fathers out of Egypt, you came to the sea, and the Egyptians pursued them with chariots and horsemen as far as the Red Sea. 7But they cried to the LORD for help, and he put darkness between you and the Egyptians; he brought the sea over them and covered them. You saw with your own eyes what I did to the Egyptians. Then you lived in the desert for a long time.

8" 'I brought you to the land of the Amorites who lived east of the Jordan. They fought against you, but I gave them into your hands. I destroyed them from before you, and you took possession of their land. 9When Balak son of Zippor, the king of Moab, prepared to fight against Israel, he sent for Balaam son of Beor to put a curse on you. 10But I would not listen to Balaam, so he blessed you again and again, and I delivered you out of his hand.

11" 'Then you crossed the Jordan and came to Jericho. The citizens of Jericho fought against you, as did also the Amorites, Perizzites, Canaanites, Hittites, Girgashites, Hivites and Jebusites, but I gave them into your hands. 12I sent the hornet ahead of you, which drove them out before you—also the two Amorite kings. You did not do it with your own sword and bow. 13So I gave you a land on which you did not toil and cities you did not build; and you live in them and eat from vineyards and olive groves that you did not plant.'

14"Now fear the LORD and serve him with all faithfulness. Throw away the gods your forefathers worshipped beyond the River and in Egypt, and serve the LORD. 15But if serving the LORD seems undesirable to you, then choose for yourselves this day whom you will serve, whether the gods your forefathers served beyond the River, or the gods of the Amorites, in whose land you are living. But as for me and my household, we will serve the LORD."

16Then the people answered, "Far be it from us to forsake the LORD to serve other gods! 17It was the LORD our God himself who brought us and our fathers up out of Egypt, from that land of slavery, and performed those great signs before our eyes. He protected us on our entire journey and among all the nations through which we travelled. 18And the LORD drove out before us all the nations, including the Amorites, who lived in the land. We too will serve the LORD, because he is our God."

19Joshua said to the people, "You are not able to serve the LORD. He is a holy God; he is a jealous God. He will not forgive your rebellion and your sins. 20If you forsake the LORD and serve foreign gods, he will turn and bring disaster on you and make an end of you, after he has been good to you."

21But the people said to Joshua, "No! We will serve the LORD."

22Then Joshua said, "You are witnesses against yourselves that you have chosen to serve the LORD."

"Yes, we are witnesses," they replied.

23"Now then," said Joshua, "throw away the foreign gods that are among you and yield your hearts to the LORD, the God of Israel."

24And the people said to Joshua, "We will serve the LORD our God and obey him."

25On that day Joshua made a covenant for the people, and there at Shechem he drew up for them decrees and laws. 26And Joshua recorded these things in the Book of the Law of God.

Then he took a large stone and set it up there under the oak near the holy place of the LORD.

27"See!" he said to all the people. "This stone will be a witness against us. It has heard all the words the LORD has said to us. It will be a witness against you if you are untrue to your God."

Buried in the Promised Land

28Then Joshua sent the people away, each to his own inheritance.

29After these things, Joshua son of Nun, the servant of the LORD, died at the age of a hundred and ten. 30And they buried him in the land of his inheritance, at Timnath Serah in the hill country of Ephraim, north of Mount Gaash.

31Israel served the LORD throughout the lifetime of Joshua and of the elders who outlived him and who had experienced everything the LORD had done for Israel.

32And Joseph's bones, which the Israelites had brought up from Egypt, were buried at Shechem in the tract of land that Jacob bought for a hundred pieces of silver from the sons of Hamor, the father of Shechem. This became the inheritance of Joseph's descendants.

33And Eleazar son of Aaron died and was buried at Gibeah, which had been allotted to his son Phinehas in the hill country of Ephraim.

NEW TESTAMENT READING
John 3:22-36

John the Baptist's Testimony About Jesus

22After this, Jesus and his disciples went out into the Judean countryside, where he spent some time with them, and baptised. 23Now John also was baptising at Aenon near Salim, because there was plenty of water, and people were constantly coming to be baptised. 24(This was before John was put in prison.) 25An argument developed between some of John's disciples and a certain Jew over the matter of ceremonial washing. 26They came to John and said to him, "Rabbi, that man who was with you on the other side of the Jordan—the one you testified about—well, he is baptising, and everyone is going to him."

27To this John replied, "A man can receive only what is given him from heaven. 28You yourselves can testify that I said, 'I am not the Christ but am sent ahead of him.' 29The bride belongs to the bridegroom. The friend who attends the bridegroom waits and listens for him, and is full of joy when he hears the bridegroom's voice. That joy is mine, and it is now complete. 30He must become greater; I must become less.

31"The one who comes from above is above all; the one who is from the earth belongs to the earth, and speaks as one from the earth. The one who comes from heaven is above all. 32He testifies to what he has seen and heard, but no-one accepts his testimony. 33The man who has accepted it has certified that God is truthful. 34For the one whom God has sent speaks the words of God, for God gives the Spirit without limit. 35The Father loves the Son and has placed everything in his hands. 36Whoever believes in the Son has eternal life, but whoever rejects the Son will not see life, for God's wrath remains on him."

READING FROM PSALMS
Psalm 55:12-23

12If an enemy were insulting me,
　　I could endure it;
if a foe were raising himself against
　　me,
　　I could hide from him.
13But it is you, a man like myself,
　　my companion, my close friend,
14with whom I once enjoyed sweet
　　fellowship
　　as we walked with the throng at the
　　house of God.

¹⁵Let death take my enemies by
       surprise;
   let them go down alive to the grave,
   for evil finds lodging among them.

¹⁶But I call to God,
   and the LORD saves me.
¹⁷Evening, morning and noon
   I cry out in distress,
   and he hears my voice.
¹⁸He ransoms me unharmed
   from the battle waged against me,
   even though many oppose me.
¹⁹God, who is enthroned for ever,
   will hear them and afflict
   them—   *Selah*
   men who never change their ways
   and have no fear of God.

²⁰My companion attacks his friends;
   he violates his covenant.
²¹His speech is smooth as butter,
   yet war is in his heart;
   his words are more soothing than oil,
   yet they are drawn swords.

²²Cast your cares on the LORD
   and he will sustain you;
   he will never let the righteous fall.
²³But you, O God, will bring down the
       wicked
   into the pit of corruption;
   bloodthirsty and deceitful men
   will not live out half their days.

But as for me, I trust in you.

MAY 4   DAY 124

OLD TESTAMENT READING
Judges 1:1–2:5

Israel Fights the Remaining Canaanites

1 After the death of Joshua, the
   Israelites asked the LORD, "Who
will be the first to go up and fight for us
against the Canaanites?"

²The LORD answered, "Judah is to
go; I have given the land into their
hands."

³Then the men of Judah said to the
Simeonites their brothers, "Come up
with us into the territory allotted to us,
to fight against the Canaanites. We in
turn will go with you into yours." So the
Simeonites went with them.

⁴When Judah attacked, the LORD
gave the Canaanites and Perizzites into
their hands and they struck down ten
thousand men at Bezek. ⁵It was there
that they found Adoni-Bezek and
fought against him, putting to rout the
Canaanites and Perizzites. ⁶Adoni-
Bezek fled, but they chased him and
caught him, and cut off his thumbs and
big toes.

⁷Then Adoni-Bezek said, "Seventy
kings with their thumbs and big toes cut
off have picked up scraps under my
table. Now God has paid me back for
what I did to them." They brought him
to Jerusalem, and he died there.

⁸The men of Judah attacked Jerusalem also and took it. They put the city
to the sword and set it on fire.

⁹After that, the men of Judah went
down to fight against the Canaanites
living in the hill country, the Negev and
the western foothills. ¹⁰They advanced
against the Canaanites living in Hebron
(formerly called Kiriath Arba) and defeated Sheshai, Ahiman and Talmai.

¹¹From there they advanced against
the people living in Debir (formerly
called Kiriath Sepher). ¹²And Caleb
said, "I will give my daughter Acsah in
marriage to the man who attacks and
captures Kiriath Sepher." ¹³Othniel son
of Kenaz, Caleb's younger brother,
took it; so Caleb gave his daughter
Acsah to him in marriage.

¹⁴One day when she came to Othniel,
she urged him to ask her father for a

field. When she got off her donkey, Caleb asked her, "What can I do for you?"

15She replied, "Do me a special favour. Since you have given me land in the Negev, give me also springs of water." Then Caleb gave her the upper and lower springs.

16The descendants of Moses' father-in-law, the Kenite, went up from the City of Palms with the men of Judah to live among the people of the Desert of Judah in the Negev near Arad.

17Then the men of Judah went with the Simeonites their brothers and attacked the Canaanites living in Zephath, and they totally destroyed the city. Therefore it was called Hormah. 18The men of Judah also took Gaza, Ashkelon and Ekron—each city with its territory.

19The LORD was with the men of Judah. They took possession of the hill country, but they were unable to drive the people from the plains, because they had iron chariots. 20As Moses had promised, Hebron was given to Caleb, who drove from it the three sons of Anak. 21The Benjamites, however, failed to dislodge the Jebusites, who were living in Jerusalem; to this day the Jebusites live there with the Benjamites.

22Now the house of Joseph attacked Bethel, and the LORD was with them. 23When they sent men to spy out Bethel (formerly called Luz), 24the spies saw a man coming out of the city and they said to him, "Show us how to get into the city and we will see that you are treated well." 25So he showed them, and they put the city to the sword but spared the man and his whole family. 26He then went to the land of the Hittites, where he built a city and called it Luz, which is its name to this day.

27But Manasseh did not drive out the people of Beth Shan or Taanach or Dor or Ibleam or Megiddo and their surrounding settlements, for the Canaanites were determined to live in that land. 28When Israel became strong, they pressed the Canaanites into forced labour but never drove them out completely. 29Nor did Ephraim drive out the Canaanites living in Gezer, but the Canaanites continued to live there among them. 30Neither did Zebulun drive out the Canaanites living in Kitron or Nahalol, who remained among them; but they did subject them to forced labour. 31Nor did Asher drive out those living in Acco or Sidon or Ahlab or Aczib or Helbah or Aphek or Rehob, 32and because of this the people of Asher lived among the Canaanite inhabitants of the land. 33Neither did Naphtali drive out those living in Beth Shemesh or Beth Anath; but the Naphtalites too lived among the Canaanite inhabitants of the land, and those living in Beth Shemesh and Beth Anath became forced labourers for them. 34The Amorites confined the Danites to the hill country, not allowing them to come down into the plain. 35And the Amorites were determined also to hold out in Mount Heres, Aijalon and Shaalbim, but when the power of the house of Joseph increased, they too were pressed into forced labour. 36The boundary of the Amorites was from Scorpion Pass to Sela and beyond.

The Angel of the LORD at Bokim

2 The angel of the LORD went up from Gilgal to Bokim and said, "I brought you up out of Egypt and led you into the land that I swore to give to your forefathers. I said, 'I will never break my covenant with you, 2and you shall not make a covenant with the people of this land, but you shall break down their altars.' Yet you have disobeyed me. Why have you done this? 3Now therefore I tell you that I will not drive them out before you; they will be ⌊thorns⌋ in your sides and their gods will be a snare to you."

4When the angel of the LORD had spoken these things to all the Israelites, the people wept aloud, 5and they called that place Bokim. There they offered sacrifices to the LORD.

NEW TESTAMENT READING
John 4:1–26

Jesus Talks With a Samaritan Woman

4 The Pharisees heard that Jesus was gaining and baptising more disciples than John, ²although in fact it was not Jesus who baptised, but his disciples. ³When the Lord learned of this, he left Judea and went back once more to Galilee.

⁴Now he had to go through Samaria. ⁵So he came to a town in Samaria called Sychar, near the plot of ground Jacob had given to his son Joseph. ⁶Jacob's well was there, and Jesus, tired as he was from the journey, sat down by the well. It was about the sixth hour.

⁷When a Samaritan woman came to draw water, Jesus said to her, "Will you give me a drink?" ⁸(His disciples had gone into the town to buy food.)

⁹The Samaritan woman said to him, "You are a Jew and I am a Samaritan woman. How can you ask me for a drink?" (For Jews do not associate with Samaritans.)

¹⁰Jesus answered her, "If you knew the gift of God and who it is that asks you for a drink, you would have asked him and he would have given you living water."

¹¹"Sir," the woman said, "you have nothing to draw with and the well is deep. Where can you get this living water? ¹²Are you greater than our father Jacob, who gave us the well and drank from it himself, as did also his sons and his flocks and herds?"

¹³Jesus answered, "Everyone who drinks this water will be thirsty again, ¹⁴but whoever drinks the water I give him will never thirst. Indeed, the water I give him will become in him a spring of water welling up to eternal life."

¹⁵The woman said to him, "Sir, give me this water so that I won't get thirsty and have to keep coming here to draw water."

¹⁶He told her, "Go, call your husband and come back."

¹⁷"I have no husband," she replied.

Jesus said to her, "You are right when you say you have no husband. ¹⁸The fact is, you have had five husbands, and the man you now have is not your husband. What you have just said is quite true."

¹⁹"Sir," the woman said, "I can see that you are a prophet. ²⁰Our fathers worshipped on this mountain, but you Jews claim that the place where we must worship is in Jerusalem."

²¹Jesus declared, "Believe me, woman, a time is coming when you will worship the Father neither on this mountain nor in Jerusalem. ²²You Samaritans worship what you do not know; we worship what we do know, for salvation is from the Jews. ²³Yet a time is coming and has now come when the true worshippers will worship the Father in spirit and truth, for they are the kind of worshippers the Father seeks. ²⁴God is spirit, and his worshippers must worship in spirit and in truth."

²⁵The woman said, "I know that Messiah" (called Christ) "is coming. When he comes, he will explain everything to us."

²⁶Then Jesus declared, "I who speak to you am he."

READING FROM PROVERBS
Proverbs 11:9–18

⁹With his mouth the godless destroys
      his neighbour,
   but through knowledge the
      righteous escape.

¹⁰When the righteous prosper, the city
      rejoices;
   when the wicked perish, there are
      shouts of joy.

¹¹Through the blessing of the upright a
      city is exalted,
   but by the mouth of the wicked it is
      destroyed.

¹²A man who lacks judgment derides
        his neighbour,
    but a man of understanding holds
        his tongue.

¹³A gossip betrays a confidence,
    but a trustworthy man keeps a
        secret.

¹⁴For lack of guidance a nation falls,
    but many advisers make victory
        sure.

¹⁵He who puts up security for another
    will surely suffer,

but whoever refuses to strike hands
    in pledge is safe.

¹⁶A kind-hearted woman gains respect,
    but ruthless men gain only wealth.

¹⁷A kind man benefits himself,
    but a cruel man brings trouble on
        himself.

¹⁸The wicked man earns deceptive
        wages,
    but he who sows righteousness
        reaps a sure reward.

DAY 125   # MAY 5

OLD TESTAMENT READING
Judges 2:6–3:31

Disobedience and Defeat

⁶After Joshua had dismissed the
Israelites, they went to take possession
of the land, each to his own inheritance.
⁷The people served the LORD throughout the lifetime of Joshua and of the
elders who outlived him and who had
seen all the great things the LORD had
done for Israel.

⁸Joshua son of Nun, the servant of the
LORD, died at the age of a hundred and
ten. ⁹And they buried him in the land of
his inheritance, at Timnath Heres in the
hill country of Ephraim, north of Mount
Gaash.

¹⁰After that whole generation had
been gathered to their fathers, another
generation grew up, who knew neither
the LORD nor what he had done for
Israel. ¹¹Then the Israelites did evil in
the eyes of the LORD and served the
Baals. ¹²They forsook the LORD, the
God of their fathers, who had brought
them out of Egypt. They followed and
worshipped various gods of the peoples
around them. They provoked the LORD

to anger ¹³because they forsook him and
served Baal and the Ashtoreths. ¹⁴In his
anger against Israel the LORD handed
them over to raiders who plundered
them. He sold them to their enemies all
around, whom they were no longer able
to resist. ¹⁵Whenever Israel went out to
fight, the hand of the LORD was against
them to defeat them, just as he had
sworn to them. They were in great
distress.

¹⁶Then the LORD raised up judges,
who saved them out of the hands of
these raiders. ¹⁷Yet they would not listen to their judges but prostituted themselves to other gods and worshipped
them. Unlike their fathers, they quickly
turned from the way in which their
fathers had walked, the way of obedience to the LORD's commands. ¹⁸When-
ever the LORD raised up a judge for
them, he was with the judge and saved
them out of the hands of their enemies
as long as the judge lived; for the LORD
had compassion on them as they
groaned under those who oppressed
and afflicted them. ¹⁹But when the
judge died, the people returned to ways
even more corrupt than those of their

fathers, following other gods and serving and worshipping them. They refused to give up their evil practices and stubborn ways.

20Therefore the LORD was very angry with Israel and said, "Because this nation has violated the covenant that I laid down for their forefathers and has not listened to me, 21I will no longer drive out before them any of the nations Joshua left when he died. 22I will use them to test Israel and see whether they will keep the way of the LORD and walk in it as their forefathers did." 23The LORD had allowed those nations to remain; he did not drive them out at once by giving them into the hands of Joshua.

3 These are the nations the LORD left to test all those Israelites who had not experienced any of the wars in Canaan 2(he did this only to teach warfare to the descendants of the Israelites who had not had previous battle experience): 3the five rulers of the Philistines, all the Canaanites, the Sidonians, and the Hivites living in the Lebanon mountains from Mount Baal Hermon to Lebo Hamath. 4They were left to test the Israelites to see whether they would obey the LORD's commands, which he had given their forefathers through Moses.

5The Israelites lived among the Canaanites, Hittites, Amorites, Perizzites, Hivites and Jebusites. 6They took their daughters in marriage and gave their own daughters to their sons, and served their gods.

Othniel

7The Israelites did evil in the eyes of the LORD; they forgot the LORD their God and served the Baals and the Asherahs. 8The anger of the LORD burned against Israel so that he sold them into the hands of Cushan-Rishathaim king of Aram Naharaim, to whom the Israelites were subject for eight years. 9But when they cried out to the LORD, he raised up for them a deliverer, Othniel son of Kenaz, Caleb's younger brother, who saved them. 10The Spirit of the LORD came upon him, so that he became Israel's judge and went to war. The LORD gave Cushan-Rishathaim king of Aram into the hands of Othniel, who overpowered him. 11So the land had peace for forty years, until Othniel son of Kenaz died.

Ehud

12Once again the Israelites did evil in the eyes of the LORD, and because they did this evil the LORD gave Eglon king of Moab power over Israel. 13Getting the Ammonites and Amalekites to join him, Eglon came and attacked Israel, and they took possession of the City of Palms. 14The Israelites were subject to Eglon king of Moab for eighteen years.

15Again the Israelites cried out to the LORD, and he gave them a deliverer —Ehud, a left-handed man, the son of Gera the Benjamite. The Israelites sent him with tribute to Eglon king of Moab. 16Now Ehud had made a double-edged sword about a foot and a half long, which he strapped to his right thigh under his clothing. 17He presented the tribute to Eglon king of Moab, who was a very fat man. 18After Ehud had presented the tribute, he sent on their way the men who had carried it. 19At the idols near Gilgal he himself turned back and said, "I have a secret message for you, O king."

The king said, "Quiet!" And all his attendants left him.

20Ehud then approached him while he was sitting alone in the upper room of his summer palace and said, "I have a message from God for you." As the king rose from his seat, 21Ehud reached with his left hand, drew the sword from his right thigh and plunged it into the king's belly. 22Even the handle sank in after the blade, which came out of his back. Ehud did not pull the sword out, and the fat closed in over it. 23Then Ehud went out to the porch; he shut the doors of the upper room behind him and locked them.

24After he had gone, the servants came and found the doors of the upper room locked. They said, "He must be relieving himself in the inner room of the house." 25They waited to the point of embarrassment, but when he did not open the doors of the room, they took a key and unlocked them. There they saw their lord fallen to the floor, dead.

26While they waited, Ehud got away. He passed by the idols and escaped to Seirah. 27When he arrived there, he blew a trumpet in the hill country of Ephraim, and the Israelites went down with him from the hills, with him leading them.

28"Follow me," he ordered, "for the LORD has given Moab, your enemy, into your hands." So they followed him down and, taking possession of the fords of the Jordan that led to Moab, they allowed no-one to cross over. 29At that time they struck down about ten thousand Moabites, all vigorous and strong; not a man escaped. 30That day Moab was made subject to Israel, and the land had peace for eighty years.

Shamgar

31After Ehud came Shamgar son of Anath, who struck down six hundred Philistines with an ox-goad. He too saved Israel.

NEW TESTAMENT READING
John 4:27–42

The Disciples Rejoin Jesus

27Just then his disciples returned and were surprised to find him talking with a woman. But no-one asked, "What do you want?" or "Why are you talking with her?"

28Then, leaving her water jar, the woman went back to the town and said to the people, 29"Come, see a man who told me everything I ever did. Could this be the Christ?" 30They came out of the town and made their way towards him.

31Meanwhile his disciples urged him, "Rabbi, eat something."

32But he said to them, "I have food to eat that you know nothing about."

33Then his disciples said to each other, "Could someone have brought him food?"

34"My food," said Jesus, "is to do the will of him who sent me and to finish his work. 35Do you not say, 'Four months more and then the harvest'? I tell you, open your eyes and look at the fields! They are ripe for harvest. 36Even now the reaper draws his wages, even now he harvests the crop for eternal life, so that the sower and the reaper may be glad together. 37Thus the saying 'One sows and another reaps' is true. 38I sent you to reap what you have not worked for. Others have done the hard work, and you have reaped the benefits of their labour."

Many Samaritans Believe

39Many of the Samaritans from that town believed in him because of the woman's testimony, "He told me everything I ever did." 40So when the Samaritans came to him, they urged him to stay with them, and he stayed two days. 41And because of his words many more became believers.

42They said to the woman, "We no longer believe just because of what you said; now we have heard for ourselves, and we know that this man really is the Saviour of the world."

READING FROM PSALMS
Psalm 56:1–13

For the director of music. To the tune of "A Dove on Distant Oaks". Of David. A *miktam*. When the Philistines had seized him in Gath.

1Be merciful to me, O God, for men
hotly pursue me;
all day long they press their attack.

²My slanderers pursue me all day
    long;
  many are attacking me in their
    pride.

³When I am afraid,
  I will trust in you.
⁴In God, whose word I praise,
  in God I trust; I will not be
    afraid.
  What can mortal man do to me?

⁵All day long they twist my words;
  they are always plotting to harm
    me.
⁶They conspire, they lurk,
  they watch my steps,
  eager to take my life.

⁷On no account let them escape;
  in your anger, O God, bring down
    the nations.

⁸Record my lament;
  list my tears on your scroll—
  are they not in your record?

⁹Then my enemies will turn back
  when I call for help.
  By this I will know that God is for
    me.
¹⁰In God, whose word I praise,
  in the LORD, whose word I
    praise—
¹¹in God I trust; I will not be afraid.
  What can man do to me?

¹²I am under vows to you, O God;
  I will present my thank-offerings to
    you.
¹³For you have delivered me from
    death
  and my feet from stumbling,
  that I may walk before God
  in the light of life.

MAY 6   DAY 126

OLD TESTAMENT READING
Judges 4:1–5:31

Deborah

4 After Ehud died, the Israelites
  once again did evil in the eyes of
the LORD. ²So the LORD sold them into
the hands of Jabin, a king of Canaan,
who reigned in Hazor. The commander
of his army was Sisera, who lived in
Harosheth Haggoyim. ³Because he had
nine hundred iron chariots and had
cruelly oppressed the Israelites for
twenty years, they cried to the LORD for
help.

⁴Deborah, a prophetess, the wife of
Lappidoth, was leading Israel at that
time. ⁵She held court under the Palm of
Deborah between Ramah and Bethel in
the hill country of Ephraim, and the
Israelites came to her to have their disputes decided. ⁶She sent for Barak son

of Abinoam from Kedesh in Naphtali
and said to him, "The LORD, the God of
Israel, commands you: 'Go, take with
you ten thousand men of Naphtali and
Zebulun and lead the way to Mount
Tabor. ⁷I will lure Sisera, the commander of Jabin's army, with his chariots
and his troops to the Kishon River and
give him into your hands.'"

⁸Barak said to her, "If you go with
me, I will go; but if you don't go with
me, I won't go."

⁹"Very well," Deborah said, "I will
go with you. But because of the way you
are going about this, the honour will not
be yours, for the LORD will hand Sisera
over to a woman." So Deborah went
with Barak to Kedesh, ¹⁰where he
summoned Zebulun and Naphtali. Ten
thousand men followed him, and
Deborah also went with him.

¹¹Now Heber the Kenite had left the

other Kenites, the descendants of Hobab, Moses' brother-in-law, and pitched his tent by the great tree in Zaanannim near Kedesh.

¹²When they told Sisera that Barak son of Abinoam had gone up to Mount Tabor, ¹³Sisera gathered together his nine hundred iron chariots and all the men with him, from Harosheth Haggoyim to the Kishon River.

¹⁴Then Deborah said to Barak, "Go! This is the day the LORD has given Sisera into your hands. Has not the LORD gone ahead of you?" So Barak went down Mount Tabor, followed by ten thousand men. ¹⁵At Barak's advance, the LORD routed Sisera and all his chariots and army by the sword, and Sisera abandoned his chariot and fled on foot. ¹⁶But Barak pursued the chariots and army as far as Harosheth Haggoyim. All the troops of Sisera fell by the sword; not a man was left.

¹⁷Sisera, however, fled on foot to the tent of Jael, the wife of Heber the Kenite, because there were friendly relations between Jabin king of Hazor and the clan of Heber the Kenite.

¹⁸Jael went out to meet Sisera and said to him, "Come, my lord, come right in. Don't be afraid." So he entered her tent, and she put a covering over him.

¹⁹"I'm thirsty," he said. "Please give me some water." She opened a skin of milk, gave him a drink, and covered him up.

²⁰"Stand in the doorway of the tent," he told her. "If someone comes by and asks you, 'Is anyone here?' say 'No.'"

²¹But Jael, Heber's wife, picked up a tent peg and a hammer and went quietly to him while he lay fast asleep, exhausted. She drove the peg through his temple into the ground, and he died.

²²Barak came by in pursuit of Sisera, and Jael went out to meet him. "Come," she said, "I will show you the man you're looking for." So he went in with her, and there lay Sisera with the tent peg through his temple—dead.

²³On that day God subdued Jabin, the Canaanite king, before the Israelites. ²⁴And the hand of the Israelites grew stronger and stronger against Jabin, the Canaanite king, until they destroyed him.

The Song of Deborah

5 On that day Deborah and Barak son of Abinoam sang this song:

²"When the princes in Israel take the lead,
  when the people willingly offer themselves—
  praise the LORD!

³"Hear this, you kings! Listen, you rulers!
  I will sing to the LORD, I will sing;
  I will make music to the LORD, the God of Israel.

⁴"O LORD, when you went out from Seir,
  when you marched from the land of Edom,
the earth shook, the heavens poured,
  the clouds poured down water.
⁵The mountains quaked before the LORD, the One of Sinai,
  before the LORD, the God of Israel.

⁶"In the days of Shamgar son of Anath,
  in the days of Jael, the roads were abandoned;
  travellers took to winding paths.
⁷Village life in Israel ceased,
  ceased until I, Deborah, arose,
  arose a mother in Israel.
⁸When they chose new gods,
  war came to the city gates,
and not a shield or spear was seen
  among forty thousand in Israel.
⁹My heart is with Israel's princes,
  with the willing volunteers among the people.
  Praise the LORD!

10"You who ride on white donkeys,
    sitting on your saddle blankets,
    and you who walk along the road,
consider 11the voice of the singers at
        the watering places.
    They recite the righteous acts of
        the LORD,
    the righteous acts of his warriors in
        Israel.

"Then the people of the LORD
    went down to the city gates.
12'Wake up, wake up, Deborah!
    Wake up, wake up, break out in
        song!
    Arise, O Barak!
    Take captive your captives, O son
        of Abinoam.'

13"Then the men who were left
    came down to the nobles;
    the people of the LORD
    came to me with the mighty.
14Some came from Ephraim, whose
        roots were in Amalek;
    Benjamin was with the people who
        followed you.
    From Makir captains came down,
    from Zebulun those who bear a
        commander's staff.
15The princes of Issachar were with
        Deborah;
    yes, Issachar was with Barak,
    rushing after him into the valley.
    In the districts of Reuben
    there was much searching of heart.
16Why did you stay among the
        campfires
    to hear the whistling for the flocks?
    In the districts of Reuben
    there was much searching of heart.
17Gilead stayed beyond the Jordan.
    And Dan, why did he linger by the
        ships?
    Asher remained on the coast
    and stayed in his coves.
18The people of Zebulun risked their
        very lives;
    so did Naphtali on the heights of
        the field.

19"Kings came, they fought;
    the kings of Canaan fought

at Taanach by the waters of Megiddo,
    but they carried off no silver, no
        plunder.
20From the heavens the stars fought,
    from their courses they fought
        against Sisera.
21The river Kishon swept them away,
    the age-old river, the river Kishon.
    March on, my soul; be strong!
22Then thundered the horses' hoofs—
    galloping, galloping go his mighty
        steeds.
23'Curse Meroz,' said the angel of the
        LORD.
    'Curse its people bitterly,
    because they did not come to help the
        LORD,
    to help the LORD against the
        mighty.'

24"Most blessed of women be Jael,
    the wife of Heber the Kenite,
    most blessed of tent-dwelling
        women.
25He asked for water, and she gave him
        milk;
    in a bowl fit for nobles she brought
        him curdled milk.
26Her hand reached for the tent peg,
    her right hand for the workman's
        hammer.
    She struck Sisera, she crushed his
        head,
    she shattered and pierced his
        temple.
27At her feet he sank,
    he fell; there he lay.
    At her feet he sank, he fell;
    where he sank, there he
        fell—dead.

28"Through the window peered Sisera's
        mother;
    behind the lattice she cried out,
    'Why is his chariot so long in coming?
    Why is the clatter of his chariots
        delayed?'
29The wisest of her ladies answer her;
    indeed, she keeps saying to herself,
30'Are they not finding and dividing the
        spoils:
    a girl or two for each man,

colourful garments as plunder for
　　Sisera,
colourful garments embroidered,
highly embroidered garments for
　　my neck—
all this as plunder?'

31"So may all your enemies perish, O
　　LORD!
But may they who love you be like
　　the sun
when it rises in its strength."

Then the land had peace for forty
years.

NEW TESTAMENT READING
John 4:43–5:15

Jesus Heals the Official's Son

43After the two days he left for
Galilee. 44(Now Jesus himself had
pointed out that a prophet has no
honour in his own country.) 45When he
arrived in Galilee, the Galileans welcomed him. They had seen all that he
had done in Jerusalem at the Passover
Feast, for they also had been there.

46Once more he visited Cana in
Galilee, where he had turned the water
into wine. And there was a certain royal
official whose son lay sick at Capernaum. 47When this man heard that
Jesus had arrived in Galilee from Judea,
he went to him and begged him to come
and heal his son, who was close to
death.

48"Unless you people see miraculous
signs and wonders," Jesus told him,
"you will never believe."

49The royal official said, "Sir, come
down before my child dies."

50Jesus replied, "You may go. Your
son will live."

The man took Jesus at his word and
departed. 51While he was still on the
way, his servants met him with the news
that his boy was living. 52When he enquired as to the time when his son got

better, they said to him, "The fever left
him yesterday at the seventh hour."

53Then the father realised that this
was the exact time at which Jesus had
said to him, "Your son will live." So he
and all his household believed.

54This was the second miraculous sign
that Jesus performed, having come
from Judea to Galilee.

The Healing at the Pool

5 Some time later, Jesus went up to
Jerusalem for a feast of the Jews.
2Now there is in Jerusalem near the
Sheep Gate a pool, which in Aramaic is
called Bethesda and which is surrounded by five covered colonnades.
3Here a great number of disabled people used to lie—the blind, the lame, the
paralysed. 5One who was there had
been an invalid for thirty-eight years.
6When Jesus saw him lying there and
learned that he had been in this condition for a long time, he asked him,
"Do you want to get well?"

7"Sir," the invalid replied, "I have
no-one to help me into the pool when
the water is stirred. While I am trying to
get in, someone else goes down ahead
of me."

8Then Jesus said to him, "Get up!
Pick up your mat and walk." 9At once
the man was cured; he picked up his mat
and walked.

The day on which this took place was
a Sabbath, 10and so the Jews said to the
man who had been healed, "It is the
Sabbath; the law forbids you to carry
your mat."

11But he replied, "The man who
made me well said to me, 'Pick up your
mat and walk.'"

12So they asked him, "Who is this
fellow who told you to pick it up and
walk?"

13The man who was healed had no
idea who it was, for Jesus had slipped
away into the crowd that was there.

14Later Jesus found him at the temple
and said to him, "See, you are well
again. Stop sinning or something worse

may happen to you." ¹⁵The man went away and told the Jews that it was Jesus who had made him well.

READING FROM PSALMS
Psalm 57:1–6

For the director of music. ⌊To the tune of⌋ "Do Not Destroy". Of David. A *miktam*. When he had fled from Saul into the cave.

¹Have mercy on me, O God, have
      mercy on me,
   for in you my soul takes refuge.
I will take refuge in the shadow of
      your wings
   until the disaster has passed.

²I cry out to God Most High,
   to God, who fulfils ⌊his purpose⌋
      for me.

³He sends from heaven and saves me,
   rebuking those who hotly pursue
      me;   *Selah*
God sends his love and his
   faithfulness.

⁴I am in the midst of lions;
   I lie among ravenous beasts—
men whose teeth are spears and
   arrows,
   whose tongues are sharp swords.

⁵Be exalted, O God, above the
   heavens;
   let your glory be over all the earth.

⁶They spread a net for my feet—
   I was bowed down in distress.
They dug a pit in my path—
   but they have fallen into it
      themselves.   *Selah*

MAY 7   DAY 127

OLD TESTAMENT READING
Judges 6:1–7:8a

Gideon

6 Again the Israelites did evil in the eyes of the LORD, and for seven years he gave them into the hands of the Midianites. ²Because the power of Midian was so oppressive, the Israelites prepared shelters for themselves in mountain clefts, caves and strongholds. ³Whenever the Israelites planted their crops, the Midianites, Amalekites and other eastern peoples invaded the country. ⁴They camped on the land and ruined the crops all the way to Gaza and did not spare a living thing for Israel, neither sheep nor cattle nor donkeys. ⁵They came up with their livestock and their tents like swarms of locusts. It was impossible to count the men and

their camels; they invaded the land to ravage it. ⁶Midian so impoverished the Israelites that they cried out to the LORD for help.

⁷When the Israelites cried to the LORD because of Midian, ⁸he sent them a prophet, who said, "This is what the LORD, the God of Israel, says: I brought you up out of Egypt, out of the land of slavery. ⁹I snatched you from the power of Egypt and from the hand of all your oppressors. I drove them from before you and gave you their land. ¹⁰I said to you, 'I am the LORD your God; do not worship the gods of the Amorites, in whose land you live.' But you have not listened to me."

¹¹The angel of the LORD came and sat down under the oak in Ophrah that belonged to Joash the Abiezrite, where his son Gideon was threshing wheat in a winepress to keep it from the

Midianites. 12When the angel of the LORD appeared to Gideon, he said, "The LORD is with us, mighty warrior."

13"But sir," Gideon replied, "if the LORD is with us, why has all this happened to us? Where are all his wonders that our fathers told us about when they said, 'Did not the LORD bring us up out of Egypt?' But now the LORD has abandoned us and put us into the hand of Midian."

14The LORD turned to him and said, "Go in the strength you have and save Israel out of Midian's hand. Am I not sending you?"

15"But Lord," Gideon asked, "how can I save Israel? My clan is the weakest in Manasseh, and I am the least in my family."

16The LORD answered, "I will be with you, and you will strike down all the Midianites together."

17Gideon replied, "If now I have found favour in your eyes, give me a sign that it is really you talking to me. 18Please do not go away until I come back and bring my offering and set it before you."

And the LORD said, "I will wait until you return."

19Gideon went in, prepared a young goat, and from an ephah of flour he made bread without yeast. Putting the meat in a basket and its broth in a pot, he brought them out and offered them to him under the oak.

20The angel of God said to him, "Take the meat and the unleavened bread, place them on this rock, and pour out the broth." And Gideon did so. 21With the tip of the staff that was in his hand, the angel of the LORD touched the meat and the unleavened bread. Fire flared from the rock, consuming the meat and the bread. And the angel of the LORD disappeared. 22When Gideon realised that it was the angel of the LORD, he exclaimed, "Ah, Sovereign LORD! I have seen the angel of the LORD face to face!"

23But the LORD said to him, "Peace! Do not be afraid. You are not going to die."

24So Gideon built an altar to the LORD there and called it The LORD is Peace. To this day it stands in Ophrah of the Abiezrites.

25That same night the LORD said to him, "Take the second bull from your father's herd, the one seven years old. Tear down your father's altar to Baal and cut down the Asherah pole beside it. 26Then build a proper kind of altar to the LORD your God on the top of this height. Using the wood of the Asherah pole that you cut down, offer the second bull as a burnt offering."

27So Gideon took ten of his servants and did as the LORD told him. But because he was afraid of his family and the men of the town, he did it at night rather than in the daytime.

28In the morning when the men of the town got up, there was Baal's altar, demolished, with the Asherah pole beside it cut down and the second bull sacrificed on the newly-built altar!

29They asked each other, "Who did this?"

When they carefully investigated, they were told, "Gideon son of Joash did it."

30The men of the town demanded of Joash, "Bring out your son. He must die, because he has broken down Baal's altar and cut down the Asherah pole beside it."

31But Joash replied to the hostile crowd around him, "Are you going to plead Baal's cause? Are you trying to save him? Whoever fights for him shall be put to death by morning! If Baal really is a god, he can defend himself when someone breaks down his altar." 32So that day they called Gideon "Jerub-Baal", saying, "Let Baal contend with him," because he broke down Baal's altar.

33Now all the Midianites, Amalekites and other eastern peoples joined forces and crossed over the Jordan and camped in the Valley of Jezreel. 34Then the Spirit of the LORD came upon

Gideon, and he blew a trumpet, summoning the Abiezrites to follow him. 35He sent messengers throughout Manasseh, calling them to arms, and also into Asher, Zebulun and Naphtali, so that they too went up to meet them.

36Gideon said to God, "If you will save Israel by my hand as you have promised—37look, I will place a wool fleece on the threshing-floor. If there is dew only on the fleece and all the ground is dry, then I will know that you will save Israel by my hand, as you said." 38And that is what happened. Gideon rose early the next day; he squeezed the fleece and wrung out the dew—a bowlful of water.

39Then Gideon said to God, "Do not be angry with me. Let me make just one more request. Allow me one more test with the fleece. This time make the fleece dry and the ground covered with dew." 40That night God did so. Only the fleece was dry; all the ground was covered with dew.

Gideon Defeats the Midianites

7 Early in the morning, Jerub-Baal (that is, Gideon) and all his men camped at the spring of Harod. The camp of Midian was north of them in the valley near the hill of Moreh. 2The LORD said to Gideon, "You have too many men for me to deliver Midian into their hands. In order that Israel may not boast against me that her own strength has saved her, 3announce now to the people, 'Anyone who trembles with fear may turn back and leave Mount Gilead.'" So twenty-two thousand men left, while ten thousand remained.

4But the LORD said to Gideon, "There are still too many men. Take them down to the water, and I will sift them out for you there. If I say, 'This one shall go with you,' he shall go; but if I say, 'This one shall not go with you,' he shall not go."

5So Gideon took the men down to the water. There the LORD told him, "Separate those who lap the water with their tongues like a dog from those who kneel down to drink." 6Three hundred men lapped with their hands to their mouths. All the rest got down on their knees to drink.

7The LORD said to Gideon, "With the three hundred men that lapped I will save you and give the Midianites into your hands. Let all the other men go, each to his own place." 8So Gideon sent the rest of the Israelites to their tents but kept the three hundred, who took over the provisions and trumpets of the others.

NEW TESTAMENT READING
John 5:16–30

Life Through the Son

16So, because Jesus was doing these things on the Sabbath, the Jews persecuted him. 17Jesus said to them, "My Father is always at his work to this very day, and I, too, am working." 18For this reason the Jews tried all the harder to kill him; not only was he breaking the Sabbath, but he was even calling God his own Father, making himself equal with God.

19Jesus gave them this answer: "I tell you the truth, the Son can do nothing by himself; he can do only what he sees his Father doing, because whatever the Father does the Son also does. 20For the Father loves the Son and shows him all he does. Yes, to your amazement he will show him even greater things than these. 21For just as the Father raises the dead and gives them life, even so the Son gives life to whom he is pleased to give it. 22Moreover, the Father judges no-one, but has entrusted all judgment to the Son, 23that all may honour the Son just as they honour the Father. He who does not honour the Son does not honour the Father, who sent him.

24"I tell you the truth, whoever hears my word and believes him who sent me has eternal life and will not be condemned; he has crossed over from death to life. 25I tell you the truth, a time is coming and has now come when the dead will hear the voice of the Son of God and those who hear will live. 26For as the Father has life in himself, so he has granted the Son to have life in himself. 27And he has given him authority to judge because he is the Son of Man.

28"Do not be amazed at this, for a time is coming when all who are in their graves will hear his voice 29and come out—those who have done good will rise to live, and those who have done evil will rise to be condemned. 30By myself I can do nothing; I judge only as I hear, and my judgment is just, for I seek not to please myself but him who sent me.

READING FROM PSALMS
Psalm 57:7–11

7My heart is steadfast, O God,
  my heart is steadfast;
  I will sing and make music.
8Awake, my soul!
  Awake, harp and lyre!
  I will awaken the dawn.

9I will praise you, O Lord, among the
    nations;
  I will sing of you among the
    peoples.
10For great is your love, reaching to the
    heavens;
  your faithfulness reaches to the
    skies.

11Be exalted, O God, above the
    heavens;
  let your glory be over all the earth.

DAY 128

MAY 8

OLD TESTAMENT READING
Judges 7:8b–8:35

Now the camp of Midian lay below him in the valley. 9During that night the LORD said to Gideon, "Get up, go down against the camp, because I am going to give it into your hands. 10If you are afraid to attack, go down to the camp with your servant Purah, 11and listen to what they are saying. Afterwards, you will be encouraged to attack the camp." So he and Purah his servant went down to the outposts of the camp. 12The Midianites, the Amalekites and all the other eastern peoples had settled in the valley, thick as locusts. Their camels could no more be counted than the sand on the seashore.

13Gideon arrived just as a man was telling a friend his dream. "I had a dream," he was saying. "A round loaf of barley bread came tumbling into the Midianite camp. It struck the tent with such force that the tent overturned and collapsed."

14His friend responded, "This can be nothing other than the sword of Gideon son of Joash, the Israelite. God has given the Midianites and the whole camp into his hands."

15When Gideon heard the dream and its interpretation, he worshiped God. He returned to the camp of Israel and called out, "Get up! The LORD has given the Midianite camp into your hands." 16Dividing the three hundred men into three companies, he placed trumpets and empty jars in the hands of all of them, with torches inside.

17"Watch me," he told them. "Follow my lead. When I get to the edge of the camp, do exactly as I do. 18When I and all who are with me blow our trumpets, then from all around the camp blow yours and shout, 'For the LORD and for Gideon.'"

19Gideon and the hundred men with him reached the edge of the camp at the beginning of the middle watch, just after they had changed the guard. They blew their trumpets and broke the jars that were in their hands. 20The three companies blew the trumpets and smashed the jars. Grasping the torches in their left hands and holding in their right hands the trumpets they were to blow, they shouted, "A sword for the LORD and for Gideon!" 21While each man held his position around the camp, all the Midianites ran, crying out as they fled.

22When the three hundred trumpets sounded, the LORD caused the men throughout the camp to turn on each other with their swords. The army fled to Beth Shittah towards Zererah as far as the border of Abel Meholah near Tabbath. 23Israelites from Naphtali, Asher and all Manasseh were called out, and they pursued the Midianites. 24Gideon sent messengers throughout the hill country of Ephraim, saying, "Come down against the Midianites and seize the waters of the Jordan ahead of them as far as Beth Barah."

So all the men of Ephraim were called out and they took the waters of the Jordan as far as Beth Barah. 25They also captured two of the Midianite leaders, Oreb and Zeeb. They killed Oreb at the rock of Oreb, and Zeeb at the winepress of Zeeb. They pursued the Midianites and brought the heads of Oreb and Zeeb to Gideon, who was by the Jordan.

Zebah and Zalmunna

8 Now the Ephraimites asked Gideon, "Why have you treated us like this? Why didn't you call us when you went to fight Midian?" And they criticised him sharply.

2But he answered them, "What have I accomplished compared to you? Aren't the gleanings of Ephraim's grapes better than the full grape harvest of Abiezer? 3God gave Oreb and Zeeb, the Midianite leaders, into your hands. What was I able to do compared to you?" At this, their resentment against him subsided.

4Gideon and his three hundred men, exhausted yet keeping up the pursuit, came to the Jordan and crossed it. 5He said to the men of Succoth, "Give my troops some bread; they are worn out, and I am still pursuing Zebah and Zalmunna, the kings of Midian."

6But the officials of Succoth said, "Do you already have the hands of Zebah and Zalmunna in your possession? Why should we give bread to your troops?"

7Then Gideon replied, "Just for that, when the LORD has given Zebah and Zalmunna into my hand, I will tear your flesh with desert thorns and briers."

8From there he went up to Peniel and made the same request of them, but they answered as the men of Succoth had. 9So he said to the men of Peniel, "When I return in triumph, I will tear down this tower."

10Now Zebah and Zalmunna were in Karkor with a force of about fifteen thousand men, all that were left of the armies of the eastern peoples; a hundred and twenty thousand swordsmen had fallen. 11Gideon went up by the route of the nomads east of Nobah and Jogbehah and fell upon the unsuspecting army. 12Zebah and Zalmunna, the two kings of Midian, fled, but he pursued them and captured them, routing their entire army.

13Gideon son of Joash then returned from the battle by the Pass of Heres. 14He caught a young man of Succoth and questioned him, and the young man wrote down for him the names of the seventy-seven officials of Succoth, the elders of the town. 15Then Gideon came and said to the men of Succoth, "Here are Zebah and Zalmunna, about whom you taunted me by saying, 'Do you already have the hands of Zebah and Zalmunna in your possession? Why should we give bread to your exhausted men?'' 16He took the elders of the town and taught the men of Succoth a lesson by punishing them with desert thorns and briers. 17He also pulled down the tower of Peniel and killed the men of the town.

18Then he asked Zebah and Zalmunna, ''What kind of men did you kill at Tabor?''

''Men like you,'' they answered, ''each one with the bearing of a prince.''

19Gideon replied, ''Those were my brothers, the sons of my own mother. As surely as the LORD lives, if you had spared their lives, I would not kill you.'' 20Turning to Jether, his oldest son, he said, ''Kill them!'' But Jether did not draw his sword, because he was only a boy and was afraid.

21Zebah and Zalmunna said, ''Come, do it yourself. 'As is the man, so is his strength.''' So Gideon stepped forward and killed them, and took the ornaments off their camels' necks.

Gideon's Ephod

22The Israelites said to Gideon, ''Rule over us—you, your son and your grandson—because you have saved us out of the hand of Midian.''

23But Gideon told them, ''I will not rule over you, nor will my son rule over you. The LORD will rule over you.'' 24And he said, ''I do have one request, that each of you give me an ear-ring from your share of the plunder.'' (It was the custom of the Ishmaelites to wear gold ear-rings.)

25They answered, ''We'll be glad to give them.'' So they spread out a garment, and each man threw a ring from his plunder onto it. 26The weight of the gold rings he asked for came to seventeen hundred shekels, not counting the ornaments, the pendants and the purple garments worn by the kings of Midian or the chains that were on their camels' necks. 27Gideon made the gold into an ephod, which he placed in Ophrah, his town. All Israel prostituted themselves

by worshipping it there, and it became a snare to Gideon and his family.

Gideon's Death

28Thus Midian was subdued before the Israelites and did not raise its head again. During Gideon's lifetime, the land enjoyed peace for forty years.

29Jerub-Baal son of Joash went back home to live. 30He had seventy sons of his own, for he had many wives. 31His concubine, who lived in Shechem, also bore him a son, whom he named Abimelech. 32Gideon son of Joash died at a good old age and was buried in the tomb of his father Joash in Ophrah of the Abiezrites.

33No sooner had Gideon died than the Israelites again prostituted themselves to the Baals. They set up Baal-Berith as their god and 34did not remember the LORD their God, who had rescued them from the hands of all their enemies on every side. 35They also failed to show kindness to the family of Jerub-Baal (that is, Gideon) for all the good things he had done for them.

NEW TESTAMENT READING
John 5:31–47

Testimonies About Jesus

31''If I testify about myself, my testimony is not valid. 32There is another who testifies in my favour, and I know that his testimony about me is valid.

33''You have sent to John and he has testified to the truth. 34Not that I accept human testimony; but I mention it that you may be saved. 35John was a lamp that burned and gave light, and you chose for a time to enjoy his light.

36''I have testimony weightier than that of John. For the very work that the Father has given me to finish, and which I am doing, testifies that the Father has sent me. 37And the Father who sent me has himself testified concerning me. You have never heard his voice nor seen his form, 38nor does his word dwell in you, for you do not believe the one he sent. 39You diligently study the Scriptures because you think that by them you possess eternal life. These are the Scriptures that testify about me, 40yet you refuse to come to me to have life.

41"I do not accept praise from men, 42but I know you. I know that you do not have the love of God in your hearts. 43I have come in my Father's name, and you do not accept me; but if someone else comes in his own name, you will accept him. 44How can you believe if you accept praise from one another, yet make no effort to obtain the praise that comes from the only God?

45"But do not think I will accuse you before the Father. Your accuser is Moses, on whom your hopes are set. 46If you believed Moses, you would believe me, for he wrote about me. 47But since you do not believe what he wrote, how are you going to believe what I say?"

READING FROM PROVERBS
Proverbs 11:19–28

19The truly righteous man attains life,
but he who pursues evil goes to his death.

20The LORD detests men of perverse heart
but he delights in those whose ways are blameless.

21Be sure of this: The wicked will not go unpunished,
but those who are righteous will go free.

22Like a gold ring in a pig's snout
is a beautiful woman who shows no discretion.

23The desire of the righteous ends only in good,
but the hope of the wicked only in wrath.

24One man gives freely, yet gains even more;
another withholds unduly, but comes to poverty.

25A generous man will prosper;
he who refreshes others will himself be refreshed.

26People curse the man who hoards grain,
but blessing crowns him who is willing to sell.

27He who seeks good finds goodwill,
but evil comes to him who searches for it.

28Whoever trusts in his riches will fall,
but the righteous will thrive like a green leaf.

MAY 9

OLD TESTAMENT READING
Judges 9:1–57

Abimelech

9 Abimelech son of Jerub-Baal went to his mother's brothers in Shechem and said to them and to all his mother's clan, 2"Ask all the citizens of Shechem, 'Which is better for you: to have all seventy of Jerub-Baal's sons rule over you, or just one man?' Remember, I am your flesh and blood."

3When the brothers repeated all this to the citizens of Shechem, they were inclined to follow Abimelech, for they said, "He is our brother." 4They gave him seventy shekels of silver from the temple of Baal-Berith, and Abimelech used it to hire reckless adventurers, who became his followers. 5He went to his father's home in Ophrah and on one stone murdered his seventy brothers, the sons of Jerub-Baal. But Jotham, the youngest son of Jerub-Baal, escaped by hiding. 6Then all the citizens of Shechem and Beth Millo gathered beside the great tree at the pillar in Shechem to crown Abimelech king.

7When Jotham was told about this, he climbed up on the top of Mount Gerizim and shouted to them, "Listen to me, citizens of Shechem, so that God may listen to you. 8One day the trees went out to anoint a king for themselves. They said to the olive tree, 'Be our king.'

9"But the olive tree answered, 'Should I give up my oil, by which both gods and men are honoured, to hold sway over the trees?'

10"Next, the trees said to the fig-tree, 'Come and be our king.'

11"But the fig-tree replied, 'Should I give up my fruit, so good and sweet, to hold sway over the trees?'

12"Then the trees said to the vine, 'Come and be our king.'

13"But the vine answered, 'Should I give up my wine, which cheers both gods and men, to hold sway over the trees?'

14"Finally all the trees said to the thornbush, 'Come and be our king.'

15"The thornbush said to the trees, 'If you really want to anoint me king over you, come and take refuge in my shade; but if not, then let fire come out of the thornbush and consume the cedars of Lebanon!'

16"Now if you have acted honourably and in good faith when you made Abimelech king, and if you have been fair to Jerub-Baal and his family, and if you have treated him as he deserves —17and to think that my father fought for you, and risked his life to rescue you from the hand of Midian 18(but today you have revolted against my father's family, murdered his seventy sons on a single stone, and made Abimelech, the son of his slave girl, king over the citizens of Shechem because he is your brother)—19if then you have acted honourably and in good faith towards Jerub-Baal and his family today, may Abimelech be your joy, and may you be his, too! 20But if you have not, let fire come out from Abimelech and consume you, citizens of Shechem and Beth Millo, and let fire come out from you, citizens of Shechem and Beth Millo, and consume Abimelech!"

21Then Jotham fled, escaping to Beer, and he lived there because he was afraid of his brother Abimelech.

22After Abimelech had governed Israel for three years, 23God sent an evil spirit between Abimelech and the citizens of Shechem, who acted treacherously against Abimelech. 24God did this in order that the crime against Jerub-Baal's seventy sons, the shedding of their blood, might be avenged on their brother Abimelech and on the citizens of Shechem, who had helped him murder his brothers. ²⁵In opposition to him these citizens of Shechem set men on the hilltops to ambush and rob everyone who passed by, and this was reported to Abimelech.

²⁶Now Gaal son of Ebed moved with his brothers into Shechem, and its citizens put their confidence in him. ²⁷After they had gone out into the fields and gathered the grapes and trodden them, they held a festival in the temple of their god. While they were eating and drinking, they cursed Abimelech. ²⁸Then Gaal son of Ebed said, "Who is Abimelech, and who is Shechem, that we should be subject to him? Isn't he Jerub-Baal's son, and isn't Zebul his deputy? Serve the men of Hamor, Shechem's father! Why should we serve Abimelech? ²⁹If only this people were under my command! Then I would get rid of him. I would say to Abimelech, 'Call out your whole army!'"

³⁰When Zebul the governor of the city heard what Gaal son of Ebed said, he was very angry. ³¹Under cover he sent messengers to Abimelech, saying, "Gaal son of Ebed and his brothers have come to Shechem and are stirring up the city against you. ³²Now then, during the night you and your men should come and lie in wait in the fields. ³³In the morning at sunrise, advance against the city. When Gaal and his men come out against you, do whatever your hand finds to do."

³⁴So Abimelech and all his troops set out by night and took up concealed positions near Shechem in four companies. ³⁵Now Gaal son of Ebed had gone out and was standing at the entrance to the city gate just as Abimelech and his soldiers came out from their hiding-place.

³⁶When Gaal saw them, he said to Zebul, "Look, people are coming down from the tops of the mountains!"

Zebul replied, "You mistake the shadows of the mountains for men."

³⁷But Gaal spoke up again: "Look, people are coming down from the centre of the land, and a company is coming from the direction of the soothsayers' tree."

³⁸Then Zebul said to him, "Where is your big talk now, you who said, 'Who is Abimelech that we should be subject to him?' Aren't these the men you ridiculed? Go out and fight them!"

³⁹So Gaal led out the citizens of Shechem and fought Abimelech. ⁴⁰Abimelech chased him, and many fell wounded in the flight—all the way to the entrance to the gate. ⁴¹Abimelech stayed in Arumah, and Zebul drove Gaal and his brothers out of Shechem.

⁴²The next day the people of Shechem went out to the fields, and this was reported to Abimelech. ⁴³So he took his men, divided them into three companies and set an ambush in the fields. When he saw the people coming out of the city, he rose to attack them. ⁴⁴Abimelech and the companies with him rushed forward to a position at the entrance to the city gate. Then two companies rushed upon those in the fields and struck them down. ⁴⁵All that day Abimelech pressed his attack against the city until he had captured it and killed its people. Then he destroyed the city and scattered salt over it.

⁴⁶On hearing this, the citizens in the tower of Shechem went into the stronghold of the temple of El-Berith. ⁴⁷When Abimelech heard that they had assembled there, ⁴⁸he and all his men went up Mount Zalmon. He took an axe and cut off some branches, which he lifted to his shoulders. He ordered the men with him, "Quick! Do what you have seen me do!" ⁴⁹So all the men cut branches and followed Abimelech. They piled them against the stronghold and set it on fire over the people inside. So all the people in the tower of Shechem, about a thousand men and women, also died.

⁵⁰Next Abimelech went to Thebez and besieged it and captured it. ⁵¹Inside the city, however, was a strong tower, to which all the men and women—all the people of the city—fled. They locked themselves in and climbed up on the tower roof. ⁵²Abimelech went

to the tower and stormed it. But as he approached the entrance to the tower to set it on fire, ⁵³a woman dropped an upper millstone on his head and cracked his skull.

⁵⁴Hurriedly he called to his armour-bearer, "Draw your sword and kill me, so that they can't say, 'A woman killed him.'" So his servant ran him through, and he died. ⁵⁵When the Israelites saw that Abimelech was dead, they went home.

⁵⁶Thus God repaid the wickedness that Abimelech had done to his father by murdering his seventy brothers. ⁵⁷God also made the men of Shechem pay for all their wickedness. The curse of Jotham son of Jerub-Baal came on them.

NEW TESTAMENT READING
John 6:1–24

Jesus Feeds the Five Thousand

6 Some time after this, Jesus crossed to the far shore of the Sea of Galilee (that is, the Sea of Tiberias), ²and a great crowd of people followed him because they saw the miraculous signs he had performed on the sick. ³Then Jesus went up on a mountainside and sat down with his disciples. ⁴The Jewish Passover Feast was near.

⁵When Jesus looked up and saw a great crowd coming towards him, he said to Philip, "Where shall we buy bread for these people to eat?" ⁶He asked this only to test him, for he already had in mind what he was going to do.

⁷Philip answered him, "Eight months' wages would not buy enough bread for each one to have a bite!"

⁸Another of his disciples, Andrew, Simon Peter's brother, spoke up, ⁹"Here is a boy with five small barley loaves and two small fish, but how far will they go among so many?"

¹⁰Jesus said, "Make the people sit down." There was plenty of grass in that place, and the men sat down, about five thousand of them. ¹¹Jesus then took the loaves, gave thanks, and distributed to those who were seated as much as they wanted. He did the same with the fish.

¹²When they had all had enough to eat, he said to his disciples, "Gather the pieces that are left over. Let nothing be wasted." ¹³So they gathered them and filled twelve baskets with the pieces of the five barley loaves left over by those who had eaten.

¹⁴After the people saw the miraculous sign that Jesus did, they began to say, "Surely this is the Prophet who is to come into the world." ¹⁵Jesus, knowing that they intended to come and make him king by force, withdrew again to a mountain by himself.

Jesus Walks on the Water

¹⁶When evening came, his disciples went down to the lake, ¹⁷where they got into a boat and set off across the lake for Capernaum. By now it was dark, and Jesus had not yet joined them. ¹⁸A strong wind was blowing and the waters grew rough. ¹⁹When they had rowed three or three and a half miles, they saw Jesus approaching the boat, walking on the water; and they were terrified. ²⁰But he said to them, "It is I; don't be afraid." ²¹Then they were willing to take him into the boat, and immediately the boat reached the shore where they were heading.

²²The next day the crowd that had stayed on the opposite shore of the lake realised that only one boat had been there, and that Jesus had not entered it with his disciples, but that they had gone away alone. ²³Then some boats from Tiberias landed near the place where the people had eaten the bread after the Lord had given thanks. ²⁴Once the crowd realised that neither Jesus nor his disciples were there, they got into the boats and went to Capernaum in search of Jesus.

READING FROM PSALMS
Psalm 58:1–11

For the director of music. ⌊To the tune of⌋ "Do Not Destroy". Of David. A *miktam*.

¹Do you rulers indeed speak justly?
  Do you judge uprightly among
    men?
²No, in your heart you devise
    injustice,
  and your hands mete out violence
    on the earth.
³Even from birth the wicked go
    astray;
  from the womb they are wayward
    and speak lies.
⁴Their venom is like the venom of a
    snake,
  like that of a cobra that has
    stopped its ears,
⁵that will not heed the tune of the
    charmer,
  however skilful the enchanter may
    be.

⁶Break the teeth in their mouths, O
    God;
  tear out, O LORD, the fangs of the
    lions!
⁷Let them vanish like water that flows
    away;
  when they draw the bow, let their
    arrows be blunted.
⁸Like a slug melting away as it moves
    along,
  like a stillborn child, may they not
    see the sun.

⁹Before your pots can feel ⌊the heat
    of⌋ the thorns—
  whether they be green or dry—the
    wicked will be swept away.
¹⁰The righteous will be glad when they
    are avenged,
  when they bathe their feet in the
    blood of the wicked.
¹¹Then men will say,
  "Surely the righteous still are
    rewarded;
  surely there is a God who judges
    the earth."

MAY 10   DAY 130

OLD TESTAMENT READING
Judges 10:1–11:40

Tola

10 After the time of Abimelech a man of Issachar, Tola son of Puah, the son of Dodo, rose to save Israel. He lived in Shamir, in the hill country of Ephraim. ²He led Israel for twenty-three years; then he died, and was buried in Shamir.

Jair

³He was followed by Jair of Gilead, who led Israel for twenty-two years.
⁴He had thirty sons, who rode thirty donkeys. They controlled thirty towns in Gilead, which to this day are called Havvoth Jair. ⁵When Jair died, he was buried in Kamon.

Jephthah

⁶Again the Israelites did evil in the eyes of the LORD. They served the Baals and the Ashtoreths, and the gods of Aram, the gods of Sidon, the gods of Moab, the gods of the Ammonites and the gods of the Philistines. And because the Israelites forsook the LORD and no longer served him, ⁷he became angry

with them. He sold them into the hands of the Philistines and the Ammonites, [8]who that year shattered and crushed them. For eighteen years they oppressed all the Israelites on the east side of the Jordan in Gilead, the land of the Amorites. [9]The Ammonites also crossed the Jordan to fight against Judah, Benjamin and the house of Ephraim; and Israel was in great distress. [10]Then the Israelites cried out to the LORD, "We have sinned against you, forsaking our God and serving the Baals."

[11]The LORD replied, "When the Egyptians, the Amorites, the Ammonites, the Philistines, [12]the Sidonians, the Amalekites and the Maonites oppressed you and you cried to me for help, did I not save you from their hands? [13]But you have forsaken me and served other gods, so I will no longer save you. [14]Go and cry out to the gods you have chosen. Let them save you when you are in trouble!"

[15]But the Israelites said to the LORD, "We have sinned. Do with us whatever you think best, but please rescue us now." [16]Then they got rid of the foreign gods among them and served the LORD. And he could bear Israel's misery no longer.

[17]When the Ammonites were called to arms and camped in Gilead, the Israelites assembled and camped at Mizpah. [18]The leaders of the people of Gilead said to each other, "Whoever will launch the attack against the Ammonites will be the head of all those living in Gilead."

11 Jephthah the Gileadite was a mighty warrior. His father was Gilead; his mother was a prostitute. [2]Gilead's wife also bore him sons, and when they were grown up, they drove Jephthah away. "You are not going to get any inheritance in our family," they said, "because you are the son of another woman." [3]So Jephthah fled from his brothers and settled in the land of Tob, where a group of adventurers gathered around him and followed him.

[4]Some time later, when the Ammonites made war on Israel, [5]the elders of Gilead went to get Jephthah from the land of Tob. [6]"Come," they said, "be our commander, so we can fight the Ammonites."

[7]Jephthah said to them, "Didn't you hate me and drive me from my father's house? Why do you come to me now, when you're in trouble?"

[8]The elders of Gilead said to him, "Nevertheless, we are turning to you now; come with us to fight the Ammonites, and you will be our head over all who live in Gilead."

[9]Jephthah answered, "Suppose you take me back to fight the Ammonites and the LORD gives them to me—will I really be your head?"

[10]The elders of Gilead replied, "The LORD is our witness; we will certainly do as you say." [11]So Jephthah went with the elders of Gilead, and the people made him head and commander over them. And he repeated all his words before the LORD in Mizpah.

[12]Then Jephthah sent messengers to the Ammonite king with the question: "What do you have against us that you have attacked our country?"

[13]The king of the Ammonites answered Jephthah's messengers, "When Israel came up out of Egypt, they took away my land from the Arnon to the Jabbok, all the way to the Jordan. Now give it back peaceably."

[14]Jephthah sent back messengers to the Ammonite king, [15]saying:

"This is what Jephthah says: Israel did not take the land of Moab or the land of the Ammonites. [16]But when they came up out of Egypt, Israel went through the desert to the Red Sea and on to Kadesh. [17]Then Israel sent messengers to the king of Edom, saying, 'Give us permission to go through your country,' but the king of Edom would not listen. They sent also to the king of Moab, and he refused. So Israel stayed at Kadesh.

18"Next they travelled through the desert, skirted the lands of Edom and Moab, passed along the eastern side of the country of Moab, and camped on the other side of the Arnon. They did not enter the territory of Moab, for the Arnon was its border.

19"Then Israel sent messengers to Sihon king of the Amorites, who ruled in Heshbon, and said to him, 'Let us pass through your country to our own place.' 20Sihon, however, did not trust Israel to pass through his territory. He mustered all his men and encamped at Jahaz and fought with Israel.

21"Then the LORD, the God of Israel, gave Sihon and all his men into Israel's hands, and they defeated them. Israel took over all the land of the Amorites who lived in that country, 22capturing all of it from the Arnon to the Jabbok and from the desert to the Jordan.

23"Now since the LORD, the God of Israel, has driven the Amorites out before his people Israel, what right have you to take it over? 24Will you not take what your god Chemosh gives you? Likewise, whatever the LORD our God has given us, we will possess. 25Are you better than Balak son of Zippor, king of Moab? Did he ever quarrel with Israel or fight with them? 26For three hundred years Israel occupied Heshbon, Aroer, the surrounding settlements and all the towns along the Arnon. Why didn't you retake them during that time? 27I have not wronged you, but you are doing me wrong by waging war against me. Let the LORD, the Judge, decide the dispute this day between the Israelites and the Ammonites."

28The king of Ammon, however, paid no attention to the message Jephthah sent him.

29Then the Spirit of the LORD came upon Jephthah. He crossed Gilead and Manasseh, passed through Mizpah of Gilead, and from there he advanced against the Ammonites. 30And Jephthah made a vow to the LORD: "If you give the Ammonites into my hands, 31whatever comes out of the door of my house to meet me when I return in triumph from the Ammonites will be the LORD's, and I will sacrifice it as a burnt offering."

32Then Jephthah went over to fight the Ammonites, and the LORD gave them into his hands. 33He devastated twenty towns from Aroer to the vicinity of Minnith, as far as Abel Karamim. Thus Israel subdued Ammon.

34When Jephthah returned to his home in Mizpah, who should come out to meet him but his daughter, dancing to the sound of tambourines! She was an only child. Except for her he had neither son nor daughter. 35When he saw her, he tore his clothes and cried, "Oh! My daughter! You have made me miserable and wretched, because I have made a vow to the LORD that I cannot break."

36"My father," she replied, "you have given your word to the LORD. Do to me just as you promised, now that the LORD has avenged you of your enemies, the Ammonites. 37But grant me this one request," she said. "Give me two months to roam the hills and weep with my friends, because I will never marry."

38"You may go," he said. And he let her go for two months. She and the girls went into the hills and wept because she would never marry. 39After the two months, she returned to her father and he did to her as he had vowed. And she was a virgin.

From this comes the Israelite custom 40that each year the young women of Israel go out for four days to commemorate the daughter of Jephthah the Gileadite.

NEW TESTAMENT READING
John 6:25–59

Jesus the Bread of Life

25When they found him on the other side of the lake, they asked him, "Rabbi, when did you get here?"

26Jesus answered, "I tell you the truth, you are looking for me, not because you saw miraculous signs but because you ate the loaves and had your fill. 27Do not work for food that spoils, but for food that endures to eternal life, which the Son of Man will give you. On him God the Father has placed his seal of approval."

28Then they asked him, "What must we do to do the works God requires?"

29Jesus answered, "The work of God is this: to believe in the one he has sent."

30So they asked him, "What miraculous sign then will you give that we may see it and believe you? What will you do? 31Our forefathers ate the manna in the desert; as it is written: 'He gave them bread from heaven to eat.'"

32Jesus said to them, "I tell you the truth, it is not Moses who has given you the bread from heaven, but it is my Father who gives you the true bread from heaven. 33For the bread of God is he who comes down from heaven and gives life to the world."

34"Sir," they said, "from now on give us this bread."

35Then Jesus declared, "I am the bread of life. He who comes to me will never go hungry, and he who believes in me will never be thirsty. 36But as I told you, you have seen me and still you do not believe. 37All that the Father gives me will come to me, and whoever comes to me I will never drive away. 38For I have come down from heaven not to do my will but to do the will of him who sent me. 39And this is the will of him who sent me, that I shall lose none of all that he has given me, but raise them up at the last day. 40For my Father's will is that everyone who looks to the Son and believes in him shall have eternal life, and I will raise him up at the last day."

41At this the Jews began to grumble about him because he said, "I am the bread that came down from heaven." 42They said, "Is this not Jesus, the son of Joseph, whose father and mother we know? How can he now say, 'I came down from heaven'?"

43"Stop grumbling among yourselves," Jesus answered. 44"No-one can come to me unless the Father who sent me draws him, and I will raise him up at the last day. 45It is written in the Prophets: 'They will all be taught by God.' Everyone who listens to the Father and learns from him comes to me. 46No-one has seen the Father except the one who is from God; only he has seen the Father. 47I tell you the truth, he who believes has everlasting life. 48I am the bread of life. 49Your forefathers ate the manna in the desert, yet they died. 50But here is the bread that comes down from heaven, which a man may eat and not die. 51I am the living bread that came down from heaven. If anyone eats of this bread, he will live for ever. This bread is my flesh, which I will give for the life of the world."

52Then the Jews began to argue sharply among themselves, "How can this man give us his flesh to eat?"

53Jesus said to them, "I tell you the truth, unless you can eat the flesh of the Son of Man and drink his blood, you have no life in you. 54Whoever eats my flesh and drinks my blood has eternal life, and I will raise him up at the last day. 55For my flesh is real food and my blood is real drink. 56Whoever eats my flesh and drinks my blood remains in me, and I in him. 57Just as the living Father sent me and I live because of the Father, so the one who feeds on me will live because of me. 58This is the bread that came down from heaven. Your forefathers ate manna and died, but he who feeds on this bread will live for ever." 59He said this while teaching in the synagogue in Capernaum.

READING FROM PSALMS
Psalm 59:1–8

For the director of music. ⌐To the tune of⌐
"Do Not Destroy". Of David. A *miktam*.
When Saul had sent men to watch David's
house in order to kill him.

¹Deliver me from my enemies, O
      God;
   protect me from those who rise up
      against me.
²Deliver me from evildoers
   and save me from bloodthirsty
      men.

³See how they lie in wait for me!
   Fierce men conspire against me
   for no offence or sin of mine, O
      LORD.

⁴I have done no wrong, yet they are
      ready to attack me.
   Arise to help me; look on my
      plight!
⁵O LORD God Almighty, the God of
      Israel,
   rouse yourself to punish all the
      nations;
   show no mercy to wicked traitors.
                                    Selah

⁶They return at evening,
   snarling like dogs,
   and prowl about the city.
⁷See what they spew from their
      mouths—
   they spew out swords from their
      lips,
   and they say, "Who can hear us?"
⁸But you, O LORD, laugh at them;
   you scoff at all those nations.

MAY 11   DAY 131

OLD TESTAMENT READING
Judges 12:1–13:25

Jephthah and Ephraim

12 The men of Ephraim called out
their forces, crossed over to
Zaphon and said to Jephthah, "Why did
you go to fight the Ammonites without
calling us to go with you? We're going to
burn down your house over your head."

²Jephthah answered, "I and my people were engaged in a great struggle
with the Ammonites, and although I
called, you didn't save me out of their
hands. ³When I saw that you wouldn't
help, I took my life in my hands and
crossed over to fight the Ammonites,
and the LORD gave me the victory over
them. Now why have you come up today to fight me?"

⁴Jephthah then called together the
men of Gilead and fought against
Ephraim. The Gileadites struck them

down because the Ephraimites had
said, "You Gileadites are renegades
from Ephraim and Manasseh." ⁵The
Gileadites captured the fords of the Jordan leading to Ephraim, and whenever
a survivor of Ephraim said, "Let me
cross over," the men of Gilead asked
him, "Are you an Ephraimite?" If he
replied, "No," ⁶they said, "All right,
say 'Shibboleth'." If he said, "Sib-
boleth", because he could not pronounce the word correctly, they seized
him and killed him at the fords of
the Jordan. Forty-two thousand
Ephraimites were killed at that time.

⁷Jephthah led Israel for six years.
Then Jephthah the Gileadite died, and
was buried in a town in Gilead.

Ibzan, Elon and Abdon

⁸After him, Ibzan of Bethlehem led
Israel. ⁹He had thirty sons and thirty
daughters. He gave his daughters away

in marriage to those outside his clan, and for his sons he brought in thirty young women as wives from outside his clan. Ibzan led Israel for seven years. ¹⁰Then Ibzan died, and was buried in Bethlehem.

¹¹After him, Elon the Zebulunite led Israel for ten years. ¹²Then Elon died, and was buried in Aijalon in the land of Zebulun.

¹³After him, Abdon son of Hillel, from Pirathon, led Israel. ¹⁴He had forty sons and thirty grandsons, who rode on seventy donkeys. He led Israel for eight years. ¹⁵Then Abdon son of Hillel died, and was buried at Pirathon in Ephraim, in the hill country of the Amalekites.

The Birth of Samson

13 Again the Israelites did evil in the eyes of the LORD, so the LORD delivered them into the hands of the Philistines for forty years.

²A certain man of Zorah, named Manoah, from the clan of the Danites, had a wife who was sterile and remained childless. ³The angel of the LORD appeared to her and said, "You are sterile and childless, but you are going to conceive and have a son. ⁴Now see to it that you drink no wine or other fermented drink and that you do not eat anything unclean, ⁵because you will conceive and give birth to a son. No razor may be used on his head, because the boy is to be a Nazirite, set apart to God from birth, and he will begin the deliverance of Israel from the hands of the Philistines."

⁶Then the woman went to her husband and told him, "A man of God came to me. He looked like an angel of God, very awesome. I didn't ask him where he came from, and he didn't tell me his name. ⁷But he said to me, 'You will conceive and give birth to a son. Now then, drink no wine or other fermented drink and do not eat anything unclean, because the boy will be a Nazirite of God from birth until the day of his death.'"

⁸Then Manoah prayed to the LORD: "O Lord, I beg you, let the man of God you sent to us come again to teach us how to bring up the boy who is to be born."

⁹God heard Manoah, and the angel of God came again to the woman while she was out in the field; but her husband Manoah was not with her. ¹⁰The woman hurried to tell her husband, "He's here! The man who appeared to me the other day!"

¹¹Manoah got up and followed his wife. When he came to the man, he said, "Are you the one who talked to my wife?"

"I am," he said.

¹²So Manoah asked him, "When your words are fulfilled, what is to be the rule for the boy's life and work?"

¹³The angel of the LORD answered, "Your wife must do all that I have told her. ¹⁴She must not eat anything that comes from the grapevine, nor drink any wine or other fermented drink nor eat anything unclean. She must do everything I have commanded her."

¹⁵Manoah said to the angel of the LORD, "We would like you to stay until we prepare a young goat for you."

¹⁶The angel of the LORD replied, "Even though you detain me, I will not eat any of your food. But if you prepare a burnt offering, offer it to the LORD." (Manoah did not realise that it was the angel of the LORD.)

¹⁷Then Manoah enquired of the angel of the LORD, "What is your name, so that we may honour you when your word comes true?"

¹⁸He replied, "Why do you ask my name? It is beyond understanding." ¹⁹Then Manoah took a young goat, together with the grain offering, and sacrificed it on a rock to the LORD. And the LORD did an amazing thing while Manoah and his wife watched: ²⁰As the flame blazed up from the altar towards heaven, the angel of the LORD ascended in the flame. Seeing this, Manoah and his wife fell with their faces to the ground. ²¹When the angel of the LORD

did not show himself again to Manoah and his wife, Manoah realised that it was the angel of the LORD.

22"We are doomed to die!" he said to his wife. "We have seen God!"

23But his wife answered, "If the LORD had meant to kill us, he would not have accepted a burnt offering and grain offering from our hands, nor shown us all these things or now told us this."

24The woman gave birth to a boy and named him Samson. He grew and the LORD blessed him, 25and the Spirit of the LORD began to stir him while he was in Mahaneh Dan, between Zorah and Eshtaol.

NEW TESTAMENT READING
John 6:60–7:13

Many Disciples Desert Jesus

60On hearing it, many of his disciples said, "This is a hard teaching. Who can accept it?"

61Aware that his disciples were grumbling about this, Jesus said to them, "Does this offend you? 62What if you see the Son of Man ascend to where he was before! 63The Spirit gives life; the flesh counts for nothing. The words I have spoken to you are spirit and they are life. 64Yet there are some of you who do not believe." For Jesus had known from the beginning which of them did not believe and who would betray him. 65He went on to say, "This is why I told you that no-one can come to me unless the Father has enabled him."

66From this time many of his disciples turned back and no longer followed him.

67"You do not want to leave too, do you?" Jesus asked the Twelve.

68Simon Peter answered him, "Lord, to whom shall we go? You have the words of eternal life. 69We believe and know that you are the Holy One of God."

70Then Jesus replied, "Have I not chosen you, the Twelve? Yet one of you is a devil!" 71(He meant Judas, the son of Simon Iscariot, who, though one of the Twelve, was later to betray him.)

Jesus Goes to the Feast of Tabernacles

7 After this, Jesus went around in Galilee, purposely staying away from Judea because the Jews there were waiting to take his life. 2But when the Jewish Feast of Tabernacles was near, 3Jesus' brothers said to him, "You ought to leave here and go to Judea, so that your disciples may see the miracles you do. 4No-one who wants to become a public figure acts in secret. Since you are doing these things, show yourself to the world." 5For even his own brothers did not believe in him.

6Therefore Jesus told them, "The right time for me has not yet come; for you any time is right. 7The world cannot hate you, but it hates me because I testify that what it does is evil. 8You go to the Feast. I am not yet going up to this Feast, because for me the right time has not yet come." 9Having said this, he stayed in Galilee.

10However, after his brothers had left for the Feast, he went also, not publicly, but in secret. 11Now at the Feast the Jews were watching for him and asking, "Where is that man?"

12Among the crowds there was widespread whispering about him. Some said, "He is a good man."

Others replied, "No, he deceives the people." 13But no-one would say anything publicly about him for fear of the Jews.

READING FROM PSALMS
Psalm 59:9–17

9O my Strength, I watch for you;
    you, O God, are my fortress, 10my loving God.

God will go before me
    and will let me gloat over those who slander me.

11But do not kill them, O Lord our
          shield,
     or my people will forget.
  In your might make them wander
          about,
     and bring them down.
12For the sins of their mouths,
     for the words of their lips,
     let them be caught in their pride.
  For the curses and lies they utter,
13   consume them in wrath,
     consume them till they are no more.
  Then it will be known to the ends of
          the earth
     that God rules over Jacob.   *Selah*

14They return at evening,
     snarling like dogs,
     and prowl about the city.
15They wander about for food
     and howl if not satisfied.
16But I will sing of your strength,
     in the morning I will sing of your
          love;
  for you are my fortress,
     my refuge in times of trouble.

17O my Strength, I sing praise to
          you;
     you, O God, are my fortress, my
          loving God.

MAY 12

OLD TESTAMENT READING
Judges 14:1–15:20

Samson's Marriage

14 Samson went down to Timnah
          and saw there a young Philistine
woman. 2When he returned, he said to
his father and mother, "I have seen a
Philistine woman in Timnah; now get
her for me as my wife."

3His father and mother replied, "Isn't
there an acceptable woman among your
relatives or among all our people? Must
you go to the uncircumcised Philistines
to get a wife?"

But Samson said to his father, "Get
her for me. She's the right one for me."
4(His parents did not know that this
was from the LORD, who was seeking an
occasion to confront the Philistines; for
at that time they were ruling over
Israel.) 5Samson went down to Timnah
together with his father and mother. As
they approached the vineyards of Timnah, suddenly a young lion came roaring towards him. 6The Spirit of the
LORD came upon him in power so that
he tore the lion apart with his bare
hands as he might have torn a young

goat. But he told neither his father nor
his mother what he had done. 7Then he
went down and talked with the woman,
and he liked her.

8Some time later, when he went back
to marry her, he turned aside to look at
the lion's carcass. In it was a swarm of
bees and some honey, 9which he
scooped out with his hands and ate as he
went along. When he rejoined his
parents, he gave them some, and they
too ate it. But he did not tell them that
he had taken the honey from the lion's
carcass.

10Now his father went down to see the
woman. And Samson made a feast
there, as was customary for bride-
grooms. 11When he appeared, he was
given thirty companions.

12"Let me tell you a riddle," Samson
said to them. "If you can give me the
answer within the seven days of the
feast, I will give you thirty linen garments and thirty sets of clothes. 13If you
can't tell me the answer, you must give
me thirty linen garments and thirty sets
of clothes."

"Tell us your riddle," they said.
"Let's hear it."

14He replied,

"Out of the eater, something to eat;
out of the strong, something
sweet."

For three days they could not give the answer.

¹⁵On the fourth day, they said to Samson's wife, "Coax your husband into explaining the riddle for us, or we will burn you and your father's household to death. Did you invite us here to rob us?"

¹⁶Then Samson's wife threw herself on him, sobbing, "You hate me! You don't really love me. You've given my people a riddle, but you haven't told me the answer."

"I haven't even explained it to my father or mother," he replied, "so why should I explain it to you?" ¹⁷She cried the whole seven days of the feast. So on the seventh day he finally told her, because she continued to press him. She in turn explained the riddle to her people.

¹⁸Before sunset on the seventh day the men of the town said to him,

"What is sweeter than honey?
What is stronger than a lion?"

Samson said to them,

"If you had not ploughed with my
heifer,
you would not have solved my
riddle."

¹⁹Then the Spirit of the LORD came upon him in power. He went down to Ashkelon, struck down thirty of their men, stripped them of their belongings and gave their clothes to those who had explained the riddle. Burning with anger, he went up to his father's house. ²⁰And Samson's wife was given to the friend who had attended him at his wedding.

Samson's Vengeance on the Philistines

15 Later on, at the time of wheat harvest, Samson took a young goat and went to visit his wife. He said,

"I'm going to my wife's room." But her father would not let him go in.

²"I was so sure you thoroughly hated her," he said, "that I gave her to your friend. Isn't her younger sister more attractive? Take her instead."

³Samson said to them, "This time I have a right to get even with the Philistines; I will really harm them." ⁴So he went out and caught three hundred foxes and tied them tail to tail in pairs. He then fastened a torch to every pair of tails, ⁵lit the torches and let the foxes loose in the standing corn of the Philistines. He burned up the shocks and standing corn, together with the vineyards and olive groves.

⁶When the Philistines asked, "Who did this?" they were told, "Samson, the Timnite's son-in-law, because his wife was given to his friend."

So the Philistines went up and burned her and her father to death. ⁷Samson said to them, "Since you've acted like this, I won't stop until I get my revenge on you." ⁸He attacked them viciously and slaughtered many of them. Then he went down and stayed in a cave in the rock of Etam.

⁹The Philistines went up and camped in Judah, spreading out near Lehi. ¹⁰The men of Judah asked, "Why have you come to fight us?"

"We have come to take Samson prisoner," they answered, "to do to him as he did to us."

¹¹Then three thousand men from Judah went down to the cave in the rock of Etam and said to Samson, "Don't you realise that the Philistines are rulers over us? What have you done to us?"

He answered, "I merely did to them what they did to me."

¹²They said to him, "We've come to tie you up and hand you over to the Philistines."

Samson said, "Swear to me that you won't kill me yourselves."

¹³"Agreed," they answered. "We will only tie you up and hand you over to them. We will not kill you." So they bound him with two new ropes and led

him up from the rock. ¹⁴As he approached Lehi, the Philistines came towards him shouting. The Spirit of the LORD came upon him in power. The ropes on his arms became like charred flax, and the bindings dropped from his hands. ¹⁵Finding a fresh jaw-bone of a donkey, he grabbed it and struck down a thousand men.

¹⁶Then Samson said,

"With a donkey's jaw-bone
    I have made donkeys of them.
With a donkey's jaw-bone
    I have killed a thousand men."

¹⁷When he finished speaking, he threw away the jaw-bone; and the place was called Ramath Lehi.

¹⁸Because he was very thirsty, he cried out to the LORD, "You have given your servant this great victory. Must I now die of thirst and fall into the hands of the uncircumcised?" ¹⁹Then God opened up the hollow place in Lehi, and water came out of it. When Samson drank, his strength returned and he revived. So the spring was called En Hakkore, and it is still there in Lehi.

²⁰Samson led Israel for twenty years in the days of the Philistines.

NEW TESTAMENT READING
John 7:14–44

Jesus Teaches at the Feast

¹⁴Not until halfway through the Feast did Jesus go up to the temple courts and begin to teach. ¹⁵The Jews were amazed and asked, "How did this man get such learning without having studied?"

¹⁶Jesus answered, "My teaching is not my own. It comes from him who sent me. ¹⁷If anyone chooses to do God's will, he will find out whether my teaching comes from God or whether I speak on my own. ¹⁸He who speaks on his own does so to gain honour for himself, but he who works for the honour of the one who sent him is a man of truth; there is nothing false about

him. ¹⁹Has not Moses given you the law? Yet not one of you keeps the law. Why are you trying to kill me?"

²⁰"You are demon-possessed," the crowd answered. "Who is trying to kill you?"

²¹Jesus said to them, "I did one miracle, and you are all astonished. ²²Yet, because Moses gave you circumcision (though actually it did not come from Moses, but from the patriarchs), you circumcise a child on the Sabbath. ²³Now if a child can be circumcised on the Sabbath so that the law of Moses may not be broken, why are you angry with me for healing the whole man on the Sabbath? ²⁴Stop judging by mere appearances, and make a right judgment."

Is Jesus the Christ?

²⁵At that point some of the people of Jerusalem began to ask, "Isn't this the man they are trying to kill? ²⁶Here he is, speaking publicly, and they are not saying a word to him. Have the authorities really concluded that he is the Christ? ²⁷But we know where this man is from; when the Christ comes, no-one will know where he is from."

²⁸Then Jesus, still teaching in the temple courts, cried out, "Yes, you know me, and you know where I am from. I am not here on my own, but he who sent me is true. You do not know him, ²⁹but I know him because I am from him and he sent me."

³⁰At this they tried to seize him, but no-one laid a hand on him, because his time had not yet come. ³¹Still, many in the crowd put their faith in him. They said, "When the Christ comes, will he do more miraculous signs than this man?"

³²The Pharisees heard the crowd whispering such things about him. Then the chief priests and the Pharisees sent temple guards to arrest him.

³³Jesus said, "I am with you for only a short time, and then I go to the one who sent me. ³⁴You will look for me, but you

will not find me; and where I am, you cannot come."

35The Jews said to one another, "Where does this man intend to go that we cannot find him? Will he go where our people live scattered among the Greeks, and teach the Greeks? 36What did he mean when he said, 'You will look for me, but you will not find me', and 'Where I am, you cannot come'?"

37On the last and greatest day of the Feast, Jesus stood and said in a loud voice, "If anyone is thirsty, let him come to me and drink. 38Whoever believes in me, as the Scripture has said, streams of living water will flow from within him." 39By this he meant the Spirit, whom those who believed in him were later to receive. Up to that time the Spirit had not been given, since Jesus had not yet been glorified.

40On hearing his words, some of the people said, "Surely this man is the Prophet."

41Others said, "He is the Christ."

Still others asked, "How can the Christ come from Galilee? 42Does not the Scripture say that the Christ will come from David's family and from Bethlehem, the town where David lived?" 43Thus the people were divided because of Jesus. 44Some wanted to seize him, but no-one laid a hand on him.

READING FROM PROVERBS
Proverbs 11:29–12:7

29He who brings trouble on his family
    will inherit only wind,
  and the fool will be servant to the
    wise.

30The fruit of the righteous is a tree of
    life,
  and he who wins souls is wise.

31If the righteous receive their due on
    earth,
  how much more the ungodly and
    the sinner!

12 Whoever loves discipline loves
    knowledge,
  but he who hates correction is
    stupid.

2A good man obtains favour from the
    LORD,
  but the LORD condemns a crafty
    man.

3A man cannot be established through
    wickedness,
  but the righteous cannot be
    uprooted.

4A wife of noble character is her
    husband's crown,
  but a disgraceful wife is like decay
    in his bones.

5The plans of the righteous are just,
  but the advice of the wicked is
    deceitful.

6The words of the wicked lie in wait
    for blood,
  but the speech of the upright
    rescues them.

7Wicked men are overthrown and are
    no more,
  but the house of the righteous
    stands firm.

OLD TESTAMENT READING
Judges 16:1–17:13

Samson and Delilah

16 One day Samson went to Gaza, where he saw a prostitute. He went in to spend the night with her. ²The people of Gaza were told, "Samson is here!" So they surrounded the place and lay in wait for him all night at the city gate. They made no move during the night, saying, "At dawn we'll kill him."

³But Samson lay there only until the middle of the night. Then he got up and took hold of the doors of the city gate, together with the two posts, and tore them loose, bar and all. He lifted them to his shoulders and carried them to the top of the hill that faces Hebron.

⁴Some time later, he fell in love with a woman in the Valley of Sorek whose name was Delilah. ⁵The rulers of the Philistines went to her and said, "See if you can lure him into showing you the secret of his great strength and how we can overpower him so that we may tie him up and subdue him. Each one of us will give you eleven hundred shekels of silver."

⁶So Delilah said to Samson, "Tell me the secret of your great strength and how you can be tied up and subdued."

⁷Samson answered her, "If anyone ties me with seven fresh thongs that have not been dried, I'll become as weak as any other man."

⁸Then the rulers of the Philistines brought her seven fresh thongs that had not been dried, and she tied him with them. ⁹With men hidden in the room, she called to him, "Samson, the Philistines are upon you!" But he snapped the thongs as easily as a piece of string snaps when it comes close to a flame. So the secret of his strength was not discovered.

¹⁰Then Delilah said to Samson, "You have made a fool of me; you lied to me. Come now, tell me how you can be tied."

¹¹He said, "If anyone ties me securely with new ropes that have never been used, I'll become as weak as any other man."

¹²So Delilah took new ropes and tied him with them. Then, with men hidden in the room, she called to him, "Samson, the Philistines are upon you!" But he snapped the ropes off his arms as if they were threads.

¹³Delilah then said to Samson, "Until now, you have been making a fool of me and lying to me. Tell me how you can be tied."

He replied, "If you weave the seven braids of my head into the fabric on the loom, and tighten it with the pin, I'll become as weak as any other man." So while he was sleeping, Delilah took the seven braids of his head, wove them into the fabric ¹⁴and tightened it with the pin.

Again she called to him, "Samson, the Philistines are upon you!" He awoke from his sleep and pulled up the pin and the loom, with the fabric.

¹⁵Then she said to him, "How can you say, 'I love you,' when you won't confide in me? This is the third time you have made a fool of me and haven't told me the secret of your great strength." ¹⁶With such nagging she prodded him day after day until he was tired to death.

¹⁷So he told her everything. "No razor has ever been used on my head," he said, "because I have been a Nazirite set apart to God since birth. If my head were shaved, my strength would leave me, and I would become as weak as any other man."

¹⁸When Delilah saw that he had told her everything, she sent word to the rulers of the Philistines, "Come back once more; he has told me everything."

So the rulers of the Philistines returned with the silver in their hands. 19Having put him to sleep on her lap, she called a man to shave off the seven braids of his hair, and so began to subdue him. And his strength left him.

20Then she called, "Samson, the Philistines are upon you!"

He awoke from his sleep and thought, "I'll go out as before and shake myself free." But he did not know that the LORD had left him.

21Then the Philistines seized him, gouged out his eyes and took him down to Gaza. Binding him with bronze shackles, they set him to grinding in the prison. 22But the hair on his head began to grow again after it had been shaved.

The Death of Samson

23Now the rulers of the Philistines assembled to offer a great sacrifice to Dagon their god and to celebrate, saying, "Our god has delivered Samson, our enemy, into our hands."

24When the people saw him, they praised their god, saying,

"Our god has delivered our enemy
    into our hands,
the one who laid waste our land
    and multiplied our slain."

25While they were in high spirits, they shouted, "Bring out Samson to entertain us." So they called Samson out of the prison, and he performed for them. When they stood him among the pillars, 26Samson said to the servant who held his hand, "Put me where I can feel the pillars that support the temple, so that I may lean against them." 27Now the temple was crowded with men and women; all the rulers of the Philistines were there, and on the roof were about three thousand men and women watching Samson perform. 28Then Samson prayed to the LORD, "O Sovereign LORD, remember me. O God, please strengthen me just once more, and let me with one blow get revenge on the Philistines for my two eyes." 29Then Samson reached towards the two central pillars on which the temple stood. Bracing himself against them, his right hand on the one and his left hand on the other, 30Samson said, "Let me die with the Philistines!" Then he pushed with all his might, and down came the temple on the rulers and all the people in it. Thus he killed many more when he died than while he lived.

31Then his brothers and his father's whole family went down to get him. They brought him back and buried him between Zorah and Eshtaol in the tomb of Manoah his father. He had led Israel twenty years.

Micah's Idols

17 Now a man named Micah from the hill country of Ephraim 2said to his mother, "The eleven hundred shekels of silver that were taken from you and about which I heard you utter a curse—I have that silver with me; I took it."

Then his mother said, "The LORD bless you, my son!"

3When he returned the eleven hundred shekels of silver to his mother, she said, "I solemnly consecrate my silver to the LORD for my son to make a carved image and a cast idol. I will give it back to you."

4So he returned the silver to his mother, and she took two hundred shekels of silver and gave them to a silversmith, who made them into the image and the idol. And they were put in Micah's house.

5Now this man Micah had a shrine, and he made an ephod and some idols and installed one of his sons as his priest. 6In those days Israel had no king; everyone did as he saw fit.

7A young Levite from Bethlehem in Judah, who had been living within the clan of Judah, 8left that town in search of some other place to stay. On his way he came to Micah's house in the hill country of Ephraim.

9Micah asked him, "Where are you from?"

"I'm a Levite from Bethlehem in Judah," he said, "and I'm looking for a place to stay."

10Then Micah said to him, "Live with me and be my father and priest, and I'll give you ten shekels of silver a year, your clothes and your food." 11So the Levite agreed to live with him, and the young man was to him like one of his sons. 12Then Micah installed the Levite, and the young man became his priest and lived in his house. 13And Micah said, "Now I know that the LORD will be good to me, since this Levite has become my priest."

NEW TESTAMENT READING
John 7:45–8:11

Unbelief of the Jewish Leaders

45Finally the temple guards went back to the chief priests and Pharisees, who asked them, "Why didn't you bring him in?"

46"No-one ever spoke the way this man does," the guards declared.

47"You mean he has deceived you also?" the Pharisees retorted. 48"Has any of the rulers or of the Pharisees believed in him? 49No! But this mob that knows nothing of the law—there is a curse on them."

50Nicodemus, who had gone to Jesus earlier and who was one of their own number, asked, 51"Does our law condemn a man without first hearing him to find out what he is doing?"

52They replied, "Are you from Galilee, too? Look into it, and you will find that a prophet does not come out of Galilee."

[The earliest and most reliable manuscripts and other ancient witnesses do not have John 7:53–8:11]

53Then each went to his own home.
8 But Jesus went to the Mount of Olives. 2At dawn he appeared again in the temple courts, where all the people gathered round him, and he sat down to teach them. 3The teachers of the law and the Pharisees brought in a woman caught in adultery. They made her stand before the group 4and said to Jesus, "Teacher, this woman was caught in the act of adultery. 5In the Law Moses commanded us to stone such women. Now what do you say?" 6They were using this question as a trap, in order to have a basis for accusing him.

But Jesus bent down and started to write on the ground with his finger. 7When they kept on questioning him, he straightened up and said to them, "If any one of you is without sin, let him be the first to throw a stone at her." 8Again he stooped down and wrote on the ground.

9At this, those who heard began to go away one at a time, the older ones first, until only Jesus was left, with the woman still standing there. 10Jesus straightened up and asked her, "Woman, where are they? Has no-one condemned you?"

11"No-one, sir," she said.

"Then neither do I condemn you," Jesus declared. "Go now and leave your life of sin."

READING FROM PSALMS
Psalm 60:1–4

For the director of music. To ˎthe tune of˼ "The Lily of the Covenant". A *miktam* of David. For teaching. When he fought Aram Naharaim and Aram Zobah, and when Joab returned and struck down twelve thousand Edomites in the Valley of Salt.

1You have rejected us, O God, and
    burst forth upon us;
  you have been angry—now restore
    us!
2You have shaken the land and torn it
    open;
  mend its fractures, for it is
    quaking.

³You have shown your people
    desperate times;
  you have given us wine that makes
    us stagger.

⁴But for those who fear you, you have
    raised a banner
  to be unfurled against the bow.
                                    Selah

MAY 14   DAY 134

OLD TESTAMENT READING
Judges 18:1–19:30

Danites Settle in Laish

18 In those days Israel had no king.
    And in those days the tribe of
the Danites was seeking a place of their
own where they might settle, because
they had not yet come into an inheritance among the tribes of Israel. ²So the
Danites sent five warriors from Zorah
and Eshtaol to spy out the land and
explore it. These men represented all
their clans. They told them, "Go,
explore the land."

  The men entered the hill country of
Ephraim and came to the house of
Micah, where they spent the night.
³When they were near Micah's house,
they recognised the voice of the young
Levite; so they turned in there and
asked him, "Who brought you here?
What are you doing in this place? Why
are you here?"

  ⁴He told them what Micah had done
for him, and said, "He has hired me and
I am his priest."

  ⁵Then they said to him, "Please
enquire of God to learn whether our
journey will be successful."

  ⁶The priest answered them, "Go in
peace. Your journey has the LORD's
approval."

  ⁷So the five men left and came to
Laish, where they saw that the people
were living in safety, like the Sidonians,
unsuspecting and secure. And since
their land lacked nothing, they were
prosperous. Also, they lived a long way

from the Sidonians and had no relationship with anyone else.

  ⁸When they returned to Zorah and
Eshtaol, their brothers asked them,
"How did you find things?"

  ⁹They answered, "Come on, let's
attack them! We have seen that the land
is very good. Aren't you going to do
something? Don't hesitate to go there
and take it over. ¹⁰When you get there,
you will find an unsuspecting people
and a spacious land that God has put
into your hands, a land that lacks
nothing whatever."

  ¹¹Then six hundred men from the clan
of the Danites, armed for battle, set out
from Zorah and Eshtaol. ¹²On their way
they set up camp near Kiriath Jearim in
Judah. This is why the place west of
Kiriath Jearim is called Mahaneh Dan
to this day. ¹³From there they went on
to the hill country of Ephraim and
came to Micah's house.

  ¹⁴Then the five men who had spied
out the land of Laish said to their
brothers, "Do you know that one of
these houses has an ephod, other household gods, a carved image and a cast
idol? Now you know what to do." ¹⁵So
they turned in there and went to the
house of the young Levite at Micah's
place and greeted him. ¹⁶The six hundred Danites, armed for battle, stood at
the entrance to the gate. ¹⁷The five men
who had spied out the land went inside
and took the carved image, the ephod,
the other household gods and the cast
idol while the priest and the six hundred
armed men stood at the entrance to the
gate.

18When these men went into Micah's house and took the carved image, the ephod, the other household gods and the cast idol, the priest said to them, "What are you doing?"

19They answered him, "Be quiet! Don't say a word. Come with us, and be our father and priest. Isn't it better that you serve a tribe and clan in Israel as priest rather than just one man's household?" 20Then the priest was glad. He took the ephod, the other household gods and the carved image and went along with the people. 21Putting their little children, their livestock and their possessions in front of them, they turned away and left.

22When they had gone some distance from Micah's house, the men who lived near Micah were called together and overtook the Danites. 23As they shouted after them, the Danites turned and said to Micah, "What's the matter with you that you called out your men to fight?"

24He replied, "You took the gods I made, and my priest, and went away. What else do I have? How can you ask, 'What's the matter with you?'"

25The Danites answered, "Don't argue with us, or some hot-tempered men will attack you, and you and your family will lose your lives." 26So the Danites went their way, and Micah, seeing that they were too strong for him, turned round and went back home.

27Then they took what Micah had made, and his priest, and went on to Laish, against a peaceful and unsuspecting people. They attacked them with the sword and burned down their city. 28There was no-one to rescue them because they lived a long way from Sidon and had no relationship with anyone else. The city was in a valley near Beth Rehob.

The Danites rebuilt the city and settled there. 29They named it Dan after their forefather Dan, who was born to Israel—though the city used to be called Laish. 30There the Danites set up for themselves the idols, and Jonathan son of Gershom, the son of Moses, and his sons were priests for the tribe of Dan until the time of the captivity of the land. 31They continued to use the idols Micah had made, all the time the house of God was in Shiloh.

A Levite and His Concubine

19 In those days Israel had no king. Now a Levite who lived in a remote area in the hill country of Ephraim took a concubine from Bethlehem in Judah. 2But she was unfaithful to him. She left him and went back to her father's house in Bethlehem, Judah. After she had been there for four months, 3her husband went to her to persuade her to return. He had with him his servant and two donkeys. She took him into her father's house, and when her father saw him, he gladly welcomed him. 4His father-in-law, the girl's father, prevailed upon him to stay; so he remained with them three days, eating and drinking, and sleeping there.

5On the fourth day they got up early and he prepared to leave, but the girl's father said to his son-in-law, "Refresh yourself with something to eat; then you can go." 6So the two of them sat down to eat and drink together. Afterwards the girl's father said, "Please stay tonight and enjoy yourself." 7And when the man got up to go, his father-in-law persuaded him, so he stayed there that night. 8On the morning of the fifth day, when he rose to go, the girl's father said, "Refresh yourself. Wait till afternoon!" So the two of them ate together.

9Then when the man, with his concubine and his servant, got up to leave, his father-in-law, the girl's father, said, "Now look, it's almost evening. Spend the night here; the day is nearly over. Stay and enjoy yourself. Early tomorrow morning you can get up and be on your way home." 10But, unwilling to stay another night, the man left and went towards Jebus (that is, Jerusalem), with his two saddled donkeys and his concubine.

[11]When they were near Jebus and the day was almost gone, the servant said to his master, "Come, let's stop at this city of the Jebusites and spend the night."

[12]His master replied, "No. We won't go into an alien city, whose people are not Israelites. We will go on to Gibeah." [13]He added, "Come, let's try to reach Gibeah or Ramah and spend the night in one of those places." [14]So they went on, and the sun set as they neared Gibeah in Benjamin. [15]There they stopped to spend the night. They went and sat in the city square, but no-one took them into his home for the night.

[16]That evening an old man from the hill country of Ephraim, who was living in Gibeah (the men of the place were Benjamites), came in from his work in the fields. [17]When he looked and saw the traveller in the city square, the old man asked, "Where are you going? Where did you come from?"

[18]He answered, "We are on our way from Bethlehem in Judah to a remote area in the hill country of Ephraim where I live. I have been to Bethlehem in Judah and now I am going to the house of the LORD. No-one has taken me into his house. [19]We have both straw and fodder for our donkeys and bread and wine for ourselves your servants —me, your maidservant, and the young man with us. We don't need anything."

[20]"You are welcome at my house," the old man said. "Let me supply whatever you need. Only don't spend the night in the square." [21]So he took him into his house and fed his donkeys. After they had washed their feet, they had something to eat and drink.

[22]While they were enjoying themselves, some of the wicked men of the city surrounded the house. Pounding on the door, they shouted to the old man who owned the house, "Bring out the man who came to your house so we can have sex with him."

[23]The owner of the house went outside and said to them, "No, my friends, don't be so vile. Since this man is my guest, don't do this disgraceful thing. [24]Look, here is my virgin daughter, and his concubine. I will bring them out to you now, and you can use them and do to them whatever you wish. But to this man, don't do such a disgraceful thing."

[25]But the men would not listen to him. So the man took his concubine and sent her outside to them, and they raped her and abused her throughout the night, and at dawn they let her go. [26]At daybreak the woman went back to the house where her master was staying, fell down at the door and lay there until daylight.

[27]When her master got up in the morning and opened the door of the house and stepped out to continue on his way, there lay his concubine, fallen in the doorway of the house, with her hands on the threshold. [28]He said to her, "Get up; let's go." But there was no answer. Then the man put her on his donkey and set out for home.

[29]When he reached home, he took a knife and cut up his concubine, limb by limb, into twelve parts and sent them into all the areas of Israel. [30]Everyone who saw it said, "Such a thing has never been seen or done, not since the day the Israelites came up out of Egypt. Think about it! Consider it! Tell us what to do!"

NEW TESTAMENT READING
John 8:12–30

The Validity of Jesus' Testimony

[12]When Jesus spoke again to the people, he said, "I am the light of the world. Whoever follows me will never walk in darkness, but will have the light of life."

[13]The Pharisees challenged him, "Here you are, appearing as your own witness; your testimony is not valid."

[14]Jesus answered, "Even if I testify

on my own behalf, my testimony is valid, for I know where I came from and where I am going. But you have no idea where I come from or where I am going. ¹⁵You judge by human standards; I pass judgment on no-one. ¹⁶But if I do judge, my decisions are right, because I am not alone. I stand with the Father, who sent me. ¹⁷In your own Law it is written that the testimony of two men is valid. ¹⁸I am one who testifies for myself; my other witness is the Father, who sent me."

¹⁹Then they asked him, "Where is your father?"

"You do not know me or my Father," Jesus replied. "If you knew me, you would know my Father also." ²⁰He spoke these words while teaching in the temple area near the place where the offerings were put. Yet no-one seized him, because his time had not yet come.

²¹Once more Jesus said to them, "I am going away, and you will look for me, and you will die in your sin. Where I go, you cannot come."

²²This made the Jews ask, "Will he kill himself? Is that why he says, 'Where I go, you cannot come'?"

²³But he continued, "You are from below; I am from above. You are of this world; I am not of this world. ²⁴I told you that you would die in your sins; if you do not believe that I am ₍the one I claim to be₎, you will indeed die in your sins."

²⁵"Who are you?" they asked.

"Just what I have been claiming all along," Jesus replied. ²⁶"I have much to say in judgment of you. But he who sent me is reliable, and what I have heard from him I tell the world."

²⁷They did not understand that he was telling them about his Father. ²⁸So Jesus said, "When you have lifted up the Son of Man, then you will know that I am ₍the one I claim to be₎, and that I do nothing on my own but speak just what the Father has taught me. ²⁹The one who sent me is with me; he has not left me alone, for I always do what pleases him." ³⁰Even as he spoke, many put their faith in him.

READING FROM PSALMS
Psalm 60:5–12

⁵Save us and help us with your right hand,
   that those you love may be delivered.
⁶God has spoken from his sanctuary:
   "In triumph I will parcel out Shechem
   and measure off the Valley of Succoth.
⁷Gilead is mine, and Manasseh is mine;
   Ephraim is my helmet,
   Judah my sceptre.
⁸Moab is my washbasin,
   upon Edom I toss my sandal;
   over Philistia I shout in triumph."

⁹Who will bring me to the fortified city?
   Who will lead me to Edom?
¹⁰Is it not you, O God, you who have rejected us
   and no longer go out with our armies?
¹¹Give us aid against the enemy,
   for the help of man is worthless.
¹²With God we shall gain the victory,
   and he will trample down our enemies.

OLD TESTAMENT READING
Judges 20:1–21:25

Israelites Fight the Benjamites

20 Then all the Israelites from Dan to Beersheba and from the land of Gilead came out as one man and assembled before the LORD in Mizpah. ²The leaders of all the people of the tribes of Israel took their places in the assembly of the people of God, four hundred thousand soldiers armed with swords. ³(The Benjamites heard that the Israelites had gone up to Mizpah.) Then the Israelites said, "Tell us how this awful thing happened."

⁴So the Levite, the husband of the murdered woman, said, "I and my concubine came to Gibeah in Benjamin to spend the night. ⁵During the night the men of Gibeah came after me and surrounded the house, intending to kill me. They raped my concubine, and she died. ⁶I took my concubine, cut her into pieces and sent one piece to each region of Israel's inheritance, because they committed this lewd and disgraceful act in Israel. ⁷Now, all you Israelites, speak up and give your verdict."

⁸All the people rose as one man, saying, "None of us will go home. No, not one of us will return to his house. ⁹But now this is what we'll do to Gibeah: We'll go up against it as the lot directs. ¹⁰We'll take ten men out of every hundred from all the tribes of Israel, and a hundred from a thousand, and a thousand from ten thousand, to get provisions for the army. Then, when the army arrives at Gibeah in Benjamin, it can give them what they deserve for all this vileness done in Israel." ¹¹So all the men of Israel got together and united as one man against the city.

¹²The tribes of Israel sent men throughout the tribe of Benjamin, saying, "What about this awful crime that was committed among you? ¹³Now surrender those wicked men of Gibeah so that we may put them to death and purge the evil from Israel."

But the Benjamites would not listen to their fellow Israelites. ¹⁴From their towns they came together at Gibeah to fight against the Israelites. ¹⁵At once the Benjamites mobilised twenty-six thousand swordsmen from their towns, in addition to seven hundred chosen men from those living in Gibeah. ¹⁶Among all these soldiers there were seven hundred chosen men who were left-handed, each of whom could sling a stone at a hair and not miss.

¹⁷Israel, apart from Benjamin, mustered four hundred thousand swordsmen, all of them fighting men.

¹⁸The Israelites went up to Bethel and enquired of God. They said, "Who of us shall go first to fight against the Benjamites?"

The LORD replied, "Judah shall go first."

¹⁹The next morning the Israelites got up and pitched camp near Gibeah. ²⁰The men of Israel went out to fight the Benjamites and took up battle positions against them at Gibeah. ²¹The Benjamites came out of Gibeah and cut down twenty-two thousand Israelites on the battlefield that day. ²²But the men of Israel encouraged one another and again took up their positions where they had stationed themselves the first day. ²³The Israelites went up and wept before the LORD until evening, and they enquired of the LORD. They said, "Shall we go up again to battle against the Benjamites, our brothers?"

The LORD answered, "Go up against them."

²⁴Then the Israelites drew near to Benjamin the second day. ²⁵This time, when the Benjamites came out from Gibeah to oppose them, they cut down another eighteen thousand Israelites, all of them armed with swords.

²⁶Then the Israelites, all the people, went up to Bethel, and there they sat weeping before the LORD. They fasted that day until evening and presented burnt offerings and fellowship offerings to the LORD. ²⁷And the Israelites enquired of the LORD. (In those days the ark of the covenant of God was there, ²⁸with Phinehas son of Eleazar, the son of Aaron, ministering before it.) They asked, "Shall we go up again to battle with Benjamin our brother, or not?"

The LORD responded, "Go, for tomorrow I will give them into your hands."

²⁹Then Israel set an ambush around Gibeah. ³⁰They went up against the Benjamites on the third day and took up positions against Gibeah as they had done before. ³¹The Benjamites came out to meet them and were drawn away from the city. They began to inflict casualties on the Israelites as before, so that about thirty men fell in the open field and on the roads—the one leading to Bethel and the other to Gibeah.

³²While the Benjamites were saying, "We are defeating them as before," the Israelites were saying, "Let's retreat and draw them away from the city to the roads."

³³All the men of Israel moved from their places and took up positions at Baal Tamar, and the Israelite ambush charged out of its place on the west of Gibeah. ³⁴Then ten thousand of Israel's finest men made a frontal attack on Gibeah. The fighting was so heavy that the Benjamites did not realise how near disaster was. ³⁵The LORD defeated Benjamin before Israel, and on that day the Israelites struck down 25,100 Benjamites, all armed with swords. ³⁶Then the Benjamites saw that they were beaten.

Now the men of Israel had given way before Benjamin, because they relied on the ambush they had set near Gibeah. ³⁷The men who had been in ambush made a sudden dash into Gibeah, spread out and put the whole city to the sword. ³⁸The men of Israel had arranged with the ambush that they should send up a great cloud of smoke from the city, ³⁹and then the men of Israel would turn in the battle.

The Benjamites had begun to inflict casualties on the men of Israel (about thirty), and they said, "We are defeating them as in the first battle." ⁴⁰But when the column of smoke began to rise from the city, the Benjamites turned and saw the smoke of the whole city going up into the sky. ⁴¹Then the men of Israel turned on them, and the men of Benjamin were terrified, because they realised that disaster had come upon them. ⁴²So they fled before the Israelites in the direction of the desert, but they could not escape the battle. And the men of Israel who came out of the towns cut them down there. ⁴³They surrounded the Benjamites, chased them and easily overran them in the vicinity of Gibeah on the east. ⁴⁴Eighteen thousand Benjamites fell, all of them valiant fighters. ⁴⁵As they turned and fled towards the desert to the rock of Rimmon, the Israelites cut down five thousand men along the roads. They kept pressing after the Benjamites as far as Gidom and struck down two thousand more.

⁴⁶On that day twenty-five thousand Benjamite swordsmen fell, all of them valiant fighters. ⁴⁷But six hundred men turned and fled into the desert to the rock of Rimmon, where they stayed for four months. ⁴⁸The men of Israel went back to Benjamin and put all the towns to the sword, including the animals and everything else they found. All the towns they came across they set on fire.

Wives for the Benjamites

21 The men of Israel had taken an oath at Mizpah: "Not one of us will give his daughter in marriage to a Benjamite."

²The people went to Bethel, where they sat before God until evening, raising their voices and weeping bitterly.

³"O LORD, the God of Israel," they cried, "why has this happened to Israel? Why should one tribe be missing from Israel today?"

⁴Early the next day the people built an altar and presented burnt offerings and fellowship offerings.

⁵Then the Israelites asked, "Who from all the tribes of Israel has failed to assemble before the LORD?" For they had taken a solemn oath that anyone who failed to assemble before the LORD at Mizpah should certainly be put to death.

⁶Now the Israelites grieved for their brothers, the Benjamites. "Today one tribe is cut off from Israel," they said. ⁷"How can we provide wives for those who are left, since we have taken an oath by the LORD not to give them any of our daughters in marriage?" ⁸Then they asked, "Which one of the tribes of Israel failed to assemble before the LORD at Mizpah?" They discovered that no-one from Jabesh Gilead had come to the camp for the assembly. ⁹For when they counted the people, they found that none of the people of Jabesh Gilead were there.

¹⁰So the assembly sent twelve thousand fighting men with instructions to go to Jabesh Gilead and put to the sword those living there, including the women and children. ¹¹"This is what you are to do," they said. "Kill every male and every woman who is not a virgin." ¹²They found among the people living in Jabesh Gilead four hundred young women who had never slept with a man, and they took them to the camp at Shiloh in Canaan.

¹³Then the whole assembly sent an offer of peace to the Benjamites at the rock of Rimmon. ¹⁴So the Benjamites returned at that time and were given the women of Jabesh Gilead who had been spared. But there were not enough for all of them.

¹⁵The people grieved for Benjamin, because the LORD had made a gap in the tribes of Israel. ¹⁶And the elders of the assembly said, "With the women of Benjamin destroyed, how shall we provide wives for the men who are left? ¹⁷The Benjamite survivors must have heirs," they said, "so that a tribe of Israel will not be wiped out. ¹⁸We can't give them our daughters as wives, since we Israelites have taken this oath: 'Cursed be anyone who gives a wife to a Benjamite.' ¹⁹But look, there is the annual festival of the LORD in Shiloh, to the north of Bethel, and east of the road that goes from Bethel to Shechem, and to the south of Lebonah."

²⁰So they instructed the Benjamites, saying, "Go and hide in the vineyards ²¹and watch. When the girls of Shiloh come out to join in the dancing, then rush from the vineyards and each of you seize a wife from the girls of Shiloh and go to the land of Benjamin. ²²When their fathers or brothers complain to us, we will say to them, 'Do us a kindness by helping them, because we did not get wives for them during the war, and you are innocent, since you did not give your daughters to them.'"

²³So that is what the Benjamites did. While the girls were dancing, each man caught one and carried her off to be his wife. Then they returned to their inheritance and rebuilt the towns and settled in them.

²⁴At that time the Israelites left that place and went home to their tribes and clans, each to his own inheritance.

²⁵In those days Israel had no king; everyone did as he saw fit.

NEW TESTAMENT READING
John 8:31–59

The Children of Abraham

³¹To the Jews who had believed him, Jesus said, "If you hold to my teaching, you are really my disciples. ³²Then you will know the truth, and the truth will set you free."

³³They answered him, "We are Abraham's descendants and have never been

slaves of anyone. How can you say that we shall be set free?"

34Jesus replied, "I tell you the truth, everyone who sins is a slave to sin. 35Now a slave has no permanent place in the family, but a son belongs to it for ever. 36So if the Son sets you free, you will be free indeed. 37I know you are Abraham's descendants. Yet you are ready to kill me, because you have no room for my word. 38I am telling you what I have seen in the Father's presence, and you do what you have heard from your father."

39"Abraham is our father," they answered.

"If you were Abraham's children," said Jesus, "then you would do the things Abraham did. 40As it is, you are determined to kill me, a man who has told you the truth that I heard from God. Abraham did not do such things. 41You are doing the things your own father does."

"We are not illegitimate children," they protested. "The only Father we have is God himself."

The Children of the Devil

42Jesus said to them, "If God were your Father, you would love me, for I came from God and now am here. I have not come on my own; but he sent me. 43Why is my language not clear to you? Because you are unable to hear what I say. 44You belong to your father, the devil, and you want to carry out your father's desire. He was a murderer from the beginning, not holding to the truth, for there is no truth in him. When he lies, he speaks his native language, for he is a liar and the father of lies. 45Yet because I tell the truth, you do not believe me! 46Can any of you prove me guilty of sin? If I am telling the truth, why don't you believe me? 47He who belongs to God hears what God says. The reason you do not hear is that you do not belong to God."

The Claims of Jesus About Himself

48The Jews answered him, "Aren't we right in saying that you are a Samaritan and demon-possessed?"

49"I am not possessed by a demon," said Jesus, "but I honour my Father and you dishonour me. 50I am not seeking glory for myself; but there is one who seeks it, and he is the judge. 51I tell you the truth, if anyone keeps my word, he will never see death."

52At this the Jews exclaimed, "Now we know that you are demon-possessed! Abraham died and so did the prophets, yet you say that if anyone keeps your word, he will never taste death. 53Are you greater than our father Abraham? He died, and so did the prophets. Who do you think you are?"

54Jesus replied, "If I glorify myself, my glory means nothing. My Father, whom you claim as your God, is the one who glorifies me. 55Though you do not know him, I know him. If I said I did not, I would be a liar like you, but I do know him and keep his word. 56Your father Abraham rejoiced at the thought of seeing my day; he saw it and was glad."

57"You are not yet fifty years old," the Jews said to him, "and you have seen Abraham!"

58"I tell you the truth," Jesus answered, "before Abraham was born, I am!" 59At this, they picked up stones to stone him, but Jesus hid himself, slipping away from the temple grounds.

READING FROM PSALMS
Psalm 61:1–8

For the director of music. With stringed instruments. Of David.

1Hear my cry, O God;
    listen to my prayer.

2From the ends of the earth I call to
        you,
    I call as my heart grows faint;

lead me to the rock that is higher
    than I.
³For you have been my refuge,
    a strong tower against the foe.

⁴I long to dwell in your tent for ever
    and take refuge in the shelter of
        your wings.   *Selah*
⁵For you have heard my vows, O God;
    you have given me the heritage of
        those who fear your name.

⁶Increase the days of the king's life,
    his years for many generations.
⁷May he be enthroned in God's
        presence for ever;
    appoint your love and faithfulness
        to protect him.

⁸Then will I ever sing praise to your
        name
    and fulfil my vows day after day.

MAY 16   DAY 136

OLD TESTAMENT READING
Ruth 1:1–2:23

Naomi and Ruth

1 In the days when the judges ruled,
there was a famine in the land, and
a man from Bethlehem in Judah,
together with his wife and two sons,
went to live for a while in the country of
Moab. ²The man's name was
Elimelech, his wife's name Naomi, and
the names of his two sons were Mahlon
and Kilion. They were Ephrathites
from Bethlehem, Judah. And they went
to Moab and lived there.

³Now Elimelech, Naomi's husband,
died, and she was left with her two sons.
⁴They married Moabite women, one
named Orpah and the other Ruth.
After they had lived there about ten
years, ⁵both Mahlon and Kilion also
died, and Naomi was left without her
two sons and her husband.

⁶When she heard in Moab that the
LORD had come to the aid of his people
by providing food for them, Naomi and
her daughters-in-law prepared to return
home from there. ⁷With her two daughters-in-law she left the place where she
had been living and set out on the road
that would take them back to the land of
Judah.

⁸Then Naomi said to her two daughters-in-law, "Go back, each of you, to
your mother's home. May the LORD
show kindness to you, as you have
shown to your dead and to me. ⁹May the
LORD grant that each of you will find
rest in the home of another husband."

Then she kissed them and they wept
aloud ¹⁰and said to her, "We will go
back with you to your people."

¹¹But Naomi said, "Return home, my
daughters. Why would you come with
me? Am I going to have any more sons,
who could become your husbands?
¹²Return home, my daughters; I am too
old to have another husband. Even if I
thought there was still hope for me—
even if I had a husband tonight and then
gave birth to sons—¹³would you wait
until they grew up? Would you remain
unmarried for them? No, my daughters.
It is more bitter for me than for you,
because the LORD's hand has gone out
against me!"

¹⁴At this they wept again. Then
Orpah kissed her mother-in-law good-
bye, but Ruth clung to her.

¹⁵"Look," said Naomi, "your sister-
in-law is going back to her people and
her gods. Go back with her."

¹⁶But Ruth replied, "Don't urge me
to leave you or to turn back from you.
Where you go I will go, and where you

stay I will stay. Your people will be my people and your God my God. ¹⁷Where you die I will die, and there I will be buried. May the LORD deal with me, be it ever so severely, if anything but death separates you and me." ¹⁸When Naomi realised that Ruth was determined to go with her, she stopped urging her.

¹⁹So the two women went on until they came to Bethlehem. When they arrived in Bethlehem, the whole town was stirred because of them, and the women exclaimed, "Can this be Naomi?"

²⁰"Don't call me Naomi," she told them. "Call me Mara, because the Almighty has made my life very bitter. ²¹I went away full, but the LORD has brought me back empty. Why call me Naomi? The LORD has afflicted me; the Almighty has brought misfortune upon me."

²²So Naomi returned from Moab accompanied by Ruth the Moabitess, her daughter-in-law, arriving in Bethlehem as the barley harvest was beginning.

Ruth Meets Boaz

2 Now Naomi had a relative on her husband's side from the clan of Elimelech, a man of standing, whose name was Boaz.

²And Ruth the Moabitess said to Naomi, "Let me go to the fields and pick up the leftover grain behind anyone in whose eyes I find favour."

Naomi said to her, "Go ahead, my daughter." ³So she went out and began to glean in the fields behind the harvesters. As it turned out, she found herself working in a field belonging to Boaz, who was from the clan of Elimelech.

⁴Just then Boaz arrived from Bethlehem and greeted the harvesters, "The LORD be with you!"

"The LORD bless you!" they called back.

⁵Boaz asked the foreman of his harvesters, "Whose young woman is that?"

⁶The foreman replied, "She is the Moabitess who came back from Moab with Naomi. ⁷She said, 'Please let me glean and gather among the sheaves behind the harvesters.' She went into the field and has worked steadily from morning till now, except for a short rest in the shelter."

⁸So Boaz said to Ruth, "My daughter, listen to me. Don't go and glean in another field and don't go away from here. Stay here with my servant girls. ⁹Watch the field where the men are harvesting, and follow along after the girls. I have told the men not to touch you. And whenever you are thirsty, go and get a drink from the water jars the men have filled."

¹⁰At this, she bowed down with her face to the ground. She exclaimed, "Why have I found such favour in your eyes that you notice me—a foreigner?"

¹¹Boaz replied, "I've been told all about what you have done for your mother-in-law since the death of your husband—how you left your father and mother and your homeland and came to live with a people you did not know before. ¹²May the LORD repay you for what you have done. May you be richly rewarded by the LORD, the God of Israel, under whose wings you have come to take refuge."

¹³"May I continue to find favour in your eyes, my lord," she said. "You have given me comfort and have spoken kindly to your servant—though I do not have the standing of one of your servant girls."

¹⁴At mealtime Boaz said to her, "Come over here. Have some bread and dip it in the wine vinegar."

When she sat down with the harvesters, he offered her some roasted grain. She ate all she wanted and had some left over. ¹⁵As she got up to leave, Boaz gave orders to his men, "Even if she gathers among the sheaves, don't embarrass her. ¹⁶Rather, pull out some stalks for her from the bundles and leave them for her to pick up, and don't rebuke her."

17So Ruth gleaned in the field until evening. Then she threshed the barley she had gathered, and it amounted to about an ephah. 18She carried it back to town, and her mother-in-law saw how much she had gathered. Ruth also brought out and gave her what she had left over after she had eaten enough.

19Her mother-in-law asked her, "Where did you glean today? Where did you work? Blessed be the man who took notice of you!"

Then Ruth told her mother-in-law about the one at whose place she had been working. "The name of the man I worked with today is Boaz," she said.

20"The LORD bless him!" Naomi said to her daughter-in-law. "He has not stopped showing his kindness to the living and the dead." She added, "That man is our close relative; he is one of our kinsman-redeemers."

21Then Ruth the Moabitess said, "He even said to me, 'Stay with my workers until they finish harvesting all my grain.'"

22Naomi said to Ruth her daughter-in-law, "It will be good for you, my daughter, to go with his girls, because in someone else's field you might be harmed."

23So Ruth stayed close to the servant girls of Boaz to glean until the barley and wheat harvests were finished. And she lived with her mother-in-law.

NEW TESTAMENT READING
John 9:1–34

Jesus Heals a Man Born Blind

9 As he went along, he saw a man blind from birth. 2His disciples asked him, "Rabbi, who sinned, this man or his parents, that he was born blind?"

3"Neither this man nor his parents sinned," said Jesus, "but this happened so that the work of God might be displayed in his life. 4As long as it is day, we must do the work of him who sent me. Night is coming, when no-one can work. 5While I am in the world, I am the light of the world."

6Having said this, he spat on the ground, made some mud with the saliva, and put it on the man's eyes. 7"Go," he told him, "wash in the Pool of Siloam" (this word means Sent). So the man went and washed, and came home seeing.

8His neighbours and those who had formerly seen him begging asked, "Isn't this the same man who used to sit and beg?" 9Some claimed that he was.

Others said, "No, he only looks like him."

But he himself insisted, "I am the man."

10"How then were your eyes opened?" they demanded.

11He replied, "The man they call Jesus made some mud and put it on my eyes. He told me to go to Siloam and wash. So I went and washed, and then I could see."

12"Where is this man?" they asked him.

"I don't know," he said.

The Pharisees Investigate the Healing

13They brought to the Pharisees the man who had been blind. 14Now the day on which Jesus had made the mud and opened the man's eyes was a Sabbath. 15Therefore the Pharisees also asked him how he had received his sight. "He put mud on my eyes," the man replied, "and I washed, and now I see."

16Some of the Pharisees said, "This man is not from God, for he does not keep the Sabbath."

But others asked, "How can a sinner do such miraculous signs?" So they were divided.

17Finally they turned again to the blind man, "What have you to say about him? It was your eyes he opened."

The man replied, "He is a prophet."

18The Jews still did not believe that he had been blind and had received his sight until they sent for the man's parents. 19"Is this your son?" they asked. "Is this the one you say was born blind? How is it that now he can see?"

20"We know he is our son," the parents answered, "and we know he was born blind. 21But how he can see now, or who opened his eyes, we don't know. Ask him. He is of age; he will speak for himself." 22His parents said this because they were afraid of the Jews, for already the Jews had decided that anyone who acknowledged that Jesus was the Christ would be put out of the synagogue. 23That was why his parents said, "He is of age; ask him."

24A second time they summoned the man who had been blind. "Give glory to God," they said. "We know this man is a sinner."

25He replied, "Whether he is a sinner or not, I don't know. One thing I do know. I was blind but now I see!"

26Then they asked him, "What did he do to you? How did he open your eyes?"

27He answered, "I have told you already and you did not listen. Why do you want to hear it again? Do you want to become his disciples, too?"

28Then they hurled insults at him and said, "You are this fellow's disciple! We are disciples of Moses! 29We know that God spoke to Moses, but as for this fellow, we don't even know where he comes from."

30The man answered, "Now that is remarkable! You don't know where he comes from, yet he opened my eyes. 31We know that God does not listen to sinners. He listens to the godly man who does his will. 32Nobody has ever heard of opening the eyes of a man born blind. 33If this man were not from God, he could do nothing."

34To this they replied, "You were steeped in sin at birth; how dare you lecture us!" And they threw him out.

READING FROM PROVERBS
Proverbs 12:8–17

8A man is praised according to his wisdom,
  but men with warped minds are despised.

9Better to be a nobody and yet have a servant
  than pretend to be somebody and have no food.

10A righteous man cares for the needs of his animal,
  but the kindest acts of the wicked are cruel.

11He who works his land will have abundant food,
  but he who chases fantasies lacks judgment.

12The wicked desire the plunder of evil men,
  but the root of the righteous flourishes.

13An evil man is trapped by his sinful talk,
  but a righteous man escapes trouble.

14From the fruit of his lips a man is filled with good things
  as surely as the work of his hands rewards him.

15The way of a fool seems right to him,
  but a wise man listens to advice.

16A fool shows his annoyance at once,
  but a prudent man overlooks an insult.

17A truthful witness gives honest testimony,
  but a false witness tells lies.

OLD TESTAMENT READING
Ruth 3:1–4:22

Ruth and Boaz at the Threshing-Floor

3 One day Naomi her mother-in-law said to her, "My daughter, should I not try to find a home for you, where you will be well provided for? ²Is not Boaz, with whose servant girls you have been, a kinsman of ours? Tonight he will be winnowing barley on the threshing-floor. ³Wash and perfume yourself, and put on your best clothes. Then go down to the threshing-floor, but don't let him know you are there until he has finished eating and drinking. ⁴When he lies down, note the place where he is lying. Then go and uncover his feet and lie down. He will tell you what to do."

⁵"I will do whatever you say," Ruth answered. ⁶So she went down to the threshing-floor and did everything her mother-in-law told her to do.

⁷When Boaz had finished eating and drinking and was in good spirits, he went over to lie down at the far end of the grain pile. Ruth approached quietly, uncovered his feet and lay down. ⁸In the middle of the night something startled the man, and he turned and discovered a woman lying at his feet.

⁹"Who are you?" he asked.

"I am your servant Ruth," she said. "Spread the corner of your garment over me, since you are a kinsman-redeemer."

¹⁰"The LORD bless you, my daughter," he replied. "This kindness is greater than that which you showed earlier: You have not run after the younger men, whether rich or poor. ¹¹And now, my daughter, don't be afraid. I will do for you all you ask. All my fellow townsmen know that you are a woman of noble character.

¹²Although it is true that I am near of kin, there is a kinsman-redeemer nearer than I. ¹³Stay here for the night, and in the morning if he wants to redeem, good; let him redeem. But if he is not willing, as surely as the LORD lives I will do it. Lie here until morning."

¹⁴So she lay at his feet until morning, but got up before anyone could be recognised; and he said, "Don't let it be known that a woman came to the threshing-floor."

¹⁵He also said, "Bring me the shawl you are wearing and hold it out." When she did so, he poured into it six measures of barley and put it on her. Then he went back to town.

¹⁶When Ruth came to her mother-in-law, Naomi asked, "How did it go, my daughter?"

Then she told her everything Boaz had done for her ¹⁷and added, "He gave me these six measures of barley, saying, 'Don't go back to your mother-in-law empty-handed.'"

¹⁸Then Naomi said, "Wait, my daughter, until you find out what happens. For the man will not rest until the matter is settled today."

Boaz Marries Ruth

4 Meanwhile Boaz went up to the town gate and sat there. When the kinsman-redeemer he had mentioned came along, Boaz said, "Come over here, my friend, and sit down." So he went over and sat down.

²Boaz took ten of the elders of the town and said, "Sit here," and they did so. ³Then he said to the kinsman-redeemer, "Naomi, who has come back from Moab, is selling the piece of land that belonged to our brother Elimelech. ⁴I thought I should bring the matter to your attention and suggest that you buy it in the presence of these seated here and in the presence of the elders of my

people. If you will redeem it, do so. But if you will not, tell me, so that I will know. For no-one has the right to do it except you, and I am next in line."

"I will redeem it," he said.

⁵Then Boaz said, "On the day you buy the land from Naomi and from Ruth the Moabitess, you acquire the dead man's widow, in order to maintain the name of the dead with his property."

⁶At this, the kinsman-redeemer said, "Then I cannot redeem it because I might endanger my own estate. You redeem it yourself. I cannot do it."

⁷(Now in earlier times in Israel, for the redemption and transfer of property to become final, one party took off his sandal and gave it to the other. This was the method of legalising transactions in Israel.)

⁸So the kinsman-redeemer said to Boaz, "Buy it yourself." And he removed his sandal.

⁹Then Boaz announced to the elders and all the people, "Today you are witnesses that I have bought from Naomi all the property of Elimelech, Kilion and Mahlon. ¹⁰I have also acquired Ruth the Moabitess, Mahlon's widow, as my wife, in order to maintain the name of the dead with his property, so that his name will not disappear from among his family or from the town records. Today you are witnesses!"

¹¹Then the elders and all those at the gate said, "We are witnesses. May the LORD make the woman who is coming into your home like Rachel and Leah, who together built up the house of Israel. May you have standing in Ephrathah and be famous in Bethlehem. ¹²Through the offspring the LORD gives you by this young woman, may your family be like that of Perez, whom Tamar bore to Judah."

The Genealogy of David

¹³So Boaz took Ruth and she became his wife. Then he went to her, and the LORD enabled her to conceive, and she gave birth to a son. ¹⁴The women said to Naomi: "Praise be to the LORD, who this day has not let you without a kinsman-redeemer. May he become famous throughout Israel! ¹⁵He will renew your life and sustain you in your old age. For your daughter-in-law, who loves you and who is better to you than seven sons, has given him birth."

¹⁶Then Naomi took the child, laid him in her lap and cared for him. ¹⁷The women living there said, "Naomi has a son." And they named him Obed. He was the father of Jesse, the father of David.

¹⁸This, then, is the family line of Perez:

Perez was the father of Hezron,
¹⁹Hezron the father of Ram,
Ram the father of Amminadab,
²⁰Amminadab the father of Nahshon,
Nahshon the father of Salmon,
²¹Salmon the father of Boaz,
Boaz the father of Obed,
²²Obed the father of Jesse,
and Jesse the father of David.

NEW TESTAMENT READING
John 9:35–10:21

Spiritual Blindness

³⁵Jesus heard that they had thrown him out, and when he found him, he said, "Do you believe in the Son of Man?"

³⁶"Who is he, sir?" the man asked. "Tell me so that I may believe in him."

³⁷Jesus said, "You have now seen him; in fact, he is the one speaking with you."

³⁸Then the man said, "Lord, I believe," and he worshipped him.

³⁹Jesus said, "For judgment I have come into this world, so that the blind will see and those who see will become blind."

⁴⁰Some Pharisees who were with him heard him say this and asked, "What? Are we blind too?"

41Jesus said, "If you were blind, you would not be guilty of sin; but now that you claim you can see, your guilt remains.

The Shepherd and His Flock

10 "I tell you the truth, the man who does not enter the sheep pen by the gate, but climbs in by some other way, is a thief and a robber. 2The man who enters by the gate is the shepherd of his sheep. 3The watchman opens the gate for him, and the sheep listen to his voice. He calls his own sheep by name and leads them out. 4When he has brought out all his own, he goes on ahead of them, and his sheep follow him because they know his voice. 5But they will never follow a stranger; in fact, they will run away from him because they do not recognise a stranger's voice." 6Jesus used this figure of speech, but they did not understand what he was telling them.

7Therefore Jesus said again, "I tell you the truth, I am the gate for the sheep. 8All who ever came before me were thieves and robbers, but the sheep did not listen to them. 9I am the gate; whoever enters through me will be saved. He will come in and go out, and find pasture. 10The thief comes only to steal and kill and destroy; I have come that they may have life, and have it to the full.

11"I am the good shepherd. The good shepherd lays down his life for the sheep. 12The hired hand is not the shepherd who owns the sheep. So when he sees the wolf coming, he abandons the sheep and runs away. Then the wolf attacks the flock and scatters it. 13The man runs away because he is a hired hand and cares nothing for the sheep.

14"I am the good shepherd; I know my sheep and my sheep know me— 15just as the Father knows me and I know the Father—and I lay down my life for the sheep. 16I have other sheep that are not of this sheep pen. I must bring them also. They too will listen to my voice, and there shall be one flock and one shepherd. 17The reason my Father loves me is that I lay down my life—only to take it up again. 18No-one takes it from me, but I lay it down of my own accord. I have authority to lay it down and authority to take it up again. This command I received from my Father."

19At these words the Jews were again divided. 20Many of them said, "He is demon-possessed and raving mad. Why listen to him?"

21But others said, "These are not the sayings of a man possessed by a demon. Can a demon open the eyes of the blind?"

READING FROM PSALMS
Psalm 62:1–12

For the director of music. For Jeduthun. A psalm of David.

1My soul finds rest in God alone;
    my salvation comes from him.
2He alone is my rock and my salvation;
    he is my fortress, I shall never be shaken.

3How long will you assault a man?
    Would all of you throw him down—
    this leaning wall, this tottering fence?
4They fully intend to topple him
    from his lofty place;
    they take delight in lies.
With their mouths they bless,
    but in their hearts they curse.
                                                    Selah

5Find rest, O my soul, in God alone;
    my hope comes from him.
6He alone is my rock and my salvation;
    he is my fortress, I shall not be shaken.

7My salvation and my honour depend
    on God;
  he is my mighty rock, my refuge.
8Trust in him at all times, O people;
  pour out your hearts to him,
    for God is our refuge.   *Selah*

9Lowborn men are but a breath,
    the highborn are but a lie;
  if weighed on a balance, they are
    nothing;
      together they are only a breath.

10Do not trust in extortion
    or take pride in stolen goods;
  though your riches increase,
    do not set your heart on them.

11One thing God has spoken,
    two things have I heard:
  that you, O God, are strong,
12 and that you, O Lord, are loving.
  Surely you will reward each person
    according to what he has done.

DAY 138   # MAY 18

OLD TESTAMENT READING
1 Samuel 1:1–2:26

The Birth of Samuel

1 There was a certain man from
Ramathaim, a Zuphite from the
hill country of Ephraim, whose name
was Elkanah son of Jeroham, the son of
Elihu, the son of Tohu, the son of Zuph,
an Ephraimite. 2He had two wives; one
was called Hannah and the other Peninnah. Peninnah had children, but Hannah had none.

3Year after year this man went up
from his town to worship and sacrifice to
the LORD Almighty at Shiloh, where
Hophni and Phinehas, the two sons of
Eli, were priests of the LORD.
4Whenever the day came for Elkanah to
sacrifice, he would give portions of the
meat to his wife Peninnah and to all her
sons and daughters. 5But to Hannah he
gave a double portion because he loved
her, and the LORD had closed her
womb. 6And because the LORD had
closed her womb, her rival kept provoking her in order to irritate her. 7This
went on year after year. Whenever
Hannah went up to the house of the
LORD, her rival provoked her till she
wept and would not eat. 8Elkanah her
husband would say to her, "Hannah,

why are you weeping? Why don't you
eat? Why are you downhearted? Don't
I mean more to you than ten sons?"

9Once when they had finished eating
and drinking in Shiloh, Hannah stood
up. Now Eli the priest was sitting on a
chair by the doorpost of the LORD's
temple. 10In bitterness of soul Hannah
wept much and prayed to the LORD.
11And she made a vow, saying, "O
LORD Almighty, if you will only look
upon your servant's misery and remember me, and not forget your servant but
give her a son, then I will give him to the
LORD for all the days of his life, and no
razor will ever be used on his head."

12As she kept on praying to the LORD,
Eli observed her mouth. 13Hannah was
praying in her heart, and her lips were
moving but her voice was not heard. Eli
thought she was drunk 14and said to her,
"How long will you keep on getting
drunk? Get rid of your wine."

15"Not so, my lord," Hannah replied,
"I am a woman who is deeply troubled.
I have not been drinking wine or beer; I
was pouring out my soul to the LORD.
16Do not take your servant for a wicked
woman; I have been praying here out of
my great anguish and grief."

17Eli answered, "Go in peace, and
may the God of Israel grant you what
you have asked of him."

¹⁸She said, "May your servant find favour in your eyes." Then she went her way and ate something, and her face was no longer downcast.

¹⁹Early the next morning they arose and worshipped before the LORD and then went back to their home at Ramah. Elkanah lay with Hannah his wife, and the LORD remembered her. ²⁰So in the course of time Hannah conceived and gave birth to a son. She named him Samuel, saying, "Because I asked the LORD for him."

Hannah Dedicates Samuel

²¹When the man Elkanah went up with all his family to offer the annual sacrifice to the LORD and to fulfil his vow, ²²Hannah did not go. She said to her husband, "After the boy is weaned, I will take him and present him before the LORD, and he will live there always."

²³"Do what seems best to you," Elkanah her husband told her. "Stay here until you have weaned him; only may the LORD make good his word." So the woman stayed at home and nursed her son until she had weaned him.

²⁴After he was weaned, she took the boy with her, young as he was, along with a three-year-old bull, an ephah of flour and a skin of wine, and brought him to the house of the LORD at Shiloh. ²⁵When they had slaughtered the bull, they brought the boy to Eli, ²⁶and she said to him, "As surely as you live, my lord, I am the woman who stood here beside you praying to the LORD. ²⁷I prayed for this child, and the LORD has granted me what I asked of him. ²⁸So now I give him to the LORD. For his whole life he shall be given over to the LORD." And he worshipped the LORD there.

Hannah's Prayer

2 Then Hannah prayed and said:

"My heart rejoices in the LORD;
in the LORD my horn is lifted high.

My mouth boasts over my enemies,
for I delight in your deliverance.

²"There is no-one holy like the LORD;
there is no-one besides you;
there is no Rock like our God.

³"Do not keep talking so proudly
or let your mouth speak such
arrogance,
for the LORD is a God who knows,
and by him deeds are weighed.

⁴"The bows of the warriors are
broken,
but those who stumbled are armed
with strength.

⁵Those who were full hire themselves
out for food,
but those who were hungry hunger
no more.
She who was barren has borne seven
children,
but she who has had many sons
pines away.

⁶"The LORD brings death and makes
alive;
he brings down to the grave and
raises up.

⁷The LORD sends poverty and wealth;
he humbles and he exalts.

⁸He raises the poor from the dust
and lifts the needy from the ash
heap;
he seats them with princes
and has them inherit a throne of
honour.

"For the foundations of the earth are
the LORD's;
upon them he has set the world.

⁹He will guard the feet of his saints,
but the wicked will be silenced in
darkness.

"It is not by strength that one
prevails;

¹⁰ those who oppose the LORD will be
shattered.
He will thunder against them from
heaven;
the LORD will judge the ends of the
earth.

"He will give strength to his king
and exalt the horn of his
anointed."

11Then Elkanah went home to
Ramah, but the boy ministered before
the LORD under Eli the priest.

Eli's Wicked Sons

12Eli's sons were wicked men; they
had no regard for the LORD. 13Now it
was the practice of the priests with the
people that whenever anyone offered a
sacrifice and while the meat was being
boiled, the servant of the priest would
come with a three-pronged fork in his
hand. 14He would plunge it into the pan
or kettle or cauldron or pot, and the
priest would take for himself whatever
the fork brought up. This is how they
treated all the Israelites who came to
Shiloh. 15But even before the fat was
burned, the servant of the priest would
come and say to the man who was sacrificing, "Give the priest some meat to
roast; he won't accept boiled meat from
you, but only raw."

16If the man said to him, "Let the fat
be burned up first, and then take whatever you want," the servant would then
answer, "No, hand it over now; if you
don't, I'll take it by force."

17This sin of the young men was very
great in the LORD's sight, for they
were treating the LORD's offering with
contempt.

18But Samuel was ministering before
the LORD—a boy wearing a linen
ephod. 19Each year his mother made
him a little robe and took it to him when
she went up with her husband to offer
the annual sacrifice. 20Eli would bless
Elkanah and his wife, saying, "May the
LORD give you children by this woman
to take the place of the one she prayed
for and gave to the LORD." Then they
would go home. 21And the LORD was
gracious to Hannah; she conceived and
gave birth to three sons and two daughters. Meanwhile, the boy Samuel grew
up in the presence of the LORD.

22Now Eli, who was very old, heard
about everything his sons were doing to
all Israel and how they slept with the
women who served at the entrance to
the Tent of Meeting. 23So he said to
them, "Why do you do such things? I
hear from all the people about these
wicked deeds of yours. 24No, my sons; it
is not a good report that I hear spreading among the LORD's people. 25If a
man sins against another man, God may
mediate for him; but if a man sins
against the LORD, who will intercede for
him?" His sons, however, did not listen
to their father's rebuke, for it was the
LORD's will to put them to death.

26And the boy Samuel continued to
grow in stature and in favour with the
LORD and with men.

NEW TESTAMENT READING
John 10:22–42

The Unbelief of the Jews

22Then came the Feast of Dedication
at Jerusalem. It was winter, 23and Jesus
was in the temple area walking in
Solomon's Colonnade. 24The Jews
gathered round him, saying, "How long
will you keep us in suspense? If you are
the Christ, tell us plainly."

25Jesus answered, "I did tell you, but
you do not believe. The miracles I do in
my Father's name speak for me, 26but
you do not believe because you are not
my sheep. 27My sheep listen to my
voice; I know them, and they follow me.
28I give them eternal life, and they shall
never perish; no-one can snatch them
out of my hand. 29My Father, who has
given them to me, is greater than all;
no-one can snatch them out of my
Father's hand. 30I and the Father are
one."

31Again the Jews picked up stones to
stone him, 32but Jesus said to them, "I
have shown you many great miracles
from the Father. For which of these do
you stone me?"

33"We are not stoning you for any
of these," replied the Jews, "but for

blasphemy, because you, a mere man, claim to be God."

34Jesus answered them, "Is it not written in your Law, 'I have said you are gods'? 35If he called them 'gods', to whom the word of God came—and the Scripture cannot be broken—36what about the one whom the Father set apart as his very own and sent into the world? Why then do you accuse me of blasphemy because I said, 'I am God's Son'? 37Do not believe me unless I do what my Father does. 38But if I do it, even though you do not believe me, believe the miracles, that you may know and understand that the Father is in me, and I in the Father." 39Again they tried to seize him, but he escaped their grasp.

40Then Jesus went back across the Jordan to the place where John had been baptising in the early days. Here he stayed 41and many people came to him. They said, "Though John never performed a miraculous sign, all that John said about this man was true." 42And in that place many believed in Jesus.

READING FROM PSALMS
Psalm 63:1–11

A psalm of David. When he was in the Desert of Judah.

1O God, you are my God,
    earnestly I seek you;
my soul thirsts for you,
    my body longs for you,
in a dry and weary land
    where there is no water.

2I have seen you in the sanctuary
    and beheld your power and your
        glory.
3Because your love is better than life,
    my lips will glorify you.
4I will praise you as long as I live,
    and in your name I will lift up my
        hands.
5My soul will be satisfied as with the
        richest of foods;
    with singing lips my mouth will
        praise you.

6On my bed I remember you;
    I think of you through the watches
        of the night.
7Because you are my help,
    I sing in the shadow of your wings.
8My soul clings to you;
    your right hand upholds me.

9They who seek my life will be
        destroyed;
    they will go down to the depths of
        the earth.
10They will be given over to the sword
    and become food for jackals.

11But the king will rejoice in God;
    all who swear by God's name will
        praise him,
    while the mouths of liars will be
        silenced.

MAY 19

OLD TESTAMENT READING
1 Samuel 2:27–4:22

Prophecy Against the House of Eli

²⁷Now a man of God came to Eli and said to him, "This is what the LORD says: 'Did I not clearly reveal myself to your father's house when they were in Egypt under Pharaoh? ²⁸I chose your father out of all the tribes of Israel to be my priest, to go up to my altar, to burn incense, and to wear an ephod in my presence. I also gave your father's house all the offerings made with fire by the Israelites. ²⁹Why do you scorn my sacrifice and offering that I prescribed for my dwelling? Why do you honour your sons more than me by fattening yourselves on the choice parts of every offering made by my people Israel?'

³⁰"Therefore the LORD, the God of Israel, declares: 'I promised that your house and your father's house would minister before me for ever.' But now the LORD declares: 'Far be it from me! Those who honour me I will honour, but those who despise me will be disdained. ³¹The time is coming when I will cut short your strength and the strength of your father's house, so that there will not be an old man in your family line ³²and you will see distress in my dwelling. Although good will be done to Israel, in your family line there will never be an old man. ³³Every one of you that I do not cut off from my altar will be spared only to blind your eyes with tears and to grieve your heart, and all your descendants will die in the prime of life.

³⁴"'And what happens to your two sons, Hophni and Phinehas, will be a sign to you—they will both die on the same day. ³⁵I will raise up for myself a faithful priest, who will do according to what is in my heart and mind. I will firmly establish his house, and he will minister before my anointed one

always. ³⁶Then everyone left in your family line will come and bow down before him for a piece of silver and a crust of bread and plead, "Appoint me to some priestly office so that I can have food to eat."'"

The LORD Calls Samuel

3 The boy Samuel ministered before the LORD under Eli. In those days the word of the LORD was rare; there were not many visions.

²One night Eli, whose eyes were becoming so weak that he could barely see, was lying down in his usual place. ³The lamp of God had not yet gone out, and Samuel was lying down in the temple of the LORD, where the ark of God was. ⁴Then the LORD called Samuel.

Samuel answered, "Here I am." ⁵And he ran to Eli and said, "Here I am; you called me."

But Eli said, "I did not call; go back and lie down." So he went and lay down.

⁶Again the LORD called, "Samuel!" And Samuel got up and went to Eli and said, "Here I am; you called me."

"My son," Eli said, "I did not call; go back and lie down."

⁷Now Samuel did not yet know the LORD: The word of the LORD had not yet been revealed to him.

⁸The LORD called Samuel a third time, and Samuel got up and went to Eli and said, "Here I am; you called me."

Then Eli realised that the LORD was calling the boy. ⁹So Eli told Samuel, "Go and lie down, and if he calls you, say, 'Speak, LORD, for your servant is listening.'" So Samuel went and lay down in his place.

¹⁰The LORD came and stood there, calling as at the other times, "Samuel! Samuel!"

Then Samuel said, "Speak, for your servant is listening."

[11]And the LORD said to Samuel: "See, I am about to do something in Israel that will make the ears of everyone who hears of it tingle. [12]At that time I will carry out against Eli everything I spoke against his family—from beginning to end. [13]For I told him that I would judge his family for ever because of the sin he knew about; his sons made themselves contemptible, and he failed to restrain them. [14]Therefore, I swore to the house of Eli, 'The guilt of Eli's house will never be atoned for by sacrifice or offering.'"

[15]Samuel lay down until morning and then opened the doors of the house of the LORD. He was afraid to tell Eli the vision, [16]but Eli called him and said, "Samuel, my son."

Samuel answered, "Here I am."

[17]"What was it he said to you?" Eli asked. "Do not hide it from me. May God deal with you, be it ever so severely, if you hide from me anything he told you." [18]So Samuel told him everything, hiding nothing from him. Then Eli said, "He is the LORD; let him do what is good in his eyes."

[19]The LORD was with Samuel as he grew up, and he let none of his words fall to the ground. [20]And all Israel from Dan to Beersheba recognised that Samuel was attested as a prophet of the LORD. [21]The LORD continued to appear at Shiloh, and there he revealed himself to Samuel through his word.

4 And Samuel's word came to all Israel.

The Philistines Capture the Ark

Now the Israelites went out to fight against the Philistines. The Israelites camped at Ebenezer, and the Philistines at Aphek. [2]The Philistines deployed their forces to meet Israel, and as the battle spread, Israel was defeated by the Philistines, who killed about four thousand of them on the battlefield. [3]When the soldiers returned to camp, the elders of Israel asked, "Why did the LORD bring defeat upon us today before the Philistines? Let us bring the ark of the LORD's covenant from Shiloh, so that it may go with us and save us from the hand of our enemies."

[4]So the people sent men to Shiloh, and they brought back the ark of the covenant of the LORD Almighty, who is enthroned between the cherubim. And Eli's two sons, Hophni and Phinehas, were there with the ark of the covenant of God.

[5]When the ark of the LORD's covenant came into the camp, all Israel raised such a great shout that the ground shook. [6]Hearing the uproar, the Philistines asked, "What's all this shouting in the Hebrew camp?"

When they learned that the ark of the LORD had come into the camp, [7]the Philistines were afraid. "A god has come into the camp," they said. "We're in trouble! Nothing like this has happened before. [8]Woe to us! Who will deliver us from the hand of these mighty gods? They are the gods who struck the Egyptians with all kinds of plagues in the desert. [9]Be strong, Philistines! Be men, or you will be subject to the Hebrews, as they have been to you. Be men, and fight!"

[10]So the Philistines fought, and the Israelites were defeated and every man fled to his tent. The slaughter was very great; Israel lost thirty thousand foot soldiers. [11]The ark of God was captured, and Eli's two sons, Hophni and Phinehas, died.

Death of Eli

[12]That same day a Benjamite ran from the battle line and went to Shiloh, his clothes torn and dust on his head. [13]When he arrived, there was Eli sitting on his chair by the side of the road, watching, because his heart feared for the ark of God. When the man entered the town and told what had happened, the whole town sent up a cry.

[14]Eli heard the outcry and asked,

"What is the meaning of this uproar?"

The man hurried over to Eli, [15]who was ninety-eight years old and whose eyes were set so that he could not see. [16]He told Eli, "I have just come from the battle line; I fled from it this very day."

Eli asked, "What happened, my son?"

[17]The man who brought the news replied, "Israel fled before the Philistines, and the army has suffered heavy losses. Also your two sons, Hophni and Phinehas, are dead, and the ark of God has been captured."

[18]When he mentioned the ark of God, Eli fell backwards off his chair by the side of the gate. His neck was broken and he died, for he was an old man and heavy. He had led Israel for forty years.

[19]His daughter-in-law, the wife of Phinehas, was pregnant and near the time of delivery. When she heard the news that the ark of God had been captured and that her father-in-law and her husband were dead, she went into labour and gave birth, but was overcome by her labour pains. [20]As she was dying, the women attending her said, "Don't despair; you have given birth to a son." But she did not respond or pay any attention.

[21]She named the boy Ichabod, saying, "The glory has departed from Israel" —because of the capture of the ark of God and the deaths of her father-in-law and her husband. [22]She said, "The glory has departed from Israel, for the ark of God has been captured."

NEW TESTAMENT READING
John 11:1–44

The Death of Lazarus

11 Now a man named Lazarus was sick. He was from Bethany, the village of Mary and her sister Martha. [2]This Mary, whose brother Lazarus now lay sick, was the same one who poured perfume on the Lord and wiped his feet with her hair. [3]So the sisters sent word to Jesus, "Lord, the one you love is sick."

[4]When he heard this, Jesus said, "This sickness will not end in death. No, it is for God's glory so that God's Son may be glorified through it." [5]Jesus loved Martha and her sister and Lazarus. [6]Yet when he heard that Lazarus was sick, he stayed where he was two more days.

[7]Then he said to his disciples, "Let us go back to Judea."

[8]"But Rabbi," they said, "a short while ago the Jews tried to stone you, and yet you are going back there?"

[9]Jesus answered, "Are there not twelve hours of daylight? A man who walks by day will not stumble, for he sees by this world's light. [10]It is when he walks by night that he stumbles, for he has no light."

[11]After he had said this, he went on to tell them, "Our friend Lazarus has fallen asleep; but I am going there to wake him up."

[12]His disciples replied, "Lord, if he sleeps, he will get better." [13]Jesus had been speaking of his death, but his disciples thought he meant natural sleep.

[14]So then he told them plainly, "Lazarus is dead, [15]and for your sake I am glad I was not there, so that you may believe. But let us go to him."

[16]Then Thomas (called Didymus) said to the rest of the disciples, "Let us also go, that we may die with him."

Jesus Comforts the Sisters

[17]On his arrival, Jesus found that Lazarus had already been in the tomb for four days. [18]Bethany was less than two miles from Jerusalem, [19]and many Jews had come to Martha and Mary to comfort them in the loss of their brother. [20]When Martha heard that Jesus was coming, she went out to meet him, but Mary stayed at home.

[21]"Lord," Martha said to Jesus, "if you had been here, my brother would

not have died. 22But I know that even now God will give you whatever you ask."

23Jesus said to her, "Your brother will rise again."

24Martha answered, "I know he will rise again in the resurrection at the last day."

25Jesus said to her, "I am the resurrection and the life. He who believes in me will live, even though he dies; 26and whoever lives and believes in me will never die. Do you believe this?"

27"Yes, Lord," she told him, "I believe that you are the Christ, the Son of God, who was to come into the world."

28And after she had said this, she went back and called her sister Mary aside. "The Teacher is here," she said, "and is asking for you." 29When Mary heard this, she got up quickly and went to him. 30Now Jesus had not yet entered the village, but was still at the place where Martha had met him. 31When the Jews who had been with Mary in the house, comforting her, noticed how quickly she got up and went out, they followed her, supposing she was going to the tomb to mourn there.

32When Mary reached the place where Jesus was and saw him, she fell at his feet and said, "Lord, if you had been here, my brother would not have died."

33When Jesus saw her weeping, and the Jews who had come along with her also weeping, he was deeply moved in spirit and troubled. 34"Where have you laid him?" he asked.

"Come and see, Lord," they replied.

35Jesus wept.

36Then the Jews said, "See how he loved him!"

37But some of them said, "Could not he who opened the eyes of the blind man have kept this man from dying?"

Jesus Raises Lazarus From the Dead

38Jesus, once more deeply moved, came to the tomb. It was a cave with a stone laid across the entrance. 39"Take away the stone," he said.

"But, Lord," said Martha, the sister of the dead man, "by this time there is a bad odour, for he has been there four days."

40Then Jesus said, "Did I not tell you that if you believed, you would see the glory of God?"

41So they took away the stone. Then Jesus looked up and said, "Father, I thank you that you have heard me. 42I knew that you always hear me, but I said this for the benefit of the people standing here, that they may believe that you sent me."

43When he had said this, Jesus called in a loud voice, "Lazarus, come out!" 44The dead man came out, his hands and feet wrapped with strips of linen, and a cloth around his face.

Jesus said to them, "Take off the grave clothes and let him go."

READING FROM PSALMS
Psalm 64:1–10

For the director of music. A psalm of
David.

1Hear me, O God, as I voice my
    complaint;
  protect my life from the threat of
    the enemy.
2Hide me from the conspiracy of the
    wicked,
  from that noisy crowd of evildoers.

3They sharpen their tongues like
    swords
  and aim their words like deadly
    arrows.
4They shoot from ambush at the
    innocent man;
  they shoot at him suddenly,
    without fear.

5They encourage each other in evil
    plans,
  they talk about hiding their snares;
  they say, "Who will see them?"

6They plot injustice and say,
  "We have devised a perfect plan!"
Surely the mind and heart of man
    are cunning.

7But God will shoot them with arrows;
  suddenly they will be struck down.
8He will turn their own tongues
    against them
  and bring them to ruin;

all who see them will shake their
    heads in scorn.

9All mankind will fear;
  they will proclaim the works of God
  and ponder what he has done.
10Let the righteous rejoice in the LORD
  and take refuge in him;
  let all the upright in heart praise
    him!

DAY 140   MAY 20

OLD TESTAMENT READING
1 Samuel 5:1–7:17

The Ark in Ashdod and Ekron

5 After the Philistines had captured
  the ark of God, they took it from
Ebenezer to Ashdod. 2Then they carried the ark into Dagon's temple and set
it beside Dagon. 3When the people of
Ashdod rose early the next day, there
was Dagon, fallen on his face on the
ground before the ark of the LORD!
They took Dagon and put him back in
his place. 4But the following morning
when they rose, there was Dagon, fallen
on his face on the ground before the ark
of the LORD! His head and hands had
been broken off and were lying on the
threshold; only his body remained.
5That is why to this day neither the
priests of Dagon nor any others who
enter Dagon's temple at Ashdod step
on the threshold.

6The LORD's hand was heavy upon
the people of Ashdod and its vicinity; he
brought devastation upon them and
afflicted them with tumours. 7When the
men of Ashdod saw what was happening, they said, "The ark of the god of
Israel must not stay here with us, because his hand is heavy upon us and
upon Dagon our god." 8So they called
together all the rulers of the Philistines
and asked them, "What shall we do with
the ark of the god of Israel?"

They answered, "Have the ark of the
god of Israel moved to Gath." So they
moved the ark of the God of Israel.

9But after they had moved it, the
LORD's hand was against that city,
throwing it into a great panic. He
afflicted the people of the city, both
young and old, with an outbreak of
tumours. 10So they sent the ark of God
to Ekron.

As the ark of God was entering
Ekron, the people of Ekron cried out,
"They have brought the ark of the god
of Israel round to us to kill us and our
people." 11So they called together all
the rulers of the Philistines and said,
"Send the ark of the god of Israel away;
let it go back to its own place, or it will
kill us and our people." For death had
filled the city with panic; God's hand
was very heavy upon it. 12Those who did
not die were afflicted with tumours, and
the outcry of the city went up to heaven.

The Ark Returned to Israel

6 When the ark of the LORD had
  been in Philistine territory for
seven months, 2the Philistines called for
the priests and the diviners and said,
"What shall we do with the ark of the
LORD? Tell us how we should send it
back to its place."

3They answered, "If you return the
ark of the god of Israel, do not send it

away empty, but by all means send a guilt offering to him. Then you will be healed, and you will know why his hand has not been lifted from you."

⁴The Philistines asked, "What guilt offering should we send to him?"

They replied, "Five gold tumours and five gold rats, according to the number of the Philistine rulers, because the same plague has struck both you and your rulers. ⁵Make models of the tumours and of the rats that are destroying the country, and pay honour to Israel's god. Perhaps he will lift his hand from you and your gods and your land. ⁶Why do you harden your hearts as the Egyptians and Pharaoh did? When he treated them harshly, did they not send the Israelites out so that they could go on their way?

⁷"Now then, get a new cart ready, with two cows that have calved and have never been yoked. Hitch the cows to the cart, but take their calves away and pen them up. ⁸Take the ark of the LORD and put it on the cart, and in a chest beside it put the gold objects you are sending back to him as a guilt offering. Send it on its way, ⁹but keep watching it. If it goes up to its own territory, towards Beth Shemesh, then the LORD has brought this great disaster on us. But if it does not, then we shall know that it was not his hand that struck us and that it happened to us by chance."

¹⁰So they did this. They took two such cows and hitched them to the cart and penned up their calves. ¹¹They placed the ark of the LORD on the cart and along with it the chest containing the gold rats and the models of the tumours. ¹²Then the cows went straight up towards Beth Shemesh, keeping on the road and lowing all the way; they did not turn to the right or to the left. The rulers of the Philistines followed them as far as the border of Beth Shemesh.

¹³Now the people of Beth Shemesh were harvesting their wheat in the valley, and when they looked up and saw the ark, they rejoiced at the sight. ¹⁴The cart came to the field of Joshua of Beth

Shemesh, and there it stopped beside a large rock. The people chopped up the wood of the cart and sacrificed the cows as a burnt offering to the LORD. ¹⁵The Levites took down the ark of the LORD, together with the chest containing the gold objects, and placed them on the large rock. On that day the people of Beth Shemesh offered burnt offerings and made sacrifices to the LORD. ¹⁶The five rulers of the Philistines saw all this and then returned that same day to Ekron.

¹⁷These are the gold tumours the Philistines sent as a guilt offering to the LORD—one each for Ashdod, Gaza, Ashkelon, Gath and Ekron. ¹⁸And the number of the gold rats was according to the number of Philistine towns belonging to the five rulers—the fortified towns with their country villages. The large rock, on which they set the ark of the LORD, is a witness to this day in the field of Joshua of Beth Shemesh.

¹⁹But God struck down some of the men of Beth Shemesh, putting seventy of them to death because they had looked into the ark of the LORD. The people mourned because of the heavy blow the LORD had dealt them, ²⁰and the men of Beth Shemesh asked, "Who can stand in the presence of the LORD, this holy God? To whom will the ark go up from here?"

²¹Then they sent messengers to the people of Kiriath Jearim, saying, "The Philistines have returned the ark of the LORD. Come down and take it up to your place." ¹So the men of Kiriath Jearim came and took up the ark of the LORD. They took it up to Abinadab's house on the hill and consecrated Eleazar his son to guard the ark of the LORD.

Samuel Subdues the Philistines at Mizpah

²It was a long time, twenty years in all, that the ark remained at Kiriath Jearim, and all the people of Israel mourned and sought after the LORD.

3And Samuel said to the whole house of Israel, "If you are returning to the LORD with all your hearts, then rid yourselves of the foreign gods and the Ashtoreths and commit yourselves to the LORD and serve him only, and he will deliver you out of the hand of the Philistines." 4So the Israelites put away their Baals and Ashtoreths, and served the LORD only.

5Then Samuel said, "Assemble all Israel at Mizpah and I will intercede with the LORD for you." 6When they had assembled at Mizpah, they drew water and poured it out before the LORD. On that day they fasted and there they confessed, "We have sinned against the LORD." And Samuel was leader of Israel at Mizpah.

7When the Philistines heard that Israel had assembled at Mizpah, the rulers of the Philistines came up to attack them. And when the Israelites heard of it, they were afraid because of the Philistines. 8They said to Samuel, "Do not stop crying out to the LORD our God for us, that he may rescue us from the hand of the Philistines." 9Then Samuel took a suckling lamb and offered it up as a whole burnt offering to the LORD. He cried out to the LORD on Israel's behalf, and the LORD answered him.

10While Samuel was sacrificing the burnt offering, the Philistines drew near to engage Israel in battle. But that day the LORD thundered with loud thunder against the Philistines and threw them into such a panic that they were routed before the Israelites. 11The men of Israel rushed out of Mizpah and pursued the Philistines, slaughtering them along the way to a point below Beth Car.

12Then Samuel took a stone and set it up between Mizpah and Shen. He named it Ebenezer, saying, "Thus far has the LORD helped us." 13So the Philistines were subdued and did not invade Israelite territory again.

Throughout Samuel's lifetime, the hand of the LORD was against the Philistines. 14The towns from Ekron to Gath that the Philistines had captured from Israel were restored to her, and Israel delivered the neighbouring territory from the power of the Philistines. And there was peace between Israel and the Amorites.

15Samuel continued as judge over Israel all the days of his life. 16From year to year he went on a circuit from Bethel to Gilgal to Mizpah, judging Israel in all those places. 17But he always went back to Ramah, where his home was, and there he also judged Israel. And he built an altar there to the LORD.

NEW TESTAMENT READING
John 11:45–12:11

The Plot to Kill Jesus

45Therefore many of the Jews who had come to visit Mary, and had seen what Jesus did, put their faith in him. 46But some of them went to the Pharisees and told them what Jesus had done. 47Then the chief priests and the Pharisees called a meeting of the Sanhedrin.

"What are we accomplishing?" they asked. "Here is this man performing many miraculous signs. 48If we let him go on like this, everyone will believe in him, and then the Romans will come and take away both our place and our nation."

49Then one of them, named Caiaphas, who was high priest that year, spoke up, "You know nothing at all! 50You do not realise that it is better for you that one man die for the people than that the whole nation perish."

51He did not say this on his own, but as high priest that year he prophesied that Jesus would die for the Jewish nation, 52and not only for that nation but also for the scattered children of God, to bring them together and make them one. 53So from that day on they plotted to take his life.

54Therefore Jesus no longer moved about publicly among the Jews. Instead he withdrew to a region near the desert, to a village called Ephraim, where he stayed with his disciples.

⁵⁵When it was almost time for the Jewish Passover, many went up from the country to Jerusalem for their ceremonial cleansing before the Passover. ⁵⁶They kept looking for Jesus, and as they stood in the temple area they asked one another, "What do you think? Isn't he coming to the Feast at all?" ⁵⁷But the chief priests and Pharisees had given orders that if anyone found out where Jesus was, he should report it so that they might arrest him.

Jesus Anointed at Bethany

12 Six days before the Passover, Jesus arrived at Bethany, where Lazarus lived, whom Jesus had raised from the dead. ²Here a dinner was given in Jesus' honour. Martha served, while Lazarus was among those reclining at the table with him. ³Then Mary took about a pint of pure nard, an expensive perfume; she poured it on Jesus' feet and wiped his feet with her hair. And the house was filled with the fragrance of the perfume.

⁴But one of his disciples, Judas Iscariot, who was later to betray him, objected, ⁵"Why wasn't this perfume sold and the money given to the poor? It was worth a year's wages." ⁶He did not say this because he cared about the poor but because he was a thief; as keeper of the money bag, he used to help himself to what was put into it.

⁷"Leave her alone," Jesus replied. "⌐It was intended⌐ that she should save this perfume for the day of my burial. ⁸You will always have the poor among you, but you will not always have me."

⁹Meanwhile a large crowd of Jews found out that Jesus was there and came, not only because of him but also to see Lazarus, whom he had raised from the dead. ¹⁰So the chief priests made plans to kill Lazarus as well, ¹¹for on account of him many of the Jews were going over to Jesus and putting their faith in him.

READING FROM PROVERBS
Proverbs 12:18–27

¹⁸Reckless words pierce like a sword,
    but the tongue of the wise brings
        healing.

¹⁹Truthful lips endure for ever,
    but a lying tongue lasts only a
        moment.

²⁰There is deceit in the hearts of those
        who plot evil,
    but joy for those who promote
        peace.

²¹No harm befalls the righteous,
    but the wicked have their fill of
        trouble.

²²The LORD detests lying lips,
    but he delights in men who are
        truthful.

²³A prudent man keeps his knowledge
        to himself,
    but the heart of fools blurts out
        folly.

²⁴Diligent hands will rule,
    but laziness ends in slave labour.

²⁵An anxious heart weighs a man
        down,
    but a kind word cheers him up.

²⁶A righteous man is cautious in
        friendship,
    but the way of the wicked leads
        them astray.

²⁷The lazy man does not roast his
        game,
    but the diligent man prizes his
        possessions.

OLD TESTAMENT READING
1 Samuel 8:1–10:8

Israel Asks for a King

8 When Samuel grew old, he appointed his sons as judges for Israel. 2The name of his firstborn was Joel and the name of his second was Abijah, and they served at Beersheba. 3But his sons did not walk in his ways. They turned aside after dishonest gain and accepted bribes and perverted justice.

4So all the elders of Israel gathered together and came to Samuel at Ramah. 5They said to him, "You are old, and your sons do not walk in your ways; now appoint a king to lead us, such as all the other nations have."

6But when they said, "Give us a king to lead us," this displeased Samuel; so he prayed to the LORD. 7And the LORD told him: "Listen to all that the people are saying to you; it is not you they have rejected, but they have rejected me as their king. 8As they have done from the day I brought them up out of Egypt until this day, forsaking me and serving other gods, so they are doing to you. 9Now listen to them; but warn them solemnly and let them know what the king who will reign over them will do."

10Samuel told all the words of the LORD to the people who were asking him for a king. 11He said, "This is what the king who will reign over you will do: He will take your sons and make them serve with his chariots and horses, and they will run in front of his chariots. 12Some he will assign to be commanders of thousands and commanders of fifties, and others to plough his ground and reap his harvest, and still others to make weapons of war and equipment for his chariots. 13He will take your daughters to be perfumers and cooks and bakers. 14He will take the best of your fields and vineyards and olive groves and give

them to his attendants. 15He will take a tenth of your grain and of your vintage and give it to his officials and attendants. 16Your menservants and maidservants and the best of your cattle and donkeys he will take for his own use. 17He will take a tenth of your flocks, and you yourselves will become his slaves. 18When that day comes, you will cry out for relief from the king you have chosen, and the LORD will not answer you in that day."

19But the people refused to listen to Samuel. "No!" they said. "We want a king over us. 20Then we shall be like all the other nations, with a king to lead us and to go out before us and fight our battles."

21When Samuel heard all that the people said, he repeated it before the LORD. 22The LORD answered, "Listen to them and give them a king."

Then Samuel said to the men of Israel, "Everyone is to go back to his town."

Samuel Anoints Saul

9 There was a Benjamite, a man of standing, whose name was Kish son of Abiel, the son of Zeror, the son of Becorath, the son of Aphiah of Benjamin. 2He had a son named Saul, an impressive young man without equal among the Israelites—a head taller than any of the others.

3Now the donkeys belonging to Saul's father Kish were lost, and Kish said to his son Saul, "Take one of the servants with you and go and look for the donkeys." 4So he passed through the hill country of Ephraim and through the area around Shalisha, but they did not find them. They went on into the district of Shaalim, but the donkeys were not there. Then he passed through the territory of Benjamin, but they did not find them.

5When they reached the district of

Zuph, Saul said to the servant who was with him, "Come, let's go back, or my father will stop thinking about the donkeys and start worrying about us."

6But the servant replied, "Look, in this town there is a man of God; he is highly respected, and everything he says comes true. Let's go there now. Perhaps he will tell us what way to take."

7Saul said to his servant, "If we go, what can we give the man? The food in our sacks is gone. We have no gift to take to the man of God. What do we have?"

8The servant answered him again. "Look," he said, "I have a quarter of a shekel of silver. I will give it to the man of God so that he will tell us what way to take." 9(Formerly in Israel, if a man went to enquire of God, he would say, "Come, let us go to the seer," because the prophet of today used to be called a seer.)

10"Good," Saul said to his servant. "Come, let's go." So they set out for the town where the man of God was.

11As they were going up the hill to the town, they met some girls coming out to draw water, and they asked them, "Is the seer here?"

12"He is," they answered. "He's ahead of you. Hurry now; he has just come to our town today, for the people have a sacrifice at the high place. 13As soon as you enter the town, you will find him before he goes up to the high place to eat. The people will not begin eating until he comes, because he must bless the sacrifice; afterwards, those who are invited will eat. Go up now; you should find him about this time."

14They went up to the town, and as they were entering it, there was Samuel, coming towards them on his way up to the high place.

15Now the day before Saul came, the LORD had revealed this to Samuel: 16"About this time tomorrow I will send you a man from the land of Benjamin. Anoint him leader over my people Israel; he will deliver my people from

the hand of the Philistines. I have looked upon my people, for their cry has reached me."

17When Samuel caught sight of Saul, the LORD said to him, "This is the man I spoke to you about; he will govern my people."

18Saul approached Samuel in the gateway and asked, "Would you please tell me where the seer's house is?"

19"I am the seer," Samuel replied. "Go up ahead of me to the high place, for today you are to eat with me, and in the morning I will let you go and will tell you all that is in your heart. 20As for the donkeys you lost three days ago, do not worry about them; they have been found. And to whom is all the desire of Israel turned, if not to you and all your father's family?"

21Saul answered, "But am I not a Benjamite, from the smallest tribe of Israel, and is not my clan the least of all the clans of the tribe of Benjamin? Why do you say such a thing to me?"

22Then Samuel brought Saul and his servant into the hall and seated them at the head of those who were invited —about thirty in number. 23Samuel said to the cook, "Bring the piece of meat I gave you, the one I told you to lay aside."

24So the cook took up the leg with what was on it and set it in front of Saul. Samuel said, "Here is what has been kept for you. Eat, because it was set aside for you for this occasion, from the time I said, 'I have invited guests.'" And Saul dined with Samuel that day.

25After they came down from the high place to the town, Samuel talked with Saul on the roof of his house. 26They rose about daybreak and Samuel called to Saul on the roof, "Get ready, and I will send you on your way." When Saul got ready, he and Samuel went outside together. 27As they were going down to the edge of the town, Samuel said to Saul, "Tell the servant to go on ahead of us"—and the servant did so —"but you stay here awhile, so that I may give you a message from God."

10 Then Samuel took a flask of oil and poured it on Saul's head and kissed him, saying, "Has not the LORD anointed you leader over his inheritance? ²When you leave me today, you will meet two men near Rachel's tomb, at Zelzah on the border of Benjamin. They will say to you, 'The donkeys you set out to look for have been found. And now your father has stopped thinking about them and is worried about you. He is asking, "What shall I do about my son?"'

³"Then you will go on from there until you reach the great tree of Tabor. Three men going up to God at Bethel will meet you there. One will be carrying three young goats, another three loaves of bread, and another a skin of wine. ⁴They will greet you and offer you two loaves of bread, which you will accept from them.

⁵"After that you will go to Gibeah of God, where there is a Philistine outpost. As you approach the town, you will meet a procession of prophets coming down from the high place with lyres, tambourines, flutes and harps being played before them, and they will be prophesying. ⁶The Spirit of the LORD will come upon you in power, and you will prophesy with them; and you will be changed into a different person. ⁷Once these signs are fulfilled, do whatever your hand finds to do, for God is with you.

⁸"Go down ahead of me to Gilgal. I will surely come down to you to sacrifice burnt offerings and fellowship offerings, but you must wait seven days until I come to you and tell you what you are to do."

NEW TESTAMENT READING
John 12:12–36

The Triumphal Entry

¹²The next day the great crowd that had come for the Feast heard that Jesus was on his way to Jerusalem. ¹³They took palm branches and went out to meet him, shouting,

"Hosanna!"

"Blessed is he who comes in the name of the Lord!"

"Blessed is the King of Israel!"

¹⁴Jesus found a young donkey and sat upon it, as it is written,

¹⁵"Do not be afraid, O Daughter of Zion;
   see, your king is coming,
   seated on a donkey's colt."

¹⁶At first his disciples did not understand all this. Only after Jesus was glorified did they realise that these things had been written about him and that they had done these things to him.

¹⁷Now the crowd that was with him when he called Lazarus from the tomb and raised him from the dead continued to spread the word. ¹⁸Many people, because they had heard that he had given this miraculous sign, went out to meet him. ¹⁹So the Pharisees said to one another, "See, this is getting us nowhere. Look how the whole world has gone after him!"

Jesus Predicts His Death

²⁰Now there were some Greeks among those who went up to worship at the Feast. ²¹They came to Philip, who was from Bethsaida in Galilee, with a request. "Sir," they said, "we would like to see Jesus." ²²Philip went to tell Andrew; Andrew and Philip in turn told Jesus.

²³Jesus replied, "The hour has come for the Son of Man to be glorified. ²⁴I tell you the truth, unless a grain of wheat falls to the ground and dies, it remains only a single seed. But if it dies, it produces many seeds. ²⁵The man who loves his life will lose it, while the man who hates his life in this world will keep

it for eternal life. ²⁶Whoever serves me must follow me; and where I am, my servant also will be. My Father will honour the one who serves me.

²⁷"Now my heart is troubled, and what shall I say? 'Father, save me from this hour'? No, it was for this very reason I came to this hour. ²⁸Father, glorify your name!"

Then a voice came from heaven, "I have glorified it, and will glorify it again." ²⁹The crowd that was there and heard it said it had thundered; others said an angel had spoken to him.

³⁰Jesus said, "This voice was for your benefit, not mine. ³¹Now is the time for judgment on this world; now the prince of this world will be driven out. ³²But I, when I am lifted up from the earth, will draw all men to myself." ³³He said this to show the kind of death he was going to die.

³⁴The crowd spoke up, "We have heard from the Law that the Christ will remain for ever, so how can you say, 'The Son of Man must be lifted up'? Who is this 'Son of Man'?"

³⁵Then Jesus told them, "You are going to have the light just a little while longer. Walk while you have the light, before darkness overtakes you. The man who walks in the dark does not know where he is going. ³⁶Put your trust in the light while you have it, so that you may become sons of light." When he had finished speaking, Jesus left and hid himself from them.

READING FROM PSALMS
Psalm 65:1–13

For the director of music. A psalm of David. A song.

¹Praise awaits you, O God, in Zion;
　to you our vows will be fulfilled.
²O you who hear prayer,
　to you all men will come.

³When we were overwhelmed by sins,
　you forgave our transgressions.
⁴Blessed are those you choose
　and bring near to live in your
　　courts!
We are filled with the good things of
　your house,
　of your holy temple.

⁵You answer us with awesome deeds
　of righteousness,
　O God our Saviour,
the hope of all the ends of the earth
　and of the farthest seas,
⁶who formed the mountains by your
　power,
　having armed yourself with
　　strength,
⁷who stilled the roaring of the seas,
　the roaring of their waves,
　and the turmoil of the nations.
⁸Those living far away fear your
　wonders;
　where morning dawns and evening
　　fades
　you call forth songs of joy.

⁹You care for the land and water it;
　you enrich it abundantly.
The streams of God are filled with
　water
　to provide the people with corn,
　for so you have ordained it.
¹⁰You drench its furrows
　and level its ridges;
　you soften it with showers
　and bless its crops.
¹¹You crown the year with your
　bounty,
　and your carts overflow with
　　abundance.
¹²The grasslands of the desert
　overflow;
　the hills are clothed with gladness.
¹³The meadows are covered with flocks
　and the valleys are mantled with
　　corn;
　they shout for joy and sing.

OLD TESTAMENT READING
1 Samuel 10:9–12:25

Saul Made King

⁹As Saul turned to leave Samuel, God changed Saul's heart, and all these signs were fulfilled that day. ¹⁰When they arrived at Gibeah, a procession of prophets met him; the Spirit of God came upon him in power, and he joined in their prophesying. ¹¹When all those who had formerly known him saw him prophesying with the prophets, they asked each other, "What is this that has happened to the son of Kish? Is Saul also among the prophets?"

¹²A man who lived there answered, "And who is their father?" So it became a saying: "Is Saul also among the prophets?" ¹³After Saul stopped prophesying, he went to the high place.

¹⁴Now Saul's uncle asked him and his servant, "Where have you been?"

"Looking for the donkeys," he said. "But when we saw they were not to be found, we went to Samuel."

¹⁵Saul's uncle said, "Tell me what Samuel said to you."

¹⁶Saul replied, "He assured us that the donkeys had been found." But he did not tell his uncle what Samuel had said about the kingship.

¹⁷Samuel summoned the people of Israel to the LORD at Mizpah ¹⁸and said to them, "This is what the LORD, the God of Israel, says: 'I brought Israel up out of Egypt, and I delivered you from the power of Egypt and all the kingdoms that oppressed you.' ¹⁹But you have now rejected your God, who saves you out of all your calamities and distresses. And you have said, 'No, set a king over us.' So now present yourselves before the LORD by your tribes and clans."

²⁰When Samuel brought all the tribes of Israel near, the tribe of Benjamin was chosen. ²¹Then he brought forward the tribe of Benjamin, clan by clan, and Matri's clan was chosen. Finally Saul son of Kish was chosen. But when they looked for him, he was not to be found. ²²So they enquired further of the LORD, "Has the man come here yet?"

And the LORD said, "Yes, he has hidden himself among the baggage."

²³They ran and brought him out, and as he stood among the people he was a head taller than any of the others. ²⁴Samuel said to all the people, "Do you see the man the LORD has chosen? There is no-one like him among all the people."

Then the people shouted, "Long live the king!"

²⁵Samuel explained to the people the regulations of the kingship. He wrote them down on a scroll and deposited it before the LORD. Then Samuel dismissed the people, each to his own home.

²⁶Saul also went to his home in Gibeah, accompanied by valiant men whose hearts God had touched. ²⁷But some troublemakers said, "How can this fellow save us?" They despised him and brought him no gifts. But Saul kept silent.

Saul Rescues the City of Jabesh

11 Nahash the Ammonite went up and besieged Jabesh Gilead. And all the men of Jabesh said to him, "Make a treaty with us, and we will be subject to you."

²But Nahash the Ammonite replied, "I will make a treaty with you only on the condition that I gouge out the right eye of every one of you and so bring disgrace on all Israel."

³The elders of Jabesh said to him, "Give us seven days so that we can send messengers throughout Israel; if no-one comes to rescue us, we will surrender to you."

[4]When the messengers came to Gibeah of Saul and reported these terms to the people, they all wept aloud. [5]Just then Saul was returning from the fields, behind his oxen, and he asked, "What is wrong with the people? Why are they weeping?" Then they repeated to him what the men of Jabesh had said.

[6]When Saul heard their words, the Spirit of God came upon him in power, and he burned with anger. [7]He took a pair of oxen, cut them into pieces, and sent the pieces by messengers throughout Israel, proclaiming, "This is what will be done to the oxen of anyone who does not follow Saul and Samuel." Then the terror of the LORD fell on the people, and they turned out as one man. [8]When Saul mustered them at Bezek, the men of Israel numbered three hundred thousand and the men of Judah thirty thousand.

[9]They told the messengers who had come, "Say to the men of Jabesh Gilead, 'By the time the sun is hot tomorrow, you will be delivered.'" When the messengers went and reported this to the men of Jabesh, they were elated. [10]They said to the Ammonites, "Tomorrow we will surrender to you, and you can do to us whatever seems good to you."

[11]The next day Saul separated his men into three divisions; during the last watch of the night they broke into the camp of the Ammonites and slaughtered them until the heat of the day. Those who survived were scattered, so that no two of them were left together.

Saul Confirmed as King

[12]The people then said to Samuel, "Who was it that asked, 'Shall Saul reign over us?' Bring these men to us and we will put them to death." [13]But Saul said, "No-one shall be put to death today, for this day the LORD has rescued Israel." [14]Then Samuel said to the people, "Come, let us go to Gilgal and there

reaffirm the kingship." [15]So all the people went to Gilgal and confirmed Saul as king in the presence of the LORD. There they sacrificed fellowship offerings before the LORD, and Saul and all the Israelites held a great celebration.

Samuel's Farewell Speech

12 Samuel said to all Israel, "I have listened to everything you said to me and have set a king over you. [2]Now you have a king as your leader. As for me, I am old and grey, and my sons are here with you. I have been your leader from my youth until now. [3]Here I stand. Testify against me in the presence of the LORD and his anointed. Whose ox have I taken? Whose donkey have I taken? Whom have I cheated? Whom have I oppressed? From whose hand have I accepted a bribe to make me shut my eyes? If I have done any of these, I will make it right."

[4]"You have not cheated or oppressed us," they replied. "You have not taken anything from anyone's hand."

[5]Samuel said to them, "The LORD is witness against you, and also his anointed is witness this day, that you have not found anything in my hand."

"He is witness," they said.

[6]Then Samuel said to the people, "It is the LORD who appointed Moses and Aaron and brought your forefathers up out of Egypt. [7]Now then, stand here, because I am going to confront you with evidence before the LORD as to all the righteous acts performed by the LORD for you and your fathers.

[8]"After Jacob entered Egypt, they cried to the LORD for help, and the LORD sent Moses and Aaron, who brought your forefathers out of Egypt and settled them in this place.

[9]"But they forgot the LORD their God; so he sold them into the hands of Sisera, the commander of the army of Hazor, and into the hands of the Philistines and the king of Moab, who fought against them. [10]They cried out to the LORD and said, 'We have sinned; we

have forsaken the LORD and served the Baals and the Ashtoreths. But now deliver us from the hands of our enemies, and we will serve you.' [11]Then the LORD sent Jerub-Baal, Barak, Jephthah and Samuel, and he delivered you from the hands of your enemies on every side, so that you lived securely.

[12]"But when you saw that Nahash king of the Ammonites was moving against you, you said to me, 'No, we want a king to rule over us'—even though the LORD your God was your king. [13]Now here is the king you have chosen, the one you asked for; see, the LORD has set a king over you. [14]If you fear the LORD and serve and obey him and do not rebel against his commands, and if both you and the king who reigns over you follow the LORD your God —good! [15]But if you do not obey the LORD, and if you rebel against his commands, his hand will be against you, as it was against your fathers.

[16]"Now then, stand still and see this great thing the LORD is about to do before your eyes! [17]Is it not wheat harvest now? I will call upon the LORD to send thunder and rain. And you will realise what an evil thing you did in the eyes of the LORD when you asked for a king."

[18]Then Samuel called upon the LORD, and that same day the LORD sent thunder and rain. So all the people stood in awe of the LORD and of Samuel.

[19]The people all said to Samuel, "Pray to the LORD your God for your servants so that we will not die, for we have added to all our other sins the evil of asking for a king."

[20]"Do not be afraid," Samuel replied. "You have done all this evil; yet do not turn away from the LORD, but serve the LORD with all your heart. [21]Do not turn away after useless idols. They can do you no good, nor can they rescue you, because they are useless. [22]For the sake of his great name the LORD will not reject his people, because the LORD was pleased to make you his own. [23]As for me, far be it from me that I should sin

against the LORD by failing to pray for you. And I will teach you the way that is good and right. [24]But be sure to fear the LORD and serve him faithfully with all your heart; consider what great things he has done for you. [25]Yet if you persist in doing evil, both you and your king will be swept away."

NEW TESTAMENT READING
John 12:37–13:17

The Jews Continue in Their Unbelief

[37]Even after Jesus had done all these miraculous signs in their presence, they still would not believe in him. [38]This was to fulfil the word of Isaiah the prophet:

"Lord, who has believed our message
  and to whom has the arm of the
    Lord been revealed?"

[39]For this reason they could not believe, because, as Isaiah says elsewhere:

[40]"He has blinded their eyes
  and deadened their hearts,
so they can neither see with their
    eyes,
  nor understand with their hearts,
  nor turn—and I would heal them."

[41]Isaiah said this because he saw Jesus' glory and spoke about him.

[42]Yet at the same time many even among the leaders believed in him. But because of the Pharisees they would not confess their faith for fear they would be put out of the synagogue; [43]for they loved praise from men more than praise from God.

[44]Then Jesus cried out, "When a man believes in me, he does not believe in me only, but in the one who sent me. [45]When he looks at me, he sees the one who sent me. [46]I have come into the world as a light, so that no-one who believes in me should stay in darkness.

[47]"As for the person who hears my

words but does not keep them, I do not judge him. For I did not come to judge the world, but to save it. 48There is a judge for the one who rejects me and does not accept my words; that very word which I spoke will condemn him at the last day. 49For I did not speak of my own accord, but the Father who sent me commanded me what to say and how to say it. 50I know that his command leads to eternal life. So whatever I say is just what the Father has told me to say.''

Jesus Washes His Disciples' Feet

13 It was just before the Passover Feast. Jesus knew that the time had come for him to leave this world and go to the Father. Having loved his own who were in the world, he now showed them the full extent of his love.

2The evening meal was being served, and the devil had already prompted Judas Iscariot, son of Simon, to betray Jesus. 3Jesus knew that the Father had put all things under his power, and that he had come from God and was returning to God; 4so he got up from the meal, took off his outer clothing, and wrapped a towel round his waist. 5After that, he poured water into a basin and began to wash his disciples' feet, drying them with the towel that was wrapped round him.

6He came to Simon Peter, who said to him, "Lord, are you going to wash my feet?"

7Jesus replied, "You do not realise now what I am doing, but later you will understand."

8"No," said Peter, "you shall never wash my feet."

Jesus answered, "Unless I wash you, you have no part with me."

9"Then, Lord," Simon Peter replied, "not just my feet but my hands and my head as well!"

10Jesus answered, "A person who has had a bath needs only to wash his feet; his whole body is clean. And you are clean, though not every one of you." 11For he knew who was going to betray

him, and that was why he said not every one was clean.

12When he had finished washing their feet, he put on his clothes and returned to his place. "Do you understand what I have done for you?" he asked them. 13"You call me 'Teacher' and 'Lord', and rightly so, for that is what I am. 14Now that I, your Lord and Teacher, have washed your feet, you also should wash one another's feet. 15I have set you an example that you should do as I have done for you. 16I tell you the truth, no servant is greater than his master, nor is a messenger greater than the one who sent him. 17Now that you know these things, you will be blessed if you do them.

READING FROM PSALMS
Psalm 66:1–12

For the director of music. A song. A psalm.

1Shout with joy to God, all the earth!
2   Sing the glory of his name;
    make his praise glorious!
3Say to God, "How awesome are your deeds!
  So great is your power
    that your enemies cringe before you.
4All the earth bows down to you;
  they sing praise to you,
  they sing praise to your name."
             Selah

5Come and see what God has done,
  how awesome his works on man's behalf!
6He turned the sea into dry land,
  they passed through the waters on foot—
  come, let us rejoice in him.
7He rules for ever by his power,
  his eyes watch the nations—
  let not the rebellious rise up
    against him.   *Selah*

8Praise our God, O peoples,
     let the sound of his praise be
          heard;
9he has preserved our lives
     and kept our feet from slipping.
10For you, O God, tested us;
     you refined us like silver.

11You brought us into prison
     and laid burdens on our backs.
12You let men ride over our heads;
     we went through fire and
          water,
     but you brought us to a place of
          abundance.

DAY 143   # MAY 23

OLD TESTAMENT READING
1 Samuel 13:1–14:23

Samuel Rebukes Saul

13 Saul was ⌊thirty⌋ years old when he became king, and he reigned over Israel for ⌊forty-⌋two years.

2Saul chose three thousand men from Israel; two thousand were with him at Michmash and in the hill country of Bethel, and a thousand were with Jonathan at Gibeah in Benjamin. The rest of the men he sent back to their homes.

3Jonathan attacked the Philistine outpost at Geba, and the Philistines heard about it. Then Saul had the trumpet blown throughout the land and said, "Let the Hebrews hear!" 4So all Israel heard the news: "Saul has attacked the Philistine outpost, and now Israel has become an offence to the Philistines." And the people were summoned to join Saul at Gilgal.

5The Philistines assembled to fight Israel, with three thousand chariots, six thousand charioteers, and soldiers as numerous as the sand on the seashore. They went up and camped at Michmash, east of Beth Aven. 6When the men of Israel saw that their situation was critical and that their army was hard pressed, they hid in caves and thickets, among the rocks, and in pits and cisterns. 7Some Hebrews even crossed the Jordan to the land of Gad and Gilead.

Saul remained at Gilgal, and all the troops with him were quaking with fear. 8He waited for seven days, the time set by Samuel; but Samuel did not come to Gilgal, and Saul's men began to scatter. 9So he said, "Bring me the burnt offering and the fellowship offerings." And Saul offered up the burnt offering. 10Just as he finished making the offering, Samuel arrived, and Saul went out to greet him.

11"What have you done?" asked Samuel.

Saul replied, "When I saw that the men were scattering, and that you did not come at the set time, and that the Philistines were assembling at Michmash, 12I thought, 'Now the Philistines will come down against me at Gilgal, and I have not sought the LORD's favour.' So I felt compelled to offer the burnt offering."

13"You acted foolishly," Samuel said. "You have not kept the command the LORD your God gave you; if you had, he would have established your kingdom over Israel for all time. 14But now your kingdom will not endure; the LORD has sought out a man after his own heart and appointed him leader of his people, because you have not kept the LORD's command."

15Then Samuel left Gilgal and went up to Gibeah in Benjamin, and Saul counted the men who were with him. They numbered about six hundred.

Israel Without Weapons

¹⁶Saul and his son Jonathan and the men with them were staying in Gibeah of Benjamin, while the Philistines camped at Michmash. ¹⁷Raiding parties went out from the Philistine camp in three detachments. One turned towards Ophrah in the vicinity of Shual, ¹⁸another towards Beth Horon, and the third towards the borderland overlooking the Valley of Zeboim facing the desert.

¹⁹Not a blacksmith could be found in the whole land of Israel, because the Philistines had said, "Otherwise the Hebrews will make swords or spears!" ²⁰So all Israel went down to the Philistines to have their ploughshares, mattocks, axes and sickles sharpened. ²¹The price was two thirds of a shekel for sharpening ploughshares and mattocks, and a third of a shekel for sharpening forks and axes and for repointing goads.

²²So on the day of the battle not a soldier with Saul and Jonathan had a sword or spear in his hand; only Saul and his son Jonathan had them.

Jonathan Attacks the Philistines

²³Now a detachment of Philistines had gone out to the pass at Michmash.

14 ¹One day Jonathan son of Saul said to the young man bearing his armour, "Come, let's go over to the Philistine outpost on the other side." But he did not tell his father.

²Saul was staying on the outskirts of Gibeah under a pomegranate tree in Migron. With him were about six hundred men, ³among whom was Ahijah, who was wearing an ephod. He was a son of Ichabod's brother Ahitub son of Phinehas, the son of Eli, the LORD's priest in Shiloh. No-one was aware that Jonathan had left.

⁴On each side of the pass that Jonathan intended to cross to reach the Philistine outpost was a cliff; the one was called Bozez, and the other Seneh. ⁵One cliff stood to the north towards Michmash, the other to the south towards Geba.

⁶Jonathan said to his young armour-bearer, "Come, let's go over to the outpost of those uncircumcised fellows. Perhaps the LORD will act on our behalf. Nothing can hinder the LORD from saving, whether by many or by few."

⁷"Do all that you have in mind," his armour-bearer said. "Go ahead; I am with you heart and soul."

⁸Jonathan said, "Come, then; we will cross over towards the men and let them see us. ⁹If they say to us, 'Wait there until we come to you,' we will stay where we are and not go up to them. ¹⁰But if they say, 'Come up to us,' we will climb up, because that will be our sign that the LORD has given them into our hands."

¹¹So both of them showed themselves to the Philistine outpost. "Look!" said the Philistines. "The Hebrews are crawling out of the holes they were hiding in." ¹²The men of the outpost shouted to Jonathan and his armour-bearer, "Come up to us and we'll teach you a lesson."

So Jonathan said to his armour-bearer, "Climb up after me; the LORD has given them into the hand of Israel."

¹³Jonathan climbed up, using his hands and feet, with his armour-bearer right behind him. The Philistines fell before Jonathan, and his armour-bearer followed and killed behind him. ¹⁴In that first attack Jonathan and his armour-bearer killed some twenty men in an area of about half an acre.

Israel Routs the Philistines

¹⁵Then panic struck the whole army —those in the camp and field, and those in the outposts and raiding parties— and the ground shook. It was a panic sent by God.

¹⁶Saul's lookouts at Gibeah in Benjamin saw the army melting away in all directions. ¹⁷Then Saul said to the men who were with him, "Muster the forces

and see who has left us.'' When they did, it was Jonathan and his armour-bearer who were not there.

18Saul said to Ahijah, ''Bring the ark of God.'' (At that time it was with the Israelites.) 19While Saul was talking to the priest, the tumult in the Philistine camp increased more and more. So Saul said to the priest, ''Withdraw your hand.''

20Then Saul and all his men assembled and went to the battle. They found the Philistines in total confusion, striking each other with their swords. 21Those Hebrews who had previously been with the Philistines and had gone up with them to their camp went over to the Israelites who were with Saul and Jonathan. 22When all the Israelites who had hidden in the hill country of Ephraim heard that the Philistines were on the run, they joined the battle in hot pursuit. 23So the LORD rescued Israel that day, and the battle moved on beyond Beth Aven.

NEW TESTAMENT READING
John 13:18–38

Jesus Predicts His Betrayal

18''I am not referring to all of you; I know those I have chosen. But this is to fulfil the scripture: 'He who shares my bread has lifted up his heel against me.'

19''I am telling you now before it happens, so that when it does happen you will believe that I am He. 20I tell you the truth, whoever accepts anyone I send accepts me; and whoever accepts me accepts the one who sent me.''

21After he had said this, Jesus was troubled in spirit and testified, ''I tell you the truth, one of you is going to betray me.''

22His disciples stared at one another, at a loss to know which of them he meant. 23One of them, the disciple whom Jesus loved, was reclining next to him. 24Simon Peter motioned to this disciple and said, ''Ask him which one he means.''

25Leaning back against Jesus, he asked him, ''Lord, who is it?''

26Jesus answered, ''It is the one to whom I will give this piece of bread when I have dipped it in the dish.'' Then, dipping the piece of bread, he gave it to Judas Iscariot, son of Simon. 27As soon as Judas took the bread, Satan entered into him.

''What you are about to do, do quickly,'' Jesus told him, 28but no-one at the meal understood why Jesus said this to him. 29Since Judas had charge of the money, some thought Jesus was telling him to buy what was needed for the Feast, or to give something to the poor. 30As soon as Judas had taken the bread, he went out. And it was night.

Jesus Predicts Peter's Denial

31When he was gone, Jesus said, ''Now is the Son of Man glorified and God is glorified in him. 32If God is glorified in him, God will glorify the Son in himself, and will glorify him at once.

33''My children, I will be with you only a little longer. You will look for me, and just as I told the Jews, so I tell you now: Where I am going, you cannot come.

34''A new command I give you: Love one another. As I have loved you, so you must love one another. 35By this all men will know that you are my disciples, if you love one another.''

36Simon Peter asked him, ''Lord, where are you going?''

Jesus replied, ''Where I am going, you cannot follow now, but you will follow later.''

37Peter asked, ''Lord, why can't I follow now? I will lay down my life for you.''

38Then Jesus answered, ''Will you really lay down your life for me? I tell you the truth, before the cock crows, you will disown me three times!

READING FROM PSALMS
Psalm 66:13–20

13I will come to your temple with burnt
     offerings
   and fulfil my vows to you—
14vows my lips promised and my mouth
     spoke
   when I was in trouble.
15I will sacrifice fat animals to you
   and an offering of rams;
   I will offer bulls and goats.   *Selah*

16Come and listen, all you who fear
     God;
   let me tell you what he has done for
     me.
17I cried out to him with my mouth;
   his praise was on my tongue.
18If I had cherished sin in my heart,
   the Lord would not have listened;
19but God has surely listened
   and heard my voice in prayer.
20Praise be to God,
   who has not rejected my prayer
   or withheld his love from me!

MAY 24   DAY 144

OLD TESTAMENT READING
1 Samuel 14:24–15:35

Jonathan Eats Honey

24Now the men of Israel were in distress that day, because Saul had bound
the people under an oath, saying,
"Cursed be any man who eats food
before evening comes, before I have
avenged myself on my enemies!" So
none of the troops tasted food.

25The entire army entered the woods,
and there was honey on the ground.
26When they went into the woods, they
saw the honey oozing out, yet no-one
put his hand to his mouth, because they
feared the oath. 27But Jonathan had not
heard that his father had bound the
people with the oath, so he reached out
the end of the staff that was in his hand
and dipped it into the honeycomb. He
raised his hand to his mouth, and his
eyes brightened. 28Then one of the soldiers told him, "Your father bound the
army under a strict oath, saying,
'Cursed be any man who eats food today!' That is why the men are faint."

29Jonathan said, "My father has
made trouble for the country. See how
my eyes brightened when I tasted a little
of this honey. 30How much better it

would have been if the men had eaten
today some of the plunder they took
from their enemies. Would not the
slaughter of the Philistines have been
even greater?"

31That day, after the Israelites had
struck down the Philistines from Michmash to Aijalon, they were exhausted.
32They pounced on the plunder and,
taking sheep, cattle and calves, they
butchered them on the ground and ate
them, together with the blood. 33Then
someone said to Saul, "Look, the men
are sinning against the Lord by eating
meat that has blood in it."

"You have broken faith," he said.
"Roll a large stone over here at once."
34Then he said, "Go out among the men
and tell them, 'Each of you bring me
your cattle and sheep, and slaughter
them here and eat them. Do not sin
against the Lord by eating meat with
blood still in it.'"

So everyone brought his ox that night
and slaughtered it there. 35Then Saul
built an altar to the Lord; it was the first
time he had done this.

36Saul said, "Let us go down after the
Philistines by night and plunder them
till dawn, and let us not leave one of
them alive."

"Do whatever seems best to you," they replied.

But the priest said, "Let us enquire of God here."

37So Saul asked God, "Shall I go down after the Philistines? Will you give them into Israel's hand?" But God did not answer him that day.

38Saul therefore said, "Come here, all you who are leaders of the army, and let us find out what sin has been committed today. 39As surely as the LORD who rescues Israel lives, even if it lies with my son Jonathan, he must die." But not one of the men said a word.

40Saul then said to all the Israelites, "You stand over there; I and Jonathan my son will stand over here."

"Do what seems best to you," the men replied.

41Then Saul prayed to the LORD, the God of Israel, "Give me the right answer." And Jonathan and Saul were taken by lot, and the men were cleared.

42Saul said, "Cast the lot between me and Jonathan my son." And Jonathan was taken.

43Then Saul said to Jonathan, "Tell me what you have done."

So Jonathan told him, "I merely tasted a little honey with the end of my staff. And now must I die?"

44Saul said, "May God deal with me, be it ever so severely, if you do not die, Jonathan."

45But the men said to Saul, "Should Jonathan die—he who has brought about this great deliverance in Israel? Never! As surely as the LORD lives, not a hair of his head shall fall to the ground, for he did this today with God's help." So the men rescued Jonathan, and he was not put to death.

46Then Saul stopped pursuing the Philistines, and they withdrew to their own land.

47After Saul had assumed rule over Israel, he fought against their enemies on every side: Moab, the Ammonites, Edom, the kings of Zobah, and the Philistines. Wherever he turned, he inflicted punishment on them. 48He fought valiantly and defeated the Amalekites, delivering Israel from the hands of those who had plundered them.

Saul's Family

49Saul's sons were Jonathan, Ishvi and Malki-Shua. The name of his older daughter was Merab, and that of the younger was Michal. 50His wife's name was Ahinoam daughter of Ahimaaz. The name of the commander of Saul's army was Abner son of Ner, and Ner was Saul's uncle. 51Saul's father Kish and Abner's father Ner were sons of Abiel.

52All the days of Saul there was bitter war with the Philistines, and whenever Saul saw a mighty or brave man, he took him into his service.

The LORD Rejects Saul as King

15 Samuel said to Saul, "I am the one the LORD sent to anoint you king over his people Israel; so listen now to the message from the LORD. 2This is what the LORD Almighty says: 'I will punish the Amalekites for what they did to Israel when they waylaid them as they came up from Egypt. 3Now go, attack the Amalekites and totally destroy everything that belongs to them. Do not spare them; put to death men and women, children and infants, cattle and sheep, camels and donkeys.'"

4So Saul summoned the men and mustered them at Telaim—two hundred thousand foot soldiers and ten thousand men from Judah. 5Saul went to the city of Amalek and set an ambush in the ravine. 6Then he said to the Kenites, "Go away, leave the Amalekites so that I do not destroy you along with them; for you showed kindness to all the Israelites when they came up out of Egypt." So the Kenites moved away from the Amalekites.

7Then Saul attacked the Amalekites

all the way from Havilah to Shur, to the east of Egypt. [8]He took Agag king of the Amalekites alive, and all his people he totally destroyed with the sword. [9]But Saul and the army spared Agag and the best of the sheep and cattle, the fat calves and lambs—everything that was good. These they were unwilling to destroy completely, but everything that was despised and weak they totally destroyed.

[10]Then the word of the LORD came to Samuel: [11]"I am grieved that I have made Saul king, because he has turned away from me and has not carried out my instructions." Samuel was troubled, and he cried out to the LORD all that night.

[12]Early in the morning Samuel got up and went to meet Saul, but he was told, "Saul has gone to Carmel. There he has set up a monument in his own honour and has turned and gone on down to Gilgal."

[13]When Samuel reached him, Saul said, "The LORD bless you! I have carried out the LORD's instructions."

[14]But Samuel said, "What then is this bleating of sheep in my ears? What is this lowing of cattle that I hear?"

[15]Saul answered, "The soldiers brought them from the Amalekites; they spared the best of the sheep and cattle to sacrifice to the LORD your God, but we totally destroyed the rest."

[16]"Stop!" Samuel said to Saul. "Let me tell you what the LORD said to me last night."

"Tell me," Saul replied.

[17]Samuel said, "Although you were once small in your own eyes, did you not become the head of the tribes of Israel? The LORD anointed you king over Israel. [18]And he sent you on a mission, saying, 'Go and completely destroy those wicked people, the Amalekites; make war on them until you have wiped them out.' [19]Why did you not obey the LORD? Why did you pounce on the plunder and do evil in the eyes of the LORD?"

[20]"But I did obey the LORD," Saul said. "I went on the mission the LORD assigned me. I completely destroyed the Amalekites and brought back Agag their king. [21]The soldiers took sheep and cattle from the plunder, the best of what was devoted to God, in order to sacrifice them to the LORD your God at Gilgal."

[22]But Samuel replied:

"Does the LORD delight in burnt
     offerings and sacrifices
  as much as in obeying the voice of
     the LORD?
To obey is better than sacrifice,
  and to heed is better than the fat of
     rams.
[23]For rebellion is like the sin of
     divination,
  and arrogance like the evil of
     idolatry.
Because you have rejected the word
     of the LORD,
  he has rejected you as king."

[24]Then Saul said to Samuel, "I have sinned. I violated the LORD's command and your instructions. I was afraid of the people and so I gave in to them. [25]Now I beg you, forgive my sin and come back with me, so that I may worship the LORD."

[26]But Samuel said to him, "I will not go back with you. You have rejected the word of the LORD, and the LORD has rejected you as king over Israel!"

[27]As Samuel turned to leave, Saul caught hold of the hem of his robe, and it tore. [28]Samuel said to him, "The LORD has torn the kingdom of Israel from you today and has given it to one of your neighbours—to one better than you. [29]He who is the Glory of Israel does not lie or change his mind; for he is not a man, that he should change his mind."

[30]Saul replied, "I have sinned. But please honour me before the elders of my people and before Israel; come back with me, so that I may worship the LORD your God." [31]So Samuel went

back with Saul, and Saul worshipped the LORD.

32Then Samuel said, "Bring me Agag king of the Amalekites."

Agag came to him confidently, thinking, "Surely the bitterness of death is past."

33But Samuel said,

"As your sword has made women
        childless,
    so will your mother be childless
        among women."

And Samuel put Agag to death before the LORD at Gilgal.

34Then Samuel left for Ramah, but Saul went up to his home in Gibeah of Saul. 35Until the day Samuel died, he did not go to see Saul again, though Samuel mourned for him. And the LORD was grieved that he had made Saul king over Israel.

NEW TESTAMENT READING
John 14:1–31

Jesus Comforts His Disciples

14 "Do not let your hearts be troubled. Trust in God; trust also in me. 2In my Father's house are many rooms; if it were not so, I would have told you. I am going there to prepare a place for you. 3And if I go and prepare a place for you, I will come back and take you to be with me that you also may be where I am. 4You know the way to the place where I am going."

Jesus the Way to the Father

5Thomas said to him, "Lord, we don't know where you are going, so how can we know the way?"

6Jesus answered, "I am the way and the truth and the life. No-one comes to the Father except through me. 7If you really knew me, you would know my Father as well. From now on, you do know him and have seen him."

8Philip said, "Lord, show us the Father and that will be enough for us."

9Jesus answered: "Don't you know me, Philip, even after I have been among you such a long time? Anyone who has seen me has seen the Father. How can you say, 'Show us the Father'? 10Don't you believe that I am in the Father, and that the Father is in me? The words I say to you are not just my own. Rather, it is the Father, living in me, who is doing his work. 11Believe me when I say that I am in the Father and the Father is in me; or at least believe on the evidence of the miracles themselves. 12I tell you the truth, anyone who has faith in me will do what I have been doing. He will do even greater things than these, because I am going to the Father. 13And I will do whatever you ask in my name, so that the Son may bring glory to the Father. 14You may ask me for anything in my name, and I will do it.

Jesus Promises the Holy Spirit

15"If you love me, you will obey what I command. 16And I will ask the Father, and he will give you another Counsellor to be with you for ever—17the Spirit of truth. The world cannot accept him, because it neither sees him nor knows him. But you know him, for he lives with you and will be in you. 18I will not leave you as orphans; I will come to you. 19Before long, the world will not see me any more, but you will see me. Because I live, you also will live. 20On that day you will realise that I am in my Father, and you are in me, and I am in you. 21Whoever has my commands and obeys them, he is the one who loves me. He who loves me will be loved by my Father, and I too will love him and show myself to him."

22Then Judas (not Judas Iscariot) said, "But, Lord, why do you intend to show yourself to us and not to the world?"

²³Jesus replied, "If anyone loves me, he will obey my teaching. My Father will love him, and we will come to him and make our home with him. ²⁴He who does not love me will not obey my teaching. These words you hear are not my own; they belong to the Father who sent me.

²⁵"All this I have spoken while still with you. ²⁶But the Counsellor, the Holy Spirit, whom the Father will send in my name, will teach you all things and will remind you of everything I have said to you. ²⁷Peace I leave with you; my peace I give you. I do not give to you as the world gives. Do not let your hearts be troubled and do not be afraid.

²⁸"You heard me say, 'I am going away and I am coming back to you.' If you loved me, you would be glad that I am going to the Father, for the Father is greater than I. ²⁹I have told you now before it happens, so that when it does happen you will believe. ³⁰I will not speak with you much longer, for the prince of this world is coming. He has no hold on me, ³¹but the world must learn that I love the Father and that I do exactly what my Father has commanded me.

"Come now; let us leave.

READING FROM PROVERBS
Proverbs 12:28–13:9

²⁸In the way of righteousness there is
  life;
    along that path is immortality.

13 A wise son heeds his father's
  instruction,
    but a mocker does not listen to
      rebuke.

²From the fruit of his lips a man
    enjoys good things,
  but the unfaithful have a craving
    for violence.

³He who guards his lips guards his life,
  but he who speaks rashly will come
    to ruin.

⁴The sluggard craves and gets nothing,
  but the desires of the diligent are
    fully satisfied.

⁵The righteous hate what is false,
  but the wicked bring shame and
    disgrace.

⁶Righteousness guards the man of
    integrity,
  but wickedness overthrows the
    sinner.

⁷One man pretends to be rich, yet has
    nothing;
  another pretends to be poor, yet
    has great wealth.

⁸A man's riches may ransom his life,
  but a poor man hears no threat.

⁹The light of the righteous shines
    brightly,
  but the lamp of the wicked is
    snuffed out.

OLD TESTAMENT READING
1 Samuel 16:1–17:37

Samuel Anoints David

16 The LORD said to Samuel, "How long will you mourn for Saul, since I have rejected him as king over Israel? Fill your horn with oil and be on your way; I am sending you to Jesse of Bethlehem. I have chosen one of his sons to be king."

²But Samuel said, "How can I go? Saul will hear about it and kill me."

The LORD said, "Take a heifer with you and say, 'I have come to sacrifice to the LORD.' ³Invite Jesse to the sacrifice, and I will show you what to do. You are to anoint for me the one I indicate."

⁴Samuel did what the LORD said. When he arrived at Bethlehem, the elders of the town trembled when they met him. They asked, "Do you come in peace?"

⁵Samuel replied, "Yes, in peace; I have come to sacrifice to the LORD. Consecrate yourselves and come to the sacrifice with me." Then he consecrated Jesse and his sons and invited them to the sacrifice.

⁶When they arrived, Samuel saw Eliab and thought, "Surely the LORD's anointed stands here before the LORD."

⁷But the LORD said to Samuel, "Do not consider his appearance or his height, for I have rejected him. The LORD does not look at the things man looks at. Man looks at the outward appearance, but the LORD looks at the heart."

⁸Then Jesse called Abinadab and made him pass in front of Samuel. But Samuel said, "The LORD has not chosen this one either." ⁹Jesse then made Shammah pass by, but Samuel said, "Nor has the LORD chosen this one." ¹⁰Jesse made seven of his sons pass before Samuel, but Samuel said to him, "The LORD has not chosen these." ¹¹So he asked Jesse, "Are these all the sons you have?"

"There is still the youngest," Jesse answered, "but he is tending the sheep."

Samuel said, "Send for him; we will not sit down until he arrives."

¹²So he sent and had him brought in. He was ruddy, with a fine appearance and handsome features.

Then the LORD said, "Rise and anoint him; he is the one."

¹³So Samuel took the horn of oil and anointed him in the presence of his brothers, and from that day on the Spirit of the LORD came upon David in power. Samuel then went to Ramah.

David in Saul's Service

¹⁴Now the Spirit of the LORD had departed from Saul, and an evil spirit from the LORD tormented him.

¹⁵Saul's attendants said to him, "See, an evil spirit from God is tormenting you. ¹⁶Let our lord command his servants here to search for someone who can play the harp. He will play when the evil spirit from God comes upon you, and you will feel better."

¹⁷So Saul said to his attendants, "Find someone who plays well and bring him to me."

¹⁸One of the servants answered, "I have seen a son of Jesse of Bethlehem who knows how to play the harp. He is a brave man and a warrior. He speaks well and is a fine-looking man. And the LORD is with him."

¹⁹Then Saul sent messengers to Jesse and said, "Send me your son David, who is with the sheep." ²⁰So Jesse took a donkey loaded with bread, a skin of wine and a young goat and sent them with his son David to Saul.

²¹David came to Saul and entered his service. Saul liked him very much, and

David became one of his armour-bearers. 22Then Saul sent word to Jesse, saying, "Allow David to remain in my service, for I am pleased with him."

23Whenever the spirit from God came upon Saul, David would take his harp and play. Then relief would come to Saul; he would feel better, and the evil spirit would leave him.

David and Goliath

17 Now the Philistines gathered their forces for war and assembled at Socoh in Judah. They pitched camp at Ephes Dammim, between Socoh and Azekah. 2Saul and the Israelites assembled and camped in the Valley of Elah and drew up their battle line to meet the Philistines. 3The Philistines occupied one hill and the Israelites another, with the valley between them.

4A champion named Goliath, who was from Gath, came out of the Philistine camp. He was over nine feet tall. 5He had a bronze helmet on his head and wore a coat of scale armour of bronze weighing five thousand shekels; 6on his legs he wore bronze greaves, and a bronze javelin was slung on his back. 7His spear shaft was like a weaver's rod, and its iron point weighed six hundred shekels. His shield-bearer went ahead of him.

8Goliath stood and shouted to the ranks of Israel, "Why do you come out and line up for battle? Am I not a Philistine, and are you not the servants of Saul? Choose a man and have him come down to me. 9If he is able to fight and kill me, we will become your subjects; but if I overcome him and kill him, you will become our subjects and serve us." 10Then the Philistine said, "This day I defy the ranks of Israel! Give me a man and let us fight each other." 11On hearing the Philistine's words, Saul and all the Israelites were dismayed and terrified.

12Now David was the son of an Ephrathite named Jesse, who was from Bethlehem in Judah. Jesse had eight sons, and in Saul's time he was old and well advanced in years. 13Jesse's three oldest sons had followed Saul to the war: The firstborn was Eliab; the second, Abinadab; and the third, Shammah. 14David was the youngest. The three oldest followed Saul, 15but David went back and forth from Saul to tend his father's sheep at Bethlehem.

16For forty days the Philistine came forward every morning and evening and took his stand.

17Now Jesse said to his son David, "Take this ephah of roasted grain and these ten loaves of bread for your brothers and hurry to their camp. 18Take along these ten cheeses to the commander of their unit. See how your brothers are and bring back some assurance from them. 19They are with Saul and all the men of Israel in the Valley of Elah, fighting against the Philistines."

20Early in the morning David left the flock with a shepherd, loaded up and set out, as Jesse had directed. He reached the camp as the army was going out to its battle positions, shouting the war cry. 21Israel and the Philistines were drawing up their lines facing each other. 22David left his things with the keeper of supplies, ran to the battle lines and greeted his brothers. 23As he was talking with them, Goliath, the Philistine champion from Gath, stepped out from his lines and shouted his usual defiance, and David heard it. 24When the Israelites saw the man, they all ran from him in great fear.

25Now the Israelites had been saying, "Do you see how this man keeps coming out? He comes out to defy Israel. The king will give great wealth to the man who kills him. He will also give him his daughter in marriage and will exempt his father's family from taxes in Israel."

26David asked the men standing near him, "What will be done for the man who kills this Philistine and removes this disgrace from Israel? Who is this uncircumcised Philistine that he should defy the armies of the living God?"

²⁷They repeated to him what they had been saying and told him, "This is what will be done for the man who kills him."

²⁸When Eliab, David's oldest brother, heard him speaking with the men, he burned with anger at him and asked, "Why have you come down here? And with whom did you leave those few sheep in the desert? I know how conceited you are and how wicked your heart is; you came down only to watch the battle."

²⁹"Now what have I done?" said David. "Can't I even speak?" ³⁰He then turned away to someone else and brought up the same matter, and the men answered him as before. ³¹What David said was overheard and reported to Saul, and Saul sent for him.

³²David said to Saul, "Let no-one lose heart on account of this Philistine; your servant will go and fight him."

³³Saul replied, "You are not able to go out against this Philistine and fight him; you are only a boy, and he has been a fighting man from his youth."

³⁴But David said to Saul, "Your servant has been keeping his father's sheep. When a lion or a bear came and carried off a sheep from the flock, ³⁵I went after it, struck it and rescued the sheep from its mouth. When it turned on me, I seized it by its hair, struck it and killed it. ³⁶Your servant has killed both the lion and the bear; this uncircumcised Philistine will be like one of them, because he has defied the armies of the living God. ³⁷The LORD who delivered me from the paw of the lion and the paw of the bear will deliver me from the hand of this Philistine."

Saul said to David, "Go, and the LORD be with you."

NEW TESTAMENT READING
John 15:1–16:4

The Vine and the Branches

15 "I am the true vine, and my Father is the gardener. ²He cuts off every branch in me that bears no fruit, while every branch that does bear fruit he prunes so that it will be even more fruitful. ³You are already clean because of the word I have spoken to you. ⁴Remain in me, and I will remain in you. No branch can bear fruit by itself; it must remain in the vine. Neither can you bear fruit unless you remain in me.

⁵"I am the vine; you are the branches. If a man remains in me and I in him, he will bear much fruit; apart from me you can do nothing. ⁶If anyone does not remain in me, he is like a branch that is thrown away and withers; such branches are picked up, thrown into the fire and burned. ⁷If you remain in me and my words remain in you, ask whatever you wish, and it will be given you. ⁸This is to my Father's glory, that you bear much fruit, showing yourselves to be my disciples.

⁹"As the Father has loved me, so have I loved you. Now remain in my love. ¹⁰If you obey my commands, you will remain in my love, just as I have obeyed my Father's commands and remain in his love. ¹¹I have told you this so that my joy may be in you and that your joy may be complete. ¹²My command is this: Love each other as I have loved you. ¹³Greater love has no-one than this, that he lay down his life for his friends. ¹⁴You are my friends if you do what I command. ¹⁵I no longer call you servants, because a servant does not know his master's business. Instead, I have called you friends, for everything that I learned from my Father I have made known to you. ¹⁶You did not choose me, but I chose you and appointed you to go and bear fruit—fruit that will last. Then the Father will give you whatever you ask in my name. ¹⁷This is my command: Love each other.

The World Hates the Disciples

¹⁸"If the world hates you, keep in mind that it hated me first. ¹⁹If you belonged to the world, it would love you

as its own. As it is, you do not belong to the world, but I have chosen you out of the world. That is why the world hates you. ²⁰Remember the words I spoke to you: 'No servant is greater than his master. If they persecuted me, they will persecute you also. If they obeyed my teaching, they will obey yours also. ²¹They will treat you this way because of my name, for they do not know the One who sent me. ²²If I had not come and spoken to them, they would not be guilty of sin. Now, however, they have no excuse for their sin. ²³He who hates me hates my Father as well. ²⁴If I had not done among them what no-one else did, they would not be guilty of sin. But now they have seen these miracles, and yet they have hated both me and my Father. ²⁵But this is to fulfil what is written in their Law: 'They hated me without reason.'

²⁶"When the Counsellor comes, whom I will send to you from the Father, the Spirit of truth who goes out from the Father, he will testify about me. ²⁷And you also must testify, for you have been with me from the beginning.

16 "All this I have told you so that you will not go astray. ²They will put you out of the synagogue; in fact, a time is coming when anyone who kills you will think he is offering a service to God. ³They will do such things because they have not known the Father or me.

⁴I have told you this, so that when the time comes you will remember that I warned you. I did not tell you this at first because I was with you.

READING FROM PSALMS
Psalm 67:1–7

For the director of music. With stringed instruments. A psalm. A song.

¹May God be gracious to us and bless us
    and make his face shine upon us,
                                    Selah
²that your ways may be known on earth,
    your salvation among all nations.

³May the peoples praise you, O God;
    may all the peoples praise you.
⁴May the nations be glad and sing for joy,
    for you rule the peoples justly
    and guide the nations of the earth.
                                    Selah
⁵May the peoples praise you, O God;
    may all the peoples praise you.

⁶Then the land will yield its harvest,
    and God, our God, will bless us.
⁷God will bless us,
    and all the ends of the earth will fear him.

MAY 26   DAY 146

OLD TESTAMENT READING
1 Samuel 17:38–18:30

³⁸Then Saul dressed David in his own tunic. He put a coat of armour on him and a bronze helmet on his head. ³⁹David fastened on his sword over the tunic and tried walking around, because he was not used to them.

"I cannot go in these," he said to

Saul, "because I am not used to them." So he took them off. ⁴⁰Then he took his staff in his hand, chose five smooth stones from the stream, put them in the pouch of his shepherd's bag and, with his sling in his hand, approached the Philistine.

⁴¹Meanwhile, the Philistine, with his shield-bearer in front of him, kept coming closer to David. ⁴²He looked David

over and saw that he was only a boy, ruddy and handsome, and he despised him. ⁴³He said to David, "Am I a dog, that you come at me with sticks?" And the Philistine cursed David by his gods. ⁴⁴"Come here," he said, "and I'll give your flesh to the birds of the air and the beasts of the field!"

⁴⁵David said to the Philistine, "You come against me with sword and spear and javelin, but I come against you in the name of the LORD Almighty, the God of the armies of Israel, whom you have defied. ⁴⁶This day the LORD will hand you over to me, and I'll strike you down and cut off your head. Today I will give the carcasses of the Philistine army to the birds of the air and the beasts of the earth, and the whole world will know that there is a God in Israel. ⁴⁷All those gathered here will know that it is not by sword or spear that the LORD saves; for the battle is the LORD's, and he will give all of you into our hands."

⁴⁸As the Philistine moved closer to attack him, David ran quickly towards the battle line to meet him. ⁴⁹Reaching into his bag and taking out a stone, he slung it and struck the Philistine on the forehead. The stone sank into his forehead, and he fell face down on the ground.

⁵⁰So David triumphed over the Philistine with a sling and a stone; without a sword in his hand he struck down the Philistine and killed him.

⁵¹David ran and stood over him. He took hold of the Philistine's sword and drew it from the scabbard. After he killed him, he cut off his head with the sword.

When the Philistines saw that their hero was dead, they turned and ran. ⁵²Then the men of Israel and Judah surged forward with a shout and pursued the Philistines to the entrance of Gath and to the gates of Ekron. Their dead were strewn along the Shaaraim road to Gath and Ekron. ⁵³When the Israelites returned from chasing the Philistines, they plundered their camp. ⁵⁴David took the Philistine's head and brought it to Jerusalem, and he put the Philistine's weapons in his own tent.

⁵⁵As Saul watched David going out to meet the Philistine, he said to Abner, commander of the army, "Abner, whose son is that young man?"

Abner replied, "As surely as you live, O king, I don't know."

⁵⁶The king said, "Find out whose son this young man is."

⁵⁷As soon as David returned from killing the Philistine, Abner took him and brought him before Saul, with David still holding the Philistine's head.

⁵⁸"Whose son are you, young man?" Saul asked him.

David said, "I am the son of your servant Jesse of Bethlehem."

Saul's Jealousy of David

18 After David had finished talking with Saul, Jonathan became one in spirit with David, and he loved him as himself. ²From that day Saul kept David with him and did not let him return to his father's house. ³And Jonathan made a covenant with David because he loved him as himself. ⁴Jonathan took off the robe he was wearing and gave it to David, along with his tunic, and even his sword, his bow and his belt.

⁵Whatever Saul sent him to do, David did it so successfully that Saul gave him a high rank in the army. This pleased all the people, and Saul's officers as well.

⁶When the men were returning home after David had killed the Philistine, the women came out from all the towns of Israel to meet King Saul with singing and dancing, with joyful songs and with tambourines and lutes. ⁷As they danced, they sang:

"Saul has slain his thousands,
 and David his tens of thousands."

⁸Saul was very angry; this refrain galled him. "They have credited David with tens of thousands," he thought, "but me with only thousands. What

more can he get but the kingdom?" 9And from that time on Saul kept a jealous eye on David.

10The next day an evil spirit from God came forcefully upon Saul. He was prophesying in his house, while David was playing the harp, as he usually did. Saul had a spear in his hand 11and he hurled it, saying to himself, "I'll pin David to the wall." But David eluded him twice.

12Saul was afraid of David, because the LORD was with David but had left Saul. 13So he sent David away from him and gave him command over a thousand men, and David led the troops in their campaigns. 14In everything he did he had great success, because the LORD was with him. 15When Saul saw how successful he was, he was afraid of him. 16But all Israel and Judah loved David, because he led them in their campaigns.

17Saul said to David, "Here is my elder daughter Merab. I will give her to you in marriage; only serve me bravely and fight the battles of the LORD." For Saul said to himself, "I will not raise a hand against him. Let the Philistines do that!"

18But David said to Saul, "Who am I, and what is my family or my father's clan in Israel, that I should become the king's son-in-law?" 19So when the time came for Merab, Saul's daughter, to be given to David, she was given in marriage to Adriel of Meholah.

20Now Saul's daughter Michal was in love with David, and when they told Saul about it, he was pleased. 21"I will give her to him," he thought, "so that she may be a snare to him and so that the hand of the Philistines may be against him." So Saul said to David, "Now you have a second opportunity to become my son-in-law."

22Then Saul ordered his attendants: "Speak to David privately and say, 'Look, the king is pleased with you, and his attendants all like you; now become his son-in-law.'"

23They repeated these words to David. But David said, "Do you think it is a small matter to become the king's son-in-law? I'm only a poor man and little known."

24When Saul's servants told him what David had said, 25Saul replied, "Say to David, 'The king wants no other price for the bride than a hundred Philistine foreskins, to take revenge on his enemies.'" Saul's plan was to have David fall by the hands of the Philistines.

26When the attendants told David these things, he was pleased to become the king's son-in-law. So before the allotted time elapsed, 27David and his men went out and killed two hundred Philistines. He brought their foreskins and presented the full number to the king so that he might become the king's son-in-law. Then Saul gave him his daughter Michal in marriage.

28When Saul realised that the LORD was with David and that his daughter Michal loved David, 29Saul became still more afraid of him, and he remained his enemy for the rest of his days.

30The Philistine commanders continued to go out to battle, and as often as they did, David met with more success than the rest of Saul's officers, and his name became well known.

NEW TESTAMENT READING
John 16:5–17:5

The Work of the Holy Spirit

5"Now I am going to him who sent me, yet none of you asks me, 'Where are you going?' 6Because I have said these things, you are filled with grief. 7But I tell you the truth: It is for your good that I am going away. Unless I go away, the Counsellor will not come to you; but if I go, I will send him to you. 8When he comes, he will convict the world of guilt in regard to sin and righteousness and judgment: 9in regard to sin, because men do not believe in me; 10in regard to righteousness, because I am going to the Father, where you can see me no longer; 11and in regard to judgment, because the prince of this world now stands condemned.

¹²"I have much more to say to you, more than you can now bear. ¹³But when he, the Spirit of truth, comes, he will guide you into all truth. He will not speak on his own; he will speak only what he hears, and he will tell you what is yet to come. ¹⁴He will bring glory to me by taking from what is mine and making it known to you. ¹⁵All that belongs to the Father is mine. That is why I said the Spirit will take from what is mine and make it known to you.

¹⁶"In a little while you will see me no more, and then after a little while you will see me."

The Disciples' Grief Will Turn to Joy

¹⁷Some of his disciples said to one another, "What does he mean by saying, 'In a little while you will see me no more, and then after a little while you will see me,' and 'Because I am going to the Father'?" ¹⁸They kept asking, "What does he mean by 'a little while'? We don't understand what he is saying."

¹⁹Jesus saw that they wanted to ask him about this, so he said to them, "Are you asking one another what I meant when I said, 'In a little while you will see me no more, and then after a little while you will see me'? ²⁰I tell you the truth, you will weep and mourn while the world rejoices. You will grieve, but your grief will turn to joy. ²¹A woman giving birth to a child has pain because her time has come; but when her baby is born she forgets the anguish because of her joy that a child is born into the world. ²²So with you: Now is your time of grief, but I will see you again and you will rejoice, and no-one will take away your joy. ²³In that day you will no longer ask me anything. I tell you the truth, my Father will give you whatever you ask in my name. ²⁴Until now you have not asked for anything in my name. Ask and you will receive, and your joy will be complete.

²⁵"Though I have been speaking figuratively, a time is coming when I will no longer use this kind of language but will tell you plainly about my Father. ²⁶In that day you will ask in my name. I am not saying that I will ask the Father on your behalf. ²⁷No, the Father himself loves you because you have loved me and have believed that I came from God. ²⁸I came from the Father and entered the world; now I am leaving the world and going back to the Father."

²⁹Then Jesus' disciples said, "Now you are speaking clearly and without figures of speech. ³⁰Now we can see that you know all things and that you do not even need to have anyone ask you questions. This makes us believe that you came from God."

³¹"You believe at last!" Jesus answered. ³²"But a time is coming, and has come, when you will be scattered, each to his own home. You will leave me all alone. Yet I am not alone, for my Father is with me.

³³"I have told you these things, so that in me you may have peace. In this world you will have trouble. But take heart! I have overcome the world."

Jesus Prays for Himself

17 After Jesus said this, he looked towards heaven and prayed:

"Father, the time has come. Glorify your Son, that your Son may glorify you. ²For you granted him authority over all people that he might give eternal life to all those you have given him. ³Now this is eternal life: that they may know you, the only true God, and Jesus Christ, whom you have sent. ⁴I have brought you glory on earth by completing the work you gave me to do. ⁵And now, Father, glorify me in your presence with the glory I had with you before the world began.

READING FROM PSALMS
Psalm 68:1–6

For the director of music. Of David. A
psalm. A song.

[1]May God arise, may his enemies be
scattered;
may his foes flee before him.
[2]As smoke is blown away by the wind,
may you blow them away;
as wax melts before the fire,
may the wicked perish before God.
[3]But may the righteous be glad
and rejoice before God;

may they be happy and joyful.

[4]Sing to God, sing praise to his name,
extol him who rides on the
clouds—
his name is the LORD—
and rejoice before him.
[5]A father to the fatherless, a defender
of widows,
is God in his holy dwelling.
[6]God sets the lonely in families,
he leads forth the prisoners with
singing;
but the rebellious live in a
sun-scorched land.

MAY 27 DAY 147

OLD TESTAMENT READING
1 Samuel 19:1–20:42

Saul Tries to Kill David

19 Saul told his son Jonathan and
all the attendants to kill David.
But Jonathan was very fond of David
[2]and warned him, "My father Saul is
looking for a chance to kill you. Be on
your guard tomorrow morning; go into
hiding and stay there. [3]I will go out and
stand with my father in the field where
you are. I'll speak to him about you and
will tell you what I find out."

[4]Jonathan spoke well of David to
Saul his father and said to him, "Let not
the king do wrong to his servant David;
he has not wronged you, and what he
has done has benefited you greatly. [5]He
took his life in his hands when he killed
the Philistine. The LORD won a great
victory for all Israel, and you saw it and
were glad. Why then would you do
wrong to an innocent man like David by
killing him for no reason?"

[6]Saul listened to Jonathan and took
this oath: "As surely as the LORD lives,
David will not be put to death."

[7]So Jonathan called David and told
him the whole conversation. He
brought him to Saul, and David was
with Saul as before.

[8]Once more war broke out, and
David went out and fought the Philistines. He struck them with such force
that they fled before him.

[9]But an evil spirit from the LORD
came upon Saul as he was sitting in his
house with his spear in his hand. While
David was playing the harp, [10]Saul tried
to pin him to the wall with his spear, but
David eluded him as Saul drove the
spear into the wall. That night David
made good his escape.

[11]Saul sent men to David's house to
watch it and to kill him in the morning.
But Michal, David's wife, warned him,
"If you don't run for your life tonight,
tomorrow you'll be killed." [12]So Michal
let David down through a window, and
he fled and escaped. [13]Then Michal
took an idol and laid it on the bed,
covering it with a garment and putting
some goats' hair at the head.

[14]When Saul sent the men to capture
David, Michal said, "He is ill."

¹⁵Then Saul sent the men back to see David and told them, "Bring him up to me in his bed so that I may kill him." ¹⁶But when the men entered, there was the idol in the bed, and at the head was some goats' hair.

¹⁷Saul said to Michal, "Why did you deceive me like this and send my enemy away so that he escaped?"

Michal told him, "He said to me, 'Let me get away. Why should I kill you?'"

¹⁸When David had fled and made his escape, he went to Samuel at Ramah and told him all that Saul had done to him. Then he and Samuel went to Naioth and stayed there. ¹⁹Word came to Saul: "David is in Naioth at Ramah"; ²⁰so he sent men to capture him. But when they saw a group of prophets prophesying, with Samuel standing there as their leader, the Spirit of God came upon Saul's men and they also prophesied. ²¹Saul was told about it, and he sent more men, and they prophesied too. Saul sent men a third time, and they also prophesied. ²²Finally, he himself left for Ramah and went to the great cistern at Secu. And he asked, "Where are Samuel and David?"

"Over in Naioth at Ramah," they said.

²³So Saul went to Naioth at Ramah. But the Spirit of God came even upon him, and he walked along prophesying until he came to Naioth. ²⁴He stripped off his robes and also prophesied in Samuel's presence. He lay that way all that day and night. This is why people say, "Is Saul also among the prophets?"

David and Jonathan

20 Then David fled from Naioth at Ramah and went to Jonathan and asked, "What have I done? What is my crime? How have I wronged your father, that he is trying to take my life?"

²"Never!" Jonathan replied. "You are not going to die! Look, my father doesn't do anything, great or small, without confiding in me. Why should he hide this from me? It's not so!"

³But David took an oath and said, "Your father knows very well that I have found favour in your eyes, and he has said to himself, 'Jonathan must not know this or he will be grieved.' Yet as surely as the LORD lives and as you live, there is only a step between me and death."

⁴Jonathan said to David, "Whatever you want me to do, I'll do for you."

⁵So David said, "Look, tomorrow is the New Moon festival, and I am supposed to dine with the king; but let me go and hide in the field until the evening of the day after tomorrow. ⁶If your father misses me at all, tell him, 'David earnestly asked my permission to hurry to Bethlehem, his home town, because an annual sacrifice is being made there for his whole clan.' ⁷If he says, 'Very well,' then your servant is safe. But if he loses his temper, you can be sure that he is determined to harm me. ⁸As for you, show kindness to your servant, for you have brought him into a covenant with you before the LORD. If I am guilty, then kill me yourself! Why hand me over to your father?"

⁹"Never!" Jonathan said. "If I had the least inkling that my father was determined to harm you, wouldn't I tell you?"

¹⁰David asked, "Who will tell me if your father answers you harshly?"

¹¹"Come," Jonathan said, "let's go out into the field." So they went there together.

¹²Then Jonathan said to David: "By the LORD, the God of Israel, I will surely sound out my father by this time the day after tomorrow! If he is favourably disposed towards you, will I not send you word and let you know? ¹³But if my father is inclined to harm you, may the LORD deal with me, be it ever so severely, if I do not let you know and send you away safely. May the LORD be with you as he has been with my father. ¹⁴But show me unfailing kindness like that of the LORD as long as I live, so that

I may not be killed, [15]and do not ever cut off your kindness from my family—not even when the LORD has cut off every one of David's enemies from the face of the earth."

[16]So Jonathan made a covenant with the house of David, saying, "May the LORD call David's enemies to account." [17]And Jonathan made David reaffirm his oath of love for him, because he loved him as he loved himself.

[18]Then Jonathan said to David: "Tomorrow is the New Moon festival. You will be missed, because your seat will be empty. [19]The day after tomorrow, towards evening, go to the place where you hid when this trouble began, and wait by the stone Ezel. [20]I will shoot three arrows to the side of it, as though I were shooting at a target. [21]Then I will send a boy and say, 'Go, find the arrows.' If I say to him, 'Look, the arrows are on this side of you; bring them here,' then come, because, as surely as the LORD lives, you are safe; there is no danger. [22]But if I say to the boy, 'Look, the arrows are beyond you,' then you must go, because the LORD has sent you away. [23]And about the matter you and I discussed—remember, the LORD is witness between you and me for ever."

[24]So David hid in the field, and when the New Moon festival came, the king sat down to eat. [25]He sat in his customary place by the wall, opposite Jonathan, and Abner sat next to Saul, but David's place was empty. [26]Saul said nothing that day, for he thought, "Something must have happened to David to make him ceremonially unclean—surely he is unclean." [27]But the next day, the second day of the month, David's place was empty again. Then Saul said to his son Jonathan, "Why hasn't the son of Jesse come to the meal, either yesterday or today?"

[28]Jonathan answered, "David earnestly asked me for permission to go to Bethlehem. [29]He said, 'Let me go, because our family is observing a sacrifice in the town and my brother has ordered me to be there. If I have found favour in your eyes, let me go to see my brothers.' That is why he has not come to the king's table."

[30]Saul's anger flared up at Jonathan and he said to him, "You son of a perverse and rebellious woman! Don't I know that you have sided with the son of Jesse to your own shame and to the shame of the mother who bore you? [31]As long as the son of Jesse lives on this earth, neither you nor your kingdom will be established. Now send and bring him to me, for he must die!"

[32]"Why should he be put to death? What has he done?" Jonathan asked his father. [33]But Saul hurled his spear at him to kill him. Then Jonathan knew that his father intended to kill David.

[34]Jonathan got up from the table in fierce anger; on that second day of the month he did not eat, because he was grieved at his father's shameful treatment of David.

[35]In the morning Jonathan went out to the field for his meeting with David. He had a small boy with him, [36]and he said to the boy, "Run and find the arrows I shoot." As the boy ran, he shot an arrow beyond him. [37]When the boy came to the place where Jonathan's arrow had fallen, Jonathan called out after him, "Isn't the arrow beyond you?" [38]Then he shouted, "Hurry! Go quickly! Don't stop!" The boy picked up the arrow and returned to his master. [39](The boy knew nothing of all this; only Jonathan and David knew.) [40]Then Jonathan gave his weapons to the boy and said, "Go, carry them back to town."

[41]After the boy had gone, David got up from the south side ⌊of the stone⌋ and bowed down before Jonathan three times, with his face to the ground. Then they kissed each other and wept together—but David wept the most.

[42]Jonathan said to David, "Go in peace, for we have sworn friendship with each other in the name of the LORD, saying, 'The LORD is witness between you and me, and between your

descendants and my descendants for ever.'" Then David left, and Jonathan went back to the town.

NEW TESTAMENT READING
John 17:6–26

Jesus Prays for His Disciples

6"I have revealed you to those whom you gave me out of the world. They were yours; you gave them to me and they have obeyed your word. 7Now they know that everything you have given me comes from you. 8For I gave them the words you gave me and they accepted them. They knew with certainty that I came from you, and they believed that you sent me. 9I pray for them. I am not praying for the world, but for those you have given me, for they are yours. 10All I have is yours, and all you have is mine. And glory has come to me through them. 11I will remain in the world no longer, but they are still in the world, and I am coming to you. Holy Father, protect them by the power of your name—the name you gave me—so that they may be one as we are one. 12While I was with them, I protected them and kept them safe by that name you gave me. None has been lost except the one doomed to destruction so that Scripture would be fulfilled.

13"I am coming to you now, but I say these things while I am still in the world, so that they may have the full measure of my joy within them. 14I have given them your word and the world has hated them, for they are not of the world any more than I am of the world. 15My prayer is not that you take them out of the world but that you protect them from the evil one. 16They are not of the world, even as I am not of it. 17Sanctify them by the truth; your word is truth. 18As you sent me into the world, I have sent them into the world. 19For them I sanctify myself, that they too may be truly sanctified.

Jesus Prays for All Believers

20"My prayer is not for them alone. I pray also for those who will believe in me through their message, 21that all of them may be one, Father, just as you are in me and I am in you. May they also be in us so that the world may believe that you have sent me. 22I have given them the glory that you gave me, that they may be one as we are one: 23I in them and you in me. May they be brought to complete unity to let the world know that you sent me and have loved them even as you have loved me.

24"Father, I want those you have given me to be with me where I am, and to see my glory, the glory you have given me because you loved me before the creation of the world.

25"Righteous Father, though the world does not know you, I know you, and they know that you have sent me. 26I have made you known to them, and will continue to make you known in order that the love you have for me may be in them and that I myself may be in them."

READING FROM PSALMS
Psalm 68:7–14

7When you went out before your people, O God,
    when you marched through the wasteland, *Selah*
8the earth shook,
    the heavens poured down rain,
before God, the One of Sinai,
    before God, the God of Israel.
9You gave abundant showers,
    O God;

you refreshed your weary
　　inheritance.
¹⁰Your people settled in it,
　　and from your bounty, O God, you
　　　provided for the poor.

¹¹The Lord announced the word,
　　and great was the company of
　　　those who proclaimed it:
¹²"Kings and armies flee in haste;

in the camps men divide the
　　plunder.
¹³Even while you sleep among the
　　campfires,
　　the wings of ⌐my⌐ dove are
　　　sheathed with silver,
　　its feathers shine with shining gold."
¹⁴When the Almighty scattered the
　　kings in the land,
　　it was like snow fallen on Zalmon.

MAY 28　　　　　　　　　　　DAY 148

OLD TESTAMENT READING
1 Samuel 21:1–23:29

David at Nob

21 David went to Nob, to Ahimelech the priest. Ahimelech trembled when he met him, and asked, "Why are you alone? Why is no-one with you?"

²David answered Ahimelech the priest, "The king charged me with a certain matter and said to me, 'No-one is to know anything about your mission and your instructions.' As for my men, I have told them to meet me at a certain place. ³Now then, what have you to hand? Give me five loaves of bread, or whatever you can find."

⁴But the priest answered David, "I don't have any ordinary bread to hand; however, there is some consecrated bread here—provided the men have kept themselves from women."

⁵David replied, "Indeed women have been kept from us, as usual whenever I set out. The men's things are holy even on missions that are not holy. How much more so today!" ⁶So the priest gave him the consecrated bread, since there was no bread there except the bread of the Presence that had been removed from before the LORD and replaced by hot bread on the day it was taken away.

⁷Now one of Saul's servants was there that day, detained before the LORD; he was Doeg the Edomite, Saul's head shepherd.

⁸David asked Ahimelech, "Don't you have a spear or sword here? I haven't brought my sword or any other weapon, because the king's business was urgent."

⁹The priest replied, "The sword of Goliath the Philistine, whom you killed in the Valley of Elah, is here; it is wrapped in a cloth behind the ephod. If you want it, take it; there is no sword here but that one."

David said, "There is none like it; give it to me."

David at Gath

¹⁰That day David fled from Saul and went to Achish king of Gath. ¹¹But the servants of Achish said to him, "Isn't this David, the king of the land? Isn't he the one they sing about in their dances:

"'Saul has slain his thousands,
　　and David his tens of thousands'?"

¹²David took these words to heart and was very much afraid of Achish king of Gath. ¹³So he feigned insanity in their presence; and while he was in their hands he acted like a madman, making

marks on the doors of the gate and letting saliva run down his beard.

14Achish said to his servants, "Look at the man! He is insane! Why bring him to me? 15Am I so short of madmen that you have to bring this fellow here to carry on like this in front of me? Must this man come into my house?"

David at Adullam and Mizpah

22 David left Gath and escaped to the cave of Adullam. When his brothers and his father's household heard about it, they went down to him there. 2All those who were in distress or in debt or discontented gathered round him, and he became their leader. About four hundred men were with him.

3From there David went to Mizpah in Moab and said to the king of Moab, "Would you let my father and mother come and stay with you until I learn what God will do for me?" 4So he left them with the king of Moab, and they stayed with him as long as David was in the stronghold.

5But the prophet Gad said to David, "Do not stay in the stronghold. Go into the land of Judah." So David left and went to the forest of Hereth.

Saul Kills the Priests of Nob

6Now Saul heard that David and his men had been discovered. And Saul, spear in hand, was seated under the tamarisk tree on the hill at Gibeah, with all his officials standing round him. 7Saul said to them, "Listen, men of Benjamin! Will the son of Jesse give all of you fields and vineyards? Will he make all of you commanders of thousands and commanders of hundreds? 8Is that why you have all conspired against me? No-one tells me when my son makes a covenant with the son of Jesse. None of you is concerned about me or tells me that my son has incited my servant to lie in wait for me, as he does today."

9But Doeg the Edomite, who was standing with Saul's officials, said, "I saw the son of Jesse come to Ahimelech son of Ahitub at Nob. 10Ahimelech enquired of the LORD for him; he also gave him provisions and the sword of Goliath the Philistine."

11Then the king sent for the priest Ahimelech son of Ahitub and his father's whole family, who were the priests at Nob, and they all came to the king. 12Saul said, "Listen now, son of Ahitub."

"Yes, my lord," he answered.

13Saul said to him, "Why have you conspired against me, you and the son of Jesse, giving him bread and a sword and enquiring of God for him, so that he has rebelled against me and lies in wait for me, as he does today?"

14Ahimelech answered the king, "Who of all your servants is as loyal as David, the king's son-in-law, captain of your bodyguard and highly respected in your household? 15Was that day the first time I enquired of God for him? Of course not! Let not the king accuse your servant or any of his father's family, for your servant knows nothing at all about this whole affair."

16But the king said, "You shall surely die, Ahimelech, you and your father's whole family."

17Then the king ordered the guards at his side: "Turn and kill the priests of the LORD, because they too have sided with David. They knew he was fleeing, yet they did not tell me."

But the king's officials were not willing to raise a hand to strike the priests of the LORD.

18The king then ordered Doeg, "You turn and strike down the priests." So Doeg the Edomite turned and struck them down. That day he killed eighty-five men who wore the linen ephod. 19He also put to the sword Nob, the town of the priests, with its men and women, its children and infants, and its cattle, donkeys and sheep.

20But Abiathar, son of Ahimelech son of Ahitub, escaped and fled to join David. 21He told David that Saul had killed the priests of the LORD. 22Then David said to Abiathar: "That day, when Doeg the Edomite was there, I knew he would be sure to tell Saul. I am responsible for the death of your father's whole family. 23Stay with me; don't be afraid; the man who is seeking your life is seeking mine also. You will be safe with me."

David Saves Keilah

23 When David was told, "Look, the Philistines are fighting against Keilah and are looting the threshing-floors," 2he enquired of the LORD, saying, "Shall I go and attack these Philistines?"

The LORD answered him, "Go, attack the Philistines and save Keilah."

3But David's men said to him, "Here in Judah we are afraid. How much more, then, if we go to Keilah against the Philistine forces!"

4Once again David enquired of the LORD, and the LORD answered him, "Go down to Keilah, for I am going to give the Philistines into your hand." 5So David and his men went to Keilah, fought the Philistines and carried off their livestock. He inflicted heavy losses on the Philistines and saved the people of Keilah. 6(Now Abiathar son of Ahimelech had brought the ephod down with him when he fled to David at Keilah.)

Saul Pursues David

7Saul was told that David had gone to Keilah, and he said, "God has handed him over to me, for David has imprisoned himself by entering a town with gates and bars." 8And Saul called up all his forces for battle, to go down to Keilah to besiege David and his men.

9When David learned that Saul was plotting against him, he said to Abiathar the priest, "Bring the ephod." 10David said, "O LORD, God of Israel, your servant has heard definitely that Saul plans to come to Keilah and destroy the town on account of me. 11Will the citizens of Keilah surrender me to him? Will Saul come down, as your servant has heard? O LORD, God of Israel, tell your servant."

And the LORD said, "He will."

12Again David asked, "Will the citizens of Keilah surrender me and my men to Saul?"

And the LORD said, "They will."

13So David and his men, about six hundred in number, left Keilah and kept moving from place to place. When Saul was told that David had escaped from Keilah, he did not go there.

14David stayed in the desert strongholds and in the hills of the Desert of Ziph. Day after day Saul searched for him, but God did not give David into his hands.

15While David was at Horesh in the Desert of Ziph, he learned that Saul had come out to take his life. 16And Saul's son Jonathan went to David at Horesh and helped him to find strength in God. 17"Don't be afraid," he said. "My father Saul will not lay a hand on you. You shall be king over Israel, and I will be second to you. Even my father Saul knows this." 18The two of them made a covenant before the LORD. Then Jonathan went home, but David remained at Horesh.

19The Ziphites went up to Saul at Gibeah and said, "Is not David hiding among us in the strongholds at Horesh, on the hill of Hakilah, south of Jeshimon? 20Now, O king, come down whenever it pleases you to do so, and we will be responsible for handing him over to the king."

21Saul replied, "The LORD bless you for your concern for me. 22Go and make further preparation. Find out where David usually goes and who has seen him there. They tell me he is very crafty. 23Find out about all the hiding-places he uses and come back to me with definite information. Then I will go with you; if he is in the area, I will track him down among all the clans of Judah." 24So they set out and went to Ziph ahead of Saul. Now David and his men were in the Desert of Maon, in the Arabah south of Jeshimon. 25Saul and his men began the search, and when David was told about it, he went down to the rock and stayed in the Desert of Maon. When Saul heard this, he went into the Desert of Maon in pursuit of David.

26Saul was going along one side of the mountain, and David and his men were on the other side, hurrying to get away from Saul. As Saul and his forces were closing in on David and his men to capture them, 27a messenger came to Saul, saying, "Come quickly! The Philistines are raiding the land." 28Then Saul broke off his pursuit of David and went to meet the Philistines. That is why they call this place Sela Hammahlekoth. 29And David went up from there and lived in the strongholds of En Gedi.

NEW TESTAMENT READING
John 18:1–24

Jesus Arrested

18 When he had finished praying, Jesus left with his disciples and crossed the Kidron Valley. On the other side there was an olive grove, and he and his disciples went into it.

2Now Judas, who betrayed him, knew the place, because Jesus had often met there with his disciples. 3So Judas came to the grove, guiding a detachment of soldiers and some officials from the chief priests and Pharisees. They were carrying torches, lanterns and weapons.

4Jesus, knowing all that was going to happen to him, went out and asked them, "Who is it you want?"

5"Jesus of Nazareth," they replied.

"I am he," Jesus said. (And Judas the traitor was standing there with them.) 6When Jesus said, "I am he," they drew back and fell to the ground.

7Again he asked them, "Who is it you want?"

And they said, "Jesus of Nazareth."

8"I told you that I am he," Jesus answered. "If you are looking for me, then let these men go." 9This happened so that the words he had spoken would be fulfilled: "I have not lost one of those you gave me."

10Then Simon Peter, who had a sword, drew it and struck the high priest's servant, cutting off his right ear. (The servant's name was Malchus.)

11Jesus commanded Peter, "Put your sword away! Shall I not drink the cup the Father has given me?"

Jesus Taken to Annas

12Then the detachment of soldiers with its commander and the Jewish officials arrested Jesus. They bound him 13and brought him first to Annas, who was the father-in-law of Caiaphas, the high priest that year. 14Caiaphas was the one who had advised the Jews that it would be good if one man died for the people.

Peter's First Denial

15Simon Peter and another disciple were following Jesus. Because this disciple was known to the high priest, he went with Jesus into the high priest's courtyard, 16but Peter had to wait outside at the door. The other disciple, who was known to the high priest, came back, spoke to the girl on duty there and brought Peter in.

17"You are not one of his disciples, are you?" the girl at the door asked Peter.

He replied, "I am not."

18It was cold, and the servants and officials stood round a fire they had made to keep warm. Peter also was standing with them, warming himself.

The High Priest Questions Jesus

19Meanwhile, the high priest questioned Jesus about his disciples and his teaching.

20"I have spoken openly to the world," Jesus replied. "I always taught in synagogues or at the temple, where all the Jews come together. I said nothing in secret. 21Why question me? Ask those who heard me. Surely they know what I said."

22When Jesus said this, one of the officials near by struck him in the face. "Is this the way you answer the high priest?" he demanded.

23"If I said something wrong," Jesus replied, "testify as to what is wrong. But if I spoke the truth, why did you strike me?" 24Then Annas sent him, still bound, to Caiaphas the high priest.

READING FROM PROVERBS
Proverbs 13:10–19

10Pride only breeds quarrels,
    but wisdom is found in those who
        take advice.

11Dishonest money dwindles away,
    but he who gathers money little by
        little makes it grow.

12Hope deferred makes the heart sick,
    but a longing fulfilled is a tree of
        life.

13He who scorns instruction will pay for
        it,
    but he who respects a command is
        rewarded.

14The teaching of the wise is a fountain
        of life,
    turning a man from the snares of
        death.

15Good understanding wins favour,
    but the way of the unfaithful is
        hard.

16Every prudent man acts out of
        knowledge,
    but a fool exposes his folly.

17A wicked messenger falls into
        trouble,
    but a trustworthy envoy brings
        healing.

18He who ignores discipline comes to
        poverty and shame,
    but whoever heeds correction is
        honoured.

19A longing fulfilled is sweet to the
        soul,
    but fools detest turning from evil.

MAY 29   DAY 149

OLD TESTAMENT READING
1 Samuel 24:1–25:44

David Spares Saul's Life

24 After Saul returned from pursuing the Philistines, he was told, "David is in the Desert of En Gedi." 2So Saul took three thousand chosen men from all Israel and set out to look for David and his men near the Crags of the Wild Goats.

3He came to the sheep pens along the way; a cave was there, and Saul went in to relieve himself. David and his men were far back in the cave. 4The men said, "This is the day the LORD spoke of when he said to you, 'I will give your enemy into your hands for you to deal with as you wish.'" Then David crept up unnoticed and cut off a corner of Saul's robe.

5Afterwards, David was conscience-stricken for having cut off a corner of his robe. 6He said to his men, "The LORD forbid that I should do such a thing to my master, the LORD's anointed, or lift my hand against him; for he is the anointed of the LORD." ⁷With these words David rebuked his men and did not allow them to attack Saul. And Saul left the cave and went his way.

⁸Then David went out of the cave and called out to Saul, "My lord the king!" When Saul looked behind him, David bowed down and prostrated himself with his face to the ground. ⁹He said to Saul, "Why do you listen when men say, 'David is bent on harming you'? ¹⁰This day you have seen with your own eyes how the LORD gave you into my hands in the cave. Some urged me to kill you, but I spared you; I said, 'I will not lift my hand against my master, because he is the LORD's anointed.' ¹¹See, my father, look at this piece of your robe in my hand! I cut off the corner of your robe but did not kill you. Now understand and recognise that I am not guilty of wrongdoing or rebellion. I have not wronged you, but you are hunting me down to take my life. ¹²May the LORD judge between you and me. And may the LORD avenge the wrongs you have done to me, but my hand will not touch you. ¹³As the old saying goes, 'From evildoers come evil deeds,' so my hand will not touch you.

¹⁴"Against whom has the king of Israel come out? Whom are you pursuing? A dead dog? A flea? ¹⁵May the LORD be our judge and decide between us. May he consider my cause and uphold it; may he vindicate me by delivering me from your hand."

¹⁶When David finished saying this, Saul asked, "Is that your voice, David my son?" And he wept aloud. ¹⁷"You are more righteous than I," he said. "You have treated me well, but I have treated you badly. ¹⁸You have just now told me of the good you did to me; the LORD gave me into your hands, but you did not kill me. ¹⁹When a man finds his enemy, does he let him get away unharmed? May the LORD reward you well for the way you treated me today. ²⁰I know that you will surely be king and

that the kingdom of Israel will be established in your hands. ²¹Now swear to me by the LORD that you will not cut off my descendants or wipe out my name from my father's family."

²²So David gave his oath to Saul. Then Saul returned home, but David and his men went up to the stronghold.

David, Nabal and Abigail

25 Now Samuel died, and all Israel assembled and mourned for him; and they buried him at his home in Ramah.

Then David moved down into the Desert of Maon. ²A certain man in Maon, who had property there at Carmel, was very wealthy. He had a thousand goats and three thousand sheep, which he was shearing in Carmel. ³His name was Nabal and his wife's name was Abigail. She was an intelligent and beautiful woman, but her husband, a Calebite, was surly and mean in his dealings.

⁴While David was in the desert, he heard that Nabal was shearing sheep. ⁵So he sent ten young men and said to them, "Go up to Nabal at Carmel and greet him in my name. ⁶Say to him: 'Long life to you! Good health to you and your household! And good health to all that is yours!

⁷"'Now I hear that it is sheepshearing time. When your shepherds were with us, we did not ill-treat them, and the whole time they were at Carmel nothing of theirs was missing. ⁸Ask your own servants and they will tell you. Therefore be favourable towards my young men, since we come at a festive time. Please give your servants and your son David whatever you can find for them.'"

⁹When David's men arrived, they gave Nabal this message in David's name. Then they waited.

¹⁰Nabal answered David's servants, "Who is this David? Who is this son of Jesse? Many servants are breaking away from their masters these days.

¹¹Why should I take my bread and water, and the meat I have slaughtered for my shearers, and give it to men coming from who knows where?"

¹²David's men turned round and went back. When they arrived, they reported every word. ¹³David said to his men, "Put on your swords!" So they put on their swords, and David put on his. About four hundred men went up with David, while two hundred stayed with the supplies.

¹⁴One of the servants told Nabal's wife Abigail: "David sent messengers from the desert to give our master his greetings, but he hurled insults at them. ¹⁵Yet these men were very good to us. They did not ill-treat us, and the whole time we were out in the fields near them nothing was missing. ¹⁶Night and day they were a wall around us all the time we were herding our sheep near them. ¹⁷Now think it over and see what you can do, because disaster is hanging over our master and his whole household. He is such a wicked man that no-one can talk to him."

¹⁸Abigail lost no time. She took two hundred loaves of bread, two skins of wine, five dressed sheep, five seahs of roasted grain, a hundred cakes of raisins and two hundred cakes of pressed figs, and loaded them on donkeys. ¹⁹Then she told her servants, "Go on ahead; I'll follow you." But she did not tell her husband Nabal.

²⁰As she came riding her donkey into a mountain ravine, there were David and his men descending towards her, and she met them. ²¹David had just said, "It's been useless—all my watching over this fellow's property in the desert so that nothing of his was missing. He has paid me back evil for good. ²²May God deal with David, be it ever so severely, if by morning I leave alive one male of all who belong to him!"

²³When Abigail saw David, she quickly got off her donkey and bowed down before David with her face to the ground. ²⁴She fell at his feet and said: "My lord, let the blame be on me alone. Please let your servant speak to you; hear what your servant has to say. ²⁵May my lord pay no attention to that wicked man Nabal. He is just like his name—his name is Fool, and folly goes with him. But as for me, your servant, I did not see the men my master sent.

²⁶"Now since the LORD has kept you, my master, from bloodshed and from avenging yourself with your own hands, as surely as the LORD lives and as you live, may your enemies and all who intend to harm my master be like Nabal. ²⁷And let this gift, which your servant has brought to my master, be given to the men who follow you. ²⁸Please forgive your servant's offence, for the LORD will certainly make a lasting dynasty for my master, because he fights the LORD's battles. Let no wrongdoing be found in you as long as you live. ²⁹Even though someone is pursuing you to take your life, the life of my master will be bound securely in the bundle of the living by the LORD your God. But the lives of your enemies he will hurl away as from the pocket of a sling. ³⁰When the LORD has done for my master every good thing he promised concerning him and has appointed him leader over Israel, ³¹my master will not have on his conscience the staggering burden of needless bloodshed or of having avenged himself. And when the LORD has brought my master success, remember your servant."

³²David said to Abigail, "Praise be to the LORD, the God of Israel, who has sent you today to meet me. ³³May you be blessed for your good judgment and for keeping me from bloodshed this day and from avenging myself with my own hands. ³⁴Otherwise, as surely as the LORD, the God of Israel, lives, who has kept me from harming you, if you had not come quickly to meet me, not one male belonging to Nabal would have been left alive by daybreak."

³⁵Then David accepted from her hand what she had brought to him and said, "Go home in peace. I have heard your words and granted your request."

36When Abigail went to Nabal, he was in the house holding a banquet like that of a king. He was in high spirits and very drunk. So she told him nothing until daybreak. 37Then in the morning, when Nabal was sober, his wife told him all these things, and his heart failed him and he became like a stone. 38About ten days later, the LORD struck Nabal and he died.

39When David heard that Nabal was dead, he said, "Praise be to the LORD, who has upheld my cause against Nabal for treating me with contempt. He has kept his servant from doing wrong and has brought Nabal's wrongdoing down on his own head."

Then David sent word to Abigail, asking her to become his wife. 40His servants went to Carmel and said to Abigail, "David has sent us to you to take you to become his wife."

41She bowed down with her face to the ground and said, "Here is your maidservant, ready to serve you and wash the feet of my master's servants." 42Abigail quickly got on a donkey and, attended by her five maids, went with David's messengers and became his wife. 43David had also married Ahinoam of Jezreel, and they both were his wives. 44But Saul had given his daughter Michal, David's wife, to Paltiel son of Laish, who was from Gallim.

NEW TESTAMENT READING
John 18:25–40

Peter's Second and Third Denials

25As Simon Peter stood warming himself, he was asked, "You are not one of his disciples, are you?"

He denied it, saying, "I am not."

26One of the high priest's servants, a relative of the man whose ear Peter had cut off, challenged him, "Didn't I see you with him in the olive grove?" 27Again Peter denied it, and at that moment a cock began to crow.

Jesus Before Pilate

28Then the Jews led Jesus from Caiaphas to the palace of the Roman governor. By now it was early morning, and to avoid ceremonial uncleanness the Jews did not enter the palace; they wanted to be able to eat the Passover. 29So Pilate came out to them and asked, "What charges are you bringing against this man?"

30"If he were not a criminal," they replied, "we would not have handed him over to you."

31Pilate said, "Take him yourselves and judge him by your own law."

"But we have no right to execute anyone," the Jews objected. 32This happened so that the words Jesus had spoken indicating the kind of death he was going to die would be fulfilled.

33Pilate then went back inside the palace, summoned Jesus and asked him, "Are you the king of the Jews?"

34"Is that your own idea," Jesus asked, "or did others talk to you about me?"

35"Am I a Jew?" Pilate replied. "It was your people and your chief priests who handed you over to me. What is it you have done?"

36Jesus said, "My kingdom is not of this world. If it were, my servants would fight to prevent my arrest by the Jews. But now my kingdom is from another place."

37"You are a king, then!" said Pilate.

Jesus answered, "You are right in saying I am a king. In fact, for this reason I was born, and for this I came into the world, to testify to the truth. Everyone on the side of truth listens to me."

38"What is truth?" Pilate asked. With this he went out again to the Jews and said, "I find no basis for a charge against him. 39But it is your custom for me to release to you one prisoner at the time of the Passover. Do you want me to release 'the king of the Jews'?"

40They shouted back, "No, not him! Give us Barabbas!" Now Barabbas had taken part in a rebellion.

READING FROM PSALMS
Psalm 68:15–20

15The mountains of Bashan are
    majestic mountains;
  rugged are the mountains of
    Bashan.
16Why gaze in envy, O rugged
    mountains,
  at the mountain where God
    chooses to reign,
  where the LORD himself will dwell
    for ever?
17The chariots of God are tens of
    thousands
  and thousands of thousands;

  the Lord ⌊has come⌋ from Sinai
    into his sanctuary.
18When you ascended on high,
  you led captives in your train;
  you received gifts from men,
  even from the rebellious—
  that you, O LORD God, might
    dwell there.

19Praise be to the Lord, to God our
    Saviour,
  who daily bears our burdens.
             Selah
20Our God is a God who saves;
  from the Sovereign LORD comes
    escape from death.

MAY 30
DAY 150

OLD TESTAMENT READING
1 Samuel 26:1–28:25

David Again Spares Saul's Life

26 The Ziphites went to Saul at Gibeah and said, "Is not David hiding on the hill of Hakilah, which faces Jeshimon?"

2So Saul went down to the Desert of Ziph, with his three thousand chosen men of Israel, to search there for David. 3Saul made his camp beside the road on the hill of Hakilah facing Jeshimon, but David stayed in the desert. When he saw that Saul had followed him there, 4he sent out scouts and learned that Saul had definitely arrived.

5Then David set out and went to the place where Saul had camped. He saw where Saul and Abner son of Ner, the commander of the army, had lain down. Saul was lying inside the camp, with the army encamped around him.

6David then asked Ahimelech the Hittite and Abishai son of Zeruiah, Joab's brother, "Who will go down into the camp with me to Saul?"

"I'll go with you," said Abishai.

7So David and Abishai went to the army by night, and there was Saul, lying asleep inside the camp with his spear stuck in the ground near his head. Abner and the soldiers were lying round him.

8Abishai said to David, "Today God has given your enemy into your hands. Now let me pin him to the ground with one thrust of my spear; I won't strike him twice."

9But David said to Abishai, "Don't destroy him! Who can lay a hand on the LORD's anointed and be guiltless? 10As surely as the LORD lives," he said, "the LORD himself will strike him; either his time will come and he will die, or he will go into battle and perish. 11But the LORD forbid that I should lay a hand on the LORD's anointed. Now get the spear and water jug that are near his head, and let's go."

12So David took the spear and water jug near Saul's head, and they left. No-one saw or knew about it, nor did anyone wake up. They were all sleeping, because the LORD had put them into a deep sleep.

¹³Then David crossed over to the other side and stood on top of the hill some distance away; there was a wide space between them. ¹⁴He called out to the army and to Abner son of Ner, "Aren't you going to answer me, Abner?"

Abner replied, "Who are you who calls to the king?"

¹⁵David said, "You're a man, aren't you? And who is like you in Israel? Why didn't you guard your lord the king? Someone came to destroy your lord the king. ¹⁶What you have done is not good. As surely as the LORD lives, you and your men deserve to die, because you did not guard your master, the LORD's anointed. Look around you. Where are the king's spear and water jug that were near his head?"

¹⁷Saul recognised David's voice and said, "Is that your voice, David my son?"

David replied, "Yes it is, my lord the king." ¹⁸And he added, "Why is my lord pursuing his servant? What have I done, and what wrong am I guilty of? ¹⁹Now let my lord the king listen to his servant's words. If the LORD has incited you against me, then may he accept an offering. If, however, men have done it, may they be cursed before the LORD! They have now driven me from my share in the LORD's inheritance and have said, 'Go, serve other gods.' ²⁰Now do not let my blood fall to the ground far from the presence of the LORD. The king of Israel has come out to look for a flea—as one hunts a partridge in the mountains."

²¹Then Saul said, "I have sinned. Come back, David my son. Because you considered my life precious today, I will not try to harm you again. Surely I have acted like a fool and have erred greatly."

²²"Here is the king's spear," David answered. "Let one of your young men come over and get it. ²³The LORD rewards every man for his righteousness and faithfulness. The LORD gave you into my hands today, but I would not lay

a hand on the LORD's anointed. ²⁴As surely as I valued your life today, so may the LORD value my life and deliver me from all trouble."

²⁵Then Saul said to David, "May you be blessed, my son David; you will do great things and surely triumph."

So David went on his way, and Saul returned home.

David Among the Philistines

27 But David thought to himself, "One of these days I shall be destroyed by the hand of Saul. The best thing I can do is to escape to the land of the Philistines. Then Saul will give up searching for me anywhere in Israel, and I will slip out of his hand."

²So David and the six hundred men with him left and went over to Achish son of Maoch king of Gath. ³David and his men settled in Gath with Achish. Each man had his family with him, and David had his two wives: Ahinoam of Jezreel and Abigail of Carmel, the widow of Nabal. ⁴When Saul was told that David had fled to Gath, he no longer searched for him.

⁵Then David said to Achish, "If I have found favour in your eyes, let a place be assigned to me in one of the country towns, that I may live there. Why should your servant live in the royal city with you?"

⁶So on that day Achish gave him Ziklag, and it has belonged to the kings of Judah ever since. ⁷David lived in Philistine territory for a year and four months.

⁸Now David and his men went up and raided the Geshurites, the Girzites and the Amalekites. (From ancient times these peoples had lived in the land extending to Shur and Egypt.) ⁹Whenever David attacked an area, he did not leave a man or woman alive, but took sheep and cattle, donkeys and camels, and clothes. Then he returned to Achish.

¹⁰When Achish asked, "Where did you go raiding today?" David would say, "Against the Negev of Judah" or

"Against the Negev of Jerahmeel" or "Against the Negev of the Kenites." [11]He did not leave a man or woman alive to be brought to Gath, for he thought, "They might inform on us and say, 'This is what David did.'" And such was his practice as long as he lived in Philistine territory. [12]Achish trusted David and said to himself, "He has become so odious to his people, the Israelites, that he will be my servant for ever."

Saul and the Witch of Endor

28 In those days the Philistines gathered their forces to fight against Israel. Achish said to David, "You must understand that you and your men will accompany me in the army."

[2]David said, "Then you will see for yourself what your servant can do."

Achish replied, "Very well, I will make you my bodyguard for life."

[3]Now Samuel was dead, and all Israel had mourned for him and buried him in his own town of Ramah. Saul had expelled the mediums and spiritists from the land.

[4]The Philistines assembled and came and set up camp at Shunem, while Saul gathered all the Israelites and set up camp at Gilboa. [5]When Saul saw the Philistine army, he was afraid; terror filled his heart. [6]He enquired of the LORD, but the LORD did not answer him by dreams or Urim or prophets. [7]Saul then said to his attendants, "Find me a woman who is a medium, so that I may go and enquire of her."

"There is one in Endor," they said.

[8]So Saul disguised himself, putting on other clothes, and at night he and two men went to the woman. "Consult a spirit for me," he said, "and bring up for me the one I name."

[9]But the woman said to him, "Surely you know what Saul has done. He has cut off the mediums and spiritists from the land. Why have you set a trap for my life to bring about my death?"

[10]Saul swore to her by the LORD, "As surely as the LORD lives, you will not be punished for this."

[11]Then the woman asked, "Whom shall I bring up for you?"

"Bring up Samuel," he said.

[12]When the woman saw Samuel, she cried out at the top of her voice and said to Saul, "Why have you deceived me? You are Saul!"

[13]The king said to her, "Don't be afraid. What do you see?"

The woman said, "I see a spirit coming up out of the ground."

[14]"What does he look like?" he asked.

"An old man wearing a robe is coming up," she said.

Then Saul knew it was Samuel, and he bowed down and prostrated himself with his face to the ground.

[15]Samuel said to Saul, "Why have you disturbed me by bringing me up?"

"I am in great distress," Saul said. "The Philistines are fighting against me, and God has turned away from me. He no longer answers me, either by prophets or by dreams. So I have called on you to tell me what to do."

[16]Samuel said, "Why do you consult me, now that the LORD has turned away from you and become your enemy? [17]The LORD has done what he predicted through me. The LORD has torn the kingdom out of your hands and given it to one of your neighbours—to David. [18]Because you did not obey the LORD or carry out his fierce wrath against the Amalekites, the LORD has done this to you today. [19]The LORD will hand over both Israel and you to the Philistines, and tomorrow you and your sons will be with me. The LORD will also hand over the army of Israel to the Philistines."

[20]Immediately Saul fell full length on the ground, filled with fear because of Samuel's words. His strength was gone, for he had eaten nothing all that day and night.

[21]When the woman came to Saul and saw that he was greatly shaken, she said, "Look, your maidservant has

obeyed you. I took my life in my hands and did what you told me to do. 22Now please listen to your servant and let me give you some food so that you may eat and have the strength to go on your way."

23He refused and said, "I will not eat."

But his men joined the woman in urging him, and he listened to them. He got up from the ground and sat on the couch.

24The woman had a fattened calf at the house, which she slaughtered at once. She took some flour, kneaded it and baked bread without yeast. 25Then she set it before Saul and his men, and they ate. That same night they got up and left.

NEW TESTAMENT READING
John 19:1–27

Jesus Sentenced to be Crucified

19 Then Pilate took Jesus and had him flogged. 2The soldiers twisted together a crown of thorns and put it on his head. They clothed him in a purple robe 3and went up to him again and again, saying, "Hail, king of the Jews!" And they struck him in the face.

4Once more Pilate came out and said to the Jews, "Look, I am bringing him out to you to let you know that I find no basis for a charge against him." 5When Jesus came out wearing the crown of thorns and the purple robe, Pilate said to them, "Here is the man!"

6As soon as the chief priests and their officials saw him, they shouted, "Crucify! Crucify!"

But Pilate answered, "You take him and crucify him. As for me, I find no basis for a charge against him."

7The Jews insisted, "We have a law, and according to that law he must die, because he claimed to be the Son of God."

8When Pilate heard this, he was even more afraid, 9and he went back inside the palace. "Where do you come from?" he asked Jesus, but Jesus gave him no answer. 10"Do you refuse to speak to me?" Pilate said. "Don't you realise I have power either to free you or to crucify you?"

11Jesus answered, "You would have no power over me if it were not given to you from above. Therefore the one who handed me over to you is guilty of a greater sin."

12From then on, Pilate tried to set Jesus free, but the Jews kept shouting, "If you let this man go, you are no friend of Caesar. Anyone who claims to be a king opposes Caesar."

13When Pilate heard this, he brought Jesus out and sat down on the judge's seat at a place known as the Stone Pavement (which in Aramaic is Gabbatha). 14It was the day of Preparation of Passover Week, about the sixth hour.

"Here is your king," Pilate said to the Jews.

15But they shouted, "Take him away! Take him away! Crucify him!"

"Shall I crucify your king?" Pilate asked.

"We have no king but Caesar," the chief priests answered.

16Finally Pilate handed him over to them to be crucified.

The Crucifixion

So the soldiers took charge of Jesus. 17Carrying his own cross, he went out to the place of the Skull (which in Aramaic is called Golgotha). 18Here they crucified him, and with him two others —one on each side and Jesus in the middle.

19Pilate had a notice prepared and fastened to the cross. It read: JESUS OF NAZARETH, THE KING OF THE JEWS. 20Many of the Jews read this sign, for the place where Jesus was crucified was near the city, and the sign was written in Aramaic, Latin and Greek. 21The chief priests of the Jews protested to Pilate, "Do not write 'The King of the Jews', but that this man claimed to be king of the Jews."

22Pilate answered, "What I have written, I have written."

23When the soldiers crucified Jesus, they took his clothes, dividing them into four shares, one for each of them, with the undergarment remaining. This garment was seamless, woven in one piece from top to bottom.

24"Let's not tear it," they said to one another. "Let's decide by lot who will get it."

This happened that the scripture might be fulfilled which said,

"They divided my garments among them
    and cast lots for my clothing."

So this is what the soldiers did.

25Near the cross of Jesus stood his mother, his mother's sister, Mary the wife of Clopas, and Mary Magdalene. 26When Jesus saw his mother there, and the disciple whom he loved standing near by, he said to his mother, "Dear woman, here is your son," 27and to the disciple, "Here is your mother." From that time on, this disciple took her into his home.

READING FROM PSALMS
Psalm 68:21–27

21Surely God will crush the heads of his enemies,
    the hairy crowns of those who go on in their sins.
22The Lord says, "I will bring them from Bashan;
    I will bring them from the depths of the sea,
23that you may plunge your feet in the blood of your foes,
    while the tongues of your dogs have their share."

24Your procession has come into view, O God,
    the procession of my God and King into the sanctuary.
25In front are the singers, after them the musicians;
    with them are the maidens playing tambourines.
26Praise God in the great congregation;
    praise the LORD in the assembly of Israel.
27There is the little tribe of Benjamin, leading them,
    there the great throng of Judah's princes,
    and there the princes of Zebulun and of Naphtali.

MAY 31   DAY 151

OLD TESTAMENT READING
1 Samuel 29:1–31:13

Achish Sends David Back to Ziklag

29 The Philistines gathered all their forces at Aphek, and Israel camped by the spring in Jezreel. 2As the Philistine rulers marched with their units of hundreds and thousands, David and his men were marching at the rear with Achish. 3The commanders of the

Philistines asked, "What about these Hebrews?"

Achish replied, "Is this not David, who was an officer of Saul king of Israel? He has already been with me for over a year, and from the day he left Saul until now, I have found no fault in him."

4But the Philistine commanders were angry with him and said, "Send the man back, that he may return to the place you assigned him. He must not go with us into battle, or he will turn against us during the fighting. How better could he regain his master's favour than by taking the heads of our own men? ⁵Isn't this the David they sang about in their dances:

"'Saul has slain his thousands,
   and David his tens of thousands'?"

⁶So Achish called David and said to him, "As surely as the LORD lives, you have been reliable, and I would be pleased to have you serve with me in the army. From the day you came to me until now, I have found no fault in you, but the rulers don't approve of you. ⁷Turn back and go in peace; do nothing to displease the Philistine rulers."

⁸"But what have I done?" asked David. "What have you found against your servant from the day I came to you until now? Why can't I go and fight against the enemies of my lord the king?"

⁹Achish answered, "I know that you have been as pleasing in my eyes as an angel of God; nevertheless, the Philistine commanders have said, 'He must not go up with us into battle.' ¹⁰Now get up early, along with your master's servants who have come with you, and leave in the morning as soon as it is light."

¹¹So David and his men got up early in the morning to go back to the land of the Philistines, and the Philistines went up to Jezreel.

David Destroys the Amalekites

30 David and his men reached Ziklag on the third day. Now the Amalekites had raided the Negev and Ziklag. They had attacked Ziklag and burned it, ²and had taken captive the women and all who were in it, both young and old. They killed none of them, but carried them off as they went on their way.

³When David and his men came to Ziklag, they found it destroyed by fire

and their wives and sons and daughters taken captive. ⁴So David and his men wept aloud until they had no strength left to weep. ⁵David's two wives had been captured—Ahinoam of Jezreel and Abigail, the widow of Nabal of Carmel. ⁶David was greatly distressed because the men were talking of stoning him; each one was bitter in spirit because of his sons and daughters. But David found strength in the LORD his God.

⁷Then David said to Abiathar the priest, the son of Ahimelech, "Bring me the ephod." Abiathar brought it to him, ⁸and David enquired of the LORD, "Shall I pursue this raiding party? Will I overtake them?"

"Pursue them," he answered. "You will certainly overtake them and succeed in the rescue."

⁹David and the six hundred men with him came to the Besor Ravine, where some stayed behind, ¹⁰for two hundred men were too exhausted to cross the ravine. But David and four hundred men continued the pursuit.

¹¹They found an Egyptian in a field and brought him to David. They gave him water to drink and food to eat —¹²part of a cake of pressed figs and two cakes of raisins. He ate and was revived, for he had not eaten any food or drunk any water for three days and three nights.

¹³David asked him, "To whom do you belong, and where do you come from?"

He said, "I am an Egyptian, the slave of an Amalekite. My master abandoned me when I became ill three days ago. ¹⁴We raided the Negev of the Kerethites and the territory belonging to Judah and the Negev of Caleb. And we burned Ziklag."

¹⁵David asked him, "Can you lead me down to this raiding party?"

He answered, "Swear to me before God that you will not kill me or hand me over to my master, and I will take you down to them."

¹⁶He led David down, and there they

were, scattered over the countryside, eating, drinking and revelling because of the great amount of plunder they had taken from the land of the Philistines and from Judah. ¹⁷David fought them from dusk until the evening of the next day, and none of them got away, except four hundred young men who rode off on camels and fled. ¹⁸David recovered everything the Amalekites had taken, including his two wives. ¹⁹Nothing was missing: young or old, boy or girl, plunder or anything else they had taken. David brought everything back. ²⁰He took all the flocks and herds, and his men drove them ahead of the other livestock, saying, "This is David's plunder."

²¹Then David came to the two hundred men who had been too exhausted to follow him and who were left behind at the Besor Ravine. They came out to meet David and the people with him. As David and his men approached, he greeted them. ²²But all the evil men and troublemakers among David's followers said, "Because they did not go out with us, we will not share with them the plunder we recovered. However, each man may take his wife and children and go."

²³David replied, "No, my brothers, you must not do that with what the LORD has given us. He has protected us and handed over to us the forces that came against us. ²⁴Who will listen to what you say? The share of the man who stayed with the supplies is to be the same as that of him who went down to the battle. All shall share alike." ²⁵David made this a statute and ordinance for Israel from that day to this.

²⁶When David arrived in Ziklag, he sent some of the plunder to the elders of Judah, who were his friends, saying, "Here is a present for you from the plunder of the LORD's enemies."

²⁷He sent it to those who were in Bethel, Ramoth Negev and Jattir; ²⁸to those in Aroer, Siphmoth, Eshtemoa ²⁹and Racal; to those in the towns of the Jerahmeelites and the Kenites; ³⁰to those in Hormah, Bor Ashan, Athach ³¹and Hebron; and to those in all the other places where David and his men had roamed.

Saul Takes His Life

31 Now the Philistines fought against Israel; the Israelites fled before them, and many fell slain on Mount Gilboa. ²The Philistines pressed hard after Saul and his sons, and they killed his sons Jonathan, Abinadab and Malki-Shua. ³The fighting grew fierce around Saul, and when the archers overtook him, they wounded him critically.

⁴Saul said to his armour-bearer, "Draw your sword and run me through, or these uncircumcised fellows will come and run me through and abuse me."

But the armour-bearer was terrified and would not do it; so Saul took his own sword and fell on it. ⁵When the armour-bearer saw that Saul was dead, he too fell on his sword and died with him. ⁶So Saul and his three sons and his armour-bearer and all his men died together that same day.

⁷When the Israelites along the valley and those across the Jordan saw that the Israelite army had fled and that Saul and his sons had died, they abandoned their towns and fled. And the Philistines came and occupied them.

⁸The next day, when the Philistines came to strip the dead, they found Saul and his three sons fallen on Mount Gilboa. ⁹They cut off his head and stripped off his armour, and they sent messengers throughout the land of the Philistines to proclaim the news in the temple of their idols and among their people. ¹⁰They put his armour in the temple of the Ashtoreths and fastened his body to the wall of Beth Shan.

¹¹When the people of Jabesh Gilead heard of what the Philistines had done to Saul, ¹²all their valiant men journeyed through the night to Beth Shan. They took down the bodies of Saul and

his sons from the wall of Beth Shan and went to Jabesh, where they burned them. 13Then they took their bones and buried them under a tamarisk tree at Jabesh, and they fasted seven days.

NEW TESTAMENT READING
John 19:28–20:9

The Death of Jesus

28Later, knowing that all was now completed, and so that the Scripture would be fulfilled, Jesus said, "I am thirsty." 29A jar of wine vinegar was there, so they soaked a sponge in it, put the sponge on a stalk of the hyssop plant, and lifted it to Jesus' lips. 30When he had received the drink, Jesus said, "It is finished." With that, he bowed his head and gave up his spirit.

31Now it was the day of Preparation, and the next day was to be a special Sabbath. Because the Jews did not want the bodies left on the crosses during the Sabbath, they asked Pilate to have the legs broken and the bodies taken down. 32The soldiers therefore came and broke the legs of the first man who had been crucified with Jesus, and then those of the other. 33But when they came to Jesus and found that he was already dead, they did not break his legs. 34Instead, one of the soldiers pierced Jesus' side with a spear, bringing a sudden flow of blood and water. 35The man who saw it has given testimony, and his testimony is true. He knows that he tells the truth, and he testifies so that you also may believe. 36These things happened so that the scripture would be fulfilled: "Not one of his bones will be broken," 37and, as another scripture says, "They will look on the one they have pierced."

The Burial of Jesus

38Later, Joseph of Arimathea asked Pilate for the body of Jesus. Now Joseph was a disciple of Jesus, but secretly because he feared the Jews. With Pilate's permission, he came and took the body away. 39He was accompanied by Nicodemus, the man who earlier had visited Jesus at night. Nicodemus brought a mixture of myrrh and aloes, about seventy-five pounds. 40Taking Jesus' body, the two of them wrapped it, with the spices, in strips of linen. This was in accordance with Jewish burial customs. 41At the place where Jesus was crucified, there was a garden, and in the garden a new tomb, in which no-one had ever been laid. 42Because it was the Jewish day of Preparation and since the tomb was near by, they laid Jesus there.

The Empty Tomb

20 Early on the first day of the week, while it was still dark, Mary Magdalene went to the tomb and saw that the stone had been removed from the entrance. 2So she came running to Simon Peter and the other disciple, the one Jesus loved, and said, "They have taken the Lord out of the tomb, and we don't know where they have put him!"

3So Peter and the other disciple started for the tomb. 4Both were running, but the other disciple outran Peter and reached the tomb first. 5He bent over and looked in at the strips of linen lying there but did not go in. 6Then Simon Peter, who was behind him, arrived and went into the tomb. He saw the strips of linen lying there, 7as well as the burial cloth that had been around Jesus' head. The cloth was folded up by itself, separate from the linen. 8Finally the other disciple, who had reached the tomb first, also went inside. He saw and believed. 9(They still did not understand from Scripture that Jesus had to rise from the dead.)

READING FROM PSALMS
Psalm 68:28–35

28Summon your power, O God;
    show us your strength, O God, as
        you have done before.

²⁹Because of your temple at Jerusalem
  kings will bring you gifts.
³⁰Rebuke the beast among the reeds,
  the herd of bulls among the
    calves of the nations.
  Humbled, may it bring bars of silver.
  Scatter the nations who delight in
    war.
³¹Envoys will come from Egypt;
  Cush will submit herself to God.

³²Sing to God, O kingdoms of the
  earth,

  sing praise to the Lord,   *Selah*
³³to him who rides the ancient skies
    above,
  who thunders with mighty voice.
³⁴Proclaim the power of God,
  whose majesty is over Israel,
  whose power is in the skies.
³⁵You are awesome, O God, in your
    sanctuary;
  the God of Israel gives power and
    strength to his people.

  Praise be to God!

JUNE 1   DAY 152

OLD TESTAMENT READING
2 Samuel 1:1–2:7

David Hears of Saul's Death

1 After the death of Saul, David returned from defeating the Amalekites and stayed in Ziklag two days. ²On
the third day a man arrived from Saul's
camp, with his clothes torn and with
dust on his head. When he came to
David, he fell to the ground to pay him
honour.

³"Where have you come from?"
David asked him.

He answered, "I have escaped from
the Israelite camp."

⁴"What happened?" David asked.
"Tell me."

He said, "The men fled from the battle. Many of them fell and died. And
Saul and his son Jonathan are dead."

⁵Then David said to the young man
who brought him the report, "How do
you know that Saul and his son
Jonathan are dead?"

⁶"I happened to be on Mount Gilboa," the young man said, "and there
was Saul, leaning on his spear, with the
chariots and riders almost upon him.
⁷When he turned round and saw me, he

called out to me, and I said, 'What can I
do?'

⁸"He asked me, 'Who are you?'
"'An Amalekite,' I answered.

⁹"Then he said to me, 'Stand over me
and kill me! I am in the throes of death,
but I'm still alive.'

¹⁰"So I stood over him and killed him,
because I knew that after he had fallen
he could not survive. And I took the
crown that was on his head and the band
on his arm and have brought them here
to my lord."

¹¹Then David and all the men with
him took hold of their clothes and tore
them. ¹²They mourned and wept and
fasted till evening for Saul and his son
Jonathan, and for the army of the LORD
and the house of Israel, because they
had fallen by the sword.

¹³David said to the young man who
brought him the report, "Where are
you from?"

"I am the son of an alien, an Amalekite," he answered.

¹⁴David asked him, "Why were you
not afraid to lift your hand to destroy
the LORD's anointed?"

¹⁵Then David called one of his men
and said, "Go, strike him down!" So he
struck him down, and he died. ¹⁶For

David had said to him, "Your blood be on your own head. Your own mouth testified against you when you said, 'I killed the LORD's anointed.'"

David's Lament for Saul and Jonathan

[17]David took up this lament concerning Saul and his son Jonathan, [18]and ordered that the men of Judah be taught this lament of the bow (it is written in the Book of Jashar):

[19]"Your glory, O Israel, lies slain on
        your heights.
    How the mighty have fallen!

[20]"Tell it not in Gath,
        proclaim it not in the streets of
        Ashkelon,
    lest the daughters of the Philistines
        be glad,
    lest the daughters of the
        uncircumcised rejoice.

[21]"O mountains of Gilboa,
    may you have neither dew nor
        rain,
    nor fields that yield offerings ⌊of
        grain⌋.
    For there the shield of the mighty
        was defiled,
    the shield of Saul—no longer
        rubbed with oil.
[22]From the blood of the slain,
    from the flesh of the mighty,
    the bow of Jonathan did not turn
        back,
    the sword of Saul did not return
        unsatisfied.

[23]"Saul and Jonathan—
    in life they were loved and
        gracious,
    and in death they were not
        parted.
    They were swifter than eagles,
    they were stronger than lions.

[24]"O daughters of Israel,
    weep for Saul,

who clothed you in scarlet and
        finery,
    who adorned your garments with
        ornaments of gold.

[25]"How the mighty have fallen in
        battle!
    Jonathan lies slain on your
        heights.
[26]I grieve for you, Jonathan my
        brother;
    you were very dear to me.
    Your love for me was wonderful,
    more wonderful than that of
        women.

[27]"How the mighty have fallen!
    The weapons of war have
        perished!"

David Anointed King Over Judah

2 In the course of time, David enquired of the LORD. "Shall I go up to one of the towns of Judah?" he asked.

The LORD said, "Go up."

David asked, "Where shall I go?"

"To Hebron," the LORD answered.

[2]So David went up there with his two wives, Ahinoam of Jezreel and Abigail, the widow of Nabal of Carmel. [3]David also took the men who were with him, each with his family, and they settled in Hebron and its towns. [4]Then the men of Judah came to Hebron and there they anointed David king over the house of Judah.

When David was told that it was the men of Jabesh Gilead who had buried Saul, [5]he sent messengers to the men of Jabesh Gilead to say to them, "The LORD bless you for showing this kindness to Saul your master by burying him. [6]May the LORD now show you kindness and faithfulness, and I too will show you the same favour because you have done this. [7]Now then, be strong and brave, for Saul your master is dead, and the house of Judah has anointed me king over them."

NEW TESTAMENT READING
John 20:10–31

Jesus Appears to Mary Magdalene

10Then the disciples went back to their homes, 11but Mary stood outside the tomb crying. As she wept, she bent over to look into the tomb 12and saw two angels in white, seated where Jesus' body had been, one at the head and the other at the foot.

13They asked her, "Woman, why are you crying?"

"They have taken my Lord away," she said, "and I don't know where they have put him." 14At this, she turned round and saw Jesus standing there, but she did not realise that it was Jesus.

15"Woman," he said, "why are you crying? Who is it you are looking for?"

Thinking he was the gardener, she said, "Sir, if you have carried him away, tell me where you have put him, and I will get him."

16Jesus said to her, "Mary."

She turned towards him and cried out in Aramaic, "Rabboni!" (which means Teacher).

17Jesus said, "Do not hold on to me, for I have not yet returned to the Father. Go instead to my brothers and tell them, 'I am returning to my Father and your Father, to my God and your God.'"

18Mary Magdalene went to the disciples with the news: "I have seen the Lord!" And she told them that he had said these things to her.

Jesus Appears to His Disciples

19On the evening of that first day of the week, when the disciples were together, with the doors locked for fear of the Jews, Jesus came and stood among them and said, "Peace be with you!" 20After he said this, he showed them his hands and side. The disciples were overjoyed when they saw the Lord.

21Again Jesus said, "Peace be with you! As the Father has sent me, I am sending you." 22And with that he breathed on them and said, "Receive the Holy Spirit. 23If you forgive anyone his sins, they are forgiven; if you do not forgive them, they are not forgiven."

Jesus Appears to Thomas

24Now Thomas (called Didymus), one of the Twelve, was not with the disciples when Jesus came. 25So the other disciples told him, "We have seen the Lord!"

But he said to them, "Unless I see the nail marks in his hands and put my finger where the nails were, and put my hand into his side, I will not believe it."

26A week later his disciples were in the house again, and Thomas was with them. Though the doors were locked, Jesus came and stood among them and said, "Peace be with you!" 27Then he said to Thomas, "Put your finger here; see my hands. Reach out your hand and put it into my side. Stop doubting and believe."

28Thomas said to him, "My Lord and my God!"

29Then Jesus told him, "Because you have seen me, you have believed; blessed are those who have not seen and yet have believed."

30Jesus did many other miraculous signs in the presence of his disciples, which are not recorded in this book. 31But these are written that you may believe that Jesus is the Christ, the Son of God, and that by believing you may have life in his name.

READING FROM PROVERBS
Proverbs 13:20–14:4

20He who walks with the wise grows wise,
　　but a companion of fools suffers harm.

21Misfortune pursues the sinner,
　　but prosperity is the reward of the righteous.

22A good man leaves an inheritance for
      his children's children,
   but a sinner's wealth is stored up
      for the righteous.

23A poor man's field may produce
      abundant food,
   but injustice sweeps it away.

24He who spares the rod hates his son,
   but he who loves him is careful to
      discipline him.

25The righteous eat to their hearts'
      content,
   but the stomach of the wicked goes
      hungry.

14 The wise woman builds her
      house,
   but with her own hands the foolish
      one tears hers down.

2He whose walk is upright fears the
      LORD,
   but he whose ways are devious
      despises him.

3A fool's talk brings a rod to his back,
   but the lips of the wise protect
      them.

4Where there are no oxen, the manger
      is empty,
   but from the strength of an ox
      comes an abundant harvest.

DAY 153

JUNE 2

OLD TESTAMENT READING
2 Samuel 2:8–3:21

*War Between the Houses of David and
Saul*

8Meanwhile, Abner son of Ner, the
commander of Saul's army, had taken
Ish-Bosheth son of Saul and brought
him over to Mahanaim. 9He made him
king over Gilead, Ashuri and Jezreel,
and also over Ephraim, Benjamin and
all Israel.

10Ish-Bosheth son of Saul was forty
years old when he became king over
Israel, and he reigned two years. The
house of Judah, however, followed
David. 11The length of time David was
king in Hebron over the house of Judah
was seven years and six months.

12Abner son of Ner, together with the
men of Ish-Bosheth son of Saul, left
Mahanaim and went to Gibeon. 13Joab
son of Zeruiah and David's men went
out and met them at the pool of Gibeon.
One group sat down on one side of the
pool and one group on the other side.

14Then Abner said to Joab, "Let's
have some of the young men get up and
fight hand to hand in front of us."

"All right, let them do it," Joab said.

15So they stood up and were counted
off—twelve men for Benjamin and Ish-
Bosheth son of Saul, and twelve for
David. 16Then each man grabbed his
opponent by the head and thrust his
dagger into his opponent's side, and
they fell down together. So that place in
Gibeon was called Helkath Hazzurim.

17The battle that day was very fierce,
and Abner and the men of Israel were
defeated by David's men.

18The three sons of Zeruiah were
there: Joab, Abishai and Asahel. Now
Asahel was as fleet-footed as a wild
gazelle. 19He chased Abner, turning
neither to the right nor to the left as
he pursued him. 20Abner looked
behind him and asked, "Is that you,
Asahel?"

"It is," he answered.

21Then Abner said to him, "Turn
aside to the right or to the left; take on
one of the young men and strip him of

his weapons." But Asahel would not stop chasing him.

²²Again Abner warned Asahel, "Stop chasing me! Why should I strike you down? How could I look your brother Joab in the face?"

²³But Asahel refused to give up the pursuit; so Abner thrust the butt of his spear into Asahel's stomach, and the spear came out through his back. He fell there and died on the spot. And every man stopped when he came to the place where Asahel had fallen and died.

²⁴But Joab and Abishai pursued Abner, and as the sun was setting, they came to the hill of Ammah, near Giah on the way to the wasteland of Gibeon. ²⁵Then the men of Benjamin rallied behind Abner. They formed themselves into a group and took their stand on top of a hill.

²⁶Abner called out to Joab, "Must the sword devour for ever? Don't you realise that this will end in bitterness? How long before you order your men to stop pursuing their brothers?"

²⁷Joab answered, "As surely as God lives, if you had not spoken, the men would have continued the pursuit of their brothers until morning."

²⁸So Joab blew the trumpet, and all the men came to a halt; they no longer pursued Israel, nor did they fight any more.

²⁹All that night Abner and his men marched through the Arabah. They crossed the Jordan, continued through the whole Bithron and came to Mahanaim.

³⁰Then Joab returned from pursuing Abner and assembled all his men. Besides Asahel, nineteen of David's men were found missing. ³¹But David's men had killed 360 Benjamites who were with Abner. ³²They took Asahel and buried him in his father's tomb at Bethlehem. Then Joab and his men marched all night and arrived at Hebron by daybreak.

3 The war between the house of Saul and the house of David lasted a long time. David grew stronger and stronger, while the house of Saul grew weaker and weaker.

²Sons were born to David in Hebron:

His firstborn was Amnon the son of Ahinoam of Jezreel;

³his second, Kileab the son of Abigail the widow of Nabal of Carmel;

the third, Absalom the son of Maacah daughter of Talmai king of Geshur;

⁴the fourth, Adonijah the son of Haggith;

the fifth, Shephatiah the son of Abital;

⁵and the sixth, Ithream the son of David's wife Eglah.

These were born to David in Hebron.

Abner Goes Over to David

⁶During the war between the house of Saul and the house of David, Abner had been strengthening his own position in the house of Saul. ⁷Now Saul had had a concubine named Rizpah daughter of Aiah. And Ish-Bosheth said to Abner, "Why did you sleep with my father's concubine?"

⁸Abner was very angry because of what Ish-Bosheth said and he answered, "Am I a dog's head—on Judah's side? This very day I am loyal to the house of your father Saul and to his family and friends. I haven't handed you over to David. Yet now you accuse me of an offence involving this woman! ⁹May God deal with Abner, be it ever so severely, if I do not do for David what the LORD promised him on oath ¹⁰and transfer the kingdom from the house of Saul and establish David's throne over Israel and Judah from Dan to Beersheba." ¹¹Ish-Bosheth did not dare to say another word to Abner, because he was afraid of him.

¹²Then Abner sent messengers on his behalf to say to David, "Whose land is it? Make an agreement with me, and I

will help you bring all Israel over to you."

13"Good," said David. "I will make an agreement with you. But I demand one thing of you: Do not come into my presence unless you bring Michal daughter of Saul when you come to see me." 14Then David sent messengers to Ish-Bosheth son of Saul, demanding, "Give me my wife Michal, whom I betrothed to myself for the price of a hundred Philistine foreskins."

15So Ish-Bosheth gave orders and had her taken away from her husband Paltiel son of Laish. 16Her husband, however, went with her, weeping behind her all the way to Bahurim. Then Abner said to him, "Go back home!" So he went back.

17Abner conferred with the elders of Israel and said, "For some time you have wanted to make David your king. 18Now do it! For the LORD promised David, 'By my servant David I will rescue my people Israel from the hand of the Philistines and from the hand of all their enemies.'"

19Abner also spoke to the Benjamites in person. Then he went to Hebron to tell David everything that Israel and the whole house of Benjamin wanted to do. 20When Abner, who had twenty men with him, came to David at Hebron, David prepared a feast for him and his men. 21Then Abner said to David, "Let me go at once and assemble all Israel for my lord the king, so that they may make a compact with you, and that you may rule over all that your heart desires." So David sent Abner away, and he went in peace.

NEW TESTAMENT READING
John 21:1–25

Jesus and the Miraculous Catch of Fish

21 Afterwards Jesus appeared again to his disciples, by the Sea of Tiberias. It happened this way: 2Simon Peter, Thomas (called Didymus), Nathanael from Cana in Galilee, the sons of Zebedee, and two other disciples were together. 3"I'm going out to fish," Simon Peter told them, and they said, "We'll go with you." So they went out and got into the boat, but that night they caught nothing.

4Early in the morning, Jesus stood on the shore, but the disciples did not realise that it was Jesus.

5He called out to them, "Friends, haven't you any fish?"

"No," they answered.

6He said, "Throw your net on the right side of the boat and you will find some." When they did, they were unable to haul the net in because of the large number of fish.

7Then the disciple whom Jesus loved said to Peter, "It is the Lord!" As soon as Simon Peter heard him say, "It is the Lord," he wrapped his outer garment around him (for he had taken it off) and jumped into the water. 8The other disciples followed in the boat, towing the net full of fish, for they were not far from shore, about a hundred yards. 9When they landed, they saw a fire of burning coals there with fish on it, and some bread.

10Jesus said to them, "Bring some of the fish you have just caught."

11Simon Peter climbed aboard and dragged the net ashore. It was full of large fish, 153, but even with so many the net was not torn. 12Jesus said to them, "Come and have breakfast." None of the disciples dared ask him, "Who are you?" They knew it was the Lord. 13Jesus came, took the bread and gave it to them, and did the same with the fish. 14This was now the third time Jesus appeared to his disciples after he was raised from the dead.

Jesus Reinstates Peter

15When they had finished eating, Jesus said to Simon Peter, "Simon son of John, do you truly love me more than these?"

"Yes, Lord," he said, "you know that I love you."

Jesus said, "Feed my lambs."

16Again Jesus said, "Simon son of John, do you truly love me?"

He answered, "Yes, Lord, you know that I love you."

Jesus said, "Take care of my sheep."

17The third time he said to him, "Simon son of John, do you love me?" Peter was hurt because Jesus asked him the third time, "Do you love me?" He said, "Lord, you know all things; you know that I love you."

Jesus said, "Feed my sheep. 18I tell you the truth, when you were younger you dressed yourself and went where you wanted; but when you are old you will stretch out your hands, and someone else will dress you and lead you where you do not want to go." 19Jesus said this to indicate the kind of death by which Peter would glorify God. Then he said to him, "Follow me!"

20Peter turned and saw that the disciple whom Jesus loved was following them. (This was the one who had leaned back against Jesus at the supper and had said, "Lord, who is going to betray you?") 21When Peter saw him, he asked, "Lord, what about him?"

22Jesus answered, "If I want him to remain alive until I return, what is that to you? You must follow me." 23Because of this, the rumour spread among the brothers that this disciple would not die. But Jesus did not say that he would not die; he only said, "If I want him to remain alive until I return, what is that to you?"

24This is the disciple who testifies to these things and who wrote them down. We know that his testimony is true.

25Jesus did many other things as well. If every one of them were written down, I suppose that even the whole world would not have room for the books that would be written.

READING FROM PSALMS
Psalm 69:1–12

For the director of music. To ⌐the tune of⌐ "Lilies". Of David.

1Save me, O God,
 for the waters have come up to my
  neck.
2I sink in the miry depths,
 where there is no foothold.
I have come into the deep waters;
 the floods engulf me.
3I am worn out calling for help;
 my throat is parched.
My eyes fail,
 looking for my God.
4Those who hate me without reason
 outnumber the hairs of my head;
many are my enemies without cause,
 those who seek to destroy me.
I am forced to restore
 what I did not steal.

5You know my folly, O God;
 my guilt is not hidden from you.

6May those who hope in you
 not be disgraced because of me,
 O Lord, the LORD Almighty;
may those who seek you
 not be put to shame because of me,
 O God of Israel.
7For I endure scorn for your sake,
 and shame covers my face.
8I am a stranger to my brothers,
 an alien to my own mother's sons;
9for zeal for your house consumes me,
 and the insults of those who insult
  you fall on me.
10When I weep and fast,
 I must endure scorn;
11when I put on sackcloth,
 people make sport of me.
12Those who sit at the gate mock me,
 and I am the song of the
  drunkards.

OLD TESTAMENT READING
2 Samuel 3:22–5:5

Joab Murders Abner

22Just then David's men and Joab returned from a raid and brought with them a great deal of plunder. But Abner was no longer with David in Hebron, because David had sent him away, and he had gone in peace. 23When Joab and all the soldiers with him arrived, he was told that Abner son of Ner had come to the king and that the king had sent him away and that he had gone in peace.

24So Joab went to the king and said, "What have you done? Look, Abner came to you. Why did you let him go? Now he is gone! 25You know Abner son of Ner; he came to deceive you and observe your movements and find out everything you are doing."

26Joab then left David and sent messengers after Abner, and they brought him back from the well of Sirah. But David did not know it. 27Now when Abner returned to Hebron, Joab took him aside into the gateway, as though to speak with him privately. And there, to avenge the blood of his brother Asahel, Joab stabbed him in the stomach, and he died.

28Later, when David heard about this, he said, "I and my kingdom are for ever innocent before the LORD concerning the blood of Abner son of Ner. 29May his blood fall upon the head of Joab and upon all his father's house! May Joab's house never be without someone who has a running sore or leprosy or who leans on a crutch or who falls by the sword or who lacks food."

30(Joab and his brother Abishai murdered Abner because he had killed their brother Asahel in the battle of Gibeon.)

31Then David said to Joab and all the people with him, "Tear your clothes and put on sackcloth and walk in mourning in front of Abner." King David himself walked behind the bier. 32They buried Abner in Hebron, and the king wept aloud at Abner's tomb. All the people wept also.

33The king sang this lament for Abner:

"Should Abner have died as the
    lawless die?
34 Your hands were not bound,
    your feet were not fettered.
You fell as one falls before wicked
    men."

And all the people wept over him again.

35Then they all came and urged David to eat something while it was still day; but David took an oath, saying, "May God deal with me, be it ever so severely, if I taste bread or anything else before the sun sets!"

36All the people took note and were pleased; indeed, everything the king did pleased them. 37So on that day all the people and all Israel knew that the king had no part in the murder of Abner son of Ner.

38Then the king said to his men, "Do you not realise that a prince and a great man has fallen in Israel this day? 39And today, though I am the anointed king, I am weak, and these sons of Zeruiah are too strong for me. May the LORD repay the evildoer according to his evil deeds!"

Ish-Bosheth Murdered

4 When Ish-Bosheth son of Saul heard that Abner had died in Hebron, he lost courage, and all Israel became alarmed. 2Now Saul's son had two men who were leaders of raiding bands. One was named Baanah and the other Recab; they were sons of Rimmon the Beerothite from the tribe of Benjamin

—Beeroth is considered part of Benjamin, ³because the people of Beeroth fled to Gittaim and have lived there as aliens to this day.

⁴(Jonathan son of Saul had a son who was lame in both feet. He was five years old when the news about Saul and Jonathan came from Jezreel. His nurse picked him up and fled, but as she hurried to leave, he fell and became crippled. His name was Mephibosheth.)

⁵Now Recab and Baanah, the sons of Rimmon the Beerothite, set out for the house of Ish-Bosheth, and they arrived there in the heat of the day while he was taking his noonday rest. ⁶They went into the inner part of the house as if to get some wheat, and they stabbed him in the stomach. Then Recab and his brother Baanah slipped away.

⁷They had gone into the house while he was lying on the bed in his bedroom. After they stabbed and killed him, they cut off his head. Taking it with them, they travelled all night by way of the Arabah. ⁸They brought the head of Ish-Bosheth to David at Hebron and said to the king, "Here is the head of Ish-Bosheth son of Saul, your enemy, who tried to take your life. This day the LORD has avenged my lord the king against Saul and his offspring."

⁹David answered Recab and his brother Baanah, the sons of Rimmon the Beerothite, "As surely as the LORD lives, who has delivered me out of all trouble, ¹⁰when a man told me, 'Saul is dead,' and thought he was bringing good news, I seized him and put him to death in Ziklag. That was the reward I gave him for his news! ¹¹How much more—when wicked men have killed an innocent man in his own house and on his own bed—should I not now demand his blood from your hand and rid the earth of you!"

¹²So David gave an order to his men, and they killed them. They cut off their hands and feet and hung the bodies by the pool in Hebron. But they took the head of Ish-Bosheth and buried it in Abner's tomb at Hebron.

David Becomes King Over Israel

5 All the tribes of Israel came to David at Hebron and said, "We are your own flesh and blood. ²In the past, while Saul was king over us, you were the one who led Israel on their military campaigns. And the LORD said to you, 'You shall shepherd my people Israel, and you shall become their ruler.'"

³When all the elders of Israel had come to King David at Hebron, the king made a compact with them at Hebron before the LORD, and they anointed David king over Israel.

⁴David was thirty years old when he became king, and he reigned for forty years. ⁵In Hebron he reigned over Judah for seven years and six months, and in Jerusalem he reigned over all Israel and Judah for thirty-three years.

NEW TESTAMENT READING
Acts 1:1–22

Jesus Taken Up Into Heaven

1 In my former book, Theophilus, I wrote about all that Jesus began to do and to teach ²until the day he was taken up to heaven, after giving instructions through the Holy Spirit to the apostles he had chosen. ³After his suffering, he showed himself to these men and gave many convincing proofs that he was alive. He appeared to them over a period of forty days and spoke about the kingdom of God. ⁴On one occasion, while he was eating with them, he gave them this command: "Do not leave Jerusalem, but wait for the gift my Father promised, which you have heard me speak about. ⁵For John baptised with water, but in a few days you will be baptised with the Holy Spirit."

⁶So when they met together, they asked him, "Lord, are you at this time going to restore the kingdom to Israel?"

⁷He said to them: "It is not for you to know the times or dates the Father has set by his own authority. ⁸But you will receive power when the Holy Spirit

comes on you; and you will be my witnesses in Jerusalem, and in all Judea and Samaria, and to the ends of the earth."

⁹After he said this, he was taken up before their very eyes, and a cloud hid him from their sight.

¹⁰They were looking intently up into the sky as he was going, when suddenly two men dressed in white stood beside them. ¹¹"Men of Galilee," they said, "why do you stand here looking into the sky? This same Jesus, who has been taken from you into heaven, will come back in the same way you have seen him go into heaven."

Matthias Chosen to Replace Judas

¹²Then they returned to Jerusalem from the hill called the Mount of Olives, a Sabbath day's walk from the city. ¹³When they arrived, they went upstairs to the room where they were staying. Those present were Peter, John, James and Andrew; Philip and Thomas, Bartholomew and Matthew; James son of Alphaeus and Simon the Zealot, and Judas son of James. ¹⁴They all joined together constantly in prayer, along with the women and Mary the mother of Jesus, and with his brothers.

¹⁵In those days Peter stood up among the believers (a group numbering about a hundred and twenty) ¹⁶and said, "Brothers, the Scripture had to be fulfilled which the Holy Spirit spoke long ago through the mouth of David concerning Judas, who served as guide for those who arrested Jesus—¹⁷he was one of our number and shared in this ministry."

¹⁸(With the reward he got for his wickedness, Judas bought a field; there he fell headlong, his body burst open and all his intestines spilled out. ¹⁹Everyone in Jerusalem heard about this, so they called that field in their language Akeldama, that is, Field of Blood.)

²⁰"For," said Peter, "it is written in the Book of Psalms,

"'May his place be deserted;
    let there be no-one to dwell in it,'

and,

"'May another take his place of
    leadership.'

²¹Therefore it is necessary to choose one of the men who have been with us the whole time the Lord Jesus went in and out among us, ²²beginning from John's baptism to the time when Jesus was taken up from us. For one of these must become a witness with us of his resurrection."

READING FROM PSALMS
Psalm 69:13–28

¹³But I pray to you, O LORD,
    in the time of your favour;
in your great love, O God,
    answer me with your sure
        salvation.
¹⁴Rescue me from the mire,
    do not let me sink;
deliver me from those who hate me,
    from the deep waters.
¹⁵Do not let the floodwaters engulf me
    or the depths swallow me up
    or the pit close its mouth over me.
¹⁶Answer me, O LORD, out of the
        goodness of your love;
    in your great mercy turn to me.
¹⁷Do not hide your face from your
        servant;
    answer me quickly, for I am in
        trouble.
¹⁸Come near and rescue me;
    redeem me because of my foes.

¹⁹You know how I am scorned,
        disgraced and shamed;
    all my enemies are before you.
²⁰Scorn has broken my heart
    and has left me helpless;
I looked for sympathy, but there was
        none,
    for comforters, but I found none.

²¹They put gall in my food
    and gave me vinegar for my thirst.

²²May the table set before them
    become a snare;
    may it become retribution and a
      trap.
²³May their eyes be darkened so that
    they cannot see,
    and their backs be bent for ever.
²⁴Pour out your wrath on them;
    let your fierce anger overtake
      them.

²⁵May their place be deserted;
    let there be no-one to dwell in their
      tents.
²⁶For they persecute those you wound
    and talk about the pain of those
      you hurt.
²⁷Charge them with crime upon crime;
    do not let them share in your
      salvation.
²⁸May they be blotted out of the book
    of life
    and not be listed with the
      righteous.

JUNE 4   DAY 155

OLD TESTAMENT READING
2 Samuel 5:6–6:23

David Conquers Jerusalem

⁶The king and his men marched to Jerusalem to attack the Jebusites, who lived there. The Jebusites said to David, "You will not get in here; even the blind and the lame can ward you off." They thought, "David cannot get in here." ⁷Nevertheless, David captured the fortress of Zion, the City of David.

⁸On that day, David said, "Anyone who conquers the Jebusites will have to use the water shaft to reach those 'lame and blind' who are David's enemies." That is why they say, "The 'blind and lame' will not enter the palace."

⁹David then took up residence in the fortress and called it the City of David. He built up the area around it, from the supporting terraces inward. ¹⁰And he became more and more powerful, because the LORD God Almighty was with him.

¹¹Now Hiram king of Tyre sent messengers to David, along with cedar logs and carpenters and stonemasons, and they built a palace for David. ¹²And David knew that the LORD had established him as king over Israel and had

exalted his kingdom for the sake of his people Israel.

¹³After he left Hebron, David took more concubines and wives in Jerusalem, and more sons and daughters were born to him. ¹⁴These are the names of the children born to him there: Shammua, Shobab, Nathan, Solomon, ¹⁵Ibhar, Elishua, Nepheg, Japhia, ¹⁶Elishama, Eliada and Eliphelet.

David Defeats the Philistines

¹⁷When the Philistines heard that David had been anointed king over Israel, they went up in full force to search for him, but David heard about it and went down to the stronghold. ¹⁸Now the Philistines had come and spread out in the Valley of Rephaim; ¹⁹so David enquired of the LORD, "Shall I go and attack the Philistines? Will you hand them over to me?"

The LORD answered him, "Go, for I will surely hand the Philistines over to you."

²⁰So David went to Baal Perazim, and there he defeated them. He said, "As waters break out, the LORD has broken out against my enemies before me." So that place was called Baal Perazim. ²¹The Philistines abandoned their idols

there, and David and his men carried them off.

22Once more the Philistines came up and spread out in the Valley of Rephaim; 23so David enquired of the LORD, and he answered, "Do not go straight up, but circle round behind them and attack them in front of the balsam trees. 24As soon as you hear the sound of marching in the tops of the balsam trees, move quickly, because that will mean the LORD has gone out in front of you to strike the Philistine army." 25So David did as the LORD commanded him, and he struck down the Philistines all the way from Gibeon to Gezer.

The Ark Brought to Jerusalem

6 David again brought together out of Israel chosen men, thirty thousand in all. 2He and all his men set out from Baalah of Judah to bring up from there the ark of God, which is called by the Name, the name of the LORD Almighty, who is enthroned between the cherubim that are on the ark. 3They set the ark of God on a new cart and brought it from the house of Abinadab, which was on the hill. Uzzah and Ahio, sons of Abinadab, were guiding the new cart 4with the ark of God on it, and Ahio was walking in front of it. 5David and the whole house of Israel were celebrating with all their might before the LORD, with songs and with harps, lyres, tambourines, sistrums and cymbals.

6When they came to the threshing-floor of Nacon, Uzzah reached out and took hold of the ark of God, because the oxen stumbled. 7The LORD's anger burned against Uzzah because of his irreverent act; therefore God struck him down and he died there beside the ark of God.

8Then David was angry because the LORD's wrath had broken out against Uzzah, and to this day that place is called Perez Uzzah.

9David was afraid of the LORD that day and said, "How can the ark of the LORD ever come to me?" 10He was not willing to take the ark of the LORD to be with him in the City of David. Instead, he took it aside to the house of Obed-Edom the Gittite. 11The ark of the LORD remained in the house of Obed-Edom the Gittite for three months, and the LORD blessed him and his entire household.

12Now King David was told, "The LORD has blessed the household of Obed-Edom and everything he has, because of the ark of God." So David went down and brought up the ark of God from the house of Obed-Edom to the City of David with rejoicing. 13When those who were carrying the ark of the LORD had taken six steps, he sacrificed a bull and a fattened calf. 14David, wearing a linen ephod, danced before the LORD with all his might, 15while he and the entire house of Israel brought up the ark of the LORD with shouts and the sound of trumpets.

16As the ark of the LORD was entering the City of David, Michal daughter of Saul watched from a window. And when she saw King David leaping and dancing before the LORD, she despised him in her heart.

17They brought the ark of the LORD and set it in its place inside the tent that David had pitched for it, and David sacrificed burnt offerings and fellowship offerings before the LORD. 18After he had finished sacrificing the burnt offerings and fellowship offerings, he blessed the people in the name of the LORD Almighty. 19Then he gave a loaf of bread, a cake of dates and a cake of raisins to each person in the whole crowd of Israelites, both men and women. And all the people went to their homes.

20When David returned home to bless his household, Michal daughter of Saul came out to meet him and said, "How the king of Israel has distinguished himself today, disrobing in the sight of the slave girls of his servants as any vulgar fellow would."

21David said to Michal, "It was before the LORD, who chose me rather than your father or anyone from his house when he appointed me ruler over the LORD's people Israel—I will celebrate before the LORD. 22I will become even more undignified than this, and I will be humiliated in my own eyes. But by these slave girls you spoke of, I will be held in honour."

23And Michal daughter of Saul had no children to the day of her death.

NEW TESTAMENT READING
Acts 1:23–2:21

23So they proposed two men: Joseph called Barsabbas (also known as Justus) and Matthias. 24Then they prayed, "Lord, you know everyone's heart. Show us which of these two you have chosen 25to take over this apostolic ministry, which Judas left to go where he belongs." 26Then they cast lots, and the lot fell to Matthias; so he was added to the eleven apostles.

The Holy Spirit Comes at Pentecost

2 When the day of Pentecost came, they were all together in one place. 2Suddenly a sound like the blowing of a violent wind came from heaven and filled the whole house where they were sitting. 3They saw what seemed to be tongues of fire that separated and came to rest on each of them. 4All of them were filled with the Holy Spirit and began to speak in other tongues as the Spirit enabled them.

5Now there were staying in Jerusalem God-fearing Jews from every nation under heaven. 6When they heard this sound, a crowd came together in bewilderment, because each one heard them speaking in his own language. 7Utterly amazed, they asked: "Are not all these men who are speaking Galileans? 8Then how is it that each of us hears them in his own native language?

9Parthians, Medes and Elamites; residents of Mesopotamia, Judea and Cappadocia, Pontus and Asia, 10Phrygia and Pamphylia, Egypt and the parts of Libya near Cyrene; visitors from Rome 11(both Jews and converts to Judaism); Cretans and Arabs—we hear them declaring the wonders of God in our own tongues!" 12Amazed and perplexed, they asked one another, "What does this mean?"

13Some, however, made fun of them and said, "They have had too much wine."

Peter Addresses the Crowd

14Then Peter stood up with the Eleven, raised his voice and addressed the crowd: "Fellow Jews and all of you who live in Jerusalem, let me explain this to you; listen carefully to what I say. 15These men are not drunk, as you suppose. It's only nine in the morning! 16No, this is what was spoken by the prophet Joel:

17"'In the last days, God says,
　I will pour out my Spirit on all
　　people.
　Your sons and daughters will
　　prophesy,
　　your young men will see visions,
　　your old men will dream dreams.
18Even on my servants, both men and
　　women,
　I will pour out my Spirit in those
　　days,
　　and they will prophesy.
19I will show wonders in the heaven
　　above
　　and signs on the earth below,
　　blood and fire and billows of
　　　smoke.
20The sun will be turned to darkness
　　and the moon to blood
　　before the coming of the great and
　　　glorious day of the Lord.
21And everyone who calls
　　on the name of the Lord will be
　　　saved.'

READING FROM PSALMS
Psalm 69:29–36

29I am in pain and distress;
　　may your salvation, O God,
　　　　protect me.

30I will praise God's name in song
　　and glorify him with thanksgiving.
31This will please the LORD more than
　　　　an ox,
　　more than a bull with its horns and
　　　　hoofs.
32The poor will see and be glad—
　　you who seek God, may your
　　　　hearts live!

33The LORD hears the needy
　　and does not despise his captive
　　　　people.

34Let heaven and earth praise him,
　　the seas and all that move in
　　　　them,
35for God will save Zion
　　and rebuild the cities of Judah.
　　Then people will settle there and
　　　　possess it;
36　the children of his servants will
　　　　inherit it,
　　and those who love his name will
　　　　dwell there.

DAY 156

JUNE 5

OLD TESTAMENT READING
2 Samuel 7:1–8:18

God's Promise to David

7 After the king was settled in his palace and the LORD had given him rest from all his enemies around him, 2he said to Nathan the prophet, "Here I am, living in a palace of cedar, while the ark of God remains in a tent."

3Nathan replied to the king, "Whatever you have in mind, go ahead and do it, for the LORD is with you."

4That night the word of the LORD came to Nathan, saying:

5"Go and tell my servant David, 'This is what the LORD says: Are you the one to build me a house to dwell in? 6I have not dwelt in a house from the day I brought the Israelites up out of Egypt to this day. I have been moving from place to place with a tent as my dwelling. 7Wherever I have moved with all the Israelites, did I ever say to any of their rulers whom I commanded to shepherd my people Israel, "Why have you not built me a house of cedar?"'

8"Now then, tell my servant David, 'This is what the LORD Almighty says: I took you from the pasture and from following the flock to be ruler over my people Israel. 9I have been with you wherever you have gone, and I have cut off all your enemies from before you. Now I will make your name great, like the names of the greatest men of the earth. 10And I will provide a place for my people Israel and will plant them so that they can have a home of their own and no longer be disturbed. Wicked people shall not oppress them any more, as they did at the beginning 11and have done ever since the time I appointed leaders over my people Israel. I will also give you rest from all your enemies.

"'The LORD declares to you that the LORD himself will establish a house for you: 12When your days are over and you rest with your fathers, I will raise up your offspring to succeed you, who will come from your own body, and I will establish his kingdom. [13]He is the one who will build a house for my Name, and I will establish the throne of his kingdom for ever. [14]I will be his father, and he shall be my son. When he does wrong, I will punish him with the rod of men, with floggings inflicted by men. [15]But my love will never be taken away from him, as I took it away from Saul, whom I removed from before you. [16]Your house and your kingdom shall endure for ever before me; your throne shall be established for ever.'"

[17]Nathan reported to David all the words of this entire revelation.

David's Prayer

[18]Then King David went in and sat before the LORD, and he said:

"Who am I, O Sovereign LORD, and what is my family, that you have brought me this far? [19]And as if this were not enough in your sight, O Sovereign LORD, you have also spoken about the future of the house of your servant. Is this your usual way of dealing with man, O Sovereign LORD?

[20]"What more can David say to you? For you know your servant, O Sovereign LORD. [21]For the sake of your word and according to your will, you have done this great thing and made it known to your servant.

[22]"How great you are, O Sovereign LORD! There is no-one like you, and there is no God but you, as we have heard with our own ears. [23]And who is like your people Israel—the one nation on earth that God went out to redeem as a people for himself, and to make a name for himself, and to perform great and awesome wonders by driving out nations and their gods from before your people, whom you redeemed from Egypt? [24]You have established your people Israel as your very own for ever, and you, O LORD, have become their God.

[25]"And now, LORD God, keep for ever the promise you have made concerning your servant and his house. Do as you promised, [26]so that your name will be great for ever. Then men will say, 'The LORD Almighty is God over Israel!' And the house of your servant David will be established before you.

[27]"O LORD Almighty, God of Israel, you have revealed this to your servant, saying, 'I will build a house for you.' So your servant has found courage to offer you this prayer. [28]O Sovereign LORD, you are God! Your words are trustworthy, and you have promised these good things to your servant. [29]Now be pleased to bless the house of your servant, that it may continue for ever in your sight; for you, O Sovereign LORD, have spoken, and with your blessing the house of your servant will be blessed for ever."

David's Victories

8 In the course of time, David defeated the Philistines and subdued them, and he took Metheg Ammah from the control of the Philistines.

[2]David also defeated the Moabites. He made them lie down on the ground and measured them off with a length of cord. Every two lengths of them were put to death, and the third length was allowed to live. So the Moabites became subject to David and brought tribute.

[3]Moreover, David fought Hadadezer son of Rehob, king of Zobah, when he went to restore his control along the Euphrates River. [4]David captured a thousand of his chariots, seven thousand charioteers and twenty

thousand foot soldiers. He hamstrung all but a hundred of the chariot horses.

5When the Arameans of Damascus came to help Hadadezer king of Zobah, David struck down twenty-two thousand of them. 6He put garrisons in the Aramean kingdom of Damascus, and the Arameans became subject to David and brought tribute. The LORD gave David victory wherever he went.

7David took the gold shields that belonged to the officers of Hadadezer and brought them to Jerusalem. 8From Tebah and Berothai, towns that belonged to Hadadezer, King David took a great quantity of bronze.

9When Tou king of Hamath heard that David had defeated the entire army of Hadadezer, 10he sent his son Joram to King David to greet him and congratulate him on his victory in battle over Hadadezer, who had been at war with Tou. Joram brought with him articles of silver and gold and bronze.

11King David dedicated these articles to the LORD, as he had done with the silver and gold from all the nations he had subdued: 12Edom and Moab, the Ammonites and the Philistines, and Amalek. He also dedicated the plunder taken from Hadadezer son of Rehob, king of Zobah.

13And David became famous after he returned from striking down eighteen thousand Edomites in the Valley of Salt.

14He put garrisons throughout Edom, and all the Edomites became subject to David. The LORD gave David victory wherever he went.

David's Officials

15David reigned over all Israel, doing what was just and right for all his people. 16Joab son of Zeruiah was over the army; Jehoshaphat son of Ahilud was recorder; 17Zadok son of Ahitub and Ahimelech son of Abiathar were priests; Seraiah was secretary; 18Benaiah son of Jehoiada was over the Kerethites and Pelethites; and David's sons were royal advisers.

NEW TESTAMENT READING
Acts 2:22–47

22"Men of Israel, listen to this: Jesus of Nazareth was a man accredited by God to you by miracles, wonders and signs, which God did among you through him, as you yourselves know. 23This man was handed over to you by God's set purpose and foreknowledge; and you, with the help of wicked men, put him to death by nailing him to the cross. 24But God raised him from the dead, freeing him from the agony of death, because it was impossible for death to keep its hold on him. 25David said about him:

"'I saw the Lord always before me.
  Because he is at my right hand,
  I will not be shaken.
26Therefore my heart is glad and my
    tongue rejoices;
  my body also will live in hope,
27because you will not abandon me to
    the grave,
  nor will you let your Holy One see
    decay.
28You have made known to me the
    paths of life;
  you will fill me with joy in your
    presence.'

29"Brothers, I can tell you confidently that the patriarch David died and was buried, and his tomb is here to this day. 30But he was a prophet and knew that God had promised him on oath that he would place one of his descendants on his throne. 31Seeing what was ahead, he spoke of the resurrection of the Christ, that he was not abandoned to the grave, nor did his body see decay. 32God has raised this Jesus to life, and we are all witnesses of the fact. 33Exalted to the right hand of God, he has received from the Father the promised Holy Spirit and has poured out what you now see and hear. 34For David did not ascend to heaven, and yet he said,

"'The Lord said to my Lord:
  "Sit at my right hand

35until I make your enemies
　　a footstool for your feet.'"'

36"Therefore let all Israel be assured of this: God has made this Jesus, whom you crucified, both Lord and Christ."

37When the people heard this, they were cut to the heart and said to Peter and the other apostles, "Brothers, what shall we do?"

38Peter replied, "Repent and be baptised, every one of you, in the name of Jesus Christ for the forgiveness of your sins. And you will receive the gift of the Holy Spirit. 39The promise is for you and your children and for all who are far off—for all whom the Lord our God will call."

40With many other words he warned them; and he pleaded with them, "Save yourselves from this corrupt generation." 41Those who accepted his message were baptised, and about three thousand were added to their number that day.

The Fellowship of the Believers

42They devoted themselves to the apostles' teaching and to the fellowship, to the breaking of bread and to prayer. 43Everyone was filled with awe, and many wonders and miraculous signs were done by the apostles. 44All the believers were together and had everything in common. 45Selling their possessions and goods, they gave to anyone as he had need. 46Every day they continued to meet together in the temple courts. They broke bread in their homes and ate together with glad and sincere hearts, 47praising God and enjoying the favour of all the people. And the Lord added to their number daily those who were being saved.

READING FROM PROVERBS
Proverbs 14:5–14

5A truthful witness does not deceive,
　　but a false witness pours out lies.

6The mocker seeks wisdom and finds none,
　　but knowledge comes easily to the discerning.

7Stay away from a foolish man,
　　for you will not find knowledge on his lips.

8The wisdom of the prudent is to give thought to their ways,
　　but the folly of fools is deception.

9Fools mock at making amends for sin,
　　but goodwill is found among the upright.

10Each heart knows its own bitterness,
　　and no-one else can share its joy.

11The house of the wicked will be destroyed,
　　but the tent of the upright will flourish.

12There is a way that seems right to a man,
　　but in the end it leads to death.

13Even in laughter the heart may ache,
　　and joy may end in grief.

14The faithless will be fully repaid for their ways,
　　and the good man rewarded for his.

OLD TESTAMENT READING
2 Samuel 9:1–10:19

David and Mephibosheth

9 David asked, "Is there anyone still left of the house of Saul to whom I can show kindness for Jonathan's sake?"

²Now there was a servant of Saul's household named Ziba. They called him to appear before David, and the king said to him, "Are you Ziba?"

"Your servant," he replied.

³The king asked, "Is there no-one still left of the house of Saul to whom I can show God's kindness?"

Ziba answered the king, "There is still a son of Jonathan; he is crippled in both feet."

⁴"Where is he?" the king asked.

Ziba answered, "He is at the house of Makir son of Ammiel in Lo Debar."

⁵So King David had him brought from Lo Debar, from the house of Makir son of Ammiel.

⁶When Mephibosheth son of Jonathan, the son of Saul, came to David, he bowed down to pay him honour.

David said, "Mephibosheth!"

"Your servant," he replied.

⁷"Don't be afraid," David said to him, "for I will surely show you kindness for the sake of your father Jonathan. I will restore to you all the land that belonged to your grandfather Saul, and you will always eat at my table."

⁸Mephibosheth bowed down and said, "What is your servant, that you should notice a dead dog like me?"

⁹Then the king summoned Ziba, Saul's servant, and said to him, "I have given your master's grandson everything that belonged to Saul and his family. ¹⁰You and your sons and your servants are to farm the land for him and bring in the crops, so that your master's grandson may be provided for. And Mephibosheth, grandson of your master, will always eat at my table." (Now Ziba had fifteen sons and twenty servants.)

¹¹Then Ziba said to the king, "Your servant will do whatever my lord the king commands his servant to do." So Mephibosheth ate at David's table like one of the king's sons.

¹²Mephibosheth had a young son named Mica, and all the members of Ziba's household were servants of Mephibosheth. ¹³And Mephibosheth lived in Jerusalem, because he always ate at the king's table, and he was crippled in both feet.

David Defeats the Ammonites

10 In the course of time, the king of the Ammonites died, and his son Hanun succeeded him as king. ²David thought, "I will show kindness to Hanun son of Nahash, just as his father showed kindness to me." So David sent a delegation to express his sympathy to Hanun concerning his father.

When David's men came to the land of the Ammonites, ³the Ammonite nobles said to Hanun their lord, "Do you think David is honouring your father by sending men to you to express sympathy? Hasn't David sent them to you to explore the city and spy it out and overthrow it?" ⁴So Hanun seized David's men, shaved off half of each man's beard, cut off their garments in the middle at the buttocks, and sent them away.

⁵When David was told about this, he sent messengers to meet the men, for they were greatly humiliated. The king said, "Stay at Jericho till your beards have grown, and then come back."

⁶When the Ammonites realised that

they had become an offence to David's nostrils, they hired twenty thousand Aramean foot soldiers from Beth Rehob and Zobah, as well as the king of Maacah with a thousand men, and also twelve thousand men from Tob.

7On hearing this, David sent Joab out with the entire army of fighting men. 8The Ammonites came out and drew up in battle formation at the entrance to their city gate, while the Arameans of Zobah and Rehob and the men of Tob and Maacah were by themselves in the open country.

9Joab saw that there were battle lines in front of him and behind him; so he selected some of the best troops in Israel and deployed them against the Arameans. 10He put the rest of the men under the command of Abishai his brother and deployed them against the Ammonites. 11Joab said, "If the Arameans are too strong for me, then you are to come to my rescue; but if the Ammonites are too strong for you, then I will come to rescue you. 12Be strong and let us fight bravely for our people and the cities of our God. The LORD will do what is good in his sight."

13Then Joab and the troops with him advanced to fight the Arameans, and they fled before him. 14When the Ammonites saw that the Arameans were fleeing, they fled before Abishai and went inside the city. So Joab returned from fighting the Ammonites and came to Jerusalem.

15After the Arameans saw that they had been routed by Israel, they regrouped. 16Hadadezer had Arameans brought from beyond the River; they went to Helam, with Shobach the commander of Hadadezer's army leading them.

17When David was told of this, he gathered all Israel, crossed the Jordan and went to Helam. The Arameans formed their battle lines to meet David and fought against him. 18But they fled before Israel, and David killed seven hundred of their charioteers and forty thousand of their foot soldiers. He also struck down Shobach the commander of their army, and he died there. 19When all the kings who were vassals of Hadadezer saw that they had been defeated by Israel, they made peace with the Israelites and became subject to them.

So the Arameans were afraid to help the Ammonites any more.

NEW TESTAMENT READING
Acts 3:1–26

Peter Heals the Crippled Beggar

3 One day Peter and John were going up to the temple at the time of prayer—at three in the afternoon. 2Now a man crippled from birth was being carried to the temple gate called Beautiful, where he was put every day to beg from those going into the temple courts. 3When he saw Peter and John about to enter, he asked them for money. 4Peter looked straight at him, as did John. Then Peter said, "Look at us!" 5So the man gave them his attention, expecting to get something from them.

6Then Peter said, "Silver or gold I do not have, but what I have I give you. In the name of Jesus Christ of Nazareth, walk." 7Taking him by the right hand, he helped him up, and instantly the man's feet and ankles became strong. 8He jumped to his feet and began to walk. Then he went with them into the temple courts, walking and jumping, and praising God. 9When all the people saw him walking and praising God, 10they recognised him as the same man who used to sit begging at the temple gate called Beautiful, and they were filled with wonder and amazement at what had happened to him.

Peter Speaks to the Onlookers

11While the beggar held on to Peter and John, all the people were astonished and came running to them in the place called Solomon's Colonnade. ¹²When Peter saw this, he said to them: "Men of Israel, why does this surprise you? Why do you stare at us as if by our own power or godliness we had made this man walk? ¹³The God of Abraham, Isaac and Jacob, the God of our fathers, has glorified his servant Jesus. You handed him over to be killed, and you disowned him before Pilate, though he had decided to let him go. ¹⁴You disowned the Holy and Righteous One and asked that a murderer be released to you. ¹⁵You killed the author of life, but God raised him from the dead. We are witnesses of this. ¹⁶By faith in the name of Jesus, this man whom you see and know was made strong. It is Jesus' name and the faith that comes through him that has given this complete healing to him, as you can all see.

¹⁷"Now, brothers, I know that you acted in ignorance, as did your leaders. ¹⁸But this is how God fulfilled what he had foretold through all the prophets, saying that his Christ would suffer. ¹⁹Repent, then, and turn to God, so that your sins may be wiped out, that times of refreshing may come from the Lord, ²⁰and that he may send the Christ, who has been appointed for you—even Jesus. ²¹He must remain in heaven until the time comes for God to restore everything, as he promised long ago through his holy prophets. ²²For Moses said, 'The Lord your God will raise up for you a prophet like me from among your own people; you must listen to everything he tells you. ²³Anyone who does not listen to him will be completely cut off from among his people.'

²⁴"Indeed, all the prophets from Samuel on, as many as have spoken, have foretold these days. ²⁵And you are heirs of the prophets and of the covenant God made with your fathers. He said to Abraham, 'Through your offspring all peoples on earth will be blessed.' ²⁶When God raised up his servant, he sent him first to you to bless you by turning each of you from your wicked ways."

READING FROM PSALMS
Psalm 70:1–5

For the director of music. Of David.
A petition.

¹Hasten, O God, to save me;
O LORD, come quickly to help me.
²May those who seek my life
be put to shame and confusion;
may all who desire my ruin
be turned back in disgrace.
³May those who say to me, "Aha!
Aha!"
turn back because of their shame.
⁴But may all who seek you
rejoice and be glad in you;
may those who love your salvation
always say,
"Let God be exalted!"

⁵Yet I am poor and needy;
come quickly to me, O God.
You are my help and my deliverer;
O LORD, do not delay.

OLD TESTAMENT READING
2 Samuel 11:1–12:31

David and Bathsheba

11 In the spring, at the time when kings go off to war, David sent Joab out with the king's men and the whole Israelite army. They destroyed the Ammonites and besieged Rabbah. But David remained in Jerusalem.

²One evening David got up from his bed and walked around on the roof of the palace. From the roof he saw a woman bathing. The woman was very beautiful, ³and David sent someone to find out about her. The man said, "Isn't this Bathsheba, the daughter of Eliam and the wife of Uriah the Hittite?" ⁴Then David sent messengers to get her. She came to him, and he slept with her. (She had purified herself from her uncleanness.) Then she went back home. ⁵The woman conceived and sent word to David, saying, "I am pregnant."

⁶So David sent this word to Joab: "Send me Uriah the Hittite." And Joab sent him to David. ⁷When Uriah came to him, David asked him how Joab was, how the soldiers were and how the war was going. ⁸Then David said to Uriah, "Go down to your house and wash your feet." So Uriah left the palace, and a gift from the king was sent after him. ⁹But Uriah slept at the entrance to the palace with all his master's servants and did not go down to his house.

¹⁰When David was told, "Uriah did not go home," he asked him, "Haven't you just come from a distance? Why didn't you go home?" ¹¹Uriah said to David, "The ark and Israel and Judah are staying in tents, and my master Joab and my lord's men are camped in the open fields. How could I go to my house to eat and drink and lie with my wife? As surely as you live, I will not do such a thing!"

¹²Then David said to him, "Stay here one more day, and tomorrow I will send you back." So Uriah remained in Jerusalem that day and the next. ¹³At David's invitation, he ate and drank with him, and David made him drunk. But in the evening Uriah went out to sleep on his mat among his master's servants; he did not go home.

¹⁴In the morning David wrote a letter to Joab and sent it with Uriah. ¹⁵In it he wrote, "Put Uriah in the front line where the fighting is fiercest. Then withdraw from him so that he will be struck down and die."

¹⁶So while Joab had the city under siege, he put Uriah at a place where he knew the strongest defenders were. ¹⁷When the men of the city came out and fought against Joab, some of the men in David's army fell; moreover, Uriah the Hittite died.

¹⁸Joab sent David a full account of the battle. ¹⁹He instructed the messenger: "When you have finished giving the king this account of the battle, ²⁰the king's anger may flare up, and he may ask you, 'Why did you get so close to the city to fight? Didn't you know they would shoot arrows from the wall? ²¹Who killed Abimelech son of Jerub-Besheth? Didn't a woman throw an upper millstone on him from the wall, so that he died in Thebez? Why did you get so close to the wall?' If he asks you this, then say to him, 'Also, your servant Uriah the Hittite is dead.'"

²²The messenger set out, and when he arrived he told David everything Joab had sent him to say. ²³The messenger said to David, "The men overpowered us and came out against us in the open, but we drove them back to the entrance to the city gate. ²⁴Then the archers shot arrows at your servants from the wall,

and some of the king's men died. Moreover, your servant Uriah the Hittite is dead.''

25David told the messenger, "Say this to Joab: 'Don't let this upset you; the sword devours one as well as another. Press the attack against the city and destroy it.' Say this to encourage Joab."

26When Uriah's wife heard that her husband was dead, she mourned for him. 27After the time of mourning was over, David had her brought to his house, and she became his wife and bore him a son. But the thing David had done displeased the LORD.

Nathan Rebukes David

12 The LORD sent Nathan to David. When he came to him, he said, "There were two men in a certain town, one rich and the other poor. 2The rich man had a very large number of sheep and cattle, 3but the poor man had nothing except one little ewe lamb that he had bought. He raised it, and it grew up with him and his children. It shared his food, drank from his cup and even slept in his arms. It was like a daughter to him.

4"Now a traveller came to the rich man, but the rich man refrained from taking one of his own sheep or cattle to prepare a meal for the traveller who had come to him. Instead, he took the ewe lamb that belonged to the poor man and prepared it for the one who had come to him."

5David burned with anger against the man and said to Nathan, "As surely as the LORD lives, the man who did this deserves to die! 6He must pay for that lamb four times over, because he did such a thing and had no pity."

7Then Nathan said to David, "You are the man! This is what the LORD, the God of Israel, says: 'I anointed you king over Israel, and I delivered you from the hand of Saul. 8I gave your master's house to you, and your master's wives into your arms. I gave you the house of Israel and Judah. And if all this had been too little, I would have given you even more. 9Why did you despise the word of the LORD by doing what is evil in his eyes? You struck down Uriah the Hittite with the sword and took his wife to be your own. You killed him with the sword of the Ammonites. 10Now, therefore, the sword shall never depart from your house, because you despised me and took the wife of Uriah the Hittite to be your own.'

11"This is what the LORD says: 'Out of your own household I am going to bring calamity upon you. Before your very eyes I will take your wives and give them to one who is close to you, and he will lie with your wives in broad daylight. 12You did it in secret, but I will do this thing in broad daylight before all Israel.'"

13Then David said to Nathan, "I have sinned against the LORD."

Nathan replied, "The LORD has taken away your sin. You are not going to die. 14But because by doing this you have made the enemies of the LORD show utter contempt, the son born to you will die."

15After Nathan had gone home, the LORD struck the child that Uriah's wife had borne to David, and he became ill. 16David pleaded with God for the child. He fasted and went into his house and spent the nights lying on the ground. 17The elders of his household stood beside him to get him up from the ground, but he refused, and he would not eat any food with them.

18On the seventh day the child died. David's servants were afraid to tell him that the child was dead, for they thought, "While the child was still living, we spoke to David but he would not listen to us. How can we tell him the child is dead? He may do something desperate."

19David noticed that his servants were whispering among themselves and he realised that the child was dead. "Is the child dead?" he asked.

"Yes," they replied, "he is dead."

²⁰Then David got up from the ground. After he had washed, put on lotions and changed his clothes, he went into the house of the LORD and worshipped. Then he went to his own house, and at his request they served him food, and he ate.

²¹His servants asked him, "Why are you acting in this way? While the child was alive, you fasted and wept, but now that the child is dead, you get up and eat!"

²²He answered, "While the child was still alive, I fasted and wept. I thought, 'Who knows? The LORD may be gracious to me and let the child live.' ²³But now that he is dead, why should I fast? Can I bring him back again? I will go to him, but he will not return to me."

²⁴Then David comforted his wife Bathsheba, and he went to her and lay with her. She gave birth to a son, and they named him Solomon. The LORD loved him; ²⁵and because the LORD loved him, he sent word through Nathan the prophet to name him Jedidiah.

²⁶Meanwhile Joab fought against Rabbah of the Ammonites and captured the royal citadel. ²⁷Joab then sent messengers to David, saying, "I have fought against Rabbah and taken its water supply. ²⁸Now muster the rest of the troops and besiege the city and capture it. Otherwise I shall take the city, and it will be named after me."

²⁹So David mustered the entire army and went to Rabbah, and attacked and captured it. ³⁰He took the crown from the head of their king—its weight was a talent of gold, and it was set with precious stones—and it was placed on David's head. He took a great quantity of plunder from the city ³¹and brought out the people who were there, consigning them to labour with saws and with iron picks and axes, and he made them work at brickmaking. He did this to all the Ammonite towns. Then David and his entire army returned to Jerusalem.

NEW TESTAMENT READING
Acts 4:1–22

Peter and John Before the Sanhedrin

4 The priests and the captain of the temple guard and the Sadducees came up to Peter and John while they were speaking to the people. ²They were greatly disturbed because the apostles were teaching the people and proclaiming in Jesus the resurrection of the dead. ³They seized Peter and John, and because it was evening, they put them in jail until the next day. ⁴But many who heard the message believed, and the number of men grew to about five thousand.

⁵The next day the rulers, elders and teachers of the law met in Jerusalem. ⁶Annas the high priest was there, and so were Caiaphas, John, Alexander and the other men of the high priest's family. ⁷They had Peter and John brought before them and began to question them: "By what power or what name did you do this?"

⁸Then Peter, filled with the Holy Spirit, said to them: "Rulers and elders of the people! ⁹If we are being called to account today for an act of kindness shown to a cripple and are asked how he was healed, ¹⁰then know this, you and all the people of Israel: It is by the name of Jesus Christ of Nazareth, whom you crucified but whom God raised from the dead, that this man stands before you healed. ¹¹He is

"'the stone you builders rejected,
   which has become the capstone.'

¹²Salvation is found in no-one else, for there is no other name under heaven given to men by which we must be saved."

¹³When they saw the courage of Peter and John and realised that they were unschooled, ordinary men, they were astonished and they took note that

these men had been with Jesus. ¹⁴But since they could see the man who had been healed standing there with them, there was nothing they could say. ¹⁵So they ordered them to withdraw from the Sanhedrin and then conferred together. ¹⁶"What are we going to do with these men?" they asked. "Everybody living in Jerusalem knows they have done an outstanding miracle, and we cannot deny it. ¹⁷But to stop this thing from spreading any further among the people, we must warn these men not to speak no longer to anyone in this name."

¹⁸Then they called them in again and commanded them not to speak or teach at all in the name of Jesus. ¹⁹But Peter and John replied, "Judge for yourselves whether it is right in God's sight to obey you rather than God. ²⁰For we cannot help speaking about what we have seen and heard."

²¹After further threats they let them go. They could not decide how to punish them, because all the people were praising God for what had happened. ²²For the man who was miraculously healed was over forty years old.

READING FROM PSALMS
Psalm 71:1–8

¹In you, O LORD, I have taken refuge;
  let me never be put to shame.
²Rescue me and deliver me in your
    righteousness;
  turn your ear to me and save me.
³Be my rock of refuge,
  to which I can always go;
give the command to save me,
  for you are my rock and my fortress.
⁴Deliver me, O my God, from the
    hand of the wicked,
  from the grasp of evil and cruel men.

⁵For you have been my hope, O
    Sovereign LORD,
  my confidence since my youth.
⁶From my birth I have relied on you;
  you brought me forth from my
    mother's womb.
  I will ever praise you.
⁷I have become like a portent to many,
  but you are my strong refuge.
⁸My mouth is filled with your praise,
  declaring your splendour all day
    long.

DAY 159

JUNE 8

OLD TESTAMENT READING
2 Samuel 13:1–39

Amnon and Tamar

13 In the course of time, Amnon son of David fell in love with Tamar, the beautiful sister of Absalom son of David.

²Amnon became frustrated to the point of illness on account of his sister Tamar, for she was a virgin, and it seemed impossible for him to do anything to her.

³Now Amnon had a friend named Jonadab son of Shimeah, David's brother. Jonadab was a very shrewd man. ⁴He asked Amnon, "Why do you, the king's son, look so haggard morning after morning? Won't you tell me?"

Amnon said to him, "I'm in love with Tamar, my brother Absalom's sister."

⁵"Go to bed and pretend to be ill," Jonadab said. "When your father comes to see you, say to him, 'I would like my sister Tamar to come and give me something to eat. Let her prepare the food in my sight so that I may watch her and then eat it from her hand.'"

6So Amnon lay down and pretended to be ill. When the king came to see him, Amnon said to him, "I would like my sister Tamar to come and make some special bread in my sight, so that I may eat from her hand."

7David sent word to Tamar at the palace: "Go to the house of your brother Amnon and prepare some food for him." 8So Tamar went to the house of her brother Amnon, who was lying down. She took some dough, kneaded it, made the bread in his sight and baked it. 9Then she took the pan and served him the bread, but he refused to eat.

"Send everyone out of here," Amnon said. So everyone left him. 10Then Amnon said to Tamar, "Bring the food into my bedroom so that I may eat from your hand." And Tamar took the bread she had prepared and brought it to her brother Amnon in his bedroom. 11But when she took it to him to eat, he grabbed her and said, "Come to bed with me, my sister."

12"Don't, my brother!" she said to him. "Don't force me. Such a thing should not be done in Israel! Don't do this wicked thing. 13What about me? Where could I get rid of my disgrace? And what about you? You would be like one of the wicked fools in Israel. Please speak to the king; he will not keep me from being married to you." 14But he refused to listen to her, and since he was stronger than she, he raped her.

15Then Amnon hated her with intense hatred. In fact, he hated her more than he had loved her. Amnon said to her, "Get up and get out!"

16"No!" she said to him. "Sending me away would be a greater wrong than what you have already done to me."

But he refused to listen to her. 17He called his personal servant and said, "Get this woman out of here and bolt the door after her." 18So his servant put her out and bolted the door after her. She was wearing a richly ornamented robe, for this was the kind of garment the virgin daughters of the king wore.

19Tamar put ashes on her head and tore the ornamented robe she was wearing. She put her hand on her head and went away, weeping aloud as she went.

20Her brother Absalom said to her, "Has that Amnon, your brother, been with you? Be quiet now, my sister; he is your brother. Don't take this thing to heart." And Tamar lived in her brother Absalom's house, a desolate woman.

21When King David heard all this, he was furious. 22Absalom never said a word to Amnon, either good or bad; he hated Amnon because he had disgraced his sister Tamar.

Absalom Kills Amnon

23Two years later, when Absalom's sheep-shearers were at Baal Hazor near the border of Ephraim, he invited all the king's sons to come there. 24Absalom went to the king and said, "Your servant has had shearers come. Will the king and his officials please join me?"

25"No, my son," the king replied. "All of us should not go; we would only be a burden to you." Although Absalom urged him, he still refused to go, but gave him his blessing. 26Then Absalom said, "If not, please let my brother Amnon come with us."

The king asked him, "Why should he go with you?" 27But Absalom urged him, so he sent with him Amnon and the rest of the king's sons.

28Absalom ordered his men, "Listen! When Amnon is in high spirits from drinking wine and I say to you, 'Strike Amnon down,' then kill him. Don't be afraid. Have not I given you this order? Be strong and brave." 29So Absalom's men did to Amnon what Absalom had ordered. Then all the king's sons got up, mounted their mules and fled.

30While they were on their way, the report came to David: "Absalom has struck down all the king's sons; not one of them is left." 31The king stood up, tore his clothes and lay down on the ground; and all his servants stood by with their clothes torn.

³²But Jonadab son of Shimeah, David's brother, said, "My lord should not think that they killed all the princes; only Amnon is dead. This has been Absalom's expressed intention ever since the day that Amnon raped his sister Tamar. ³³My lord the king should not be concerned about the report that all the king's sons are dead. Only Amnon is dead."

³⁴Meanwhile, Absalom had fled.

Now the man standing watch looked up and saw many people on the road west of him, coming down the side of the hill. The watchman went and told the king, "I see men in the direction of Horonaim, on the side of the hill."

³⁵Jonadab said to the king, "See, the king's sons are here; it has happened just as your servant said."

³⁶As he finished speaking, the king's sons came in, wailing loudly. The king, too, and all his servants wept very bitterly.

³⁷Absalom fled and went to Talmai son of Ammihud, the king of Geshur. But King David mourned for his son every day.

³⁸After Absalom fled and went to Geshur, he stayed there for three years. ³⁹And the spirit of the king longed to go to Absalom, for he was consoled concerning Amnon's death.

NEW TESTAMENT READING
Acts 4:23–5:11

The Believers' Prayer

²³On their release, Peter and John went back to their own people and reported all that the chief priests and elders had said to them. ²⁴When they heard this, they raised their voices together in prayer to God. "Sovereign Lord," they said, "you made the heaven and the earth and the sea, and everything in them. ²⁵You spoke by the Holy Spirit through the mouth of your servant, our father David:

" 'Why do the nations rage
    and the peoples plot in vain?
²⁶The kings of the earth take their
    stand
    and the rulers gather together
against the Lord
    and against his Anointed One.'

²⁷Indeed Herod and Pontius Pilate met together with the Gentiles and the people of Israel in this city to conspire against your holy servant Jesus, whom you anointed. ²⁸They did what your power and will had decided beforehand should happen. ²⁹Now, Lord, consider their threats and enable your servants to speak your word with great boldness. ³⁰Stretch out your hand to heal and perform miraculous signs and wonders through the name of your holy servant Jesus."

³¹After they prayed, the place where they were meeting was shaken. And they were all filled with the Holy Spirit and spoke the word of God boldly.

The Believers Share Their Possessions

³²All the believers were one in heart and mind. No-one claimed that any of his possessions was his own, but they shared everything they had. ³³With great power the apostles continued to testify to the resurrection of the Lord Jesus, and much grace was upon them all. ³⁴There were no needy persons among them. For from time to time those who owned lands or houses sold them, brought the money from the sales ³⁵and put it at the apostles' feet, and it was distributed to anyone as he had need.

³⁶Joseph, a Levite from Cyprus, whom the apostles called Barnabas (which means Son of Encouragement), ³⁷sold a field he owned and brought the money and put it at the apostles' feet.

Ananias and Sapphira

5 Now a man named Ananias, together with his wife Sapphira, also sold a piece of property. ²With his wife's full knowledge he kept back part of the money for himself, but brought the rest and put it at the apostles' feet.

³Then Peter said, "Ananias, how is it that Satan has so filled your heart that you have lied to the Holy Spirit and have kept for yourself some of the money you received for the land? ⁴Didn't it belong to you before it was sold? And after it was sold, wasn't the money at your disposal? What made you think of doing such a thing? You have not lied to men but to God."

⁵When Ananias heard this, he fell down and died. And great fear seized all who heard what had happened. ⁶Then the young men came forward, wrapped up his body, and carried him out and buried him.

⁷About three hours later his wife came in, not knowing what had happened. ⁸Peter asked her, "Tell me, is this the price you and Ananias got for the land?"

"Yes," she said, "that is the price."

⁹Peter said to her, "How could you agree to test the Spirit of the Lord? Look! The feet of the men who buried your husband are at the door, and they will carry you out also."

¹⁰At that moment she fell down at his feet and died. Then the young men came in and, finding her dead, carried her out and buried her beside her husband. ¹¹Great fear seized the whole church and all who heard about these events.

READING FROM PSALMS
Psalm 71:9–18

⁹Do not cast me away when I am old;
  do not forsake me when my
    strength is gone.
¹⁰For my enemies speak against me;
  those who wait to kill me conspire
    together.
¹¹They say, "God has forsaken him;
  pursue him and seize him,
  for no-one will rescue him."
¹²Be not far from me, O God;
  come quickly, O my God, to help
    me.
¹³May my accusers perish in shame;
  may those who want to harm me
  be covered with scorn and
    disgrace.

¹⁴But as for me, I shall always have
    hope;
  I will praise you more and more.
¹⁵My mouth will tell of your
    righteousness,
  of your salvation all day long,
  though I know not its measure.
¹⁶I will come and proclaim your mighty
    acts, O Sovereign LORD;
  I will proclaim your righteousness,
    yours alone.
¹⁷Since my youth, O God, you have
    taught me,
  and to this day I declare your
    marvellous deeds.
¹⁸Even when I am old and grey,
  do not forsake me, O God,
  till I declare your power to the next
    generation,
    your might to all who are to come.

JUNE 9

OLD TESTAMENT READING
2 Samuel 14:1–15:12

Absalom Returns to Jerusalem

14 Joab son of Zeruiah knew that the king's heart longed for Absalom. ²So Joab sent someone to Tekoa and had a wise woman brought from there. He said to her, "Pretend you are in mourning. Dress in mourning clothes, and don't use any cosmetic lotions. Act like a woman who has spent many days grieving for the dead. ³Then go to the king and speak these words to him." And Joab put the words in her mouth.

⁴When the woman from Tekoa went to the king, she fell with her face to the ground to pay him honour, and she said, "Help me, O king!"

⁵The king asked her, "What is troubling you?"

She said, "I am indeed a widow; my husband is dead. ⁶I your servant had two sons. They got into a fight with each other in the field, and no-one was there to separate them. One struck the other and killed him. ⁷Now the whole clan has risen up against your servant; they say, 'Hand over the one who struck his brother down, so that we may put him to death for the life of his brother whom he killed; then we will get rid of the heir as well.' They would put out the only burning coal I have left, leaving my husband neither name nor descendant on the face of the earth."

⁸The king said to the woman, "Go home, and I will issue an order on your behalf."

⁹But the woman from Tekoa said to him, "My lord the king, let the blame rest on me and on my father's family, and let the king and his throne be without guilt."

¹⁰The king replied, "If anyone says anything to you, bring him to me, and he will not bother you again."

¹¹She said, "Then let the king invoke the LORD his God to prevent the avenger of blood from adding to the destruction, so that my son shall not be destroyed."

"As surely as the LORD lives," he said, "not one hair of your son's head will fall to the ground."

¹²Then the woman said, "Let your servant speak a word to my lord the king."

"Speak," he replied.

¹³The woman said, "Why then have you devised a thing like this against the people of God? When the king says this, does he not convict himself, for the king has not brought back his banished son? ¹⁴Like water spilled on the ground, which cannot be recovered, so we must die. But God does not take away life; instead, he devises ways so that a banished person may not remain estranged from him.

¹⁵"And now I have come to say this to my lord the king because the people have made me afraid. Your servant thought, 'I will speak to the king; perhaps he will do what his servant asks. ¹⁶Perhaps the king will agree to deliver his servant from the hand of the man who is trying to cut off both me and my son from the inheritance God gave us.'

¹⁷"And now your servant says, 'May the word of my lord the king bring me rest, for my lord the king is like an angel of God in discerning good and evil. May the LORD your God be with you.'"

¹⁸Then the king said to the woman, "Do not keep from me the answer to what I am going to ask you."

"Let my lord the king speak," the woman said.

¹⁹The king asked, "Isn't the hand of Joab with you in all this?"

The woman answered, "As surely as you live, my lord the king, no-one can turn to the right or to the left from anything my lord the king says. Yes, it was your servant Joab who instructed me to do this and who put all these words into the mouth of your servant. [20]Your servant Joab did this to change the present situation. My lord the king has wisdom like that of an angel of God—he knows everything that happens in the land."

[21]The king said to Joab, "Very well, I will do it. Go, bring back the young man Absalom."

[22]Joab fell with his face to the ground to pay him honour, and he blessed the king. Joab said, "Today your servant knows that he has found favour in your eyes, my lord the king, because the king has granted his servant's request."

[23]Then Joab went to Geshur and brought Absalom back to Jerusalem. [24]But the king said, "He must go to his own house; he must not see my face." So Absalom went to his own house and did not see the face of the king.

[25]In all Israel there was not a man so highly praised for his handsome appearance as Absalom. From the top of his head to the sole of his foot there was no blemish in him. [26]Whenever he cut the hair of his head—he used to cut his hair from time to time when it became too heavy for him—he would weigh it, and its weight was two hundred shekels by the royal standard.

[27]Three sons and a daughter were born to Absalom. The daughter's name was Tamar, and she became a beautiful woman.

[28]Absalom lived for two years in Jerusalem without seeing the king's face. [29]Then Absalom sent for Joab in order to send him to the king, but Joab refused to come to him. So he sent a second time, but he refused to come. [30]Then he said to his servants, "Look, Joab's field is next to mine, and he has barley there. Go and set it on fire." So Absalom's servants set the field on fire.

[31]Then Joab did go to Absalom's house and he said to him, "Why have your servants set my field on fire?"

[32]Absalom said to Joab, "Look, I sent word to you and said, 'Come here so that I can send you to the king to ask, "Why have I come from Geshur? It would be better for me if I were still there!"' Now then, I want to see the king's face, and if I am guilty of anything, let him put me to death."

[33]So Joab went to the king and told him this. Then the king summoned Absalom, and he came in and bowed down with his face to the ground before the king. And the king kissed Absalom.

Absalom's Conspiracy

15 In the course of time, Absalom provided himself with a chariot and horses and with fifty men to run ahead of him. [2]He would get up early and stand by the side of the road leading to the city gate. Whenever anyone came with a complaint to be placed before the king for a decision, Absalom would call out to him, "What town are you from?" He would answer, "Your servant is from one of the tribes of Israel." [3]Then Absalom would say to him, "Look, your claims are valid and proper, but there is no representative of the king to hear you." [4]And Absalom would add, "If only I were appointed judge in the land! Then everyone who has a complaint or case could come to me and I would see that he receives justice."

[5]Also, whenever anyone approached him to bow down before him, Absalom would reach out his hand, take hold of him and kiss him. [6]Absalom behaved in this way towards all the Israelites who came to the king asking for justice, and so he stole the hearts of the men of Israel.

[7]At the end of four years, Absalom said to the king, "Let me go to Hebron and fulfil a vow I made to the LORD. [8]While your servant was living at Geshur in Aram, I made this vow: 'If the LORD takes me back to Jerusalem, I will worship the LORD in Hebron.'"

⁹The king said to him, "Go in peace." So he went to Hebron.

¹⁰Then Absalom sent secret messengers throughout the tribes of Israel to say, "As soon as you hear the sound of the trumpets, then say, 'Absalom is king in Hebron.'" ¹¹Two hundred men from Jerusalem had accompanied Absalom. They had been invited as guests and went quite innocently, knowing nothing about the matter. ¹²While Absalom was offering sacrifices, he also sent for Ahithophel the Gilonite, David's counsellor, to come from Giloh, his home town. And so the conspiracy gained strength, and Absalom's following kept on increasing.

NEW TESTAMENT READING
Acts 5:12–42

The Apostles Heal Many

¹²The apostles performed many miraculous signs and wonders among the people. And all the believers used to meet together in Solomon's Colonnade. ¹³No-one else dared join them, even though they were highly regarded by the people. ¹⁴Nevertheless, more and more men and women believed in the Lord and were added to their number. ¹⁵As a result, people brought the sick into the streets and laid them on beds and mats so that at least Peter's shadow might fall on some of them as he passed by. ¹⁶Crowds gathered also from the towns around Jerusalem, bringing their sick and those tormented by evil spirits, and all of them were healed.

The Apostles Persecuted

¹⁷Then the high priest and all his associates, who were members of the party of the Sadducees, were filled with jealousy. ¹⁸They arrested the apostles and put them in the public jail. ¹⁹But during the night an angel of the Lord opened the doors of the jail and brought them out. ²⁰"Go, stand in the temple courts," he said, "and tell the people the full message of this new life."

²¹At daybreak they entered the temple courts, as they had been told, and began to teach the people.

When the high priest and his associates arrived, they called together the Sanhedrin—the full assembly of the elders of Israel—and sent to the jail for the apostles. ²²But on arriving at the jail, the officers did not find them there. So they went back and reported, ²³"We found the jail securely locked, with the guards standing at the doors; but when we opened them, we found no-one inside." ²⁴On hearing this report, the captain of the temple guard and the chief priests were puzzled, wondering what would come of this.

²⁵Then someone came and said, "Look! The men you put in jail are standing in the temple courts teaching the people." ²⁶At that, the captain went with his officers and brought the apostles. They did not use force, because they feared that the people would stone them.

²⁷Having brought the apostles, they made them appear before the Sanhedrin to be questioned by the high priest. ²⁸"We gave you strict orders not to teach in this name," he said. "Yet you have filled Jerusalem with your teaching and are determined to make us guilty of this man's blood."

²⁹Peter and the other apostles replied: "We must obey God rather than men! ³⁰The God of our fathers raised Jesus from the dead—whom you had killed by hanging him on a tree. ³¹God exalted him to his own right hand as Prince and Saviour that he might give repentance and forgiveness of sins to Israel. ³²We are witnesses of these things, and so is the Holy Spirit, whom God has given to those who obey him."

³³When they heard this, they were furious and wanted to put them to death. ³⁴But a Pharisee named Gamaliel, a teacher of the law, who was honoured by all the people, stood up in the Sanhedrin and ordered that the men be put outside for a little while. ³⁵Then he

addressed them: "Men of Israel, consider carefully what you intend to do to these men. ³⁶Some time ago Theudas appeared, claiming to be somebody, and about four hundred men rallied to him. He was killed, all his followers were dispersed, and it all came to nothing. ³⁷After him, Judas the Galilean appeared in the days of the census and led a band of people in revolt. He too was killed, and all his followers were scattered. ³⁸Therefore, in the present case I advise you: Leave these men alone! Let them go! For if their purpose or activity is of human origin, it will fail. ³⁹But if it is from God, you will not be able to stop these men; you will only find yourselves fighting against God."

⁴⁰His speech persuaded them. They called the apostles in and had them flogged. Then they ordered them not to speak in the name of Jesus, and let them go.

⁴¹The apostles left the Sanhedrin, rejoicing because they had been counted worthy of suffering disgrace for the Name. ⁴²Day after day, in the temple courts and from house to house, they never stopped teaching and proclaiming the good news that Jesus is the Christ.

READING FROM PROVERBS
Proverbs 14:15–24

¹⁵A simple man believes anything,
  but a prudent man gives thought to
    his steps.

¹⁶A wise man fears the LORD and shuns
    evil,
  but a fool is hotheaded and
    reckless.

¹⁷A quick-tempered man does foolish
    things,
  and a crafty man is hated.

¹⁸The simple inherit folly,
  but the prudent are crowned with
    knowledge.

¹⁹Evil men will bow down in the
    presence of the good,
  and the wicked at the gates of the
    righteous.

²⁰The poor are shunned even by their
    neighbours,
  but the rich have many friends.

²¹He who despises his neighbour sins,
  but blessed is he who is kind to the
    needy.

²²Do not those who plot evil go astray?
  But those who plan what is good
    find love and faithfulness.

²³All hard work brings a profit,
  but mere talk leads only to
    poverty.

²⁴The wealth of the wise is their crown,
  but the folly of fools yields folly.

OLD TESTAMENT READING
2 Samuel 15:13–16:14

David Flees

¹³A messenger came and told David, "The hearts of the men of Israel are with Absalom."

¹⁴Then David said to all his officials who were with him in Jerusalem, "Come! We must flee, or none of us will escape from Absalom. We must leave immediately, or he will move quickly to overtake us and bring ruin upon us and put the city to the sword."

¹⁵The king's officials answered him, "Your servants are ready to do whatever our lord the king chooses."

¹⁶The king set out, with his entire household following him; but he left ten concubines to take care of the palace. ¹⁷So the king set out, with all the people following him, and they halted at a place some distance away. ¹⁸All his men marched past him, along with all the Kerethites and Pelethites; and all the six hundred Gittites who had accompanied him from Gath marched before the king.

¹⁹The king said to Ittai the Gittite, "Why should you come along with us? Go back and stay with King Absalom. You are a foreigner, an exile from your homeland. ²⁰You came only yesterday. And today shall I make you wander about with us, when I do not know where I am going? Go back, and take your countrymen. May kindness and faithfulness be with you."

²¹But Ittai replied to the king, "As surely as the LORD lives, and as my lord the king lives, wherever my lord the king may be, whether it means life or death, there will your servant be."

²²David said to Ittai, "Go ahead, march on." So Ittai the Gittite marched on with all his men and the families that were with him.

²³The whole countryside wept aloud as all the people passed by. The king also crossed the Kidron Valley, and all the people moved on towards the desert.

²⁴Zadok was there, too, and all the Levites who were with him were carrying the ark of the covenant of God. They set down the ark of God, and Abiathar offered sacrifices until all the people had finished leaving the city.

²⁵Then the king said to Zadok, "Take the ark of God back into the city. If I find favour in the LORD's eyes, he will bring me back and let me see it and his dwelling-place again. ²⁶But if he says, 'I am not pleased with you,' then I am ready; let him do to me whatever seems good to him."

²⁷The king also said to Zadok the priest, "Aren't you a seer? Go back to the city in peace, with your son Ahimaaz and Jonathan son of Abiathar. You and Abiathar take your two sons with you. ²⁸I will wait at the fords in the desert until word comes from you to inform me." ²⁹So Zadok and Abiathar took the ark of God back to Jerusalem and stayed there.

³⁰But David continued up the Mount of Olives, weeping as he went; his head was covered and he was barefoot. All the people with him covered their heads too and were weeping as they went up. ³¹Now David had been told, "Ahithophel is among the conspirators with Absalom." So David prayed, "O LORD, turn Ahithophel's counsel into foolishness."

³²When David arrived at the summit, where people used to worship God, Hushai the Arkite was there to meet him, his robe torn and dust on his head. ³³David said to him, "If you go with me, you will be a burden to me. ³⁴But if you return to the city and say to Absalom, 'I will be your servant, O king; I was your father's servant in the past, but now I will be your servant,' then you can help

me by frustrating Ahithophel's advice.
35Won't the priests Zadok and Abiathar
be there with you? Tell them anything
you hear in the king's palace. 36Their
two sons, Ahimaaz son of Zadok and
Jonathan son of Abiathar, are there
with them. Send them to me with anything you hear."

37So David's friend Hushai arrived at
Jerusalem as Absalom was entering the
city.

David and Ziba

16 When David had gone a short
distance beyond the summit,
there was Ziba, the steward of Mephibosheth, waiting to meet him. He had a
string of donkeys saddled and loaded
with two hundred loaves of bread, a
hundred cakes of raisins, a hundred
cakes of figs and a skin of wine.

2The king asked Ziba, "Why have
you brought these?"

Ziba answered, "The donkeys are for
the king's household to ride on, the
bread and fruit are for the men to eat,
and the wine is to refresh those who
become exhausted in the desert."

3The king then asked, "Where is your
master's grandson?"

Ziba said to him, "He is staying in
Jerusalem, because he thinks, 'Today
the house of Israel will give me back my
grandfather's kingdom.'"

4Then the king said to Ziba, "All that
belonged to Mephibosheth is now
yours."

"I humbly bow," Ziba said. "May I
find favour in your eyes, my lord the
king."

Shimei Curses David

5As King David approached Bahurim, a man from the same clan as
Saul's family came out from there. His
name was Shimei son of Gera, and he
cursed as he came out. 6He pelted
David and all the king's officials with
stones, though all the troops and the
special guard were on David's right and
left. 7As he cursed, Shimei said, "Get
out, get out, you man of blood, you

scoundrel! 8The LORD has repaid you
for all the blood you shed in the household of Saul, in whose place you have
reigned. The LORD has handed the
kingdom over to your son Absalom.
You have come to ruin because you are
a man of blood!"

9Then Abishai son of Zeruiah said to
the king, "Why should this dead dog
curse my lord the king? Let me go over
and cut off his head."

10But the king said, "What do you
and I have in common, you sons of
Zeruiah? If he is cursing because the
LORD said to him, 'Curse David,' who
can ask, 'Why do you do this?'"

11David then said to Abishai and all
his officials, "My son, who is of my own
flesh, is trying to take my life. How
much more, then, this Benjamite!
Leave him alone; let him curse, for the
LORD has told him to. 12It may be that
the LORD will see my distress and repay
me with good for the cursing I am receiving today."

13So David and his men continued
along the road while Shimei was going
along the hillside opposite him, cursing
as he went and throwing stones at him
and showering him with dirt. 14The king
and all the people with him arrived at
their destination exhausted. And there
he refreshed himself.

NEW TESTAMENT READING
Acts 6:1–7:19

The Choosing of the Seven

6 In those days when the number of
disciples was increasing, the Grecian Jews among them complained
against the Hebraic Jews because their
widows were being overlooked in the
daily distribution of food. 2So the
Twelve gathered all the disciples
together and said, "It would not be right
for us to neglect the ministry of the word
of God in order to wait on tables.
3Brothers, choose seven men from
among you who are known to be full of
the Spirit and wisdom. We will turn this

responsibility over to them ⁴and will give our attention to prayer and the ministry of the word."

⁵This proposal pleased the whole group. They chose Stephen, a man full of faith and of the Holy Spirit; also Philip, Procorus, Nicanor, Timon, Parmenas, and Nicolas from Antioch, a convert to Judaism. ⁶They presented these men to the apostles, who prayed and laid their hands on them.

⁷So the word of God spread. The number of disciples in Jerusalem increased rapidly, and a large number of priests became obedient to the faith.

Stephen Seized

⁸Now Stephen, a man full of God's grace and power, did great wonders and miraculous signs among the people. ⁹Opposition arose, however, from members of the Synagogue of the Freedmen (as it was called)—Jews of Cyrene and Alexandria as well as the provinces of Cilicia and Asia. These men began to argue with Stephen, ¹⁰but they could not stand up against his wisdom or the Spirit by whom he spoke.

¹¹Then they secretly persuaded some men to say, "We have heard Stephen speak words of blasphemy against Moses and against God."

¹²So they stirred up the people and the elders and the teachers of the law. They seized Stephen and brought him before the Sanhedrin. ¹³They produced false witnesses, who testified, "This fellow never stops speaking against this holy place and against the law. ¹⁴For we have heard him say that this Jesus of Nazareth will destroy this place and change the customs Moses handed down to us."

¹⁵All who were sitting in the Sanhedrin looked intently at Stephen, and they saw that his face was like the face of an angel.

Stephen's Speech to the Sanhedrin

7 Then the high priest asked him, "Are these charges true?"

²To this he replied: "Brothers and fathers, listen to me! The God of glory appeared to our father Abraham while he was still in Mesopotamia, before he lived in Haran. ³'Leave your country and your people,' God said, 'and go to the land I will show you.'

⁴"So he left the land of the Chaldeans and settled in Haran. After the death of his father, God sent him to this land where you are now living. ⁵He gave him no inheritance here, not even a foot of ground. But God promised him that he and his descendants after him would possess the land, even though at that time Abraham had no child. ⁶God spoke to him in this way: 'Your descendants will be strangers in a country not their own, and they will be enslaved and ill-treated for four hundred years. ⁷But I will punish the nation they serve as slaves,' God said, 'and afterwards they will come out of that country and worship me in this place.'⁸Then he gave Abraham the covenant of circumcision. And Abraham became the father of Isaac and circumcised him eight days after his birth. Later Isaac became the father of Jacob, and Jacob became the father of the twelve patriarchs.

⁹"Because the patriarchs were jealous of Joseph, they sold him as a slave into Egypt. But God was with him ¹⁰and rescued him from all his troubles. He gave Joseph wisdom and enabled him to gain the goodwill of Pharaoh king of Egypt; so he made him ruler over Egypt and all his palace.

¹¹"Then a famine struck all Egypt and Canaan, bringing great suffering, and our fathers could not find food. ¹²When Jacob heard that there was grain in Egypt, he sent our fathers on their first visit. ¹³On their second visit, Joseph told his brothers who he was, and Pharaoh learned about Joseph's family. ¹⁴After this, Joseph sent for his father Jacob and his whole family, seventy-five in all. ¹⁵Then Jacob went down to Egypt, where he and our fathers died. ¹⁶Their bodies were brought back to Shechem and placed in the tomb that Abraham had bought from the sons of

Hamor at Shechem for a certain sum of money.

17"As the time drew near for God to fulfil his promise to Abraham, the number of our people in Egypt greatly increased. 18Then another king, who knew nothing about Joseph, became ruler of Egypt. 19He dealt treacherously with our people and oppressed our forefathers by forcing them to throw out their newborn babies so that they would die.

READING FROM PSALMS
Psalm 71:19–24

19Your righteousness reaches to the
     skies, O God,
  you who have done great things.
  Who, O God, is like you?

20Though you have made me see
        troubles, many and bitter,
     you will restore my life again;
  from the depths of the earth
     you will again bring me up.
21You will increase my honour
     and comfort me once again.

22I will praise you with the harp
     for your faithfulness, O my God;
  I will sing praise to you with the lyre,
     O Holy One of Israel.
23My lips will shout for joy
     when I sing praise to you—
  I, whom you have redeemed.
24My tongue will tell of your righteous
        acts
     all day long,
  for those who wanted to harm me
     have been put to shame and
        confusion.

JUNE 11   DAY 162

OLD TESTAMENT READING
2 Samuel 16:15–18:18

The Advice of Hushai and Ahithophel

15Meanwhile, Absalom and all the men of Israel came to Jerusalem, and Ahithophel was with him. 16Then Hushai the Arkite, David's friend, went to Absalom and said to him, "Long live the king! Long live the king!"

17Absalom asked Hushai, "Is this the love you show your friend? Why didn't you go with your friend?"

18Hushai said to Absalom, "No, the one chosen by the LORD, by these people and by all the men of Israel—his I will be, and I will remain with him. 19Furthermore, whom should I serve? Should I not serve the son? Just as I served your father, so I will serve you."

20Absalom said to Ahithophel, "Give us your advice. What should we do?"

21Ahithophel answered, "Lie with your father's concubines whom he left to take care of the palace. Then all Israel will hear that you have made yourself an offence to your father's nostrils, and the hands of everyone with you will be strengthened." 22So they pitched a tent for Absalom on the roof, and he lay with his father's concubines in the sight of all Israel.

23Now in those days the advice Ahithophel gave was like that of one who enquires of God. That was how both David and Absalom regarded all of Ahithophel's advice.

17 Ahithophel said to Absalom, "I would choose twelve thousand men and set out tonight in pursuit of David. 2I would attack him while he is weary and weak. I would strike him with terror, and then all the people with him will flee. I would strike down only the king 3and bring all the people back to you. The death of the man you seek will

mean the return of all; all the people will be unharmed." ⁴This plan seemed good to Absalom and to all the elders of Israel.

⁵But Absalom said, "Summon also Hushai the Arkite, so that we can hear what he has to say." ⁶When Hushai came to him, Absalom said, "Ahithophel has given this advice. Should we do what he says? If not, give us your opinion."

⁷Hushai replied to Absalom, "The advice Ahithophel has given is not good this time. ⁸You know your father and his men; they are fighters, and as fierce as a wild bear robbed of her cubs. Besides, your father is an experienced fighter; he will not spend the night with the troops. ⁹Even now, he is hidden in a cave or some other place. If he should attack your troops first, whoever hears about it will say, 'There is a slaughter among the troops who follow Absalom.' ¹⁰Then even the bravest soldier, whose heart is like the heart of a lion, will melt with fear, for all Israel knows that your father is a fighter and that those with him are brave.

¹¹"So I advise you: Let all Israel, from Dan to Beersheba—as numerous as the sand on the seashore—be gathered to you, with you yourself leading them into battle. ¹²Then we will attack him wherever he may be found, and we will fall on him as dew settles on the ground. Neither he nor any of his men will be left alive. ¹³If he withdraws into a city, then all Israel will bring ropes to that city, and we will drag it down to the valley until not even a piece of it can be found."

¹⁴Absalom and all the men of Israel said, "The advice of Hushai the Arkite is better than that of Ahithophel." For the LORD had determined to frustrate the good advice of Ahithophel in order to bring disaster on Absalom.

¹⁵Hushai told Zadok and Abiathar, the priests, "Ahithophel has advised Absalom and the elders of Israel to do such and such, but I have advised them to do so and so. ¹⁶Now send a message

immediately and tell David, 'Do not spend the night at the fords in the desert; cross over without fail, or the king and all the people with him will be swallowed up.'"

¹⁷Jonathan and Ahimaaz were staying at En Rogel. A servant girl was to go and inform them, and they were to go and tell King David, for they could not risk being seen entering the city. ¹⁸But a young man saw them and told Absalom. So the two of them left quickly and went to the house of a man in Bahurim. He had a well in his courtyard, and they climbed down into it. ¹⁹His wife took a covering and spread it out over the opening of the well and scattered grain over it. No-one knew anything about it.

²⁰When Absalom's men came to the woman at the house, they asked, "Where are Ahimaaz and Jonathan?"

The woman answered them, "They crossed over the brook." The men searched but found no-one, so they returned to Jerusalem.

²¹After the men had gone, the two climbed out of the well and went to inform King David. They said to him, "Set out and cross the river at once; Ahithophel has advised such and such against you." ²²So David and all the people with him set out and crossed the Jordan. By daybreak, no-one was left who had not crossed the Jordan.

²³When Ahithophel saw that his advice had not been followed, he saddled his donkey and set out for his house in his home town. He put his house in order and then hanged himself. So he died and was buried in his father's tomb.

²⁴David went to Mahanaim, and Absalom crossed the Jordan with all the men of Israel. ²⁵Absalom had appointed Amasa over the army in place of Joab. Amasa was the son of a man named Jether, an Israelite who had married Abigail, the daughter of Nahash and sister of Zeruiah the mother of Joab. ²⁶The Israelites and Absalom camped in the land of Gilead.

27When David came to Mahanaim, Shobi son of Nahash from Rabbah of the Ammonites, and Makir son of Ammiel from Lo Debar, and Barzillai the Gileadite from Rogelim 28brought bedding and bowls and articles of pottery. They also brought wheat and barley, flour and roasted grain, beans and lentils, 29honey and curds, sheep, and cheese from cows' milk for David and his people to eat. For they said, "The people have become hungry and tired and thirsty in the desert."

Absalom's Death

18 David mustered the men who were with him and appointed over them commanders of thousands and commanders of hundreds. 2David sent the troops out—a third under the command of Joab, a third under Joab's brother Abishai son of Zeruiah, and a third under Ittai the Gittite. The king told the troops, "I myself will surely march out with you."

3But the men said, "You must not go out; if we are forced to flee, they won't care about us. Even if half of us die, they won't care; but you are worth ten thousand of us. It would be better now for you to give us support from the city."

4The king answered, "I will do whatever seems best to you."

So the king stood beside the gate while all the men marched out in units of hundreds and of thousands. 5The king commanded Joab, Abishai and Ittai, "Be gentle with the young man Absalom for my sake." And all the troops heard the king giving orders concerning Absalom to each of the commanders.

6The army marched into the field to fight Israel, and the battle took place in the forest of Ephraim. 7There the army of Israel was defeated by David's men, and the casualties that day were great —twenty thousand men. 8The battle spread out over the whole countryside, and the forest claimed more lives that day than the sword.

9Now Absalom happened to meet David's men. He was riding his mule, and as the mule went under the thick branches of a large oak, Absalom's head got caught in the tree. He was left hanging in mid-air, while the mule he was riding kept on going.

10When one of the men saw this, he told Joab, "I have just seen Absalom hanging in an oak tree."

11Joab said to the man who had told him this, "What! You saw him? Why didn't you strike him to the ground right there? Then I would have had to give you ten shekels of silver and a warrior's belt."

12But the man replied, "Even if a thousand shekels were weighed out into my hands, I would not lift my hand against the king's son. In our hearing the king commanded you and Abishai and Ittai, 'Protect the young man Absalom for my sake.' 13And if I had put my life in jeopardy—and nothing is hidden from the king—you would have kept your distance from me."

14Joab said, "I am not going to wait like this for you." So he took three javelins in his hand and plunged them into Absalom's heart while Absalom was still alive in the oak tree. 15And ten of Joab's armour-bearers surrounded Absalom, struck him and killed him.

16Then Joab sounded the trumpet, and the troops stopped pursuing Israel, for Joab halted them. 17They took Absalom, threw him into a big pit in the forest and piled up a large heap of rocks over him. Meanwhile, all the Israelites fled to their homes.

18During his life-time Absalom had taken a pillar and erected it in the King's Valley as a monument to himself, for he thought, "I have no son to carry on the memory of my name." He named the pillar after himself, and it is called Absalom's Monument to this day.

NEW TESTAMENT READING
Acts 7:20–43

20"At that time Moses was born, and he was no ordinary child. For three months he was cared for in his father's house. 21When he was placed outside, Pharaoh's daughter took him and brought him up as her own son. 22Moses was educated in all the wisdom of the Egyptians and was powerful in speech and action.

23"When Moses was forty years old, he decided to visit his fellow Israelites. 24He saw one of them being ill-treated by an Egyptian, so he went to his defence and avenged him by killing the Egyptian. 25Moses thought that his own people would realise that God was using him to rescue them, but they did not. 26The next day Moses came upon two Israelites who were fighting. He tried to reconcile them by saying, 'Men, you are brothers; why do you want to hurt each other?'

27"But the man who was ill-treating the other pushed Moses aside and said, 'Who made you ruler and judge over us? 28Do you want to kill me as you killed the Egyptian yesterday?' 29When Moses heard this, he fled to Midian, where he settled as a foreigner and had two sons.

30"After forty years had passed, an angel appeared to Moses in the flames of a burning bush in the desert near Mount Sinai. 31When he saw this, he was amazed at the sight. As he went over to look more closely, he heard the Lord's voice: 32'I am the God of your fathers, the God of Abraham, Isaac and Jacob.' Moses trembled with fear and did not dare to look.

33"Then the Lord said to him, 'Take off your sandals; the place where you are standing is holy ground. 34I have indeed seen the oppression of my people in Egypt. I have heard their groaning and have come down to set them free. Now come, I will send you back to Egypt.'

35"This is the same Moses whom they had rejected with the words, 'Who made you ruler and judge?' He was sent to be their ruler and deliverer by God himself, through the angel who appeared to him in the bush. 36He led them out of Egypt and did wonders and miraculous signs in Egypt, at the Red Sea and for forty years in the desert.

37"This is that Moses who told the Israelites, 'God will send you a prophet like me from your own people.' 38He was in the assembly in the desert, with the angel who spoke to him on Mount Sinai, and with our fathers; and he received living words to pass on to us.

39"But our fathers refused to obey him. Instead, they rejected him and in their hearts turned back to Egypt. 40They told Aaron, 'Make us gods who will go before us. As for this fellow Moses who led us out of Egypt—we don't know what has happened to him!' 41That was the time they made an idol in the form of a calf. They brought sacrifices to it and held a celebration in honour of what their hands had made. 42But God turned away and gave them over to the worship of the heavenly bodies. This agrees with what is written in the book of the prophets:

" 'Did you bring me sacrifices and
    offerings
    for forty years in the desert, O
    house of Israel?
43You have lifted up the shrine of
    Molech
    and the star of your god Rephan,
    the idols you made to worship.
Therefore I will send you into exile'
    beyond Babylon.

READING FROM PSALMS
Psalm 72:1–20

Of Solomon.

1Endow the king with your justice, O
    God,
    the royal son with your
    righteousness.

2He will judge your people in
righteousness,
  your afflicted ones with justice.
3The mountains will bring prosperity
to the people,
  the hills the fruit of righteousness.
4He will defend the afflicted among
the people
  and save the children of the needy;
  he will crush the oppressor.

5He will endure as long as the sun,
  as long as the moon, through all
generations.
6He will be like rain falling on a mown
field,
  like showers watering the earth.
7In his days the righteous will flourish;
  prosperity will abound till the
moon is no more.

8He will rule from sea to sea
  and from the River to the ends of
the earth.
9The desert tribes will bow before him
  and his enemies will lick the dust.
10The kings of Tarshish and of distant
shores
  will bring tribute to him;
  the kings of Sheba and Seba
  will present him gifts.
11All kings will bow down to him
  and all nations will serve him.

12For he will deliver the needy who cry
out,
  the afflicted who have no-one to
help.

13He will take pity on the weak and the
needy
  and save the needy from death.
14He will rescue them from oppression
and violence,
  for precious is their blood in his
sight.

15Long may he live!
  May gold from Sheba be given to
him.
  May people ever pray for him
  and bless him all day long.
16Let corn abound throughout the
land;
  on the tops of the hills may it sway.
  Let its fruit flourish like Lebanon;
  let it thrive like the grass of the
field.
17May his name endure for ever;
  may it continue as long as the sun.

All nations will be blessed through
him,
  and they will call him blessed.

18Praise be to the LORD God, the God
of Israel,
  who alone does marvellous deeds.
19Praise be to his glorious name for
ever;
  may the whole earth be filled with
his glory.
      Amen and Amen.

20This concludes the prayers of David
son of Jesse.

JUNE 12

OLD TESTAMENT READING
2 Samuel 18:19–19:43

David Mourns

¹⁹Now Ahimaaz son of Zadok said, "Let me run and take the news to the king that the LORD has delivered him from the hand of his enemies."

²⁰"You are not the one to take the news today," Joab told him. "You may take the news another time, but you must not do so today, because the king's son is dead."

²¹Then Joab said to a Cushite, "Go, tell the king what you have seen." The Cushite bowed down before Joab and ran off.

²²Ahimaaz son of Zadok again said to Joab, "Come what may, please let me run behind the Cushite."

But Joab replied, "My son, why do you want to go? You don't have any news that will bring you a reward."

²³He said, "Come what may, I want to run."

So Joab said, "Run!" Then Ahimaaz ran by way of the plain and outran the Cushite.

²⁴While David was sitting between the inner and outer gates, the watchman went up to the roof of the gateway by the wall. As he looked out, he saw a man running alone. ²⁵The watchman called out to the king and reported it.

The king said, "If he is alone, he must have good news." And the man came closer and closer.

²⁶Then the watchman saw another man running, and he called down to the gatekeeper, "Look, another man running alone!"

The king said, "He must be bringing good news, too."

²⁷The watchman said, "It seems to me that the first one runs like Ahimaaz son of Zadok."

"He's a good man," the king said. "He comes with good news."

²⁸Then Ahimaaz called out to the king, "All is well!" He bowed down before the king with his face to the ground and said, "Praise be to the LORD your God! He has delivered up the men who lifted their hands against my lord the king."

²⁹The king asked, "Is the young man Absalom safe?"

Ahimaaz answered, "I saw great confusion just as Joab was about to send the king's servant and me, your servant, but I don't know what it was."

³⁰The king said, "Stand aside and wait here." So he stepped aside and stood there.

³¹Then the Cushite arrived and said, "My lord the king, hear the good news! The LORD has delivered you today from all who rose up against you."

³²The king asked the Cushite, "Is the young man Absalom safe?"

The Cushite replied, "May the enemies of my lord the king and all who rise up to harm you be like that young man."

³³The king was shaken. He went up to the room over the gateway and wept. As he went, he said: "O my son Absalom! My son, my son Absalom! If only I had died instead of you—O Absalom, my son, my son!"

19 Joab was told, "The king is weeping and mourning for Absalom." ²And for the whole army the victory that day was turned into mourning, because on that day the troops heard it said, "The king is grieving for his son." ³The men stole into the city that day as men steal in who are ashamed when they flee from battle. ⁴The king covered his face and cried aloud, "O my son Absalom! O Absalom, my son, my son!"

⁵Then Joab went into the house to the

king and said, "Today you have humiliated all your men, who have just saved your life and the lives of your sons and daughters and the lives of your wives and concubines. 6You love those who hate you and hate those who love you. You have made it clear today that the commanders and their men mean nothing to you. I see that you would be pleased if Absalom were alive today and all of us were dead. 7Now go out and encourage your men. I swear by the LORD that if you don't go out, not a man will be left with you by nightfall. This will be worse for you than all the calamities that have come upon you from your youth till now."

8So the king got up and took his seat in the gateway. When the men were told, "The king is sitting in the gateway," they all came before him.

David Returns to Jerusalem

Meanwhile, the Israelites had fled to their homes. 9Throughout the tribes of Israel, the people were all arguing with each other, saying, "The king delivered us from the hand of our enemies; he is the one who rescued us from the hand of the Philistines. But now he has fled the country because of Absalom; 10and Absalom, whom we anointed to rule over us, has died in battle. So why do you say nothing about bringing the king back?"

11King David sent this message to Zadok and Abiathar, the priests: "Ask the elders of Judah, 'Why should you be the last to bring the king back to his palace, since what is being said throughout Israel has reached the king at his quarters? 12You are my brothers, my own flesh and blood. So why should you be the last to bring back the king?' 13And say to Amasa, 'Are you not my own flesh and blood? May God deal with me, be it ever so severely, if from now on you are not the commander of my army in place of Joab.' "

14He won over the hearts of all the men of Judah as though they were one man. They sent word to the king, "Return, you and all your men." 15Then the king returned and went as far as the Jordan.

Now the men of Judah had come to Gilgal to go out and meet the king and bring him across the Jordan. 16Shimei son of Gera, the Benjamite from Bahurim, hurried down with the men of Judah to meet King David. 17With him were a thousand Benjamites, along with Ziba, the steward of Saul's household, and his fifteen sons and twenty servants. They rushed to the Jordan, where the king was. 18They crossed at the ford to take the king's household over and to do whatever he wished.

When Shimei son of Gera crossed the Jordan, he fell prostrate before the king 19and said to him, "May my lord not hold me guilty. Do not remember how your servant did wrong on the day my lord the king left Jerusalem. May the king put it out of his mind. 20For I your servant know that I have sinned, but today I have come here as the first of the whole house of Joseph to come down and meet my lord the king."

21Then Abishai son of Zeruiah said, "Shouldn't Shimei be put to death for this? He cursed the LORD's anointed."

22David replied, "What do you and I have in common, you sons of Zeruiah? This day you have become my adversaries! Should anyone be put to death in Israel today? Do I not know that today I am king over Israel?" 23So the king said to Shimei, "You shall not die." And the king promised him on oath.

24Mephibosheth, Saul's grandson, also went down to meet the king. He had not taken care of his feet or trimmed his moustache or washed his clothes from the day the king left until the day he returned safely. 25When he came from Jerusalem to meet the king, the king asked him, "Why didn't you go with me, Mephibosheth?"

26He said, "My lord the king, since I your servant am lame, I said, 'I will have my donkey saddled and will ride on it, so that I can go with the king.' But Ziba my servant betrayed me. 27And he has slandered your servant to my lord the king. My lord the king is like an angel of God; so do whatever pleases you. 28All my grandfather's descendants deserved nothing but death from my lord the king, but you gave your servant a place among those who sat at your table. So what right do I have to make any more appeals to the king?"

29The king said to him, "Why say more? I order you and Ziba to divide the fields."

30Mephibosheth said to the king, "Let him take everything, now that my lord the king has arrived home safely."

31Barzillai the Gileadite also came down from Rogelim to cross the Jordan with the king and to send him on his way from there. 32Now Barzillai was a very old man, eighty years of age. He had provided for the king during his stay in Mahanaim, for he was a very wealthy man. 33The king said to Barzillai, "Cross over with me and stay with me in Jerusalem, and I will provide for you."

34But Barzillai answered the king, "How many more years shall I live, that I should go up to Jerusalem with the king? 35I am now eighty years old. Can I tell the difference between what is good and what is not? Can your servant taste what he eats and drinks? Can I still hear the voices of men and women singers? Why should your servant be an added burden to my lord the king? 36Your servant will cross over the Jordan with the king for a short distance, but why should the king reward me in this way? 37Let your servant return, that I may die in my own town near the tomb of my father and mother. But here is your servant Kimham. Let him cross over with my lord the king. Do for him whatever pleases you."

38The king said, "Kimham shall cross over with me, and I will do for him whatever pleases you. And anything you desire from me I will do for you."

39So all the people crossed the Jordan, and then the king crossed over. The king kissed Barzillai and gave him his blessing, and Barzillai returned to his home.

40When the king crossed over to Gilgal, Kimham crossed over with him. All the troops of Judah and half the troops of Israel had taken the king over.

41Soon all the men of Israel were coming to the king and saying to him, "Why did our brothers, the men of Judah, steal the king away and bring him and his household across the Jordan, together with all his men?"

42All the men of Judah answered the men of Israel, "We did this because the king is closely related to us. Why are you angry about it? Have we eaten any of the king's provisions? Have we taken anything for ourselves?"

43Then the men of Israel answered the men of Judah, "We have ten shares in the king; and besides, we have a greater claim on David than you have. So why do you treat us with contempt? Were we not the first to speak of bringing back our king?"

But the men of Judah responded even more harshly than the men of Israel.

NEW TESTAMENT READING
Acts 7:44–8:3

44"Our forefathers had the tabernacle of the Testimony with them in the desert. It had been made as God directed Moses, according to the pattern he had seen. 45Having received the tabernacle, our fathers under Joshua brought it with them when they took the land from the nations God drove out before them. It remained in the land until the time of David, 46who enjoyed God's favour and asked that he might provide a dwelling-place for the God of Jacob. 47But it was Solomon who built the house for him.

48"However, the Most High does not live in houses made by men. As the prophet says:

49" 'Heaven is my throne,
     and the earth is my footstool.

What kind of house will you build for
me?

says the Lord.
Or where will my resting place be?
⁵⁰Has not my hand made all these
things?'

⁵¹"You stiff-necked people, with uncircumcised hearts and ears! You are
just like your fathers: You always resist
the Holy Spirit! ⁵²Was there ever a
prophet your fathers did not persecute?
They even killed those who predicted
the coming of the Righteous One. And
now you have betrayed and murdered
him—⁵³you who have received the law
that was put into effect through angels
but have not obeyed it."

The Stoning of Stephen

⁵⁴When they heard this, they were
furious and gnashed their teeth at him.
⁵⁵But Stephen, full of the Holy Spirit,
looked up to heaven and saw the glory
of God, and Jesus standing at the right
hand of God. ⁵⁶"Look," he said, "I see
heaven open and the Son of Man standing at the right hand of God."

⁵⁷At this they covered their ears and,
yelling at the top of their voices, they all
rushed at him, ⁵⁸dragged him out of the
city and began to stone him. Meanwhile, the witnesses laid their clothes at
the feet of a young man named Saul.

⁵⁹While they were stoning him,
Stephen prayed, "Lord Jesus, receive
my spirit." ⁶⁰Then he fell on his knees
and cried out, "Lord, do not hold this
sin against them." When he had said
this, he fell asleep.

8 And Saul was there, giving approval to his death.

The Church Persecuted and Scattered

On that day a great persecution broke
out against the church at Jerusalem, and
all except the apostles were scattered
throughout Judea and Samaria. ²Godly
men buried Stephen and mourned
deeply for him. ³But Saul began to
destroy the church. Going from house
to house, he dragged off men and
women and put them in prison.

READING FROM PSALMS
Psalm 73:1–14

A psalm of Asaph.

¹Surely God is good to Israel,
  to those who are pure in heart.

²But as for me, my feet had almost
    slipped;
  I had nearly lost my foothold.
³For I envied the arrogant
  when I saw the prosperity of the
    wicked.

⁴They have no struggles;
  their bodies are healthy and strong.
⁵They are free from the burdens
    common to man;
  they are not plagued by human ills.
⁶Therefore pride is their necklace;
  they clothe themselves with
    violence.
⁷From their callous hearts comes
    iniquity;
  the evil conceits of their minds
    know no limits.
⁸They scoff, and speak with malice;
  in their arrogance they threaten
    oppression.
⁹Their mouths lay claim to heaven,
  and their tongues take possession
    of the earth.
¹⁰Therefore their people turn to them
  and drink up waters in abundance.
¹¹They say, "How can God know?
  Does the Most High have
    knowledge?"

¹²This is what the wicked are like—
    always carefree, they increase in
    wealth.

¹³Surely in vain have I kept my heart
    pure;
  in vain have I washed my hands in
    innocence.
¹⁴All day long I have been plagued;
  I have been punished every
    morning.

JUNE 13

OLD TESTAMENT READING
2 Samuel 20:1–21:22

Sheba Rebels Against David

20 Now a troublemaker named Sheba son of Bicri, a Benjamite, happened to be there. He sounded the trumpet and shouted,

"We have no share in David,
    no part in Jesse's son!
Every man to his tent, O Israel!"

²So all the men of Israel deserted David to follow Sheba son of Bicri. But the men of Judah stayed by their king all the way from the Jordan to Jerusalem.

³When David returned to his palace in Jerusalem, he took the ten concubines he had left to take care of the palace and put them in a house under guard. He provided for them, but did not lie with them. They were kept in confinement till the day of their death, living as widows.

⁴Then the king said to Amasa, "Summon the men of Judah to come to me within three days, and be here yourself." ⁵But when Amasa went to summon Judah, he took longer than the time the king had set for him.

⁶David said to Abishai, "Now Sheba son of Bicri will do us more harm than Absalom did. Take your master's men and pursue him, or he will find fortified cities and escape from us." ⁷So Joab's men and the Kerethites and Pelethites and all the mighty warriors went out under the command of Abishai. They marched out from Jerusalem to pursue Sheba son of Bicri.

⁸While they were at the great rock in Gibeon, Amasa came to meet them. Joab was wearing his military tunic, and strapped over it at his waist was a belt with a dagger in its sheath. As he stepped forward, it dropped out of its sheath.

⁹Joab said to Amasa, "How are you, my brother?" Then Joab took Amasa by the beard with his right hand to kiss him. ¹⁰Amasa was not on his guard against the dagger in Joab's hand, and Joab plunged it into his belly, and his intestines spilled out on the ground. Without being stabbed again, Amasa died. Then Joab and his brother Abishai pursued Sheba son of Bicri.

¹¹One of Joab's men stood beside Amasa and said, "Whoever favours Joab, and whoever is for David, let him follow Joab!" ¹²Amasa lay wallowing in his blood in the middle of the road, and the man saw that all the troops came to a halt there. When he realised that everyone who came up to Amasa stopped, he dragged him from the road into a field and threw a garment over him. ¹³After Amasa had been removed from the road, all the men went on with Joab to pursue Sheba son of Bicri.

¹⁴Sheba passed through all the tribes of Israel to Abel Beth Maacah and through the entire region of the Berites, who gathered together and followed him. ¹⁵All the troops with Joab came and besieged Sheba in Abel Beth Maacah. They built a siege ramp up to the city, and it stood against the outer fortifications. While they were battering the wall to bring it down, ¹⁶a wise woman called from the city, "Listen! Listen! Tell Joab to come here so that I can speak to him." ¹⁷He went towards her, and she asked, "Are you Joab?"

"I am," he answered.

She said, "Listen to what your servant has to say."

"I'm listening," he said.

¹⁸She continued, "Long ago they used to say, 'Get your answer at Abel,' and that settled it. ¹⁹We are the peaceful and faithful in Israel. You are trying to destroy a city that is a mother in Israel. Why do you want to swallow up the LORD's inheritance?"

20"Far be it from me!" Joab replied, "Far be it from me to swallow up or destroy! 21That is not the case. A man named Sheba son of Bicri, from the hill country of Ephraim, has lifted up his hand against the king, against David. Hand over this one man, and I'll withdraw from the city."

The woman said to Joab, "His head will be thrown to you from the wall."

22Then the woman went to all the people with her wise advice, and they cut off the head of Sheba son of Bicri and threw it to Joab. So he sounded the trumpet, and his men dispersed from the city, each returning to his home. And Joab went back to the king in Jerusalem.

23Joab was over Israel's entire army; Benaiah son of Jehoiada was over the Kerethites and Pelethites; 24Adoniram was in charge of forced labour; Jehoshaphat son of Ahilud was recorder; 25Sheva was secretary; Zadok and Abiathar were priests; 26and Ira the Jairite was David's priest.

The Gibeonites Avenged

21 During the reign of David, there was a famine for three successive years; so David sought the face of the LORD. The LORD said, "It is on account of Saul and his blood-stained house; it is because he put the Gibeonites to death."

2The king summoned the Gibeonites and spoke to them. (Now the Gibeonites were not a part of Israel but were survivors of the Amorites; the Israelites had sworn to ⌊spare⌋ them, but Saul in his zeal for Israel and Judah had tried to annihilate them.) 3David asked the Gibeonites, "What shall I do for you? How shall I make amends so that you will bless the LORD's inheritance?"

4The Gibeonites answered him, "We have no right to demand silver or gold from Saul or his family, nor do we have the right to put anyone in Israel to death."

"What do you want me to do for you?" David asked.

5They answered the king, "As for the man who destroyed us and plotted against us so that we have been decimated and have no place anywhere in Israel, 6let seven of his male descendants be given to us to be killed and exposed before the LORD at Gibeah of Saul—the LORD's chosen one."

So the king said, "I will give them to you."

7The king spared Mephibosheth son of Jonathan, the son of Saul, because of the oath before the LORD between David and Jonathan son of Saul. 8But the king took Armoni and Mephibosheth, the two sons of Aiah's daughter Rizpah, whom she had borne to Saul, together with the five sons of Saul's daughter Merab, whom she had borne to Adriel son of Barzillai the Meholathite. 9He handed them over to the Gibeonites, who killed and exposed them on a hill before the LORD. All seven of them fell together; they were put to death during the first days of harvest, just as the barley harvest was beginning.

10Rizpah daughter of Aiah took sackcloth and spread it out for herself on a rock. From the beginning of the harvest till the rain poured down from the heavens on the bodies, she did not let the birds of the air touch them by day or the wild animals by night. 11When David was told what Aiah's daughter Rizpah, Saul's concubine, had done, 12he went and took the bones of Saul and his son Jonathan from the citizens of Jabesh Gilead. (They had taken them secretly from the public square at Beth Shan, where the Philistines had hung them after they struck Saul down on Gilboa.) 13David brought the bones of Saul and his son Jonathan from there, and the bones of those who had been killed and exposed were gathered up.

14They buried the bones of Saul and his son Jonathan in the tomb of Saul's father Kish, at Zela in Benjamin, and did everything the king commanded.

After that, God answered prayer on behalf of the land.

Wars Against the Philistines

15Once again there was a battle between the Philistines and Israel. David went down with his men to fight against the Philistines, and he became exhausted. 16And Ishbi-Benob, one of the descendants of Rapha, whose bronze spearhead weighed three hundred shekels and who was armed with a new ⌊sword⌋, said he would kill David. 17But Abishai son of Zeruiah came to David's rescue; he struck the Philistine down and killed him. Then David's men swore to him, saying, "Never again will you go out with us to battle, so that the lamp of Israel will not be extinguished."

18In the course of time, there was another battle with the Philistines, at Gob. At that time Sibbecai the Hushathite killed Saph, one of the descendants of Rapha.

19In another battle with the Philistines at Gob, Elhanan son of Jaare-Oregim the Bethlehemite killed Goliath the Gittite, who had a spear with a shaft like a weaver's rod.

20In still another battle, which took place at Gath, there was a huge man with six fingers on each hand and six toes on each foot—twenty-four in all. He also was descended from Rapha. 21When he taunted Israel, Jonathan son of Shimeah, David's brother, killed him.

22These four were descendants of Rapha in Gath, and they fell at the hands of David and his men.

NEW TESTAMENT READING
Acts 8:4–40

Philip in Samaria

4Those who had been scattered preached the word wherever they went. 5Philip went down to a city in Samaria and proclaimed the Christ there. 6When the crowds heard Philip and saw the miraculous signs he did, they all paid close attention to what he said. 7With shrieks, evil spirits came out of many, and many paralytics and cripples were healed. 8So there was great joy in that city.

Simon the Sorcerer

9Now for some time a man named Simon had practised sorcery in the city and amazed all the people of Samaria. He boasted that he was someone great, 10and all the people, both high and low, gave him their attention and exclaimed, "This man is the divine power known as the Great Power." 11They followed him because he had amazed them for a long time with his magic. 12But when they believed Philip as he preached the good news of the kingdom of God and the name of Jesus Christ, they were baptised, both men and women. 13Simon himself believed and was baptised. And he followed Philip everywhere, astonished by the great signs and miracles he saw.

14When the apostles in Jerusalem heard that Samaria had accepted the word of God, they sent Peter and John to them. 15When they arrived, they prayed for them that they might receive the Holy Spirit, 16because the Holy Spirit had not yet come upon any of them; they had simply been baptised into the name of the Lord Jesus. 17Then Peter and John placed their hands on them, and they received the Holy Spirit.

18When Simon saw that the Spirit was given at the laying on of the apostles' hands, he offered them money 19and said, "Give me also this ability so that everyone on whom I lay my hands may receive the Holy Spirit."

20Peter answered: "May your money perish with you, because you thought you could buy the gift of God with money! 21You have no part or share in this ministry, because your heart is not right before God. 22Repent of this wickedness and pray to the Lord. Perhaps he will forgive you for having such a thought in your heart. 23For I see that you are full of bitterness and captive to sin."

24Then Simon answered, "Pray to the Lord for me so that nothing you have said may happen to me."

25When they had testified and proclaimed the word of the Lord, Peter and John returned to Jerusalem, preaching the gospel in many Samaritan villages.

Philip and the Ethiopian

26Now an angel of the Lord said to Philip, "Go south to the road—the desert road—that goes down from Jerusalem to Gaza." 27So he started out, and on his way he met an Ethiopian eunuch, an important official in charge of all the treasury of Candace, queen of the Ethiopians. This man had gone to Jerusalem to worship, 28and on his way home was sitting in his chariot reading the book of Isaiah the prophet. 29The Spirit told Philip, "Go to that chariot and stay near it."

30Then Philip ran up to the chariot and heard the man reading Isaiah the prophet. "Do you understand what you are reading?" Philip asked.

31"How can I," he said, "unless someone explains it to me?" So he invited Philip to come up and sit with him.

32The eunuch was reading this passage of Scripture:

"He was led like a sheep to the
    slaughter,
  and as a lamb before the shearer is
    silent,
so he did not open his mouth.
33In his humiliation he was deprived of
    justice.
  Who can speak of his descendants?
  For his life was taken from the
    earth."

34The eunuch asked Philip, "Tell me, please, who is the prophet talking about, himself or someone else?"

35Then Philip began with that very passage of Scripture and told him the good news about Jesus.

36As they travelled along the road, they came to some water and the eunuch said, "Look, here is water. Why shouldn't I be baptised?" 38And he gave orders to stop the chariot. Then both Philip and the eunuch went down into the water and Philip baptised him. 39When they came up out of the water, the Spirit of the Lord suddenly took Philip away, and the eunuch did not see him again, but went on his way rejoicing. 40Philip, however, appeared at Azotus and travelled about, preaching the gospel in all the towns until he reached Caesarea.

READING FROM PROVERBS
Proverbs 14:25–35

25A truthful witness saves lives,
  but a false witness is deceitful.

26He who fears the LORD has a secure
    fortress,
  and for his children it will be a
    refuge.

27The fear of the LORD is a fountain of
    life,
  turning a man from the snares of
    death.

28A large population is a king's glory,
  but without subjects a prince is
    ruined.

29A patient man has great
    understanding,
  but a quick-tempered man displays
    folly.

30A heart at peace gives life to the
    body,
  but envy rots the bones.

31He who oppresses the poor shows
  contempt for their Maker,

but whoever is kind to the needy
honours God.

³²When calamity comes, the wicked are
brought down,
but even in death the righteous
have a refuge.

³³Wisdom reposes in the heart of the
discerning

and even among fools she lets
herself be known.

³⁴Righteousness exalts a nation,
but sin is a disgrace to any people.

³⁵A king delights in a wise servant,
but a shameful servant incurs his
wrath.

DAY 165 # JUNE 14

OLD TESTAMENT READING
2 Samuel 22:1–23:7

David's Song of Praise

22 David sang to the LORD the
words of this song when the
LORD delivered him from the hand of all
his enemies and from the hand of Saul.
²He said:

"The LORD is my rock, my fortress
and my deliverer;
3   my God is my rock, in whom I take
refuge,
my shield and the horn of my
salvation.
He is my stronghold, my refuge and
my saviour—
from violent men you save me.
⁴I call to the LORD, who is worthy of
praise,
and I am saved from my enemies.

⁵"The waves of death swirled about
me;
the torrents of destruction
overwhelmed me.
⁶The cords of the grave coiled around
me;
the snares of death confronted me.
⁷In my distress I called to the LORD;
I called out to my God.
From his temple he heard my voice;
my cry came to his ears.

⁸"The earth trembled and quaked,
the foundations of the heavens
shook;
they trembled because he was
angry.
⁹Smoke rose from his nostrils;
consuming fire came from his
mouth,
burning coals blazed out of it.
¹⁰He parted the heavens and came
down;
dark clouds were under his feet.
¹¹He mounted the cherubim and flew;
he soared on the wings of the wind.
¹²He made darkness his canopy around
him—
the dark rain clouds of the sky.
¹³Out of the brightness of his presence
bolts of lightning blazed forth.
¹⁴The LORD thundered from heaven;
the voice of the Most High
resounded.
¹⁵He shot arrows and scattered ⌞the
enemies⌟,
bolts of lightning and routed them.
¹⁶The valleys of the sea were exposed
and the foundations of the earth
laid bare
at the rebuke of the LORD,
at the blast of breath from his
nostrils.

¹⁷"He reached down from on high and
took hold of me;
he drew me out of deep waters.

¹⁸He rescued me from my powerful
    enemy,
  from my foes, who were too strong
    for me.
¹⁹They confronted me in the day of my
    disaster,
  but the LORD was my support.
²⁰He brought me out into a spacious
    place;
  he rescued me because he
    delighted in me.

²¹"The LORD has dealt with me
    according to my righteousness;
  according to the cleanness of my
    hands he has rewarded me.
²²For I have kept the ways of the LORD;
  I have not done evil by turning
    from my God.
²³All his laws are before me;
  I have not turned away from his
    decrees.
²⁴I have been blameless before him
  and have kept myself from sin.
²⁵The LORD has rewarded me
    according to my righteousness,
  according to my cleanness in his
    sight.

²⁶"To the faithful you show yourself
    faithful,
  to the blameless you show yourself
    blameless,
²⁷to the pure you show yourself pure,
  but to the crooked you show
    yourself shrewd.
²⁸You save the humble,
  but your eyes are on the haughty to
    bring them low.
²⁹You are my lamp, O LORD;
  the LORD turns my darkness into
    light.
³⁰With your help I can advance against
    a troop;
  with my God I can scale a wall.

³¹"As for God, his way is perfect;
  the word of the LORD is flawless.
He is a shield
  for all who take refuge in him.
³²For who is God besides the LORD?
  And who is the Rock except our
    God?

³³It is God who arms me with strength
  and makes my way perfect.
³⁴He makes my feet like the feet of a
    deer;
  he enables me to stand on the
    heights.
³⁵He trains my hands for battle;
  my arms can bend a bow of bronze.
³⁶You give me your shield of victory;
  you stoop down to make me great.
³⁷You broaden the path beneath me,
  so that my ankles do not turn over.

³⁸"I pursued my enemies and crushed
    them;
  I did not turn back till they were
    destroyed.
³⁹I crushed them completely, and they
    could not rise;
  they fell beneath my feet.
⁴⁰You armed me with strength for
    battle;
  you made my adversaries bow at
    my feet.
⁴¹You made my enemies turn their
    backs in flight,
  and I destroyed my foes.
⁴²They cried for help, but there was
    no-one to save them—
  to the LORD, but he did not
    answer.
⁴³I beat them as fine as the dust of the
    earth;
  I pounded and trampled them like
    mud in the streets.

⁴⁴"You have delivered me from the
    attacks of my people;
  you have preserved me as the head
    of nations.
  People I did not know are subject to
    me,
⁴⁵ and foreigners come cringing to
    me;
  as soon as they hear me, they obey
    me.
⁴⁶They all lose heart;
  they come trembling from their
    strongholds.

⁴⁷"The LORD lives! Praise be to my
    Rock!

Exalted be God, the Rock, my
Saviour!
48He is the God who avenges me,
who puts the nations under me,
49 who sets me free from my enemies.
You exalted me above my foes;
from violent men you rescued me.
50Therefore I will praise you, O LORD,
among the nations;
I will sing praises to your name.
51He gives his king great victories;
he shows unfailing kindness to his
anointed,
to David and his descendants for
ever."

The Last Words of David

23 These are the last words of
David:

"The oracle of David son of Jesse,
the oracle of the man exalted by
the Most High,
the man anointed by the God of
Jacob,
Israel's singer of songs:

2"The Spirit of the LORD spoke
through me;
his word was on my tongue.
3The God of Israel spoke,
the Rock of Israel said to me:
'When one rules over men in
righteousness,
when he rules in the fear of God,
4he is like the light of morning at
sunrise
on a cloudless morning,
like the brightness after rain
that brings the grass from the
earth.'

5"Is not my house right with God?
Has he not made with me an
everlasting covenant,
arranged and secured in every
part?
Will he not bring to fruition my
salvation
and grant me my every desire?

6But evil men are all to be cast aside
like thorns,
which are not gathered with the
hand.
7Whoever touches thorns
uses a tool of iron or the shaft of a
spear;
they are burned up where they
lie."

NEW TESTAMENT READING
Acts 9:1–31

Saul's Conversion

9 Meanwhile, Saul was still breathing out murderous threats against
the Lord's disciples. He went to the
high priest 2and asked him for letters
to the synagogues in Damascus, so that
if he found any there who belonged to
the Way, whether men or women, he
might take them as prisoners to Jerusalem. 3As he neared Damascus on his
journey, suddenly a light from heaven
flashed around him. 4He fell to the
ground and heard a voice say to him,
"Saul, Saul, why do you persecute
me?"

5"Who are you, Lord?" Saul asked.
"I am Jesus, whom you are persecuting," he replied. 6"Now get up and
go into the city, and you will be told
what you must do."

7The men travelling with Saul stood
there speechless; they heard the sound
but did not see anyone. 8Saul got up
from the ground, but when he opened
his eyes he could see nothing. So they
led him by the hand into Damascus.
9For three days he was blind, and did
not eat or drink anything.

10In Damascus there was a disciple
named Ananias. The Lord called to him
in a vision, "Ananias!"

"Yes, Lord," he answered.
11The Lord told him, "Go to the
house of Judas on Straight Street and
ask for a man from Tarsus named Saul,
for he is praying. 12In a vision he has
seen a man named Ananias come and

place his hands on him to restore his sight."

13"Lord," Ananias answered, "I have heard many reports about this man and all the harm he has done to your saints in Jerusalem. 14And he has come here with authority from the chief priests to arrest all who call on your name."

15But the Lord said to Ananias, "Go! This man is my chosen instrument to carry my name before the Gentiles and their kings and before the people of Israel. 16I will show him how much he must suffer for my name."

17Then Ananias went to the house and entered it. Placing his hands on Saul, he said, "Brother Saul, the Lord —Jesus, who appeared to you on the road as you were coming here—has sent me so that you may see again and be filled with the Holy Spirit." 18Immediately, something like scales fell from Saul's eyes, and he could see again. He got up and was baptised, 19and after taking some food, he regained his strength.

Saul in Damascus and Jerusalem

Saul spent several days with the disciples in Damascus. 20At once he began to preach in the synagogues that Jesus is the Son of God. 21All those who heard him were astonished and asked, "Isn't he the man who caused havoc in Jerusalem among those who call on this name? And hasn't he come here to take them as prisoners to the chief priests?" 22Yet Saul grew more and more powerful and baffled the Jews living in Damascus by proving that Jesus is the Christ.

23After many days had gone by, the Jews conspired to kill him, 24but Saul learned of their plan. Day and night they kept close watch on the city gates in order to kill him. 25But his followers took him by night and lowered him in a basket through an opening in the wall.

26When he came to Jerusalem, he tried to join the disciples, but they were all afraid of him, not believing that he really was a disciple. 27But Barnabas took him and brought him to the apostles. He told them how Saul on his journey had seen the Lord and that the Lord had spoken to him, and how in Damascus he had preached fearlessly in the name of Jesus. 28So Saul stayed with them and moved about freely in Jerusalem, speaking boldly in the name of the Lord. 29He talked and debated with the Grecian Jews, but they tried to kill him. 30When the brothers learned of this, they took him down to Caesarea and sent him off to Tarsus.

31Then the church throughout Judea, Galilee and Samaria enjoyed a time of peace. It was strengthened; and encouraged by the Holy Spirit, it grew in numbers, living in the fear of the Lord.

READING FROM PSALMS
Psalm 73:15–28

15If I had said, "I will speak thus,"
    I would have betrayed your
       children.
16When I tried to understand all this,
    it was oppressive to me
17till I entered the sanctuary of God;
    then I understood their final
       destiny.

18Surely you place them on slippery
       ground;
    you cast them down to ruin.
19How suddenly are they destroyed,
    completely swept away by terrors!
20As a dream when one awakes,
    so when you arise, O Lord,
    you will despise them as fantasies.

21When my heart was grieved
    and my spirit embittered,
22I was senseless and ignorant;
    I was a brute beast before you.

23Yet I am always with you;
    you hold me by my right hand.

²⁴You guide me with your counsel,
    and afterwards you will take me
        into glory.
²⁵Whom have I in heaven but you?
    And earth has nothing I desire
        besides you.
²⁶My flesh and my heart may fail,
    but God is the strength of my heart
    and my portion for ever.

²⁷Those who are far from you will
        perish;
    you destroy all who are unfaithful
        to you.
²⁸But as for me, it is good to be near
        God.
    I have made the Sovereign LORD
        my refuge;
    I will tell of all your deeds.

DAY 166

JUNE 15

OLD TESTAMENT READING
2 Samuel 23:8–24:25

David's Mighty Men

⁸These are the names of David's
mighty men:

Josheb-Basshebeth, a Tahkemonite,
was chief of the Three; he raised his
spear against eight hundred men, whom
he killed in one encounter.

⁹Next to him was Eleazar son of
Dodai the Ahohite. As one of the three
mighty men, he was with David when
they taunted the Philistines gathered ⌊at
Pas Dammim⌋ for battle. Then the men
of Israel retreated, ¹⁰but he stood his
ground and struck down the Philistines
till his hand grew tired and froze to the
sword. The LORD brought about a great
victory that day. The troops returned to
Eleazar, but only to strip the dead.

¹¹Next to him was Shammah son of
Agee the Hararite. When the Philistines banded together at a place where
there was a field full of lentils, Israel's
troops fled from them. ¹²But Shammah
took his stand in the middle of the field.
He defended it and struck the Philistines down, and the LORD brought
about a great victory.

¹³During harvest time, three of the
thirty chief men came down to David at
the cave of Adullam, while a band of
Philistines was encamped in the Valley

of Rephaim. ¹⁴At that time David was
in the stronghold, and the Philistine
garrison was at Bethlehem. ¹⁵David
longed for water and said, "Oh, that
someone would get me a drink of water
from the well near the gate of Bethlehem!" ¹⁶So the three mighty men
broke through the Philistine lines, drew
water from the well near the gate of
Bethlehem and carried it back to David.
But he refused to drink it; instead, he
poured it out before the LORD. ¹⁷"Far
be it from me, O LORD, to do this!" he
said. "Is it not the blood of men who
went at the risk of their lives?" And
David would not drink it.

Such were the exploits of the three
mighty men.

¹⁸Abishai the brother of Joab son of
Zeruiah was chief of the Three. He
raised his spear against three hundred
men, whom he killed, and so he became
as famous as the Three. ¹⁹Was he not
held in greater honour than the Three?
He became their commander, even
though he was not included among
them.

²⁰Benaiah son of Jehoiada was a
valiant fighter from Kabzeel, who performed great exploits. He struck down
two of Moab's best men. He also went
down into a pit on a snowy day and
killed a lion. ²¹And he struck down a
huge Egyptian. Although the Egyptian
had a spear in his hand, Benaiah went

against him with a club. He snatched the spear from the Egyptian's hand and killed him with his own spear. ²²Such were the exploits of Benaiah son of Jehoiada; he too was as famous as the three mighty men. ²³He was held in greater honour than any of the Thirty, but he was not included among the Three. And David put him in charge of his bodyguard.

²⁴Among the Thirty were:

Asahel the brother of Joab,
Elhanan son of Dodo from Bethlehem,
²⁵Shammah the Harodite,
Elika the Harodite,
²⁶Helez the Paltite,
Ira son of Ikkesh from Tekoa,
²⁷Abiezer from Anathoth,
Mebunnai the Hushathite,
²⁸Zalmon the Ahohite,
Maharai the Netophathite,
²⁹Heled son of Baanah the Netophathite,
Ithai son of Ribai from Gibeah of Benjamin,
³⁰Benaiah the Pirathonite,
Hiddai from the ravines of Gaash,
³¹Abi-Albon the Arbathite,
Azmaveth the Barhumite,
³²Eliahba the Shaalbonite,
the sons of Jashen,
Jonathan ³³son of Shammah the Hararite,
Ahiam son of Sharar the Hararite,
³⁴Eliphelet son of Ahasbai the Maacathite,
Eliam son of Ahithophel the Gilonite,
³⁵Hezro the Carmelite,
Paarai the Arbite,
³⁶Igal son of Nathan from Zobah, the son of Hagri,
³⁷Zelek the Ammonite,
Naharai the Beerothite, the armour-bearer of Joab son of Zeruiah,
³⁸Ira the Ithrite,
Gareb the Ithrite

³⁹and Uriah the Hittite.
There were thirty-seven in all.

David Counts the Fighting Men

24 Again the anger of the LORD burned against Israel, and he incited David against them, saying, "Go and take a census of Israel and Judah."

²So the king said to Joab and the army commanders with him, "Go throughout the tribes of Israel from Dan to Beersheba and enrol the fighting men, so that I may know how many there are."

³But Joab replied to the king, "May the LORD your God multiply the troops a hundred times over, and may the eyes of my lord the king see it. But why does my lord the king want to do such a thing?"

⁴The king's word, however, overruled Joab and the army commanders; so they left the presence of the king to enrol the fighting men of Israel.

⁵After crossing the Jordan, they camped near Aroer, south of the town in the gorge, and then went through Gad and on to Jazer. ⁶They went to Gilead and the region of Tahtim Hodshi, and on to Dan Jaan and around towards Sidon. ⁷Then they went towards the fortress of Tyre and all the towns of the Hivites and Canaanites. Finally, they went on to Beersheba in the Negev of Judah.

⁸After they had gone through the entire land, they came back to Jerusalem at the end of nine months and twenty days.

⁹Joab reported the number of the fighting men to the king: In Israel there were eight hundred thousand able-bodied men who could handle a sword, and in Judah five hundred thousand.

¹⁰David was conscience-stricken after he had counted the fighting men, and he said to the LORD, "I have sinned greatly in what I have done. Now, O LORD, I beg you, take away the guilt of your servant. I have done a very foolish thing."

¹¹Before David got up the next morning, the word of the LORD had come to Gad the prophet, David's seer: ¹²"Go and tell David, 'This is what the LORD says: I am giving you three options. Choose one of them for me to carry out against you.'"

¹³So Gad went to David and said to him, "Shall there come upon you three years of famine in your land? Or three months of fleeing from your enemies while they pursue you? Or three days of plague in your land? Now then, think it over and decide how I should answer the one who sent me."

¹⁴David said to Gad, "I am in deep distress. Let us fall into the hands of the LORD, for his mercy is great; but do not let me fall into the hands of men."

¹⁵So the LORD sent a plague on Israel from that morning until the end of the time designated, and seventy thousand of the people from Dan to Beersheba died. ¹⁶When the angel stretched out his hand to destroy Jerusalem, the LORD was grieved because of the calamity and said to the angel who was afflicting the people, "Enough! Withdraw your hand." The angel of the LORD was then at the threshing-floor of Araunah the Jebusite.

¹⁷When David saw the angel who was striking down the people, he said to the LORD, "I am the one who has sinned and done wrong. These are but sheep. What have they done? Let your hand fall upon me and my family."

David Builds an Altar

¹⁸On that day Gad went to David and said to him, "Go up and build an altar to the LORD on the threshing-floor of Araunah the Jebusite." ¹⁹So David went up, as the LORD had commanded through Gad. ²⁰When Araunah looked and saw the king and his men coming towards him, he went out and bowed down before the king with his face to the ground.

²¹Araunah said, "Why has my lord the king come to his servant?"

"To buy your threshing-floor," David answered, "so that I can build an altar to the LORD, that the plague on the people may be stopped."

²²Araunah said to David, "Let my lord the king take whatever pleases him and offer it up. Here are oxen for the burnt offering, and here are threshing-sledges and ox yokes for the wood. ²³O king, Araunah gives all this to the king." Araunah also said to him, "May the LORD your God accept you."

²⁴But the king replied to Araunah, "No, I insist on paying you for it. I will not sacrifice to the LORD my God burnt offerings that cost me nothing."

So David bought the threshing-floor and the oxen and paid fifty shekels of silver for them. ²⁵David built an altar to the LORD there and sacrificed burnt offerings and fellowship offerings. Then the LORD answered prayer on behalf of the land, and the plague on Israel was stopped.

NEW TESTAMENT READING
Acts 9:32–10:23a

Aeneas and Dorcas

³²As Peter travelled about the country, he went to visit the saints in Lydda. ³³There he found a man named Aeneas, a paralytic who had been bedridden for eight years. ³⁴"Aeneas," Peter said to him, "Jesus Christ heals you. Get up and tidy up your mat." Immediately Aeneas got up. ³⁵All those who lived in Lydda and Sharon saw him and turned to the Lord.

³⁶In Joppa there was a disciple named Tabitha (which, when translated, is Dorcas), who was always doing good and helping the poor. ³⁷About that time she became sick and died, and her body was washed and placed in an upstairs room. ³⁸Lydda was near Joppa; so when the disciples heard that Peter was in Lydda, they sent two men to him and urged him, "Please come at once!"

³⁹Peter went with them, and when he arrived he was taken upstairs to the

room. All the widows stood around him, crying and showing him the robes and other clothing that Dorcas had made while she was still with them.

⁴⁰Peter sent them all out of the room; then he got down on his knees and prayed. Turning towards the dead woman, he said, "Tabitha, get up." She opened her eyes, and seeing Peter she sat up. ⁴¹He took her by the hand and helped her to her feet. Then he called the believers and the widows and presented her to them alive. ⁴²This became known all over Joppa, and many people believed in the Lord. ⁴³Peter stayed in Joppa for some time with a tanner named Simon.

Cornelius Calls for Peter

10 At Caesarea there was a man named Cornelius, a centurion in what was known as the Italian Regiment. ²He and all his family were devout and God-fearing; he gave generously to those in need and prayed to God regularly. ³One day at about three in the afternoon he had a vision. He distinctly saw an angel of God, who came to him and said, "Cornelius!"

⁴Cornelius stared at him in fear. "What is it, Lord?" he asked.

The angel answered, "Your prayers and gifts to the poor have come up as a memorial offering before God. ⁵Now send men to Joppa to bring back a man named Simon who is called Peter. ⁶He is staying with Simon the tanner, whose house is by the sea."

⁷When the angel who spoke to him had gone, Cornelius called two of his servants and a devout soldier who was one of his attendants. ⁸He told them everything that had happened and sent them to Joppa.

Peter's Vision

⁹About noon the following day as they were on their journey and approaching the city, Peter went up on the roof to pray. ¹⁰He became hungry and wanted something to eat, and while the meal was being prepared, he fell into a trance. ¹¹He saw heaven opened and something like a large sheet being let down to earth by its four corners. ¹²It contained all kinds of four-footed animals, as well as reptiles of the earth and birds of the air. ¹³Then a voice told him, "Get up, Peter. Kill and eat."

¹⁴"Surely not, Lord!" Peter replied. "I have never eaten anything impure or unclean."

¹⁵The voice spoke to him a second time, "Do not call anything impure that God has made clean."

¹⁶This happened three times, and immediately the sheet was taken back to heaven.

¹⁷While Peter was wondering about the meaning of the vision, the men sent by Cornelius found out where Simon's house was and stopped at the gate. ¹⁸They called out, asking if Simon who was known as Peter was staying there.

¹⁹While Peter was still thinking about the vision, the Spirit said to him, "Simon, three men are looking for you. ²⁰So get up and go downstairs. Do not hesitate to go with them, for I have sent them."

²¹Peter went down and said to the men, "I'm the one you're looking for. Why have you come?"

²²The men replied, "We have come from Cornelius the centurion. He is a righteous and God-fearing man, who is respected by all the Jewish people. A holy angel told him to have you come to his house so that he could hear what you have to say." ²³Then Peter invited the men into the house to be his guests.

READING FROM PSALMS
Psalm 74:1–9

A maskil of Asaph.

¹Why have you rejected us for ever, O God?
  Why does your anger smoulder against the sheep of your pasture?

²Remember the people you purchased
of old,
the tribe of your inheritance,
whom you redeemed—
Mount Zion, where you dwelt.
³Turn your steps towards these
everlasting ruins,
all this destruction the enemy has
brought on the sanctuary.

⁴Your foes roared in the place where
you met with us;
they set up their standards as signs.
⁵They behaved like men wielding axes
to cut through a thicket of trees.

⁶They smashed all the carved
panelling
with their axes and hatchets.
⁷They burned your sanctuary to the
ground;
they defiled the dwelling-place of
your Name.
⁸They said in their hearts, "We will
crush them completely!"
They burned every place where
God was worshipped in the
land.
⁹We are given no miraculous signs;
no prophets are left,
and none of us knows how long this
will be.

DAY 167

JUNE 16

OLD TESTAMENT READING
1 Kings 1:1–2:12

Adonijah Sets Himself Up as King

1 When King David was old and well
advanced in years, he could not
keep warm even when they put covers
over him. ²So his servants said to him,
"Let us look for a young virgin to attend
the king and take care of him. She can
lie beside him so that our lord the king
may keep warm."

³Then they searched throughout
Israel for a beautiful girl and found
Abishag, a Shunammite, and brought
her to the king. ⁴The girl was very
beautiful; she took care of the king and
waited on him, but the king had no
intimate relations with her.

⁵Now Adonijah, whose mother was
Haggith, put himself forward and said,
"I will be king." So he got chariots and
horses ready, with fifty men to run
ahead of him. ⁶(His father had never
interfered with him by asking, "Why do
you behave as you do?" He was also
very handsome and was born next after
Absalom.)

⁷Adonijah conferred with Joab son of
Zeruiah and with Abiathar the priest,
and they gave him their support. ⁸But
Zadok the priest, Benaiah son of
Jehoiada, Nathan the prophet, Shimei
and Rei and David's special guard did
not join Adonijah.

⁹Adonijah then sacrificed sheep, cattle and fattened calves at the Stone of
Zoheleth near En Rogel. He invited all
his brothers, the king's sons, and all the
men of Judah who were royal officials,
¹⁰but he did not invite Nathan the
prophet or Benaiah or the special guard
or his brother Solomon.

¹¹Then Nathan asked Bathsheba,
Solomon's mother, "Have you not
heard that Adonijah, the son of Haggith, has become king without our lord
David's knowing it? ¹²Now then, let me
advise you how you can save your own
life and the life of your son Solomon.
¹³Go in to King David and say to him,
'My lord the king, did you not swear to
me your servant: "Surely Solomon your
son shall be king after me, and he will sit
on my throne"? Why then has Adonijah
become king?' ¹⁴While you are still

there talking to the king, I will come in and confirm what you have said."

¹⁵So Bathsheba went to see the aged king in his room, where Abishag the Shunammite was attending him. ¹⁶Bathsheba bowed low and knelt before the king.

"What is it you want?" the king asked.

¹⁷She said to him, "My lord, you yourself swore to me your servant by the LORD your God: 'Solomon your son shall become king after me, and he will sit on my throne.' ¹⁸But now Adonijah has become king, and you, my lord the king, do not know about it. ¹⁹He has sacrificed great numbers of cattle, fattened calves, and sheep, and has invited all the king's sons, Abiathar the priest and Joab the commander of the army, but he has not invited Solomon your servant. ²⁰My lord the king, the eyes of all Israel are on you, to learn from you who will sit on the throne of my lord the king after him. ²¹Otherwise, as soon as my lord the king is laid to rest with his fathers, I and my son Solomon will be treated as criminals."

²²While she was still speaking with the king, Nathan the prophet arrived. ²³And they told the king, "Nathan the prophet is here." So he went before the king and bowed with his face to the ground.

²⁴Nathan said, "Have you, my lord the king, declared that Adonijah shall be king after you, and that he will sit on your throne? ²⁵Today he has gone down and sacrificed great numbers of cattle, fattened calves, and sheep. He has invited all the king's sons, the commanders of the army and Abiathar the priest. Right now they are eating and drinking with him and saying, 'Long live King Adonijah!' ²⁶But me your servant, and Zadok the priest, and Benaiah son of Jehoiada, and your servant Solomon he did not invite. ²⁷Is this something my lord the king has done without letting his servants know who should sit on the throne of my lord the king after him?"

David Makes Solomon King

²⁸Then King David said, "Call in Bathsheba." So she came into the king's presence and stood before him.

²⁹The king then took an oath: "As surely as the LORD lives, who has delivered me out of every trouble, ³⁰I will surely carry out today what I swore to you by the LORD, the God of Israel: Solomon your son shall be king after me, and he will sit on my throne in my place."

³¹Then Bathsheba bowed low with her face to the ground and, kneeling before the king, said, "May my lord King David live for ever!"

³²King David said, "Call in Zadok the priest, Nathan the prophet and Benaiah son of Jehoiada." When they came before the king, ³³he said to them: "Take your lord's servants with you and set Solomon my son on my own mule and take him down to Gihon. ³⁴There shall Zadok the priest and Nathan the prophet anoint him king over Israel. Blow the trumpet and shout, 'Long live King Solomon!' ³⁵Then you are to go up with him, and he is to come and sit on my throne and reign in my place. I have appointed him ruler over Israel and Judah."

³⁶Benaiah son of Jehoiada answered the king, "Amen! May the LORD, the God of my lord the king, so declare it. ³⁷As the LORD was with my lord the king, so may he be with Solomon to make his throne even greater than the throne of my lord King David!"

³⁸So Zadok the priest, Nathan the prophet, Benaiah son of Jehoiada, the Kerethites and the Pelethites went down and put Solomon on King David's mule and escorted him to Gihon. ³⁹Zadok the priest took the horn of oil from the sacred tent and anointed Solomon. Then they sounded the trumpet and all the people shouted, "Long live King Solomon!" ⁴⁰And all the people went up after him, playing flutes and rejoicing greatly, so that the ground shook with the sound.

⁴¹Adonijah and all the guests who were with him heard it as they were finishing their feast. On hearing the sound of the trumpet, Joab asked, "What's the meaning of all the noise in the city?"

⁴²Even as he was speaking, Jonathan son of Abiathar the priest arrived. Adonijah said, "Come in. A worthy man like you must be bringing good news."

⁴³"Not at all!" Jonathan answered. "Our lord King David has made Solomon king. ⁴⁴The king has sent with him Zadok the priest, Nathan the prophet, Benaiah son of Jehoiada, the Kerethites and the Pelethites, and they have put him on the king's mule, ⁴⁵and Zadok the priest and Nathan the prophet have anointed him king at Gihon. From there they have gone up cheering, and the city resounds with it. That's the noise you hear. ⁴⁶Moreover, Solomon has taken his seat on the royal throne. ⁴⁷Also, the royal officials have come to congratulate our lord King David, saying, 'May your God make Solomon's name more famous than yours and his throne greater than yours!' And the king bowed in worship on his bed ⁴⁸and said, 'Praise be to the LORD, the God of Israel, who has allowed my eyes to see a successor on my throne today.'"

⁴⁹At this, all Adonijah's guests rose in alarm and dispersed. ⁵⁰But Adonijah, in fear of Solomon, went and took hold of the horns of the altar. ⁵¹Then Solomon was told, "Adonijah is afraid of King Solomon and is clinging to the horns of the altar. He says, 'Let King Solomon swear to me today that he will not put his servant to death with the sword.'"

⁵²Solomon replied, "If he shows himself to be a worthy man, not a hair of his head will fall to the ground; but if evil is found in him, he will die." ⁵³Then King Solomon sent men, and they brought him down from the altar. And Adonijah came and bowed down to King Solomon, and Solomon said, "Go to your home."

David's Charge to Solomon

2 When the time drew near for David to die, he gave a charge to Solomon his son.

²"I am about to go the way of all the earth," he said. "So be strong, show yourself a man, ³and observe what the LORD your God requires: Walk in his ways, and keep his decrees and commands, his laws and requirements, as written in the Law of Moses, so that you may prosper in all you do and wherever you go, ⁴and that the LORD may keep his promise to me: 'If your descendants watch how they live, and if they walk faithfully before me with all their heart and soul, you will never fail to have a man on the throne of Israel.'

⁵"Now you yourself know what Joab son of Zeruiah did to me—what he did to the two commanders of Israel's armies, Abner son of Ner and Amasa son of Jether. He killed them, shedding their blood in peacetime as if in battle, and with that blood stained the belt round his waist and the sandals on his feet. ⁶Deal with him according to your wisdom, but do not let his grey head go down to the grave in peace.

⁷"But show kindness to the sons of Barzillai of Gilead and let them be among those who eat at your table. They stood by me when I fled from your brother Absalom.

⁸"And remember, you have with you Shimei son of Gera, the Benjamite from Bahurim, who called down bitter curses on me the day I went to Mahanaim. When he came down to meet me at the Jordan, I swore to him by the LORD: 'I will not put you to death by the sword.' ⁹But now, do not consider him innocent. You are a man of wisdom; you will know what to do to him. Bring his grey head down to the grave in blood."

¹⁰Then David rested with his fathers and was buried in the City of David. ¹¹He had reigned for forty years over Israel—seven years in Hebron and

thirty-three in Jerusalem. [12]So Solomon sat on the throne of his father David, and his rule was firmly established.

NEW TESTAMENT READING
Acts 10:23b–11:18

Peter at Cornelius' House

The next day Peter started out with them, and some of the brothers from Joppa went along. [24]The following day he arrived in Caesarea. Cornelius was expecting them and had called together his relatives and close friends. [25]As Peter entered the house, Cornelius met him and fell at his feet in reverence. [26]But Peter made him get up. "Stand up," he said, "I am only a man myself."

[27]Talking with him, Peter went inside and found a large gathering of people. [28]He said to them: "You are well aware that it is against our law for a Jew to associate with a Gentile or visit him. But God has shown me that I should not call any man impure or unclean. [29]So when I was sent for, I came without raising any objection. May I ask why you sent for me?"

[30]Cornelius answered: "Four days ago I was in my house praying at this hour, at three in the afternoon. Suddenly a man in shining clothes stood before me [31]and said, 'Cornelius, God has heard your prayer and remembered your gifts to the poor. [32]Send to Joppa for Simon who is called Peter. He is a guest in the home of Simon the tanner, who lives by the sea.' [33]So I sent for you immediately, and it was good of you to come. Now we are all here in the presence of God to listen to everything the Lord has commanded you to tell us."

[34]Then Peter began to speak: "I now realise how true it is that God does not show favouritism [35]but accepts men from every nation who fear him and do what is right. [36]You know the message God sent to the people of Israel, telling the good news of peace through Jesus Christ, who is Lord of all. [37]You know what has happened throughout Judea,

beginning in Galilee after the baptism that John preached—[38]how God anointed Jesus of Nazareth with the Holy Spirit and power, and how he went around doing good and healing all who were under the power of the devil, because God was with him.

[39]"We are witnesses of everything he did in the country of the Jews and in Jerusalem. They killed him by hanging him on a tree, [40]but God raised him from the dead on the third day and caused him to be seen. [41]He was not seen by all the people, but by witnesses whom God had already chosen—by us who ate and drank with him after he rose from the dead. [42]He commanded us to preach to the people and to testify that he is the one whom God appointed as judge of the living and the dead. [43]All the prophets testify about him that everyone who believes in him receives forgiveness of sins through his name."

[44]While Peter was still speaking these words, the Holy Spirit came on all who heard the message. [45]The circumcised believers who had come with Peter were astonished that the gift of the Holy Spirit had been poured out even on the Gentiles. [46]For they heard them speaking in tongues and praising God.

Then Peter said, [47]"Can anyone keep these people from being baptised with water? They have received the Holy Spirit just as we have." [48]So he ordered that they be baptised in the name of Jesus Christ. Then they asked Peter to stay with them for a few days.

Peter Explains His Actions

11 The apostles and the brothers throughout Judea heard that the Gentiles also had received the word of God. [2]So when Peter went up to Jerusalem, the circumcised believers criticised him [3]and said, "You went into the house of uncircumcised men and ate with them."

[4]Peter began and explained everything to them precisely as it had happened: [5]"I was in the city of Joppa

praying, and in a trance I saw a vision. I saw something like a large sheet being let down from heaven by its four corners, and it came down to where I was. 6I looked into it and saw four-footed animals of the earth, wild beasts, reptiles, and birds of the air. 7Then I heard a voice telling me, 'Get up, Peter. Kill and eat.'

8"I replied, 'Surely not, Lord! Nothing impure or unclean has ever entered my mouth.'

9"The voice spoke from heaven a second time, 'Do not call anything impure that God has made clean.' 10This happened three times, and then it was pulled up to heaven again.

11"Right then three men who had been sent to me from Caesarea stopped at the house where I was staying. 12The Spirit told me to have no hesitation about going with them. These six brothers also went with me, and we entered the man's house. 13He told us how he had seen an angel appear in his house and say, 'Send to Joppa for Simon who is called Peter. 14He will bring you a message through which you and all your household will be saved.'

15"As I began to speak, the Holy Spirit came on them as he had come on us at the beginning. 16Then I remembered what the Lord had said: 'John baptised with water, but you will be baptised with the Holy Spirit.' 17So if God gave them the same gift as he gave us, who believed in the Lord Jesus Christ, who was I to think that I could oppose God?"

18When they heard this, they had no further objections and praised God, saying, "So then, God has granted even the Gentiles repentance unto life."

READING FROM PSALMS
Psalm 74:10–17

10How long will the enemy mock you, O God?
Will the foe revile your name for ever?
11Why do you hold back your hand, your right hand?
Take it from the folds of your garment and destroy them!

12But you, O God, are my king from of old;
you bring salvation upon the earth.
13It was you who split open the sea by your power;
you broke the heads of the monster in the waters.
14It was you who crushed the heads of Leviathan
and gave him as food to the creatures of the desert.
15It was you who opened up springs and streams;
you dried up the ever-flowing rivers.
16The day is yours, and yours also the night;
you established the sun and moon.
17It was you who set all the boundaries of the earth;
you made both summer and winter.

OLD TESTAMENT READING
1 Kings 2:13–3:15

Solomon's Throne Established

13Now Adonijah, the son of Haggith, went to Bathsheba, Solomon's mother. Bathsheba asked him, "Do you come peacefully?"

He answered, "Yes, peacefully." 14Then he added, "I have something to say to you."

"You may say it," she replied.

15"As you know," he said, "the kingdom was mine. All Israel looked to me as their king. But things changed, and the kingdom has gone to my brother; for it has come to him from the LORD. 16Now I have one request to make of you. Do not refuse me."

"You may make it," she said.

17So he continued, "Please ask King Solomon—he will not refuse you—to give me Abishag the Shunammite as my wife."

18"Very well," Bathsheba replied, "I will speak to the king for you."

19When Bathsheba went to King Solomon to speak to him for Adonijah, the king stood up to meet her, bowed down to her and sat down on his throne. He had a throne brought for the king's mother, and she sat down at his right hand.

20"I have one small request to make of you," she said. "Do not refuse me."

The king replied, "Make it, my mother; I will not refuse you."

21So she said, "Let Abishag the Shunammite be given in marriage to your brother Adonijah."

22King Solomon answered his mother, "Why do you request Abishag the Shunammite for Adonijah? You might as well request the kingdom for him—after all, he is my older brother—yes, for him and for Abiathar the priest and Joab son of Zeruiah!"

23Then King Solomon swore by the LORD: "May God deal with me, be it ever so severely, if Adonijah does not pay with his life for this request! 24And now, as surely as the LORD lives—he who has established me securely on the throne of my father David and has founded a dynasty for me as he promised—Adonijah shall be put to death today!" 25So King Solomon gave orders to Benaiah son of Jehoiada, and he struck down Adonijah and he died.

26To Abiathar the priest the king said, "Go back to your fields in Anathoth. You deserve to die, but I will not put you to death now, because you carried the ark of the Sovereign LORD before my father David and shared all my father's hardships." 27So Solomon removed Abiathar from the priesthood of the LORD, fulfilling the word the LORD had spoken at Shiloh about the house of Eli.

28When the news reached Joab, who had conspired with Adonijah though not with Absalom, he fled to the tent of the LORD and took hold of the horns of the altar. 29King Solomon was told that Joab had fled to the tent of the LORD and was beside the altar. Then Solomon ordered Benaiah son of Jehoiada, "Go, strike him down!"

30So Benaiah entered the tent of the LORD and said to Joab, "The king says, 'Come out!'"

But he answered, "No, I will die here."

Benaiah reported to the king, "This is how Joab answered me."

31Then the king commanded Benaiah, "Do as he says. Strike him down and bury him, and so clear me and my father's house of the guilt of the innocent blood that Joab shed. 32The LORD will repay him for the blood he shed, because without the knowledge of my father David he attacked two men and killed them with the sword. Both of them—Abner son of Ner, commander of Israel's army, and Amasa son of Jether, commander of Judah's army—were better men and more upright than he. [33]May the guilt of their blood rest on the head of Joab and his descendants for ever. But on David and his descendants, his house and his throne, may there be the LORD's peace for ever."

[34]So Benaiah son of Jehoiada went up and struck down Joab and killed him, and he was buried on his own land in the desert. [35]The king put Benaiah son of Jehoiada over the army in Joab's position and replaced Abiathar with Zadok the priest.

[36]Then the king sent for Shimei and said to him, "Build yourself a house in Jerusalem and live there, but do not go anywhere else. [37]The day you leave and cross the Kidron Valley, you can be sure you will die; your blood will be on your own head."

[38]Shimei answered the king, "What you say is good. Your servant will do as my lord the king has said." And Shimei stayed in Jerusalem for a long time.

[39]But three years later, two of Shimei's slaves ran off to Achish son of Maacah, king of Gath, and Shimei was told, "Your slaves are in Gath." [40]At this, he saddled his donkey and went to Achish at Gath in search of his slaves. So Shimei went away and brought the slaves back from Gath.

[41]When Solomon was told that Shimei had gone from Jerusalem to Gath and had returned, [42]the king summoned Shimei and said to him, "Did I not make you swear by the LORD and warn you, 'On the day you leave to go anywhere else, you can be sure you will die'? At that time you said to me, 'What you say is good. I will obey.' [43]Why then did you not keep your oath to the LORD and obey the command I gave you?"

[44]The king also said to Shimei, "You know in your heart all the wrong you did to my father David. Now the LORD will repay you for your wrongdoing. [45]But King Solomon will be blessed, and David's throne will remain secure before the LORD for ever."

[46]Then the king gave the order to Benaiah son of Jehoiada, and he went out and struck Shimei down and killed him.

The kingdom was now firmly established in Solomon's hands.

Solomon Asks for Wisdom

3 Solomon made an alliance with Pharaoh king of Egypt and married his daughter. He brought her to the City of David until he finished building his palace and the temple of the LORD, and the wall around Jerusalem. [2]The people, however, were still sacrificing at the high places, because a temple had not yet been built for the Name of the LORD. [3]Solomon showed his love for the LORD by walking according to the statutes of his father David, except that he offered sacrifices and burned incense on the high places.

[4]The king went to Gibeon to offer sacrifices, for that was the most important high place, and Solomon offered a thousand burnt offerings on that altar. [5]At Gibeon the LORD appeared to Solomon during the night in a dream, and God said, "Ask for whatever you want me to give you."

[6]Solomon answered, "You have shown great kindness to your servant, my father David, because he was faithful to you and righteous and upright in heart. You have continued this great kindness to him and have given him a son to sit on his throne this very day.

[7]"Now, O LORD my God, you have made your servant king in place of my father David. But I am only a little child and do not know how to carry out my duties. [8]Your servant is here among the people you have chosen, a great people, too numerous to count or number. [9]So give your servant a discerning heart to govern your people and to distinguish between right and wrong. For who is able to govern this great people of yours?"

¹⁰The Lord was pleased that Solomon had asked for this. ¹¹So God said to him, "Since you have asked for this and not for long life or wealth for yourself, nor have asked for the death of your enemies but for discernment in administering justice, ¹²I will do what you have asked. I will give you a wise and discerning heart, so that there will never have been anyone like you, nor will there ever be. ¹³Moreover, I will give you what you have not asked for—both riches and honour—so that in your lifetime you will have no equal among kings. ¹⁴And if you walk in my ways and obey my statutes and commands as David your father did, I will give you a long life." ¹⁵Then Solomon awoke—and he realised it had been a dream.

He returned to Jerusalem, stood before the ark of the Lord's covenant and sacrificed burnt offerings and fellowship offerings. Then he gave a feast for all his court.

NEW TESTAMENT READING
Acts 11:19–12:19a

The Church in Antioch

¹⁹Now those who had been scattered by the persecution in connection with Stephen travelled as far as Phoenicia, Cyprus and Antioch, telling the message only to Jews. ²⁰Some of them, however, men from Cyprus and Cyrene, went to Antioch and began to speak to Greeks also, telling them the good news about the Lord Jesus. ²¹The Lord's hand was with them, and a great number of people believed and turned to the Lord.

²²News of this reached the ears of the church at Jerusalem, and they sent Barnabas to Antioch. ²³When he arrived and saw the evidence of the grace of God, he was glad and encouraged them all to remain true to the Lord with all their hearts. ²⁴He was a good man, full of the Holy Spirit and faith, and a great number of people were brought to the Lord.

²⁵Then Barnabas went to Tarsus to look for Saul, ²⁶and when he found him, he brought him to Antioch. So for a whole year Barnabas and Saul met with the church and taught great numbers of people. The disciples were called Christians first at Antioch.

²⁷During this time some prophets came down from Jerusalem to Antioch. ²⁸One of them, named Agabus, stood up and through the Spirit predicted that a severe famine would spread over the entire Roman world. (This happened during the reign of Claudius.) ²⁹The disciples, each according to his ability, decided to provide help for the brothers living in Judea. ³⁰This they did, sending their gift to the elders by Barnabas and Saul.

Peter's Miraculous Escape From Prison

12 It was about this time that King Herod arrested some who belonged to the church, intending to persecute them. ²He had James, the brother of John, put to death with the sword. ³When he saw that this pleased the Jews, he proceeded to seize Peter also. This happened during the Feast of Unleavened Bread. ⁴After arresting him, he put him in prison, handing him over to be guarded by four squads of four soldiers each. Herod intended to bring him out for public trial after the Passover.

⁵So Peter was kept in prison, but the church was earnestly praying to God for him.

⁶The night before Herod was to bring him to trial, Peter was sleeping between two soldiers, bound with two chains, and sentries stood guard at the entrance. ⁷Suddenly an angel of the Lord appeared and a light shone in the cell. He struck Peter on the side and woke him up. "Quick, get up!" he said, and the chains fell off Peter's wrists.

⁸Then the angel said to him, "Put on your clothes and sandals." And Peter

did so. "Wrap your cloak around you and follow me," the angel told him. [9]Peter followed him out of the prison, but he had no idea that what the angel was doing was really happening; he thought he was seeing a vision. [10]They passed the first and second guards and came to the iron gate leading to the city. It opened for them by itself, and they went through it. When they had walked the length of one street, suddenly the angel left him.

[11]Then Peter came to himself and said, "Now I know without a doubt that the Lord sent his angel and rescued me from Herod's clutches and from everything the Jewish people were anticipating."

[12]When this had dawned on him, he went to the house of Mary the mother of John, also called Mark, where many people had gathered and were praying. [13]Peter knocked at the outer entrance, and a servant girl named Rhoda came to answer the door. [14]When she recognised Peter's voice, she was so overjoyed she ran back without opening it and exclaimed, "Peter is at the door!"

[15]"You're out of your mind," they told her. When she kept insisting that it was so, they said, "It must be his angel."

[16]But Peter kept on knocking, and when they opened the door and saw him, they were astonished. [17]Peter motioned with his hand for them to be quiet and described how the Lord had brought him out of prison. "Tell James and the brothers about this," he said, and then he left for another place.

[18]In the morning, there was no small commotion among the soldiers as to what had become of Peter. [19]After Herod had a thorough search made for him and did not find him, he cross-examined the guards and ordered that they be executed.

READING FROM PROVERBS
Proverbs 15:1–10

15 A gentle answer turns away wrath,
but a harsh word stirs up anger.

[2]The tongue of the wise commends knowledge,
but the mouth of the fool gushes folly.

[3]The eyes of the LORD are everywhere,
keeping watch on the wicked and the good.

[4]The tongue that brings healing is a tree of life,
but a deceitful tongue crushes the spirit.

[5]A fool spurns his father's discipline,
but whoever heeds correction shows prudence.

[6]The house of the righteous contains great treasure,
but the income of the wicked brings them trouble.

[7]The lips of the wise spread knowledge;
not so the hearts of fools.

[8]The LORD detests the sacrifice of the wicked,
but the prayer of the upright pleases him.

[9]The LORD detests the way of the wicked
but he loves those who pursue righteousness.

[10]Stern discipline awaits him who leaves the path;
he who hates correction will die.

OLD TESTAMENT READING
1 Kings 3:16–5:18

A Wise Ruling

16Now two prostitutes came to the king and stood before him. 17One of them said, "My lord, this woman and I live in the same house. I had a baby while she was there with me. 18The third day after my child was born, this woman also had a baby. We were alone; there was no-one in the house but the two of us.

19"During the night this woman's son died because she lay on him. 20So she got up in the middle of the night and took my son from my side while your servant was asleep. She put him by her breast and put her dead son by my breast. 21The next morning, I got up to nurse my son—and he was dead! But when I looked at him closely in the morning light, I saw that it wasn't the son I had borne."

22The other woman said, "No! The living one is my son; the dead one is yours."

But the first one insisted, "No! The dead one is yours; the living one is mine." And so they argued before the king.

23The king said, "This one says, 'My son is alive and your son is dead,' while that one says, 'No! Your son is dead and mine is alive.'"

24Then the king said, "Bring me a sword." So they brought a sword for the king. 25He then gave an order: "Cut the living child in two and give half to one and half to the other."

26The woman whose son was alive was filled with compassion for her son and said to the king, "Please, my lord, give her the living baby! Don't kill him!"

But the other said, "Neither I nor you shall have him. Cut him in two!"

27Then the king gave his ruling: "Give the living baby to the first woman. Do not kill him; she is his mother."

28When all Israel heard the verdict the king had given, they held the king in awe, because they saw that he had wisdom from God to administer justice.

Solomon's Officials and Governors

4 So King Solomon ruled over all Israel. 2And these were his chief officials:

Azariah son of Zadok—the priest;
3Elihoreph and Ahijah, sons of Shisha—secretaries;
Jehoshaphat son of Ahilud—recorder;
4Benaiah son of Jehoiada—commander-in-chief;
Zadok and Abiathar—priests;
5Azariah son of Nathan—in charge of the district officers;
Zabud son of Nathan—a priest and personal adviser to the king;
6Ahishar—in charge of the palace;
Adoniram son of Abda—in charge of forced labour.

7Solomon also had twelve district governors over all Israel, who supplied provisions for the king and the royal household. Each one had to provide supplies for one month in the year. 8These are their names:

Ben-Hur—in the hill country of Ephraim;
9Ben-Deker—in Makaz, Shaalbim, Beth Shemesh and Elon Beth-hanan;
10Ben-Hesed—in Arubboth (Socoh and all the land of Hepher were his);
11Ben-Abinadab—in Naphoth Dor

(he was married to Taphath daughter of Solomon);

¹²Baana son of Ahilud—in Taanach and Megiddo, and in all of Beth Shan next to Zarethan below Jezreel, from Beth Shan to Abel Meholah across to Jokmeam;

¹³Ben-Geber—in Ramoth Gilead (the settlements of Jair son of Manasseh in Gilead were his, as well as the district of Argob in Bashan and its sixty large walled cities with bronze gate bars);

¹⁴Ahinadab son of Iddo—in Mahanaim;

¹⁵Ahimaaz—in Naphtali (he had married Basemath daughter of Solomon);

¹⁶Baana son of Hushai—in Asher and in Aloth;

¹⁷Jehoshaphat son of Paruah—in Issachar;

¹⁸Shimei son of Ela—in Benjamin;

¹⁹Geber son of Uri—in Gilead (the country of Sihon king of the Amorites and the country of Og king of Bashan). He was the only governor over the district.

Solomon's Daily Provisions

²⁰The people of Judah and Israel were as numerous as the sand on the seashore; they ate, they drank and they were happy. ²¹And Solomon ruled over all the kingdoms from the River to the land of the Philistines, as far as the border of Egypt. These countries brought tribute and were Solomon's subjects all his life.

²²Solomon's daily provisions were thirty cors of fine flour and sixty cors of meal, ²³ten head of stall-fed cattle, twenty of pasture-fed cattle and a hundred sheep and goats, as well as deer, gazelles, roebucks and choice fowl. ²⁴For he ruled over all the kingdoms west of the River, from Tiphsah to Gaza, and had peace on all sides. ²⁵During Solomon's lifetime Judah and Israel, from Dan to Beersheba, lived in safety, each man under his own vine and fig-tree.

²⁶Solomon had four thousand stalls for chariot horses, and twelve thousand horses.

²⁷The district officers, each in his month, supplied provisions for King Solomon and all who came to the king's table. They saw to it that nothing was lacking. ²⁸They also brought to the proper place their quotas of barley and straw for the chariot horses and the other horses.

Solomon's Wisdom

²⁹God gave Solomon wisdom and very great insight, and a breadth of understanding as measureless as the sand on the seashore. ³⁰Solomon's wisdom was greater than the wisdom of all the men of the East, and greater than all the wisdom of Egypt. ³¹He was wiser than any other man, including Ethan the Ezrahite—wiser than Heman, Calcol and Darda, the sons of Mahol. And his fame spread to all the surrounding nations. ³²He spoke three thousand proverbs and his songs numbered a thousand and five. ³³He described plant life, from the cedar of Lebanon to the hyssop that grows out of walls. He also taught about animals and birds, reptiles and fish. ³⁴Men of all nations came to listen to Solomon's wisdom, sent by all the kings of the world, who had heard of his wisdom.

Preparations for Building the Temple

5 When Hiram king of Tyre heard that Solomon had been anointed king to succeed his father David, he sent his envoys to Solomon, because he had always been on friendly terms with David. ²Solomon sent back this message to Hiram:

³"You know that because of the wars waged against my father

David from all sides, he could not build a temple for the Name of the LORD his God until the LORD put his enemies under his feet. [4]But now the LORD my God has given me rest on every side, and there is no adversary or disaster. [5]I intend, therefore, to build a temple for the Name of the LORD my God, as the LORD told my father David, when he said, 'Your son whom I will put on the throne in your place will build the temple for my Name.'

[6]"So give orders that cedars of Lebanon be cut for me. My men will work with yours, and I will pay you for your men whatever wages you set. You know that we have no-one so skilled in felling timber as the Sidonians."

[7]When Hiram heard Solomon's message, he was greatly pleased and said, "Praise be to the LORD today, for he has given David a wise son to rule over this great nation."

[8]So Hiram sent word to Solomon:

"I have received the message you sent me and will do all you want in providing the cedar and pine logs. [9]My men will haul them down from Lebanon to the sea, and I will float them in rafts by sea to the place you specify. There I will separate them and you can take them away. And you are to grant my wish by providing food for my royal household."

[10]In this way Hiram kept Solomon supplied with all the cedar and pine logs he wanted, [11]and Solomon gave Hiram twenty thousand cors of wheat as food for his household, in addition to twenty thousand baths of pressed olive oil. Solomon continued to do this for Hiram year after year. [12]The LORD gave Solomon wisdom, just as he had promised him. There were peaceful relations between Hiram and Solomon, and the two of them made a treaty.

[13]King Solomon conscripted labourers from all Israel—thirty thousand men. [14]He sent them off to Lebanon in shifts of ten thousand a month, so that they spent one month in Lebanon and two months at home. Adoniram was in charge of the forced labour. [15]Solomon had seventy thousand carriers and eighty thousand stonecutters in the hills, [16]as well as thirty-three hundred foremen who supervised the project and directed the workmen. [17]At the king's command they removed from the quarry large blocks of quality stone to provide a foundation of dressed stone for the temple. [18]The craftsmen of Solomon and Hiram and the men of Gebal cut and prepared the timber and stone for the building of the temple.

NEW TESTAMENT READING
Acts 12:19b–13:12

Herod's Death

Then Herod went from Judea to Caesarea and stayed there a while. [20]He had been quarrelling with the people of Tyre and Sidon; they now joined together and sought an audience with him. Having secured the support of Blastus, a trusted personal servant of the king, they asked for peace, because they depended on the king's country for their food supply.

[21]On the appointed day Herod, wearing his royal robes, sat on his throne and delivered a public address to the people. [22]They shouted, "This is the voice of a god, not of a man." [23]Immediately, because Herod did not give praise to God, an angel of the Lord struck him down, and he was eaten by worms and died.

[24]But the word of God continued to increase and spread.

[25]When Barnabas and Saul had finished their mission, they returned from Jerusalem, taking with them John, also called Mark.

Barnabas and Saul Sent Off

13 In the church at Antioch there were prophets and teachers: Barnabas, Simeon called Niger, Lucius of Cyrene, Manaen (who had been brought up with Herod the tetrarch) and Saul. ²While they were worshipping the Lord and fasting, the Holy Spirit said, "Set apart for me Barnabas and Saul for the work to which I have called them." ³So after they had fasted and prayed, they placed their hands on them and sent them off.

On Cyprus

⁴The two of them, sent on their way by the Holy Spirit, went down to Seleucia and sailed from there to Cyprus. ⁵When they arrived at Salamis, they proclaimed the word of God in the Jewish synagogues. John was with them as their helper.

⁶They travelled through the whole island until they came to Paphos. There they met a Jewish sorcerer and false prophet named Bar-Jesus, ⁷who was an attendant of the proconsul, Sergius Paulus. The proconsul, an intelligent man, sent for Barnabas and Saul because he wanted to hear the word of God. ⁸But Elymas the sorcerer (for that is what his name means) opposed them and tried to turn the proconsul from the faith. ⁹Then Saul, who was also called Paul, filled with the Holy Spirit, looked straight at Elymas and said, ¹⁰"You are a child of the devil and an enemy of everything that is right! You are full of all kinds of deceit and trickery. Will you never stop perverting the right ways of the Lord? ¹¹Now the hand of the Lord is against you. You are going to be blind, and for a time you will be unable to see the light of the sun."

Immediately mist and darkness came over him, and he groped about, seeking someone to lead him by the hand. ¹²When the proconsul saw what had happened, he believed, for he was amazed at the teaching about the Lord.

READING FROM PSALMS
Psalm 74:18–23

¹⁸Remember how the enemy has
  mocked you, O LORD,
  how foolish people have reviled
    your name.
¹⁹Do not hand over the life of your
    dove to wild beasts;
  do not forget the lives of your
    afflicted people for ever.
²⁰Have regard for your covenant,
  because haunts of violence fill the
    dark places of the land.
²¹Do not let the oppressed retreat in
    disgrace;
  may the poor and needy praise
    your name.

²²Rise up, O God, and defend your
    cause;
  remember how fools mock you all
    day long.
²³Do not ignore the clamour of your
    adversaries,
  the uproar of your enemies, which
    rises continually.

OLD TESTAMENT READING
1 Kings 6:1–7:22

Solomon Builds the Temple

6 In the four hundred and eightieth year after the Israelites had come out of Egypt, in the fourth year of Solomon's reign over Israel, in the month of Ziv, the second month, he began to build the temple of the LORD.

²The temple that King Solomon built for the LORD was sixty cubits long, twenty wide and thirty high. ³The portico at the front of the main hall of the temple extended the width of the temple, that is twenty cubits, and projected ten cubits from the front of the temple. ⁴He made narrow clerestory windows in the temple. ⁵Against the walls of the main hall and inner sanctuary he built a structure around the building, in which there were side rooms. ⁶The lowest floor was five cubits wide, the middle floor six cubits and the third floor seven. He made offset ledges around the outside of the temple so that nothing would be inserted into the temple walls.

⁷In building the temple, only blocks dressed at the quarry were used, and no hammer, chisel or any other iron tool was heard at the temple site while it was being built.

⁸The entrance to the lowest floor was on the south side of the temple; a stairway led up to the middle level and from there to the third. ⁹So he built the temple and completed it, roofing it with beams and cedar planks. ¹⁰And he built the side rooms all along the temple. The height of each was five cubits, and they were attached to the temple by beams of cedar.

¹¹The word of the LORD came to Solomon: ¹²"As for this temple you are building, if you follow my decrees, carry out my regulations and keep all my commands and obey them, I will fulfil through you the promise I gave to David your father. ¹³And I will live among the Israelites and will not abandon my people Israel."

¹⁴So Solomon built the temple and completed it. ¹⁵He lined its interior walls with cedar boards, panelling them from the floor of the temple to the ceiling, and covered the floor of the temple with planks of pine. ¹⁶He partitioned off twenty cubits at the rear of the temple with cedar boards from floor to ceiling to form within the temple an inner sanctuary, the Most Holy Place. ¹⁷The main hall in front of this room was forty cubits long. ¹⁸The inside of the temple was cedar, carved with gourds and open flowers. Everything was cedar; no stone was to be seen.

¹⁹He prepared the inner sanctuary within the temple to set the ark of the covenant of the LORD there. ²⁰The inner sanctuary was twenty cubits long, twenty wide and twenty high. He overlaid the inside with pure gold, and he also overlaid the altar of cedar. ²¹Solomon covered the inside of the temple with pure gold, and he extended gold chains across the front of the inner sanctuary, which was overlaid with gold. ²²So he overlaid the whole interior with gold. He also overlaid with gold the altar that belonged to the inner sanctuary.

²³In the inner sanctuary he made a pair of cherubim of olive wood, each ten cubits high. ²⁴One wing of the first cherub was five cubits long, and the other wing five cubits—ten cubits from wing tip to wing tip. ²⁵The second cherub also measured ten cubits, for the two cherubim were identical in size and shape. ²⁶The height of each cherub was ten cubits. ²⁷He placed the cherubim inside the innermost room of the temple, with their wings spread out. The wing of one cherub touched one wall, while the wing of

the other touched the other wall, and their wings touched each other in the middle of the room. ²⁸He overlaid the cherubim with gold.

²⁹On the walls all round the temple, in both the inner and outer rooms, he carved cherubim, palm trees and open flowers. ³⁰He also covered the floors of both the inner and outer rooms of the temple with gold.

³¹For the entrance of the inner sanctuary he made doors of olive wood with five-sided jambs. ³²And on the two olive wood doors he carved cherubim, palm trees and open flowers, and overlaid the cherubim and palm trees with beaten gold. ³³In the same way he made four-sided jambs of olive wood for the entrance to the main hall. ³⁴He also made two pine doors, each having two leaves that turned in sockets. ³⁵He carved cherubim, palm trees and open flowers on them and overlaid them with gold hammered evenly over the carvings.

³⁶And he built the inner courtyard of three courses of dressed stone and one course of trimmed cedar beams.

³⁷The foundation of the temple of the LORD was laid in the fourth year, in the month of Ziv. ³⁸In the eleventh year in the month of Bul, the eighth month, the temple was finished in all its details according to its specifications. He had spent seven years building it.

Solomon Builds His Palace

7 It took Solomon thirteen years, however, to complete the construction of his palace. ²He built the Palace of the Forest of Lebanon a hundred cubits long, fifty wide and thirty high, with four rows of cedar columns supporting trimmed cedar beams. ³It was roofed with cedar above the beams that rested on the columns—forty-five beams, fifteen to a row. ⁴Its windows were placed high in sets of three, facing each other. ⁵All the doorways had rectangular frames; they were in the front part in sets of three, facing each other.

⁶He made a colonnade fifty cubits long and thirty wide. In front of it was a portico, and in front of that were pillars and an overhanging roof.

⁷He built the throne hall, the Hall of Justice, where he was to judge, and he covered it with cedar from floor to ceiling. ⁸And the palace in which he was to live, set farther back, was similar in design. Solomon also made a palace like this hall for Pharaoh's daughter, whom he had married.

⁹All these structures, from the outside to the great courtyard and from foundation to eaves, were made of blocks of high-grade stone cut to size and trimmed with a saw on their inner and outer faces. ¹⁰The foundations were laid with large stones of good quality, some measuring ten cubits and some eight. ¹¹Above were high-grade stones, cut to size, and cedar beams. ¹²The great courtyard was surrounded by a wall of three courses of dressed stone and one course of trimmed cedar beams, as was the inner courtyard of the temple of the LORD with its portico.

The Temple's Furnishings

¹³King Solomon sent to Tyre and brought Huram, ¹⁴whose mother was a widow from the tribe of Naphtali and whose father was a man of Tyre and a craftsman in bronze. Huram was highly skilled and experienced in all kinds of bronze work. He came to King Solomon and did all the work assigned to him.

¹⁵He cast two bronze pillars, each eighteen cubits high and twelve cubits round, by line. ¹⁶He also made two capitals of cast bronze to set on the tops of the pillars; each capital was five cubits high. ¹⁷A network of interwoven chains festooned the capitals on top of the pillars, seven for each capital. ¹⁸He made pomegranates in two rows encircling each network to decorate the capitals on top of the pillars. He did the same for each capital. ¹⁹The capitals on top of the pillars in the portico were in the shape of lilies, four cubits high. ²⁰On

the capitals of both pillars, above the bowl-shaped part next to the network, were the two hundred pomegranates in rows all around. ²¹He erected the pillars at the portico of the temple. The pillar to the south he named Jakin and the one to the north Boaz. ²²The capitals on top were in the shape of lilies. And so the work on the pillars was completed.

NEW TESTAMENT READING
Acts 13:13–41

In Pisidian Antioch

¹³From Paphos, Paul and his companions sailed to Perga in Pamphylia, where John left them to return to Jerusalem. ¹⁴From Perga they went on to Pisidian Antioch. On the Sabbath they entered the synagogue and sat down. ¹⁵After the reading from the Law and the Prophets, the synagogue rulers sent word to them, saying, "Brothers, if you have a message of encouragement for the people, please speak."

¹⁶Standing up, Paul motioned with his hand and said: "Men of Israel and you Gentiles who worship God, listen to me! ¹⁷The God of the people of Israel chose our fathers; he made the people prosper during their stay in Egypt, with mighty power he led them out of that country, ¹⁸he endured their conduct for about forty years in the desert, ¹⁹he overthrew seven nations in Canaan and gave their land to his people as their inheritance. ²⁰All this took about 450 years.

"After this, God gave them judges until the time of Samuel the prophet. ²¹Then the people asked for a king, and he gave them Saul son of Kish, of the tribe of Benjamin, who ruled for forty years. ²²After removing Saul, he made David their king. He testified concerning him: 'I have found David son of Jesse a man after my own heart; he will do everything I want him to do.'

²³"From this man's descendants God has brought to Israel the Saviour Jesus,

as he promised. ²⁴Before the coming of Jesus, John preached repentance and baptism to all the people of Israel. ²⁵As John was completing his work, he said: 'Who do you think I am? I am not that one. No, but he is coming after me, whose sandals I am not worthy to untie.'

²⁶"Brothers, children of Abraham, and you God-fearing Gentiles, it is to us that this message of salvation has been sent. ²⁷The people of Jerusalem and their rulers did not recognise Jesus, yet in condemning him they fulfilled the words of the prophets that are read every Sabbath. ²⁸Though they found no proper ground for a death sentence, they asked Pilate to have him executed. ²⁹When they had carried out all that was written about him, they took him down from the tree and laid him in a tomb. ³⁰But God raised him from the dead, ³¹and for many days he was seen by those who had travelled with him from Galilee to Jerusalem. They are now his witnesses to our people.

³²"We tell you the good news: What God promised our fathers ³³he has fulfilled for us, their children, by raising up Jesus. As it is written in the second Psalm:

"'You are my Son;
    today I have become your Father.'

³⁴The fact that God raised him from the dead, never to decay, is stated in these words:

"'I will give you the holy and sure
    blessings promised to David.'

³⁵So it is stated elsewhere:

"'You will not let your Holy One see
    decay.'

³⁶"For when David had served God's purpose in his own generation, he fell asleep; he was buried with his fathers and his body decayed. ³⁷But the one whom God raised from the dead did not see decay.

38"Therefore, my brothers, I want you to know that through Jesus the forgiveness of sins is proclaimed to you. 39Through him everyone who believes is justified from everything you could not be justified from by the law of Moses. 40Take care that what the prophets have said does not happen to you:

41"'Look, you scoffers,
    wonder and perish,
  for I am going to do something in
      your days
    that you would never believe,
    even if someone told you.'"

READING FROM PSALMS
Psalm 75:1–10

For the director of music. ⌊To the tune of⌋ "Do Not Destroy". A psalm of Asaph. A song.

1We give thanks to you, O God,
    we give thanks, for your Name is
      near;
    men tell of your wonderful deeds.

2You say, "I choose the appointed
      time;
    it is I who judge uprightly.

3When the earth and all its people
      quake,
    it is I who hold its pillars firm.
                                    Selah

4To the arrogant I say, 'Boast no
      more,'
  and to the wicked, 'Do not lift up
      your horns.
5Do not lift your horns against
      heaven;
    do not speak with outstretched
      neck.'"

6No-one from the east or the west
    or from the desert can exalt a man.
7But it is God who judges:
    He brings one down, he exalts
      another.
8In the hand of the LORD is a cup
    full of foaming wine mixed with
      spices;
  he pours it out, and all the wicked of
      the earth
    drink it down to its very dregs.

9As for me, I will declare this for ever;
    I will sing praise to the God of
      Jacob.
10I will cut off the horns of all the
      wicked,
    but the horns of the righteous shall
      be lifted up.

DAY 171   # JUNE 20

OLD TESTAMENT READING
1 Kings 7:23–8:21

23He made the Sea of cast metal, circular in shape, measuring ten cubits from rim to rim and five cubits high. It took a line of thirty cubits to measure round it. 24Below the rim, gourds encircled it—ten to a cubit. The gourds were cast in two rows in one piece with the Sea. 25The Sea stood on twelve bulls, three facing north, three facing west, three facing south and three facing east. The Sea rested on top of them, and their hindquarters were towards the centre. 26It was a handbreadth in thickness, and its rim was like the rim of a cup, like a lily blossom. It held two thousand baths.

27He also made ten movable stands of bronze; each was four cubits long, four wide and three high. 28This is how the stands were made: They had side panels attached to uprights. ²⁹On the panels between the uprights were lions, bulls and cherubim—and on the uprights as well. Above and below the lions and bulls were wreaths of hammered work. ³⁰Each stand had four bronze wheels with bronze axles, and each had a basin resting on four supports, cast with wreaths on each side. ³¹On the inside of the stand there was an opening that had a circular frame one cubit deep. This opening was round, and with its basework it measured a cubit and a half. Around its opening there was engraving. The panels of the stands were square, not round. ³²The four wheels were under the panels, and the axles of the wheels were attached to the stand. The diameter of each wheel was a cubit and a half. ³³The wheels were made like chariot wheels; the axles, rims, spokes and hubs were all of cast metal.

³⁴Each stand had four handles, one on each corner, projecting from the stand. ³⁵At the top of the stand there was a circular band half a cubit deep. The supports and panels were attached to the top of the stand. ³⁶He engraved cherubim, lions and palm trees on the surfaces of the supports and on the panels, in every available space, with wreaths all around. ³⁷This is the way he made the ten stands. They were all cast in the same moulds and were identical in size and shape.

³⁸He then made ten bronze basins, each holding forty baths and measuring four cubits across, one basin to go on each of the ten stands. ³⁹He placed five of the stands on the south side of the temple and five on the north. He placed the Sea on the south side, at the southeast corner of the temple. ⁴⁰He also made the basins and shovels and sprinkling bowls.

So Huram finished all the work he had undertaken for King Solomon in the temple of the LORD:

⁴¹the two pillars;
the two bowl-shaped capitals on top of the pillars;
the two sets of network decorating the two bowl-shaped capitals on top of the pillars;
⁴²the four hundred pomegranates for the two sets of network (two rows of pomegranates for each network, decorating the bowl-shaped capitals on top of the pillars);
⁴³the ten stands with their ten basins;
⁴⁴the Sea and the twelve bulls under it;
⁴⁵the pots, shovels and sprinkling bowls.

All these objects that Huram made for King Solomon for the temple of the LORD were of burnished bronze. ⁴⁶The king had them cast in clay moulds in the plain of the Jordan between Succoth and Zarethan. ⁴⁷Solomon left all these things unweighed, because there were so many; the weight of the bronze was not determined.

⁴⁸Solomon also made all the furnishings that were in the LORD's temple:

the golden altar;
the golden table on which was the bread of the Presence;
⁴⁹the lampstands of pure gold (five on the right and five on the left, in front of the inner sanctuary);
the gold floral work and lamps and tongs;
⁵⁰the pure gold dishes, wick trimmers, sprinkling bowls, dishes and censers;
and the gold sockets for the doors of the innermost room, the Most Holy Place, and also for the doors of the main hall of the temple.

⁵¹When all the work King Solomon had done for the temple of the LORD was finished, he brought in the things his father David had dedicated—the silver and gold and the furnishings—and he placed them in the treasuries of the LORD's temple.

The Ark Brought to the Temple

8 Then King Solomon summoned into his presence at Jerusalem the elders of Israel, all the heads of the tribes and the chiefs of the Israelite families, to bring up the ark of the LORD's covenant from Zion, the City of David. ²All the men of Israel came together to King Solomon at the time of the festival in the month of Ethanim, the seventh month.

³When all the elders of Israel had arrived, the priests took up the ark, ⁴and they brought up the ark of the LORD and the Tent of Meeting and all the sacred furnishings in it. The priests and Levites carried them up, ⁵and King Solomon and the entire assembly of Israel that had gathered about him were before the ark, sacrificing so many sheep and cattle that they could not be recorded or counted.

⁶The priests then brought the ark of the LORD's covenant to its place in the inner sanctuary of the temple, the Most Holy Place, and put it beneath the wings of the cherubim. ⁷The cherubim spread their wings over the place of the ark and overshadowed the ark and its carrying poles. ⁸These poles were so long that their ends could be seen from the Holy Place in front of the inner sanctuary, but not from outside the Holy Place; and they are still there today. ⁹There was nothing in the ark except the two stone tablets that Moses had placed in it at Horeb, where the LORD made a covenant with the Israelites after they came out of Egypt.

¹⁰When the priests withdrew from the Holy Place, the cloud filled the temple of the LORD. ¹¹And the priests could not perform their service because of the cloud, for the glory of the LORD filled his temple.

¹²Then Solomon said, "The LORD has said that he would dwell in a dark cloud; ¹³I have indeed built a magnificent temple for you, a place for you to dwell for ever."

¹⁴While the whole assembly of Israel was standing there, the king turned round and blessed them. ¹⁵Then he said:

"Praise be to the LORD, the God of Israel, who with his own hand has fulfilled what he promised with his own mouth to my father David. For he said, ¹⁶'Since the day I brought my people Israel out of Egypt, I have not chosen a city in any tribe of Israel to have a temple built for my Name to be there, but I have chosen David to rule my people Israel.'

¹⁷"My father David had it in his heart to build a temple for the Name of the LORD, the God of Israel. ¹⁸But the LORD said to my father David, 'Because it was in your heart to build a temple for my Name, you did well to have this in your heart. ¹⁹Nevertheless, you are not the one to build the temple, but your son, who is your own flesh and blood—he is the one who will build the temple for my Name.'

²⁰"The LORD has kept the promise he made: I have succeeded David my father and now I sit on the throne of Israel, just as the LORD promised, and I have built the temple for the Name of the LORD, the God of Israel. ²¹I have provided a place there for the ark, in which is the covenant of the LORD that he made with our fathers when he brought them out of Egypt."

NEW TESTAMENT READING
Acts 13:42–14:7

⁴²As Paul and Barnabas were leaving the synagogue, the people invited them to speak further about these things on the next Sabbath. ⁴³When the congregation was dismissed, many of the Jews and devout converts to Judaism followed Paul and Barnabas, who talked with them and urged them to continue in the grace of God.

⁴⁴On the next Sabbath almost the whole city gathered to hear the word of the Lord. ⁴⁵When the Jews saw the crowds, they were filled with jealousy and talked abusively against what Paul was saying.

⁴⁶Then Paul and Barnabas answered them boldly: "We had to speak the word of God to you first. Since you reject it and do not consider yourselves worthy of eternal life, we now turn to the Gentiles. ⁴⁷For this is what the Lord has commanded us:

"'I have made you a light for the
Gentiles,
that you may bring salvation to the
ends of the earth.'"

⁴⁸When the Gentiles heard this, they were glad and honoured the word of the Lord; and all who were appointed for eternal life believed.

⁴⁹The word of the Lord spread through the whole region. ⁵⁰But the Jews incited the God-fearing women of high standing and the leading men of the city. They stirred up persecution against Paul and Barnabas, and expelled them from their region. ⁵¹So they shook the dust from their feet in protest against them and went to Iconium. ⁵²And the disciples were filled with joy and with the Holy Spirit.

In Iconium

14 At Iconium Paul and Barnabas went as usual into the Jewish synagogue. There they spoke so effectively that a great number of Jews and Gentiles believed. ²But the Jews who refused to believe stirred up the Gentiles and poisoned their minds against the brothers. ³So Paul and Barnabas spent considerable time there, speaking boldly for the Lord, who confirmed the message of his grace by enabling them to do miraculous signs and wonders. ⁴The people of the city were divided; some sided with the Jews, others with the apostles. ⁵There was a plot afoot among the Gentiles and Jews, together with their leaders, to ill-treat them and stone them. ⁶But they found out about it and fled to the Lycaonian cities of Lystra and Derbe and to the surrounding country, ⁷where they continued to preach the good news.

READING FROM PSALMS
Psalm 76:1–12

For the director of music. With stringed instruments. A psalm of Asaph. A song.

¹In Judah God is known;
his name is great in Israel.
²His tent is in Salem,
his dwelling-place in Zion.
³There he broke the flashing arrows,
the shields and the swords, the
weapons of war.   *Selah*

⁴You are resplendent with light,
more majestic than mountains rich
with game.
⁵Valiant men lie plundered,
they sleep their last sleep;
not one of the warriors
can lift his hands.
⁶At your rebuke, O God of Jacob,
both horse and chariot lie still.
⁷You alone are to be feared.
Who can stand before you when
you are angry?
⁸From heaven you pronounced
judgment,
and the land feared and was
quiet—
⁹when you, O God, rose up to judge,
to save all the afflicted of the land.
          Selah
¹⁰Surely your wrath against men brings
you praise,
and the survivors of your wrath are
restrained.

¹¹Make vows to the LORD your God
and fulfil them;
let all the neighbouring lands
bring gifts to the One to be feared.
¹²He breaks the spirit of rulers;
he is feared by the kings of the
earth.

OLD TESTAMENT READING
1 Kings 8:22–9:9

Solomon's Prayer of Dedication

²²Then Solomon stood before the altar of the LORD in front of the whole assembly of Israel, spread out his hands towards heaven ²³and said:

"O LORD, God of Israel, there is no God like you in heaven above or on earth below—you who keep your covenant of love with your servants who continue whole-heartedly in your way. ²⁴You have kept your promise to your servant David my father; with your mouth you have promised and with your hand you have fulfilled it—as it is today.

²⁵"Now LORD, God of Israel, keep for your servant David my father the promises you made to him when you said, 'You shall never fail to have a man to sit before me on the throne of Israel, if only your sons are careful in all they do to walk before me as you have done.' ²⁶And now, O God of Israel, let your word that you promised your servant David my father come true.

²⁷"But will God really dwell on earth? The heavens, even the highest heaven, cannot contain you. How much less this temple I have built! ²⁸Yet give attention to your servant's prayer and his plea for mercy, O LORD my God. Hear the cry and the prayer that your servant is praying in your presence this day. ²⁹May your eyes be open towards this temple night and day, this place of which you said, 'My Name shall be there,' so that you will hear the prayer your servant prays towards this place. ³⁰Hear the supplication of your servant and of your people Israel when they pray towards this place. Hear from heaven, your dwelling-place, and when you hear, forgive.

³¹"When a man wrongs his neighbour and is required to take an oath and he comes and swears the oath before your altar in this temple, ³²then hear from heaven and act. Judge between your servants, condemning the guilty and bringing down on his own head what he has done. Declare the innocent not guilty, and so establish his innocence.

³³"When your people Israel have been defeated by an enemy because they have sinned against you, and when they turn back to you and confess your name, praying and making supplication to you in this temple, ³⁴then hear from heaven and forgive the sin of your people Israel and bring them back to the land you gave to their fathers.

³⁵"When the heavens are shut up and there is no rain because your people have sinned against you, and when they pray towards this place and confess your name and turn from their sin because you have afflicted them, ³⁶then hear from heaven and forgive the sin of your servants, your people Israel. Teach them the right way to live, and send rain on the land you gave your people for an inheritance.

³⁷"When famine or plague comes to the land, or blight or mildew, locusts or grasshoppers, or when an enemy besieges them in any of their cities, whatever disaster or disease may come, ³⁸and when a prayer or plea is made by any of your people Israel—each one aware of the afflictions of his own heart, and spreading out his

hands towards this temple— [39]then hear from heaven, your dwelling-place. Forgive and act; deal with each man according to all he does, since you know his heart (for you alone know the hearts of all men), [40]so that they will fear you all the time they live in the land you gave our fathers.

[41]"As for the foreigner who does not belong to your people Israel but has come from a distant land because of your name— [42]for men will hear of your great name and your mighty hand and your out-stretched arm—when he comes and prays towards this temple, [43]then hear from heaven, your dwelling-place, and do whatever the foreigner asks of you, so that all the peoples of the earth may know your name and fear you, as do your own people Israel, and may know that this house I have built bears your Name.

[44]"When your people go to war against their enemies, wherever you send them, and when they pray to the LORD towards the city you have chosen and the temple I have built for your Name, [45]then hear from heaven their prayer and their plea, and uphold their cause.

[46]"When they sin against you— for there is no-one who does not sin—and you become angry with them and give them over to the enemy, who takes them captive to his own land, far away or near; [47]and if they have a change of heart in the land where they are held captive, and repent and plead with you in the land of their conquerors and say, 'We have sinned, we have done wrong, we have acted wickedly'; [48]and if they turn back to you with all their heart and soul in the land of their enemies who took them captive, and pray to you towards the land you gave their fathers, towards the city you have chosen and the temple I have built

for your Name; [49]then from heaven, your dwelling-place, hear their prayer and their plea, and uphold their cause. [50]And forgive your people, who have sinned against you; forgive all the offences they have committed against you, and cause their conquerors to show them mercy; [51]for they are your people and your inheritance, whom you brought out of Egypt, out of that iron-smelting furnace.

[52]"May your eyes be open to your servant's plea and to the plea of your people Israel, and may you listen to them whenever they cry out to you. [53]For you singled them out from all the nations of the world to be your own inheritance, just as you declared through your servant Moses when you, O Sovereign LORD, brought our fathers out of Egypt."

[54]When Solomon had finished all these prayers and supplications to the LORD, he rose from before the altar of the LORD, where he had been kneeling with his hands spread out towards heaven. [55]He stood and blessed the whole assembly of Israel in a loud voice, saying:

[56]"Praise be to the LORD, who has given rest to his people Israel just as he promised. Not one word has failed of all the good promises he gave through his servant Moses. [57]May the LORD our God be with us as he was with our fathers; may he never leave us nor forsake us. [58]May he turn our hearts to him, to walk in all his ways and to keep the commands, decrees and regulations he gave our fathers. [59]And may these words of mine, which I have prayed before the LORD, be near to the LORD our God day and night, that he may uphold the cause of his servant and the cause of his people Israel according to each day's need, [60]so that all the peoples

of the earth may know that the LORD is God and that there is no other. ⁶¹But your hearts must be fully committed to the LORD our God, to live by his decrees and obey his commands, as at this time."

The Dedication of the Temple

⁶²Then the king and all Israel with him offered sacrifices before the LORD. ⁶³Solomon offered a sacrifice of fellowship offerings to the LORD: twenty-two thousand cattle and a hundred and twenty thousand sheep and goats. So the king and all the Israelites dedicated the temple of the LORD.

⁶⁴On that same day the king consecrated the middle part of the courtyard in front of the temple of the LORD, and there he offered burnt offerings, grain offerings and the fat of the fellowship offerings, because the bronze altar before the LORD was too small to hold the burnt offerings, the grain offerings and the fat of the fellowship offerings.

⁶⁵So Solomon observed the festival at that time, and all Israel with him—a vast assembly, people from Lebo Hamath to the Wadi of Egypt. They celebrated it before the LORD our God for seven days and seven days more, fourteen days in all. ⁶⁶On the following day he sent the people away. They blessed the king and then went home, joyful and glad in heart for all the good things the LORD had done for his servant David and his people Israel.

The LORD Appears to Solomon

9 When Solomon had finished building the temple of the LORD and the royal palace, and had achieved all he had desired to do, ²the LORD appeared to him a second time, as he had appeared to him at Gibeon. ³The LORD said to him:

"I have heard the prayer and plea you have made before me; I have consecrated this temple, which you have built, by putting my Name there for ever. My eyes and my heart will always be there.

⁴"As for you, if you walk before me in integrity of heart and uprightness, as David your father did, and do all I command and observe my decrees and laws, ⁵I will establish your royal throne over Israel for ever, as I promised David your father when I said, 'You shall never fail to have a man on the throne of Israel.'

⁶"But if you or your sons turn away from me and do not observe the commands and decrees I have given you and go off to serve other gods and worship them, ⁷then I will cut off Israel from the land I have given them and will reject this temple I have consecrated for my Name. Israel will then become a byword and an object of ridicule among all peoples. ⁸And though this temple is now imposing, all who pass by will be appalled and will scoff and say, 'Why has the LORD done such a thing to this land and to this temple?' ⁹People will answer, 'Because they have forsaken the LORD their God, who brought their fathers out of Egypt, and have embraced other gods, worshipping and serving them— that is why the LORD brought all this disaster on them.'"

NEW TESTAMENT READING
Acts 14:8–28

In Lystra and Derbe

⁸In Lystra there sat a man crippled in his feet, who was lame from birth and had never walked. ⁹He listened to Paul as he was speaking. Paul looked directly at him, saw that he had faith to be healed ¹⁰and called out, "Stand up on your feet!" At that, the man jumped up and began to walk.

¹¹When the crowd saw what Paul had done, they shouted in the Lycaonian language, "The gods have come down to us in human form!" ¹²Barnabas they called Zeus, and Paul they called Hermes because he was the chief speaker. ¹³The priest of Zeus, whose temple was just outside the city, brought bulls and wreaths to the city gates because he and the crowd wanted to offer sacrifices to them.

¹⁴But when the apostles Barnabas and Paul heard of this, they tore their clothes and rushed out into the crowd, shouting: ¹⁵"Men, why are you doing this? We too are only men, human like you. We are bringing you good news, telling you to turn from these worthless things to the living God, who made heaven and earth and sea and everything in them. ¹⁶In the past, he let all nations go their own way. ¹⁷Yet he has not left himself without testimony: He has shown kindness by giving you rain from heaven and crops in their seasons; he provides you with plenty of food and fills your hearts with joy." ¹⁸Even with these words, they had difficulty keeping the crowd from sacrificing to them.

¹⁹Then some Jews came from Antioch and Iconium and won the crowd over. They stoned Paul and dragged him outside the city, thinking he was dead. ²⁰But after the disciples had gathered round him, he got up and went back into the city. The next day he and Barnabas left for Derbe.

The Return to Antioch in Syria

²¹They preached the good news in that city and won a large number of disciples. Then they returned to Lystra, Iconium and Antioch, ²²strengthening the disciples and encouraging them to remain true to the faith. "We must go through many hardships to enter the kingdom of God," they said. ²³Paul and Barnabas appointed elders for them in each church and, with prayer and fasting, committed them to the Lord, in whom they had put their trust. ²⁴After going through Pisidia, they came into Pamphylia, ²⁵and when they had preached the word in Perga, they went down to Attalia.

²⁶From Attalia they sailed back to Antioch, where they had been committed to the grace of God for the work they had now completed. ²⁷On arriving there, they gathered the church together and reported all that God had done through them and how he had opened the door of faith to the Gentiles. ²⁸And they stayed there a long time with the disciples.

READING FROM PROVERBS
Proverbs 15:11–20

¹¹Death and Destruction lie open
    before the LORD—
  how much more the hearts of men!

¹²A mocker resents correction;
  he will not consult the wise.

¹³A happy heart makes the face
    cheerful,
  but heartache crushes the spirit.

¹⁴The discerning heart seeks
    knowledge,
  but the mouth of a fool feeds on
    folly.

¹⁵All the days of the oppressed are
    wretched,
  but the cheerful heart has a
    continual feast.

¹⁶Better a little with the fear of the
    LORD
  than great wealth with turmoil.

¹⁷Better a meal of vegetables where
    there is love
  than a fattened calf with hatred.

¹⁸A hot-tempered man stirs up
    dissension,
  but a patient man calms a quarrel.

¹⁹The way of the sluggard is blocked
with thorns,
but the path of the upright is a
highway.

²⁰A wise son brings joy to his
father,
but a foolish man despises his
mother.

DAY 173

JUNE 22

OLD TESTAMENT READING
1 Kings 9:10–11:13

Solomon's Other Activities

¹⁰At the end of twenty years, during which Solomon built these two buildings—the temple of the LORD and the royal palace—¹¹King Solomon gave twenty towns in Galilee to Hiram king of Tyre, because Hiram had supplied him with all the cedar and pine and gold he wanted. ¹²But when Hiram went from Tyre to see the towns that Solomon had given him, he was not pleased with them. ¹³"What kind of towns are these you have given me, my brother?" he asked. And he called them the Land of Cabul, a name they have to this day. ¹⁴Now Hiram had sent to the king 120 talents of gold.

¹⁵Here is the account of the forced labour King Solomon conscripted to build the LORD's temple, his own palace, the supporting terraces, the wall of Jerusalem, and Hazor, Megiddo and Gezer. ¹⁶(Pharaoh king of Egypt had attacked and captured Gezer. He had set it on fire. He killed its Canaanite inhabitants, and then gave it as a wedding gift to his daughter, Solomon's wife. ¹⁷And Solomon rebuilt Gezer.) He built up Lower Beth Horon, ¹⁸Baalath, and Tadmor in the desert, within his land, ¹⁹as well as all his store cities and the towns for his chariots and for his horses—whatever he desired to build in Jerusalem, in Lebanon and throughout all the territory he ruled.

²⁰All the people left from the Amorites, Hittites, Perizzites, Hivites and Jebusites (these peoples were not Israelites), ²¹that is, their descendants remaining in the land, whom the Israelites could not exterminate—these Solomon conscripted for his slave labour force, as it is to this day. ²²But Solomon did not make slaves of any of the Israelites; they were his fighting men, his government officials, his officers, his captains, and the commanders of his chariots and charioteers. ²³They were also the chief officials in charge of Solomon's projects—550 officials supervising the men who did the work.

²⁴After Pharaoh's daughter had come up from the City of David to the palace Solomon had built for her, he constructed the supporting terraces.

²⁵Three times a year Solomon sacrificed burnt offerings and fellowship offerings on the altar he had built for the LORD, burning incense before the LORD along with them, and so fulfilled the temple obligations.

²⁶King Solomon also built ships at Ezion Geber, which is near Elath in Edom, on the shore of the Red Sea. ²⁷And Hiram sent his men—sailors who knew the sea—to serve in the fleet with Solomon's men. ²⁸They sailed to Ophir and brought back 420 talents of gold, which they delivered to King Solomon.

The Queen of Sheba Visits Solomon

10 When the queen of Sheba heard about the fame of Solomon and his relation to the name of the LORD, she came to test him with hard questions. ²Arriving at Jerusalem with a very great caravan—with camels carrying spices, large quantities of gold, and precious stones—she came to Solomon and talked with him about all that she had on her mind. ³Solomon answered all her questions; nothing was too hard for the king to explain to her. ⁴When the queen of Sheba saw all the wisdom of Solomon and the palace he had built, ⁵the food on his table, the seating of his officials, the attending servants in their robes, his cupbearers, and the burnt offerings he made at the temple of the LORD, she was overwhelmed.

⁶She said to the king, "The report I heard in my own country about your achievements and your wisdom is true. ⁷But I did not believe these things until I came and saw with my own eyes. Indeed, not even half was told me; in wisdom and wealth you have far exceeded the report I heard. ⁸How happy your men must be! How happy your officials, who continually stand before you and hear your wisdom! ⁹Praise be to the LORD your God, who has delighted in you and placed you on the throne of Israel. Because of the LORD's eternal love for Israel, he has made you king, to maintain justice and righteousness."

¹⁰And she gave the king 120 talents of gold, large quantities of spices, and precious stones. Never again were so many spices brought in as those the queen of Sheba gave to King Solomon.

¹¹(Hiram's ships brought gold from Ophir; and from there they brought great cargoes of almug-wood and precious stones. ¹²The king used the almug-wood to make supports for the temple of the LORD and for the royal palace, and to make harps and lyres for the musicians. So much almug-wood has never been imported or seen since that day.)

¹³King Solomon gave the queen of Sheba all she desired and asked for, besides what he had given her out of his royal bounty. Then she left and returned with her retinue to her own country.

Solomon's Splendour

¹⁴The weight of the gold that Solomon received yearly was 666 talents, ¹⁵not including the revenues from merchants and traders and from all the Arabian kings and the governors of the land.

¹⁶King Solomon made two hundred large shields of hammered gold; six hundred bekas of gold went into each shield. ¹⁷He also made three hundred small shields of hammered gold, with three minas of gold in each shield. The king put them in the Palace of the Forest of Lebanon.

¹⁸Then the king made a great throne inlaid with ivory and overlaid with fine gold. ¹⁹The throne had six steps, and its back had a rounded top. On both sides of the seat were armrests, with a lion standing beside each of them. ²⁰Twelve lions stood on the six steps, one at either end of each step. Nothing like it had ever been made for any other kingdom. ²¹All King Solomon's goblets were gold, and all the household articles in the Palace of the Forest of Lebanon were pure gold. Nothing was made of silver, because silver was considered of little value in Solomon's days. ²²The king had a fleet of trading ships at sea along with the ships of Hiram. Once every three years it returned carrying gold, silver and ivory, and apes and baboons.

²³King Solomon was greater in riches and wisdom than all the other kings of the earth. ²⁴The whole world sought audience with Solomon to hear the wisdom God had put in his heart. ²⁵Year after year, everyone who came brought a gift—articles of silver and gold, robes, weapons and spices, and horses and mules.

²⁶Solomon accumulated chariots and horses; he had fourteen hundred chariots and twelve thousand horses, which he kept in the chariot cities and also with him in Jerusalem. ²⁷The king made silver as common in Jerusalem as stones, and cedar as plentiful as

sycamore-fig trees in the foothills. [28]Solomon's horses were imported from Egypt and from Kue—the royal merchants purchased them from Kue. [29]They imported a chariot from Egypt for six hundred shekels of silver, and a horse for a hundred and fifty. They also exported them to all the kings of the Hittites and of the Arameans.

Solomon's Wives

11 King Solomon, however, loved many foreign women besides Pharaoh's daughter—Moabites, Ammonites, Edomites, Sidonians and Hittites. [2]They were from nations about which the LORD had told the Israelites, "You must not intermarry with them, because they will surely turn your hearts after their gods." Nevertheless, Solomon held fast to them in love. [3]He had seven hundred wives of royal birth and three hundred concubines, and his wives led him astray. [4]As Solomon grew old, his wives turned his heart after other gods, and his heart was not fully devoted to the LORD his God, as the heart of David his father had been. [5]He followed Ashtoreth the goddess of the Sidonians, and Molech the detestable god of the Ammonites. [6]So Solomon did evil in the eyes of the LORD; he did not follow the LORD completely, as David his father had done.

[7]On a hill east of Jerusalem, Solomon built a high place for Chemosh the detestable god of Moab, and for Molech the detestable god of the Ammonites. [8]He did the same for all his foreign wives, who burned incense and offered sacrifices to their gods.

[9]The LORD became angry with Solomon because his heart had turned away from the LORD, the God of Israel, who had appeared to him twice. [10]Although he had forbidden Solomon to follow other gods, Solomon did not keep the LORD's command. [11]So the LORD said to Solomon, "Since this is your attitude and you have not kept my covenant and my decrees, which I commanded you, I will most certainly tear the kingdom away from you and give it to one of your subordinates. [12]Nevertheless, for the sake of David your father, I will not do it during your lifetime. I will tear it out of the hand of your son. [13]Yet I will not tear the whole kingdom from him, but will give him one tribe for the sake of David my servant and for the sake of Jerusalem, which I have chosen."

NEW TESTAMENT READING
Acts 15:1–21

The Council at Jerusalem

15 Some men came down from Judea to Antioch and were teaching the brothers: "Unless you are circumcised, according to the custom taught by Moses, you cannot be saved." [2]This brought Paul and Barnabas into sharp dispute and debate with them. So Paul and Barnabas were appointed, along with some other believers, to go up to Jerusalem to see the apostles and elders about this question. [3]The church sent them on their way, and as they travelled through Phoenicia and Samaria, they told how the Gentiles had been converted. This news made all the brothers very glad. [4]When they came to Jerusalem, they were welcomed by the church and the apostles and elders, to whom they reported everything God had done through them.

[5]Then some of the believers who belonged to the party of the Pharisees stood up and said, "The Gentiles must be circumcised and required to obey the law of Moses."

[6]The apostles and elders met to consider this question. [7]After much discussion, Peter got up and addressed them: "Brothers, you know that some time ago God made a choice among you that the Gentiles might hear from my lips the message of the gospel and believe. [8]God, who knows the heart, showed that he accepted them by giving the Holy Spirit to them, just as he did to us. [9]He made no distinction between us and

them, for he purified their hearts by faith. [10]Now then, why do you try to test God by putting on the necks of the disciples a yoke that neither we nor our fathers have been able to bear? [11]No! We believe it is through the grace of our Lord Jesus that we are saved, just as they are."

[12]The whole assembly became silent as they listened to Barnabas and Paul telling about the miraculous signs and wonders God had done among the Gentiles through them. [13]When they finished, James spoke up: "Brothers, listen to me. [14]Simon has described to us how God at first showed his concern by taking from the Gentiles a people for himself. [15]The words of the prophets are in agreement with this, as it is written:

[16]" 'After this I will return
    and rebuild David's fallen tent.
  Its ruins I will rebuild,
    and I will restore it,
[17]that the remnant of men may seek the
      Lord,
    and all the Gentiles who bear my
      name,
  says the Lord, who does these things'
[18] that have been known for ages.

[19]"It is my judgment, therefore, that we should not make it difficult for the Gentiles who are turning to God. [20]Instead we should write to them, telling them to abstain from food polluted by idols, from sexual immorality, from the meat of strangled animals and from blood. [21]For Moses has been preached

in every city from the earliest times and is read in the synagogues on every Sabbath."

READING FROM PSALMS
Psalm 77:1–9

For the director of music. For Jeduthun. Of
Asaph. A psalm.

[1]I cried out to God for help;
  I cried out to God to hear me.
[2]When I was in distress, I sought the
      Lord;
  at night I stretched out untiring
      hands
  and my soul refused to be
      comforted.

[3]I remembered you, O God, and I
      groaned;
  I mused, and my spirit grew
      faint.   *Selah*
[4]You kept my eyes from closing;
  I was too troubled to speak.
[5]I thought about the former days,
  the years of long ago;
[6]I remembered my songs in the night.
  My heart mused and my spirit
      enquired:

[7]"Will the Lord reject for ever?
  Will he never show his favour
      again?
[8]Has his unfailing love vanished for
      ever?
  Has his promise failed for all time?
[9]Has God forgotten to be merciful?
  Has he in anger withheld his
      compassion?"   *Selah*

OLD TESTAMENT READING
1 Kings 11:14–12:24

Solomon's Adversaries

¹⁴Then the LORD raised up against Solomon an adversary, Hadad the Edomite, from the royal line of Edom. ¹⁵Earlier when David was fighting with Edom, Joab the commander of the army, who had gone up to bury the dead, had struck down all the men in Edom. ¹⁶Joab and all the Israelites stayed there for six months, until they had destroyed all the men in Edom. ¹⁷But Hadad, still only a boy, fled to Egypt with some Edomite officials who had served his father. ¹⁸They set out from Midian and went to Paran. Then taking men from Paran with them, they went to Egypt, to Pharaoh king of Egypt, who gave Hadad a house and land and provided him with food.

¹⁹Pharaoh was so pleased with Hadad that he gave him a sister of his own wife, Queen Tahpenes, in marriage. ²⁰The sister of Tahpenes bore him a son named Genubath, whom Tahpenes brought up in the royal palace. There Genubath lived with Pharaoh's own children.

²¹While he was in Egypt, Hadad heard that David rested with his fathers and that Joab the commander of the army was also dead. Then Hadad said to Pharaoh, "Let me go, so that I may return to my own country."

²²"What have you lacked here that you want to go back to your own country?" Pharaoh asked.

"Nothing," Hadad replied, "but do let me go!"

²³And God raised up against Solomon another adversary, Rezon son of Eliada, who had fled from his master, Hadadezer king of Zobah. ²⁴He gathered men around him and became the leader of a band of rebels when David destroyed the forces ̣of Zobah ̣; the rebels went to Damascus, where they settled and took control. ²⁵Rezon was Israel's adversary as long as Solomon lived, adding to the trouble caused by Hadad. So Rezon ruled in Aram and was hostile towards Israel.

Jeroboam Rebels Against Solomon

²⁶Also, Jeroboam son of Nebat rebelled against the king. He was one of Solomon's officials, an Ephraimite from Zeredah, and his mother was a widow named Zeruah.

²⁷Here is the account of how he rebelled against the king: Solomon had built the supporting terraces and had filled in the gap in the wall of the city of David his father. ²⁸Now Jeroboam was a man of standing, and when Solomon saw how well the young man did his work, he put him in charge of the whole labour force of the house of Joseph.

²⁹About that time Jeroboam was going out of Jerusalem, and Ahijah the prophet of Shiloh met him on the way, wearing a new cloak. The two of them were alone out in the country, ³⁰and Ahijah took hold of the new cloak he was wearing and tore it into twelve pieces. ³¹Then he said to Jeroboam, "Take ten pieces for yourself, for this is what the LORD, the God of Israel, says: 'See, I am going to tear the kingdom out of Solomon's hand and give you ten tribes. ³²But for the sake of my servant David and the city of Jerusalem, which I have chosen out of all the tribes of Israel, he will have one tribe. ³³I will do this because they have forsaken me and worshipped Ashtoreth the goddess of the Sidonians, Chemosh the god of the Moabites, and Molech the god of the Ammonites, and have not walked in my ways, nor done what is right in my eyes, nor kept my statutes and laws as David, Solomon's father, did.

³⁴"'But I will not take the whole kingdom out of Solomon's hand; I have made him ruler all the days of his life for the sake of David my servant, whom I chose and who observed my commands and statutes. ³⁵I will take the kingdom from his son's hands and give you ten tribes. ³⁶I will give one tribe to his son so that David my servant may always have a lamp before me in Jerusalem, the city where I chose to put my Name. ³⁷However, as for you, I will take you, and you will rule over all that your heart desires; you will be king over Israel. ³⁸If you do whatever I command you and walk in my ways and do what is right in my eyes by keeping my statutes and commands, as David my servant did, I will be with you. I will build you a dynasty as enduring as the one I built for David and will give Israel to you. ³⁹I will humble David's descendants because of this, but not for ever.'"

⁴⁰Solomon tried to kill Jeroboam, but Jeroboam fled to Egypt, to Shishak the king, and stayed there until Solomon's death.

Solomon's Death

⁴¹As for the other events of Solomon's reign—all he did and the wisdom he displayed—are they not written in the book of the annals of Solomon? ⁴²Solomon reigned in Jerusalem over all Israel for forty years. ⁴³Then he rested with his fathers and was buried in the city of David his father. And Rehoboam his son succeeded him as king.

Israel Rebels Against Rehoboam

12 Rehoboam went to Shechem, for all the Israelites had gone there to make him king. ²When Jeroboam son of Nebat heard this (he was still in Egypt, where he had fled from King Solomon), he returned from Egypt. ³So they sent for Jeroboam, and he and the whole assembly of Israel went to Rehoboam and said to him: ⁴"Your father put a heavy yoke on us,

but now lighten the harsh labour and the heavy yoke he put on us, and we will serve you."

⁵Rehoboam answered, "Go away for three days and then come back to me." So the people went away.

⁶Then King Rehoboam consulted the elders who had served his father Solomon during his lifetime. "How would you advise me to answer these people?" he asked.

⁷They replied, "If today you will be a servant to these people and serve them and give them a favourable answer, they will always be your servants."

⁸But Rehoboam rejected the advice the elders gave him and consulted the young men who had grown up with him and were serving him. ⁹He asked them, "What is your advice? How should we answer these people who say to me, 'Lighten the yoke your father put on us'?"

¹⁰The young men who had grown up with him replied, "Tell these people who have said to you, 'Your father put a heavy yoke on us, but make our yoke lighter'—tell them, 'My little finger is thicker than my father's waist. ¹¹My father laid on you a heavy yoke; I will make it even heavier. My father scourged you with whips; I will scourge you with scorpions.'"

¹²Three days later Jeroboam and all the people returned to Rehoboam, as the king had said, "Come back to me in three days." ¹³The king answered the people harshly. Rejecting the advice given him by the elders, ¹⁴he followed the advice of the young men and said, "My father made your yoke heavy; I will make it even heavier. My father scourged you with whips; I will scourge you with scorpions." ¹⁵So the king did not listen to the people, for this turn of events was from the LORD, to fulfil the word the LORD had spoken to Jeroboam son of Nebat through Ahijah the Shilonite.

¹⁶When all Israel saw that the king refused to listen to them, they answered the king:

"What share do we have in David,
    what part in Jesse's son?
  To your tents, O Israel!
    Look after your own house, O
      David!"

So the Israelites went home. [17]But as for the Israelites who were living in the towns of Judah, Rehoboam still ruled over them.

[18]King Rehoboam sent out Adoniram, who was in charge of forced labour, but all Israel stoned him to death. King Rehoboam, however, managed to get into his chariot and escape to Jerusalem. [19]So Israel has been in rebellion against the house of David to this day.

[20]When all the Israelites heard that Jeroboam had returned, they sent and called him to the assembly and made him king over all Israel. Only the tribe of Judah remained loyal to the house of David.

[21]When Rehoboam arrived in Jerusalem, he mustered the whole house of Judah and the tribe of Benjamin—a hundred and eighty thousand fighting men—to make war against the house of Israel and to regain the kingdom for Rehoboam son of Solomon.

[22]But this word of God came to Shemaiah the man of God: [23]"Say to Rehoboam son of Solomon king of Judah, to the whole house of Judah and Benjamin, and to the rest of the people, [24]'This is what the LORD says: Do not go up to fight against your brothers, the Israelites. Go home, every one of you, for this is my doing.'" So they obeyed the word of the LORD and went home again, as the LORD had ordered.

NEW TESTAMENT READING
Acts 15:22–41

The Council's Letter to Gentile Believers

[22]Then the apostles and elders, with the whole church, decided to choose some of their own men and send them to Antioch with Paul and Barnabas. They chose Judas (called Barsabbas) and Silas, two men who were leaders among the brothers. [23]With them they sent the following letter:

The apostles and elders, your brothers,

To the Gentile believers in Antioch, Syria and Cilicia:

Greetings.

[24]We have heard that some went out from us without our authorisation and disturbed you, troubling your minds by what they said. [25]So we all agreed to choose some men and send them to you with our dear friends Barnabas and Paul—[26]men who have risked their lives for the name of our Lord Jesus Christ. [27]Therefore we are sending Judas and Silas to confirm by word of mouth what we are writing. [28]It seemed good to the Holy Spirit and to us not to burden you with anything beyond the following requirements: [29]You are to abstain from food sacrificed to idols, from blood, from the meat of strangled animals and from sexual immorality. You will do well to avoid these things.

Farewell.

[30]The men were sent off and went down to Antioch, where they gathered the church together and delivered the letter. [31]The people read it and were glad for its encouraging message. [32]Judas and Silas, who themselves were prophets, said much to encourage and strengthen the brothers. [33]After spending some time there, they were sent off by the brothers with the blessing of peace to return to those who had sent them. [35]But Paul and Barnabas remained in Antioch, where they and many others taught and preached the word of the Lord.

Disagreement Between Paul and Barnabas

36Some time later Paul said to Barnabas, "Let us go back and visit the brothers in all the towns where we preached the word of the Lord and see how they are doing." 37Barnabas wanted to take John, also called Mark, with them, 38but Paul did not think it wise to take him, because he had deserted them in Pamphylia and had not continued with them in the work. 39They had such a sharp disagreement that they parted company. Barnabas took Mark and sailed for Cyprus, 40but Paul chose Silas and left, commended by the brothers to the grace of the Lord. 41He went through Syria and Cilicia, strengthening the churches.

READING FROM PSALMS
Psalm 77:10–20

10Then I thought, "To this I will appeal:
the years of the right hand of the Most High."
11I will remember the deeds of the LORD;
yes, I will remember your miracles of long ago.

12I will meditate on all your works
and consider all your mighty deeds.

13Your ways, O God, are holy.
What god is so great as our God?
14You are the God who performs miracles;
you display your power among the peoples.
15With your mighty arm you redeemed your people,
the descendants of Jacob and Joseph. *Selah*

16The waters saw you, O God,
the waters saw you and writhed;
the very depths were convulsed.
17The clouds poured down water,
the skies resounded with thunder;
your arrows flashed back and forth.
18Your thunder was heard in the whirlwind,
your lightning lit up the world;
the earth trembled and quaked.
19Your path led through the sea,
your way through the mighty waters,
though your footprints were not seen.

20You led your people like a flock
by the hand of Moses and Aaron.

JUNE 24
DAY 175

OLD TESTAMENT READING
1 Kings 12:25–14:20

Golden Calves at Bethel and Dan

25Then Jeroboam fortified Shechem in the hill country of Ephraim and lived there. From there he went out and built up Peniel.

26Jeroboam thought to himself, "The kingdom is now likely to revert to the house of David. 27If these people go up to offer sacrifices at the temple of the LORD in Jerusalem, they will again give their allegiance to their lord, Rehoboam king of Judah. They will kill me and return to King Rehoboam."

28After seeking advice, the king made two golden calves. He said to the people, "It is too much for you to go up to Jerusalem. Here are your gods, O Israel, who brought you up out of Egypt." 29One he set up in Bethel, and the other in Dan. 30And this thing became a sin; the people went even as far as Dan to worship the one there.

31Jeroboam built shrines on high places and appointed priests from all sorts of people, even though they were not Levites. 32He instituted a festival on the fifteenth day of the eighth month, like the festival held in Judah, and offered sacrifices on the altar. This he did in Bethel, sacrificing to the calves he had made. And at Bethel he also installed priests at the high places he had made. 33On the fifteenth day of the eighth month, a month of his own choosing, he offered sacrifices on the altar he had built at Bethel. So he instituted the festival for the Israelites and went up to the altar to make offerings.

The Man of God From Judah

13 By the word of the LORD a man of God came from Judah to Bethel, as Jeroboam was standing by the altar to make an offering. 2He cried out against the altar by the word of the LORD: "O altar, altar! This is what the LORD says: 'A son named Josiah will be born to the house of David. On you he will sacrifice the priests of the high places who now make offerings here, and human bones will be burned on you.'" 3That same day the man of God gave a sign: "This is the sign the LORD has declared: The altar will be split apart and the ashes on it will be poured out."

4When King Jeroboam heard what the man of God cried out against the altar at Bethel, he stretched out his hand from the altar and said, "Seize him!" But the hand he stretched out towards the man shrivelled up, so that he could not pull it back. 5Also, the altar was split apart and its ashes poured out according to the sign given by the man of God by the word of the LORD.

6Then the king said to the man of God, "Intercede with the LORD your God and pray for me that my hand may be restored." So the man of God interceded with the LORD, and the king's hand was restored and became as it was before.

7The king said to the man of God, "Come home with me and have something to eat, and I will give you a gift."

8But the man of God answered the king, "Even if you were to give me half your possessions, I would not go with you, nor would I eat bread or drink water here. 9For I was commanded by the word of the LORD: 'You must not eat bread or drink water or return by the way you came.'" 10So he took another road and did not return by the way he had come to Bethel.

11Now there was a certain old prophet living in Bethel, whose sons came and told him all that the man of God had done there that day. They also told their father what he had said to the king. 12Their father asked them, "Which way did he go?" And his sons showed him which road the man of God from Judah had taken. 13So he said to his sons, "Saddle the donkey for me." And when they had saddled the donkey for him, he mounted it 14and rode after the man of God. He found him sitting under an oak tree and asked, "Are you the man of God who came from Judah?"

"I am," he replied.

15So the prophet said to him, "Come home with me and eat."

16The man of God said, "I cannot turn back and go with you, nor can I eat bread or drink water with you in this place. 17I have been told by the word of the LORD: 'You must not eat bread or drink water there or return by the way you came.'"

18The old prophet answered, "I too am a prophet, as you are. And an angel said to me by the word of the LORD: 'Bring him back with you to your house so that he may eat bread and drink water.'" (But he was lying to him.) 19So the man of God returned with him and ate and drank in his house.

20While they were sitting at the table, the word of the LORD came to the old prophet who had brought him back. 21He cried out to the man of God who had come from Judah, "This is what the LORD says: 'You have defied the word of the LORD and have not kept the command the LORD your God gave you. 22You came back and ate bread and drank water in the place where he told you not to eat or drink. Therefore your body will not be buried in the tomb of your fathers.'"

23When the man of God had finished eating and drinking, the prophet who had brought him back saddled his donkey for him. 24As he went on his way, a lion met him on the road and killed him, and his body was thrown down on the road, with both the donkey and the lion standing beside it. 25Some people who passed by saw the body thrown down there, with the lion standing beside the body, and they went and reported it in the city where the old prophet lived.

26When the prophet who had brought him back from his journey heard of it, he said, "It is the man of God who defied the word of the LORD. The LORD has given him over to the lion, which has mauled him and killed him, as the word of the LORD had warned him."

27The prophet said to his sons, "Saddle the donkey for me," and they did so. 28Then he went out and found the body thrown down on the road, with the donkey and the lion standing beside it. The lion had neither eaten the body nor mauled the donkey. 29So the prophet picked up the body of the man of God, laid it on the donkey, and brought it back to his own city to mourn for him and bury him. 30Then he laid the body in his own tomb, and they mourned over him and said, "Oh, my brother!"

31After burying him, he said to his sons, "When I die, bury me in the grave where the man of God is buried; lay my bones beside his bones. 32For the message he declared by the word of the LORD against the altar in Bethel and against all the shrines on the high places in the towns of Samaria will certainly come true."

33Even after this, Jeroboam did not change his evil ways, but once more appointed priests for the high places from all sorts of people. Anyone who wanted to become a priest he consecrated for the high places. 34This was the sin of the house of Jeroboam that led to its downfall and to its destruction from the face of the earth.

Ahijah's Prophecy Against Jeroboam

14 At that time Abijah son of Jeroboam became ill, 2and Jeroboam said to his wife, "Go, disguise yourself, so that you won't be recognised as the wife of Jeroboam. Then go to Shiloh. Ahijah the prophet is there —the one who told me I would be king over this people. 3Take ten loaves of bread with you, some cakes and a jar of honey, and go to him. He will tell you what will happen to the boy." 4So Jeroboam's wife did what he said and went to Ahijah's house in Shiloh.

Now Ahijah could not see; his sight was gone because of his age. 5But the LORD had told Ahijah, "Jeroboam's wife is coming to ask you about her son, for he is ill, and you are to give her such and such an answer. When she arrives, she will pretend to be someone else."

6So when Ahijah heard the sound of her footsteps at the door, he said, "Come in, wife of Jeroboam. Why this pretence? I have been sent to you with bad news. 7Go, tell Jeroboam that this is what the LORD, the God of Israel, says: 'I raised you up from among the people and made you a leader over my people Israel. 8I tore the kingdom away from the house of David and gave it to you, but you have not been like my servant David, who kept my commands and followed me with all his heart, doing only what was right in my eyes. 9You have done more evil than all who lived before you. You have made for yourself other gods, idols made of metal; you have provoked me to anger and thrust me behind your back.

10"'Because of this, I am going to bring disaster on the house of Jeroboam. I will cut off from Jeroboam every last male in Israel—slave or free.

I will burn up the house of Jeroboam as one burns dung, until it is all gone. ¹¹Dogs will eat those belonging to Jeroboam who die in the city, and the birds of the air will feed on those who die in the country. The LORD has spoken!'

¹²"As for you, go back home. When you set foot in your city, the boy will die. ¹³All Israel will mourn for him and bury him. He is the only one belonging to Jeroboam who will be buried, because he is the only one in the house of Jeroboam in whom the LORD, the God of Israel, has found anything good.

¹⁴"The LORD will raise up for himself a king over Israel who will cut off the family of Jeroboam. This is the day! What? Yes, even now. ¹⁵And the LORD will strike Israel, so that it will be like a reed swaying in the water. He will uproot Israel from this good land that he gave to their forefathers and scatter them beyond the River, because they provoked the LORD to anger by making Asherah poles. ¹⁶And he will give Israel up because of the sins Jeroboam has committed and has caused Israel to commit."

¹⁷Then Jeroboam's wife got up and left and went to Tirzah. As soon as she stepped over the threshold of the house, the boy died. ¹⁸They buried him, and all Israel mourned for him, as the LORD had said through his servant the prophet Ahijah.

¹⁹The other events of Jeroboam's reign, his wars and how he ruled, are written in the book of the annals of the kings of Israel. ²⁰He reigned for twenty-two years and then rested with his fathers. And Nadab his son succeeded him as king.

NEW TESTAMENT READING
Acts 16:1–15

Timothy Joins Paul and Silas

16 He came to Derbe and then to Lystra, where a disciple named Timothy lived, whose mother was a Jewess and a believer, but whose father was a Greek. ²The brothers at Lystra and Iconium spoke well of him. ³Paul wanted to take him along on the journey, so he circumcised him because of the Jews who lived in that area, for they all knew that his father was a Greek. ⁴As they travelled from town to town, they delivered the decisions reached by the apostles and elders in Jerusalem for the people to obey. ⁵So the churches were strengthened in the faith and grew daily in numbers.

Paul's Vision of the Man of Macedonia

⁶Paul and his companions travelled throughout the region of Phrygia and Galatia, having been kept by the Holy Spirit from preaching the word in the province of Asia. ⁷When they came to the border of Mysia, they tried to enter Bithynia, but the Spirit of Jesus would not allow them to. ⁸So they passed by Mysia and went down to Troas. ⁹During the night Paul had a vision of a man of Macedonia standing and begging him, "Come over to Macedonia and help us." ¹⁰After Paul had seen the vision, we got ready at once to leave for Macedonia, concluding that God had called us to preach the gospel to them.

Lydia's Conversion in Philippi

¹¹From Troas we put out to sea and sailed straight for Samothrace, and the next day on to Neapolis. ¹²From there we travelled to Philippi, a Roman colony and the leading city of that district of Macedonia. And we stayed there several days.

¹³On the Sabbath we went outside the city gate to the river, where we expected to find a place of prayer. We sat down and began to speak to the women who had gathered there. ¹⁴One of those listening was a woman named Lydia, a dealer in purple cloth from the city of Thyatira, who was a worshipper of God. The Lord opened her heart to respond to Paul's message. ¹⁵When she

and the members of her household were baptised, she invited us to her home. "If you consider me a believer in the Lord," she said, "come and stay at my house." And she persuaded us.

READING FROM PSALMS
Psalm 78:1–8

A maskil of Asaph.

¹O my people, hear my teaching;
    listen to the words of my mouth.
²I will open my mouth in parables,
    I will utter hidden things, things
        from of old—
³what we have heard and known,
    what our fathers have told us.
⁴We will not hide them from their
        children;
    we will tell the next generation

the praiseworthy deeds of the LORD,
    his power, and the wonders he has
        done.
⁵He decreed statutes for Jacob
    and established the law in Israel,
which he commanded our forefathers
    to teach their children,
⁶so that the next generation would
        know them,
    even the children yet to be born,
    and they in turn would tell their
        children.
⁷Then they would put their trust in
        God
    and would not forget his deeds
    but would keep his commands.
⁸They would not be like their
        forefathers—
    a stubborn and rebellious
        generation,
whose hearts were not loyal to God,
    whose spirits were not faithful to
        him.

JUNE 25   DAY 176

OLD TESTAMENT READING
1 Kings 14:21–16:7

Rehoboam King of Judah

²¹Rehoboam son of Solomon was king in Judah. He was forty-one years old when he became king, and he reigned for seventeen years in Jerusalem, the city the LORD had chosen out of all the tribes of Israel in which to put his Name. His mother's name was Naamah; she was an Ammonite.

²²Judah did evil in the eyes of the LORD. By the sins they committed they stirred up his jealous anger more than their fathers had done. ²³They also set up for themselves high places, sacred stones and Asherah poles on every high hill and under every spreading tree. ²⁴There were even male

shrine-prostitutes in the land; the people engaged in all the detestable practices of the nations the LORD had driven out before the Israelites.

²⁵In the fifth year of King Rehoboam, Shishak king of Egypt attacked Jerusalem. ²⁶He carried off the treasures of the temple of the LORD and the treasures of the royal palace. He took everything, including all the gold shields Solomon had made. ²⁷So King Rehoboam made bronze shields to replace them and assigned these to the commanders of the guard on duty at the entrance to the royal palace. ²⁸Whenever the king went to the LORD's temple, the guards bore the shields, and afterwards they returned them to the guardroom.

²⁹As for the other events of Rehoboam's reign, and all he did, are they

not written in the book of the annals of the kings of Judah? ³⁰There was continual warfare between Rehoboam and Jeroboam. ³¹And Rehoboam rested with his fathers and was buried with them in the City of David. His mother's name was Naamah; she was an Ammonite. And Abijah his son succeeded him as king.

Abijah King of Judah

15 In the eighteenth year of the reign of Jeroboam son of Nebat, Abijah became king of Judah, ²and he reigned in Jerusalem for three years. His mother's name was Maacah daughter of Abishalom.

³He committed all the sins his father had done before him; his heart was not fully devoted to the LORD his God, as the heart of David his forefather had been. ⁴Nevertheless, for David's sake the LORD his God gave him a lamp in Jerusalem by raising up a son to succeed him and by making Jerusalem strong. ⁵For David had done what was right in the eyes of the LORD and had not failed to keep any of the LORD's commands all the days of his life—except in the case of Uriah the Hittite.

⁶There was war between Rehoboam and Jeroboam throughout ⌊Abijah's⌋ lifetime. ⁷As for the other events of Abijah's reign, and all he did, are they not written in the book of the annals of the kings of Judah? There was war between Abijah and Jeroboam. ⁸And Abijah rested with his fathers and was buried in the City of David. And Asa his son succeeded him as king.

Asa King of Judah

⁹In the twentieth year of Jeroboam king of Israel, Asa became king of Judah, ¹⁰and he reigned in Jerusalem for forty-one years. His grandmother's name was Maacah daughter of Abishalom.

¹¹Asa did what was right in the eyes of the LORD, as his father David had done.

¹²He expelled the male shrine-prostitutes from the land and got rid of all the idols his fathers had made. ¹³He even deposed his grandmother Maacah from her position as queen mother, because she had made a repulsive Asherah pole. Asa cut the pole down and burned it in the Kidron Valley. ¹⁴Although he did not remove the high places, Asa's heart was fully committed to the LORD all his life. ¹⁵He brought into the temple of the LORD the silver and gold and the articles that he and his father had dedicated.

¹⁶There was war between Asa and Baasha king of Israel throughout their reigns. ¹⁷Baasha king of Israel went up against Judah and fortified Ramah to prevent anyone from leaving or entering the territory of Asa king of Judah.

¹⁸Asa then took all the silver and gold that was left in the treasuries of the LORD's temple and of his own palace. He entrusted it to his officials and sent them to Ben-Hadad son of Tabrimmon, the son of Hezion, the king of Aram, who was ruling in Damascus. ¹⁹"Let there be a treaty between me and you," he said, "as there was between my father and your father. See, I am sending you a gift of silver and gold. Now break your treaty with Baasha king of Israel so that he will withdraw from me."

²⁰Ben-Hadad agreed with King Asa and sent the commanders of his forces against the towns of Israel. He conquered Ijon, Dan, Abel Beth Maacah and all Kinnereth in addition to Naphtali. ²¹When Baasha heard this, he stopped building Ramah and withdrew to Tirzah. ²²Then King Asa issued an order to all Judah—no-one was exempt—and they carried away from Ramah the stones and timber Baasha had been using there. With them King Asa built up Geba in Benjamin, and also Mizpah.

²³As for all the other events of Asa's reign, all his achievements, all he did and the cities he built, are they not written in the book of the annals of the kings of Judah? In his old age, however,

his feet became diseased. 24Then Asa rested with his fathers and was buried with them in the city of his father David. And Jehoshaphat his son succeeded him as king.

Nadab King of Israel

25Nadab son of Jeroboam became king of Israel in the second year of Asa king of Judah, and he reigned over Israel for two years. 26He did evil in the eyes of the LORD, walking in the ways of his father and in his sin, which he had caused Israel to commit.

27Baasha son of Ahijah of the house of Issachar plotted against him, and he struck him down at Gibbethon, a Philistine town, while Nadab and all Israel were besieging it. 28Baasha killed Nadab in the third year of Asa king of Judah and succeeded him as king.

29As soon as he began to reign, he killed Jeroboam's whole family. He did not leave Jeroboam anyone that breathed, but destroyed them all, according to the word of the LORD given through his servant Ahijah the Shilonite—30because of the sins Jeroboam had committed and had caused Israel to commit, and because he provoked the LORD, the God of Israel, to anger.

31As for the other events of Nadab's reign, and all he did, are they not written in the book of the annals of the kings of Israel? 32There was war between Asa and Baasha king of Israel throughout their reigns.

Baasha King of Israel

33In the third year of Asa king of Judah, Baasha son of Ahijah became king of all Israel in Tirzah, and he reigned for twenty-four years. 34He did evil in the eyes of the LORD, walking in the ways of Jeroboam and in his sin, which he had caused Israel to commit.

16 Then the word of the LORD came to Jehu son of Hanani against Baasha: 2"I lifted you up from the dust and made you leader of my people Israel, but you walked in the ways of Jeroboam and caused my people Israel to sin and to provoke me to anger by their sins. 3So I am about to consume Baasha and his house, and I will make your house like that of Jeroboam son of Nebat. 4Dogs will eat those belonging to Baasha who die in the city, and the birds of the air will feed on those who die in the country."

5As for the other events of Baasha's reign, what he did and his achievements, are they not written in the book of the annals of the kings of Israel? 6Baasha rested with his fathers and was buried in Tirzah. And Elah his son succeeded him as king.

7Moreover, the word of the LORD came through the prophet Jehu son of Hanani to Baasha and his house, because of all the evil he had done in the eyes of the LORD, provoking him to anger by the things he did, and becoming like the house of Jeroboam—and also because he destroyed it.

NEW TESTAMENT READING
Acts 16:16–40

Paul and Silas in Prison

16Once when we were going to the place of prayer, we were met by a slave girl who had a spirit by which she predicted the future. She earned a great deal of money for her owners by fortune-telling. 17This girl followed Paul and the rest of us, shouting, "These men are servants of the Most High God, who are telling you the way to be saved." 18She kept this up for many days. Finally Paul became so troubled that he turned round and said to the spirit, "In the name of Jesus Christ I command you to come out of her!" At that moment the spirit left her.

19When the owners of the slave girl realised that their hope of making money was gone, they seized Paul and Silas and dragged them into the marketplace to face the authorities. 20They brought them before the magistrates and said, "These men are Jews, and are throwing our city into an uproar 21by advocating customs unlawful for us Romans to accept or practise."

22The crowd joined in the attack against Paul and Silas, and the magistrates ordered them to be stripped and beaten. 23After they had been severely flogged, they were thrown into prison, and the jailer was commanded to guard them carefully. 24Upon receiving such orders, he put them in the inner cell and fastened their feet in the stocks.

25About midnight Paul and Silas were praying and singing hymns to God, and the other prisoners were listening to them. 26Suddenly there was such a violent earthquake that the foundations of the prison were shaken. At once all the prison doors flew open, and everybody's chains came loose. 27The jailer woke up, and when he saw the prison doors open, he drew his sword and was about to kill himself because he thought the prisoners had escaped. 28But Paul shouted, "Don't harm yourself! We are all here!"

29The jailer called for lights, rushed in and fell trembling before Paul and Silas. 30He then brought them out and asked, "Sirs, what must I do to be saved?"

31They replied, "Believe in the Lord Jesus, and you will be saved—you and your household. 32Then they spoke the word of the Lord to him and to all the others in his house. 33At that hour of the night the jailer took them and washed their wounds; then immediately he and all his family were baptised. 34The jailer brought them into his house and set a meal before them; he was filled with joy because he had come to believe in God—he and his whole family.

35When it was daylight, the magistrates sent their officers to the jailer with the order: "Release those men." 36The jailer told Paul, "The magistrates have ordered that you and Silas be released. Now you can leave. Go in peace."

37But Paul said to the officers: "They beat us publicly without a trial, even though we are Roman citizens, and threw us into prison. And now do they want to get rid of us quietly? No! Let them come themselves and escort us out."

38The officers reported this to the magistrates, and when they heard that Paul and Silas were Roman citizens, they were alarmed. 39They came to appease them and escorted them from the prison, requesting them to leave the city. 40After Paul and Silas came out of the prison, they went to Lydia's house, where they met with the brothers and encouraged them. Then they left.

READING FROM PROVERBS
Proverbs 15:21–30

21Folly delights a man who lacks
　　judgment,
　　but a man of understanding keeps a
　　　straight course.

22Plans fail for lack of counsel,
　　but with many advisers they
　　　succeed.

23A man finds joy in giving an apt
　　reply—
　　and how good is a timely word!

24The path of life leads upward for the
　　wise
　　to keep him from going down to
　　　the grave.

25The LORD tears down the proud
　　man's house
　　but he keeps the widow's
　　　boundaries intact.

26The LORD detests the thoughts of the
　　wicked,
　　but those of the pure are pleasing
　　　to him.

27A greedy man brings trouble to his
　　family,
　　but he who hates bribes will live.

²⁸The heart of the righteous weighs its
  answers,
    but the mouth of the wicked gushes
      evil.

²⁹The LORD is far from the
  wicked

but he hears the prayer of the
  righteous.

³⁰A cheerful look brings joy to the
  heart,
    and good news gives health to the
      bones.

JUNE 26   DAY 177

OLD TESTAMENT READING
1 Kings 16:8–18:15

Elah King of Israel

⁸In the twenty-sixth year of Asa king
of Judah, Elah son of Baasha became
king of Israel, and he reigned in Tirzah
for two years.

⁹Zimri, one of his officials, who had
command of half his chariots, plotted
against him. Elah was in Tirzah at the
time, getting drunk in the home of
Arza, the man in charge of the palace at
Tirzah. ¹⁰Zimri came in, struck him
down and killed him in the twenty-
seventh year of Asa king of Judah. Then
he succeeded him as king.

¹¹As soon as he began to reign and
was seated on the throne, he killed off
Baasha's whole family. He did not spare
a single male, whether relative or
friend. ¹²So Zimri destroyed the whole
family of Baasha, in accordance with
the word of the LORD spoken against
Baasha through the prophet Jehu—
¹³because of all the sins Baasha and his
son Elah had committed and had caused
Israel to commit, so that they provoked
the LORD, the God of Israel, to anger by
their worthless idols.

¹⁴As for the other events of Elah's
reign, and all he did, are they not written in the book of the annals of the kings
of Israel?

Zimri King of Israel

¹⁵In the twenty-seventh year of Asa
king of Judah, Zimri reigned in Tirzah

for seven days. The army was encamped
near Gibbethon, a Philistine town.
¹⁶When the Israelites in the camp heard
that Zimri had plotted against the king
and murdered him, they proclaimed
Omri, the commander of the army, king
over Israel that very day there in the
camp. ¹⁷Then Omri and all the Israelites
with him withdrew from Gibbethon and
laid siege to Tirzah. ¹⁸When Zimri saw
that the city was taken, he went into the
citadel of the royal palace and set the
palace on fire around him. So he died,
¹⁹because of the sins he had committed,
doing evil in the eyes of the LORD and
walking in the ways of Jeroboam and in
the sin he had committed and had
caused Israel to commit.

²⁰As for the other events of Zimri's
reign, and the rebellion he carried out,
are they not written in the book of the
annals of the kings of Israel?

Omri King of Israel

²¹Then the people of Israel were split
into two factions; half supported Tibni
son of Ginath for king, and the other
half supported Omri. ²²But Omri's followers proved stronger than those of
Tibni son of Ginath. So Tibni died and
Omri became king.

²³In the thirty-first year of Asa king of
Judah, Omri became king of Israel, and
he reigned for twelve years, six of them
in Tirzah. ²⁴He bought the hill of
Samaria from Shemer for two talents of
silver and built a city on the hill, calling

it Samaria, after Shemer, the name of the former owner of the hill.

25But Omri did evil in the eyes of the LORD and sinned more than all those before him. 26He walked in all the ways of Jeroboam son of Nebat and in his sin, which he had caused Israel to commit, so that they provoked the LORD, the God of Israel, to anger by their worthless idols.

27As for the other events of Omri's reign, what he did and the things he achieved, are they not written in the book of the annals of the kings of Israel? 28Omri rested with his fathers and was buried in Samaria. And Ahab his son succeeded him as king.

Ahab Becomes King of Israel

29In the thirty-eighth year of Asa king of Judah, Ahab son of Omri became king of Israel, and he reigned in Samaria over Israel for twenty-two years. 30Ahab son of Omri did more evil in the eyes of the LORD than any of those before him. 31He not only considered it trivial to commit the sins of Jeroboam son of Nebat, but he also married Jezebel daughter of Ethbaal king of the Sidonians, and began to serve Baal and worship him. 32He set up an altar for Baal in the temple of Baal that he built in Samaria. 33Ahab also made an Asherah pole and did more to provoke the LORD, the God of Israel, to anger than did all the kings of Israel before him.

34In Ahab's time, Hiel of Bethel rebuilt Jericho. He laid its foundations at the cost of his firstborn son Abiram, and he set up its gates at the cost of his youngest son Segub, in accordance with the word of the LORD spoken by Joshua son of Nun.

Elijah Fed by Ravens

17 Now Elijah the Tishbite, from Tishbe in Gilead, said to Ahab, "As the LORD, the God of Israel, lives, whom I serve, there will be neither dew nor rain in the next few years except at my word."

2Then the word of the LORD came to Elijah: 3"Leave here, turn eastward and hide in the Kerith Ravine, east of the Jordan. 4You will drink from the brook, and I have ordered the ravens to feed you there."

5So he did what the LORD had told him. He went to the Kerith Ravine, east of the Jordan, and stayed there. 6The ravens brought him bread and meat in the morning and bread and meat in the evening, and he drank from the brook.

The Widow at Zarephath

7Some time later the brook dried up because there had been no rain in the land. 8Then the word of the LORD came to him: 9"Go at once to Zarephath of Sidon and stay there. I have commanded a widow in that place to supply you with food." 10So he went to Zarephath. When he came to the town gate, a widow was there gathering sticks. He called to her and asked, "Would you bring me a little water in a jar so I may have a drink?" 11As she was going to get it, he called, "And bring me, please, a piece of bread."

12"As surely as the LORD your God lives," she replied, "I don't have any bread—only a handful of flour in a jar and a little oil in a jug. I am gathering a few sticks to take home and make a meal for myself and my son, that we may eat it—and die."

13Elijah said to her, "Don't be afraid. Go home and do as you have said. But first make a small cake of bread for me from what you have and bring it to me, and then make something for yourself and your son. 14For this is what the LORD, the God of Israel, says: 'The jar of flour will not be used up and the jug of oil will not run dry until the day the LORD gives rain on the land.'"

15She went away and did as Elijah had told her. So there was food every day for Elijah and for the woman and her family. ¹⁶For the jar of flour was not used up and the jug of oil did not run dry, in keeping with the word of the LORD spoken by Elijah.

¹⁷Some time later the son of the woman who owned the house became ill. He grew worse and worse, and finally stopped breathing. ¹⁸She said to Elijah, "What do you have against me, man of God? Did you come to remind me of my sin and kill my son?"

¹⁹"Give me your son," Elijah replied. He took him from her arms, carried him to the upper room where he was staying, and laid him on his bed. ²⁰Then he cried out to the LORD, "O LORD my God, have you brought tragedy also upon this widow I am staying with, by causing her son to die?" ²¹Then he stretched himself out on the boy three times and cried to the LORD, "O LORD my God, let this boy's life return to him!"

²²The LORD heard Elijah's cry, and the boy's life returned to him, and he lived. ²³Elijah picked up the child and carried him down from the room into the house. He gave him to his mother and said, "Look, your son is alive!" ²⁴Then the woman said to Elijah, "Now I know that you are a man of God and that the word of the LORD from your mouth is the truth."

Elijah and Obadiah

18 After a long time, in the third year, the word of the LORD came to Elijah: "Go and present yourself to Ahab, and I will send rain on the land." ²So Elijah went to present himself to Ahab.

Now the famine was severe in Samaria, ³and Ahab had summoned Obadiah, who was in charge of his palace. (Obadiah was a devout believer in the LORD. ⁴While Jezebel was killing off the LORD's prophets, Obadiah had taken a hundred prophets and hidden them in two caves, fifty in each, and had supplied them with food and water.) ⁵Ahab

had said to Obadiah, "Go through the land to all the springs and valleys. Maybe we can find some grass to keep the horses and mules alive so we will not have to kill any of our animals." ⁶So they divided the land they were to cover, Ahab going in one direction and Obadiah in another.

⁷As Obadiah was walking along, Elijah met him. Obadiah recognised him, bowed down to the ground, and said, "Is it really you, my lord Elijah?"

⁸"Yes," he replied. "Go tell your master, 'Elijah is here.'"

⁹"What have I done wrong," asked Obadiah, "that you are handing your servant over to Ahab to be put to death? ¹⁰As surely as the LORD your God lives, there is not a nation or kingdom where my master has not sent someone to look for you. And whenever a nation or kingdom claimed you were not there, he made them swear they could not find you. ¹¹But now you tell me to go to my master and say, 'Elijah is here.' ¹²I don't know where the Spirit of the LORD may carry you when I leave you. If I go and tell Ahab and he doesn't find you, he will kill me. Yet I your servant have worshipped the LORD since my youth. ¹³Haven't you heard, my lord, what I did while Jezebel was killing the prophets of the LORD? I hid a hundred of the LORD's prophets in two caves, fifty in each, and supplied them with food and water. ¹⁴And now you tell me to go to my master and say, 'Elijah is here.' He will kill me!"

¹⁵Elijah said, "As the LORD Almighty lives, whom I serve, I will surely present myself to Ahab today."

NEW TESTAMENT READING
Acts 17:1–21

In Thessalonica

17 When they had passed through Amphipolis and Apollonia, they came to Thessalonica, where there was a Jewish synagogue. ²As his custom was, Paul went into the synagogue, and on three Sabbath days he reasoned with them from the Scriptures, ³explaining and proving that the Christ had to suffer and rise from the dead. "This Jesus I am proclaiming to you is the Christ," he said. ⁴Some of the Jews were persuaded and joined Paul and Silas, as did a large number of God-fearing Greeks and not a few prominent women.

⁵But the Jews were jealous; so they rounded up some bad characters from the market-place, formed a mob and started a riot in the city. They rushed to Jason's house in search of Paul and Silas in order to bring them out to the crowd. ⁶But when they did not find them, they dragged Jason and some other brothers before the city officials, shouting: "These men who have caused trouble all over the world have now come here, ⁷and Jason has welcomed them into his house. They are all defying Caesar's decrees, saying that there is another king, one called Jesus." ⁸When they heard this, the crowd and the city officials were thrown into turmoil. ⁹Then they put Jason and the others on bail and let them go.

In Berea

¹⁰As soon as it was night, the brothers sent Paul and Silas away to Berea. On arriving there, they went to the Jewish synagogue. ¹¹Now the Bereans were of more noble character than the Thessalonians, for they received the message with great eagerness and examined the Scriptures every day to see if what Paul said was true. ¹²Many of the Jews believed, as did also a number of prominent Greek women and many Greek men.

¹³When the Jews in Thessalonica learned that Paul was preaching the word of God at Berea, they went there too, agitating the crowds and stirring them up. ¹⁴The brothers immediately sent Paul to the coast, but Silas and Timothy stayed at Berea. ¹⁵The men who escorted Paul brought him to Athens and then left with instructions for Silas and Timothy to join him as soon as possible.

In Athens

¹⁶While Paul was waiting for them in Athens, he was greatly distressed to see that the city was full of idols. ¹⁷So he reasoned in the synagogue with the Jews and the God-fearing Greeks, as well as in the market-place day by day with those who happened to be there. ¹⁸A group of Epicurean and Stoic philosophers began to dispute with him. Some of them asked, "What is this babbler trying to say?" Others remarked, "He seems to be advocating foreign gods." They said this because Paul was preaching the good news about Jesus and the resurrection. ¹⁹Then they took him and brought him to a meeting of the Areopagus, where they said to him, "May we know what this new teaching is that you are presenting? ²⁰You are bringing some strange ideas to our ears, and we want to know what they mean." ²¹(All the Athenians and the foreigners who lived there spent their time doing nothing but talking about and listening to the latest ideas.)

READING FROM PSALMS
Psalm 78:9–16

⁹The men of Ephraim, though armed
          with bows,
    turned back on the day of battle;
¹⁰they did not keep God's covenant
    and refused to live by his law.
¹¹They forgot what he had done,
    the wonders he had shown them.
¹²He did miracles in the sight of their
          fathers
    in the land of Egypt, in the region
          of Zoan.
¹³He divided the sea and led them
          through;
    he made the water stand firm like a
          wall.

14He guided them with the cloud by
day
and with light from the fire all
night.
15He split the rocks in the desert

and gave them water as abundant
as the seas;
16he brought streams out of a rocky crag
and made water flow down like
rivers.

JUNE 27   DAY 178

OLD TESTAMENT READING
1 Kings 18:16–19:21

Elijah on Mount Carmel

16So Obadiah went to meet Ahab and told him, and Ahab went to meet Elijah. 17When he saw Elijah, he said to him, "Is that you, you troubler of Israel?"

18"I have not made trouble for Israel," Elijah replied. "But you and your father's family have. You have abandoned the LORD's commands and have followed the Baals. 19Now summon the people from all over Israel to meet me on Mount Carmel. And bring the four hundred and fifty prophets of Baal and the four hundred prophets of Asherah, who eat at Jezebel's table."

20So Ahab sent word throughout all Israel and assembled the prophets on Mount Carmel. 21Elijah went before the people and said, "How long will you waver between two opinions? If the LORD is God, follow him; but if Baal is God, follow him."

But the people said nothing.

22Then Elijah said to them, "I am the only one of the LORD's prophets left, but Baal has four hundred and fifty prophets. 23Get two bulls for us. Let them choose one for themselves, and let them cut it into pieces and put it on the wood but not set fire to it. I will prepare the other bull and put it on the wood but not set fire to it. 24Then you call on the name of your god, and I will call on the name of the LORD. The god who answers by fire—he is God."

Then all the people said, "What you say is good."

25Elijah said to the prophets of Baal, "Choose one of the bulls and prepare it first, since there are so many of you. Call on the name of your god, but do not light the fire." 26So they took the bull given them and prepared it.

Then they called on the name of Baal from morning till noon. "O Baal, answer us!" they shouted. But there was no response; no-one answered. And they danced around the altar they had made.

27At noon Elijah began to taunt them. "Shout louder!" he said. "Surely he is a god! Perhaps he is deep in thought, or busy, or travelling. Maybe he is sleeping and must be awakened." 28So they shouted louder and slashed themselves with swords and spears, as was their custom, until their blood flowed. 29Midday passed, and they continued their frantic prophesying until the time for the evening sacrifice. But there was no response, no-one answered, no-one paid attention.

30Then Elijah said to all the people, "Come here to me." They came to him, and he repaired the altar of the LORD, which was in ruins. 31Elijah took twelve stones, one for each of the tribes descended from Jacob, to whom the word of the LORD had come, saying, "Your name shall be Israel." 32With the stones he built an altar in the name of the LORD, and he dug a trench round it large enough to hold two seahs of seed. 33He arranged the wood, cut the bull into pieces and laid it on the wood. Then he said to them, "Fill four large jars with water and pour it on the offering and on the wood."

34"Do it again," he said, and they did it again.

"Do it a third time," he ordered, and they did it the third time. 35The water ran down around the altar and even filled the trench.

36At the time of sacrifice, the prophet Elijah stepped forward and prayed: "O LORD, God of Abraham, Isaac and Israel, let it be known today that you are God in Israel and that I am your servant and have done all these things at your command. 37Answer me, O LORD, answer me, so these people will know that you, O LORD, are God, and that you are turning their hearts back again."

38Then the fire of the LORD fell and burned up the sacrifice, the wood, the stones and the soil, and also licked up the water in the trench.

39When all the people saw this, they fell prostrate and cried, "The LORD— he is God! The LORD—he is God!"

40Then Elijah commanded them, "Seize the prophets of Baal. Don't let anyone get away!" They seized them, and Elijah had them brought down to the Kishon Valley and slaughtered there.

41And Elijah said to Ahab, "Go, eat and drink, for there is the sound of a heavy rain." 42So Ahab went off to eat and drink, but Elijah climbed to the top of Carmel, bent down to the ground and put his face between his knees.

43"Go and look towards the sea," he told his servant. And he went up and looked.

"There is nothing there," he said.

Seven times Elijah said, "Go back."

44The seventh time the servant reported, "A cloud as small as a man's hand is rising from the sea."

So Elijah said, "Go and tell Ahab, 'Hitch up your chariot and go down before the rain stops you.'"

45Meanwhile, the sky grew black with clouds, the wind rose, a heavy rain came on and Ahab rode off to Jezreel. 46The power of the LORD came upon Elijah and, tucking his cloak into his belt, he ran ahead of Ahab all the way to Jezreel.

Elijah Flees to Horeb

19 Now Ahab told Jezebel everything Elijah had done and how he had killed all the prophets with the sword. 2So Jezebel sent a messenger to Elijah to say, "May the gods deal with me, be it ever so severely, if by this time tomorrow I do not make your life like that of one of them."

3Elijah was afraid and ran for his life. When he came to Beersheba in Judah, he left his servant there, 4while he himself went a day's journey into the desert. He came to a broom tree, sat down under it and prayed that he might die. "I have had enough, LORD," he said. "Take my life; I am no better than my ancestors." 5Then he lay down under the tree and fell asleep.

All at once an angel touched him and said, "Get up and eat." 6He looked around, and there by his head was a cake of bread baked over hot coals, and a jar of water. He ate and drank and then lay down again.

7The angel of the LORD came back a second time and touched him and said, "Get up and eat, for the journey is too much for you." 8So he got up and ate and drank. Strengthened by that food, he travelled for forty days and forty nights until he reached Horeb, the mountain of God. 9There he went into a cave and spent the night.

The LORD Appears to Elijah

And the word of the LORD came to him: "What are you doing here, Elijah?"

10He replied, "I have been very zealous for the LORD God Almighty. The Israelites have rejected your covenant, broken down your altars, and put your prophets to death with the sword. I am the only one left, and now they are trying to kill me too."

11The LORD said, "Go out and stand on the mountain in the presence of the LORD, for the LORD is about to pass by."

Then a great and powerful wind tore the mountains apart and shattered the rocks before the LORD, but the LORD was not in the wind. After the wind there was an earthquake, but the LORD was not in the earthquake. 12After the earthquake came a fire, but the LORD was not in the fire. And after the fire came a gentle whisper. 13When Elijah heard it, he pulled his cloak over his face and went out and stood at the mouth of the cave.

Then a voice said to him, "What are you doing here, Elijah?"

14He replied, "I have been very zealous for the LORD God Almighty. The Israelites have rejected your covenant, broken down your altars, and put your prophets to death with the sword. I am the only one left, and now they are trying to kill me too."

15The LORD said to him, "Go back the way you came, and go to the Desert of Damascus. When you get there, anoint Hazael king over Aram. 16Also, anoint Jehu son of Nimshi king over Israel, and anoint Elisha son of Shaphat from Abel Meholah to succeed you as prophet. 17Jehu will put to death any who escape the sword of Hazael, and Elisha will put to death any who escape the sword of Jehu. 18Yet I reserve seven thousand in Israel—all whose knees have not bowed down to Baal and all whose mouths have not kissed him."

The Call of Elisha

19So Elijah went from there and found Elisha son of Shaphat. He was ploughing with twelve yoke of oxen, and he himself was driving the twelfth pair. Elijah went up to him and threw his cloak around him. 20Elisha then left his oxen and ran after Elijah. "Let me

kiss my father and mother good-bye," he said, "and then I will come with you."

"Go back," Elijah replied. "What have I done to you?"

21So Elisha left him and went back. He took his yoke of oxen and slaughtered them. He burned the ploughing equipment to cook the meat and gave it to the people, and they ate. Then he set out to follow Elijah and became his attendant.

NEW TESTAMENT READING
Acts 17:22–18:8

22Paul then stood up in the meeting of the Areopagus and said: "Men of Athens! I see that in every way you are very religious. 23For as I walked around and looked carefully at your objects of worship, I even found an altar with this inscription: TO AN UNKNOWN GOD. Now what you worship as something unknown I am going to proclaim to you.

24"The God who made the world and everything in it is the Lord of heaven and earth and does not live in temples built by hands. 25And he is not served by human hands, as if he needed anything, because he himself gives all men life and breath and everything else. 26From one man he made every nation of men, that they should inhabit the whole earth; and he determined the times set for them and the exact places where they should live. 27God did this so that men would seek him and perhaps reach out for him and find him, though he is not far from each one of us. 28For in him we live and move and have our being.' As some of your own poets have said, 'We are his offspring.'

29"Therefore since we are God's offspring, we should not think that the divine being is like gold or silver or stone—an image made by man's design and skill. 30In the past God overlooked such ignorance, but now he commands all people everywhere to repent. 31For he has set a day when he will judge the world with justice by the man he has appointed. He has given proof of this to all men by raising him from the dead."

32When they heard about the resurrection of the dead, some of them sneered, but others said, "We want to hear you again on this subject." 33At that, Paul left the Council. 34A few men became followers of Paul and believed. Among them was Dionysius, a member of the Areopagus, also a woman named Damaris, and a number of others.

In Corinth

18 After this, Paul left Athens and went to Corinth. 2There he met a Jew named Aquila, a native of Pontus, who had recently come from Italy with his wife Priscilla, because Claudius had ordered all the Jews to leave Rome. Paul went to see them, 3and because he was a tentmaker as they were, he stayed and worked with them. 4Every Sabbath he reasoned in the synagogue, trying to persuade Jews and Greeks.

5When Silas and Timothy came from Macedonia, Paul devoted himself exclusively to preaching, testifying to the Jews that Jesus was the Christ. 6But when the Jews opposed Paul and became abusive, he shook out his clothes in protest and said to them, "Your blood be on your own heads! I am clear of my responsibility. From now on I will go to the Gentiles."

7Then Paul left the synagogue and went next door to the house of Titius Justus, a worshipper of God. 8Crispus, the synagogue ruler, and his entire household believed in the Lord; and many of the Corinthians who heard him believed and were baptised.

READING FROM PSALMS
Psalm 78:17–31

17But they continued to sin against him,
　　rebelling in the desert against the Most High.

18They wilfully put God to the test by demanding the food they craved.
19They spoke against God, saying, "Can God spread a table in the desert?
20When he struck the rock, water gushed out,
　　and streams flowed abundantly.
But can he also give us food?
　　Can he supply meat for his people?"
21When the Lord heard them, he was very angry;
　　his fire broke out against Jacob, and his wrath rose against Israel,
22for they did not believe in God or trust in his deliverance.
23Yet he gave a command to the skies above
　　and opened the doors of the heavens;
24he rained down manna for the people to eat,
　　he gave them the grain of heaven.
25Men ate the bread of angels;
　　he sent them all the food they could eat.
26He let loose the east wind from the heavens
　　and led forth the south wind by his power.
27He rained meat down on them like dust,
　　flying birds like sand on the seashore.
28He made them come down inside their camp,
　　all around their tents.
29They ate till they had more than enough,
　　for he had given them what they craved.
30But before they turned from the food they craved,
　　even while it was still in their mouths,
31God's anger rose against them;
　　he put to death the sturdiest among them,
　　cutting down the young men of Israel.

OLD TESTAMENT READING
1 Kings 20:1–21:29

Ben-Hadad Attacks Samaria

20 Now Ben-Hadad king of Aram mustered his entire army. Accompanied by thirty-two kings with their horses and chariots, he went up and besieged Samaria and attacked it. ²He sent messengers into the city to Ahab king of Israel, saying, "This is what Ben-Hadad says: ³'Your silver and gold are mine, and the best of your wives and children are mine.'"

⁴The king of Israel answered, "Just as you say, my lord the king. I and all I have are yours."

⁵The messengers came again and said, "This is what Ben-Hadad says: 'I sent to demand your silver and gold, your wives and your children. ⁶But about this time tomorrow I am going to send my officials to search your palace and the houses of your officials. They will seize everything you value and carry it away.'"

⁷The king of Israel summoned all the elders of the land and said to them, "See how this man is looking for trouble! When he sent for my wives and my children, my silver and my gold, I did not refuse him."

⁸The elders and the people all answered, "Don't listen to him or agree to his demands."

⁹So he replied to Ben-Hadad's messengers, "Tell my lord the king, 'Your servant will do all you demanded the first time, but this demand I cannot meet.'" They left and took the answer back to Ben-Hadad.

¹⁰Then Ben-Hadad sent another message to Ahab: "May the gods deal with me, be it ever so severely, if enough dust remains in Samaria to give each of my men a handful."

¹¹The king of Israel answered, "Tell him: 'One who puts on his armour should not boast like one who takes it off.'"

¹²Ben-Hadad heard this message while he and the kings were drinking in their tents, and he ordered his men: "Prepare to attack." So they prepared to attack the city.

Ahab Defeats Ben-Hadad

¹³Meanwhile a prophet came to Ahab king of Israel and announced, "This is what the LORD says: 'Do you see this vast army? I will give it into your hand today, and then you will know that I am the LORD.'"

¹⁴"But who will do this?" asked Ahab.

The prophet replied, "This is what the LORD says: 'The young officers of the provincial commanders will do it.'"

"And who will start the battle?" he asked.

The prophet answered, "You will."

¹⁵So Ahab summoned the young officers of the provincial commanders, 232 men. Then he assembled the rest of the Israelites, 7,000 in all. ¹⁶They set out at noon while Ben-Hadad and the 32 kings allied with him were in their tents getting drunk. ¹⁷The young officers of the provincial commanders went out first.

Now Ben-Hadad had dispatched scouts, who reported, "Men are advancing from Samaria."

¹⁸He said, "If they have come out for peace, take them alive; if they have come out for war, take them alive."

¹⁹The young officers of the provincial commanders marched out of the city with the army behind them ²⁰and each one struck down his opponent. At that, the Arameans fled, with the Israelites in pursuit. But Ben-Hadad king of Aram escaped on horseback with some of his

horsemen. [21]The king of Israel advanced and overpowered the horses and chariots and inflicted heavy losses on the Arameans.

[22]Afterwards, the prophet came to the king of Israel and said, "Strengthen your position and see what must be done, because next spring the king of Aram will attack you again."

[23]Meanwhile, the officials of the king of Aram advised him, "Their gods are gods of the hills. That is why they were too strong for us. But if we fight them on the plains, surely we will be stronger than they. [24]Do this: Remove all the kings from their commands and replace them with other officers. [25]You must also raise an army like the one you lost—horse for horse and chariot for chariot—so we can fight Israel on the plains. Then surely we will be stronger than they." He agreed with them and acted accordingly.

[26]The next spring Ben-Hadad mustered the Arameans and went up to Aphek to fight against Israel. [27]When the Israelites were also mustered and given provisions, they marched out to meet them. The Israelites camped opposite them like two small flocks of goats, while the Arameans covered the countryside.

[28]The man of God came up and told the king of Israel, "This is what the LORD says: 'Because the Arameans think the LORD is a god of the hills and not a god of the valleys, I will deliver this vast army into your hands, and you will know that I am the LORD.'"

[29]For seven days they camped opposite each other, and on the seventh day the battle was joined. The Israelites inflicted a hundred thousand casualties on the Aramean foot soldiers in one day. [30]The rest of them escaped to the city of Aphek, where the wall collapsed on twenty-seven thousand of them. And Ben-Hadad fled to the city and hid in an inner room.

[31]His officials said to him, "Look, we have heard that the kings of the house of Israel are merciful. Let us go to the king of Israel with sackcloth round our waists and ropes round our heads. Perhaps he will spare your life."

[32]Wearing sackcloth round their waists and ropes round their heads, they went to the king of Israel and said, "Your servant Ben-Hadad says: 'Please let me live.'"

The king answered, "Is he still alive? He is my brother."

[33]The men took this as a good sign and were quick to pick up his word. "Yes, your brother Ben-Hadad!" they said.

"Go and get him," the king said. When Ben-Hadad came out, Ahab had him come up into his chariot.

[34]"I will return the cities my father took from your father," Ben-Hadad offered. "You may set up your own market areas in Damascus, as my father did in Samaria."

Ahab said, "On the basis of a treaty I will set you free." So he made a treaty with him, and let him go.

A Prophet Condemns Ahab

[35]By the word of the LORD one of the sons of the prophets said to his companion, "Strike me with your weapon," but the man refused.

[36]So the prophet said, "Because you have not obeyed the LORD, as soon as you leave me a lion will kill you." And after the man went away, a lion found him and killed him.

[37]The prophet found another man and said, "Strike me, please." So the man struck him and wounded him. [38]Then the prophet went and stood by the road waiting for the king. He disguised himself with his headband down over his eyes. [39]As the king passed by, the prophet called out to him, "Your servant went into the thick of the battle, and someone came to me with a captive and said, 'Guard this man. If he is missing, it will be your life for his life, or you must pay a talent of silver.' [40]While your servant was busy here and there, the man disappeared."

"That is your sentence," the king of Israel said. "You have pronounced it yourself."

41Then the prophet quickly removed the headband from his eyes, and the king of Israel recognised him as one of the prophets. 42He said to the king, "This is what the LORD says: 'You have set free a man I had determined should die. Therefore it is your life for his life, your people for his people.'" 43Sullen and angry, the king of Israel went to his palace in Samaria.

Naboth's Vineyard

21 Some time later there was an incident involving a vineyard belonging to Naboth the Jezreelite. The vineyard was in Jezreel, close to the palace of Ahab king of Samaria. 2Ahab said to Naboth, "Let me have your vineyard to use for a vegetable garden, since it is close to my palace. In exchange I will give you a better vineyard or, if you prefer, I will pay you whatever it is worth."

3But Naboth replied, "The LORD forbid that I should give you the inheritance of my fathers."

4So Ahab went home, sullen and angry because Naboth the Jezreelite had said, "I will not give you the inheritance of my fathers." He lay on his bed sulking and refused to eat.

5His wife Jezebel came in and asked him, "Why are you so sullen? Why won't you eat?"

6He answered her, "Because I said to Naboth the Jezreelite, 'Sell me your vineyard; or if you prefer, I will give you another vineyard in its place.' But he said, 'I will not give you my vineyard.'"

7Jezebel his wife said, "Is this how you act as king over Israel? Get up and eat! Cheer up. I'll get you the vineyard of Naboth the Jezreelite."

8So she wrote letters in Ahab's name, placed his seal on them, and sent them to the elders and nobles who lived in Naboth's city with him. 9In those letters she wrote:

"Proclaim a day of fasting and seat Naboth in a prominent place among the people. 10But seat two scoundrels opposite him and have them testify that he has cursed both God and the king. Then take him out and stone him to death."

11So the elders and nobles who lived in Naboth's city did as Jezebel directed in the letters she had written to them. 12They proclaimed a fast and seated Naboth in a prominent place among the people. 13Then two scoundrels came and sat opposite him and brought charges against Naboth before the people, saying, "Naboth has cursed both God and the king." So they took him outside the city and stoned him to death. 14Then they sent word to Jezebel: "Naboth has been stoned and is dead."

15As soon as Jezebel heard that Naboth had been stoned to death, she said to Ahab, "Get up and take possession of the vineyard of Naboth the Jezreelite that he refused to sell you. He is no longer alive, but dead." 16When Ahab heard that Naboth was dead, he got up and went down to take possession of Naboth's vineyard.

17Then the word of the LORD came to Elijah the Tishbite: 18"Go down to meet Ahab king of Israel, who rules in Samaria. He is now in Naboth's vineyard, where he has gone to take possession of it. 19Say to him, 'This is what the LORD says: Have you not murdered a man and seized his property?' Then say to him, 'This is what the LORD says: In the place where dogs licked up Naboth's blood, dogs will lick up your blood—yes, yours!'"

20Ahab said to Elijah, "So you have found me, my enemy!"

"I have found you," he answered, "because you have sold yourself to do evil in the eyes of the LORD. 21'I am going to bring disaster on you. I will consume your descendants and cut off from Ahab every last male in Israel —slave or free. 22I will make your house like that of Jeroboam son of Nebat and that of Baasha son of Ahijah, because you have provoked me to anger and have caused Israel to sin.'

²³"And also concerning Jezebel the LORD says: 'Dogs will devour Jezebel by the wall of Jezreel.'

²⁴"Dogs will eat those belonging to Ahab who die in the city, and the birds of the air will feed on those who die in the country."

²⁵(There was never a man like Ahab, who sold himself to do evil in the eyes of the LORD, urged on by Jezebel his wife. ²⁶He behaved in the vilest manner by going after idols, like the Amorites the LORD drove out before Israel.)

²⁷When Ahab heard these words, he tore his clothes, put on sackcloth and fasted. He lay in sackcloth and went around meekly.

²⁸Then the word of the LORD came to Elijah the Tishbite: ²⁹"Have you noticed how Ahab has humbled himself before me? Because he has humbled himself, I will not bring this disaster in his day, but I will bring it on his house in the days of his son."

NEW TESTAMENT READING
Acts 18:9–19:13

⁹One night the Lord spoke to Paul in a vision: "Do not be afraid; keep on speaking, do not be silent. ¹⁰For I am with you, and no-one is going to attack and harm you, because I have many people in this city." ¹¹So Paul stayed for a year and a half, teaching them the word of God.

¹²While Gallio was proconsul of Achaia, the Jews made a united attack on Paul and brought him into court. ¹³"This man," they charged, "is persuading the people to worship God in ways contrary to the law."

¹⁴Just as Paul was about to speak, Gallio said to the Jews, "If you Jews were making a complaint about some misdemeanour or serious crime, it would be reasonable for me to listen to

you. ¹⁵But since it involves questions about words and names and your own law—settle the matter yourselves. I will not be a judge of such things." ¹⁶So he had them ejected from the court. ¹⁷Then they all turned on Sosthenes the synagogue ruler and beat him in front of the court. But Gallio showed no concern whatever.

Priscilla, Aquila and Apollos

¹⁸Paul stayed on in Corinth for some time. Then he left the brothers and sailed for Syria, accompanied by Priscilla and Aquila. Before he sailed, he had his hair cut off at Cenchrea because of a vow he had taken. ¹⁹They arrived at Ephesus, where Paul left Priscilla and Aquila. He himself went into the synagogue and reasoned with the Jews. ²⁰When they asked him to spend more time with them, he declined. ²¹But as he left, he promised, "I will come back if it is God's will." Then he set sail from Ephesus. ²²When he landed at Caesarea, he went up and greeted the church and then went down to Antioch.

²³After spending some time in Antioch, Paul set out from there and travelled from place to place throughout the region of Galatia and Phrygia, strengthening all the disciples.

²⁴Meanwhile a Jew named Apollos, a native of Alexandria, came to Ephesus. He was a learned man, with a thorough knowledge of the Scriptures. ²⁵He had been instructed in the way of the Lord, and he spoke with great fervour and taught about Jesus accurately, though he knew only the baptism of John. ²⁶He began to speak boldly in the synagogue. When Priscilla and Aquila heard him, they invited him to their home and explained to him the way of God more adequately.

²⁷When Apollos wanted to go to Achaia, the brothers encouraged him and wrote to the disciples there to welcome him. On arriving, he was a great help to those who by grace had believed. ²⁸For he vigorously refuted the

Jews in public debate, proving from the Scriptures that Jesus was the Christ.

Paul in Ephesus

19 While Apollos was at Corinth, Paul took the road through the interior and arrived at Ephesus. There he found some disciples 2and asked them, "Did you receive the Holy Spirit when you believed?"

They answered, "No, we have not even heard that there is a Holy Spirit."

3So Paul asked, "Then what baptism did you receive?"

"John's baptism," they replied.

4Paul said, "John's baptism was a baptism of repentance. He told the people to believe in the one coming after him, that is, in Jesus." 5On hearing this, they were baptised into the name of the Lord Jesus. 6When Paul placed his hands on them, the Holy Spirit came on them, and they spoke in tongues and prophesied. 7There were about twelve men in all.

8Paul entered the synagogue and spoke boldly there for three months, arguing persuasively about the kingdom of God. 9But some of them became obstinate; they refused to believe and publicly maligned the Way. So Paul left them. He took the disciples with him and had discussions daily in the lecture hall of Tyrannus. 10This went on for two years, so that all the Jews and Greeks who lived in the province of Asia heard the word of the Lord.

11God did extraordinary miracles through Paul, 12so that even handkerchiefs and aprons that had touched him were taken to the sick, and their illnesses were cured and the evil spirits left them.

13Some Jews who went around driving out evil spirits tried to invoke the name of the Lord Jesus over those who were demon-possessed. They would say, "In the name of Jesus, whom Paul preaches, I command you to come out."

READING FROM PSALMS
Psalm 78:32-39

32In spite of all this, they kept on
　　sinning;
　　in spite of his wonders, they did not
　　　believe.
33So he ended their days in futility
　　and their years in terror.
34Whenever God slew them, they
　　would seek him;
　　they eagerly turned to him again.
35They remembered that God was their
　　Rock,
　　that God Most High was their
　　　Redeemer.
36But then they would flatter him with
　　their mouths,
　　lying to him with their tongues;
37their hearts were not loyal to him,
　　they were not faithful to his
　　　covenant.
38Yet he was merciful;
　　he forgave their iniquities
　　and did not destroy them.
　Time after time he restrained his
　　anger
　　and did not stir up his full wrath.
39He remembered that they were but
　　flesh,
　　a passing breeze that does not
　　　return.

OLD TESTAMENT READING
1 Kings 22:1–53

Micaiah Prophesies Against Ahab

22 For three years there was no war between Aram and Israel. ²But in the third year Jehoshaphat king of Judah went down to see the king of Israel. ³The king of Israel had said to his officials, "Don't you know that Ramoth Gilead belongs to us and yet we are doing nothing to retake it from the king of Aram?"

⁴So he asked Jehoshaphat, "Will you go with me to fight against Ramoth Gilead?"

Jehoshaphat replied to the king of Israel, "I am as you are, my people as your people, my horses as your horses." ⁵But Jehoshaphat also said to the king of Israel, "First seek the counsel of the LORD."

⁶So the king of Israel brought together the prophets—about four hundred men—and asked them, "Shall I go to war against Ramoth Gilead, or shall I refrain?"

"Go," they answered, "for the Lord will give it into the king's hand."

⁷But Jehoshaphat asked, "Is there not a prophet of the LORD here whom we can enquire of?"

⁸The king of Israel answered Jehoshaphat, "There is still one man through whom we can enquire of the LORD, but I hate him because he never prophesies anything good about me, but always bad. He is Micaiah son of Imlah."

"The king should not say that," Jehoshaphat replied.

⁹So the king of Israel called one of his officials and said, "Bring Micaiah son of Imlah at once."

¹⁰Dressed in their royal robes, the king of Israel and Jehoshaphat king of Judah were sitting on their thrones at the threshing-floor by the entrance of the gate of Samaria, with all the prophets prophesying before them. ¹¹Now Zedekiah son of Kenaanah had made iron horns and he declared, "This is what the LORD says: 'With these you will gore the Arameans until they are destroyed.'"

¹²All the other prophets were prophesying the same thing. "Attack Ramoth Gilead and be victorious," they said, "for the LORD will give it into the king's hand."

¹³The messenger who had gone to summon Micaiah said to him, "Look, as one man the other prophets are predicting success for the king. Let your word agree with theirs, and speak favourably."

¹⁴But Micaiah said, "As surely as the LORD lives, I can tell him only what the LORD tells me."

¹⁵When he arrived, the king asked him, "Micaiah, shall we go to war against Ramoth Gilead, or shall I refrain?"

"Attack and be victorious," he answered, "for the LORD will give it into the king's hand."

¹⁶The king said to him, "How many times must I make you swear to tell me nothing but the truth in the name of the LORD?"

¹⁷Then Micaiah answered, "I saw all Israel scattered on the hills like sheep without a shepherd, and the LORD said, 'These people have no master. Let each one go home in peace.'"

¹⁸The king of Israel said to Jehoshaphat, "Didn't I tell you that he never prophesies anything good about me, but only bad?"

¹⁹Micaiah continued, "Therefore hear the word of the LORD: I saw the LORD sitting on his throne with all the host of heaven standing round him on his right and on his left. ²⁰And the LORD said, 'Who will entice Ahab into

attacking Ramoth Gilead and going to his death there?'

"One suggested this, and another that. 21Finally, a spirit came forward, stood before the LORD and said, 'I will entice him.'

22"'By what means?' the LORD asked.

"'I will go out and be a lying spirit in the mouths of all his prophets,' he said.

"'You will succeed in enticing him,' said the LORD. 'Go and do it.'

23"So now the LORD has put a lying spirit in the mouths of all these prophets of yours. The LORD has decreed disaster for you."

24Then Zedekiah son of Kenaanah went up and slapped Micaiah in the face. "Which way did the spirit from the LORD go when he went from me to speak to you?" he asked.

25Micaiah replied, "You will find out on the day you go to hide in an inner room."

26The king of Israel then ordered, "Take Micaiah and send him back to Amon the ruler of the city and to Joash the king's son 27and say, 'This is what the king says: Put this fellow in prison and give him nothing but bread and water until I return safely.'"

28Micaiah declared, "If you ever return safely, the LORD has not spoken through me." Then he added, "Mark my words, all you people!"

Ahab Killed at Ramoth Gilead

29So the king of Israel and Jehoshaphat king of Judah went up to Ramoth Gilead. 30The king of Israel said to Jehoshaphat, "I will enter the battle in disguise, but you wear your royal robes." So the king of Israel disguised himself and went into battle.

31Now the king of Aram had ordered his thirty-two chariot commanders, "Do not fight with anyone, small or great, except the king of Israel." 32When the chariot commanders saw Jehoshaphat, they thought, "Surely this is the king of Israel." So they turned to

attack him, but when Jehoshaphat cried out, 33the chariot commanders saw he was not the king of Israel and stopped pursuing him.

34But someone drew his bow at random and hit the king of Israel between the sections of his armour. The king told his chariot driver, "Wheel round and get me out of the fighting. I've been wounded." 35All day long the battle raged, and the king was propped up in his chariot facing the Arameans. The blood from his wound ran onto the floor of the chariot, and that evening he died. 36As the sun was setting, a cry spread through the army: "Every man to his town; everyone to his land!"

37So the king died and was brought to Samaria, and they buried him there. 38They washed the chariot at a pool in Samaria (where the prostitutes bathed), and the dogs licked up his blood, as the word of the LORD had declared.

39As for the other events of Ahab's reign, including all he did, the palace he built and inlaid with ivory, and the cities he fortified, are they not written in the book of the annals of the kings of Israel? 40Ahab rested with his fathers. And Ahaziah his son succeeded him as king.

Jehoshaphat King of Judah

41Jehoshaphat son of Asa became king of Judah in the fourth year of Ahab king of Israel. 42Jehoshaphat was thirty-five years old when he became king, and he reigned in Jerusalem for twenty-five years. His mother's name was Azubah daughter of Shilhi. 43In everything he walked in the ways of his father Asa and did not stray from them; he did what was right in the eyes of the LORD. The high places, however, were not removed, and the people continued to offer sacrifices and burn incense there. 44Jehoshaphat was also at peace with the king of Israel.

45As for the other events of Jehoshaphat's reign, the things he achieved and his military exploits, are they not written in the book of the annals of the kings of Judah? [46]He rid the land of the rest of the male shrine-prostitutes who remained there even after the reign of his father Asa. [47]There was then no king in Edom; a deputy ruled.

[48]Now Jehoshaphat built a fleet of trading ships to go to Ophir for gold, but they never set sail—they were wrecked at Ezion Geber. [49]At that time Ahaziah son of Ahab said to Jehoshaphat, "Let my men sail with your men," but Jehoshaphat refused.

[50]Then Jehoshaphat rested with his fathers and was buried with them in the city of David his father. And Jehoram his son succeeded him.

Ahaziah King of Israel

[51]Ahaziah son of Ahab became king of Israel in Samaria in the seventeenth year of Jehoshaphat king of Judah, and he reigned over Israel for two years. [52]He did evil in the eyes of the LORD, because he walked in the ways of his father and mother and in the ways of Jeroboam son of Nebat, who caused Israel to sin. [53]He served and worshipped Baal and provoked the LORD, the God of Israel, to anger, just as his father had done.

NEW TESTAMENT READING
Acts 19:14–41

[14]Seven sons of Sceva, a Jewish chief priest, were doing this. [15]One day, the evil spirit answered them, "Jesus I know, and I know about Paul, but who are you?" [16]Then the man who had the evil spirit jumped on them and overpowered them all. He gave them such a beating that they ran out of the house naked and bleeding.

[17]When this became known to the Jews and Greeks living in Ephesus, they were all seized with fear, and the name of the Lord Jesus was held in high honour. [18]Many of those who believed now came and openly confessed their evil deeds. [19]A number who had practised sorcery brought their scrolls together and burned them publicly. When they calculated the value of the scrolls, the total came to fifty thousand drachmas. [20]In this way the word of the Lord spread widely and grew in power.

[21]After all this had happened, Paul decided to go to Jerusalem, passing through Macedonia and Achaia. "After I have been there," he said, "I must visit Rome also." [22]He sent two of his helpers, Timothy and Erastus, to Macedonia, while he stayed in the province of Asia a little longer.

The Riot in Ephesus

[23]About that time there arose a great disturbance about the Way. [24]A silversmith named Demetrius, who made silver shrines of Artemis, brought in no little business for the craftsmen. [25]He called them together, along with the workmen in related trades, and said: "Men, you know we receive a good income from this business. [26]And you see and hear how this fellow Paul has convinced and led astray large numbers of people here in Ephesus and in practically the whole province of Asia. He says that man-made gods are no gods at all. [27]There is danger not only that our trade will lose its good name, but also that the temple of the great goddess Artemis will be discredited, and the goddess herself, who is worshipped throughout the province of Asia and the world, will be robbed of her divine majesty."

[28]When they heard this, they were furious and began shouting: "Great is Artemis of the Ephesians!" [29]Soon the whole city was in an uproar. The people seized Gaius and Aristarchus, Paul's travelling companions from Macedonia, and rushed as one man into the theatre. [30]Paul wanted to appear before the crowd, but the disciples would not let him. [31]Even some of the officials of the province, friends of Paul, sent him a message begging him not to venture into the theatre.

³²The assembly was in confusion: Some were shouting one thing, some another. Most of the people did not even know why they were there. ³³The Jews pushed Alexander to the front, and some of the crowd shouted instructions to him. He motioned for silence in order to make a defence before the people. ³⁴But when they realised he was a Jew, they all shouted in unison for about two hours: "Great is Artemis of the Ephesians!"

³⁵The city clerk quietened the crowd and said: "Men of Ephesus, doesn't all the world know that the city of Ephesus is the guardian of the temple of the great Artemis and of her image, which fell from heaven? ³⁶Therefore, since these facts are undeniable, you ought to be quiet and not do anything rash. ³⁷You have brought these men here, though they have neither robbed temples nor blasphemed our goddess. ³⁸If, then, Demetrius and his fellow craftsmen have a grievance against anybody, the courts are open and there are proconsuls. They can press charges. ³⁹If there is anything further you want to bring up, it must be settled in a legal assembly. ⁴⁰As it is, we are in danger of being charged with rioting because of today's events. In that case we would not be able to account for this commotion, since there is no reason for it." ⁴¹After he had said this, he dismissed the assembly.

READING FROM PROVERBS
Proverbs 15:31–16:7

³¹He who listens to a life-giving rebuke
    will be at home among the wise.

³²He who ignores discipline despises himself,
    but whoever heeds correction gains understanding.

³³The fear of the LORD teaches a man wisdom,
    and humility comes before honour.

16 To man belong the plans of the heart,
    but from the LORD comes the reply of the tongue.

²All a man's ways seem innocent to him,
    but motives are weighed by the LORD.

³Commit to the LORD whatever you do,
    and your plans will succeed.

⁴The LORD works out everything for his own ends—
    even the wicked for a day of disaster.

⁵The LORD detests all the proud of heart.
    Be sure of this: They will not go unpunished.

⁶Through love and faithfulness sin is atoned for;
    through the fear of the LORD a man avoids evil.

⁷When a man's ways are pleasing to the LORD,
    he makes even his enemies live at peace with him.

JUNE 30

OLD TESTAMENT READING
2 Kings 1:1–2:25

The LORD's Judgment on Ahaziah

1 After Ahab's death, Moab rebelled against Israel. ²Now Ahaziah had fallen through the lattice of his upper room in Samaria and injured himself. So he sent messengers, saying to them, "Go and consult Baal-Zebub, the god of Ekron, to see if I will recover from this injury."

³But the angel of the LORD said to Elijah the Tishbite, "Go up and meet the messengers of the king of Samaria and ask them, 'Is it because there is no God in Israel that you are going off to consult Baal-Zebub, the god of Ekron?' ⁴Therefore this is what the LORD says: 'You will not leave the bed you are lying on. You will certainly die!'" So Elijah went.

⁵When the messengers returned to the king, he asked them, "Why have you come back?"

⁶"A man came to meet us," they replied. "And he said to us, 'Go back to the king who sent you and tell him, "This is what the LORD says: Is it because there is no God in Israel that you are sending men to consult Baal-Zebub, the god of Ekron? Therefore you will not leave the bed you are lying on. You will certainly die!"'"

⁷The king asked them, "What kind of man was it who came to meet you and told you this?"

⁸They replied, "He was a man with a garment of hair and with a leather belt round his waist."

The king said, "That was Elijah the Tishbite."

⁹Then he sent to Elijah a captain with his company of fifty men. The captain went up to Elijah, who was sitting on the top of a hill, and said to him, "Man of God, the king says, 'Come down!'"

¹⁰Elijah answered the captain, "If I am a man of God, may fire come down from heaven and consume you and your fifty men!" Then the fire fell from heaven and consumed the captain and his men.

¹¹At this the king sent to Elijah another captain with his fifty men. The captain said to him, "Man of God, this is what the king says, 'Come down at once!'"

¹²"If I am a man of God," Elijah replied, "may fire come down from heaven and consume you and your fifty men!" Then the fire of God fell from heaven and consumed him and his fifty men.

¹³So the king sent a third captain with his fifty men. This third captain went up and fell on his knees before Elijah. "Man of God," he begged, "please have respect for my life and the lives of these fifty men, your servants! ¹⁴See, fire has fallen from heaven and consumed the first two captains and all their men. But now have respect for my life!"

¹⁵The angel of the LORD said to Elijah, "Go down with him; do not be afraid of him." So Elijah got up and went down with him to the king.

¹⁶He told the king, "This is what the LORD says: Is it because there is no God in Israel for you to consult that you have sent messengers to consult Baal-Zebub, the god of Ekron? Because you have done this, you will never leave the bed you are lying on. You will certainly die!" ¹⁷So he died, according to the word of the LORD that Elijah had spoken.

Because Ahaziah had no son, Joram succeeded him as king in the second year of Jehoram son of Jehoshaphat king of Judah. ¹⁸As for all the other events of Ahaziah's reign, and what he did, are they not written in the book of the annals of the kings of Israel?

Elijah Taken Up to Heaven

2 When the LORD was about to take Elijah up to heaven in a whirlwind, Elijah and Elisha were on their way from Gilgal. ²Elijah said to Elisha, "Stay here; the LORD has sent me to Bethel."

But Elisha said, "As surely as the LORD lives and as you live, I will not leave you." So they went down to Bethel.

³The company of the prophets at Bethel came out to Elisha and asked, "Do you know that the LORD is going to take your master from you today?"

"Yes, I know," Elisha replied, "but do not speak of it."

⁴Then Elijah said to him, "Stay here, Elisha; the LORD has sent me to Jericho."

And he replied, "As surely as the LORD lives and as you live, I will not leave you." So they went to Jericho.

⁵The company of the prophets at Jericho went up to Elisha and asked him, "Do you know that the LORD is going to take your master from you today?"

"Yes, I know," he replied, "but do not speak of it."

⁶Then Elijah said to him, "Stay here; the LORD has sent me to the Jordan."

And he replied, "As surely as the LORD lives and as you live, I will not leave you." So the two of them walked on.

⁷Fifty men of the company of the prophets went and stood at a distance, facing the place where Elijah and Elisha had stopped at the Jordan. ⁸Elijah took his cloak, rolled it up and struck the water with it. The water divided to the right and to the left, and the two of them crossed over on dry ground.

⁹When they had crossed, Elijah said to Elisha, "Tell me, what can I do for you before I am taken from you?"

"Let me inherit a double portion of your spirit," Elisha replied.

¹⁰"You have asked a difficult thing," Elijah said, "yet if you see me when I am taken from you, it will be yours —otherwise not."

¹¹As they were walking along and talking together, suddenly a chariot of fire and horses of fire appeared and separated the two of them, and Elijah went up to heaven in a whirlwind. ¹²Elisha saw this and cried out, "My father! My father! The chariots and horsemen of Israel!" And Elisha saw him no more. Then he took hold of his own clothes and tore them apart.

¹³He picked up the cloak that had fallen from Elijah and went back and stood on the bank of the Jordan. ¹⁴Then he took the cloak that had fallen from him and struck the water with it. "Where now is the LORD, the God of Elijah?" he asked. When he struck the water, it divided to the right and to the left, and he crossed over.

¹⁵The company of the prophets from Jericho, who were watching, said, "The spirit of Elijah is resting on Elisha." And they went to meet him and bowed to the ground before him. ¹⁶"Look," they said, "we your servants have fifty able men. Let them go and look for your master. Perhaps the Spirit of the LORD has picked him up and set him down on some mountain or in some valley."

"No," Elisha replied, "do not send them."

¹⁷But they persisted until he was too ashamed to refuse. So he said, "Send them." And they sent fifty men, who searched for three days but did not find him. ¹⁸When they returned to Elisha, who was staying in Jericho, he said to them, "Didn't I tell you not to go?"

Healing of the Water

¹⁹The men of the city said to Elisha, "Look, our lord, this town is well situated, as you can see, but the water is bad and the land is unproductive."

²⁰"Bring me a new bowl," he said, "and put salt in it." So they brought it to him.

²¹Then he went out to the spring and

threw the salt into it, saying, "This is what the LORD says: 'I have healed this water. Never again will it cause death or make the land unproductive.'" ²²And the water has remained wholesome to this day, according to the word Elisha had spoken.

Elisha Is Jeered

²³From there Elisha went up to Bethel. As he was walking along the road, some youths came out of the town and jeered at him. "Go on up, you baldhead!" they said. "Go on up, you baldhead!" ²⁴He turned round, looked at them and called down a curse on them in the name of the LORD. Then two bears came out of the woods and mauled forty-two of the youths. ²⁵And he went on to Mount Carmel and from there returned to Samaria.

NEW TESTAMENT READING
Acts 20:1–38

Through Macedonia and Greece

20 When the uproar had ended, Paul sent for the disciples and, after encouraging them, said good-bye and set out for Macedonia. ²He travelled through that area, speaking many words of encouragement to the people, and finally arrived in Greece, ³where he stayed three months. Because the Jews made a plot against him just as he was about to sail for Syria, he decided to go back through Macedonia. ⁴He was accompanied by Sopater son of Pyrrhus from Berea, Aristarchus and Secundus from Thessalonica, Gaius from Derbe, Timothy also, and Tychicus and Trophimus from the province of Asia. ⁵These men went on ahead and waited for us at Troas. ⁶But we sailed from Philippi after the Feast of Unleavened Bread, and five days later joined the others at Troas, where we stayed seven days.

Eutychus Raised From the Dead at Troas

⁷On the first day of the week we came together to break bread. Paul spoke to the people and, because he intended to leave the next day, kept on talking until midnight. ⁸There were many lamps in the upstairs room where we were meeting. ⁹Seated in a window was a young man named Eutychus, who was sinking into a deep sleep as Paul talked on and on. When he was sound asleep, he fell to the ground from the third storey and was picked up dead. ¹⁰Paul went down, threw himself on the young man and put his arms around him. "Don't be alarmed," he said. "He's alive!" ¹¹Then he went upstairs again and broke bread and ate. After talking until daylight, he left. ¹²The people took the young man home alive and were greatly comforted.

Paul's Farewell to the Ephesian Elders

¹³We went on ahead to the ship and sailed for Assos, where we were going to take Paul aboard. He had made this arrangement because he was going there on foot. ¹⁴When he met us at Assos, we took him aboard and went on to Mitylene. ¹⁵The next day we set sail from there and arrived off Kios. The day after that we crossed over to Samos, and on the following day arrived at Miletus. ¹⁶Paul had decided to sail past Ephesus to avoid spending time in the province of Asia, for he was in a hurry to reach Jerusalem, if possible, by the day of Pentecost.

¹⁷From Miletus, Paul sent to Ephesus for the elders of the church. ¹⁸When they arrived, he said to them: "You know how I lived the whole time I was with you, from the first day I came into the province of Asia. ¹⁹I served the Lord with great humility and with tears, although I was severely tested by the plots of the Jews. ²⁰You know that I have not hesitated to preach anything that would be helpful to you but have

taught you publicly and from house to house. ²¹I have declared to both Jews and Greeks that they must turn to God in repentance and have faith in our Lord Jesus.

²²"And now, compelled by the Spirit, I am going to Jerusalem, not knowing what will happen to me there. ²³I only know that in every city the Holy Spirit warns me that prison and hardships are facing me. ²⁴However, I consider my life worth nothing to me, if only I may finish the race and complete the task the Lord Jesus has given me—the task of testifying to the gospel of God's grace.

²⁵"Now I know that none of you among whom I have gone about preaching the kingdom will ever see me again. ²⁶Therefore, I declare to you today that I am innocent of the blood of all men. ²⁷For I have not hesitated to proclaim to you the whole will of God. ²⁸Keep watch over yourselves and all the flock of which the Holy Spirit has made you overseers. Be shepherds of the church of God, which he bought with his own blood. ²⁹I know that after I leave, savage wolves will come in among you and will not spare the flock. ³⁰Even from your own number men will arise and distort the truth in order to draw away disciples after them. ³¹So be on your guard! Remember that for three years I never stopped warning each of you night and day with tears.

³²"Now I commit you to God and to the word of his grace, which can build you up and give you an inheritance among all those who are sanctified. ³³I have not coveted anyone's silver or gold or clothing. ³⁴You yourselves know that these hands of mine have supplied my own needs and the needs of my companions. ³⁵In everything I did, I showed you that by this kind of hard work we must help the weak, remembering the words the Lord Jesus himself said: 'It is more blessed to give than to receive.'"

³⁶When he had said this, he knelt down with all of them and prayed. ³⁷They all wept as they embraced him and kissed him. ³⁸What grieved them most was his statement that they would never see his face again. Then they accompanied him to the ship.

READING FROM PSALMS
Psalm 78:40–55

⁴⁰How often they rebelled against him
    in the desert
  and grieved him in the wasteland!
⁴¹Again and again they put God to the
    test;
  they vexed the Holy One of Israel.
⁴²They did not remember his power—
  the day he redeemed them from
    the oppressor,
⁴³the day he displayed his miraculous
    signs in Egypt,
  his wonders in the region of Zoan.
⁴⁴He turned their rivers to blood;
  they could not drink from their
    streams.
⁴⁵He sent swarms of flies that devoured
    them,
  and frogs that devastated them.
⁴⁶He gave their crops to the
    grasshopper,
  their produce to the locust.
⁴⁷He destroyed their vines with hail
  and their sycamore-figs with sleet.
⁴⁸He gave over their cattle to the hail,
  their livestock to bolts of lightning.
⁴⁹He unleashed against them his hot
    anger,
  his wrath, indignation and
    hostility—
  a band of destroying angels.
⁵⁰He prepared a path for his anger;
  he did not spare them from death
  but gave them over to the plague.
⁵¹He struck down all the firstborn of
    Egypt,
  the firstfruits of manhood in the
    tents of Ham.
⁵²But he brought his people out like a
    flock;
  he led them like sheep through the
    desert.
⁵³He guided them safely, so they were
    unafraid;

but the sea engulfed their enemies.
⁵⁴Thus he brought them to the border
    of his holy land,
to the hill country his right hand
    had taken.

⁵⁵He drove out nations before them
    and allotted their lands to them as
        an inheritance;
he settled the tribes of Israel in
    their homes.

DAY 182

JULY 1

OLD TESTAMENT READING
2 Kings 3:1–4:37

Moab Revolts

3 Joram son of Ahab became king of
Israel in Samaria in the eighteenth
year of Jehoshaphat king of Judah, and
he reigned for twelve years. ²He did evil
in the eyes of the LORD, but not as his
father and mother had done. He got rid
of the sacred stone of Baal that his
father had made. ³Nevertheless he
clung to the sins of Jeroboam son of
Nebat, which he had caused Israel to
commit; he did not turn away from
them.

⁴Now Mesha king of Moab raised
sheep, and he had to supply the king of
Israel with a hundred thousand lambs
and with the wool of a hundred
thousand rams. ⁵But after Ahab died,
the king of Moab rebelled against the
king of Israel. ⁶So at that time King
Joram set out from Samaria and mobilised all Israel. ⁷He also sent this message to Jehoshaphat king of Judah:
"The king of Moab has rebelled against
me. Will you go with me to fight against
Moab?"

"I will go with you," he replied. "I am
as you are, my people as your people,
my horses as your horses."

⁸"By what route shall we attack?" he
asked.

"Through the Desert of Edom," he
answered.

⁹So the king of Israel set out with the
king of Judah and the king of Edom.
After a roundabout march of seven

days, the army had no more water for
themselves or for the animals with
them.

¹⁰"What!" exclaimed the king of
Israel. "Has the LORD called us three
kings together only to hand us over to
Moab?"

¹¹But Jehoshaphat asked, "Is there
no prophet of the LORD here, that we
may enquire of the LORD through
him?"

An officer of the king of Israel
answered, "Elisha son of Shaphat is
here. He used to pour water on the
hands of Elijah."

¹²Jehoshaphat said, "The word of the
LORD is with him." So the king of Israel
and Jehoshaphat and the king of Edom
went down to him.

¹³Elisha said to the king of Israel,
"What do we have to do with each
other? Go to the prophets of your father
and the prophets of your mother."

"No," the king of Israel answered,
"because it was the LORD who called us
three kings together to hand us over to
Moab."

¹⁴Elisha said, "As surely as the LORD
Almighty lives, whom I serve, if I did
not have respect for the presence of
Jehoshaphat king of Judah, I would not
look at you or even notice you. ¹⁵But
now bring me a harpist."

While the harpist was playing, the
hand of the LORD came upon Elisha
¹⁶and he said, "This is what the LORD
says: Make this valley full of ditches.
¹⁷For this is what the LORD says: You
will see neither wind nor rain, yet this
valley will be filled with water, and you,

your cattle and your other animals will drink. ¹⁸This is an easy thing in the eyes of the LORD; he will also hand Moab over to you. ¹⁹You will overthrow every fortified city and every major town. You will cut down every good tree, stop up all the springs, and ruin every good field with stones."

²⁰The next morning, about the time for offering the sacrifice, there it was —water flowing from the direction of Edom! And the land was filled with water.

²¹Now all the Moabites had heard that the kings had come to fight against them; so every man, young and old, who could bear arms was called up and stationed on the border. ²²When they got up early in the morning, the sun was shining on the water. To the Moabites across the way, the water looked red —like blood. ²³"That's blood!" they said. "Those kings must have fought and slaughtered each other. Now to the plunder, Moab!"

²⁴But when the Moabites came to the camp of Israel, the Israelites rose up and fought them until they fled. And the Israelites invaded the land and slaughtered the Moabites. ²⁵They destroyed the towns, and each man threw a stone on every good field until it was covered. They stopped up all the springs and cut down every good tree. Only Kir Hareseth was left with its stones in place, but men armed with slings surrounded it and attacked it as well.

²⁶When the king of Moab saw that the battle had gone against him, he took with him seven hundred swordsmen to break through to the king of Edom, but they failed. ²⁷Then he took his firstborn son, who was to succeed him as king, and offered him as a sacrifice on the city wall. The fury against Israel was great; they withdrew and returned to their own land.

The Widow's Oil

4 The wife of a man from the company of the prophets cried out to Elisha, "Your servant my husband is dead, and you know that he revered the LORD. But now his creditor is coming to take my two boys as his slaves."

²Elisha replied to her, "How can I help you? Tell me, what do you have in your house?"

"Your servant has nothing there at all," she said, "except a little oil."

³Elisha said, "Go round and ask all your neighbours for empty jars. Don't ask for just a few. ⁴Then go inside and shut the door behind you and your sons. Pour oil into all the jars, and as each is filled, put it to one side."

⁵She left him and afterwards shut the door behind her and her sons. They brought the jars to her and she kept pouring. ⁶When all the jars were full, she said to her son, "Bring me another one."

But he replied, "There is not a jar left." Then the oil stopped flowing.

⁷She went and told the man of God, and he said, "Go, sell the oil and pay your debts. You and your sons can live on what is left."

The Shunammite's Son Restored to Life

⁸One day Elisha went to Shunem. And a well-to-do woman was there, who urged him to stay for a meal. So whenever he came by, he stopped there to eat. ⁹She said to her husband, "I know that this man who often comes our way is a holy man of God. ¹⁰Let's make a small room on the roof and put in it a bed and a table, a chair and a lamp for him. Then he can stay there whenever he comes to us."

¹¹One day when Elisha came, he went up to his room and lay down there. ¹²He said to his servant Gehazi, "Call the Shunammite." So he called her, and she stood before him. ¹³Elisha said to him, "Tell her, 'You have gone to all this trouble for us. Now what can be done for you? Can we speak on your behalf to the king or the commander of the army?'"

She replied, "I have a home among my own people."

¹⁴"What can be done for her?" Elisha asked.

Gehazi said, "Well, she has no son and her husband is old."

¹⁵Then Elisha said, "Call her." So he called her, and she stood in the doorway. ¹⁶"About this time next year," Elisha said, "you will hold a son in your arms."

"No, my lord," she objected. "Don't mislead your servant, O man of God!"

¹⁷But the woman became pregnant, and the next year about that same time she gave birth to a son, just as Elisha had told her.

¹⁸The child grew, and one day he went out to his father, who was with the reapers. ¹⁹"My head! My head!" he said to his father.

His father told a servant, "Carry him to his mother." ²⁰After the servant had lifted him up and carried him to his mother, the boy sat on her lap until noon, and then he died. ²¹She went up and laid him on the bed of the man of God, then shut the door and went out.

²²She called her husband and said, "Please send me one of the servants and a donkey so I can go to the man of God quickly and return."

²³"Why go to him today?" he asked. "It's not the New Moon or the Sabbath."

"It's all right," she said.

²⁴She saddled the donkey and said to her servant, "Lead on; don't slow down for me unless I tell you." ²⁵So she set out and came to the man of God at Mount Carmel.

When she saw her in the distance, the man of God said to his servant Gehazi, "Look! There's the Shunammite! ²⁶Run to meet her and ask her, 'Are you all right? Is your husband all right? Is your child all right?'"

"Everything is all right," she said.

²⁷When she reached the man of God at the mountain, she took hold of his feet. Gehazi came over to push her away, but the man of God said, "Leave her alone! She is in bitter distress, but the LORD has hidden it from me and has not told me why."

²⁸"Did I ask you for a son, my lord?" she said. "Didn't I tell you, 'Don't raise my hopes'?"

²⁹Elisha said to Gehazi, "Tuck your cloak into your belt, take my staff in your hand and run. If you meet anyone, do not greet him, and if anyone greets you, do not answer. Lay my staff on the boy's face."

³⁰But the child's mother said, "As surely as the LORD lives and as you live, I will not leave you." So he got up and followed her.

³¹Gehazi went on ahead and laid the staff on the boy's face, but there was no sound or response. So Gehazi went back to meet Elisha and told him, "The boy has not awakened."

³²When Elisha reached the house, there was the boy lying dead on his couch. ³³He went in, shut the door on the two of them and prayed to the LORD. ³⁴Then he got on the bed and lay upon the boy, mouth to mouth, eyes to eyes, hands to hands. As he stretched himself out upon him, the boy's body grew warm. ³⁵Elisha turned away and walked back and forth in the room and then got onto the bed and stretched out upon him once more. The boy sneezed seven times and opened his eyes.

³⁶Elisha summoned Gehazi and said, "Call the Shunammite." And he did. When she came, he said, "Take your son." ³⁷She came in, fell at his feet and bowed to the ground. Then she took her son and went out.

NEW TESTAMENT READING
Acts 21:1–26

On to Jerusalem

21 After we had torn ourselves away from them, we put out to sea and sailed straight to Cos. The next day we went to Rhodes and from there to Patara. ²We found a ship crossing over to Phoenicia, went on board and set sail. ³After sighting Cyprus and passing to the south of it, we sailed on to Syria. We landed at Tyre, where our ship was to unload its cargo. 4Finding the disciples there, we stayed with them seven days. Through the Spirit they urged Paul not to go on to Jerusalem. 5But when our time was up, we left and continued on our way. All the disciples and their wives and children accompanied us out of the city, and there on the beach we knelt to pray. 6After saying good-bye to each other, we went aboard the ship, and they returned home.

7We continued our voyage from Tyre and landed at Ptolemais, where we greeted the brothers and stayed with them for a day. 8Leaving the next day, we reached Caesarea and stayed at the house of Philip the evangelist, one of the Seven. 9He had four unmarried daughters who prophesied.

10After we had been there a number of days, a prophet named Agabus came down from Judea. 11Coming over to us, he took Paul's belt, tied his own hands and feet with it and said, "The Holy Spirit says, 'In this way the Jews of Jerusalem will bind the owner of this belt and will hand him over to the Gentiles.'"

12When we heard this, we and the people there pleaded with Paul not to go up to Jerusalem. 13Then Paul answered, "Why are you weeping and breaking my heart? I am ready not only to be bound, but also to die in Jerusalem for the name of the Lord Jesus." 14When he would not be dissuaded, we gave up and said, "The Lord's will be done."

15After this, we got ready and went up to Jerusalem. 16Some of the disciples from Caesarea accompanied us and brought us to the home of Mnason, where we were to stay. He was a man from Cyprus and one of the early disciples.

Paul's Arrival at Jerusalem

17When we arrived at Jerusalem, the brothers received us warmly. 18The next day Paul and the rest of us went to see James, and all the elders were present. 19Paul greeted them and reported in detail what God had done among the Gentiles through his ministry.

20When they heard this, they praised God. Then they said to Paul: "You see, brother, how many thousands of Jews have believed, and all of them are zealous for the law. 21They have been informed that you teach all the Jews who live among the Gentiles to turn away from Moses, telling them not to circumcise their children or live according to our customs. 22What shall we do? They will certainly hear that you have come, 23so do what we tell you. There are four men with us who have made a vow. 24Take these men, join in their purification rites and pay their expenses, so that they can have their heads shaved. Then everybody will know there is no truth in these reports about you, but that you yourself are living in obedience to the law. 25As for the Gentile believers, we have written to them our decision that they should abstain from food sacrificed to idols, from blood, from the meat of strangled animals and from sexual immorality."

26The next day Paul took the men and purified himself along with them. Then he went to the temple to give notice of the date when the days of purification would end and the offering would be made for each of them.

READING FROM PSALMS
Psalm 78:56–72

56But they put God to the test
and rebelled against the Most
High;
they did not keep his statutes.
57Like their fathers they were disloyal
and faithless,
as unreliable as a faulty bow.
58They angered him with their high
places;

they aroused his jealousy with their
  idols.

⁵⁹When God heard them, he was very
  angry;
  he rejected Israel completely.

⁶⁰He abandoned the tabernacle of
  Shiloh,
  the tent he had set up among men.

⁶¹He sent ⌊the ark of⌋ his might into
  captivity,
  his splendour into the hands of the
  enemy.

⁶²He gave his people over to the sword;
  he was very angry with his
  inheritance.

⁶³Fire consumed their young men,
  and their maidens had no wedding
  songs;

⁶⁴their priests were put to the sword,
  and their widows could not weep.

⁶⁵Then the Lord awoke as from
  sleep,

as a man wakes from the stupor of
  wine.

⁶⁶He beat back his enemies;
  he put them to everlasting shame.

⁶⁷Then he rejected the tents of Joseph,
  he did not choose the tribe of
  Ephraim;

⁶⁸but he chose the tribe of Judah,
  Mount Zion, which he loved.

⁶⁹He built his sanctuary like the
  heights,
  like the earth that he established
  for ever.

⁷⁰He chose David his servant
  and took him from the sheep pens;

⁷¹from tending the sheep he brought
  him
  to be the shepherd of his people
  Jacob,
  of Israel his inheritance.

⁷²And David shepherded them with
  integrity of heart;
  with skilful hands he led them.

DAY 183

JULY 2

OLD TESTAMENT READING
2 Kings 4:38–6:23

Death in the Pot

³⁸Elisha returned to Gilgal and there
was a famine in that region. While the
company of the prophets was meeting
with him, he said to his servant, "Put on
the large pot and cook some stew for
these men."

³⁹One of them went out into the fields
to gather herbs and found a wild vine.
He gathered some of its gourds and
filled the fold of his cloak. When he
returned, he cut them up into the pot of
stew, though no-one knew what they
were. ⁴⁰The stew was poured out for the
men, but as they began to eat it, they
cried out, "O man of God, there is
death in the pot!" And they could not
eat it.

⁴¹Elisha said, "Get some flour." He
put it into the pot and said, "Serve it to
the people to eat." And there was nothing harmful in the pot.

Feeding of a Hundred

⁴²A man came from Baal Shalishah,
bringing the man of God twenty loaves
of barley bread baked from the first ripe
corn, along with some ears of new corn.
"Give it to the people to eat," Elisha
said.

⁴³"How can I set this before a hundred men?" his servant asked.

But Elisha answered, "Give it to the
people to eat. For this is what the LORD
says: 'They will eat and have some left
over.'" ⁴⁴Then he set it before them,
and they ate and had some left over,
according to the word of the LORD.

Naaman Healed of Leprosy

5 Now Naaman was commander of the army of the king of Aram. He was a great man in the sight of his master and highly regarded, because through him the LORD had given victory to Aram. He was a valiant soldier, but he had leprosy.

2Now bands from Aram had gone out and had taken captive a young girl from Israel, and she served Naaman's wife. 3She said to her mistress, "If only my master would see the prophet who is in Samaria! He would cure him of his leprosy."

4Naaman went to his master and told him what the girl from Israel had said. 5"By all means, go," the king of Aram replied. "I will send a letter to the king of Israel." So Naaman left, taking with him ten talents of silver, six thousand shekels of gold and ten sets of clothing. 6The letter that he took to the king of Israel read: "With this letter I am sending my servant Naaman to you so that you may cure him of his leprosy."

7As soon as the king of Israel read the letter, he tore his robes and said, "Am I God? Can I kill and bring back to life? Why does this fellow send someone to me to be cured of his leprosy? See how he is trying to pick a quarrel with me!"

8When Elisha the man of God heard that the king of Israel had torn his robes, he sent him this message: "Why have you torn your robes? Make the man come to me and he will know that there is a prophet in Israel." 9So Naaman went with his horses and chariots and stopped at the door of Elisha's house. 10Elisha sent a messenger to say to him, "Go, wash yourself seven times in the Jordan, and your flesh will be restored and you will be cleansed."

11But Naaman went away angry and said, "I thought that he would surely come out to me and stand and call on the name of the LORD his God, wave his hand over the spot and cure me of my leprosy. 12Are not Abana and Pharpar, the rivers of Damascus, better than any

of the waters of Israel? Couldn't I wash in them and be cleansed?" So he turned and went off in a rage.

13Naaman's servants went to him and said, "My father, if the prophet had told you to do some great thing, would you not have done it? How much more, then, when he tells you, 'Wash and be cleansed'?" 14So he went down and dipped himself in the Jordan seven times, as the man of God had told him, and his flesh was restored and became clean like that of a young boy.

15Then Naaman and all his attendants went back to the man of God. He stood before him and said, "Now I know that there is no God in all the world except in Israel. Please accept now a gift from your servant."

16The prophet answered, "As surely as the LORD lives, whom I serve, I will not accept a thing." And even though Naaman urged him, he refused.

17"If you will not," said Naaman, "please let me, your servant, be given as much earth as a pair of mules can carry, for your servant will never again make burnt offerings and sacrifices to any other god but the LORD. 18But may the LORD forgive your servant for this one thing: When my master enters the temple of Rimmon to bow down and he is leaning on my arm and I bow there also—when I bow down in the temple of Rimmon, may the LORD forgive your servant for this."

19"Go in peace," Elisha said.

After Naaman had travelled some distance, 20Gehazi, the servant of Elisha the man of God, said to himself, "My master was too easy on Naaman, this Aramean, by not accepting from him what he brought. As surely as the LORD lives, I will run after him and get something from him."

21So Gehazi hurried after Naaman. When Naaman saw him running towards him, he got down from the chariot to meet him. "Is everything all right?" he asked.

22"Everything is all right," Gehazi answered. "My master sent me to say,

'Two young men from the company of the prophets have just come to me from the hill country of Ephraim. Please give them a talent of silver and two sets of clothing.'"

23"By all means, take two talents," said Naaman. He urged Gehazi to accept them, and then tied up the two talents of silver in two bags, with two sets of clothing. He gave them to two of his servants, and they carried them ahead of Gehazi. 24When Gehazi came to the hill, he took the things from the servants and put them away in the house. He sent the men away and they left. 25Then he went in and stood before his master Elisha.

"Where have you been, Gehazi?" Elisha asked.

"Your servant didn't go anywhere," Gehazi answered.

26But Elisha said to him, "Was not my spirit with you when the man got down from his chariot to meet you? Is this the time to take money, or to accept clothes, olive groves, vineyards, flocks, herds, or menservants and maidservants? 27Naaman's leprosy will cling to you and to your descendants for ever." Then Gehazi went from Elisha's presence and he was leprous, as white as snow.

An Axe-Head Floats

6 The company of the prophets said to Elisha, "Look, the place where we meet with you is too small for us. 2Let us go to the Jordan, where each of us can get a pole; and let us build a place there for us to live."

And he said, "Go."

3Then one of them said, "Won't you please come with your servants?"

"I will," Elisha replied. 4And he went with them.

They went to the Jordan and began to cut down trees. 5As one of them was cutting down a tree, the iron axe-head fell into the water. "Oh, my lord," he cried out, "it was borrowed!"

6The man of God asked, "Where did it fall?" When he showed him the place, Elisha cut a stick and threw it there, and made the iron float. 7"Lift it out," he said. Then the man reached out his hand and took it.

Elisha Traps Blinded Arameans

8Now the king of Aram was at war with Israel. After conferring with his officers, he said, "I will set up my camp in such and such a place."

9The man of God sent word to the king of Israel: "Beware of passing that place, because the Arameans are going down there." 10So the king of Israel checked on the place indicated by the man of God. Time and again Elisha warned the king, so that he was on his guard in such places.

11This enraged the king of Aram. He summoned his officers and demanded of them, "Will you not tell me which of us is on the side of the king of Israel?"

12"None of us, my lord the king," said one of his officers, "but Elisha, the prophet who is in Israel, tells the king of Israel the very words you speak in your bedroom."

13"Go, find out where he is," the king ordered, "so that I can send men and capture him." The report came back: "He is in Dothan." 14Then he sent horses and chariots and a strong force there. They went by night and surrounded the city.

15When the servant of the man of God got up and went out early the next morning, an army with horses and chariots had surrounded the city. "Oh, my lord, what shall we do?" the servant asked.

16"Don't be afraid," the prophet answered. "Those who are with us are more than those who are with them."

17And Elisha prayed, "O LORD, open his eyes so that he may see." Then the LORD opened the servant's eyes, and he looked and saw the hills full of horses and chariots of fire all round Elisha. 18As the enemy came down towards him, Elisha prayed to the LORD, "Strike these people with blindness." So he struck them with blindness, as Elisha had asked.

19Elisha told them, "This is not the road and this is not the city. Follow me, and I will lead you to the man you are looking for." And he led them to Samaria.

20After they entered the city, Elisha said, "LORD, open the eyes of these men so that they can see." Then the LORD opened their eyes and they looked, and there they were, inside Samaria.

21When the king of Israel saw them, he asked Elisha, "Shall I kill them, my father? Shall I kill them?"

22"Do not kill them," he answered. "Would you kill men you have captured with your own sword or bow? Set food and water before them so that they may eat and drink and then go back to their master." 23So he prepared a great feast for them, and after they had finished eating and drinking, he sent them away, and they returned to their master. So the bands from Aram stopped raiding Israel's territory.

NEW TESTAMENT READING
Acts 21:27–22:21

Paul Arrested

27When the seven days were nearly over, some Jews from the province of Asia saw Paul at the temple. They stirred up the whole crowd and seized him, 28shouting, "Men of Israel, help us! This is the man who teaches all men everywhere against our people and our law and this place. And besides, he has brought Greeks into the temple area and defiled this holy place." 29(They had previously seen Trophimus the Ephesian in the city with Paul and assumed that Paul had brought him into the temple area.)

30The whole city was aroused, and the people came running from all directions. Seizing Paul, they dragged him

from the temple, and immediately the gates were shut. 31While they were trying to kill him, news reached the commander of the Roman troops that the whole city of Jerusalem was in an uproar. 32He at once took some officers and soldiers and ran down to the crowd. When the rioters saw the commander and his soldiers, they stopped beating Paul.

33The commander came up and arrested him and ordered him to be bound with two chains. Then he asked who he was and what he had done. 34Some in the crowd shouted one thing and some another, and since the commander could not get at the truth because of the uproar, he ordered that Paul be taken into the barracks. 35When Paul reached the steps, the violence of the mob was so great he had to be carried by the soldiers. 36The crowd that followed kept shouting, "Away with him!"

Paul Speaks to the Crowd

37As the soldiers were about to take Paul into the barracks, he asked the commander, "May I say something to you?"

"Do you speak Greek?" he replied. 38"Aren't you the Egyptian who started a revolt and led four thousand terrorists out into the desert some time ago?"

39Paul answered, "I am a Jew, from Tarsus in Cilicia, a citizen of no ordinary city. Please let me speak to the people."

40Having received the commander's permission, Paul stood on the steps and motioned to the crowd. When they were all silent, he said to them 22 in Aramaic: 1"Brothers and fathers, listen now to my defence."

2When they heard him speak to them in Aramaic, they became very quiet.

Then Paul said: 3"I am a Jew, born in Tarsus of Cilicia, but brought up in this city. Under Gamaliel I was thoroughly trained in the law of our fathers and was just as zealous for God as any of you are today. [4]I persecuted the followers of this Way to their death, arresting both men and women and throwing them into prison, [5]as also the high priest and all the Council can testify. I even obtained letters from them to their brothers in Damascus, and went there to bring these people as prisoners to Jerusalem to be punished.

[6]"About noon as I came near Damascus, suddenly a bright light from heaven flashed around me. [7]I fell to the ground and heard a voice say to me, 'Saul! Saul! Why do you persecute me?'

[8]"'Who are you, Lord?' I asked.

"'I am Jesus of Nazareth, whom you are persecuting,' he replied. [9]My companions saw the light, but they did not understand the voice of him who was speaking to me.

[10]"'What shall I do, Lord?' I asked.

"'Get up,' the Lord said, 'and go into Damascus. There you will be told all that you have been assigned to do.' [11]My companions led me by the hand into Damascus, because the brilliance of the light had blinded me.

[12]"A man named Ananias came to see me. He was a devout observer of the law and highly respected by all the Jews living there. [13]He stood beside me and said, 'Brother Saul, receive your sight!' And at that very moment I was able to see him.

[14]"Then he said: 'The God of our fathers has chosen you to know his will and to see the Righteous One and to hear words from his mouth. [15]You will be his witness to all men of what you have seen and heard. [16]And now what are you waiting for? Get up, be baptised and wash your sins away, calling on his name.'

[17]"When I returned to Jerusalem and was praying at the temple, I fell into a trance [18]and saw the Lord speaking. 'Quick!' he said to me. 'Leave Jerusalem immediately, because they will not accept your testimony about me.'

[19]"'Lord,' I replied, 'these men know that I went from one synagogue to another to imprison and beat those who believe in you. [20]And when the blood of your martyr Stephen was shed, I stood there giving my approval and guarding the clothes of those who were killing him.'

[21]"Then the Lord said to me, 'Go; I will send you far away to the Gentiles.'"

READING FROM PSALMS
Psalm 79:1–13

A psalm of Asaph.

[1]O God, the nations have invaded
your inheritance;
they have defiled your holy temple,
they have reduced Jerusalem to
rubble.
[2]They have given the dead bodies of
your servants
as food to the birds of the air,
the flesh of your saints to the beasts
of the earth.
[3]They have poured out blood like
water
all around Jerusalem,
and there is no-one to bury the
dead.
[4]We are objects of reproach to our
neighbours,
of scorn and derision to those
around us.

[5]How long, O LORD? Will you be
angry for ever?
How long will your jealousy burn
like fire?
[6]Pour out your wrath on the nations
that do not acknowledge you,
on the kingdoms
that do not call on your name;
[7]for they have devoured Jacob
and destroyed his homeland.
[8]Do not hold against us the sins of the
fathers;
may your mercy come quickly to
meet us,
for we are in desperate need.

9Help us, O God our Saviour,
  for the glory of your name;
 deliver us and forgive our sins
  for your name's sake.
10Why should the nations say,
  "Where is their God?"
 Before our eyes, make known among
  the nations
  that you avenge the outpoured
  blood of your servants.
11May the groans of the prisoners come
  before you;

by the strength of your arm
 preserve those condemned to die.

12Pay back into the laps of our
  neighbours seven times
 the reproach they have hurled at
  you, O Lord.
13Then we your people, the sheep of
  your pasture,
 will praise you for ever;
 from generation to generation
  we will recount your praise.

JULY 3 DAY 184

OLD TESTAMENT READING
2 Kings 6:24—8:15

Famine in Besieged Samaria

24Some time later, Ben-Hadad king
of Aram mobilised his entire army and
marched up and laid siege to Samaria.
25There was a great famine in the city;
the siege lasted so long that a donkey's
head sold for eighty shekels of silver,
and a fourth of a cab of seed pods for five
shekels.

26As the king of Israel was passing by
on the wall, a woman cried to him,
"Help me, my lord the king!"

27The king replied, "If the LORD does
not help you, where can I get help for
you? From the threshing-floor? From
the winepress?" 28Then he asked her,
"What's the matter?"

She answered, "This woman said to
me, 'Give up your son so that we may
eat him today, and tomorrow we'll eat
my son.' 29So we cooked my son and ate
him. The next day I said to her, 'Give up
your son so that we may eat him,' but
she had hidden him."

30When the king heard the woman's
words, he tore his robes. As he went
along the wall, the people looked, and
there, underneath, he had sackcloth on
his body. 31He said, "May God deal

with me, be it ever so severely, if the
head of Elisha son of Shaphat remains
on his shoulders today!"

32Now Elisha was sitting in his house,
and the elders were sitting with him.
The king sent a messenger ahead, but
before he arrived, Elisha said to the
elders, "Don't you see how this murderer is sending someone to cut off
my head? Look, when the messenger
comes, shut the door and hold it shut
against him. Is not the sound of his
master's footsteps behind him?"

33While he was still talking to them,
the messenger came down to him. And
ˌthe kingˌ said, "This disaster is from
the LORD. Why should I wait for the
LORD any longer?"

7 Elisha said, "Hear the word of the
LORD. This is what the LORD says:
About this time tomorrow, a seah of
flour will sell for a shekel and two seahs
of barley for a shekel at the gate of
Samaria."

2The officer on whose arm the king
was leaning said to the man of God,
"Look, even if the LORD should open
the floodgates of the heavens, could this
happen?"

"You will see it with your own eyes,"
answered Elisha, "but you will not eat
any of it!"

The Siege Lifted

3Now there were four men with leprosy at the entrance of the city gate. They said to each other, "Why stay here until we die? 4If we say, 'We'll go into the city'—the famine is there, and we will die. And if we stay here, we will die. So let's go over to the camp of the Arameans and surrender. If they spare us, we live; if they kill us, then we die."

5At dusk they got up and went to the camp of the Arameans. When they reached the edge of the camp, not a man was there, 6for the Lord had caused the Arameans to hear the sound of chariots and horses and a great army, so that they said to one another, "Look, the king of Israel has hired the Hittite and Egyptian kings to attack us!" 7So they got up and fled in the dusk and abandoned their tents and their horses and donkeys. They left the camp as it was and ran for their lives.

8The men who had leprosy reached the edge of the camp and entered one of the tents. They ate and drank, and carried away silver, gold and clothes, and went off and hid them. They returned and entered another tent and took some things from it and hid them also.

9Then they said to each other, "We're not doing right. This is a day of good news and we are keeping it to ourselves. If we wait until daylight, punishment will overtake us. Let's go at once and report this to the royal palace."

10So they went and called out to the city gatekeepers and told them, "We went into the Aramean camp and not a man was there—not a sound of anyone —only tethered horses and donkeys, and the tents left just as they were."

11The gatekeepers shouted the news, and it was reported within the palace.

12The king got up in the night and said to his officers, "I will tell you what the Arameans have done to us. They know we are starving; so they have left the camp to hide in the countryside, thinking, 'They will surely come out, and then we will take them alive and get into the city.'"

13One of his officers answered, "Make some men take five of the horses that are left in the city. Their plight will be like that of all the Israelites left here —yes, they will only be like all these Israelites who are doomed. So let us send them to find out what happened."

14So they selected two chariots with their horses, and the king sent them after the Aramean army. He commanded the drivers, "Go and find out what has happened." 15They followed them as far as the Jordan, and they found the whole road strewn with the clothing and equipment the Arameans had thrown away in their headlong flight. So the messengers returned and reported to the king. 16Then the people went out and plundered the camp of the Arameans. So a seah of flour sold for a shekel, and two seahs of barley sold for a shekel, as the LORD had said.

17Now the king had put the officer on whose arm he leaned in charge of the gate, and the people trampled him in the gateway, and he died, just as the man of God had foretold when the king came down to his house. 18It happened as the man of God had said to the king: "About this time tomorrow, a seah of flour will sell for a shekel and two seahs of barley for a shekel at the gate of Samaria."

19The officer had said to the man of God, "Look, even if the LORD should open the floodgates of the heavens, could this happen?" The man of God had replied, "You will see it with your own eyes, but you will not eat any of it!" 20And that is exactly what happened to him, for the people trampled him in the gateway, and he died.

The Shunammite's Land Restored

8 Now Elisha had said to the woman whose son he had restored to life, "Go away with your family and stay for a while wherever you can, because the LORD has decreed a famine in the land

that will last seven years." [2]The woman proceeded to do as the man of God said. She and her family went away and stayed in the land of the Philistines for seven years.

[3]At the end of the seven years she came back from the land of the Philistines and went to the king to beg for her house and land. [4]The king was talking to Gehazi, the servant of the man of God, and had said, "Tell me about all the great things Elisha has done." [5]Just as Gehazi was telling the king how Elisha had restored the dead to life, the woman whose son Elisha had brought back to life came to beg the king for her house and land.

Gehazi said, "This is the woman, my lord the king, and this is her son whom Elisha restored to life." [6]The king asked the woman about it, and she told him.

Then he assigned an official to her case and said to him, "Give back everything that belonged to her, including all the income from her land from the day she left the country until now."

Hazael Murders Ben-Hadad

[7]Elisha went to Damascus, and Ben-Hadad king of Aram was ill. When the king was told, "The man of God has come all the way up here," [8]he said to Hazael, "Take a gift with you and go to meet the man of God. Consult the LORD through him; ask him, 'Will I recover from this illness?'"

[9]Hazael went to meet Elisha, taking with him as a gift forty camel-loads of all the finest wares of Damascus. He went in and stood before him, and said, "Your son Ben-Hadad king of Aram has sent me to ask, 'Will I recover from this illness?'"

[10]Elisha answered, "Go and say to him, 'You will certainly recover'; but the LORD has revealed to me that he will in fact die." [11]He stared at him with a fixed gaze until Hazael felt ashamed. Then the man of God began to weep.

[12]"Why is my lord weeping?" asked Hazael.

"Because I know the harm you will do to the Israelites," he answered. "You will set fire to their fortified places, kill their young men with the sword, dash their little children to the ground, and rip open their pregnant women."

[13]Hazael said, "How could your servant, a mere dog, accomplish such a feat?"

"The LORD has shown me that you will become king of Aram," answered Elisha.

[14]Then Hazael left Elisha and returned to his master. When Ben-Hadad asked, "What did Elisha say to you?" Hazael replied, "He told me that you would certainly recover." [15]But the next day he took a thick cloth, soaked it in water and spread it over the king's face, so that he died. Then Hazael succeeded him as king.

NEW TESTAMENT READING
Acts 22:22–23:11

Paul the Roman Citizen

[22]The crowd listened to Paul until he said this. Then they raised their voices and shouted, "Rid the earth of him! He's not fit to live!"

[23]As they were shouting and throwing off their cloaks and flinging dust into the air, [24]the commander ordered Paul to be taken into the barracks. He directed that he be flogged and questioned in order to find out why the people were shouting at him like this. [25]As they stretched him out to flog him, Paul said to the centurion standing there, "Is it legal for you to flog a Roman citizen who hasn't even been found guilty?"

[26]When the centurion heard this, he went to the commander and reported it. "What are you going to do?" he asked. "This man is a Roman citizen."

[27]The commander went to Paul and asked, "Tell me, are you a Roman citizen?"

"Yes, I am," he answered.

28Then the commander said, "I had to pay a big price for my citizenship."

"But I was born a citizen," Paul replied.

29Those who were about to question him withdrew immediately. The commander himself was alarmed when he realised that he had put Paul, a Roman citizen, in chains.

Before the Sanhedrin

30The next day, since the commander wanted to find out exactly why Paul was being accused by the Jews, he released him and ordered the chief priests and all the Sanhedrin to assemble. Then he brought Paul and had him stand before them.

23 Paul looked straight at the Sanhedrin and said, "My brothers, I have fulfilled my duty to God in all good conscience to this day." 2At this the high priest Ananias ordered those standing near Paul to strike him on the mouth. 3Then Paul said to him, "God will strike you, you whitewashed wall! You sit there to judge me according to the law, yet you yourself violate the law by commanding that I be struck!"

4Those who were standing near Paul said, "You dare to insult God's high priest?"

5Paul replied, "Brothers, I did not realise that he was the high priest; for it is written: 'Do not speak evil about the ruler of your people.'"

6Then Paul, knowing that some of them were Sadducees and the others Pharisees, called out in the Sanhedrin, "My brothers, I am a Pharisee, the son of a Pharisee. I stand on trial because of my hope in the resurrection of the dead." 7When he said this, a dispute broke out between the Pharisees and the Sadducees, and the assembly was divided. 8(The Sadducees say that there is no resurrection, and that there are neither angels nor spirits, but the Pharisees acknowledge them all.)

9There was a great uproar, and some of the teachers of the law who were Pharisees stood up and argued vigorously. "We find nothing wrong with this man," they said. "What if a spirit or an angel has spoken to him?" 10The dispute became so violent that the commander was afraid Paul would be torn to pieces by them. He ordered the troops to go down and take him away from them by force and bring him into the barracks.

11The following night the Lord stood near Paul and said, "Take courage! As you have testified about me in Jerusalem, so you must also testify in Rome."

READING FROM PROVERBS
Proverbs 16:8–17

8Better a little with righteousness
     than much gain with injustice.

9In his heart a man plans his course,
     but the LORD determines his steps.

10The lips of a king speak as an oracle,
     and his mouth should not betray
     justice.

11Honest scales and balances are from
     the LORD;
     all the weights in the bag are of his
     making.

12Kings detest wrongdoing,
     for a throne is established through
     righteousness.

13Kings take pleasure in honest lips;
     they value a man who speaks the
     truth.

14A king's wrath is a messenger of
     death,
     but a wise man will appease it.

15When a king's face brightens, it
     means life;
     his favour is like a rain cloud in
     spring.

16How much better to get wisdom than
    gold,
  to choose understanding rather
    than silver!

17The highway of the upright avoids
    evil;
  he who guards his way guards his
    life.

JULY 4   DAY 185

OLD TESTAMENT READING
2 Kings 8:16–9:37

Jehoram King of Judah

16In the fifth year of Joram son of
Ahab king of Israel, when Jehoshaphat
was king of Judah, Jehoram son of
Jehoshaphat began his reign as king of
Judah. 17He was thirty-two years old
when he became king, and he reigned in
Jerusalem for eight years. 18He walked
in the ways of the kings of Israel, as the
house of Ahab had done, for he married
a daughter of Ahab. He did evil in the
eyes of the LORD. 19Nevertheless, for
the sake of his servant David, the LORD
was not willing to destroy Judah. He
had promised to maintain a lamp for
David and his descendants for ever.

20In the time of Jehoram, Edom rebelled against Judah and set up its own
king. 21So Jehoram went to Zair with all
his chariots. The Edomites surrounded
him and his chariot commanders; but he
rose up and broke through by night; his
army, however, fled back home. 22To
this day Edom has been in rebellion
against Judah. Libnah revolted at the
same time.

23As for the other events of Jehoram's reign, and all he did, are they
not written in the book of the annals of
the kings of Judah? 24Jehoram rested
with his fathers and was buried with
them in the City of David. And Ahaziah
his son succeeded him as king.

Ahaziah King of Judah

25In the twelfth year of Joram son of
Ahab king of Israel, Ahaziah son of

Jehoram king of Judah began to reign.
26Ahaziah was twenty-two years old
when he became king, and he reigned in
Jerusalem for one year. His mother's
name was Athaliah, a granddaughter of
Omri king of Israel. 27He walked in the
ways of the house of Ahab and did evil
in the eyes of the LORD, as the house of
Ahab had done, for he was related by
marriage to Ahab's family.

28Ahaziah went with Joram son of
Ahab to war against Hazael king of
Aram at Ramoth Gilead. The Arameans wounded Joram; 29so King
Joram returned to Jezreel to recover
from the wounds the Arameans had
inflicted on him at Ramoth in his battle
with Hazael king of Aram.

Then Ahaziah son of Jehoram king of
Judah went down to Jezreel to see
Joram son of Ahab, because he had
been wounded.

Jehu Anointed King of Israel

9 The prophet Elisha summoned a
    man from the company of the
prophets and said to him, "Tuck your
cloak into your belt, take this flask of oil
with you and go to Ramoth Gilead.
2When you get there, look for Jehu son
of Jehoshaphat, the son of Nimshi. Go
to him, get him away from his companions and take him into an inner room.
3Then take the flask and pour the oil on
his head and declare, 'This is what the
LORD says: I anoint you king over
Israel.' Then open the door and run;
don't delay!"

4So the young man, the prophet,

went to Ramoth Gilead. ⁵When he arrived, he found the army officers sitting together. "I have a message for you, commander," he said.

"For which of us?" asked Jehu.

"For you, commander," he replied.

⁶Jehu got up and went into the house. Then the prophet poured the oil on Jehu's head and declared, "This is what the LORD, the God of Israel, says: 'I anoint you king over the LORD's people Israel. ⁷You are to destroy the house of Ahab your master, and I will avenge the blood of my servants the prophets and the blood of all the LORD's servants shed by Jezebel. ⁸The whole house of Ahab will perish. I will cut off from Ahab every last male in Israel—slave or free. ⁹I will make the house of Ahab like the house of Jeroboam son of Nebat and like the house of Baasha son of Ahijah. ¹⁰As for Jezebel, dogs will devour her on the plot of ground at Jezreel, and no-one will bury her.'" Then he opened the door and ran.

¹¹When Jehu went out to his fellow officers, one of them asked him, "Is everything all right? Why did this madman come to you?"

"You know the man and the sort of things he says," Jehu replied.

¹²"That's not true!" they said. "Tell us."

Jehu said, "Here is what he told me: 'This is what the LORD says: I anoint you king over Israel.'"

¹³They hurried and took their cloaks and spread them under him on the bare steps. Then they blew the trumpet and shouted, "Jehu is king!"

Jehu Kills Joram and Ahaziah

¹⁴So Jehu son of Jehoshaphat, the son of Nimshi, conspired against Joram. (Now Joram and all Israel had been defending Ramoth Gilead against Hazael king of Aram, ¹⁵but King Joram had returned to Jezreel to recover from the wounds the Arameans had inflicted on him in the battle with Hazael king of Aram.) Jehu said, "If this is the way you

feel, don't let anyone slip out of the city to go and tell the news in Jezreel." ¹⁶Then he got into his chariot and rode to Jezreel, because Joram was resting there and Ahaziah king of Judah had gone down to see him.

¹⁷When the lookout standing on the tower in Jezreel saw Jehu's troops approaching, he called out, "I see some troops coming."

"Get a horseman," Joram ordered. "Send him to meet them and ask, 'Do you come in peace?'"

¹⁸The horseman rode off to meet Jehu and said, "This is what the king says: 'Do you come in peace?'"

"What do you have to do with peace?" Jehu replied. "Fall in behind me."

The lookout reported, "The messenger has reached them, but he isn't coming back."

¹⁹So the king sent out a second horseman. When he came to them he said, "This is what the king says: 'Do you come in peace?'"

Jehu replied, "What do you have to do with peace? Fall in behind me."

²⁰The lookout reported, "He has reached them, but he isn't coming back either. The driving is like that of Jehu son of Nimshi—he drives like a madman."

²¹"Hitch up my chariot," Joram ordered. And when it was hitched up, Joram king of Israel and Ahaziah king of Judah rode out, each in his own chariot, to meet Jehu. They met him at the plot of ground that had belonged to Naboth the Jezreelite. ²²When Joram saw Jehu he asked, "Have you come in peace, Jehu?"

"How can there be peace," Jehu replied, "as long as all the idolatry and witchcraft of your mother Jezebel abound?"

²³Joram turned about and fled, calling out to Ahaziah, "Treachery, Ahaziah!"

²⁴Then Jehu drew his bow and shot Joram between the shoulders. The arrow pierced his heart and he slumped

down in his chariot. ²⁵Jehu said to Bidkar, his chariot officer, "Pick him up and throw him on the field that belonged to Naboth the Jezreelite. Remember how you and I were riding together in chariots behind Ahab his father when the LORD made this prophecy about him: ²⁶'Yesterday I saw the blood of Naboth and the blood of his sons, declares the LORD, and I will surely make you pay for it on this plot of ground, declares the LORD.' Now then, pick him up and throw him on that plot, in accordance with the word of the LORD."

²⁷When Ahaziah king of Judah saw what had happened, he fled up the road to Beth Haggan. Jehu chased him, shouting, "Kill him too!" They wounded him in his chariot on the way up to Gur near Ibleam, but he escaped to Megiddo and died there. ²⁸His servants took him by chariot to Jerusalem and buried him with his fathers in his tomb in the City of David. ²⁹(In the eleventh year of Joram son of Ahab, Ahaziah had become king of Judah.)

Jezebel Killed

³⁰Then Jehu went to Jezreel. When Jezebel heard about it, she painted her eyes, arranged her hair and looked out of a window. ³¹As Jehu entered the gate, she asked, "Have you come in peace, Zimri, you murderer of your master?"

³²He looked up at the window and called out, "Who is on my side? Who?" Two or three eunuchs looked down at him. ³³"Throw her down!" Jehu said. So they threw her down, and some of her blood spattered the wall and the horses as they trampled her underfoot.

³⁴Jehu went in and ate and drank. "Take care of that cursed woman," he said, "and bury her, for she was a king's daughter." ³⁵But when they went out to bury her, they found nothing except her skull, her feet and her hands. ³⁶They went back and told Jehu, who said, "This is the word of the LORD that he

spoke through his servant Elijah the Tishbite: On the plot of ground at Jezreel dogs will devour Jezebel's flesh. ³⁷Jezebel's body will be like refuse on the ground in the plot at Jezreel, so that no-one will be able to say, 'This is Jezebel.'"

NEW TESTAMENT READING
Acts 23:12–35

The Plot to Kill Paul

¹²The next morning the Jews formed a conspiracy and bound themselves with an oath not to eat or drink until they had killed Paul. ¹³More than forty men were involved in this plot. ¹⁴They went to the chief priests and elders and said, "We have taken a solemn oath not to eat anything until we have killed Paul. ¹⁵Now then, you and the Sanhedrin petition the commander to bring him before you on the pretext of wanting more accurate information about his case. We are ready to kill him before he gets here."

¹⁶But when the son of Paul's sister heard of this plot, he went into the barracks and told Paul.

¹⁷Then Paul called one of the centurions and said, "Take this young man to the commander; he has something to tell him." ¹⁸So he took him to the commander.

The centurion said, "Paul, the prisoner, sent for me and asked me to bring this young man to you because he has something to tell you."

¹⁹The commander took the young man by the hand, drew him aside and asked, "What is it you want to tell me?"

²⁰He said: "The Jews have agreed to ask you to bring Paul before the Sanhedrin tomorrow on the pretext of wanting more accurate information about him. ²¹Don't give in to them, because more than forty of them are waiting in ambush for him. They have taken an oath not to eat or drink until they have killed him. They are ready

now, waiting for your consent to their request."

²²The commander dismissed the young man and cautioned him, "Don't tell anyone that you have reported this to me."

Paul Transferred to Caesarea

²³Then he called two of his centurions and ordered them, "Get ready a detachment of two hundred soldiers, seventy horsemen and two hundred spearmen to go to Caesarea at nine tonight. ²⁴Provide mounts for Paul so that he may be taken safely to Governor Felix."

²⁵He wrote a letter as follows:

²⁶Claudius Lysias,

To His Excellency, Governor Felix:

Greetings.

²⁷This man was seized by the Jews and they were about to kill him, but I came with my troops and rescued him, for I had learned that he is a Roman citizen. ²⁸I wanted to know why they were accusing him, so I brought him to their Sanhedrin. ²⁹I found that the accusation had to do with questions about their law, but there was no charge against him that deserved death or imprisonment. ³⁰When I was informed of a plot to be carried out against the man, I sent him to you at once. I also ordered his accusers to present to you their case against him.

³¹So the soldiers, carrying out their orders, took Paul with them during the night and brought him as far as Antipatris. ³²The next day they let the cavalry go on with him, while they returned to the barracks. ³³When the cavalry arrived in Caesarea, they delivered the letter to the governor and handed Paul over to him. ³⁴The governor read the letter and asked what province he was from. Learning that he was from Cilicia, ³⁵he said, "I will hear your case when your accusers get here." Then he ordered that Paul be kept under guard in Herod's palace.

READING FROM PSALMS
Psalm 80:1–7

For the director of music. To the tune of "The Lilies of the Covenant". Of Asaph. A psalm.

¹Hear us, O Shepherd of Israel,
   you who lead Joseph like a flock;
you who sit enthroned between the
     cherubim, shine forth
² before Ephraim, Benjamin and
     Manasseh.
Awaken your might;
   come and save us.

³Restore us, O God;
   make your face shine upon us,
   that we may be saved.

⁴O Lord God Almighty,
   how long will your anger smoulder
   against the prayers of your people?
⁵You have fed them with the bread of
     tears;
   you have made them drink tears by
     the bowlful.
⁶You have made us a source of
     contention to our neighbours,
   and our enemies mock us.

⁷Restore us, O God Almighty;
   make your face shine upon us,
   that we may be saved.

OLD TESTAMENT READING
2 Kings 10:1–11:21

Ahab's Family Killed

10 Now there were in Samaria seventy sons of the house of Ahab. So Jehu wrote letters and sent them to Samaria: to the officials of Jezreel, to the elders and to the guardians of Ahab's children. He said, ²"As soon as this letter reaches you, since your master's sons are with you and you have chariots and horses, a fortified city and weapons, ³choose the best and most worthy of your master's sons and set him on his father's throne. Then fight for your master's house."

⁴But they were terrified and said, "If two kings could not resist him, how can we?"

⁵So the palace administrator, the city governor, the elders and the guardians sent this message to Jehu: "We are your servants and we will do anything you say. We will not appoint anyone as king; you do whatever you think best."

⁶Then Jehu wrote them a second letter, saying, "If you are on my side and will obey me, take the heads of your master's sons and come to me in Jezreel by this time tomorrow."

Now the royal princes, seventy of them, were with the leading men of the city, who were bringing them up. ⁷When the letter arrived, these men took the princes and slaughtered all seventy of them. They put their heads in baskets and sent them to Jehu in Jezreel. ⁸When the messenger arrived, he told Jehu, "They have brought the heads of the princes."

Then Jehu ordered, "Put them in two piles at the entrance of the city gate until morning."

⁹The next morning Jehu went out. He stood before all the people and said,

"You are innocent. It was I who conspired against my master and killed him, but who killed all these? ¹⁰Know then, that not a word the LORD has spoken against the house of Ahab will fail. The LORD has done what he promised through his servant Elijah." ¹¹So Jehu killed everyone in Jezreel who remained of the house of Ahab, as well as all his chief men, his close friends and his priests, leaving him no survivor.

¹²Jehu then set out and went towards Samaria. At Beth Eked of the Shepherds, ¹³he met some relatives of Ahaziah king of Judah and asked, "Who are you?"

They said, "We are relatives of Ahaziah, and we have come down to greet the families of the king and of the queen mother."

¹⁴"Take them alive!" he ordered. So they took them alive and slaughtered them by the well of Beth Eked—forty-two men. He left no survivor.

¹⁵After he left there, he came upon Jehonadab son of Recab, who was on his way to meet him. Jehu greeted him and said, "Are you in accord with me, as I am with you?"

"I am," Jehonadab answered.

"If so," said Jehu, "give me your hand." So he did, and Jehu helped him up into the chariot. ¹⁶Jehu said, "Come with me and see my zeal for the LORD." Then he had him ride along in his chariot.

¹⁷When Jehu came to Samaria, he killed all who were left there of Ahab's family; he destroyed them, according to the word of the LORD spoken to Elijah.

Ministers of Baal Killed

¹⁸Then Jehu brought all the people together and said to them, "Ahab served Baal a little; Jehu will serve him much. ¹⁹Now summon all the prophets of Baal, all his ministers and all his

priests. See that no-one is missing, because I am going to hold a great sacrifice for Baal. Anyone who fails to come will no longer live." But Jehu was acting deceptively in order to destroy the ministers of Baal.

20Jehu said, "Call an assembly in honour of Baal." So they proclaimed it. 21Then he sent word throughout Israel, and all the ministers of Baal came; not one stayed away. They crowded into the temple of Baal until it was full from one end to the other. 22And Jehu said to the keeper of the wardrobe, "Bring robes for all the ministers of Baal." So he brought out robes for them.

23Then Jehu and Jehonadab son of Recab went into the temple of Baal. Jehu said to the ministers of Baal, "Look around and see that no servants of the LORD are here with you—only ministers of Baal." 24So they went in to make sacrifices and burnt offerings. Now Jehu had posted eighty men outside with this warning: "If one of you lets any of the men I am placing in your hands escape, it will be your life for his life."

25As soon as Jehu had finished making the burnt offering, he ordered the guards and officers: "Go in and kill them; let no-one escape." So they cut them down with the sword. The guards and officers threw the bodies out and then entered the inner shrine of the temple of Baal. 26They brought the sacred stone out of the temple of Baal and burned it. 27They demolished the sacred stone of Baal and tore down the temple of Baal, and people have used it for a latrine to this day.

28So Jehu destroyed Baal worship in Israel. 29However, he did not turn away from the sins of Jeroboam son of Nebat, which he had caused Israel to commit —the worship of the golden calves at Bethel and Dan.

30The LORD said to Jehu, "Because you have done well in accomplishing what is right in my eyes and have done to the house of Ahab all I had in mind to do, your descendants will sit on the throne of Israel to the fourth generation." 31Yet Jehu was not careful to keep the law of the LORD, the God of Israel, with all his heart. He did not turn away from the sins of Jeroboam, which he had caused Israel to commit.

32In those days the LORD began to reduce the size of Israel. Hazael overpowered the Israelites throughout their territory 33east of the Jordan in all the land of Gilead (the region of Gad, Reuben and Manasseh), from Aroer by the Arnon Gorge through Gilead to Bashan.

34As for the other events of Jehu's reign, all he did, and all his achievements, are they not written in the book of the annals of the kings of Israel?

35Jehu rested with his fathers and was buried in Samaria. And Jehoahaz his son succeeded him as king. 36The time that Jehu reigned over Israel in Samaria was twenty-eight years.

Athaliah and Joash

11 When Athaliah the mother of Ahaziah saw that her son was dead, she proceeded to destroy the whole royal family. 2But Jehosheba, the daughter of King Jehoram and sister of Ahaziah, took Joash son of Ahaziah and stole him away from among the royal princes, who were about to be murdered. She put him and his nurse in a bedroom to hide him from Athaliah; so he was not killed. 3He remained hidden with his nurse at the temple of the LORD for six years while Athaliah ruled the land.

4In the seventh year Jehoiada sent for the commanders of units of a hundred, the Carites and the guards and had them brought to him at the temple of the LORD. He made a covenant with them and put them under oath at the temple of the LORD. Then he showed them the king's son. 5He commanded them, saying, "This is what you are to do: You who are in the three companies that are going on duty on the Sabbath—a third of you guarding the royal palace, 6a third at the Sur Gate, and a third at the gate behind the guard, who take turns guarding the temple—7and you who are in the other two companies that normally go off Sabbath duty are all to guard the temple for the king. 8Station yourselves round the king, each man with his weapon in his hand. Anyone who approaches your ranks must be put to death. Stay close to the king wherever he goes."

9The commanders of units of a hundred did just as Jehoiada the priest ordered. Each one took his men—those who were going on duty on the Sabbath and those who were going off duty—and came to Jehoiada the priest. 10Then he gave the commanders the spears and shields that had belonged to King David and that were in the temple of the LORD. 11The guards, each with his weapon in his hand, stationed themselves round the king—near the altar and the temple, from the south side to the north side of the temple.

12Jehoiada brought out the king's son and put the crown on him; he presented him with a copy of the covenant and proclaimed him king. They anointed him, and the people clapped their hands and shouted, "Long live the king!"

13When Athaliah heard the noise made by the guards and the people, she went to the people at the temple of the LORD. 14She looked and there was the king, standing by the pillar, as the custom was. The officers and the trumpeters were beside the king, and all the people of the land were rejoicing and blowing trumpets. Then Athaliah tore her robes and called out, "Treason! Treason!"

15Jehoiada the priest ordered the commanders of units of a hundred, who were in charge of the troops: "Bring her out between the ranks and put to the sword anyone who follows her." For the priest had said, "She must not be put to death in the temple of the LORD." 16So they seized her as she reached the place where the horses enter the palace

grounds, and there she was put to death.

17Jehoiada then made a covenant between the LORD and the king and people that they would be the LORD's people. He also made a covenant between the king and the people. 18All the people of the land went to the temple of Baal and tore it down. They smashed the altars and idols to pieces and killed Mattan the priest of Baal in front of the altars.

Then Jehoiada the priest posted guards at the temple of the LORD. 19He took with him the commanders of hundreds, the Carites, the guards and all the people of the land, and together they brought the king down from the temple of the LORD and went into the palace, entering by way of the gate of the guards. The king then took his place on the royal throne, 20and all the people of the land rejoiced. And the city was quiet, because Athaliah had been slain with the sword at the palace.

21Joash was seven years old when he began his reign.

NEW TESTAMENT READING
Acts 24:1–27

The Trial Before Felix

24 Five days later the high priest Ananias went down to Caesarea with some of the elders and a lawyer named Tertullus, and they brought their charges against Paul before the governor. 2When Paul was called in, Tertullus presented his case before Felix: "We have enjoyed a long period of peace under you, and your foresight has brought about reforms in this nation. 3Everywhere and in every way, most excellent Felix, we acknowledge this with profound gratitude. 4But in order not to weary you further, I would request that you be kind enough to hear us briefly.

5"We have found this man to be a troublemaker, stirring up riots among the Jews all over the world. He is a ringleader of the Nazarene sect [6]and even tried to desecrate the temple; so we seized him. [8]By examining him yourself you will be able to learn the truth about all these charges we are bringing against him."

[9]The Jews joined in the accusation, asserting that these things were true.

[10]When the governor motioned for him to speak, Paul replied: "I know that for a number of years you have been a judge over this nation; so I gladly make my defence. [11]You can easily verify that no more than twelve days ago I went up to Jerusalem to worship. [12]My accusers did not find me arguing with anyone at the temple, or stirring up a crowd in the synagogues or anywhere else in the city. [13]And they cannot prove to you the charges they are now making against me. [14]However, I admit that I worship the God of our fathers as a follower of the Way, which they call a sect. I believe everything that agrees with the Law and that is written in the Prophets, [15]and I have the same hope in God as these men, that there will be a resurrection of both the righteous and the wicked. [16]So I strive always to keep my conscience clear before God and man.

[17]"After an absence of several years, I came to Jerusalem to bring my people gifts for the poor and to present offerings. [18]I was ceremonially clean when they found me in the temple courts doing this. There was no crowd with me, nor was I involved in any disturbance. [19]But there are some Jews from the province of Asia, who ought to be here before you and bring charges if they have anything against me. [20]Or these who are here should state what crime they found in me when I stood before the Sanhedrin—[21]unless it was this one thing I shouted as I stood in their presence: 'It is concerning the resurrection of the dead that I am on trial before you today.'"

[22]Then Felix, who was well acquainted with the Way, adjourned the proceedings. "When Lysias the commander comes," he said, "I will decide your case." [23]He ordered the centurion to keep Paul under guard but to give him some freedom and permit his friends to take care of his needs.

[24]Several days later Felix came with his wife Drusilla, who was a Jewess. He sent for Paul and listened to him as he spoke about faith in Christ Jesus. [25]As Paul discoursed on righteousness, self-control and the judgment to come, Felix was afraid and said, "That's enough for now! You may leave. When I find it convenient, I will send for you." [26]At the same time he was hoping that Paul would offer him a bribe, so he sent for him frequently and talked with him.

[27]When two years had passed, Felix was succeeded by Porcius Festus, but because Felix wanted to grant a favour to the Jews, he left Paul in prison.

READING FROM PSALMS
Psalm 80:8–19

[8]You brought a vine out of Egypt;
   you drove out the nations and
      planted it.
[9]You cleared the ground for it,
   and it took root and filled the land.
[10]The mountains were covered with its
         shade,
   the mighty cedars with its
      branches.
[11]It sent out its boughs to the Sea,
   its shoots as far as the River.

[12]Why have you broken down its walls
   so that all who pass by pick its
      grapes?
[13]Boars from the forest ravage it
   and the creatures of the field feed
      on it.
[14]Return to us, O God Almighty!
   Look down from heaven and see!
   Watch over this vine,
[15]   the root your right hand has
         planted,
   the son you have raised up for
      yourself.

16Your vine is cut down, it is burned
    with fire;
  at your rebuke your people perish.
17Let your hand rest on the man at your
    right hand,
  the son of man you have raised up
    for yourself.

18Then we will not turn away from you;
    revive us, and we will call on your
    name.

19Restore us, O Lord God Almighty;
    make your face shine upon us,
    that we may be saved.

JULY 6   DAY 187

OLD TESTAMENT READING
2 Kings 12:1–14:22

Joash Repairs the Temple

12 In the seventh year of Jehu,
Joash became king, and he
reigned in Jerusalem for forty years. His
mother's name was Zibiah; she was
from Beersheba. 2Joash did what was
right in the eyes of the Lord all the
years Jehoiada the priest instructed
him. 3The high places, however, were
not removed; the people continued
to offer sacrifices and burn incense
there.

4Joash said to the priests, "Collect all
the money that is brought as sacred
offerings to the temple of the Lord
—the money collected in the census,
the money received from personal vows
and the money brought voluntarily
to the temple. 5Let every priest receive the
money from one of the treasurers, and
let it be used to repair whatever damage
is found in the temple."

6But by the twenty-third year of King
Joash the priests still had not repaired
the temple. 7Therefore King Joash summoned Jehoiada the priest and the
other priests and asked them, "Why
aren't you repairing the damage done to
the temple? Take no more money from
your treasurers, but hand it over for
repairing the temple." 8The priests
agreed that they would not collect
any more money from the people and

that they would not repair the temple
themselves.

9Jehoiada the priest took a chest and
bored a hole in its lid. He placed it
beside the altar, on the right side as one
enters the temple of the Lord. The
priests who guarded the entrance put
into the chest all the money that was
brought to the temple of the Lord.
10Whenever they saw that there was a
large amount of money in the chest, the
royal secretary and the high priest
came, counted the money that had been
brought into the temple of the Lord
and put it into bags. 11When the amount
had been determined, they gave the
money to the men appointed to supervise the work on the temple. With it
they paid those who worked on the
temple of the Lord—the carpenters
and builders, 12the masons and
stonecutters. They purchased timber
and dressed stone for the repair of the
temple of the Lord, and met all the
other expenses of restoring the temple.

13The money brought into the temple
was not spent for making silver basins,
wick trimmers, sprinkling bowls, trumpets or any other articles of gold or
silver for the temple of the Lord; 14it
was paid to the workmen, who used it to
repair the temple. 15They did not require an accounting from those to
whom they gave the money to pay the
workers, because they acted with complete honesty. 16The money from the
guilt offerings and sin offerings was not

brought into the temple of the LORD; it belonged to the priests.

¹⁷About this time Hazael king of Aram went up and attacked Gath and captured it. Then he turned to attack Jerusalem. ¹⁸But Joash king of Judah took all the sacred objects dedicated by his fathers—Jehoshaphat, Jehoram and Ahaziah, the kings of Judah—and the gifts he himself had dedicated and all the gold found in the treasuries of the temple of the LORD and of the royal palace, and he sent them to Hazael king of Aram, who then withdrew from Jerusalem.

¹⁹As for the other events of the reign of Joash, and all he did, are they not written in the book of the annals of the kings of Judah? ²⁰His officials conspired against him and assassinated him at Beth Millo, on the road down to Silla. ²¹The officials who murdered him were Jozabad son of Shimeath and Jehozabad son of Shomer. He died and was buried with his fathers in the City of David. And Amaziah his son succeeded him as king.

Jehoahaz King of Israel

13 In the twenty-third year of Joash son of Ahaziah king of Judah, Jehoahaz son of Jehu became king of Israel in Samaria, and he reigned for seventeen years. ²He did evil in the eyes of the LORD by following the sins of Jeroboam son of Nebat, which he had caused Israel to commit, and he did not turn away from them. ³So the LORD's anger burned against Israel, and for a long time he kept them under the power of Hazael king of Aram and Ben-Hadad his son.

⁴Then Jehoahaz sought the LORD's favour, and the LORD listened to him, for he saw how severely the king of Aram was oppressing Israel. ⁵The LORD provided a deliverer for Israel, and they escaped from the power of Aram. So the Israelites lived in their own homes as they had before. ⁶But they did not turn away from the sins of the house of Jeroboam, which he had caused Israel to commit; they continued in them. Also, the Asherah pole remained standing in Samaria.

⁷Nothing had been left of the army of Jehoahaz except fifty horsemen, ten chariots and ten thousand foot soldiers, for the king of Aram had destroyed the rest and made them like the dust at threshing time.

⁸As for the other events of the reign of Jehoahaz, all he did and his achievements, are they not written in the book of the annals of the kings of Israel? ⁹Jehoahaz rested with his fathers and was buried in Samaria. And Jehoash his son succeeded him as king.

Jehoash King of Israel

¹⁰In the thirty-seventh year of Joash king of Judah, Jehoash son of Jehoahaz became king of Israel in Samaria, and he reigned for sixteen years. ¹¹He did evil in the eyes of the LORD and did not turn away from any of the sins of Jeroboam son of Nebat, which he had caused Israel to commit; he continued in them.

¹²As for the other events of the reign of Jehoash, all he did and his achievements, including his war against Amaziah king of Judah, are they not written in the book of the annals of the kings of Israel? ¹³Jehoash rested with his fathers, and Jeroboam succeeded him on the throne. Jehoash was buried in Samaria with the kings of Israel.

¹⁴Now Elisha was suffering from the illness from which he died. Jehoash king of Israel went down to see him and wept over him. "My father! My father!" he cried. "The chariots and horsemen of Israel!"

¹⁵Elisha said, "Get a bow and some arrows," and he did so. ¹⁶"Take the bow in your hands," he said to the king of Israel. When he had taken it, Elisha put his hands on the king's hands.

¹⁷"Open the east window," he said, and he opened it. "Shoot!" Elisha said,

and he shot. "The LORD's arrow of victory, the arrow of victory over Aram!" Elisha declared. "You will completely destroy the Arameans at Aphek."

18Then he said, "Take the arrows," and the king took them. Elisha told him, "Strike the ground." He struck it three times and stopped. 19The man of God was angry with him and said, "You should have struck the ground five or six times; then you would have defeated Aram and completely destroyed it. But now you will defeat it only three times."

20Elisha died and was buried.

Now Moabite raiders used to enter the country every spring. 21Once while some Israelites were burying a man, suddenly they saw a band of raiders; so they threw the man's body into Elisha's tomb. When the body touched Elisha's bones, the man came to life and stood up on his feet.

22Hazael king of Aram oppressed Israel throughout the reign of Jehoahaz. 23But the LORD was gracious to them and had compassion and showed concern for them because of his covenant with Abraham, Isaac and Jacob. To this day he has been unwilling to destroy them or banish them from his presence.

24Hazael king of Aram died, and Ben-Hadad his son succeeded him as king. 25Then Jehoash son of Jehoahaz recaptured from Ben-Hadad son of Hazael the towns he had taken in battle from his father Jehoahaz. Three times Jehoash defeated him, and so he recovered the Israelite towns.

Amaziah King of Judah

14 In the second year of Jehoash son of Jehoahaz king of Israel, Amaziah son of Joash king of Judah began to reign. 2He was twenty-five years old when he became king, and he reigned in Jerusalem for twenty-nine years. His mother's name was Jehoaddin; she was from Jerusalem. 3He did what was right in the eyes of the LORD, but not as his father David had done. In everything he followed the example of his father Joash. 4The high places, however, were not removed; the people continued to offer sacrifices and burn incense there.

5After the kingdom was firmly in his grasp, he executed the officials who had murdered his father the king. 6Yet he did not put the sons of the assassins to death, in accordance with what is written in the Book of the Law of Moses where the LORD commanded: "Fathers shall not be put to death for their children, nor children put to death for their fathers; each is to die for his own sins."

7He was the one who defeated ten thousand Edomites in the Valley of Salt and captured Sela in battle, calling it Joktheel, the name it has to this day.

8Then Amaziah sent messengers to Jehoash son of Jehoahaz, the son of Jehu, king of Israel, with the challenge: "Come, meet me face to face."

9But Jehoash king of Israel replied to Amaziah king of Judah: "A thistle in Lebanon sent a message to a cedar in Lebanon, 'Give your daughter to my son in marriage.' Then a wild beast in Lebanon came along and trampled the thistle underfoot. 10You have indeed defeated Edom and now you are arrogant. Glory in your victory, but stay at home! Why ask for trouble and cause your own downfall and that of Judah also?"

11Amaziah, however, would not listen, so Jehoash king of Israel attacked. He and Amaziah king of Judah faced each other at Beth Shemesh in Judah. 12Judah was routed by Israel, and every man fled to his home. 13Jehoash king of Israel captured Amaziah king of Judah, the son of Joash, the son of Ahaziah, at Beth Shemesh. Then Jehoash went to Jerusalem and broke down the wall of Jerusalem from the Ephraim Gate to the Corner Gate—a section about six hundred feet long. 14He took all the gold and silver and all the articles found in the temple of the LORD and in the treasuries of the royal palace. He also took hostages and returned to Samaria.

15As for the other events of the reign of Jehoash, what he did and his achievements, including his war against Amaziah king of Judah, are they not written in the book of the annals of the kings of Israel? 16Jehoash rested with his fathers and was buried in Samaria with the kings of Israel. And Jeroboam his son succeeded him as king.

17Amaziah son of Joash king of Judah lived for fifteen years after the death of Jehoash son of Jehoahaz king of Israel. 18As for the other events of Amaziah's reign, are they not written in the book of the annals of the kings of Judah?

19They conspired against him in Jerusalem, and he fled to Lachish, but they sent men after him to Lachish and killed him there. 20He was brought back by horse and was buried in Jerusalem with his fathers, in the City of David.

21Then all the people of Judah took Azariah, who was sixteen years old, and made him king in place of his father Amaziah. 22He was the one who rebuilt Elath and restored it to Judah after Amaziah rested with his fathers.

NEW TESTAMENT READING
Acts 25:1–22

The Trial Before Festus

25 Three days after arriving in the province, Festus went up from Caesarea to Jerusalem, 2where the chief priests and Jewish leaders appeared before him and presented the charges against Paul. 3They urgently requested Festus, as a favour to them, to have Paul transferred to Jerusalem, for they were preparing an ambush to kill him along the way. 4Festus answered, "Paul is being held at Caesarea, and I myself am going there soon. 5Let some of your leaders come with me and press charges against the man there, if he has done anything wrong."

6After spending eight or ten days with them, he went down to Caesarea, and the next day he convened the court and ordered that Paul be brought before him. 7When Paul appeared, the Jews who had come down from Jerusalem stood around him, bringing many serious charges against him, which they could not prove.

8Then Paul made his defence: "I have done nothing wrong against the law of the Jews or against the temple or against Caesar."

9Festus, wishing to do the Jews a favour, said to Paul, "Are you willing to go up to Jerusalem and stand trial before me there on these charges?"

10Paul answered: "I am now standing before Caesar's court, where I ought to be tried. I have not done any wrong to the Jews, as you yourself know very well. 11If, however, I am guilty of doing anything deserving death, I do not refuse to die. But if the charges brought against me by these Jews are not true, no-one has the right to hand me over to them. I appeal to Caesar!"

12After Festus had conferred with his council, he declared: "You have appealed to Caesar. To Caesar you will go!"

Festus Consults King Agrippa

13A few days later King Agrippa and Bernice arrived at Caesarea to pay their respects to Festus. 14Since they were spending many days there, Festus discussed Paul's case with the king. He said: "There is a man here whom Felix left as a prisoner. 15When I went to Jerusalem, the chief priests and elders of the Jews brought charges against him and asked that he be condemned.

16"I told them that it is not the Roman custom to hand over any man before he has faced his accusers and has had an opportunity to defend himself against their charges. 17When they came here with me, I did not delay the case, but convened the court the next day and ordered the man to be brought in. 18When his accusers got up to speak, they did not charge him with any of the crimes I had expected. ¹⁹Instead, they had some points of dispute with him about their own religion and about a dead man named Jesus whom Paul claimed was alive. ²⁰I was at a loss how to investigate such matters; so I asked if he would be willing to go to Jerusalem and stand trial there on these charges. ²¹When Paul made his appeal to be held over for the Emperor's decision, I ordered him to be held until I could send him to Caesar."

²²Then Agrippa said to Festus, "I would like to hear this man myself."

He replied, "Tomorrow you will hear him."

READING FROM PSALMS
Psalm 81:1–7

For the director of music. According to *gittith*. Of Asaph.

¹Sing for joy to God our strength;
  shout aloud to the God of Jacob!

²Begin the music, strike the tambourine,
  play the melodious harp and lyre.

³Sound the ram's horn at the New Moon,
  and when the moon is full, on the day of our Feast;
⁴this is a decree for Israel,
  an ordinance of the God of Jacob.
⁵He established it as a statute for Joseph
  when he went out against Egypt,
  where we heard a language we did not understand.

⁶He says, "I removed the burden from their shoulders;
  their hands were set free from the basket.
⁷In your distress you called and I rescued you,
  I answered you out of a thundercloud;
  I tested you at the waters of Meribah.   *Selah*

JULY 7   DAY 188

OLD TESTAMENT READING
2 Kings 14:23–15:38

Jeroboam II King of Israel

²³In the fifteenth year of Amaziah son of Joash king of Judah, Jeroboam son of Jehoash king of Israel became king in Samaria, and he reigned for forty-one years. ²⁴He did evil in the eyes of the LORD and did not turn away from any of the sins of Jeroboam son of Nebat, which he had caused Israel to commit. ²⁵He was the one who restored the boundaries of Israel from Lebo Hamath to the Sea of the Arabah, in accordance with the word of the LORD, the God of Israel, spoken through his servant Jonah son of Amittai, the prophet from Gath Hepher.

²⁶The LORD had seen how bitterly everyone in Israel, whether slave or free, was suffering; there was no-one to help them. ²⁷And since the LORD had not said he would blot out the name of Israel from under heaven, he saved them by the hand of Jeroboam son of Jehoash.

²⁸As for the other events of Jeroboam's reign, all he did, and his military achievements, including how he recovered for Israel both Damascus and Hamath, which had belonged to Yaudi, are they not written in the book of the annals of the kings of Israel? ²⁹Jeroboam rested with his fathers, the

kings of Israel. And Zechariah his son succeeded him as king.

Azariah King of Judah

15 In the twenty-seventh year of Jeroboam king of Israel, Azariah son of Amaziah king of Judah began to reign. 2He was sixteen years old when he became king, and he reigned in Jerusalem for fifty-two years. His mother's name was Jecoliah; she was from Jerusalem. 3He did what was right in the eyes of the LORD, just as his father Amaziah had done. 4The high places, however, were not removed; the people continued to offer sacrifices and burn incense there.

5The LORD afflicted the king with leprosy until the day he died, and he lived in a separate house. Jotham the king's son had charge of the palace and governed the people of the land.

6As for the other events of Azariah's reign, and all he did, are they not written in the book of the annals of the kings of Judah? 7Azariah rested with his fathers and was buried near them in the City of David. And Jotham his son succeeded him as king.

Zechariah King of Israel

8In the thirty-eighth year of Azariah king of Judah, Zechariah son of Jeroboam became king of Israel in Samaria, and he reigned for six months. 9He did evil in the eyes of the LORD, as his fathers had done. He did not turn away from the sins of Jeroboam son of Nebat, which he had caused Israel to commit.

10Shallum son of Jabesh conspired against Zechariah. He attacked him in front of the people, assassinated him and succeeded him as king. 11The other events of Zechariah's reign are written in the book of the annals of the kings of Israel. 12So the word of the LORD spoken to Jehu was fulfilled: "Your descendants will sit on the throne of Israel to the fourth generation."

Shallum King of Israel

13Shallum son of Jabesh became king in the thirty-ninth year of Uzziah king of Judah, and he reigned in Samaria for one month. 14Then Menahem son of Gadi went from Tirzah up to Samaria. He attacked Shallum son of Jabesh in Samaria, assassinated him and succeeded him as king.

15The other events of Shallum's reign, and the conspiracy he led, are written in the book of the annals of the kings of Israel.

16At that time Menahem, starting out from Tirzah, attacked Tiphsah and everyone in the city and its vicinity, because they refused to open their gates. He sacked Tiphsah and ripped open all the pregnant women.

Menahem King of Israel

17In the thirty-ninth year of Azariah king of Judah, Menahem son of Gadi became king of Israel, and he reigned in Samaria for ten years. 18He did evil in the eyes of the LORD. During his entire reign he did not turn away from the sins of Jeroboam son of Nebat, which he had caused Israel to commit.

19Then Pul king of Assyria invaded the land, and Menahem gave him a thousand talents of silver to gain his support and strengthen his own hold on the kingdom. 20Menahem exacted this money from Israel. Every wealthy man had to contribute fifty shekels of silver to be given to the king of Assyria. So the king of Assyria withdrew and stayed in the land no longer.

21As for the other events of Menahem's reign, and all he did, are they not written in the book of the annals of the kings of Israel? 22Menahem rested with his fathers. And Pekahiah his son succeeded him as king.

Pekahiah King of Israel

23In the fiftieth year of Azariah king of Judah, Pekahiah son of Menahem became king of Israel in Samaria, and he reigned for two years. ²⁴Pekahiah did evil in the eyes of the LORD. He did not turn away from the sins of Jeroboam son of Nebat, which he had caused Israel to commit. ²⁵One of his chief officers, Pekah son of Remaliah, conspired against him. Taking fifty men of Gilead with him, he assassinated Pekahiah, along with Argob and Arieh, in the citadel of the royal palace at Samaria. So Pekah killed Pekahiah and succeeded him as king.

²⁶The other events of Pekahiah's reign, and all he did, are written in the book of the annals of the kings of Israel.

Pekah King of Israel

²⁷In the fifty-second year of Azariah king of Judah, Pekah son of Remaliah became king of Israel in Samaria, and he reigned for twenty years. ²⁸He did evil in the eyes of the LORD. He did not turn away from the sins of Jeroboam son of Nebat, which he had caused Israel to commit.

²⁹In the time of Pekah king of Israel, Tiglath-Pileser king of Assyria came and took Ijon, Abel Beth Maacah, Janoah, Kedesh and Hazor. He took Gilead and Galilee, including all the land of Naphtali, and deported the people to Assyria. ³⁰Then Hoshea son of Elah conspired against Pekah son of Remaliah. He attacked and assassinated him, and then succeeded him as king in the twentieth year of Jotham son of Uzziah.

³¹As for the other events of Pekah's reign, and all he did, are they not written in the book of the annals of the kings of Israel?

Jotham King of Judah

³²In the second year of Pekah son of Remaliah king of Israel, Jotham son of Uzziah king of Judah began to reign. ³³He was twenty-five years old when he became king, and he reigned in Jerusalem for sixteen years. His mother's name was Jerusha daughter of Zadok. ³⁴He did what was right in the eyes of the LORD, just as his father Uzziah had done. ³⁵The high places, however, were not removed; the people continued to offer sacrifices and burn incense there. Jotham rebuilt the Upper Gate of the temple of the LORD.

³⁶As for the other events of Jotham's reign, and what he did, are they not written in the book of the annals of the kings of Judah? ³⁷(In those days the LORD began to send Rezin king of Aram and Pekah son of Remaliah against Judah.) ³⁸Jotham rested with his fathers and was buried with them in the City of David, the city of his father. And Ahaz his son succeeded him as king.

NEW TESTAMENT READING
Acts 25:23–26:23

Paul Before Agrippa

²³The next day Agrippa and Bernice came with great pomp and entered the audience room with the high ranking officers and the leading men of the city. At the command of Festus, Paul was brought in. ²⁴Festus said: "King Agrippa, and all who are present with us, you see this man! The whole Jewish community has petitioned me about him in Jerusalem and here in Caesarea, shouting that he ought not to live any longer. ²⁵I found he had done nothing deserving of death, but because he made his appeal to the Emperor I decided to send him to Rome. ²⁶But I have nothing definite to write to His Majesty about him. Therefore I have brought him before all of you, and especially before you, King Agrippa, so that as a result of this investigation I may have something to write. ²⁷For I think it is unreasonable to send on a prisoner without specifying the charges against him."

26 Then Agrippa said to Paul, "You have permission to speak for yourself."

So Paul motioned with his hand and began his defence: [2]"King Agrippa, I consider myself fortunate to stand before you today as I make my defence against all the accusations of the Jews, [3]and especially so because you are well acquainted with all the Jewish customs and controversies. Therefore, I beg you to listen to me patiently.

[4]"The Jews all know the way I have lived ever since I was a child, from the beginning of my life in my own country, and also in Jerusalem. [5]They have known me for a long time and can testify, if they are willing, that according to the strictest sect of our religion, I lived as a Pharisee. [6]And now it is because of my hope in what God has promised our fathers that I am on trial today. [7]This is the promise our twelve tribes are hoping to see fulfilled as they earnestly serve God day and night. O King, it is because of this hope that the Jews are accusing me. [8]Why should any of you consider it incredible that God raises the dead?

[9]"I too was convinced that I ought to do all that was possible to oppose the name of Jesus of Nazareth. [10]And that is just what I did in Jerusalem. On the authority of the chief priests I put many of the saints in prison, and when they were put to death, I cast my vote against them. [11]Many a time I went from one synagogue to another to have them punished, and I tried to force them to blaspheme. In my obsession against them, I even went to foreign cities to persecute them.

[12]"On one of these journeys I was going to Damascus with the authority and commission of the chief priests. [13]About noon, O King, as I was on the road, I saw a light from heaven, brighter than the sun, blazing around me and my companions. [14]We all fell to the ground, and I heard a voice saying to me in Aramaic, 'Saul, Saul, why do you persecute me? It is hard for you to kick against the goads.'

[15]"Then I asked, 'Who are you, Lord?'

"'I am Jesus, whom you are persecuting,' the Lord replied. [16]'Now get up and stand on your feet. I have appeared to you to appoint you as a servant and as a witness of what you have seen of me and what I will show you. [17]I will rescue you from your own people and from the Gentiles. I am sending you to them [18]to open their eyes and turn them from darkness to light, and from the power of Satan to God, so that they may receive forgiveness of sins and a place among those who are sanctified by faith in me.'

[19]"So then, King Agrippa, I was not disobedient to the vision from heaven. [20]First to those in Damascus, then to those in Jerusalem and in all Judea, and to the Gentiles also, I preached that they should repent and turn to God and prove their repentance by their deeds. [21]That is why the Jews seized me in the temple courts and tried to kill me. [22]But I have had God's help to this very day, and so I stand here and testify to small and great alike. I am saying nothing beyond what the prophets and Moses said would happen— [23]that the Christ would suffer and, as the first to rise from the dead, would proclaim light to his own people and to the Gentiles."

READING FROM PROVERBS
Proverbs 16:18–27

[18]Pride goes before destruction,
    a haughty spirit before a fall.

[19]Better to be lowly in spirit and among
        the oppressed
    than to share plunder with the
        proud.

[20]Whoever gives heed to instruction
        prospers,
    and blessed is he who trusts in the
        LORD.

[21]The wise in heart are called
        discerning,
    and pleasant words promote
        instruction.

22Understanding is a fountain of life to
　　those who have it,
　but folly brings punishment to
　　fools.

23A wise man's heart guides his mouth,
　and his lips promote instruction.

24Pleasant words are a honeycomb,
　sweet to the soul and healing to the
　　bones.

25There is a way that seems right to a
　　man,
　but in the end it leads to death.

26The labourer's appetite works for
　　him;
　his hunger drives him on.

27A scoundrel plots evil,
　and his speech is like a scorching
　　fire.

JULY 8   DAY 189

OLD TESTAMENT READING
2 Kings 16:1–17:41

Ahaz King of Judah

16 In the seventeenth year of
Pekah son of Remaliah, Ahaz
son of Jotham king of Judah began to
reign. 2Ahaz was twenty years old when
he became king, and he reigned in Jerusalem for sixteen years. Unlike David
his father, he did not do what was right
in the eyes of the LORD his God. 3He
walked in the ways of the kings of Israel
and even sacrificed his son in the fire,
following the detestable ways of the
nations the LORD had driven out before
the Israelites. 4He offered sacrifices and
burned incense at the high places, on
the hilltops and under every spreading
tree.

5Then Rezin king of Aram and Pekah
son of Remaliah king of Israel marched
up to fight against Jerusalem and besieged Ahaz, but they could not overpower him. 6At that time, Rezin king of
Aram recovered Elath for Aram by
driving out the men of Judah. Edomites
then moved into Elath and have lived
there to this day.

7Ahaz sent messengers to say to Tiglath-Pileser king of Assyria, "I am your
servant and vassal. Come up and save
me out of the hand of the king of Aram

and of the king of Israel who are attacking me." 8And Ahaz took the silver and
gold found in the temple of the LORD
and in the treasuries of the royal palace
and sent it as a gift to the king of Assyria. 9The king of Assyria complied by
attacking Damascus and capturing it.
He deported its inhabitants to Kir and
put Rezin to death.

10Then King Ahaz went to Damascus
to meet Tiglath-Pileser king of Assyria.
He saw an altar in Damascus and sent to
Uriah the priest a sketch of the altar,
with detailed plans for its construction.
11So Uriah the priest built an altar in
accordance with all the plans that King
Ahaz had sent from Damascus and
finished it before King Ahaz returned.
12When the king came back from
Damascus and saw the altar, he
approached it and presented offerings
on it. 13He offered up his burnt offering
and grain offering, poured out his drink
offering, and sprinkled the blood of his
fellowship offerings on the altar. 14The
bronze altar that stood before the LORD
he brought from the front of the temple
—from between the new altar and the
temple of the LORD—and put it on the
north side of the new altar.

15King Ahaz then gave these orders
to Uriah the priest: "On the large new
altar, offer the morning burnt offering

and the evening grain offering, the king's burnt offering and his grain offering, and the burnt offering of all the people of the land, and their grain offering and their drink offering. Sprinkle on the altar all the blood of the burnt offerings and sacrifices. But I will use the bronze altar for seeking guidance." 16And Uriah the priest did just as King Ahaz had ordered.

17King Ahaz took away the side panels and removed the basins from the movable stands. He removed the Sea from the bronze bulls that supported it and set it on a stone base. 18He took away the Sabbath canopy that had been built at the temple and removed the royal entrance outside the temple of the LORD, in deference to the king of Assyria.

19As for the other events of the reign of Ahaz, and what he did, are they not written in the book of the annals of the kings of Judah? 20Ahaz rested with his fathers and was buried with them in the City of David. And Hezekiah his son succeeded him as king.

Hoshea Last King of Israel

17 In the twelfth year of Ahaz king of Judah, Hoshea son of Elah became king of Israel in Samaria, and he reigned for nine years. 2He did evil in the eyes of the LORD, but not like the kings of Israel who preceded him.

3Shalmaneser king of Assyria came up to attack Hoshea, who had been Shalmaneser's vassal and had paid him tribute. 4But the king of Assyria discovered that Hoshea was a traitor, for he had sent envoys to So king of Egypt, and he no longer paid tribute to the king of Assyria, as he had done year by year. Therefore Shalmaneser seized him and put him in prison. 5The king of Assyria invaded the entire land, marched against Samaria and laid siege to it for three years. 6In the ninth year of Hoshea, the king of Assyria captured Samaria and deported the Israelites to Assyria. He settled them in Halah, in

Gozan on the Habor River and in the towns of the Medes.

Israel Exiled Because of Sin

7All this took place because the Israelites had sinned against the LORD their God, who had brought them out of Egypt from under the power of Pharaoh king of Egypt. They worshipped other gods 8and followed the practices of the nations the LORD had driven out before them, as well as the practices that the kings of Israel had introduced. 9The Israelites secretly did things against the LORD their God that were not right. From watchtower to fortified city they built themselves high places in all their towns. 10They set up sacred stones and Asherah poles on every high hill and under every spreading tree. 11At every high place they burned incense, as the nations whom the LORD had driven out before them had done. They did wicked things that provoked the LORD to anger. 12They worshipped idols, though the LORD had said, "You shall not do this." 13The LORD warned Israel and Judah through all his prophets and seers: "Turn from your evil ways. Observe my commands and decrees, in accordance with the entire Law that I commanded your fathers to obey and that I delivered to you through my servants the prophets."

14But they would not listen and were as stiff-necked as their fathers, who did not trust in the LORD their God. 15They rejected his decrees and the covenant he had made with their fathers and the warnings he had given them. They followed worthless idols and themselves became worthless. They imitated the nations around them although the LORD had ordered them, "Do not do as they do," and they did the things the LORD had forbidden them to do.

16They forsook all the commands of the LORD their God and made for themselves two idols cast in the shape of calves, and an Asherah pole. They bowed down to all the starry hosts, and they worshipped Baal. [17]They sacrificed their sons and daughters in the fire. They practised divination and sorcery and sold themselves to do evil in the eyes of the LORD, provoking him to anger.

[18]So the LORD was very angry with Israel and removed them from his presence. Only the tribe of Judah was left, [19]and even Judah did not keep the commands of the LORD their God. They followed the practices Israel had introduced. [20]Therefore the LORD rejected all the people of Israel; he afflicted them and gave them into the hands of plunderers, until he thrust them from his presence.

[21]When he tore Israel away from the house of David, they made Jeroboam son of Nebat their king. Jeroboam enticed Israel away from following the LORD and caused them to commit a great sin. [22]The Israelites persisted in all the sins of Jeroboam and did not turn away from them [23]until the LORD removed them from his presence, as he had warned through all his servants the prophets. So the people of Israel were taken from their homeland into exile in Assyria, and they are still there.

Samaria Resettled

[24]The king of Assyria brought people from Babylon, Cuthah, Avva, Hamath and Sepharvaim and settled them in the towns of Samaria to replace the Israelites. They took over Samaria and lived in its towns. [25]When they first lived there, they did not worship the LORD; so he sent lions among them and they killed some of the people. [26]It was reported to the king of Assyria: "The people you deported and resettled in the towns of Samaria do not know what the god of that country requires. He has sent lions among them, which are killing them off, because the people do not know what he requires."

[27]Then the king of Assyria gave this order: "Make one of the priests you took captive from Samaria go back to live there and teach the people what the god of the land requires." [28]So one of the priests who had been exiled from Samaria came to live in Bethel and taught them how to worship the LORD.

[29]Nevertheless, each national group made its own gods in the several towns where they settled, and set them up in the shrines the people of Samaria had made at the high places. [30]The men from Babylon made Succoth Benoth, the men from Cuthah made Nergal, and the men from Hamath made Ashima; [31]the Avvites made Nibhaz and Tartak, and the Sepharvites burned their children in the fire as sacrifices to Adrammelech and Anammelech, the gods of Sepharvaim. [32]They worshipped the LORD, but they also appointed all sorts of their own people to officiate for them as priests in the shrines at the high places. [33]They worshipped the LORD, but they also served their own gods in accordance with the customs of the nations from which they had been brought.

[34]To this day they persist in their former practices. They neither worship the LORD nor adhere to the decrees and ordinances, the laws and commands that the LORD gave the descendants of Jacob, whom he named Israel. [35]When the LORD made a covenant with the Israelites, he commanded them: "Do not worship any other gods or bow down to them, serve them or sacrifice to them. [36]But the LORD, who brought you up out of Egypt with mighty power and outstretched arm, is the one you must worship. To him you shall bow down and to him offer sacrifices. [37]You must always be careful to keep the decrees and ordinances, the laws and commands he wrote for you. Do not worship other gods. [38]Do not forget the covenant I have made with you, and do not worship other gods. [39]Rather, worship the LORD your God; it is he who will deliver you from the hand of all your enemies."

[40]They would not listen, however, but persisted in their former practices.

41Even while these people were worshipping the LORD, they were serving their idols. To this day their children and grandchildren continue to do as their fathers did.

NEW TESTAMENT READING
Acts 26:24–27:12

24At this point Festus interrupted Paul's defence. "You are out of your mind, Paul!" he shouted. "Your great learning is driving you insane."

25"I am not insane, most excellent Festus," Paul replied. "What I am saying is true and reasonable. 26The king is familiar with these things, and I can speak freely to him. I am convinced that none of this has escaped his notice, because it was not done in a corner. 27King Agrippa, do you believe the prophets? I know you do."

28Then Agrippa said to Paul, "Do you think that in such a short time you can persuade me to be a Christian?"

29Paul replied, "Short time or long —I pray God that not only you but all who are listening to me today may become what I am, except for these chains."

30The king rose, and with him the governor and Bernice and those sitting with them. 31They left the room, and while talking with one another, they said, "This man is not doing anything that deserves death or imprisonment."

32Agrippa said to Festus, "This man could have been set free if he had not appealed to Caesar."

Paul Sails for Rome

27 When it was decided that we would sail for Italy, Paul and some other prisoners were handed over to a centurion named Julius, who belonged to the Imperial Regiment. 2We boarded a ship from Adramyttium about to sail for ports along the coast of the province of Asia, and we put out to sea. Aristarchus, a Macedonian from Thessalonica, was with us.

3The next day we landed at Sidon; and Julius, in kindness to Paul, allowed him to go to his friends so they might provide for his needs. 4From there we put out to sea again and passed to the lee of Cyprus because the winds were against us. 5When we had sailed across the open sea off the coast of Cilicia and Pamphylia, we landed at Myra in Lycia. 6There the centurion found an Alexandrian ship sailing for Italy and put us on board. 7We made slow headway for many days and had difficulty arriving off Cnidus. When the wind did not allow us to hold our course, we sailed to the lee of Crete, opposite Salmone. 8We moved along the coast with difficulty and came to a place called Fair Havens, near the town of Lasea.

9Much time had been lost, and sailing had already become dangerous because by now it was after the Fast. So Paul warned them, 10"Men, I can see that our voyage is going to be disastrous and bring great loss to ship and cargo, and to our own lives also." 11But the centurion, instead of listening to what Paul said, followed the advice of the pilot and of the owner of the ship. 12Since the harbour was unsuitable to winter in, the majority decided that we should sail on, hoping to reach Phoenix and winter there. This was a harbour in Crete, facing both south-west and north-west.

READING FROM PSALMS
Psalm 81:8–16

8"Hear, O my people, and I will warn you—
    if you would but listen to me, O Israel!
9You shall have no foreign god among you;
    you shall not bow down to an alien god.
10I am the LORD your God,
    who brought you up out of Egypt.

Open wide your mouth and I will
  fill it.

¹¹"But my people would not listen to
  me;
  Israel would not submit to me.
¹²So I gave them over to their stubborn
  hearts
  to follow their own devices.

¹³"If my people would but listen to me,
  if Israel would follow my ways,

¹⁴how quickly would I subdue their
  enemies
  and turn my hand against their
  foes!
¹⁵Those who hate the LORD would
  cringe before him,
  and their punishment would last
  for ever.
¹⁶But you would be fed with the finest
  of wheat;
  with honey from the rock I would
  satisfy you."

JULY 9

OLD TESTAMENT READING
2 Kings 18:1–19:13

Hezekiah King of Judah

18 In the third year of Hoshea son
  of Elah king of Israel, Hezekiah
son of Ahaz king of Judah began to
reign. ²He was twenty-five years old
when he became king, and he reigned in
Jerusalem for twenty-nine years. His
mother's name was Abijah daughter of
Zechariah. ³He did what was right in
the eyes of the LORD, just as his father
David had done. ⁴He removed the high
places, smashed the sacred stones and
cut down the Asherah poles. He broke
into pieces the bronze snake Moses had
made, for up to that time the Israelites
had been burning incense to it. (It was
called Nehushtan.)

⁵Hezekiah trusted in the LORD, the
God of Israel. There was no-one like
him among all the kings of Judah, either
before him or after him. ⁶He held fast to
the LORD and did not cease to follow
him; he kept the commands the LORD
had given Moses. ⁷And the LORD was
with him; he was successful in whatever
he undertook. He rebelled against the
king of Assyria and did not serve him.
⁸From watchtower to fortified city, he

defeated the Philistines, as far as Gaza
and its territory.

⁹In King Hezekiah's fourth year,
which was the seventh year of Hoshea
son of Elah king of Israel, Shalmaneser
king of Assyria marched against Samaria and laid siege to it. ¹⁰At the end of
three years the Assyrians took it. So
Samaria was captured in Hezekiah's
sixth year, which was the ninth year of
Hoshea king of Israel. ¹¹The king of
Assyria deported Israel to Assyria and
settled them in Halah, in Gozan on the
Habor River, and in towns of the
Medes. ¹²This happened because they
had not obeyed the LORD their God, but
had violated his covenant—all that
Moses the servant of the LORD commanded. They neither listened to the
commands nor carried them out.

¹³In the fourteenth year of King
Hezekiah's reign, Sennacherib king of
Assyria attacked all the fortified cities
of Judah and captured them. ¹⁴So Hezekiah king of Judah sent this message to
the king of Assyria at Lachish: "I have
done wrong. Withdraw from me, and I
will pay whatever you demand of me."
The king of Assyria exacted from Hezekiah king of Judah three hundred talents
of silver and thirty talents of gold. ¹⁵So
Hezekiah gave him all the silver that

was found in the temple of the LORD and in the treasuries of the royal palace.

16At this time Hezekiah king of Judah stripped off the gold with which he had covered the doors and doorposts of the temple of the LORD, and gave it to the king of Assyria.

Sennacherib Threatens Jerusalem

17The king of Assyria sent his supreme commander, his chief officer and his field commander with a large army, from Lachish to King Hezekiah at Jerusalem. They came up to Jerusalem and stopped at the aqueduct of the Upper Pool, on the road to the Washerman's Field. 18They called for the king; and Eliakim son of Hilkiah the palace administrator, Shebna the secretary, and Joah son of Asaph the recorder went out to them.

19The field commander said to them, "Tell Hezekiah:

" 'This is what the great king, the king of Assyria, says: On what are you basing this confidence of yours? 20You say you have strategy and military strength—but you speak only empty words. On whom are you depending, that you rebel against me? 21Look now, you are depending on Egypt, that splintered reed of a staff, which pierces a man's hand and wounds him if he leans on it! Such is Pharaoh king of Egypt to all who depend on him. 22And if you say to me, "We are depending on the LORD our God" —isn't he the one whose high places and altars Hezekiah removed, saying to Judah and Jerusalem, "You must worship before this altar in Jerusalem"?

23" 'Come now, make a bargain with my master, the king of Assyria: I will give you two thousand horses—if you can put riders on them! 24How can you repulse one officer of the least of my master's officials, even though you are depending on Egypt for chariots and horsemen? 25Furthermore, have I come to attack and destroy this place without word from the LORD? The LORD himself told me to march against this country and destroy it.' "

26Then Eliakim son of Hilkiah, and Shebna and Joah said to the field commander, "Please speak to your servants in Aramaic, since we understand it. Don't speak to us in Hebrew in the hearing of the people on the wall."

27But the commander replied, "Was it only to your master and you that my master sent me to say these things, and not to the men sitting on the wall— who, like you, will have to eat their own filth and drink their own urine?"

28Then the commander stood and called out in Hebrew: "Hear the word of the great king, the king of Assyria! 29This is what the king says: Do not let Hezekiah deceive you. He cannot deliver you from my hand. 30Do not let Hezekiah persuade you to trust in the LORD when he says, 'The LORD will surely deliver us; this city will not be given into the hand of the king of Assyria.'

31"Do not listen to Hezekiah. This is what the king of Assyria says: Make peace with me and come out to me. Then every one of you will eat from his own vine and fig-tree and drink water from his own cistern, 32until I come and take you to a land like your own, a land of grain and new wine, a land of bread and vineyards, a land of olive trees and honey. Choose life and not death!

"Do not listen to Hezekiah, for he is misleading you when he says, 'The LORD will deliver us.' 33Has the god of any nation ever delivered his land from the hand of the king of Assyria? 34Where are the gods of Hamath and Arpad? Where are the gods of Sepharvaim, Hena and Ivvah? Have they rescued Samaria from my hand? 35Who of all the gods of these countries has been able to save his land from me? How then can the LORD deliver Jerusalem from my hand?"

³⁶But the people remained silent and said nothing in reply, because the king had commanded, "Do not answer him."

³⁷Then Eliakim son of Hilkiah the palace administrator, Shebna the secretary and Joah son of Asaph the recorder went to Hezekiah, with their clothes torn, and told him what the field commander had said.

Jerusalem's Deliverance Foretold

19 When King Hezekiah heard this, he tore his clothes and put on sackcloth and went into the temple of the LORD. ²He sent Eliakim the palace administrator, Shebna the secretary and the leading priests, all wearing sackcloth, to the prophet Isaiah son of Amoz. ³They told him, "This is what Hezekiah says: This day is a day of distress and rebuke and disgrace, as when children come to the point of birth and there is no strength to deliver them. ⁴It may be that the LORD your God will hear all the words of the field commander, whom his master, the king of Assyria, has sent to ridicule the living God, and that he will rebuke him for the words the LORD your God has heard. Therefore pray for the remnant that still survives."

⁵When King Hezekiah's officials came to Isaiah, ⁶Isaiah said to them, "Tell your master, 'This is what the LORD says: Do not be afraid of what you have heard—those words with which the underlings of the king of Assyria have blasphemed me. ⁷Listen! I am going to put such a spirit in him that when he hears a certain report, he will return to his own country, and there I will have him cut down with the sword.'"

⁸When the field commander heard that the king of Assyria had left Lachish, he withdrew and found the king fighting against Libnah.

⁹Now Sennacherib received a report that Tirhakah, the Cushite king of Egypt, was marching out to fight against him. So he again sent messengers to Hezekiah with this word: ¹⁰"Say to Hezekiah king of Judah: Do not let the god you depend on deceive you when he says, 'Jerusalem will not be handed over to the king of Assyria.' ¹¹Surely you have heard what the kings of Assyria have done to all the countries, destroying them completely. And will you be delivered? ¹²Did the gods of the nations that were destroyed by my forefathers deliver them: the gods of Gozan, Haran, Rezeph and the people of Eden who were in Tel Assar? ¹³Where is the king of Hamath, the king of Arpad, the king of the city of Sepharvaim, or of Hena or Ivvah?"

NEW TESTAMENT READING
Acts 27:13–44

The Storm

¹³When a gentle south wind began to blow, they thought they had obtained what they wanted; so they weighed anchor and sailed along the shore of Crete. ¹⁴Before very long, a wind of hurricane force, called the "northeaster", swept down from the island. ¹⁵The ship was caught by the storm and could not head into the wind; so we gave way to it and were driven along. ¹⁶As we passed to the lee of a small island called Cauda, we were hardly able to make the lifeboat secure. ¹⁷When the men had hoisted it aboard, they passed ropes under the ship itself to hold it together. Fearing that they would run aground on the sand-bars of Syrtis, they lowered the sea anchor and let the ship be driven along. ¹⁸We took such a violent battering from the storm that the next day they began to throw the cargo overboard. ¹⁹On the third day, they threw the ship's tackle overboard with their own hands. ²⁰When neither sun nor stars appeared for many days and the

storm continued raging, we finally gave up all hope of being saved.

21After the men had gone a long time without food, Paul stood up before them and said: "Men, you should have taken my advice not to sail from Crete; then you would have spared yourselves this damage and loss. 22But now I urge you to keep up your courage, because not one of you will be lost; only the ship will be destroyed. 23Last night an angel of the God whose I am and whom I serve stood beside me 24and said, 'Do not be afraid, Paul. You must stand trial before Caesar; and God has graciously given you the lives of all who sail with you.' 25So keep up your courage, men, for I have faith in God that it will happen just as he told me. 26Nevertheless, we must run aground on some island."

The Shipwreck

27On the fourteenth night we were still being driven across the Adriatic Sea, when about midnight the sailors sensed they were approaching land. 28They took soundings and found that the water was one hundred and twenty feet deep. A short time later they took soundings again and found it was ninety feet deep. 29Fearing that we would be dashed against the rocks, they dropped four anchors from the stern and prayed for daylight. 30In an attempt to escape from the ship, the sailors let the lifeboat down into the sea, pretending they were going to lower some anchors from the bow. 31Then Paul said to the centurion and the soldiers, "Unless these men stay with the ship, you cannot be saved." 32So the soldiers cut the ropes that held the lifeboat and let it fall away.

33Just before dawn Paul urged them all to eat. "For the last fourteen days," he said, "you have been in constant suspense and have gone without food —you haven't eaten anything. 34Now I urge you to take some food. You need it to survive. Not one of you will lose a single hair from his head." 35After he said this, he took some bread and gave

thanks to God in front of them all. Then he broke it and began to eat. 36They were all encouraged and ate some food themselves. 37Altogether there were 276 of us on board. 38When they had eaten as much as they wanted, they lightened the ship by throwing the grain into the sea.

39When daylight came, they did not recognise the land, but they saw a bay with a sandy beach, where they decided to run the ship aground if they could. 40Cutting loose the anchors, they left them in the sea and at the same time untied the ropes that held the rudders. Then they hoisted the foresail to the wind and made for the beach. 41But the ship struck a sand-bar and ran aground. The bow stuck fast and would not move, and the stern was broken to pieces by the pounding of the surf.

42The soldiers planned to kill the prisoners to prevent any of them from swimming away and escaping. 43But the centurion wanted to spare Paul's life and kept them from carrying out their plan. He ordered those who could swim to jump overboard first and get to land. 44The rest were to get there on planks or on pieces of the ship. In this way everyone reached land in safety.

READING FROM PSALMS
Psalm 82:1–8

A psalm of Asaph.

1God presides in the great assembly;
  he gives judgment among the
    "gods":

2"How long will you defend the unjust
  and show partiality to the wicked?
                              Selah
3Defend the cause of the weak and
    fatherless;
  maintain the rights of the poor and
    oppressed.
4Rescue the weak and needy;
  deliver them from the hand of the
    wicked.

5"They know nothing, they
    understand nothing.
    They walk about in darkness;
    all the foundations of the earth are
        shaken.

6"I said, 'You are "gods";
    you are all sons of the Most High.'

7But you will die like mere men;
    you will fall like every other
        ruler."

8Rise up, O God, judge the earth,
    for all the nations are your
        inheritance.

JULY 10   DAY 191

OLD TESTAMENT READING
2 Kings 19:14–20:21

Hezekiah's Prayer

14Hezekiah received the letter from
the messengers and read it. Then he
went up to the temple of the LORD and
spread it out before the LORD. 15And
Hezekiah prayed to the LORD: "O
LORD, God of Israel, enthroned between the cherubim, you alone are God
over all the kingdoms of the earth. You
have made heaven and earth. 16Give
ear, O LORD, and hear; open your eyes,
O LORD, and see; listen to the words
Sennacherib has sent to insult the living
God.

17"It is true, O LORD, that the Assyrian kings have laid waste these
nations and their lands. 18They have
thrown their gods into the fire and destroyed them, for they were not gods
but only wood and stone, fashioned by
men's hands. 19Now, O LORD our God,
deliver us from his hand, so that you
alone, O LORD, are God."

Isaiah Prophesies Sennacherib's Fall

20Then Isaiah son of Amoz sent a
message to Hezekiah: "This is what the
LORD, the God of Israel, says: I have
heard your prayer concerning Sennacherib king of Assyria. 21This is the

word that the LORD has spoken against
him:

"'The Virgin Daughter of Zion
    despises you and mocks you.
The Daughter of Jerusalem
    tosses her head as you flee.
22Who is it you have insulted and
        blasphemed?
    Against whom have you raised
        your voice
and lifted your eyes in pride?
    Against the Holy One of Israel!
23By your messengers
    you have heaped insults on the
        Lord.
And you have said,
    "With my many chariots
I have ascended the heights of the
        mountains,
    the utmost heights of Lebanon.
I have cut down its tallest cedars,
    the choicest of its pines.
I have reached its remotest parts,
    the finest of its forests.
24I have dug wells in foreign lands
    and drunk the water there.
With the soles of my feet
    I have dried up all the streams of
        Egypt."

25"'Have you not heard?
    Long ago I ordained it.
In days of old I planned it;
    now I have brought it to pass,
that you have turned fortified cities
    into piles of stone.

26Their people, drained of power,
    are dismayed and put to shame.
They are like plants in the field,
    like tender green shoots,
like grass sprouting on the roof,
    scorched before it grows up.

27" 'But I know where you stay
    and when you come and go
    and how you rage against me.
28Because you rage against me
    and your insolence has reached my
        ears,
I will put my hook in your nose
    and my bit in your mouth,
and I will make you return
    by the way you came.'

29"This will be the sign for you, O
Hezekiah:

This year you will eat what grows by
      itself,
    and the second year what springs
      from that.
But in the third year sow and reap,
    plant vineyards and eat their fruit.
30Once more a remnant of the house of
      Judah
will take root below and bear fruit
    above.
31For out of Jerusalem will come a
      remnant,
    and out of Mount Zion a band of
      survivors.

The zeal of the LORD Almighty will
accomplish this.

32"Therefore this is what the LORD
says concerning the king of Assyria:

"He will not enter this city
    or shoot an arrow here.
He will not come before it with shield
    or build a siege ramp against it.
33By the way that he came he will
      return;
    he will not enter this city,
           declares the LORD.
34I will defend this city and save it,
    for my sake and for the sake of
      David my servant."

35That night the angel of the LORD
went out and put to death a hundred
and eighty-five thousand men in the
Assyrian camp. When the people got up
the next morning—there were all the
dead bodies! 36So Sennacherib king of
Assyria broke camp and withdrew. He
returned to Nineveh and stayed there.

37One day, while he was worshipping
in the temple of his god Nisroch, his
sons Adrammelech and Sharezer cut
him down with the sword, and they
escaped to the land of Ararat. And
Esarhaddon his son succeeded him as
king.

Hezekiah's Illness

20 In those days Hezekiah became
ill and was at the point of death.
The prophet Isaiah son of Amoz went to
him and said, "This is what the LORD
says: Put your house in order, because
you are going to die; you will not
recover."

2Hezekiah turned his face to the wall
and prayed to the LORD, 3"Remember,
O LORD, how I have walked before you
faithfully and with wholehearted devotion and have done what is good in your
eyes." And Hezekiah wept bitterly.

4Before Isaiah had left the middle
court, the word of the LORD came to
him: 5"Go back and tell Hezekiah, the
leader of my people, 'This is what the
LORD, the God of your father David,
says: I have heard your prayer and seen
your tears; I will heal you. On the third
day from now you will go up to the
temple of the LORD. 6I will add fifteen
years to your life. And I will deliver you
and this city from the hand of the king of
Assyria. I will defend this city for my
sake and for the sake of my servant
David.' "

7Then Isaiah said, "Prepare a poultice of figs." They did so and applied it
to the boil, and he recovered.

8Hezekiah had asked Isaiah, "What
will be the sign that the LORD will heal
me and that I will go up to the temple of
the LORD on the third day from now?"

9Isaiah answered, "This is the LORD's sign to you that the LORD will do what he has promised: Shall the shadow go forward ten steps, or shall it go back ten steps?"

10"It is a simple matter for the shadow to go forward ten steps," said Hezekiah. "Rather, have it go back ten steps."

11Then the prophet Isaiah called upon the LORD, and the LORD made the shadow go back the ten steps it had gone down on the stairway of Ahaz.

Envoys From Babylon

12At that time Merodach-Baladan son of Baladan king of Babylon sent Hezekiah letters and a gift, because he had heard of Hezekiah's illness. 13Hezekiah received the messengers and showed them all that was in his storehouses—the silver, the gold, the spices and the fine oil—his armoury and everything found among his treasures. There was nothing in his palace or in all his kingdom that Hezekiah did not show them.

14Then Isaiah the prophet went to King Hezekiah and asked, "What did those men say, and where did they come from?"

"From a distant land," Hezekiah replied. "They came from Babylon."

15The prophet asked, "What did they see in your palace?"

"They saw everything in my palace," Hezekiah said. "There is nothing among my treasures that I did not show them."

16Then Isaiah said to Hezekiah, "Hear the word of the LORD: 17The time will surely come when everything in your palace, and all that your fathers have stored up until this day, will be carried off to Babylon. Nothing will be left, says the LORD. 18And some of your descendants, your own flesh and blood, that will be born to you, will be taken away, and they will become eunuchs in the palace of the king of Babylon."

19"The word of the LORD you have spoken is good," Hezekiah replied. For he thought, "Will there not be peace and security in my lifetime?"

20As for the other events of Hezekiah's reign, all his achievements and how he made the pool and the tunnel by which he brought water into the city, are they not written in the book of the annals of the kings of Judah? 21Hezekiah rested with his fathers. And Manasseh his son succeeded him as king.

NEW TESTAMENT READING
Acts 28:1–16

Ashore on Malta

28 Once safely on shore, we found out that the island was called Malta. 2The islanders showed us unusual kindness. They built a fire and welcomed us all because it was raining and cold. 3Paul gathered a pile of brushwood and, as he put it on the fire, a viper, driven out by the heat, fastened itself on his hand. 4When the islanders saw the snake hanging from his hand, they said to each other, "This man must be a murderer; for though he escaped from the sea, Justice has not allowed him to live." 5But Paul shook the snake off into the fire and suffered no ill effects. 6The people expected him to swell up or suddenly fall dead, but after waiting a long time and seeing nothing unusual happen to him, they changed their minds and said he was a god.

7There was an estate near by that belonged to Publius, the chief official of the island. He welcomed us to his home and for three days entertained us hospitably. 8His father was sick in bed, suffering from fever and dysentery. Paul went in to see him and, after prayer, placed his hands on him and healed him. 9When this had happened, the rest of the sick on the island came and were cured. 10They honoured us in many ways and when we were ready to sail, they furnished us with the supplies we needed.

Arrival at Rome

¹¹After three months we put out to sea in a ship that had wintered in the island. It was an Alexandrian ship with the figurehead of the twin gods Castor and Pollux. ¹²We put in at Syracuse and stayed there three days. ¹³From there we set sail and arrived at Rhegium. The next day the south wind came up, and on the following day we reached Puteoli. ¹⁴There we found some brothers who invited us to spend a week with them. And so we came to Rome. ¹⁵The brothers there had heard that we were coming, and they travelled as far as the Forum of Appius and the Three Taverns to meet us. At the sight of these men Paul thanked God and was encouraged. ¹⁶When we got to Rome, Paul was allowed to live by himself, with a soldier to guard him.

READING FROM PSALMS
Psalm 83:1–18

A song. A psalm of Asaph.

¹O God, do not keep silent;
　　be not quiet, O God, be not still.
²See how your enemies are astir,
　　how your foes rear their heads.
³With cunning they conspire against
　　your people;
　　they plot against those you cherish.
⁴"Come," they say, "let us destroy
　　them as a nation,
　　that the name of Israel be
　　remembered no more."

⁵With one mind they plot together;
　　they form an alliance against you—
⁶the tents of Edom and the
　　Ishmaelites,
　　of Moab and the Hagrites,
⁷Gebal, Ammon and Amalek,
　　Philistia, with the people of Tyre.
⁸Even Assyria has joined them
　　to lend strength to the descendants
　　of Lot.　　　　　*Selah*

⁹Do to them as you did to Midian,
　　as you did to Sisera and Jabin at
　　the river Kishon,
¹⁰who perished at Endor
　　and became like refuse on the
　　ground.
¹¹Make their nobles like Oreb and
　　Zeeb,
　　all their princes like Zebah and
　　Zalmunna,
¹²who said, "Let us take possession
　　of the pasture-lands of God."

¹³Make them like tumble-weed, O my
　　God,
　　like chaff before the wind.
¹⁴As fire consumes the forest
　　or a flame sets the mountains
　　ablaze,
¹⁵so pursue them with your tempest
　　and terrify them with your storm.
¹⁶Cover their faces with shame
　　so that men will seek your name, O
　　LORD.

¹⁷May they ever be ashamed and
　　dismayed;
　　may they perish in disgrace.
¹⁸Let them know that you, whose name
　　is the LORD—
　　that you alone are the Most High
　　over all the earth.

OLD TESTAMENT READING
2 Kings 21:1–22:20

Manasseh King of Judah

21 Manasseh was twelve years old when he became king, and he reigned in Jerusalem for fifty-five years. His mother's name was Hephzibah. ²He did evil in the eyes of the LORD, following the detestable practices of the nations the LORD had driven out before the Israelites. ³He rebuilt the high places his father Hezekiah had destroyed; he also erected altars to Baal and made an Asherah pole, as Ahab king of Israel had done. He bowed down to all the starry hosts and worshipped them. ⁴He built altars in the temple of the LORD, of which the LORD had said, "In Jerusalem I will put my Name." ⁵In both courts of the temple of the LORD, he built altars to all the starry hosts. ⁶He sacrificed his own son in the fire, practised sorcery and divination, and consulted mediums and spiritists. He did much evil in the eyes of the LORD, provoking him to anger.

⁷He took the carved Asherah pole he had made and put it in the temple, of which the LORD had said to David and to his son Solomon, "In this temple and in Jerusalem, which I have chosen out of all the tribes of Israel, I will put my Name for ever. ⁸I will not again make the feet of the Israelites wander from the land I gave their forefathers, if only they will be careful to do everything I commanded them and will keep the whole Law that my servant Moses gave them." ⁹But the people did not listen. Manasseh led them astray, so that they did more evil than the nations the LORD had destroyed before the Israelites.

¹⁰The LORD said through his servants the prophets: ¹¹"Manasseh king of Judah has committed these detestable sins. He has done more evil than the Amorites who preceded him and has led Judah into sin with his idols. ¹²Therefore this is what the LORD, the God of Israel, says: I am going to bring such disaster on Jerusalem and Judah that the ears of everyone who hears of it will tingle. ¹³I will stretch out over Jerusalem the measuring line used against Samaria and the plumb-line used against the house of Ahab. I will wipe out Jerusalem as one wipes out a dish, wiping it and turning it upside-down. ¹⁴I will forsake the remnant of my inheritance and hand them over to their enemies. They will be looted and plundered by all their foes, ¹⁵because they have done evil in my eyes and have provoked me to anger from the day their forefathers came out of Egypt until this day."

¹⁶Moreover, Manasseh also shed so much innocent blood that he filled Jerusalem from end to end—besides the sin that he had caused Judah to commit, so that they did evil in the eyes of the LORD.

¹⁷As for the other events of Manasseh's reign, and all he did, including the sin he committed, are they not written in the book of the annals of the kings of Judah? ¹⁸Manasseh rested with his fathers and was buried in his palace garden, the garden of Uzza. And Amon his son succeeded him as king.

Amon King of Judah

¹⁹Amon was twenty-two years old when he became king, and he reigned in Jerusalem for two years. His mother's name was Meshullemeth daughter of Haruz; she was from Jotbah. ²⁰He did evil in the eyes of the LORD, as his father Manasseh had done. ²¹He walked in all the ways of his father; he worshipped the idols his father had worshipped, and bowed down to them. ²²He forsook the

LORD, the God of his fathers, and did not walk in the way of the LORD.

²³Amon's officials conspired against him and assassinated the king in his palace. ²⁴Then the people of the land killed all who had plotted against King Amon, and they made Josiah his son king in his place.

²⁵As for the other events of Amon's reign, and what he did, are they not written in the book of the annals of the kings of Judah? ²⁶He was buried in his grave in the garden of Uzza. And Josiah his son succeeded him as king.

The Book of the Law Found

22 Josiah was eight years old when he became king, and he reigned in Jerusalem for thirty-one years. His mother's name was Jedidah daughter of Adaiah; she was from Bozkath. ²He did what was right in the eyes of the LORD and walked in all the ways of his father David, not turning aside to the right or to the left.

³In the eighteenth year of his reign, King Josiah sent the secretary, Shaphan son of Azaliah, the son of Meshullam, to the temple of the LORD. He said: ⁴"Go up to Hilkiah the high priest and make him get ready the money that has been brought into the temple of the LORD, which the doorkeepers have collected from the people. ⁵Make them entrust it to the men appointed to supervise the work on the temple. And make these men pay the workers who repair the temple of the LORD—⁶the carpenters, the builders and the masons. Also make them purchase timber and dressed stone to repair the temple. ⁷But they need not account for the money entrusted to them, because they are acting faithfully."

⁸Hilkiah the high priest said to Shaphan the secretary, "I have found the Book of the Law in the temple of the LORD." He gave it to Shaphan, who read it. ⁹Then Shaphan the secretary went to the king and reported to him: "Your officials have paid out the money that was in the temple of the LORD and have entrusted it to the workers and supervisors at the temple." ¹⁰Then Shaphan the secretary informed the king, "Hilkiah the priest has given me a book." And Shaphan read from it in the presence of the king.

¹¹When the king heard the words of the Book of the Law, he tore his robes. ¹²He gave these orders to Hilkiah the priest, Ahikam son of Shaphan, Acbor son of Micaiah, Shaphan the secretary and Asaiah the king's attendant: ¹³"Go and enquire of the LORD for me and for the people and for all Judah about what is written in this book that has been found. Great is the LORD's anger that burns against us because our fathers have not obeyed the words of this book; they have not acted in accordance with all that is written there concerning us."

¹⁴Hilkiah the priest, Ahikam, Acbor, Shaphan and Asaiah went to speak to the prophetess Huldah, who was the wife of Shallum son of Tikvah, the son of Harhas, keeper of the wardrobe. She lived in Jerusalem, in the Second District.

¹⁵She said to them, "This is what the LORD, the God of Israel, says: Tell the man who sent you to me, ¹⁶'This is what the LORD says: I am going to bring disaster on this place and its people, according to everything written in the book the king of Judah has read. ¹⁷Because they have forsaken me and burned incense to other gods and provoked me to anger by all the idols their hands have made, my anger will burn against this place and will not be quenched.' ¹⁸Tell the king of Judah, who sent you to enquire of the LORD, 'This is what the LORD, the God of Israel, says concerning the words you heard: ¹⁹Because your heart was responsive and you humbled yourself before the LORD when you heard what I have spoken against this place and its people, that they would become accursed and laid waste, and because you tore your robes and wept in my presence, I have heard you, declares the LORD.

²⁰Therefore I will gather you to your fathers, and you will be buried in peace. Your eyes will not see all the disaster I am going to bring on this place.'"

So they took her answer back to the king.

NEW TESTAMENT READING
Acts 28:17–31

Paul Preaches at Rome Under Guard

¹⁷Three days later he called together the leaders of the Jews. When they had assembled, Paul said to them: "My brothers, although I have done nothing against our people or against the customs of our ancestors, I was arrested in Jerusalem and handed over to the Romans. ¹⁸They examined me and wanted to release me, because I was not guilty of any crime deserving death. ¹⁹But when the Jews objected, I was compelled to appeal to Caesar—not that I had any charge to bring against my own people. ²⁰For this reason I have asked to see you and talk with you. It is because of the hope of Israel that I am bound with this chain."

²¹They replied, "We have not received any letters from Judea concerning you, and none of the brothers who have come from there has reported or said anything bad about you. ²²But we want to hear what your views are, for we know that people everywhere are talking against this sect."

²³They arranged to meet Paul on a certain day, and came in even larger numbers to the place where he was staying. From morning till evening he explained and declared to them the kingdom of God and tried to convince them about Jesus from the Law of Moses and from the Prophets. ²⁴Some were convinced by what he said, but others would not believe. ²⁵They disagreed among themselves and began to leave after Paul had made this final statement: "The Holy Spirit spoke the truth to your forefathers when he said through Isaiah the prophet:

²⁶"'Go to this people and say,
"You will be ever hearing but never
  understanding;
  you will be ever seeing but never
    perceiving."
²⁷For this people's heart has become
  calloused;
  they hardly hear with their ears,
  and they have closed their eyes.
Otherwise they might see with their
  eyes,
  hear with their ears,
  understand with their hearts
and turn, and I would heal them.'

²⁸"Therefore I want you to know that God's salvation has been sent to the Gentiles, and they will listen!"

³⁰For two whole years Paul stayed there in his own rented house and welcomed all who came to see him. ³¹Boldly and without hindrance he preached the kingdom of God and taught about the Lord Jesus Christ.

READING FROM PROVERBS
Proverbs 16:28–17:4

²⁸A perverse man stirs up dissension,
  and a gossip separates close
    friends.

²⁹A violent man entices his neighbour
  and leads him down a path that is
    not good.

³⁰He who winks with his eye is plotting
  perversity;
  he who purses his lips is bent on
    evil.

³¹Grey hair is a crown of splendour;
  it is attained by a righteous life.

³²Better a patient man than a warrior,
  a man who controls his temper
  than one who takes a city.

33The lot is cast into the lap,
   but its every decision is from the
   LORD.

17 Better a dry crust with peace
     and quiet
   than a house full of feasting, with
     strife.

2A wise servant will rule over a
   disgraceful son,

and will share the inheritance as
   one of the brothers.

3The crucible for silver and the
   furnace for gold,
   but the LORD tests the heart.

4A wicked man listens to evil lips;
   a liar pays attention to a malicious
     tongue.

JULY 12

OLD TESTAMENT READING
2 Kings 23:1–24:7

Josiah Renews the Covenant

23 Then the king called together all
     the elders of Judah and Jeru-
salem. 2He went up to the temple of
the LORD with the men of Judah, the people
of Jerusalem, the priests and the
prophets—all the people from the least
to the greatest. He read in their hearing
all the words of the Book of the Covenant, which had been found in the
temple of the LORD. 3The king stood by
the pillar and renewed the covenant
in the presence of the LORD—to follow the
LORD and keep his commands, regulations and decrees with all his heart and
all his soul, thus confirming the words of
the covenant written in this book. Then
all the people pledged themselves to the
covenant.

4The king ordered Hilkiah the high
priest, the priests next in rank and the
doorkeepers to remove from the temple
of the LORD all the articles made for
Baal and Asherah and all the starry
hosts. He burned them outside Jerusalem in the fields of the Kidron Valley
and took the ashes to Bethel. 5He did
away with the pagan priests appointed
by the kings of Judah to burn incense on
the high places of the towns of Judah
and on those around Jerusalem—those
who burned incense to Baal, to the sun
and moon, to the constellations and to
all the starry hosts. 6He took the Asherah pole from the temple of the LORD
to the Kidron Valley outside Jerusalem
and burned it there. He ground it to
powder and scattered the dust over the
graves of the common people. 7He also
tore down the quarters of the male
shrine-prostitutes, which were in the
temple of the LORD and where women
did weaving for Asherah.

8Josiah brought all the priests from
the towns of Judah and desecrated the
high places, from Geba to Beersheba,
where the priests had burned incense.
He broke down the shrines at the gates
—at the entrance to the Gate of Joshua,
the city governor, which is on the left of
the city gate. 9Although the priests
of the high places did not serve at the
altar of the LORD in Jerusalem, they ate
unleavened bread with their fellow
priests.

10He desecrated Topheth, which was
in the Valley of Ben Hinnom, so no-one
could use it to sacrifice his son or daughter in the fire to Molech. 11He removed
from the entrance to the temple of the
LORD the horses that the kings of Judah
had dedicated to the sun. They were in

the court near the room of an official named Nathan-Melech. Josiah then burned the chariots dedicated to the sun.

12He pulled down the altars the kings of Judah had erected on the roof near the upper room of Ahaz, and the altars Manasseh had built in the two courts of the temple of the LORD. He removed them from there, smashed them to pieces and threw the rubble into the Kidron Valley. 13The king also desecrated the high places that were east of Jerusalem on the south of the Hill of Corruption—the ones Solomon king of Israel had built for Ashtoreth the vile goddess of the Sidonians, for Chemosh the vile god of Moab, and for Molech the detestable god of the people of Ammon. 14Josiah smashed the sacred stones and cut down the Asherah poles and covered the sites with human bones.

15Even the altar at Bethel, the high place made by Jeroboam son of Nebat, who had caused Israel to sin—even that altar and high place he demolished. He burned the high place and ground it to powder, and burned the Asherah pole also. 16Then Josiah looked around, and when he saw the tombs that were there on the hillside, he had the bones removed from them and burned on the altar to defile it, in accordance with the word of the LORD proclaimed by the man of God who foretold these things.

17The king asked, "What is that tombstone I see?"

The men of the city said, "It marks the tomb of the man of God who came from Judah and pronounced against the altar of Bethel the very things you have done to it."

18"Leave it alone," he said. "Don't let anyone disturb his bones." So they spared his bones and those of the prophet who had come from Samaria.

19Just as he had done at Bethel, Josiah removed and defiled all the shrines at the high places that the kings of Israel had built in the towns of Samaria that had provoked the LORD to anger. 20Josiah slaughtered all the priests of those high places on the altars and burned human bones on them. Then he went back to Jerusalem.

21The king gave this order to all the people: "Celebrate the Passover to the LORD your God, as it is written in this Book of the Covenant." 22Not since the days of the judges who led Israel, nor throughout the days of the kings of Israel and the kings of Judah, had any such Passover been observed. 23But in the eighteenth year of King Josiah, this Passover was celebrated to the LORD in Jerusalem.

24Furthermore, Josiah got rid of the mediums and spiritists, the household gods, the idols and all the other detestable things seen in Judah and Jerusalem. This he did to fulfil the requirements of the law written in the book that Hilkiah the priest had discovered in the temple of the LORD. 25Neither before nor after Josiah was there a king like him who turned to the LORD as he did—with all his heart and with all his soul and with all his strength, in accordance with all the Law of Moses.

26Nevertheless, the LORD did not turn away from the heat of his fierce anger, which burned against Judah because of all that Manasseh had done to provoke him to anger. 27So the LORD said, "I will remove Judah also from my presence as I removed Israel, and I will reject Jerusalem, the city I chose, and this temple, about which I said, 'There shall my Name be.'"

28As for the other events of Josiah's reign, and all he did, are they not written in the book of the annals of the kings of Judah?

29While Josiah was king, Pharaoh Neco king of Egypt went up to the Euphrates River to help the king of Assyria. King Josiah marched out to meet him in battle, but Neco faced him and killed him at Megiddo. 30Josiah's servants brought his body in a chariot from Megiddo to Jerusalem and buried him in his own tomb. And the people of the land took Jehoahaz son of Josiah and anointed him and made him king in place of his father.

Jehoahaz King of Judah

31Jehoahaz was twenty-three years old when he became king, and he reigned in Jerusalem for three months. His mother's name was Hamutal daughter of Jeremiah; she was from Libnah. 32He did evil in the eyes of the LORD, just as his fathers had done. 33Pharaoh Neco put him in chains at Riblah in the land of Hamath so that he might not reign in Jerusalem, and he imposed on Judah a levy of a hundred talents of silver and a talent of gold. 34Pharaoh Neco made Eliakim son of Josiah king in place of his father Josiah and changed Eliakim's name to Jehoiakim. But he took Jehoahaz and carried him off to Egypt, and there he died. 35Jehoiakim paid Pharaoh Neco the silver and gold he demanded. In order to do so, he taxed the land and exacted the silver and gold from the people of the land according to their assessments.

Jehoiakim King of Judah

36Jehoiakim was twenty-five years old when he became king, and he reigned in Jerusalem for eleven years. His mother's name was Zebidah daughter of Pedaiah; she was from Rumah. 37And he did evil in the eyes of the LORD, just as his fathers had done.

24 During Jehoiakim's reign, Nebuchadnezzar king of Babylon invaded the land, and Jehoiakim became his vassal for three years. But then he changed his mind and rebelled against Nebuchadnezzar. 2The LORD sent Babylonian, Aramean, Moabite and Ammonite raiders against him. He sent them to destroy Judah, in accordance with the word of the LORD proclaimed by his servants the prophets. 3Surely these things happened to Judah

according to the LORD's command, in order to remove them from his presence because of the sins of Manasseh and all he had done, 4including the shedding of innocent blood. For he had filled Jerusalem with innocent blood, and the LORD was not willing to forgive.

5As for the other events of Jehoiakim's reign, and all he did, are they not written in the book of the annals of the kings of Judah? 6Jehoiakim rested with his fathers. And Jehoiachin his son succeeded him as king.

7The king of Egypt did not march out from his own country again, because the king of Babylon had taken all his territory, from the Wadi of Egypt to the Euphrates River.

NEW TESTAMENT READING
Romans 1:1–17

1 Paul, a servant of Christ Jesus, called to be an apostle and set apart for the gospel of God—2the gospel he promised beforehand through his prophets in the Holy Scriptures 3regarding his Son, who as to his human nature was a descendant of David, 4and who through the Spirit of holiness was declared with power to be the Son of God, by his resurrection from the dead: Jesus Christ our Lord. 5Through him and for his name's sake, we received grace and apostleship to call people from among all the Gentiles to the obedience that comes from faith. 6And you also are among those who are called to belong to Jesus Christ.

7To all in Rome who are loved by God and called to be saints:

Grace and peace to you from God our Father and from the Lord Jesus Christ.

Paul's Longing to Visit Rome

8First, I thank my God through Jesus Christ for all of you, because your faith is being reported all over the world. 9God, whom I serve with my whole heart in preaching the gospel of his Son, is my witness that constantly I remember you 10in my prayers at all times; and I pray that now at last by God's will the way may be opened for me to come to you.

11I long to see you so that I may impart to you some spiritual gift to make you strong—12that is, that you and I may be mutually encouraged by each other's faith. 13I do not want you to be unaware, brothers, that I planned many times to come to you (but have been prevented from doing so until now) in order that I might have a harvest among you, just as I have had among the other Gentiles.

14I am bound both to Greeks and non-Greeks, both to the wise and the foolish. 15That is why I am so eager to preach the gospel also to you who are at Rome.

16I am not ashamed of the gospel, because it is the power of God for the salvation of everyone who believes: first for the Jew, then for the Gentile. 17For in the gospel a righteousness from God is revealed, a righteousness that is by faith from first to last, just as it is written: "The righteous will live by faith."

READING FROM PSALMS
Psalm 84:1–7

For the director of music. According to *gittith*. Of the Sons of Korah. A psalm.

1How lovely is your dwelling-place,
    O LORD Almighty!
2My soul yearns, even faints,
    for the courts of the LORD;
my heart and my flesh cry out
    for the living God.

3Even the sparrow has found a home,
    and the swallow a nest for herself,
    where she may have her young—
a place near your altar,
    O LORD Almighty, my King and
        my God.
4Blessed are those who dwell in your
        house;
    they are ever praising you.   *Selah*

5Blessed are those whose strength is in
        you,
    who have set their hearts on
        pilgrimage.
6As they pass through the Valley of
        Baca,
    they make it a place of springs;
    the autumn rains also cover it with
        pools.
7They go from strength to strength,
    till each appears before God in
        Zion.

JULY 13   DAY 194

OLD TESTAMENT READING
2 Kings 24:8–25:30

Jehoiachin King of Judah

8Jehoiachin was eighteen years old when he became king, and he reigned in Jerusalem for three months. His mother's name was Nehushta daughter of Elnathan; she was from Jerusalem. 9He did evil in the eyes of the LORD, just as his father had done.

10At that time the officers of Nebuchadnezzar king of Babylon advanced on Jerusalem and laid siege to it, 11and Nebuchadnezzar himself came up to the city while his officers were besieging it. 12Jehoiachin king of Judah, his mother, his attendants, his nobles and his officials all surrendered to him.

In the eighth year of the reign of the king of Babylon, he took Jehoiachin prisoner. 13As the LORD had declared, Nebuchadnezzar removed all the treasures from the temple of the LORD and from the royal palace, and took away all the gold articles that Solomon king of Israel had made for the temple of the LORD. 14He carried into exile all Jerusalem: all the officers and fighting men, and all the craftsmen and artisans—a total of ten thousand. Only the poorest people of the land were left.

15Nebuchadnezzar took Jehoiachin captive to Babylon. He also took from Jerusalem to Babylon the king's mother, his wives, his officials and the leading men of the land. 16The king of Babylon also deported to Babylon the entire force of seven thousand fighting men, strong and fit for war, and a thousand craftsmen and artisans. 17He made Mattaniah, Jehoiachin's uncle, king in his place and changed his name to Zedekiah.

Zedekiah King of Judah

18Zedekiah was twenty-one years old when he became king, and he reigned in Jerusalem for eleven years. His mother's name was Hamutal daughter of Jeremiah; she was from Libnah. 19He did evil in the eyes of the LORD, just as Jehoiakim had done. 20It was because of the LORD's anger that all this happened to Jerusalem and Judah, and in the end he thrust them from his presence.

The Fall of Jerusalem

Now Zedekiah rebelled against the king of Babylon.

25 So in the ninth year of Zedekiah's reign, on the tenth day of the tenth month, Nebuchadnezzar king of Babylon marched against Jerusalem with his whole army. He encamped outside the city and built siege works all around it. 2The city was kept under siege until the eleventh year of King Zedekiah. 3By the ninth day of the fourth month the famine in the city had become so severe that there was no food for the people to eat. 4Then the city wall was broken through, and the whole army fled at night through the gate between the two walls near the king's garden, though the Babylonians were surrounding the city. They fled towards the Arabah, 5but the Babylonian army pursued the king and overtook him in the plains of Jericho. All his soldiers were separated from him and scattered, 6and he was captured. He was taken to the king of Babylon at Riblah, where sentence was pronounced on him. 7They killed the sons of Zedekiah before his eyes. Then they put out his eyes, bound him with bronze shackles and took him to Babylon.

8On the seventh day of the fifth month, in the nineteenth year of Nebuchadnezzar king of Babylon, Nebuzaradan commander of the imperial guard, an official of the king of Babylon, came to Jerusalem. 9He set fire to the temple of the LORD, the royal palace and all the houses of Jerusalem. Every important building he burned down. 10The whole Babylonian army, under the commander of the imperial guard, broke down the walls around Jerusalem. 11Nebuzaradan the commander of the guard carried into exile the people who remained in the city, along with the rest of the populace and those who had gone over to the king of Babylon. 12But the commander left behind some of the poorest people of the land to work the vineyards and fields.

13The Babylonians broke up the bronze pillars, the movable stands and the bronze Sea that were at the temple of the LORD and they carried the bronze to Babylon. 14They also took away the pots, shovels, wick trimmers, dishes and all the bronze articles used in the temple service. 15The commander of the imperial guard took away the censers and sprinkling bowls—all that were made of pure gold or silver.

16The bronze from the two pillars, the Sea and the movable stands, which Solomon had made for the temple of the LORD, was more than could be weighed. 17Each pillar was twenty-seven feet high. The bronze capital on top of one pillar was four and a half feet high and was decorated with a network and pomegranates of bronze all around. The other pillar, with its network, was similar.

18The commander of the guard took as prisoners Seraiah the chief priest, Zephaniah the priest next in rank and the three doorkeepers. 19Of those still in the city, he took the officer in charge of the fighting men and five royal advisers. He also took the secretary who was chief officer in charge of conscripting the people of the land and sixty of his men who were found in the city. 20Nebuzaradan the commander took them all and brought them to the king of Babylon at Riblah. 21There at Riblah, in the land of Hamath, the king had them executed.

So Judah went into captivity, away from her land.

22Nebuchadnezzar king of Babylon appointed Gedaliah son of Ahikam, the son of Shaphan, to be over the people he had left behind in Judah. 23When all the army officers and their men heard that the king of Babylon had appointed Gedaliah as governor, they came to Gedaliah at Mizpah—Ishmael son of Nethaniah, Johanan son of Kareah, Seraiah son of Tanhumeth the Netophathite, Jaazaniah the son of the Maacathite, and their men. 24Gedaliah took an oath to reassure them and their men. "Do not be afraid of the Babylonian officials," he said. "Settle down in the land and serve the king of Babylon, and it will go well with you."

25In the seventh month, however, Ishmael son of Nethaniah, the son of Elishama, who was of royal blood, came with ten men and assassinated Gedaliah and also the men of Judah and the Babylonians who were with him at Mizpah. 26At this, all the people from

the least to the greatest, together with the army officers, fled to Egypt for fear of the Babylonians.

Jehoiachin Released

27In the thirty-seventh year of the exile of Jehoiachin king of Judah, in the year Evil-Merodach became king of Babylon, he released Jehoiachin from prison on the twenty-seventh day of the twelfth month. 28He spoke kindly to him and gave him a seat of honour higher than those of the other kings who were with him in Babylon. 29So Jehoiachin put aside his prison clothes and for the rest of his life ate regularly at the king's table. 30Day by day the king gave Jehoiachin a regular allowance as long as he lived.

NEW TESTAMENT READING
Romans 1:18–32

God's Wrath Against Mankind

18The wrath of God is being revealed from heaven against all the godlessness and wickedness of men who suppress the truth by their wickedness, 19since what may be known about God is plain to them, because God has made it plain to them. 20For since the creation of the world God's invisible qualities—his eternal power and divine nature—have been clearly seen, being understood from what has been made, so that men are without excuse.

21For although they knew God, they neither glorified him as God nor gave thanks to him, but their thinking became futile and their foolish hearts became darkened. 22Although they claimed to be wise, they became fools 23and exchanged the glory of the immortal God for images made to look like mortal man and birds and animals and reptiles.

24Therefore God gave them over in

the sinful desires of their hearts to sexual impurity for the degrading of their bodies with one another. 25They exchanged the truth of God for a lie, and worshipped and served created things rather than the Creator—who is for ever praised. Amen.

26Because of this, God gave them over to shameful lusts. Even their women exchanged natural relations for unnatural ones. 27In the same way the men also abandoned natural relations with women and were inflamed with lust for one another. Men committed indecent acts with other men, and received in themselves the due penalty for their perversion.

28Furthermore, since they did not think it worth while to retain the knowledge of God, he gave them over to a depraved mind, to do what ought not to be done. 29They have become filled with every kind of wickedness, evil, greed and depravity. They are full of envy, murder, strife, deceit and malice. They are gossips, 30slanderers, God-haters, insolent, arrogant and boastful; they invent ways of doing evil; they disobey their parents; 31they are senseless, faithless, heartless, ruthless. 32Although they know God's righteous decree that those who do such things deserve death,

they not only continue to do these very things but also approve of those who practise them.

READING FROM PSALMS
Psalm 84:8–12

8Hear my prayer, O LORD God Almighty;
　listen to me, O God of Jacob.
　　　　　　　　　　　　Selah
9Look upon our shield, O God;
　look with favour on your anointed one.

10Better is one day in your courts
　than a thousand elsewhere;
　I would rather be a doorkeeper in the house of my God
　than dwell in the tents of the wicked.
11For the LORD God is a sun and shield;
　the LORD bestows favour and honour;
　no good thing does he withhold from those whose walk is blameless.

12O LORD Almighty,
　blessed is the man who trusts in you.

DAY 195

JULY 14

OLD TESTAMENT READING
Jonah 1:1–4:11

Jonah Flees From the LORD

1 The word of the LORD came to Jonah son of Amittai: 2"Go to the great city of Nineveh and preach against it, because its wickedness has come up before me."

3But Jonah ran away from the LORD and headed for Tarshish. He went down

to Joppa, where he found a ship bound for that port. After paying the fare, he went aboard and sailed for Tarshish to flee from the LORD.

4Then the LORD sent a great wind on the sea, and such a violent storm arose that the ship threatened to break up. 5All the sailors were afraid and each cried out to his own god. And they threw the cargo into the sea to lighten the ship.

But Jonah had gone below deck,

where he lay down and fell into a deep sleep. 6The captain went to him and said, "How can you sleep? Get up and call on your god! Maybe he will take notice of us, and we will not perish."

7Then the sailors said to each other, "Come, let us cast lots to find out who is responsible for this calamity." They cast lots and the lot fell on Jonah.

8So they asked him, "Tell us, who is responsible for making all this trouble for us? What do you do? Where do you come from? What is your country? From what people are you?"

9He answered, "I am a Hebrew and I worship the LORD, the God of heaven, who made the sea and the land."

10This terrified them and they asked, "What have you done?" (They knew he was running away from the LORD, because he had already told them so.)

11The sea was getting rougher and rougher. So they asked him, "What should we do to you to make the sea calm down for us?"

12"Pick me up and throw me into the sea," he replied, "and it will become calm. I know that it is my fault that this great storm has come upon you."

13Instead, the men did their best to row back to land. But they could not, for the sea grew even wilder than before. 14Then they cried to the LORD, "O LORD, please do not let us die for taking this man's life. Do not hold us accountable for killing an innocent man, for you, O LORD, have done as you pleased." 15Then they took Jonah and threw him overboard, and the raging sea grew calm. 16At this the men greatly feared the LORD, and they offered a sacrifice to the LORD and made vows to him.

17But the LORD provided a great fish to swallow Jonah, and Jonah was inside the fish three days and three nights.

Jonah's Prayer

2 From inside the fish Jonah prayed to the LORD his God. 2He said:

"In my distress I called to the LORD,
  and he answered me.
From the depths of the grave I called
    for help,
  and you listened to my cry.
3You hurled me into the deep,
  into the very heart of the seas,
  and the currents swirled about me;
all your waves and breakers
  swept over me.
4I said, 'I have been banished
    from your sight;
  yet I will look again
    towards your holy temple.'
5The engulfing waters threatened me,
  the deep surrounded me;
  seaweed was wrapped around my
    head.
6To the roots of the mountains I sank
    down;
  the earth beneath barred me in for
    ever.
But you brought my life up from the
    pit,
  O LORD my God.

7"When my life was ebbing away,
  I remembered you, LORD,
and my prayer rose to you,
  to your holy temple.

8"Those who cling to worthless idols
  forfeit the grace that could be
    theirs.
9But I, with a song of thanksgiving,
  will sacrifice to you.
What I have vowed I will make good.
  Salvation comes from the LORD."

10And the LORD commanded the fish, and it vomited Jonah onto dry land.

Jonah Goes to Nineveh

3 Then the word of the LORD came to Jonah a second time: 2"Go to the great city of Nineveh and proclaim to it the message I give you."

3Jonah obeyed the word of the LORD and went to Nineveh. Now Nineveh was a very important city—a visit required three days. 4On the first day, Jonah started into the city. He proclaimed: "Forty more days and Nineveh will be overturned." 5The Ninevites believed God. They declared a fast, and all of them, from the greatest to the least, put on sackcloth.

6When the news reached the king of Nineveh, he rose from his throne, took off his royal robes, covered himself with sackcloth and sat down in the dust. 7Then he issued a proclamation in Nineveh:

"By the decree of the king and his nobles:

Do not let any man or beast, herd or flock, taste anything; do not let them eat or drink. 8But let man and beast be covered with sackcloth. Let everyone call urgently on God. Let them give up their evil ways and their violence. 9Who knows? God may yet relent and with compassion turn from his fierce anger so that we will not perish."

10When God saw what they did and how they turned from their evil ways, he had compassion and did not bring upon them the destruction he had threatened.

Jonah's Anger at the LORD's Compassion

4 But Jonah was greatly displeased and became angry. 2He prayed to the LORD, "O LORD, is this not what I said when I was still at home? That is why I was so quick to flee to Tarshish. I knew that you are a gracious and compassionate God, slow to anger and abounding in love, a God who relents from sending calamity. 3Now, O LORD, take away my life, for it is better for me to die than to live."

4But the LORD replied, "Have you any right to be angry?"

5Jonah went out and sat down at a place east of the city. There he made himself a shelter, sat in its shade and waited to see what would happen to the city. 6Then the LORD God provided a vine and made it grow up over Jonah to give shade for his head to ease his discomfort, and Jonah was very happy about the vine. 7But at dawn the next day God provided a worm, which chewed the vine so that it withered. 8When the sun rose, God provided a scorching east wind, and the sun blazed on Jonah's head so that he grew faint. He wanted to die, and said, "It would be better for me to die than to live."

9But God said to Jonah, "Do you have a right to be angry about the vine?"

"I do," he said. "I am angry enough to die."

10But the LORD said, "You have been concerned about this vine, though you did not tend it or make it grow. It sprang up overnight and died overnight. 11But Nineveh has more than a hundred and twenty thousand people who cannot tell their right hand from their left, and many cattle as well. Should I not be concerned about that great city?"

NEW TESTAMENT READING
Romans 2:1–16

God's Righteous Judgment

2 You, therefore, have no excuse, you who pass judgment on someone else, for at whatever point you judge the other, you are condemning yourself, because you who pass judgment do the same things. 2Now we know that God's judgment against those who do such things is based on truth. 3So when you, a mere man, pass judgment on them and yet do the same things, do you think you will escape God's judgment? 4Or do you show contempt for the riches of his kindness, tolerance and patience, not realising that God's kindness leads you towards repentance?

5But because of your stubbornness

and your unrepentant heart, you are storing up wrath against yourself for the day of God's wrath, when his righteous judgment will be revealed. 6God "will give to each person according to what he has done". 7To those who by persistence in doing good seek glory, honour and immortality, he will give eternal life. 8But for those who are self-seeking and who reject the truth and follow evil, there will be wrath and anger. 9There will be trouble and distress for every human being who does evil: first for the Jew, then for the Gentile; 10but glory, honour and peace for everyone who does good: first for the Jew, then for the Gentile. 11For God does not show favouritism.

12All who sin apart from the law will also perish apart from the law, and all who sin under the law will be judged by the law. 13For it is not those who hear the law who are righteous in God's sight, but it is those who obey the law who will be declared righteous. 14(Indeed, when Gentiles, who do not have the law, do by nature things required by the law, they are a law for themselves, even though they do not have the law, 15since they show that the requirements of the law are written on their hearts, their consciences also bearing witness, and their thoughts now accusing, now even defending them.)

16This will take place on the day when God will judge men's secrets through Jesus Christ, as my gospel declares.

READING FROM PSALMS
Psalm 85:1–7

For the director of music. Of the Sons of Korah. A psalm.

1You showed favour to your land, O LORD;
　you restored the fortunes of Jacob.
2You forgave the iniquity of your people
　and covered all their sins. *Selah*
3You set aside all your wrath
　and turned from your fierce anger.

4Restore us again, O God our Saviour,
　and put away your displeasure towards us.
5Will you be angry with us for ever?
　Will you prolong your anger through all generations?
6Will you not revive us again,
　that your people may rejoice in you?
7Show us your unfailing love, O LORD,
　and grant us your salvation.

JULY 15

OLD TESTAMENT READING
Amos 1:1–2:16

1 The words of Amos, one of the shepherds of Tekoa—what he saw concerning Israel two years before the earthquake, when Uzziah was king of Judah and Jeroboam son of Jehoash was king of Israel.

2He said:

"The LORD roars from Zion
　and thunders from Jerusalem;
the pastures of the shepherds dry up,
　and the top of Carmel withers."

Judgment on Israel's Neighbours

3This is what the LORD says:

"For three sins of Damascus,
　even for four, I will not turn back
⌊my wrath⌋.

Because she threshed Gilead
　with sledges having iron teeth,
[4]I will send fire upon the house of
　Hazael
　that will consume the fortresses of
　Ben-Hadad.
[5]I will break down the gate of
　Damascus;
　I will destroy the king who is in the
　Valley of Aven
and the one who holds the sceptre in
　Beth Eden.
　The people of Aram will go into
　exile to Kir,"
　　　　　　　　says the LORD.

[6]This is what the LORD says:

"For three sins of Gaza,
　even for four, I will not turn back
　⌞my wrath⌟.
Because she took captive whole
　communities
　and sold them to Edom,
[7]I will send fire upon the walls of Gaza
　that will consume her fortresses.
[8]I will destroy the king of Ashdod
　and the one who holds the sceptre
　in Ashkelon.
I will turn my hand against Ekron,
　till the last of the Philistines is
　dead,"
　　　　　says the Sovereign LORD.

[9]This is what the LORD says:

"For three sins of Tyre,
　even for four, I will not turn back
　⌞my wrath⌟.
Because she sold whole communities
　of captives to Edom,
　disregarding a treaty of
　brotherhood,
[10]I will send fire upon the walls of Tyre
　that will consume her fortresses."

[11]This is what the LORD says:

"For three sins of Edom,
　even for four, I will not turn back
　⌞my wrath⌟.

Because he pursued his brother with
　a sword,
　stifling all compassion,
because his anger raged continually
　and his fury flamed unchecked,
[12]I will send fire upon Teman
　that will consume the fortresses of
　Bozrah."

[13]This is what the LORD says:

"For three sins of Ammon,
　even for four, I will not turn back
　⌞my wrath⌟.
Because he ripped open the pregnant
　women of Gilead
　in order to extend his borders,
[14]I will set fire to the walls of Rabbah
　that will consume her fortresses
amid war cries on the day of battle,
　amid violent winds on a stormy
　day.
[15]Her king will go into exile,
　he and his officials together,"
　　　　　　　　says the LORD.

2 This is what the LORD says:

"For three sins of Moab,
　even for four, I will not turn back
　⌞my wrath⌟.
Because he burned, as if to lime,
　the bones of Edom's king,
[2]I will send fire upon Moab
　that will consume the fortresses of
　Kerioth.
Moab will go down in great tumult
　amid war cries and the blast of the
　trumpet.
[3]I will destroy her ruler
　and kill all her officials with him,"
　　　　　　　　says the LORD.

[4]This is what the LORD says:

"For three sins of Judah,
　even for four, I will not turn back
　⌞my wrath⌟.
Because they have rejected the law of
　the LORD
　and have not kept his decrees,

because they have been led astray by
false gods,
the gods their ancestors followed,
⁵I will send fire upon Judah
that will consume the fortresses of
Jerusalem."

Judgment on Israel

⁶This is what the LORD says:

"For three sins of Israel,
even for four, I will not turn back
⌊my wrath⌋.
They sell the righteous for silver,
and the needy for a pair of sandals.
⁷They trample on the heads of the
poor
as upon the dust of the ground
and deny justice to the oppressed.
Father and son use the same girl
and so profane my holy name.
⁸They lie down beside every altar
on garments taken in pledge.
In the house of their god
they drink wine taken as fines.

⁹"I destroyed the Amorite before
them,
though he was tall as the cedars
and strong as the oaks.
I destroyed his fruit above
and his roots below.

¹⁰"I brought you up out of Egypt,
and I led you for forty years in the
desert
to give you the land of the
Amorites.

¹¹I also raised up prophets from among
your sons
and Nazirites from among your
young men.
Is this not true, people of Israel?"
declares the LORD.

¹²"But you made the Nazirites drink
wine
and commanded the prophets not
to prophesy.

¹³"Now then, I will crush you
as a cart crushes when loaded with
grain.

¹⁴The swift will not escape,
the strong will not muster their
strength,
and the warrior will not save his
life.
¹⁵The archer will not stand his ground,
the fleet-footed soldier will not get
away,
and the horseman will not save his
life.
¹⁶Even the bravest warriors
will flee naked on that day,"
declares the LORD.

NEW TESTAMENT READING
Romans 2:17–3:8

The Jews and the Law

¹⁷Now you, if you call yourself a Jew;
if you rely on the law and brag about
your relationship to God; ¹⁸if you know
his will and approve of what is superior
because you are instructed by the law;
¹⁹if you are convinced that you are a
guide for the blind, a light for those who
are in the dark, ²⁰an instructor of the
foolish, a teacher of infants, because
you have in the law the embodiment of
knowledge and truth—²¹you, then,
who teach others, do you not teach
yourself? You who preach against
stealing, do you steal? ²²You who say
that people should not commit adultery, do you commit adultery? You who
abhor idols, do you rob temples? ²³You
who brag about the law, do you dishonour God by breaking the law? ²⁴As
it is written: "God's name is blasphemed among the Gentiles because of
you."

²⁵Circumcision has value if you
observe the law, but if you break the
law, you have become as though you
had not been circumcised. ²⁶If those
who are not circumcised keep the law's
requirements, will they not be regarded
as though they were circumcised? ²⁷The
one who is not circumcised physically
and yet obeys the law will condemn you

who, even though you have the written code and circumcision, are a law-breaker.

28A man is not a Jew if he is only one outwardly, nor is circumcision merely outward and physical. 29No, a man is a Jew if he is one inwardly; and circumcision is circumcision of the heart, by the Spirit, not by the written code. Such a man's praise is not from men, but from God.

God's Faithfulness

3 What advantage, then, is there in being a Jew, or what value is there in circumcision? 2Much in every way! First of all, they have been entrusted with the very words of God.

3What if some did not have faith? Will their lack of faith nullify God's faithfulness? 4Not at all! Let God be true, and every man a liar. As it is written:

"So that you may be proved right
    when you speak
and prevail when you judge."

5But if our unrighteousness brings out God's righteousness more clearly, what shall we say? That God is unjust in bringing his wrath on us? (I am using a human argument.) 6Certainly not! If that were so, how could God judge the world? 7Someone might argue, "If my falsehood enhances God's truthfulness and so increases his glory, why am I still condemned as a sinner?" 8Why not say—as we are being slanderously reported as saying and as some claim that we say—"Let us do evil that good may result"? Their condemnation is deserved.

READING FROM PROVERBS
Proverbs 17:5–14

5He who mocks the poor shows
    contempt for their Maker;
whoever gloats over disaster will
    not go unpunished.

6Children's children are a crown to the
    aged,
and parents are the pride of their
    children.

7Arrogant lips are unsuited to a fool—
how much worse lying lips to a
    ruler!

8A bribe is a charm to the one who
    gives it;
wherever he turns, he succeeds.

9He who covers over an offence
    promotes love,
but whoever repeats the matter
    separates close friends.

10A rebuke impresses a man of
    discernment
more than a hundred lashes a fool.

11An evil man is bent only on rebellion;
a merciless official will be sent
    against him.

12Better to meet a bear robbed of her
    cubs
than a fool in his folly.

13If a man pays back evil for good,
evil will never leave his house.

14Starting a quarrel is like breaching a
    dam;
so drop the matter before a dispute
    breaks out.

OLD TESTAMENT READING
Amos 3:1–4:13

Witnesses Summoned Against Israel

3 Hear this word the LORD has spoken against you, O people of Israel—against the whole family I brought up out of Egypt:

²"You only have I chosen
of all the families of the earth;
therefore I will punish you
for all your sins."

³Do two walk together
unless they have agreed to do so?
⁴Does a lion roar in the thicket
when he has no prey?
Does he growl in his den
when he has caught nothing?
⁵Does a bird fall into a trap on the ground
where no snare has been set?
Does a trap spring up from the earth
when there is nothing to catch?
⁶When a trumpet sounds in a city,
do not the people tremble?
When disaster comes to a city,
has not the LORD caused it?

⁷Surely the Sovereign LORD does nothing
without revealing his plan
to his servants the prophets.

⁸The lion has roared—
who will not fear?
The Sovereign LORD has spoken—
who can but prophesy?

⁹Proclaim to the fortresses of Ashdod
and to the fortresses of Egypt:
"Assemble yourselves on the
mountains of Samaria;
see the great unrest within her
and the oppression among her
people."

¹⁰"They do not know how to do right,"
declares the LORD,
"who hoard plunder and loot in
their fortresses."

¹¹Therefore this is what the Sovereign LORD says:

"An enemy will overrun the land;
he will pull down your strongholds
and plunder your fortresses."

¹²This is what the LORD says:

"As a shepherd saves from the lion's
mouth
only two leg bones or a piece of an
ear,
so will the Israelites be saved,
those who sit in Samaria
on the edge of their beds
and in Damascus on their
couches."

¹³"Hear this and testify against the house of Jacob," declares the Lord, the LORD God Almighty.

¹⁴"On the day I punish Israel for her
sins,
I will destroy the altars of Bethel;
the horns of the altar will be cut off
and fall to the ground.
¹⁵I will tear down the winter house
along with the summer house;
the houses adorned with ivory will be
destroyed
and the mansions will be
demolished,"
declares the LORD.

Israel Has Not Returned to God

4 Hear this word, you cows of Bashan on Mount Samaria,
you women who oppress the poor
and crush the needy

and say to your husbands, "Bring
us some drinks!"
[2]The Sovereign LORD has sworn by his
holiness:
"The time will surely come
when you will be taken away with
hooks,
the last of you with fish-hooks.
[3]You will each go straight out
through breaks in the wall,
and you will be cast out towards
Harmon,"
           declares the LORD.
[4]"Go to Bethel and sin;
go to Gilgal and sin yet more.
Bring your sacrifices every morning,
your tithes every three years.
[5]Burn leavened bread as a
thank-offering
and brag about your freewill
offerings—
boast about them, you Israelites,
for this is what you love to do,"
           declares the Sovereign LORD.

[6]"I gave you empty stomachs in every
city
and lack of bread in every town,
yet you have not returned to me,"
           declares the LORD.

[7]"I also withheld rain from you
when the harvest was still three
months away.
I sent rain on one town,
but withheld it from another.
One field had rain;
another had none and dried up.
[8]People staggered from town to town
for water
but did not get enough to drink,
yet you have not returned to me,"
           declares the LORD.

[9]"Many times I struck your gardens
and vineyards,
I struck them with blight and
mildew.
Locusts devoured your fig and olive
trees,
yet you have not returned to me,"
           declares the LORD.

[10]"I sent plagues among you
as I did to Egypt.
I killed your young men with the
sword,
along with your captured horses.
I filled your nostrils with the stench of
your camps,
yet you have not returned to me,"
           declares the LORD.

[11]"I overthrew some of you
as I overthrew Sodom and
Gomorrah.
You were like a burning stick
snatched from the fire,
yet you have not returned to me,"
           declares the LORD.

[12]"Therefore this is what I will do to
you, Israel,
and because I will do this to you,
prepare to meet your God, O
Israel."

[13]He who forms the mountains,
creates the wind,
and reveals his thoughts to man,
he who turns dawn to darkness,
and treads the high places of the
earth—
the LORD God Almighty is his
name.

NEW TESTAMENT READING
Romans 3:9–31

No-one Is Righteous

[9]What shall we conclude then? Are
we any better? Not at all! We have
already made the charge that Jews and
Gentiles alike are all under sin. [10]As it is
written:

"There is no-one righteous, not even
one;
[11]   there is no-one who understands,
no-one who seeks God.
[12]All have turned away,
they have together become
worthless;

there is no-one who does good,
  not even one."
13"Their throats are open graves;
  their tongues practise deceit."
  "The poison of vipers is on their
  lips."
14 "Their mouths are full of cursing
  and bitterness."
15"Their feet are swift to shed blood;
16 ruin and misery mark their ways,
17and the way of peace they do not
  know."
18 "There is no fear of God before
  their eyes."

19Now we know that whatever the law
says, it says to those who are under
the law, so that every mouth may be
silenced and the whole world held
accountable to God. 20Therefore no-
one will be declared righteous in his
sight by observing the law; rather,
through the law we become conscious of
sin.

Righteousness Through Faith

21But now a righteousness from God,
apart from law, has been made known,
to which the Law and the Prophets testify. 22This righteousness from God
comes through faith in Jesus Christ to
all who believe. There is no difference,
23for all have sinned and fall short of the
glory of God, 24and are justified freely
by his grace through the redemption
that came by Christ Jesus. 25God presented him as a sacrifice of atonement,
through faith in his blood. He did this to
demonstrate his justice, because in his
forbearance he had left the sins committed beforehand unpunished26—he did
it to demonstrate his justice at the
present time, so as to be just and the one
who justifies those who have faith in
Jesus.

27Where, then, is boasting? It is excluded. On what principle? On that of
observing the law? No, but on that of
faith. 28For we maintain that a man is
justified by faith apart from observing
the law. 29Is God the God of Jews only?
Is he not the God of Gentiles too? Yes,
of Gentiles too, 30since there is only one
God, who will justify the circumcised by
faith and the uncircumcised through
that same faith. 31Do we, then, nullify
the law by this faith? Not at all! Rather,
we uphold the law.

READING FROM PSALMS
Psalm 85:8–13

8I will listen to what God the LORD
  will say;
  he promises peace to his people,
  his saints—
  but let them not return to folly.
9Surely his salvation is near those who
  fear him,
  that his glory may dwell in our
  land.

10Love and faithfulness meet together;
  righteousness and peace kiss each
  other.
11Faithfulness springs forth from the
  earth,
  and righteousness looks down from
  heaven.
12The LORD will indeed give what is
  good,
  and our land will yield its harvest.
13Righteousness goes before him
  and prepares the way for his steps.

JULY 17

OLD TESTAMENT READING
Amos 5:1–27

A Lament and Call to Repentance

5 Hear this word, O house of Israel, this lament I take up concerning you:

2"Fallen is Virgin Israel,
    never to rise again,
deserted in her own land,
    with no-one to lift her up."

3This is what the Sovereign LORD says:

"The city that marches out a
        thousand strong for Israel
    will have only a hundred left;
the town that marches out a hundred
        strong
    will have only ten left."

4This is what the LORD says to the house of Israel:

"Seek me and live;
5   do not seek Bethel,
do not go to Gilgal,
    do not journey to Beersheba.
For Gilgal will surely go into exile,
    and Bethel will be reduced to
        nothing."
6Seek the LORD and live,
    or he will sweep through the house
        of Joseph like a fire;
it will devour,
    and Bethel will have no-one to
        quench it.

7You who turn justice into bitterness
    and cast righteousness to the
        ground
8(he who made the Pleiades and
        Orion,
    who turns blackness into dawn
    and darkens day into night,

who calls for the waters of the sea
    and pours them out over the face
        of the land—
    the LORD is his name—
9he flashes destruction on the
        stronghold
    and brings the fortified city to
        ruin),
10you hate the one who reproves in
        court
    and despise him who tells the truth.

11You trample on the poor
    and force him to give you grain.
Therefore, though you have built
        stone mansions,
    you will not live in them;
though you have planted lush
        vineyards,
    you will not drink their wine.
12For I know how many are your
        offences
    and how great your sins.

You oppress the righteous and take
        bribes
    and you deprive the poor of justice
        in the courts.
13Therefore the prudent man keeps
        quiet in such times,
    for the times are evil.

14Seek good, not evil,
    that you may live.
Then the LORD God Almighty will be
        with you,
    just as you say he is.
15Hate evil, love good;
    maintain justice in the courts.
Perhaps the LORD God Almighty will
        have mercy
    on the remnant of Joseph.

16Therefore this is what the Lord, the
LORD God Almighty, says:

"There will be wailing in all the
        streets

and cries of anguish in every public
square.
The farmers will be summoned to
weep
and the mourners to wail.
¹⁷There will be wailing in all the
vineyards,
for I will pass through your midst,"
says the LORD.

The Day of the LORD

¹⁸Woe to you who long
for the day of the LORD!
Why do you long for the day of the
LORD?
That day will be darkness, not
light.
¹⁹It will be as though a man fled from a
lion
only to meet a bear,
as though he entered his house
and rested his hand on the wall
only to have a snake bite him.
²⁰Will not the day of the LORD be
darkness, not light—
pitch-dark, without a ray of
brightness?

²¹"I hate, I despise your religious
feasts;
I cannot stand your assemblies.
²²Even though you bring me burnt
offerings and grain offerings,
I will not accept them.
Though you bring choice fellowship
offerings,
I will have no regard for them.
²³Away with the noise of your songs!
I will not listen to the music of your
harps.
²⁴But let justice roll on like a river,
righteousness like a never-failing
stream!

²⁵"Did you bring me sacrifices and
offerings
for forty years in the desert, O
house of Israel?
²⁶You have lifted up the shrine of your
king,
the pedestal of your idols,
the star of your god—
which you made for yourselves.
²⁷Therefore I will send you into exile
beyond Damascus,"
says the LORD, whose name is God
Almighty.

NEW TESTAMENT READING
Romans 4:1–15

Abraham Justified by Faith

4 What then shall we say that Abraham, our forefather, discovered in
this matter? ²If, in fact, Abraham was
justified by works, he had something to
boast about—but not before God.
³What does the Scripture say? "Abraham believed God, and it was credited
to him as righteousness."

⁴Now when a man works, his wages
are not credited to him as a gift, but as
an obligation. ⁵However, to the man
who does not work but trusts God who
justifies the wicked, his faith is credited
as righteousness. ⁶David says the same
thing when he speaks of the blessedness
of the man to whom God credits righteousness apart from works:

⁷"Blessed are they
whose transgressions are forgiven,
whose sins are covered.
⁸Blessed is the man
whose sin the Lord will never
count against him."

⁹Is this blessedness only for the circumcised, or also for the uncircumcised? We have been saying that
Abraham's faith was credited to him as
righteousness. ¹⁰Under what circumstances was it credited? Was it after he
was circumcised, or before? It was not
after, but before! ¹¹And he received the
sign of circumcision, a seal of the righteousness that he had by faith while he
was still uncircumcised. So then, he is
the father of all who believe but have
not been circumcised, in order that

righteousness might be credited to them. ¹²And he is also the father of the circumcised who not only are circumcised but who also walk in the footsteps of the faith that our father Abraham had before he was circumcised.

¹³It was not through law that Abraham and his offspring received the promise that he would be heir of the world, but through the righteousness that comes by faith. ¹⁴For if those who live by law are heirs, faith has no value and the promise is worthless, ¹⁵because law brings wrath. And where there is no law there is no transgression.

READING FROM PSALMS
Psalm 86:1–10

A prayer of David.

¹Hear, O Lᴏʀᴅ, and answer me,
    for I am poor and needy.
²Guard my life, for I am devoted to
    you.

You are my God; save your
    servant
    who trusts in you.
³Have mercy on me, O Lord,
    for I call to you all day long.
⁴Bring joy to your servant,
    for to you, O Lord,
    I lift up my soul.

⁵You are forgiving and good, O Lord,
    abounding in love to all who call to
    you.
⁶Hear my prayer, O Lᴏʀᴅ;
    listen to my cry for mercy.
⁷In the day of my trouble I will call to
    you,
    for you will answer me.

⁸Among the gods there is none like
    you, O Lord;
    no deeds can compare with yours.
⁹All the nations you have made
    will come and worship before you,
    O Lord;
    they will bring glory to your name.
¹⁰For you are great and do marvellous
    deeds;
    you alone are God.

DAY 199

JULY 18

OLD TESTAMENT READING
Amos 6:1–7:17

Woe to the Complacent

6 Woe to you who are complacent in
    Zion,
    and to you who feel secure on
      Mount Samaria,
you notable men of the foremost
    nation,
    to whom the people of Israel
      come!
²Go to Calneh and look at it;
    go from there to great Hamath,
    and then go down to Gath in
      Philistia.

Are they better off than your two
    kingdoms?
    Is their land larger than yours?
³You put off the evil day
    and bring near a reign of terror.
⁴You lie on beds inlaid with ivory
    and lounge on your couches.
You dine on choice lambs
    and fattened calves.
⁵You strum away on your harps like
    David
    and improvise on musical
      instruments.
⁶You drink wine by the bowlful
    and use the finest lotions,
    but you do not grieve over the ruin
      of Joseph.

7Therefore you will be among the first
    to go into exile;
  your feasting and lounging will
    end.

The Lord Abhors the Pride of Israel

8The Sovereign LORD has sworn by
himself—the LORD God Almighty
declares:

  "I abhor the pride of Jacob
    and detest his fortresses;
  I will deliver up the city
    and everything in it."

9If ten men are left in one house, they
too will die. 10And if a relative who is to
burn the bodies comes to carry them out
of the house and asks anyone still hiding
there, "Is anyone with you?" and he
says, "No," then he will say, "Hush!
We must not mention the name of the
LORD."

11For the LORD has given the
    command,
  and he will smash the great house
    into pieces
  and the small house into bits.

12Do horses run on the rocky crags?
  Does one plough there with oxen?
But you have turned justice into
    poison
  and the fruit of righteousness into
    bitterness—

13you who rejoice in the conquest of Lo
    Debar
  and say, "Did we not take Karnaim
    by our own strength?"

14For the LORD God Almighty
    declares,
  "I will stir up a nation against you,
    O house of Israel,
  that will oppress you all the way
    from Lebo Hamath to the valley of
    the Arabah."

Locusts, Fire and a Plumb-Line

7 This is what the Sovereign LORD
  showed me: He was preparing
swarms of locusts after the king's share
had been harvested and just as the
second crop was coming up. 2When
they had stripped the land clean, I cried
out, "Sovereign LORD, forgive! How
can Jacob survive? He is so small!"

3So the LORD relented.

"This will not happen," the LORD
said.

4This is what the Sovereign LORD
showed me: The Sovereign LORD was
calling for judgment by fire; it dried up
the great deep and devoured the land.
5Then I cried out, "Sovereign LORD, I
beg you, stop! How can Jacob survive?
He is so small!"

6So the LORD relented.

"This will not happen either," the
Sovereign LORD said.

7This is what he showed me: The
Lord was standing by a wall that had
been built true to plumb, with a plumb-
line in his hand. 8And the LORD asked
me, "What do you see, Amos?"

"A plumb-line," I replied.

Then the Lord said, "Look, I am
setting a plumb-line among my people
Israel; I will spare them no longer.

9"The high places of Isaac will be
    destroyed
  and the sanctuaries of Israel will be
    ruined;
  with my sword I will rise against
    the house of Jeroboam."

Amos and Amaziah

10Then Amaziah the priest of Bethel
sent a message to Jeroboam king of
Israel: "Amos is raising a conspiracy
against you in the very heart of Israel.
The land cannot bear all his words.
11For this is what Amos is saying:

  "'Jeroboam will die by the sword,
    and Israel will surely go into exile,
    away from their native land.'"

¹²Then Amaziah said to Amos, "Get out, you seer! Go back to the land of Judah. Earn your bread there and do your prophesying there. ¹³Don't prophesy any more at Bethel, because this is the king's sanctuary and the temple of the kingdom."

¹⁴Amos answered Amaziah, "I was neither a prophet nor a prophet's son, but I was a shepherd, and I also took care of sycamore-fig trees. ¹⁵But the LORD took me from tending the flock and said to me, 'Go, prophesy to my people Israel.' ¹⁶Now then, hear the word of the LORD. You say,

"'Do not prophesy against Israel,
    and stop preaching against the
      house of Isaac.'

¹⁷"Therefore this is what the LORD says:

"'Your wife will become a prostitute
    in the city,
  and your sons and daughters will
    fall by the sword.
Your land will be measured and
    divided up,
  and you yourself will die in a pagan
    country.
And Israel will certainly go into exile,
    away from their native land.'"

NEW TESTAMENT READING
Romans 4:16–5:11

¹⁶Therefore, the promise comes by faith, so that it may be by grace and may be guaranteed to all Abraham's offspring—not only to those who are of the law but also to those who are of the faith of Abraham. He is the father of us all. ¹⁷As it is written: "I have made you a father of many nations." He is our father in the sight of God, in whom he believed—the God who gives life to the dead and calls things that are not as though they were.

¹⁸Against all hope, Abraham in hope believed and so became the father of many nations, just as it had been said to him, "So shall your offspring be." ¹⁹Without weakening in his faith, he faced the fact that his body was as good as dead—since he was about a hundred years old—and that Sarah's womb was also dead. ²⁰Yet he did not waver through unbelief regarding the promise of God, but was strengthened in his faith and gave glory to God, ²¹being fully persuaded that God had power to do what he had promised. ²²This is why "it was credited to him as righteousness." ²³The words "it was credited to him" were written not for him alone, ²⁴but also for us, to whom God will credit righteousness—for us who believe in him who raised Jesus our Lord from the dead. ²⁵He was delivered over to death for our sins and was raised to life for our justification.

Peace and Joy

5 Therefore, since we have been justified through faith, we have peace with God through our Lord Jesus Christ, ²through whom we have gained access by faith into this grace in which we now stand. And we rejoice in the hope of the glory of God. ³Not only so, but we also rejoice in our sufferings, because we know that suffering produces perseverance; ⁴perseverance, character; and character, hope. ⁵And hope does not disappoint us, because God has poured out his love into our hearts by the Holy Spirit, whom he has given us.

⁶You see, at just the right time, when we were still powerless, Christ died for the ungodly. ⁷Very rarely will anyone die for a righteous man, though for a good man someone might possibly dare to die. ⁸But God demonstrates his own love for us in this: While we were still sinners, Christ died for us.

⁹Since we have now been justified by his blood, how much more shall we be saved from God's wrath through him! ¹⁰For if, when we were God's enemies, we were reconciled to him through the

death of his Son, how much more, having been reconciled, shall we be saved through his life! 11Not only is this so, but we also rejoice in God through our Lord Jesus Christ, through whom we have now received reconciliation.

READING FROM PSALMS
Psalm 86:11–17

11Teach me your way, O LORD,
 and I will walk in your truth;
 give me an undivided heart,
 that I may fear your name.
12I will praise you, O Lord my God,
 with all my heart;
 I will glorify your name for ever.
13For great is your love towards me;
 you have delivered me from the
 depths of the grave.

14The arrogant are attacking me, O
 God;
 a band of ruthless men seeks my
 life—
 men without regard for you.
15But you, O Lord, are a
 compassionate and gracious
 God,
 slow to anger, abounding in love
 and faithfulness.
16Turn to me and have mercy on me;
 grant your strength to your servant
 and save the son of your
 maidservant.
17Give me a sign of your goodness,
 that my enemies may see it and be
 put to shame,
 for you, O LORD, have helped me
 and comforted me.

JULY 19   DAY 200

OLD TESTAMENT READING
Amos 8:1–9:15

A Basket of Ripe Fruit

8 This is what the Sovereign LORD showed me: a basket of ripe fruit. 2"What do you see, Amos?" he asked.

 "A basket of ripe fruit," I answered.

 Then the LORD said to me, "The time is ripe for my people Israel; I will spare them no longer.

 3"In that day," declares the Sovereign LORD, "the songs in the temple will turn to wailing. Many, many bodies—flung everywhere! Silence!"

4Hear this, you who trample the
 needy
 and do away with the poor of the
 land,

5saying,

 "When will the New Moon be over
 that we may sell grain,
 and the Sabbath be ended
 that we may market wheat?"—
 skimping the measure,
 boosting the price
 and cheating with dishonest scales,
6buying the poor with silver
 and the needy for a pair of sandals,
 selling even the sweepings with the
 wheat.

7The LORD has sworn by the Pride of Jacob: "I will never forget anything they have done.

8"Will not the land tremble for this,
 and all who live in it mourn?
 The whole land will rise like the Nile;
 it will be stirred up and then sink
 like the river of Egypt.

9"In that day," declares the Sovereign LORD,

"I will make the sun go down at noon
    and darken the earth in broad
    daylight.
10I will turn your religious feasts into
    mourning
    and all your singing into weeping.
I will make all of you wear sackcloth
    and shave your heads.
I will make that time like mourning
    for an only son
    and the end of it like a bitter day.

11"The days are coming," declares the
    Sovereign LORD,
    "when I will send a famine through
    the land—
not a famine of food or a thirst for
    water,
    but a famine of hearing the words
    of the LORD.
12Men will stagger from sea to sea
    and wander from north to east,
searching for the word of the LORD,
    but they will not find it.

13"In that day

"the lovely young women and strong
    young men
    will faint because of thirst.
14They who swear by the shame of
    Samaria,
    or say, 'As surely as your god lives,
    O Dan,'
    or, 'As surely as the god of
    Beersheba lives'—
they will fall,
    never to rise again."

Israel to Be Destroyed

9 I saw the Lord standing by the
    altar, and he said:

"Strike the tops of the pillars
    so that the thresholds shake.
Bring them down on the heads of all
    the people;

those who are left I will kill with
    the sword.
Not one will get away,
    none will escape.
2Though they dig down to the depths
    of the grave,
    from there my hand will take them.
Though they climb up to the heavens,
    from there I will bring them down.
3Though they hide themselves on the
    top of Carmel,
    there I will hunt them down and
    seize them.
Though they hide from me at the
    bottom of the sea,
    there I will command the serpent
    to bite them.
4Though they are driven into exile by
    their enemies,
    there I will command the sword to
    slay them.
I will fix my eyes upon them
    for evil and not for good."

5The Lord, the LORD Almighty,
    he who touches the earth and it
    melts,
    and all who live in it mourn—
the whole land rises like the Nile,
    then sinks like the river of Egypt—
6he who builds his lofty palace in the
    heavens
    and sets its foundation on the
    earth,
who calls for the waters of the sea
    and pours them out over the face
    of the land—
    the LORD is his name.

7"Are not you Israelites
    the same to me as the Cushites?"
    declares the LORD.
"Did I not bring Israel up from
    Egypt,
    the Philistines from Caphtor
    and the Arameans from Kir?

8"Surely the eyes of the Sovereign
    LORD
    are on the sinful kingdom.
I will destroy it
    from the face of the earth—

yet I will not totally destroy
    the house of Jacob,"
                declares the LORD.
⁹"For I will give the command,
    and I will shake the house of Israel
    among all the nations
as grain is shaken in a sieve,
    and not a pebble will reach the
      ground.
¹⁰All the sinners among my people
    will die by the sword,
all those who say,
    'Disaster will not overtake or
      meet us.'

Israel's Restoration

¹¹"In that day I will restore
    David's fallen tent.
I will repair its broken places,
    restore its ruins,
    and build it as it used to be,
¹²so that they may possess the remnant
    of Edom
and all the nations that bear my
    name,"
          declares the LORD,
      who will do these things.

¹³"The days are coming," declares
the LORD,

    "when the reaper will be overtaken
      by the ploughman
    and the planter by the one treading
      grapes.
New wine will drip from the
    mountains
    and flow from all the hills.
¹⁴I will bring back my exiled people
    Israel;
    they will rebuild the ruined cities
      and live in them.
They will plant vineyards and drink
    their wine;
    they will make gardens and eat
      their fruit.
¹⁵I will plant Israel in their own land,
    never again to be uprooted
    from the land I have given them,"
        says the LORD your God.

NEW TESTAMENT READING
Romans 5:12–21

Death Through Adam, Life Through Christ

¹²Therefore, just as sin entered the world through one man, and death through sin, and in this way death came to all men, because all sinned—¹³for before the law was given, sin was in the world. But sin is not taken into account when there is no law. ¹⁴Nevertheless, death reigned from the time of Adam to the time of Moses, even over those who did not sin by breaking a command, as did Adam, who was a pattern of the one to come.

¹⁵But the gift is not like the trespass. For if the many died by the trespass of the one man, how much more did God's grace and the gift that came by the grace of the one man, Jesus Christ, overflow to the many! ¹⁶Again, the gift of God is not like the result of the one man's sin: The judgment followed one sin and brought condemnation, but the gift followed many trespasses and brought justification. ¹⁷For if, by the trespass of the one man, death reigned through that one man, how much more will those who receive God's abundant provision of grace and of the gift of righteousness reign in life through the one man, Jesus Christ.

¹⁸Consequently, just as the result of one trespass was condemnation for all men, so also the result of one act of righteousness was justification that brings life for all men. ¹⁹For just as through the disobedience of the one man the many were made sinners, so also through the obedience of the one man the many will be made righteous.

²⁰The law was added so that the trespass might increase. But where sin increased, grace increased all the more, ²¹so that, just as sin reigned in death, so also grace might reign through righteousness to bring eternal life through Jesus Christ our Lord.

READING FROM PROVERBS
Proverbs 17:15–24

15Acquitting the guilty and
          condemning the innocent—
    the LORD detests them both.

16Of what use is money in the hand of a
        fool,
    since he has no desire to get
        wisdom?

17A friend loves at all times,
    and a brother is born for adversity.

18A man lacking in judgment strikes
        hands in pledge
    and puts up security for his
        neighbour.

19He who loves a quarrel loves sin;
    he who builds a high gate invites
        destruction.

20A man of perverse heart does not
        prosper;
    he whose tongue is deceitful falls
        into trouble.

21To have a fool for a son brings grief;
    there is no joy for the father of a
        fool.

22A cheerful heart is good medicine,
    but a crushed spirit dries up the
        bones.

23A wicked man accepts a bribe in
        secret
    to pervert the course of justice.

24A discerning man keeps wisdom in
        view,
    but a fool's eyes wander to the ends
        of the earth.

DAY 201

JULY 20

OLD TESTAMENT READING
Hosea 1:1–2:23

1 The word of the LORD that came to
  Hosea son of Beeri during the
reigns of Uzziah, Jotham, Ahaz and
Hezekiah, kings of Judah, and during
the reign of Jeroboam son of Joash king
of Israel:

Hosea's Wife and Children

2When the LORD began to speak
through Hosea, the LORD said to him,
"Go, take to yourself an adulterous
wife and children of unfaithfulness, because the land is guilty of the vilest
adultery in departing from the LORD."
3So he married Gomer daughter of Dib-
laim, and she conceived and bore him a
son.

4Then the LORD said to Hosea, "Call
him Jezreel, because I will soon punish
the house of Jehu for the massacre at
Jezreel, and I will put an end to the
kingdom of Israel. 5In that day I will
break Israel's bow in the Valley of
Jezreel."

6Gomer conceived again and gave
birth to a daughter. Then the LORD said
to Hosea, "Call her Lo-Ruhamah, for I
will no longer show love to the house of
Israel, that I should at all forgive them.
7Yet I will show love to the house of
Judah; and I will save them—not by
bow, sword or battle, or by horses and
horsemen, but by the LORD their God."

8After she had weaned Lo-Ruhamah,
Gomer had another son. 9Then the
LORD said, "Call him Lo-Ammi, for you
are not my people, and I am not your
God.

¹⁰"Yet the Israelites will be like the sand on the seashore, which cannot be measured or counted. In the place where it was said to them, 'You are not my people', they will be called 'sons of the living God'. ¹¹The people of Judah and the people of Israel will be reunited, and they will appoint one leader and will come up out of the land, for great will be the day of Jezreel.

2 "Say of your brothers, 'My people', and of your sisters, 'My loved one'.

Israel Punished and Restored

²"Rebuke your mother, rebuke her,
  for she is not my wife,
  and I am not her husband.
Let her remove the adulterous look
    from her face
  and the unfaithfulness from
    between her breasts.
³Otherwise I will strip her naked
  and make her as bare as on the day
    she was born;
I will make her like a desert,
  turn her into a parched land,
  and slay her with thirst.
⁴I will not show my love to her
    children,
  because they are the children of
    adultery.
⁵Their mother has been unfaithful
  and has conceived them in
    disgrace.
She said, 'I will go after my lovers,
  who give me my food and my
    water,
  my wool and my linen, my oil and
    my drink.'
⁶Therefore I will block her path with
    thornbushes;
  I will wall her in so that she cannot
    find her way.
⁷She will chase after her lovers but not
    catch them;
  she will look for them but not find
    them.
Then she will say,
  'I will go back to my husband as at
    first,
  for then I was better off than now.'

⁸She has not acknowledged that I was
    the one
  who gave her the grain, the new
    wine and oil,
  who lavished on her the silver and
    gold—
  which they used for Baal.

⁹"Therefore I will take away my grain
    when it ripens,
  and my new wine when it is ready.
I will take back my wool and my
    linen,
  intended to cover her nakedness.
¹⁰So now I will expose her lewdness
  before the eyes of her lovers;
  no-one will take her out of my
    hands.
¹¹I will stop all her celebrations:
  her yearly festivals, her New
    Moons,
  her Sabbath days—all her
    appointed feasts.
¹²I will ruin her vines and her fig-trees,
  which she said were her pay from
    her lovers;
I will make them a thicket,
  and wild animals will devour them.
¹³I will punish her for the days
  she burned incense to the Baals;
she decked herself with rings and
    jewellery,
  and went after her lovers,
  but me she forgot,"
                    declares the LORD.

¹⁴"Therefore I am now going to allure
    her;
  I will lead her into the desert
  and speak tenderly to her.
¹⁵There I will give her back her
    vineyards,
  and will make the Valley of Achor
    a door of hope.
There she will sing as in the days of
    her youth,
  as in the day she came up out of
    Egypt.

¹⁶"In that day," declares the LORD,
  "you will call me 'my husband';
  you will no longer call me 'my
    master'.

17I will remove the names of the Baals
    from her lips;
no longer will their names be
    invoked.
18In that day I will make a covenant for
    them
    with the beasts of the field and the
        birds of the air
    and the creatures that move along
        the ground.
Bow and sword and battle
    I will abolish from the land,
so that all may lie down in safety.
19I will betroth you to me for ever;
    I will betroth you in righteousness
        and justice,
    in love and compassion.
20I will betroth you in faithfulness,
    and you will acknowledge the
        LORD.

21"In that day I will respond,"
    declares the LORD—
"I will respond to the skies,
    and they will respond to the earth;
22and the earth will respond to the
    grain,
    the new wine and oil,
    and they will respond to Jezreel.
23I will plant her for myself in the land;
    I will show my love to the one I
        called 'Not my loved one'.
I will say to those called 'Not my
    people', 'You are my people';
    and they will say, 'You are my
        God.'"

NEW TESTAMENT READING
Romans 6:1–14

Dead to Sin, Alive in Christ

6 What shall we say, then? Shall we
go on sinning, so that grace may
increase? 2By no means! We died to sin;
how can we live in it any longer? 3Or
don't you know that all of us who were
baptised into Christ Jesus were baptised
into his death? 4We were therefore
buried with him through baptism into
death in order that, just as Christ was
raised from the dead through the glory
of the Father, we too may live a new
life.

5If we have been united with him like
this in his death, we will certainly also
be united with him in his resurrection.
6For we know that our old self was
crucified with him so that the body of sin
might be done away with, that we
should no longer be slaves to sin—
7because anyone who has died has been
freed from sin.

8Now if we died with Christ, we believe that we will also live with him. 9For
we know that since Christ was raised
from the dead, he cannot die again;
death no longer has mastery over him.
10The death he died, he died to sin once
for all; but the life he lives, he lives to
God.

11In the same way, count yourselves
dead to sin but alive to God in Christ
Jesus. 12Therefore do not let sin reign in
your mortal body so that you obey its
evil desires. 13Do not offer the parts of
your body to sin, as instruments of wickedness, but rather offer yourselves to
God, as those who have been brought
from death to life; and offer the parts of
your body to him as instruments of
righteousness. 14For sin shall not be
your master, because you are not under
law, but under grace.

READING FROM PSALMS
Psalm 87:1–7

Of the Sons of Korah. A psalm. A song.

1He has set his foundation on the holy
    mountain;
2   the LORD loves the gates of Zion
    more than all the dwellings of
        Jacob.
3Glorious things are said of you,
    O city of God: *Selah*
4"I will record Rahab and Babylon
    among those who acknowledge
        me—

Philistia too, and Tyre, along with
    Cush—
  and will say, 'This one was born in
    Zion.'"

⁵Indeed, of Zion it will be said,
  "This one and that one were born
    in her,

and the Most High himself will
    establish her."
⁶The LORD will write in the register of
    the peoples:
  "This one was born in Zion."

Selah

⁷As they make music they will sing,
  "All my fountains are in you."

JULY 21   DAY 202

OLD TESTAMENT READING
Hosea 3:1–5:15

Hosea's Reconciliation With His Wife

3 The LORD said to me, "Go, show
  your love to your wife again,
though she is loved by another and is an
adulteress. Love her as the LORD loves
the Israelites, though they turn to other
gods and love the sacred raisin cakes."

²So I bought her for fifteen shekels of
silver and about a homer and a lethek of
barley. ³Then I told her, "You are to
live with me for many days; you must
not be a prostitute or be intimate with
any man, and I will live with you."

⁴For the Israelites will live for many
days without king or prince, without
sacrifice or sacred stones, without
ephod or idol. ⁵Afterwards the Israelites will return and seek the LORD their
God and David their king. They will
come trembling to the LORD and to his
blessings in the last days.

The Charge Against Israel

4 Hear the word of the LORD,
  you Israelites,
  because the LORD has a charge to
    bring
  against you who live in the land:
  "There is no faithfulness, no love,
    no acknowledgment of God in the
      land.

²There is only cursing, lying and
    murder,
  stealing and adultery;
they break all bounds,
  and bloodshed follows bloodshed.
³Because of this the land mourns,
  and all who live in it waste away;
the beasts of the field and the birds of
    the air
  and the fish of the sea are dying.

⁴"But let no man bring a charge,
  let no man accuse another,
for your people are like those
  who bring charges against a priest.
⁵You stumble day and night,
  and the prophets stumble with you.
So I will destroy your mother—
⁶   my people are destroyed from lack
      of knowledge.

  "Because you have rejected
      knowledge,
  I also reject you as my priests;
because you have ignored the law of
      your God,
  I also will ignore your children.
⁷The more the priests increased,
  the more they sinned against me;
  they exchanged their Glory for
      something disgraceful.
⁸They feed on the sins of my people
  and relish their wickedness.
⁹And it will be: Like people, like
    priests.

I will punish both of them for their
    ways
and repay them for their deeds.

10"They will eat but not have enough;
    they will engage in prostitution but
        not increase,
because they have deserted the LORD
    to give themselves 11to
        prostitution,
to old wine and new,
    which take away the understanding
        12of my people.
They consult a wooden idol
    and are answered by a stick of
        wood.
A spirit of prostitution leads them
    astray;
they are unfaithful to their God.
13They sacrifice on the mountaintops
    and burn offerings on the hills,
under oak, poplar and terebinth,
    where the shade is pleasant.
Therefore your daughters turn to
    prostitution
    and your daughters-in-law to
        adultery.

14"I will not punish your daughters
    when they turn to prostitution,
nor your daughters-in-law
    when they commit adultery,
because the men themselves consort
    with harlots
    and sacrifice with
        shrine-prostitutes—
a people without understanding
    will come to ruin!

15"Though you commit adultery, O
    Israel,
    let not Judah become guilty.

"Do not go to Gilgal;
    do not go up to Beth Aven.
    And do not swear, 'As surely as the
        LORD lives!'
16The Israelites are stubborn,
    like a stubborn heifer.
How then can the LORD pasture them
    like lambs in a meadow?

17Ephraim is joined to idols;
    leave him alone!
18Even when their drinks are gone,
    they continue their prostitution;
    their rulers dearly love shameful
        ways.
19A whirlwind will sweep them away,
    and their sacrifices will bring them
        shame.

Judgment Against Israel

5 "Hear this, you priests!
    Pay attention, you Israelites!
Listen, O royal house!
    This judgment is against you:
You have been a snare at Mizpah,
    a net spread out on Tabor.
2The rebels are deep in slaughter.
    I will discipline all of them.
3I know all about Ephraim;
    Israel is not hidden from me.
Ephraim, you have now turned to
    prostitution;
    Israel is corrupt.

4"Their deeds do not permit them
    to return to their God.
A spirit of prostitution is in their
    heart;
    they do not acknowledge the
        LORD.
5Israel's arrogance testifies against
    them;
    the Israelites, even Ephraim,
        stumble in their sin;
    Judah also stumbles with them.
6When they go with their flocks and
    herds
    to seek the LORD,
they will not find him;
    he has withdrawn himself from
        them.
7They are unfaithful to the LORD;
    they give birth to illegitimate
        children.
Now their New Moon festivals
    will devour them and their fields.

8"Sound the trumpet in Gibeah,
    the horn in Ramah.

Raise the battle cry in Beth Aven;
    lead on, O Benjamin.
[9]Ephraim will be laid waste
    on the day of reckoning.
Among the tribes of Israel
    I proclaim what is certain.
[10]Judah's leaders are like those
    who move boundary stones.
I will pour out my wrath on them
    like a flood of water.
[11]Ephraim is oppressed,
    trampled in judgment,
    intent on pursuing idols.
[12]I am like a moth to Ephraim,
    like rot to the people of Judah.

[13]"When Ephraim saw his sickness,
    and Judah his sores,
then Ephraim turned to Assyria,
    and sent to the great king for help.
But he is not able to cure you,
    not able to heal your sores.
[14]For I will be like a lion to Ephraim,
    like a great lion to Judah.
I will tear them to pieces and go
    away;
I will carry them off, with no-one
    to rescue them.
[15]Then I will go back to my place
    until they admit their guilt.
And they will seek my face;
    in their misery they will earnestly
    seek me."

NEW TESTAMENT READING
Romans 6:15–7:6

Slaves to Righteousness

[15]What then? Shall we sin because we
are not under law but under grace? By
no means! [16]Don't you know that when
you offer yourselves to someone to
obey him as slaves, you are slaves to the
one whom you obey—whether you are
slaves to sin, which leads to death, or to
obedience, which leads to righteousness? [17]But thanks be to God that,
though you used to be slaves to sin, you
wholeheartedly obeyed the form of

teaching to which you were entrusted.
[18]You have been set free from sin and
have become slaves to righteousness.

[19]I put this in human terms because
you are weak in your natural selves. Just
as you used to offer the parts of your
body in slavery to impurity and to ever-
increasing wickedness, so now offer
them in slavery to righteousness leading
to holiness. [20]When you were slaves to
sin, you were free from the control of
righteousness. [21]What benefit did you
reap at that time from the things you are
now ashamed of? Those things result in
death! [22]But now that you have been set
free from sin and have become slaves to
God, the benefit you reap leads to holiness, and the result is eternal life. [23]For
the wages of sin is death, but the gift of
God is eternal life in Christ Jesus our
Lord.

An Illustration From Marriage

7 Do you not know, brothers—for I
    am speaking to men who know the
law—that the law has authority over a
man only as long as he lives? [2]For example, by law a married woman is
bound to her husband as long as he
is alive, but if her husband dies, she is
released from the law of marriage. [3]So
then, if she marries another man while
her husband is still alive, she is called an
adulteress. But if her husband dies, she
is released from that law and is not an
adulteress, even though she marries
another man.

[4]So, my brothers, you also died to the
law through the body of Christ, that you
might belong to another, to him who
was raised from the dead, in order that
we might bear fruit to God. [5]For when
we were controlled by the sinful nature,
the sinful passions aroused by the law
were at work in our bodies, so that we
bore fruit for death. [6]But now, by dying
to what once bound us, we have been
released from the law so that we serve in
the new way of the Spirit, and not in the
old way of the written code.

READING FROM PSALMS
Psalm 88:1–9a

A song. A psalm of the Sons of Korah. For the director of music. According to *mahalath leannoth*. A *maskil* of Heman the Ezrahite.

¹O LORD, the God who saves me,
    day and night I cry out before you.
²May my prayer come before you;
    turn your ear to my cry.

³For my soul is full of trouble
    and my life draws near the grave.
⁴I am counted among those who go
    down to the pit;
    I am like a man without strength.
⁵I am set apart with the dead,
    like the slain who lie in the grave,
whom you remember no more,
    who are cut off from your care.

⁶You have put me in the lowest pit,
    in the darkest depths.
⁷Your wrath lies heavily upon me;
    you have overwhelmed me with all
      your waves.   *Selah*
⁸You have taken from me my closest
    friends
    and have made me repulsive to
      them.
  I am confined and cannot escape;
⁹ my eyes are dim with grief.

DAY 203

JULY 22

OLD TESTAMENT READING
Hosea 6:1–7:16

Israel Unrepentant

6 "Come, let us return to the LORD.
    He has torn us to pieces
  but he will heal us;
he has injured us
  but he will bind up our wounds.
²After two days he will revive us;
  on the third day he will restore us,
  that we may live in his presence.
³Let us acknowledge the LORD;
  let us press on to acknowledge
    him.
As surely as the sun rises,
  he will appear;
he will come to us like the winter
    rains,
  like the spring rains that water the
    earth."

⁴"What can I do with you, Ephraim?
  What can I do with you, Judah?
Your love is like the morning mist,
  like the early dew that disappears.
⁵Therefore I cut you in pieces with my
    prophets,
  I killed you with the words of my
    mouth;
  my judgments flashed like
    lightning upon you.
⁶For I desire mercy, not sacrifice,
  and acknowledgment of God
    rather than burnt offerings.
⁷Like Adam, they have broken the
    covenant—
  they were unfaithful to me there.
⁸Gilead is a city of wicked men,
  stained with footprints of blood.
⁹As marauders lie in ambush for a
    man,
  so do bands of priests;
they murder on the road to Shechem,
  committing shameful crimes.
¹⁰I have seen a horrible thing
  in the house of Israel.
There Ephraim is given to
    prostitution
  and Israel is defiled.

¹¹"Also for you, Judah,
  a harvest is appointed.

"Whenever I would restore the
fortunes of my people,
7 ¹whenever I would heal Israel,
the sins of Ephraim are exposed
and the crimes of Samaria
revealed.
They practise deceit,
thieves break into houses,
bandits rob in the streets;
²but they do not realise
that I remember all their evil
deeds.
Their sins engulf them;
they are always before me.

³"They delight the king with their
wickedness,
the princes with their lies.
⁴They are all adulterers,
burning like an oven
whose fire the baker need not stir
from the kneading of the dough till
it rises.
⁵On the day of the festival of our king
the princes become inflamed with
wine,
and he joins hands with the
mockers.
⁶Their hearts are like an oven;
they approach him with intrigue.
Their passion smoulders all night;
in the morning it blazes like a
flaming fire.
⁷All of them are hot as an oven;
they devour their rulers.
All their kings fall,
and none of them calls on me.

⁸"Ephraim mixes with the nations;
Ephraim is a flat cake not turned
over.
⁹Foreigners sap his strength,
but he does not realise it.
His hair is sprinkled with grey,
but he does not notice.
¹⁰Israel's arrogance testifies against
him,
but despite all this
he does not return to the LORD his
God
or search for him.

¹¹"Ephraim is like a dove,
easily deceived and senseless—
now calling to Egypt,
now turning to Assyria.
¹²When they go, I will throw my net
over them;
I will pull them down like birds of
the air.
When I hear them flocking together,
I will catch them.
¹³Woe to them,
because they have strayed from
me!
Destruction to them,
because they have rebelled against
me!
I long to redeem them
but they speak lies against me.
¹⁴They do not cry out to me from their
hearts
but wail upon their beds.
They gather together for grain and
new wine
but turn away from me.
¹⁵I trained them and strengthened
them,
but they plot evil against me.
¹⁶They do not turn to the Most High;
they are like a faulty bow.
Their leaders will fall by the sword
because of their insolent words.
For this they will be ridiculed
in the land of Egypt.

NEW TESTAMENT READING
Romans 7:7–25

Struggling With Sin

⁷What shall we say, then? Is the law
sin? Certainly not! Indeed I would not
have known what sin was except
through the law. For I would not have
known what coveting really was if the
law had not said, "Do not covet." ⁸But
sin, seizing the opportunity afforded by
the commandment, produced in me
every kind of covetous desire. For apart
from law, sin is dead. ⁹Once I was alive
apart from law; but when the commandment came, sin sprang to life and I died.

¹⁰I found that the very commandment that was intended to bring life actually brought death. ¹¹For sin, seizing the opportunity afforded by the commandment, deceived me, and through the commandment put me to death. ¹²So then, the law is holy, and the commandment is holy, righteous and good.

¹³Did that which is good, then, become death to me? By no means! But in order that sin might be recognised as sin, it produced death in me through what was good, so that through the commandment sin might become utterly sinful.

¹⁴We know that the law is spiritual; but I am unspiritual, sold as a slave to sin. ¹⁵I do not understand what I do. For what I want to do I do not do, but what I hate I do. ¹⁶And if I do what I do not want to do, I agree that the law is good. ¹⁷As it is, it is no longer I myself who do it, but it is sin living in me. ¹⁸I know that nothing good lives in me, that is, in my sinful nature. For I have the desire to do what is good, but I cannot carry it out. ¹⁹For what I do is not the good I want to do; no, the evil I do not want to do —this I keep on doing. ²⁰Now if I do what I do not want to do, it is no longer I who do it, but it is sin living in me that does it.

²¹So I find this law at work: When I want to do good, evil is right there with me. ²²For in my inner being I delight in God's law; ²³but I see another law at work in the members of my body, waging war against the law of my mind and making me a prisoner of the law of sin at work within my members. ²⁴What a wretched man I am! Who will rescue me from this body of death? ²⁵Thanks be to God—through Jesus Christ our Lord!

So then, I myself in my mind am a slave to God's law, but in the sinful nature a slave to the law of sin.

READING FROM PSALMS
Psalm 88:9b–18

I call to you, O LORD, every day;
    I spread out my hands to you.
¹⁰Do you show your wonders to the
        dead?
    Do those who are dead rise up and
        praise you?   *Selah*
¹¹Is your love declared in the grave,
    your faithfulness in Destruction?
¹²Are your wonders known in the place
        of darkness,
    or your righteous deeds in the land
        of oblivion?

¹³But I cry to you for help, O LORD;
    in the morning my prayer comes
        before you.
¹⁴Why, O LORD, do you reject me
    and hide your face from me?

¹⁵From my youth I have been afflicted
        and close to death;
    I have suffered your terrors and am
        in despair.
¹⁶Your wrath has swept over me;
    your terrors have destroyed me.
¹⁷All day long they surround me like a
        flood;
    they have completely engulfed me.
¹⁸You have taken my companions and
        loved ones from me;
    the darkness is my closest friend.

OLD TESTAMENT READING
Hosea 8:1–9:17

Israel to Reap the Whirlwind

8 "Put the trumpet to your lips!
An eagle is over the house of the
LORD
because the people have broken my
covenant
and rebelled against my law.
²Israel cries out to me,
'O our God, we acknowledge you!'
³But Israel has rejected what is good;
an enemy will pursue him.
⁴They set up kings without my
consent;
they choose princes without my
approval.
With their silver and gold
they make idols for themselves
to their own destruction.
⁵Throw out your calf-idol, O Samaria!
My anger burns against them.
How long will they be incapable of
purity?
6 They are from Israel!
This calf—a craftsman has made it;
it is not God.
It will be broken in pieces,
that calf of Samaria.

⁷"They sow the wind
and reap the whirlwind.
The stalk has no head;
it will produce no flour.
Were it to yield grain,
foreigners would swallow it up.
⁸Israel is swallowed up;
now she is among the nations
like a worthless thing.
⁹For they have gone up to Assyria
like a wild donkey wandering
alone.
Ephraim has sold herself to lovers.
¹⁰Although they have sold themselves
among the nations,
I will now gather them together.
They will begin to waste away
under the oppression of the mighty
king.

¹¹"Though Ephraim built many altars
for sin offerings,
these have become altars for
sinning.
¹²I wrote for them the many things of
my law,
but they regarded them as
something alien.
¹³They offer sacrifices given to me
and they eat the meat,
but the LORD is not pleased with
them.
Now he will remember their
wickedness
and punish their sins:
They will return to Egypt.
¹⁴Israel has forgotten his Maker
and built palaces;
Judah has fortified many towns.
But I will send fire upon their cities
that will consume their fortresses."

Punishment for Israel

9 Do not rejoice, O Israel;
do not be jubilant like the other
nations.
For you have been unfaithful to your
God;
you love the wages of a prostitute
at every threshing-floor.
²Threshing-floors and winepresses will
not feed the people;
the new wine will fail them.
³They will not remain in the LORD's
land;
Ephraim will return to Egypt
and eat unclean food in Assyria.
⁴They will not pour out wine offerings
to the LORD,
nor will their sacrifices please him.
Such sacrifices will be to them like
the bread of mourners;
all who eat them will be unclean.

This food will be for themselves;
    it will not come into the temple of
        the LORD.

5What will you do on the day of your
    appointed feasts,
    on the festival days of the LORD?
6Even if they escape from destruction,
    Egypt will gather them,
    and Memphis will bury them.
Their treasures of silver will be taken
    over by briers,
    and thorns will overrun their tents.
7The days of punishment are coming,
    the days of reckoning are at hand.
    Let Israel know this.
Because your sins are so many
    and your hostility so great,
the prophet is considered a fool,
    the inspired man a maniac.
8The prophet, along with my God,
    is the watchman over Ephraim,
yet snares await him on all his paths,
    and hostility in the house of his
        God.
9They have sunk deep into corruption,
    as in the days of Gibeah.
God will remember their wickedness
    and punish them for their sins.

10"When I found Israel,
    it was like finding grapes in the
        desert;
when I saw your fathers,
    it was like seeing the early fruit on
        the fig-tree.
But when they came to Baal Peor,
    they consecrated themselves to
        that shameful idol
    and became as vile as the thing
        they loved.
11Ephraim's glory will fly away like a
    bird—
no birth, no pregnancy, no
    conception.
12Even if they bring up children,
    I will bereave them of every one.
Woe to them
    when I turn away from them!
13I have seen Ephraim, like Tyre,
    planted in a pleasant place.
But Ephraim will bring out
    their children to the slayer."

14Give them, O LORD—
    what will you give them?
Give them wombs that miscarry
    and breasts that are dry.

15"Because of all their wickedness in
    Gilgal,
    I hated them there.
Because of their sinful deeds,
    I will drive them out of my house.
I will no longer love them;
    all their leaders are rebellious.
16Ephraim is blighted,
    their root is withered,
    they yield no fruit.
Even if they bear children,
    I will slay their cherished
        offspring."

17My God will reject them
    because they have not obeyed him;
    they will be wanderers among the
        nations.

NEW TESTAMENT READING
Romans 8:1–17

Life Through the Spirit

8 Therefore, there is now no condemnation for those who are in
Christ Jesus, 2because through Christ
Jesus the law of the Spirit of life set me
free from the law of sin and death. 3For
what the law was powerless to do in that
it was weakened by the sinful nature,
God did by sending his own Son in the
likeness of sinful man to be a sin offering. And so he condemned sin in sinful
man, 4in order that the righteous requirements of the law might be fully met
in us, who do not live according to the
sinful nature but according to the Spirit.

5Those who live according to the sinful nature have their minds set on what
that nature desires; but those who live
in accordance with the Spirit have their
minds set on what the Spirit desires.
6The mind of sinful man is death, but
the mind controlled by the Spirit is life
and peace; 7the sinful mind is hostile to
God. It does not submit to God's law,

nor can it do so. ⁸Those controlled by the sinful nature cannot please God.

⁹You, however, are controlled not by the sinful nature but by the Spirit, if the Spirit of God lives in you. And if anyone does not have the Spirit of Christ, he does not belong to Christ. ¹⁰But if Christ is in you, your body is dead because of sin, yet your spirit is alive because of righteousness. ¹¹And if the Spirit of him who raised Jesus from the dead is living in you, he who raised Christ from the dead will also give life to your mortal bodies through his Spirit, who lives in you.

¹²Therefore, brothers, we have an obligation—but it is not to the sinful nature, to live according to it. ¹³For if you live according to the sinful nature, you will die; but if by the Spirit you put to death the misdeeds of the body, you will live, ¹⁴because those who are led by the Spirit of God are sons of God. ¹⁵For you did not receive a spirit that makes you a slave again to fear, but you received the Spirit of sonship. And by him we cry, "Abba, Father." ¹⁶The Spirit himself testifies with our spirit that we are God's children. ¹⁷Now if we are children, then we are heirs—heirs of God and co-heirs with Christ, if indeed we share in his sufferings in order that we may also share in his glory.

READING FROM PROVERBS
Proverbs 17:25–18:6

²⁵A foolish son brings grief to his father
   and bitterness to the one who bore
      him.

²⁶It is not good to punish an innocent
      man,
   or to flog officials for their
      integrity.

²⁷A man of knowledge uses words with
      restraint,
   and a man of understanding is
      even-tempered.

²⁸Even a fool is thought wise if he
      keeps silent,
   and discerning if he holds his
      tongue.

18 An unfriendly man pursues
   selfish ends;
   he defies all sound judgment.

²A fool finds no pleasure in
      understanding
   but delights in airing his own
      opinions.

³When wickedness comes, so does
      contempt,
   and with shame comes disgrace.

⁴The words of a man's mouth are deep
      waters,
   but the fountain of wisdom is a
      bubbling brook.

⁵It is not good to be partial to the
      wicked
   or to deprive the innocent of
      justice.

⁶A fool's lips bring him strife,
   and his mouth invites a beating.

JULY 24

OLD TESTAMENT READING
Hosea 10:1–11:11

10 Israel was a spreading vine;
he brought forth fruit for
himself.
As his fruit increased,
he built more altars;
as his land prospered,
he adorned his sacred stones.
2Their heart is deceitful,
and now they must bear their guilt.
The LORD will demolish their altars
and destroy their sacred stones.

3Then they will say, "We have no king
because we did not revere the
LORD.
But even if we had a king,
what could he do for us?"
4They make many promises,
take false oaths
and make agreements;
therefore lawsuits spring up
like poisonous weeds in a ploughed
field.
5The people who live in Samaria fear
for the calf-idol of Beth Aven.
Its people will mourn over it,
and so will its idolatrous priests,
those who had rejoiced over its
splendour,
because it is taken from them into
exile.
6It will be carried to Assyria
as tribute for the great king.
Ephraim will be disgraced;
Israel will be ashamed of its
wooden idols.
7Samaria and its king will float away
like a twig on the surface of the
waters.
8The high places of wickedness will be
destroyed—
it is the sin of Israel.
Thorns and thistles will grow up
and cover their altars.

Then they will say to the mountains,
"Cover us!"
and to the hills, "Fall on us!"

9"Since the days of Gibeah, you have
sinned, O Israel,
and there you have remained.
Did not war overtake
the evildoers in Gibeah?
10When I please, I will punish them;
nations will be gathered against
them
to put them in bonds for their
double sin.
11Ephraim is a trained heifer
that loves to thresh;
so I will put a yoke
on her fair neck.
I will drive Ephraim,
Judah must plough,
and Jacob must break up the
ground.
12Sow for yourselves righteousness,
reap the fruit of unfailing love,
and break up your unploughed
ground;
for it is time to seek the LORD,
until he comes
and showers righteousness on
you.
13But you have planted wickedness,
you have reaped evil,
you have eaten the fruit of
deception.
Because you have depended on your
own strength
and on your many warriors,
14the roar of battle will rise against
your people,
so that all your fortresses will be
devastated—
as Shalman devastated Beth Arbel on
the day of battle,
when mothers were dashed to the
ground with their children.
15Thus will it happen to you, O Bethel,
because your wickedness is great.

When that day dawns,
the king of Israel will be
completely destroyed.

God's Love for Israel

11 "When Israel was a child, I
loved him,
and out of Egypt I called my son.
[2]But the more I called Israel,
the further they went from me.
They sacrificed to the Baals
and they burned incense to images.
[3]It was I who taught Ephraim to walk,
taking them by the arms;
but they did not realise
it was I who healed them.
[4]I led them with cords of human
kindness,
with ties of love;
I lifted the yoke from their neck
and bent down to feed them.

[5]"Will they not return to Egypt
and will not Assyria rule over them
because they refuse to repent?
[6]Swords will flash in their cities,
will destroy the bars of their gates
and put an end to their plans.
[7]My people are determined to turn
from me.
Even if they call to the Most High,
he will by no means exalt them.

[8]"How can I give you up, Ephraim?
How can I hand you over, Israel?
How can I treat you like Admah?
How can I make you like Zeboiim?
My heart is changed within me;
all my compassion is aroused.
[9]I will not carry out my fierce anger,
nor will I turn and devastate
Ephraim.
For I am God, and not man—
the Holy One among you.
I will not come in wrath.
[10]They will follow the LORD;
he will roar like a lion.
When he roars,
his children will come trembling
from the west.

[11]They will come trembling
like birds from Egypt,
like doves from Assyria.
I will settle them in their homes,"
declares the LORD.

NEW TESTAMENT READING
Romans 8:18–39

Future Glory

[18]I consider that our present sufferings are not worth comparing with the glory that will be revealed in us. [19]The creation waits in eager expectation for the sons of God to be revealed. [20]For the creation was subjected to frustration, not by its own choice, but by the will of the one who subjected it, in hope [21]that the creation itself will be liberated from its bondage to decay and brought into the glorious freedom of the children of God.

[22]We know that the whole creation has been groaning as in the pains of childbirth right up to the present time. [23]Not only so, but we ourselves, who have the firstfruits of the Spirit, groan inwardly as we wait eagerly for our adoption as sons, the redemption of our bodies. [24]For in this hope we were saved. But hope that is seen is no hope at all. Who hopes for what he already has? [25]But if we hope for what we do not yet have, we wait for it patiently.

[26]In the same way, the Spirit helps us in our weakness. We do not know what we ought to pray for, but the Spirit himself intercedes for us with groans that words cannot express. [27]And he who searches our hearts knows the mind of the Spirit, because the Spirit intercedes for the saints in accordance with God's will.

More Than Conquerors

[28]And we know that in all things God works for the good of those who love him, who have been called according to his purpose. [29]For those God foreknew

he also predestined to be conformed to the likeness of his Son, that he might be the firstborn among many brothers. [30]And those he predestined, he also called; those he called, he also justified; those he justified, he also glorified.

[31]What, then, shall we say in response to this? If God is for us, who can be against us? [32]He who did not spare his own Son, but gave him up for us all —how will he not also, along with him, graciously give us all things? [33]Who will bring any charge against those whom God has chosen? It is God who justifies. [34]Who is he that condemns? Christ Jesus, who died—more than that, who was raised to life—is at the right hand of God and is also interceding for us. [35]Who shall separate us from the love of Christ? Shall trouble or hardship or persecution or famine or nakedness or danger or sword? [36]As it is written:

"For your sake we face death all day long;
   we are considered as sheep to be slaughtered."

[37]No, in all these things we are more than conquerors through him who loved us. [38]For I am convinced that neither death nor life, neither angels nor demons, neither the present nor the future, nor any powers, [39]neither height nor depth, nor anything else in all creation, will be able to separate us from the love of God that is in Christ Jesus our Lord.

READING FROM PSALMS
Psalm 89:1–8

A *maskil* of Ethan the Ezrahite.

[1]I will sing of the LORD's great love for ever;
   with my mouth I will make your faithfulness known through all generations.
[2]I will declare that your love stands firm for ever,
   that you established your faithfulness in heaven itself.

[3]You said, "I have made a covenant with my chosen one,
   I have sworn to David my servant,
[4]'I will establish your line for ever and make your throne firm through all generations.'"   *Selah*

[5]The heavens praise your wonders, O LORD,
   your faithfulness too, in the assembly of the holy ones.
[6]For who in the skies above can compare with the LORD?
   Who is like the LORD among the heavenly beings?
[7]In the council of the holy ones God is greatly feared;
   he is more awesome than all who surround him.
[8]O LORD God Almighty, who is like you?
   You are mighty, O LORD, and your faithfulness surrounds you.

JULY 25

OLD TESTAMENT READING
Hosea 11:12–14:9

Israel's Sin

¹²Ephraim has surrounded me with
lies,
  the house of Israel with deceit.
And Judah is unruly against God,
  even against the faithful Holy One.

12 ¹Ephraim feeds on the wind;
  he pursues the east wind all day
and multiplies lies and violence.
He makes a treaty with Assyria
  and sends olive oil to Egypt.
²The LORD has a charge to bring
  against Judah;
he will punish Jacob according to
  his ways
and repay him according to his
  deeds.
³In the womb he grasped his brother's
  heel;
  as a man he struggled with God.
⁴He struggled with the angel and
  overcame him;
  he wept and begged for his favour.
He found him at Bethel
  and talked with him there—
⁵the LORD God Almighty,
  the LORD is his name of renown!
⁶But you must return to your God;
  maintain love and justice,
  and wait for your God always.

⁷The merchant uses dishonest scales;
  he loves to defraud.
⁸Ephraim boasts,
  "I am very rich; I have become
  wealthy.
With all my wealth they will not find
  in me
  any iniquity or sin."

⁹"I am the LORD your God,
  ⌊who brought you⌋ out of Egypt;
I will make you live in tents again,
  as in the days of your appointed
  feasts.

¹⁰I spoke to the prophets,
  gave them many visions
  and told parables through them."

¹¹Is Gilead wicked?
  Its people are worthless!
Do they sacrifice bulls in Gilgal?
  Their altars will be like piles of
  stones
  on a ploughed field.
¹²Jacob fled to the country of Aram;
  Israel served to get a wife,
  and to pay for her he tended sheep.
¹³The LORD used a prophet to bring
  Israel up from Egypt,
  by a prophet he cared for him.
¹⁴But Ephraim has bitterly provoked
  him to anger;
  his Lord will leave upon him the
  guilt of his bloodshed
  and will repay him for his
  contempt.

The LORD's Anger Against Israel

13 ¹When Ephraim spoke, men
  trembled;
  he was exalted in Israel.
But he became guilty of Baal
  worship and died.
²Now they sin more and more;
  they make idols for themselves
  from their silver,
cleverly fashioned images,
  all of them the work of craftsmen.
It is said of these people,
  "They offer human sacrifice
  and kiss the calf-idols."
³Therefore they will be like the
  morning mist,
  like the early dew that disappears,
  like chaff swirling from a
  threshing-floor,
  like smoke escaping through a
  window.

⁴"But I am the LORD your God,
  ⌊who brought you⌋ out of Egypt.

You shall acknowledge no God but
me,
no Saviour except me.
⁵I cared for you in the desert,
in the land of burning heat.
⁶When I fed them, they were satisfied;
when they were satisfied, they
became proud;
then they forgot me.
⁷So I will come upon them like a lion,
like a leopard I will lurk by the
path.
⁸Like a bear robbed of her cubs,
I will attack them and rip them
open.
Like a lion I will devour them;
a wild animal will tear them apart.

⁹"You are destroyed, O Israel,
because you are against me,
against your helper.
¹⁰Where is your king, that he may save
you?
Where are your rulers in all your
towns,
of whom you said,
'Give me a king and princes'?
¹¹So in my anger I gave you a king,
and in my wrath I took him away.
¹²The guilt of Ephraim is stored up,
his sins are kept on record.
¹³Pains as of a woman in childbirth
come to him,
but he is a child without wisdom;
when the time arrives,
he does not come to the opening of
the womb.

¹⁴"I will ransom them from the power
of the grave;
I will redeem them from death.
Where, O death, are your plagues?
Where, O grave, is your
destruction?

"I will have no compassion,
15 even though he thrives among his
brothers.
An east wind from the LORD will
come,
blowing in from the desert;

his spring will fail
and his well dry up.
His storehouse will be plundered
of all its treasures.
¹⁶The people of Samaria must bear
their guilt,
because they have rebelled against
their God.
They will fall by the sword;
their little ones will be dashed to
the ground,
their pregnant women ripped
open."

Repentance to Bring Blessing

14 Return, O Israel, to the LORD
your God.
Your sins have been your
downfall!
²Take words with you
and return to the LORD.
Say to him:
"Forgive all our sins
and receive us graciously,
that we may offer the fruit of our
lips.
³Assyria cannot save us;
we will not mount war-horses.
We will never again say 'Our gods'
to what our own hands have made,
for in you the fatherless find
compassion."

⁴"I will heal their waywardness
and love them freely,
for my anger has turned away from
them.
⁵I will be like the dew to Israel;
he will blossom like a lily.
Like a cedar of Lebanon
he will send down his roots;
6 his young shoots will grow.
His splendour will be like an olive
tree,
his fragrance like a cedar of
Lebanon.
⁷Men will dwell again in his shade.
He will flourish like the corn.
He will blossom like a vine,
and his fame will be like the wine
from Lebanon.

8O Ephraim, what more have I to do
    with idols?
  I will answer him and care for him.
  I am like a green pine tree;
    your fruitfulness comes from me."

9Who is wise? He will realise these
      things.
    Who is discerning? He will
      understand them.
  The ways of the LORD are right;
    the righteous walk in them,
    but the rebellious stumble in them.

NEW TESTAMENT READING
Romans 9:1–21

God's Sovereign Choice

9 I speak the truth in Christ—I am
    not lying, my conscience confirms
it in the Holy Spirit—2I have great sorrow and unceasing anguish in my heart.
3For I could wish that I myself were
cursed and cut off from Christ for the
sake of my brothers, those of my own
race, 4the people of Israel. Theirs is the
adoption as sons; theirs the divine
glory, the covenants, the receiving of
the law, the temple worship and the
promises. 5Theirs are the patriarchs,
and from them is traced the human
ancestry of Christ, who is God over all,
for ever praised! Amen.

6It is not as though God's word had
failed. For not all who are descended
from Israel are Israel. 7Nor because
they are his descendants are they all
Abraham's children. On the contrary,
"It is through Isaac that your offspring
will be reckoned." 8In other words, it is
not the natural children who are God's
children, but it is the children of the
promise who are regarded as Abraham's offspring. 9For this was how the
promise was stated: "At the appointed
time I will return, and Sarah will have a
son."

10Not only that, but Rebekah's children had one and the same father, our
father Isaac. 11Yet, before the twins

were born or had done anything good or
bad—in order that God's purpose in
election might stand: 12not by works but
by him who calls—she was told, "The
older will serve the younger." 13Just as it
is written: "Jacob I loved, but Esau I
hated."

14What then shall we say? Is God
unjust? Not at all! 15For he says to
Moses,

  "I will have mercy on whom I have
      mercy,
    and I will have compassion on
      whom I have compassion."

16It does not, therefore, depend on
man's desire or effort, but on God's
mercy. 17For the Scripture says to Pharaoh: "I raised you up for this very purpose, that I might display my power in
you and that my name might be proclaimed in all the earth." 18Therefore
God has mercy on whom he wants to
have mercy, and he hardens whom he
wants to harden.

19One of you will say to me: "Then
why does God still blame us? For who
resists his will?" 20But who are you, O
man, to talk back to God? "Shall what is
formed say to him who formed it, 'Why
did you make me like this?'" 21Does not
the potter have the right to make out of
the same lump of clay some pottery for
noble purposes and some for common
use?

READING FROM PSALMS
Psalm 89:9–13

9You rule over the surging sea;
    when its waves mount up, you still
      them.
10You crushed Rahab like one of the
      slain;
    with your strong arm you scattered
      your enemies.
11The heavens are yours, and yours
      also the earth;
    you founded the world and all that
      is in it.

¹²You created the north and the south;
Tabor and Hermon sing for joy at
your name.

¹³Your arm is endued with power;
your hand is strong, your right
hand exalted.

DAY 207

JULY 26

OLD TESTAMENT READING
1 Chronicles 1:1–2:17

Historical Records From Adam to Abraham

To Noah's Sons

1 Adam, Seth, Enosh, ²Kenan, Mahalalel, Jared, ³Enoch, Methuselah, Lamech, Noah.

⁴The sons of Noah:
Shem, Ham and Japheth.

The Japhethites

⁵The sons of Japheth:
Gomer, Magog, Madai, Javan, Tubal, Meshech and Tiras.

⁶The sons of Gomer:
Ashkenaz, Riphath and Togarmah.

⁷The sons of Javan:
Elishah, Tarshish, the Kittim and the Rodanim.

The Hamites

⁸The sons of Ham:
Cush, Mizraim, Put and Canaan.

⁹The sons of Cush:
Seba, Havilah, Sabta, Raamah and Sabteca.

The sons of Raamah:
Sheba and Dedan.

¹⁰Cush was the father of
Nimrod, who grew to be a mighty warrior on earth.

¹¹Mizraim was the father of
the Ludites, Anamites, Lehabites, Naphtuhites, ¹²Pathrusites, Casluhites (from whom the Philistines came) and Caphtorites.

¹³Canaan was the father of
Sidon his firstborn, and of the Hittites, ¹⁴Jebusites, Amorites, Girgashites, ¹⁵Hivites, Arkites, Sinites, ¹⁶Arvadites, Zemarites and Hamathites.

The Semites

¹⁷The sons of Shem:
Elam, Asshur, Arphaxad, Lud and Aram.

The sons of Aram:
Uz, Hul, Gether and Meshech.

¹⁸Arphaxad was the father of Shelah, and Shelah the father of Eber.

¹⁹Two sons were born to Eber:
One was named Peleg, because in his time the earth was divided; his brother was named Joktan.

²⁰Joktan was the father of
Almodad, Sheleph, Hazarmaveth, Jerah, ²¹Hadoram, Uzal, Diklah, ²²Obal, Abimael, Sheba, ²³Ophir, Havilah and Jobab. All these were sons of Joktan.

²⁴Shem, Arphaxad, Shelah,
²⁵Eber, Peleg, Reu,
²⁶Serug, Nahor, Terah
²⁷and Abram (that is, Abraham).

The Family of Abraham

²⁸The sons of Abraham:
Isaac and Ishmael.

Descendants of Hagar

²⁹These were their descendants:
Nebaioth the firstborn of

Ishmael, Kedar, Adbeel, Mibsam, [30]Mishma, Dumah, Massa, Hadad, Tema, [31]Jetur, Naphish and Kedemah. These were the sons of Ishmael.

Descendants of Keturah

[32]The sons born to Keturah, Abraham's concubine:
Zimran, Jokshan, Medan, Midian, Ishbak and Shuah.
The sons of Jokshan:
Sheba and Dedan.
[33]The sons of Midian:
Ephah, Epher, Hanoch, Abida and Eldaah.
All these were descendants of Keturah.

Descendants of Sarah

[34]Abraham was the father of Isaac.
The sons of Isaac:
Esau and Israel.

Esau's Sons

[35]The sons of Esau:
Eliphaz, Reuel, Jeush, Jalam and Korah.
[36]The sons of Eliphaz:
Teman, Omar, Zepho, Gatam and Kenaz;
by Timna: Amalek.
[37]The sons of Reuel:
Nahath, Zerah, Shammah and Mizzah.

The People of Seir in Edom

[38]The sons of Seir:
Lotan, Shobal, Zibeon, Anah, Dishon, Ezer and Dishan.
[39]The sons of Lotan:
Hori and Homam. Timna was Lotan's sister.
[40]The sons of Shobal:
Alvan, Manahath, Ebal, Shepho and Onam.
The sons of Zibeon:
Aiah and Anah.
[41]The son of Anah:
Dishon.

The sons of Dishon:
Hemdan, Eshban, Ithran and Keran.
[42]The sons of Ezer:
Bilhan, Zaavan and Akan.
The sons of Dishan:
Uz and Aran.

The Rulers of Edom

[43]These were the kings who reigned in Edom before any Israelite king reigned:
Bela son of Beor, whose city was named Dinhabah.
[44]When Bela died, Jobab son of Zerah from Bozrah succeeded him as king.
[45]When Jobab died, Husham from the land of the Temanites succeeded him as king.
[46]When Husham died, Hadad son of Bedad, who defeated Midian in the country of Moab, succeeded him as king. His city was named Avith.
[47]When Hadad died, Samlah from Masrekah succeeded him as king.
[48]When Samlah died, Shaul from Rehoboth on the river succeeded him as king.
[49]When Shaul died, Baal-Hanan son of Acbor succeeded him as king.
[50]When Baal-Hanan died, Hadad succeeded him as king. His city was named Pau, and his wife's name was Mehetabel daughter of Matred, the daughter of Me-Zahab. [51]Hadad also died.

The chiefs of Edom were:
Timna, Alvah, Jetheth, [52]Oholibamah, Elah, Pinon, [53]Kenaz, Teman, Mibzar, [54]Magdiel and Iram. These were the chiefs of Edom.

Israel's Sons

2 These were the sons of Israel:
Reuben, Simeon, Levi, Judah, Issachar, Zebulun, [2]Dan,

Joseph, Benjamin, Naphtali, Gad and Asher.

Judah

To Hezron's Sons

³The sons of Judah:

Er, Onan and Shelah. These three were born to him by a Canaanite woman, the daughter of Shua. Er, Judah's firstborn, was wicked in the LORD's sight; so the LORD put him to death. ⁴Tamar, Judah's daughter-in-law, bore him Perez and Zerah. Judah had five sons in all.

⁵The sons of Perez:

Hezron and Hamul.

⁶The sons of Zerah:

Zimri, Ethan, Heman, Calcol and Darda—five in all.

⁷The son of Carmi:

Achar, who brought trouble on Israel by violating the ban on taking devoted things.

⁸The son of Ethan:

Azariah.

⁹The sons born to Hezron were:

Jerahmeel, Ram and Caleb.

From Ram Son of Hezron

¹⁰Ram was the father of Amminadab, and Amminadab the father of Nahshon, the leader of the people of Judah. ¹¹Nahshon was the father of Salmon, Salmon the father of Boaz, ¹²Boaz the father of Obed and Obed the father of Jesse.

¹³Jesse was the father of

Eliab his firstborn; the second son was Abinadab, the third Shimea, ¹⁴the fourth Nethanel, the fifth Raddai, ¹⁵the sixth Ozem and the seventh David. ¹⁶Their sisters were Zeruiah and Abigail. Zeruiah's three sons were Abishai, Joab and Asahel. ¹⁷Abigail was the mother of Amasa, whose father was Jether the Ishmaelite.

NEW TESTAMENT READING
Romans 9:22–10:4

²²What if God, choosing to show his wrath and make his power known, bore with great patience the objects of his wrath—prepared for destruction? ²³What if he did this to make the riches of his glory known to the objects of his mercy, whom he prepared in advance for glory—²⁴even us, whom he also called, not only from the Jews but also from the Gentiles? ²⁵As he says in Hosea:

"I will call them 'my people' who are
    not my people;
and I will call her 'my loved one'
    who is not my loved one,"

²⁶and,

"It will happen that in the very place
    where it was said to them,
    'You are not my people,'
they will be called 'sons of the living
    God.' ."

²⁷Isaiah cries out concerning Israel:

"Though the number of the Israelites
    be like the sand by the sea,
    only the remnant will be saved.
²⁸For the Lord will carry out
    his sentence on earth with speed
    and finality."

²⁹It is just as Isaiah said previously:

"Unless the Lord Almighty
    had left us descendants,
we would have become like Sodom,
    we would have been like
    Gomorrah."

Israel's Unbelief

³⁰What then shall we say? That the Gentiles, who did not pursue righteousness, have obtained it, a righteousness that is by faith; ³¹but Israel, who pursued a law of righteousness, has not attained it. ³²Why not? Because they

pursued it not by faith but as if it were by works. They stumbled over the "stumbling-stone". [33]As it is written:

"See, I lay in Zion a stone that causes
      men to stumble
   and a rock that makes them fall,
and the one who trusts in him will
      never be put to shame."

10 Brothers, my heart's desire and prayer to God for the Israelites is that they may be saved. [2]For I can testify about them that they are zealous for God, but their zeal is not based on knowledge. [3]Since they did not know the righteousness that comes from God and sought to establish their own, they did not submit to God's righteousness. [4]Christ is the end of the law so that there may be righteousness for everyone who believes.

READING FROM PSALMS
Psalm 89:14–18

[14]Righteousness and justice are the
      foundation of your throne;
   love and faithfulness go before
      you.
[15]Blessed are those who have learned
      to acclaim you,
   who walk in the light of your
      presence, O LORD.
[16]They rejoice in your name all day
      long;
   they exult in your righteousness.
[17]For you are their glory and
      strength,
   and by your favour you exalt our
      horn.
[18]Indeed, our shield belongs to the
      LORD,
   our king to the Holy One of Israel.

JULY 27 DAY 208

OLD TESTAMENT READING
1 Chronicles 2:18–4:8

Caleb Son of Hezron

[18]Caleb son of Hezron had children by his wife Azubah (and by Jerioth). These were her sons: Jesher, Shobab and Ardon. [19]When Azubah died, Caleb married Ephrath, who bore him Hur. [20]Hur was the father of Uri, and Uri the father of Bezalel.

[21]Later, Hezron lay with the daughter of Makir the father of Gilead (he had married her when he was sixty years old), and she bore him Segub. [22]Segub was the father of Jair, who controlled twenty-three towns in Gilead. [23](But Geshur and Aram captured Havvoth Jair, as well as Kenath with its surrounding

settlements—sixty towns.) All these were descendants of Makir the father of Gilead.

[24]After Hezron died in Caleb Ephrathah, Abijah the wife of Hezron bore him Ashhur the father of Tekoa.

Jerahmeel Son of Hezron

[25]The sons of Jerahmeel the firstborn of Hezron:
   Ram his firstborn, Bunah, Oren, Ozem and Ahijah. [26]Jerahmeel had another wife, whose name was Atarah; she was the mother of Onam.

[27]The sons of Ram the firstborn of Jerahmeel:
   Maaz, Jamin and Eker.
[28]The sons of Onam:
   Shammai and Jada.

The sons of Shammai:
Nadab and Abishur.

²⁹Abishur's wife was named Abihail, who bore him Ahban and Molid.
³⁰The sons of Nadab:
Seled and Appaim. Seled died without children.
³¹The son of Appaim:
Ishi, who was the father of Sheshan.
Sheshan was the father of Ahlai.
³²The sons of Jada, Shammai's brother:
Jether and Jonathan. Jether died without children.
³³The sons of Jonathan:
Peleth and Zaza.
These were the descendants of Jerahmeel.

³⁴Sheshan had no sons—only daughters.
He had an Egyptian servant named Jarha. ³⁵Sheshan gave his daughter in marriage to his servant Jarha, and she bore him Attai.

³⁶Attai was the father of Nathan,
Nathan the father of Zabad,
³⁷Zabad the father of Ephlal,
Ephlal the father of Obed,
³⁸Obed the father of Jehu,
Jehu the father of Azariah,
³⁹Azariah the father of Helez,
Helez the father of Eleasah,
⁴⁰Eleasah the father of Sismai,
Sismai the father of Shallum,
⁴¹Shallum the father of Jekamiah,
and Jekamiah the father of Elishama.

The Clans of Caleb

⁴²The sons of Caleb the brother of Jerahmeel:
Mesha his firstborn, who was the father of Ziph, and his son Mareshah, who was the father of Hebron.
⁴³The sons of Hebron:
Korah, Tappuah, Rekem and Shema. ⁴⁴Shema was the father of Raham, and Raham the father of Jorkeam. Rekem was the

father of Shammai. ⁴⁵The son of Shammai was Maon, and Maon was the father of Beth Zur.

⁴⁶Caleb's concubine Ephah was the mother of Haran, Moza and Gazez. Haran was the father of Gazez.
⁴⁷The sons of Jahdai:
Regem, Jotham, Geshan, Pelet, Ephah and Shaaph.
⁴⁸Caleb's concubine Maacah was the mother of Sheber and Tirhanah. ⁴⁹She also gave birth to Shaaph the father of Madmannah and to Sheva the father of Macbenah and Gibea. Caleb's daughter was Acsah. ⁵⁰These were the descendants of Caleb.

The sons of Hur the firstborn of Ephrathah:
Shobal the father of Kiriath Jearim, ⁵¹Salma the father of Bethlehem, and Hareph the father of Beth Gader.
⁵²The descendants of Shobal the father of Kiriath Jearim were:
Haroeh, half the Manahathites, ⁵³and the clans of Kiriath Jearim: the Ithrites, Puthites, Shumathites and Mishraites. From these descended the Zorathites and Eshtaolites.
⁵⁴The descendants of Salma:
Bethlehem, the Netophathites, Atroth Beth Joab, half the Manahathites, the Zorites, ⁵⁵and the clans of scribes who lived at Jabez: the Tirathites, Shimeathites and Sucathites. These are the Kenites who came from Hammath, the father of the house of Recab.

The Sons of David

3 These were the sons of David born to him in Hebron:
The firstborn was Amnon the son of Ahinoam of Jezreel;
the second, Daniel the son of Abigail of Carmel;
²the third, Absalom the son of

Maacah daughter of Talmai king of Geshur;

the fourth, Adonijah the son of Haggith;

[3]the fifth, Shephatiah the son of Abital;

and the sixth, Ithream, by his wife Eglah.

[4]These six were born to David in Hebron, where he reigned for seven years and six months.

David reigned in Jerusalem for thirty-three years, [5]and these were the children born to him there:

Shammua, Shobab, Nathan and Solomon. These four were by Bathsheba daughter of Ammiel. [6]There were also Ibhar, Elishua, Eliphelet, [7]Nogah, Nepheg, Japhia, [8]Elishama, Eliada and Eliphelet—nine in all. [9]All these were the sons of David, besides his sons by his concubines. And Tamar was their sister.

The Kings of Judah

[10]Solomon's son was Rehoboam,
Abijah his son,
Asa his son,
Jehoshaphat his son,
[11]Jehoram his son,
Ahaziah his son,
Joash his son,
[12]Amaziah his son,
Azariah his son,
Jotham his son,
[13]Ahaz his son,
Hezekiah his son,
Manasseh his son,
[14]Amon his son,
Josiah his son.

[15]The sons of Josiah:
Johanan the firstborn,
Jehoiakim the second son,
Zedekiah the third,
Shallum the fourth.

[16]The successors of Jehoiakim:
Jehoiachin his son,
and Zedekiah.

The Royal Line After the Exile

[17]The descendants of Jehoiachin the captive:

Shealtiel his son, [18]Malkiram, Pedaiah, Shenazzar, Jekamiah, Hoshama and Nedabiah.

[19]The sons of Pedaiah:
Zerubbabel and Shimei.

The sons of Zerubbabel:
Meshullam and Hananiah. Shelomith was their sister. [20]There were also five others: Hashubah, Ohel, Berekiah, Hasadiah and Jushab-Hesed.

[21]The descendants of Hananiah:
Pelatiah and Jeshaiah, and the sons of Rephaiah, of Arnan, of Obadiah and of Shecaniah.

[22]The descendants of Shecaniah:
Shemaiah and his sons:
Hattush, Igal, Bariah, Neariah and Shaphat—six in all.

[23]The sons of Neariah:
Elioenai, Hizkiah and Azrikam —three in all.

[24]The sons of Elioenai:
Hodaviah, Eliashib, Pelaiah, Akkub, Johanan, Delaiah and Anani—seven in all.

Other Clans of Judah

4 The descendants of Judah:
Perez, Hezron, Carmi, Hur and Shobal.

[2]Reaiah son of Shobal was the father of Jahath, and Jahath the father of Ahumai and Lahad. These were the clans of the Zorathites.

[3]These were the sons of Etam:
Jezreel, Ishma and Idbash. Their sister was named Hazzelelponi. [4]Penuel was the father of Gedor, and Ezer the father of Hushah.

These were the descendants of Hur, the firstborn of Ephrathah and father of Bethlehem.

[5]Ashhur the father of Tekoa had two wives, Helah and Naarah.

[6]Naarah bore him Ahuzzam, Hepher, Temeni and Haahashtari. These were the descendants of Naarah.

[7]The sons of Helah:
Zereth, Zohar, Ethnan, [8]and

Koz, who was the father of Anub and Hazzobebah and of the clans of Aharhel son of Harum.

NEW TESTAMENT READING
Romans 10:5–11:10

5Moses describes in this way the righteousness that is by the law: "The man who does these things will live by them." 6But the righteousness that is by faith says: "Do not say in your heart, 'Who will ascend into heaven?'" (that is, to bring Christ down) 7"or 'Who will descend into the deep?'" (that is, to bring Christ up from the dead). 8But what does it say? "The word is near you; it is in your mouth and in your heart," that is, the word of faith we are proclaiming: 9That if you confess with your mouth, "Jesus is Lord," and believe in your heart that God raised him from the dead, you will be saved. 10For it is with your heart that you believe and are justified, and it is with your mouth that you confess and are saved. 11As the Scripture says, "Anyone who trusts in him will never be put to shame." 12For there is no difference between Jew and Gentile—the same Lord is Lord of all and richly blesses all who call on him, 13for, "Everyone who calls on the name of the Lord will be saved."

14How, then, can they call on the one they have not believed in? And how can they believe in the one of whom they have not heard? And how can they hear without someone preaching to them? 15And how can they preach unless they are sent? As it is written, "How beautiful are the feet of those who bring good news!"

16But not all the Israelites accepted the good news. For Isaiah says, "Lord, who has believed our message?" 17Consequently, faith comes from hearing the message, and the message is heard through the word of Christ. 18But I ask: Did they not hear? Of course they did:

"Their voice has gone out into all the earth,
   their words to the ends of the world."

19Again I ask: Did Israel not understand? First, Moses says,

"I will make you envious by those who are not a nation;
I will make you angry by a nation that has no understanding."

20And Isaiah boldly says,

"I was found by those who did not seek me;
I revealed myself to those who did not ask for me."

21But concerning Israel he says,

"All day long I have held out my hands
   to a disobedient and obstinate people."

The Remnant of Israel

11 I ask then: Did God reject his people? By no means! I am an Israelite myself, a descendant of Abraham, from the tribe of Benjamin. 2God did not reject his people, whom he foreknew. Don't you know what the Scripture says in the passage about Elijah—how he appealed to God against Israel: 3"Lord, they have killed your prophets and torn down your altars; I am the only one left, and they are trying to kill me"? 4And what was God's answer to him? "I have reserved for myself seven thousand who have not bowed the knee to Baal." 5So too, at the present time there is a remnant chosen by grace. 6And if by grace, then it is no longer by works; if it were, grace would no longer be grace.

7What then? What Israel sought so earnestly it did not obtain, but the elect did. The others were hardened, 8as it is written:

"God gave them a spirit of stupor,
eyes so that they could not see
and ears so that they could not
hear,
to this very day."

⁹And David says:

"May their table become a snare and
a trap,
a stumbling-block and a retribution
for them.
¹⁰May their eyes be darkened so they
cannot see,
and their backs be bent for ever."

READING FROM PROVERBS
Proverbs 18:7–16

⁷A fool's mouth is his undoing,
and his lips are a snare to his soul.

⁸The words of a gossip are like choice
morsels;
they go down to a man's inmost
parts.

⁹One who is slack in his work
is brother to one who destroys.

¹⁰The name of the LORD is a strong
tower;
the righteous run to it and are safe.

¹¹The wealth of the rich is their
fortified city;
they imagine it an unscalable wall.

¹²Before his downfall a man's heart is
proud,
but humility comes before honour.

¹³He who answers before listening—
that is his folly and his shame.

¹⁴A man's spirit sustains him in
sickness,
but a crushed spirit who can bear?

¹⁵The heart of the discerning acquires
knowledge;
the ears of the wise seek it out.

¹⁶A gift opens the way for the giver
and ushers him into the presence of
the great.

JULY 28   DAY 209

OLD TESTAMENT READING
1 Chronicles 4:9–5:26

⁹Jabez was more honourable than his brothers. His mother had named him Jabez, saying, "I gave birth to him in pain." ¹⁰Jabez cried out to the God of Israel, "Oh, that you would bless me and enlarge my territory! Let your hand be with me, and keep me from harm so that I will be free from pain." And God granted his request.

¹¹Kelub, Shuhah's brother, was the father of Mehir, who was the father of Eshton. ¹²Eshton was the father of Beth Rapha, Paseah and Tehinnah the father of Ir Nahash. These were the men of Recah.

¹³The sons of Kenaz:
Othniel and Seraiah.
The sons of Othniel:
Hathath and Meonothai.
¹⁴Meonothai was the father of Ophrah.
Seraiah was the father of Joab,
the father of Ge Harashim. It was called this because its people were craftsmen.

¹⁵The sons of Caleb son of Jephunneh:

Iru, Elah and Naam.

The son of Elah:

Kenaz.

¹⁶The sons of Jehallelel:

Ziph, Ziphah, Tiria and Asarel.

¹⁷The sons of Ezrah:

Jether, Mered, Epher and Jalon. One of Mered's wives gave birth to Miriam, Shammai and Ishbah the father of Eshtemoa. ¹⁸(His Judean wife gave birth to Jered the father of Gedor, Heber the father of Soco, and Jekuthiel the father of Zanoah.) These were the children of Pharaoh's daughter Bithiah, whom Mered had married.

¹⁹The sons of Hodiah's wife, the sister of Naham:

the father of Keilah the Garmite, and Eshtemoa the Maacathite.

²⁰The sons of Shimon:

Amnon, Rinnah, Ben-Hanan and Tilon.

The descendants of Ishi:

Zoheth and Ben-Zoheth.

²¹The sons of Shelah son of Judah:

Er the father of Lecah, Laadah the father of Mareshah and the clans of the linen workers at Beth Ashbea, ²²Jokim, the men of Cozeba, and Joash and Saraph, who ruled in Moab and Jashubi Lehem. (These records are from ancient times.) ²³They were the potters who lived at Netaim and Gederah; they stayed there and worked for the king.

Simeon

²⁴The descendants of Simeon:

Nemuel, Jamin, Jarib, Zerah and Shaul;

²⁵Shallum was Shaul's son, Mibsam his son and Mishma his son.

²⁶The descendants of Mishma:

Hammuel his son, Zaccur his son and Shimei his son.

²⁷Shimei had sixteen sons and six daughters, but his brothers did not have many children; so their entire clan did not become as numerous as the people of Judah. ²⁸They lived in Beersheba, Moladah, Hazar Shual, ²⁹Bilhah, Ezem, Tolad, ³⁰Bethuel, Hormah, Ziklag, ³¹Beth Marcaboth, Hazar Susim, Beth Biri and Shaaraim. These were their towns until the reign of David. ³²Their surrounding villages were Etam, Ain, Rimmon, Token and Ashan—five towns—³³and all the villages around these towns as far as Baalath. These were their settlements. And they kept a genealogical record.

³⁴Meshobab, Jamlech, Joshah son of Amaziah, ³⁵Joel, Jehu son of Joshibiah, the son of Seraiah, the son of Asiel, ³⁶also Elioenai, Jaakobah, Jeshohaiah, Asaiah, Adiel, Jesimiel, Benaiah, ³⁷and Ziza son of Shiphi, the son of Allon, the son of Jedaiah, the son of Shimri, the son of Shemaiah.

³⁸The men listed above by name were leaders of their clans. Their families increased greatly, ³⁹and they went to the outskirts of Gedor to the east of the valley in search of pasture for their flocks. ⁴⁰They found rich, good pasture, and the land was spacious, peaceful and quiet. Some Hamites had lived there formerly.

⁴¹The men whose names were listed came in the days of Hezekiah king of Judah. They attacked the Hamites in their dwellings and also the Meunites who were there and completely destroyed them, as is evident to this day. Then they settled in their place, because there was pasture for their flocks. ⁴²And five hundred of these Simeonites, led by Pelatiah, Neariah, Rephaiah and Uzziel, the sons of Ishi, invaded the hill country of Seir. ⁴³They killed the remaining Amalekites who had escaped, and they have lived there to this day.

Reuben

5 The sons of Reuben the firstborn of Israel (he was the firstborn, but when he defiled his father's marriage bed, his rights as firstborn were given to the sons of Joseph son of Israel; so he could not be listed in the genealogical record in accordance with his birthright, [2]and though Judah was the strongest of his brothers and a ruler came from him, the rights of the firstborn belonged to Joseph)—[3]the sons of Reuben the firstborn of Israel:

Hanoch, Pallu, Hezron and Carmi.

[4]The descendants of Joel:

Shemaiah his son, Gog his son, Shimei his son, [5]Micah his son, Reaiah his son, Baal his son, [6]and Beerah his son, whom Tiglath-Pileser king of Assyria took into exile. Beerah was a leader of the Reubenites.

[7]Their relatives by clans, listed according to their genealogical records:

Jeiel the chief, Zechariah, [8]and Bela son of Azaz, the son of Shema, the son of Joel. They settled in the area from Aroer to Nebo and Baal Meon. [9]To the east they occupied the land up to the edge of the desert that extends to the Euphrates River, because their livestock had increased in Gilead.

[10]During Saul's reign they waged war against the Hagrites, who were defeated at their hands; they occupied the dwellings of the Hagrites throughout the entire region east of Gilead.

Gad

[11]The Gadites lived next to them in Bashan, as far as Salecah:

[12]Joel was the chief, Shapham the second, then Janai and Shaphat, in Bashan.

[13]Their relatives, by families, were:

Michael, Meshullam, Sheba, Jorai, Jacan, Zia and Eber—seven in all. [14]These were the sons of Abihail son of Huri, the son of Jaroah, the son of Gilead, the son of Michael, the son of Jeshishai, the son of Jahdo, the son of Buz.

[15]Ahi son of Abdiel, the son of Guni, was head of their family.

[16]The Gadites lived in Gilead, in Bashan and its outlying villages, and on all the pasture-lands of Sharon as far as they extended.

[17]All these were entered in the genealogical records during the reigns of Jotham king of Judah and Jeroboam king of Israel.

[18]The Reubenites, the Gadites and the half-tribe of Manasseh had 44,760 men ready for military service—able-bodied men who could handle shield and sword, who could use a bow, and who were trained for battle. [19]They waged war against the Hagrites, Jetur, Naphish and Nodab. [20]They were helped in fighting them, and God handed the Hagrites and all their allies over to them, because they cried out to him during the battle. He answered their prayers, because they trusted in him. [21]They seized the livestock of the Hagrites—fifty thousand camels, two hundred and fifty thousand sheep and two thousand donkeys. They also took one hundred thousand people captive, [22]and many others fell slain, because the battle was God's. And they occupied the land until the exile.

The Half-Tribe of Manasseh

[23]The people of the half-tribe of Manasseh were numerous; they settled in the land from Bashan to Baal Hermon, that is, to Senir (Mount Hermon).

[24]These were the heads of their families: Epher, Ishi, Eliel, Azriel, Jeremiah, Hodaviah and Jahdiel. They were brave warriors, famous men, and heads of their families. [25]But they were unfaithful to the God of their fathers and prostituted themselves to the gods of

the peoples of the land, whom God had destroyed before them. 26So the God of Israel stirred up the spirit of Pul king of Assyria (that is, Tiglath-Pileser king of Assyria), who took the Reubenites, the Gadites and the half-tribe of Manasseh into exile. He took them to Halah, Habor, Hara and the river of Gozan, where they are to this day.

NEW TESTAMENT READING
Romans 11:11–32

Ingrafted Branches

11Again I ask: Did they stumble so as to fall beyond recovery? Not at all! Rather, because of their transgression, salvation has come to the Gentiles to make Israel envious. 12But if their transgression means riches for the world, and their loss means riches for the Gentiles, how much greater riches will their fulness bring!

13I am talking to you Gentiles. Inasmuch as I am the apostle to the Gentiles, I make much of my ministry 14in the hope that I may somehow arouse my own people to envy and save some of them. 15For if their rejection is the reconciliation of the world, what will their acceptance be but life from the dead? 16If the part of the dough offered as firstfruits is holy, then the whole batch is holy; if the root is holy, so are the branches.

17If some of the branches have been broken off, and you, though a wild olive shoot, have been grafted in among the others and now share in the nourishing sap from the olive root, 18do not boast over those branches. If you do, consider this: You do not support the root, but the root supports you. 19You will say then, "Branches were broken off so that I could be grafted in." 20Granted. But they were broken off because of unbelief, and you stand by faith. Do not be arrogant, but afraid. 21For if God did not spare the natural branches, he will not spare you either.

22Consider therefore the kindness and sternness of God: sternness to those who fell, but kindness to you, provided that you continue in his kindness. Otherwise, you also will be cut off. 23And if they do not persist in unbelief, they will be grafted in, for God is able to graft them in again. 24After all, if you were cut out of an olive tree that is wild by nature, and contrary to nature were grafted into a cultivated olive tree, how much more readily will these, the natural branches, be grafted into their own olive tree!

All Israel Will Be Saved

25I do not want you to be ignorant of this mystery, brothers, so that you may not be conceited: Israel has experienced a hardening in part until the full number of the Gentiles has come in. 26And so all Israel will be saved, as it is written:

"The deliverer will come from Zion;
    he will turn godlessness away from
        Jacob.
27And this is my covenant with them
    when I take away their sins."

28As far as the gospel is concerned, they are enemies on your account; but as far as election is concerned, they are loved on account of the patriarchs, 29for God's gifts and his call are irrevocable. 30Just as you who were at one time disobedient to God have now received mercy as a result of their disobedience, 31so they too have now become disobedient in order that they too may now receive mercy as a result of God's mercy to you. 32For God has bound all men over to disobedience so that he may have mercy on them all.

READING FROM PSALMS
Psalm 89:19–29

19Once you spoke in a vision,
    to your faithful people you said:
    "I have bestowed strength on a
        warrior;

I have exalted a young man from
among the people.
²⁰I have found David my servant;
with my sacred oil I have anointed
him.
²¹My hand will sustain him;
surely my arm will strengthen him.
²²No enemy will subject him to
tribute;
no wicked man will oppress him.
²³I will crush his foes before him
and strike down his adversaries.
²⁴My faithful love will be with him,
and through my name his horn will
be exalted.

²⁵I will set his hand over the sea,
his right hand over the rivers.
²⁶He will call out to me, 'You are my
Father,
my God, the Rock my Saviour.'
²⁷I will also appoint him my firstborn,
the most exalted of the kings of the
earth.
²⁸I will maintain my love to him for
ever,
and my covenant with him will
never fail.
²⁹I will establish his line for ever,
his throne as long as the heavens
endure.

JULY 29   DAY 210

OLD TESTAMENT READING
1 Chronicles 6:1–81

Levi

6 The sons of Levi:
Gershon, Kohath and Merari.
²The sons of Kohath:
Amram, Izhar, Hebron and
Uzziel.
³The children of Amram:
Aaron, Moses and Miriam.
The sons of Aaron:
Nadab, Abihu, Eleazar and
Ithamar.
⁴Eleazar was the father of
Phinehas,
Phinehas the father of Abishua,
⁵Abishua the father of Bukki,
Bukki the father of Uzzi,
⁶Uzzi the father of Zerahiah,
Zerahiah the father of Meraioth,
⁷Meraioth the father of Amariah,
Amariah the father of Ahitub,
⁸Ahitub the father of Zadok,
Zadok the father of Ahimaaz,
⁹Ahimaaz the father of Azariah,
Azariah the father of Johanan,
¹⁰Johanan the father of Azariah (it
was he who served as priest in

the temple Solomon built in
Jerusalem),
¹¹Azariah the father of Amariah,
Amariah the father of Ahitub,
¹²Ahitub the father of Zadok,
Zadok the father of Shallum,
¹³Shallum the father of Hilkiah,
Hilkiah the father of Azariah,
¹⁴Azariah the father of Seraiah,
and Seraiah the father of Jehozadak.
¹⁵Jehozadak was deported when the
Lord sent Judah and Jerusalem
into exile by the hand of
Nebuchadnezzar.

¹⁶The sons of Levi:
Gershon, Kohath and Merari.
¹⁷These are the names of the sons of
Gershon:
Libni and Shimei.
¹⁸The sons of Kohath:
Amram, Izhar, Hebron and
Uzziel.
¹⁹The sons of Merari:
Mahli and Mushi.
These are the clans of the Levites
listed according to their fathers:

²⁰Of Gershon:

Libni his son, Jehath his son,
Zimmah his son, ²¹Joah his son,
Iddo his son, Zerah his son
and Jeatherai his son.

²²The descendants of Kohath:

Amminadab his son, Korah his
son,
Assir his son, ²³Elkanah his son,
Ebiasaph his son, Assir his son,
²⁴Tahath his son, Uriel his son,
Uzziah his son and Shaul his son.

²⁵The descendants of Elkanah:

Amasai, Ahimoth,
²⁶Elkanah his son, Zophai his son,
Nahath his son, ²⁷Eliab his son,
Jeroham his son, Elkanah his
son
and Samuel his son.

²⁸The sons of Samuel:

Joel the firstborn
and Abijah the second son.

²⁹The descendants of Merari:

Mahli, Libni his son,
Shimei his son, Uzzah his son,
³⁰Shimea his son, Haggiah his son
and Asaiah his son.

The Temple Musicians

³¹These are the men David put in
charge of the music in the house of the
LORD after the ark came to rest there.
³²They ministered with music before the
tabernacle, the Tent of Meeting, until
Solomon built the temple of the LORD in
Jerusalem. They performed their duties
according to the regulations laid down
for them.

³³Here are the men who served,
together with their sons:

From the Kohathites:

Heman, the musician,
the son of Joel, the son of
Samuel,
³⁴the son of Elkanah, the son of
Jeroham,
the son of Eliel, the son of Toah,
³⁵the son of Zuph, the son of Elka-
nah,
the son of Mahath, the son of
Amasai,
³⁶the son of Elkanah, the son of
Joel,
the son of Azariah, the son of
Zephaniah,
³⁷the son of Tahath, the son of
Assir,
the son of Ebiasaph, the son of
Korah,
³⁸the son of Izhar, the son of
Kohath,
the son of Levi, the son of Israel;

³⁹and Heman's associate Asaph,
who served at his right hand:
Asaph son of Berekiah, the son
of Shimea,
⁴⁰the son of Michael, the son of
Baaseiah,
the son of Malkijah, ⁴¹the son of
Ethni,
the son of Zerah, the son of
Adaiah,
⁴²the son of Ethan, the son of Zim-
mah,
the son of Shimei, ⁴³the son of
Jahath,
the son of Gershon, the son of
Levi;

⁴⁴and from their associates, the
Merarites, at his left hand:
Ethan son of Kishi, the son of
Abdi,
the son of Malluch, ⁴⁵the son of
Hashabiah,
the son of Amaziah, the son of
Hilkiah,
⁴⁶the son of Amzi, the son of Bani,
the son of Shemer, ⁴⁷the son of
Mahli,
the son of Mushi, the son of
Merari,
the son of Levi.

⁴⁸Their fellow Levites were assigned
to all the other duties of the tabernacle,
the house of God. ⁴⁹But Aaron and his
descendants were the ones who presented offerings on the altar of burnt
offering and on the altar of incense
in connection with all that was done in
the Most Holy Place, making atonement for Israel, in accordance with

769 JULY 29

all that Moses the servant of God had commanded.

⁵⁰These were the descendants of Aaron:

Eleazar his son, Phinehas his son,

Abishua his son, ⁵¹Bukki his son, Uzzi his son, Zerahiah his son,

⁵²Meraioth his son, Amariah his son,

Ahitub his son, ⁵³Zadok his son and Ahimaaz his son.

⁵⁴These were the locations of their settlements allotted as their territory (they were assigned to the descendants of Aaron who were from the Kohathite clan, because the first lot was for them):

⁵⁵They were given Hebron in Judah with its surrounding pasture-lands. ⁵⁶But the fields and villages around the city were given to Caleb son of Jephunneh.

⁵⁷So the descendants of Aaron were given Hebron (a city of refuge), and Libnah, Jattir, Eshtemoa, ⁵⁸Hilen, Debir, ⁵⁹Ashan, Juttah and Beth Shemesh, together with their pasture-lands. ⁶⁰And from the tribe of Benjamin they were given Gibeon, Geba, Alemeth and Anathoth, together with their pasture-lands.

These towns, which were distributed among the Kohathite clans, were thirteen in all.

⁶¹The rest of Kohath's descendants were allotted ten towns from the clans of half the tribe of Manasseh.

⁶²The descendants of Gershon, clan by clan, were allotted thirteen towns from the tribes of Issachar, Asher and Naphtali, and from the part of the tribe of Manasseh that is in Bashan.

⁶³The descendants of Merari, clan by clan, were allotted twelve towns from the tribes of Reuben, Gad and Zebulun.

⁶⁴So the Israelites gave the Levites these towns and their pasture-lands.

⁶⁵From the tribes of Judah, Simeon and Benjamin they allotted the previously named towns.

⁶⁶Some of the Kohathite clans were given as their territory towns from the tribe of Ephraim.

⁶⁷In the hill country of Ephraim they were given Shechem (a city of refuge), and Gezer, ⁶⁸Jokmeam, Beth Horon, ⁶⁹Aijalon and Gath Rimmon, together with their pasture-lands.

⁷⁰And from half the tribe of Manasseh the Israelites gave Aner and Bileam, together with their pasture-lands, to the rest of the Kohathite clans.

⁷¹The Gershonites received the following:

From the clan of the half-tribe of Manasseh

they received Golan in Bashan and also Ashtaroth, together with their pasture-lands:

⁷²from the tribe of Issachar

they received Kedesh, Daberath, ⁷³Ramoth and Anem, together with their pasture-lands;

⁷⁴from the tribe of Asher

they received Mashal, Abdon, ⁷⁵Hukok and Rehob, together with their pasture-lands;

⁷⁶and from the tribe of Naphtali

they received Kedesh in Galilee, Hammon and Kiriathaim, together with their pasture-lands.

⁷⁷The Merarites (the rest of the Levites) received the following:

From the tribe of Zebulun

they received Jokneam, Kartah, Rimmono and Tabor, together with their pasture-lands;

⁷⁸from the tribe of Reuben across the Jordan east of Jericho

they received Bezer in the desert, Jahzah, ⁷⁹Kedemoth and Mephaath, together with their pasture-lands;

⁸⁰and from the tribe of Gad
they received Ramoth in Gilead,
Mahanaim, ⁸¹Heshbon and
Jazer, together with their
pasture-lands.

NEW TESTAMENT READING
Romans 11:33–12:21

Doxology

³³Oh, the depth of the riches of the
wisdom and knowledge of God!
How unsearchable his judgments,
and his paths beyond tracing out!

³⁴"Who has known the mind of the
Lord?
Or who has been his counsellor?"

³⁵"Who has ever given to God,
that God should repay him?"

³⁶For from him and through him and to
him are all things.
To him be the glory for ever!
Amen.

Living Sacrifices

12 Therefore, I urge you, brothers,
in view of God's mercy, to offer
your bodies as living sacrifices, holy and
pleasing to God—this is your spiritual
act of worship. ²Do not conform any
longer to the pattern of this world, but
be transformed by the renewing of your
mind. Then you will be able to test and
approve what God's will is—his good,
pleasing and perfect will.

³For by the grace given me I say to
every one of you: Do not think of yourself more highly than you ought, but
rather think of yourself with sober judgment, in accordance with the measure
of faith God has given you. ⁴Just as each
of us has one body with many members,
and these members do not all have the
same function, ⁵so in Christ we who are
many form one body, and each member
belongs to all the others. ⁶We have
different gifts, according to the grace
given us. If a man's gift is prophesying,
let him use it in proportion to his faith.
⁷If it is serving, let him serve; if it is
teaching, let him teach; ⁸if it is encouraging, let him encourage; if it is

contributing to the needs of others, let
him give generously; if it is leadership,
let him govern diligently; if it is showing
mercy, let him do it cheerfully.

Love

⁹Love must be sincere. Hate what is
evil; cling to what is good. ¹⁰Be devoted
to one another in brotherly love.
Honour one another above yourselves.
¹¹Never be lacking in zeal, but keep
your spiritual fervour, serving the Lord.
¹²Be joyful in hope, patient in affliction,
faithful in prayer. ¹³Share with God's
people who are in need. Practise
hospitality.

¹⁴Bless those who persecute you;
bless and do not curse. ¹⁵Rejoice with
those who rejoice; mourn with those
who mourn. ¹⁶Live in harmony with
one another. Do not be proud, but be
willing to associate with people of low
position. Do not be conceited.

¹⁷Do not repay anyone evil for evil.
Be careful to do what is right in the eyes
of everybody. ¹⁸If it is possible, as far as
it depends on you, live at peace with
everyone. ¹⁹Do not take revenge, my
friends, but leave room for God's
wrath, for it is written: "It is mine to
avenge; I will repay," says the Lord.
²⁰On the contrary:

"If your enemy is hungry, feed him;
if he is thirsty, give him something
to drink.
In doing this, you will heap burning
coals on his head."

²¹Do not be overcome by evil, but overcome evil with good.

READING FROM PSALMS
Psalm 89:30–37

³⁰"If his sons forsake my law
and do not follow my statutes,
³¹if they violate my decrees
and fail to keep my commands,
³²I will punish their sin with the rod,
their iniquity with flogging;

33but I will not take my love from him,
    nor will I ever betray my
    faithfulness.
34I will not violate my covenant
    or alter what my lips have
    uttered.
35Once for all, I have sworn by my
    holiness—

and I will not lie to David—
36that his line will continue for ever
    and his throne endure before me
    like the sun;
37it will be established for ever like the
    moon,
    the faithful witness in the sky.''

Selah

JULY 30   DAY 211

OLD TESTAMENT READING
1 Chronicles 7:1–9:1a

Issachar

7 The sons of Issachar:
    Tola, Puah, Jashub and Shimron
    —four in all.
2The sons of Tola:
    Uzzi, Rephaiah, Jeriel, Jahmai,
    Ibsam and Samuel—heads of
    their families. During the reign
    of David, the descendants of
    Tola listed as fighting men in
    their   genealogy   numbered
    22,600.
3The son of Uzzi:
    Izrahiah.
    The sons of Izrahiah:
    Michael, Obadiah, Joel and
    Isshiah. All five of them were
    chiefs. 4According to their fam-
    ily genealogy, they had 36,000
    men ready for battle, for they
    had many wives and children.
5The relatives who were fighting
    men belonging to all the clans of
    Issachar, as listed in their gen-
    ealogy, were 87,000 in all.

Benjamin

6Three sons of Benjamin:
    Bela, Beker and Jediael.
7The sons of Bela:
    Ezbon, Uzzi, Uzziel, Jerimoth
    and Iri, heads of families—five

in all. Their genealogical record
listed 22,034 fighting men.
8The sons of Beker:
    Zemirah,   Joash,   Eliezer,
    Elioenai, Omri, Jeremoth, Abi-
    jah, Anathoth and Alemeth. All
    these were the sons of Beker.
9Their genealogical record listed
    the heads of families and 20,200
    fighting men.
10The son of Jediael:
    Bilhan.
    The sons of Bilhan:
    Jeush,   Benjamin,   Ehud,
    Kenaanah, Zethan, Tarshish
    and Ahishahar. 11All these sons
    of Jediael were heads of families.
    There were 17,200 fighting men
    ready to go out to war.
12The Shuppites and Huppites were
    the descendants of Ir, and the
    Hushites the descendants of
    Aher.

Naphtali

13The sons of Naphtali:
    Jahziel, Guni, Jezer and Shil-
    lem—the descendants of Bilhah.

Manasseh

14The descendants of Manasseh:
    Asriel   was   his   descendant
    through his Aramean concubine.
    She gave birth to Makir the father
    of Gilead. 15Makir took a wife from

among the Huppites and Shuppites. His sister's name was Maacah.

Another descendant was named Zelophehad, who had only daughters.

¹⁶Makir's wife Maacah gave birth to a son and named him Peresh. His brother was named Sheresh, and his sons were Ulam and Rakem.

¹⁷The son of Ulam:

Bedan.

These were the sons of Gilead son of Makir, the son of Manasseh. ¹⁸His sister Hammoleketh gave birth to Ishhod, Abiezer and Mahlah.

¹⁹The sons of Shemida were:

Ahian, Shechem, Likhi and Aniam.

Ephraim

²⁰The descendants of Ephraim:

Shuthelah, Bered his son,
Tahath his son, Eleadah his son,
Tahath his son, ²¹Zabad his son
and Shuthelah his son.

Ezer and Elead were killed by the native-born men of Gath, when they went down to seize their livestock. ²²Their father Ephraim mourned for them many days, and his relatives came to comfort him. ²³Then he lay with his wife again, and she became pregnant and gave birth to a son. He named him Beriah, because there had been misfortune in his family. ²⁴His daughter was Sheerah, who built Lower and Upper Beth Horon as well as Uzzen Sheerah.

²⁵Rephah was his son, Resheph his son,

Telah his son, Tahan his son,
²⁶Ladan his son, Ammihud his son,

Elishama his son, ²⁷Nun his son and Joshua his son.

²⁸Their lands and settlements included Bethel and its surrounding villages, Naaran to the east, Gezer and its villages to the west, and Shechem and its villages all the way to Ayyah and its villages. ²⁹Along the borders of Manasseh were Beth Shan, Taanach, Megiddo and Dor, together with their villages. The descendants of Joseph son of Israel lived in these towns.

Asher

³⁰The sons of Asher:

Imnah, Ishvah, Ishvi and Beriah. Their sister was Serah.

³¹The sons of Beriah:

Heber and Malkiel, who was the father of Birzaith.

³²Heber was the father of Japhlet, Shomer and Hotham and of their sister Shua.

³³The sons of Japhlet:

Pasach, Bimhal and Ashvath. These were Japhlet's sons.

³⁴The sons of Shomer:

Ahi, Rohgah, Hubbah and Aram.

³⁵The sons of his brother Helem:

Zophah, Imna, Shelesh and Amal.

³⁶The sons of Zophah:

Suah, Harnepher, Shual, Beri, Imrah, ³⁷Bezer, Hod, Shamma, Shilshah, Ithran and Beera.

³⁸The sons of Jether:

Jephunneh, Pispah and Ara.

³⁹The sons of Ulla:

Arah, Hanniel and Rizia.

⁴⁰All these were descendants of Asher—heads of families, choice men, brave warriors and outstanding leaders. The number of men ready for battle, as listed in their genealogy, was 26,000.

The Genealogy of Saul the Benjamite

8 Benjamin was the father of Bela his firstborn,

Ashbel the second son, Aharah the third,

²Nohah the fourth and Rapha the fifth.

³The sons of Bela were:

Addar,   Gera,   Abihud,

[4] Abishua, Naaman, Ahoah, [5] Gera, Shephuphan and Huram.

[6] These were the descendants of Ehud, who were heads of families of those living in Geba and were deported to Manahath: [7] Naaman, Ahijah and Gera, who deported them and who was the father of Uzza and Ahihud.

[8] Sons were born to Shaharaim in Moab after he had divorced his wives Hushim and Baara. [9] By his wife Hodesh he had Jobab, Zibia, Mesha, Malcam, [10] Jeuz, Sakia and Mirmah. These were his sons, heads of families. [11] By Hushim he had Abitub and Elpaal.

[12] The sons of Elpaal:

Eber, Misham, Shemed (who built Ono and Lod with its surrounding villages), [13] and Beriah and Shema, who were heads of families of those living in Aijalon and who drove out the inhabitants of Gath.

[14] Ahio, Shashak, Jeremoth, [15] Zebadiah, Arad, Eder, [16] Michael, Ishpah and Joha were the sons of Beriah.

[17] Zebadiah, Meshullam, Hizki, Heber, [18] Ishmerai, Izliah and Jobab were the sons of Elpaal.

[19] Jakim, Zicri, Zabdi, [20] Elienai, Zillethai, Eliel, [21] Adaiah, Beraiah and Shimrath were the sons of Shimei.

[22] Ishpan, Eber, Eliel, [23] Abdon, Zicri, Hanan, [24] Hananiah, Elam, Anthothijah, [25] Iphdeiah and Penuel were the sons of Shashak.

[26] Shamsherai, Shehariah, Athaliah, [27] Jaareshiah, Elijah and Zicri were the sons of Jeroham.

[28] All these were heads of families, chiefs as listed in their genealogy, and they lived in Jerusalem.

[29] Jeiel the father of Gibeon lived in Gibeon.

His wife's name was Maacah, [30] and his firstborn son was Abdon, followed by Zur, Kish, Baal, Ner, Nadab, [31] Gedor, Ahio, Zeker [32] and Mikloth, who was the father of Shimeah. They too lived near their relatives in Jerusalem.

[33] Ner was the father of Kish, Kish the father of Saul, and Saul the father of Jonathan, Malki-Shua, Abinadab and Esh-Baal.

[34] The son of Jonathan:

Merib-Baal, who was the father of Micah.

[35] The sons of Micah:

Pithon, Melech, Tarea and Ahaz.

[36] Ahaz was the father of Jehoaddah, Jehoaddah was the father of Alemeth, Azmaveth and Zimri, and Zimri was the father of Moza. [37] Moza was the father of Binea; Raphah was his son, Eleasah his son and Azel his son.

[38] Azel had six sons, and these were their names:

Azrikam, Bokeru, Ishmael, Sheariah, Obadiah and Hanan. All these were the sons of Azel.

[39] The sons of his brother Eshek:

Ulam his firstborn, Jeush the second son and Eliphelet the third. [40] The sons of Ulam were brave warriors who could handle the bow. They had many sons and grandsons—150 in all.

All these were descendants of Benjamin.

9 All Israel was listed in the genealogies in the book of the kings of Israel.

NEW TESTAMENT READING
Romans 13:1–14

Submission to the Authorities

13 Everyone must submit himself to the governing authorities, for there is no authority except that which

God has established. The authorities that exist have been established by God. 2Consequently, he who rebels against the authority is rebelling against what God has instituted, and those who do so will bring judgment on themselves. 3For rulers hold no terror for those who do right, but for those who do wrong. Do you want to be free from fear of the one in authority? Then do what is right and he will commend you. 4For he is God's servant to do you good. But if you do wrong, be afraid, for he does not bear the sword for nothing. He is God's servant, an agent of wrath to bring punishment on the wrongdoer. 5Therefore, it is necessary to submit to the authorities, not only because of possible punishment but also because of conscience.

6This is also why you pay taxes, for the authorities are God's servants, who give their full time to governing. 7Give everyone what you owe him: If you owe taxes, pay taxes; if revenue, then revenue; if respect, then respect; if honour, then honour.

Love, for the Day Is Near

8Let no debt remain outstanding, except the continuing debt to love one another, for he who loves his fellow-man has fulfilled the law. 9The commandments, "Do not commit adultery," "Do not murder," "Do not steal," "Do not covet," and whatever other commandment there may be, are summed up in this one rule: "Love your neighbour as yourself." 10Love does no harm to its neighbour. Therefore love is the fulfilment of the law.

11And do this, understanding the present time. The hour has come for you to wake up from your slumber, because our salvation is nearer now than when we first believed. 12The night is nearly over; the day is almost here. So let us put aside the deeds of darkness and put on the armour of light. 13Let us behave decently, as in the daytime, not in orgies and drunkenness, not in sexual immorality and debauchery, not in dissension and jealousy. 14Rather, clothe yourselves with the Lord Jesus Christ, and do not think about how to gratify the desires of the sinful nature.

READING FROM PSALMS
Psalm 89:38–45

38But you have rejected, you have spurned,
   you have been very angry with
      your anointed one.
39You have renounced the covenant
      with your servant
   and have defiled his crown in the
      dust.
40You have broken through all his walls
   and reduced his strongholds to
      ruins.
41All who pass by have plundered him;
   he has become the scorn of his
      neighbours.
42You have exalted the right hand of
      his foes;
   you have made all his enemies
      rejoice.
43You have turned back the edge of his
      sword
   and have not supported him in
      battle.
44You have put an end to his splendour
   and cast his throne to the ground.
45You have cut short the days of his
      youth;
   you have covered him with a
      mantle of shame.   *Selah*

OLD TESTAMENT READING
1 Chronicles 9:1b–10:14

The People in Jerusalem

The people of Judah were taken captive to Babylon because of their unfaithfulness. ²Now the first to resettle on their own property in their own towns were some Israelites, priests, Levites and temple servants.

³Those from Judah, from Benjamin, and from Ephraim and Manasseh who lived in Jerusalem were:

⁴Uthai son of Ammihud, the son of Omri, the son of Imri, the son of Bani, a descendant of Perez son of Judah.

⁵Of the Shilonites:
Asaiah the firstborn and his sons.

⁶Of the Zerahites:
Jeuel.
The people from Judah numbered 690.

⁷Of the Benjamites:
Sallu son of Meshullam, the son of Hodaviah, the son of Hassenuah;

⁸Ibneiah son of Jeroham; Elah son of Uzzi, the son of Micri; and Meshullam son of Shephatiah, the son of Reuel, the son of Ibnijah.

⁹The people from Benjamin, as listed in their genealogy, numbered 956. All these men were heads of their families.

¹⁰Of the priests:
Jedaiah; Jehoiarib; Jakin;

¹¹Azariah son of Hilkiah, the son of Meshullam, the son of Zadok, the son of Meraioth, the son of Ahitub, the official in charge of the house of God;

¹²Adaiah son of Jeroham, the son of Pashhur, the son of Malkijah; and Maasai son of Adiel, the son of Jahzerah, the son of Meshullam, the son of Meshillemith, the son of Immer.

¹³The priests, who were heads of families, numbered 1,760. They were able men, responsible for ministering in the house of God.

¹⁴Of the Levites:
Shemaiah son of Hasshub, the son of Azrikam, the son of Hashabiah, a Merarite; ¹⁵Bakbakkar, Heresh, Galal and Mattaniah son of Mica, the son of Zicri, the son of Asaph; ¹⁶Obadiah son of Shemaiah, the son of Galal, the son of Jeduthun; and Berekiah son of Asa, the son of Elkanah, who lived in the villages of the Netophathites.

¹⁷The gatekeepers:
Shallum, Akkub, Talmon, Ahiman and their brothers, Shallum their chief ¹⁸being stationed at the King's Gate on the east, up to the present time. These were the gatekeepers belonging to the camp of the Levites. ¹⁹Shallum son of Kore, the son of Ebiasaph, the son of Korah, and his fellow gatekeepers from his family (the Korahites) were responsible for guarding the thresholds of the Tent just as their fathers had been responsible for guarding the entrance to the dwelling of the LORD. ²⁰In earlier times Phinehas son of Eleazar was in charge of the gatekeepers, and the LORD was with him. ²¹Zechariah son of Meshelemiah was the gatekeeper at the entrance to the Tent of Meeting. ²²Altogether, those chosen to be gatekeepers at the thresholds numbered 212. They were registered by genealogy in their villages. The

gatekeepers had been assigned to their positions of trust by David and Samuel the seer. [23]They and their descendants were in charge of guarding the gates of the house of the LORD—the house called the Tent. [24]The gatekeepers were on the four sides: east, west, north and south. [25]Their brothers in their villages had to come from time to time and share their duties for seven-day periods. [26]But the four principal gatekeepers, who were Levites, were entrusted with the responsibility for the rooms and treasuries in the house of God. [27]They would spend the night stationed round the house of God, because they had to guard it; and they had charge of the key for opening it each morning.

[28]Some of them were in charge of the articles used in the temple service; they counted them when they were brought in and when they were taken out. [29]Others were assigned to take care of the furnishings and all the other articles of the sanctuary, as well as the flour and wine, and the oil, incense and spices. [30]But some of the priests took care of mixing the spices. [31]A Levite named Mattithiah, the firstborn son of Shallum the Korahite, was entrusted with the responsibility for baking the offering bread. [32]Some of their Kohathite brothers were in charge of preparing for every Sabbath the bread set out on the table.

[33]Those who were musicians, heads of Levite families, stayed in the rooms of the temple and were exempt from other duties because they were responsible for the work day and night.

[34]All these were heads of Levite families, chiefs as listed in their genealogy, and they lived in Jerusalem.

The Genealogy of Saul

[35]Jeiel the father of Gibeon lived in Gibeon.

His wife's name was Maacah, [36]and his firstborn son was Abdon, followed by Zur, Kish, Baal, Ner, Nadab, [37]Gedor, Ahio, Zechariah and Mikloth. [38]Mikloth was the father of Shimeam. They too lived near their relatives in Jerusalem.

[39]Ner was the father of Kish, Kish the father of Saul, and Saul the father of Jonathan, Malki-Shua, Abinadab and Esh-Baal.

[40]The son of Jonathan:

Merib-Baal, who was the father of Micah.

[41]The sons of Micah:

Pithon, Melech, Tahrea and Ahaz.

[42]Ahaz was the father of Jadah, Jadah was the father of Alemeth, Azmaveth and Zimri, and Zimri was the father of Moza. [43]Moza was the father of Binea; Rephaiah was his son, Eleasah his son and Azel his son.

[44]Azel had six sons, and these were their names:

Azrikam, Bokeru, Ishmael, Sheariah, Obadiah and Hanan. These were the sons of Azel.

Saul Takes His Life

10 Now the Philistines fought against Israel; the Israelites fled before them, and many fell slain on Mount Gilboa. [2]The Philistines pressed hard after Saul and his sons, and they killed his sons Jonathan, Abinadab and Malki-Shua. [3]The fighting grew fierce around Saul, and when the archers overtook him, they wounded him.

[4]Saul said to his armour-bearer, "Draw your sword and run me through, or these uncircumcised fellows will come and abuse me."

But his armour-bearer was terrified and would not do it; so Saul took his own sword and fell on it. [5]When the armour-bearer saw that Saul was dead, he too fell on his sword and died. [6]So Saul and his three sons died, and all his house died together.

[7]When all the Israelites in the valley saw that the army had fled and that Saul and his sons had died, they abandoned

their towns and fled. And the Philistines came and occupied them.

[8]The next day, when the Philistines came to strip the dead, they found Saul and his sons fallen on Mount Gilboa. [9]They stripped him and took his head and his armour, and sent messengers throughout the land of the Philistines to proclaim the news among their idols and their people. [10]They put his armour in the temple of their gods and hung up his head in the temple of Dagon.

[11]When all the inhabitants of Jabesh Gilead heard of everything the Philistines had done to Saul, [12]all their valiant men went and took the bodies of Saul and his sons and brought them to Jabesh. Then they buried their bones under the great tree in Jabesh, and they fasted seven days.

[13]Saul died because he was unfaithful to the LORD; he did not keep the word of the LORD, and even consulted a medium for guidance, [14]and did not enquire of the LORD. So the LORD put him to death and turned the kingdom over to David son of Jesse.

[5]One man considers one day more sacred than another; another man considers every day alike. Each one should be fully convinced in his own mind. [6]He who regards one day as special, does so to the Lord. He who eats meat, eats to the Lord, for he gives thanks to God; and he who abstains, does so to the Lord and gives thanks to God. [7]For none of us lives to himself alone and none of us dies to himself alone. [8]If we live, we live to the Lord; and if we die, we die to the Lord. So, whether we live or die, we belong to the Lord.

[9]For this very reason, Christ died and returned to life so that he might be the Lord of both the dead and the living. [10]You, then, why do you judge your brother? Or why do you look down on your brother? For we will all stand before God's judgment seat. [11]It is written:

> "'As surely as I live,' says the Lord,
> 'Every knee will bow before me;
> every tongue will confess to
> God.'"

[12]So then, each of us will give an account of himself to God.

[13]Therefore let us stop passing judgment on one another. Instead, make up your mind not to put any stumbling-block or obstacle in your brother's way. [14]As one who is in the Lord Jesus, I am fully convinced that no food is unclean in itself. But if anyone regards something as unclean, then for him it is unclean. [15]If your brother is distressed because of what you eat, you are no longer acting in love. Do not by your eating destroy your brother for whom Christ died. [16]Do not allow what you consider good to be spoken of as evil. [17]For the kingdom of God is not a matter of eating and drinking, but of righteousness, peace and joy in the Holy Spirit, [18]because anyone who serves Christ in this way is pleasing to God and approved by men.

NEW TESTAMENT READING
Romans 14:1–18

The Weak and the Strong

14 Accept him whose faith is weak, without passing judgment on disputable matters. [2]One man's faith allows him to eat everything, but another man, whose faith is weak, eats only vegetables. [3]The man who eats everything must not look down on him who does not, and the man who does not eat everything must not condemn the man who does, for God has accepted him. [4]Who are you to judge someone else's servant? To his own master he stands or falls. And he will stand, for the Lord is able to make him stand.

READING FROM PROVERBS
Proverbs 18:17–19:2

17The first to present his case seems
right,
  till another comes forward and
  questions him.

18Casting the lot settles disputes
  and keeps strong opponents apart.

19An offended brother is more
  unyielding than a fortified city,
  and disputes are like the barred
  gates of a citadel.

20From the fruit of his mouth a man's
  stomach is filled;
  with the harvest from his lips he is
  satisfied.

21The tongue has the power of life and
death,

and those who love it will eat its
fruit.

22He who finds a wife finds what is
good
  and receives favour from the
  LORD.

23A poor man pleads for mercy,
  but a rich man answers harshly.

24A man of many companions may
  come to ruin,
  but there is a friend who sticks
  closer than a brother.

19 Better a poor man whose walk
is blameless
  than a fool whose lips are perverse.

2It is not good to have zeal without
knowledge,
  nor to be hasty and miss the way.

DAY 213

AUGUST 1

OLD TESTAMENT READING
1 Chronicles 11:1–12:22

David Becomes King Over Israel

11 All Israel came together to
David at Hebron and said, "We
are your own flesh and blood. 2In the
past, even while Saul was king, you
were the one who led Israel on their
military campaigns. And the LORD your
God said to you, 'You will shepherd my
people Israel, and you will become their
ruler.'"

3When all the elders of Israel had
come to King David at Hebron, he
made a compact with them at Hebron
before the LORD, and they anointed
David king over Israel, as the LORD had
promised through Samuel.

David Conquers Jerusalem

4David and all the Israelites marched
to Jerusalem (that is, Jebus). The Jebusites who lived there 5said to David,
"You will not get in here." Nevertheless, David captured the fortress of
Zion, the City of David.

6David had said, "Whoever leads the
attack on the Jebusites will become
commander-in-chief." Joab son of
Zeruiah went up first, and so he received the command.

7David then took up residence in the
fortress, and so it was called the City of
David. 8He built up the city around it,
from the supporting terraces to the surrounding wall, while Joab restored the
rest of the city. 9And David became
more and more powerful, because the
LORD Almighty was with him.

David's Mighty Men

[10]These were the chiefs of David's mighty men—they, together with all Israel, gave his kingship strong support to extend it over the whole land, as the LORD had promised—[11]this is the list of David's mighty men:

Jashobeam, a Hacmonite, was chief of the officers; he raised his spear against three hundred men, whom he killed in one encounter.

[12]Next to him was Eleazar son of Dodai the Ahohite, one of the three mighty men. [13]He was with David at Pas Dammim when the Philistines gathered there for battle. At a place where there was a field full of barley, the troops fled from the Philistines. [14]But they took their stand in the middle of the field. They defended it and struck the Philistines down, and the LORD brought about a great victory.

[15]Three of the thirty chiefs came down to David to the rock at the cave of Adullam, while a band of Philistines was encamped in the Valley of Rephaim. [16]At that time David was in the stronghold, and the Philistine garrison was at Bethlehem. [17]David longed for water and said, "Oh, that someone would get me a drink of water from the well near the gate of Bethlehem!" [18]So the Three broke through the Philistine lines, drew water from the well near the gate of Bethlehem and carried it back to David. But he refused to drink it; instead, he poured it out before the LORD. [19]"God forbid that I should do this!" he said. "Should I drink the blood of these men who went at the risk of their lives?" Because they risked their lives to bring it back, David would not drink it.

Such were the exploits of the three mighty men.

[20]Abishai the brother of Joab was chief of the Three. He raised his spear against three hundred men, whom he killed, and so he became as famous as the Three. [21]He was doubly honoured above the Three and became their commander, even though he was not included among them.

[22]Benaiah son of Jehoiada was a valiant fighter from Kabzeel, who performed great exploits. He struck down two of Moab's best men. He also went down into a pit on a snowy day and killed a lion. [23]And he struck down an Egyptian who was seven and a half feet tall. Although the Egyptian had a spear like a weaver's rod in his hand, Benaiah went against him with a club. He snatched the spear from the Egyptian's hand and killed him with his own spear. [24]Such were the exploits of Benaiah son of Jehoiada; he too was as famous as the three mighty men. [25]He was held in greater honour than any of the Thirty, but he was not included among the Three. And David put him in charge of his bodyguard.

[26]The mighty men were:
Asahel the brother of Joab,
Elhanan son of Dodo from Bethlehem,
[27]Shammoth the Harorite,
Helez the Pelonite,
[28]Ira son of Ikkesh from Tekoa,
Abiezer from Anathoth,
[29]Sibbecai the Hushathite,
Ilai the Ahohite,
[30]Maharai the Netophathite,
Heled son of Baanah the Netophathite,
[31]Ithai son of Ribai from Gibeah in Benjamin,
Benaiah the Pirathonite,
[32]Hurai from the ravines of Gaash,
Abiel the Arbathite,
[33]Azmaveth the Baharumite,
Eliahba the Shaalbonite,
[34]the sons of Hashem the Gizonite,
Jonathan son of Shagee the Hararite,
[35]Ahiam son of Sacar the Hararite,
Eliphal son of Ur,
[36]Hepher the Mekerathite,
Ahijah the Pelonite,

37Hezro the Carmelite,
Naarai son of Ezbai,

38Joel the brother of Nathan,
Mibhar son of Hagri,

39Zelek the Ammonite,
Naharai the Berothite, the
armour-bearer of Joab son of
Zeruiah,

40Ira the Ithrite,
Gareb the Ithrite,

41Uriah the Hittite,
Zabad son of Ahlai,

42Adina son of Shiza the Reubenite, who was chief of the Reubenites, and the thirty with him,

43Hanan son of Maacah,
Joshaphat the Mithnite,

44Uzzia the Ashterathite,
Shama and Jeiel the sons of
Hotham the Aroerite,

45Jediael son of Shimri,
his brother Joha the Tizite,

46Eliel the Mahavite,
Jeribai and Joshaviah the sons of
Elnaam,
Ithmah the Moabite,

47Eliel, Obed and Jaasiel the
Mezobaite.

Warriors Join David

12 These were the men who came to David at Ziklag, while he was banished from the presence of Saul son of Kish (they were among the warriors who helped him in battle; 2they were armed with bows and were able to shoot arrows or to sling stones right-handed or left-handed; they were kinsmen of Saul from the tribe of Benjamin):

3Ahiezer their chief and Joash the sons of Shemaah the Gibeathite; Jeziel and Pelet the sons of Azmaveth; Beracah, Jehu the Anathothite, 4and Ishmaiah the Gibeonite, a mighty man among the Thirty, who was a leader of the Thirty; Jeremiah, Jahaziel, Johanan, Jozabad the Gederathite, 5Eluzai, Jerimoth, Bealiah, Shemariah and Shephatiah the

Haruphite; 6Elkanah, Isshiah, Azarel, Joezer and Jashobeam the Korahites; 7and Joelah and Zebadiah the sons of Jeroham from Gedor.

8Some Gadites defected to David at his stronghold in the desert. They were brave warriors, ready for battle and able to handle the shield and spear. Their faces were the faces of lions, and they were as swift as gazelles in the mountains.

9Ezer was the chief,
Obadiah the second in command,
Eliab the third,

10Mishmannah the fourth, Jeremiah
the fifth,

11Attai the sixth, Eliel the seventh,

12Johanan the eighth, Elzabad the
ninth,

13Jeremiah the tenth and Macbannai
the eleventh.

14These Gadites were army commanders; the least was a match for a hundred, and the greatest for a thousand. 15It was they who crossed the Jordan in the first month when it was overflowing all its banks, and they put to flight everyone living in the valleys, to the east and to the west.

16Other Benjamites and some men from Judah also came to David in his stronghold. 17David went out to meet them and said to them, "If you have come to me in peace, to help me, I am ready to have you unite with me. But if you have come to betray me to my enemies when my hands are free from violence, may the God of our fathers see it and judge you."

18Then the Spirit came upon Amasai, chief of the Thirty, and he said:

"We are yours, O David!
We are with you, O son of Jesse!
Success, success to you,
and success to those who help you,
for your God will help you."

So David received them and made them leaders of his raiding bands.

¹⁹Some of the men of Manasseh defected to David when he went with the Philistines to fight against Saul. (He and his men did not help the Philistines because, after consultation, their rulers sent him away. They said, "It will cost us our heads if he deserts to his master Saul.") ²⁰When David went to Ziklag, these were the men of Manasseh who defected to him: Adnah, Jozabad, Jediael, Michael, Jozabad, Elihu and Zillethai, leaders of units of a thousand in Manasseh. ²¹They helped David against raiding bands, for all of them were brave warriors, and they were commanders in his army. ²²Day after day men came to help David, until he had a great army, like the army of God.

NEW TESTAMENT READING
Romans 14:19–15:13

¹⁹Let us therefore make every effort to do what leads to peace and to mutual edification. ²⁰Do not destroy the work of God for the sake of food. All food is clean, but it is wrong for a man to eat anything that causes someone else to stumble. ²¹It is better not to eat meat or drink wine or to do anything else that will cause your brother to fall.

²²So whatever you believe about these things keep between yourself and God. Blessed is the man who does not condemn himself by what he approves. ²³But the man who has doubts is condemned if he eats, because his eating is not from faith; and everything that does not come from faith is sin.

15 We who are strong ought to bear with the failings of the weak and not to please ourselves. ²Each of us should please his neighbour for his good, to build him up. ³For even Christ did not please himself but, as it is written: "The insults of those who insult you have fallen on me." ⁴For everything that was written in the past was written to teach us, so that through endurance and the encouragement of the Scriptures we might have hope.

⁵May the God who gives endurance and encouragement give you a spirit of unity among yourselves as you follow Christ Jesus, ⁶so that with one heart and mouth you may glorify the God and Father of our Lord Jesus Christ.

⁷Accept one another, then, just as Christ accepted you, in order to bring praise to God. ⁸For I tell you that Christ has become a servant of the Jews on behalf of God's truth, to confirm the promises made to the patriarchs ⁹so that the Gentiles may glorify God for his mercy, as it is written:

"Therefore I will praise you among
    the Gentiles;
  I will sing hymns to your name."

¹⁰Again, it says,

"Rejoice, O Gentiles, with his
    people."

¹¹And again,

"Praise the Lord, all you Gentiles,
    and sing praises to him, all you
    peoples."

¹²And again, Isaiah says,

"The Root of Jesse will spring up,
    one who will arise to rule over the
      nations;
  the Gentiles will hope in him."

¹³May the God of hope fill you with all joy and peace as you trust in him, so that you may overflow with hope by the power of the Holy Spirit.

READING FROM PSALMS
Psalm 89:46–52

⁴⁶How long, O LORD? Will you hide
    yourself for ever?
  How long will your wrath burn like
    fire?
⁴⁷Remember how fleeting is my life.

For what futility you have created
all men!
48What man can live and not see death,
or save himself from the power of
the grave?   *Selah*
49O Lord, where is your former great
love,
which in your faithfulness you
swore to David?
50Remember, Lord, how your servant
has been mocked,

how I bear in my heart the taunts
of all the nations,
51the taunts with which your enemies
have mocked, O LORD,
with which they have mocked
every step of your anointed
one.

52Praise be to the LORD for ever!
Amen and Amen.

AUGUST 2

OLD TESTAMENT READING
1 Chronicles 12:23–14:17

Others Join David at Hebron

23These are the numbers of the men
armed for battle who came to David at
Hebron to turn Saul's kingdom over to
him, as the LORD had said:
24men of Judah, carrying shield and
spear—6,800 armed for battle;
25men of Simeon, warriors ready for
battle—7,100;
26men of Levi—4,600, 27including
Jehoiada, leader of the family of
Aaron with 3,700 men, 28and
Zadok, a brave young warrior,
with 22 officers from his family;
29men of Benjamin, Saul's kinsmen
—3,000, most of whom had
remained loyal to Saul's house
until then;
30men of Ephraim, brave warriors,
famous in their own clans—
20,800;
31men of half the tribe of Manasseh,
designated by name to come and
make David king—18,000;
32men of Issachar, who understood
the times and knew what Israel
should do—200 chiefs, with
all their relatives under their
command;

33men of Zebulun, experienced
soldiers prepared for battle with
every type of weapon, to help
David with undivided loyalty—
50,000;
34men of Naphtali—1,000 officers,
together with 37,000 men carrying shields and spears;
35men of Dan, ready for battle—
28,600;
36men of Asher, experienced soldiers prepared for battle—
40,000;
37and from east of the Jordan, men
of Reuben, Gad, and the half-
tribe of Manasseh, armed with
every type of weapon—120,000.

38All these were fighting men who
volunteered to serve in the ranks. They
came to Hebron fully determined to
make David king over all Israel. All the
rest of the Israelites were also of one
mind to make David king. 39The men
spent three days there with David, eating and drinking, for their families had
supplied provisions for them. 40Also,
their neighbours from as far away as
Issachar, Zebulun and Naphtali came
bringing food on donkeys, camels,
mules and oxen. There were plentiful
supplies of flour, fig cakes, raisin cakes,
wine, oil, cattle and sheep, for there was
joy in Israel.

Bringing Back the Ark

13 David conferred with each of his officers, the commanders of thousands and commanders of hundreds. [2]He then said to the whole assembly of Israel, "If it seems good to you and if it is the will of the LORD our God, let us send word far and wide to the rest of our brothers throughout the territories of Israel, and also to the priests and Levites who are with them in their towns and pasture-lands, to come and join us. [3]Let us bring the ark of our God back to us, for we did not enquire of it during the reign of Saul." [4]The whole assembly agreed to do this, because it seemed right to all the people.

[5]So David assembled all the Israelites, from the Shihor River in Egypt to Lebo Hamath, to bring the ark of God from Kiriath Jearim. [6]David and all the Israelites with him went to Baalah of Judah (Kiriath Jearim) to bring up from there the ark of God the LORD, who is enthroned between the cherubim—the ark that is called by the Name.

[7]They moved the ark of God from Abinadab's house on a new cart, with Uzzah and Ahio guiding it. [8]David and all the Israelites were celebrating with all their might before God, with songs and with harps, lyres, tambourines, cymbals and trumpets.

[9]When they came to the threshing-floor of Kidon, Uzzah reached out his hand to steady the ark, because the oxen stumbled. [10]The LORD's anger burned against Uzzah, and he struck him down because he had put his hand on the ark. So he died there before God.

[11]Then David was angry because the LORD's wrath had broken out against Uzzah, and to this day that place is called Perez Uzzah.

[12]David was afraid of God that day and asked, "How can I ever bring the ark of God to me?" [13]He did not take the ark to be with him in the City of David. Instead, he took it aside to the house of Obed-Edom the Gittite. [14]The ark of God remained with the family of Obed-Edom in his house for three months, and the LORD blessed his household and everything he had.

David's House and Family

14 Now Hiram king of Tyre sent messengers to David, along with cedar logs, stonemasons and carpenters to build a palace for him. [2]And David knew that the LORD had established him as king over Israel and that his kingdom had been highly exalted for the sake of his people Israel.

[3]In Jerusalem David took more wives and became the father of more sons and daughters. [4]These are the names of the children born to him there: Shammua, Shobab, Nathan, Solomon, [5]Ibhar, Elishua, Elpelet, [6]Nogah, Nepheg, Japhia, [7]Elishama, Beeliada and Eliphelet.

David Defeats the Philistines

[8]When the Philistines heard that David had been anointed king over all Israel, they went up in full force to search for him, but David heard about it and went out to meet them. [9]Now the Philistines had come and raided the Valley of Rephaim; [10]so David enquired of God: "Shall I go and attack the Philistines? Will you hand them over to me?"

The LORD answered him, "Go, I will hand them over to you."

[11]So David and his men went up to Baal Perazim, and there he defeated them. He said, "As waters break out, God has broken out against my enemies by my hand." So that place was called Baal Perazim. [12]The Philistines had abandoned their gods there, and David gave orders to burn them in the fire.

[13]Once more the Philistines raided the valley; [14]so David enquired of God again, and God answered him, "Do not go straight up, but circle round them and attack them in front of the balsam

trees. 15As soon as you hear the sound of marching in the tops of the balsam trees, move out to battle, because that will mean God has gone out in front of you to strike the Philistine army." 16So David did as God commanded him, and they struck down the Philistine army, all the way from Gibeon to Gezer.

17So David's fame spread throughout every land, and the LORD made all the nations fear him.

NEW TESTAMENT READING
Romans 15:14–33

Paul the Minister to the Gentiles

14I myself am convinced, my brothers, that you yourselves are full of goodness, complete in knowledge and competent to instruct one another. 15I have written to you quite boldly on some points, as if to remind you of them again, because of the grace God gave me 16to be a minister of Christ Jesus to the Gentiles with the priestly duty of proclaiming the gospel of God, so that the Gentiles might become an offering acceptable to God, sanctified by the Holy Spirit.

17Therefore I glory in Christ Jesus in my service to God. 18I will not venture to speak of anything except what Christ has accomplished through me in leading the Gentiles to obey God by what I have said and done—19by the power of signs and miracles, through the power of the Spirit. So from Jerusalem all the way around to Illyricum, I have fully proclaimed the gospel of Christ. 20It has always been my ambition to preach the gospel where Christ was not known, so that I would not be building on someone else's foundation. 21Rather, as it is written:

"Those who were not told about him
    will see,
and those who have not heard will
    understand."

22This is why I have often been hindered from coming to you.

Paul's Plan to Visit Rome

23But now that there is no more place for me to work in these regions, and since I have been longing for many years to see you, 24I plan to do so when I go to Spain. I hope to visit you while passing through and to have you assist me on my journey there, after I have enjoyed your company for a while. 25Now, however, I am on my way to Jerusalem in the service of the saints there. 26For Macedonia and Achaia were pleased to make a contribution for the poor among the saints in Jerusalem. 27They were pleased to do it, and indeed they owe it to them. For if the Gentiles have shared in the Jews' spiritual blessings, they owe it to the Jews to share with them their material blessings. 28So after I have completed this task and have made sure that they have received this fruit, I will go to Spain and visit you on the way. 29I know that when I come to you, I will come in the full measure of the blessing of Christ.

30I urge you, brothers, by our Lord Jesus Christ and by the love of the Spirit, to join me in my struggle by praying to God for me. 31Pray that I may be rescued from the unbelievers in Judea and that my service to Jerusalem may be acceptable to the saints there, 32so that by God's will I may come to you with joy and together with you be refreshed. 33The God of peace be with you all. Amen.

READING FROM PSALMS
Psalm 90:1–10

A prayer of Moses the man of God.

1Lord, you have been our
    dwelling-place
throughout all generations.

²Before the mountains were born
  or you brought forth the earth and
    the world,
  from everlasting to everlasting you
    are God.

³You turn men back to dust,
  saying, "Return to dust, O sons of
    men."
⁴For a thousand years in your sight
  are like a day that has just gone
    by,
  or like a watch in the night.
⁵You sweep men away in the sleep of
    death;
  they are like the new grass of the
    morning—
⁶though in the morning it springs up
    new,

by evening it is dry and
    withered.

⁷We are consumed by your anger
  and terrified by your indignation.
⁸You have set our iniquities before
    you,
  our secret sins in the light of your
    presence.
⁹All our days pass away under your
    wrath;
  we finish our years with a moan.
¹⁰The length of our days is seventy
    years—
  or eighty, if we have the strength;
yet their span is but trouble and
    sorrow,
  for they quickly pass, and we fly
    away.

AUGUST 3   DAY 215

OLD TESTAMENT READING
1 Chronicles 15:1–16:36

The Ark Brought to Jerusalem

15 After David had constructed
buildings for himself in the City
of David, he prepared a place for the
ark of God and pitched a tent for it.
²Then David said, "No-one but the Levites may carry the ark of God, because
the LORD chose them to carry the ark of
the LORD and to minister before him for
ever."

³David assembled all Israel in Jerusalem to bring up the ark of the LORD to
the place he had prepared for it. ⁴He
called together the descendants of
Aaron and the Levites:

⁵From the descendants of Kohath,
  Uriel the leader and 120 rela-
    tives;
⁶from the descendants of Merari,
  Asaiah the leader and 220 rela-
    tives;

⁷from the descendants of Gershon,
  Joel the leader and 130 relatives;
⁸from the descendants of Eli-
    zaphan,
  Shemaiah the leader and 200
    relatives;
⁹from the descendants of Hebron,
  Eliel the leader and 80 relatives;
¹⁰from the descendants of Uzziel,
  Amminadab the leader and 112
    relatives.

¹¹Then David summoned Zadok and
Abiathar the priests, and Uriel, Asaiah,
Joel, Shemaiah, Eliel and Amminadab
the Levites. ¹²He said to them, "You
are the heads of the Levitical families;
you and your fellow Levites are to consecrate yourselves and bring up the ark
of the LORD, the God of Israel, to the
place I have prepared for it. ¹³It was
because you, the Levites, did not bring
it up the first time that the LORD our
God broke out in anger against us. We
did not enquire of him about how to do
it in the prescribed way." ¹⁴So the

priests and Levites consecrated themselves in order to bring up the ark of the LORD, the God of Israel. 15And the Levites carried the ark of God with the poles on their shoulders, as Moses had commanded in accordance with the word of the LORD.

16David told the leaders of the Levites to appoint their brothers as singers to sing joyful songs, accompanied by musical instruments: lyres, harps and cymbals.

17So the Levites appointed Heman son of Joel; from his brothers, Asaph son of Berekiah; and from their brothers the Merarites, Ethan son of Kushaiah; 18and with them their brothers next in rank: Zechariah, Jaaziel, Shemiramoth, Jehiel, Unni, Eliab, Benaiah, Maaseiah, Mattithiah, Eliphelehu, Mikneiah, Obed-Edom and Jeiel, the gatekeepers.

19The musicians Heman, Asaph and Ethan were to sound the bronze cymbals; 20Zechariah, Aziel, Shemiramoth, Jehiel, Unni, Eliab, Maaseiah and Benaiah were to play the lyres according to *alamoth*, 21and Mattithiah, Eliphelehu, Mikneiah, Obed-Edom, Jeiel and Azaziah were to play the harps, directing according to *sheminith*. 22Kenaniah the head Levite was in charge of the singing; that was his responsibility because he was skilful at it.

23Berekiah and Elkanah were to be doorkeepers for the ark. 24Shebaniah, Joshaphat, Nethanel, Amasai, Zechariah, Benaiah and Eliezer the priests were to blow trumpets before the ark of God. Obed-Edom and Jehiah were also to be doorkeepers for the ark.

25So David and the elders of Israel and the commanders of units of a thousand went to bring up the ark of the covenant of the LORD from the house of Obed-Edom, with rejoicing. 26Because God had helped the Levites who were carrying the ark of the covenant of the LORD, seven bulls and seven rams were sacrificed. 27Now David was clothed in a robe of fine linen, as were all the Levites who were carrying the ark, and as were

the singers, and Kenaniah, who was in charge of the singing of the choirs. David also wore a linen ephod. 28So all Israel brought up the ark of the covenant of the LORD with shouts, with the sounding of rams' horns and trumpets, and of cymbals, and the playing of lyres and harps.

29As the ark of the covenant of the LORD was entering the City of David, Michal daughter of Saul watched from a window. And when she saw King David dancing and celebrating, she despised him in her heart.

16 They brought the ark of God and set it inside the tent that David had pitched for it, and they presented burnt offerings and fellowship offerings before God. 2After David had finished sacrificing the burnt offerings and fellowship offerings, he blessed the people in the name of the LORD. 3Then he gave a loaf of bread, a cake of dates and a cake of raisins to each Israelite man and woman.

4He appointed some of the Levites to minister before the ark of the LORD, to make petition, to give thanks, and to praise the LORD, the God of Israel: 5Asaph was the chief, Zechariah second, then Jeiel, Shemiramoth, Jehiel, Mattithiah, Eliab, Benaiah, Obed-Edom and Jeiel. They were to play the lyres and harps, Asaph was to sound the cymbals, 6and Benaiah and Jahaziel the priests were to blow the trumpets regularly before the ark of the covenant of God.

David's Psalm of Thanks

7That day David first committed to Asaph and his associates this psalm of thanks to the LORD:

8Give thanks to the LORD, call on his
    name;
  make known among the nations
    what he has done.
9Sing to him, sing praise to him;
  tell of all his wonderful acts.
10Glory in his holy name;

let the hearts of those who seek the
LORD rejoice.
[11] Look to the LORD and his strength;
seek his face always.
[12] Remember the wonders he has done,
his miracles, and the judgments he
pronounced,
[13] O descendants of Israel his servant,
O sons of Jacob, his chosen ones.

[14] He is the LORD our God;
his judgments are in all the earth.
[15] He remembers his covenant for ever,
the word he commanded, for a
thousand generations,
[16] the covenant he made with Abraham,
the oath he swore to Isaac.
[17] He confirmed it to Jacob as a decree,
to Israel as an everlasting
covenant:
[18] "To you I will give the land of
Canaan
as the portion you will inherit."

[19] When they were but few in number,
few indeed, and strangers in it,
[20] they wandered from nation to nation,
from one kingdom to another.
[21] He allowed no man to oppress them;
for their sake he rebuked kings:
[22] "Do not touch my anointed ones;
do my prophets no harm."

[23] Sing to the LORD, all the earth;
proclaim his salvation day after
day.
[24] Declare his glory among the nations,
his marvellous deeds among all
peoples.
[25] For great is the LORD and most
worthy of praise;
he is to be feared above all gods.
[26] For all the gods of the nations are
idols,
but the LORD made the heavens.
[27] Splendour and majesty are before
him;
strength and joy in his
dwelling-place.
[28] Ascribe to the LORD, O families of
nations,
ascribe to the LORD glory and
strength,

[29] ascribe to the LORD the glory due
to his name.
Bring an offering and come before
him;
worship the LORD in the splendour
of his holiness.
[30] Tremble before him, all the earth!
The world is firmly established; it
cannot be moved.
[31] Let the heavens rejoice, let the earth
be glad;
let them say among the nations,
"The LORD reigns!"
[32] Let the sea resound, and all that is in
it;
let the fields be jubilant, and
everything in them!
[33] Then the trees of the forest will sing,
they will sing for joy before the
LORD,
for he comes to judge the earth.

[34] Give thanks to the LORD, for he is
good;
his love endures for ever.
[35] Cry out, "Save us, O God our
Saviour;
gather us and deliver us from the
nations,
that we may give thanks to your holy
name,
that we may glory in your praise."
[36] Praise be to the LORD, the God of
Israel,
from everlasting to everlasting.

Then all the people said "Amen" and
"Praise the LORD."

NEW TESTAMENT READING
Romans 16:1–27

Personal Greetings

16 I commend to you our sister
Phoebe, a servant of the church
in Cenchrea. [2] I ask you to receive her in
the Lord in a way worthy of the saints
and to give her any help she may need
from you, for she has been a great help
to many people, including me.

³Greet Priscilla and Aquila, my fellow-workers in Christ Jesus. ⁴They risked their lives for me. Not only I but all the churches of the Gentiles are grateful to them.

⁵Greet also the church that meets at their house.

Greet my dear friend Epenetus, who was the first convert to Christ in the province of Asia.

⁶Greet Mary, who worked very hard for you.

⁷Greet Andronicus and Junias, my relatives who have been in prison with me. They are outstanding among the apostles, and they were in Christ before I was.

⁸Greet Ampliatus, whom I love in the Lord.

⁹Greet Urbanus, our fellow-worker in Christ, and my dear friend Stachys.

¹⁰Greet Apelles, tested and approved in Christ.

Greet those who belong to the household of Aristobulus.

¹¹Greet Herodion, my relative.

Greet those in the household of Narcissus who are in the Lord.

¹²Greet Tryphena and Tryphosa, those women who work hard in the Lord.

Greet my dear friend Persis, another woman who has worked very hard in the Lord.

¹³Greet Rufus, chosen in the Lord, and his mother, who has been a mother to me, too.

¹⁴Greet Asyncritus, Phlegon, Hermes, Patrobas, Hermas and the brothers with them.

¹⁵Greet Philologus, Julia, Nereus and his sister, and Olympas and all the saints with them.

¹⁶Greet one another with a holy kiss.

All the churches of Christ send greetings.

¹⁷I urge you, brothers, to watch out for those who cause divisions and put obstacles in your way that are contrary to the teaching you have learned. Keep away from them. ¹⁸For such people are not serving our Lord Christ, but their own appetites. By smooth talk and flattery they deceive the minds of naïve people. ¹⁹Everyone has heard about your obedience, so I am full of joy over you; but I want you to be wise about what is good, and innocent about what is evil.

²⁰The God of peace will soon crush Satan under your feet.

The grace of our Lord Jesus be with you.

²¹Timothy, my fellow-worker, sends his greetings to you, as do Lucius, Jason and Sosipater, my relatives.

²²I, Tertius, who wrote down this letter, greet you in the Lord.

²³Gaius, whose hospitality I and the whole church here enjoy, sends you his greetings.

Erastus, who is the city's director of public works, and our brother Quartus send you their greetings.

²⁵Now to him who is able to establish you by my gospel and the proclamation of Jesus Christ, according to the revelation of the mystery hidden for long ages past, ²⁶but now revealed and made known through the prophetic writings by the command of the eternal God, so that all nations might believe and obey him—²⁷to the only wise God be glory for ever through Jesus Christ! Amen.

READING FROM PSALMS
Psalm 90:11–17

¹¹Who knows the power of your anger?
For your wrath is as great as the
fear that is due to you.
¹²Teach us to number our days aright,
that we may gain a heart of
wisdom.

¹³Relent, O Lord! How long will it be?
Have compassion on your servants.
¹⁴Satisfy us in the morning with your
unfailing love,
that we may sing for joy and be
glad all our days.
¹⁵Make us glad for as many days as you
have afflicted us,

for as many years as we have seen
trouble.
¹⁶May your deeds be shown to your
servants,
your splendour to their
children.

¹⁷May the favour of the Lord our God
rest upon us;
establish the work of our hands for
us—
yes, establish the work of our
hands.

AUGUST 4   DAY 216

OLD TESTAMENT READING
1 Chronicles 16:37–18:17

³⁷David left Asaph and his associates
before the ark of the covenant of the
LORD to minister there regularly,
according to each day's requirements.
³⁸He also left Obed-Edom and his sixty-
eight associates to minister with them.
Obed-Edom son of Jeduthun, and also
Hosah, were gatekeepers.

³⁹David left Zadok the priest and his
fellow priests before the tabernacle of
the LORD at the high place in Gibeon
⁴⁰to present burnt offerings to the LORD
on the altar of burnt offering regularly,
morning and evening, in accordance
with everything written in the Law of
the LORD, which he had given Israel.
⁴¹With them were Heman and Jeduthun
and the rest of those chosen and designated by name to give thanks to the
LORD, "for his love endures for ever."
⁴²Heman and Jeduthun were responsible for the sounding of the trumpets and
cymbals and for the playing of the other
instruments for sacred song. The sons of
Jeduthun were stationed at the gate.

⁴³Then all the people left, each for his
own home, and David returned home to
bless his family.

God's Promise to David

17 After David was settled in his
palace, he said to Nathan the
prophet, "Here I am, living in a palace

of cedar, while the ark of the covenant
of the LORD is under a tent."
²Nathan replied to David, "Whatever you have in mind, do it, for God is
with you."
³That night the word of God came to
Nathan, saying:

⁴"Go and tell my servant David,
'This is what the LORD says: You
are not the one to build me a house
to dwell in. ⁵I have not dwelt in a
house from the day I brought Israel
up out of Egypt to this day. I have
moved from one tent site to
another, from one dwelling-place
to another. ⁶Wherever I have
moved with all the Israelites, did I
ever say to any of their leaders
whom I commanded to shepherd
my people, "Why have you not
built me a house of cedar?"'

⁷"Now then, tell my servant
David, 'This is what the LORD
Almighty says: I took you from the
pasture and from following the
flock, to be ruler over my people
Israel. ⁸I have been with you
wherever you have gone, and I
have cut off all your enemies from
before you. Now I will make your
name like the names of the greatest
men of the earth. ⁹And I will provide a place for my people Israel
and will plant them so that they can
have a home of their own and no
longer be disturbed. Wicked people will not oppress them any

more, as they did at the beginning [10]and have done ever since the time I appointed leaders over my people Israel. I will also subdue all your enemies.

"'I declare to you that the LORD will build a house for you: [11]When your days are over and you go to be with your fathers, I will raise up your offspring to succeed you, one of your own sons, and I will establish his kingdom. [12]He is the one who will build a house for me, and I will establish his throne for ever. [13]I will be his father, and he will be my son. I will never take my love away from him, as I took it away from your predecessor. [14]I will set him over my house and my kingdom for ever; his throne will be established for ever.'"

[15]Nathan reported to David all the words of this entire revelation.

David's Prayer

[16]Then King David went in and sat before the LORD, and he said:

"Who am I, O LORD God, and what is my family, that you have brought me this far? [17]And as if this were not enough in your sight, O God, you have spoken about the future of the house of your servant. You have looked on me as though I were the most exalted of men, O LORD God.

[18]"What more can David say to you for honouring your servant? For you know your servant, [19]O LORD. For the sake of your servant and according to your will, you have done this great thing and made known all these great promises.

[20]"There is no-one like you, O LORD, and there is no God but you, as we have heard with our own ears. [21]And who is like your people Israel—the one nation on earth whose God went out to redeem a people for himself, and to make a name for yourself, and to perform great and awesome wonders by driving out nations from before your people, whom you redeemed from Egypt? [22]You made your people Israel your very own for ever, and you, O LORD, have become their God.

[23]"And now, LORD, let the promise you have made concerning your servant and his house be established for ever. Do as you promised, [24]so that it will be established and that your name will be great for ever. Then men will say, 'The LORD Almighty, the God over Israel, is Israel's God!' And the house of your servant David will be established before you.

[25]"You, my God, have revealed to your servant that you will build a house for him. So your servant has found courage to pray to you. [26]O LORD, you are God! You have promised these good things to your servant. [27]Now you have been pleased to bless the house of your servant, that it may continue for ever in your sight; for you, O LORD, have blessed it, and it will be blessed for ever."

David's Victories

18 In the course of time, David defeated the Philistines and subdued them, and he took Gath and its surrounding villages from the control of the Philistines.

[2]David also defeated the Moabites, and they became subject to him and brought tribute.

[3]Moreover, David fought Hadadezer king of Zobah, as far as Hamath, when he went to establish his control along the Euphrates River. [4]David captured a thousand of his chariots, seven thousand charioteers and twenty thousand foot soldiers. He hamstrung all but a hundred of the chariot horses.

5When the Arameans of Damascus came to help Hadadezer king of Zobah, David struck down twenty-two thousand of them. 6He put garrisons in the Aramean kingdom of Damascus, and the Arameans became subject to him and brought tribute. The LORD gave David victory everywhere he went.

7David took the gold shields carried by the officers of Hadadezer and brought them to Jerusalem. 8From Tebah and Cun, towns that belonged to Hadadezer, David took a great quantity of bronze, which Solomon used to make the bronze Sea, the pillars and various bronze articles.

9When Tou king of Hamath heard that David had defeated the entire army of Hadadezer king of Zobah, 10he sent his son Hadoram to King David to greet him and congratulate him on his victory in battle over Hadadezer, who had been at war with Tou. Hadoram brought all kinds of articles of gold and silver and bronze.

11King David dedicated these articles to the LORD, as he had done with the silver and gold he had taken from all these nations: Edom and Moab, the Ammonites and the Philistines, and Amalek.

12Abishai son of Zeruiah struck down eighteen thousand Edomites in the Valley of Salt. 13He put garrisons in Edom, and all the Edomites became subject to David. The LORD gave David victory everywhere he went.

David's Officials

14David reigned over all Israel, doing what was just and right for all his people. 15Joab son of Zeruiah was over the army; Jehoshaphat son of Ahilud was recorder; 16Zadok son of Ahitub and Ahimelech son of Abiathar were priests; Shavsha was secretary; 17Benaiah son of Jehoiada was over the Kerethites and Pelethites; and David's sons were chief officials at the king's side.

NEW TESTAMENT READING
1 Corinthians 1:1–17

1 Paul, called to be an apostle of Christ Jesus by the will of God, and our brother Sosthenes,

2To the church of God in Corinth, to those sanctified in Christ Jesus and called to be holy, together with all those everywhere who call on the name of our Lord Jesus Christ—their Lord and ours:

3Grace and peace to you from God our Father and the Lord Jesus Christ.

Thanksgiving

4I always thank God for you because of his grace given you in Christ Jesus. 5For in him you have been enriched in every way—in all your speaking and in all your knowledge—6because our testimony about Christ was confirmed in you. 7Therefore you do not lack any spiritual gift as you eagerly wait for our Lord Jesus Christ to be revealed. 8He will keep you strong to the end, so that you will be blameless on the day of our Lord Jesus Christ. 9God, who has called you into fellowship with his Son Jesus Christ our Lord, is faithful.

Divisions in the Church

10I appeal to you, brothers, in the name of our Lord Jesus Christ, that all of you agree with one another so that there may be no divisions among you and that you may be perfectly united in mind and thought. 11My brothers, some from Chloe's household have informed me that there are quarrels among you. 12What I mean is this: One of you says, "I follow Paul"; another, "I follow Apollos"; another, "I follow Cephas"; still another, "I follow Christ."

13Is Christ divided? Was Paul crucified for you? Were you baptised into the name of Paul? 14I am thankful that I did not baptise any of you except Crispus and Gaius, ¹⁵so no-one can say that you were baptised into my name. (¹⁶Yes, I also baptised the household of Stephanas; beyond that, I don't remember if I baptised anyone else.) ¹⁷For Christ did not send me to baptise, but to preach the gospel—not with words of human wisdom, lest the cross of Christ be emptied of its power.

READING FROM PROVERBS
Proverbs 19:3–12

³A man's own folly ruins his life,
    yet his heart rages against the
    LORD.

⁴Wealth brings many friends,
    but a poor man's friend deserts
    him.

⁵A false witness will not go
    unpunished,
    and he who pours out lies will not
    go free.

⁶Many curry favour with a ruler,
    and everyone is the friend of a man
    who gives gifts.

⁷A poor man is shunned by all his
    relatives—
    how much more do his friends
    avoid him!
Though he pursues them with
    pleading,
    they are nowhere to be found.

⁸He who gets wisdom loves his own
    soul;
    he who cherishes understanding
    prospers.

⁹A false witness will not go
    unpunished,
    and he who pours out lies will
    perish.

¹⁰It is not fitting for a fool to live in
    luxury—
    how much worse for a slave to rule
    over princes!

¹¹A man's wisdom gives him patience;
    it is to his glory to overlook an
    offence.

¹²A king's rage is like the roar of a lion,
    but his favour is like dew on the
    grass.

DAY 217

AUGUST 5

OLD TESTAMENT READING
1 Chronicles 19:1–22:1

The Battle Against the Ammonites

19 In the course of time, Nahash king of the Ammonites died, and his son succeeded him as king. ²David thought, "I will show kindness to Hanun son of Nahash, because his father showed kindness to me." So David sent a delegation to express his sympathy to Hanun concerning his father.

When David's men came to Hanun in the land of the Ammonites to express sympathy to him, ³the Ammonite nobles said to Hanun, "Do you think David is honouring your father by sending men to you to express sympathy? Haven't his men come to you to explore and spy out the country and overthrow it?" ⁴So Hanun seized David's men, shaved them, cut off their garments in the middle at the buttocks, and sent them away.

⁵When someone came and told David about the men, he sent messengers to meet them, for they were greatly

humiliated. The king said, "Stay at Jericho till your beards have grown, and then come back."

⁶When the Ammonites realised that they had become an offence to David's nostrils, Hanun and the Ammonites sent a thousand talents of silver to hire chariots and charioteers from Aram Naharaim, Aram Maacah and Zobah. ⁷They hired thirty-two thousand chariots and charioteers, as well as the king of Maacah with his troops, who came and camped near Medeba, while the Ammonites were mustered from their towns and moved out for battle.

⁸On hearing this, David sent Joab out with the entire army of fighting men. ⁹The Ammonites came out and drew up in battle formation at the entrance to their city, while the kings who had come were by themselves in the open country.

¹⁰Joab saw that there were battle lines in front of him and behind him; so he selected some of the best troops in Israel and deployed them against the Arameans. ¹¹He put the rest of the men under the command of Abishai his brother, and they were deployed against the Ammonites. ¹²Joab said, "If the Arameans are too strong for me, then you are to rescue me; but if the Ammonites are too strong for you, then I will rescue you. ¹³Be strong and let us fight bravely for our people and the cities of our God. The LORD will do what is good in his sight."

¹⁴Then Joab and the troops with him advanced to fight the Arameans, and they fled before him. ¹⁵When the Ammonites saw that the Arameans were fleeing, they too fled before his brother Abishai and went inside the city. So Joab went back to Jerusalem.

¹⁶After the Arameans saw that they had been routed by Israel, they sent messengers and had Arameans brought from beyond the River, with Shophach the commander of Hadadezer's army leading them.

¹⁷When David was told of this, he gathered all Israel and crossed the Jordan; he advanced against them and formed his battle lines opposite them. David formed his lines to meet the Arameans in battle, and they fought against him. ¹⁸But they fled before Israel, and David killed seven thousand of their charioteers and forty thousand of their foot soldiers. He also killed Shophach the commander of their army.

¹⁹When the vassals of Hadadezer saw that they had been defeated by Israel, they made peace with David and became subject to him.

So the Arameans were not willing to help the Ammonites any more.

The Capture of Rabbah

20 In the spring, at the time when kings go off to war, Joab led out the armed forces. He laid waste the land of the Ammonites and went to Rabbah and besieged it, but David remained in Jerusalem. Joab attacked Rabbah and left it in ruins. ²David took the crown from the head of their king—its weight was found to be a talent of gold, and it was set with precious stones—and it was placed on David's head. He took a great quantity of plunder from the city ³and brought out the people who were there, consigning them to labour with saws and with iron picks and axes. David did this to all the Ammonite towns. Then David and his entire army returned to Jerusalem.

War With the Philistines

⁴In the course of time, war broke out with the Philistines, at Gezer. At that time Sibbecai the Hushathite killed Sippai, one of the descendants of the Rephaites, and the Philistines were subjugated.

⁵In another battle with the Philistines, Elhanan son of Jair killed Lahmi the brother of Goliath the Gittite, who had a spear with a shaft like a weaver's rod.

⁶In still another battle, which took place at Gath, there was a huge man with six fingers on each hand and six toes on each foot—twenty-four in all. He also was descended from Rapha.

7When he taunted Israel, Jonathan son of Shimea, David's brother, killed him.

8These were descendants of Rapha in Gath, and they fell at the hands of David and his men.

David Numbers the Fighting Men

21 Satan rose up against Israel and incited David to take a census of Israel. 2So David said to Joab and the commanders of the troops, "Go and count the Israelites from Beersheba to Dan. Then report back to me so that I may know how many there are."

3But Joab replied, "May the LORD multiply his troops a hundred times over. My lord the king, are they not all my lord's subjects? Why does my lord want to do this? Why should he bring guilt on Israel?"

4The king's word, however, overruled Joab; so Joab left and went throughout Israel and then came back to Jerusalem. 5Joab reported the number of the fighting men to David: In all Israel there were one million one hundred thousand men who could handle a sword, including four hundred and seventy thousand in Judah.

6But Joab did not include Levi and Benjamin in the numbering, because the king's command was repulsive to him. 7This command was also evil in the sight of God; so he punished Israel.

8Then David said to God, "I have sinned greatly by doing this. Now, I beg you, take away the guilt of your servant. I have done a very foolish thing."

9The LORD said to Gad, David's seer, 10"Go and tell David, 'This is what the LORD says: I am giving you three options. Choose one of them for me to carry out against you.'"

11So Gad went to David and said to him, "This is what the LORD says: 'Take your choice: 12three years of famine, three months of being swept away before your enemies, with their swords overtaking you, or three days of the sword of the LORD—days of plague in the land with the angel of the LORD ravaging every part of Israel.' Now

then, decide how I should answer the one who sent me."

13David said to Gad, "I am in deep distress. Let me fall into the hands of the LORD, for his mercy is very great; but do not let me fall into the hands of men."

14So the LORD sent a plague on Israel, and seventy thousand men of Israel fell dead. 15And God sent an angel to destroy Jerusalem. But as the angel was doing so, the LORD saw it and was grieved because of the calamity and said to the angel who was destroying the people, "Enough! Withdraw your hand." The angel of the LORD was then standing at the threshing-floor of Araunah the Jebusite.

16David looked up and saw the angel of the LORD standing between heaven and earth, with a drawn sword in his hand extended over Jerusalem. Then David and the elders, clothed in sackcloth, fell face down.

17David said to God, "Was it not I who ordered the fighting men to be counted? I am the one who has sinned and done wrong. These are but sheep. What have they done? O LORD my God, let your hand fall upon me and my family, but do not let this plague remain on your people."

18Then the angel of the LORD ordered Gad to tell David to go up and build an altar to the LORD on the threshing-floor of Araunah the Jebusite. 19So David went up in obedience to the word that Gad had spoken in the name of the LORD.

20While Araunah was threshing wheat, he turned and saw the angel; his four sons who were with him hid themselves. 21Then David approached, and when Araunah looked and saw him, he left the threshing-floor and bowed down before David with his face to the ground.

22David said to him, "Let me have the site of your threshing-floor so that I can build an altar to the LORD, that the plague on the people may be stopped. Sell it to me at the full price."

²³Araunah said to David, "Take it! Let my lord the king do whatever pleases him. Look, I will give the oxen for the burnt offerings, the threshing-sledges for the wood, and the wheat for the grain offering. I will give all this."

²⁴But King David replied to Araunah, "No, I insist on paying the full price. I will not take for the LORD what is yours, or sacrifice a burnt offering that costs me nothing."

²⁵So David paid Araunah six hundred shekels of gold for the site. ²⁶David built an altar to the LORD there and sacrificed burnt offerings and fellowship offerings. He called on the LORD, and the LORD answered him with fire from heaven on the altar of burnt offering.

²⁷Then the LORD spoke to the angel, and he put his sword back into its sheath. ²⁸At that time, when David saw that the LORD had answered him on the threshing-floor of Araunah the Jebusite, he offered sacrifices there. ²⁹The tabernacle of the LORD, which Moses had made in the desert, and the altar of burnt offering were at that time on the high place at Gibeon. ³⁰But David could not go before it to enquire of God, because he was afraid of the sword of the angel of the LORD.

22 Then David said, "The house of the LORD God is to be here, and also the altar of burnt offering for Israel."

NEW TESTAMENT READING
1 Corinthians 1:18–2:5

Christ the Wisdom and Power of God

¹⁸For the message of the cross is foolishness to those who are perishing, but to us who are being saved it is the power of God. ¹⁹For it is written:

"I will destroy the wisdom of the
 wise;
 the intelligence of the intelligent I
 will frustrate."

²⁰Where is the wise man? Where is the scholar? Where is the philosopher of this age? Has not God made foolish the wisdom of the world? ²¹For since in the wisdom of God the world through its wisdom did not know him, God was pleased through the foolishness of what was preached to save those who believe. ²²Jews demand miraculous signs and Greeks look for wisdom, ²³but we preach Christ crucified: a stumbling-block to Jews and foolishness to Gentiles, ²⁴but to those whom God has called, both Jews and Greeks, Christ the power of God and the wisdom of God. ²⁵For the foolishness of God is wiser than man's wisdom, and the weakness of God is stronger than man's strength.

²⁶Brothers, think of what you were when you were called. Not many of you were wise by human standards; not many were influential; not many were of noble birth. ²⁷But God chose the foolish things of the world to shame the wise; God chose the weak things of the world to shame the strong. ²⁸He chose the lowly things of this world and the despised things—and the things that are not—to nullify the things that are, ²⁹so that no-one may boast before him. ³⁰It is because of him that you are in Christ Jesus, who has become for us wisdom from God—that is, our righteousness, holiness and redemption. ³¹Therefore, as it is written: "Let him who boasts boast in the Lord."

2 When I came to you, brothers, I did not come with eloquence or superior wisdom as I proclaimed to you the testimony about God. ²For I resolved to know nothing while I was with you except Jesus Christ and him crucified. ³I came to you in weakness and fear, and with much trembling. ⁴My message and my preaching were not with wise and persuasive words, but with a demonstration of the Spirit's power, ⁵so that your faith might not rest on men's wisdom, but on God's power.

READING FROM PSALMS
Psalm 91:1–8

¹He who dwells in the shelter of the
    Most High
  will rest in the shadow of the
    Almighty.
²I will say of the LORD, "He is my
    refuge and my fortress,
  my God, in whom I trust."

³Surely he will save you from the
    fowler's snare
  and from the deadly pestilence.
⁴He will cover you with his feathers,

and under his wings you will find
    refuge;
  his faithfulness will be your shield
    and rampart.
⁵You will not fear the terror of night,
  nor the arrow that flies by day,
⁶nor the pestilence that stalks in the
    darkness,
  nor the plague that destroys at
    midday.
⁷A thousand may fall at your side,
  ten thousand at your right hand,
  but it will not come near you.
⁸You will only observe with your eyes
  and see the punishment of the
    wicked.

DAY 218

AUGUST 6

OLD TESTAMENT READING
1 Chronicles 22:2–23:32

Preparations for the Temple

²So David gave orders to assemble
the aliens living in Israel, and from
among them he appointed stonecutters
to prepare dressed stone for building
the house of God. ³He provided a large
amount of iron to make nails for the
doors of the gateways and for the
fittings, and more bronze than could be
weighed. ⁴He also provided more cedar
logs than could be counted, for the
Sidonians and Tyrians had brought
large numbers of them to David.

⁵David said, "My son Solomon is
young and inexperienced, and the
house to be built for the LORD should be
of great magnificence and fame and
splendour in the sight of all the nations.
Therefore I will make preparations for
it." So David made extensive preparations before his death.

⁶Then he called for his son Solomon
and charged him to build a house for the
LORD, the God of Israel. ⁷David said to
Solomon: "My son, I had it in my heart

to build a house for the Name of the
LORD my God. ⁸But this word of the
LORD came to me: 'You have shed
much blood and have fought many
wars. You are not to build a house for
my Name, because you have shed much
blood on the earth in my sight. ⁹But you
will have a son who will be a man of
peace and rest, and I will give him rest
from all his enemies on every side. His
name will be Solomon, and I will grant
Israel peace and quiet during his reign.
¹⁰He is the one who will build a house
for my Name. He will be my son, and I
will be his father. And I will establish
the throne of his kingdom over Israel
for ever.'

¹¹"Now, my son, the LORD be with
you, and may you have success and
build the house of the LORD your God,
as he said you would. ¹²May the LORD
give you discretion and understanding
when he puts you in command over
Israel, so that you may keep the law of
the LORD your God. ¹³Then you will
have success if you are careful to
observe the decrees and laws that the
LORD gave to Moses for Israel. Be

strong and courageous. Do not be afraid or discouraged.

14"I have taken great pains to provide for the temple of the LORD a hundred thousand talents of gold, a million talents of silver, quantities of bronze and iron too great to be weighed, and wood and stone. And you may add to them. 15You have many workmen: stonecutters, masons and carpenters, as well as men skilled in every kind of work 16in gold and silver, bronze and iron—craftsmen beyond number. Now begin the work, and the LORD be with you."

17Then David ordered all the leaders of Israel to help his son Solomon. 18He said to them, "Is not the LORD your God with you? And has he not granted you rest on every side? For he has handed the inhabitants of the land over to me, and the land is subject to the LORD and to his people. 19Now devote your heart and soul to seeking the LORD your God. Begin to build the sanctuary of the LORD God, so that you may bring the ark of the covenant of the LORD and the sacred articles belonging to God into the temple that will be built for the Name of the LORD."

The Levites

23 When David was old and full of years, he made his son Solomon king over Israel.

2He also gathered together all the leaders of Israel, as well as the priests and Levites. 3The Levites thirty years old or more were counted, and the total number of men was thirty-eight thousand. 4David said, "Of these, twenty-four thousand are to supervise the work of the temple of the LORD and six thousand are to be officials and judges. 5Four thousand are to be gatekeepers and four thousand are to praise the LORD with the musical instruments I have provided for that purpose."

6David divided the Levites into groups corresponding to the sons of Levi: Gershon, Kohath and Merari.

Gershonites

7Belonging to the Gershonites:
Ladan and Shimei.

8The sons of Ladan:
Jehiel the first, Zetham and Joel—three in all.

9The sons of Shimei:
Shelomoth, Haziel and Haran—three in all.
These were the heads of the families of Ladan.

10And the sons of Shimei:
Jahath, Ziza, Jeush and Beriah.
These were the sons of Shimei—four in all.

11Jahath was the first and Ziza the second, but Jeush and Beriah did not have many sons; so they were counted as one family with one assignment.

Kohathites

12The sons of Kohath:
Amram, Izhar, Hebron and Uzziel—four in all.

13The sons of Amram:
Aaron and Moses.
Aaron was set apart, he and his descendants for ever, to consecrate the most holy things, to offer sacrifices before the LORD, to minister before him and to pronounce blessings in his name for ever. 14The sons of Moses the man of God were counted as part of the tribe of Levi.

15The sons of Moses:
Gershom and Eliezer.

16The descendants of Gershom:
Shubael was the first.

17The descendants of Eliezer:
Rehabiah was the first.
Eliezer had no other sons, but the sons of Rehabiah were very numerous.

18The sons of Izhar:
Shelomith was the first.

19The sons of Hebron:
Jeriah the first, Amariah the second, Jahaziel the third and Jekameam the fourth.

²⁰The sons of Uzziel:
Micah the first and Isshiah the
second.

Merarites

²¹The sons of Merari:
Mahli and Mushi.
The sons of Mahli:
Eleazar and Kish.
²²Eleazar died without having
sons: he had only daughters.
Their cousins, the sons of Kish,
married them.
²³The sons of Mushi:
Mahli, Eder and Jerimoth—
three in all.

²⁴These were the descendants of Levi
by their families—the heads of families
as they were registered under their
names and counted individually, that is,
the workers twenty years old or more
who served in the temple of the Lord.
²⁵For David had said, "Since the Lord,
the God of Israel, has granted rest to his
people and has come to dwell in Jerusalem for ever, ²⁶the Levites no longer
need to carry the tabernacle or any of
the articles used in its service."
²⁷According to the last instructions of
David, the Levites were counted from
those twenty years old or more.

²⁸The duty of the Levites was to help
Aaron's descendants in the service of
the temple of the Lord: to be in charge
of the courtyards, the side rooms, the
purification of all sacred things and the
performance of other duties at the
house of God. ²⁹They were in charge of
the bread set out on the table, the flour
for the grain offerings, the unleavened
wafers, the baking and the mixing, and
all measurements of quantity and size.
³⁰They were also to stand every morning to thank and praise the Lord. They
were to do the same in the evening ³¹and
whenever burnt offerings were presented to the Lord on Sabbaths and at
New Moon festivals and at appointed
feasts. They were to serve before the
Lord regularly in the proper number
and in the way prescribed for them.

³²And so the Levites carried out their
responsibilities for the Tent of Meeting,
for the Holy Place and, under their
brothers the descendants of Aaron, for
the service of the temple of the Lord.

NEW TESTAMENT READING
1 Corinthians 2:6–16

Wisdom From the Spirit

⁶We do, however, speak a message of
wisdom among the mature, but not the
wisdom of this age or of the rulers of this
age, who are coming to nothing. ⁷No,
we speak of God's secret wisdom, a
wisdom that has been hidden and that
God destined for our glory before time
began. ⁸None of the rulers of this age
understood it, for if they had, they
would not have crucified the Lord of
glory. ⁹However, as it is written:

"No eye has seen,
no ear has heard,
no mind has conceived
what God has prepared for those
who love him"—

¹⁰but God has revealed it to us by his
Spirit.
The Spirit searches all things, even
the deep things of God. ¹¹For who
among men knows the thoughts of a
man except the man's spirit within him?
In the same way no-one knows the
thoughts of God except the Spirit of
God. ¹²We have not received the spirit
of the world but the Spirit who is from
God, that we may understand what God
has freely given us. ¹³This is what we
speak, not in words taught us by human
wisdom but in words taught by the
Spirit, expressing spiritual truths in
spiritual words. ¹⁴The man without the
Spirit does not accept the things that
come from the Spirit of God, for they
are foolishness to him, and he cannot
understand them, because they are
spiritually discerned. ¹⁵The spiritual
man makes judgments about all things,

but he himself is not subject to any man's judgment:

16"For who has known the mind of the
 Lord
  that he may instruct him?"

But we have the mind of Christ.

READING FROM PSALMS
Psalm 91:9–16

9If you make the Most High your
 dwelling—
  even the Lord, who is my refuge—
10then no harm will befall you,
  no disaster will come near your
  tent.

11For he will command his angels
  concerning you
  to guard you in all your ways;
12they will lift you up in their hands,
  so that you will not strike your foot
   against a stone.
13You will tread upon the lion and the
  cobra;
  you will trample the great lion and
   the serpent.

14"Because he loves me," says the
 Lord, "I will rescue him;
  I will protect him, for he
   acknowledges my name.
15He will call upon me, and I will
  answer him;
  I will be with him in trouble,
  I will deliver him and honour him.
16With long life will I satisfy him
  and show him my salvation."

AUGUST 7   DAY 219

OLD TESTAMENT READING
1 Chronicles 24:1–26:19

The Divisions of Priests

24 These were the divisions of the sons of Aaron:

The sons of Aaron were Nadab, Abihu, Eleazar and Ithamar. 2But Nadab and Abihu died before their father did, and they had no sons; so Eleazar and Ithamar served as the priests. 3With the help of Zadok a descendant of Eleazar and Ahimelech a descendant of Ithamar, David separated them into divisions for their appointed order of ministering. 4A larger number of leaders were found among Eleazar's descendants than among Ithamar's, and they were divided accordingly: sixteen heads of families from Eleazar's descendants and eight heads of families from Ithamar's descendants. 5They divided them impartially by drawing lots, for there were officials of the sanctuary and officials of God among the descendants of both Eleazar and Ithamar.

6The scribe Shemaiah son of Nethanel, a Levite, recorded their names in the presence of the king and of the officials: Zadok the priest, Ahimelech son of Abiathar and the heads of families of the priests and the Levites—one family being taken from Eleazar and then one from Ithamar.

7The first lot fell to Jehoiarib,
 the second to Jedaiah,
8the third to Harim,
 the fourth to Seorim,
9the fifth to Malkijah,
 the sixth to Mijamin,
10the seventh to Hakkoz,
 the eighth to Abijah,
11the ninth to Jeshua,
 the tenth to Shecaniah,

¹²the eleventh to Eliashib,
   the twelfth to Jakim,
¹³the thirteenth to Huppah,
   the fourteenth to Jeshebeab,
¹⁴the fifteenth to Bilgah,
   the sixteenth to Immer,
¹⁵the seventeenth to Hezir,
   the eighteenth to Happizzez,
¹⁶the nineteenth to Pethahiah,
   the twentieth to Jehezkel,
¹⁷the twenty-first to Jakin,
   the twenty-second to Gamul,
¹⁸the twenty-third to Delaiah
   and the twenty-fourth to Maaziah.

¹⁹This was their appointed order of ministering when they entered the temple of the LORD, according to the regulations prescribed for them by their forefather Aaron, as the LORD, the God of Israel, had commanded him.

The Rest of the Levites

²⁰As for the rest of the descendants of Levi:
   from the sons of Amram: Shubael;
      from the sons of Shubael: Jehdeiah.
   ²¹As for Rehabiah, from his sons: Isshiah was the first.
²²From the Izharites: Shelomoth;
      from the sons of Shelomoth: Jahath.
²³The sons of Hebron: Jeriah the first, Amariah the second, Jahaziel the third and Jekameam the fourth.
²⁴The son of Uzziel: Micah;
   from the sons of Micah: Shamir.
²⁵The brother of Micah: Isshiah;
   from the sons of Isshiah: Zechariah.
²⁶The sons of Merari: Mahli and Mushi.
   The son of Jaaziah: Beno.
²⁷The sons of Merari:
   from Jaaziah: Beno, Shoham, Zaccur and Ibri.
²⁸From Mahli: Eleazar, who had no sons.

²⁹From Kish: the son of Kish: Jerahmeel.
³⁰And the sons of Mushi: Mahli, Eder and Jerimoth.

These were the Levites, according to their families. ³¹They also cast lots, just as their brothers the descendants of Aaron did, in the presence of King David and of Zadok, Ahimelech, and the heads of families of the priests and of the Levites. The families of the eldest brother were treated the same as those of the youngest.

The Singers

25 David, together with the commanders of the army, set apart some of the sons of Asaph, Heman and Jeduthun for the ministry of prophesying, accompanied by harps, lyres and cymbals. Here is the list of the men who performed this service:

²From the sons of Asaph:
   Zaccur, Joseph, Nethaniah and Asarelah. The sons of Asaph were under the supervision of Asaph, who prophesied under the king's supervision.
³As for Jeduthun, from his sons:
   Gedaliah, Zeri, Jeshaiah, Shimei, Hashabiah and Mattithiah, six in all, under the supervision of their father Jeduthun, who prophesied, using the harp in thanking and praising the LORD.
⁴As for Heman, from his sons:
   Bukkiah, Mattaniah, Uzziel, Shubael and Jerimoth; Hananiah, Hanani, Eliathah, Giddalti and Romamti-Ezer; Joshbekashah, Mallothi, Hothir and Mahazioth.
⁵All these were sons of Heman the king's seer. They were given to him through the promises of God to exalt him. God gave Heman fourteen sons and three daughters.

⁶All these men were under the supervision of their fathers for the music of

the temple of the LORD, with cymbals, lyres and harps, for the ministry at the house of God. Asaph, Jeduthun and Heman were under the supervision of the king. [7]Along with their relatives —all of them trained and skilled in music for the LORD—they numbered 288. [8]Young and old alike, teacher as well as student, cast lots for their duties.

[9]The first lot, which was for Asaph, fell to Joseph,
his sons and relatives,   12
the second to Gedaliah,
he and his relatives
and sons,   12
[10]the third to Zaccur,
his sons and relatives,   12
[11]the fourth to Izri,
his sons and relatives,   12
[12]the fifth to Nethaniah,
his sons and relatives,   12
[13]the sixth to Bukkiah,
his sons and relatives,   12
[14]the seventh to Jesarelah,
his sons and relatives,   12
[15]the eighth to Jeshaiah,
his sons and relatives,   12
[16]the ninth to Mattaniah,
his sons and relatives,   12
[17]the tenth to Shimei,
his sons and relatives,   12
[18]the eleventh to Azarel,
his sons and relatives,   12
[19]the twelfth to Hashabiah,
his sons and relatives,   12
[20]the thirteenth to Shubael,
his sons and relatives,   12
[21]the fourteenth to Mattithiah,
his sons and relatives,   12
[22]the fifteenth to Jerimoth,
his sons and relatives,   12
[23]the sixteenth to Hananiah,
his sons and relatives,   12
[24]the seventeenth to Joshbakashah,
his sons and relatives,   12
[25]the eighteenth to Hanani,
his sons and relatives,   12
[26]the nineteenth to Mallothi,
his sons and relatives,   12

[27]the twentieth to Eliathah,
his sons and relatives,   12
[28]the twenty-first to Hothir,
his sons and relatives,   12
[29]the twenty-second to Giddalti,
his sons and relatives,   12
[30]the twenty-third to Mahazioth,
his sons and relatives,   12
[31]the twenty-fourth to Romamti-Ezer,
his sons and relatives,   12

The Gatekeepers

26 The divisions of the gatekeepers:

From the Korahites: Meshelemiah son of Kore, one of the sons of Asaph.
[2]Meshelemiah had sons:
Zechariah the firstborn,
Jediael the second,
Zebadiah the third,
Jathniel the fourth,
[3]Elam the fifth,
Jehohanan the sixth
and Eliehoenai the seventh.
[4]Obed-Edom also had sons:
Shemaiah the firstborn,
Jehozabad the second,
Joah the third,
Sacar the fourth,
Nethanel the fifth,
[5]Ammiel the sixth,
Issachar the seventh
and Peullethai the eighth.
(For God had blessed Obed-Edom.)

[6]His son Shemaiah also had sons, who were leaders in their father's family because they were very capable men. [7]The sons of Shemaiah: Othni, Rephael, Obed and Elzabad; his relatives Elihu and Semakiah were also able men. [8]All these were descendants of Obed-Edom; they and their sons and

their relatives were capable men with the strength to do the work —descendants of Obed-Edom, 62 in all.

⁹Meshelemiah had sons and relatives, who were able men—18 in all.

¹⁰Hosah the Merarite had sons: Shimri the first (although he was not the firstborn, his father had appointed him the first), ¹¹Hilkiah the second, Tabaliah the third and Zechariah the fourth. The sons and relatives of Hosah were 13 in all.

¹²These divisions of the gatekeepers, through their chief men, had duties for ministering in the temple of the LORD, just as their relatives had. ¹³Lots were cast for each gate, according to their families, young and old alike.

¹⁴The lot for the East Gate fell to Shelemiah. Then lots were cast for his son Zechariah, a wise counsellor, and the lot for the North Gate fell to him. ¹⁵The lot for the South Gate fell to Obed-Edom, and the lot for the storehouse fell to his sons. ¹⁶The lots for the West Gate and the Shalleketh Gate on the upper road fell to Shuppim and Hosah.

Guard was alongside guard: ¹⁷There were six Levites a day on the east, four a day on the north, four a day on the south and two at a time at the storehouse. ¹⁸As for the court to the west, there were four at the road and two at the court itself.

¹⁹These were the divisions of the gatekeepers who were descendants of Korah and Merari.

NEW TESTAMENT READING
1 Corinthians 3:1–23

On Divisions in the Church

3 Brothers, I could not address you as spiritual but as worldly—mere infants in Christ. ²I gave you milk, not solid food, for you were not yet ready for it. Indeed, you are still not ready. ³You are still worldly. For since there is jealousy and quarrelling among you, are you not worldly? Are you not acting like mere men? ⁴For when one says, "I follow Paul," and another, "I follow Apollos," are you not mere men?

⁵What, after all, is Apollos? And what is Paul? Only servants, through whom you came to believe—as the Lord has assigned to each his task. ⁶I planted the seed, Apollos watered it, but God made it grow. ⁷So neither he who plants nor he who waters is anything, but only God, who makes things grow. ⁸The man who plants and the man who waters have one purpose, and each will be rewarded according to his own labour. ⁹For we are God's fellowworkers; you are God's field, God's building.

¹⁰By the grace God has given me, I laid a foundation as an expert builder, and someone else is building on it. But each one should be careful how he builds. ¹¹For no-one can lay any foundation other than the one already laid, which is Jesus Christ. ¹²If any man builds on this foundation using gold, silver, costly stones, wood, hay or straw, ¹³his work will be shown for what it is, because the Day will bring it to light. It will be revealed with fire, and the fire will test the quality of each man's work. ¹⁴If what he has built survives, he will receive his reward. ¹⁵If it is burned up, he will suffer loss; he himself will be saved, but only as one escaping through the flames.

¹⁶Don't you know that you yourselves are God's temple and that God's Spirit lives in you? ¹⁷If anyone destroys God's temple, God will destroy him; for God's temple is sacred, and you are that temple.

¹⁸Do not deceive yourselves. If any one of you thinks he is wise by the standards of this age, he should become a "fool" so that he may become wise. ¹⁹For the wisdom of this world is foolishness in God's sight. As it is

written: "He catches the wise in their craftiness"; [20]and again, "The Lord knows that the thoughts of the wise are futile." [21]So then, no more boasting about men! All things are yours, [22]whether Paul or Apollos or Cephas or the world or life or death or the present or the future—all are yours, [23]and you are of Christ, and Christ is of God.

READING FROM PSALMS
Psalm 92:1–15

A psalm. A song. For the Sabbath day.

[1]It is good to praise the LORD
    and make music to your name, O
        Most High,
[2]to proclaim your love in the morning
    and your faithfulness at night,
[3]to the music of the ten-stringed lyre
    and the melody of the harp.

[4]For you make me glad by your deeds,
        O LORD;
    I sing for joy at the work of your
        hands.
[5]How great are your works, O LORD,
    how profound your thoughts!
[6]The senseless man does not know,
    fools do not understand,

[7]that though the wicked spring up like
        grass
    and all evildoers flourish,
    they will be for ever destroyed.

[8]But you, O LORD, are exalted for
        ever.

[9]For surely your enemies, O LORD,
    surely your enemies will perish;
    all evildoers will be scattered.
[10]You have exalted my horn like that of
        a wild ox;
    fine oils have been poured upon
        me.
[11]My eyes have seen the defeat of my
        adversaries;
    my ears have heard the rout of my
        wicked foes.

[12]The righteous will flourish like a palm
        tree,
    they will grow like a cedar of
        Lebanon;
[13]planted in the house of the LORD,
    they will flourish in the courts of
        our God.
[14]They will still bear fruit in old age,
    they will stay fresh and green,
[15]proclaiming, "The LORD is upright;
    he is my Rock, and there is no
        wickedness in him."

AUGUST 8   DAY 220

OLD TESTAMENT READING
1 Chronicles 26:20–27:34

The Treasurers and Other Officials

[20]Their fellow Levites were in charge of the treasuries of the house of God and the treasuries for the dedicated things.

[21]The descendants of Ladan, who were Gershonites through Ladan and who were heads of families belonging to Ladan the Gershonite, were Jehieli, [22]the sons of Jehieli, Zetham and his brother Joel. They were in charge of the treasuries of the temple of the LORD.

[23]From the Amramites, the Izharites, the Hebronites and the Uzzielites:

[24]Shubael, a descendant of Gershom son of Moses, was the officer in charge of the treasuries. [25]His relatives through Eliezer: Rehabiah his son, Jeshaiah his son, Joram his son, Zicri his son and Shelomith his son. [26]Shelomith

and his relatives were in charge of all the treasuries for the things dedicated by King David, by the heads of families who were the commanders of thousands and commanders of hundreds, and by the other army commanders. ²⁷Some of the plunder taken in battle they dedicated for the repair of the temple of the LORD. ²⁸And everything dedicated by Samuel the seer and by Saul son of Kish, Abner son of Ner and Joab son of Zeruiah, and all the other dedicated things were in the care of Shelomith and his relatives.

²⁹From the Izharites: Kenaniah and his sons were assigned duties away from the temple, as officials and judges over Israel.

³⁰From the Hebronites: Hashabiah and his relatives—seventeen hundred able men—were responsible in Israel west of the Jordan for all the work of the LORD and for the king's service. ³¹As for the Hebronites, Jeriah was their chief according to the genealogical records of their families. In the fortieth year of David's reign a search was made in the records, and capable men among the Hebronites were found at Jazer in Gilead. ³²Jeriah had two thousand seven hundred relatives, who were able men and heads of families, and King David put them in charge of the Reubenites, the Gadites and the half-tribe of Manasseh for every matter pertaining to God and for the affairs of the king.

Army Divisions

27 This is the list of the Israelites —heads of families, commanders of thousands and commanders of hundreds, and their officers, who served the king in all that concerned the army divisions that were on duty month by month throughout the year. Each division consisted of 24,000 men.

²In charge of the first division, for the first month, was Jashobeam son of Zabdiel. There were 24,000 men in his division. ³He was a descendant of Perez and chief of all the army officers for the first month.

⁴In charge of the division for the second month was Dodai the Ahohite; Mikloth was the leader of his division. There were 24,000 men in his division.

⁵The third army commander, for the third month, was Benaiah son of Jehoiada the priest. He was chief and there were 24,000 men in his division. ⁶This was the Benaiah who was a mighty man among the Thirty and was over the Thirty. His son Ammizabad was in charge of his division.

⁷The fourth, for the fourth month, was Asahel the brother of Joab; his son Zebadiah was his successor. There were 24,000 men in his division.

⁸The fifth, for the fifth month, was the commander Shamhuth the Izrahite. There were 24,000 men in his division.

⁹The sixth, for the sixth month, was Ira the son of Ikkesh the Tekoite. There were 24,000 men in his division.

¹⁰The seventh, for the seventh month, was Helez the Pelonite, an Ephraimite. There were 24,000 men in his division.

¹¹The eighth, for the eighth month, was Sibbecai the Hushathite, a Zerahite. There were 24,000 men in his division.

¹²The ninth, for the ninth month, was Abiezer the Anathothite, a Benjamite. There were 24,000 men in his division.

¹³The tenth, for the tenth month, was Maharai the Netophathite, a Zerahite. There were 24,000 men in his division.

¹⁴The eleventh, for the eleventh month,

was Benaiah the Pirathonite, an Ephraimite. There were 24,000 men in his division.

[15]The twelfth, for the twelfth month, was Heldai the Netophathite, from the family of Othniel. There were 24,000 men in his division.

Officers of the Tribes

[16]The officers over the tribes of Israel:

over the Reubenites: Eliezer son of Zicri;

over the Simeonites: Shephatiah son of Maacah;

[17]over Levi: Hashabiah son of Kemuel;

over Aaron: Zadok;

[18]over Judah: Elihu, a brother of David;

over Issachar: Omri son of Michael;

[19]over Zebulun: Ishmaiah son of Obadiah;

over Naphtali: Jerimoth son of Azriel;

[20]over the Ephraimites: Hoshea son of Azaziah;

over half the tribe of Manasseh: Joel son of Pedaiah;

[21]over the half-tribe of Manasseh in Gilead: Iddo son of Zechariah;

over Benjamin: Jaasiel son of Abner;

[22]over Dan: Azarel son of Jeroham. These were the officers over the tribes of Israel.

[23]David did not take the number of the men twenty years old or less, because the LORD had promised to make Israel as numerous as the stars in the sky. [24]Joab son of Zeruiah began to count the men but did not finish. Wrath came on Israel on account of this numbering, and the number was not entered in the book of the annals of King David.

The King's Overseers

[25]Azmaveth son of Adiel was in charge of the royal storehouses.

Jonathan son of Uzziah was in charge of the storehouses in the outlying districts, in the towns, the villages and the watchtowers.

[26]Ezri son of Kelub was in charge of the field workers who farmed the land.

[27]Shimei the Ramathite was in charge of the vineyards.

Zabdi the Shiphmite was in charge of the produce of the vineyards for the wine vats.

[28]Baal-Hanan the Gederite was in charge of the olive and sycamore-fig trees in the western foothills.

Joash was in charge of the supplies of olive oil.

[29]Shitrai the Sharonite was in charge of the herds grazing in Sharon.

Shaphat son of Adlai was in charge of the herds in the valleys.

[30]Obil the Ishmaelite was in charge of the camels.

Jehdeiah the Meronothite was in charge of the donkeys.

[31]Jaziz the Hagrite was in charge of the flocks.

All these were the officials in charge of King David's property.

[32]Jonathan, David's uncle, was a counsellor, a man of insight and a scribe. Jehiel son of Hacmoni took care of the king's sons.

[33]Ahithophel was the king's counsellor.

Hushai the Arkite was the king's friend. [34]Ahithophel was succeeded by Jehoiada son of Benaiah and by Abiathar.

Joab was the commander of the royal army.

NEW TESTAMENT READING
1 Corinthians 4:1–21

Apostles of Christ

4 So then, men ought to regard us as servants of Christ and as those entrusted with the secret things of God. [2]Now it is required that those who have

been given a trust must prove faithful. ³I care very little if I am judged by you or by any human court; indeed, I do not even judge myself. ⁴My conscience is clear, but that does not make me innocent. It is the Lord who judges me. ⁵Therefore judge nothing before the appointed time; wait till the Lord comes. He will bring to light what is hidden in darkness and will expose the motives of men's hearts. At that time each will receive his praise from God.

⁶Now, brothers, I have applied these things to myself and Apollos for your benefit, so that you may learn from us the meaning of the saying, "Do not go beyond what is written." Then you will not take pride in one man over against another. ⁷For who makes you different from anyone else? What do you have that you did not receive? And if you did receive it, why do you boast as though you did not?

⁸Already you have all you want! Already you have become rich! You have become kings—and that without us! How I wish that you really had become kings so that we might be kings with you! ⁹For it seems to me that God has put us apostles on display at the end of the procession, like men condemned to die in the arena. We have been made a spectacle to the whole universe, to angels as well as to men. ¹⁰We are fools for Christ, but you are so wise in Christ! We are weak, but you are strong! You are honoured, we are dishonoured! ¹¹To this very hour we go hungry and thirsty, we are in rags, we are brutally treated, we are homeless. ¹²We work hard with our own hands. When we are cursed, we bless; when we are persecuted, we endure it; ¹³when we are slandered, we answer kindly. Up to this moment we have become the scum of the earth, the refuse of the world.

¹⁴I am not writing this to shame you, but to warn you, as my dear children. ¹⁵Even though you have ten thousand guardians in Christ, you do not have many fathers, for in Christ Jesus I became your father through the gospel.

¹⁶Therefore I urge you to imitate me. ¹⁷For this reason I am sending to you Timothy, my son whom I love, who is faithful in the Lord. He will remind you of my way of life in Christ Jesus, which agrees with what I teach everywhere in every church.

¹⁸Some of you have become arrogant, as if I were not coming to you. ¹⁹But I will come to you very soon, if the Lord is willing, and then I will find out not only how these arrogant people are talking, but what power they have. ²⁰For the kingdom of God is not a matter of talk but of power. ²¹What do you prefer? Shall I come to you with a whip, or in love and with a gentle spirit?

READING FROM PROVERBS
Proverbs 19:13–22

¹³A foolish son is his father's ruin,
    and a quarrelsome wife is like a
        constant dripping.

¹⁴Houses and wealth are inherited from
        parents,
    but a prudent wife is from the
        LORD.

¹⁵Laziness brings on deep sleep,
    and the shiftless man goes hungry.

¹⁶He who obeys instructions guards his
        life,
    but he who is contemptuous of his
        ways will die.

¹⁷He who is kind to the poor lends to
        the LORD,
    and he will reward him for what he
        has done.

¹⁸Discipline your son, for in that there
        is hope;
    do not be a willing party to his
        death.

¹⁹A hot-tempered man must pay the
        penalty;

if you rescue him, you will have to do it again.

20Listen to advice and accept instruction,
    and in the end you will be wise.

21Many are the plans in a man's heart,
    but it is the LORD's purpose that prevails.

22What a man desires is unfailing love;
    better to be poor than a liar.

AUGUST 9   DAY 221

OLD TESTAMENT READING
1 Chronicles 28:1–29:30

David's Plans for the Temple

28 David summoned all the officials of Israel to assemble at Jerusalem: the officers over the tribes, the commanders of the divisions in the service of the king, the commanders of thousands and commanders of hundreds, and the officials in charge of all the property and livestock belonging to the king and his sons, together with the palace officials, the mighty men and all the brave warriors.

2King David rose to his feet and said: "Listen to me, my brothers and my people. I had it in my heart to build a house as a place of rest for the ark of the covenant of the LORD, for the footstool of our God, and I made plans to build it. 3But God said to me, 'You are not to build a house for my Name, because you are a warrior and have shed blood.'

4"Yet the LORD, the God of Israel, chose me from my whole family to be king over Israel for ever. He chose Judah as leader, and from the house of Judah he chose my family, and from my father's sons he was pleased to make me king over all Israel. 5Of all my sons —and the LORD has given me many —he has chosen my son Solomon to sit on the throne of the kingdom of the LORD over Israel. 6He said to me, 'Solomon your son is the one who will build my house and my courts, for I have chosen him to be my son, and I will be his father. 7I will establish his kingdom for ever if he is unswerving in carrying out my commands and laws, as is being done at this time.'

8"So now I charge you in the sight of all Israel and of the assembly of the LORD, and in the hearing of our God: Be careful to follow all the commands of the LORD your God, that you may possess this good land and pass it on as an inheritance to your descendants for ever.

9"And you, my son Solomon, acknowledge the God of your father, and serve him with wholehearted devotion and with a willing mind, for the LORD searches every heart and understands every motive behind the thoughts. If you seek him, he will be found by you; but if you forsake him, he will reject you for ever. 10Consider now, for the LORD has chosen you to build a temple as a sanctuary. Be strong and do the work."

11Then David gave his son Solomon the plans for the portico of the temple, its buildings, its storerooms, its upper parts, its inner rooms and the place of atonement. 12He gave him the plans of all that the Spirit had put in his mind for the courts of the temple of the LORD and all the surrounding rooms, for the treasuries of the temple of God and for the treasuries for the dedicated things. 13He gave him instructions for the divisions of the priests and Levites, and for all the work of serving in the temple of the LORD, as well as for all the articles to be used in its service. [14]He designated the weight of gold for all the gold articles to be used in various kinds of service, and the weight of silver for all the silver articles to be used in various kinds of service: [15]the weight of gold for the gold lampstands and their lamps, with the weight for each lampstand and its lamps; and the weight of silver for each silver lampstand and its lamps, according to the use of each lampstand; [16]the weight of gold for each table for consecrated bread; the weight of silver for the silver tables; [17]the weight of pure gold for the forks, sprinkling bowls and pitchers; the weight of gold for each gold dish; the weight of silver for each silver dish; [18]and the weight of the refined gold for the altar of incense. He also gave him the plan for the chariot, that is, the cherubim of gold that spread their wings and shelter the ark of the covenant of the LORD.

[19]"All this," David said, "I have in writing from the hand of the LORD upon me, and he gave me understanding in all the details of the plan."

[20]David also said to Solomon his son, "Be strong and courageous, and do the work. Do not be afraid or discouraged, for the LORD God, my God, is with you. He will not fail you or forsake you until all the work for the service of the temple of the LORD is finished. [21]The divisions of the priests and Levites are ready for all the work on the temple of God, and every willing man skilled in any craft will help you in all the work. The officials and all the people will obey your every command."

Gifts for Building the Temple

29 Then King David said to the whole assembly: "My son Solomon, the one whom God has chosen, is young and inexperienced. The task is great, because this palatial structure is not for man but for the LORD God. [2]With all my resources I have provided for the temple of my God—gold for the gold work, silver for the silver, bronze

for the bronze, iron for the iron and wood for the wood, as well as onyx for the settings, turquoise, stones of various colours, and all kinds of fine stone and marble—all of these in large quantities. [3]Besides, in my devotion to the temple of my God I now give my personal treasures of gold and silver for the temple of my God, over and above everything I have provided for this holy temple: [4]three thousand talents of gold (gold of Ophir) and seven thousand talents of refined silver, for the overlaying of the walls of the buildings, [5]for the gold work and the silver work, and for all the work to be done by the craftsmen. Now, who is willing to consecrate himself today to the LORD?"

[6]Then the leaders of families, the officers of the tribes of Israel, the commanders of thousands and commanders of hundreds, and the officials in charge of the king's work gave willingly. [7]They gave towards the work on the temple of God five thousand talents and ten thousand darics of gold, ten thousand talents of silver, eighteen thousand talents of bronze and a hundred thousand talents of iron. [8]Any who had precious stones gave them to the treasury of the temple of the LORD in the custody of Jehiel the Gershonite. [9]The people rejoiced at the willing response of their leaders, for they had given freely and wholeheartedly to the LORD. David the king also rejoiced greatly.

David's Prayer

[10]David praised the LORD in the presence of the whole assembly, saying,

"Praise be to you, O LORD,
    God of our father Israel,
    from everlasting to everlasting.
[11]Yours, O LORD, is the greatness and
        the power
    and the glory and the majesty and
        the splendour,
    for everything in heaven and earth
        is yours.

Yours, O Lord, is the kingdom;
  you are exalted as head over all.
[12]Wealth and honour come from you;
  you are the ruler of all things.
In your hands are strength and power
  to exalt and give strength to all.
[13]Now, our God, we give you thanks,
  and praise your glorious name.

[14]"But who am I, and who are my people, that we should be able to give as generously as this? Everything comes from you, and we have given you only what comes from your hand. [15]We are aliens and strangers in your sight, as were all our forefathers. Our days on earth are like a shadow, without hope. [16]O Lord our God, as for all this abundance that we have provided for building you a temple for your Holy Name, it comes from your hand, and all of it belongs to you. [17]I know, my God, that you test the heart and are pleased with integrity. All these things have I given willingly and with honest intent. And now I have seen with joy how willingly your people who are here have given to you. [18]O Lord, God of our fathers Abraham, Isaac and Israel, keep this desire in the hearts of your people for ever, and keep their hearts loyal to you. [19]And give my son Solomon the wholehearted devotion to keep your commands, requirements and decrees and to do everything to build the palatial structure for which I have provided."

[20]Then David said to the whole assembly, "Praise the Lord your God." So they all praised the Lord, the God of their fathers; they bowed low and fell prostrate before the Lord and the king.

Solomon Acknowledged as King

[21]The next day they made sacrifices to the Lord and presented burnt offerings to him: a thousand bulls, a thousand rams and a thousand male lambs, together with their drink offerings, and other sacrifices in abundance for all Israel. [22]They ate and drank with great joy in the presence of the Lord that day.

Then they acknowledged Solomon son of David as king a second time, anointing him before the Lord to be ruler and Zadok to be priest. [23]So Solomon sat on the throne of the Lord as king in place of his father David. He prospered and all Israel obeyed him. [24]All the officers and mighty men, as well as all of King David's sons, pledged their submission to King Solomon.

[25]The Lord highly exalted Solomon in the sight of all Israel and bestowed on him royal splendour such as no king over Israel ever had before.

The Death of David

[26]David son of Jesse was king over all Israel. [27]He ruled over Israel for forty years—seven in Hebron and thirty-three in Jerusalem. [28]He died at a good old age, having enjoyed long life, wealth and honour. His son Solomon succeeded him as king.

[29]As for the events of King David's reign, from beginning to end, they are written in the records of Samuel the seer, the records of Nathan the prophet and the records of Gad the seer, [30]together with the details of his reign and power, and the circumstances that surrounded him and Israel and the kingdoms of all the other lands.

NEW TESTAMENT READING
1 Corinthians 5:1–13

Expel the Immoral Brother!

5 It is actually reported that there is sexual immorality among you, and of a kind that does not occur even among pagans: A man has his father's wife. [2]And you are proud! Shouldn't you rather have been filled with grief and have put out of your fellowship the man who did this? [3]Even though I am not physically present, I am with you in

spirit. And I have already passed judgment on the one who did this, just as if I were present. ⁴When you are assembled in the name of our Lord Jesus and I am with you in spirit, and the power of our Lord Jesus is present, ⁵hand this man over to Satan, so that the sinful nature may be destroyed and his spirit saved on the day of the Lord.

⁶Your boasting is not good. Don't you know that a little yeast works through the whole batch of dough? ⁷Get rid of the old yeast that you may be a new batch without yeast—as you really are. For Christ, our Passover lamb, has been sacrificed. ⁸Therefore let us keep the Festival, not with the old yeast, the yeast of malice and wickedness, but with bread without yeast, the bread of sincerity and truth.

⁹I have written to you in my letter not to associate with sexually immoral people—¹⁰not at all meaning the people of this world who are immoral, or the greedy and swindlers, or idolaters. In that case you would have to leave this world. ¹¹But now I am writing to you that you must not associate with anyone who calls himself a brother but is sexually immoral or greedy, an idolater or a slanderer, a drunkard or a swindler. With such a man do not even eat.

¹²What business is it of mine to judge those outside the church? Are you not to judge those inside? ¹³God will judge those outside. "Expel the wicked man from among you."

READING FROM PSALMS
Psalm 93:1–5

¹The LORD reigns, he is robed in
majesty;
the LORD is robed in majesty
and is armed with strength.
The world is firmly established;
it cannot be moved.
²Your throne was established long
ago;
you are from all eternity.

³The seas have lifted up, O LORD,
the seas have lifted up their voice;
the seas have lifted up their
pounding waves.
⁴Mightier than the thunder of the
great waters,
mightier than the breakers of the
sea—
the LORD on high is mighty.

⁵Your statutes stand firm;
holiness adorns your house
for endless days, O LORD.

DAY 222

AUGUST 10

OLD TESTAMENT READING
2 Chronicles 1:1–17

Solomon Asks for Wisdom

1 Solomon son of David established himself firmly over his kingdom, for the LORD his God was with him and made him exceedingly great.

²Then Solomon spoke to all Israel —to the commanders of thousands and commanders of hundreds, to the judges and to all the leaders in Israel, the heads of families—³and Solomon and the whole assembly went to the high place at Gibeon, for God's Tent of Meeting was there, which Moses the LORD's servant had made in the desert. ⁴Now David had brought up the ark of God from Kiriath Jearim to the place he had prepared for it, because he had pitched a tent for it in Jerusalem. ⁵But the bronze altar that Bezalel son of Uri, the son of Hur, had made was in Gibeon in

front of the tabernacle of the LORD; so Solomon and the assembly enquired of him there. 6Solomon went up to the bronze altar before the LORD in the Tent of Meeting and offered a thousand burnt offerings on it.

7That night God appeared to Solomon and said to him, "Ask for whatever you want me to give you."

8Solomon answered God, "You have shown great kindness to David my father and have made me king in his place. 9Now, LORD God, let your promise to my father David be confirmed, for you have made me king over a people who are as numerous as the dust of the earth. 10Give me wisdom and knowledge, that I may lead this people, for who is able to govern this great people of yours?"

11God said to Solomon, "Since this is your heart's desire and you have not asked for wealth, riches or honour, nor for the death of your enemies, and since you have not asked for a long life but for wisdom and knowledge to govern my people over whom I have made you king, 12therefore wisdom and knowledge will be given you. And I will also give you wealth, riches and honour, such as no king who was before you ever had and none after you will have."

13Then Solomon went to Jerusalem from the high place at Gibeon, from before the Tent of Meeting. And he reigned over Israel.

14Solomon accumulated chariots and horses; he had fourteen hundred chariots and twelve thousand horses, which he kept in the chariot cities and also with him in Jerusalem. 15The king made silver and gold as common in Jerusalem as stones, and cedar as plentiful as sycamore-fig trees in the foothills. 16Solomon's horses were imported from Egypt and from Kue—the royal merchants purchased them from Kue. 17They imported a chariot from Egypt for six hundred shekels of silver, and a horse for a hundred and fifty. They also exported them to all the kings of the Hittites and of the Arameans.

NEW TESTAMENT READING
1 Corinthians 6:1–20

Lawsuits Among Believers

6 If any of you has a dispute with another, dare he take it before the ungodly for judgment instead of before the saints? 2Do you not know that the saints will judge the world? And if you are to judge the world, are you not competent to judge trivial cases? 3Do you not know that we will judge angels? How much more the things of this life! 4Therefore, if you have disputes about such matters, appoint as judges even men of little account in the church! 5I say this to shame you. Is it possible that there is nobody among you wise enough to judge a dispute between believers? 6But instead, one brother goes to law against another—and this in front of unbelievers!

7The very fact that you have lawsuits among you means you have been completely defeated already. Why not rather be wronged? Why not rather be cheated? 8Instead, you yourselves cheat and do wrong, and you do this to your brothers.

9Do you not know that the wicked will not inherit the kingdom of God? Do not be deceived: Neither the sexually immoral nor idolaters nor adulterers nor male prostitutes nor homosexual offenders 10nor thieves nor the greedy nor drunkards nor slanderers nor swindlers will inherit the kingdom of God. 11And that is what some of you were. But you were washed, you were sanctified, you were justified in the name of the Lord Jesus Christ and by the Spirit of our God.

Sexual Immorality

12"Everything is permissible for me" —but not everything is beneficial. "Everything is permissible for me"— but I will not be mastered by anything. 13"Food for the stomach and the stomach for food"—but God will destroy them both. The body is not meant for sexual immorality, but for the Lord, and the Lord for the body. [14]By his power God raised the Lord from the dead, and he will raise us also. [15]Do you not know that your bodies are members of Christ himself? Shall I then take the members of Christ and unite them with a prostitute? Never! [16]Do you not know that he who unites himself with a prostitute is one with her in body? For it is said, "The two will become one flesh." [17]But he who unites himself with the Lord is one with him in spirit.

[18]Flee from sexual immorality. All other sins a man commits are outside his body, but he who sins sexually sins against his own body. [19]Do you not know that your body is a temple of the Holy Spirit, who is in you, whom you have received from God? You are not your own; [20]you were bought at a price. Therefore honour God with your body.

READING FROM PSALMS
Psalm 94:1–11

[1]O Lord, the God who avenges,
    O God who avenges, shine forth.
[2]Rise up, O Judge of the earth;

pay back to the proud what they
    deserve.
[3]How long will the wicked, O Lord,
    how long will the wicked be
    jubilant?

[4]They pour out arrogant words;
    all the evildoers are full of
    boasting.
[5]They crush your people, O Lord;
    they oppress your inheritance.
[6]They slay the widow and the alien;
    they murder the fatherless.
[7]They say, "The Lord does not see;
    the God of Jacob pays no heed."

[8]Take heed, you senseless ones among
    the people;
    you fools, when will you become
    wise?
[9]Does he who implanted the ear not
    hear?
    Does he who formed the eye not
    see?
[10]Does he who disciplines nations not
    punish?
    Does he who teaches man lack
    knowledge?
[11]The Lord knows the thoughts of
    man;
    he knows that they are futile.

DAY 223

AUGUST 11

OLD TESTAMENT READING
Ecclesiastes 1:1–3:22

Everything Is Meaningless

1   The words of the Teacher, son of
    David, king of Jerusalem:

[2]"Meaningless! Meaningless!"
    says the Teacher.
  "Utterly meaningless!
    Everything is meaningless."

[3]What does man gain from all his
    labour
    at which he toils under the sun?
[4]Generations come and generations
    go,
    but the earth remains for ever.
[5]The sun rises and the sun sets,
    and hurries back to where it rises.
[6]The wind blows to the south
    and turns to the north;
  round and round it goes,
    ever returning on its course.

7All streams flow into the sea,
  yet the sea is never full.
To the place the streams come from,
  there they return again.
8All things are wearisome,
  more than one can say.
The eye never has enough of seeing,
  nor the ear its fill of hearing.
9What has been will be again,
  what has been done will be done
    again;
  there is nothing new under the sun.
10Is there anything of which one can
    say,
  "Look! This is something new"?
It was here already, long ago;
  it was here before our time.
11There is no remembrance of men of
    old,
  and even those who are yet to
    come
will not be remembered
  by those who follow.

Wisdom Is Meaningless

12I, the Teacher, was king over Israel in Jerusalem. 13I devoted myself to study and to explore by wisdom all that is done under heaven. What a heavy burden God has laid on men! 14I have seen all the things that are done under the sun; all of them are meaningless, a chasing after the wind.

15What is twisted cannot be
    straightened;
  what is lacking cannot be counted.

16I thought to myself, "Look, I have grown and increased in wisdom more than anyone who has ruled over Jerusalem before me; I have experienced much of wisdom and knowledge." 17Then I applied myself to the understanding of wisdom, and also of madness and folly, but I learned that this, too, is a chasing after the wind.

18For with much wisdom comes much
    sorrow;
  the more knowledge, the more
    grief.

Pleasures Are Meaningless

2 I thought in my heart, "Come now, I will test you with pleasure to find out what is good." But that also proved to be meaningless. 2"Laughter," I said, "is foolish. And what does pleasure accomplish?" 3I tried cheering myself with wine, and embracing folly—my mind still guiding me with wisdom. I wanted to see what was worth while for men to do under heaven during the few days of their lives.

4I undertook great projects: I built houses for myself and planted vineyards. 5I made gardens and parks and planted all kinds of fruit trees in them. 6I made reservoirs to water groves of flourishing trees. 7I bought male and female slaves and had other slaves who were born in my house. I also owned more herds and flocks than anyone in Jerusalem before me. 8I amassed silver and gold for myself, and the treasure of kings and provinces. I acquired men and women singers, and a harem as well—the delights of the heart of man. 9I became greater by far than anyone in Jerusalem before me. In all this my wisdom stayed with me.

10I denied myself nothing my eyes
    desired;
  I refused my heart no pleasure.
My heart took delight in all my work,
  and this was the reward for all my
    labour.
11Yet when I surveyed all that my
    hands had done
  and what I had toiled to achieve,
everything was meaningless, a
    chasing after the wind;
  nothing was gained under the sun.

Wisdom and Folly Are Meaningless

12Then I turned my thoughts to
    consider wisdom,
  and also madness and folly.
What more can the king's successor
    do
  than what has already been done?

13I saw that wisdom is better than folly,
just as light is better than darkness.
14The wise man has eyes in his head,
while the fool walks in the
darkness;
but I came to realise
that the same fate overtakes them
both.

15Then I thought in my heart,

"The fate of the fool will overtake me
also.
What then do I gain by being
wise?"
I said in my heart,
"This too is meaningless."
16For the wise man, like the fool, will
not be long remembered;
in days to come both will be
forgotten.
Like the fool, the wise man too must
die!

Toil Is Meaningless

17So I hated life, because the work
that is done under the sun was grievous
to me. All of it is meaningless, a chasing
after the wind. 18I hated all the things I
had toiled for under the sun, because I
must leave them to the one who comes
after me. 19And who knows whether he
will be a wise man or a fool? Yet he will
have control over all the work into
which I have poured my effort and skill
under the sun. This too is meaningless.
20So my heart began to despair over all
my toilsome labour under the sun. 21For
a man may do his work with wisdom,
knowledge and skill, and then he must
leave all he owns to someone who has
not worked for it. This too is meaningless and a great misfortune. 22What
does a man get for all the toil and
anxious striving with which he labours
under the sun? 23All his days his work is
pain and grief; even at night his mind
does not rest. This too is meaningless.

24A man can do nothing better than to
eat and drink and find satisfaction in his
work. This too, I see, is from the hand

of God, 25for without him, who can eat
or find enjoyment? 26To the man who
pleases him, God gives wisdom, knowledge and happiness, but to the sinner he
gives the task of gathering and storing
up wealth to hand it over to the one who
pleases God. This too is meaningless, a
chasing after the wind.

A Time for Everything

3 There is a time for everything,
and a season for every activity
under heaven:

2 a time to be born and a time to die,
a time to plant and a time to
uproot,
3 a time to kill and a time to heal,
a time to tear down and a time to
build,
4 a time to weep and a time to laugh,
a time to mourn and a time to
dance,
5 a time to scatter stones and a time
to gather them,
a time to embrace and a time to
refrain,
6 a time to search and a time to give
up,
a time to keep and a time to throw
away,
7 a time to tear and a time to mend,
a time to be silent and a time to
speak,
8 a time to love and a time to hate,
a time for war and a time for
peace.

9What does the worker gain from his
toil? 10I have seen the burden God has
laid on men. 11He has made everything
beautiful in its time. He has also set
eternity in the hearts of men; yet they
cannot fathom what God has done from
beginning to end. 12I know that there is
nothing better for men than to be happy
and do good while they live. 13That
everyone may eat and drink, and find
satisfaction in all his toil—this is the gift
of God. 14I know that everything God
does will endure for ever; nothing can

be added to it and nothing taken from it. God does it so that men will revere him.

15Whatever is has already been,
   and what will be has been before;
   and God will call the past to
      account.

16And I saw something else under the sun:

In the place of judgment—
   wickedness was there,
  in the place of justice—wickedness
   was there.

17I thought in my heart,

"God will bring to judgment
  both the righteous and the wicked,
for there will be a time for every
   activity,
a time for every deed."

18I also thought, "As for men, God tests them so that they may see that they are like the animals. 19Man's fate is like that of the animals; the same fate awaits them both: As one dies, so dies the other. All have the same breath; man has no advantage over the animal. Everything is meaningless. 20All go to the same place; all come from dust, and to dust all return. 21Who knows if the spirit of man rises upward and if the spirit of the animal goes down into the earth?"

22So I saw that there is nothing better for a man than to enjoy his work, because that is his lot. For who can bring him to see what will happen after him?

NEW TESTAMENT READING
1 Corinthians 7:1–16

Marriage

7 Now for the matters you wrote about: It is good for a man not to marry. 2But since there is so much immorality, each man should have his own wife, and each woman her own husband. 3The husband should fulfil his marital duty to his wife, and likewise the wife to her husband. 4The wife's body does not belong to her alone but also to her husband. In the same way, the husband's body does not belong to him alone but also to his wife. 5Do not deprive each other except by mutual consent and for a time, so that you may devote yourselves to prayer. Then come together again so that Satan will not tempt you because of your lack of self-control. 6I say this as a concession, not as a command. 7I wish that all men were as I am. But each man has his own gift from God; one has this gift, another has that.

8Now to the unmarried and the widows I say: It is good for them to stay unmarried, as I am. 9But if they cannot control themselves, they should marry, for it is better to marry than to burn with passion.

10To the married I give this command (not I, but the Lord): A wife must not separate from her husband. 11But if she does, she must remain unmarried or else be reconciled to her husband. And a husband must not divorce his wife.

12To the rest I say this (I, not the Lord): If any brother has a wife who is not a believer and she is willing to live with him, he must not divorce her. 13And if a woman has a husband who is not a believer and he is willing to live with her, she must not divorce him. 14For the unbelieving husband has been sanctified through his wife, and the unbelieving wife has been sanctified through her believing husband. Otherwise your children would be unclean, but as it is, they are holy.

15But if the unbeliever leaves, let him do so. A believing man or woman is not bound in such circumstances; God has called us to live in peace. 16How do you know, wife, whether you will save your husband? Or, how do you know, husband, whether you will save your wife?

READING FROM PSALMS
Psalm 94:12–23

¹²Blessed is the man you discipline, O
　　LORD,
　　the man you teach from your law;
¹³you grant him relief from days of
　　trouble,
　　till a pit is dug for the wicked.
¹⁴For the LORD will not reject his
　　people;
　　he will never forsake his
　　inheritance.
¹⁵Judgment will again be founded on
　　righteousness,
　　and all the upright in heart will
　　follow it.

¹⁶Who will rise up for me against the
　　wicked?
　　Who will take a stand for me
　　against evildoers?
¹⁷Unless the LORD had given me help,
　　I would soon have dwelt in the
　　silence of death.

¹⁸When I said, "My foot is slipping,"
　　your love, O LORD, supported
　　me.
¹⁹When anxiety was great within me,
　　your consolation brought joy to my
　　soul.

²⁰Can a corrupt throne be allied with
　　you—
　　one that brings on misery by its
　　decrees?
²¹They band together against the
　　righteous
　　and condemn the innocent to
　　death.
²²But the LORD has become my
　　fortress,
　　and my God the rock in whom I
　　take refuge.
²³He will repay them for their sins
　　and destroy them for their
　　wickedness;
　　the LORD our God will destroy
　　them.

DAY 224

AUGUST 12

OLD TESTAMENT READING
Ecclesiastes 4:1–6:12

Oppression, Toil, Friendlessness

4 Again I looked and saw all the
　oppression that was taking place
under the sun:

　I saw the tears of the oppressed—
　　and they have no comforter;
　power was on the side of their
　　oppressors—
　　and they have no comforter.
²And I declared that the dead,
　who had already died,
　are happier than the living,
　who are still alive.
³But better than both
　is he who has not yet been,
who has not seen the evil
　that is done under the sun.

⁴And I saw that all labour and all
achievement spring from man's envy of
his neighbour. This too is meaningless,
a chasing after the wind.

⁵The fool folds his hands
　and ruins himself.
⁶Better one handful with tranquillity
　than two handfuls with toil
　and chasing after the wind.

⁷Again I saw something meaningless
under the sun:

⁸There was a man all alone;
　he had neither son nor brother.

There was no end to his toil,
yet his eyes were not content with
his wealth.
"For whom am I toiling," he asked,
"and why am I depriving myself of
enjoyment?"
This too is meaningless—
a miserable business!

9Two are better than one,
because they have a good return
for their work:
10If one falls down,
his friend can help him up.
But pity the man who falls
and has no-one to help him up!
11Also, if two lie down together, they
will keep warm.
But how can one keep warm
alone?
12Though one may be overpowered,
two can defend themselves.
A cord of three strands is not quickly
broken.

Advancement Is Meaningless

13Better a poor but wise youth than
an old but foolish king who no longer
knows how to take warning. 14The
youth may have come from prison to the
kingship, or he may have been born in
poverty within his kingdom. 15I saw that
all who lived and walked under the sun
followed the youth, the king's successor. 16There was no end to all the
people who were before them. But
those who came later were not pleased
with the successor. This too is meaningless, a chasing after the wind.

Stand in Awe of God

5 Guard your steps when you go to
the house of God. Go near to listen
rather than to offer the sacrifice of fools,
who do not know that they do wrong.

2Do not be quick with your mouth,
do not be hasty in your heart
to utter anything before God.

God is in heaven
and you are on earth,
so let your words be few.
3As a dream comes when there are
many cares,
so the speech of a fool when there
are many words.

4When you make a vow to God, do
not delay in fulfilling it. He has no
pleasure in fools; fulfil your vow. 5It is
better not to vow than to make a vow
and not fulfil it. 6Do not let your mouth
lead you into sin. And do not protest to
the ˪temple˩ messenger, "My vow was a
mistake." Why should God be angry at
what you say and destroy the work of
your hands? 7Much dreaming and many
words are meaningless. Therefore stand
in awe of God.

Riches Are Meaningless

8If you see the poor oppressed in a
district, and justice and rights denied,
do not be surprised at such things; for
one official is eyed by a higher one, and
over them both are others higher still.
9The increase from the land is taken by
all; the king himself profits from the
fields.

10Whoever loves money never has
money enough;
whoever loves wealth is never
satisfied with his income.
This too is meaningless.

11As goods increase,
so do those who consume them.
And what benefit are they to the
owner
except to feast his eyes on them?

12The sleep of a labourer is sweet,
whether he eats little or much,
but the abundance of a rich man
permits him no sleep.

13I have seen a grievous evil under the
sun:

wealth hoarded to the harm of its
    owner,
14   or wealth lost through some
    misfortune,
so that when he has a son
    there is nothing left for him.
15Naked a man comes from his
    mother's womb,
    and as he comes, so he departs.
He takes nothing from his labour
    that he can carry in his hand.

16This too is a grievous evil:

As a man comes, so he departs,
    and what does he gain,
    since he toils for the wind?
17All his days he eats in darkness,
    with great frustration, affliction
        and anger.

18Then I realised that it is good and
proper for a man to eat and drink, and
to find satisfaction in his toilsome
labour under the sun during the few
days of life God has given him—for this
is his lot. 19Moreover, when God gives
any man wealth and possessions, and
enables him to enjoy them, to accept his
lot and be happy in his work—this is a
gift of God. 20He seldom reflects on the
days of his life, because God keeps him
occupied with gladness of heart.

6 I have seen another evil under the
sun, and it weighs heavily on men:
2God gives a man wealth, possessions
and honour, so that he lacks nothing his
heart desires, but God does not enable
him to enjoy them, and a stranger enjoys them instead. This is meaningless,
a grievous evil.

3A man may have a hundred children
and live many years; yet no matter how
long he lives, if he cannot enjoy his
prosperity and does not receive proper
burial, I say that a stillborn child is
better off than he. 4It comes without
meaning, it departs in darkness, and in
darkness its name is shrouded. 5Though
it never saw the sun or knew anything, it
has more rest than does that man—

6even if he lives a thousand years twice
over but fails to enjoy his prosperity.
Do not all go to the same place?

7All man's efforts are for his mouth,
    yet his appetite is never satisfied.
8What advantage has a wise man
    over a fool?
What does a poor man gain
    by knowing how to conduct himself
        before others?
9Better what the eye sees
    than the roving of the appetite.
This too is meaningless,
    a chasing after the wind.

10Whatever exists has already been
    named,
    and what man is has been known;
no man can contend
    with one who is stronger than he.
11The more the words,
    the less the meaning,
    and how does that profit anyone?

12For who knows what is good for a
man in life, during the few and
meaningless days he passes through like
a shadow? Who can tell him what will
happen under the sun after he is gone?

NEW TESTAMENT READING
1 Corinthians 7:17–35

17Nevertheless, each one should retain the place in life that the Lord
assigned to him and to which God has
called him. This is the rule I lay down in
all the churches. 18Was a man already
circumcised when he was called? He
should not become uncircumcised. Was
a man uncircumcised when he was
called? He should not be circumcised.
19Circumcision is nothing and uncircumcision is nothing. Keeping God's
commands is what counts. 20Each one
should remain in the situation which he
was in when God called him. 21Were
you a slave when you were called?
Don't let it trouble you—although if

you can gain your freedom, do so. 22For he who was a slave when he was called by the Lord is the Lord's freedman; similarly, he who was a free man when he was called is Christ's slave. 23You were bought at a price; do not become slaves of men. 24Brothers, each man, as responsible to God, should remain in the situation God called him to.

25Now about virgins: I have no command from the Lord, but I give a judgment as one who by the Lord's mercy is trustworthy. 26Because of the present crisis, I think that it is good for you to remain as you are. 27Are you married? Do not seek a divorce. Are you unmarried? Do not look for a wife. 28But if you do marry, you have not sinned; and if a virgin marries, she has not sinned. But those who marry will face many troubles in this life, and I want to spare you this.

29What I mean, brothers, is that the time is short. From now on those who have wives should live as if they had none; 30those who mourn, as if they did not; those who are happy, as if they were not; those who buy something, as if it were not theirs to keep; 31those who use the things of the world, as if not engrossed in them. For this world in its present form is passing away.

32I would like you to be free from concern. An unmarried man is concerned about the Lord's affairs—how he can please the Lord. 33But a married man is concerned about the affairs of this world—how he can please his wife —34and his interests are divided. An unmarried woman or virgin is concerned about the Lord's affairs: Her aim is to be devoted to the Lord in both body and spirit. But a married woman is concerned about the affairs of this world—how she can please her husband. 35I am saying this for your own good, not to restrict you, but that you may live in a right way in undivided devotion to the Lord.

READING FROM PROVERBS
Proverbs 19:23—20:4

23The fear of the LORD leads to life:
Then one rests content, untouched
by trouble.

24The sluggard buries his hand in the
dish;
he will not even bring it back to his
mouth!

25Flog a mocker, and the simple will
learn prudence;
rebuke a discerning man, and he
will gain knowledge.

26He who robs his father and drives out
his mother
is a son who brings shame and
disgrace.

27Stop listening to instruction, my son,
and you will stray from the words
of knowledge.

28A corrupt witness mocks at justice,
and the mouth of the wicked gulps
down evil.

29Penalties are prepared for mockers,
and beatings for the backs of fools.

20 Wine is a mocker and beer a
brawler;
whoever is led astray by them is
not wise.

2A king's wrath is like the roar of a
lion;
he who angers him forfeits his life.

3It is to a man's honour to avoid strife,
but every fool is quick to quarrel.

4A sluggard does not plough in
season;
so at harvest time he looks but
finds nothing.

OLD TESTAMENT READING
Ecclesiastes 7:1–9:12

Wisdom

7 A good name is better than fine
perfume,
  and the day of death better than
  the day of birth.
2It is better to go to a house of
mourning
  than to go to a house of feasting,
for death is the destiny of every man;
  the living should take this to heart.
3Sorrow is better than laughter,
  because a sad face is good for the
  heart.
4The heart of the wise is in the house
of mourning,
  but the heart of fools is in the
  house of pleasure.
5It is better to heed a wise man's
rebuke
  than to listen to the song of fools.
6Like the crackling of thorns under
the pot,
  so is the laughter of fools.
  This too is meaningless.

7Extortion turns a wise man into a
fool,
  and a bribe corrupts the heart.

8The end of a matter is better than its
beginning,
  and patience is better than pride.
9Do not be quickly provoked in your
spirit,
  for anger resides in the lap of fools.

10Do not say, "Why were the old days
better than these?"
  For it is not wise to ask such
  questions.

11Wisdom, like an inheritance, is a
good thing
  and benefits those who see the sun.

12Wisdom is a shelter
  as money is a shelter,
but the advantage of knowledge is
this:
  that wisdom preserves the life of its
  possessor.

13Consider what God has done:

Who can straighten
  what he has made crooked?
14When times are good, be happy;
  but when times are bad, consider:
God has made the one
  as well as the other.
Therefore, a man cannot discover
  anything about his future.

15In this meaningless life of mine I
have seen both of these:

a righteous man perishing in his
righteousness,
  and a wicked man living long in his
  wickedness.
16Do not be over-righteous,
  neither be overwise—
  why destroy yourself?
17Do not be overwicked,
  and do not be a fool—
  why die before your time?
18It is good to grasp the one
  and not let go of the other.
  The man who fears God will avoid
  all ⌊extremes⌋.

19Wisdom makes one wise man more
powerful
  than ten rulers in a city.

20There is not a righteous man on earth
  who does what is right and never
  sins.

21Do not pay attention to every word
people say,
  or you may hear your servant
  cursing you—

22for you know in your heart
  that many times you yourself have
    cursed others.

23All this I tested by wisdom and I said,

"I am determined to be wise"—
  but this was beyond me.
24Whatever wisdom may be,
  it is far off and most profound—
    who can discover it?
25So I turned my mind to understand,
  to investigate and to search out
    wisdom and the scheme of
    things
and to understand the stupidity of
    wickedness
  and the madness of folly.

26I find more bitter than death
  the woman who is a snare,
whose heart is a trap
  and whose hands are chains.
The man who pleases God will escape
    her,
  but the sinner she will ensnare.

27"Look," says the Teacher, "this is
what I have discovered:

"Adding one thing to another to
    discover the scheme of things—
28 while I was still searching
    but not finding—
I found one ⌐upright⌐ man among a
    thousand,
  but not one ⌐upright⌐ woman
    among them all.
29This only have I found:
  God made mankind upright,
  but men have gone in search of
    many schemes."

8 Who is like the wise man?
   Who knows the explanation of
   things?
Wisdom brightens a man's face
  and changes its hard appearance.

Obey the King

2Obey the king's command, I say,
because you took an oath before God.

3Do not be in a hurry to leave the king's
presence. Do not stand up for a bad
cause, for he will do whatever he
pleases. 4Since a king's word is
supreme, who can say to him, "What
are you doing?"

5Whoever obeys his command will
    come to no harm,
  and the wise heart will know the
    proper time and procedure.
6For there is a proper time and
    procedure for every matter,
  though a man's misery weighs
    heavily upon him.

7Since no man knows the future,
  who can tell him what is to come?
8No man has power over the wind to
    contain it;
  so no-one has power over the day
    of his death.
As no-one is discharged in time of
    war,
  so wickedness will not release
    those who practise it.

9All this I saw, as I applied my mind
to everything done under the sun.
There is a time when a man lords it over
others to his own hurt. 10Then too, I saw
the wicked buried—those who used to
come and go from the holy place and
receive praise in the city where they did
this. This too is meaningless.
11When the sentence for a crime is not
quickly carried out, the hearts of the
people are filled with schemes to do
wrong. 12Although a wicked man commits a hundred crimes and still lives a
long time, I know that it will go better
with God-fearing men, who are reverent before God. 13Yet because the
wicked do not fear God, it will not go
well with them, and their days will not
lengthen like a shadow.
14There is something else meaningless that occurs on earth: righteous men
who get what the wicked deserve, and
wicked men who get what the righteous
deserve. This too, I say, is meaningless.
15So I commend the enjoyment of life,

because nothing is better for a man under the sun than to eat and drink and be glad. Then joy will accompany him in his work all the days of the life God has given him under the sun.

16When I applied my mind to know wisdom and to observe man's labour on earth—his eyes not seeing sleep day or night—17then I saw all that God has done. No-one can comprehend what goes on under the sun. Despite all his efforts to search it out, man cannot discover its meaning. Even if a wise man claims he knows, he cannot really comprehend it.

A Common Destiny for All

9 So I reflected on all this and concluded that the righteous and the wise and what they do are in God's hands, but no man knows whether love or hate awaits him. 2All share a common destiny—the righteous and the wicked, the good and the bad, the clean and the unclean, those who offer sacrifices and those who do not.

As it is with the good man,
　　so with the sinner;
as it is with those who take oaths,
　　so with those who are afraid to
　　　　take them.

3This is the evil in everything that happens under the sun: The same destiny overtakes all. The hearts of men, moreover, are full of evil and there is madness in their hearts while they live, and afterwards they join the dead. 4Anyone who is among the living has hope—even a live dog is better off than a dead lion!

5For the living know that they will die,
　　but the dead know nothing;
they have no further reward,
　　and even the memory of them is
　　　　forgotten.

6Their love, their hate
　　and their jealousy have long since
　　　　vanished;

never again will they have a part
　　in anything that happens under the
　　　　sun.

7Go, eat your food with gladness, and drink your wine with a joyful heart, for it is now that God favours what you do. 8Always be clothed in white, and always anoint your head with oil. 9Enjoy life with your wife, whom you love, all the days of this meaningless life that God has given you under the sun—all your meaningless days. For this is your lot in life and in your toilsome labour under the sun. 10Whatever your hand finds to do, do it with all your might, for in the grave, where you are going, there is neither working nor planning nor knowledge nor wisdom.

11I have seen something else under the sun:

The race is not to the swift
　　or the battle to the strong,
nor does food come to the wise
　　or wealth to the brilliant
　　or favour to the learned;
but time and chance happen to them
　　all.

12Moreover, no man knows when his hour will come:

As fish are caught in a cruel net,
　　or birds are taken in a snare,
so men are trapped by evil times
　　that fall unexpectedly upon them.

NEW TESTAMENT READING
1 Corinthians 7:36—8:13

36If anyone thinks he is acting improperly towards the virgin he is engaged to, and if she is getting on in years and he feels he ought to marry, he should do as he wants. He is not sinning. They should get married. 37But the man who has settled the matter in his own mind, who is under no compulsion but has control over his own will, and who has made up his mind not to marry the virgin—this man also does the right thing. 38So then, he who marries the virgin does right, but he who does not marry her does even better.

39A woman is bound to her husband as long as he lives. But if her husband dies, she is free to marry anyone she wishes, but he must belong to the Lord. 40In my judgment, she is happier if she stays as she is—and I think that I too have the Spirit of God.

Food Sacrificed to Idols

8 Now about food sacrificed to idols: We know that we all possess knowledge. Knowledge puffs up, but love builds up. 2The man who thinks he knows something does not yet know as he ought to know. 3But the man who loves God is known by God.

4So then, about eating food sacrificed to idols: We know that an idol is nothing at all in the world and that there is no God but one. 5For even if there are so-called gods, whether in heaven or on earth (as indeed there are many "gods" and many "lords"), 6yet for us there is but one God, the Father, from whom all things came and for whom we live; and there is but one Lord, Jesus Christ, through whom all things came and through whom we live.

7But not everyone knows this. Some people are still so accustomed to idols that when they eat such food they think of it as having been sacrificed to an idol, and since their conscience is weak, it is defiled. 8But food does not bring us near to God; we are no worse if we do not eat, and no better if we do.

9Be careful, however, that the exercise of your freedom does not become a stumbling-block to the weak. 10For if anyone with a weak conscience sees you who have this knowledge eating in an idol's temple, won't he be emboldened to eat what has been sacrificed to idols? 11So this weak brother, for whom Christ died, is destroyed by your knowledge.

12When you sin against your brothers in this way and wound their weak conscience, you sin against Christ. 13Therefore, if what I eat causes my brother to fall into sin, I will never eat meat again, so that I will not cause him to fall.

READING FROM PSALMS
Psalm 95:1–11

1Come, let us sing for joy to the LORD;
　　let us shout aloud to the Rock of
　　　　our salvation.
2Let us come before him with
　　thanksgiving
　　and extol him with music and song.

3For the LORD is the great God,
　　the great King above all gods.
4In his hand are the depths of the
　　earth,
　　and the mountain peaks belong to
　　　　him.
5The sea is his, for he made it,
　　and his hands formed the dry land.

6Come, let us bow down in worship,
　　let us kneel before the LORD our
　　　　Maker;
7for he is our God
　　and we are the people of his
　　　　pasture,
　　the flock under his care.

Today, if you hear his voice,
8　do not harden your hearts as you
　　　　did at Meribah,
　　as you did that day at Massah in the
　　　　desert,
9where your fathers tested and tried
　　　　me,
　　though they had seen what I did.
10For forty years I was angry with that
　　generation;
　　I said, "They are a people whose
　　　　hearts go astray,
　　and they have not known my
　　　　ways."
11So I declared on oath in my anger,
　　"They shall never enter my rest."

AUGUST 14

OLD TESTAMENT READING
Ecclesiastes 9:13–12:14

Wisdom Better Than Folly

13I also saw under the sun this example of wisdom that greatly impressed me: 14There was once a small city with only a few people in it. And a powerful king came against it, surrounded it and built huge siegeworks against it. 15Now there lived in that city a man poor but wise, and he saved the city by his wisdom. But nobody remembered that poor man. 16So I said, "Wisdom is better than strength." But the poor man's wisdom is despised, and his words are no longer heeded.

17The quiet words of the wise are more to be heeded
    than the shouts of a ruler of fools.
18Wisdom is better than weapons of war,
    but one sinner destroys much good.

10 As dead flies give perfume a bad smell,
    so a little folly outweighs wisdom and honour.
2The heart of the wise inclines to the right,
    but the heart of the fool to the left.
3Even as he walks along the road,
    the fool lacks sense
    and shows everyone how stupid he is.
4If a ruler's anger rises against you,
    do not leave your post;
    calmness can lay great errors to rest.

5There is an evil I have seen under the sun,
    the sort of error that arises from a ruler:
6Fools are put in many high positions,
    while the rich occupy the low ones.

7I have seen slaves on horseback,
    while princes go on foot like slaves.

8Whoever digs a pit may fall into it;
    whoever breaks through a wall
    may be bitten by a snake.
9Whoever quarries stones may be injured by them;
    whoever splits logs may be endangered by them.

10If the axe is dull
    and its edge unsharpened,
more strength is needed
    but skill will bring success.

11If a snake bites before it is charmed,
    there is no profit for the charmer.

12Words from a wise man's mouth are gracious,
    but a fool is consumed by his own lips.
13At the beginning his words are folly;
    at the end they are wicked madness—
14   and the fool multiplies words.

No-one knows what is coming—
    who can tell him what will happen after him?

15A fool's work wearies him;
    he does not know the way to town.

16Woe to you, O land whose king was a servant
    and whose princes feast in the morning.
17Blessed are you, O land whose king is of noble birth
    and whose princes eat at a proper time—
    for strength and not for drunkenness.

18If a man is lazy, the rafters sag;
    if his hands are idle, the house leaks.

¹⁹A feast is made for laughter,
and wine makes life merry,
but money is the answer for
everything.

²⁰Do not revile the king even in your
thoughts,
or curse the rich in your bedroom,
because a bird of the air may carry
your words,
and a bird on the wing may report
what you say.

Bread Upon the Waters

11 Cast your bread upon the
waters,
for after many days you will find it
again.
²Give portions to seven, yes to eight,
for you do not know what disaster
may come upon the land.

³If clouds are full of water,
they pour rain upon the earth.
Whether a tree falls to the south or to
the north,
in the place where it falls, there
will it lie.
⁴Whoever watches the wind will not
plant;
whoever looks at the clouds will
not reap.

⁵As you do not know the path of the
wind,
or how the body is formed in a
mother's womb,
so you cannot understand the work of
God,
the Maker of all things.

⁶Sow your seed in the morning,
and at evening let not your hands
be idle,
for you do not know which will
succeed,
whether this or that,
or whether both will do equally
well.

Remember Your Creator While Young

⁷Light is sweet,
and it pleases the eyes to see the
sun.
⁸However many years a man may live,
let him enjoy them all.
But let him remember the days of
darkness,
for they will be many.
Everything to come is meaningless.

⁹Be happy, young man, while you are
young,
and let your heart give you joy in
the days of your youth.
Follow the ways of your heart
and whatever your eyes see,
but know that for all these things
God will bring you to judgment.
¹⁰So then, banish anxiety from your
heart
and cast off the troubles of your
body,
for youth and vigour are
meaningless.

12 Remember your Creator
in the days of your youth,
before the days of trouble come
and the years approach when you
will say,
"I find no pleasure in them"—
²before the sun and the light
and the moon and the stars grow
dark,
and the clouds return after the
rain;
³when the keepers of the house
tremble,
and the strong men stoop,
when the grinders cease because they
are few,
and those looking through the
windows grow dim;
⁴when the doors to the street are
closed
and the sound of grinding fades;
when men rise up at the sound of
birds,
but all their songs grow faint;

5when men are afraid of heights
and of dangers in the streets;
when the almond tree blossoms
and the grasshopper drags himself
along
and desire no longer is stirred.
Then man goes to his eternal home
and mourners go about the streets.

6Remember him—before the silver
cord is severed,
or the golden bowl is broken;
before the pitcher is shattered at the
spring,
or the wheel broken at the well,
7and the dust returns to the ground it
came from,
and the spirit returns to God who
gave it.

8"Meaningless! Meaningless!" says
the Teacher.
"Everything is meaningless!"

The Conclusion of the Matter

9Not only was the Teacher wise, but
also he imparted knowledge to the people. He pondered and searched out
and set in order many proverbs. 10The
Teacher searched to find just the right
words, and what he wrote was upright
and true.

11The words of the wise are like
goads, their collected sayings like firmly
embedded nails—given by one
Shepherd. 12Be warned, my son, of anything in addition to them.

Of making many books there is no
end, and much study wearies the body.

13Now all has been heard;
here is the conclusion of the
matter:
Fear God and keep his
commandments,
for this is the whole ˌduty˩ of man.
14For God will bring every deed into
judgment,
including every hidden thing,
whether it is good or evil.

NEW TESTAMENT READING
1 Corinthians 9:1–18

The Rights of an Apostle

9 Am I not free? Am I not an
apostle? Have I not seen Jesus our
Lord? Are you not the result of my
work in the Lord? 2Even though I may
not be an apostle to others, surely I am
to you! For you are the seal of my
apostleship in the Lord.

3This is my defence to those who sit in
judgment on me. 4Don't we have the
right to food and drink? 5Don't we have
the right to take a believing wife along
with us, as do the other apostles and the
Lord's brothers and Cephas? 6Or is it
only I and Barnabas who must work for
a living?

7Who serves as a soldier at his own
expense? Who plants a vineyard and
does not eat of its grapes? Who tends a
flock and does not drink of the milk?
8Do I say this merely from a human
point of view? Doesn't the Law say the
same thing? 9For it is written in the Law
of Moses: "Do not muzzle an ox while it
is treading out the grain." Is it about
oxen that God is concerned? 10Surely he
says this for us, doesn't he? Yes, this
was written for us, because when the
ploughman ploughs and the thresher
threshes, they ought to do so in the hope
of sharing in the harvest. 11If we have
sown spiritual seed among you, is it too
much if we reap a material harvest from
you? 12If others have this right of support from you, shouldn't we have it all
the more?

But we did not use this right. On the
contrary, we put up with anything
rather than hinder the gospel of Christ.
13Don't you know that those who work
in the temple get their food from the
temple, and those who serve at the altar
share in what is offered on the altar?
14In the same way, the Lord has commanded that those who preach the gospel should receive their living from the
gospel.

15But I have not used any of these

rights. And I am not writing this in the hope that you will do such things for me. I would rather die than have anyone deprive me of this boast. 16Yet when I preach the gospel, I cannot boast, for I am compelled to preach. Woe to me if I do not preach the gospel! 17If I preach voluntarily, I have a reward; if not voluntarily, I am simply discharging the trust committed to me. 18What then is my reward? Just this: that in preaching the gospel I may offer it free of charge, and so not make use of my rights in preaching it.

READING FROM PSALMS
Psalm 96:1–13

1Sing to the LORD a new song;
　　sing to the LORD, all the earth.
2Sing to the LORD, praise his name;
　　proclaim his salvation day after
　　　day.
3Declare his glory among the nations,
　　his marvellous deeds among all
　　　peoples.

4For great is the LORD and most
　　worthy of praise;
　　he is to be feared above all gods.
5For all the gods of the nations are
　　idols,
　　but the LORD made the heavens.
6Splendour and majesty are before
　　him;
　　strength and glory are in his
　　　sanctuary.

7Ascribe to the LORD, O families of
　　nations,
　　ascribe to the LORD glory and
　　　strength.
8Ascribe to the LORD the glory due to
　　his name;
　　bring an offering and come into his
　　　courts.
9Worship the LORD in the splendour
　　of his holiness;
　　tremble before him, all the earth.

10Say among the nations, "The LORD
　　reigns."
　　The world is firmly established, it
　　　cannot be moved;
　　he will judge the peoples with
　　　equity.
11Let the heavens rejoice, let the earth
　　be glad;
　　let the sea resound, and all that is
　　　in it;
12　let the fields be jubilant, and
　　　everything in them.
　　Then all the trees of the forest will
　　　sing for joy;
13　they will sing before the LORD, for
　　　he comes,
　　he comes to judge the earth.
　　He will judge the world in
　　　righteousness
　　　and the peoples in his truth.

AUGUST 15　　　　　　　　DAY 227

OLD TESTAMENT READING
2 Chronicles 2:1–5:1

Preparations for Building the Temple

2 Solomon gave orders to build a temple for the Name of the LORD and a royal palace for himself. 2He conscripted seventy thousand men as carriers and eighty thousand as stone-cutters in the hills and thirty-six hundred as foremen over them.
3Solomon sent this message to Hiram king of Tyre:

　"Send me cedar logs as you did for my father David when you sent him cedar to build a palace to live in. ⁴Now I am about to build a temple for the Name of the LORD my God and to dedicate it to him for burning fragrant incense before him, for setting out the consecrated bread regularly, and for making burnt offerings every morning and evening and on Sabbaths and New Moons and at the appointed feasts of the LORD our God. This is a lasting ordinance for Israel.

⁵"The temple I am going to build will be great, because our God is greater than all other gods. ⁶But who is able to build a temple for him, since the heavens, even the highest heavens, cannot contain him? Who then am I to build a temple for him, except as a place to burn sacrifices before him?

⁷"Send me, therefore, a man skilled to work in gold and silver, bronze and iron, and in purple, crimson and blue yarn, and experienced in the art of engraving, to work in Judah and Jerusalem with my skilled craftsmen, whom my father David provided.

⁸"Send me also cedar, pine and algum logs from Lebanon, for I know that your men are skilled in cutting timber there. My men shall work with yours ⁹to provide me with plenty of timber, because the temple I build must be large and magnificent. ¹⁰I will give your servants, the woodsmen who cut the timber, twenty thousand cors of ground wheat, twenty thousand cors of barley, twenty thousand baths of wine and twenty thousand baths of olive oil."

¹¹Hiram king of Tyre replied by letter to Solomon:

"Because the LORD loves his people, he has made you their king."

¹²And Hiram added:

"Praise be to the LORD, the God of Israel, who made heaven and earth! He has given King David a wise son, endowed with intelligence and discernment, who will build a temple for the LORD and a palace for himself.

¹³"I am sending you Huram-Abi, a man of great skill, ¹⁴whose mother was from Dan and whose father was from Tyre. He is trained to work in gold and silver, bronze and iron, stone and wood, and with purple and blue and crimson yarn and fine linen. He is experienced in all kinds of engraving and can execute any design given to him. He will work with your craftsmen and with those of my lord, David your father.

¹⁵"Now let my lord send his servants the wheat and barley and the olive oil and wine he promised, ¹⁶and we will cut all the logs from Lebanon that you need and will float them in rafts by sea down to Joppa. You can then take them up to Jerusalem."

¹⁷Solomon took a census of all the aliens who were in Israel, after the census his father David had taken; and they were found to be 153,600. ¹⁸He assigned 70,000 of them to be carriers and 80,000 to be stonecutters in the hills, with 3,600 foremen over them to keep the people working.

Solomon Builds the Temple

3 Then Solomon began to build the temple of the LORD in Jerusalem on Mount Moriah, where the LORD had appeared to his father David. It was on the threshing-floor of Araunah the Jebusite, the place provided by David. ²He began building on the second day of the second month in the fourth year of his reign.

³The foundation Solomon laid for building the temple of God was sixty cubits long and twenty cubits wide

(using the cubit of the old standard). ⁴The portico at the front of the temple was twenty cubits long across the width of the building and twenty cubits high.

He overlaid the inside with pure gold. ⁵He panelled the main hall with pine and covered it with fine gold and decorated it with palm tree and chain designs. ⁶He adorned the temple with precious stones. And the gold he used was gold of Parvaim. ⁷He overlaid the ceiling beams, door-frames, walls and doors of the temple with gold, and he carved cherubim on the walls.

⁸He built the Most Holy Place, its length corresponding to the width of the temple—twenty cubits long and twenty cubits wide. He overlaid the inside with six hundred talents of fine gold. ⁹The gold nails weighed fifty shekels. He also overlaid the upper parts with gold.

¹⁰In the Most Holy Place he made a pair of sculptured cherubim and overlaid them with gold. ¹¹The total wingspan of the cherubim was twenty cubits. One wing of the first cherub was five cubits long and touched the temple wall, while its other wing, also five cubits long, touched the wing of the other cherub. ¹²Similarly one wing of the second cherub was five cubits long and touched the other temple wall, and its other wing, also five cubits long, touched the wing of the first cherub. ¹³The wings of these cherubim extended twenty cubits. They stood on their feet, facing the main hall.

¹⁴He made the curtain of blue, purple and crimson yarn and fine linen, with cherubim worked into it.

¹⁵In the front of the temple he made two pillars, which ⌊together⌋ were thirty-five cubits long, each with a capital on top measuring five cubits. ¹⁶He made interwoven chains and put them on top of the pillars. He also made a hundred pomegranates and attached them to the chains. ¹⁷He erected the pillars in the front of the temple, one to the south and one to the north. The one to the south he named Jakin and the one to the north Boaz.

The Temple's Furnishings

4 He made a bronze altar twenty cubits long, twenty cubits wide and ten cubits high. ²He made the Sea of cast metal, circular in shape, measuring ten cubits from rim to rim and five cubits high. It took a line of thirty cubits to measure round it. ³Below the rim, figures of bulls encircled it—ten to a cubit. The bulls were cast in two rows in one piece with the Sea.

⁴The Sea stood on twelve bulls, three facing north, three facing west, three facing south and three facing east. The Sea rested on top of them, and their hindquarters were towards the centre. ⁵It was a handbreadth in thickness, and its rim was like the rim of a cup, like a lily blossom. It held three thousand baths.

⁶He then made ten basins for washing and placed five on the south side and five on the north. In them the things to be used for the burnt offerings were rinsed, but the Sea was to be used by the priests for washing.

⁷He made ten gold lampstands according to the specifications for them and placed them in the temple, five on the south side and five on the north.

⁸He made ten tables and placed them in the temple, five on the south side and five on the north. He also made a hundred gold sprinkling bowls.

⁹He made the courtyard of the priests, and the large court and the doors for the court, and overlaid the doors with bronze. ¹⁰He placed the Sea on the south side, at the south-east corner.

¹¹He also made the pots and shovels and sprinkling bowls.

So Huram finished the work he had undertaken for King Solomon in the temple of God:

¹²the two pillars;
   the two bowl-shaped capitals on top of the pillars;
   the two sets of network decorating

the two bowl-shaped capitals on top of the pillars;

¹³the four hundred pomegranates for the two sets of network (two rows of pomegranates for each network, decorating the bowl-shaped capitals on top of the pillars);

¹⁴the stands with their basins;

¹⁵the Sea and the twelve bulls under it;

¹⁶the pots, shovels, meat forks and all related articles.

All the objects that Huram-Abi made for King Solomon for the temple of the LORD were of polished bronze. ¹⁷The king had them cast in clay moulds in the plain of the Jordan between Succoth and Zarethan. ¹⁸All these things that Solomon made amounted to so much that the weight of the bronze was not determined.

¹⁹Solomon also made all the furnishings that were in God's temple:

the golden altar;
the tables on which was the bread of the Presence;

²⁰the lampstands of pure gold with their lamps, to burn in front of the inner sanctuary as prescribed;

²¹the gold floral work and lamps and tongs (they were solid gold);

²²the pure gold wick trimmers, sprinkling bowls, dishes and censers; and the gold doors of the temple: the inner doors to the Most Holy Place and the doors of the main hall.

5 When all the work Solomon had done for the temple of the LORD was finished, he brought in the things his father David had dedicated—the silver and gold and all the furnishings—and he placed them in the treasuries of God's temple.

NEW TESTAMENT READING
1 Corinthians 9:19–10:13

¹⁹Though I am free and belong to no man, I make myself a slave to everyone, to win as many as possible. ²⁰To the Jews I became like a Jew, to win the Jews. To those under the law I became like one under the law (though I myself am not under the law), so as to win those under the law. ²¹To those not having the law I became like one not having the law (though I am not free from God's law but am under Christ's law), so as to win those not having the law. ²²To the weak I became weak, to win the weak. I have become all things to all men so that by all possible means I might save some. ²³I do all this for the sake of the gospel, that I may share in its blessings.

²⁴Do you not know that in a race all the runners run, but only one gets the prize? Run in such a way as to get the prize. ²⁵Everyone who competes in the games goes into strict training. They do it to get a crown that will not last; but we do it to get a crown that will last for ever. ²⁶Therefore I do not run like a man running aimlessly; I do not fight like a man beating the air. ²⁷No, I beat my body and make it my slave so that after I have preached to others, I myself will not be disqualified for the prize.

Warnings From Israel's History

10 For I do not want you to be ignorant of the fact, brothers, that our forefathers were all under the cloud and that they all passed through the sea. ²They were all baptised into Moses in the cloud and in the sea. ³They all ate the same spiritual food ⁴and drank the same spiritual drink; for they drank from the spiritual rock that accompanied them, and that rock was Christ. ⁵Nevertheless, God was not pleased with most of them; their bodies were scattered over the desert.

⁶Now these things occurred as examples to keep us from setting our hearts

on evil things as they did. 7Do not be idolaters, as some of them were; as it is written: "The people sat down to eat and drink and got up to indulge in pagan revelry." 8We should not commit sexual immorality, as some of them did—and in one day twenty-three thousand of them died. 9We should not test the Lord, as some of them did—and were killed by snakes. 10And do not grumble, as some of them did—and were killed by the destroying angel.

11These things happened to them as examples and were written down as warnings for us, on whom the fulfilment of the ages has come. 12So, if you think you are standing firm, be careful that you don't fall! 13No temptation has seized you except what is common to man. And God is faithful; he will not let you be tempted beyond what you can bear. But when you are tempted, he will also provide a way out so that you can stand up under it.

READING FROM PSALMS
Psalm 97:1–12

1The LORD reigns, let the earth be glad;
  let the distant shores rejoice.

2Clouds and thick darkness surround him;
  righteousness and justice are the foundation of his throne.
3Fire goes before him
  and consumes his foes on every side.
4His lightning lights up the world;
  the earth sees and trembles.
5The mountains melt like wax before the LORD,
  before the Lord of all the earth.
6The heavens proclaim his righteousness,
  and all the peoples see his glory.

7All who worship images are put to shame,
  those who boast in idols—
  worship him, all you gods!

8Zion hears and rejoices
  and the villages of Judah are glad
  because of your judgments, O LORD.
9For you, O LORD, are the Most High over all the earth;
  you are exalted far above all gods.

10Let those who love the LORD hate evil,
  for he guards the lives of his faithful ones
  and delivers them from the hand of the wicked.
11Light is shed upon the righteous
  and joy on the upright in heart.
12Rejoice in the LORD, you who are righteous,
  and praise his holy name.

OLD TESTAMENT READING
2 Chronicles 5:2–7:10

The Ark Brought to the Temple

²Then Solomon summoned to Jerusalem the elders of Israel, all the heads of the tribes and the chiefs of the Israelite families, to bring up the ark of the LORD's covenant from Zion, the City of David. ³And all the men of Israel came together to the king at the time of the festival in the seventh month.

⁴When all the elders of Israel had arrived, the Levites took up the ark, ⁵and they brought up the ark and the Tent of Meeting and all the sacred furnishings in it. The priests, who were Levites, carried them up; ⁶and King Solomon and the entire assembly of Israel that had gathered about him were before the ark, sacrificing so many sheep and cattle that they could not be recorded or counted.

⁷The priests then brought the ark of the LORD's covenant to its place in the inner sanctuary of the temple, the Most Holy Place, and put it beneath the wings of the cherubim. ⁸The cherubim spread their wings over the place of the ark and covered the ark and its carrying poles. ⁹These poles were so long that their ends, extending from the ark, could be seen in front of the inner sanctuary, but not from outside the Holy Place; and they are still there today. ¹⁰There was nothing in the ark except the two tablets that Moses had placed in it at Horeb, where the LORD made a covenant with the Israelites after they came out of Egypt.

¹¹The priests then withdrew from the Holy Place. All the priests who were there had consecrated themselves, regardless of their divisions. ¹²All the Levites who were musicians—Asaph, Heman, Jeduthun and their sons and relatives—stood on the east side of the altar, dressed in fine linen and playing cymbals, harps and lyres. They were accompanied by 120 priests sounding trumpets. ¹³The trumpeters and singers joined in unison, as with one voice, to give praise and thanks to the LORD. Accompanied by trumpets, cymbals and other instruments, they raised their voices in praise to the LORD and sang:

"He is good;
  his love endures for ever."

Then the temple of the LORD was filled with a cloud, ¹⁴and the priests could not perform their service because of the cloud, for the glory of the LORD filled the temple of God.

6 Then Solomon said, "The LORD has said that he would dwell in a dark cloud; ²I have built a magnificent temple for you, a place for you to dwell for ever."

³While the whole assembly of Israel was standing there, the king turned round and blessed them. ⁴Then he said:

"Praise be to the LORD, the God of Israel, who with his hands has fulfilled what he promised with his mouth to my father David. For he said, ⁵'Since the day I brought my people out of Egypt, I have not chosen a city in any tribe of Israel to have a temple built for my Name to be there, nor have I chosen anyone to be the leader over my people Israel. ⁶But now I have chosen Jerusalem for my Name to be there, and I have chosen David to rule my people Israel.'

⁷"My father David had it in his heart to build a temple for the Name of the LORD, the God of Israel. ⁸But the LORD said to my father David, 'Because it was in your heart to build a temple for my

Name, you did well to have this in your heart. 9Nevertheless, you are not the one to build the temple, but your son, who is your own flesh and blood—he is the one who will build the temple for my Name.'

10"The LORD has kept the promise he made. I have succeeded David my father and now I sit on the throne of Israel, just as the LORD promised, and I have built the temple for the Name of the LORD, the God of Israel. 11There I have placed the ark, in which is the covenant of the LORD that he made with the people of Israel."

Solomon's Prayer of Dedication

12Then Solomon stood before the altar of the LORD in front of the whole assembly of Israel and spread out his hands. 13Now he had made a bronze platform, five cubits long, five cubits wide and three cubits high, and had placed it in the centre of the outer court. He stood on the platform and then knelt down before the whole assembly of Israel and spread out his hands towards heaven. 14He said:

"O LORD, God of Israel, there is no God like you in heaven or on earth—you who keep your covenant of love with your servants who continue wholeheartedly in your way. 15You have kept your promise to your servant David my father; with your mouth you have promised and with your hand you have fulfilled it—as it is today.

16"Now LORD, God of Israel, keep for your servant David my father the promises you made to him when you said, 'You shall never fail to have a man to sit before me on the throne of Israel, if only your sons are careful in all they do to walk before me according to my law, as you have done.' 17And now, O LORD, God of Israel, let your word that you

promised your servant David come true.

18"But will God really dwell on earth with men? The heavens, even the highest heavens, cannot contain you. How much less this temple that I have built! 19Yet give attention to your servant's prayer and his plea for mercy, O LORD my God. Hear the cry and the prayer that your servant is praying in your presence. 20May your eyes be open towards this temple day and night, this place of which you said you would put your Name there. May you hear the prayer your servant prays towards this place. 21Hear the supplications of your servant and of your people Israel when they pray towards this place. Hear from heaven, your dwelling-place; and when you hear, forgive.

22"When a man wrongs his neighbour and is required to take an oath and he comes and swears the oath before your altar in this temple, 23then hear from heaven and act. Judge between your servants, repaying the guilty by bringing down on his own head what he has done. Declare the innocent not guilty and so establish his innocence.

24"When your people Israel have been defeated by an enemy because they have sinned against you and when they turn back and confess your name, praying and making supplication before you in this temple, 25then hear from heaven and forgive the sin of your people Israel and bring them back to the land you gave to them and their fathers.

26"When the heavens are shut up and there is no rain because your people have sinned against you, and when they pray towards this place and confess your name and turn from their sin because you have afflicted them, 27then hear from heaven and forgive the sin of your servants, your people Israel. Teach them the right way to live, and send rain on the land that you gave your people for an inheritance.

28"When famine or plague comes to the land, or blight or mildew, locusts or grasshoppers, or when enemies besiege them in any of their cities, whatever disaster or disease may come, 29and when a prayer or plea is made by any of your people Israel—each one aware of his afflictions and pains, and spreading out his hands towards this temple—30then hear from heaven, your dwelling-place. Forgive, and deal with each man according to all he does, since you know his heart (for you alone know the hearts of men), 31so that they will fear you and walk in your ways all the time they live in the land that you gave our fathers.

32"As for the foreigner who does not belong to your people Israel but has come from a distant land because of your great name and your mighty hand and your outstretched arm—when he comes and prays towards this temple, 33then hear from heaven, your dwelling-place, and do whatever the foreigner asks of you, so that all the peoples of the earth may know your name and fear you, as do your own people Israel, and may know that this house that I have built bears your Name.

34"When your people go to war against their enemies, wherever you send them, and when they pray to you towards this city you have chosen and the temple I have built for your Name, 35then hear from heaven their prayer and their plea, and uphold their cause.

36"When they sin against you— for there is no-one who does not sin—and you become angry with them and give them over to the enemy, who takes them captive to

a land far away or near; 37and if they have a change of heart in the land where they are held captive, and repent and plead with you in the land of their captivity and say, 'We have sinned, we have done wrong and acted wickedly'; 38and if they turn back to you with all their heart and soul in the land of their captivity where they were taken, and pray towards the land that you gave their fathers, towards the city you have chosen and towards the temple that I have built for your Name; 39then from heaven, your dwelling-place, hear their prayer and their pleas, and uphold their cause. And forgive your people, who have sinned against you.

40"Now, my God, may your eyes be open and your ears attentive to the prayers offered in this place.

41"Now arise, O LORD God, and
come to your resting place,
    you and the ark of your might.
May your priests, O LORD God,
    be clothed with salvation,
    may your saints rejoice in your
        goodness.
42O LORD God, do not reject your
    anointed one.
    Remember the great love
        promised to David your
        servant."

The Dedication of the Temple

7 When Solomon finished praying, fire came down from heaven and consumed the burnt offering and the sacrifices, and the glory of the LORD filled the temple. 2The priests could not enter the temple of the LORD because the glory of the LORD filled it. 3When all the Israelites saw the fire coming down and the glory of the LORD above the temple, they knelt on the pavement with their faces to the ground, and they worshipped and gave thanks to the LORD, saying,

"He is good;
    his love endures for ever."

4Then the king and all the people offered sacrifices before the LORD. 5And King Solomon offered a sacrifice of twenty-two thousand head of cattle and a hundred and twenty thousand sheep and goats. So the king and all the people dedicated the temple of God. 6The priests took their positions, as did the Levites with the LORD's musical instruments, which King David had made for praising the LORD and which were used when he gave thanks, saying, "His love endures for ever." Opposite the Levites, the priests blew their trumpets, and all the Israelites were standing.

7Solomon consecrated the middle part of the courtyard in front of the temple of the LORD, and there he offered burnt offerings and the fat of the fellowship offerings, because the bronze altar he had made could not hold the burnt offerings, the grain offerings and the fat portions.

8So Solomon observed the festival at that time for seven days, and all Israel with him—a vast assembly, people from Lebo Hamath to the Wadi of Egypt. 9On the eighth day they held an assembly, for they had celebrated the dedication of the altar for seven days and the festival for seven days more. 10On the twenty-third day of the seventh month he sent the people to their homes, joyful and glad in heart for the good things the LORD had done for David and Solomon and for his people Israel.

NEW TESTAMENT READING
1 Corinthians 10:14–11:1

Idol Feasts and the Lord's Supper

14Therefore, my dear friends, flee from idolatry. 15I speak to sensible people; judge for yourselves what I say. 16Is not the cup of thanksgiving for which we give thanks a participation in the blood of Christ? And is not the bread that we break a participation in the body of Christ? 17Because there is one loaf, we, who are many, are one body, for we all partake of the one loaf.

18Consider the people of Israel: Do not those who eat the sacrifices participate in the altar? 19Do I mean then that a sacrifice offered to an idol is anything, or that an idol is anything? 20No, but the sacrifices of pagans are offered to demons, not to God, and I do not want you to be participants with demons. 21You cannot drink the cup of the Lord and the cup of demons too; you cannot have a part in both the Lord's table and the table of demons. 22Are we trying to arouse the Lord's jealousy? Are we stronger than he?

The Believer's Freedom

23"Everything is permissible"—but not everything is beneficial. "Everything is permissible"—but not everything is constructive. 24Nobody should seek his own good, but the good of others.

25Eat anything sold in the meat market without raising questions of conscience, 26for, "The earth is the Lord's, and everything in it."

27If some unbeliever invites you to a meal and you want to go, eat whatever is put before you without raising questions of conscience. 28But if anyone says to you, "This has been offered in sacrifice," then do not eat it, both for the sake of the man who told you and for conscience' sake—29the other man's conscience, I mean, not yours. For why should my freedom be judged by another's conscience? 30If I take part in the meal with thankfulness, why am I denounced because of something I thank God for?

31So whether you eat or drink or whatever you do, do it all for the glory of God. 32Do not cause anyone to stumble, whether Jews, Greeks or the church of God—33even as I try to please everybody in every way. For I am not seeking my own good but the good of many, so that they may be saved.

11 ¹Follow my example, as I follow the example of Christ.

READING FROM PROVERBS
Proverbs 20:5–14

⁵The purposes of a man's heart are
    deep waters,
  but a man of understanding draws
    them out.

⁶Many a man claims to have unfailing
    love,
  but a faithful man who can find?

⁷The righteous man leads a blameless
    life;
  blessed are his children after him.

⁸When a king sits on his throne to
    judge,
  he winnows out all evil with his
    eyes.

⁹Who can say, "I have kept my heart
    pure;
  I am clean and without sin"?

¹⁰Differing weights and differing
    measures—
  the LORD detests them both.

¹¹Even a child is known by his actions,
  by whether his conduct is pure and
    right.

¹²Ears that hear and eyes that see—
  the LORD has made them both.

¹³Do not love sleep or you will grow
    poor;
  stay awake and you will have food
    to spare.

¹⁴"It's no good, it's no good!" says the
    buyer;
  then off he goes and boasts about
    his purchase.

DAY 229

AUGUST 17

OLD TESTAMENT READING
2 Chronicles 7:11–9:31

The LORD Appears to Solomon

¹¹When Solomon had finished the temple of the LORD and the royal palace, and had succeeded in carrying out all he had in mind to do in the temple of the LORD and in his own palace, ¹²the LORD appeared to him at night and said:

"I have heard your prayer and have chosen this place for myself as a temple for sacrifices.

¹³"When I shut up the heavens so that there is no rain, or command locusts to devour the land or send a plague among my people, ¹⁴if my people, who are called by my name, will humble themselves and pray and seek my face and turn from their wicked ways, then will I hear from heaven and will forgive their sin and will heal their land. ¹⁵Now my eyes will be open and my ears attentive to the prayers offered in this place. ¹⁶I have chosen and consecrated this temple so that my Name may be there for ever. My eyes and my heart will always be there.

¹⁷"As for you, if you walk before me as David your father did, and do all I command, and observe my decrees and laws, ¹⁸I will establish your royal throne, as I covenanted with David your father when I said, 'You shall never fail to have a man to rule over Israel.'

[19]"But if you turn away and forsake the decrees and commands I have given you and go off to serve other gods and worship them, [20]then I will uproot Israel from my land, which I have given them, and will reject this temple which I have consecrated for my Name. I will make it a byword and an object of ridicule among all peoples. [21]And though this temple is now so imposing, all who pass by will be appalled and say, 'Why has the LORD done such a thing to this land and to this temple?' [22]People will answer, 'Because they have forsaken the LORD, the God of their fathers, who brought them out of Egypt, and have embraced other gods, worshipping and serving them—that is why he brought all this disaster on them.'"

Solomon's Other Activities

8 At the end of twenty years, during which Solomon built the temple of the LORD and his own palace, [2]Solomon rebuilt the villages that Hiram had given him, and settled Israelites in them. [3]Solomon then went to Hamath Zobah and captured it. [4]He also built up Tadmor in the desert and all the store cities he had built in Hamath. [5]He rebuilt Upper Beth Horon and Lower Beth Horon as fortified cities, with walls and with gates and bars, [6]as well as Baalath and all his store cities, and all the cities for his chariots and for his horses—whatever he desired to build in Jerusalem, in Lebanon and throughout all the territory that he ruled.

[7]All the people left from the Hittites, Amorites, Perizzites, Hivites and Jebusites (these peoples were not Israelites), [8]that is, their descendants remaining in the land, whom the Israelites had not destroyed—these Solomon conscripted for his slave labour force, as it is to this day. [9]But Solomon did not make slaves of the Israelites for his work; they were his fighting men, commanders of his

captains, and commanders of his chariots and charioteers. [10]They were also King Solomon's chief officials—two hundred and fifty officials supervising the men.

[11]Solomon brought Pharaoh's daughter up from the City of David to the palace he had built for her, for he said, "My wife must not live in the palace of David king of Israel, because the places the ark of the LORD has entered are holy."

[12]On the altar of the LORD that he had built in front of the portico, Solomon sacrificed burnt offerings to the LORD, [13]according to the daily requirement for offerings commanded by Moses for Sabbaths, New Moons and the three annual feasts—the Feast of Unleavened Bread, the Feast of Weeks and the Feast of Tabernacles. [14]In keeping with the ordinance of his father David, he appointed the divisions of the priests for their duties and the Levites to lead the praise and to assist the priests according to each day's requirement. He also appointed the gatekeepers by divisions for the various gates, because this was what David the man of God had ordered. [15]They did not deviate from the king's commands to the priests or to the Levites in any matter, including that of the treasuries.

[16]All Solomon's work was carried out, from the day the foundation of the temple of the LORD was laid until its completion. So the temple of the LORD was finished.

[17]Then Solomon went to Ezion Geber and Elath on the coast of Edom. [18]And Hiram sent him ships commanded by his own officers, men who knew the sea. These with Solomon's men, sailed to Ophir and brought back four hundred and fifty talents of gold, which they delivered to King Solomon.

The Queen of Sheba Visits Solomon

9 When the queen of Sheba heard of Solomon's fame, she came to Jerusalem to test him with hard questions. Arriving with a very great caravan—

with camels carrying spices, large quantities of gold, and precious stones—she came to Solomon and talked with him about all she had on her mind. ²Solomon answered all her questions; nothing was too hard for him to explain to her. ³When the queen of Sheba saw the wisdom of Solomon, as well as the palace he had built, ⁴the food on his table, the seating of his officials, the attending servants in their robes, the cupbearers in their robes and the burnt offerings he made at the temple of the LORD, she was overwhelmed.

⁵She said to the king, "The report I heard in my own country about your achievements and your wisdom is true. ⁶But I did not believe what they said until I came and saw with my own eyes. Indeed, not even half the greatness of your wisdom was told me; you have far exceeded the report I heard. ⁷How happy your men must be! How happy your officials, who continually stand before you and hear your wisdom! ⁸Praise be to the LORD your God, who has delighted in you and placed you on his throne as king to rule for the LORD your God. Because of the love of your God for Israel and his desire to uphold them for ever, he has made you king over them, to maintain justice and righteousness."

⁹Then she gave the king 120 talents of gold, large quantities of spices, and precious stones. There had never been such spices as those the queen of Sheba gave to King Solomon.

¹⁰(The men of Hiram and the men of Solomon brought gold from Ophir; they also brought algum-wood and precious stones. ¹¹The king used the algum-wood to make steps for the temple of the LORD and for the royal palace, and to make harps and lyres for the musicians. Nothing like them had ever been seen in Judah.)

¹²King Solomon gave the queen of Sheba all she desired and asked for; he gave her more than she had brought to him. Then she left and returned with her retinue to her own country.

Solomon's Splendour

¹³The weight of the gold that Solomon received yearly was 666 talents, ¹⁴not including the revenues brought in by merchants and traders. Also all the kings of Arabia and the governors of the land brought gold and silver to Solomon.

¹⁵King Solomon made two hundred large shields of hammered gold; six hundred bekas of hammered gold went into each shield. ¹⁶He also made three hundred small shields of hammered gold, with three hundred bekas of gold in each shield. The king put them in the Palace of the Forest of Lebanon.

¹⁷Then the king made a great throne inlaid with ivory and overlaid with pure gold. ¹⁸The throne had six steps, and a footstool of gold was attached to it. On both sides of the seat were armrests, with a lion standing beside each of them. ¹⁹Twelve lions stood on the six steps, one at either end of each step. Nothing like it had ever been made for any other kingdom. ²⁰All King Solomon's goblets were gold, and all the household articles in the Palace of the Forest of Lebanon were pure gold. Nothing was made of silver, because silver was considered of little value in Solomon's day. ²¹The king had a fleet of trading ships manned by Hiram's men. Once every three years it returned, carrying gold, silver and ivory, and apes and baboons.

²²King Solomon was greater in riches and wisdom than all the other kings of the earth. ²³All the kings of the earth sought audience with Solomon to hear the wisdom God had put in his heart. ²⁴Year after year, everyone who came brought a gift—articles of silver and gold, and robes, weapons and spices, and horses and mules.

²⁵Solomon had four thousand stalls for horses and chariots, and twelve thousand horses, which he kept in the chariot cities and also with him in Jerusalem. ²⁶He ruled over all the kings from the River to the land of

the Philistines, as far as the border of Egypt. ²⁷The king made silver as common in Jerusalem as stones, and cedar as plentiful as sycamore-fig trees in the foothills. ²⁸Solomon's horses were imported from Egypt and from all other countries.

Solomon's Death

²⁹As for the other events of Solomon's reign, from beginning to end, are they not written in the records of Nathan the prophet, in the prophecy of Ahijah the Shilonite and in the visions of Iddo the seer concerning Jeroboam son of Nebat? ³⁰Solomon reigned in Jerusalem over all Israel for forty years. ³¹Then he rested with his fathers and was buried in the city of David his father. And Rehoboam his son succeeded him as king.

NEW TESTAMENT READING
1 Corinthians 11:2–34

Propriety in Worship

²I praise you for remembering me in everything and for holding to the teachings, just as I passed them on to you.

³Now I want you to realise that the head of every man is Christ, and the head of the woman is man, and the head of Christ is God. ⁴Every man who prays or prophesies with his head covered dishonours his head. ⁵And every woman who prays or prophesies with her head uncovered dishonours her head—it is just as though her head were shaved. ⁶If a woman does not cover her head, she should have her hair cut off; and if it is a disgrace for a woman to have her hair cut or shaved off, she should cover her head. ⁷A man ought not to cover his head, since he is the image and glory of God; but the woman is the glory of man. ⁸For man did not come from woman, but woman from man; ⁹neither was man created for

woman, but woman for man. ¹⁰For this reason, and because of the angels, the woman ought to have a sign of authority on her head.

¹¹In the Lord, however, woman is not independent of man, nor is man independent of woman. ¹²For as woman came from man, so also man is born of woman. But everything comes from God. ¹³Judge for yourselves: Is it proper for a woman to pray to God with her head uncovered? ¹⁴Does not the very nature of things teach you that if a man has long hair, it is a disgrace to him, ¹⁵but that if a woman has long hair, it is her glory? For long hair is given to her as a covering. ¹⁶If anyone wants to be contentious about this, we have no other practice—nor do the churches of God.

The Lord's Supper

¹⁷In the following directives I have no praise for you, for your meetings do more harm than good. ¹⁸In the first place, I hear that when you come together as a church, there are divisions among you, and to some extent I believe it. ¹⁹No doubt there have to be differences among you to show which of you have God's approval. ²⁰When you come together, it is not the Lord's Supper you eat, ²¹for as you eat, each of you goes ahead without waiting for anybody else. One remains hungry, another gets drunk. ²²Don't you have homes to eat and drink in? Or do you despise the church of God and humiliate those who have nothing? What shall I say to you? Shall I praise you for this? Certainly not!

²³For I received from the Lord what I also passed on to you: The Lord Jesus, on the night he was betrayed, took bread, ²⁴and when he had given thanks, he broke it and said, "This is my body, which is for you; do this in remembrance of me." ²⁵In the same way, after supper he took the cup, saying, "This cup is the new covenant in my blood; do this, whenever you drink it,

in remembrance of me." ²⁶For whenever you eat this bread and drink this cup, you proclaim the Lord's death until he comes.

²⁷Therefore, whoever eats the bread or drinks the cup of the Lord in an unworthy manner will be guilty of sinning against the body and blood of the Lord. ²⁸A man ought to examine himself before he eats of the bread and drinks of the cup. ²⁹For anyone who eats and drinks without recognising the body of the Lord eats and drinks judgment on himself. ³⁰That is why many among you are weak and sick, and a number of you have fallen asleep. ³¹But if we judged ourselves, we would not come under judgment. ³²When we are judged by the Lord, we are being disciplined so that we will not be condemned with the world.

³³So then, my brothers, when you come together to eat, wait for each other. ³⁴If anyone is hungry, he should eat at home, so that when you meet together it may not result in judgment.

And when I come I will give further directions.

READING FROM PSALMS
Psalm 98:1–9

A psalm.

¹Sing to the LORD a new song,
  for he has done marvellous
    things;

his right hand and his holy arm
  have worked salvation for him.
²The LORD has made his salvation
    known
  and revealed his righteousness to
    the nations.
³He has remembered his love
  and his faithfulness to the house of
    Israel;
all the ends of the earth have seen
  the salvation of our God.

⁴Shout for joy to the LORD, all the
    earth,
  burst into jubilant song with
    music;
⁵make music to the LORD with the
    harp,
  with the harp and the sound of
    singing,
⁶with trumpets and the blast of the
    ram's horn—
  shout for joy before the LORD, the
    King.

⁷Let the sea resound, and everything
    in it,
  the world, and all who live in it.
⁸Let the rivers clap their hands,
  let the mountains sing together for
    joy;
⁹let them sing before the LORD,
  for he comes to judge the earth.
He will judge the world in
    righteousness
  and the peoples with equity.

OLD TESTAMENT READING
Song of Songs 1:1–4:16

1   Solomon's Song of Songs.

Beloved

²Let him kiss me with the kisses of his
    mouth—
  for your love is more delightful
    than wine.
³Pleasing is the fragrance of your
    perfumes;
  your name is like perfume poured
    out.
No wonder the maidens love you!
⁴Take me away with you—let us
    hurry!
Let the king bring me into his
    chambers.

Friends

We rejoice and delight in you;
  we will praise your love more than
    wine.

Beloved

How right they are to adore you!

⁵Dark am I, yet lovely,
  O daughters of Jerusalem!
dark like the tents of Kedar,
  like the tent curtains of Solomon.
⁶Do not stare at me because I am
    dark,
because I am darkened by the sun.
My mother's sons were angry with
    me
and made me take care of the
    vineyards;
  my own vineyard I have neglected.
⁷Tell me, you whom I love, where you
    graze your flock
and where you rest your sheep at
    midday.

Why should I be like a veiled woman
  beside the flocks of your friends?

Friends

⁸If you do not know, most beautiful of
    women,
  follow the tracks of the sheep
and graze your young goats
  by the tents of the shepherds.

Lover

⁹I liken you, my darling, to a mare
  harnessed to one of the chariots of
    Pharaoh.
¹⁰Your cheeks are beautiful with
    ear-rings,
  your neck with strings of jewels.
¹¹We will make you ear-rings of gold,
  studded with silver.

Beloved

¹²While the king was at his table,
  my perfume spread its fragrance.
¹³My lover is to me a sachet of myrrh
  resting between my breasts.
¹⁴My lover is to me a cluster of henna
    blossoms
  from the vineyards of En Gedi.

Lover

¹⁵How beautiful you are, my darling!
  Oh, how beautiful!
  Your eyes are doves.

Beloved

¹⁶How handsome you are, my lover!
  Oh, how charming!
  And our bed is verdant.

Lover

¹⁷The beams of our house are cedars;
  our rafters are firs.

Beloved

2 I am a rose of Sharon,
    a lily of the valleys.

Lover

²Like a lily among thorns
    is my darling among the maidens.

Beloved

³Like an apple tree among the trees of
        the forest
    is my lover among the young men.
I delight to sit in his shade,
    and his fruit is sweet to my taste.
⁴He has taken me to the banquet hall,
    and his banner over me is love.
⁵Strengthen me with raisins,
    refresh me with apples,
    for I am faint with love.
⁶His left arm is under my head,
    and his right arm embraces me.
⁷Daughters of Jerusalem, I charge you
    by the gazelles and by the does of
        the field:
Do not arouse or awaken love
    until it so desires.

⁸Listen! My lover!
    Look! Here he comes,
leaping across the mountains,
    bounding over the hills.
⁹My lover is like a gazelle or a young
        stag.
    Look! There he stands behind our
        wall,
gazing through the windows,
    peering through the lattice.
¹⁰My lover spoke and said to me,
    "Arise, my darling,
    my beautiful one, and come with
        me.
¹¹See! The winter is past;
    the rains are over and gone.
¹²Flowers appear on the earth;
    the season of singing has come,
    the cooing of doves
    is heard in our land.
¹³The fig-tree forms its early fruit;
    the blossoming vines spread their
        fragrance.

Arise, come, my darling;
    my beautiful one, come with me."

Lover

¹⁴My dove in the clefts of the rock,
    in the hiding-places on the
        mountainside,
show me your face,
    let me hear your voice;
for your voice is sweet,
    and your face is lovely.
¹⁵Catch for us the foxes,
    the little foxes
    that ruin the vineyards,
    our vineyards that are in bloom.

Beloved

¹⁶My lover is mine and I am his;
    he browses among the lilies.
¹⁷Until the day breaks
    and the shadows flee,
turn, my lover,
    and be like a gazelle
or like a young stag
    on the rugged hills.

3 All night long on my bed
    I looked for the one my heart
        loves;
    I looked for him but did not find
        him.
²I will get up now and go about the
        city,
    through its streets and squares;
I will search for the one my heart
        loves.
    So I looked for him but did not find
        him.
³The watchmen found me
    as they made their rounds in the
        city.
    "Have you seen the one my heart
        loves?"
⁴Scarcely had I passed them
    when I found the one my heart
        loves.
I held his hand and would not let him go
    till I had brought him to my
        mother's house,
    to the room of the one who
        conceived me.

⁵Daughters of Jerusalem, I charge you
  by the gazelles and by the does of
    the field:
Do not arouse or awaken love
  until it so desires.

⁶Who is this coming up from the
    desert
  like a column of smoke,
perfumed with myrrh and incense
  made from all the spices of the
    merchant?
⁷Look! It is Solomon's carriage,
  escorted by sixty warriors,
    the noblest of Israel,
⁸all of them wearing the sword,
  all experienced in battle,
each with his sword at his side,
  prepared for the terrors of the
    night.
⁹King Solomon made for himself the
    carriage;
  he made it of wood from Lebanon.
¹⁰Its posts he made of silver,
  its base of gold.
Its seat was upholstered with purple,
  its interior lovingly inlaid
by the daughters of Jerusalem.
¹¹Come out, you daughters of Zion,
  and look at King Solomon wearing
    the crown,
  the crown with which his mother
    crowned him
on the day of his wedding,
  the day his heart rejoiced.

Lover

4 How beautiful you are, my
    darling!
  Oh, how beautiful!
  Your eyes behind your veil are
    doves.
Your hair is like a flock of goats
  descending from Mount Gilead.
²Your teeth are like a flock of sheep
    just shorn,
  coming up from the washing.
Each has its twin;
  not one of them is alone.
³Your lips are like a scarlet ribbon;
  your mouth is lovely.

Your temples behind your veil
  are like the halves of a
    pomegranate.
⁴Your neck is like the tower of David,
  built with elegance;
on it hang a thousand shields,
  all of them shields of warriors.
⁵Your two breasts are like two fawns,
  like twin fawns of a gazelle
    that browse among the lilies.
⁶Until the day breaks
  and the shadows flee,
I will go to the mountain of myrrh
  and to the hill of incense.
⁷All beautiful you are, my darling;
  there is no flaw in you.

⁸Come with me from Lebanon, my
    bride,
  come with me from Lebanon.
Descend from the crest of Amana,
  from the top of Senir, the summit
    of Hermon,
from the lions' dens
  and the mountain haunts of the
    leopards.
⁹You have stolen my heart, my sister,
    my bride;
  you have stolen my heart
with one glance of your eyes,
  with one jewel of your necklace.
¹⁰How delightful is your love, my
    sister, my bride!
  How much more pleasing is your
    love than wine,
and the fragrance of your perfume
    than any spice!
¹¹Your lips drop sweetness as the
    honeycomb, my bride;
  milk and honey are under your
    tongue.
The fragrance of your garments is
  like that of Lebanon.
¹²You are a garden locked up, my
    sister, my bride;
  you are a spring enclosed, a sealed
    fountain.
¹³Your plants are an orchard of
    pomegranates
  with choice fruits,
  with henna and nard,

14 nard and saffron,
  calamus and cinnamon,
  with every kind of incense tree,
  with myrrh and aloes
  and all the finest spices.

15You are a garden fountain,
  a well of flowing water
  streaming down from Lebanon.

Beloved

16Awake, north wind,
  and come, south wind!
Blow on my garden,
  that its fragrance may spread
   abroad.
Let my lover come into his garden
  and taste its choice fruits.

NEW TESTAMENT READING
1 Corinthians 12:1–26

Spiritual Gifts

12 Now about spiritual gifts, brothers, I do not want you to be ignorant. 2You know that when you were pagans, somehow or other you were influenced and led astray to mute idols. 3Therefore I tell you that no-one who is speaking by the Spirit of God says, "Jesus is cursed," and no-one can say, "Jesus is Lord," except by the Holy Spirit.

4There are different kinds of gifts, but the same Spirit. 5There are different kinds of service, but the same Lord. 6There are different kinds of working, but the same God works all of them in all men.

7Now to each one the manifestation of the Spirit is given for the common good. 8To one there is given through the Spirit the message of wisdom, to another the message of knowledge by means of the same Spirit, 9to another faith by the same Spirit, to another gifts of healing by that one Spirit, 10to another miraculous powers, to another prophecy, to another distinguishing between spirits, to another speaking in different kinds of tongues, and to still

another the interpretation of tongues. 11All these are the work of one and the same Spirit, and he gives them to each one, just as he determines.

One Body, Many Parts

12The body is a unit, though it is made up of many parts; and though all its parts are many, they form one body. So it is with Christ. 13For we were all baptised by one Spirit into one body—whether Jews or Greeks, slave or free—and we were all given the one Spirit to drink.

14Now the body is not made up of one part but of many. 15If the foot should say, "Because I am not a hand, I do not belong to the body," it would not for that reason cease to be part of the body. 16And if the ear should say, "Because I am not an eye, I do not belong to the body," it would not for that reason cease to be part of the body. 17If the whole body were an eye, where would the sense of hearing be? If the whole body were an ear, where would the sense of smell be? 18But in fact God has arranged the parts in the body, every one of them, just as he wanted them to be. 19If they were all one part, where would the body be? 20As it is, there are many parts, but one body.

21The eye cannot say to the hand, "I don't need you!" And the head cannot say to the feet, "I don't need you!" 22On the contrary, those parts of the body that seem to be weaker are indispensable, 23and the parts that we think are less honourable we treat with special honour. And the parts that are unpresentable are treated with special modesty, 24while our presentable parts need no special treatment. But God has combined the members of the body and has given greater honour to the parts that lacked it, 25so that there should be no division in the body, but that its parts should have equal concern for each other. 26If one part suffers, every part suffers with it; if one part is honoured, every part rejoices with it.

READING FROM PSALMS
Psalm 99:1–9

¹The LORD reigns,
  let the nations tremble;
he sits enthroned between the
    cherubim,
  let the earth shake.
²Great is the LORD in Zion;
  he is exalted over all the nations.
³Let them praise your great and
    awesome name—
  he is holy.

⁴The King is mighty, he loves
    justice—
  you have established equity;
in Jacob you have done
  what is just and right.
⁵Exalt the LORD our God

and worship at his footstool;
  he is holy.

⁶Moses and Aaron were among his
    priests,
  Samuel was among those who
    called on his name;
they called on the LORD
  and he answered them.
⁷He spoke to them from the pillar of
    cloud;
  they kept his statutes and the
    decrees he gave them.

⁸O LORD our God,
  you answered them;
you were to Israel a forgiving God,
  though you punished their
    misdeeds.
⁹Exalt the LORD our God
  and worship at his holy mountain,
  for the LORD our God is holy.

AUGUST 19   DAY 231

OLD TESTAMENT READING
Song of Songs 5:1–8:14

Lover

5 I have come into my garden, my
  sister, my bride;
  I have gathered my myrrh with my
    spice.
  I have eaten my honeycomb and my
    honey;
  I have drunk my wine and my milk.

Friends

  Eat, O friends, and drink;
    drink your fill, O lovers.

Beloved

²I slept but my heart was awake.
  Listen! My lover is knocking:

"Open to me, my sister, my darling,
  my dove, my flawless one.
My head is drenched with dew,
  my hair with the dampness of the
    night."
³I have taken off my robe—
  must I put it on again?
I have washed my feet—
  must I soil them again?
⁴My lover thrust his hand through the
    latch-opening;
  my heart began to pound for him.
⁵I arose to open for my lover,
  and my hands dripped with myrrh,
my fingers with flowing myrrh,
  on the handles of the lock.
⁶I opened for my lover,
  but my lover had left; he was
    gone.
  My heart sank at his departure.
I looked for him but did not find him.
  I called him but he did not answer.

7The watchmen found me
    as they made their rounds in the
        city.
They beat me, they bruised me;
    they took away my cloak,
    those watchmen of the walls!
8O daughters of Jerusalem, I charge
        you—
    if you find my lover,
what will you tell him?
    Tell him I am faint with love.

Friends

9How is your beloved better than
        others,
    most beautiful of women?
How is your beloved better than
        others,
    that you charge us so?

Beloved

10My lover is radiant and ruddy,
    outstanding among ten
        thousand.
11His head is purest gold;
    his hair is wavy
    and black as a raven.
12His eyes are like doves
    by the water streams,
    washed in milk,
    mounted like jewels.
13His cheeks are like beds of spice
    yielding perfume.
His lips are like lilies
    dripping with myrrh.
14His arms are rods of gold
    set with chrysolite.
His body is like polished ivory
    decorated with sapphires.
15His legs are pillars of marble
    set on bases of pure gold.
His appearance is like Lebanon,
    choice as its cedars.
16His mouth is sweetness itself;
    he is altogether lovely.
This is my lover, this my friend,
    O daughters of Jerusalem.

Friends

6 Where has your lover gone,
    most beautiful of women?
Which way did your lover turn,
    that we may look for him with you?

Beloved

2My lover has gone down to his
        garden,
    to the beds of spices,
to browse in the gardens
    and to gather lilies.
3I am my lover's and my lover is mine;
    he browses among the lilies.

Lover

4You are beautiful, my darling, as
        Tirzah,
    lovely as Jerusalem,
    majestic as troops with banners.
5Turn your eyes from me;
    they overwhelm me.
Your hair is like a flock of goats
    descending from Gilead.
6Your teeth are like a flock of sheep
    coming up from the washing.
Each has its twin,
    not one of them is alone.
7Your temples behind your veil
    are like the halves of a
        pomegranate.
8Sixty queens there may be,
    and eighty concubines,
    and virgins beyond number;
9but my dove, my perfect one, is
        unique,
    the only daughter of her mother,
    the favourite of the one who bore
        her.
The maidens saw her and called her
        blessed;
    the queens and concubines praised
        her.

Friends

10Who is this that appears like the
        dawn,
    fair as the moon, bright as the sun,
    majestic as the stars in procession?

Lover

11I went down to the grove of nut trees
    to look at the new growth in the
    valley,
  to see if the vines had budded
    or the pomegranates were in
    bloom.
12Before I realised it,
    my desire set me among the royal
    chariots of my people.

Friends

13Come back, come back, O
    Shulammite;
  come back, come back, that we
    may gaze on you!

Lover

  Why would you gaze on the
    Shulammite
  as on the dance of Mahanaim?

7 How beautiful your sandalled feet,
    O prince's daughter!
  Your graceful legs are like jewels,
    the work of a craftsman's hands.
2Your navel is a rounded goblet
    that never lacks blended wine.
  Your waist is a mound of wheat
    encircled by lilies.
3Your breasts are like two fawns,
    twins of a gazelle.
4Your neck is like an ivory tower.
  Your eyes are the pools of Heshbon
    by the gate of Bath Rabbim.
  Your nose is like the tower of
    Lebanon
    looking towards Damascus.
5Your head crowns you like Mount
    Carmel.
  Your hair is like royal tapestry;
    the king is held captive by its
    tresses.
6How beautiful you are and how
    pleasing,
  O love, with your delights!
7Your stature is like that of the palm,
    and your breasts like clusters of
    fruit.

8I said, "I will climb the palm tree;
    I will take hold of its fruit."
  May your breasts be like the clusters
    of the vine,
    the fragrance of your breath like
    apples,
9 and your mouth like the best wine.

Beloved

  May the wine go straight to my lover,
    flowing gently over lips and teeth.
10I belong to my lover,
    and his desire is for me.
11Come, my lover, let us go to the
    countryside,
    let us spend the night in the
    villages.
12Let us go early to the vineyards
    to see if the vines had budded,
  if their blossoms have opened,
    and if the pomegranates are in
    bloom—
    there I will give you my love.
13The mandrakes send out their
    fragrance,
    and at our door is every delicacy,
  both new and old,
    that I have stored up for you, my
    lover.

8 If only you were to me like a
    brother,
  who was nursed at my mother's
    breasts!
  Then, if I found you outside,
    I would kiss you,
    and no-one would despise me.
2I would lead you
    and bring you to my mother's
    house—
    she who has taught me.
  I would give you spiced wine to
    drink,
    the nectar of my pomegranates.
3His left arm is under my head
    and his right arm embraces me.
4Daughters of Jerusalem, I charge
    you:
  Do not arouse or awaken love
    until it so desires.

Friends

5Who is this coming up from the
  desert
    leaning on her lover?

Beloved

  Under the apple tree I roused you;
    there your mother conceived you,
    there she who was in labour gave
      you birth.
6Place me like a seal over your heart,
    like a seal on your arm;
  for love is as strong as death,
    its jealousy unyielding as the grave.
  It burns like blazing fire,
    like a mighty flame.
7Many waters cannot quench love;
    rivers cannot wash it away.
  If one were to give
    all the wealth of his house for love,
    it would be utterly scorned.

Friends

8We have a young sister,
    and her breasts are not yet grown.
  What shall we do for our sister
    for the day she is spoken for?
9If she is a wall,
    we will build towers of silver on
      her.
  If she is a door,
    we will enclose her with panels of
      cedar.

Beloved

10I am a wall,
    and my breasts are like towers.
  Thus I have become in his eyes
    like one bringing contentment.
11Solomon had a vineyard in Baal
    Hamon;
  he let out his vineyard to tenants.
  Each was to bring for its fruit
    a thousand shekels of silver.
12But my own vineyard is mine to give;
    the thousand shekels are for you,
      O Solomon,
    and two hundred are for those who
      tend its fruit.

Lover

13You who dwell in the gardens
    with friends in attendance,
    let me hear your voice!

Beloved

14Come away, my lover,
    and be like a gazelle
    or like a young stag
      on the spice-laden mountains.

NEW TESTAMENT READING
1 Corinthians 12:27–13:13

27Now you are the body of Christ, and
each one of you is a part of it. 28And in
the church God has appointed first of
all apostles, second prophets, third
teachers, then workers of miracles, also
those having gifts of healing, those able
to help others, those with gifts of
administration, and those speaking in
different kinds of tongues. 29Are all
apostles? Are all prophets? Are all
teachers? Do all work miracles? 30Do
all have gifts of healing? Do all speak in
tongues? Do all interpret? 31But eagerly
desire the greater gifts.

Love

And now I will show you the most excellent way.

13 If I speak in the tongues of men
  and of angels, but have not love,
I am only a resounding gong or a clang-
ing cymbal. 2If I have the gift of prophecy and can fathom all mysteries and
all knowledge, and if I have a faith that
can move mountains, but have not love,
I am nothing. 3If I give all I possess to
the poor and surrender my body to the
flames, but have not love, I gain
nothing.

4Love is patient, love is kind. It does
not envy, it does not boast, it is not
proud. 5It is not rude, it is not self-
seeking, it is not easily angered, it keeps

no record of wrongs. 6Love does not delight in evil but rejoices with the truth. 7It always protects, always trusts, always hopes, always perseveres.

8Love never fails. But where there are prophecies, they will cease; where there are tongues, they will be stilled; where there is knowledge, it will pass away. 9For we know in part and we prophesy in part, 10but when perfection comes, the imperfect disappears. 11When I was a child, I talked like a child, I thought like a child, I reasoned like a child. When I became a man, I put childish ways behind me. 12Now we see but a poor reflection as in a mirror; then we shall see face to face. Now I know in part; then I shall know fully, even as I am fully known.

13And now these three remain: faith, hope and love. But the greatest of these is love.

READING FROM PSALMS
Psalm 100:1–5

> A psalm. For giving thanks.

1Shout for joy to the LORD, all the earth.
2   Worship the LORD with gladness;
       come before him with joyful songs.
3Know that the LORD is God.
   It is he who made us, and we are his;
   we are his people, the sheep of his pasture.

4Enter his gates with thanksgiving
       and his courts with praise;
   give thanks to him and praise his name.
5For the LORD is good and his love endures for ever;
   his faithfulness continues through all generations.

AUGUST 20 DAY 232

OLD TESTAMENT READING
2 Chronicles 10:1–12:16

Israel Rebels Against Rehoboam

10 Rehoboam went to Shechem, for all the Israelites had gone there to make him king. 2When Jeroboam son of Nebat heard this (he was in Egypt, where he had fled from King Solomon), he returned from Egypt. 3So they sent for Jeroboam, and he and all Israel went to Rehoboam and said to him: 4"Your father put a heavy yoke on us, but now lighten the harsh labour and the heavy yoke he put on us, and we will serve you."

5Rehoboam answered, "Come back to me in three days." So the people went away.

6Then King Rehoboam consulted the elders who had served his father Solomon during his lifetime. "How would

you advise me to answer these people?" he asked.

7They replied, "If you will be kind to these people and please them and give them a favourable answer, they will always be your servants."

8But Rehoboam rejected the advice the elders gave him and consulted the young men who had grown up with him and were serving him. 9He asked them, "What is your advice? How should we answer these people who say to me, 'Lighten the yoke your father put on us'?"

10The young men who had grown up with him replied, "Tell the people who have said to you, 'Your father put a heavy yoke on us, but make our yoke lighter'—tell them, 'My little finger is thicker than my father's waist. 11My father laid on you a heavy yoke; I will make it even heavier. My father scourged you with whips; I will scourge you with scorpions.'"

¹²Three days later Jeroboam and all the people returned to Rehoboam, as the king had said, "Come back to me in three days." ¹³The king answered them harshly. Rejecting the advice of the elders, ¹⁴he followed the advice of the young men and said, "My father made your yoke heavy; I will make it even heavier. My father scourged you with whips; I will scourge you with scorpions." ¹⁵So the king did not listen to the people, for this turn of events was from God, to fulfil the word that the LORD had spoken to Jeroboam son of Nebat through Ahijah the Shilonite.

¹⁶When all Israel saw that the king refused to listen to them, they answered the king:

"What share do we have in David,
    what part in Jesse's son?
To your tents, O Israel!
    Look after your own house, O
        David!"

So all the Israelites went home. ¹⁷But as for the Israelites who were living in the towns of Judah, Rehoboam still ruled over them.

¹⁸King Rehoboam sent out Adoniram, who was in charge of forced labour, but the Israelites stoned him to death. King Rehoboam, however, managed to get into his chariot and escape to Jerusalem. ¹⁹So Israel has been in rebellion against the house of David to this day.

11 When Rehoboam arrived in Jerusalem, he mustered the house of Judah and Benjamin—a hundred and eighty thousand fighting men —to make war against Israel and to regain the kingdom for Rehoboam.

²But this word of the LORD came to Shemaiah the man of God: ³"Say to Rehoboam son of Solomon king of Judah and to all the Israelites in Judah and Benjamin, ⁴This is what the LORD says: Do not go up to fight against your brothers. Go home, every one of you, for this is my doing.'" So they obeyed the words of the LORD and turned back from marching against Jeroboam.

Rehoboam Fortifies Judah

⁵Rehoboam lived in Jerusalem and built up towns for defence in Judah: ⁶Bethlehem, Etam, Tekoa, ⁷Beth Zur, Soco, Adullam, ⁸Gath, Mareshah, Ziph, ⁹Adoraim, Lachish, Azekah, ¹⁰Zorah, Aijalon and Hebron. These were fortified cities in Judah and Benjamin. ¹¹He strengthened their defences and put commanders in them, with supplies of food, olive oil and wine. ¹²He put shields and spears in all the cities, and made them very strong. So Judah and Benjamin were his.

¹³The priests and Levites from all their districts throughout Israel sided with him. ¹⁴The Levites even abandoned their pasture-lands and property, and came to Judah and Jerusalem because Jeroboam and his sons had rejected them as priests of the LORD. ¹⁵And he appointed his own priests for the high places and for the goat and calf idols he had made. ¹⁶Those from every tribe of Israel who set their hearts on seeking the LORD, the God of Israel, followed the Levites to Jerusalem to offer sacrifices to the LORD, the God of their fathers. ¹⁷They strengthened the kingdom of Judah and supported Rehoboam son of Solomon for three years, walking in the ways of David and Solomon during this time.

Rehoboam's Family

¹⁸Rehoboam married Mahalath, who was the daughter of David's son Jerimoth and of Abihail, the daughter of Jesse's son Eliab. ¹⁹She bore him sons: Jeush, Shemariah and Zaham. ²⁰Then he married Maacah daughter of Absalom, who bore him Abijah, Attai, Ziza and Shelomith. ²¹Rehoboam loved Maacah daughter of Absalom more than any of his other wives and concubines. In all he had eighteen wives

and sixty concubines, twenty-eight sons and sixty daughters.

²²Rehoboam appointed Abijah son of Maacah to be the chief prince among his brothers, in order to make him king. ²³He acted wisely, dispersing some of his sons throughout the districts of Judah and Benjamin, and to all the fortified cities. He gave them abundant provisions and took many wives for them.

Shishak Attacks Jerusalem

12 After Rehoboam's position as king was established and he had become strong, he and all Israel with him abandoned the law of the Lord. ²Because they had been unfaithful to the Lord, Shishak king of Egypt attacked Jerusalem in the fifth year of King Rehoboam. ³With twelve hundred chariots and sixty thousand horsemen and the innumerable troops of Libyans, Sukkites and Cushites that came with him from Egypt, ⁴he captured the fortified cities of Judah and came as far as Jerusalem.

⁵Then the prophet Shemaiah came to Rehoboam and to the leaders of Judah who had assembled in Jerusalem for fear of Shishak, and he said to them, "This is what the Lord says: 'You have abandoned me; therefore I now abandon you to Shishak.'"

⁶The leaders of Israel and the king humbled themselves and said, "The Lord is just."

⁷When the Lord saw that they humbled themselves, this word of the Lord came to Shemaiah: "Since they have humbled themselves, I will not destroy them but will soon give them deliverance. My wrath will not be poured out on Jerusalem through Shishak. ⁸They will, however, become subject to him, so that they may learn the difference between serving me and serving the kings of other lands."

⁹When Shishak king of Egypt attacked Jerusalem, he carried off the treasures of the temple of the Lord and the treasures of the royal palace. He took everything, including the gold shields that Solomon had made. ¹⁰So King Rehoboam made bronze shields to replace them and assigned these to the commanders of the guard on duty at the entrance to the royal palace. ¹¹Whenever the king went to the Lord's temple, the guards went with him, bearing the shields, and afterwards they returned them to the guardroom.

¹²Because Rehoboam humbled himself, the Lord's anger turned from him, and he was not totally destroyed. Indeed, there was some good in Judah.

¹³King Rehoboam established himself firmly in Jerusalem and continued as king. He was forty-one years old when he became king, and he reigned for seventeen years in Jerusalem, the city the Lord had chosen out of all the tribes of Israel in which to put his Name. His mother's name was Naamah; she was an Ammonite. ¹⁴He did evil because he had not set his heart on seeking the Lord.

¹⁵As for the events of Rehoboam's reign, from beginning to end, are they not written in the records of Shemaiah the prophet and of Iddo the seer that deal with genealogies? There was continual warfare between Rehoboam and Jeroboam. ¹⁶Rehoboam rested with his fathers and was buried in the City of David. And Abijah his son succeeded him as king.

NEW TESTAMENT READING
1 Corinthians 14:1–19

Gifts of Prophecy and Tongues

14 Follow the way of love and eagerly desire spiritual gifts, especially the gift of prophecy. ²For anyone who speaks in a tongue does not speak to men but to God. Indeed, no one understands him; he utters mysteries with his spirit. ³But everyone who prophesies speaks to men for their strengthening, encouragement and

comfort. [4]He who speaks in a tongue edifies himself, but he who prophesies edifies the church. [5]I would like every one of you to speak in tongues, but I would rather have you prophesy. He who prophesies is greater than one who speaks in tongues, unless he interprets, so that the church may be edified.

[6]Now, brothers, if I come to you and speak in tongues, what good will I be to you, unless I bring you some revelation or knowledge or prophecy or word of instruction? [7]Even in the case of lifeless things that make sounds, such as the flute or harp, how will anyone know what tune is being played unless there is a distinction in the notes? [8]Again, if the trumpet does not sound a clear call, who will get ready for battle? [9]So it is with you. Unless you speak intelligible words with your tongue, how will anyone know what you are saying? You will just be speaking into the air. [10]Undoubtedly there are all sorts of languages in the world, yet none of them is without meaning. [11]If then I do not grasp the meaning of what someone is saying, I am a foreigner to the speaker, and he is a foreigner to me. [12]So it is with you. Since you are eager to have spiritual gifts, try to excel in gifts that build up the church.

[13]For this reason anyone who speaks in a tongue should pray that he may interpret what he says. [14]For if I pray in a tongue, my spirit prays, but my mind is unfruitful. [15]So what shall I do? I will pray with my spirit, but I will also pray with my mind; I will sing with my spirit, but I will also sing with my mind. [16]If you are praising God with your spirit, how can one who finds himself among those who do not understand say "Amen" to your thanksgiving, since he does not know what you are saying? [17]You may be giving thanks well enough, but the other man is not edified.

[18]I thank God that I speak in tongues more than all of you. [19]But in the church I would rather speak five intelligible words to instruct others than ten thousand words in a tongue.

READING FROM PROVERBS
Proverbs 20:15–24

[15]Gold there is, and rubies in
    abundance,
  but lips that speak knowledge are a
    rare jewel.

[16]Take the garment of one who puts up
    security for a stranger;
  hold it in pledge if he does it for a
    wayward woman.

[17]Food gained by fraud tastes sweet to
    a man,
  but he ends up with a mouth full of
    gravel.

[18]Make plans by seeking advice;
  if you wage war, obtain guidance.

[19]A gossip betrays a confidence;
  so avoid a man who talks too
    much.

[20]If a man curses his father or mother,
  his lamp will be snuffed out in pitch
    darkness.

[21]An inheritance quickly gained at the
    beginning
  will not be blessed at the end.

[22]Do not say, "I'll pay you back for this
    wrong!"
  Wait for the LORD, and he will
    deliver you.

[23]The LORD detests differing weights,
  and dishonest scales do not please
    him.

[24]A man's steps are directed by the
    LORD.
  How then can anyone understand
    his own way?

OLD TESTAMENT READING
2 Chronicles 13:1–15:19

Abijah King of Judah

13 In the eighteenth year of the reign of Jeroboam, Abijah became king of Judah, ²and he reigned in Jerusalem for three years. His mother's name was Maacah, a daughter of Uriel of Gibeah.

There was war between Abijah and Jeroboam. ³Abijah went into battle with a force of four hundred thousand able fighting men, and Jeroboam drew up a battle line against him with eight hundred thousand able troops.

⁴Abijah stood on Mount Zemaraim, in the hill country of Ephraim, and said, "Jeroboam and all Israel, listen to me! ⁵Don't you know that the LORD, the God of Israel, has given the kingship of Israel to David and his descendants for ever by a covenant of salt? ⁶Yet Jeroboam son of Nebat, an official of Solomon son of David, rebelled against his master. ⁷Some worthless scoundrels gathered around him and opposed Rehoboam son of Solomon when he was young and indecisive and not strong enough to resist them.

⁸"And now you plan to resist the kingdom of the LORD, which is in the hands of David's descendants. You are indeed a vast army and have with you the golden calves that Jeroboam made to be your gods. ⁹But didn't you drive out the priests of the LORD, the sons of Aaron, and the Levites, and make priests of your own as the peoples of other lands do? Whoever comes to consecrate himself with a young bull and seven rams may become a priest of what are not gods.

¹⁰"As for us, the LORD is our God, and we have not forsaken him. The priests who serve the LORD are sons of Aaron, and the Levites assist them. ¹¹Every morning and evening they present burnt offerings and fragrant incense to the LORD. They set out the bread on the ceremonially clean table and light the lamps on the gold lampstand every evening. We are observing the requirements of the LORD our God. But you have forsaken him. ¹²God is with us; he is our leader. His priests with their trumpets will sound the battle cry against you. Men of Israel, do not fight against the LORD, the God of your fathers, for you will not succeed."

¹³Now Jeroboam had sent troops round to the rear, so that while he was in front of Judah the ambush was behind them. ¹⁴Judah turned and saw that they were being attacked at both front and rear. Then they cried out to the LORD. The priests blew their trumpets ¹⁵and the men of Judah raised the battle cry. At the sound of their battle cry, God routed Jeroboam and all Israel before Abijah and Judah. ¹⁶The Israelites fled before Judah, and God delivered them into their hands. ¹⁷Abijah and his men inflicted heavy losses on them, so that there were five hundred thousand casualties among Israel's able men. ¹⁸The men of Israel were subdued on that occasion, and the men of Judah were victorious because they relied on the LORD, the God of their fathers.

¹⁹Abijah pursued Jeroboam and took from him the towns of Bethel, Jeshanah and Ephron, with their surrounding villages. ²⁰Jeroboam did not regain power during the time of Abijah. And the LORD struck him down and he died.

²¹But Abijah grew in strength. He married fourteen wives and had twenty-two sons and sixteen daughters.

²²The other events of Abijah's reign, what he did and what he said, are written in the annotations of the prophet Iddo.

14 And Abijah rested with his fathers and was buried in the City of David. Asa his son succeeded him as king, and in his days the country was at peace for ten years.

Asa King of Judah

2Asa did what was good and right in the eyes of the LORD his God. 3He removed the foreign altars and the high places, smashed the sacred stones and cut down the Asherah poles. 4He commanded Judah to seek the LORD, the God of their fathers, and to obey his laws and commands. 5He removed the high places and incense altars in every town in Judah, and the kingdom was at peace under him. 6He built up the fortified cities of Judah, since the land was at peace. No-one was at war with him during those years, for the LORD gave him rest.

7"Let us build up these towns," he said to Judah, "and put walls round them, with towers, gates and bars. The land is still ours, because we have sought the LORD our God; we sought him and he has given us rest on every side." So they built and prospered.

8Asa had an army of three hundred thousand men from Judah, equipped with large shields and with spears, and two hundred and eighty thousand from Benjamin, armed with small shields and with bows. All these were brave fighting men.

9Zerah the Cushite marched out against them with a vast army and three hundred chariots, and came as far as Mareshah. 10Asa went out to meet him, and they took up battle positions in the Valley of Zephathah near Mareshah.

11Then Asa called to the LORD his God and said, "LORD, there is no-one like you to help the powerless against the mighty. Help us, O LORD our God, for we rely on you, and in your name we have come against this vast army. O LORD, you are our God; do not let man prevail against you."

12The LORD struck down the Cushites before Asa and Judah. The Cushites fled, 13and Asa and his army pursued them as far as Gerar. Such a great number of Cushites fell that they could not

recover; they were crushed before the LORD and his forces. The men of Judah carried off a large amount of plunder. 14They destroyed all the villages around Gerar, for the terror of the LORD had fallen upon them. They plundered all these villages, since there was much booty there. 15They also attacked the camps of the herdsmen and carried off droves of sheep and goats and camels. Then they returned to Jerusalem.

Asa's Reform

15 The Spirit of God came upon Azariah son of Oded. 2He went out to meet Asa and said to him, "Listen to me, Asa and all Judah and Benjamin. The LORD is with you when you are with him. If you seek him, he will be found by you, but if you forsake him, he will forsake you. 3For a long time Israel was without the true God, without a priest to teach and without the law. 4But in their distress they turned to the LORD, the God of Israel, and sought him, and he was found by them. 5In those days it was not safe to travel about, for all the inhabitants of the lands were in great turmoil. 6One nation was being crushed by another and one city by another, because God was troubling them with every kind of distress. 7But as for you, be strong and do not give up, for your work will be rewarded."

8When Asa heard these words and the prophecy of Azariah son of Oded the prophet, he took courage. He removed the detestable idols from the whole land of Judah and Benjamin and from the towns he had captured in the hills of Ephraim. He repaired the altar of the LORD that was in front of the portico of the LORD's temple.

9Then he assembled all Judah and Benjamin and the people from Ephraim, Manasseh and Simeon who had settled among them, for large numbers had come over to him from Israel when they saw that the LORD his God was with him.

[10]They assembled at Jerusalem in the third month of the fifteenth year of Asa's reign. [11]At that time they sacrificed to the LORD seven hundred head of cattle and seven thousand sheep and goats from the plunder they had brought back. [12]They entered into a covenant to seek the LORD, the God of their fathers, with all their heart and soul. [13]All who would not seek the LORD, the God of Israel, were to be put to death, whether small or great, man or woman. [14]They took an oath to the LORD with loud acclamation, with shouting and with trumpets and horns. [15]All Judah rejoiced about the oath because they had sworn it wholeheartedly. They sought God eagerly, and he was found by them. So the LORD gave them rest on every side.

[16]King Asa also deposed his grandmother Maacah from her position as queen mother, because she had made a repulsive Asherah pole. Asa cut the pole down, broke it up and burned it in the Kidron Valley. [17]Although he did not remove the high places from Israel, Asa's heart was fully committed to the LORD all his life. [18]He brought into the temple of God the silver and gold and the articles that he and his father had dedicated.

[19]There was no more war until the thirty-fifth year of Asa's reign.

NEW TESTAMENT READING
1 Corinthians 14:20–40

[20]Brothers, stop thinking like children. In regard to evil be infants, but in your thinking be adults. [21]In the Law it is written:

"Through men of strange tongues
    and through the lips of foreigners
I will speak to this people,
    but even then they will not listen to
        me,"

says the Lord.

[22]Tongues, then, are a sign, not for believers but for unbelievers; prophecy, however, is for believers, not for unbelievers. [23]So if the whole church comes together and everyone speaks in tongues, and some who do not understand or some unbelievers come in, will they not say that you are out of your mind? [24]But if an unbeliever or someone who does not understand comes in while everybody is prophesying, he will be convinced by all that he is a sinner and will be judged by all, [25]and the secrets of his heart will be laid bare. So he will fall down and worship God, exclaiming, "God is really among you!"

Orderly Worship

[26]What then shall we say, brothers? When you come together, everyone has a hymn, or a word of instruction, a revelation, a tongue or an interpretation. All of these must be done for the strengthening of the church. [27]If anyone speaks in a tongue, two—or at the most three—should speak, one at a time, and someone must interpret. [28]If there is no interpreter, the speaker should keep quiet in the church and speak to himself and God.

[29]Two or three prophets should speak, and the others should weigh carefully what is said. [30]And if a revelation comes to someone who is sitting down, the first speaker should stop. [31]For you can all prophesy in turn so that everyone may be instructed and encouraged. [32]The spirits of prophets are subject to the control of prophets. [33]For God is not a God of disorder but of peace.

As in all the congregations of the saints, [34]women should remain silent in the churches. They are not allowed to speak, but must be in submission, as the Law says. [35]If they want to enquire about something, they should ask their own husbands at home; for it is disgraceful for a woman to speak in the church.

[36]Did the word of God originate with you? Or are you the only people it has reached? [37]If anybody thinks he is a

prophet or spiritually gifted, let him acknowledge that what I am writing to you is the Lord's command. [38]If he ignores this, he himself will be ignored.

[39]Therefore, my brothers, be eager to prophesy, and do not forbid speaking in tongues. [40]But everything should be done in a fitting and orderly way.

READING FROM PSALMS
Psalm 101:1–8

Of David. A psalm.

[1]I will sing of your love and justice;
　to you, O LORD, I will sing praise.
[2]I will be careful to lead a blameless
　　life—
　when will you come to me?

I will walk in my house
　with blameless heart.
[3]I will set before my eyes
　no vile thing.

The deeds of faithless men I hate;
　they shall not cling to me.

[4]Men of perverse heart shall be far
　from me;
　I will have nothing to do with evil.

[5]Whoever slanders his neighbour in
　　secret,
　him will I put to silence;
whoever has haughty eyes and a
　　proud heart,
　him will I not endure.

[6]My eyes will be on the faithful in the
　　land,
　that they may dwell with me;
he whose walk is blameless
　will minister to me.

[7]No-one who practises deceit
　will dwell in my house;
no-one who speaks falsely
　will stand in my presence.

[8]Every morning I will put to silence
　all the wicked in the land;
I will cut off every evildoer
　from the city of the LORD.

AUGUST 22

OLD TESTAMENT READING
2 Chronicles 16:1–18:27

Asa's Last Years

16 In the thirty-sixth year of Asa's reign Baasha king of Israel went up against Judah and fortified Ramah to prevent anyone from leaving or entering the territory of Asa king of Judah.

[2]Asa then took the silver and gold out of the treasuries of the LORD's temple and of his own palace and sent it to Ben-Hadad king of Aram, who was ruling in Damascus. [3]"Let there be a treaty between me and you," he said, "as there was between my father and your father. See, I am sending you silver and gold. Now break your treaty with Baasha king of Israel so that he will withdraw from me."

[4]Ben-Hadad agreed with King Asa and sent the commanders of his forces against the towns of Israel. They conquered Ijon, Dan, Abel Maim and all the store cities of Naphtali. [5]When Baasha heard this, he stopped building Ramah and abandoned his work. [6]Then King Asa brought all the men of Judah, and they carried away from Ramah the stones and timber Baasha had been using. With them he built up Geba and Mizpah.

⁷At that time Hanani the seer came to Asa king of Judah and said to him: "Because you relied on the king of Aram and not on the LORD your God, the army of the king of Aram has escaped from your hand. ⁸Were not the Cushites and Libyans a mighty army with great numbers of chariots and horsemen? Yet when you relied on the LORD, he delivered them into your hand. ⁹For the eyes of the LORD range throughout the earth to strengthen those whose hearts are fully committed to him. You have done a foolish thing, and from now on you will be at war."

¹⁰Asa was angry with the seer because of this; he was so enraged that he put him in prison. At the same time Asa brutally oppressed some of the people.

¹¹The events of Asa's reign, from beginning to end, are written in the book of the kings of Judah and Israel. ¹²In the thirty-ninth year of his reign Asa was afflicted with a disease in his feet. Though his disease was severe, even in his illness he did not seek help from the LORD, but only from the physicians. ¹³Then in the forty-first year of his reign Asa died and rested with his fathers. ¹⁴They buried him in the tomb that he had cut out for himself in the City of David. They laid him on a bier covered with spices and various blended perfumes, and they made a huge fire in his honour.

Jehoshaphat King of Judah

17 Jehoshaphat his son succeeded him as king and strengthened himself against Israel. ²He stationed troops in all the fortified cities of Judah and put garrisons in Judah and in the towns of Ephraim that his father Asa had captured.

³The LORD was with Jehoshaphat because in his early years he walked in the ways that his father David had followed. He did not consult the Baals ⁴but sought the God of his father and followed his commands rather than the practices of Israel. ⁵The LORD established the kingdom under his control; and all Judah brought gifts to Jehoshaphat, so that he had great wealth and honour. ⁶His heart was devoted to the ways of the LORD; furthermore, he removed the high places and the Asherah poles from Judah.

⁷In the third year of his reign he sent his officials Ben-Hail, Obadiah, Zechariah, Nethanel and Micaiah to teach in the towns of Judah. ⁸With them were certain Levites—Shemaiah, Nethaniah, Zebadiah, Asahel, Shemiramoth, Jehonathan, Adonijah, Tobijah and Tob-Adonijah—and the priests Elishama and Jehoram. ⁹They taught throughout Judah, taking with them the Book of the Law of the LORD; they went round to all the towns of Judah and taught the people.

¹⁰The fear of the LORD fell on all the kingdoms of the lands surrounding Judah, so that they did not make war with Jehoshaphat. ¹¹Some Philistines brought Jehoshaphat gifts and silver as tribute, and the Arabs brought him flocks: seven thousand seven hundred rams and seven thousand seven hundred goats.

¹²Jehoshaphat became more and more powerful; he built forts and store cities in Judah ¹³and had large supplies in the towns of Judah. He also kept experienced fighting men in Jerusalem. ¹⁴Their enrolment by families was as follows:

From Judah, commanders of units of 1,000:
Adnah the commander, with 300,000 fighting men;
¹⁵next, Jehohanan the commander, with 280,000;
¹⁶next, Amasiah son of Zicri, who volunteered himself for the service of the LORD, with 200,000.
¹⁷From Benjamin:
Eliada, a valiant soldier, with 200,000 men armed with bows and shields;

18next, Jehozabad, with 180,000 men armed for battle.

19These were the men who served the king, besides those he stationed in the fortified cities throughout Judah.

Micaiah Prophesies Against Ahab

18 Now Jehoshaphat had great wealth and honour, and he allied himself with Ahab by marriage. 2Some years later he went down to visit Ahab in Samaria. Ahab slaughtered many sheep and cattle for him and the people with him and urged him to attack Ramoth Gilead. 3Ahab king of Israel asked Jehoshaphat king of Judah, "Will you go with me against Ramoth Gilead?"

Jehoshaphat replied, "I am as you are, and my people as your people; we will join you in the war." 4But Jehoshaphat also said to the king of Israel, "First seek the counsel of the LORD."

5So the king of Israel brought together the prophets—four hundred men—and asked them, "Shall we go to war against Ramoth Gilead, or shall I refrain?"

"Go," they answered, "for God will give it into the king's hand."

6But Jehoshaphat asked, "Is there not a prophet of the LORD here whom we can enquire of?"

7The king of Israel answered Jehoshaphat, "There is still one man through whom we can enquire of the LORD, but I hate him because he never prophesies anything good about me, but always bad. He is Micaiah son of Imlah."

"The king should not say that," Jehoshaphat replied.

8So the king of Israel called one of his officials and said, "Bring Micaiah son of Imlah at once."

9Dressed in their royal robes, the king of Israel and Jehoshaphat king of Judah were sitting on their thrones at the threshing-floor by the entrance to the gate of Samaria, with all the prophets prophesying before them. 10Now Zedekiah son of Kenaanah had made iron horns, and he declared, "This is what the LORD says: 'With these you will gore the Arameans until they are destroyed.'"

11All the other prophets were prophesying the same thing. "Attack Ramoth Gilead and be victorious," they said, "for the LORD will give it into the king's hand."

12The messenger who had gone to summon Micaiah said to him, "Look, as one man the other prophets are predicting success for the king. Let your word agree with theirs, and speak favourably."

13But Micaiah said, "As surely as the LORD lives, I can tell him only what my God says."

14When he arrived, the king asked him, "Micaiah, shall we go to war against Ramoth Gilead, or shall I refrain?"

"Attack and be victorious," he answered, "for they will be given into your hand."

15The king said to him, "How many times must I make you swear to tell me nothing but the truth in the name of the LORD?"

16Then Micaiah answered, "I saw all Israel scattered on the hills like sheep without a shepherd, and the LORD said, 'These people have no master. Let each one go home in peace.'"

17The king of Israel said to Jehoshaphat, "Didn't I tell you that he never prophesies anything good about me, but only bad?"

18Micaiah continued, "Therefore hear the word of the LORD: I saw the LORD sitting on his throne with all the host of heaven standing on his right and on his left. 19And the LORD said, 'Who will entice Ahab king of Israel into attacking Ramoth Gilead and going to his death there?'

"One suggested this, and another that. 20Finally, a spirit came forward, stood before the LORD and said, 'I will entice him.'

"'By what means?' the LORD asked.

21"'I will go and be a lying spirit in the mouths of all his prophets,' he said.

"'You will succeed in enticing him,' said the LORD. 'Go and do it.'

22"So now the LORD has put a lying spirit in the mouths of these prophets of yours. The LORD has decreed disaster for you."

23Then Zedekiah son of Kenaanah went up and slapped Micaiah in the face. "Which way did the spirit from the LORD go when he went from me to speak to you?" he asked.

24Micaiah replied, "You will find out on the day you go to hide in an inner room."

25The king of Israel then ordered, "Take Micaiah and send him back to Amon the ruler of the city and to Joash the king's son, 26and say, 'This is what the king says: Put this fellow in prison and give him nothing but bread and water until I return safely.'"

27Micaiah declared, "If you ever return safely, the LORD has not spoken through me." Then he added, "Mark my words, all you people!"

NEW TESTAMENT READING
1 Corinthians 15:1–34

The Resurrection of Christ

15 Now, brothers, I want to remind you of the gospel I preached to you, which you received and on which you have taken your stand. 2By this gospel you are saved, if you hold firmly to the word I preached to you. Otherwise, you have believed in vain.

3For what I received I passed on to you as of first importance: that Christ died for our sins according to the Scriptures, 4that he was buried, that he was raised on the third day according to the Scriptures, 5and that he appeared to Peter, and then to the Twelve. 6After that, he appeared to more than five hundred of the brothers at the same time, most of whom are still living, though some have fallen asleep. 7Then he appeared to James, then to all the apostles, 8and last of all he appeared to me also, as to one abnormally born.

9For I am the least of the apostles and do not even deserve to be called an apostle, because I persecuted the church of God. 10But by the grace of God I am what I am, and his grace to me was not without effect. No, I worked harder than all of them—yet not I, but the grace of God that was with me. 11Whether, then, it was I or they, this is what we preach, and this is what you believed.

The Resurrection of the Dead

12But if it is preached that Christ has been raised from the dead, how can some of you say that there is no resurrection of the dead? 13If there is no resurrection of the dead, then not even Christ has been raised. 14And if Christ has not been raised, our preaching is useless and so is your faith. 15More than that, we are then found to be false witnesses about God, for we have testified about God that he raised Christ from the dead. But he did not raise him if in fact the dead are not raised. 16For if the dead are not raised, then Christ has not been raised either. 17And if Christ has not been raised, your faith is futile; you are still in your sins. 18Then those also who have fallen asleep in Christ are lost. 19If only for this life we have hope in Christ, we are to be pitied more than all men.

20But Christ has indeed been raised from the dead, the firstfruits of those who have fallen asleep. 21For since death came through a man, the resurrection of the dead comes also through a man. 22For as in Adam all die, so in Christ all will be made alive. 23But each in his own turn: Christ, the firstfruits; then, when he comes, those who belong to him. 24Then the end will come, when he hands over the kingdom to God the

Father after he has destroyed all dominion, authority and power. 25For he must reign until he has put all his enemies under his feet. 26The last enemy to be destroyed is death. 27For he "has put everything under his feet". Now when it says that "everything" has been put under him, it is clear that this does not include God himself, who put everything under Christ. 28When he has done this, then the Son himself will be made subject to him who put everything under him, so that God may be all in all.

29Now if there is no resurrection, what will those do who are baptised for the dead? If the dead are not raised at all, why are people baptised for them? 30And as for us, why do we endanger ourselves every hour? 31I die every day —I mean that, brothers—just as surely as I glory over you in Christ Jesus our Lord. 32If I fought wild beasts in Ephesus for merely human reasons, what have I gained? If the dead are not raised,

"Let us eat and drink,
   for tomorrow we die."

33Do not be misled: "Bad company corrupts good character." 34Come back to your senses as you ought, and stop sinning; for there are some who are ignorant of God—I say this to your shame.

READING FROM PSALMS
Psalm 102:1–11

A prayer of an afflicted man. When he is faint and pours out his lament before the LORD.

1Hear my prayer, O LORD;
   let my cry for help come to you.
2Do not hide your face from me
   when I am in distress.
Turn your ear to me;
   when I call, answer me quickly.

3For my days vanish like smoke;
   my bones burn like glowing
     embers.
4My heart is blighted and withered
   like grass;
   I forget to eat my food.
5Because of my loud groaning
   I am reduced to skin and bones.
6I am like a desert owl,
   like an owl among the ruins.
7I lie awake; I have become
   like a bird alone on a roof.
8All day long my enemies taunt me;
   those who rail against me use my
     name as a curse.
9For I eat ashes as my food
   and mingle my drink with tears
10because of your great wrath,
   for you have taken me up and
     thrown me aside.
11My days are like the evening shadow;
   I wither away like grass.

DAY 235

AUGUST 23

OLD TESTAMENT READING
2 Chronicles 18:28–21:3

Ahab Killed at Ramoth Gilead

28So the king of Israel and Jehoshaphat king of Judah went up to Ramoth Gilead. 29The king of Israel said to Jehoshaphat, "I will enter the battle in disguise, but you wear your royal robes." So the king of Israel disguised himself and went into battle.

30Now the king of Aram had ordered his chariot commanders, "Do not fight with anyone, small or great, except the king of Israel." 31When the chariot commanders saw Jehoshaphat, they thought, "This is the king of Israel." So they turned to attack him, but Jehoshaphat cried out, and the LORD helped him. God drew them away from him, [32]for when the chariot commanders saw that he was not the king of Israel, they stopped pursuing him.

[33]But someone drew his bow at random and hit the king of Israel between the sections of his armour. The king told the chariot driver, "Wheel around and get me out of the fighting. I've been wounded." [34]All day long the battle raged, and the king of Israel propped himself up in his chariot facing the Arameans until evening. Then at sunset he died.

19 When Jehoshaphat king of Judah returned safely to his palace in Jerusalem, [2]Jehu the seer, the son of Hanani, went out to meet him and said to the king, "Should you help the wicked and love those who hate the LORD? Because of this, the wrath of the LORD is upon you. [3]There is, however, some good in you, for you have rid the land of the Asherah poles and have set your heart on seeking God."

Jehoshaphat Appoints Judges

[4]Jehoshaphat lived in Jerusalem, and he went out again among the people from Beersheba to the hill country of Ephraim and turned them back to the LORD, the God of their fathers. [5]He appointed judges in the land, in each of the fortified cities of Judah. [6]He told them, "Consider carefully what you do, because you are not judging for man but for the LORD, who is with you whenever you give a verdict. [7]Now let the fear of the LORD be upon you. Judge carefully, for with the LORD our God there is no injustice or partiality or bribery."

[8]In Jerusalem also, Jehoshaphat appointed some of the Levites, priests and heads of Israelite families to administer the law of the LORD and to settle disputes. And they lived in Jerusalem. [9]He gave them these orders: "You must serve faithfully and wholeheartedly in the fear of the LORD. [10]In every case that comes before you from your fellow countrymen who live in the cities—

whether bloodshed or other concerns of the law, commands, decrees or ordinances—you are to warn them not to sin against the LORD; otherwise his wrath will come on you and your brothers. Do this, and you will not sin.

[11]"Amariah the chief priest will be over you in any matter concerning the LORD, and Zebadiah son of Ishmael, the leader of the tribe of Judah, will be over you in any matter concerning the king, and the Levites will serve as officials before you. Act with courage, and may the LORD be with those who do well."

Jehoshaphat Defeats Moab and Ammon

20 After this, the Moabites and Ammonites with some of the Meunites came to make war on Jehoshaphat.

[2]Some men came and told Jehoshaphat, "A vast army is coming against you from Edom, from the other side of the Sea. It is already in Hazazon Tamar" (that is, En Gedi). [3]Alarmed, Jehoshaphat resolved to enquire of the LORD, and he proclaimed a fast for all Judah. [4]The people of Judah came together to seek help from the LORD; indeed, they came from every town in Judah to seek him.

[5]Then Jehoshaphat stood up in the assembly of Judah and Jerusalem at the temple of the LORD in the front of the new courtyard [6]and said:

"O LORD, God of our fathers, are you not the God who is in heaven? You rule over all the kingdoms of the nations. Power and might are in your hand, and no-one can withstand you. [7]O our God, did you not drive out the inhabitants of this land before your people Israel and give it for ever to the descendants of Abraham your friend? [8]They have lived in it and have built in it a sanctuary for your Name, saying, [9]'If calamity comes upon us, whether the sword of judgment, or plague or famine, we will stand in your presence before this temple that bears your Name and will cry out to you in our distress, and you will hear us and save us.'

10"But now here are men from Ammon, Moab and Mount Seir, whose territory you would not allow Israel to invade when they came from Egypt; so they turned away from them and did not destroy them. 11See how they are repaying us by coming to drive us out of the possession you gave us as an inheritance. 12O our God, will you not judge them? For we have no power to face this vast army that is attacking us. We do not know what to do, but our eyes are upon you."

13All the men of Judah, with their wives and children and little ones, stood there before the LORD.

14Then the Spirit of the LORD came upon Jahaziel son of Zechariah, the son of Benaiah, the son of Jeiel, the son of Mattaniah, a Levite and descendant of Asaph, as he stood in the assembly.

15He said, "Listen, King Jehoshaphat and all who live in Judah and Jerusalem! This is what the LORD says to you: 'Do not be afraid or discouraged because of this vast army. For the battle is not yours, but God's. 16Tomorrow march down against them. They will be climbing up by the Pass of Ziz, and you will find them at the end of the gorge in the Desert of Jeruel. 17You will not have to fight this battle. Take up your positions; stand firm and see the deliverance the LORD will give you, O Judah and Jerusalem. Do not be afraid; do not be discouraged. Go out to face them tomorrow, and the LORD will be with you.'"

18Jehoshaphat bowed with his face to the ground, and all the people of Judah and Jerusalem fell down in worship before the LORD. 19Then some Levites from the Kohathites and Korahites stood up and praised the LORD, the God of Israel, with a very loud voice.

20Early in the morning they left for the Desert of Tekoa. As they set out, Jehoshaphat stood and said, "Listen to me, Judah and people of Jerusalem! Have faith in the LORD your God and you will be upheld; have faith in his prophets and you will be successful." 21After consulting the people, Jehoshaphat appointed men to sing to the LORD and to praise him for the splendour of his holiness as they went out at the head of the army, saying:

"Give thanks to the LORD,
    for his love endures for ever."

22As they began to sing and praise, the LORD set ambushes against the men of Ammon and Moab and Mount Seir who were invading Judah, and they were defeated. 23The men of Ammon and Moab rose up against the men from Mount Seir to destroy and annihilate them. After they finished slaughtering the men from Seir, they helped to destroy one another.

24When the men of Judah came to the place that overlooks the desert and looked towards the vast army, they saw only dead bodies lying on the ground; no-one had escaped. 25So Jehoshaphat and his men went to carry off their plunder, and they found among them a great amount of equipment and clothing and also articles of value—more than they could take away. There was so much plunder that it took three days to collect it. 26On the fourth day they assembled in the Valley of Beracah, where they praised the LORD. This is why it is called the Valley of Beracah to this day.

27Then, led by Jehoshaphat, all the men of Judah and Jerusalem returned joyfully to Jerusalem, for the LORD had given them cause to rejoice over their enemies. 28They entered Jerusalem and went to the temple of the LORD with harps and lutes and trumpets.

²⁹The fear of God came upon all the kingdoms of the countries when they heard how the LORD had fought against the enemies of Israel. ³⁰And the kingdom of Jehoshaphat was at peace, for his God had given him rest on every side.

The End of Jehoshaphat's Reign

³¹So Jehoshaphat reigned over Judah. He was thirty-five years old when he became king of Judah, and he reigned in Jerusalem for twenty-five years. His mother's name was Azubah daughter of Shilhi. ³²He walked in the ways of his father Asa and did not stray from them; he did what was right in the eyes of the LORD. ³³The high places, however, were not removed, and the people still had not set their hearts on the God of their fathers.

³⁴The other events of Jehoshaphat's reign, from beginning to end, are written in the annals of Jehu son of Hanani, which are recorded in the book of the kings of Israel.

³⁵Later, Jehoshaphat king of Judah made an alliance with Ahaziah king of Israel, who was guilty of wickedness. ³⁶He agreed with him to construct a fleet of trading ships. After these were built at Ezion Geber, ³⁷Eliezer son of Dodavahu of Mareshah prophesied against Jehoshaphat, saying, "Because you have made an alliance with Ahaziah, the LORD will destroy what you have made." The ships were wrecked and were not able to set sail to trade.

21 Then Jehoshaphat rested with his fathers and was buried with them in the City of David. And Jehoram his son succeeded him as king. ²Jehoram's brothers, the sons of Jehoshaphat, were Azariah, Jehiel, Zechariah, Azariahu, Michael and Shephatiah. All these were sons of Jehoshaphat king of Israel. ³Their father had given them many gifts of silver and gold and articles of value, as well as fortified cities in Judah, but he had given the kingdom to Jehoram because he was his firstborn son.

NEW TESTAMENT READING
1 Corinthians 15:35-49

The Resurrection Body

³⁵But someone may ask, "How are the dead raised? With what kind of body will they come?" ³⁶How foolish! What you sow does not come to life unless it dies. ³⁷When you sow, you do not plant the body that will be, but just a seed, perhaps of wheat or of something else. ³⁸But God gives it a body as he has determined, and to each kind of seed he gives its own body. ³⁹All flesh is not the same: Men have one kind of flesh, animals have another, birds another and fish another. ⁴⁰There are also heavenly bodies and there are earthly bodies; but the splendour of the heavenly bodies is one kind, and the splendour of the earthly bodies is another. ⁴¹The sun has one kind of splendour, the moon another and the stars another; and star differs from star in splendour.

⁴²So will it be with the resurrection of the dead. The body that is sown is perishable, it is raised imperishable; ⁴³it is sown in dishonour, it is raised in glory; it is sown in weakness, it is raised in power; ⁴⁴it is sown a natural body, it is raised a spiritual body.

If there is a natural body, there is also a spiritual body. ⁴⁵So it is written: "The first man Adam became a living being"; the last Adam, a life-giving spirit. ⁴⁶The spiritual did not come first, but the natural, and after that the spiritual. ⁴⁷The first man was of the dust of the earth, the second man from heaven. ⁴⁸As was the earthly man, so are those who are of the earth; and as is the man from heaven, so also are those who are of heaven. ⁴⁹And just as we have borne the likeness of the earthly man, so shall we bear the likeness of the man from heaven.

READING FROM PSALMS
Psalm 102:12–17

¹²But you, O LORD, sit enthroned for
     ever;
     your renown endures through all
       generations.
¹³You will arise and have compassion
     on Zion,
     for it is time to show favour to her;
     the appointed time has come.

¹⁴For her stones are dear to your
     servants;
     her very dust moves them to pity.
¹⁵The nations will fear the name of the
     LORD,
     all the kings of the earth will revere
       your glory.
¹⁶For the LORD will rebuild Zion
     and appear in his glory.
¹⁷He will respond to the prayer of the
     destitute;
     he will not despise their plea.

DAY 236

AUGUST 24

OLD TESTAMENT READING
2 Chronicles 21:4–23:21

Jehoram King of Judah

⁴When Jehoram established himself
firmly over his father's kingdom, he put
all his brothers to the sword along with
some of the princes of Israel. ⁵Jehoram
was thirty-two years old when he became king, and he reigned in Jerusalem
for eight years. ⁶He walked in the ways
of the kings of Israel, as the house of
Ahab had done, for he married a daughter of Ahab. He did evil in the eyes of
the LORD. ⁷Nevertheless, because of
the covenant the LORD had made with
David, the LORD was not willing to destroy the house of David. He had promised to maintain a lamp for him and his
descendants for ever.

⁸In the time of Jehoram, Edom rebelled against Judah and set up its own
king. ⁹So Jehoram went there with his
officers and all his chariots. The Edomites surrounded him and his chariot
commanders, but he rose up and broke
through by night. ¹⁰To this day Edom
has been in rebellion against Judah.

Libnah revolted at the same time,
because Jehoram had forsaken the
LORD, the God of his fathers. ¹¹He had
also built high places on the hills of

Judah and had caused the people of
Jerusalem to prostitute themselves and
had led Judah astray.

¹²Jehoram received a letter from Elijah the prophet, which said:

"This is what the LORD, the God of
your father David, says: 'You have
not walked in the ways of your
father Jehoshaphat or of Asa king
of Judah. ¹³But you have walked in
the ways of the kings of Israel, and
you have led Judah and the people
of Jerusalem to prostitute themselves, just as the house of Ahab
did. You have also murdered your
own brothers, members of your
father's house, men who were better than you. ¹⁴So now the LORD is
about to strike your people, your
sons, your wives and everything
that is yours, with a heavy blow.
¹⁵You yourself will be very ill with a
lingering disease of the bowels, until the disease causes your bowels
to come out.'"

¹⁶The LORD aroused against Jehoram
the hostility of the Philistines and of the
Arabs who lived near the Cushites.
¹⁷They attacked Judah, invaded it and
carried off all the goods found in the
king's palace, together with his sons and

wives. Not a son was left to him except Ahaziah, the youngest.

18After all this, the LORD afflicted Jehoram with an incurable disease of the bowels. 19In the course of time, at the end of the second year, his bowels came out because of the disease, and he died in great pain. His people made no fire in his honour, as they had for his fathers.

20Jehoram was thirty-two years old when he became king, and he reigned in Jerusalem for eight years. He passed away, to no-one's regret, and was buried in the City of David, but not in the tombs of the kings.

Ahaziah King of Judah

22 The people of Jerusalem made Ahaziah, Jehoram's youngest son, king in his place, since the raiders, who came with the Arabs into the camp, had killed all the older sons. So Ahaziah son of Jehoram king of Judah began to reign.

2Ahaziah was twenty-two years old when he became king, and he reigned in Jerusalem for one year. His mother's name was Athaliah, a granddaughter of Omri.

3He too walked in the ways of the house of Ahab, for his mother encouraged him in doing wrong. 4He did evil in the eyes of the LORD, as the house of Ahab had done, for after his father's death they became his advisers, to his undoing. 5He also followed their counsel when he went with Joram son of Ahab king of Israel to war against Hazael king of Aram at Ramoth Gilead. 6so he returned to Jezreel to recover from the wounds they had inflicted on him at Ramoth in his battle with Hazael king of Aram.

Then Ahaziah son of Jehoram king of Judah went down to Jezreel to see Joram son of Ahab because he had been wounded.

7Through Ahaziah's visit to Joram, God brought about Ahaziah's downfall. When Ahaziah arrived, he went out with Joram to meet Jehu son of Nimshi, whom the LORD had anointed to destroy the house of Ahab. 8While Jehu was executing judgment on the house of Ahab, he found the princes of Judah and the sons of Ahaziah's relatives, who had been attending Ahaziah, and he killed them. 9He then went in search of Ahaziah, and his men captured him while he was hiding in Samaria. He was brought to Jehu and put to death. They buried him, for they said, "He was a son of Jehoshaphat, who sought the LORD with all his heart." So there was no-one in the house of Ahaziah powerful enough to retain the kingdom.

Athaliah and Joash

10When Athaliah the mother of Ahaziah saw that her son was dead, she proceeded to destroy the whole royal family of the house of Judah. 11But Jehosheba, the daughter of King Jehoram, took Joash son of Ahaziah and stole him away from among the royal princes who were about to be murdered and put him and his nurse in a bedroom. Because Jehosheba, the daughter of King Jehoram and wife of the priest Jehoiada, was Ahaziah's sister, she hid the child from Athaliah so that she could not kill him. 12He remained hidden with them at the temple of God for six years while Athaliah ruled the land.

23 In the seventh year Jehoiada showed his strength. He made a covenant with the commanders of units of a hundred: Azariah son of Jeroham, Ishmael son of Jehohanan, Azariah son of Obed, Maaseiah son of Adaiah, and Elishaphat son of Zicri. 2They went throughout Judah and gathered the Levites and the heads of Israelite families from all the towns. When they came to Jerusalem, 3the whole assembly made a covenant with the king at the temple of God.

Jehoiada said to them, "The king's son shall reign, as the LORD promised concerning the descendants of David.

4Now this is what you are to do: A third of you priests and Levites who are going on duty on the Sabbath are to keep watch at the doors, 5a third of you at the royal palace and a third at the Foundation Gate, and all the other men are to be in the courtyards of the temple of the LORD. 6No-one is to enter the temple of the LORD except the priests and Levites on duty; they may enter because they are consecrated, but all the other men are to guard what the LORD has assigned to them. 7The Levites are to station themselves round the king, each man with his weapons in his hand. Anyone who enters the temple must be put to death. Stay close to the king wherever he goes."

8The Levites and all the men of Judah did just as Jehoiada the priest ordered. Each one took his men—those who were going on duty on the Sabbath and those who were going off duty—for Jehoiada the priest had not released any of the divisions. 9Then he gave the commanders of units of a hundred the spears and the large and small shields that had belonged to King David and that were in the temple of God. 10He stationed all the men, each with his weapon in his hand, round the king —near the altar and the temple, from the south side to the north side of the temple.

11Jehoiada and his sons brought out the king's son and put the crown on him; they presented him with a copy of the covenant and proclaimed him king. They anointed him and shouted, "Long live the king!"

12When Athaliah heard the noise of the people running and cheering the king, she went to them at the temple of the LORD. 13She looked, and there was the king, standing by his pillar at the entrance. The officers and the trumpeters were beside the king, and all the people of the land were rejoicing and blowing trumpets, and singers with musical instruments were leading the praises. Then Athaliah tore her robes and shouted, "Treason! Treason!"

14Jehoiada the priest sent out the commanders of units of a hundred, who were in charge of the troops, and said to them: "Bring her out between the ranks and put to the sword anyone who follows her." For the priest had said, "Do not put her to death at the temple of the LORD." 15So they seized her as she reached the entrance of the Horse Gate on the palace grounds, and there they put her to death.

16Jehoiada then made a covenant that he and the people and the king would be the LORD's people. 17All the people went to the temple of Baal and tore it down. They smashed the altars and idols and killed Mattan the priest of Baal in front of the altars.

18Then Jehoiada placed the oversight of the temple of the LORD in the hands of the priests, who were Levites, to whom David had made assignments in the temple, to present the burnt offerings of the LORD as written in the Law of Moses, with rejoicing and singing, as David had ordered. 19He also stationed doorkeepers at the gates of the LORD's temple so that no-one who was in any way unclean might enter.

20He took with him the commanders of hundreds, the nobles, the rulers of the people and all the people of the land and brought the king down from the temple of the LORD. They went into the palace through the Upper Gate and seated the king on the royal throne, 21and all the people of the land rejoiced. And the city was quiet, because Athaliah had been slain with the sword.

NEW TESTAMENT READING
1 Corinthians 15:50–16:4

50I declare to you, brothers, that flesh and blood cannot inherit the kingdom of God, nor does the perishable inherit the imperishable. 51Listen, I tell you a mystery: We will not all sleep, but we will all be changed—52in a flash, in the twinkling of an eye, at the last trumpet.

For the trumpet will sound, the dead will be raised imperishable, and we will be changed. ⁵³For the perishable must clothe itself with the imperishable, and the mortal with immortality. ⁵⁴When the perishable has been clothed with the imperishable, and the mortal with immortality, then the saying that is written will come true: "Death has been swallowed up in victory."

⁵⁵"Where, O death, is your victory?
      Where, O death, is your sting?"

⁵⁶The sting of death is sin, and the power of sin is the law. ⁵⁷But thanks be to God! He gives us the victory through our Lord Jesus Christ.

⁵⁸Therefore, my dear brothers, stand firm. Let nothing move you. Always give yourselves fully to the work of the Lord, because you know that your labour in the Lord is not in vain.

The Collection for God's People

16 Now about the collection for God's people: Do what I told the Galatian churches to do. ²On the first day of every week, each one of you should set aside a sum of money in keeping with his income, saving it up, so that when I come no collections will have to be made. ³Then, when I arrive, I will give letters of introduction to the men you approve and send them with your gift to Jerusalem. ⁴If it seems advisable for me to go also, they will accompany me.

READING FROM PROVERBS
Proverbs 20:25–21:4

²⁵It is a trap for a man to dedicate
      something rashly
  and only later to consider his vows.

²⁶A wise king winnows out the wicked;
  he drives the threshing wheel over
      them.

²⁷The lamp of the LORD searches the
      spirit of a man;
  it searches out his inmost being.

²⁸Love and faithfulness keep a king
      safe;
  through love his throne is made
      secure.

²⁹The glory of young men is their
      strength,
  grey hair the splendour of the old.

³⁰Blows and wounds cleanse away evil,
  and beatings purge the inmost
      being.

21 The king's heart is in the hand of the LORD;
  he directs it like a watercourse
      wherever he pleases.

²All a man's ways seem right to him,
  but the LORD weighs the heart.

³To do what is right and just
  is more acceptable to the LORD
      than sacrifice.

⁴Haughty eyes and a proud heart,
  the lamp of the wicked, are sin!

AUGUST 25

OLD TESTAMENT READING
2 Chronicles 24:1–25:28

Joash Repairs the Temple

24 Joash was seven years old when he became king, and he reigned in Jerusalem for forty years. His mother's name was Zibiah; she was from Beersheba. ²Joash did what was right in the eyes of the LORD all the years of Jehoiada the priest. ³Jehoiada chose two wives for him, and he had sons and daughters.

⁴Some time later Joash decided to restore the temple of the LORD. ⁵He called together the priests and Levites and said to them, "Go to the towns of Judah and collect the money due annually from all Israel, to repair the temple of your God. Do it now." But the Levites did not act at once.

⁶Therefore the king summoned Jehoiada the chief priest and said to him, "Why haven't you required the Levites to bring in from Judah and Jerusalem the tax imposed by Moses the servant of the LORD and by the assembly of Israel for the Tent of the Testimony?"

⁷Now the sons of that wicked woman Athaliah had broken into the temple of God and had used even its sacred objects for the Baals.

⁸At the king's command, a chest was made and placed outside, at the gate of the temple of the LORD. ⁹A proclamation was then issued in Judah and Jerusalem that they should bring to the LORD the tax that Moses the servant of God had required of Israel in the desert. ¹⁰All the officials and all the people brought their contributions gladly, dropping them into the chest until it was full. ¹¹Whenever the chest was brought in by the Levites to the king's officials and they saw that there was a large amount of money, the royal secretary and the officer of the chief priest would come and empty the chest and carry it back to its place. They did this regularly and collected a great amount of money. ¹²The king and Jehoiada gave it to the men who carried out the work required for the temple of the LORD. They hired masons and carpenters to restore the LORD's temple, and also workers in iron and bronze to repair the temple.

¹³The men in charge of the work were diligent, and the repairs progressed under them. They rebuilt the temple of God according to its original design and reinforced it. ¹⁴When they had finished, they brought the rest of the money to the king and Jehoiada, and with it were made articles for the LORD's temple: articles for the service and for the burnt offerings, and also dishes and other objects of gold and silver. As long as Jehoiada lived, burnt offerings were presented continually in the temple of the LORD.

¹⁵Now Jehoiada was old and full of years, and he died at the age of a hundred and thirty. ¹⁶He was buried with the kings in the City of David, because of the good he had done in Israel for God and his temple.

The Wickedness of Joash

¹⁷After the death of Jehoiada, the officials of Judah came and paid homage to the king, and he listened to them. ¹⁸They abandoned the temple of the LORD, the God of their fathers, and worshiped Asherah poles and idols. Because of their guilt, God's anger came upon Judah and Jerusalem. ¹⁹Although the LORD sent prophets to the people to bring them back to him, and though they testified against them, they would not listen.

²⁰Then the Spirit of God came upon Zechariah son of Jehoiada the priest. He stood before the people and said, "This is what God says: 'Why do you disobey the LORD's commands? You

will not prosper. Because you have forsaken the LORD, he has forsaken you.'"

²¹But they plotted against him, and by order of the king they stoned him to death in the courtyard of the LORD's temple. ²²King Joash did not remember the kindness Zechariah's father Jehoiada had shown him but killed his son, who said as he lay dying, "May the LORD see this and call you to account."

²³At the turn of the year, the army of Aram marched against Joash; it invaded Judah and Jerusalem and killed all the leaders of the people. They sent all the plunder to their king in Damascus. ²⁴Although the Aramean army had come with only a few men, the LORD delivered into their hands a much larger army. Because Judah had forsaken the LORD, the God of their fathers, judgment was executed on Joash. ²⁵When the Arameans withdrew, they left Joash severely wounded. His officials conspired against him for murdering the son of Jehoiada the priest, and they killed him in his bed. So he died and was buried in the City of David, but not in the tombs of the kings.

²⁶Those who conspired against him were Zabad, son of Shimeath an Ammonite woman, and Jehozabad, son of Shimrith a Moabite woman. ²⁷The account of his sons, the many prophecies about him, and the record of the restoration of the temple of God are written in the annotations on the book of the kings. And Amaziah his son succeeded him as king.

Amaziah King of Judah

25 Amaziah was twenty-five years old when he became king, and he reigned in Jerusalem for twenty-nine years. His mother's name was Jehoaddin; she was from Jerusalem. ²He did what was right in the eyes of the LORD, but not wholeheartedly. ³After the kingdom was firmly in his control, he executed the officials who had murdered his father the king. ⁴Yet he did not put their sons to death, but acted in accordance with what is written in the Law, in the Book of Moses, where the LORD commanded: "Fathers shall not be put to death for their children, nor children put to death for their fathers; each is to die for his own sins."

⁵Amaziah called the people of Judah together and assigned them according to their families to commanders of thousands and commanders of hundreds for all Judah and Benjamin. He then mustered those twenty years old or more and found that there were three hundred thousand men ready for military service, able to handle the spear and shield. ⁶He also hired a hundred thousand fighting men from Israel for a hundred talents of silver.

⁷But a man of God came to him and said, "O king, these troops from Israel must not march with you, for the LORD is not with Israel—not with any of the people of Ephraim. ⁸Even if you go and fight courageously in battle, God will overthrow you before the enemy, for God has the power to help or to overthrow."

⁹Amaziah asked the man of God, "But what about the hundred talents I paid for these Israelite troops?"

The man of God replied, "The LORD can give you much more than that."

¹⁰So Amaziah dismissed the troops who had come to him from Ephraim and sent them home. They were furious with Judah and left for home in a great rage.

¹¹Amaziah then marshalled his strength and led his army to the Valley of Salt, where he killed ten thousand men of Seir. ¹²The army of Judah also captured ten thousand men alive, took them to the top of a cliff and threw them down so that all were dashed to pieces.

¹³Meanwhile the troops that Amaziah had sent back and had not allowed to take part in the war raided Judean towns from Samaria to Beth Horon. They killed three thousand people and carried off great quantities of plunder.

¹⁴When Amaziah returned from slaughtering the Edomites, he brought

back the gods of the people of Seir. He set them up as his own gods, bowed down to them and burned sacrifices to them. 15The anger of the LORD burned against Amaziah, and he sent a prophet to him, who said, "Why do you consult this people's gods, which could not save their own people from your hand?"

16While he was still speaking, the king said to him, "Have we appointed you an adviser to the king? Stop! Why be struck down?"

So the prophet stopped but said, "I know that God has determined to destroy you, because you have done this and have not listened to my counsel."

17After Amaziah king of Judah consulted his advisers, he sent this challenge to Jehoash son of Jehoahaz, the son of Jehu, king of Israel: "Come, meet me face to face."

18But Jehoash king of Israel replied to Amaziah king of Judah, "A thistle in Lebanon sent a message to a cedar in Lebanon, 'Give your daughter to my son in marriage.' Then a wild beast in Lebanon came along and trampled the thistle underfoot. 19You say to yourself that you have defeated Edom, and now you are arrogant and proud. But stay at home! Why ask for trouble and cause your own downfall and that of Judah also?"

20Amaziah, however, would not listen, for God so worked that he might hand them over to Jehoash, because they sought the gods of Edom. 21So Jehoash king of Israel attacked. He and Amaziah king of Judah faced each other at Beth Shemesh in Judah. 22Judah was routed by Israel, and every man fled to his home. 23Jehoash king of Israel captured Amaziah king of Judah, the son of Joash, the son of Ahaziah, at Beth Shemesh. Then Jehoash brought him to Jerusalem and broke down the wall of Jerusalem from the Ephraim Gate to the Corner Gate—a section about six hundred feet long. 24He took all the gold and silver and all the articles found in the temple of God that had been in the care of Obed-Edom, together with

the palace treasures and the hostages, and returned to Samaria.

25Amaziah son of Joash king of Judah lived for fifteen years after the death of Jehoash son of Jehoahaz king of Israel. 26As for the other events of Amaziah's reign, from beginning to end, are they not written in the book of the kings of Judah and Israel? 27From the time that Amaziah turned away from following the LORD, they conspired against him in Jerusalem and he fled to Lachish, but they sent men after him to Lachish and killed him there. 28He was brought back by horse and was buried with his fathers in the City of Judah.

NEW TESTAMENT READING
1 Corinthians 16:5–24

Personal Requests

5After I go through Macedonia, I will come to you—for I will be going through Macedonia. 6Perhaps I will stay with you awhile, or even spend the winter, so that you can help me on my journey, wherever I go. 7I do not want to see you now and make only a passing visit; I hope to spend some time with you, if the Lord permits. 8But I will stay on at Ephesus until Pentecost, 9because a great door for effective work has opened to me, and there are many who oppose me.

10If Timothy comes, see to it that he has nothing to fear while he is with you, for he is carrying on the work of the Lord, just as I am. 11No-one, then, should refuse to accept him. Send him on his way in peace so that he may return to me. I am expecting him along with the brothers.

12Now about our brother Apollos: I strongly urged him to go to you with the brothers. He was quite unwilling to go now, but he will go when he has the opportunity.

13Be on your guard; stand firm in the faith; be men of courage; be strong. 14Do everything in love.

15You know that the household of

Stephanas were the first converts in Achaia, and they have devoted themselves to the service of the saints. I urge you, brothers, 16to submit to such as these and to everyone who joins in the work, and labours at it. 17I was glad when Stephanas, Fortunatus and Achaicus arrived, because they have supplied what was lacking from you. 18For they refreshed my spirit and yours also. Such men deserve recognition.

Final Greetings

19The churches in the province of Asia send you greetings. Aquila and Priscilla greet you warmly in the Lord, and so does the church that meets at their house. 20All the brothers here send you greetings. Greet one another with a holy kiss.

21I, Paul, write this greeting in my own hand.

22If anyone does not love the Lord —a curse be on him. Come, O Lord!

23The grace of the Lord Jesus be with you.

24My love to all of you in Christ Jesus. Amen.

READING FROM PSALMS
Psalm 102:18–28

18Let this be written for a future generation,
that a people not yet created may praise the LORD:

19"The LORD looked down from his sanctuary on high,
from heaven he viewed the earth,
20to hear the groans of the prisoners and release those condemned to death."
21So the name of the LORD will be declared in Zion
and his praise in Jerusalem
22when the peoples and the kingdoms assemble to worship the LORD.

23In the course of my life he broke my strength;
he cut short my days.
24So I said:
"Do not take me away, O my God, in the midst of my days;
your years go on through all generations.
25In the beginning you laid the foundations of the earth,
and the heavens are the work of your hands.
26They will perish, but you remain;
they will all wear out like a garment.
Like clothing you will change them and they will be discarded.
27But you remain the same,
and your years will never end.
28The children of your servants will live in your presence;
their descendants will be established before you."

OLD TESTAMENT READING
2 Chronicles 26:1–28:27

Uzziah King of Judah

26 Then all the people of Judah took Uzziah, who was sixteen years old, and made him king in place of his father Amaziah. ²He was the one who rebuilt Elath and restored it to Judah after Amaziah rested with his fathers.

³Uzziah was sixteen years old when he became king, and he reigned in Jerusalem for fifty-two years. His mother's name was Jecoliah; she was from Jerusalem. ⁴He did what was right in the eyes of the LORD, just as his father Amaziah had done. ⁵He sought God during the days of Zechariah, who instructed him in the fear of God. As long as he sought the LORD, God gave him success.

⁶He went to war against the Philistines and broke down the walls of Gath, Jabneh and Ashdod. He then rebuilt towns near Ashdod and elsewhere among the Philistines. ⁷God helped him against the Philistines and against the Arabs who lived in Gur Baal and against the Meunites. ⁸The Ammonites brought tribute to Uzziah, and his fame spread as far as the border of Egypt, because he had become very powerful.

⁹Uzziah built towers in Jerusalem at the Corner Gate, at the Valley Gate and at the angle of the wall, and he fortified them. ¹⁰He also built towers in the desert and dug many cisterns, because he had much livestock in the foothills and in the plain. He had people working his fields and vineyards in the hills and in the fertile lands, for he loved the soil.

¹¹Uzziah had a well-trained army, ready to go out by divisions according to their numbers as mustered by Jeiel the secretary and Maaseiah the officer under the direction of Hananiah, one of the royal officials. ¹²The total number of family leaders over the fighting men was 2,600. ¹³Under their command was an army of 307,500 men trained for war, a powerful force to support the king against his enemies. ¹⁴Uzziah provided shields, spears, helmets, coats of armour, bows and slingstones for the entire army. ¹⁵In Jerusalem he made machines designed by skilful men for use on the towers and on the corner defences to shoot arrows and hurl large stones. His fame spread far and wide, for he was greatly helped until he became powerful.

¹⁶But after Uzziah became powerful, his pride led to his downfall. He was unfaithful to the LORD his God, and entered the temple of the LORD to burn incense on the altar of incense. ¹⁷Azariah the priest with eighty other courageous priests of the LORD followed him in. ¹⁸They confronted him and said, "It is not right for you, Uzziah, to burn incense to the LORD. That is for the priests, the descendants of Aaron, who have been consecrated to burn incense. Leave the sanctuary, for you have been unfaithful; and you will not be honoured by the LORD God."

¹⁹Uzziah, who had a censer in his hand ready to burn incense, became angry. While he was raging at the priests in their presence before the incense altar in the LORD's temple, leprosy broke out on his forehead. ²⁰When Azariah the chief priest and all the other priests looked at him, they saw that he had leprosy on his forehead, so they hurried him out. Indeed, he himself was eager to leave, because the LORD had afflicted him.

²¹King Uzziah had leprosy until the day he died. He lived in a separate house—leprous, and excluded from the temple of the LORD. Jotham his son had charge of the palace and governed the people of the land.

22The other events of Uzziah's reign, from beginning to end, are recorded by the prophet Isaiah son of Amoz. 23Uzziah rested with his fathers and was buried near them in a field for burial that belonged to the kings, for people said, "He had leprosy." And Jotham his son succeeded him as king.

Jotham King of Judah

27 Jotham was twenty-five years old when he became king, and he reigned in Jerusalem for sixteen years. His mother's name was Jerusha daughter of Zadok. 2He did what was right in the eyes of the LORD, just as his father Uzziah had done, but unlike him he did not enter the temple of the LORD. The people, however, continued their corrupt practices. 3Jotham rebuilt the Upper Gate of the temple of the LORD and did extensive work on the wall at the hill of Ophel. 4He built towns in the Judean hills and forts and towers in the wooded areas.

5Jotham made war on the king of the Ammonites and conquered them. That year the Ammonites paid him a hundred talents of silver, ten thousand cors of wheat and ten thousand cors of barley. The Ammonites brought him the same amount also in the second and third years.

6Jotham grew powerful because he walked steadfastly before the LORD his God.

7The other events in Jotham's reign, including all his wars and the other things he did, are written in the book of the kings of Israel and Judah. 8He was twenty-five years old when he became king, and he reigned in Jerusalem for sixteen years. 9Jotham rested with his fathers and was buried in the City of David. And Ahaz his son succeeded him as king.

Ahaz King of Judah

28 Ahaz was twenty years old when he became king, and he reigned in Jerusalem for sixteen years. Unlike David his father, he did not do what was right in the eyes of the LORD. 2He walked in the ways of the kings of Israel and also made cast idols for worshiping the Baals. 3He burned sacrifices in the Valley of Ben Hinnom and sacrificed his sons in the fire, following the detestable ways of the nations that the LORD had driven out before the Israelites. 4He offered sacrifices and burned incense at the high places, on the hilltops and under every spreading tree.

5Therefore the LORD his God handed him over to the king of Aram. The Arameans defeated him and took many of his people as prisoners and brought them to Damascus.

He was also given into the hands of the king of Israel, who inflicted heavy casualties on him. 6In one day Pekah son of Remaliah killed a hundred and twenty thousand soldiers in Judah—because Judah had forsaken the LORD, the God of their fathers. 7Zicri, an Ephraimite warrior, killed Maaseiah the king's son, Azrikam the officer in charge of the palace, and Elkanah, second to the king. 8The Israelites took captive from their kinsmen two hundred thousand wives, sons and daughters. They also took a great deal of plunder, which they carried back to Samaria.

9But a prophet of the LORD named Oded was there, and he went out to meet the army when it returned to Samaria. He said to them, "Because the LORD, the God of your fathers, was angry with Judah, he gave them into your hand. But you have slaughtered them in a rage that reaches to heaven. 10And now you intend to make the men and women of Judah and Jerusalem your slaves. But aren't you also guilty of sins against the LORD your God? 11Now listen to me! Send back your fellow countrymen that you have taken as prisoners, for the LORD's fierce anger rests on you."

12Then some of the leaders in Ephraim—Azariah son of Jehohanan,

Berekiah son of Meshillemoth, Jehizkiah son of Shallum, and Amasa son of Hadlai—confronted those who were arriving from the war. 13"You must not bring those prisoners here," they said, "or we will be guilty before the LORD. Do you intend to add to our sin and guilt? For our guilt is already great, and his fierce anger rests on Israel."

14So the soldiers gave up the prisoners and plunder in the presence of the officials and all the assembly. 15The men designated by name took the prisoners, and from the plunder they clothed all who were naked. They provided them with clothes and sandals, food and drink, and healing balm. All those who were weak they put on donkeys. So they took them back to their fellow countrymen at Jericho, the City of Palms, and returned to Samaria.

16At that time King Ahaz sent to the king of Assyria for help. 17The Edomites had again come and attacked Judah and carried away prisoners, 18while the Philistines had raided towns in the foothills and in the Negev of Judah. They captured and occupied Beth Shemesh, Aijalon and Gederoth, as well as Soco, Timnah and Gimzo, with their surrounding villages. 19The LORD had humbled Judah because of Ahaz king of Israel, for he had promoted wickedness in Judah and had been most unfaithful to the LORD. 20Tiglath-Pileser king of Assyria came to him, but gave him trouble instead of help. 21Ahaz took some of the things from the temple of the LORD and from the royal palace and from the princes and presented them to the king of Assyria, but that did not help him.

22In his time of trouble King Ahaz became even more unfaithful to the LORD. 23He offered sacrifices to the gods of Damascus, who had defeated him; for he thought, "Since the gods of the kings of Aram have helped them, I will sacrifice to them so that they will help me." But they were his downfall and the downfall of all Israel.

24Ahaz gathered together the furnishings from the temple of God and took them away. He shut the doors of the LORD's temple and set up altars at every street corner in Jerusalem. 25In every town in Judah he built high places to burn sacrifices to other gods and provoked the LORD, the God of his fathers, to anger.

26The other events of his reign and all his ways, from beginning to end, are written in the book of the kings of Judah and Israel. 27Ahaz rested with his fathers and was buried in the city of Jerusalem, but he was not placed in the tombs of the kings of Israel. And Hezekiah his son succeeded him as king.

NEW TESTAMENT READING
2 Corinthians 1:1–11

1 Paul, an apostle of Christ Jesus by the will of God, and Timothy our brother,

To the church of God in Corinth, together with all the saints throughout Achaia:

2Grace and peace to you from God our Father and the Lord Jesus Christ.

The God of All Comfort

3Praise be to the God and Father of our Lord Jesus Christ, the Father of compassion and the God of all comfort, 4who comforts us in all our troubles, so that we can comfort those in any trouble with the comfort we ourselves have received from God. 5For just as the sufferings of Christ flow over into our lives, so also through Christ our comfort overflows. 6If we are distressed, it is for your comfort and salvation; if we are comforted, it is for your comfort, which produces in you patient endurance of the same sufferings we suffer. 7And our hope for you is firm, because we know that just as you share in our sufferings, so also you share in our comfort.

8We do not want you to be uninformed, brothers, about the hardships we suffered in the province of Asia. We were under great pressure, far beyond our ability to endure, so that we despaired even of life. 9Indeed, in our hearts we felt the sentence of death. But this happened that we might not rely on ourselves but on God, who raises the dead. 10He has delivered us from such a deadly peril, and he will deliver us. On him we have set our hope that he will continue to deliver us, 11as you help us by your prayers. Then many will give thanks on our behalf for the gracious favour granted us in answer to the prayers of many.

READING FROM PSALMS
Psalm 103:1–12

Of David.

1Praise the LORD, O my soul;
    all my inmost being, praise his holy
        name.
2Praise the LORD, O my soul,
    and forget not all his benefits—

3who forgives all your sins
    and heals all your diseases,
4who redeems your life from the pit
    and crowns you with love and
        compassion,
5who satisfies your desires with good
        things
    so that your youth is renewed like
        the eagle's.

6The LORD works righteousness
    and justice for all the oppressed.

7He made known his ways to Moses,
    his deeds to the people of Israel:
8The LORD is compassionate and
        gracious,
    slow to anger, abounding in love.
9He will not always accuse,
    nor will he harbour his anger for
        ever;
10he does not treat us as our sins
        deserve
    or repay us according to our
        iniquities.
11For as high as the heavens are above
        the earth,
    so great is his love for those who
        fear him;
12as far as the east is from the west,
    so far has he removed our
        transgressions from us.

AUGUST 27   DAY 239

OLD TESTAMENT READING
2 Chronicles 29:1–31:1

Hezekiah Purifies the Temple

29 Hezekiah was twenty-five years old when he became king, and he reigned in Jerusalem for twenty-nine years. His mother's name was Abijah daughter of Zechariah. 2He did what was right in the eyes of the LORD, just as his father David had done.

3In the first month of the first year of his reign, he opened the doors of the temple of the LORD and repaired them. 4He brought in the priests and the Levites, assembled them in the square on the east side 5and said, "Listen to me, Levites! Consecrate yourselves now and consecrate the temple of the LORD, the God of your fathers. Remove all defilement from the sanctuary. 6Our fathers were unfaithful; they did evil in the eyes of the LORD our God and forsook him. They turned their faces away from the LORD's dwelling-place and turned their backs on him. 7They also shut the doors of the portico and put out the lamps. They did not burn incense or present any burnt offerings at the sanctuary to the God of Israel. 8Therefore, the anger of the LORD has fallen on Judah and Jerusalem; he has made them an object of dread and horror and scorn, as you can see with your own eyes. 9This is why our fathers have fallen by the sword and why our sons and daughters and our wives are in captivity. 10Now I intend to make a covenant with the LORD, the God of Israel, so that his fierce anger will turn away from us. 11My sons, do not be negligent now, for the LORD has chosen you to stand before him and serve him, to minister before him and to burn incense."

12Then these Levites set to work:

from the Kohathites,
> Mahath son of Amasai and Joel son of Azariah;

from the Merarites,
> Kish son of Abdi and Azariah son of Jehallelel;

from the Gershonites,
> Joah son of Zimmah and Eden son of Joah;

13from the descendants of Elizaphan,
> Shimri and Jeiel;

from the descendants of Asaph,
> Zechariah and Mattaniah;

14from the descendants of Heman,
> Jehiel and Shimei;

from the descendants of Jeduthun,
> Shemaiah and Uzziel.

15When they had assembled their brothers and consecrated themselves, they went in to purify the temple of the LORD, as the king had ordered, following the word of the LORD. 16The priests went into the sanctuary of the LORD to purify it. They brought out to the courtyard of the LORD's temple everything unclean that they found in the temple of the LORD. The Levites took it and carried it out to the Kidron Valley. 17They began the consecration on the first day of the first month, and by the eighth day of the month they reached the portico of the LORD. For eight more days they consecrated the temple of the LORD

itself, finishing in the sixteenth day of the first month.

18Then they went in to King Hezekiah and reported: "We have purified the entire temple of the LORD, the altar of burnt offering with all its utensils, and the table for setting out the consecrated bread, with all its articles. 19We have prepared and consecrated all the articles that King Ahaz removed in his unfaithfulness while he was king. They are now in front of the LORD's altar."

20Early the next morning King Hezekiah gathered the city officials together and went up to the temple of the LORD. 21They brought seven bulls, seven rams, seven male lambs and seven male goats as a sin offering for the kingdom, for the sanctuary and for Judah. The king commanded the priests, the descendants of Aaron, to offer these on the altar of the LORD. 22So they slaughtered the bulls, and the priests took the blood and sprinkled it on the altar; next they slaughtered the rams and sprinkled their blood on the altar; then they slaughtered the lambs and sprinkled their blood on the altar. 23The goats for the sin offering were brought before the king and the assembly, and they laid their hands on them. 24The priests then slaughtered the goats and presented their blood on the altar for a sin offering to atone for all Israel, because the king had ordered the burnt offering and the sin offering for all Israel.

25He stationed the Levites in the temple of the LORD with cymbals, harps and lyres in the way prescribed by David and Gad the king's seer and Nathan the prophet; this was commanded by the LORD through his prophets. 26So the Levites stood ready with David's instruments, and the priests with their trumpets.

27Hezekiah gave the order to sacrifice the burnt offering on the altar. As the offering began, singing to the LORD began also, accompanied by trumpets and the instruments of David king of Israel. 28The whole assembly bowed in worship, while the singers sang and the trumpeters played. All this continued until the sacrifice of the burnt offering was completed.

29When the offerings were finished, the king and everyone present with him knelt down and worshipped. 30King Hezekiah and his officials ordered the Levites to praise the LORD with the words of David and of Asaph the seer. So they sang praises with gladness and bowed their heads and worshipped.

31Then Hezekiah said, "You have now dedicated yourselves to the LORD. Come and bring sacrifices and thank-offerings to the temple of the LORD." So the assembly brought sacrifices and thank-offerings, and all whose hearts were willing brought burnt offerings.

32The number of burnt offerings the assembly brought was seventy bulls, a hundred rams and two hundred male lambs—all of them for burnt offerings to the LORD. 33The animals consecrated as sacrifices amounted to six hundred bulls and three thousand sheep and goats. 34The priests, however, were too few to skin all the burnt offerings; so their kinsmen the Levites helped them until the task was finished and until other priests had been consecrated, for the Levites had been more conscientious in consecrating themselves than the priests had been. 35There were burnt offerings in abundance, together with the fat of the fellowship offerings and the drink offerings that accompanied the burnt offerings.

So the service of the temple of the LORD was re-established. 36Hezekiah and all the people rejoiced at what God had brought about for his people, because it was done so quickly.

Hezekiah Celebrates the Passover

30 Hezekiah sent word to all Israel and Judah and also wrote letters to Ephraim and Manasseh, inviting them to come to the temple of the LORD in Jerusalem and celebrate the Passover to the LORD, the God of Israel. 2The king and his officials and the whole assembly in Jerusalem decided to celebrate the Passover in the second month. 3They had not been able to celebrate it at the regular time because not enough priests had consecrated themselves and the people had not assembled in Jerusalem. 4The plan seemed right both to the king and to the whole assembly. 5They decided to send a proclamation throughout Israel, from Beersheba to Dan, calling the people to come to Jerusalem and celebrate the Passover to the LORD, the God of Israel. It had not been celebrated in large numbers according to what was written.

6At the king's command, couriers went throughout Israel and Judah with letters from the king and from his officials, which read:

"People of Israel, return to the LORD, the God of Abraham, Isaac and Israel, that he may return to you who are left, who have escaped from the hand of the kings of Assyria. 7Do not be like your fathers and brothers, who were unfaithful to the LORD, the God of their fathers, so that he made them an object of horror, as you see. 8Do not be stiff-necked, as your fathers were; submit to the LORD. Come to the sanctuary, which he has consecrated for ever. Serve the LORD your God, so that his fierce anger will turn away from you. 9If you return to the LORD, then your brothers and your children will be shown compassion by their captors and will come back to this land, for the LORD your God is gracious and compassionate. He will not turn his face from you if you return to him."

10The couriers went from town to town in Ephraim and Manasseh, as far as Zebulun, but the people scorned and ridiculed them. 11Nevertheless, some men of Asher, Manasseh and Zebulun humbled themselves and went to Jerusalem. 12Also in Judah the hand of God was on the people to give them unity of mind to carry out what the king and his officials had ordered, following the word of the LORD.

¹³A very large crowd of people assembled in Jerusalem to celebrate the Feast of Unleavened Bread in the second month. ¹⁴They removed the altars in Jerusalem and cleared away the incense altars and threw them into the Kidron Valley.

¹⁵They slaughtered the Passover lamb on the fourteenth day of the second month. The priests and the Levites were ashamed and consecrated themselves and brought burnt offerings to the temple of the LORD. ¹⁶Then they took up their regular positions as prescribed in the Law of Moses the man of God. The priests sprinkled the blood handed to them by the Levites. ¹⁷Since many in the crowd had not consecrated themselves, the Levites had to kill the Passover lambs for all those who were not ceremonially clean and could not consecrate ⌊their lambs⌋ to the LORD. ¹⁸Although most of the many people who came from Ephraim, Manasseh, Issachar and Zebulun had not purified themselves, yet they ate the Passover, contrary to what was written. But Hezekiah prayed for them, saying, "May the LORD, who is good, pardon everyone ¹⁹who sets his heart on seeking God —the LORD, the God of his fathers —even if he is not clean according to the rules of the sanctuary." ²⁰And the LORD heard Hezekiah and healed the people.

²¹The Israelites who were present in Jerusalem celebrated the Feast of Unleavened Bread for seven days with great rejoicing, while the Levites and priests sang to the LORD every day, accompanied by the LORD's instruments of praise.

²²Hezekiah spoke encouragingly to all the Levites, who showed good understanding of the service of the LORD. For the seven days they ate their assigned portion and offered fellowship offerings and praised the LORD, the God of their fathers.

²³The whole assembly then agreed to celebrate the festival seven more days; so for another seven days they celebrated joyfully. ²⁴Hezekiah king of Judah provided a thousand bulls and seven thousand sheep and goats for the assembly, and the officials provided them with a thousand bulls and ten thousand sheep and goats. A great number of priests consecrated themselves. ²⁵The entire assembly of Judah rejoiced, along with the priests and Levites and all who had assembled from Israel, including the aliens who had come from Israel and those who lived in Judah. ²⁶There was great joy in Jerusalem, for since the days of Solomon son of David king of Israel there had been nothing like this in Jerusalem. ²⁷The priests and the Levites stood to bless the people, and God heard them, for their prayer reached heaven, his holy dwelling-place.

31 When all this had ended, the Israelites who were there went out to the towns of Judah, smashed the sacred stones and cut down the Asherah poles. They destroyed the high places and the altars throughout Judah and Benjamin and in Ephraim and Manasseh. After they had destroyed all of them, the Israelites returned to their own towns and to their own property.

NEW TESTAMENT READING
2 Corinthians 1:12–22

Paul's Change of Plans

¹²Now this is our boast: Our conscience testifies that we have conducted ourselves in the world, and especially in our relations with you, in the holiness and sincerity that are from God. We have done so not according to worldly wisdom but according to God's grace. ¹³For we do not write to you anything you cannot read or understand. And I hope that, ¹⁴as you have understood us in part, you will come to understand fully that you can boast of us just as we will boast of you in the day of the Lord Jesus.

¹⁵Because I was confident of this, I planned to visit you first so that you might benefit twice. ¹⁶I planned to visit you on my way to Macedonia and to come back to you from Macedonia, and then to have you send me on my way to Judea. ¹⁷When I planned this, did I do it lightly? Or do I make my plans in a worldly manner so that in the same breath I say, "Yes, yes" and "No, no"?

¹⁸But as surely as God is faithful, our message to you is not "Yes" and "No". ¹⁹For the Son of God, Jesus Christ, who was preached among you by me and Silas and Timothy, was not "Yes" and "No", but in him it has always been "Yes". ²⁰For no matter how many promises God has made, they are "Yes" in Christ. And so through him the "Amen" is spoken by us to the glory of God. ²¹Now it is God who makes both us and you stand firm in Christ. He anointed us, ²²set his seal of ownership on us, and put his Spirit in our hearts as a deposit, guaranteeing what is to come.

READING FROM PSALMS
Psalm 103:13–22

¹³As a father has compassion on his children,
    so the LORD has compassion on those who fear him;

¹⁴for he knows how we are formed,
    he remembers that we are dust.
¹⁵As for man, his days are like grass,
    he flourishes like a flower of the field;
¹⁶the wind blows over it and it is gone,
    and its place remembers it no more.
¹⁷But from everlasting to everlasting
    the LORD's love is with those who fear him,
    and his righteousness with their children's children—
¹⁸with those who keep his covenant
    and remember to obey his precepts.

¹⁹The LORD has established his throne in heaven,
    and his kingdom rules over all.

²⁰Praise the LORD, you his angels,
    you mighty ones who do his bidding,
    who obey his word.
²¹Praise the LORD, all his heavenly hosts,
    you his servants who do his will.
²²Praise the LORD, all his works
    everywhere in his dominion.

Praise the LORD, O my soul.

AUGUST 28   DAY 240

OLD TESTAMENT READING
2 Chronicles 31:2–33:20

Contributions for Worship

²Hezekiah assigned the priests and Levites to divisions—each of them according to their duties as priests or Levites—to offer burnt offerings and fellowship offerings, to minister, to give thanks and to sing praises at the gates of the LORD's dwelling. ³The king contributed from his own possessions for the morning and evening burnt offerings and for the burnt offerings on the Sabbaths, New Moons and appointed feasts as written in the Law of the LORD. ⁴He ordered the people living in Jerusalem to give the portion due to the priests and Levites so that they could devote themselves to the Law of the LORD. ⁵As soon as the order went out, the Israelites

generously gave the firstfruits of their grain, new wine, oil and honey and all that the fields produced. They brought a great amount, a tithe of everything. [6]The men of Israel and Judah who lived in the towns of Judah also brought a tithe of their herds and flocks and a tithe of the holy things dedicated to the LORD their God, and they piled them in heaps. [7]They began doing this in the third month and finished in the seventh month. [8]When Hezekiah and his officials came and saw the heaps, they praised the LORD and blessed his people Israel.

[9]Hezekiah asked the priests and Levites about the heaps; [10]and Azariah the chief priest, from the family of Zadok, answered, "Since the people began to bring their contributions to the temple of the LORD, we have had enough to eat and plenty to spare, because the LORD has blessed his people, and this great amount is left over."

[11]Hezekiah gave orders to prepare storerooms in the temple of the LORD, and this was done. [12]Then they faithfully brought in the contributions, tithes and dedicated gifts. Conaniah, a Levite, was in charge of these things, and his brother Shimei was next in rank. [13]Jehiel, Azaziah, Nahath, Asahel, Jerimoth, Jozabad, Eliel, Ismakiah, Mahath and Benaiah were supervisors under Conaniah and Shimei his brother, by appointment of King Hezekiah and Azariah the official in charge of the temple of God.

[14]Kore son of Imnah the Levite, keeper of the East Gate, was in charge of the freewill offerings given to God, distributing the contributions made to the LORD and also the consecrated gifts. [15]Eden, Miniamin, Jeshua, Shemaiah, Amariah and Shecaniah assisted him faithfully in the towns of the priests, distributing to their fellow priests according to their divisions, old and young alike.

[16]In addition, they distributed to the males three years old or more whose names were in the genealogical records

—all who would enter the temple of the LORD to perform the daily duties of their various tasks, according to their responsibilities and their divisions. [17]And they distributed to the priests enrolled by their families in the genealogical records and likewise to the Levites twenty years old or more, according to their responsibilities and their divisions. [18]They included all the little ones, the wives, and the sons and daughters of the whole community listed in these genealogical records. For they were faithful in consecrating themselves.

[19]As for the priests, the descendants of Aaron, who lived on the farm lands around their towns or in any other towns, men were designated by name to distribute portions to every male among them and to all who were recorded in the genealogies of the Levites.

[20]This is what Hezekiah did throughout Judah, doing what was good and right and faithful before the LORD his God. [21]In everything that he undertook in the service of God's temple and in obedience to the law and the commands, he sought his God and worked wholeheartedly. And so he prospered.

Sennacherib Threatens Jerusalem

32 After all that Hezekiah had so faithfully done, Sennacherib king of Assyria came and invaded Judah. He laid siege to the fortified cities, thinking to conquer them for himself. [2]When Hezekiah saw that Sennacherib had come and that he intended to make war on Jerusalem, [3]he consulted with his officials and military staff about blocking off the water from the springs outside the city, and they helped him. [4]A large force of men assembled, and they blocked all the springs and the stream that flowed through the land. "Why should the kings of Assyria come and find plenty of water?" they said. [5]Then he worked hard repairing all the broken sections of the wall and building towers on it. He built another wall outside that one and reinforced the supporting terraces of the City of David. He also made large numbers of weapons and shields.

⁶He appointed military officers over the people and assembled them before him in the square at the city gate and encouraged them with these words: ⁷"Be strong and courageous. Do not be afraid or discouraged because of the king of Assyria and the vast army with him, for there is a greater power with us than with him. ⁸With him is only the arm of flesh, but with us is the LORD our God to help us and to fight our battles." And the people gained confidence from what Hezekiah the king of Judah said.

⁹Later, when Sennacherib king of Assyria and all his forces were laying siege to Lachish, he sent his officers to Jerusalem with this message for Hezekiah king of Judah and for all the people of Judah who were there:

¹⁰"This is what Sennacherib king of Assyria says: On what are you basing your confidence, that you remain in Jerusalem under siege? ¹¹When Hezekiah says, 'The LORD our God will save us from the hand of the king of Assyria,' he is misleading you, to let you die of hunger and thirst. ¹²Did not Hezekiah himself remove this god's high places and altars, saying to Judah and Jerusalem, 'You must worship before one altar and burn sacrifices on it'?

¹³"Do you not know what I and my fathers have done to all the peoples of the other lands? Were the gods of those nations ever able to deliver their land from my hand? ¹⁴Who of all the gods of these nations that my fathers destroyed has been able to save his people from me? How then can your god deliver you from my hand? ¹⁵Now do not let Hezekiah deceive you and mislead you like this. Do not believe him, for no god of any nation or

kingdom has been able to deliver his people from my hand or the hand of my fathers. How much less will your god deliver you from my hand!"

¹⁶Sennacherib's officers spoke further against the LORD God and against his servant Hezekiah. ¹⁷The king also wrote letters insulting the LORD, the God of Israel, and saying this against him: "Just as the gods of the peoples of the other lands did not rescue their people from my hand, so the god of Hezekiah will not rescue his people from my hand." ¹⁸Then they called out in Hebrew to the people of Jerusalem who were on the wall, to terrify them and make them afraid in order to capture the city. ¹⁹They spoke about the God of Jerusalem as they did about the gods of the other peoples of the world—the work of men's hands.

²⁰King Hezekiah and the prophet Isaiah son of Amoz cried out in prayer to heaven about this. ²¹And the LORD sent an angel, who annihilated all the fighting men and the leaders and officers in the camp of the Assyrian king. So he withdrew to his own land in disgrace. And when he went into the temple of his god, some of his sons cut him down with the sword.

²²So the LORD saved Hezekiah and the people of Jerusalem from the hand of Sennacherib king of Assyria and from the hand of all others. He took care of them on every side. ²³Many brought offerings to Jerusalem for the LORD and valuable gifts for Hezekiah king of Judah. From then on he was highly regarded by all the nations.

Hezekiah's Pride, Success and Death

²⁴In those days Hezekiah became ill and was at the point of death. He prayed to the LORD, who answered him and gave him a miraculous sign. ²⁵But Hezekiah's heart was proud and he did not respond to the kindness shown him; therefore the LORD's wrath was on him

and on Judah and Jerusalem. 26Then Hezekiah repented of the pride of his heart, as did the people of Jerusalem; therefore the LORD's wrath did not come upon them during the days of Hezekiah.

27Hezekiah had very great riches and honour, and he made treasuries for his silver and gold and for his precious stones, spices, shields and all kinds of valuables. 28He also made buildings to store the harvest of grain, new wine and oil; and he made stalls for various kinds of cattle, and pens for the flocks. 29He built villages and acquired great numbers of flocks and herds, for God had given him very great riches.

30It was Hezekiah who blocked the upper outlet of the Gihon spring and channelled the water down to the west side of the City of David. He succeeded in everything he undertook. 31But when envoys were sent by the rulers of Babylon to ask him about the miraculous sign that had occurred in the land, God left him to test him and to know everything that was in his heart.

32The other events of Hezekiah's reign and his acts of devotion are written in the vision of the prophet Isaiah son of Amoz in the book of the kings of Judah and Israel. 33Hezekiah rested with his fathers and was buried on the hill where the tombs of David's descendants are. All Judah and the people of Jerusalem honoured him when he died. And Manasseh his son succeeded him as king.

Manasseh King of Judah

33 Manasseh was twelve years old when he became king, and he reigned in Jerusalem for fifty-five years. 2He did evil in the eyes of the LORD, following the detestable practices of the nations the LORD had driven out before the Israelites. 3He rebuilt the high places his father Hezekiah had demolished; he also erected altars to the Baals and made Asherah poles. He bowed down to all the starry hosts and worshipped them. 4He built altars in the temple of the LORD, of which the LORD had said, "My Name will remain in Jerusalem for ever." 5In both courts of the temple of the LORD, he built altars to all the starry hosts. 6He sacrificed his sons in the fire in the Valley of Ben Hinnom, practised sorcery, divination and witchcraft, and consulted mediums and spiritists. He did much evil in the eyes of the LORD, provoking him to anger.

7He took the carved image he had made and put it in God's temple, of which God had said to David and to his son Solomon, "In this temple and in Jerusalem, which I have chosen out of all the tribes of Israel, I will put my Name for ever. 8I will not again make the feet of the Israelites leave the land I assigned to your forefathers, if only they will be careful to do everything that I commanded them concerning all the laws, decrees and ordinances given through Moses." 9But Manasseh led Judah and the people of Jerusalem astray, so that they did more evil than the nations the LORD had destroyed before the Israelites.

10The LORD spoke to Manasseh and his people, but they paid no attention. 11So the LORD brought against them the army commanders of the king of Assyria, who took Manasseh prisoner, put a hook in his nose, bound him with bronze shackles and took him to Babylon. 12In his distress he sought the favour of the LORD his God and humbled himself greatly before the God of his fathers. 13And when he prayed to him, the LORD was moved by his entreaty and listened to his plea; so he brought him back to Jerusalem and to his kingdom. Then Manasseh knew that the LORD is God.

14Afterwards he rebuilt the outer wall of the City of David, west of the Gihon spring in the valley, as far as the entrance of the Fish Gate and encircling the hill of Ophel; he also made it much higher. He stationed military commanders in all the fortified cities in Judah.

15He got rid of the foreign gods and removed the image from the temple of the LORD, as well as all the altars he had built on the temple hill and in Jerusalem; and he threw them out of the city. 16Then he restored the altar of the LORD and sacrificed fellowship offerings and thank-offerings on it, and told Judah to serve the LORD, the God of Israel. 17The people, however, continued to sacrifice at the high places, but only to the LORD their God.

18The other events of Manasseh's reign, including his prayer to his God and the words the seers spoke to him in the name of the LORD, the God of Israel, are written in the annals of the kings of Israel. 19His prayer and how God was moved by his entreaty, as well as all his sins and unfaithfulness, and the sites where he built high places and set up Asherah poles and idols before he humbled himself—all are written in the records of the seers. 20Manasseh rested with his fathers and was buried in his palace. And Amon his son succeeded him as king.

NEW TESTAMENT READING
2 Corinthians 1:23–2:11

23I call God as my witness that it was in order to spare you that I did not return to Corinth. 24Not that we lord it over your faith, but we work with you for your joy, because it is by faith you stand firm. 2 1So I made up my mind that I would not make another painful visit to you. 2For if I grieve you, who is left to make me glad but you whom I have grieved? 3I wrote as I did so that when I came I should not be distressed by those who ought to make me rejoice. I had confidence in all of you, that you would all share my joy. 4For I wrote to you out of great distress and anguish of heart and with many tears, not to grieve you but to let you know the depth of my love for you.

Forgiveness for the Sinner

5If anyone has caused grief, he has not so much grieved me as he has grieved all of you, to some extent—not to put it too severely. 6The punishment inflicted on him by the majority is sufficient for him. 7Now instead, you ought to forgive and comfort him, so that he will not be overwhelmed by excessive sorrow. 8I urge you, therefore, to reaffirm your love for him. 9The reason I wrote to you was to see if you would stand the test and be obedient in everything. 10If you forgive anyone, I also forgive him. And what I have forgiven —if there was anything to forgive—I have forgiven in the sight of Christ for your sake, 11in order that Satan might not outwit us. For we are not unaware of his schemes.

READING FROM PROVERBS
Proverbs 21:5–16

5The plans of the diligent lead to profit
as surely as haste leads to poverty.

6A fortune made by a lying tongue
is a fleeting vapour and a deadly snare.

7The violence of the wicked will drag them away,
for they refuse to do what is right.

8The way of the guilty is devious,
but the conduct of the innocent is upright.

9Better to live on a corner of the roof
than share a house with a quarrelsome wife.

10The wicked man craves evil;
his neighbour gets no mercy from him.

11When a mocker is punished, the simple gain wisdom;

when a wise man is instructed, he
gets knowledge.

12The Righteous One takes note of the
house of the wicked
and brings the wicked to ruin.

13If a man shuts his ears to the cry of
the poor,
he too will cry out and not be
answered.

14A gift given in secret soothes anger,
and a bribe concealed in the cloak
pacifies great wrath.

15When justice is done, it brings joy to
the righteous
but terror to evildoers.

16A man who strays from the path of
understanding
comes to rest in the company of the
dead.

AUGUST 29

OLD TESTAMENT READING
2 Chronicles 33:21–35:19

Amon King of Judah

21Amon was twenty-two years old
when he became king, and he reigned in
Jerusalem for two years. 22He did evil in
the eyes of the LORD, as his father Manasseh had done. Amon worshipped
and offered sacrifices to all the idols
Manasseh had made. 23But unlike his
father Manasseh, he did not humble
himself before the LORD; Amon increased his guilt.

24Amon's officials conspired against
him and assassinated him in his palace.
25Then the people of the land killed all
who had plotted against King Amon,
and they made Josiah his son king in his
place.

Josiah's Reforms

34 Josiah was eight years old when
he became king, and he reigned
in Jerusalem for thirty-one years. 2He
did what was right in the eyes of the
LORD and walked in the ways of his
father David, not turning aside to the
right or to the left.

3In the eighth year of his reign, while
he was still young, he began to seek the
God of his father David. In his twelfth
year he began to purge Judah and Jerusalem of high places, Asherah poles,
carved idols and cast images. 4Under his
direction the altars of the Baals were
torn down; he cut to pieces the incense
altars that were above them, and
smashed the Asherah poles, the idols
and the images. These he broke to
pieces and scattered over the graves of
those who had sacrificed to them. 5He
burned the bones of the priests on their
altars, and so he purged Judah and Jerusalem. 6In the towns of Manasseh,
Ephraim and Simeon, as far as Naphtali, and in the ruins around them, 7he
tore down the altars and the Asherah
poles and crushed the idols to powder
and cut to pieces all the incense altars
throughout Israel. Then he went back
to Jerusalem.

8In the eighteenth year of Josiah's
reign, to purify the land and the temple,
he sent Shaphan son of Azaliah and
Maaseiah the ruler of the city, with Joah
son of Joahaz, the recorder, to repair
the temple of the LORD his God.

9They went to Hilkiah the high
priest and gave him the money that had
been brought into the temple of God,
which the Levites who were the doorkeepers had collected from the people

of Manasseh, Ephraim and the entire remnant of Israel and from all the people of Judah and Benjamin and the inhabitants of Jerusalem. [10]Then they entrusted it to the men appointed to supervise the work on the LORD's temple. These men paid the workers who repaired and restored the temple. [11]They also gave money to the carpenters and builders to purchase dressed stone, and timber for joists and beams for the buildings that the kings of Judah had allowed to fall into ruin.

[12]The men did the work faithfully. Over them to direct them were Jahath and Obadiah, Levites descended from Merari, and Zechariah and Meshullam, descended from Kohath. The Levites —all who were skilled in playing musical instruments—[13]had charge of the labourers and supervised all the workers from job to job. Some of the Levites were secretaries, scribes and doorkeepers.

The Book of the Law Found

[14]While they were bringing out the money that had been taken into the temple of the LORD, Hilkiah the priest found the Book of the Law of the LORD that had been given through Moses. [15]Hilkiah said to Shaphan the secretary, "I have found the Book of the Law in the temple of the LORD." He gave it to Shaphan.

[16]Then Shaphan took the book to the king and reported to him: "Your officials are doing everything that has been committed to them. [17]They have paid out the money that was in the temple of the LORD and have entrusted it to the supervisors and workers." [18]Then Shaphan the secretary informed the king, "Hilkiah the priest has given me a book." And Shaphan read from it in the presence of the king.

[19]When the king heard the words of the Law, he tore his robes. [20]He gave these orders to Hilkiah, Ahikam son of Shaphan, Abdon son of Micah, Shaphan the secretary and Asaiah the

king's attendant: [21]"Go and enquire of the LORD for me and for the remnant in Israel and Judah about what is written in this book that has been found. Great is the LORD's anger that is poured out on us because our fathers have not kept the word of the LORD; they have not acted in accordance with all that is written in this book."

[22]Hilkiah and those the king had sent with him went to speak to the prophetess Huldah, who was the wife of Shallum son of Tokhath, the son of Hasrah, keeper of the wardrobe. She lived in Jerusalem, in the Second District.

[23]She said to them, "This is what the LORD, the God of Israel, says: Tell the man who sent you to me, [24]'This is what the LORD says: I am going to bring disaster on this place and its people —all the curses written in the book that has been read in the presence of the king of Judah. [25]Because they have forsaken me and burned incense to other gods and provoked me to anger by all that their hands have made, my anger will be poured out on this place and will not be quenched.' [26]Tell the king of Judah, who sent you to enquire of the LORD, 'This is what the LORD, the God of Israel, says concerning the words you heard: [27]Because your heart was responsive and you humbled yourself before God when you heard what he spoke against this place and its people, and because you humbled yourself before me and tore your robes and wept in my presence, I have heard you, declares the LORD. [28]Now I will gather you to your fathers, and you will be buried in peace. Your eyes will not see all the disaster I am going to bring on this place and on those who live here.'"

So they took her answer back to the king.

[29]Then the king called together all the elders of Judah and Jerusalem. [30]He went up to the temple of the LORD with the men of Judah, the people of Jerusalem, the priests and the Levites—all the people from the least to the

greatest. He read in their hearing all the words of the Book of the Covenant, which had been found in the temple of the LORD. [31]The king stood by his pillar and renewed the covenant in the presence of the LORD—to follow the LORD and keep his commands, regulations and decrees with all his heart and all his soul, and to obey the words of the covenant written in this book.

[32]Then he made everyone in Jerusalem and Benjamin pledge themselves to it; the people of Jerusalem did this in accordance with the covenant of God, the God of their fathers.

[33]Josiah removed all the detestable idols from all the territory belonging to the Israelites, and he made all who were present in Israel serve the LORD their God. As long as he lived, they did not fail to follow the LORD, the God of their fathers.

Josiah Celebrates the Passover

35 Josiah celebrated the Passover to the LORD in Jerusalem, and the Passover lamb was slaughtered on the fourteenth day of the first month. [2]He appointed the priests to their duties and encouraged them in the service of the LORD's temple. [3]He said to the Levites, who instructed all Israel and who had been consecrated to the LORD: "Put the sacred ark in the temple that Solomon son of David king of Israel built. It is not to be carried about on your shoulders. Now serve the LORD your God and his people Israel. [4]Prepare yourselves by families in your divisions, according to the directions written by David king of Israel and by his son Solomon.

[5]"Stand in the holy place with a group of Levites for each sub-division of the families of your fellow countrymen, the lay people. [6]Slaughter the Passover lambs, consecrate yourselves and prepare the lambs for your fellow countrymen, doing what the LORD commanded through Moses."

[7]Josiah provided for all the lay people who were there a total of thirty thousand sheep and goats for the Passover offerings, and also three thousand cattle—all from the king's own possessions.

[8]His officials also contributed voluntarily to the people and the priests and Levites. Hilkiah, Zechariah and Jehiel, the administrators of God's temple, gave the priests two thousand six hundred Passover offerings and three hundred cattle. [9]Also Conaniah along with Shemaiah and Nethanel, his brothers, and Hashabiah, Jeiel and Jozabad, the leaders of the Levites, provided five thousand Passover offerings and five hundred head of cattle for the Levites.

[10]The service was arranged and the priests stood in their places with the Levites in their divisions as the king had ordered. [11]The Passover lambs were slaughtered, and the priests sprinkled the blood handed to them, while the Levites skinned the animals. [12]They set aside the burnt offerings to give them to the sub-divisions of the families of the people to offer to the LORD, as is written in the Book of Moses. They did the same with the cattle. [13]They roasted the Passover animals over the fire as prescribed, and boiled the holy offerings in pots, cauldrons and pans and served them quickly to all the people. [14]After this, they made preparations for themselves and for the priests, because the priests, the descendants of Aaron, were sacrificing the burnt offerings and the fat portions until nightfall. So the Levites made preparations for themselves and for the Aaronic priests.

[15]The musicians, the descendants of Asaph, were in the places prescribed by David, Asaph, Heman and Jeduthun the king's seer. The gatekeepers at each gate did not need to leave their posts, because their fellow Levites made the preparations for them.

[16]So at that time the entire service of the LORD was carried out for the celebration of the Passover and the offering of burnt offerings on the altar of the LORD, as King Josiah had

ordered. ¹⁷The Israelites who were present celebrated the Passover at that time and observed the Feast of Unleavened Bread for seven days. ¹⁸The Passover had not been observed like this in Israel since the days of the prophet Samuel; and none of the kings of Israel had ever celebrated such a Passover as did Josiah, with the priests, the Levites and all Judah and Israel who were there with the people of Jerusalem. ¹⁹This Passover was celebrated in the eighteenth year of Josiah's reign.

NEW TESTAMENT READING
2 Corinthians 2:12–3:6

Ministers of the New Covenant

¹²Now when I went to Troas to preach the gospel of Christ and found that the Lord had opened a door for me, ¹³I still had no peace of mind, because I did not find my brother Titus there. So I said good-bye to them and went on to Macedonia.

¹⁴But thanks be to God, who always leads us in triumphal procession in Christ and through us spreads everywhere the fragrance of the knowledge of him. ¹⁵For we are to God the aroma of Christ among those who are being saved and those who are perishing. ¹⁶To the one we are the smell of death; to the other, the fragrance of life. And who is equal to such a task? ¹⁷Unlike so many, we do not peddle the word of God for profit. On the contrary, in Christ we speak before God with sincerity, like men sent from God.

3 Are we beginning to commend ourselves again? Or do we need, like some people, letters of recommendation to you or from you? ²You yourselves are our letter, written on our hearts, known and read by everybody. ³You show that you are a letter from Christ, the result of our ministry, written not with ink but with the Spirit of the living God, not on tablets of stone but on tablets of human hearts.

⁴Such confidence as this is ours through Christ before God. ⁵Not that we are competent in ourselves to claim anything for ourselves, but our competence comes from God. ⁶He has made us competent as ministers of a new covenant—not of the letter but of the Spirit; for the letter kills, but the Spirit gives life.

READING FROM PSALMS
Psalm 104:1–18

¹Praise the LORD, O my soul.

O LORD my God, you are very great;
    you are clothed with splendour and
      majesty.
²He wraps himself in light as with a
    garment;
    he stretches out the heavens like a
      tent
³ and lays the beams of his upper
    chambers on their waters.
He makes the clouds his chariot
    and rides on the wings of the wind.
⁴He makes winds his messengers,
    flames of fire his servants.

⁵He set the earth on its foundations;
    it can never be moved.
⁶You covered it with the deep as with
    a garment;
    the waters stood above the
      mountains.
⁷But at your rebuke the waters fled,
    at the sound of your thunder they
      took to flight;
⁸they flowed over the mountains,
    they went down into the valleys,
    to the place you assigned for them.
⁹You set a boundary they cannot
    cross;
    never again will they cover the
      earth.

¹⁰He makes springs pour water into the
    ravines;
    it flows between the mountains.

11They give water to all the beasts of
       the field;
   the wild donkeys quench their
       thirst.
12The birds of the air nest by the
       waters;
   they sing among the branches.
13He waters the mountains from his
       upper chambers;
   the earth is satisfied by the fruit of
       his work.
14He makes grass grow for the cattle,
   and plants for man to cultivate—
       bringing forth food from the earth:

15wine that gladdens the heart of man,
   oil to make his face shine,
   and bread that sustains his heart.
16The trees of the LORD are well
       watered,
   the cedars of Lebanon that he
       planted.
17There the birds make their nests;
   the stork has its home in the pine
       trees.
18The high mountains belong to the
       wild goats;
   the crags are a refuge for the
       conies.

DAY 242

AUGUST 30

OLD TESTAMENT READING
2 Chronicles 35:20—36:23

The Death of Josiah

20After all this, when Josiah had set
the temple in order, Neco king of Egypt
went up to fight at Carchemish on the
Euphrates, and Josiah marched out to
meet him in battle. 21But Neco sent
messengers to him saying, "What quarrel is there between you and me, O king
of Judah? It is not you I am attacking at
this time, but the house with which I am
at war. God has told me to hurry; so
stop opposing God, who is with me, or
he will destroy you."

22Josiah, however, would not turn
away from him, but disguised himself to
engage him in battle. He would not
listen to what Neco had said at God's
command but went to fight him on the
plain of Megiddo.

23Archers shot King Josiah, and he
told his officers, "Take me away; I am
badly wounded." 24So they took him
out of his chariot, put him in the other
chariot he had and brought him to Jerusalem, where he died. He was buried in
the tombs of his fathers, and all Judah
and Jerusalem mourned for him.

25Jeremiah composed laments for
Josiah, and to this day all the men and
women singers commemorate Josiah
in the laments. These became a tradition
in Israel and are written in the Laments.

26The other events of Josiah's reign
and his acts of devotion, according to
what is written in the Law of the LORD
—27all the events, from beginning to
end, are written in the book of the kings
of Israel and Judah. 36 1And the
people of the land took
Jehoahaz son of Josiah and made him
king in Jerusalem in place of his father.

Jehoahaz King of Judah

2Jehoahaz was twenty-three years old
when he became king, and he reigned in
Jerusalem for three months. 3The king
of Egypt dethroned him in Jerusalem
and imposed on Judah a levy of a hundred talents of silver and a talent of gold.
4The king of Egypt made Eliakim, a
brother of Jehoahaz, king over Judah
and Jerusalem and changed Eliakim's
name to Jehoiakim. But Neco took
Eliakim's brother Jehoahaz and carried
him off to Egypt.

Jehoiakim King of Judah

⁵Jehoiakim was twenty-five years old when he became king, and he reigned in Jerusalem for eleven years. He did evil in the eyes of the LORD his God. ⁶Nebuchadnezzar king of Babylon attacked him and bound him with bronze shackles to take him to Babylon. ⁷Nebuchadnezzar also took to Babylon articles from the temple of the LORD and put them in his temple there.

⁸The other events of Jehoiakim's reign, the detestable things he did and all that was found against him, are written in the book of the kings of Israel and Judah. And Jehoiachin his son succeeded him as king.

Jehoiachin King of Judah

⁹Jehoiachin was eighteen years old when he became king, and he reigned in Jerusalem for three months and ten days. He did evil in the eyes of the LORD. ¹⁰In the spring, King Nebuchadnezzar sent for him and brought him to Babylon, together with articles of value from the temple of the LORD, and he made Jehoiachin's uncle, Zedekiah, king over Judah and Jerusalem.

Zedekiah King of Judah

¹¹Zedekiah was twenty-one years old when he became king, and he reigned in Jerusalem for eleven years. ¹²He did evil in the eyes of the LORD his God and did not humble himself before Jeremiah the prophet, who spoke the word of the LORD. ¹³He also rebelled against King Nebuchadnezzar, who had made him take an oath in God's name. He became stiff-necked and hardened his heart and would not turn to the LORD, the God of Israel. ¹⁴Furthermore, all the leaders of the priests and the people became more and more unfaithful, following all the detestable practices of the nations and defiling the temple of the LORD, which he had consecrated in Jerusalem.

The Fall of Jerusalem

¹⁵The LORD, the God of their fathers, sent word to them through his messengers again and again, because he had pity on his people and on his dwelling-place. ¹⁶But they mocked God's messengers, despised his words and scoffed at his prophets until the wrath of the LORD was aroused against his people and there was no remedy. ¹⁷He brought up against them the king of the Babylonians, who killed their young men with the sword in the sanctuary, and spared neither young man nor young woman, old man or aged. God handed all of them over to Nebuchadnezzar. ¹⁸He carried to Babylon all the articles from the temple of God, both large and small, and the treasures of the LORD's temple and the treasures of the king and his officials. ¹⁹They set fire to God's temple and broke down the wall of Jerusalem; they burned all the palaces and destroyed everything of value there.

²⁰He carried into exile to Babylon the remnant who escaped from the sword, and they became servants to him and his sons until the kingdom of Persia came to power. ²¹The land enjoyed its sabbath rests; all the time of its desolation it rested, until the seventy years were completed in fulfilment of the word of the LORD spoken by Jeremiah.

²²In the first year of Cyrus king of Persia, in order to fulfil the word of the LORD spoken by Jeremiah, the LORD moved the heart of Cyrus king of Persia to make a proclamation throughout his realm and to put it in writing:

²³"This is what Cyrus king of Persia says:

" 'The LORD, the God of heaven, has given me all the kingdoms of the earth and he has appointed me to build a temple for him at Jerusalem in Judah. Anyone of his people among you—may the LORD his God be with him, and let him go up.' "

NEW TESTAMENT READING
2 Corinthians 3:7–18

The Glory of the New Covenant

[7]Now if the ministry that brought death, which was engraved in letters on stone, came with glory, so that the Israelites could not look steadily at the face of Moses because of its glory, fading though it was, [8]will not the ministry of the Spirit be even more glorious? [9]If the ministry that condemns men is glorious, how much more glorious is the ministry that brings righteousness! [10]For what was glorious has no glory now in comparison with the surpassing glory. [11]And if what was fading away came with glory, how much greater is the glory of that which lasts!

[12]Therefore, since we have such a hope, we are very bold. [13]We are not like Moses, who would put a veil over his face to keep the Israelites from gazing at it while the radiance was fading away. [14]But their minds were made dull, for to this day the same veil remains when the old covenant is read. It has not been removed, because only in Christ is it taken away. [15]Even to this day when Moses is read, a veil covers their hearts. [16]But whenever anyone turns to the Lord, the veil is taken away. [17]Now the Lord is the Spirit, and where the Spirit of the Lord is, there is freedom. [18]And we, who with unveiled faces all reflect the Lord's glory, are being transformed into his likeness with ever-increasing glory, which comes from the Lord, who is the Spirit.

READING FROM PSALMS
Psalm 104:19–30

[19]The moon marks off the seasons,
    and the sun knows when to go
      down.
[20]You bring darkness, it becomes night,
    and all the beasts of the forest
      prowl.
[21]The lions roar for their prey
    and seek their food from God.
[22]The sun rises, and they steal away;
    they return and lie down in their
      dens.
[23]Then man goes out to his work,
    to his labour until evening.

[24]How many are your works, O LORD!
    In wisdom you made them all;
    the earth is full of your creatures.
[25]There is the sea, vast and spacious,
    teeming with creatures beyond
      number—
    living things both large and small.
[26]There the ships go to and fro,
    and the leviathan, which you
      formed to frolic there.

[27]These all look to you
    to give them their food at the
      proper time.
[28]When you give it to them,
    they gather it up;
  when you open your hand,
    they are satisfied with good things.
[29]When you hide your face,
    they are terrified;
  when you take away their breath,
    they die and return to the dust.
[30]When you send your Spirit,
    they are created,
    and you renew the face of the earth.

OLD TESTAMENT READING
Micah 1:1–4:13

1 The word of the LORD that came to
Micah of Moresheth during the
reigns of Jotham, Ahaz and Hezekiah,
kings of Judah—the vision he saw concerning Samaria and Jerusalem.

²Hear, O peoples, all of you,
listen, O earth and all who are in it,
that the Sovereign LORD may witness
against you,
the Lord from his holy temple.

Judgment Against Samaria and Jerusalem

³Look! The LORD is coming from his
dwelling-place;
he comes down and treads the high
places of the earth.
⁴The mountains melt beneath him
and the valleys split apart,
like wax before the fire,
like water rushing down a slope.
⁵All this is because of Jacob's
transgression,
because of the sins of the house of
Israel.
What is Jacob's transgression?
Is it not Samaria?
What is Judah's high place?
Is it not Jerusalem?

⁶"Therefore I will make Samaria a
heap of rubble,
a place for planting vineyards.
I will pour her stones into the valley
and lay bare her foundations.
⁷All her idols will be broken to pieces;
all her temple gifts will be burned
with fire;
I will destroy all her images.
Since she gathered her gifts from the
wages of prostitutes,
as the wages of prostitutes they will
again be used."

Weeping and Mourning

⁸Because of this I will weep and wail;
I will go about barefoot and naked.
I will howl like a jackal
and moan like an owl.
⁹For her wound is incurable;
it has come to Judah.
It has reached the very gate of my
people,
even to Jerusalem itself.
¹⁰Tell it not in Gath;
weep not at all.
In Beth Ophrah
roll in the dust.
¹¹Pass on in nakedness and shame,
you who live in Shaphir.
Those who live in Zaanan
will not come out.
Beth Ezel is in mourning;
its protection is taken from you.
¹²Those who live in Maroth writhe in
pain,
waiting for relief,
because disaster has come from the
LORD,
even to the gate of Jerusalem.
¹³You who live in Lachish,
harness the team to the chariot.
You were the beginning of sin
to the Daughter of Zion,
for the transgressions of Israel
were found in you.
¹⁴Therefore you will give parting gifts
to Moresheth Gath.
The town of Aczib will prove
deceptive
to the kings of Israel.
¹⁵I will bring a conqueror against you
who live in Mareshah.
He who is the glory of Israel
will come to Adullam.
¹⁶Shave your heads in mourning
for the children in whom you
delight;
make yourselves as bald as the
vulture,
for they will go from you into exile.

Man's Plans and God's

2 Woe to those who plan iniquity,
to those who plot evil on their
beds!
At morning's light they carry it out
because it is in their power to do it.
[2]They covet fields and seize them,
and houses, and take them.
They defraud a man of his home,
a fellow-man of his inheritance.

[3]Therefore, the LORD says:

"I am planning disaster against this
people,
from which you cannot save
yourselves.
You will no longer walk proudly,
for it will be a time of calamity.
[4]In that day men will ridicule you;
they will taunt you with this
mournful song:
'We are utterly ruined;
my people's possession is divided
up.
He takes it from me!
He assigns our fields to traitors.' "

[5]Therefore you will have no-one in the
assembly of the LORD
to divide the land by lot.

False Prophets

[6]"Do not prophesy," their prophets
say.
"Do not prophesy about these
things;
disgrace will not overtake us."
[7]Should it be said, O house of Jacob:
"Is the Spirit of the LORD angry?
Does he do such things?"

"Do not my words do good
to him whose ways are upright?
[8]Lately my people have risen up
like an enemy.
You strip off the rich robe
from those who pass by without a
care,
like men returning from battle.

[9]You drive the women of my people
from their pleasant homes.
You take away my blessing
from their children for ever.
[10]Get up, go away!
For this is not your resting place,
because it is defiled,
it is ruined, beyond all remedy.
[11]If a liar and deceiver comes and says,
'I will prophesy for you plenty of
wine and beer,'
he would be just the prophet for
this people!

Deliverance Promised

[12]"I will surely gather all of you, O
Jacob;
I will surely bring together the
remnant of Israel.
I will bring them together like sheep
in a pen,
like a flock in its pasture;
the place will throng with people.
[13]One who breaks open the way will go
up before them;
they will break through the gate
and go out.
Their king will pass through before
them,
the LORD at their head."

Leaders and Prophets Rebuked

3 Then I said,

"Listen, you leaders of Jacob,
you rulers of the house of Israel.
Should you not know justice;
[2] you who hate good and love evil;
who tear the skin from my people
and the flesh from their bones;
[3]who eat my people's flesh,
strip off their skin
and break their bones in pieces;
who chop them up like meat for the
pan,
like flesh for the pot."

[4]Then they will cry out to the LORD,
but he will not answer them.
At that time he will hide his face from
them
because of the evil they have done.

⁵This is what the LORD says:

"As for the prophets
　who lead my people astray,
if one feeds them,
　they proclaim 'peace';
if he does not,
　they prepare to wage war against
　　him.
⁶Therefore night will come over you,
　without visions,
　and darkness, without divination.
The sun will set for the prophets,
　and the day will go dark for them.
⁷The seers will be ashamed
　and the diviners disgraced.
They will all cover their faces
　because there is no answer from
　　God."

⁸But as for me, I am filled with power,
　with the Spirit of the LORD,
　and with justice and might,
to declare to Jacob his transgression,
　to Israel his sin.
⁹Hear this, you leaders of the house of
　　Jacob,
　you rulers of the house of Israel,
who despise justice
　and distort all that is right;
¹⁰who build Zion with bloodshed,
　and Jerusalem with wickedness.
¹¹Her leaders judge for a bribe,
　her priests teach for a price,
　and her prophets tell fortunes for
　　money.
Yet they lean upon the LORD and say,
　"Is not the LORD among us?
　No disaster will come upon us."
¹²Therefore because of you,
　Zion will be ploughed like a field,
Jerusalem will become a heap of
　　rubble,
　the temple hill a mound overgrown
　　with thickets.

The Mountain of the LORD

4 In the last days

the mountain of the LORD's temple
　will be established
　as chief among the mountains;

it will be raised above the hills,
　and peoples will stream to it.

²Many nations will come and say,

"Come, let us go up to the mountain
　of the LORD,
　to the house of the God of Jacob.
He will teach us his ways,
　so that we may walk in his paths."
The law will go out from Zion,
　the word of the LORD from
　　Jerusalem.
³He will judge between many peoples
　and will settle disputes for strong
　　nations far and wide.
They will beat their swords into
　　ploughshares
　and their spears into pruning
　　hooks.
Nation will not take up sword against
　　nation,
　nor will they train for war any
　　more.
⁴Every man will sit under his own vine
　and under his own fig-tree,
and no-one will make them afraid,
　for the LORD Almighty has spoken.
⁵All the nations may walk
　in the name of their gods;
we will walk in the name of the LORD
　our God for ever and ever.

The LORD's Plan

⁶"In that day," declares the LORD,

"I will gather the lame;
　I will assemble the exiles
　and those I have brought to grief.
⁷I will make the lame a remnant,
　those driven away a strong nation.
The LORD will rule over them in
　　Mount Zion
　from that day and for ever.
⁸As for you, O watchtower of the
　　flock,
　O stronghold of the Daughter of
　　Zion,
the former dominion will be restored
　to you;

kingship will come to the Daughter
of Jerusalem."

⁹Why do you now cry aloud—
have you no king?
Has your counsellor perished,
that pain seizes you like that of a
woman in labour?
¹⁰Writhe in agony, O Daughter of
Zion,
like a woman in labour,
for now you must leave the city
to camp in the open field.
You will go to Babylon;
there you will be rescued.
There the LORD will redeem you
out of the hand of your enemies.

¹¹But now many nations
are gathered against you.
They say, "Let her be defiled,
let our eyes gloat over Zion!"
¹²But they do not know
the thoughts of the LORD;
they do not understand his plan,
he who gathers them like sheaves
to the threshing-floor.

¹³"Rise and thresh, O Daughter of
Zion,
for I will give you horns of iron;
I will give you hoofs of bronze
and you will break to pieces many
nations."

You will devote their ill-gotten gains
to the LORD,
their wealth to the Lord of all the
earth.

NEW TESTAMENT READING
2 Corinthians 4:1–18

Treasures in Jars of Clay

4 Therefore, since through God's
mercy we have this ministry, we do
not lose heart. ²Rather, we have renounced secret and shameful ways; we
do not use deception, nor do we distort
the word of God. On the contrary, by
setting forth the truth plainly we commend ourselves to every man's con-
science in the sight of God. ³And even if
our gospel is veiled, it is veiled to those
who are perishing. ⁴The god of this age
has blinded the minds of unbelievers, so
that they cannot see the light of the
gospel of the glory of Christ, who is the
image of God. ⁵For we do not preach
ourselves, but Jesus Christ as Lord, and
ourselves as your servants for Jesus'
sake. ⁶For God, who said, "Let light
shine out of darkness," made his light
shine in our hearts to give us the light of
the knowledge of the glory of God in the
face of Christ.

⁷But we have this treasure in jars of
clay to show that this all-surpassing
power is from God and not from us.
⁸We are hard pressed on every side, but
not crushed; perplexed, but not in despair; ⁹persecuted, but not abandoned;
struck down, but not destroyed. ¹⁰We
always carry around in our body the
death of Jesus, so that the life of Jesus
may also be revealed in our body. ¹¹For
we who are alive are always being given
over to death for Jesus' sake, so that his
life may be revealed in our mortal body.
¹²So then, death is at work in us, but life
is at work in you.

¹³It is written: "I believed; therefore I
have spoken." With that same spirit of
faith we also believe and therefore
speak, ¹⁴because we know that the one
who raised the Lord Jesus from the
dead will also raise us with Jesus and
present us with you in his presence.
¹⁵All this is for your benefit, so that the
grace that is reaching more and more
people may cause thanksgiving to overflow to the glory of God.

¹⁶Therefore we do not lose heart.
Though outwardly we are wasting
away, yet inwardly we are being renewed day by day. ¹⁷For our light and
momentary troubles are achieving for
us an eternal glory that far outweighs
them all. ¹⁸So we fix our eyes not on
what is seen, but on what is unseen. For
what is seen is temporary, but what is
unseen is eternal.

READING FROM PSALMS
Psalm 104:31–35

31May the glory of the LORD endure for
    ever;
    may the LORD rejoice in his
      works—
32he who looks at the earth, and it
    trembles,
    who touches the mountains, and
    they smoke.

33I will sing to the LORD all my life;

34May my meditation be pleasing to
    him,
    as I rejoice in the LORD.
35But may sinners vanish from the
    earth
    and the wicked be no more.

Praise the LORD, O my soul.

Praise the LORD.

SEPTEMBER 1   DAY 244

OLD TESTAMENT READING
Micah 5:1–7:20

A Promised Ruler From Bethlehem

5 Marshal your troops, O city of
    troops,
    for a siege is laid against us.
They will strike Israel's ruler
    on the cheek with a rod.

2"But you, Bethlehem Ephrathah,
    though you are small among the
      clans of Judah,
out of you will come for me
    one who will be ruler over Israel,
    whose origins are from of old,
    from ancient times."

3Therefore Israel will be abandoned
    until the time when she who is in
      labour gives birth
and the rest of his brothers return
    to join the Israelites.

4He will stand and shepherd his flock
    in the strength of the LORD,
    in the majesty of the name of the
      LORD his God.
And they will live securely, for then
    his greatness
    will reach to the ends of the earth.
5   And he will be their peace.

Deliverance and Destruction

When the Assyrian invades our land
    and marches through our
      fortresses,
we will raise against him seven
    shepherds,
    even eight leaders of men.
6They will rule the land of Assyria
    with the sword,
    the land of Nimrod with drawn
      sword.
He will deliver us from the Assyrian
    when he invades our land
    and marches into our borders.

7The remnant of Jacob will be
    in the midst of many peoples
like dew from the LORD,
    like showers on the grass,
which do not wait for man
    or linger for mankind.
8The remnant of Jacob will be among
    the nations,
    in the midst of many peoples,
like a lion among the beasts of the
    forest,
    like a young lion among flocks of
      sheep,
which mauls and mangles as it goes,
    and no-one can rescue.

⁹Your hand will be lifted up in
       triumph over your enemies,
   and all your foes will be destroyed.

¹⁰"In that day," declares the LORD,

"I will destroy your horses from
       among you
   and demolish your chariots.
¹¹I will destroy the cities of your land
   and tear down all your strongholds.
¹²I will destroy your witchcraft
   and you will no longer cast spells.
¹³I will destroy your carved images
   and your sacred stones from among
       you;
you will no longer bow down
   to the work of your hands.
¹⁴I will uproot from among you your
       Asherah poles
   and demolish your cities.
¹⁵I will take vengeance in anger and
       wrath
   upon the nations that have not
       obeyed me."

The LORD's Case Against Israel

6   Listen to what the LORD says:

"Stand up, plead your case before the
       mountains;
   let the hills hear what you have to
       say.
²Hear, O mountains, the LORD's
       accusation;
   listen, you everlasting foundations
       of the earth.
For the LORD has a case against his
       people;
   he is lodging a charge against
       Israel.

³"My people, what have I done to
       you?
   How have I burdened you?
       Answer me.
⁴I brought you up out of Egypt
   and redeemed you from the land of
       slavery.
I sent Moses to lead you,
   also Aaron and Miriam.

⁵My people, remember
   what Balak king of Moab
       counselled
   and what Balaam son of Beor
       answered.
Remember ⌊your journey⌋ from
       Shittim to Gilgal,
   that you may know the righteous
       acts of the LORD."

⁶With what shall I come before the
       LORD
   and bow down before the exalted
       God?
Shall I come before him with burnt
       offerings,
   with calves a year old?
⁷Will the LORD be pleased with
       thousands of rams,
   with ten thousand rivers of oil?
Shall I offer my firstborn for my
       transgression,
   the fruit of my body for the sin of
       my soul?
⁸He has showed you, O man, what is
       good.
   And what does the LORD require
       of you?
To act justly and to love mercy
   and to walk humbly with your
       God.

Israel's Guilt and Punishment

⁹Listen! The LORD is calling to the
       city—
   and to fear your name is wisdom—
"Heed the rod and the One who
       appointed it.
¹⁰Am I still to forget, O wicked house,
   your ill-gotten treasures
   and the short ephah, which is
       accursed?
¹¹Shall I acquit a man with dishonest
       scales,
   with a bag of false weights?
¹²Her rich men are violent;
   her people are liars
   and their tongues speak
       deceitfully.
¹³Therefore, I have begun to destroy
       you,
   to ruin you because of your sins.

[14]You will eat but not be satisfied;
    your stomach will still be empty.
You will store up but save nothing,
    because what you save I will give to
        the sword.
[15]You will plant but not harvest;
    you will press olives but not use the
        oil on yourselves,
    you will crush grapes but not drink
        the wine.
[16]You have observed the statutes of
        Omri
    and all the practices of Ahab's
        house,
    and you have followed their
        traditions.
Therefore I will give you over to ruin
    and your people to derision;
    you will bear the scorn of the
        nations."

Israel's Misery

7 What misery is mine!
    I am like one who gathers summer
        fruit
    at the gleaning of the vineyard;
there is no cluster of grapes to eat,
    none of the early figs that I crave.
[2]The godly have been swept from the
        land;
    not one upright man remains.
All men lie in wait to shed blood;
    each hunts his brother with a net.
[3]Both hands are skilled in doing evil;
    the ruler demands gifts,
the judge accepts bribes,
    the powerful dictate what they
        desire—
    they all conspire together.
[4]The best of them is like a brier,
    the most upright worse than a
        thorn hedge.
The day of your watchmen has come,
    the day God visits you.
    Now is the time of their confusion.
[5]Do not trust a neighbour;
    put no confidence in a friend.
Even with her who lies in your
        embrace
    be careful of your words.
[6]For a son dishonours his father,

a daughter rises up against her
        mother,
a daughter-in-law against her
        mother-in-law—
    a man's enemies are the members
        of his own household.

[7]But as for me, I watch in hope for the
        LORD,
    I wait for God my Saviour;
    my God will hear me.

Israel Will Rise

[8]Do not gloat over me, my enemy!
    Though I have fallen, I will rise.
Though I sit in darkness,
    the LORD will be my light.
[9]Because I have sinned against him,
    I will bear the LORD's wrath,
until he pleads my case
    and establishes my right.
He will bring me out into the light;
    I will see his righteousness.
[10]Then my enemy will see it
    and will be covered with shame,
    she who said to me,
    "Where is the LORD your God?"
My eyes will see her downfall;
    even now she will be trampled
        underfoot
    like mire in the streets.

[11]The day for building your walls will
        come,
    the day for extending your
        boundaries.
[12]In that day people will come to you
    from Assyria and the cities of
        Egypt,
    even from Egypt to the Euphrates
    and from sea to sea
    and from mountain to mountain.
[13]The earth will become desolate
    because of its inhabitants,
    as the result of their deeds.

Prayer and Praise

[14]Shepherd your people with your
        staff,
    the flock of your inheritance,

which lives by itself in a forest,
in fertile pasture-lands.
Let them feed in Bashan and Gilead
as in days long ago.

¹⁵"As in the days when you came out of
Egypt,
I will show them my wonders."

¹⁶Nations will see and be ashamed,
deprived of all their power.
They will lay their hands on their
mouths
and their ears will become deaf.
¹⁷They will lick dust like a snake,
like creatures that crawl on the
ground.
They will come trembling out of their
dens;
they will turn in fear to the LORD
our God
and will be afraid of you.
¹⁸Who is a God like you,
who pardons sin and forgives the
transgression
of the remnant of his inheritance?
You do not stay angry for ever
but delight to show mercy.
¹⁹You will again have compassion on
us;
you will tread our sins underfoot
and hurl all our iniquities into the
depths of the sea.
²⁰You will be true to Jacob,
and show mercy to Abraham,
as you pledged on oath to our fathers
in days long ago.

NEW TESTAMENT READING
2 Corinthians 5:1–10

Our Heavenly Dwelling

5 Now we know that if the earthly
tent we live in is destroyed, we
have a building from God, an eternal
house in heaven, not built by human
hands. ²Meanwhile we groan, longing
to be clothed with our heavenly dwelling, ³because when we are clothed, we
will not be found naked. ⁴For while we

are in this tent, we groan and are burdened, because we do not wish to be
unclothed but to be clothed with our
heavenly dwelling, so that what is mortal may be swallowed up by life. ⁵Now it
is God who has made us for this very
purpose and has given us the Spirit as a
deposit, guaranteeing what is to come.
⁶Therefore we are always confident
and know that as long as we are at home
in the body we are away from the Lord.
⁷We live by faith, not by sight. ⁸We are
confident, I say, and would prefer to be
away from the body and at home with
the Lord. ⁹So we make it our goal to
please him, whether we are at home in
the body or away from it. ¹⁰For we must
all appear before the judgment seat of
Christ, that each one may receive what
is due to him for the things done while in
the body, whether good or bad.

READING FROM PROVERBS
Proverbs 21:17–26

¹⁷He who loves pleasure will become
poor;
whoever loves wine and oil will
never be rich.

¹⁸The wicked become a ransom for the
righteous,
and the unfaithful for the upright.

¹⁹Better to live in a desert
than with a quarrelsome and
ill-tempered wife.

²⁰In the house of the wise are stores of
choice food and oil,
but a foolish man devours all he
has.

²¹He who pursues righteousness and
love
finds life, prosperity and honour.

²²A wise man attacks the city of the
mighty

and pulls down the stronghold in
which they trust.

23He who guards his mouth and his
tongue
keeps himself from calamity.

24The proud and arrogant man—
"Mocker" is his name;

25The sluggard's craving will be the
death of him,
because his hands refuse to work.

26All day long he craves for more,
but the righteous give without
sparing.

SEPTEMBER 2

DAY 245

OLD TESTAMENT READING
Isaiah 1:1–2:22

1 The vision concerning Judah and
Jerusalem that Isaiah son of Amoz
saw during the reigns of Uzziah,
Jotham, Ahaz and Hezekiah, kings of
Judah.

A Rebellious Nation

2Hear, O heavens! Listen, O earth!
For the LORD has spoken:
"I reared children and brought them
up,
but they have rebelled against me.

3The ox knows his master,
the donkey his owner's manger,
but Israel does not know,
my people do not understand."

4Ah, sinful nation,
a people loaded with guilt,
a brood of evildoers,
children given to corruption!
They have forsaken the LORD;
they have spurned the Holy One of
Israel
and turned their backs on him.

5Why should you be beaten any more?
Why do you persist in rebellion?
Your whole head is injured,
your whole heart afflicted.

6From the sole of your foot to the top
of your head
there is no soundness—

only wounds and bruises
and open sores,
not cleansed or bandaged
or soothed with oil.

7Your country is desolate,
your cities burned with fire;
your fields are being stripped by
foreigners
right before you,
laid waste as when overthrown by
strangers.

8The Daughter of Zion is left
like a shelter in a vineyard,
like a hut in a field of melons,
like a city under siege.

9Unless the LORD Almighty
had left us some survivors,
we would have become like Sodom,
we would have been like
Gomorrah.

10Hear the word of the LORD,
you rulers of Sodom;
listen to the law of our God,
you people of Gomorrah!

11"The multitude of your sacrifices—
what are they to me?" says the
LORD.
"I have more than enough of burnt
offerings,
of rams and the fat of fattened
animals;
I have no pleasure
in the blood of bulls and lambs and
goats.

¹²When you come to appear before me,
  who has asked this of you,
  this trampling of my courts?
¹³Stop bringing meaningless offerings!
  Your incense is detestable to me.
New Moons, Sabbaths and
    convocations—
  I cannot bear your evil assemblies.
¹⁴Your New Moon festivals and your
    appointed feasts
  my soul hates.
They have become a burden to me;
  I am weary of bearing them.
¹⁵When you spread out your hands in
    prayer,
  I will hide my eyes from you;
even if you offer many prayers,
  I will not listen.
Your hands are full of blood;
¹⁶ wash and make yourselves clean.
Take your evil deeds
  out of my sight!
Stop doing wrong,
¹⁷ learn to do right!
Seek justice,
  encourage the oppressed.
Defend the cause of the fatherless,
  plead the case of the widow.

¹⁸"Come now, let us reason together,"
  says the LORD.
"Though your sins are like scarlet,
  they shall be as white as snow;
though they are red as crimson,
  they shall be like wool.
¹⁹If you are willing and obedient,
  you will eat the best from the land;
²⁰but if you resist and rebel,
  you will be devoured by the
    sword."
          For the mouth of the LORD has
            spoken.

²¹See how the faithful city
  has become a harlot!
She once was full of justice;
  righteousness used to dwell in
    her—
  but now murderers!
²²Your silver has become dross,
  your choice wine is diluted with
    water.

²³Your rulers are rebels,
  companions of thieves;
they all love bribes
  and chase after gifts.
They do not defend the cause of the
    fatherless;
  the widow's case does not come
    before them.
²⁴Therefore the Lord, the LORD
    Almighty,
  the Mighty One of Israel, declares:
"Ah, I will get relief from my foes
  and avenge myself on my enemies.
²⁵I will turn my hand against you;
  I will thoroughly purge away your
    dross
  and remove all your impurities.
²⁶I will restore your judges as in days of
    old,
  your counsellors as at the
    beginning.
Afterwards you will be called
  the City of Righteousness,
  the Faithful City."

²⁷Zion will be redeemed with justice,
  her penitent ones with
    righteousness.
²⁸But rebels and sinners will both be
    broken,
  and those who forsake the LORD
    will perish.
²⁹"You will be ashamed because of the
    sacred oaks
  in which you have delighted;
you will be disgraced because of the
    gardens
  that you have chosen.
³⁰You will be like an oak with fading
    leaves,
  like a garden without water.
³¹The mighty man will become tinder
  and his work a spark;
both will burn together,
  with no-one to quench the fire."

The Mountain of the LORD

2 This is what Isaiah son of Amoz
  saw concerning Judah and Jerusalem:

²In the last days

the mountain of the LORD's temple
    will be established
as chief among the mountains;
it will be raised above the hills,
    and all nations will stream to it.

³Many peoples will come and say,

"Come, let us go up to the mountain
    of the LORD,
to the house of the God of Jacob.
He will teach us his ways,
    so that we may walk in his paths."
The law will go out from Zion,
    the word of the LORD from
      Jerusalem.
⁴He will judge between the nations
    and will settle disputes for many
      peoples.
They will beat their swords into
    ploughshares
    and their spears into pruning
      hooks.
Nation will not take up sword against
    nation,
    nor will they train for war any
      more.

⁵Come, O house of Jacob,
    let us walk in the light of the LORD.

The Day of the LORD

⁶You have abandoned your people,
    the house of Jacob.
They are full of superstitions from
    the East;
    they practise divination like the
      Philistines
    and clasp hands with pagans.
⁷Their land is full of silver and gold;
    there is no end to their treasures.
Their land is full of horses;
    there is no end to the chariots.
⁸Their land is full of idols;
    they bow down to the work of their
      hands,
    to what their fingers have made.
⁹So man will be brought low

and mankind humbled—
    do not forgive them.

¹⁰Go into the rocks,
    hide in the ground
from dread of the LORD
    and the splendour of his majesty!
¹¹The eyes of the arrogant man will be
    humbled
    and the pride of men brought low;
the LORD alone will be exalted in that
    day.

¹²The LORD Almighty has a day in
    store
    for all the proud and lofty,
    for all that is exalted
    (and they will be humbled),
¹³for all the cedars of Lebanon, tall and
    lofty,
    and all the oaks of Bashan,
¹⁴for all the towering mountains
    and all the high hills,
¹⁵for every lofty tower
    and every fortified wall,
¹⁶for every trading ship
    and every stately vessel.
¹⁷The arrogance of man will be brought
    low
    and the pride of men humbled;
the LORD alone will be exalted in that
    day,
¹⁸   and the idols will totally disappear.

¹⁹Men will flee to caves in the rocks
    and to holes in the ground
from the dread of the LORD
    and the splendour of his majesty,
    when he rises to shake the earth.
²⁰In that day men will throw away
    to the rodents and bats
their idols of silver and idols of gold,
    which they made to worship.
²¹They will flee to caverns in the rocks
    and to the overhanging crags
from dread of the LORD
    and the splendour of his majesty,
    when he rises to shake the earth.

²²Stop trusting in man,
    who has but a breath in his nostrils.
Of what account is he?

NEW TESTAMENT READING
2 Corinthians 5:11–6:2

The Ministry of Reconciliation

¹¹Since, then, we know what it is to fear the Lord, we try to persuade men. What we are is plain to God, and I hope it is also plain to your conscience. ¹²We are not trying to commend ourselves to you again, but are giving you an opportunity to take pride in us, so that you can answer those who take pride in what is seen rather than in what is in the heart. ¹³If we are out of our mind, it is for the sake of God; if we are in our right mind, it is for you. ¹⁴For Christ's love compels us, because we are convinced that one died for all, and therefore all died. ¹⁵And he died for all, that those who live should no longer live for themselves but for him who died for them and was raised again.

¹⁶So from now on we regard no-one from a worldly point of view. Though we once regarded Christ in this way, we do so no longer. ¹⁷Therefore, if anyone is in Christ, he is a new creation; the old has gone, the new has come! ¹⁸All this is from God, who reconciled us to himself through Christ and gave us the ministry of reconciliation: ¹⁹that God was reconciling the world to himself in Christ, not counting men's sins against them. And he has committed to us the message of reconciliation. ²⁰We are therefore Christ's ambassadors, as though God were making his appeal through us. We implore you on Christ's behalf: Be reconciled to God. ²¹God made him who had no sin to be sin for us, so that in him we might become the righteousness of God.

6 As God's fellow-workers we urge you not to receive God's grace in vain. ²For he says,

"In the time of my favour I heard
    you,
and in the day of salvation I helped
    you."

I tell you, now is the time of God's favour, now is the day of salvation.

READING FROM PSALMS
Psalm 105:1–11

¹Give thanks to the LORD, call on his
    name;
    make known among the nations
      what he has done.
²Sing to him, sing praise to him;
    tell of all his wonderful acts.
³Glory in his holy name;
    let the hearts of those who seek the
      LORD rejoice.
⁴Look to the LORD and his strength;
    seek his face always.

⁵Remember the wonders he has done,
    his miracles, and the judgments he
      pronounced,
⁶O descendants of Abraham his
    servant,
    O sons of Jacob, his chosen ones.
⁷He is the LORD our God;
    his judgments are in all the earth.

⁸He remembers his covenant for ever,
    the word he commanded, for a
      thousand generations,
⁹the covenant he made with
    Abraham,
    the oath he swore to Isaac.
¹⁰He confirmed it to Jacob as a decree,
    to Israel as an everlasting
      covenant:
¹¹"To you I will give the land of
    Canaan
    as the portion you will inherit."

OLD TESTAMENT READING
Isaiah 3:1–5:7

Judgment on Jerusalem and Judah

3 See now, the Lord,
    the LORD Almighty,
is about to take from Jerusalem and
    Judah
both supply and support:
all supplies of food and all supplies of
    water,
² the hero and warrior,
the judge and prophet,
    the soothsayer and elder,
³the captain of fifty and man of rank,
    the counsellor, skilled craftsman
    and clever enchanter.

⁴I will make boys their officials;
    mere children will govern them.
⁵People will oppress each other—
    man against man, neighbour
    against neighbour.
The young will rise up against the
    old,
the base against the honourable.

⁶A man will seize one of his brothers
    at his father's home, and say,
"You have a cloak, you be our
    leader;
take charge of this heap of ruins!"
⁷But in that day he will cry out,
    "I have no remedy.
I have no food or clothing in my
    house;
do not make me the leader of the
    people."

⁸Jerusalem staggers,
    Judah is falling;
their words and deeds are against the
    LORD,
defying his glorious presence.
⁹The look on their faces testifies
    against them;

they parade their sin like Sodom;
    they do not hide it.
Woe to them!
    They have brought disaster upon
    themselves.

¹⁰Tell the righteous it will be well with
    them,
for they will enjoy the fruit of their
    deeds.
¹¹Woe to the wicked! Disaster is upon
    them!
They will be paid back for what
    their hands have done.

¹²Youths oppress my people,
    women rule over them.
O my people, your guides lead you
    astray;
they turn you from the path.

¹³The LORD takes his place in court;
    he rises to judge the people.
¹⁴The LORD enters into judgment
    against the elders and leaders of his
    people:
"It is you who have ruined my
    vineyard;
the plunder from the poor is in
    your houses.
¹⁵What do you mean by crushing my
    people
and grinding the faces of the
    poor?"
        declares the Lord, the LORD
        Almighty.

¹⁶The LORD says,
    "The women of Zion are haughty,
walking along with outstretched
    necks,
    flirting with their eyes,
tripping along with mincing
    with ornaments jingling on
    ankles.
¹⁷Therefore the J
    on the '
    Zi

the LORD will make their scalps
    bald."

18In that day the Lord will snatch
away their finery: the bangles and headbands and crescent necklaces, 19the
ear-rings and bracelets and veils, 20the
head-dresses and ankle chains and
sashes, the perfume bottles and charms,
21the signet rings and nose rings, 22the
fine robes and the capes and cloaks, the
purses 23and mirrors, and the linen garments and tiaras and shawls.

24Instead of fragrance there will be a
    stench;
  instead of a sash, a rope;
instead of well-dressed hair,
    baldness;
instead of fine clothing, sackcloth;
  instead of beauty, branding.
25Your men will fall by the sword,
  your warriors in battle.
26The gates of Zion will lament and
    mourn;
  destitute, she will sit on the
    ground.

4 In that day seven women
  will take hold of one man
and say, "We will eat our own food
  and provide our own clothes;
only let us be called by your name.
  Take away our disgrace!"

The Branch of the LORD

2In that day the Branch of the LORD
will be beautiful and glorious, and the
fruit of the land will be the pride and
glory of the survivors in Israel. 3Those
who are left in Zion, who remain in
Jerusalem, will be called holy, all who
are recorded among the living in Jerusalem. 4The LORD will wash away the
filth of the women of Zion; he will
cleanse the bloodstains from Jerusalem
[b]y a spirit of judgment and a spirit of
[fire.] Then the LORD will create over all
[of Mount] Zion and over those who
[assemble there a c]loud of smoke by day
[and a glow of blazing fire] by night; over

all the glory will be a canopy. 6It will be
a shelter and shade from the heat of the
day, and a refuge and hiding-place from
the storm and rain.

The Song of the Vineyard

5 I will sing for the one I love
  a song about his vineyard:
My loved one had a vineyard
  on a fertile hillside.
2He dug it up and cleared it of stones
  and planted it with the choicest
    vines.
He built a watchtower in it
  and cut out a winepress as well.
Then he looked for a crop of good
    grapes,
  but it yielded only bad fruit.

3"Now you dwellers in Jerusalem and
  men of Judah,
judge between me and my
    vineyard.
4What more could have been done for
  my vineyard
than I have done for it?
When I looked for good grapes,
  why did it yield only bad?
5Now I will tell you
  what I am going to do to my
    vineyard:
I will take away its hedge,
  and it will be destroyed;
I will break down its wall,
  and it will be trampled.
6I will make it a wasteland,
  neither pruned nor cultivated,
  and briers and thorns will grow
    there.
I will command the clouds
  not to rain on it."

7The vineyard of the LORD Almighty
  is the house of Israel,
and the men of Judah
  are the garden of his delight.
And he looked for justice, but saw
    bloodshed;
for righteousness, but heard cries
  of distress.

NEW TESTAMENT READING
2 Corinthians 6:3–7:1

Paul's Hardships

³We put no stumbling-block in anyone's path, so that our ministry will not be discredited. ⁴Rather, as servants of God we commend ourselves in every way: in great endurance; in troubles, hardships and distresses; ⁵in beatings, imprisonments and riots; in hard work, sleepless nights and hunger; ⁶in purity, understanding, patience and kindness; in the Holy Spirit and in sincere love; ⁷in truthful speech and in the power of God; with weapons of righteousness in the right hand and in the left; ⁸through glory and dishonour, bad report and good report; genuine, yet regarded as impostors; ⁹known, yet regarded as unknown; dying, and yet we live on; beaten, and yet not killed; ¹⁰sorrowful, yet always rejoicing; poor, yet making many rich; having nothing, and yet possessing everything.

¹¹We have spoken freely to you, Corinthians, and opened wide our hearts to you. ¹²We are not withholding our affection from you, but you are withholding yours from us. ¹³As a fair exchange—I speak as to my children—open wide your hearts also.

Do Not Be Yoked With Unbelievers

¹⁴Do not be yoked together with unbelievers. For what do righteousness and wickedness have in common? Or what fellowship can light have with darkness? ¹⁵What harmony is there between Christ and Belial? What does a believer have in common with an unbeliever? ¹⁶What agreement is there between the temple of God and idols? For we are the temple of the living God. As God has said: "I will live with them and walk among them, and I will be their God, and they will be my people."

¹⁷"Therefore come out from them
     and be separate,
              says the Lord.
Touch no unclean thing,
     and I will receive you."
¹⁸"I will be a Father to you,
     and you will be my sons and
         daughters,
              says the Lord Almighty."

7 Since we have these promises, dear friends, let us purify ourselves from everything that contaminates body and spirit, perfecting holiness out of reverence for God.

READING FROM PSALMS
Psalm 105:12–22

¹²When they were but few in number,
     few indeed, and strangers in it,
¹³they wandered from nation to nation,
     from one kingdom to another.
¹⁴He allowed no-one to oppress them;
     for their sake he rebuked kings:
¹⁵"Do not touch my anointed ones;
     do my prophets no harm."

¹⁶He called down famine on the land
     and destroyed all their supplies of
         food;
¹⁷and he sent a man before them—
     Joseph, sold as a slave.
¹⁸They bruised his feet with shackles,
     his neck was put in irons,
¹⁹till what he foretold came to pass,
     till the word of the LORD proved
         him true.
²⁰The king sent and released him,
     the ruler of peoples set him free.
²¹He made him master of his
         household,
     ruler over all he possessed,
²²to instruct his princes as he pleased
     and teach his elders wisdom.

SEPTEMBER 4

OLD TESTAMENT READING
Isaiah 5:8–8:10

Woes and Judgments

⁸Woe to you who add house to house
    and join field to field
till no space is left
    and you live alone in the land.

⁹The LORD Almighty has declared in
my hearing:

"Surely the great houses will become
        desolate,
    the fine mansions left without
        occupants.
¹⁰A ten-acre vineyard will produce only
        a bath of wine,
    a homer of seed only an ephah of
        grain."

¹¹Woe to those who rise early in the
        morning
    to run after their drinks,
who stay up late at night
    till they are inflamed with wine.
¹²They have harps and lyres at their
        banquets,
    tambourines and flutes and wine,
but they have no regard for the deeds
        of the LORD,
    no respect for the work of his
        hands.
¹³Therefore my people will go into
        exile
    for lack of understanding;
their men of rank will die of hunger
    and their masses will be parched
        with thirst.
¹⁴Therefore the grave enlarges its
        appetite
    and opens its mouth without limit;
into it will descend their nobles and
        masses
    with all their brawlers and
        revellers.

¹⁵So man will be brought low
    and mankind humbled,
    the eyes of the arrogant humbled.
¹⁶But the LORD Almighty will be
        exalted by his justice,
    and the holy God will show himself
        holy by his righteousness.
¹⁷Then sheep will graze as in their own
        pasture;
    lambs will feed among the ruins of
        the rich.

¹⁸Woe to those who draw sin along
        with cords of deceit,
    and wickedness as with cart ropes,
¹⁹to those who say, "Let God hurry,
    let him hasten his work
    so that we may see it.
Let it approach,
    let the plan of the Holy One of
        Israel come,
    so that we may know it."

²⁰Woe to those who call evil good
        and good evil,
    who put darkness for light
        and light for darkness,
    who put bitter for sweet
        and sweet for bitter.

²¹Woe to those who are wise in their
        own eyes
    and clever in their own sight.

²²Woe to those who are heroes at
        drinking wine
    and champions at mixing drinks,
²³who acquit the guilty for a bribe,
    but deny justice to the innocent.

²⁴Therefore, as tongues of fire lick up
        straw
    and as dry grass sinks down in the
        flames,
so their roots will decay
    and their flowers blow away like
        dust;

for they have rejected the law of the
    LORD Almighty
  and spurned the word of the Holy
    One of Israel.
25Therefore the LORD's anger burns
    against his people;
  his hand is raised and he strikes
    them down.
The mountains shake,
  and the dead bodies are like refuse
    in the streets.

Yet for all this, his anger is not turned
    away,
  his hand is still upraised.

26He lifts up a banner for the distant
    nations,
  he whistles for those at the ends of
    the earth.
Here they come,
  swiftly and speedily!
27Not one of them grows tired or
    stumbles,
  not one slumbers or sleeps;
not a belt is loosened at the waist,
  not a sandal thong is broken.
28Their arrows are sharp,
  all their bows are strung;
their horses' hoofs seem like flint,
  their chariot wheels like a
    whirlwind.
29Their roar is like that of the lion,
  they roar like young lions;
they growl as they seize their prey
  and carry it off with no-one to
    rescue.
30In that day they will roar over it
  like the roaring of the sea.
And if one looks at the land,
  he will see darkness and distress;
  even the light will be darkened by
    the clouds.

Isaiah's Commission

6 In the year that King Uzziah died, I
saw the Lord seated on a throne,
high and exalted, and the train of his
robe filled the temple. 2Above him were
seraphs, each with six wings: With two
wings they covered their faces, with
two they covered their feet, and with
two they were flying. 3And they were
calling to one another:

  "Holy, holy, holy is the LORD
    Almighty;
  the whole earth is full of his glory."

4At the sound of their voices the doorposts and thresholds shook and the
temple was filled with smoke.

5"Woe to me!" I cried. "I am ruined!
For I am a man of unclean lips, and I live
among a people of unclean lips, and my
eyes have seen the King, the LORD
Almighty."

6Then one of the seraphs flew to me
with a live coal in his hand, which he had
taken with tongs from the altar. 7With it
he touched my mouth and said, "See,
this has touched your lips; your guilt is
taken away and your sin atoned for."

8Then I heard the voice of the Lord
saying, "Whom shall I send? And who
will go for us?"

And I said, "Here am I. Send me!"

9He said, "Go and tell this people:

  "'Be ever hearing, but never
    understanding;
  be ever seeing, but never
    perceiving.'
10Make the heart of this people
    calloused;
  make their ears dull
  and close their eyes.
Otherwise they might see with their
    eyes,
  hear with their ears,
  understand with their hearts,
and turn and be healed."

11Then I said, "For how long, O
Lord?"

And he answered:

  "Until the cities lie ruined
    and without inhabitant,
  until the houses are left deserted
    and the fields ruined and ravaged,
12until the LORD has sent everyone far
    away
  and the land is utterly forsaken.

¹³And though a tenth remains in the
land,
it will again be laid waste.
But as the terebinth and oak
leave stumps when they are cut
down,
so the holy seed will be the stump
in the land."

The Sign of Immanuel

7 When Ahaz son of Jotham, the son
of Uzziah, was king of Judah, King
Rezin of Aram and Pekah son of Remaliah king of Israel marched up to
fight against Jerusalem, but they could
not overpower it.

²Now the house of David was told,
"Aram has allied itself with Ephraim";
so the hearts of Ahaz and his people
were shaken, as the trees of the forest
are shaken by the wind.

³Then the LORD said to Isaiah, "Go
out, you and your son Shear-Jashub, to
meet Ahaz at the end of the aqueduct of
the Upper Pool, on the road to the
Washerman's Field. ⁴Say to him, 'Be
careful, keep calm and don't be afraid.
Do not lose heart because of these two
smouldering stubs of firewood—
because of the fierce anger of Rezin and
Aram and of the son of Remaliah.
⁵Aram, Ephraim and Remaliah's son
have plotted your ruin, saying, ⁶"Let us
invade Judah; let us tear it apart and
divide it among ourselves, and make the
son of Tabeel king over it." ⁷Yet this is
what the Sovereign LORD says:

"'It will not take place,
it will not happen,
⁸for the head of Aram is Damascus,
and the head of Damascus is only
Rezin.
Within sixty-five years
Ephraim will be too shattered to be
a people.
⁹The head of Ephraim is Samaria,
and the head of Samaria is only
Remaliah's son.
If you do not stand firm in your faith,
you will not stand at all.'"

¹⁰Again the LORD spoke to Ahaz,
¹¹"Ask the LORD your God for a sign,
whether in the deepest depths or in the
highest heights."

¹²But Ahaz said, "I will not ask; I will
not put the LORD to the test."

¹³Then Isaiah said, "Hear now, you
house of David! Is it not enough to try
the patience of men? Will you try the
patience of my God also? ¹⁴Therefore
the Lord himself will give you a sign:
The virgin will be with child and will
give birth to a son, and will call him
Immanuel. ¹⁵He will eat curds and
honey when he knows enough to reject
the wrong and choose the right. ¹⁶But
before the boy knows enough to reject
the wrong and choose the right, the
land of the two kings you dread will
be laid waste. ¹⁷The LORD will bring
on you and on your people and on
the house of your father a time unlike
any since Ephraim broke away from
Judah—he will bring the king of
Assyria."

¹⁸In that day the LORD will whistle for
flies from the distant streams of Egypt
and for bees from the land of Assyria.
¹⁹They will all come and settle in the
steep ravines and in the crevices in the
rocks, on all the thornbushes and at all
the water holes. ²⁰In that day the Lord
will use a razor hired from beyond the
River—the king of Assyria—to shave
your head and the hair of your legs, and
to take off your beards also. ²¹In that
day, a man will keep alive a young cow
and two goats. ²²And because of the
abundance of the milk they give, he will
have curds to eat. All who remain in the
land will eat curds and honey. ²³In that
day, in every place where there were a
thousand vines worth a thousand silver
shekels, there will be only briers and
thorns. ²⁴Men will go there with bow
and arrow, for the land will be covered
with briers and thorns. ²⁵As for all the
hills once cultivated by the hoe, you will
no longer go there for fear of the briers
and thorns; they will become places
where cattle are turned loose and where
sheep run.

Assyria, the LORD's Instrument

8 The LORD said to me, "Take a large scroll and write on it with an ordinary pen: Maher-Shalal-Hash-Baz. ²And I will call in Uriah the priest and Zechariah son of Jeberekiah as reliable witnesses for me."

³Then I went to the prophetess, and she conceived and gave birth to a son. And the LORD said to me, "Name him Maher-Shalal-Hash-Baz. ⁴Before the boy knows how to say 'My father' or 'My mother', the wealth of Damascus and the plunder of Samaria will be carried off by the king of Assyria."

⁵The LORD spoke to me again:

⁶"Because this people has rejected
    the gently flowing waters of
        Shiloah
and rejoices over Rezin
    and the son of Remaliah,
⁷therefore the Lord is about to bring
        against them
    the mighty floodwaters of the
        River—
    the king of Assyria with all his
        pomp.
It will overflow all its channels,
    run over all its banks
⁸and sweep on into Judah, swirling
        over it,
    passing through it and reaching up
        to the neck.
Its outspread wings will cover the
        breadth of your land,
    O Immanuel!"

⁹Raise the war cry, you nations, and
        be shattered!
    Listen, all you distant lands.
Prepare for battle, and be shattered!
    Prepare for battle, and be
        shattered!
¹⁰Devise your strategy, but it will be
        thwarted;
    propose your plan, but it will not
        stand,
for God is with us.

NEW TESTAMENT READING
2 Corinthians 7:2–16

Paul's Joy

²Make room for us in your hearts. We have wronged no-one, we have corrupted no-one, we have exploited no-one. ³I do not say this to condemn you; I have said before that you have such a place in our hearts that we would live or die with you. ⁴I have great confidence in you; I take great pride in you. I am greatly encouraged; in all our troubles my joy knows no bounds.

⁵For when we came into Macedonia, this body of ours had no rest, but we were harassed at every turn—conflicts on the outside, fears within. ⁶But God, who comforts the downcast, comforted us by the coming of Titus, ⁷and not only by his coming but also by the comfort you had given him. He told us about your longing for me, your deep sorrow, your ardent concern for me, so that my joy was greater than ever.

⁸Even if I caused you sorrow by my letter, I do not regret it. Though I did regret it—I see that my letter hurt you, but only for a little while—⁹yet now I am happy, not because you were made sorry, but because your sorrow led you to repentance. For you became sorrowful as God intended and so were not harmed in any way by us. ¹⁰Godly sorrow brings repentance that leads to salvation and leaves no regret, but worldly sorrow brings death. ¹¹See what this godly sorrow has produced in you: what earnestness, what eagerness to clear yourselves, what indignation, what alarm, what longing, what concern, what readiness to see justice done. At every point you have proved yourselves to be innocent in this matter. ¹²So even though I wrote to you, it was not on account of the one who did the wrong or of the injured party, but rather that before God you could see for yourselves how devoted to us you are. ¹³By all this we are encouraged.

In addition to our own encouragement, we were especially delighted to see how happy Titus was, because his spirit has been refreshed by all of you. [14]I had boasted to him about you, and you have not embarrassed me. But just as everything we said to you was true, so our boasting about you to Titus has proved to be true as well. [15]And his affection for you is all the greater when he remembers that you were all obedient, receiving him with fear and trembling. [16]I am glad I can have complete confidence in you.

READING FROM PSALMS
Psalm 105:23–36

[23]Then Israel entered Egypt;
  Jacob lived as an alien in the land of Ham.
[24]The LORD made his people very fruitful;
  he made them too numerous for their foes,
[25]whose hearts he turned to hate his people,
  to conspire against his servants.
[26]He sent Moses his servant,
  and Aaron, whom he had chosen.

[27]They performed his miraculous signs among them,
  his wonders in the land of Ham.
[28]He sent darkness and made the land dark—
  for had they not rebelled against his words?
[29]He turned their waters into blood,
  causing their fish to die.
[30]Their land teemed with frogs,
  which went up into the bedrooms of their rulers.
[31]He spoke, and there came swarms of flies,
  and gnats throughout their country.
[32]He turned their rain into hail,
  with lightning throughout their land;
[33]he struck down their vines and fig-trees
  and shattered the trees of their country.
[34]He spoke, and the locusts came,
  grasshoppers without number;
[35]they ate up every green thing in their land,
  ate up the produce of their soil.
[36]Then he struck down all the firstborn in their land,
  the firstfruits of all their manhood.

SEPTEMBER 5

OLD TESTAMENT READING
Isaiah 8:11–10:19

Fear God

[11]The LORD spoke to me with his strong hand upon me, warning me not to follow the way of this people. He said:

[12]"Do not call conspiracy everything that these people call conspiracy;
  do not fear what they fear, and do not dread it.
[13]The LORD Almighty is the one you are to regard as holy,
  he is the one you are to fear,
  he is the one you are to dread,
[14]and he will be a sanctuary;
  but for both houses of Israel he will be
a stone that causes men to stumble
  and a rock that makes them fall.
And for the people of Jerusalem he will be
a trap and a snare.

¹⁵Many of them will stumble;
    they will fall and be broken,
    they will be snared and captured."

¹⁶Bind up the testimony
    and seal up the law among my
        disciples.
¹⁷I will wait for the LORD,
    who is hiding his face from the
        house of Jacob.
I will put my trust in him.

¹⁸Here am I, and the children the
LORD has given me. We are signs and
symbols in Israel from the LORD
Almighty, who dwells on Mount Zion.
    ¹⁹When men tell you to consult
mediums and spiritists, who whisper
and mutter, should not a people enquire
of their God? Why consult the dead on
behalf of the living? ²⁰To the law and to
the testimony! If they do not speak
according to this word, they have no
light of dawn. ²¹Distressed and hungry,
they will roam through the land; when
they are famished, they will become
enraged and, looking upward, will curse
their king and their God. ²²Then they
will look towards the earth and see only
distress and darkness and fearful
gloom, and they will be thrust into utter
darkness.

To Us a Child Is Born

9 Nevertheless, there will be no
    more gloom for those who were in
distress. In the past he humbled the land
of Zebulun and the land of Naphtali,
but in the future he will honour Galilee
of the Gentiles, by the way of the sea,
along the Jordan—

²The people walking in darkness
    have seen a great light;
on those living in the land of the
        shadow of death
    a light has dawned.
³You have enlarged the nation
    and increased their joy;
they rejoice before you
    as people rejoice at the harvest,

as men rejoice
    when dividing the plunder.
⁴For as in the day of Midian's defeat,
    you have shattered
the yoke that burdens them,
    the bar across their shoulders,
    the rod of their oppressor.
⁵Every warrior's boot used in battle
    and every garment rolled in blood
will be destined for burning,
    will be fuel for the fire.
⁶For to us a child is born,
    to us a son is given,
    and the government will be on his
        shoulders.
And he will be called
    Wonderful Counsellor, Mighty
        God,
    Everlasting Father, Prince of
        Peace.
⁷Of the increase of his government
        and peace
    there will be no end.
He will reign on David's throne
    and over his kingdom,
establishing and upholding it
    with justice and righteousness
    from that time on and for ever.
The zeal of the LORD Almighty
    will accomplish this.

The LORD's Anger Against Israel

⁸The Lord has sent a message against
        Jacob;
    it will fall on Israel.
⁹All the people will know it—
    Ephraim and the inhabitants of
        Samaria—
who say with pride
    and arrogance of heart,
¹⁰"The bricks have fallen down,
    but we will rebuild with dressed
        stone;
the fig-trees have been felled,
    but we will replace them with
        cedars."
¹¹But the LORD has strengthened
        Rezin's foes against them
    and has spurred their enemies on.
¹²Arameans from the east and
    Philistines from the west

have devoured Israel with open
mouth.

Yet for all this, his anger is not turned
away,
his hand is still upraised.

13But the people have not returned to
him who struck them,
nor have they sought the LORD
Almighty.
14So the LORD will cut off from Israel
both head and tail,
both palm branch and reed in a
single day;
15the elders and prominent men are the
head,
the prophets who teach lies are the
tail.
16Those who guide this people mislead
them,
and those who are guided are led
astray.
17Therefore the Lord will take no
pleasure in the young men,
nor will he pity the fatherless and
widows,
for everyone is ungodly and wicked,
every mouth speaks vileness.

Yet for all this, his anger is not turned
away,
his hand is still upraised.

18Surely wickedness burns like a fire;
it consumes briers and thorns,
it sets the forest thickets ablaze,
so that it rolls upward in a column
of smoke.
19By the wrath of the LORD Almighty
the land will be scorched
and the people will be fuel for the
fire;
no-one will spare his brother.
20On the right they will devour,
but still be hungry;
on the left they will eat,
but not be satisfied.
Each will feed on the flesh of his own
offspring:
21 Manasseh will feed on Ephraim,
and Ephraim on Manasseh;

together they will turn against
Judah.

Yet for all this, his anger is not turned
away,
his hand is still upraised.

10 Woe to those who make unjust
laws,
to those who issue oppressive
decrees,
2to deprive the poor of their rights
and withhold justice from the
oppressed of my people,
making widows their prey
and robbing the fatherless.
3What will you do on the day of
reckoning,
when disaster comes from afar?
To whom will you run for help?
Where will you leave your riches?
4Nothing will remain but to cringe
among the captives
or fall among the slain.

Yet for all this, his anger is not
turned away,
his hand is still upraised.

God's Judgment on Assyria

5"Woe to the Assyrian, the rod of my
anger,
in whose hand is the club of my
wrath!
6I send him against a godless nation,
I dispatch him against a people
who anger me,
to seize loot and snatch plunder,
and to trample them down like
mud in the streets.
7But this is not what he intends,
this is not what he has in mind;
his purpose is to destroy,
to put an end to many nations.
8'Are not my commanders all kings?'
he says.
9 'Has not Calno fared like
Carchemish?
Is not Hamath like Arpad,
and Samaria like Damascus?
10As my hand seized the kingdoms of
the idols,

kingdoms whose images excelled
   those of Jerusalem and
   Samaria—
11shall I not deal with Jerusalem and
   her images
   as I dealt with Samaria and her
   idols?' "

12When the Lord has finished all his
work against Mount Zion and Jerusalem, he will say, "I will punish the
king of Assyria for the wilful pride of his
heart and the haughty look in his eyes.
13For he says:

   " 'By the strength of my hand I have
      done this,
   and by my wisdom, because I have
      understanding.
   I removed the boundaries of nations,
   I plundered their treasures;
   like a mighty one I subdued their
      kings.
14As one reaches into a nest,
   so my hand reached for the wealth
      of the nations;
   as men gather abandoned eggs,
   so I gathered all the countries;
   not one flapped a wing,
   or opened its mouth to chirp.' "

15Does the axe raise itself above him
   who swings it,
   or the saw boast against him who
      uses it?
As if a rod were to wield him who lifts
   it up,
   or a club brandish him who is not
      wood!
16Therefore, the Lord, the LORD
   Almighty,
   will send a wasting disease upon his
      sturdy warriors;
under his pomp a fire will be kindled
   like a blazing flame.
17The Light of Israel will become a fire,
   their Holy One a flame;
in a single day it will burn and
   consume
   his thorns and his briers.
18The splendour of his forests and
   fertile fields

it will completely destroy,
   as when a sick man wastes away.
19And the remaining trees of his forests
   will be so few
   that a child could write them down.

NEW TESTAMENT READING
2 Corinthians 8:1–15

Generosity Encouraged

8 And now, brothers, we want you to
   know about the grace that God has
given the Macedonian churches. 2Out
of the most severe trial, their overflowing joy and their extreme poverty
welled up in rich generosity. 3For I
testify that they gave as much as they
were able, and even beyond their
ability. Entirely on their own, 4they
urgently pleaded with us for the privilege of sharing in this service to the
saints. 5And they did not do as we expected, but they gave themselves first to
the Lord and then to us in keeping with
God's will. 6So we urged Titus, since he
had earlier made a beginning, to bring
also to completion this act of grace on
your part. 7But just as you excel in
everything—in faith, in speech, in
knowledge, in complete earnestness
and in your love for us—see that you
also excel in this grace of giving.

8I am not commanding you, but I
want to test the sincerity of your love by
comparing it with the earnestness of
others. 9For you know the grace of our
Lord Jesus Christ, that though he was
rich, yet for your sakes he became poor,
so that you through his poverty might
become rich.

10And here is my advice about what is
best for you in this matter: Last year you
were the first not only to give but also to
have the desire to do so. 11Now finish
the work, so that your eager willingness
to do it may be matched by your completion of it, according to your means.
12For if the willingness is there, the gift
is acceptable according to what one has,
not according to what he does not have.

¹³Our desire is not that others might be relieved while you are hard pressed, but that there might be equality. ¹⁴At the present time your plenty will supply what they need, so that in turn their plenty will supply what you need. Then there will be equality, ¹⁵as it is written: "He who gathered much did not have too much, and he who gathered little did not have too little."

READING FROM PROVERBS
Proverbs 21:27–22:6

²⁷The sacrifice of the wicked is
    detestable—
  how much more so when brought
    with evil intent!

²⁸A false witness will perish,
  and whoever listens to him will be
    destroyed for ever.

²⁹A wicked man puts up a bold front,
  but an upright man gives thought
    to his ways.

³⁰There is no wisdom, no insight, no
    plan

that can succeed against the
    LORD.

³¹The horse is made ready for the day
    of battle,
  but victory rests with the LORD.

22 A good name is more desirable
    than great riches;
  to be esteemed is better than silver
    or gold.

²Rich and poor have this in common:
  The LORD is the Maker of them all.

³A prudent man sees danger and takes
    refuge,
  but the simple keep going and
    suffer for it.

⁴Humility and the fear of the LORD
  bring wealth and honour and life.

⁵In the paths of the wicked lie thorns
    and snares,
  but he who guards his soul stays far
    from them.

⁶Train a child in the way he should go,
  and when he is old he will not turn
    from it.

DAY 249

SEPTEMBER 6

OLD TESTAMENT READING
Isaiah 10:20–13:22

The Remnant of Israel

²⁰In that day the remnant of Israel,
    the survivors of the house of Jacob,
  will no longer rely on him
    who struck them down
  but will truly rely on the LORD,
    the Holy One of Israel.
²¹A remnant will return, a remnant of
    Jacob

will return to the Mighty God.
²²Though your people, O Israel, be like
    the sand by the sea,
  only a remnant will return.
  Destruction has been decreed,
    overwhelming and righteous.
²³The Lord, the LORD Almighty, will
    carry out
  the destruction decreed upon the
    whole land.

²⁴Therefore, this is what the Lord, the LORD Almighty, says:

"O my people who live in Zion,
    do not be afraid of the Assyrians,
who beat you with a rod
    and lift up a club against you, as
        Egypt did.
²⁵Very soon my anger against you will
        end
    and my wrath will be directed to
        their destruction."

²⁶The LORD Almighty will lash them
        with a whip,
    as when he struck down Midian at
        the rock of Oreb;
and he will raise his staff over the
        waters,
    as he did in Egypt.
²⁷In that day their burden will be lifted
        from your shoulders,
    their yoke from your neck;
the yoke will be broken
    because you have grown so fat.

²⁸They enter Aiath;
    they pass through Migron;
    they store supplies at Michmash.
²⁹They go over the pass, and say,
    "We will camp overnight at
        Geba."
    Ramah trembles;
    Gibeah of Saul flees.
³⁰Cry out, O Daughter of Gallim!
    Listen, O Laishah!
    Poor Anathoth!
³¹Madmenah is in flight;
    the people of Gebim take cover.
³²This day they will halt at Nob;
    they will shake their fist
at the mount of the Daughter of
        Zion,
    at the hill of Jerusalem.

³³See, the Lord, the LORD Almighty,
    will lop off the boughs with great
        power.
The lofty trees will be felled,
    the tall ones will be brought low.
³⁴He will cut down the forest thickets
        with an axe;
    Lebanon will fall before the Mighty
        One.

The Branch From Jesse

11 A shoot will come up from the
        stump of Jesse;
    from his roots a Branch will bear
        fruit.
²The Spirit of the LORD will rest on
        him—
    the Spirit of wisdom and of
        understanding,
    the Spirit of counsel and of power,
    the Spirit of knowledge and of the
        fear of the LORD—
³and he will delight in the fear of the
        LORD.

He will not judge by what he sees
        with his eyes,
    or decide by what he hears with his
        ears;
⁴but with righteousness he will judge
        the needy,
    with justice he will give decisions
        for the poor of the earth.
He will strike the earth with the rod
        of his mouth;
    with the breath of his lips he will
        slay the wicked.
⁵Righteousness will be his belt
    and faithfulness the sash round his
        waist.

⁶The wolf will live with the lamb,
    the leopard will lie down with the
        goat,
the calf and the lion and the yearling
        together;
    and a little child will lead them.
⁷The cow will feed with the bear,
    their young will lie down together,
    and the lion will eat straw like the
        ox.
⁸The infant will play near the hole of
        the cobra,
    and the young child put his hand
        into the viper's nest.
⁹They will neither harm nor destroy
    on all my holy mountain,
for the earth will be full of the
        knowledge of the LORD
    as the waters cover the sea.

10In that day the Root of Jesse will stand as a banner for the peoples; the nations will rally to him, and his place of rest will be glorious. 11In that day the Lord will reach out his hand a second time to reclaim the remnant that is left of his people from Assyria, from Lower Egypt, from Upper Egypt, from Cush, from Elam, from Babylonia, from Hamath and from the islands of the sea.

12He will raise a banner for the nations
    and gather the exiles of Israel;
he will assemble the scattered people
    of Judah
from the four quarters of the earth.
13Ephraim's jealousy will vanish,
    and Judah's enemies will be cut off;
Ephraim will not be jealous of Judah,
    nor Judah hostile towards
    Ephraim.
14They will swoop down on the slopes
    of Philistia to the west;
together they will plunder the
    people to the east.
They will lay hands on Edom and
    Moab,
    and the Ammonites will be subject
    to them.
15The Lord will dry up
    the gulf of the Egyptian sea;
with a scorching wind he will sweep
    his hand
    over the Euphrates River.
He will break it up into seven streams
    so that men can cross over in
    sandals.
16There will be a highway for the
    remnant of his people
    that is left from Assyria,
as there was for Israel
    when they came up from Egypt.

Songs of Praise

12 In that day you will say:

"I will praise you, O Lord.
    Although you were angry with me,
your anger has turned away
    and you have comforted me.
2Surely God is my salvation;
    I will trust and not be afraid.

The Lord, the Lord, is my strength
    and my song;
he has become my salvation."
3With joy you will draw water
    from the wells of salvation.

4In that day you will say:

"Give thanks to the Lord, call on his
    name;
    make known among the nations
    what he has done,
and proclaim that his name is
    exalted.
5Sing to the Lord, for he has done
    glorious things;
    let this be known to all the world.
6Shout aloud and sing for joy, people
    of Zion,
for great is the Holy One of Israel
    among you."

A Prophecy Against Babylon

13 An oracle concerning Babylon that Isaiah son of Amoz saw:

2Raise a banner on a bare hilltop,
    shout to them;
beckon to them
    to enter the gates of the nobles.
3I have commanded my holy ones;
    I have summoned my warriors to
    carry out my wrath—
    those who rejoice in my triumph.

4Listen, a noise on the mountains,
    like that of a great multitude!
Listen, an uproar among the
    kingdoms,
    like nations massing together!
The Lord Almighty is mustering
    an army for war.
5They come from faraway lands,
    from the ends of the heavens—
the Lord and the weapons of his
    wrath—
    to destroy the whole country.

6Wail, for the day of the Lord is near;
    it will come like destruction from
    the Almighty.

7Because of this, all hands will go
     limp,
  every man's heart will melt.
8Terror will seize them,
     pain and anguish will grip them;
  they will writhe like a woman in
     labour.
They will look aghast at each other,
     their faces aflame.

9See, the day of the LORD is coming
  —a cruel day, with wrath and
     fierce anger—
to make the land desolate
  and destroy the sinners within it.
10The stars of heaven and their
     constellations
  will not show their light.
The rising sun will be darkened
  and the moon will not give its light.
11I will punish the world for its evil,
  the wicked for their sins.
I will put an end to the arrogance of
     the haughty
  and will humble the pride of the
     ruthless.
12I will make man scarcer than pure
     gold,
  more rare than the gold of Ophir.
13Therefore I will make the heavens
     tremble;
  and the earth will shake from its
     place
at the wrath of the LORD Almighty,
  in the day of his burning anger.

14Like a hunted gazelle,
  like sheep without a shepherd,
each will return to his own people,
  each will flee to his native land.
15Whoever is captured will be thrust
     through;
  all who are caught will fall by the
     sword.
16Their infants will be dashed to pieces
     before their eyes;
  their houses will be looted and
     their wives ravished.
17See, I will stir up against them the
     Medes,
  who do not care for silver
  and have no delight in gold.

18Their bows will strike down the
     young men;
  they will have no mercy on infants
  nor will they look with compassion
     on children.
19Babylon, the jewel of kingdoms,
  the glory of the Babylonians' pride,
will be overthrown by God
  like Sodom and Gomorrah.
20She will never be inhabited
  or lived in through all generations;
no Arab will pitch his tent there,
  no shepherd will rest his flocks
     there.
21But desert creatures will lie there,
  jackals will fill her houses;
  there the owls will dwell,
  and there the wild goats will leap
     about.
22Hyenas will howl in her strongholds,
  jackals in her luxurious palaces.
Her time is at hand,
  and her days will not be prolonged.

NEW TESTAMENT READING
2 Corinthians 8:16–9:5

Titus Sent to Corinth

16I thank God, who put into the heart
of Titus the same concern I have for
you. 17For Titus not only welcomed our
appeal, but he is coming to you with
much enthusiasm and on his own initia-
tive. 18And we are sending along with
him the brother who is praised by all the
churches for his service to the gospel.
19What is more, he was chosen by the
churches to accompany us as we carry
the offering, which we administer in
order to honour the Lord himself and to
show our eagerness to help. 20We want
to avoid any criticism of the way we
administer this liberal gift. 21For we are
taking pains to do what is right, not only
in the eyes of the Lord but also in the
eyes of men.

22In addition, we are sending with
them our brother who has often proved

to us in many ways that he is zealous, and now even more so because of his great confidence in you. 23As for Titus, he is my partner and fellow-worker among you; as for our brothers, they are representatives of the churches and an honour to Christ. 24Therefore show these men the proof of your love and the reason for your pride in you, so that the churches can see it.

9 There is no need for me to write to you about this service to the saints. 2For I know your eagerness to help, and I have been boasting about it to the Macedonians, telling them that since last year you in Achaia were ready to give; and your enthusiasm has stirred most of them to action. 3But I am sending the brothers in order that our boasting about you in this matter should not prove hollow, but that you may be ready, as I said you would be. 4For if any Macedonians come with me and find you unprepared, we—not to say anything about you—would be ashamed of having been so confident. 5So I thought it necessary to urge the brothers to visit you in advance and finish the arrangements for the generous gift you had promised. Then it will be ready as a generous gift, not as one grudgingly given.

READING FROM PSALMS
Psalm 105:37–45

37He brought out Israel, laden with
       silver and gold,
   and from among their tribes
       no-one faltered.
38Egypt was glad when they left,
   because dread of Israel had fallen
       on them.
39He spread out a cloud as a covering,
   and a fire to give light at night.
40They asked, and he brought them
       quail
   and satisfied them with the bread
       of heaven.
41He opened the rock, and water
       gushed out;
   like a river it flowed in the desert.

42For he remembered his holy promise
   given to his servant Abraham.
43He brought out his people with
       rejoicing,
   his chosen ones with shouts of joy;
44he gave them the lands of the nations,
   and they fell heir to what others
       had toiled for—
45that they might keep his precepts
   and observe his laws.

Praise the LORD.

DAY 250

SEPTEMBER 7

OLD TESTAMENT READING
Isaiah 14:1–16:14

14 The LORD will have compassion
       on Jacob;
   once again he will choose Israel
   and will settle them in their own
       land.
   Aliens will join them
       and unite with the house of Jacob.
2Nations will take them
   and bring them to their own place.

And the house of Israel will possess
       the nations
   as menservants and maidservants
       in the LORD's land.
   They will make captives of their
       captors
   and rule over their oppressors.

3On the day the LORD gives you relief
from suffering and turmoil and cruel
bondage, 4you will take up this taunt
against the king of Babylon:

How the oppressor has come to an
end!
How his fury has ended!
5The Lord has broken the rod of the
wicked,
the sceptre of the rulers,
6which in anger struck down peoples
with unceasing blows,
and in fury subdued nations
with relentless aggression.
7All the lands are at rest and at peace;
they break into singing.
8Even the pine trees and the cedars of
Lebanon
exult over you and say,
"Now that you have been laid low,
no woodsman comes to cut us
down."

9The grave below is all astir
to meet you at your coming;
it rouses the spirits of the departed to
greet you—
all those who were leaders in the
world;
it makes them rise from their
thrones—
all those who were kings over the
nations.
10They will all respond,
they will say to you,
"You also have become weak, as we
are;
you have become like us."
11All your pomp has been brought
down to the grave,
along with the noise of your harps;
maggots are spread out beneath you
and worms cover you.

12How you have fallen from heaven,
O morning star, son of the dawn!
You have been cast down to the earth,
you who once laid low the nations!
13You said in your heart,
"I will ascend to heaven;
I will raise my throne
above the stars of God;
I will sit enthroned on the mount of
assembly,
on the utmost heights of the sacred
mountain.
14I will ascend above the tops of the
clouds;
I will make myself like the Most
High."
15But you are brought down to the
grave,
to the depths of the pit.

16Those who see you stare at you,
they ponder your fate:
"Is this the man who shook the earth
and made kingdoms tremble,
17the man who made the world a
desert,
who overthrew its cities
and would not let his captives go
home?"

18All the kings of the nations lie in
state,
each in his own tomb.
19But you are cast out of your tomb
like a rejected branch;
you are covered with the slain,
with those pierced by the sword,
those who descend to the stones of
the pit.
Like a corpse trampled underfoot,
20   you will not join them in burial,
for you have destroyed your land
and killed your people.

The offspring of the wicked
will never be mentioned again.
21Prepare a place to slaughter his sons
for the sins of their forefathers;
they are not to rise to inherit the land
and cover the earth with their
cities.

22"I will rise up against them,"
declares the Lord Almighty.
"I will cut off from Babylon her name
and survivors,
her offspring and descendants,"
declares the Lord.
23"I will turn her into a place for owls
and into swampland;
I will sweep her with the broom of
destruction,"
declares the Lord Almighty.

A Prophecy Against Assyria

24The LORD Almighty has sworn,

"Surely, as I have planned, so it will
    be,
  and as I have purposed, so it will
    stand.
25I will crush the Assyrian in my land;
  on my mountains I will trample
    him down.
His yoke will be taken from my
    people,
  and his burden removed from their
    shoulders."

26This is the plan determined for the
    whole world;
  this is the hand stretched out over
    all nations.
27For the LORD Almighty has
    purposed, and who can thwart
    him?
His hand is stretched out, and who
    can turn it back?

A Prophecy Against the Philistines

28This oracle came in the year King
Ahaz died:

29Do not rejoice, all you Philistines,
  that the rod that struck you is
    broken;
from the root of that snake will spring
    up a viper,
  its fruit will be a darting, venomous
    serpent.
30The poorest of the poor will find
    pasture,
  and the needy will lie down in
    safety.
But your root I will destroy by
    famine;
  it will slay your survivors.

31Wail, O gate! Howl, O city!
  Melt away, all you Philistines!
A cloud of smoke comes from the
    north,
  and there is not a straggler in its
    ranks.

32What answer shall be given
  to the envoys of that nation?
"The LORD has established Zion,
  and in her his afflicted people will
    find refuge."

A Prophecy Against Moab

15 An oracle concerning Moab:

Ar in Moab is ruined,
  destroyed in a night!
Kir in Moab is ruined,
  destroyed in a night!
2Dibon goes up to its temple,
  to its high places to weep;
Moab wails over Nebo and
    Medeba.
Every head is shaved
  and every beard cut off.
3In the streets they wear sackcloth;
  on the roofs and in the public
    squares
they all wail,
  prostrate with weeping.
4Heshbon and Elealeh cry out,
  their voices are heard all the way to
    Jahaz.
Therefore the armed men of Moab
    cry out,
  and their hearts are faint.

5My heart cries out over Moab;
  her fugitives flee as far as Zoar,
  as far as Eglath Shelishiyah.
They go up the way to Luhith,
  weeping as they go;
on the road to Horonaim
  they lament their destruction.
6The waters of Nimrim are dried up
  and the grass is withered;
the vegetation is gone
  and nothing green is left.
7So the wealth they have acquired and
    stored up
  they carry away over the Ravine of
    the Poplars.
8Their outcry echoes along the border
    of Moab;
  their wailing reaches as far as
    Eglaim,
  their lamentation as far as Beer
    Elim.

⁹Dimon's waters are full of blood,
    but I will bring still more upon
        Dimon—
a lion upon the fugitives of Moab
    and upon those who remain in the
        land.

16 Send lambs as tribute to the
    ruler of the land,
from Sela, across the desert,
    to the mount of the Daughter of
        Zion.
²Like fluttering birds
    pushed from the nest,
so are the women of Moab
    at the fords of the Arnon.

³"Give us counsel,
    render a decision.
Make your shadow like night—
    at high noon.
Hide the fugitives,
    do not betray the refugees.
⁴Let the Moabite fugitives stay with
        you;
    be their shelter from the
        destroyer."

The oppressor will come to an end,
    and destruction will cease;
the aggressor will vanish from the
        land.
⁵In love a throne will be established;
    in faithfulness a man will sit on it—
    one from the house of David—
one who in judging seeks justice
    and speeds the cause of
        righteousness.

⁶We have heard of Moab's pride—
    her overweening pride and conceit,
her pride and her insolence—
    but her boasts are empty.
⁷Therefore the Moabites wail,
    they wail together for Moab.
Lament and grieve
    for the men of Kir Hareseth.
⁸The fields of Heshbon wither,
    the vines of Sibmah also.
The rulers of the nations
    have trampled down the choicest
        vines,

which once reached Jazer
    and spread towards the desert.
Their shoots spread out
    and went as far as the sea.
⁹So I weep, as Jazer weeps,
    for the vines of Sibmah.
O Heshbon, O Elealeh,
    I drench you with tears!
The shouts of joy over your ripened
        fruit
    and over your harvests have been
        stilled.
¹⁰Joy and gladness are taken away from
        the orchards;
    no-one sings or shouts in the
        vineyards;
no-one treads out wine at the presses,
    for I have put an end to the
        shouting.
¹¹My heart laments for Moab like a
        harp,
    my inmost being for Kir Hareseth.
¹²When Moab appears at her high
        place,
    she only wears herself out;
when she goes to her shrine to pray,
    it is to no avail.

¹³This is the word the LORD has
already spoken concerning Moab. ¹⁴But
now the LORD says: "Within three
years, as a servant bound by contract
would count them, Moab's splendour
and all her many people will be despised, and her survivors will be very
few and feeble."

NEW TESTAMENT READING
2 Corinthians 9:6–15

Sowing Generously

⁶Remember this: Whoever sows
sparingly will also reap sparingly, and
whoever sows generously will also reap
generously. ⁷Each man should give
what he has decided in his heart to give,
not reluctantly or under compulsion,
for God loves a cheerful giver. ⁸And
God is able to make all grace abound to
you, so that in all things at all times,

having all that you need, you will abound in every good work. ⁹As it is written:

"He has scattered abroad his gifts to the poor;
    his righteousness endures for ever."

¹⁰Now he who supplies seed to the sower and bread for food will also supply and increase your store of seed and will enlarge the harvest of your righteousness. ¹¹You will be made rich in every way so that you can be generous on every occasion, and through us your generosity will result in thanksgiving to God.

¹²This service that you perform is not only supplying the needs of God's people but is also overflowing in many expressions of thanks to God. ¹³Because of the service by which you have proved yourselves, men will praise God for the obedience that accompanies your confession of the gospel of Christ, and for your generosity in sharing with them and with everyone else. ¹⁴And in their prayers for you their hearts will go out to you, because of the surpassing grace God has given you. ¹⁵Thanks be to God for his indescribable gift!

READING FROM PSALMS
Psalm 106:1–15

¹Praise the LORD.

Give thanks to the LORD, for he is good;
    his love endures for ever.
²Who can proclaim the mighty acts of the LORD
    or fully declare his praise?
³Blessed are they who maintain justice,
    who constantly do what is right.
⁴Remember me, O LORD, when you show favour to your people,
    come to my aid when you save them,
⁵that I may enjoy the prosperity of your chosen ones,
    that I may share in the joy of your nation
    and join your inheritance in giving praise.

⁶We have sinned, even as our fathers did;
    we have done wrong and acted wickedly.
⁷When our fathers were in Egypt,
    they gave no thought to your miracles;
    they did not remember your many kindnesses,
    and they rebelled by the sea, the Red Sea.
⁸Yet he saved them for his name's sake,
    to make his mighty power known.
⁹He rebuked the Red Sea, and it dried up;
    he led them through the depths as through a desert.
¹⁰He saved them from the hand of the foe;
    from the hand of the enemy he redeemed them.
¹¹The waters covered their adversaries;
    not one of them survived.
¹²Then they believed his promises
    and sang his praise.

¹³But they soon forgot what he had done
    and did not wait for his counsel.
¹⁴In the desert they gave in to their craving;
    in the wasteland they put God to the test.
¹⁵So he gave them what they asked for,
    but sent a wasting disease upon them.

OLD TESTAMENT READING
Isaiah 17:1–19:25

An Oracle Against Damascus

17 An oracle concerning Damascus:

"See, Damascus will no longer be a
city
but will become a heap of ruins.
²The cities of Aroer will be deserted
and left to flocks, which will lie
down,
with no-one to make them afraid.
³The fortified city will disappear from
Ephraim,
and royal power from Damascus;
the remnant of Aram will be
like the glory of the Israelites,"
declares the LORD Almighty.

⁴"In that day the glory of Jacob will
fade;
the fat of his body will waste away.
⁵It will be as when a reaper gathers the
standing corn
and harvests the corn with his
arm—
as when a man gleans ears of corn
in the Valley of Rephaim.
⁶Yet some gleanings will remain,
as when an olive tree is beaten,
leaving two or three olives on the
topmost branches,
four or five on the fruitful boughs,"
declares the LORD,
the God of Israel.

⁷In that day men will look to their
Maker
and turn their eyes to the Holy
One of Israel.
⁸They will not look to the altars,
the work of their hands,
and they will have no regard for the
Asherah poles
and the incense altars their fingers
have made.

⁹In that day their strong cities, which
they left because of the Israelites, will
be like places abandoned to thickets
and undergrowth. And all will be
desolation.

¹⁰You have forgotten God your
Saviour;
you have not remembered the
Rock, your fortress.
Therefore, though you set out the
finest plants
and plant imported vines,
¹¹though on the day you set them out,
you make them grow,
and on the morning when you plant
them, you bring them to bud,
yet the harvest will be as nothing
in the day of disease and incurable
pain.

¹²Oh, the raging of many nations—
they rage like the raging sea!
Oh, the uproar of the peoples—
they roar like the roaring of great
waters!
¹³Although the peoples roar like the
roar of surging waters,
when he rebukes them they flee far
away,
driven before the wind like chaff on
the hills,
like tumble-weed before a gale.
¹⁴In the evening, sudden terror!
Before the morning, they are
gone!
This is the portion of those who loot
us,
the lot of those who plunder us.

A Prophecy Against Cush

18 Woe to the land of whirring
wings
along the rivers of Cush,
²which sends envoys by sea
in papyrus boats over the water.

Go, swift messengers,
to a people tall and smooth-skinned,
   to a people feared far and wide,
an aggressive nation of strange
      speech,
   whose land is divided by rivers.
3All you people of the world,
   you who live on the earth,
when a banner is raised on the
      mountains,
   you will see it,
and when a trumpet sounds,
   you will hear it.
4This is what the LORD says to me:
   "I will remain quiet and will look
      on from my dwelling-place,
like shimmering heat in the sunshine,
   like a cloud of dew in the heat of
      harvest."
5For, before the harvest, when the
      blossom is gone
   and the flower becomes a ripening
      grape,
he will cut off the shoots with pruning
      knives,
   and cut down and take away the
      spreading branches.
6They will all be left to the mountain
      birds of prey
   and to the wild animals;
the birds will feed on them all
      summer,
   the wild animals all winter.

7At that time gifts will be brought to
the LORD Almighty

from a people tall and
      smooth-skinned,
   from a people feared far and wide,
an aggressive nation of strange
      speech,
   whose land is divided by rivers—

the gifts will be brought to Mount Zion,
the place of the Name of the LORD
Almighty.

A Prophecy About Egypt

19 An oracle concerning Egypt:

See, the LORD rides on a swift cloud
   and is coming to Egypt.

The idols of Egypt tremble before
      him,
   and the hearts of the Egyptians
      melt within them.

2"I will stir up Egyptian against
      Egyptian—
   brother will fight against brother,
   neighbour against neighbour,
   city against city,
   kingdom against kingdom.
3The Egyptians will lose heart,
   and I will bring their plans to
      nothing;
they will consult the idols and the
      spirits of the dead,
   the mediums and the spiritists.
4I will hand the Egyptians over
   to the power of a cruel master,
and a fierce king will rule over
      them,"
   declares the Lord, the LORD
      Almighty.

5The waters of the river will dry up,
   and the river bed will be parched
      and dry.
6The canals will stink;
   the streams of Egypt will dwindle
      and dry up.
The reeds and rushes will wither,
7   also the plants along the Nile,
      at the mouth of the river.
Every sown field along the Nile
   will become parched, will blow
      away and be no more.
8The fishermen will groan and lament,
   all who cast hooks into the Nile;
those who throw nets on the water
   will pine away.
9Those who work with combed flax
   will despair,
   the weavers of fine linen will lose
      hope.
10The workers in cloth will be dejected,
   and all the wage earners will be
      sick at heart.

11The officials of Zoan are nothing but
      fools;
   the wise counsellors of Pharaoh
      give senseless advice.

How can you say to Pharaoh,
"I am one of the wise men,
a disciple of the ancient kings"?

12Where are your wise men now?
Let them show you and make
known
what the LORD Almighty
has planned against Egypt.
13The officials of Zoan have become
fools,
the leaders of Memphis are
deceived;
the cornerstones of her peoples
have led Egypt astray.
14The LORD has poured into them
a spirit of dizziness;
they make Egypt stagger in all that
she does,
as a drunkard staggers around in
his vomit.
15There is nothing Egypt can do—
head or tail, palm branch or reed.

16In that day the Egyptians will be
like women. They will shudder with fear
at the uplifted hand that the LORD
Almighty raises against them. 17And
the land of Judah will bring terror to the
Egyptians; everyone to whom Judah is
mentioned will be terrified, because of
what the LORD Almighty is planning
against them.

18In that day five cities in Egypt will
speak the language of Canaan and
swear allegiance to the LORD Almighty.
One of them will be called the City of
Destruction.

19In that day there will be an altar to
the LORD in the heart of Egypt, and a
monument to the LORD at its border.
20It will be a sign and witness to the
LORD Almighty in the land of Egypt.
When they cry out to the LORD because
of their oppressors, he will send them a
saviour and defender, and he will rescue
them. 21So the LORD will make himself
known to the Egyptians, and in that day
they will acknowledge the LORD. They
will worship with sacrifices and grain
offerings; they will make vows to the
LORD and keep them. 22The LORD will

strike Egypt with a plague; he will strike
them and heal them. They will turn to
the LORD, and he will respond to their
pleas and heal them.

23In that day there will be a highway
from Egypt to Assyria. The Assyrians
will go to Egypt and the Egyptians to
Assyria. The Egyptians and Assyrians
will worship together. 24In that day
Israel will be the third, along with Egypt
and Assyria, a blessing on the earth.
25The LORD Almighty will bless them,
saying, "Blessed be Egypt my people,
Assyria my handiwork, and Israel my
inheritance."

NEW TESTAMENT READING
2 Corinthians 10:1–18

Paul's Defence of His Ministry

10 By the meekness and gentleness
of Christ, I appeal to you—I,
Paul, who am "timid" when face to face
with you, but "bold" when away! 2I beg
you that when I come I may not have to
be as bold as I expect to be towards
some people who think that we live by
the standards of this world. 3For though
we live in the world, we do not wage war
as the world does. 4The weapons we
fight with are not the weapons of the
world. On the contrary, they have divine power to demolish strongholds. 5We
demolish arguments and every pre-
tension that sets itself up against the
knowledge of God, and we take captive
every thought to make it obedient to
Christ. 6And we will be ready to punish
every act of disobedience, once your
obedience is complete.

7You are looking only on the surface
of things. If anyone is confident that he
belongs to Christ, he should consider
again that we belong to Christ just as
much as he. 8For even if I boast some-
what freely about the authority the
Lord gave us for building you up rather
than pulling you down, I will not be
ashamed of it. 9I do not want to seem to
be trying to frighten you with my letters.

¹⁰For some say, "His letters are weighty and forceful, but in person he is unimpressive and his speaking amounts to nothing." ¹¹Such people should realise that what we are in our letters when we are absent, we will be in our actions when we are present.

¹²We do not dare to classify or compare ourselves with some who commend themselves. When they measure themselves by themselves and compare themselves with themselves, they are not wise. ¹³We, however, will not boast beyond proper limits, but will confine our boasting to the field God has assigned to us, a field that reaches even to you. ¹⁴We are not going too far in our boasting, as would be the case if we had not come to you, for we did get as far as you with the gospel of Christ. ¹⁵Neither do we go beyond our limits by boasting of work done by others. Our hope is that, as your faith continues to grow, our area of activity among you will greatly expand, ¹⁶so that we can preach the gospel in the regions beyond you. For we do not want to boast about work already done in another man's territory. ¹⁷But, "Let him who boasts boast in the Lord." ¹⁸For it is not the one who commends himself who is approved, but the one whom the Lord commends.

READING FROM PSALMS
Psalm 106:16–31

¹⁶In the camp they grew envious of Moses
    and of Aaron, who was consecrated to the LORD.
¹⁷The earth opened up and swallowed Dathan;
    it buried the company of Abiram.
¹⁸Fire blazed among their followers;
    a flame consumed the wicked.

¹⁹At Horeb they made a calf
    and worshipped an idol cast from metal.
²⁰They exchanged their Glory
    for an image of a bull, which eats grass.
²¹They forgot the God who saved them,
    who had done great things in Egypt,
²²miracles in the land of Ham
    and awesome deeds by the Red Sea.
²³So he said he would destroy them—
    had not Moses, his chosen one, stood in the breach before him
    to keep his wrath from destroying them.

²⁴Then they despised the pleasant land;
    they did not believe his promise.
²⁵They grumbled in their tents
    and did not obey the LORD.
²⁶So he swore to them with uplifted hand
    that he would make them fall in the desert,
²⁷make their descendants fall among the nations
    and scatter them throughout the lands.

²⁸They yoked themselves to the Baal of Peor
    and ate sacrifices offered to lifeless gods;
²⁹they provoked the LORD to anger by their wicked deeds;
    and a plague broke out among them.
³⁰But Phinehas stood up and intervened,
    and the plague was checked.
³¹This was credited to him as righteousness
    for endless generations to come.

OLD TESTAMENT READING
Isaiah 20:1–23:18

A Prophecy Against Egypt and Cush

20 In the year that the supreme commander, sent by Sargon king of Assyria, came to Ashdod and attacked and captured it—²at that time the LORD spoke through Isaiah son of Amoz. He said to him, "Take off the sackcloth from your body and the sandals from your feet." And he did so, going around stripped and barefoot.

³Then the LORD said, "Just as my servant Isaiah has gone stripped and barefoot for three years, as a sign and portent against Egypt and Cush, ⁴so the king of Assyria will lead away stripped and barefoot the Egyptian captives and Cushite exiles, young and old, with buttocks bared—to Egypt's shame. ⁵Those who trusted in Cush and boasted in Egypt will be afraid and put to shame. ⁶In that day the people who live on this coast will say, 'See what has happened to those we relied on, those we fled to for help and deliverance from the king of Assyria! How then can we escape?'"

A Prophecy Against Babylon

21 An oracle concerning the Desert by the Sea:

Like whirlwinds sweeping through
    the southland,
an invader comes from the desert,
    from a land of terror.

²A dire vision has been shown to me:
    The traitor betrays, the looter
        takes loot.
Elam, attack! Media, lay siege!
    I will bring to an end all the
        groaning she caused.

³At this my body is racked with pain,
    pangs seize me, like those of a
        woman in labour;

I am staggered by what I hear,
    I am bewildered by what I see.
⁴My heart falters,
    fear makes me tremble;
the twilight I longed for
    has become a horror to me.

⁵They set the tables,
    they spread the rugs,
    they eat, they drink!
Get up, you officers,
    oil the shields!

⁶This is what the Lord says to me:

"Go, post a lookout
    and have him report what he sees.
⁷When he sees chariots
    with teams of horses,
    riders on donkeys
        or riders on camels,
let him be alert,
    fully alert."

⁸And the lookout shouted,

"Day after day, my lord, I stand on
    the watchtower;
    every night I stay at my post.
⁹Look, here comes a man in a chariot
    with a team of horses.
And he gives back the answer:
    'Babylon has fallen, has fallen!
All the images of its gods
    lie shattered on the ground!'"

¹⁰O my people, crushed on the
    threshing-floor,
    I tell you what I have heard
from the LORD Almighty,
    from the God of Israel.

A Prophecy Against Edom

¹¹An oracle concerning Dumah:

Someone calls to me from Seir,
    "Watchman, what is left of the
        night?

Watchman, what is left of the
night?"
12The watchman replies,
"Morning is coming, but also the
night.
If you would ask, then ask;
and come back yet again."

A Prophecy Against Arabia

13An oracle concerning Arabia:

You caravans of Dedanites,
who camp in the thickets of
Arabia,
14 bring water for the thirsty;
you who live in Tema,
bring food for the fugitives.
15They flee from the sword,
from the drawn sword,
from the bent bow
and from the heat of battle.

16This is what the Lord says to me:
"Within one year, as a servant bound by
contract would count it, all the pomp of
Kedar will come to an end. 17The sur-
vivors of the bowmen, the warriors of
Kedar, will be few." The LORD, the
God of Israel, has spoken.

A Prophecy About Jerusalem

22 An oracle concerning the Valley
of Vision:

What troubles you now,
that you have all gone up on the
roofs,
2O town full of commotion,
O city of tumult and revelry?
Your slain were not killed by the
sword,
nor did they die in battle.
3All your leaders have fled together;
they have been captured without
using the bow.
All you who were caught were taken
prisoner together,
having fled while the enemy was
still far away.

4Therefore I said, "Turn away from
me;
let me weep bitterly.
Do not try to console me
over the destruction of my
people."

5The Lord, the LORD Almighty, has a
day
of tumult and trampling and terror
in the Valley of Vision,
a day of battering down walls
and of crying out to the mountains.
6Elam takes up the quiver,
with her charioteers and horses;
Kir uncovers the shield.
7Your choicest valleys are full of
chariots,
and horsemen are posted at the
city gates;
8 the defences of Judah are stripped
away.

And you looked in that day
to the weapons in the Palace of the
Forest;
9you saw that the City of David
had many breaches in its defences;
you stored up water
in the Lower Pool.
10You counted the buildings in
Jerusalem
and tore down houses to
strengthen the wall.
11You built a reservoir between the two
walls
for the water of the Old Pool,
but you did not look to the One who
made it,
or have regard for the One who
planned it long ago.

12The Lord, the LORD Almighty,
called you on that day
to weep and to wail,
to tear out your hair and put on
sackcloth.
13But see, there is joy and revelry,
slaughtering of cattle and killing of
sheep,
eating of meat and drinking of
wine!

"Let us eat and drink," you say,
"for tomorrow we die!"

[14]The LORD Almighty has revealed this in my hearing: "Till your dying day this sin will not be atoned for," says the Lord, the LORD Almighty.

[15]This is what the Lord, the LORD Almighty, says:

"Go, say to this steward,
to Shebna, who is in charge of the palace:
[16]What are you doing here and who gave you permission
to cut out a grave for yourself here,
hewing your grave on the height
and chiselling your resting place in the rock?

[17]"Beware, the LORD is about to take firm hold of you
and hurl you away, O you mighty man.
[18]He will roll you up tightly like a ball
and throw you into a large country.
There you will die
and there your splendid chariots will remain—
you disgrace to your master's house!
[19]I will depose you from your office,
and you will be ousted from your position.

[20]"In that day I will summon my servant, Eliakim son of Hilkiah. [21]I will clothe him with your robe and fasten your sash around him and hand your authority over to him. He will be a father to those who live in Jerusalem and to the house of Judah. [22]I will place on his shoulder the key to the house of David; what he opens no-one can shut, and what he shuts no-one can open. [23]I will drive him like a peg into a firm place; he will be a seat of honour for the house of his father. [24]All the glory of his family will hang on him: its offspring and offshoots—all its lesser vessels, from the bowls to all the jars.

[25]"In that day," declares the LORD Almighty, "the peg driven into the firm place will give way; it will be sheared off and will fall, and the load hanging on it will be cut down." The LORD has spoken.

A Prophecy About Tyre

23 An oracle concerning Tyre:

Wail, O ships of Tarshish!
For Tyre is destroyed
and left without house or harbour.
From the land of Cyprus
word has come to them.

[2]Be silent, you people of the island
and you merchants of Sidon,
whom the seafarers have enriched.
[3]On the great waters
came the grain of the Shihor;
the harvest of the Nile was the revenue of Tyre,
and she became the market-place of the nations.

[4]Be ashamed, O Sidon, and you, O fortress of the sea,
for the sea has spoken:
"I have neither been in labour nor given birth;
I have neither reared sons nor brought up daughters."
[5]When word comes to Egypt,
they will be in anguish at the report from Tyre.

[6]Cross over to Tarshish;
wail, you people of the island.
[7]Is this your city of revelry,
the old, old city,
whose feet have taken her
to settle in far-off lands?
[8]Who planned this against Tyre,
the bestower of crowns,
whose merchants are princes,
whose traders are renowned in the earth?
[9]The LORD Almighty planned it,
to bring low the pride of all glory

and to humble all who are
renowned on the earth.

[10]Till your land as along the Nile,
O Daughter of Tarshish,
for you no longer have a harbour.
[11]The LORD has stretched out his hand
over the sea
and made its kingdoms tremble.
He has given an order concerning
Phoenicia
that her fortresses be destroyed.
[12]He said, "No more of your revelling,
O Virgin Daughter of Sidon, now
crushed!

"Up, cross over to Cyprus;
even there you will find no rest."
[13]Look at the land of the Babylonians,
this people that is now of no
account!
The Assyrians have made it
a place for desert creatures;
they raised up their siege towers,
they stripped its fortresses bare
and turned it into a ruin.

[14]Wail, you ships of Tarshish;
your fortress is destroyed!

[15]At that time Tyre will be forgotten
for seventy years, the span of a king's
life. But at the end of these seventy
years, it will happen to Tyre as in the
song of the prostitute:

[16]"Take up a harp, walk through the
city,
O prostitute forgotten;
play the harp well, sing many a song,
so that you will be remembered."

[17]At the end of seventy years, the
LORD will deal with Tyre. She will return to her hire as a prostitute and will
ply her trade with all the kingdoms on
the face of the earth. [18]Yet her profit
and her earnings will be set apart for the
LORD; they will not be stored up or
hoarded. Her profits will go to those
who live before the LORD, for abundant
food and fine clothes.

NEW TESTAMENT READING
2 Corinthians 11:1–15

Paul and the False Apostles

11 I hope you will put up with a
little of my foolishness; but you
are already doing that. [2]I am jealous for
you with a godly jealousy. I promised
you to one husband, to Christ, so that I
might present you as a pure virgin to
him. [3]But I am afraid that just as Eve
was deceived by the serpent's cunning,
your minds may somehow be led astray
from your sincere and pure devotion to
Christ. [4]For if someone comes to you
and preaches a Jesus other than the
Jesus we preached, or if you receive a
different spirit from the one you received, or a different gospel from the
one you accepted, you put up with it
easily enough. [5]But I do not think I am
in the least inferior to those "super-
apostles". [6]I may not be a trained
speaker, but I do have knowledge. We
have made this perfectly clear to you in
every way.

[7]Was it a sin for me to lower myself in
order to elevate you by preaching the
gospel of God to you free of charge? [8]I
robbed other churches by receiving support from them so as to serve you. [9]And
when I was with you and needed something, I was not a burden to anyone, for
the brothers who came from Macedonia
supplied what I needed. I have kept
myself from being a burden to you in
any way, and will continue to do so.
[10]As surely as the truth of Christ is in
me, nobody in the regions of Achaia
will stop this boasting of mine. [11]Why?
Because I do not love you? God knows I
do! [12]And I will keep on doing what I
am doing in order to cut the ground
from under those who want an opportunity to be considered equal with us in
the things they boast about.

[13]For such men are false apostles,
deceitful workmen, masquerading as
apostles of Christ. [14]And no wonder,
for Satan himself masquerades as an
angel of light. [15]It is not surprising,

then, if his servants masquerade as servants of righteousness. Their end will be what their actions deserve.

READING FROM PROVERBS
Proverbs 22:7–16

[7]The rich rule over the poor,
    and the borrower is servant to the lender.

[8]He who sows wickedness reaps trouble,
    and the rod of his fury will be destroyed.

[9]A generous man will himself be blessed,
    for he shares his food with the poor.

[10]Drive out the mocker, and out goes strife;
    quarrels and insults are ended.

[11]He who loves a pure heart and whose speech is gracious
    will have the king for his friend.

[12]The eyes of the LORD keep watch over knowledge,
    but he frustrates the words of the unfaithful.

[13]The sluggard says, "There is a lion outside!"
    or, "I will be murdered in the streets!"

[14]The mouth of an adulteress is a deep pit;
    he who is under the LORD's wrath will fall into it.

[15]Folly is bound up in the heart of a child,
    but the rod of discipline will drive it far from him.

[16]He who oppresses the poor to increase his wealth
    and he who gives gifts to the rich—both come to poverty.

SEPTEMBER 10 DAY 253

OLD TESTAMENT READING
Isaiah 24:1–26:21

The LORD's Devastation of the Earth

24 See, the LORD is going to lay waste the earth
    and devastate it;
he will ruin its face
    and scatter its inhabitants—
[2]it will be the same
    for priests as for people,
    for master as for servant,
    for mistress as for maid,
    for seller as for buyer,
    for borrower as for lender,
    for debtor as for creditor.

[3]The earth will be completely laid waste
    and totally plundered.
        The LORD has spoken
            this word.

[4]The earth dries up and withers,
    the world languishes and withers,
    the exalted of the earth languish.
[5]The earth is defiled by its people;
    they have disobeyed the laws,
    violated the statutes
    and broken the everlasting covenant.
[6]Therefore a curse consumes the earth;

its people must bear their
    guilt.
Therefore earth's inhabitants are
    burned up,
    and very few are left.
⁷The new wine dries up and the vine
    withers;
    all the merrymakers groan.
⁸The gaiety of the tambourines is
    stilled,
    the noise of the revellers has
      stopped,
    the joyful harp is silent.
⁹No longer do they drink wine with a
    song;
    the beer is bitter to its drinkers.
¹⁰The ruined city lies desolate;
    the entrance to every house is
      barred.
¹¹In the streets they cry out for wine;
    all joy turns to gloom,
    all gaiety is banished from the
      earth.
¹²The city is left in ruins,
    its gate is battered to pieces.
¹³So will it be on the earth
    and among the nations,
as when an olive tree is beaten,
    or as when gleanings are left after
    the grape harvest.

¹⁴They raise their voices, they shout for
    joy;
    from the west they acclaim the
      LORD's majesty.
¹⁵Therefore in the east give glory to the
    LORD;
    exalt the name of the LORD, the
      God of Israel,
    in the islands of the sea.
¹⁶From the ends of the earth we hear
    singing:
    "Glory to the Righteous One."

But I said, "I waste away, I waste
    away!
    Woe to me!
The treacherous betray!
    With treachery the treacherous
      betray!"
¹⁷Terror and pit and snare await you,
    O people of the earth.

¹⁸Whoever flees at the sound of terror
    will fall into a pit;
whoever climbs out of the pit
    will be caught in a snare.

The floodgates of the heavens are
    opened,
    the foundations of the earth shake.
¹⁹The earth is broken up,
    the earth is split asunder,
    the earth is thoroughly shaken.
²⁰The earth reels like a drunkard,
    it sways like a hut in the wind;
so heavy upon it is the guilt of its
    rebellion
    that it falls—never to rise again.

²¹In that day the LORD will punish
    the powers in the heavens above
    and the kings on the earth below.
²²They will be herded together
    like prisoners bound in a dungeon;
they will be shut up in prison
    and be punished after many days.
²³The moon will be abashed, the sun
    ashamed;
    for the LORD Almighty will reign
on Mount Zion and in Jerusalem,
    and before its elders, gloriously.

Praise to the LORD

25 O LORD, you are my God;
    I will exalt you and praise your
    name,
for in perfect faithfulness
    you have done marvellous things,
    things planned long ago.
²You have made the city a heap of
    rubble,
    the fortified town a ruin,
the foreigners' stronghold a city no
    more;
    it will never be rebuilt.
³Therefore strong peoples will honour
    you;
    cities of ruthless nations will revere
    you.
⁴You have been a refuge for the poor,
    a refuge for the needy in his
    distress,
a shelter from the storm
    and a shade from the heat.

For the breath of the ruthless
   is like a storm driving against a wall
5 and like the heat of the desert.
You silence the uproar of foreigners;
   as heat is reduced by the shadow of
     a cloud,
so the song of the ruthless is stilled.

⁶On this mountain the LORD Almighty
   will prepare
a feast of rich food for all peoples,
a banquet of aged wine—
   the best of meats and the finest of
     wines.
⁷On this mountain he will destroy
   the shroud that enfolds all peoples,
   the sheet that covers all nations;
8 he will swallow up death for ever.
The Sovereign LORD will wipe away
     the tears
   from all faces;
he will remove the disgrace of his
     people
   from all the earth.
             The LORD has spoken.

⁹In that day they will say,

"Surely this is our God;
   we trusted in him, and he saved us.
This is the LORD, we trusted in him;
   let us rejoice and be glad in his
     salvation."

¹⁰The hand of the LORD will rest on this
     mountain;
   but Moab will be trampled under
     him
as straw is trampled down in the
     manure.
¹¹They will spread out their hands in it,
   as a swimmer spreads out his hands
     to swim.
God will bring down their pride
   despite the cleverness of their
     hands.
¹²He will bring down your high fortified
     walls
   and lay them low;
he will bring them down to the
     ground,
   to the very dust.

A Song of Praise

26 In that day this song will be sung
    in the land of Judah:

We have a strong city;
   God makes salvation
   its walls and ramparts.
²Open the gates
   that the righteous nation may
     enter,
   the nation that keeps faith.
³You will keep in perfect peace
   him whose mind is steadfast,
   because he trusts in you.
⁴Trust in the LORD for ever,
   for the LORD, the LORD, is the
     Rock eternal.
⁵He humbles those who dwell on high,
   he lays the lofty city low;
he levels it to the ground
   and casts it down to the dust.
⁶Feet trample it down—
   the feet of the oppressed,
   the footsteps of the poor.

⁷The path of the righteous is level;
   O upright One, you make the way
     of the righteous smooth.
⁸Yes, LORD, walking in the way of
     your laws,
   we wait for you;
your name and renown
   are the desire of our hearts.
⁹My soul yearns for you in the night;
   in the morning my spirit longs for
     you.
When your judgments come upon the
     earth,
   the people of the world learn
     righteousness.
¹⁰Though grace is shown to the wicked,
   they do not learn righteousness;
even in a land of uprightness they go
     on doing evil
   and regard not the majesty of the
     LORD.
¹¹O LORD, your hand is lifted high,
   but they do not see it.
Let them see your zeal for your
     people and be put to shame;
   let the fire reserved for your
     enemies consume them.

12LORD, you establish peace for us;
all that we have accomplished you
have done for us.

13O LORD, our God, other lords
besides you have ruled over us,
but your name alone do we
honour.

14They are now dead, they live no
more;
those departed spirits do not rise.
You punished them and brought
them to ruin;
you wiped out all memory of them.

15You have enlarged the nation, O
LORD;
you have enlarged the nation.
You have gained glory for yourself;
you have extended all the borders
of the land.

16LORD, they came to you in their
distress;
when you disciplined them,
they could barely whisper a prayer.

17As a woman with child and about to
give birth
writhes and cries out in her pain,
so were we in your presence, O
LORD.

18We were with child, we writhed in
pain,
but we gave birth to wind.
We have not brought salvation to the
earth;
we have not given birth to people
of the world.

19But your dead will live;
their bodies will rise.
You who dwell in the dust,
wake up and shout for joy.
Your dew is like the dew of the
morning;
the earth will give birth to her
dead.

20Go, my people, enter your rooms
and shut the doors behind you;
hide yourselves for a little while
until his wrath has passed by.

21See, the LORD is coming out of his
dwelling
to punish the people of the earth
for their sins.
The earth will disclose the blood shed
upon her;
she will conceal her slain no longer.

NEW TESTAMENT READING
2 Corinthians 11:16–33

Paul Boasts About His Sufferings

16I repeat: Let no-one take me for a
fool. But if you do, then receive me just
as you would a fool, so that I may do a
little boasting. 17In this self-confident
boasting I am not talking as the Lord
would, but as a fool. 18Since many are
boasting in the way the world does, I too
will boast. 19You gladly put up with
fools since you are so wise! 20In fact, you
even put up with anyone who enslaves
you or exploits you or takes advantage
of you or pushes himself forward or
slaps you in the face. 21To my shame I
admit that we were too weak for that!

What anyone else dares to boast
about—I am speaking as a fool—I
also dare to boast about. 22Are they
Hebrews? So am I. Are they Israelites?
So am I. Are they Abraham's descendants? So am I. 23Are they servants of
Christ? (I am out of my mind to talk like
this.) I am more. I have worked much
harder, been in prison more frequently,
been flogged more severely, and been
exposed to death again and again.
24Five times I received from the Jews
the forty lashes minus one. 25Three
times I was beaten with rods, once I was
stoned, three times I was shipwrecked, I
spent a night and a day in the open sea,
26I have been constantly on the move. I
have been in danger from rivers, in
danger from bandits, in danger from my
own countrymen, in danger from Gentiles; in danger in the city, in danger in
the country, in danger at sea; and in
danger from false brothers. 27I have
laboured and toiled and have often
gone without sleep; I have known

hunger and thirst and have often gone without food; I have been cold and naked. ²⁸Besides everything else, I face daily the pressure of my concern for all the churches. ²⁹Who is weak, and I do not feel weak? Who is led into sin, and I do not inwardly burn?

³⁰If I must boast, I will boast of the things that show my weakness. ³¹The God and Father of the Lord Jesus, who is to be praised for ever, knows that I am not lying. ³²In Damascus the governor under King Aretas had the city of the Damascenes guarded in order to arrest me. ³³But I was lowered in a basket from a window in the wall and slipped through his hands.

READING FROM PSALMS
Psalm 106:32–39

³²By the waters of Meribah they
    angered the LORD,
  and trouble came to Moses because
    of them;
³³for they rebelled against the Spirit of
    God,
  and rash words came from Moses'
    lips.

³⁴They did not destroy the peoples
    as the LORD had commanded
    them,
³⁵but they mingled with the nations
    and adopted their customs.
³⁶They worshipped their idols,
    which became a snare to them.
³⁷They sacrificed their sons
    and their daughters to demons.
³⁸They shed innocent blood,
    the blood of their sons and
    daughters,
  whom they sacrificed to the idols of
    Canaan,
  and the land was desecrated by
    their blood.
³⁹They defiled themselves by what they
    did;
  by their deeds they prostituted
    themselves.

SEPTEMBER 11   DAY 254

OLD TESTAMENT READING
Isaiah 27:1–28:29

Deliverance of Israel

27 In that day,
  the LORD will punish with his
    sword,
  his fierce, great and powerful
    sword,
  Leviathan the gliding serpent,
  Leviathan the coiling serpent;
he will slay the monster of the sea.

²In that day—

"Sing about a fruitful vineyard:
³ I, the LORD, watch over it;
  I water it continually.
  I guard it day and night
    so that no-one may harm it.
⁴ I am not angry.
  If only there were briers and thorns
    confronting me!
  I would march against them in
    battle;
  I would set them all on fire.
⁵Or else let them come to me for
    refuge;
  let them make peace with me,
  yes, let them make peace with me."

⁶In days to come Jacob will take root,
  Israel will bud and blossom
  and fill all the world with fruit.

⁷Has ⌊the LORD⌋ struck her
  as he struck down those who struck
    her?

Has she been killed
as those were killed who killed
her?
⁸By warfare and exile you contend
with her—
with his fierce blast he drives her
out,
as on a day the east wind blows.
⁹By this, then, will Jacob's guilt be
atoned for,
and this will be the full fruitage of
the removal of his sin:
When he makes all the altar stones
to be like chalk stones crushed to
pieces,
no Asherah poles or incense altars
will be left standing.
¹⁰The fortified city stands desolate,
an abandoned settlement, forsaken
like the desert;
there the calves graze,
there they lie down;
they strip its branches bare.
¹¹When its twigs are dry, they are
broken off
and women come and make fires
with them.
For this is a people without
understanding;
so their Maker has no compassion
on them,
and their Creator shows them no
favour.

¹²In that day the LORD will thresh
from the flowing Euphrates to the Wadi
of Egypt, and you, O Israelites, will be
gathered up one by one. ¹³And in that
day a great trumpet will sound. Those
who were perishing in Assyria and those
who were exiled in Egypt will come and
worship the LORD on the holy mountain
in Jerusalem.

Woe to Ephraim

28 Woe to that wreath, the pride
of Ephraim's drunkards,
to the fading flower, his glorious
beauty,
set on the head of a fertile valley—
to that city, the pride of those laid
low by wine!

²See, the Lord has one who is
powerful and strong.
Like a hailstorm and a destructive
wind,
like a driving rain and a flooding
downpour,
he will throw it forcefully to the
ground.
³That wreath, the pride of Ephraim's
drunkards,
will be trampled underfoot.
⁴That fading flower, his glorious
beauty,
set on the head of a fertile valley,
will be like a fig ripe before harvest—
as soon as someone sees it and
takes it in his hand,
he swallows it.

⁵In that day the LORD Almighty
will be a glorious crown,
a beautiful wreath
for the remnant of his people.
⁶He will be a spirit of justice
to him who sits in judgment,
a source of strength
to those who turn back the battle at
the gate.

⁷And these also stagger from wine
and reel from beer:
Priests and prophets stagger from
beer
and are befuddled with wine;
they reel from beer,
they stagger when seeing visions,
they stumble when rendering
decisions.
⁸All the tables are covered with vomit
and there is not a spot without
filth.

⁹"Who is it he is trying to teach?
To whom is he explaining his
message?
To children weaned from their milk,
to those just taken from the
breast?
¹⁰For it is:
Do and do, do and do,
rule on rule, rule on rule;
a little here, a little there."

11 Very well then, with foreign lips and
strange tongues
God will speak to this people,
12 to whom he said,
"This is the resting-place, let the
weary rest";
and, "This is the place of repose"—
but they would not listen.
13 So then, the word of the LORD to
them will become:
Do and do, do and do,
rule on rule, rule on rule;
a little here, a little there—
so that they will go and fall
backwards,
be injured and snared and
captured.

14 Therefore hear the word of the
LORD, you scoffers
who rule this people in Jerusalem.
15 You boast, "We have entered into a
covenant with death,
with the grave we have made an
agreement.
When an overwhelming scourge
sweeps by,
it cannot touch us,
for we have made a lie our refuge
and falsehood our hiding-place."

16 So this is what the Sovereign LORD
says:

"See, I lay a stone in Zion,
a tested stone,
a precious cornerstone for a sure
foundation;
the one who trusts will never be
dismayed.
17 I will make justice the measuring line
and righteousness the plumb-line;
hail will sweep away your refuge, the
lie,
and water will overflow your
hiding-place.
18 Your covenant with death will be
annulled;
your agreement with the grave will
not stand.
When the overwhelming scourge
sweeps by,
you will be beaten down by it.

19 As often as it comes it will carry you
away;
morning after morning, by day and
by night,
it will sweep through."

The understanding of this message
will bring sheer terror.
20 The bed is too short to stretch out on,
the blanket too narrow to wrap
around you.
21 The LORD will rise up as he did at
Mount Perazim,
he will rouse himself as in the
Valley of Gibeon—
to do his work, his strange work,
and perform his task, his alien
task.
22 Now stop your mocking,
or your chains will become heavier;
the Lord, the LORD Almighty, has
told me
of the destruction decreed against
the whole land.

23 Listen and hear my voice;
pay attention and hear what I say.
24 When a farmer ploughs for planting,
does he plough continually?
Does he keep on breaking up and
harrowing the soil?
25 When he has levelled the surface,
does he not sow caraway and
scatter cummin?
Does he not plant wheat in its place,
barley in its plot,
and spelt in its field?
26 His God instructs him
and teaches him the right way.

27 Caraway is not threshed with a
sledge,
nor is a cartwheel rolled over
cummin;
caraway is beaten out with a rod,
and cummin with a stick.
28 Grain must be ground to make bread;
so one does not go on threshing it
for ever.
Though he drives the wheels of his
threshing-cart over it,
his horses do not grind it.

29All this also comes from the LORD
Almighty,
    wonderful in counsel and
        magnificent in wisdom.

NEW TESTAMENT READING
2 Corinthians 12:1–10

Paul's Vision and His Thorn

12 I must go on boasting. Although there is nothing to be gained, I will go on to visions and revelations from the Lord. 2I know a man in Christ who fourteen years ago was caught up to the third heaven. Whether it was in the body or out of the body I do not know—God knows. 3And I know that this man—whether in the body or apart from the body I do not know, but God knows—4was caught up to paradise. He heard inexpressible things, things that man is not permitted to tell. 5I will boast about a man like that, but I will not boast about myself, except about my weaknesses. 6Even if I should choose to boast, I would not be a fool, because I would be speaking the truth. But I refrain, so no-one will think more of me than is warranted by what I do or say.

7To keep me from becoming conceited because of these surpassingly great revelations, there was given me a thorn in my flesh, a messenger of Satan, to torment me. 8Three times I pleaded with the Lord to take it away from me. 9But he said to me, "My grace is sufficient for you, for my power is made perfect in weakness." Therefore I will boast all the more gladly about my weaknesses, so that Christ's power may rest on me. 10That is why, for Christ's sake, I delight in weaknesses, in insults, in hardships, in persecutions, in difficulties. For when I am weak, then I am strong.

READING FROM PSALMS
Psalm 106:40–48

40Therefore the LORD was angry with
    his people
    and abhorred his inheritance.
41He handed them over to the nations,
    and their foes ruled over them.
42Their enemies oppressed them
    and subjected them to their power.
43Many times he delivered them,
    but they were bent on rebellion
    and they wasted away in their sin.

44But he took note of their distress
    when he heard their cry;
45for their sake he remembered his
    covenant
    and out of his great love he
    relented.
46He caused them to be pitied
    by all who held them captive.

47Save us, O LORD our God,
    and gather us from the nations,
that we may give thanks to your holy
    name
    and glory in your praise.

48Praise be to the LORD, the God of
    Israel,
    from everlasting to everlasting.
Let all the people say, "Amen!"

Praise the LORD.

OLD TESTAMENT READING
Isaiah 29:1–30:18

Woe to David's City

29 Woe to you, Ariel, Ariel,
the city where David settled!
Add year to year
and let your cycle of festivals go
on.
²Yet I will besiege Ariel;
she will mourn and lament,
she will be to me like an altar
hearth.
³I will encamp against you all around;
I will encircle you with towers
and set up my siege works against
you.
⁴Brought low, you will speak from the
ground;
your speech will mumble out of the
dust.
Your voice will come ghostlike from
the earth;
out of the dust your speech will
whisper.

⁵But your many enemies will become
like fine dust,
the ruthless hordes like blown
chaff.
Suddenly, in an instant,
⁶ the LORD Almighty will come
with thunder and earthquake and
great noise,
with windstorm and tempest and
flames of a devouring fire.
⁷Then the hordes of all the nations
that fight against Ariel,
that attack her and her fortress and
besiege her,
will be as it is with a dream,
with a vision in the night—
⁸as when a hungry man dreams that he
is eating,
but he awakens, and his hunger
remains;

as when a thirsty man dreams that he
is drinking,
but he awakens faint, with his
thirst unquenched.
So will it be with the hordes of all the
nations
that fight against Mount Zion.

⁹Be stunned and amazed,
blind yourselves and be sightless;
be drunk, but not from wine,
stagger, but not from beer.
¹⁰The LORD has brought over you a
deep sleep:
He has sealed your eyes (the
prophets);
he has covered your heads (the
seers).

¹¹For you this whole vision is nothing
but words sealed in a scroll. And if you
give the scroll to someone who can
read, and say to him, "Read this,
please," he will answer, "I can't; it is
sealed." ¹²Or if you give the scroll to
someone who cannot read, and say,
"Read this, please," he will answer, "I
don't know how to read."

¹³The Lord says:

"These people come near to me with
their mouth
and honour me with their lips,
but their hearts are far from me.
Their worship of me
is made up only of rules taught by
men.
¹⁴Therefore once more I will astound
these people
with wonder upon wonder;
the wisdom of the wise will perish,
the intelligence of the intelligent
will vanish."
¹⁵Woe to those who go to great depths
to hide their plans from the LORD,

who do their work in darkness and
    think,
    "Who sees us? Who will know?"
16You turn things upside down,
    as if the potter were thought to be
        like the clay!
Shall what is formed say to him who
    formed it,
    "He did not make me"?
Can the pot say of the potter,
    "He knows nothing"?

17In a very short time, will not Lebanon
    be turned into a fertile field
and the fertile field seem like a
    forest?
18In that day the deaf will hear the
    words of the scroll,
    and out of gloom and darkness
    the eyes of the blind will see.
19Once more the humble will rejoice in
    the LORD;
    the needy will rejoice in the Holy
        One of Israel.
20The ruthless will vanish,
    the mockers will disappear,
    and all who have an eye for evil will
        be cut down—
21those who with a word make a man
    out to be guilty,
    who ensnare the defender in court
    and with false testimony deprive
        the innocent of justice.

22Therefore this is what the LORD,
who redeemed Abraham, says to the
house of Jacob:

"No longer will Jacob be ashamed;
    no longer will their faces grow
        pale.
23When they see among them their
    children,
    the work of my hands,
they will keep my name holy;
    they will acknowledge the holiness
        of the Holy One of Jacob,
    and will stand in awe of the God of
        Israel.
24Those who are wayward in spirit will
    gain understanding;
    those who complain will accept
        instruction."

Woe to the Obstinate Nation

30 "Woe to the obstinate
    children,"
    declares the LORD,
"to those who carry out plans that are
    not mine,
    forming an alliance, but not by my
        Spirit,
    heaping sin upon sin;
2who go down to Egypt
    without consulting me;
who look for help to Pharaoh's
    protection,
    to Egypt's shade for refuge.
3But Pharaoh's protection will be to
    your shame,
    Egypt's shade will bring you
        disgrace.
4Though they have officials in Zoan
    and their envoys have arrived in
        Hanes,
5everyone will be put to shame
    because of a people useless to
        them,
who bring neither help nor
    advantage,
    but only shame and disgrace."

6An oracle concerning the animals of
the Negev:

Through a land of hardship and
    distress,
    of lions and lionesses,
    of adders and darting snakes,
the envoys carry their riches on
    donkeys' backs,
    their treasures on the humps of
        camels,
    to that unprofitable nation,
7   to Egypt, whose help is utterly
        useless.
Therefore I call her
    Rahab the Do-Nothing.

8Go now, write it on a tablet for them,
    inscribe it on a scroll,
that for the days to come
    it may be an everlasting witness.
9These are rebellious people, deceitful
    children,

children unwilling to listen to the
LORD's instruction.
[10]They say to the seers,
"See no more visions!"
and to the prophets,
"Give us no more visions of what is
right!
Tell us pleasant things,
prophesy illusions.
[11]Leave this way,
get off this path,
and stop confronting us
with the Holy One of Israel!"

[12]Therefore, this is what the Holy
One of Israel says:

"Because you have rejected this
message,
relied on oppression
and depended on deceit,
[13]this sin will become for you
like a high wall, cracked and
bulging,
that collapses suddenly, in an
instant.
[14]It will break in pieces like pottery,
shattered so mercilessly
that among its pieces not a fragment
will be found
for taking coals from a hearth
or scooping water out of a cistern."

[15]This is what the Sovereign LORD,
the Holy One of Israel, says:

"In repentance and rest is your
salvation,
in quietness and trust is your
strength,
but you would have none of it.
[16]You said, 'No, we will flee on horses.'
Therefore you will flee!
You said, 'We will ride off on swift
horses.'
Therefore your pursuers will be
swift!
[17]A thousand will flee
at the threat of one;
at the threat of five
you will all flee away,

till you are left
like a flagstaff on a mountaintop,
like a banner on a hill."

[18]Yet the LORD longs to be gracious to
you;
he rises to show you compassion.
For the LORD is a God of justice.
Blessed are all who wait for him!

NEW TESTAMENT READING
2 Corinthians 12:11–21

Paul's Concern for the Corinthians

[11]I have made a fool of myself, but
you drove me to it. I ought to have been
commended by you, for I am not in the
least inferior to the "super-apostles",
even though I am nothing. [12]The things
that mark an apostle—signs, wonders
and miracles—were done among you
with great perseverance. [13]How were
you inferior to the other churches, except that I was never a burden to you?
Forgive me this wrong!

[14]Now I am ready to visit you for the
third time, and I will not be a burden to
you, because what I want is not your
possessions but you. After all, children
should not have to save up for their
parents, but parents for their children.
[15]So I will very gladly spend for you
everything I have and expend myself as
well. If I love you more, will you love
me less? [16]Be that as it may, I have not
been a burden to you. Yet, crafty fellow
that I am, I caught you by trickery!
[17]Did I exploit you through any of the
men I sent you? [18]I urged Titus to go to
you and I sent our brother with him.
Titus did not exploit you, did he? Did
we not act in the same spirit and follow
the same course?

[19]Have you been thinking all along
that we have been defending ourselves
to you? We have been speaking in the
sight of God as those in Christ; and
everything we do, dear friends, is for
your strengthening. [20]For I am afraid
that when I come I may not find you as I

want you to be, and you may not find me as you want me to be. I fear that there may be quarrelling, jealousy, outbursts of anger, factions, slander, gossip, arrogance and disorder. 21I am afraid that when I come again my God will humble me before you, and I will be grieved over many who have sinned earlier and have not repented of the impurity, sexual sin and debauchery in which they have indulged.

READING FROM PSALMS
Psalm 107:1–9

1Give thanks to the LORD, for he is good;
  his love endures for ever.
2Let the redeemed of the LORD say this—

those he redeemed from the hand of the foe,
3those he gathered from the lands,
  from east and west, from north and south.

4Some wandered in desert wastelands,
  finding no way to a city where they could settle.
5They were hungry and thirsty,
  and their lives ebbed away.
6Then they cried out to the LORD in their trouble,
  and he delivered them from their distress.
7He led them by a straight way
  to a city where they could settle.
8Let them give thanks to the LORD for his unfailing love
  and his wonderful deeds for men,
9for he satisfies the thirsty
  and fills the hungry with good things.

DAY 256

SEPTEMBER 13

OLD TESTAMENT READING
Isaiah 30:19–32:20

19O people of Zion, who live in Jerusalem, you will weep no more. How gracious he will be when you cry for help! As soon as he hears, he will answer you. 20Although the Lord gives you the bread of adversity and the water of affliction, your teachers will be hidden no more; with your own eyes you will see them. 21Whether you turn to the right or to the left, your ears will hear a voice behind you, saying, "This is the way; walk in it." 22Then you will defile your idols overlaid with silver and your images covered with gold; you will throw them away like a menstrual cloth and say to them, "Away with you!"

23He will also send you rain for the seed you sow in the ground, and the food that comes from the land will be rich and plentiful. In that day your cattle will graze in broad meadows. 24The oxen and donkeys that work the soil will eat fodder and mash, spread out with fork and shovel. 25In the day of great slaughter, when the towers fall, streams of water will flow on every high mountain and every lofty hill. 26The moon will shine like the sun, and the sunlight will be seven times brighter, like the light of seven full days, when the LORD binds up the bruises of his people and heals the wounds he inflicted.

27See, the Name of the LORD comes from afar,
  with burning anger and dense clouds of smoke;
his lips are full of wrath,
  and his tongue is a consuming fire.

28His breath is like a rushing torrent,
    rising up to the neck.
  He shakes the nations in the sieve of
    destruction;
  he places in the jaws of the peoples
    a bit that leads them astray.
29And you will sing
    as on the night you celebrate a holy
      festival;
  your hearts will rejoice
    as when people go up with flutes
  to the mountain of the LORD,
    to the Rock of Israel.
30The LORD will cause men to hear his
    majestic voice
  and will make them see his arm
    coming down
  with raging anger and consuming fire,
    with cloudburst, thunderstorm and
      hail.
31The voice of the LORD will shatter
    Assyria;
  with his sceptre he will strike them
    down.
32Every stroke the LORD lays on them
    with his punishing rod
  will be to the music of tambourines
    and harps,
  as he fights them in battle with the
    blows of his arm.
33Topheth has long been prepared;
    it has been made ready for the king.
  Its fire pit has been made deep and
    wide,
  with an abundance of fire and
    wood;
  the breath of the LORD,
    like a stream of burning sulphur,
    sets it ablaze.

Woe to Those Who Rely on Egypt

31 Woe to those who go down to
    Egypt for help,
  who rely on horses,
  who trust in the multitude of their
    chariots
  and in the great strength of their
    horsemen,
  but do not look to the Holy One of
    Israel,
  or seek help from the LORD.

2Yet he too is wise and can bring
    disaster;
  he does not take back his words.
  He will rise up against the house of
    the wicked,
  against those who help evildoers.
3But the Egyptians are men and not
    God;
  their horses are flesh and not spirit.
  When the LORD stretches out his
    hand,
  he who helps will stumble,
  he who is helped will fall;
  both will perish together.

4This is what the LORD says to me:

"As a lion growls,
    a great lion over his prey—
  and though a whole band of
    shepherds
  is called together against him,
  he is not frightened by their shouts
    or disturbed by their clamour—
  so the LORD Almighty will come
    down
  to do battle on Mount Zion and on
    its heights.
5Like birds hovering overhead,
    the LORD Almighty will shield
      Jerusalem;
  he will shield it and deliver it,
  he will 'pass over' it and will rescue
    it."

6Return to him you have so greatly
revolted against, O Israelites. 7For in
that day every one of you will reject the
idols of silver and gold your sinful hands
have made.

8"Assyria will fall by a sword that is
    not of man;
  a sword, not of mortals, will
    devour them.
  They will flee before the sword
    and their young men will be put to
      forced labour.
9Their stronghold will fall because of
    terror;

at sight of the battle standard their
    commanders will panic,"
declares the LORD,
    whose fire is in Zion,
    whose furnace is in Jerusalem.

The Kingdom of Righteousness

32 See, a king will reign in
    righteousness
    and rulers will rule with justice.
[2]Each man will be like a shelter from
    the wind
    and a refuge from the storm,
like streams of water in the desert
    and the shadow of a great rock in a
    thirsty land.

[3]Then the eyes of those who see will
    no longer be closed,
    and the ears of those who hear will
    listen.
[4]The mind of the rash will know and
    understand,
    and the stammering tongue will be
    fluent and clear.
[5]No longer will the fool be called
    noble
    nor the scoundrel be highly
    respected.
[6]For the fool speaks folly,
    his mind is busy with evil:
He practises ungodliness
    and spreads error concerning the
    LORD;
the hungry he leaves empty
    and from the thirsty he withholds
    water.
[7]The scoundrel's methods are wicked,
    he makes up evil schemes
to destroy the poor with lies,
    even when the plea of the needy is
    just.
[8]But the noble man makes noble
    plans,
    and by noble deeds he stands.

The Women of Jerusalem

[9]You women who are so complacent,
    rise up and listen to me;

you daughters who feel secure,
    hear what I have to say!
[10]In little more than a year
    you who feel secure will tremble;
the grape harvest will fail,
    and the harvest of fruit will not
    come.
[11]Tremble, you complacent women;
    shudder, you daughters who feel
    secure!
Strip off your clothes,
    put sackcloth round your waists.
[12]Beat your breasts for the pleasant
    fields,
    for the fruitful vines
[13]and for the land of my people,
    a land overgrown with thorns and
    briers—
    yes, mourn for all houses of
    merriment
    and for this city of revelry.
[14]The fortress will be abandoned,
    the noisy city deserted;
citadel and watchtower will become a
    wasteland for ever,
    the delight of donkeys, a pasture
    for flocks,
[15]till the Spirit is poured upon us from
    on high,
    and the desert becomes a fertile
    field,
    and the fertile field seems like a
    forest.
[16]Justice will dwell in the desert
    and righteousness live in the fertile
    field.
[17]The fruit of righteousness will be
    peace;
    the effect of righteousness will be
    quietness and confidence for
    ever.
[18]My people will live in peaceful
    dwelling-places,
    in secure homes,
    in undisturbed places of rest.
[19]Though hail flattens the forest
    and the city is levelled
    completely,
[20]how blessed you will be,
    sowing your seed by every stream,
    and letting your cattle and donkeys
    range free.

NEW TESTAMENT READING
2 Corinthians 13:1–14

Final Warnings

13 This will be my third visit to you. "Every matter must be established by the testimony of two or three witnesses." [2]I already gave you a warning when I was with you the second time. I now repeat it while absent: On my return I will not spare those who sinned earlier or any of the others, [3]since you are demanding proof that Christ is speaking through me. He is not weak in dealing with you, but is powerful among you. [4]For to be sure, he was crucified in weakness, yet he lives by God's power. Likewise, we are weak in him, yet by God's power we will live with him to serve you.

[5]Examine yourselves to see whether you are in the faith; test yourselves. Do you not realise that Christ Jesus is in you—unless, of course, you fail the test? [6]And I trust that you will discover that we have not failed the test. [7]Now we pray to God that you will not do anything wrong. Not that people will see that we have stood the test but that you will do what is right even though we may seem to have failed. [8]For we cannot do anything against the truth, but only for the truth. [9]We are glad whenever we are weak but you are strong; and our prayer is for your perfection. [10]This is why I write these things when I am absent, that when I come I may not have to be harsh in my use of authority —the authority the Lord gave me for building you up, not for tearing you down.

Final Greetings

[11]Finally, brothers, good-bye. Aim for perfection, listen to my appeal, be of one mind, live in peace. And the God of love and peace will be with you.

[12]Greet one another with a holy kiss. [13]All the saints send their greetings.

[14]May the grace of the Lord Jesus Christ, and the love of God, and the fellowship of the Holy Spirit be with you all.

READING FROM PROVERBS
Proverbs 22:17–27

Sayings of the Wise

[17]Pay attention and listen to the sayings of the wise;
  apply your heart to what I teach,
[18]for it is pleasing when you keep them in your heart
  and have all of them ready on your lips.
[19]So that your trust may be in the LORD,
  I teach you today, even you.
[20]Have I not written thirty sayings for you,
  sayings of counsel and knowledge,
[21]teaching you true and reliable words,
  so that you can give sound answers to him who sent you?

[22]Do not exploit the poor because they are poor
  and do not crush the needy in court,
[23]for the LORD will take up their case
  and will plunder those who plunder them.
[24]Do not make friends with a hot-tempered man,
  do not associate with one easily angered,
[25]or you may learn his ways
  and get yourself ensnared.
[26]Do not be a man who strikes hands in pledge
  or puts up security for debts;
[27]if you lack the means to pay,
  your very bed will be snatched from under you.

OLD TESTAMENT READING
Isaiah 33:1–35:10

Distress and Help

33 Woe to you, O destroyer,
you who have not been
destroyed!
Woe to you, O traitor,
you who have not been betrayed!
When you stop destroying,
you will be destroyed;
when you stop betraying,
you will be betrayed.

2O LORD, be gracious to us;
we long for you.
Be our strength every morning,
our salvation in time of distress.
3At the thunder of your voice, the
peoples flee;
when you rise up, the nations
scatter.
4Your plunder, O nations, is
harvested as by young locusts;
like a swarm of locusts men pounce
on it.

5The LORD is exalted, for he dwells on
high;
he will fill Zion with justice and
righteousness.
6He will be the sure foundation for
your times,
a rich store of salvation and
wisdom and knowledge;
the fear of the LORD is the key to
this treasure.

7Look, their brave men cry aloud in
the streets;
the envoys of peace weep bitterly.
8The highways are deserted,
no travellers are on the roads.
The treaty is broken,
its witnesses are despised,
no-one is respected.
9The land mourns and wastes away;
Lebanon is ashamed and withers;

Sharon is like the Arabah,
and Bashan and Carmel drop their
leaves.

10"Now will I arise," says the LORD.
"Now will I be exalted;
now will I be lifted up.
11You conceive chaff,
you give birth to straw;
your breath is a fire that consumes
you.
12The peoples will be burned as if to
lime;
like cut thornbushes they will be
set ablaze."

13You who are far away, hear what I
have done;
you who are near, acknowledge my
power!
14The sinners in Zion are terrified;
trembling grips the godless:
"Who of us can dwell with the
consuming fire?
Who of us can dwell with
everlasting burning?"
15He who walks righteously
and speaks what is right,
who rejects gain from extortion
and keeps his hand from accepting
bribes,
who stops his ears against plots of
murder
and shuts his eyes against
contemplating evil—
16this is the man who will dwell on the
heights,
whose refuge will be the mountain
fortress.
His bread will be supplied,
and water will not fail him.

17Your eyes will see the king in his
beauty
and view a land that stretches afar.
18In your thoughts you will ponder the
former terror:
"Where is that chief officer?

Where is the one who took the
revenue?
Where is the officer in charge of
the towers?"
¹⁹You will see those arrogant people no
more,
those people of an obscure speech,
with their strange,
incomprehensible tongue.

²⁰Look upon Zion, the city of our
festivals;
your eyes will see Jerusalem,
a peaceful abode, a tent that will
not be moved;
its stakes will never be pulled up,
nor any of its ropes broken.
²¹There the LORD will be our Mighty
One.
It will be like a place of broad
rivers and streams.
No galley with oars will ride them,
no mighty ship will sail them.
²²For the LORD is our judge,
the LORD is our lawgiver,
the LORD is our king;
it is he who will save us.

²³Your rigging hangs loose:
The mast is not held secure,
the sail is not spread.
Then an abundance of spoils will be
divided
and even the lame will carry off
plunder.
²⁴No-one living in Zion will say, "I am
ill";
and the sins of those who dwell
there will be forgiven.

Judgment Against the Nations

34 Come near, you nations, and
listen;
pay attention, you peoples!
Let the earth hear, and all that is
in it,
the world, and all that comes out
of it!
²The LORD is angry with all nations;
his wrath is upon all their armies.
He will totally destroy them,

he will give them over to slaughter.
³Their slain will be thrown out,
their dead bodies will send up a
stench;
the mountains will be soaked with
their blood.
⁴All the stars of the heavens will be
dissolved
and the sky rolled up like a scroll;
all the starry host will fall
like withered leaves from the vine,
like shrivelled figs from the
fig-tree.

⁵My sword has drunk its fill in the
heavens;
see, it descends in judgment on
Edom,
the people I have totally
destroyed.
⁶The sword of the LORD is bathed in
blood,
it is covered with fat—
the blood of lambs and goats,
fat from the kidneys of rams.
For the LORD has a sacrifice in
Bozrah
and a great slaughter in Edom.
⁷And the wild oxen will fall with them,
the bull calves and the great bulls.
Their land will be drenched with
blood,
and the dust will be soaked with
fat.

⁸For the LORD has a day of vengeance,
a year of retribution, to uphold
Zion's cause.
⁹Edom's streams will be turned into
pitch,
her dust into burning sulphur;
her land will become blazing pitch!
¹⁰It will not be quenched night and day;
its smoke will rise for ever.
From generation to generation it will
lie desolate;
no-one will ever pass through it
again.
¹¹The desert owl and screech owl will
possess it;
the great owl and the raven will
nest there.

God will stretch out over Edom
the measuring line of chaos
and the plumb-line of desolation.
12Her nobles will have nothing there to
be called a kingdom,
all her princes will vanish away.
13Thorns will overrun her citadels,
nettles and brambles her
strongholds.
She will become a haunt for jackals,
a home for owls.
14Desert creatures will meet with
hyenas,
and wild goats will bleat to each
other;
there the night creatures will also
repose
and find for themselves places of
rest.
15The owl will nest there and lay eggs,
she will hatch them, and care for
her young under the shadow of
her wings;
there also the falcons will gather,
each with its mate.

16Look in the scroll of the LORD and
read:

None of these will be missing,
not one will lack her mate.
For it is his mouth that has given the
order,
and his Spirit will gather them
together.
17He allots their portions;
his hand distributes them by
measure.
They will possess it for ever
and dwell there from generation to
generation.

Joy of the Redeemed

35 The desert and the parched
land will be glad;
the wilderness will rejoice and
blossom.
Like the crocus, 2it will burst into
bloom;
it will rejoice greatly and shout for
joy.

The glory of Lebanon will be given to
it,
the splendour of Carmel and
Sharon;
they will see the glory of the LORD,
the splendour of our God.

3Strengthen the feeble hands,
steady the knees that give way;
4say to those with fearful hearts,
"Be strong, do not fear;
your God will come,
he will come with vengeance;
with divine retribution
he will come to save you."

5Then will the eyes of the blind be
opened
and the ears of the deaf unstopped.
6Then will the lame leap like a deer,
and the mute tongue shout for joy.
Water will gush forth in the
wilderness
and streams in the desert.
7The burning sand will become a pool,
the thirsty ground bubbling
springs.
In the haunts where jackals once lay,
grass and reeds and papyrus will
grow.

8And a highway will be there;
it will be called the Way of
Holiness.
The unclean will not journey on it;
it will be for those who walk in that
Way;
wicked fools will not go about on it.
9No lion will be there,
nor will any ferocious beast get up
on it;
they will not be found there.
But only the redeemed will walk
there,
10 and the ransomed of the LORD will
return.
They will enter Zion with singing;
everlasting joy will crown their
heads.
Gladness and joy will overtake them,
and sorrow and sighing will flee
away.

NEW TESTAMENT READING
Galatians 1:1–24

1 Paul, an apostle—sent not from men nor by man, but by Jesus Christ and God the Father, who raised him from the dead—²and all the brothers with me,

To the churches in Galatia:

³Grace and peace to you from God our Father and the Lord Jesus Christ, ⁴who gave himself for our sins to rescue us from the present evil age, according to the will of our God and Father, ⁵to whom be glory for ever and ever. Amen.

No Other Gospel

⁶I am astonished that you are so quickly deserting the one who called you by the grace of Christ and are turning to a different gospel—⁷which is really no gospel at all. Evidently some people are throwing you into confusion and are trying to pervert the gospel of Christ. ⁸But even if we or an angel from heaven should preach a gospel other than the one we preached to you, let him be eternally condemned! ⁹As we have already said, so now I say again: If anybody is preaching to you a gospel other than what you accepted, let him be eternally condemned!

¹⁰Am I now trying to win the approval of men, or of God? Or am I trying to please men? If I were still trying to please men, I would not be a servant of Christ.

Paul Called by God

¹¹I want you to know, brothers, that the gospel I preached is not something that man made up. ¹²I did not receive it from any man, nor was I taught it; rather, I received it by revelation from Jesus Christ.

¹³For you have heard of my previous way of life in Judaism, how intensely I persecuted the church of God and tried to destroy it. ¹⁴I was advancing in Judaism beyond many Jews of my own age and was extremely zealous for the traditions of my fathers. ¹⁵But when God, who set me apart from birth and called me by his grace, was pleased ¹⁶to reveal his Son in me so that I might preach him among the Gentiles, I did not consult any man, ¹⁷nor did I go up to Jerusalem to see those who were apostles before I was, but I went immediately into Arabia and later returned to Damascus.

¹⁸Then after three years, I went up to Jerusalem to get acquainted with Peter and stayed with him fifteen days. ¹⁹I saw none of the other apostles—only James, the Lord's brother. ²⁰I assure you before God that what I am writing to you is no lie. ²¹Later I went to Syria and Cilicia. ²²I was personally unknown to the churches of Judea that are in Christ. ²³They only heard the report: "The man who formerly persecuted us is now preaching the faith he once tried to destroy." ²⁴And they praised God because of me.

READING FROM PSALMS
Psalm 107:10–22

¹⁰Some sat in darkness and the deepest gloom,
  prisoners suffering in iron chains,
¹¹for they had rebelled against the words of God
  and despised the counsel of the Most High.
¹²So he subjected them to bitter labour;
  they stumbled, and there was no-one to help.
¹³Then they cried to the LORD in their trouble,
  and he saved them from their distress.
¹⁴He brought them out of darkness and the deepest gloom
  and broke away their chains.

15Let them give thanks to the LORD for
　　his unfailing love
　and his wonderful deeds for men,
16for he breaks down gates of bronze
　　and cuts through bars of iron.

17Some became fools through their
　　rebellious ways
　and suffered affliction because of
　　their iniquities.
18They loathed all food
　　and drew near the gates of death.

19Then they cried to the LORD in their
　　trouble,
　and he saved them from their
　　distress.
20He sent forth his word and healed
　　them;
　he rescued them from the grave.
21Let them give thanks to the LORD for
　　his unfailing love
　and his wonderful deeds for men.
22Let them give sacrifice thank-offerings
　　and tell of his works with songs of
　　joy.

DAY 258　　　**SEPTEMBER 15**

OLD TESTAMENT READING
Isaiah 36:1–37:38

Sennacherib Threatens Jerusalem

36 In the fourteenth year of King
Hezekiah's reign, Sennacherib
king of Assyria attacked all the fortified
cities of Judah and captured them.
2Then the king of Assyria sent his field
commander with a large army from
Lachish to King Hezekiah at Jerusalem.
When the commander stopped at the
aqueduct of the Upper Pool, on the
road to the Washerman's Field,
3Eliakim son of Hilkiah the palace
administrator, Shebna the secretary,
and Joah son of Asaph the recorder
went out to him.

4The field commander said to them,
"Tell Hezekiah,

　"'This is what the great king, the
king of Assyria, says: On what are
you basing this confidence of
yours? 5You say you have strategy
and military strength—but you
speak only empty words. On whom
are you depending, that you rebel
against me? 6Look now, you are
depending on Egypt, that splintered reed of a staff, which pierces

a man's hand and wounds him if he
leans on it! Such is Pharaoh king of
Egypt to all who depend on him.
7And if you say to me, "We are
depending on the LORD our God"
—isn't he the one whose high
places and altars Hezekiah removed, saying to Judah and Jerusalem, "You must worship before
this altar"?

8"'Come now, make a bargain
with my master, the king of Assyria: I will give you two thousand
horses—if you can put riders on
them! 9How then can you repulse
one officer of the least of my master's officials, even though you are
depending on Egypt for chariots
and horsemen? 10Furthermore,
have I come to attack and destroy
this land without the LORD? The
LORD himself told me to march
against this country and destroy
it.'"

11Then Eliakim, Shebna and Joah
said to the field commander, "Please
speak to your servants in Aramaic,
since we understand it. Don't speak to
us in Hebrew in the hearing of the
people on the wall."

12But the commander replied, "Was

it only to your master and you that my master sent me to say these things, and not to the men sitting on the wall—who, like you, will have to eat their own filth and drink their own urine?"

[13]Then the commander stood and called out in Hebrew, "Hear the words of the great king, the king of Assyria! [14]This is what the king says: Do not let Hezekiah deceive you. He cannot deliver you! [15]Do not let Hezekiah persuade you to trust in the LORD when he says, 'The LORD will surely deliver us; this city will not be given into the hand of the king of Assyria.'

[16]"Do not listen to Hezekiah. This is what the king of Assyria says: Make peace with me and come out to me. Then every one of you will eat from his own vine and fig-tree and drink water from his own cistern, [17]until I come and take you to a land like your own—a land of corn and new wine, a land of bread and vineyards.

[18]"Do not let Hezekiah mislead you when he says, 'The LORD will deliver us.' Has the god of any nation ever delivered his land from the hand of the king of Assyria? [19]Where are the gods of Hamath and Arpad? Where are the gods of Sepharvaim? Have they rescued Samaria from my hand? [20]Who of all the gods of these countries have been able to save his land from me? How then can the LORD deliver Jerusalem from my hand?"

[21]But the people remained silent and said nothing in reply, because the king had commanded, "Do not answer him."

[22]Then Eliakim son of Hilkiah the palace administrator, Shebna the secretary, and Joah son of Asaph the recorder went to Hezekiah, with their clothes torn, and told him what the field commander had said.

Jerusalem's Deliverance Foretold

37 When King Hezekiah heard this, he tore his clothes and put on sackcloth and went into the temple of the LORD. [2]He sent Eliakim the palace administrator, Shebna the secretary, and the leading priests, all wearing sackcloth, to the prophet Isaiah son of Amoz. [3]They told him, "This is what Hezekiah says: This day is a day of distress and rebuke and disgrace, as when children come to the point of birth and there is no strength to deliver them. [4]It may be that the LORD your God will hear the words of the field commander, whom his master, the king of Assyria, has sent to ridicule the living God, and that he will rebuke him for the words the LORD your God has heard. Therefore pray for the remnant that still survives."

[5]When King Hezekiah's officials came to Isaiah, [6]Isaiah said to them, "Tell your master, 'This is what the LORD says: Do not be afraid of what you have heard—those words with which the underlings of the king of Assyria have blasphemed me. [7]Listen! I am going to put a spirit in him so that when he hears a certain report, he will return to his own country, and there I will have him cut down with the sword.'"

[8]When the field commander heard that the king of Assyria had left Lachish, he withdrew and found the king fighting against Libnah.

[9]Now Sennacherib received a report that Tirhakah, the Cushite king ⌊of Egypt⌋, was marching out to fight against him. When he heard it, he sent messengers to Hezekiah with this word: [10]"Say to Hezekiah king of Judah: Do not let the god you depend on deceive you when he says, 'Jerusalem will not be handed over to the king of Assyria.' [11]Surely you have heard what the kings of Assyria have done to all the countries, destroying them completely. And will you be delivered? [12]Did the gods of the nations that were destroyed by my forefathers deliver them—the gods of Gozan, Haran, Rezeph and the people of Eden who were in Tel Assar? [13]Where is the king of Hamath, the king of Arpad, the king of the city of Sepharvaim, or of Hena or Ivvah?

Hezekiah's Prayer

[14]Hezekiah received the letter from the messengers and read it. Then he went up to the temple of the LORD and spread it out before the LORD. [15]And Hezekiah prayed to the LORD: [16]"O LORD Almighty, God of Israel, enthroned between the cherubim, you alone are God over all the kingdoms of the earth. You have made heaven and earth. [17]Give ear, O LORD, and hear; open your eyes, O LORD, and see; listen to all the words Sennacherib has sent to insult the living God.

[18]"It is true, O LORD, that the Assyrian kings have laid waste all these peoples and their lands. [19]They have thrown their gods into the fire and destroyed them, for they were not gods but only wood and stone, fashioned by human hands. [20]Now, O LORD our God, deliver us from his hand, so that all kingdoms on earth may know that you alone, O LORD, are God."

Sennacherib's Fall

[21]Then Isaiah son of Amoz sent a message to Hezekiah: "This is what the LORD, the God of Israel, says: Because you have prayed to me concerning Sennacherib king of Assyria, [22]this is the word the LORD has spoken against him:

"The Virgin Daughter of Zion
    despises and mocks you.
The Daughter of Jerusalem
    tosses her head as you flee.
[23]Who is it you have insulted and
        blasphemed?
    Against whom have you raised
        your voice
and lifted your eyes in pride?
    Against the Holy One of Israel!
[24]By your messengers
    you have heaped insults on the
        Lord.
And you have said,
    'With my many chariots
I have ascended the heights of the
        mountains,
    the utmost heights of Lebanon.

I have cut down its tallest cedars,
    the choicest of its pines.
I have reached its remotest heights,
    the finest of its forests.
[25]I have dug wells in foreign lands
    and drunk the water there.
With the soles of my feet
    I have dried up all the streams of
        Egypt.'

[26]"Have you not heard?
    Long ago I ordained it.
In days of old I planned it;
    now I have brought it to pass,
that you have turned fortified cities
    into piles of stone.
[27]Their people, drained of power,
    are dismayed and put to shame.
They are like plants in the field,
    like tender green shoots,
like grass sprouting on the roof,
    scorched before it grows up.

[28]"But I know where you stay
    and when you come and go
    and how you rage against me.
[29]Because you rage against me
    and because your insolence has
        reached my ears,
I will put my hook in your nose
    and my bit in your mouth,
and I will make you return
    by the way you came.

[30]"This will be the sign for you, O Hezekiah:

"This year you will eat what grows by
        itself,
    and the second year what springs
        from that.
But in the third year sow and reap,
    plant vineyards and eat their fruit.
[31]Once more a remnant of the house of
        Judah
    will take root below and bear fruit
        above.
[32]For out of Jerusalem will come a
        remnant,
    and out of Mount Zion a band of
        survivors.

The zeal of the LORD Almighty
　　will accomplish this.

33"Therefore this is what the LORD
says concerning the king of Assyria:

"He will not enter this city
　　or shoot an arrow here.
He will not come before it with shield
　　or build a siege ramp against it.
34By the way that he came he will
　　　　return;
　　he will not enter this city,"
　　　　　　　　declares the LORD.
35"I will defend this city and save it,
　　for my sake and for the sake of
　　　　David my servant!"

36Then the angel of the LORD went
out and put to death a hundred and
eighty-five thousand men in the Assyrian camp. When the people got up
the next morning—there were all the
dead bodies! 37So Sennacherib king of
Assyria broke camp and withdrew. He
returned to Nineveh and stayed there.

38One day, while he was worshipping
in the temple of his god Nisroch, his
sons Adrammelech and Sharezer cut
him down with the sword, and they
escaped to the land of Ararat. And
Esarhaddon his son succeeded him as
king.

NEW TESTAMENT READING
Galatians 2:1–10

Paul Accepted by the Apostles

2 Fourteen years later I went up
again to Jerusalem, this time with
Barnabas. I took Titus along also. 2I
went in response to a revelation and set
before them the gospel that I preach
among the Gentiles. But I did this
privately to those who seemed to be
leaders, for fear that I was running or
had run my race in vain. 3Yet not even
Titus, who was with me, was compelled

to be circumcised, even though he was a
Greek. 4⌐This matter arose⌐ because
some false brothers had infiltrated our
ranks to spy on the freedom we have in
Christ Jesus and to make us slaves. 5We
did not give in to them for a moment, so
that the truth of the gospel might remain with you.

6As for those who seemed to be important—whatever they were makes no
difference to me; God does not judge
by external appearance—those men
added nothing to my message. 7On the
contrary, they saw that I had been entrusted with the task of preaching the
gospel to the Gentiles, just as Peter had
been to the Jews. 8For God, who was at
work in the ministry of Peter as an
apostle to the Jews, was also at work in
my ministry as an apostle to the Gentiles. 9James, Peter and John, those
reputed to be pillars, gave me and Barnabas the right hand of fellowship when
they recognised the grace given to me.
They agreed that we should go to the
Gentiles, and they to the Jews. 10All
they asked was that we should continue
to remember the poor, the very thing I
was eager to do.

READING FROM PSALMS
Psalm 107:23–32

23Others went out on the sea in ships;
　　they were merchants on the mighty
　　　　waters.
24They saw the works of the LORD,
　　his wonderful deeds in the deep.
25For he spoke and stirred up a tempest
　　that lifted high the waves.
26They mounted up to the heavens and
　　　　went down to the depths;
　　in their peril their courage melted
　　　　away.
27They reeled and staggered like
　　　　drunken men;
　　they were at their wits' end.
28Then they cried out to the LORD in
　　　　their trouble,

and he brought them out of their
    distress.
²⁹He stilled the storm to a whisper;
    the waves of the sea were hushed.
³⁰They were glad when it grew calm,
    and he guided them to their desired
    haven.

³¹Let them give thanks to the LORD for
    his unfailing love
    and his wonderful deeds for men.
³²Let them exalt him in the assembly of
    the people
    and praise him in the council of the
    elders.

DAY 259   # SEPTEMBER 16

OLD TESTAMENT READING
Isaiah 38:1–40:31

Hezekiah's Illness

38 In those days Hezekiah became
    ill and was at the point of death.
The prophet Isaiah son of Amoz went to
him and said, "This is what the LORD
says: Put your house in order, because
you are going to die; you will not
recover."

²Hezekiah turned his face to the wall
and prayed to the LORD, ³"Remember,
O LORD, how I have walked before you
faithfully and with wholehearted devotion and have done what is good in
your eyes." And Hezekiah wept
bitterly.

⁴Then the word of the LORD came to
Isaiah: ⁵"Go and tell Hezekiah, 'This is
what the LORD, the God of your father
David, says: I have heard your prayer
and seen your tears; I will add fifteen
years to your life. ⁶And I will deliver
you and this city from the hand of the
king of Assyria. I will defend this city.

⁷"'This is the LORD's sign to you that
the LORD will do what he has promised:
⁸I will make the shadow cast by the sun
go back the ten steps it has gone down
on the stairway of Ahaz.'" So the sunlight went back the ten steps it had gone
down.

⁹A writing of Hezekiah king of Judah
after his illness and recovery:

¹⁰I said, "In the prime of my life
    must I go through the gates of
        death
    and be robbed of the rest of my
        years?"
¹¹I said, "I will not again see the LORD,
    the LORD, in the land of the living;
no longer will I look on mankind,
    or be with those who now dwell in
        this world.
¹²Like a shepherd's tent my house
    has been pulled down and taken
        from me.
Like a weaver I have rolled up my
    life,
    and he has cut me off from the
        loom;
    day and night you made an end of
        me.
¹³I waited patiently till dawn,
    but like a lion he broke all my
        bones;
    day and night you made an end of
        me.
¹⁴I cried like a swift or thrush,
    I moaned like a mourning dove.
My eyes grew weak as I looked to the
    heavens.
    I am troubled; O Lord, come to my
        aid!"

¹⁵But what can I say?
    He has spoken to me, and he
        himself has done this.
I will walk humbly all my years
    because of this anguish of my soul.
¹⁶Lord, by such things men live;
    and my spirit finds life in them too.

You restored me to health
and let me live.
[17]Surely it was for my benefit
that I suffered such anguish.
In your love you kept me
from the pit of destruction;
you have put all my sins
behind your back.

[18]For the grave cannot praise you,
death cannot sing your praise;
those who go down to the pit
cannot hope for your faithfulness.

[19]The living, the living—they praise
you,
as I am doing today;
fathers tell their children
about your faithfulness.

[20]The LORD will save me,
and we will sing with stringed
instruments
all the days of our lives
in the temple of the LORD.

[21]Isaiah had said, "Prepare a poultice
of figs and apply it to the boil, and he
will recover."

[22]Hezekiah had asked, "What will be
the sign that I will go up to the temple of
the LORD?"

Envoys From Babylon

39 At that time Merodach-Baladan
son of Baladan king of Babylon
sent Hezekiah letters and a gift, because
he had heard of his illness and recovery.
[2]Hezekiah received the envoys gladly
and showed them what was in his storehouses—the silver, the gold, the spices,
the fine oil, his entire armoury and
everything found among his treasures.
There was nothing in his palace or in all
his kingdom that Hezekiah did not show
them.

[3]Then Isaiah the prophet went to
King Hezekiah and asked, "What did
those men say, and where did they come
from?"

"From a distant land," Hezekiah
replied. "They came to me from
Babylon."

[4]The prophet asked, "What did they
see in your palace?"

"They saw everything in my palace,"
Hezekiah said. "There is nothing
among my treasures that I did not show
them."

[5]Then Isaiah said to Hezekiah, "Hear
the word of the LORD Almighty: [6]The
time will surely come when everything
in your palace, and all that your fathers
have stored up until this day, will be
carried off to Babylon. Nothing will be
left, says the LORD. [7]And some of your
descendants, your own flesh and blood
who will be born to you, will be taken
away, and they will become eunuchs in
the palace of the king of Babylon."

[8]"The word of the LORD you have
spoken is good," Hezekiah replied. For
he thought, "There will be peace and
security in my lifetime."

Comfort for God's People

40 Comfort, comfort my people,
says your God.
[2]Speak tenderly to Jerusalem,
and proclaim to her
that her hard service has been
completed,
that her sin has been paid for,
that she has received from the LORD's
hand
double for all her sins.

[3]A voice of one calling:
"In the desert prepare
the way for the LORD;
make straight in the wilderness
a highway for our God.
[4]Every valley shall be raised up,
every mountain and hill made low;
the rough ground shall become level,
the rugged places a plain.
[5]And the glory of the LORD will be
revealed,
and all mankind together will
see it.
For the mouth of the
LORD has spoken."

[6]A voice says, "Cry out."
And I said, "What shall I cry?"

"All men are like grass,
    and all their glory is like the
        flowers of the field.
7The grass withers and the flowers fall,
    because the breath of the LORD
        blows on them.
    Surely the people are grass.
8The grass withers and the flowers fall,
    but the word of our God stands for
        ever."

9You who bring good tidings to Zion,
    go up on a high mountain.
You who bring good tidings to
        Jerusalem,
    lift up your voice with a shout,
lift it up, do not be afraid;
    say to the towns of Judah,
    "Here is your God!"
10See, the Sovereign LORD comes with
        power,
    and his arm rules for him.
See, his reward is with him,
    and his recompense accompanies
        him.
11He tends his flock like a shepherd:
    He gathers the lambs in his arms
and carries them close to his heart;
    he gently leads those that have
        young.

12Who has measured the waters in the
        hollow of his hand,
    or with the breadth of his hand
        marked off the heavens?
Who has held the dust of the earth in
        a basket,
    or weighed the mountains on the
        scales
    and the hills in a balance?
13Who has understood the mind of the
        LORD,
    or instructed him as his counsellor?
14Whom did the LORD consult to
        enlighten him,
    and who taught him the right way?
Who was it that taught him
        knowledge
    or showed him the path of
        understanding?

15Surely the nations are like a drop in a
        bucket;

they are regarded as dust on the
        scales;
    he weighs the islands as though
        they were fine dust.
16Lebanon is not sufficient for altar
        fires,
    nor its animals enough for burnt
        offerings.
17Before him all the nations are as
        nothing;
    they are regarded by him as
        worthless
    and less than nothing.

18To whom, then, will you compare
        God?
    What image will you compare him
        to?
19As for an idol, a craftsman casts it,
    and a goldsmith overlays it with
        gold
    and fashions silver chains for it.
20A man too poor to present such an
        offering
    selects wood that will not rot.
He looks for a skilled craftsman
    to set up an idol that will not
        topple.

21Do you not know?
    Have you not heard?
Has it not been told you from the
        beginning?
    Have you not understood since the
        earth was founded?
22He sits enthroned above the circle of
        the earth,
    and its people are like
        grasshoppers.
He stretches out the heavens like a
        canopy,
    and spreads them out like a tent to
        live in.
23He brings princes to naught
    and reduces the rulers of this world
        to nothing.
24No sooner are they planted,
    no sooner are they sown,
    no sooner do they take root in the
        ground,
than he blows on them and they
        wither,

and a whirlwind sweeps them away
　　like chaff.

25"To whom will you compare me?
　　Or who is my equal?" says the
　　　Holy One.
26Lift your eyes and look to the
　　heavens:
　　Who created all these?
He who brings out the starry host one
　　by one,
　　and calls them each by name.
Because of his great power and
　　mighty strength,
　　not one of them is missing.

27Why do you say, O Jacob,
　　and complain, O Israel,
　　"My way is hidden from the LORD;
　　my cause is disregarded by my
　　　God"?
28Do you not know?
　　Have you not heard?
The LORD is the everlasting God,
　　the Creator of the ends of the
　　earth.
He will not grow tired or weary,
　　and his understanding no-one can
　　fathom.
29He gives strength to the weary
　　and increases the power of the
　　weak.
30Even youths grow tired and weary,
　　and young men stumble and fall;
31but those who hope in the LORD
　　will renew their strength.
They will soar on wings like eagles;
　　they will run and not grow weary,
　　they will walk and not be faint.

NEW TESTAMENT READING
Galatians 2:11–3:9

Paul Opposes Peter

11When Peter came to Antioch, I
opposed him to his face, because he was
clearly in the wrong. 12Before certain
men came from James, he used to eat

with the Gentiles. But when they arrived, he began to draw back and separate himself from the Gentiles because
he was afraid of those who belonged to
the circumcision group. 13The other
Jews joined him in his hypocrisy, so that
by their hypocrisy even Barnabas was
led astray.

14When I saw that they were not
acting in line with the truth of the gospel, I said to Peter in front of them all,
"You are a Jew, yet you live like a
Gentile and not like a Jew. How is it,
then, that you force Gentiles to follow
Jewish customs?

15"We who are Jews by birth and not
'Gentile sinners' 16know that a man is
not justified by observing the law, but
by faith in Jesus Christ. So we, too, have
put our faith in Christ Jesus that we may
be justified by faith in Christ and not by
observing the law, because by observing
the law no-one will be justified.

17"If, while we seek to be justified in
Christ, it becomes evident that we
ourselves are sinners, does that mean
that Christ promotes sin? Absolutely
not! 18If I rebuild what I destroyed, I
prove that I am a law-breaker. 19For
through the law I died to the law so that
I might live for God. 20I have been
crucified with Christ and I no longer
live, but Christ lives in me. The life I live
in the body, I live by faith in the Son of
God, who loved me and gave himself
for me. 21I do not set aside the grace of
God, for if righteousness could be
gained through the law, Christ died for
nothing!"

Faith or Observance of the Law

3 You foolish Galatians! Who has
bewitched you? Before your very
eyes Jesus Christ was clearly portrayed
as crucified. 2I would like to learn just
one thing from you: Did you receive the
Spirit by observing the law, or by believing what you heard? 3Are you so foolish? After beginning with the Spirit, are
you now trying to attain your goal by
human effort? 4Have you suffered so

much for nothing—if it really was for nothing? 5Does God give you his Spirit and work miracles among you because you observe the law, or because you believe what you heard?

6Consider Abraham: "He believed God, and it was credited to him as righteousness." 7Understand, then, that those who believe are children of Abraham. 8The Scripture foresaw that God would justify the Gentiles by faith, and announced the gospel in advance to Abraham: "All nations will be blessed through you." 9So those who have faith are blessed along with Abraham, the man of faith.

READING FROM PSALMS
Psalm 107:33–43

33He turned rivers into a desert,
    flowing springs into thirsty ground,
34and fruitful land into a salt waste,
    because of the wickedness of those
        who lived there.
35He turned the desert into pools of
        water
    and the parched ground into
        flowing springs;
36there he brought the hungry to live,
    and they founded a city where they
        could settle.
37They sowed fields and planted
        vineyards
    that yielded a fruitful harvest;
38he blessed them, and their numbers
        greatly increased,
    and he did not let their herds
        diminish.

39Then their numbers decreased, and
        they were humbled
    by oppression, calamity and
        sorrow;
40he who pours contempt on nobles
    made them wander in a trackless
        waste.
41But he lifted the needy out of their
        affliction
    and increased their families like
        flocks.
42The upright see and rejoice,
    but all the wicked shut their
        mouths.

43Whoever is wise, let him heed these
        things
    and consider the great love of the
        LORD.

SEPTEMBER 17

OLD TESTAMENT READING
Isaiah 41:1–42:25

The Helper of Israel

41 "Be silent before me, you islands!
    Let the nations renew their
        strength!
Let them come forward and speak;
    let us meet together at the place of
        judgment.

2"Who has stirred up one from the
        east,
calling him in righteousness to his
        service?
He hands nations over to him
    and subdues kings before him.
He turns them to dust with his sword,
    to wind-blown chaff with his bow.
3He pursues them and moves on
        unscathed,
    by a path his feet have not
        travelled before.
4Who has done this and carried it
        through,
    calling forth the generations from
        the beginning?

I, the Lord—with the first of them
and with the last—I am he."

[5]The islands have seen it and fear;
the ends of the earth tremble.
They approach and come forward;
[6]   each helps the other
and says to his brother, "Be
strong!"
[7]The craftsman encourages the
goldsmith,
and he who smooths with the
hammer
spurs on him who strikes the anvil.
He says of the welding, "It is good."
He nails down the idol so that it
will not topple.

[8]"But you, O Israel, my servant,
Jacob, whom I have chosen,
you descendants of Abraham my
friend,
[9]I took you from the ends of the earth,
from its farthest corners I called
you.
I said, 'You are my servant';
I have chosen you and have not
rejected you.
[10]So do not fear, for I am with you;
do not be dismayed, for I am your
God.
I will strengthen you and help you;
I will uphold you with my righteous
right hand.

[11]"All who rage against you
will surely be ashamed and
disgraced;
those who oppose you
will be as nothing and perish.
[12]Though you search for your enemies,
you will not find them.
Those who wage war against you
will be as nothing at all.
[13]For I am the Lord, your God,
who takes hold of your right hand
and says to you, Do not fear;
I will help you.
[14]Do not be afraid, O worm Jacob,
O little Israel,
for I myself will help you," declares
the Lord,

your Redeemer, the Holy One of
Israel.
[15]"See, I will make you into a
threshing-sledge,
new and sharp, with many teeth.
You will thresh the mountains and
crush them,
and reduce the hills to chaff.
[16]You will winnow them, the wind will
pick them up,
and a gale will blow them away.
But you will rejoice in the Lord
and glory in the Holy One of
Israel.

[17]"The poor and needy search for
water,
but there is none;
their tongues are parched with
thirst.
But I the Lord will answer them;
I, the God of Israel, will not
forsake them.
[18]I will make rivers flow on barren
heights,
and springs within the valleys.
I will turn the desert into pools of
water,
and the parched ground into
springs.
[19]I will put in the desert
the cedar and the acacia, the
myrtle and the olive.
I will set pines in the wasteland,
the fir and the cypress together,
[20]so that people may see and know,
may consider and understand,
that the hand of the Lord has done
this,
that the Holy One of Israel has
created it.

[21]"Present your case," says the Lord.
"Set forth your arguments," says
Jacob's King.
[22]"Bring in ⸤your idols⸥ to tell us
what is going to happen.
Tell us what the former things were,
so that we may consider them
and know their final outcome.
Or declare to us the things to come,

23 tell us what the future holds,
  so that we may know you are gods.
Do something, whether good or bad,
  so that we will be dismayed and
  filled with fear.
24But you are less than nothing
  and your works are utterly
  worthless;
  he who chooses you is detestable.

25"I have stirred up one from the
  north, and he comes—
  one from the rising sun who calls
  on my name.
He treads on rulers as if they were
  mortar,
  as if he were a potter treading the
  clay.
26Who told of this from the beginning,
  so that we could know,
  or beforehand, so that we could
  say, 'He was right'?
No-one told of this,
  no-one foretold it,
  no-one heard any words from you.
27I was the first to tell Zion, 'Look,
  here they are!'
  I gave to Jerusalem a messenger of
  good tidings.
28I look but there is no-one—
  no-one among them to give
  counsel,
  no-one to give answer when I ask
  them.
29See, they are all false!
  Their deeds amount to nothing;
  their images are but wind and
  confusion.

The Servant of the Lord

42 "Here is my servant, whom I
  uphold,
  my chosen one in whom I delight;
I will put my Spirit on him
  and he will bring justice to the
  nations.
2He will not shout or cry out,
  or raise his voice in the streets.
3A bruised reed he will not break,
  and a smouldering wick he will not
  snuff out.

In faithfulness he will bring forth
  justice;
4 he will not falter or be discouraged
till he establishes justice on earth.
  In his law the islands will put their
  hope."

5This is what God the Lord says—
he who created the heavens and
  stretched them out,
  who spread out the earth and all
  that comes out of it,
who gives breath to its people,
  and life to those who walk on it:
6"I, the Lord, have called you in
  righteousness;
  I will take hold of your hand.
I will keep you and will make you
  to be a covenant for the people
  and a light for the Gentiles,
7to open eyes that are blind,
  to free captives from prison
  and to release from the dungeon
  those who sit in darkness.

8"I am the Lord; that is my name!
  I will not give my glory to another
  or my praise to idols.
9See, the former things have taken
  place,
  and new things I declare;
before they spring into being
  I announce them to you."

Song of Praise to the Lord

10Sing to the Lord a new song,
  his praise from the ends of the
  earth,
you who go down to the sea, and all
  that is in it,
  you islands, and all who live in
  them.
11Let the desert and its towns raise
  their voices;
  let the settlements where Kedar
  lives rejoice.
Let the people of Sela sing for joy;
  let them shout from the
  mountaintops.
12Let them give glory to the Lord
  and proclaim his praise in the
  islands.

13The LORD will march out like a
  mighty man,
  like a warrior he will stir up his
    zeal;
  with a shout he will raise the battle
    cry
  and will triumph over his enemies.

14"For a long time I have kept silent,
  I have been quiet and held myself
    back.
  But now, like a woman in childbirth,
  I cry out, I gasp and pant.
15I will lay waste the mountains and
    hills
  and dry up all their vegetation;
  I will turn rivers into islands
  and dry up the pools.
16I will lead the blind by ways they have
    not known,
  along unfamiliar paths I will guide
    them;
  I will turn the darkness into light
    before them
  and make the rough places smooth.
  These are the things I will do;
  I will not forsake them.
17But those who trust in idols,
  who say to images, 'You are our
    gods,'
  will be turned back in utter shame.

Israel Blind and Deaf

18"Hear, you deaf;
  look, you blind, and see!
19Who is blind but my servant,
  and deaf like the messenger I send?
  Who is blind like the one committed
    to me,
  blind like the servant of the LORD?
20You have seen many things, but have
    paid no attention;
  your ears are open, but you hear
    nothing."
21It pleased the LORD
  for the sake of his righteousness
  to make his law great and glorious.
22But this is a people plundered and
    looted,
  all of them trapped in pits
  or hidden away in prisons.

They have become plunder,
  with no-one to rescue them;
they have been made loot,
  with no-one to say, "Send them
    back."

23Which of you will listen to this
  or pay close attention in time to
    come?
24Who handed Jacob over to become
    loot,
  and Israel to the plunderers?
  Was it not the LORD,
  against whom we have sinned?
  For they would not follow his ways;
  they did not obey his law.
25So he poured out on them his burning
    anger,
  the violence of war.
  It enveloped them in flames, yet they
    did not understand;
  it consumed them, but they did not
    take it to heart.

NEW TESTAMENT READING
Galatians 3:10–25

10All who rely on observing the law
are under a curse, for it is written:
"Cursed is everyone who does not continue to do everything written in the
Book of the Law." 11Clearly no-one is
justified before God by the law, because, "The righteous will live by faith."
12The law is not based on faith; on the
contrary, "The man who does these
things will live by them." 13Christ redeemed us from the curse of the law by
becoming a curse for us, for it is written:
"Cursed is everyone who is hung on a
tree." 14He redeemed us in order that
the blessing given to Abraham might
come to the Gentiles through Christ
Jesus, so that by faith we might receive
the promise of the Spirit.

The Law and the Promise

15Brothers, let me take an example
from everyday life. Just as no-one can

set aside or add to a human covenant that has been duly established, so it is in this case. [16]The promises were spoken to Abraham and to his seed. The Scripture does not say "and to seeds", meaning many people, but "and to your seed", meaning one person, who is Christ. [17]What I mean is this: The law, introduced 430 years later, does not set aside the covenant previously established by God and thus do away with the promise. [18]For if the inheritance depends on the law, then it no longer depends on a promise; but God in his grace gave it to Abraham through a promise.

[19]What, then, was the purpose of the law? It was added because of transgressions until the Seed to whom the promise referred had come. The law was put into effect through angels by a mediator. [20]A mediator, however, does not represent just one party; but God is one.

[21]Is the law, therefore, opposed to the promises of God? Absolutely not! For if a law had been given that could impart life, then righteousness would certainly have come by the law. [22]But the Scripture declares that the whole world is a prisoner of sin, so that what was promised, being given through faith in Jesus Christ, might be given to those who believe.

[23]Before this faith came, we were held prisoners by the law, locked up until faith should be revealed. [24]So the law was put in charge to lead us to Christ that we might be justified by faith. [25]Now that faith has come, we are no longer under the supervision of the law.

READING FROM PROVERBS
Proverbs 22:28–23:9

[28]Do not move an ancient boundary stone
set up by your forefathers.

[29]Do you see a man skilled in his work?
He will serve before kings;
he will not serve before obscure men.

23 When you sit to dine with a ruler,
note well what is before you,
[2]and put a knife to your throat
if you are given to gluttony.
[3]Do not crave his delicacies,
for that food is deceptive.

[4]Do not wear yourself out to get rich;
have the wisdom to show restraint.
[5]Cast but a glance at riches, and they are gone,
for they will surely sprout wings
and fly off to the sky like an eagle.

[6]Do not eat the food of a stingy man,
do not crave his delicacies;
[7]for he is the kind of man
who is always thinking about the cost.
"Eat and drink," he says to you,
but his heart is not with you.
[8]You will vomit up the little you have eaten
and will have wasted your compliments.

[9]Do not speak to a fool,
for he will scorn the wisdom of your words.

OLD TESTAMENT READING
Isaiah 43:1–44:23

Israel's Only Saviour

43 But now, this is what the LORD says—
he who created you, O Jacob,
he who formed you, O Israel:
"Fear not, for I have redeemed you;
I have summoned you by name;
you are mine.
2When you pass through the waters,
I will be with you;
and when you pass through the
rivers,
they will not sweep over you.
When you walk through the fire,
you will not be burned;
the flames will not set you ablaze.
3For I am the LORD, your God,
the Holy One of Israel, your
Saviour;
I give Egypt for your ransom,
Cush and Seba in your stead.
4Since you are precious and honoured
in my sight,
and because I love you,
I will give men in exchange for you,
and people in exchange for your
life.
5Do not be afraid, for I am with you;
I will bring your children from the
east
and gather you from the west.
6I will say to the north, 'Give them
up!'
and to the south, 'Do not hold
them back.'
Bring my sons from afar
and my daughters from the ends of
the earth—
7everyone who is called by my name,
whom I created for my glory,
whom I formed and made."

8Lead out those who have eyes but are
blind,
who have ears but are deaf.
9All the nations gather together
and the peoples assemble.
Which of them foretold this
and proclaimed to us the former
things?
Let them bring in their witnesses to
prove they were right,
so that others may hear and say,
"It is true."
10"You are my witnesses," declares the
LORD,
"and my servant whom I have
chosen,
so that you may know and believe me
and understand that I am he.
Before me no god was formed,
nor will there be one after me.
11I, even I, am the LORD,
and apart from me there is no
saviour.
12I have revealed and saved and
proclaimed—
I, and not some foreign god among
you.
You are my witnesses," declares the
LORD, "that I am God.
13 Yes, and from ancient days I am
he.
No-one can deliver out of my hand.
When I act, who can reverse it?"

*God's Mercy and Israel's
Unfaithfulness*

14This is what the LORD says—
your Redeemer, the Holy One of
Israel:
"For your sake I will send to Babylon
and bring down as fugitives all the
Babylonians,
in the ships in which they took
pride.
15I am the LORD, your Holy One,
Israel's Creator, your King."

16This is what the LORD says—
he who made a way through the sea,
a path through the mighty waters,

17who drew out the chariots and
    horses,
  the army and reinforcements
    together,
and they lay there, never to rise
    again,
  extinguished, snuffed out like a
    wick:
18"Forget the former things;
  do not dwell on the past.
19See, I am doing a new thing!
  Now it springs up; do you not
    perceive it?
I am making a way in the desert
  and streams in the wasteland.
20The wild animals honour me,
  the jackals and the owls,
because I provide water in the desert
  and streams in the wasteland,
  to give drink to my people, my
    chosen,
21 the people I formed for myself
  that they may proclaim my praise.

22"Yet you have not called upon me, O
    Jacob,
  you have not wearied yourselves
    for me, O Israel.
23You have not brought me sheep for
    burnt offerings,
  nor honoured me with your
    sacrifices.
I have not burdened you with grain
    offerings
  nor wearied you with demands for
    incense.
24You have not bought any fragrant
    calamus for me,
  or lavished on me the fat of your
    sacrifices.
But you have burdened me with your
    sins
  and wearied me with your
    offences.

25"I, even I, am he who blots out
  your transgressions, for my own
    sake,
  and remembers your sins no more.
26Review the past for me,
  let us argue the matter together;
  state the case for your innocence.

27Your first father sinned;
  your spokesmen rebelled against
    me.
28So I will disgrace the dignitaries of
  your temple,
  and I will consign Jacob to
    destruction
  and Israel to scorn.

Israel the Chosen

44 "But now listen, O Jacob, my
    servant,
  Israel, whom I have chosen.
2This is what the LORD says—
  he who made you, who formed you
    in the womb,
  and who will help you:
Do not be afraid, O Jacob, my
    servant,
  Jeshurun, whom I have chosen.
3For I will pour water on the thirsty
    land,
  and streams on the dry ground;
I will pour out my Spirit on your
    offspring,
  and my blessing on your
    descendants.
4They will spring up like grass in a
    meadow,
  like poplar trees by flowing
    streams.
5One will say, 'I belong to the LORD';
  another will call himself by the
    name of Jacob;
still another will write on his hand,
    'The LORD's',
  and will take the name Israel.

The Lord, Not Idols

6"This is what the LORD says—
  Israel's King and Redeemer, the
    LORD Almighty:
I am the first and I am the last;
  apart from me there is no God.
7Who then is like me? Let him
    proclaim it.
  Let him declare and lay out before
    me
what has happened since I
    established my ancient people,

and what is yet to come—
    yes, let him foretell what will
        come.
8Do not tremble, do not be afraid.
    Did I not proclaim this and foretell
        it long ago?
You are my witnesses. Is there any
        God besides me?
    No, there is no other Rock; I know
        not one."

9All who make idols are nothing,
    and the things they treasure are
        worthless.
Those who would speak up for them
        are blind;
    they are ignorant, to their own
        shame.
10Who shapes a god and casts an idol,
    which can profit him nothing?
11He and his kind will be put to shame;
    craftsmen are nothing but men.
Let them all come together and take
        their stand;
    they will be brought down to terror
        and infamy.

12The blacksmith takes a tool
    and works with it in the coals;
he shapes an idol with hammers,
    he forges it with the might of his
        arm.
He gets hungry and loses his strength;
    he drinks no water and grows faint.
13The carpenter measures with a line
    and makes an outline with a
        marker;
he roughs it out with chisels
    and marks it with compasses.
He shapes it in the form of man,
    of man in all his glory,
    that it may dwell in a shrine.
14He cut down cedars,
    or perhaps took a cypress or oak.
He let it grow among the trees of the
        forest,
    or planted a pine, and the rain
        made it grow.
15It is man's fuel for burning;
    some of it he takes and warms
        himself,
    he kindles a fire and bakes bread.

But he also fashions a god and
        worships it;
    he makes an idol and bows down
        to it.
16Half of the wood he burns in the fire;
    over it he prepares his meal,
    he roasts his meat and eats his fill.
He also warms himself and says,
    "Ah! I am warm; I see the fire."
17From the rest he makes a god, his
        idol;
    he bows down to it and worships.
He prays to it and says,
    "Save me; you are my god."
18They know nothing, they understand
        nothing;
    their eyes are plastered over so that
        they cannot see,
    and their minds closed so that they
        cannot understand.
19No-one stops to think,
    no-one has the knowledge or
        understanding to say,
"Half of it I used for fuel;
    I even baked bread over its coals,
    I roasted meat and I ate.
Shall I make a detestable thing from
        what is left?
    Shall I bow down to a block of
        wood?"
20He feeds on ashes, a deluded heart
        misleads him;
    he cannot save himself, or say,
    "Is not this thing in my right hand a
        lie?"

21"Remember these things, O Jacob,
    for you are my servant, O Israel.
I have made you, you are my servant;
    O Israel, I will not forget you.
22I have swept away your offences like
        a cloud,
    your sins like the morning mist.
Return to me,
    for I have redeemed you."

23Sing for joy, O heavens, for the LORD
        has done this;
    shout aloud, O earth beneath.
Burst into song, you mountains,
    you forests and all your trees,
for the LORD has redeemed Jacob,
    he displays his glory in Israel.

NEW TESTAMENT READING
Galatians 3:26–4:20

Sons of God

²⁶You are all sons of God through faith in Christ Jesus, ²⁷for all of you who were baptised into Christ have clothed yourselves with Christ. ²⁸There is neither Jew nor Greek, slave nor free, male nor female, for you are all one in Christ Jesus. ²⁹If you belong to Christ, then you are Abraham's seed, and heirs according to the promise.

⁴What I am saying is that as long as the heir is a child, he is no different from a slave, although he owns the whole estate. ²He is subject to guardians and trustees until the time set by his father. ³So also, when we were children, we were in slavery under the basic principles of the world. ⁴But when the time had fully come, God sent his Son, born of a woman, born under law, ⁵to redeem those under law, that we might receive the full rights of sons. ⁶Because you are sons, God sent the Spirit of his Son into our hearts, the Spirit who calls out, "*Abba*, Father." ⁷So you are no longer a slave, but a son; and since you are a son, God has made you also an heir.

Paul's Concern for the Galatians

⁸Formerly, when you did not know God, you were slaves to those who by nature are not gods. ⁹But now that you know God—or rather are known by God—how is it that you are turning back to those weak and miserable principles? Do you wish to be enslaved by them all over again? ¹⁰You are observing special days and months and seasons and years! ¹¹I fear for you, that somehow I have wasted my efforts on you.

¹²I plead with you, brothers, become like me, for I became like you. You have done me no wrong. ¹³As you know, it was because of an illness that I first preached the gospel to you. ¹⁴Even though my illness was a trial to you, you did not treat me with contempt or scorn. Instead, you welcomed me as if I were an angel of God, as if I were Christ Jesus himself. ¹⁵What has happened to all your joy? I can testify that, if you could have done so, you would have torn out your eyes and given them to me. ¹⁶Have I now become your enemy by telling you the truth?

¹⁷Those people are zealous to win you over, but for no good. What they want is to alienate you ⌐from us⌐, so that you may be zealous for them. ¹⁸It is fine to be zealous, provided the purpose is good, and to be so always and not just when I am with you. ¹⁹My dear children, for whom I am again in the pains of childbirth until Christ is formed in you, ²⁰how I wish I could be with you now and change my tone, because I am perplexed about you!

READING FROM PSALMS
Psalm 108:1–5

A song. A psalm of David.

¹My heart is steadfast, O God;
   I will sing and make music with all
      my soul.
²Awake, harp and lyre!
   I will awaken the dawn.
³I will praise you, O LORD, among the
      nations;
   I will sing of you among the
      peoples.
⁴For great is your love, higher than
      the heavens;
   your faithfulness reaches to the
      skies.
⁵Be exalted, O God, above the
      heavens,
   and let your glory be over all the
      earth.

OLD TESTAMENT READING
Isaiah 44:24–46:13

Jerusalem to Be Inhabited

24"This is what the LORD says—
   your Redeemer, who formed you
      in the womb:

I am the LORD,
who has made all things,
who alone stretched out the heavens,
who spread out the earth by myself,

25who foils the signs of false prophets
   and makes fools of diviners,
who overthrows the learning of the
      wise
   and turns it into nonsense,
26who carries out the words of his
      servants
   and fulfils the predictions of his
      messengers,

who says of Jerusalem, 'It shall be
      inhabited,'
   of the towns of Judah, 'They shall
      be built,'
   and of their ruins, 'I will restore
      them,'
27who says to the watery deep, 'Be dry,
   and I will dry up your streams,'
28who says of Cyrus, 'He is my
      shepherd
   and will accomplish all that I
      please;
he will say of Jerusalem, "Let it be
      rebuilt,"
   and of the temple, "Let its
      foundations be laid."'

45 "This is what the LORD says to
      his anointed,
   to Cyrus, whose right hand I take
      hold of
to subdue nations before him
   and to strip kings of their armour,
to open doors before him
   so that gates will not be shut:

2I will go before you
   and will level the mountains;
I will break down gates of bronze
   and cut through bars of iron.
3I will give you the treasures of
      darkness,
   riches stored in secret places,
so that you may know that I am the
      LORD,
   the God of Israel, who summons
      you by name.
4For the sake of Jacob my servant,
   of Israel my chosen,
I summon you by name
   and bestow on you a title of
      honour,
   though you do not acknowledge
      me.
5I am the LORD, and there is no other;
   apart from me there is no God.
I will strengthen you,
   though you have not
      acknowledged me,
6so that from the rising of the sun
   to the place of its setting
men may know there is none besides
      me.
   I am the LORD, and there is no
      other.
7I form the light and create darkness,
   I bring prosperity and create
      disaster;
I, the LORD, do all these things.

8"You heavens above, rain down
      righteousness;
   let the clouds shower it down.
Let the earth open wide,
   let salvation spring up,
let righteousness grow with it;
   I, the LORD, have created it.

9"Woe to him who quarrels with his
      Maker,
   to him who is but a potsherd
      among the potsherds on the
      ground.

Does the clay say to the potter,
  'What are you making?'
Does your work say,
  'He has no hands'?
¹⁰Woe to him who says to his father,
  'What have you begotten?'
or to his mother,
  'What have you brought to birth?'

¹¹"This is what the LORD says—
  the Holy One of Israel, and its
    Maker:
Concerning things to come,
  do you question me about my
    children,
  or give me orders about the work
    of my hands?
¹²It is I who made the earth
  and created mankind upon it.
My own hands stretched out the
    heavens;
  I marshalled their starry hosts.
¹³I will raise up Cyrus in my
    righteousness;
  I will make all his ways straight.
He will rebuild my city
  and set my exiles free,
but not for a price or reward,
  says the LORD Almighty."

¹⁴This is what the LORD says:

"The products of Egypt and the
    merchandise of Cush,
  and those tall Sabeans—
they will come over to you
  and will be yours;
they will trudge behind you,
  coming over to you in chains.
They will bow down before you
  and plead with you, saying,
'Surely God is with you, and there is
    no other;
  there is no other god.'"

¹⁵Truly you are a God who hides
    himself,
  O God and Saviour of Israel.
¹⁶All the makers of idols will be put to
    shame and disgraced;
  they will go off into disgrace
    together.

¹⁷But Israel will be saved by the LORD
  with an everlasting salvation;
you will never be put to shame or
    disgraced,
  to ages everlasting.

¹⁸For this is what the LORD says—
  he who created the heavens,
    he is God;
he who fashioned and made the
    earth,
  he founded it;
he did not create it to be empty,
  but formed it to be inhabited—
he says:
"I am the LORD,
  and there is no other.
¹⁹I have not spoken in secret,
  from somewhere in a land of
    darkness;
I have not said to Jacob's
    descendants,
  'Seek me in vain.'
I, the LORD, speak the truth;
  I declare what is right.

²⁰"Gather together and come;
  assemble, you fugitives from the
    nations.
Ignorant are those who carry about
    idols of wood,
  who pray to gods that cannot save.
²¹Declare what is to be, present it—
  let them take counsel together.
Who foretold this long ago,
  who declared it from the distant
    past?
Was it not I, the LORD?
  And there is no God apart from
    me,
a righteous God and a Saviour;
  there is none but me.

²²"Turn to me and be saved,
  all you ends of the earth;
for I am God, and there is no
    other.
²³By myself I have sworn,
  my mouth has uttered in all
    integrity
  a word that will not be revoked:
Before me every knee will bow;
  by me every tongue will swear.

[24]They will say of me, 'In the LORD alone
are righteousness and strength.'"
All who have raged against him
will come to him and be put to shame.
[25]But in the LORD all the descendants of Israel
will be found righteous and will exult.

Gods of Babylon

46 Bel bows down, Nebo stoops low;
their idols are borne by beasts of burden.
The images that are carried about are burdensome,
a burden for the weary.
[2]They stoop and bow down together;
unable to rescue the burden,
they themselves go off into captivity.

[3]"Listen to me, O house of Jacob,
all you who remain of the house of Israel,
you whom I have upheld since you were conceived,
and have carried since your birth.
[4]Even to your old age and grey hairs
I am he, I am he who will sustain you.
I have made you and I will carry you;
I will sustain you and I will rescue you.

[5]"To whom will you compare me or count me equal?
To whom will you liken me that we may be compared?
[6]Some pour out gold from their bags
and weigh out silver on the scales;
they hire a goldsmith to make it into a god,
and they bow down and worship it.
[7]They lift it to their shoulders and carry it;
they set it up in its place, and there it stands.
From that spot it cannot move.

Though one cries out to it, it does not answer;
it cannot save him from his troubles.

[8]"Remember this, fix it in mind,
take it to heart, you rebels.
[9]Remember the former things, those of long ago;
I am God, and there is no other;
I am God, and there is none like me.
[10]I make known the end from the beginning,
from ancient times, what is still to come.
I say: My purpose will stand,
and I will do all that I please.
[11]From the east I summon a bird of prey;
from a far-off land, a man to fulfil my purpose.
What I have said, that will I bring about;
what I have planned, that will I do.
[12]Listen to me, you stubborn-hearted,
you who are far from righteousness.
[13]I am bringing my righteousness near,
it is not far away;
and my salvation will not be delayed.
I will grant salvation to Zion,
my splendour to Israel.

NEW TESTAMENT READING
Galatians 4:21–5:6

Hagar and Sarah

[21]Tell me, you who want to be under the law, are you not aware of what the law says? [22]For it is written that Abraham had two sons, one by the slave woman and the other by the free woman. [23]His son by the slave woman was born in the ordinary way; but his son by the free woman was born as the result of a promise.

[24]These things may be taken figuratively, for the women represent two

covenants. One covenant is from Mount Sinai and bears children who are to be slaves: This is Hagar. ²⁵Now Hagar stands for Mount Sinai in Arabia and corresponds to the present city of Jerusalem, because she is in slavery with her children. ²⁶But the Jerusalem that is above is free, and she is our mother. ²⁷For it is written:

"Be glad, O barren woman,
    who bears no children;
break forth and cry aloud,
    you who have no labour pains;
because more are the children of the
      desolate woman
    than of her who has a husband."

²⁸Now you, brothers, like Isaac, are children of promise. ²⁹At that time the son born in the ordinary way persecuted the son born by the power of the Spirit. It is the same now. ³⁰But what does the Scripture say? "Get rid of the slave woman and her son, for the slave woman's son will never share in the inheritance with the free woman's son." ³¹Therefore, brothers, we are not children of the slave woman, but of the free woman.

Freedom in Christ

5 It is for freedom that Christ has set us free. Stand firm, then, and do not let yourselves be burdened again by a yoke of slavery.

²Mark my words! I, Paul, tell you that if you let yourselves be circumcised, Christ will be of no value to you at all. ³Again I declare to every man who lets himself be circumcised that he is required to obey the whole law. ⁴You who are trying to be justified by law have been alienated from Christ; you have fallen away from grace. ⁵But by faith we eagerly await through the Spirit the righteousness for which we hope. ⁶For in Christ Jesus neither circumcision nor uncircumcision has any value. The only thing that counts is faith expressing itself through love.

READING FROM PSALMS
Psalm 108:6–13

⁶Save us and help us with your right
    hand,
    that those you love may be
      delivered.
⁷God has spoken from his sanctuary:
    "In triumph I will parcel out
      Shechem
    and measure off the Valley of
      Succoth.
⁸Gilead is mine, Manasseh is mine;
    Ephraim is my helmet,
    Judah my sceptre.
⁹Moab is my washbasin,
    upon Edom I toss my sandal;
    over Philistia I shout in triumph."

¹⁰Who will bring me to the fortified
    city?
    Who will lead me to Edom?
¹¹Is it not you, O God, you who have
    rejected us
    and no longer go out with our
      armies?
¹²Give us aid against the enemy,
    for the help of man is worthless.
¹³With God we shall gain the victory,
    and he will trample down our
      enemies.

OLD TESTAMENT READING
Isaiah 47:1–49:7

The Fall of Babylon

47 "Go down, sit in the dust,
   Virgin Daughter of Babylon;
sit on the ground without a throne,
   Daughter of the Babylonians.
No more will you be called
   tender or delicate.
²Take millstones and grind flour;
   take off your veil.
Lift up your skirts, bare your legs,
   and wade through the streams.
³Your nakedness will be exposed
   and your shame uncovered.
I will take vengeance;
   I will spare no-one."

⁴Our Redeemer—the LORD Almighty
      is his name—
is the Holy One of Israel.

⁵"Sit in silence, go into darkness,
   Daughter of the Babylonians;
no more will you be called
   queen of kingdoms.
⁶I was angry with my people
   and desecrated my inheritance;
I gave them into your hand,
   and you showed them no mercy.
Even on the aged
   you laid a very heavy yoke.
⁷You said, 'I will continue for ever—
   the eternal queen!'
But you did not consider these things
   or reflect on what might happen.

⁸"Now then, listen, you wanton
      creature,
   lounging in your security
and saying to yourself,
   'I am, and there is none besides
      me.
I will never be a widow
   or suffer the loss of children.'
⁹Both of these will overtake you

in a moment, on a single day:
   loss of children and widowhood.
They will come upon you in full
      measure,
   in spite of your many sorceries
      and all your potent spells.
¹⁰You have trusted in your wickedness
   and have said, 'No-one sees me.'
Your wisdom and knowledge mislead
      you
   when you say to yourself,
   'I am, and there is none besides
      me.'
¹¹Disaster will come upon you,
   and you will not know how to
      conjure it away.
A calamity will fall upon you
   that you cannot ward off with a
      ransom;
a catastrophe you cannot foresee
   will suddenly come upon you.

¹²"Keep on, then, with your magic
      spells
   and with your many sorceries,
   which you have laboured at since
      childhood.
Perhaps you will succeed,
   perhaps you will cause terror.
¹³All the counsel you have received has
   only worn you out!
Let your astrologers come forward,
   those stargazers who make
      predictions month by month,
let them save you from what is
   coming upon you.
¹⁴Surely they are like stubble;
   the fire will burn them up.
They cannot even save themselves
   from the power of the flame.
Here are no coals to warm anyone;
   here is no fire to sit by.
¹⁵That is all they can do for you—
   these you have laboured with
      and trafficked with since
      childhood.
Each of them goes on in his error;
   there is not one that can save you.

Stubborn Israel

48

"Listen to this, O house of
Jacob,
you who are called by the name of
Israel
and come from the line of Judah,
you who take oaths in the name of
the LORD
and invoke the God of Israel—
but not in truth or righteousness—
²you who call yourselves citizens of
the holy city
and rely on the God of Israel—
the LORD Almighty is his name:
³I foretold the former things long ago,
my mouth announced them and I
made them known;
then suddenly I acted, and they
came to pass.
⁴For I knew how stubborn you were;
the sinews of your neck were iron,
your forehead was bronze.
⁵Therefore I told you these things long
ago;
before they happened I announced
them to you
so that you could not say,
'My idols did them;
my wooden image and metal god
ordained them.'
⁶You have heard these things; look at
them all.
Will you not admit them?

"From now on I will tell you of new
things,
of hidden things unknown to you.
⁷They are created now, and not long
ago;
you have not heard of them before
today.
So you cannot say,
'Yes, I knew of them.'
⁸You have neither heard nor
understood;
from of old your ear has not been
open.
Well do I know how treacherous you
are;
you were called a rebel from birth.
⁹For my own name's sake I delay my
wrath;

for the sake of my praise I hold it
back from you,
so as not to cut you off.
¹⁰See, I have refined you, though not as
silver;
I have tested you in the furnace of
affliction.
¹¹For my own sake, for my own sake, I
do this.
How can I let myself be defamed?
I will not yield my glory to another.

Israel Freed

¹²"Listen to me, O Jacob,
Israel, whom I have called:
I am he;
I am the first and I am the last.
¹³My own hand laid the foundations of
the earth,
and my right hand spread out the
heavens;
when I summon them,
they all stand up together.

¹⁴"Come together, all of you, and
listen:
Which of ₍the idols₎ has foretold
these things?
The LORD's chosen ally
will carry out his purpose against
Babylon;
his arm will be against the
Babylonians.
¹⁵I, even I, have spoken;
yes, I have called him.
I will bring him,
and he will succeed in his mission.

¹⁶"Come near me and listen to this:

"From the first announcement I have
not spoken in secret;
at the time it happens, I am there."

And now the Sovereign LORD has
sent me,
with his Spirit.

¹⁷This is what the LORD says—
your Redeemer, the Holy One of
Israel:

"I am the LORD your God,
  who teaches you what is best for
    you,
  who directs you in the way you
    should go.
[18]If only you had paid attention to my
    commands,
  your peace would have been like a
    river,
  your righteousness like the waves
    of the sea.
[19]Your descendants would have been
    like the sand,
  your children like its numberless
    grains;
  their name would never be cut off
    nor destroyed from before me."

[20]Leave Babylon,
  flee from the Babylonians!
Announce this with shouts of joy
  and proclaim it.
Send it out to the ends of the earth;
  say, "The LORD has redeemed his
    servant Jacob."
[21]They did not thirst when he led them
    through the deserts;
  he made water flow for them from
    the rock;
  he split the rock
    and water gushed out.

[22]"There is no peace," says the LORD,
    "for the wicked."

The Servant of the LORD

49 Listen to me, you islands;
      hear this, you distant nations:
Before I was born the LORD called
    me;
  from my birth he has made
    mention of my name.
[2]He made my mouth like a sharpened
    sword,
  in the shadow of his hand he hid
    me;
  he made me into a polished arrow
    and concealed me in his quiver.
[3]He said to me, "You are my servant,

Israel, in whom I will display my
    splendour."
[4]But I said, "I have laboured to no
    purpose;
  I have spent my strength in vain
    and for nothing.
Yet what is due to me is in the LORD's
    hand,
  and my reward is with my God."

[5]And now the LORD says—
  he who formed me in the womb to
    be his servant
to bring Jacob back to him
  and gather Israel to himself,
for I am honoured in the eyes of the
    LORD
  and my God has been my
    strength—
[6]he says:
"It is too small a thing for you to be
    my servant
  to restore the tribes of Jacob
  and bring back those of Israel I
    have kept.
I will also make you a light for the
    Gentiles,
  that you may bring my salvation to
    the ends of the earth."

[7]This is what the LORD says—
  the Redeemer and Holy One of
    Israel—
to him who was despised and
    abhorred by the nation,
  to the servant of rulers:
"Kings will see you and rise up,
  princes will see and bow down,
because of the LORD, who is faithful,
  the Holy One of Israel, who has
    chosen you."

NEW TESTAMENT READING
Galatians 5:7–26

[7]You were running a good race. Who
cut in on you and kept you from obeying
the truth? [8]That kind of persuasion does
not come from the one who calls you.
[9]"A little yeast works through the

whole batch of dough." [10]I am confident in the Lord that you will take no other view. The one who is throwing you into confusion will pay the penalty, whoever he may be. [11]Brothers, if I am still preaching circumcision, why am I still being persecuted? In that case the offence of the cross has been abolished. [12]As for those agitators, I wish they would go the whole way and emasculate themselves!

[13]You, my brothers, were called to be free. But do not use your freedom to indulge the sinful nature; rather, serve one another in love. [14]The entire law is summed up in a single command: "Love your neighbour as yourself." [15]If you keep on biting and devouring each other, watch out or you will be destroyed by each other.

Life by the Spirit

[16]So I say, live by the Spirit, and you will not gratify the desires of the sinful nature. [17]For the sinful nature desires what is contrary to the Spirit, and the Spirit what is contrary to the sinful nature. They are in conflict with each other, so that you do not do what you want. [18]But if you are led by the Spirit, you are not under law.

[19]The acts of the sinful nature are obvious: sexual immorality, impurity and debauchery; [20]idolatry and witchcraft; hatred, discord, jealousy, fits of rage, selfish ambition, dissensions, factions [21]and envy; drunkenness, orgies, and the like. I warn you, as I did before, that those who live like this will not inherit the kingdom of God.

[22]But the fruit of the Spirit is love, joy, peace, patience, kindness, goodness, faithfulness, [23]gentleness and self-control. Against such things there is no law. [24]Those who belong to Christ Jesus have crucified the sinful nature with its passions and desires. [25]Since we live by the Spirit, let us keep in step with the Spirit. [26]Let us not become conceited, provoking and envying each other.

READING FROM PSALMS
Psalm 109:1–20

For the director of music. Of David. A psalm.

[1]O God, whom I praise,
    do not remain silent,
[2]for wicked and deceitful men
    have opened their mouths against
    me;
  they have spoken against me with
    lying tongues.
[3]With words of hatred they surround
    me;
  they attack me without cause.
[4]In return for my friendship they
    accuse me,
  but I am a man of prayer.
[5]They repay me evil for good,
    and hatred for my friendship.

[6]Appoint an evil man to oppose him;
    let an accuser stand at his right
    hand.
[7]When he is tried, let him be found
    guilty,
  and may his prayers condemn him.
[8]May his days be few;
    may another take his place of
    leadership.
[9]May his children be fatherless
    and his wife a widow.
[10]May his children be wandering
    beggars;
  may they be driven from their
    ruined homes.
[11]May a creditor seize all he has;
    may strangers plunder the fruits of
    his labour.
[12]May no-one extend kindness to him
    or take pity on his fatherless
    children.
[13]May his descendants be cut off,
    their names blotted out from the
    next generation.
[14]May the iniquity of his fathers be
    remembered before the LORD;
  may the sin of his mother never be
    blotted out.
[15]May their sins always remain before
    the LORD,

that he may cut off the memory of
   them from the earth.

16For he never thought of doing a
      kindness,
   but hounded to death the poor
      and the needy and the
      broken-hearted.
17He loved to pronounce a curse—
   may it come on him;

he found no pleasure in blessing—
   may it be far from him.
18He wore cursing as his garment;
   it entered into his body like water,
      into his bones like oil.
19May it be like a cloak wrapped about
      him,
   like a belt tied for ever round him.
20May this be the LORD's payment to
      my accusers,
   to those who speak evil of me.

SEPTEMBER 21   DAY 264

OLD TESTAMENT READING
Isaiah 49:8–51:16

Restoration of Israel

   8This is what the LORD says:

   "In the time of my favour I will
         answer you,
      and in the day of salvation I will
         help you;
   I will keep you and will make you
      to be a covenant for the people,
   to restore the land
      and to reassign its desolate
         inheritances,
   9to say to the captives, 'Come out,'
      and to those in darkness,
         'Be free!'

   "They will feed beside the roads
      and find pasture on every barren
         hill.
   10They will neither hunger nor thirst,
      nor will the desert heat or the sun
         beat upon them.
   He who has compassion on them will
         guide them
      and lead them beside springs of
         water.
   11I will turn all my mountains into
         roads,
      and my highways will be raised up.

   12See, they will come from afar—
      some from the north, some from
         the west,
      some from the region of Aswan."

   13Shout for joy, O heavens;
      rejoice, O earth;
      burst into song, O mountains!
   For the LORD comforts his people
      and will have compassion on his
         afflicted ones.

   14But Zion said, "The LORD has
         forsaken me,
      the Lord has forgotten me."

   15"Can a mother forget the baby at her
         breast
      and have no compassion on the
         child she has borne?
   Though she may forget,
      I will not forget you!
   16See, I have engraved you on the
         palms of my hands;
      your walls are ever before me.
   17Your sons hasten back,
      and those who laid you waste
         depart from you.
   18Lift up your eyes and look around;
      all your sons gather and come to
         you.
   As surely as I live," declares the
      LORD,

"you will wear them all as
   ornaments;
   you will put them on, like a bride.

19"Though you were ruined and made
   desolate
   and your land laid waste,
now you will be too small for your
   people,
   and those who devoured you will
   be far away.
20The children born during your
   bereavement
   will yet say in your hearing,
'This place is too small for us;
   give us more space to live in.'
21Then you will say in your heart,
   'Who bore me these?
I was bereaved and barren;
   I was exiled and rejected.
   Who brought these up?
I was left all alone,
   but these—where have they come
   from?'"

22This is what the Sovereign LORD
says:

"See, I will beckon to the Gentiles,
   I will lift up my banner to the
   peoples;
they will bring your sons in their arms
   and carry your daughters on their
   shoulders.
23Kings will be your foster fathers,
   and their queens your nursing
   mothers.
They will bow down before you with
   their faces to the ground;
   they will lick the dust at your feet.
Then you will know that I am the
   LORD;
   those who hope in me will not be
   disappointed."

24Can plunder be taken from warriors,
   or captives rescued from the fierce?

25But this is what the LORD says:

"Yes, captives will be taken from
   warriors,

and plunder retrieved from the
   fierce;
I will contend with those who
   contend with you,
   and your children I will save.
26I will make your oppressors eat their
   own flesh;
   they will be drunk on their own
   blood, as with wine.
Then all mankind will know
   that I, the LORD, am your Saviour,
   your Redeemer, the Mighty One of
   Jacob."

Israel's Sin and the Servant's Obedience

50 This is what the LORD says:

"Where is your mother's certificate
   of divorce
   with which I sent her away?
Or to which of my creditors
   did I sell you?
Because of your sins you were sold;
   because of your transgressions
   your mother was sent away.
2When I came, why was there no-one?
   When I called, why was there
   no-one to answer?
Was my arm too short to ransom
   you?
   Do I lack the strength to rescue
   you?
By a mere rebuke I dry up the sea,
   I turn rivers into a desert;
their fish rot for lack of water
   and die of thirst.
3I clothe the sky with darkness
   and make sackcloth its covering."

4The Sovereign LORD has given me an
   instructed tongue,
   to know the word that sustains the
   weary.
He wakens me morning by morning,
   wakens my ear to listen like one
   being taught.
5The Sovereign LORD has opened my
   ears,
   and I have not been rebellious;
   I have not drawn back.

⁶I offered my back to those who beat
    me,
  my cheeks to those who pulled out
    my beard;
I did not hide my face
  from mocking and spitting.
⁷Because the Sovereign Lord helps
    me,
  I will not be disgraced.
Therefore have I set my face like
    flint,
  and I know I will not be put to
    shame.
⁸He who vindicates me is near.
  Who then will bring charges
    against me?
Let us face each other!
  Who is my accuser?
Let him confront me!
⁹It is the Sovereign Lord who helps
    me.
  Who is he who will condemn me?
They will all wear out like a garment;
  the moths will eat them up.

¹⁰Who among you fears the Lord
  and obeys the word of his servant?
Let him who walks in the dark,
  who has no light,
trust in the name of the Lord
  and rely on his God.
¹¹But now, all you who light fires
  and provide yourselves with
    flaming torches,
go, walk in the light of your fires
  and of the torches you have set
    ablaze.
This is what you shall receive from
    my hand:
  You will lie down in torment.

Everlasting Salvation for Zion

51   "Listen to me, you who pursue
    righteousness
  and who seek the Lord:
Look to the rock from which you
    were cut
  and to the quarry from which you
    were hewn;
²look to Abraham, your father,
  and to Sarah, who gave you birth.

When I called him he was but one,
  and I blessed him and made him
    many.
³The Lord will surely comfort Zion
  and will look with compassion on
    all her ruins;
he will make her deserts like Eden,
  her wastelands like the garden of
    the Lord.
Joy and gladness will be found in her,
  thanksgiving and the sound of
    singing.

⁴"Listen to me, my people;
  hear me, my nation:
The law will go out from me;
  my justice will become a light to
    the nations.
⁵My righteousness draws near
    speedily,
  my salvation is on the way,
  and my arm will bring justice to the
    nations.
The islands will look to me
  and wait in hope for my arm.
⁶Lift up your eyes to the heavens,
  look at the earth beneath;
the heavens will vanish like smoke,
  the earth will wear out like a
    garment
  and its inhabitants die like flies.
But my salvation will last for ever,
  my righteousness will never fail.

⁷"Hear me, you who know what is
    right,
  you people who have my law in
    your hearts:
Do not fear the reproach of men
  or be terrified by their insults.
⁸For the moth will eat them up like a
    garment;
  the worm will devour them like
    wool.
But my righteousness will last for
    ever,
  my salvation through all
    generations."

⁹Awake, awake! Clothe yourself with
    strength,
  O arm of the Lord;

awake, as in days gone by,
    as in generations of old.
Was it not you who cut Rahab to
    pieces,
    who pierced that monster through?
[10]Was it not you who dried up the sea,
    the waters of the great deep,
who made a road in the depths of the
    sea
    so that the redeemed might cross
      over?
[11]The ransomed of the LORD will
    return.
They will enter Zion with singing;
    everlasting joy will crown their
    heads.
Gladness and joy will overtake them,
    and sorrow and sighing will flee
    away.

[12]"I, even I, am he who comforts you.
    Who are you that you fear mortal
    men,
    the sons of men, who are but grass,
[13]that you forget the LORD your
    Maker,
who stretched out the heavens
    and laid the foundations of the
      earth,
that you live in constant terror every
    day
    because of the wrath of the
      oppressor,
    who is bent on destruction?
For where is the wrath of the
    oppressor?
[14]   The cowering prisoners will soon
    be set free;
they will not die in their dungeon,
    nor will they lack bread.
[15]For I am the LORD your God,
    who churns up the sea so that its
    waves roar—
    the LORD Almighty is his name.
[16]I have put my words in your mouth
    and covered you with the shadow
    of my hand—
I who set the heavens in place,
    who laid the foundations of the
      earth,
    and who say to Zion, 'You are my
      people.'"

NEW TESTAMENT READING
Galatians 6:1–18

Doing Good to All

6 Brothers, if someone is caught in a sin, you who are spiritual should restore him gently. But watch yourself, or you also may be tempted. [2]Carry each other's burdens, and in this way you will fulfil the law of Christ. [3]If anyone thinks he is something when he is nothing, he deceives himself. [4]Each one should test his own actions. Then he can take pride in himself, without comparing himself to somebody else, [5]for each one should carry his own load.

[6]Anyone who receives instruction in the word must share all good things with his instructor.

[7]Do not be deceived: God cannot be mocked. A man reaps what he sows. [8]The one who sows to please his sinful nature, from that nature will reap destruction; the one who sows to please the Spirit, from the Spirit will reap eternal life. [9]Let us not become weary in doing good, for at the proper time we will reap a harvest if we do not give up. [10]Therefore, as we have opportunity, let us do good to all people, especially to those who belong to the family of believers.

Not Circumcision but a New Creation

[11]See what large letters I use as I write to you with my own hand!

[12]Those who want to make a good impression outwardly are trying to compel you to be circumcised. The only reason they do this is to avoid being persecuted for the cross of Christ. [13]Not even those who are circumcised obey the law, yet they want you to be circumcised that they may boast about your flesh. [14]May I never boast except in the cross of our Lord Jesus Christ, through which the world has been crucified to me, and I to the world. [15]Neither circumcision nor uncircumcision means anything; what counts is a new creation.

16Peace and mercy to all who follow this rule, even to the Israel of God.

17Finally, let no-one cause me trouble, for I bear on my body the marks of Jesus.

18The grace of our Lord Jesus Christ be with your spirit, brothers. Amen.

READING FROM PROVERBS
Proverbs 23:10–18

10Do not move an ancient boundary stone
or encroach on the fields of the fatherless,
11for their Defender is strong;
he will take up their case against you.

12Apply your heart to instruction
and your ears to words of knowledge.

13Do not withhold discipline from a child;
if you punish him with the rod, he will not die.
14Punish him with the rod
and save his soul from death.

15My son, if your heart is wise,
then my heart will be glad;
16my inmost being will rejoice
when your lips speak what is right.

17Do not let your heart envy sinners,
but always be zealous for the fear of the LORD.
18There is surely a future hope for you,
and your hope will not be cut off.

SEPTEMBER 22   DAY 265

OLD TESTAMENT READING
Isaiah 51:17–54:17

The Cup of the LORD's Wrath

17Awake, awake!
Rise up, O Jerusalem,
you who have drunk from the hand of the LORD
the cup of his wrath,
you who have drained to its dregs
the goblet that makes men stagger.
18Of all the sons she bore
there was none to guide her;
of all the sons she brought up
there was none to take her by the hand.
19These double calamities have come upon you—
who can comfort you?—
ruin and destruction, famine and sword—
who can console you?

20Your sons have fainted;
they lie at the head of every street,
like antelope caught in a net.
They are filled with the wrath of the LORD
and the rebuke of your God.

21Therefore hear this, you afflicted one,
made drunk, but not with wine.
22This is what your Sovereign LORD says,
your God, who defends his people:
"See, I have taken out of your hand
the cup that made you stagger;
from that cup, the goblet of my wrath,
you will never drink again.
23I will put it into the hands of your tormentors,
who said to you,
'Fall prostrate that we may walk over you.'

And you made your back like the
    ground,
    like a street to be walked over."

52 Awake, awake, O Zion,
    clothe yourself with strength.
Put on your garments of splendour,
    O Jerusalem, the holy city.
The uncircumcised and defiled
    will not enter you again.
²Shake off your dust;
    rise up, sit enthroned, O
      Jerusalem.
Free yourself from the chains on your
    neck,
    O captive Daughter of Zion.

³For this is what the LORD says:

"You were sold for nothing,
    and without money you will be
      redeemed."

⁴For this is what the Sovereign LORD
says:

"At first my people went down to
    Egypt to live;
    lately, Assyria has oppressed
      them.

⁵"And now what do I have here?"
declares the LORD.

"For my people have been taken
    away for nothing,
    and those who rule them mock,"
             declares the LORD.
"And all day long
    my name is constantly
      blasphemed.
⁶Therefore my people will know my
    name;
    therefore in that day they will
      know
that it is I who foretold it.
    Yes, it is I."

⁷How beautiful on the mountains
    are the feet of those who bring
      good news,

who proclaim peace,
    who bring good tidings,
    who proclaim salvation,
who say to Zion,
    "Your God reigns!"
⁸Listen! Your watchmen lift up their
    voices;
    together they shout for joy.
When the LORD returns to Zion,
    they will see it with their own eyes.
⁹Burst into songs of joy together,
    you ruins of Jerusalem,
for the LORD has comforted his
    people,
he has redeemed Jerusalem.
¹⁰The LORD will lay bare his holy arm
    in the sight of all the nations,
and all the ends of the earth will see
    the salvation of our God.

¹¹Depart, depart, go out from there!
    Touch no unclean thing!
Come out from it and be pure,
    you who carry the vessels of the
      LORD.
¹²But you will not leave in haste
    or go in flight;
for the LORD will go before you,
    the God of Israel will be your rear
      guard.

The Suffering and Glory of the Servant

¹³See, my servant will act wisely;
    he will be raised and lifted up and
      highly exalted.
¹⁴Just as there were many who were
    appalled at him—
    his appearance was so disfigured
      beyond that of any man
    and his form marred beyond
      human likeness—
¹⁵so will he sprinkle many nations,
    and kings will shut their mouths
      because of him.
For what they were not told, they will
    see,
    and what they have not heard, they
      will understand.

53 Who has believed our message
    and to whom has the arm of the
      LORD been revealed?

2He grew up before him like a tender
       shoot,
   and like a root out of dry ground.
He had no beauty or majesty to
       attract us to him,
   nothing in his appearance that we
       should desire him.
3He was despised and rejected by
       men,
   a man of sorrows, and familiar with
       suffering.
Like one from whom men hide their
       faces
   he was despised, and we esteemed
       him not.

4Surely he took up our infirmities
   and carried our sorrows,
yet we considered him stricken by
       God,
   smitten by him, and afflicted.
5But he was pierced for our
       transgressions,
   he was crushed for our iniquities;
the punishment that brought us peace
       was upon him,
   and by his wounds we are healed.
6We all, like sheep, have gone astray,
   each of us has turned to his own
       way;
and the LORD has laid on him
   the iniquity of us all.

7He was oppressed and afflicted,
   yet he did not open his mouth;
he was led like a lamb to the
       slaughter,
   and as a sheep before her shearers
       is silent,
so he did not open his mouth.
8By oppression and judgment he was
       taken away.
   And who can speak of his
       descendants?
For he was cut off from the land of
       the living;
   for the transgression of my people
       he was stricken.
9He was assigned a grave with the
       wicked,
   and with the rich in his death,
though he had done no violence,
   nor was any deceit in his mouth.

10Yet it was the LORD's will to crush
       him and cause him to suffer,
   and though the LORD makes his life
       a guilt offering,
he will see his offspring and prolong
       his days,
   and the will of the LORD will
       prosper in his hand.
11After the suffering of his soul,
   he will see the light ⌊of life⌋ and be
       satisfied;
by his knowledge my righteous
       servant will justify many,
   and he will bear their iniquities.
12Therefore I will give him a portion
       among the great,
   and he will divide the spoils with
       the strong,
because he poured out his life unto
       death,
   and was numbered with the
       transgressors.
For he bore the sin of many,
   and made intercession for the
       transgressors.

The Future Glory of Zion

54 "Sing, O barren woman,
       you who never bore a child;
burst into song, shout for joy,
   you who were never in labour;
because more are the children of the
       desolate woman
   than of her who has a husband,"
                           says the LORD.
2"Enlarge the place of your tent,
   stretch your tent curtains wide,
       do not hold back;
lengthen your cords,
   strengthen your stakes.
3For you will spread out to the right
       and to the left;
   your descendants will dispossess
       nations
and settle in their desolate cities.

4"Do not be afraid; you will not suffer
       shame.
   Do not fear disgrace; you will not
       be humiliated.
You will forget the shame of your
       youth

and remember no more the
    reproach of your widowhood.
5For your Maker is your husband—
    the LORD Almighty is his name—
the Holy One of Israel is your
    Redeemer;
he is called the God of all the
    earth.
6The LORD will call you back
    as if you were a wife deserted and
      distressed in spirit—
a wife who married young,
    only to be rejected," says your
    God.
7"For a brief moment I abandoned
    you,
but with deep compassion I will
    bring you back.
8In a surge of anger
    I hid my face from you for a
      moment,
but with everlasting kindness
    I will have compassion on you,"
says the LORD your Redeemer.

9"To me this is like the days of Noah,
    when I swore that the waters of
      Noah would never again cover
      the earth.
So now I have sworn not to be angry
    with you,
never to rebuke you again.
10Though the mountains be shaken
    and the hills be removed,
yet my unfailing love for you will not
    be shaken
nor my covenant of peace be
    removed,"
says the LORD, who has
    compassion on you.

11"O afflicted city, lashed by storms
    and not comforted,
I will build you with stones of
    turquoise,
your foundations with sapphires.
12I will make your battlements of
    rubies,
your gates of sparkling jewels,
and all your walls of precious
    stones.

13All your sons will be taught by the
    LORD,
    and great will be your children's
      peace.
14In righteousness you will be
    established:
Tyranny will be far from you;
    you will have nothing to fear.
Terror will be far removed;
    it will not come near you.
15If anyone does attack you, it will not
    be my doing;
whoever attacks you will surrender
    to you.

16"See, it is I who created the
    blacksmith
who fans the coals into flame
    and forges a weapon fit for its
      work.
And it is I who have created the
    destroyer to work havoc;
17 no weapon forged against you will
    prevail,
    and you will refute every tongue
      that accuses you.
This is the heritage of the servants of
    the LORD,
    and this is their vindication from
      me,"
             declares the LORD.

NEW TESTAMENT READING
Ephesians 1:1–23

1 Paul, an apostle of Christ Jesus by
   the will of God,

To the saints in Ephesus, the faithful
in Christ Jesus:

2Grace and peace to you from God
our Father and the Lord Jesus Christ.

Spiritual Blessings in Christ

3Praise be to the God and Father of
our Lord Jesus Christ, who has blessed

us in the heavenly realms with every spiritual blessing in Christ. ⁴For he chose us in him before the creation of the world to be holy and blameless in his sight. In love ⁵he predestined us to be adopted as his sons through Jesus Christ, in accordance with his pleasure and will—⁶to the praise of his glorious grace, which he has freely given us in the One he loves. ⁷In him we have redemption through his blood, the forgiveness of sins, in accordance with the riches of God's grace ⁸that he lavished on us with all wisdom and understanding. ⁹And he made known to us the mystery of his will according to his good pleasure, which he purposed in Christ, ¹⁰to be put into effect when the times will have reached their fulfilment—to bring all things in heaven and on earth together under one head, even Christ.

¹¹In him we were also chosen, having been predestined according to the plan of him who works out everything in conformity with the purpose of his will, ¹²in order that we, who were the first to hope in Christ, might be for the praise of his glory. ¹³And you also were included in Christ when you heard the word of truth, the gospel of your salvation. Having believed, you were marked in him with a seal, the promised Holy Spirit, ¹⁴who is a deposit guaranteeing our inheritance until the redemption of those who are God's possession —to the praise of his glory.

Thanksgiving and Prayer

¹⁵For this reason, ever since I heard about your faith in the Lord Jesus and your love for all the saints, ¹⁶I have not stopped giving thanks for you, remembering you in my prayers. ¹⁷I keep asking that the God of our Lord Jesus Christ, the glorious Father, may give you the Spirit of wisdom and revelation, so that you may know him better. ¹⁸I pray also that the eyes of your heart may be enlightened in order that you may know the hope to which he has called

you, the riches of his glorious inheritance in the saints, ¹⁹and his incomparably great power for us who believe. That power is like the working of his mighty strength, ²⁰when he exerted in Christ when he raised him from the dead and seated him at his right hand in the heavenly realms, ²¹far above all rule and authority, power and dominion, and every title that can be given, not only in the present age but also in the one to come. ²²And God placed all things under his feet and appointed him to be head over everything for the church, ²³which is his body, the fulness of him who fills everything in every way.

READING FROM PSALMS
Psalm 109:21–31

²¹But you, O Sovereign LORD,
     deal well with me for your name's sake;
  out of the goodness of your love,
     deliver me.
²²For I am poor and needy,
     and my heart is wounded within me.
²³I fade away like an evening shadow;
     I am shaken off like a locust.
²⁴My knees give way from fasting;
     my body is thin and gaunt.
²⁵I am an object of scorn to my accusers;
     when they see me, they shake their heads.

²⁶Help me, O LORD my God;
     save me in accordance with your love.
²⁷Let them know that it is your hand,
     that you, O LORD, have done it.
²⁸They may curse, but you will bless;
     when they attack they will be put to shame,
  but your servant will rejoice.
²⁹My accusers will be clothed with disgrace
     and wrapped in shame as in a cloak.

30With my mouth I will greatly extol
    the LORD;
  in the great throng I will praise
    him.

31For he stands at the right hand of the
    needy one,
  to save his life from those who
    condemn him.

SEPTEMBER 23

OLD TESTAMENT READING
Isaiah 55:1–57:13

Invitation to the Thirsty

55 "Come, all you who are thirsty,
        come to the waters;
  and you who have no money,
    come, buy and eat!
  Come, buy wine and milk
    without money and without cost.
2Why spend money on what is not
    bread,
  and your labour on what does not
    satisfy?
Listen, listen to me, and eat what is
    good,
  and your soul will delight in the
    richest of fare.
3Give ear and come to me;
  hear me, that your soul may live.
I will make an everlasting covenant
    with you,
  my faithful love promised to
    David.
4See, I have made him a witness to the
    peoples,
  a leader and commander of the
    peoples.
5Surely you will summon nations you
    know not,
  and nations that do not know you
    will hasten to you,
because of the LORD your God,
    the Holy One of Israel,
  for he has endowed you with
    splendour."

6Seek the LORD while he may be
    found;
  call on him while he is near.

7Let the wicked forsake his way
  and the evil man his thoughts.
Let him turn to the LORD, and he will
    have mercy on him,
  and to our God, for he will freely
    pardon.

8"For my thoughts are not your
    thoughts,
  neither are your ways my ways,"
    declares the LORD.
9"As the heavens are higher than the
    earth,
  so are my ways higher than your
    ways
  and my thoughts than your
    thoughts.
10As the rain and the snow
  come down from heaven,
and do not return to it
  without watering the earth
and making it bud and flourish,
  so that it yields seed for the sower
    and bread for the eater,
11so is my word that goes out from my
    mouth:
  It will not return to me empty,
but will accomplish what I desire
  and achieve the purpose for which
    I sent it.
12You will go out in joy
  and be led forth in peace;
the mountains and hills
  will burst into song before you,
and all the trees of the field
  will clap their hands.
13Instead of the thornbush will grow
    the pine tree,
  and instead of briers the myrtle will
    grow.

This will be for the LORD's renown,
   for an everlasting sign,
   which will not be destroyed.''

Salvation for Others

56 This is what the LORD says:

"Maintain justice
   and do what is right,
for my salvation is close at hand
   and my righteousness will soon be
     revealed.
[2]Blessed is the man who does this,
   the man who holds it fast,
who keeps the Sabbath without
     desecrating it,
   and keeps his hand from doing any
     evil.''

[3]Let no foreigner who has bound
   himself to the LORD say,
   "The LORD will surely exclude me
     from his people.''
And let not any eunuch complain,
   "I am only a dry tree.''

[4]For this is what the LORD says:

"To the eunuchs who keep my
     Sabbaths,
who choose what pleases me
   and hold fast to my covenant—
[5]to them I will give within my temple
   and its walls
a memorial and a name
   better than sons and daughters;
I will give them an everlasting name
   that will not be cut off.
[6]And foreigners who bind themselves
   to the LORD
to serve him,
to love the name of the LORD,
   and to worship him,
all who keep the Sabbath without
     desecrating it
   and who hold fast to my
     covenant—
[7]these I will bring to my holy
     mountain
   and give them joy in my house of
     prayer.

Their burnt offerings and sacrifices
   will be accepted on my altar;
for my house will be called
   a house of prayer for all nations.''
[8]The Sovereign LORD declares—
   he who gathers the exiles of Israel:
"I will gather still others to them
   besides those already gathered.''

God's Accusation Against the Wicked

[9]Come, all you beasts of the field,
   come and devour, all you beasts of
     the forest!
[10]Israel's watchmen are blind,
   they all lack knowledge;
they are all mute dogs,
   they cannot bark;
they lie around and dream,
   they love to sleep.
[11]They are dogs with mighty appetites;
   they never have enough.
They are shepherds who lack
     understanding;
   they all turn to their own way,
   each seeks his own gain.
[12]"Come,'' each one cries, "let me get
     wine!
Let us drink our fill of beer!
And tomorrow will be like today,
   or even far better.''

57 The righteous perish,
   and no-one ponders it in his
     heart;
devout men are taken away,
   and no-one understands
that the righteous are taken away
   to be spared from evil.
[2]Those who walk uprightly
   enter into peace;
   they find rest as they lie in death.

[3]"But you—come here, you sons of a
     sorceress,
   you offspring of adulterers and
     prostitutes!
[4]Whom are you mocking?
   At whom do you sneer
   and stick out your tongue?
Are you not a brood of rebels,
   the offspring of liars?

[5]You burn with lust among the oaks
    and under every spreading tree;
you sacrifice your children in the
    ravines
    and under the overhanging crags.

[6]⌞The idols⌟ among the smooth stones
    of the ravines are your portion;
they, they are your lot.
Yes, to them you have poured out
    drink offerings
    and offered grain offerings.
In the light of these things, should I
    relent?
[7]You have made your bed on a high
    and lofty hill;
there you went up to offer your
    sacrifices.
[8]Behind your doors and your
    doorposts
    you have put your pagan symbols.
Forsaking me, you uncovered your
    bed,
    you climbed into it and opened it
    wide;
you made a pact with those whose
    beds you love,
    and you looked on their
    nakedness.
[9]You went to Molech with olive oil
    and increased your perfumes.
You sent your ambassadors far
    away;
    you descended to the grave itself!
[10]You were wearied by all your ways,
    but you would not say, 'It is
    hopeless.'
You found renewal of your strength,
    and so you did not faint.

[11]"Whom have you so dreaded and
    feared
    that you have been false to me,
and have neither remembered me
    nor pondered this in your hearts?
Is it not because I have long been
    silent
    that you do not fear me?
[12]I will expose your righteousness and
    your works,
    and they will not benefit you.

[13]When you cry out for help,
    let your collection ⌞of idols⌟ save
    you!
The wind will carry all of them off,
    a mere breath will blow them
    away.
But the man who makes me his
    refuge
    will inherit the land
    and possess my holy mountain."

NEW TESTAMENT READING
Ephesians 2:1–22

Made Alive in Christ

2 As for you, you were dead in your
transgressions and sins, [2]in which
you used to live when you followed the
ways of this world and of the ruler of the
kingdom of the air, the spirit who is now
at work in those who are disobedient.
[3]All of us also lived among them at one
time, gratifying the cravings of our sinful nature and following its desires and
thoughts. Like the rest, we were by
nature objects of wrath. [4]But because of
his great love for us, God, who is rich in
mercy, [5]made us alive with Christ even
when we were dead in transgressions
—it is by grace you have been saved.
[6]And God raised us up with Christ and
seated us with him in the heavenly
realms in Christ Jesus, [7]in order that in
the coming ages he might show the
incomparable riches of his grace, expressed in his kindness to us in Christ
Jesus. [8]For it is by grace you have been
saved, through faith—and this not from
yourselves, it is the gift of God—[9]not by
works, so that no-one can boast. [10]For
we are God's workmanship, created in
Christ Jesus to do good works, which
God prepared in advance for us to do.

One in Christ

[11]Therefore, remember that formerly
you who are Gentiles by birth and called
"uncircumcised" by those who call
themselves "the circumcision" (that

done in the body by the hands of men)
—¹²remember that at that time you
were separate from Christ, excluded
from citizenship in Israel and foreigners
to the covenants of the promise, without hope and without God in the world.
¹³But now in Christ Jesus you who once
were far away have been brought near
through the blood of Christ.

¹⁴For he himself is our peace, who has
made the two one and has destroyed the
barrier, the dividing wall of hostility,
¹⁵by abolishing in his flesh the law with
its commandments and regulations. His
purpose was to create in himself one
new man out of the two, thus making
peace, ¹⁶and in this one body to reconcile both of them to God through the
cross, by which he put to death their
hostility. ¹⁷He came and preached
peace to you who were far away and
peace to those who were near. ¹⁸For
through him we both have access to the
Father by one Spirit.

¹⁹Consequently, you are no longer
foreigners and aliens, but fellow-
citizens with God's people and members of God's household, ²⁰built on
the foundation of the apostles and
prophets, with Christ Jesus himself as
the chief cornerstone. ²¹In him the
whole building is joined together and
rises to become a holy temple in the
Lord. ²²And in him you too are being
built together to become a dwelling in
which God lives by his Spirit.

READING FROM PSALMS
Psalm 110:1–7

Of David. A psalm.

¹The LORD says to my Lord:
  "Sit at my right hand
until I make your enemies
  a footstool for your feet."

²The LORD will extend your mighty
    sceptre from Zion;
  you will rule in the midst of your
    enemies.
³Your troops will be willing
  on your day of battle.
Arrayed in holy majesty,
  from the womb of the dawn
you will receive the dew of your
    youth.

⁴The LORD has sworn
  and will not change his mind:
"You are a priest for ever,
  in the order of Melchizedek."

⁵The Lord is at your right hand;
  he will crush kings on the day of his
    wrath.
⁶He will judge nations, heaping up the
    dead
  and crushing the rulers of the
    whole earth.
⁷He will drink from a brook beside the
    way;
  therefore he will lift up his head.

SEPTEMBER 24

OLD TESTAMENT READING
Isaiah 57:14–59:21

Comfort for the Contrite

¹⁴And it will be said:

"Build up, build up, prepare the
    road!
  Remove the obstacles out of the
    way of my people."
¹⁵For this is what the high and lofty
    One says—
  he who lives for ever, whose name
    is holy:
"I live in a high and holy place,
  but also with him who is contrite
    and lowly in spirit,
to revive the spirit of the lowly
  and to revive the heart of the
    contrite.
¹⁶I will not accuse for ever,
  nor will I always be angry,
for then the spirit of man would grow
    faint before me—
  the breath of man that I have
    created.
¹⁷I was enraged by his sinful greed;
  I punished him, and hid my face in
    anger,
yet he kept on in his wilful ways.
¹⁸I have seen his ways, but I will heal
    him;
  I will guide him and restore
    comfort to him,
¹⁹ creating praise on the lips of the
    mourners in Israel.
  Peace, peace, to those far and near,"
    says the LORD. "And I will heal
    them."
²⁰But the wicked are like the tossing
    sea,
  which cannot rest,
  whose waves cast up mire and
    mud.
²¹"There is no peace," says my God,
  "for the wicked."

True Fasting

58 "Shout it aloud, do not hold
    back.
  Raise your voice like a trumpet.
Declare to my people their rebellion
  and to the house of Jacob their
    sins.
²For day after day they seek me out;
  they seem eager to know my ways,
as if they were a nation that does
    what is right
  and has not forsaken the
    commands of its God.
They ask me for just decisions
  and seem eager for God to come
    near them.
³'Why have we fasted,' they say,
  'and you have not seen it?
Why have we humbled ourselves,
  and you have not noticed?'

"Yet on the day of your fasting, you
    do as you please
  and exploit all your workers.
⁴Your fasting ends in quarrelling and
    strife,
  and in striking each other with
    wicked fists.
You cannot fast as you do today
  and expect your voice to be heard
    on high.
⁵Is this the kind of fast I have chosen,
  only a day for a man to humble
    himself?
Is it only for bowing one's head like a
    reed
  and for lying on sackcloth and
    ashes?
Is that what you call a fast,
  a day acceptable to the LORD?

⁶"Is not this the kind of fasting I have
    chosen:
to loose the chains of injustice
  and untie the cords of the yoke,
to set the oppressed free
  and break every yoke?

[7]Is it not to share your food with the
hungry
and to provide the poor wanderer
with shelter—
when you see the naked, to clothe
him,
and not to turn away from your
own flesh and blood?
[8]Then your light will break forth like
the dawn,
and your healing will quickly
appear;
then your righteousness will go
before you,
and the glory of the LORD will be
your rear guard.
[9]Then you will call, and the LORD will
answer;
you will cry for help, and he will
say: Here am I.

"If you do away with the yoke of
oppression,
with the pointing finger and
malicious talk,
[10]and if you spend yourselves on behalf
of the hungry
and satisfy the needs of the
oppressed,
then your light will rise in the
darkness,
and your night will become like the
noonday.
[11]The LORD will guide you always;
he will satisfy your needs in a
sun-scorched land
and will strengthen your frame.
You will be like a well-watered
garden,
like a spring whose waters never
fail.
[12]Your people will rebuild the ancient
ruins
and will raise up the age-old
foundations;
you will be called Repairer of Broken
Walls,
Restorer of Streets with Dwellings.

[13]"If you keep your feet from breaking
the Sabbath
and from doing as you please on
my holy day,
if you call the Sabbath a delight
and the LORD's holy day
honourable,
and if you honour it by not going your
own way
and not doing as you please or
speaking idle words,
[14]then you will find your joy in the
LORD,
and I will cause you to ride on the
heights of the land
and to feast on the inheritance of
your father Jacob."
The mouth of the LORD
has spoken.

Sin, Confession and Redemption

59 Surely the arm of the LORD is
not too short to save,
nor his ear too dull to hear.
[2]But your iniquities have separated
you from your God;
your sins have hidden his face from
you,
so that he will not hear.
[3]For your hands are stained with
blood,
your fingers with guilt.
Your lips have spoken lies,
and your tongue mutters wicked
things.
[4]No-one calls for justice;
no-one pleads his case with
integrity.
They rely on empty arguments and
speak lies;
they conceive trouble and give
birth to evil.
[5]They hatch the eggs of vipers
and spin a spider's web.
Whoever eats their eggs will die,
and when one is broken, an adder
is hatched.
[6]Their cobwebs are useless for
clothing;
they cannot cover themselves with
what they make.
Their deeds are evil deeds,
and acts of violence are in their
hands.
[7]Their feet rush into sin;

they are swift to shed innocent
        blood.
Their thoughts are evil thoughts;
    ruin and destruction mark their
        ways.
⁸The way of peace they do not know;
    there is no justice in their paths.
They have turned them into crooked
        roads;
    no-one who walks in them will
        know peace.

⁹So justice is far from us,
    and righteousness does not reach
        us.
We look for light, but all is darkness;
    for brightness, but we walk in deep
        shadows.
¹⁰Like the blind we grope along the
        wall,
    feeling our way like men without
        eyes.
At midday we stumble as if it were
        twilight;
    among the strong, we are like the
        dead.
¹¹We all growl like bears;
    we moan mournfully like doves.
We look for justice, but find none;
    for deliverance, but it is far away.

¹²For our offences are many in your
        sight,
    and our sins testify against us.
Our offences are ever with us,
    and we acknowledge our iniquities:
¹³rebellion and treachery against the
        LORD,
    turning our backs on our God,
fomenting oppression and revolt,
    uttering lies our hearts have
        conceived.
¹⁴So justice is driven back,
    and righteousness stands at a
        distance;
truth has stumbled in the streets,
    honesty cannot enter.
¹⁵Truth is nowhere to be found,
    and whoever shuns evil becomes a
        prey.

The LORD looked and was displeased
    that there was no justice.

¹⁶He saw that there was no-one,
    he was appalled that there was
        no-one to intervene;
so his own arm worked salvation for
        him,
    and his own righteousness
        sustained him.
¹⁷He put on righteousness as his
        breastplate,
    and the helmet of salvation on his
        head;
he put on the garments of vengeance
    and wrapped himself in zeal as in a
        cloak.
¹⁸According to what they have done,
    so will he repay
wrath to his enemies
    and retribution to his foes;
he will repay the islands their due.
¹⁹From the west, men will fear the
    name of the LORD,
    and from the rising of the sun, they
        will revere his glory.
For he will come like a pent-up flood
    that the breath of the LORD drives
        along.

²⁰"The Redeemer will come to Zion,
    to those in Jacob who repent of
        their sins,"

                    declares the LORD.

²¹"As for me, this is my covenant with
them," says the LORD. "My Spirit, who
is on you, and my words that I have put
in your mouth will not depart from your
mouth, or from the mouths of your
children, or from the mouths of their
descendants from this time on and for
ever," says the LORD.

NEW TESTAMENT READING
Ephesians 3:1–21

Paul the Preacher to the Gentiles

3 For this reason I, Paul, the prisoner
    of Christ Jesus for the sake of you
Gentiles—
²Surely you have heard about the administration of God's grace that was

given to me for you, ³that is, the mystery made known to me by revelation, as I have already written briefly. ⁴In reading this, then, you will be able to understand my insight into the mystery of Christ, ⁵which was not made known to men in other generations as it has now been revealed by the Spirit to God's holy apostles and prophets. ⁶This mystery is that through the gospel the Gentiles are heirs together with Israel, members together of one body, and sharers together in the promise in Christ Jesus.

⁷I became a servant of this gospel by the gift of God's grace given me through the working of his power. ⁸Although I am less than the least of all God's people, this grace was given me: to preach to the Gentiles the unsearchable riches of Christ, ⁹and to make plain to everyone the administration of this mystery, which for ages past was kept hidden in God, who created all things. ¹⁰His intent was that now, through the church, the manifold wisdom of God should be made known to the rulers and authorities in the heavenly realms, ¹¹according to his eternal purpose which he accomplished in Christ Jesus our Lord. ¹²In him and through faith in him we may approach God with freedom and confidence. ¹³I ask you, therefore, not to be discouraged because of my sufferings for you, which are your glory.

A Prayer for the Ephesians

¹⁴For this reason I kneel before the Father, ¹⁵from whom his whole family in heaven and on earth derives its name. ¹⁶I pray that out of his glorious riches he may strengthen you with power through his Spirit in your inner being, ¹⁷so that Christ may dwell in your hearts through faith. And I pray that you, being rooted and established in love, ¹⁸may have power, together with all the saints, to grasp how wide and long and high and deep is the love of Christ, ¹⁹and to know this love that surpasses knowledge—that you may be filled to the measure of all the fulness of God.

²⁰Now to him who is able to do immeasurably more than all we ask or imagine, according to his power that is at work within us, ²¹to him be glory in the church and in Christ Jesus throughout all generations, for ever and ever! Amen.

READING FROM PSALMS
Psalm 111:1–10

¹Praise the LORD.

I will extol the LORD with all my
    heart
      in the council of the upright and in
      the assembly.

²Great are the works of the LORD;
    they are pondered by all who
      delight in them.

³Glorious and majestic are his deeds,
    and his righteousness endures for
      ever.

⁴He has caused his wonders to be
    remembered;
    the LORD is gracious and
      compassionate.

⁵He provides food for those who fear
    him;
    he remembers his covenant for
      ever.

⁶He has shown his people the power
    of his works,
    giving them the lands of other
      nations.

⁷The works of his hands are faithful
    and just;
    all his precepts are trustworthy.

⁸They are steadfast for ever and ever,
    done in faithfulness and
      uprightness.

⁹He provided redemption for his
    people;
    he ordained his covenant for
      ever—
    holy and awesome is his name.

¹⁰The fear of the LORD is the beginning
    of wisdom;
    all who follow his precepts have
      good understanding.
To him belongs eternal praise.

SEPTEMBER 25

OLD TESTAMENT READING
Isaiah 60:1–62:12

The Glory of Zion

60 "Arise, shine, for your light has
come,
and the glory of the LORD rises
upon you.
²See, darkness covers the earth
and thick darkness is over the
peoples,
but the LORD rises upon you
and his glory appears over you.
³Nations will come to your light,
and kings to the brightness of your
dawn.

⁴"Lift up your eyes and look about
you:
All assemble and come to you;
your sons come from afar,
and your daughters are carried on
the arm.
⁵Then you will look and be radiant,
your heart will throb and swell with
joy;
the wealth on the seas will be brought
to you,
to you the riches of the nations will
come.
⁶Herds of camels will cover your
land,
young camels of Midian and
Ephah.
And all from Sheba will come,
bearing gold and incense
and proclaiming the praise of the
LORD.
⁷All Kedar's flocks will be gathered to
you,
the rams of Nebaioth will serve
you;
they will be accepted as offerings on
my altar,
and I will adorn my glorious
temple.

⁸"Who are these that fly along like
clouds,
like doves to their nests?
⁹Surely the islands look to me;
in the lead are the ships of
Tarshish,
bringing your sons from afar,
with their silver and gold,
to the honour of the LORD your God,
the Holy One of Israel,
for he has endowed you with
splendour.

¹⁰"Foreigners will rebuild your walls,
and their kings will serve you.
Though in anger I struck you,
in favour I will show you
compassion.
¹¹Your gates will always stand open,
they will never be shut, day or
night,
so that men may bring you the wealth
of the nations—
their kings led in triumphal
procession.
¹²For the nation or kingdom that will
not serve you will perish;
it will be utterly ruined.

¹³"The glory of Lebanon will come to
you,
the pine, the fir and the cypress
together,
to adorn the place of my sanctuary;
and I will glorify the place of my
feet.
¹⁴The sons of your oppressors will
come bowing before you;
all who despise you will bow down
at your feet
and will call you the City of the
LORD,
Zion of the Holy One of Israel.

¹⁵"Although you have been forsaken
and hated,
with no-one travelling through,

I will make you the everlasting pride
and the joy of all generations.
¹⁶You will drink the milk of nations
and be nursed at royal breasts.
Then you will know that I, the LORD,
am your Saviour,
your Redeemer, the Mighty One of
Jacob.
¹⁷Instead of bronze I will bring you
gold,
and silver in place of iron.
Instead of wood I will bring you
bronze,
and iron in place of stones.
I will make peace your governor
and righteousness your ruler.
¹⁸No longer will violence be heard in
your land,
nor ruin or destruction within your
borders,
but you will call your walls Salvation
and your gates Praise.
¹⁹The sun will no more be your light by
day,
nor will the brightness of the moon
shine on you,
for the LORD will be your everlasting
light,
and your God will be your glory.
²⁰Your sun will never set again,
and your moon will wane no more;
the LORD will be your everlasting
light,
and your days of sorrow will end.
²¹Then will all your people be righteous
and they will possess the land for
ever.
They are the shoot I have planted,
the work of my hands,
for the display of my splendour.
²²The least of you will become a
thousand,
the smallest a mighty nation.
I am the LORD;
in its time I will do this swiftly."

The Year of the LORD's Favour

61 The Spirit of the Sovereign
LORD is on me,
because the LORD has anointed me
to preach good news to the poor.
He has sent me to bind up the
broken-hearted,
to proclaim freedom for the
captives
and release from darkness for the
prisoners,
²to proclaim the year of the LORD's
favour
and the day of vengeance of our
God,
to comfort all who mourn,
³ and provide for those who grieve in
Zion—
to bestow on them a crown of beauty
instead of ashes,
the oil of gladness
instead of mourning,
and a garment of praise
instead of a spirit of despair.
They will be called oaks of
righteousness,
a planting of the LORD
for the display of his splendour.

⁴They will rebuild the ancient ruins
and restore the places long
devastated;
they will renew the ruined cities
that have been devastated for
generations.
⁵Aliens will shepherd your flocks;
foreigners will work your fields and
vineyards.
⁶And you will be called priests of the
LORD,
you will be named ministers of our
God.
You will feed on the wealth of
nations,
and in their riches you will boast.

⁷Instead of their shame
my people will receive a double
portion,
and instead of disgrace
they will rejoice in their
inheritance;
and so they will inherit a double
portion in their land,
and everlasting joy will be theirs.

⁸"For I, the LORD, love justice;
  I hate robbery and iniquity.
In my faithfulness I will reward them
  and make an everlasting covenant
    with them.
⁹Their descendants will be known
    among the nations
  and their offspring among the
    peoples.
All who see them will acknowledge
  that they are a people the LORD
    has blessed."

¹⁰I delight greatly in the LORD;
  my soul rejoices in my God.
For he has clothed me with garments
    of salvation
  and arrayed me in a robe of
    righteousness,
as a bridegroom adorns his head like
    a priest,
  and as a bride adorns herself with
    her jewels.
¹¹For as the soil makes the young plant
    come up
  and a garden causes seeds to grow,
so the Sovereign LORD will make
    righteousness and praise
  spring up before all nations.

Zion's New Name

62 For Zion's sake I will not keep
    silent,
  for Jerusalem's sake I will not
    remain quiet,
till her righteousness shines out like
    the dawn,
  her salvation like a blazing torch.
²The nations will see your
    righteousness,
  and all kings your glory;
you will be called by a new name
  that the mouth of the LORD will
    bestow.
³You will be a crown of splendour in
    the LORD's hand,
  a royal diadem in the hand of your
    God.
⁴No longer will they call you
    Deserted,
  or name your land Desolate.

But you will be called Hephzibah,
  and your land Beulah;
for the LORD will take delight in you,
  and your land will be married.
⁵As a young man marries a maiden,
  so will your sons marry you;
as a bridegroom rejoices over his
    bride,
  so will your God rejoice over you.

⁶I have posted watchmen on your
    walls, O Jerusalem;
  they will never be silent day or
    night.
You who call on the LORD,
  give yourselves no rest,
⁷and give him no rest till he establishes
    Jerusalem
  and makes her the praise of the
    earth.

⁸The LORD has sworn by his right
    hand
  and by his mighty arm:
"Never again will I give your grain
    as food for your enemies,
and never again will foreigners drink
    the new wine
  for which you have toiled;
⁹but those who harvest it will eat it
    and praise the LORD,
and those who gather the grapes will
    drink it
  in the courts of my sanctuary."

¹⁰Pass through, pass through the gates!
  Prepare the way for the people.
Build up, build up the highway!
  Remove the stones.
Raise a banner for the nations.

¹¹The LORD has made proclamation
    to the ends of the earth:
  "Say to the Daughter of Zion,
  'See, your Saviour comes!
See, his reward is with him,
  and his recompense accompanies
    him.'"
¹²They will be called the Holy People,
    the Redeemed of the LORD;
and you will be called Sought After,
    the City No Longer Deserted.

NEW TESTAMENT READING
Ephesians 4:1–16

Unity in the Body of Christ

4 As a prisoner for the Lord, then, I urge you to live a life worthy of the calling you have received. ²Be completely humble and gentle; be patient, bearing with one another in love. ³Make every effort to keep the unity of the Spirit through the bond of peace. ⁴There is one body and one Spirit—just as you were called to one hope when you were called—⁵one Lord, one faith, one baptism; ⁶one God and Father of all, who is over all and through all and in all.

⁷But to each one of us grace has been given as Christ apportioned it. ⁸This is why it says:

"When he ascended on high,
    he led captives in his train
    and gave gifts to men."

⁹(What does "he ascended" mean except that he also descended to the lower, earthly regions? ¹⁰He who descended is the very one who ascended higher than all the heavens, in order to fill the whole universe.) ¹¹It was he who gave some to be apostles, some to be prophets, some to be evangelists, and some to be pastors and teachers, ¹²to prepare God's people for works of service, so that the body of Christ may be built up ¹³until we all reach unity in the faith and in the knowledge of the Son of God and become mature, attaining to the whole measure of the fulness of Christ.

¹⁴Then we will no longer be infants, tossed back and forth by the waves, and blown here and there by every wind of teaching and by the cunning and craftiness of men in their deceitful scheming.

¹⁵Instead, speaking the truth in love, we will in all things grow up into him who is the Head, that is, Christ. ¹⁶From him the whole body, joined and held together by every supporting ligament, grows and builds itself up in love, as each part does its work.

READING FROM PROVERBS
Proverbs 23:19–28

¹⁹Listen, my son, and be wise,
    and keep your heart on the right
        path.
²⁰Do not join those who drink too
        much wine
    or gorge themselves on meat,
²¹for drunkards and gluttons become
        poor,
    and drowsiness clothes them in
        rags.

²²Listen to your father, who gave you
        life,
    and do not despise your mother
        when she is old.
²³Buy the truth and do not sell it;
    get wisdom, discipline and
        understanding.
²⁴The father of a righteous man has
        great joy;
    he who has a wise son delights in
        him.
²⁵May your father and mother be glad;
    may she who gave you birth
        rejoice!

²⁶My son, give me your heart
    and let your eyes keep to my ways,
²⁷for a prostitute is a deep pit
    and a wayward wife is a narrow
        well.
²⁸Like a bandit she lies in wait,
    and multiplies the unfaithful
        among men.

SEPTEMBER 26

OLD TESTAMENT READING
Isaiah 63:1–65:16

God's Day of Vengeance and Redemption

63 Who is this coming from Edom,
from Bozrah, with his garments
stained crimson?
Who is this, robed in splendour,
striding forward in the greatness of
his strength?

"It is I, speaking in righteousness,
mighty to save."

²Why are your garments red,
like those of one treading the
winepress?

³"I have trodden the winepress alone;
from the nations no-one was with
me.
I trampled them in my anger
and trod them down in my wrath;
their blood spattered my garments,
and I stained all my clothing.
⁴For the day of vengeance was in my
heart,
and the year of my redemption has
come.
⁵I looked, but there was no-one to
help,
I was appalled that no-one gave
support;
so my own arm worked salvation for
me,
and my own wrath sustained me.
⁶I trampled the nations in my anger;
in my wrath I made them drunk
and poured their blood on the
ground."

Praise and Prayer

⁷I will tell of the kindnesses of the
LORD,
the deeds for which he is to be
praised,
according to all the LORD has done
for us—
yes, the many good things he has
done
for the house of Israel,
according to his compassion and
many kindnesses.
⁸He said, "Surely they are my people,
sons who will not be false to me";
and so he became their Saviour.
⁹In all their distress he too was
distressed,
and the angel of his presence saved
them.
In his love and mercy he redeemed
them;
he lifted them up and carried them
all the days of old.
¹⁰Yet they rebelled
and grieved his Holy Spirit.
So he turned and became their enemy
and he himself fought against
them.

¹¹Then his people recalled the days of
old,
the days of Moses and his people—
where is he who brought them
through the sea,
with the shepherd of his flock?
Where is he who set
his Holy Spirit among them,
¹²who sent his glorious arm of power
to be at Moses' right hand,
who divided the waters before them,
to gain for himself everlasting
renown,
¹³who led them through the depths?
Like a horse in open country,
they did not stumble;
¹⁴like cattle that go down to the plain,
they were given rest by the Spirit of
the LORD.
This is how you guided your people
to make for yourself a glorious
name.

¹⁵Look down from heaven and see
    from your lofty throne, holy and
        glorious.
  Where are your zeal and your might?
  Your tenderness and compassion
        are withheld from us.
¹⁶But you are our Father,
    though Abraham does not know us
        or Israel acknowledge us;
  you, O Lord, are our Father,
    our Redeemer from of old is your
        name.
¹⁷Why, O Lord, do you make us
        wander from your ways
  and harden our hearts so that we
        do not revere you?
  Return for the sake of your servants,
    the tribes that are your inheritance.
¹⁸For a little while your people
        possessed your holy place,
  but now our enemies have
        trampled down your sanctuary.
¹⁹We are yours from of old;
    but you have not ruled over them,
  they have not been called by your
        name.

64 Oh, that you would rend the
    heavens and come down,
  that the mountains would tremble
        before you!
²As when fire sets twigs ablaze
    and causes water to boil,
  come down to make your name
        known to your enemies
  and cause the nations to quake
        before you!
³For when you did awesome things
        that we did not expect,
  you came down, and the
        mountains trembled before
        you.
⁴Since ancient times no-one has
        heard,
    no ear has perceived,
  no eye has seen any God besides you,
    who acts on behalf of those who
        wait for him.
⁵You come to the help of those who
        gladly do right,
  who remember your ways.

But when we continued to sin against
        them,
    you were angry.
  How then can we be saved?
⁶All of us have become like one who is
        unclean,
    and all our righteous acts are like
        filthy rags;
  we all shrivel up like a leaf,
    and like the wind our sins sweep us
        away.
⁷No-one calls on your name
    or strives to lay hold of you;
  for you have hidden your face from
        us
  and made us waste away because
        of our sins.

⁸Yet, O Lord, you are our Father.
    We are the clay, you are the
        potter;
  we are all the work of your hand.
⁹Do not be angry beyond measure, O
        Lord;
  do not remember our sins for ever.
  Oh, look upon us we pray,
    for we are all your people.
¹⁰Your sacred cities have become a
        desert;
  even Zion is a desert, Jerusalem a
        desolation.
¹¹Our holy and glorious temple, where
        our fathers praised you,
  has been burned with fire,
  and all that we treasured lies in
        ruins.
¹²After all this, O Lord, will you hold
        yourself back?
  Will you keep silent and punish us
        beyond measure?

Judgment and Salvation

65 "I revealed myself to those who
    did not ask for me;
  I was found by those who did not
        seek me.
  To a nation that did not call on my
        name,
    I said, 'Here am I, here am I.'
²All day long I have held out my
        hands
  to an obstinate people,

who walk in ways not good,
  pursuing their own imaginations—
³a people who continually provoke me
    to my very face,
  offering sacrifices in gardens
  and burning incense on altars of
    brick;
⁴who sit among the graves
  and spend their nights keeping
    secret vigil;
who eat the flesh of pigs,
  and whose pots hold broth of
    unclean meat;
⁵who say, 'Keep away; don't come
    near me,
  for I am too sacred for you!'
Such people are smoke in my
    nostrils,
  a fire that keeps burning all day.

⁶"See, it stands written before me;
  I will not keep silent but will pay
    back in full;
  I will pay it back into their laps—
⁷both your sins and the sins of your
    fathers,"
  says the LORD.
"Because they burned sacrifices on
    the mountains
  and defied me on the hills,
I will measure into their laps
  the full payment for their former
    deeds."

⁸This is what the LORD says:

"As when juice is still found in a
    cluster of grapes
  and men say, 'Don't destroy it,
    there is yet some good in it,'
so will I do on behalf of my servants;
  I will not destroy them all.
⁹I will bring forth descendants from
    Jacob,
  and from Judah those who will
    possess my mountains;
my chosen people will inherit them,
  and there will my servants live.
¹⁰Sharon will become a pasture for
    flocks,
  and the Valley of Achor a resting
    place for herds,
  for my people who seek me.

¹¹"But as for you who forsake the
    LORD
  and forget my holy mountain,
who spread a table for Fortune
  and fill bowls of mixed wine for
    Destiny,
¹²I will destine you for the sword,
  and you will all bend down for the
    slaughter;
for I called but you did not answer,
  I spoke but you did not listen.
You did evil in my sight
  and chose what displeases me."

¹³Therefore this is what the Sovereign
LORD says:

"My servants will eat,
  but you will go hungry;
my servants will drink,
  but you will go thirsty;
my servants will rejoice,
  but you will be put to shame.
¹⁴My servants will sing
  out of the joy of their hearts,
but you will cry out
  from anguish of heart
  and wail in brokenness of spirit.
¹⁵You will leave your name
  to my chosen ones as a curse;
the Sovereign LORD will put you to
    death,
  but to his servants he will give
    another name.
¹⁶Whoever invokes a blessing in the
    land
  will do so by the God of truth;
he who takes an oath in the land
  will swear by the God of truth.
For the past troubles will be forgotten
  and hidden from my eyes.

NEW TESTAMENT READING
Ephesians 4:17—5:7

Living as Children of Light

¹⁷So I tell you this, and insist on it in
the Lord, that you must no longer live as
the Gentiles do, in the futility of their

thinking. [18]They are darkened in their understanding and separated from the life of God because of the ignorance that is in them due to the hardening of their hearts. [19]Having lost all sensitivity, they have given themselves over to sensuality so as to indulge in every kind of impurity, with a continual lust for more.

[20]You, however, did not come to know Christ that way. [21]Surely you heard of him and were taught in him in accordance with the truth that is in Jesus. [22]You were taught, with regard to your former way of life, to put off your old self, which is being corrupted by its deceitful desires; [23]to be made new in the attitude of your minds; [24]and to put on the new self, created to be like God in true righteousness and holiness.

[25]Therefore each of you must put off falsehood and speak truthfully to his neighbour, for we are all members of one body. [26]"In your anger do not sin": Do not let the sun go down while you are still angry, [27]and do not give the devil a foothold. [28]He who has been stealing must steal no longer, but must work, doing something useful with his own hands, that he may have something to share with those in need.

[29]Do not let any unwholesome talk come out of your mouths, but only what is helpful for building others up according to their needs, that it may benefit those who listen. [30]And do not grieve the Holy Spirit of God, with whom you were sealed for the day of redemption. [31]Get rid of all bitterness, rage and anger, brawling and slander, along with every form of malice. [32]Be kind and compassionate to one another, forgiving each other, just as in Christ God forgave you.

5 Be imitators of God, therefore, as dearly loved children [2]and live a life of love, just as Christ loved us and gave himself up for us as a fragrant offering and sacrifice to God.

[3]But among you there must not be even a hint of sexual immorality, or of any kind of impurity, or of greed, because these are improper for God's holy people. [4]Nor should there be obscenity, foolish talk or coarse joking, which are out of place, but rather thanksgiving. [5]For of this you can be sure: No immoral, impure or greedy person—such a man is an idolater—has any inheritance in the kingdom of Christ and of God. [6]Let no-one deceive you with empty words, for because of such things God's wrath comes on those who are disobedient. [7]Therefore do not be partners with them.

READING FROM PSALMS
Psalm 112:1–10

[1]Praise the LORD.

Blessed is the man who fears the
    LORD,
  who finds great delight in his
    commands.

[2]His children will be mighty in the
    land;
  the generation of the upright will
    be blessed.

[3]Wealth and riches are in his house,
  and his righteousness endures for
    ever.

[4]Even in darkness light dawns for the
    upright,
  for the gracious and compassionate
    and righteous man.

[5]Good will come to him who is
    generous and lends freely,
  who conducts his affairs with
    justice.

[6]Surely he will never be shaken;
  a righteous man will be
    remembered for ever.

[7]He will have no fear of bad news;
  his heart is steadfast, trusting in the
    LORD.

[8]His heart is secure, he will have no
    fear;
  in the end he will look in triumph
    on his foes.

⁹He has scattered abroad his gifts to
 the poor,
 his righteousness endures for
  ever;
 his horn will be lifted high in
  honour.

¹⁰The wicked man will see and be
 vexed,
 he will gnash his teeth and waste
  away;
 the longings of the wicked will
  come to nothing.

DAY 270   SEPTEMBER 27

OLD TESTAMENT READING
Isaiah 65:17—66:24

New Heavens and a New Earth

¹⁷"Behold, I will create
 new heavens and a new earth.
The former things will not be
 remembered,
 nor will they come to mind.
¹⁸But be glad and rejoice for ever
 in what I will create,
for I will create Jerusalem to be a
 delight
 and its people a joy.
¹⁹I will rejoice over Jerusalem
 and take delight in my people;
the sound of weeping and of crying
 will be heard in it no more.

²⁰"Never again will there be in it
 an infant who lives but a few days,
 or an old man who does not live
  out his years;
he who dies at a hundred
 will be thought a mere youth;
he who fails to reach a hundred
 will be considered accursed.
²¹They will build houses and dwell in
 them;
 they will plant vineyards and eat
  their fruit.
²²No longer will they build houses and
 others live in them,
 or plant and others eat.
For as the days of a tree,
 so will be the days of my people;
my chosen ones will long enjoy
 the works of their hands.

²³They will not toil in vain
 or bear children doomed to
  misfortune;
for they will be a people blessed by
 the LORD,
 they and their descendants with
  them.
²⁴Before they call I will answer;
 while they are still speaking I will
  hear.
²⁵The wolf and the lamb will feed
 together,
 and the lion will eat straw like the
  ox,
 but dust will be the serpent's food.
They will neither harm nor destroy
 on all my holy mountain,"
     says the LORD.

Judgment and Hope

66 This is what the LORD says:

"Heaven is my throne,
 and the earth is my footstool.
Where is the house you will build for
 me?
 Where will my resting place be?
²Has not my hand made all these
 things,
 and so they came into being?"
    declares the LORD.

"This is the one I esteem:
 he who is humble and contrite in
  spirit,
 and trembles at my word.
³But whoever sacrifices a bull
 is like one who kills a man,

and whoever offers a lamb,
    like one who breaks a dog's neck;
whoever makes a grain offering
    is like one who presents pig's
        blood,
and whoever burns memorial
    incense,
    like one who worships an idol.
They have chosen their own ways,
    and their souls delight in their
        abominations;
⁴so I also will choose harsh treatment
    for them
    and will bring upon them what they
        dread.
For when I called, no-one answered,
    when I spoke, no-one listened.
They did evil in my sight
    and chose what displeases me."

⁵Hear the word of the LORD,
    you who tremble at his word;
"Your brothers who hate you,
    and exclude you because of my
        name, have said,
'Let the LORD be glorified,
    that we may see your joy!'
    Yet they will be put to shame.
⁶Hear that uproar from the city,
    hear that noise from the temple!
It is the sound of the LORD
    repaying his enemies all they
        deserve.

⁷"Before she goes into labour,
    she gives birth;
before the pains come upon her,
    she delivers a son.
⁸Who has ever heard of such a thing?
    Who has ever seen such things?
Can a country be born in a day
    or a nation be brought forth in a
        moment?
Yet no sooner is Zion in labour
    than she gives birth to her children.
⁹Do I bring to the moment of birth
    and not give delivery?" says
        the LORD.
"Do I close up the womb
    when I bring to delivery?" says
        your God.

¹⁰"Rejoice with Jerusalem and be glad
    for her,
    all you who love her;
rejoice greatly with her,
    all you who mourn over her.
¹¹For you will nurse and be satisfied
    at her comforting breasts;
you will drink deeply
    and delight in her overflowing
        abundance."

¹²For this is what the LORD says:

"I will extend peace to her like a
    river,
    and the wealth of nations like a
        flooding stream;
you will nurse and be carried on her
    arm
    and dandled on her knees.
¹³As a mother comforts her child,
    so will I comfort you;
    and you will be comforted over
        Jerusalem."

¹⁴When you see this, your heart will
    rejoice
    and you will flourish like grass;
the hand of the LORD will be made
    known to his servants,
    but his fury will be shown to his
        foes.
¹⁵See, the LORD is coming with fire,
    and his chariots are like a
        whirlwind;
he will bring down his anger with
    fury,
    and his rebuke with flames of fire.
¹⁶For with fire and with his sword
    the LORD will execute judgment
    upon all men,
    and many will be those slain by the
        LORD.

¹⁷"Those who consecrate and purify
themselves to go into the gardens, following the one in the midst of those who
eat the flesh of pigs and rats and other
abominable things—they will meet
their end together," declares the LORD.

¹⁸"And I, because of their actions and
their imaginations, am about to come

and gather all nations and tongues, and they will come and see my glory.

19"I will set a sign among them, and I will send some of those who survive to the nations—to Tarshish, to the Libyans and Lydians (famous as archers), to Tubal and Greece, and to the distant islands that have not heard of my fame or seen my glory. They will proclaim my glory among the nations. 20And they will bring all your brothers, from all the nations, to my holy mountain in Jerusalem as an offering to the LORD—on horses, in chariots and wagons, and on mules and camels," says the LORD. "They will bring them, as the Israelites bring their grain offerings, to the temple of the LORD in ceremonially clean vessels. 21And I will select some of them also to be priests and Levites," says the LORD.

22"As the new heavens and the new earth that I make will endure before me," declares the LORD, "so will your name and descendants endure. 23From one New Moon to another and from one Sabbath to another, all mankind will come and bow down before me," says the LORD. 24"And they will go out and look upon the dead bodies of those who rebelled against me; their worm will not die, nor will their fire be quenched, and they will be loathsome to all mankind."

NEW TESTAMENT READING
Ephesians 5:8–33

8For you were once darkness, but now you are light in the Lord. Live as children of light 9(for the fruit of the light consists in all goodness, righteousness and truth) 10and find out what pleases the Lord. 11Have nothing to do with the fruitless deeds of darkness, but rather expose them. 12For it is shameful even to mention what the disobedient do in secret. 13But everything exposed by the light becomes visible, 14for it is light that makes everything visible. This is why it is said:

"Wake up, O sleeper,
rise from the dead,
and Christ will shine on you."

15Be very careful, then, how you live—not as unwise but as wise, 16making the most of every opportunity, because the days are evil. 17Therefore do not be foolish, but understand what the Lord's will is. 18Do not get drunk on wine, which leads to debauchery. Instead, be filled with the Spirit. 19Speak to one another with psalms, hymns and spiritual songs. Sing and make music in your heart to the Lord, 20always giving thanks to God the Father for everything, in the name of our Lord Jesus Christ.

21Submit to one another out of reverence for Christ.

Wives and Husbands

22Wives, submit to your husbands as to the Lord. 23For the husband is the head of the wife as Christ is the head of the church, his body, of which he is the Saviour. 24Now as the church submits to Christ, so also wives should submit to their husbands in everything.

25Husbands, love your wives, just as Christ loved the church and gave himself up for her 26to make her holy, cleansing her by the washing with water through the word, 27and to present her to himself as a radiant church, without stain or wrinkle or any other blemish, but holy and blameless. 28In this same way, husbands ought to love their wives as their own bodies. He who loves his wife loves himself. 29After all, no-one ever hated his own body, but he feeds and cares for it, just as Christ does the church—30for we are members of his body. 31"For this reason a man will leave his father and mother and be united to his wife, and the two will become one flesh." 32This is a profound mystery—but I am talking about Christ and the church. 33However, each one of you also must love his wife as he loves himself, and the wife must respect her husband.

READING FROM PSALMS
Psalm 113:1–9

[1]Praise the LORD.

Praise, O servants of the LORD,
    praise the name of the LORD.
[2]Let the name of the LORD be praised,
    both now and for evermore.
[3]From the rising of the sun to the
      place where it sets,
    the name of the LORD is to be
      praised.

[4]The LORD is exalted over all the
      nations,
    his glory above the heavens.

[5]Who is like the LORD our God,
    the One who sits enthroned on
      high,
[6]who stoops down to look
    on the heavens and the earth?

[7]He raises the poor from the dust
    and lifts the needy from the ash
      heap;
[8]he seats them with princes,
    with the princes of their people.
[9]He settles the barren woman in her
      home
    as a happy mother of children.

Praise the LORD.

SEPTEMBER 28   DAY 271

OLD TESTAMENT READING
Nahum 1:1–3:19

1 An oracle concerning Nineveh.
The book of the vision of Nahum
the Elkoshite.

The LORD's Anger Against Nineveh

[2]The LORD is a jealous and avenging
      God;
    the LORD takes vengeance and is
      filled with wrath.
The LORD takes vengeance on his
      foes
    and maintains his wrath against his
      enemies.
[3]The LORD is slow to anger and great
      in power;
    the LORD will not leave the guilty
      unpunished.
His way is in the whirlwind and the
      storm,
    and clouds are the dust of his feet.
[4]He rebukes the sea and dries it up;
    he makes all the rivers run dry.
Bashan and Carmel wither
    and the blossoms of Lebanon fade.

[5]The mountains quake before him
    and the hills melt away.
The earth trembles at his presence,
    the world and all who live in it.
[6]Who can withstand his indignation?
    Who can endure his fierce anger?
His wrath is poured out like fire;
    the rocks are shattered before him.

[7]The LORD is good,
    a refuge in times of trouble.
He cares for those who trust in him,
[8]   but with an overwhelming flood
he will make an end of ⌊Nineveh⌋;
    he will pursue his foes into
      darkness.

[9]Whatever they plot against the LORD
    he will bring to an end;
    trouble will not come a second
      time.
[10]They will be entangled among thorns
    and drunk from their wine;
    they will be consumed like dry
      stubble.
[11]From you, ⌊O Nineveh,⌋ has one
      come forth
who plots evil against the LORD
    and counsels wickedness.

¹²This is what the LORD says:

"Although they have allies and are
    numerous,
  they will be cut off and pass away.
Although I have afflicted you, ⸀O
    Judah⸀,
  I will afflict you no more.
¹³Now I will break their yoke from
    your neck
  and tear your shackles away."

¹⁴The LORD has given a command
    concerning you, ⸀Nineveh⸀:
  "You will have no descendants to
    bear your name.
I will destroy the carved images and
    cast idols
  that are in the temple of your gods.
I will prepare your grave,
  for you are vile."

¹⁵Look, there on the mountains,
  the feet of one who brings good
    news,
  who proclaims peace!
Celebrate your festivals, O Judah,
  and fulfil your vows.
No more will the wicked invade you;
  they will be completely destroyed.

Nineveh to Fall

2 An attacker advances against you,
    ⸀Nineveh⸀.
  Guard the fortress,
  watch the road,
  brace yourselves,
  marshal all your strength!

²The LORD will restore the splendour
    of Jacob
  like the splendour of Israel,
though destroyers have laid them
    waste
  and have ruined their vines.

³The shields of his soldiers are red;
  the warriors are clad in scarlet.
The metal on the chariots flashes
  on the day they are made ready;
  the spears of pine are brandished.

⁴The chariots storm through the
    streets,
  rushing back and forth through the
    squares.
They look like flaming torches;
  they dart about like lightning.

⁵He summons his picked troops,
  yet they stumble on their way.
They dash to the city wall;
  the protective shield is put in
    place.
⁶The river gates are thrown open
  and the palace collapses.
⁷It is decreed that ⸀the city⸀
  be exiled and carried away.
Its slave girls moan like doves
  and beat upon their breasts.
⁸Nineveh is like a pool,
  and its water is draining away.
"Stop! Stop!" they cry,
  but no-one turns back.
⁹Plunder the silver!
  Plunder the gold!
The supply is endless,
  the wealth from all its treasures!
¹⁰She is pillaged, plundered, stripped!
  Hearts melt, knees give way,
  bodies tremble, every face grows
    pale.

¹¹Where now is the lions' den,
  the place where they fed their
    young,
where the lion and lioness went,
  and the cubs, with nothing to fear?
¹²The lion killed enough for his cubs
  and strangled the prey for his mate,
filling his lairs with the kill
  and his dens with the prey.

¹³"I am against you,"
  declares the LORD Almighty.
"I will burn up your chariots in
    smoke,
  and the sword will devour your
    young lions.
I will leave you no prey on the
    earth.
The voices of your messengers
  will no longer be heard."

Woe to Nineveh

3 Woe to the city of blood,
full of lies,
full of plunder,
never without victims!
²The crack of whips,
the clatter of wheels,
galloping horses
and jolting chariots!
³Charging cavalry,
flashing swords
and glittering spears!
Many casualties,
piles of dead,
bodies without number,
people stumbling over the
corpses—
⁴all because of the wanton lust of a
harlot,
alluring, the mistress of sorceries,
who enslaved nations by her
prostitution
and peoples by her witchcraft.

⁵"I am against you," declares the
LORD Almighty.
"I will lift your skirts over your
face.
I will show the nations your
nakedness
and the kingdoms your shame.
⁶I will pelt you with filth,
I will treat you with contempt
and make you a spectacle.
⁷All who see you will flee from you
and say,
'Nineveh is in ruins—who will
mourn for her?'
Where can I find anyone to
comfort you?"

⁸Are you better than Thebes,
situated on the Nile,
with water around her?
The river was her defence,
the waters her wall.
⁹Cush and Egypt were her boundless
strength;
Put and Libya were among her
allies.
¹⁰Yet she was taken captive
and went into exile.

Her infants were dashed to pieces
at the head of every street.
Lots were cast for her nobles,
and all her great men were put in
chains.
¹¹You too will become drunk;
you will go into hiding
and seek refuge from the enemy.

¹²All your fortresses are like fig-trees
with their first ripe fruit;
when they are shaken,
the figs fall into the mouth of the
eater.
¹³Look at your troops—
they are all women!
The gates of your land
are wide open to your enemies;
fire has consumed their bars.

¹⁴Draw water for the siege,
strengthen your defences!
Work the clay,
tread the mortar,
repair the brickwork!
¹⁵There the fire will devour you;
the sword will cut you down
and, like grasshoppers, consume
you.
Multiply like grasshoppers,
multiply like locusts!
¹⁶You have increased the number of
your merchants
till they are more than the stars of
the sky,
but like locusts they strip the land
and then fly away.
¹⁷Your guards are like locusts,
your officials like swarms of locusts
that settle in the walls on a cold
day—
but when the sun appears they fly
away,
and no-one knows where.

¹⁸O king of Assyria, your shepherds
slumber;
your nobles lie down to rest.
Your people are scattered on the
mountains
with no-one to gather them.

19Nothing can heal your wound;
  your injury is fatal.
Everyone who hears the news about
    you
  claps his hands at your fall,
for who has not felt
  your endless cruelty?

NEW TESTAMENT READING
Ephesians 6:1–24

Children and Parents

6 Children, obey your parents in the
  Lord, for this is right. 2"Honour
your father and mother"—which is the
first commandment with a promise—
3"that it may go well with you and that
you may enjoy long life on the earth."

4Fathers, do not exasperate your children; instead, bring them up in the training and instruction of the Lord.

Slaves and Masters

5Slaves, obey your earthly masters with respect and fear, and with sincerity of heart, just as you would obey Christ. 6Obey them not only to win their favour when their eye is on you, but like slaves of Christ, doing the will of God from your heart. 7Serve wholeheartedly, as if you were serving the Lord, not men, 8because you know that the Lord will reward everyone for whatever good he does, whether he is slave or free.

9And masters, treat your slaves in the same way. Do not threaten them, since you know that he who is both their Master and yours is in heaven, and there is no favouritism with him.

The Armour of God

10Finally, be strong in the Lord and in his mighty power. 11Put on the full armour of God so that you can take your stand against the devil's schemes. 12For our struggle is not against flesh and blood, but against the rulers, against the authorities, against the powers of this dark world and against the spiritual forces of evil in the heavenly realms. 13Therefore put on the full armour of God, so that when the day of evil comes, you may be able to stand your ground, and after you have done everything, to stand. 14Stand firm then, with the belt of truth buckled round your waist, with the breastplate of righteousness in place, 15and with your feet fitted with the readiness that comes from the gospel of peace. 16In addition to all this, take up the shield of faith, with which you can extinguish all the flaming arrows of the evil one. 17Take the helmet of salvation and the sword of the Spirit, which is the word of God. 18And pray in the Spirit on all occasions with all kinds of prayers and requests. With this in mind, be alert and always keep on praying for all the saints.

19Pray also for me, that whenever I open my mouth, words may be given me so that I will fearlessly make known the mystery of the gospel, 20for which I am an ambassador in chains. Pray that I may declare it fearlessly, as I should.

Final Greetings

21Tychicus, the dear brother and faithful servant in the Lord, will tell you everything, so that you also may know how I am and what I am doing. 22I am sending him to you for this very purpose, that you may know how we are, and that he may encourage you.

23Peace to the brothers, and love with faith from God the Father and the Lord Jesus Christ. 24Grace to all who love our Lord Jesus Christ with an undying love.

READING FROM PSALMS
Psalm 114:1–8

1When Israel came out of Egypt,
  the house of Jacob from a people
    of foreign tongue,

2Judah became God's sanctuary,
  Israel his dominion.

3The sea looked and fled,
  the Jordan turned back;
4the mountains skipped like rams,
  the hills like lambs.

5Why was it, O sea, that you fled,
  O Jordan, that you turned back,

6you mountains, that you skipped like
  rams,
    you hills, like lambs?

7Tremble, O earth, at the presence of
  the Lord,
    at the presence of the God of
    Jacob,
8who turned the rock into a pool,
  the hard rock into springs of water.

SEPTEMBER 29   DAY 272

OLD TESTAMENT READING
Zephaniah 1:1–3:20

1 The word of the Lord that came to
  Zephaniah son of Cushi, the son of
Gedaliah, the son of Amariah, the son
of Hezekiah, during the reign of Josiah
son of Amon king of Judah:

Warning of Coming Destruction

2"I will sweep away everything
  from the face of the earth,"
                    declares the Lord.
3"I will sweep away both men and
  animals;
  I will sweep away the birds of the
  air
  and the fish of the sea.
The wicked will have only heaps of
  rubble
  when I cut off man from the face of
  the earth,"
                    declares the Lord.

Against Judah

4"I will stretch out my hand against
  Judah
  and against all who live in
  Jerusalem.
I will cut off from this place every
  remnant of Baal,
  the names of the pagan and the
  idolatrous priests—

5those who bow down on the roofs
  to worship the starry host,
  those who bow down and swear by
  the Lord
  and who also swear by Molech,
6those who turn back from following
  the Lord
  and neither seek the Lord nor
  enquire of him.
7Be silent before the Sovereign Lord,
  for the day of the Lord is near.
The Lord has prepared a sacrifice;
  he has consecrated those he has
  invited.
8On the day of the Lord's sacrifice
  I will punish the princes
  and the king's sons
and all those clad
  in foreign clothes.
9On that day I will punish
  all who avoid stepping on the
  threshold,
who fill the temple of their gods
  with violence and deceit.

10"On that day," declares the Lord,
  "a cry will go up from the Fish
  Gate,
  wailing from the New Quarter,
  and a loud crash from the hills.
11Wail, you who live in the market
  district;
  all your merchants will be wiped
  out,

all who trade with silver will be
    ruined.'
[12]At that time I will search Jerusalem
        with lamps
    and punish those who are
        complacent,
    who are like wine left on its dregs,
who think, 'The LORD will do
        nothing,
    either good or bad.'
[13]Their wealth will be plundered,
    their houses demolished.
They will build houses
    but not live in them;
they will plant vineyards
    but not drink the wine.

The Great Day of the LORD

[14]"The great day of the LORD is near—
    near and coming quickly.
Listen! The cry on the day of the
        LORD will be bitter,
    the shouting of the warrior there.
[15]That day will be a day of wrath,
    a day of distress and anguish,
a day of trouble and ruin,
    a day of darkness and gloom,
    a day of clouds and blackness,
[16]a day of trumpet and battle cry
    against the fortified cities
    and against the corner towers.
[17]I will bring distress on the people
    and they will walk like blind men,
    because they have sinned against
        the LORD.
Their blood will be poured out like
        dust
    and their entrails like filth.
[18]Neither their silver nor their gold
    will be able to save them
    on the day of the LORD's wrath.
In the fire of his jealousy
    the whole world will be consumed,
for he will make a sudden end
    of all who live in the earth."

2   Gather together, gather together,
        O shameful nation,
[2]before the appointed time arrives
    and that day sweeps on like chaff,

before the fierce anger of the LORD
    comes upon you,
    before the day of the LORD's wrath
    comes upon you.
[3]Seek the LORD, all you humble of the
        land,
    you who do what he commands.
Seek righteousness, seek humility;
    perhaps you will be sheltered
    on the day of the LORD's anger.

Against Philistia

[4]Gaza will be abandoned
    and Ashkelon left in ruins.
At midday Ashdod will be emptied
    and Ekron uprooted.
[5]Woe to you who live by the sea,
    O Kerethite people;
the word of the LORD is against you,
    O Canaan, land of the Philistines.

"I will destroy you,
    and none will be left."

[6]The land by the sea, where the
        Kerethites dwell,
    will be a place for shepherds and
        sheep pens.
[7]It will belong to the remnant of the
        house of Judah;
    there they will find pasture.
In the evening they will lie down
    in the houses of Ashkelon.
The LORD their God will care for
        them;
    he will restore their fortunes.

Against Moab and Ammon

[8]"I have heard the insults of Moab
    and the taunts of the Ammonites,
who insulted my people
    and made threats against their
        land.
[9]Therefore, as surely as I live,"
    declares the LORD Almighty, the
        God of Israel,

"surely Moab will become like
        Sodom,
    the Ammonites like Gomorrah—
a place of weeds and salt pits,
    a wasteland for ever.

The remnant of my people will
   plunder them;
 the survivors of my nation will
   inherit their land."

[10] This is what they will get in return for
   their pride,
 for insulting and mocking the
   people of the LORD Almighty.
[11] The LORD will be awesome to them
 when he destroys all the gods of the
   land.
 The nations on every shore will
   worship him,
 every one in its own land.

Against Cush

[12] "You too, O Cushites,
 will be slain by my sword."

Against Assyria

[13] He will stretch out his hand against
   the north
 and destroy Assyria,
 leaving Nineveh utterly desolate
 and dry as the desert.
[14] Flocks and herds will lie down there,
 creatures of every kind.
 The desert owl and the screech owl
 will roost on her columns.
 Their calls will echo through the
   windows,
 rubble will be in the doorways,
 the beams of cedar will be exposed.
[15] This is the carefree city
 that lived in safety.
 She said to herself,
 "I am, and there is none besides
   me."
 What a ruin she has become,
 a lair for wild beasts!
 All who pass by her scoff
 and shake their fists.

The Future of Jerusalem

3 Woe to the city of oppressors,
   rebellious and defiled!
[2] She obeys no-one,
 she accepts no correction.

She does not trust in the LORD,
 she does not draw near to her God.
[3] Her officials are roaring lions,
 her rulers are evening wolves,
 who leave nothing for the morning.
[4] Her prophets are arrogant;
 they are treacherous men.
 Her priests profane the sanctuary
 and do violence to the law.
[5] The LORD within her is righteous;
 he does no wrong.
 Morning by morning he dispenses his
   justice,
 and every new day he does not fail,
 yet the unrighteous know no
   shame.

[6] "I have cut off nations;
 their strongholds are demolished.
 I have left their streets deserted,
 with no-one passing through.
 Their cities are destroyed;
 no-one will be left—no-one
   at all.
[7] I said to the city,
 'Surely you will fear me
 and accept correction!'
 Then her dwelling would not be cut
   off,
 nor all my punishments come upon
   her.
 But they were still eager
 to act corruptly in all they did.
[8] Therefore wait for me," declares the
   LORD,
 "for the day I will stand up to
   testify.
 I have decided to assemble the
   nations,
 to gather the kingdoms
 and to pour out my wrath on them—
 all my fierce anger.
 The whole world will be consumed
 by the fire of my jealous anger.

[9] "Then will I purify the lips of the
   peoples,
 that all of them may call on the
   name of the LORD
 and serve him shoulder to
   shoulder.

¹⁰From beyond the rivers of Cush
my worshippers, my scattered
people,
will bring me offerings.
¹¹On that day you will not be put to
shame
for all the wrongs you have done to
me,
because I will remove from this city
those who rejoice in their pride.
Never again will you be haughty
on my holy hill.
¹²But I will leave within you
the meek and humble,
who trust in the name of the LORD.
¹³The remnant of Israel will do no
wrong;
they will speak no lies,
nor will deceit be found in their
mouths.
They will eat and lie down
and no-one will make them
afraid."

¹⁴Sing, O Daughter of Zion;
shout aloud, O Israel!
Be glad and rejoice with all your
heart,
O Daughter of Jerusalem!
¹⁵The LORD has taken away your
punishment,
he has turned back your enemy.
The LORD, the King of Israel, is with
you;
never again will you fear any harm.
¹⁶On that day they will say to
Jerusalem,

"Do not fear, O Zion;
do not let your hands hang limp.
¹⁷The LORD your God is with you,
he is mighty to save.
He will take great delight in you,
he will quiet you with his love,
he will rejoice over you with
singing."

¹⁸"The sorrows for the appointed feasts
I will remove from you;
they are a burden and a reproach
to you.
¹⁹At that time I will deal
with all who oppressed you;

I will rescue the lame
and gather those who have been
scattered.
I will give them praise and honour
in every land where they were put
to shame.
²⁰At that time I will gather you;
at that time I will bring you home.
I will give you honour and praise
among all the peoples of the earth
when I restore your fortunes
before your very eyes,"
says the LORD.

NEW TESTAMENT READING
Philippians 1:1–26

1 Paul and Timothy, servants of
Christ Jesus,

To all the saints in Christ Jesus at
Philippi, together with the overseers
and deacons:

²Grace and peace to you from God
our Father and the Lord Jesus Christ.

Thanksgiving and Prayer

³I thank my God every time I remember you. ⁴In all my prayers for all of you,
I always pray with joy ⁵because of your
partnership in the gospel from the first
day until now, ⁶being confident of this,
that he who began a good work in you
will carry it on to completion until the
day of Christ Jesus.

⁷It is right for me to feel this way
about all of you, since I have you in my
heart; for whether I am in chains or
defending and confirming the gospel, all
of you share in God's grace with me.
⁸God can testify how I long for all of you
with the affection of Christ Jesus.

⁹And this is my prayer: that your love
may abound more and more in knowledge and depth of insight, ¹⁰so that you
may be able to discern what is best and
may be pure and blameless until the day
of Christ, ¹¹filled with the fruit of righteousness that comes through Jesus
Christ—to the glory and praise of God.

Paul's Chains Advance the Gospel

12Now I want you to know, brothers, that what has happened to me has really served to advance the gospel. 13As a result, it has become clear throughout the whole palace guard and to everyone else that I am in chains for Christ. 14Because of my chains, most of the brothers in the Lord have been encouraged to speak the word of God more courageously and fearlessly.

15It is true that some preach Christ out of envy and rivalry, but others out of goodwill. 16The latter do so in love, knowing that I am put here for the defence of the gospel. 17The former preach Christ out of selfish ambition, not sincerely, supposing that they can stir up trouble for me while I am in chains. 18But what does it matter? The important thing is that in every way, whether from false motives or true, Christ is preached. And because of this I rejoice.

Yes, and I will continue to rejoice, 19for I know that through your prayers and the help given by the Spirit of Jesus Christ, what has happened to me will turn out for my deliverance. 20I eagerly expect and hope that I will in no way be ashamed, but will have sufficient courage so that now as always Christ will be exalted in my body, whether by life or by death. 21For to me, to live is Christ and to die is gain. 22If I am to go on living in the body, this will mean fruitful labour for me. Yet what shall I choose? I do not know! 23I am torn between the two: I desire to depart and be with Christ, which is better by far; 24but it is more necessary for you that I remain in the body. 25Convinced of this, I know that I will remain, and I will continue with all of you for your progress and joy in the faith, 26so that through my being with you again your joy in Christ Jesus will overflow on account of me.

READING FROM PROVERBS
Proverbs 23:29–24:4

29Who has woe? Who has sorrow?
　　Who has strife? Who has
　　complaints?
　　Who has needless bruises? Who
　　has bloodshot eyes?
30Those who linger over wine,
　　who go to sample bowls of mixed
　　wine.
31Do not gaze at wine when it is red,
　　when it sparkles in the cup,
　　when it goes down smoothly!
32In the end it bites like a snake
　　and poisons like a viper.
33Your eyes will see strange sights
　　and your mind imagine confusing
　　things.
34You will be like one sleeping on the
　　high seas,
　　lying on top of the rigging.
35"They hit me," you will say, "but I'm
　　not hurt!
　　They beat me, but I don't feel it!
　　When will I wake up
　　so I can find another drink?"

24 Do not envy wicked men,
　　do not desire their company;
2for their hearts plot violence,
　　and their lips talk about making
　　trouble.

3By wisdom a house is built,
　　and through understanding it is
　　established;
4through knowledge its rooms are
　　filled
　　with rare and beautiful treasures.

OLD TESTAMENT READING
Jeremiah 1:1–2:30

1 The words of Jeremiah son of Hilkiah, one of the priests at Anathoth in the territory of Benjamin. ²The word of the LORD came to him in the thirteenth year of the reign of Josiah son of Amon king of Judah, ³and through the reign of Jehoiakim son of Josiah king of Judah, down to the fifth month of the eleventh year of Zedekiah son of Josiah king of Judah, when the people of Jerusalem went into exile.

The Call of Jeremiah

⁴The word of the LORD came to me, saying,

⁵"Before I formed you in the womb I knew you,
before you were born I set you apart;
I appointed you as a prophet to the nations."

⁶"Ah, Sovereign LORD," I said, "I do not know how to speak; I am only a child."

⁷But the LORD said to me, "Do not say, 'I am only a child.' You must go to everyone I send you to and say whatever I command you. ⁸Do not be afraid of them, for I am with you and will rescue you," declares the LORD.

⁹Then the LORD reached out his hand and touched my mouth and said to me, "Now, I have put my words in your mouth. ¹⁰See, today I appoint you over nations and kingdoms to uproot and tear down, to destroy and overthrow, to build and to plant."

¹¹The word of the LORD came to me: "What do you see, Jeremiah?"

"I see the branch of an almond tree," I replied.

¹²The LORD said to me, "You have seen correctly, for I am watching to see that my word is fulfilled."

¹³The word of the LORD came to me again: "What do you see?"

"I see a boiling pot, tilting away from the north," I answered.

¹⁴The LORD said to me, "From the north disaster will be poured out on all who live in the land. ¹⁵I am about to summon all the peoples of the northern kingdoms," declares the LORD.

"Their kings will come and set up their thrones
in the entrance of the gates of Jerusalem;
they will come against all her surrounding walls
and against all the towns of Judah.
¹⁶I will pronounce my judgments on my people
because of their wickedness in forsaking me,
in burning incense to other gods
and in worshipping what their hands have made.

¹⁷"Get yourself ready! Stand up and say to them whatever I command you. Do not be terrified by them, or I will terrify you before them. ¹⁸Today I have made you a fortified city, an iron pillar and a bronze wall to stand against the whole land—against the kings of Judah, its officials, its priests and the people of the land. ¹⁹They will fight against you but will not overcome you, for I am with you and will rescue you," declares the LORD.

Israel Forsakes God

2 The word of the LORD came to me: ²"Go and proclaim in the hearing of Jerusalem:

"'I remember the devotion of your youth,
how as a bride you loved me

and followed me through the desert,
    through a land not sown.
³Israel was holy to the LORD,
    the firstfruits of his harvest;
all who devoured her were held
        guilty,
    and disaster overtook them,'"
                    declares the LORD.

⁴Hear the word of the LORD, O house
        of Jacob,
    all you clans of the house of Israel.

⁵This is what the LORD says:

"What fault did your fathers find in
        me,
    that they strayed so far from me?
They followed worthless idols
    and became worthless themselves.
⁶They did not ask, 'Where is the
        LORD,
    who brought us up out of Egypt
and led us through the barren
        wilderness,
    through a land of deserts and rifts,
a land of drought and darkness,
    a land where no-one travels and
        no-one lives?'
⁷I brought you into a fertile land
    to eat its fruit and rich produce.
But you came and defiled my land
    and made my inheritance
        detestable.
⁸The priests did not ask,
    'Where is the LORD?'
Those who deal with the law did not
        know me;
    the leaders rebelled against me.
The prophets prophesied by Baal,
    following worthless idols.

⁹"Therefore I bring charges against
        you again,"
                    declares the LORD.
"And I will bring charges against
    your children's children.
¹⁰Cross over to the coasts of Kittim and
        look,
    send to Kedar and observe closely;
    see if there has ever been anything
        like this:

¹¹Has a nation ever changed its gods?
    (Yet they are not gods at all.)
But my people have exchanged their
        Glory
    for worthless idols.
¹²Be appalled at this, O heavens,
    and shudder with great horror,"
                    declares the LORD.
¹³"My people have committed two
        sins:
They have forsaken me,
    the spring of living water,
and have dug their own cisterns,
    broken cisterns that cannot hold
        water.
¹⁴Is Israel a servant, a slave by birth?
    Why then has he become plunder?
¹⁵Lions have roared;
    they have growled at him.
They have laid waste his land;
    his towns are burned and deserted.
¹⁶Also, the men of Memphis and
        Tahpanhes
    have shaved the crown of your
        head.
¹⁷Have you not brought this on
        yourselves
    by forsaking the LORD your God
        when he led you in the way?
¹⁸Now why go to Egypt
    to drink water from the Shihor?
And why go to Assyria
    to drink water from the River?
¹⁹Your wickedness will punish you;
    your backsliding will rebuke you.
Consider then and realise
    how evil and bitter it is for you
when you forsake the LORD your God
    and have no awe of me,"
                    declares the Lord,
                        the LORD Almighty.

²⁰"Long ago you broke off your yoke
    and tore off your bonds;
    you said, 'I will not serve you!'
Indeed, on every high hill
    and under every spreading tree
    you lay down as a prostitute.
²¹I had planted you like a choice vine
    of sound and reliable stock.
How then did you turn against me
    into a corrupt, wild vine?

22Although you wash yourself with
    soda
  and use an abundance of soap,
  the stain of your guilt is still before
    me,"
      declares the Sovereign LORD.
23"How can you say, 'I am not defiled;
  I have not run after the Baals'?
See how you behaved in the valley;
  consider what you have done.
You are a swift she-camel
  running here and there,
24a wild donkey accustomed to the
    desert,
  sniffing the wind in her craving—
  in her heat who can restrain her?
Any males that pursue her need not
  tire themselves;
  at mating time they will find her.
25Do not run until your feet are bare
  and your throat is dry.
But you said, 'It's no use!
  I love foreign gods,
  and I must go after them.'

26"As a thief is disgraced when he is
    caught,
  so the house of Israel is
    disgraced—
they, their kings and their officials,
  their priests and their prophets.
27They say to wood, 'You are my
    father,'
  and to stone, 'You gave me birth.'
They have turned their backs to me
  and not their faces;
yet when they are in trouble, they
  say,
  'Come and save us!'
28Where then are the gods you made
  for yourselves?
  Let them come if they can save you
  when you are in trouble!
For you have as many gods
  as you have towns, O Judah.

29"Why do you bring charges against
    me?
  You have all rebelled against me,"
      declares the LORD.
30"In vain I punished your people;
  they did not respond to correction.

Your sword has devoured your
    prophets
  like a ravening lion.

NEW TESTAMENT READING
Philippians 1:27–2:11

27Whatever happens, conduct yourselves in a manner worthy of the gospel
of Christ. Then, whether I come and see
you or only hear about you in my absence, I will know that you stand firm in
one spirit, contending as one man for
the faith of the gospel 28without being
frightened in any way by those who
oppose you. This is a sign to them that
they will be destroyed, but that you will
be saved—and that by God. 29For it has
been granted to you on behalf of Christ
not only to believe on him, but also to
suffer for him, 30since you are going
through the same struggle you saw I
had, and now hear that I still have.

Imitating Christ's Humility

2 If you have any encouragement
  from being united with Christ, if
any comfort from his love, if any fellowship with the Spirit, if any tenderness and compassion, 2then make my
joy complete by being like-minded,
having the same love, being one in spirit
and purpose. 3Do nothing out of selfish
ambition or vain conceit, but in humility
consider others better than yourselves.
4Each of you should look not only to
your own interests, but also to the interests of others.

5Your attitude should be the same as
that of Christ Jesus:

6Who, being in very nature God,
  did not consider equality with God
    something to be grasped,
7but made himself nothing,
  taking the very nature of a servant,
  being made in human likeness.
8And being found in appearance as a
    man,

he humbled himself
and became obedient to
death—even death on a cross!
⁹Therefore God exalted him to the
highest place
and gave him the name that is
above every name,
¹⁰that at the name of Jesus every knee
should bow,
in heaven and on earth and under
the earth,
¹¹and every tongue confess that Jesus
Christ is Lord,
to the glory of God the Father.

READING FROM PSALMS
Psalm 115:1–11

¹Not to us, O LORD, not to us
but to your name be the glory,
because of your love and
faithfulness.

²Why do the nations say,
"Where is their God?"

³Our God is in heaven;
he does whatever pleases him.
⁴But their idols are silver and gold,
made by the hands of men.
⁵They have mouths, but cannot speak,
eyes, but they cannot see;
⁶they have ears, but cannot hear,
noses, but they cannot smell;
⁷they have hands, but cannot feel,
feet, but they cannot walk;
nor can they utter a sound with
their throats.
⁸Those who make them will be like
them,
and so will all who trust in them.

⁹O house of Israel, trust in the
LORD—
he is their help and shield.
¹⁰O house of Aaron, trust in the
LORD—
he is their help and shield.
¹¹You who fear him, trust in the
LORD—
he is their help and shield.

OCTOBER 1   DAY 274

OLD TESTAMENT READING
Jeremiah 2:31–4:9

³¹"You of this generation, consider
the word of the LORD:

"Have I been a desert to Israel
or a land of great darkness?
Why do my people say, 'We are free
to roam;
we will come to you no more'?
³²Does a maiden forget her jewellery,
a bride her wedding ornaments?
Yet my people have forgotten me,
days without number.
³³How skilled you are at pursuing love!
Even the worst of women can learn
from your ways.

³⁴On your clothes men find
the lifeblood of the innocent poor,
though you did not catch them
breaking in.
Yet in spite of all this
³⁵ you say, 'I am innocent;
he is not angry with me.'
But I will pass judgment on you
because you say, 'I have not
sinned.'
³⁶Why do you go about so much,
changing your ways?
You will be disappointed by Egypt
as you were by Assyria.
³⁷You will also leave that place
with your hands on your head,
for the LORD has rejected those you
trust;
you will not be helped by them.

3 "If a man divorces his wife
and she leaves him and marries
another man,
should he return to her again?
Would not the land be completely
defiled?
But you have lived as a prostitute
with many lovers—
would you now return to me?"
declares the LORD.
²"Look up to the barren heights and
see.
Is there any place where you have
not been ravished?
By the roadside you sat waiting for
lovers,
sat like a nomad in the desert.
You have defiled the land
with your prostitution and
wickedness.
³Therefore the showers have been
withheld,
and no spring rains have fallen.
Yet you have the brazen look of a
prostitute;
you refuse to blush with shame.
⁴Have you not just called to me:
'My Father, my friend from my
youth,
⁵will you always be angry?
Will your wrath continue for ever?'
This is how you talk,
but you do all the evil you can."

Unfaithful Israel

⁶During the reign of King Josiah, the
LORD said to me, "Have you seen what
faithless Israel has done? She has gone
up on every high hill and under every
spreading tree and has committed adultery there. ⁷I thought that after she had
done all this she would return to me but
she did not, and her unfaithful sister
Judah saw it. ⁸I gave faithless Israel her
certificate of divorce and sent her away
because of all her adulteries. Yet I saw
that her unfaithful sister Judah had no
fear; she also went out and committed
adultery. ⁹Because Israel's immorality
mattered so little to her, she defiled the
land and committed adultery with stone

and wood. ¹⁰In spite of all this, her
unfaithful sister Judah did not return to
me with all her heart, but only in pretence," declares the LORD.

¹¹The LORD said to me, "Faithless
Israel is more righteous than unfaithful
Judah. ¹²Go, proclaim this message
towards the north:

"'Return, faithless Israel,' declares
the LORD,
'I will frown on you no longer,
for I am merciful,' declares the
LORD,
'I will not be angry for ever.
¹³Only acknowledge your guilt—
you have rebelled against the LORD
your God,
you have scattered your favours to
foreign gods
under every spreading tree,
and have not obeyed me,'"
declares the LORD.

¹⁴"Return, faithless people," declares the LORD, "for I am your husband. I will choose you—one from a
town and two from a clan—and bring
you to Zion. ¹⁵Then I will give you
shepherds after my own heart, who will
lead you with knowledge and understanding. ¹⁶In those days, when your
numbers have increased greatly in the
land," declares the LORD, "men will no
longer say, 'The ark of the covenant of
the LORD.' It will never enter their
minds or be remembered; it will not be
missed, nor will another one be made.
¹⁷At that time they will call Jerusalem
The Throne of the LORD, and all nations
will gather in Jerusalem to honour the
name of the LORD. No longer will they
follow the stubbornness of their evil
hearts. ¹⁸In those days the house of
Judah will join the house of Israel, and
together they will come from a northern
land to the land I gave your forefathers
as an inheritance.

¹⁹"I myself said,

"'How gladly would I treat you like
sons

and give you a desirable land,
   the most beautiful inheritance of
     any nation.'
I thought you would call me 'Father'
   and not turn away from following
     me.
20But like a woman unfaithful to her
   husband,
  so you have been unfaithful to me,
   O house of Israel,"
              declares the LORD.

21A cry is heard on the barren heights,
   the weeping and pleading of the
     people of Israel,
because they have perverted their
   ways
  and have forgotten the LORD their
   God.

22"Return, faithless people;
   I will cure you of backsliding."

"Yes, we will come to you,
   for you are the LORD our God.
23Surely the ⌞idolatrous⌟ commotion on
   the hills
  and mountains is a deception;
surely in the LORD our God
   is the salvation of Israel.
24From our youth shameful gods have
   consumed
  the fruits of our fathers' labour—
   their flocks and herds,
   their sons and daughters.
25Let us lie down in our shame,
   and let our disgrace cover us.
We have sinned against the LORD our
   God,
  both we and our fathers;
from our youth till this day
  we have not obeyed the LORD our
   God."

4 "If you will return, O Israel,
   return to me,"
              declares the LORD.
"If you put your detestable idols out
   of my sight
  and no longer go astray,
2and if in a truthful, just and righteous
   way

you swear, 'As surely as the LORD
   lives,'
then the nations will be blessed by
   him
  and in him they will glory."

3This is what the LORD says to the
men of Judah and to Jerusalem:

"Break up your unploughed ground
   and do not sow among thorns.
4Circumcise yourselves to the LORD,
   circumcise your hearts,
  you men of Judah and people of
   Jerusalem,
or my wrath will break out and burn
   like fire
  because of the evil you have
   done—
  burn with no-one to quench it.

Disaster From the North

5"Announce in Judah and proclaim in
   Jerusalem and say:
  'Sound the trumpet throughout the
   land!'
  Cry aloud and say:
  'Gather together!
  Let us flee to the fortified cities!'
6Raise the signal to go to Zion!
  Flee for safety without delay!
For I am bringing disaster from the
   north,
  even terrible destruction."

7A lion has come out of his lair;
  a destroyer of nations has set out.
He has left his place
  to lay waste your land.
Your towns will lie in ruins
  without inhabitant.
8So put on sackcloth,
  lament and wail,
for the fierce anger of the LORD
  has not turned away from us.

9"In that day," declares the LORD,
  "the king and the officials will lose
   heart,
the priests will be horrified,
  and the prophets will be appalled."

NEW TESTAMENT READING
Philippians 2:12–30

Shining as Stars

12Therefore, my dear friends, as you have always obeyed—not only in my presence, but now much more in my absence—continue to work out your salvation with fear and trembling, 13for it is God who works in you to will and to act according to his good purpose.

14Do everything without complaining or arguing, 15so that you may become blameless and pure, children of God without fault in a crooked and depraved generation, in which you shine like stars in the universe 16as you hold out the word of life—in order that I may boast on the day of Christ that I did not run or labour for nothing. 17But even if I am being poured out like a drink offering on the sacrifice and service coming from your faith, I am glad and rejoice with all of you. 18So you too should be glad and rejoice with me.

Timothy and Epaphroditus

19I hope in the Lord Jesus to send Timothy to you soon, that I also may be cheered when I receive news about you. 20I have no-one else like him, who takes a genuine interest in your welfare. 21For everyone looks out for his own interests, not those of Jesus Christ. 22But you know that Timothy has proved himself, because as a son with his father he has served with me in the work of the gospel. 23I hope, therefore, to send him as soon as I see how things go with me. 24And I am confident in the Lord that I myself will come soon.

25But I think it is necessary to send back to you Epaphroditus, my brother, fellow-worker and fellow-soldier, who is also your messenger, whom you sent to take care of my needs. 26For he longs for all of you and is distressed because you heard he was ill. 27Indeed he was ill, and almost died. But God had mercy on him, and not on him only but also on me, to spare me sorrow upon sorrow. 28Therefore I am all the more eager to send him, so that when you see him again you may be glad and I may be less anxiety. 29Welcome him in the Lord with great joy, and honour men like him, 30because he almost died for the work of Christ, risking his life to make up for the help you could not give me.

READING FROM PSALMS
Psalm 115:12–18

12The LORD remembers us and will bless us:
   He will bless the house of Israel,
   he will bless the house of Aaron,
13he will bless those who fear the LORD—
   small and great alike.

14May the LORD make you increase,
   both you and your children.
15May you be blessed by the LORD,
   the Maker of heaven and earth.

16The highest heavens belong to the LORD,
   but the earth he has given to man.
17It is not the dead who praise the LORD,
   those who go down to silence;
18it is we who extol the LORD,
   both now and for evermore.

   Praise the LORD.

OLD TESTAMENT READING
Jeremiah 4:10–5:31

¹⁰Then I said, "Ah, Sovereign Lord, how completely you have deceived this people and Jerusalem by saying, 'You will have peace,' when the sword is at our throats."

¹¹At that time this people and Jerusalem will be told, "A scorching wind from the barren heights in the desert blows towards my people, but not to winnow or cleanse; ¹²a wind too strong for that comes from me. Now I pronounce my judgments against them."

¹³Look! He advances like the clouds,
      his chariots come like a whirlwind,
his horses are swifter than eagles.
      Woe to us! We are ruined!
¹⁴O Jerusalem, wash the evil from your
         heart and be saved.
      How long will you harbour wicked
         thoughts?
¹⁵A voice is announcing from Dan,
      proclaiming disaster from the hills
         of Ephraim.
¹⁶"Tell this to the nations,
      proclaim it to Jerusalem:
   'A besieging army is coming from a
         distant land,
      raising a war cry against the cities
         of Judah.
¹⁷They surround her like men guarding
         a field,
      because she has rebelled against
         me,'"
                        declares the Lord.
¹⁸"Your own conduct and actions
      have brought this upon you.
   This is your punishment.
      How bitter it is!
      How it pierces to the heart!"

¹⁹Oh, my anguish, my anguish!
      I writhe in pain.
   Oh, the agony of my heart!
      My heart pounds within me,
      I cannot keep silent.

For I have heard the sound of the
         trumpet;
      I have heard the battle cry.
²⁰Disaster follows disaster;
      the whole land lies in ruins.
   In an instant my tents are destroyed,
      my shelter in a moment.
²¹How long must I see the battle
         standard
      and hear the sound of the trumpet?

²²"My people are fools;
      they do not know me.
   They are senseless children;
      they have no understanding.
   They are skilled in doing evil;
      they know not how to do good."

²³I looked at the earth,
      and it was formless and empty;
   and at the heavens,
      and their light was gone.
²⁴I looked at the mountains,
      and they were quaking;
   all the hills were swaying.
²⁵I looked, and there were no people;
      every bird in the sky had flown
         away.
²⁶I looked, and the fruitful land was a
         desert;
      all its towns lay in ruins
   before the Lord, before his fierce
         anger.

²⁷This is what the Lord says:

   "The whole land will be ruined,
      though I will not destroy it
         completely.
²⁸Therefore the earth will mourn
      and the heavens above grow dark,
   because I have spoken and will not
         relent,
      I have decided and will not turn
         back."

²⁹At the sound of horsemen and
         archers
      every town takes to flight.

Some go into the thickets;
    some climb up among the rocks.
All the towns are deserted;
    no-one lives in them.

30What are you doing, O devastated
      one?
    Why dress yourself in scarlet
      and put on jewels of gold?
    Why shade your eyes with paint?
      You adorn yourself in vain.
Your lovers despise you;
    they seek your life.

31I hear a cry as of a woman in labour,
    a groan as of one bearing her first
      child—
the cry of the Daughter of Zion
      gasping for breath,
    stretching out her hands and
      saying,
"Alas! I am fainting;
    my life is given over to murderers."

Not One Is Upright

5   "Go up and down the streets of
    Jerusalem,
    look around and consider,
    search through her squares.
If you can find but one person
    who deals honestly and seeks the
      truth,
    I will forgive this city.
2Although they say, 'As surely as the
      Lord lives,'
    still they are swearing falsely."

3O Lord, do not your eyes look for
      truth?
    You struck them, but they felt no
      pain;
    you crushed them but they refused
      correction.
They made their faces harder than
      stone
    and refused to repent.
4I thought, "These are only the poor;
    they are foolish,
for they do not know the way of the
      Lord,
    the requirements of their God.

5So I will go to the leaders
    and speak to them;
surely they know the way of the
      Lord,
    the requirements of their God."
But with one accord they too had
      broken off the yoke
    and torn off the bonds.
6Therefore a lion from the forest will
      attack them,
    a wolf from the desert will ravage
      them,
a leopard will lie in wait near their
      towns
    to tear to pieces any who venture
      out,
for their rebellion is great
    and their backslidings many.

7"Why should I forgive you?
    Your children have forsaken me
    and sworn by gods that are not
      gods.
I supplied all their needs,
    yet they committed adultery
    and thronged to the houses of
      prostitutes.
8They are well-fed, lusty stallions,
    each neighing for another man's
      wife.
9Should I not punish them for this?"
    declares the Lord.
"Should I not avenge myself
    on such a nation as this?

10"Go through her vineyards and
      ravage them,
    but do not destroy them
      completely.
Strip off her branches,
    for these people do not belong to
      the Lord.
11The house of Israel and the house of
      Judah
    have been utterly unfaithful to
      me,"
             declares the Lord.

12They have lied about the Lord;
    they said, "He will do nothing!
No harm will come to us;
    we will never see sword or famine.

¹³The prophets are but wind
  and the word is not in them;
so let what they say be done to
  them."

¹⁴Therefore this is what the LORD
God Almighty says:

"Because the people have spoken
  these words,
  I will make my words in your
  mouth a fire
and these people the wood it
  consumes.
¹⁵O house of Israel," declares the
  LORD,
  "I am bringing a distant nation
  against you—
an ancient and enduring nation,
  a people whose language you do
  not know,
  whose speech you do not
  understand.
¹⁶Their quivers are like an open grave;
  all of them are mighty warriors.
¹⁷They will devour your harvests and
  food,
  devour your sons and daughters;
they will devour your flocks and
  herds,
  devour your vines and fig-trees.
With the sword they will destroy
  the fortified cities in which you
  trust.

¹⁸"Yet even in those days," declares
the LORD, "I will not destroy you completely. ¹⁹And when the people ask,
'Why has the LORD our God done all
this to us?' you will tell them, 'As you
have forsaken me and served foreign
gods in your own land, so now you will
serve foreigners in a land not your own.'

²⁰"Announce this to the house of Jacob
  and proclaim it in Judah:
²¹Hear this, you foolish and senseless
  people,
  who have eyes but do not see,
  who have ears but do not hear:
²²Should you not fear me?" declares
  the LORD.

"Should you not tremble in my
  presence?
I made the sand a boundary for the
  sea,
  an everlasting barrier it cannot
  cross.
The waves may roll, but they cannot
  prevail;
  they may roar, but they cannot
  cross it.
²³But these people have stubborn and
  rebellious hearts;
  they have turned aside and gone
  away.
²⁴They do not say to themselves,
  'Let us fear the LORD our God,
who gives autumn and spring rains in
  season,
  who assures us of the regular weeks
  of harvest.'
²⁵Your wrongdoings have kept these
  away;
  your sins have deprived you of
  good.

²⁶"Among my people are wicked men
  who lie in wait like men who snare
  birds
  and like those who set traps to
  catch men.
²⁷Like cages full of birds,
  their houses are full of deceit;
they have become rich and powerful
²⁸ and have grown fat and sleek.
Their evil deeds have no limit;
  they do not plead the case of the
  fatherless to win it,
  they do not defend the rights of the
  poor.
²⁹Should I not punish them for this?"
  declares the LORD.
"Should I not avenge myself
  on such a nation as this?

³⁰"A horrible and shocking thing
  has happened in the land:
³¹The prophets prophesy lies,
  the priests rule by their own
  authority,
and my people love it this way.
  But what will you do in the end?

NEW TESTAMENT READING
Philippians 3:1–4:1

No Confidence in the Flesh

3 Finally, my brothers, rejoice in the Lord! It is no trouble for me to write the same things to you again, and it is a safeguard for you.

²Watch out for those dogs, those men who do evil, those mutilators of the flesh. ³For it is we who are the circumcision, we who worship by the Spirit of God, who glory in Christ Jesus, and who put no confidence in the flesh—⁴though I myself have reasons for such confidence.

If anyone else thinks he has reasons to put confidence in the flesh, I have more: ⁵circumcised on the eighth day, of the people of Israel, of the tribe of Benjamin, a Hebrew of Hebrews; in regard to the law, a Pharisee; ⁶as for zeal, persecuting the church; as for legalistic righteousness, faultless.

⁷But whatever was to my profit I now consider loss for the sake of Christ. ⁸What is more, I consider everything a loss compared to the surpassing greatness of knowing Christ Jesus my Lord, for whose sake I have lost all things. I consider them rubbish, that I may gain Christ ⁹and be found in him, not having a righteousness of my own that comes from the law, but that which is through faith in Christ—the righteousness that comes from God and is by faith. ¹⁰I want to know Christ and the power of his resurrection and the fellowship of sharing in his sufferings, becoming like him in his death, ¹¹and so, somehow, to attain to the resurrection from the dead.

Pressing on Towards the Goal

¹²Not that I have already obtained all this, or have already been made perfect, but I press on to take hold of that for which Christ Jesus took hold of me. ¹³Brothers, I do not consider myself yet to have taken hold of it. But one thing I do: Forgetting what is behind and straining towards what is ahead, ¹⁴I press on towards the goal to win the prize for which God has called me heavenwards in Christ Jesus.

¹⁵All of us who are mature should take such a view of things. And if on some point you think differently, that too God will make clear to you. ¹⁶Only let us live up to what we have already attained.

¹⁷Join with others in following my example, brothers, and take note of those who live according to the pattern we gave you. ¹⁸For, as I have often told you before and now say again even with tears, many live as enemies of the cross of Christ. ¹⁹Their destiny is destruction, their god is their stomach, and their glory is in their shame. Their mind is on earthly things. ²⁰But our citizenship is in heaven. And we eagerly await a Saviour from there, the Lord Jesus Christ, ²¹who, by the power that enables him to bring everything under his control, will transform our lowly bodies so that they will be like his glorious body.

4 Therefore, my brothers, you whom I love and long for, my joy and crown, that is how you should stand firm in the Lord, dear friends!

READING FROM PSALMS
Psalm 116:1–11

¹I love the LORD, for he heard my voice;
  he heard my cry for mercy.
²Because he turned his ear to me,
  I will call on him as long as I live.

³The cords of death entangled me,
  the anguish of the grave came upon me;
  I was overcome by trouble and sorrow.
⁴Then I called on the name of the LORD:
  "O LORD, save me!"

⁵The LORD is gracious and righteous;
　　our God is full of compassion.
⁶The LORD protects the
　　simple-hearted;
　　when I was in great need, he saved
　　　me.

⁷Be at rest once more, O my soul,
　　for the LORD has been good to you.

⁸For you, O LORD, have delivered my
　　soul from death,
　　my eyes from tears,
　　my feet from stumbling,
⁹that I may walk before the LORD
　　in the land of the living.
¹⁰I believed; therefore I said,
　　"I am greatly afflicted."
¹¹And in my dismay I said,
　　"All men are liars."

OCTOBER 3

OLD TESTAMENT READING
Jeremiah 6:1–7:29

Jerusalem Under Siege

6 "Flee for safety, people of
　　Benjamin!
　　Flee from Jerusalem!
　Sound the trumpet in Tekoa!
　　Raise the signal over Beth
　　　Hakkerem!
　For disaster looms out of the north,
　　even terrible destruction.
²I will destroy the Daughter of Zion,
　　so beautiful and delicate.
³Shepherds with their flocks will come
　　against her;
　　they will pitch their tents round
　　　her,
　　each tending his own portion."

⁴"Prepare for battle against her!
　　Arise, let us attack at noon!
　But, alas, the daylight is fading,
　　and the shadows of evening grow
　　　long.
⁵So arise, let us attack at night
　　and destroy her fortresses!"

⁶This is what the LORD Almighty
says:

　"Cut down the trees
　　and build siege ramps against
　　　Jerusalem.

This city must be punished;
　it is filled with oppression.
⁷As a well pours out its water,
　so she pours out her wickedness.
Violence and destruction resound in
　　her;
　her sickness and wounds are ever
　　　before me.
⁸Take warning, O Jerusalem,
　or I will turn away from you
and make your land desolate
　so that no-one can live in it."

⁹This is what the LORD Almighty
says:

"Let them glean the remnant of
　　Israel
　as thoroughly as a vine;
pass your hand over the branches
　　again,
　like one gathering grapes."

¹⁰To whom can I speak and give
　　warning?
　Who will listen to me?
Their ears are closed
　so that they cannot hear.
The word of the LORD is offensive to
　　them;
　they find no pleasure in it.
¹¹But I am full of the wrath of the
　　LORD,
　and I cannot hold it in.

"Pour it out on the children in the
    street
    and on the young men gathered
        together;
both husband and wife will be caught
    in it,
    and the old, those weighed down
        with years.
¹²Their houses will be turned over to
        others,
    together with their fields and their
        wives,
    when I stretch out my hand
        against those who live in the land,"
                        declares the LORD.
¹³"From the least to the greatest,
    all are greedy for gain;
prophets and priests alike,
    all practise deceit.
¹⁴They dress the wound of my people
    as though it were not serious.
'Peace, peace,' they say,
    when there is no peace.
¹⁵Are they ashamed of their loathsome
        conduct?
    No, they have no shame at all;
    they do not even know how to
        blush.
So they will fall among the fallen;
    they will be brought down when I
        punish them,"
                        says the LORD.

¹⁶This is what the LORD says:

"Stand at the crossroads and look;
    ask for the ancient paths,
ask where the good way is, and walk
        in it,
    and you will find rest for your
        souls.
    But you said, 'We will not walk in
        it.'
¹⁷I appointed watchmen over you and
        said,
    'Listen to the sound of the
        trumpet!'
    But you said, 'We will not listen.'
¹⁸Therefore hear, O nations;
    observe, O witnesses,
    what will happen to them.
¹⁹Hear, O earth:

I am bringing disaster on this people,
    the fruit of their schemes,
because they have not listened to my
        words
    and have rejected my law.
²⁰What do I care about incense from
        Sheba
    or sweet calamus from a distant
        land?
Your burnt offerings are not
        acceptable;
    your sacrifices do not please me."

²¹Therefore this is what the LORD
says:

"I will put obstacles before this
        people.
    Fathers and sons alike will stumble
        over them;
    neighbours and friends will
        perish."

²²This is what the LORD says:

"Look, an army is coming
    from the land of the north;
a great nation is being stirred up
    from the ends of the earth.
²³They are armed with bow and spear;
    they are cruel and show no mercy.
They sound like the roaring sea
    as they ride on their horses;
they come like men in battle
        formation
    to attack you, O Daughter of
        Zion."

²⁴We have heard reports about them,
    and our hands hang limp.
Anguish has gripped us,
    pain like that of a woman in
        labour.
²⁵Do not go out to the fields
    or walk on the roads,
for the enemy has a sword,
    and there is terror on every side.
²⁶O my people, put on sackcloth
    and roll in ashes;
mourn with bitter wailing
    as for an only son,
for suddenly the destroyer
    will come upon us.

27"I have made you a tester of metals
    and my people the ore,
that you may observe
    and test their ways.
28They are all hardened rebels,
    going about to slander.
They are bronze and iron;
    they all act corruptly.
29The bellows blow fiercely
    to burn away the lead with fire,
    but the refining goes on in vain;
        the wicked are not purged out.
30They are called rejected silver,
    because the LORD has rejected
        them."

False Religion Worthless

7 This is the word that came to Jeremiah from the LORD: 2"Stand at the gate of the LORD's house and there proclaim this message:

"'Hear the word of the LORD, all you people of Judah who come through these gates to worship the LORD. 3This is what the LORD Almighty, the God of Israel, says: Reform your ways and your actions, and I will let you live in this place. 4Do not trust in deceptive words and say, "This is the temple of the LORD, the temple of the LORD, the temple of the LORD!" 5If you really change your ways and your actions and deal with each other justly, 6if you do not oppress the alien, the fatherless or the widow and do not shed innocent blood in this place, and if you do not follow other gods to your own harm, 7then I will let you live in this place, in the land I gave to your forefathers for ever and ever. 8But look, you are trusting in deceptive words that are worthless.

9"'Will you steal and murder, commit adultery and perjury, burn incense to Baal and follow other gods you have not known, 10and then come and stand before me in this house, which bears my Name, and say, "We are safe"—safe to do all these detestable things? 11Has this house, which bears my Name, become a den of robbers to you? But I have been watching! declares the LORD.

12"'Go now to the place in Shiloh where I first made a dwelling for my Name, and see what I did to it because of the wickedness of my people Israel. 13While you were doing all these things, declares the LORD, I spoke to you again and again, but you did not listen; I called you, but you did not answer. 14Therefore, what I did to Shiloh I will now do to the house that bears my Name, the temple you trust in, the place I gave to you and your fathers. 15I will thrust you from my presence, just as I did all your brothers, the people of Ephraim.'

16"So do not pray for this people nor offer any plea or petition for them; do not plead with me, for I will not listen to you. 17Do you not see what they are doing in the towns of Judah and in the streets of Jerusalem? 18The children gather wood, the fathers light the fire, and the women knead the dough and make cakes of bread for the Queen of Heaven. They pour out drink offerings to other gods to provoke me to anger. 19But am I the one they are provoking? declares the LORD. Are they not rather harming themselves, to their own shame?

20"'Therefore this is what the Sovereign LORD says: My anger and my wrath will be poured out on this place, on man and beast, on the trees of the field and on the fruit of the ground, and it will burn and not be quenched.

21"'This is what the LORD Almighty, the God of Israel, says: Go ahead, add your burnt offerings to your other sacrifices and eat the meat yourselves! 22For when I brought your forefathers out of Egypt and spoke to them, I did not just give them commands about burnt offerings and sacrifices, 23but I gave them this command: Obey me, and I will be your God and you will be my people. Walk in all the ways I command you, that it may go well with you. 24But they did not listen or pay attention; instead, they followed the stubborn inclinations of their evil hearts. They went backward and not forward.

25From the time your forefathers left Egypt until now, day after day, again and again I sent you my servants the prophets. 26But they did not listen to me or pay attention. They were stiff-necked and did more evil than their forefathers.'

27"When you tell them all this, they will not listen to you; when you call to them, they will not answer. 28Therefore say to them, 'This is the nation that has not obeyed the LORD its God or responded to correction. Truth has perished; it has vanished from their lips.' 29Cut off your hair and throw it away; take up a lament on the barren heights, for the LORD has rejected and abandoned this generation that is under his wrath.

NEW TESTAMENT READING
Philippians 4:2–23

Exhortations

2I plead with Euodia and I plead with Syntyche to agree with each other in the Lord. 3Yes, and I ask you, loyal yoke-fellow, help these women who have contended at my side in the cause of the gospel, along with Clement and the rest of my fellow-workers, whose names are in the book of life.

4Rejoice in the Lord always. I will say it again: Rejoice! 5Let your gentleness be evident to all. The Lord is near. 6Do not be anxious about anything, but in everything, by prayer and petition, with thanksgiving, present your requests to God. 7And the peace of God, which transcends all understanding, will guard your hearts and your minds in Christ Jesus.

8Finally, brothers, whatever is true, whatever is noble, whatever is right, whatever is pure, whatever is lovely, whatever is admirable—if anything is excellent or praiseworthy—think about such things. 9Whatever you have learned or received or heard from me, or seen in me—put it into practice. And the God of peace will be with you.

Thanks for Their Gifts

10I rejoice greatly in the Lord that at last you have renewed your concern for me. Indeed, you have been concerned, but you had no opportunity to show it. 11I am not saying this because I am in need, for I have learned to be content whatever the circumstances. 12I know what it is to be in need, and I know what it is to have plenty. I have learned the secret of being content in any and every situation, whether well fed or hungry, whether living in plenty or in want. 13I can do everything through him who gives me strength.

14Yet it was good of you to share in my troubles. 15Moreover, as you Philippians know, in the early days of your acquaintance with the gospel, when I set out from Macedonia, not one church shared with me in the matter of giving and receiving, except you only; 16for even when I was in Thessalonica, you sent me aid again and again when I was in need. 17Not that I am looking for a gift, but I am looking for what may be credited to your account. 18I have received full payment and even more; I am amply supplied, now that I have received from Epaphroditus the gifts you sent. They are a fragrant offering, an acceptable sacrifice, pleasing to God. 19And my God will meet all your needs according to his glorious riches in Christ Jesus.

20To our God and Father be glory for ever and ever. Amen.

Final Greetings

21Greet all the saints in Christ Jesus. The brothers who are with me send greetings. 22All the saints send you greetings, especially those who belong to Caesar's household.

23The grace of the Lord Jesus Christ be with your spirit. Amen.

READING FROM PROVERBS
Proverbs 24:5–14

[5] A wise man has great power,
    and a man of knowledge increases
      strength;
[6] for waging war you need guidance,
    and for victory many advisers.

[7] Wisdom is too high for a fool;
    in the assembly at the gate he has
      nothing to say.

[8] He who plots evil
    will be known as a schemer.
[9] The schemes of folly are sin,
    and men detest a mocker.

[10] If you falter in times of trouble,
    how small is your strength!

[11] Rescue those being led away to
      death;
    hold back those staggering towards
      slaughter.
[12] If you say, "But we knew nothing
      about this,"
    does not he who weighs the heart
      perceive it?
Does not he who guards your life
      know it?
    Will he not repay each person
      according to what he has done?

[13] Eat honey, my son, for it is good;
    honey from the comb is sweet to
      your taste.
[14] Know also that wisdom is sweet to
      your soul;
    if you find it, there is a future hope
      for you,
    and your hope will not be cut off.

OCTOBER 4   DAY 277

OLD TESTAMENT READING
Jeremiah 7:30–9:16

The Valley of Slaughter

[30] "'The people of Judah have done evil in my eyes, declares the LORD. They have set up their detestable idols in the house that bears my Name and have defiled it. [31] They have built the high places of Topheth in the Valley of Ben Hinnom to burn their sons and daughters in the fire—something I did not command, nor did it enter my mind. [32] So beware, the days are coming, declares the LORD, when people will no longer call it Topheth or the Valley of Ben Hinnom, but the Valley of Slaughter, for they will bury the dead in Topheth until there is no more room. [33] Then the carcasses of this people will become food for the birds of the air and the beasts of the earth, and there will be no-one to frighten them away. [34] I will bring an end to the sounds of joy and gladness and to the voices of bride and bridegroom in the towns of Judah and the streets of Jerusalem, for the land will become desolate.

8 "'At that time, declares the LORD, the bones of the kings and officials of Judah, the bones of the priests and prophets, and the bones of the people of Jerusalem will be removed from their graves. [2] They will be exposed to the sun and the moon and all the stars of the heavens, which they have loved and served and which they have followed and consulted and worshipped. They will not be gathered up or buried, but will be like refuse lying on the ground. [3] Wherever I banish them, all the survivors of this evil nation will prefer death to life, declares the LORD Almighty.'

Sin and Punishment

4"Say to them, 'This is what the LORD says:

"'When men fall down, do they not
    get up?
When a man turns away, does he
    not return?
5Why then have these people turned
    away?
  Why does Jerusalem always turn
    away?
They cling to deceit;
  they refuse to return.
6I have listened attentively,
  but they do not say what is right.
No-one repents of his wickedness,
  saying, "What have I done?"
Each pursues his own course
  like a horse charging into battle.
7Even the stork in the sky
  knows her appointed seasons,
and the dove, the swift and the thrush
  observe the time of their
    migration.
But my people do not know
  the requirements of the LORD.

8"'How can you say, "We are wise,
  for we have the law of the LORD,"
when actually the lying pen of the
    scribes
  has handled it falsely?
9The wise will be put to shame;
  they will be dismayed and trapped.
Since they have rejected the word of
    the LORD,
  what kind of wisdom do they have?
10Therefore I will give their wives to
    other men
  and their fields to new owners.
From the least to the greatest,
  all are greedy for gain;
prophets and priests alike,
  all practise deceit.
11They dress the wound of my people
  as though it were not serious.
"Peace, peace," they say,
  when there is no peace.
12Are they ashamed of their loathsome
    conduct?

No, they have no shame at all;
  they do not even know how to
    blush.
So they will fall among the fallen;
  they will be brought down when
    they are punished,
                    says the LORD.

13"I will take away their harvest,
                    declares the LORD.
  There will be no grapes on the
    vine.
There will be no figs on the tree,
  and their leaves will wither.
What I have given them
  will be taken from them.'"

14"Why are we sitting here?
  Gather together!
Let us flee to the fortified cities
  and perish there!
For the LORD our God has doomed
    us to perish
  and given us poisoned water to
    drink,
because we have sinned against
    him.
15We hoped for peace
  but no good has come,
for a time of healing
  but there was only terror.
16The snorting of the enemy's horses
  is heard from Dan;
at the neighing of their stallions
  the whole land trembles.
They have come to devour
  the land and everything in it,
  the city and all who live there."

17"See, I will send venomous snakes
    among you,
  vipers that cannot be charmed,
  and they will bite you,"
                    declares the LORD.

18O my Comforter in sorrow,
  my heart is faint within me.
19Listen to the cry of my people
  from a land far away:
"Is the LORD not in Zion?
  Is her King no longer there?"

"Why have they provoked me to
    anger with their images,
  with their worthless foreign idols?"

20"The harvest is past,
    the summer has ended,
    and we are not saved."

21Since my people are crushed, I am
    crushed;
  I mourn, and horror grips me.
22Is there no balm in Gilead?
  Is there no physician there?
  Why then is there no healing
    for the wound of my people?

9 1Oh, that my head were a spring
    of water
  and my eyes a fountain of tears!
  I would weep day and night
    for the slain of my people.
2Oh, that I had in the desert
    a lodging place for travellers,
  so that I might leave my people
    and go away from them;
  for they are all adulterers,
    a crowd of unfaithful people.

3"They make ready their tongue
    like a bow, to shoot lies;
  it is not by truth
    that they triumph in the land.
  They go from one sin to another;
    they do not acknowledge me,"
                        declares the LORD.
4"Beware of your friends;
    do not trust your brothers.
  For every brother is a deceiver,
    and every friend a slanderer.
5Friend deceives friend,
    and no-one speaks the truth.
  They have taught their tongues to lie;
    they weary themselves with
      sinning.
6You live in the midst of deception;
    in their deceit they refuse to
      acknowledge me,"
                        declares the LORD.

7Therefore this is what the LORD
Almighty says:

"See, I will refine and test them,
  for what else can I do
  because of the sin of my people?
8Their tongue is a deadly arrow;
    it speaks with deceit.
  With his mouth each speaks cordially
    to his neighbour,
  but in his heart he sets a trap for
    him.
9Should I not punish them for this?"
    declares the LORD.
  "Should I not avenge myself
    on such a nation as this?"

10I will weep and wail for the
    mountains
  and take up a lament concerning
    the desert pastures.
  They are desolate and untravelled,
    and the lowing of cattle is not
      heard.
  The birds of the air have fled
    and the animals are gone.

11"I will make Jerusalem a heap of
    ruins,
    a haunt of jackals;
  and I will lay waste the towns of
    Judah
  so that no-one can live there."

12What man is wise enough to understand this? Who has been instructed by
the LORD and can explain it? Why has
the land been ruined and laid waste like
a desert that no-one can cross?

13The LORD said, "It is because they
have forsaken my law, which I set before them; they have not obeyed me or
followed my law. 14Instead, they have
followed the stubbornness of their
hearts; they have followed the Baals,
as their fathers taught them."
15Therefore, this is what the LORD
Almighty, the God of Israel, says: "See,
I will make this people eat bitter food
and drink poisoned water. 16I will scatter them among nations that neither
they nor their fathers have known, and I
will pursue them with the sword until I
have destroyed them."

NEW TESTAMENT READING
Colossians 1:1–23

1 Paul, an apostle of Christ Jesus by the will of God, and Timothy our brother,

²To the holy and faithful brothers in Christ at Colosse:

Grace and peace to you from God our Father.

Thanksgiving and Prayer

³We always thank God, the Father of our Lord Jesus Christ, when we pray for you, ⁴because we have heard of your faith in Christ Jesus and of the love you have for all the saints—⁵the faith and love that spring from the hope that is stored up for you in heaven and that you have already heard about in the word of truth, the gospel ⁶that has come to you. All over the world this gospel is bearing fruit and growing, just as it has been doing among you since the day you heard it and understood God's grace in all its truth. ⁷You learned it from Epaphras, our dear fellow-servant, who is a faithful minister of Christ on our behalf, ⁸and who also told us of your love in the Spirit.

⁹For this reason, since the day we heard about you, we have not stopped praying for you and asking God to fill you with the knowledge of his will through all spiritual wisdom and understanding. ¹⁰And we pray this in order that you may live a life worthy of the Lord and may please him in every way: bearing fruit in every good work, growing in the knowledge of God, ¹¹being strengthened with all power according to his glorious might so that you may have great endurance and patience, and joyfully ¹²giving thanks to the Father, who has qualified you to share in the inheritance of the saints in the kingdom of light. ¹³For he has rescued us from the dominion of darkness and brought us into the kingdom of the Son he loves,

¹⁴in whom we have redemption, the forgiveness of sins.

The Supremacy of Christ

¹⁵He is the image of the invisible God, the firstborn over all creation. ¹⁶For by him all things were created: things in heaven and on earth, visible and invisible, whether thrones or powers or rulers or authorities; all things were created by him and for him. ¹⁷He is before all things, and in him all things hold together. ¹⁸And he is the head of the body, the church; he is the beginning and the firstborn from among the dead, so that in everything he might have the supremacy. ¹⁹For God was pleased to have all his fulness dwell in him, ²⁰and through him to reconcile to himself all things, whether things on earth or things in heaven, by making peace through his blood, shed on the cross.

²¹Once you were alienated from God and were enemies in your minds because of your evil behaviour. ²²But now he has reconciled you by Christ's physical body through death to present you holy in his sight, without blemish and free from accusation—²³if you continue in your faith, established and firm, not moved from the hope held out in the gospel. This is the gospel that you heard and that has been proclaimed to every creature under heaven, and of which I, Paul, have become a servant.

READING FROM PSALMS
Psalm 116:12–19

¹²How can I repay the LORD
for all his goodness to me?
¹³I will lift up the cup of salvation
and call on the name of the LORD.
¹⁴I will fulfil my vows to the LORD
in the presence of all his people.

¹⁵Precious in the sight of the LORD
is the death of his saints.

16O Lᴏʀᴅ, truly I am your servant;
   I am your servant, the son of your
      maidservant;
   you have freed me from my chains.

17I will sacrifice a thank-offering to you
   and call on the name of the Lᴏʀᴅ.

18I will fulfil my vows to the Lᴏʀᴅ
   in the presence of all his people,
19in the courts of the house of the
     Lᴏʀᴅ—
   in your midst, O Jerusalem.

Praise the Lᴏʀᴅ.

OCTOBER 5   DAY 278

OLD TESTAMENT READING
Jeremiah 9:17–11:17

17This is what the Lᴏʀᴅ Almighty
says:

"Consider now! Call for the wailing
   women to come;
   send for the most skilful of them.
18Let them come quickly
   and wail over us
till our eyes overflow with tears
   and water streams from our
     eyelids.
19The sound of wailing is heard from
   Zion:
   'How ruined we are!
   How great is our shame!
We must leave our land
   because our houses are in ruins.'"

20Now, O women, hear the word of the
   Lᴏʀᴅ;
   open your ears to the words of his
     mouth.
Teach your daughters how to wail;
   teach one another a lament.
21Death has climbed in through our
   windows
   and has entered our fortresses;
it has cut off the children from the
   streets
   and the young men from the public
     squares.

22Say, "This is what the Lᴏʀᴅ declares:

"'The dead bodies of men will lie
   like refuse on the open field,
like cut corn behind the reaper,
   with no-one to gather them.'"

23This is what the Lᴏʀᴅ says:

"Let not the wise man boast of his
   wisdom
   or the strong man boast of his
     strength
   or the rich man boast of his riches,
24but let him who boasts boast about
   this:
   that he understands and knows me,
that I am the Lᴏʀᴅ, who exercises
   kindness,
   justice and righteousness on earth,
   for in these I delight,"
              declares the Lᴏʀᴅ.

25"The days are coming," declares
the Lᴏʀᴅ, "when I will punish all who
are circumcised only in the flesh—
26Egypt, Judah, Edom, Ammon, Moab
and all who live in the desert in distant
places. For all these nations are really
uncircumcised, and even the whole
house of Israel is uncircumcised in
heart."

God and Idols

10 Hear what the Lᴏʀᴅ says to you,
O house of Israel. 2This is what
the Lᴏʀᴅ says:

"Do not learn the ways of the nations
or be terrified by signs in the sky,
though the nations are terrified by
them.
3For the customs of the peoples are
worthless;
they cut a tree out of the forest,
and a craftsman shapes it with his
chisel.
4They adorn it with silver and gold;
they fasten it with hammer and
nails
so that it will not totter.
5Like a scarecrow in a melon patch,
their idols cannot speak;
they must be carried
because they cannot walk.
Do not fear them;
they can do no harm
nor can they do any good."

6No-one is like you, O LORD;
you are great,
and your name is mighty in power.
7Who should not revere you,
O King of the nations?
This is your due.
Among all the wise men of the
nations
and in all their kingdoms,
there is no-one like you.
8They are all senseless and foolish;
they are taught by worthless
wooden idols.
9Hammered silver is brought from
Tarshish
and gold from Uphaz.
What the craftsman and goldsmith
have made
is then dressed in blue and
purple—
all made by skilled workers.
10But the LORD is the true God;
he is the living God, the eternal
King.
When he is angry, the earth trembles;
the nations cannot endure his
wrath.

11"Tell them this: 'These gods, who
did not make the heavens and the earth,
will perish from the earth and from
under the heavens.'"

12But God made the earth by his
power;
he founded the world by his
wisdom
and stretched out the heavens by
his understanding.
13When he thunders, the waters in the
heavens roar;
he makes clouds rise from the ends
of the earth.
He sends lightning with the rain
and brings out the wind from his
storehouses.

14Everyone is senseless and without
knowledge;
every goldsmith is shamed by his
idols.
His images are a fraud;
they have no breath in them.
15They are worthless, the objects of
mockery;
when their judgment comes, they
will perish.
16He who is the Portion of Jacob is not
like these,
for he is the Maker of all things,
including Israel, the tribe of his
inheritance—
the LORD Almighty is his name.

Coming Destruction

17Gather up your belongings to leave
the land,
you who live under siege.
18For this is what the LORD says:
"At this time I will hurl out
those who live in this land;
I will bring distress on them
so that they may be captured."

19Woe to me because of my injury!
My wound is incurable!
Yet I said to myself,
"This is my sickness, and I must
endure it."
20My tent is destroyed;
all its ropes are snapped.

My sons are gone from me and are no
　　more;
　　no-one is left now to pitch my tent
　　or to set up my shelter.
²¹The shepherds are senseless
　　and do not enquire of the LORD;
so they do not prosper
　　and all their flock is scattered.
²²Listen! The report is coming—
　　a great commotion from the land of
　　　the north!
It will make the towns of Judah
　　desolate,
　　a haunt of jackals.

Jeremiah's Prayer

²³I know, O LORD, that a man's life is
　　not his own;
　　it is not for man to direct his steps.
²⁴Correct me, LORD, but only with
　　justice—
　　not in your anger,
　　lest you reduce me to nothing.
²⁵Pour out your wrath on the nations
　　that do not acknowledge you,
　　on the peoples who do not call on
　　　your name.
For they have devoured Jacob;
　　they have devoured him
　　completely
　　and destroyed his homeland.

The Covenant Is Broken

11 This is the word that came to
Jeremiah from the LORD:
²"Listen to the terms of this covenant
and tell them to the people of Judah and
to those who live in Jerusalem. ³Tell
them that this is what the LORD, the
God of Israel, says: 'Cursed is the man
who does not obey the terms of this
covenant—⁴the terms I commanded
your forefathers when I brought them
out of Egypt, out of the iron-smelting
furnace.' I said, 'Obey me and do everything I command you, and you will be
my people, and I will be your God.
⁵Then I will fulfil the oath I swore to
your forefathers, to give them a land

flowing with milk and honey'—the land
you possess today."

I answered, "Amen, LORD."

⁶The LORD said to me, "Proclaim all
these words in the towns of Judah and in
the streets of Jerusalem: 'Listen to the
terms of this covenant and follow them.
⁷From the time I brought your fore-
fathers up from Egypt until today, I
warned them again and again, saying,
"Obey me." ⁸But they did not listen or
pay attention; instead, they followed
the stubbornness of their evil hearts. So
I brought on them all the curses of the
covenant I had commanded them to
follow but that they did not keep.'"

⁹Then the LORD said to me, "There is
a conspiracy among the people of Judah
and those who live in Jerusalem. ¹⁰They
have returned to the sins of their forefathers, who refused to listen to my
words. They have followed other gods
to serve them. Both the house of Israel
and the house of Judah have broken the
covenant I made with their forefathers.
¹¹Therefore this is what the LORD says:
'I will bring on them a disaster they
cannot escape. Although they cry out to
me, I will not listen to them. ¹²The
towns of Judah and the people of Jerusalem will go and cry out to the gods to
whom they burn incense, but they will
not help them at all when disaster
strikes. ¹³You have as many gods as you
have towns, O Judah; and the altars you
have set up to burn incense to that
shameful god Baal are as many as the
streets of Jerusalem.'

¹⁴"Do not pray for this people nor
offer any plea or petition for them, because I will not listen when they call to
me in the time of their distress.

¹⁵"What is my beloved doing in my
　　temple
　　as she works out her evil schemes
　　　with many?
　　Can consecrated meat avert ⌊your
　　　punishment⌋?
When you engage in your
　　wickedness,
　　then you rejoice."

16The LORD called you a thriving olive
    tree
  with fruit beautiful in form.
But with the roar of a mighty storm
  he will set it on fire,
  and its branches will be broken.

17The LORD Almighty, who planted
you, has decreed disaster for you, because the house of Israel and the house
of Judah have done evil and provoked
me to anger by burning incense to Baal.

NEW TESTAMENT READING
Colossians 1:24–2:5

Paul's Labour for the Church

24Now I rejoice in what was suffered
for you, and I fill up in my flesh what is
still lacking in regard to Christ's afflictions, for the sake of his body, which is
the church. 25I have become its servant
by the commission God gave me to
present to you the word of God in its
fulness—26the mystery that has been
kept hidden for ages and generations,
but is now disclosed to the saints. 27To
them God has chosen to make known
among the Gentiles the glorious riches
of this mystery, which is Christ in you,
the hope of glory.

28We proclaim him, admonishing and

teaching everyone with all wisdom, so
that we may present everyone perfect in
Christ. 29To this end I labour, struggling
with all his energy, which so powerfully
works in me.

2 I want you to know how much I am
  struggling for you and for those at
Laodicea, and for all who have not met
me personally. 2My purpose is that they
may be encouraged in heart and united
in love, so that they may have the full
riches of complete understanding, in
order that they may know the mystery
of God, namely, Christ, 3in whom are
hidden all the treasures of wisdom and
knowledge. 4I tell you this so that no-
one may deceive you by fine-sounding
arguments. 5For though I am absent
from you in body, I am present with you
in spirit and delight to see how orderly
you are and how firm your faith in
Christ is.

READING FROM PSALMS
Psalm 117:1–2

1Praise the LORD, all you nations;
  extol him, all you peoples.
2For great is his love towards us,
  and the faithfulness of the LORD
    endures for ever.

Praise the LORD.

DAY 279   # OCTOBER 6

OLD TESTAMENT READING
Jeremiah 11:18–13:27

Plot Against Jeremiah

18Because the LORD revealed their
plot to me, I knew it, for at that time he
showed me what they were doing. 19I
had been like a gentle lamb led to the
slaughter; I did not realise that they had
plotted against me, saying,

"Let us destroy the tree and its fruit;
  let us cut him off from the land of
    the living,
  that his name be remembered no
    more."

20But, O LORD Almighty, you who
  judge righteously
and test the heart and mind,
let me see your vengeance upon them,
  for to you I have committed my
    cause.

21"Therefore this is what the LORD says about the men of Anathoth who are seeking your life and saying, 'Do not prophesy in the name of the LORD or you will die by our hands'—22therefore this is what the LORD Almighty says: 'I will punish them. Their young men will die by the sword, their sons and daughters by famine. 23Not even a remnant will be left to them, because I will bring disaster on the men of Anathoth in the year of their punishment.'"

Jeremiah's Complaint

12

You are always righteous, O LORD,
    when I bring a case before you.
Yet I would speak with you about your justice:
    Why does the way of the wicked prosper?
    Why do all the faithless live at ease?
2You have planted them, and they have taken root;
    they grow and bear fruit.
You are always on their lips
    but far from their hearts.
3Yet you know me, O LORD;
    you see me and test my thoughts about you.
Drag them off like sheep to be butchered!
    Set them apart for the day of slaughter!
4How long will the land lie parched
    and the grass in every field be withered?
Because those who live in it are wicked,
    the animals and birds have perished.
Moreover, the people are saying,
    "He will not see what happens to us."

God's Answer

5"If you have raced with men on foot
    and they have worn you out,
    how can you compete with horses?

If you stumble in safe country,
    how will you manage in the thickets by the Jordan?
6Your brothers, your own family—
    even they have betrayed you;
    they have raised a loud cry against you.
Do not trust them,
    though they speak well of you.

7"I will forsake my house,
    abandon my inheritance;
I will give the one I love
    into the hands of her enemies.
8My inheritance has become to me
    like a lion in the forest.
She roars at me;
    therefore I hate her.
9Has not my inheritance become to me
    like a speckled bird of prey
    that other birds of prey surround and attack?
Go and gather all the wild beasts;
    bring them to devour.
10Many shepherds will ruin my vineyard
    and trample down my field;
they will turn my pleasant field
    into a desolate wasteland.
11It will be made a wasteland,
    parched and desolate before me;
the whole land will be laid waste
    because there is no-one who cares.
12Over all the barren heights in the desert
    destroyers will swarm,
for the sword of the LORD will devour
    from one end of the land to the other;
    no-one will be safe.
13They will sow wheat but reap thorns;
    they will wear themselves out but gain nothing.
So bear the shame of your harvest
    because of the LORD's fierce anger."

14This is what the LORD says: "As for all my wicked neighbours who seize the inheritance I gave to my people Israel, I will uproot them from their lands and I will uproot the house of Judah from among them. 15But after I uproot them, I will again have compassion and will bring each of them back to his own inheritance and his own country. 16And if they learn well the ways of my people and swear by my name, saying, 'As surely as the LORD lives'—even as they once taught my people to swear by Baal —then they will be established among my people. 17But if any nation does not listen, I will completely uproot and destroy it," declares the LORD.

A Linen Belt

13 This is what the LORD said to me: "Go and buy a linen belt and put it round your waist, but do not let it touch water. 2So I bought a belt, as the LORD directed, and put it round my waist.

3Then the word of the LORD came to me a second time: 4"Take the belt you bought and are wearing round your waist, and go now to Perath and hide it there in a crevice in the rocks." 5So I went and hid it at Perath, as the LORD told me.

6Many days later the LORD said to me, "Go now to Perath and get the belt I told you to hide there." 7So I went to Perath and dug up the belt and took it from the place where I had hidden it, but now it was ruined and completely useless.

8Then the word of the LORD came to me: 9"This is what the LORD says: 'In the same way I will ruin the pride of Judah and the great pride of Jerusalem. 10These wicked people, who refuse to listen to my words, who follow the stubbornness of their hearts and go after other gods to serve and worship them, will be like this belt—completely useless! 11For as a belt is bound round a man's waist, so I bound the whole house of Israel and the whole house of Judah to me,' declares the LORD, 'to be my people for my renown and praise and honour. But they have not listened.'

Wineskins

12"Say to them: 'This is what the LORD, the God of Israel, says: Every wineskin should be filled with wine.' And if they say to you, 'Don't we know that every wineskin should be filled with wine?' 13then tell them, 'This is what the LORD says: I am going to fill with drunkenness all who live in this land, including the kings who sit on David's throne, the priests, the prophets and all those living in Jerusalem. 14I will smash them one against the other, fathers and sons alike, declares the LORD. I will allow no pity or mercy or compassion to keep me from destroying them.'"

Threat of Captivity

15Hear and pay attention,
    do not be arrogant,
    for the LORD has spoken.
16Give glory to the LORD your God
    before he brings the darkness,
before your feet stumble
    on the darkening hills.
You hope for light,
    but he will turn it to thick darkness
    and change it to deep gloom.
17But if you do not listen,
    I will weep in secret
    because of your pride;
my eyes will weep bitterly,
    overflowing with tears,
    because the LORD's flock will be
        taken captive.

18Say to the king and to the queen
    mother,
    "Come down from your thrones,
for your glorious crowns
    will fall from your heads."
19The cities in the Negev will be shut
        up,
    and there will be no-one to open
        them.
All Judah will be carried into exile,
    carried completely away.

20Lift up your eyes and see
    those who are coming from the
        north.

Where is the flock that was entrusted
    to you,
  the sheep of which you boasted?
[21]What will you say when ⌊the LORD⌋
    sets over you
    those you cultivated as your special
      allies?
Will not pain grip you
  like that of a woman in labour?
[22]And if you ask yourself,
    "Why has this happened to
      me?"—
  it is because of your many sins
    that your skirts have been torn off
    and your body ill-treated.
[23]Can the Ethiopian change his skin
    or the leopard its spots?
Neither can you do good
  who are accustomed to doing evil.

[24]"I will scatter you like chaff
    driven by the desert wind.
[25]This is your lot,
    the portion I have decreed for
      you,"
                    declares the LORD,
  "because you have forgotten me
    and trusted in false gods.
[26]I will pull up your skirts over your
    face
    that your shame may be seen—
[27]your adulteries and lustful neighings,
    your shameless prostitution!
  I have seen your detestable acts
    on the hills and in the fields.
  Woe to you, O Jerusalem!
    How long will you be unclean?"

NEW TESTAMENT READING
Colossians 2:6–23

*Freedom From Human Regulations
Through Life With Christ*

[6]So then, just as you received Christ
Jesus as Lord, continue to live in him,
[7]rooted and built up in him, strengthened in the faith as you were taught,
and overflowing with thankfulness.

[8]See to it that no-one takes you captive through hollow and deceptive
philosophy, which depends on human
tradition and the basic principles of this
world rather than on Christ.

[9]For in Christ all the fulness of the
Deity lives in bodily form, [10]and you
have been given fulness in Christ, who is
the Head over every power and authority. [11]In him you were also circumcised,
in the putting off of the sinful nature,
not with a circumcision done by the
hands of men but with the circumcision
done by Christ, [12]having been buried
with him in baptism and raised with him
through your faith in the power of God,
who raised him from the dead.

[13]When you were dead in your sins
and in the uncircumcision of your sinful
nature, God made you alive with Christ.
He forgave us all our sins, [14]having cancelled the written code, with its regulations, that was against us and that
stood opposed to us; he took it away,
nailing it to the cross. [15]And having
disarmed the powers and authorities,
he made a public spectacle of them, tri-
umphing over them by the cross.

[16]Therefore do not let anyone judge
you by what you eat or drink, or with
regard to a religious festival, a New
Moon celebration or a Sabbath day.
[17]These are a shadow of the things that
were to come; the reality, however, is
found in Christ. [18]Do not let anyone
who delights in false humility and the
worship of angels disqualify you for the
prize. Such a person goes into great
detail about what he has seen, and his
unspiritual mind puffs him up with idle
notions. [19]He has lost connection with
the Head, from whom the whole body,
supported and held together by its liga-
ments and sinews, grows as God causes
it to grow.

[20]Since you died with Christ to the
basic principles of this world, why, as
though you still belonged to it, do you
submit to its rules: [21]"Do not handle!
Do not taste! Do not touch!"? [22]These
are all destined to perish with use,
because they are based on human
commands and teachings. [23]Such regulations indeed have an appearance of

wisdom, with their self-imposed worship, their false humility and their harsh treatment of the body, but they lack any value in restraining sensual indulgence.

READING FROM PSALMS
Psalm 118:1–16

[1]Give thanks to the Lord, for he is good;
  his love endures for ever.

[2]Let Israel say:
  "His love endures for ever."
[3]Let the house of Aaron say:
  "His love endures for ever."
[4]Let those who fear the Lord say:
  "His love endures for ever."

[5]In my anguish I cried to the Lord,
  and he answered by setting me free.
[6]The Lord is with me; I will not be afraid.
  What can man do to me?
[7]The Lord is with me; he is my helper.
  I will look in triumph on my enemies.

[8]It is better to take refuge in the Lord
  than to trust in man.
[9]It is better to take refuge in the Lord
  than to trust in princes.

[10]All the nations surrounded me,
  but in the name of the Lord I cut them off.
[11]They surrounded me on every side,
  but in the name of the Lord I cut them off.
[12]They swarmed around me like bees,
  but they died out as quickly as burning thorns;
  in the name of the Lord I cut them off.

[13]I was pushed back and about to fall,
  but the Lord helped me.
[14]The Lord is my strength and my song;
  he has become my salvation.

[15]Shouts of joy and victory
  resound in the tents of the righteous:
  "The Lord's right hand has done mighty things!
[16] The Lord's right hand is lifted high;
  the Lord's right hand has done mighty things!"

DAY 280

OCTOBER 7

OLD TESTAMENT READING
Jeremiah 14:1–15:21

Drought, Famine, Sword

14 This is the word of the Lord to Jeremiah concerning the drought:

[2]"Judah mourns,
  her cities languish;
they wail for the land,
  and a cry goes up from Jerusalem.

[3]The nobles send their servants for water;
  they go to the cisterns
  but find no water.
They return with their jars unfilled;
  dismayed and despairing,
  they cover their heads.
[4]The ground is cracked
  because there is no rain in the land;
the farmers are dismayed
  and cover their heads.
[5]Even the doe in the field

deserts her newborn fawn
because there is no grass.
⁶Wild donkeys stand on the barren
heights
and pant like jackals;
their eyesight fails
for lack of pasture."

⁷Although our sins testify against us,
O LORD, do something for the sake
of your name.
For our backsliding is great;
we have sinned against you.
⁸O Hope of Israel,
its Saviour in times of distress,
why are you like a stranger in the
land,
like a traveller who stays only a
night?
⁹Why are you like a man taken by
surprise,
like a warrior powerless to save?
You are among us, O LORD,
and we bear your name;
do not forsake us!

¹⁰This is what the LORD says about
this people:

"They greatly love to wander;
they do not restrain their feet.
So the LORD does not accept them;
he will now remember their
wickedness
and punish them for their sins."

¹¹Then the LORD said to me, "Do not
pray for the well-being of this people.
¹²Although they fast, I will not listen to
their cry; though they offer burnt offerings and grain offerings, I will not
accept them. Instead, I will destroy
them with the sword, famine and
plague."

¹³But I said, "Ah, Sovereign LORD,
the prophets keep telling them, 'You
will not see the sword or suffer famine.
Indeed, I will give you lasting peace in
this place.'"

¹⁴Then the LORD said to me, "The
prophets are prophesying lies in my
name. I have not sent them or

appointed them or spoken to them.
They are prophesying to you false
visions, divinations, idolatries and the
delusions of their own minds. ¹⁵Therefore, this is what the LORD says about
the prophets who are prophesying in my
name: I did not send them, yet they are
saying, 'No sword or famine will touch
this land.' Those same prophets will
perish by sword and famine. ¹⁶And the
people they are prophesying to will be
thrown out into the streets of Jerusalem
because of the famine and sword. There
will be no-one to bury them or their
wives, their sons or their daughters. I
will pour out on them the calamity they
deserve.

¹⁷"Speak this word to them:

"'Let my eyes overflow with tears
night and day without ceasing;
for my virgin daughter—my
people—
has suffered a grievous wound,
a crushing blow.
¹⁸If I go into the country,
I see those slain by the sword;
if I go into the city,
I see the ravages of famine.
Both prophet and priest
have gone to a land they know
not.'"

¹⁹Have you rejected Judah completely?
Do you despise Zion?
Why have you afflicted us
so that we cannot be healed?
We hoped for peace
but no good has come,
for a time of healing
but there is only terror.
²⁰O LORD, we acknowledge our
wickedness
and the guilt of our fathers;
we have indeed sinned against you.
²¹For the sake of your name do not
despise us;
do not dishonour your glorious
throne.
Remember your covenant with us
and do not break it.

²²Do any of the worthless idols of the
    nations bring rain?
  Do the skies themselves send down
    showers?
No, it is you, O LORD our God.
  Therefore our hope is in you,
  for you are the one who does all
    this.

15 Then the LORD said to me:
"Even if Moses and Samuel
were to stand before me, my heart
would not go out to this people. Send
them away from my presence! Let them
go! ²And if they ask you, 'Where shall
we go?' tell them, 'This is what the
LORD says:

  " 'Those destined for death, to death;
    those for the sword, to the sword;
    those for starvation, to starvation;
    those for captivity, to captivity.'

³"I will send four kinds of destroyers
against them," declares the LORD, "the
sword to kill and the dogs to drag away
and the birds of the air and the beasts of
the earth to devour and destroy. ⁴I will
make them abhorrent to all the kingdoms of the earth because of what Manasseh son of Hezekiah king of Judah
did in Jerusalem.

⁵"Who will have pity on you, O
    Jerusalem?
  Who will mourn for you?
  Who will stop to ask how you are?
⁶You have rejected me," declares the
    LORD.
  "You keep on backsliding.
So I will lay hands on you and destroy
    you;
  I can no longer show compassion.
⁷I will winnow them with a winnowing
    fork
  at the city gates of the land.
I will bring bereavement and
    destruction on my people,
  for they have not changed their
    ways.
⁸I will make their widows more
    numerous
  than the sand of the sea.

At midday I will bring a destroyer
  against the mothers of their young
    men;
  suddenly I will bring down on them
    anguish and terror.
⁹The mother of seven will grow faint
  and breathe her last.
  Her sun will set while it is still day;
  she will be disgraced and
    humiliated.
I will put the survivors to the sword
  before their enemies,"
            declares the LORD.

¹⁰Alas, my mother, that you gave me
    birth,
  a man with whom the whole land
    strives and contends!
I have neither lent nor borrowed,
  yet everyone curses me.

¹¹The LORD said,

"Surely I will deliver you for a good
    purpose;
  surely I will make your enemies
    plead with you
  in times of disaster and times of
    distress.

¹²"Can a man break iron—
  iron from the north—or bronze?
¹³Your wealth and your treasures
  I will give as plunder, without
    charge,
  because of all your sins
    throughout your country.
¹⁴I will enslave you to your enemies
  in a land you do not know,
  for my anger will kindle a fire
    that will burn against you."

¹⁵You understand, O LORD;
  remember me and care for me.
  Avenge me on my persecutors.
You are long-suffering—do not take
    me away;
  think of how I suffer reproach for
    your sake.
¹⁶When your words came, I ate them;
  they were my joy and my heart's
    delight,

for I bear your name,
   O LORD God Almighty.
¹⁷I never sat in the company of
   revellers,
   never made merry with them;
I sat alone because your hand was on
   me
   and you had filled me with
     indignation.
¹⁸Why is my pain unending
   and my wound grievous and
     incurable?
Will you be to me like a deceptive
   brook,
   like a spring that fails?

¹⁹Therefore this is what the LORD
says:

"If you repent, I will restore you
   that you may serve me;
if you utter worthy, not worthless,
   words,
   you will be my spokesman.
Let this people turn to you,
   but you must not turn to them.
²⁰I will make you to be a wall to this people,
   a fortified wall of bronze;
they will fight against you
   but will not overcome you,
for I am with you
   to rescue and save you,"
     declares the LORD.
²¹"I will save you from the hands of the
   wicked
   and redeem you from the grasp of
     the cruel."

NEW TESTAMENT READING
Colossians 3:1–4:1

Rules for Holy Living

3 Since, then, you have been raised
with Christ, set your hearts on
things above, where Christ is seated at
the right hand of God. ²Set your minds
on things above, not on earthly things.
³For you died, and your life is now
hidden with Christ in God. ⁴When

Christ, who is your life, appears, then
you also will appear with him in glory.

⁵Put to death, therefore, whatever
belongs to your earthly nature: sexual
immorality, impurity, lust, evil desires
and greed, which is idolatry. ⁶Because
of these, the wrath of God is coming.
⁷You used to walk in these ways, in the
life you once lived. ⁸But now you must
rid yourselves of all such things as these:
anger, rage, malice, slander and filthy
language from your lips. ⁹Do not lie to
each other, since you have taken off
your old self with its practices ¹⁰and
have put on the new self, which is being
renewed in knowledge in the image of
its Creator. ¹¹Here there is no Greek or
Jew, circumcised or uncircumcised,
barbarian, Scythian, slave or free, but
Christ is all, and is in all.

¹²Therefore, as God's chosen people,
holy and dearly loved, clothe yourselves
with compassion, kindness, humility,
gentleness and patience. ¹³Bear with
each other and forgive whatever griev-
ances you may have against one
another. Forgive as the Lord forgave
you. ¹⁴And over all these virtues put on
love, which binds them all together in
perfect unity.

¹⁵Let the peace of Christ rule in your
hearts, since as members of one body
you were called to peace. And be thank-
ful. ¹⁶Let the word of Christ dwell in you
richly as you teach and admonish one
another with all wisdom, and as you sing
psalms, hymns and spiritual songs with
gratitude in your hearts to God. ¹⁷And
whatever you do, whether in word or
deed, do it all in the name of the Lord
Jesus, giving thanks to God the Father
through him.

Rules for Christian Households

¹⁸Wives, submit to your husbands, as
is fitting in the Lord.

¹⁹Husbands, love your wives and do
not be harsh with them.

²⁰Children, obey your parents in
everything, for this pleases the Lord.

²¹Fathers, do not embitter your chil-
dren, or they will become discouraged.

22Slaves, obey your earthly masters in everything; and do it, not only when their eye is on you and to win their favour, but with sincerity of heart and reverence for the Lord. 23Whatever you do, work at it with all your heart, as working for the Lord, not for men, 24since you know that you will receive an inheritance from the Lord as a reward. It is the Lord Christ you are serving. 25Anyone who does wrong will be repaid for his wrong, and there is no favouritism.

4 Masters, provide your slaves with what is right and fair, because you know that you also have a Master in heaven.

READING FROM PROVERBS
Proverbs 24:15–22

15Do not lie in wait like an outlaw
    against a righteous man's
    house,
do not raid his dwelling-place;
16for though a righteous man falls
    seven times, he rises again,
but the wicked are brought down
    by calamity.

17Do not gloat when your enemy falls;
    when he stumbles, do not let your
    heart rejoice,
18or the LORD will see and disapprove
    and turn his wrath away from him.

19Do not fret because of evil men
    or be envious of the wicked,
20for the evil man has no future hope,
    and the lamp of the wicked will be
    snuffed out.

21Fear the LORD and the king, my son,
    and do not join with the rebellious,
22for those two will send sudden
    destruction upon them,
and who knows what calamities
    they can bring?

DAY 281

OCTOBER 8

OLD TESTAMENT READING
Jeremiah 16:1–17:27

Day of Disaster

16 Then the word of the LORD came to me: 2"You must not marry and have sons or daughters in this place." 3For this is what the LORD says about the sons and daughters born in this land and about the women who are their mothers and the men who are their fathers: 4"They will die of deadly diseases. They will not be mourned or buried but will be like refuse lying on the ground. They will perish by sword and famine, and their dead bodies will become food for the birds of the air and the beasts of the earth."

5For this is what the LORD says: "Do not enter a house where there is a funeral meal; do not go to mourn or show sympathy, because I have withdrawn my blessing, my love and my pity from this people," declares the LORD. 6"Both high and low will die in this land. They will not be buried or mourned, and no-one will cut himself or shave his head for them. 7No-one will offer food to comfort those who mourn for the dead—not even for a father or a mother —nor will anyone give them a drink to console them.

8"And do not enter a house where there is feasting and sit down to eat and drink. 9For this is what the LORD Almighty, the God of Israel, says: Before your eyes and in your days I will bring an end to the sounds of joy and gladness and to the voices of bride and bridegroom in this place.

10"When you tell these people all this and they ask you, 'Why has the LORD decreed such a great disaster against us? What wrong have we done? What sin have we committed against the LORD our God?' 11then say to them, 'It is because your fathers forsook me,' declares the LORD, 'and followed other gods and served and worshipped them. They forsook me and did not keep my law. 12But you have behaved more wickedly than your fathers. See how each of you is following the stubbornness of his evil heart instead of obeying me. 13So I will throw you out of this land into a land neither you nor your fathers have known, and there you will serve other gods day and night, for I will show you no favour.'

14"However, the days are coming," declares the LORD, "when men will no longer say, 'As surely as the LORD lives, who brought the Israelites up out of Egypt,' 15but they will say, 'As surely as the LORD lives, who brought the Israelites up out of the land of the north and out of all the countries where he had banished them.' For I will restore them to the land I gave to their forefathers.

16"But now I will send for many fishermen," declares the LORD, "and they will catch them. After that I will send for many hunters, and they will hunt them down on every mountain and hill and from the crevices of the rocks. 17My eyes are on all their ways; they are not hidden from me, nor is their sin concealed from my eyes. 18I will repay them double for their wickedness and their sin, because they have defiled my land with the lifeless forms of their vile images and have filled my inheritance with their detestable idols."

19O LORD, my strength and my
        fortress,
    my refuge in time of distress,
to you the nations will come
    from the ends of the earth and say,
"Our fathers possessed nothing but
        false gods,
    worthless idols that did them no
        good.
20Do men make their own gods?
    Yes, but they are not gods!"

21"Therefore I will teach them—
    this time I will teach them
    my power and might.
Then they will know
    that my name is the LORD.

17

        "Judah's sin is engraved with an
        iron tool,
    inscribed with a flint point,
on the tablets of their hearts
    and on the horns of their altars.
2Even their children remember
    their altars and Asherah poles
beside the spreading trees
    and on the high hills.
3My mountain in the land
    and your wealth and all your
        treasures
I will give away as plunder,
    together with your high places,
    because of sin throughout your
        country.
4Through your own fault you will lose
    the inheritance I gave you.
I will enslave you to your enemies
    in a land you do not know,
for you have kindled my anger,
    and it will burn for ever."

5This is what the LORD says:

"Cursed is the one who trusts in man,
    who depends on flesh for his
        strength
    and whose heart turns away from
        the LORD.
6He will be like a bush in the
        wastelands;
    he will not see prosperity when it
        comes.
He will dwell in the parched places of
        the desert,
    in a salt land where no-one lives.
7"But blessed is the man who trusts in
        the LORD,
    whose confidence is in him.

⁸He will be like a tree planted by the
water
  that sends out its roots by the
  stream.
It does not fear when heat comes;
  its leaves are always green.
It has no worries in a year of drought
  and never fails to bear fruit.”

⁹The heart is deceitful above all things
  and beyond cure.
  Who can understand it?

¹⁰“I the LORD search the heart
  and examine the mind,
to reward a man according to his
  conduct,
  according to what his deeds
  deserve.”

¹¹Like a partridge that hatches eggs it
  did not lay
  is the man who gains riches by
  unjust means.
When his life is half gone, they will
  desert him,
  and in the end he will prove to be a
  fool.

¹²A glorious throne, exalted from the
  beginning,
  is the place of our sanctuary.

¹³O LORD, the hope of Israel,
  all who forsake you will be put to
  shame.
Those who turn away from you will
  be written in the dust
because they have forsaken the
  LORD,
  the spring of living water.

¹⁴Heal me, O LORD, and I shall be
  healed;
  save me and I shall be saved,
  for you are the one I praise.

¹⁵They keep saying to me,
  “Where is the word of the LORD?
  Let it now be fulfilled!”

¹⁶I have not run away from being your
  shepherd;
  you know I have not desired the
  day of despair.

What passes my lips is open before
  you.
¹⁷Do not be a terror to me;
  you are my refuge in the day of
  disaster.
¹⁸Let my persecutors be put to shame,
  but keep me from shame;
let them be terrified,
  but keep me from terror.
Bring on them the day of disaster;
  destroy them with double
  destruction.

Keeping the Sabbath Holy

¹⁹This is what the LORD said to me:
“Go and stand at the gate of the people,
through which the kings of Judah go in
and out; stand also at all the other gates
of Jerusalem. ²⁰Say to them, ‘Hear the
word of the LORD, O kings of Judah and
all people of Judah and everyone living
in Jerusalem who come through these
gates. ²¹This is what the LORD says: Be
careful not to carry a load on the Sabbath day or bring it through the gates of
Jerusalem. ²²Do not bring a load out of
your houses or do any work on the
Sabbath, but keep the Sabbath day
holy, as I commanded your forefathers.
²³Yet they did not listen or pay attention; they were stiff-necked and would
not listen or respond to discipline. ²⁴But
if you are careful to obey me, declares
the LORD, and bring no load through
the gates of this city on the Sabbath, but
keep the Sabbath day holy by not doing
any work on it, ²⁵then kings who sit on
David’s throne will come through the
gates of this city with their officials.
They and their officials will come riding
in chariots and on horses, accompanied
by the men of Judah and those living in
Jerusalem, and this city will be inhabited for ever. ²⁶People will come from
the towns of Judah and the villages
around Jerusalem, from the territory of
Benjamin and the western foothills,
from the hill country and the Negev,
bringing burnt offerings and sacrifices,
grain offerings, incense and thank-
offerings to the house of the LORD.

27But if you do not obey me to keep the Sabbath day holy by not carrying any load as you come through the gates of Jerusalem on the Sabbath day, then I will kindle an unquenchable fire in the gates of Jerusalem that will consume her fortresses.'"

NEW TESTAMENT READING
Colossians 4:2–18

Further Instructions

2Devote yourselves to prayer, being watchful and thankful. 3And pray for us, too, that God may open a door for our message, so that we may proclaim the mystery of Christ, for which I am in chains. 4Pray that I may proclaim it clearly, as I should. 5Be wise in the way you act towards outsiders; make the most of every opportunity. 6Let your conversation be always full of grace, seasoned with salt, so that you may know how to answer everyone.

Final Greetings

7Tychicus will tell you all the news about me. He is a dear brother, a faithful minister and fellow-servant in the Lord. 8I am sending him to you for the express purpose that you may know about our circumstances and that he may encourage your hearts. 9He is coming with Onesimus, our faithful and dear brother, who is one of you. They will tell you everything that is happening here.

10My fellow-prisoner Aristarchus sends you his greetings, as does Mark, the cousin of Barnabas. (You have received instructions about him; if he comes to you, welcome him.) 11Jesus, who is called Justus, also sends greetings. These are the only Jews among my fellow-workers for the kingdom of God, and they have proved a comfort to me. 12Epaphras, who is one of you and a servant of Christ Jesus, sends greetings. He is always wrestling in prayer for you,

that you may stand firm in all the will of God, mature and fully assured. 13I vouch for him that he is working hard for you and for those at Laodicea and Hierapolis. 14Our dear friend Luke, the doctor, and Demas send greetings. 15Give my greetings to the brothers at Laodicea, and to Nympha and the church in her house.

16After this letter has been read to you, see that it is also read in the church of the Laodiceans and that you in turn read the letter from Laodicea.

17Tell Archippus: "See to it that you complete the work you have received in the Lord."

18I, Paul, write this greeting in my own hand. Remember my chains. Grace be with you.

READING FROM PSALMS
Psalm 118:17–29

17I will not die but live,
  and will proclaim what the LORD
    has done.
18The LORD has chastened me severely,
  but he has not given me over to
    death.

19Open for me the gates of
    righteousness;
  I will enter and give thanks to the
    LORD.
20This is the gate of the LORD
  through which the righteous may
    enter.
21I will give you thanks, for you
    answered me;
  you have become my salvation.

22The stone the builders rejected
  has become the capstone;
23the LORD has done this,
  and it is marvellous in our eyes.
24This is the day the LORD has made;
  let us rejoice and be glad in it.

25O LORD, save us;
  O LORD, grant us success.
26Blessed is he who comes in the name
    of the LORD.

From the house of the LORD we
  bless you.
27The LORD is God,
  and he has made his light shine
    upon us.
With boughs in hand, join in the
    festal procession
  up to the horns of the altar.

28You are my God, and I will give
    thanks;
  you are my God, and I will exalt
    you.

29Give thanks to the LORD, for he is
    good;
  his love endures for ever.

DAY 282

OCTOBER 9

OLD TESTAMENT READING
Jeremiah 18:1–20:18

At the Potter's House

18 This is the word that came to
    Jeremiah from the LORD: 2"Go
down to the potter's house, and there I
will give you my message." 3So I went
down to the potter's house, and I saw
him working at the wheel. 4But the
pot he was shaping from the clay was
marred in his hands; so the potter
formed it into another pot, shaping it as
seemed best to him.

5Then the word of the LORD came to
me: 6"O house of Israel, can I not do
with you as this potter does?" declares
the LORD. "Like clay in the hand of the
potter, so are you in my hand, O house
of Israel. 7If at any time I announce that
a nation or kingdom is to be uprooted,
torn down and destroyed, 8and if that
nation I warned repents of its evil, then
I will relent and not inflict on it the
disaster I had planned. 9And if at
another time I announce that a nation
or kingdom is to be built up and
planted, 10and if it does evil in my sight
and does not obey me, then I will re-
consider the good I had intended to do
for it.

11"Now therefore say to the people of
Judah and those living in Jerusalem,
'This is what the LORD says: Look! I am
preparing a disaster for you and de-
vising a plan against you. So turn from
your evil ways, each one of you, and

reform your ways and your actions.'
12But they will reply, 'It's no use. We
will continue with our own plans; each
of us will follow the stubbornness of his
evil heart.'"

13Therefore this is what the LORD
says:

"Enquire among the nations:
  Who has ever heard anything like
    this?
A most horrible thing has been done
  by Virgin Israel.
14Does the snow of Lebanon
  ever vanish from its rocky slopes?
Do its cool waters from distant
    sources
  ever cease to flow?
15Yet my people have forgotten me;
  they burn incense to worthless
    idols,
  which made them stumble in their
    ways
  and in the ancient paths.
They made them walk in bypaths
  and on roads not built up.
16Their land will be laid waste,
  an object of lasting scorn;
all who pass by will be appalled
  and will shake their heads.
17Like a wind from the east,
  I will scatter them before their
    enemies;
I will show them my back and not my
    face
  in the day of their disaster."

18They said, "Come, let's make plans against Jeremiah; for the teaching of the law by the priest will not be lost, nor will counsel from the wise, nor the word from the prophets. So come, let's attack him with our tongues and pay no attention to anything he says."

19Listen to me, O LORD;
  hear what my accusers are saying!
20Should good be repaid with evil?
  Yet they have dug a pit for me.
  Remember that I stood before you
  and spoke on their behalf
  to turn your wrath away from
    them.
21So give their children over to famine;
  hand them over to the power of the
    sword.
  Let their wives be made childless and
    widows;
  let their men be put to death,
  their young men slain by the sword
    in battle.
22Let a cry be heard from their houses
  when you suddenly bring invaders
    against them,
  for they have dug a pit to capture me
  and have hidden snares for my
    feet.
23But you know, O LORD,
  all their plots to kill me.
  Do not forgive their crimes
  or blot out their sins from your
    sight.
  Let them be overthrown before you;
  deal with them in the time of your
    anger.

19 This is what the LORD says: "Go and buy a clay jar from a potter. Take along some of the elders of the people and of the priests 2and go out to the Valley of Ben Hinnom, near the entrance of the Potsherd Gate. There proclaim the words I tell you, 3and say, 'Hear the word of the LORD, O kings of Judah and people of Jerusalem. This is what the LORD Almighty, the God of Israel, says: Listen! I am going to bring a disaster on this place that will make the ears of everyone who hears of it

tingle. 4For they have forsaken me and made this a place of foreign gods; they have burned sacrifices in it to gods that neither they nor their fathers nor the kings of Judah ever knew, and they have filled this place with the blood of the innocent. 5They have built the high places of Baal to burn their sons in the fire as offerings to Baal—something I did not command or mention, nor did it enter my mind. 6So beware, the days are coming, declares the LORD, when people will no longer call this place Topheth or the Valley of Ben Hinnom, but the Valley of Slaughter.

7" 'In this place I will ruin the plans of Judah and Jerusalem. I will make them fall by the sword before their enemies, at the hands of those who seek their lives, and I will give their carcasses as food to the birds of the air and the beasts of the earth. 8I will devastate this city and make it an object of scorn; all who pass by will be appalled and will scoff because of all its wounds. 9I will make them eat the flesh of their sons and daughters, and they will eat one another's flesh during the stress of the siege imposed on them by the enemies who seek their lives.'

10"Then break the jar while those who go with you are watching, 11and say to them, 'This is what the LORD Almighty says: I will smash this nation and this city just as this potter's jar is smashed and cannot be repaired. They will bury the dead in Topheth until there is no more room. 12This is what I will do to this place and to those who live here, declares the LORD. I will make this city like Topheth. 13The houses in Jerusalem and those of the kings of Judah will be defiled like this place, Topheth—all the houses where they burned incense on the roofs to all the starry hosts and poured out drink offerings to other gods.'"

14Jeremiah then returned from Topheth, where the LORD had sent him to prophesy, and stood in the court of the LORD's temple and said to all the people, 15"This is what the LORD

Almighty, the God of Israel, says: 'Listen! I am going to bring on this city and the villages around it every disaster I pronounced against them, because they were stiff-necked and would not listen to my words.'"

Jeremiah and Pashhur

20 When the priest Pashhur son of Immer, the chief officer in the temple of the LORD, heard Jeremiah prophesying these things, ²he had Jeremiah the prophet beaten and put in the stocks at the Upper Gate of Benjamin at the LORD's temple. ³The next day, when Pashhur released him from the stocks, Jeremiah said to him, "The LORD's name for you is not Pashhur, but Magor-Missabib. ⁴For this is what the LORD says: 'I will make you a terror to yourself and to all your friends; with your own eyes you will see them fall by the sword of their enemies. I will hand all Judah over to the king of Babylon, who will carry them away to Babylon or put them to the sword. ⁵I will hand over to their enemies all the wealth of this city—all its products, all its valuables and all the treasures of the kings of Judah. They will take it away as plunder and carry it off to Babylon. ⁶And you, Pashhur, and all who live in your house will go into exile to Babylon. There you will die and be buried, you and all your friends to whom you have prophesied lies.'"

Jeremiah's Complaint

⁷O LORD, you deceived me, and I was deceived;
    you overpowered me and prevailed.
I am ridiculed all day long;
    everyone mocks me.
⁸Whenever I speak, I cry out
    proclaiming violence and destruction.
So the word of the LORD has brought me
    insult and reproach all day long.

⁹But if I say, "I will not mention him
    or speak any more in his name,"
his word is in my heart like a fire,
    a fire shut up in my bones.
I am weary of holding it in;
    indeed, I cannot.
¹⁰I hear many whispering,
    "Terror on every side!
    Report him! Let's report him!"
All my friends
    are waiting for me to slip, saying,
"Perhaps he will be deceived;
    then we will prevail over him
    and take our revenge on him."

¹¹But the LORD is with me like a mighty warrior;
    so my persecutors will stumble and not prevail.
They will fail and be thoroughly disgraced;
    their dishonour will never be forgotten.
¹²O LORD Almighty, you who examine the righteous
    and probe the heart and mind,
let me see your vengeance upon them,
    for to you I have committed my cause.

¹³Sing to the LORD!
    Give praise to the LORD!
He rescues the life of the needy
    from the hands of the wicked.

¹⁴Cursed be the day I was born!
    May the day my mother bore me not be blessed!
¹⁵Cursed be the man who brought my father the news,
    who made him very glad, saying,
    "A child is born to you—a son!"
¹⁶May that man be like the towns
    the LORD overthrew without pity.
May he hear wailing in the morning,
    a battle cry at noon.
¹⁷For he did not kill me in the womb,
    with my mother as my grave,
    her womb enlarged for ever.
¹⁸Why did I ever come out of the womb
    to see trouble and sorrow
    and to end my days in shame?

NEW TESTAMENT READING
1 Thessalonians 1:1–2:16

1 Paul, Silas and Timothy,

To the church of the Thessalonians in God the Father and the Lord Jesus Christ:

Grace and peace to you.

Thanksgiving for the Thessalonians' Faith

2We always thank God for all of you, mentioning you in our prayers. 3We continually remember before our God and Father your work produced by faith, your labour prompted by love, and your endurance inspired by hope in our Lord Jesus Christ.

4For we know, brothers loved by God, that he has chosen you, 5because our gospel came to you not simply with words, but also with power, with the Holy Spirit and with deep conviction. You know how we lived among you for your sake. 6You became imitators of us and of the Lord; in spite of severe suffering, you welcomed the message with the joy given by the Holy Spirit. 7And so you became a model to all the believers in Macedonia and Achaia. 8The Lord's message rang out from you not only in Macedonia and Achaia—your faith in God has become known everywhere. Therefore we do not need to say anything about it, 9for they themselves report what kind of reception you gave us. They tell how you turned to God from idols to serve the living and true God, 10and to wait for his Son from heaven, whom he raised from the dead —Jesus, who rescues us from the coming wrath.

Paul's Ministry in Thessalonica

2 You know, brothers, that our visit to you was not a failure. 2We had previously suffered and been insulted in Philippi, as you know, but with the help of our God we dared to tell you his gospel in spite of strong opposition. 3For the appeal we make does not spring from error or impure motives, nor are we trying to trick you. 4On the contrary, we speak as men approved by God to be entrusted with the gospel. We are not trying to please men but God, who tests our hearts. 5You know we never used flattery, nor did we put on a mask to cover up greed—God is our witness. 6We were not looking for praise from men, not from you or anyone else.

As apostles of Christ we could have been a burden to you, 7but we were gentle among you, like a mother caring for her little children. 8We loved you so much that we were delighted to share with you not only the gospel of God but our lives as well, because you had become so dear to us. 9Surely you remember, brothers, our toil and hardship; we worked night and day in order not to be a burden to anyone while we preached the gospel of God to you.

10You are witnesses, and so is God, of how holy, righteous and blameless we were among you who believed. 11For you know that we dealt with each of you as a father deals with his own children, 12encouraging, comforting and urging you to live lives worthy of God, who calls you into his kingdom and glory.

13And we also thank God continually because, when you received the word of God, which you heard from us, you accepted it not as the word of men, but as it actually is, the word of God, which is at work in you who believe. 14For you, brothers, became imitators of God's churches in Judea, which are in Christ Jesus: You suffered from your own countrymen the same things those churches suffered from the Jews, 15who killed the Lord Jesus and the prophets and also drove us out. They displease God and are hostile to all men 16in their effort to keep us from speaking to the Gentiles so that they may be saved. In this way they always heap up their sins to the limit. The wrath of God has come upon them at last.

READING FROM PSALMS
Psalm 119:1–8

א Aleph

¹Blessed are they whose ways are
　　blameless,
　　who walk according to the law of
　　　the LORD.

²Blessed are they who keep his
　　statutes
　　and seek him with all their heart.
³They do nothing wrong;
　　they walk in his ways.
⁴You have laid down precepts
　　that are to be fully obeyed.
⁵Oh, that my ways were steadfast
　　in obeying your decrees!
⁶Then I would not be put to shame
　　when I consider all your
　　　commands.
⁷I will praise you with an upright heart
　　as I learn your righteous laws.
⁸I will obey your decrees;
　　do not utterly forsake me.

DAY 283

OCTOBER 10

OLD TESTAMENT READING
Jeremiah 21:1–23:8

God Rejects Zedekiah's Request

21 The word came to Jeremiah from the LORD when King Zedekiah sent to him Pashhur son of Malkijah and the priest Zephaniah son of Maaseiah. They said: ²"Enquire now of the LORD for us because Nebuchadnezzar king of Babylon is attacking us. Perhaps the LORD will perform wonders for us as in times past so that he will withdraw from us."

³But Jeremiah answered them, "Tell Zedekiah, ⁴'This is what the LORD, the God of Israel, says: I am about to turn against you the weapons of war that are in your hands, which you are using to fight the king of Babylon and the Babylonians who are outside the wall besieging you. And I will gather them inside this city. ⁵I myself will fight against you with an outstretched hand and a mighty arm in anger and fury and great wrath. ⁶I will strike down those who live in this city—both men and animals—and they will die of a terrible plague. ⁷After that, declares the LORD,

I will hand over Zedekiah king of Judah, his officials and the people in this city who survive the plague, sword and famine, to Nebuchadnezzar king of Babylon and to their enemies who seek their lives. He will put them to the sword; he will show them no mercy or pity or compassion.'

⁸"Furthermore, tell the people, 'This is what the LORD says: See, I am setting before you the way of life and the way of death. ⁹Whoever stays in this city will die by the sword, famine or plague. But whoever goes out and surrenders to the Babylonians who are besieging you will live; he will escape with his life. ¹⁰I have determined to do this city harm and not good, declares the LORD. It will be given into the hands of the king of Babylon, and he will destroy it with fire.'

¹¹"Moreover, say to the royal house of Judah, 'Hear the word of the LORD; ¹²O house of David, this is what the LORD says:

　　"'Administer justice every morning;
　　　rescue from the hand of his
　　　　oppressor
　　　the one who has been robbed,

or my wrath will break out and burn
like fire
because of the evil you have
done—
burn with no-one to quench it.
13I am against you, ⌊Jerusalem,⌋
you who live above this valley
on the rocky plateau,
declares the LORD—
you who say, "Who can come against
us?
Who can enter our refuge?"
14I will punish you as your deeds
deserve,
declares the LORD.
I will kindle a fire in your forests
that will consume everything
around you.'"

Judgment Against Evil Kings

22 This is what the LORD says: "Go
down to the palace of the king of
Judah and proclaim this message there:
2'Hear the word of the LORD, O king of
Judah, you who sit on David's throne
—you, your officials and your people
who come through these gates. 3This is
what the LORD says: Do what is just
and right. Rescue from the hand of
his oppressor the one who has been
robbed. Do no wrong or violence to the
alien, the fatherless or the widow, and
do not shed innocent blood in this place.
4For if you are careful to carry out these
commands, then kings who sit on
David's throne will come through the
gates of this palace, riding in chariots
and on horses, accompanied by their
officials and their people. 5But if you do
not obey these commands, declares the
LORD, I swear by myself that this palace
will become a ruin.'"

6For this is what the LORD says about
the palace of the king of Judah:

"Though you are like Gilead to me,
like the summit of Lebanon,
I will surely make you like a desert,
like towns not inhabited.
7I will send destroyers against you,
each man with his weapons,

and they will cut up your fine cedar
beams
and throw them into the fire.

8"People from many nations will pass
by this city and will ask one another,
'Why has the LORD done such a thing to
this great city?' 9And the answer will be:
'Because they have forsaken the covenant of the LORD their God and have
worshipped and served other gods.'"

10Do not weep for the dead ⌊king⌋ or
mourn his loss;
rather, weep bitterly for him who is
exiled,
because he will never return
nor see his native land again.

11For this is what the LORD says about
Shallum son of Josiah, who succeeded
his father as king of Judah but has gone
from this place: "He will never return.
12He will die in the place where they
have led him captive; he will not see this
land again."

13"Woe to him who builds his palace by
unrighteousness,
his upper rooms by injustice,
making his countrymen work for
nothing,
not paying them for their labour.
14He says, 'I will build myself a great
palace
with spacious upper rooms.'
So he makes large windows in it,
panels it with cedar
and decorates it in red.

15Does it make you a king
to have more and more cedar?
Did not your father have food and
drink?
He did what was right and just,
so all went well with him.
16He defended the cause of the poor
and needy,
and so all went well.
Is that not what it means to know
me?"
declares the LORD.

¹⁷"But your eyes and your heart
    are set only on dishonest gain,
on shedding innocent blood
    and on oppression and extortion."

¹⁸Therefore this is what the LORD says about Jehoiakim son of Josiah king of Judah:

"They will not mourn for him:
    'Alas, my brother! Alas, my sister!'
They will not mourn for him:
    'Alas, my master! Alas, his
        splendour!'
¹⁹He will have the burial of a donkey—
    dragged away and thrown
        outside the gates of Jerusalem."

²⁰"Go up to Lebanon and cry out,
    let your voice be heard in Bashan,
    cry out from Abarim,
for all your allies are crushed.
²¹I warned you when you felt secure,
    but you said, 'I will not listen!'
This has been your way from your
        youth;
    you have not obeyed me.
²²The wind will drive all your
        shepherds away,
    and your allies will go into exile.
Then you will be ashamed and
        disgraced
    because of all your wickedness.
²³You who live in 'Lebanon',
    who are nestled in cedar buildings,
how you will groan when pangs come
        upon you,
    pain like that of a woman in
        labour!

²⁴"As surely as I live," declares the LORD, "even if you, Jehoiachin son of Jehoiakim king of Judah, were a signet ring on my right hand, I would still pull you off. ²⁵I will hand you over to those who seek your life, those you fear—to Nebuchadnezzar king of Babylon and to the Babylonians. ²⁶I will hurl you and the mother who gave you birth into another country, where neither of you was born, and there you both will die. ²⁷You will never come back to the land you long to return to."

²⁸Is this man Jehoiachin a despised,
        broken pot,
    an object no-one wants?
Why will he and his children be
        hurled out,
    cast into a land they do not know?
²⁹O land, land, land,
    hear the word of the LORD!
³⁰This is what the LORD says:
    "Record this man as if childless,
        a man who will not prosper in his
            lifetime,
for none of his offspring will prosper,
    none will sit on the throne of David
        or rule any more in Judah."

The Righteous Branch

23 "Woe to the shepherds who are destroying and scattering the sheep of my pasture!" declares the LORD. ²Therefore this is what the LORD, the God of Israel, says to the shepherds who tend my people: "Because you have scattered my flock and driven them away and have not bestowed care on them, I will bestow punishment on you for the evil you have done," declares the LORD. ³"I myself will gather the remnant of my flock out of all the countries where I have driven them and will bring them back to their pasture, where they will be fruitful and increase in number. ⁴I will place shepherds over them who will tend them, and they will no longer be afraid or terrified, nor will any be missing," declares the LORD.

⁵"The days are coming," declares the
        LORD,
    "when I will raise up to David a
        righteous Branch,
    a King who will reign wisely
        and do what is just and right in the
            land.
⁶In his days Judah will be saved
    and Israel will live in safety.
This is the name by which he will be
        called:
    The LORD Our Righteousness.

⁷"So then, the days are coming," declares the LORD, "when people will no

longer say, 'As surely as the LORD lives, who brought the Israelites up out of Egypt,' [8]but they will say, 'As surely as the LORD lives, who brought the descendants of Israel up out of the land of the north and out of all the countries where he had banished them.' Then they will live in their own land."

NEW TESTAMENT READING
1 Thessalonians 2:17–3:13

Paul's Longing to See the Thessalonians

[17]But, brothers, when we were torn away from you for a short time (in person, not in thought), out of our intense longing we made every effort to see you. [18]For we wanted to come to you —certainly I, Paul, did, again and again —but Satan stopped us. [19]For what is our hope, our joy, or the crown in which we will glory in the presence of our Lord Jesus Christ when he comes? Is it not you? [20]Indeed, you are our glory and joy.

3 So when we could stand it no longer, we thought it best to be left by ourselves in Athens. [2]We sent Timothy, who is our brother and God's fellow-worker in spreading the gospel of Christ, to strengthen and encourage you in your faith, [3]so that no-one would be unsettled by these trials. You know quite well that we were destined for them. [4]In fact, when we were with you, we kept telling you that we would be persecuted. And it turned out that way, as you well know. [5]For this reason, when I could stand it no longer, I sent to find out about your faith. I was afraid that in some way the tempter might have tempted you and our efforts might have been useless.

Timothy's Encouraging Report

[6]But Timothy has just now come to us from you and has brought good news about your faith and love. He has told us that you always have pleasant memories of us and that you long to see us, just as we also long to see you. [7]Therefore, brothers, in all our distress and persecution we were encouraged about you because of your faith. [8]For now we really live, since you are standing firm in the Lord. [9]How can we thank God enough for you in return for all the joy we have in the presence of our God because of you? [10]Night and day we pray most earnestly that we may see you again and supply what is lacking in your faith.

[11]Now may our God and Father himself and our Lord Jesus clear the way for us to come to you. [12]May the Lord make your love increase and overflow for each other and for everyone else, just as ours does for you. [13]May he strengthen your hearts so that you will be blameless and holy in the presence of our God and Father when our Lord Jesus comes with all his holy ones.

READING FROM PSALMS
Psalm 119:9–16

ב Beth

[9]How can a young man keep his way pure?
  By living according to your word.
[10]I seek you with all my heart;
    do not let me stray from your commands.
[11]I have hidden your word in my heart
    that I might not sin against you.
[12]Praise be to you, O LORD;
    teach me your decrees.
[13]With my lips I recount
    all the laws that come from your mouth.
[14]I rejoice in following your statutes
    as one rejoices in great riches.
[15]I meditate on your precepts
    and consider your ways.
[16]I delight in your decrees;
    I will not neglect your word.

OCTOBER 11

OLD TESTAMENT READING
Jeremiah 23:9–25:14

Lying Prophets

⁹Concerning the prophets:

My heart is broken within me;
 all my bones tremble.
I am like a drunken man,
 like a man overcome by wine,
because of the LORD
 and his holy words.
¹⁰The land is full of adulterers;
 because of the curse the land lies
 parched
 and the pastures in the desert are
 withered.
The ˻prophets˼ follow an evil course
 and use their power unjustly.

¹¹"Both prophet and priest are godless;
 even in my temple I find their
 wickedness,"
  declares the LORD.
¹²"Therefore their path will become
 slippery;
 they will be banished to darkness
 and there they will fall.
I will bring disaster on them
 in the year they are punished,"
  declares the LORD.

¹³"Among the prophets of Samaria
 I saw this repulsive thing:
They prophesied by Baal
 and led my people Israel astray.
¹⁴And among the prophets of
 Jerusalem
 I have seen something horrible:
 They commit adultery and live a
 lie.
They strengthen the hands of
 evildoers,
 so that no-one turns from his
 wickedness.
They are all like Sodom to me;
 the people of Jerusalem are like
 Gomorrah."

¹⁵Therefore, this is what the LORD
Almighty says concerning the prophets:

"I will make them eat bitter food
 and drink poisoned water,
because from the prophets of
 Jerusalem
 ungodliness has spread throughout
 the land."

¹⁶This is what the LORD Almighty
says:

"Do not listen to what the prophets
 are prophesying to you;
 they fill you with false hopes.
They speak visions from their own
 minds,
 not from the mouth of the LORD.
¹⁷They keep saying to those who
 despise me,
 'The LORD says: You will have
 peace.'
And to all who follow the
 stubbornness of their hearts
 they say, 'No harm will come to
 you.'
¹⁸But which of them has stood in the
 council of the LORD
 to see or to hear his word?
 Who has listened and heard his
 word?
¹⁹See, the storm of the LORD
 will burst out in wrath,
a whirlwind swirling down
 on the heads of the wicked.
²⁰The anger of the LORD will not turn
 back
 until he fully accomplishes
 the purposes of his heart.
In days to come
 you will understand it clearly.
²¹I did not send these prophets,
 yet they have run with their
 message;
I did not speak to them,
 yet they have prophesied.
²²But if they had stood in my council,

they would have proclaimed my
> words to my people
and would have turned them from
> their evil ways
> and from their evil deeds.

23"Am I only a God nearby,"
> declares the LORD,
"and not a God far away?
24Can anyone hide in secret places
> so that I cannot see him?"
> declares the LORD.
"Do not I fill heaven and earth?"
> declares the LORD.

25"I have heard what the prophets say who prophesy lies in my name. They say, 'I had a dream! I had a dream!' 26How long will this continue in the hearts of these lying prophets, who prophesy the delusions of their own minds? 27They think the dreams they tell one another will make my people forget my name, just as their fathers forgot my name through Baal worship. 28Let the prophet who has a dream tell his dream, but let the one who has my word speak it faithfully. For what has straw to do with grain?" declares the LORD. 29"Is not my word like fire," declares the LORD, "and like a hammer that breaks a rock in pieces?

30"Therefore," declares the LORD, "I am against the prophets who steal from one another words supposedly from me." 31Yes," declares the LORD, "I am against the prophets who wag their own tongues and yet declare, 'The LORD declares.' 32Indeed, I am against those who prophesy false dreams," declares the LORD. "They tell them and lead my people astray with their reckless lies, yet I did not send or appoint them. They do not benefit these people in the least," declares the LORD.

False Oracles and False Prophets

33"When these people, or a prophet or a priest, ask you, 'What is the oracle of the LORD?' say to them, 'What oracle? I will forsake you, declares the

LORD.' 34If a prophet or a priest or anyone else claims, 'This is the oracle of the LORD,' I will punish that man and his household. 35This is what each of you keeps on saying to his friend or relative: 'What is the LORD's answer?' or 'What has the LORD spoken?' 36But you must not mention 'the oracle of the LORD' again, because every man's own word becomes his oracle and so you distort the words of the living God, the LORD Almighty, our God. 37This is what you keep saying to a prophet: 'What is the LORD's answer to you?' or 'What has the LORD spoken?' 38Although you claim, 'This is the oracle of the LORD,' this is what the LORD says: You used the words, 'This is the oracle of the LORD,' even though I told you that you must not claim, 'This is the oracle of the LORD.' 39Therefore, I will surely forget you and cast you out of my presence along with the city I gave to you and your fathers. 40I will bring upon you everlasting disgrace —everlasting shame that will not be forgotten."

Two Baskets of Figs

24 After Jehoiachin son of Jehoiakim king of Judah and the officials, the craftsmen and the artisans of Judah were carried into exile from Jerusalem to Babylon by Nebuchadnezzar king of Babylon, the LORD showed me two baskets of figs placed in front of the temple of the LORD. 2One basket had very good figs, like those that ripen early; the other basket had very poor figs, so bad that they could not be eaten.

3Then the LORD asked me, "What do you see, Jeremiah?"

"Figs," I answered. "The good ones are very good, but the poor ones are so bad that they cannot be eaten."

4Then the word of the LORD came to me: 5"This is what the LORD, the God of Israel, says: 'Like these good figs, I regard as good the exiles from Judah, whom I sent away from this place to the land of the Babylonians. 6My eyes will watch over them for their good, and I will bring them back to this land. I will build them up and not tear them down; I will plant them and not uproot them. 7I will give them a heart to know me, that I am the LORD. They will be my people, and I will be their God, for they will return to me with all their heart.

8" 'But like the poor figs, which are so bad that they cannot be eaten,' says the LORD, 'so will I deal with Zedekiah king of Judah, his officials and the survivors from Jerusalem, whether they remain in this land or live in Egypt. 9I will make them abhorrent and an offence to all the kingdoms of the earth, a reproach and a byword, an object of ridicule and cursing, wherever I banish them. 10I will send the sword, famine and plague against them until they are destroyed from the land I gave to them and their fathers.'"

Seventy Years of Captivity

25 The word came to Jeremiah concerning all the people of Judah in the fourth year of Jehoiakim son of Josiah king of Judah, which was the first year of Nebuchadnezzar king of Babylon. 2So Jeremiah the prophet said to all the people of Judah and to all those living in Jerusalem: 3For twenty-three years—from the thirteenth year of Josiah son of Amon king of Judah until this very day—the word of the LORD has come to me and I have spoken to you again and again, but you have not listened.

4And though the LORD has sent all his servants the prophets to you again and again, you have not listened or paid any attention. 5They said, "Turn now, each of you, from your evil ways and your evil practices, and you can stay in the land the LORD gave to you and your fathers for ever and ever. 6Do not follow other gods to serve and worship them; do not provoke me to anger with what your hands have made. Then I will not harm you."

7"But you did not listen to me," declares the LORD, "and you have provoked me with what your hands have made, and you have brought harm to yourselves."

8Therefore the LORD Almighty says this: "Because you have not listened to my words, 9I will summon all the peoples of the north and my servant Nebuchadnezzar king of Babylon," declares the LORD, "and I will bring them against this land and its inhabitants and against all the surrounding nations. I will completely destroy them and make them an object of horror and scorn, and an everlasting ruin. 10I will banish from them the sounds of joy and gladness, the voices of bride and bridegroom, the sound of millstones and the light of the lamp. 11This whole country will become a desolate wasteland, and these nations will serve the king of Babylon for seventy years.

12"But when the seventy years are fulfilled, I will punish the king of Babylon and his nation, the land of the Babylonians, for their guilt," declares the LORD, "and will make it desolate for ever. 13I will bring upon that land all the things I have spoken against it, all that are written in this book and prophesied by Jeremiah against all the nations. 14They themselves will be enslaved by many nations and great kings; I will repay them according to their deeds and the work of their hands."

NEW TESTAMENT READING
1 Thessalonians 4:1–18

Living to Please God

4 Finally, brothers, we instructed you how to live in order to please God, as in fact you are living. Now we ask you and urge you in the Lord Jesus to do this more and more. 2For you know what instructions we gave you by the authority of the Lord Jesus.

3It is God's will that you should be sanctified: that you should avoid sexual immorality; 4that each of you should learn to control his own body in a way that is holy and honourable, 5not in passionate lust like the heathen, who do not know God; 6and that in this matter no-one should wrong his brother or take advantage of him. The Lord will punish men for all such sins, as we have already told you and warned you. 7For God did not call us to be impure, but to live a holy life. 8Therefore, he who rejects this instruction does not reject man but God, who gives you his Holy Spirit.

9Now about brotherly love we do not need to write to you, for you yourselves have been taught by God to love each other. 10And in fact, you do love all the brothers throughout Macedonia. Yet we urge you, brothers, to do so more and more.

11Make it your ambition to lead a quiet life, to mind your own business and to work with your hands, just as we told you, 12so that your daily life may win the respect of outsiders and so that you will not be dependent on anybody.

The Coming of the Lord

13Brothers, we do not want you to be ignorant about those who fall asleep, or to grieve like the rest of men, who have no hope. 14We believe that Jesus died and rose again and so we believe that God will bring with Jesus those who have fallen asleep in him. 15According to the Lord's own word, we tell you that we who are still alive, who are left till the coming of the Lord, will certainly not precede those who have fallen asleep. 16For the Lord himself will come down from heaven, with a loud command, with the voice of the archangel and with the trumpet call of God, and the dead in Christ will rise first. 17After that, we who are still alive and are left will be caught up together with them in the clouds to meet the Lord in the air. And so we will be with the Lord for ever. 18Therefore encourage each other with these words.

READING FROM PROVERBS
Proverbs 24:23–34

Further Sayings of the Wise

23These also are sayings of the wise:

To show partiality in judging is not
    good:
24Whoever says to the guilty, "You are
    innocent"—
  peoples will curse him and nations
    denounce him.
25But it will go well with those who
    convict the guilty,
  and rich blessing will come upon
    them.

26An honest answer
  is like a kiss on the lips.

27Finish your outdoor work
  and get your fields ready;
  after that, build your house.

28Do not testify against your neighbour
    without cause,
  or use your lips to deceive.
29Do not say, "I'll do to him as he has
    done to me;
  I'll pay that man back for what he
    did."

30I went past the field of the sluggard,
  past the vineyard of the man who
    lacks judgment;
31thorns had come up everywhere,
  the ground was covered with
    weeds,
  and the stone wall was in ruins.
32I applied my heart to what I observed
  and learned a lesson from what I
    saw:
33A little sleep, a little slumber,
  a little folding of the hands to
    rest—
34and poverty will come on you like a
    bandit
  and scarcity like an armed man.

OCTOBER 12

OLD TESTAMENT READING
Jeremiah 25:15–26:24

The Cup of God's Wrath

¹⁵This is what the LORD, the God of Israel, said to me: "Take from my hand this cup filled with the wine of my wrath and make all the nations to whom I send you drink it. ¹⁶When they drink it, they will stagger and go mad because of the sword I will send among them."

¹⁷So I took the cup from the LORD's hand and made all the nations to whom he sent me drink it: ¹⁸Jerusalem and the towns of Judah, its kings and officials, to make them a ruin and an object of horror and scorn and cursing, as they are today; ¹⁹Pharaoh king of Egypt, his attendants, his officials and all his people, ²⁰and all the foreign people there; all the kings of Uz; all the kings of the Philistines (those of Ashkelon, Gaza, Ekron, and the people left at Ashdod); ²¹Edom, Moab and Ammon; ²²all the kings of Tyre and Sidon; the kings of the coastlands across the sea; ²³Dedan, Tema, Buz and all who are in distant places; ²⁴all the kings of Arabia and all the kings of the foreign people who live in the desert; ²⁵all the kings of Zimri, Elam and Media; ²⁶and all the kings of the north, near and far, one after the other—all the kingdoms on the face of the earth. And after all of them, the king of Sheshach will drink it too.

²⁷"Then tell them, 'This is what the LORD Almighty, the God of Israel, says: Drink, get drunk and vomit, and fall to rise no more because of the sword I will send among you.' ²⁸But if they refuse to take the cup from your hand and drink, tell them, 'This is what the LORD Almighty says: You must drink it! ²⁹See, I am beginning to bring disaster on the city that bears my Name, and will you indeed go unpunished? You will not go unpunished, for I am calling down a sword upon all who live on the earth, declares the LORD Almighty.'

³⁰"Now prophesy all these words against them and say to them:

"'The LORD will roar from on high;
    he will thunder from his holy
        dwelling
    and roar mightily against his land.
He will shout like those who tread
        the grapes,
    shout against all who live on the
        earth.
³¹The tumult will resound to the ends
        of the earth,
    for the LORD will bring charges
        against the nations;
he will bring judgment on all
        mankind
    and put the wicked to the sword,'"
                    declares the LORD.

³²This is what the LORD Almighty says:

"Look! Disaster is spreading
    from nation to nation;
a mighty storm is rising
    from the ends of the earth."

³³At that time those slain by the LORD will be everywhere—from one end of the earth to the other. They will not be mourned or gathered up or buried, but will be like refuse lying on the ground.

³⁴Weep and wail, you shepherds;
    roll in the dust, you leaders of the
        flock.
For your time to be slaughtered has
        come;
    you will fall and be shattered like
        fine pottery.
³⁵The shepherds will have nowhere to
        flee,
    the leaders of the flock no place to
        escape.
³⁶Hear the cry of the shepherds,

the wailing of the leaders of the
flock,
for the LORD is destroying their
pasture.
37The peaceful meadows will be laid
waste
because of the fierce anger of the
LORD.
38Like a lion he will leave his lair,
and their land will become desolate
because of the sword of the oppressor
and because of the LORD's fierce
anger.

Jeremiah Threatened With Death

26 Early in the reign of Jehoiakim
son of Josiah king of Judah, this
word came from the LORD: 2"This is
what the LORD says: Stand in the courtyard of the LORD's house and speak to
all the people of the towns of Judah who
come to worship in the house of the
LORD. Tell them everything I command
you; do not omit a word. 3Perhaps they
will listen and each will turn from his
evil way. Then I will relent and not
bring on them the disaster I was planning because of the evil they have done.
4Say to them, 'This is what the LORD
says: If you do not listen to me and
follow my law, which I have set before
you, 5and if you do not listen to the
words of my servants the prophets,
whom I have sent to you again and again
(though you have not listened), 6then I
will make this house like Shiloh and this
city an object of cursing among all the
nations of the earth.'"

7The priests, the prophets and all the
people heard Jeremiah speak these
words in the house of the LORD. 8But as
soon as Jeremiah finished telling all the
people everything the LORD had commanded him to say, the priests, the
prophets and all the people seized him
and said, "You must die! 9Why do you
prophesy in the LORD's name that this
house will be like Shiloh and this city
will be desolate and deserted?" And all
the people crowded around Jeremiah in
the house of the LORD.

10When the officials of Judah heard
about these things, they went up from
the royal palace to the house of the
LORD and took their places at the entrance of the New Gate of the LORD's
house. 11Then the priests and the
prophets said to the officials and all the
people, "This man should be sentenced
to death because he has prophesied
against this city. You have heard it with
your own ears!"

12Then Jeremiah said to all the officials and all the people: "The LORD
sent me to prophesy against this house
and this city all the things you have
heard. 13Now reform your ways and
your actions and obey the LORD your
God. Then the LORD will relent and not
bring the disaster he has pronounced
against you. 14As for me, I am in your
hands; do with me whatever you think is
good and right. 15Be assured, however,
that if you put me to death, you will
bring the guilt of innocent blood on
yourselves and on this city and on those
who live in it, for in truth the LORD has
sent me to you to speak all these words
in your hearing."

16Then the officials and all the people
said to the priests and the prophets,
"This man should not be sentenced to
death! He has spoken to us in the name
of the LORD our God."

17Some of the elders of the land
stepped forward and said to the entire
assembly of people, 18"Micah of
Moresheth prophesied in the days of
Hezekiah king of Judah. He told all the
people of Judah, 'This is what the LORD
Almighty says:

"'Zion will be ploughed like a field,
Jerusalem will become a heap of
rubble,
the temple hill a mound overgrown
with thickets.'

19"Did Hezekiah king of Judah or anyone else in Judah put him to death? Did
not Hezekiah fear the LORD and seek
his favour? And did not the LORD relent, so that he did not bring the disaster
he pronounced against them? We are

about to bring a terrible disaster on ourselves!"

20(Now Uriah son of Shemaiah from Kiriath Jearim was another man who prophesied in the name of the LORD; he prophesied the same things against this city and this land as Jeremiah did. 21When King Jehoiakim and all his officers and officials heard his words, the king sought to put him to death. But Uriah heard of it and fled in fear to Egypt. 22King Jehoiakim, however, sent Elnathan son of Acbor to Egypt, along with some other men. 23They brought Uriah out of Egypt and took him to King Jehoiakim, who had him struck down with a sword and his body thrown into the burial place of the common people.)

24Furthermore, Ahikam son of Shaphan supported Jeremiah, and so he was not handed over to the people to be put to death.

NEW TESTAMENT READING
1 Thessalonians 5:1–28

5 Now, brothers, about times and dates we do not need to write to you, 2for you know very well that the day of the Lord will come like a thief in the night. 3While people are saying, "Peace and safety", destruction will come on them suddenly, as labour pains on a pregnant woman, and they will not escape.

4But you, brothers, are not in darkness so that this day should surprise you like a thief. 5You are all sons of the light and sons of the day. We do not belong to the night or to the darkness. 6So then, let us not be like others, who are asleep, but let us be alert and self-controlled. 7For those who sleep, sleep at night, and those who get drunk, get drunk at night. 8But since we belong to the day, let us be self-controlled, putting on faith and love as a breastplate, and the hope of salvation as a helmet. 9For God did not appoint us to suffer wrath but to receive salvation through our Lord

Jesus Christ. 10He died for us so that, whether we are awake or asleep, we may live together with him. 11Therefore encourage one another and build each other up, just as in fact you are doing.

Final Instructions

12Now we ask you, brothers, to respect those who work hard among you, who are over you in the Lord and who admonish you. 13Hold them in the highest regard in love because of their work. Live in peace with each other. 14And we urge you, brothers, warn those who are idle, encourage the timid, help the weak, be patient with everyone. 15Make sure that nobody pays back wrong for wrong, but always try to be kind to each other and to everyone else.

16Be joyful always; 17pray continually; 18give thanks in all circumstances, for this is God's will for you in Christ Jesus.

19Do not put out the Spirit's fire; 20do not treat prophecies with contempt. 21Test everything. Hold on to the good. 22Avoid every kind of evil.

23May God himself, the God of peace, sanctify you through and through. May your whole spirit, soul and body be kept blameless at the coming of our Lord Jesus Christ. 24The one who calls you is faithful and he will do it.

25Brothers, pray for us. 26Greet all the brothers with a holy kiss. 27I charge you before the Lord to have this letter read to all the brothers.

28The grace of our Lord Jesus Christ be with you.

READING FROM PSALMS
Psalm 119:17–24

ג Gimel

17Do good to your servant, and I will live;
   I will obey your word.
18Open my eyes that I may see
   wonderful things in your law.

¹⁹I am a stranger on earth;
  do not hide your commands from
  me.
²⁰My soul is consumed with longing
  for your laws at all times.
²¹You rebuke the arrogant, who are
  cursed
  and who stray from your
  commands.

²²Remove from me scorn and
  contempt,
  for I keep your statutes.
²³Though rulers sit together and
  slander me,
  your servant will meditate on your
  decrees.
²⁴Your statutes are my delight;
  they are my counsellors.

OCTOBER 13

DAY 286

OLD TESTAMENT READING
Jeremiah 27:1–29:23

Judah to Serve Nebuchadnezzar

27 Early in the reign of Zedekiah son of Josiah king of Judah, this word came to Jeremiah from the LORD: ²This is what the LORD said to me: "Make a yoke out of straps and crossbars and put it on your neck. ³Then send word to the kings of Edom, Moab, Ammon, Tyre and Sidon through the envoys who have come to Jerusalem to Zedekiah king of Judah. ⁴Give them a message for their masters and say, 'This is what the LORD Almighty, the God of Israel, says: "Tell this to your masters: ⁵With my great power and outstretched arm I made the earth and its people and the animals that are on it, and I give it to anyone I please. ⁶Now I will hand all your countries over to my servant Nebuchadnezzar king of Babylon; I will make even the wild animals subject to him. ⁷All nations will serve him and his son and his grandson until the time for his land comes; then many nations and great kings will subjugate him.

⁸"'"If, however, any nation or kingdom will not serve Nebuchadnezzar king of Babylon or bow its neck under his yoke, I will punish that nation with the sword, famine and plague, declares the LORD, until I destroy it by his hand. ⁹So do not listen to your prophets, your

diviners, your interpreters of dreams, your mediums or your sorcerers who tell you, 'You will not serve the king of Babylon.' ¹⁰They prophesy lies to you that will only serve to remove you far from your lands; I will banish you and you will perish. ¹¹But if any nation will bow its neck under the yoke of the king of Babylon and serve him, I will let that nation remain in its own land to till it and to live there, declares the LORD."'"

¹²I gave the same message to Zedekiah king of Judah. I said, "Bow your neck under the yoke of the king of Babylon; serve him and his people, and you will live. ¹³Why will you and your people die by the sword, famine and plague with which the LORD has threatened any nation that will not serve the king of Babylon? ¹⁴Do not listen to the words of the prophets who say to you, 'You will not serve the king of Babylon,' for they are prophesying lies to you. ¹⁵'I have not sent them,' declares the LORD. 'They are prophesying lies in my name. Therefore, I will banish you and you will perish, both you and the prophets who prophesy to you.'"

¹⁶Then I said to the priests and all these people, "This is what the LORD says: Do not listen to the prophets who say, 'Very soon now the articles from the LORD's house will be brought back

from Babylon.' They are prophesying lies to you. [17]Do not listen to them. Serve the king of Babylon, and you will live. Why should this city become a ruin? [18]If they are prophets and have the word of the LORD, let them plead with the LORD Almighty that the furnishings remaining in the house of the LORD and in the palace of the king of Judah and in Jerusalem not be taken to Babylon. [19]For this is what the LORD Almighty says about the pillars, the Sea, the movable stands and the other furnishings that are left in this city, [20]which Nebuchadnezzar king of Babylon did not take away when he carried Jehoiachin son of Jehoiakim king of Judah into exile from Jerusalem to Babylon, along with all the nobles of Judah and Jerusalem—[21]yes, this is what the LORD Almighty, the God of Israel, says about the things that are left in the house of the LORD and in the palace of the king of Judah and in Jerusalem: [22]'They will be taken to Babylon and there they will remain until the day I come for them,' declares the LORD. 'Then I will bring them back and restore them to this place.'"

The False Prophet Hananiah

28 In the fifth month of that same year, the fourth year, early in the reign of Zedekiah king of Judah, the prophet Hananiah son of Azzur, who was from Gibeon, said to me in the house of the LORD in the presence of the priests and all the people: [2]"This is what the LORD Almighty, the God of Israel, says: 'I will break the yoke of the king of Babylon. [3]Within two years I will bring back to this place all the articles of the LORD's house that Nebuchadnezzar king of Babylon removed from here and took to Babylon. [4]I will also bring back to this place Jehoiachin son of Jehoiakim king of Judah and all the other exiles from Judah who went to Babylon,' declares the LORD, 'for I will break the yoke of the king of Babylon.'"

[5]Then the prophet Jeremiah replied to the prophet Hananiah before the priests and all the people who were standing in the house of the LORD. [6]He said, "Amen! May the LORD do so! May the LORD fulfil the words you have prophesied by bringing the articles of the LORD's house and all the exiles back to this place from Babylon. [7]Nevertheless, listen to what I have to say in your hearing and in the hearing of all the people: [8]From early times the prophets who preceded you and me have prophesied war, disaster and plague against many countries and great kingdoms. [9]But the prophet who prophesies peace will be recognised as one truly sent by the LORD only if his prediction comes true."

[10]Then the prophet Hananiah took the yoke off the neck of the prophet Jeremiah and broke it, [11]and he said before all the people, "This is what the LORD says: 'In the same way will I break the yoke of Nebuchadnezzar king of Babylon off the neck of all the nations within two years.'" At this, the prophet Jeremiah went on his way.

[12]Shortly after the prophet Hananiah had broken the yoke off the neck of the prophet Jeremiah, the word of the LORD came to Jeremiah: [13]"Go and tell Hananiah, 'This is what the LORD says: You have broken a wooden yoke, but in its place you will get a yoke of iron. [14]This is what the LORD Almighty, the God of Israel, says: I will put an iron yoke on the necks of all these nations to make them serve Nebuchadnezzar king of Babylon, and they will serve him. I will even give him control over the wild animals.'"

[15]Then the prophet Jeremiah said to Hananiah the prophet, "Listen, Hananiah! The LORD has not sent you, yet you have persuaded this nation to trust in lies. [16]Therefore, this is what the LORD says: 'I am about to remove you from the face of the earth. This very year you are going to die, because you have preached rebellion against the LORD.'"

17In the seventh month of that same year, Hananiah the prophet died.

A Letter to the Exiles

29 This is the text of the letter that the prophet Jeremiah sent from Jerusalem to the surviving elders among the exiles and to the priests, the prophets and all the other people Nebuchadnezzar had carried into exile from Jerusalem to Babylon. 2(This was after King Jehoiachin and the queen mother, the court officials and the leaders of Judah and Jerusalem, the craftsmen and the artisans had gone into exile from Jerusalem.) 3He entrusted the letter to Elasah son of Shaphan and to Gemariah son of Hilkiah, whom Zedekiah king of Judah sent to King Nebuchadnezzar in Babylon. It said:

4This is what the LORD Almighty, the God of Israel, says to all those I carried into exile from Jerusalem to Babylon: 5"Build houses and settle down; plant gardens and eat what they produce. 6Marry and have sons and daughters; find wives for your sons and give your daughters in marriage, so that they too may have sons and daughters. Increase in number there; do not decrease. 7Also, seek the peace and prosperity of the city to which I have carried you into exile. Pray to the LORD for it, because if it prospers, you too will prosper." 8Yes, this is what the LORD Almighty, the God of Israel, says: "Do not let the prophets and diviners among you deceive you. Do not listen to the dreams you encourage them to have. 9They are prophesying lies to you in my name. I have not sent them," declares the LORD.

10This is what the LORD says: "When seventy years are completed for Babylon, I will come to you and fulfil my gracious promise to bring you back to this place.

11For I know the plans I have for you," declares the LORD, "plans to prosper you and not to harm you, plans to give you hope and a future. 12Then you will call upon me and come and pray to me, and I will listen to you. 13You will seek me and find me when you seek me with all your heart. 14I will be found by you," declares the LORD, "and will bring you back from captivity. I will gather you from all the nations and places where I have banished you," declares the LORD, "and will bring you back to the place from which I carried you into exile."

15You may say, "The LORD has raised up prophets for us in Babylon," 16but this is what the LORD says about the king who sits on David's throne and all the people who remain in this city, your countrymen who did not go with you into exile—17yes, this is what the LORD Almighty says: "I will send the sword, famine and plague against them and I will make them like poor figs that are so bad they cannot be eaten. 18I will pursue them with the sword, famine and plague and will make them abhorrent to all the kingdoms of the earth and an object of cursing and horror, of scorn and reproach, among all the nations where I drive them. 19For they have not listened to my words," declares the LORD, "words that I sent to them again and again by my servants the prophets. And you exiles have not listened either," declares the LORD.

20Therefore, hear the word of the LORD, all you exiles whom I have sent away from Jerusalem to Babylon. 21This is what the LORD Almighty, the God of Israel, says about Ahab son of Kolaiah and Zedekiah son of Maaseiah, who are prophesying lies to you in my name: "I will hand them over to Nebuchadnezzar king of Babylon, and he will put them to death before your very eyes. 22Because of them, all the exiles from Judah who are in Babylon will use this curse: 'The LORD treat you like Zedekiah and Ahab, whom the king of Babylon burned in the fire.' 23For they have done outrageous things in Israel; they have committed adultery with their neighbours' wives and in my name have spoken lies, which I did not tell them to do. I know it and am a witness to it," declares the LORD.

NEW TESTAMENT READING
2 Thessalonians 1:1–12

1 Paul, Silas and Timothy,

To the church of the Thessalonians in God our Father and the Lord Jesus Christ:

2Grace and peace to you from God the Father and the Lord Jesus Christ.

Thanksgiving and Prayer

3We ought always to thank God for you, brothers, and rightly so, because your faith is growing more and more, and the love every one of you has for each other is increasing. 4Therefore among God's churches we boast about your perseverance and faith in all the persecutions and trials you are enduring.

5All this is evidence that God's judgment is right, and as a result you will be counted worthy of the kingdom of God, for which you are suffering. 6God is just: He will pay back trouble to those who trouble you 7and give relief to you who are troubled, and to us as well. This will happen when the Lord Jesus is revealed from heaven in blazing fire with his powerful angels. 8He will punish those who do not know God and do not obey the gospel of our Lord Jesus. 9They will be punished with everlasting destruction and shut out from the presence of the Lord and from the majesty of his power 10on the day he comes to be glorified in his holy people and to be marvelled at among all those who have believed. This includes you, because you believed our testimony to you.

11With this in mind, we constantly pray for you, that our God may count you worthy of his calling, and that by his power he may fulfil every good purpose of yours and every act prompted by your faith. 12We pray this so that the name of our Lord Jesus may be glorified in you, and you in him, according to the grace of our God and the Lord Jesus Christ.

READING FROM PSALMS
Psalm 119:25–32

ℸ Daleth

25I am laid low in the dust;
        preserve my life according to your
        word.
26I recounted my ways and you
        answered me;
        teach me your decrees.
27Let me understand the teaching of
        your precepts;
        then I will meditate on your
        wonders.
28My soul is weary with sorrow;
        strengthen me according to your
        word.
29Keep me from deceitful ways;
        be gracious to me through your
        law.
30I have chosen the way of truth;
        I have set my heart on your laws.
31I hold fast to your statutes, O LORD;
        do not let me be put to shame.
32I run in the path of your commands,
        for you have set my heart free.

OLD TESTAMENT READING
Jeremiah 29:24–31:14

Message to Shemaiah

²⁴Tell Shemaiah the Nehelamite, ²⁵"This is what the LORD Almighty, the God of Israel, says: You sent letters in your own name to all the people in Jerusalem, to Zephaniah son of Maaseiah the priest, and to all the other priests. You said to Zephaniah, ²⁶'The LORD has appointed you priest in place of Jehoiada to be in charge of the house of the LORD; you should put any madman who acts like a prophet into the stocks and neck-irons. ²⁷So why have you not reprimanded Jeremiah from Anathoth, who poses as a prophet among you? ²⁸He has sent this message to us in Babylon: It will be a long time. Therefore build houses and settle down; plant gardens and eat what they produce.'"

²⁹Zephaniah the priest, however, read the letter to Jeremiah the prophet. ³⁰Then the word of the LORD came to Jeremiah: ³¹"Send this message to all the exiles: 'This is what the LORD says about Shemaiah the Nehelamite: Because Shemaiah has prophesied to you, even though I did not send him, and has led you to believe a lie, ³²this is what the LORD says: I will surely punish Shemaiah the Nehelamite and his descendants. He will have no-one left among his people, nor will he see the good things I will do for my people, declares the LORD, because he has preached rebellion against me.'"

Restoration of Israel

30 This is the word that came to Jeremiah from the LORD: ²"This is what the LORD, the God of Israel, says: 'Write in a book all the words I have spoken to you. ³The days are coming,' declares the LORD, 'when I will bring my people Israel and Judah back from captivity and restore them to the land I gave to their forefathers to possess,' says the LORD."

⁴These are the words the LORD spoke concerning Israel and Judah: ⁵"This is what the LORD says:

"'Cries of fear are heard—
    terror, not peace.
⁶Ask and see:
    Can a man bear children?
Then why do I see every strong man
    with his hands on his stomach like
        a woman in labour,
    every face turned deathly pale?
⁷How awful that day will be!
    None will be like it.
It will be a time of trouble for Jacob,
    but he will be saved out of it.

⁸"'In that day,' declares the LORD
        Almighty,
    'I will break the yoke off their
        necks
and will tear off their bonds;
    no longer will foreigners enslave
        them.
⁹Instead, they will serve the LORD
        their God
    and David their king,
    whom I will raise up for them.

¹⁰"'So do not fear, O Jacob my
        servant;
    do not be dismayed, O Israel,'
            declares the LORD.
'I will surely save you out of a distant
        place,
    your descendants from the land of
        their exile.
Jacob will again have peace and
        security,
    and no-one will make him afraid.
¹¹I am with you and will save you,'
    declares the LORD.

'Though I completely destroy all the
  nations
    among which I scatter you,
  I will not completely destroy you.
I will discipline you but only with
  justice;
  I will not let you go entirely
    unpunished.'

12"This is what the LORD says:

"'Your wound is incurable,
  your injury beyond healing.
13There is no-one to plead your cause,
  no remedy for your sore,
  no healing for you.
14All your allies have forgotten you;
  they care nothing for you.
I have struck you as an enemy would
  and punished you as would the
    cruel,
because your guilt is so great
  and your sins so many.
15Why do you cry out over your
    wound,
  your pain that has no cure?
Because of your great guilt and many
    sins
  I have done these things to you.

16"But all who devour you will be
    devoured;
  all your enemies will go into exile.
Those who plunder you will be
    plundered;
  all who make spoil of you I will
    despoil.
17But I will restore you to health
  and heal your wounds,'
                        declares the LORD,
'because you are called an outcast,
  Zion for whom no-one cares.'

18"This is what the LORD says:

"'I will restore the fortunes of
    Jacob's tents
  and have compassion on his
    dwellings;
the city will be rebuilt on her ruins,
  and the palace will stand in its
    proper place.

19From them will come songs of
    thanksgiving
  and the sound of rejoicing.
I will add to their numbers,
  and they will not be decreased;
I will bring them honour,
  and they will not be disdained.
20Their children will be as in days of
    old,
  and their community will be
    established before me;
I will punish all who oppress them.
21Their leader will be one of their own;
  their ruler will arise from among
    them.
I will bring him near and he will come
    close to me,
  for who is he who will devote
    himself
  to be close to me?'
                        declares the LORD.
22"'So you will be my people,
  and I will be your God.'"

23See, the storm of the LORD
  will burst out in wrath,
a driving wind swirling down
  on the heads of the wicked.
24The fierce anger of the LORD will not
    turn back
  until he fully accomplishes
    the purposes of his heart.
In days to come
  you will understand this.

31 "At that time," declares the
    LORD, "I will be the God of all
the clans of Israel, and they will be my
people."
  2This is what the LORD says:

"The people who survive the sword
  will find favour in the desert;
  I will come to give rest to Israel."

3The LORD appeared to us in the past,
saying:

"I have loved you with an everlasting
    love;
  I have drawn you with
    loving-kindness.

⁴I will build you up again
    and you will be rebuilt, O Virgin
      Israel.
  Again you will take up your
      tambourines
    and go out to dance with the
      joyful.
⁵Again you will plant vineyards
    on the hills of Samaria;
  the farmers will plant them
    and enjoy their fruit.
⁶There will be a day when watchmen
      cry out
    on the hills of Ephraim,
  'Come, let us go up to Zion,
    to the LORD our God.'"

⁷This is what the LORD says:

"Sing with joy for Jacob;
    shout for the foremost of the
      nations.
  Make your praises heard, and say,
    'O LORD, save your people,
      the remnant of Israel.'
⁸See, I will bring them from the land
      of the north
    and gather them from the ends of
      the earth.
  Among them will be the blind and
      the lame,
    expectant mothers and women in
      labour;
    a great throng will return.
⁹They will come with weeping;
    they will pray as I bring them back.
  I will lead them beside streams of
      water
    on a level path where they will not
      stumble,
  because I am Israel's father,
    and Ephraim is my firstborn son.

¹⁰"Hear the word of the LORD, O
      nations;
    proclaim it in distant coastlands:
  'He who scattered Israel will gather
      them
    and will watch over his flock like a
      shepherd.'
¹¹For the LORD will ransom Jacob
    and redeem them from the hand of
      those stronger than they.

¹²They will come and shout for joy on
      the heights of Zion;
    they will rejoice in the bounty of
      the LORD—
  the grain, the new wine and the oil,
    the young of the flocks and herds.
  They will be like a well-watered
      garden,
    and they will sorrow no more.
¹³Then maidens will dance and be glad,
    young men and old as well.
  I will turn their mourning into
      gladness;
    I will give them comfort and joy
      instead of sorrow.
¹⁴I will satisfy the priests with
      abundance,
    and my people will be filled with
      my bounty,"

                    declares the LORD.

NEW TESTAMENT READING
2 Thessalonians 2:1–17

The Man of Lawlessness

2 Concerning the coming of our Lord
  Jesus Christ and our being
gathered to him, we ask you, brothers,
²not to become easily unsettled or
alarmed by some prophecy, report or
letter supposed to have come from us,
saying that the day of the Lord has
already come. ³Don't let anyone deceive you in any way, for ⌊that day will
not come⌋ until the rebellion occurs and
the man of lawlessness is revealed, the
man doomed to destruction. ⁴He will
oppose and will exalt himself over
everything that is called God or is
worshipped, so that he sets himself
up in God's temple, proclaiming himself to be God.

⁵Don't you remember that when I
was with you I used to tell you these
things? ⁶And now you know what is
holding him back, so that he may be
revealed at the proper time. ⁷For the
secret power of lawlessness is already at
work; but the one who now holds it back
will continue to do so till he is taken out

of the way. 8And then the lawless one will be revealed, whom the Lord Jesus will overthrow with the breath of his mouth and destroy by the splendour of his coming. 9The coming of the lawless one will be in accordance with the work of Satan displayed in all kinds of counterfeit miracles, signs and wonders, 10and in every sort of evil that deceives those who are perishing. They perish because they refused to love the truth and so be saved. 11For this reason God sends them a powerful delusion so that they will believe the lie 12and so that all will be condemned who have not believed the truth but have delighted in wickedness.

Stand Firm

13But we ought always to thank God for you, brothers loved by the Lord, because from the beginning God chose you to be saved through the sanctifying work of the Spirit and through belief in the truth. 14He called you to this through our gospel, that you might share in the glory of our Lord Jesus Christ. 15So then, brothers, stand firm and hold to the teachings we passed on to you, whether by word of mouth or by letter.

16May our Lord Jesus Christ himself and God our Father, who loved us and by his grace gave us eternal encouragement and good hope, 17encourage your hearts and strengthen you in every good deed and word.

READING FROM PSALMS
Psalm 119:33–40

ח He

33Teach me, O LORD, to follow your decrees;
    then I will keep them to the end.
34Give me understanding, and I will keep your law
    and obey it with all my heart.
35Direct me in the path of your commands,
    for there I find delight.
36Turn my heart towards your statutes
    and not towards selfish gain.
37Turn my eyes away from worthless things;
    preserve my life according to your word.
38Fulfil your promise to your servant,
    so that you may be feared.
39Take away the disgrace I dread,
    for your laws are good.
40How I long for your precepts!
    Preserve my life in your righteousness.

DAY 288

OCTOBER 15

OLD TESTAMENT READING
Jeremiah 31:15–32:25

15This is what the LORD says:

"A voice is heard in Ramah,
    mourning and great weeping,
Rachel weeping for her children
    and refusing to be comforted,
because her children are no more."

16This is what the LORD says:

"Restrain your voice from weeping
    and your eyes from tears,
for your work will be rewarded,"
            declares the LORD.
    "They will return from the land of
        the enemy.
17So there is hope for your future,"
            declares the LORD.

"Your children will return to their
own land.

18"I have surely heard Ephraim's
moaning:
'You disciplined me like an unruly
calf,
and I have been disciplined.
Restore me, and I will return,
because you are the LORD my God.
19After I strayed,
I repented;
after I came to understand,
I beat my breast.
I was ashamed and humiliated
because I bore the disgrace of my
youth.'
20Is not Ephraim my dear son,
the child in whom I delight?
Though I often speak against him,
I still remember him.
Therefore my heart yearns for him;
I have great compassion for him,"
declares the LORD.

21"Set up road signs;
put up guideposts.
Take note of the highway,
the road that you take.
Return, O Virgin Israel,
return to your towns.
22How long will you wander,
O unfaithful daughter?
The LORD will create a new thing on
earth—
a woman will surround a man."

23This is what the LORD Almighty,
the God of Israel, says: "When I bring
them back from captivity, the people in
the land of Judah and in its towns will
once again use these words: 'The LORD
bless you, O righteous dwelling, O
sacred mountain.' 24People will live
together in Judah and all its towns—
farmers and those who move about with
their flocks. 25I will refresh the weary
and satisfy the faint."

26At this I awoke and looked around.
My sleep had been pleasant to me.

27"The days are coming," declares
the LORD, "when I will plant the house
of Israel and the house of Judah with the

offspring of men and of animals. 28Just
as I watched over them to uproot and
tear down, and to overthrow, destroy
and bring disaster, so I will watch over
them to build and to plant," declares
the LORD. 29"In those days people will
no longer say,

'The fathers have eaten sour grapes,
and the children's teeth are set on
edge.'

30Instead, everyone will die for his own
sin; whoever eats sour grapes—his own
teeth will be set on edge.

31"The time is coming," declares the
LORD,
"when I will make a new covenant
with the house of Israel
and with the house of Judah.
32It will not be like the covenant
I made with their forefathers
when I took them by the hand
to lead them out of Egypt,
because they broke my covenant,
though I was a husband to them,"
declares the LORD.
33"This is the covenant that I will make
with the house of Israel
after that time," declares the
LORD.
"I will put my law in their minds
and write it on their hearts.
I will be their God,
and they will be my people.
34No longer will a man teach his
neighbour,
or a man his brother, saying,
'Know the LORD,'
because they will all know me,
from the least of them to the
greatest,"
declares the LORD.
"For I will forgive their wickedness
and will remember their sins no
more."

35This is what the LORD says,

he who appoints the sun
to shine by day,
who decrees the moon and stars
to shine by night,

who stirs up the sea
so that its waves roar—
the LORD Almighty is his name:
36"Only if these decrees vanish from
my sight,"
declares the LORD,
"will the descendants of Israel ever
cease
to be a nation before me."

37This is what the LORD says:

"Only if the heavens above can be
measured
and the foundations of the earth
below be searched out
will I reject all the descendants of
Israel
because of all they have done,"
declares the LORD.

38"The days are coming," declares
the LORD, "when this city will be rebuilt
for me from the Tower of Hananel to
the Corner Gate. 39The measuring line
will stretch from there straight to the hill
of Gareb and then turn to Goah. 40The
whole valley where dead bodies and
ashes are thrown, and all the terraces
out to the Kidron Valley on the east as
far as the corner of the Horse Gate, will
be holy to the LORD. The city will never
again be uprooted or demolished."

Jeremiah Buys a Field

32 This is the word that came to
Jeremiah from the LORD in the
tenth year of Zedekiah king of Judah,
which was the eighteenth year of
Nebuchadnezzar. 2The army of the king
of Babylon was then besieging Jerusalem, and Jeremiah the prophet was
confined in the courtyard of the guard in
the royal palace of Judah.

3Now Zedekiah king of Judah had
imprisoned him there, saying, "Why do
you prophesy as you do? You say, 'This
is what the LORD says: I am about to
hand this city over to the king of Babylon, and he will capture it. 4Zedekiah
king of Judah will not escape out of the
hands of the Babylonians but will certainly be handed over to the king of

Babylon, and will speak with him face
to face and see him with his own eyes.
5He will take Zedekiah to Babylon,
where he will remain until I deal with
him, declares the LORD. If you fight
against the Babylonians, you will not
succeed.'"

6Jeremiah said, "The word of the
LORD came to me: 7Hanamel son of
Shallum your uncle is going to come to
you and say, 'Buy my field at Anathoth,
because as nearest relative it is your
right and duty to buy it.'

8"Then, just as the LORD had said, my
cousin Hanamel came to me in the
courtyard of the guard and said, 'Buy
my field at Anathoth in the territory
of Benjamin. Since it is your right to
redeem it and possess it, buy it for
yourself.'

"I knew that this was the word of the
LORD; 9so I bought the field at Anathoth
from my cousin Hanamel and weighed
out for him seventeen shekels of silver.
10I signed and sealed the deed, had it
witnessed, and weighed out the silver
on the scales. 11I took the deed of purchase—the sealed copy containing the
terms and conditions, as well as the
unsealed copy—12and I gave this deed
to Baruch son of Neriah, the son of
Mahseiah, in the presence of my cousin
Hanamel and of the witnesses who had
signed the deed and of all the Jews
sitting in the courtyard of the guard.

13"In their presence I gave Baruch
these instructions: 14'This is what the
LORD Almighty, the God of Israel, says:
Take these documents, both the sealed
and unsealed copies of the deed of
purchase, and put them in a clay jar so
that they will last a long time. 15For this
is what the LORD Almighty, the God of
Israel, says: Houses, fields and
vineyards will again be bought in this
land.'

16"After I had given the deed of purchase to Baruch son of Neriah, I prayed
to the LORD:

17"Ah, Sovereign LORD, you have
made the heavens and the earth by

your great power and outstretched arm. Nothing is too hard for you. [18]You show love to thousands but bring the punishment for the fathers' sins into the laps of their children after them. O great and powerful God, whose name is the LORD Almighty, [19]great are your purposes and mighty are your deeds. Your eyes are open to all the ways of men; you reward everyone according to his conduct and as his deeds deserve. [20]You performed miraculous signs and wonders in Egypt and have continued them to this day, both in Israel and among all mankind, and have gained the renown that is still yours. [21]You brought your people Israel out of Egypt with signs and wonders, by a mighty hand and an outstretched arm and with great terror. [22]You gave them this land you had sworn to give to their forefathers, a land flowing with milk and honey. [23]They came in and took possession of it, but they did not obey you or follow your law; they did not do what you commanded them to do. So you brought all this disaster upon them.

[24]"See how the siege ramps are built up to take the city. Because of the sword, famine and plague, the city will be handed over to the Babylonians who are attacking it. What you said has happened, as you now see. [25]And though the city will be handed over to the Babylonians, you, O Sovereign LORD, say to me, 'Buy the field with silver and have the transaction witnessed.'"

NEW TESTAMENT READING
2 Thessalonians 3:1–18

Request for Prayer

3 Finally, brothers, pray for us that the message of the Lord may spread rapidly and be honoured, just as it was with you. [2]And pray that we may be delivered from wicked and evil men, for not everyone has faith. [3]But the Lord is faithful, and he will strengthen and protect you from the evil one. [4]We have confidence in the Lord that you are doing and will continue to do the things we command. [5]May the Lord direct your hearts into God's love and Christ's perseverance.

Warning Against Idleness

[6]In the name of the Lord Jesus Christ, we command you, brothers, to keep away from every brother who is idle and does not live according to the teaching you received from us. [7]For you yourselves know how you ought to follow our example. We were not idle when we were with you, [8]nor did we eat anyone's food without paying for it. On the contrary, we worked night and day, labouring and toiling so that we would not be a burden to any of you. [9]We did this, not because we do not have the right to such help, but in order to make ourselves a model for you to follow. [10]For even when we were with you, we gave you this rule: "If a man will not work, he shall not eat."

[11]We hear that some among you are idle. They are not busy; they are busybodies. [12]Such people we command and urge in the Lord Jesus Christ to settle down and earn the bread they eat. [13]And as for you, brothers, never tire of doing what is right.

[14]If anyone does not obey our instruction in this letter, take special note of him. Do not associate with him, in order that he may feel ashamed. [15]Yet do not regard him as an enemy, but warn him as a brother.

Final Greetings

[16]Now may the Lord of peace himself give you peace at all times and in every way. The Lord be with all of you.

[17]I, Paul, write this greeting in my own hand, which is the distinguishing

mark in all my letters. This is how I write.

[18]The grace of our Lord Jesus Christ be with you all.

READING FROM PROVERBS
Proverbs 25:1–10

More Proverbs of Solomon

25 These are more proverbs of Solomon, copied by the men of Hezekiah king of Judah:

[2]It is the glory of God to conceal a
    matter;
  to search out a matter is the glory
    of kings.

[3]As the heavens are high and the earth
    is deep,
  so the hearts of kings are
    unsearchable.

[4]Remove the dross from the silver,
  and out comes material for the
    silversmith;

[5]remove the wicked from the king's
    presence,
  and his throne will be established
    through righteousness.

[6]Do not exalt yourself in the king's
    presence,
  and do not claim a place among
    great men;
[7]it is better for him to say to you,
    "Come up here,"
  than for him to humiliate you
    before a nobleman.

What you have seen with your eyes
[8] do not bring hastily to court,
for what will you do in the end
  if your neighbour puts you to
    shame?

[9]If you argue your case with a
    neighbour,
  do not betray another man's
    confidence,
[10]or he who hears it may shame you
  and you will never lose your bad
    reputation.

DAY 289

OCTOBER 16

OLD TESTAMENT READING
Jeremiah 32:26–34:22

[26]Then the word of the LORD came to Jeremiah: [27]"I am the LORD, the God of all mankind. Is anything too hard for me? [28]Therefore, this is what the LORD says: I am about to hand this city over to the Babylonians and to Nebuchadnezzar king of Babylon, who will capture it. [29]The Babylonians who are attacking this city will come in and set it on fire; they will burn it down, along with the houses where the people provoked me to anger by burning incense on the roofs to Baal and by pouring out drink offerings to other gods.

[30]"The people of Israel and Judah have done nothing but evil in my sight from their youth; indeed, the people of Israel have done nothing but provoke me with what their hands have made, declares the LORD. [31]From the day it was built until now, this city has so aroused my anger and wrath that I must remove it from my sight. [32]The people of Israel and Judah have provoked me by all the evil they have done—they, their kings and officials, their priests and prophets, the men of Judah and the people of Jerusalem. [33]They turned their backs to me and not their faces; though I taught them again and again, they would not listen or respond to discipline. [34]They set up their abominable idols in the house that bears my Name

and defiled it. 35They built high places for Baal in the Valley of Ben Hinnom to sacrifice their sons and daughters to Molech, though I never commanded, nor did it enter my mind, that they should do such a detestable thing and so make Judah sin.

36"You are saying about this city, 'By the sword, famine and plague it will be handed over to the king of Babylon'; but this is what the LORD, the God of Israel, says: 37I will surely gather them from all the lands where I banish them in my furious anger and great wrath; I will bring them back to this place and let them live in safety. 38They will be my people, and I will be their God. 39I will give them singleness of heart and action, so that they will always fear me for their own good and the good of their children after them. 40I will make an everlasting covenant with them: I will never stop doing good to them, and I will inspire them to fear me, so that they will never turn away from me. 41I will rejoice in doing them good and will assuredly plant them in this land with all my heart and soul.

42"This is what the LORD says: As I have brought all this great calamity on this people, so I will give them all the prosperity I have promised them. 43Once more fields will be bought in this land of which you say, 'It is a desolate waste, without men or animals, for it has been handed over to the Babylonians.' 44Fields will be bought for silver, and deeds will be signed, sealed and witnessed in the territory of Benjamin, in the villages around Jerusalem, in the towns of Judah and in the towns of the hill country, of the western foothills and of the Negev, because I will restore their fortunes, declares the LORD."

Promise of Restoration

33 While Jeremiah was still confined in the courtyard of the guard, the word of the LORD came to him a second time: 2"This is what the LORD says, he who made the earth, the LORD who formed it and established it—the LORD is his name: 3'Call to me and I will answer you and tell you great and unsearchable things you do not know.' 4For this is what the LORD, the God of Israel, says about the houses in this city and the royal palaces of Judah that have been torn down to be used against the siege ramps and the sword 5in the fight with the Babylonians: 'They will be filled with the dead bodies of the men I will slay in my anger and wrath. I will hide my face from this city because of all its wickedness.

6"'Nevertheless, I will bring health and healing to it; I will heal my people and will let them enjoy abundant peace and security. 7I will bring Judah and Israel back from captivity and will rebuild them as they were before. 8I will cleanse them from all the sin they have committed against me and will forgive all their sins of rebellion against me. 9Then this city will bring me renown, joy, praise and honour before all nations on earth that hear of all the good things I do for it; and they will be in awe and will tremble at the abundant prosperity and peace I provide for it.'

10"This is what the LORD says: 'You say about this place, "It is a desolate waste, without men or animals." Yet in the towns of Judah and the streets of Jerusalem that are deserted, inhabited by neither men nor animals, there will be heard once more 11the sounds of joy and gladness, the voices of bride and bridegroom, and the voices of those who bring thank-offerings to the house of the LORD, saying,

"Give thanks to the LORD Almighty,
   for the LORD is good;
   his love endures for ever."

For I will restore the fortunes of the land as they were before,' says the LORD.

12"This is what the LORD Almighty says: 'In this place, desolate and without men or animals—in all its towns there will again be pastures for shepherds to rest their flocks. [13]In the towns of the hill country, of the western foothills and of the Negev, in the territory of Benjamin, in the villages around Jerusalem and in the towns of Judah, flocks will again pass under the hand of the one who counts them,' says the LORD.

[14]"'The days are coming,' declares the LORD, 'when I will fulfil the gracious promise I made to the house of Israel and to the house of Judah.

[15]"'In those days and at that time
   I will make a righteous Branch
      sprout from David's line;
   he will do what is just and right in
      the land.
[16]In those days Judah will be saved
   and Jerusalem will live in safety.
This is the name by which it will be
      called:
   The LORD Our Righteousness.'

[17]For this is what the LORD says: 'David will never fail to have a man to sit on the throne of the house of Israel, [18]nor will the priests, who are Levites, ever fail to have a man to stand before me continually to offer burnt offerings, to burn grain offerings and to present sacrifices.'"

[19]The word of the LORD came to Jeremiah: [20]"This is what the LORD says: 'If you can break my covenant with the day and my covenant with the night, so that day and night no longer come at their appointed time, [21]then my covenant with David my servant—and my covenant with the Levites who are priests ministering before me—can be broken and David will no longer have a descendant to reign on his throne. [22]I will make the descendants of David my servant and the Levites who minister before me as countless as the stars of the sky and as measureless as the sand on the seashore.'"

[23]The word of the LORD came to Jeremiah: [24]"Have you not noticed that these people are saying, 'The LORD has rejected the two kingdoms he chose'? So they despise my people and no longer regard them as a nation. [25]This is what the LORD says: 'If I have not established my covenant with day and night and the fixed laws of heaven and earth, [26]then I will reject the descendants of Jacob and David my servant and will not choose one of his sons to rule over the descendants of Abraham, Isaac and Jacob. For I will restore their fortunes and have compassion on them.'"

Warning to Zedekiah

34 While Nebuchadnezzar king of Babylon and all his army and all the kingdoms and peoples in the empire he ruled were fighting against Jerusalem and all its surrounding towns, this word came to Jeremiah from the LORD: [2]"This is what the LORD, the God of Israel, says: Go to Zedekiah king of Judah and tell him, 'This is what the LORD says: I am about to hand this city over to the king of Babylon, and he will burn it down. [3]You will not escape from his grasp but will surely be captured and handed over to him. You will see the king of Babylon with your own eyes, and he will speak with you face to face. And you will go to Babylon.

[4]"'Yet hear the promise of the LORD, O Zedekiah king of Judah. This is what the LORD says concerning you: You will not die by the sword; [5]you will die peacefully. As people made a funeral fire in honour of your fathers, the former kings who preceded you, so they will make a fire in your honour and lament, "Alas, O master!" I myself make this promise, declares the LORD.'"

[6]Then Jeremiah the prophet told all this to Zedekiah king of Judah, in Jerusalem, [7]while the army of the king of Babylon was fighting against Jerusalem and the other cities of Judah that were still holding out—Lachish and Azekah. These were the only fortified cities left in Judah.

Freedom for Slaves

[8]The word came to Jeremiah from the LORD after King Zedekiah had made a covenant with all the people in Jerusalem to proclaim freedom for the slaves. [9]Everyone was to free his Hebrew slaves, both male and female; no-one was to hold a fellow Jew in bondage. [10]So all the officials and people who entered into this covenant agreed that they would free their male and female slaves and no longer hold them in bondage. They agreed, and set them free. [11]But afterwards they changed their minds and took back the slaves they had freed and enslaved them again.

[12]Then the word of the LORD came to Jeremiah: [13]"This is what the LORD, the God of Israel, says: I made a covenant with your forefathers when I brought them out of Egypt, out of the land of slavery. I said, [14]'Every seventh year each of you must free any fellow Hebrew who has sold himself to you. After he has served you for six years, you must let him go free.' Your fathers, however, did not listen to me or pay attention to me. [15]Recently you repented and did what is right in my sight: Each of you proclaimed freedom to his countrymen. You even made a covenant before me in the house that bears my Name. [16]But now you have turned round and profaned my name; each of you has taken back the male and female slaves you had set free to go where they wished. You have forced them to become your slaves again.

[17]"Therefore, this is what the LORD says: You have not obeyed me; you have not proclaimed freedom for your fellow countrymen. So I now proclaim 'freedom' for you, declares the LORD —'freedom' to fall by the sword, plague and famine. I will make you abhorrent to all the kingdoms of the earth. [18]The men who have violated my covenant and have not fulfilled the terms of the covenant they made before me, I will treat like the calf they cut in two and

then walked between its pieces. [19]The leaders of Judah and Jerusalem, the court officials, the priests and all the people of the land who walked between the pieces of the calf, [20]I will hand over to their enemies who seek their lives. Their dead bodies will become food for the birds of the air and the beasts of the earth.

[21]"I will hand Zedekiah king of Judah and his officials over to their enemies who seek their lives, to the army of the king of Babylon, which has withdrawn from you. [22]I am going to give the order, declares the LORD, and I will bring them back to this city. They will fight against it, take it and burn it down. And I will lay waste the towns of Judah so that no-one can live there.'"

NEW TESTAMENT READING
1 Timothy 1:1–20

1 Paul, an apostle of Christ Jesus by the command of God our Saviour and of Christ Jesus our hope,

[2]To Timothy my true son in the faith:

Grace, mercy and peace from God the Father and Christ Jesus our Lord.

Warning Against False Teachers of the Law

[3]As I urged you when I went into Macedonia, stay there in Ephesus so that you may command certain men not to teach false doctrines any longer [4]nor to devote themselves to myths and endless genealogies. These promote controversies rather than God's work —which is by faith. [5]The goal of this command is love, which comes from a pure heart and a good conscience and a sincere faith. [6]Some have wandered away from these and turned to meaningless talk. [7]They want to be teachers of the law, but they do not know what they are talking about or what they so confidently affirm.

8We know that the law is good if one uses it properly. 9We also know that law is made not for the righteous but for lawbreakers and rebels, the ungodly and sinful, the unholy and irreligious; for those who kill their fathers or mothers, for murderers, 10for adulterers and perverts, for slave traders and liars and perjurers—and for whatever else is contrary to the sound doctrine 11that conforms to the glorious gospel of the blessed God, which he entrusted to me.

The Lord's Grace to Paul

12I thank Christ Jesus our Lord, who has given me strength, that he considered me faithful, appointing me to his service. 13Even though I was once a blasphemer and a persecutor and a violent man, I was shown mercy because I acted in ignorance and unbelief. 14The grace of our Lord was poured out on me abundantly, along with the faith and love that are in Christ Jesus.

15Here is a trustworthy saying that deserves full acceptance: Christ Jesus came into the world to save sinners—of whom I am the worst. 16But for that very reason I was shown mercy so that in me, the worst of sinners, Christ Jesus might display his unlimited patience as an example for those who would believe on him and receive eternal life. 17Now to the King eternal, immortal, invisible, the only God, be honour and glory for ever and ever. Amen.

18Timothy, my son, I give you this instruction in keeping with the prophecies once made about you, so that by following them you may fight the good fight, 19holding on to faith and a good conscience. Some have rejected these and so have shipwrecked their faith. 20Among them are Hymenaeus and Alexander, whom I have handed over to Satan to be taught not to blaspheme.

READING FROM PSALMS
Psalm 119:41–48

ﬨ Waw

41May your unfailing love come to me,
    O LORD,
    your salvation according to your
       promise;
42then I will answer the one who taunts
       me,
    for I trust in your word.
43Do not snatch the word of truth from
       my mouth,
    for I have put my hope in your
       laws.
44I will always obey your law,
    for ever and ever.
45I will walk about in freedom,
    for I have sought out your
       precepts.
46I will speak of your statutes before
       kings
    and will not be put to shame,
47for I delight in your commands
    because I love them.
48I lift up my hands to your commands,
    which I love,
    and I meditate on your decrees.

OLD TESTAMENT READING
Jeremiah 35:1–37:21

The Recabites

35 This is the word that came to Jeremiah from the LORD during the reign of Jehoiakim son of Josiah king of Judah: ²"Go to the Recabite family and invite them to come to one of the side rooms of the house of the LORD and give them wine to drink."

³So I went to get Jaazaniah son of Jeremiah, the son of Habazziniah, and his brothers and all his sons—the whole family of the Recabites. ⁴I brought them into the house of the LORD, into the room of the sons of Hanan son of Igdaliah the man of God. It was next to the room of the officials, which was over that of Maaseiah son of Shallum the door-keeper. ⁵Then I set bowls full of wine and some cups before the men of the Recabite family and said to them, "Drink some wine."

⁶But they replied, "We do not drink wine, because our forefather Jonadab son of Recab gave us this command: 'Neither you nor your descendants must ever drink wine. ⁷Also you must never build houses, sow seed or plant vineyards; you must never have any of these things; you must always live in tents. Then you will live a long time in the land where you are nomads.' ⁸We have obeyed everything our forefather Jonadab son of Recab commanded us. Neither we nor our wives nor our sons and daughters have ever drunk wine ⁹or built houses to live in or had vineyards, fields or crops. ¹⁰We have lived in tents and have fully obeyed everything our forefather Jonadab commanded us. ¹¹But when Nebuchadnezzar king of Babylon invaded this land, we said, 'Come, we must go to Jerusalem to escape the Babylonian and Aramean armies.' So we have remained in Jerusalem."

¹²Then the word of the LORD came to Jeremiah, saying: ¹³"This is what the LORD Almighty, the God of Israel, says: Go and tell the men of Judah and the people of Jerusalem, 'Will you not learn a lesson and obey my words?' declares the LORD. ¹⁴Jonadab son of Recab ordered his sons not to drink wine and this command has been kept. To this day they do not drink wine, because they obey their forefather's command. But I have spoken to you again and again, yet you have not obeyed me. ¹⁵Again and again I sent all my servants the prophets to you. They said, "Each of you must turn from your wicked ways and reform your actions; do not follow other gods to serve them. Then you shall live in the land I have given to you and your fathers." But you have not paid attention or listened to me. ¹⁶The descendants of Jonadab son of Recab have carried out the command their forefather gave them, but these people have not obeyed me.'

¹⁷"Therefore, this is what the LORD God Almighty, the God of Israel, says: 'Listen! I am going to bring on Judah and on everyone living in Jerusalem every disaster I pronounced against them. I spoke to them, but they did not listen; I called to them, but they did not answer.'"

¹⁸Then Jeremiah said to the family of the Recabites, "This is what the LORD Almighty, the God of Israel, says: 'You have obeyed the command of your forefather Jonadab and have followed all his instructions and have done everything he ordered.' ¹⁹Therefore, this is what the LORD Almighty, the God of Israel, says: 'Jonadab son of Recab shall never fail to have a man to serve me.'"

Jehoiakim Burns Jeremiah's Scroll

36 In the fourth year of Jehoiakim son of Josiah king of Judah, this word came to Jeremiah from the LORD:

2"Take a scroll and write on it all the words I have spoken to you concerning Israel, Judah and all the other nations from the time I began speaking to you in the reign of Josiah till now. 3Perhaps when the people of Judah hear about every disaster I plan to inflict on them, each of them will turn from his wicked way; then I will forgive their wickedness and their sin."

4So Jeremiah called Baruch son of Neriah, and while Jeremiah dictated all the words the Lord had spoken to him, Baruch wrote them on the scroll. 5Then Jeremiah told Baruch, "I am restricted; I cannot go to the Lord's temple. 6So you go to the house of the Lord on a day of fasting and read to the people from the scroll the words of the Lord that you wrote as I dictated. Read them to all the people of Judah who come in from their towns. 7Perhaps they will bring their petition before the Lord, and each will turn from his wicked ways, for the anger and wrath pronounced against this people by the Lord are great."

8Baruch son of Neriah did everything Jeremiah the prophet told him to do; at the Lord's temple he read the words of the Lord from the scroll. 9In the ninth month of the fifth year of Jehoiakim son of Josiah king of Judah, a time of fasting before the Lord was proclaimed for all the people in Jerusalem and those who had come from the towns of Judah. 10From the room of Gemariah son of Shaphan the secretary, which was in the upper courtyard at the entrance of the New Gate of the temple, Baruch read to all the people at the Lord's temple the words of Jeremiah from the scroll.

11When Micaiah son of Gemariah, the son of Shaphan, heard all the words of the Lord from the scroll, 12he went down to the secretary's room in the royal palace, where all the officials were sitting: Elishama the secretary, Delaiah son of Shemaiah, Elnathan son of Acbor, Gemariah son of Shaphan, Zedekiah son of Hananiah, and all the other officials. 13After Micaiah told

them everything he had heard Baruch read to the people from the scroll, 14all the officials sent Jehudi son of Nethaniah, the son of Shelemiah, the son of Cushi, to say to Baruch, "Bring the scroll from which you have read to the people and come." So Baruch son of Neriah went to them with the scroll in his hand. 15They said to him, "Sit down, please, and read it to us."

So Baruch read it to them. 16When they heard all these words, they looked at each other in fear and said to Baruch, "We must report all these words to the king." 17Then they asked Baruch, "Tell us, how did you come to write all this? Did Jeremiah dictate it?"

18"Yes," Baruch replied, "he dictated all these words to me, and I wrote them in ink on the scroll."

19Then the officials said to Baruch, "You and Jeremiah, go and hide. Don't let anyone know where you are."

20After they put the scroll in the room of Elishama the secretary, they went to the king in the courtyard and reported everything to him. 21The king sent Jehudi to get the scroll, and Jehudi brought it from the room of Elishama the secretary and read it to the king and all the officials standing beside him. 22It was the ninth month and the king was sitting in the winter apartment, with a fire burning in the brazier in front of him. 23Whenever Jehudi had read three or four columns of the scroll, the king cut them off with a scribe's knife and threw them into the brazier, until the entire scroll was burned in the fire. 24The king and all his attendants who heard all these words showed no fear, nor did they tear their clothes. 25Even though Elnathan, Delaiah and Gemariah urged the king not to burn the scroll, he would not listen to them. 26Instead, the king commanded Jerahmeel, a son of the king, Seraiah son of Azriel and Shelemiah son of Abdeel to arrest Baruch the scribe and Jeremiah the prophet. But the Lord had hidden them.

27After the king burned the scroll

containing the words that Baruch had written at Jeremiah's dictation, the word of the LORD came to Jeremiah: 28"Take another scroll and write on it all the words that were on the first scroll, which Jehoiakim king of Judah burned up. 29Also tell Jehoiakim king of Judah, 'This is what the LORD says: You burned that scroll and said, "Why did you write on it that the king of Babylon would certainly come and destroy this land and cut off both men and animals from it?" 30Therefore, this is what the LORD says about Jehoiakim king of Judah: He will have no-one to sit on the throne of David; his body will be thrown out and exposed to the heat by day and the frost by night. 31I will punish him and his children and his attendants for their wickedness; I will bring on them and those living in Jerusalem and the people of Judah every disaster I pronounced against them, because they have not listened.'"

32So Jeremiah took another scroll and gave it to the scribe Baruch son of Neriah, and as Jeremiah dictated, Baruch wrote on it all the words of the scroll that Jehoiakim king of Judah had burned in the fire. And many similar words were added to them.

Jeremiah in Prison

37 Zedekiah son of Josiah was made king of Judah by Nebuchadnezzar king of Babylon; he reigned in place of Jehoiachin son of Jehoiakim. 2Neither he nor his attendants nor the people of the land paid any attention to the words the LORD had spoken through Jeremiah the prophet.

3King Zedekiah, however, sent Jehucal son of Shelemiah with the priest Zephaniah son of Maaseiah to Jeremiah the prophet with this message: "Please pray to the LORD our God for us."

4Now Jeremiah was free to come and go among the people, for he had not yet been put in prison. 5Pharaoh's army had marched out of Egypt, and when the Babylonians who were besieging Jerusalem heard the report about them, they withdrew from Jerusalem.

6Then the word of the LORD came to Jeremiah the prophet: 7"This is what the LORD, the God of Israel, says: Tell the king of Judah, who sent you to enquire of me, 'Pharaoh's army, which has marched out to support you, will go back to its own land, to Egypt. 8Then the Babylonians will return and attack this city; they will capture it and burn it down.'

9"This is what the LORD says: Do not deceive yourselves, thinking, 'The Babylonians will surely leave us.' They will not! 10Even if you were to defeat the entire Babylonian army that is attacking you and only wounded men were left in their tents, they would come out and burn this city down."

11After the Babylonian army had withdrawn from Jerusalem because of Pharaoh's army, 12Jeremiah started to leave the city to go to the territory of Benjamin to get his share of the property among the people there. 13But when he reached the Benjamin Gate, the captain of the guard, whose name was Irijah son of Shelemiah, the son of Hananiah, arrested him and said, "You are deserting to the Babylonians!"

14"That's not true!" Jeremiah said. "I am not deserting to the Babylonians." But Irijah would not listen to him; instead, he arrested Jeremiah and brought him to the officials. 15They were angry with Jeremiah and had him beaten and imprisoned in the house of Jonathan the secretary, which they had made into a prison.

16Jeremiah was put into a vaulted cell in a dungeon, where he remained a long time. 17Then King Zedekiah sent for him and had him brought to the palace, where he asked him privately, "Is there any word from the LORD?"

"Yes," Jeremiah replied, "you will be handed over to the king of Babylon."

18Then Jeremiah said to King Zedekiah, "What crime have I committed against you or your officials or this people, that you have put me in prison? ¹⁹Where are your prophets who prophesied to you, 'The king of Babylon will not attack you or this land'? ²⁰But now, my lord the king, please listen. Let me bring my petition before you: Do not send me back to the house of Jonathan the secretary, or I shall die there."

²¹King Zedekiah then gave orders for Jeremiah to be placed in the courtyard of the guard and given bread from the street of the bakers each day until all the bread in the city was gone. So Jeremiah remained in the courtyard of the guard.

NEW TESTAMENT READING
1 Timothy 2:1–15

Instructions on Worship

2 I urge, then, first of all, that requests, prayers, intercession and thanksgiving be made for everyone— ²for kings and all those in authority, that we may live peaceful and quiet lives in all godliness and holiness. ³This is good, and pleases God our Saviour, ⁴who wants all men to be saved and to come to a knowledge of the truth. ⁵For there is one God and one mediator between God and men, the man Christ Jesus, ⁶who gave himself as a ransom for all men—the testimony given in its proper time. ⁷And for this purpose I was appointed a herald and an apostle—I am telling the truth, I am not lying —and a teacher of the true faith to the Gentiles.

⁸I want men everywhere to lift up holy hands in prayer, without anger or disputing.

⁹I also want women to dress modestly, with decency and propriety, not with braided hair or gold or pearls or expensive clothes, ¹⁰but with good deeds, appropriate for women who profess to worship God.

¹¹A woman should learn in quietness and full submission. ¹²I do not permit a woman to teach or to have authority over a man; she must be silent. ¹³For Adam was formed first, then Eve. ¹⁴And Adam was not the one deceived; it was the woman who was deceived and became a sinner. ¹⁵But women will be saved through childbearing—if they continue in faith, love and holiness with propriety.

READING FROM PSALMS
Psalm 119:49–56

ז Zayin

⁴⁹Remember your word to your servant,
  for you have given me hope.
⁵⁰My comfort in my suffering is this:
  Your promise preserves my life.
⁵¹The arrogant mock me without restraint,
  but I do not turn from your law.
⁵²I remember your ancient laws, O LORD,
  and I find comfort in them.
⁵³Indignation grips me because of the wicked,
  who have forsaken your law.
⁵⁴Your decrees are the theme of my song
  wherever I lodge.
⁵⁵In the night I remember your name, O LORD,
  and I will keep your law.
⁵⁶This has been my practice:
  I obey your precepts.

OLD TESTAMENT READING
Jeremiah 38:1–40:6

Jeremiah Thrown Into a Cistern

38 Shephatiah son of Mattan, Gedaliah son of Pashhur, Jehucal son of Shelemiah, and Pashhur son of Malkijah heard what Jeremiah was telling all the people when he said, 2"This is what the LORD says: 'Whoever stays in this city will die by the sword, famine or plague, but whoever goes over to the Babylonians will live. He will escape with his life; he will live.' 3And this is what the LORD says: 'This city will certainly be handed over to the army of the king of Babylon, who will capture it.'"

4Then the officials said to the king, "This man should be put to death. He is discouraging the soldiers who are left in this city, as well as all the people, by the things he is saying to them. This man is not seeking the good of these people but their ruin."

5"He is in your hands," King Zedekiah answered. "The king can do nothing to oppose you."

6So they took Jeremiah and put him into the cistern of Malkijah, the king's son, which was in the courtyard of the guard. They lowered Jeremiah by ropes into the cistern; it had no water in it, only mud, and Jeremiah sank down into the mud.

7But Ebed-Melech, a Cushite, an official in the royal palace, heard that they had put Jeremiah into the cistern. While the king was sitting in the Benjamin Gate, 8Ebed-Melech went out of the palace and said to him, 9"My lord the king, these men have acted wickedly in all they have done to Jeremiah the prophet. They have thrown him into a cistern, where he will starve to death when there is no longer any bread in the city."

10Then the king commanded Ebed-Melech the Cushite, "Take thirty men from here with you and lift Jeremiah the prophet out of the cistern before he dies."

11So Ebed-Melech took the men with him and went to a room under the treasury in the palace. He took some old rags and worn-out clothes from there and let them down with ropes to Jeremiah in the cistern. 12Ebed-Melech the Cushite said to Jeremiah, "Put these old rags and worn-out clothes under your arms to pad the ropes." Jeremiah did so, 13and they pulled him up with the ropes and lifted him out of the cistern. And Jeremiah remained in the courtyard of the guard.

Zedekiah Questions Jeremiah Again

14Then King Zedekiah sent for Jeremiah the prophet and had him brought to the third entrance to the temple of the LORD. "I am going to ask you something," the king said to Jeremiah. "Do not hide anything from me."

15Jeremiah said to Zedekiah, "If I give you an answer, will you not kill me? Even if I did give you counsel, you would not listen to me."

16But King Zedekiah swore this oath secretly to Jeremiah: "As surely as the LORD lives, who has given us breath, I will neither kill you nor hand you over to those who are seeking your life."

17Then Jeremiah said to Zedekiah, "This is what the LORD God Almighty, the God of Israel, says: 'If you surrender to the officers of the king of Babylon, your life will be spared and this city will not be burned down; you and your family will live. 18But if you will not surrender to the officers of the king of Babylon, this city will be handed over to the Babylonians and they will burn it down; you yourself will not escape from their hands.'"

¹⁹King Zedekiah said to Jeremiah, "I am afraid of the Jews who have gone over to the Babylonians, for the Babylonians may hand me over to them and they will ill-treat me."

²⁰"They will not hand you over," Jeremiah replied. "Obey the LORD by doing what I tell you. Then it will go well with you, and your life will be spared. ²¹But if you refuse to surrender, this is what the LORD has revealed to me: ²²All the women left in the palace of the king of Judah will be brought out to the officials of the king of Babylon. Those women will say to you:

" 'They misled you and overcame you—
       those trusted friends of yours.
Your feet are sunk in the mud;
       your friends have deserted you.'

²³"All your wives and children will be brought out to the Babylonians. You yourself will not escape from their hands but will be captured by the king of Babylon; and this city will be burned down."

²⁴Then Zedekiah said to Jeremiah, "Do not let anyone know about this conversation, or you may die. ²⁵If the officials hear that I talked with you, and they come to you and say, 'Tell us what you said to the king and what the king said to you; do not hide it from us or we will kill you,' ²⁶then tell them, 'I was pleading with the king not to send me back to Jonathan's house to die there.'"

²⁷All the officials did come to Jeremiah and question him, and he told them everything the king had ordered him to say. So they said no more to him, for no-one had heard his conversation with the king.

²⁸And Jeremiah remained in the courtyard of the guard until the day Jerusalem was captured.

The Fall of Jerusalem

39 This is how Jerusalem was taken: ¹In the ninth year of Zedekiah king of Judah, in the tenth month, Nebuchadnezzar king of Babylon marched against Jerusalem with his whole army and laid siege to it. ²And on the ninth day of the fourth month of Zedekiah's eleventh year, the city wall was broken through. ³Then all the officials of the king of Babylon came and took seats in the Middle Gate: Nergal-Sharezer of Samgar, Nebo-Sarsekim a chief officer, Nergal-Sharezer a high official and all the other officials of the king of Babylon. ⁴When Zedekiah king of Judah and all the soldiers saw them, they fled; they left the city at night by way of the king's garden, through the gate between the two walls, and headed towards the Arabah.

⁵But the Babylonian army pursued them and overtook Zedekiah in the plains of Jericho. They captured him and took him to Nebuchadnezzar king of Babylon at Riblah in the land of Hamath, where he pronounced sentence on him. ⁶There at Riblah the king of Babylon slaughtered the sons of Zedekiah before his eyes and also killed all the nobles of Judah. ⁷Then he put out Zedekiah's eyes and bound him with bronze shackles to take him to Babylon.

⁸The Babylonians set fire to the royal palace and the houses of the people and broke down the walls of Jerusalem. ⁹Nebuzaradan commander of the imperial guard carried into exile to Babylon the people who remained in the city, along with those who had gone over to him, and the rest of the people. ¹⁰But Nebuzaradan the commander of the guard left behind in the land of Judah some of the poor people, who owned nothing; and at that time he gave them vineyards and fields.

¹¹Now Nebuchadnezzar king of Babylon had given these orders about Jeremiah through Nebuzaradan commander of the imperial guard: ¹²"Take

him and look after him; don't harm him but do for him whatever he asks." [13]So Nebuzaradan the commander of the guard, Nebushazban a chief officer, Nergal-Sharezer a high official and all the other officers of the king of Babylon [14]sent and had Jeremiah taken out of the courtyard of the guard. They handed him over to Gedaliah son of Ahikam, the son of Shaphan, to take him back to his home. So he remained among his own people.

[15]While Jeremiah had been confined in the courtyard of the guard, the word of the LORD came to him: [16]"Go and tell Ebed-Melech the Cushite, 'This is what the LORD Almighty, the God of Israel, says: I am about to fulfil my words against this city through disaster, not prosperity. At that time they will be fulfilled before your eyes. [17]But I will rescue you on that day, declares the LORD; you will not be handed over to those you fear. [18]I will save you; you will not fall by the sword but will escape with your life, because you trust in me, declares the LORD.'"

Jeremiah Freed

40 The word came to Jeremiah from the LORD after Nebuzaradan commander of the imperial guard had released him at Ramah. He had found Jeremiah bound in chains among all the captives from Jerusalem and Judah who were being carried into exile to Babylon. [2]When the commander of the guard found Jeremiah, he said to him, "The LORD your God decreed this disaster for this place. [3]And now the LORD has brought it about; he has done just as he said he would. All this happened because you people sinned against the LORD and did not obey him. [4]But today I am freeing you from the chains on your wrists. Come with me to Babylon, if you like, and I will look after you; but if you do not want to, then don't come. Look, the whole country

lies before you; go wherever you please." [5]However, before Jeremiah turned to go, Nebuzaradan added, "Go back to Gedaliah son of Ahikam, the son of Shaphan, whom the king of Babylon has appointed over the towns of Judah, and live with him among the people, or go anywhere else you please."

Then the commander gave him provisions and a present and let him go. [6]So Jeremiah went to Gedaliah son of Ahikam at Mizpah and stayed with him among the people who were left behind in the land.

NEW TESTAMENT READING
1 Timothy 3:1–16

Overseers and Deacons

3 Here is a trustworthy saying: If anyone sets his heart on being an overseer, he desires a noble task. [2]Now the overseer must be above reproach, the husband of but one wife, temperate, self-controlled, respectable, hospitable, able to teach, [3]not given to drunkenness, not violent but gentle, not quarrelsome, not a lover of money. [4]He must manage his own family well and see that his children obey him with proper respect. [5](If anyone does not know how to manage his own family, how can he take care of God's church?) [6]He must not be a recent convert, or he may become conceited and fall under the same judgment as the devil. [7]He must also have a good reputation with outsiders, so that he will not fall into disgrace and into the devil's trap.

[8]Deacons, likewise, are to be men worthy of respect, sincere, not indulging in much wine, and not pursuing dishonest gain. [9]They must keep hold of the deep truths of the faith with a clear conscience. [10]They must first be tested;

and then if there is nothing against them, let them serve as deacons.

[11]In the same way, their wives are to be women worthy of respect, not malicious talkers but temperate and trustworthy in everything.

[12]A deacon must be the husband of but one wife and must manage his children and his household well. [13]Those who have served well gain an excellent standing and great assurance in their faith in Christ Jesus.

[14]Although I hope to come to you soon, I am writing you these instructions so that, [15]if I am delayed, you will know how people ought to conduct themselves in God's household, which is the church of the living God, the pillar and foundation of the truth. [16]Beyond all question, the mystery of godliness is great:

He appeared in a body,
    was vindicated by the Spirit,
was seen by angels,
    was preached among the nations,
    was believed on in the world,
    was taken up in glory.

READING FROM PSALMS
Psalm 119:57–64

ן Heth

[57]You are my portion, O LORD;
    I have promised to obey your
        words.
[58]I have sought your face with all my
        heart;
    be gracious to me according to
        your promise.
[59]I have considered my ways
    and have turned my steps to your
        statutes.
[60]I will hasten and not delay
    to obey your commands.
[61]Though the wicked bind me with
        ropes,
    I will not forget your law.
[62]At midnight I rise to give you thanks
    for your righteous laws.
[63]I am a friend to all who fear you,
    to all who follow your precepts.
[64]The earth is filled with your love, O
        LORD;
    teach me your decrees.

DAY 292

OCTOBER 19

OLD TESTAMENT READING
Jeremiah 40:7–42:22

Gedaliah Assassinated

[7]When all the army officers and their men who were still in the open country heard that the king of Babylon had appointed Gedaliah son of Ahikam as governor over the land and had put him in charge of the men, women and children who were the poorest in the land and who had not been carried into exile to Babylon, [8]they came to Gedaliah at Mizpah—Ishmael son of Nethaniah, Johanan and Jonathan the sons of

Kareah, Seraiah son of Tanhumeth, the sons of Ephai the Netophathite, and Jaazaniah the son of the Maacathite, and their men. [9]Gedaliah son of Ahikam, the son of Shaphan, took an oath to reassure them and their men. "Do not be afraid to serve the Babylonians," he said. "Settle down in the land and serve the king of Babylon, and it will go well with you. [10]I myself will stay in Mizpah to represent you before the Babylonians who come to us, but you are to harvest the wine, summer fruit and oil, and put them in your storage jars, and live in the towns you have taken over."

¹¹When all the Jews in Moab, Ammon, Edom and all the other countries heard that the king of Babylon had left a remnant in Judah and had appointed Gedaliah son of Ahikam, the son of Shaphan, as governor over them, ¹²they all came back to the land of Judah, to Gedaliah at Mizpah, from all the countries where they had been scattered. And they harvested an abundance of wine and summer fruit.

¹³Johanan son of Kareah and all the army officers still in the open country came to Gedaliah at Mizpah ¹⁴and said to him, "Don't you know that Baalis king of the Ammonites has sent Ishmael son of Nethaniah to take your life?" But Gedaliah son of Ahikam did not believe them.

¹⁵Then Johanan son of Kareah said privately to Gedaliah in Mizpah, "Let me go and kill Ishmael son of Nethaniah, and no-one will know it. Why should he take your life and cause all the Jews who are gathered around you to be scattered and the remnant of Judah to perish?"

¹⁶But Gedaliah son of Ahikam said to Johanan son of Kareah, "Don't do such a thing! What you are saying about Ishmael is not true."

41 In the seventh month Ishmael son of Nethaniah, the son of Elishama, who was of royal blood and had been one of the king's officers, came with ten men to Gedaliah son of Ahikam at Mizpah. While they were eating together there, ²Ishmael son of Nethaniah and the ten men who were with him got up and struck down Gedaliah son of Ahikam, the son of Shaphan, with the sword, killing the one whom the king of Babylon had appointed as governor over the land. ³Ishmael also killed all the Jews who were with Gedaliah at Mizpah, as well as the Babylonian soldiers who were there.

⁴The day after Gedaliah's assassination, before anyone knew about it, ⁵eighty men who had shaved off their beards, torn their clothes and cut themselves came from Shechem, Shiloh and Samaria, bringing grain offerings and incense with them to the house of the LORD. ⁶Ishmael son of Nethaniah went out from Mizpah to meet them, weeping as he went. When he met them, he said, "Come to Gedaliah son of Ahikam." ⁷When they went into the city, Ishmael son of Nethaniah and the men who were with him slaughtered them and threw them into a cistern. ⁸But ten of them said to Ishmael, "Don't kill us! We have wheat and barley, oil and honey, hidden in a field." So he let them alone and did not kill them with the others. ⁹Now the cistern where he threw all the bodies of the men he had killed along with Gedaliah was the one King Asa had made as part of his defence against Baasha king of Israel. Ishmael son of Nethaniah filled it with the dead.

¹⁰Ishmael made captives of all the rest of the people who were in Mizpah—the king's daughters along with all the others who were left there, over whom Nebuzaradan commander of the imperial guard had appointed Gedaliah son of Ahikam. Ishmael son of Nethaniah took them captive and set out to cross over to the Ammonites.

¹¹When Johanan son of Kareah and all the army officers who were with him heard about all the crimes Ishmael son of Nethaniah had committed, ¹²they took all their men and went to fight Ishmael son of Nethaniah. They caught up with him near the great pool in Gibeon. ¹³When all the people Ishmael had with him saw Johanan son of Kareah and the army officers who were with him, they were glad. ¹⁴All the people Ishmael had taken captive at Mizpah turned and went over to Johanan son of Kareah. ¹⁵But Ishmael son of Nethaniah and eight of his men escaped from Johanan and fled to the Ammonites.

Flight to Egypt

¹⁶Then Johanan son of Kareah and all the army officers who were with him led

away all the survivors from Mizpah whom he had recovered from Ishmael son of Nethaniah after he had assassinated Gedaliah son of Ahikam: the soldiers, women, children and court officials he had brought from Gibeon. ¹⁷And they went on, stopping at Geruth Kimham near Bethlehem on their way to Egypt ¹⁸to escape the Babylonians. They were afraid of them because Ishmael son of Nethaniah had killed Gedaliah son of Ahikam, whom the king of Babylon had appointed as governor over the land.

42 Then all the army officers, including Johanan son of Kareah and Jezaniah son of Hoshaiah, and all the people from the least to the greatest approached ²Jeremiah the prophet and said to him, "Please hear our petition and pray to the LORD your God for this entire remnant. For as you now see, though we were once many, now only a few are left. ³Pray that the LORD your God will tell us where we should go and what we should do."

⁴"I have heard you," replied Jeremiah the prophet. "I will certainly pray to the LORD your God as you have requested; I will tell you everything the LORD says and will keep nothing back from you."

⁵Then they said to Jeremiah, "May the LORD be a true and faithful witness against us if we do not act in accordance with everything the LORD your God sends you to tell us. ⁶Whether it is favourable or unfavourable, we will obey the LORD our God, to whom we are sending you, so that it will go well with us, for we will obey the LORD our God."

⁷Ten days later the word of the LORD came to Jeremiah. ⁸So he called together Johanan son of Kareah and all the army officers who were with him and all the people from the least to the greatest. ⁹He said to them, "This is what the LORD, the God of Israel, to whom you sent me to present your petition, says: ¹⁰If you stay in this land, I will build you up and not tear you down; I will plant you and not uproot you, for I am grieved over the disaster I have inflicted on you. ¹¹Do not be afraid of the king of Babylon, whom you now fear. Do not be afraid of him, declares the LORD, for I am with you and will save you and deliver you from his hands. ¹²I will show you compassion so that he will have compassion on you and restore you to your land.'

¹³"However, if you say, 'We will not stay in this land,' and so disobey the LORD your God, ¹⁴and if you say, 'No, we will go and live in Egypt, where we will not see war or hear the trumpet or be hungry for bread,' ¹⁵then hear the word of the LORD, O remnant of Judah. This is what the LORD Almighty, the God of Israel, says: 'If you are determined to go to Egypt and you do go to settle there, ¹⁶then the sword you fear will overtake you there, and the famine you dread will follow you into Egypt, and there you will die. ¹⁷Indeed, all who are determined to go to Egypt to settle there will die by the sword, famine and plague; not one of them will survive or escape the disaster I will bring on them.' ¹⁸This is what the LORD Almighty, the God of Israel, says: 'As my anger and wrath have been poured out on those who lived in Jerusalem, so will my wrath be poured out on you when you go to Egypt. You will be an object of cursing and horror, of condemnation and reproach; you will never see this place again.'

¹⁹"O remnant of Judah, the LORD has told you, 'Do not go to Egypt.' Be sure of this: I warn you today ²⁰that you made a fatal mistake when you sent me to the LORD your God and said, 'Pray to the LORD our God for us; tell us everything he says and we will do it.' ²¹I have told you today, but you still have not obeyed the LORD your God in all he sent me to tell you. ²²So now, be sure of this: You will die by the sword, famine and plague in the place where you want to go to settle."

NEW TESTAMENT READING
1 Timothy 4:1–16

Instructions to Timothy

4 The Spirit clearly says that in later times some will abandon the faith and follow deceiving spirits and things taught by demons. ²Such teachings come through hypocritical liars, whose consciences have been seared as with a hot iron. ³They forbid people to marry and order them to abstain from certain foods, which God created to be received with thanksgiving by those who believe and who know the truth. ⁴For everything God created is good, and nothing is to be rejected if it is received with thanksgiving, ⁵because it is consecrated by the word of God and prayer.

⁶If you point these things out to the brothers, you will be a good minister of Christ Jesus, brought up in the truths of the faith and of the good teaching that you have followed. ⁷Have nothing to do with godless myths and old wives' tales; rather, train yourself to be godly. ⁸For physical training is of some value, but godliness has value for all things, holding promise for both the present life and the life to come.

⁹This is a trustworthy saying that deserves full acceptance ¹⁰(and for this we labour and strive), that we have put our hope in the living God, who is the Saviour of all men, and especially of those who believe.

¹¹Command and teach these things. ¹²Don't let anyone look down on you because you are young, but set an example for the believers in speech, in life, in love, in faith and in purity. ¹³Until I come, devote yourself to the public reading of Scripture, to preaching and to teaching. ¹⁴Do not neglect your gift, which was given you through a prophetic message when the body of elders laid their hands on you.

¹⁵Be diligent in these matters; give yourself wholly to them, so that everyone may see your progress. ¹⁶Watch your life and doctrine closely. Persevere in them, because if you do, you will save both yourself and your hearers.

READING FROM PROVERBS
Proverbs 25:11–20

¹¹A word aptly spoken
    is like apples of gold in settings of
        silver.

¹²Like an ear-ring of gold or an
        ornament of fine gold
    is a wise man's rebuke to a listening
        ear.

¹³Like the coolness of snow at harvest
        time
    is a trustworthy messenger to those
        who send him;
    he refreshes the spirit of his
        masters.

¹⁴Like clouds and wind without rain
    is a man who boasts of gifts he does
        not give.

¹⁵Through patience a ruler can be
        persuaded,
    and a gentle tongue can break a
        bone.

¹⁶If you find honey, eat just enough—
    too much of it, and you will vomit.

¹⁷Seldom set foot in your neighbour's
        house—
    too much of you, and he will hate
        you.

¹⁸Like a club or a sword or a sharp
        arrow
    is the man who gives false
        testimony against his
        neighbour.

¹⁹Like a bad tooth or a lame foot
    is reliance on the unfaithful in
        times of trouble.

²⁰Like one who takes away a garment
        on a cold day,
    or like vinegar poured on soda,
    is one who sings songs to a heavy
        heart.

OCTOBER 20

OLD TESTAMENT READING
Jeremiah 43:1–45:5

43 When Jeremiah finished telling the people all the words of the LORD their God—everything the LORD had sent him to tell them—²Azariah son of Hoshaiah and Johanan son of Kareah and all the arrogant men said to Jeremiah, "You are lying! The LORD our God has not sent you to say, 'You must not go to Egypt to settle there.' ³But Baruch son of Neriah is inciting you against us to hand us over to the Babylonians, so that they may kill us or carry us into exile to Babylon."

⁴So Johanan son of Kareah and all the army officers and all the people disobeyed the LORD's command to stay in the land of Judah. ⁵Instead, Johanan son of Kareah and all the army officers led away all the remnant of Judah who had come back to live in the land of Judah from all the nations where they had been scattered. ⁶They also led away all the men, women and children and the king's daughters whom Nebuzaradan commander of the imperial guard had left with Gedaliah son of Ahikam, the son of Shaphan, and Jeremiah the prophet and Baruch son of Neriah. ⁷So they entered Egypt in disobedience to the LORD and went as far as Tahpanhes.

⁸In Tahpanhes the word of the LORD came to Jeremiah: ⁹"While the Jews are watching, take some large stones with you and bury them in clay in the brick pavement at the entrance to Pharaoh's palace in Tahpanhes. ¹⁰Then say to them, 'This is what the LORD Almighty, the God of Israel, says: I will send for my servant Nebuchadnezzar king of Babylon, and I will set his throne over these stones I have buried here; he will spread his royal canopy above them. ¹¹He will come and attack Egypt, bringing death to those destined for death, captivity to those destined for captivity, and the sword to those destined for the sword. ¹²He will set fire to the temples of the gods of Egypt; he will burn their temples and take their gods captive. As a shepherd wraps his garment round him, so will he wrap Egypt round himself and depart from there unscathed. ¹³There in the temple of the sun in Egypt he will demolish the sacred pillars and will burn down the temples of the gods of Egypt.'"

Disaster Because of Idolatry

44 This word came to Jeremiah concerning all the Jews living in Lower Egypt—in Migdol, Tahpanhes and Memphis—and in Upper Egypt: ²"This is what the LORD Almighty, the God of Israel, says: You saw the great disaster I brought on Jerusalem and on all the towns of Judah. Today they lie deserted and in ruins ³because of the evil they have done. They provoked me to anger by burning incense and by worshipping other gods that neither they nor you nor your fathers ever knew. ⁴Again and again I sent my servants the prophets, who said, 'Do not do this detestable thing that I hate!' ⁵But they did not listen or pay attention; they did not turn from their wickedness or stop burning incense to other gods. ⁶Therefore, my fierce anger was poured out; it raged against the towns of Judah and the streets of Jerusalem and made them the desolate ruins they are today.

⁷"Now this is what the LORD God Almighty, the God of Israel, says: Why bring such great disaster on yourselves by cutting off from Judah the men and women, the children and infants, and so leave yourselves without a remnant? ⁸Why provoke me to anger with what your hands have made, burning incense to other gods in Egypt, where you have come to live? You will destroy yourselves and make yourselves an object of

cursing and reproach among all the nations on earth. 9Have you forgotten the wickedness committed by your fathers and by the kings and queens of Judah and the wickedness committed by you and your wives in the land of Judah and the streets of Jerusalem? 10To this day they have not humbled themselves or shown reverence, nor have they followed my law and the decrees I set before you and your fathers.

11"Therefore, this is what the LORD Almighty, the God of Israel, says: I am determined to bring disaster on you and to destroy all Judah. 12I will take away the remnant of Judah who were determined to go to Egypt to settle there. They will all perish in Egypt; they will fall by the sword or die from famine. From the least to the greatest, they will die by sword or famine. They will become an object of cursing and horror, of condemnation and reproach. 13I will punish those who live in Egypt with the sword, famine and plague, as I punished Jerusalem. 14None of the remnant of Judah who have gone to live in Egypt will escape or survive to return to the land of Judah, to which they long to return and live; none will return except a few fugitives."

15Then all the men who knew that their wives were burning incense to other gods, along with all the women who were present—a large assembly —and all the people living in Lower and Upper Egypt, said to Jeremiah, 16"We will not listen to the message you have spoken to us in the name of the LORD! 17We will certainly do everything we said we would: We will burn incense to the Queen of Heaven and will pour out drink offerings to her just as we and our fathers, our kings and our officials did in the towns of Judah and in the streets of Jerusalem. At that time we had plenty of food and were well off and suffered no harm. 18But ever since we stopped burning incense to the Queen of Heaven and pouring out drink offerings to her, we have had nothing and have been perishing by sword and famine."

19The women added, "When we burned incense to the Queen of Heaven and poured out drink offerings to her, did not our husbands know that we were making cakes like her image and pouring out drink offerings to her?"

20Then Jeremiah said to all the people, both men and women, who were answering him, 21"Did not the LORD remember and think about the incense burned in the towns of Judah and the streets of Jerusalem by you and your fathers, your kings and your officials and the people of the land? 22When the LORD could no longer endure your wicked actions and the detestable things you did, your land became an object of cursing and a desolate waste without inhabitants, as it is today. 23Because you have burned incense and have sinned against the LORD and have not obeyed him or followed his law or his decrees or his stipulations, this disaster has come upon you, as you now see."

24Then Jeremiah said to all the people, including the women, "Hear the word of the LORD, all you people of Judah in Egypt. 25This is what the LORD Almighty, the God of Israel, says: You and your wives have shown by your actions what you promised when you said, 'We will certainly carry out the vows we made to burn incense and pour out drink offerings to the Queen of Heaven.'

"Go ahead then, do what you promised! Keep your vows! 26But hear the word of the LORD, all Jews living in Egypt: 'I swear by my great name,' says the LORD, 'that no-one from Judah living anywhere in Egypt shall ever again invoke my name or swear, "As surely as the Sovereign LORD lives." 27For I am watching over them for harm, not for good; the Jews in Egypt will perish by sword and famine until they are all destroyed. 28Those who escape the sword and return to the land of Judah from Egypt will be very few. Then the whole remnant of Judah who came to live in Egypt will know whose word will stand —mine or theirs.

29"'This will be the sign to you that I will punish you in this place,' declares the LORD, 'so that you will know that my threats of harm against you will surely stand.' 30This is what the LORD says: 'I am going to hand Pharaoh Hophra king of Egypt over to his enemies who seek his life, just as I handed Zedekiah king of Judah over to Nebuchadnezzar king of Babylon, the enemy who was seeking his life.'"

A Message to Baruch

45 This is what Jeremiah the prophet told Baruch son of Neriah in the fourth year of Jehoiakim son of Josiah king of Judah, after Baruch had written on a scroll the words Jeremiah was then dictating: 2"This is what the LORD, the God of Israel, says to you, Baruch: 3You said, 'Woe to me! The LORD has added sorrow to my pain; I am worn out with groaning and find no rest.'"

4 The LORD said, "Say this to him: 'This is what the LORD says: I will overthrow what I have built and uproot what I have planted, throughout the land. 5Should you then seek great things for yourself? Seek them not. For I will bring disaster on all people, declares the LORD, but wherever you go I will let you escape with your life.'"

NEW TESTAMENT READING
1 Timothy 5:1–6:2

Advice About Widows, Elders and Slaves

5 Do not rebuke an older man harshly, but exhort him as if he were your father. Treat younger men as brothers, 2older women as mothers, and younger women as sisters, with absolute purity.

3Give proper recognition to those widows who are really in need. 4But if a widow has children or grandchildren, these should learn first of all to put their religion into practice by caring for their own family and so repaying their parents and grandparents, for this is pleasing to God. 5The widow who is really in need and left all alone puts her hope in God and continues night and day to pray and to ask God for help. 6But the widow who lives for pleasure is dead even while she lives. 7Give the people these instructions, too, so that no-one may be open to blame. 8If anyone does not provide for his relatives, and especially for his immediate family, he has denied the faith and is worse than an unbeliever.

9No widow may be put on the list of widows unless she is over sixty, has been faithful to her husband, 10and is well known for her good deeds, such as bringing up children, showing hospitality, washing the feet of the saints, helping those in trouble and devoting herself to all kinds of good deeds.

11As for younger widows, do not put them on such a list. For when their sensual desires overcome their dedication to Christ, they want to marry. 12Thus they bring judgment on themselves, because they have broken their first pledge. 13Besides, they get into the habit of being idle and going about from house to house. And not only do they become idlers, but also gossips and busybodies, saying things they ought not to. 14So I counsel younger widows to marry, to have children, to manage their homes and to give the enemy no opportunity for slander. 15Some have in fact already turned away to follow Satan.

16If any woman who is a believer has widows in her family, she should help them and not let the church be burdened with them, so that the church can help those widows who are really in need.

17The elders who direct the affairs of the church well are worthy of double honour, especially those whose work is preaching and teaching. 18For the Scripture says, "Do not muzzle the ox while it is treading out the grain," and "The worker deserves his wages." ¹⁹Do not entertain an accusation against an elder unless it is brought by two or three witnesses. ²⁰Those who sin are to be rebuked publicly, so that the others may take warning.

²¹I charge you, in the sight of God and Christ Jesus and the elect angels, to keep these instructions without partiality, and to do nothing out of favouritism.

²²Do not be hasty in the laying on of hands, and do not share in the sins of others. Keep yourself pure.

²³Stop drinking only water, and use a little wine because of your stomach and your frequent illnesses.

²⁴The sins of some men are obvious, reaching the place of judgment ahead of them; the sins of others trail behind them. ²⁵In the same way, good deeds are obvious, and even those that are not cannot be hidden.

6 All who are under the yoke of slavery should consider their masters worthy of full respect, so that God's name and our teaching may not be slandered. ²Those who have believing masters are not to show less respect for them because they are brothers. Instead, they are to serve them even better, because those who benefit from their service are believers, and dear to them. These are the things you are to teach and urge on them.

READING FROM PSALMS
Psalm 119:65–72

ט Teth

⁶⁵Do good to your servant
 according to your word, O LORD.
⁶⁶Teach me knowledge and good judgment,
 for I believe in your commands.
⁶⁷Before I was afflicted I went astray,
 but now I obey your word.
⁶⁸You are good, and what you do is good;
 teach me your decrees.
⁶⁹Though the arrogant have smeared me with lies,
 I keep your precepts with all my heart.
⁷⁰Their hearts are callous and unfeeling,
 but I delight in your law.
⁷¹It was good for me to be afflicted
 so that I might learn your decrees.
⁷²The law from your mouth is more precious to me
 than thousands of pieces of silver and gold.

OCTOBER 21   DAY 294

OLD TESTAMENT READING
Jeremiah 46:1–47:7

A Message About Egypt

46 This is the word of the LORD that came to Jeremiah the prophet concerning the nations:

²Concerning Egypt:

This is the message against the army of Pharaoh Neco king of Egypt, which was defeated at Carchemish on the Euphrates River by Nebuchadnezzar king of Babylon in the fourth year of Jehoiakim son of Josiah king of Judah:

³"Prepare your shields, both large and small,
 and march out for battle!
⁴Harness the horses,
 mount the steeds!
 Take your positions
 with helmets on!

Polish your spears,
  put on your armour!
5What do I see?
  They are terrified,
  they are retreating,
  their warriors are defeated.
They flee in haste
  without looking back,
  and there is terror on every side,"
                    declares the LORD.
6"The swift cannot flee
  nor the strong escape.
In the north by the River Euphrates
  they stumble and fall.

7"Who is this that rises like the Nile,
  like rivers of surging waters?
8Egypt rises like the Nile,
  like rivers of surging waters.
She says, 'I will rise and cover the
    earth;
  I will destroy cities and their
    people.'
9Charge, O horses!
  Drive furiously, O charioteers!
March on, O warriors—
  men of Cush and Put who carry
    shields,
  men of Lydia who draw the bow.
10But that day belongs to the Lord, the
    LORD Almighty—
  a day of vengeance, for vengeance
    on his foes.
The sword will devour till it is
    satisfied,
  till it has quenched its thirst with
    blood.
For the Lord, the LORD Almighty,
    will offer sacrifice
  in the land of the north by the
    River Euphrates.

11"Go up to Gilead and get balm,
  O Virgin Daughter of Egypt.
But you multiply remedies in vain;
  there is no healing for you.
12The nations will hear of your shame;
  your cries will fill the earth.
One warrior will stumble over
    another;
  both will fall down together."

13This is the message the LORD spoke
to Jeremiah the prophet about the
coming of Nebuchadnezzar king of
Babylon to attack Egypt:

14"Announce this in Egypt, and
    proclaim it in Migdol;
  proclaim it also in Memphis and
    Tahpanhes:
'Take your positions and get ready,
  for the sword devours those around
    you.'
15Why will your warriors be laid low?
  They cannot stand, for the LORD
    will push them down.
16They will stumble repeatedly;
  they will fall over each other.
They will say, 'Get up, let us go back
  to our own people and our native
    lands,
  away from the sword of the
    oppressor.'
17There they will exclaim,
  'Pharaoh king of Egypt is only a
    loud noise;
  he has missed his opportunity.'

18"As surely as I live," declares the
    King,
  whose name is the LORD Almighty,
"one will come who is like Tabor
    among the mountains,
  like Carmel by the sea.
19Pack your belongings for exile,
  you who live in Egypt,
for Memphis will be laid waste
  and lie in ruins without inhabitant.

20"Egypt is a beautiful heifer,
  but a gadfly is coming
    against her from the north.
21The mercenaries in her ranks
  are like fattened calves.
They too will turn and flee together,
  they will not stand their ground,
for the day of disaster is coming upon
    them,
  the time for them to be punished.
22Egypt will hiss like a fleeing serpent
  as the enemy advances in force;
they will come against her with axes,
  like men who cut down trees.

²³They will chop down her forest,"
          declares the LORD,
    "dense though it be.
They are more numerous than
          locusts,
    they cannot be counted.
²⁴The Daughter of Egypt will be put to
          shame,
    handed over to the people of the
          north."

²⁵The LORD Almighty, the God of
Israel, says: "I am about to bring
punishment on Amon god of Thebes,
on Pharaoh, on Egypt and her gods and
her kings, and on those who rely on
Pharaoh. ²⁶I will hand them over to
those who seek their lives, to
Nebuchadnezzar king of Babylon and
his officers. Later, however, Egypt will
be inhabited as in times past," declares
the LORD.

²⁷"Do not fear, O Jacob my servant;
    do not be dismayed, O Israel.
I will surely save you out of a distant
          place,
    and your descendants from the
          land of their exile.
Jacob will again have peace and
          security,
    and no-one will make him afraid.
²⁸Do not fear, O Jacob my servant,
    for I am with you," declares the
          LORD.
"Though I completely destroy all the
          nations
    among which I scatter you,
    I will not completely destroy you.
I will discipline you but only with
          justice;
    I will not let you go entirely
          unpunished."

A Message About the Philistines

47 This is the word of the LORD that
came to Jeremiah the prophet
concerning the Philistines before Pharaoh attacked Gaza:

²This is what the LORD says:

"See how the waters are rising in the
          north;
    they will become an overflowing
          torrent.
They will overflow the land and
          everything in it,
    the towns and those who live in
          them.
The people will cry out;
    all who dwell in the land will wail
³at the sound of the hoofs of galloping
          steeds,
    at the noise of enemy chariots
    and the rumble of their wheels.
Fathers will not turn to help their
          children;
    their hands will hang limp.
⁴For the day has come
    to destroy all the Philistines
and to cut off all survivors
    who could help Tyre and Sidon.
The LORD is about to destroy the
          Philistines,
    the remnant from the coasts of
          Caphtor.
⁵Gaza will shave her head in
          mourning;
    Ashkelon will be silenced.
O remnant on the plain,
    how long will you cut yourselves?

⁶"'Ah, sword of the LORD,' ⌐you cry,⌐
    'how long till you rest?
Return to your scabbard;
    cease and be still.'
⁷But how can it rest
    when the LORD has commanded it,
when he has ordered it
    to attack Ashkelon and the coast?"

NEW TESTAMENT READING
1 Timothy 6:3–21

Love of Money

³If anyone teaches false doctrines and
does not agree to the sound instruction
of our Lord Jesus Christ and to godly
teaching, ⁴he is conceited and understands nothing. He has an unhealthy

interest in controversies and quarrels about words that result in envy, strife, malicious talk, evil suspicions [5]and constant friction between men of corrupt mind, who have been robbed of the truth and who think that godliness is a means to financial gain.

[6]But godliness with contentment is great gain. [7]For we brought nothing into the world, and we can take nothing out of it. [8]But if we have food and clothing, we will be content with that. [9]People who want to get rich fall into temptation and a trap and into many foolish and harmful desires that plunge men into ruin and destruction. [10]For the love of money is a root of all kinds of evil. Some people, eager for money, have wandered from the faith and pierced themselves with many griefs.

Paul's Charge to Timothy

[11]But you, man of God, flee from all this, and pursue righteousness, godliness, faith, love, endurance and gentleness. [12]Fight the good fight of the faith. Take hold of the eternal life to which you were called when you made your good confession in the presence of many witnesses. [13]In the sight of God, who gives life to everything, and of Christ Jesus, who while testifying before Pontius Pilate made the good confession, I charge you [14]to keep this command without spot or blame until the appearing of our Lord Jesus Christ, [15]which God will bring about in his own time—God, the blessed and only Ruler, the King of kings and Lord of lords, [16]who alone is immortal and who lives in unapproachable light, whom no-one has seen or can see. To him be honour and might for ever. Amen.

[17]Command those who are rich in this present world not to be arrogant nor to put their hope in wealth, which is so uncertain, but to put their hope in God, who richly provides us with everything for our enjoyment. [18]Command them to do good, to be rich in good deeds, and to be generous and willing to share. [19]In this way they will lay up treasure for themselves as a firm foundation for the coming age, so that they may take hold of the life that is truly life.

[20]Timothy, guard what has been entrusted to your care. Turn away from godless chatter and the opposing ideas of what is falsely called knowledge, [21]which some have professed and in so doing have wandered from the faith.

Grace be with you.

READING FROM PSALMS
Psalm 119:73–80

ʼ Yodh

[73]Your hands made me and formed me;
  give me understanding to learn your commands.
[74]May those who fear you rejoice when they see me,
  for I have put my hope in your word.
[75]I know, O LORD, that your laws are righteous,
  and in faithfulness you have afflicted me.
[76]May your unfailing love be my comfort,
  according to your promise to your servant.
[77]Let your compassion come to me that I may live,
  for your law is my delight.
[78]May the arrogant be put to shame for wronging me without cause;
  but I will meditate on your precepts.
[79]May those who fear you turn to me,
  those who understand your statutes.
[80]May my heart be blameless towards your decrees,
  that I may not be put to shame.

OLD TESTAMENT READING
Jeremiah 48:1–49:6

A Message About Moab

48 Concerning Moab:

This is what the LORD Almighty, the God of Israel, says:

"Woe to Nebo, for it will be ruined.
Kiriathaim will be disgraced and
captured;
the stronghold will be disgraced
and shattered.
2Moab will be praised no more;
in Heshbon men will plot her
downfall:
'Come, let us put an end to that
nation.'
You too, O Madmen, will be
silenced;
the sword will pursue you.
3Listen to the cries from Horonaim,
cries of great havoc and
destruction.
4Moab will be broken;
her little ones will cry out.
5They go up the way to Luhith,
weeping bitterly as they go;
on the road down to Horonaim
anguished cries over the
destruction are heard.
6Flee! Run for your lives;
become like a bush in the desert.
7Since you trust in your deeds and
riches,
you too will be taken captive,
and Chemosh will go into exile,
together with his priests and
officials.
8The destroyer will come against
every town,
and not a town will escape.
The valley will be ruined
and the plateau destroyed,
because the LORD has spoken.

9Put salt on Moab,
for she will be laid waste;
her towns will become desolate,
with no-one to live in them.

10"A curse on him who is lax in doing
the LORD's work!
A curse on him who keeps his
sword from bloodshed!

11"Moab has been at rest from youth,
like wine left on its dregs,
not poured from one jar to another—
she has not gone into exile.
So she tastes as she did,
and her aroma is unchanged.
12But days are coming,"
declares the LORD,
"when I will send men who pour from
jars,
and they will pour her out;
they will empty her jars
and smash her jugs.
13Then Moab will be ashamed of
Chemosh,
as the house of Israel was ashamed
when they trusted in Bethel.

14"How can you say, 'We are warriors,
men valiant in battle'?
15Moab will be destroyed and her
towns invaded;
her finest young men will go down
in the slaughter,"
declares the King, whose name is
the LORD Almighty.
16"The fall of Moab is at hand;
her calamity will come quickly.
17Mourn for her, all who live around
her,
all who know her fame;
say, 'How broken is the mighty
sceptre,
how broken the glorious staff!'

18"Come down from your glory
and sit on the parched ground,

O inhabitants of the Daughter of
Dibon,
for he who destroys Moab
will come up against you
and ruin your fortified cities.
19Stand by the road and watch,
you who live in Aroer.
Ask the man fleeing and the woman
escaping,
ask them, 'What has happened?'
20Moab is disgraced, for she is
shattered.
Wail and cry out!
Announce by the Arnon
that Moab is destroyed.
21Judgment has come to the plateau—
to Holon, Jahzah and Mephaath,
22 to Dibon, Nebo and Beth
Diblathaim,
23 to Kiriathaim, Beth Gamul and
Beth Meon,
24 to Kerioth and Bozrah—
to all the towns of Moab, far and
near.
25Moab's horn is cut off;
her arm is broken,
declares the LORD.

26"Make her drunk,
for she has defied the LORD.
Let Moab wallow in her vomit;
let her be an object of ridicule.
27Was not Israel the object of your
ridicule?
Was she caught among thieves,
that you shake your head in scorn
whenever you speak of her?
28Abandon your towns and dwell
among the rocks,
you who live in Moab.
Be like a dove that makes its nest
at the mouth of a cave.

29"We have heard of Moab's pride—
her overweening pride and conceit,
her pride and arrogance
and the haughtiness of her heart.
30I know her insolence but it is futile,"
declares the LORD,
"and her boasts accomplish
nothing.
31Therefore I wail over Moab,
for all Moab I cry out,

I moan for the men of Kir
Hareseth.
32I weep for you, as Jazer weeps,
O vines of Sibmah.
Your branches spread as far as the
sea;
they reached as far as the sea of
Jazer.
The destroyer has fallen
on your ripened fruit and grapes.
33Joy and gladness are gone
from the orchards and fields of
Moab.
I have stopped the flow of wine from
the presses;
no-one treads them with shouts of
joy.
Although there are shouts,
they are not shouts of joy.

34"The sound of their cry rises
from Heshbon to Elealeh and
Jahaz,
from Zoar as far as Horonaim and
Eglath Shelishiyah,
for even the waters of Nimrim are
dried up.
35In Moab I will put an end
to those who make offerings on the
high places
and burn incense to their gods,"
declares the LORD.
36"So my heart laments for Moab like a
flute;
it laments like a flute for the men of
Kir Hareseth.
The wealth they acquired is gone.
37Every head is shaved
and every beard cut off;
every hand is slashed
and every waist is covered with
sackcloth.
38On all the roofs in Moab
and in the public squares
there is nothing but mourning,
for I have broken Moab
like a jar that no-one wants,"
declares the LORD.
39"How shattered she is! How they
wail!
How Moab turns her back in
shame!

OLD TESTAMENT READING
Jeremiah 49:7–50:10

A Message About Edom

⁷Concerning Edom:

This is what the LORD Almighty says:

"Is there no longer wisdom in
    Teman?
  Has counsel perished from the
    prudent?
  Has their wisdom decayed?
⁸Turn and flee, hide in deep caves,
  you who live in Dedan,
for I will bring disaster on Esau
  at the time I punish him.
⁹If grape-pickers came to you,
  would they not leave a few grapes?
If thieves came during the night,
  would they not steal only as much
    as they wanted?
¹⁰But I will strip Esau bare;
  I will uncover his hiding-places,
  so that he cannot conceal himself.
His children, relatives and
    neighbours will perish,
  and he will be no more.
¹¹Leave your orphans; I will protect
    their lives.
  Your widows too can trust in me."

¹²This is what the LORD says: "If
those who do not deserve to drink the
cup must drink it, why should you go
unpunished? You will not go unpunished, but must drink it. ¹³I swear by
myself," declares the LORD, "that Bozrah will become a ruin and an object of
horror, of reproach and of cursing; and
all its towns will be in ruins for ever."

¹⁴I have heard a message from the
    LORD:
  An envoy was sent to the nations to
    say,
"Assemble yourselves to attack it!
  Rise up for battle!"

¹⁵"Now I will make you small among
    the nations,
  despised among men.
¹⁶The terror you inspire
  and the pride of your heart have
    deceived you,
you who live in the clefts of the rocks,
  who occupy the heights of the hill.
Though you build your nest as high as
    the eagle's,
  from there I will bring you down,"
            declares the LORD.
¹⁷"Edom will become an object of
    horror;
  all who pass by will be appalled and
    will scoff
  because of all its wounds.
¹⁸As Sodom and Gomorrah were
    overthrown,
  along with their neighbouring
    towns,"
            says the LORD,
"so no-one will live there;
  no man will dwell in it.

¹⁹"Like a lion coming up from Jordan's
    thickets
  to a rich pasture-land,
I will chase Edom from its land in an
    instant.
  Who is the chosen one I will
    appoint for this?
Who is like me and who can
    challenge me?
  And what shepherd can stand
    against me?"
²⁰Therefore, hear what the LORD has
    planned against Edom,
  what he has purposed against those
    who live in Teman:
The young of the flock will be
    dragged away;
  he will completely destroy their
    pasture because of them.
²¹At the sound of their fall the earth
    will tremble;
  their cry will resound to the Red
    Sea.

22Look! An eagle will soar and swoop
down,
    spreading its wings over Bozrah.
In that day the hearts of Edom's
    warriors
    will be like the heart of a woman in
      labour.

A Message About Damascus

23Concerning Damascus:

"Hamath and Arpad are dismayed,
    for they have heard bad news.
They are disheartened,
    troubled like the restless sea.
24Damascus has become feeble,
    she has turned to flee
    and panic has gripped her;
anguish and pain have seized her,
    pain like that of a woman in labour.
25Why has the city of renown not been
    abandoned,
    the town in which I delight?
26Surely, her young men will fall in the
    streets;
    all her soldiers will be silenced in
      that day,"
           declares the LORD Almighty.
27"I will set fire to the walls of
    Damascus;
    it will consume the fortresses of
      Ben-Hadad."

A Message About Kedar and Hazor

28Concerning Kedar and the kingdoms of Hazor, which Nebuchadnezzar
king of Babylon attacked:

This is what the LORD says:

"Arise, and attack Kedar
    and destroy the people of the East.
29Their tents and their flocks will be
    taken;
    their shelters will be carried off
    with all their goods and camels.
Men will shout to them,
    'Terror on every side!'

30"Flee quickly away!
    Stay in deep caves, you who live in
      Hazor,"
           declares the LORD.

"Nebuchadnezzar king of Babylon
    has plotted against you;
    he has devised a plan against you.

31"Arise and attack a nation at ease,
    which lives in confidence,"
           declares the LORD,

"a nation that has neither gates nor
    bars;
    its people live alone.
32Their camels will become plunder,
    and their large herds will be booty.
I will scatter to the winds those who
    are in distant places
    and will bring disaster on them
      from every side,"
           declares the LORD.
33"Hazor will become a haunt of
    jackals,
    a desolate place for ever.
No-one will live there;
    no man will dwell in it."

A Message About Elam

34This is the word of the LORD that
came to Jeremiah the prophet concerning Elam, early in the reign of Zedekiah
king of Judah:

35This is what the LORD Almighty
says:

"See, I will break the bow of Elam,
    the mainstay of their might.
36I will bring against Elam the four
    winds
    from the four quarters of the
      heavens;
I will scatter them to the four winds,
    and there will not be a nation
    where Elam's exiles do not go.
37I will shatter Elam before their foes,
    before those who seek their lives;
I will bring disaster upon them,
    even my fierce anger,"
           declares the LORD.
"I will pursue them with the sword
    until I have made an end of them.
38I will set my throne in Elam
    and destroy her king and officials,"
           declares the LORD.

³⁹"Yet I will restore the fortunes of
Elam
in days to come,"
declares the LORD.

A Message About Babylon

50 This is the word the LORD spoke
through Jeremiah the prophet
concerning Babylon and the land of the
Babylonians:

²"Announce and proclaim among the
nations,
lift up a banner and proclaim it;
keep nothing back, but say,
'Babylon will be captured;
Bel will be put to shame,
Marduk filled with terror.
Her images will be put to shame
and her idols filled with terror.'
³A nation from the north will attack
her
and lay waste her land.
No-one will live in it;
both men and animals will flee
away.

⁴"In those days, at that time,"
declares the LORD,
"the people of Israel and the people
of Judah together
will go in tears to seek the LORD
their God.
⁵They will ask the way to Zion
and turn their faces towards it.
They will come and bind themselves
to the LORD
in an everlasting covenant
that will not be forgotten.

⁶"My people have been lost sheep;
their shepherds have led them
astray
and caused them to roam on the
mountains.
They wandered over mountain and
hill
and forgot their own resting place.
⁷Whoever found them devoured
them;
their enemies said, 'We are not
guilty,

for they sinned against the LORD,
their true pasture,
the LORD, the hope of their
fathers.'

⁸"Flee out of Babylon;
leave the land of the Babylonians,
and be like the goats that lead the
flock.
⁹For I will stir up and bring against
Babylon
an alliance of great nations from
the land of the north.
They will take up their positions
against her,
and from the north she will be
captured.
Their arrows will be like skilled
warriors
who do not return empty-handed.
¹⁰So Babylonia will be plundered;
all who plunder her will have their
fill,"
declares the LORD.

NEW TESTAMENT READING
2 Timothy 2:1–26

2 You then, my son, be strong in the
grace that is in Christ Jesus. ²And
the things you have heard me say in the
presence of many witnesses entrust to
reliable men who will also be qualified
to teach others. ³Endure hardship with
us like a good soldier of Christ Jesus.
⁴No-one serving as a soldier gets in-
volved in civilian affairs—he wants to
please his commanding officer.
⁵Similarly, if anyone competes as an
athlete, he does not receive the victor's
crown unless he competes according to
the rules. ⁶The hardworking farmer
should be the first to receive a share of
the crops. ⁷Reflect on what I am saying,
for the Lord will give you insight into all
this.

⁸Remember Jesus Christ, raised from
the dead, descended from David. This
is my gospel, ⁹for which I am suffering
even to the point of being chained
like a criminal. But God's word is
not chained. ¹⁰Therefore I endure

everything for the sake of the elect, that they too may obtain the salvation that is in Christ Jesus, with eternal glory.

[11]Here is a trustworthy saying:

If we died with him,
  we will also live with him;
[12]if we endure,
  we will also reign with him.
If we disown him,
  he will also disown us;
[13]if we are faithless,
  he will remain faithful,
  for he cannot disown himself.

A Workman Approved by God

[14]Keep reminding them of these things. Warn them before God against quarrelling about words; it is of no value, and only ruins those who listen. [15]Do your best to present yourself to God as one approved, a workman who does not need to be ashamed and who correctly handles the word of truth. [16]Avoid godless chatter, because those who indulge in it will become more and more ungodly. [17]Their teaching will spread like gangrene. Among them are Hymenaeus and Philetus, [18]who have wandered away from the truth. They say that the resurrection has already taken place, and they destroy the faith of some. [19]Nevertheless, God's solid foundation stands firm, sealed with this inscription: "The Lord knows those who are his," and, "Everyone who confesses the name of the Lord must turn away from wickedness."

[20]In a large house there are articles not only of gold and silver, but also of wood and clay; some are for noble purposes and some for ignoble. [21]If a man cleanses himself from the latter, he will be an instrument for noble purposes, made holy, useful to the Master and prepared to do any good work.

[22]Flee the evil desires of youth, and pursue righteousness, faith, love and peace, along with those who call on the Lord out of a pure heart. [23]Don't have anything to do with foolish and stupid arguments, because you know they produce quarrels. [24]And the Lord's servant must not quarrel; instead, he must be kind to everyone, able to teach, not resentful. [25]Those who oppose him he must gently instruct, in the hope that God will grant them repentance leading them to a knowledge of the truth, [26]and that they will come to their senses and escape from the trap of the devil, who has taken them captive to do his will.

READING FROM PROVERBS
Proverbs 25:21–26:2

[21]If your enemy is hungry, give him
    food to eat;
  if he is thirsty, give him water to
    drink.
[22]In doing this, you will heap burning
    coals on his head,
  and the LORD will reward you.

[23]As a north wind brings rain,
  so a sly tongue brings angry looks.

[24]Better to live on a corner of the roof
  than share a house with a
    quarrelsome wife.

[25]Like cold water to a weary soul
  is good news from a distant land.

[26]Like a muddied spring or a polluted
    well
  is a righteous man who gives way to
    the wicked.

[27]It is not good to eat too much honey,
  nor is it honourable to seek one's
    own honour.

[28]Like a city whose walls are broken
    down
  is a man who lacks self-control.

26 Like snow in summer or rain in
    harvest,
  honour is not fitting for a fool.

[2]Like a fluttering sparrow or a darting
    swallow,
  an undeserved curse does not come
    to rest.

OLD TESTAMENT READING
Jeremiah 50:11–51:14

¹¹"Because you rejoice and are glad,
　you who pillage my inheritance,
because you frolic like a heifer
　　threshing corn
and neigh like stallions,
¹²your mother will be greatly ashamed;
　she who gave you birth will be
　　disgraced.
She will be the least of the nations—
　a wilderness, a dry land, a desert.
¹³Because of the LORD's anger she will
　not be inhabited
but will be completely desolate.
All who pass Babylon will be
　horrified and scoff
because of all her wounds.

¹⁴"Take up your positions round
　Babylon,
all you who draw the bow.
Shoot at her! Spare no arrows,
　for she has sinned against the
　LORD.
¹⁵Shout against her on every side!
　She surrenders, her towers fall,
　her walls are torn down.
Since this is the vengeance of the
　LORD,
　take vengeance on her;
　do to her as she has done to others.
¹⁶Cut off from Babylon the sower,
　and the reaper with his sickle at
　harvest.
Because of the sword of the
　oppressor
let everyone return to his own
　people,
let everyone flee to his own land.

¹⁷"Israel is a scattered flock
　that lions have chased away.
The first to devour him
　was the king of Assyria;
the last to crush his bones
　was Nebuchadnezzar king of
　Babylon."

¹⁸Therefore this is what the LORD
Almighty, the God of Israel, says:

"I will punish the king of Babylon
　and his land
　as I punished the king of Assyria.
¹⁹But I will bring Israel back to his own
　pasture
　and he will graze on Carmel and
　Bashan;
his appetite will be satisfied
　on the hills of Ephraim and Gilead.
²⁰In those days, at that time,"
　declares the LORD,
"search will be made for Israel's
　guilt,
　but there will be none,
and for the sins of Judah,
　but none will be found,
　for I will forgive the remnant I
　spare.

²¹"Attack the land of Merathaim
　and those who live in Pekod.
Pursue, kill and completely destroy
　them,"
　　　　　　　　declares the LORD.
"Do everything I have commanded
　you.
²²The noise of battle is in the land,
　the noise of great destruction!
²³How broken and shattered
　is the hammer of the whole earth!
How desolate is Babylon
　among the nations!
²⁴I set a trap for you, O Babylon,
　and you were caught before you
　knew it;
you were found and captured
　because you opposed the LORD.
²⁵The LORD has opened his arsenal
　and brought out the weapons of his
　wrath,
for the Sovereign LORD Almighty has
　work to do
　in the land of the Babylonians.
²⁶Come against her from afar.
　Break open her granaries;
　pile her up like heaps of grain.

Completely destroy her
  and leave her no remnant.
27Kill all her young bulls;
  let them go down to the slaughter!
Woe to them! For their day has
    come,
  the time for them to be punished.
28Listen to the fugitives and refugees
    from Babylon
declaring in Zion
how the LORD our God has taken
    vengeance,
  vengeance for his temple.

29"Summon archers against Babylon,
  all those who draw the bow.
Encamp all round her;
  let no-one escape.
Repay her for her deeds;
  do to her as she has done.
For she defied the LORD,
  the Holy One of Israel.
30Therefore, her young men will fall in
    the streets;
  all her soldiers will be silenced in
    that day,"
                    declares the LORD.
31"See, I am against you, O arrogant
    one,"
  declares the Lord, the LORD
    Almighty,
"for your day has come,
  the time for you to be punished.
32The arrogant one will stumble and
    fall
  and no-one will help her up;
I will kindle a fire in her towns
  that will consume all who are
    around her."

33This is what the LORD Almighty
says:

  "The people of Israel are oppressed,
    and the people of Judah as well.
  All their captors hold them fast,
    refusing to let them go.
34Yet their Redeemer is strong;
  the LORD Almighty is his name.
He will vigorously defend their cause
  so that he may bring rest to their
    land,

but unrest to those who live in
    Babylon.

35"A sword against the Babylonians!"
    declares the LORD—
  "against those who live in Babylon
    and against her officials and wise
    men!
36A sword against her false prophets!
  They will become fools.
A sword against her warriors!
  They will be filled with terror.
37A sword against her horses and
    chariots
  and all the foreigners in her ranks!
  They will become women.
A sword against her treasures!
  They will be plundered.
38A drought on her waters!
  They will dry up.
For it is a land of idols,
  idols that will go mad with terror.

39"So desert creatures and hyenas will
    live there,
  and there the owl will dwell.
It will never again be inhabited
  or lived in from generation to
    generation.
40As God overthrew Sodom and
    Gomorrah
  along with their neighbouring
    towns,"
                    declares the LORD,
  "so no-one will live there;
  no man will dwell in it.

41"Look! An army is coming from the
    north;
  a great nation and many kings
  are being stirred up from the ends
    of the earth.
42They are armed with bows and
    spears;
  they are cruel and without mercy.
They sound like the roaring sea
  as they ride on their horses;
they come like men in battle
    formation
  to attack you, O Daughter of
    Babylon.

⁴³The king of Babylon has heard
reports about them,
and his hands hang limp.
Anguish has gripped him,
pain like that of a woman in
labour.
⁴⁴Like a lion coming up from Jordan's
thickets
to a rich pasture-land,
I will chase Babylon from its land in
an instant.
Who is the chosen one I will
appoint for this?
Who is like me and who can
challenge me?
And what shepherd can stand
against me?"
⁴⁵Therefore, hear what the LORD has
planned against Babylon,
what he has purposed against the
land of the Babylonians:
The young of the flock will be
dragged away;
he will completely destroy their
pasture because of them.
⁴⁶At the sound of Babylon's capture
the earth will tremble;
its cry will resound among the
nations.

51

This is what the LORD says:

"See, I will stir up the spirit of a
destroyer
against Babylon and the people of
Leb Kamai.
²I will send foreigners to Babylon
to winnow her and to devastate her
land;
they will oppose her on every side
in the day of her disaster.
³Let not the archer string his bow,
nor let him put on his armour.
Do not spare her young men;
completely destroy her army.
⁴They will fall down slain in Babylon,
fatally wounded in her streets.
⁵For Israel and Judah have not been
forsaken
by their God, the LORD Almighty,
though their land is full of guilt
before the Holy One of Israel.

⁶"Flee from Babylon!
Run for your lives!
Do not be destroyed because of
her sins.
It is time for the LORD's vengeance;
he will pay her what she deserves.
⁷Babylon was a gold cup in the LORD's
hand;
she made the whole earth drunk.
The nations drank her wine;
therefore they have now gone
mad.
⁸Babylon will suddenly fall and be
broken.
Wail over her!
Get balm for her pain;
perhaps she can be healed.

⁹"'We would have healed Babylon,
but she cannot be healed;
let us leave her and each go to his
own land,
for her judgment reaches to the
skies,
it rises as high as the clouds.'

¹⁰"'The LORD has vindicated us;
come, let us tell in Zion
what the LORD our God has done.'

¹¹"Sharpen the arrows,
take up the shields!
The LORD has stirred up the kings of
the Medes,
because his purpose is to destroy
Babylon.
The LORD will take vengeance,
vengeance for his temple.
¹²Lift up a banner against the walls of
Babylon!
Reinforce the guard,
station the watchmen,
prepare an ambush!
The LORD will carry out his purpose,
his decree against the people of
Babylon.
¹³You who live by many waters
and are rich in treasures,
your end has come,
the time for you to be cut off.
¹⁴The LORD Almighty has sworn by
himself:

I will surely fill you with men, as
    with a swarm of locusts,
and they will shout in triumph over
    you.

NEW TESTAMENT READING
2 Timothy 3:1–17

Godlessness in the Last Days

3 But mark this: There will be terrible times in the last days. [2]People
will be lovers of themselves, lovers of
money, boastful, proud, abusive, disobedient to their parents, ungrateful,
unholy, [3]without love, unforgiving,
slanderous, without self-control, brutal,
not lovers of the good, [4]treacherous,
rash, conceited, lovers of pleasure
rather than lovers of God—[5]having a
form of godliness but denying its power.
Have nothing to do with them.

[6]They are the kind who worm their
way into homes and gain control over
weak-willed women, who are loaded
down with sins and are swayed by all
kinds of evil desires, [7]always learning
but never able to acknowledge the
truth. [8]Just as Jannes and Jambres
opposed Moses, so also these men
oppose the truth—men of depraved
minds, who, as far as the faith is concerned, are rejected. [9]But they will not
get very far because, as in the case of
those men, their folly will be clear to
everyone.

Paul's Charge to Timothy

[10]You, however, know all about my
teaching, my way of life, my purpose,
faith, patience, love, endurance, [11]per-
secutions, sufferings—what kinds of
things happened to me in Antioch, Iconium and Lystra, the persecutions I endured. Yet the Lord rescued me from

all of them. [12]In fact, everyone who
wants to live a godly life in Christ Jesus
will be persecuted, [13]while evil men and
impostors will go from bad to worse,
deceiving and being deceived. [14]But as
for you, continue in what you have
learned and have become convinced of,
because you know those from whom
you learned it, [15]and how from infancy
you have known the holy Scriptures,
which are able to make you wise for
salvation through faith in Christ Jesus.
[16]All Scripture is God-breathed and is
useful for teaching, rebuking, correct-
ing and training in righteousness, [17]so
that the man of God may be thoroughly
equipped for every good work.

READING FROM PSALMS
Psalm 119:89–96

ל Lamedh

[89]Your word, O Lord, is eternal;
    it stands firm in the heavens.
[90]Your faithfulness continues through
    all generations;
    you established the earth, and it
    endures.
[91]Your laws endure to this day,
    for all things serve you.
[92]If your law had not been my delight,
    I would have perished in my
    affliction.
[93]I will never forget your precepts,
    for by them you have preserved my
    life.
[94]Save me, for I am yours;
    I have sought out your precepts.
[95]The wicked are waiting to destroy
    me,
    but I will ponder your statutes.
[96]To all perfection I see a limit;
    but your commands are boundless.

OLD TESTAMENT READING
Jeremiah 51:15–64

¹⁵"He made the earth by his power;
  he founded the world by his
    wisdom
  and stretched out the heavens by
    his understanding.
¹⁶When he thunders, the waters in the
    heavens roar;
  he makes clouds rise from the ends
    of the earth.
He sends lightning with the rain
  and brings out the wind from his
    storehouses.

¹⁷"Every man is senseless and without
    knowledge;
  every goldsmith is shamed by his
    idols.
His images are a fraud;
  they have no breath in them.
¹⁸They are worthless, the objects of
    mockery;
  when their judgment comes, they
    will perish.
¹⁹He who is the Portion of Jacob is not
    like these,
  for he is the Maker of all things,
including the tribe of his
    inheritance—
  the LORD Almighty is his name.

²⁰"You are my war club,
  my weapon for battle—
with you I shatter nations,
  with you I destroy kingdoms,
²¹with you I shatter horse and rider,
  with you I shatter chariot and
    driver,
²²with you I shatter man and woman,
  with you I shatter old man and
    youth,
  with you I shatter young man and
    maiden,
²³with you I shatter shepherd and flock,
  with you I shatter farmer and oxen,

with you I shatter governors and
    officials.

²⁴"Before your eyes I will repay
Babylon and all who live in Babylonia
for all the wrong they have done in
Zion," declares the LORD.

²⁵"I am against you, O destroying
    mountain,
  you who destroy the whole earth,"
    declares the LORD.
  "I will stretch out my hand against
    you,
  roll you off the cliffs,
  and make you a burnt-out
    mountain.
²⁶No rock will be taken from you for a
    cornerstone,
  nor any stone for a foundation,
  for you will be desolate for ever,"
    declares the LORD.

²⁷"Lift up a banner in the land!
  Blow the trumpet among the
    nations!
Prepare the nations for battle against
    her;
  summon against her these
    kingdoms:
  Ararat, Minni and Ashkenaz.
Appoint a commander against her;
  send up horses like a swarm of
    locusts.
²⁸Prepare the nations for battle against
    her—
  the kings of the Medes,
their governors and all their officials,
  and all the countries they rule.
²⁹The land trembles and writhes,
  for the LORD's purposes against
    Babylon stand—
to lay waste the land of Babylon
  so that no-one will live there.
³⁰Babylon's warriors have stopped
    fighting;
  they remain in their strongholds.

Their strength is exhausted;
   they have become like women.
Her dwellings are set on fire;
   the bars of her gates are broken.
[31]One courier follows another
   and messenger follows messenger
to announce to the king of Babylon
   that his entire city is captured,
[32]the river crossings seized,
   the marshes set on fire,
   and the soldiers terrified."

[33]This is what the LORD Almighty,
the God of Israel, says:

"The Daughter of Babylon is like a
   threshing-floor
   at the time it is trampled;
   the time to harvest her will soon
     come."

[34]"Nebuchadnezzar king of Babylon
   has devoured us,
he has thrown us into confusion,
   he has made us an empty jar.
Like a serpent he has swallowed us
   and filled his stomach with our
     delicacies,
   and then has spewed us out.
[35]May the violence done to our flesh be
   upon Babylon,"
   say the inhabitants of Zion.
"May our blood be on those who live
   in Babylonia,"
   says Jerusalem.

[36]Therefore, this is what the LORD
says:

"See, I will defend your cause
   and avenge you;
I will dry up her sea
   and make her springs dry.
[37]Babylon will be a heap of ruins,
   a haunt of jackals,
an object of horror and scorn,
   a place where no-one lives.
[38]Her people all roar like young lions,
   they growl like lion cubs.
[39]But while they are aroused,
   I will set out a feast for them
   and make them drunk,

so that they shout with laughter—
   then sleep for ever and not
     awake,"
           declares the LORD.
[40]"I will bring them down
   like lambs to the slaughter,
   like rams and goats.

[41]"How Sheshach will be captured,
   the boast of the whole earth seized!
What a horror Babylon will be
   among the nations!
[42]The sea will rise over Babylon;
   its roaring waves will cover her.
[43]Her towns will be desolate,
   a dry and desert land,
a land where no-one lives,
   through which no man travels.
[44]I will punish Bel in Babylon
   and make him spew out what he
     has swallowed.
The nations will no longer stream to
   him.
   And the wall of Babylon will fall.

[45]"Come out of her, my people!
   Run for your lives!
Run from the fierce anger of the
   LORD.
[46]Do not lose heart or be afraid
   when rumours are heard in the
     land;
one rumour comes this year, another
   the next,
rumours of violence in the land
   and of ruler against ruler.
[47]For the time will surely come
   when I will punish the idols of
     Babylon;
her whole land will be disgraced
   and her slain will all lie fallen
     within her.
[48]Then heaven and earth and all that is
   in them
will shout for joy over Babylon,
   for out of the north
destroyers will attack her,"
           declares the LORD.

[49]"Babylon must fall because of Israel's
   slain,
just as the slain in all the earth
   have fallen because of Babylon.

⁵⁰You who have escaped the sword,
leave and do not linger!
Remember the LORD in a distant
land,
and think on Jerusalem."

⁵¹"We are disgraced,
for we have been insulted
and shame covers our faces,
because foreigners have entered
the holy places of the LORD's
house."

⁵²"But days are coming," declares the
LORD,
"when I will punish her idols,
and throughout her land
the wounded will groan.
⁵³Even if Babylon reaches the sky
and fortifies her lofty stronghold,
I will send destroyers against her,"
declares the LORD.

⁵⁴"The sound of a cry comes from
Babylon,
the sound of great destruction
from the land of the Babylonians.
⁵⁵The LORD will destroy Babylon;
he will silence her noisy din.
Waves ⌊of enemies⌋ will rage like
great waters;
the roar of their voices will
resound.
⁵⁶A destroyer will come against
Babylon;
her warriors will be captured,
and their bows will be broken.
For the LORD is a God of retribution;
he will repay in full.
⁵⁷I will make her officials and wise men
drunk,
her governors, officers and
warriors as well;
they will sleep for ever and not
awake,"
declares the King, whose name is
the LORD Almighty.

⁵⁸This is what the LORD Almighty
says:

"Babylon's thick wall will be levelled
and her high gates set on fire;

the peoples exhaust themselves for
nothing,
the nations' labour is only fuel for
the flames."

⁵⁹This is the message Jeremiah gave
to the staff officer Seraiah son of
Neriah, the son of Mahseiah, when he
went to Babylon with Zedekiah king of
Judah in the fourth year of his reign.
⁶⁰Jeremiah had written on a scroll about
all the disasters that would come upon
Babylon—all that had been recorded
concerning Babylon. ⁶¹He said to
Seraiah, "When you get to Babylon, see
that you read all these words aloud.
⁶²Then say, 'O LORD, you have said you
will destroy this place, so that neither
man nor animal will live in it; it will be
desolate for ever.' ⁶³When you finish
reading this scroll, tie a stone to it and
throw it into the Euphrates. ⁶⁴Then say,
'So will Babylon sink to rise no more
because of the disaster I will bring upon
her. And her people will fall.'"

The words of Jeremiah end here.

NEW TESTAMENT READING
2 Timothy 4:1–22

4 In the presence of God and of
Christ Jesus, who will judge the
living and the dead, and in view of his
appearing and his kingdom, I give you
this charge: ²Preach the Word; be prepared in season and out of season;
correct, rebuke and encourage—with
great patience and careful instruction.
³For the time will come when men will
not put up with sound doctrine. Instead,
to suit their own desires, they will
gather around them a great number of
teachers to say what their itching ears
want to hear. ⁴They will turn their ears
away from the truth and turn aside to
myths. ⁵But you, keep your head in all
situations, endure hardship, do the
work of an evangelist, discharge all the
duties of your ministry.

⁶For I am already being poured out like a drink offering, and the time has come for my departure. ⁷I have fought the good fight, I have finished the race, I have kept the faith. ⁸Now there is in store for me the crown of righteousness, which the Lord, the righteous Judge, will award to me on that day—and not only to me, but also to all who have longed for his appearing.

Personal Remarks

⁹Do your best to come to me quickly, ¹⁰for Demas, because he loved this world, has deserted me and has gone to Thessalonica. Crescens has gone to Galatia, and Titus to Dalmatia. ¹¹Only Luke is with me. Get Mark and bring him with you, because he is helpful to me in my ministry. ¹²I sent Tychicus to Ephesus. ¹³When you come, bring the cloak that I left with Carpus at Troas, and my scrolls, especially the parchments.

¹⁴Alexander the metalworker did me a great deal of harm. The Lord will repay him for what he has done. ¹⁵You too should be on your guard against him, because he strongly opposed our message.

¹⁶At my first defence, no-one came to my support, but everyone deserted me. May it not be held against them. ¹⁷But the Lord stood at my side and gave me strength, so that through me the message might be fully proclaimed and all the Gentiles might hear it. And I was delivered from the lion's mouth. ¹⁸The Lord will rescue me from every evil attack and will bring me safely to his heavenly kingdom. To him be glory for ever and ever. Amen.

Final Greetings

¹⁹Greet Priscilla and Aquila and the household of Onesiphorus. ²⁰Erastus stayed in Corinth, and I left Trophimus sick in Miletus. ²¹Do your best to get here before winter. Eubulus greets you, and so do Pudens, Linus, Claudia and all the brothers.

²²The Lord be with your spirit. Grace be with you.

READING FROM PSALMS
Psalm 119:97–104

מ Mem

⁹⁷Oh, how I love your law!
    I meditate on it all day long.
⁹⁸Your commands make me wiser than
        my enemies,
    for they are ever with me.
⁹⁹I have more insight than all my
        teachers,
    for I meditate on your statutes.
¹⁰⁰I have more understanding than the
        elders,
    for I obey your precepts.
¹⁰¹I have kept my feet from every evil
        path
    so that I might obey your word.
¹⁰²I have not departed from your laws,
    for you yourself have taught me.
¹⁰³How sweet are your words to my
        taste,
    sweeter than honey to my mouth!
¹⁰⁴I gain understanding from your
        precepts;
    therefore I hate every wrong path.

OLD TESTAMENT READING
Jeremiah 52:1–34

The Fall of Jerusalem

52 Zedekiah was twenty-one years old when he became king, and he reigned in Jerusalem for eleven years. His mother's name was Hamutal daughter of Jeremiah; she was from Libnah. ²He did evil in the eyes of the LORD, just as Jehoiakim had done. ³It was because of the LORD's anger that all this happened to Jerusalem and Judah, and in the end he thrust them from his presence.

Now Zedekiah rebelled against the king of Babylon.

⁴So in the ninth year of Zedekiah's reign, on the tenth day of the tenth month, Nebuchadnezzar king of Babylon marched against Jerusalem with his whole army. They camped outside the city and built siege works all around it. ⁵The city was kept under siege until the eleventh year of King Zedekiah.

⁶By the ninth day of the fourth month the famine in the city had become so severe that there was no food for the people to eat. ⁷Then the city wall was broken through, and the whole army fled. They left the city at night through the gate between the two walls near the king's garden, though the Babylonians were surrounding the city. They fled towards the Arabah, ⁸but the Babylonian army pursued King Zedekiah and overtook him in the plains of Jericho. All his soldiers were separated from him and scattered, ⁹and he was captured.

He was taken to the king of Babylon at Riblah in the land of Hamath, where he pronounced sentence on him. ¹⁰There at Riblah the king of Babylon slaughtered the sons of Zedekiah before his eyes; he also killed all the officials of Judah. ¹¹Then he put out Zedekiah's eyes, bound him with bronze shackles and took him to Babylon, where he put him in prison till the day of his death.

¹²On the tenth day of the fifth month, in the nineteenth year of Nebuchadnezzar king of Babylon, Nebuzaradan commander of the imperial guard, who served the king of Babylon, came to Jerusalem. ¹³He set fire to the temple of the LORD, the royal palace and all the houses of Jerusalem. Every important building he burned down. ¹⁴The whole Babylonian army under the commander of the imperial guard broke down all the walls around Jerusalem. ¹⁵Nebuzaradan the commander of the guard carried into exile some of the poorest people and those who remained in the city, along with the rest of the craftsmen and those who had gone over to the king of Babylon. ¹⁶But Nebuzaradan left behind the rest of the poorest people of the land to work the vineyards and fields.

¹⁷The Babylonians broke up the bronze pillars, the movable stands and the bronze Sea that were at the temple of the LORD and they carried all the bronze to Babylon. ¹⁸They also took away the pots, shovels, wick trimmers, sprinkling bowls, dishes and all the bronze articles used in the temple service. ¹⁹The commander of the imperial guard took away the basins, censers, sprinkling bowls, pots, lampstands, dishes and bowls used for drink offerings—all that were made of pure gold or silver.

²⁰The bronze from the two pillars, the Sea and the twelve bronze bulls under it, and the movable stands, which King Solomon had made for the temple of the LORD, was more than could be weighed. ²¹Each of the pillars was eighteen cubits high and twelve cubits in circumference; each was four fingers thick, and hollow. ²²The bronze capital on the top

of the one pillar was five cubits high and was decorated with a network and pomegranates of bronze all around. The other pillar, with its pomegranates, was similar. 23There were ninety-six pomegranates on the sides; the total number of pomegranates above the surrounding network was a hundred.

24The commander of the guard took as prisoners Seraiah the chief priest, Zephaniah the priest next in rank and the three doorkeepers. 25Of those still in the city, he took the officer in charge of the fighting men, and seven royal advisers. He also took the secretary who was chief officer in charge of conscripting the people of the land and sixty of his men who were found in the city. 26Nebuzaradan the commander took them all and brought them to the king of Babylon at Riblah. 27There at Riblah, in the land of Hamath, the king had them executed.

So Judah went into captivity, away from her land. 28This is the number of the people Nebuchadnezzar carried into exile:

in the seventh year, 3,023 Jews;
29in Nebuchadnezzar's eighteenth year, 832 people from Jerusalem;
30in his twenty-third year,
745 Jews taken into exile by Nebuzaradan
the commander of the imperial guard.
There were 4,600 people in all.

Jehoiachin Released

31In the thirty-seventh year of the exile of Jehoiachin king of Judah, in the year Evil-Merodach became king of Babylon, he released Jehoiachin king of Judah and freed him from prison on the twenty-fifth day of the twelfth month. 32He spoke kindly to him and gave him a seat of honour higher than those of the other kings who were with him in Babylon. 33So Jehoiachin put aside his prison clothes and for the rest of his life ate regularly at the king's table. 34Day by day the king of Babylon gave Jehoiachin a regular allowance as long as he lived, till the day of his death.

NEW TESTAMENT READING
Titus 1:1–16

1 Paul, a servant of God and an apostle of Jesus Christ for the faith of God's elect and the knowledge of the truth that leads to godliness—2a faith and knowledge resting on the hope of eternal life, which God, who does not lie, promised before the beginning of time, 3and at his appointed season he brought his word to light through the preaching entrusted to me by the command of God our Saviour,

4To Titus, my true son in our common faith:

Grace and peace from God the Father and Christ Jesus our Saviour.

Titus' Task on Crete

5The reason I left you in Crete was that you might straighten out what was left unfinished and appoint elders in every town, as I directed you. 6An elder must be blameless, the husband of but one wife, a man whose children believe and are not open to the charge of being wild and disobedient. 7Since an overseer is entrusted with God's work, he must be blameless—not overbearing, not quick-tempered, not given to drunkenness, not violent, not pursuing dishonest gain. 8Rather he must be hospitable, one who loves what is good, who is self-controlled, upright, holy and disciplined. 9He must hold firmly to the trustworthy message as it has been taught, so that he can encourage others by sound doctrine and refute those who oppose it.

10For there are many rebellious people, mere talkers and deceivers, especially those of the circumcision group. 11They must be silenced, because they are ruining whole households by teaching things they ought not to teach —and that for the sake of dishonest gain. 12Even one of their own prophets has said, "Cretans are always liars, evil brutes, lazy gluttons." [13]This testimony is true. Therefore, rebuke them sharply, so that they will be sound in the faith [14]and will pay no attention to Jewish myths or to the commands of those who reject the truth. [15]To the pure, all things are pure, but to those who are corrupted and do not believe, nothing is pure. In fact, both their minds and consciences are corrupted. [16]They claim to know God, but by their actions they deny him. They are detestable, disobedient and unfit for doing anything good.

READING FROM PSALMS
Psalm 119:105–112

﬩ Nun

[105]Your word is a lamp to my feet
and a light for my path.

[106]I have taken an oath and confirmed it,
that I will follow your righteous laws.
[107]I have suffered much;
preserve my life, O LORD,
according to your word.
[108]Accept, O LORD, the willing praise of my mouth,
and teach me your laws.
[109]Though I constantly take my life in my hands,
I will not forget your law.
[110]The wicked have set a snare for me,
but I have not strayed from your precepts.
[111]Your statutes are my heritage for ever;
they are the joy of my heart.
[112]My heart is set on keeping your decrees
to the very end.

OCTOBER 27   DAY 300

OLD TESTAMENT READING
Habakkuk 1:1–3:19

1 The oracle that Habakkuk the prophet received.

Habakkuk's Complaint

[2]How long, O LORD, must I call for help,
but you do not listen?
Or cry out to you, "Violence!"
but you do not save?
[3]Why do you make me look at injustice?
Why do you tolerate wrong?
Destruction and violence are before me;
there is strife, and conflict abounds.
[4]Therefore the law is paralysed,
and justice never prevails.

The wicked hem in the righteous,
so that justice is perverted.

The LORD's Answer

[5]"Look at the nations and watch—
and be utterly amazed.
For I am going to do something in your days
that you would not believe,
even if you were told.
[6]I am raising up the Babylonians,
that ruthless and impetuous people,
who sweep across the whole earth
to seize dwelling-places not their own.
[7]They are a feared and dreaded people;
they are a law to themselves
and promote their own honour.

8Their horses are swifter than
    leopards,
  fiercer than wolves at dusk.
Their cavalry gallops headlong;
  their horsemen come from afar.
They fly like a vulture swooping to
    devour;
9 they all come bent on violence.
Their hordes advance like a desert
    wind
  and gather prisoners like sand.
10They deride kings
  and scoff at rulers.
They laugh at all fortified cities;
  they build earthen ramps and
    capture them.
11Then they sweep past like the wind
  and go on—
  guilty men, whose own strength is
    their god."

Habakkuk's Second Complaint

12O LORD, are you not from
    everlasting?
My God, my Holy One, we will not
    die.
O LORD, you have appointed them to
    execute judgment;
O Rock, you have ordained them
    to punish.
13Your eyes are too pure to look on
    evil;
  you cannot tolerate wrong.
Why then do you tolerate the
    treacherous?
Why are you silent while the
    wicked
swallow up those more righteous
    than themselves?
14You have made men like fish in the
    sea,
like sea creatures that have no
    ruler.
15The wicked foe pulls all of them up
    with hooks,
  he catches them in his net,
he gathers them up in his drag-net;
  and so he rejoices and is glad.
16Therefore he sacrifices to his net
  and burns incense to his drag-net,

for by his net he lives in luxury
  and enjoys the choicest food.
17Is he to keep on emptying his net,
  destroying nations without mercy?

2 I will stand at my watch
  and station myself on the ramparts;
I will look to see what he will say to
    me,
  and what answer I am to give to
    this complaint.

The LORD's Answer

2Then the LORD replied:

"Write down the revelation
  and make it plain on tablets
  so that a herald may run with it.
3For the revelation awaits an
    appointed time;
  it speaks of the end
  and will not prove false.
Though it linger, wait for it;
  it will certainly come and will not
    delay.

4"See, he is puffed up;
  his desires are not upright—
  but the righteous will live by his
    faith—
5indeed, wine betrays him;
  he is arrogant and never at rest.
Because he is as greedy as the grave
  and like death is never satisfied,
he gathers to himself all the nations
  and takes captive all the peoples.

6"Will not all of them taunt him with
ridicule and scorn, saying,

"'Woe to him who piles up stolen
    goods
  and makes himself wealthy by
    extortion!
  How long must this go on?'
7Will not your debtors suddenly arise?
  Will not they wake up and make
    you tremble?
  Then you will become their victim.
8Because you have plundered many
    nations,

the peoples who are left will
    plunder you.
For you have shed man's blood;
    you have destroyed lands and cities
        and everyone in them.

⁹"Woe to him who builds his realm by
    unjust gain
    to set his nest on high,
    to escape the clutches of ruin!
¹⁰You have plotted the ruin of many
    peoples,
    shaming your own house and
        forfeiting your life.
¹¹The stones of the wall will cry out,
    and the beams of the woodwork
        will echo it.

¹²"Woe to him who builds a city with
    bloodshed
    and establishes a town by crime!
¹³Has not the LORD Almighty
    determined
    that the people's labour is only fuel
        for the fire,
    that nations exhaust themselves for
        nothing?
¹⁴For the earth will be filled with the
    knowledge of the glory of the
    LORD,
    as the waters cover the sea.

¹⁵"Woe to him who gives drink to his
    neighbours,
    pouring it from the wineskin till
        they are drunk,
    so that he can gaze on their naked
        bodies.
¹⁶You will be filled with shame instead
    of glory.
    Now it is your turn! Drink and be
        exposed!
The cup from the LORD's right hand
    is coming round to you,
    and disgrace will cover your glory.
¹⁷The violence you have done to
    Lebanon will overwhelm you,
    and your destruction of animals
        will terrify you.
For you have shed man's blood;
    you have destroyed lands and cities
        and everyone in them.

¹⁸"Of what value is an idol, since a man
    has carved it?
    Or an image that teaches lies?
For he who makes it trusts in his own
    creation;
    he makes idols that cannot speak.
¹⁹Woe to him who says to wood, 'Come
    to life!'
    Or to lifeless stone, 'Wake up!'
Can it give guidance?
    It is covered with gold and silver;
        there is no breath in it.
²⁰But the LORD is in his holy temple;
    let all the earth be silent before
        him."

Habakkuk's Prayer

3 A prayer of Habakkuk the
prophet. On *shigionoth*.

²LORD, I have heard of your fame;
    I stand in awe of your deeds, O
    LORD.
Renew them in our day,
    in our time make them known;
    in wrath remember mercy.

³God came from Teman,
    the Holy One from Mount Paran.
                                    Selah
His glory covered the heavens
    and his praise filled the earth.
⁴His splendour was like the sunrise;
    rays flashed from his hand,
    where his power was hidden.
⁵Plague went before him;
    pestilence followed his steps.
⁶He stood, and shook the earth;
    he looked, and made the nations
        tremble.
The ancient mountains crumbled
    and the age-old hills collapsed.
    His ways are eternal.
⁷I saw the tents of Cushan in distress,
    the dwellings of Midian in anguish.

⁸Were you angry with the rivers, O
    LORD?
    Was your wrath against the
        streams?

Did you rage against the sea
    when you rode with your horses
    and your victorious chariots?
9You uncovered your bow,
    you called for many arrows.   *Selah*
You split the earth with rivers;
10   the mountains saw you and
        writhed.
Torrents of water swept by;
    the deep roared
    and lifted its waves on high.

11Sun and moon stood still in the
        heavens
    at the glint of your flying arrows,
    at the lightning of your flashing
        spear.
12In wrath you strode through the earth
    and in anger you threshed the
        nations.
13You came out to deliver your people,
    to save your anointed one.
You crushed the leader of the land of
        wickedness,
    you stripped him from head to
        foot.   *Selah*
14With his own spear you pierced his
        head
    when his warriors stormed out to
        scatter us,
gloating as though about to devour
    the wretched who were in hiding.
15You trampled the sea with your
        horses,
    churning the great waters.

16I heard and my heart pounded,
    my lips quivered at the sound;
decay crept into my bones,
    and my legs trembled.
Yet I will wait patiently for the day of
        calamity
    to come on the nation invading us.
17Though the fig-tree does not bud
    and there are no grapes on the
        vines,
though the olive crop fails
    and the fields produce no food,
though there are no sheep in the pen
    and no cattle in the stalls,
18yet I will rejoice in the LORD,
    I will be joyful in God my Saviour.

19The Sovereign LORD is my strength;
    he makes my feet like the feet of a
        deer,
    he enables me to go on the heights.

For the director of music. On my
    stringed instruments.

NEW TESTAMENT READING
Titus 2:1–15

*What Must Be Taught to Various
Groups*

2 You must teach what is in accord
    with sound doctrine. 2Teach the
older men to be temperate, worthy of
respect, self-controlled, and sound in
faith, in love and endurance.

3Likewise, teach the older women to
be reverent in the way they live, not to
be slanderers or addicted to much wine,
but to teach what is good. 4Then they
can train the younger women to love
their husbands and children, 5to be self-
controlled and pure, to be busy at
home, to be kind, and to be subject to
their husbands, so that no-one will
malign the word of God.

6Similarly, encourage the young men
to be self-controlled. 7In everything set
them an example by doing what is
good. In your teaching show integrity,
seriousness 8and soundness of speech
that cannot be condemned, so that
those who oppose you may be ashamed
because they have nothing bad to say
about us.

9Teach slaves to be subject to their
masters in everything, to try to please
them, not to talk back to them, 10and
not to steal from them, but to show that
they can be fully trusted, so that in every
way they will make the teaching about
God our Saviour attractive.

11For the grace of God that brings
salvation has appeared to all men. 12It
teaches us to say "No" to ungodliness
and worldly passions, and to live self-
controlled, upright and godly lives in
this present age, 13while we wait for the

blessed hope—the glorious appearing of our great God and Saviour, Jesus Christ, ¹⁴who gave himself for us to redeem us from all wickedness and to purify for himself a people that are his very own, eager to do what is good.

¹⁵These, then, are the things you should teach. Encourage and rebuke with all authority. Do not let anyone despise you.

READING FROM PROVERBS
Proverbs 26:3–12

³A whip for the horse, a halter for the
    donkey,
  and a rod for the backs of fools!

⁴Do not answer a fool according to his
    folly,
  or you will be like him yourself.

⁵Answer a fool according to his folly,
  or he will be wise in his own eyes.

⁶Like cutting off one's feet or drinking
    violence
is the sending of a message by the
    hand of a fool.

⁷Like a lame man's legs that hang limp
  is a proverb in the mouth of a fool.

⁸Like tying a stone in a sling
  is the giving of honour to a fool.

⁹Like a thornbush in a drunkard's
    hand
is a proverb in the mouth of a fool.

¹⁰Like an archer who wounds at
    random
is he who hires a fool or any
    passer-by.

¹¹As a dog returns to its vomit,
  so a fool repeats his folly.

¹²Do you see a man wise in his own
    eyes?
There is more hope for a fool than
    for him.

OCTOBER 28   DAY 301

OLD TESTAMENT READING
Lamentations 1:1–2:6

1 How deserted lies the city,
  once so full of people!
How like a widow is she,
  who once was great among the
    nations!
She who was queen among the
    provinces
has now become a slave.

²Bitterly she weeps at night,
  tears are upon her cheeks.
Among all her lovers
  there is none to comfort her.
All her friends have betrayed her;
  they have become her enemies.

³After affliction and harsh labour,
  Judah has gone into exile.
She dwells among the nations;
  she finds no resting place.
All who pursue her have overtaken
    her
in the midst of her distress.

⁴The roads to Zion mourn,
  for no-one comes to her appointed
    feasts.
All her gateways are desolate,
  her priests groan,
her maidens grieve,
  and she is in bitter anguish.

⁵Her foes have become her masters;
  her enemies are at ease.

The LORD has brought her grief
   because of her many sins.
Her children have gone into exile,
   captive before the foe.

6All the splendour has departed
   from the Daughter of Zion.
Her princes are like deer
   that find no pasture;
in weakness they have fled
   before the pursuer.

7In the days of her affliction and
      wandering
   Jerusalem remembers all the
      treasures
   that were hers in days of old.
When her people fell into enemy
      hands,
   there was no-one to help her.
Her enemies looked at her
   and laughed at her destruction.

8Jerusalem has sinned greatly
   and so has become unclean.
All who honoured her despise her,
   for they have seen her nakedness;
she herself groans
   and turns away.

9Her filthiness clung to her skirts;
   she did not consider her future.
Her fall was astounding;
   there was none to comfort her.
"Look, O LORD, on my affliction,
   for the enemy has triumphed."

10The enemy laid hands
   on all her treasures;
she saw pagan nations
   enter her sanctuary—
those you had forbidden
   to enter your assembly.

11All her people groan
   as they search for bread;
they barter their treasures for food
   to keep themselves alive.
"Look, O LORD, and consider,
   for I am despised."

12"Is it nothing to you, all you who pass
      by?

Look around and see.
Is any suffering like my suffering
   that was inflicted on me,
that the LORD brought on me
   in the day of his fierce anger?

13"From on high he sent fire,
   sent it down into my bones.
He spread a net for my feet
   and turned me back.
He made me desolate,
   faint all the day long.

14"My sins have been bound into a
      yoke;
   by his hands they were woven
      together.
They have come upon my neck
   and the Lord has sapped my
      strength.
He has handed me over
   to those I cannot withstand.

15"The Lord has rejected
   all the warriors in my midst;
he has summoned an army against me
   to crush my young men.
In his winepress the Lord has
      trampled
   the Virgin Daughter of Judah.

16"This is why I weep
   and my eyes overflow with tears.
No-one is near to comfort me,
   no-one to restore my spirit.
My children are destitute
   because the enemy has prevailed."

17Zion stretches out her hands,
   but there is no-one to comfort her.
The LORD has decreed for Jacob
   that his neighbours become his
      foes;
Jerusalem has become
   an unclean thing among them.

18"The LORD is righteous,
   yet I rebelled against his command.
Listen, all you peoples;
   look upon my suffering.
My young men and maidens
   have gone into exile.

19"I called to my allies
   but they betrayed me.
My priests and my elders
   perished in the city
while they searched for food
   to keep themselves alive.

20"See, O LORD, how distressed I am!
   I am in torment within,
and in my heart I am disturbed,
   for I have been most rebellious.
Outside, the sword bereaves;
   inside, there is only death.

21"People have heard my groaning,
   but there is no-one to comfort me.
All my enemies have heard of my
      distress;
   they rejoice at what you have
      done.
May you bring the day you have
      announced
   so that they may become like me.

22"Let all their wickedness come
      before you;
   deal with them
as you have dealt with me
   because of all my sins.
My groans are many
   and my heart is faint."

2   How the Lord has covered the
     Daughter of Zion
   with the cloud of his anger!
He has hurled down the splendour of
      Israel
   from heaven to earth;
he has not remembered his footstool
   in the day of his anger.

2Without pity the Lord has swallowed
      up
   all the dwellings of Jacob;
in his wrath he has torn down
   the strongholds of the Daughter of
      Judah.
He has brought her kingdom and its
      princes
   down to the ground in dishonour.

3In fierce anger he has cut off
   every horn of Israel.

He has withdrawn his right hand
   at the approach of the enemy.
He has burned in Jacob like a flaming
      fire
   that consumes everything around
      it.

4Like an enemy he has strung his bow;
   his right hand is ready.
Like a foe he has slain
   all who were pleasing to the eye;
he has poured out his wrath like fire
   on the tent of the Daughter of
      Zion.

5The Lord is like an enemy;
   he has swallowed up Israel.
He has swallowed up all her palaces
   and destroyed her strongholds.
He has multiplied mourning and
      lamentation
   for the Daughter of Judah.

6He has laid waste his dwelling like a
      garden;
   he has destroyed his place of
      meeting.
The LORD has made Zion forget
   her appointed feasts and her
      Sabbaths;
in his fierce anger he has spurned
   both king and priest.

NEW TESTAMENT READING
Titus 3:1-15

Doing What is Good

3   Remind the people to be subject to
     rulers and authorities, to be obedi-
ent, to be ready to do whatever is good,
2to slander no-one, to be peaceable and
considerate, and to show true humility
towards all men.

3At one time we too were foolish,
disobedient, deceived and enslaved by
all kinds of passions and pleasures. We
lived in malice and envy, being hated
and hating one another. 4But when the
kindness and love of God our Saviour
appeared, 5he saved us, not because of

righteous things we had done, but because of his mercy. He saved us through the washing of rebirth and renewal by the Holy Spirit, 6whom he poured out on us generously through Jesus Christ our Saviour, 7so that, having been justified by his grace, we might become heirs having the hope of eternal life. 8This is a trustworthy saying. And I want you to stress these things, so that those who have trusted in God may be careful to devote themselves to doing what is good. These things are excellent and profitable for everyone.

9But avoid foolish controversies and genealogies and arguments and quarrels about the law, because these are unprofitable and useless. 10Warn a divisive person once, and then warn him a second time. After that, have nothing to do with him. 11You may be sure that such a man is warped and sinful; he is self-condemned.

Final Remarks

12As soon as I send Artemas or Tychicus to you, do your best to come to me at Nicopolis, because I have decided to winter there. 13Do everything you can to help Zenas the lawyer and Apollos on their way and see that they have everything they need. 14Our people must learn to devote themselves to doing what is good, in order that they may provide for daily necessities and not live unproductive lives.

15Everyone with me sends you greetings. Greet those who love us in the faith.

Grace be with you all.

READING FROM PSALMS
Psalm 119:113–120

ס Samekh

113I hate double-minded men,
    but I love your law.
114You are my refuge and my shield;
    I have put my hope in your word.
115Away from me, you evildoers,
    that I may keep the commands of
        my God!
116Sustain me according to your
        promise, and I shall live;
    do not let my hopes be dashed.
117Uphold me, and I shall be delivered;
    I shall always have regard for your
        decrees.
118You reject all who stray from your
        decrees,
    for their deceitfulness is in vain.
119All the wicked of the earth you
        discard like dross;
    therefore I love your statutes.
120My flesh trembles in fear of you;
    I stand in awe of your laws.

OCTOBER 29

OLD TESTAMENT READING
Lamentations 2:7–3:39

7The Lord has rejected his altar
    and abandoned his sanctuary.
He has handed over to the enemy
    the walls of her palaces;
they have raised a shout in the house
        of the LORD
    as on the day of an appointed feast.

8The LORD determined to tear down
    the wall around the Daughter of
        Zion.
He stretched out a measuring line
    and did not withhold his hand from
        destroying.
He made ramparts and walls
    lament;
    together they wasted away.

⁹Her gates have sunk into the ground;
    their bars he has broken and
    destroyed.
Her king and her princes are exiled
    among the nations,
    the law is no more,
and her prophets no longer find
    visions from the LORD.

¹⁰The elders of the Daughter of Zion
    sit on the ground in silence;
they have sprinkled dust on their
    heads
    and put on sackcloth.
The young women of Jerusalem
    have bowed their heads to the
    ground.

¹¹My eyes fail from weeping,
    I am in torment within,
my heart is poured out on the ground
    because my people are destroyed,
    because children and infants faint
    in the streets of the city.

¹²They say to their mothers,
    "Where is bread and wine?"
as they faint like wounded men
    in the streets of the city,
as their lives ebb away
    in their mothers' arms.

¹³What can I say for you?
    With what can I compare you,
    O Daughter of Jerusalem?
To what can I liken you,
    that I may comfort you,
    O Virgin Daughter of Zion?
Your wound is as deep as the sea.
    Who can heal you?

¹⁴The visions of your prophets
    were false and worthless;
they did not expose your sin
    to ward off your captivity.
The oracles they gave you
    were false and misleading.

¹⁵All who pass your way
    clap their hands at you;
they scoff and shake their heads
    at the Daughter of Jerusalem:

"Is this the city that was called
    the perfection of beauty,
    the joy of the whole earth?"

¹⁶All your enemies open their mouths
    wide against you;
they scoff and gnash their teeth
    and say, "We have swallowed her
    up.
This is the day we have waited for;
    we have lived to see it."

¹⁷The LORD has done what he planned;
    he has fulfilled his word,
    which he decreed long ago.
He has overthrown you without pity,
    he has let the enemy gloat over
    you,
he has exalted the horn of your
    foes.

¹⁸The hearts of the people
    cry out to the Lord.
O wall of the Daughter of Zion,
    let your tears flow like a river
    day and night;
give yourself no relief,
    your eyes no rest.

¹⁹Arise, cry out in the night,
    as the watches of the night begin;
pour out your heart like water
    in the presence of the Lord.
Lift up your hands to him
    for the lives of your children,
who faint from hunger
    at the head of every street.

²⁰"Look, O LORD, and consider:
    Whom have you ever treated like
    this?
Should women eat their offspring,
    the children they have cared for?
Should priest and prophet be killed
    in the sanctuary of the Lord?

²¹"Young and old lie together
    in the dust of the streets;
my young men and maidens
    have fallen by the sword.
You have slain them in the day of
    your anger;
    you have slaughtered them without
    pity.

22"As you summon to a feast day,
  so you summoned against me
    terrors on every side.
In the day of the LORD's anger
  no-one escaped or survived;
those I cared for and reared,
  my enemy has destroyed."

3 I am the man who has seen
    affliction
  by the rod of his wrath.
²He has driven me away and made me
    walk
  in darkness rather than light;
³indeed, he has turned his hand
    against me
  again and again, all day long.

⁴He has made my skin and my flesh
    grow old
  and has broken my bones.
⁵He has besieged me and surrounded
    me
  with bitterness and hardship.
⁶He has made me dwell in darkness
  like those long dead.

⁷He has walled me in so that I cannot
    escape;
  he has weighed me down with
    chains.
⁸Even when I call out or cry for help,
  he shuts out my prayer.
⁹He has barred my way with blocks of
    stone;
  he has made my paths crooked.

¹⁰Like a bear lying in wait,
  like a lion in hiding,
¹¹he dragged me from the path and
    mangled me
  and left me without help.
¹²He drew his bow
  and made me the target for his
    arrows.

¹³He pierced my heart
  with arrows from his quiver.
¹⁴I became the laughing-stock of all my
    people;
  they mock me in song all day long.
¹⁵He has filled me with bitter herbs
  and sated me with gall.

¹⁶He has broken my teeth with gravel;
  he has trampled me in the dust.
¹⁷I have been deprived of peace;
  I have forgotten what prosperity is.
¹⁸So I say, "My splendour is gone
  and all that I had hoped from the
    LORD."

¹⁹I remember my affliction and my
    wandering,
  the bitterness and the gall.
²⁰I well remember them,
  and my soul is downcast within me.
²¹Yet this I call to mind
  and therefore I have hope:

²²Because of the LORD's great love we
    are not consumed,
  for his compassions never fail.
²³They are new every morning;
  great is your faithfulness.
²⁴I say to myself, "The LORD is my
    portion;
  therefore I will wait for him."

²⁵The LORD is good to those whose
    hope is in him,
  to the one who seeks him;
²⁶it is good to wait quietly
  for the salvation of the LORD.
²⁷It is good for a man to bear the yoke
  while he is young.

²⁸Let him sit alone in silence,
  for the LORD has laid it on him.
²⁹Let him bury his face in the dust—
  there may yet be hope.
³⁰Let him offer his cheek to one who
    would strike him,
  and let him be filled with disgrace.

³¹For men are not cast off
  by the Lord for ever.
³²Though he brings grief, he will show
    compassion,
  so great is his unfailing love.
³³For he does not willingly bring
    affliction
  or grief to the children of men.

³⁴To crush underfoot
  all prisoners in the land,

³⁵to deny a man his rights
before the Most High,
³⁶to deprive a man of justice—
would not the Lord see such
things?

³⁷Who can speak and have it happen
if the Lord has not decreed it?
³⁸Is it not from the mouth of the Most
High
that both calamities and good
things come?
³⁹Why should any living man complain
when punished for his sins?

NEW TESTAMENT READING
Philemon 1–25

¹Paul, a prisoner of Christ Jesus, and
Timothy our brother,

To Philemon our dear friend and
fellow-worker, ²to Apphia our sister,
to Archippus our fellow-soldier and to
the church that meets in your home:

³Grace to you and peace from God
our Father and the Lord Jesus Christ.

Thanksgiving and Prayer

⁴I always thank my God as I remem-
ber you in my prayers, ⁵because I hear
about your faith in the Lord Jesus and
your love for all the saints. ⁶I pray that
you may be active in sharing your faith,
so that you will have a full understanding of every good thing we have in
Christ. ⁷Your love has given me great
joy and encouragement, because you,
brother, have refreshed the hearts of
the saints.

Paul's Plea for Onesimus

⁸Therefore, although in Christ I
could be bold and order you to do what
you ought to do, ⁹yet I appeal to you on
the basis of love. I then, as Paul—an old
man and now also a prisoner of Christ
Jesus—¹⁰I appeal to you for my son

Onesimus, who became my son while I
was in chains. ¹¹Formerly he was useless
to you, but now he has become useful
both to you and to me.

¹²I am sending him—who is my very
heart—back to you. ¹³I would have
liked to keep him with me so that he
could take your place in helping me
while I am in chains for the gospel.
¹⁴But I did not want to do anything
without your consent, so that any
favour you do will be spontaneous and
not forced. ¹⁵Perhaps the reason he was
separated from you for a little while was
that you might have him back for good
—¹⁶no longer as a slave, but better than
a slave, as a dear brother. He is very
dear to me but even dearer to you, both
as a man and as a brother in the Lord.

¹⁷So if you consider me a partner,
welcome him as you would welcome
me. ¹⁸If he has done you any wrong or
owes you anything, charge it to me. ¹⁹I,
Paul, am writing this with my own hand.
I will pay it back—not to mention that
you owe me your very self. ²⁰I do wish,
brother, that I may have some benefit
from you in the Lord; refresh my heart
in Christ. ²¹Confident of your obedience, I write to you, knowing that you
will do even more than I ask.

²²And one thing more: Prepare a
guest room for me, because I hope to be
restored to you in answer to your
prayers.

²³Epaphras, my fellow-prisoner in
Christ Jesus, sends you greetings.
²⁴And so do Mark, Aristarchus, Demas
and Luke, my fellow-workers.
²⁵The grace of the Lord Jesus Christ
be with your spirit.

READING FROM PSALMS
Psalm 119:121–128

י Ayin

¹²¹I have done what is righteous and
just;
do not leave me to my oppressors.

¹²²Ensure your servant's well-being;
   let not the arrogant oppress me.
¹²³My eyes fail, looking for your
   salvation,
   looking for your righteous promise.
¹²⁴Deal with your servant according to
   your love
   and teach me your decrees.
¹²⁵I am your servant; give me
   discernment

that I may understand your
   statutes.
¹²⁶It is time for you to act, O LORD;
   your law is being broken.
¹²⁷Because I love your commands
   more than gold, more than pure
   gold,
¹²⁸and because I consider all your
   precepts right,
   I hate every wrong path.

DAY 303   # OCTOBER 30

OLD TESTAMENT READING
Lamentations 3:40–5:22

⁴⁰Let us examine our ways and test
   them,
   and let us return to the LORD.
⁴¹Let us lift up our hearts and our
   hands
   to God in heaven, and say:
⁴²"We have sinned and rebelled
   and you have not forgiven.

⁴³"You have covered yourself with
   anger and pursued us;
   you have slain without pity.
⁴⁴You have covered yourself with a
   cloud
   so that no prayer can get through.
⁴⁵You have made us scum and refuse
   among the nations.

⁴⁶"All our enemies have opened their
   mouths
   wide against us.
⁴⁷We have suffered terror and pitfalls,
   ruin and destruction."
⁴⁸Streams of tears flow from my eyes
   because my people are destroyed.

⁴⁹My eyes will flow unceasingly,
   without relief,
⁵⁰until the LORD looks down
   from heaven and sees.
⁵¹What I see brings grief to my soul

because of all the women of my
   city.
⁵²Those who were my enemies without
   cause
   hunted me like a bird.
⁵³They tried to end my life in a pit
   and threw stones at me;
⁵⁴the waters closed over my head,
   and I thought I was about to be cut
   off.

⁵⁵I called on your name, O LORD,
   from the depths of the pit.
⁵⁶You heard my plea: "Do not close
   your ears
   to my cry for relief."
⁵⁷You came near when I called you,
   and you said, "Do not fear."

⁵⁸O Lord, you took up my case;
   you redeemed my life.
⁵⁹You have seen, O LORD, the wrong
   done to me.
   Uphold my cause!
⁶⁰You have seen the depth of their
   vengeance,
   all their plots against me.

⁶¹O LORD, you have heard their insults,
   all their plots against me—
⁶²what my enemies whisper and mutter
   against me all day long.
⁶³Look at them! Sitting or standing,
   they mock me in their songs.

⁶⁴Pay them back what they deserve, O
   LORD,
   for what their hands have done.
⁶⁵Put a veil over their hearts,
   and may your curse be on them!
⁶⁶Pursue them in anger and destroy
   them
   from under the heavens of the
   LORD.

4 How the gold has lost its lustre,
   the fine gold become dull!
   The sacred gems are scattered
   at the head of every street.

²How the precious sons of Zion,
   once worth their weight in gold,
   are now considered as pots of clay,
   the work of a potter's hands!

³Even jackals offer their breasts
   to nurse their young,
   but my people have become heartless
   like ostriches in the desert.

⁴Because of thirst the infant's tongue
   sticks to the roof of its mouth;
   the children beg for bread,
   but no-one gives it to them.

⁵Those who once ate delicacies
   are destitute in the streets.
   Those nurtured in purple
   now lie on ash heaps.

⁶The punishment of my people
   is greater than that of Sodom,
   which was overthrown in a moment
   without a hand turned to help her.

⁷Their princes were brighter than
   snow
   and whiter than milk,
   their bodies more ruddy than rubies,
   their appearance like sapphires.

⁸But now they are blacker than soot;
   they are not recognised in the
   streets.
   Their skin has shrivelled on their
   bones;
   it has become as dry as a stick.

⁹Those killed by the sword are better
   off
   than those who die of famine;
   racked with hunger, they waste away
   for lack of food from the field.

¹⁰With their own hands compassionate
   women
   have cooked their own children,
   who became their food
   when my people were destroyed.

¹¹The LORD has given full vent to his
   wrath;
   he has poured out his fierce anger.
   He kindled a fire in Zion
   that consumed her foundations.

¹²The kings of the earth did not
   believe,
   nor did any of the world's people,
   that enemies and foes could enter
   the gates of Jerusalem.

¹³But it happened because of the sins of
   her prophets
   and the iniquities of her priests,
   who shed within her
   the blood of the righteous.

¹⁴Now they grope through the streets
   like men who are blind.
   They are so defiled with blood
   that no-one dares to touch their
   garments.

¹⁵"Go away! You are unclean!" men
   cry to them.
   "Away! Away! Don't touch us!"
   When they flee and wander about,
   people among the nations say,
   "They can stay here no longer."

¹⁶The LORD himself has scattered
   them;
   he no longer watches over them.
   The priests are shown no honour,
   the elders no favour.

¹⁷Moreover, our eyes failed,
   looking in vain for help;
   from our towers we watched
   for a nation that could not save us.

¹⁸Men stalked us at every step,
   so we could not walk in our streets.
Our end was near, our days were
      numbered,
   for our end had come.

¹⁹Our pursuers were swifter
      than eagles in the sky;
   they chased us over the mountains
   and lay in wait for us in the desert.

²⁰The LORD's anointed, our very life
      breath,
   was caught in their traps.
We thought that under his shadow
   we would live among the nations.

²¹Rejoice and be glad, O Daughter of
      Edom,
   you who live in the land of Uz.
But to you also the cup will be
      passed;
   you will be drunk and stripped
      naked.

²²O Daughter of Zion, your
      punishment will end;
   he will not prolong your exile.
But, O Daughter of Edom, he will
      punish your sin
   and expose your wickedness.

5 Remember, O LORD, what has
   happened to us;
   look, and see our disgrace.
²Our inheritance has been turned over
      to aliens,
   our homes to foreigners.
³We have become orphans and
      fatherless,
   our mothers like widows.
⁴We must buy the water we drink;
   our wood can be had only at a
      price.
⁵Those who pursue us are at our heels;
   we are weary and find no rest.
⁶We submitted to Egypt and Assyria
   to get enough bread.
⁷Our fathers sinned and are no more,
   and we bear their punishment.
⁸Slaves rule over us,
   and there is none to free us from
      their hands.

⁹We get our bread at the risk of our
      lives
   because of the sword in the desert.
¹⁰Our skin is hot as an oven,
   feverish from hunger.
¹¹Women have been ravished in Zion,
   and virgins in the towns of Judah.
¹²Princes have been hung up by their
      hands;
   elders are shown no respect.
¹³Young men toil at the millstones;
   boys stagger under loads of wood.
¹⁴The elders are gone from the city
      gate;
   the young men have stopped their
      music.
¹⁵Joy is gone from our hearts;
   our dancing has turned to
      mourning.
¹⁶The crown has fallen from our head.
   Woe to us, for we have sinned!
¹⁷Because of this our hearts are faint;
   because of these things our eyes
      grow dim
¹⁸for Mount Zion, which lies desolate,
   with jackals prowling over it.

¹⁹You, O LORD, reign for ever;
   your throne endures from
      generation to generation.
²⁰Why do you always forget us?
   Why do you forsake us so long?
²¹Restore us to yourself, O LORD, that
      we may return;
   renew our days as of old
²²unless you have utterly rejected us
   and are angry with us beyond
      measure.

NEW TESTAMENT READING
Hebrews 1:1–14

The Son Superior to Angels

1 In the past God spoke to our forefathers through the prophets at
many times and in various ways, ²but in
these last days he has spoken to us by his
Son, whom he appointed heir of all
things, and through whom he made the
universe. ³The Son is the radiance of

God's glory and the exact representation of his being, sustaining all things by his powerful word. After he had provided purification for sins, he sat down at the right hand of the Majesty in heaven. [4]So he became as much superior to the angels as the name he has inherited is superior to theirs.

[5]For to which of the angels did God ever say,

"You are my Son;
    today I have become your
        Father"?

Or again,

"I will be his Father,
    and he will be my Son"?

[6]And again, when God brings his firstborn into the world, he says,

"Let all God's angels worship him."

[7]In speaking of the angels he says,

"He makes his angels winds,
    his servants flames of fire."

[8]But about the Son he says,

"Your throne, O God, will last for
        ever and ever,
    and righteousness will be the
        sceptre of your kingdom.
[9]You have loved righteousness and
        hated wickedness;
    therefore God, your God, has set
        you above your companions
    by anointing you with the oil of
        joy."

[10]He also says,

"In the beginning, O Lord, you laid
        the foundations of the earth,
    and the heavens are the work of
        your hands.

[11]They will perish, but you remain;
    they will all wear out like a
        garment.
[12]You will roll them up like a robe;
    like a garment they will be
        changed.
But you remain the same,
    and your years will never end."

[13]To which of the angels did God ever say,

"Sit at my right hand
until I make your enemies
    a footstool for your feet"?

[14]Are not all angels ministering spirits sent to serve those who will inherit salvation?

READING FROM PSALMS
Psalm 119:129–136

ⅾ Pe

[129]Your statutes are wonderful;
    therefore I obey them.
[130]The unfolding of your words gives
        light;
    it gives understanding to the
        simple.
[131]I open my mouth and pant,
    longing for your commands.
[132]Turn to me and have mercy on me,
    as you always do to those who love
        your name.
[133]Direct my footsteps according to
        your word;
    let no sin rule over me.
[134]Redeem me from the oppression of
        men,
    that I may obey your precepts.
[135]Make your face shine upon your
        servant
    and teach me your decrees.
[136]Streams of tears flow from my eyes,
    for your law is not obeyed.

OCTOBER 31

OLD TESTAMENT READING
Obadiah 1–21

¹The vision of Obadiah.

This is what the Sovereign LORD says about Edom—

We have heard a message from the
LORD:
An envoy was sent to the nations
to say,
"Rise, and let us go against her for
battle"—

²"See, I will make you small among
the nations;
you will be utterly despised.
³The pride of your heart has deceived
you,
you who live in the clefts of the
rocks
and make your home on the
heights,
you who say to yourself,
'Who can bring me down to the
ground?'
⁴Though you soar like the eagle
and make your nest among the
stars,
from there I will bring you down,"
declares the LORD.
⁵"If thieves came to you,
if robbers in the night—
Oh, what a disaster awaits you—
would they not steal only as much
as they wanted?
If grape pickers came to you,
would they not leave a few grapes?
⁶But how Esau will be ransacked,
his hidden treasures pillaged!
⁷All your allies will force you to the
border;
your friends will deceive and
overpower you;
those who eat your bread will set a
trap for you,
but you will not detect it.

⁸"In that day," declares the LORD,
"will I not destroy the wise men of
Edom,
men of understanding in the
mountains of Esau?
⁹Your warriors, O Teman, will be
terrified,
and everyone in Esau's mountains
will be cut down in the slaughter.
¹⁰Because of the violence against your
brother Jacob,
you will be covered with shame;
you will be destroyed for ever.
¹¹On the day you stood aloof
while strangers carried off his
wealth
and foreigners entered his gates
and cast lots for Jerusalem,
you were like one of them.
¹²You should not look down on your
brother
in the day of his misfortune,
nor rejoice over the people of Judah
in the day of their destruction,
nor boast so much
in the day of their trouble.
¹³You should not march through the
gates of my people
in the day of their disaster,
nor look down on them in their
calamity
in the day of their disaster,
nor seize their wealth
in the day of their disaster.
¹⁴You should not wait at the crossroads
to cut down their fugitives,
nor hand over their survivors
in the day of their trouble.

¹⁵"The day of the LORD is near
for all nations.
As you have done, it will be done to
you;
your deeds will return upon your
own head.
¹⁶Just as you drank on my holy hill,
so all the nations will drink
continually;

they will drink and drink
and be as if they had never been.
¹⁷But on Mount Zion will be
deliverance;
it will be holy,
and the house of Jacob
will possess its inheritance.
¹⁸The house of Jacob will be a fire
and the house of Joseph a flame;
the house of Esau will be stubble,
and they will set it on fire and
consume it.
There will be no survivors
from the house of Esau."
The LORD has spoken.

¹⁹People from the Negev will occupy
the mountains of Esau,
and people from the foothills will
possess
the land of the Philistines.
They will occupy the fields of
Ephraim and Samaria,
and Benjamin will possess Gilead.
²⁰This company of Israelite exiles who
are in Canaan
will possess ⌊the land⌋ as far as
Zarephath;
the exiles from Jerusalem who are in
Sepharad
will possess the towns of the
Negev.
²¹Deliverers will go up on Mount Zion
to govern the mountains of Esau.
And the kingdom will be the
LORD's.

NEW TESTAMENT READING
Hebrews 2:1–18

Warning to Pay Attention

2 We must pay more careful attention, therefore, to what we have
heard, so that we do not drift away. ²For
if the message spoken by angels was
binding, and every violation and disobedience received its just punishment,
³how shall we escape if we ignore such a
great salvation? This salvation, which
was first announced by the Lord, was

confirmed to us by those who heard
him. ⁴God also testified to it by signs,
wonders and various miracles, and gifts
of the Holy Spirit distributed according
to his will.

Jesus Made Like His Brothers

⁵It is not to angels that he has subjected the world to come, about which
we are speaking. ⁶But there is a place
where someone has testified:

"What is man that you are mindful of
him,
the son of man that you care for
him?
⁷You made him a little lower than the
angels;
you crowned him with glory and
honour
⁸ and put everything under his feet."

In putting everything under him, God
left nothing that is not subject to him.
Yet at present we do not see everything
subject to him. ⁹But we see Jesus, who
was made a little lower than the angels,
now crowned with glory and honour
because he suffered death, so that by
the grace of God he might taste death
for everyone.

¹⁰In bringing many sons to glory, it
was fitting that God, for whom and
through whom everything exists, should
make the author of their salvation perfect through suffering. ¹¹Both the one
who makes men holy and those who are
made holy are of the same family. So
Jesus is not ashamed to call them
brothers. ¹²He says,

"I will declare your name to my
brothers;
in the presence of the congregation
I will sing your praises."

¹³And again,

"I will put my trust in him."

And again he says,

"Here am I, and the children God
    has given me."

14Since the children have flesh and
blood, he too shared in their humanity
so that by his death he might destroy
him who holds the power of death—
that is, the devil—15and free those who
all their lives were held in slavery by
their fear of death. 16For surely it is not
angels he helps, but Abraham's descendants. 17For this reason he had to
be made like his brothers in every way,
in order that he might become a merciful and faithful high priest in service to
God, and that he might make atonement for the sins of the people.
18Because he himself suffered when he
was tempted, he is able to help those
who are being tempted.

READING FROM PROVERBS
Proverbs 26:13–22

13The sluggard says, "There is a lion in
    the road,
    a fierce lion roaming the streets!"

14As a door turns on its hinges,
    so a sluggard turns on his bed.

15The sluggard buries his hand in the
    dish;
    he is too lazy to bring it back to his
    mouth.

16The sluggard is wiser in his own eyes
    than seven men who answer
    discreetly.

17Like one who seizes a dog by the ears
    is a passer-by who meddles in a
    quarrel not his own.

18Like a madman shooting
    firebrands or deadly arrows
19is a man who deceives his neighbour
    and says, "I was only joking!"

20Without wood a fire goes out;
    without gossip a quarrel dies down.

21As charcoal to embers and as wood to
    fire,
    so is a quarrelsome man for
    kindling strife.

22The words of a gossip are like choice
    morsels;
    they go down to a man's inmost
    parts.

DAY 305   # NOVEMBER 1

OLD TESTAMENT READING
Joel 1:1–2:17

1   The word of the LORD that came to
    Joel son of Pethuel.

An Invasion of Locusts

2Hear this, you elders;
    listen, all who live in the land.
Has anything like this ever happened
    in your days
    or in the days of your forefathers?

3Tell it to your children,
    and let your children tell it to their
    children,
    and their children to the next
    generation.
4What the locust swarm has left
    the great locusts have eaten;
what the great locusts have left
    the young locusts have eaten;
what the young locusts have left
    other locusts have eaten.

5Wake up, you drunkards, and weep!
    Wail, all you drinkers of wine;

wail because of the new wine,
　　for it has been snatched from your
　　　lips.
[6]A nation has invaded my land,
　　powerful and without number;
it has the teeth of a lion,
　　the fangs of a lioness.
[7]It has laid waste my vines
　　and ruined my fig-trees.
It has stripped off their bark
　　and thrown it away,
　　leaving their branches white.

[8]Mourn like a virgin in sackcloth
　　grieving for the husband of her
　　　youth.
[9]Grain offerings and drink offerings
　　are cut off from the house of the
　　　LORD.
The priests are in mourning,
　　those who minister before the
　　　LORD.
[10]The fields are ruined,
　　the ground is dried up;
the grain is destroyed,
　　the new wine is dried up,
　　the oil fails.
[11]Despair, you farmers,
　　wail, you vine growers;
grieve for the wheat and the barley,
　　because the harvest of the field is
　　　destroyed.
[12]The vine is dried up
　　and the fig-tree is withered;
the pomegranate, the palm and the
　　apple tree—
　　all the trees of the field—are dried
　　　up.
Surely the joy of mankind
　　is withered away.

A Call to Repentance

[13]Put on sackcloth, O priests, and
　　mourn;
　　wail, you who minister before the
　　　altar.
Come, spend the night in sackcloth,
　　you who minister before my God;
for the grain offerings and drink
　　offerings
　　are withheld from the house of
　　　your God.

[14]Declare a holy fast;
　　call a sacred assembly.
Summon the elders
　　and all who live in the land
to the house of the LORD your God,
　　and cry out to the LORD.

[15]Alas for that day!
　　For the day of the LORD is near;
　　it will come like destruction from
　　　the Almighty.

[16]Has not the food been cut off
　　before our very eyes—
joy and gladness
　　from the house of our God?
[17]The seeds are shrivelled
　　beneath the clods.
The storehouses are in ruins,
　　the granaries have been broken
　　　down,
for the grain has dried up.
[18]How the cattle moan!
　　The herds mill about
because they have no pasture;
　　even the flocks of sheep are
　　　suffering.

[19]To you, O LORD, I call,
　　for fire has devoured the open
　　　pastures
　　and flames have burned up all the
　　　trees of the field.
[20]Even the wild animals pant for you;
　　the streams of water have dried up
　　and fire has devoured the open
　　　pastures.

An Army of Locusts

2 Blow the trumpet in Zion;
　　sound the alarm on my holy hill.
Let all who live in the land tremble,
　　for the day of the LORD is coming.
It is close at hand—
[2]　a day of darkness and gloom,
　　a day of clouds and blackness.
Like dawn spreading across the
　　mountains
　　a large and mighty army comes,
such as never was of old
　　nor ever will be in ages to come.

³Before them fire devours,
  behind them a flame blazes.
Before them the land is like the
    garden of Eden,
  behind them, a desert waste—
    nothing escapes them.
⁴They have the appearance of horses;
  they gallop along like cavalry.
⁵With a noise like that of chariots
  they leap over the mountaintops,
like a crackling fire consuming
    stubble,
  like a mighty army drawn up for
    battle.

⁶At the sight of them, nations are in
    anguish;
  every face turns pale.
⁷They charge like warriors;
  they scale walls like soldiers.
They all march in line,
  not swerving from their course.
⁸They do not jostle each other;
  each marches straight ahead.
They plunge through defences
  without breaking ranks.
⁹They rush upon the city;
  they run along the wall.
They climb into the houses;
  like thieves they enter through the
    windows.

¹⁰Before them the earth shakes,
  the sky trembles,
the sun and moon are darkened,
  and the stars no longer shine.
¹¹The LORD thunders
  at the head of his army;
his forces are beyond number,
  and mighty are those who obey his
    command.
The day of the LORD is great;
  it is dreadful.
  Who can endure it?

Rend Your Heart

¹²"Even now," declares the LORD,
  "return to me with all your heart,
    with fasting and weeping and
    mourning."

¹³Rend your heart
  and not your garments.
Return to the LORD your God,
  for he is gracious and
    compassionate,
slow to anger and abounding in love,
  and he relents from sending
    calamity.
¹⁴Who knows? He may turn and have
    pity
  and leave behind a blessing—
grain offerings and drink offerings
  for the LORD your God.

¹⁵Blow the trumpet in Zion,
  declare a holy fast,
  call a sacred assembly.
¹⁶Gather the people,
  consecrate the assembly;
bring together the elders,
  gather the children,
    those nursing at the breast.
Let the bridegroom leave his room
  and the bride her chamber.
¹⁷Let the priests, who minister before
    the LORD,
  weep between the temple porch
    and the altar.
Let them say, "Spare your people,
    O LORD.
  Do not make your inheritance an
    object of scorn,
  a byword among the nations.
Why should they say among the
    peoples,
  'Where is their God?'"

NEW TESTAMENT READING
Hebrews 3:1–19

Jesus Greater Than Moses

3 Therefore, holy brothers, who
  share in the heavenly calling, fix
your thoughts on Jesus, the apostle and
high priest whom we confess. ²He was
faithful to the one who appointed him,
just as Moses was faithful in all God's
house. ³Jesus has been found worthy of
greater honour than Moses, just as the

builder of a house has greater honour than the house itself. [4]For every house is built by someone, but God is the builder of everything. [5]Moses was faithful as a servant in all God's house, testifying to what would be said in the future. [6]But Christ is faithful as a son over God's house. And we are his house, if we hold on to our courage and the hope of which we boast.

Warning Against Unbelief

[7]So, as the Holy Spirit says:

"Today, if you hear his voice,
[8] do not harden your hearts
as you did in the rebellion,
    during the time of testing in the
      desert,
[9]where your fathers tested and tried
      me
and for forty years saw what I did.
[10]That is why I was angry with that
      generation,
    and I said, 'Their hearts are always
      going astray,
    and they have not known my
      ways.'
[11]So I declared on oath in my anger,
    'They shall never enter my rest.' "

[12]See to it, brothers, that none of you has a sinful, unbelieving heart that turns away from the living God. [13]But encourage one another daily, as long as it is called Today, so that none of you may be hardened by sin's deceitfulness. [14]We have come to share in Christ if we hold firmly till the end the confidence we had at first. [15]As has just been said:

"Today, if you hear his voice,
    do not harden your hearts
as you did in the rebellion."

[16]Who were they who heard and rebelled? Were they not all those Moses led out of Egypt? [17]And with whom was he angry for forty years? Was it not with those who sinned, whose bodies fell in the desert? [18]And to whom did God swear that they would never enter his rest if not to those who disobeyed? [19]So we see that they were not able to enter, because of their unbelief.

READING FROM PSALMS
Psalm 119:137–144

‏צ‎ Tsadhe

[137]Righteous are you, O LORD,
    and your laws are right.
[138]The statutes you have laid down are
      righteous;
    they are fully trustworthy.
[139]My zeal wears me out,
    for my enemies ignore your words.
[140]Your promises have been
      thoroughly tested,
    and your servant loves them.
[141]Though I am lowly and despised,
    I do not forget your precepts.
[142]Your righteousness is everlasting
    and your law is true.
[143]Trouble and distress have come
      upon me,
    but your commands are my delight.
[144]Your statutes are for ever right;
    give me understanding that I may
      live.

NOVEMBER 2

OLD TESTAMENT READING
Joel 2:18–3:21

The Lord's Answer

18Then the Lord will be jealous for his land
and take pity on his people.

19The Lord will reply to them:

"I am sending you grain, new wine and oil,
enough to satisfy you fully;
never again will I make you
an object of scorn to the nations.

20"I will drive the northern army far from you,
pushing it into a parched and barren land,
with its front columns going into the eastern sea
and those in the rear into the western sea.
And its stench will go up;
its smell will rise."

Surely he has done great things.
21 Be not afraid, O land;
be glad and rejoice.
Surely the Lord has done great things.
22 Be not afraid, O wild animals,
for the open pastures are becoming green.
The trees are bearing fruit;
the fig-tree and the vine yield their riches.
23Be glad, O people of Zion,
rejoice in the Lord your God,
for he has given you
the autumn rains in righteousness.
He sends you abundant showers,
both autumn and spring rains, as before.
24The threshing-floors will be filled with grain;
the vats will overflow with new wine and oil.

25"I will repay you for the years the locusts have eaten—
the great locust and the young locust,
the other locusts and the locust swarm—
my great army that I sent among you.
26You will have plenty to eat, until you are full,
and you will praise the name of the Lord your God,
who has worked wonders for you;
never again will my people be shamed.
27Then you will know that I am in Israel,
that I am the Lord your God,
and that there is no other;
never again will my people be shamed.

The Day of the Lord

28"And afterwards,
I will pour out my Spirit on all people.
Your sons and daughters will prophesy,
your old men will dream dreams,
your young men will see visions.
29Even on my servants, both men and women,
I will pour out my Spirit in those days.
30I will show wonders in the heavens
and on the earth,
blood and fire and billows of smoke.
31The sun will be turned to darkness
and the moon to blood
before the coming of the great and dreadful day of the Lord.
32And everyone who calls
on the name of the Lord will be saved;
for on Mount Zion and in Jerusalem
there will be deliverance,
as the Lord has said,

among the survivors
whom the LORD calls.

The Nations Judged

3 "In those days and at that time,
when I restore the fortunes of
Judah and Jerusalem,
²I will gather all nations
and bring them down to the Valley
of Jehoshaphat.
There I will enter into judgment
against them
concerning my inheritance, my
people Israel,
for they scattered my people among
the nations
and divided up my land.
³They cast lots for my people
and traded boys for prostitutes;
they sold girls for wine
that they might drink.

⁴"Now what have you against me, O
Tyre and Sidon and all you regions of
Philistia? Are you repaying me for
something I have done? If you are
paying me back, I will swiftly and
speedily return on your own heads what
you have done. ⁵For you took my silver
and my gold and carried off my finest
treasures to your temples. ⁶You sold the
people of Judah and Jerusalem to the
Greeks, that you might send them far
from their homeland.

⁷"See, I am going to rouse them out
of the places to which you sold them,
and I will return on your own heads
what you have done. ⁸I will sell your
sons and daughters to the people of
Judah, and they will sell them to the
Sabeans, a nation far away." The LORD
has spoken.

⁹Proclaim this among the nations:
Prepare for war!
Rouse the warriors!
Let all the fighting men draw near
and attack.
¹⁰Beat your ploughshares into swords
and your pruning hooks into
spears.

Let the weakling say,
"I am strong!"
¹¹Come quickly, all you nations from
every side,
and assemble there.

Bring down your warriors, O LORD!

¹²"Let the nations be roused;
let them advance into the Valley of
Jehoshaphat,
for there I will sit
to judge all the nations on every
side.
¹³Swing the sickle,
for the harvest is ripe.
Come, trample the grapes,
for the winepress is full
and the vats overflow—
so great is their wickedness!"

¹⁴Multitudes, multitudes
in the valley of decision!
For the day of the LORD is near
in the valley of decision.
¹⁵The sun and moon will be darkened,
and the stars no longer shine.
¹⁶The LORD will roar from Zion
and thunder from Jerusalem;
the earth and the sky will tremble.
But the LORD will be a refuge for his
people,
a stronghold for the people of
Israel.

Blessings for God's People

¹⁷"Then you will know that I, the LORD
your God,
dwell in Zion, my holy hill.
Jerusalem will be holy;
never again will foreigners invade
her.

¹⁸"In that day the mountains will drip
new wine,
and the hills will flow with milk;
all the ravines of Judah will run
with water.
A fountain will flow out of the LORD's
house
and will water the valley of acacias.
¹⁹But Egypt will be desolate,
Edom a desert waste,

because of violence done to the
people of Judah,
   in whose land they shed innocent
blood.
20Judah will be inhabited for ever
and Jerusalem through all
generations.
21Their bloodguilt, which I have not
pardoned,
   I will pardon."

The LORD dwells in Zion!

NEW TESTAMENT READING
Hebrews 4:1–13

A Sabbath-rest for the People of God

4 Therefore, since the promise of entering his rest still stands, let us be
careful that none of you be found to
have fallen short of it. 2For we also have
had the gospel preached to us, just as
they did; but the message they heard
was of no value to them, because those
who heard did not combine it with faith.
3Now we who have believed enter that
rest, just as God has said,

"So I declared on oath in my anger,
   'They shall never enter my rest.'"

And yet his work has been finished since
the creation of the world. 4For somewhere he has spoken about the seventh
day in these words: "And on the
seventh day God rested from all his
work." 5And again in the passage above
he says, "They shall never enter my
rest."

6It still remains that some will enter
that rest, and those who formerly had
the gospel preached to them did not
go in, because of their disobedience.
7Therefore God again set a certain day,
calling it Today, when a long time later
he spoke through David, as was said
before:

"Today, if you hear his voice,
   do not harden your hearts."

8For if Joshua had given them rest, God
would not have spoken later about
another day. 9There remains, then, a
Sabbath-rest for the people of God;
10for anyone who enters God's rest also
rests from his own work, just as God did
from his. 11Let us, therefore, make
every effort to enter that rest, so that
no-one will fall by following their example of disobedience.

12For the word of God is living and
active. Sharper than any double-edged
sword, it penetrates even to dividing
soul and spirit, joints and marrow; it
judges the thoughts and attitudes of the
heart. 13Nothing in all creation is hidden
from God's sight. Everything is uncovered and laid bare before the eyes of
him to whom we must give account.

READING FROM PSALMS
Psalm 119:145–152

ק Qoph

145I call with all my heart; answer me,
   O LORD,
   and I will obey your decrees.
146I call out to you; save me
   and I will keep your statutes.
147I rise before dawn and cry for help;
   I have put my hope in your word.
148My eyes stay open through the
   watches of the night,
   that I may meditate on your
   promises.
149Hear my voice in accordance with
   your love;
   preserve my life, O LORD,
   according to your laws.
150Those who devise wicked schemes
   are near,
   but they are far from your law.
151Yet you are near, O LORD,
   and all your commands are true.
152Long ago I learned from your
   statutes
   that you established them to last
   for ever.

OLD TESTAMENT READING
Ezekiel 1:1–3:27

*The Living Creatures and the
Glory of the LORD*

1 In the thirtieth year, in the fourth month on the fifth day, while I was among the exiles by the Kebar River, the heavens were opened and I saw visions of God.

²On the fifth of the month—it was the fifth year of the exile of King Jehoiachin —³the word of the LORD came to Ezekiel the priest, the son of Buzi, by the Kebar River in the land of the Babylonians. There the hand of the LORD was upon him.

⁴I looked, and I saw a windstorm coming out of the north—an immense cloud with flashing lightning and surrounded by brilliant light. The centre of the fire looked like glowing metal, ⁵and in the fire was what looked like four living creatures. In appearance their form was that of a man, ⁶but each of them had four faces and four wings. ⁷Their legs were straight; their feet were like those of a calf and gleamed like burnished bronze. ⁸Under their wings on their four sides they had the hands of a man. All four of them had faces and wings, ⁹and their wings touched one another. Each one went straight ahead; they did not turn as they moved.

¹⁰Their faces looked like this: Each of the four had the face of a man, and on the right side each had the face of a lion, and on the left the face of an ox; each also had the face of an eagle. ¹¹Such were their faces. Their wings were spread out upwards; each had two wings, one touching the wing of another creature on either side, and two wings covering its body. ¹²Each one went straight ahead. Wherever the spirit would go, they would go, without turning as they went. ¹³The appearance of the living creatures was like burning coals of fire or like torches. Fire moved back and forth among the creatures; it was bright, and lightning flashed out of it. ¹⁴The creatures sped back and forth like flashes of lightning.

¹⁵As I looked at the living creatures, I saw a wheel on the ground beside each creature with its four faces. ¹⁶This was the appearance and structure of the wheels: They sparkled like chrysolite, and all four looked alike. Each appeared to be made like a wheel intersecting a wheel. ¹⁷As they moved, they would go in any one of the four directions the creatures faced; the wheels did not turn about as the creatures went. ¹⁸Their rims were high and awesome, and all four rims were full of eyes all around.

¹⁹When the living creatures moved, the wheels beside them moved; and when the living creatures rose from the ground, the wheels also rose. ²⁰Wherever the spirit would go, they would go, and the wheels would rise along with them, because the spirit of the living creatures was in the wheels. ²¹When the creatures moved, they also moved; when the creatures stood still, they also stood still; and when the creatures rose from the ground, the wheels rose along with them, because the spirit of the living creatures was in the wheels.

²²Spread out above the heads of the living creatures was what looked like an expanse, sparkling like ice, and awesome. ²³Under the expanse their wings were stretched out one towards the other, and each had two wings covering its body. ²⁴When the creatures moved, I heard the sound of their wings, like the roar of rushing waters, like the voice of the Almighty, like the tumult of an army. When they stood still, they lowered their wings.

²⁵Then there came a voice from above the expanse over their heads as they stood with lowered wings. ²⁶Above

the expanse over their heads was what looked like a throne of sapphire, and high above on the throne was a figure like that of a man. 27I saw that from what appeared to be his waist up he looked like glowing metal, as if full of fire, and that from there down he looked like fire; and brilliant light surrounded him. 28Like the appearance of a rainbow in the clouds on a rainy day, so was the radiance around him.

This was the appearance of the likeness of the glory of the LORD. When I saw it, I fell face down, and I heard the voice of one speaking.

Ezekiel's Call

2 He said to me, "Son of man, stand up on your feet and I will speak to you." 2As he spoke, the Spirit came into me and raised me to my feet, and I heard him speaking to me.

3He said: "Son of man, I am sending you to the Israelites, to a rebellious nation that has rebelled against me; they and their fathers have been in revolt against me to this very day. 4The people to whom I am sending you are obstinate and stubborn. Say to them, 'This is what the Sovereign LORD says.' 5And whether they listen or fail to listen—for they are a rebellious house—they will know that a prophet has been among them. 6And you, son of man, do not be afraid of them or their words. Do not be afraid, though briers and thorns are all around you and you live among scorpions. Do not be afraid of what they say or terrified by them, though they are a rebellious house. 7You must speak my words to them, whether they listen or fail to listen, for they are rebellious. 8But you, son of man, listen to what I say to you. Do not rebel like that rebellious house; open your mouth and eat what I give you."

9Then I looked, and I saw a hand stretched out to me. In it was a scroll, 10which he unrolled before me. On both sides of it were written words of lament and mourning and woe.

3 And he said to me, "Son of man, eat what is before you, eat this scroll; then go and speak to the house of Israel." 2So I opened my mouth, and he gave me the scroll to eat.

3Then he said to me, "Son of man, eat this scroll I am giving you and fill your stomach with it." So I ate it, and it tasted as sweet as honey in my mouth.

4He then said to me: "Son of man, go now to the house of Israel and speak my words to them. 5You are not being sent to a people of obscure speech and difficult language, but to the house of Israel—6not to many peoples of obscure speech and difficult language, whose words you cannot understand. Surely if I had sent you to them, they would have listened to you. 7But the house of Israel is not willing to listen to you because they are not willing to listen to me, for the whole house of Israel is hardened and obstinate. 8But I will make you as unyielding and hardened as they are. 9I will make your forehead like the hardest stone, harder than flint. Do not be afraid of them or terrified by them, though they are a rebellious house."

10And he said to me, "Son of man, listen carefully and take to heart all the words I speak to you. 11Go now to your countrymen in exile and speak to them. Say to them, 'This is what the Sovereign LORD says,' whether they listen or fail to listen."

12Then the Spirit lifted me up, and I heard behind me a loud rumbling sound—May the glory of the LORD be praised in his dwelling-place!—13the sound of the wings of the living creatures brushing against each other and the sound of the wheels beside them, a loud rumbling sound. 14The Spirit then lifted me up and took me away, and I went in bitterness and in the anger of my spirit, with the strong hand of the LORD upon me. 15I came to the exiles who lived at Tel Abib near the Kebar River. And there, where they were living, I sat among them for seven days—overwhelmed.

Warning to Israel

¹⁶At the end of seven days the word of the LORD came to me. ¹⁷"Son of man, I have made you a watchman for the house of Israel; so hear the word I speak and give them warning from me. ¹⁸When I say to a wicked man, 'You will surely die,' and you do not warn him or speak out to dissuade him from his evil ways in order to save his life, that wicked man will die for his sin, and I will hold you accountable for his blood. ¹⁹But if you do warn the wicked man and he does not turn from his wickedness or from his evil ways, he will die for his sin; but you will have saved yourself.

²⁰"Again, when a righteous man turns from his righteousness and does evil, and I put a stumbling-block before him, he will die. Since you did not warn him, he will die for his sin. The righteous things he did will not be remembered, and I will hold you accountable for his blood. ²¹But if you do warn the righteous man not to sin and he does not sin, he will surely live because he took warning, and you will have saved yourself."

²²The hand of the LORD was upon me there, and he said to me, "Get up and go out to the plain, and there I will speak to you." ²³So I got up and went out to the plain. And the glory of the LORD was standing there, like the glory I had seen by the Kebar River, and I fell face down.

²⁴Then the Spirit came into me and raised me to my feet. He spoke to me and said: "Go, shut yourself inside your house. ²⁵And you, son of man, they will tie with ropes; you will be bound so that you cannot go out among the people. ²⁶I will make your tongue stick to the roof of your mouth so that you will be silent and unable to rebuke them, though they are a rebellious house. ²⁷But when I speak to you, I will open your mouth and you shall say to them, 'This is what the Sovereign LORD says.' Whoever will listen let him listen, and whoever will refuse let him refuse; for they are a rebellious house.

NEW TESTAMENT READING
Hebrews 4:14—5:10

Jesus the Great High Priest

¹⁴Therefore, since we have a great high priest who has gone through the heavens, Jesus the Son of God, let us hold firmly to the faith we profess. ¹⁵For we do not have a high priest who is unable to sympathise with our weaknesses, but we have one who has been tempted in every way, just as we are —yet was without sin. ¹⁶Let us then approach the throne of grace with confidence, so that we may receive mercy and find grace to help us in our time of need.

5 Every high priest is selected from among men and is appointed to represent them in matters related to God, to offer gifts and sacrifices for sins. ²He is able to deal gently with those who are ignorant and are going astray, since he himself is subject to weakness. ³This is why he has to offer sacrifices for his own sins, as well as for the sins of the people.

⁴No-one takes this honour upon himself; he must be called by God, just as Aaron was. ⁵So Christ also did not take upon himself the glory of becoming a high priest. But God said to him,

"You are my Son;
   today I have become your Father."

⁶And he says in another place,

"You are a priest for ever,
   in the order of Melchizedek."

⁷During the days of Jesus' life on earth, he offered up prayers and petitions with loud cries and tears to the one who could save him from death, and he was heard because of his reverent submission. ⁸Although he was a son, he learned obedience from what he suffered ⁹and, once made perfect, he became the source of eternal salvation for all who obey him ¹⁰and was designated by God to be high priest in the order of Melchizedek.

READING FROM PSALMS
Psalm 119:153–160

ר Resh

153Look upon my suffering and deliver
me,
for I have not forgotten your law.
154Defend my cause and redeem me;
preserve my life according to your
promise.
155Salvation is far from the wicked,
for they do not seek out your
decrees.

156Your compassion is great, O LORD;
preserve my life according to your
laws.
157Many are the foes who persecute
me,
but I have not turned from your
statutes.
158I look on the faithless with loathing,
for they do not obey your word.
159See how I love your precepts;
preserve my life, O LORD,
according to your love.
160All your words are true;
all your righteous laws are eternal.

DAY 308

NOVEMBER 4

OLD TESTAMENT READING
Ezekiel 4:1–6:14

Siege of Jerusalem Symbolised

4 "Now, son of man, take a clay tablet, put it in front of you and draw
the city of Jerusalem on it. 2Then lay
siege to it: Erect siege works against it,
build a ramp up to it, set up camps
against it and put battering-rams
around it. 3Then take an iron pan, place
it as an iron wall between you and the
city and turn your face towards it. It will
be under siege, and you shall besiege it.
This will be a sign to the house of Israel.

4"Then lie on your left side and put
the sin of the house of Israel upon yourself. You are to bear their sin for the
number of days you lie on your side. 5I
have assigned you the same number of
days as the years of their sin. So for 390
days you will bear the sin of the house of
Israel.

6"After you have finished this, lie
down again, this time on your right side,
and bear the sin of the house of Judah. I
have assigned you 40 days, a day for
each year. 7Turn your face towards the
siege of Jerusalem and with bared arm
prophesy against her. 8I will tie you up

with ropes so that you cannot turn from
one side to the other until you have
finished the days of your siege.

9"Take wheat and barley, beans and
lentils, millet and spelt; put them in a
storage jar and use them to make bread
for yourself. You are to eat it during the
390 days you lie on your side. 10Weigh
out twenty shekels of food to eat each
day and eat it at set times. 11Also measure out a sixth of a hin of water and
drink it at set times. 12Eat the food as
you would a barley cake; bake it in the
sight of the people, using human excrement for fuel." 13The LORD said, "In
this way the people of Israel will eat
defiled food among the nations where I
will drive them."

14Then I said, "Not so, Sovereign
LORD! I have never defiled myself.
From my youth until now I have never
eaten anything found dead or torn by
wild animals. No unclean meat has ever
entered my mouth."

15"Very well," he said, "I will let you
bake your bread over cow manure in-
stead of human excrement." 16He then said to me: "Son of man, I
will cut off the supply of food in Jeru-
salem. The people will eat rationed
food in anxiety and drink rationed

water in despair, 17for food and water will be scarce. They will be appalled at the sight of each other and will waste away because of their sin.

5 "Now, son of man, take a sharp sword and use it as a barber's razor to shave your head and your beard. Then take a set of scales and divide up the hair. 2When the days of your siege come to an end, burn a third of the hair with fire inside the city. Take a third and strike it with the sword all around the city. And scatter a third to the wind. For I will pursue them with drawn sword. 3But take a few strands of hair and tuck them away in the folds of your garment. 4Again, take a few of these and throw them into the fire and burn them up. A fire will spread from there to the whole house of Israel.

5"This is what the Sovereign LORD says: This is Jerusalem, which I have set in the centre of the nations, with countries all around her. 6Yet in her wickedness she has rebelled against my laws and decrees more than the nations and countries around her. She has rejected my laws and has not followed my decrees.

7"Therefore this is what the Sovereign LORD says: You have been more unruly than the nations around you and have not followed my decrees or kept my laws. You have not even conformed to the standards of the nations around you.

8"Therefore this is what the Sovereign LORD says: I myself am against you, Jerusalem, and I will inflict punishment on you in the sight of the nations. 9Because of all your detestable idols, I will do to you what I have never done before and will never do again. 10Therefore in your midst fathers will eat their children, and children will eat their fathers. I will inflict punishment on you and will scatter all your survivors to the winds. 11Therefore as surely as I live, declares the Sovereign LORD, because you have defiled my sanctuary with all your vile images and detestable practices, I myself will withdraw my favour; I will not look on you with pity or spare you. 12A third of your people will die of the plague or perish by famine inside you; a third will fall by the sword outside your walls; and a third I will scatter to the winds and pursue with drawn sword.

13"Then my anger will cease and my wrath against them will subside, and I will be avenged. And when I have spent my wrath upon them, they will know that I the LORD have spoken in my zeal.

14"I will make you a ruin and a reproach among the nations around you, in the sight of all who pass by. 15You will be a reproach and a taunt, a warning and an object of horror to the nations around you when I inflict punishment on you in anger and in wrath and with stinging rebuke. I the LORD have spoken. 16When I shoot at you with my deadly and destructive arrows of famine, I will shoot to destroy you. I will bring more and more famine upon you and cut off your supply of food. 17I will send famine and wild beasts against you, and they will leave you childless. Plague and bloodshed will sweep through you, and I will bring the sword against you. I the LORD have spoken."

A Prophecy Against the Mountains of Israel

6 The word of the LORD came to me: 2"Son of man, set your face against the mountains of Israel; prophesy against them 3and say: 'O mountains of Israel, hear the word of the Sovereign LORD. This is what the Sovereign LORD says to the mountains and hills, to the ravines and valleys: I am about to bring a sword against you, and I will destroy your high places. 4Your altars will be demolished and your incense altars will be smashed; and I will slay your people in front of your idols. 5I will lay the dead bodies of the Israelites in front of their idols, and I will scatter your bones around your altars. 6Wherever you live, the towns will be laid waste and the high places demolished, so that your altars will be laid waste and devastated, your

idols smashed and ruined, your incense altars broken down, and what you have made wiped out. 7Your people will fall slain among you, and you will know that I am the LORD.

8"But I will spare some, for some of you will escape the sword when you are scattered among the lands and nations. 9Then in the nations where they have been carried captive, those who escape will remember me—how I have been grieved by their adulterous hearts, which have turned away from me, and by their eyes, which have lusted after their idols. They will loathe themselves for the evil they have done and for all their detestable practices. 10And they will know that I am the LORD; I did not threaten in vain to bring this calamity on them.

11"'This is what the Sovereign LORD says: Strike your hands together and stamp your feet and cry out "Alas!" because of all the wicked and detestable practices of the house of Israel, for they will fall by the sword, famine and plague. 12He that is far away will die of the plague, and he that is near will fall by the sword, and he that survives and is spared will die of famine. So will I spend my wrath upon them. 13And they will know that I am the LORD, when their people lie slain among their idols around their altars, on every high hill and on all the mountaintops, under every spreading tree and every leafy oak—places where they offered fragrant incense to all their idols. 14And I will stretch out my hand against them and make the land a desolate waste from the desert to Diblah—wherever they live. Then they will know that I am the LORD.'"

NEW TESTAMENT READING
Hebrews 5:11–6:12

Warning Against Falling Away

11We have much to say about this, but it is hard to explain because you are slow to learn. 12In fact, though by this time you ought to be teachers, you need someone to teach you the elementary truths of God's word all over again. You need milk, not solid food! 13Anyone who lives on milk, being still an infant, is not acquainted with the teaching about righteousness. 14But solid food is for the mature, who by constant use have trained themselves to distinguish good from evil.

6 Therefore let us leave the elementary teachings about Christ and go on to maturity, not laying again the foundation of repentance from acts that lead to death, and of faith in God, 2instruction about baptisms, the laying on of hands, the resurrection of the dead, and eternal judgment. 3And God permitting, we will do so.

4It is impossible for those who have once been enlightened, who have tasted the heavenly gift, who have shared in the Holy Spirit, 5who have tasted the goodness of the word of God and the powers of the coming age, 6if they fall away, to be brought back to repentance, because to their loss they are crucifying the Son of God all over again and subjecting him to public disgrace.

7Land that drinks in the rain often falling on it and that produces a crop useful to those for whom it is farmed receives the blessing of God. 8But land that produces thorns and thistles is worthless and is in danger of being cursed. In the end it will be burned.

9Even though we speak like this, dear friends, we are confident of better things in your case—things that accompany salvation. 10God is not unjust; he will not forget your work and the love you have shown him as you have helped his people and continue to help them. 11We want each of you to show this same diligence to the very end, in order to make your hope sure. 12We do not want you to become lazy, but to imitate those who through faith and patience inherit what has been promised.

READING FROM PROVERBS
Proverbs 26:23–27:4

23Like a coating of glaze over
   earthenware
   are fervent lips with an evil heart.

24A malicious man disguises himself
   with his lips,
   but in his heart he harbours
      deceit.
25Though his speech is charming, do
   not believe him,
   for seven abominations fill his
      heart.
26His malice may be concealed by
      deception,
   but his wickedness will be exposed
      in the assembly.

27If a man digs a pit, he will fall
      into it;

if a man rolls a stone, it will roll
   back on him.

28A lying tongue hates those it hurts,
   and a flattering mouth works ruin.

27 Do not boast about tomorrow,
   for you do not know what a day
   may bring forth.

2Let another praise you, and not your
      own mouth;
   someone else, and not your own
      lips.

3Stone is heavy and sand a burden,
   but provocation by a fool is heavier
      than both.

4Anger is cruel and fury
      overwhelming,
   but who can stand before jealousy?

NOVEMBER 5

OLD TESTAMENT READING
Ezekiel 7:1–9:11

The End Has Come

7 The word of the LORD came to me:
2"Son of man, this is what the
Sovereign LORD says to the land of
Israel: The end! The end has come upon
the four corners of the land. 3The end is
now upon you and I will unleash my
anger against you. I will judge you
according to your conduct and repay
you for all your detestable practices. 4I
will not look on you with pity or spare
you; I will surely repay you for your
conduct and the detestable practices
among you. Then you will know that I
am the LORD.

5"This is what the Sovereign LORD
says: Disaster! An unheard-of disaster
is coming. 6The end has come! The end
has come! It has roused itself against
you. It has come! 7Doom has come

upon you—you who dwell in the land.
The time has come, the day is near;
there is panic, not joy, upon the mountains. 8I am about to pour out my wrath
on you and spend my anger against you;
I will judge you according to your conduct and repay you for all your detestable practices. 9I will not look on you
with pity or spare you; I will repay you
in accordance with your conduct and
the detestable practices among you.
Then you will know that it is I the LORD
who strikes the blow.

10"The day is here! It has come!
Doom has burst forth, the rod has
budded, arrogance has blossomed!
11Violence has grown into a rod to punish wickedness; none of the people will
be left, none of that crowd—no wealth,
nothing of value. 12The time has come,
the day has arrived. Let not the buyer
rejoice nor the seller grieve, for wrath is
upon the whole crowd. 13The seller will

not recover the land he has sold as long as both of them live, for the vision concerning the whole crowd will not be reversed. Because of their sins, not one of them will preserve his life. 14Though they blow the trumpet and get everything ready, no-one will go into battle, for my wrath is upon the whole crowd.

15"Outside is the sword, inside are plague and famine; those in the country will die by the sword, and those in the city will be devoured by famine and plague. 16All who survive and escape will be in the mountains, moaning like doves of the valleys, each because of his sins. 17Every hand will go limp, and every knee will become as weak as water. 18They will put on sackcloth and be clothed with terror. Their faces will be covered with shame and their heads will be shaved. 19They will throw their silver into the streets, and their gold will be an unclean thing. Their silver and gold will not be able to save them in the day of the LORD's wrath. They will not satisfy their hunger or fill their stomachs with it, for it has made them stumble into sin. 20They were proud of their beautiful jewellery and used it to make their detestable idols and vile images. Therefore I will turn these into an unclean thing for them. 21I will hand it all over as plunder to foreigners and as loot to the wicked of the earth, and they will defile it. 22I will turn my face away from them, and they will desecrate my treasured place; robbers will enter it and desecrate it.

23"Prepare chains, because the land is full of bloodshed and the city is full of violence. 24I will bring the most wicked of the nations to take possession of their houses; I will put an end to the pride of the mighty, and their sanctuaries will be desecrated. 25When terror comes, they will seek peace, but there will be none. 26Calamity upon calamity will come, and rumour upon rumour. They will try to get a vision from the prophet; the teaching of the law by the priest will be lost, as will the counsel of the elders. 27The king will mourn, the prince will be

clothed with despair, and the hands of the people of the land will tremble. I will deal with them according to their conduct, and by their own standards I will judge them. Then they will know that I am the LORD."

Idolatry in the Temple

8 In the sixth year, in the sixth month on the fifth day, while I was sitting in my house and the elders of Judah were sitting before me, the hand of the Sovereign LORD came upon me there. 2I looked, and I saw a figure like that of a man. From what appeared to be his waist down he was like fire, and from there up his appearance was as bright as glowing metal. 3He stretched out what looked like a hand and took me by the hair of my head. The Spirit lifted me up between earth and heaven and in visions of God he took me to Jerusalem, to the entrance to the north gate of the inner court, where the idol that provokes to jealousy stood. 4And there before me was the glory of the God of Israel, as in the vision I had seen in the plain.

5Then he said to me, "Son of man, look towards the north." So I looked, and in the entrance north of the gate of the altar I saw this idol of jealousy.

6And he said to me, "Son of man, do you see what they are doing—the utterly detestable things the house of Israel is doing here, things that will drive me far from my sanctuary? But you will see things that are even more detestable."

7Then he brought me to the entrance to the court. I looked, and I saw a hole in the wall. 8He said to me, "Son of man, now dig into the wall." So I dug into the wall and saw a doorway there.

9And he said to me, "Go in and see the wicked and detestable things they are doing here." 10So I went in and looked, and I saw portrayed all over the walls all kinds of crawling things and detestable animals and all the idols of the house of Israel. 11In front of them stood seventy elders of the house of Israel, and Jaazaniah son of Shaphan was standing among them. Each had a censer in his hand, and a fragrant cloud of incense was rising.

[12] He said to me, "Son of man, have you seen what the elders of the house of Israel are doing in the darkness, each at the shrine of his own idol? They say, 'The LORD does not see us; the LORD has forsaken the land.'" [13] Again, he said, "You will see them doing things that are even more detestable."

[14] Then he brought me to the entrance to the north gate of the house of the LORD, and I saw women sitting there, mourning for Tammuz. [15] He said to me, "Do you see this, son of man? You will see things that are even more detestable than this."

[16] He then brought me into the inner court of the house of the LORD, and there at the entrance to the temple, between the portico and the altar, were about twenty-five men. With their backs towards the temple of the LORD and their faces towards the east, they were bowing down to the sun in the east.

[17] He said to me, "Have you seen this, son of man? Is it a trivial matter for the house of Judah to do the detestable things they are doing here? Must they also fill the land with violence and continually provoke me to anger? Look at them putting the branch to their nose! [18] Therefore I will deal with them in anger; I will not look on them with pity or spare them. Although they shout in my ears, I will not listen to them."

Idolaters Killed

9 Then I heard him call out in a loud voice, "Bring the guards of the city here, each with a weapon in his hand." [2] And I saw six men coming from the direction of the upper gate, which faces north, each with a deadly weapon in his hand. With them was a man clothed in linen who had a writing kit at his side. They came in and stood beside the bronze altar.

[3] Now the glory of the God of Israel went up from above the cherubim, where it had been, and moved to the threshold of the temple. Then the LORD called to the man clothed in linen who had the writing kit at his side [4] and said to him, "Go throughout the city of Jerusalem and put a mark on the foreheads of those who grieve and lament over all the detestable things that are done in it."

[5] As I listened, he said to the others, "Follow him through the city and kill, without showing pity or compassion. [6] Slaughter old men, young men and maidens, women and children, but do not touch anyone who has the mark. Begin at my sanctuary." So they began with the elders who were in front of the temple.

[7] Then he said to them, "Defile the temple and fill the courts with the slain. Go!" So they went out and began killing throughout the city. [8] While they were killing and I was left alone, I fell face down, crying out, "Ah, Sovereign LORD! Are you going to destroy the entire remnant of Israel in this outpouring of your wrath on Jerusalem?"

[9] He answered me, "The sin of the house of Israel and Judah is exceedingly great; the land is full of bloodshed and the city is full of injustice. They say, 'The LORD has forsaken the land; the LORD does not see.' [10] So I will not look on them with pity or spare them, but I will bring down on their own heads what they have done."

[11] Then the man in linen with the writing kit at his side brought back word, saying, "I have done as you commanded."

NEW TESTAMENT READING
Hebrews 6:13–7:10

The Certainty of God's Promise

[13] When God made his promise to Abraham, since there was no-one greater for him to swear by, he swore by

himself, [14]saying, "I will surely bless you and give you many descendants." [15]And so after waiting patiently, Abraham received what was promised.

[16]Men swear by someone greater than themselves, and the oath confirms what is said and puts an end to all argument. [17]Because God wanted to make the unchanging nature of his purpose very clear to the heirs of what was promised, he confirmed it with an oath. [18]God did this so that, by two unchangeable things in which it is impossible for God to lie, we who have fled to take hold of the hope offered to us may be greatly encouraged. [19]We have this hope as an anchor for the soul, firm and secure. It enters the inner sanctuary behind the curtain, [20]where Jesus, who went before us, has entered on our behalf. He has become a high priest for ever, in the order of Melchizedek.

Melchizedek the Priest

7 This Melchizedek was king of Salem and priest of God Most High. He met Abraham returning from the defeat of the kings and blessed him, [2]and Abraham gave him a tenth of everything. First, his name means "king of righteousness"; then also, "king of Salem" means "king of peace". [3]Without father or mother, without genealogy, without beginning of days or end of life, like the Son of God he remains a priest for ever.

[4]Just think how great he was: Even the patriarch Abraham gave him a tenth of the plunder! [5]Now the law requires the descendants of Levi who become priests to collect a tenth from the people —that is, their brothers—even though their brothers are descended from Abraham. [6]This man, however, did not trace his descent from Levi, yet he collected a tenth from Abraham and blessed him who had the promises. [7]And without doubt the lesser person is blessed by the greater. [8]In the one case, the tenth is collected by men who die; but in the other case, by him who is declared to be living. [9]One might even say that Levi, who collects the tenth, paid the tenth through Abraham, [10]because when Melchizedek met Abraham, Levi was still in the body of his ancestor.

READING FROM PSALMS
Psalm 119:161–168

ש Sin and Shin

[161]Rulers persecute me without cause,
  but my heart trembles at your
    word.
[162]I rejoice in your promise
  like one who finds great spoil.
[163]I hate and abhor falsehood
  but I love your law.
[164]Seven times a day I praise you
  for your righteous laws.
[165]Great peace have they who love
    your law,
  and nothing can make them
    stumble.
[166]I wait for your salvation, O LORD,
  and I follow your commands.
[167]I obey your statutes,
  for I love them greatly.
[168]I obey your precepts and your
    statutes,
  for all my ways are known to you.

OLD TESTAMENT READING
Ezekiel 10:1–12:28

The Glory Departs From the Temple

10 I looked, and I saw the likeness of a throne of sapphire above the expanse that was over the heads of the cherubim. ²The LORD said to the man clothed in linen, "Go in among the wheels beneath the cherubim. Fill your hands with burning coals from among the cherubim and scatter them over the city." And as I watched, he went in.

³Now the cherubim were standing on the south side of the temple when the man went in, and a cloud filled the inner court. ⁴Then the glory of the LORD rose from above the cherubim and moved to the threshold of the temple. The cloud filled the temple, and the court was full of the radiance of the glory of the LORD. ⁵The sound of the wings of the cherubim could be heard as far away as the outer court, like the voice of God Almighty when he speaks.

⁶When the LORD commanded the man in linen, "Take fire from among the wheels, from among the cherubim," the man went in and stood beside a wheel. ⁷Then one of the cherubim reached out his hand to the fire that was among them. He took up some of it and put it into the hands of the man in linen, who took it and went out. ⁸(Under the wings of the cherubim could be seen what looked like the hands of a man.)

⁹I looked, and I saw beside the cherubim four wheels, one beside each of the cherubim; the wheels sparkled like chrysolite. ¹⁰As for their appearance, the four of them looked alike; each was like a wheel intersecting a wheel. ¹¹As they moved, they would go in any one of the four directions the cherubim faced; the wheels did not turn about as the cherubim went. The cherubim went in whatever direction the head faced, without turning as they went. ¹²Their entire bodies, including their backs, their hands and their wings, were completely full of eyes, as were their four wheels. ¹³I heard the wheels being called "the whirling wheels". ¹⁴Each of the cherubim had four faces: One face was that of a cherub, the second face of a man, the third the face of a lion, and the fourth the face of an eagle.

¹⁵Then the cherubim rose upwards. These were the living creatures I had seen by the Kebar River. ¹⁶When the cherubim moved, the wheels beside them moved; and when the cherubim spread their wings to rise from the ground, the wheels did not leave their side. ¹⁷When the cherubim stood still, they also stood still; and when the cherubim rose, they rose with them, because the spirit of the living creatures was in them.

¹⁸Then the glory of the LORD departed from over the threshold of the temple and stopped above the cherubim. ¹⁹While I watched, the cherubim spread their wings and rose from the ground, and as they went, the wheels went with them. They stopped at the entrance to the east gate of the LORD's house, and the glory of the God of Israel was above them.

²⁰These were the living creatures I had seen beneath the God of Israel by the Kebar River, and I realised that they were cherubim. ²¹Each had four faces and four wings, and under their wings was what looked like the hands of a man. ²²Their faces had the same appearance as those I had seen by the Kebar River. Each one went straight ahead.

Judgment on Israel's Leaders

11 Then the Spirit lifted me up and brought me to the gate of the house of the LORD that faces east. There at the entrance to the gate were twenty-five men, and I saw among them Jaaza-niah son of Azzur and Pelatiah son of Benaiah, leaders of the people. ²The LORD said to me, "Son of man, these are the men who are plotting evil and giving wicked advice in this city. ³They say, 'Will it not soon be time to build houses? This city is a cooking pot, and we are the meat.' ⁴Therefore prophesy against them; prophesy, son of man."

⁵Then the Spirit of the LORD came upon me, and he told me to say: "This is what the LORD says: That is what you are saying, O house of Israel, but I know what is going through your mind. ⁶You have killed many people in this city and filled its streets with the dead.

⁷"Therefore this is what the Sovereign LORD says: The bodies you have thrown there are the meat and this city is the pot, but I will drive you out of it. ⁸You fear the sword, and the sword is what I will bring against you, declares the Sovereign LORD. ⁹I will drive you out of the city and hand you over to foreigners and inflict punishment on you. ¹⁰You will fall by the sword, and I will execute judgment on you at the borders of Israel. Then you will know that I am the LORD. ¹¹This city will not be a pot for you, nor will you be the meat in it; I will execute judgment on you at the borders of Israel. ¹²And you will know that I am the LORD, for you have not followed my decrees or kept my laws but have conformed to the standards of the nations around you."

¹³Now as I was prophesying, Pelatiah son of Benaiah died. Then I fell face down and cried out in a loud voice, "Ah, Sovereign LORD! Will you completely destroy the remnant of Israel?"

¹⁴The word of the LORD came to me: ¹⁵"Son of man, your brothers—your brothers who are your blood-relatives and the whole house of Israel—are those of whom the people of Jerusalem have said, 'They are far away from the LORD; this land was given to us as our possession.'

Promised Return of Israel

¹⁶"Therefore say: 'This is what the Sovereign LORD says: Although I sent them far away among the nations and scattered them among the countries, yet for a little while I have been a sanctuary for them in the countries where they have gone.'

¹⁷"Therefore say: 'This is what the Sovereign LORD says: I will gather you from the nations and bring you back from the countries where you have been scattered, and I will give you back the land of Israel again.'

¹⁸"They will return to it and remove all its vile images and detestable idols. ¹⁹I will give them an undivided heart and put a new spirit in them; I will remove from them their heart of stone and give them a heart of flesh. ²⁰Then they will follow my decrees and be careful to keep my laws. They will be my people, and I will be their God. ²¹But as for those whose hearts are devoted to their vile images and detestable idols, I will bring down on their own heads what they have done, declares the Sovereign LORD."

²²Then the cherubim, with the wheels beside them, spread their wings, and the glory of the God of Israel was above them. ²³The glory of the LORD went up from within the city and stopped above the mountain east of it. ²⁴The Spirit lifted me up and brought me to the exiles in Babylonia in the vision given by the Spirit of God.

Then the vision I had seen went up from me, ²⁵and I told the exiles everything the LORD had shown me.

The Exile Symbolised

12 The word of the LORD came to me: ²"Son of man, you are living among a rebellious people. They have eyes to see but do not see and ears to hear but do not hear, for they are a rebellious people.

³"Therefore, son of man, pack your belongings for exile and in the daytime, as they watch, set out and go from

where you are to another place. Perhaps they will understand, though they are a rebellious house. [4]During the daytime, while they watch, bring out your belongings packed for exile. Then in the evening, while they are watching, go out like those who go into exile. [5]While they watch, dig through the wall and take your belongings out through it. [6]Put them on your shoulder as they are watching and carry them out at dusk. Cover your face so that you cannot see the land, for I have made you a sign to the house of Israel."

[7]So I did as I was commanded. During the day I brought out my things packed for exile. Then in the evening I dug through the wall with my hands. I took my belongings out at dusk, carrying them on my shoulders while they watched.

[8]In the morning the word of the LORD came to me: [9]"Son of man, did not that rebellious house of Israel ask you, 'What are you doing?'

[10]"Say to them, 'This is what the Sovereign LORD says: This oracle concerns the prince in Jerusalem and the whole house of Israel who are there.' [11]Say to them, 'I am a sign to you.'

"As I have done, so it will be done to them. They will go into exile as captives.

[12]"The prince among them will put his things on his shoulder at dusk and leave, and a hole will be dug in the wall for him to go through. He will cover his face so that he cannot see the land. [13]I will spread my net for him, and he will be caught in my snare; I will bring him to Babylonia, the land of the Chaldeans, but he will not see it, and there he will die. [14]I will scatter to the winds all those around him—his staff and all his troops—and I will pursue them with drawn sword.

[15]"They will know that I am the LORD, when I disperse them among the nations and scatter them through the countries. [16]But I will spare a few of them from the sword, famine and plague, so that in the nations where they go they may acknowledge all their detestable practices. Then they will know that I am the LORD."

[17]The word of the LORD came to me: [18]"Son of man, tremble as you eat your food, and shudder in fear as you drink your water. [19]Say to the people of the land: 'This is what the Sovereign LORD says about those living in Jerusalem and in the land of Israel: They will eat their food in anxiety and drink their water in despair, for their land will be stripped of everything in it because of the violence of all who live there. [20]The inhabited towns will be laid waste and the land will be desolate. Then you will know that I am the LORD.'"

[21]The word of the LORD came to me: [22]"Son of man, what is this proverb you have in the land of Israel: 'The days go by and every vision comes to nothing'? [23]Say to them, 'This is what the Sovereign LORD says: I am going to put an end to this proverb, and they will no longer quote it in Israel.' Say to them, 'The days are near when every vision will be fulfilled. [24]For there will be no more false visions or flattering divinations among the people of Israel. [25]But I the LORD will speak what I will, and it shall be fulfilled without delay. For in your days, you rebellious house, I will fulfil whatever I say, declares the Sovereign LORD.'"

[26]The word of the LORD came to me: [27]"Son of man, the house of Israel is saying, 'The vision he sees is for many years from now, and he prophesies about the distant future.'

[28]"Therefore say to them, 'This is what the Sovereign LORD says: None of my words will be delayed any longer; whatever I say will be fulfilled, declares the Sovereign LORD.'"

NEW TESTAMENT READING
Hebrews 7:11–28

Jesus Like Melchizedek

[11]If perfection could have been attained through the Levitical priesthood (for on the basis of it the law was

given to the people), why was there still need for another priest to come—one in the order of Melchizedek, not in the order of Aaron? [12]For when there is a change of the priesthood, there must also be a change of the law. [13]He of whom these things are said belonged to a different tribe, and no-one from that tribe has ever served at the altar. [14]For it is clear that our Lord descended from Judah, and in regard to that tribe Moses said nothing about priests. [15]And what we have said is even more clear if another priest like Melchizedek appears, [16]one who has become a priest not on the basis of a regulation as to his ancestry but on the basis of the power of an indestructible life. [17]For it is declared:

"You are a priest for ever,
    in the order of Melchizedek."

[18]The former regulation is set aside because it was weak and useless [19](for the law made nothing perfect), and a better hope is introduced, by which we draw near to God.

[20]And it was not without an oath! Others became priests without any oath, [21]but he became a priest with an oath when God said to him:

"The Lord has sworn
    and will not change his mind:
'You are a priest for ever.'"

[22]Because of this oath, Jesus has become the guarantee of a better covenant.

[23]Now there have been many of those priests, since death prevented them from continuing in office; [24]but because Jesus lives for ever, he has a permanent priesthood. [25]Therefore he is able to save completely those who come to God through him, because he always lives to intercede for them.

[26]Such a high priest meets our need —one who is holy, blameless, pure, set apart from sinners, exalted above the heavens. [27]Unlike the other high priests, he does not need to offer sacrifices day after day, first for his own sins, and then for the sins of the people. He sacrificed for their sins once for all when he offered himself. [28]For the law appoints as high priests men who are weak; but the oath, which came after the law, appointed the Son, who has been made perfect for ever.

READING FROM PSALMS
Psalm 119:169–176

ת Taw

[169]May my cry come before you, O
    LORD;
    give me understanding according
        to your word.
[170]May my supplication come before
    you;
    deliver me according to your
        promise.
[171]May my lips overflow with praise,
    for you teach me your decrees.
[172]May my tongue sing of your word,
    for all your commands are
        righteous.
[173]May your hand be ready to help me,
    for I have chosen your precepts.
[174]I long for your salvation, O LORD,
    and your law is my delight.
[175]Let me live that I may praise you,
    and may your laws sustain me.
[176]I have strayed like a lost sheep.
    Seek your servant,
    for I have not forgotten your
        commands.

OLD TESTAMENT READING
Ezekiel 13:1–15:8

False Prophets Condemned

13 The word of the LORD came to me: ²"Son of man, prophesy against the prophets of Israel who are now prophesying. Say to those who prophesy out of their own imagination: 'Hear the word of the LORD! ³This is what the Sovereign LORD says: Woe to the foolish prophets who follow their own spirit and have seen nothing! ⁴Your prophets, O Israel, are like jackals among ruins. ⁵You have not gone up to the breaks in the wall to repair it for the house of Israel so that it will stand firm in the battle on the day of the LORD. ⁶Their visions are false and their divinations a lie. They say, "The LORD declares", when the LORD has not sent them; yet they expect their words to be fulfilled. ⁷Have you not seen false visions and uttered lying divinations when you say, "The LORD declares", though I have not spoken?

⁸"'Therefore this is what the Sovereign LORD says: Because of your false words and lying visions, I am against you, declares the Sovereign LORD. ⁹My hand will be against the prophets who see false visions and utter lying divinations. They will not belong to the council of my people or be listed in the records of the house of Israel, nor will they enter the land of Israel. Then you will know that I am the Sovereign LORD.

¹⁰"'Because they lead my people astray, saying, "Peace", when there is no peace, and because, when a flimsy wall is built, they cover it with whitewash, ¹¹therefore tell those who cover it with whitewash that it is going to fall. Rain will come in torrents, and I will send hailstones hurtling down, and violent winds will burst forth. ¹²When the wall collapses, will people not ask you, "Where is the whitewash you covered it with?"

¹³"'Therefore this is what the Sovereign LORD says: In my wrath I will unleash a violent wind, and in my anger hailstones and torrents of rain will fall with destructive fury. ¹⁴I will tear down the wall you have covered with whitewash and will level it to the ground so that its foundation will be laid bare. When it falls, you will be destroyed in it; and you will know that I am the LORD. ¹⁵So I will spend my wrath against the wall and against those who covered it with whitewash. I will say to you, "The wall is gone and so are those who whitewashed it, ¹⁶those prophets of Israel who prophesied to Jerusalem and saw visions of peace for her when there was no peace, declares the Sovereign LORD."'

¹⁷"Now, son of man, set your face against the daughters of your people who prophesy out of their own imagination. Prophesy against them ¹⁸and say, 'This is what the Sovereign LORD says: Woe to the women who sew magic charms on all their wrists and make veils of various lengths for their heads in order to ensnare people. Will you ensnare the lives of my people but preserve your own? ¹⁹You have profaned me among my people for a few handfuls of barley and scraps of bread. By lying to my people, who listen to lies, you have killed those who should not have died and have spared those who should not live.

²⁰"'Therefore this is what the Sovereign LORD says: I am against your magic charms with which you ensnare people like birds and I will tear them from your arms; I will set free the people that you ensnare like birds. ²¹I will tear off your veils and save my people from your hands, and they will no longer fall prey to your power. Then you will know that I am the LORD.

²²Because you disheartened the righteous with your lies, when I had brought them no grief, and because you encouraged the wicked not to turn from their evil ways and so save their lives, ²³therefore you will no longer see false visions or practise divination. I will save my people from your hands. And then you will know that I am the LORD.'"

Idolaters Condemned

14 Some of the elders of Israel came to me and sat down in front of me. ²Then the word of the LORD came to me: ³"Son of man, these men have set up idols in their hearts and put wicked stumbling-blocks before their faces. Should I let them enquire of me at all? ⁴Therefore speak to them and tell them, 'This is what the Sovereign LORD says: When any Israelite sets up idols in his heart and puts a wicked stumbling-block before his face and then goes to a prophet, I the LORD will answer him myself in keeping with his great idolatry. ⁵I will do this to recapture the hearts of the people of Israel, who have all deserted me for their idols.'

⁶"Therefore say to the house of Israel, 'This is what the Sovereign LORD says: Repent! Turn from your idols and renounce all your detestable practices!

⁷"When any Israelite or any alien living in Israel separates himself from me and sets up idols in his heart and puts a wicked stumbling-block before his face and then goes to a prophet to enquire of me, I the LORD will answer him myself. ⁸I will set my face against that man and make him an example and a byword. I will cut him off from my people. Then you will know that I am the LORD.

⁹"And if the prophet is enticed to utter a prophecy, I the LORD have enticed that prophet, and I will stretch out my hand against him and destroy him from among my people Israel. ¹⁰They will bear their guilt—the prophet will be as guilty as the one who consults him.

¹¹Then the people of Israel will no longer stray from me, nor will they defile themselves any more with all their sins. They will be my people, and I will be their God, declares the Sovereign LORD.'"

Judgment Inescapable

¹²The word of the LORD came to me: ¹³"Son of man, if a country sins against me by being unfaithful and I stretch out my hand against it to cut off its food supply and send famine upon it and kill its men and their animals, ¹⁴even if these three men—Noah, Daniel and Job—were in it, they could save only themselves by their righteousness, declares the Sovereign LORD.

¹⁵"Or if I send wild beasts through that country and they leave it childless and it becomes desolate so that no-one can pass through it because of the beasts, ¹⁶as surely as I live, declares the Sovereign LORD, even if these three men were in it, they could not save their own sons or daughters. They alone would be saved, but the land would be desolate.

¹⁷"Or if I bring a sword against that country and say, 'Let the sword pass throughout the land,' and I kill its men and their animals, ¹⁸as surely as I live, declares the Sovereign LORD, even if these three men were in it, they could not save their own sons or daughters. They alone would be saved.

¹⁹"Or if I send a plague into that land and pour out my wrath upon it through bloodshed, killing its men and their animals, ²⁰as surely as I live, declares the Sovereign LORD, even if Noah, Daniel and Job were in it, they could save neither son nor daughter. They would save only themselves by their righteousness.

²¹"For this is what the Sovereign LORD says: How much worse will it be when I send against Jerusalem my four dreadful judgments—sword and famine and wild beasts and plague—to kill its men and their animals! ²²Yet

there will be some survivors—sons and daughters who will be brought out of it. They will come to you, and when you see their conduct and their actions, you will be consoled regarding the disaster I have brought upon Jerusalem—every disaster I have brought upon it. ²³You will be consoled when you see their conduct and their actions, for you will know that I have done nothing in it without cause, declares the Sovereign Lord."

Jerusalem, a Useless Vine

15 The word of the Lord came to me: ²"Son of man, how is the wood of a vine better than that of a branch on any of the trees in the forest? ³Is wood ever taken from it to make anything useful? Do they make pegs from it to hang things on? ⁴And after it is thrown on the fire as fuel and the fire burns both ends and chars the middle, is it then useful for anything? ⁵If it was not useful for anything when it was whole, how much less can it be made into something useful when the fire has burned it and it is charred?

⁶"Therefore this is what the Sovereign Lord says: As I have given the wood of the vine among the trees of the forest as fuel for the fire, so will I treat the people living in Jerusalem. ⁷I will set my face against them. Although they have come out of the fire, the fire will yet consume them. And when I set my face against them, you will know that I am the Lord. ⁸I will make the land desolate because they have been unfaithful, declares the Sovereign Lord."

NEW TESTAMENT READING
Hebrews 8:1–13

The High Priest of a New Covenant

8 The point of what we are saying is this: We do have such a high priest, who sat down at the right hand of the throne of the Majesty in heaven, ²and who serves in the sanctuary, the true tabernacle set up by the Lord, not by man.

³Every high priest is appointed to offer both gifts and sacrifices, and so it was necessary for this one also to have something to offer. ⁴If he were on earth, he would not be a priest, for there are already men who offer the gifts prescribed by the law. ⁵They serve at a sanctuary that is a copy and shadow of what is in heaven. This is why Moses was warned when he was about to build the tabernacle: "See to it that you make everything according to the pattern shown you on the mountain." ⁶But the ministry Jesus has received is as superior to theirs as the covenant of which he is mediator is superior to the old one, and it is founded on better promises.

⁷For if there had been nothing wrong with that first covenant, no place would have been sought for another. ⁸But God found fault with the people and said:

> "The time is coming, declares the Lord,
>   when I will make a new covenant
> with the house of Israel
>   and with the house of Judah.
> ⁹It will not be like the covenant
>   I made with their forefathers
> when I took them by the hand
>   to lead them out of Egypt,
> because they did not remain faithful
>   to my covenant,
>   and I turned away from them,
>   declares the Lord.
> ¹⁰This is the covenant I will make with
>   the house of Israel
>   after that time, declares the Lord.
> I will put my laws in their minds
>   and write them on their hearts.
> I will be their God,
>   and they will be my people.
> ¹¹No longer will a man teach his
>   neighbour,
>   or a man his brother, saying,
>   'Know the Lord,'
> because they will all know me,

from the least of them to the greatest.

12For I will forgive their wickedness and will remember their sins no more."

13By calling this covenant "new", he has made the first one obsolete; and what is obsolete and ageing will soon disappear.

READING FROM PSALMS
Psalm 120:1–7

A song of ascents.

1I call on the LORD in my distress,
and he answers me.

2Save me, O LORD, from lying lips
and from deceitful tongues.

3What will he do to you,
and what more besides, O deceitful tongue?
4He will punish you with a warrior's sharp arrows,
with burning coals of the broom tree.

5Woe to me that I dwell in Meshech,
that I live among the tents of Kedar!
6Too long have I lived
among those who hate peace.
7I am a man of peace;
but when I speak, they are for war.

DAY 312

NOVEMBER 8

OLD TESTAMENT READING
Ezekiel 16:1–63

An Allegory of Unfaithful Jerusalem

16 The word of the LORD came to me: 2"Son of man, confront Jerusalem with her detestable practices 3and say, 'This is what the Sovereign LORD says to Jerusalem: Your ancestry and birth were in the land of the Canaanites; your father was an Amorite and your mother a Hittite. 4On the day you were born your cord was not cut, nor were you washed with water to make you clean, nor were you rubbed with salt or wrapped in cloths. 5No-one looked on you with pity or had compassion enough to do any of these things for you. Rather, you were thrown out into the open field, for on the day you were born you were despised.

6"'Then I passed by and saw you kicking about in your blood, and as you lay there in your blood I said to you, "Live!" 7I made you grow like a plant of the field. You grew up and developed and became the most beautiful of jewels. Your breasts were formed and your hair grew, you who were naked and bare.

8"'Later I passed by, and when I looked at you and saw that you were old enough for love, I spread the corner of my garment over you and covered your nakedness. I gave you my solemn oath and entered into a covenant with you, declares the Sovereign LORD, and you became mine.

9"'I bathed you with water and washed the blood from you and put ointments on you. 10I clothed you with an embroidered dress and put leather sandals on you. I dressed you in fine linen and covered you with costly garments. 11I adorned you with jewellery: I put bracelets on your arms and a necklace around your neck, 12and I put a ring on your nose, ear-rings on your ears and a beautiful crown on your head. 13So you were adorned with gold and silver;

your clothes were of fine linen and costly fabric and embroidered cloth. Your food was fine flour, honey and olive oil. You became very beautiful and rose to be a queen. ¹⁴And your fame spread among the nations on account of your beauty, because the splendour I had given you made your beauty perfect, declares the Sovereign LORD.

¹⁵"'But you trusted in your beauty and used your fame to become a prostitute. You lavished your favours on anyone who passed by and your beauty became his. ¹⁶You took some of your garments to make gaudy high places, where you carried on your prostitution. Such things should not happen, nor should they ever occur. ¹⁷You also took the fine jewellery I gave you, the jewellery made of my gold and silver, and you made for yourself male idols and engaged in prostitution with them. ¹⁸And you took your embroidered clothes to put on them, and you offered my oil and incense before them. ¹⁹Also the food I provided for you—the fine flour, olive oil and honey I gave you to eat—you offered as fragrant incense before them. That is what happened, declares the Sovereign LORD.

²⁰"'And you took your sons and daughters whom you bore to me and sacrificed them as food to the idols. Was your prostitution not enough? ²¹You slaughtered my children and sacrificed them to the idols. ²²In all your detestable practices and your prostitution you did not remember the days of your youth, when you were naked and bare, kicking about in your blood.

²³"'Woe! Woe to you, declares the Sovereign LORD. In addition to all your other wickedness, ²⁴you built a mound for yourself and made a lofty shrine in every public square. ²⁵At the head of every street you built your lofty shrines and degraded your beauty, offering your body with increasing promiscuity to anyone who passed by. ²⁶You engaged in prostitution with the Egyptians, your lustful neighbours, and

provoked me to anger with your increasing promiscuity. ²⁷So I stretched out my hand against you and reduced your territory; I gave you over to the greed of your enemies, the daughters of the Philistines, who were shocked by your lewd conduct. ²⁸You engaged in prostitution with the Assyrians too, because you were insatiable; and even after that, you still were not satisfied. ²⁹Then you increased your promiscuity to include Babylonia, a land of merchants, but even with this you were not satisfied.

³⁰"'How weak-willed you are, declares the Sovereign LORD, when you do all these things, acting like a brazen prostitute! ³¹When you built your mounds at the head of every street and made your lofty shrines in every public square, you were unlike a prostitute, because you scorned payment.

³²"'You adulterous wife! You prefer strangers to your own husband! ³³Every prostitute receives a fee, but you give gifts to all your lovers, bribing them to come to you from everywhere for your illicit favours. ³⁴So in your prostitution you are the opposite of others; no-one runs after you for your favours. You are the very opposite, for you give payment and none is given to you.

³⁵"'Therefore, you prostitute, hear the word of the LORD! ³⁶This is what the Sovereign LORD says: Because you poured out your wealth and exposed your nakedness in your promiscuity with your lovers, and because of all your detestable idols, and because you gave them your children's blood, ³⁷therefore I am going to gather all your lovers, with whom you found pleasure, those you loved as well as those you hated. I will gather them against you from all around and will strip you in front of them, and they will see all your nakedness. ³⁸I will sentence you to the punishment of women who commit adultery and who shed blood; I will bring upon you the blood vengeance of my wrath and jealous anger. ³⁹Then I will hand you over to your lovers, and they will tear

down your mounds and destroy your lofty shrines. They will strip you of your clothes and take your fine jewellery and leave you naked and bare. 40They will bring a mob against you, who will stone you and hack you to pieces with their swords. 41They will burn down your houses and inflict punishment on you in the sight of many women. I will put a stop to your prostitution, and you will no longer pay your lovers. 42Then my wrath against you will subside and my jealous anger will turn away from you; I will be calm and no longer angry.

43"'Because you did not remember the days of your youth but enraged me with all these things, I will surely bring down on your head what you have done, declares the Sovereign LORD. Did you not add lewdness to all your other detestable practices?

44"'Everyone who quotes proverbs will quote this proverb about you: "Like mother, like daughter." 45You are a true daughter of your mother, who despised her husband and her children; and you are a true sister of your sisters, who despised their husbands and their children. Your mother was a Hittite and your father an Amorite. 46Your older sister was Samaria, who lived to the north of you with her daughters; and your younger sister, who lived to the south of you with her daughters, was Sodom. 47You not only walked in their ways and copied their detestable practices, but in all your ways you soon became more depraved than they. 48As surely as I live, declares the Sovereign LORD, your sister Sodom and her daughters never did what you and your daughters have done.

49"'Now this was the sin of your sister Sodom: She and her daughters were arrogant, overfed and unconcerned; they did not help the poor and needy. 50They were haughty and did detestable things before me. Therefore I did away with them as you have seen. 51Samaria did not commit half the sins you did. You have done more detestable things than they, and have made your sisters seem righteous by all these things you have done. 52Bear your disgrace, for you have furnished some justification for your sisters. Because your sins were more vile than theirs, they appear more righteous than you. So then, be ashamed and bear your disgrace, for you have made your sisters appear righteous.

53"'However, I will restore the fortunes of Sodom and her daughters and of Samaria and her daughters, and your fortunes along with them, 54so that you may bear your disgrace and be ashamed of all you have done in giving them comfort. 55And your sisters, Sodom with her daughters and Samaria with her daughters, will return to what they were before; and you and your daughters will return to what you were before. 56You would not even mention your sister Sodom in the day of your pride, 57before your wickedness was uncovered. Even so, you are now scorned by the daughters of Edom and all her neighbours and the daughters of the Philistines—all those around you who despise you. 58You will bear the consequences of your lewdness and your detestable practices, declares the LORD.

59"'This is what the Sovereign LORD says: I will deal with you as you deserve, because you have despised my oath by breaking the covenant. 60Yet I will remember the covenant I made with you in the days of your youth, and I will establish an everlasting covenant with you. 61Then you will remember your ways and be ashamed when you receive your sisters, both those who are older than you and those who are younger. I will give them to you as daughters, but not on the basis of my covenant with you. 62So I will establish my covenant with you, and you will know that I am the LORD. 63Then, when I make atonement for you for all you have done, you will remember and be ashamed and never again open your mouth because of your humiliation, declares the Sovereign LORD.'"

NEW TESTAMENT READING
Hebrews 9:1–15

Worship in the Earthly Tabernacle

9 Now the first covenant had regulations for worship and also an earthly sanctuary. [2]A tabernacle was set up. In its first room were the lampstand, the table and the consecrated bread; this was called the Holy Place. [3]Behind the second curtain was a room called the Most Holy Place, [4]which had the golden altar of incense and the gold-covered ark of the covenant. This ark contained the gold jar of manna, Aaron's staff that had budded, and the stone tablets of the covenant. [5]Above the ark were the cherubim of the Glory, overshadowing the atonement cover. But we cannot discuss these things in detail now.

[6]When everything had been arranged like this, the priests entered regularly into the outer room to carry on their ministry. [7]But only the high priest entered the inner room, and that only once a year, and never without blood, which he offered for himself and for the sins the people had committed in ignorance. [8]The Holy Spirit was showing by this that the way into the Most Holy Place had not yet been disclosed as long as the first tabernacle was still standing. [9]This is an illustration for the present time, indicating that the gifts and sacrifices being offered were not able to clear the conscience of the worshipper. [10]They are only a matter of food and drink and various ceremonial washings —external regulations applying until the time of the new order.

The Blood of Christ

[11]When Christ came as high priest of the good things that are already here, he went through the greater and more perfect tabernacle that is not man-made, that is to say, not a part of this creation. [12]He did not enter by means of the blood of goats and calves; but he entered the Most Holy Place once for all

by his own blood, having obtained eternal redemption. [13]The blood of goats and bulls and the ashes of a heifer sprinkled on those who are ceremonially unclean sanctify them so that they are outwardly clean. [14]How much more, then, will the blood of Christ, who through the eternal Spirit offered himself unblemished to God, cleanse our consciences from acts that lead to death, so that we may serve the living God!

[15]For this reason Christ is the mediator of a new covenant, that those who are called may receive the promised eternal inheritance—now that he has died as a ransom to set them free from the sins committed under the first covenant.

READING FROM PROVERBS
Proverbs 27:5–14

[5]Better is open rebuke
    than hidden love.

[6]Wounds from a friend can be trusted,
    but an enemy multiplies kisses.

[7]He who is full loathes honey,
    but to the hungry even what is
        bitter tastes sweet.

[8]Like a bird that strays from its nest
    is a man who strays from his home.

[9]Perfume and incense bring joy to the
        heart,
    and the pleasantness of one's
        friend springs from his earnest
        counsel.

[10]Do not forsake your friend and the
        friend of your father,
    and do not go to your brother's
        house when disaster strikes
        you—
    better a neighbour nearby than a
        brother far away.

11Be wise, my son, and bring joy to my
    heart;
  then I can answer anyone who
    treats me with contempt.

12The prudent see danger and take
    refuge,
  but the simple keep going and
    suffer for it.

13Take the garment of one who puts up
    security for a stranger;
  hold it in pledge if he does it for a
    wayward woman.

14If a man loudly blesses his neighbour
    early in the morning,
  it will be taken as a curse.

DAY 313   # NOVEMBER 9

OLD TESTAMENT READING
Ezekiel 17:1–18:32

Two Eagles and a Vine

17 The word of the LORD came to
me: 2"Son of man, set forth an
allegory and tell the house of Israel a
parable. 3Say to them, 'This is what the
Sovereign LORD says: A great eagle
with powerful wings, long feathers and
full plumage of varied colours came to
Lebanon. Taking hold of the top of a
cedar, 4he broke off its topmost shoot
and carried it away to a land of merchants, where he planted it in a city of
traders.

5"'He took some of the seed of your
land and put it in fertile soil. He planted
it like a willow by abundant water, 6and
it sprouted and became a low, spreading
vine. Its branches turned towards him,
but its roots remained under it. So it
became a vine and produced branches
and put out leafy boughs.

7"'But there was another great eagle
with powerful wings and full plumage.
The vine now sent out its roots towards
him from the plot where it was planted
and stretched out its branches to him for
water. 8It had been planted in good soil
by abundant water so that it would produce branches, bear fruit and become a
splendid vine.'

9"Say to them, 'This is what the
Sovereign LORD says: Will it thrive?

Will it not be uprooted and stripped of
its fruit so that it withers? All its new
growth will wither. It will not take a
strong arm or many people to pull it up
by the roots. 10Even if it is transplanted,
will it thrive? Will it not wither completely when the east wind strikes it
—wither away in the plot where it
grew?'"

11Then the word of the LORD came to
me: 12"Say to this rebellious house, 'Do
you not know what these things mean?'
Say to them: 'The king of Babylon went
to Jerusalem and carried off her king
and her nobles, bringing them back with
him to Babylon. 13Then he took a member of the royal family and made a
treaty with him, putting him under
oath. He also carried away the leading
men of the land, 14so that the kingdom
would be brought low, unable to rise
again, surviving only by keeping his
treaty. 15But the king rebelled against
him by sending his envoys to Egypt to
get horses and a large army. Will he
succeed? Will he who does such things
escape? Will he break the treaty and yet
escape?

16"'As surely as I live, declares the
Sovereign LORD, he shall die in Babylon, in the land of the king who put him
on the throne, whose oath he despised
and whose treaty he broke. 17Pharaoh
with his mighty army and great horde
will be of no help to him in war, when

ramps are built and siege works erected to destroy many lives. [18]He despised the oath by breaking the covenant. Because he had given his hand in pledge and yet did all these things, he shall not escape.

[19]"Therefore this is what the Sovereign LORD says: As surely as I live, I will bring down on his head my oath that he despised and my covenant that he broke. [20]I will spread my net for him, and he will be caught in my snare. I will bring him to Babylon and execute judgment upon him there because he was unfaithful to me. [21]All his fleeing troops will fall by the sword, and the survivors will be scattered to the winds. Then you will know that I the LORD have spoken.

[22]"This is what the Sovereign LORD says: I myself will take a shoot from the very top of a cedar and plant it; I will break off a tender sprig from its topmost shoots and plant it on a high and lofty mountain. [23]On the mountain heights of Israel I will plant it; it will produce branches and bear fruit and become a splendid cedar. Birds of every kind will nest in it; they will find shelter in the shade of its branches. [24]All the trees of the field will know that I the LORD bring down the tall tree and make the low tree grow tall. I dry up the green tree and make the dry tree flourish.

" 'I the LORD have spoken, and I will do it.' "

The Soul Who Sins Will Die

18 The word of the LORD came to me: [2]"What do you people mean by quoting this proverb about the land of Israel:

" 'The fathers eat sour grapes,
    and the children's teeth are set on edge'?

[3]"As surely as I live, declares the Sovereign LORD, you will no longer quote this proverb in Israel. [4]For every living soul belongs to me, the father as well as the son—both alike belong to

me. The soul who sins is the one who will die.

[5]"Suppose there is a righteous man
    who does what is just and right.
[6]He does not eat at the mountain shrines
    or look to the idols of the house of Israel.
He does not defile his neighbour's wife
    or lie with a woman during her period.
[7]He does not oppress anyone,
    but returns what he took in pledge for a loan.
He does not commit robbery,
    but gives his food to the hungry
    and provides clothing for the naked.
[8]He does not lend at usury
    or take excessive interest.
He withholds his hand from doing wrong
    and judges fairly between man and man.
[9]He follows my decrees
    and faithfully keeps my laws.
That man is righteous;
    he will surely live,
        declares the Sovereign LORD.

[10]"Suppose he has a violent son, who sheds blood or does any of these other things [11](though the father has done none of them):

"He eats at the mountain shrines.
He defiles his neighbour's wife.
[12]He oppresses the poor and needy.
He commits robbery.
He does not return what he took in pledge.
He looks to the idols.
He does detestable things.
[13]He lends at usury and takes excessive interest.

Will such a man live? He will not! Because he has done all these detestable things, he will surely be put to death and his blood will be on his own head.

14"But suppose this son has a son who sees all the sins his father commits, and, though he sees them, he does not do such things:

15"He does not eat at the mountain shrines
   or look to the idols of the house of Israel.
He does not defile his neighbour's wife.
16He does not oppress anyone
   or require a pledge for a loan.
He does not commit robbery,
   but gives his food to the hungry
   and provides clothing for the naked.
17He withholds his hand from sin
   and takes no usury or excessive interest.
He keeps my laws and follows my decrees.

He will not die for his father's sin; he will surely live. 18But his father will die for his own sin, because he practised extortion, robbed his brother and did what was wrong among his people.

19"Yet you ask, 'Why does the son not share the guilt of his father?' Since the son has done what is just and right and has been careful to keep all my decrees, he will surely live. 20The one who sins is the one who will die. The son will not share the guilt of the father, nor will the father share the guilt of the son. The righteousness of the righteous man will be credited to him, and the wickedness of the wicked will be charged against him.

21"But if a wicked man turns away from all the sins he has committed and keeps all my decrees and does what is just and right, he will surely live; he will not die. 22None of the offences he has committed will be remembered against him. Because of the righteous things he has done, he will live. 23Do I take any pleasure in the death of the wicked? declares the Sovereign LORD. Rather, am I not pleased when they turn from their ways and live?

24"But if a righteous man turns from his righteousness and commits sin and does the same detestable things the wicked man does, will he live? None of the righteous things he has done will be remembered. Because of the unfaithfulness he is guilty of and because of the sins he has committed, he will die. 25"Yet you say, 'The way of the Lord is not just.' Hear, O house of Israel: Is my way unjust? Is it not your ways that are unjust? 26If a righteous man turns from his righteousness and commits sin, he will die for it; because of the sin he has committed he will die. 27But if a wicked man turns away from the wickedness he has committed and does what is just and right, he will save his life. 28Because he considers all the offences he has committed and turns away from them, he will surely live; he will not die. 29Yet the house of Israel says, 'The way of the Lord is not just.' Are my ways unjust, O house of Israel? Is it not your ways that are unjust?

30"Therefore, O house of Israel, I will judge you, each one according to his ways, declares the Sovereign LORD. Repent! Turn away from all your offences; then sin will not be your downfall. 31Rid yourselves of all the offences you have committed, and get a new heart and a new spirit. Why will you die, O house of Israel? 32For I take no pleasure in the death of anyone, declares the Sovereign LORD. Repent and live!

NEW TESTAMENT READING
Hebrews 9:16–28

16In the case of a will, it is necessary to prove the death of the one who made it, 17because a will is in force only when somebody has died; it never takes effect while the one who made it is living. 18This is why even the first covenant was not put into effect without blood. 19When Moses had proclaimed every commandment of the law to all the people, he took the blood of calves, together with water, scarlet wool and branches of hyssop, and sprinkled the scroll and all the people. 20He said, "This is the blood of the covenant, which God has commanded you to keep." 21In the same way, he sprinkled with the blood both the tabernacle and everything used in its ceremonies. 22In fact, the law requires that nearly everything be cleansed with blood, and without the shedding of blood there is no forgiveness.

23It was necessary, then, for the copies of the heavenly things to be purified with these sacrifices, but the heavenly things themselves with better sacrifices than these. 24For Christ did not enter a man-made sanctuary that was only a copy of the true one; he entered heaven itself, now to appear for us in God's presence. 25Nor did he enter heaven to offer himself again and again, the way the high priest enters the Most Holy Place every year with blood that is not his own. 26Then Christ would have had to suffer many times since the creation of the world. But now he has appeared once for all at the end of the ages to do away with sin by the sacrifice of himself. 27Just as man is destined to die once, and after that to face judgment, 28so Christ was sacrificed once to take away the sins of many people; and

he will appear a second time, not to bear sin, but to bring salvation to those who are waiting for him.

READING FROM PSALMS
Psalm 121:1–8

A song of ascents.

1I lift up my eyes to the hills—
    where does my help come from?
2My help comes from the LORD,
    the Maker of heaven and earth.

3He will not let your foot slip—
    he who watches over you will not
        slumber;
4indeed, he who watches over Israel
    will neither slumber nor sleep.

5The LORD watches over you—
    the LORD is your shade at your
        right hand;
6the sun will not harm you by day,
    nor the moon by night.

7The LORD will keep you from all
        harm—
    he will watch over your life;
8the LORD will watch over your
        coming and going
    both now and for evermore.

NOVEMBER 10   DAY 314

OLD TESTAMENT READING
Ezekiel 19:1–20:44

A Lament for Israel's Princes

19 "Take up a lament concerning the princes of Israel 2and say:

"'What a lioness was your mother
        among the lions!
    She lay down among the young lions
        and reared her cubs.
3She brought up one of her cubs,
    and he became a strong lion.

He learned to tear the prey
        and he devoured men.
4The nations heard about him,
    and he was trapped in their pit.
    They led him with hooks
        to the land of Egypt.

5"'When she saw her hope unfulfilled,
        her expectation gone,
    she took another of her cubs
        and made him a strong lion.
6He prowled among the lions,
    for he was now a strong lion.

He learned to tear the prey
and he devoured men.
⁷He broke down their strongholds
and devastated their towns.
The land and all who were in it
were terrified by his roaring.
⁸Then the nations came against him,
those from regions round about.
They spread their net for him,
and he was trapped in their pit.
⁹With hooks they pulled him into a
cage
and brought him to the king of
Babylon.
They put him in prison,
so his roar was heard no longer
on the mountains of Israel.

¹⁰"'Your mother was like a vine in
your vineyard
planted by the water;
it was fruitful and full of branches
because of abundant water.
¹¹Its branches were strong,
fit for a ruler's sceptre.
It towered high
above the thick foliage,
conspicuous for its height
and for its many branches.
¹²But it was uprooted in fury
and thrown to the ground.
The east wind made it shrivel,
it was stripped of its fruit;
its strong branches withered
and fire consumed them.
¹³Now it is planted in the desert,
in a dry and thirsty land.
¹⁴Fire spread from one of its main
branches
and consumed its fruit.
No strong branch is left on it
fit for a ruler's sceptre.'

This is a lament and is to be used as a
lament."

Rebellious Israel

20 In the seventh year, in the fifth
month on the tenth day, some of
the elders of Israel came to enquire of
the LORD, and they sat down in front
of me.

²Then the word of the LORD came to
me: ³"Son of man, speak to the elders of
Israel and say to them, 'This is what the
Sovereign LORD says: Have you come
to enquire of me? As surely as I live, I
will not let you enquire of me, declares
the Sovereign LORD.'

⁴"Will you judge them? Will you
judge them, son of man? Then confront
them with the detestable practices of
their fathers ⁵and say to them: 'This is
what the Sovereign LORD says: On the
day I chose Israel, I swore with uplifted
hand to the descendants of the house of
Jacob and revealed myself to them in
Egypt. With uplifted hand I said to
them, "I am the LORD your God." ⁶On
that day I swore to them that I would
bring them out of Egypt into a land I
had searched out for them, a land flowing with milk and honey, the most
beautiful of all lands. ⁷And I said to
them, "Each of you, get rid of the vile
images you have set your eyes on, and
do not defile yourselves with the idols of
Egypt. I am the LORD your God."

⁸"'But they rebelled against me and
would not listen to me; they did not get
rid of the vile images they had set their
eyes on, nor did they forsake the idols of
Egypt. So I said I would pour out my
wrath on them and spend my anger
against them in Egypt. ⁹But for the sake
of my name I did what would keep it
from being profaned in the eyes of the
nations they lived among and in whose
sight I had revealed myself to the
Israelites by bringing them out of
Egypt. ¹⁰Therefore I led them out of
Egypt and brought them into the desert.
¹¹I gave them my decrees and made
known to them my laws, for the man
who obeys them will live by them.
¹²Also I gave them my Sabbaths as a
sign between us, so they would know
that I the LORD made them holy.

¹³"'Yet the people of Israel rebelled
against me in the desert. They did not
follow my decrees but rejected my laws
—although the man who obeys them
will live by them—and they utterly
desecrated my Sabbaths. So I said I

would pour out my wrath on them and destroy them in the desert. 14But for the sake of my name I did what would keep it from being profaned in the eyes of the nations in whose sight I had brought them out. 15Also with uplifted hand I swore to them in the desert that I would not bring them into the land I had given them—a land flowing with milk and honey, most beautiful of all lands— 16because they rejected my laws and did not follow my decrees and desecrated my Sabbaths. For their hearts were devoted to their idols. 17Yet I looked on them with pity and did not destroy them or put an end to them in the desert. 18I said to their children in the desert, "Do not follow the statutes of your fathers or keep their laws or defile yourselves with their idols. 19I am the LORD your God; follow my decrees and be careful to keep my laws. 20Keep my Sabbaths holy, that they may be a sign between us. Then you will know that I am the LORD your God."

21"But the children rebelled against me: They did not follow my decrees, they were not careful to keep my laws —although the man who obeys them will live by them—and they desecrated my Sabbaths. So I said I would pour out my wrath on them and spend my anger against them in the desert. 22But I withheld my hand, and for the sake of my name I did what would keep it from being profaned in the eyes of the nations in whose sight I had brought them out. 23Also with uplifted hand I swore to them in the desert that I would disperse them among the nations and scatter them through the countries, 24because they had not obeyed my laws but had rejected my decrees and desecrated my Sabbaths, and their eyes ⌊lusted⌋ after their fathers' idols. 25I also gave them over to statutes that were not good and laws they could not live by; 26I let them become defiled through their gifts—the sacrifice of every firstborn —that I might fill them with horror so that they would know that I am the LORD.'

27"Therefore, son of man, speak to the people of Israel and say to them, 'This is what the Sovereign LORD says: In this also your fathers blasphemed me by forsaking me: 28When I brought them into the land I had sworn to give them and they saw any high hill or any leafy tree, there they offered their sacrifices, made offerings that provoked me to anger, presented their fragrant incense and poured out their drink offerings. 29Then I said to them: What is this high place you go to?'" (It is called Bamah to this day.)

Judgment and Restoration

30"Therefore say to the house of Israel: 'This is what the Sovereign LORD says: Will you defile yourselves the way your fathers did and lust after their vile images? 31When you offer your gifts —the sacrifice of your sons in the fire —you continue to defile yourselves with all your idols to this day. Am I to let you enquire of me, O house of Israel? As surely as I live, declares the Sovereign LORD, I will not let you enquire of me. 32'You say, "We want to be like the nations, like the peoples of the world, who serve wood and stone." But what you have in mind will never happen. 33As surely as I live, declares the Sovereign LORD, I will rule over you with a mighty hand and an outstretched arm and with outpoured wrath. 34I will bring you from the nations and gather you from the countries where you have been scattered—with a mighty hand and an outstretched arm and with outpoured wrath. 35I will bring you into the desert of the nations and there, face to face, I will execute judgment upon you. 36As I judged your fathers in the desert of the land of Egypt, so I will judge you, declares the Sovereign LORD. 37I will take note of you as you pass under my rod, and I will bring you into the bond of the covenant. 38I will purge you of those who revolt and rebel against me. Although I will bring them out of the land where they are living, yet they will not enter the land of Israel. Then you will know that I am the LORD.

39"'As for you, O house of Israel, this is what the Sovereign LORD says: Go and serve your idols, every one of you! But afterwards you will surely listen to me and no longer profane my holy name with your gifts and idols. 40For on my holy mountain, the high mountain of Israel, declares the Sovereign LORD, there in the land the entire house of Israel will serve me, and there I will accept them. There I will require your offerings and your choice gifts, along with all your holy sacrifices. 41I will accept you as fragrant incense when I bring you out from the nations and gather you from the countries where you have been scattered, and I will show myself holy among you in the sight of the nations. 42Then you will know that I am the LORD, when I bring you into the land of Israel, the land I had sworn with uplifted hand to give to your fathers. 43There you will remember your conduct and all the actions by which you have defiled yourselves, and you will loathe yourselves for all the evil you have done. 44You will know that I am the LORD, when I deal with you for my name's sake and not according to your evil ways and your corrupt practices, O house of Israel, declares the Sovereign LORD.'"

NEW TESTAMENT READING
Hebrews 10:1-18

Christ's Sacrifice Once for All

10 The law is only a shadow of the good things that are coming—not the realities themselves. For this reason it can never, by the same sacrifices repeated endlessly year after year, make perfect those who draw near to worship. 2If it could, would they not have stopped being offered? For the worshippers would have been cleansed once for all, and would no longer have felt guilty for their sins. 3But those sacrifices are an annual reminder of sins,

4because it is impossible for the blood of bulls and goats to take away sins.

5Therefore, when Christ came into the world, he said:

"Sacrifice and offering you did not desire,
    but a body you prepared for me;
6with burnt offerings and sin offerings
    you were not pleased.
7Then I said, 'Here I am—it is written about me in the scroll—
    I have come to do your will, O God.'"

8First he said, "Sacrifices and offerings, burnt offerings and sin offerings you did not desire, nor were you pleased with them" (although the law required them to be made). 9Then he said, "Here I am, I have come to do your will." He sets aside the first to establish the second. 10And by that will, we have been made holy through the sacrifice of the body of Jesus Christ once for all.

11Day after day every priest stands and performs his religious duties; again and again he offers the same sacrifices, which can never take away sins. 12But when this priest had offered for all time one sacrifice for sins, he sat down at the right hand of God. 13Since that time he waits for his enemies to be made his footstool, 14because by one sacrifice he has made perfect for ever those who are being made holy.

15The Holy Spirit also testifies to us about this. First he says:

16"This is the covenant I will make with them
    after that time, says the Lord.
I will put my laws in their hearts,
    and I will write them on their minds."

17Then he adds:

"Their sins and lawless acts
    I will remember no more."

18And where these have been forgiven, there is no longer any sacrifice for sin.

READING FROM PSALMS
Psalm 122:1–9

A song of ascents. Of David.

1 I rejoiced with those who said to me,
   "Let us go to the house of the
   LORD."
2 Our feet are standing
   in your gates, O Jerusalem.

3 Jerusalem is built like a city
   that is closely compacted together.
4 That is where the tribes go up,
   the tribes of the LORD,
   to praise the name of the LORD
   according to the statute given to
   Israel.

5 There the thrones for judgment
   stand,
   the thrones of the house of
   David.

6 Pray for the peace of Jerusalem:
   "May those who love you be
   secure.
7 May there be peace within your walls
   and security within your
   citadels."
8 For the sake of my brothers and
   friends,
   I will say, "Peace be within you."
9 For the sake of the house of the LORD
   our God,
   I will seek your prosperity.

NOVEMBER 11   DAY 315

OLD TESTAMENT READING
Ezekiel 20:45–22:22

Prophecy Against the South

45 The word of the LORD came to me:
46 "Son of man, set your face towards
the south; preach against the south and
prophesy against the forest of the south-
land. 47 Say to the southern forest: 'Hear
the word of the LORD. This is what the
Sovereign LORD says: I am about to set
fire to you, and it will consume all your
trees, both green and dry. The blazing
flame will not be quenched, and every
face from south to north will be scorched by it. 48 Everyone will see that I the
LORD have kindled it; it will not be
quenched.'"

49 Then I said, "Ah, Sovereign LORD!
They are saying of me, 'Isn't he just
telling parables?'"

Babylon, God's Sword of Judgment

21 The word of the LORD came to
me: 2 "Son of man, set your face
against Jerusalem and preach against

the sanctuary. Prophesy against the
land of Israel 3 and say to her: 'This is
what the LORD says: I am against you. I
will draw my sword from its scabbard
and cut off from you both the righteous
and the wicked. 4 Because I am going to
cut off the righteous and the wicked, my
sword will be unsheathed against everyone from south to north. 5 Then all people will know that I the LORD have
drawn my sword from its scabbard; it
will not return again.'

6 "Therefore groan, son of man!
Groan before them with broken heart
and bitter grief. 7 And when they ask
you, 'Why are you groaning?' you shall
say, 'Because of the news that is coming. Every heart will melt and every
hand go limp; every spirit will become
faint and every knee become as weak as
water.' It is coming! It will surely take
place, declares the Sovereign LORD.'"

8 The word of the LORD came to me:
9 "Son of man, prophesy and say, 'This
is what the Lord says:

"'A sword, a sword,
sharpened and polished—

¹⁰sharpened for the slaughter,
    polished to flash like lightning!

   "'Shall we rejoice in the sceptre of
my son ⌊Judah⌋? The sword despises
every such stick.

¹¹"'The sword is appointed to be
    polished,
    to be grasped with the hand;
it is sharpened and polished,
    made ready for the hand of the
      slayer.
¹²Cry out and wail, son of man,
    for it is against my people;
    it is against all the princes of Israel.
They are thrown to the sword
    along with my people.
Therefore beat your breast.

¹³"'Testing will surely come. And
what if the sceptre ⌊of Judah⌋, which
the sword despises, does not continue?
declares the Sovereign LORD.'

¹⁴"So then, son of man, prophesy
    and strike your hands together.
Let the sword strike twice,
    even three times.
It is a sword for slaughter—
    a sword for great slaughter,
    closing in on them from every side.
¹⁵So that hearts may melt
    and the fallen be many,
I have stationed the sword for
      slaughter
    at all their gates.
Oh! It is made to flash like lightning,
    it is grasped for slaughter.
¹⁶O sword, slash to the right,
    then to the left,
    wherever your blade is turned.
¹⁷I too will strike my hands together,
    and my wrath will subside.
I the LORD have spoken."

¹⁸The word of the LORD came to me:
¹⁹"Son of man, mark out two roads for
the sword of the king of Babylon to
take, both starting from the same country. Make a signpost where the road
branches off to the city. ²⁰Mark out one

road for the sword to come against Rabbah of the Ammonites and another
against Judah and fortified Jerusalem.
²¹For the king of Babylon will stop at
the fork in the road, at the junction of
the two roads, to seek an omen: He will
cast lots with arrows, he will consult his
idols, he will examine the liver. ²²Into
his right hand will come the lot for
Jerusalem, where he is to set up battering-rams, to give the command to
slaughter, to sound the battle cry, to set
battering-rams against the gates, to
build a ramp and to erect siege works.
²³It will seem like a false omen to those
who have sworn allegiance to him, but
he will remind them of their guilt and
take them captive.

²⁴"Therefore this is what the
Sovereign LORD says: 'Because you
people have brought to mind your guilt
by your open rebellion, revealing your
sins in all that you do—because you
have done this, you will be taken
captive.

²⁵"'O profane and wicked prince of
Israel, whose day has come, whose time
of punishment has reached its climax,
²⁶this is what the Sovereign LORD says:
Take off the turban, remove the crown.
It will not be as it was: The lowly will be
exalted and the exalted will be brought
low. ²⁷A ruin! A ruin! I will make it a
ruin! It will not be restored until he
comes to whom it rightfully belongs; to
him I will give it.'

²⁸"And you, son of man, prophesy
and say, 'This is what the Sovereign
LORD says about the Ammonites and
their insults:

   "'A sword, a sword,
    drawn for the slaughter,
polished to consume
    and to flash like lightning!
²⁹Despite false visions concerning you
    and lying divinations about you,
it will be laid on the necks
    of the wicked who are to be slain,
    whose day has come,
    whose time of punishment has
      reached its climax.

30Return the sword to its scabbard.
  In the place where you were
    created,
  in the land of your ancestry,
    I will judge you.
31I will pour out my wrath upon you
    and breathe out my fiery anger
      against you;
  I will hand you over to brutal men,
    men skilled in destruction.
32You will be fuel for the fire,
    your blood will be shed in your
      land,
  you will be remembered no more;
    for I the LORD have spoken.'"

Jerusalem's Sins

22 The word of the LORD came to me: 2"Son of man, will you judge her? Will you judge this city of bloodshed? Then confront her with all her detestable practices 3and say: 'This is what the Sovereign LORD says: O city that brings on herself doom by shedding blood in her midst and defiles herself by making idols, 4you have become guilty because of the blood you have shed and have become defiled by the idols you have made. You have brought your days to a close, and the end of your years has come. Therefore I will make you an object of scorn to the nations and a laughing-stock to all the countries. 5Those who are near and those who are far away will mock you, O infamous city, full of turmoil.

6"'See how each of the princes of Israel who are in you uses his power to shed blood. 7In you they have treated father and mother with contempt; in you they have oppressed the alien and ill-treated the fatherless and the widow. 8You have despised my holy things and desecrated my Sabbaths. 9In you are slanderous men bent on shedding blood; in you are those who eat at the mountain shrines and commit lewd acts. 10In you are those who dishonour their fathers' bed; in you are those who violate women during their period, when they are ceremonially unclean.

11In you one man commits a detestable offence with his neighbour's wife, another shamefully defiles his daughter-in-law, and another violates his sister, his own father's daughter. 12In you men accept bribes to shed blood; you take usury and excessive interest and make unjust gain from your neighbours by extortion. And you have forgotten me, declares the Sovereign LORD.

13"'I will surely strike my hands together at the unjust gain you have made and at the blood you have shed in your midst. 14Will your courage endure or your hands be strong in the day I deal with you? I the LORD have spoken, and I will do it. 15I will disperse you among the nations and scatter you through the countries; and I will put an end to your uncleanness. 16When you have been defiled in the eyes of the nations, you will know that I am the LORD.'"

17Then the word of the LORD came to me: 18"Son of man, the house of Israel has become dross to me; all of them are the copper, tin, iron and lead left inside a furnace. They are but the dross of silver. 19Therefore this is what the Sovereign LORD says: 'Because you have all become dross, I will gather you into Jerusalem. 20As men gather silver, copper, iron, lead and tin into a furnace to melt it with a fiery blast, so will I gather you in my anger and my wrath and put you inside the city and melt you. 21I will gather you and I will blow on you with my fiery wrath, and you will be melted inside her. 22As silver is melted in a furnace, so you will be melted inside her, and you will know that I the LORD have poured out my wrath upon you.'"

NEW TESTAMENT READING
Hebrews 10:19–39

A Call to Persevere

19Therefore, brothers, since we have confidence to enter the Most Holy Place by the blood of Jesus, 20by a new and living way opened for us through the curtain, that is, his body, 21and since we have a great priest over the house of God, 22let us draw near to God with a sincere heart in full assurance of faith, having our hearts sprinkled to cleanse us from a guilty conscience and having our bodies washed with pure water. 23Let us hold unswervingly to the hope we profess, for he who promised is faithful. 24And let us consider how we may spur one another on towards love and good deeds. 25Let us not give up meeting together, as some are in the habit of doing, but let us encourage one another—and all the more as you see the Day approaching.

26If we deliberately keep on sinning after we have received the knowledge of the truth, no sacrifice for sins is left, 27but only a fearful expectation of judgment and of raging fire that will consume the enemies of God. 28Anyone who rejected the law of Moses died without mercy on the testimony of two or three witnesses. 29How much more severely do you think a man deserves to be punished who has trampled the Son of God under foot, who has treated as an unholy thing the blood of the covenant that sanctified him, and who has insulted the Spirit of grace? 30For we know him who said, "It is mine to avenge; I will repay," and again, "The Lord will judge his people." 31It is a dreadful thing to fall into the hands of the living God.

32Remember those earlier days after you had received the light, when you stood your ground in a great contest in the face of suffering. 33Sometimes you were publicly exposed to insult and persecution; at other times you stood side by side with those who were so treated. 34You sympathised with those in prison and joyfully accepted the confiscation of your property, because you knew that you yourselves had better and lasting possessions.

35So do not throw away your confidence; it will be richly rewarded. 36You need to persevere so that when you have done the will of God, you will receive what he has promised. 37For in just a very little while,

"He who is coming will come and will not delay.
38   But my righteous one will live by faith.
And if he shrinks back,
    I will not be pleased with him."

39But we are not of those who shrink back and are destroyed, but of those who believe and are saved.

READING FROM PSALMS
Psalm 123:1–4

A song of ascents.

1I lift up my eyes to you,
    to you whose throne is in heaven.
2As the eyes of slaves look to the hand of their master,
    as the eyes of a maid look to the hand of her mistress,
so our eyes look to the LORD our God,
    till he shows us his mercy.

3Have mercy on us, O LORD, have mercy on us,
    for we have endured much contempt.
4We have endured much ridicule from the proud,
    much contempt from the arrogant.

OLD TESTAMENT READING
Ezekiel 22:23–23:49

²³Again the word of the LORD came to me: ²⁴"Son of man, say to the land, 'You are a land that has had no rain or showers in the day of wrath.' ²⁵There is a conspiracy of her princes within her like a roaring lion tearing its prey; they devour people, take treasures and precious things and make many widows within her. ²⁶Her priests do violence to my law and profane my holy things; they do not distinguish between the holy and the common; they teach that there is no difference between the unclean and the clean; and they shut their eyes to the keeping of my Sabbaths, so that I am profaned among them. ²⁷Her officials within her are like wolves tearing their prey; they shed blood and kill people to make unjust gain. ²⁸Her prophets whitewash these deeds for them by false visions and lying divinations. They say, 'This is what the Sovereign LORD says'—when the LORD has not spoken. ²⁹The people of the land practise extortion and commit robbery; they oppress the poor and needy and ill-treat the alien, denying them justice.

³⁰"I looked for a man among them who would build up the wall and stand before me in the gap on behalf of the land so that I would not have to destroy it, but I found none. ³¹So I will pour out my wrath on them and consume them with my fiery anger, bringing down on their own heads all they have done, declares the Sovereign LORD."

Two Adulterous Sisters

23 The word of the LORD came to me: ²"Son of man, there were two women, daughters of the same mother. ³They became prostitutes in Egypt, engaging in prostitution from their youth. In that land their breasts were fondled and their virgin bosoms caressed. ⁴The older was named Oholah, and her sister was Oholibah. They were mine and gave birth to sons and daughters. Oholah is Samaria, and Oholibah is Jerusalem.

⁵"Oholah engaged in prostitution while she was still mine; and she lusted after her lovers, the Assyrians—warriors ⁶clothed in blue, governors and commanders, all of them handsome young men, and mounted horsemen. ⁷She gave herself as a prostitute to all the elite of the Assyrians and defiled herself with all the idols of everyone she lusted after. ⁸She did not give up the prostitution she began in Egypt, when during her youth men slept with her, caressed her virgin bosom and poured out their lust upon her.

⁹"Therefore I handed her over to her lovers, the Assyrians, for whom she lusted. ¹⁰They stripped her naked, took away her sons and daughters and killed her with the sword. She became a byword among women, and punishment was inflicted on her.

¹¹"Her sister Oholibah saw this, yet in her lust and prostitution she was more depraved than her sister. ¹²She too lusted after the Assyrians—governors and commanders, warriors in full dress, mounted horsemen, all handsome young men. ¹³I saw that she too defiled herself; both of them went the same way.

¹⁴"But she carried her prostitution still further. She saw men portrayed on a wall, figures of Chaldeans portrayed in red, ¹⁵with belts round their waists and flowing turbans on their heads; all of them looked like Babylonian chariot officers, natives of Chaldea. ¹⁶As soon as she saw them, she lusted after them and sent messengers to them in Chaldea. ¹⁷Then the Babylonians came to her, to the bed of love, and in their lust

they defiled her. After she had been defiled by them, she turned away from them in disgust. [18]When she carried on her prostitution openly and exposed her nakedness, I turned away from her in disgust, just as I had turned away from her sister. [19]Yet she became more and more promiscuous as she recalled the days of her youth, when she was a prostitute in Egypt. [20]There she lusted after her lovers, whose genitals were like those of donkeys and whose emission was like that of horses. [21]So you longed for the lewdness of your youth, when in Egypt your bosom was caressed and your young breasts fondled.

[22]"Therefore, Oholibah, this is what the Sovereign LORD says: I will stir up your lovers against you, those you turned away from in disgust, and I will bring them against you from every side —[23]the Babylonians and all the Chaldeans, the men of Pekod and Shoa and Koa, and all the Assyrians with them, handsome young men, all of them governors and commanders, chariot officers and men of high rank, all mounted on horses. [24]They will come against you with weapons, chariots and wagons and with a throng of people; they will take up positions against you on every side with large and small shields and with helmets. I will turn you over to them for punishment, and they will punish you according to their standards. [25]I will direct my jealous anger against you, and they will deal with you in fury. They will cut off your noses and your ears, and those of you who are left will fall by the sword. They will take away your sons and daughters, and those of you who are left will be consumed by fire. [26]They will also strip you of your clothes and take your fine jewellery. [27]So I will put a stop to the lewdness and prostitution you began in Egypt. You will not look on these things with longing or remember Egypt any more.

[28]"For this is what the Sovereign LORD says: I am about to hand you over to those you hate, to those you turned

away from in disgust. [29]They will deal with you in hatred and take away everything you have worked for. They will leave you naked and bare, and the shame of your prostitution will be exposed. Your lewdness and promiscuity [30]have brought this upon you, because you lusted after the nations and defiled yourself with their idols. [31]You have gone the way of your sister; so I will put her cup into your hand.

[32]"This is what the Sovereign LORD says:

"You will drink your sister's cup,
    a cup large and deep;
it will bring scorn and derision,
    for it holds so much.
[33]You will be filled with drunkenness
    and sorrow,
    the cup of ruin and desolation,
    the cup of your sister Samaria.
[34]You will drink it and drain it dry;
    you will dash it to pieces
    and tear your breasts.

I have spoken, declares the Sovereign LORD.

[35]"Therefore this is what the Sovereign LORD says: Since you have forgotten me and thrust me behind your back, you must bear the consequences of your lewdness and prostitution."

[36]The LORD said to me: "Son of man, will you judge Oholah and Oholibah? Then confront them with their detestable practices, [37]for they have committed adultery and blood is on their hands. They committed adultery with their idols; they even sacrificed their children, whom they bore to me, as food for them. [38]They have also done this to me: At that same time they defiled my sanctuary and desecrated my Sabbaths. [39]On the very day they sacrificed their children to their idols, they entered my sanctuary and desecrated it. That is what they did in my house.

[40]"They even sent messengers for men who came from far away, and when they arrived you bathed yourself for

them, painted your eyes and put on your jewellery. 41You sat on an elegant couch, with a table spread before it on which you had placed the incense and oil that belonged to me.

42"The noise of a carefree crowd was around her; Sabeans were brought from the desert along with men from the rabble, and they put bracelets on the arms of the woman and her sister and beautiful crowns on their heads. 43Then I said about the one worn out by adultery, 'Now let them use her as a prostitute, for that is all she is.' 44And they slept with her. As men sleep with a prostitute, so they slept with those lewd women, Oholah and Oholibah. 45But righteous men will sentence them to the punishment of women who commit adultery and shed blood, because they are adulterous and blood is on their hands.

46"This is what the Sovereign LORD says: Bring a mob against them and give them over to terror and plunder. 47The mob will stone them and cut them down with their swords; they will kill their sons and daughters and burn down their houses.

48"So I will put an end to lewdness in the land, that all women may take warning and not imitate you. 49You will suffer the penalty for your lewdness and bear the consequences of your sins of idolatry. Then you will know that I am the Sovereign LORD.' "

NEW TESTAMENT READING
Hebrews 11:1–16

By Faith

11 Now faith is being sure of what we hope for and certain of what we do not see. 2This is what the ancients were commended for.

3By faith we understand that the universe was formed at God's command, so that what is seen was not made out of what was visible.

4By faith Abel offered God a better sacrifice than Cain did. By faith he was commended as a righteous man, when God spoke well of his offerings. And by faith he still speaks, even though he is dead.

5By faith Enoch was taken from this life, so that he did not experience death; he could not be found, because God had taken him away. For before he was taken, he was commended as one who pleased God. 6And without faith it is impossible to please God, because anyone who comes to him must believe that he exists and that he rewards those who earnestly seek him.

7By faith Noah, when warned about things not yet seen, in holy fear built an ark to save his family. By his faith he condemned the world and became heir of the righteousness that comes by faith.

8By faith Abraham, when called to go to a place he would later receive as his inheritance, obeyed and went, even though he did not know where he was going. 9By faith he made his home in the promised land like a stranger in a foreign country; he lived in tents, as did Isaac and Jacob, who were heirs with him of the same promise. 10For he was looking forward to the city with foundations, whose architect and builder is God.

11By faith Abraham, even though he was past age—and Sarah herself was barren—was enabled to become a father because he considered him faithful who had made the promise. 12And so from this one man, and he as good as dead, came descendants as numerous as the stars in the sky and as countless as the sand on the seashore.

13All these people were still living by faith when they died. They did not receive the things promised; they only saw them and welcomed them from a distance. And they admitted that they were aliens and strangers on earth. 14People who say such things show that they are looking for a country of their own. 15If they had been thinking of the country they had left, they would have had opportunity to return. 16Instead, they were longing for a better country —a heavenly one. Therefore God is not ashamed to be called their God, for he has prepared a city for them.

READING FROM PROVERBS
Proverbs 27:15–22

15A quarrelsome wife is like
    a constant dripping on a rainy day;
16restraining her is like restraining the
        wind
    or grasping oil with the hand.

17As iron sharpens iron,
    so one man sharpens another.

18He who tends a fig-tree will eat its
        fruit,

and he who looks after his master
        will be honoured.

19As water reflects a face,
    so a man's heart reflects the man.

20Death and Destruction are never
        satisfied,
    and neither are the eyes of man.

21The crucible for silver and the
        furnace for gold,
    but man is tested by the praise he
        receives.

22Though you grind a fool in a mortar,
        grinding him like grain with a
        pestle,
    you will not remove his folly from
        him.

DAY 317

NOVEMBER 13

OLD TESTAMENT READING
Ezekiel 24:1–25:17

The Cooking Pot

24 In the ninth year, in the tenth month on the tenth day, the word of the LORD came to me: 2"Son of man, record this date, this very date, because the king of Babylon has laid siege to Jerusalem this very day. 3Tell this rebellious house a parable and say to them: 'This is what the Sovereign LORD says:

    "'Put on the cooking pot; put it on
        and pour water into it.
4Put into it the pieces of meat,
    all the choice pieces—the leg and
        the shoulder.
Fill it with the best of these bones;
5   take the pick of the flock.
Pile wood beneath it for the bones;
    bring it to the boil
    and cook the bones in it.

6"'For this is what the Sovereign LORD says:

    "'Woe to the city of bloodshed,
        to the pot now encrusted,
        whose deposit will not go away!
Empty it piece by piece
    without casting lots for them.

7"'For the blood she shed is in her
        midst:
    She poured it on the bare rock;
she did not pour it on the ground,
    where the dust would cover it.
8To stir up wrath and take revenge
    I put her blood on the bare rock,
    so that it would not be covered.

9"'Therefore this is what the Sovereign LORD says:

    "'Woe to the city of bloodshed!
        I, too, will pile the wood high.
10So heap on the wood
    and kindle the fire.

Cook the meat well,
    mixing in the spices;
    and let the bones be charred.
[11]Then set the empty pot on the coals
    till it becomes hot and its copper
    glows
so its impurities may be melted
    and its deposit burned away.
[12]It has frustrated all efforts;
    its heavy deposit has not been
    removed,
    not even by fire.

[13]"'Now your impurity is lewdness. Because I tried to cleanse you but you would not be cleansed from your impurity, you will not be clean again until my wrath against you has subsided.

[14]"'I the LORD have spoken. The time has come for me to act. I will not hold back; I will not have pity, nor will I relent. You will be judged according to your conduct and your actions, declares the Sovereign LORD.'"

Ezekiel's Wife Dies

[15]The word of the LORD came to me: [16]"Son of man, with one blow I am about to take away from you the delight of your eyes. Yet do not lament or weep or shed any tears. [17]Groan quietly; do not mourn for the dead. Keep your turban fastened and your sandals on your feet; do not cover the lower part of your face or eat the customary food ⌊of mourners⌋."

[18]So I spoke to the people in the morning, and in the evening my wife died. The next morning I did as I had been commanded.

[19]Then the people asked me, "Won't you tell us what these things have to do with us?"

[20]So I said to them, "The word of the LORD came to me: [21]Say to the house of Israel, 'This is what the Sovereign LORD says: I am about to desecrate my sanctuary—the stronghold in which you take pride, the delight of your eyes, the object of your affection. The sons and daughters you left behind will fall by the sword. [22]And you will do as I have done. You will not cover the lower part of your face or eat the customary food ⌊of mourners⌋. [23]You will keep your turbans on your heads and your sandals on your feet. You will not mourn or weep but will waste away because of your sins and groan among yourselves. [24]Ezekiel will be a sign to you; you will do just as he has done. When this happens, you will know that I am the Sovereign LORD.'

[25]"And you, son of man, on the day I take away their stronghold, their joy and glory, the delight of their eyes, their heart's desire, and their sons and daughters as well—[26]on that day a fugitive will come to tell you the news. [27]At that time your mouth will be opened; you will speak with him and will no longer be silent. So you will be a sign to them, and they will know that I am the LORD."

A Prophecy Against Ammon

25 The word of the LORD came to me: [2]"Son of man, set your face against the Ammonites and prophesy against them. [3]Say to them, 'Hear the word of the Sovereign LORD. This is what the Sovereign LORD says: Because you said "Aha!" over my sanctuary when it was desecrated and over the land of Israel when it was laid waste and over the people of Judah when they went into exile, [4]therefore I am going to give you to the people of the East as a possession. They will set up their camps and pitch their tents among you; they will eat your fruit and drink your milk. [5]I will turn Rabbah into a pasture for camels and Ammon into a resting place for sheep. Then you will know that I am the LORD. [6]For this is what the Sovereign LORD says: Because you have clapped your hands and stamped your feet, rejoicing with all the malice of your heart against the land of Israel, [7]therefore I will stretch out my hand against you and give you as plunder to

the nations. I will cut you off from the nations and exterminate you from the countries. I will destroy you, and you will know that I am the LORD.'"

A Prophecy Against Moab

8"This is what the Sovereign LORD says: 'Because Moab and Seir said, "Look, the house of Judah has become like all the other nations," 9therefore I will expose the flank of Moab, beginning at its frontier towns—Beth Jeshimoth, Baal Meon and Kiriathaim—the glory of that land. 10I will give Moab along with the Ammonites to the people of the East as a possession, so that the Ammonites will not be remembered among the nations; 11and I will inflict punishment on Moab. Then they will know that I am the LORD.'"

A Prophecy Against Edom

12"This is what the Sovereign LORD says: 'Because Edom took revenge on the house of Judah and became very guilty by doing so, 13therefore this is what the Sovereign LORD says: I will stretch out my hand against Edom and kill its men and their animals. I will lay it waste, and from Teman to Dedan they will fall by the sword. 14I will take vengeance on Edom by the hand of my people Israel, and they will deal with Edom in accordance with my anger and my wrath; they will know my vengeance, declares the Sovereign LORD.'"

A Prophecy Against Philistia

15"This is what the Sovereign LORD says: 'Because the Philistines acted in vengeance and took revenge with malice in their hearts, and with ancient hostility sought to destroy Judah, 16therefore this is what the Sovereign LORD says: I am about to stretch out my hand against the Philistines, and I will cut off the Kerethites and destroy those remaining along the coast. 17I will carry out great vengeance on them and punish them in my wrath. Then they will know that I am the LORD, when I take vengeance on them.'"

NEW TESTAMENT READING
Hebrews 11:17–40

17By faith Abraham, when God tested him, offered Isaac as a sacrifice. He who had received the promises was about to sacrifice his one and only son, 18even though God had said to him, "It is through Isaac that your offspring will be reckoned." 19Abraham reasoned that God could raise the dead, and figuratively speaking, he did receive Isaac back from death.

20By faith Isaac blessed Jacob and Esau in regard to their future.

21By faith Jacob, when he was dying, blessed each of Joseph's sons, and worshipped as he leaned on the top of his staff.

22By faith Joseph, when his end was near, spoke about the exodus of the Israelites from Egypt and gave instructions about his bones.

23By faith Moses' parents hid him for three months after he was born, because they saw he was no ordinary child, and they were not afraid of the king's edict.

24By faith Moses, when he had grown up, refused to be known as the son of Pharaoh's daughter. 25He chose to be ill-treated along with the people of God rather than to enjoy the pleasures of sin for a short time. 26He regarded disgrace for the sake of Christ as of greater value than the treasures of Egypt, because he was looking ahead to his reward. 27By faith he left Egypt, not fearing the king's anger; he persevered because he saw him who is invisible. 28By faith he kept the Passover and the sprinkling of blood, so that the destroyer of the firstborn would not touch the firstborn of Israel.

29By faith the people passed through the Red Sea as on dry land; but when the Egyptians tried to do so, they were drowned.

30By faith the walls of Jericho fell, after the people had marched around them for seven days.

31By faith the prostitute Rahab, because she welcomed the spies, was not killed with those who were disobedient.

32And what more shall I say? I do not have time to tell about Gideon, Barak, Samson, Jephthah, David, Samuel and the prophets, 33who through faith conquered kingdoms, administered justice, and gained what was promised; who shut the mouths of lions, 34quenched the fury of the flames, and escaped the edge of the sword; whose weakness was turned to strength; and who became powerful in battle and routed foreign armies. 35Women received back their dead, raised to life again. Others were tortured and refused to be released, so that they might gain a better resurrection. 36Some faced jeers and flogging, while still others were chained and put in prison. 37They were stoned; they were sawn in two; they were put to death by the sword. They went about in sheepskins and goatskins, destitute, persecuted and ill-treated—38the world was not worthy of them. They wandered in deserts and mountains, and in caves and holes in the ground.

39These were all commended for their faith, yet none of them received what had been promised. 40God had planned something better for us so that only together with us would they be made perfect.

READING FROM PSALMS
Psalm 124:1–8

A song of ascents. Of David.

1If the LORD had not been on our side—
  let Israel say—
2if the LORD had not been on our side
  when men attacked us,
3when their anger flared against us,
  they would have swallowed us alive;
4the flood would have engulfed us,
  the torrent would have swept over us,
5the raging waters
  would have swept us away.

6Praise be to the LORD,
  who has not let us be torn by their teeth.
7We have escaped like a bird
  out of the fowler's snare;
  the snare has been broken,
  and we have escaped.
8Our help is in the name of the LORD,
  the Maker of heaven and earth.

NOVEMBER 14   DAY 318

OLD TESTAMENT READING
Ezekiel 26:1–27:36

A Prophecy Against Tyre

26 In the eleventh year, on the first day of the month, the word of the LORD came to me: 2"Son of man, because Tyre has said of Jerusalem, 'Aha! The gate to the nations is broken, and its doors have swung open to me; now that she lies in ruins I will prosper,' 3therefore this is what the Sovereign LORD says: I am against you, O Tyre, and I will bring many nations against you, like the sea casting up its waves. 4They will destroy the walls of Tyre and pull down her towers; I will scrape away her rubble and make her a bare rock. 5Out in the sea she will become a place

to spread fishing nets, for I have spoken, declares the Sovereign LORD. She will become plunder for the nations, ⁶and her settlements on the mainland will be ravaged by the sword. Then they will know that I am the LORD.

⁷"For this is what the Sovereign LORD says: From the north I am going to bring against Tyre Nebuchadnezzar king of Babylon, king of kings, with horses and chariots, with horsemen and a great army. ⁸He will ravage your settlements on the mainland with the sword; he will set up siege works against you, build a ramp up to your walls and raise his shields against you. ⁹He will direct the blows of his battering-rams against your walls and demolish your towers with his weapons. ¹⁰His horses will be so many that they will cover you with dust. Your walls will tremble at the noise of the war horses, wagons and chariots when he enters your gates as men enter a city whose walls have been broken through. ¹¹The hoofs of his horses will trample all your streets; he will kill your people with the sword, and your strong pillars will fall to the ground. ¹²They will plunder your wealth and loot your merchandise; they will break down your walls and demolish your fine houses and throw your stones, timber and rubble into the sea. ¹³I will put an end to your noisy songs, and the music of your harps will be heard no more. ¹⁴I will make you a bare rock, and you will become a place to spread fishing nets. You will never be rebuilt, for I the LORD have spoken, declares the Sovereign LORD.

¹⁵"This is what the Sovereign LORD says to Tyre: Will not the coastlands tremble at the sound of your fall, when the wounded groan and the slaughter takes place in you? ¹⁶Then all the princes of the coast will step down from their thrones and lay aside their robes and take off their embroidered garments. Clothed with terror, they will sit on the ground, trembling every moment, appalled at you. ¹⁷Then they will take up a lament concerning you and say to you:

" 'How you are destroyed, O city of
 renown,
 peopled by men of the sea!
You were a power on the seas,
 you and your citizens;
you put your terror
 on all who lived there.
¹⁸Now the coastlands tremble
 on the day of your fall;
the islands in the sea
 are terrified at your collapse.'

¹⁹"This is what the Sovereign LORD says: When I make you a desolate city, like cities no longer inhabited, and when I bring the ocean depths over you and its vast waters cover you, ²⁰then I will bring you down with those who go down to the pit, to the people of long ago. I will make you dwell in the earth below, as in ancient ruins, with those who go down to the pit, and you will not return or take your place in the land of the living. ²¹I will bring you to a horrible end and you will be no more. You will be sought, but you will never again be found, declares the Sovereign LORD."

A Lament for Tyre

27 The word of the LORD came to me: ²"Son of man, take up a lament concerning Tyre. ³Say to Tyre, situated at the gateway to the sea, merchant of peoples on many coasts, 'This is what the Sovereign LORD says:

" 'You say, O Tyre,
 "I am perfect in beauty."
⁴Your domain was on the high seas;
 your builders brought your beauty
 to perfection.
⁵They made all your timbers
 of pine trees from Senir;
they took a cedar from Lebanon
 to make a mast for you.
⁶Of oaks from Bashan
 they made your oars;
of cypress wood from the coasts of
 Cyprus
 they made your deck, inlaid with
 ivory.

⁷Fine embroidered linen from Egypt
    was your sail
    and served as your banner;
    your awnings were of blue and purple
      from the coasts of Elishah.
⁸Men of Sidon and Arvad were your
    oarsmen;
    your skilled men, O Tyre, were
      aboard as your seamen.
⁹Veteran craftsmen of Gebal were on
    board
    as shipwrights to caulk your seams.
All the ships of the sea and their
    sailors
    came alongside to trade for your
      wares.

¹⁰'' Men of Persia, Lydia and Put
    served as soldiers in your army.
They hung their shields and helmets
    on your walls,
    bringing you splendour.
¹¹Men of Arvad and Helech
    manned your walls on every side;
    men of Gammad
    were in your towers.
They hung their shields around your
    walls;
    they brought your beauty to
      perfection.

¹²'' Tarshish did business with you
because of your great wealth of goods;
they exchanged silver, iron, tin and lead
for your merchandise.
¹³'' Greece, Tubal and Meshech
traded with you; they exchanged slaves
and articles of bronze for your wares.
¹⁴'' Men of Beth Togarmah exchanged work horses, war horses and
mules for your merchandise.
¹⁵'' The men of Rhodes traded with
you, and many coastlands were your
customers; they paid you with ivory
tusks and ebony.
¹⁶'' Aram did business with you because of your many products; they
exchanged turquoise, purple fabric,
embroidered work, fine linen, coral
and rubies for your merchandise.
¹⁷'' Judah and Israel traded with you;
they exchanged wheat from Minnith

and confections, honey, oil and balm for
your wares.
¹⁸'' Damascus, because of your many
products and great wealth of goods, did
business with you in wine from Helbon
and wool from Zahar.
¹⁹'' Danites and Greeks from Uzal
bought your merchandise; they exchanged wrought iron, cassia and calamus for your wares.
²⁰'' Dedan traded in saddle blankets
with you.
²¹'' 'Arabia and all the princes of
Kedar were your customers; they did
business with you in lambs, rams and
goats.
²²'' The merchants of Sheba and
Raamah traded with you; for your merchandise they exchanged the finest of all
kinds of spices and precious stones, and
gold.
²³'' Haran, Canneh and Eden and
merchants of Sheba, Asshur and Kil-
mad traded with you. ²⁴In your market-
place they traded with you beautiful
garments, blue fabric, embroidered
work and multicoloured rugs with cords
twisted and tightly knotted.

²⁵'' The ships of Tarshish serve
    as carriers for your wares.
You are filled with heavy cargo
    in the heart of the sea.
²⁶Your oarsmen take you
    out to the high seas.
But the east wind will break you to
    pieces
    in the heart of the sea.
²⁷Your wealth, merchandise and
    wares,
    your mariners, seamen and
      shipwrights,
    your merchants and all your soldiers,
    and everyone else on board
will sink into the heart of the sea
    on the day of your shipwreck.
²⁸The shorelands will quake
    when your seamen cry out.
²⁹All who handle the oars
    will abandon their ships;
    the mariners and all the seamen
    will stand on the shore.

30They will raise their voice
  and cry bitterly over you;
they will sprinkle dust on their heads
    and roll in ashes.
31They will shave their heads because
      of you
  and will put on sackcloth.
They will weep over you with anguish
      of soul
  and with bitter mourning.
32As they wail and mourn over you,
  they will take up a lament
      concerning you:
"Who was ever silenced like Tyre,
  surrounded by the sea?"
33When your merchandise went out on
      the seas,
  you satisfied many nations;
with your great wealth and your
      wares
  you enriched the kings of the earth.
34Now you are shattered by the sea
    in the depths of the waters;
  your wares and all your company
    have gone down with you.
35All who live in the coastlands
    are appalled at you;
  their kings shudder with horror
    and their faces are distorted with
      fear.
36The merchants among the nations
    hiss at you;
  you have come to a horrible end
    and will be no more.'"

NEW TESTAMENT READING
Hebrews 12:1–13

God Disciplines His Sons

12 Therefore, since we are surrounded by such a great cloud of witnesses, let us throw off everything that hinders and the sin that so easily entangles, and let us run with perseverance the race marked out for us. 2Let us fix our eyes on Jesus, the author and perfecter of our faith, who for the joy set before him endured the cross, scorning its shame, and sat down at the right hand of the throne of God. 3Consider him who endured such opposition from sinful men, so that you will not grow weary and lose heart.

4In your struggle against sin, you have not yet resisted to the point of shedding your blood. 5And you have forgotten that word of encouragement that addresses you as sons:

"My son, do not make light of the
    Lord's discipline,
  and do not lose heart when he
    rebukes you,
6because the Lord disciplines those he
    loves,
  and he punishes everyone he
    accepts as a son."

7Endure hardship as discipline; God is treating you as sons. For what son is not disciplined by his father? 8If you are not disciplined (and everyone undergoes discipline), then you are illegitimate children and not true sons. 9Moreover, we have all had human fathers who disciplined us and we respected them for it. How much more should we submit to the Father of our spirits and live! 10Our fathers disciplined us for a little while as they thought best; but God disciplines us for our good, that we may share in his holiness. 11No discipline seems pleasant at the time, but painful. Later on, however, it produces a harvest of righteousness and peace for those who have been trained by it.

12Therefore, strengthen your feeble arms and weak knees! 13"Make level paths for your feet," so that the lame may not be disabled, but rather healed.

READING FROM PSALMS
Psalm 125:1–5

A song of ascents.

1Those who trust in the LORD are like
    Mount Zion,
  which cannot be shaken but
    endures for ever.

²As the mountains surround
    Jerusalem,
so the LORD surrounds his
    people
both now and for evermore.

³The sceptre of the wicked will not
    remain
over the land allotted to the
    righteous,

for then the righteous might use
    their hands to do evil.
⁴Do good, O LORD, to those who are
    good,
to those who are upright in heart.
⁵But those who turn to crooked ways
    the LORD will banish with the
    evildoers.

Peace be upon Israel.

NOVEMBER 15   DAY 319

OLD TESTAMENT READING
Ezekiel 28:1–29:21

A Prophecy Against the King of Tyre

28 The word of the LORD came to
me: ²"Son of man, say to the
ruler of Tyre, 'This is what the
Sovereign LORD says:

"'In the pride of your heart
    you say, "I am a god;
I sit on the throne of a god
    in the heart of the seas."
But you are a man and not a god,
    though you think you are as wise as
    a god.
³Are you wiser than Daniel?
    Is no secret hidden from you?
⁴By your wisdom and understanding
    you have gained wealth for
    yourself
and amassed gold and silver
    in your treasuries.
⁵By your great skill in trading
    you have increased your wealth,
and because of your wealth
    your heart has grown proud.

⁶"'Therefore this is what the
Sovereign LORD says:

"'Because you think you are wise,
    as wise as a god,

⁷I am going to bring foreigners against
    you,
the most ruthless of nations;
they will draw their swords against
    your beauty and wisdom
and pierce your shining splendour.
⁸They will bring you down to the pit,
    and you will die a violent death
    in the heart of the seas.
⁹Will you then say, "I am a god,"
    in the presence of those who kill
    you?
You will be but a man, not a god,
    in the hands of those who slay you.
¹⁰You will die the death of the
    uncircumcised
    at the hands of foreigners.

I have spoken, declares the Sovereign
LORD.'"

¹¹The word of the LORD came to me:
¹²"Son of man, take up a lament concerning the king of Tyre and say to him:
'This is what the Sovereign LORD says:

"'You were the model of perfection,
    full of wisdom and perfect in
    beauty.
¹³You were in Eden,
    the garden of God;
every precious stone adorned you:
    ruby, topaz and emerald,
    chrysolite, onyx and jasper,
    sapphire, turquoise and beryl.

Your settings and mountings were
    made of gold;
  on the day you were created they
    were prepared.
14You were anointed as a guardian
    cherub,
  for so I ordained you.
You were on the holy mount of God;
  you walked among the fiery stones.
15You were blameless in your ways
  from the day you were created
  till wickedness was found in you.
16Through your widespread trade
  you were filled with violence,
  and you sinned.
So I drove you in disgrace from the
    mount of God,
  and I expelled you, O guardian
    cherub,
  from among the fiery stones.
17Your heart became proud
  on account of your beauty,
  and you corrupted your wisdom
    because of your splendour.
So I threw you to the earth;
  I made a spectacle of you before
    kings.
18By your many sins and dishonest
    trade
  you have desecrated your
    sanctuaries.
So I made a fire come out from you,
  and it consumed you,
and I reduced you to ashes on the
    ground
  in the sight of all who were
    watching.
19All the nations who knew you
  are appalled at you;
  you have come to a horrible end
  and will be no more.'"

A Prophecy Against Sidon

20The word of the LORD came to me:
21"Son of man, set your face against
Sidon; prophesy against her 22and say:
'This is what the Sovereign LORD says:

  "'I am against you, O Sidon,
    and I will gain glory within you.
  They will know that I am the LORD,

when I inflict punishment on her
  and show myself holy within her.
23I will send a plague upon her
  and make blood flow in her streets.
The slain will fall within her,
  with the sword against her on every
    side.
Then they will know that I am the
    LORD.

24"'No longer will the people of
Israel have malicious neighbours who
are painful briers and sharp thorns.
Then they will know that I am the
Sovereign LORD.

25"'This is what the Sovereign LORD
says: When I gather the people of Israel
from the nations where they have been
scattered, I will show myself holy
among them in the sight of the nations.
Then they will live in their own land,
which I gave to my servant Jacob.
26They will live there in safety and will
build houses and plant vineyards; they
will live in safety when I inflict punishment on all their neighbours who
maligned them. Then they will know
that I am the LORD their God.'"

A Prophecy Against Egypt

29 In the tenth year, in the tenth
month on the twelfth day, the
word of the LORD came to me: 2"Son of
man, set your face against Pharaoh king
of Egypt and prophesy against him and
against all Egypt. 3Speak to him and
say: 'This is what the Sovereign LORD
says:

  "'I am against you, Pharaoh king of
    Egypt,
  you great monster lying among
    your streams.
You say, "The Nile is mine;
  I made it for myself."
4But I will put hooks in your jaws
  and make the fish of your streams
    stick to your scales.
I will pull you out from among your
    streams,
  with all the fish sticking to your
    scales.

5I will leave you in the desert,
    you and all the fish of your
        streams.
You will fall on the open field
    and not be gathered or picked up.
I will give you as food
    to the beasts of the earth and the
        birds of the air.

6Then all who live in Egypt will know
that I am the LORD.

"'You have been a staff of reed for
the house of Israel. 7When they grasped
you with their hands, you splintered and
you tore open their shoulders; when
they leaned on you, you broke and their
backs were wrenched.

8"'Therefore this is what the
Sovereign LORD says: I will bring a
sword against you and kill your men
and their animals. 9Egypt will become
a desolate wasteland. Then they will
know that I am the LORD.

"'Because you said, "The Nile is
mine; I made it," 10therefore I am
against you and against your streams,
and I will make the land of Egypt a ruin
and a desolate waste from Migdol to
Aswan, as far as the border of Cush.
11No foot of man or animal will pass
through it; no-one will live there for
forty years. 12I will make the land of
Egypt desolate among devastated
lands, and her cities will lie desolate for
forty years among ruined cities. And I
will disperse the Egyptians among the
nations and scatter them through the
countries.

13"'Yet this is what the Sovereign
LORD says: At the end of forty years I
will gather the Egyptians from the nations where they were scattered. 14I will
bring them back from captivity and return them to Upper Egypt, the land of
their ancestry. There they will be a
lowly kingdom. 15It will be the lowliest
of kingdoms and will never again exalt
itself above the other nations. I will
make it so weak that it will never again
rule over the nations. 16Egypt will no
longer be a source of confidence for the

people of Israel but will be a reminder
of their sin in turning to her for help.
Then they will know that I am the
Sovereign LORD.'"

17In the twenty-seventh year, in the
first month on the first day, the word of
the LORD came to me. 18"Son of man,
Nebuchadnezzar king of Babylon drove
his army in a hard campaign against
Tyre; every head was rubbed bare and
every shoulder made raw. Yet he and
his army got no reward from the campaign he led against Tyre. 19Therefore
this is what the Sovereign LORD says: I
am going to give Egypt to Nebuchadnezzar king of Babylon, and he will
carry off its wealth. He will loot and
plunder the land as pay for his army. 20I
have given him Egypt as a reward for his
efforts because he and his army did it for
me, declares the Sovereign LORD.
21"On that day I will make a horn
grow for the house of Israel, and I will
open your mouth among them. Then
they will know that I am the LORD."

NEW TESTAMENT READING
Hebrews 12:14–29

Warning Against Refusing God

14Make every effort to live in peace
with all men and to be holy; without
holiness no-one will see the Lord. 15See
to it that no-one misses the grace of God
and that no bitter root grows up to cause
trouble and defile many. 16See that no-
one is sexually immoral, or is godless
like Esau, who for a single meal sold his
inheritance rights as the oldest son.
17Afterwards, as you know, when he
wanted to inherit this blessing, he was
rejected. He could bring about no
change of mind, though he sought the
blessing with tears.

18You have not come to a mountain
that can be touched and that is burning
with fire; to darkness, gloom and storm;
19to a trumpet blast or to such a voice
speaking words that those who heard it

begged that no further word be spoken to them, [20]because they could not bear what was commanded: "If even an animal touches the mountain, it must be stoned." [21]The sight was so terrifying that Moses said, "I am trembling with fear."

[22]But you have come to Mount Zion, to the heavenly Jerusalem, the city of the living God. You have come to thousands upon thousands of angels in joyful assembly, [23]to the church of the firstborn, whose names are written in heaven. You have come to God, the judge of all men, to the spirits of righteous men made perfect, [24]to Jesus the mediator of a new covenant, and to the sprinkled blood that speaks a better word than the blood of Abel.

[25]See to it that you do not refuse him who speaks. If they did not escape when they refused him who warned them on earth, how much less will we, if we turn away from him who warns us from heaven? [26]At that time his voice shook the earth, but now he has promised, "Once more I will shake not only the earth but also the heavens." [27]The words "once more" indicate the removing of what can be shaken—that is, created things—so that what cannot be shaken may remain.

[28]Therefore, since we are receiving a kingdom that cannot be shaken, let us be thankful, and so worship God acceptably with reverence and awe, [29]for our "God is a consuming fire."

READING FROM PSALMS
Psalm 126:1–6

A song of ascents.

[1]When the LORD brought back the
    captives to Zion,
  we were like men who dreamed.
[2]Our mouths were filled with laughter,
    our tongues with songs of joy.
  Then it was said among the nations,
    "The LORD has done great things
      for them."
[3]The LORD has done great things for
    us,
  and we are filled with joy.

[4]Restore our fortunes, O LORD,
    like streams in the Negev.
[5]Those who sow in tears
    will reap with songs of joy.
[6]He who goes out weeping,
    carrying seed to sow,
  will return with songs of joy,
    carrying sheaves with him.

NOVEMBER 16

OLD TESTAMENT READING
Ezekiel 30:1–31:18

A Lament for Egypt

30 The word of the LORD came to me: [2]"Son of man, prophesy and say: 'This is what the Sovereign LORD says:

  "'Wail and say,
    "Alas for that day!"

[3]For the day is near,
    the day of the LORD is near—
  a day of clouds,
    a time of doom for the nations.
[4]A sword will come against Egypt,
    and anguish will come upon Cush.
  When the slain fall in Egypt,
    her wealth will be carried away
    and her foundations torn down.

[5]Cush and Put, Lydia and all Arabia,
  Libya and the people of the covenant

land will fall by the sword along with Egypt.

6"This is what the LORD says:

"'The allies of Egypt will fall
and her proud strength will fail.
From Migdol to Aswan
they will fall by the sword within
her,
declares the Sovereign LORD.
7"'They will be desolate
among desolate lands,
and their cities will lie
among ruined cities.
8Then they will know that I am the
LORD,
when I set fire to Egypt
and all her helpers are crushed.

9"'On that day messengers will go out from me in ships to frighten Cush out of her complacency. Anguish will take hold of them on the day of Egypt's doom, for it is sure to come.

10"'This is what the Sovereign LORD says:

"'I will put an end to the hordes of
Egypt
by the hand of Nebuchadnezzar
king of Babylon.
11He and his army—the most ruthless
of nations—
will be brought in to destroy the
land.
They will draw their swords against
Egypt
and fill the land with the slain.
12I will dry up the streams of the Nile
and sell the land to evil men;
by the hand of foreigners
I will lay waste the land and
everything in it.

I the LORD have spoken.

13"'This is what the Sovereign LORD says:

"'I will destroy the idols
and put an end to the images in
Memphis.

No longer will there be a prince in
Egypt,
and I will spread fear throughout
the land.
14I will lay waste Upper Egypt,
set fire to Zoan
and inflict punishment on Thebes.
15I will pour out my wrath on Pelusium,
the stronghold of Egypt,
and cut off the hordes of Thebes.
16I will set fire to Egypt;
Pelusium will writhe in agony.
Thebes will be taken by storm;
Memphis will be in constant
distress.
17The young men of Heliopolis and
Bubastis
will fall by the sword,
and the cities themselves will go
into captivity.
18Dark will be the day at Tahpanhes
when I break the yoke of Egypt;
there her proud strength will come
to an end.
She will be covered with clouds,
and her villages will go into
captivity.
19So I will inflict punishment on Egypt,
and they will know that I am the
LORD.'"

20In the eleventh year, in the first month on the seventh day, the word of the LORD came to me: 21"Son of man, I have broken the arm of Pharaoh king of Egypt. It has not been bound up for healing or put in a splint so as to become strong enough to hold a sword. 22Therefore this is what the Sovereign LORD says: I am against Pharaoh king of Egypt. I will break both his arms, the good arm as well as the broken one, and make the sword fall from his hand. 23I will disperse the Egyptians among the nations and scatter them through the countries. 24I will strengthen the arms of the king of Babylon and put my sword in his hand, but I will break the arms of Pharaoh, and he will groan before him like a mortally wounded man. 25I will strengthen the arms of the king of Babylon, but the arms of Pharaoh will fall limp. Then they will know that I am the LORD, when I put my sword into the hand of the king of Babylon and he brandishes it against Egypt. ²⁶I will disperse the Egyptians among the nations and scatter them through the countries. Then they will know that I am the LORD."

A Cedar in Lebanon

31 In the eleventh year, in the third month on the first day, the word of the LORD came to me: ²"Son of man, say to Pharaoh king of Egypt and to his hordes:

"'Who can be compared with you in
    majesty?
³Consider Assyria, once a cedar in
    Lebanon,
  with beautiful branches
    overshadowing the forest;
it towered on high,
  its top above the thick foliage.
⁴The waters nourished it,
  deep springs made it grow tall;
their streams flowed
  all around its base
and sent their channels
  to all the trees of the field.
⁵So it towered higher
  than all the trees of the field;
its boughs increased
  and its branches grew long,
    spreading because of abundant
      waters.
⁶All the birds of the air
  nested in its boughs,
all the beasts of the field
  gave birth under its branches;
all the great nations
  lived in its shade.
⁷It was majestic in beauty,
  with its spreading boughs,
for its roots went down
  to abundant waters.
⁸The cedars in the garden of God
  could not rival it,
nor could the pine trees
  equal its boughs,
nor could the plane trees
  compare with its branches—

no tree in the garden of God
  could match its beauty.
⁹I made it beautiful
  with abundant branches,
the envy of all the trees of Eden
  in the garden of God.

¹⁰"'Therefore this is what the Sovereign LORD says: Because it towered on high, lifting its top above the thick foliage, and because it was proud of its height, ¹¹I handed it over to the ruler of the nations, for him to deal with according to its wickedness. I cast it aside, ¹²and the most ruthless of foreign nations cut it down and left it. Its boughs fell on the mountains and in all the valleys; its branches lay broken in all the ravines of the land. All the nations of the earth came out from under its shade and left it. ¹³All the birds of the air settled on the fallen tree, and all the beasts of the field were among its branches. ¹⁴Therefore no other trees by the waters are ever to tower proudly on high, lifting their tops above the thick foliage. No other trees so well-watered are ever to reach such a height; they are all destined for death, for the earth below, among mortal men, with those who go down to the pit.

¹⁵"'This is what the Sovereign LORD says: On the day it was brought down to the grave I covered the deep springs with mourning for it; I held back its streams, and its abundant waters were restrained. Because of it I clothed Lebanon with gloom, and all the trees of the field withered away. ¹⁶I made the nations tremble at the sound of its fall when I brought it down to the grave with those who go down to the pit. Then all the trees of Eden, the choicest and best of Lebanon, all the trees that were well-watered, were consoled in the earth below. ¹⁷Those who lived in its shade, its allies among the nations, had also gone down to the grave with it, joining those killed by the sword.

¹⁸"'Which of the trees of Eden can be compared with you in splendour and majesty? Yet you, too, will be brought

down with the trees of Eden to the earth below; you will lie among the uncircumcised, with those killed by the sword.

" 'This is Pharaoh and all his hordes, declares the Sovereign LORD.' "

NEW TESTAMENT READING
Hebrews 13:1–25

Concluding Exhortations

13 Keep on loving each other as brothers. ²Do not forget to entertain strangers, for by so doing some people have entertained angels without knowing it. ³Remember those in prison as if you were their fellow-prisoners, and those who are ill-treated as if you yourselves were suffering.

⁴Marriage should be honoured by all, and the marriage bed kept pure, for God will judge the adulterer and all the sexually immoral. ⁵Keep your lives free from the love of money and be content with what you have, because God has said,

"Never will I leave you;
    never will I forsake you."

⁶So we say with confidence,

"The Lord is my helper; I will not be afraid.
    What can man do to me?"

⁷Remember your leaders, who spoke the word of God to you. Consider the outcome of their way of life and imitate their faith. ⁸Jesus Christ is the same yesterday and today and for ever. ⁹Do not be carried away by all kinds of strange teachings. It is good for our hearts to be strengthened by grace, not by ceremonial foods, which are of no value to those who eat them. ¹⁰We have an altar from which those who minister at the tabernacle have no right to eat. ¹¹The high priest carries the blood of animals into the Most Holy Place as a sin offering, but the bodies are burned outside the camp. ¹²And so Jesus also

suffered outside the city gate to make the people holy through his own blood. ¹³Let us, then, go to him outside the camp, bearing the disgrace he bore. ¹⁴For here we do not have an enduring city, but we are looking for the city that is to come.

¹⁵Through Jesus, therefore, let us continually offer to God a sacrifice of praise—the fruit of lips that confess his name. ¹⁶And do not forget to do good and to share with others, for with such sacrifices God is pleased.

¹⁷Obey your leaders and submit to their authority. They keep watch over you as men who must give an account. Obey them so that their work will be a joy, not a burden, for that would be of no advantage to you.

¹⁸Pray for us. We are sure that we have a clear conscience and desire to live honourably in every way. ¹⁹I particularly urge you to pray so that I may be restored to you soon.

²⁰May the God of peace, who through the blood of the eternal covenant brought back from the dead our Lord Jesus, that great Shepherd of the sheep, ²¹equip you with everything good for doing his will, and may he work in us what is pleasing to him, through Jesus Christ, to whom be glory for ever and ever. Amen.

²²Brothers, I urge you to bear with my word of exhortation, for I have written you only a short letter.

²³I want you to know that our brother Timothy has been released. If he arrives soon, I will come with him to see you.

²⁴Greet all your leaders and all God's people. Those from Italy send you their greetings.

²⁵Grace be with you all.

READING FROM PROVERBS
Proverbs 27:23–28:6

²³Be sure you know the condition of
    your flocks,
        give careful attention to your
            herds;

²⁴for riches do not endure for ever,
>   and a crown is not secure for all
>   generations.
²⁵When the hay is removed and new
>   growth appears
>   and the grass from the hills is
>   gathered in,
²⁶the lambs will provide you with
>   clothing,
>   and the goats with the price of a
>   field.
²⁷You will have plenty of goats' milk
>   to feed you and your family
>   and to nourish your servant girls.

28 The wicked man flees
>   though no-one pursues,
>   but the righteous are as bold as a
>   lion.

²When a country is rebellious, it has
>   many rulers,

but a man of understanding and
>   knowledge maintains order.

³A ruler who oppresses the poor
>   is like a driving rain that leaves no
>   crops.

⁴Those who forsake the law praise the
>   wicked,
>   but those who keep the law resist
>   them.

⁵Evil men do not understand justice,
>   but those who seek the LORD
>   understand it fully.

⁶Better a poor man whose walk is
>   blameless
>   than a rich man whose ways are
>   perverse.

DAY 321

NOVEMBER 17

OLD TESTAMENT READING
Ezekiel 32:1–33:20

A Lament for Pharaoh

32 In the twelfth year, in the
twelfth month on the first day,
the word of the LORD came to me:
²"Son of man, take up a lament concerning Pharaoh king of Egypt and say
to him:

"'You are like a lion among the
>   nations;
>   you are like a monster in the seas
>   thrashing about in your streams,
>   churning the water with your feet
>   and muddying the streams.

³"'This is what the Sovereign LORD
says:

"'With a great throng of people
>   I will cast my net over you,

and they will haul you up in my
>   net.
⁴I will throw you on the land
>   and hurl you on the open field.
I will let all the birds of the air settle
>   on you
>   and all the beasts of the earth
>   gorge themselves on you.
⁵I will spread your flesh on the
>   mountains
>   and fill the valleys with your
>   remains.
⁶I will drench the land with your
>   flowing blood
>   all the way to the mountains,
>   and the ravines will be filled with
>   your flesh.
⁷When I snuff you out, I will cover the
>   heavens
>   and darken their stars;
I will cover the sun with a cloud,
>   and the moon will not give its light.

8All the shining lights in the heavens
    I will darken over you;
    I will bring darkness over your land,
        declares the Sovereign LORD.
9I will trouble the hearts of many
      peoples
    when I bring about your
      destruction among the nations,
    among lands you have not known.
10I will cause many peoples to be
      appalled at you,
    and their kings will shudder with
      horror because of you
    when I brandish my sword before
      them.
On the day of your downfall
    each of them will tremble
    every moment for his life.

11"'For this is what the Sovereign
LORD says:

"'The sword of the king of Babylon
    will come against you.
12I will cause your hordes to fall
    by the swords of mighty men—
      the most ruthless of all nations.
They will shatter the pride of Egypt,
    and all her hordes will be
      overthrown.
13I will destroy all her cattle
    from beside abundant waters
    no longer to be stirred by the foot of
      man
    or muddied by the hoofs of cattle.
14Then I will let her waters settle
    and make her streams flow like oil,
      declares the Sovereign LORD.
15When I make Egypt desolate
    and strip the land of everything in
      it,
    when I strike down all who live there,
    then they will know that I am the
      LORD.'

16"This is the lament they will chant
for her. The daughters of the nations
will chant it; for Egypt and all her
hordes they will chant it, declares the
Sovereign LORD."

17In the twelfth year, on the fifteenth
day of the month, the word of the LORD
came to me: 18"Son of man, wail for the
hordes of Egypt and consign to the
earth below both her and the daughters
of mighty nations, with those who go
down to the pit. 19Say to them, 'Are you
more favoured than others? Go down
and be laid among the uncircumcised.'
20They will fall among those killed by
the sword. The sword is drawn; let her
be dragged off with all her hordes.
21From within the grave the mighty
leaders will say of Egypt and her allies,
'They have come down and they lie with
the uncircumcised, with those killed by
the sword.'

22"Assyria is there with her whole
army; she is surrounded by the graves of
all her slain, all who have fallen by the
sword. 23Their graves are in the depths
of the pit and her army lies around her
grave. All who had spread terror in the
land of the living are slain, fallen by the
sword.

24"Elam is there, with all her hordes
around her grave. All of them are slain,
fallen by the sword. All who had spread
terror in the land of the living went
down uncircumcised to the earth below.
They bear their shame with those who
go down to the pit. 25A bed is made for
her among the slain, with all her hordes
around her grave. All of them are uncircumcised, killed by the sword. Because
their terror had spread in the land of the
living, they bear their shame with those
who go down to the pit; they are laid
among the slain.

26"Meshech and Tubal are there,
with all their hordes around their
graves. All of them are uncircumcised,
killed by the sword because they spread
their terror in the land of the living.
27Do they not lie with the other uncircumcised warriors who have fallen, who
went down to the grave with their
weapons of war, whose swords were
placed under their heads? The punishment for their sins rested on their
bones, though the terror of these warriors had stalked through the land of the
living.

28"You too, O Pharaoh, will be

broken and will lie among the uncircumcised, with those killed by the sword.

²⁹"Edom is there, her kings and all her princes; despite their power, they are laid with those killed by the sword. They lie with the uncircumcised, with those who go down to the pit.

³⁰"All the princes of the north and all the Sidonians are there; they went down with the slain in disgrace despite the terror caused by their power. They lie uncircumcised with those killed by the sword and bear their shame with those who go down to the pit.

³¹"Pharaoh—he and all his army—will see them and he will be consoled for all his hordes that were killed by the sword, declares the Sovereign Lord. ³²Although I had him spread terror in the land of the living, Pharaoh and all his hordes will be laid among the uncircumcised, with those killed by the sword, declares the Sovereign Lord."

Ezekiel a Watchman

33 The word of the Lord came to me: ²"Son of man, speak to your countrymen and say to them: 'When I bring the sword against a land, and the people of the land choose one of their men and make him their watchman, ³and he sees the sword coming against the land and blows the trumpet to warn the people, ⁴then if anyone hears the trumpet but does not take warning and the sword comes and takes his life, his blood will be on his own head. ⁵Since he heard the sound of the trumpet but did not take warning, his blood will be on his own head. If he had taken warning, he would have saved himself. ⁶But if the watchman sees the sword coming and does not blow the trumpet to warn the people and the sword comes and takes the life of one of them, that man will be taken away because of his sin, but I will hold the watchman accountable for his blood.'

⁷"Son of man, I have made you a watchman for the house of Israel; so hear the word I speak and give them warning from me. ⁸When I say to the wicked, 'O wicked man, you will surely die,' and you do not speak out to dissuade him from his ways, that wicked man will die for his sin, and I will hold you accountable for his blood. ⁹But if you do warn the wicked man to turn from his ways and he does not do so, he will die for his sin, but you will be saved yourself.

¹⁰"Son of man, say to the house of Israel, 'This is what you are saying: "Our offences and sins weigh us down, and we are wasting away because of them. How then can we live?"' ¹¹Say to them, 'As surely as I live, declares the Sovereign Lord, I take no pleasure in the death of the wicked, but rather that they turn from their ways and live. Turn! Turn from your evil ways! Why will you die, O house of Israel?'

¹²"Therefore, son of man, say to your countrymen, 'The righteousness of the righteous man will not save him when he disobeys, and the wickedness of the wicked man will not cause him to fall when he turns from it. The righteous man, if he sins, will not be allowed to live because of his former righteousness.' ¹³If I tell the righteous man that he will surely live, but then he trusts in his righteousness and does evil, none of the righteous things he has done will be remembered; he will die for the evil he has done. ¹⁴And if I say to the wicked man, 'You will surely die,' but he then turns away from his sin and does what is just and right—¹⁵if he gives back what he took in pledge for a loan, returns what he has stolen, follows the decrees that give life, and does no evil, he will surely live; he will not die. ¹⁶None of the sins he has committed will be remembered against him. He has done what is just and right; he will surely live.

¹⁷"Yet your countrymen say, 'The way of the Lord is not just.' But it is their way that is not just. ¹⁸If a righteous man turns from his righteousness and does evil, he will die for it. ¹⁹And if a

wicked man turns away from his wickedness and does what is just and right, he will live by doing so. [20]Yet, O house of Israel, you say, 'The way of the Lord is not just.' But I will judge each of you according to his own ways."

NEW TESTAMENT READING
James 1:1–27

1 James, a servant of God and of the Lord Jesus Christ,

To the twelve tribes scattered among the nations:

Greetings.

Trials and Temptations

[2]Consider it pure joy, my brothers, whenever you face trials of many kinds, [3]because you know that the testing of your faith develops perseverance. [4]Perseverance must finish its work so that you may be mature and complete, not lacking anything. [5]If any of you lacks wisdom, he should ask God, who gives generously to all without finding fault, and it will be given to him. [6]But when he asks, he must believe and not doubt, because he who doubts is like a wave of the sea, blown and tossed by the wind. [7]That man should not think he will receive anything from the Lord; [8]he is a double-minded man, unstable in all he does.

[9]The brother in humble circumstances ought to take pride in his high position. [10]But the one who is rich should take pride in his low position, because he will pass away like a wild flower. [11]For the sun rises with scorching heat and withers the plant; its blossom falls and its beauty is destroyed. In the same way, the rich man will fade away even while he goes about his business.

[12]Blessed is the man who perseveres under trial, because when he has stood the test, he will receive the crown of life that God has promised to those who love him.

[13]When tempted, no-one should say, "God is tempting me." For God cannot be tempted by evil, nor does he tempt anyone; [14]but each one is tempted when, by his own evil desire, he is dragged away and enticed. [15]Then, after desire has conceived, it gives birth to sin; and sin, when it is full-grown, gives birth to death.

[16]Don't be deceived, my dear brothers. [17]Every good and perfect gift is from above, coming down from the Father of the heavenly lights, who does not change like shifting shadows. [18]He chose to give us birth through the word of truth, that we might be a kind of firstfruits of all he created.

Listening and Doing

[19]My dear brothers, take note of this: Everyone should be quick to listen, slow to speak and slow to become angry, [20]for man's anger does not bring about the righteous life that God desires. [21]Therefore, get rid of all moral filth and the evil that is so prevalent, and humbly accept the word planted in you, which can save you.

[22]Do not merely listen to the word, and so deceive yourselves. Do what it says. [23]Anyone who listens to the word but does not do what it says is like a man who looks at his face in a mirror [24]and, after looking at himself, goes away and immediately forgets what he looks like. [25]But the man who looks intently into the perfect law that gives freedom, and continues to do this, not forgetting what he has heard, but doing it—he will be blessed in what he does.

[26]If anyone considers himself religious and yet does not keep a tight rein on his tongue, he deceives himself and his religion is worthless. [27]Religion that God our Father accepts as pure and faultless is this: to look after orphans and widows in their distress and to keep oneself from being polluted by the world.

READING FROM PSALMS
Psalm 127:1–5

A song of ascents. Of Solomon.

¹Unless the LORD builds the house,
its builders labour in vain.
Unless the LORD watches over the
city,
the watchmen stand guard in vain.
²In vain you rise early
and stay up late,
toiling for food to eat—

for he grants sleep to those he
loves.

³Sons are a heritage from the LORD,
children a reward from him.
⁴Like arrows in the hands of a warrior
are sons born in one's youth.
⁵Blessed is the man
whose quiver is full of them.
They will not be put to shame
when they contend with their
enemies in the gate.

NOVEMBER 18

OLD TESTAMENT READING
Ezekiel 33:21–35:15

Jerusalem's Fall Explained

²¹In the twelfth year of our exile, in
the tenth month on the fifth day, a man
who had escaped from Jerusalem came
to me and said, "The city has fallen!"
²²Now the evening before the man arrived, the hand of the LORD was upon
me, and he opened my mouth before
the man came to me in the morning. So
my mouth was opened and I was no
longer silent.

²³Then the word of the LORD came to
me: ²⁴"Son of man, the people living in
those ruins in the land of Israel are
saying, 'Abraham was only one man,
yet he possessed the land. But we are
many; surely the land has been given to
us as our possession.' ²⁵Therefore say to
them, 'This is what the Sovereign LORD
says: Since you eat meat with the blood
still in it and look to your idols and shed
blood, should you then possess the
land? ²⁶You rely on your sword, you do
detestable things, and each of you defiles his neighbour's wife. Should you
then possess the land?'

²⁷"Say this to them: 'This is what the
Sovereign LORD says: As surely as I

live, those who are left in the ruins will
fall by the sword, those out in the country I will give to the wild animals to be
devoured, and those in strongholds and
caves will die of a plague. ²⁸I will make
the land a desolate waste, and her proud
strength will come to an end, and the
mountains of Israel will become desolate so that no-one will cross them.
²⁹Then they will know that I am the
LORD, when I have made the land a
desolate waste because of all the detestable things they have done.'

³⁰"As for you, son of man, your countrymen are talking together about you
by the walls and at the doors of the
houses, saying to each other, 'Come
and hear the message that has come
from the LORD.' ³¹My people come to
you, as they usually do, and sit before
you to listen to your words, but they do
not put them into practice. With their
mouths they express devotion, but their
hearts are greedy for unjust gain.
³²Indeed, to them you are nothing more
than one who sings love songs with a
beautiful voice and plays an instrument
well, for they hear your words but do
not put them into practice.

³³"When all this comes true—and it
surely will—then they will know that a
prophet has been among them."

Shepherds and Sheep

34 The word of the LORD came to me: 2"Son of man, prophesy against the shepherds of Israel; prophesy and say to them: 'This is what the Sovereign LORD says: Woe to the shepherds of Israel who only take care of themselves! Should not shepherds take care of the flock? 3You eat the curds, clothe yourselves with the wool and slaughter the choice animals, but you do not take care of the flock. 4You have not strengthened the weak or healed the sick or bound up the injured. You have not brought back the strays or searched for the lost. You have ruled them harshly and brutally. 5So they were scattered because there was no shepherd, and when they were scattered they became food for all the wild animals. 6My sheep wandered over all the mountains and on every high hill. They were scattered over the whole earth, and no-one searched or looked for them.

7"'Therefore, you shepherds, hear the word of the LORD: 8As surely as I live, declares the Sovereign LORD, because my flock lacks a shepherd and so has been plundered and has become food for all the wild animals, and because my shepherds did not search for my flock but cared for themselves rather than for my flock, 9therefore, O shepherds, hear the word of the LORD: 10This is what the Sovereign LORD says: I am against the shepherds and will hold them accountable for my flock. I will remove them from tending the flock so that the shepherds can no longer feed themselves. I will rescue my flock from their mouths, and it will no longer be food for them.

11"'For this is what the Sovereign LORD says: I myself will search for my sheep and look after them. 12As a shepherd looks after his scattered flock when he is with them, so will I look after my sheep. I will rescue them from all the places where they were scattered on a day of clouds and darkness. 13I will

bring them out from the nations and gather them from the countries, and I will bring them into their own land. I will pasture them on the mountains of Israel, in the ravines and in all the settlements in the land. 14I will tend them in a good pasture, and the mountain heights of Israel will be their grazing land. There they will lie down in good grazing land, and there they will feed in a rich pasture on the mountains of Israel. 15I myself will tend my sheep and make them lie down, declares the Sovereign LORD. 16I will search for the lost and bring back the strays. I will bind up the injured and strengthen the weak, but the sleek and the strong I will destroy. I will shepherd the flock with justice.

17"'As for you, my flock, this is what the Sovereign LORD says: I will judge between one sheep and another, and between rams and goats. 18Is it not enough for you to feed on the good pasture? Must you also trample the rest of your pasture with your feet? Is it not enough for you to drink clear water? Must you also muddy the rest with your feet? 19Must my flock feed on what you have trampled and drink what you have muddied with your feet?

20"'Therefore this is what the Sovereign LORD says to them: See, I myself will judge between the fat sheep and the lean sheep. 21Because you shove with flank and shoulder, butting all the weak sheep with your horns until you have driven them away, 22I will save my flock, and they will no longer be plundered. I will judge between one sheep and another. 23I will place over them one shepherd, my servant David, and he will tend them; he will tend them and be their shepherd. 24I the LORD will be their God, and my servant David will be prince among them. I the LORD have spoken.

25"'I will make a covenant of peace with them and rid the land of wild beasts so that they may live in the desert and sleep in the forests in safety. 26I will bless them and the places surrounding my hill. I will send down showers in season; there will be showers of blessing. 27The trees of the field will yield their fruit and the ground will yield its crops; the people will be secure in their land. They will know that I am the LORD, when I break the bars of their yoke and rescue them from the hands of those who enslaved them. 28They will no longer be plundered by the nations, nor will wild animals devour them. They will live in safety, and no-one will make them afraid. 29I will provide for them a land renowned for its crops, and they will no longer be victims of famine in the land or bear the scorn of the nations. 30Then they will know that I, the LORD their God, am with them and that they, the house of Israel, are my people, declares the Sovereign LORD. 31You my sheep, the sheep of my pasture, are people, and I am your God, declares the Sovereign LORD.'"

A Prophecy Against Edom

35 The word of the LORD came to me: 2"Son of man, set your face against Mount Seir; prophesy against it 3and say: 'This is what the Sovereign LORD says: I am against you, Mount Seir, and I will stretch out my hand against you and make you a desolate waste. 4I will turn your towns into ruins and you will be desolate. Then you will know that I am the LORD.

5"'Because you harboured an ancient hostility and delivered the Israelites over to the sword at the time of their calamity, the time their punishment reached its climax, 6therefore as surely as I live, declares the Sovereign LORD, I will give you over to bloodshed and it will pursue you. Since you did not hate bloodshed, bloodshed will pursue you. 7I will make Mount Seir a desolate waste and cut off from it all who come and go. 8I will fill your mountains with the slain; those killed by the sword will fall on your hills and in your valleys and in all your ravines. 9I will make you desolate for ever; your towns will not be inhabited. Then you will know that I am the LORD.

10"'Because you have said, "These two nations and countries will be ours and we will take possession of them," even though I the LORD was there, 11therefore as surely as I live, declares the Sovereign LORD, I will treat you in accordance with the anger and jealousy you showed in your hatred of them and I will make myself known among them when I judge you. 12Then you will know that I the LORD have heard all the contemptible things you have said against the mountains of Israel. You said, "They have been laid waste and have been given over to us to devour." 13You boasted against me and spoke against me without restraint, and I heard it. 14This is what the Sovereign LORD says: While the whole earth rejoices, I will make you desolate. 15Because you rejoiced when the inheritance of the house of Israel became desolate, that is how I will treat you. You will be desolate, O Mount Seir, you and all of Edom. Then they will know that I am the LORD.'"

NEW TESTAMENT READING
James 2:1–26

Favouritism Forbidden

2 My brothers, as believers in our glorious Lord Jesus Christ, don't show favouritism. 2Suppose a man comes into your meeting wearing a gold ring and fine clothes, and a poor man in shabby clothes also comes in. 3If you show special attention to the man wearing fine clothes and say, "Here's a good seat for you," but say to the poor man, "You stand there" or "Sit on the floor by my feet," 4have you not discriminated among yourselves and become judges with evil thoughts?

5Listen, my dear brothers: Has not God chosen those who are poor in the eyes of the world to be rich in faith and to inherit the kingdom he promised those who love him? 6But you have insulted the poor. Is it not the rich who are exploiting you? Are they not the ones who are dragging you into court? 7Are they not the ones who are slandering the noble name of him to whom you belong?

8If you really keep the royal law found in Scripture, "Love your neighbour as yourself," you are doing right. 9But if you show favouritism, you sin and are convicted by the law as law-breakers. 10For whoever keeps the whole law and yet stumbles at just one point is guilty of breaking all of it. 11For he who said, "Do not commit adultery," also said, "Do not murder." If you do not commit adultery but do commit murder, you have become a law-breaker.

12Speak and act as those who are going to be judged by the law that gives freedom, 13because judgment without mercy will be shown to anyone who has not been merciful. Mercy triumphs over judgment!

Faith and Deeds

14What good is it, my brothers, if a man claims to have faith but has no deeds? Can such faith save him? 15Suppose a brother or sister is without clothes and daily food. 16If one of you says to him, "Go, I wish you well; keep warm and well fed," but does nothing about his physical needs, what good is it? 17In the same way, faith by itself, if it is not accompanied by action, is dead.

18But someone will say, "You have faith; I have deeds."

Show me your faith without deeds, and I will show you my faith by what I do. 19You believe that there is one God. Good! Even the demons believe that —and shudder.

20You foolish man, do you want evidence that faith without deeds is useless? 21Was not our ancestor Abraham considered righteous for what he did when he offered his son Isaac on the altar? 22You see that his faith and his actions were working together, and his faith was made complete by what he did. 23And the scripture was fulfilled that says, "Abraham believed God, and it was credited to him as righteousness," and he was called God's friend. 24You see that a person is justified by what he does and not by faith alone.

25In the same way, was not even Rahab the prostitute considered righteous for what she did when she gave lodging to the spies and sent them off in a different direction? 26As the body without the spirit is dead, so faith without deeds is dead.

READING FROM PSALMS
Psalm 128:1–6

A song of ascents.

1Blessed are all who fear the LORD,
    who walk in his ways.
2You will eat the fruit of your labour;
    blessings and prosperity will be
      yours.
3Your wife will be like a fruitful vine
    within your house;
    your sons will be like olive shoots
      round your table.
4Thus is the man blessed
    who fears the LORD.

5May the LORD bless you from Zion
    all the days of your life;
    may you see the prosperity of
      Jerusalem,
6   and may you live to see your
      children's children.

Peace be upon Israel.

NOVEMBER 19

OLD TESTAMENT READING
Ezekiel 36:1–37:28

A Prophecy to the Mountains of Israel

36 "Son of man, prophesy to the mountains of Israel and say, 'O mountains of Israel, hear the word of the LORD. ²This is what the Sovereign LORD says: The enemy said of you, "Aha! The ancient heights have become our possession."' ³Therefore prophesy and say, 'This is what the Sovereign LORD says: Because they ravaged and hounded you from every side so that you became the possession of the rest of the nations and the object of people's malicious talk and slander, ⁴therefore, O mountains of Israel, hear the word of the Sovereign LORD: This is what the Sovereign LORD says to the mountains and hills, to the ravines and valleys, to the desolate ruins and the deserted towns that have been plundered and ridiculed by the rest of the nations around you—⁵this is what the Sovereign LORD says: In my burning zeal I have spoken against the rest of the nations, and against Edom, for with glee and with malice in their hearts they made my land their own possession so that they might plunder its pastureland.' ⁶Therefore prophesy concerning the land of Israel and say to the mountains and hills, to the ravines and valleys: 'This is what the Sovereign LORD says: I speak in my jealous wrath because you have suffered the scorn of the nations. ⁷Therefore this is what the Sovereign LORD says: I swear with uplifted hand that the nations around you will also suffer scorn.

⁸"'But you, O mountains of Israel, will produce branches and fruit for my people Israel, for they will soon come home. ⁹I am concerned for you and will look on you with favour; you will be ploughed and sown, ¹⁰and I will multiply the number of people upon you, even the whole house of Israel. The towns will be inhabited and the ruins rebuilt. ¹¹I will increase the number of men and animals upon you, and they will be fruitful and become numerous. I will settle people on you as in the past and will make you prosper more than before. Then you will know that I am the LORD. ¹²I will cause people, my people Israel, to walk upon you. They will possess you, and you will be their inheritance; you will never again deprive them of their children.

¹³"'This is what the Sovereign LORD says: Because people say to you, "You devour men and deprive your nation of its children," ¹⁴therefore you will no longer devour men or make your nation childless, declares the Sovereign LORD. ¹⁵No longer will I make you hear the taunts of the nations, and no longer will you suffer the scorn of the peoples or cause your nation to fall, declares the Sovereign LORD.'"

¹⁶Again the word of the LORD came to me: ¹⁷"Son of man, when the people of Israel were living in their own land, they defiled it by their conduct and their actions. Their conduct was like a woman's monthly uncleanness in my sight. ¹⁸So I poured out my wrath on them because they had shed blood in the land and because they had defiled it with their idols. ¹⁹I dispersed them among the nations, and they were scattered through the countries; I judged them according to their conduct and their actions. ²⁰And wherever they went among the nations they profaned my holy name, for it was said of them, 'These are the LORD's people, and yet they had to leave his land.' ²¹So I had concern for my holy name, which the house of Israel profaned among the nations where they had gone.

²²"Therefore say to the house of

Israel, 'This is what the Sovereign LORD says: It is not for your sake, O house of Israel, that I am going to do these things, but for the sake of my holy name, which you have profaned among the nations where you have gone. 23I will show the holiness of my great name, which has been profaned among the nations, the name you have profaned among them. Then the nations will know that I am the LORD, declares the Sovereign LORD, when I show myself holy through you before their eyes.

24"'For I will take you out of the nations; I will gather you from all the countries and bring you back into your own land. 25I will sprinkle clean water on you, and you will be clean; I will cleanse you from all your impurities and from all your idols. 26I will give you a new heart and put a new spirit in you; I will remove from you your heart of stone and give you a heart of flesh. 27And I will put my Spirit in you and move you to follow my decrees and be careful to keep my laws. 28You will live in the land I gave your forefathers; you will be my people, and I will be your God. 29I will save you from all your uncleanness. I will call for the corn and make it plentiful and will not bring famine upon you. 30I will increase the fruit of the trees and the crops of the field, so that you will no longer suffer disgrace among the nations because of famine. 31Then you will remember your evil ways and wicked deeds, and you will loathe yourselves for your sins and detestable practices. 32I want you to know that I am not doing this for your sake, declares the Sovereign LORD. Be ashamed and disgraced for your conduct, O house of Israel!

33"'This is what the Sovereign LORD says: On the day I cleanse you from all your sins, I will resettle your towns, and the ruins will be rebuilt. 34The desolate land will be cultivated instead of lying desolate in the sight of all who pass through it. 35They will say, "This land that was laid waste has become like the garden of Eden; the cities that were lying in ruins, desolate and destroyed, are now fortified and inhabited." 36Then the nations around you that remain will know that I the LORD have rebuilt what was destroyed and have replanted what was desolate. I the LORD have spoken, and I will do it.'

37"'This is what the Sovereign LORD says: Once again I will yield to the plea of the house of Israel and do this for them: I will make their people as numerous as sheep, 38as numerous as the flocks for offerings at Jerusalem during her appointed feasts. So will the ruined cities be filled with flocks of people. Then they will know that I am the LORD."

The Valley of Dry Bones

37 The hand of the LORD was upon me, and he brought me out by the Spirit of the LORD and set me in the middle of a valley; it was full of bones. 2He led me to and fro among them, and I saw a great many bones on the floor of the valley, bones that were very dry. 3He asked me, "Son of man, can these bones live?"

I said, "O Sovereign LORD, you alone know."

4Then he said to me, "Prophesy to these bones and say to them, 'Dry bones, hear the word of the LORD! 5This is what the Sovereign LORD says to these bones: I will make breath enter you, and you will come to life. 6I will attach tendons to you and make flesh come upon you and cover you with skin; I will put breath in you, and you will come to life. Then you will know that I am the LORD.'"

7So I prophesied as I was commanded. And as I was prophesying, there was a noise, a rattling sound, and the bones came together, bone to bone. 8I looked, and tendons and flesh appeared on them and skin covered them, but there was no breath in them.

9Then he said to me, "Prophesy to the breath; prophesy, son of man, and say to it, 'This is what the Sovereign

LORD says: Come from the four winds, O breath, and breathe into these slain, that they may live.'" [10]So I prophesied as he commanded me, and breath entered them; they came to life and stood up on their feet—a vast army.

[11]Then he said to me: "Son of man, these bones are the whole house of Israel. They say, 'Our bones are dried up and our hope is gone; we are cut off.' [12]Therefore prophesy and say to them: 'This is what the Sovereign LORD says: O my people, I am going to open your graves and bring you up from them; I will bring you back to the land of Israel. [13]Then you, my people, will know that I am the LORD, when I open your graves and bring you up from them. [14]I will put my Spirit in you and you will live, and I will settle you in your own land. Then you will know that I the LORD have spoken, and I have done it, declares the LORD.'"

One Nation Under One King

[15]The word of the LORD came to me: [16]"Son of man, take a stick of wood and write on it, 'Belonging to Judah and the Israelites associated with him.' Then take another stick of wood, and write on it, 'Ephraim's stick, belonging to Joseph and all the house of Israel associated with him.' [17]Join them together into one stick so that they will become one in your hand.

[18]"When your countrymen ask you, 'Won't you tell us what you mean by this?' [19]say to them, 'This is what the Sovereign LORD says: I am going to take the stick of Joseph—which is in Ephraim's hand—and of the Israelite tribes associated with him, and join it to Judah's stick, making them a single stick of wood, and they will become one in my hand.' [20]Hold before their eyes the sticks you have written on [21]and say to them, 'This is what the Sovereign LORD says: I will take the Israelites out of the nations where they have gone. I will gather them from all around and bring them back into their own land. [22]I

will make them one nation in the land, on the mountains of Israel. There will be one king over all of them and they will never again be two nations or be divided into two kingdoms. [23]They will no longer defile themselves with their idols and vile images or with any of their offences, for I will save them from all their sinful backsliding, and I will cleanse them. They will be my people, and I will be their God.

[24]"'My servant David will be king over them, and they will all have one shepherd. They will follow my laws and be careful to keep my decrees. [25]They will live in the land I gave to my servant Jacob, the land where your fathers lived. They and their children and their children's children will live there for ever, and David my servant will be their prince for ever. [26]I will make a covenant of peace with them; it will be an everlasting covenant. I will establish them and increase their numbers, and I will put my sanctuary among them for ever. [27]My dwelling-place will be with them; I will be their God, and they will be my people. [28]Then the nations will know that I the LORD make Israel holy, when my sanctuary is among them for ever.'"

NEW TESTAMENT READING
James 3:1–18

Taming the Tongue

3 Not many of you should presume to be teachers, my brothers, because you know that we who teach will be judged more strictly. [2]We all stumble in many ways. If anyone is never at fault in what he says, he is a perfect man, able to keep his whole body in check.

[3]When we put bits into the mouths of horses to make them obey us, we can turn the whole animal. [4]Or take ships as an example. Although they are so large and are driven by strong winds, they are steered by a very small rudder wherever the pilot wants to go. [5]Likewise the

tongue is a small part of the body, but it makes great boasts. Consider what a great forest is set on fire by a small spark. 6The tongue also is a fire, a world of evil among the parts of the body. It corrupts the whole person, sets the whole course of his life on fire, and is itself set on fire by hell.

7All kinds of animals, birds, reptiles and creatures of the sea are being tamed and have been tamed by man, 8but no man can tame the tongue. It is a restless evil, full of deadly poison.

9With the tongue we praise our Lord and Father, and with it we curse men, who have been made in God's likeness. 10Out of the same mouth come praise and cursing. My brothers, this should not be. 11Can both fresh water and salt water flow from the same spring? 12My brothers, can a fig-tree bear olives, or a grapevine bear figs? Neither can a salt spring produce fresh water.

Two Kinds of Wisdom

13Who is wise and understanding among you? Let him show it by his good life, by deeds done in the humility that comes from wisdom. 14But if you harbour bitter envy and selfish ambition in your hearts, do not boast about it or deny the truth. 15Such "wisdom" does not come down from heaven but is earthly, unspiritual, of the devil. 16For where you have envy and selfish ambition, there you find disorder and every evil practice.

17But the wisdom that comes from heaven is first of all pure; then peace-loving, considerate, submissive, full of mercy and good fruit, impartial and sincere. 18Peacemakers who sow in peace raise a harvest of righteousness.

READING FROM PSALMS
Psalm 129:1–8

A song of ascents.

1They have greatly oppressed me from
        my youth—
    let Israel say—
2they have greatly oppressed me from
        my youth,
    but they have not gained the
        victory over me.
3Ploughmen have ploughed my back
    and made their furrows long.
4But the LORD is righteous;
    he has cut me free from the cords
        of the wicked.

5May all who hate Zion
    be turned back in shame.
6May they be like grass on the roof,
    which withers before it can grow;
7with it the reaper cannot fill his
        hands,
    nor the one who gathers fill his
        arms.
8May those who pass by not say,
    "The blessing of the LORD be upon
        you;
    we bless you in the name of the
        LORD."

OLD TESTAMENT READING
Ezekiel 38:1–39:29

A Prophecy Against Gog

38 The word of the LORD came to me: [2]"Son of man, set your face against Gog, of the land of Magog, the chief prince of Meshech and Tubal; prophesy against him [3]and say: 'This is what the Sovereign LORD says: I am against you, O Gog, chief prince of Meshech and Tubal. [4]I will turn you around, put hooks in your jaws and bring you out with your whole army —your horses, your horsemen fully armed, and a great horde with large and small shields, all of them brandishing their swords. [5]Persia, Cush and Put will be with them, all with shields and helmets, [6]also Gomer with all its troops, and Beth Togarmah from the far north with all its troops—the many nations with you.

[7]"'Get ready; be prepared, you and all the hordes gathered about you, and take command of them. [8]After many days you will be called to arms. In future years you will invade a land that has recovered from war, whose people were gathered from many nations to the mountains of Israel, which had long been desolate. They had been brought out from the nations, and now all of them live in safety. [9]You and all your troops and the many nations with you will go up, advancing like a storm; you will be like a cloud covering the land.

[10]"'This is what the Sovereign LORD says: On that day thoughts will come into your mind and you will devise an evil scheme. [11]You will say, "I will invade a land of unwalled villages; I will attack a peaceful and unsuspecting people—all of them living without walls and without gates and bars. [12]I will plunder and loot and turn my hand against the resettled ruins and the people gathered from the nations, rich in livestock and goods, living at the centre of the land." [13]Sheba and Dedan and the merchants of Tarshish and all her villages will say to you, "Have you come to plunder? Have you gathered your hordes to loot, to carry off silver and gold, to take away livestock and goods and to seize much plunder?"'

[14]"Therefore, son of man, prophesy and say to Gog: 'This is what the Sovereign LORD says: In that day, when my people Israel are living in safety, will you not take notice of it? [15]You will come from your place in the far north, you and many nations with you, all of them riding on horses, a great horde, a mighty army. [16]You will advance against my people Israel like a cloud that covers the land. In days to come, O Gog, I will bring you against my land, so that the nations may know me when I show myself holy through you before their eyes.

[17]"'This is what the Sovereign LORD says: Are you not the one I spoke of in former days by my servants the prophets of Israel? At that time they prophesied for years that I would bring you against them. [18]This is what will happen in that day: When Gog attacks the land of Israel, my hot anger will be aroused, declares the Sovereign LORD. [19]In my zeal and fiery wrath I declare that at that time there shall be a great earthquake in the land of Israel. [20]The fish of the sea, the birds of the air, the beasts of the field, every creature that moves along the ground, and all the people on the face of the earth will tremble at my presence. The mountains will be overturned, the cliffs will crumble and every wall will fall to the ground. [21]I will summon a sword against Gog on all my mountains, declares the Sovereign LORD. Every man's sword

will be against his brother. ²²I will execute judgment upon him with plague and bloodshed; I will pour down torrents of rain, hailstones and burning sulphur on him and on his troops and on the many nations with him. ²³And so I will show my greatness and my holiness, and I will make myself known in the sight of many nations. Then they will know that I am the LORD.'

39 "Son of man, prophesy against Gog and say: 'This is what the Sovereign LORD says: I am against you, O Gog, chief prince of Meshech and Tubal. ²I will turn you around and drag you along. I will bring you from the far north and send you against the mountains of Israel. ³Then I will strike your bow from your left hand and make your arrows drop from your right hand. ⁴On the mountains of Israel you will fall, and all your troops and the nations with you. I will give you as food to all kinds of carrion birds and to the wild animals. ⁵You will fall in the open field, for I have spoken, declares the Sovereign LORD. ⁶I will send fire on Magog and on those who live in safety in the coastlands, and they will know that I am the LORD.

⁷" 'I will make known my holy name among my people Israel. I will no longer let my holy name be profaned, and the nations will know that I the LORD am the Holy One in Israel. ⁸It is coming! It will surely take place, declares the Sovereign LORD. This is the day I have spoken of.

⁹" 'Then those who live in the towns of Israel will go out and use the weapons for fuel and burn them up—the small and large shields, the bows and arrows, the war clubs and spears. For seven years they will use them for fuel. ¹⁰They will not need to gather wood from the fields or cut it from the forests, because they will use the weapons for fuel. And they will plunder those who plundered them and loot those who looted them, declares the Sovereign LORD.

¹¹" 'On that day I will give Gog a burial place in Israel, in the valley of those who travel east towards the Sea. It will block the way of travellers, because Gog and all his hordes will be buried there. So it will be called the Valley of Hamon Gog.

¹²" 'For seven months the house of Israel will be burying them in order to cleanse the land. ¹³All the people of the land will bury them, and the day I am glorified will be a memorable day for them, declares the Sovereign LORD.

¹⁴" 'Men will be regularly employed to cleanse the land. Some will go throughout the land and, in addition to them, others will bury those that remain on the ground. At the end of the seven months they will begin their search. ¹⁵As they go through the land and one of them sees a human bone, he will set up a marker beside it until the gravediggers have buried it in the Valley of Hamon Gog. ¹⁶(Also a town called Hamonah will be there.) And so they will cleanse the land.'

¹⁷"Son of man, this is what the Sovereign LORD says: Call out to every kind of bird and all the wild animals: 'Assemble and come together from all around to the sacrifice I am preparing for you, the great sacrifice on the mountains of Israel. There you will eat flesh and drink blood. ¹⁸You will eat the flesh of mighty men and drink the blood of the princes of the earth as if they were rams and lambs, goats and bulls—all of them fattened animals from Bashan. ¹⁹At the sacrifice I am preparing for you, you will eat fat till you are glutted and drink blood till you are drunk. ²⁰At my table you will eat your fill of horses and riders, mighty men and soldiers of every kind,' declares the Sovereign LORD.

²¹"I will display my glory among the nations, and all the nations will see the punishment I inflict and the hand I lay upon them. ²²From that day forward the house of Israel will know that I am the LORD their God. ²³And the nations will know that the people of Israel went into exile for their sin, because they were unfaithful to me. So I hid my face from

them and handed them over to their enemies, and they all fell by the sword. ²⁴I dealt with them according to their uncleanness and their offences, and I hid my face from them.

²⁵"Therefore this is what the Sovereign LORD says: I will now bring Jacob back from captivity and will have compassion on all the people of Israel, and I will be zealous for my holy name. ²⁶They will forget their shame and all the unfaithfulness they showed towards me when they lived in safety in their land with no-one to make them afraid. ²⁷When I have brought them back from the nations and have gathered them from the countries of their enemies, I will show myself holy through them in the sight of many nations. ²⁸Then they will know that I am the LORD their God, for though I sent them into exile among the nations, I will gather them to their own land, not leaving any behind. ²⁹I will no longer hide my face from them, for I will pour out my Spirit on the house of Israel, declares the Sovereign LORD."

NEW TESTAMENT READING
James 4:1–17

Submit Yourselves to God

4 What causes fights and quarrels among you? Don't they come from your desires that battle within you? ²You want something but don't get it. You kill and covet, but you cannot have what you want. You quarrel and fight. You do not have, because you do not ask God. ³When you ask, you do not receive, because you ask with wrong motives, that you may spend what you get on your pleasures.

⁴You adulterous people, don't you know that friendship with the world is hatred towards God? Anyone who chooses to be a friend of the world becomes an enemy of God. ⁵Or do you think Scripture says without reason that the spirit he caused to live in us envies intensely? ⁶But he gives us more grace. That is why Scripture says:

"God opposes the proud
  but gives grace to the humble."

⁷Submit yourselves, then, to God. Resist the devil, and he will flee from you. ⁸Come near to God and he will come near to you. Wash your hands, you sinners, and purify your hearts, you double-minded. ⁹Grieve, mourn and wail. Change your laughter to mourning and your joy to gloom. ¹⁰Humble yourselves before the Lord, and he will lift you up.

¹¹Brothers, do not slander one another. Anyone who speaks against his brother or judges him speaks against the law and judges it. When you judge the law, you are not keeping it, but sitting in judgment on it. ¹²There is only one Lawgiver and Judge, the one who is able to save and destroy. But you—who are you to judge your neighbour?

Boasting About Tomorrow

¹³Now listen, you who say, "Today or tomorrow we will go to this or that city, spend a year there, carry on business and make money." ¹⁴Why, you do not even know what will happen tomorrow. What is your life? You are a mist that appears for a little while and then vanishes. ¹⁵Instead, you ought to say, "If it is the Lord's will, we will live and do this or that." ¹⁶As it is, you boast and brag. All such boasting is evil. ¹⁷Anyone, then, who knows the good he ought to do and doesn't do it, sins.

READING FROM PROVERBS
Proverbs 28:7–17

⁷He who keeps the law is a discerning son,
  but a companion of gluttons disgraces his father.

8He who increases his wealth by
      exorbitant interest
   amasses it for another, who will be
      kind to the poor.

9If anyone turns a deaf ear to the law,
   even his prayers are detestable.

10He who leads the upright along an
      evil path
   will fall into his own trap,
   but the blameless will receive a
      good inheritance.

11A rich man may be wise in his own
      eyes,
   but a poor man who has
      discernment sees through him.

12When the righteous triumph, there is
      great elation;
   but when the wicked rise to power,
      men go into hiding.

13He who conceals his sins does not
      prosper,
   but whoever confesses and
      renounces them finds mercy.

14Blessed is the man who always fears
      the LORD,
   but he who hardens his heart falls
      into trouble.

15Like a roaring lion or a charging bear
   is a wicked man ruling over a
      helpless people.

16A tyrannical ruler lacks judgment,
   but he who hates ill-gotten gain will
      enjoy a long life.

17A man tormented by the guilt of
      murder
   will be a fugitive till death;
   let no-one support him.

NOVEMBER 21   DAY 325

OLD TESTAMENT READING
Ezekiel 40:1–49

The New Temple Area

40 In the twenty-fifth year of our
      exile, at the beginning of the
year, on the tenth of the month, in the
fourteenth year after the fall of the city
—on that very day the hand of the LORD
was upon me and he took me there. 2In
visions of God he took me to the land of
Israel and set me on a very high mountain, on whose south side were some
buildings that looked like a city. 3He
took me there, and I saw a man whose
appearance was like bronze; he was
standing in the gateway with a linen
cord and a measuring rod in his hand.
4The man said to me, "Son of man, look
with your eyes and hear with your ears
and pay attention to everything I am

going to show you, for that is why you
have been brought here. Tell the house
of Israel everything you see."

The East Gate to the Outer Court

5I saw a wall completely surrounding
the temple area. The length of the
measuring rod in the man's hand was six
long cubits, each of which was a cubit
and a handbreadth. He measured the
wall; it was one measuring rod thick and
one rod high.
6Then he went to the gate facing east.
He climbed its steps and measured the
threshold of the gate; it was one rod
deep. 7The alcoves for the guards were
one rod long and one rod wide, and the
projecting walls between the alcoves
were five cubits thick. And the
threshold of the gate next to the portico
facing the temple was one rod deep.

[8]Then he measured the portico of the gateway; [9]it was eight cubits deep and its jambs were two cubits thick. The portico of the gateway faced the temple.

[10]Inside the east gate were three alcoves on each side; the three had the same measurements, and the faces of the projecting walls on each side had the same measurements. [11]Then he measured the width of the entrance to the gateway; it was ten cubits and its length was thirteen cubits. [12]In front of each alcove was a wall one cubit high, and the alcoves were six cubits square. [13]Then he measured the gateway from the top of the rear wall of one alcove to the top of the opposite one; the distance was twenty-five cubits from one parapet opening to the opposite one. [14]He measured along the faces of the projecting walls all around the inside of the gateway—sixty cubits. The measurement was up to the portico facing the courtyard. [15]The distance from the entrance of the gateway to the far end of its portico was fifty cubits. [16]The alcoves and the projecting walls inside the gateway were surmounted by narrow parapet openings all round, as was the portico; the openings all round faced inward. The faces of the projecting walls were decorated with palm trees.

The Outer Court

[17]Then he brought me into the outer court. There I saw some rooms and a pavement that had been constructed all round the court; there were thirty rooms along the pavement. [18]It abutted the sides of the gateways and was as wide as they were long; this was the lower pavement. [19]Then he measured the distance from the inside of the lower gateway to the outside of the inner court; it was a hundred cubits on the east side as well as on the north.

The North Gate

[20]Then he measured the length and width of the gate facing north, leading into the outer court. [21]Its alcoves—three on each side—its projecting walls and its portico had the same measurements as those of the first gateway. It was fifty cubits long and twenty-five cubits wide. [22]Its openings, its portico and its palm tree decorations had the same measurements as those of the gate facing east. Seven steps led up to it, with its portico opposite them. [23]There was a gate to the inner court facing the north gate, just as there was on the east. He measured from one gate to the opposite one; it was a hundred cubits.

The South Gate

[24]Then he led me to the south side and I saw a gate facing south. He measured its jambs and its portico, and they had the same measurements as the others. [25]The gateway and its portico had narrow openings all round, like the openings of the others. It was fifty cubits long and twenty-five cubits wide. [26]Seven steps led up to it, with its portico opposite them; it had palm tree decorations on the faces of the projecting walls on each side. [27]The inner court also had a gate facing south, and he measured from this gate to the outer gate on the south side; it was a hundred cubits.

Gates to the Inner Court

[28]Then he brought me into the inner court through the south gate, and he measured the south gate; it had the same measurements as the others. [29]Its alcoves, its projecting walls and its portico had the same measurements as the others. The gateway and its portico had openings all round. It was fifty cubits long and twenty-five cubits wide. [30](The porticoes of the gateways around the inner court were twenty-five cubits wide and five cubits deep.) [31]Its portico faced the outer court; palm trees decorated its jambs, and eight steps led up to it.

[32]Then he brought me to the inner court on the east side, and he measured

the gateway; it had the same measurements as the others. ³³Its alcoves, its projecting walls and its portico had the same measurements as the others. The gateway and its portico had openings all round. It was fifty cubits long and twenty-five cubits wide. ³⁴Its portico faced the outer court; palm trees decorated the jambs on either side, and eight steps led up to it.

³⁵Then he brought me to the north gate and measured it. It had the same measurements as the others, ³⁶as did its alcoves, its projecting walls and its portico, and it had openings all round. It was fifty cubits long and twenty-five cubits wide. ³⁷Its portico faced the outer court; palm trees decorated the jambs on either side, and eight steps led up to it.

The Rooms for Preparing Sacrifices

³⁸A room with a doorway was by the portico in each of the inner gateways, where the burnt offerings were washed. ³⁹In the portico of the gateway were two tables on each side, on which the burnt offerings, sin offerings and guilt offerings were slaughtered. ⁴⁰By the outside wall of the portico of the gateway, near the steps at the entrance to the north gateway were two tables, and on the other side of the steps were two tables. ⁴¹So there were four tables on one side of the gateway and four on the other—eight tables in all—on which the sacrifices were slaughtered. ⁴²There were also four tables of dressed stone for the burnt offerings, each a cubit and a half long, a cubit and a half wide and a cubit high. On them were placed the utensils for slaughtering the burnt offerings and the other sacrifices. ⁴³And double-pronged hooks, each a handbreadth long, were attached to the wall all around. The tables were for the flesh of the offerings.

Rooms for the Priests

⁴⁴Outside the inner gate, within the inner court, were two rooms, one at the side of the north gate and facing south, and another at the side of the south gate and facing north. ⁴⁵He said to me, "The room facing south is for the priests who have charge of the temple, ⁴⁶and the room facing north is for the priests who have charge of the altar. These are the sons of Zadok, who are the only Levites who may draw near to the Lord to minister before him."

⁴⁷Then he measured the court: It was square—a hundred cubits long and a hundred cubits wide. And the altar was in front of the temple.

The Temple

⁴⁸He brought me to the portico of the temple and measured the jambs of the portico; they were five cubits wide on either side. The width of the entrance was fourteen cubits and its projecting walls were three cubits wide on either side. ⁴⁹The portico was twenty cubits wide, and twelve cubits from front to back. It was reached by a flight of stairs, and there were pillars on each side of the jambs.

NEW TESTAMENT READING
James 5:1–20

Warning to Rich Oppressors

5 Now listen, you rich people, weep and wail because of the misery that is coming upon you. ²Your wealth has rotted, and moths have eaten your clothes. ³Your gold and silver are corroded. Their corrosion will testify against you and eat your flesh like fire. You have hoarded wealth in the last days. ⁴Look! The wages you failed to pay the workmen who mowed your fields are crying out against you. The cries of the harvesters have reached the ears of the Lord Almighty. ⁵You have lived on earth in luxury and self-indulgence. You have fattened yourselves in the day of slaughter. ⁶You

have condemned and murdered innocent men, who were not opposing you.

Patience in Suffering

7Be patient, then, brothers, until the Lord's coming. See how the farmer waits for the land to yield its valuable crop and how patient he is for the autumn and spring rains. 8You too, be patient and stand firm, because the Lord's coming is near. 9Don't grumble against each other, brothers, or you will be judged. The Judge is standing at the door!

10Brothers, as an example of patience in the face of suffering, take the prophets who spoke in the name of the Lord. 11As you know, we consider blessed those who have persevered. You have heard of Job's perseverance and have seen what the Lord finally brought about. The Lord is full of compassion and mercy.

12Above all, my brothers, do not swear—not by heaven or by earth or by anything else. Let your "Yes" be yes, and your "No", no, or you will be condemned.

The Prayer of Faith

13Is any one of you in trouble? He should pray. Is anyone happy? Let him sing songs of praise. 14Is any one of you sick? He should call the elders of the church to pray over him and anoint him with oil in the name of the Lord. 15And the prayer offered in faith will make the sick person well; the Lord will raise him up. If he has sinned, he will be forgiven. 16Therefore confess your sins to each other and pray for each other so that you may be healed. The prayer of a righteous man is powerful and effective.

17Elijah was a man just like us. He prayed earnestly that it would not rain, and it did not rain on the land for three and a half years. 18Again he prayed, and the heavens gave rain, and the earth produced its crops.

19My brothers, if one of you should wander from the truth and someone should bring him back, 20remember this: Whoever turns a sinner from the error of his way will save him from death and cover over a multitude of sins.

READING FROM PSALMS
Psalm 130:1–8

A song of ascents.

1Out of the depths I cry to you, O
    LORD;
2 O Lord, hear my voice.
Let your ears be attentive
    to my cry for mercy.

3If you, O LORD, kept a record of sins,
    O Lord, who could stand?
4But with you there is forgiveness;
    therefore you are feared.

5I wait for the LORD, my soul waits,
    and in his word I put my hope.
6My soul waits for the Lord
    more than watchmen wait for the
        morning,
    more than watchmen wait for the
        morning.

7O Israel, put your hope in the LORD,
    for with the LORD is unfailing love
    and with him is full redemption.
8He himself will redeem Israel
    from all their sins.

OLD TESTAMENT READING
Ezekiel 41:1–42:20

41 Then the man brought me to the outer sanctuary and measured the jambs; the width of the jambs was six cubits on each side. ²The entrance was ten cubits wide, and the projecting walls on each side of it were five cubits wide. He also measured the outer sanctuary; it was forty cubits long and twenty cubits wide.

³Then he went into the inner sanctuary and measured the jambs of the entrance; each was two cubits wide. The entrance was six cubits wide, and the projecting walls on each side of it were seven cubits wide. ⁴And he measured the length of the inner sanctuary; it was twenty cubits, and its width was twenty cubits across the end of the outer sanctuary. He said to me, "This is the Most Holy Place."

⁵Then he measured the wall of the temple; it was six cubits thick, and each side room round the temple was four cubits wide. ⁶The side rooms were on three levels, one above another, thirty on each level. There were ledges all round the wall of the temple to serve as supports for the side rooms, so that the supports were not inserted into the wall of the temple. ⁷The side rooms all round the temple were wider at each successive level. The structure surrounding the temple was built in ascending stages, so that the rooms widened as one went upward. A stairway went up from the lowest floor to the top floor through the middle floor.

⁸I saw that the temple had a raised base all round it, forming the foundation of the side rooms. It was the length of the rod, six long cubits. ⁹The outer wall of the side rooms was five cubits thick. The open area between the side rooms of the temple ¹⁰and the ⌊priests'⌋ rooms was twenty cubits wide all round

the temple. ¹¹There were entrances to the side rooms from the open area, one on the north and another on the south; and the base adjoining the open area was five cubits wide all round.

¹²The building facing the temple courtyard on the west side was seventy cubits wide. The wall of the building was five cubits thick all round, and its length was ninety cubits.

¹³Then he measured the temple; it was a hundred cubits long, and the temple courtyard and the building with its walls were also a hundred cubits long. ¹⁴The width of the temple courtyard on the east, including the front of the temple, was a hundred cubits.

¹⁵Then he measured the length of the building facing the courtyard at the rear of the temple, including its galleries on each side; it was a hundred cubits.

The outer sanctuary, the inner sanctuary and the portico facing the court, ¹⁶as well as the thresholds and the narrow windows and galleries round the three of them—everything beyond and including the threshold was covered with wood. The floor, the wall up to the windows, and the windows were covered. ¹⁷In the space above the outside of the entrance to the inner sanctuary and on the walls at regular intervals all round the inner and outer sanctuary ¹⁸were carved cherubim and palm trees. Palm trees alternated with cherubim. Each cherub had two faces: ¹⁹the face of a man towards the palm tree on one side and the face of a lion towards the palm tree on the other. They were carved all round the whole temple. ²⁰From the floor to the area above the entrance, cherubim and palm trees were carved on the wall of the outer sanctuary.

²¹The outer sanctuary had a rectangular door-frame, and the one at the front of the Most Holy Place was similar. ²²There was a wooden altar three cubits high and two cubits square; its corners,

its base and its sides were of wood. The man said to me, "This is the table that is before the LORD." ²³Both the outer sanctuary and the Most Holy Place had double doors. ²⁴Each door had two leaves—two hinged leaves for each door. ²⁵And on the doors of the outer sanctuary were carved cherubim and palm trees like those carved on the walls, and there was a wooden overhang on the front of the portico. ²⁶On the side walls of the portico were narrow windows with palm trees carved on each side. The side rooms of the temple also had overhangs.

Rooms for the Priests

42 Then the man led me northward into the outer court and brought me to the rooms opposite the temple courtyard and opposite the outer wall on the north side. ²The building whose door faced north was a hundred cubits long and fifty cubits wide. ³Both in the section twenty cubits from the inner court and in the section opposite the pavement of the outer court, gallery faced gallery at the three levels. ⁴In front of the rooms was an inner passageway ten cubits wide and a hundred cubits long. Their doors were on the north. ⁵Now the upper rooms were narrower, for the galleries took more space from them than from the rooms on the lower and middle floors of the building. ⁶The rooms on the third floor had no pillars, as the courts had; so they were smaller in floor space than those on the lower and middle floors. ⁷There was an outer wall parallel to the rooms and the outer court; it extended in front of the rooms for fifty cubits. ⁸While the row of rooms on the side next to the outer court was fifty cubits long, the row on the side nearest the sanctuary was a hundred cubits long. ⁹The lower rooms had an entrance on the east side as one enters them from the outer court.

¹⁰On the south side along the length of the wall of the outer court, adjoining the temple courtyard and opposite the outer wall, were rooms ¹¹with a passageway in front of them. These were like the rooms on the north; they had the same length and width, with similar exits and dimensions. Similar to the doorways on the north ¹²were the doorways of the rooms on the south. There was a doorway at the beginning of the passageway that was parallel to the corresponding wall extending eastward, by which one enters the rooms.

¹³Then he said to me, "The north and south rooms facing the temple courtyard are the priests' rooms, where the priests who approach the LORD will eat the most holy offerings. There they will put the most holy offerings—the grain offerings, the sin offerings and the guilt offerings—for the place is holy. ¹⁴Once the priests enter the holy precincts, they are not to go into the outer court until they leave behind the garments in which they minister, for these are holy. They are to put on other clothes before they go near the places that are for the people."

¹⁵When he had finished measuring what was inside the temple area, he led me out by the east gate and measured the area all around: ¹⁶He measured the east side with the measuring rod; it was five hundred cubits. ¹⁷He measured the north side; it was five hundred cubits by the measuring rod. ¹⁸He measured the south side; it was five hundred cubits by the measuring rod. ¹⁹Then he turned to the west side and measured; it was five hundred cubits by the measuring rod. ²⁰So he measured the area on all four sides. It had a wall round it, five hundred cubits long and five hundred cubits wide, to separate the holy from the common.

NEW TESTAMENT READING
1 Peter 1:1—2:3

1 Peter, an apostle of Jesus Christ,

To God's elect, strangers in the world, scattered throughout Pontus,

Galatia, Cappadocia, Asia and Bithynia, ²who have been chosen according to the foreknowledge of God the Father, through the sanctifying work of the Spirit, for obedience to Jesus Christ and sprinkling by his blood:

Grace and peace be yours in abundance.

Praise to God for a Living Hope

³Praise be to the God and Father of our Lord Jesus Christ! In his great mercy he has given us new birth into a living hope through the resurrection of Jesus Christ from the dead, ⁴and into an inheritance that can never perish, spoil or fade—kept in heaven for you, ⁵who through faith are shielded by God's power until the coming of the salvation that is ready to be revealed in the last time. ⁶In this you greatly rejoice, though now for a little while you may have had to suffer grief in all kinds of trials. ⁷These have come so that your faith—of greater worth than gold, which perishes even though refined by fire—may be proved genuine and may result in praise, glory and honour when Jesus Christ is revealed. ⁸Though you have not seen him, you love him; and even though you do not see him now, you believe in him and are filled with an inexpressible and glorious joy, ⁹for you are receiving the goal of your faith, the salvation of your souls.

¹⁰Concerning this salvation, the prophets, who spoke of the grace that was to come to you, searched intently and with the greatest care, ¹¹trying to find out the time and circumstances to which the Spirit of Christ in them was pointing when he predicted the sufferings of Christ and the glories that would follow. ¹²It was revealed to them that they were not serving themselves but you, when they spoke of the things that have now been told you by those who have preached the gospel to you by the Holy Spirit sent from heaven. Even angels long to look into these things.

Be Holy

¹³Therefore, prepare your minds for action; be self-controlled; set your hope fully on the grace to be given you when Jesus Christ is revealed. ¹⁴As obedient children, do not conform to the evil desires you had when you lived in ignorance. ¹⁵But just as he who called you is holy, so be holy in all you do; ¹⁶for it is written: "Be holy, because I am holy."

¹⁷Since you call on a Father who judges each man's work impartially, live your lives as strangers here in reverent fear. ¹⁸For you know that it was not with perishable things such as silver or gold that you were redeemed from the empty way of life handed down to you from your forefathers, ¹⁹but with the precious blood of Christ, a lamb without blemish or defect. ²⁰He was chosen before the creation of the world, but was revealed in these last times for your sake. ²¹Through him you believe in God, who raised him from the dead and glorified him, and so your faith and hope are in God.

²²Now that you have purified yourselves by obeying the truth so that you have sincere love for your brothers, love one another deeply, from the heart. ²³For you have been born again, not of perishable seed, but of imperishable, through the living and enduring word of God. ²⁴For,

"All men are like grass,
     and all their glory is like the
         flowers of the field;
  the grass withers and the flowers fall,
²⁵ but the word of the Lord stands for
         ever."

And this is the word that was preached to you.

2 Therefore, rid yourselves of all malice and all deceit, hypocrisy, envy, and slander of every kind. ²Like newborn babies, crave pure spiritual milk, so that by it you may grow up in your salvation, ³now that you have tasted that the Lord is good.

READING FROM PSALMS
Psalm 131:1–3

A song of ascents. Of David.

[1]My heart is not proud, O LORD,
   my eyes are not haughty;
   I do not concern myself with great
      matters
   or things too wonderful for me.

[2]But I have stilled and quietened my
      soul;
   like a weaned child with its
      mother,
   like a weaned child is my soul
      within me.

[3]O Israel, put your hope in the LORD
   both now and for evermore.

DAY 327   # NOVEMBER 23

OLD TESTAMENT READING
Ezekiel 43:1–44:31

The Glory Returns to the Temple

43 Then the man brought me to the gate facing east, [2]and I saw the glory of the God of Israel coming from the east. His voice was like the roar of rushing waters, and the land was radiant with his glory. [3]The vision I saw was like the vision I had seen when he came to destroy the city and like the visions I had seen by the Kebar River, and I fell face down. [4]The glory of the LORD entered the temple through the gate facing east. [5]Then the Spirit lifted me up and brought me into the inner court, and the glory of the LORD filled the temple.

[6]While the man was standing beside me, I heard someone speaking to me from inside the temple. [7]He said: "Son of man, this is the place of my throne and the place for the soles of my feet. This is where I will live among the Israelites for ever. The house of Israel will never again defile my holy name —neither they nor their kings—by their prostitution and the lifeless idols of their kings at their high places. [8]When they placed their threshold next to my threshold and their doorposts beside my doorposts, with only a wall between me and them, they defiled my holy name by their detestable practices. So I destroyed them in my anger. [9]Now let

them put away from me their prostitution and the lifeless idols of their kings, and I will live among them for ever.

[10]"Son of man, describe the temple to the people of Israel, that they may be ashamed of their sins. Let them consider the plan, [11]and if they are ashamed of all they have done, make known to them the design of the temple—its arrangement, its exits and entrances— its whole design and all its regulations and laws. Write these down before them so that they may be faithful to its design and follow all its regulations.

[12]"This is the law of the temple: All the surrounding area on top of the mountain will be most holy. Such is the law of the temple.

The Altar

[13]"These are the measurements of the altar in long cubits, that cubit being a cubit and a handbreadth: Its gutter is a cubit deep and a cubit wide, with a rim of one span around the edge. And this is the height of the altar: [14]From the gutter on the ground up to the lower edge is two cubits high and a cubit wide, and from the smaller ledge up to the larger ledge it is four cubits high and a cubit wide. [15]The altar hearth is four cubits high, and four horns project upward from the hearth. [16]The altar hearth is square, twelve cubits long and twelve

cubits wide. ¹⁷The upper ledge also is square, fourteen cubits long and fourteen cubits wide, with a rim of half a cubit and a gutter of a cubit all round. The steps of the altar face east."

¹⁸Then he said to me, "Son of man, this is what the Sovereign LORD says: These will be the regulations for sacrificing burnt offerings and sprinkling blood upon the altar when it is built: ¹⁹You are to give a young bull as a sin offering to the priests, who are Levites, of the family of Zadok, who come near to minister before me, declares the Sovereign LORD. ²⁰You are to take some of its blood and put it on the four horns of the altar and on the four corners of the upper ledge and all round the rim, and so purify the altar and make atonement for it. ²¹You are to take the bull for the sin offering and burn it in the designated part of the temple area outside the sanctuary.

²²"On the second day you are to offer a male goat without defect for a sin offering, and the altar is to be purified as it was purified with the bull. ²³When you have finished purifying it, you are to offer a young bull and a ram from the flock, both without defect. ²⁴You are to offer them before the LORD, and the priests are to sprinkle salt on them and sacrifice them as a burnt offering to the LORD.

²⁵"For seven days you are to provide a male goat daily for a sin offering; you are also to provide a young bull and a ram from the flock, both without defect. ²⁶For seven days they are to make atonement for the altar and cleanse it; thus they will dedicate it. ²⁷At the end of these days, from the eighth day on, the priests are to present your burnt offerings and fellowship offerings on the altar. Then I will accept you, declares the Sovereign LORD."

The Prince, the Levites, the Priests

44 Then the man brought me back to the outer gate of the sanctuary, the one facing east, and it was shut.

²The LORD said to me, "This gate is to remain shut. It must not be opened; no-one may enter through it. It is to remain shut because the LORD, the God of Israel, has entered through it. ³The prince himself is the only one who may sit inside the gateway to eat in the presence of the LORD. He is to enter by way of the portico of the gateway and go out the same way."

⁴Then the man brought me by way of the north gate to the front of the temple. I looked and saw the glory of the LORD filling the temple of the LORD, and I fell face down.

⁵The LORD said to me, "Son of man, look carefully, listen closely and give attention to everything I tell you concerning all the regulations regarding the temple of the LORD. Give attention to the entrance of the temple and all the exits of the sanctuary. ⁶Say to the rebellious house of Israel, 'This is what the Sovereign LORD says: Enough of your detestable practices, O house of Israel! ⁷In addition to all your other detestable practices, you brought foreigners uncircumcised in heart and flesh into my sanctuary, desecrating my temple while you offered me food, fat and blood, and you broke my covenant. ⁸Instead of carrying out your duty in regard to my holy things, you put others in charge of my sanctuary. ⁹This is what the Sovereign LORD says: No foreigner uncircumcised in heart and flesh is to enter my sanctuary, not even the foreigners who live among the Israelites.

¹⁰"'The Levites who went far from me when Israel went astray and who wandered from me after their idols must bear the consequences of their sin. ¹¹They may serve in my sanctuary, having charge of the gates of the temple and serving in it; they may slaughter the burnt offerings and sacrifices for the people and stand before the people and serve them. ¹²But because they served them in the presence of their idols and made the house of Israel fall into sin, therefore I have sworn with uplifted hand that they must bear the

consequences of their sin, declares the Sovereign LORD. [13]They are not to come near to serve me as priests or come near any of my holy things or my most holy offerings; they must bear the shame of their detestable practices. [14]Yet I will put them in charge of the duties of the temple and all the work that is to be done in it.

[15]"'But the priests, who are Levites and descendants of Zadok and who faithfully carried out the duties of my sanctuary when the Israelites went astray from me, are to come near to minister before me; they are to stand before me to offer sacrifices of fat and blood, declares the Sovereign LORD. [16]They alone are to enter my sanctuary; they alone are to come near my table to minister before me and perform my service.

[17]"'When they enter the gates of the inner court, they are to wear linen clothes; they must not wear any woollen garment while ministering at the gates of the inner court or inside the temple. [18]They are to wear linen turbans on their heads and linen undergarments round their waists. They must not wear anything that makes them perspire. [19]When they go out into the outer court where the people are, they are to take off the clothes they have been ministering in and leave them in the sacred rooms, and put on other clothes, so that they do not consecrate the people by means of their garments.

[20]"'They must not shave their heads or let their hair grow long, but they are to keep the hair of their heads trimmed. [21]No priest is to drink wine when he enters the inner court. [22]They must not marry widows or divorced women; they may marry only virgins of Israelite descent or widows of priests. [23]They are to teach my people the difference between the holy and the common and show them how to distinguish between the unclean and the clean.

[24]"'In any dispute, the priests are to serve as judges and decide it according to my ordinances. They are to keep my laws and my decrees for all my appointed feasts, and they are to keep my Sabbaths holy.

[25]"'A priest must not defile himself by going near a dead person; however, if the dead person was his father or mother, son or daughter, brother or unmarried sister, then he may defile himself. [26]After he is cleansed, he must wait seven days. [27]On the day he goes into the inner court of the sanctuary to minister in the sanctuary, he is to offer a sin offering for himself, declares the Sovereign LORD.

[28]"'I am to be the only inheritance the priests have. You are to give them no possession in Israel; I will be their possession. [29]They will eat the grain offerings, the sin offerings and the guilt offerings; and everything in Israel devoted to the LORD will belong to them. [30]The best of all the firstfruits and of all your special gifts will belong to the priests. You are to give them the first portion of your ground meal so that a blessing may rest on your household. [31]The priests must not eat anything, bird or animal, found dead or torn by wild animals.

NEW TESTAMENT READING
1 Peter 2:4–25

The Living Stone and a Chosen People

[4]As you come to him, the living Stone —rejected by men but chosen by God and precious to him—[5]you also, like living stones, are being built into a spiritual house to be a holy priesthood, offering spiritual sacrifices acceptable to God through Jesus Christ. [6]For in Scripture it says:

"See, I lay a stone in Zion,
    a chosen and precious cornerstone,
and the one who trusts in him
    will never be put to shame."

[7]Now to you who believe, this stone is precious. But to those who do not believe,

"The stone the builders rejected
has become the capstone,"

⁸and,

"A stone that causes men to stumble
and a rock that makes them fall."

They stumble because they disobey the message—which is also what they were destined for.

⁹But you are a chosen people, a royal priesthood, a holy nation, a people belonging to God, that you may declare the praises of him who called you out of darkness into his wonderful light. ¹⁰Once you were not a people, but now you are the people of God; once you had not received mercy, but now you have received mercy.

¹¹Dear friends, I urge you, as aliens and strangers in the world, to abstain from sinful desires, which war against your soul. ¹²Live such good lives among the pagans that, though they accuse you of doing wrong, they may see your good deeds and glorify God on the day he visits us.

Submission to Rulers and Masters

¹³Submit yourselves for the Lord's sake to every authority instituted among men: whether to the king, as the supreme authority, ¹⁴or to governors, who are sent by him to punish those who do wrong and to commend those who do right. ¹⁵For it is God's will that by doing good you should silence the ignorant talk of foolish men. ¹⁶Live as free men, but do not use your freedom as a cover-up for evil; live as servants of God. ¹⁷Show proper respect to everyone: Love the brotherhood of believers, fear God, honour the king.

¹⁸Slaves, submit yourselves to your masters with all respect, not only to those who are good and considerate, but also to those who are harsh. ¹⁹For it is commendable if a man bears up under the pain of unjust suffering because he is conscious of God. ²⁰But how is it to

your credit if you receive a beating for doing wrong and endure it? But if you suffer for doing good and you endure it, this is commendable before God. ²¹To this you were called, because Christ suffered for you, leaving you an example, that you should follow in his steps.

²²"He committed no sin,
and no deceit was found in his
mouth."

²³When they hurled their insults at him, he did not retaliate; when he suffered, he made no threats. Instead, he entrusted himself to him who judges justly. ²⁴He himself bore our sins in his body on the tree, so that we might die to sins and live for righteousness; by his wounds you have been healed. ²⁵For you were like sheep going astray, but now you have returned to the Shepherd and Overseer of your souls.

READING FROM PSALMS
Psalm 132:1–18

A song of ascents.

¹O LORD, remember David
and all the hardships he endured.

²He swore an oath to the LORD
and made a vow to the Mighty One
of Jacob:

³"I will not enter my house
or go to my bed—

⁴I will allow no sleep to my eyes,
no slumber to my eyelids,

⁵till I find a place for the LORD,
a dwelling for the Mighty One of
Jacob."

⁶We heard it in Ephrathah,
we came upon it in the fields of
Jaar:

⁷"Let us go to his dwelling-place;
let us worship at his footstool—

⁸arise, O LORD, and come to your
resting place,

you and the ark of your might.
⁹May your priests be clothed with
    righteousness;
    may your saints sing for joy.”

¹⁰For the sake of David your servant,
    do not reject your anointed one.

¹¹The LORD swore an oath to David,
    a sure oath that he will not revoke:
“One of your own descendants
    I will place on your throne—

¹²if your sons keep my covenant
    and the statutes I teach them,
    then their sons shall sit
    on your throne for ever and ever.”

¹³For the LORD has chosen Zion,
    he has desired it for his dwelling:

¹⁴“This is my resting place for ever and
    ever;
    here I will sit enthroned, for I have
    desired it—

¹⁵I will bless her with abundant
    provisions;
    her poor will I satisfy with food.

¹⁶I will clothe her priests with
    salvation,
    and her saints shall ever sing for
    joy.

¹⁷“Here I will make a horn grow for
    David
    and set up a lamp for my anointed
    one.

¹⁸I will clothe his enemies with shame,
    but the crown on his head shall be
    resplendent.”

DAY 328

NOVEMBER 24

OLD TESTAMENT READING
Ezekiel 45:1–46:24

Division of the Land

45 ¹ “‘When you allot the land as an
inheritance, you are to present
to the LORD a portion of the land as a
sacred district, 25,000 cubits long and
20,000 cubits wide; the entire area will
be holy. ²Of this, a section 500 cubits
square is to be for the sanctuary, with 50
cubits around it for open land. ³In the
sacred district, measure off a section
25,000 cubits long and 10,000 cubits
wide. In it will be the sanctuary, the
Most Holy Place. ⁴It will be the sacred
portion of the land for the priests, who
minister in the sanctuary and who draw
near to minister before the LORD. It will
be a place for their houses as well as a
holy place for the sanctuary. ⁵An area
25,000 cubits long and 10,000 cubits
wide will belong to the Levites, who
serve in the temple, as their possession
for towns to live in.

⁶“‘You are to give the city as its property an area 5,000 cubits wide and
25,000 cubits long, adjoining the sacred
portion; it will belong to the whole
house of Israel.

⁷“‘The prince will have the land
bordering each side of the area formed
by the sacred district and the property
of the city. It will extend westward from
the west side and eastward from the east
side, running lengthwise from the western to the eastern border parallel to one
of the tribal portions. ⁸This land will be
his possession in Israel. And my princes
will no longer oppress my people but
will allow the house of Israel to possess
the land according to their tribes.

⁹“‘This is what the Sovereign LORD
says: You have gone far enough, O
princes of Israel! Give up your violence
and oppression and do what is just and
right. Stop dispossessing my people, declares the Sovereign LORD. ¹⁰You are to
use accurate scales, an accurate ephah
and an accurate bath. ¹¹The ephah and

the bath are to be the same size, the bath containing a tenth of a homer and the ephah a tenth of a homer; the homer is to be the standard measure for both. [12]The shekel is to consist of twenty gerahs. Twenty shekels plus twenty-five shekels plus fifteen shekels equal one mina.

Offerings and Holy Days

[13]"'This is the special gift you are to offer: a sixth of an ephah from each homer of wheat and a sixth of an ephah from each homer of barley. [14]The prescribed portion of oil, measured by the bath, is a tenth of a bath from each cor (which consists of ten baths or one homer, for ten baths are equivalent to a homer). [15]Also one sheep is to be taken from every flock of two hundred from the well-watered pastures of Israel. These will be used for the grain offerings, burnt offerings and fellowship offerings to make atonement for the people, declares the Sovereign LORD. [16]All the people of the land will participate in this special gift for the use of the prince in Israel. [17]It will be the duty of the prince to provide the burnt offerings, grain offerings and drink offerings at the festivals, the New Moons and the Sabbaths—at all the appointed feasts of the house of Israel. He will provide the sin offerings, grain offerings, burnt offerings and fellowship offerings to make atonement for the house of Israel.

[18]"'This is what the Sovereign LORD says: In the first month on the first day you are to take a young bull without defect and purify the sanctuary. [19]The priest is to take some of the blood of the sin offering and put it on the doorposts of the temple, on the four corners of the upper ledge of the altar and on the gateposts of the inner court. [20]You are to do the same on the seventh day of the month for anyone who sins unintentionally or through ignorance; so you are to make atonement for the temple.

[21]"'In the first month on the fourteenth day you are to observe the Passover, a feast lasting seven days, during which you shall eat bread made without yeast. [22]On that day the prince is to provide a bull as a sin offering for himself and for all the people of the land. [23]Every day during the seven days of the Feast he is to provide seven bulls and seven rams without defect as a burnt offering to the LORD, and a male goat for a sin offering. [24]He is to provide as a grain offering an ephah for each bull and an ephah for each ram, along with a hin of oil for each ephah.

[25]"'During the seven days of the Feast, which begins in the seventh month on the fifteenth day, he is to make the same provision for sin offerings, burnt offerings, grain offerings and oil.

46 "'This is what the Sovereign LORD says: The gate of the inner court facing east is to be shut on the six working days, but on the Sabbath day and on the day of the New Moon it is to be opened. [2]The prince is to enter from the outside through the portico of the gateway and stand by the gatepost. The priests are to sacrifice his burnt offering and his fellowship offerings. He is to worship at the threshold of the gateway and then go out, but the gate will not be shut until evening. [3]On the Sabbaths and New Moons the people of the land are to worship in the presence of the LORD at the entrance to that gateway. [4]The burnt offering the prince brings to the LORD on the Sabbath day is to be six male lambs and a ram, all without defect. [5]The grain offering given with the ram is to be an ephah, and the grain offering with the lambs is to be as much as he pleases, along with a hin of oil for each ephah. [6]On the day of the New Moon he is to offer a young bull, six lambs and a ram, all without defect. [7]He is to provide as a grain offering one ephah with the bull, one ephah with the ram, and with the lambs as much as he wants to give, along with a hin of oil with each ephah. [8]When the prince enters, he is to go in through the portico of the gateway, and he is to come out the same way.

9 "'When the people of the land come before the LORD at the appointed feasts, whoever enters by the north gate to worship is to go out by the south gate; and whoever enters by the south gate is to go out by the north gate. No-one is to return through the gate by which he entered, but each is to go out by the opposite gate. 10The prince is to be among them, going in when they go in and going out when they go out.

11 "'At the festivals and the appointed feasts, the grain offering is to be an ephah with a bull, an ephah with a ram, and with the lambs as much as one pleases, along with a hin of oil for each ephah. 12When the prince provides a freewill offering to the LORD—whether a burnt offering or fellowship offerings —the gate facing east is to be opened for him. He shall offer his burnt offering or his fellowship offerings as he does on the Sabbath day. Then he shall go out, and after he has gone out, the gate will be shut.

13 "'Every day you are to provide a year-old lamb without defect for a burnt offering to the LORD; morning by morning you shall provide it. 14You are also to provide with it morning by morning a grain offering, consisting of a sixth of an ephah with a third of a hin of oil to moisten the flour. The presenting of this grain offering to the LORD is a lasting ordinance. 15So the lamb and the grain offering and the oil shall be provided morning by morning for a regular burnt offering.

16 "'This is what the Sovereign LORD says: If the prince makes a gift from his inheritance to one of his sons, it will also belong to his descendants; it is to be their property by inheritance. 17If, however, he makes a gift from his inheritance to one of his servants, the servant may keep it until the year of freedom; then it will revert to the prince. His inheritance belongs to his sons only; it is theirs. 18The prince must not take any of the inheritance of the people, driving them off their property. He is to give his sons their inheritance out of his own property, so that none of my people will be separated from his property.'"

19Then the man brought me through the entrance at the side of the gate to the sacred rooms facing north, which belonged to the priests, and showed me a place at the western end. 20He said to me, "This is the place where the priests will cook the guilt offering and the sin offering and bake the grain offering, to avoid bringing them into the outer court and consecrating the people."

21He then brought me to the outer court and led me round to its four corners, and I saw in each corner another court. 22In the four corners of the outer court were enclosed courts, forty cubits long and thirty cubits wide; each of the courts in the four corners was the same size. 23Around the inside of each of the four courts was a ledge of stone, with places for fire built all round under the ledge. 24He said to me, "These are the kitchens where those who minister at the temple will cook the sacrifices of the people."

NEW TESTAMENT READING
1 Peter 3:1–22

Wives and Husbands

3 Wives, in the same way be submissive to your husbands so that, if any of them do not believe the word, they may be won over without words by the behaviour of their wives, 2when they see the purity and reverence of your lives. 3Your beauty should not come from outward adornment, such as braided hair and the wearing of gold jewellery and fine clothes. 4Instead, it should be that of your inner self, the unfading beauty of a gentle and quiet spirit, which is of great worth in God's sight. 5For this is the way the holy women of the past who put their hope in God used to make themselves beautiful. They were submissive to their own

husbands, [6]like Sarah, who obeyed Abraham and called him her master. You are her daughters if you do what is right and do not give way to fear.

[7]Husbands, in the same way be considerate as you live with your wives, and treat them with respect as the weaker partner and as heirs with you of the gracious gift of life, so that nothing will hinder your prayers.

Suffering for Doing Good

[8]Finally, all of you, live in harmony with one another; be sympathetic, love as brothers, be compassionate and humble. [9]Do not repay evil with evil or insult with insult, but with blessing, because to this you were called so that you may inherit a blessing. [10]For,

"Whoever would love life
　and see good days
must keep his tongue from evil
　and his lips from deceitful speech.
[11]He must turn from evil and do good;
　he must seek peace and pursue it.
[12]For the eyes of the Lord are on the
　　righteous
　and his ears are attentive to their
　　prayer,
　but the face of the Lord is against
　　those who do evil."

[13]Who is going to harm you if you are eager to do good? [14]But even if you should suffer for what is right, you are blessed. "Do not fear what they fear; do not be frightened." [15]But in your hearts set apart Christ as Lord. Always be prepared to give an answer to everyone who asks you to give the reason for the hope that you have. But do this with gentleness and respect, [16]keeping a clear conscience, so that those who speak maliciously against your good behaviour in Christ may be ashamed of their slander. [17]It is better, if it is God's will, to suffer for doing good than for doing evil. [18]For Christ died for sins once for all, the righteous for the unrighteous, to bring you to God. He was

put to death in the body but made alive by the Spirit, [19]through whom also he went and preached to the spirits in prison [20]who disobeyed long ago when God waited patiently in the days of Noah while the ark was being built. In it only a few people, eight in all, were saved through water, [21]and this water symbolises baptism that now saves you also—not the removal of dirt from the body but the pledge of a good conscience towards God. It saves you by the resurrection of Jesus Christ, [22]who has gone into heaven and is at God's right hand—with angels, authorities and powers in submission to him.

READING FROM PROVERBS
Proverbs 28:18–28

[18]He whose walk is blameless is kept
　　safe,
　but he whose ways are perverse
　　will suddenly fall.

[19]He who works his land will have
　　abundant food,
　but the one who chases fantasies
　　will have his fill of poverty.

[20]A faithful man will be richly blessed,
　but one eager to get rich will not go
　　unpunished.

[21]To show partiality is not good—
　yet a man will do wrong for a piece
　　of bread.

[22]A stingy man is eager to get rich
　and is unaware that poverty awaits
　　him.

[23]He who rebukes a man will in the end
　　gain more favour
　than he who has a flattering
　　tongue.

[24]He who robs his father or mother
　and says, "It's not wrong"—

he is partner to him who
  destroys.

25A greedy man stirs up dissension,
  but he who trusts in the LORD will
    prosper.

26He who trusts in himself is a fool,
  but he who walks in wisdom is kept
    safe.

27He who gives to the poor will lack
    nothing,
  but he who closes his eyes to them
    receives many curses.

28When the wicked rise to power,
    people go into hiding;
  but when the wicked perish, the
    righteous thrive.

DAY 329   **NOVEMBER 25**

OLD TESTAMENT READING
Ezekiel 47:1–48:35

The River From the Temple

47 The man brought me back to the
   entrance of the temple, and I
saw water coming out from under the
threshold of the temple towards the east
(for the temple faced east). The water
was coming down from under the south
side of the temple, south of the altar.
2He then brought me out through the
north gate and led me round the outside
to the outer gate facing east, and the
water was flowing from the south side.

3As the man went eastward with a
measuring line in his hand, he measured
off a thousand cubits and then led me
through water that was ankle-deep. 4He
measured off another thousand cubits
and led me through water that was
knee-deep. He measured off another
thousand and led me through water that
was up to the waist. 5He measured off
another thousand, but now it was a river
that I could not cross, because the water
had risen and was deep enough to swim
in—a river that no-one could cross. 6He
asked me, "Son of man, do you see
this?"

Then he led me back to the bank of
the river. 7When I arrived there, I saw a
great number of trees on each side of
the river. 8He said to me, "This water

flows towards the eastern region and
goes down into the Arabah, where it
enters the Sea. When it empties into the
Sea, the water there becomes fresh.
9Swarms of living creatures will live
wherever the river flows. There will be
large numbers of fish, because this
water flows there and makes the salt
water fresh; so where the river flows
everything will live. 10Fishermen will
stand along the shore; from En Gedi to
En Eglaim there will be places for
spreading nets. The fish will be of many
kinds—like the fish of the Great Sea.
11But the swamps and marshes will not
become fresh; they will be left for salt.
12Fruit trees of all kinds will grow on
both banks of the river. Their leaves will
not wither, nor will their fruit fail.
Every month they will bear, because the
water from the sanctuary flows to them.
Their fruit will serve for food and their
leaves for healing."

The Boundaries of the Land

13This is what the Sovereign LORD
says: "These are the boundaries by
which you are to divide the land for an
inheritance among the twelve tribes of
Israel, with two portions for Joseph.
14You are to divide it equally among
them. Because I swore with uplifted
hand to give it to your forefathers, this
land will become your inheritance.

¹⁵"This is to be the boundary of the land:

"On the north side it will run from the Great Sea by the Hethlon road past Lebo Hamath to Zedad, ¹⁶Berothah and Sibraim (which lies on the border between Damascus and Hamath), as far as Hazer Hatticon, which is on the border of Hauran. ¹⁷The boundary will extend from the sea to Hazar Enan, along the northern border of Damascus, with the border of Hamath to the north. This will be the north boundary.

¹⁸"On the east side the boundary will run between Hauran and Damascus, along the Jordan between Gilead and the land of Israel, to the eastern sea and as far as Tamar. This will be the east boundary.

¹⁹"On the south side it will run from Tamar as far as the waters of Meribah Kadesh, then along the Wadi ⌞of Egypt⌟ to the Great Sea. This will be the south boundary.

²⁰"On the west side, the Great Sea will be the boundary to a point opposite Lebo Hamath. This will be the west boundary.

²¹"You are to distribute this land among yourselves according to the tribes of Israel. ²²You are to allot it as an inheritance for yourselves and for the aliens who have settled among you and who have children. You are to consider them as native-born Israelites; along with you they are to be allotted an inheritance among the tribes of Israel. ²³In whatever tribe the alien settles, there you are to give him his inheritance," declares the Sovereign LORD.

The Division of the Land

48 "These are the tribes, listed by name: At the northern frontier, Dan will have one portion; it will follow the Hethlon road to Lebo Hamath; Hazar Enan and the northern border of Damascus next to Hamath will be part of its border from the east side to the west side.

²"Asher will have one portion; it will border the territory of Dan from east to west.

³"Naphtali will have one portion; it will border the territory of Asher from east to west.

⁴"Manasseh will have one portion; it will border the territory of Naphtali from east to west.

⁵"Ephraim will have one portion; it will border the territory of Manasseh from east to west.

⁶"Reuben will have one portion; it will border the territory of Ephraim from east to west.

⁷"Judah will have one portion; it will border the territory of Reuben from east to west.

⁸"Bordering the territory of Judah from east to west will be the portion you are to present as a special gift. It will be 25,000 cubits wide, and its length from east to west will equal one of the tribal portions; the sanctuary will be in the centre of it.

⁹"The special portion you are to offer to the LORD will be 25,000 cubits long and 10,000 cubits wide. ¹⁰This will be the sacred portion for the priests. It will be 25,000 cubits long on the north side, 10,000 cubits wide on the west side, 10,000 cubits wide on the east side and 25,000 cubits long on the south side. In the centre of it will be the sanctuary of the LORD. ¹¹This will be for the consecrated priests, the Zadokites, who were faithful in serving me and did not go astray as the Levites did when the Israelites went astray. ¹²It will be a special gift to them from the sacred portion of the land, a most holy portion, bordering the territory of the Levites.

¹³"Alongside the territory of the priests, the Levites will have an allotment 25,000 cubits long and 10,000 cubits wide. Its total length will be 25,000 cubits and its width 10,000 cubits. ¹⁴They must not sell or exchange any of it. This is the best of the land, and

must not pass into other hands, because it is holy to the LORD.

15"The remaining area, 5,000 cubits wide and 25,000 cubits long, will be for the common use of the city, for houses and for pasture-land. The city will be in the centre of it 16and will have these measurements: the north side 4,500 cubits, the south side 4,500 cubits, the east side 4,500 cubits, and the west side 4,500 cubits. 17The pasture-land for the city will be 250 cubits on the north, 250 cubits on the south, 250 cubits on the east, and 250 cubits on the west. 18What remains of the area, bordering on the sacred portion and running the length of it, will be 10,000 cubits on the east side and 10,000 cubits on the west side. Its produce will supply food for the workers of the city. 19The workers from the city who farm it will come from all the tribes of Israel. 20The entire portion will be a square, 25,000 cubits on each side. As a special gift you will set aside the sacred portion, along with the property of the city.

21"What remains on both sides of the area formed by the sacred portion and the city property will belong to the prince. It will extend eastward from the 25,000 cubits of the sacred portion to the eastern border, and westward from the 25,000 cubits to the western border. Both these areas running the length of the tribal portions will belong to the prince, and the sacred portion with the temple sanctuary will be in the centre of them. 22So the property of the Levites and the property of the city will lie in the centre of the area that belongs to the prince. The area belonging to the prince will lie between the border of Judah and the border of Benjamin.

23"As for the rest of the tribes: Benjamin will have one portion; it will extend from the east side to the west side.

24"Simeon will have one portion; it will border the territory of Benjamin from east to west.

25"Issachar will have one portion; it will border the territory of Simeon from east to west.

26"Zebulun will have one portion; it will border the territory of Issachar from east to west.

27"Gad will have one portion; it will border the territory of Zebulun from east to west.

28"The southern boundary of Gad will run south from Tamar to the waters of Meribah Kadesh, then along the Wadi ⌐of Egypt⌐ to the Great Sea.

29"This is the land you are to allot as an inheritance to the tribes of Israel, and these will be their portions," declares the Sovereign LORD.

The Gates of the City

30"These will be the exits of the city: Beginning on the north side, which is 4,500 cubits long, 31the gates of the city will be named after the tribes of Israel. The three gates on the north side will be the gate of Reuben, the gate of Judah and the gate of Levi.

32"On the east side, which is 4,500 cubits long, will be three gates: the gate of Joseph, the gate of Benjamin and the gate of Dan.

33"On the south side, which measures 4,500 cubits, will be three gates: the gate of Simeon, the gate of Issachar and the gate of Zebulun.

34"On the west side, which is 4,500 cubits long, will be three gates: the gate of Gad, the gate of Asher and the gate of Naphtali.

35"The distance all around will be 18,000 cubits.

"And the name of the city from that time on will be:

THE LORD IS THERE."

NEW TESTAMENT READING
1 Peter 4:1–19

Living for God

4 Therefore, since Christ suffered in his body, arm yourselves also with the same attitude, because he who has

suffered in his body is done with sin. ²As a result, he does not live the rest of his earthly life for evil human desires, but rather for the will of God. ³For you have spent enough time in the past doing what pagans choose to do—living in debauchery, lust, drunkenness, orgies, carousing and detestable idolatry. ⁴They think it strange that you do not plunge with them into the same flood of dissipation, and they heap abuse on you. ⁵But they will have to give account to him who is ready to judge the living and the dead. ⁶For this is the reason the gospel was preached even to those who are now dead, so that they might be judged according to men in regard to the body, but live according to God in regard to the spirit.

⁷The end of all things is near. Therefore be clear minded and self-controlled so that you can pray. ⁸Above all, love each other deeply, because love covers over a multitude of sins. ⁹Offer hospitality to one another without grumbling. ¹⁰Each one should use whatever gift he has received to serve others, faithfully administering God's grace in its various forms. ¹¹If anyone speaks, he should do it as one speaking the very words of God. If anyone serves, he should do it with the strength God provides, so that in all things God may be praised through Jesus Christ. To him be the glory and the power for ever and ever. Amen.

Suffering for Being a Christian

¹²Dear friends, do not be surprised at the painful trial you are suffering, as though something strange were happening to you. ¹³But rejoice that you participate in the sufferings of Christ, so that you may be overjoyed when his glory is revealed. ¹⁴If you are insulted because of the name of Christ, you are blessed, for the Spirit of glory and of God rests on you. ¹⁵If you suffer, it should not be as a murderer or thief or any other kind of criminal, or even as a meddler. ¹⁶However, if you suffer as a Christian, do not be ashamed, but praise God that you bear that name. ¹⁷For it is time for judgment to begin with the family of God; and if it begins with us, what will the outcome be for those who do not obey the gospel of God? ¹⁸And,

> "If it is hard for the righteous to be saved,
>   what will become of the ungodly and the sinner?"

¹⁹So then, those who suffer according to God's will should commit themselves to their faithful Creator and continue to do good.

READING FROM PSALMS
Psalm 133:1–3

A song of ascents. Of David.

¹How good and pleasant it is
    when brothers live together in unity!
²It is like precious oil poured on the head,
    running down on the beard,
    running down on Aaron's beard,
    down upon the collar of his robes.
³It is as if the dew of Hermon
    were falling on Mount Zion.
For there the LORD bestows his blessing,
    even life for evermore.

OLD TESTAMENT READING
Daniel 1:1–2:23

Daniel's Training in Babylon

1 In the third year of the reign of Jehoiakim king of Judah, Nebuchadnezzar king of Babylon came to Jerusalem and besieged it. ²And the Lord delivered Jehoiakim king of Judah into his hand, along with some of the articles from the temple of God. These he carried off to the temple of his god in Babylonia and put in the treasure-house of his god.

³Then the king ordered Ashpenaz, chief of his court officials, to bring in some of the Israelites from the royal family and the nobility—⁴young men without any physical defect, handsome, showing aptitude for every kind of learning, well informed, quick to understand, and qualified to serve in the king's palace. He was to teach them the language and literature of the Babylonians. ⁵The king assigned them a daily amount of food and wine from the king's table. They were to be trained for three years, and after that they were to enter the king's service.

⁶Among these were some from Judah: Daniel, Hananiah, Mishael and Azariah. ⁷The chief official gave them new names: to Daniel, the name Belteshazzar; to Hananiah, Shadrach; to Mishael, Meshach; and to Azariah, Abednego.

⁸But Daniel resolved not to defile himself with the royal food and wine, and he asked the chief official for permission not to defile himself in this way. ⁹Now God had caused the official to show favour and sympathy to Daniel, ¹⁰but the official told Daniel, "I am afraid of my lord the king, who has assigned your food and drink. Why should he see you looking worse than the other young men of your age? The king would then have my head because of you."

¹¹Daniel then said to the guard whom the chief official had appointed over Daniel, Hananiah, Mishael and Azariah, ¹²"Please test your servants for ten days: Give us nothing but vegetables to eat and water to drink. ¹³Then compare our appearance with that of the young men who eat the royal food, and treat your servants in accordance with what you see." ¹⁴So he agreed to this and tested them for ten days.

¹⁵At the end of the ten days they looked healthier and better nourished than any of the young men who ate the royal food. ¹⁶So the guard took away their choice food and the wine they were to drink and gave them vegetables instead.

¹⁷To these four young men God gave knowledge and understanding of all kinds of literature and learning. And Daniel could understand visions and dreams of all kinds.

¹⁸At the end of the time set by the king to bring them in, the chief official presented them to Nebuchadnezzar. ¹⁹The king talked with them, and he found none equal to Daniel, Hananiah, Mishael and Azariah; so they entered the king's service. ²⁰In every matter of wisdom and understanding about which the king questioned them, he found them ten times better than all the magicians and enchanters in his whole kingdom.

²¹And Daniel remained there until the first year of King Cyrus.

Nebuchadnezzar's Dream

2 In the second year of his reign, Nebuchadnezzar had dreams; his mind was troubled and he could not sleep. ²So the king summoned the magicians, enchanters, sorcerers and astrologers to tell him what he had

dreamed. When they came in and stood before the king, [3]he said to them, "I have had a dream that troubles me and I want to know what it means."

[4]Then the astrologers answered the king in Aramaic, "O king, live for ever! Tell your servants the dream, and we will interpret it."

[5]The king replied to the astrologers, "This is what I have firmly decided: If you do not tell me what my dream was and interpret it, I will have you cut into pieces and your houses turned into piles of rubble. [6]But if you tell me the dream and explain it, you will receive from me gifts and rewards and great honour. So tell me the dream and interpret it for me."

[7]Once more they replied, "Let the king tell his servants the dream, and we will interpret it."

[8]Then the king answered, "I am certain that you are trying to gain time, because you realise that this is what I have firmly decided: [9]If you do not tell me the dream, there is just one penalty for you. You have conspired to tell me misleading and wicked things, hoping the situation will change. So then, tell me the dream, and I will know that you can interpret it for me."

[10]The astrologers answered the king, "There is not a man on earth who can do what the king asks! No king, however great and mighty, has ever asked such a thing of any magician or enchanter or astrologer. [11]What the king asks is too difficult. No-one can reveal it to the king except the gods, and they do not live among men."

[12]This made the king so angry and furious that he ordered the execution of all the wise men of Babylon. [13]So the decree was issued to put the wise men to death, and men were sent to look for Daniel and his friends to put them to death.

[14]When Arioch, the commander of the king's guard, had gone out to put to death the wise men of Babylon, Daniel spoke to him with wisdom and tact. [15]He asked the king's officer, "Why did the king issue such a harsh decree?" Arioch then explained the matter to Daniel. [16]At this, Daniel went in to the king and asked for time, so that he might interpret the dream for him.

[17]Then Daniel returned to his house and explained the matter to his friends Hananiah, Mishael and Azariah. [18]He urged them to plead for mercy from the God of heaven concerning this mystery, so that he and his friends might not be executed with the rest of the wise men of Babylon. [19]During the night the mystery was revealed to Daniel in a vision. Then Daniel praised the God of heaven [20]and said:

"Praise be to the name of God for
        ever and ever;
    wisdom and power are his.
[21]He changes times and seasons;
    he sets up kings and deposes them.
  He gives wisdom to the wise
    and knowledge to the discerning.
[22]He reveals deep and hidden things;
    he knows what lies in darkness,
    and light dwells with him.
[23]I thank and praise you, O God of my
        fathers:
    You have given me wisdom and
        power,
  you have made known to me what we
        asked of you,
    you have made known to us the
        dream of the king."

NEW TESTAMENT READING
1 Peter 5:1–14

To Elders and Young Men

5 To the elders among you, I appeal as a fellow-elder, a witness of Christ's sufferings and one who also will share in the glory to be revealed: [2]Be shepherds of God's flock that is under your care, serving as overseers—not because you must, but because you are willing, as God wants you to be; not greedy for money, but eager to serve; [3]not lording it over those entrusted to

you, but being examples to the flock. [4]And when the Chief Shepherd appears, you will receive the crown of glory that will never fade away.

[5]Young men, in the same way be submissive to those who are older. All of you, clothe yourselves with humility towards one another, because,

"God opposes the proud
    but gives grace to the humble."

[6]Humble yourselves, therefore, under God's mighty hand, that he may lift you up in due time. [7]Cast all your anxiety on him because he cares for you.

[8]Be self-controlled and alert. Your enemy the devil prowls around like a roaring lion looking for someone to devour. [9]Resist him, standing firm in the faith, because you know that your brothers throughout the world are undergoing the same kind of sufferings.

[10]And the God of all grace, who called you to his eternal glory in Christ, after you have suffered a little while, will himself restore you and make you strong, firm and steadfast. [11]To him be the power for ever and ever. Amen.

Final Greetings

[12]With the help of Silas, whom I regard as a faithful brother, I have written to you briefly, encouraging you and testifying that this is the true grace of God. Stand fast in it.

[13]She who is in Babylon, chosen together with you, sends you her greetings, and so does my son Mark. [14]Greet one another with a kiss of love.

Peace to all of you who are in Christ.

READING FROM PSALMS
Psalm 134:1–3

A song of ascents.

[1]Praise the LORD, all you servants of
        the LORD
    who minister by night in the house
        of the LORD.
[2]Lift up your hands in the sanctuary
    and praise the LORD.

[3]May the LORD, the Maker of heaven
        and earth,
    bless you from Zion.

DAY 331

NOVEMBER 27

OLD TESTAMENT READING
Daniel 2:24–3:12

Daniel Interprets the Dream

[24]Then Daniel went to Arioch, whom the king had appointed to execute the wise men of Babylon, and said to him, "Do not execute the wise men of Babylon. Take me to the king, and I will interpret his dream for him."

[25]Arioch took Daniel to the king at once and said, "I have found a man among the exiles from Judah who can tell the king what his dream means."

[26]The king asked Daniel (also called Belteshazzar), "Are you able to tell me what I saw in my dream and interpret it?"

[27]Daniel replied, "No wise man, enchanter, magician or diviner can explain to the king the mystery he has asked about, [28]but there is a God in heaven who reveals mysteries. He has shown King Nebuchadnezzar what will happen in days to come. Your dream and the visions that passed through your mind as you lay on your bed are these:

[29]"As you were lying there, O king, your mind turned to things to come, and

the revealer of mysteries showed you what is going to happen. [30]As for me, this mystery has been revealed to me, not because I have greater wisdom than other living men, but so that you, O king, may know the interpretation and that you may understand what went through your mind.

[31]"You looked, O king, and there before you stood a large statue—an enormous, dazzling statue, awesome in appearance. [32]The head of the statue was made of pure gold, its chest and arms of silver, its belly and thighs of bronze, [33]its legs of iron, its feet partly of iron and partly of baked clay. [34]While you were watching, a rock was cut out, but not by human hands. It struck the statue on its feet of iron and clay and smashed them. [35]Then the iron, the clay, the bronze, the silver and the gold were broken to pieces at the same time and became like chaff on a threshing-floor in the summer. The wind swept them away without leaving a trace. But the rock that struck the statue became a huge mountain and filled the whole earth.

[36]"This was the dream, and now we will interpret it to the king. [37]You, O king, are the king of kings. The God of heaven has given you dominion and power and might and glory; [38]in your hands he has placed mankind and the beasts of the field and the birds of the air. Wherever they live, he has made you ruler over them all. You are that head of gold.

[39]"After you, another kingdom will rise, inferior to yours. Next, a third kingdom, one of bronze, will rule over the whole earth. [40]Finally, there will be a fourth kingdom, strong as iron—for iron breaks and smashes everything—and as iron breaks things to pieces, so it will crush and break all the others. [41]Just as you saw that the feet and toes were partly of baked clay and partly of iron, so this will be a divided kingdom; yet it will have some of the strength of iron in it, even as you saw iron mixed with clay. [42]As the toes were partly iron

and partly clay, so this kingdom will be partly strong and partly brittle. [43]And just as you saw the iron mixed with baked clay, so the people will be a mixture and will not remain united, any more than iron mixes with clay.

[44]"In the time of those kings, the God of heaven will set up a kingdom that will never be destroyed, nor will it be left to another people. It will crush all those kingdoms and bring them to an end, but it will itself endure for ever. [45]This is the meaning of the vision of the rock cut out of a mountain, but not by human hands—a rock that broke the iron, the bronze, the clay, the silver and the gold to pieces.

"The great God has shown the king what will take place in the future. The dream is true and the interpretation is trustworthy."

[46]Then King Nebuchadnezzar fell prostrate before Daniel and paid him honour and ordered that an offering and incense be presented to him. [47]The king said to Daniel, "Surely your God is the God of gods and the Lord of kings and a revealer of mysteries, for you were able to reveal this mystery."

[48]Then the king placed Daniel in a high position and lavished many gifts on him. He made him ruler over the entire province of Babylon and placed him in charge of all its wise men. [49]Moreover, at Daniel's request the king appointed Shadrach, Meshach and Abednego administrators over the province of Babylon, while Daniel himself remained at the royal court.

The Image of Gold and the Fiery Furnace

3 King Nebuchadnezzar made an image of gold, ninety feet high and nine feet wide, and set it up on the plain of Dura in the province of Babylon. [2]He then summoned the satraps, prefects, governors, advisers, treasurers, judges, magistrates and all the other provincial officials to come to the dedication of the image he had set up. [3]So the satraps, prefects, governors, advisers, treasurers, judges, magistrates and all the other provincial officials assembled for the dedication of the image that King Nebuchadnezzar had set up, and they stood before it.

⁴Then the herald loudly proclaimed, "This is what you are commanded to do, O peoples, nations and men of every language: ⁵As soon as you hear the sound of the horn, flute, zither, lyre, harp, pipes and all kinds of music, you must fall down and worship the image of gold that King Nebuchadnezzar has set up. ⁶Whoever does not fall down and worship will immediately be thrown into a blazing furnace."

⁷Therefore, as soon as they heard the sound of the horn, flute, zither, lyre, harp and all kinds of music, all the peoples, nations and men of every language fell down and worshipped the image of gold that King Nebuchadnezzar had set up.

⁸At this time some astrologers came forward and denounced the Jews. ⁹They said to King Nebuchadnezzar, "O king, live for ever! ¹⁰You have issued a decree, O king, that everyone who hears the sound of the horn, flute, zither, lyre, harp, pipes and all kinds of music must fall down and worship the image of gold, ¹¹and that whoever does not fall down and worship will be thrown into a blazing furnace. ¹²But there are some Jews whom you have set over the affairs of the province of Babylon—Shadrach, Meshach and Abednego—who pay no attention to you, O king. They neither serve your gods nor worship the image of gold you have set up."

NEW TESTAMENT READING
2 Peter 1:1–21

1 Simon Peter, a servant and apostle of Jesus Christ,

To those who through the righteousness of our God and Saviour Jesus Christ have received a faith as precious as ours:

²Grace and peace be yours in abundance through the knowledge of God and of Jesus our Lord.

Making One's Calling and Election Sure

³His divine power has given us everything we need for life and godliness through our knowledge of him who called us by his own glory and goodness. ⁴Through these he has given us his very great and precious promises, so that through them you may participate in the divine nature and escape the corruption in the world caused by evil desires.

⁵For this very reason, make every effort to add to your faith goodness; and to goodness, knowledge; ⁶and to knowledge, self-control; and to self-control, perseverance; and to perseverance, godliness; ⁷and to godliness, brotherly kindness; and to brotherly kindness, love. ⁸For if you possess these qualities in increasing measure, they will keep you from being ineffective and unproductive in your knowledge of our Lord Jesus Christ. ⁹But if anyone does not have them, he is short-sighted and blind, and has forgotten that he has been cleansed from his past sins.

¹⁰Therefore, my brothers, be all the more eager to make your calling and election sure. For if you do these things, you will never fall, ¹¹and you will receive a rich welcome into the eternal kingdom of our Lord and Saviour Jesus Christ.

Prophecy of Scripture

¹²So I will always remind you of these things, even though you know them and are firmly established in the truth you now have. ¹³I think it is right to refresh your memory as long as I live in the tent of this body, ¹⁴because I know that I will soon put it aside, as our Lord Jesus Christ has made clear to me. ¹⁵And I

will make every effort to see that after my departure you will always be able to remember these things.

¹⁶We did not follow cleverly invented stories when we told you about the power and coming of our Lord Jesus Christ, but we were eye-witnesses of his majesty. ¹⁷For he received honour and glory from God the Father when the voice came to him from the Majestic Glory, saying, "This is my Son, whom I love; with him I am well pleased." ¹⁸We ourselves heard this voice that came from heaven when we were with him on the sacred mountain.

¹⁹And we have the word of the prophets made more certain, and you will do well to pay attention to it, as to a light shining in a dark place, until the day dawns and the morning star rises in your hearts. ²⁰Above all, you must understand that no prophecy of Scripture came about by the prophet's own interpretation. ²¹For prophecy never had its origin in the will of man, but men spoke from God as they were carried along by the Holy Spirit.

READING FROM PSALMS
Psalm 135:1–12

¹Praise the LORD.

Praise the name of the LORD;
  praise him, you servants of the
    LORD,
²you who minister in the house of the
    LORD,

in the courts of the house of our
    God.

³Praise the LORD, for the LORD is
    good;
  sing praise to his name, for that is
    pleasant.
⁴For the LORD has chosen Jacob to be
    his own,
  Israel to be his treasured
    possession.

⁵I know that the LORD is great,
  that our Lord is greater than all
    gods.
⁶The LORD does whatever pleases
    him,
  in the heavens and on the earth,
  in the seas and all their depths.
⁷He makes clouds rise from the ends
    of the earth;
  he sends lightning with the rain
  and brings out the wind from his
    storehouses.

⁸He struck down the firstborn of
    Egypt,
  the firstborn of men and animals.
⁹He sent his signs and wonders into
    your midst, O Egypt,
  against Pharaoh and all his
    servants.
¹⁰He struck down many nations
  and killed mighty kings—
¹¹Sihon king of the Amorites,
  Og king of Bashan
  and all the kings of Canaan—
¹²and he gave their land as an
    inheritance,
  an inheritance to his people Israel.

NOVEMBER 28

OLD TESTAMENT READING
Daniel 3:13–4:18

13Furious with rage, Nebuchadnezzar summoned Shadrach, Meshach and Abednego. So these men were brought before the king, 14and Nebuchadnezzar said to them, "Is it true, Shadrach, Meshach and Abednego, that you do not serve my gods or worship the image of gold I have set up? 15Now when you hear the sound of the horn, flute, zither, lyre, harp, pipes and all kinds of music, if you are ready to fall down and worship the image I made, very good. But if you do not worship it, you will be thrown immediately into a blazing furnace. Then what god will be able to rescue you from my hand?"

16Shadrach, Meshach and Abednego replied to the king, "O Nebuchadnezzar, we do not need to defend ourselves before you in this matter. 17If we are thrown into the blazing furnace, the God we serve is able to save us from it, and he will rescue us from your hand, O king. 18But even if he does not, we want you to know, O king, that we will not serve your gods or worship the image of gold you have set up."

19Then Nebuchadnezzar was furious with Shadrach, Meshach and Abednego, and his attitude towards them changed. He ordered the furnace to be heated seven times hotter than usual 20and commanded some of the strongest soldiers in his army to tie up Shadrach, Meshach and Abednego and throw them into the blazing furnace. 21So these men, wearing their robes, trousers, turbans and other clothes, were bound and thrown into the blazing furnace. 22The king's command was so urgent and the furnace so hot that the flames of the fire killed the soldiers who took up Shadrach, Meshach and Abednego, 23and these three men, firmly tied, fell into the blazing furnace.

24Then King Nebuchadnezzar leaped to his feet in amazement and asked his advisers, "Weren't there three men that we tied up and threw into the fire?"

They replied, "Certainly, O king."

25He said, "Look! I see four men walking around in the fire, unbound and unharmed, and the fourth looks like a son of the gods."

26Nebuchadnezzar then approached the opening of the blazing furnace and shouted, "Shadrach, Meshach and Abednego, servants of the Most High God, come out! Come here!"

So Shadrach, Meshach and Abednego came out of the fire, 27and the satraps, prefects, governors and royal advisers crowded around them. They saw that the fire had not harmed their bodies, nor was a hair of their heads singed; their robes were not scorched, and there was no smell of fire on them.

28Then Nebuchadnezzar said, "Praise be to the God of Shadrach, Meshach and Abednego, who has sent his angel and rescued his servants! They trusted in him and defied the king's command and were willing to give up their lives rather than serve or worship any god except their own God. 29Therefore I decree that the people of any nation or language who say anything against the God of Shadrach, Meshach and Abednego be cut into pieces and their houses be turned into piles of rubble, for no other god can save in this way." 30Then the king promoted Shadrach, Meshach and Abednego in the province of Babylon.

Nebuchadnezzar's Dream of a Tree

4 King Nebuchadnezzar,

To the peoples, nations and men of every language, who live in all the world:

May you prosper greatly!

[2] It is my pleasure to tell you about the miraculous signs and wonders that the Most High God has performed for me.

3 How great are his signs,
   how mighty his wonders!
His kingdom is an eternal
   kingdom;
   his dominion endures from
      generation to generation.

[4] I, Nebuchadnezzar, was at home in my palace, contented and prosperous. [5] I had a dream that made me afraid. As I was lying in my bed, the images and visions that passed through my mind terrified me. [6] So I commanded that all the wise men of Babylon be brought before me to interpret the dream for me. [7] When the magicians, enchanters, astrologers and diviners came, I told them the dream, but they could not interpret it for me. [8] Finally, Daniel came into my presence and I told him the dream. (He is called Belteshazzar, after the name of my god, and the spirit of the holy gods is in him.)

[9] I said, "Belteshazzar, chief of the magicians, I know that the spirit of the holy gods is in you, and no mystery is too difficult for you. Here is my dream; interpret it for me. [10] These are the visions I saw while lying in my bed: I looked, and there before me stood a tree in the middle of the land. Its height was enormous. [11] The tree grew large and strong and its top touched the sky; it was visible to the ends of the earth. [12] Its leaves were beautiful, its fruit abundant, and on it was food for all. Under it the beasts of the field found shelter, and the birds of the air lived in its branches; from it every creature was fed.

[13] "In the visions I saw while lying in my bed, I looked, and there before me was a messenger, a holy one, coming down from heaven. [14] He called in a loud voice: 'Cut down the tree and trim off its branches; strip off its leaves and scatter its fruit. Let the animals flee from under it and the birds from its branches. [15] But let the stump and its roots, bound with iron and bronze, remain in the ground, in the grass of the field.

"'Let him be drenched with the dew of heaven, and let him live with the animals among the plants of the earth. [16] Let his mind be changed from that of a man and let him be given the mind of an animal, till seven times pass by for him.

[17] "'The decision is announced by messengers, the holy ones declare the verdict, so that the living may know that the Most High is sovereign over the kingdoms of men and gives them to anyone he wishes and sets over them the lowliest of men.'

[18] "This is the dream that I, King Nebuchadnezzar, had. Now, Belteshazzar, tell me what it means, for none of the wise men in my kingdom can interpret it for me. But you can, because the spirit of the holy gods is in you."

NEW TESTAMENT READING
2 Peter 2:1–22

False Teachers and Their Destruction

2 But there were also false prophets among the people, just as there will be false teachers among you. They will secretly introduce destructive heresies, even denying the sovereign Lord who bought them—bringing swift destruction on themselves. [2] Many will follow their shameful ways and will bring the way of truth into disrepute. [3] In their

greed these teachers will exploit you with stories they have made up. Their condemnation has long been hanging over them, and their destruction has not been sleeping.

⁴For if God did not spare angels when they sinned, but sent them to hell, putting them into gloomy dungeons to be held for judgment; ⁵if he did not spare the ancient world when he brought the flood on its ungodly people, but protected Noah, a preacher of righteousness, and seven others; ⁶if he condemned the cities of Sodom and Gomorrah by burning them to ashes, and made them an example of what is going to happen to the ungodly; ⁷and if he rescued Lot, a righteous man, who was distressed by the filthy lives of lawless men ⁸(for that righteous man, living among them day after day, was tormented in his righteous soul by the lawless deeds he saw and heard)—⁹if this is so, then the Lord knows how to rescue godly men from trials and to hold the unrighteous for the day of judgment, while continuing their punishment. ¹⁰This is especially true of those who follow the corrupt desire of the sinful nature and despise authority.

Bold and arrogant, these men are not afraid to slander celestial beings; ¹¹yet even angels, although they are stronger and more powerful, do not bring slanderous accusations against such beings in the presence of the Lord. ¹²But these men blaspheme in matters they do not understand. They are like brute beasts, creatures of instinct, born only to be caught and destroyed, and like beasts they too will perish.

¹³They will be paid back with harm for the harm they have done. Their idea of pleasure is to carouse in broad daylight. They are blots and blemishes, revelling in their pleasures while they feast with you. ¹⁴With eyes full of adultery, they never stop sinning; they seduce the unstable; they are experts in greed—an accursed brood! ¹⁵They have left the straight way and wandered off to follow the way of Balaam son of Beor, who loved the wages of wickedness. ¹⁶But he was rebuked for his wrongdoing by a donkey—a beast without speech—who spoke with a man's voice and restrained the prophet's madness.

¹⁷These men are springs without water and mists driven by a storm. Blackest darkness is reserved for them. ¹⁸For they mouth empty, boastful words and, by appealing to the lustful desires of sinful human nature, they entice people who are just escaping from those who live in error. ¹⁹They promise them freedom, while they themselves are slaves of depravity—for a man is a slave to whatever has mastered him. ²⁰If they have escaped the corruption of the world by knowing our Lord and Saviour Jesus Christ and are again entangled in it and overcome, they are worse off at the end than they were at the beginning. ²¹It would have been better for them not to have known the way of righteousness, than to have known it and then to turn their backs on the sacred command that was passed on to them. ²²Of them the proverbs are true: "A dog returns to its vomit," and, "A sow that is washed goes back to her wallowing in the mud."

READING FROM PROVERBS
Proverbs 29:1–9

29 A man who remains
stiff-necked after many rebukes
will suddenly be destroyed—
without remedy.

²When the righteous thrive, the
people rejoice;
when the wicked rule, the people
groan.

³A man who loves wisdom brings joy
to his father,
but a companion of prostitutes
squanders his wealth.

⁴By justice a king gives a country
    stability,
  but one who is greedy for bribes
    tears it down.

⁵Whoever flatters his neighbour
  is spreading a net for his feet.

⁶An evil man is snared by his own sin,
  but a righteous one can sing and be
    glad.

⁷The righteous care about justice for
    the poor,
  but the wicked have no such
    concern.

⁸Mockers stir up a city,
  but wise men turn away anger.

⁹If a wise man goes to court with a
    fool,
  the fool rages and scoffs, and there
    is no peace.

NOVEMBER 29   DAY 333

OLD TESTAMENT READING
Daniel 4:19–5:16

Daniel Interprets the Dream

¹⁹Then Daniel (also called Bel-
teshazzar) was greatly perplexed
for a time, and his thoughts terrified him. So the king said, "Belteshazzar, do not let the dream or
its meaning alarm you."

Belteshazzar answered, "My
lord, if only the dream applied to
your enemies and its meaning to
your adversaries! ²⁰The tree you
saw, which grew large and strong,
with its top touching the sky, visible to the whole earth, ²¹with
beautiful leaves and abundant
fruit, providing food for all, giving
shelter to the beasts of the field,
and having nesting places in its
branches for the birds of the air
—²²you, O king, are that tree! You
have become great and strong;
your greatness has grown until it
reaches the sky, and your dominion extends to distant parts of the
earth.

²³"You, O king, saw a messen-
ger, a holy one, coming down from
heaven and saying, 'Cut down the
tree and destroy it, but leave the
stump, bound with iron and

bronze, in the grass of the field,
while its roots remain in the
ground. Let him be drenched with
the dew of heaven; let him live like
the wild animals, until seven times
pass by for him.'

²⁴"This is the interpretation, O
king, and this is the decree the
Most High has issued against my
lord the king: ²⁵You will be driven
away from people and will live with
the wild animals; you will eat grass
like cattle and be drenched with the
dew of heaven. Seven times will
pass by for you until you acknowledge that the Most High is
sovereign over the kingdoms of
men and gives them to anyone he
wishes. ²⁶The command to leave
the stump of the tree with its roots
means that your kingdom will be
restored to you when you acknowledge that Heaven rules. ²⁷There-
fore, O king, be pleased to accept
my advice: Renounce your sins by
doing what is right, and your wickedness by being kind to the oppressed. It may be that then your
prosperity will continue."

The Dream Is Fulfilled

²⁸All this happened to King Ne-
buchadnezzar. ²⁹Twelve months

later, as the king was walking on the roof of the royal palace of Babylon, [30]he said, "Is not this the great Babylon I have built as the royal residence, by my mighty power and for the glory of my majesty?"

[31]The words were still on his lips when a voice came from heaven, "This is what is decreed for you, King Nebuchadnezzar: Your royal authority has been taken from you. [32]You will be driven away from people and will live with the wild animals; you will eat grass like cattle. Seven times will pass by for you until you acknowledge that the Most High is sovereign over the kingdoms of men and gives them to anyone he wishes."

[33]Immediately what had been said about Nebuchadnezzar was fulfilled. He was driven away from people and ate grass like cattle. His body was drenched with the dew of heaven until his hair grew like the feathers of an eagle and his nails like the claws of a bird.

[34]At the end of that time, I, Nebuchadnezzar, raised my eyes towards heaven, and my sanity was restored. Then I praised the Most High; I honoured and glorified him who lives for ever.

His dominion is an eternal dominion;
> his kingdom endures from generation to generation.
[35] All the peoples of the earth are regarded as nothing.
He does as he pleases with the powers of heaven and the peoples of the earth.
No-one can hold back his hand or say to him: "What have you done?"

[36]At the same time that my sanity was restored, my honour and splendour were returned to me for the glory of my kingdom. My advisers and nobles sought me out, and I was restored to my throne and became even greater than before. [37]Now I, Nebuchadnezzar, praise and exalt and glorify the King of heaven, because everything he does is right and all his ways are just. And those who walk in pride he is able to humble.

The Writing on the Wall

5 King Belshazzar gave a great banquet for a thousand of his nobles and drank wine with them. [2]While Belshazzar was drinking his wine, he gave orders to bring in the gold and silver goblets that Nebuchadnezzar his father had taken from the temple in Jerusalem, so that the king and his nobles, his wives and his concubines might drink from them. [3]So they brought in the gold goblets that had been taken from the temple of God in Jerusalem, and the king and his nobles, his wives and his concubines drank from them. [4]As they drank the wine, they praised the gods of gold and silver, of bronze, iron, wood and stone.

[5]Suddenly the fingers of a human hand appeared and wrote on the plaster of the wall, near the lampstand in the royal palace. The king watched the hand as it wrote. [6]His face turned pale and he was so frightened that his knees knocked together and his legs gave way.

[7]The king called out for the enchanters, astrologers and diviners to be brought and said to these wise men of Babylon, "Whoever reads this writing and tells me what it means will be clothed in purple and have a gold chain placed around his neck, and he will be made the third highest ruler in the kingdom."

[8]Then all the king's wise men came in, but they could not read the writing or tell the king what it meant. [9]So King Belshazzar became even more terrified and his face grew more pale. His nobles were baffled.

¹⁰The queen, hearing the voices of the king and his nobles, came into the banquet hall. "O king, live for ever!" she said. "Don't be alarmed! Don't look so pale! ¹¹There is a man in your kingdom who has the spirit of the holy gods in him. In the time of your father he was found to have insight and intelligence and wisdom like that of the gods. King Nebuchadnezzar your father—your father the king, I say—appointed him chief of the magicians, enchanters, astrologers and diviners. ¹²This man Daniel, whom the king called Belteshazzar, was found to have a keen mind and knowledge and understanding, and also the ability to interpret dreams, explain riddles and solve difficult problems. Call for Daniel, and he will tell you what the writing means."

¹³So Daniel was brought before the king, and the king said to him, "Are you Daniel, one of the exiles my father the king brought from Judah? ¹⁴I have heard that the spirit of the gods is in you and that you have insight, intelligence and outstanding wisdom. ¹⁵The wise men and enchanters were brought before me to read this writing and tell me what it means, but they could not explain it. ¹⁶Now I have heard that you are able to give interpretations and to solve difficult problems. If you can read this writing and tell me what it means, you will be clothed in purple and have a gold chain placed around your neck, and you will be made the third highest ruler in the kingdom."

NEW TESTAMENT READING
2 Peter 3:1–18

The Day of the Lord

3 Dear friends, this is now my second letter to you. I have written both of them as reminders to stimulate you to wholesome thinking. ²I want you to recall the words spoken in the past by the holy prophets and the command given by our Lord and Saviour through your apostles.

³First of all, you must understand that in the last days scoffers will come, scoffing and following their own evil desires. ⁴They will say, "Where is this 'coming' he promised? Ever since our fathers died, everything goes on as it has since the beginning of creation." ⁵But they deliberately forget that long ago by God's word the heavens existed and the earth was formed out of water and by water. ⁶By these waters also the world of that time was deluged and destroyed. ⁷By the same word the present heavens and earth are reserved for fire, being kept for the day of judgment and destruction of ungodly men.

⁸But do not forget this one thing, dear friends: With the Lord a day is like a thousand years, and a thousand years are like a day. ⁹The Lord is not slow in keeping his promise, as some understand slowness. He is patient with you, not wanting anyone to perish, but everyone to come to repentance.

¹⁰But the day of the Lord will come like a thief. The heavens will disappear with a roar; the elements will be destroyed by fire, and the earth and everything in it will be laid bare. ¹¹Since everything will be destroyed in this way, what kind of people ought you to be? You ought to live holy and godly lives ¹²as you look forward to the day of God and speed its coming. That day will bring about the destruction of the heavens by fire, and the elements will melt in the heat. ¹³But in keeping with his promise we are looking forward to a new heaven and a new earth, the home of righteousness.

¹⁴So then, dear friends, since you are looking forward to this, make every effort to be found spotless, blameless and at peace with him. ¹⁵Bear in mind that our Lord's patience means salvation, just as our dear brother Paul also wrote to you with the wisdom that God gave him. ¹⁶He writes the same way in all his letters, speaking in them of these matters. His letters contain some things that are hard to understand, which ignorant and unstable people

distort, as they do the other Scriptures, to their own destruction. 17Therefore, dear friends, since you already know this, be on your guard so that you may not be carried away by the error of lawless men and fall from your secure position. 18But grow in the grace and knowledge of our Lord and Saviour Jesus Christ. To him be glory both now and for ever! Amen.

READING FROM PSALMS
Psalm 135:13–21

13Your name, O LORD, endures for
  ever,
    your renown, O LORD, through all
    generations.
14For the LORD will vindicate his
  people

and have compassion on his
  servants.

15The idols of the nations are silver and
  gold,
    made by the hands of men.
16They have mouths, but cannot speak,
    eyes, but they cannot see;
17they have ears, but cannot hear,
    nor is there breath in their mouths.
18Those who make them will be like
  them,
    and so will all who trust in them.

19O house of Israel, praise the LORD;
    O house of Aaron, praise the
    LORD;
20O house of Levi, praise the LORD;
    you who fear him, praise the LORD.
21Praise be to the LORD from Zion,
    to him who dwells in Jerusalem.

Praise the LORD.

DAY 334

NOVEMBER 30

OLD TESTAMENT READING
Daniel 5:17–6:28

17Then Daniel answered the king, "You may keep your gifts for yourself and give your rewards to someone else. Nevertheless, I will read the writing for the king and tell him what it means.

18"O king, the Most High God gave your father Nebuchadnezzar sovereignty and greatness and glory and splendour. 19Because of the high position he gave him, all the peoples and nations and men of every language dreaded and feared him. Those the king wanted to put to death, he put to death; those he wanted to spare, he spared; those he wanted to promote, he promoted; and those he wanted to humble, he humbled. 20But when his heart became arrogant and hardened with pride, he was deposed from his royal

throne and stripped of his glory. 21He was driven away from people and given the mind of an animal; he lived with the wild donkeys and ate grass like cattle; and his body was drenched with the dew of heaven, until he acknowledged that the Most High God is sovereign over the kingdoms of men and sets over them anyone he wishes.

22"But you his son, O Belshazzar, have not humbled yourself, though you knew all this. 23Instead, you have set yourself up against the Lord of heaven. You had the goblets from his temple brought to you, and you and your nobles, your wives and your concubines drank wine from them. You praised the gods of silver and gold, of bronze, iron, wood and stone, which cannot see or hear or understand. But you did not honour the God who holds in his hand your life and all your ways. 24Therefore he sent the hand that wrote the inscription.

25"This is the inscription that was written:

MENE, MENE, TEKEL, PARSIN

26"This is what these words mean:

Mene: God has numbered the days of your reign and brought it to an end.

27*Tekel*: You have been weighed on the scales and found wanting.

28*Peres*: Your kingdom is divided and given to the Medes and Persians."

29Then at Belshazzar's command, Daniel was clothed in purple, a gold chain was placed around his neck, and he was proclaimed the third highest ruler in the kingdom.

30That very night Belshazzar, king of the Babylonians, was slain, 31and Darius the Mede took over the kingdom, at the age of sixty-two.

Daniel in the Den of Lions

6 It pleased Darius to appoint 120 satraps to rule throughout the kingdom, 2with three administrators over them, one of whom was Daniel. The satraps were made accountable to them so that the king might not suffer loss. 3Now Daniel so distinguished himself among the administrators and the satraps by his exceptional qualities that the king planned to set him over the whole kingdom. 4At this, the administrators and the satraps tried to find grounds for charges against Daniel in his conduct of government affairs, but they were unable to do so. They could find no corruption in him, because he was trustworthy and neither corrupt nor negligent. 5Finally these men said, "We will never find any basis for charges against this man Daniel unless it has something to do with the law of his God."

6So the administrators and the satraps went as a group to the king and said: "O King Darius, live for ever! 7The royal administrators, prefects, satraps, advisers and governors have all agreed that the king should issue an edict and enforce the decree that anyone who prays to any god or man during the next thirty days, except to you, O king, shall be thrown into the lions' den. 8Now, O king, issue the decree and put it in writing so that it cannot be altered —in accordance with the laws of the Medes and Persians, which cannot be repealed." 9So King Darius put the decree in writing.

10Now when Daniel learned that the decree had been published, he went home to his upstairs room where the windows opened towards Jerusalem. Three times a day he got down on his knees and prayed, giving thanks to his God, just as he had done before. 11Then these men went as a group and found Daniel praying and asking God for help. 12So they went to the king and spoke to him about his royal decree: "Did you not publish a decree that during the next thirty days anyone who prays to any god or man except to you, O king, would be thrown into the lions' den?"

The king answered, "The decree stands—in accordance with the laws of the Medes and Persians, which cannot be repealed."

13Then they said to the king, "Daniel, who is one of the exiles from Judah, pays no attention to you, O king, or to the decree you put in writing. He still prays three times a day." 14When the king heard this, he was greatly distressed; he was determined to rescue Daniel and made every effort until sundown to save him.

15Then the men went as a group to the king and said to him, "Remember, O king, that according to the law of the Medes and Persians no decree or edict that the king issues can be changed."

16So the king gave the order, and they brought Daniel and threw him into the lions' den. The king said to Daniel, "May your God, whom you serve continually, rescue you!"

17A stone was brought and placed over the mouth of the den, and the king sealed it with his own signet ring and with the rings of his nobles, so that Daniel's situation might not be changed. 18Then the king returned to his palace and spent the night without eating and without any entertainment being brought to him. And he could not sleep.

19At the first light of dawn, the king got up and hurried to the lions' den. 20When he came near the den, he called to Daniel in an anguished voice, "Daniel, servant of the living God, has your God, whom you serve continually, been able to rescue you from the lions?"

21Daniel answered, "O king, live for ever! 22My God sent his angel, and he shut the mouths of the lions. They have not hurt me, because I was found innocent in his sight. Nor have I ever done any wrong before you, O king."

23The king was overjoyed and gave orders to lift Daniel out of the den. And when Daniel was lifted from the den, no wound was found on him, because he had trusted in his God.

24At the king's command, the men who had falsely accused Daniel were brought in and thrown into the lions' den, along with their wives and children. And before they reached the floor of the den, the lions overpowered them and crushed all their bones.

25Then King Darius wrote to all the peoples, nations and men of every language throughout the land:

"May you prosper greatly!

26"I issue a decree that in every part of my kingdom people must fear and reverence the God of Daniel.

"For he is the living God
and he endures for ever;
his kingdom will not be destroyed,
his dominion will never end.

27He rescues and he saves;
he performs signs and wonders
in the heavens and on the earth.
He has rescued Daniel
from the power of the lions."

28So Daniel prospered during the reign of Darius and the reign of Cyrus the Persian.

NEW TESTAMENT READING
1 John 1:1–2:11

The Word of Life

1 That which was from the beginning, which we have heard, which we have seen with our eyes, which we have looked at and our hands have touched—this we proclaim concerning the Word of life. 2The life appeared; we have seen it and testify to it, and we proclaim to you the eternal life, which was with the Father and has appeared to us. 3We proclaim to you what we have seen and heard, so that you also may have fellowship with us. And our fellowship is with the Father and with his Son, Jesus Christ. 4We write this to make our joy complete.

Walking in the Light

5This is the message we have heard from him and declare to you: God is light; in him there is no darkness at all. 6If we claim to have fellowship with him yet walk in the darkness, we lie and do not live by the truth. 7But if we walk in the light, as he is in the light, we have fellowship with one another, and the blood of Jesus, his Son, purifies us from all sin.

8If we claim to be without sin, we deceive ourselves and the truth is not in us. 9If we confess our sins, he is faithful and just and will forgive us our sins and purify us from all unrighteousness. 10If we claim we have not sinned, we make him out to be a liar and his word has no place in our lives.

2 My dear children, I write this to you so that you will not sin. But if anybody does sin, we have one who speaks to the Father in our defence —Jesus Christ, the Righteous One. [2]He is the atoning sacrifice for our sins, and not only for ours but also for the sins of the whole world.

[3]We know that we have come to know him if we obey his commands. [4]The man who says, "I know him," but does not do what he commands is a liar, and the truth is not in him. [5]But if anyone obeys his word, God's love is truly made complete in him. This is how we know we are in him: [6]Whoever claims to live in him must walk as Jesus did.

[7]Dear friends, I am not writing you a new command but an old one, which you have had since the beginning. This old command is the message you have heard. [8]Yet I am writing you a new command; its truth is seen in him and you, because the darkness is passing and the true light is already shining.

[9]Anyone who claims to be in the light but hates his brother is still in the darkness. [10]Whoever loves his brother lives in the light, and there is nothing in him to make him stumble. [11]But whoever hates his brother is in the darkness and walks around in the darkness; he does not know where he is going, because the darkness has blinded him.

READING FROM PSALMS
Psalm 136:1–12

[1]Give thanks to the LORD, for he is good.
> *His love endures for ever.*

[2]Give thanks to the God of gods.
> *His love endures for ever.*

[3]Give thanks to the Lord of lords:
> *His love endures for ever.*

[4]to him who alone does great wonders,
> *His love endures for ever.*

[5]who by his understanding made the heavens,
> *His love endures for ever.*

[6]who spread out the earth upon the waters,
> *His love endures for ever.*

[7]who made the great lights—
> *His love endures for ever.*

[8]the sun to govern the day,
> *His love endures for ever.*

[9]the moon and stars to govern the night;
> *His love endures for ever.*

[10]to him who struck down the firstborn of Egypt
> *His love endures for ever.*

[11]and brought Israel out from among them
> *His love endures for ever.*

[12]with a mighty hand and outstretched arm;
> *His love endures for ever.*

DECEMBER 1

OLD TESTAMENT READING
Daniel 7:1–8:14

Daniel's Dream of Four Beasts

7 In the first year of Belshazzar king of Babylon, Daniel had a dream, and visions passed through his mind as he was lying on his bed. He wrote down the substance of his dream.

²Daniel said: "In my vision at night I looked, and there before me were the four winds of heaven churning up the great sea. ³Four great beasts, each different from the others, came up out of the sea.

⁴"The first was like a lion, and it had the wings of an eagle. I watched until its wings were torn off and it was lifted from the ground so that it stood on two feet like a man, and the heart like a man was given to it.

⁵"And there before me was a second beast, which looked like a bear. It was raised up on one of its sides, and it had three ribs in its mouth between its teeth. It was told, 'Get up and eat your fill of flesh!'

⁶"After that, I looked, and there before me was another beast, one that looked like a leopard. And on its back it had four wings like those of a bird. This beast had four heads, and it was given authority to rule.

⁷"After that, in my vision at night I looked, and there before me was a fourth beast—terrifying and frightening and very powerful. It had large iron teeth; it crushed and devoured its victims and trampled underfoot whatever was left. It was different from all the former beasts, and it had ten horns.

⁸"While I was thinking about the horns, there before me was another horn, a little one, which came up among them; and three of the first horns were uprooted before it. This horn had eyes

like the eyes of a man and a mouth that spoke boastfully.

⁹"As I looked,

"thrones were set in place,
   and the Ancient of Days took his
      seat.
His clothing was as white as snow;
   the hair of his head was white like
      wool.
His throne was flaming with fire,
   and its wheels were all ablaze.
¹⁰A river of fire was flowing,
   coming out from before him.
Thousands upon thousands attended
      him;
   ten thousand times ten thousand
      stood before him.
The court was seated,
   and the books were opened.

¹¹"Then I continued to watch because of the boastful words the horn was speaking. I kept looking until the beast was slain and its body destroyed and thrown into the blazing fire. ¹²(The other beasts had been stripped of their authority, but were allowed to live for a period of time.)

¹³"In my vision at night I looked, and there before me was one like a son of man, coming with the clouds of heaven. He approached the Ancient of Days and was led into his presence. ¹⁴He was given authority, glory and sovereign power; all peoples, nations and men of every language worshipped him. His dominion is an everlasting dominion that will not pass away, and his kingdom is one that will never be destroyed.

The Interpretation of the Dream

¹⁵"I, Daniel, was troubled in spirit, and the visions that passed through my mind disturbed me. ¹⁶I approached one of those standing there and asked him the true meaning of all this.

"So he told me and gave me the interpretation of these things: [17]'The four great beasts are four kingdoms that will rise from the earth. [18]But the saints of the Most High will receive the kingdom and will possess it for ever—yes, for ever and ever.'

[19]"Then I wanted to know the true meaning of the fourth beast, which was different from all the others and most terrifying, with its iron teeth and bronze claws—the beast that crushed and devoured its victims and trampled underfoot whatever was left. [20]I also wanted to know about the ten horns on its head and about the other horn that came up, before which three of them fell—the horn that looked more imposing than the others and that had eyes and a mouth that spoke boastfully. [21]As I watched, this horn was waging war against the saints and defeating them, [22]until the Ancient of Days came and pronounced judgment in favour of the saints of the Most High, and the time came when they possessed the kingdom.

[23]"He gave me this explanation: 'The fourth beast is a fourth kingdom that will appear on earth. It will be different from all the other kingdoms and will devour the whole earth, trampling it down and crushing it. [24]The ten horns are ten kings who will come from this kingdom. After them another king will arise, different from the earlier ones; he will subdue three kings. [25]He will speak against the Most High and oppress his saints and try to change the set times and the laws. The saints will be handed over to him for a time, times and half a time.

[26]"'But the court will sit, and his power will be taken away and completely destroyed for ever. [27]Then the sovereignty, power and greatness of the kingdoms under the whole heaven will be handed over to the saints, the people of the Most High. His kingdom will be an everlasting kingdom, and all rulers will worship and obey him.'

[28]"This is the end of the matter. I, Daniel, was deeply troubled by my thoughts, and my face turned pale, but I kept the matter to myself."

Daniel's Vision of a Ram and a Goat

8 In the third year of King Belshazzar's reign, I, Daniel, had a vision, after the one that had already appeared to me. [2]In my vision I saw myself in the citadel of Susa in the province of Elam; in the vision I was beside the Ulai Canal. [3]I looked up, and there before me was a ram with two horns, standing beside the canal, and the horns were long. One of the horns was longer than the other but grew up later. [4]I watched the ram as he charged towards the west and the north and the south. No animal could stand against him, and none could rescue from his power. He did as he pleased and became great.

[5]As I was thinking about this, suddenly a goat with a prominent horn between his eyes came from the west, crossing the whole earth without touching the ground. [6]He came towards the two-horned ram I had seen standing beside the canal and charged at him in great rage. [7]I saw him attack the ram furiously, striking the ram and shattering his two horns. The ram was powerless to stand against him; the goat knocked him to the ground and trampled on him, and none could rescue the ram from his power. [8]The goat became very great, but at the height of his power his large horn was broken off, and in its place four prominent horns grew up towards the four winds of heaven.

[9]Out of one of them came another horn, which started small but grew in power to the south and to the east and towards the Beautiful Land. [10]It grew until it reached the host of the heavens, and it threw some of the starry host down to the earth and trampled on them. [11]It set itself up to be as great as the Prince of the host; it took away the daily sacrifice from him, and the place of his sanctuary was brought low. [12]Because of rebellion, the host of the

saints, and the daily sacrifice were given over to it. It prospered in everything it did, and truth was thrown to the ground.

¹³Then I heard a holy one speaking, and another holy one said to him, "How long will it take for the vision to be fulfilled—the vision concerning the daily sacrifice, the rebellion that causes desolation, and the surrender of the sanctuary and of the host that will be trampled underfoot?"

¹⁴He said to me, "It will take 2,300 evenings and mornings; then the sanctuary will be reconsecrated."

NEW TESTAMENT READING
1 John 2:12–27

¹²I write to you, dear children,
    because your sins have been
      forgiven on account of his
      name.
¹³I write to you, fathers,
    because you have known him who
      is from the beginning.
I write to you, young men,
    because you have overcome the
      evil one.
I write to you, dear children,
    because you have known the
      Father.
¹⁴I write to you, fathers,
    because you have known him who
      is from the beginning.
I write to you, young men,
    because you are strong,
    and the word of God lives in you,
    and you have overcome the evil
      one.

Do Not Love the World

¹⁵Do not love the world or anything in the world. If anyone loves the world, the love of the Father is not in him. ¹⁶For everything in the world—the cravings of sinful man, the lust of his eyes and the boasting of what he has and does—comes not from the Father but from the world. ¹⁷The world and its desires pass away, but the man who does the will of God lives for ever.

Warning Against Antichrists

¹⁸Dear children, this is the last hour; and as you have heard that the antichrist is coming, even now many antichrists have come. This is how we know it is the last hour. ¹⁹They went out from us, but they did not really belong to us. For if they had belonged to us, they would have remained with us; but their going showed that none of them belonged to us.

²⁰But you have an anointing from the Holy One, and all of you know the truth. ²¹I do not write to you because you do not know the truth, but because you do know it and because no lie comes from the truth. ²²Who is the liar? It is the man who denies that Jesus is the Christ. Such a man is the antichrist—he denies the Father and the Son. ²³No-one who denies the Son has the Father; whoever acknowledges the Son has the Father also.

²⁴See that what you have heard from the beginning remains in you. If it does, you also will remain in the Son and in the Father. ²⁵And this is what he promised us—even eternal life.

²⁶I am writing these things to you about those who are trying to lead you astray. ²⁷As for you, the anointing you received from him remains in you, and you do not need anyone to teach you. But as his anointing teaches you about all things and as that anointing is real, not counterfeit—just as it has taught you, remain in him.

READING FROM PSALMS
Psalm 136:13–26

¹³to him who divided the Red Sea
    asunder
      His love endures for ever.
¹⁴and brought Israel through the midst
    of it,
      His love endures for ever.

¹⁵but swept Pharaoh and his army into
    the Red Sea;
      His love endures for ever.

¹⁶to him who led his people through the
    desert,
      His love endures for ever.
¹⁷who struck down great kings,
      His love endures for ever.
¹⁸and killed mighty kings—
      His love endures for ever.
¹⁹Sihon king of the Amorites
      His love endures for ever.
²⁰and Og king of Bashan—
      His love endures for ever.

²¹and gave their land as an inheritance,
      His love endures for ever.
²²an inheritance to his servant Israel;
      His love endures for ever.

²³to the One who remembered us in
    our low estate
      His love endures for ever.
²⁴and freed us from our enemies,
      His love endures for ever.
²⁵and who gives food to every creature.
      His love endures for ever.

²⁶Give thanks to the God of heaven.
      His love endures for ever.

DECEMBER 2   DAY 336

OLD TESTAMENT READING
Daniel 8:15–9:19

The Interpretation of the Vision

¹⁵While I, Daniel, was watching the vision and trying to understand it, there before me stood one who looked like a man. ¹⁶And I heard a man's voice from the Ulai calling, "Gabriel, tell this man the meaning of the vision."

¹⁷As he came near the place where I was standing, I was terrified and fell prostrate. "Son of man," he said to me, "understand that the vision concerns the time of the end."

¹⁸While he was speaking to me, I was in a deep sleep, with my face to the ground. Then he touched me and raised me to my feet.

¹⁹He said: "I am going to tell you what will happen later in the time of wrath, because the vision concerns the appointed time of the end. ²⁰The two-horned ram that you saw represents the kings of Media and Persia. ²¹The shaggy goat is the king of Greece, and the large horn between his eyes is the first king. ²²The four horns that replaced the one that was broken off represent four kingdoms that will emerge from his nation but will not have the same power.

²³"In the latter part of their reign, when rebels have become completely wicked, a stern-faced king, a master of intrigue, will arise. ²⁴He will become very strong, but not by his own power. He will cause astounding devastation and will succeed in whatever he does. He will destroy the mighty men and the holy people. ²⁵He will cause deceit to prosper, and he will consider himself superior. When they feel secure, he will destroy many and take his stand against the Prince of princes. Yet he will be destroyed, but not by human power.

²⁶"The vision of the evenings and mornings that has been given you is true, but seal up the vision, for it concerns the distant future."

²⁷I, Daniel, was exhausted and lay ill for several days. Then I got up and went about the king's business. I was appalled by the vision; it was beyond understanding.

Daniel's Prayer

9 In the first year of Darius son of Xerxes (a Mede by descent), who was made ruler over the Babylonian kingdom—²in the first year of his reign, I, Daniel, understood from the Scriptures, according to the word of the LORD given to Jeremiah the prophet, that the desolation of Jerusalem would last seventy years. ³So I turned to the Lord God and pleaded with him in prayer and petition, in fasting, and in sackcloth and ashes.

⁴I prayed to the LORD my God and confessed:

"O Lord, the great and awesome God, who keeps his covenant of love with all who love him and obey his commands, ⁵we have sinned and done wrong. We have been wicked and have rebelled; we have turned away from your commands and laws. ⁶We have not listened to your servants the prophets, who spoke in your name to our kings, our princes and our fathers, and to all the people of the land.

⁷"Lord, you are righteous, but this day we are covered with shame—the men of Judah and people of Jerusalem and all Israel, both near and far, in all the countries where you have scattered us because of our unfaithfulness to you. ⁸O LORD, we and our kings, our princes and our fathers are covered with shame because we have sinned against you. ⁹The Lord our God is merciful and forgiving, even though we have rebelled against him; ¹⁰we have not obeyed the LORD our God or kept the laws he gave us through his servants the prophets. ¹¹All Israel has transgressed your law and turned away, refusing to obey you.

"Therefore the curses and sworn judgments written in the Law of Moses, the servant of God, have been poured out on us, because we have sinned against you. ¹²You have fulfilled the words spoken against us and against our rulers by bringing upon us great disaster. Under the whole heaven nothing has ever been done like what has been done to Jerusalem. ¹³Just as it is written in the Law of Moses, all this disaster has come upon us, yet we have not sought the favour of the LORD our God by turning from our sins and giving attention to your truth. ¹⁴The LORD did not hesitate to bring the disaster upon us, for the LORD our God is righteous in everything he does; yet we have not obeyed him.

¹⁵"Now, O Lord our God, who brought your people out of Egypt with a mighty hand and who made for yourself a name that endures to this day, we have sinned, we have done wrong. ¹⁶O Lord, in keeping with all your righteous acts, turn away your anger and your wrath from Jerusalem, your city, your holy hill. Our sins and the iniquities of our fathers have made Jerusalem and your people an object of scorn to all those around us.

¹⁷"Now, our God, hear the prayers and petitions of your servant. For your sake, O Lord, look with favour on your desolate sanctuary. ¹⁸Give ear, O God, and hear; open your eyes and see the desolation of the city that bears your Name. We do not make requests of you because we are righteous, but because of your great mercy. ¹⁹O Lord, listen! O Lord, forgive! O Lord, hear and act! For your sake, O my God, do not delay, because your city and your people bear your Name."

NEW TESTAMENT READING
1 John 2:28–3:10

Children of God

²⁸And now, dear children, continue in him, so that when he appears we may be confident and unashamed before him at his coming.

²⁹If you know that he is righteous,

you know that everyone who does what is right has been born of him.

3 How great is the love the Father has lavished on us, that we should be called children of God! And that is what we are! The reason the world does not know us is that it did not know him. ²Dear friends, now we are children of God, and what we will be has not yet been made known. But we know that when he appears, we shall be like him, for we shall see him as he is. ³Everyone who has this hope in him purifies himself, just as he is pure.

⁴Everyone who sins breaks the law; in fact, sin is lawlessness. ⁵But you know that he appeared so that he might take away our sins. And in him is no sin. ⁶No-one who lives in him keeps on sinning. No-one who continues to sin has either seen him or known him.

⁷Dear children, do not let anyone lead you astray. He who does what is right is righteous, just as he is righteous. ⁸He who does what is sinful is of the devil, because the devil has been sinning from the beginning. The reason the Son of God appeared was to destroy the devil's work. ⁹No-one who is born of God will continue to sin, because God's seed remains in him; he cannot go on sinning, because he has been born of God. ¹⁰This is how we know who the children of God are and who the children of the devil are: Anyone who does not do what is right is not a child of God; nor is anyone who does not love his brother.

READING FROM PROVERBS
Proverbs 29:10–18

¹⁰Bloodthirsty men hate a man of integrity
and seek to kill the upright.

¹¹A fool gives full vent to his anger,
but a wise man keeps himself under control.

¹²If a ruler listens to lies,
all his officials become wicked.

¹³The poor man and the oppressor have this in common:
The LORD gives sight to the eyes of both.

¹⁴If a king judges the poor with fairness,
his throne will always be secure.

¹⁵The rod of correction imparts wisdom,
but a child left to himself disgraces his mother.

¹⁶When the wicked thrive, so does sin,
but the righteous will see their downfall.

¹⁷Discipline your son, and he will give you peace;
he will bring delight to your soul.

¹⁸Where there is no revelation, the people cast off restraint;
but blessed is he who keeps the law.

DECEMBER 3

OLD TESTAMENT READING
Daniel 9:20–11:1

The Seventy "Sevens"

20While I was speaking and praying, confessing my sin and the sin of my people Israel and making my request to the LORD my God for his holy hill— 21while I was still in prayer, Gabriel, the man I had seen in the earlier vision, came to me in swift flight about the time of the evening sacrifice. 22He instructed me and said to me, "Daniel, I have now come to give you insight and understanding. 23As soon as you began to pray, an answer was given, which I have come to tell you, for you are highly esteemed. Therefore, consider the message and understand the vision:

24"Seventy 'sevens' are decreed for your people and your holy city to finish transgression, to put an end to sin, to atone for wickedness, to bring in everlasting righteousness, to seal up vision and prophecy and to anoint the most holy.

25"Know and understand this: From the issuing of the decree to restore and rebuild Jerusalem until the Anointed One, the ruler, comes, there will be seven 'sevens', and sixty-two 'sevens'. It will be rebuilt with streets and a trench, but in times of trouble. 26After the sixty-two 'sevens', the Anointed One will be cut off and will have nothing. The people of the ruler who will come will destroy the city and the sanctuary. The end will come like a flood: War will continue until the end, and desolations have been decreed. 27He will confirm a covenant with many for one 'seven'. In the middle of the 'seven' he will put an end to sacrifice and offering. And on a wing⌊of the temple⌋ he will set up an abomination that causes desolation, until the end that is decreed is poured out on him."

Daniel's Vision of a Man

10 In the third year of Cyrus king of Persia, a revelation was given to Daniel (who was called Belteshazzar). Its message was true and it concerned a great war. The understanding of the message came to him in a vision.

2At that time I, Daniel, mourned for three weeks. 3I ate no choice food; no meat or wine touched my lips; and I used no lotions at all until the three weeks were over.

4On the twenty-fourth day of the first month, as I was standing on the bank of the great river, the Tigris, 5I looked up and there before me was a man dressed in linen, with a belt of the finest gold round his waist. 6His body was like chrysolite, his face like lightning, his eyes like flaming torches, his arms and legs like the gleam of burnished bronze, and his voice like the sound of a multitude.

7I, Daniel, was the only one who saw the vision; the men with me did not see it, but such terror overwhelmed them that they fled and hid themselves. 8So I was left alone, gazing at this great vision; I had no strength left, my face turned deathly pale and I was helpless. 9Then I heard him speaking, and as I listened to him, I fell into a deep sleep, my face to the ground.

10A hand touched me and set me trembling on my hands and knees. 11He said, "Daniel, you who are highly esteemed, consider carefully the words I am about to speak to you, and stand up, for I have now been sent to you." And when he said this to me, I stood up trembling.

12Then he continued, "Do not be afraid, Daniel. Since the first day that you set your mind to gain understanding and to humble yourself before your God, your words were heard, and I have come in response to them. 13But the prince of the Persian kingdom resisted me twenty-one days. Then Michael, one of the chief princes, came to help me, because I was detained there with the king of Persia. [14]Now I have come to explain to you what will happen to your people in the future, for the vision concerns a time yet to come."

[15]While he was saying this to me, I bowed with my face towards the ground and was speechless. [16]Then one who looked like a man touched my lips, and I opened my mouth and began to speak. I said to the one standing before me, "I am overcome with anguish because of the vision, my lord, and I am helpless. [17]How can I, your servant, talk with you, my lord? My strength is gone and I can hardly breathe."

[18]Again the one who looked like a man touched me and gave me strength. [19]"Do not be afraid, O man highly esteemed," he said. "Peace! Be strong now; be strong."

When he spoke to me, I was strengthened and said, "Speak, my lord, since you have given me strength."

[20]So he said, "Do you know why I have come to you? Soon I will return to fight against the prince of Persia, and when I go, the prince of Greece will come; [21]but first I will tell you what is written in the Book of Truth. (No-one supports me against them except Michael, your prince. [1]And in the first year of Darius the Mede, I took my stand to support and protect him.)

NEW TESTAMENT READING
1 John 3:11–4:6

Love One Another

[11]This is the message you heard from the beginning: We should love one another. [12]Do not be like Cain, who belonged to the evil one and murdered his brother. And why did he murder him? Because his own actions were evil

and his brother's were righteous. [13]Do not be surprised, my brothers, if the world hates you. [14]We know that we have passed from death to life, because we love our brothers. Anyone who does not love remains in death. [15]Anyone who hates his brother is a murderer, and you know that no murderer has eternal life in him.

[16]This is how we know what love is: Jesus Christ laid down his life for us. And we ought to lay down our lives for our brothers. [17]If anyone has material possessions and sees his brother in need but has no pity on him, how can the love of God be in him? [18]Dear children, let us not love with words or tongue but with actions and in truth. [19]This then is how we know that we belong to the truth, and how we set our hearts at rest in his presence [20]whenever our hearts condemn us. For God is greater than our hearts, and he knows everything.

[21]Dear friends, if our hearts do not condemn us, we have confidence before God [22]and receive from him anything we ask, because we obey his commands and do what pleases him. [23]And this is his command: to believe in the name of his Son, Jesus Christ, and to love one another as he commanded us. [24]Those who obey his commands live in him, and he in them. And this is how we know that he lives in us: We know it by the Spirit he gave us.

Test the Spirits

4 Dear friends, do not believe every spirit, but test the spirits to see whether they are from God, because many false prophets have gone out into the world. [2]This is how you can recognise the Spirit of God: Every spirit that acknowledges that Jesus Christ has come in the flesh is from God, [3]but every spirit that does not acknowledge Jesus is not from God. This is the spirit of the antichrist, which you have heard is coming and even now is already in the world.

4You, dear children, are from God and have overcome them, because the one who is in you is greater than the one who is in the world. 5They are from the world and therefore speak from the viewpoint of the world, and the world listens to them. 6We are from God, and whoever knows God listens to us; but whoever is not from God does not listen to us. This is how we recognise the Spirit of truth and the spirit of falsehood.

READING FROM PSALMS
Psalm 137:1–9

1By the rivers of Babylon we sat and wept
  when we remembered Zion.
2There on the poplars
  we hung our harps,
3for there our captors asked us for songs,
  our tormentors demanded songs of joy;

they said, "Sing us one of the songs of Zion!"

4How can we sing the songs of the Lord
  while in a foreign land?
5If I forget you, O Jerusalem,
  may my right hand forget ⌊its skill⌋.
6May my tongue cling to the roof of my mouth
  if I do not remember you,
if I do not consider Jerusalem
  my highest joy.

7Remember, O Lord, what the Edomites did
  on the day Jerusalem fell.
"Tear it down," they cried,
  "tear it down to its foundations!"

8O Daughter of Babylon, doomed to destruction,
  happy is he who repays you
  for what you have done to us—
9he who seizes your infants
  and dashes them against the rocks.

DAY 338

DECEMBER 4

OLD TESTAMENT READING
Daniel 11:2–35

The Kings of the South and the North

2"Now then, I tell you the truth: Three more kings will appear in Persia, and then a fourth, who will be far richer than all the others. When he has gained power by his wealth, he will stir up everyone against the kingdom of Greece. 3Then a mighty king will appear, who will rule with great power and do as he pleases. 4After he has appeared, his empire will be broken up and parcelled out towards the four winds of heaven. It will not go to his descendants, nor will it have the power he exercised, because his empire will be uprooted and given to others.

5"The king of the South will become strong, but one of his commanders will become even stronger than he and will rule his own kingdom with great power. 6After some years, they will become allies. The daughter of the king of the South will go to the king of the North to make an alliance, but she will not retain her power, and he and his power will not last. In those days she will be handed over, together with her royal escort and her father and the one who supported her.

7"One from her family line will arise to take her place. He will attack the forces of the king of the North and enter his fortress; he will fight against them and be victorious. 8He will also seize their gods, their metal images and their valuable articles of silver and gold and carry them off to Egypt. For some years he will leave the king of the North alone. 9Then the king of the North will invade the realm of the king of the South but will retreat to his own country. 10His sons will prepare for war and assemble a great army, which will sweep on like an irresistible flood and carry the battle as far as his fortress.

11"Then the king of the South will march out in rage and fight against the king of the North, who will raise a large army, but it will be defeated. 12When the army is carried off, the king of the South will be filled with pride and will slaughter many thousands, yet he will not remain triumphant. 13For the king of the North will muster another army, larger than the first; and after several years, he will advance with a huge army fully equipped.

14"In those times many will rise against the king of the South. The violent men among your own people will rebel in fulfilment of the vision, but without success. 15Then the king of the North will come and build up siege ramps and will capture a fortified city. The forces of the South will be powerless to resist; even their best troops will not have the strength to stand. 16The invader will do as he pleases; no-one will be able to stand against him. He will establish himself in the Beautiful Land and will have the power to destroy it. 17He will determine to come with the might of his entire kingdom and will make an alliance with the king of the South. And he will give him a daughter in marriage in order to overthrow the kingdom, but his plans will not succeed or help him. 18Then he will turn his attention to the coastlands and will take many of them, but a commander will put an end to his insolence and will turn his insolence back upon him. 19After this, he will turn back towards the fortresses of his own country but will stumble and fall, to be seen no more.

20"His successor will send out a tax collector to maintain the royal splendour. In a few years, however, he will be destroyed, yet not in anger or in battle.

21"He will be succeeded by a contemptible person who has not been given the honour of royalty. He will invade the kingdom when its people feel secure, and he will seize it through intrigue. 22Then an overwhelming army will be swept away before him; both it and a prince of the covenant will be destroyed. 23After coming to an agreement with him, he will act deceitfully, and with only a few people he will rise to power. 24When the richest provinces feel secure, he will invade them and will achieve what neither his fathers nor his forefathers did. He will distribute plunder, loot and wealth among his followers. He will plot the overthrow of fortresses—but only for a time.

25"With a large army he will stir up his strength and courage against the king of the South. The king of the South will wage war with a large and very powerful army, but he will not be able to stand because of the plots devised against him. 26Those who eat from the king's provisions will try to destroy him; his army will be swept away, and many will fall in battle. 27The two kings, with their hearts bent on evil, will sit at the same table and lie to each other, but to no avail, because an end will still come at the appointed time. 28The king of the North will return to his own country with great wealth, but his heart will be set against the holy covenant. He will take action against it and then return to his own country.

29"At the appointed time he will invade the South again, but this time the outcome will be different from what it was before. 30Ships of the western coastlands will oppose him, and he will lose heart. Then he will turn back and vent his fury against the holy covenant. He will return and show favour to those who forsake the holy covenant.

31"His armed forces will rise up to desecrate the temple fortress and will abolish the daily sacrifice. Then they will set up the abomination that causes desolation. 32With flattery he will corrupt those who have violated the covenant, but the people who know their God will firmly resist him.

33"Those who are wise will instruct many, though for a time they will fall by the sword or be burned or captured or plundered. 34When they fall, they will receive a little help, and many who are not sincere will join them. 35Some of the wise will stumble, so that they may be refined, purified and made spotless until the time of the end, for it will still come at the appointed time.

NEW TESTAMENT READING
1 John 4:7–21

God's Love and Ours

7Dear friends, let us love one another, for love comes from God. Everyone who loves has been born of God and knows God. 8Whoever does not love does not know God, because God is love. 9This is how God showed his love among us: He sent his one and only Son into the world that we might live through him. 10This is love: not that we loved God, but that he loved us and sent his Son as an atoning sacrifice for our sins. 11Dear friends, since God so loved us, we also ought to love one another. 12No-one has ever seen God; but if we love one another, God lives in us and his love is made complete in us.

13We know that we live in him and he in us, because he has given us of his Spirit. 14And we have seen and testify that the Father has sent his Son to be the Saviour of the world. 15If anyone acknowledges that Jesus is the Son of God, God lives in him and he in God. 16And so we know and rely on the love God has for us.

God is love. Whoever lives in love lives in God, and God in him. 17In this way, love is made complete among us so that we will have confidence on the day

of judgment, because in this world we are like him. 18There is no fear in love. But perfect love drives out fear, because fear has to do with punishment. The one who fears is not made perfect in love.

19We love because he first loved us. 20If anyone says, "I love God," yet hates his brother, he is a liar. For anyone who does not love his brother, whom he has seen, cannot love God, whom he has not seen. 21And he has given us this command: Whoever loves God must also love his brother.

READING FROM PSALMS
Psalm 138:1–8

Of David.

1I will praise you, O LORD, with all my heart;
   before the "gods" I will sing your praise.
2I will bow down towards your holy temple
   and will praise your name
   for your love and your faithfulness,
for you have exalted above all things
   your name and your word.
3When I called, you answered me;
   you made me bold and
   stout-hearted.

4May all the kings of the earth praise you, O LORD,
   when they hear the words of your mouth.
5May they sing of the ways of the LORD,
   for the glory of the LORD is great.

6Though the LORD is on high, he looks upon the lowly,
   but the proud he knows from afar.
7Though I walk in the midst of trouble,
   you preserve my life;
you stretch out your hand against the anger of my foes,

with your right hand you save me.

⁸The LORD will fulfil ⸤his purpose⸥ for me;

your love, O LORD, endures for ever—

do not abandon the works of your hands.

DECEMBER 5   DAY 339

OLD TESTAMENT READING
Daniel 11:36–12:13

The King Who Exalts Himself

³⁶"The king will do as he pleases. He will exalt and magnify himself above every god and will say unheard-of things against the God of gods. He will be successful until the time of wrath is completed, for what has been determined must take place. ³⁷He will show no regard for the gods of his fathers or for the one desired by women, nor will he regard any god, but will exalt himself above them all. ³⁸Instead of them, he will honour a god of fortresses; a god unknown to his fathers he will honour with gold and silver, with precious stones and costly gifts. ³⁹He will attack the mightiest fortresses with the help of a foreign god and will greatly honour those who acknowledge him. He will make them rulers over many people and will distribute the land at a price.

⁴⁰"At the time of the end the king of the South will engage him in battle, and the king of the North will storm out against him with chariots and cavalry and a great fleet of ships. He will invade many countries and sweep through them like a flood. ⁴¹He will also invade the Beautiful Land. Many countries will fall, but Edom, Moab and the leaders of Ammon will be delivered from his hand. ⁴²He will extend his power over many countries; Egypt will not escape. ⁴³He will gain control of the treasures of gold and silver and all the riches of Egypt, with the Libyans and Nubians in submission. ⁴⁴But reports from the east and the north will alarm him, and he will set out in a great rage to destroy and annihilate many. ⁴⁵He will pitch his royal tents between the seas at the beautiful holy mountain. Yet he will come to his end, and no-one will help him.

The End Times

12 "At that time Michael, the great prince who protects your people, will arise. There will be a time of distress such as has not happened from the beginning of nations until then. But at that time your people—everyone whose name is found written in the book—will be delivered. ²Multitudes who sleep in the dust of the earth will awake: some to everlasting life, others to shame and everlasting contempt. ³Those who are wise will shine like the brightness of the heavens, and those who lead many to righteousness, like the stars for ever and ever. ⁴But you, Daniel, close up and seal the words of the scroll until the time of the end. Many will go here and there to increase knowledge."

⁵Then I, Daniel, looked, and there before me stood two others, one on this bank of the river and one on the opposite bank. ⁶One of them said to the man clothed in linen, who was above the waters of the river, "How long will it be before these astonishing things are fulfilled?"

⁷The man clothed in linen, who was

above the waters of the river, lifted his right hand and his left hand towards heaven, and I heard him swear by him who lives for ever, saying, "It will be for a time, times and half a time. When the power of the holy people has been finally broken, all these things will be completed."

⁸I heard, but I did not understand. So I asked, "My lord, what will the outcome of all this be?"

⁹He replied, "Go your way, Daniel, because the words are closed up and sealed until the time of the end. ¹⁰Many will be purified, made spotless and refined, but the wicked will continue to be wicked. None of the wicked will understand, but those who are wise will understand.

¹¹"From the time that the daily sacrifice is abolished and the abomination that causes desolation is set up, there will be 1,290 days. ¹²Blessed is the one who waits for and reaches the end of the 1,335 days.

¹³"As for you, go your way till the end. You will rest, and then at the end of the days you will rise to receive your allotted inheritance."

NEW TESTAMENT READING
1 John 5:1–21

Faith in the Son of God

5 Everyone who believes that Jesus is the Christ is born of God, and everyone who loves the father loves his child as well. ²This is how we know that we love the children of God: by loving God and carrying out his commands. ³This is love for God: to obey his commands. And his commands are not burdensome, ⁴for everyone born of God overcomes the world. This is the victory that has overcome the world, even our faith. ⁵Who is it that overcomes the world? Only he who believes that Jesus is the Son of God.

⁶This is the one who came by water and blood—Jesus Christ. He did not come by water only, but by water and blood. And it is the Spirit who testifies, because the Spirit is the truth. ⁷For there are three that testify: ⁸the Spirit, the water and the blood; and the three are in agreement. ⁹We accept man's testimony, but God's testimony is greater because it is the testimony of God, which he has given about his Son. ¹⁰Anyone who believes in the Son of God has this testimony in his heart. Anyone who does not believe God has made him out to be a liar, because he has not believed the testimony God has given about his Son. ¹¹And this is the testimony: God has given us eternal life, and this life is in his Son. ¹²He who has the Son has life; he who does not have the Son of God does not have life.

Concluding Remarks

¹³I write these things to you who believe in the name of the Son of God so that you may know that you have eternal life. ¹⁴This is the confidence we have in approaching God: that if we ask anything according to his will, he hears us. ¹⁵And if we know that he hears us—whatever we ask—we know that we have what we asked of him.

¹⁶If anyone sees his brother commit a sin that does not lead to death, he should pray and God will give him life. I refer to those whose sin does not lead to death. There is a sin that leads to death. I am not saying that he should pray about that. ¹⁷All wrongdoing is sin, and there is a sin that does not lead to death.

¹⁸We know that anyone born of God does not continue to sin; the one who was born of God keeps him safe, and the evil one cannot harm him. ¹⁹We know that we are children of God, and that the whole world is under the control of the evil one. ²⁰We know also that the Son of God has come and has given us understanding, so that we may know him who is true. And we are in him who is true—even in his Son Jesus Christ. He is the true God and eternal life.

²¹Dear children, keep yourselves from idols.

READING FROM PSALMS
Psalm 139:1–10

For the director of music. Of David.
A psalm.

¹O LORD, you have searched me
and you know me.
²You know when I sit and when I
rise;
you perceive my thoughts from
afar.
³You discern my going out and my
lying down;
you are familiar with all my ways.
⁴Before a word is on my tongue
you know it completely, O LORD.

⁵You hem me in—behind and before;
you have laid your hand upon me.
⁶Such knowledge is too wonderful for
me,
too lofty for me to attain.

⁷Where can I go from your Spirit?
Where can I flee from your
presence?
⁸If I go up to the heavens, you are
there;
if I make my bed in the depths, you
are there.
⁹If I rise on the wings of the dawn,
if I settle on the far side of the sea,
¹⁰even there your hand will guide me,
your right hand will hold me fast.

DECEMBER 6   DAY 340

OLD TESTAMENT READING
Haggai 1:1–2:23

A Call to Build the House of the LORD

1 In the second year of King Darius,
on the first day of the sixth month,
the word of the LORD came through the
prophet Haggai to Zerubbabel son of
Shealtiel, governor of Judah, and to
Joshua son of Jehozadak, the high
priest:

²This is what the LORD Almighty
says: "These people say, 'The time has
not yet come for the LORD's house to be
built.'"

³Then the word of the LORD came
through the prophet Haggai: ⁴"Is it a
time for you yourselves to be living in
your panelled houses, while this house
remains a ruin?"

⁵Now this is what the LORD Almighty
says: "Give careful thought to your
ways. ⁶You have planted much, but
have harvested little. You eat, but
never have enough. You drink,
but never have your fill. You put on
clothes, but are not warm. You earn

wages, only to put them in a purse with
holes in it."

⁷This is what the LORD Almighty
says: "Give careful thought to your
ways. ⁸Go up into the mountains and
bring down timber and build the house,
so that I may take pleasure in it and be
honoured," says the LORD. ⁹"You
expected much, but see, it turned out to
be little. What you brought home, I
blew away. Why?" declares the LORD
Almighty. "Because of my house,
which remains a ruin, while each of you
is busy with his own house. ¹⁰Therefore,
because of you the heavens have with-
held their dew and the earth its crops.
¹¹I called for a drought on the fields and
the mountains, on the grain, the new
wine, the oil and whatever the ground
produces, on men and cattle, and on the
labour of your hands."

¹²Then Zerubbabel son of Shealtiel,
Joshua son of Jehozadak, the high
priest, and the whole remnant of the
people obeyed the voice of the LORD
their God and the message of the
prophet Haggai, because the LORD

their God had sent him. And the people feared the LORD.

¹³Then Haggai, the LORD's messenger, gave this message of the LORD to the people: "I am with you," declares the LORD. ¹⁴So the LORD stirred up the spirit of Zerubbabel son of Shealtiel, governor of Judah, and the spirit of Joshua son of Jehozadak, the high priest, and the spirit of the whole remnant of the people. They came and began work on the house of the LORD Almighty, their God, ¹⁵on the twenty-fourth day of the sixth month in the second year of King Darius.

The Promised Glory of the New House

2 On the twenty-first day of the seventh month, the word of the LORD came through the prophet Haggai: ²"Speak to Zerubbabel, governor of Judah, to Joshua son of Jehozadak, the high priest, and to the remnant of the people. Ask them, ³'Who of you is left who saw this house in its former glory? How does it look to you now? Does it not seem to you like nothing? ⁴But now be strong, O Zerubbabel,' declares the LORD. 'Be strong, O Joshua son of Jehozadak, the high priest. Be strong, all you people of the land,' declares the LORD, 'and work. For I am with you,' declares the LORD Almighty. ⁵'This is what I covenanted with you when you came out of Egypt. And my Spirit remains among you. Do not fear.'

⁶"This is what the LORD Almighty says: 'In a little while I will once more shake the heavens and the earth, the sea and the dry land. ⁷I will shake all nations, and the desired of all nations will come, and I will fill this house with glory,' says the LORD Almighty. ⁸'The silver is mine and the gold is mine,' declares the LORD Almighty. ⁹'The glory of this present house will be greater than the glory of the former house,' says the LORD Almighty. 'And in this place I will grant peace,' declares the LORD Almighty."

Blessings for a Defiled People

¹⁰On the twenty-fourth day of the ninth month, in the second year of Darius, the word of the LORD came to the prophet Haggai: ¹¹"This is what the LORD Almighty says: 'Ask the priests what the law says: ¹²If a person carries consecrated meat in the fold of his garment, and that fold touches some bread or stew, some wine, oil or other food, does it become consecrated?'"

The priests answered, "No."

¹³Then Haggai said, "If a person defiled by contact with a dead body touches one of these things, does it become defiled?"

"Yes," the priests replied, "it becomes defiled."

¹⁴Then Haggai said, "'So it is with this people and this nation in my sight,' declares the LORD. 'Whatever they do and whatever they offer there is defiled.

¹⁵"'Now give careful thought to this from this day on—consider how things were before one stone was laid on another in the LORD's temple. ¹⁶When anyone came to a heap of twenty measures, there were only ten. When anyone went to a wine vat to draw fifty measures, there were only twenty. ¹⁷I struck all the work of your hands with blight, mildew and hail, yet you did not turn to me,' declares the LORD. ¹⁸'From this day on, from this twenty-fourth day of the ninth month, give careful thought to the day when the foundation of the LORD's temple was laid. Give careful thought: ¹⁹Is there yet any seed left in the barn? Until now, the vine and the fig-tree, the pomegranate and the olive tree have not borne fruit.

"'From this day on I will bless you.'"

Zerubbabel the LORD's Signet Ring

²⁰The word of the LORD came to Haggai a second time on the twenty-fourth day of the month: ²¹"Tell Zerubbabel governor of Judah that I will shake the heavens and the earth. ²²I will overturn royal thrones and shatter the power of

the foreign kingdoms. I will overthrow chariots and their drivers; horses and their riders will fall, each by the sword of his brother.

²³"'On that day,' declares the LORD Almighty, 'I will take you, my servant Zerubbabel son of Shealtiel,' declares the LORD, 'and I will make you like my signet ring, for I have chosen you,' declares the LORD Almighty.'"

NEW TESTAMENT READING
2 John 1–13

¹The elder,

To the chosen lady and her children, whom I love in the truth—and not I only, but also all who know the truth —²because of the truth, which lives in us and will be with us for ever:

³Grace, mercy and peace from God the Father and from Jesus Christ, the Father's Son, will be with us in truth and love.

⁴It has given me great joy to find some of your children walking in the truth, just as the Father commanded us. ⁵And now, dear lady, I am not writing you a new command but one we have had from the beginning. I ask that we love one another. ⁶And this is love: that we walk in obedience to his commands. As you have heard from the beginning, his command is that you walk in love.

⁷Many deceivers, who do not acknowledge Jesus Christ as coming in the flesh, have gone out into the world. Any such person is the deceiver and the antichrist. ⁸Watch out that you do not lose what you have worked for, but that you may be rewarded fully. ⁹Anyone who runs ahead and does not continue in the teaching of Christ does not have God; whoever continues in the teaching has both the Father and the Son. ¹⁰If anyone comes to you and does not bring this teaching, do not take him into your house or welcome him. ¹¹Anyone who

welcomes him shares in his wicked work.

¹²I have much to write to you, but I do not want to use paper and ink. Instead, I hope to visit you and talk with you face to face, so that our joy may be complete.

¹³The children of your chosen sister send their greetings.

READING FROM PROVERBS
Proverbs 29:19–27

¹⁹A servant cannot be corrected by mere words;
though he understands, he will not respond.

²⁰Do you see a man who speaks in haste?
There is more hope for a fool than for him.

²¹If a man pampers his servant from youth,
he will bring grief in the end.

²²An angry man stirs up dissension,
and a hot-tempered one commits many sins.

²³A man's pride brings him low,
but a man of lowly spirit gains honour.

²⁴The accomplice of a thief is his own enemy;
he is put under oath and dare not testify.

²⁵Fear of man will prove to be a snare,
but whoever trusts in the LORD is kept safe.

²⁶Many seek an audience with a ruler,
but it is from the LORD that man gets justice.

²⁷The righteous detest the dishonest;
the wicked detest the upright.

OLD TESTAMENT READING
Zechariah 1:1–4:14

A Call to Return to the LORD

1 In the eighth month of the second year of Darius, the word of the LORD came to the prophet Zechariah son of Berekiah, the son of Iddo:

2"The LORD was very angry with your forefathers. 3Therefore tell the people: This is what the LORD Almighty says: 'Return to me,' declares the LORD Almighty, 'and I will return to you,' says the LORD Almighty. 4Do not be like your forefathers, to whom the earlier prophets proclaimed: This is what the LORD Almighty says: 'Turn from your evil ways and your evil practices.' But they would not listen or pay attention to me, declares the LORD. 5Where are your forefathers now? And the prophets, do they live for ever? 6But did not my words and my decrees, which I commanded my servants the prophets, overtake your forefathers?

"Then they repented and said, 'The LORD Almighty has done to us what our ways and practices deserve, just as he determined to do.'"

The Man Among the Myrtle Trees

7On the twenty-fourth day of the eleventh month, the month of Shebat, in the second year of Darius, the word of the LORD came to the prophet Zechariah son of Berekiah, the son of Iddo.

8During the night I had a vision—and there before me was a man riding a red horse! He was standing among the myrtle trees in a ravine. Behind him were red, brown and white horses.

9I asked, "What are these, my lord?"

The angel who was talking with me answered, "I will show you what they are."

10Then the man standing among the myrtle trees explained, "They are the ones the LORD has sent to go throughout the earth."

11And they reported to the angel of the LORD, who was standing among the myrtle trees, "We have gone throughout the earth and found the whole world at rest and in peace."

12Then the angel of the LORD said, "LORD Almighty, how long will you withhold mercy from Jerusalem and from the towns of Judah, which you have been angry with these seventy years?" 13So the LORD spoke kind and comforting words to the angel who talked with me.

14Then the angel who was speaking to me said, "Proclaim this word: This is what the LORD Almighty says: 'I am very jealous for Jerusalem and Zion, 15but I am very angry with the nations that feel secure. I was only a little angry, but they added to the calamity.'

16"Therefore, this is what the LORD says: 'I will return to Jerusalem with mercy, and there my house will be rebuilt. And the measuring line will be stretched out over Jerusalem,' declares the LORD Almighty.

17"Proclaim further: This is what the LORD Almighty says: 'My towns will again overflow with prosperity, and the LORD will again comfort Zion and choose Jerusalem.'"

Four Horns and Four Craftsmen

18Then I looked up—and there before me were four horns! 19I asked the angel who was speaking to me, "What are these?"

He answered me, "These are the horns that scattered Judah, Israel and Jerusalem."

20Then the LORD showed me four craftsmen. 21I asked, "What are these coming to do?"

He answered, "These are the horns that scattered Judah so that no-one could raise his head, but the craftsmen have come to terrify them and throw down these horns of the nations who lifted up their horns against the land of Judah to scatter its people."

A Man With a Measuring Line

2 Then I looked up—and there before me was a man with a measuring line in his hand! ²I asked, "Where are you going?"

He answered me, "To measure Jerusalem, to find out how wide and how long it is."

³Then the angel who was speaking to me left, and another angel came to meet him ⁴and said to him: "Run, tell that young man, 'Jerusalem will be a city without walls because of the great number of men and livestock in it. ⁵And I myself will be a wall of fire around it,' declares the LORD, 'and I will be its glory within.'

⁶"Come! Come! Flee from the land of the north," declares the LORD, "for I have scattered you to the four winds of heaven," declares the LORD.

⁷"Come, O Zion! Escape, you who live in the Daughter of Babylon!" ⁸For this is what the LORD Almighty says: "After he has honoured me and has sent me against the nations that have plundered you—for whoever touches you touches the apple of his eye—⁹I will surely raise my hand against them so that their slaves will plunder them. Then you will know that the LORD Almighty has sent me.

¹⁰"Shout and be glad, O Daughter of Zion. For I am coming, and I will live among you," declares the LORD. ¹¹"Many nations will be joined with the LORD in that day and will become my people. I will live among you and you will know that the LORD Almighty has sent me to you. ¹²The LORD will inherit Judah as his portion in the holy land and will again choose Jerusalem. ¹³Be still before the LORD, all mankind, because he has roused himself from his holy dwelling."

Clean Garments for the High Priest

3 Then he showed me Joshua the high priest standing before the angel of the LORD, and Satan standing at his right side to accuse him. ²The LORD said to Satan, "The LORD rebuke you, Satan! The LORD, who has chosen Jerusalem, rebuke you! Is not this man a burning stick snatched from the fire?"

³Now Joshua was dressed in filthy clothes as he stood before the angel. ⁴The angel said to those who were standing before him, "Take off his filthy clothes."

Then he said to Joshua, "See, I have taken away your sin, and I will put rich garments on you."

⁵Then I said, "Put a clean turban on his head." So they put a clean turban on his head and clothed him, while the angel of the LORD stood by.

⁶The angel of the LORD gave this charge to Joshua: ⁷"This is what the LORD Almighty says: 'If you will walk in my ways and keep my requirements, then you will govern my house and have charge of my courts, and I will give you a place among these standing here.

⁸"'Listen, O high priest Joshua and your associates seated before you, who are men symbolic of things to come: I am going to bring my servant, the Branch. ⁹See, the stone I have set in front of Joshua! There are seven eyes on that one stone, and I will engrave an inscription on it,' says the LORD Almighty, 'and I will remove the sin of this land in a single day.

¹⁰"'In that day each of you will invite his neighbour to sit under his vine and fig-tree,' declares the LORD Almighty."

The Gold Lampstand and the Two Olive Trees

4 Then the angel who talked with me returned and wakened me, as a man is wakened from his sleep. ²He asked me, "What do you see?"

I answered, "I see a solid gold lampstand with a bowl at the top and seven lights on it, with seven channels to the lights. ³Also there are two olive trees by it, one on the right of the bowl and the other on its left."

⁴I asked the angel who talked with me, "What are these, my lord?"

⁵He answered, "Do you not know what these are?"

"No, my lord," I replied.

⁶So he said to me, "This is the word of the LORD to Zerubbabel: 'Not by might nor by power, but by my Spirit,' says the LORD Almighty.

⁷"What are you, O mighty mountain? Before Zerubbabel you will become level ground. Then he will bring out the capstone to shouts of 'God bless it! God bless it!'"

⁸Then the word of the LORD came to me: ⁹"The hands of Zerubbabel have laid the foundation of this temple; his hands will also complete it. Then you will know that the LORD Almighty has sent me to you.

¹⁰"Who despises the day of small things? Men will rejoice when they see the plumb-line in the hand of Zerubbabel.

"(These seven are the eyes of the LORD, which range throughout the earth.)"

¹¹Then I asked the angel, "What are these two olive trees on the right and the left of the lampstand?"

¹²Again I asked him, "What are these two olive branches beside the two gold pipes that pour out golden oil?"

¹³He replied, "Do you not know what these are?"

"No, my lord," I said.

¹⁴So he said, "These are the two who are anointed to serve the Lord of all the earth."

NEW TESTAMENT READING
3 John 1–14

¹The elder,

To my dear friend Gaius, whom I love in the truth.

²Dear friend, I pray that you may enjoy good health and that all may go well with you, even as your soul is getting along well. ³It gave me great joy to have some brothers come and tell about your faithfulness to the truth and how you continue to walk in the truth. ⁴I have no greater joy than to hear that my children are walking in the truth.

⁵Dear friend, you are faithful in what you are doing for the brothers, even though they are strangers to you. ⁶They have told the church about your love. You will do well to send them on their way in a manner worthy of God. ⁷It was for the sake of the Name that they went out, receiving no help from the pagans. ⁸We ought therefore to show hospitality to such men so that we may work together for the truth.

⁹I wrote to the church, but Diotrephes, who loves to be first, will have nothing to do with us. ¹⁰So if I come, I will call attention to what he is doing, gossiping maliciously about us. Not satisfied with that, he refuses to welcome the brothers. He also stops those who want to do so and puts them out of the church.

¹¹Dear friend, do not imitate what is evil but what is good. Anyone who does what is good is from God. Anyone who does what is evil has not seen God. ¹²Demetrius is well spoken of by everyone—and even by the truth itself. We also speak well of him, and you know that our testimony is true.

¹³I have much to write to you, but I do not want to do so with pen and ink. ¹⁴I hope to see you soon, and we will talk face to face.

Peace to you. The friends here send their greetings. Greet the friends there by name.

READING FROM PSALMS
Psalm 139:11–16

¹¹If I say, "Surely the darkness will hide me
and the light become night around me,"

12even the darkness will not be dark to
you;
the night will shine like the day,
for darkness is as light to you.

13For you created my inmost being;
you knit me together in my
mother's womb.

14I praise you because I am fearfully
and wonderfully made;

your works are wonderful,
I know that full well.

15My frame was not hidden from you
when I was made in the secret
place.
When I was woven together in the
depths of the earth,

16 your eyes saw my unformed body.
All the days ordained for me
were written in your book
before one of them came to be.

DECEMBER 8   DAY 342

OLD TESTAMENT READING
Zechariah 5:1–8:23

The Flying Scroll

5 I looked again—and there before
me was a flying scroll!

2He asked me, "What do you see?"

I answered, "I see a flying scroll,
thirty feet long and fifteen feet wide."

3And he said to me, "This is the curse
that is going out over the whole land; for
according to what it says on one side,
every thief will be banished, and
according to what it says on the other,
everyone who swears falsely will be
banished. 4The LORD Almighty declares, 'I will send it out, and it will enter
the house of the thief and the house of
him who swears falsely by my name. It
will remain in his house and destroy it,
both its timbers and its stones.'"

The Woman in a Basket

5Then the angel who was speaking
to me came forward and said to me,
"Look up and see what this is that is
appearing."

6I asked, "What is it?"

He replied, "It is a measuring basket." And he added, "This is the iniquity of the people throughout the
land."

7Then the cover of lead was raised,
and there in the basket sat a woman!
8He said, "This is wickedness," and he
pushed her back into the basket and
pushed the lead cover down over its
mouth.

9Then I looked up—and there before
me were two women, with the wind in
their wings! They had wings like those
of a stork, and they had lifted up the basket
between heaven and earth.

10"Where are they taking the basket?" I asked the angel who was speaking to me.

11He replied, "To the country of
Babylonia to build a house for it. When
it is ready, the basket will be set there in
its place."

Four Chariots

6 I looked up again—and there before me were four chariots coming
out from between two mountains—
mountains of bronze! 2The first chariot
had red horses, the second black, 3the
third white, and the fourth dappled—
all of them powerful. 4I asked the angel
who was speaking to me, "What are
these, my lord?"

5The angel answered me, "These are
the four spirits of heaven, going out
from standing in the presence of the
Lord of the whole world. 6The one with

the black horses is going towards the north country, the one with the white horses towards the west, and the one with the dappled horses towards the south."

⁷When the powerful horses went out, they were straining to go throughout the earth. And he said, "Go throughout the earth!" So they went throughout the earth.

⁸Then he called to me, "Look, those going towards the north country have given my Spirit rest in the land of the north."

A Crown for Joshua

⁹The word of the LORD came to me: ¹⁰"Take silver and gold from the exiles Heldai, Tobijah and Jedaiah, who have arrived from Babylon. Go the same day to the house of Josiah son of Zephaniah. ¹¹Take the silver and gold and make a crown, and set it on the head of the high priest, Joshua son of Jehozadak. ¹²Tell him this is what the LORD Almighty says: 'Here is the man whose name is the Branch, and he will branch out from his place and build the temple of the LORD. ¹³It is he who will build the temple of the LORD, and he will be clothed with majesty and will sit and rule on his throne. And he will be a priest on his throne. And there will be harmony between the two.' ¹⁴The crown will be given to Heldai, Tobijah, Jedaiah and Hen son of Zephaniah as a memorial in the temple of the LORD. ¹⁵Those who are far away will come and help to build the temple of the LORD, and you will know that the LORD Almighty has sent me to you. This will happen if you diligently obey the LORD your God."

Justice and Mercy, Not Fasting

7 In the fourth year of King Darius, the word of the LORD came to Zechariah on the fourth day of the ninth month, the month of Kislev. ²The people of Bethel had sent Sharezer and Regem-Melech, together with their men, to entreat the LORD ³by asking the priests of the house of the LORD Almighty and the prophets, "Should I mourn and fast in the fifth month, as I have done for so many years?"

⁴Then the word of the LORD Almighty came to me: ⁵"Ask all the people of the land and the priests, 'When you fasted and mourned in the fifth and seventh months for the past seventy years, was it really for me that you fasted? ⁶And when you were eating and drinking, were you not just feasting for yourselves? ⁷Are these not the words the LORD proclaimed through the earlier prophets when Jerusalem and its surrounding towns were at rest and prosperous, and the Negev and the western foothills were settled?'"

⁸And the word of the LORD came again to Zechariah: ⁹"This is what the LORD Almighty says: 'Administer true justice; show mercy and compassion to one another. ¹⁰Do not oppress the widow or the fatherless, the alien or the poor. In your hearts do not think evil of each other.'

¹¹"But they refused to pay attention; stubbornly they turned their backs and stopped up their ears. ¹²They made their hearts as hard as flint and would not listen to the law or to the words that the LORD Almighty had sent by his Spirit through the earlier prophets. So the LORD Almighty was very angry.

¹³" 'When I called, they did not listen; so when they called, I would not listen,' says the LORD Almighty. ¹⁴'I scattered them with a whirlwind among all the nations, where they were strangers. The land was left so desolate behind them that no-one could come or go. This is how they made the pleasant land desolate.'"

The LORD Promises to Bless Jerusalem

8 Again the word of the LORD Almighty came to me. ²This is what the LORD Almighty says: "I am very jealous for Zion; I am burning with jealousy for her."

³This is what the LORD says: "I will return to Zion and dwell in Jerusalem. Then Jerusalem will be called the City of Truth, and the mountain of the LORD Almighty will be called the Holy Mountain."

⁴This is what the LORD Almighty says: "Once again men and women of ripe old age will sit in the streets of Jerusalem, each with cane in hand because of his age. ⁵The city streets will be filled with boys and girls playing there."

⁶This is what the LORD Almighty says: "It may seem marvellous to the remnant of this people at that time, but will it seem marvellous to me?" declares the LORD Almighty.

⁷This is what the LORD Almighty says: "I will save my people from the countries of the east and the west. ⁸I will bring them back to live in Jerusalem; they will be my people, and I will be faithful and righteous to them as their God."

⁹This is what the LORD Almighty says: "You who now hear these words spoken by the prophets who were there when the foundation was laid for the house of the LORD Almighty, let your hands be strong so that the temple may be built. ¹⁰Before that time there were no wages for man or beast. No-one could go about his business safely because of his enemy, for I had turned every man against his neighbour. ¹¹But now I will not deal with the remnant of this people as I did in the past," declares the LORD Almighty.

¹²"The seed will grow well, the vine will yield its fruit, the ground will produce its crops, and the heavens will drop their dew. I will give all these things as an inheritance to the remnant of this people. ¹³As you have been an object of cursing among the nations, O Judah and Israel, so will I save you, and you will be a blessing. Do not be afraid, but let your hands be strong."

¹⁴This is what the LORD Almighty says: "Just as I had determined to bring disaster upon you and showed no pity when your fathers angered me," says the LORD Almighty, ¹⁵"so now I have determined to do good again to Jerusalem and Judah. Do not be afraid. ¹⁶These are the things you are to do: Speak the truth to each other, and render true and sound judgment in your courts; ¹⁷do not plot evil against your neighbour, and do not love to swear falsely. I hate all this," declares the LORD.

¹⁸Again the word of the LORD Almighty came to me. ¹⁹This is what the LORD Almighty says: "The fasts of the fourth, fifth, seventh and tenth months will become joyful and glad occasions and happy festivals for Judah. Therefore love truth and peace."

²⁰This is what the LORD Almighty says: "Many peoples and the inhabitants of many cities will yet come, ²¹and the inhabitants of one city will go to another and say, 'Let us go at once to entreat the LORD and seek the LORD Almighty. I myself am going.' ²²And many peoples and powerful nations will come to Jerusalem to seek the LORD Almighty and to entreat him."

²³This is what the LORD Almighty says: "In those days ten men from all languages and nations will take firm hold of one Jew by the hem of his robe and say, 'Let us go with you, because we have heard that God is with you.'"

NEW TESTAMENT READING
Jude 1–25

¹Jude, a servant of Jesus Christ and a brother of James,

To those who have been called, who are loved by God the Father and kept by Jesus Christ:

²Mercy, peace and love be yours in abundance.

The Sin and Doom of Godless Men

³Dear friends, although I was very eager to write to you about the salvation we share, I felt I had to write and urge you to contend for the faith that was

once for all entrusted to the saints. ⁴For certain men whose condemnation was written about long ago have secretly slipped in among you. They are godless men, who change the grace of our God into a licence for immorality and deny Jesus Christ our only Sovereign and Lord.

⁵Though you already know all this, I want to remind you that the Lord delivered his people out of Egypt, but later destroyed those who did not believe. ⁶And the angels who did not keep their positions of authority but abandoned their own home—these he has kept in darkness, bound with everlasting chains for judgment on the great Day. ⁷In a similar way, Sodom and Gomorrah and the surrounding towns gave themselves up to sexual immorality and perversion. They serve as an example of those who suffer the punishment of eternal fire.

⁸In the very same way, these dreamers pollute their own bodies, reject authority and slander celestial beings. ⁹But even the archangel Michael, when he was disputing with the devil about the body of Moses, did not dare to bring a slanderous accusation against him, but said, "The Lord rebuke you!" ¹⁰Yet these men speak abusively against whatever they do not understand; and what things they do understand by instinct, like unreasoning animals—these are the very things that destroy them.

¹¹Woe to them! They have taken the way of Cain; they have rushed for profit into Balaam's error; they have been destroyed in Korah's rebellion.

¹²These men are blemishes at your love feasts, eating with you without the slightest qualm—shepherds who feed only themselves. They are clouds without rain, blown along by the wind; autumn trees, without fruit and uprooted—twice dead. ¹³They are wild waves of the sea, foaming up their shame; wandering stars, for whom blackest darkness has been reserved for ever.

¹⁴Enoch, the seventh from Adam, prophesied about these men: "See, the Lord is coming with thousands upon thousands of his holy ones ¹⁵to judge everyone, and to convict all the ungodly of all the ungodly acts they have done in the ungodly way, and of all the harsh words ungodly sinners have spoken against him." ¹⁶These men are grumblers and fault-finders; they follow their own evil desires; they boast about themselves and flatter others for their own advantage.

A Call to Persevere

¹⁷But, dear friends, remember what the apostles of our Lord Jesus Christ foretold. ¹⁸They said to you, "In the last times there will be scoffers who will follow their own ungodly desires." ¹⁹These are the men who divide you, who follow mere natural instincts and do not have the Spirit.

²⁰But you, dear friends, build yourselves up in your most holy faith and pray in the Holy Spirit. ²¹Keep yourselves in God's love as you wait for the mercy of our Lord Jesus Christ to bring you to eternal life.

²²Be merciful to those who doubt; ²³snatch others from the fire and save them; to others show mercy, mixed with fear—hating even the clothing stained by corrupted flesh.

Doxology

²⁴To him who is able to keep you from falling and to present you before his glorious presence without fault and with great joy—²⁵to the only God our Saviour be glory, majesty, power and authority, through Jesus Christ our Lord, before all ages, now and for evermore! Amen.

READING FROM PSALMS
Psalm 139:17–24

¹⁷How precious to me are your
    thoughts, O God!
  How vast is the sum of them!

18Were I to count them,
     they would outnumber the grains
          of sand.
When I awake,
     I am still with you.

19If only you would slay the wicked, O
          God!
     Away from me, you bloodthirsty
          men!
20They speak of you with evil intent;
     your adversaries misuse your
          name.

21Do I not hate those who hate you, O
          LORD,
     and abhor those who rise up
          against you?
22I have nothing but hatred for them;
     I count them my enemies.

23Search me, O God, and know my
          heart;
     test me and know my anxious
          thoughts.
24See if there is any offensive way in
          me,
     and lead me in the way everlasting.

DECEMBER 9 DAY 343

OLD TESTAMENT READING
Zechariah 9:1–11:17

Judgment on Israel's Enemies

An Oracle

9 The word of the LORD is against
     the land of Hadrach
     and will rest upon Damascus—
for the eyes of men and all the tribes
          of Israel
     are on the LORD—
2and upon Hamath too, which borders
          on it,
     and upon Tyre and Sidon, though
          they are very skilful.
3Tyre has built herself a stronghold;
     she has heaped up silver like dust,
     and gold like the dirt of the streets.
4But the Lord will take away her
          possessions
     and destroy her power on the sea,
     and she will be consumed by fire.
5Ashkelon will see it and fear;
     Gaza will writhe in agony,
     and Ekron too, for her hope will
          wither.
Gaza will lose her king
     and Ashkelon will be deserted.
6Foreigners will occupy Ashdod,

and I will cut off the pride of the
          Philistines.
7I will take the blood from their
          mouths,
     the forbidden food from between
          their teeth.
Those who are left will belong to our
          God
     and become leaders in Judah,
     and Ekron will be like the
          Jebusites.
8But I will defend my house
     against marauding forces.
Never again will an oppressor
     overrun my people,
for now I am keeping watch.

The Coming of Zion's King

9Rejoice greatly, O Daughter of Zion!
     Shout, Daughter of Jerusalem!
See, your king comes to you,
     righteous and having salvation,
gentle and riding on a donkey,
     on a colt, the foal of a donkey.
10I will take away the chariots from
          Ephraim
     and the war-horses from Jerusalem,
     and the battle-bow will be broken.
He will proclaim peace to the
          nations.

His rule will extend from sea to sea
    and from the River to the ends of
    the earth.

[11] As for you, because of the blood of
    my covenant with you,
    I will free your prisoners from the
    waterless pit.

[12] Return to your fortress, O prisoners
    of hope;
    even now I announce that I will
    restore twice as much to you.

[13] I will bend Judah as I bend my bow
    and fill it with Ephraim.
    I will rouse your sons, O Zion,
    against your sons, O Greece,
    and make you like a warrior's
    sword.

The LORD Will Appear

[14] Then the LORD will appear over
    them;
    his arrow will flash like lightning.
    The Sovereign LORD will sound the
    trumpet;
    he will march in the storms of the
    south,

[15] and the LORD Almighty will shield
    them.
    They will destroy
    and overcome with slingstones.
    They will drink and roar as with wine;
    they will be full like a bowl
    used for sprinkling the corners of
    the altar.

[16] The LORD their God will save them
    on that day
    as the flock of his people.
    They will sparkle in his land
    like jewels in a crown.

[17] How attractive and beautiful they will
    be!
    Grain will make the young men
    thrive,
    and new wine the young women.

The LORD Will Care for Judah

10 Ask the LORD for rain in the
    springtime;
    it is the LORD who makes the storm
    clouds.

He gives showers of rain to men,
    and plants of the field to everyone.
[2] The idols speak deceit,
    diviners see visions that lie;
    they tell dreams that are false,
    they give comfort in vain.
    Therefore the people wander like
    sheep
    oppressed for lack of a shepherd.

[3] "My anger burns against the
    shepherds,
    and I will punish the leaders;
    for the LORD Almighty will care
    for his flock, the house of Judah,
    and make them like a proud horse
    in battle.
[4] From Judah will come the
    cornerstone,
    from him the tent peg,
    from him the battle-bow,
    from him every ruler.
[5] Together they will be like mighty men
    trampling the muddy streets in
    battle.
    Because the LORD is with them,
    they will fight and overthrow the
    horsemen.

[6] "I will strengthen the house of Judah
    and save the house of Joseph.
    I will restore them
    because I have compassion on
    them.
    They will be as though
    I had not rejected them,
    for I am the LORD their God
    and I will answer them.
[7] The Ephraimites will become like
    mighty men,
    and their hearts will be glad as with
    wine.
    Their children will see it and be
    joyful;
    their hearts will rejoice in the
    LORD.
[8] I will signal for them
    and gather them in.
    Surely I will redeem them;
    they will be as numerous as before.
[9] Though I scatter them among the
    peoples,

yet in distant lands they will
remember me.
They and their children will survive,
and they will return.
[10]I will bring them back from Egypt
and gather them from Assyria.
I will bring them to Gilead and
Lebanon,
and there will not be room enough
for them.
[11]They will pass through the sea of
trouble;
the surging sea will be subdued
and all the depths of the Nile will
dry up.
Assyria's pride will be brought down
and Egypt's sceptre will pass away.
[12]I will strengthen them in the LORD
and in his name they will walk,"
declares the LORD.

11 Open your doors, O Lebanon,
so that fire may devour your
cedars!
[2]Wail, O pine tree, for the cedar has
fallen;
the stately trees are ruined!
Wail, oaks of Bashan;
the dense forest has been cut
down!
[3]Listen to the wail of the shepherds:
their rich pastures are destroyed!
Listen to the roar of the lions;
the lush thicket of the Jordan is
ruined!

Two Shepherds

[4]This is what the LORD my God says:
"Pasture the flock marked for slaughter. [5]Their buyers slaughter them and
go unpunished. Those who sell them
say, 'Praise the LORD, I am rich!' Their
own shepherds do not spare them. [6]For
I will no longer have pity on the people
of the land," declares the LORD. "I will
hand everyone over to his neighbour
and his king. They will oppress the land,
and I will not rescue them from their
hands."

[7]So I pastured the flock marked for
slaughter, particularly the oppressed of
the flock. Then I took two staffs and
called one Favour and the other Union,
and I pastured the flock. [8]In one month
I got rid of the three shepherds.

The flock detested me, and I grew
weary of them [9]and said, "I will not be
your shepherd. Let the dying die, and
the perishing perish. Let those who are
left eat one another's flesh."

[10]Then I took my staff called Favour
and broke it, revoking the covenant I
had made with all the nations. [11]It was
revoked on that day, and so the afflicted
of the flock who were watching me
knew it was the word of the LORD.

[12]I told them, "If you think it best,
give me my pay; but if not, keep it." So
they paid me thirty pieces of silver.

[13]And the LORD said to me, "Throw it
to the potter"—the handsome price at
which they priced me! So I took the
thirty pieces of silver and threw them
into the house of the LORD to the potter.

[14]Then I broke my second staff called
Union, breaking the brotherhood between Judah and Israel.

[15]Then the LORD said to me, "Take
again the equipment of a foolish shepherd. [16]For I am going to raise up a
shepherd over the land who will not
care for the lost, or seek the young, or
heal the injured, or feed the healthy,
but will eat the meat of the choice
sheep, tearing off their hoofs.

[17]"Woe to the worthless shepherd,
who deserts the flock!
May the sword strike his arm and his
right eye!
May his arm be completely
withered,
his right eye totally blinded!"

NEW TESTAMENT READING
Revelation 1:1–20

Prologue

1 The revelation of Jesus Christ,
which God gave him to show his
servants what must soon take place. He

made it known by sending his angel to his servant John, ²who testifies to everything he saw—that is, the word of God and the testimony of Jesus Christ. ³Blessed is the one who reads the words of this prophecy, and blessed are those who hear it and take to heart what is written in it, because the time is near.

Greetings and Doxology

⁴John,

To the seven churches in the province of Asia:

Grace and peace to you from him who is, and who was, and who is to come, and from the seven spirits before his throne, ⁵and from Jesus Christ, who is the faithful witness, the firstborn from the dead, and the ruler of the kings of the earth.

To him who loves us and has freed us from our sins by his blood, ⁶and has made us to be a kingdom and priests to serve his God and Father—to him be glory and power for ever and ever! Amen.

⁷Look, he is coming with the clouds,
    and every eye will see him,
even those who pierced him;
    and all the peoples of the earth will
        mourn because of him.
            So shall it be! Amen.

⁸"I am the Alpha and the Omega," says the Lord God, "who is, and who was, and who is to come, the Almighty."

One Like a Son of Man

⁹I, John, your brother and companion in the suffering and kingdom and patient endurance that are ours in Jesus, was on the island of Patmos because of the word of God and the testimony of Jesus. ¹⁰On the Lord's Day I was in the Spirit, and I heard behind me a loud voice like a trumpet, ¹¹which said: "Write on a scroll what you see and send it to the seven churches: to Ephesus, Smyrna, Pergamum, Thyatira, Sardis, Philadelphia and Laodicea."

¹²I turned round to see the voice that was speaking to me. And when I turned I saw seven golden lampstands, ¹³and among the lampstands was someone "like a son of man", dressed in a robe reaching down to his feet and with a golden sash round his chest. ¹⁴His head and hair were white like wool, as white as snow, and his eyes were like blazing fire. ¹⁵His feet were like bronze glowing in a furnace, and his voice was like the sound of rushing waters. ¹⁶In his right hand he held seven stars, and out of his mouth came a sharp double-edged sword. His face was like the sun shining in all its brilliance.

¹⁷When I saw him, I fell at his feet as though dead. Then he placed his right hand on me and said: "Do not be afraid. I am the First and the Last. ¹⁸I am the Living One; I was dead, and behold I am alive for ever and ever! And I hold the keys of death and Hades.

¹⁹"Write, therefore, what you have seen, what is now and what will take place later. ²⁰The mystery of the seven stars that you saw in my right hand and of the seven golden lampstands is this: The seven stars are the angels of the seven churches, and the seven lampstands are the seven churches.

READING FROM PSALMS
Psalm 140:1–5

For the director of music. A psalm of David.

¹Rescue me, O LORD, from evil men;
    protect me from men of violence,
²who devise evil plans in their hearts
    and stir up war every day.

³They make their tongues as sharp as
  a serpent's;
   the poison of vipers is on their lips.
                                    Selah

⁴Keep me, O LORD, from the hands of
   the wicked;

protect me from men of violence
  who plan to trip my feet.
⁵Proud men have hidden a snare for
  me;
   they have spread out the cords of
    their net
and have set traps for me along my
   path.   *Selah*

DECEMBER 10   DAY 344

OLD TESTAMENT READING
Zechariah 12:1–14:21

Jerusalem's Enemies to Be Destroyed

An Oracle

12 This is the word of the LORD
   concerning Israel. The LORD,
who stretches out the heavens, who lays
the foundation of the earth, and who
forms the spirit of man within him, declares: ²"I am going to make Jerusalem
a cup that sends all the surrounding
peoples reeling. Judah will be besieged
as well as Jerusalem. ³On that day,
when all the nations of the earth are
gathered against her, I will make Jerusalem an immovable rock for all the
nations. All who try to move it will
injure themselves. ⁴On that day I will
strike every horse with panic and its
rider with madness," declares the
LORD. "I will keep a watchful eye over
the house of Judah, but I will blind all
the horses of the nations. ⁵Then the
leaders of Judah will say in their hearts,
'The people of Jerusalem are strong,
because the LORD Almighty is their
God.'

⁶"On that day I will make the leaders
of Judah like a brazier in a woodpile,
like a flaming torch among sheaves.
They will consume right and left all the
surrounding peoples, but Jerusalem will
remain intact in her place.

⁷The LORD will save the dwellings of
Judah first, so that the honour of the

house of David and of Jerusalem's inhabitants may not be greater than that
of Judah. ⁸On that day the LORD will
shield those who live in Jerusalem, so
that the feeblest among them will be
like David, and the house of David will
be like God, like the Angel of the LORD
going before them. ⁹On that day I will
set out to destroy all the nations that
attack Jerusalem.

Mourning for the One They Pierced

¹⁰"And I will pour out on the house of
David and the inhabitants of Jerusalem
a spirit of grace and supplication. They
will look on me, the one they have
pierced, and they will mourn for him as
one mourns for an only child, and grieve
bitterly for him as one grieves for a
firstborn son. ¹¹On that day the weeping
in Jerusalem will be great, like the
weeping of Hadad Rimmon in the plain
of Megiddo. ¹²The land will mourn,
each clan by itself, with their wives by
themselves: the clan of the house of
David and their wives, the clan of the
house of Nathan and their wives, ¹³the
clan of the house of Levi and their
wives, the clan of Shimei and their
wives, ¹⁴and all the rest of the clans and
their wives.

Cleansing From Sin

13 "On that day a fountain will be
   opened to the house of David
and the inhabitants of Jerusalem, to
cleanse them from sin and impurity.

²"On that day, I will banish the names of the idols from the land, and they will be remembered no more," declares the LORD Almighty. "I will remove both the prophets and the spirit of impurity from the land. ³And if anyone still prophesies, his father and mother, to whom he was born, will say to him, 'You must die, because you have told lies in the LORD's name.' When he prophesies, his own parents will stab him.

⁴"On that day every prophet will be ashamed of his prophetic vision. He will not put on a prophet's garment of hair in order to deceive. ⁵He will say, 'I am not a prophet. I am a farmer; the land has been my livelihood since my youth.' ⁶If someone asks him, 'What are these wounds on your body?' he will answer, 'The wounds I was given at the house of my friends.'

The Shepherd Struck, the Sheep Scattered

⁷"Awake, O sword, against my
    shepherd,
    against the man who is close to
      me!"
  declares the LORD Almighty.
"Strike the shepherd,
    and the sheep will be scattered,
    and I will turn my hand against the
      little ones.
⁸In the whole land," declares the
    LORD,
  "two-thirds will be struck down
      and perish;
    yet one-third will be left in it.
⁹This third I will bring into the fire;
    I will refine them like silver
    and test them like gold.
They will call on my name
    and I will answer them;
I will say, 'They are my people,'
    and they will say, 'The LORD is our
      God.'"

The LORD Comes and Reigns

14 A day of the LORD is coming when your plunder will be divided among you.

²I will gather all the nations to Jerusalem to fight against it; the city will be captured, the houses ransacked, and the women raped. Half of the city will go into exile, but the rest of the people will not be taken from the city.

³Then the LORD will go out and fight against those nations, as he fights in the day of battle. ⁴On that day his feet will stand on the Mount of Olives, east of Jerusalem, and the Mount of Olives will be split in two from east to west, forming a great valley, with half of the mountain moving north and half moving south. ⁵You will flee by my mountain valley, for it will extend to Azel. You will flee as you fled from the earthquake in the days of Uzziah king of Judah. Then the LORD my God will come, and all the holy ones with him.

⁶On that day there will be no light, no cold or frost. ⁷It will be a unique day, without daytime or night-time—a day known to the LORD. When evening comes, there will be light.

⁸On that day living water will flow out from Jerusalem, half to the eastern sea and half to the western sea, in summer and in winter.

⁹The LORD will be king over the whole earth. On that day there will be one LORD, and his name the only name.

¹⁰The whole land, from Geba to Rimmon, south of Jerusalem, will become like the Arabah. But Jerusalem will be raised up and remain in its place, from the Benjamin Gate to the site of the First Gate, to the Corner Gate, and from the Tower of Hananel to the royal winepresses. ¹¹It will be inhabited; never again will it be destroyed. Jerusalem will be secure.

¹²This is the plague with which the LORD will strike all the nations that fought against Jerusalem: Their flesh will rot while they are still standing on their feet, their eyes will rot in their sockets, and their tongues will rot in their mouths. ¹³On that day men will be stricken by the LORD with great panic. Each man will seize the hand of another, and they will attack each

other. [14]Judah too will fight at Jerusalem. The wealth of all the surrounding nations will be collected—great quantities of gold and silver and clothing. [15]A similar plague will strike the horses and mules, the camels and donkeys, and all the animals in those camps.

[16]Then the survivors from all the nations that have attacked Jerusalem will go up year after year to worship the King, the LORD Almighty, and to celebrate the Feast of Tabernacles. [17]If any of the peoples of the earth do not go up to Jerusalem to worship the King, the LORD Almighty, they will have no rain. [18]If the Egyptian people do not go up and take part, they will have no rain. The LORD will bring on them the plague he inflicts on the nations that do not go up to celebrate the Feast of Tabernacles. [19]This will be the punishment of Egypt and the punishment of all the nations that do not go up to celebrate the Feast of Tabernacles.

[20]On that day HOLY TO THE LORD will be inscribed on the bells of the horses, and the cooking pots in the LORD's house will be like the sacred bowls in front of the altar. [21]Every pot in Jerusalem and Judah will be holy to the LORD Almighty, and all who come to sacrifice will take some of the pots and cook in them. And on that day there will no longer be a Canaanite in the house of the LORD Almighty.

NEW TESTAMENT READING
Revelation 2:1–17

To the Church in Ephesus

2 "To the angel of the church in Ephesus write:

These are the words of him who holds the seven stars in his right hand and walks among the seven golden lampstands: [2]I know your deeds, your hard work and your perseverance. I know that you cannot tolerate wicked men, that you have tested those who claim to be apostles but are not, and have found them false. [3]You have persevered and have endured hardships for my name, and have not grown weary.

[4]Yet I hold this against you: You have forsaken your first love. [5]Remember the height from which you have fallen! Repent and do the things you did at first. If you do not repent, I will come to you and remove your lampstand from its place. [6]But you have this in your favour: You hate the practices of the Nicolaitans, which I also hate.

[7]He who has an ear, let him hear what the Spirit says to the churches. To him who overcomes, I will give the right to eat from the tree of life, which is in the paradise of God.

To the Church in Smyrna

[8]"To the angel of the church in Smyrna write:

These are the words of him who is the First and the Last, who died and came to life again. [9]I know your afflictions and your poverty —yet you are rich! I know the slander of those who say they are Jews and are not, but are a synagogue of Satan. [10]Do not be afraid of what you are about to suffer. I tell you, the devil will put some of you in prison to test you, and you will suffer persecution for ten days. Be faithful, even to the point of death, and I will give you the crown of life.

[11]He who has an ear, let him hear what the Spirit says to the churches. He who overcomes will not be hurt at all by the second death.

To the Church in Pergamum

[12]"To the angel of the church in Pergamum write:

These are the words of him who has the sharp, double-edged sword. ¹³I know where you live—where Satan has his throne. Yet you remain true to my name. You did not renounce your faith in me, even in the days of Antipas, my faithful witness, who was put to death in your city—where Satan lives.

¹⁴Nevertheless, I have a few things against you: You have people there who hold to the teaching of Balaam, who taught Balak to entice the Israelites to sin by eating food sacrificed to idols and by committing sexual immorality. ¹⁵Likewise you also have those who hold to the teaching of the Nicolaitans. ¹⁶Repent therefore! Otherwise, I will soon come to you and will fight against them with the sword of my mouth.

¹⁷He who has an ear, let him hear what the Spirit says to the churches. To him who overcomes, I will give some of the hidden manna. I will also give him a white stone with a new name written on it, known only to him who receives it.

READING FROM PROVERBS
Proverbs 30:1–10

Sayings of Agur

30 The sayings of Agur son of Jakeh—an oracle:

This man declared to Ithiel,
    to Ithiel and to Ucal:

²"I am the most ignorant of men;
    I do not have a man's
        understanding.
³I have not learned wisdom,
    nor have I knowledge of the Holy
        One.
⁴Who has gone up to heaven and
        come down?
    Who has gathered up the wind in
        the hollow of his hands?
    Who has wrapped up the waters in
        his cloak?
    Who has established all the ends of
        the earth?
    What is his name, and the name of
        his son?
    Tell me if you know!

⁵"Every word of God is flawless;
    he is a shield to those who take
        refuge in him.
⁶Do not add to his words,
    or he will rebuke you and prove
        you a liar.

⁷"Two things I ask of you, O Lord;
    do not refuse me before I die:
⁸Keep falsehood and lies far from me;
    give me neither poverty nor riches,
    but give me only my daily bread.
⁹Otherwise, I may have too much and
        disown you
    and say, 'Who is the Lord?'
    Or I may become poor and steal,
    and so dishonour the name of my
        God.

¹⁰"Do not slander a servant to his
        master,
    or he will curse you, and you will
        pay for it.

OLD TESTAMENT READING
Esther 1:1–2:18

Queen Vashti Deposed

1 This is what happened during the time of Xerxes, the Xerxes who ruled over 127 provinces stretching from India to Cush: ²At that time King Xerxes reigned from his royal throne in the citadel of Susa, ³and in the third year of his reign he gave a banquet for all his nobles and officials. The military leaders of Persia and Media, the princes, and the nobles of the provinces were present.

⁴For a full 180 days he displayed the vast wealth of his kingdom and the splendour and glory of his majesty. ⁵When these days were over, the king gave a banquet, lasting seven days, in the enclosed garden of the king's palace, for all the people from the least to the greatest, who were in the citadel of Susa. ⁶The garden had hangings of white and blue linen, fastened with cords of white linen and purple material to silver rings on marble pillars. There were couches of gold and silver on a mosaic pavement of porphyry, marble, mother-of-pearl and other costly stones. ⁷Wine was served in goblets of gold, each one different from the other, and the royal wine was abundant, in keeping with the king's liberality. ⁸By the king's command each guest was allowed to drink in his own way, for the king instructed all the wine stewards to serve each man what he wished.

⁹Queen Vashti also gave a banquet for the women in the royal palace of King Xerxes.

¹⁰On the seventh day, when King Xerxes was in high spirits from wine, he commanded the seven eunuchs who served him—Mehuman, Biztha, Harbona, Bigtha, Abagtha, Zethar and Carcas—¹¹to bring before him Queen Vashti, wearing her royal crown, in order to display her beauty to the people and nobles, for she was lovely to look at. ¹²But when the attendants delivered the king's command, Queen Vashti refused to come. Then the king became furious and burned with anger.

¹³Since it was customary for the king to consult experts in matters of law and justice, he spoke with the wise men who understood the times ¹⁴and were closest to the king—Carshena, Shethar, Admatha, Tarshish, Meres, Marsena and Memucan, the seven nobles of Persia and Media who had special access to the king and were highest in the kingdom.

¹⁵"According to law, what must be done to Queen Vashti?" he asked. "She has not obeyed the command of King Xerxes that the eunuchs have taken to her."

¹⁶Then Memucan replied in the presence of the king and the nobles, "Queen Vashti has done wrong, not only against the king but also against all the nobles and the peoples of all the provinces of King Xerxes. ¹⁷For the queen's conduct will become known to all the women, and so they will despise their husbands and say, 'King Xerxes commanded Queen Vashti to be brought before him, but she would not come.' ¹⁸This very day the Persian and Median women of the nobility who have heard about the queen's conduct will respond to all the king's nobles in the same way. There will be no end of disrespect and discord.

¹⁹"Therefore, if it pleases the king, let him issue a royal decree and let it be written in the laws of Persia and Media, which cannot be repealed, that Vashti is never again to enter the presence of King Xerxes. Also let the king give her royal position to someone else who is better than she. ²⁰Then when the king's edict is proclaimed throughout all his vast realm, all the women will respect

their husbands, from the least to the greatest.''

²¹The king and his nobles were pleased with this advice, so the king did as Memucan proposed. ²²He sent dispatches to all parts of the kingdom, to each province in its own script and to each people in its own language, proclaiming in each people's tongue that every man should be ruler over his own household.

Esther Made Queen

2 Later when the anger of King Xerxes had subsided, he remembered Vashti and what she had done and what he had decreed about her. ²Then the king's personal attendants proposed, ''Let a search be made for beautiful young virgins for the king. ³Let the king appoint commissioners in every province of his realm to bring all these beautiful girls into the harem at the citadel of Susa. Let them be placed under the care of Hegai, the king's eunuch, who is in charge of the women; and let beauty treatments be given to them. ⁴Then let the girl who pleases the king be queen instead of Vashti.'' This advice appealed to the king, and he followed it.

⁵Now there was in the citadel of Susa a Jew of the tribe of Benjamin, named Mordecai son of Jair, the son of Shimei, the son of Kish, ⁶who had been carried into exile from Jerusalem by Nebuchadnezzar king of Babylon, among those taken captive with Jehoiachin king of Judah. ⁷Mordecai had a cousin named Hadassah, whom he had brought up because she had neither father nor mother. This girl, who was also known as Esther, was lovely in form and features, and Mordecai had taken her as his own daughter when her father and mother died.

⁸When the king's order and edict had been proclaimed, many girls were brought to the citadel of Susa and put under the care of Hegai. Esther also was taken to the king's palace and entrusted to Hegai, who had charge of the harem.

⁹The girl pleased him and won his favour. Immediately he provided her with her beauty treatments and special food. He assigned to her seven maids selected from the king's palace and moved her and her maids into the best place in the harem.

¹⁰Esther had not revealed her nationality and family background, because Mordecai had forbidden her to do so. ¹¹Every day he walked to and fro near the courtyard of the harem to find out how Esther was and what was happening to her.

¹²Before a girl's turn came to go in to King Xerxes, she had to complete twelve months of beauty treatments prescribed for the women, six months with oil of myrrh and six with perfumes and cosmetics. ¹³And this is how she would go to the king: Anything she wanted was given to her to take with her from the harem to the king's palace. ¹⁴In the evening she would go there and in the morning return to another part of the harem to the care of Shaashgaz, the king's eunuch who was in charge of the concubines. She would not return to the king unless he was pleased with her and summoned her by name.

¹⁵When the turn came for Esther (the girl Mordecai had adopted, the daughter of his uncle Abihail) to go to the king, she asked for nothing other than what Hegai, the king's eunuch who was in charge of the harem, suggested. And Esther won the favour of everyone who saw her. ¹⁶She was taken to King Xerxes in the royal residence in the tenth month, the month of Tebeth, in the seventh year of his reign.

¹⁷Now the king was attracted to Esther more than to any of the other women, and she won his favour and approval more than any of the other virgins. So he set a royal crown on her head and made her queen instead of Vashti. ¹⁸And the king gave a great banquet, Esther's banquet, for all his nobles and officials. He proclaimed a holiday throughout the provinces and distributed gifts with royal liberality.

NEW TESTAMENT READING
Revelation 2:18–3:6

To the Church in Thyatira

18"To the angel of the church in Thyatira write:

These are the words of the Son of God, whose eyes are like blazing fire and whose feet are like burnished bronze. 19I know your deeds, your love and faith, your service and perseverance, and that you are now doing more than you did at first.

20Nevertheless, I have this against you: You tolerate that woman Jezebel, who calls herself a prophetess. By her teaching she misleads my servants into sexual immorality and the eating of food sacrificed to idols. 21I have given her time to repent of her immorality, but she is unwilling. 22So I will cast her on a bed of suffering, and I will make those who commit adultery with her suffer intensely, unless they repent of her ways. 23I will strike her children dead. Then all the churches will know that I am he who searches hearts and minds, and I will repay each of you according to your deeds. 24Now I say to the rest of you in Thyatira, to you who do not hold to her teaching and have not learned Satan's so-called deep secrets (I will not impose any other burden on you): 25Only hold on to what you have until I come.

26To him who overcomes and does my will to the end, I will give authority over the nations—

27'He will rule them with an iron sceptre;
   he will dash them to pieces like pottery'—

just as I have received authority from my Father. 28I will also give

him the morning star. 29He who has an ear, let him hear what the Spirit says to the churches.

To the Church in Sardis

3 "To the angel of the church in Sardis write:

These are the words of him who holds the seven spirits of God and the seven stars. I know your deeds; you have a reputation of being alive, but you are dead. 2Wake up! Strengthen what remains and is about to die, for I have not found your deeds complete in the sight of my God. 3Remember, therefore, what you have received and heard; obey it, and repent. But if you do not wake up, I will come like a thief, and you will not know at what time I will come to you.

4Yet you have a few people in Sardis who have not soiled their clothes. They will walk with me, dressed in white, for they are worthy. 5He who overcomes will, like them, be dressed in white. I will never blot out his name from the book of life, but will acknowledge his name before my Father and his angels. 6He who has an ear, let him hear what the Spirit says to the churches.

READING FROM PSALMS
Psalm 140:6–13

6O LORD, I say to you, "You are my God."
   Hear, O LORD, my cry for mercy.
7O Sovereign LORD, my strong deliverer,
   who shields my head in the day of battle—
8do not grant the wicked their desires, O LORD;
   do not let their plans succeed, or they will become proud.   *Selah*

9Let the heads of those who surround
me
be covered with the trouble their
lips have caused.
10Let burning coals fall upon them;
may they be thrown into the fire,
into miry pits, never to rise.
11Let slanderers not be established in
the land;

may disaster hunt down men of
violence.

12I know that the LORD secures justice
for the poor
and upholds the cause of the needy.
13Surely the righteous will praise your
name
and the upright will live before you.

DAY 346 # DECEMBER 12

OLD TESTAMENT READING
Esther 2:19–5:14

Mordecai Uncovers a Conspiracy

19When the virgins were assembled a
second time, Mordecai was sitting at
the king's gate. 20But Esther had kept
secret her family background and
nationality just as Mordecai had told
her to do, for she continued to follow
Mordecai's instructions as she had done
when he was bringing her up.

21During the time Mordecai was sitting at the king's gate, Bigthana and
Teresh, two of the king's officers who
guarded the doorway, became angry
and conspired to assassinate King
Xerxes. 22But Mordecai found out
about the plot and told Queen Esther,
who in turn reported it to the king,
giving credit to Mordecai. 23And when
the report was investigated and found to
be true, the two officials were hanged
on a gallows. All this was recorded in
the book of the annals in the presence of
the king.

Haman's Plot to Destroy the Jews

3 After these events, King Xerxes
honoured Haman son of Hammedatha, the Agagite, elevating him and
giving him a seat of honour higher than
that of all the other nobles. 2All the

royal officials at the king's gate knelt
down and paid honour to Haman, for
the king had commanded this concerning him. But Mordecai would not kneel
down or pay him honour.

3Then the royal officials at the king's
gate asked Mordecai, "Why do you disobey the king's command?" 4Day after
day they spoke to him but he refused to
comply. Therefore they told Haman
about it to see whether Mordecai's
behaviour would be tolerated, for he
had told them he was a Jew.

5When Haman saw that Mordecai
would not kneel down or pay him honour, he was enraged. 6Yet having
learned who Mordecai's people were,
he scorned the idea of killing only Mordecai. Instead Haman looked for a way
to destroy all Mordecai's people, the
Jews, throughout the whole kingdom of
Xerxes.

7In the twelfth year of King Xerxes,
in the first month, the month of Nisan,
they cast the *pur* (that is, the lot) in the
presence of Haman to select a day and
month. And the lot fell on the twelfth
month, the month of Adar.

8Then Haman said to King Xerxes,
"There is a certain people dispersed and
scattered among the peoples in all the
provinces of your kingdom whose customs are different from those of all
other people and who do not obey the
king's laws; it is not in the king's best

interest to tolerate them. ⁹If it pleases the king, let a decree be issued to destroy them, and I will put ten thousand talents of silver into the royal treasury for the men who carry out this business."

¹⁰So the king took his signet ring from his finger and gave it to Haman son of Hammedatha, the Agagite, the enemy of the Jews. ¹¹"Keep the money," the king said to Haman, "and do with the people as you please."

¹²Then on the thirteenth day of the first month the royal secretaries were summoned. They wrote out in the script of each province and in the language of each people all Haman's orders to the king's satraps, the governors of the various provinces and the nobles of the various peoples. These were written in the name of King Xerxes himself and sealed with his own ring. ¹³Dispatches were sent by couriers to all the king's provinces with the order to destroy, kill and annihilate all the Jews—young and old, women and little children—on a single day, the thirteenth day of the twelfth month, the month of Adar, and to plunder their goods. ¹⁴A copy of the text of the edict was to be issued as law in every province and made known to the people of every nationality so that they would be ready for that day.

¹⁵Spurred on by the king's command, the couriers went out, and the edict was issued in the citadel of Susa. The king and Haman sat down to drink, but the city of Susa was bewildered.

Mordecai Persuades Esther to Help

4 When Mordecai learned of all that had been done, he tore his clothes, put on sackcloth and ashes, and went out into the city, wailing loudly and bitterly. ²But he went only as far as the king's gate, because no-one clothed in sackcloth was allowed to enter it. ³In every province to which the edict and order of the king came, there was great mourning among the Jews, with fasting, weeping and wailing. Many lay in sackcloth and ashes.

⁴When Esther's maids and eunuchs came and told her about Mordecai, she was in great distress. She sent clothes for him to put on instead of his sackcloth, but he would not accept them. ⁵Then Esther summoned Hathach, one of the king's eunuchs assigned to attend her, and ordered him to find out what was troubling Mordecai and why.

⁶So Hathach went out to Mordecai in the open square of the city in front of the king's gate. ⁷Mordecai told him everything that had happened to him, including the exact amount of money Haman had promised to pay into the royal treasury for the destruction of the Jews. ⁸He also gave him a copy of the text of the edict for their annihilation, which had been published in Susa, to show to Esther and explain it to her, and he told him to urge her to go into the king's presence to beg for mercy and plead with him for her people.

⁹Hathach went back and reported to Esther what Mordecai had said. ¹⁰Then she instructed him to say to Mordecai, ¹¹"All the king's officials and the people of the royal provinces know that for any man or woman who approaches the king in the inner court without being summoned the king has but one law: that he be put to death. The only exception to this is for the king to extend the gold sceptre to him and spare his life. But thirty days have passed since I was called to go to the king."

¹²When Esther's words were reported to Mordecai, ¹³he sent back this answer: "Do not think that because you are in the king's house you alone of all the Jews will escape. ¹⁴For if you remain silent at this time, relief and deliverance for the Jews will arise from another place, but you and your father's family will perish. And who knows but that you have come to royal position for such a time as this?"

¹⁵Then Esther sent this reply to Mordecai: ¹⁶"Go, gather together all the Jews who are in Susa, and fast for me. Do not eat or drink for three days, night or day. I and my maids will fast as you

do. When this is done, I will go to the king, even though it is against the law. And if I perish, I perish."

17So Mordecai went away and carried out all of Esther's instructions.

Esther's Request to the King

5 On the third day Esther put on her royal robes and stood in the inner court of the palace, in front of the king's hall. The king was sitting on his royal throne in the hall, facing the entrance. 2When he saw Queen Esther standing in the court, he was pleased with her and held out to her the gold sceptre that was in his hand. So Esther approached and touched the tip of the sceptre.

3Then the king asked, "What is it, Queen Esther? What is your request? Even up to half the kingdom, it will be given you."

4"If it pleases the king," replied Esther, "let the king, together with Haman, come today to a banquet I have prepared for him."

5"Bring Haman at once," the king said, "so that we may do what Esther asks."

So the king and Haman went to the banquet Esther had prepared. 6As they were drinking wine, the king again asked Esther, "Now what is your petition? It will be given you. And what is your request? Even up to half the kingdom, it will be granted."

7Esther replied, "My petition and my request is this: 8If the king regards me with favour and if it pleases the king to grant my petition and fulfil my request, let the king and Haman come tomorrow to the banquet I will prepare for them. Then I will answer the king's question."

Haman's Rage Against Mordecai

9Haman went out that day happy and in high spirits. But when he saw Mordecai at the king's gate and observed that he neither rose nor showed fear in his presence, he was filled with rage against Mordecai. 10Nevertheless, Haman restrained himself and went home.

Calling together his friends and Zeresh, his wife, 11Haman boasted to them about his vast wealth, his many sons, and all the ways the king had honoured him and how he had elevated him above the other nobles and officials. 12"And that's not all," Haman added. "I'm the only person Queen Esther invited to accompany the king to the banquet she gave. And she has invited me along with the king tomorrow. 13But all this gives me no satisfaction as long as I see that Jew Mordecai sitting at the king's gate."

14His wife Zeresh and all his friends said to him, "Have a gallows built, seventy-five feet high, and ask the king in the morning to have Mordecai hanged on it. Then go with the king to the dinner and be happy." This suggestion delighted Haman, and he had the gallows built.

NEW TESTAMENT READING
Revelation 3:7–22

To the Church in Philadelphia

7"To the angel of the church in Philadelphia write:

These are the words of him who is holy and true, who holds the key of David. What he opens no-one can shut, and what he shuts no-one can open. 8I know your deeds. See, I have placed before you an open door no-one can shut. I know that you have little strength, yet you have kept my word and have not denied my name. 9I will make those who are of the synagogue of Satan, who claim to be Jews though they are not, but are liars—I will make them come and fall down at your feet and acknowledge that I have loved you. 10Since you have kept my command to endure patiently, I will also keep you from the hour of trial that is going to come upon the whole world to test those who live on the earth.

¹¹I am coming soon. Hold on to what you have, so that no-one will take your crown. ¹²Him who overcomes I will make a pillar in the temple of my God. Never again will he leave it. I will write on him the name of my God and the name of the city of my God, the new Jerusalem, which is coming down out of heaven from my God; and I will also write on him my new name. ¹³He who has an ear, let him hear what the Spirit says to the churches.

To the Church in Laodicea

¹⁴"To the angel of the church in Laodicea write:

These are the words of the Amen, the faithful and true witness, the ruler of God's creation. ¹⁵I know your deeds, that you are neither cold nor hot. I wish you were either one or the other! ¹⁶So, because you are lukewarm—neither hot nor cold—I am about to spit you out of my mouth. ¹⁷You say, 'I am rich; I have acquired wealth and do not need a thing.' But you do not realise that you are wretched, pitiful, poor, blind and naked. ¹⁸I counsel you to buy from me gold refined in the fire, so that you can become rich; and white clothes to wear, so that you can cover your shameful nakedness; and salve to put on your eyes, so that you can see.

¹⁹Those whom I love I rebuke and discipline. So be earnest, and repent. ²⁰Here I am! I stand at the door and knock. If anyone hears my voice and opens the door, I will come in and eat with him, and he with me.

²¹To him who overcomes I will give the right to sit with me on my throne, just as I overcame and sat down with my Father on his throne. ²²He who has an ear, let him hear what the Spirit says to the churches."

READING FROM PSALMS
Psalm 141:1–10

A psalm of David.

¹O LORD, I call to you; come quickly to me.
  Hear my voice when I call to you.
²May my prayer be set before you like incense;
  may the lifting up of my hands be like the evening sacrifice.

³Set a guard over my mouth, O LORD;
  keep watch over the door of my lips.
⁴Let not my heart be drawn to what is evil,
  to take part in wicked deeds
  with men who are evildoers;
  let me not eat of their delicacies.

⁵Let a righteous man strike me—it is a kindness;
  let him rebuke me—it is oil on my head.
  My head will not refuse it.

Yet my prayer is ever against the deeds of evildoers;
6   their rulers will be thrown down from the cliffs,
  and the wicked will learn that my words were well spoken.
⁷ They will say, ⌐ "As one ploughs and breaks up the earth,
  so our bones have been scattered at the mouth of the grave."

⁸But my eyes are fixed on you, O Sovereign LORD;
  in you I take refuge—do not give me over to death.
⁹Keep me from the snares they have laid for me,
  from the traps set by evildoers.
¹⁰Let the wicked fall into their own nets,
  while I pass by in safety.

DECEMBER 13

OLD TESTAMENT READING
Esther 6:1–8:17

Mordecai Honoured

6 That night the king could not sleep; so he ordered the book of the chronicles, the record of his reign, to be brought in and read to him. ²It was found recorded there that Mordecai had exposed Bigthana and Teresh, two of the king's officers who guarded the doorway, who had conspired to assassinate King Xerxes.

³"What honour and recognition has Mordecai received for this?" the king asked.

"Nothing has been done for him," his attendants answered.

⁴The king said, "Who is in the court?" Now Haman had just entered the outer court of the palace to speak to the king about hanging Mordecai on the gallows he had erected for him.

⁵His attendants answered, "Haman is standing in the court."

"Bring him in," the king ordered.

⁶When Haman entered, the king asked him, "What should be done for the man the king delights to honour?"

Now Haman thought to himself, "Who is there that the king would rather honour than me?" ⁷So he answered the king, "For the man the king delights to honour, ⁸have them bring a royal robe the king has worn and a horse the king has ridden, one with a royal crest placed on its head. ⁹Then let the robe and horse be entrusted to one of the king's most noble princes. Let them robe the man the king delights to honour, and lead him on the horse through the city streets, proclaiming before him, 'This is what is done for the man the king delights to honour!'"

¹⁰"Go at once," the king commanded Haman. "Get the robe and the horse and do just as you have suggested for Mordecai the Jew, who sits at the king's gate. Do not neglect anything you have recommended."

¹¹So Haman got the robe and the horse. He robed Mordecai, and led him on horseback through the city streets, proclaiming before him, "This is what is done for the man the king delights to honour!"

¹²Afterwards Mordecai returned to the king's gate. But Haman rushed home, with his head covered, in grief, ¹³and told Zeresh his wife and all his friends everything that had happened to him.

His advisers and his wife Zeresh said to him, "Since Mordecai, before whom your downfall has started, is of Jewish origin, you cannot stand against him —you will surely come to ruin!" ¹⁴While they were still talking with him, the king's eunuchs arrived and hurried Haman away to the banquet Esther had prepared.

Haman Hanged

7 So the king and Haman went to dine with Queen Esther, ²and as they were drinking wine on that second day, the king again asked, "Queen Esther, what is your petition? It will be given you. What is your request? Even up to half the kingdom, it will be granted."

³Then Queen Esther answered, "If I have found favour with you, O king, and if it pleases your majesty, grant me my life—this is my petition. And spare my people—this is my request. ⁴For I and my people have been sold for destruction and slaughter and annihilation. If we had merely been sold as male and female slaves, I would have kept quiet, because no such distress would justify disturbing the king."

⁵King Xerxes asked Queen Esther, "Who is he? Where is the man who has dared to do such a thing?"

⁶Esther said, "The adversary and enemy is this vile Haman."

Then Haman was terrified before the king and queen. ⁷The king got up in a rage, left his wine and went out into the palace garden. But Haman, realising that the king had already decided his fate, stayed behind to beg Queen Esther for his life.

⁸Just as the king returned from the palace garden to the banquet hall, Haman was falling on the couch where Esther was reclining.

The king exclaimed, "Will he even molest the queen while she is with me in the house?"

As soon as the word left the king's mouth, they covered Haman's face. ⁹Then Harbona, one of the eunuchs attending the king, said, "A gallows seventy-five feet high stands by Haman's house. He had it made for Mordecai, who spoke up to help the king."

The king said, "Hang him on it!" ¹⁰So they hanged Haman on the gallows he had prepared for Mordecai. Then the king's fury subsided.

The King's Edict on Behalf of the Jews

8 That same day King Xerxes gave Queen Esther the estate of Haman, the enemy of the Jews. And Mordecai came into the presence of the king, for Esther had told how he was related to her. ²The king took off his signet ring, which he had reclaimed from Haman, and presented it to Mordecai. And Esther appointed him over Haman's estate.

³Esther again pleaded with the king, falling at his feet and weeping. She begged him to put an end to the evil plan of Haman the Agagite, which he had devised against the Jews. ⁴Then the king extended the gold sceptre to Esther and she arose and stood before him.

⁵"If it pleases the king," she said, "and if he regards me with favour and thinks it the right thing to do, and if he is pleased with me, let an order be written overruling the dispatches that Haman

son of Hammedatha, the Agagite, devised and wrote to destroy the Jews in all the king's provinces. ⁶For how can I bear to see disaster fall on my people? How can I bear to see the destruction of my family?"

⁷King Xerxes replied to Queen Esther and to Mordecai the Jew, "Because Haman attacked the Jews, I have given his estate to Esther, and they have hanged him on the gallows. ⁸Now write another decree in the king's name on behalf of the Jews as seems best to you, and seal it with the king's signet ring —for no document written in the king's name and sealed with his ring can be revoked."

⁹At once the royal secretaries were summoned—on the twenty-third day of the third month, the month of Sivan. They wrote out all Mordecai's orders to the Jews, and to the satraps, governors and nobles of the 127 provinces stretching from India to Cush. These orders were written in the script of each province and the language of each people and also to the Jews in their own script and language. ¹⁰Mordecai wrote in the name of King Xerxes, sealed the dispatches with the king's signet ring, and sent them by mounted couriers, who rode fast horses especially bred for the king.

¹¹The king's edict granted the Jews in every city the right to assemble and protect themselves; to destroy, kill and annihilate any armed force of any nationality or province that might attack them and their women and children; and to plunder the property of their enemies. ¹²The day appointed for the Jews to do this in all the provinces of King Xerxes was the thirteenth day of the twelfth month, the month of Adar. ¹³A copy of the text of the edict was to be issued as law in every province and made known to the people of every nationality so that the Jews would be ready on that day to avenge themselves on their enemies.

¹⁴The couriers, riding the royal horses, raced out, spurred on by the

king's command. And the edict was also issued in the citadel of Susa.

¹⁵Mordecai left the king's presence wearing royal garments of blue and white, a large crown of gold and a purple robe of fine linen. And the city of Susa held a joyous celebration. ¹⁶For the Jews it was a time of happiness and joy, gladness and honour. ¹⁷In every province and in every city, wherever the edict of the king went, there was joy and gladness among the Jews, with feasting and celebrating. And many people of other nationalities became Jews because fear of the Jews had seized them.

NEW TESTAMENT READING
Revelation 4:1–11

The Throne in Heaven

4 After this I looked, and there before me was a door standing open in heaven. And the voice I had first heard speaking to me like a trumpet said, "Come up here, and I will show you what must take place after this." ²At once I was in the Spirit, and there before me was a throne in heaven with someone sitting on it. ³And the one who sat there had the appearance of jasper and carnelian. A rainbow, resembling an emerald, encircled the throne. ⁴Surrounding the throne were twenty-four other thrones, and seated on them were twenty-four elders. They were dressed in white and had crowns of gold on their heads. ⁵From the throne came flashes of lightning, rumblings and peals of thunder. Before the throne, seven lamps were blazing. These are the seven spirits of God. ⁶Also before the throne there was what looked like a sea of glass, clear as crystal.

In the centre, around the throne, were four living creatures, and they were covered with eyes, in front and behind. ⁷The first living creature was like a lion, the second was like an ox, the third had a face like a man, the fourth was like a flying eagle. ⁸Each of the four living creatures had six wings and was covered with eyes all around, even under his wings. Day and night they never stop saying:

"Holy, holy, holy
is the Lord God Almighty,
who was, and is, and is to come."

⁹Whenever the living creatures give glory, honour and thanks to him who sits on the throne and who lives for ever and ever, ¹⁰the twenty-four elders fall down before him who sits on the throne, and worship him who lives for ever and ever. They lay their crowns before the throne and say:

¹¹"You are worthy, our Lord and God,
to receive glory and honour and
power,
for you created all things,
and by your will they were created
and have their being."

READING FROM PSALMS
Psalm 142:1–7

A maskil of David. When he was in the cave. A prayer.

¹I cry aloud to the LORD;
I lift up my voice to the LORD for
mercy.
²I pour out my complaint before him;
before him I tell my trouble.

³When my spirit grows faint within
me,
it is you who know my way.
In the path where I walk
men have hidden a snare for me.
⁴Look to my right and see;
no-one is concerned for me.
I have no refuge;
no-one cares for my life.

⁵I cry to you, O LORD;
I say, "You are my refuge,
my portion in the land of the
living."

6Listen to my cry,
  for I am in desperate need;
rescue me from those who pursue
    me,
  for they are too strong
    for me.

7Set me free from my prison,
  that I may praise your name.

Then the righteous will gather about
    me
  because of your goodness to me.

DECEMBER 14 DAY 348

OLD TESTAMENT READING
Esther 9:1–10:3

Triumph of the Jews

9 On the thirteenth day of the twelfth
  month, the month of Adar, the
edict commanded by the king was to be
carried out. On this day the enemies of
the Jews had hoped to overpower them,
but now the tables were turned and the
Jews got the upper hand over those who
hated them. 2The Jews assembled in
their cities in all the provinces of King
Xerxes to attack those seeking their
destruction. No-one could stand against
them, because the people of all the
other nationalities were afraid of them.
3And all the nobles of the provinces, the
satraps, the governors and the king's
administrators helped the Jews, because fear of Mordecai had seized them.
4Mordecai was prominent in the palace;
his reputation spread throughout the
provinces, and he became more and
more powerful.

5The Jews struck down all their
enemies with the sword, killing and
destroying them, and they did what
they pleased to those who hated them.
6In the citadel of Susa, the Jews killed
and destroyed five hundred men. 7They
also killed Parshandatha, Dalphon,
Aspatha, 8Poratha, Adalia, Aridatha,
9Parmashta, Arisai, Aridai and
Vaizatha, 10the ten sons of Haman son
of Hammedatha, the enemy of the
Jews. But they did not lay their hands
on the plunder.

11The number of those slain in the
citadel of Susa was reported to the king
that same day. 12The king said to Queen
Esther, "The Jews have killed and destroyed five hundred men and the ten
sons of Haman in the citadel of Susa.
What have they done in the rest of the
king's provinces? Now what is your
petition? It will be given you. What is
your request? It will also be granted."

13"If it pleases the king," Esther
answered, "give the Jews in Susa permission to carry out this day's edict
tomorrow also, and let Haman's ten
sons be hanged on gallows."

14So the king commanded that this be
done. An edict was issued in Susa, and
they hanged the ten sons of Haman.
15The Jews in Susa came together on the
fourteenth day of the month of Adar,
and they put to death in Susa three
hundred men, but they did not lay their
hands on the plunder.

16Meanwhile, the remainder of the
Jews who were in the king's provinces
also assembled to protect themselves
and get relief from their enemies. They
killed seventy-five thousand of them but
did not lay their hands on the plunder.
17This happened on the thirteenth day
of the month of Adar, and on the fourteenth they rested and made it a day of
feasting and joy.

Purim Celebrated

18The Jews in Susa, however, had
assembled on the thirteenth and fourteenth, and then on the fifteenth they

rested and made it a day of feasting and joy.

¹⁹That is why rural Jews—those living in villages—observe the fourteenth of the month of Adar as a day of joy and feasting, a day for giving presents to each other.

²⁰Mordecai recorded these events, and he sent letters to all the Jews throughout the provinces of King Xerxes, near and far, ²¹to have them celebrate annually the fourteenth and fifteenth days of the month of Adar ²²as the time when the Jews got relief from their enemies, and as the month when their sorrow was turned into joy and their mourning into a day of celebration. He wrote to them to observe the days as days of feasting and joy and giving presents of food to one another and gifts to the poor.

²³So the Jews agreed to continue the celebration they had begun, doing what Mordecai had written to them. ²⁴For Haman son of Hammedatha, the Agagite, the enemy of all the Jews, had plotted against the Jews to destroy them and had cast the *pur* (that is, the lot) for their ruin and destruction. ²⁵But when the plot came to the king's attention, he issued written orders that the evil scheme Haman had devised against the Jews should come back on to his own head, and that he and his sons should be hanged on the gallows. ²⁶(Therefore these days were called Purim, from the word *pur*.) Because of everything written in this letter and because of what they had seen and what had happened to them, ²⁷the Jews took it upon themselves to establish the custom that they and their descendants and all who join them should without fail observe these two days every year, in the way prescribed and at the time appointed. ²⁸These days should be remembered and observed in every generation by every family, and in every province and in every city. And these days of Purim should never cease to be celebrated by the Jews, nor should the memory of them die out among their descendants.

²⁹So Queen Esther, daughter of Abihail, along with Mordecai the Jew, wrote with full authority to confirm this second letter concerning Purim. ³⁰And Mordecai sent letters to all the Jews in the 127 provinces of the kingdom of Xerxes—words of goodwill and assurance—³¹to establish these days of Purim at their designated times, as Mordecai the Jew and Queen Esther had decreed for them, and as they had established for themselves and their descendants in regard to their times of fasting and lamentation. ³²Esther's decree confirmed these regulations about Purim, and it was written down in the records.

The Greatness of Mordecai

10 King Xerxes imposed tribute throughout the empire, to its distant shores. ²And all his acts of power and might, together with a full account of the greatness of Mordecai to which the king had raised him, are they not written in the book of the annals of the kings of Media and Persia? ³Mordecai the Jew was second in rank to King Xerxes, pre-eminent among the Jews, and held in high esteem by his many fellow Jews, because he worked for the good of his people and spoke up for the welfare of all the Jews.

NEW TESTAMENT READING
Revelation 5:1–14

The Scroll and the Lamb

5 Then I saw in the right hand of him who sat on the throne a scroll with writing on both sides and sealed with seven seals. ²And I saw a mighty angel proclaiming in a loud voice, "Who is worthy to break the seals and open the scroll?" ³But no-one in heaven or on earth or under the earth could open the scroll or even look inside it. ⁴I wept and wept because no-one was found who was worthy to open the scroll or look inside. ⁵Then one of the elders said to me, "Do not weep! See, the Lion of the tribe of Judah, the Root of David, has triumphed. He is able to open the scroll and its seven seals."

6Then I saw a Lamb, looking as if it had been slain, standing in the centre of the throne, encircled by the four living creatures and the elders. He had seven horns and seven eyes, which are the seven spirits of God sent out into all the earth. 7He came and took the scroll from the right hand of him who sat on the throne. 8And when he had taken it, the four living creatures and the twenty-four elders fell down before the Lamb. Each one had a harp and they were holding golden bowls full of incense, which are the prayers of the saints. 9And they sang a new song:

"You are worthy to take the scroll
    and to open its seals,
because you were slain,
    and with your blood you purchased
        men for God
    from every tribe and language and
        people and nation.
10You have made them to be a
        kingdom and priests to serve
        our God,
    and they will reign on the earth."

11Then I looked and heard the voice of many angels, numbering thousands upon thousands, and ten thousand times ten thousand. They encircled the throne and the living creatures and the elders. 12In a loud voice they sang:

"Worthy is the Lamb, who was slain,
    to receive power and wealth and
        wisdom and strength
    and honour and glory and praise!"

13Then I heard every creature in heaven and on earth and under the earth and on the sea, and all that is in them, singing:

"To him who sits on the throne and
    to the Lamb

be praise and honour and glory and
    power,
        for ever and ever!"

14The four living creatures said, "Amen", and the elders fell down and worshipped.

READING FROM PROVERBS
Proverbs 30:11–23

11"There are those who curse their
        fathers
    and do not bless their mothers;
12those who are pure in their own eyes
    and yet are not cleansed of their
        filth;
13those whose eyes are ever so
        haughty,
    whose glances are so disdainful;
14those whose teeth are swords
    and whose jaws are set with knives
to devour the poor from the earth,
    the needy from among mankind.

15"The leech has two daughters.
    'Give! Give!' they cry.

"There are three things that are
        never satisfied,
    four that never say, 'Enough!':
16the grave, the barren womb,
    land, which is never satisfied with
        water,
    and fire, which never says,
        'Enough!'

17"The eye that mocks a father,
    that scorns obedience to a mother,
will be pecked out by the ravens of
        the valley,
    will be eaten by the vultures.

18"There are three things that are too
        amazing for me,
    four that I do not understand:

19the way of an eagle in the sky,
    the way of a snake on a rock,
the way of a ship on the high seas,
    and the way of a man with a maiden.

20"This is the way of an adulteress:
    She eats and wipes her mouth
    and says, 'I've done nothing
      wrong.'

21"Under three things the earth
      trembles,
    under four it cannot bear up:
22a servant who becomes king,
    a fool who is full of food,
23an unloved woman who is
      married,
    and a maidservant who displaces
      her mistress.

DAY 349

DECEMBER 15

OLD TESTAMENT READING
Malachi 1:1–2:16

1 An oracle: The word of the LORD
to Israel through Malachi.

Jacob Loved, Esau Hated

2"I have loved you," says the LORD.

"But you ask, 'How have you loved
us?'

"Was not Esau Jacob's brother?" the
LORD says. "Yet I have loved Jacob,
3but Esau I have hated, and I have
turned his mountains into a wasteland
and left his inheritance to the desert
jackals."

4Edom may say, "Though we have
been crushed, we will rebuild the
ruins."

But this is what the LORD Almighty
says: "They may build, but I will demolish. They will be called the Wicked
Land, a people always under the wrath
of the LORD. 5You will see it with your
own eyes and say, 'Great is the LORD
—even beyond the borders of Israel!'

Blemished Sacrifices

6"A son honours his father, and a
servant his master. If I am a father,
where is the honour due to me? If I am a
master, where is the respect due to

me?" says the LORD Almighty. "It is
you, O priests, who show contempt for
my name.

"But you ask, 'How have we shown
contempt for your name?'

7"You place defiled food on my altar.

"But you ask, 'How have we defiled
you?'

"By saying that the LORD's table is
contemptible. 8When you bring blind
animals for sacrifice, is that not wrong?
When you sacrifice crippled or diseased
animals, is that not wrong? Try offering
them to your governor! Would he be
pleased with you? Would he accept
you?" says the LORD Almighty.

9"Now implore God to be gracious to
us. With such offerings from your
hands, will he accept you?"—says the
LORD Almighty.

10"Oh, that one of you would shut the
temple doors, so that you would not
light useless fires on my altar! I am not
pleased with you," says the LORD
Almighty, "and I will accept no offering
from your hands. 11My name will be
great among the nations, from the rising
to the setting of the sun. In every place
incense and pure offerings will be
brought to my name, because my name
will be great among the nations," says
the LORD Almighty.

12"But you profane it by saying of the
Lord's table, 'It is defiled', and of its

food, 'It is contemptible.' [13]And you say, 'What a burden!' and you sniff at it contemptuously," says the LORD Almighty.

"When you bring injured, crippled or diseased animals and offer them as sacrifices, should I accept them from your hands?" says the LORD. [14]"Cursed is the cheat who has an acceptable male in his flock and vows to give it, but then sacrifices a blemished animal to the Lord. For I am a great king," says the LORD Almighty, "and my name is to be feared among the nations.

Admonition for the Priests

2 "And now this admonition is for you, O priests. [2]If you do not listen, and if you do not set your heart to honour my name," says the LORD Almighty, "I will send a curse upon you, and I will curse your blessings. Yes, I have already cursed them, because you have not set your heart to honour me.

[3]"Because of you I will rebuke your descendants; I will spread on your faces the offal from your festival sacrifices, and you will be carried off with it. [4]And you will know that I have sent you this admonition so that my covenant with Levi may continue," says the LORD Almighty. [5]"My covenant was with him, a covenant of life and peace, and I gave them to him; this called for reverence and he revered me and stood in awe of my name. [6]True instruction was in his mouth and nothing false was found on his lips. He walked with me in peace and uprightness, and turned many from sin.

[7]"For the lips of a priest ought to preserve knowledge, and from his mouth men should seek instruction— because he is the messenger of the LORD Almighty. [8]But you have turned from the way and by your teaching have caused many to stumble; you have violated the covenant with Levi," says the LORD Almighty. [9]"So I have caused

you to be despised and humiliated before all the people, because you have not followed my ways but have shown partiality in matters of the law."

Judah Unfaithful

[10]Have we not all one Father? Did not one God create us? Why do we profane the covenant of our fathers by breaking faith with one another?

[11]Judah has broken faith. A detestable thing has been committed in Israel and in Jerusalem: Judah has desecrated the sanctuary the LORD loves, by marrying the daughter of a foreign god. [12]As for the man who does this, whoever may be, may the LORD cut him off from the tents of Jacob—even though he brings offerings to the LORD Almighty.

[13]Another thing you do: You flood the LORD's altar with tears. You weep and wail because he no longer pays attention to your offerings or accepts them with pleasure from your hands. [14]You ask, "Why?" It is because the LORD is acting as the witness between you and the wife of your youth, because you have broken faith with her, though she is your partner, the wife of your marriage covenant.

[15]Has not ⌊the LORD⌋ made them one? In flesh and spirit they are his. And why one? Because he was seeking godly offspring. So guard yourself in your spirit, and do not break faith with the wife of your youth.

[16]"I hate divorce," says the LORD God of Israel, "and I hate a man's covering himself with violence as well as with his garment," says the LORD Almighty.

So guard yourself in your spirit, and do not break faith.

NEW TESTAMENT READING
Revelation 6:1–17

The Seals

6 I watched as the Lamb opened the first of the seven seals. Then I heard one of the four living creatures

say in a voice like thunder, "Come!" ²I looked, and there before me was a white horse! Its rider held a bow, and he was given a crown, and he rode out as a conqueror bent on conquest.

³When the Lamb opened the second seal, I heard the second living creature say, "Come!" ⁴Then another horse came out, a fiery red one. Its rider was given power to take peace from the earth and to make men slay each other. To him was given a large sword.

⁵When the Lamb opened the third seal, I heard the third living creature say, "Come!" I looked, and there before me was a black horse! Its rider was holding a pair of scales in his hand. ⁶Then I heard what sounded like a voice among the four living creatures, saying, "A quart of wheat for a day's wages, and three quarts of barley for a day's wages, and do not damage the oil and the wine!"

⁷When the Lamb opened the fourth seal, I heard the voice of the fourth living creature say, "Come!" ⁸I looked, and there before me was a pale horse! Its rider was named Death, and Hades was following close behind him. They were given power over a fourth of the earth to kill by sword, famine and plague, and by the wild beasts of the earth.

⁹When he opened the fifth seal, I saw under the altar the souls of those who had been slain because of the word of God and the testimony they had maintained. ¹⁰They called out in a loud voice, "How long, Sovereign Lord, holy and true, until you judge the inhabitants of the earth and avenge our blood?" ¹¹Then each of them was given a white robe, and they were told to wait a little longer, until the number of their fellow-servants and brothers who were to be killed as they had been was completed.

¹²I watched as he opened the sixth seal. There was a great earthquake. The sun turned black like sackcloth made of goat hair, the whole moon turned blood red, ¹³and the stars in the sky fell to earth, as late figs drop from a fig-tree when shaken by a strong wind. ¹⁴The sky receded like a scroll, rolling up, and every mountain and island was removed from its place.

¹⁵Then the kings of the earth, the princes, the generals, the rich, the mighty, and every slave and every free man hid in caves and among the rocks of the mountains. ¹⁶They called to the mountains and the rocks, "Fall on us and hide us from the face of him who sits on the throne and from the wrath of the Lamb! ¹⁷For the great day of their wrath has come, and who can stand?"

READING FROM PSALMS
Psalm 143:1–12

A psalm of David.

¹O Lᴏʀᴅ, hear my prayer,
    listen to my cry for mercy;
in your faithfulness and righteousness
    come to my relief.
²Do not bring your servant into
    judgment,
    for no-one living is righteous
      before you.

³The enemy pursues me,
    he crushes me to the ground;
he makes me dwell in darkness
    like those long dead.
⁴So my spirit grows faint within me;
    my heart within me is dismayed.

⁵I remember the days of long ago;
    I meditate on all your works
    and consider what your hands have
      done.
⁶I spread out my hands to you;
    my soul thirsts for you like a
      parched land.   *Selah*

⁷Answer me quickly, O Lᴏʀᴅ;
    my spirit fails.
Do not hide your face from me
    or I will be like those who go down
      to the pit.

8Let the morning bring me word of
your unfailing love,
for I have put my trust in
you.
Show me the way I should go,
for to you I lift up my soul.
9Rescue me from my enemies, O
LORD,
for I hide myself in you.
10Teach me to do your will,
for you are my God;

may your good Spirit
lead me on level ground.

11For your name's sake, O LORD,
preserve my life;
in your righteousness, bring me out
of trouble.
12In your unfailing love, silence my
enemies;
destroy all my foes,
for I am your servant.

DECEMBER 16 DAY 350

OLD TESTAMENT READING
Malachi 2:17—4:6

The Day of Judgment

17You have wearied the LORD with
your words.

"How have we wearied him?" you
ask.

By saying, "All who do evil are good
in the eyes of the LORD, and he is
pleased with them" or "Where is the
God of justice?"

3 "See, I will send my messenger,
who will prepare the way before
me. Then suddenly the Lord you are
seeking will come to his temple; the
messenger of the covenant, whom you
desire, will come," says the Lord
Almighty.

2But who can endure the day of his
coming? Who can stand when he
appears? For he will be like a refiner's
fire or a launderer's soap. 3He will sit as
a refiner and purifier of silver; he will
purify the Levites and refine them like
gold and silver. Then the LORD will
have men who will bring offerings in
righteousness, 4and the offerings of
Judah and Jerusalem will be acceptable
to the LORD, as in days gone by, as in
former years.

5"So I will come near to you for judgment. I will be quick to testify against
sorcerers, adulterers and perjurers,
against those who defraud labourers of
their wages, who oppress the widows
and the fatherless, and deprive aliens of
justice, but do not fear me," says the
LORD Almighty.

Robbing God

6"I the LORD do not change. So you,
O descendants of Jacob, are not destroyed. 7Ever since the time of your
forefathers you have turned away from
my decrees and have not kept them.
Return to me, and I will return to you,"
says the LORD Almighty.

"But you ask, 'How are we to
return?'

8"Will a man rob God? Yet you rob
me.

"But you ask, 'How do we rob you?'

"In tithes and offerings. 9You are
under a curse—the whole nation of you
—because you are robbing me. 10Bring
the whole tithe into the storehouse, that
there may be food in my house. Test me
in this," says the LORD Almighty, "and
see if I will not throw open the floodgates of heaven and pour out so much
blessing that you will not have room

enough for it. ¹¹I will prevent pests from devouring your crops, and the vines in your fields will not cast their fruit," says the LORD Almighty. ¹²"Then all the nations will call you blessed, for yours will be a delightful land," says the LORD Almighty.

¹³"You have said harsh things against me," says the LORD.

"Yet you ask, 'What have we said against you?'

¹⁴"You have said, 'It is futile to serve God. What did we gain by carrying out his requirements and going about like mourners before the LORD Almighty? ¹⁵But now we call the arrogant blessed. Certainly the evildoers prosper, and even those who challenge God escape.'"

¹⁶Then those who feared the LORD talked with each other, and the LORD listened and heard. A scroll of remembrance was written in his presence concerning those who feared the LORD and honoured his name.

¹⁷"They will be mine," says the LORD Almighty, "in the day when I make up my treasured possession. I will spare them, just as in compassion a man spares his son who serves him. ¹⁸And you will again see the distinction between the righteous and the wicked, between those who serve God and those who do not.

The Day of the LORD

4 "Surely the day is coming; it will burn like a furnace. All the arrogant and every evildoer will be stubble, and that day that is coming will set them on fire," says the LORD Almighty. "Not a root or a branch will be left to them. ²But for you who revere my name, the sun of righteousness will rise with healing in its wings. And you will go out and leap like calves released from the stall. ³Then you will trample down the wicked; they will be ashes under the soles of your feet on the day when I do these things," says the LORD Almighty.

⁴"Remember the law of my servant Moses, the decrees and laws I gave him at Horeb for all Israel.

⁵"See, I will send you the prophet Elijah before that great and dreadful day of the LORD comes. ⁶He will turn the hearts of the fathers to their children, and the hearts of the children to their fathers; or else I will come and strike the land with a curse."

NEW TESTAMENT READING
Revelation 7:1–17

144,000 Sealed

7 After this I saw four angels standing at the four corners of the earth, holding back the four winds of the earth to prevent any wind from blowing on the land or on the sea or on any tree. ²Then I saw another angel coming up from the east, having the seal of the living God. He called out in a loud voice to the four angels who had been given power to harm the land and the sea: ³"Do not harm the land or the sea or the trees until we put a seal on the foreheads of the servants of our God." ⁴Then I heard the number of those who were sealed: 144,000 from all the tribes of Israel.

⁵From the tribe of Judah 12,000 were sealed,
from the tribe of Reuben 12,000,
from the tribe of Gad 12,000,
⁶from the tribe of Asher 12,000,
from the tribe of Naphtali 12,000,
from the tribe of Manasseh 12,000,
⁷from the tribe of Simeon 12,000,
from the tribe of Levi 12,000,
from the tribe of Issachar 12,000,
⁸from the tribe of Zebulun 12,000,
from the tribe of Joseph 12,000,
from the tribe of Benjamin 12,000.

The Great Multitude in White Robes

⁹After this I looked and there before me was a great multitude that no-one

could count, from every nation, tribe, people and language, standing before the throne and in front of the Lamb. They were wearing white robes and were holding palm branches in their hands. ¹⁰And they cried out in a loud voice:

"Salvation belongs to our God,
who sits on the throne,
and to the Lamb."

¹¹All the angels were standing round the throne and around the elders and the four living creatures. They fell down on their faces before the throne and worshipped God, ¹²saying:

"Amen!
Praise and glory
and wisdom and thanks and honour
and power and strength
be to our God for ever and ever.
Amen!"

¹³Then one of the elders asked me, "These in white robes—who are they, and where did they come from?"

¹⁴I answered, "Sir, you know."

And he said, "These are they who have come out of the great tribulation; they have washed their robes and made them white in the blood of the Lamb. ¹⁵Therefore,

"they are before the throne of God
and serve him day and night in his
temple;
and he who sits on the throne will
spread his tent over them.
¹⁶Never again will they hunger;
never again will they thirst.
The sun will not beat upon them,
nor any scorching heat.

¹⁷For the Lamb at the centre of the
throne will be their shepherd;
he will lead them to springs of
living water.
And God will wipe away every tear
from their eyes."

READING FROM PSALMS
Psalm 144:1–8

Of David.

¹Praise be to the LORD my Rock,
who trains my hands for war,
my fingers for battle.
²He is my loving God and my fortress,
my stronghold and my deliverer,
my shield, in whom I take refuge,
who subdues peoples under me.

³O LORD, what is man that you care
for him,
the son of man that you think of
him?
⁴Man is like a breath;
his days are like a fleeting shadow.

⁵Part your heavens, O LORD, and
come down;
touch the mountains, so that they
smoke.
⁶Send forth lightning and scatter ⌊the
enemies⌋;
shoot your arrows and rout them.
⁷Reach down your hand from on high;
deliver me and rescue me
from the mighty waters,
from the hands of foreigners
⁸whose mouths are full of lies,
whose right hands are deceitful.

DECEMBER 17

OLD TESTAMENT READING
Ezra 1:1–2:67

Cyrus Helps the Exiles to Return

1 In the first year of Cyrus king of Persia, in order to fulfil the word of the LORD spoken by Jeremiah, the LORD moved the heart of Cyrus king of Persia to make a proclamation throughout his realm and to put it in writing:

²"This is what Cyrus king of Persia says:

"'The LORD, the God of heaven, has given me all the kingdoms of the earth and he has appointed me to build a temple for him at Jerusalem in Judah. ³Anyone of his people among you—may his God be with you—let him go up to Jerusalem in Judah and build the temple of the LORD, the God of Israel, the God who is in Jerusalem. ⁴And the people of any place where survivors may now be living are to provide him with silver and gold, with goods and livestock, and with freewill offerings for the temple of God in Jerusalem.'"

⁵Then the family heads of Judah and Benjamin, and the priests and Levites —everyone whose heart God had moved—prepared to go up and build the house of the LORD in Jerusalem. ⁶All their neighbours assisted them with articles of silver and gold, with goods and livestock, and with valuable gifts, in addition to all the freewill offerings. ⁷Moreover, King Cyrus brought out the articles belonging to the temple of the LORD, which Nebuchadnezzar had carried away from Jerusalem and had placed in the temple of his god. ⁸Cyrus king of Persia had them brought by Mithredath the treasurer, who counted them out to Sheshbazzar the prince of Judah.

⁹This was the inventory:

gold dishes	30
silver dishes	1,000
silver pans	29
¹⁰gold bowls	30
matching silver bowls	410
other articles	1,000

¹¹In all, there were 5,400 articles of gold and of silver. Sheshbazzar brought all these along when the exiles came up from Babylon to Jerusalem.

The List of the Exiles Who Returned

2 Now these are the people of the province who came up from the captivity of the exiles, whom Nebuchadnezzar king of Babylon had taken captive to Babylon (they returned to Jerusalem and Judah, each to his own town, ²in company with Zerubbabel, Jeshua, Nehemiah, Seraiah, Reelaiah, Mordecai, Bilshan, Mispar, Bigvai, Rehum and Baanah):

The list of the men of the people of Israel:

³the descendants of Parosh	2,172
⁴of Shephatiah	372
⁵of Arah	775
⁶of Pahath-Moab (through the line of Jeshua and Joab)	2,812
⁷of Elam	1,254
⁸of Zattu	945
⁹of Zaccai	760
¹⁰of Bani	642
¹¹of Bebai	623
¹²of Azgad	1,222
¹³of Adonikam	666
¹⁴of Bigvai	2,056
¹⁵of Adin	454
¹⁶of Ater (through Hezekiah)	98
¹⁷of Bezai	323
¹⁸of Jorah	112
¹⁹of Hashum	223
²⁰of Gibbar	95

21the men of Bethlehem   123
22of Netophah   56
23of Anathoth   128
24of Azmaveth   42
25of Kiriath Jearim,
   Kephirah and Beeroth   743
26of Ramah and Geba   621
27of Michmash   122
28of Bethel and Ai   223
29of Nebo   52
30of Magbish   156
31of the other Elam   1,254
32of Harim   320
33of Lod, Hadid and Ono   725
34of Jericho   345
35of Senaah   3,630

36The priests:

the descendants of Jedaiah
   (through the family of
   Jeshua)   973
37of Immer   1,052
38of Pashhur   1,247
39of Harim   1,017

40The Levites:

the descendants of Jeshua
   and Kadmiel (through
   the line of Hodaviah)   74

41The singers:

the descendants of Asaph   128

42The gatekeepers of the temple:

the descendants of
   Shallum, Ater, Talmon,
   Akkub, Hatita and
   Shobai   139

43The temple servants:

the descendants of
   Ziha, Hasupha, Tabbaoth,
44Keros, Siaha, Padon,
45Lebanah, Hagabah, Akkub,
46Hagab, Shalmai, Hanan,
47Giddel, Gahar, Reaiah,
48Rezin, Nekoda, Gazzam,

49Uzza, Paseah, Besai,
50Asnah, Meunim, Nephussim,
51Bakbuk, Hakupha, Harhur,
52Bazluth, Mehida, Harsha,
53Barkos, Sisera, Temah,
54Neziah and Hatipha

55The descendants of the servants
   of Solomon:

the descendants of
   Sotai, Hassophereth, Peruda,
56Jaala, Darkon, Giddel,
57Shephatiah, Hattil,
   Pokereth-Hazzebaim and Ami

58The temple servants and
   the descendants of the
   servants of Solomon   392

59The following came up from
the towns of Tel Melah, Tel Harsha, Kerub, Addon and Immer,
but they could not show that their
families were descended from
Israel:

60The descendants of
   Delaiah, Tobiah and
   Nekoda   652

61And from among the priests:

The descendants of
   Hobaiah, Hakkoz and Barzillai
   (a man who had married a
   daughter of Barzillai the
   Gileadite and was called by that
   name).
62These searched for their family
records, but they could not find
them and so were excluded from
the priesthood as unclean. 63The
governor ordered them not to eat
any of the most sacred food until
there was a priest ministering with
the Urim and Thummim.

64The whole company numbered
42,360, 65besides their 7,337 menservants and maidservants; and
they also had 200 men and women

singers. 66They had 736 horses, 245 mules, 67435 camels and 6,720 donkeys.

NEW TESTAMENT READING
Revelation 8:1–9:12

The Seventh Seal and the Golden Censer

8 When he opened the seventh seal, there was silence in heaven for about half an hour.

2And I saw the seven angels who stand before God, and to them were given seven trumpets.

3Another angel, who had a golden censer, came and stood at the altar. He was given much incense to offer, with the prayers of all the saints, on the golden altar before the throne. 4The smoke of the incense, together with the prayers of the saints, went up before God from the angel's hand. 5Then the angel took the censer, filled it with fire from the altar, and hurled it on the earth; and there came peals of thunder, rumblings, flashes of lightning and an earthquake.

The Trumpets

6Then the seven angels who had the seven trumpets prepared to sound them.

7The first angel sounded his trumpet, and there came hail and fire mixed with blood, and it was hurled down upon the earth. A third of the earth was burned up, a third of the trees were burned up, and all the green grass was burned up.

8The second angel sounded his trumpet, and something like a huge mountain, all ablaze, was thrown into the sea. A third of the sea turned into blood, 9a third of the living creatures in the sea died, and a third of the ships were destroyed.

10The third angel sounded his trumpet, and a great star, blazing like a torch, fell from the sky on a third of the rivers and on the springs of water— 11the name of the star is Wormwood. A third of the waters turned bitter, and many people died from the waters that had become bitter.

12The fourth angel sounded his trumpet, and a third of the sun was struck, a third of the moon, and a third of the stars, so that a third of them turned dark. A third of the day was without light, and also a third of the night.

13As I watched, I heard an eagle that was flying in mid-air call out in a loud voice: "Woe! Woe! Woe to the inhabitants of the earth, because of the trumpet blasts about to be sounded by the other three angels!"

9 The fifth angel sounded his trumpet, and I saw a star that had fallen from the sky to the earth. The star was given the key to the shaft of the Abyss. 2When he opened the Abyss, smoke rose from it like the smoke from a gigantic furnace. The sun and sky were darkened by the smoke from the Abyss. 3And out of the smoke locusts came down upon the earth and were given power like that of scorpions of the earth. 4They were told not to harm the grass of the earth or any plant or tree, but only those people who did not have the seal of God on their foreheads. 5They were not given power to kill them, but only to torture them for five months. And the agony they suffered was like that of the sting of a scorpion when it strikes a man. 6During those days men will seek death, but will not find it; they will long to die, but death will elude them.

7The locusts looked like horses prepared for battle. On their heads they wore something like crowns of gold, and their faces resembled human faces. 8Their hair was like women's hair, and their teeth were like lions' teeth. 9They had breastplates like breastplates of iron, and the sound of their wings was like the thundering of many horses and chariots rushing into battle. 10They had tails and stings like scorpions, and in their tails they had power to torment people for five months. [11]They had as king over them the angel of the Abyss, whose name in Hebrew is Abaddon, and in Greek, Apollyon.

[12]The first woe is past; two other woes are yet to come.

READING FROM PSALMS
Psalm 144:9–15

[9]I will sing a new song to you, O God;
on the ten-stringed lyre I will make
music to you,
[10]to the One who gives victory to kings,
who delivers his servant David
from the deadly sword.

[11]Deliver me and rescue me
from the hands of foreigners

whose mouths are full of lies,
whose right hands are deceitful.

[12]Then our sons in their youth
will be like well-nurtured plants,
and our daughters will be like pillars
carved to adorn a palace.
[13]Our barns will be filled
with every kind of provision.
Our sheep will increase by thousands,
by tens of thousands in our fields;
[14]   our oxen will draw heavy loads.
There will be no breaching of walls,
no going into captivity,
no cry of distress in our streets.

[15]Blessed are the people of whom this
is true;
blessed are the people whose God
is the LORD.

DECEMBER 18 DAY 352

OLD TESTAMENT READING
Ezra 2:68–4:5

[68]When they arrived at the house of the LORD in Jerusalem, some of the heads of the families gave freewill offerings towards the rebuilding of the house of God on its site. [69]According to their ability they gave to the treasury for this work 61,000 drachmas of gold, 5,000 minas of silver and 100 priestly garments.

[70]The priests, the Levites, the singers, the gatekeepers and the temple servants settled in their own towns, along with some of the other people, and the rest of the Israelites settled in their towns.

Rebuilding the Altar

3 When the seventh month came and the Israelites had settled in their towns, the people assembled as one

man in Jerusalem. [2]Then Jeshua son of Jozadak and his fellow priests and Zerubbabel son of Shealtiel and his associates began to build the altar of the God of Israel to sacrifice burnt offerings on it, in accordance with what is written in the Law of Moses the man of God. [3]Despite their fear of the peoples around them, they built the altar on its foundation and sacrificed burnt offerings on it to the LORD, both the morning and evening sacrifices. [4]Then in accordance with what is written, they celebrated the Feast of Tabernacles with the required number of burnt offerings prescribed for each day. [5]After that, they presented the regular burnt offerings, the New Moon sacrifices and the sacrifices for all the appointed sacred feasts of the LORD, as well as those brought as freewill offerings to the LORD. [6]On the first day of the seventh month they began to offer burnt offerings to the LORD, though the foundation of the LORD's temple had not yet been laid.

Rebuilding the Temple

⁷Then they gave money to the masons and carpenters, and gave food and drink and oil to the people of Sidon and Tyre, so that they would bring cedar logs by sea from Lebanon to Joppa, as authorised by Cyrus king of Persia.

⁸In the second month of the second year after their arrival at the house of God in Jerusalem, Zerubbabel son of Shealtiel, Jeshua son of Jozadak and the rest of their brothers (the priests and the Levites and all who had returned from the captivity to Jerusalem) began the work, appointing Levites twenty years of age and older to supervise the building of the house of the LORD. ⁹Jeshua and his sons and brothers and Kadmiel and his sons (descendants of Hodaviah) and the sons of Henadad and their sons and brothers—all Levites—joined together in supervising those working on the house of God.

¹⁰When the builders laid the foundation of the temple of the LORD, the priests in their vestments and with trumpets, and the Levites (the sons of Asaph) with cymbals, took their places to praise the LORD, as prescribed by David king of Israel. ¹¹With praise and thanksgiving they sang to the LORD:

"He is good;
   his love to Israel endures for
      ever."

And all the people gave a great shout of praise to the LORD, because the foundation of the house of the LORD was laid. ¹²But many of the older priests and Levites and family heads, who had seen the former temple, wept aloud when they saw the foundation of this temple being laid, while many others shouted for joy. ¹³No-one could distinguish the sound of the shouts of joy from the sound of weeping, because the people

made so much noise. And the sound was heard far away.

Opposition to the Rebuilding

4 When the enemies of Judah and Benjamin heard that the exiles were building a temple for the LORD, the God of Israel, ²they came to Zerubbabel and to the heads of the families and said, "Let us help you build because, like you, we seek your God and have been sacrificing to him since the time of Esarhaddon king of Assyria, who brought us here."

³But Zerubbabel, Jeshua and the rest of the heads of the families of Israel answered, "You have no part with us in building a temple to our God. We alone will build it for the LORD, the God of Israel, as King Cyrus, the king of Persia, commanded us."

⁴Then the peoples around them set out to discourage the people of Judah and make them afraid to go on building. ⁵They hired counsellors to work against them and frustrate their plans during the entire reign of Cyrus king of Persia and down to the reign of Darius king of Persia.

NEW TESTAMENT READING
Revelation 9:13–10:11

¹³The sixth angel sounded his trumpet, and I heard a voice coming from the horns of the golden altar that is before God. ¹⁴It said to the sixth angel who had the trumpet, "Release the four angels who are bound at the great river Euphrates." ¹⁵And the four angels who had been kept ready for this very hour and day and month and year were released to kill a third of mankind. ¹⁶The number of the mounted troops was two hundred million. I heard their number.

¹⁷The horses and riders I saw in my vision looked like this: Their breastplates were fiery red, dark blue, and yellow as sulphur. The heads of the

horses resembled the heads of lions, and out of their mouths came fire, smoke and sulphur. [18]A third of mankind was killed by the three plagues of fire, smoke and sulphur that came out of their mouths. [19]The power of the horses was in their mouths and in their tails; for their tails were like snakes, having heads with which they inflict injury.

[20]The rest of mankind that were not killed by these plagues still did not repent of the work of their hands; they did not stop worshipping demons, and idols of gold, silver, bronze, stone and wood —idols that cannot see or hear or walk. [21]Nor did they repent of their murders, their magic arts, their sexual immorality or their thefts.

The Angel and the Little Scroll

10 Then I saw another mighty angel coming down from heaven. He was robed in a cloud, with a rainbow above his head; his face was like the sun, and his legs were like fiery pillars. [2]He was holding a little scroll, which lay open in his hand. He planted his right foot on the sea and his left foot on the land, [3]and he gave a loud shout like the roar of a lion. When he shouted, the voices of the seven thunders spoke. [4]And when the seven thunders spoke, I was about to write; but I heard a voice from heaven say, "Seal up what the seven thunders have said and do not write it down."

[5]Then the angel I had seen standing on the sea and on the land raised his right hand to heaven. [6]And he swore by him who lives for ever and ever, who created the heavens and all that is in them, the earth and all that is in it, and the sea and all that is in it, and said, "There will be no more delay! [7]But in the days when the seventh angel is about to sound his trumpet, the mystery of God will be accomplished, just as he announced to his servants the prophets."

[8]Then the voice that I had heard from heaven spoke to me once more: "Go, take the scroll that lies open in the hand of the angel who is standing on the sea and on the land."

[9]So I went to the angel and asked him to give me the little scroll. He said to me, "Take it and eat it. It will turn your stomach sour, but in your mouth it will be as sweet as honey." [10]I took the little scroll from the angel's hand and ate it. It tasted as sweet as honey in my mouth, but when I had eaten it, my stomach turned sour. [11]Then I was told, "You must prophesy again about many peoples, nations, languages and kings."

READING FROM PROVERBS
Proverbs 30:24–33

[24]"Four things on earth are small,
 yet they are extremely wise:
[25]Ants are creatures of little strength,
 yet they store up their food in the
  summer;
[26]conies are creatures of little power,
 yet they make their home in the
  crags;
[27]locusts have no king,
 yet they advance together in ranks;
[28]a lizard can be caught with the hand,
 yet it is found in kings' palaces.

[29]"There are three things that are
  stately in their stride,
 four that move with stately
  bearing:
[30]a lion, mighty among beasts,
 who retreats before nothing;
[31]a strutting cock, a he-goat,
 and a king with his army around
  him.

[32]"If you have played the fool and
  exalted yourself,
 or if you have planned evil,
  clap your hand over your mouth!
[33]For as churning the milk produces
  butter,
 and as twisting the nose produces
  blood,
 so stirring up anger produces
  strife."

DECEMBER 19

OLD TESTAMENT READING
Ezra 4:6–5:17

Later Opposition Under Xerxes and Artaxerxes

6At the beginning of the reign of Xerxes, they lodged an accusation against the people of Judah and Jerusalem.

7And in the days of Artaxerxes king of Persia, Bishlam, Mithredath, Tabeel and the rest of his associates wrote a letter to Artaxerxes. The letter was written in Aramaic script and in the Aramaic language.

8Rehum the commanding officer and Shimshai the secretary wrote a letter against Jerusalem to Artaxerxes the king as follows:

9Rehum the commanding officer and Shimshai the secretary, together with the rest of their associates—the judges and officials over the men from Tripolis, Persia, Erech and Babylon, the Elamites of Susa, 10and the other people whom the great and honourable Ashurbanipal deported and settled in the city of Samaria and elsewhere in Trans-Euphrates.

11(This is a copy of the letter they sent him.)

To King Artaxerxes,

From your servants, the men of Trans-Euphrates:

12The king should know that the Jews who came up to us from you have gone to Jerusalem and are rebuilding that rebellious and wicked city. They are restoring the walls and repairing the foundations.

13Furthermore, the king should know that if this city is built and its walls are restored, no more taxes, tribute or duty will be paid, and the royal revenues will suffer. 14Now since we are under obligation to the palace and it is not proper for us to see the king dishonoured, we are sending this message to inform the king, 15so that a search may be made in the archives of your predecessors. In these records you will find that this city is a rebellious city, troublesome to kings and provinces, a place of rebellion from ancient times. That is why this city was destroyed. 16We inform the king that if this city is built and its walls are restored, you will be left with nothing in Trans-Euphrates.

17The king sent this reply:

To Rehum the commanding officer, Shimshai the secretary and the rest of their associates living in Samaria and elsewhere in Trans-Euphrates:

Greetings.

18The letter you sent us has been read and translated in my presence. 19I issued an order and a search was made, and it was found that this city has a long history of revolt against kings and has been a place of rebellion and sedition. 20Jerusalem has had powerful kings ruling over the whole of Trans-Euphrates, and taxes, tribute and duty were paid to them. 21Now issue an order to these men to stop work, so that this city will not be rebuilt until I so order. 22Be careful not to neglect this matter. Why let this threat grow, to the detriment of the royal interests?

²³As soon as the copy of the letter of King Artaxerxes was read to Rehum and Shimshai the secretary and their associates, they went immediately to the Jews in Jerusalem and compelled them by force to stop.

²⁴Thus the work on the house of God in Jerusalem came to a standstill until the second year of the reign of Darius king of Persia.

Tattenai's Letter to Darius

5 Now Haggai the prophet and Zechariah the prophet, a descendant of Iddo, prophesied to the Jews in Judah and Jerusalem in the name of the God of Israel, who was over them. ²Then Zerubbabel son of Shealtiel and Jeshua son of Jozadak set to work to rebuild the house of God in Jerusalem. And the prophets of God were with them, helping them. ³At that time Tattenai, governor of Trans-Euphrates, and Shethar-Bozenai and their associates went to them and asked, "Who authorised you to rebuild this temple and restore this structure?" ⁴They also asked, "What are the names of the men constructing this building?" ⁵But the eye of their God was watching over the elders of the Jews, and they were not stopped until a report could go to Darius and his written reply be received.

⁶This is a copy of the letter that Tattenai, governor of Trans-Euphrates, and Shethar-Bozenai and their associates, the officials of Trans-Euphrates, sent to King Darius. ⁷The report they sent him read as follows:

To King Darius:

Cordial greetings.

⁸The king should know that we went to the district of Judah, to the temple of the great God. The people are building it with large stones and placing the timbers in the walls. The work is being carried on with diligence and is making rapid progress under their direction.

⁹We questioned the elders and asked them, "Who authorised you to rebuild this temple and restore this structure?" ¹⁰We also asked them their names, so that we could write down the names of their leaders for your information.

¹¹This is the answer they gave us:

"We are the servants of the God of heaven and earth, and we are rebuilding the temple that was built many years ago, one that a great king of Israel built and finished. ¹²But because our fathers angered the God of heaven, he handed them over to Nebuchadnezzar the Chaldean, king of Babylon, who destroyed this temple and deported the people to Babylon.

¹³"However, in the first year of Cyrus king of Babylon, King Cyrus issued a decree to rebuild this house of God. ¹⁴He even removed from the temple of Babylon the gold and silver articles of the house of God, which Nebuchadnezzar had taken from the temple in Jerusalem and brought to the temple in Babylon.

"Then King Cyrus gave them to a man named Sheshbazzar, whom he had appointed governor, ¹⁵and he told him, 'Take these articles and go and deposit them in the temple in Jerusalem. And rebuild the house of God on its site.' ¹⁶So this Sheshbazzar came and laid the foundations of the house of God in Jerusalem. From that day to the present it has been under construction but is not yet finished."

¹⁷Now if it pleases the king, let a search be made in the royal archives of Babylon to see if King Cyrus did in fact issue a decree to rebuild this house of God in Jerusalem. Then let the king send us his decision in this matter.

NEW TESTAMENT READING
Revelation 11:1–19

The Two Witnesses

11 I was given a reed like a measuring rod and was told, "Go and measure the temple of God and the altar, and count the worshippers there. ²But exclude the outer court; do not measure it, because it has been given to the Gentiles. They will trample on the holy city for 42 months. ³And I will give power to my two witnesses, and they will prophesy for 1,260 days, clothed in sackcloth." ⁴These are the two olive trees and the two lampstands that stand before the Lord of the earth. ⁵If anyone tries to harm them, fire comes from their mouths and devours their enemies. This is how anyone who wants to harm them must die. ⁶These men have power to shut up the sky so that it will not rain during the time they are prophesying; and they have power to turn the waters into blood and to strike the earth with every kind of plague as often as they want.

⁷Now when they have finished their testimony, the beast that comes up from the Abyss will attack them, and overpower and kill them. ⁸Their bodies will lie in the street of the great city, which is figuratively called Sodom and Egypt, where also their Lord was crucified. ⁹For three and a half days men from every people, tribe, language and nation will gaze on their bodies and refuse them burial. ¹⁰The inhabitants of the earth will gloat over them and will celebrate by sending each other gifts, because these two prophets had tormented those who live on earth.

¹¹But after the three and a half days a breath of life from God entered them, and they stood on their feet, and terror struck those who saw them. ¹²Then they heard a loud voice from heaven saying to them, "Come up here." And they went up to heaven in a cloud, while their enemies looked on.

¹³At that very hour there was a severe earthquake and a tenth of the city collapsed. Seven thousand people were killed in the earthquake, and the survivors were terrified and gave glory to the God of heaven.

¹⁴The second woe has passed; the third woe is coming soon.

The Seventh Trumpet

¹⁵The seventh angel sounded his trumpet, and there were loud voices in heaven, which said:

"The kingdom of the world has
     become the kingdom of our
     Lord and of his Christ,
 and he will reign for ever and
     ever."

¹⁶And the twenty-four elders, who were seated on their thrones before God, fell on their faces and worshipped God, ¹⁷saying:

"We give thanks to you, Lord God
     Almighty,
 the One who is and who was,
 because you have taken your great
     power
 and have begun to reign.
¹⁸The nations were angry;
 and your wrath has come.
 The time has come for judging the
     dead,
 and for rewarding your servants
     the prophets
 and your saints and those who
     reverence your name,
 both small and great—
 and for destroying those who destroy
     the earth."

¹⁹Then God's temple in heaven was opened, and within his temple was seen the ark of his covenant. And there came flashes of lightning, rumblings, peals of thunder, an earthquake and a great hailstorm.

READING FROM PSALMS
Psalm 145:1–7

A psalm of praise. Of David.

¹I will exalt you, my God the King;
    I will praise your name for ever
        and ever.
²Every day I will praise you
    and extol your name for ever and
        ever.

³Great is the LORD and most worthy
        of praise;
    his greatness no-one can fathom.

⁴One generation will commend your
        works to another;
    they will tell of your mighty acts.
⁵They will speak of the glorious
        splendour of your majesty,
    and I will meditate on your
        wonderful works.
⁶They will tell of the power of your
        awesome works,
    and I will proclaim your great
        deeds.
⁷They will celebrate your abundant
        goodness
    and joyfully sing of your
        righteousness.

DECEMBER 20   DAY 354

OLD TESTAMENT READING
Ezra 6:1–7:10

The Decree of Darius

6 King Darius then issued an order,
    and they searched in the archives
stored in the treasury at Babylon. ²A
scroll was found in the citadel of Ecba-
tana in the province of Media, and this
was written on it:

Memorandum:

³In the first year of King Cyrus,
the king issued a decree concerning
the temple of God in Jerusalem:

    Let the temple be rebuilt as a
    place to present sacrifices, and let
    its foundations be laid. It is to be
    ninety feet high and ninety feet
    wide, ⁴with three courses of large
    stones and one of timbers. The
    costs are to be paid by the royal
    treasury. ⁵Also, the gold and silver
    articles of the house of God, which
    Nebuchadnezzar took from the
    temple in Jerusalem and brought to
    Babylon, are to be returned to

their places in the temple in Jerusalem; they are to be deposited in
the house of God.

⁶Now then, Tattenai, governor
of Trans-Euphrates, and Shethar-
Bozenai and you, their fellow officials of that province, stay away
from there. ⁷Do not interfere with
the work on this temple of God.
Let the governor of the Jews and
the Jewish elders rebuild this house
of God on its site.

⁸Moreover, I hereby decree
what you are to do for these elders
of the Jews in the construction of
this house of God:

    The expenses of these men are to
    be fully paid out of the royal treas-
    ury, from the revenues of Trans-
    Euphrates, so that the work will
    not stop. ⁹Whatever is needed—
    young bulls, rams, male lambs for
    burnt offerings to the God of
    heaven and wheat, salt, wine and
    oil, as requested by the priests in
    Jerusalem—must be given them
    daily without fail, ¹⁰so that they
    may offer sacrifices pleasing to the
    God of heaven and pray for the

well-being of the king and his sons. ¹¹Furthermore, I decree that if anyone changes this edict, a beam is to be pulled from his house and he is to be lifted up and impaled on it. And for this crime his house is to be made a pile of rubble. ¹²May God, who has caused his Name to dwell there, overthrow any king or people who lifts a hand to change this decree or to destroy this temple in Jerusalem.

I Darius have decreed it. Let it be carried out with diligence.

Completion and Dedication of the Temple

¹³Then, because of the decree King Darius had sent, Tattenai, governor of Trans-Euphrates, and Shethar-Bozenai and their associates carried it out with diligence. ¹⁴So the elders of the Jews continued to build and prosper under the preaching of Haggai the prophet and Zechariah, a descendant of Iddo. They finished building the temple according to the command of the God of Israel and the decrees of Cyrus, Darius and Artaxerxes, kings of Persia. ¹⁵The temple was completed on the third day of the month Adar, in the sixth year of the reign of King Darius.

¹⁶Then the people of Israel—the priests, the Levites and the rest of the exiles—celebrated the dedication of the house of God with joy. ¹⁷For the dedication of this house of God they offered a hundred bulls, two hundred rams, four hundred male lambs and, as a sin offering for all Israel, twelve male goats, one for each of the tribes of Israel. ¹⁸And they installed the priests in their divisions and the Levites in their groups for the service of God at Jerusalem, according to what is written in the Book of Moses.

The Passover

¹⁹On the fourteenth day of the first month, the exiles celebrated the Passover. ²⁰The priests and Levites had purified themselves and were all ceremonially clean. The Levites slaughtered the Passover lamb for all the exiles, for their brothers the priests and for themselves. ²¹So the Israelites who had returned from the exile ate it, together with all who had separated themselves from the unclean practices of their Gentile neighbours in order to seek the LORD, the God of Israel. ²²For seven days they celebrated with joy the Feast of Unleavened Bread, because the LORD had filled them with joy by changing the attitude of the king of Assyria, so that he assisted them in the work on the house of God, the God of Israel.

Ezra Comes to Jerusalem

7 After these things, during the reign of Artaxerxes king of Persia, Ezra son of Seraiah, the son of Azariah, the son of Hilkiah, ²the son of Shallum, the son of Zadok, the son of Ahitub, ³the son of Amariah, the son of Azariah, the son of Meraioth, ⁴the son of Zerahiah, the son of Uzzi, the son of Bukki, ⁵the son of Abishua, the son of Phinehas, the son of Eleazar, the son of Aaron the chief priest—⁶this Ezra came up from Babylon. He was a teacher well versed in the Law of Moses, which the LORD, the God of Israel, had given. The king had granted him everything he asked, for the hand of the LORD his God was on him. ⁷Some of the Israelites, including priests, Levites, singers, gate-keepers and temple servants, also came up to Jerusalem in the seventh year of King Artaxerxes.

⁸Ezra arrived in Jerusalem in the fifth month of the seventh year of the king. ⁹He had begun his journey from Babylon on the first day of the first month, and he arrived in Jerusalem on the first day of the fifth month, for the gracious hand of his God was on him. ¹⁰For Ezra had devoted himself to the study and observance of the Law of the LORD, and to teaching its decrees and laws in Israel.

NEW TESTAMENT READING
Revelation 12:1–13:1a

The Woman and the Dragon

12 A great and wondrous sign appeared in heaven: a woman clothed with the sun, with the moon under her feet and a crown of twelve stars on her head. ²She was pregnant and cried out in pain as she was about to give birth. ³Then another sign appeared in heaven: an enormous red dragon with seven heads and ten horns and seven crowns on his heads. ⁴His tail swept a third of the stars out of the sky and flung them to the earth. The dragon stood in front of the woman who was about to give birth, so that he might devour her child the moment it was born. ⁵She gave birth to a son, a male child, who will rule all the nations with an iron sceptre. And her child was snatched up to God and to his throne. ⁶The woman fled into the desert to a place prepared for her by God, where she might be taken care of for 1,260 days.

⁷And there was war in heaven. Michael and his angels fought against the dragon, and the dragon and his angels fought back. ⁸But he was not strong enough, and they lost their place in heaven. ⁹The great dragon was hurled down—that ancient serpent called the devil, or Satan, who leads the whole world astray. He was hurled to the earth, and his angels with him.

¹⁰Then I heard a loud voice in heaven say:

"Now have come the salvation and
    the power and the kingdom of
    our God,
and the authority of his Christ.
For the accuser of our brothers,
    who accuses them before our God
    day and night,
    has been hurled down.
¹¹They overcame him
    by the blood of the Lamb
    and by the word of their testimony;

they did not love their lives so much
    as to shrink from death.
¹²Therefore rejoice, you heavens
    and you who dwell in them!
But woe to the earth and the sea,
    because the devil has gone down to
    you!
He is filled with fury,
    because he knows that his time is
    short."

¹³When the dragon saw that he had been hurled to the earth, he pursued the woman who had given birth to the male child. ¹⁴The woman was given the two wings of a great eagle, so that she might fly to the place prepared for her in the desert, where she would be taken care of for a time, times and half a time, out of the serpent's reach. ¹⁵Then from his mouth the serpent spewed water like a river, to overtake the woman and sweep her away with the torrent. ¹⁶But the earth helped the woman by opening its mouth and swallowing the river that the dragon had spewed out of his mouth. ¹⁷Then the dragon was enraged at the woman and went off to make war against the rest of her offspring—those who obey God's commandments and hold to the testimony of Jesus.

13 ¹And the dragon stood on the shore of the sea.

READING FROM PSALMS
Psalm 145:8–13a

⁸The LORD is gracious and
    compassionate,
    slow to anger and rich in love.
⁹The LORD is good to all;
    he has compassion on all he has
    made.
¹⁰All you have made will praise you, O
    LORD;
    your saints will extol you.
¹¹They will tell of the glory of your
    kingdom
    and speak of your might,

¹²so that all men may know of your
    mighty acts
and the glorious splendour of your
    kingdom.

¹³Your kingdom is an everlasting
    kingdom,
and your dominion endures
    through all generations.

DAY 355

DECEMBER 21

OLD TESTAMENT READING
Ezra 7:11—8:14

King Artaxerxes' Letter to Ezra

¹¹This is a copy of the letter King
Artaxerxes had given to Ezra the priest
and teacher, a man learned in matters
concerning the commands and decrees
of the LORD for Israel:

¹²Artaxerxes, king of kings,

To Ezra the priest, a teacher of the
Law of the God of heaven:

Greetings.

¹³Now I decree that any of the
Israelites in my kingdom, including
priests and Levites, who wish to go
to Jerusalem with you, may go.
¹⁴You are sent by the king and his
seven advisers to enquire about
Judah and Jerusalem with regard
to the Law of your God, which is in
your hand. ¹⁵Moreover, you are to
take with you the silver and gold
that the king and his advisers have
freely given to the God of Israel,
whose dwelling is in Jerusalem,
¹⁶together with all the silver and
gold you may obtain from the province of Babylon, as well as the
freewill offerings of the people and
priests for the temple of their God
in Jerusalem. ¹⁷With this money be
sure to buy bulls, rams and male
lambs, together with their grain
offerings and drink offerings, and
sacrifice them on the altar of the
temple of your God in Jerusalem.

¹⁸You and your brother Jews
may then do whatever seems best
with the rest of the silver and gold,
in accordance with the will of your
God. ¹⁹Deliver to the God of Jerusalem all the articles entrusted to
you for worship in the temple of
your God. ²⁰And anything else
needed for the temple of your God
that you may have occasion to
supply, you may provide from the
royal treasury.

²¹Now I, King Artaxerxes, order
all the treasurers of Trans-
Euphrates to provide with diligence whatever Ezra the priest, a
teacher of the Law of the God of
heaven, may ask of you—²²up to a
hundred talents of silver, a hundred
cors of wheat, a hundred baths of
wine, a hundred baths of olive oil,
and salt without limit. ²³Whatever
the God of heaven has prescribed,
let it be done with diligence for the
temple of the God of heaven. Why
should there be wrath against the
realm of the king and of his sons?
²⁴You are also to know that you
have no authority to impose taxes,
tribute or duty on any of the
priests, Levites, singers, gatekeepers, temple servants or other
workers at this house of God.

²⁵And you, Ezra, in accordance
with the wisdom of your God,
which you possess, appoint magistrates and judges to administer
justice to all the people of Trans-
Euphrates—all who know the laws
of your God. And you are to teach
any who do not know them.

26Whoever does not obey the law of your God and the law of the king must surely be punished by death, banishment, confiscation of property, or imprisonment.

27Praise be to the LORD, the God of our fathers, who has put it into the king's heart to bring honour to the house of the LORD in Jerusalem in this way 28and who has extended his good favour to me before the king and his advisers and all the king's powerful officials. Because the hand of the LORD my God was on me, I took courage and gathered leading men from Israel to go up with me.

List of the Family Heads Returning With Ezra

8 These are the family heads and those registered with them who came up with me from Babylon during the reign of King Artaxerxes:

2of the descendants of Phinehas, Gershom;

of the descendants of Ithamar, Daniel;

of the descendants of David, Hattush 3of the descendants of Shecaniah;

of the descendants of Parosh, Zechariah, and with him were registered 150 men;

4of the descendants of Pahath-Moab, Eliehoenai son of Zerahiah, and with him 200 men;

5of the descendants of Zattu, Shecaniah son of Jahaziel, and with him 300 men;

6of the descendants of Adin, Ebed son of Jonathan, and with him 50 men;

7of the descendants of Elam, Jeshaiah son of Athaliah, and with him 70 men;

8of the descendants of Shephatiah, Zebadiah son of Michael, and with him 80 men;

9of the descendants of Joab, Obadiah son of Jehiel; and with him 218 men;

10of the descendants of Bani, Shelomith son of Josiphiah, and with him 160 men;

11of the descendants of Bebai, Zechariah son of Bebai, and with him 28 men;

12of the descendants of Azgad, Johanan son of Hakkatan, and with him 110 men;

13of the descendants of Adonikam, the last ones, whose names were Eliphelet, Jeuel and Shemaiah, and with them 60 men;

14of the descendants of Bigvai, Uthai and Zaccur, and with them 70 men.

NEW TESTAMENT READING
Revelation 13:1b–18

The Beast out of the Sea

And I saw a beast coming out of the sea. He had ten horns and seven heads, with ten crowns on his horns, and on each head a blasphemous name. 2The beast I saw resembled a leopard, but had feet like those of a bear and a mouth like that of a lion. The dragon gave the beast his power and his throne and great authority. 3One of the heads of the beast seemed to have had a fatal wound, but the fatal wound had been healed. The whole world was astonished and followed the beast. 4Men worshipped the dragon because he had given authority to the beast, and they also worshipped the beast and asked, "Who is like the beast? Who can make war against him?"

5The beast was given a mouth to utter proud words and blasphemies and to exercise his authority for forty-two months. 6He opened his mouth to blaspheme God, and to slander his name and his dwelling-place and those who live in heaven. 7He was given power to make war against the saints and to conquer them. And he was given authority over every tribe, people, language and nation. [8]All inhabitants of the earth will worship the beast—all whose names have not been written in the book of life belonging to the Lamb that was slain from the creation of the world.

[9]He who has an ear, let him hear.

[10]If anyone is to go into captivity,
  into captivity he will go.
If anyone is to be killed with the
    sword,
  with the sword he will be killed.

This calls for patient endurance and faithfulness on the part of the saints.

The Beast out of the Earth

[11]Then I saw another beast, coming out of the earth. He had two horns like a lamb, but he spoke like a dragon. [12]He exercised all the authority of the first beast on his behalf, and made the earth and its inhabitants worship the first beast, whose fatal wound had been healed. [13]And he performed great and miraculous signs, even causing fire to come down from heaven to earth in full view of men. [14]Because of the signs he was given power to do on behalf of the first beast, he deceived the inhabitants of the earth. He ordered them to set up an image in honour of the beast who was wounded by the sword and yet lived. [15]He was given power to give breath to the image of the first beast, so that it could speak and cause all who refused to worship the image to be killed. [16]He also forced everyone, small and great, rich and poor, free and slave, to receive a mark on his right hand or on his forehead, [17]so that no-one could buy or sell unless he had the mark, which is the name of the beast or the number of his name.

[18]This calls for wisdom. If anyone has insight, let him calculate the number of the beast, for it is man's number. His number is 666.

READING FROM PSALMS
Psalm 145:13b–21

The LORD is faithful to all his
    promises
  and loving towards all he has made.
[14]The LORD upholds all those who fall
  and lifts up all who are bowed
    down.
[15]The eyes of all look to you,
  and you give them their food at the
    proper time.
[16]You open your hand
  and satisfy the desires of every
    living thing.

[17]The LORD is righteous in all his ways
  and loving towards all he has
    made.
[18]The LORD is near to all who call on
    him,
  to all who call on him in truth.
[19]He fulfils the desires of those who
    fear him;
  he hears their cry and saves them.
[20]The LORD watches over all who love
    him,
  but all the wicked he will destroy.

[21]My mouth will speak in praise of the
    LORD.
  Let every creature praise his holy
    name
  for ever and ever.

OLD TESTAMENT READING
Ezra 8:15–9:15

The Return to Jerusalem

¹⁵I assembled them at the canal that flows towards Ahava, and we camped there three days. When I checked among the people and the priests, I found no Levites there. ¹⁶So I summoned Eliezer, Ariel, Shemaiah, Elnathan, Jarib, Elnathan, Nathan, Zechariah and Meshullam, who were leaders, and Joiarib and Elnathan, who were men of learning, ¹⁷and I sent them to Iddo, the leader in Casiphia. I told them what to say to Iddo and his kinsmen, the temple servants in Casiphia, so that they might bring attendants to us for the house of our God. ¹⁸Because the gracious hand of our God was on us, they brought us Sherebiah, a capable man, from the descendants of Mahli son of Levi, the son of Israel, and Sherebiah's sons and brothers, 18 men; ¹⁹and Hashabiah, together with Jeshaiah from the descendants of Merari, and his brothers and nephews, 20 men. ²⁰They also brought 220 of the temple servants —a body that David and the officials had established to assist the Levites. All were registered by name.

²¹There, by the Ahava Canal, I proclaimed a fast, so that we might humble ourselves before our God and ask him for a safe journey for us and our children, with all our possessions. ²²I was ashamed to ask the king for soldiers and horsemen to protect us from enemies on the road, because we had told the king, "The gracious hand of our God is on everyone who looks to him, but his great anger is against all who forsake him." ²³So we fasted and petitioned our God about this, and he answered our prayer.

²⁴Then I set apart twelve of the leading priests, together with Sherebiah, Hashabiah and ten of their brothers, ²⁵and I weighed out to them the offering of silver and gold and the articles that the king, his advisers, his officials and all Israel present there had donated for the house of our God. ²⁶I weighed out to them 650 talents of silver, silver articles weighing 100 talents, 100 talents of gold, ²⁷20 bowls of gold valued at 1,000 darics, and two fine articles of polished bronze, as precious as gold.

²⁸I said to them, "You as well as these articles are consecrated to the LORD. The silver and gold are a freewill offering to the LORD, the God of your fathers. ²⁹Guard them carefully until you weigh them out in the chambers of the house of the LORD in Jerusalem before the leading priests and the Levites and the family heads of Israel." ³⁰Then the priests and Levites received the silver and gold and sacred articles that had been weighed out to be taken to the house of our God in Jerusalem.

³¹On the twelfth day of the first month we set out from the Ahava Canal to go to Jerusalem. The hand of our God was on us, and he protected us from enemies and bandits along the way. ³²So we arrived in Jerusalem, where we rested three days.

³³On the fourth day, in the house of our God, we weighed out the silver and gold and the sacred articles into the hands of Meremoth son of Uriah, the priest. Eleazar son of Phinehas was with him, and so were the Levites Jozabad son of Jeshua and Noadiah son of Binnui. ³⁴Everything was accounted for by number and weight, and the entire weight was recorded at that time.

³⁵Then the exiles who had returned from captivity sacrificed burnt offerings to the God of Israel: twelve bulls for all Israel, ninety-six rams, seventy-seven male lambs and, as a sin offering, twelve male goats. All this was a burnt offering

to the LORD. 36They also delivered the king's orders to the royal satraps and to the governors of Trans-Euphrates who then gave assistance to the people and to the house of God.

Ezra's Prayer About Intermarriage

9 After these things had been done, the leaders came to me and said, "The people of Israel, including the priests and the Levites, have not kept themselves separate from the neighbouring peoples with their detestable practices, like those of the Canaanites, Hittites, Perizzites, Jebusites, Ammonites, Moabites, Egyptians and Amorites. 2They have taken some of their daughters as wives for themselves and their sons, and have mingled the holy race with the peoples around them. And the leaders and officials have led the way in this unfaithfulness."

3When I heard this, I tore my tunic and cloak, pulled hair from my head and beard and sat down appalled. 4Then everyone who trembled at the words of the God of Israel gathered round me because of this unfaithfulness of the exiles. And I sat there appalled until the evening sacrifice.

5Then, at the evening sacrifice, I rose from my self-abasement, with my tunic and cloak torn, and fell on my knees with my hands spread out to the LORD my God 6and prayed:

"O my God, I am too ashamed and disgraced to lift up my face to you, my God, because our sins are higher than our heads and our guilt has reached to the heavens. 7From the days of our forefathers until now, our guilt has been great. Because of our sins, we and our kings and our priests have been subjected to the sword and captivity, to pillage and humiliation at the hand of foreign kings, as it is today.

8"But now, for a brief moment, the LORD our God has been gracious in leaving us a remnant and giving us a firm place in his sanctuary, and so our God gives light to our eyes and a little relief in our bondage. 9Though we are slaves, our God has not deserted us in our bondage. He has shown us kindness in the sight of the kings of Persia: He has granted us new life to rebuild the house of our God and repair its ruins, and he has given us a wall of protection in Judah and Jerusalem.

10"But now, O our God, what can we say after this? For we have disregarded the commands 11you gave through your servants the prophets when you said: 'The land you are entering to possess is a land polluted by the corruption of its peoples. By their detestable practices they have filled it with their impurity from one end to the other. 12Therefore, do not give your daughters in marriage to their sons or take their daughters for your sons. Do not seek a treaty of friendship with them at any time, that you may be strong and eat the good things of the land and leave it to your children as an everlasting inheritance.'

13"What has happened to us is a result of our evil deeds and our great guilt, and yet, our God, you have punished us less than our sins have deserved and have given us a remnant like this. 14Shall we again break your commands and intermarry with the peoples who commit such detestable practices? Would you not be angry enough with us to destroy us, leaving us no remnant or survivor? 15O LORD, God of Israel, you are righteous! We are left this day as a remnant. Here we are before you in our guilt, though because of it not one of us can stand in your presence."

NEW TESTAMENT READING
Revelation 14:1–13

The Lamb and the 144,000

14 Then I looked, and there before me was the Lamb, standing on Mount Zion, and with him 144,000 who had his name and his Father's name written on their foreheads. ²And I heard a sound from heaven like the roar of rushing waters and like a loud peal of thunder. The sound I heard was like that of harpists playing their harps. ³And they sang a new song before the throne and before the four living creatures and the elders. No-one could learn the song except the 144,000 who had been redeemed from the earth. ⁴These are those who did not defile themselves with women, for they kept themselves pure. They follow the Lamb wherever he goes. They were purchased from among men and offered as firstfruits to God and the Lamb. ⁵No lie was found in their mouths; they are blameless.

The Three Angels

⁶Then I saw another angel flying in mid-air, and he had the eternal gospel to proclaim to those who live on the earth—to every nation, tribe, language and people. ⁷He said in a loud voice, "Fear God and give him glory, because the hour of his judgment has come. Worship him who made the heavens, the earth, the sea and the springs of water."

⁸A second angel followed and said, "Fallen! Fallen is Babylon the Great, which made all the nations drink the maddening wine of her adulteries."

⁹A third angel followed them and said in a loud voice: "If anyone worships the beast and his image and receives his mark on the forehead or on the hand, ¹⁰he, too, will drink of the wine of God's fury, which has been poured full strength into the cup of his wrath. He will be tormented with burning sulphur in the presence of the holy angels and of the Lamb. ¹¹And the smoke of their torment rises for ever and ever. There is no rest day or night for those who worship the beast and his image, or for anyone who receives the mark of his name." ¹²This calls for patient endurance on the part of the saints who obey God's commandments and remain faithful to Jesus.

¹³Then I heard a voice from heaven say, "Write: Blessed are the dead who die in the Lord from now on."

"Yes," says the Spirit, "they will rest from their labour, for their deeds will follow them."

READING FROM PROVERBS
Proverbs 31:1–9

Sayings of King Lemuel

31 The sayings of King Lemuel— an oracle his mother taught him:

²"O my son, O son of my womb,
    O son of my vows,
³do not spend your strength on women,
    your vigour on those who ruin kings.

⁴"It is not for kings, O Lemuel—
    not for kings to drink wine,
    not for rulers to crave beer,
⁵lest they drink and forget what the law decrees,
    and deprive all the oppressed of their rights.
⁶Give beer to those who are perishing,
    wine to those who are in anguish;
⁷let them drink and forget their poverty
    and remember their misery no more.

⁸"Speak up for those who cannot speak for themselves,
    for the rights of all who are destitute.
⁹Speak up and judge fairly;
    defend the rights of the poor and needy."

DECEMBER 23

Ezra 10:1–44

The People's Confession of Sin

10 While Ezra was praying and confessing, weeping and throwing himself down before the house of God, a large crowd of Israelites—men, women and children—gathered round him. They too wept bitterly. ²Then Shecaniah son of Jehiel, one of the descendants of Elam, said to Ezra, "We have been unfaithful to our God by marrying foreign women from the peoples around us. But in spite of this, there is still hope for Israel. ³Now let us make a covenant before our God to send away all these women and their children, in accordance with the counsel of my lord and of those who fear the commands of our God. Let it be done according to the Law. ⁴Rise up; this matter is in your hands. We will support you, so take courage and do it."

⁵So Ezra rose up and put the leading priests and Levites and all Israel under oath to do what had been suggested. And they took the oath. ⁶Then Ezra withdrew from before the house of God and went to the room of Jehohanan son of Eliashib. While he was there, he ate no food and drank no water, because he continued to mourn over the unfaithfulness of the exiles.

⁷A proclamation was then issued throughout Judah and Jerusalem for all the exiles to assemble in Jerusalem. ⁸Anyone who failed to appear within three days would forfeit all his property, in accordance with the decision of the officials and elders, and would himself be expelled from the assembly of the exiles.

⁹Within the three days, all the men of Judah and Benjamin had gathered in Jerusalem. And on the twentieth day of the ninth month, all the people were sitting in the square before the house of God, greatly distressed by the occasion and because of the rain. ¹⁰Then Ezra the priest stood up and said to them, "You have been unfaithful; you have married foreign women, adding to Israel's guilt. ¹¹Now make confession to the LORD, the God of your fathers, and do his will. Separate yourselves from the peoples around you and from your foreign wives."

¹²The whole assembly responded with a loud voice: "You are right! We must do as you say. ¹³But there are many people here and it is the rainy season; so we cannot stand outside. Besides, this matter cannot be taken care of in a day or two, because we have sinned greatly in this thing. ¹⁴Let our officials act for the whole assembly. Then let everyone in our towns who has married a foreign woman come at a set time, along with the elders and judges of each town, until the fierce anger of our God in this matter is turned away from us." ¹⁵Only Jonathan son of Asahel and Jahzeiah son of Tikvah, supported by Meshullam and Shabbethai the Levite, opposed this.

¹⁶So the exiles did as proposed. Ezra the priest selected men who were family heads, one from each family division, and all of them designated by name. On the first day of the tenth month they sat down to investigate the cases, ¹⁷and by the first day of the first month they finished dealing with all the men who had married foreign women.

Those Guilty of Intermarriage

¹⁸Among the descendants of the priests, the following had married foreign women:

From the descendants of Jeshua son of Jozadak, and his brothers:

Maaseiah, Eliezer, Jarib and Gedaliah. 19(They all gave their hands in pledge to put away their wives, and for their guilt they each presented a ram from the flock as a guilt offering.)

20From the descendants of Immer:
Hanani and Zebadiah.

21From the descendants of Harim:
Maaseiah, Elijah, Shemaiah, Jehiel and Uzziah.

22From the descendants of Pashhur:
Elioenai, Maaseiah, Ishmael, Nethanel, Jozabad and Elasah.

23Among the Levites:

Jozabad, Shimei, Kelaiah (that is Kelita), Pethahiah, Judah and Eliezer.

24From the singers:
Eliashib.

From the gatekeepers:
Shallum, Telem and Uri.

25And among the other Israelites:

From the descendants of Parosh:
Ramiah, Izziah, Malkijah, Mijamin, Eleazar, Malkijah and Benaiah.

26From the descendants of Elam:
Mattaniah, Zechariah, Jehiel, Abdi, Jeremoth and Elijah.

27From the descendants of Zattu:
Elioenai, Eliashib, Mattaniah, Jeremoth, Zabad and Aziza.

28From the descendants of Bebai:
Jehohanan, Hananiah, Zabbai and Athlai.

29From the descendants of Bani:
Meshullam, Malluch, Adaiah, Jashub, Sheal and Jeremoth.

30From the descendants of Pahath-Moab:
Adna, Kelal, Benaiah, Maaseiah, Mattaniah, Bezalel, Binnui and Manasseh.

31From the descendants of Harim:
Eliezer, Ishijah, Malkijah, Shemaiah, Shimeon, 32Benjamin, Malluch and Shemariah.

33From the descendants of Hashum:
Mattenai, Mattattah, Zabad, Eliphelet, Jeremai, Manasseh and Shimei.

34From the descendants of Bani:
Maadai, Amram, Uel, 35Benaiah, Bedeiah, Keluhi, 36Vaniah, Meremoth, Eliashib, 37Mattaniah, Mattenai and Jaasu.

38From the descendants of Binnui:
Shimei, 39Shelemiah, Nathan, Adaiah, 40Macnadebai, Shashai, Sharai, 41Azarel, Shelemiah, Shemariah, 42Shallum, Amariah and Joseph.

43From the descendants of Nebo:
Jeiel, Mattithiah, Zabad, Zebina, Jaddai, Joel and Benaiah.

44All these had married foreign women, and some of them had children by these wives.

NEW TESTAMENT READING
Revelation 14:14–15:8

The Harvest of the Earth

14I looked, and there before me was a white cloud, and seated on the cloud was one "like a son of man" with a crown of gold on his head and a sharp sickle in his hand. 15Then another angel came out of the temple and called in a loud voice to him who was sitting on the cloud, "Take your sickle and reap, because the time to reap has come, for the harvest of the earth is ripe." 16So he who was seated on the cloud swung his sickle over the earth, and the earth was harvested.

17Another angel came out of the temple in heaven, and he too had a sharp sickle. 18Still another angel, who had charge of the fire, came from the altar and called in a loud voice to him who had the sharp sickle, "Take your sharp sickle and gather the clusters of grapes from the earth's vine, because its grapes are ripe." 19The angel swung his sickle on the earth, gathered its grapes and threw them into the great winepress of God's wrath. 20They were trampled in the winepress outside the city, and blood flowed out of the press, rising as high as the horses' bridles for a distance of 1,600 stadia.

Seven Angels With Seven Plagues

15 I saw in heaven another great and marvellous sign: seven angels with the seven last plagues—last, because with them God's wrath is completed. 2And I saw what looked like a sea of glass mixed with fire and, standing beside the sea, those who had been victorious over the beast and his image and over the number of his name. They held harps given them by God 3and sang the song of Moses the servant of God and the song of the Lamb:

"Great and marvellous are your
        deeds,
    Lord God Almighty.
Just and true are your ways,
    King of the ages.
4Who will not fear you, O Lord,
    and bring glory to your name?
For you alone are holy.
All nations will come
    and worship before you,
for your righteous acts have been
        revealed."

5After this I looked and in heaven the temple, that is, the tabernacle of the Testimony, was opened. 6Out of the temple came the seven angels with the seven plagues. They were dressed in clean, shining linen and wore golden sashes round their chests. 7Then one of the four living creatures gave to the seven angels seven golden bowls filled with the wrath of God, who lives for ever and ever. 8And the temple was filled with smoke from the glory of God

and from his power, and no-one could enter the temple until the seven plagues of the seven angels were completed.

READING FROM PSALMS
Psalm 146:1–10

1Praise the LORD.

Praise the LORD, O my soul.
2   I will praise the LORD all my life;
    I will sing praise to my God as long
        as I live.

3Do not put your trust in princes,
    in mortal men, who cannot save.
4When their spirit departs, they return
        to the ground;
    on that very day their plans come
        to nothing.

5Blessed is he whose help is the God
        of Jacob,
    whose hope is in the LORD his
        God,
6the Maker of heaven and earth,
    the sea, and everything in them—
    the LORD, who remains faithful for
        ever.
7He upholds the cause of the
        oppressed
    and gives food to the hungry.
The LORD sets prisoners free,
8   the LORD gives sight to the blind,
    the LORD lifts up those who are
        bowed down,
    the LORD loves the righteous.
9The LORD watches over the alien
    and sustains the fatherless and the
        widow,
    but he frustrates the ways of the
        wicked.

10The LORD reigns for ever,
    your God, O Zion, for all
        generations.

Praise the LORD.

OLD TESTAMENT READING
Nehemiah 1:1–2:20

Nehemiah's Prayer

1 The words of Nehemiah son of Hacaliah:

In the month of Kislev in the twentieth year, while I was in the citadel of Susa, ²Hanani, one of my brothers, came from Judah with some other men, and I questioned them about the Jewish remnant that survived the exile, and also about Jerusalem.

³They said to me, "Those who survived the exile and are back in the province are in great trouble and disgrace. The wall of Jerusalem is broken down, and its gates have been burned with fire."

⁴When I heard these things, I sat down and wept. For some days I mourned and fasted and prayed before the God of heaven. ⁵Then I said:

"O LORD, God of heaven, the great and awesome God, who keeps his covenant of love with those who love him and obey his commands, ⁶let your ear be attentive and your eyes open to hear the prayer your servant is praying before you day and night for your servants, the people of Israel. I confess the sins we Israelites, including myself and my father's house, have committed against you. ⁷We have acted very wickedly towards you. We have not obeyed the commands, decrees and laws you gave your servant Moses.

⁸"Remember the instruction you gave your servant Moses, saying, 'If you are unfaithful, I will scatter you among the nations, ⁹but if you return to me and obey my commands, then even if your exiled people are at the farthest horizon, I will gather them from there and bring them to the place I have chosen as a dwelling for my Name.'

¹⁰"They are your servants and your people, whom you redeemed by your great strength and your mighty hand. ¹¹O Lord, let your ear be attentive to the prayer of this your servant and to the prayer of your servants who delight in revering your name. Give your servant success today by granting him favour in the presence of this man."

I was cupbearer to the king.

Artaxerxes Sends Nehemiah to Jerusalem

2 In the month of Nisan in the twentieth year of King Artaxerxes, when wine was brought for him, I took the wine and gave it to the king. I had not been sad in his presence before; ²so the king asked me, "Why does your face look so sad when you are not ill? This can be nothing but sadness of heart."

I was very much afraid, ³but I said to the king, "May the king live for ever! Why should my face not look sad when the city where my fathers are buried lies in ruins, and its gates have been destroyed by fire?"

⁴The king said to me, "What is it you want?"

Then I prayed to the God of heaven, ⁵and I answered the king, "If it pleases the king and if your servant has found favour in his sight, let him send me to the city in Judah where my fathers are buried so that I can rebuild it."

⁶Then the king, with the queen sitting beside him, asked me, "How long will your journey take, and when will you get back?" It pleased the king to send me; so I set a time.

7I also said to him, "If it pleases the king, may I have letters to the governors of Trans-Euphrates, so that they will provide me safe-conduct until I arrive in Judah? 8And may I have a letter to Asaph, keeper of the king's forest, so he will give me timber to make beams for the gates of the citadel by the temple and for the city wall and for the residence I will occupy?" And because the gracious hand of my God was upon me, the king granted my requests. 9So I went to the governors of Trans-Euphrates and gave them the king's letters. The king had also sent army officers and cavalry with me.

10When Sanballat the Horonite and Tobiah the Ammonite official heard about this, they were very much disturbed that someone had come to promote the welfare of the Israelites.

Nehemiah Inspects Jerusalem's Walls

11I went to Jerusalem, and after staying there three days 12I set out during the night with a few men. I had not told anyone what my God had put in my heart to do for Jerusalem. There were no mounts with me except the one I was riding on.

13By night I went out through the Valley Gate towards the Jackal Well and the Dung Gate, examining the walls of Jerusalem, which had been broken down, and its gates, which had been destroyed by fire. 14Then I moved on towards the Fountain Gate and the King's Pool, but there was not enough room for my mount to get through; 15so I went up the valley by night, examining the wall. Finally, I turned back and re-entered through the Valley Gate. 16The officials did not know where I had gone or what I was doing, because as yet I had said nothing to the Jews or the priests or nobles or officials or any others who would be doing the work.

17Then I said to them, "You see the trouble we are in: Jerusalem lies in ruins, and its gates have been burned with fire. Come, let us rebuild the wall of Jerusalem, and we will no longer be in disgrace." 18I also told them about the gracious hand of my God upon me and what the king had said to me.

They replied, "Let us start rebuilding." So they began this good work.

19But when Sanballat the Horonite, Tobiah the Ammonite official and Geshem the Arab heard about it, they mocked and ridiculed us. "What is this you are doing?" they asked. "Are you rebelling against the king?"

20I answered them by saying, "The God of heaven will give us success. We his servants will start rebuilding, but as for you, you have no share in Jerusalem or any claim or historic right to it."

NEW TESTAMENT READING
Revelation 16:1–21

The Seven Bowls of God's Wrath

16 Then I heard a loud voice from the temple saying to the seven angels, "Go, pour out the seven bowls of God's wrath on the earth."

2The first angel went and poured out his bowl on the land, and ugly and painful sores broke out on the people who had the mark of the beast and worshipped his image.

3The second angel poured out his bowl on the sea, and it turned into blood like that of a dead man, and every living thing in the sea died.

4The third angel poured out his bowl on the rivers and springs of water, and they became blood. 5Then I heard the angel in charge of the waters say:

"You are just in these judgments,
    you who are and who were, the
        Holy One,
because you have so judged;
6for they have shed the blood of your
        saints and prophets,
    and you have given them blood to
        drink as they deserve."

7And I heard the altar respond:

> "Yes, Lord God Almighty,
>   true and just are your judgments."

8The fourth angel poured out his bowl on the sun, and the sun was given power to scorch people with fire. 9They were seared by the intense heat and they cursed the name of God, who had control over these plagues, but they refused to repent and glorify him.

10The fifth angel poured out his bowl on the throne of the beast, and his kingdom was plunged into darkness. Men gnawed their tongues in agony 11and cursed the God of heaven because of their pains and their sores, but they refused to repent of what they had done.

12The sixth angel poured out his bowl on the great river Euphrates, and its water was dried up to prepare the way for the kings from the East. 13Then I saw three evil spirits that looked like frogs; they came out of the mouth of the dragon, out of the mouth of the beast and out of the mouth of the false prophet. 14They are spirits of demons performing miraculous signs, and they go out to the kings of the whole world, to gather them for the battle on the great day of God Almighty.

15"Behold, I come like a thief! Blessed is he who stays awake and keeps his clothes with him, so that he may not go naked and be shamefully exposed."

16Then they gathered the kings together to the place that in Hebrew is called Armageddon.

17The seventh angel poured out his bowl into the air, and out of the temple came a loud voice from the throne, saying, "It is done!" 18Then there came flashes of lightning, rumblings, peals of thunder and a severe earthquake. No earthquake like it has ever occurred since man has been on earth, so tremendous was the quake. 19The great city split into three parts, and the cities of the nations collapsed. God remembered Babylon the Great and gave her

the cup filled with the wine of the fury of his wrath. 20Every island fled away and the mountains could not be found. 21From the sky huge hailstones of about a hundred pounds each fell upon men. And they cursed God on account of the plague of hail, because the plague was so terrible.

READING FROM PSALMS
Psalm 147:1–11

1Praise the LORD.

> How good it is to sing praises to our
>   God,
>   how pleasant and fitting to praise
>   him!

2The LORD builds up Jerusalem;
    he gathers the exiles of Israel.
3He heals the broken-hearted
    and binds up their wounds.

4He determines the number of the
        stars
    and calls them each by name.
5Great is our Lord and mighty in
        power;
    his understanding has no limit.
6The LORD sustains the humble
    but casts the wicked to the ground.

7Sing to the LORD with thanksgiving;
    make music to our God on the
        harp.
8He covers the sky with clouds;
    he supplies the earth with rain
    and makes grass grow on the hills.
9He provides food for the cattle
    and for the young ravens when
        they call.

10His pleasure is not in the strength of
        the horse,
    nor his delight in the legs of a man;
11the LORD delights in those who fear
        him,
    who put their hope in his unfailing
        love.

OLD TESTAMENT READING
Nehemiah 3:1–4:23

Builders of the Wall

3 Eliashib the high priest and his fellow priests went to work and rebuilt the Sheep Gate. They dedicated it and set its doors in place, building as far as the Tower of the Hundred, which they dedicated, and as far as the Tower of Hananel. ²The men of Jericho built the adjoining section, and Zaccur son of Imri built next to them.

³The Fish Gate was rebuilt by the sons of Hassenaah. They laid its beams and put its doors and bolts and bars in place. ⁴Meremoth son of Uriah, the son of Hakkoz, repaired the next section. Next to him Meshullam son of Berekiah, the son of Meshezabel, made repairs, and next to him Zadok son of Baana also made repairs. ⁵The next section was repaired by the men of Tekoa, but their nobles would not put their shoulders to the work under their supervisors.

⁶The Jeshanah Gate was repaired by Joiada son of Paseah and Meshullam son of Besodeiah. They laid its beams and put its doors and bolts and bars in place. ⁷Next to them, repairs were made by men from Gibeon and Mizpah —Melatiah of Gibeon and Jadon of Meronoth—places under the authority of the governor of Trans-Euphrates. ⁸Uzziel son of Harhaiah, one of the goldsmiths, repaired the next section; and Hananiah, one of the perfumemakers, made repairs next to that. They restored Jerusalem as far as the Broad Wall. ⁹Rephaiah son of Hur, ruler of a half-district of Jerusalem, repaired the next section. ¹⁰Adjoining this, Jedaiah son of Harumaph made repairs opposite his house, and Hattush son of Hashabneiah made repairs next to him. ¹¹Malkijah son of Harim and Hasshub

son of Pahath-Moab repaired another section and the Tower of the Ovens. ¹²Shallum son of Hallohesh, ruler of a half-district of Jerusalem, repaired the next section with the help of his daughters.

¹³The Valley Gate was repaired by Hanun and the residents of Zanoah. They rebuilt it and put its doors and bolts and bars in place. They also repaired five hundred yards of the wall as far as the Dung Gate.

¹⁴The Dung Gate was repaired by Malkijah son of Recab, ruler of the district of Beth Hakkerem. He rebuilt it and put its doors and bolts and bars in place.

¹⁵The Fountain Gate was repaired by Shallun son of Col-Hozeh, ruler of the district of Mizpah. He rebuilt it, roofing it over and putting its doors and bolts and bars in place. He also repaired the wall of the Pool of Siloam, by the King's Garden, as far as the steps going down from the City of David. ¹⁶Beyond him, Nehemiah son of Azbuk, ruler of a half-district of Beth Zur, made repairs up to a point opposite the tombs of David, as far as the artificial pool and the House of the Heroes.

¹⁷Next to him, the repairs were made by the Levites under Rehum son of Bani. Beside him, Hashabiah, ruler of half the district of Keilah, carried out repairs for his district. ¹⁸Next to him, the repairs were made by their countrymen under Binnui son of Henadad, ruler of the other half-district of Keilah. ¹⁹Next to him, Ezer son of Jeshua, ruler of Mizpah, repaired another section, from a point facing the ascent to the armoury as far as the angle. ²⁰Next to him, Baruch son of Zabbai zealously repaired another section, from the angle to the entrance of the house of

Eliashib the high priest. 21Next to him, Meremoth son of Uriah, the son of Hakkoz, repaired another section, from the entrance of Eliashib's house to the end of it.

22The repairs next to him were made by the priests from the surrounding region. 23Beyond them, Benjamin and Hasshub made repairs in front of their house; and next to them, Azariah son of Maaseiah, the son of Ananiah, made repairs beside his house. 24Next to him, Binnui son of Henadad repaired another section, from Azariah's house to the angle and the corner, 25and Palal son of Uzai worked opposite the angle and the tower projecting from the upper palace near the court of the guard. Next to him, Pedaiah son of Parosh 26and the temple servants living on the hill of Ophel made repairs up to a point opposite the Water Gate towards the east and the projecting tower. 27Next to them, the men of Tekoa repaired another section, from the great projecting tower to the wall of Ophel.

28Above the Horse Gate, the priests made repairs, each in front of his own house. 29Next to them, Zadok son of Immer made repairs opposite his house. Next to him, Shemaiah son of Shecaniah, the guard at the East Gate, made repairs. 30Next to him, Hananiah son of Shelemiah, and Hanun, the sixth son of Zalaph, repaired another section. Next to him, Meshullam son of Berekiah made repairs opposite his living quarters. 31Next to him, Malkijah, one of the goldsmiths, made repairs as far as the house of the temple servants and the merchants, opposite the Inspection Gate, and as far as the room above the corner; 32and between the room above the corner and the Sheep Gate the goldsmiths and merchants made repairs.

Opposition to the Rebuilding

4 When Sanballat heard that we were rebuilding the wall, he be-

He ridiculed the Jews, 2and in the presence of his associates and the army of Samaria, he said, "What are those feeble Jews doing? Will they restore their wall? Will they offer sacrifices? Will they finish in a day? Can they bring the stones back to life from those heaps of rubble—burned as they are?"

3Tobiah the Ammonite, who was at his side, said, "What they are building —if even a fox climbed up on it, it would break down their wall of stones!"

4Hear us, O our God, for we are despised. Turn their insults back on their own heads. Give them over as plunder in a land of captivity. 5Do not cover up their guilt or blot out their sins from your sight, for they have thrown insults in the face of the builders.

6So we rebuilt the wall till all of it reached half its height, for the people worked with all their heart.

7But when Sanballat, Tobiah, the Arabs, the Ammonites and the men of Ashdod heard that the repairs to Jerusalem's walls had gone ahead and that the gaps were being closed, they were very angry. 8They all plotted together to come and fight against Jerusalem and stir up trouble against it. 9But we prayed to our God and posted a guard day and night to meet this threat.

10Meanwhile, the people in Judah said, "The strength of the labourers is giving out, and there is so much rubble that we cannot rebuild the wall."

11Also our enemies said, "Before they know it or see us, we will be right there among them and will kill them and put an end to the work."

12Then the Jews who lived near them came and told us ten times over, "Wherever you turn, they will attack us."

13Therefore I stationed some of the people behind the lowest points of the wall at the exposed places, posting them by families, with their swords, spears and bows. 14After I looked things over, I stood up and said to the nobles, the

'Don't be afraid of them. Remember the Lord, who is great and awesome, and fight for your brothers, your sons and your daughters, your wives and your homes."

15When our enemies heard that we were aware of their plot and that God had frustrated it, we all returned to the wall, each to his own work.

16From that day on, half of my men did the work, while the other half were equipped with spears, shields, bows and armour. The officers posted themselves behind all the people of Judah 17who were building the wall. Those who carried materials did their work with one hand and held a weapon in the other, 18and each of the builders wore his sword at his side as he worked. But the man who sounded the trumpet stayed with me.

19Then I said to the nobles, the officials and the rest of the people, "The work is extensive and spread out, and we are widely separated from each other along the wall. 20Wherever you hear the sound of the trumpet, join us there. Our God will fight for us!"

21So we continued the work with half the men holding spears, from the first light of dawn till the stars came out. 22At that time I also said to the people, "Have every man and his helper stay inside Jerusalem at night, so that they can serve us as guards by night and workmen by day." 23Neither I nor my brothers nor my men nor the guards with me took off our clothes; each had his weapon, even when he went for water.

NEW TESTAMENT READING
Revelation 17:1–18

The Woman on the Beast

17 One of the seven angels who had the seven bowls came and said

punishment of the great prostitute, who sits on many waters. 2With her the kings of the earth committed adultery and the inhabitants of the earth were intoxicated with the wine of her adulteries."

3Then the angel carried me away in the Spirit into a desert. There I saw a woman sitting on a scarlet beast that was covered with blasphemous names and had seven heads and ten horns. 4The woman was dressed in purple and scarlet, and was glittering with gold, precious stones and pearls. She held a golden cup in her hand, filled with abominable things and the filth of her adulteries. 5This title was written on her forehead:

MYSTERY
BABYLON THE GREAT
THE MOTHER OF PROSTITUTES
AND OF THE ABOMINATIONS
OF THE EARTH.

6I saw that the woman was drunk with the blood of the saints, the blood of those who bore testimony to Jesus.

When I saw her, I was greatly astonished. 7Then the angel said to me: "Why are you astonished? I will explain to you the mystery of the woman and of the beast she rides, which has the seven heads and ten horns. 8The beast, which you saw, once was, now is not, and will come up out of the Abyss and go to his destruction. The inhabitants of the earth whose names have not been written in the book of life from the creation of the world will be astonished when they see the beast, because he once was, now is not, and yet will come.

9"This calls for a mind with wisdom. The seven heads are seven hills on which the woman sits. 10They are also seven kings. Five have fallen, one is, the other has not yet come; but when he does come, he must remain for a little now is not, is an eighth king. He belongs to the seven and is going to his destruction.

12"The ten horns you saw are ten kings who have not yet received a kingdom, but who for one hour will receive authority as kings along with the beast. 13They have one purpose and will give their power and authority to the beast. 14They will make war against the Lamb, but the Lamb will overcome them because he is Lord of lords and King of kings—and with him will be his called, chosen and faithful followers."

15Then the angel said to me, "The waters you saw, where the prostitute sits, are peoples, multitudes, nations and languages. 16The beast and the ten horns you saw will hate the prostitute. They will bring her to ruin and leave her naked; they will eat her flesh and burn her with fire. 17For God has put it into their hearts to accomplish his purpose by agreeing to give the beast their power to rule, until God's words are fulfilled. 18The woman you saw is the great city that rules over the kings of the earth."

READING FROM PSALMS
Psalm 147:12–20

12Extol the LORD, O Jerusalem;
    praise your God, O Zion,
13for he strengthens the bars of your
        gates
    and blesses your people within
        you.
14He grants peace to your borders
    and satisfies you with the finest of
        wheat.

15He sends his command to the earth;
    his word runs swiftly.
16He spreads the snow like wool
    and scatters the frost like ashes.
17He hurls down hail like pebbles.
    Who can withstand his icy blast?
18He sends his word and melts them;
    he stirs up his breezes, and the
        waters flow.

19He has revealed his word to Jacob,
    his laws and decrees to Israel.
20He has done this for no other nation;
    they do not know his laws.

Praise the LORD.

DECEMBER 26   DAY 360

OLD TESTAMENT READING
Nehemiah 5:1–7:3

Nehemiah Helps the Poor

5 Now the men and their wives raised a great outcry against their Jewish brothers. 2Some were saying, "We and our sons and daughters are numerous; in order for us to eat and stay alive, we must get grain."

3Others were saying, "We are mortgaging our fields, our vineyards and our homes to get grain during the famine."

4Still others were saying, "We have

tax on our fields and vineyards. 5Although we are of the same flesh and blood as our countrymen and though our sons are as good as theirs, yet we have to subject our sons and daughters to slavery. Some of our daughters have already been enslaved, but we are powerless, because our fields and our vineyards belong to others."

6When I heard their outcry and these charges, I was very angry. 7I pondered them in my mind and then accused the nobles and officials. I told them, "You are exacting usury from your own counmeeting to deal with them [8]and said: "As far as possible, we have bought back our Jewish brothers who were sold to the Gentiles. Now you are selling your brothers, only for them to be sold back to us!" They kept quiet, because they could find nothing to say.

[9]So I continued, "What you are doing is not right. Shouldn't you walk in the fear of our God to avoid the reproach of our Gentile enemies? [10]I and my brothers and my men are also lending the people money and grain. But let the exacting of usury stop! [11]Give back to them immediately their fields, vineyards, olive groves and houses, and also the usury you are charging them —the hundredth part of the money, grain, new wine and oil."

[12]"We will give it back," they said. "And we will not demand anything more from them. We will do as you say."

Then I summoned the priests and made the nobles and officials take an oath to do what they had promised. [13]I also shook out the folds of my robe and said, "In this way may God shake out of his house and possessions every man who does not keep this promise. So may such a man be shaken out and emptied!"

At this the whole assembly said, "Amen," and praised the LORD. And the people did as they had promised.

[14]Moreover, from the twentieth year of King Artaxerxes, when I was appointed to be their governor in the land of Judah, until his thirty-second year—twelve years—neither I nor my brothers ate the food allotted to the governor. [15]But the earlier governors —those preceding me—placed a heavy burden on the people and took forty shekels of silver from them in addition to food and wine. Their assistants also lorded it over the people. But out of reverence for God I did not act like that. [16]Instead, I devoted myself to the work on this wall. All my men were assembled there for the work; we did not

[17]Furthermore, a hundred and fifty Jews and officials ate at my table, as well as those who came to us from the surrounding nations. [18]Each day one ox, six choice sheep and some poultry were prepared for me, and every ten days an abundant supply of wine of all kinds. In spite of all this, I never demanded the food allotted to the governor, because the demands were heavy on these people.

[19]Remember me with favour, O my God, for all I have done for these people.

Further Opposition to the Rebuilding

6 When word came to Sanballat, Tobiah, Geshem the Arab and the rest of our enemies that I had rebuilt the wall and not a gap was left in it— though up to that time I had not set up the doors in the gates—[2]Sanballat and Geshem sent me this message: "Come, let us meet together in one of the villages on the plain of Ono."

But they were scheming to harm me; [3]so I sent messengers to them with this reply: "I am carrying on a great project and cannot go down. Why should the work stop while I leave it and go down to you?" [4]Four times they sent me the same message, and each time I gave them the same answer.

[5]Then, the fifth time, Sanballat sent his assistant to me with the same message, and in his hand was an unsealed letter [6]in which was written:

"It is reported among the nations—and Geshem says it is true —that you and the Jews are plotting to revolt, and therefore you are building the wall. Moreover, according to these reports you are about to become their king [7]and have even appointed prophets to make this proclamation about you in Jerusalem: 'There is a king in Judah!' Now this report will get back to the king; so come, let us

⁸I sent him this reply: "Nothing like what you are saying is happening; you are just making it up out of your head."

⁹They were all trying to frighten us, thinking, "Their hands will get too weak for the work, and it will not be completed."

⌊But I prayed,⌋ "Now strengthen my hands."

¹⁰One day I went to the house of Shemaiah son of Delaiah, the son of Mehetabel, who was shut in at his home. He said, "Let us meet in the house of God, inside the temple, and let us close the temple doors, because men are coming to kill you—by night they are coming to kill you."

¹¹But I said, "Should a man like me run away? Or should one like me go into the temple to save his life? I will not go!" ¹²I realised that God had not sent him, but that he had prophesied against me because Tobiah and Sanballat had hired him. ¹³He had been hired to intimidate me so that I would commit a sin by doing this, and then they would give me a bad name to discredit me.

¹⁴Remember Tobiah and Sanballat, O my God, because of what they have done; remember also the prophetess Noadiah and the rest of the prophets who have been trying to intimidate me.

The Completion of the Wall

¹⁵So the wall was completed on the twenty-fifth of Elul, in fifty-two days. ¹⁶When all our enemies heard about this, all the surrounding nations were afraid and lost their self-confidence, because they realised that this work had been done with the help of our God.

¹⁷Also, in those days the nobles of Judah were sending many letters to Tobiah, and replies from Tobiah kept coming to them. ¹⁸For many in Judah were under oath to him, since he was son-in-law to Shecaniah son of Arah, and his son Jehohanan had married the daughter of Meshullam son of Berekiah. ¹⁹Moreover, they kept reporting to me his good deeds and then telling him what I said. And Tobiah sent letters to intimidate me.

7 After the wall had been rebuilt and I had set the doors in place, the gatekeepers and the singers and the Levites were appointed. ²I put in charge of Jerusalem my brother Hanani, along with Hananiah the commander of the citadel, because he was a man of integrity and feared God more than most men do. ³I said to them, "The gates of Jerusalem are not to be opened until the sun is hot. While the gatekeepers are still on duty, make them shut the doors and bar them. Also appoint residents of Jerusalem as guards, some at their posts and some near their own houses."

NEW TESTAMENT READING
Revelation 18:1–17a

The Fall of Babylon

18 After this I saw another angel coming down from heaven. He had great authority, and the earth was illuminated by his splendour. ²With a mighty voice he shouted:

"Fallen! Fallen is Babylon the Great!
    She has become a home for
        demons
and a haunt for every evil spirit,
    a haunt for every unclean and
        detestable bird.
³For all the nations have drunk
    the maddening wine of her
        adulteries.
The kings of the earth committed
    adultery with her,
    and the merchants of the earth
        grew rich from her excessive
        luxuries."

⁴Then I heard another voice from heaven say:

"Come out of her, my people,
    so that you will not share in her
        sins,

so that you will not receive any of
her plagues;
[5]for her sins are piled up to heaven,
and God has remembered her
crimes.
[6]Give back to her as she has given;
pay her back double for what she
has done.
Mix her a double portion from her
own cup.
[7]Give her as much torture and grief
as the glory and luxury she gave
herself.
In her heart she boasts,
'I sit as queen; I am not a widow,
and I will never mourn.'
[8]Therefore in one day her plagues will
overtake her:
death, mourning and famine.
She will be consumed by fire,
for mighty is the Lord God who
judges her.

[9]"When the kings of the earth who
committed adultery with her and shared
her luxury see the smoke of her burning, they will weep and mourn over her.
[10]Terrified at her torment, they will
stand far off and cry:

"'Woe! Woe, O great city,
O Babylon, city of power!
In one hour your doom has come!'

[11]"The merchants of the earth will
weep and mourn over her because no-
one buys their cargoes any more—
[12]cargoes of gold, silver, precious stones
and pearls; fine linen, purple, silk and
scarlet cloth; every sort of citron wood,
and articles of every kind made of ivory,
costly wood, bronze, iron and marble;
[13]cargoes of cinnamon and spice, of incense, myrrh and frankincense, of wine
and olive oil, of fine flour and wheat;
cattle and sheep; horses and carriages;
and bodies and souls of men.

[14]"They will say, 'The fruit you
longed for is gone from you. All your
riches and splendour have vanished,

never to be recovered.' [15]The merchants who sold these things and gained
their wealth from her will stand far off,
terrified at her torment. They will weep
and mourn [16]and cry out:

"'Woe! Woe, O great city,
dressed in fine linen, purple and
scarlet,
and glittering with gold, precious
stones and pearls!
[17]In one hour such great wealth has
been brought to ruin!'

READING FROM PROVERBS
Proverbs 31:10-20

Epilogue: The Wife of Noble
Character

[10]A wife of noble character who can
find?
She is worth far more than rubies.
[11]Her husband has full confidence in
her
and lacks nothing of value.
[12]She brings him good, not harm,
all the days of her life.
[13]She selects wool and flax
and works with eager hands.
[14]She is like the merchant ships,
bringing her food from afar.
[15]She gets up while it is still dark;
she provides food for her family
and portions for her servant girls.
[16]She considers a field and buys it;
out of her earnings she plants a
vineyard.
[17]She sets about her work vigorously;
her arms are strong for her tasks.
[18]She sees that her trading is profitable,
and her lamp does not go out at
night.
[19]In her hand she holds the distaff
and grasps the spindle with her
fingers.
[20]She opens her arms to the poor
and extends her hands to the
needy.

OLD TESTAMENT READING
Nehemiah 7:4–8:18

The List of the Exiles Who Returned

⁴Now the city was large and spacious, but there were few people in it, and the houses had not yet been rebuilt. ⁵So my God put it into my heart to assemble the nobles, the officials and the common people for registration by families. I found the genealogical record of those who had been the first to return. This is what I found written there:

⁶These are the people of the province who came up from the captivity of the exiles whom Nebuchadnezzar king of Babylon had taken captive (they returned to Jerusalem and Judah, each to his own town, ⁷in company with Zerubbabel, Jeshua, Nehemiah, Azariah, Raamiah, Nahamani, Mordecai, Bilshan, Mispereth, Bigvai, Nehum and Baanah):

The list of the men of Israel:

⁸the descendants of Parosh	2,172
⁹of Shephatiah	372
¹⁰of Arah	652
¹¹of Pahath-Moab (through the line of Jeshua and Joab)	2,818
¹²of Elam	1,254
¹³of Zattu	845
¹⁴of Zaccai	760
¹⁵of Binnui	648
¹⁶of Bebai	628
¹⁷of Azgad	2,322
¹⁸of Adonikam	667
¹⁹of Bigvai	2,067
²⁰of Adin	655
²¹of Ater (through Hezekiah)	98
²²of Hashum	328
²³of Bezai	324
²⁴of Hariph	112
²⁵of Gibeon	95
²⁶the men of Bethlehem and Netophah	188
²⁷of Anathoth	128
²⁸of Beth Azmaveth	42
²⁹of Kiriath Jearim, Kephirah and Beeroth	743
³⁰of Ramah and Geba	621
³¹of Michmash	122
³²of Bethel and Ai	123
³³of the other Nebo	52
³⁴of the other Elam	1,254
³⁵of Harim	320
³⁶of Jericho	345
³⁷of Lod, Hadid and Ono	721
³⁸of Senaah	3,930

³⁹The priests:

the descendants of Jedaiah (through the family of Jeshua)	973
⁴⁰of Immer	1,052
⁴¹of Pashhur	1,247
⁴²of Harim	1,017

⁴³The Levites:

the descendants of Jeshua (through Kadmiel through the line of Hodaviah)	74

⁴⁴The singers:

the descendants of Asaph	148

⁴⁵The gatekeepers:

the descendants of Shallum, Ater, Talmon, Akkub, Hatita and Shobai	138

⁴⁶The temple servants:

the descendants of
Ziha, Hasupha, Tabbaoth,
⁴⁷Keros, Sia, Padon,
⁴⁸Lebana, Hagaba, Shalmai,
⁴⁹Hanan, Giddel, Gahar,

[50]Reaiah, Rezin, Nekoda,
[51]Gazzam, Uzza, Paseah,
[52]Besai, Meunim, Nephussim,
[53]Bakbuk, Hakupha, Harhur,
[54]Bazluth, Mehida, Harsha,
[55]Barkos, Sisera, Temah,
[56]Neziah and Hatipha

[57]The descendants of the servants
of Solomon:

the descendants of
  Sotai, Sophereth, Perida,
[58]Jaala, Darkon, Giddel,
[59]Shephatiah, Hattil, Pokereth-
  Hazzebaim and Amon

[60]The temple servants and
  the descendants of the
  servants of Solomon   392

[61]The following came up from
the towns of Tel Melah, Tel Harsha, Kerub, Addon and Immer,
but they could not show that their
families were descended from
Israel:

[62]the descendants of
  Delaiah, Tobiah and
  Nekoda   642

[63]And from among the priests:

  the descendants of
  Hobaiah, Hakkoz and Barzillai
  (a man who had married a
  daughter of Barzillai the
  Gileadite and was called by that
  name).
[64]These searched for their family
records, but they could not find
them and so were excluded from
the priesthood as unclean. [65]The
governor, therefore, ordered them
not to eat any of the most sacred
food until there should be a priest
ministering with the Urim and
Thummim.

[66]The whole company numbered
42,360, [67]besides their 7,337 menservants and maidservants; and

they also had 245 men and women
singers. [68]There were 736 horses,
245 mules, [69]435 camels and 6,720
donkeys.

[70]Some of the heads of the families contributed to the work. The
governor gave to the treasury 1,000
drachmas of gold, 50 bowls and 530
garments for priests. [71]Some of the
heads of the families gave to the
treasury for the work 20,000 drachmas of gold and 2,200 minas of
silver. [72]The total given by the rest
of the people was 20,000 drachmas
of gold, 2,000 minas of silver and 67
garments for priests.

[73]The priests, the Levites, the
gatekeepers, the singers and the
temple servants, along with certain
of the people and the rest of the
Israelites, settled in their own
towns.

Ezra Reads the Law

When the seventh month came and the
Israelites had settled in their towns,
8 [1]all the people assembled as one
man in the square before the Water
Gate. They told Ezra the scribe to bring
out the Book of the Law of Moses,
which the LORD had commanded for
Israel.

[2]So on the first day of the seventh
month, Ezra the priest brought the Law
before the assembly, which was made
up of men and women and all who were
able to understand. [3]He read it aloud
from daybreak till noon as he faced the
square before the Water Gate in the
presence of the men, women and others
who could understand. And all the people listened attentively to the Book of
the Law.

[4]Ezra the scribe stood on a high
wooden platform built for the occasion.
Beside him on his right stood Mat-
tithiah, Shema, Anaiah, Uriah, Hilkiah
and Maaseiah; and on his left were
Pedaiah, Mishael, Malkijah, Hashum,
Hashbaddanah, Zechariah and
Meshullam.

[5]Ezra opened the book. All the people could see him because he was standing above them; and as he opened it, the people all stood up. [6]Ezra praised the LORD, the great God; and all the people lifted their hands and responded, "Amen! Amen!" Then they bowed down and worshiped the LORD with their faces to the ground.

[7]The Levites—Jeshua, Bani, Sherebiah, Jamin, Akkub, Shabbethai, Hodiah, Maaseiah, Kelita, Azariah, Jozabad, Hanan and Pelaiah—instructed the people in the Law while the people were standing there. [8]They read from the Book of the Law of God, making it clear and giving the meaning so that the people could understand what was being read.

[9]Then Nehemiah the governor, Ezra the priest and scribe, and the Levites who were instructing the people said to them all, "This day is sacred to the LORD your God. Do not mourn or weep." For all the people had been weeping as they listened to the words of the Law.

[10]Nehemiah said, "Go and enjoy choice food and sweet drinks, and send some to those who have nothing prepared. This day is sacred to our Lord. Do not grieve, for the joy of the LORD is your strength."

[11]The Levites calmed all the people saying, "Be still, for this is a sacred day. Do not grieve."

[12]Then all the people went away to eat and drink, to send portions of food and to celebrate with great joy, because they now understood the words that had been made known to them.

[13]On the second day of the month, the heads of all the families, along with the priests and the Levites, gathered round Ezra the scribe to give attention to the words of the Law. [14]They found written in the Law, which the LORD had commanded through Moses, that the Israelites were to live in booths during the feast of the seventh month [15]and that they should proclaim this word and spread it throughout their towns and in Jerusalem: "Go out into the hill country and bring back branches from olive and wild olive trees, and from myrtles, palms and shade trees, to make booths"—as it is written.

[16]So the people went out and brought back branches and built themselves booths on their own roofs, in their courtyards, in the courts of the house of God and in the square by the Water Gate and the one by the Gate of Ephraim. [17]The whole company that had returned from exile built booths and lived in them. From the days of Joshua son of Nun until that day, the Israelites had not celebrated it like this. And their joy was very great.

[18]Day after day, from the first day to the last, Ezra read from the Book of the Law of God. They celebrated the feast for seven days, and on the eighth day, in accordance with the regulation, there was an assembly.

NEW TESTAMENT READING
Revelation 18:17b–19:10

"Every sea captain, and all who travel by ship, the sailors, and all who earn their living from the sea, will stand far off. [18]When they see the smoke of her burning, they will exclaim, 'Was there ever a city like this great city?' [19]They will throw dust on their heads, and with weeping and mourning cry out:

"'Woe! Woe, O great city,
    where all who had ships on the sea
    became rich through her wealth!
In one hour she has been brought to
    ruin!
[20]Rejoice over her, O heaven!
    Rejoice, saints and apostles and
        prophets!
God has judged her for the way she
        treated you.'"

[21]Then a mighty angel picked up a boulder the size of a large millstone and threw it into the sea, and said:

"With such violence
   the great city of Babylon will be
       thrown down,
   never to be found again.
²²The music of harpists and musicians,
   flute players and trumpeters,
   will never be heard in you again.
No workman of any trade
   will ever be found in you again.
The sound of a millstone
   will never be heard in you again.
²³The light of a lamp
   will never shine in you again.
The voice of bridegroom and bride
   will never be heard in you again.
Your merchants were the world's
   great men.
   By your magic spell all the nations
       were led astray.
²⁴In her was found the blood of
   prophets and of the saints,
   and of all who have been killed on
       the earth."

Hallelujah!

19 After this I heard what sounded
       like the roar of a great multitude
in heaven shouting:

"Hallelujah!
Salvation and glory and power
   belong to our God,
2   for true and just are his judgments.
He has condemned the great
       prostitute
   who corrupted the earth by her
       adulteries.
He has avenged on her the blood of
   his servants."

³And again they shouted:

"Hallelujah!
The smoke from her goes up for ever
   and ever."

⁴The twenty-four elders and the four
living creatures fell down and worshipped God, who was seated on the throne.
And they cried:

"Amen, Hallelujah!"

⁵Then a voice came from the throne,
saying:

"Praise our God,
   all you his servants,
you who fear him,
   both small and great!"

⁶Then I heard what sounded like a
great multitude, like the roar of rushing
waters and like loud peals of thunder,
shouting:

"Hallelujah!
   For our Lord God Almighty
       reigns.
⁷Let us rejoice and be glad
   and give him glory!
For the wedding of the Lamb has
       come,
   and his bride has made herself
       ready.
⁸Fine linen, bright and clean,
   was given her to wear."

(Fine linen stands for the righteous acts
of the saints.)

⁹Then the angel said to me, "Write:
'Blessed are those who are invited to the
wedding supper of the Lamb!'" And he
added, "These are the true words of
God."
¹⁰At this I fell at his feet to worship
him. But he said to me, "Do not do it! I
am a fellow-servant with you and with
your brothers who hold to the testimony
of Jesus. Worship God! For the testimony of Jesus is the spirit of prophecy."

READING FROM PSALMS
Psalm 148:1–6

¹Praise the LORD.

Praise the LORD from the heavens,
   praise him in the heights above.
²Praise him, all his angels,
   praise him, all his heavenly hosts.

³Praise him, sun and moon,
   praise him, all you shining stars.
⁴Praise him, you highest heavens
   and you waters above the skies.
⁵Let them praise the name of the
   LORD,

for he commanded and they were
   created.
⁶He set them in place for ever and
   ever;
   he gave a decree that will never
   pass away.

DECEMBER 28   DAY 362

OLD TESTAMENT READING
Nehemiah 9:1–37

The Israelites Confess Their Sins

9 On the twenty-fourth day of the same month, the Israelites gathered together, fasting and wearing sackcloth and having dust on their heads. ²Those of Israelite descent had separated themselves from all foreigners. They stood in their places and confessed their sins and the wickedness of their fathers. ³They stood where they were and read from the Book of the Law of the LORD their God for a quarter of the day, and spent another quarter in confession and in worshipping the LORD their God. ⁴Standing on the stairs were the Levites—Jeshua, Bani, Kadmiel, Shebaniah, Bunni, Sherebiah, Bani and Kenani—who called with loud voices to the LORD their God. ⁵And the Levites —Jeshua, Kadmiel, Bani, Hashabneiah, Sherebiah, Hodiah, Shebaniah and Pethahiah—said: "Stand up and praise the LORD your God, who is from everlasting to everlasting."

"Blessed be your glorious name, and may it be exalted above all blessing and praise. ⁶You alone are the LORD. You made the heavens, even the highest heavens, and all their starry host, the earth and all that is on it, the seas and all that is in them. You give life to everything, and the multitudes of heaven worship you.

⁷"You are the LORD God, who chose Abram and brought him out of Ur of the Chaldeans and named him Abraham. ⁸You found his heart faithful to you, and you made a covenant with him to give to his descendants the land of the Canaanites, Hittites, Amorites, Perizzites, Jebusites and Girgashites. You have kept your promise because you are righteous.

⁹"You saw the suffering of our forefathers in Egypt; you heard their cry at the Red Sea. ¹⁰You sent miraculous signs and wonders against Pharaoh, against all his officials and all the people of his land, for you knew how arrogantly the Egyptians treated them. You made a name for yourself, which remains to this day. ¹¹You divided the sea before them, so that they passed through it on dry ground, but you hurled their pursuers into the depths, like a stone into mighty waters. ¹²By day you led them with a pillar of cloud, and by night with a pillar of fire to give them light on the way they were to take.

¹³"You came down on Mount Sinai; you spoke to them from heaven. You gave them regulations and laws that are just and right, and decrees and commands that are good. ¹⁴You made known to them your holy Sabbath and gave them commands, decrees and laws through your servant Moses.

[15]In their hunger you gave them bread from heaven and in their thirst you brought them water from the rock; you told them to go in and take possession of the land you had sworn with uplifted hand to give them.

[16]"But they, our forefathers, became arrogant and stiff-necked, and did not obey your commands. [17]They refused to listen and failed to remember the miracles you performed among them. They became stiff-necked and in their rebellion appointed a leader in order to return to their slavery. But you are a forgiving God, gracious and compassionate, slow to anger and abounding in love. Therefore you did not desert them, [18]even when they cast for themselves an image of a calf and said, 'This is your god, who brought you up out of Egypt,' or when they committed awful blasphemies.

[19]"Because of your great compassion you did not abandon them in the desert. By day the pillar of cloud did not cease to guide them on their path, nor the pillar of fire by night to shine on the way they were to take. [20]You gave your good Spirit to instruct them. You did not withhold your manna from their mouths, and you gave them water for their thirst. [21]For forty years you sustained them in the desert; they lacked nothing, their clothes did not wear out nor did their feet become swollen.

[22]"You gave them kingdoms and nations, allotting to them even the remotest frontiers. They took over the country of Sihon king of Heshbon and the country of Og king of Bashan. [23]You made their sons as numerous as the stars in the sky, and you brought them into the land that you told their fathers to enter and possess. [24]Their sons went in and took possession of the land. You subdued before them the

Canaanites, who lived in the land; you handed the Canaanites over to them, along with their kings and the peoples of the land, to deal with them as they pleased. [25]They captured fortified cities and fertile land; they took possession of houses filled with all kinds of good things, wells already dug, vineyards, olive groves and fruit trees in abundance. They ate to the full and were well-nourished; they revelled in your great goodness.

[26]"But they were disobedient and rebelled against you; they put your law behind their backs. They killed your prophets, who had admonished them in order to turn them back to you; they committed awful blasphemies. [27]So you handed them over to their enemies, who oppressed them. But when they were oppressed they cried out to you. From heaven you heard them, and in your great compassion you gave them deliverers, who rescued them from the hand of their enemies.

[28]"But as soon as they were at rest, they again did what was evil in your sight. Then you abandoned them to the hand of their enemies so that they ruled over them. And when they cried out to you again, you heard from heaven, and in your compassion you delivered them time after time.

[29]"You warned them to return to your law, but they became arrogant and disobeyed your commands. They sinned against your ordinances, by which a man will live if he obeys them. Stubbornly they turned their backs on you, became stiff-necked and refused to listen. [30]For many years you were patient with them. By your Spirit you admonished them through your prophets. Yet they paid no attention, so you handed them over to the neighbouring peoples. [31]But in your great mercy you did

not put an end to them or abandon them, for you are a gracious and merciful God.

32"Now therefore, O our God, the great, mighty and awesome God, who keeps his covenant of love, do not let all this hardship seem trifling in your eyes—the hardship that has come upon us, upon our kings and leaders, upon our priests and prophets, upon our fathers and all your people, from the days of the kings of Assyria until today. 33In all that has happened to us, you have been just; you have acted faithfully, while we did wrong. 34Our kings, our leaders, our priests and our fathers did not follow your law; they did not pay attention to your commands or the warnings you gave them. 35Even while they were in their kingdom, enjoying your great goodness to them in the spacious and fertile land you gave them, they did not serve you or turn from their evil ways.

36"But see, we are slaves today, slaves in the land you gave our forefathers so that they could eat its fruit and the other good things it produces. 37Because of our sins, its abundant harvest goes to the kings you have placed over us. They rule over our bodies and our cattle as they please. We are in great distress.

NEW TESTAMENT READING
Revelation 19:11–21

The Rider on the White Horse

11I saw heaven standing open and there before me was a white horse, whose rider is called Faithful and True. With justice he judges and makes war. 12His eyes are like blazing fire, and on his head are many crowns. He has a name written on him that no-one knows

but he himself. 13He is dressed in a robe dipped in blood, and his name is the Word of God. 14The armies of heaven were following him, riding on white horses and dressed in fine linen, white and clean. 15Out of his mouth comes a sharp sword with which to strike down the nations. "He will rule them with an iron sceptre." He treads the winepress of the fury of the wrath of God Almighty. 16On his robe and on his thigh he has this name written:

KING OF KINGS AND LORD OF LORDS.

17And I saw an angel standing in the sun, who cried in a loud voice to all the birds flying in mid-air, "Come, gather together for the great supper of God, 18so that you may eat the flesh of kings, generals, and mighty men, of horses and their riders, and the flesh of all people, free and slave, small and great."

19Then I saw the beast and the kings of the earth and their armies gathered together to make war against the rider on the horse and his army. 20But the beast was captured, and with him the false prophet who had performed the miraculous signs on his behalf. With these signs he had deluded those who had received the mark of the beast and worshipped his image. The two of them were thrown alive into the fiery lake of burning sulphur. 21The rest of them were killed with the sword that came out of the mouth of the rider on the horse, and all the birds gorged themselves on their flesh.

READING FROM PSALMS
Psalm 148:7–14

7Praise the LORD from the earth,
　　you great sea creatures and all
　　　　ocean depths,
8lightning and hail, snow and clouds,
　　stormy winds that do his bidding,
9you mountains and all hills,
　　fruit trees and all cedars,

¹⁰wild animals and all cattle,
　　small creatures and flying birds,
¹¹kings of the earth and all nations,
　　you princes and all rulers on
　　　earth,
¹²young men and maidens,
　　old men and children.

¹³Let them praise the name of the
　　LORD,

for his name alone is exalted;
　　his splendour is above the earth
　　　and the heavens.
¹⁴He has raised up for his people a
　　horn,
　　the praise of all his saints,
　　of Israel, the people close to his
　　　heart.

Praise the LORD.

DAY 363

DECEMBER 29

OLD TESTAMENT READING
Nehemiah 9:38–11:21

The Agreement of the People

³⁸"In view of all this, we are making a binding agreement, putting it in writing, and our leaders, our Levites and our priests are affixing their seals to it."

10 Those who sealed it were:

Nehemiah the governor, the son
　　of Hacaliah.

Zedekiah, ²Seraiah, Azariah,
　　Jeremiah,
³Pashhur, Amariah, Malkijah,
⁴Hattush, Shebaniah, Malluch,
⁵Harim, Meremoth, Obadiah,
⁶Daniel, Ginnethon, Baruch,
⁷Meshullam, Abijah, Mijamin,
⁸Maaziah, Bilgai and Shemaiah.
　　These were the priests.

⁹The Levites:

Jeshua son of Azaniah,
　　Binnui of the sons of
　　　Henadad, Kadmiel,
¹⁰and their associates:
　　Shebaniah, Hodiah, Kelita,
　　　Pelaiah, Hanan,
¹¹Mica, Rehob, Hashabiah,

¹²Zaccur, Sherebiah, Shebaniah,
¹³Hodiah, Bani and Beninu.

¹⁴The leaders of the people:

Parosh, Pahath-Moab, Elam,
　　Zattu, Bani,
¹⁵Bunni, Azgad, Bebai,
¹⁶Adonijah, Bigvai, Adin,
¹⁷Ater, Hezekiah, Azzur,
¹⁸Hodiah, Hashum, Bezai,
¹⁹Hariph, Anathoth, Nebai,
²⁰Magpiash, Meshullam, Hezir,
²¹Meshezabel, Zadok, Jaddua,
²²Pelatiah, Hanan, Anaiah,
²³Hoshea, Hananiah, Hasshub,
²⁴Hallohesh, Pilha, Shobek,
²⁵Rehum, Hashabnah, Maaseiah,
²⁶Ahiah, Hanan, Anan,
²⁷Malluch, Harim and Baanah.

²⁸"The rest of the people—priests, Levites, gatekeepers, singers, temple servants and all who separated themselves from the neighbouring peoples for the sake of the Law of God, together with their wives and all their sons and daughters who are able to understand—²⁹all these now join their brothers the nobles, and bind themselves with a curse and an oath to follow the Law of God given through Moses the servant of

God and to obey carefully all the commands, regulations and decrees of the LORD our Lord.

30"We promise not to give our daughters in marriage to the peoples around us or take their daughters for our sons.

31"When the neighbouring peoples bring merchandise or grain to sell on the Sabbath, we will not buy from them on the Sabbath or on any holy day. Every seventh year we will forgo working the land and will cancel all debts.

32"We assume the responsibility for carrying out the commands to give a third of a shekel each year for the service of the house of our God: 33for the bread set out on the table; for the regular grain offerings and burnt offerings; for the offerings on the Sabbaths, New Moon festivals and appointed feasts; for the holy offerings; for sin offerings to make atonement for Israel; and for all the duties of the house of our God.

34"We—the priests, the Levites and the people—have cast lots to determine when each of our families is to bring to the house of our God at set times each year a contribution of wood to burn on the altar of the LORD our God, as it is written in the Law.

35"We also assume responsibility for bringing to the house of the LORD each year the firstfruits of our crops and of every fruit tree.

36"As it is also written in the Law, we will bring the firstborn of our sons and of our cattle, of our herds and of our flocks to the house of our God, to the priests ministering there.

37"Moreover, we will bring to the storerooms of the house of our God, to the priests, the first of our ground meal, of our ⸢grain⸣ offerings, of the fruit of all our trees and of our new wine and oil. And we will bring a tithe of our crops to the Levites, for it is the Levites who collect the tithes in all the towns where we work. 38A priest descended from Aaron is to accompany the Levites when they receive the tithes, and the Levites are to bring a tenth of the tithes up to the house of our God, to the storerooms of the treasury. 39The people of Israel, including the Levites, are to bring their contributions of grain, new wine and oil to the storerooms where the articles for the sanctuary are kept and where the ministering priests, the gatekeepers and the singers stay.

"We will not neglect the house of our God."

The New Residents of Jerusalem

11 Now the leaders of the people settled in Jerusalem, and the rest of the people cast lots to bring one out of every ten to live in Jerusalem, the holy city, while the remaining nine were to stay in their own towns. 2The people commended all the men who volunteered to live in Jerusalem.

3These are the provincial leaders who settled in Jerusalem (now some Israelites, priests, Levites, temple servants and descendants of Solomon's servants lived in the towns of Judah, each on his own property in the various towns, 4while other people from both Judah and Benjamin lived in Jerusalem):

From the descendants of Judah:

Athaiah son of Uzziah, the son of Zechariah, the son of Amariah, the son of Shephatiah, the son of Mahalalel, a descendant of Perez; 5and Maaseiah son of Baruch, the son of Col-Hozeh, the son of Hazaiah, the son of Adaiah, the son of Joiarib, the son of Zechariah, a descendant of Shelah. 6The descendants of Perez who lived in Jerusalem totalled 468 able men.

⁷From the descendants of Benjamin:

Sallu son of Meshullam, the son of Joed, the son of Pedaiah, the son of Kolaiah, the son of Maaseiah, the son of Ithiel, the son of Jeshaiah, ⁸and his followers, Gabbai and Sallai—928 men. ⁹Joel son of Zicri was their chief officer, and Judah son of Hassenuah was over the Second District of the city.

¹⁰From the priests:

Jedaiah; the son of Joiarib; Jakin; ¹¹Seraiah son of Hilkiah, the son of Meshullam, the son of Zadok, the son of Meraioth, the son of Ahitub, supervisor in the house of God, ¹²and their associates, who carried on work for the temple—822 men; Adaiah son of Jeroham, the son of Pelaliah, the son of Amzi, the son of Zechariah, the son of Pashhur, the son of Malkijah, ¹³and his associates, who were heads of families—242 men; Amashsai son of Azarel, the son of Ahzai, the son of Meshillemoth, the son of Immer, ¹⁴and his associates, who were able men—128 men. Their chief officer was Zabdiel son of Haggedolim.

¹⁵From the Levites:

Shemaiah son of Hasshub, the son of Azrikam, the son of Hashabiah, the son of Bunni; ¹⁶Shabbethai and Jozabad, two of the heads of the Levites, who had charge of the outside work of the house of God; ¹⁷Mattaniah son of Mica, the son of Zabdi, the son of Asaph, the director who led in thanksgiving and prayer; Bakbukiah, second among his associates; and Abda son of Shammua, the son of Galal, the son of Jeduthun. ¹⁸The Levites in the holy city totalled 284.

¹⁹The gatekeepers:

Akkub, Talmon and their associates, who kept watch at the gates —172 men.

²⁰The rest of the Israelites, with the priests and Levites, were in all the towns of Judah, each on his ancestral property.

²¹The temple servants lived on the hill of Ophel, and Ziha and Gishpa were in charge of them.

NEW TESTAMENT READING
Revelation 20:1–15

The Thousand Years

20 And I saw an angel coming down out of heaven, having the key to the Abyss and holding in his hand a great chain. ²He seized the dragon, that ancient serpent, who is the devil, or Satan, and bound him for a thousand years. ³He threw him into the Abyss, and locked and sealed it over him, to keep him from deceiving the nations any more until the thousand years were ended. After that, he must be set free for a short time.

⁴I saw thrones on which were seated those who had been given authority to judge. And I saw the souls of those who had been beheaded because of their testimony for Jesus and because of the word of God. They had not worshipped the beast or his image and had not received his mark on their foreheads or their hands. They came to life and reigned with Christ for a thousand years. ⁵(The rest of the dead did not come to life until the thousand years were ended.) This is the first resurrection. ⁶Blessed and holy are those who have part in the first resurrection. The second death has no power over them, but they will be priests of God and of Christ and will reign with him for a thousand years.

Satan's Doom

⁷When the thousand years are over, Satan will be released from his prison

8and will go out to deceive the nations in the four corners of the earth—Gog and Magog—to gather them for battle. In number they are like the sand on the seashore. 9They marched across the breadth of the earth and surrounded the camp of God's people, the city he loves. But fire came down from heaven and devoured them. 10And the devil, who deceived them, was thrown into the lake of burning sulphur, where the beast and the false prophet had been thrown. They will be tormented day and night for ever and ever.

The Dead Are Judged

11Then I saw a great white throne and him who was seated on it. Earth and sky fled from his presence, and there was no place for them. 12And I saw the dead, great and small, standing before the throne, and books were opened. Another book was opened, which is the book of life. The dead were judged according to what they had done as recorded in the books. 13The sea gave up the dead that were in it, and death and Hades gave up the dead that were in them, and each person was judged according to what he had done. 14Then death and Hades were thrown into the lake of fire. The lake of fire is the second death. 15If anyone's name was not found written in the book of life, he was thrown into the lake of fire.

READING FROM PSALMS
Psalm 149:1–9

1Praise the LORD.

Sing to the LORD a new song,
   his praise in the assembly of the
      saints.

2Let Israel rejoice in their Maker;
   let the people of Zion be glad in
      their King.
3Let them praise his name with
      dancing
   and make music to him with
      tambourine and harp.
4For the LORD takes delight in his
      people;
   he crowns the humble with
      salvation.
5Let the saints rejoice in this honour
   and sing for joy on their beds.

6May the praise of God be in their
      mouths
   and a double-edged sword in their
      hands,
7to inflict vengeance on the nations
   and punishment on the peoples,
8to bind their kings with fetters,
   their nobles with shackles of iron,
9to carry out the sentence written
      against them.
   This is the glory of all his saints.

Praise the LORD.

DECEMBER 30   DAY 364

OLD TESTAMENT READING
Nehemiah 11:22–12:47

22The chief officer of the Levites in Jerusalem was Uzzi son of Bani, the son of Hashabiah, the son of Mattaniah, the son of Mica. Uzzi was one of Asaph's descendants, who were the singers responsible for the service of the house of

God. 23The singers were under the king's orders, which regulated their daily activity.

24Pethahiah son of Meshezabel, one of the descendants of Zerah son of Judah, was the king's agent in all affairs relating to the people.

25As for the villages with their fields, some of the people of Judah lived in

Kiriath Arba and its surrounding settlements, in Dibon and its settlements, in Jekabzeel and its villages, 26in Jeshua, in Moladah, in Beth Pelet, 27in Hazar Shual, in Beersheba and its settlements, 28in Ziklag, in Meconah and its settlements, 29in En Rimmon, in Zorah, in Jarmuth, 30Zanoah, Adullam and their villages, in Lachish and its fields, and in Azekah and its settlements. So they were living all the way from Beersheba to the Valley of Hinnom.

31The descendants of the Benjamites from Geba lived in Michmash, Aija, Bethel and its settlements, 32in Anathoth, Nob and Ananiah, 33in Hazor, Ramah and Gittaim, 34in Hadid, Zeboim and Neballat, 35in Lod and Ono, and in the Valley of the Craftsmen.

36Some of the divisions of the Levites of Judah settled in Benjamin.

Priests and Levites

12 These were the priests and Levites who returned with Zerubbabel son of Shealtiel and with Jeshua:
Seraiah, Jeremiah, Ezra,
2Amariah, Malluch, Hattush,
3Shecaniah, Rehum, Meremoth,
4Iddo, Ginnethon, Abijah,
5Mijamin, Moadiah, Bilgah,
6Shemaiah, Joiarib, Jedaiah,
7Sallu, Amok, Hilkiah and Jedaiah.
These were the leaders of the priests and their associates in the days of Jeshua.

8The Levites were Jeshua, Binnui, Kadmiel, Sherebiah, Judah, and also Mattaniah, who, together with his associates, was in charge of the songs of thanksgiving. 9Bakbukiah and Unni, their associates, stood opposite them in the services.

10Jeshua was the father of Joiakim, Joiakim the father of Eliashib, Eliashib the father of Joiada, 11Joiada the father of Jonathan, and Jonathan the father of Jaddua.

12In the days of Joiakim, these were the heads of the priestly families:

of Seraiah's family, Meraiah;
of Jeremiah's, Hananiah;
13of Ezra's, Meshullam;
of Amariah's, Jehohanan;
14of Malluch's, Jonathan;
of Shecaniah's, Joseph;
15of Harim's, Adna;
of Meremoth's, Helkai;
16of Iddo's, Zechariah;
of Ginnethon's, Meshullam;
17of Abijah's, Zicri;
of Miniamin's and of Moadiah's, Piltai;
18of Bilgah's, Shammua;
of Shemaiah's, Jehonathan;
19of Joiarib's, Mattenai;
of Jedaiah's, Uzzi;
20of Sallu's, Kallai;
of Amok's, Eber;
21of Hilkiah's, Hashabiah;
of Jedaiah's, Nethanel.

22The family heads of the Levites in the days of Eliashib, Joiada, Johanan and Jaddua, as well as those of the priests, were recorded in the reign of Darius the Persian. 23The family heads among the descendants of Levi up to the time of Johanan son of Eliashib were recorded in the book of the annals. 24And the leaders of the Levites were Hashabiah, Sherebiah, Jeshua son of Kadmiel, and their associates, who stood opposite them to give praise and thanksgiving, one section responding to the other, as prescribed by David the man of God.

25Mattaniah, Bakbukiah, Obadiah, Meshullam, Talmon and Akkub were gatekeepers who guarded the storerooms at the gates. 26They served in the days of Joiakim son of Jeshua, the son of Jozadak, and in the days of Nehemiah the governor and of Ezra the priest and scribe.

Dedication of the Wall of Jerusalem

27At the dedication of the wall of Jerusalem, the Levites were sought out from where they lived and were brought to Jerusalem to celebrate joyfully the dedication with songs of thanksgiving and with the music of cymbals, harps and lyres. 28The singers also were brought together from the region around Jerusalem—from the villages of the Netophathites, 29from Beth Gilgal, and from the area of Geba and Azmaveth, for the singers had built villages for themselves around Jerusalem. 30When the priests and Levites had purified themselves ceremonially, they purified the people, the gates and the wall.

31I had the leaders of Judah go up on top of the wall. I also assigned two large choirs to give thanks. One was to proceed on top of the wall to the right, towards the Dung Gate. 32Hoshaiah and half the leaders of Judah followed them, 33along with Azariah, Ezra, Meshullam, 34Judah, Benjamin, Shemaiah, Jeremiah, 35as well as some priests with trumpets, and also Zechariah son of Jonathan, the son of Shemaiah, the son of Mattaniah, the son of Micaiah, the son of Zaccur, the son of Asaph, 36and his associates—Shemaiah, Azarel, Milalai, Gilalai, Maai, Nethanel, Judah and Hanani—with musical instruments ₍prescribed by₎ David the man of God. Ezra the scribe led the procession. 37At the Fountain Gate they continued directly up the steps of the City of David on the ascent to the wall and passed above the house of David to the Water Gate on the east.

38The second choir proceeded in the opposite direction. I followed them on top of the wall, together with half the people—past the Tower of the Ovens to the Broad Wall, 39over the Gate of Ephraim, the Jeshanah Gate, the Fish Gate, the Tower of Hananel and the Tower of the Hundred, as far as the Sheep Gate. At the Gate of the Guard they stopped.

40The two choirs that gave thanks then took their places in the house of God; so did I, together with half the officials, 41as well as the priests—Eliakim, Maaseiah, Miniamin, Micaiah, Elioenai, Zechariah and

Hananiah with their trumpets—42and also Maaseiah, Shemaiah, Eleazar, Uzzi, Jehohanan, Malkijah, Elam and Ezer. The choirs sang under the direction of Jezrahiah. 43And on that day they offered great sacrifices, rejoicing because God had given them great joy. The women and children also rejoiced. The sound of rejoicing in Jerusalem could be heard far away.

44At that time men were appointed to be in charge of the storerooms for the contributions, firstfruits and tithes. From the fields around the towns they were to bring into the storerooms the portions required by the Law for the priests and the Levites, for Judah was pleased with the ministering priests and Levites. 45They performed the service of their God and the service of purification, as did also the singers and gatekeepers, according to the commands of David and his son Solomon. 46For long ago, in the days of David and Asaph, there had been directors for the singers and for the songs of praise and thanksgiving to God. 47So in the days of Zerubbabel and of Nehemiah, all Israel contributed the daily portions for the singers and gatekeepers. They also set aside the portion for the other Levites, and the Levites set aside the portion for the descendants of Aaron.

NEW TESTAMENT READING
Revelation 21:1–27

The New Jerusalem

21 Then I saw a new heaven and a new earth, for the first heaven and the first earth had passed away, and there was no longer any sea. 2I saw the Holy City, the new Jerusalem, coming down out of heaven from God, prepared as a bride beautifully dressed for her husband. 3And I heard a loud voice from the throne saying, "Now the dwelling of God is with men, and he will live with them. They will be his people,

and God himself will be with them and be their God. [4]He will wipe every tear from their eyes. There will be no more death or mourning or crying or pain, for the old order of things has passed away."

[5]He who was seated on the throne said, "I am making everything new!" Then he said, "Write this down, for these words are trustworthy and true."

[6]He said to me: "It is done. I am the Alpha and the Omega, the Beginning and the End. To him who is thirsty I will give to drink without cost from the spring of the water of life. [7]He who overcomes will inherit all this, and I will be his God and he will be my son. [8]But the cowardly, the unbelieving, the vile, the murderers, the sexually immoral, those who practise magic arts, the idolaters and all liars—their place will be in the fiery lake of burning sulphur. This is the second death."

[9]One of the seven angels who had the seven bowls full of the seven last plagues came and said to me, "Come, I will show you the bride, the wife of the Lamb." [10]And he carried me away in the Spirit to a mountain great and high, and showed me the Holy City, Jerusalem, coming down out of heaven from God. [11]It shone with the glory of God, and its brilliance was like that of a very precious jewel, like a jasper, clear as crystal. [12]It had a great, high wall with twelve gates, and with twelve angels at the gates. On the gates were written the names of the twelve tribes of Israel. [13]There were three gates on the east, three on the north, three on the south and three on the west. [14]The wall of the city had twelve foundations, and on them were the names of the twelve apostles of the Lamb.

[15]The angel who talked with me had a measuring rod of gold to measure the city, its gates and its walls. [16]The city was laid out like a square, as long as it was wide. He measured the city with the rod and found it to be 12,000 stadia in length, and as wide and high as it is long. [17]He measured its wall and it was 144 cubits thick, by man's measurement, which the angel was using. [18]The wall was made of jasper, and the city of pure gold, as pure as glass. [19]The foundations of the city walls were decorated with every kind of precious stone. The first foundation was jasper, the second sapphire, the third chalcedony, the fourth emerald, [20]the fifth sardonyx, the sixth carnelian, the seventh chrysolite, the eighth beryl, the ninth topaz, the tenth chrysoprase, the eleventh jacinth, and the twelfth amethyst. [21]The twelve gates were twelve pearls, each gate made of a single pearl. The great street of the city was of pure gold, like transparent glass.

[22]I did not see a temple in the city, because the Lord God Almighty and the Lamb are its temple. [23]The city does not need the sun or the moon to shine on it, for the glory of God gives it light, and the Lamb is its lamp. [24]The nations will walk by its light, and the kings of the earth will bring their splendour into it. [25]On no day will its gates ever be shut, for there will be no night there. [26]The glory and honour of the nations will be brought into it. [27]Nothing impure will ever enter it, nor will anyone who does what is shameful or deceitful, but only those whose names are written in the Lamb's book of life.

READING FROM PROVERBS
Proverbs 31:21–31

[21]When it snows, she has no fear for her household;
    for all of them are clothed in scarlet.
[22]She makes coverings for her bed;
    she is clothed in fine linen and purple.
[23]Her husband is respected at the city gate,
    where he takes his seat among the elders of the land.
[24]She makes linen garments and sells them,

and supplies the merchants with
    sashes.
25She is clothed with strength and
    dignity;
    she can laugh at the days to
    come.
26She speaks with wisdom,
    and faithful instruction is on her
    tongue.
27She watches over the affairs of her
    household
    and does not eat the bread of
    idleness.

28Her children arise and call her
    blessed;
    her husband also, and he praises
    her:
29"Many women do noble things,
    but you surpass them all."
30Charm is deceptive, and beauty is
    fleeting;
    but a woman who fears the LORD is
    to be praised.
31Give her the reward she has earned,
    and let her works bring her praise
    at the city gate.

DECEMBER 31 DAY 365

OLD TESTAMENT READING
Nehemiah 13:1–31

Nehemiah's Final Reforms

13 On that day the Book of Moses was read aloud in the hearing of the people and there it was found written that no Ammonite or Moabite should ever be admitted into the assembly of God, 2because they had not met the Israelites with food and water but had hired Balaam to call a curse down on them. (Our God, however, turned the curse into a blessing.) 3When the people heard this law, they excluded from Israel all who were of foreign descent.

4Before this, Eliashib the priest had been put in charge of the storerooms of the house of our God. He was closely associated with Tobiah, 5and he had provided him with a large room formerly used to store the grain offerings and incense and temple articles, and also the tithes of grain, new wine and oil prescribed for the Levites, singers and gatekeepers, as well as the contributions for the priests.

6But while all this was going on, I was not in Jerusalem, for in the thirty-second year of Artaxerxes king of Babylon I had returned to the king. Some time later I asked his permission 7and came back to Jerusalem. Here I learned about the evil thing Eliashib had done in providing Tobiah a room in the courts of the house of God. 8I was greatly displeased and threw all Tobiah's household goods out of the room. 9I gave orders to purify the rooms, and then I put back into them the equipment of the house of God, with the grain offerings and the incense.

10I also learned that the portions assigned to the Levites had not been given to them, and that all the Levites and singers responsible for the service had gone back to their own fields. 11So I rebuked the officials and asked them, "Why is the house of God neglected?" Then I called them together and stationed them at their posts.

12All Judah brought the tithes of grain, new wine and oil into the storerooms. 13I put Shelemiah the priest, Zadok the scribe, and a Levite named Pedaiah in charge of the storerooms and made Hanan son of Zaccur, the son of Mattaniah, their assistant, because these men were considered trustworthy. They were made responsible for distributing the supplies to their brothers.

¹⁴Remember me for this, O my God, and do not blot out what I have so faithfully done for the house of my God and its services.

¹⁵In those days I saw men in Judah treading winepresses on the Sabbath and bringing in grain and loading it on donkeys, together with wine, grapes, figs and all other kinds of loads. And they were bringing all this into Jerusalem on the Sabbath. Therefore I warned them against selling food on that day. ¹⁶Men from Tyre who lived in Jerusalem were bringing in fish and all kinds of merchandise and selling them in Jerusalem on the Sabbath to the people of Judah. ¹⁷I rebuked the nobles of Judah and said to them, "What is this wicked thing you are doing—desecrating the Sabbath day? ¹⁸Didn't your forefathers do the same things, so that our God brought all this calamity upon us and upon this city? Now you are stirring up more wrath against Israel by desecrating the Sabbath."

¹⁹When evening shadows fell on the gates of Jerusalem before the Sabbath, I ordered the doors to be shut and not opened until the Sabbath was over. I stationed some of my own men at the gates so that no load could be brought in on the Sabbath day. ²⁰Once or twice the merchants and sellers of all kinds of goods spent the night outside Jerusalem. ²¹But I warned them and said, "Why do you spend the night by the wall? If you do this again, I will lay hands on you." From that time on they no longer came on the Sabbath. ²²Then I commanded the Levites to purify themselves and go and guard the gates in order to keep the Sabbath day holy.

Remember me for this also, O my God, and show mercy to me according to your great love.

²³Moreover, in those days I saw men of Judah who had married women from Ashdod, Ammon and Moab. ²⁴Half of their children spoke the language of Ashdod or the language of one of the other peoples, and did not know how to speak the language of Judah. ²⁵I rebuked them and called curses down on them. I beat some of the men and pulled out their hair. I made them take an oath in God's name and said: "You are not to give your daughters in marriage to their sons, nor are you to take their daughters in marriage for your sons or for yourselves. ²⁶Was it not because of marriages like these that Solomon king of Israel sinned? Among the many nations there was no king like him. He was loved by his God, and God made him king over all Israel, but even he was led into sin by foreign women. ²⁷Must we hear now that you too are doing all this terrible wickedness and are being unfaithful to our God by marrying foreign women?"

²⁸One of the sons of Joiada son of Eliashib the high priest was son-in-law to Sanballat the Horonite. And I drove him away from me.

²⁹Remember them, O my God, because they defiled the priestly office and the covenant of the priesthood and of the Levites.

³⁰So I purified the priests and the Levites of everything foreign, and assigned them duties, each to his own task. ³¹I also made provision for contributions of wood at designated times, and for the firstfruits.

Remember me with favour, O my God.

NEW TESTAMENT READING
Revelation 22:1–21

The River of Life

22 Then the angel showed me the river of the water of life, as clear as crystal, flowing from the throne of God and of the Lamb ²down the middle of the great street of the city. On each side of the river stood the tree of life, bearing twelve crops of fruit, yielding its fruit every month. And the leaves of the tree are for the healing of the nations. ³No longer will there be any curse. The throne of God and of the Lamb will be in the city, and his servants will serve him. ⁴They will see his face, and his name will be on their foreheads. ⁵There will be no more night. They will not need the light of a lamp or the light of the sun, for the Lord God will give them light. And they will reign for ever and ever.

⁶The angel said to me, "These words are trustworthy and true. The Lord, the God of the spirits of the prophets, sent his angel to show his servants the things that must soon take place."

Jesus Is Coming

⁷"Behold, I am coming soon! Blessed is he who keeps the words of the prophecy in this book."

⁸I, John, am the one who heard and saw these things. And when I had heard and seen them, I fell down to worship at the feet of the angel who had been showing them to me. ⁹But he said to me, "Do not do it! I am a fellow-servant with you and with your brothers the prophets and of all who keep the words of this book. Worship God!"

¹⁰Then he told me, "Do not seal up the words of the prophecy of this book, because the time is near. ¹¹Let him who does wrong continue to do wrong; let him who is vile continue to be vile; let him who does right continue to do right; and let him who is holy continue to be holy."

¹²"Behold, I am coming soon! My reward is with me, and I will give to everyone according to what he has done. ¹³I am the Alpha and the Omega, the First and the Last, the Beginning and the End.

¹⁴"Blessed are those who wash their robes, that they may have the right to the tree of life and may go through the gates into the city. ¹⁵Outside are the dogs, those who practise magic arts, the sexually immoral, the murderers,

the idolaters and everyone who loves and practises falsehood.

¹⁶"I, Jesus, have sent my angel to give you this testimony for the churches. I am the Root and the Offspring of David, and the bright Morning Star."

¹⁷The Spirit and the bride say, "Come!" And let him who hears say, "Come!" Whoever is thirsty, let him come; and whoever wishes, let him take the free gift of the water of life.

¹⁸I warn everyone who hears the words of the prophecy of this book: If anyone adds anything to them, God will add to him the plagues described in this book. ¹⁹And if anyone takes words away from this book of prophecy, God will take away from him his share in the tree of life and in the holy city, which are described in this book.

²⁰He who testifies to these things says, "Yes, I am coming soon."

Amen. Come, Lord Jesus.

²¹The grace of the Lord Jesus be with God's people. Amen.

READING FROM PSALMS
Psalm 150:1–6

¹Praise the LORD.

Praise God in his sanctuary;
  ʼ praise him in his mighty heavens.
²Praise him for his acts of power;
  praise him for his surpassing
    greatness.
³Praise him with the sounding of the
    trumpet,
  praise him with the harp and lyre,
⁴praise him with tambourine and
    dancing,
  praise him with the strings and
    flute,
⁵praise him with the clash of cymbals,
  praise him with resounding
    cymbals.

⁶Let everything that has breath praise
    the LORD.

Praise the LORD.

NEW INTERNATIONAL VERSION

Notes and Maps

TABLE OF CONTENTS

THE BIBLE AT A GLANCE

BIBLE REFERENCE	SETTING AND IMPORTANT CHARACTERS	IMPORTANT EVENTS	APPROXIMATE DATE
Genesis 1-11	*'Eden'* *Mesopotamia* Adam & Eve Noah	Creation Flood	
Genesis 12-36	*'Israel'* Abraham Isaac Jacob		1800 B.C.
Genesis 37 – Exodus 12	*Egypt* Joseph Moses	'Exodus' Giving of the Law	1400 B.C.
Exodus 13 – Deuteronomy 34	*Desert Wanderings* Moses		
Joshua – 1 Samuel 7 Ruth	*Israel* Joshua Samuel	Conquest Settlement	1200 B.C.
1 Samuel 8 – 1 Kings 11 1 Chronicles – 2 Chronicles 11	*Israel* Saul David Solomon	Founding of the monarchy	1000 B.C.
1 Kings 12 – 2 Kings 25 2 Chronicles 12-36 Jonah Joel Nahum Zephaniah Lamentations Habakkuk Obadiah	*Israel* Elijah Elisha Amos Hosea Isaiah Micah	Kingdom of Israel divided into Israel and Judah	900 B.C.
	Babylon Jeremiah Ezekiel Daniel	Israel 'ended' Judah exiled	587 B.C.
Ezra Nehemiah Esther	*Israel* Haggai Zechariah Malachi	'Return'	400 B.C.
Matthew Mark Luke John	*Israel* Jesus Christ	Birth, death, resurrection	
Acts Letters Revelation	*'All the World'* Peter John Paul	Birth & growth of the churches	100 A.D.

Psalms, Proverbs, Job, Song of Songs, Ecclesiastes

TIME CHART

INTRODUCTORY NOTES

Over the last hundred years or so we have gained a better understanding of the history of the Jewish nation as it relates to world history. This is partly a result of the work of archaeologists combined with scientific ways of dating their discoveries. Thus we can be more accurate in dating biblical events.

Nevertheless, the further back into history we go the less is it possible to pinpoint a precise date. After about 1000 B.C. we can be more definite about dates, but before this (2000–1000 B.C.) there may be differences of up to 100 years. The dates marked with * on the chart overleaf are those which are particularly debated although generally accepted. The abbreviation *c.* means 'about' (Latin 'circa'). ** means 'somewhere within this period'.

Surprisingly, it is harder to pinpoint many New Testament dates! The New Testament itself gives us fewer clues than the Old Testament about historical details. It is especially difficult to say precisely when many of the books were written, so all the dates in the chart are not the only dates suggested.

INTRODUCTORY NOTE

Biblical Period and where it is recorded	World Events
BEGINNINGS OF TIME Genesis	
Abraham c.2000 – 1825**	Middle Bronze Age
Isaac c. 1900 – 1725**	1950 – 1550
Jacob c. 1800 – 1700**	
Joseph c. 1720 – 1550**	
Jacob and his eleven sons join Joseph in Egypt c.1700	

2000 B.C.

EXODUS FROM EGYPT AND CONQUEST OF CANAAN Exodus – Joshua	
Moses	Pharaoh Rameses II
Exodus 1280/1260*	1290 – 1224
Desert Wanderings	
Joshua	
Fall of Jericho 1240/1220*	

1300 B.C.

DEATH OF JOSHUA TO THE FIRST KING Judges – 1 Samuel 12	
Joshua 1300 –1190*	PHILISTINES
The Judges 1220/1200 – 1050/1045	Iron Age
Samuel 1075 –1035	
Saul 1050/1045 –1010	

1200 B.C.

ISRAEL'S GOLDEN AGE 1 Samuel 13 – 1 Kings 11 (1 Chronicles 10 – 2 Chronicles 9)	
David 1010 – 970	PHILISTINES
Solomon 970 – 930	

1000 B.C.

THE TWO KINGDOMS	1 Kings 12 – 2 Kings 17 (2 Chronicles 10 – 28)		930 B.C.
Israel: The Northern Kingdom	Prophets		
930 – 909 Jeroboam I			
909 – 908 Nadab			
908 – 885 Baasha			
885 – 884 Elah			
884　　Zimri			
884　　Tibni			
884 – 873 Omri			
873 – 853 Ahab	Elijah		
853 – 852 Ahaziah			
852 – 841 Joram	Elisha		
841 – 813 Jehu			
813 – 798 Jehoahaz			800 B.C.
798 – 781 Jehoash			
781 – 753 Jeroboam II	?Jonah		
753 – 752 Zechariah	Amos c. 760 – 750	Tiglath Pileser III	
752　　Shallum	Hosea c. 750 – 725	of ASSYRIA 745 – 727	
752 – 741 Menahem	''		
741 – 739 Pekahiah	''		
739 – 731 Pekah	''		
731 – 722 Hoshea	''	Shalmanezer V of	
		ASSYRIA 727 – 722	
Fall of Samaria, capital of Israel 722			

930 B.C.

Judah: The Southern Kingdom	Prophets	
930 – 913 Rehoboam		
913 – 910 Abijah		
910 – 869 Asa		
869 – 848 Jehoshaphat		
848 – 841 Jehoram		
841 Ahaziah		
841 – 835 Athaliah		
835 – 796 Joash		
796 – 767 Amaziah		
767 – 739 Azariah (Uzziah)	Isaiah 740 – 701	Tiglath Pileser III of ASSYRIA 745 – 727
739 – 731 Jotham		Shalmanezer V of ASSYRIA 727 – 722
731 – 715 Ahaz	Micah 725 – 701	

800 B.C.

LAST DAYS OF JUDAH 1 Kings 18 – 25 (2 Chronicles 29 – 36)

	Prophets	
715 – 686 Hezekiah	Isaiah/Micah	Sennacherib of ASSYRIA
710 Siege of Jerusalem		
686 – 641 Manasseh		
641 – 639 Amon	Jeremiah/?Zephaniah/?Jonah	Fall of Nineveh, capital of ASSYRIA 612
639 – 609 Josiah	?Nahum/?Habakkuk/?Joel	
	Lamentations	
609 Jehoahaz		Nebuchadnezzar of BABYLON
609 – 597 Jehoiakim		
605 Daniel deported to Babylon		
597 Jehoiachin	Ezekiel 593 – 571	
First deportation to Babylon		
597 – 587 Zedekiah	Obadiah	
Second deportation to Babylon		

700 B.C.

600 B.C.

562	Further deportation to Babylon	

EXILE AND RETURN Ezra, Nehemiah, Esther, Haggai, Zechariah, Malachi, Isaiah 40 – 66

Cyrus of PERSIA

Prophets

Artaxerxes of PERSIA

539	Fall of Babylon		
538	Cyrus' Decree		
	First Return to Jerusalem		
515	Dedication of second Jerusalem temple	Haggai	520
		Zechariah	520
		Malachi	c.500 – 450
445	Nehemiah arrives in Jerusalem		
428**	Ezra arrives in Jerusalem		

500 B.C.

BETWEEN THE TESTAMENTS (1 & 2 Maccabees, in the APOCRYPHA)

336 – 323	Alexander the Great of GREECE

Fall of PERSIA 331

323	Greek Empire divided into Ptolemaic (Egypt) and Seleucid (Syria and Mesopotamia)
323 – 198	Israel a Ptolemaic state
198 – 166	Israel a Seleucid state
167	Desecration of Jerusalem temple
	Maccabean Revolt
165	Jerusalem temple rededicated
142	Jewish Independence
63	Pompey of Rome annexes Jerusalem
40 B.C. – 4 A.D.	Herod the Great

Antiochus Epiphanes,
SELEUCID king 175 – 163

300 B.C.

200 B.C.

100 B.C.

LIFE OF JESUS Matthew, Mark, Luke, John

?4 B.C.	Birth of John the Baptist	27 B.C. – 14 A.D. Caesar Augustus of ROME
?4	Birth of Jesus	26 – 30 A.D. Pontius Pilate
?29 A.D.	Baptism of Jesus	
30/33 A.D.	Crucifixion	

30 A.D.

→

THE EARLY CHURCH Acts & Letters

		Literature		
35	Paul's conversion	49/50	Galatians	41 – 54 Claudius
47	Paul's first missionary journey	50 – 51	1&2 Thessalonians	
49	Important Church Council	55 – 56	1&2 Corinthians	
50 – 52	Paul's second missionary journey	58	Romans	
		**50 – 62	James	
53 – 57	Paul's third missionary journey	61	Philemon, Colossians, Ephesians, Philippians	54 – 68 Nero
64	Death of Paul in Rome	**62 – 64	1 Peter	
70	Fall of Jerusalem to Rome	62	1&2 Timothy, Titus	
		**63/64	Mark	
		64 – 68	2 Peter	81 – 96 Domitian
		**65 – 68	Hebrews	
		70	Matthew	
		80	Jude	
		**65 – 80	Luke, Acts	
		**75 – 85	John	
		**70 – 100	1,2,3 John	
		**90 – 100	Revelation	
		**90 – 95		

50 A.D.

100 A.D.

WELL-KNOWN EVENTS
IN THE BIBLE

Creation **Genesis** 1–2
The first sin **Genesis** 3
Cain kills Abel **Genesis** 4
Noah and the Ark **Genesis** 6–9
Sodom and Gomorrah **Genesis** 18–19
Abraham prepares to sacrifice Isaac **Genesis** 22
Jacob's Dream **Genesis** 28:10–22
Joseph's coat of many colours **Genesis** 37
Moses in the bulrushes **Exodus** 2
Moses and the burning bush **Exodus** 3
Plagues on Egypt **Exodus** 7–11
The first Passover **Exodus** 12
The Exodus **Exodus** 12–13
Crossing the Red Sea **Exodus** 13–14
Manna and quail **Exodus** 16
Water from the rock **Exodus** 17
The Ten Commandments **Exodus** 20
Balaam's donkey **Numbers** 22
Death of Moses **Deuteronomy** 34
Crossing the Jordan **Joshua** 3
The Battle of Jericho **Joshua** 6
Gideon and the fleece **Judges** 6–7
Samson and Delilah **Judges** 13–16
Samuel called by God **1 Samuel** 1–3
David and Goliath **1 Samuel** 17
David and Bathsheba **2 Samuel** 11
Solomon builds the Temple **1 Kings** 6–7, **2 Chronicles** 3–4
Elijah and the priests of Baal **1 Kings** 18
The miracles of Elisha **2 Kings** 4–5
'The Lord is my Shepherd' **Psalm** 23
Benefits of Wisdom **Proverbs** 3
Sayings of the wise **Proverbs** 22
The Wife of noble character **Proverbs** 31
'To us a child is born' **Isaiah** 9
Ezekiel and the dry bones **Ezekiel** 37
The fiery furnace **Daniel** 3
Writing on the wall **Daniel** 5
Daniel in the lions' den **Daniel** 6
Hosea and his adulterous wife **Hosea** 1–3
Jonah and the fish **Jonah** 1
Coming of the Holy Spirit at Pentecost **Acts** 2
Death of Stephen **Acts** 6–7
Conversion of Saul **Acts** 9:1–31
Paul's shipwreck **Acts** 27–28

WELL-KNOWN EVENTS
IN THE LIFE OF JESUS

Birth   **Matthew 1–2; Luke 1–2**

Baptism   **Matthew 3:13–17; Mark 1:9–11; Luke 3:21–22**

Temptation   **Matthew 4:1–11; Mark 1:12–13; Luke 4:1–13**

The transfiguration   **Matthew 17:1–13; Mark 9:2–13; Luke 9:28–36**

The triumphal entry into Jerusalem   **Matthew 21:1–11; Mark 11:1–11;
   Luke 19:28–44; John 12:12–19**

Jesus clears the temple   **Matthew 21:12–13; Mark 11:15–19;
   Luke 19:45–48; John 2:12–25**

The widow's offering   **Mark 12:41–44; Luke 21:1–4**

The last supper   **Matthew 26:17–30; Mark 14:12–26; Luke 22:7–38;
   John 13:21–30**

Jesus washes his disciples' feet   **John 13:1–17**

Jesus at Gethsemane   **Matthew 26:36–46; Mark 14:32–42; Luke 22:39–46**

Judas betrays Jesus   **Matthew 26:47–56; Mark 14:43–50; Luke 22:1–6, 47–53;
   John 18:1–11**

Peter denies Jesus   **Matthew 26:69–75; Mark 14:66–72; Luke 22:54–62;
   John 18:15–18, 25–27**

The trial and crucifixion   **Matthew 26:57–27:66; Mark 15:1–47;
   Luke 22:66–23:56; John 18:28–19:42**

Resurrection and ascension   **Matthew 28:1–20; Mark 16:1–20; Luke 24:1–53;
   John 20:1–21:25**

SELECTED MIRACLES OF JESUS

Man with leprosy   **Matthew 8:2–4; Mark 1:40–42; Luke 5:12–13**

Roman centurion's servant   **Matthew 8:5–13; Luke 7:1–10**

Calming the storm   **Matthew 8:23–27; Mark 4:37–41; Luke 8:22–25**

Two demon-possessed men   **Matthew 8:28–34; Mark 5:1–15; Luke 8:26–39**

Paralysed man   **Matthew 9:2–7; Mark 2:3–12; Luke 5:18–25**

Jairus's daughter   **Matthew 9:18–19, 23–25; Mark 5:22–24, 38–42;
   Luke 8:41–42, 49–56**

Woman with bleeding   **Matthew 9:20–22; Mark 5:25–29; Luke 8:43–48**

Walking on water   **Matthew 14:25; Mark 6:48–51; John 6:19–21**

5000 people fed   **Matthew 14:15–21; Mark 6:35–44; Luke 9:12–17;
   John 6:5–13**

Canaanite woman's daughter   **Matthew 15:21–28; Mark 7:24–30**

4000 people fed   **Matthew 15:32–38; Mark 8:1–9**

Boy with a demon   **Matthew 17:14–18; Mark 9:17–29; Luke 9:38–43**

Fig-tree withered   **Matthew 21:18–22; Mark 11:12–14, 20–25**

Man possessed (in synagogue)   **Mark 1:23–26; Luke 4:33–35**

Catch of fish   **Luke 5:4–11**

Widow's son at Nain   **Luke 7:11–15**

Crippled woman   **Luke 13:11–13**

Ten men with leprosy   **Luke** 17:11–19
The high-priest's servant   **Luke** 22:50–51
Water turned to wine   **John** 2:1–11
Official's son at Capernaum   **John** 4:46–54
Sick man at pool of Bethesda   **John** 5:1–9
Man born blind   **John** 9:1–7
Lazarus   **John** 11:1–44
Another catch of fish   **John** 21:1–11

SELECTED PARABLES OF JESUS

Lamp under a bowl   **Matthew** 5:14–15; **Mark** 4:21–22; **Luke** 8:16; 11:33
House on the rock   **Matthew** 7:24–27; **Luke** 6:47–49
New cloth   **Matthew** 9:16; **Mark** 2:21; **Luke** 5:36
New wine in old wineskins   **Matthew** 9:17; **Mark** 2:22; **Luke** 5:37–38
Sower   **Matthew** 13:3–8, 18–23; **Mark** 4:3–8, 14–20; **Luke** 8:5–8, 11–15
Weeds   **Matthew** 13:24–30, 36–43
Mustard seed   **Matthew** 13:31–32; **Mark** 4:30–32; **Luke** 13:18–19
Yeast   **Matthew** 13:33; **Luke** 13:20–21
Hidden treasure   **Matthew** 13:44
Valuable pearl   **Matthew** 13:45–46
Owner of a house   **Matthew** 13:52
Lost sheep   **Matthew** 18:12–14; **Luke** 15:4–7
Unforgiving servant   **Matthew** 18:23–34
Workers in the vineyard   **Matthew** 20:1–16
Wicked tenants   **Matthew** 21:33–44; **Mark** 12:1–11; **Luke** 20:9–18
Wedding feast   **Matthew** 22:2–14
Faithful and wise servant   **Matthew** 24:45–51; **Luke** 12:42–48
Ten virgins   **Matthew** 25:1–13
Talents   **Matthew** 25:14–30; **Luke** 19:12–27
Sheep and goats   **Matthew** 25:31–46
Watchful servants   **Mark** 13:35–37; **Luke** 12:35–40
Good Samaritan   **Luke** 10:30–37
Friend at midnight   **Luke** 11:5–8
Rich fool   **Luke** 12:16–21
Wedding feast   **Luke** 14:7–14
Great banquet   **Luke** 14:16–24
Cost of discipleship   **Luke** 14:28–33
Lost coin   **Luke** 15:8–10
Lost (prodigal) son   **Luke** 15:11–32
Rich man and Lazarus   **Luke** 16:19–31
Pharisee and tax collector   **Luke** 18:10–14

WHAT IS THE BIBLE?

Although one book, the Bible contains sixty-six individual books. Within each of these there is often a variety of writing such as poetry, prose, biography, letters, family trees, official records, songs and prayers. It is important to recognise the type of writing when we are reading so that we read the Bible on its own terms. To read poetry, for example, as if it was an excerpt from an official record, would make it very difficult to understand.

POETRY

The main division is between prose and poetry. Several of the Old Testament books are written completely in poetic form: Psalms, the Song of Songs and Lamentations for instance. Most of the book of Job is written in poetic form, and other poems are found in prose passages, for example, Exodus 15; Judges 5 and 1 Samuel 2. Modern translations show quite clearly where poetry is used and it is easy to see that most of the prophetic books are written in poetic form. In the New Testament there is some poetry, for example, Mary's Song (Luke 1:46–55), Zechariah's Song (Luke 1:68–79) and Philippians 2:6–11.

There is an important difference between Hebrew/Jewish poetry and modern poetry. Hebrew poetry uses **rhythm** and not rhyme. It also uses **'parallelism'** which means that the idea or thought in one line is repeated in the next line in a different way and using different words. A glance at any poetic passage will illustrate this, for example:

Job 33:4 'The Spirit of God has made me;
the breath of the Almighty
gives me life.'

There are also many **different types of poetry**. The Song of Songs and the book of Job are each written as a play with various actors. In the Psalms there are poetic songs and prayers for many different occasions: songs of thanksgiving, songs for pilgrims, songs for the coronation of a king, prayers for the congregation and prayers for individuals. In the New Testament it is probable that Philippians 2:6–11, for example, was a hymn sung by the first Christians.

LAW

Israel's laws are found in the books of Exodus through to Deuteronomy. These formed the foundation of the life of the nation and of its relationship with God. Thus the law is regarded as an expression of God's character and will; the law shows how God wants his people to behave, to worship, and to live in society.

The best known list of laws is the Ten Commandments (Exodus 20). These are a summary of the essential points of the many laws contained in Exodus through to Deuteronomy. Three groups of laws have been drawn out: Covenant Law or the **Book of the Covenant** (Exodus 21–23), which contains moral, civil and religious laws. **The Holiness Code** (Leviticus 17–26) which, as its name suggests, arises from the frequent

statements, 'I the LORD am holy—I who make you holy' (Leviticus 21:8). This law 'book' sets out rules for worship, especially about priests and sacrifices. The **Deuteronomic Code** (Deuteronomy 12–25) is set out like a sermon and includes warnings about the consequences of breaking the laws.

These laws touch on every area of life, not only religion. There are laws about family life (marriage etc.), human rights, theft, damage to property, personal and food hygiene and so on. Many of them are uncompromising, or absolute statements: 'You shall/shall not' (as in Exodus 20), but many are what we call 'case laws': 'if . . . then'—what to do in particular situations.

There are no new lists of commandments in the New Testament, though some regard the **Sermon on the Mount** (Matthew 5–7) as the new law for Christians. The standards set out there are even more difficult to achieve than in the Old Testament law. Some Christians therefore regard these as ideals to be aimed at, even if they can never fully attain them. Paul has much to say about the law (and uses the word in different ways), but basically he teaches that while it is good, it is limited. This is because people can never earn God's love—it is given freely.

A SPECIAL KIND OF HISTORY

There is much in the Bible which helps us to piece together the early history of the Jewish nation and later, the early church. The history books of the Old Testament are Joshua through to 2 Kings, and 1 and 2 Chronicles record some of the same events. There are historical passages in Isaiah and Jeremiah, and parts of Genesis, Exodus and Numbers could be described as 'history'. In the New Testament there are some historical references in the Gospels and Acts.

In the Hebrew Bible Joshua–2 Kings are grouped together and called 'The Former Prophets'. This will help us to understand that biblical history is not history told for its own sake, but history told from a particular point of view. It does not tell us everything that happened but only those events which show how God is at work in his world, developing his plan in the Jewish nation and later in the church. This does not mean that this history is unreliable, for archaeology and comparative studies of other nations show it to be trustworthy.

There are many references in the Old Testament books of history which show that the writers and editors used older writings and records. For example Joshua 10:13 and 2 Samuel 1:18 refer to 'The Book of Jashar'; 1 Kings 11:41 to the 'annals of Solomon' and 1 Chronicles 29:29 to 'the records of Nathan the prophet and the records of Gad the seer'. Reference is also made to particular people writing down God's words: Exodus 24:4 (Moses); 1 Samuel 10:25 (Samuel). The many family trees (genealogies) were other sources used by the writers. In the New Testament the writer of Luke and Acts indicates that he has investigated other accounts (Luke 1:3).

PROPHECY

There are many prophetic books in the Old Testament and they are grouped together from Isaiah through to Malachi. The popular idea of prophecy is that it is the prediction of future events, but biblical prophecy is much more than this. The prophets announced God's message not only, or necessarily, about the future, but very often about the present. Frequently they began with the words, 'This is what the Lord says'. They spoke God's word and that meant that they condemned social injustice and sham worship. They exposed mistaken, cosy ideas about God and his laws and warned the people that God must punish them if they did not mend their ways.

The prophets communicated what they had to say in many different ways: dialogue, narrative, poetry, picture language and drama. Many prophets have given us an account of how God called them to their work. Their conviction was that they said what God had told them to say, but how they received those words we do not know.

There are a few references to prophets writing down at least some of their message: Isaiah 30:8 (Isaiah), and Jeremiah 30:2 (Jeremiah). Jeremiah 36 also tells us that Jeremiah dictated some of his message to Baruch who must have been a follower of his.

Other prophecies have both an immediate and a long term meaning; they were fulfilled in the prophet's lifetime or soon after, but only partly so. The New Testament writers understood this and show how many of the Old Testament promises were finally fulfilled in the life, death and resurrection of Jesus.

APOCALYPTIC

This is a particular type of prophetic literature found notably in Daniel (chapters 6–12) and Revelation, but also in Isaiah 24–27, Ezekiel 38–39, Zechariah 9–14 (the first part of the book is apocalyptic in thought) and Mark 13, which is known as 'the little Apocalypse'. The word comes from Greek, and means 'unveiling' or 'revealing' and the book of Revelation is often called 'The Apocalypse' since it is the unveiling or revealing of the future. Apocalyptic writing is full of strange symbols and creatures, as well as angels. The interpretation of apocalyptic writing gives rise to a variety of points of view.

WISDOM

We know that many ancient nations had 'wisdom writings'. Job, Ecclesiastes and Proverbs are the main biblical Wisdom books, but many of the Psalms belong to this type of writing (for example, 1, 34, 37, 73 etc). Wisdom writing was interested in the problems of existence: why are we here? why are things the way they are? why do people suffer? In its simplest and earliest form wisdom was communicated in riddles (Judges 14:14; 1 Samuel 24:13 for example) and the proverbs found in the biblical book of that name. The book of Proverbs is full of statements and observations, often amusing, about life. Sometimes they are presented as if a father or teacher were talking to his son or student, teaching him how to behave in various situations.

GOSPEL

Although there are four Gospels the word actually applies to what they contain, for the announcement that a new age has begun with Jesus **is** the gospel, which means 'good news'. The Gospels are, nevertheless, a new and particular kind of biblical literature. It is important to understand that the Gospels are not biographies; they do not simply recount the life of Jesus. Rather, each Gospel presents the story of Jesus from a particular viewpoint, and each has a distinctive way of telling the story. Matthew has grouped Jesus' teaching together; Mark is a vivid, fast-moving story; Luke has beautiful pen sketches of many of the people who featured in the story of Jesus; John is a deeply religious, almost otherworldly study.

Scholars have discussed the writing of the Gospels a great deal. A very early record tells us that Mark wrote down Peter's memories of Jesus. Luke was probably written by the man who helped Paul in some of his missionary work.

LETTERS

The writers of the New Testament letters follow the 'rules' for letter writing of the first century A.D. This began with an opening sentence giving the name of the writer and the recipient. Then followed a general greeting and enquiry into the health of the recipient. The main section of the letter was concluded with a personal greeting. However, the New Testament letters are much longer than the average 150–200 words of the letters of that period. Even Philemon, the shortest, is 470 words. Paul's letters are usually characterised by a main section which deals first with teaching and then with the way Christians should put into practice what they have learned. Although most of the New Testament letters tell us the name of the author some do not.

There are some interesting letters in the Old Testament. The best example is in Jeremiah 29, but others are found in 1 Kings 21; 2 Chronicles 30; Ezra 4 and 5 and Nehemiah 6.

THE LAND AND PEOPLE OF THE BIBLE

GEOGRAPHY

NAME: The place in which the story of the Bible is set has been known by different names in its history:

Canaan is the earliest reference to the country (Genesis 10:19; 11:31). As Genesis 12:6 shows, the name is associated with the people who lived there: Canaanites.

Israel or 'the land of Israel', is the name used as the Old Testament progresses (e.g. 1 Samuel 13:19). When the nation was divided the northern part was called '**Israel**', and the southern area '**Judah**'. In the New Testament period under the Romans, the land was divided into provinces such as 'Judea' and 'Galilee'.

Palestine has also been used, as for example, in the earlier part of this century. It is associated with the '**Philistines**' who once occupied the coastal area to the west of Israel—the 'land of the Philistines' or '**Philistia**'.

Today, the whole area is so divided that the various titles only confuse!

PHYSICAL FEATURES: The land of Israel is small, roughly the size of Wales, 150–200 miles long and 100 miles at its widest point. It is a land of great contrasts. Travelling in an easterly direction from the Mediterranean Sea there is a coastal plain from which the land slopes gently at first, then more steeply to the central highlands of Judea. It then drops sharply to the Jordan rift valley and rises again to a mountainous plateau in the Trans-Jordan area. Travelling from north to south the land descends steadily from Mount Hermon (9000 feet) to the Dead Sea (1275 feet below sea level).

LANDSCAPE: The present landscape is very different from what it was in the early Old Testament period. Then the northern central area and Trans-Jordan were covered by lush forest, and the plains nearer the coast were sand dunes, lagoons, swamp and forest. In the north-west and central areas (where most of the Bible story is set) there were fertile plains. The southern area was desert scrub.

CLIMATE: There are great variations in the climate which falls roughly between temperate and tropical, with wet winters and hot, dry summers (May/June–September/October). Climate varies with the height above sea level, distance from the coast, etc. **Rainfall** is vital and while the rainy season is predictable the are great variations from year to year. In the Bible there are references to:

'**the early rains**'–mid-October: (Autumn) which make ploughing possible. This is followed by the rainy season proper, November–March, with most rain falling in December and January. '**the latter rains**' or 'spring rains'–vital to mature the grain.

Rainfall averages lessen from north to south and from west to east. During the summer, dew and morning mist bring moisture to the coastal areas and the plains, and this is of vital importance. Drought and famine were constant factors which had to be reckoned with.

OCCUPATIONS:

Agriculture. The people of the Bible, and particularly of Old Testament times, were farmers. Almost everyone would have had their own smallholding, growing what was needed for food, and keeping sheep, goats and cattle. Goats provided milk, and their skins were used to make tents. Sheep provided milk and wool, and occasionally meat. By New Testament times it was fairly common to keep chickens.

Though a large part of the land was desert and rock, and therefore unsuitable for farming, the areas of lower Galilee were fertile. Barley was grown in the fertile valleys (such as the Jordan valley), and wheat in the Plain of Jezreel. Flax for making linen, and millet were also grown. Pomegranates, melons, dates, cucumbers, figs and nuts were important crops providing a supplement to water in the long hot season. On the lower hills there were vineyards—the vine is an important symbol in the Bible (e.g. Isaiah 5:7; John 15:1). Olives were eaten for food, and their oil was used for lighting, cooking, medicine, and soap for washing. **Harvesting** began in March (Flax) and proceeded with barley (April/May), wheat (May/June), grapes (July–October), figs (August/September) and olives (October/November).

Other Occupations

FISHING: Whole communities made their living from fishing, as the New Testament Gospels show. Lake Galilee was the focus for this.

MINING: The mining of iron and copper in the area of Ezion Geber began around 1000 B.C. Chemical salts and pitch were found in the Dead Sea area.

POTTERY: Although there are several references to potters and their craft in the Bible, there was nothing distinctive about Israelite pottery.

FROM TENTS TO TOWNS

THE TRIBE: The story of Israel begins with Abraham. He lived a 'semi-nomadic' life (i.e. travelling from place to place and living in tents) much as the modern Bedouin today. The tribe would include the entire family, from the head of the family/tribe, through the various generations to the youngest member. Servants and large numbers of animals would be included.

EARLY COMMUNITIES: After the settlement in Canaan under Joshua's leadership, the twelve tribes gradually settled into small farming communities or villages, which later became walled towns and cities. Towns were small with about 150–200 houses.

LATER DEVELOPMENTS: Under the kings, and especially Solomon, towns became larger and the gap between rich and poor widened as farms were taken over, and even tenant farmers were forced off their land.

NEW TESTAMENT TIMES: By New Testament times towns were planned more carefully, though life was still quite rural. Jerusalem probably had a quarter of a million inhabitants in the time of Jesus. The Romans, famed for their civil engineering, did much to improve conditions by building drainage schemes, aqueducts etc. They also created 'provinces', some of which were governed by a governor or proconsul, and others (where troops were stationed) by a procurator. Some cities were given special status as Roman colonies and were governed by magistrates. Philippi was one of these. Roman citizenship was another privilege and Paul was proud of his.

HOW PEOPLE LIVED

The Bible covers a period of some 2000 years so there were changes in some customs and in the way people lived. It is only possible to look at a few of these customs in this section.

FAMILY LIFE:

Circumcision. Eight days after birth a boy was circumcised. Other races practised circumcision but it had religious meaning for the Jews. It reminded them that God had chosen them and that they were different from other people.

Education. Learning was based on 'the Scriptures', particularly the Laws in the Pentateuch. The many festivals helped children to learn about the history of Israel. Children were taught at home, but by New Testament times boys would go to the synagogue school.

The eldest son succeeded his father. While both boys and girls would help on the farm, girls would also help in the home. Women did all the food preparation, water carrying, spinning, weaving, and the making of clothes.

Marriage. This was arranged by parents, and throughout biblical times there was an insistence that marriage should take place only between fellow Israelites, though many disregarded this, as the Old Testament shows. The **engagement** was binding and a 'bride price' (mohar) would be paid to the bride's father, and a dowry by the bride's father. These could be paid in servants, land, property or work, not only in money. **Divorce** was allowed, but the actual grounds for this were not

clear and were still being debated in Jesus' time.

Death. There were clear mourning rites which lasted seven days. The body had to be buried within 24 hours, either in a cave, or for the rich, a specially prepared tomb. There was no clear understanding of a **life beyond death** in the Old Testament. It was believed that the dead went to a 'place of shadows' called 'Sheol'. By the New Testament period the Pharisees believed in a physical resurrection, and certainly many of the ordinary people did as well (see John 11).

JUSTICE AND ADMINISTRATION:

Early period. After the settlement, when towns began to be established, the entrance ('the gate') became the meeting place and a kind of law-court, where cases were heard and judgment given. Under Solomon an organised administration and government began to emerge, and community and military service was introduced.

Later period. Towards the end of the Old Testament period families of priests began to emerge with wide powers and influence. Together with 'elders' these priests formed a central governing body called **'the Sanhedrin'** or 'the Council'. It had wide civil and administrative powers and its own police force. It was this court that tried Jesus, and later, some of his followers.

ISRAEL AND HER NEIGHBOURS

Although Israel was a tiny country its position in relation to the nations surrounding it gave it a strategic importance. This is because it formed a kind of land bridge between powerful nations: Egypt in the south and Mesopotamia in the north were constantly struggling with each other for possession, influence and control of vital trade routes. An understanding of this helps us to see why, in the Old Testament in particular, there was constant warfare and threat of invasion.

SUMERIA. This probably forms the background culture to Genesis 1–11. It is the oldest culture of which we know, and dates to at least 4500 B.C., so that Sumeria is often called 'the cradle of civilisation'. It lay near the Persian Gulf, between the Tigris and Euphrates rivers (modern S. Iraq). Its largest city was Ur from which Abraham's family came. Sumerians were scientists, mathematicians and astronomers, but their greatest contribution to civilisation was **writing**, which they seem to have invented. The earliest understandable writing dates from 3200 B.C., and many later languages developed from this. Sumeria had been finally absorbed by the Semites by 1750 B.C., but its legacy of writings lived on.

EGYPT. In Genesis and Exodus the founding fathers of Israel (Abraham, Isaac etc.) travelled constantly to and from Egypt. Egyptian civilisation is very old and reaches back at least to 3000 B.C. It was an advanced culture and Egyptians had special interest in dreams and their interpretation, as well as in poetry, proverbs and story-writing. Their king was called 'Pharaoh' (his Majesty) and was regarded as a god.

At the end of the Old Testament period Egypt's power had dwindled so that she often tried to form political alliances with other nations, including Israel, to keep herself going.

CANAANITES. These were the main racial group in Palestine at the time of the Conquest. They lived in small 'city-states' or 'fortress towns', built on hill summits. Other tribal groups lived alongside them, such as Amorites, Perizzites, etc. (see Exodus 33:2). The significance of the Canaanites for Israel's history is in their religion. This was a nature religion, its chief god being Baal, the storm god, and provider (or withholder) of rain.

PHILISTINES. They appear to have been part of a general movement of tribes known as 'Sea People', who came to the coastal areas of Palestine from Crete, Cyprus and the Aegean Islands. The territory was known as 'the land of the Philistines' or 'Philistia'. They had five settlements or 'city-states': Gaza, Ashkelon, Gath, Ashdod and Ekron which formed a closely knit and very efficient social and military unit. Their chief god was Dagon.

There was constant border warfare between Israel and the Philistines throughout the period of the Judges and until King David finally defeated them.

SYRIA. Also called Aram (after the Aramean tribes who settled here), Syria lay to the north of Israel. Its chief city was Damascus. Aramaic was probably the language of these early settlers. Relationships between Israel and Syria varied between border warfare, independent existence and alliance.

In the New Testament Antioch in Syria was an important centre of early Christianity, and it was there that the followers of Jesus were first called Christians.

ASSYRIA. This lay in north Mesopotamia (the northern part of modern Iraq). It was an ancient nation, settled at least by c. 2300 B.C., but its importance for the history of Israel spans a period of some 200 years (850–650 B.C.) during which Israel became part of the Assyrian empire. Their capital city was Asshur (their chief god had the same name), but later Nineveh became the capital city until Assyria fell to the Babylonians in 612 B.C. Assyria was a cruel, but very efficient, military nation who resettled conquered peoples away from their own land, thus breaking their national identity. This fate befell the Northern Kingdom of Israel in 722 B.C. Kings mentioned in the OT are **Tiglath-Pileser I** (744–727 B.C.—2 Ki 15:29), **Shalmaneser V** (726–722 B.C.—2 Ki 17:3), **Sargon II** (721–705 B.C.—Isa 20:1), **Sennacherib** (704–681 B.C.—2 Ki 18:13), **Esarhaddon** (681–669 B.C.—2 Ki 19:37) and **Ashurbanipal** (660–627 B.C.—Ezr 4:10).

BABYLON. Babylonian history reaches back to the Sumerian period from which it derives many of its cultural traditions. It lay in what is now Southern Iraq. The Assyrian Empire passed to Babylon under king Nebuchadnezzar. Both Ezekiel and Daniel were exiled to Babylon, and Ezra the scribe returned to Israel from Babylon, although by then Babylon had itself fallen to the Persian king, Cyrus, in 539 B.C.

PERSIA. Persians were originally travelling Indo-Europeans from Southern Russia, who settled in what is now modern Iran about 1000 B.C. Their capital was Susa, where Nehemiah was based, while the book of Esther gives an inside view of life in the royal palace there. We learn about Persian policy towards conquered peoples from 2 Chronicles and Ezra, both of which contain a decree of king Cyrus. It shows that Persia encouraged subject nations to continue their own religion and culture. Kings mentioned in the OT are **Cyrus II**, the Great (or Darius the Mede, 559–530 B.C.; 2 Ch 36:22–23; Ezr 1:1–4; Da 1:21); **Darius I**, the Great (522–486 B.C.; Ezr 4:5; Ne 12:22; Hag 1:1; Zec 1:1); **Artaxerxes** (465–424 B.C.; Ezr 7:1, 21–26; Ne 2:1–8), **Darius II** (424–404 B.C.; Ne 12:22).

Persian power was overthrown by Alexander the Great of Greece in 331 B.C.

GREECE. It was Alexander the Great who was responsible for the spread of Greek civilisation throughout the vast Greek empire. Greek cities were established all over the empire, and Greek philosophy, science, morality, customs and language spread everywhere (including Israel) even after Alexander's death when his empire was divided between his four generals.

ROME. In 63 B.C. much of Israel was incorporated into the Roman province of Syria when Pompey marched into Jerusalem. Over the next few decades there was a lot of rivalry among Roman leaders, but in 31 B.C. Octavian emerged as sole ruler of the Empire. In 27 B.C. he took the name Augustus and it was during his rule that Jesus was born (Luke 2:1). Rome brought many benefits to the world: for example, roads which made travelling and trade so much easier. Latin and Greek were the official language throughout the empire and this helped the early Christian missionaries as they went everywhere preaching.

Despite the fact that subject nations were allowed to follow their own customs and religion, the Jews hated Rome. In the time of Jesus Roman troops were stationed in Judea, and Jewish hopes that God would intervene and deliver them became very strong. Resistance to Roman rule increased during the period A.D. 60–70 and in A.D. 70. Rome retaliated by destroying the Temple in Jerusalem.

Persecution of Christians seems to have been unusual, but the book of Revelation may indicate a firmer line being taken against the Christian church.

PLAN OF THE BIBLE

GENESIS

As its name implies this book is about origins or beginnings—of the universe, of the different nations, of sin, and of the Jewish people. The first eleven chapters reach back to the beginning of time and deal with questions that we all ask: who made the world? where did we come from? why is there suffering and evil in the world?

In chapters 12–50 we move from the general (the human race) to the particular as we learn how God moved into the chaos and confusion and chose one man, Abraham. God directed him to settle in the land of Israel and he and his descendants, Isaac and Jacob, are known as the patriarchs (fathers) or founders of Israel. Jacob's twelve sons are the beginnings of the twelve tribes. Through Joseph, one of his sons, the whole family settle in Egypt.

EXODUS

The centre-piece of this book is God's deliverance of emergent Israel from Egypt and the book's name means 'going out'. Some four hundred years separate Genesis and Exodus, during which time Egyptian attitudes to the settlers changed from peaceful co-existence to hostility and oppression. Moses emerged to lead God's people out of Egypt, their destination being the land of Israel. At the mountain of Sinai God gave Moses the laws which were to form the basis of the newly-formed nation's life. These are summed up in the Ten Commandments.

LEVITICUS

This is a book of further laws or rules, mainly for Israel's worship, and in particular about sacrifice and the priesthood. A keyword is 'holiness', for the intention of the laws was to help the people relate to God and in so doing to reflect his character in daily life.

NUMBERS

The first ten chapters continue in the legal atmosphere of Leviticus. The name of the book arises from the various censuses or numberings taken prior to breaking camp and leaving Sinai. The remaining chapters are a sad record of almost forty years wandering in the desert and of complaints and rebellion against Moses and God.

DEUTERONOMY

The setting of the book is the border of the land of Israel. It is presented as three sermons of Moses in which he surveys the journey from Egypt, the people's rebellion and God's patient loyalty. He restates and underlines some of the laws of Exodus, Leviticus and Numbers (thus the book's title, which means 'second law-giving'), and stresses the need for obedience after they have settled in Israel. The book closes with some final words of Moses and his death.

JOSHUA

The first twelve chapters tell us about the initial occupation of Israel under its new leader, Joshua. The remaining chapters outline the planned territorial division among the twelve tribes. Many of the native people still had to be conquered.

JUDGES

This book continues the story of the conquest of the land of Israel which involved conflict with various tribes both in and around Israel. Interwoven in the account is the constant disobedience to God alternating with a turning back to him, and his patient loyalty which is demonstrated in various leaders (called 'judges') who emerged to rally the tribes to fight their enemies.

RUTH

This is a story of family loyalty and loyalty to God and to his laws. It is set in the same period as Judges. The central character, Ruth, was not an Israelite but came to believe in God and, through her marriage to an Israelite called Boaz, became the great-grandmother of David and an ancestor of Jesus.

1 SAMUEL

The first and second books of Samuel recount Israel's history in the crucial transition from intermittent leadership to monarchy. The books take their name from the prophet who appointed the first two kings, Saul and David.

1 Samuel picks up from the book of Judges and shows how the continued harassment from neighbouring tribes made the people ask for a king.

2 SAMUEL

This is about Israel's second, and best known king, David. The book opens against a background of civil war following the death of Saul in battle. Later in the book we read of intrigue among David's sons over the succession. It was David who established Jerusalem as Israel's capital.

1 KINGS

The two books of Kings cover the history of Israel over a period of almost four hundred years.

The first eleven chapters of 1 Kings concern David's son, Solomon, the third king of Israel. His importance centres on his building of the Jerusalem Temple, the focal point of Israel's worship. His son, Rehoboam, inherited a dissatisfied nation and due to his foolish attitude ten of the tribes formed themselves into a separate state under a former official of Solomon's called Jeroboam. Subsequently this state is known as Israel, or the Northern Kingdom, and the remaining two tribes as Judah, or the Southern Kingdom. The history of these two states is recounted in interwoven accounts in the remaining chapters of 1 and 2 Kings. Elijah, an important prophet, dominates the end of 1 Kings.

2 KINGS

The death of Elijah and the emergence of the prophet Elisha occupy the early chapters of 2 Kings. The remaining sweep of the history covers some three hundred years, and from a religious point of view is all downhill apart from one or two religious revivals promoted by the reigning monarch. The end of the Northern Kingdom comes a century and a half before that of Judah, but in both cases it is understood as the inevitable punishment for turning away from God.

1 CHRONICLES

The two books of Chronicles cover the same period as Samuel and Kings but from a particular point of view. The writer, known as 'The Chronicler', shows that David laid the foundations of Israel's worship even though he did not build the Temple. In the first nine chapters he uses family trees to trace the history of Israel from Adam to the return from Exile to show that Judah is the true people of God.

2 CHRONICLES

Solomon, the builder of the Temple, is the subject of chapters 1–9. It becomes obvious in the remaining chapters that interest lies only in the history of Judah, through whom God would continue his purpose. Special attention is also given to kings who promoted religious reform. The end of the book goes beyond 2 Kings as it hints that the period in exile in Babylon is about to end. Persia has taken over the Babylonian empire.

EZRA

This follows on in time immediately from 2 Chronicles. The Persian king has issued a decree which allows the Jews to return to Israel and to rebuild the Jerusalem Temple. In chapters 3–6 we learn that initially the altar was rebuilt and sacrifices resumed but opposition halted the temple rebuilding for many years. Finally, it was completed and dedicated. Some time later (chapters 7–10) Ezra, an expert on the Jewish law, was sent from Babylon to help and guide the newly-established community. The main problem was that the Jews were intermarrying with other nations, thereby threatening the survival of national identity.

NEHEMIAH

Another leader in establishing the new community, Nehemiah organised the rebuilding of the walls round Jerusalem, so vital to its security (chapters 1–7). Once this was done Ezra read the law (from the first five books of the Bible) to the people and led them in a

confession of their disobedience to God and then to a promise to obey him in the future (chapters 8–10). Nehemiah also carried through several social reforms (chapters 11–13).

ESTHER

The setting of this story is the Persian king's palace in the same period as Ezra–Nehemiah. Esther, a Jew, became a Persian queen and was able to save the Jews in the Persian empire from a plot to exterminate them.

JOB

The story of Job is found in the first two and the last chapter of the book. Satan is allowed to bring several major tragedies into the life of this good and religious man. The main section of the book is a discussion between Job and three friends (a fourth makes a brief appearance) as to why Job has suffered so much trouble. The questions raised are not only about human suffering but about God: is he fair? is he even good? Traditional, trite answers are shown to be inadequate.

PSALMS

Here are sacred songs, poems and prayers which originated in Israel's worship and her experience of God. They are traditionally associated with David but reflect centuries of individual and corporate responses to God. Human emotions of anger, despair, sadness, guilt, doubt, joy, praise and adoration are expressed. Themes include the Law, Jerusalem and its Temple, Israel's history, the natural world, human suffering and God's justice.

PROVERBS

The first nine chapters are written as though a father, or perhaps a teacher, is giving advice to a son or student. After this each verse presents a proverb as we know proverbs today—concise, common sense and often witty statements about wise, successful living. Dominant themes include: poverty, justice, pride, self-control, drunkenness, anger, speaking wisely.

ECCLESIASTES

The name of this book means something like 'The Teacher' and the central word is 'meaningless'. The writer examines every aspect of life: wealth, social position, professional success and pleasure and concludes that they are futile because of the fact of death which comes to everyone. The only positive suggestion is that we should enjoy whatever God has given us, and in 12:13 the Teacher states his conclusion: 'Fear God and keep his Commandments'.

SONG OF SONGS

This is presented in poetic form as a 'song' about the wonder of sexual love. There are at least two individual speakers, a man and a woman, and a group called 'friends'. There are conversations between them, but also thoughts of each lover about the other. Many see the Song as a symbol of God's love for his people.

ISAIAH

This book relates to a period of some three hundred years. Chapters 1–39 are set in the closing years of the Northern Kingdom when Judah was still relatively safe. Isaiah worked in Jerusalem warning its people that God's judgment must fall on them because of social injustice and religious hypocrisy. To successive kings of Judah he advised dependence on God's guidance and protection rather than on political alliances with foreign nations. Jerusalem is spared the same fate as the Northern Kingdom for the time being.

Chapters 40–55 are concerned with the Jewish exiles in Babylon. The message is one of comfort: God is about to do something new and the punishment and pain of the past are over. The return to the land of Israel will recall the deliverance from Egypt.

In the final section of the book, which is set in the period after the temple had been rebuilt, there is evidence that the new community is in danger of slipping back into old patterns of behaviour. Alongside warnings is a vision of the greatness of God and his plans for the blessing of the Jews, and through them, of all nations.

JEREMIAH

This prophet worked in the closing years of Judah. His message was one of warning: God's judgment must come if the people persist in rebelling against him. Indeed, judgment has become inevitable and they would be wise to recognise that God was using Babylon to punish them. When the ruling classes were exiled to Babylon Jeremiah told them that God would work out his plans through the exiles. At the same time he tried to encourage those who remained in Judah to accept their fate, but his words fell on deaf ears. Within the book we have several insights into what this unpopular prophet was thinking and feeling.

LAMENTATIONS

This is a funeral song about the devastated city of Jerusalem, possibly written by Jeremiah. Each chapter is a complete poem and in each the mood changes from anguish and despair in the recognition that punishment was deserved, to hope in God's love and mercy. Prayer is made that God will once again show these to his people.

EZEKIEL

This prophet was exiled to Babylon and his work was among the exiles there. He may have been a priest and a key theme of the book is God's holiness. The book is full of strange symbolism, visions and accounts of how the prophet often presented his message through drama. Roughly, the first thirty-three chapters convey a similar message to that of Jeremiah and at a similar period: Jerusalem will be captured by Babylon and the temple will be destroyed. Once this had

taken place Ezekiel's message was one of comfort (chapters 33–39): God will bring back his people to their own country one day. Meanwhile, in Babylon they will learn that God can be worshipped even though there is no temple or they cannot offer sacrifice. Chapters 40–48 are a detailed vision of the future which centres on the Temple.

DANIEL

Daniel was also an exile in Babylon but was chosen to live in the Babylonian court and to train for the civil service. Despite this privilege we learn that Daniel, and later three of his friends, refused to give up their Jewish faith. God blessed their loyalty and Daniel was respected and consulted by the Babylonian, and later the Persian kings, particularly because of his ability to interpret dreams. The second part of the book (chapters 7–12) includes some detailed visions full of strange symbols and not always easy to interpret.

HOSEA

This prophet lived and worked in the Northern Kingdom in the closing years of its existence. Through his own experience of a broken marriage Hosea gained a deep insight into Israel's relationship to God. The covenant made at Sinai was like a marriage, but like Hosea's own wife Israel had left God to worship Canaanite gods. Hosea speaks movingly of the sadness God feels because of his love for Israel even though she deserves to be punished.

JOEL

We are not sure when Joel lived. In chapter 1 he speaks of the devastation caused by a plague of locusts. This may have been a real event or a vision but in either case it is a symbol of the invading army which God will use to punish his people (2:1–11). Joel calls the people to turn back to God while there is still time and speaks of a special outpouring of God's Spirit (2:12–32). Chapter 3 concerns a final and universal judgment.

AMOS

This prophet came from the Southern Kingdom but worked in the Northern Kingdom slightly earlier than Hosea. In chapters 1–2 he speaks of God's judgment on the surrounding nations but also on the complacent Northern Kingdom. In chapter 3 he announces that God has broken off the covenant agreement with his people in the Northern Kingdom and the next few chapters show why: oppression, social injustice, religious hypocrisy. Five visions (chapters 7–9) show that there is still time to turn back to God, but in the last two visions punishment is inevitable. A hope for something beyond God's judgment is expressed in the last few verses.

OBADIAH

This is the shortest Old Testament book and we know nothing about the prophet. The theme is the punishment of Edom, which lay to the south-east of the Dead Sea. The

Edomites were descendants of Esau and thus related to the Israelites, yet they were long-standing enemies. The reference in this book suggests that when Jerusalem fell to the Babylonian army in 587 B.C. the Edomites did nothing to help and maybe even took some advantage of Judah's fate. While Edom disappeared from history Obadiah foretells the return of Israel to her own land.

JONAH

God told the prophet Jonah to go and warn the people of Nineveh, capital of Assyria (a cruel enemy of Israel) that God was going to punish them. After attempts to evade God's orders Jonah reluctantly preached in the city and the Ninevites turned to God. Jonah was furious with God for showing mercy to such wicked people and God tries to demonstrate to the prophet that he feels compassion even for Israel's enemies.

MICAH

This prophet lived and worked a little later than Amos and Hosea and about the same time as Isaiah and what he has to say is very similar to them. He worked in the Southern Kingdom and condemned social injustice and inequality, and corruption among the political and religious leaders. God must punish his people but beyond this Micah speaks of a future which will centre on the Jerusalem temple when a descendant of David will emerge to lead God's people against her enemies (chapters 4–7). 6:6–8 seems to sum up the message, not only of Micah, but of all the prophets of this period.

NAHUM

This prophet announces the destruction of Nineveh, capital of Assyria. In the opening verses Nahum speaks of God as 'slow to anger' but also that he will 'not leave the guilty unpunished'. It is for this reason that God must now punish Nineveh for extreme cruelty. Chapters 2 and 3 are a poem about the siege of Nineveh. This took place in 612 B.C.

HABAKKUK

Because Habakkuk mentions Babylon (1:6) it is assumed that he worked at the end of the seventh century B.C. The prophet questions God about his justice: why does he turn a blind eye to cruelty and wickedness? How can he use wicked people to punish people who are better than them? God gives no direct answer (chapter 2) but promises that one day he will punish all oppression and injustice. Chapter 3 is a poem about God coming to punish all wickedness and concludes with a statement by the prophet of his trust in God, no matter what happens.

ZEPHANIAH

Zephaniah worked just before Jeremiah. The theme of the book is God's universal judgment. Chapter 1 deals with the judgment of Israel but 2:1–3 promises that this may be averted if they turn back to God. The remainder of chapter 2 foretells the punishment of

some of Israel's neighbours. Beyond the judgment of Jerusalem the prophet sees hope (chapter 3).

HAGGAI

Haggai and Zechariah belong to the same period (520 B.C.). Many Jews had returned to Israel to rebuild their national life. Initially they worked with enthusiasm but opposition brought the work of rebuilding the Temple to a standstill. Haggai rallied the people, showing that the economic difficulties they were experiencing were because they had their priorities wrong. The important thing for their national life was God's 'house' and God had greater things in store if they would only learn to put him first.

ZECHARIAH

Like Haggai, this prophet encouraged the people to take up the work they had left off and complete the Temple building. His messages are given in a series of visions in chapters 1–8 and concern other issues as well as the rebuilding. Chapters 9–14 are in a different form, more typical of prophetic messages. Their theme is the future age: Israel's deliverance, God's triumph and the work of the Messiah.

MALACHI

This book indicates that after the time of Haggai and Zechariah things deteriorated again. The people felt disappointed with God (1:2–5), the religious leaders were corrupt and slipshod in their duties (1:6–2:9), and everybody disobedient to God's laws (2:10–16) while at the same time treating him with contempt (2:17–3:18). Chapter 4 looks forward to the time when injustice will be dealt with and those who are loyal to God will be restored.

MATTHEW

The first three Gospels follow a similar pattern and are often known as the 'Synoptic Gospels' because they 'see together' the life of Jesus. Yet each has its own particular emphasis.

Matthew begins by tracing Jesus' family history back to Abraham and recounts various incidents concerned with Jesus' birth (chapters 1–2). His is a carefully organised Gospel and is especially interested in what Jesus said: the Sermon on the Mount (chapters 5–7), parables about the kingdom of heaven (chapter 13) and parables about the end of time (chapter 25). He also shows that Jesus is the Messiah spoken of in the Old Testament.

MARK

This Gospel concentrates mainly on what Jesus did, although the writer does include some of Jesus' teaching. Within the first few chapters several miracles are recorded. He does not speak about Jesus' birth but begins with John the Baptist's work and Jesus' baptism and temptations. Chapters 1–9 are about Jesus' work in Galilee, chapters 10–15 his journey to Jerusalem ending in his death, and chapter 16 about his resurrection. 16:9–20 was added later, probably by the early church.

LUKE

The first two chapters of this Gospel contain several unique incidents related to Jesus' birth and early life. Luke traces Jesus' family tree to Adam, which underlines the emphasis on Jesus as the Saviour of the whole world. He stresses that Jesus is concerned for minority groups, for the poor and the oppressed. Other prominent themes are prayer, joy and the Holy Spirit. He often cross-references events to dates in secular history. He is also the author of Acts.

JOHN

It is obvious from the first verse that this Gospel is very different in atmosphere to the other three. Jesus' miracles are called 'signs', Jesus does not speak of the 'king-dom' but of 'eternal life'. There are no parables but several long, rather complex sermons which are usually linked to one of the signs. Thus when Jesus heals a blind man he speaks of himself as 'the light of the world'. These 'I am' sayings are quite dis-tinctive to this Gospel and the accounts of Jesus' appearances after his resurrection are also unique.

ACTS

This is the 'second instalment' of the story begun in Luke's Gospel and tells us what happened in the early church in the first thirty years or so. It begins with the ascension of Jesus (chapter 1) and the coming of the Holy Spirit at Pentecost (chapter 2). The next ten chapters show how the gospel spread beyond the locality of Jerusalem as far as Samaria. Peter, Stephen and James are the main char-acters. Chapters 13–28 centre on Paul and his three missionary tours taking the gospel to Greece and Europe. The whole book shows that the main source of opposition to the 'new religion' came from the Jews, not the Roman government.

ROMANS

This is the first of twenty-one letters found in the New Testament. They are very important because they give us an inside view of life in the earliest Christian churches and the teaching of their leaders. Paul had not been to Rome when he wrote this letter. It is the most detailed account of an important part of his teaching: that the only way to be accepted by God is to rely on what Jesus did through his death and resurrection (chapters 1–8). In chapters 9–11 Paul expresses the hope that although the Jews have largely refused this teaching they will one day accept it. Romans follows the pattern of most of Paul's letters: the first part is teaching and the second prac-tical application in real life. Thus chapters 12–16 speak of how Christians should behave in the church and in the world.

1 CORINTHIANS

This and the following letter were written to a church in the Greek city of Corinth which Paul had visited (Acts 18:1–21). Paul had heard that there were various problems in the church: party politics (chapters 1–4), moral problems (chapter 5), Christians taking each other to court (chapter 6), marriage (chapter 7), special difficulties arising from living in a city full of temples to various gods (chapters 8–10), the organisation of worship (chapters 11–14) and intellectual problems with life after death (chapter 15).

2 CORINTHIANS

Between this and the previous letter Paul visited the church. There had been a lot of criticism and even hostility shown to him, and his authority as a leader had been called into question. Relationships had improved but Paul finds it necessary to stress the genuineness of his authority as an apostle (chapters 2–3, 10–13). The letter shows how deeply Paul felt (chapter 7). Chapter 5 con-tains further teaching on life after death, and chapters 8–9 give details about an appeal for financial help for a group of churches facing hardship.

GALATIANS

This is probably the first of Paul's letters and its theme is similar to that of Romans. It is apparent that many Jews felt that non-Jews becoming Christians should keep the Jewish law and in particular the food laws, and be circumcised. (Acts also tells us this.) The heart of Paul's teaching on this view is found in 2:14–21: a right relationship with God is possible only through Jesus, and nothing else is required. Chapters 5–6 show that this does not mean we can do as we like. Christians are called to 'serve one another in love' and the Holy Spirit is given to help them do this.

EPHESIANS

This letter may have been written to several churches in and around the important city of Ephesus. Paul founded this church on his third missionary tour (Acts 18:23–20:1). The clear theme of the letter is unity: God's plan is to bring to an end all that divides men and women, social classes, nations and religions. Jesus Christ is the unifying force, as the head 'unites' the human body. Chap-ters 4–6 show that this unity is very practical: it is worked out in good relationships in the family, the church and the work place.

PHILIPPIANS

Paul established this church on his second missionary tour (Acts 16:6–40), and this letter was written some ten or twelve years after that visit. It is a warm, personal letter to a church for which he felt a deep affection. He speaks of his imprisonment which has resulted in the gospel being preached to Roman personnel (chapter 1). Chapter 2 contains an important statement about Jesus as the servant who was willing to give up his rights for the good of others, and Paul encourages the church to follow that example.

COLOSSIANS

The church was founded by Epaphras, one of Paul's converts. The contents of the letter make it clear that wrong teaching was creeping into the church. In the face of this Paul stresses the true gospel: Jesus is absolutely central. He existed before time began and he is the one who brings God and the human race together again (chapter 1). Rituals, regulations, philosophical reasonings and self-denial are not what is required (chapter 2) but right relationships and attitudes in the church, the family, the work place and the world (chapters 3–4).

1 THESSALONIANS

Paul founded this church on his second missionary tour (Acts 17:1–9) amid a lot of opposition from Jews. This and 2 Thessalonians are among Paul's earliest letters. No doubt because the Jews had continued to undermine his reputation Paul begins by insisting that he is a true apostle (chapters 1–2). From chapter 3 we learn that Timothy had been sent to the church and had returned to Paul with an encouraging report. In chapters 4 and 5 Paul deals with two questions: what happens to Christians when they die? and when will Jesus return?

2 THESSALONIANS

The Thessalonian church did not fully understand what Paul had said in his first letter (1 Thessalonians) about Jesus' return. They had also been confused by other teachers who said that Jesus had already returned. Furthermore, some church members had even opted out of responsibilities on the basis that if Jesus was about to return there was not much point in going to work! Paul deals with all these difficulties.

1 TIMOTHY

Paul had met Timothy on his second missionary tour (Acts 16:1–3) and Timothy had worked with him. Now he was a leader in the church at Ephesus and Paul writes to encourage him and give him advice about organising the church there. He writes about public prayer, the appointment of leaders, help for widows and attitudes to slaves (chapters 2–5). He warns about those who teach differently to what has been taught by recognised leaders.

2 TIMOTHY

This is more personal than 1 Timothy and was written at the end of Paul's life. He warns Timothy that wrong teaching is on the increase and people will easily be deceived. In the face of this Timothy must stand by the truth, which will take courage.

TITUS

In a similar way to Timothy, Titus was a leader in the church on the island of Crete. Paul writes as he did in 1 Timothy, about the organisation and leadership of the church, correct teaching in the face of error and right attitudes in the church, the work place and the world.

PHILEMON

Philemon was probably a convert of Paul's and now a church worker. Onesimus, one of his slaves, had run away but had met Paul and become a Christian. Paul writes to Philemon to say that he is sending Onesimus back to his master and appeals to Philemon to do what would have been unusual in those days—to forgive and reinstate Onesimus.

HEBREWS

We do not know who wrote this letter, nor who the readers were. Since the writer's theme is that the Temple and its ceremonies were temporary pointers to Christianity it is probable that the original readers were Jews. The keyword for this letter is 'better'. Jesus has offered a better (and the last) sacrifice (chapters 4–7). He is 'better' than all that has gone before: greater than the angels (chapters 1–2), greater than Moses (chapter 3). The New Covenant has replaced the Old (chapters 8–10). In the closing chapters he writes to encourage his readers to keep going in the face of difficulties and hostility. The people of the Old Testament did wonderful things because they relied on God (chapter 11). Christians must follow their example and the example of Jesus (chapter 12).

JAMES

James may have been Jesus' brother who was also the first leader of the church in Jerusalem. It could be the first of the New Testament letters to be written, and it is very practical. The main themes are: if we say we are Christians we must also live like Christians; discrimination of any kind is wrong, as is oppression of the poor and the weak; Christians should be self-controlled, especially in what they say.

1 PETER

This letter was written to Christians in the Black Sea coastal area, probably in the early 60s A.D. The theme is suffering, and probably the readers were facing real persecution because they were Christians. Christians must not be surprised if they experience opposition and persecution; Jesus, their example, certainly did! Indeed, they may be full of hope and joy because they are sharing with Jesus in this way. Throughout the letter there are also practical guidelines on Christian behaviour.

2 PETER

The letter opens with the same emphasis as in 1 Peter on Christian behaviour. Chapters 2 and 3 are a strong onslaught against those who mislead by wrong teaching and the writer speaks in detail of their future punishment. This leads him to speak of the return of Jesus.

1 JOHN

It is probable that the writer of this letter and 2 and 3 John was also the writer of the Gospel of John and the book of Revelation. It is clear that the Christians to whom he wrote 1 John